ST. CHARLES COUNTY COMMUNITY COLLEGE
3 9835 00003017 5

S0-AYE-120

# STRUCTURED SOCIAL INEQUALITY

# Structured Social Inequality

## A Reader in Comparative Social Stratification

EDITED AND WITH INTRODUCTIONS BY

*Celia S. Heller*

HUNTER COLLEGE OF THE CITY UNIVERSITY OF NEW YORK





**The Macmillan Company**
NEW YORK
**Collier-Macmillan Limited**
LONDON

First Printing



Library of Congress catalog card number: 69-10021

THE MACMILLAN COMPANY, NEW YORK
COLLIER-MACMILLAN CANADA, LTD., TORONTO, ONTARIO

Printed in the United States of America

To my sister Ann

# PREFACE

This volume is intended to serve as a textbook for both undergraduate and graduate levels. The introductions to the eight parts of the book together aim to cover the major areas of stratification. Each introduction places the articles of that section into the larger context of the particular area to which they pertain. Thus an instructor can rely entirely on this book as the textbook for his course. Or, if he prefers, he can use it as a supplement to a standard textbook, selecting from among the readings those that correspond to the topics in that textbook. To conserve space and to make possible the inclusion of more readings, I have abridged slightly the selections from scholarly journals. In those selections from books the abridgment of material has also facilitated a wider coverage of ideas from each author. (Where passages have been omitted, the conventional ellipsis sign appears.) In a number of readings I have added editorial footnotes, and these carry my initials to distinguish them from the author's original footnotes.

Before I close, I would like to acknowledge my debts to those who have directly or indirectly influenced this work. I am most grateful to my grandfather, Saul Rosenman, for opening the door to the magic world of ideas for me when I was still a child and for directing my eyes to the injustices of inequality. As a sociologist, I am deeply indebted intellectually to my teachers: Conrad Arensberg, Robert K. Merton, Paul Lazarsfeld, Herbert Hyman, and Hans Zetterberg. In preparing this book, I benefited from the discussions with and advice from my friends and colleagues: Alfonso Pinkney, Suzanne Keller, Richard A. Schermerhorn, George Fischer, Judith Kramer, Wanda Wendt, Philip Weintraub, Barbara Bauman, Gerda Lorenz, and Sarah Karant. The comments by Dennis Wrong on the introductions to and choices of selections—a number of which led to revisions—are much appreciated. And I am very grateful to John Moore, an ally in this venture, for his patience, encouragement, generosity, and editorial help.

C. S. H.

# CONTENTS

**GENERAL INTRODUCTION** 1

Part I
**THEORIES OF STRATIFICATION—THE CLASSIC TRADITION**
**Introduction** 7
On Class KARL MARX 14
Class, Status, Party MAX WEBER 24
Elites and Their Circulation VILFREDO PARETO 34
The Rise and Fall of Whole Classes JOSEPH SCHUMPETER 39

Part II
**PRINCIPAL TYPES OF STRATIFICATION SYSTEMS**
**Introduction** 51
Interpretations of Slavery:
The Slave Status in the Americas ARNOLD A. SIO 63
Caste in India and the United States GERALD D. BERREMAN 74
Feudal Society MARC BLOCH 81
Class Society in the Melting Pot THEODOR GEIGER
(translated for this volume by Celia S. Heller) 91

Part III
**MAJOR DIMENSIONS OF SOCIAL STRATIFICATION**
**Introduction** 105
**Objective**
*Economic Inequality*
What's Happening to Our Income Revolution? HERMAN P. MILLER 133
Challenge to Affluence—The Emergence of an "Under-class"
GUNNAR MYRDAL 138
The Soviet Income Revolution MURRAY YANOWITCH 143
*Power Inequality*
The New Class MILOVAN DJILAS 154
From the Ruling Class to the Power Elite T. B. BOTTOMORE 160
Power in the Local Community RICHARD A. SCHERMERHORN 168

*Status Inequality*
What Social Class Is in America
W. LLOYD WARNER with MARCHIA MEEKER and KENNETH EELLS 175
Social Stratification of the Jewish Community in a Small Polish Town CELIA STOPNICKA HELLER 183
Occupational Prestige in the United States, 1925–1963
ROBERT W. HODGE, PAUL M. SIEGEL, and PETER H. ROSSI 192
Status Consistency and Inconsistency GERHARD E. LENSKI 204
**Subjective**
Non-egalitarian Classlessness—Similarities in Interpreting Mutually Opposed Systems STANISLAW OSSOWSKI 206
Social Class, Ideology, and Voting Preference: An Analysis of the 1964 Presidential Election
GERTRUDE J. SELZNICK and STEPHEN STEINBERG 216
Relative Deprivation—Attitudes to Class and Status Inequality in England W. G. RUNCIMAN 226
Changes of Social Structure in Social Consciousness STEFAN NOWAK 235

Part IV
**CONSEQUENCES OF STRATIFICATION: DIFFERENTIAL LIFE CHANCES AND WAYS OF LIFE**
**Introduction** 249
Social Class, Life Expectancy, and Overall Mortality
AARON ANTONOVSKY 257
Class Subcultures in American Society HERBERT J. GANS 270
Blue-collar Marriage—Barriers to Marital Communication
MIRRA KOMAROVSKY 276
Social Class Differences in Family Life in the USSR H. KENT GEIGER 284
Social Class and Success EPHRAIM H. MIZRUCHI 296

Part V
**SOCIAL MOBILITY**
**Introduction** 309
Social Mobility PITIRIM SOROKIN 317
Comparative Social Mobility S. M. MILLER 325
Occupational Mobility in the United States
PETER M. BLAU and OTIS DUDLEY DUNCAN 340
Sponsored and Contest Mobility and the School System
RALPH H. TURNER 353
Psychological Factors in Social Mobility: Intelligence and Motivation
SEYMOUR MARTIN LIPSET and REINHARD BENDIX 362

Part VI
**ETHNICITY, RACE, AND CLASS**
**Introduction** 375
Race, Color, and Class in Central America and the Andes
JULIAN PITT-RIVERS 380

The Negro American—Community and Class Realities: The Ordeal of Change G. FRANKLIN EDWARDS 387
Class as an Explanation of Ethnic Differences in Upward Mobility—The Case of Mexican Americans CELIA STOPNICKA HELLER 396
The Protestant Establishment—Aristocracy and Caste in America E. DIGBY BALTZELL 403

Part VII
**CHANGE IN STRATIFICATION SYSTEMS**
**Introduction** 415
Interaction Between Industrial and Pre-industrial Stratification Systems BERT F. HOSELITZ 421
Peruvian Stratification and Mobility—Revolutionary and Developmental Potential DAVID CHAPLIN 427
The Emerging Pattern of Israeli Stratification S. N. EISENSTADT 438
Social Stratification in Industrial Society JOHN H. GOLDTHORPE 452
Strata and Strata Interests in Socialist Society WLODZIMIERZ WESOLOWSKI 465

Part VIII
**UNRESOLVED ISSUES IN STRATIFICATION THEORY**
**Introduction** 479
Social Structure, Group Interests, and Conflict Groups RALF DAHRENDORF 488
Some Principles of Stratification KINGSLEY DAVIS and WILBERT E. MOORE 496
Some Notes on the Functional Theory of Stratification WLODZIMIERZ WESOLOWSKI 503
The Tumin-Moore Polemics—Remaining Points of Argument WILBERT E. MOORE 511
Social Inequality Without Stratification DENNIS H. WRONG 513
Beyond the Ruling Class—Strategic Elites SUZANNE KELLER 520
Classes in Modern Society T. B. BOTTOMORE 524

**NAME INDEX** 533

**SUBJECT INDEX** 541

# GENERAL INTRODUCTION

The study of social stratification is one of the most flourishing areas of American sociology today. Hardly an issue of the leading sociological journals appears that does not contain one or more articles on this topic. However, this field, now well developed and thriving as a basic branch of sociology, was long neglected as a subject of systematic investigation in the United States. The systematic study of social stratification is a phenomenon of only the last three decades. It is reflected in the fact that in 1929 the authors of the book *Trends in American Sociology,* much acclaimed in its day, found no materials on social stratification worthy of a chapter.[1] Another indicator of the neglect is the late appearance of textbooks on this subject. The first general work suitable for university students was the collection of readings by Bendix and Lipset that was issued in 1953.[2] Then, in 1955, came the short but succinct paperback *Class and Society* by Kurt B. Mayer.[3] But the first textbooks in the traditional sense of the word did not appear until 1957.[4]

The growth of empirical studies of social stratification can be traced to the Great Depression and to the influence of Marxist thought on the intellectuals of that epoch. But even if the systematic study of stratification in the United States goes back only that far, the interest in this phenomenon is as old as sociology itself. Auguste Comte touched on it in his discussion of division of labor and social solidarity. It was at the heart of Saint-Simon's preoccupation with how industrial society is to be organized to bring about a moral regeneration. Herbert Spencer gave it some attention, particularly in his *Study of Sociology* when he wrote about *class bias* as a serious obstacle to sociological thought. He made the "modern" sounding observation that the ideas and sentiments of the class to which the sociologist himself belongs "affect alike his conceptions of the past, his interpretations of present, his anticipations of the future."[5] The same could be said about early American sociologists—Lester F. Ward, William Graham Sumner, Charles H. Cooley—for, as has been convincingly demonstrated by Charles Page, they too were concerned with the subject of social stratification.[6] And it was at the very center of the thought of those theorists from whose writings constitute the first readings of this book: Marx, Weber, Pareto, and Schumpeter.

[1] G. A. Lundberg, *et al., Trends in American Sociology,* New York: Harpers, 1929, as reported by Charles H. Page, *Class in Amercian Sociology,* New York: Dial Press, 1940.

[2] Reinhard Bendix and Seymour Martin Lipset, eds., *Class, Status and Power,* Glencoe, Illinois: Free Press, 1953.

[3] Kurt B. Mayer, *Class and Society*, New York: Random House, 1955.

[4] Bernard Barber, *Social Stratification*, New York: Harcourt, Brace and Company, 1957; Joseph A. Kahl, *The American Class Structure*, New York: Holt, Rinehart and Winston, 1957.

[5] Herbert Spencer, "The Class Bias," in C. Wright Mills, ed., *Images of Man*, New York: George Braziller, 1960, p. 64.

[6] Page, *op. cit.*

It is not enough to indicate that interest in social stratification is as old as sociology itself, for, as a matter of fact, it preceded the nineteenth-century beginnings of sociology.

Among the earliest written thoughts and judgments about social inequality were those of the Hebrew prophets who denounced the excesses of the rich and mighty. And as could easily be guessed—because there is hardly a subject that cannot be traced to them—Plato and Aristotle paid attention to this phenomenon. Plato was preoccupied with the conception of a society in which social inequality would correspond perfectly to the inherent inequality of men. Thus, his Republic is a utopian society where each man assumes the occupation for which he is best fitted. Aristotle, the great classifier, gave us the scheme of three classes present in all states: "One class is very rich, another very poor, and a third is a mean."[7] Knowing his preference for the *mean* in all things, it is not surprising that he thought the middle class the best of the three and those states possessing a large middle class the best administered. In his *Politics* we also find differing dichotomous schemes: One is the basic division of people everywhere into free and slave; and the other is the division of every population into those who work and those who do not.

From his selection of written materials on social inequality spanning several thousand years, the Polish sociologist Stanislaw Ossowski isolated two major perspectives:

1. Those who approve of the existing social order: They see social inequality as basically just, for it consists of everyone getting his due. In this view, social inequality is a natural scheme of things in which one gets what he deserves. Approval of the existing order, says Ossowski, has somehow always developed into apologetics for it.
2. Those who question the existing social order: They see inequality as unjust, measuring it against the ideal of equality: ". . . an ideal which over the centuries has been extinguished and reborn, aroused people to action, taken the form of unrealizable dreams or glimmered in the mists of an afterworld, but which has always managed to emerge from the recesses of the social consciousness to disturb the existing state of affairs."[8]

In both instances, Ossowski shows, it is not merely a question of perspective: each suggests "different practical policies." If so, then the increasingly frequent argument that the above two contrasting perspectives also run through the contemporary sociological theories of stratification assume special significance. According to them, the *functionalist* theory stems from the first, the *conservative tradition* and its competitor, conflict theory, grows out of the latter, the *radical tradition.*[9] To oversimplify for the sake of brevity, functional theory holds that stratification is a necessary requirement for the existence of society. According to conflict theory, *power* not functional necessity is the key to stratification. The differential distribution of power accounts for the inequality in valued goods and services. (Expositions of these competing theories appear in the final part of this book). What makes these theories different from all the conservative and radical

[7] Aristotle, *Politics,* trans. by Benjamin Jowett, New York: Modern Library, 1943, p. 190.

[8] Stanislaw Ossowski, *Class Structure in the Social Consciousness,* New York: Free Press, 1963, p. 179.

[9] See Gerhard E. Lenski, *Power and Privilege*, New York: McGraw-Hill Book Company, 1966, pp. 14–17; Also Ralf Dahrendorf, *Class and Class Conflict in Industrial Society*, Stanford: Stanford University Press, 1959, p. 158. For an earlier statement to the same effect, see S. M. Lipset and Reinhard Bendix, "Social Status and Social Structure," *British Journal of Sociology*, Vol. II, 1952, p. 150.

formulations that preceded them—say some sociologists in the role of critics—is that they are phrased in morally neutral terms. But beyond that façade, as it were, are premises no different from those inherent in the other formulations.

In light of such assertions, it would seem only proper for the editor of a volume such as this to make explicit to which "camp" she belongs. But a third alternative is emerging: Voices are beginning to be raised about the need for a synthesis of functionalist and conflict theories and some even claim that much has already been achieved toward developing such a synthesis. These voices reflect an explicit or implicit adherence to the Hegelian dialectic, to the concept that the historical process is characterized by the principle of the struggle of opposites (*thesis* and *antithesis*) and their continual resolution (*synthesis*). Convinced of the dialectical principle in intellectual development—that ideas give rise to opposite ideas and that the struggle between them results in an eventual synthesis, a new and different entity containing elements of both within it—I am confident that ultimately such a synthesis will emerge in stratification theory. Clearly, however, it would be foolish at this point to attempt a premature collection of readings in stratification to represent such a synthesis. This book after all is intended primarily as a textbook for courses on social stratification. That is why it is eclectic (hopefully in the better sense of the word) in its selections: It espouses no one sociological position to the exclusion of others. The reader will find both major theoretical viewpoints and the attempts at synthesis represented here.

What consciously guided me in the selection of articles was first of all a concern for excellence. A second concern was to cover the major aspects of the field of stratification as it has so far developed. And a third consideration was to represent the comparative orientation in its coverage. To accomplish these aims, I have not confined myself to the work of sociologists, but occasionally have drawn on that of anthropologists, economists, historians, and political scientists. I have also included a few readings that appear in print for the first time here. To these, insofar as this is its first appearance in English, belongs the portion from Theodor Geiger's *Die Klassengesellschaft im Schmelztiegel,* which has exercised a profound influence on European sociological thought, but is little known in the United States.

The book consists of eight parts. It begins with classical theory and finishes with contemporary theory. The logic behind it is, first, that classical theory—represented in this book by Weber, Marx, and Pareto—has exercised a profound influence on the empirical studies in stratification. And such studies heavily dominate the next six parts of the book. Secondly, the reason contemporary theory is placed at the end of the book rather than together with classical theory is, as has already been indicated, that it is dominated by controversy. The reader should be able to judge the merits of each position better, armed with the knowledge of the empirical studies.

Social stratification is too often treated as if it were synonymous with social differentiation, which it is not. Social differentiation is a universal phenomenon: In all societies we have a separation of positions and roles, some division of functions and labor. But social differentiation alone does not constitute stratification. First of all, social differentiation does not always involve differential evaluation or ranking of positions, whereas stratification does. Positions may be differentiated from one another and yet not *ranked* relative to each other. For example, in our society the position of the adolescent is generally not considered superior to that of infant, merely different.

Social stratification, however, can be considered a certain type of social differentiation. To put it differently, whenever you have stratification you have social differentiation, but not the other way around. Although the universality of social differentiation is undisputed, there is some controversy about whether stratification is universal. Scattered throughout this book, the reader will find statements declaring that it is. Those making the statements generally also consider stratification *necessary* in all social systems. But others point to some primitive societies without stratification. There is, however, general agreement among sociologists that stratification has been present in all complex societies to date. Although many deduce from this and argue that stratification is a necessary *condition* for complex society, the proposition is a bit shaky. It could just as well be that stratification is a *consequence* of complexity and that therefore mechanisms might evolve or consciously be introduced that could counteract this consequence. What I am suggesting is that it is a logical fallacy to deduce, as many do, inevitability from universality.

To this writer the crucial question in examining a society at a given time is not whether it is stratified or not but the degree to and way in which it is stratified. Minimally stratified systems must be distinguished from highly stratified ones, because they involve social relations that are qualitatively different and because they have qualitatively different consequences for their members. Despite the manifold variations in the phenomenon of stratification, through time and space, the following ideal types can be distinguished: slave, caste, estate, and class and stratification in advanced industrial society. The readings in Part II of this book deal with principal types of stratification systems.

Although we have specified that stratification is not synonymous with social differentiation and that it involves differential ranking, we have not yet made clear what stratification means. To say that this is the subject of this book is not to beg the question but rather to point to the great complexity of the phenomenon known as stratification. As the reader will gather from the following selections, and especially those in the first part, there is no uniform definition of social stratification. Perhaps the most common meaning that runs through the numerous contemporary definitions is that it refers to an arrangement of positions in a graded hierarchy of socially superior and inferior ranks.[10] As suggested by the title of this book I find it convenient to think of stratification as a system of structured inequality in the things that count in a given society, that is, both tangible and symbolic goods of that society. The term *structured* indicates an arrangement of elements: the inequality is not random but follows a pattern, displays relative constancy and stability, and is backed by ideas that legitimize and justify it. The various forms of patterning, the degree of stability, and the extent of institutionalization vary from one system to another. But several principal types, as has already been said, can be distinguished. They are the subject of the readings in the Part II of this book. The nature of the things that count and how unequal is their distribution in modern society, is treated in Part III, "Major Dimensions of Stratification." The readings deal with the actual inequalities—in income, wealth, power, and prestige—as well as how the members of society perceive, interpret, and evaluate these inequalities.

When we say that the preceding—wealth, power, prestige—are things that count,

[10] Mayer, *op. cit.*, p. 4.

we have in mind the consequences for the people who have or lack them, who possess more or less of these goods. The consequences manifest themselves in almost every aspect of life. The readings in Part IV, "Differential Life Chances and Ways of Life," cover some of them: how strata differ in the basic chance to stay alive, in value orientations, family organization, type of home socialization, the quality of formal education, and so on.

Although we conceptualize these differential patterns of social behavior as consequences of stratification, we are nevertheless fully aware that they in turn affect the stratification system. The pattern of mutual dependence is operating here as in social phenomena in general.[11] Effects of conditions react on the conditions themselves or, as Homans expressed it, "they wax and wane together."[12] Where this manifests itself dramatically is in the realm of social mobility. The same pattern of behavior that may represent a positive adjustment to one's situation in the stratification system may be dysfunctional for social mobility. For example, the low aspiration levels of youths in the lower strata helps to avoid inevitable frustrations, because there is not enough room "on top" for many of them. At the same time, however, such low aspirations eliminate from the race, individuals who might be able to achieve the positions that are open.

Social mobility—the transition from one social position to another in the stratification system—is the subject of Part VI of this book. The readings deal with extent of social mobility, its types, factors that affect it, and modes of mobility. They lead rather easily to the selections in Part VI on ethnicity (including race) and social stratification. Ethnicity and social stratification are two major and related features of a number of contemporary societies and it is therefore important to explore the connection between them. Mindful that such exploration is especially crucial in understanding the Negro revolts in contemporary American cities, we have purposefully included in this part, in contrast to the rest of the book, selections primarily concerning stratification and ethnicity in the United States.

To reiterate then, this book aims to be comparative in its approach, a perspective that is gaining ground in contemporary American sociology. Perhaps in no other area of sociology have we moved as far away from parochialism as in the study of stratification. Hopefully these selections will reflect it. In so far as it was possible, an attempt was made to include, in all those parts of the book that deal with modern stratification, readings about the various aspects of the Soviet type of stratification as well as the Western type.

The comparative approach manifests itself perhaps most fully in Part VII, "Change in Stratification Systems." It begins with a general article about change in preindustrial stratification systems and concludes with one dealing with change in the stratification systems of advanced industrial societies.

The last part of this book, "Unresolved Issues in Stratification Theory," consists of articles concerning the two major issues: (1) the old, and as yet unresolved, question of the nature of stratification in general and (2) the new question of the nature of the now emerging stratification system in advanced industrial society. We already referred to the readings dealing with the first in explaining why this book begins and ends with theoretical statements. As for the selections

[11] For the classic criticism of the concept of one-sided causation in the study of social phenomena, see Vilfredo Pareto: *The Mind and Society*, New York: Harcourt, Brace and Co., 1935, pp. 68–74; 254–256.

[12] George C. Homans, *The Human Group*, New York: Harcourt, Brace and Co., 1950, p. 7.

regarding the latter issue, they struggle to grasp the outline of the new system of structured inequality that is now shaping. Perhaps it is only fitting that the readings on both of these issues constitute our final readings, for they help us to pinpoint what we know and what we do not yet know about structured social inequality.

# PART I
# Theories of Stratification— The Classic Tradition

The readings in the first part of this book are not the only theoretical ones included. Such statements are to some extent dispersed throughout and are concentrated again in Part VIII. What distinguishes the first readings in theory from the rest is that they are, to borrow C. Wright Mills' designation, in the "classic tradition"[1] and as such are indispensable to the student of stratification. They have served in the past and continue to serve even today as points of orientation for the work of others. The extent to which the theorists represented here have influenced research and thought will become clear when one encounters the numerous references to them in the rest of the readings on the many aspects of stratification.

The two giants of stratification theory are Karl Marx (1818–1883) and Max Weber (1864–1920). We begin with Marx not only because his work chronologically preceded Weber's but also because it was part of Weber's intellectual tradition. To Weber, Marxism in general seemed an "untenable monocausal theory": It reduced the multiplicity of causal factors to a single-factor theorem.[2] Yet Weber's theory of stratification could not be well understood by one ignorant of Marx's ideas on class. In a sense all Weber's work (and particularly that on stratification) was shaped by his *intellectual dialogue* with Marx.

In contrast to Weber's concise statement on stratification—the second selection here—Marx's extensive writings do not contain an explicit exposition of his class theory.[3] (He undertook this task for the last chapter of *Capital,* entitled "The

[1] C. Wright Mills, *Images of Man,* New York: George Braziller, 1960, p. 2.

[2] H. H. Gerth and C. Wright Mills, "Intellectual Orientation," in *From Max Weber: Essays in Sociology,* New York: Oxford University Press, 1958, pp. 46–47.

[3] Among the best known essays written by sociologists on Marx's theory of class are Reinhard Bendix and Seymour Martin Lipset, "Karl Marx's Theory of Social Classes," in *Class, Status and Power,* Glencoe:, Illinois: Free Press, 1953, pp. 26–35; Ralf Dahrendorf, "Karl Marx's Model of the Class Society," in *Class and Class Conflict in Industrial Society,* Stanford: Stanford University Press, 1959, pp. 3–36 and Stanislaw Ossowski, "The Marxian Synthesis," in *Class Structure in the Social Consciousness,* New York: Free Press, 1963, pp. 69–88.

Classes," but he had written only a little more than a page when death interrupted him).

However, there is hardly a work by Marx in which he did not make generalizaitons about class or analyze concrete social structures or historical events in terms of his class theory. Included here are excerpts from four of them that convey the essential elements of his thought on class. The first is the beginning of the systematic and scholarly exposition that he never finished (p. 14). Right here we become aware that Marx did not always employ a two-class model (capitalists, alternately termed the "bourgeoisie," and the proletarians) for which he is often accused. He speaks of the "three big classes" in the modern society of his day. In this brief beginning he did pose the question "What constitutes a class?" but the manuscript broke off just when he was about to provide the answer. His collaborator Engels did not take up the unanswered question.[4]

It is hoped that the reader will find at least a partial answer in the portion of the *Communist Manifesto* reprinted here (pp. 14–21), although this is an early work by Marx. His thoughts on class gained in precision in later writings. Despite this and despite its propagandistic rather than scholarly tone the *Manifesto* possesses a historical importance on which there is no need to elaborate. Furthermore, it contains almost all the elements of Marx's concept of class developed in his later works—even if often in less precise form. Wresting the theory from the propaganda is not easy, for the text is full of ambiguous generalizations. Take, for example, the opening sentence: What does it really mean that the ". . . history of all hitherto existing society is the history of class struggle?" It is clearly fallacious if it signifies that there has not been cooperation among classes. If it means that the class struggle is the only factor in social change, it is again wrong.[5] We may set it aside as expressing in the categorical rhetoric of propaganda Marx's theory of class, which is to be discovered from the rest of the selection.

Marx uses the term *class* in a generic sense, in the modern sense of stratum in general rather than type of stratum characteristic of capitalism. Thus he speaks of "classes" under slavery and feudalism as well as capitalism. He sees these classes not as monolithic structures but as containing distinct subdivisions whose interests often diverge. For the latter he sometimes uses the term *gradations* and other times *fractions* so that, for example, "the *lower* middle class" is such a fraction of the middle class (p. 20). He also designates these subdivisions as *strata* and thus speaks of the "lower strata of the middle class" (p. 18).

In the excerpt here from the *Manifesto,* the dichotomous conception of class appears to contradict the fragment of *Capital* where Marx referred to three classes. Marx employs the term class in two different ways, depending on context: (1) as a designation of concrete entities—strata at a given time—for example, wage laborers, capitalists, and landowners as the three "big classes" of his day (p. 14) and (2) as an analytic concept. In the latter sense, class is presented as a dichotomous scheme used to explain change from one social system to another, as well as to project the direction in which capitalist society would develop. Throughout history two dominant classes are in conflict with each other and this generates change. Capitalist society, according to Marx, was moving in the direction of the

[4] Recently Dahrendorf, *op. cit.*, made an effort to reconstruct this answer by stringing together quotations from the various writings by Marx.

[5] Pitirim Sorokin, *Contemporary Sociological Theories,* New York: Harper Brothers, 1928, pp. 540–543.

elimination of all other classes but the bourgeoisie and the proletariat. The other classes would "decay and finally disappear in the face of modern industry" (p. 20). He predicted that capitalist society would achieve "this dichotomy in full in the penultimate act of the drama," in the period that precedes the collapse of capitalism.[6]

Because Marx's dichotomous conception of class has been subject to much criticism, it may be interesting to note that such formulations have long preceded him. As Ossowski demonstrates, throughout cultural history there has been a tendency to conceive of hierarchical divisions of society in dichotomous terms. Aristotle, for example, saw the basic division in the social structure as the distinction between free men and slaves. In the writings of the Fathers of the Church society was divided into two strata: the rich and the poor.[7] And as we think of the history of the United States, the words of Alexander Hamilton come to mind: "All communities divide themselves into the few and the many. The first are the rich and well-born and the other the mass of the people who seldom judge or determine right."[8] This last example could also serve to illustrate the proposition that dichotomous conceptions of stratification are not necessarily the products of radical thought. Hamilton was supporting his argument for an aristocratic Senate elected for life.

By reading the section from the *Manifesto* the discerning will also discover that, contrary to what some sociology textbooks assert,[9] Marx did not disregard other aspects of stratification by emphasizing the economic one. On the contrary, the essential feature of social inequality, according to him, is power. Society is divided into those who have it, *the oppressors* and those who do not have it *the oppressed.* Marx's "economic interpretation" is an explanation of what accounts for this inequality in power. He maintains that the relation to the means of production is the determining factor. Those who own the means of production have the power to rule and oppress those who do not own it. The idea of the *ruling class* encountered in the *Manifesto* is elaborated in the pages here reprinted from *The German Ideology,* especially the thesis on how this class controls the prevailing ideas in a given society.

In the *Manifesto* one also finds Marx's important concept of class consciousness. Although he does spell out in this pamphlet the conditions under which such consciousness arises, also included here are some pages from his *Poverty of Philosophy,* where additional subjective aspects of class are delineated. Here also the two separate concepts that the sociologist of today would designate as *objective class* and *subjective class* are found. Individuals in the same economic situation constitute a class (objective) even when no awareness of its distinctive interests exists among them. To this Marx elsewhere refers as "class in itself," *Klasse an sich.* When such a class develops consciousness of its distinct interests it becomes a "class for itself," *Klasse für sich* (subjective class).

We turn next to the Max Weber selection, "Class, Status, Party." Of all the theoretical writings about stratification, this essay is probably the one most often referred to in American articles and books on this subject. That Weber's theory

[6] Ossowski, *op. cit.*, p. 75.
[7] *Ibid.*, pp. 19–37.
[8] Quoted in Arthur Schlessinger, Jr., *Age of Jackson*, Boston: Little Brown, 1945, p. 10.
[9] For example, Chinoy says that Marx "overlooked" other factors of stratification and "seriously neglected the ubiquitous problem of political power." See Ely Chinoy, *Society—An Introduction to Sociology*, New York: Random House, 1962, p. 133.

has had a much larger influence on stratification studies in the United States than has the theory of Marx may be partly because of the fact that Weber, in sharp contrast to Marx, set forth his entire theory in a single essay. But the more important reason lies in the nature of the concepts: those of Weber are narrower and lend themselves more to the technique of modern research.

What Marx assumed—that those who had the economic means also had the power and prestige—Weber made problematical by creating three distinct concepts: class, status, and power. In studying a given stratification system, the sociologist—if he has learned his leason from Weber—will not assume that the distribution of the above three factors coincides. The burden will rest on him to investigate to what degree prestige and power correlate with class.

Weber's concept of class resembles Marx's only in so far as it refers to an economic stratum. But even here it must not be overlooked that for Weber the importance of the economic factor lies elsewhere than in the relation to the means of production. His concept of class is narrower than that of Marx because it denotes only one type of strata in such a system. The other important type, based on prestige rather than economic criteria, is the *status group*.

A substantial part of the reprinted essay deals with status stratification and especially its relation to economic stratification. However, reading Weber critically one may discover that he is quite ambiguous about the latter. On one hand he stresses that status groups and classes are *empirically* distinct from each other, asserting that "'status groups' hinder the strict carrying through of the sheer market principle" (p. 27) and that "Both propertied and propertyless people can belong to the same status group, and frequently they do" (p. 28). But on the other hand, he qualified statements of this kind in a way that makes one conclude that class and status are in fact very much connected. Take, for example, his generalization that "Property as such is not always recognized as a status qualification, but in the long run it is, and with extraordinary regularity" (p. 28). What Weber fails to make explicit in this essay is that one has to separate *analytically* the economic and status factors that *actually* are closely joined together, precisely in order to understand the nature of the connection in a given society at a given time. Perhaps the ambiguity could be traced to Weber's failure to differentiate the competing bases of honor in Europe during the transition from feudalism to capitalism. The rising bourgoisie did claim honor based on sheer economic considerations, but the aristocracy refused at first to recognize it. The latter had a vested interest in honor based on feudal values such as chivalry and lineage. In America, with no background of feudalism, the "self-made man" was accorded honor from the outset.

Weber perhaps expressed the relation between class and status more succintly in his *Religion of India* than in the reprinted essay when he stated that "Social honor [status] can adhere directly to a class situation and it is also, indeed most of the time, determined by the average class situation of the status group members. This, however, is not necessarily the case. Status membership, in turn, influences the class situation in that the style of life required by status groups makes them prefer special kinds of property or gainful pursuits and reject others."[10]

As for power, the reprinted essay begins with an explanation and definition of it, but Weber does not elaborate on the distribution of power. It should be noted,

[10] Max Weber, *Religion of India,* Glencoe, Illinois: Free Press, 1958, p. 39.

however, that his definition lends itself to the concept of a continuum in the distribution of power, contrasting with Marx's dichotomous conception.

Power is the main subject of our third selection from the lengthy work of Vilfredo Pareto (1848–1923), the *Tratado di Sociologia Generale,* which appeared in its English edition under the title *Mind and Society.* The pages reprinted here contain perhaps the best known part of this magnum opus and the thoughts contained in them are often referred to as his *theory of circulation of elites.*

It is particularly important to pay attention to Pareto's concept of *elite,* for this term is common in the current literature and yet is used in a variety of meanings. Although Pareto defines elite in terms of the distribution of certain attributes, he does not operate with this concept in his theory of elite circulation but with the narrower one of *governing elite.* The theory deals with the relation between those who have power, the governing elite, and those who do not, the nonelite.

In this it resembles closely the thoughts of Mosca,[11] another "Machiavellian," as James Burnham labeled him. First of all, the concepts of political or ruling class (Mosca) and governing elite (Pareto) are very similar. Then, too, we encounter in both of them, as in Marx, a dichotomous conception of power. They see power as the universal aspect of stratification: all societies are divided into two strata—the rulers and the ruled. (This similarity between the Machiavellians and Marx are especially noteworthy because they opposed and sharply criticized Marx's social theory).

From a historical perspective, it may be interesting to recall here that the similarities in the theories of Pareto and Mosca gave rise to heated polemics as to who borrowed from whom; they were begun by Mosca himself who first raised the question of indebtedness.[12] By now we know enough about the sociology of knowledge to recognize that similarities do not necessarily imply "borrowing," often a euphemism for stealing. The intellectual climate of a given time focuses the attention of thinkers on certain problems.

In the Marx selection are some comments on what would go today under the heading of social mobility: how individuals rise or sink from one class to another. Such mobility in Marx's theory is connected with social change: with the transformation from feudalism to capitalism or with the development of capitalism. Pareto's contribution is toward the understanding of social mobility as a universal phenomenon, present in all societies to a larger or smaller extent.

He begins the exposition of his theory with the empirical generalization—the truth of which has withstood the test of time—that no stratification system, even that of caste, is completely closed. Systems do, however, differ in amount of inter-strata mobility. In addition, he makes the important distinction between the normative and factual state (p. 37), which could serve us well later when we come to the readings about various types of stratification systems (Part II of this book). To rephrase Pareto, the norms of a given society may preclude mobility and yet mobility will take place (caste society). Conversely, the norms may postulate unlimited mobility (capitalist society) while actually the amount is limited.

Here too we find a similarity to Mosca. Mosca's contention, translated into current sociological terms, is that society makes use of both ascribed and achieved status, but that societies differ in the degree in which they rely on one or the other.

[11] Gaetano Mosca, *The Ruling Class,* New York: McGraw-Hill Book Company, 1939.
[12] Arthur Livingston, "Introduction," *Ibid.,* pp. ix–xvi.

He declares that in every society there are two tendencies in conflict with each other. One he calls democratic, the tendency toward an open structure that allows able people to rise. The other is aristocratic, the tendency toward closure: those on top set up barriers for those who want to climb.[13]

In criticizing Pareto's theory of elite circulation, Bottomore asserts, and we could take issue with this, that its analytical quality is less impressive than the glamour of the style. He considers it a major difficulty of this theory that it does not differentiate clearly and precisely between the process in which *individuals* circulate between the elite and nonelite and the process in which *one governing elite* is replaced by another.[14]

Although Pareto does refer to both processes by the same designation—circulation of elites—the preceding criticism may not be entirely valid. Pareto makes clear that he is primarily interested in the first process. Furthermore, he shows that the second process is dependent on the first (p. 38). A governing elite "crashes to ruin" when upward movement into it and downward movement out of it are severely curtailed. The reason is that it retains those members who are not capable of exercising power (no downward movement out of the elite) and fails to absorb capable nonelite individuals who eventually bring about its downfall and replace it (no upward movement into the elite). Pareto also points to force as an important element in the change of governing elites. The replacement of such an elite, he maintains, may be the result of its failure to use force.

Again one might point to the resemblence between Pareto's and Mosca's thought. Mosca also speaks of the disastrous consequences for the ruling classes that result from their being too closed to individuals from below. For when they are open to such individuals they ". . . are continually replenished through the admission of new elements who have inborn talents for leadership and will to lead". And this ". . . prevents that exhaustion of aristocracies of birth which usually paves the way for great social cataclysms."[15]

Joseph Schumpeter (1883–1950) also sees the aforenamed processes as connected, but analytically he differentiates one from the other more sharply than does Pareto. Thus his essay "Social Classes in an Ethnically Homogenous Environment," contains two separate sections: one dealing with the "Movement Across Class Lines,"[16] and the other—Part 2 of the Schumpeter selection—with the "Rise and Fall of Whole Classes."

First we should note that Schumpeter uses the term *classes* in the broad sense of strata, rather than in the Weberian sense. Hence he speaks of classes in feudal as well as capitalist society. His theory of the rise and fall of strata, as well as their relative rank, is a functional one. He explains the connection between the rank of a stratum, which he calls class, and its function in society. Its rank depends on the significance that *is attributed* to that function and how successfully it performs that function. Every class that has once enjoyed an elevated position, Schumpeter tells us, is greatly aided in seizing new functions "because the sources and gains of its prior function survive for some time."

Although Schumpeter's theory is a functional one, it does not suffer in my estimation from the shortcoming of current functional theories which cannot be

[13] *Ibid.*, pp. 56–68; 116–119; 405–420.
[14] T. B. Bottomore, *Elites and Society*, New York: Basic Books, 1964, pp. 42–43.
[15] Mosca, *op. cit.*, p. 416.
[16] Joseph Schumpeter, *Imperialism and Social Classes*, New York: Meridian Books, 1955, pp. 124–134.

used to explain change adequately. The Schumpeter theory of rise and fall of classes is precisely a theory of how stratification systems change and become replaced.

The historical case Schumpeter uses in detail to illustrate his theory is that of the rise and fall of the feudal aristocracy in Europe and more specifically in Germany. It would serve us well to acquaint ourselves with this material because feudalism is included in the next part of our book, Major Types of Stratification Systems. And in proceeding to that part we will also benefit from Schumpeter's historical perspective. He demonstrates convincingly that a stratification system at a given time cannot be understood without taking into account the system that preceded it.

# ON CLASS

## *Karl Marx*

### I.

The owners merely of labour-power, owners of capital, and landowners, whose respective sources of income are wages, profit, and ground-rent, in other words, wage-labourers, capitalists, and land-owners constitute the three big classes of modern society based upon the capitalist mode of production.

In England, modern society is indisputably most highly and classically developed in economic structure. Nevertheless, even here the stratification of classes does not appear in its pure form. Middle and intermediate strata even here obliterate lines of demarcation everywhere (although incomparably less in rural districts than in the cities). However, this is immaterial for our analysis. We have seen that the continual tendency and law of development of the capitalist mode of production is more and more to divorce the means of production from labour, and more and more to concentrate the scattered means of production into large groups, thereby transforming labour into wage-labour and the means of production into capital. And to this tendency, on the other hand, corresponds the independent separation of landed property from capital and labour,[1] or the transformation of all landed property into the form of landed property corresponding to the capitalist mode of production.

The first question to be answered is this: What constitutes a class?—and the reply to this follows naturally from the reply to another question, namely: What makes wage-labourers, capitalists, and landlords constitute the three great social classes?

At first glance—the identity of revenues and sources of revenue. There are three great social groups whose members, the individuals forming them, live on wages, profit, and ground-rent respectively, on the realization of their labour-power, their capital, and their landed property.

However, from this standpoint, physicians and officials, e.g., would also constitute two classes, for they belong to two distinct social groups, the members of each of these groups receiving their revenue from one and the same source. The same would also be true of the infinite fragmentation of interest and rank into which the division of social labour splits labourers as well as capitalists and landlords—the latter, e.g., into owners of vineyards, farm owners, owners of forests, mine owners, and owners of fisheries.

[Here the manuscript breaks off.]

### II.

#### BOURGEOIS AND PROLETARIANS[2]

The history of all hitherto existing society[3] is the history of class struggles.

Section I is the unfinished last chapter from *Capital: A Critique of Political Economy*. Section II consists of pages from Part I of the *Manifesto of the Communist Party* by Karl Marx and Friedrich Engels. Section III is from Karl Marx and Friedrich Engels, *The German Ideology*. Section IV is from *The Poverty of Philosophy*.

[1] F. List remarks correctly: "The prevalence of a self-sufficient economy on large estates demonstrates solely the lack of civilization, means of communication, domestic trades and wealthy cities. It is to be encountered, therefore, throughout Russia, Poland, Hungary and Mecklenburg. Formerly, it was also prevalent in England; with the advance of trades and commerce, however, this was replaced by the breaking up into middle estates and the leasing of land." (*Die Ackerverfassung, die Zwergwirtschaft und die Auswanderung*, 1842, p. 10.)

[2] By bourgeoisie is meant the class of modern capitalists, owners of the means of social production and employers of wage-labour; by proletariat, the class of modern wage-labourers who, having no means of production of their own, are reduced to selling their labour power in order to live.

[3] That is, all *written* history. In 1837, the pre-history of society, the social organisation existing previous to recorded history, was all but unknown. Since then Haxthausen [August von, 1792-1866] discovered common ownership of land in Russia, Maurer [Georg Ludwig von] proved it to be the social foundation from which all Teutonic races started in history, and, by and by, village communities were found to be, or to have been, the primitive form of society everywhere from India to Ireland. The inner organisation of this primitive communistic society was laid bare, in its typical form, by Morgan's [Lewis H., 1818-1881] crowning discovery of the true nature of the *gens* and its relation to the *tribe*. With the dissolution of these primæval communities, society begins to be differentiated into separate and finally antagonistic classes. I have attempted to retrace this process of dissolution in *The Origin of the Family, Private Property and the State.*

Freeman and slave, patrician and plebeian, lord and serf, guild-master[4] and journeyman, in a word, oppressor and oppressed, stood in constant opposition to one another, carried on an uninterrupted, now hidden, now open fight, a fight that each time ended, either in a revolutionary reconstitution of society at large, or in the common ruin of the contending classes.

In the earlier epochs of history, we find almost everywhere a complicated arrangement of society into various orders, a manifold gradation of social rank. In ancient Rome we have patricians, knights, plebeians, slaves; in the Middle Ages, feudal lords, vassals, guild-masters, journeymen, apprentices, serfs; in almost all of these classes, again, subordinate gradations.

The modern bourgeois society that has sprouted from the ruins of feudal society, has not done away with class antagonisms. It has but established new classes, new conditions of oppression, new forms of struggle in place of the old ones.

Our epoch, the epoch of the bourgeoisie, possesses, however, this distinctive feature: It has simplified the class antagonisms. Society as a whole is more and more splitting up into two great hostile camps, into two great classes directly facing each other—bourgeoisie and proletariat.

From the serfs of the Middle Ages sprang the chartered burghers of the earliest towns. From these burgesses the first elements of the bourgeoisie were developed.

The discovery of America, the rounding of the Cape, opened up fresh ground for the rising bourgeoisie. The East-Indian and Chinese markets, the colonisation of America, trade with the colonies, the increase in the means of exchange and in commodities generally, gave to commerce, to navigation, to industry, an impulse never before known, and thereby, to the revolutionary element in the tottering feudal society, a rapid development.

The feudal system of industry, in which industrial production was monopolised by closed guilds, now no longer sufficed for the growing wants of the new markets. The manufacturing system took its place. The guild-masters were pushed aside by the manufacturing middle class; division of labour between the different corporate guilds vanished in the face of division of labour in each single workshop.

Meantime the markets kept ever growing, the demand ever rising. Even manufacture no longer sufficed. Thereupon, steam and machinery revolutionised industrial production. The place of manufacture was taken by the giant, modern industry, the place of the industrial middle class, by industrial millionaires—the leaders of whole industrial armies, the modern bourgeois.

Modern industry has established the world market, for which the discovery of America paved the way. This market has given an immense development to commerce, to navigation, to communication by land. This development has, in its turn, reacted on the extension of industry; and in proportion as industry, commerce, navigation, railways extended, in the same proportion the bourgeoisie developed, increased its capital, and pushed into the background every class handed down from the Middle Ages.

We see, therefore, how the modern bourgeoisie is itself the product of a long course of development, of a series of revolutions in the modes of production and of exchange.

Each step in the development of the bourgeoisie was accompanied by a corresponding political advance of that class. An oppressed class under the sway of the feudal nobility, it became an armed and self-governing association in the mediæval commune;[5] here independent urban republic (as in Italy and Germany), there taxable "third estate" of the monarchy (as in France); afterwards, in the period of manufacture proper, serving either the semi-feudal or the absolute monarchy as a counterpoise against the nobility, and, in fact, corner-stone of the great monarchies in

[4] Guild-master, that is a full member of a guild, a master within, not a head of a guild.

[5] "Commune" was the name taken in France by the nascent towns even before they had conquered from their feudal lords and masters local self-government and political rights as the "Third Estate." Generally speaking, for the economic development of the bourgeoisie, England is here taken as the typical country, for its political development, France.

general—the bourgeoisie has at last, since the establishment of modern industry and of the world market, conquered for itself, in the modern representative state, exclusive political sway. The executive of the modern state is but a committee for managing the common affairs of the whole bourgeoisie.

The bourgeoisie has played a most revolutionary rôle in history.

The bourgeoisie, wherever it has got the upper hand, has put an end to all feudal, patriarchal, idyllic relations. It has pitilessly torn asunder the motley feudal ties that bound man to his "natural superiors," and has left no other bond between man and man than naked self-interest, than callous "cash payment." It has drowned the most heavenly ecstasies of religious fervour, of chivalrous enthusiasm, of philistine sentimentalism, in the icy water of egotistical calculation. It has resolved personal worth into exchange value, and in place of the numberless indefeasible chartered freedoms, has set up that single, unconscionable freedom—Free Trade. In one word, for exploitation, veiled by religious and political illusions, it has substituted naked, shameless, direct, brutal exploitation.

The bourgeoisie has stripped of its halo every occupation hitherto honoured and looked up to with reverent awe. It has converted the physician, the lawyer, the priest, the poet, the man of science, into its paid wage-labourers.

The bourgeoisie has torn away from the family its sentimental veil, and has reduced the family relation to a mere money relation.

The bourgeoisie has disclosed how it came to pass that the brutal display of vigour in the Middle Ages, which reactionaries so much admire, found its fitting complement in the most slothful indolence. It has been the first to show what man's activity can bring about. It has accomplished wonders far surpassing Egyptian pyramids, Roman aqueducts, and Gothic cathedrals; it has conducted expeditions that put in the shade all former migrations of nations and crusades.

The bourgeoisie cannot exist without constantly revolutionising the instruments of production, and thereby the relations of production, and with them the whole relations of society. Conservation of the old modes of production in unaltered form, was, on the contrary, the first condition of existence for all earlier industrial classes. Constant revolutionising of production, uninterrupted disturbance of all social conditions, everlasting uncertainty and agitation distinguish the bourgeois epoch from all earlier ones. All fixed, fast-frozen relations, with their train of ancient and venerable prejudices and opinions, are swept away, all new-formed ones become antiquated before they can ossify. All that is solid melts into air, all that is holy is profaned, and man is at last compelled to face with sober senses his real conditions of life and his relations with his kind.

The need of a constantly expanding market for its products chases the bourgeoisie over the whole surface of the globe. It must nestle everywhere, settle everywhere, establish connections everywhere.

The bourgeoisie has through its exploitation of the world market given a cosmopolitan character to production and consumption in every country. To the great chagrin of reactionaries, it has drawn from under the feet of industry the national ground on which it stood. All old-established national industries have been destroyed or are daily being destroyed. They are dislodged by new industries, whose introduction becomes a life and death question for all civilised nations, by industries that no longer work up indigenous raw material, but raw material drawn from the remotest zones; industries whose products are consumed, not only at home, but in every quarter of the globe. In place of the old wants, satisfied by the production of the country, we find new wants, requiring for their satisfaction the products of distant lands and climes. In place of the old local and national seclusion and self-sufficiency, we have intercourse in every direction, universal inter-dependence of nations. And as in material, so also in intellectual production. The intellectual creations of individual nations become common property. National one-sidedness and narrow-mindedness become more and more impossible, and from the numerous national and local literatures there arises a world literature.

The bourgeoisie, by the rapid improvement of all instruments of production, by the immensely facilitated means of communication, draws all nations, even the most barbarian, into civilisation. The cheap prices of its commodities are the heavy artillery with which it batters down all Chinese walls, with which it forces the barbarians' intensely obstinate hatred of foreigners to capitulate. It compels all nations, on pain of extinction to adopt the bourgeois mode of production; it compels them to introduce what it calls civilisation into their midst, *i.e.*, to become bourgeois themselves. In a word, it creates a world after its own image.

The bourgeoisie has subjected the country to the rule of the towns. It has created enormous cities, has greatly increased the urban population as compared with the rural, and has thus rescued a considerable part of the population from the idiocy of rural life. Just as it has made the country dependent on the towns, so it has made barbarian and semi-barbarian countries dependent on the civilised ones, nations of peasants on nations of bourgeois, the East on the West.

More and more the bourgeoisie keeps doing away with the scattered state of the population, of the means of production, and of property. It has agglomerated population, centralised means of production, and has concentrated property in a few hands. The necessary consequence of this was political centralisation. Independent, or but loosely connected provinces, with separate interests, laws, governments and systems of taxation, became lumped together into one nation, with one government, one code of laws, one national class interest, one frontier and one customs tariff.

The bourgeoisie, during its rule of scarce one hundred years, has created more massive and more colossal productive forces than have all preceding generations together. Subjection of nature's forces to man, machinery, application of chemistry to industry and agriculture, steam-navigation, railways, electric telegraphs, clearing of whole continents for cultivation, canalisation of rivers, whole populations conjured out of the ground—what earlier century had even a presentiment that such productive forces slumbered in the lap of social labour?

We see then that the means of production and of exchange, which served as the foundation for the growth of the bourgeoisie were generated in feudal society. At a certain stage in the development of these means of production and of exchange, the conditions under which feudal society produced and exchanged, the feudal organisation of agriculture and manufacturing industry, in a word, the feudal relations of property became no longer compatible with the already developed productive forces; they became so many fetters. They had to be burst asunder; they were burst asunder.

Into their place stepped free competition, accompanied by a social and political constitution adapted to it, and by the economic and political sway of the bourgeois class.

A similar movement is going on before our own eyes. Modern bourgeois society with its relations of production, of exchange and of property, a society that has conjured up such gigantic means of production and of exchange, is like the sorcerer who is no longer able to control the powers of the nether world whom he has called up by his spells. For many a decade past the history of industry and commerce is but the history of the revolt of modern productive forces against modern conditions of production, against the property relations that are the conditions for the existence of the bourgeoisie and of its rule. It is enough to mention the commercial crises that by their periodical return put the existence of the entire bourgeois society on trial, each time more threateningly. In these crises a great part not only of the existing products, but also of the previously created productive forces, are periodically destroyed. In these crises there breaks out an epidemic that, in all earlier epochs, would have seemed an absurdity—the epidemic of overproduction. Society suddenly finds itself put back into a state of momentary barbarism; it appears as if a famine, a universal war of devastation had cut off the supply of every means of subsistence; industry and commerce seem to be destroyed. And why? Because there is too much civilisation, too much means of subsistence, too much industry, too much commerce. The productive forces at the disposal of society no longer tend to further the development of the conditions of bourgeois property; on the contrary, they have become too powerful for these conditions, by which they are fettered, and no sooner do they overcome these fetters than they bring disorder into the whole of bourgeois society, endanger the existence of bourgeois property. The conditions of bourgeois society are too narrow to comprise the wealth created by them. And how does the bourgeoisie get over these crises? On the one hand by enforced destruction of a mass of productive forces; on the other, by the conquest of new markets, and by the more thorough exploitation of the old ones. That is to say, by paving the way for more extensive and more destructive crises, and by diminishing the means whereby crises are prevented.

The weapons with which the bourgeoisie felled feudalism to the ground are now turned against the bourgeoisie itself.

But not only has the bourgeoisie forged the weapons that bring death to itself; it has also called into existence the men who are to wield those weapons—the modern working class—the proletarians.

In proportion as the bourgeoisie, *i.e.*, capital, is developed, in the same proportion is the probetariat, the modern working class, developed—a class of labourers, who live only so long as they find work, and who find work only so long as their labour increases capital. These labourers, who must sell themselves piecemeal, are a commodity, like every other article of commerce, and are consequently exposed to all the vicissitudes of competition, to all the fluctuations of the market.

Owing to the extensive use of machinery and to division of labour, the work of the proletarians has lost all individual character, and, consequently, all charm for the workman. He becomes an appendage of the machine, and it is only the most simple, most montonous, and most easily acquired knack, that is required of him. Hence, the cost of production of a workman is restricted, almost entirely, to the means of subsistence that he requires for his maintenance, and for the propagation of his race. But the price of a commodity, and therefore also of labour, is equal to its cost of production. In proportion, therefore, as the repulsiveness of the work increases, the wage decreases. Nay more, in proportion as the use of machinery and division of labour increases, in the same proportion the burden of toil also increases, whether by prolongation of the working hours, by increase of the work exacted in a given time, or by increased speed of the machinery, etc.

Modern industry has converted the little workshop of the patriarchal master into the great factory of the industrial capitalist. Masses of labourers, crowded into the factory, are organised like soldiers. As privates of the industrial army they are placed under the command of a perfect hierarchy of officers and sergeants. Not only are they slaves of the bourgeois class, and of the bourgeois state; they are daily and hourly enslaved by the machine, by the overlooker, and, above all, by the individual bourgeois manufacturer himself. The more openly this despotism proclaims gain to be its end and aim, the more petty, the more hateful and the more embittering it is.

The less the skill and exertion of strength implied in manual labour, in other words, the more modern industry develops, the more is the labour of men superseded by that of women. Differences of age and sex have no longer any distinctive social validity for the working class. All are instruments of labour, more or less expensive to use, according to their age and sex.

No sooner has the labourer received his wages in cash, for the moment escaping exploitation by the manufacturer, than he is set upon by the other portions of the bourgeoisie, the landlord, the shopkeeper, the pawnbroker, etc.

The lower strata of the middle class—the small tradespeople, shopkeepers, and retired tradesmen generally, the handicraftsmen and peasants—all these sink gradually into the proletariat, partly because their diminutive capital does not suffice for the scale on which modern industry is carried on, and is swamped in the competition with the large capitalists, partly because their specialised skill is rendered worthless by new methods of production. Thus the proletariat is recruited from all classes of the population.

The proletariat goes through various

stages of development. With its birth begins its struggle with the bourgeoisie. At first the contest is carried on by individual labourers, then by the work people of a factory, then by the operatives of one trade, in one locality against the individual bourgeois who directly exploits them. They direct their attacks not against the bourgeois conditions of production, but against the instruments of production themselves; they destroy imported wares that compete with their labour, they smash machinery to pieces, they set factories ablaze, they seek to restore by force this vanished status of the workman of the Middle Ages.

At this stage the labourers still form an incoherent mass scattered over the whole country, and broken up by their mutual competition. If anywhere they unite to form more compact bodies, this is not yet the consequence of their own active union, but of the union of the bourgeoisie, which class, in order to attain its own political ends, is compelled to set the whole proletariat in motion, and is moreover still able to do so for a time. At this stage, therefore, the proletarians do not fight their enemies, but the enemies of their enemies, the remnants of absolute monarchy, the landowners, the non-industrial bourgeois, the petty bourgeoisie. Thus the whole historical movement is concentrated in the hands of the bourgeoisie; every victory so obtained is a victory for the bourgeoisie.

But with the development of industry the proletariat not only increases in number; it becomes concentrated in greater masses, its strength grows, and it feels that strength more. The various interests and conditions of life within the ranks of the proletariat are more and more equalised, in proportion as machinery obliterates all distinctions of labour and nearly everywhere reduces wages to the same low level. The growing competition among the bourgeois, and the resulting commercial crises, make the wages of the workers ever more fluctuating. The unceasing improvement of machinery, ever more rapidly developing, makes their livelihood more and more precarious; the collisions between individual workmen and individual bourgeois take more and more the character of collisions between two classes. Thereupon the workers begin to form combinations (trade unions) against the bourgeoisie; they club together in order to keep up the rate of wages; they found permanent associations in order to make provision beforehand for these occasional revolts. Here and there the contest breaks out into riots.

Now and then the workers are victorious, but only for a time. The real fruit of their battles lies, not in the immediate result, but in the ever expanding union of the workers. This union is furthered by the improved means of communication which are created by modern industry, and which place the workers of different localities in contact with one another. It was just this contact that was needed to centralise the numerous local struggles, all of the same character, into one national struggle between classes. But every class struggle is a political struggle. And that union, to attain which the burghers of the Middle Ages, with their miserable highways, required centuries, the modern proletarians, thanks to railways, achieve in a few years.

This organisation of the proletarians into a class, and consequently into a political party, is continually being upset again by the competition between the workers themselves. But it ever rises up again, stronger, firmer, mightier. It compels legislative recognition of particular interests of the workers, by taking advantage of the divisions among the bourgeoisie itself. Thus the ten-hour bill in England was carried.

Altogether, collisions between the classes of the old society further the course of development of the proletariat in many ways. The bourgeoisie finds itself involved in a constant battle. At first with the aristocracy; later on, with those portions of the bourgeoisie itself whose interests have become antagonistic to the progress of industry at all times with the bourgeoisie of foreign countries. In all these battles it sees itself compelled to appeal to the proletariat, to ask for its help, and thus, to drag it into the political arena. The bourgeoisie itself, therefore, supplies the proletariat with its own elements of political and general education, in other words, it furnishes the proletariat with weapons for fighting the bourgeoisie.

Further, as we have already seen, entire

sections of the ruling classes are, by the advance of industry, precipitated into the proletariat, or are at least threatened in their conditions of existence. These also supply the proletariat with fresh elements of enlightenment and progress.

Finally, in times when the class struggle nears the decisive hour, the process of dissolution going on within the ruling class, in fact within the whole range of old society, assumes such a violent, glaring character, that a small section of the ruling class cuts itself adrift, and joins the revolutionary class, the class that holds the future in its hands. Just as, therefore, at an earlier period, a section of the nobility went over to the bourgeoisie, so now a portion of the bourgeoisie goes over to the proletariat, and in particular, a portion of the bourgeois ideologists, who have raised themselves to the level of comprehending theoretically the historical movement as a whole.

Of all the classes that stand face to face with the bourgeoisie today, the proletariat alone is a really revolutionary class. The other classes decay and finally disappear in the face of modern industry; the proletariat is its special and essential product.

The lower middle class, the small manufacturer, the shopkeeper, the artisan, the peasant, all these fight against the bourgeoisie, to save from extinction their existence as fractions of the middle class. They are therefore not revolutionary, but conservative. Nay more, they are reactionary, for they try to roll back the wheel of history. If by chance they are revolutionary, they are so only in view of their impending transfer into the proletariat; they thus defend not their present, but their future interests; they desert their own standpoint to adopt that of the proletariat.

The "dangerous class," the social scum (*Lumpenproletariat*), that passively rotting mass thrown off by the lowest layers of old society, may, here and there, be swept into the movement by a proletarian revolution; its conditions of life, however, prepare it far more for the part of a bribed tool of reactionary intrigue.

The social conditions of the old society no longer exist for the proletariat. The proletarian is without property; his relation to his wife and children has no longer anything in common with bourgeois family relations; modern industrial labour, modern subjection to capital, the same in England as in France, in America as in Germany, has stripped him of every trace of national character. Law, morality, religion, are to him so many bourgeois prejudices, behind which lurk in ambush just as many bourgeois interests.

All the preceding classes that got the upper hand, sought to fortify their already acquired status by subjecting society at large to their conditions of appropriation. The proletarians cannot become masters of the productive forces of society, except by abolishing their own previous mode of appropriation, and thereby also every other previous mode of appropriation. They have nothing of their own to secure and to fortify; their mission is to destroy all previous securities for, and insurance of, individual property.

All previous historical movements were movements of minorities, or in the interest of minorities. The proletarian movement is the self-conscious, independent movement of the immense majority, in the interest of the immense majority. The proletariat, the lowest stratum of our present society, cannot stir, cannot raise itself up, without the whole superincumbent strata of official society being sprung into the air.

Though not in substance, yet in form, the struggle of the proletariat with the bourgeoisie is at first a national struggle. The proletariat of each country must, of course, first of all settle matters with its own bourgeoisie.

In depicting the most general phases of the development of the proletariat, we traced the more or less veiled civil war, raging within existing society, up to the point where that war breaks out into open revolution, and where the violent overthrow of the bourgeoisie lays the foundation for the sway of the proletariat.

Hitherto, every form of society has been based, as we have already seen, on the antagonism of oppressing and oppressed classes. But in order to oppress a class, certain conditions must be assured to it under which it can, at least, continue its slavish existence. The serf, in the period of serfdom, raised himself to membership in the commune, just as the petty bourgeois under the yoke of feudal absolutism, managed to develop into a bourgeois. The modern labourer, on the contrary, instead of rising with the progress of industry, sinks deeper and deeper below the conditions of existence of his own class. He becomes a pauper, and pauperism develops more rapidly than population and wealth. And here it becomes evident, that the bourgeoisie is unfit any longer to be the ruling class in society, and to impose its conditions of existence upon society as an over-riding law. It is unfit to rule because it is incompetent to assure an existence to its slave within his slavery, because it cannot help letting him sink into such a state, that it has to feed him, instead of being fed by him. Society can no longer live under this bourgeoisie, in other words, its existence is no longer compatible with society.

The essential condition for the existence and sway of the bourgeois class, is the formation and augmentation of capital; the condition for capital is wage-labour. Wage-labour rests exclusively on competition between the labourers. The advance of industry, whose involuntary promoter is the bourgeoisie, replaces the isolation of the labourers, due to competition, by their revolutionary combination, due to association. The development of modern industry, therefore, cuts from under its feet the very foundation on which the bourgeoisie produces and appropriates products. What the bourgeoisie therefore produces, above all, are its own grave-diggers. Its fall and the victory of the proletariat are equally inevitable.

. . . . . . . . . . . . . . . . . . . . . . . . . . . . . . . . . . . .

III.

The ideas of the ruling class are in every epoch the ruling ideas: i.e. the class, which is the ruling material force of society, is at the same time its ruling intellectual force. The class which has the means of material production at its disposal, has control at the same time over the means of mental production, so that thereby, generally speaking, the ideas of those who lack the means of mental production are subject to it. The ruling ideas are nothing more than the ideal expression of the dominant material relationships, the dominant material relationships grasped as ideas; hence of the relationships which make the one class the ruling one, therefore the ideas of its dominance. The individuals composing the ruling class possess among other things consciousness, and therefore think. In so far, therefore, as they rule as a class and determine the extent and compass of an epoch, it is self-evident that they do this in their whole range, hence among other things rule also as thinkers, as producers of ideas, and regulate the production and distribution of the ideas of their age: thus their ideas are the ruling ideas of the epoch. For instance, in an age and in a country where royal power, aristocracy and bourgeoisie are contending for mastery and where, therefore, mastery is shared, the doctrine of the separation of powers proves to be the dominant idea and is expressed as an "eternal law." The division of labour, which we saw above as one of the chief forces of history up till now, manifests itself also in the ruling class as the division of mental and material labour, so that inside this class one part appears as the thinkers of the class (its active, conceptive ideologists, who make the perfecting of the illusion of the class about itself their chief source of livelihood), while the others' attitude to these ideas and illusions is more passive and receptive, because they are in reality the active members of this class and have less time to make up illusions and ideas about themselves. Within this class this cleavage can even develop into a certain opposition and hostility between the two parts, which, however, in the case of a practical collision, in which the class itself is endangered, automatically comes to nothing, in which case there also vanishes the semblance that the ruling ideas were not the ideas of the ruling class and had a power distinct from the power of this class. The existence of revolutionary ideas in a particular period presupposes the existence of a revolutionary class; about the premises for the latter sufficient has already been said above.

If now in considering the course of history we detach the ideas of the ruling class from the ruling class itself and attribute to them an independent existence, if we confine ourselves to saying that these or those ideas were dominant, without bothering ourselves about the conditions of production and the producers of these ideas, if we then ignore the individuals and world conditions which are the source of the ideas, we can say, for instance, that during the time that the aristocracy was dominant, the concepts honour, loyalty, etc., were dominant, during the dominance of the bourgeoisie the concepts freedom, equality, etc. The ruling class itself on the whole imagines this to be so. This conception of history, which is common to all historians, particularly since the eighteenth century, will necessarily come up against the phenomenon that increasingly abstract ideas hold sway, i.e. ideas which increasingly take on the form of universality. For each new class which puts itself in the place of one ruling before it, is compelled, merely in order to carry through its aim, to represent its interest as the common interest of all the members of society, put in an ideal form; it will give its ideas the form of universality, and represent them as the only rational, universally valid ones. The class making a revolution appears from the very start, merely because it is opposed to a *class*, not as a class but as the representative of the whole of society; it appears as the whole mass of society confronting the one ruling class. It can do this because, to start with, its interest really is more connected with the common interest of all other non-ruling classes, because under the pressure of conditions its interest has not yet been able to develop as the particular interest of a particular class. Its victory, therefore, benefits also many individuals of the other classes which are not winning a dominant position, but only in so far as it now puts these individuals in a position to raise themselves into the ruling class. When the French bourgeoisie overthrew the power of the aristocracy, it thereby made it possible for many proletarians to raise themselves above the proletariat, but only in so far as they became bourgeois. Every new class, therefore, achieves its hegemony only on a broader basis than that of the class ruling previously, in return for which the opposition of the non-ruling class against the new ruling class later develops all the more sharply and profoundly. Both these things determine the fact that the struggle to be waged against this new ruling class, in its turn, aims at a more decided and radical negation of the previous conditions of society than could all previous classes which sought to rule.

This whole semblance, that the rule of a certain class is only the rule of certain ideas, comes to a natural end, of course, as soon as society ceases at last to be organized in the form of class-rule, that is to say as soon as it is no longer necessary to represent a particular interest as general or "the general interest" as ruling.

. . . . . . . . . . . . . . . . . . . . . . . . . . . . . . . . . . .

## IV.

Feudalism also had its proletariat—serfdom, which contained all the germs of the bourgeoisie. Feudal production also had two antagonistic elements which are likewise designated by the name of the *good side* and the *bad side* of feudalism, irrespective of the fact that it is always the bad side that in the end triumphs over the good side. It is the bad side that produces the movement which makes history, by providing a struggle. If, during the epoch of the domination of feudalism, the economists, enthusiastic over the knightly virtues, the beautiful harmony between rights and duties, the patriarchal life of the towns, the prosperous condition of domestic industry in the countryside, the development of industry organized into corporations, guilds and fraternities, in short, everything that constitutes the good side of feudalism, had set themselves the problem of eliminating everything that cast a shadow on this picture—serfdom, privileges, anarchy—what would have happened? All the elements which called forth the struggle would have been destroyed, and the development of the bourgeoisie nipped in the bud. One would have set oneself the absurd problem of eliminating history.

After the triumph of the bourgeoisie there was no longer any question of the good or the bad side of feudalism. The bourgeoisie took possession of the productive forces it had developed under feudalism. All the old economic forms, the corresponding civil relations, the political state which was the official expression of the old civil society, were smashed.

Thus feudal production, to be judged properly, must be considered as a mode of production founded on antagonism. It must be shown how wealth was produced within this antagonism, how the productive forces were developed at the same time as class antagonisms, how one of the classes, the bad side, the drawback of society, went on growing until the material conditions for its emancipation had attained full maturity. Is not this as good as saying that the mode of production, the relations in which productive forces are developed, are anything but eternal laws, but that they correspond to a definite development of men and of their productive forces, and that a change in men's productive forces necessarily brings about a change in their relations of production? As the main thing is not to be deprived of the fruits of civilization, of the acquired productive forces, the traditional forms in which they were produced must be smashed. From this moment the revolutionary class becomes conservative.

The bourgeoisie begins with a proletariat which is itself a relic of the proletariat of feudal times. In the course of its historical development, the bourgeoisie necessarily develops its antagonistic character, which at first is more or less disguised, existing only in a latent state. As the bourgeoisie develops, there develops in its bosom a new proletariat, a modern proletariat; there develops a struggle between the proletarian class and the bourgeois class, a struggle which, before being felt, perceived, appreciated, understood, avowed and proclaimed aloud by both sides, expresses itself, to start with, merely in partial and momentary conflicts, in subversive acts. On the other hand, if all the members of the modern bourgeoisie have the same interests inasmuch as they form a class as against another class; they have opposite, antagonistic interests inasmuch as they stand face to face with one another. This opposition of interests results from the economic conditions of their bourgeois life. From day to day it thus becomes clearer that the production relations in which the bourgeoisie moves have not a simple, uniform character, but a dual character; that in the selfsame relations in which wealth is produced, poverty is produced also; that in the selfsame relations in which there is a development of the productive forces, there is also a force producing repression; that these relations produce *bourgeois wealth*, i.e., the wealth of the bourgeois class, only by continually annihilating the wealth of the individual members of this class and by producing an evergrowing proletariat.

. . . . . . . . . . . . . . . . . . . . . . . . . . . . . . . . .

Economic conditions had first transformed the mass of the people of the country into workers. The combination of capital has created for this mass a common situation, common interests. *This mass is thus already a class as against capital, but not yet for itself.* [Italics supplied.] In the struggle, of which we have noted only a few phases, this mass becomes united, and constitutes itself as a *class for itself.* [Italics supplied][6] The interests it defends become class interests. But the struggle of class against class is a political struggle.

In the bourgeoisie we have two phases to distinguish: that in which it constituted itself as a class under the regime of feudalism and absolute monarchy, and that in which, already constituted as a class, it overthrew feudalism and monarchy to make society into a bourgeois society. The first of these phases was the longer and necessitated the greater efforts. This too began by partial combinations against the feudal lords.

Much research has been carried out to trace the different historical phases that the bourgeoisie has passed through, from the commune up to its constitution as a class.

[6] The two last sentences are often cited and here they are in the German original: "So ist die Masse bereits eine Klasse gegenüber dem Kapital aber noch nicht für sich selbst. In dem Kampf . . . findet sich diese Masse zusammen, konstituiert sie sich als Klasse für sich selbst." *Das Elend der Philosophie* in *Karl Marx, Friedrich Engels Werke,* Berlin: Dietz Verlag, 1959, 4, p. 181. (C. S. H.)

But when it is a question of making a precise study of strikes, combinations[7] and other forms in which the proletarians carry out before our eyes their organization as a class, some are seized with real fear and others display a *transcendental* disdain.

An oppressed class is the vital condition for every society founded on the antagonism of classes. The emancipation of the oppressed class thus implies necessarily the creation of a new society. For the oppressed class to be able to emancipate itself it is necessary that the productive powers already acquired and the existing social relations should no longer be capable of existing side by side. Of all the instruments of production, the greatest productive power is the revolutionary class itself. The organization of revolutionary elements as a class supposes the existence of all the productive forces which could be engendered in the bosom of the old society.

Does this mean that after the fall of the old society there will be a new class domination culminating in a new political power? No.

The condition for the emancipation of the working class is the abolition of every class, just as the condition for the liberation of the third estate, of the bourgeois order, was the abolition of all estates[8] and all orders.

The working class, in the course of its development, will substitute for the old civil society an association which will exclude classes and their antagonism, and there will be no more political power properly so-called, since political power is precisely the official expression of antagonism in civil society.

. . . . . . . . . . . . . . . . . . . . . . . . . . . . . . . . . . .

[7] Trade Unions. (C. S. H.)

[8] Estates here in the historical sense of the estates of feudalism, estates with definite and limited privileges. The revolution of the bourgeoisie abolished the estates and their privileges. Bourgeois society knows only *classes*. It was, therefore, absolutely in contradiction with history to describe the proletariat as the "fourth estate." [*Note by F. Engels to the German edition,* 1885].

# CLASS, STATUS, PARTY

## *Max Weber*

### ECONOMICALLY DETERMINED POWER AND THE SOCIAL ORDER

Law exists when there is a probability that an order will be upheld by a specific staff of men who will use physical or psychical compulsion with the intention of obtaining conformity with the order, or of inflicting sanctions for infringement of it.[1] The structure of every legal order directly influences the distribution of power, economic or otherwise, within its respective community. This is true of all legal orders and not only that of the state. In general, we understand by "power" the chance of a man or of a number of men to realize their own will in a communal action even against the resistance of others who are not participating in the action.

"Economically conditioned" power is not, of course, identical with "power" as such. On the contrary, the emergence of economic power may be the consequence of power existing on other grounds. Man does not strive for power only in order to enrich himself economically. Power, including economic power, may be valued "for its own sake." Very frequently the striving for power is also conditioned by the social "honor" it entails. Not all power, however, entails social honor: The typical American Boss, as well as the typical big speculator, deliberately relinquishes social honor. Quite generally, "mere economic" power, and especially "naked" money power, is by no means a recognized basis of social honor. Nor is power the only basis of social honor. Indeed, social honor, or prestige, may even be the basis of political or economic power, and very frequently has been. Power, as well as honor, may be

From *From Max Weber: Essays in Sociology,* edited and translated by H. H. Gerth and C. Wright Mills. 

[1] *Wirtschaft und Gesellschaft,* Part III, Chap. 4, pp. 631–640. The first sentence in paragraph one and the several definitions in this chapter in brackets do not appear in the original text. They have been taken from other contexts of *Wirtschaft und Gesellschaft.*

guaranteed by the legal order, but, at least normally, it is not their primary source. The legal order is rather an additional factor that enhances the chance to hold power or honor; but it cannot always secure them.

The way in which social honor is distributed in a community between typical groups participating in this distribution we may call the "social order." The social order and the economic order are, of course, similarly related to the "legal order." However, the social and the economic order are not identical. The economic order is for us merely the way in which economic goods and services are distributed and used. The social order is of course conditioned by the economic order to a high degree, and in its turn reacts upon it.

Now: "classes," "status groups," and "parties" are phenomena of the distribution of power within a community.

## DETERMINATION OF CLASS-SITUATION BY MARKET-SITUATION

In our terminology, "classes" are not communities; they merely represent possible, and frequent bases for communal action. We may speak of a "class" when (1) a number of people have in common a specific causal component of their life chances, in so far as (2) this component is represented exclusively by economic interests in the possession of goods and opportunities for income, and (3) is represented under the conditions of the commodity or labor markets. [These points refer to "class situation," which we may express more briefly as the typical chance for a supply of goods, external living conditions, and personal life experiences, in so far as this chance is determined by the amount and kind of power, or lack of such, to dispose of goods or skills for the sake of income in a given economic order. The term "class" refers to any group of people that is found in the same class situation.]

It is the most elemental economic fact that the way in which the disposition over material property is distributed among a plurality of people meeting competitively in the market for the purpose of exchange, in itself creates specific life chances. According to the law of marginal utility this mode of distribution excludes the non-owners from competing for highly valued goods; it favors the owners and, in fact, gives to them a monopoly to acquire such goods. Other things being equal, this mode of distribution monopolizes the opportunities for profitable deals for all those who, provided with goods, do not necessarily have to exchange them. It increases, at least generally, their power in price wars with those who, being propertyless, have nothing to offer but their services in native form or goods in a form constituted through their own labor, and who above all are compelled to get rid of these products in order barely to subsist. This mode of distribution gives to the propertied a monopoly on the possibility of transferring property from the sphere of use as a "fortune," to the sphere of "capital goods"; that is, it gives them the entrepreneurial function and all chances to share directly or indirectly in returns on capital. All this holds true within the area in which pure market conditions prevail. "Property" and "lack of property" are, therefore, the basic categories of all class situations. It does not matter whether these two categories become effective in price wars or in competitive struggles.

Within these categories, however, class situations are further differentiated: on the one hand, according to the kind of property that is usable for returns; and, on the other hand, according to the kind of services that can be offered in the market. Ownership of domestic buildings; productive establishments; warehouses; stores; agriculturally usable land, large and small holdings—quantitative differences with possibly qualitative consequences—; ownership of mines; cattle; men (slaves); disposition over mobile instruments of production, or capital goods of all sorts, especially money or objects that can be exchanged for money easily and at any time; disposition over products of one's own labor or of others' labor differing according to their various distances from consumability; disposition over transferable monopolies of any kind—all these distinctions differentiate the class situations of the propertied just as does the "meaning" which they can and do give to the utilization of property, especially to property which has money equivalence.. Accordingly, the propertied, for instance, may belong to the class of rentiers or to the class of entrepreneurs.

Those who have no property but who offer services are differentiated just as much according to their kinds of services as according to the way in which they make use of these services, in a continuous or discontinuous relation to a recipient. But always this is the generic connotation of the concept of class: that the kind of chance in the *market* is the decisive moment which presents a common condition for the individual's fate. "Class situation" is, in this sense, ultimately "market situation." The effect of naked possession *per se*, which among cattle breeders gives the non-owning slave or serf into the power of the cattle owner, is only a forerunner of real "class" formation. However, in the cattle loan and in the naked severity of the law of debts in such communities, for the first time mere "possession" as such emerges as decisive for the fate of the individual. This is very much in contrast to the agricultural communities based on labor. The creditor-debtor relation becomes the basis of "class situations" only in those cities where a "credit market," however primitive, with rates of interest increasing according to the extent of dearth and a factual monopolization of credits, is developed by a plutocracy. Therewith "class struggles" begin.

Those men whose fate is not determined by the chance of using goods or services for themselves on the market, e.g. slaves, are not, however, a "class" in the technical sense of the term. They are, rather, a "status group."

## COMMUNAL ACTION FLOWING FROM CLASS INTEREST

According to our terminology, the factor that creates "class" is unambiguously economic interest, and indeed, only those interests involved in the existence of the "market." Nevertheless, the concept of "class-interest" is an ambiguous one: even as an empirical concept it is ambiguous as soon as one understands by it something other than the factual direction of interests following with a certain probability from the class situation for a certain "average" of those people subjected to the class situation. The class situation and other circumstances remaining the same, the direction in which the individual worker, for instance, is likely to pursue his interests may vary widely, according to whether he is constitutionally qualified for the task at hand to a high, to an average, or to a low degree. In the same way, the direction of interests may vary according to whether or not a *communal* action of a larger or smaller portion of those commonly affected by the "class situation," or even an association among them, e.g. a "trade union," has grown out of the class situation from which the individual may or may not expect promising results. [Communal action refers to that action which is oriented to the feeling of the actors that they belong together. Societal action, on the other hand, is oriented to a rationally motivated adjustment of interests.] The rise of societal or even of communal action from a common class situation is by no means a universal phenomenon.

The class situation may be restricted in its effects to the generation of essentially *similar* reactions, that is to say, within our terminology, of "mass actions." However, it may not have even this result. Furthermore, often merely an amorphous communal action emerges. For example, the "murmuring" of the workers known in ancient oriental ethics: the moral disapproval of the work-master's conduct, which in its practical significance was probably equivalent to an increasingly typical phenomenon of precisely the latest industrial development, namely, the "slow down" (the deliberate limiting of work effort) of laborers by virtue of tacit agreement. The degree in which "communal action" and possibly "societal action," emerges from the "mass actions" of the members of a class is linked to general cultural conditions, especially to those of an intellectual sort. It is also linked to the extent of the contrasts that have already evolved, and is especially linked to the *transparency* of the connections between the causes and the consequences of the "class situation." For however different life chances may be, this fact in itself, according to all experience, by no means gives birth to "class action" (communal action by the members of a class). The fact of being conditioned and the results of the class situation must be distinctly recognizable. For only then the contrast of life chances can be felt not as an absolutely given fact to be accepted, but as a resultant from either (1) the given distribution of property, or (2) the structure of the concrete economic order. It is only then that people may react against the class structure not only through acts of an intermittent and irrational protest, but in the form of rational association. There have been "class situations" of the first category (1), of a specifically naked and transparent sort, in the urban centers of Antiquity and during the Middle Ages; especially then, when great fortunes were accumulated by factually monopolized trading in industrial products of these localities or in foodstuffs. Furthermore, under certain circumstances, in the rural economy of the most diverse periods, when agriculture was increasingly exploited in a profit-making manner. The most important historical example of the second category (2) is the class situation of the modern "proletariat."

## TYPES OF "CLASS STRUGGLE"

Thus every class may be the carrier of any one of the possibly innumerable forms of "class action," but this is not necessarily so. In any case, a class does not in itself constitute a community. To treat "class" conceptually as having the same value as "community" leads to distortion. That men in the same class situation regularly react in mass actions to such tangible situations as economic ones in the direction of those interests that are most adequate to their average number is an important and after all simple fact for the understanding of historical events. Above all, this fact must not lead to that kind of pseudo-scientific operation with the concepts of "class" and "class interests" so frequently found these days and which has found its most classic expression in the statement of a talented author, that the individual may be in error concerning his interests but that the "class" is "infallible" about its interests. Yet, if classes as such are not communities, nevertheless class situation emerge only on the basis of communalization. The communal action that brings forth class situations, however, is not basically action between members of the identical class; it is an action between members of different classes. Communal actions that directly determine the class situation of the worker and the entrepreneur are: the labor market, the commodities market, and the capitalistic enterprise. But, in its turn, the existence of a capitalistic enterprise presupposes that a very specific communal action exists and that it is specifically structured to protect the possession of goods *per se,* and especially the power of individuals to dispose, in principle, freely over the means of production. The existence of a capitalistic enterprise is preconditioned by a specific kind of "legal order." Each kind of class situation, and above all when it rests upon the power of property *per se*, will become most clearly efficacious, when all other determinants of reciprocal relations are, as far as possible, eliminated in their significance. It is in this way that the utilization of the power of property in the market obtains its most sovereign importance.

Now "status groups" hinder the strict carrying through of the sheer market principle. In the present context they are of interest to us only from this one point of view. Before we briefly consider them, note that not much of a general nature can be said about the more specific kinds of antagonism between "classes" (in our meaning of the term). The great shift, which has been going on continuously in the past, and up to our times, may be summarized, although at the cost of some precision: the struggle in which class situations are effective has progressively shifted from consumption credit toward, first, competitive struggles in the commodity market, and, then, toward price wars on the labor market. The "class struggles" of antiquity—to the extent that they were genuine class struggles and not struggles between status groups—were initially carried on by indebted peasants, and perhaps also by artisans threatened by debt bondage and struggling against urban creditors. For debt bondage is the normal result of the differentiation of wealth in commercial cities, especially in seaport cities. A similar situation has existed among cattle breeders. Debt relationships as such produced class action up to the time of Cataline. Along with this, and with an increase in provision of grain for the city by transporting it from the outside, the struggle over the means of sustenance emerged. It centered in the first place around the provision of bread and the determination of the price of bread. It lasted throughout antiquity and the entire Middle Ages. The propertyless as such flocked together against those who actually and supposedly were interested in the dearth of bread. This fight spread until it involved all those commodities essential to the way of life and to handicraft production. There were only incipient discussions of wage disputes in antiquity and in the Middle Ages. But they have been slowly increasing up into modern times. In the earlier periods they were completely secondary to slave rebellions as well as to fights in the commodity market.

The propertyless of antiquity and of the Middle Ages protested against monopolies, pre-emption, forestalling, and the withholding of goods from the market in order to raise prices. Today the central issue is the determination of the price of labor.

This transition is represented by the fight for access to the market and for the determination of the price of products. Such fights went on between merchants and workers in the putting-out system of domestic handicraft during the transition to modern times. Since it is quite a general phenomenon we must mention here that the class antagonisms that are conditioned through the market situation are usually most bitter between those who actually and directly participate as opponents in price wars. It is not the rentier, the shareholder, and the banker who suffer the ill will of the worker, but almost exclusively the manufacturer and the business executives who are the direct opponents of workers in price wars. This is so in spite of the fact that it is precisely the cash boxes of the rentier, the share-holder, and the banker into which the more or less "unearned" gains flow, rather than into the pockets of the manufacturers or of the business executives. This simple state of affairs has very frequently been decisive for the role the class situation has played in the formation of political parties. For example, it has made possible the varieties of patriarchal socialism and the frequent attempts—formerly, at least—of threatened status groups to form alliances with the proletariat against the "bourgeoisie."

## STATUS HONOR

In contrast to classes, *status groups* are normally communities. They are, however, often of an amorphous kind. In contrast to the purely economically determined "class situation" we wish to designate as "status situation" every typical component of the life fate of men that is determined by a specific, positive or negative, social estimation of *honor*.[2] This honor may be connected with any quality shared by a plurality, and, of course, it can be knit to a class situation: class distinctions are linked in the most varied ways with status distinctions. Property as such is not always recognized as a status qualification, but in the long run it is, and with extraordinary regularity. In the subsistence economy of the organized neighborhood, very often the richest man is simply the chieftain. However, this often means only an honorific preference. For example, in the so-called pure modern "democracy," that is, one devoid of any expressly ordered status privileges for individuals, it may be that only the families coming under approximately the same tax class dance with one another. This example is reported of certain smaller Swiss cities. But status honor need not necessarily be linked with a "class situation." On the contrary, it normally stands in sharp opposition to the pretensions of sheer property.

Both propertied and propertyless people can belong to the same status group, and frequently they do with very tangible consequences. This "equality" of social esteem may, however, in the long run become quite precarious. The "equality"

[2] Because "status situation," *Ständische Lage*, is a distinctly Weberian concept, the definition is presented here in its German original: "eine typisch wirksam im Anspruch genommene positive oder negative Privilegierung in der socialen Schätzung." *Wirtschaft und Gesellschaft*, Tübingen: Mohr, 1925, p. 179. (C. S. H.)

of status among the American "gentlemen," for instance, is expressed by the fact that outside the subordination determined by the different functions of "business," it would be considered strictly repugnant—wherever the old tradition still prevails—if even the richest "chief," while playing billiards or cards in his club in the evening, would not treat his "clerk" as in every sense fully his equal in birthright. It would be repugnant if the American "chief" would bestow upon his "clerk" the condescending "benevolence" marking a distinction of "position," which the German chief can never dissever from his attitude. This is one of the most important reasons why in America the German "clubby-ness" has never been able to attain the attraction that the American clubs have.

## GUARANTEES OF STATUS STRATIFICATION

In content, status honor is normally expressed by the fact that above all else a specific *style of life* can be expected from all those who wish to belong to the circle. Linked with this expectation are restrictions on "social" intercourse (that is, intercourse which is not subservient to economic or any other of business's "functional" purposes). These restrictions may confine normal marriages to within the status circle and may lead to complete endogamous closure. As soon as there is not a mere individual and socially irrelevant imitation of another style of life, but an agreed-upon communal action of this closing character, the "status" development is under way.

In its characteristic form, stratification by "status groups" on the basis of conventional styles of life evolves at the present time in the United States out of the traditional democracy. For example, only the resident of a certain street ("the street") is considered as belonging to "society," is qualified for social intercourse, and is visited and invited. Above all, this differentiation evolves in such a way as to make for strict submission to the fashion that is dominant at a given time in society. This submission to fashion also exists among men in America to a degree unknown in Germany. Such submission is considered to be an indication of the fact that a given man *pretends* to qualify as a gentleman. This submission decides, at least *prima facie,* that he will be treated as such. And this recognition becomes just as important for his employment chances in "swank" establishments, and above all, for social intercourse and marriage with "esteemed" families, as the qualification for dueling among Germans in the Kaiser's day. As for the rest: certain families resident for a long time, and, of course, correspondingly wealthy, e.g. "F. F. V., i.e. First Families of Virginia," or the actual or alleged descendants of the "Indian Princess" Pocahontas, of the Pilgrim Fathers, or of the Knickerbockers, the members of almost inaccessible sects and all sorts of circles setting themselves apart by means of any other characteristics and badges . . . all these elements usurp "status" honor. The development of status is essentially a question of stratification resting upon usurpation. Such usurpation is the normal origin of almost all status honor. But the road from this purely conventional situation to legal privilege, positive or negative, is easily traveled as soon as a certain stratification of the social order has in fact been "lived in" and has achieved stability by virtue of a stable distribution of economic power.

## "ETHNIC" SEGREGATION AND "CASTE"

Where the consequences have been realized to their full extent, the status group evolves into a closed "caste." Status distinctions are then guaranteed not merely by conventions and laws, but also by *rituals.* This occurs in such a way that every physical contact with a member of any caste that is considered to be "lower" by the members of a "higher" caste is considered as making for a ritualistic impurity and to be a stigma which must be expiated by a religious act. Individual castes develop quite distinct cults and gods.

In general, however, the status structure reaches such extreme consequences only where there are underlying differences which are held to be "ethnic." The "caste" is, indeed, the normal form in which ethnic communities usually live side by side in a "societalized" manner. These ethnic communities believe in blood relationship and exclude exogamous marriage and social intercourse. Such a caste situation is part of the phenomenon of "pariah" peoples and is found all over the world. These people form communities, acquire specific occupational traditions of handicrafts or of other arts, and cultivate a belief in their ethnic community. They live in a "diaspora" strictly segregated from all personal intercourse, except that of an unavoidable sort, and their situation is legally precarious. Yet, by virtue of their economic indispensability, they are tolerated, indeed, frequently privileged, and they live in interspersed political communities. The Jews are the most impressive historical example.

A "status" segregation grown into a "caste" differs in its structure from a mere "ethnic" segregation: the caste structure transforms the horizontal and unconnected coexistences of ethnically segregated groups into a vertical social system of super- and subordination. Correctly formulated: a comprehensive societalization integrates the ethnically divided communities into specific political and communal action. In their consequences they differ precisely in this way: ethnic coexistences condition a mutual repulsion and disdain but allow each ethnic community to consider its own honor as the highest one; the caste structure brings about a social subordination and an acknowledgment of "more honor" in favor of the privileged caste and status groups. This is due to the fact that in the caste structure ethnic distinctions as such have become "functional" distinctions within the political societalization (warriors, priests, artisans that are politically important for war and for building, and so on). But even pariah people who are most despised are usually apt to continue cultivating in some manner that which is equally peculiar to ethnic and to status communities: the belief in their own specific "honor." This is the case with the Jews.

Only with the negatively privileged status does the "sense of dignity" take a specific deviation. A sense of dignity is the precipitation in individuals of social honor and of conventional demands which a positively privileged status group raises for the deportment of its members. The sense of dignity that characterizes positively privileged status groups is naturally related to their "being" which does not transcend itself, that is, it is to their "beauty and excellence" (καλο-κἄγαδια). Their kingdom is "of this world." They live for the present and by exploiting their great past. The sense of dignity of the negatively privileged strata naturally refers to a future lying beyond the present, whether it is of this life or of another. In other words, it must be nurtured by the belief in a providential "mission" and by a belief in a specific honor before God. The "chosen people's" dignity is nurtured by a belief either that in the beyond "the last will be the first," or that in this life a Messiah will appear to bring forth into the light of the world which has cast them out the hidden honor of the pariah people. This simple state of affairs, and not the "resentment" which is so strongly emphasized in Nietzsche's much admired construction in the *Genealogy of Morals,* is the source of the religiosity cultivated by pariah status groups. In passing, we may note that resentment may be accurately applied only to a limited extent; for one of Nietzsche's main examples, Buddhism, it is not at all applicable.

Incidentally, the development of status groups from ethnic segregations is by no means the normal phenomenon. On the contrary, since objective "racial differences" are by no means basic to every subjective sentiment of an ethnic community, the ultimately racial foundation of status structure is rightly and absolutely a question of the concrete individual case. Very frequently a status group is instrumental in the production of a thoroughbred anthropological type. Certainly a status group is to a high degree effective in producing extreme types, for they select personally qualified individuals (e.g. the Knighthood selects those who are fit for warfare, physically and psychically). But selection is far from being the only, or the predominant, way in which status groups are formed: Political membership or class situation has at all times been at least as frequently decisive. And today the class situation is by far the predominant factor, for of course the possibility of a style of life expected for members of a status group is usually conditioned economically.

### STATUS PRIVILEGES

For all practical purposes, stratification goes hand in hand with a monopolization of ideal and material goods or opportunities, in a manner we have come to know as typical. Besides the specific status honor, which always rests upon distance and exclusiveness, we find all sorts of material monopolies. Such honorific preferences may consist of the privilege of wearing special costumes, of eating special dishes taboo to others, of carrying arms—which is most obvious in its consequences—the right to pursue certain non-professional dilettante artistic practices, e.g. to play certain musical instruments. Of course, material monopolies provide the most effective motives for the exclusiveness of a status group; although, in themselves, they are rarely sufficient, almost always they come into play to some extent. Within a status circle there is the question of intermarriage: the interest of the families in the monopolization of potential bridegrooms is at least of equal importance and is parallel to the interest in the monopolization of daughters. The daughters of the circle must be provided for. With an increased inclosure of the status group, the conventional preferential opportunities for special employment grow into a legal monopoly of special offices for the members. Certain goods become objects for monopolization by status groups. In the typical fashion these include "entailed estates" and frequently also the possessions of serfs or bondsmen and, finally, special trades. This monopolization occurs positively when the status group is exclusively entitled to own and to manage them; and negatively when, in order to maintain its specific way of life, the status group must *not* own and manage them.

The decisive role of a "style of life" in status "honor" means that status groups are the specific bearers of all "conventions." In whatever way it may be manifest, all "stylization" of life either originates in status groups or is at least conserved by them. Even if the principles of status conventions differ greatly, they reveal certain typical traits, especially among those strata which are most privileged. Quite generally, among privileged status groups there is a status disqualification that operates against the performance of common physical labor. This disqualification is now "setting in" in America against the old tradition of esteem for labor. Very frequently every rational economic pursuit, and especially "entrepreneurial activity," is looked upon as a disqualification of status. Artistic and literary activity is also considered as degrading work as soon as it is exploited for income, or at least when it is connected with hard physical exertion. An example is the sculptor working like a mason in his dusty smock as over against the painter in his salon-like "studio" and those forms of musical practice that are acceptable to the status group.

### ECONOMIC CONDITIONS AND EFFECTS OF STATUS STRATIFICATION

The frequent disqualification of the gainfully employed as such is a direct result of the principle of status stratification peculiar to the social order, and of course, of this principle's opposition to a distribution of power which is regulated exclusively through the market. These two factors operate along with various individual ones, which will be touched upon below.

We have seen above that the market and its processes "knows no personal distinctions": "functional" interests dominate it. It knows nothing of "honor." The status order means precisely the reverse, viz.: stratification in terms of "honor" and of styles of life peculiar to status groups as such. If mere economic acquisition and naked economic power still bearing the stigma of its extra-status origin could bestow upon anyone who has won it the same honor as those who are interested in status by virtue of style of life claim for themselves, the status order would be threatened at its very root. This is the more so as, given equality of status honor, property *per se* represents an addition even if it is not overtly acknowledged to be such. Yet if such economic acquisition and power gave the agent any honor at all, his wealth would result in his attaining more honor than those who successfully claim honor by virtue of style of life. Therefore all groups having interests in the status order react with special sharpness precisely against the pretensions of purely economic acquisition. In most cases they react the more vigorously the more they feel themselves threatened. Calderon's respectful treatment of the peasant, for instance, as opposed to Shakespeare's simultaneous and ostensible disdain of the *canaille* illustrates the different way in which a firmly structured status order reacts as compared with a status order that has become economically precarious. This is an example of a state of affairs that recurs everywhere. Precisely because of the rigorous reactions against the claims of property *per se*, the "parvenu" is never accepted, personally and without reservation, by the privileged status groups, no matter how completely his style of life has been adjusted to theirs. They will only accept his descendants who have been educated in the conventions of their status group and who have never besmirched its honor by their own economic labor.

As to the general *effect* of the status order, only one consequence can be stated, but it is a very important one: the hindrance of the free development of the market occurs first for those goods which status groups directly withheld from free exchange by monopolization. This monopolization may be effected either legally or conventionally. For example, in many Hellenic cities during the epoch of status groups, and also originally in Rome, the inherited estate (as is shown by the old formula for indiction against spendthrifts) was monopolized just as were the estates of knights, peasants, priests, and especially the clientele of the craft and merchant guilds. The market is restricted, and the power of naked property *per se*, which gives its stamp to "class formation," is pushed into the background. The results of this process can be most varied. Of course, they do not necessarily weaken the contrasts in the economic situation. Frequently they strengthen these contrasts, and in any case, where stratification by status permeates a community as strongly as was the case in all political communities of antiquity and of the Middle Ages, one can never speak of a genuinely free market competition as we understand it today. There are wider effects than this direct exclusion of special goods from the market. From the contrariety between the status order and the purely economic order mentioned above, it follows that in most instances the notion of honor peculiar to status absolutely abhors that which is essential to the market: higgling. Honor abhors higgling among peers and occasionally it taboos higgling for the members of a status group in general. Therefore, everywhere some status groups, and usually the most influential, consider almost any kind of overt participation in economic acquisition as absolutely stigmatizing.

With some over-simplification, one might thus say that "classes" are stratified according to their relations to the production and acquisition of goods; whereas "status groups" are stratified according to the principles of their *consumption* of goods as represented by special "styles of life."

An "occupational group" is also a status group. For normally, it successfully claims social honor only by virtue of the special style of life which may be determined by it. The differences between classes and status groups frequently overlap. It is precisely those status communities most strictly segregated in terms of honor (viz. the Indian castes) who today show, although within very rigid limits, a relatively high degree of indifference to pecuniary income. However, the Brahmins seek such income in many different ways.

As to the general economic conditions making for the predominance of stratification by "status," only very little can be said. When the bases of the acquisition and distribution of goods are relatively stable, stratification by status is favored. Every technological repercussion and economic transformation threatens stratification by status and pushes the class situation into the foreground. Epochs and countries in which the naked class situation is of predominant significance are regularly the periods of technical and economic transformations. And every slowing down of the shifting of economic stratifications leads, in due course, to the growth of status structures and makes for a resuscitation of the important role of social honor.

## PARTIES

Whereas the genuine place of "classes" is within the economic order, the place of "status groups" is within the social order, that is, within the sphere of the distribution of "honor." From within these spheres, classes and status groups influence one another and they influence the legal order and are in turn influenced by it. But "parties" live in a house of "power."

Their action is oriented toward the acquisition of social "power," that is to say, toward influencing a communal action no matter what its content may be. In principle, parties may exist in a social "club" as well as in a "state." As over against the actions of classes and status groups, for which this is not necessarily the case, the communal actions of "parties" always mean a societalization. For party actions are always directed toward a goal which is striven for in planned manner. This goal may be a "cause" (the party may aim at realizing a program for ideal or material purposes), or the goal may be "personal" (sinecures, power, and from these, honor for the leader and the followers of the party). Usually the party action aims at all these simultaneously. Parties are, therefore, only possible within communities that are societalized, that is, which have some rational order and a staff of persons available who are ready to enforce it. For parties aim precisely at influencing this staff, and if possible, to recruit it from party followers.

In any individual case, parties may represent interests determined through "class situation" or "status situation," and they may recruit their following respectively from one or the other. But they need be neither purely "class" nor purely "status" parties. In most cases they are partly class parties and partly status parties, but sometimes they are neither. They may represent ephemeral or enduring structures. Their means of attaining power may be quite varied, ranging from naked violence of any sort to canvassing for votes with coarse or subtle means: money, social influence, the force of speech, suggestion, clumsy hoax, and so on to the rougher or more artful tactics of obstruction in parliamentary bodies.

The sociological structure of parties differs in a basic way according to the kind of communal action which they struggle to influence. Parties also differ according to whether or not the community is stratified by status or by classes. Above all else, they vary according to the structure of domination within the community. For their leaders normally deal with the conquest of a community. They are, in the general concept which is maintained here, not only products of specially modern forms of domination. We shall also designate as parties the ancient and medieval "parties," despite the fact that their structure differs basically from the structure of modern parties. By virtue of these structural differences of domination it is impossible to say anything about the structure of parties without discussing the structural forms of social domination *per se*. Parties, which are always structures struggling for domination, are very frequently organized in a very strict "authoritarian" fashion . . .

Concerning "classes," "status groups," and "parties," it must be said in general that they necessarily presuppose a comprehensive societalization, and especially a political framework of communal action, within which they operate. This does not mean that parties would be confined by the frontiers of any individual political community. On the contrary, at all times it has been the order of the day that the societalization (even when it aims at the use of military force in common) reaches beyond the frontiers of politics. This has been the case in the solidarity of interests among the Oligarchs and among the democrats in Hellas, among the Guelfs and among the Ghibellines in the Middle Ages, and within the Calvinist party during the period of religious struggles. It has been the case up to the solidarity of the landlords (international congress of agrarian landlords), and has continued among princes (holy alliance, Karlsbad decrees), socialist workers, conservatives (the longing of Prussian conservatives for Russian intervention in 1850). But their aim is not necessarily the establishment of new international political, i.e. *territorial* dominion. In the main they aim to influence the existing dominion.[3]

# ELITES AND THEIR CIRCULATION

*Vilfredo Pareto*

Whether certain theorists like it or not, the fact is that human society is not a homogeneous thing, that individuals are physically, morally, and intellectually different. Here we are interested in things as they actually are. Of that fact, therefore, we have to take account. And we must also take account of another fact: that the social classes are not entirely distinct, even in countries where a caste system prevails; and that in modern civilized countries circulation among the various classes is exceedingly rapid. To consider at all exhaustively here this matter of the diversity of the vastly numerous social groups and the numberless ways in which they mix is out of the question. As usual, therefore, since we cannot have the more, we must rest content with the less and try to make the problem easier in order to have it the more manageable. That is a first step along a path that others may go on following. We shall consider the problem only in its bearing on the social equilibrium and try to reduce as far as possible the numbers of the groups and the modes of circulation, putting under one head phenomena that prove to be roughly and after a fashion similar.

Suppose we begin by giving a theoretical definition of the thing we are dealing with, making it as exact as possible, and then go on to see what practical considerations we can replace it with to get a first approximation. Let us for the moment completely disregard considerations as to the good or bad, useful or harmful, praiseworthy or reprehensible character of the various traits in individuals, and confine ourselves to degrees—to whether, in other words, the trait in a given case be slight, average, intense, or more exactly, to the index that may be assigned to each individual with reference to the degree, or intensity, in him of the trait in question.

Let us assume that in every branch of human activity each individual is given an index which stands as a sign of his capacity, very much the way grades are given in the various subjects in examinations in school. The highest type of lawyer, for instance, will be given 10. The man who does not get a client will be given 1—reserving zero for the man who is an out-and-out idiot. To the man who has made his millions—honestly or dishonestly as the case may be—we will give 10. To the man who has earned his thousands we will give 6; to such as just manage to keep out of the poor-house, 1, keeping zero for those who get in. To the woman "in politics," such as the Aspasia of Pericles, the Maintenon of Louis XIV, the Pompadour of Louis XV, who has managed to infatuate a man of power and play a part in the man's career, we shall give some higher number, such as 8 or 9; to the strumpet who merely satisfies the senses of such a man and exerts no influence on public affairs, we shall give zero. To a clever rascal who knows how to fool people and still keep clear of the penitentiary, we shall give 8, 9, or 10, according to the number of geese he has plucked and the amount of money he has been able to get out of them. To the sneak-thief who snatches a piece of silver from a restaurant table and runs away into the arms of a policeman, we shall give 1. To a poet like Carducci we shall give 8 or 9 according to our tastes; to a scribbler who puts people to rout with his sonnets we shall give zero. For chess-players we can't get very precise indices, noting what matches, and how many, they have won. And so on for all the branches of human activity.

We are speaking, remember, of an actual,

From *The Mind and Society* by Vilfredo Pareto, translated by A. Bongiorno and A. Livingston and edited by A. Livingston, Harcourt, Brace & Company, 1935. Reprinted by permission of the Pareto Fund.

[3] The posthumously published text breaks off here. We omit an incomplete sketch of types of "warrior estates."

not a potential, state. If at an English examination a pupil says: "I could know English very well if I chose to; I do not know any because I have never seen fit to learn," the examiner replies: "I am not interested in your alibi. The grade for what you know is zero." If, similarly, someone says: "So-and-so does not steal, not because he couldn't, but because he is a gentleman," we reply: "Very well, we admire him for his self-control, but his grade as a thief is zero."

There are people who worship Napoleon Bonaparte as a god. There are people who hate him as the lowest of criminals. Which are right? We do not choose to solve that question in connexion with a quite different matter. Whether Napoleon was a good man or a bad man, he was certainly not an idiot, nor a man of little account, as millions of others are. He had exceptional qualities, and that is enough for us to give him a high ranking, though without prejudice of any sort that might be raised as to the ethics of his qualities or their social utility.

In short, we are here as usual resorting to scientific analysis, which distinguishes one problem from another and studies each one separately. As usual, again, we are replacing imperceptable variations in absolutely exact numbers with the sharp variations corresponding to groupings by class, just as in examinations those who are passed are sharply and arbitrarily distinguished from those who are "failed," and just as in the matter of physical age we distinguish children from young people, the young from the aged.

So let us make a class of the people who have the highest indices in their branch of activity, and to that class give the name of *élite*.[1]

For the particular investigation with which we are engaged, a study of the social equilibrium, it will help if we further divide that class into two classes: a *governing élite*, comprising individuals who directly or indirectly play some considerable part in government, and a *non-governing élite*, comprising the rest.

A chess champion is certainly a member of the *élite*, but it is no less certain that his merits as a chess-player do not open the doors to political influence for him; and hence unless he has other qualities to win him that distinction, he is not a member of the governing *élite*. Mistresses of absolute monarchs have oftentimes been members of the *élite*, either because of their beauty or because of their intellectual endowments; but only a few of them, who have had, in addition, the particular talents required by politics, have played any part in government.

So we get two strata in a population: (1) A lower stratum, the *non-élite*, with whose possible influence on government we are not just here concerned; then (2) a higher stratum, *the élite*, which is divided into two: (*a*) a governing *élite*; (*b*) a non-governing *élite*.

In the concrete, there are no examinations whereby each person is assigned to his proper place in these various classes. That deficiency is made up for by other means, by various sorts of labels that serve the purpose after a fashion. Such labels are the rule even where there are examinations. The label "lawyer" is affixed to a man who is supposed to know something about the law and often does, though sometimes again he is an ignoramus. So, the governing *élite* contains individuals who wear labels appropriate to political offices of a certain altitude—ministers, Senators, Deputies, chief justices, generals, colonels, and so on—making the apposite exceptions for those who have found their way into that

[1] Kolabinska, *La circulation des élites en France*, p. 5: "The outstanding idea in the term '*élite*' is 'superiority'. That is the only one I keep. I disregard secondary connotations of appreciation or as to the utility of such superiority. I am not interested here in what is desirable. I am making a simple study of what is. In a broad sense I mean by the *élite* in a society people who possess in marked degree qualities of intelligence, character, skill, capacity, of whatever kind. . . . On the other hand I entirely avoid any sort of judgment on the merits and utility of such classes." [The phrase "circulation of *élites*" is well established in Continental literature. Pareto himself renders it in Italian as "circulation of the élite (selected, chosen, ruling, 'better') classes." It is a cumbersome phrase and not very exact, and I see no reason for preferring it to the more natural and, in most connexions, the more exact English phrase, class-circulation.—A.L.]

exalted company without possessing qualities corresponding to the labels they wear.

Such exceptions are much more numerous than the exceptions among lawyers, physicians, engineers, millionaires (who have made their own money), artists of distinction, and so on; for the reason, among others, that in these latter departments of human activity the labels are won directly by each individual, whereas in the *élite* some of the labels—the label of wealth, for instance—are hereditary. In former times there were hereditary labels in the governing *élite* also—in our day hardly more than the label of king remains in that status; but if direct inheritance has disappeared, inheritance is still powerful indirectly; and an individual who has inherited a sizeable patrimony can easily be named Senator in certain countries, or can get himself elected to the parliament by buying votes or, on occasion, by wheedling voters with assurances that he is a democrat of democrats, a Socialist, an Anarchist. Wealth, family, or social connexions also help in many other cases to win the label of the *élite* in general, or of the governing *élite* in particular, for persons who otherwise hold no claim upon it.

In societies where the social unit is the family the label worn by the head of the family also benefits all other members. In Rome, the man who became emperor generally raised his freedmen to the higher class, and oftentimes, in fact, to the governing *élite*. For that matter, now more, now fewer, of the freedmen taking part in the Roman government possessed qualities good or bad that justified their wearing the labels which they had won through imperial bounty. In our societies, the social unit is the individual; but the place that the individual occupies in society also benefits his wife, his children, his connexions, his friends.

If all these deviations from type were of little importance, they might be disregarded, as they are virtually disregarded in cases where a diploma is required for the practice of a profession. Everyone knows that there are persons who do not deserve their diplomas, but experience shows that on the whole such exceptions may be overlooked.

One might, further, from certain points of view at least, disregard deviations if they remained more or less constant quantitatively—if there were only a negligible variation in proportions between the total of a class and the people who wear its label without possessing the qualities corresponding.

As a matter of fact, the real cases that we have to consider in our societies differ from those two. The deviations are not so few that they can be disregarded. Then again, their number is variable, and the variations give rise to situations having an important bearing on the social equilibrium. We are therefore required to make a special study of them.

Furthermore, the manner in which the various groups in a population intermix has to be considered. In moving from one group to another an individual generally brings with him certain inclinations, sentiments, attitudes, that he has acquired in the group from which he comes, and that circumstance cannot be ignored.

To this mixing, in the particular case in which only two groups, the *élite* and the non-*élite*, are envisaged, the term "circulation of élites" has been applied[2]—in French, *circulation des élites* [or in more general terms "class-circulation"].

In conclusion we must pay special attention (1), in the case of one single group, to the proportions between the total of the group and the number of individuals who are nominally members of it but do not possess the qualities requisite for effective membership; and then (2), in the case of various groups, to the ways in which transitions from one group to the other occur, and to the intensity of that movement—that is to say, to the velocity of the circulation.

Velocity in circulation has to be considered not only absolutely but also in relation to the supply of and the demand for certain social elements. A country that is

[2] [And most inappropriately, for, in this sense, the phrase never meant more than circulation within the *élite*. Furthermore, the *élite* is not the only class to be considered, and the principles that apply to circulation within the *élite* apply to circulation within such lower classes as one may choose for one purpose or another to consider.—

always at peace does not require many soldiers in its governing class, and the production of generals may be overexuberant as compared with the demand. But when a country is in a state of continuous warfare many soldiers are necessary, and though production remains at the same level it may not meet the demand. That, we might note in passing, has been one of the causes for the collapse of many aristocracies.[3]

Another example. In a country where there is little industry and little commerce, the supply of individuals possessing in high degree the qualities requisite for those types of activity exceeds the demand. Then industry and commerce develop and the supply, though remaining the same, no longer meets the demand.

We must not confuse the state of law with the state of fact. The latter alone, or almost alone, has a bearing on the social equilibrium. There are many examples of castes that are legally closed, but into which, in point of fact, new-comers make their way, and often in large numbers. On the other hand, what difference does it make if a caste is legally open, but conditions *de facto* prevent new accessions to it? If a person who acquires wealth thereby becomes a member of the governing class, but no one gets rich, it is as if the class were closed; and if only a few get rich, it is as if the law erected serious barriers against access to the caste. Something of that sort was observable towards the end of the Roman Empire. People who acquired wealth entered the order of the curials. But only a few individuals made any money. Theoretically we might examine any number of groups. Practically we have to confine ourselves to the more important.

[3] Kolabinska, *Op. cit.*, p. 10: "Inadequate recruiting in the *élite* does not result from a mere numerical proportion between new members and old. Account has to be taken of the number of persons who possess the qualities required for membership in the governing *élite* but are refused admittance; or else, in an opposite direction, the number of new members the *élite* might require but does not get. In the first case, the production of persons possessing unusual qualities as regards education may far surpass the number of such persons that the *élite* can accommodate, and then we get what has been called an 'intellectual proletariat.'"

We shall proceed by successive approximations, starting with the simple and going on to the complex.

***Higher Class and Lower Class in General.*** The least we can do is to divide society into two strata: a higher stratum, which usually contains the rulers, and a lower stratum, which usually contains the ruled. That fact is so obvious that it has always forced itself even upon the most casual observation, and so for the circulation of individuals between the two strata. Even Plato had an inkling of class-circulation and tried to regulate it artificially. The "new man," the upstart, the *parvenu*, has always been a subject of interest, and literature has analyzed him unendingly. Here, then, we are merely giving a more exact form to things that have long been perceived more or less vaguely. Above . . . we noted a varying distribution of residues in the various social groupings, and chiefly in the higher and the lower class. Such heterogeneousness is a fact perceived by the most superficial glance. . . .

The upper stratum of society, the *élite*, nominally contains certain groups of peoples, not always very sharply defined, that are called aristocracies. There are cases in which the majority of individuals belonging to such aristocracies actually possess the qualities requisite for remaining there; and then again there are cases where considerable numbers of the individuals making up the class do not possess those requisities. Such people may occupy more or less important places in the governing *élite* or they may be barred from it.

In the beginning, military, religious, and commercial aristocracies and plutocracies —with a few exceptions not worth considering—must have constituted parts of the governing *élite* and sometimes have made up the whole of it. The victorious warrior, the prosperous merchant, the opulent plutocrat, were men of such parts, each in his own field, as to be superior to the average individual. Under those circumstances the label corresponded to an actual capacity. But as time goes by, considerable, sometimes very considerable, differences arise between the capacity and the label; while on the other hand, certain aristocracies originally figuring prominently in the rising *élite* end by constituting an insignificant element in it. That has happened especially to military aristocracies.

Aristocracies do not last. Whatever the causes, it is an incontestable fact that after a certain length of time they pass away. History is a graveyard of aristocracies. The Athenian "People" was an aristocracy as compared with the remainder of a population of resident aliens and slaves. It vanished without leaving any descent. The various aristocracies of Rome vanished in their time. So did the aristocracies of the Barbarians. Where, in France, are the descendants of the Frankish conquerors? The genealogies of the English nobility have been very exactly kept; and they show that very few families still remain to claim descent from the comrades of William the Conqueror. The rest have vanished. In Germany the aristocracy of the present day is very largely made up of descendants of vassals of the lords of old. The populations of European countries have increased enormously during the past few centuries. It is as certain as certain can be that the aristocracies have not increased in proportion.

They decay not in numbers only. They decay also in quality, in the sense that they lose their vigour, that there is a decline in the proportions of the residues which enabled them to win their power and hold it. The governing class is restored not only in numbers, but—and that is the more important thing—in quality, by families rising from the lower classes and bringing with them the vigour and the proportions of residues necessary for keeping themselves in power. It is also restored by the loss of its more degenerate members.

If one of those movements comes to an end, or worse still, if they both come to an end, the governing class crashes to ruin and often sweeps the whole of a nation along with it. Potent cause of disturbance in the equilibrium is the accumulation of superior elements in the lower classes and, conversely, of inferior elements in the higher classes. If human aristocracies were like thorough-breds among animals, which reproduce themselves over long periods of time with approximately the same traits, the history of the human race would be something altogether different from the history we know.

In virtue of class-circulation, the governing *élite* is always in a state of slow and continuous transformation. It flows on like a river, never being today what it was yesterday. From time to time sudden and violent disturbances occur. There is a flood—the river overflows its banks. Afterwards, the new governing *élite* again resumes its slow transformation. The flood has subsided, the river is again flowing normally in its wonted bed.

Revolutions come about through accumulations in the higher strata of society—either because of a slowing-down in class-circulation, or from other causes—of decadent elements no longer possessing the residues suitable for keeping them in power, and shrinking from the use of force; while meantime in the lower strata of society elements of superior quality are coming to the fore, possessing residues suitable for exercising the functions of government and willing enough to use force.

In general, in revolutions the members of the lower strata are captained by leaders from the higher strata, because the latter possess the intellectual qualities required for outlining a tactic, while lacking the combative residues supplied by the individuals from the lower strata.

Violent movements take place by fits and starts, and effects therefore do not follow immediately on their causes. After a governing class, or a nation, has maintained itself for long periods of time on force and acquired great wealth, it may subsist for some time still without using force, buying off its adversaries and paying not only in gold, but also in terms of the dignity and respect that it had formerly enjoyed and which constitute, as it were, a capital. In the first stages of decline, power is maintained by bargainings and concessions, and people are so deceived into thinking that the policy can be carried on indefinitely. So the decadent Roman Empire bought peace of the Barbarians with money and honours. So Louis XVI, in France, squandering in a very short time an ancestral inheritance of love, respect, and almost religious reverence for the monarchy, managed, by making repeated concessions, to be the King of the Revolution. So the English aristocracy managed to prolong its term of power in the second half of the nineteenth century down to the dawn of its decadence, which was heralded by the "Parliament Bill" in the first years of the twentieth.

. . . . . . . . . . . . . . . . . . . . . . . . . . . . . . . . .

# THE RISE AND FALL OF WHOLE CLASSES

*Joseph Schumpeter*

## I.

. . . Every social situation is the heritage of preceding situations and takes over from them not only their cultures, their dispositions, and their "spirit," but also elements of their social structure and concentrations of power. This fact is of itself interesting. The social pyramid is never made of a single substance, is never seamless. There is no single *Zeitgeist*, except in the sense of a construct. This means that in explaining any historical course or situation, account must be taken of the fact that much in it can be explained only by the survival of elements that are actually alien to its own trends. . . .When applied to our problem, this means, first, that any theory of class structure, in dealing with a given historical period, must include prior class structures among its data; and then, that any general theory of classes and class formation must explain the fact that classes coexisting at any given time bear the marks of different centuries on their brow, so to speak—that they stem from varying conditions. This is in the essential nature of the matter, an aspect of the nature of the class phenomenon. Classes, once they have come into being, harden in their mold and perpetuate themselves, even when the social conditions that created them have disappeared. . . .

From *Imperialism and Social Classes*, by Joseph Schumpeter, Meridian Books, 1960. Copyright 1951. Reprinted by permission.

Any study of classes and class situations therefore leads, in unending regression, to other classes and class situations, . . . Similarly—though less closely so—analysis of the economic value of goods always leads back from a use value to a cost value and back again to a use value, so that it seems to turn in a circle. Yet this very analogy points to the logical way out. The general and mutual interdependence of values and prices in an economic situation does not prevent us from finding an all-encompassing explanatory principle; and the fact of regression in our own case does not mean the non-existence of a principle that will explain the formation, nature, and basic laws of classes—though this fact naturally does not necessarily furnish us with such a principle. If we cannot derive the sought-for principle from the genesis of classes in a classless state, it may yet emerge from a study of how classes function and what happens to them especially from actual observation of the changes in the relationship of existing classes to one another and of individuals within the class structure—*provided* it can be shown that the elements explaining such changes also include the reason why classes exist at all. . . .

## II.

We observe . . . that the class structure of a people . . . changes by virtue of the fact that the relative social position of the classes as such undergoes shifts. A question now poses itself that is analogous to the question concerning the reasons for shifts of individual families within the class. Why and how do classes change their relative position?

We see such a shift most plainly, not in cases where it is the result of a slow, organic process, but in those where it occurs by a single historical event. The most important instance of the latter process is the forcible subjugation of one social entity by another that is politically alien—usually nationally as well, though that is not essential to us now. What interests us in such an upheaval is the fact that classes that appear as "upper" or "ruling" even to superficial observation—especially *the* "ruling class" —are much more deeply affected than the "lower" classes, and in an altogether different way. True, even the lower classes may often—though not always or necessarily—be put in a worse economic plight, but their position as a class, their relative social rating, is affected only slightly or not at all, usually remaining essentially unchanged under the new overlord. The upper classes, on the other hand, are likely to lose the very core of their position—the more so the nearer they are to the top of the social pyramid. Let us, for example, take the conquest of certain Romanized regions by the Germans during the Great Migration. . . . There is only one way in which the upper class can maintain its full social position under such circumstances; that is when it is received into the corresponding class of the conqueror. . . . Thus it was a common policy of the East Roman Empire to accept the nobility of subjugated peoples (of Bulgaria, for example, in the time of the Macedonian emperors) into the imperial Byzantine nobility. But it will be seen at once that this constitutes no exception to our assertion; for it was not the old class itself that retained its social validity, but merely the sum of its members in their function as members of what now came to be the upper class.

Yet even this shift in the relative position of the classes toward each other does not quite tell us what we need to know. After all, it was the result of outside influence, which was accidental from the viewpoint of the class system in existence before. Let us, nevertheless, take note of the following two elements: to be conquered always means failure, and the failure applies particularly to the ruling classes. Apparently it is this inherent character of subjugation, so destructive to prestige, that has, in turn, much to do with the forfeiture of social position. A calamity lacking this special character—a great earthquake, for example—would not have such an effect, unless it were linked in the public mind with a failure, on the part of the upper classes, to entertain, let us say, good relations with the gods. This offers an obvious analogy with the effect of personal failure of a leader—a leader of mounted nomads, for example. The position of a monarchial family is typically rooted in class. Yet nothing shakes its position so much as an unsuccessful war. It would be difficult to find any case of loss of monarchial position that did not have, at least indirectly, some connection with this element. Again, this matter of having been subjugated or of meeting with failure is not just a question of failure in general, failure in any field; the failure becomes relevant only when it occurs with respect to certain definite fields—not merely those fields which the observer, from the necessities he has grasped, deems important, but those for which the class in question is responsible in a way that other classes are not. Only when a class has thus been weighed and found wanting, in the light of the circumstances of the times, does its position toward other classes of citizens decline—all down the line, not merely in this point alone—although, of course, a position once gained may prove equal to quite a number of such tests.

Here, then, in a flash, we begin to see the underlying relationship that leads directly to an answer to our question. This is the connection between the social rank of a class and its function. Each class is always linked to such a special function. That is the real core of all theories of the division of labor and occupation in the field of class phenomena—except that these theories, in our opinion, evaluate this element incorrectly. . . . Every class, . . . has a definite function which it must fulfill according to its whole concept and orientation, and which it actually does discharge as a class and through the class conduct of its members. Moreover, the position of each class in the total national structure, depends, on the one hand, on the significance that is attributed to that function, and, on the other hand, on the degree to which the class successfully performs the function. Changes in relative class position are always explained by changes along these two lines, and in no other way. For the time being, the propositions just put forth are liable to obvious objections. Just what their meaning is will be shown by an example which at the same time may serve to demonstrate our line of reasoning for cases that are not dependent on the effect of outside forces. The proof cannot be absolute, for that would require an analysis of universal history.

. . . . . . . . . . . . . . . . . . . . . . . . . . . . . . . . . . . .

Now let us examine our example. At the time the Germans entered the limelight of history, their aristocracy was no more than the leading circle of a mounted nomad people. It was simply a circle of families of enhanced prestige—more precisely, a plurality of distinct circles, differing from one another by the degree of prestige they enjoyed. Their members had more to do with making the policies of the totality than the rest. . . . There were real or potential chieftains of larger or smaller groups and subgroups. Yet there was one distinction as against the case of the mounted nomads, a distinction which explains the sharply marked character of the picture. Even when we first catch sight of them, the Germans were in a very high stage of agriculture, normally and preeminently living by tilling the soil. . . . Agriculture, to a much higher degree than nomadic animal husbandry, destroys uniformity of behavior among the members of a community,[1] and *adds a new distinction to that between leaders and led.* Hence we encounter the Germanic aristocracy from the very outset in a more sharply circumscribed special function. We need scarcely fear contradiction when we characterize this function as that of military leadership—a leadership, however, that meant not merely the command of forces but, to an increasing degree during the ensuing centuries, the actual execution of combat actions. Nor need we fear contradiction when we assert that this is the primary explanation for the generally enhanced position of the aristocracy, for its association with further functions—presiding at group meetings, leadership in other group concerns. It is plausible that the predominance of the military function, in uncomplicated circumstances and where the group is small in numbers, inhibits the emergence of positions of a different character. In the course of the Great Migrations and the concluding Merovingian and Carolingian successes, this social class steadily rose in power and position—it is of small moment, in this connection, that actual family content may have turned over rather rapidly. There can be no doubt, after all, that we are still entitled to speak of the same class. The question now at issue is no sooner put than answered. How can we explain this rise, this shift in relative class position? Evidently from the fact that, in the circumstances of the time, the basic class function gained in actual importance—as understood by us, the observers—and that this importance was sensed, not necessarily consciously, by the rest of the people. Both aspects are essential. Without the former there would not, in the long run, be an adequate explanation, a link with the objective facts of life of the social group; without the latter the vital connections between those vital facts and the phenomenon they created would be lacking.

This enhanced importance is *reflected and objectified* in the rise of a definite institution among the Germans in their new territories--the creation of great manorial estates. This is their social meaning and they become incomprehensible when this element is left out of consideration. It is for this very reason that the problem of the rise of such estates is such a complex and controversial one in the literature of legal and social history. All of a sudden, as it were, the great estates are in existence in the Carolingian period. One can only conclude from this fact that far-reaching social transformations had taken place; and, as is often the case with problems that are more apparent than real, this one has given rise to labored theories that are not always free of unconscious humor. Actually it is no more than the expression and gradual realization of an administrative system that arose independently, under the impact of our factor of a previously shifted class structure. Like the feudal system itself, the manorial estates, in one of their aspects, are only the expression of an administrative system adapted to special outward circumstances and the special class structure of the times—to the legal system in general, to passive methods of disposing of natural resources. (The methods are not necessarily

[1] More precisely, it is independent of positional elements that are recognizable before the event occurs. For the event may be—and generally is—tied to one of these elements.

passive in every case.) With the establishment of the great estates and the development of a mode of life in keeping with their conception at the time, as well as of a body of law affecting all classes—vassalage, immunity, court privilege, village law, and so on—there commenced a great social process that was subject to many fluctuations and setbacks and that ended only in the nineteenth century with the complete abolition of manorial privileges, even then leaving a heritage of established position to later times. We shall call this process *patrimonialization.*

There are four factors that justify the proposition that, down to the threshold of the "modern age," the relative position of our class was rising rather than sinking. I think this is apparent from the fact that, for the most part, its actual and legal privileges were on the increase, while similarly those of the remaining classes were on the decline. The only exception in this respect is the urban bourgeoisie, even though its rise did not take place in a straight line. It did, however, demonstrate the ultimate impotence of legal and political restrictions, even when the outward resources of power are at the disposal of those that impose them. It burst out of the social pyramid of feudal society, slipped from the grasp of the nobility, and enhanced its own weight and function despite all class legislation.

True, in the course of the centuries there were radical upheavals within that other class. (Technically, we should really speak in the plural, or at least distinguish between high and low aristocracy, but for the sake of simplicity in presentation we shall here speak only of a single class of feudal lords). There were numerous shifts in the position of groups within the class—above all, a constant turnover of its constituents. There were losses as well as gains in all these respects, though in the long run the gains outweighed the losses, as far as concerns class position as such. This outcome is attributable to the following four reasons: In the first place, during this entire time war essentially retained its character as a mode of life—a character it has since increasingly lost. It was a normal thing, not a last resort, as it came to be later. War and instant readiness for war remained an indispensable element of survival in every walk of life, in all socially characteristic situations. Those who could not themselves function along these lines were dependent on the protection of some individual warlord. Because this class function was so vital, it served to enhance the significance of another factor we should like to adduce in explaining shifts in class position. The class in question exercised its function with signal success. For, in the second place, the warrior of that period grew into an expert mounted fighter. Success in the profession of arms required not merely an aptitude for fighting, but constant application to technical mastery. Those who had other concerns were by that fact alone disqualified from the full exercise of this function. Today, special technical skill can be confined to the few who, in case of need, can in a short time train men drawn from their regular occupations. But that was not true then. Nor could the military rest content with working out measures for mobilization. The warlord himself constituted the machine on which everything rested. These circumstances lie at the very heart of the matter. . . . This also disposes of the seemingly plausible notion that possession of certain "means of production"—horse and armor—was the factor that led to the formation of the class. It is only necessary to realize that one of the objectives of the system of benefices must have been to furnish not only these immediate means but also those required for the life and profession of a knight in general to those who had already been chosen for other reasons. Yet these material elements and and the way in which they were provided did have the effect of elevating and securing class position. There were other mere consequences that worked in the same direction. On the one hand, the class base was broadened. Even relatively, the number of professional warriors was greater than that of the members of the nobility in the time of universal liability to military service. Then again, the qualities required and developed by the chivalric life were eminently suited to the defense of class position against other segments of the population, which in turn were in the process of losing these very qualities. A third reason for rising class position lay in the elaboration of functions that were originally subsidiary to the main function but that now, by virtue of the situation, were carefully preserved and even more closely associated with it. National horizons, interests, and tasks were expanding, and the upper class found ever new sources of activity and thus of power in the great problems of empire, which assumed reality for it alone. It should be pointed out, however, that the situation is by no means exhaustively characterized by mere reference to the interrelationship of these functions with the basic function that genetically explains class position. Two other relationships must be considered and conceptually differentiated from the one described. Quite apart from the fact that aptitude for war was necessary even for the exercise of these further functions—a qualification that gradually disappeared—it is manifestly significant that the exercise of these other functions was objectively related to the military preoccupations of a person of high rank. Here too it was a matter of deciding, commanding, leading, winning. This the knights—or at least a sufficient number of them—were able and willing to do. It was from their ranks that the emerging high nobility was recruited, and by no means exclusively nor even normally from the families of the earlier high nobility; and it was this section of the knighthood that maintained and enhanced the position of the entire knightly class. No such interrelationship was apparent in the economic sphere. The knight had neither the desire nor the ability to become a trader. Later on, as we shall presently see, this was reversed, though only in a special sense—a fact which again justifies our conception and explains the emergence of the bourgeois from the feudal class structure, as well as the already mentioned relative decline of the nobility as against this new group whose ancestors had once stood far beneath the nobility, whether they had been legally subordinate or not. The fundamental significance of this relationship to class development is evident, and it will later be formulated in general terms. Another relationship exists by virtue of the fact that, quite apart, for the moment, from the two correlations described, members of an elevated class, especially when their position has materialized even outwardly into privileges, property, and organic functions, find easier access to new functions (which they may even monopolize) than members of other classes. A fourth reason for the rise in the position of our class lies in the opportunities it had to colonize frontier regions, either for its own benefit or at any rate for the benefit of small subgroups, in its capacity to exploit these opportunities, and in the fact that they *were* exploited with success. This led to rising wealth, to a position of dominance over aliens, which in turn enhanced class position at home.

Yet from the end of the fourteenth century down to the present day our class has been almost without interruption on the downgrade. This is seen not so much in its legal status which even gained rather than lost in the fifteenth, sixteenth, and seventeenth centuries and did not begin to be systematically undermined until the eighteenth century—which agrees with the general observation that of all the clearly marked elements of social life the "superstructure"[2] of law, custom, and so forth is always the last to change, always lags behind changes in the actual life situation. Nor is it expressed in a decline in "social" position which, on the contrary, has been surprisingly well maintained to the present day. Rather does this decline emerge in the invariable subjection of the class to a new social factor—new, at least, in this particular form—the state power. At first glance it may seem as though this holds nothing new from the viewpoint of our subject, as though this need not impinge on class position as such. For primarily the "state power" meant no more than the sum total of the powers of the sovereign; and subjection of this nature meant no more than subjection to a superior within the class. . . . But the fact is that the sovereign did not subjugate the nobility in his capacity as feudal overlord; he did so in his capacity as master over an entirely different power—and it was to this power that he

[2] I employ this term, suggestive of the economic interpretation of history, in order to give expression to my belief that our line of reasoning is entirely reconcilable with that approach.

bent the nobility. There arose an administrative machine, at first predominantly manned by the nobility—more of this presently—but one with which it was by no means identical. This machinery, being capable of functioning equally well and even better in other hands, could be—and was in fact wrested from the grasp of the nobility and even of the sovereign. Objectively and theoretically, this was a new kind of subordination—submission to something that *ultimately turned out to be alien and even hostile.*

What we mean by patrimonialization is the process that explains this unfavorable change in class position—a process that must itself be explained. The term, in other words, is used in a broader sense than its technical application in legal and social history. We mean, first of all, the familiar process by which, from the Carolingian period on, vital functions became hereditary. Briefly, imperfectly, and indeed incorrectly put, they tended to become objects of the law of property. This is the *patrimonialization of office.* Secondly, we mean the process by which landownership by the nobles became—at first in fact and then in law (in its extreme form this is the alodification of fiefs)—a thing apart from the unified feudal system, in time simply a source of income, a means of production, an object of traffic. This is the *patrimonialization of landed property.* Thirdly, we mean the process by which the individual emerged from the obligations and attitudes of the feudal relationship, becoming in theory a citizen left to his own devices, shaping his private sphere more or less at will, even though for the time being he was still invested with special privileges and tied to fixed social forms. This is the *patrimonialization of the individual.* The rococo period shows us an intermediate state that is highly illuminating. In many outward respects the position of the nobility was never more splendid. Socially, legally, and materially, it rested on the very extensive heritage of the feudal age, in part well preserved, for the rest showing itself highly resistant even in a state of impairment. In all three directions this position was strengthened by the fact that the new state machine, whatever it may have taken away from the old position of overlordship, still needed to be staffed by the nobility, while in financial respects it proved at first to be an almost inexhaustible object of exploitation. What the historian, often quite superficially, describes as courtly extravagance at the whim of the sovereign, was actually the very essence of a social and political system which sought to transform the nobility from an independent gentry into a pliant court aristocracy, not merely by force, but also by economic temptation. Actually the time of that independence, when the nobles stood on their own two feet, was at an end. The essence and guarantee of independence had lain in the fact that in case of need the lord would mount his horse and defend himself, sword in hand, against dangers from above or below—the last example, already adulterated by other factors, is furnished by the sixteenth-century peasant wars. The time was past when the coronation formula of Aragon was a striking expression of an actual situation, when the concept of the "peer" had real meaning. Now the servility of the estates just as strikingly expressed a new situation of dependence on the favor and protection of the state machine. More and more the position of overlordship became a derivate, even where it antedated the state and had its foundations outside the state, even though it continued to enjoy the glory of ancient—and otherwise to an increasing degree borrowed—associations. In telling confirmation of our view, the complement to this situation was that the lower nobility was primarily preoccupied with its private concerns, while the higher nobility as such had nothing whatever to do. The facts are in part obscured by the circumstance that *members* of both groups were active in the service of the state, while there was an understandable tendency to continue the old functions in form rather than in substance. The rugged pugnacity of the knight remained as an ideal, to be refined into the fine arts of wielding the foil and riding according to the tenets of the classcial school, utterly devoid of any further significance in the social struggle for survival. Intervention in the affairs of state became a skillful ritual, an end in itself without relevance to the task in hand. If the action had any meaning at all, this was determined, not by the great lords who actually figured in the proceedings, but by other persons and interests. It is this survival of social and material position on the one hand, and the extensive decay of underlying functions on the other, that explain the characteristic charm and high culture of that period. True, even then this group had not completely closed ranks, but it had far fewer motives for accepting newcomers than any class immediately embroiled in the struggle for survival where it must stand up and show its mettle. Yet for a while, during the time in question, the nobility could utterly ignore the nature of the relationship between ruling and serving, could temporarily surrender to the illusion that the world was its oyster, that fun was the only purpose of life, that any act that was not pure entertainment represented a graciously conferred boon. All classes, including the ruling class, exercise rights just for the sake of maintaining them. But the rococo period was characterized by the exercise of rights (which were more and more losing their function) for purely selfish reasons—and this meant that the overlord really ceased to be one, in the essential meaning of his class position. Obviously the course of events in the eighteenth century supports our contention that such a situation could continue only because it was the heritage of an altogether different situation, and also because it never existed in the pure state and was always subject to numerous corrective and weakening factors. The only alternatives would have been a timely, voluntary surrender or adaptation to a process marked by legal continuity, or loss of position by events that break such continuity—in other words, retreat or defeat; and both contingencies lead to the same final result.

To the degree required for our purposes, we may enumerate the essential elements and causes of the process of patrimonialization under the four headings we have set forth. The scope of our study requires, however, that in each case we rest content with only the first links in causal chains that ultimately reach very deep. Thus we cannot immediately discuss why physical, armed combat ceased to be a mode of life inside the national community, and gradually outside it as well. But the fact that this happened did pull the foundation from under the main function of our class. One has to ask oneself whether the competitive economy of the nineteenth century could have existed if industrial families had not had to be continually concerned over their survival and to give constant attention to current business decisions. Reflection will show why we assert that the occasional exercise of a function—no matter how frequent the occasion, how vital the preoccupation, how suitable the function to become the basis of a full-time vocation—is insufficient to intrench a special discipline and orientation in such a way that they become the very life of a class. Even when he serves in the army, the modern conscript remains at heart a civilian. The modern professional soldier is a soldier in the sense that a lawyer is a lawyer. He is *not* a warrior, even though the traditional officer corps, in order to engender or preserve such an orientation, cultivates a warrior ideology, even going so far as to keep alive the fiction of individual readiness for combat by tolerating or promoting the duel. But when combat is no longer a mode of life, when it is no longer imminent at any moment in defense of immediate, personal interests—then it is no longer *the* great task, foreordained and self-evident. Battle, even though it may still be frequent, soon becomes an emergency situation, foreign and disturbing to other spheres of life, and there is no longer occasion for every member of the class to be constantly trained in it with every fiber of his being. This carries two consequences. The basic cause for the slow demilitarization of the nobility must be sought in the whole trend of society, which more and more circumscribed the occasion and opportunity for defending individual and class position by force of arms. Ultimately, this demilitarization made the armed class struggle—if one wishes to use that term—altogether impossible, and thus one of the conspicuous guarantees of class position fell by the wayside. Of far greater importance was the fact that this demilitarization, and the resulting orientation toward other interests, more and more had the effect of turning the nobility against its own basic function, causing it to undermine the very foundations of its own social importance. To an ever-increasing degree military service was rejected. It was not that the obligation to render such service was denied, but it was regarded as onerous and the call to it was complied with only grudgingly, if at all. Proof is furnished by the fact that in the fifteenth and early sixteenth centuries the feudal lords used the call to military service as one of the ways of making the estates comply with their financial requirements—something that can be understood only when it is realized that such duty, while acknowledged, was also resented. In this way, a replacement was found for the nobility in that sphere where combat still remained vital to survival—a sphere in which the nobility might well have continued to play a role, preserving part of its social importance. We should not overrate the significance of technical innovations in this process. On the technical side there was nothing to keep the nobility from taking to small arms and ordnance, just as it had once, with similar social results, mastered the technique of mounted and armored combat. It is no valid objection to say that the new techniques led to an increase in the number of effectives. For apart from the fact that this was to a certain extent a consequence of the circumstance that the people replacing the nobility were available in greater numbers, the earlier introduction of the host of mounted knights had itself led to a numerical increase in the nobility, a process to which any class vigorously oriented toward its function readily submits. *It is only because this did not happen now* that we think of the nobility as clinging stubbornly to the fighting methods of the Middle Ages and that the very idea of the nobility's adapting itself to the new methods seems far-fetched and unreal. Yet the army of knighthood did not fail because the mercenary army came into being. Rather the system of mercenaries arose because the knightly host failed from inner causes. But once the new situation existed, once the mercenary system functioned—with the nobility in part furnishing the financial resources (though mostly from the pockets of its own copyholders) for the very purpose of evading military service—*then* the army of knighthood had really grown obsolete and inferior. There was a stronger power in existence now, and this meant a fundamental change in the total social-class structure. As we shall presently have occasion to discuss again, the individual knight was still the most likely candidate for positions of leadership in the mercenary army; and significantly enough, he endeavored for a long time, by his bearing and appearance, to convey the impression that he was prepared at any moment to ride out full tilt with lowered lance to meet his enemy in indvidual combat—though in the end he was likely to don armor only when his portrait was to be painted. Even though this shed glamor on the class as a whole, it was something rather different from bearing the whole burden of combat. Yet the survival of such conspicuous externals served to slow down the full effect of the internal change. And with this, we have disposed not only of the first two of the four factors we enumerated as effecting changes in position, but also of the fourth, since the possibility of private colonization is obviously associated with the warrior function as a whole.

The process by which our class relinquished its basic class function implies not merely voluntary surrender and failure of will power, but also the pressure of the objective social situation which resulted in inactivity and flagging will. It implies not only *giving up*, but also, once that had begun, *taking away*. For the nobles this process was at the same time a process of individual emancipation, and it enabled the nobility as a class to loosen all the other feudal bonds—bonds which had already begun to lose meaning and to enter into a state of atrophy. This is just what we mean, in the case of the nobility, by "patrimonialization of the individual." But it is precisely because a decline in the social importance of a class function—the inadequate exercise and ultimate surrender of that function—*sets the members of the class free* that the decline in class position which might be expected occurs only if the class is unable to adapt itself to some other function that rates the same social importance as the old one. This fact, let us remark in passing, constitutes a severe limitation on the explanatory value of the relationship between class and function. There can never be any lack of new functions, unless a people chances into a stagnant social situation, free of problems. And every class that has once enjoyed an elevated position is greatly aided in seizing on new functions, because the sources and gains of its prior function survive for some time. In our own case we see at once that two such functions automatically obtruded themselves on the nobility by virtue of their relation to its former positions as the warrior and master class, and to which it did, in fact, turn. These functions were the staffing of the state machine and the administration of its own landed estates. It is at once evident why these two functions were, on the one hand, able to slow down and soften the descent of the class, while, on the other hand, they were insufficient to preserve its old position. Orientation toward individually owned landed property did not occur everywhere at the same rate and in the same manner. The differences in this respect are highly instructive. Where the state machine arose on the basis of the princely domain [*Fürstenterritorium*]—which was the case precisely where the mercenary system was most strongly developed—this orientation took place much more rapidly and sharply than in cases where the state had other antecedents, the single important example of the latter being England. Longer than anywhere else, and to a certain extent down to the present day, the English nobility continued in a position of national leadership, though in the course of time it became an agent rather than a ruler. It was able to do so because it did not turn to agriculture as an occupation and thus, on the one hand, remained free of all economic activity, while, on the other, it never degenerated into a group of economic and political partisans, as the nobility of other countries did. Nevertheless, the causes, the broad outlines, and the ultimate results of the process were everywhere the same, except that they emerge with particular clarity where the nobleman turns husbandman, where landlordism develops in its pure form. *Just as the manorial system corresponds to the type of the knightly warrior-politician and warrior-administrator, so the system of large landed estates corresponds to the type of the aristocratic businessman.* Naturally our process was determined by economic developments. Landlordism is possible only when population density has risen and when centers of consumption exist. The declining purchasing power of feudal money rents was a sharp incentive to the exploitation of inherited feudal resources for private economic gain, even though such exploitation was destructive of prestige. But the heart of the matter lies in the conquests of the period between the Merovingians and Hohenstaufens, which led to a situation in which the administration and enjoyment of what had been gained, individually and as a class, made for a full life, weakening the incentive for further headlong action—quite apart from the fact that outward opportunities for such action began to dwindle. These developments gave a calculating, private-economic direction to the nobility's attitude toward such matters as its own property, its relation to the peasantry, and the maintenance of feudal rights and duties. And all this, in turn, led to corresponding legal forms and constitutes the social content of the "patrimonialization of landed property."

The situation is basically similar in the case of the "patrimonialization of office." It too becomes the comprehensible from the same causal nexus. Here too, in the course of time, the successful families established themselves in the positions they had temporarily acquired, as though such a situation must automatically endure—just as the bourgeoisie in the early nineteenth century established itself in the positions it had created, invested those positions with appropriate legal standing, regarded individual control of the means and fruits of production as self-evident and, indeed, the whole order as permanent, because it was "natural." Yet this analogy does not extend all the way. It deserts us because of the circumstance that the old overlords, in order to administer and maintain their position, did not always have to repeat those actions that had led to the conquest of that position, while the position of the industrialists is rapidly dissipated unless it is constantly marked by the same kind of success that created it. That is the main reason why the analogy between feudal and industrial rule breaks down when applied seriously and in detail. There are, to be sure, other reasons as well, of which we shall mention the two most important. The feudal master class was once—and the bourgeoisie was never—the supreme pinnacle of a uniformly constructed social pyramid. The feudal nobility was once lord and master in every sphere of life—which constitutes a difference in prestige that can never be made up. Moreover, the feudal nobility was once—and the bourgeoisie was never—not only the sole possessor of physical power; it *was* physical power incarnate. The aforementioned main difference, however, means, on the one hand, that in the case of the nobility, class and individual family position endured far better and longer than in the case of the bourgeoisie. It means, on the other hand, that the objective social importance of the function of the bourgeoisie as a class is not as readily destroyed by its own failure as was true in the case of the nobility. The failing bourgeois family drops out of the class so swiftly that the class itself always consists of families which are normally equal to their function. Stated in a somewhat different way, with the emphasis on another factor: the nobility *conquered* the material complement to its position, while the bourgeoisie *created* this complement for itself.

. . . . . . . . . . . . . . . . . . . . . . . . . . . . . . . . . .

Not always, but predominantly—though to a declining degree—the functions involved in the attainment of outstanding success were exercised by members of the nobility.[3] There are many reasons for this. The existing class relationship facilitated mutual understanding and concerted action. By tradition the nobility was fitted for the tasks immediately in hand—quite apart from the traditions of war, there was the lordly mode of life, the habit of command and of handling people, of much greater importance in practical action than mere technical competence; even in our own times many outstanding presidents of English railway companies have been members of the court nobility. To complete the list of the most important considerations, there was finally the need to keep the nobility occupied, to tie it to the dynasty, to maintain its prestige among the people. This led to powerful customs and taboos which strengthened the position of the nobility all the more, since they perpetuated certain feudal and patrimonial elements which created the illusion of the continued existence of the old system. These customs included the long-maintained practice of reserving high government office to the nobility, the requirement that even ordinary army officers must show descent from a certain number of aristocratic ancestors, and so on. The practices of simony and patronage were specifically patrimonial and in most countries endured deep into the eighteenth century; in the English army, for example, they were abolished only during Gladstone's second ministry. Semi-dynastic succession in office likewise disappeared but slowly. As late as Louis XIV, Colbert and Louvois were succeeded by their sons in the same or similar offices, and the fact attracted not the slightest notice. It is nevertheless important to realize that this function of the nobility, though tending to preserve its position, merely shuffling the position of families, and serving to admit an infusion of new blood (the present-day high aristocracy was largely formed in this fashion), was something altogether different from the former warrior function of the nobility—this, of course, is self-evident—and also different from its position of leadership in public affairs during the Middle Ages. That position was then filled by warlords and by the military class generally, in their own right and with their own resources, regardless of feudal subordination. Now it was exercised at the behest, not of the feudal lord, but of the sovereign, in his borrowed right and power. The core of the system had vanished, its meaning and social content had changed. What did continue, maintaining the position of the nobility, though at a steadily declining rate, were merely accessory elements—ancient prestige, access to and fitness for certain key government jobs and

3 To the extent that other persons were involved, they were "elevated" and assimilated to the nobility—not always voluntarily.

political functions (now superseded by the modern trained expert), intimate contact between class members which facilitated survival, a material basis in agriculture and sometimes industry, stemming from land ownership, incidental opportunities of all kinds which were open to the individual in an "elevated" position. All this, however, tended to be swept away in time. And, confirming our basic view, the process did not take place uniformly and mechanically, but with characteristic differences, according to whether one or the other element of position could be made the basis for social function and success.

What we have been discussing is only an example, though one that demonstrates all the important elements essential in answering our question. It shows not only how our thesis may be proved, but also how it is meant to be understood. In particular there now emerges, much more clearly than would be possible from a general discussion, the sense in which we speak of a socially necessary function, of class activity and orientation to activity which we, the observers, understand to be necessary for the survival of the social group, under a given set of circumstances and with a given disposition on the part of the people, and which the group itself senses to be vital for survival. We have only to add the following:

*All* functions that can be distinguished in the case of a given people and in a given historical situation are "socially necessary." This criterion alone, therefore, cannot decide their relative evaluation. Evidently it is a question of how important the individual class member is in a given situation more particularly, to what degree he can be replaced. The individual warrior in the Middle Ages was less replaceable and individually more "important" than the peasant. The individual industrialist is less replaceable and individually more "important" than the individual worker.

The social importance of class members varies with our two basic elements—the importance of the class function and the degree of success in carrying out that function. But the relation is not always a direct one. Other causes often appear to be far more conspicuous and immediate. Yet such causes, on their part, can always be reduced to those basic elements, just as, according to the economic interpretation of history, the flow of social events is always ultimately shaped by the inner logic of the economic machine, though very often this influence is anything but direct. It is especially the inertia of once solidly established positions that creates a discrepancy between theory and practice, opening up a long chapter of intermediate processes. But these positions themselves can be made comprehensible in accordance with our principle.

Only this latter element explains why the evaluation of a function and the evaluation (that is, the social value) of a class do not always run parallel; why, instead, changes in class evaluation tend to lag behind changes in the evaluation of functions. This also explains the fact that, on first impression, it is more correct to describe the evaluation of a function as dependent on the social rank of those who exercise it. We say, for example, that the social rank of a class depends on the evaluation of its function by the social group, or on its importance for survival. and that "function" often appears at first, not as the prime mover, but as an accessory factor, something quite separate.[4] And this impression is strengthened—but also fully explained—by still another factor: socially necessary functions are not simply coordinate specialties. They do not all have the same relation to the leadership of social groups. Quite apart from the question of the degree to which *individual* members of the class are replaceable, the *intensity* of this relation to leadership provides a criterion for ranking socially necessary functions above and below one another and not simply for placing them beside each other as mere social necessities. But social leadership can express itself in many different concrete activities, and those which are chosen by a once-dominant group will thereby achieve higher social evaluation.

When we survey the ideas set forth in this section, we see that the causes that account for shifts in the relative positions of classes also, *ipso facto,* account for the original

[4] It is more accurate, by the way, to say that class determines "occupation" than the other way round.

order of rank—the order in which we find them at the outset of any given period. We also see why it is not always easy to establish an unequivocal class hierarchy, why there cannot always be "ruling" classes. More than that, it follows immediately that the same factors which ultimately account for shifts in class position in historical time and for the existing class structure at any given point in time, also answer the question of why there is such a phenomenon as class structure at all. For a class *gains and loses position in the same way that it emerges and passes as a class;* and only because an individual class *does* emerge and pass is there the general problem of class structure.

# PART II
# Principal Types of Stratification Systems

The social strata of our day bear, to use Schumpeter's picturesque description, the marks of different centuries on their brow. One could say, more generally, that the stratification system of any given time bears marks of the systems that preceded it. Thus it is important to study the major types of stratification systems not only in order to gain knowledge about the range of variation in the phenomenon of social inequality but also to understand the patterns of inequality today. For example, the contemporary system of stratification in the United States, and particularly in the South, still shows evidence of eighteenth- and nineteenth-century slavery and cannot be fully comprehended without taking that into account.

This is one of the main reasons why the first reading in this section deals with slavery. It is surprising yet true that sociologists have almost completely neglected slavery as a system of stratification. They generally distinguish caste, estate, and class as the principal types of stratification systems and do not name slavery as one of them.[1] And yet the literate public has become aware that slavery still exists in some parts of the world. A report compiled for the United Nations Human Rights Commission by Dr. Mohamed Awad of the United Arab Republic estimates that there are more than two million slaves today in various parts of Asia, Africa, and South America.[2]

What we mean by *types* of stratification? Despite the manifold variations in social inequality, through time and space, the following ideal types can be distinguished: slave, caste, estate, class, and "modern" stratification in advanced industrial society. By designating them as ideal types we serve notice that concrete systems are never exact replicas of these; as a matter of fact they are often "mixed

[1] See, for example, Kurt B. Mayer, *Class and Society,* New York: Random House, 1955, p. 7; Kare Svalastoga, *Social Differentiation,* New York: David McKay, 1965, p. 40; T. B. Bottomore, *Classes in Modern Society*, New York: Pantheon Books, 1966, p. 9. A noteworthy exception is Egon E. Bergel's, *Social Stratification*, New York: McGraw-Hill Book Company, 1962. It includes a chapter entitled "The Basic Division: Freedom and Bondage."

[2] C. L. Sulzberger, "Foreign Affairs: Slaves and Science," *The New York Times,* March 1, 1967, p. 42. Also see "Group Urging U.N. to Halt Slavery," *The New York Times*, December 4, 1966, p. 166.

types," containing elements of different ideal types.[3] However, it is precisely in order to gain some understanding of these concrete historical structures that we focus on ideal tpyes. Admittedly, each of these types is complex and there are many unsettled questions about their distinguishing characteristics. Nevertheless, armed with the theoretical formulations in the preceding section, we can attempt to specify the criteria of relevance that are implicit in this array of principal types of stratification. The following criteria seem of paramount importance. It should be noted at the outset that some pertain to the normative side and others to the actual side of stratification.

1. *Normatively* open-closed. Do the norms call for open or closed strata? What is the degree of openness or closure that they prescribe, prefer, or permit?
2. (Related to the preceding but pertaining to recruitment or filling of positions). *Normative* ascription-achievement. How much reliance is supposed to be placed on ascription, as compared with achievement, in filling of positions. (Ascription refers to the investment of persons with distinct statuses and roles by virtue of some quality or qualities over which they have no control; achievement—statuses obtained by virtue of their own achievement.)
3. Degree and type of institutionalization of inequality. How is unequal access to positions of advantage institutionalized? On what basis? Is it buttressed, and to what extent, by custom, law, ideology, and so on?
4. The *actual* predominant factor of social inequality from which all other inequality tends to flow—is it the power factor, the economic one, or status?

In introducing the selections, which deal mostly with concrete cases, we shall pay attention to how each of them meets these criteria. We shall also try to indicate the relative weight of a discussed criterion in a given system, for even though the four criteria are relevant in all types of stratification systems, they are not of equal importance in all systems. Take, for example, slavery. The two criteria of utmost significance are three and four: a high degree of institutionalization and the type of economic inequality are its distinguishing characteristics. To use the words of the outstanding historian of Greek slavery M. J. Finley, slavery is a system of stratification in which "... a man is in the eyes of the *law* and of public opinion and with respect to all other parties a *possession* of another man." [Italics supplied].[4] It was the economic fact of being owned, of being a possession, not the nature of the work, that made one a slave. Finley demonstrates convincingly that in ancient Greece there was no type of work solely performed by slaves in which free men would not engage. "In the Greek scale of values," he tells us, "the crucial test was not so much the nature of the work as the condition [freedom or slavery] . . . under which it was carried on."

Regrettably, this fact about slavery has not been brought into the contemporary discussion of the functional explanation of stratification, as we shall have the opportunity to note later when we read some of its well-known statements. According

[3] It might be fitting to recall here Max Weber's explanation of what an ideal type is. "An ideal type is formed by the one-sided *accentuation* of one or more points of view and by the synthesis of a great many diffuse, discrete, more or less present and occasionally absent concrete individual phenomena, which are arranged to those one-sidedly emphasized view points into a unified *analytical* construct. In its conceptual purity this mental construct cannot be found anywhere in reality." Max Weber, *The Methodology of the Social Sciences*, Glencoe: Free Press, 1949, p. 90.

[4] M. J. Finley, *Slavery in Classical Antiquity*, Cambridge, England: W. Heffer & Sons, 1960, p. 145.

to the functional theory, those positions rank higher in any society that (1) have the greater importance for society, (2) require greater training.[5] It can be easily seen that this explanation does not fit the slave system. The position of a slave ranked low because he was legally a possession, whereas the free man ranked higher because he was not owned by another. With ownership of the person came complete power over him. Thus the low rank of the *slave position* was tied to both the economic and power relation inherent in it.

The prestige factor in slavery is inseparable from the economic and power factors—but only in regard to the position, not in regard to the individuals who occupied it. It was the worst position to be in, but it was not considered to reflect on the *intrinsic* worth of the person. This is tied to the ways in which slave positions were filled. The slave system relied partially on birth (slave status was inherited from the mother), but its main sources of supply were captives and victims of war and piracy.

As Finley expresses it succinctly, ". . . the condition of servitude was one which no man, woman, or child, regardless of status or wealth, could be sure to escape in case of war or some other unpredictable and uncontrollable emergency." It is understandable why under such circumstances the idea of natural slavery could not gain ground, for everyone, so to speak, was a potential slave. There were attempts to justify slavery as "part of the natural arrangement" of things but this formulation did not become prominent either in Greece or Rome. The predominating view was that slavery was a man-made arrangement, a conventional institution, universally practiced.[6] As Florentius, the Roman jurist, phrased it, "Slavery is an institution of the *ius gentium* whereby someone is subject to the *dominium* of another, contrary to nature."[7] This did not, however, make the Greeks or Romans accept slavery less or question it more than it was later in the American South. Slavery remained unchallenged for they saw it as a necessity. To the Greeks, Nietzsche said, slavery was ". . . a necessary disgrace, of which one feels *ashamed,* as a disgrace and necessity at the same time."[8] They, including their philosophers, could not imagine civilized society without slaves just as most people today, including many sociologists, cannot imagine industrial society without differential ranking of occupations.

Since the publication in 1947 of Frank Tannenbaum's *Slave and Citizen,* the most original and thoughtful studies have expounded the view that slavery in the United States had little in common with previous forms of servitude.[9] But Arnold A. Sio, in the reprinted essay, "Interpretations of Slavery: Slave Status," basing himself on recent scholarship, challenges this view. He draws a thorough comparison of slavery in the United States with slavery in Rome and more briefly compares it in the United States and in Latin America. He demonstrates convincingly that the *legal* status of the slave as property was essentially the same in Rome and in the United States. Neither did American slavery differ from ancient slavery in its pervasiveness. For there was hardly a branch of Greek life not

[5] Kingsley Davis and Wilbert E. Moore, "Some Principles of Stratification," see pp. 496–503 in this volume.

[6] Finley, *op. cit.*, pp. 145–164.

[7] *Ibid.*, p. 153.

[8] As quoted by Finley, *ibid.*, p. 70.

[9] David Brion Davis, *The Problem of Slavery in Western Culture*, Ithaca: Cornell University Press, 1966, p. 29.

affected in some way by the fact that many people in Greece were slaves or former slaves.

Sio's position is in accord with the subsequent monumental work by David Brion Davis, who minimizes the difference between ancient slave systems and the American one and maintains that ". . . a comparable analysis of historical forms of servitude reveals precedents for *most* of the striking traits of American slavery" (italics supplied).[10] Davis, however, makes clear that he is not implying that slavery in America lacked distinctive characteristics, such as its racial basis and its legal barriers against manumission. And he does assert that "In no ancient society was the distinction between slave and freedom so sharply drawn as in America."[11]

This distinction is tied to the manner of filling positions. As is shown in Sio's essay, the major difference between Southern slavery and that in Greece and Rome was that race was made the basis for filling slave positions in the United States. Greek and Roman slavery had no color line. But we gather from David Brion Davis' work that the color line in America was not entirely unique. Racial distinctions were of some importance in the Arab world and in Mameluke Egypt, where Negro slaves were far more prevalent than in the Roman Empire. According to Davis, "Moslems not only accepted the legitimacy of Negro enslavement, but were inclined to think of black Africans as a docile race who were born to be slaves." And he shows that in China during the T'ang Dynasty ". . . there was a definite connection between slavery and racial prejudice."[12]

Sio questions the widely accepted thesis of the profound differences between slavery in the United States and Latin America. However, in surveying the work done in this field, he finds it insufficient and calls for more comparative studies. Since then a number of the kind of studies he called for have appeared, such as those by Eugene Genovese, Herbert S. Klein, and David Brion Davis.[13] In a review article of these studies, Sio says that ". . . they provide us with the beginning of a significant body of scholarship on slavery in the Americas."[14] According to Genovese the slave system of the South was not unique; what was unique was the civilization of the South. As far as its slavery is concerned, it represents a case of a "mature, commercially oriented slave system."[15] David Brion Davis, too, stresses the similarities between slavery in the United States and Latin America. He challenges the assumption of modern historians that Latin Americans were more sensitive to the essential humanity of their slaves. It is true, says he, that slavery in Latin America was less affected by competitive capitalism and closer to a patriarchal system than that in North America. But evidence shows that at times an exploitative, capitalistic form of servitude existed in Brazil and Spanish America and that, on the other hand, at certain times and places the paternalistic pattern existed in North America and the humanity of slaves was openly acknowledged. He concludes therefore that ". . . it may be that the differences between Latin America and the United States were no greater than regional or temporal differences

[10] *As quoted by Finley, ibid.*, p. 31.

[11] *Ibid.*, pp. 30, 47.

[12] *Ibid.*, pp. 50–51.

[13] Eugene D. Genovese, *The Political Economy of Slavery: Studies in the Economy and Society of the Slave South*, New York: Pantheon Books, 1965; Herbert S. Klein, *Slavery in the Americas—A Comparative Study of Cuba and Virginia*, Chicago: University of Chicago Press, 1967.

[14] Arnold A. Sio, "Society, Slavery, and the Slave," *Social and Economic Studies*, Vol. 16, September, 1967, pp. 330–344.

[15] Genovese, *op. cit.*, p. 8.

within the countries themselves." And this conclusion leads him to view Negro slavery in the Americas as "a single phenomenon, or *Gestalt,* whose variations were less significant than underlying patterns of unity."[16]

Older historical treatments of slavery in the United States proceed along the thesis that the status of the Negro in America as a member of a racial minority developed concurrently, because there was neither a tradition of slavery or racial prejudice in the colonies. But this, according to Sio, is an erroneous assumption, because recent historical evidence indicates that discrimination against the Negro occurred before the slave status was fully defined.

The tie between race and slavery accounts for all other major differences between American and ancient slavery. First of all, it explains why the American slave, in contrast to the slave of ancient times, was considered *intrinsically* inferior. This supposed innate inferiority was in turn developed into an ideology, a rationalization for the tie between slavery and race. The restriction of slavery to the Negro made possible its existence in the United States, a country whose Declaration of Independence proclaimed that all men were created equal. This restriction rested on the principle that it was a position fit for Negroes, and not whites, because the first were innately inferior beings. Slavery in ancient times was not restricted to any particular group who "ought properly to occupy the legal status of slave." Thus there was no conception of the slave or former slave as innately inferior. But in America it was considered proper and fitting that Negroes be slaves because of their race.

The tie between slavery and race also accounts, to quote Sio, for "the creation of a hereditary, endogamous, and permanent group of individuals in the status of slaves." When we consider slavery in terms of the criterion of open-closed, we realize that the closure is not inherent in the norms of slavery. As Frank Tannenbaum noted, and he is quoted by Sio, slavery systems differ in terms of "ease and availability of manumission," of change from slave to free status. Manumission was a common phenomenon in the Greek world, and easy for the Roman slave but very hard for the Negro slave in America.

This joining of slave status with race also throws light on why the position of the freed Negro was low in contrast to the situation in Rome and Greece where the former slave could rise. Sio explains it in terms of "caste law as well as slave law" governing the status of the Negro in the ante-bellum South. (The fact that the law of the South restricted the status of slavery "to members of a particular group for whom slavery is defined as natural, inevitable, and permanent" makes him think of it as "caste law.") This writer prefers to formulate it differently, however: Slavery was joined with race and an ideology of inferiority developed to justify it. And these were the two seeds of the caste system that developed fully once slavery was abolished in the South. Prior to that there was the incipient caste of the small number of free Negroes in the North and South who were legally prohibited from intermarrying with the dominant group. The free Negro was a living denial that slavery followed "naturally and inevitably" from the fact of being Negro and was thus a symbolic threat to Southern slavery. This throws light on the growth of "caste laws" in the *later slavery* period. Because of them the "freedom" of the Negro turned out quite often to be limited. The caste laws and practices also strengthened pro-slavery feelings among nonslaveholders, even the

[16] Davis, *op. cit.,* pp. 223–262. Direct quotations are from pp. 224 and 229.

very poor ones whose economic opportunities were limited by slavery.[17] No matter how low his status the white person was higher than the Negro, by virtue of not being the property of another and not having the *potential* of being turned into property. It is the latter that sustained the strong commitment of the non-slaveholding free population to slavery, even if slavery was the source of economic disadvantage for many of them. The case in point is that of the unskilled laborer who had no place open for him for advancement under the system of slavery. But in the matter of prestige he was twice ahead of the slaves: he was neither a slave nor a potential slave.

The main factor in status variation among the whites was the relation to slaveholding. Among slaveholders, status varied directly with the numbers of slaves held. Among those with no slaves, "the immediacy of relationship or closeness of approximation to the goal of slaveholding was the primary relevant consideration." In the slave stratum, too, variations in prestige could be distinguished between substrata such as "house servants" and "field hands."[18]

Sociologists first became aware of caste through their studies of India. Much later came the interest in caste in the United States. When one reads detailed descriptions of caste stratification in these two societies, the similarities in codes of behavior and practices are glaring.[19] The sharp difference between them is that in the United States caste is pinned to race, whereas in India the caste line is not a color line. (Indians do seem to have skin color preferences, in that "fairness" is considered more beautiful, but this may be comparable to the present preference for blond hair in the United States).[20]

But then it is this sharp difference that has given rise to the controversy about whether the concept of caste fits the American condition. In our selection "Caste in India and the United States," Gerald D. Berreman summarizes the essential points of this controversy by defending the position that a caste structure exists in the South. The definition of the caste system with which he begins is a "hierarchy of endogamous divisions in which membership is hereditary and permanent," he adds that the "hierarchy includes inequality, both in status and access to goods and services." He then goes on to demonstrate how the system in the South is similar to that of India in the characteristics included in the definition, as well as in other features. It seems to me that it would prove useful as we read Berreman to think of how the caste system lines up on the criteria of relevance we proposed at the beginning of the introduction (p. 52) and how it differs on these from slavery.

The criterion that looms largest is the criterion of open-closed, for the norms of the caste system—in contrast to those slavery, let alone the other types of stratification systems—call for *absolute* closure of the strata. Next, in filling positions, the norms call for *exclusive* reliance on ascription. The mechanism that effectuates the preceding two norms is that membership in strata is *exclusively* hereditary. Endogamy is not necessary for assuring closure or ascription, because this could be

[17] Support for my reinterpretation is found in Wilbert E. Moore and Robin M. Williams, "Stratification in the Ante-Bellum South," *American Sociological Review*, Vol. 7, June, 1942, pp. 343–351; and in Klein, *op. cit.*

[18] *Ibid.*, Moore and Williams.

[19] John Dollard, *Caste and Class in a Southern Town*, New Haven: Yale University Press, 1957; Baidya Nath Varma, "The Caste System of India," in *Contemporary India*, London: Asia Publishing House, 1964, pp. 59–81; and Harold C. Isaacs, *India's Ex-Untouchables*, New York: John Day Company, 1965.

[20] Isaacs, *ibid.*

accomplished through a patrilineal or matrilineal inheritance of positions. I would suggest that the unconditional endogamy in the caste system is related to another criterion, that of degree of institutionalization of inequality. Of all the principal types of stratification systems, the caste system is most highly institutionalized. In the caste system the inequality between the strata is guaranteed not only by laws—which is also true of slavery—and by conventions—which is true of other stratification systems—but also by ritualism—which is not present elsewhere. If we recall our readings in theory, Max Weber drew our attention to ritualism as a characteristic feature of caste stratification. Elsewhere he spoke about ritual barriers as being essential for caste.[21] Berreman shows convincingly how this feature is present in the South as well as in India.[22] I want to suggest that unconditional endogamy is the logical consequence of the idea of ritualistic impurity just as are the "inviolable barriers against commensalism," to use Max Weber's expression. Endogamy is characteristic of all other types of stratification but is not unconditional even in slavery. American slavery departed in this respect from the ideal type and contained this feature of caste stratification.

Finally, we must consider which factor of inequality is the paramount one. It should be recalled that Weber spoke of caste as a closed status group, meaning that it was stratification in terms of prestige. The Weberian formulation can be modified by stating that prestige inequality is the most important factor from which all other inequality flows. There is a hierarchy of prestige in terms of *inherent* inferiority and superiority that applies to both the strata and the individuals who are found in them. This determines the economic and power position of the individuals in that stratum. It contrasts with slavery, where the predominant factor is the economic one. Thus it could be said that although the Marxist model of economic determinism fits slavery it does not fit the caste system. The crucial test of the weight of the status factor in caste stratification is that in those cases of discrepancy between one's economic standing and his status, states decides the caste placement. Furthermore, status in caste stratification, in contrast to the economic situation in slavery, as we already noted, is unchangeable. People of low caste who manage to advance economically, nevertheless cannot cross the caste line.

It is noteworthy that feudalism has been the subject of controversy among social scientists similar to that surrounding caste. Some historians insist that feudalism is a technical term that can be used only for Western European institutions of the Middle Ages and reject attempts to find feudalism in other places or at other times. Others, like Strayer and Coulborn, think of it as a highly abstract concept that describes a general method of political organization.[23]

To the latter belongs also Marc Bloch, even if in his book *Feudal Society*—and in the excerpt we are reprinting—he deals almost exclusively with Western European feudalism. His is a dynamic treatment of feudalism, for he deals with its emergence and its development. Bloch too sees the political aspect as primary, since power—or as he terms it, authority—is monopolized by a small group of

[21] Max Weber, *The Religion of India*, Glencoe: Illinois, Free Press, 1958, pp. 39–45.

[22] We find parallel descriptions of this phenomenon in Japan in regard to the *Eta* who today comprise about 2 per cent of the total populace and who physically are indistinguishable in any sense from the rest. See George De Vos and Hiroshi Wagatsuma, *Japan's Invisible Race*, Berkeley: University of California Press, 1966.

[23] Joseph R. Strayer and Rushton Coulborn, "The Idea of Feudalism," in *Feudalism in History*, Princeton, N.J.: Princeton University Press, 1956, p. 5.

military leaders. The main function of these leaders was as warriors, for fighting, as Bloch shows, was not merely an occasional duty, but their life's purpose. Whatever the sources of their income—mostly land, but sometimes shops and workshops—they always "Lived on the labour of other men." He therefore stresses that the characteristic feature of the top stratum was not the possession of wealth but "some form of exploitation." The men who had power also possessed important sources of wealth, but wealth alone did not confer power.

Neither did wealth confer status. Status was derived from power rather than ownership and was joined indivisibly to it. As Bloch expresses it, "If the possession of manors was the mark of a genuinely noble status . . ., the only form of wealth which seemed compatible with high rank, this was due in the first place to the authority over other men which it implied. (Could there ever be a surer basis of prestige than to be able to say: 'It is my will.')"

Bloch refers to the strata in the feudal order as classes, using the term in the generic sense that we noted in Marx. Contemporary sociological writing generally employs the term *estates,* a distinction derived from Toennies' dichotomous typology of estates as "communal and classes as societal collectives."[24] As we gather from the descriptions this fits the top stratum, if not during the period of the emergence of feudalism, certainly once it was solidified. It was "set apart by its power, by the nature of its wealth, its mode of life, by its very morals." Bloch describes in some detail the mode and style of life, the central values and code of behavior of this "dominant class" that eventually became transformed into a nobility. The facts could serve us well as points of comparison when we focus on comparable aspects of modern stratification. As far as the understanding of feudal stratification, we are now touching on the degree of institutionalization of inequality. Sociologists generally conceive of estate stratification as a system where the strata are clearly distinguished and set off from one another by *law.*[25] Bloch's treatment presses us to reconsider this point. He demonstrates that such laws did not exist during the "first feudal age" in Europe and explains the conditions under which they came into existence in the twelfth century. In that century a new power was born, the urban patriciates who aspired to noble status. The warriors recognized them as foreign to their own mentality and therefore as constituting a special threat, because their number would endanger the noble way of life. On the other hand they were farsighted enough not to exclude from their ranks the "new forces." Thus, according to Bloch, came about the transformation of the nobility into a legal class. The law did not impose a ban on new admissions, but rather subjected them to strict control. We see then that norms of the estate system call for relatively closed strata; only a limited number of new families can be admitted to the dominant stratum in accordance with firmly established rules. As Bloch picturesquely expresses it, "If the access to the circle of knights was not absolutely closed, the door was nevertheless only slightly ajar." In filling the positions, the norms stipulate chief reliance on ascription by means of inheritance but also pay heed to achievement. The enforcement of these norms may be through custom and tradition or, when these do not suffice, through formal laws.

Another common sociological formulation that requires critical scrutiny, in

[24] Ferdinand Toennies, "Estates and Classes," in Reinhard Bendix and S. M. Lipset, eds., *Class, Status and Power,* Glencoe, Illinois: 1953, p. 49.

[25] See Mayer, *loc. cit.*; see also Bernard Barber, *Social Stratification,* New York: Harcourt, Brace, 1957, p. 55.

light of Bloch's profound analysis of European feudalism, is the conclusion that the estate system consisted of "a *hierarchy* of several social strata," (italics supplied).[26] In his summary of the fundamental characteristic of European feudalism, Bloch stresses that it was an *unequal* society, rather than a hierarchical one.

Before proceeding to the discussion of the next selection it might be interesting to mention that Bottomore, basing himself on Bloch, considers, among the different types of stratification systems, feudalism as closest to Marx's model of a society because it is characterized by the rule of a warrior class that has in its hands the ownership of land and military force.[27]

But it is Marx's model of capitalist society that is subjected to thorough criticism in our last selection on types of stratification systems. Its author, Theodor Geiger, makes a distinction between stratification in capitalist society and contemporary highly industrialized society, which according to him is no longer capitalist. He sees Marx's theory as an adequate explanation of capitalist stratification but completely erroneous in relation to "postcapitalist" stratification. Geiger's distinction between capitalist and postcapitalist society is especially important because capitalism and industrial society are often treated by social scientists as if they were synonymous.[28] Capitalism is only one form of industrial society, whose distinguishing mark Geiger shows is the joining of ownership with control of the means of production. Thus the economic factor is decisive and power results from it. One might add, so does status result from it, as was noted by Max Weber, who pointed to the class situation (economic) in the society of his time (capitalist) as "by far the predominant factor, for of course the possibility of style of life expected for members of a status group is usually conditioned economically."[29]

Geiger's penetrating essay,[30] *Die Klassengesellschaft im Schmelztiegel* has exercised a profound influence on European sociological thought but is unknown in the United States.[31] I have translated parts of the book that seemed to me to convey the essential thoughts of Geiger on the differences between capitalist and postcapitalist stratification.

He puts forth clearly the thesis of the weakening of class in the Marxian sense, because in the postcapitalist society the existing interest groups are no longer determined by the social relationships within the system of production, that is, property. The old class society stands on the threshold of a new type of society that cannot be adequately understood in terms of class opposition and conflict. Certain new lines of development are taking place that were unanticipated by Marx and cannot be accounted for by his theory. The old middle class—contrary to Marx's prediction—did not become "proletarianized" and did not join the anticapitalist proletarian front. As a matter of fact it turned against it. In addition, a new propertyless middle class has arisen that has turned out to be largely aloof

[26] Mayer, *loc. cit.*, p. 7.

[27] T. B. Bottomore, see p. 160 of this volume.

[28] Ralf Dahrendorf, in *Class and Conflict in Industrial Society*, Stanford: Stanford University Press, 1959, especially pp. 36–41, is very critical of the failure to distinguish between the two. In his book he consistently uses the label postcapitalist to designate advanced industrial society.

[29] See p. 24–34 of this volume.

[30] T. H. Marshall, "General Survey of Changes in Social Stratification in the Twentieth Century," in *Transactions of the Third World Congress of Sociology*, Vol. III, London, 1956, p. 13.

[31] For example, among the prominent authors in the field of stratification the following European sociologists refer to Geiger: Ossowski, Marshall, Bottomore, Aron, and Dahrendorf. Not even in the most recent writings of Lipset, Lenski, and so on, has there been mention of the work of Geiger.

and even hostile to the proletarian front. Geiger sees fascism and Nazism as the outcome of this hostility of the middle class to socialism as well as to large capital.

The pauperization of the working class which, Marx foretold, has not taken place. On the contrary, a new line of development is evident: income distribution crosses class lines. With it comes the increasing importance of consumption. In the postcapitalist era, devoid of traditional symbols, status, according to Geiger, is determined by income. Consumption replaces ownership of the means of production as a status symbol.

Another new line of development is the "institutionalization" of class conflict, by which Geiger means the recognition by owners of the legitimacy of labor organization. The owners and trade unions face each other as two great powers of the economic structure. Galbraith's more recent concept of trade unions as a "countervailing power" resembles the Geiger formulation about the institutionalization of class conflict. So does Dahrendorf's "theory" of "institutional isolation of industrial conflict."[32]

Geiger also points to the "managerial revolution" (Burnham's thesis)[33] as a new line of development. Under this heading is found his very important analysis of the difference between ownership and control of the means of production. We are witnessing, says Geiger, the separation of control of property or the means of production from ownership. He maintains that, insofar as in the postcapitalist society of the West the owner is increasingly hampered in the control of the property, society becomes "socialist in substance," even though it has remained capitalist in name. This is largely a semantic problem, but I doubt that it is correct to think of such a society as "socialist in substance." Socialist implies both *collective ownership* and *collective control,* and the latter accounts for the fact that to this day socialism has been only possible in small groups. Because collective control is not a feature of advanced industrial society, a more appropriate designation is the one that is currently coming into usage, *welfare capitalism,* to distinguish it from the Soviet type of society. Geiger himself points out that in the latter societies, so called socialist countries, collective ownership is only a phrase, because not the public, but economic managers have control over the property. This places them in a position of power. Thus the analysis by Geiger suggests—and we shall be able to judge on the basis of empirical studies to what extent this holds true—that the stratification in contemporary Soviet-type societies and Western-type societies is essentially the same. Both are characterized by the primacy of the state over the economy, and in both a group of men controls the economic resources of the society. This group, says Geiger, is the ruling stratum of the future if society continues on the road of planned economy.

We gather from this account that power is emerging as the primary factor of inequality in advanced industrial society. If this is so—and we will be able to judge better later in light of the empirical studies in the next section of the book—then the stratification system of highly industrialized society will differ fundamentally from its predecessor capitalist stratification whose primary factor is economic. Mosca made the point that in capitalism, which he referred to as the bureaucratic state, ". . . wealth produces power just as political power has been producing

[32] John K. Galbraith, *American Capitalism: The Concept of Countervailing Power,* Boston: Houghton Mifflin, 1956, pp. 114–117; Dahrendorf, *op. cit.,* pp. 267–272.

[33] James Burnham, *The Managerial Revolution,* New York: John Day Company, 1941.

wealth" in feudalism.[34] Advanced industrial society would then resemble feudalism in the primacy of power.

It is fitting to conclude this introduction with a summary of how the principal types of stratification systems, about which you will be reading, line up on the criteria of relevance that were proposed at the beginning of the introduction. In terms of the first criterion—whether the norms call for open or closed strata—the caste system stands at one extreme and the capitalist and modern systems at the opposite extreme. The norms of the caste system ask for *absolute closure,* the norms for the latter for *absolute openness.* The norms of the estate system also prescribe closure, but not complete closure, for they provide an opening for the select few to move up to the higher estates. As for slavery, it seems to vary on this criterion.

Corresponding to the lineup on the first criterion is the lineup on the second criterion of normative reliance on achievement or ascription—and the reasons are clear, because each of the two criteria is the consequence of the other. Again the polar types are caste with its call for *exclusive reliance on ascription* and its opposite, class plus the advanced industrial system for *exclusive reliance on achievement.*

As for the third, the degree and nature of institutionalization, the highest degree corresponds to caste with its ritualistic impurity, for it imposes utmost control. Also quite binding are the laws of slavery and the customs, traditions, or laws of estates. The matter of institutionalization in capitalist and advanced industrial society is more intricate, as we shall discover from later readings. Because the norms call for absolute openness and exclusive reliance on achievement, we have to search the manner and degree to which these goals are guaranteed. Suffice it to say at this point that the factual order in caste, slavery, and possibly also the estate system comes closer to their respective normative order of closure and ascription than does the factual order of capitalist and advanced industrial societies to the norms of absolute openness and exclusive reliance on achievement.

In the matter of the fourth criterion, the actual predominant factor of social inequality from which all other inequality tends to flow, it is the economic component in the cases of slave and class stratification, status in caste, and power in the case of estate and modern stratification. Clearly, we are not implying that the economic factor in the first two stratification systems or the power factor in the two last ones is the same in nature, manifestations, or complexity. This also applies to the other factors in each stratification system: In all types of stratification systems economic, power, and status inequality are present, but they vary in their nature, manifestations, and complexity from system to system.

Where the difference lies between capitalist and modern on one hand, and the other stratification systems, on the other, is in the correlation between economic, power, and prestige inequality; although close, it is not equally tight. This is so because the relations among the three factors are considerably more complex in the first than in the latter systems.

But a common note in all stratification systems, as the readings show, is that the strata are not homogenous and in each of them substrata can be distinguished. It merits emphasis, because this characteristic is often seen as unique to the class system.

Finally, I should like to make clear that in this summary the most tentative generalizations are those concerning modern stratification in advanced industrial

[34] Gaetano Mosca, *The Ruling Class,* New York: McGraw-Hill Book Company, 1939, p. 57.

society. It resembles capitalist stratification on three of the four criteria, but this may be because it is an emerging system; new and different features may come forth in the course of its development. What the new features are or are likely to be is the subject of much controversy, as we shall learn later from the readings in the final part of this volume.

# INTERPRETATIONS OF SLAVERY: THE SLAVE STATUS IN THE AMERICAS

*Arnold A. Sio*

Recent interpretations of slavery in the United States suggest that we may be entering a new phase of scholarship on slavery as new approaches and categories are introduced by historians, and as anthropologists and sociologists again take up the study of an institution that was of such concern to their nineteenth century predecessors.

As an assessment of these interpretations, the concern of this essay is with those aspects of the legal status of the slave which appear as problematic or neglected. The purpose is to reformulate, refocus, and clarify rather than to introduce an alternative interpretation or to present new materials.

Although the scholarship on slavery has tended to shift away from the strong moral bias as well as the categories of analysis carried over for so long from the pro-slavery and anti-slavery debates, those aspects of the slavery system traditionally at issue also constitute the problematic aspects in the more recent interpretations. These are the legal status of the slave, the relations of masters and slaves, and the relationship between these two facets of the institution.[1]

## I.

The concept of slavery covers a considerable variety of social phenomena, but it is generally thought of as the practice of bringing strangers into a society for use in economic production and legally defining them in terms of the category of property. The complete subordination of the slave to the will of the master is regarded as a main defining feature of the institution.

> Subordination implies and is an aspect of authority. Authority is the socially recognized right to direct, control or manage some or all of the affairs of a person, or group, or thing. In this sense there is an overlap between property as a bundle of rights over things and the authority which is invested in some person over others as their slaves, with the result that such types of authority are treated as property at law.[2]

Slavery involves the "legal assimilation of interpersonal rights to the norm of property rights over things".[3]

This definition of the legal status of the slave has been taken in many studies as a basis for an interpretation solely in terms of the property component in the status[4]. . . . This conception obscures significant differences between the property and racial components in the status, and circumvents critical evidence pertaining to the personal component in the status.[5]

In this essay an attempt is made to distinguish between the property and racial components in the status of the ante-bellum slave through a comparison with Roman slavery where the status involved a property but not a racial component. This is followed by a consideration of the evidence for a personal component in the definition of the slave status in the United States. The essay concludes with some re-examination of the status of the slave in Latin America in terms of the three components.

The interpretations of Frank Tannen-

From *Comparative Studies in Society and History*, Vol. VII, No. 3, April, 1965, pp. 289–308. Reprinted by permission.

[1] See Stanley Elkins, *Slavery*, (Chicago, 1959), Chap. I; Kenneth Stampp, "The Historian and Southern Negro Slavery," *American Historical Review*, LVII, (April, 1952), pp. 613–24; Richard Hofstadter, "U. B. Phillips and the Plantation Legend," *Journal of Negro History*, XIXX, (April, 1944), pp. 109–25.

[2] M. G. Smith, "Slavery and Emancipation in Two Societies", *Social and Economic Studies*, III, Nos. 3 and 4 (1954), pp. 245–46.

[3] *Ibid.*, p. 246.

[4] The classic account is H. J. Nieboer, *Slavery as an Industrial System* (Rotterdam, 1910).

[5] Wilbert Moore, "Slave Law and the Social Structure", *Journal of Negro History*, XXVI April, 1941), pp. 171–202.

baum[6] and Stanley Elkins[7] exemplify the shift away from the moral approach to the institution of slavery and the introduction of new methods and categories. The treatment in both is comparative. Why did slavery in the United States differ in form and consequences from the kind of servitude developed in the Latin American colonies of Spain and Portugal? According to Tannenbaum, there were at least three traditions or historical forces in Latin America which prevented the definition of the slave there solely as property; namely, the continuance of the Roman law of slavery as it came down through the Justinian Code, the influence of the Catholic Church, and the long familiarity of the Iberians with Moors and Negroes.[8] Tannenbaum puts his emphasis on whether, "The law accepted the doctrine of the moral personality of the slave and made possible the gradual achievement of freedom implicit in such a doctrine" and on a universalistic religion, i.e. Catholicism, in preventing the definition of the slave solely as property.[9] In the United States slavery developed in a legal and moral setting in which the doctrine of the moral personality of the slave did not affect the definition of his status in the society. "Legally he was a chattel under the law, and in practice an animal to be bred for market."[10]

[6] *Slave and Citizen* (New York, 1947).

[7] *Slavery*. Chap. 2. This discussion is limited to his treatment of the legal status of the slave. Elkins proposes an alternative to the established approach to slavery in the United States which, taking its stance from the debates over slavery, has been concerned mainly with the rightness or wrongness of the institution considered in terms of categories pertaining to the health and welfare of the slaves. The historical study of slavery has alternated over the years between a pro-slavery and an anti-slavery position, but the purpose and the categories of analysis have remained unchanged. The result has been a continuing confusion of the historical study of slavery with moral judgments about slavery. Elkins proposes discarding this approach and adopting instead the method of comparison as followed by Tannenbaum. Slavery as an evil is taken for granted. Elkins' treatment of slavery as analogous to the concentration camp in its effects on Negro personality is discussed in Earle E. Thorpe, "Chattel Slavery and Concentration Camps", *The Negro History Bulletin*, XXV (May, 1962), pp. 171–76.

[8] Tannenbaum, pp. 43–65.

[9] *Ibid.*, p. 8.

[10] *Ibid.*, p. 82.

In comparing North American and Latin American slavery, Elkins adds to Tannenbaum's earlier treatment. The legal status of the slave in "the liberal, Protestant, secularized, capitalist culture of America" is contrasted with that of the slave in "the conservative, paternalistic, Catholic, quasi-medieval culture of Spain and Portugal and their New World colonies".[11] Elkins concludes that in the absence of such restraining institutions in the United States the search for private gain and profit was unlimited, and the law of slavery developed in such a way as to eliminate the slightest hindrance to the authority of the slaveholder over his slaves. The legal status of the slave developed exclusively in terms of property as the result of the demands of an emerging capitalism. Slavery in the United States was "a system conceived and evolved exclusively on the grounds of property."[12]

For Elkins and Tannenbaum the definitive feature of the legal status of the ante-bellum slave was the centrality of the property component. The rights of personality were suppressed by the law, and the legal subordination of the slave to the authority of the master in the areas of parentage and kinship, property and other private rights, and police and disciplinary power over the slave was developed to such an extent as to make slavery in the United States a unique system.[13] The entire institution became integrated around the definition of the slave as property.

Kenneth Stampp's *The Peculiar Institution*[14] has been viewed as one of the most important and provocative contributions since Ulrich B. Phillips' *American Negro Slavery*.[15] Although it is organized essentially in terms of the categories used by Phillips and other earlier students of slavery, Stampp's study exceeds the earlier work in comprehensiveness, in presenting the response of the slave to the institution, and in its use of the available scientific evidence regarding race. In contrast to Elkins and

[11] Elkins, p. 37.

[12] *Ibid.*, p. 55.

[13] *Ibid.*, p. 52. These categories are taken from Elkins, but they are also used by Stampp and Tannenbaum in describing the status of the slave.

[14] (New York, 1957).

[15] (New York, 1918).

Tannenbaum, Stampp takes up the social organization of slavery as well as its legal structure. His interpretation of the legal status of the slave is mainly in terms of economic values, and stresses the property component as do Elkins and Tannenbaum.[16] Unlike Elkins and Tannenbaum, however, he finds that the status also contained a personal element, which made for a certain degree of ambiguity in the status.[17]

In these interpretations, the initial status of the Negro is taken as having been neither that of a slave nor that of a member of a racial group against which discrimination was practised. The status of the Negro as a slave and his status as a member of a racial minority apparently developed concurrently, since there was no tradition of slavery or of racial discrimination in the colonies to inform the initial status of the Negro. The causal connection implied between slavery and racial discrimination is a widely held conception and needs to be reconsidered in the light of recent historical investigation and comparative evidence.

Much more difficult to grasp is the effect of racial discrimination on the definition of the slave status. Elkins refers to "the most implacable race-consciousness yet observed in virtually any society" as affecting the definition of the status, but the stress on economic values in his interpretation obscures any distinction that may have been intended between the property and racial components in the status[18]. . . .

Tannenbaum is clearly concerned with the consequences of racial discrimination for the legal status of the Negro as slave and as freedman. He stresses the fact that slavery in the United States meant Negro slavery. In contrast to Latin America, slavery in the ante-bellum South involved "caste", "by law of nature", or "innate inferiority".[19]

Slavery systems can be distinguished in terms of the ease and availability of manumission and the status of the freedman, as these indicate whether or not the law denied the moral personality of the slave.[20] In the United States the conception of the slave as a racial inferior led to severe restrictions on manumission and to a low status for free Negroes. At the same time, however, it is readily apparent from Tannenbaum's comparison with slavery in Latin America that in his view the conception of the ante-bellum Negro as innately inferior affected all the legal categories defining his status: the extent of the assimilation of his rights to property in law as well as manumission and the status of the freedman.[21] Racial discrimination accentuated the legal definition of the slave as property.

The slave as property is taken as the primary or exclusive component in these interpretations of the legal status of the slave in the United States. For Elkins and Stampp this is the consequence mainly of economic forces, while for Tannenbaum ideological forces are basic. The focus on the definition of the slave as property results in a tendency to fuse the property and racial components, and in a failure to consider the evidence bearing on the personal component in the legal status.

## II.

While the assimilation to property in law of the rights of slaves was common to slavery in classical antiquity and the United States, slavery in ancient society "was a type unfamiliar to Europeans and Americans of the last two centuries. It had no color line. (Therefore, *pace Aristotle,* it had no single and clearly defined race or slave caste.)"[22] Moreover, the law of slavery in ancient society did not deny the moral personality of the slave as, according to Roman law, the institution of slavery was of the *Ius Gentium* but at the same time contrary to the *Ius Naturale,* for all men

[16] Stampp, Chap. 5.

[17] *Ibid.,* pp. 192–93.

[18] Elkins, p. 61.

[19] Tannenbaum, pp. 55–56.

[20] *Ibid.,* p. 69. See also William L. Westermann, *The Slave Systems of Greek and Roman Antiquity* (Philadelphia, 1955), p. 154.

[21] Tannenbaum, p. 69.

[22] William L. Westermann, "Slavery and Elements of Freedom in Ancient Greece", *Bulletin of the Polish Institute Of Arts and Sciences in America,* I (Jan., 1943), p. 346. See also M. I. Finley, "Between Slavery and Freedom", *Comparative Studies in Society and History,* VI (Apr., 1964), p. 246.

were equal under natural law.[23] A comparison with slavery in Rome . . . thus provides a method for distinguishing between the property and the racial components in the definition of the legal status[24]. . . .

As to marriage and the family in the ante-bellum South, marriages between slaves had no legal standing. "The relation between slaves is essentially different from that of man and wife, joined in lawful wedlock . . . with slaves it may be dissolved at the pleasure of either party, or by the sale of one or both, depending on the caprice or necessity of the owners."[25] The denial of legal marriage meant, in conjunction with the rule that the child follow the conditions of the mother, that the offspring of slaves had no legal father, whether the father was slave or free. The duration of the union between slaves depended on the interests of the master or those of the slaves. The union was subject at any time to being dissolved by the sale of one or both of the slaves. The children of these "contubernial relationships", as they were termed, had no legal protection against separation from their parents. In the law there was no such thing as fornication or adultery among slaves. . . .

Roman slaves were also legally incapable of marriage. Any union between slaves or between slaves and free persons was differentiated as *contubernium* as opposed to *conubium.* A marriage was terminated if either party became enslaved. Infidelity between slaves could not be adultery. Although a slave could be guilty of adultery with a married free woman, it was not possible for an enslaved female to commit the offense, or for it to be commited with her. The inheritance of slavery followed the rule that the child follow the status of the mother, whatever the position of the father. . . . The children of slaves were the property of the owner of the mother, and, since the economic use of slaves during the Republic was at the discretion of the master, slaves were bought and sold without regard for their families. . . .[26]

According to the legal codes of the ante-bellum South, a slave "was unable to acquire title to property by purchase, gift, or devise".[27] A slave might not make a will, and he could not, by will, inherit anything. Slaves were not to hire themselves out, locate their own employment, establish their own residence, or make contracts for any purpose including, of course, marriage. A slave "can do nothing, possess nothing, nor acquire anything but what must belong to his master".[28] He could engage in financial transactions, but only as his master's agent. A slave could not be a party to a suit, except indirectly, when a free person represented him in a suit for freedom. Slaves might only be witnesses in court in cases involving slaves or free Negroes. When the testimony of a slave was allowed, he was not put under oath as a responsible person. Teaching slaves to read and write was prohibited, and instruction in religion was also subject to legal restrictions.

"Of the slave's civil position", in Rome, "it may be said that he had none."[29] A slave could not make a contract, he could be neither creditor nor debtor, he could not make a will, and if he became free, a will made in slavery was void. Slaves could in no way be concerned in civil proceedings which had to be made in the name of the master. A judgment against a slave was null and void and the pact of a slave was likewise void.

At to his participation in commerce, "his capacity here is almost purely derivative, and the texts speak of him as unqualified in

[23] Westermann, *The Slave Systems*, pp. 57, 80; W. W. Buckland, *The Roman Law of Slavery* (Cambridge, 1906), p. 1. The consequent ambiguity in the status of the slave as property and as a person in ancient society is discussed at a later point.

[24] Materials for the description of the legal status of the ante-bellum slave are standard and taken from Elkins, Chap. 2; Stampp, Chap. 5; Tannenbaum, p. 69ff; and Helen T. Catterall, *Judicial Cases Concerning Slavery and the Negro* (Washington, 1926). Those for the Roman Republic are taken from the standard work by Buckland; R. H. Barrow, *Historical Introduction to the Study of Roman Law* (Cambridge, 1932); and Rudolph Sohm, *The Institutes* (Oxford, 1907).

[25] *Howard v. Howard,* 6 Jones N.C. 235, December 1858. Catterall, II, p. 221.

[26] Buckland, p. 77.

[27] Stampp, p. 197.

[28] The Civil Code of Louisiana quoted in John C. Hurd, *The Law of Freedom and Bondage in the United States* (Boston, 1858), II, p. 160.

[29] Buckland, p. 82.

nearly every branch of law".[30] Although the Roman slave could acquire possessions for the master, "the will of the slave and, in fact, his mental faculties in general, operate in principle, where they operate at all, for the benefit of the master".[31] Legally the slave did not have possessory rights in the property acquired by him or granted to him. The *peculium* assigned to him by the master . . . did not go with the slave upon manumission unless expressly given by the master. . . .

The slave codes of the South supported the "full dominion" of the master in matters of policy and discipline. The slave's relationship with his master was expected to be one of complete subordination. Generally, homicide was the major crime that could be committed against an enslaved individual. The owner of a slave, however, could not be indicted for assault and battery on his own slave. "The power of the master must be absolute to render the submission of the slave perfect."[32] Furthermore, the master was not held responsible for the death of a slave as a consequence of "moderate correction", for "it cannot be presumed that prepensed malice (which alone makes murder felony) should induce any man to destroy his own estate".[33] The master was to recover damages caused by an assault or homicide against his slave.

During the Roman Republic there was no legal limitation on the power of the slave-owner: "his rights were unrestricted".[34] "Except in cases of revolt which endangered the government the Roman state left the problem of the discipline and punishment of slaves to their masters."[35] Sohm writes that as against his master, "a slave had no legal rights whatsoever".[36] . . . In case of injury done to a slave "the master had cause of action for damages against the perpetrator".[37] If a slave was enticed into escaping or forcibly removed the owner might resort to both criminal and civil action.

These comparisons suggest that, on the legal evidence which defines the authority of the master in the areas of parentage and kinship, property and other rights, and police and disciplinary power over slaves, there is nothing sufficiently distinctive to distinguish the legal status of the slave as property in the United States from that in Rome.

Arnold Toynbee refers to the "Negro slave immigrant" as having been "subject to the twofold penalization of racial discrimination and legal servitude".[38] A society may extensively assimilate to property in law the rights of slaves, as indeed many have, but yet not restrict the status of slavery to members of a particular group for whom slavery is defined as natural, inevitable, and permanent as occurred in the United States. This was the introduction of caste into the status of the ante-bellum Negro, slave or free. The Negro as slave occupied both a slave status and a caste status.[39] He was subject to disabilities in addition to those connected with the legal categorization of him as property, and these disabilities continued to define his status as a freedman. Caste law as well as slave law governed the status of the Negro.

The restriction of slavery to the Negro rested on the legal principle that it was a status properly belonging to the Negro as an innately (racially) inferior being. If slavery was a status attaching to a racial inferior, then it was inheritable even where one parent was white. Intermarriage between Negro slaves and whites was prohibited. Racial inferiority, legalized inheritance, and endogamy were related to another principle; namely, that slavery was the presumptive status of every Negro or person of color. The slave status was to follow naturally and inevitably from Negro ancestry.[40]

Although the slave and caste statuses were coextensive for the preponderant majority of ante-bellum Negroes, there were

[30] *Ibid.*, p. 82.
[31] *Ibid.*, p. 82.
[32] *State v. Mann*, 2 Deveroux 263, (N.C.), December 1829, Catterall, II, p. 57.
[33] Virginia Act of 1669, Hurd I, p. 232.
[34] Buckland, p. 36.
[35] Westermann, p. 75.
[36] Sohm, p. 166.
[37] Westermann, p. 83.
[38] Arnold J. Toynbee, *A Study of History* (Oxford, 1934), II, p. 218.
[39] Moore, pp. 177–9.
[40] *Ibid.*, 184–88. See also Winthrop D. Jordan, 'American Chiaroscuro: The Status and Definition of Mulattoes in the British Colonies", *William and Mary Quarterly*, XIX, No. 2 (April, 1962), pp. 183–200.

free Negroes in the North and South who, however, continued to be members of the lower caste. Caste was inclusive of the slave and free status. Thus the rule that the child follow the condition of the mother made slaves of the majority of Negroes and members of the lower caste of all Negroes. Negroes, slave or free, were legally prohibited from intermarrying with members of the dominant group. All members of the lower caste were presumed to be slaves unless they could establish that they should be legally free. There was a definite strain in the legal structure to establish slavery and caste as coextensive for all Negroes. The status of the free Negro is evidence of this strain. Although legally no longer an object of property rights, he was legally and socially a member of a lower caste and as such his life chances, whether he lived in the North or South, were held within narrow limits.[41]

Slavery in Republican Rome was not restricted to any particular group who ought properly to occupy the legal status of slaves. The legal restrictions on intermarriage of slave and free, on manumission, and on the status of freedmen, though at times severe, were not the consequence of a conception of the slave or former slave as innately inferior. Those who were enslaved in Rome did not constitute a caste in the society for whom the proper and permanent status was conceived to be slavery.[42] . . .

Setting aside the conventional question as to "why slavery produced discrimination?" Carl Degler has separated the two elements, and, still treating the question historically, asks rather "which appeared first, slavery or discrimination?" His main argument is that from the beginning "the Negro was treated as an inferior to the white man, servant or free".[43] Caste or elements of caste antedated slavery, and as the legal status evolved "it reflected and included as a part of its essence, this same discrimination the white man had practiced against the Negro" from the outset in New England as well as the South.[44]

The colonists of the early seventeenth century not only were well aware of the distinction between indentured servitude and slavery, but they had ample opportunity to acquire the prejudicial attitudes and discriminatory practices against Negroes through the slave trade and from Providence, Bermuda, Barbados, Jamaica, and the Spanish and Portuguese colonies.[45] Moreover, there was the inferior status ascribed to the non-Caucasian Indians and even their enslavement almost from the beginning of English settlement.

The evidence summarized by Degler indicates that Negroes were being set aside as a separate group because of their race before the legal status of slavery became fully crystallized in the late seventeenth century. There was legislation (1) preventing interracial marriages and sexual union; (2) declaring that the status of the offspring of a white man and a Negro would follow that of the mother; and (3) establishing civil and legal disabilities applying to Negroes either free or in servitude.[46] As to the situation of the Negro in the North, "from the earliest years a lowly differentiated status, if not slavery itself, was reserved and recognized for the Negro—and the Indian, it might be added".[47] Degler concludes that "long before slavery or black labor became an important part of the Southern economy, a special and inferior status had been worked out for the Negroes. . . . it was a demand for labor which dragged the Negro to American shores, but the status he acquired cannot be explained by reference to that economic motive."[48] . . .

[41] John Hope Franklin, *The Free Negro in North Carolina* (Chapel Hill, 1943); Leon F. Litwack, *North of Slavery* (Chicago, 1961).

[42] Westermann, pp. 15, 23.

[43] Carl N. Degler, "Slavery and the Genesis of American Race Prejudice", *Comparative Studies in Society and History*, II (Oct., 1959), p. 52. Cf. Oscar and Mary F. Handlin, "Origins of the Southern Labor System", *William and Mary Quarterly*, 3rd. Ser., VI (April, 1950), pp. 199–222; Winthrop D. Jordan, "Modern Tensions and the Origins of American Slavery", *Journal of Southern History*, XXVII (Feb., 1962). pp. 18–33.

[44] Degler, p. 52.

[45] *Ibid.*, pp. 53–56. See also Winthrop D. Jordan, "The Influence of the West Indies on the Origin of New England Slavery", *William and Mary Quarterly*, XXVIII (April, 1961), pp. 243–250.

[46] *Ibid.*, pp. 56–62. See also Moore, pp. 177–86.

[47] Degler, p. 62.

[48] *Ibid.*, p. 62. Jordan, *The Influence of the West Indies*, pp. 243–44, 250.

Kingsley Davis has observed that "slavery is extremely interesting precisely because it does attempt to fit human beings into the category of objects of property rights. . . . Always the slave is given some rights, and these rights interfere with the attempt to deal with him solely as property."[49] Westermann found this to be a "constant paradox" in Greek and Roman antiquity, and "inherent in the very nature of the institution". "Theoretically", the slave was a chattel and subject only to the laws pertaining to private property, and in "actuality" he was "also a human being and subject to protective legislation affecting human individuals".[50] . . . Under the law in Greek, Roman, and Near Eastern society the slave had an ambiguous status: he was both an object of property rights and a rudimentary legal person.

As to the personal component in the status of the slave in the United States, Elkins argues that as a consequence of the requirements of capitalistic argriculture "to operate efficiently and profitably", through the rational employment of slaves as economic instruments, any ambiguity in the legal status of the slave as property could not be tolerated.[51] Any rights of personality that remained to the Negro at the end of the seventeenth century had been suppressed by the middle of the eighteenth.[52] However they may differ as to causation, Elkins and Tannenbaum are in agreement that the status of the slave was determinate as property.[53] . . . Stampp, on the other hand, found a "dual character" in the legal codes. The legal authorities "were caught in a dilemma whenever they found that the slave's status as property was incompatible with this status as a person".[54] In a much earlier and very careful treatment of the personal component, Moore found that initially the question as to whether a slave was a person or a piece of property was involved in the difficult issue as to the status of the slave after conversion and baptism. Allowing the slave the privilege of salvation implied a recognition of him as a Christian person, and, by implication, as a legal personality. The idea that conversion and baptism altered the status of the slave as property was not easily changed, and the settling of the difficulty in favor of continued enslavement does not appear to have finally disposed of the matter.[55] . . .

There are three aspects to be considered in taking up the matter of the doubtful status of the slave before the law. The most obvious, of course, is that the dual quality is inherent in the status itself. Slaves are conscious beings defined as economic property. . . . The value of a slave as property resides in his being a person, but his value as a person rests in his status being defined as property.[56]

The second aspect involves the recognition in the law not only of the humanity of the slave, but also that he may be the subject of rights of his own. In this connection, Stampp has noted a significant juxtaposition of two clauses in the legal code of Alabama in 1853. The first defines the status of the slave as property and establishes the owner's rights to the slave's "time, labor, and services", as well as the slave's obligation to comply with the lawful demands of the master. The second contains the personal element and states the master's obligation to be humane to his slaves and to provide them with adequate food, clothing, and with care during illness and old age.[57] . . .

Cases clearly affirming that the slave was a person were also numerous during the ante-bellum period. One judgment in Tennessee held:

> A slave is not in the condition of a horse . . . he is made after the image of the Creator. He has mental capacities, and an immortal principle in his nature . . . the laws . . . cannot extinguish

[49] *Human Society* (New York, 1949), p. 456.
[50] Westermann, p. 1.
[51] Elkins, pp. 49, 53.
[52] *Ibid.*, p. 42.
[53] Tannenbaum, p. 97.
[54] Stampp, pp. 192–93.

[55] Moore, pp. 195–96. See also Charles Sellers, "The Travail of Slavery", in Charles Sellers, ed., *The Southerner as American* (Chapel Hill, 1960), pp. 40–71.
[56] Talcott Parsons and Neil J. Smelser, *Economy and Society* (Glencoe, 1956), p. 12.
[57] Stampp, pp. 192–93. The following discussion is not intended to be comprehensive. For a detailed treatment of the definition of the slave as a person see Moore, pp. 191–202.

his high born nature, nor deprive him of many rights which are inherent in man.[58]

. . . . . . . . . . . . . . . . . . . . . . . . . . . . . . . . . . . .

Many of the laws also implied that a slave was a legal person in that he was capable of committing crimes and could be held to trial. . . .

. . . Again, however, there were limits on the extent to which the personality of the slave was recognized, and in defining these limits the courts frequently expressed the indeterminate character of the status:

Because they are rational *human beings*, they are capable of committing crimes; and, in reference to acts which are crimes, are regarded as *persons*. Because they are *slaves*, they are . . . incapable of performing civil acts; and in reference to all such, they are *things*; not persons.[59]

. . . The third aspect pertains to the cases of manumission by will, deed, and legislative action; the instances of successful suits for freedom; and the cases of self-purchase—all of which implied evaluation of the slave as a person with some legal capacity. . . .[60]

Moreover, the presence of free Negroes in the population from the beginning; manumission; suits for freedom; and self-purchase indicated that slavery did not follow naturally and inevitably from Negro ancestry. The intrusion of the values of liberty and individual achievement into the legal structure meant that race and slavery were not coextensive for all Negroes. The law sanctioned the possibility of slaves legitimately aspiring to and attaining in attenuated form the culture goals of the enslaving group having to do with freedom and individual achievement. The status of the free Negro was real and symbolic evidence of the indeterminacy resulting from the attainment of goals that were presumably denied to Negroes and applicable only to whites.[61]

**III.**

. . . As the preceding discussion has indicated, in the United States where slaves were conceived of as innately inferior they constituted a caste in the society and their rights were extensively assimilated to property in law. In Republican Rome where slaves were not conceived of as innately inferior to the enslaving group and did not form a separate caste an equally extensive assimilation of their rights to property occurred. In contrast to the United States, manumission was easily available to the Roman slave, and the freedman could look forward to assimilation into Roman society.

Although the slave status in Rome was not justified in terms of the innate inferiority of the slave, the assimilation of ownership in slaves to property was comparable to that in the United States. Roman law respected the moral personality of the slave, as reflected in the rules governing manumission and the status of the freed slave, but this did not prevent the assimilation of his rights to property in law.

In so far as the legal categorization of the slave as property is concerned we are dealing with a common social form in Rome and the United States. Caste produced the contrast between the legal structures of the two systems of slavery. The consequence of racial discrimination for the legal structure of ante-bellum slavery was the creation of a hereditary, endogamous and permanent group of individuals in the status of slaves who, moreover, continued as members of a lower caste in the society after freedom. Although the conception of the slave as innately (racially) inferior to the enslaving group had important consequences for manumission and for the status of freedmen, as Tannenbaum has indicated, the comparison with Rome suggests that it did not accentuate the assimilation of ownership in slaves to property. Racial discrimination does not appear to have

[58] *Kennedy v. Williams*, 7 Humphreys, Sept., 1846 (Tenn.) *Ibid.*, II, p. 530.

[59] *Creswell's Executor v. Walker*, 37 Ala. 229, January, 1861, *Ibid.*, III, p. 247.

[60] *Catherine Bodine's Will*, 4 Dana 476, October 1836, (Ken.), *Ibid.*, I, pp. 334–35.

[61] Wilbert Moore and Robin Williams, "Stratification in the Ante-bellum South", *American Sociological Review*, VII (June, 1942), pp. 343–51. Cf. Douglas Hall, "Slaves and Slavery in the British West Indies", *Social and Economic Studies*, II, No. 4 (December, 1962), pp. 305–18.

affected the legal status of the slave as property.

Now slavery in Rome was not a single social phenomenon historically. Not until the first two centuries of the Empire did significant changes occur in the authority of the master over the rights of slaves. "In their ultimate legal formulation the changes found expression in the Codes of Theodosius and Justinian."[62] Up to that time, although Roman law respected the moral integrity of the slave, the subordination of the slave to the authority of the master was comparable to that in the United States. The slave law that came down through the Justinian Code to influence the Iberian law of slavery, later to be transferred to Latin America, contained not only the doctrine of the moral personality of the slave, but also embodied those changes in later Roman law which had "loosened the strict controls by which the slave element had formerly been bound to the will of the master group".[63]

According to the interpretations of slavery in Latin America by Tannenbaum and Elkins, it was this body of law in conjunction with certain traditions and institutional arrangements that functioned to protect the slaves both from an extensive assimilation to property in law and from a caste status. Some reference will be made in the concluding portion of this essay to the need for a revision of this interpretation on the basis of more recent research.

Considerable variation occurs among slavery systems in the extent to which the slave is assimilated to property in law. Variations in this component are generally taken to be related to "the level of technical development and the accompanying institutional apparatus, including the economic system".[64] Where slavery was a domestic system, as in China and the Near East, the assimilation of the slave to property in law was less extensive than in Rome and the United States where slavery was an industrial system.[65]

[62] Westermann, p. 140.

[63] *Ibid.*, p. 140.

[64] Sidney W. Mintz, Review of *Slavery* by Stanley Elkins, *American Anthropologist*, 63 (June, 1961), p. 580.

[65] G. Martin Wilbur, *Slavery in China During the Former Han Dynasty* (Chicago, 1943), p. 243; Mendelsohn pp. 121–22.

The property component in the status of the ante-bellum slave was undoubtedly related to economic values and the labor needs of an emerging capitalism, as Elkins and Stampp have emphasized, but the entire status cannot be derived from the operation of economic values. On the one hand, the extensive assimilation to property in law of the Roman slave did not generate a conception of him as innately inferior and create a caste of slaves and freedmen. On the other hand, the absence of certain institutions and traditions embodying values respecting the moral personality of the slave does not account for the conception of the Negro as inherently inferior and for caste. If these were absent, then the assimilation of ownership in slaves to property in law must have caused racial discrimination and caste. The historical evidence indicates rather that discrimination against the Negro occurred before the slave status was fully defined and before Negro labor became pivotal to the economic system.[66]

In the conception of the legal status of the slave as determinate in terms of property the slave has neither a juridical nor a moral personality. The values of the dominant group in the United States that had a bearing on the law of slavery were, on the one hand, those which legitimatized slavery and the rigid system of stratification, and on the other hand, those values pertaining to freedom and individual dignity and worth. Although there was no complex of laws, traditions, and institutions pertaining to the institution of slavery as such that embodied

[66] That the essential features of a caste status for the Negro may have preceded the full development of the slave status does not alter the widely accepted proposition that the initial status of the Negro was not that of a slave but rather that of an indentured servant or free man. Some aspects of caste appear to have developed later than others, but the main defining features were fixed early and before the complete development of the status of slavery. Racial segregation, although obviously foreshadowed in the status of the free Negro, did not appear as a part of the caste system until the late nineteenth and early twentieth centuries. The system of restricted contacts between Negroes and whites, clearly based on the long-standing assumption of the innate inferiority of the Negro, was simply the latest feature of caste to develop. See C. Vann Woodward, *The Strange Career of Jim Crow* (New York, 1957).

these latter values, a significant element in the general value system of the South was an ethical valuation of the individual. The legal evidence indicates that these extra-legal values of the society were expressed in the legal definition and conception of slavery. The law of slavery shows the existence of an ethical norm, however vague and rudimentary, attaching value to the individual.[67]

The interpretation of the legal status of the slave primarily or wholly in terms of property has implications as well for the conception of the pattern of relations between masters and slaves. In discussing the connection between the legal structure and the master-slave relationship, David Potter has observed that "the human relationship within this legal context was complex and multiple". The relation between masters and slaves had "two faces—a paternalistic manorial one and an exploitative commercial one".[68]

In the interpretations of Tannenbaum, Elkins, and Stampp there is a close correspondence between the legal structure and the pattern of the master-slave relationship. Since, according to these writers, the slave status was governed by instrumental and economic values and not affected by the religious and ethical convictions of the dominant group attaching value to the individual, there was nothing to impede the rational use of slaves as economic instruments. The exploitative commercial pattern was expected to be followed in organizing the relations of masters and slaves. It was normatively and numerically the predominant pattern in the South.

Given this conception of the connection between the legal structure and the relations of masters and slaves, the paternalistic manorial pattern can only be interpreted as a deviation from the expected and approved pattern of the master-slave relationship. It is not interpreted as an equally recognized and approved mode of organizing and managing the relations of masters and slaves, but rather as the result of fortuitous circumstances. It is attributed to the smallness of the plantation or to the "personal factor".[69] According to this interpretation there was nothing in the law to sanction the paternalistic manorial pattern, while the commercial exploitative pattern was clearly compatible with the instrumental use of slaves as sanctioned in the definition of the slave as an object of property rights. Yet, the paternalistic manorial pattern was widespread in the South as an accepted and approved mode of organizing the master-slave relationship and represented, as did the personal component in the legal status, the intrusion of the valuation of the individual into a categorized relationship.[70]

## IV.

Since the contrast with slavery in Latin America is central to the interpretations of

[67] Moore, pp. 201–02. For another discussion of the alternative value systems and the resulting conflicts within Southern society and within individuals see Sellers, pp. 51–67. A similar ambiguity existed in connection with slavery in ancient society. In Roman law "slavery is the only case in which, in the extant sources . . ., a conflict is declared to exist between the *Ius Gentium* and the *Ius Naturale*". Buckland, p. 1. "No society", writes Finley, "can carry such a conflict within it, around so important a set of beliefs and institutions, without the stresses erupting in some fashion, no matter how remote and extended the lines and connections may be from the original stimulus." M. I. Finley, "Was Greek Civilization Based on Slave Labour?", in M. I. Finley, ed. *Slavery in Classical Antiquity* (Cambridge, 1960), p. 162.

[68] David M. Potter, Review of *The Peculiar Institution* by Kenneth Stampp, *Yale Review*, 46 (Winter, 1957), pp. 260–61.

[69] Elkins, pp. 137–38.

[70] . . . Franklin has pointed out that the bulk of the slaves were on small plantations. If so, then the paternalistic manorial pattern must have been exceedingly widespread. On the other hand, it has also been suggested that this pattern was to be found on the larger holdings. Phillips had this conception of the master-slave relationship on large plantations. It seems likely that both patterns were normative; that is, accepted and approved ways of organizing the master-slave relationship. If this was the case, then further investigation must be directed at ascertaining the determinants of these patterns on the concrete level. Size would be one among several determinants. See John Hope Franklin, *From Slavery to Freedom* (New York, 1952), pp. 185–86. Needless to say, the pattern of the master-slave relationship is significant for the impact of slavery upon the personality of the Negro. If the paternalistic manorial pattern was widely institutionalized in the ante-bellum South, then a very significant number of Negro slaves were able to escape the tendency for the system to absorb the personality. Cf. Elkins, pp. 137–138.

slavery in the United States by Tannenbaum and Elkins, some reference may be made to the more recent studies of slavery and race relations in Latin America and the implications for a comparison with North America. The results of these studies appear to be consistent with those of this essay.

In connection with the interpretations of slavery in Latin America by Elkins and Tannenbaum, Mintz questions whether slavery in Latin America can be treated as a single phenomenon historically.[71] He points out that once slavery became a part of the industrial plantation system in Cuba and Puerto Rico, for example, an extensive assimilation to property in law of the rights of slaves occurred in spite of an institutional framework protecting the moral personality of the slave. Slavery in Cuba "dehumanized the slave as viciously as had Jamaican or North America slavery".[72] Much the same thing happened in Puerto Rico. . . .[73]

As to the racial component in the slave status, investigations of race relations in Brazil, where most of the work has been done, indicate that during the colonial period slavery also involved a caste system between whites and Negro slaves, "based on white supremacy and the institutionalized inferiority of colored slaves".[74] Concubinage was widely practiced, but inter-marriage was rare, "as the system demanded the separation of the two castes and the clearcut distinction of superiors and inferiors".[75] Colonial legislation discriminated against the free Negroes who "were often coupled with enslaved Negroes in the laws".[76] They were prevented from acquiring possessions or participating in activities in the society "which might tend to place them on a level with whites".[77] Mulattoes who attained positions of importance in Brazil "did so in spite of the official and social prejudices which existed against them throughout the whole of the colonial period".[78]

It is readily apparent from these studies that a much greater similarity existed between slavery in the United States and Latin America than here-to-fore suspected. The status of slaves in Latin America, as well as in Rome and the United States, indicates that whether or not the law respected the moral personality of the slave, an extensive assimilation of his rights to property in law occurred under slavery as an industrial system. Moreover, contrary to the widely held conception, racial discrimination was present in Latin America and had the consequence of creating a duality in the status of the slave as property and as a member of a racial caste.[79] These elements were apparently combined to some extent with a respect for the moral personality of the slave in the law.

Further comparative study of slavery in the United States and Latin America will enable us to delineate more precisely the differences and similarities in the property, racial, and personal components of the slave status in these societies. We may also expect such study to reveal, as this essay has attempted to do, that economic and ideological forces were not mutually exclusive in their consequences for the legal structure of slavery.

[71] Useful summaries are to be found in Juan Comas, "Recent Research on Race Relations—Latin America", *International Social Science Journal*, XIII, No. 2 (1961), pp. 271–99; Oracy Noguiera, "Skin Color and Social Class", *Plantation Systems of the New World* (Washington, 1959), pp. 164–83; Roger Bastide, "Race Relations in Brazil", *International Social Science Bulletin*, IX, No. 4 (1957), pp. 495–512.

[72] Mintz, p. 581.

[73] *Ibid.*, p. 583, See also O. A. Sherrard, *Freedom from Fear* (London, 1959), p. 75. *The Golden Age of Brazil* (Berkeley, 1961), p. 173. Gilberto Freyre's *The Masters and the Slaves* (New York, 1946), on which much of the existing conception of slavery in Brazil is based, wrote mainly about domestic slaves.

[74] Harley Ross Hammond, "Race, Social Mobility and Politics in Brazil", *Race*, IV, No. 2 (1962), p. 477. See Charles Wagley, "From Caste to Class in North Brazil", in Charles Wagley (ed.), *Race and Class in Rural Brazil* (New York, 1963), pp. 142–156.

[75] *Ibid.*, p. 4.

[76] Boxer, p. 17.

[77] *Ibid.*, p. 17.

[78] *Ibid.*, p. 17.

[79] Nogueira, pp. 167–176, has attempted to distinguish race prejudice in Brazil from that in the Unites States. With reference to the origin of race prejudice in Brazil, James G. Leyburn, in his dicussion of Nogueira's paper, questions whether it was slavery which produced race prejudice. *Ibid.*, p. 181.

# CASTE IN INDIA AND THE UNITED STATES[1]

*Gerald D. Berreman*

Many writers who have contributed to the vast literature on the caste system in India have emphasized its unique aspects and ignored or denied the qualities it shares with rigid systems of social stratification found in other societies. Others have claimed to find caste systems or caste groups in such widely scattered areas as Arabia, Polynesia, Africa, Guatemala, and Japan.[2] Some observers refer to Negro-white relations in the United States, and particularly in the South, as being those of caste,[3] a usage which others, including C. S. Johnson, Oliver C. Cox, and, more recently, G. E. Simpson and J. M. Yinger, have criticized. This paper will compare the relationship between "touchable," especially twice-born, and "untouchable" castes in India with that between Negroes and whites in the southern United States.

Caste can be defined so that it is applicable only to India, just as it is possible to define narrowly almost any sociocultural phenomenon. Indianists have traditionally held to specific, usually enumerative, definitions. Indeed, the caste system in India has several unique features, among which are its religious aspects, its complexity, and the degree to which the caste is a cohesive group that regulates the behavior of its members. Within India there is considerable variation in the characteristics of, and the relations among, the groups to which the term "caste", is applied.

However, caste can be accurately defined in broader terms. For many purposes similar social facts may be usefully categorized together, despite differences which, while not denied, are not crucial to the purposes at hand. For purposes of cross-cultural comparison this is necessary: for the study of social process, and with the aim of deriving generalizations, caste is a concept which might well be applied cross-culturally. For these purposes a caste system may be defined as a *hierarchy of endogamous divisions in which membership is hereditary and permanent*. Here hierarchy includes inequality both in status and in access to goods and services. Interdependence of the subdivisions, restricted contacts among them, occupational specialization, and/or a degree of cultural distinctiveness might be added as criteria, although they appear to be correlates rather than defining characteristics.

This definition is perhaps best viewed as describing an ideal type at one end of a continuum along which systems of social stratification might be ranged. There can be little doubt that the systems in India and the southern United States would fall far toward the caste extreme of the continuum.[4] It now becomes necessary to look at the differences cited as crucial by those who object to use of the term "caste" in both societies. The objections raised by those interested in structure, relationships, and interaction will be discussed here; the objections of those interested in specific content will be ignored —not because the latter objections are less cogent, but because they are less relevant

Reprinted from the *American Journal of Sociology*, Vol. LXVI, September, 1960, by permission of the University of Chicago Press. 

[1] Delivered in abbreviated form before the Fifty-eighth Annual Meeting of the American Anthropological Association in Mexico City, December, 1959, and based partly on research carried out in India under a Ford Foundation Foreign Area Training Fellowship during fifteen months of 1957-58 (reported in full in my "Kin, Caste, and Community in a Himalayan Hill Village" [unpublished Ph.D. dissertation, Cornell University, 1959]). I am indebted to Joel V. Berreman and Lloyd A. Fallers for their helpful comments.

[2] E. D. Chapple and C. S. Coon, *Principles of Anthropology* (New York: Henry Holt & Co., 1942), p. 437; S. F. Nadel, "Caste and Government in Primitive Society," *Journal of the Anthropological Society of Bombay*, New Series VIII (September, 1954), 9–22; M. M. Tumin, *Caste in a Peasant Society* (Princeton, N.J.: Princeton University Press, 1952); J. D. Donoghue, "An Eta Community in Japan: The Social Persistence of Outcaste Groups," *American Anthropologist*, LIX (December, 1957), 1000–1017.

[3] E.g., Allison Davis, Kingsley Davis, John Dollard, Buell Gallagher, Gunnar Myrdal, Kenneth Stampp, Lloyd Warner.

[4] The Tira of Africa, for example, would not fall so far toward this extreme (cf. Nadel, *op. cit.*, pp. 18 ff.).

to the comparison of social systems.[5]

Johnson sees many similarities in the two systems but objects to identifying both as caste, since "a caste system is not only a separated system, it is a stable system in which changes are socially impossible; the fact that change cannot occur is accepted by all, or practically all, participants. . . . No expenditure of psychological or physical energy is necessary to maintain a caste system."[6] Simpson and Yinger agree with Johnson and further object that, in the United States, "we lack a set of religious principles justifying a rigid system of social stratification and causing it to be willingly accepted by those at all levels."[7] Cox lists a number of features of a caste system (i.e., caste in India) which distinguish it from an interracial situation (i.e., Negro-white relations in America), important among which are its "nonconflictive," "non-pathological," and "static" nature, coupled with absence of "aspiration and progressiveness."[8]

Central to these distinctions is that caste in India is passively accepted and indorsed by all on the basis of religio-philosophical explanations which are universally subscribed to, while Negro-white relations in America are characterized by dissent, resentment, guilt, and conflict. But this contrast is invalid, resulting, as it does, from an idealized and unrealistic view of Indian caste, contrasted with a more realistic, pragmatic view of American race relations; Indian caste is viewed as it is supposed to work rather than as it does work; American race relations are seen as they do work rather than as they are supposed, by the privileged, to work. The traditional white southerner, asked to describe relations between the races, will describe the Negro as happy in his place, which he may quote science and Scripture to justify. This is similar to the explanations offered for the Indian system by the advantaged.

The point here is that ideal intercaste behavior and attitudes in India are much like those in America, while the actual interaction and attitudes are also similar. Commonly, ideal behavior and attitudes in India have been contrasted with real behavior and attitudes in America—a fact which has led to a false impression of difference. Similarly, comparisons of race relations in the rapidly changing urban or industrial South with caste relations in slowly changing rural or agrarian India lead to erroneous conclusions. Valid comparison can be made at either level, but must be with comparable data. The impact on intergroup relations of the social and economic changes which accompany urban life seems to be similar in both societies. Recent literature on village India and on the changing caste functions and caste relations in cities and industrial areas presents a realistic picture which goes far toward counteracting traditional stereotypes of Indian caste.[9]

[5] As a matter of fact, ignorance of the details of content in the patterns of relations between whites and Negroes in the United States has prevented many Indianists from seeing very striking similarities. Two contrasting views of the cross-cultural applicability of the concept of caste have appeared since this paper was written: F. C. Bailey, "For a Sociology of India?" *Contributions to Indian Sociology*, No. 3 (July, 1959), 88–101, esp. 97–98; and E. R. Leach, "Introduction: What Should We Mean by Caste?" in *Aspects of Caste in South India, Ceylon and North-west Pakistan* ("Cambridge Papers in Social Anthropology," No. 2 [Cambridge: Cambridge University Press, 1959]), pp. 1–10.

[6] C. S. Johnson, *Growing up in the Black Belt* (Washington, D.C.: American Council on Education, 1941), p. 326.

[7] G. E. Simpson and J. M. Yinger, *Racial and Cultural Minorities* (New York: Harper & Bros., 1953), p. 328.

[8] O. C. Cox, "Race and Caste: A Distinction," *American Journal of Sociology*, L (March, 1945), 360 (see also his *Caste, Class and Race* [Garden City, N.Y.: Doubleday & Co., 1948]).

[9] See, for example, the following community studies: F. G. Bailey, *Caste and the Economic Frontier* (Manchester: University of Manchester Press, 1957); Berreman, *op. cit.*; S. C. Dube, *Indian Village* (Ithaca, N.Y.: Cornell University Press, 1955); Oscar Lewis, *Village Life in Northern India* (Urbana: University of Illinois Press, 1958); McKim Marriott (ed.), *Village India* (American Anthropological Association Memoir No. 83 [Chicago: University of Chicago Press, 1955]); M. E. Opler and R. D. Singh, "The Division of Labor in an Indian Village," in *A Reader in General Anthropology*, ed. C. S. Coon (New York: Henry Holt & Co., 1948), pp. 464–96; M. N. Srinivas *et al.*, *India's Villages* (Development Department, West Bengal: West Bengal Government Press, 1955). See also, for example, the following studies of caste in the contemporary

In a study of caste functioning in Sirkanda, a hill village of northern Uttar Pradesh, India, I was struck by the similarity of relations between the twice-born and untouchable castes to race relations in the southern United States.[10] In both situations there is a genuine caste division, according to the definition above. In the two systems there are rigid rules of avoidance between castes, and certain types of contacts are defined as contaminating, while others are non-contaminating. The ideological justification for the rules differs in the two cultures, as do the definitions of the acts themselves; but these are cultural details. The tabooed contacts are symbolically rather than literally injurious as evidenced by the many inconsistencies in application of the rules.[11] Enforced deference, for example, is a prominent feature of both systems. Lack of deference from low castes is not contaminating, but it is promptly punished, for it implies equality. The essential similarity lies in the fact that the function of the rules in both cases is to maintain the caste system with institutionalized inequality as its fundamental feature. In the United States, color is a conspicuous mark of caste, while in India there are complex religious features which do not appear in America, but in both cases dwelling area, occupation, place of worship, and cultural behavior, and so on, are important symbols associated with caste status. The crucial fact is that caste status is determined, and therefore the systems are perpetuated, by birth: membership in them is ascribed and unalterable. Individuals in low castes are considered inherently inferior and are relegated to a disadvantaged position, regardless of their behavior. From the point of view of the social psychology of intergroup relations, this is probably the most important common and distinct feature of caste systems.

In both the United States and India, high castes maintain their superior position by exercising powerful sanctions, and they rationalize their status with elaborate philosophical, religious, psychological, or genetic explanations. The latter are not sufficient in themselves to maintain the systems, largely because they are incompletely accepted among those whose depressed position they are thought to justify. In both places castes are economically interdependent. In both there are great differences in power and privilege among, as well as class differences within, castes and elaborate barriers to free social intercourse among them.

Similarities in the two caste systems extend throughout the range of behavior and attitudes expressed in relations among groups. An important and conspicuous area of similarity is associated with competition for certain benefits or "gains" which are personally gratifying and/or socially valued and which by their nature or under the circumstances cannot be enjoyed by all equally. Competitive striving is, of course, not unique to caste organization; it is probably found to some extent in all societies. It is subject to a variety of social controls resulting in a variety of forms of social stratification, one of which is a caste system as defined here. However, the genesis of caste systems is not here at issue.[12]

setting: Bailey, *op. cit.,* N. K. Bose, "Some Aspects of Caste in Bengal," *American Journal of Folklore*, LXXI (July-September, 1958), 397–412; Leach, *op. cit.,*; Arthur Niehoff, *Factory Workers in India* ("Milwaukee Public Museum Publications in Anthropology," No. 5 [1959]); M. N. Srinivas, "Caste in Modern India," *Journal of Asian Studies*, XVI (August, 1957), 529–48; and the several articles comprising the symposium on "Caste in India" contained in *Man in India*, XXXIX (April–June, 1959), 92–162.

[10] The following discussion is based not exclusively on the Sirkanda materials but on observations and literature in non-hill areas as well. The hill area presents some distinct regional variations in caste structure, important among which is the absence of intermediate castes—all are either twice-born or untouchable. This leads to a dichotomous situation, as in the United States, but one which differs in that there are important caste divisions on either side of the "pollution barrier" (cf. Bailey, *op. cit.,* p. 8; Berreman, *op cit.,* pp. 389 ff.). Relations across this barrier do not differ greatly from similar relations among plains castes, although somewhat more informal contact is allowed—pollution comes about less easily—in the hills.

[11] The symbolic acts—the "etiquette" of caste relations—in India and in America are often remarkably similar. The symbolism in America is, of course, not primarily religious as much as it is in India, although the sacred aspects in India are often far from the minds of those engaging in the acts and are not infrequently unknown to them.

[12] Cf. Nadel, *op cit.*

The caste system in India and in the United States has secured gains for the groups established at the top of the hierarchy. Their desire to retain their position for themselves and their children accounts for their efforts to perpetuate the system. John Dollard, in his discussion of "Southerntown," identifies their gains as economic, sexual, and in prestige.

In the economic field, low-caste dependence is maintained in India as in America by economic and physical sanctions. This assures not only greater high-caste income but a ready supply of free service and cheap labor from the low castes. It also guarantees the continuing availability of the other gains. In India it is the most explicitly recognized high-caste advantage.

The sexual gain for the southern white caste is defined by Dollard, quoting whom I will substitute "high caste" and "low caste" for "white" and "Negro," respectively. In this form his definition fits the Indian caste system equally well.

> In simplest terms, we mean by a "sexual gain" the fact that [high-caste] men, by virtue of their caste position, have access to two classes of women, those of the [high] and [low] castes. The same condition is somewhat true of the [low-caste] women, except that they are rather the objects of the gain than the choosers, though it is a fact that they have some degree of access to [high-caste] men as well as men of their own caste. [Low-caste] men and [high-caste] women, on the other hand, are limited to their own castes in sexual choices.[13]

This arrangement is maintained in the Indian caste system, as it is in America, by severe sanctions imposed upon any low-caste man who might venture to defy the code, by the toleration accorded high-caste men who have relations with low-caste women, and by the precautions which high-caste men take to protect their women from the low castes.

High-caste people gain, by virtue of their caste status alone, deference from others, constant reinforcement of a feeling of superiority, and a permanent scapegoat in the lower castes. Dollard has stated the implications of this gain in prestige, and, again substituting a caste designation for a racial one, his statement describes the Indian system perfectly:

> The gain here . . . consists in the fact that a member of the [high] caste has an automatic right to demand forms of behavior from [low-caste people] which serve to increase his own self-esteem.
>
> It must always be remembered that in the end this deference is demanded and not merely independently given.[14]

Ideally the high-caste person is paternalistic and authoritarian, while the low-caste person responds with deferential, submissive, subservient behavior. Gallagher might have been describing India rather than America when he noted: "By the attitudes of mingled fear, hostility, deprecation, discrimination, amused patronage, friendly domination, and rigid authoritarianism, the white caste generates opposite and complementary attitudes in the Negro caste."[15]

An additional high-caste gain in India is the religious tradition which gives people of high caste promise of greater rewards in the next life than those of low caste. People can increase their rewards in the next life by fulfilling their traditional caste duty. For high castes, this generally results in increasing the economic advantages and prestige acquired in this life, while it requires that the low castes subordinate their own economic gains and prestige in this life to the service and honor of high castes. Thus, for high-caste people, behavior leading to immediate rewards is consistent with ultimate rewards, while, for low-caste people, behavior required for the two rewards is contradictory.

These advantages are significant and recognized reasons for maintenance of the

[13] John Dollard, *Caste and Class in a Southern Town* ("Anchor Books" [Garden City, N.Y.: Doubleday & Co., 1957]), p. 135 (cf. Berreman, *op cit.*, pp. 470 ff.).

[14] Dollard, *op cit.*, p. 174. Nadel speaking of caste in general, has noted that "the lower caste are despised, not only unhappily under-privileged; they bear a stigma apart from being unfortunate. Converseley, the higher castes are not merely entitled to the possession of coveted privileges, but are also in some way exalted and endowed with a higher dignity" (Nadel, *op cit.*, p. 16).

[15] B. G. Gallagher, *American Caste and the Negro College* (New York: Columbia University Press, 1938), p. 109.

system by the privileged groups.[16] They are expressed in folklore, proverbs, and jokes; for instance, a story tells that, as the funeral procession of an old landlord passed two untouchable women going for water, one hand of the corpse fell from under the shroud and flopped about. One of the women turned to the other and remarked, "You see, Takur Singh is dead, but he still beckons to us." Other stories recount the avariciousness of Brahmins in their priestly role, the hard-heartedness of landlords, and the like.

The compensatory gains for low-caste people are cited more often by high-caste advocates of the system than by those alleged to enjoy them. They are gains common to authoritarian systems everywhere and are usually subject to the will of the dominant groups.

As noted above, India is frequently cited as an example of a society in which people of deprived and subject status are content with their lot, primarily justifying it by religion and philosophy. This is the characteristic of caste in India most often cited to distinguish it from hereditary systems elsewhere, notably in the southern United States. On the basis of my research and the literature, I maintain that this is not accurate and therefore not a valid distinction. Its prevalence is attributable in part, at least, to the vested interests of the advantaged and more articulate castes in the perpetuation of the caste system and the maintenance of a favorable view of it to outsiders. The same arguments and the same biases are frequently presented by apologists for the caste system of the southern United States.

In both systems there is a tendency to look to the past as a period of halcyon amity and to view conflict and resentment as resulting from outside disturbances of the earlier normal equilibrium. Alien ideas, or large-scale economic disturbances, or both, are often blamed for reform movements and rebellion. Such explanations may account for the national and regional reform movements which find their advocates and followers primarily among the educated and social elites; they do not account for the recurrent grass-roots attempts, long endemic in India, to raise caste status; for the state of mind which has often led to low-caste defections from Hinduism when the opportunity to do so without fear of major reprisals has presented itself; nor for the chronic resentment and tension which characterizes intercaste relations in even so remote a village as Sirkanda, the one in which I worked.

Among the low or untouchable castes in Sirkanda, there was a great deal of readily expressed resentment regarding their caste position. Specific complaints revolved around economic, prestige, and sexual impositions by the high castes. Although resentment was suppressed in the presence of people of the dominant high castes, it was readily expressed where there was no fear of detection or reprisal.[17] Low-caste people felt compelled to express village loyalties in public, but in private acts and attitudes caste loyalties were consistently and intensely dominant when the two conflicted.

Caste, as such, was not often seriously questioned in the village. Objections were characteristically directed not at "caste" but at "my position in the caste hierarchy."

In the multicaste system of India, abolition of the system evidently seems impossible from the point of view of any particular caste, and a change in its rank within the system is viewed by its members as the only plausible means of improving the situation. Moreover, abolition would destroy the caste as a group which is superior to at least some other groups, and, while it would give caste members an opportunity to mingle as equals with their superiors, it would also force them to mingle as equals with their inferiors. Abolition, even if it could be

[16] Cf. Pauline M. Mahar, "Changing Caste Ideology in a North Indian Village" *Journal of Social Issues*, XIV (1958), 51–65, esp. pp. 55–56; Kailash K. Singh, "Inter-caste Tensions in Two Villages in North India" (unpublished Ph.D dissertation, Cornell University, 1957), pp. 184–85; and M. N. Srinivas, "The Dominant Caste in Rampura," *American Anthropologist*, LXI (1959), 1–16, esp. p. 4.

[17] Elaborate precautions were often taken by informants to insure against any possibility that their expressions of feeling might become known to their caste superiors, which is very similar to behavior I have observed among Negroes of Montgomery, Alabama.

accomplished, would thus create an ambivalent situation for any particular caste in contrast to the clear-cut advantages of an improvement in rank.

In the dual system of the southern United States where the high caste is clearly dominant, abolition of the caste division may be seen by the subordinate group as the only plausible remedy for their deprived position. Furthermore, they have nothing to lose but their inferior status, since there are no lower castes. There are, of course, Negroes and organized groups of Negroes, such as the black supremacist "Muslims" recently in the news in the United States, who want to invert the caste hierarchy; conversely, there are low-caste people in India who want to abolish the entire system. But these seem to be atypical viewpoints. The anticaste religions and reform movements which have from time to time appealed with some success to the lower castes in India, for example, Buddhism, Islam, Christianity, Shiism, have been unable, in practice, to remain casteless. This seems to be a point of real difference between Indian and American low-caste attitudes, for in America objection is more characteristically directed toward the system as such.[18]

In Sirkanda those low-caste people who spoke most piously against high-caste abuses were likely to be equally abusive to their caste inferiors. However, no low caste was encountered whose members did not seriously question its place in the hierarchy. A sizable literature is accumulating concerning castes which have sought to alter their status.[19] Such attempts were made in Sirkanda. A more common reaction to deprived status on the part of low-caste people was what Dollard calls "passive accommodation" coupled with occasional ingroup aggression.[20]

In both America and India there is a tendency for the person of low caste to "laugh it off" or to become resigned. In Sirkanda low-caste people could not avoid frequent contacts with their superiors, because of their proximity and relative numbers. Contacts were frequently informal, but status differences and the dangers of ritual pollution were not forgotten. An untouchable in this village who covered up his bitter resentment by playing the buffoon received favors denied to his more sullen caste fellows. The irresponsible, simple-minded untouchable is a widespread stereotype and one which he, like the Negro, has found useful. Similarly, sullen resignation, with the attendant stereotype of lazy shiftlessness, is a common response, typified in the southern Negro axiom, "Do what the man says." This, too, helps him avoid trouble, although it does little for the individual's self-respect. Aggression against the economically and numerically dominant high castes in Sirkanda was too dangerous to be a reasonable alternative. It was discussed by low-caste people in private but was rarely carried out. Even legitimate complaints to outside authority were avoided in view of the general belief that the high-caste's wealth would insure an outcome unfavorable to the low castes—a belief well grounded in experience.

Since they harbored indignation and resentment, a number of rationalizations of their status were employed by low-caste people, apparently as mechanisms to lessen the sting of reality. Thus, they often attributed their caste status to relative wealth and numbers: "If we were wealthy and in the majority, we would make the high castes untouchable."

Three more explanations of their caste status were consistently offered by low-caste people. These had the effect of denying the legitimacy of their low-caste position:

1. Members of the entire caste (or sub-caste) group would deny that they deserved the low status to which they had been assigned. One example:

> Englishmen and Muslims are untouchables because they have an alien religion and they eat beef. This is as it should be. We are Hindus and we do not eat beef, yet we, too are treated as untouchables. This is not proper. We should be accorded higher status.

[18] Whether this difference in attitude is widely correlated with multiple, as compared to dual, caste systems, or is attributable to other differences in the Indian and American situations, can be established only by further comparative work.

[19] E.g., Opler and Singh, *op. cit.*, p. 476; B. S. Cohn, "The Changing Status of a Depressed Caste," in Marriott (ed.), *op. cit.*, pp. 53–77; and Bailey, *op. cit.*, pp. 220–26.

[20] Dollard, *op. cit.*, p. 253.

No group would admit to being lowest in the caste hierarchy.

2. People might grant that the caste of their clan, lineage, or family was of low status but deny that their particular group really belonged to it. I have not encountered a low-caste group which did not claim high-caste ancestry or origin. Thus a typical comment is:

> Yes, we are drummers by occupation, but our ancestor was a Brahmin who married a drummer woman. By rights, therefore, we should be Brahmins, but in such cases the high castes here go against the usual custom and assign the child the caste of his low-caste parent rather than of his father, from whom a person inherits everything else.

3. A person might grant that his own caste and even his lineage or family were of low status, but his explanation would excuse him from responsibility for it. Such explanations were supplied by Brahmins who, as the most privileged caste and the recipients of religiously motivated charity from all castes, have a vested interest in maintenance of the system and its acceptance by those at all levels. An individual's horoscope would describe him as having been of high caste and exemplary behavior in a previous life and therefore destined for even greater things in the present life. However, in performing some religiously meritorious act in his previous existence, he inadvertently sinned (e.g., he was a raja, tricked by dishonest servants who did not give to the Brahmin the charity he intended for them). As a result he had to be punished in this life with a low rebirth.

Thus, no one said, in effect, "I am of low status and so are my family members and my caste-fellows, and justly so, because of our misdeeds in previous lives." To do so would lead to a psychologically untenable position, though one advocated by high-caste people and by orthodox Hinduism. Rationalizations or beliefs such as these form a consistent pattern—they are not isolated instances. Neither are they unique to the village or culture reported here: the literature reveals similar beliefs elsewhere in North India.[21] They evidently indicate something less than enthusiastic acceptance of caste position and, meanwhile, they perhaps alleviate or divert resentment.

That people remain in an inferior position, therefore, does not mean that they do so willingly, or that they believe it is justified, or that they would do anything in their power to change it, given the opportunity. Rationalizations of caste status which are consistent and convincing to those who are unaffected or who benefit from them seem much less so to those whose deprivation they are expected to justify or explain. Adherence to a religious principle may not significantly affect the attitudes and behavior to which logic would seem, or to which dogma attempts, to tie it. A comparison of the realities of caste attitudes and interaction in India and the United States suggests that no group of people is content to be low in a caste hierarchy—to live a life of inherited deprivation and subjection—regardless of the rationalizations offered them by their superiors or constructed by themselves. This is one of many points on which further cross-cultural comparison, and only cross-cultural comparison of caste behavior, might be conclusive.

It should be evident that the range of similarities between caste in India and race relations in America, when viewed as relations among people, is wide and that the details are remarkably similar in view of the differences in cultural context. Without denying or belittling the differences, I would hold that the term "caste system" is applicable at the present time in the southern United States, if it is applicable anywhere outside of Hindu India, and that it can be usefully applied to societies with systems of hierarchical, endogamous subdivisions whose membership is hereditary and permanent, wherever they occur. By comparing

[21] Cf. E. T. Atkinson, *The Himalayan Districts of the North-Western Provinces of India* (Allahabad: North-Western Provinces and Oudh Press, 1886), III, 446; B. S. Cohn, "The Camars of Senapur: A Study of the Changing Status of a Depressed Caste" (unpublished Ph.D. dissertation, Cornell University, 1954), pp. 112 ff.; and D. N. Majumdar, *The Fortunes of Primitive Tribes* (Lucknow: Universal Publishers Ltd., 1944), p. 193.

caste situations, so defined, it should be possible to derive further insight, not only into caste in India, but into a widespread type of relations between groups—insight which is obscured if we insist upon treating Indian caste as entirely unique.

# FEUDAL SOCIETY

*Marc Bloch*

## THE DISAPPEARANCE OF THE ANCIENT ARISTOCRACIES OF BIRTH

For the writers who first gave feudalism its name, for the men of the French Revolution, who worked to destroy it, the idea of nobility seemed inseparably linked with it. It would scarcely be possible, however, to find an association of ideas more palpably false—at least if we set any store by the exact use of historical terms. Certainly there was nothing egalitarian about the societies of the feudal era; but not every dominant class is a nobility. To deserve this name such a class must evidently combine two characteristics. First, it must have a legal status of its own, which confirms and makes effectual the superiority to which it lays claim. In the second place, this status must be hereditary—with the qualification, however, that a limited number of new families may be admitted to it, in accordance with formally established rules. In other words, actual power is not enough, nor is even that form of inheritance (effective though it is in practice) which consists as much in the advantages children enjoy through having parents of high status as in the wealth they may inherit; it is necessary, in addition, that social privileges as well as hereditary succession should be recognized by law. . . . In this sense—and it is the only legitimate one—nobility made its appearance relatively late in western Europe. The first lineaments of the institution did not begin to emerge before the twelfth century, and it took definite shape only in the following century when the fief and vassalage were already in decline. Throughout the first feudal age, and in the period immediately preceding it, it was unknown.

. . . . . . . . . . . . . . . . . . . . . . . . . . . . . . . . . . . .

The most striking feature of the history of the dominant families in the first feudal age is the shortness of their pedigrees—at least if we agree to reject not only the fables invented by the Middle Ages themselves, but also the ingenious though improbable conjectures which in our own day various scholars have founded on very hypothetical principles for the transmission of proper names. . . . To speak of nobility is to speak of pedigrees: in the case in point, pedigrees did not matter because there was no nobility.

## DIFFERENT MEANINGS OF THE WORD *NOBLE* IN THE FIRST FEUDAL AGE

This is not to say, however, that from the ninth to the eleventh century the word "noble" (in Latin *nobilis*) was not to be found fairly frequently in the documents. But it had no precise legal meaning and simply indicated an actual or an accepted pre-eminence, in accordance with a variety of different criteria. Almost invariably it involved the idea of a certain distinction of birth; but it also implied a measure of wealth. Thus we find Paul the Deacon (an eighth-century writer who is usually more lucid than in this case), in a commentary on a passage of the *Rule* of St. Benedict, hesitating between, and confusing, these two interpretations.[1] From the beginning of the feudal era these uses of the word "noble," though too fluctuating to admit of precise definition, at least reflected some major trends, and their very vicissitudes are instructive.

In days when so many men had to agree to hold their lands of a lord, the mere fact of escaping such subjection was a sign of superiority. It is not surprising therefore that the possession of an allod (even if this was no more than a peasant property) should



[1] *Bibliotheca Casinensis,* vol. IV, p. 151.

have been sometimes considered a sufficient title to the name "noble" or *edel*. It is also worth noticing that in the majority of the texts in which petty allodialists appear with this designation, we see them parading it only to surrender it immediately by becoming the tenants or serfs of a more powerful man.

If from the end of the eleventh century onwards we come across scarcely any more "nobles" of this sort—in reality rather humble folk—the crystallization of the idea of nobility which was then taking place on altogether different lines was not the only reason. In a great part of the West practically the whole social class had disappeared; it had become extinct.

In the Frankish period a great number of slaves had received their freedom. Naturally these intruders were not readily accepted as equals by families which had never been sullied by the servile taint. With the "free man" (*liber*), who might be a former slave set free or the recent descendant of a freedman, the Romans had not so long before contrasted the pure *ingenuus*; but in the Latin of the decadence the two words had become almost synonymous. An unblemished line was nevertheless genuine nobility in the vague sense in which that word was ordinarily employed. "To be noble is to count among one's ancestors no one who has been subjected to slavery." Such was the definition still given, towards the beginning of the eleventh century, by an Italian gloss, systematizing a usage of which we find more than one trace elsewhere.[2] . . .

Nevertheless, in the course of the first feudal age, the word [noble] gradually lost its humbler uses and tended more and more to be reserved for those groups of powerful men who had been able to acquire a growing dominance in society as a result of the breakdown of government and the general extension of protective ties. In this sense the word was still loosely used, without any precise definition of status or caste; but not without a very strong sense of the supremacy of the rank so described. Certainly the strong sense of a hierarchic order was present in the minds of those parties to a peace pact in 1023 who swore to refrain from attacking "noble-women"—no others were mentioned.[3] In short, if the concept of nobility as a legal class remained unknown, it is quite permissible from this period, by a slight simplification of terminology, to speak of a social class of nobles and especially, perhaps, of a noble way of life. For it was principally by the nature of its wealth, by its exercise of authority, and by its social habits that this group was defined.

## THE NOBLE CLASS A CLASS OF LORDS

This dominant class has sometimes been described as a landed class, and if by that is meant that fundamentally its members derived their revenues from their control of the soil, we may agree. From what other source could they have looked for them? Yet it must be added that, when available, tolls, market fees, and fines levied on a local trade were not the least coveted of properties. The characteristic feature was some form of exploitation. Whatever the sources of the noble's income—agricultural land or, as was much more rarely the case, shops or workshops—he always lived on the labour of other men. In other words, he was above all a manorial lord. . . .

## THE PROFESSION OF ARMS

If the possession of manors was the mark of a genuinely noble status and, along with treasure in money or jewels, the only form of wealth which seemed compatible with high rank, this was due in the first place to the authority over other men which it implied. (Could there ever be a surer basis of prestige than to be able to say: "It is my will"?) But another reason was that the very vocation of the noble prevented him from engaging in any direct economic activity. He was committed body and soul to his particular function—that of the warrior. This fact, which is of fundamental importance, explains the rôle of the military vassals in the formation of medieval aristocracy. They did not constitute the whole of it; the owners of allodial manors, quickly assimilated by social habits to the enfeoffed vassals and sometimes more powerful than they,

[2] *M.G.H., LL,* vol. IV, p. 557, col. 2, l. 6.

[3] Peace oath of Beauvais in C. Pfister, *Études sur le régne de Robert le Pieux,* 1885, p. lxi.

could hardly have been excluded. The vassal groups, nevertheless, formed the basic element in it. . . .

It was not only vassals, of course, who had the capacity or the duty to fight; nor were they the only ones with a love of fighting in that first feudal age, when society from top to bottom was imbued with the taste for violence or the fear of it. The laws which attempted to restrict or prohibit the bearing of arms by members of the lower classes did not make their appearance before the second half of the twelfth century, and they coincided both with the progress of legal differentiation between classes and with a relative abatement of disorder. But whether he was a vassal or even—where such still existed—an allodial lord, the "noble" of early feudal times, in contrast with all the temporary soldiers, had the special characteristic of being a better armed warrior and a professional warrior.

He fought on horseback; and though he might on occasion dismount during the battle, he always moved about on horseback. Moreover, he fought fully equipped; his offensive weapons were the lance and the sword, occasionally the mace, while for defence he wore a helmet and a garment made wholly or partly of metal, and he carried a round or triangular shield. Strictly speaking, it was not the horse alone which made the knight; his humbler companion, the squire, whose duty it was to look after the horses and arrange the change of mounts along the road, was also mounted. Sometimes in addition to the heavy cavalry of the knights, armies included the more lightly equipped horsemen usually known as "serjeants." The distinguishing mark of the highest class of fighting-man was the combination of horse and complete equipment.

. . . . . . . . . . . . . . . . . . . . . . . . . . . . . . . . . .

Now is it surprising that in the eyes of generations which had good reasons for exalting force in its crudest form the fighting-man *par excellence* should have been the most feared, the most sought-after and the most respected of men? A theory at that time very widely current represented the human community as being divided into three "orders": those who prayed, those who fought, and those who worked. It was unanimously agreed that the second should be placed much higher than the third. But the evidence of the epic goes farther still, showing that the soldier had little hesitation in rating his mission even higher than that of the specialist in prayer. Pride is one of the essential ingredients of all class-consciousness. That of the "nobles" of the feudal era was, above all, the pride of the warrior.

Moreover, fighting was for them not merely an occasional duty to be performed for the sake of their lord, or king, or family. It represented much more—their whole purpose in life.

. . . . . . . . . . . . . . . . . . . . . . . . . . . . . . . . . .

A supple and muscular body . . ., it is almost superfluous to say, was not enough to make the ideal knight. To these qualities he must add courage as well. And it was also because it gave scope for the exercise of this virtue that war created such joy in the hearts of men for whom daring and the contempt for death were, in a sense, professional assets. It is true that this valour did not always prevent mad panics (we have seen examples of them in face of the Vikings), nor was it above resorting to crude stratagems. Nevertheless the knightly class knew how to fight—on this point, history agrees with legend. Its unquestionable heroism was nurtured by many elements: the simple physical reaction of a healthy human being; the rage of despair—it is when he feels himself "wounded unto death" that the "cautious" Oliver strikes such terrible blows, in order "to avenge himself all he could"; the devotion to a chief or, in the case of the holy war, to a cause; the passionate desire for glory, personal or collective; the fatalistic acquiescence in face of ineluctable destiny, of which literature offers no more poignant examples than some of the last cantos of the *Nibelungenlied*; finally, the hope of reward in another world, promised not only to him who died for his God, but also to him who died for his master.

Accustomed to danger, the knight found in war yet another attraction: it offered a remedy for boredom. For these men whose culture long remained rudimentary and who—apart from a few great barons and their counsellors—were seldom occupied by very heavy administrative cares, everyday life easily slipped into a grey monotony. Thus was born an appetite for diversions which, when one's native soil failed to afford the means to gratify it, sought satisfaction in distant lands.

. . . . . . . . . . . . . . . . . . . . . . . . . . . . . . . . .

. . . it was undoubtedly considered that the finest gift the chief could bestow was the right to a share of the plunder. This was also the principal profit which the knight who fought on his own account in little local wars expected from his efforts. It was a double prize, moreover: men and things. . . .

. . . War in the feudal age was in no sense war in kid gloves. It was accompanied by actions which seem to us today anything but chivalrous; as for instance—a frequent occurrence, sometimes even in disregard of a solemn oath—the massacre or mutilation of garrisons which had held out "too long." It involved, as a natural concomitant, the devastation of the enemy's estates.

. . . . . . . . . . . . . . . . . . . . . . . . . . . . . . . . .

## THE NOBLE AT HOME

Favourite sport though it was, war had its dead seasons; but at these times the knightly class was distinguished from its neighbours by a manner of life which was essentially that of a nobility.

. . . . . . . . . . . . . . . . . . . . . . . . . . . . . . . . .

Everything tended to induce him to live in the country. First, there was the habit, which was becoming more and more widespread, of remunerating vassals by means of fiefs, consisting in the vast majority of cases of rural manors; then there was the weakening of feudal obligations, which favoured the tendency among the retainers who had now been provided with fiefs to live each in his own home, far from the kings, the great barons, and the bishops, who controlled the towns; finally, a taste for the open air, natural to these sportsmen, played its part. . . .

Thus whatever modifications it may be necessary to introduce into the picture of a nobility exclusively rural from the outset, it remains true that, ever since knights existed, a growing majority of them in the North and many even in the coastal regions of the Mediterranean ordinarily resided in a country mansion.

. . . . . . . . . . . . . . . . . . . . . . . . . . . . . . . . .

## OCCUPATIONS AND DISTRACTIONS

Though usually a countryman in the sense that his home was in the country, the noble was nevertheless no agriculturalist. To put his hand to the hoe or the plough would have been an indication that he had come down in the world—as happened to a poor knight whose history is known to us through a collection of anecdotes. And if he sometimes liked to contemplate the workers in the fields or the yellowing harvest on his estates, it does not appear that as a rule he took a very direct part in the management of the farm. The manuals of estate management, when they came to be written, were intended not for the master, but for his stewards; the "country gentleman" belongs to quite another age—after the economic revolution in the sixteenth century. Although the rights of jurisdiction which he possessed over his tenants constituted one of the essential sources of his power, the lord of the village as a rule exercised them much less frequently in person than through the agency of bailiffs, themselves of peasant extraction. Nevertheless the exercise of judicial functions was certainly one of the few peaceful occupations of the knight. As a rule he only concerned himself with judicial duties within the framework of his class, which meant that he either settled the lawsuits of his own vassals or sat as judge of his peers in the court to which he had been summoned by his feudal lord; but where public justice survived, as in England and Germany, he took his place in the court of the county or the hundred. There was enough of this activity to make the legal spirit one of the earliest cultural influences to be diffused in knightly circles.

The favourite amusements of the nobility bore the imprint of a warlike temper.

First, there was hunting. As has already been said, it was more than a sport. The people of western Europe were not yet living in surroundings from which the menace of wild beasts had been finally removed. Moreover, at a time when the flesh of cattle, inadequately fed and of poor stock, furnished only indifferent meat, much venison was eaten, especially in the homes of the rich.

. . . . . . . . . . . . . . . . . . . . . . . . . . . . . . . . . .

Then there were the tournaments. . . . The contests of young men are an almost universal feature of folklore. In the armies, moreover, the imitation of war at all times provided a training for troops as well as a pastime. . . . The distinctive contribution of the feudal age was to evolve from these contests, whether military or popular, a type of mock battle at which prizes were generally offered, confined to mounted combatants equipped with knightly arms; and hence to create a distinctive class amusement, which the nobility found more exciting than any other.

. . . . . . . . . . . . . . . . . . . . . . . . . . . . . . . . . .

Nevertheless, the passion for tournaments, as for genuine warfare, was not always disinterested. Since the victor frequently took possession of the equipment and horses of the vanquished and sometimes even of his person, releasing him only on payment of a ransom, skill and strength were profitable assets. More than one jousting knight made a profession, and a very lucrative one, out of his skill in combat. Thus the love of arms inextricably combined the ingredients of "joy" and the appetite for gain.

## RULES OF CONDUCT

It was natural that a class so clearly defined by its mode of life and its social supremacy should eventually devise a code of conduct peculiar to itself. But it was only during the second feudal age, which was in every sense the age of awakening self-consciousness, that these rules assumed a precise form and, along with it, a more refined character.

The term which, from about the year 1100, commonly served to describe the sum of noble qualities was the characteristic word "courtesy" (*courtoisie*), which is derived from *cour*. . . . It was in fact in the assemblies, temporary or permanent, which were formed round the principal barons and the kings, that these laws of conduct came to be evolved; the isolation of the knight in his "tower" would not have permitted their development. Emulation and social contacts were necessary, and that is why this advance in moral sensibility was bound up both with the consolidation of the great principalities or monarchies and with the restoration of a greater degree of intercommunication. Another term was *prudhomme,* and as "courteous" (*courtois*) gradually acquired a more commonplace meaning, this word was used more and more frequently to denote something higher: a name so great and so good that merely to pronounce it "fills the mouth," declared St. Louis, intending thereby to vindicate the secular virtues as against those of the monk.

. . . . . . . . . . . . . . . . . . . . . . . . . . . . . . . . . .

As we have seen, the nobility had never been completely illiterate; still less had it been impervious to the influence of literature, though this was listened to rather than read. But a great step forward was taken when knights themselves became literary men. It is significant that the *genre* to which they devoted themselves almost exclusively up to the thirteenth century was lyric poetry. The earliest of the troubadours known to us—it should be added that he was certainly not the first—ranked among the most powerful princes in France. . . .

Towards the pleasures of the flesh the attitude of the knightly class appears to have been frankly realistic. It was the attitude of the age as a whole. The Church imposed ascetic standards on its members and required laymen to restrict sexual intercourse to marriage and the purpose of procreation. But it did not practise its own precepts very effectively, and this was especially true of the secular clergy, among whom even the Gregorian reform purified the lives of few but the episcopate. . . .

. . . The noble's marriage, as we know, was often an ordinary business transaction, and the houses of the nobility swarmed with bastards. At first sight, the advent of "courtesy" does not seem to have effected any great change in these morals. Certain of the songs of William of Aquitaine sing the praises of sensual pleasure in barrack-room style and this attitude was to find more than one imitator among the poets who succeeded him. Nevertheless, with William, who was apparently the heir of a tradition whose origins elude us, another conception of love was already emerging—that "courtly" love, which was certainly one of the most curious products of the moral code of chivalry. Can we conceive of Don Quixote without Dulcinea?

The characteristic features of courtly love can be summarized fairly simply. It had nothing to do with marriage, or rather it was directly opposed to the legal state of marriage, since the beloved was as a rule a married woman and the lover was never her husband. This love was often bestowed upon a lady of higher rank, but in any case it always involved a strong emphasis on the man's adoration of the woman. It professed to be an all-engrossing passion, constantly frustrated, easily jealous, and nourished by its own difficulties; but its stereotyped development early acquired something of a ritual character. It was not averse to casuistry. Finally, as the troubadour Geoffrey Rudel said, in a poem which, wrongly interpreted, gave rise to the famous legend of Princess Far-away, it was, ideally, a "distant" love. It did not indeed reject carnal intercourse on principle, nor according to Andrew the Chaplain, who discoursed on the subject, did it despise minor physical gratifications if obliged to renounce "the ultimate solace". But absence or obstacles, instead of destroying it, only enriched it with a poetic melancholy. If possession, always to be desired, was seen to be quite out of the question, the sentiment none the less endured as an exciting emotion and a poignant joy.

Such is the picture drawn for us by the poets. For courtly love is only known to us through literature and for that reason it is very difficult to determine to what extent it was merely a fashionable fiction.

. . . . . . . . . . . . . . . . . . . . . . . . . . . . . . . . . . . . . . . . . .

That a knight should carefully calculate his booty or his ransoms and, on returning home, impose a heavy "tallage" on his peasants provoked little or no criticism. Gain was legitimate; but on one condition —that it should be promptly and liberally expended. "I can assure you," said a troubadour when he was reproached for his brigandage, "if I robbed, it was to give, not to hoard."[4] No doubt we are entitled to regard as a little suspect the insistence with which the minstrels, those professional parasites, extolled above all other duties that of generosity, *largesse,* "lady and queen in whose light all virtues shine." No doubt also, among the nobles of middle or lesser rank and still more perhaps among the great barons, there were always miserly or merely prudent individuals, more inclined to amass scarce coin or jewels in their coffers than to distribute them. It is none the less true that, in squandering a fortune that was easily gained and easily lost, the noble thought to affirm his superiority over classes less confident in the future or more careful in providing for it. This praiseworthy prodigality might not always stop at generosity or even luxury. A chronicler has preserved for us the record of the remarkable competition in wasteful expenditure witnessed one day at a great "court" held in Limousin. One knight had a plot of ground ploughed up and sown with small pieces of silver; another burned wax candles for his cooking; a third, "through boastfulness," ordered thirty of his horses to be burnt alive.[5] What must a merchant have thought of this struggle for prestige through extravagance—which reminds us of the practices of certain primitive races? Here again different notions of honour marked the line of separation between the social groups.

Thus set apart by its power, by the nature of its wealth and its mode of life, by its very morals, the social class of nobles was toward the middle of the twelfth century quite ready to solidify into a legal and hereditary class. The ever more frequent use which from that time onwards seems to have been made of the word *gentilhomme*—man of good *gent* or lineage—to describe

[4] Albert de Malaspina, in C. Appel, *Provenzalische Chrestomathie,* 3rd ed., no. 90, v. 19 *et seq.*

[5] Geoffroi de Vigeois, I, 69 in Labbe, *Bibliotheca,* II, p. 322.

the members of this class is an indication of the growing importance attributed to qualities of birth. With the wide adoption of the ceremony of "dubbing" or formal arming of the knight the legal class of nobility took definite shape.

## TRANSFORMATION OF THE NOBILITY INTO A LEGAL CLASS

. . . . . . . . . . . . . . . . . . . . . . . . . . . . . . . . . .

It is true that when they expressly imposed the hereditary rule sovereigns and courts of law were hardly aware that they were doing anything new, since at all times the great majority of those who were knighted were descendants of knights. In the eyes of an increasingly exclusive group opinion, only high birth—"guarantee of the continuation of ancient honour," as it was called by Ramon Lull—enabled a man to observe the code of behavior to which he was committed by the delivery of arms. "Ah, God! how badly is the good warrior rewarded who makes the son of a villein a knight!" exclaims the poet of *Girart de Roussillon,* about 1160;[6] which, however, testifies to the fact that these intruders were by no means rare. No law, no custom, could altogether exclude them. Moreover, they appeared at times to be almost necessary for the recruitment of armies; for that same class prejudice produced a strong conviction that only knights had the right to fight on horseback fully armed. In 1302, on the eve of the battle of Courtrai, the Flemish princes, desiring to have a cavalry force, knighted a number of rich burghers whose wealth enabled them to provide themselves with the necessary horses and equipment.[7] The transformation of what had long been by mere convention a hereditary vocation, liable to many setbacks, into a legalized and jealously-guarded privilege was therefore of capital importance, even if contemporaries had no clear awareness of this development. The profound social changes which were in progress at that time on the fringes of the knightly world had certainly done much to inspire these Draconian measures.

In the twelfth century a new power was born—the urban patriciate. In these rich merchants who frequently acquired manors and many of whom had aspired to "the baldric of knighthood", for themselves or their sons, the hereditary warriors could not fail to recognize elements much more foreign to their own mentality and way of life—much more disturbing also on account of their number—than the soldiers of fortune or the manorial officials who had hitherto provided most of the non-noble candidates for knighthood. We know, through Bishop Otto of Freising, the reactions of the German barons to the knighthoods which they considered were too freely distributed, in northern Italy, to "men in trades and crafts"; Beaumanoir, in France, has very clearly explained how the pressure of the new social classes, eager to invest their capital in land, led the kings to take the precautions necessary to prevent the purchase of a fief from making every *nouveau riche* the equal of a descendant of knights. When a class feels itself threatened it tends to close its ranks.

It would be a mistake, however, to imagine that there was, in theory, any insuperable obstacle. A class of powerful individuals could not transform itself completely into a hereditary caste without being compelled to exclude from its ranks the new forces whose inevitable emergence is the very law of life, thereby condemning itself, as a social group, to permanent enfeeblement. Thus the evolution of legal opinion during the feudal period tended much less to impose a strict ban on new admissions than to subject them to rigorous control. Formerly every knight could make a knight. . . . however, such action had become illegal, and a heavy fine was the just punishment for this anachronism. For a member of the knightly order no longer had the right to confer membership on others unless the aspirant was already of knightly lineage. When such was not the case he might indeed be knighted, but only by special permission from the sole authority who, according to contemporary notions, was entitled to exercise the extraordinary

[6] Raimon Lull, *Libro de la orden de Caballeria,* ed. I. R. de Luanco, III, 8; *Girart de Roussillon,* trans. P. Meyer, p. 28 (cf. ed. Foerster, *Roman. Studien,* vol. V, p. 940 *et seq.*).

[7] P. Thomas, *Textes Historiques sur Lille,* II, 1936, p. 237.

power of dispensing from customary rules: namely the king, the sole bestower, as Beaumanoir says, of "novelties." . . .

If access to the circle of knights by birth was not absolutely closed, the door was nevertheless only very slightly ajar. It was certainly very much less easy to enter than it had been before or would be in the future; hence the violent reaction against the nobility which, in France at least, broke out in the fourteenth century. What more striking proof can be found of the solidarity and exclusive spirit of a class than the fierceness of the attacks to which it is subjected? "Revolt of the non-nobles against the nobles"—the expression, which was virtually in official use at the time of the Jacquerie is revealing; and not less so is the list of combatants. Étienne Marcel, a rich burgess and the first magistrate of the first of cities, deliberately set himself up as the enemy of the nobles. Under Louis XI or Louis XIV he would have been one of them himself. In truth, the period from about 1250 to about 1400 was, on the continent, the period which witnessed the most rigid stratification of social classes.

## THE DESCENDANTS OF KNIGHTS BECOME A PRIVILEGED CLASS

By itself, however, the restriction of knighthood to members of families already confirmed in that status or to the recipients of exceptional favours would not have sufficed to form a genuine nobility. For this would have meant that the privileges which according to the conception of nobility were inseparable from noble birth would have been made dependent on a ceremony which might or might not be carried out. It was not just a question of prestige. Increasingly the pre-eminent position which it was agreed to accord to knights, both as "ordained" warriors and as vassals charged with the highest responsibilities in war and counsel, tended to take concrete shape in a precise legal code. Now, from the end of the eleventh century to the first years of the thirteenth, the same rules were reproduced throughout feudal Europe. In order to enjoy these advantages it was necessary in the first place that a man should efficiently perform his duties as a vassal, "that he have arms and horses, that, unless prevented by age, he take part in the host and in the expeditions, in the assemblies and in the courts," say the *Usages* of Catalonia. It was also necessary that he should have been knighted. The general weakening of vassal services had the result that gradually the first condition ceased to be insisted on; the later texts pass it over in silence. The second, on the other hand, remained for a long time very much in force. As late as 1238, a private family regulation, the statute of the parceners who possessed in common the castle of La Garde-Guérin in the Gévaudan, gives priority to a younger son over the eldest, if the former has received knighthood and the latter has not.

. . . . . . . . . . . . . . . . . . . . . . . . . . . . . . . . . . . . . .

In the last years of the thirteenth century, the evolution was almost everywhere complete. What henceforth made the noble was not the old rite of initiation, now reduced to the status of a polite formality and neglected by the majority because as a rule it involved great expense; it was the hereditary right to be knighted, whether or not that right was exercised. One calls a nobleman, writes Beaumanoir, whoever is "of knightly lineage". And shortly after 1284 the earliest authorization of knighthood granted by the chancellery of the kings of France to a person not of noble birth raised at one stroke, without imposing any conditions at all, the entire posterity of the recipient "to the privileges, rights and franchises which the nobles are accustomed to enjoy by virtue of the two lines of descent".

## THE LAW OF THE NOBLES

This body of private law (which with certain necessary modifications applied to women of noble birth as well as to men) varied considerably in its details from one region to another. Moreover it evolved only slowly, and in the course of time underwent important modifications. Military vassals had for a long time been governed by a law which differed from the common rules. They were not tried by the same courts as other dependents; their fiefs were not inherited in the same way as other properties. Their family status itself bore the marks of their rank. . . .

A number of other features underlined still more emphatically the social supremacy of the class as well as its character as a fighting order. If it was a question of maintaining purity of blood, there was obviously no more effective means than the complete prohibition of marriages with persons of inferior status. Only in the imported feudalism of Cyprus and the hierarchic society of Germany, however, did it come to that; and in the latter country, which was characterized, as we shall see, by a highly-developed system of gradations within the nobility itself, it was only the higher ranks and not the petty knights, sprung from former manorial officials, who were restricted in this way. Elsewhere the memory of the ancient equality of free men continued, so far as marriage was concerned, to be reflected in law, if not in practice. Everywhere, however, certain great religious communities, which hitherto had displayed their aristocratic spirit only in rejecting postulants of servile origin, decided now to admit them only if they were descended from the nobility. Everywhere also—earlier in one place, later in another—we find evidence that the noble was specially protected in his person against the non-noble; that he was subject to an exceptional penal law, with heavier fines, as a rule, than those exacted from the common people; that recourse to private vengeance, regarded as inseparable from the bearing of arms, tended to be reserved for him; that the sumptuary laws assigned to him a place apart. The importance attached to birth as the source of privilege was expressed in the transformation of the old individual signs of "recognition," painted on the knight's shield or engraved on his seal, into the armorial bearings, sometimes transmitted with the fief but more often handed down, even without the property, from generation to generation. The use of these symbols of continuity, first seen in the royal and princely dynasties, where pride of birth was particularly strong, and soon adopted by houses of lesser rank, was regarded henceforth as the monopoly of the families classed as noble. Finally, although tax exemptions were still far from being strictly defined, the military obligation—formerly the characteristic duty of the vassal, now the noble's duty *par excellence*—had henceforth the effect of relieving the nobleman of the usual pecuniary burdens; these being in his case replaced by warlike services.

However strong the rights acquired by birth, they were not so strong that they might not be lost by the exercise of certain occupations deemed to be incompatible with high rank. It is true that the conception of derogation (*dérogeance*) was as yet far from being fully developed.[8] The rule which forbade nobles to engage in trade seems at that time to have been imposed on them above all by certain urban statutes, which were intended to protect the virtual monopoly of the merchant communities rather than to serve the pride of a hostile caste. But by universal consent agricultural labor was regarded as contrary to the honor of the military class. Even with his own compliance—so the *Parlement* of Paris decided—a knight who had acquired a tenement in villeinage could not perform rural labor services. "To plough, to dig, to carry a load of wood or manure"—these were actions which, according to a Provençal ordinance, automatically involved deprivation of knightly privileges. It was also in Provence that a noblewoman was characterized as one who goes "neither to the oven, nor to the wash-house, nor to the mill".[9] The nobility had ceased to be defined by the exercise of a function—that of the armed retainer. It was no longer a class of initiates. It remained, however, a class distinguished by its mode of life.

. . . . . . . . . . . . . . . . . . . . . . . . . . . . . . . . . .

## HAS THERE BEEN MORE THAN ONE FEUDALISM?

In the eyes of Montesquieu, the establishment of "feudal laws" was a phenomenon *sui generis*, "an event which happened once in the world, and which will perhaps never happen again." Voltaire, less experienced, no doubt, in the precise formulation of legal definitions, but a man of wider outlook, demurred. "Feudalism," he wrote, "is not an event; it is a very old form which,

[8] [*Dérogeance* was an act on the part of a nobleman which constituted an impairment of his rank and led to its forfeiture.]

[9] *Olim*, I, p. 427, no. XVII (Chandeleur, 1255); F. Benoit, *Recueil des actes*, passages cited above, p. 326, n. 1; M. Z. Isnard, *Livre des privilèges de Manosque*, 1894, no. XLVII, p. 154.

with differences in its working, subsists in three-quarters of our hemisphere."[10] Modern scholarship has in general rallied to the side of Voltaire. Egyptian feudalism, Achaean feudalism, Chinese feudalism, Japanese feudalism—all these forms and more are now familiar concepts. . . . Since it is obvious that all these societies, separated by time and space, have received the name "feudal" only on account of their similarities, real or supposed, to Western feudalism, it is the characteristics of this basic type, to which all the others must be referred, that it is of primary importance to define.

. . . . . . . . . . . . . . . . . . . . . . . . . . . . . . . . .

Let us therefore try to bring in broad outline what we have learned about European feudalism, in the strict sense of the word, from its history. . . .

The simplest way will be to begin by saying what feudal society was not. Although the obligations arising from blood-relationship played a very active part in it, it did not rely on kinship alone. More precisely, feudal ties proper were developed when those of kinship proved inadequate. Again, despite the persistence of the idea of a public authority super-imposed on the multitude of petty powers, feudalism coincided with a profound weakening of the State, particularly in its protective capacity. But much as feudal society differed from societies based on kinship as well as from those dominated by the power of the State, it was their successor and bore their imprint. For while the characteristic relationships of personal subjection retained something of the quasi-family character of the original companionage, a considerable part of the political authority exercised by innumerable petty chiefs had the appearance of a usurpation of "regalian" rights.

European feudalism should therefore be seen as the outcome of the violent dissolution of older societies. It would in fact be unintelligible without the great upheaval of the Germanic invasions which, by forcibly uniting two societies originally at very different stages of development, disrupted both of them and brought to the surface a great many modes of thought and social practices of an extremely primitive character. It finally developed in the atmosphere of the last barbarian raids. It involved a far-reaching restriction of social intercourse, a circulation of money too sluggish to admit of a salaried officialdom, and a mentality attached to things tangible and local. When these conditions began to change, feudalism began to wane.

It was an unequal society, rather than a hierarchical one—with chiefs rather than nobles; and with serfs, not slaves. If slavery had not played so small a part, there would have been no need for the characteristically feudal forms of dependence, as applied to the lower orders of society. In an age of disorder, the place of the adventurer was too important, the memory of men too short, the regularity of social classifications too uncertain, to admit of the strict formation of regular castes.

Nevertheless the feudal system meant the rigorous economic subjection of a host of humble folk to a few powerful men. Having received from earlier ages the Roman *villa* (which in some respects anticipated the manor) and the German village chiefdom, it extended and consolidated these methods whereby men exploited men, and combining inextricably the right to the revenues from the land with the right to exercise authority, it fashioned from all this the true manor of medieval times. And this it did partly for the benefit of an oligarchy of priests and monks whose task it was to propitiate Heaven, but chiefly for the benefit of an oligarchy of warriors.

As even the most perfunctory comparative study will show, one of the most distinctive characteristics of feudal societies was the virtual identity of the class of chiefs with the class of professional warriors serving in the only way that then seemed effective, that is as heavily armed horsemen. . . .

In feudal society the characteristic human bond was the subordinate's link with a nearby chief. From one level to another the ties thus formed—like so many chains branching out indefinitely—joined the smallest to the greatest. Land itself was valued above all because it enabled a lord to provide himself with "men" by supplying the remuneration for them. We want lands,

[10] *Esprit des Lois*, XXX, I; Voltaire, *Fragments sur quelques révolutions dans l'Inde*, II (ed. Garnier, XXIX, p. 91).

said in effect the Norman lords who refused the gifts of jewels, arms, and horses offered by their duke. And they added among themselves: "It will thus be possible for us to maintain many knights, and the duke will no longer be able to do so."[11]

. . . . . . . . . . . . . . . . . . . . . . . . . . . . . . . . . .

A subject peasantry; widespread use of the service tenement (i.e. the fief) instead of a salary, which was out of the question; the supremacy of a class of specialized warriors; ties of obedience and protection which bind man to man and, within the warrior class, assume the distinctive form called vassalage; fragmentation of authority—leading inevitably to disorder; and, in the midst of all this, the survival of other forms of association, family and State, of which the latter, during the second feudal age, was to acquire renewed strength—such then seem to be the fundamental features of European feudalism. Like all the phenomena revealed by that science of eternal change which is history, the social structure thus characterized certainly bore the peculiar stamp of an age and an environment. Yet just as the matrilineal or agnatic clan or even certain types of economic enterprise are found in much the same forms in very different societies, it is by no means impossible that societies different from our own should have passed through a phase closely resembling that which has just been defined. If so, it is legitimate to call them feudal during that phase. . . .

# CLASS SOCIETY IN THE MELTING POT

## *Theodor Geiger*

. . . A united proletarian class front against the capitalist system has neither grown stronger nor expanded in modern times. The new proletarian sections of society—for example, the impoverished petty bourgeois groups and considerable portions of the white collar stratum—have reacted entirely differently than the industrial workers to their social situation; at any rate, they do not perceive socialism as the target of their interests. How strange it is to see a supposedly scientific train of thought[1] first assert that this attitude, deviating from the class consciousness of the industrial workers, is precisely typical for the bourgeois-infected proletarian groups, and then go on to designate this objectively described typical attitude as a false consciousness!

Within the working class itself a cooling of proletarian class consciousness and a split has taken place. There is a cooling as considerable parts of this class have risen in their income level to lower middle-class conditions. Their social attitude and thinking follows much more this changed income status than their relation to the means of production. They have become, as one says, *bourgeois* (*verbürgerlicht*). They no longer see their interests lying in the collectivization[2] of the means of production, but rather in the preservation and further improvement of their socioeconomic position within the existing society. In connection therewith a split has opened between "consciousness" and interests. Large portions of the wage-working class have found their place and have established themselves within the existing society. This class as such is a multitude of linked substrata that live in quite different circumstances. Opposite interests have therefore evolved *within* the wage-working class.

On the other hand—unexpectedly—the interest of the so-called capitalist class in the preservation of capitalism is wavering. This is connected with the previously mentioned change in the organizational form of the economy. The individuals who are in key positions in the capitalist economy, the leaders of the big enterprises, are no longer the owners but big executives

From *Die Klassengesellschaft im Schmelztiegel,* Kiepenheuer & Witsch, 1949. Reprinted by permission. (Translated by Celia S. Heller.)

[11] Dudo of Saint-Quentin, ed. Lair (*Mém. Soc. Antiquaires Normandie,* XXIII), III, 43–4 (933).

[1] Marxist thought. (C. S. H.)

[2] Geiger uses the German term "*Sozialisierung*" and I shall refer to it throughout the text as *collectivization.* I consider it closer to the German meaning than *nationalization.* (C. S. H.).

who are salaried employees. They are not directly interested in the preservation of the rights of property. Their kind will not disappear in case of full collectivization. They would pass from serving the stockholders to serving the state, but their function would continue essentially unchanged. It is very doubtful whether the far-sighted among them still think in the categories of capitalism-socialism at all. The representatives of today's capitalism are not committed to capitalism.

The true capitalist attitude, the interest in preserving the right of private property, is to be sought among the real owners—but this means today among the smaller to medium businessmen. Outright antisocialism, that is opposition to the idea of collectivization, is still widespread among the intellectuals. However, their antisocialist posture has nothing to do with the "relationship to the means of production" and is altogether divorced from their economic position. They do not stress the right of property, but economic freedom. They distrust the political conditions that appear to follow in the wake of collectivization and distrust the dictatorship that does not tolerate personal and, especially, intellectual freedom. Precisely therein the intellectuals today have found allies in all strata, not last among the working class itself. The activization of the class struggle and sharpening of psychological class contradictions anticipated and foretold by Marxism have not materialized. The interest fronts regarding the future social structure have shifted in a direction for which there is no explanation based on Marxist social theory. *"Scientific" Marxism has failed, confronted with the social reality of the twentieth century.*

. . . The Marxist model of industrial class society was presumably not inappropriate for the period of high capitalism. To be sure, a series of phenomena did not fit this model of stratification and therefore, at no time did the model give a complete picture of society. But one must consider that society has been seized by deep unrest since the breakthrough of industrialization. The structural changes no longer occur as a series of distinct conditions, each of which has its typical appearance, but rather do they form a continuous stream within which the various structures barely have time to unfold but, so to speak, are intertwined. They do not appear as consecutive states separable from one another but rather as changing trends of development. The society of Marx's time, viewed statically, was in no way dominated by the class principle. . . . What Marx saw—and adequately described—was a tendency toward the abolition of the then structural lines. What he predicted—and in this he erred—was the full development of the class structure. Class stratification never really emerged as a dominant state of stratification. Long before it was able to penetrate the whole society, other structural trends broke into the picture, deflected the stratification of "capital and labor" and obscured it. These new structural trends came to the fore before the preceding ones could mature. . . .

. . . The class society of Marxist coloring is obviously in retreat. No one can tell as yet with confidence which direction the development will take. But we can point out a number of competing trends and, with caution, venture some suggestions as to the weight and force with which they will contribute to the future formation of society. . . .

## NEW LINES OF DEVELOPMENT

*The Middle Strata.* The first shift in the stratification lines proceded from the propertied middle stratum. Marxism counted that the struggle between capital and wage labor would become the fate of the entire society and define its features. This prediction came true in fact but in a manner surprising to its authors. The expectation was that individual members of society would increasingly solidify around the two poles of capital and wage labor. . . . A minority of middle tradesmen would with energy and luck advance to the ranks of capital but the majority would sink, would become proletarianized, and would finally join the anticapitalist front in its struggle. In this manner the final point in the unfolding of capitalism would be reached; after the collapse and liquidation of that system, socialism would come into being. The actual run of events was different. The class struggle between the opposite poles of capitalism and wage labor did not by and by seize the entire society and did not divide it into two hostile camps. However, this class struggle did give rise to a new constellation of fronts on a different plane. Let us see how this came about.

The class struggle between capital and wage labor did indeed become also the fate of the propertied middle stratum. It was directly on its way to proletarianization. But those partially caught and partially threatened by it refused to draw what the Marxists considered the only "reasonable" conclusion from their social destiny. Their sociopolitical stand oscillated between dull resignation and desperate uproar. The blind hatred of the artisans and petty industrialists against the large enterprises with which they were competing and the struggle of the small traders against the department stores and the consumer organizations remind one in their reactionary-utopian absurdity of the corresponding phase in the labor movement: the attack on machines by the Luddites.[3]

The following phase almost coincided with . . . the economic recovery of the middle stratum. At that time the middle-class movement began, the realistic political (*realpolitische*) efforts of which were partly directed toward the organization of solidary self-help and partly aimed at legislative measures for the protection of the middle class, for the restoration and strengthening of the economic position of the small artisans. This realistic political struggle was not directed against the capitalistic system as such but against its development beyond the point where, through the continuous concentration of [big] enterprises, it became dangerous to the small and middle-size entrepreneurs. In this the middle-class movement proved itself hostile to progress and conservative in a narrow bourgeois way.

Curiously contradictory tendencies were at work underneath the ideological struggle of the movement. The threat to the smaller traders by the big enterprises was answered by a deep, even hostile, aversion against "capital." One protested against being considered as part of the capitalist class that one feared and hated. Here the fact that the word "capitalist" had assumed an odious sound because of the obtrusive agitation of the labor movement may have played a psychological part. The ancient talk about solid workmanship of handicraft and the cheap factory output—long since bare of its old validity—was nevertheless continued in ideological propagandist form. Pseudo-theoretical arguments were brought forth in favor of competitive morality, which recognized as proper methods of competition precisely those that the small tradesman could cope with and could himself apply, while the underbidding made possible through the higher efficiency of the big enterprises was labeled as dirty competition. In practice the then continual and heated agitation against the formation of the monopoly of big capital did not fail to make a certain impression on the public.

The repulsion against capital did not manifest itself, however, in a corresponding good will toward the class-struggling enemies of capital. On the contrary! The anticapitalism of the bourgeois middle stratum limited itself to the competitive superiority of the large enterprises, to the progressive concentration and monopolization of enterprises. In contrast, it defended with tooth and nail the right of private property of the means of production as an economic and moral article of faith. The attack of the labor movement against the right of private property was totally misunderstood by the middle stratum—it considered the idea of collectivization a real horror. In addition, other factors created a deep chasm between the middle stratum and the organized working class. The religiously conventional petit bourgeoisie was not negligibly offended by the religious hostility of the labor movement of that day. But above all it experienced as a shocking challenge the Marxist prediction of a proletarianization of the middle stratum that was then obtrusively stressed by socialist agitators. This was, from the standpoint of the labor movement, the worst

[3] A quasi-insurrectionary movement of working people in England who between 1811 and 1816 smashed new labor-saving textile machinery in a protest against reduced wages and unemployment attributed to their introduction. For a penetrating analysis of this movement, see E. P. Thompson, *The Making of the English Working Class*, New York: Vintage Books, 1966, pp. 547–602. (C. S. H.).

possible psychology of recruitment. The middle stratum reacted to it in a fully paradoxical manner. Even though it lived in state of constant fear of actually becoming proletarianized through the development of large capitalism, it turned with deepset indignation against those who predicted this very proletarianization.

Insofar as the economic and realistic political struggle of the middle stratum was mainly directed against large capital, its socio-ideological struggle was above all directed against the labor movement and its proletarian socialism. The middle stratum flattered itself in its propaganda with the fact that it was a protective "buffer" between the fronts of the class struggle but actually it felt helplessly squeezed between these fronts. It conducted a two-front struggle against both. The situation further deteriorated when a little later, right after 1900, the class struggle entered a regulated phase, partly because of the governmental social policy, partly because of legislative recognition of the wage struggle and collective bargaining. The anxious feeling grew that both powerful fronts—on one side capital and on the other side the mass organization—would fight out their class struggle upon the back of the middle class and conclude their truce at its cost. The engagement of the middle class on two fronts against both parties to the class struggle became transformed into a struggle precisely against the class struggle that threatened to pulverize it between its two fronts. . . . The class principle itself, the class society as a structural model, was a thorn in the side of the middle stratum. It is significant that from this perspective the designation middle class was experienced as an insult. The spokesmen of the movement always talked about the middle estate and thus symbolically placed their flock outside the model of a class society.

After the end of the nineteenth century this attitude received strength because the propertied middle stratum gave way to the so-called new middle stratum—that is, the private employees whose number at that time grew like an avalanche. The socio-political attitude of this new stratum was at the beginning not uniform and was insecure. On the one hand the employees recognized that their position as a paid work force demanded a mass organization corresponding to the labor movement. On the other hand, their behavior toward the "proletarian" class front was largely aloof and even hostile. Many of them stemmed from middle-class small businessmen. They were themselves victims of the proletarianization of the industrial middle stratum, but ideologically they reacted against this, contrary to their destiny, precisely because they felt *déclassé*. They had a prestige need to open and deepen a social gulf between themselves and the workers.

Another part of the salaried employees' stratum derived from working-class families. They appreciated their transition from the factory to the office, from blue-collar to white-collar clothes, from the machine to the desk as a social advance and because of this they experienced a need to maintain a distance. I omit, but do not forget, those among them who joined the socialist workers' front. There were many of them and their number grew in time, not least because of the fact that the socialist parties became socially acceptable (*salonfähig*). In terms of the class structure in Marx's sense, the salaried employee was doubtlessly closer to the worker than to anybody else in modern society. Because of his prestige need for detachment from the working class he coveted the status ideology of the industrial middle stratum.

Out of totally different—and partly directly opposite—motives the industrial middle stratum, as well as a large part of the officials, nourished an aversion against the class model as such. . . . The last result of this new front formation was the bourgeois revolution of fascism and hitlerism. The "folk community" (*Volksgemeinschaft*) and the "corporate" ideas[4] were slogans unmistakeably directed against the class struggle idea. It was among this dissatisfied industrial stratum, among the lower levels of salaried employees with their suppressed ambitions that Mussolini and Hitler—and their henchmen in all countries—recruited their first followers. Here they found that mixture of narrow-minded brutality and sentimental "idealism" that

[4] Fascist concepts. (C. S. H.)

made an impression on their half barbarian and half confused political goals. *It is the joke of history that Hitler in twelve years contributed more toward the ruin of the industrial middle stratum than capitalism during the entire past century could manage.*

The brief role of the middle strata in big politics is a paradox of social history: a class denies indignantly that it is a class and it carried on a bitter class struggle against the reality and idea of the class struggle.

***Class Structure and Income.*** The second line of development that worked against the class structure came from the distribution of wealth. Marx emphasized that the size of income had nothing to do with class position. The worker may be as well rewarded as possible, he is still cut off from the means of production. The producer may be on the verge of bankruptcy—he still disposes of the production apparatus. The class difference rests on the relation of the individual to the means of production, not his position as a consumer. This is basically so, but Marx does not underestimate the importance of income distribution. How else could he have ascribed in his theory of the development and the collapse of capitalism such an essential role to the supposedly progressive pauperization? The pauperization would sharpen the class antagonism and the class struggle. . . .

How the income distribution crossed class lines is to be described in greater detail. No matter what the doctrinaires of pauperization may claim, the actual position of workers has improved in absolute terms as well as relative to other strata. The entire picture is, however, more complex. A small group of individuals still have tremendous incomes. Apart from these few, an increasing income equalization has taken place. This was primarily accomplished in many countries by a strongly progressive income tax. Furthermore, there is the wage policy that remains limited in its effects on the relations between workers, salaried employees, and officials. Within the realm of wage and salary earners, the workers have achieved a much more favorable position through the organized struggle for better wages. In addition, within the last thirty years, the lowest wages more or less coincided with the movement of prices, and in part outstripped them, whereas the compensation of those with higher incomes did not keep up with the rising prices. . . . Inside the working class itself there was the parallel occurrence of an opposite development. Some seventy years ago all workers were at the lowest income level of society. Since then in the wake of the specialization of industrial work the wages of workers have considerably varied. On account of this, specific categories of workers have been placed in varied favorable positions as consumers. The top wage categories come near the salaries of higher employees and officials. The workers in toto are better off but there is considerable variation within. . . .

So much for the facts. In order to fully appreciate their social significance, a view into social history is indicated. The stormy development of industry and large cities in the past century disolved the old traditions of status but also broke up the traditional consumption habits. Up until then for each social position there was a corresponding standard of living. A person in a high position owed to his social appearance a certain expenditure of wealth. The same was also true the other way around: it did not behove persons in modest positions to "raise themselves above their position" in expenditures. The standard of living that one could afford was not determined primarily by the available means but by the social position. . . .

In a time that is without traditional status symbols, the income position, the position as consumer, determines social status. Next to it the Marxist "relation to production" turns pale. To be sure, one can hardly speak of an income stratum. . . . A person either has or has not a share in the means of production. Here there is a clear boundary—even if not in each case, nevertheless in principle. Income, however, divides itself along a sliding scale. There is a contrast between Croesus and the have-not. Between these two, however, lie a thousand grades, and the majority of wage and salary earners are neither Croesi nor have-nots. The income scale is a continuum. . . . Indeed, one can divide the population into poor, of low means, well-off, and rich, but the boundaries between adjacent categories are arbitrarily drawn and are in reality fluid. The lowest of those of moderate means is farther away from the highest in his category than from the highest among the poor. Thus the income distribution no longer corresponds to the former class boundaries . . . because it has put workers on an equal footing with certain groups from other classes. With that the class relation has lost much of its divisive strength. Most workers are, in terms of purchasing power and consumer habits, *petits bourgeois*. Insofar as they are not *petits bourgeois* in their political and social attitudes, it is due more to the labor-movement creed of the past century and to a doctrine that persisted because of convulsive propaganda rather than to the fact the "social consciousness is determined by social existence."

***The Institutionalization of Class Conflict.*** A fourth line of development, the tension that crosses all class fronts has its origin in late capitalism and is therefore more recent.[5] It derives from the *institutionalization of class conflict*.

The wage workers used the method of coalition in their class struggle. The basic thought was to fight monopoly with another monopoly. The propertied bourgeoisie enjoyed, thanks to the legal institution of property, a monopoly over the means of production. Counter to them, the wage workers sought to create a collective monopoly of labor power through trade-union organization. These two monopolies complemented each other. Labor could only create goods by the use of the means of production; the means of production lay fallow without labor power. Therefore capital tried during the entire nineteenth century to prevent the creation of a labor-power monopoly, but in about 1900 the struggle was decided and the trade-union movement held the palm of victory in its hand. . . .

Since then private ownership of the means of production and the mass organization of wage labor stand facing each other as the two great powers of the economic structure. The collective contract means that organized capital and organized wage labor confront one another as two closed parties of the labor market. Collective bargaining and arbitration, if necessary forced arbitration, are only the last logical steps on this road.

The invaluable significance of this process can be expressed thus: henceforth class conflict was declared respectable (*salonfähig*) and was expressed less dramatically, and the tension between capital and labor was recognized as a structural principle of the labor market and raised to a societal legal institution. I have therefore designated the aforementioned process as the "Institutionalization of Class Conflict." The weapons, the methods, and the tactics of the class struggle are recognized and thereby brought under control. The conflict proceeds in accordance with definite rules of the game. Thus class conflict is deprived of its worst sting, it is transformed into a legitimate tension between power factors that balance each other. Capital and wage labor wrestle with each other, arrive at compromises, negotiate and decide on wage levels, hours, and other conditions of work. . . .

***The Managerial Revolution.***

. . . . . . . . . . . . . . . . . . . . . . . . . . . . . . . . . . .

The connection between democracy and capitalism has been discussed for a long time and is possibly more fervently disputed today than ever before. By democracy we understand a political form of organization under whose banner the people as a whole possess the power of government so that all participate equally therein. By capitalism we mean an economic system that rests on the private initiative of the owners of enterprises. It is well known that in the eyes of some the highest task of democracy is to overcome capitalism. Others maintain that political democracy alone is a farce as long as it is not supported by economic democracy, and the latter is defined as the exact opposite of capitalism. No matter what one's attitude, however, the fact is that the democratic idea arose in its time in alliance with capitalism. Also another connection between the two may be pointed to:

[5] We omitted the third line of development, the conflict between town and country. As Dahrendorf explains, the conflict between town and country "... presumably figures so largely in Geiger's book because it was first published in and for Denmark." Dahrendorf, *op. cit.*, p. 98.

Capitalism signifies a free scope of action and therefore the abstention of government from interference in the economic sphere. Thus capitalism can only thrive in a liberal state that is assigned a minimum of functions. On the other hand, as a matter of experience, since 1914 the frictions in the operation of democracy grew with the increasing scope of functions that the state arrogated to itself. This is not surprising, because such an increase brings with it a growing number of issues of conflict in state politics. Therefore, apart from basic considerations we may assert that there is a positive connection, both in a historical and practical sense, between capitalism and political democracy.

Unmistakable signs indicate that a profound change is taking place in the social structure—and in this Burnham is surely right—in fact it is already far advanced.

The concept of social structure refers among other things and above all to the distribution of power in society. Which is the ruling stratum? From a political–institutional point of view all share equally in democracy. It has, however, correctly been objected that this formal equality is confronted with the fact that in capitalist society the capitalist class possesses superior actual power—more accurately: used to possess it. Superior power—to follow Burnham's argument—is held by those who control the access to the economic resources of society and therefore enjoy income privileges. Now then, a capitalist is the owner of the means of production. Facing him stand the broad masses who obtain access to these means of production only through the work contract with the owner. Thus the capitalists control the economic resources of society, the capitalists skim the cream from the society's income, the capitalists are the ruling class.

But even within the framework of capitalist society the preceding propositions are subject to certain limitations. To be sure, the capitalist stratum has a monopoly over the material means of production. And a counterweight was already created with the unfolding capitalist society when workers through their trade unions organized a collective monopoly of wage labor, an economic resource of no lesser significance than the material means of production. In the developed capitalist society capital and wage labor thus face each other as two organized fronts. Both are economic powerblocks and their balance shifts with the economic changes. In addition, it should be noted that political democracy shifts its center of gravity more and more in the direction of labor because the latter, thanks to its large numbers, was not only able to soften but even to cancel the privileged economic position of capital. And this then was indeed the course of affairs during the short history of democracy. Capital's freedom of movement was being noticeably diminished. We learned to view this development as social progress.

. . . . . . . . . . . . . . . . . . . . . . . . . . . . . . . . . . . .

For a long time socialism was considered the opponent and heir of capitalism. If capitalism rests on private initiative, socialism signifies that society as such steers the economic life. If the private ownership of the means of production is capitalism then socialism is the joint ownership of the means of production. Collectivization according to Marx is the expropriation if the exproprietors. The state abolishes private ownership of the means of production and thereby makes also impossible any kind of economically privileged position insofar as such advantage is based on the control of the access to the means of production by single individuals or groups of individuals. That the latter is fallacious will become clear later. First I invite you to consider the right to property and its relation to collectivization.

The capitalist age has committed idolatry with the concept of property, buttressed by the theory of natural rights. Three ideas became especially prominent in the process:

1. The right of property is conceived as the relationship of a person to a thing and the content of this relationship is the dominion of the owner over the property.
2. Property belongs to the original rights of man and is therefore regarded as independent from the legal order. The right of property is there *a priori*, and legislation must merely protect it.

3. Property is inherently an unlimited dominion and yet its exercise can be limited by law in order to preserve the human rights of others.

The newer theory of jurisprudence unmasks the preceding conception as a legend. I shall attempt to show why. Already Marx—perhaps he was not the first but nevertheless he was more impressive than his predecessors—has demonstrated that the property relationship is not a relationship of a person to a thing but a relationship between persons in regard to a thing. The property relationship is a social relationship. Paul's property is the authority to exclude Peter and John from the use of the object of property. . . .

The meaning of the concept of property consists of the guarantee by society that the owner may use the property object in certain ways and that others should not disturb him in this, especially not by their own use of the object. The meaning of the right of property is therefore, concisely expressed, the conception of the right to dispose of a thing that society guarantees to an individual. And here something quite decisive comes to light. These rights to dispose are not consequences or derivatives of the right of property but they constitute in their aggregate the entire content of the right of property. Without them nothing is left of the right of ownership.

This leads us to the question of the limits of the right of property. Nowhere is it unlimited. Even the liberalism based on the concept of natural law (*naturrechtlicher Liberalismus*) imposes limitations. But notice: it perceives the right of property as an absolute in itself, as complete dominion, and limits only its use in certain respects. Such a distinction becomes senseless once one recognizes that precisely this guaranteed right to control is the only constant of the right of property. If one limits that, one limits the very right of property.

But furthermore: according to the liberalism based on the concept of natural law, the proper understanding of the general rights of men automatically and compellingly indicates in which way and direction the exercise of the right of property is to be limited. It is, however, not possible to set up an objective and universally valid criterion as to the threshold beyond which A's exercise of his right of property would violate the presumed legitimate interests of B or the general welfare. Everything depends here on the social structure and the concept of law (*Rechtsauffassung*) in a given place and time. And indeed the right of property is very diverse and varying in societies of different times and in different lands. Because, however, as it was explained above, the meaning of the right of property is nothing else than precisely the sum of the rights to control, socially guaranteed, the preceding can be better expressed in the following way. Instead of saying that the exercise of the ("inherently absolute") right of property is variously limited, we may express it: the right of property is a concept that, in different societies, comprises different contents of the right to control things. . . . Thus the talk of governmental or legal interference with property is completely senseless. Without a positive governmental or legal order there is no right of property with which one could interfere.

What conclusions follow for the ideas of collectivization from this conception that diverges from the metaphysics of natural law? If the content of the property relation is not a mystic authority over a thing, but quite simply the totality of the rights of control that are guaranteed in a given society, then the formal abolition of the right of property is a completely unimportant gesture. It comes down to this: what right to dispose of property is guaranteed to what persons by the positive legal order of a society? On the other hand, it is quite unimportant what legal term we use to designate the formal source of this right to dispose. The right of property is one term—any other term would do just as well. Despite his attempt toward a sociological concept of law, Marx remained nevertheless a son of the nineteenth century and a disciple of the metaphysics of that time. Capitalist society is possessed by the ideal of the sanctity of private property—its opposite, socialism, is not less blinded by the notion that the right of property is the work of the devil. Both endow the concept of property with a mystic content of reality. The striking force of socialism is directed against the myth of property. Supposedly its existence keeps capitalism alive, and its abolition will result in the means of production being under the collective control of society. But when the right of property is deprived of its magic blind faith, clearly neither the former nor the latter is shown to be the case.

One can imagine a society in which the formal juridical right of property is completely maintained but where its exercise is visibly limited. This simply means that the number, scope, and intensity of the owner's rights to dispose are diminished through so called public interference. Intervention brought special restrictions in the rights to control the means of production and because of this the right of property took on a different and more modest meaning. This reduction in the content of the right of property can and has been continued through a policy of taxation, regulations, allocation of raw materials, and so forth. One can conceive of a society that remains capitalist in the sense that it formally and juridically maintains the right of property, but it is emptied of all content. It no longer guarantees, especially in regard to the means of production, any rights to dispose. Interventionism has limited only negatively the rights of control: whatever was not explicitly prohibited was allowed. However, extensive economic planning made positive decisions how and for what the owner is to use his production apparatus. He receives his directives from the outside (from above) or is driven to one kind of production and prevented from another by the allocation of raw materials, fuel, and labor as well as price regulation. What he retains then is the title of property, the designation of owner without any content to it and also that income that derives from the arrangements forced on him.

Part of this income provides for personal expenses. The owner is not a capitalist because of this income. It corresponds to the salaries of the managers in the service of a socialist society. One is a capitalist thanks to that part of the income that through savings is newly invested. In a socialist society this part of the yield of a given enterprise goes to the collective, in capitalist society it takes the form of accretion in the wealth of the owner. But also the right of ownership of this saved wealth becomes hollow in the planned society. The owner cannot invest his wealth according to his own discretion and calculation. The public authority decides through money, credit, and investment policy and through the regulation of the production of capital goods where and how newly acquired money is to be invested. Thus it is true that the capitalist is the formal owner but he is robbed of all his authority to control his property. This is plain collectivization. The right of ownership is maintained as a legal institution but no authority (*Befugnisse*) can be derived from it. One could just as well abolish the right of ownership as such. The only difference would be in the terms, not in the substance. The society is capitalist in name, socialist (*sozialisiert*) in substance.

Thus I would like to substitute another concept for Burnham's concept of socialism. He denies socialism any chance of a future because the workers are neither capable of collectivizing the societal production apparatus or of gaining by force the use of the corresponding income privilege. Socialism is thus implicitly defined as rule by workers. It seems to me that a more practical concept would be that of designating as socialism any socioeconomic arrangement in which the right to control the means of production is no longer vested in the owner but in society as such. Naturally this does not mean that the "public" exercises this control and in this Burnham was right: the expropriation of the means of production does not put the workers or the collectivity into the possession of economic power.

The analysis of the right of property and the right to control it has its reverse side. Similarly to the society in which the right of ownership is formally guaranteed but through comprehensive economic planning made hollow, the so-called collective ownership of the means of production is only a phrase. If the concept of ownership is to have any real meaning it can only be the one that the owners are guaranteed certain rights of control. The socialist society does not recognize any owners authorized to dispose of property. And yet somebody must exercise control. It cannot be the general public as such. The ones who are authorized to dispose in a socialist society are the economic officials of the commonwealth (*Gemeinwesen*). It is a different circle of persons than that in capitalist society but, as there, it is a minority. To those deprived of control it does not matter who has the legal title to control property, and on what basis. One could answer that it nevertheless does matter whether the capitalist controls in his own interest or whether the official in a socialist society controls on behalf of the public. But again these are only words. The capitalist also claims that he proceeds in the public interest. But who can actually make him do it? In a socialist society the owner is deprived of the right to dispose and therefore also of the possibility of uncontrolled misuse of that power. In his place the economic official of the commonwealth has the power to dispose—and who actually has authority over him? Higher officials and so on until the peak of the hierarchy is reached. But not the public. And it is part of human experience that the occupant of a position of power takes care to know how he can use it for his own advantage. Both the private owner in capitalist society and the economic official in socialist society enjoy a position of power because of their control of the production apparatus. Both are also privileged because of a superior share in the social product. The difference lies solely in the formal legal base of the privilege. The institutions are of a different juridical structure, the phenomenon is essentially the same.

The right of property without the right of control over it is but a phrase. But whoever is authorized to control it enjoys a superior position that corresponds to ownership even if the title of ownership is abolished.

From these conditions one can arrive at a certain picture of the structure of future society. It must be admitted that those who dispose over the means of production and control the access of others to them are the ruling social stratum. Thus far there is no doubt that the capitalists were the ruling class in nineteenth-century Western Europe, that their influence weakened in the first half of the twentieth century and that in the Soviet Union it was completely abolished. It is theoretically conceivable but highly improbable that the Western world would return to a free economy; that is, one that is autonomously regulated by its own mechanisms. If this were to happen, the power position of the owners of the means of production would become strong again. It is much more probable that we will follow the beaten track and will move toward a more systematic governmental regulation of the economy. . . .

Burnham saw well through the hollowness, that is, the purely ideological meaning of the concept of the natural right of property. He also described in certain breadth how the right of the owners to control has diminished in favor of society and has become replaced by governmental regulation of the economy. He saw quite well that in this respect the difference between Soviet Russia and the West is not one in direction as such but in methods and degree of thoroughness. Burnham also calls special attention to the fact that collectivization, which was brought about in the Soviet Union through revolution and with a bang, is proceeding in Western Europe and in America as part of a slower development. The owner of the means of production is forced out of his position of power through regulation and other interference. . . .

The nineteenth-century period of governmental restraint is at an end, the political system of trade has gained the upper hand over the economic one. We designate it as the primacy of the state over the economy. Something else is closely linked with it. In the liberal economy the single enterprise with its production apparatus is an autonomous economic unit—within the framework of economic legality. In the government-controlled economy the single enterprise becomes a dependent organ of the entire economic machinery of society. What the single enterprise produces with the help of its apparatus, how much and how it produces, what qualities, and so on—all this is decided by political channels, either directly by means of directives and orders or indirectly by the manner in which the state controls the flow of raw material, fuel, labor power, and credit that keeps production going. The single enterprise is no longer a productive autonomy.

Thus the owner of the enterprise, even though he is left with this legal title, has been robbed of his position of power. But I do not see how this power is to be transferred to the production personnel of the plant. The whole enterprise and its apparatus are organized within the total economic apparatus of society. No person whose functions are confined to a single enterprise can henceforth be assigned the right to control the production apparatus or to control the access to it by others. Economic life becomes centralized and the authority to control the total economic apparatus of society passes over to the state. Burnham is quite correct in this: that the system of economic planning corresponds to the bureaucratic form of political rule. He describes these parallels in all their breadth. But curiously he fails to see that political buraucratism (*Bürokratismus*) absorbs the economy itself—yes, that it comes into being exactly through nationalization (*Verstaatlichung*) of economic life. . . .

Now, then, our government is democratic: that is, we live under the rule of the majority. If the economy is to be subordinate to governmental authority, this could mean that the growing democratic majorities gain respective authority to control the total societal production apparatus. Economic power, in the same sense as political democracy, would thus come into the hands of "the people."

But it is known that those in whom power is vested institutionally do not necessarily possess it in actuality. The absolute prince lost his power to the professional bureaucracy whose specialized knowledge he faced as a dilettante. In democracy political power lies with the people as a whole but there are complaints everywhere that it is being slid over more and more from the hands of the people to those of the professional politician. Political affairs have become gradually so complicated that the individual is no longer able to comprehend them. The broad masses can never have power in their own hands but must entrust it to special organs. The real power position of the general public can therefore only lie in its effective control over the use of power by its trusted organs. This is its proper sense in the political sphere. So will it also be in the governmental economic sphere—probably to a more marked extent yet.

The group of individuals that controls the total economic apparatus of society can be properly designated as the governmental economic bureaucracy. This bureaucracy began to form during the period between the two world wars. Regulation of prices, allocation of raw materials and fuel, taxing investments through money and credit policy, and other measures brought new administrative bodies into being. So a whole hierarchy of employees arises . . . and grows in number with the spread of economic regulatory measures. . . . These employees manage the societal power to control the means of production. They do not lean, as capitalists do, on the legal title of ownership but on something else by the name of office mandate or office authority. If the names differ, the phenomenon is to a large extent the same. In the hands of a small group of people is concentrated the power to dispose over the economic resources of society. This group is the ruling stratum of the future if society persists on the road to a planned economy. Within this bureaucracy the production heads of single enterprises constitute only external organs, local executive organs of the central economic bureaucracy. Only through this peripheral belonging to the state economic bureaucracy do they participate in the latter's collective position of power. On the other hand, the above described development also signifies a strengthening of the hitherto existing administrative bureaucracy. First of all, the total number of the corps of officials grows with the rise of the new economic bureaucracy. Secondly, thanks to the similarity in education, status, and function a narrow solidary relationship is formed between the old and new bureaucracy. Thirdly, the hitherto existing administrative functions and the new functions of directing the economy become interlocked in such a manifold way that a sharp dividing line between the corresponding official hierarchies can hardly emerge.

One may object that the corps of officials in a democratic political system behave in accordance with the orders of the political channels; that, properly speaking, the economic bureaucracy does not decide but rather the government does, controlled by parliament that, in turn, is watched by the electorate. It has already been suggested that today there is less control by the people over parliament and government than the proponents of democracy must have wished. When the state also takes over the direction of the economy then even the position of professional politicians is diminished. The economy offers an abundance of complex connections and problems, the knowledge and mastery of which demand expert technical knowledge of the highest order. Most laymen hardly have a notion of the existence of some of these problems, let alone the capacity to solve them. To some smaller extent this also applies to professional politicians. Parliament may make its decisions, the government and each single minister may give their directives, but they become rather powerless when the technical experts of the economic bureaucracy invoke invincible economic principles. They will largely have the last word, especially because the directives can be manifoldly modified in their practical application. . . . In a centrally planned economic and social order (*Wirtschaftsgesellschaft*), power belongs to the economic officials, and if the name bureaucracy sounds too forbidding, one may substitute for it "the rule of experts."

In its peculiar, indeed impressive, course, the democratic-capitalist society transforms itself step by step. Democracy and capitalism are the offspring of the same historical hour. Political equality and economic freedom go together. The rule of the people —the governmental form of political equality—becomes, because of practical necessity, the representative rule of the majority. With the unfolding of capitalism, the propertyless strata grew in number. With the consistent application of the democratic principle of equality they win the political majority. As propertyless they seek to weaken the power of the propertied. The political power of labor as a majority built a counterweight, nearly outweighing the power of the capitalist minority: political equality thus becomes the rival of economic freedom. Through their control of the governmental power apparatus the propertyless masses clipped the owners' power to dispose over the means of production and also their autonomous initiative. Capitalism is thus being liquidated by democracy.

But next, the bell also tolls for democracy. Under the pressure of the majority, the democratic state takes hold more and more of the economic sphere: first in the form of intervention, then with regulation of the scope of enterprises, and finally through comprehensive economic planning. Democratic government becomes strong government, takes on new tasks and more of them, and also casts itself as the master over the economy. . . . Mounting governmental power breaks down the public's actual control over the governmental organs' use of power. And yet with the control of these organs by the public, democracy stands or falls. First comes the weakening of the power of voters in favor of the professional politicians. But then, apparently through the nationalization (*Verstaatlichung*) of the economy, the position of the professional politicians is weakened in favor of economic bureaucracy. The circle has been completed, a new social era gets off to its start. . . .

This prognosis naturally fits only the case of the planned economy—but this case it fits well. . . . With the elevation of open economic planning into an institution, the position of officialdom, at least economic officialdom, becomes quite different. It is a position that in the place of private entrepreneurs disposes over the economic resources and therewith gets the chance of income privileges. It is undeniable that there has risen also in Soviet Russia, in this dictatorial bureaucracy, a new stratum of both the powerful and the relatively rich. Their prosperity expresses itself not only in their salaries; it consists much more and to a growing extent of consumer privileges, apart from salary, that are connected to their function. It would indeed be remarkable if the masters of the productive apparatus were not to enjoy a rich bonus in the process of distributing the social product. . . .

In yet another respect—and with this we may conclude our reflections—it behooves us to put forth in hypothetical form the consequences of a planned economy for social stratification and to contrast them with the class theory of Marx.

Material economic factors determine, according to Marx, the social structure and especially the class structure of a society. The conflict of classes, whose members are in solidarity because of the equality in their position and social status, determines political behavior. This means, however, that the respective power constellation of the classes that are anchored in the economic plane determines the political institutions and measures of a society. Differently expressed, the material economic factors (EF) determine the class structure (CS) and the latter through the respective power constellation determines the political superstructure (PSS). This relation is shown in Figure 9.

EF --------→ CS --------→ PSS

*Figure 9*

It follows logically, as far as I can see, that this scheme of relationships can apply validly only within the boundaries of a liberal economic and social order. One could imagine that the prevailing dynamic-dialectic course of events—according to Marx's conception of history—has at a given point of time brought about a constellation of political factors that made it possible for those momentarily in possession of power to establish economic planning. . . . The productive forces will be brought under political control. . . . Consequently, let us assume that the class disposed toward planning and politically dominant in a given historical period ushers in not only what it considers a planned economy but also proves capable of keeping the officials in the planned economy under control. In this manner the whole course of dialectic change would be brought to a halt and Marx's casual relationship turned upside down (Figure 10). The political superstructure moves from the end of the chain to its beginning.

(CS ----→) PSS ----→ EF ----→ CS

*Figure 10*

A given class structure has brought about a constellation of political factors that makes possible the transition to a planned economy and is thus utilized. The authorities that, thanks to this condition (class structure and its corresponding political superstructure), control the apparatus of the planned economy therewith also direct the course of the future social structure that depends on the formation of material economic factors. Those who possess power naturally make an effort to protect their key positions and their control over the planned economy. They therefore arrange the economic and political affairs so as to preclude a shift in the material economic factors. Such a shift would, according to the doctrine, entail a change in the class structure, and thereby in the balance of power, and threaten the power position of the then ruling class. The dynamic unfolding of economic capacity is thus brought to a halt by economic planning. . . . The economic and social order is placed under a stationary legality, in any case, a legality whose change is regulated. By purposefully shaping it, the masters of economic planning are able to determine the class structure of society. Invalid would be the objection that the productive forces in Marx's sense consist not only of purely economic material factors but also of technology whose further development within the planned economy could lead to surprising changes. Technical innovations can only change the material economic structure, can only become new economic forces if they are put into service; that is, if they are utilized in the production process. Total economic planning, however, naturally also signifies the control of technical means and proceedings. Innovations become either recognized or suppressed; the degree of technical rationalization is determined by the authorities. Thus whoever controls and governs the planned economic apparatus prevents the mobilization of newly discovered technical opportunities insofar as they threaten his power position in society.

The historical dialectic materialism of Marx—if there is still a grain of truth left within its content—applies only so long as the productive forces continue to be permitted to unfold according to their internal dynamics. The material economic factors constitute the independent variable in the historical and philosophic thought of Marx. Conversely, in a society with a pervading planned economy, the political power constellation with its corresponding superstructure of political institutions becomes the independent variable, and those who possess power know how to prevent its variation.

Thus, the science of Karl Marx is nothing but the anti-ideology corresponding to the liberal social reality of his time. Its conceptual models were derived from the time-bound liberal social reality and their value is limited by it. If Marxist practice were to succeed in casting aside the remainder of the liberal reality, the Marxist theoretical principles on which such political practice is based would become valueless.

# PART III
# Major Dimensions of Social Stratification

Social inequalities are diverse and intricate, especially in the highly complex societies of today and even in those where all people are considered equal before the law. The inequalities must therefore be categorized in order to be studied and understood. The basic division along which our selections in this section are organized is one that has its roots in Marx's thought—objective and subjective dimensions. The first refers to actual inequalities—their sources, extents, and forms—whereas the latter refers to the perception, interpretation, and evaluation by the society in general, as well as by the individuals variously located in it.

In presenting the readings about the objective side of stratification, we in turn utilize the scheme adopted from Max Weber and arrange them under the subheadings (1) economic inequality (2) power inequality and (3) status inequality. The scheme served us well in the last section where, in the introduction to the readings on the principal types of stratification systems we analyzed each type in terms of its predominant dimension or factor of inequality. In studying modern societies this analytical framework is especially useful, because its stratification systems are more complex and are not characterized by such a close and visible correlation between the three dimensions—economic inequality and differences in power and prestige—that marked feudal and caste stratification.

Most of the readings in this section are based on empirical studies of stratification in the twentieth century. They will therefore, among other things, provide us with some basis for judging to what extent Geiger's generalizations about "post-capitalist society"—the last selection in the preceding section—are borne out by systematic observation. In each grouping of the present we made an effort to include materials on Soviet-type as well as Western-type societies.

## OBJECTIVE DIMENSIONS

***Economic Inequality.*** Considering that the economic factor is the predominant factor in class stratification we must note that it has been—as was brought out in the introduction to the preceeding section and some of its selections—almost completely neglected as a subject of empirical studies by sociologists. This may be partly due to the fact that it is considered the domain of economists rather than sociologists. Whatever the reason, it does explain why our selections on this subject are mostly from the works by economists.

Economic inequality must be approached in at least two important ways: in terms of distribution of both income and wealth. Before doing so it is worth noting that the representatives, defenders or ideologists of capitalism never denied the inequality of income and wealth. They simply justified its existence as representing just rewards for initiative, effort, intelligence, frugality, etc.—qualities which they held in great esteem and considered as meriting rewards. But after World War II we witness in Western societies (which still tend to be called capitalist but for which social scientists are increasingly adopting the name "welfare capitalism", the designation of their structures as egalitarian and the claims of a trend toward leveling in income and wealth. The latter was based on both common sense observations of post-World War II "prosperity" and affluence as well as elaborate analyses of official statistics. In England, for example, until the 1960s a remarkable agreement existed among economists and statisticians about a continuous movement toward greater equality in incomes since 1938. Then Richard T. Titmuss raised the important issue—which has been posed again and again in regard to many other problems, starting with Durkheim's concern about the statistics on suicide—about the validity of official figures on income and wealth. Reexamining the data on which the conclusions about greater equality were based, Titmuss found that tax returns were mostly used. But tax returns, he says, do not provide a complete picture of income distribution. *Yearly income* in the traditional sense of disposable cash gives a delusive picture of the state of affairs of the upper class because of a number of widespread practices such as the transformation of cash into benefits in kind, the spreading of "income" over life and over the lives of a few generations, and the transformation of income into capital. As he expresses it, ". . . all these make 'cash in hand' less necessary for the business of daily life for certain classes and living on overdrafts, trusts, and other forms of command over resources more fiscally rewarding if, at times, perhaps a little irksome."[1]

After examining the statistics and the validity of the conclusions that economists and statisticians drew from them, he infers that less is known about economic inequality today than is generally thought or admitted. Inequality has according to him, assumed new and subtle forms and the old statistical tools are not adequate for measuring it. Thus he warns that one needs to be more hesitant in suggesting that long-range equalizing tendencies are operating in Britain.

To judge from the evidence presented in our first reading, "What's Happening to Our Income Revolution?" by Herman P. Miller, neither do we have any basis for asserting that such a trend exists in the United States. True, we have the indisputable facts that real incomes are higher today in the United States than anywhere else in the world and that they have been growing steadily. But these facts are often used as if they were indicative of reduced inequality, which they are not. To talk about the latter, one has to compare relative income through time. Miller does

[1] Richard M. Titmuss, *Income Distribution and Social Change,* London: George Allen and Unwin, 1962, p. 293.

that and comes up with the finding that although inequality was being reduced during the war years and the immediate postwar years, income distribution has remained stable during the last twenty years.

What is particularly interesting is the reason Miller gives for studying the gap between the poor and the rich even though conditions are improving in America. He gives as his reason the feelings of relative deprivation on the part of those who have less, although he does not use this expression. Proceeding from the theories of Marx, Toynbee, and Veblen, he assumes that these feelings are widespread. Looking critically at this, one must point out that it is largely an empirical question—that is, only empirical studies can ascertain to what extent such feelings prevail today. Theoretically one can hypothesize that feelings of relative well-being are just as extensive or even outweigh those of relative deprivation, because a generation has experienced a marked improvement in its standard of living and is reminding its children of this improvement. However, all this is in the realm of the subjective aspect of stratification and we want to deal with the objective factors first, keeping them analytically separate from the subjective. In studying the objective side of economic inequality, the basic question is what the actual extent of inequality is —not how do people perceive it or experience it.

The technique used by Miller for comparing income distribution through time would also be appropriate in this kind of approach. Also suitable are cross-societal comparisons, which Miller pursues in the opening chapter of his book, and they show that incomes are about as evenly distributed in the United States as in Great Britain and more evenly distributed than in most other countries for which such figures are available.[2] But one could go beyond that by introducing an equalitarian model and measuring the extent of inequality in a given society at a given time or through time, as well as by comparing different societies, against this model. Thus, for example, taking the data presented by Miller, we would see that the lowest fifth of families and individuals in the United States has been receiving since 1944 only one-fourth of the income that would be theirs if there were income equality, whereas to the top 5 per cent went four times the income that they would receive under income equality. Interestingly, the next to the highest fifth of families and individuals has been receiving the share (22–23 per cent) that approximately corresponds to the equalitarian model. (See Table 2, p. 13.)

After exposing as a myth the contention that incomes in general are becoming gradually more evenly distributed, Miller goes on to deal with other misrepresentations on the theme of "a trend toward equalization." He shows that in the last ten years the income gap between whites and nonwhites has not been narrowing: on the contrary, there is some evidence of its having widened again. The same applies to the income differentials between skilled and unskilled workers.

In the last part of his essay, subheaded "Where Do We Go From Here?", Miller raises the issues of technological unemployment, of the American economy being plagued by relatively high unemployment since late 1957, and of the unskilled finding it increasingly difficult to find jobs. And these issues are the main subject of the selection by Gunnar Myrdal, who sees a trend in America toward the

[2] Herman P. Miller, *Rich Man, Poor Man,* New York: Thomas Y. Crowell Co., 1964, chap. 1, and summary on p. 31.

development of an *underclass* that is really not an integrated part of the nation. It is composed of unemployed, unemployable and underemployed persons and families at the bottom, to whom opportunities are becoming more closed while they are growing more plentiful for the rest of the nation. They are generally referred to as the poor, but social scientists have variously designated them as lower class (distinguished from the working class), the lower-lower class and more recently "the unstable poor," "the clinically dependent," and "the disreputable poor."[3] Whatever the designation, the descriptions of the characteristics of this group resemble Marx's references to the *Lumpenproletariat*. Here one finds demoralization and social pathology on a grand scale and the root of it, Myrdal argues, is unemployment. The aid given to these people, such as unemployment compensation, may keep them alive, but it is not the solution to the problems of demoralization and pathology bred by unemployment; on the contrary, it breeds more pathology. As Myrdal expresses it, ". . . there is no real cure for unemployment," and this cure is not forthcoming on a large enough scale.

That this phenomenon is not unique to the United States we gather from studies in Great Britain. There too you find poverty ". . . confined to particular groups in the population—mainly old people and workers in certain occupations or regions that have been left behind as a result of technological progress," groups separated from the working class at large whose material conditions have improved in the last decades.[4] However, if an underclass of unemployed, unemployable, and underemployed is thought of as a characteristic feature of highly industrial societies then the proposition has to be confined to so-called capitalist countries, for this phenomenon is absent in the Soviet Union and Soviet-type societies. It could be argued that there is in the Soviet Union an underclass, but then one would have to make clear that its origin, in contrast to that of the West, is not primarily economic but political. I am referring to the large numbers in the forced-labor camps of Siberia—widely known as slave laborers. They are there because they are deemed politically or socially undesirable. They are not underemployed, but, on the contrary, they constitute a source of cheap labor for the Soviet authorities. The plight of these captive laborers has gained some new attention as a result of the lately published memoirs and autobiographical novels of former camp inmates.[5] But exact studies of this Soviet underclass are nonexistant.

Such studies even if few, do exist about economic inequality among the population at large in the Soviet Union (excluding the forced laborers). In his article "The Soviet Income Revolution," which is reprinted here, Murray Yanowitch focuses on income inequality since 1956, since de-Stalinization. The extent of actual inequality in the Soviet Union is of particular interest, because the Soviet regime came into power on slogans of economic equality. But the equalization that was brought about by the revolution was soon reversed by differential wages

[3] S. M. Miller uses the term "unstable poor," Hyland Lewis "clinically dependent," David Matza "the disreputable poor" See David Matza, "The Disreputable Poor," in Neil J. Smelser and S. M. Lipset, *Social Structure and Mobility in Economic Development*, Chicago: Aldine Co., 1966, pp. 311–340. S. M. Miller "The American Lower Classes: A Typological Approach," *Sociology and Social Research*, Vol. 48, No. 3, April, 1964. Hylan Lewis "Child Rearing Among Low Income Families" Washington Center for Metropolitan Studies, 1961.

[4] T. B. Bottomore, *Classes in Modern Society*, New York: Pantheon Books, 1966, pp. 42–43.

[5] See, for example, Alexander Solzhenitsyn, *One day in the Life of Ivan Denisovich*, New York: E. P. Dutton & Co., 1963.

as incentives for increased production.[6] As the inequality grew so did the ideological rationalizations that denounced equalitarianism as non- or antisocialist by labeling it petty bourgoeis, and so on. By 1931, and until de-Stalinization, Yanowitch tells us, every major statement of Soviet wage policy contained such denunciations.[7] Thus, a government that called itself socialist promoted inequality in its territories while its admirers abroad were criticizing the economic inequalities in their own countries.

With de-Stalinization came a new wage policy that put much emphasis on *narrowing* the income gap between high- and low-paid personnel (not on eliminating inequality). Yanowitch examines the extent to which this policy has been implemented since 1956. The measures that he used to ascertain the trends in Soviet wages, as he points out and as the reader will soon learn, are summary measures of wage dispersion that, in contrast to Miller's measures, tell nothing about the share of total income received by a given percentage of the working population. But in footnote 9 of his article we find some data, based on Soviet sources, that make it possible to derive rough estimates of the shares of total income and to compare them cautiously to the data on income distribution in the United States. On the basis of the figures found there we calculate that since 1934 the bottom fifth of the working population received 10.2 per cent; the second fifth 14.9 per cent; the third fifth 19.1, the fourth 24.6, and the top fifth 31.2 per cent of the total wages. If one compares it to the distribution in the United States (see Table 2, p. 134), there seems to be in this respect less inequality in the Soviet Union. One must however, be very cautious in making such a comparison, for a number of reasons. First of all, the figures are not strictly comparable. If the American figures are only conservative estimates of inequality, the Soviet figures are even more so. The monetary bonuses and nonmonetary supplements of the top-income group are way out of proportion to those of the lower groups. This leads us to a more fundamental and more difficult problem of comparing inequality in the Soviet Union and the United States, which has been well captured in another connection by Andreski. He points out that the difference between a family that has to live in a corner of a room that it shares with two others and a family that has one room per person is greater than the difference between the latter and a family that possesses one hundred rooms. The difference between freezing and having adequate clothing is larger than between having, let us say, three suits and three hundred.[8] Need we say

[6] The question of incentives is again arising today in such countries as China and Cuba. It seems that in the latter it is a source of controversy between Castro and the pro-Soviet old-guard Communists. The latter are for financial incentives, which Castro opposes as fostering inequality. To promote greater equality he proposed a plan to abolish rent by 1970. As harbingers of the future, the following are now free: public telephones, funerals, and admission to ballparks. Castro champions "moral incentives" for increasing production insisting that "Men are capable of responding to moral factors." See "Castro Assails Old-Guard Reds," *The New York Times,* September 30, 1966; Juan de Onis, "Castro's Migrant Labor," *The New York Times,* February 10, 1968. In an interview with Mr. Mathews, a former correspondent and editorial writer for the New York Times, Castro said, "Communist countries like Russia are becoming more capitalistic because they are relying on material incentives more and more." But in Cuba, "We do not believe in the materialistic concepts of capitalism and other types of communism in which money is the incentive." He added that "Men live for more things than money" and went on to explain that in Cuba the ". . . . economic system is being planned, gradually and with much success, to create a society in which money will become unnecessary." See "Castro, an Interview, Confirms Soviet-Cuban Rift," *The New York Times,* December 21, 1967, p. 17.

[7] For a general article on Soviet stratification under the reign of Stalin, see Alex Inkeles, "Social Stratification and Mobility in the Soviet Union: 1940–1950," *American Sociological Review,* Vol. 15, 1950, pp. 465–479.

[8] Stanislav Andreski, *The Uses of Comparative Sociology,* Berkeley: University of California Press, 1964, p. 347.

that the first alternatives symbolize the conditions in the Soviet Union and the second in America? Lest we should become too philosophical for the taste of some readers, let us finish on a note of certainty. Even on the basis of the official figures there is a considerable amount of inequality in the Soviet Union if measured against the equalitarian model we proposed as a heuristic device.

To return to the subject of new trends, which is the main theme of the Yanowitch article, it is particularly worth noticing that since 1956 a narrowing of wage differentials between skilled and unskilled workers has been taking place in the Soviet Union (in contrast to the United States). But then it seems that the USSR has a shortage of unskilled labor, as compared with its recent overabundance in the United States. As for his measures of general wage inequality, Yanowitch found since 1956 a reversal of the 1934–1956 trend of growing inequality, so that wage inequality has been decreasing but still has remained greater in 1959 (his last figures) than in the late 1920s and 1930s. If the planned changes were to be realized, he says, the inequality would be further reduced. Subsequent studies indicate that by 1965 it was less reduced than was anticipated for that date by Yanowitch on the basis of the Soviet government pronouncements.[9] However, even if the plans were realized, the Soviet Union, as Yanowitch underlines, would still be far from an equalitarian society. One could add that equalitarianism continues to be condemned in the Soviet Union as a goal for now. For instance, the March 4, 1966, *Izvestia* column, "Talks with Readers," was devoted to comments on "Ours and 'Mine' in Theory and Life." Here we find such statements as: ". . . there is not and cannot be yet complete equality here because people's labor is not equal. . . . There is not and cannot be as yet equality in income and in the amount of personal property here. The CPSU [Communist Party of the Soviet Union] has never assented and will never assent to the principle of leveling since it reflects petty bourgeois attitudes and operates against the interests of the working people. The Party is taking all possible steps to *reduce* the difference between high paid and low paid categories of workers. But this difference can be reduced to a minimum *only gradually*." (Italics supplied.)[10]

Whether or not the Party is "taking all possible steps," we gather from Yanowitch's objective analysis that the inequality in income distribution is being reduced. He finished, however, on an important note that it is not "at all clear . . . that inequality in the distribution of political power is moving in the same direction." And it is this inequality in power that, according to many sociologists, is the most significant factor of Soviet stratification.

***Power Inequality.*** In the selection from his book, *The New Class,* Milovan Djilas maintains that in the Communist states a governing class exercises complete control over the society through power, ownership, and ideology. Of these three factors, power is the one that played and still plays the most important part: it constitutes "the basic characteristic of communism." What distinguishes Communist power is its being almost exclusively an end in itself "because it is both the source and guarantee of all privilege." This power is in the hands of a new class, a political bureaucracy resembling the ruling classes of other societies, except that its power is more complete and less subject to restraint. It developed gradually from the very

[9] See Janet G. Chapman, "The Minimum Wage in the USSR," *Problems of Communism,* Vol. XIII, No. 5, September-October, 1964, pp. 76–79.

[10] Condensed text reprinted in: *Current Digest of the Soviet Press,* Vol. XVIII, No. 9, March 23, 1966, p. 5.

narrow group of "professional revolutionaries" into a "class of owners and exploiters." Here Djilas pursues a Marxist analysis by arguing that the new class is the actual owner of the means of production. Collective ownership is but a façade, because the new class disposes with property and exercises exclusive control over it. (Note the similarity to Theodor Geiger's analysis.) The monopoly it establishes in the name of the working class turns out to be primarily a monopoly over the working class itself. Finally, Djilas predicts at the end of the excerpt that, as did other ruling classes, this one will have its end. And when this occurs ". . . there will be less sorrow over its passing than there was for any other class before it." It is noteworthy that these words come from a person who helped to bring this "class" into being in Yugoslavia and who was for some time one of its prominent members. This leading Communist, former vice-president of Yugoslavia and friend of Tito, was expelled from the Party in 1954 and in 1956 sentenced to serve a ten-year prison term for expressing the ideas contained in the *New Class.*

When we shift our attention to power inequality in the United States, we are struck by it complexity as compared with the Soviet type of power. Numerous empirical studies have been conducted on the power structure of various American communities and they present a far from uniform picture. Richard A. Schermerhorn reviews under four headings the findings of these studies in the selection on "Power in the Local Community." First comes the question of governmental versus nongovernmental control, and here the findings are fairly consistent. American communities that have been studied display more reliance on nongovernmental rather than governmental control, on private rather than official leaders, on business leaders rather than men from other walks of life. When it comes to the second theme, the pattern of power distribution, the studies show wide differences. Subsequent to the Schermerhorn analysis, Peter Rossi has nevertheless discerned three main types of community power structure, the first two being very similar and differing only in the number of decision makers who share power among themselves. (1) Pyramidal—the ultimate source of power is in one man or a very small number of men. He (or they) makes major policy decisions that are carried out by the lower echelons. Examples are the Lynds' Middletown and Hunter's Regional City. (2) Caucus rule—"Lines of power tend to end in a relatively large group of men who make decisions through consensus. Decision making tends to be a matter of manufacturing consent among the 'cozy few' who make up the caucus." An example is Rossi's Mediana. (3) Polylith—there are separate power structures for major spheres of community activity, such as local government in the hands of professional politicians and community service organizations in the hands of businessman and professionals.[11]

The third heading under which Schermerhorn reviews the findings of various studies is, "What issues are decided at what levels in American Communities?" Here the primary concern is with the nature of the issues that are kept out of the arena of public discussion, as compared with those that are allowed to reach the attention of the public. Again, there is no uniformity in the findings. And finally he examines the role-images of the leaders in the communities. Public opinion, community confidence in leadership—he argues—may determine what can or cannot be

[11] Peter H. Rossi, "Power and Community Structures," in Lewis A. Coser, ed., *Political Sociology,* New York: Harper & Row Publishers, 1966, pp. 132–145, especially pp. 142–143.

done by those who wield one type of authority or another. But the information on this score is far from conclusive.

One should add that the studies of community power have been criticized on methological grounds. Because many of them employed the reputational method in order to ascertain the distribution power, the issue has been raised whether reputations of power are an adequate index of its distribution.[12]

It is worth remembering that at first those who have studied the power structure in given communities were convinced that they were getting by this means at the power structure of the country at large. With time this optimistic view was challenged and voices were heard that the power distribution in the United States was not merely the sum of its distributions in local communities. After all, the focus of those studies was on community decisions, for the basic question about community power is who has more to say, or can have more to say, about things that affect people in that particular community. These decisions are quite minor as compared with those on the national scale that determines the future of the society at large.[13] Even if we had a thorough knowledge of community decision making, we would gain from it very little knowledge about the decisions that affect the whole nation. And yet despite the wide recognition that community and national power refer to different "orders of phenomena," few sociological studies of the national power structure have been made. Thus C. Wright Mills' *The Power Elite* remains the significant but highly criticized work in this area.[14] Mills interprets the American power system in terms of a power elite that makes the top decisions in the economic, political, and military spheres and a powerless mass at the bottom. His interpretation has been and continues to be subject to much controversy. It's validity has been challenged on both theoretical and factual grounds.

Talcott Parsons, for example, characterized C. Wright Mills' approach to power as a "zero-sum" conception and criticized it as not fitting the actual phenomenon of power in complex societies. According to this conception, Parsons explains, ". . . there is a fixed 'quantity' of power in any relational system and hence any gain of power on the part of A must by definition occur by diminishing the power at the disposal of the other units B, C, D." But, believes Parsons, this is not how power operates in "advanced" national societies. He conceptualizes power as a circulating medium, analogous to money, so that a "systematic extension of power spheres without sacrifice of the power of other units" often occurs.[15]

Suzanne Keller, on the other hand, criticizes the validity of the data and their interpretation in *The Power Elite*. According to her, there is a marked inconsistency between elaborate empirical documentation and sweeping generalizations without sufficient evidence. Where empirical evidence is presented it is not always thoroughly examined. She maintains that "Mills' own data do not firmly support his conclusions concerning the increasing social uniformity and ascending power of the leading elites in American society."[16] Perhaps most surprising of all criticisms is the one by Dahrendorf who designates *The Power Elite* as showing traces of a

[12] Raymond E. Wolfinger, "Reputation and Reality in the Study of 'Community Power'," *America Sociological Review*, 25, October, 1960, pp. 636–644.

[13] William Spinard, "Power in Local Communities," *Social Problems*, 12, Winter, 1965, pp. 335–356.

[14] C. Wright Mills, *The Power Elite*, New York: Oxford University Press, 1967.

[15] Talcot Parsons, "On the Concept of Political Power," Reinhard Bendix and Seymour Martin Lipsett, eds., *Class, Status and Power*, 2nd ed., New York: Free Press, 1966, pp. 240–265. Direct quotation from p. 261.

[16] Suzanne Keller, *Beyond the Ruling Class*, New York: Random House, 1963, p. 109.

conservative view. (This work, as well as many of Mills' other writings, has been often characterized as leftist in position). Dahrendorf labels it conservative in charging that Mills does not take full cognizance of the consequences of separation of ownership and control in American society.[17] But irrespective of the nature of critisicm, the striking fact remains that no serious sociological discussion of power in America or in modern society in general fails to refer to Mills' work.

Foremost among such discussions is T. B. Bottomore's *Elites and Society*. The excerpt here, "From the Ruling Class to the Power Elite," represents his much-applauded effort of clarifying and reconciling the two competing concepts of ruling class and power elite. In his critical examination of the two concepts he points to the work of Mills as exemplifying most clearly the difficulties in the concept of governing—or power elite. (As Bottomore rightfully reminds us, Mills was influenced by theories that are considered contradictory, on the one hand by Marx and on the other by Mosca and Pareto). In Mills' study of the power elite there is an explanation of the power position and its three principal components. The power position of business executives is explained by the growth in size and complexity of business corporations, of the military chiefs by the growth in scale and expense of the weapons of war, and of the national political leaders by the decline of the legislature. But, says Bottomore—and this writer does not entirely agree with him—Mills does not explain why there is not one but three power elites. I disagree because Mills does concern himself with the basis of its unity. He talks about their easy intermingling because of similarity in origin, education, and style of life. But what is perhaps even more compelling is Mills' contention that they have many "points of coinciding interest" and that at times their unity is that of "explicit coordination" for the purpose of common interests.[18]

However, if we return to the main aims of Bottomore's essay, we do find that he successfully solves for us the riddle of which way the two concepts—ruling class and governing or power elite—are alike and in which way they differ. Both, says he, emphasize the division between rulers and ruled as one of the most important facts of social structure. But the division is stated differently: ". . . the concept of a 'governing elite' contrasts the organized, ruling minority with the unorganized majority, or masses, while the concept of a 'ruling class' contrasts the dominant class with subject classes, which may themselves be organized, or be creating organizations." From these different conceptions, Bottomore adds, come the differences in the way of conceiving the relations between ruler and ruled. One could add that they are also the bases of contrasting views of the future. We noted the optimism of Djilas, which we can now see as being tied to his conception of the ruling group as a class rather than elite and the bottom as a subject class with the potential of becoming organized. In comparison, Mills' view of the future is a pessimistic one, for at the bottom is a mass of politically uninterested beings, shortsighted concerning events outside their immediate experiences.

But if we were to agree with all that Bottomore says we would have to conclude that Djilas' optimism has no basis in the reality situation, for his concept of new class does not fit the reality of Soviet-type societies. According to Bottomore the actual power structure of the Communist countries approaches the "pure type of a 'power elite'." It is regrettable that he does not deal at this point with the Djilas

[17] Ralf Dahrendorf, *Class and Class Conflict in Industrial Society*, Stanford: Stanford University Press, 1959, p. 43.

[18] Mills, *op. cit.*, p. 19.

argument, a crucial one: that the power group in these countries is a class because it exercises complete control over property.

Conceivably one could resolve the dilemma of whether the ruling group in a Soviet-type society is a class or an elite by concretely applying in the analysis of these societies an idea found in the conclusion of Bottomore's essay. I have in mind the thought that the ruling class and power elite "may be seen as complementary concepts which refer . . . to different aspects of the *same* political system" (italics supplied), as well as to different types of political systems. As far as I know, no one has pursued successfully this sort of analysis in regard to Communist countries.

Also worthy of being stressed in the conclusion is the author's explicit program of what can be accomplished with these two concepts. As he expresses it, "With their help we can attempt to distinguish between societies [a] in which there is a ruling class, and at the same time elites which represent particular aspects of its interests; [b] societies in which there is no ruling class, but a political elite which founds its power upon the control of administration, or upon military force, rather than upon property ownership and inheritance; [c] and societies in which there exists a multiplicity of elites among which no cohesive and enduring group of powerful individuals or families seems to discoverable at all."

Yes, we can attempt to classify in the above suggested manner and, in dealing with past societies, perhaps achieve some consensus. But when we deal with contemporary society, different social scientists, with perhaps equal devotion to objectivity, place the same society in different categories of this classification. This is vividly exemplified in the two contrasting pictures of the structure of power in American society drawn by two American sociologists writing in the 1950s—C. Wright Mills and David Riesman. Riesman's picture is not that of a power elite but of "'veto groups' among which power is dispersed."[19] Thus, according to him, there is no single unified power at the top of the structure, as asserted by Mills, but an "amorphous power structure." It consists of a ". . . series of groups, each of which has struggled and finally attained a power to stop things conceivably inimical to its interests and, within far narrower limits, to start things."[20] Riesman's picture of the American power structure resembles then type C, whereas Mills' is type B in the Bottomore classification. Which is right? Regrettably the question remains unanswered, for the evidence on both sides of the controversy is rather sketchy. Thus, one cannot do better than finish on the usual note that more disciplined historical and comparative research is needed as a solid empirical basis for evaluating who is right, Mills or Riesman.[21]

***Status Inequality.*** Where the research is rather plentiful is on the dimension of status inequality. This becomes especially interesting if one holds the view that the power and economic aspects are more important factors of stratification. It is the position of Lenski, among others, who made little attempt in his book on stratification to examine prestige inequality. He justified it partly on the grounds ". . . that

[19] David Riesman, "The Images of Power," in *The Lonely Crowd*, New York: Doubleday Anchor Edition, 1953, pp. 239–271. Later, two books have appeared, continuing the controversy—the first is consistent with the thesis of Mills and the second with that of Riesman: G. William Dornhoff, *Who Rules America?*, New Jersey: Prentice Hall, 1967; Arnold M. Rose, *The Power Structure*, New York: Oxford University Press, 1967.

[20] *Ibid.*, p. 247.

[21] William Kornhauser, "'Power Elite' or 'Veto Groups'?" in S. M. Lipset and Leo Lowenthal, eds., *Culture and Social Character*, New York: Free Press, 1961, p. 267.

prestige can be understood more readily as a function of power and privilege than the other way around." He holds that while "... there is a certain element of feedback, the major causal flow ... [is] from power and privilege to prestige."[22] Although we might take some issue with this generalization, based on the analysis of caste in the preceding section of this book, it nevertheless fits well the system of contemporary stratification in industrial society. The future historian of knowledge may be puzzled that the stratification studies of the most industrial country of our time concentrated so heavily on status to the neglect of power. The fact that empirical investigations of stratification in America began with small towns—and small towns in New England at that—may hold the key to this puzzle. (We use here and throughout this discussion the term *status* in Weber's sense or, as Mayer rephrased it, as "... the *differentiation* of prestige and deference among individuals and groups in a society.")[23]

It was W. Lloyd Warner who opened the floodgates of empirical studies, to borrow Hodges' metaphor,[24] when he led a research team of social anthropologists into the New England seaport of Newburyport, a town of 17,000 inhabitants, which he called Yankee City. That is why, mindful of the methodological criticisms to which Warner's work has been subjected,[25] I nevertheless agree with Milton Gordon's conclusion that "All in all, American sociology owes more of a debt of gratitude to this social anthropologist who transferred his attention from the aborigines of the Australian bush to the good citizens of Yankee City than has hitherto been acknowledged."[26] Other studies of stratification in small towns in America by Warner and his colleagues followed the Yankee City series. He summarizes the findings of all in the excerpt from the book *Social Class In America,* which is reprinted here.

In the first part of the selection is found the theoretical orientation of Warner and his collaborators. They make clear that in talking about social class they refer to a status of rank hierarchy. (Later in the book from which this selection is taken, this is made even more explicit in the authors' formal definition of class as "two or more orders of people who are believed to be, and are accordingly ranked by all members of the community in socially superior or inferior positions.")[27] Then the authors proceed to a functional explanation of social class in America. It exists, according to them, because the social structure of complex societies "must have rank orders to perform certain functions necessary for group survival." The main function of stratification, they elaborate, is an integrative one. This is the very opposite of the view of class found in Marx: in Marx's conception, class divides society; in the above functionalist view, social class unites and solidifies society. But then one must recall that Warner's meaning of social class is different from that of Marx. This is especially worth noting because Warner claims to have

[22] Gerhard E. Lenski, *Power and Privilege,* New York: McGraw-Hill Book Company, 1966, p. 430.

[23] Kurt B. Mayer, *Class and Society,* New York: Random House, 1955, p. 24.

[24] Harold M. Hodges, *Social Stratification,* Cambridge: Schenkman Publishing Company, 1964. p. 63.

[25] See, for example, Harold P. Pfautz and O. D. Duncan, "A Critical Evaluation of Warner's Work in Community, Stratification," *American Sociological Review,* 15, April, 1950, pp. 205–215; Ruth Kornhauser, "The Warner Approach to Social Stratification," in R. Bendix and S. M. Lipset, eds., *Class, Status and Power,* Glencoe, Illinois: Free Press, 1953, pp. 224–255.

[26] Milton M. Gordon, *Social Class in American Sociology,* Durham, N. C.: Duke University Press, 1958, p. 123.

[27] W. Lloyd Warner, with Marchia Meeker and Kenneth Eells, *Social Class in America,* Chicago: Social Science Research Associates, 1949, p. 129.

begun his studies with an economic conception of class borrowed from Marx.

He explains that his concept was changed when he discovered in Yankee City that the divisions were not strictly along economic lines and that money alone did not guarantee high social position. And yet, when we examine critically what he tells us about the highest stratum among the six he delineates—the upper-upper, whose rank is determined by lineage,—we discern that the ultimate source of the status is nevertheless money, even if it is only a certain kind: "old money" that has been in the family for generations. What I am suggesting is that Warner's evidence, contrary to what he claims, shows wealth to be the basis of status in Yankee City and the other towns, but in order to be at the top of the status hierarchy one must either have old money or "translate new money" into socially approved behavior and possessions.

In this respect Yankee City and the *stetl* in prewar Poland bear some similarity, as can be observed in our next selection: "Social Stratification of the Jewish Community in a Small Polish Town," by Celia Stopnicka Heller. Wealth alone did not assure a person of status in the Jewish community. It was a source of prestige only insofar as it enabled a man to contribute to the welfare of the community, to do "good deeds" and to give to charity. But no matter how it was used, it was a source of power. Those wealthy individuals who did not use a part of their money in the prescribed manner were nevertheless accorded deference, even if it were spurious, in order to prevent them from exercising power against one. This suggests that, contrary to numerous sociological formulations, including the preceding definition of status by Kurt Mayer, deference is tied not only to prestige but also to power. Deference accorded because of power superiority may, however, be either real or spurious. It is likely to be only spurious if power ranks low in the normative system of a society, as it did in the Jewish culture of Poland.

The power of money and material goods also throws light on the pronounced manifestation of conspicuous consumption in the Jewish community. Since Veblen's formulation, conspicuous consumption has been largely seen by sociologists as a symbolic claim of status.[28] And yet in the small town Jewish community of Poland conspicuous consumption was more tied to power than status. First of all, by parading one's money in terms of conspicuous consumption one was not likely to win prestige because, as we have noted, money alone was not the source of it. Furthermore, ostentation was strongly discouraged in the process of home socialization on the grounds that it would make others jealous and would strengthen the hostile attitudes of the Gentiles. Despite this it was quite prominent. Conspicuous consumption performed two functions: it served notice that one was powerful enough to deal with the hostile outside world and that one was capable of dispensing favors.

Because money was considered an unstable commodity, it was expected that one would use it to obtain the greater and more lasting sources of status: lineage and learning. The traditional meaning of education in the *stetl* (small town) deserves special attention; it was very different from that in modern industrial society. In modern industrial society, education, perhaps even more than money, needs to be translated into socially approved behavior—proper occupation—to be a source of prestige. Thus the observation that Warner made about money and prestige in Yankee City applies, I think, even more to education. In contrast with

[28] Thorstein Veblen, *The Theory of the Leisure Class*, New York: Macmillan, 1899; new ed., New York: Mentor Books, 1953.

this, in the *stetl*, education needed no further validation to yield prestige: it was an unqualified source of it.

The pattern of stratification described in this article involved most of the Jews in prewar Poland, because three-fourths of the Jewish population lived in small towns. But the critics have increasingly questioned whether the small town represents America, a claim made by Warner and picturesquely expressed in his phrase "Jonesville is in all Americans and all Americans are in Jonesville. . . . To Study Jonesville is to study America."[29] After all, census data show that the big cities and their suburbia are increasingly more representative of America, and sociological analysis reveals that the dominant forces of society are located there, rather than in small towns.

Now, as Kurt Mayer explains, prestige rests on interpersonal recognition that always involves at least one individual who claims deference and another who honors this claim.[30] The description of status hierarchy in small towns, where every one knows everyone else, is therefore far from a description of prestige stratification of American society at large. How does it operate in the anonymous, impersonal city, with its fleeting social contacts and segmented activities? What about prestige and stratification in the metropolis or megalopolis? We do lack systematic studies that tackle such questions, but they are beginning to be explored.

Bensman points to the existence of status communities as the vehicle of prestige differentiation in urban society. These are not territorial communities but what he calls communities "of shared meanings."[31] Perhaps it is an awkward designation and *nonterritorial* would have sufficed, for what is most significant here is that in contrast to small towns, territory is not relevant.[32] As Bensman expresses it in terms of the musical community, his case study, the professional musician may be more at home in the concert halls of New York or Moscow than in the apartment of his next-door neighbor. It is a community in the sense that in it "the individual chooses to live out his major life interests."[33]

He talks about the "multidimensionality" of prestige or status in urban society. It refers to the contended fact that there are different sets of prestige values within the same society, each status community having its own set of prestige values. Thus there is a vast array of prestige values or sources of status that, in their totality, may be interrelated but often are in conflict. According to Bensman, the prestige one receives in the society at large is based on how one's status community rates in the society and on his imputed position in that status community.

Bensman maintains that in a complex urban society, status communities are not only the "basic vehicle" of prestige stratification, but also of "the total pattern of life for much of the urban population at large."[34] I would take issue with both of these, for I doubt that status communities are characteristic of the

[29] W. Lloyd Warner, *Democracy in Jonesville*, New York: Harper & Brothers, 1949, p. xv.

[30] Kurt B. Mayer, *op. cit.*, p. 24.

[31] Joseph Bensman, "Status Communities in an Urban Society: The Musical Community," paper delivered at the Annual Meeting of the American Sociological Association, August, 1967.

[32] Similarly, Charles Kadushin, tracing himself to Simmel, points to "social circles" as units of mass society. They are "nongeographical communities" of "like-minded persons." See his "The Friends and Supporters of Psychotherapy: On Social Circles in Urban Life," *American Sociological Review*, Vol. 31, December, 1966, pp. 786–802.

[33] Bensman, *loc. cit.*,

[34] *Ibid.*

working class. If anything, territorial communities are the pattern, as is reflected dramatically in the fights of juvenile gangs over the boundaries of territories. In contrast to the professional musicians who, the author tells us, draw their friends from among professional musicians and devoted amateurs and find their marriage partners among them, workers, and especially their children, tend to make friends among neighbors and marry the girl or boy next door or the high school sweetheart. Much of the social pathology of urban areas may, however, be the result of the breakup of lower-class territorial communities with no corresponding development of nonterritorial status communities.

But Bensman's contention (and my criticism of it), could only be settled through empirical research into the problem of how representative status communities are of the society at large or of certain layers of society. Such research is, of course, lacking, because the concept of the status community is a recent one. In contrast, the aspects of status stratification that has been thoroughly investigated is occupational ranking. As a matter of fact, the prestige hierarchy of occupations is probably the best-studied aspect of stratification systems of contemporary societies. Extensive empirical investigations have been conducted on this subject in different types of societies, so-called capitalist and socialist, developed and developing. A few studies have also appeared comparing the occupational hierarchies of different countries, starting with the pioneering and influential work of Inkeles and Rossi that appeared in 1956.[35] Inkeles and Rossi examined comparable occupations in six industrialized countries: (the only ones for which data were available then) the United States, Great Britain, New Zealand, Japan, Germany, and the Soviet Union, in order to test two contrasting positions—the *structuralist* and *culturalist*—on the relation between the standardized modern occupational system and the value system of a given nation. The structuralist position holds that the modern industrial occupational system is a highly coherent one, tied to the requirements of industrial society and little influenced by traditional values. In contrast, the culturalist position is that the particular values of a nation would result in a differential evaluation of modern occupations within that nation. Inkeles and Rossi found much evidence to support the structuralist position. There was remarkable agreement on the prestige accorded by popular opinion to comparable occupations in the six countries (twelve of the fifteen coefficients of correlation were above 0.9), despite differences in culture—especially pronounced between Japan and the rest—and differences in form of government—especially marked between the Soviet Union and the rest. Actually, the author's explanation of the similarity was expressed in terms of two causal factors: First, there "... is a relatively invariable hierarchy of prestige associated with the industrial system" and secondly, the countries compared have in common the characteristic of a national state.[36]

The influential and widely accepted thesis presented in this article was a bit shaken when studies in developing nations came forth, showing rankings of occupations similar to those in industrialized countries.[37] Subsequently Hodge, Treiman, and Rossi addressed themselves to an explanation of this uniformity in

[35] Alex Inkeles and Peter H. Rossi, "National Comparisons of Occupational Prestige," *American Journal of Sociology*, Vol. 61, January, 1956, pp. 329–339.

[36] *Ibid.*, p. 339.

[37] See, for example, on occupational ranking in Indonesia, Murray Thomas, "Reinspecting a Structural Position on Occupational Prestige," *American Journal of Sociology*, Vol. 67, March, 1962, pp. 561–565.

occupational ranking of industrialized and developing nations.[38] They examined data from twenty-four nations, underdeveloped as well as developed. Their findings show "... that it is impossible to argue at least for newly developing countries that similarities in levels of industrialization induced similarities in the hierarchical evaluation of occupations, since without any substantial progress toward industrialization many new nations have achieved a structure of occupational evaluations quite similar to that observed in the United States."[39] (This is noteworthy because it was precisely what was argued in the essay by Inkeles and Rossi, and because Rossi is the coauthor of the article we are now discussing). The data, as they make explicit, did not fall in a simple structuralist or a simple culturalist position. According to them, their data suggest that occupational evaluations may be a causal factor in industrialization, and not merely the effect of industrialization. The "appropriate" kind of occupational evaluations, either native or borrowed, may lead to economic expansion, "providing a necessary though not sufficient condition for development rather than being a simple consequence of it."[40] In other words, if occupations that are necessary to industrialization are valued, people are more likely to train for them, thus hastening industrialization.

Obviously the authors of the study were convinced that their data were valid, that the comparisons were valid despite the technical defects. They do mention that in light of the great heterogeneity of the occupational studies in various lands and the problems involved in matching occupational titles, there may be some question about the wisdom of comparing them at all, but they dismiss this question and move on to comparisons. The question has, however, subsequently been taken up by Archibald Haller and David Lewis.[41] They examined the statistical limitations of the data, including the deficiencies in comparability, and concluded that inferences about the similarities in the occupational prestige structures of different societies are not well established. First of all, the evidence of similarities is confined to translatable occupational titles. Then, too, the small and biased samples of both occupational titles and the people interviewed about them are subject to significant errors.

Whether the thesis of similarity of occupational prestige hierarchies from country to country has been substantially dented by Haller and Lewis awaits further scholarly appraisal. But what do we know about the stability of such hierarchies over time in the same country?

Hodge, Siegel, and Rossi address themselves to this question in our next reading, "Occupational Prestige in the United States, 1925–1963," and their data are from the various studies of occupational ranking conducted in the United States at different times. Such studies have a fairly long history in the United States. One of the first investigations was that by Counts, who, in 1925, asked a group of teachers and college and high school students to rate forty-five familiar American occupations.[42] Hodge, Siegel, and Rossi review this study, as well as the ones that followed it, and come out with the finding that no appreciable changes have

[38] Robert W. Hodge, Donald J. Treiman, and Peter H. Rossi, "A Comparative Study of Occupational Prestige," in Bendix and Lipset, *op. cit.*, 2nd ed., pp. 309–322.

[39] *Ibid.*, p. 320.

[40] *Ibid.*, p. 321.

[41] Archibald O. Haller and David M. Lewis, "The Hypothesis of Intersocietal Similarity in Occupational Prestige Hierarchies," *American Journal of Sociology*, Vol. 72, September, 1966, pp. 210–216.

[42] George S. Counts, "Social Status of Occupations," *School Review*, Vol. 33, 1926, pp. 16–27.

taken place in the prestige structure of American occupations in the last forty years.

Among these studies, the most systematic and influential was the one made by North and Hatt, shortly after World War II, of the nationwide ranking of ninety occupations.[43] And it is this study that the authors have replicated in 1963. They found an unusually high correlation of 0.99 between the prestige scores derived from the 1947 North and Hatt study and their replication. Thus, the authors conclude that few changes have occurred in the sixteen-year period. Their explanation of this stability is that there are many good reasons for its existence. However, when one examines these reasons, he finds that a number of them are not necessarily the reasons *for* stability, but merely functional consequences *of* occupational stability. We cannot simply deduce, as the authors do, that stability in occupational ranking exists because pronounced changes in the prestige structure would lead to such negative consequences as furthering ambiguities or status inconsistencies and altering fundamentally the meaning of achievement, career, seniority, and occupational prestige. (The reasoning seems circular.) Apart from these consequences, erroneously labeled reasons for stability in occupational ranking, they enumerate the following factors, which could be considered causal factors in prestige stabilty. The educational requirements and monetary rewards of occupations tend to be stable. Because prestige of occupations is largely determined by these two factors, the prestige tends to be stable.

In this connection we may recall that the North-Hatt study did attempt to find out why people ranked occupations the way they did. They discovered that *high income* was most frequently mentioned by the public as the most important criterion for an "excellent" rating.[44] Moreover, in his analysis of the North-Hatt data, Dudley Duncan shows a 0.91 correlation between occupational evaluations and a combined measure of the income and educational attainment of each of the occupations examined.[45] We get some further insight into how much importance is assigned to the income of an occupation from two questions asked in a Gallup Poll of 1951. They were, "Which of these two jobs would you personally prefer a son of yours to take, assuming he is equally qualified: a skilled laborer's job at $100 a week or a white-collar desk job at $75 a week?"; and, after the same beginning, ". . . a college professor's job at $4,000 a year or a factory foreman's job at $6,000 a year?" In answer to both of these questions, a majority of respondents, in both manual and nonmanual occupations, expressed a preference

[43] National Opinion Research Center, "Jobs and Occupations: A popular Evaluation," *Opinion News*, September 1, 1947, pp. 3–13, reprinted in Bendix and Lipset, *op. cit.*, pp. 411–426.

[44] *Ibid.*, p. 419. The study asked, "When you say certain jobs have 'excellent standing' what do you think is the one main thing about such jobs that gives this standing?" The answers were:

| | |
|---|---|
| The job pays well | 18% |
| It serves humanity; it is an essential job | 16 |
| Preparation requires much education, hard work & money | 14 |
| The job carries social prestige | 14 |
| It requires high moral standards, honesty, responsibility | 9 |
| It requires intelligence and ability | 9 |
| It provides security, steady work | 5 |
| The job has a good future; the field is not overcrowded | 3 |
| The job is pleasant, safe, and easy | 2 |
| It affords maximum chance for initiative and freedom | 0 (less than 0.5%) |
| Miscellaneous answers; don't know, no answer | 10 |
| | 100% |

[45] O. D. Duncan, "A Socioeconomic Index for All Occupations," in Albert J. Reiss, *Occupation and Social Status*, New York: Free Press, 1961, p. 124.

for the manual job. In the case of the second question, where the majority was smaller, the preference for the foreman among manual respondents was 61 per cent as against 34 per cent and among nonmanual 52 per cent as against 44 per cent.[46] These figures read like a modern rendition of *Vico's* dictum "... by the eternal common civil nature, men first seek wealth, then honors. . . ."[47]

All this suggests, and casual observation supports it, that although at an given time there may be a discrepancy between the prestige and income of an occupation, in the long run there is a high consistency. A high-ranking occupation whose relative income falls substantially will eventually go down in rank. If the income of a given occupation increases substantially, it will eventually gain in rank. We are, of course, touching on the problem referred to by the various terms of *status consistency, congruence* and *crystallization.* It was for the first time, as far as we know, subjected to quantification by Gerhard Lenski in his article "Status Crystallization: A Non-Vertical Dimension of Social Status," which appeared in 1954. This was followed by a stream of research and discussion on the subject which continues to this day. Much of the research is cited and briefly summarized in "Status Consistency and Inconsistency" the pages reprinted here from Lenski's book, *Power and Privilege.* (The term *status* in this usage is broader than in the Weberian sense. It refers to position in general rather than prestige position.)

When Lenski undertook the task of conceptualizing status crystallization in his original article, he made clear that individual or family status is approached by him not as "a single position in a uni-dimensional hierarchy" but as a "series of positions in a series of related hierarchies."[48]

Lenski focused on the relative positions in the following four hierarchies: (1) the income hierarchy, (2) the occupational hierarchy, (3) the educational hierarchy, and (4) the ethnic hierarchy. Two logical possibilities flow from this: (1) status consistency or crystallization—positions of the individual rank more or less the same, as for example all high or all low and (2) status inconsistency—one or more positions of an individual rank much higher than another or others.

But Lenski conceptualized status consistency or crystallization in terms of a continuum ranging from high to low. He developed a technique, which he describes in the article, for comparing the relative positions of an individual in several hierarchies. High status crystallization occurs when the positions rank nearly the same; low crystallization when they rank quite differently in the different hierarchies.

At this point it would be well to mention that in a later article Warner Landecker—who conducted the research project jointly with Lenski—addressed himself in part to when high crystallization is more likely to occur by devising a crystallization index and then testing the hypothesis that status crystallization is strongest at the two extremes of the stratification system. He arrived at this hypothesis by reasoning that persons who rate highest in one hierarchy will have the most power to monopolize equivalent positions in the other hierarchies. On the other hand, to be at the bottom of one hierarchy handicaps one's access to higher positions in the other hierarchies. The latter part of the hypothesis was not confirmed by the results of

[46] Quoted in W. G. Runciman, *Relative Deprivation and Social Justice*, Berkeley: University of California Press, 1966, p. 234.

[47] The rest of the sentence reads "and lastly nobility." See Thomas Goddard Bergin and Max Harold Fisch, eds., *The New Science of Giambattista Vico,* New York: Anchor Books, 1961, p. 320.

[48] Gerhard E. Lenski, "Status Crystallization: A Non-Vertical Dimension," *American Sociological Review*, Vol. 19, August, 1954, p. 405.

the tests, but the first was. The hypothesis that crystallization would be particularly strong at the highest level was supported by the fact that the index of class crystallization showed a higher score at the top status level than at any other level.[49]

Lenski's main interest was different: He was concerned with the *utility* of the concept of status crystallization. His study was aimed at testing its utility by investigating whether it could account ". . . for some of the variance in political behavior which is left unexplained by traditional methods of stratification analysis." He then treated status crystallization as the independent variable and "liberal political tendencies" as the dependent one. The analysis of the data led him to the conclusion that such tendencies ". . . are associated with low degree of status crystallization."

Extrapolating from these findings, Lenski contended that one could predict that the greater the proportion of the population suffering from acute status inconsistencies, the greater the proportion supporting programs of social change. This has been criticized by Kenkel, who demonstrated that it has not always been the case.[50] It is noteworthy that in the reprinted pages from the book that appeared about a decade later than his article, Lenski states his hypothesis about the consequences of status inconsistency in more cautious terms. Since the appearance of the book, Kelly and Chambliss have reported on their attempt to resolve the discrepancy between the findings in Lenski's initial article and the findings by Kenkel. Their study, however, relied on a mail-back questionnaire sent to a sample of Seattle residents. The responses indicated that the ". . . social class membership and ethnic background of respondents are far more important determinants of political attitudes than the degree to which persons are status consistent or inconsistent."[51]

But other empirical studies that appeared about the same time or subsequently have provided some specification as to which kinds of status inconsistency lead to which kind of liberal tendencies. For example, in a later article Lenski showed that his secondary analysis of twenty-five national surveys of voting behavior in Australia, Britain, and the United States provides support for the thesis that status inconsistency between one's occupation and religious affiliation increases liberal or left-of-center tendencies.[52] On the other hand, Treiman's study shows that status inconsistency *per se* has no effect on prejudice against Negroes.[53]

The Polish sociologist Andrzej Malewski has given further thought to this problem. contending that although status inconsistency tends to lead to support of change, this does not necessarily mean support of liberal or leftist causes, as suggested by Lenski and others. He reasons that when an individual of incongruent

[49] Werner S. Landecker, "Class Crystallization and Its Urban Pattern," *Social Research*, Vol. 27, Autumn, 1960, pp. 308–320.

[50] F. W. Kenkel, "The Relationship Between Status Consistency and Politico-Economic Attitudes," *American Sociological Review*, Vol. 21, June, 1956, pp. 365–368. See also, Gerhard Lenski, "Comment on Kenkel's Communication," same issue, p. 369.

[51] K. Dennis Kelly and William J. Chambliss, "Status Consistency and Political Attitudes," *American Sociological Review*, Vol. 31, June, 1966, p. 381.

[52] Gerhard E. Lenski, "Status Inconsistency and the Vote: A Four Nation Test," *American Journal of Sociology*, Vol. 32, April, 1967, pp. 298–302.

[53] Its data were from a representative national sample of the adult white population in the United States, and its measures of consistency involved: (1) income and education as status variables and (2) education and education of spouse. See Donald J. Treiman, "Status Discrepancy and Prejudice," *American Journal of Sociology*, Vol. 71, May, 1966, pp. 651–669.

status cannot raise himself on those hierarchies where his position is low, he will tend to "reject the system of evaluation which justifies his humiliations" and join those who oppose that system.[54] If the only group rejecting this system of evaluation is the radical Left, such individuals will tend to accept its program. However, if there are radical Right groups, whose programs promise possibilities of raising one's position in the hierarchies where one ranks low, they show great readiness to accept such programs. Malewski supports his contention with evidence from empirical studies.[55]

Later than Malewski, however, Norbert Wiley put forth the interesting hypothesis that the consequences of status inconsistency may be different for individuals and different for the social system. He argues that although status inconsistent individuals may be more radical, their existence may have an overall conservative effect on the social system. According to him, "To the people at the bottom of the system, who are all too consistent, the possibility of social ascent—even though it be only on one dimension, into an inconsistent posture—may give them a certain amount of hope which prevents them from becoming more radical."[56] Thus he concludes that in the United States, status inconsistency ". . . may contribute to keeping the whole political system in the Democratic-Republican center, at the cost of pushing some inconsistents a bit to the right or left of the main line."[57]

As we can gather, the concept of status consistency has been given considerable attention since the initial article by Lenski. To what degree it represents an important addition to the hitherto pursued analysis of political behavior as a reflection of presence or lack of class consciousness will become clearer after we have studied the subjective dimension of class.

## SUBJECTIVE DIMENSION

The study of the subjective dimension of inequality revolves around the query whether, to what extent and how, subjective awareness of stratification varies with one's objective position in the stratification system. Another central question is that of the consequences of different kinds of awaremess. In other words the problem is that of the origin, nature, forms and consequences of what is often labeled as class consciousness.

As we have learned from the readings in theory, Marx saw the objective conditions of inequality pressing for an awareness to develop. Even Marx's writings, however, imply that the objective position in the stratification system is not the only determinant of class consciousness. Basing ourselves on the work of later theorists, we can point to the other important factor, *the definition of the situation* by which the perception and thinking about the objective position, or situation is guided. Here, as is often the case when observing a wide variety of social phenomena, the W. I. Thomas theorem manifests relevance: "If men define situations as real,

[54] Andrzej Malewski, "The Degree of Status Incongruence and its Effects," *The Polish Sociological Bulletin*, Vol. 7, No. 1, 1963. Reprinted in Bendix and Lipset 2nd ed., *op. cit.*, pp. 303–308.

[55] For further support of the thesis that a relationship exists between status inconsistency and right-wing political extremism, see Gary B. Rush, "Status Consistency and Right-Wing Extremism," *American Sociological Review*, Vol. 32, February, 1967, pp. 86–92.

[56] Norbert Wiley, "The Ethnic Mobility Trap and Stratification Theory," *Social Problems*, Vol. 15, Fall, 1967, p. 159.

[57] *Ibid.*

they are real in their consequences."[58] And such definitions in regard to stratification are provided by ideologies. Thus the objective position may press for certain awareness but the prevailing ideology may constitute a counterforce against such awareness arising. All things being equal, persons who believe in the ideology that their society is classless are less likely to perceive actual class differences than the nonbelievers. For example, most observers well acquainted with both sides of the Atlantic maintain that Americans are less class conscious than Europeans. And this is often accounted for by the Americans' belief in the creed of equality.[59]

That the ideology about the stratification system as a whole is an important factor in coloring or distorting the perception of inequality is implied in the essay "Non-Equalitarian Classlessness" by the well-known Polish sociologist Stanislaw Ossowski. He concentrates on the ideologies of the two mutually opposed systems, the United States and the Soviet Union, and shows the similarities between them. Both interpret the objective social inequalities in their own system in another way than in terms of class. As a matter fact, in each ideology the rejection of the image of its own society as a class hierarchy goes hand in hand with a recognition of the existance of social inequalities and its approval as representing just rewards of merit. Ossowski draws this conclusion from a point-by-point comparison of the traditional American ideology, the American Creed, and the official Soviet ideology.

As one reads the details, the question arises in one's mind: How is it possible for such similar conceptions of social structure to be applied to countries with such different political and economic systems as the United States and the USSR? The author addresses himself to this question and answers that it is so because the two start with a different assumption, the assumption of each being incompatible with the assumption of the other. Communist doctrine assumes that the abolition of private ownership of the means of production is the necessary condition of a classless, harmonious society. The American Creed assumes that the rights guaranteed by the American Constitution are the necessary conditions.

In the beginning of the essay Ossowski shows how American sociology has been influenced by traditional ideology, by the American Creed, in its choice of problems for study, in its answers, in its concepts and interpretations. And yet toward the end he states that in the United States the American Creed can and is being questioned by sociologists and others as a valid representation of existing reality (even if rarely, I would add, as a valid set of values and goals), in sharp contrast to the Soviet Union where no conceptions at odds with the official ideology were found until 1954, when Ossowski wrote this essay. One could extend the generalization for the Soviet Union up to this day, although it would not apply to some Soviet-type societies. It is not inappropriate to mention that when Ossowski wrote the

[58] For a treatment of how ideologies in general provide definitions of situations, see Florian Znaniecki, *Cultural Sciences*, Urbana: University of Illinois Press, 1963, pp. 267–285. As for a sociological definition of ideology, a number are available. Many of them resemble in content the following definition of Talcott Parsons: "An ideology, then, is a system of beliefs, held in common by members of a collectivity, i.e., a society, or sub-collectivity of one—including a movement deviant from the main culture of the society—a system of ideas which is oriented to the evaluative integration of the collectivity, by interpretation of the empirical nature of the collectivity and the situation in which it is placed, the processes by which it has developed to its given state, the goals to which its members are collectively oriented, and their relation to the future course of events." *The Social System*, New York: Free Press, 1964, p. 349.

[59] See, for example, S. M. Lipset and Reinhard Bendix, "Ideological Equalitarianism and Social Mobility in the United States," *Transactions of the Second World Congress of Sociology*, Vol. II, London: International Sociological Association, 1954.

essay—as well as other parts of the book *Class Structure in the Social Consciousness* from which it is taken—he did not think it would be published in Poland. As he explains in the preface to the American edition of the translated book, "Its appearance in print was in a certain sense linked with the events of October 1956 in Poland, for these made it possible to publish the work on which I had been engaged for several years without hope of publication. . . . The book went to press in the post-October period of enthusiasm and hope, and the emotional climate was reflected in its final touches." Perhaps to these final touches reflecting overenthusiasm belongs the note on which the book ends. One of the important consequences of the events that took place in Poland in October, 1956, says the author ". . . was the destruction of the official myths which concealed our reality" [Poland's actual conditions]. But although Polish sociologists may not have been as free to address themselves to certain questions as they were in the short period following the so-called Polish October, they nevertheless continued up to 1968 (when the campaign against "revisionism" and "Zionism" began) to investigate problems that remain untouched in the Soviet Union. This is exemplified in the article by Nowak to be discussed soon, and the articles by Wesolowski found in Parts VII and VIII of this book.

In the reprinted essay, Ossowski does refer to Richard Centers' influential work, *The Psychology of Social Classes.* But I would like to elaborate a bit on this book because it constituted at the time of its appearance in 1949 an important breakthrough in the study of the subjective aspect of class. I am not referring to its theoretical line, which is rather weak. Even though at the beginning of the book the author expresses his indebtedness to Marx, and throughout it he maintains that his evidence supports the interest theory of class, his very definition of class, as well as of other formulations, reflects a psychological, and what would be labeled by Marxists an idealistic, position. He states that ". . . *a class is no less than what people collectively think it is. It is a psychological structuring*. . . ."[60] This explicitly denies that class is an objective phenomenon which, as we recall, was Marx's position. The following widely quoted passage from Marx's writing expresses plainly his view of the general relation between objective reality and subjective experience: "As in private life one distinguishes between what a man thinks and says of himself and what he really is and does, so still more in historical struggles must one distinguish the phrases and fancies of the parties from their real organism and their real interests, their conception of themselves from their reality."[61] Marx spoke of objective class interests, not the psychological dispositions that Centers terms interests.

When we referred to Centers' work as a breakthrough in its time, we had in mind that his work in a sense exploded the ideological myth that Americans, irrespective of socioeconomic position, considered themselves as belonging to one class, the middle class. This myth was supported by various national polls conducted prior to the Centers study which reported that 79 to 88 per cent of Americans placed themselves in the middle class. It led *Fortune Magazine*, a sponsor of one of these polls, to proclaim "America Is Middle Class."

In his book Centers explains how he came to doubt the validity of those findings.

[60] Richard Centers, *The Psychology of Social Classes,* Princeton: Princeton University Press, 1949, p. 78.

[61] Karl Marx, *The Eighteen Brumaire of Louis Bonaparte,* New York: International Publishers, n.d., p. 41.

His study demonstrated that they were a function of the alternatives that the people were given to choose from: upper, middle, and lower. Not many chose to place themselves in a class designated by the value-laden term *lower*. When given a fourth alternative by him, working class, about half placed themselves there. Centers refers to this self-placement in a specific class as *class identification* and shows that it correlates with one's occupation. Three-fourths of business, professional, and white-collar individuals placed themselves in the middle class while almost four-fifths of the manual workers placed themselves in the working or lower class. He considers the fact that most people placed themselves, as they were asked to do, in one of these four classes, and that it correlated with their occupation, as indicating class consciousness. Thus he came up with the finding that Americans are class conscious, which was contrary to the hitherto prevalent characterizations of Americans in general, and of American working class in particular, as lacking class consciousness when compared with Europeans, for example.[62]

But by now, through the discussion engendered by Centers and subsequent studies, social scientists recognize that their surveys both hide some of the ignorance that people have about their stratification system and encourage some ideological distortions. In which case they place themselves is partly an artifact of the alternatives they are given to choose from rather than the expression of their everyday way of thinking. Respondents may, for instance, for fear of appearing ignorant, hide the fact that they do not understand the question or do not know to which class they belong, and make a choice of one of the alternative answers. Then too, the different alternatives given in surveys may tap different ideologies. The three alternatives in the *Fortune* study—upper, middle, lower—may have tapped the American equalitarian ideology, discussed by Ossowski. The four-class alternatives in Centers' study may have tapped the "Work Is Good" ideology, the heritage of the Protestant Ethic.[63]

The empirical study conducted by Gross in Minneapolis, Minnesota has much bearing on what was discussed here. By administering different types of questions to the sample of respondents, he demonstrated that the degree of structuring of a question has an effect on how people "identify" themselves in terms of class. In response to the open-ended question "What class do you belong to?" every third respondent failed to place himself in a class (20 per cent answered they did not know and about 15 per cent replied that there were no social classes or that they did not belong to any class). He also used two types of closed questions: the one that appeared in the *Fortune* survey and the one from the Centers study. Having analyzed and compared the answers to the open-ended and the two closed-ended questions, Gross stated, "In short, the conclusions the investigator emerges with using upper-middle-lower or the upper-middle-working-lower forced choice questions, are of great variance with the conclusion that emerges from the use of an open-ended class identification question."[64]

Apart from class identification, Richard Centers saw the politicoeconomic orientation as the major aspect of class consciousness. The instrument that he

[62] Centers, *op. cit.*, pp. 30–38 and 78–106.

[63] Bernard Barber, *Social Stratification*, New York: Harcourt, Brace and Company, 1957, pp. 210–211.

[64] Neal Gross, "Social Class Identification in the Urban Community," *American Sociological Review*, Vol. 18, 1953, pp. 398–404.

employed for ascertaining the politicoeconomic orientation was a *conservatism-radicalism battery* of six questions. But his material by and large does not support his contention that class self-identification is the intervening variable between occupation and politicoeconomic orientation. Centers contends that not only do Americans readily identify the class to which they belong, but that the answers to the identification question are predictive of the answers to the ideology battery. His data showed that the highest percent of conservatives and ultraconservatives fall in the self-identified upper and middle classes, whereas the greater proportion of radicals and ultraradicals are in the self-identified working and lower classes. However, careful inspection of his data discloses that one gets a better prediction of the politicoeconomic orientation by varying occupation than by varying class self-identification.[65]

Subsequently Arthur Kornhauser reviewed the findings of the Centers study, as well as other public opinions studies up to 1950, and generalized that on economic issues there was a tendency for opinions to be based on class position. But questions on other issues—such as international questions, race relations, religious doctrine, and so on—". . . fail to support the conception of a neat general pattern of radicalism-conservatism in which social classes manifest consistent contrasts."[66]

This ties in rather well to our next reading, "Social Class, Ideology, and Voting Preference" by Gertrude Jaeger Selznick and Stephen Steinberg, which analyzes the 1964 presidential vote. The paper aims at two things: to clarify the relation between voting and general beliefs, which they term *ideology,* and to gain a better understanding of the reasons for Goldwater's overwhelming defeat in the 1964 election. As regards the first, they found that both objective class, indicated by occupation, and political beliefs are related to how people voted in that election. The question posed then was whether the relationship between objective class and the vote could be explained by class differences in political beliefs. But their data showed that political beliefs were not related to class. Ideological agreement and disagreement with Goldwater was fairly equally distributed throughout the class structure.

The authors then proceeded to consider whether the relation between class and the vote could be explained by immediate economic interests as perceived by the voters, what they label pocketbook concerns. Among all classes, many voters displayed the discordant combination of fairly conservative political beliefs and a pro-welfare orientation. But in such cases, the pro-welfare orientation tended to take precedence as far as voting was concerned. A pro-welfare orientation was most prevalent among workers and this explains the overwhelming vote for Johnson.

Selznick and Steinberg underline that the pro-welfare stand of many Johnson voters was not backed up by a consistent set of liberal political beliefs. Such people, they point out, could respond favorably to reactionary movements if their economic interests were not threatened and, one could add, especially if they were promised an enhancement of their economic interests. The authors conclude that class in the United States has little relation to basic political ideology. Thus in the United States the workers continue to differ from the pattern of class consciousness

[65] Joseph A. Kahl, *The American Class Structure*, New York: Holt, Rinehart and Winston, 1957, p. 165.

[66] Arthur Kornhauser, "Public Opinion and Social Class," *American Journal of Sociology*, Vol. 55, January, 1955, p. 334.

as envisaged by Karl Marx. Does this imply that growing affluence will tend to reduce even this limited class consciousness of working people now related to economic issues? The claim that this is the case falls within the thesis of the *embourgeoisment* of the working class under welfare capitalism. (Recall the early formulation of this thesis by Theodor Geiger.) But some sociologists warn against such an assumption saying that working-class affluence may sharpen class consciousness if status differences increase or harden at the same time. They point out that "... the development of marked discrepancies between income and status hierarchies tends to be productive of radical attitudes on the part of those who are unable to secure a degree of social recognition commensurate with their economic standing."[67]

But whether class consciousness would increase, I would like to add, would depend on how people perceive and experience these status differences. A work that throws much light on this is the book by W. Runciman, *Relative Deprivation and Social Justice,* in which class consciousness is explored systematically and in depth in a manner and to a degree hitherto unencountered. The author does this using both the historical and survey methods.

Our selection from this book is limited to the findings of the survey he conducted in England in 1962. (A stratified random sample of the British population, consisting of 1415, was chosen, of which 1087 respondents were interviewed.)[68] The main problem to which he addresses himself here is, "What is the relation between institutionalized inequalities and the awareness or resentment of them?" It has particular relevance in Britain, because it is a country of the following contradictions which, as the author notes in his introduction to the book, have been "variously admired or deplored according to the observer's political taste." Here is the country where the Industrial Revolution began and one of the few that is currently described as affluent. Yet its social structure is, according to Runciman, the most traditional of any industrialized country in the world. It has a Socialist government, but its hereditary monarchy has survived with undiminished prestige. The class consciousness of the working class in England led Marx to the prediction that the proletariat in advanced capitalism would revolt, yet the British Labor movement is "notorious in its gradualism."[69]

The two concepts that Runciman employs, *relative deprivation* and *reference group,* are related, in that both derive from a truism that "... people's attitudes, aspirations, and grievances largely depend on the frame of reference within which they are conceived."[70] Throughout the selection, as one comes again and again across the term relative deprivation, one must bear in mind that the author uses it as a strictly subjective concept. It refers to the sense and feeling of deprivation.

[67] John H. Goldthorpe and David Lockwood, "Affluence and the British Class Structure," *The Sociological Review,* Vol. 11, July, 1963, p. 140; Gavin Mackenzie, "The Economic Dimensions of Embourgeoisement," *The British Journal of Sociology*, Vol. XVIII, March, 1967, pp. 29–45. Other researches show that such consciousness is present to a larger degree in certain sectors of the working class—notably the unemployed who express more militant views than the employed. See: John C. Legett, "Economic Insecurity and Working-Class Consciousness," *American Sociological Review,* Vol. 29, April, 1964, pp. 226–235; John C. Legett, *Class, Race, and Labor—Working-Class Consciousness in Detroit,* New York : Oxford University Press, 1968. For similar findings in Cuba, see Maurice Zeitlin, "Economic Insecurity and the Political Attitudes of Cuban Workers," *American Sociological Review,* Vol. 31, February 1966, pp. 35–52.

[68] Runciman, *op. cit.,* p. 151.

[69] *Ibid,* p. 4.

[70] *Ibid,* p. 9.

In accordance with this meaning a person who is relatively deprived is not necessarily *objectively deprived,* in the sense of lacking certain things. Thus relative deprivation may be greater or smaller than actual deprivation. In addition, the concept of relative deprivation means that the sense and feeling of deprivation come from a comparison with the perceived situation of another person or group, which is the reference group. [71] Poverty does not in itself necessarily lead to relative deprivation. As Durkheim noted long ago, what is needed for men to be content with their lot ". . . is not that they have more or less, but that they be convinced that they have no right to more." [72] And although it is true that today in societies that are no longer traditional men tend not to be satisfied with their lot, Runciman observes that only rarely are egalitarian resentments as militant or widespread as the actual structure of inequalities would suggest to be plausible. On the basis of his more systematic examination of historical materials from 1918 to 1962, he comes to a similar conclusion concerning Great Britain during that period. The magnitude and frequency of relative deprivation seldom corresponds to the facts of economic inequality.

In his survey of 1962, Runciman investigated separately the feelings of deprivation in regard to economic inequality and status or prestige inequality. His historical investigation led him to the hypothesis that the relation between inequality and relative deprivation in each of these two dimensions would be different. The survey data confirmed it: There is a difference between attitudes toward economic and status inequality of the kind that the historical discussion suggested. Working-class people are less likely to feel relatively deprived in respect to income than middle-class people who are earning the same. (The author uses the term working class as synonymous with manual occupations and middle class with nonmanual occupations.) The class in which people place themselves—which Centers called self-identification and which Runciman calls self-rated class—does not seem to have any significant effect on such attitudes. But it does correlate independently with attitudes toward inequalities of status. Manual workers who placed themselves in the middle class showed greater relative deprivation in status than those who designated themselves as working class. These differences, as well as others, are explained by the author in terms of reference group theory.

In the conclusion to our selection, Runciman explains that he is turning in the final section of the book to the problem of how far the relative deprivation which the English people were feeling in 1962 could be vindicated by the appeal to social justice. He considered this problem an integral part of the task he undertook in his book. In the final part of his book he poses then the nonsociological question: "Which, if any of these inequalities ought to be perceived and resented—whether they are or not—by the standards of social justice." [73] We know that, to paraphrase Pareto, the subject of sociology is what *is,* not what *ought* to be. The book is concerned with both of these questions and no wonder therefore, that its author described it as a work at once of sociology and political philosophy. [74]

Although Runciman's concern with the social justice of inequalities is nonsociological, the problem of social justice and inequality can be approached

[71] The concept of reference group was first coined by Herbert H. Hyman. See his "The Psychology of Status," *Archives of Psychology,* Vol. 38, 1942, pp. 5–94.

[72] As quoted in Runciman, *op. cit.,* p. 25.

[73] Runciman, *op. cit.,* pp. 3–4.

[74] *Ibid,* p. 5.

sociologically, as demonstrated in the article by Stefan Nowak.[75] The author investigated whether in socialist Poland people perceive as just the social inequalities that exist. From this alone we can gather the originally of the article, for it is a subject to which sociologists have not been paying much attention.

It is also original because the subjective aspect of class has hitherto been unexplored *in* Poland, let alone *in* other Soviet-type societies. We only have some indirect knowledge about subjective awareness of class in the Soviet Union, such as from the earlier study conducted by Harvard University's Russian Research Center among Russian refugees at the end of World War II. That study showed that many respondents, irrespective of class, saw the interests of workers and peasants as opposed to that of the intelligentsia—the professional, managerial, and white-collar strata.[76] Of course, such indirect findings have to be approached with some caution, because the refugees differed in many ways from those who stayed behind.[77]

Stefan Nowak's article is based on a survey conducted *in* Poland in 1961 (comparable in recency to Runciman's study). The author begins the analysis of his data with the answers to the question of how respondents thought their social position ranked as compared with that of other people in Poland.

In looking at the distribution of answers that the author arranged along a seven-point scale ranging from very high to very low, it is especially interesting to note that in this socialist society only 6 per cent of the respondents were "unable" to answer how they ranked in their society. In Poland, where the official ideology maintains and insists that the workers are in power, more than half of the unskilled workers and almost one-third of the skilled workers feel relatively deprived as compared with 7 per cent of the professionals—categorized in Poland as "creative intelligentsia and free professions." (Nowak suggests that those who answered that they compared low or very low could be considered as expressing the feeling of deprivation.) Or take those who considered their position above average in this "workers' land": only 6 to 7 per cent of the workers, but half of the professionals did so.

Consistent with the above, are also the findings concerning the subjective aspect of social mobility. The higher the occupational group, the greater the proportion of those who consider themselves to have advanced to a higher position than that of their fathers. Still this might be a biased reading of the article, as well as of the Polish reality, if we fail to note the ingenious refinement in Nowak's analysis of the perception of self-advancement. He examined in turn the answers of those individuals who remained in their father's occupational category to discover how they evaluated their position in comparison with that of their fathers. The fact that a sizable proportion of workers whose fathers were workers see their position as higher than that of their fathers, Nowak interprets to mean that they thus ". . . express indirectly the conviction that the over-all position of the working class in the social structure has improved." Of course, one could easily inject a

[75] Another Polish sociologist who addresses himself to social justice and inequality is Adam Sarapata, "The *Iustum Premium* as a Criterion of Social Stratification," paper presented at the Sixth World Congress of Sociology, Evian, France, September, 1966.

[76] Alex Inkeles and Raymond Bauer, *The Soviet Citizen,* Cambridge, Mass.: Harvard University Press, 1959. The generalization here is based on the respondents' answers to the following question: "Below is given a paired list of classes in Soviet society. We would like to know for each of these pairs . . . do their interests coincide with or contradict each other? Check the condition you think correct for each group." See Tables 85 and 89.

[77] However, the authors of the study present evidence to support their contention that these difference were not extreme. See *ibid,* pp. 7–10 and 25–40.

note of doubt into this interpretation. It blurs the distinction between two areas that must be clearly distinguished from one another: first, an over-all improvement in the position of the working class and, second, an improvement in the position of individuals *within* the working class. The answers of the Polish workers could reflect the objective fact that they have *individually* advanced as compared with their fathers. Because Poland is becoming more industrialized, it is quite possible that many of these individuals have experienced upward mobility, although they have not moved out of the paternal occupational category. After all, skilled and even unskilled occupations have their own internal hierarchy. What we are suggesting is that, in contrast to Nowak's contention, the answers of those who said that they have advanced as compared with their fathers may reflect their perception of their own individual advancement, rather than the advancement of their class.

But let us turn to the important problem—with which we began this discussion of Nowak's article—of how people perceive the social inequalities existing in Poland. Again, a smaller proportion of manual workers than those in nonmanual occupations answered that the differences have diminished. (See Table 9T.) As a matter of fact, if we dichotomize the answers (Nowak does not) into those who think that social distinctions have diminished and those who do not think so, there is almost an even split among unskilled workers: 51.5 and 48.5 per cent, respectively. Still, it must not be omitted that a majority in each occupational category thought today's differences to be smaller than the prewar ones. Nevertheless, as the author states and demonstrates, the prevailing structure is ". . . regarded as marked by a fairly strong system of differentiation." The factor (among the ten enumerated in the questionnaire) on which there is most agreement as being the source of division and animosity in Poland is income and wealth inequality. (Over 80 per cent thought that it divides, and over 70 per cent that it is the cause of animosity.) But of all the ten factors, the smallest percentage pointed to differences in social origin, 21 and 17 per cent, respectively. I think the latter is especially noteworthy, because prewar Poland was marked by its aristocratic tradition.[78]

The author deepens the analysis by investigating the relationship between the perception of social animosity and the respondents objective social position. He shows that the higher the position the greater the chance that the respondent will perceive the structure as a *nonconflicting* one. Furthermore, the higher the position the more likely that he will see social animosity coming from the lower levels of society. In reverse, the lower the objective position the greater the tendency to see the animosity coming from the top levels.

We finally come to the crucial question of preferences concerning the continuation of social differences in Poland. Strikingly, over 80 per cent of all the respondents wanted to see an increase in equality, with almost half of the total sample coming out for the complete disappearance of social inequality. However, the proposition expressing the latter extreme equalitarian attitude had the smallest endorsement in the highest occupational group, the professionals.

It would be most interesting, especially in light of the Ossowski thesis, if we had comparable data from those Western-type societies marked by equalitarian ideologies, such as the United States or Australia. I cannot help but doubt that half of the population in such societies would express a desire for the complete

[78] Alexander Hertz, "The Case of an East European Intelligentsia," *Journal of Central European Affairs,* 1951, pp. 10–26; Jan Szczepanski, *Les Classes Sociales de la Société Polonaise Contemporaine, Cahiers Internationaux de Sociologie,* 1963, pp. 205–211.

disappearance of social inequality. But even if studies demonstrated that more people in Soviet-type societies than in Western societies wanted the complete disappearance of social inequality, we still could not conclude from it that the impact of socialist ideology on equalitarian attitudes is stronger. We must not forget that the Communist ideology posits a communist stage in the far-off future completely devoid of social inequality. In answering the question the way they did, the Polish respondents may have simply given back to the investigators that ideological line. One would have to ask two questions, one about the near future and one about the far-off future, to interpret with more confidence the answers on the preferences of the Polish people concerning the continuation of social inequalities.

## INDEXES OF STRATIFICATION

Because the study of the subjective dimensions of class revolves around the queries whether, to what extent, and how subjective awareness or class consciousness varies with the objective position in the stratification system, it is most important to consider briefly in this introduction the methodological problem of indicators of objective position. In scientific study we seek an indicator that, in addition to being valid, is (1) standardized—capable of application in exactly the same way to all the things it is supposed to indicate or measure; (2) reliable—giving the same results no matter who uses it; and (3) preferably scalar—that it permit determination of different amounts or degrees of the given phenomenon for which it stands; (4) economical—giving maximum results with a minimum expenditure of time and effort. An indicator that has such characteristics is usually referred to as an *index*.[79]

Now many investigators of various aspects of American stratification have devised indexes of socioeconomic position that proved useful for their researches. A study of nineteen such major indexes found a high intercorrelation among these "standard measurement tools."[80] The relatively high correlations among the variables in these indexes suggested that they all may be measuring the same factor with varying accuracy. To test this Kahl and Davis, the authors of the above study, used the statistical technique of factor analysis. They discovered that the indexes were highly correlated, because they all measured, but in differing degrees, the same underlying dimension.

Because this underlying dimension was related to occupation, it may be well to add here that in contemporary industrial society when a single-item index is used it is most often occupation. And even though a single item-index may suffer in accuracy, it has the advantages of being easier to standardize, make reliable, scale, and use economically. An occupational index has the additional advantage in that it is relatively easy to ascertain a person's occupation, although his salary or the cost of his house may be harder to obtain.

To conclude this introduction to the readings on major dimensions of stratification, it should be said that even though the intercorrelation between them is considerable it is far from perfect. There is a certain amount of overlapping among them. Both because of the complexity of modern stratification and the discrepancies in positions along one or another dimension, the readings are arranged separately for each dimension.

[79] For a thorough treatment of indices, see "Indices of Social Class Position," in Barber, *op. cit.*, pp. 168–185.

[80] Joseph A. Kahl and James A. Davis, "A Comparison of Indexes of Socio-Economic Status," *American Sociological Review*, Vol. 20, June, 1955, pp. 317–325.

# Objective Dimensions
## Economic Inequality

## WHAT'S HAPPENING TO OUR INCOME REVOLUTION?

*Herman P. Miller*

A myth has been created in the United States that incomes are gradually becoming more evenly distributed. This view is held by prominent economists of both major political parties. It is also shared by the editors of the influential mass media.

Arthur F. Burns, chief economist for the Eisenhower Administration, stated in 1951 that "the transformation in the distribution of our national income . . . may already be counted as one of the great social revolutions of history." Paul Samuelson, one of President Kennedy's leading economic advisers, stated in 1961 that "the American income pyramid is becoming less unequal. . . ."

In the preceding chapter, several basic facts were presented regarding trends in the inequality of income distribution in the United States. It was shown that there has been no appreciable change in income shares for nearly twenty years. This question will now be examined a little more intensively.

Despite the existence of much poverty in the United States, there is general agreement that real levels of living are much higher than they were only ten years ago and that the prospects for future increases are very good.[1] If $3,000 in 1962 dollars is used as

**TABLE 1 Distribution of Families and Incomes by Income (in 1962 dollars) 1929, 1947, and 1962**

| *Income Level* | 1929 | 1947 | 1962 |
|---|---|---|---|
| Under $3,000 | 51% | 30% | 21% |
| Between $3,000 and $6,000 | 34 | 40 | 31 |
| Between $6,000 and $8,000 | 7 | 14 | 18 |
| Between $8,000 and $10,000 | 3 | 7 | 11 |
| $10,000 and over | 5 | 9 | 19 |

Jeanette M. Fitzwilliams, "Size Distribution of Income in 1962," *Survey of Current Business,* April, 1963, Table 3. Figures for the under $3,000 group are based on unpublished data.

the poverty line, it can be noted that thirty years ago about half of the families and individuals lived at levels that would be regarded as substandard today. This number may be somewhat overstated because of the inclusion of unrelated individuals, but it is not grossly out of line. Of course even today there are large numbers trying to get by on very little, but the proportion at this low level has been more than cut in half. In 1962 only about one-fifth of the families and individuals had incomes under $3,000.

The figures at the other end of the income scale show why ours is called an affluent society. In 1962 about one family out of every five had an income over $10,000. In many cases this high an income is achieved only because the wife and the husband are both out working; but the income is there nonetheless and it is available for air conditioners, dishwashers, second cars, and prestige schools. Thirty years ago an income over $10,000 (in 1962 terms; much less as dollars were counted then) was achieved by only one family out of twenty.[2] Since conditions are improving you may wonder why it is important to consider the gap between the rich and the poor. Isn't it enough that the *amount* of income received by the poor has gone up substantially? Why be concerned about their share? Many who

 The chapter of the book from which most of the pages are taken is entitled, "What's Happening to Our Social Revolution?"

[1] We are here inserting the table, figures, and text from the preceding chapter to support this point (C. S. H.).

[2] We are now returning to the text of the chapter. (C. S. H.)

have thought about this problem seriously regard the *share* as the critical factor. When Karl Marx, for example, spoke about the inevitability of increasing misery among workers under capitalism he had a very special definition of misery in mind. Sumner Slichter, in summarizing the Marxian position on this point, states: " . . . Marx conceded that real wages *might* rise, but not the relative share of labor. Even if real wages rose, misery would grow, according to Marx, since workers would be worse off relative to capitalists. . . ."

In other words "needs" stem not so much from what we lack as from what our neighbors have. Veblen called this trait our "pecuniary standard of living" and modern economists refer to it as the "relative income hypothesis," but it all comes back to the same thing. Except for those rare souls who have hitched their wagons to thoughts rather than things, there is no end to "needs." So long as there are people who have more, others will "need" more. If this is indeed the basis for human behavior, then obviously the gap between the rich and the poor cannot be ignored, however high the *minimum* levels of living may be raised.

. . . . . . . . . . . . . . . . . . . . . . . . . . . . . . . . .

Most opinions regarding changes in inequality, including those held by professional economists, are based on statistical measures of income rather than on philosophical concepts. With all their limitations, the income figures may well serve as a first approximation of changes in welfare.[3]

During the depression of the thirties there was a distinct drop in the share of the income received by the upper income groups. In 1929, the last year of the prosperous twenties, the top 5 percent of the families and individuals received nearly one-third of the income. Their share dropped during the depression and amounted to about one-fourth of the income at the outbreak of World War II. During the war years there was a further decline and their share dropped to 21 percent in 1944. Since that time there has been no significant change in the percent of income received by the wealthiest group. The stability of income distribution during the past twenty years is a matter of some concern that has been generally overlooked by students in the field.

. . . The trend described for the top twentieth applies to the top fifth as well. But now let's look at the bottom groups. In 1935, the poorest fifth of the families and individuals received only 4 percent of the income. Their share rose to 5 percent in 1944 and has remained at that level ever since. The stability since 1944 of the shares received by each of the other quintiles is equally striking.[4] These figures show that the share of income received by the lower income groups has not changed for twenty years. Let us look at some other evidence that supports this view and then examine the implications of the findings.

[3] We are inserting the figures and explanatory text from the preceding chapter. (C. S. H.)

[4] We are now returning to the text of the chapter. (C. S. H.)

**TABLE 2 Percent of Income Received by Each Fifth of Families and Individuals and by Top 5%**

| *Families and individuals ranked from lowest to highest* | 1959 | 1935 | 1941 | 1944 | 1961 |
|---|---|---|---|---|---|
| Lowest fifth | 13% (lowest and second fifths combined) | 4% | 4% | 5% | 5% |
| Second fifth | | 9 | 10 | 11 | 11 |
| Middle fifth | 14 | 14 | 15 | 16 | 16 |
| Fourth fifth | 19 | 21 | 22 | 22 | 23 |
| Highest fifth | 54 | 52 | 49 | 46 | 45 |
| Top 5% | 30 | 27 | 24 | 21 | 20 |

U.S. Bureau of the Census, *Historical Statistics of the United States, Colonial Times to 1957*, p. 166, and Jeanette M. Fitzwilliams; see Table III-2.

## WHITE-NONWHITE INCOME DIFFERENTIALS ARE NOT NARROWING

The narrowing of income differentials between whites and nonwhites (92 percent of whom are Negroes) is sometimes cited as evidence of a trend toward equalization. . . .

The income gap between whites and nonwhites did narrow during World War II. During the last decade, however, it shows some evidence of having widened again (see Table 3 . . .). The census statistics demonstrate this dismaying fact.

In 1947, the median wage or salary income for nonwhite workers was 54 percent of that received by the whites. In 1962, the ratio was almost identical (55 percent). Prior to 1947 there was a substantial reduction in the earnings gap between whites and nonwhites. In view of the stability of the earnings gap during the postwar period, however, the reduction during the war years cannot be viewed as part of a continuing process, but rather as a phenomenon closely related to war-induced shortages of unskilled labor and government regulations such as those of the War Labor Board designed generally to raise the incomes of lower paid workers, and to an economy operating at full tilt.

**TABLE 3 The Income Gap: White vs. Nonwhite Male Workers Aged 14 and Over, in 1939, and 1947 to 1962[5]**

| *Year* | *White* | *Nonwhite* | *Nonwhite as percent of white* |
|---|---|---|---|
| All persons with wage or salary income: | | | |
| 1939 | $1,112 | $ 460 | 41% |
| 1947 | 2,357 | 1,279 | 54 |
| 1948 | 2,711 | 1,615 | 60 |
| 1949 | 2,735 | 1,367 | 50 |
| 1950 | 2,982 | 1,828 | 61 |
| 1951 | 3,345 | 2,060 | 62 |
| 1952 | 3,507 | 2,038 | 58 |
| 1953 | 3,760 | 2,233 | 59 |
| 1954 | 3,754 | 2,131 | 57 |
| 1955 | 3,986 | 2,342 | 59 |
| 1956 | 4,260 | 2,396 | 56 |
| 1957 | 4,396 | 2,436 | 55 |
| 1958 | 4,596 | 2,652 | 58 |
| 1959 | 4,902 | 2,844 | 58 |
| 1960 | 5,137 | 3,075 | 60 |
| 1961 | 5,287 | 3,015 | 57 |
| 1962 | 5,462 | 3,023 | 55 |

[5] These figures, as well as others throughout the selections, are expressed in terms of constant purchasing power so that the effects of inflation are eliminated. (C. S. H.)

This conclusion is reinforced by details of the 1960 census which show that in the twenty-six states (including the District of Columbia) which have 100,000 or more Negroes, the ratio of Negro to white income for sales increased between 1949 and 1959 in two states (District of Columbia and Florida) and it was unchanged in two others (New Jersey and Oklahoma). In every other state there was a widening of the gap between the incomes of whites and Negroes and in some cases it was fairly substantial.

## OCCUPATIONAL DIFFERENTIALS IN EARNINGS ARE NOT NARROWING

One of the most widely and strongly held misconceptions about income concerns the narrowing of the difference in earnings between skilled and unskilled workers. The prevailing view holds that the decrease in the earnings gap between the skilled and the unskilled in the United States is part of a historical process that has been going on since the turn of the century. The Department of Labor reports that in 1907 the median earnings of skilled workers in manufacturing industries was about twice that received by unskilled workers. By the end of World War I, it was only 75 percent greater, and by the end of World War II only 55 percent greater. Thus, during a forty-year period, this income gap was reduced by about 50 percent, an average of about 1 percent per year.

Recent trends in income differentials between skilled and unskilled workers are shown in Table 4. These figures represent the median wages and salaries received during the year in the major occupation groups for men. Women are excluded because their earnings are highly influenced by the fact that a large proportion of them work intermittently rather than full time.

There was not too much variation among occupation groups in the rate of income growth during the entire twenty-two-year period. The average income for most of the

**TABLE 4 Men's Income by Occupation: Percent Change**

| *Year* | *Professional and Managerial Workers* | *Craftsmen* | *Semiskilled Factory Workers* | *Service Workers and Nonfarm Laborers* |
|---|---|---|---|---|
| 1939–61 | 243% | 322% | 331% | 314% |
| 1939–50 | 96 | 160 | 172 | 180 |
| 1950–61 | 75 | 62 | 59 | 48 |

U.S. Bureau of the Census, *Current Population Reports—Consumer Income,* Series P-60, Nos. 9 and 39 (for Table 4).

occupations quadrupled. But an examination of the growth rate for two different periods, 1939–50, and 1950–61, reveals striking differences.

During the decade that included World War II, the lower paid occupations made the greatest relative gains in average income. Thus, laborers and service workers (waiters, barbers, janitors, and the like), two of the lowest paid groups among nonfarm workers, had increases of about 180 percent. The gains for craftsmen, who are somewhat higher paid, was 160 percent; professional and managerial workers, the highest paid workers of all, had the lowest relative gains —96 percent.

During the past decade the picture has been reversed. Laborers and service workers made the smallest relative gains, 48 percent; craftsmen had increases of 62 percent, and the professional and managerial workers had the greatest gains of all, 75 percent. The narrowing of the income gap between the skilled and the unskilled, the high-paid and the low-paid workers, which was evident up to and including the war years, has stopped during the past decade and the trend seems to be moving in the opposite direction.

The above figures are national averages in which all industries and regions are combined. They are very useful for identifying major trends, but they can also be very misleading because they average together so many different things. It is important to examine the figures for a particular industry in a particular region to get a better understanding of the underlying trends. The primary and fabricated metals industries have been selected for this purpose. The same analysis was also made for about ten other major American industries and the results are generally the same as those presented below.

About 2,200,000 men were engaged in the production of metals or the fabrication of metal products in 1960. This employment was about equally divided between production and fabrication

. . . . . . . . . . . . . . . . . . . . . . . . . . . . . . . . .

An examination of employment in this industry shows that the total number of workers increased by 24 percent between 1950 and 1960. Professional, managerial, and other white-collar workers increased 62 percent; skilled and semiskilled production workers increased by about 20 percent, but unskilled laborers decreased 9 percent. Thus, despite the general rise in employment and output in this industry, there was a drop in the demand for unskilled labor.

In view of these changes in the demand for labor in this industry, what happened to earnings? . . . In all states except Ohio and California, unskilled workers in this industry made greater relative gains than the semiskilled between 1939–49. Similar figures are not available for the higher paid "other" workers for 1939. Thus there was a tendency toward a narrowing of earnings differentials in this industry between 1939–49. But, during the decade 1949–59, the reverse was true. In every state there was a widening of differentials, with the highest paid "other" workers making the greatest relative gains, followed by the semiskilled workers and then the unskilled. . . .

## WHERE DO WE GO FROM HERE?

There was a time, not too long ago, when economists did not look for changes in income distribution because they did not expect to find any. Indeed, the stability of the income curve was so striking that it was given a name, Pareto's Law, in honor of the economist[6] who conducted some of the earliest statistical inquiries in this field.

Pareto believed that the distribution of income is fixed and that regardless of changes in economic conditions, short of a revolutionary change from a competitive to a collectivist society, the distribution of income is the same in all places and at all times.

Statistical studies in recent years have so thoroughly demolished Pareto's notions that we have now come to look for change where no change exists. The facts show that our "social revolution" ended nearly twenty years ago; yet important segments of the American public, many of them highly placed government officials and prominent educators, think and act as though it were a continuing process. Intelligent public policy demands that things be seen as they are, not as they were.

The stability of income distribution, particularly during the fifties, could be related to the fact that the decade was dominated by a political philosophy committed to stability rather than change. In a different climate income differentials might narrow further. This could be accomplished through legislation designed to raise the levels of living of the poor: expansion of unemployment insurance benefits, federal aid to dependent children of the unemployed, liberalization of social security benefits, increase in the minimum wage and extension of its coverage, federal aid under the Area Redevelopment Act to revitalize the economies of areas with large and persistent unemployment.

In opposition to political factors that seem to favor equalization, there are some very stubborn economic factors that seem to be headed in quite the other direction. For many years now unskilled workers have been a declining part of the American labor force. This fact has been documented over and over again. Between 1940 and 1950 and again between 1950 and 1960 only one nonfarm occupation group for men—laborers—declined in number at a time when all other groups were increasing. Their income changed erratically. Laborers had the greatest relative income gains during the forties and the smallest relative gains during the fifties. This could mean that unskilled labor was in very short supply during World War II, with millions of young men away in the armed forces and the economy working at full steam. This pressure, with a little help from the government, forced wage rates up more for unskilled workers than for other workers. Since the fifties, on the other hand, there is evidence that the supply of unskilled labor has far exceeded the demand. As a result the unskilled are finding it increasingly difficult to locate jobs and many who are employed live in constant fear of being replaced by machines. Moreover, the overabundance of these workers has prevented their wages from keeping pace with the others; thus the gap between the earnings of skilled and unskilled has widened.

The American economy has been plagued by relatively high unemployment since late 1957. According to the Joint Economic Committee, which has studied this problem in some detail, it is still premature to attribute this unemployment to the technological changes that are rapidly reshaping the economy. However, there can be no doubt that many thousands of unskilled workers in farming, manufacturing, mining, and railroads have been permanently displaced by machines and that this trend will continue. The labor-union leaders who represent these workers certainly tend to view the problem in this light. Even if they do not qualify as impartial observers, they know how these economic developments are interpreted at the grass-roots level. The leader of the Transport Workers Union of America, Michael Quill, is one among many who have spoken out sharply. His words carry a defiant ring that has been virtually absent from the American scene for over twenty years. He stated: "Unless something is done to put people to work despite automation, they may get rough in this country and this country may have a real upheaval, a real turmoil." The increase in racial tension and juvenile delinquency during

[6] Vilfredo Pareto, claimed by economists as well as sociologists. (C. S. H.)

the past few years may be early manifestations of trouble to come.

Labor-union leaders are not the only ones who have shown a keen awareness of both the bogey and the boon of automation. Many who have given the matter serious thought find it conceivable that, in the absence of remedial action, this nation may soon be faced with an increase in the disparity of incomes. We may then discover that our "social revolution" has not only been marking time for nearly twenty years, but that it is beginning to move backward. Justice William O. Douglas has spoken out eloquently on this subject in the pamphlet *Freedom of the Mind:* "We have a surplus of everything—including unemployed people; and the hundreds of unemployed and unemployable will increase if technology continues to be our master. We have a surplus of food and millions of hungry people at home as well as abroad. When the machine displaces man and does most of the work, who will own the machines and receive the rich dividends? Are we on the threshold of re-entering the world of feudalism which Europe left in the 15th and 16th centuries and which is fastened on much of the Middle East today?"

# CHALLENGE TO AFFLUENCE—THE EMERGENCE OF AN "UNDER-CLASS"[1]

*Gunnar Myrdal*

The facts about unemployment and its immediate causes are well known in America due to its excellent statistical reporting. . . . Less often observed and commented upon is the tendency of the changes under way to trap an "under-class"[1] of unemployed and, gradually, unemployable and underemployed persons and families at the bottom of a society, while for the majority of people above that layer the increasingly democratic structure of the educational system creates ever more real liberty and equality of opportunity, at least over the course of two generations.

The American self-image was, and is, that of a free and open society where anyone who is of a sound body and soul and has the drive can find work, at least when business is on the upturn, and where he can climb to the highest and most rewarding positions. It was this image, and the considerable degree of reality that actually corresponded to it, that induced millions of poor people in Europe to seek their opportunity in America right up to the First World War.

Reality never agreed entirely with that image. And over the last few generations a process has been under way that, while it opened more opportunities to more people, also closed ever more opportunities to some. Now in the end it threatens to split off a true "under-class" that is not really an integrated part of the nation but a useless and miserable substratum.

To start at the heights, the "self-made man" with great wealth and a supreme command over men and productive resources has been disappearing in America ever since the time when college education became so common that a man without a degree could hardly advance in business. Business itself has tended to become increasingly large-scale and highly organized. . . .

We have to remind ourselves, however, that to a considerable extent this American image was always something of a myth. Even leaving out the highest social and economic positions that have now been closed up to those starting without higher education, the opportunity to rise in society, or even to maintain a decent and respectable level of living and to participate in the nation's general culture and the solution of its problems, was not always that open in the old days. Great masses of people had no



[1] The word "under-class" does not seem to be used in English. . . . Nevertheless, the term will be used in this book as the only one adequate to the social reality discussed.

possibility of sharing in the American image of liberty and opportunity of rising economically and socially. This applied to the cotton farming Negro tenants in the South, the white hillbillies not far south of Washington, D.C., and similar groups of poor whites elsewhere in the country, the migrant workers on the big California farms, and to the workers in the sweatshops in the cities. Moreover, partly overlapping with the last category, there were the new immigrants in the city slums, handicapped in many ways, who often suffered miserable hardships before they came into their own.

Finally, in the periodic slowdowns in business activity a large number even of well integrated workers found themselves unemployed and without an income. The series of such reverses culminated in the Great Depression when up to 20 percent or more of the labor force was unemployed.

Abject destitution for millions of people is thus nothing new in America. The trend has definitely been to decrease the number suffering from it or even running a major risk of it. Major causes of this have been the rising productivity of the American economy and also the facts that educational facilities have been vastly improved and that good schools and college education have been placed at the disposal of an ever increasing portion of the people, earlier and more generously than in any other Western country.

## THE NEW THREAT

Nevertheless, there is something threatening in the very recent changes and in the trend for the foreseeable future. The displacement of unskilled and even of much skilled labor has a definiteness that must compel us to stop and think. To take advantage of the expansion of demand for highly educated and trained labor, which is occurring and would do so even more rapidly if the growth rate of the economy were higher, would require such education and training of the displaced that he simply cannot think of jumping the gap, no matter how alert and enterprising he is. He needs to be helped to do it by society or he will not be able to do it at all.

What is happening is similar to the disappearance more than half a century ago of the "self-made man" from the highest positions as a result of the widening of college education and training for leadership in business as it increasingly became large-scale, organized, and stratified. This process has continued steadily downwards, first to middle positions and then to ever lower strata of employees in industry and commerce, until it is now beginning to make unskilled and many skilled workers redundant.

This is a new threat. For when the process has proceeded that far, without a parallel change for educating and training the *whole* labor force to correspond to the new demands, there is no longer any vast space left beneath for economic advance and social mobility as when the self-made man at the top disappeared. Those not needed are true "outcasts." They simply become unemployed, and indeed largely unemployable, or underemployed. It is almost as difficult for them to get and hold a good job as it long ago became to start as a shoeshine boy and end as the president of a big corporation.

This emergence of an American "underclass" of unemployed and largely unemployable and underemployed occurs at a time when almost the last batches of immigrants from Southern and Eastern Europe and their descendants have finally become integrated in the American nation. It happens when those educated and trained to fit the new direction of labor demand are experiencing a brisk demand for their work, and when the general levels of living of the majority of well employed Americans—and thereby the general conception spread by the mass-communication industry of what the American way of life is like—have risen high above what a few generations ago were considered comfortable standards. In society at large there is more equality of opportunity today than there ever was. But for the bottom layer there is less or none.

The disappearance of the self-made man was a slight change in society compared to that now under way, closing all good jobs and soon almost all jobs worth having in affluent America to those who have happened to be born in regions, localities, or economic and social strata where education and training for life and work in this new America are not provided as a normal thing. For the larger part of America there is social and economic mobility through the educational system. Beneath that level a line is drawn to an "under-class." That class line becomes demarcated almost as a caste line, since the children in this class tend to become as poorly endowed as their parents.

In a situation of high and rising unemployment even the trade unions often, unwillingly, become instrumental in hardening the line which excludes that substratum of workers from opportunities of getting jobs. The process of automation is particularly extensive in sectors of the American economy in which there are effective trade unions. These unions are thus forced to press for job security for their own members even when this creates incentives for the employers not to engage new workers. In a situation of high unemployment the unions also often feel their bargaining strength weakened and find it difficult to dissipate too much of it by taking a consistent and strong stand for what is the main interest from all the workers' point of view, full employment. . . . To an observer it seems almost a miracle that big units of the movement, particularly the industrial unions in the C.I.O. wing, have found it possible to take such broadminded and progressive positions on national economic issues as they actually have.

The fact that the substratum is not very articulate in America and is, therefore, not much noticed by the ordinary, well educated Americans who are busily and happily enjoying both their work and their leisure, does not detract from the gravity of this development. On the contrary, it is fatal for democracy, and not only demoralizing for the individual members of this under-class that they are so mute and without initiative and that they are not becoming organized to fight for their interests. For its own health and even preservation an effective, full-fledged democracy needs movements of protest on the part of the underprivileged.

## THE CURSE OF UNEMPLOYMENT

. . . It is discouraging but probably realistic when the Kennedy administration has redefined tolerable unemployment to be as high as 4 per cent, apparently not reckoning part-time unemployment and underemployment at low productivity levels.

There is even a probability that the level of unemployment may be higher still when a boom has to be broken, ultimately, because of the scarcity of educated and trained workers, if for no other reason. This will leave a hard core of unemployment that is uncomfortably high.

Unemployment is a damaging way of life. It is particularly damaging for the young in the nation, and even more particularly when their educational and cultural level is low. Crime, prostitution, and all sorts of shady ways of passing time will thrive as they did in the slums during the depression years in the thirties and as they increasingly begin to do today.

The well meaning proposals, put forward by progressive writers, for paying greatly increased unemployment benefits or sometimes even full wages without time limit to those who have been thrown out of work through no fault of their own, have, of course, little chance of being accepted by Congress. But apart from their lack of political realism, such proposals underestimate how unhealthy and destructive it is for anybody and particularly for young people without much share in the national culture to go idle and live more permanently on doles—this tenet of old fashioned Puritanism, I believe, is also fully borne out by recent social research. Work is not only, and not even mainly, a "disutility" as conceived by the classical economist. It is, if not always a pleasure, the basis for self-respect and a dignified life. There is no real cure for unemployment except employment, which does not mean, of course, that it is not important to make it possible for people to live when they have become unemployed.

## A VICIOUS CIRCLE

The essential question when probing into the social impact of the formation of this under-class is the character of the selective process which determines whether a man comes above or beneath the dividing line. The selection operates on the criterion of education and training. When old people have failed, and young people are now failing, to get an education up to levels which correspond to national standards and the direction of the demand for labor, the explanation is usually that they have been living in an environment of poverty and squalor.

It has become customary to describe the situation in underdeveloped countries as one of a vicious circle where "poverty perpetuates itself." But the same vicious circle operates in an underprivileged class in the richest country. . . .[2]

They will become disheartened and apathetic. As parents they will not be able to pay toward such support of the education of their children that would be needed. Instead, they will have an incentive to take them out of school early if any employment, even at low wages and promising no secure future, offers itself. The home environment of the unemployed and poor will generally be less conductive for children and youth to become educated and trained for good jobs.

The unemployed will be forced to live in the slums or, more probably, they will always have lived in the slums. Whatever the regulations are, the schools will be bad in the slums as they will be in the districts where the backwoods farmer lives. And the whole way of life in the crowded slum quarters in the cities or the rural slum districts will be destructive for the will and ability to advance in life.

A remarkable tendency in America has been that parallel and prior to the rise in unemployment the efforts of slum clearance in the cities have mainly benefited the middle third of the nation who could afford to pay the rents in the new houses which only to a small extent have really been "low-cost housing." Those made homeless have been pressed into other already crowded slum districts or into districts which in this process of change became slum districts.

This perverted tendency in American housing policy has its parallel in almost all other social policies. Various social security schemes as well as to an extent the minimum wage regulations happen to stop just above the very neediest groups of people. The voluntary health insurance schemes are much too expensive for the poorest who show the highest incidence of illness and ill health, both mental and bodily. In the same way agricultural policy has mainly aided the big and progressive farmers and has done little if anything for small farmers, small tenants, and agricultural workers. It is true that most of them should be moved out of agriculture, but little is done to speed the process, to prepare them not to end up unemployed or underemployed in the slums.

There is a political factor in this vicious circle of circular causation leading to a cumulative process. The poor in America are unorganized and largely mute. They exert no pressure corresponding to their numbers and to the severity of their plight. They are the least revolutionary proletariat in the world. As the studies of registration and election participation show, they are largely responsible for the comparatively low percentage of voters in America, and this not only in the South where the Negroes are still largely kept from voting even if they wanted to, but in the rest of the country, as well.

As they represent the big unutilized reserve of potential voters, the platforms of both Democrats and Republicans worked out before every election will regularly seem to imply a radical departure from policies pursued up till then—though most often couched in general and noncommittal terms. When the elections are over, however, and many of the poor are seen to have still stayed away from the polls, actual policies return to the routine of not doing much for them.

## THE MINORITY GROUPS

Much of the rising unemployment falls upon minority groups and implies a serious setback in the process of national integration. The largest and still most handicapped minority group in America is that of the Negroes.

From about the beginning of the last war there has been a definite trend toward

[2] For an early statement of the theory of circular causation resulting in a cumulative process and of its application to an underprivileged category of people in a rich country, see *An American Dilemma* (New York, Harper, 1944), Chapter 3, Section 7, "The Theory of the Vicious Circle," pp. 78 ff., and Appendix 3, "A Methodological Note on the Principle of Cumulation," pp. 1035 ff.

improved race relations in America, a development which is the more remarkable as for sixty years up till that time there had been no great change in the status of the Negroes in America. A very important cause among others of this encouraging trend was undoubtedly the rising level of labor demand from the beginning of the war and after the Great Depression. An increasing number of Negroes were allowed to acquire skills, join trade unions, and get seniority and job protection in new fields that were opening themselves for Negroes.

But the Negroes are still the "last hired and the first fired." Negro unemployment is presently about three times as high as the average rate, which means that close to a fifth of the Negro workers are unemployed. Apart from a tiny upper and middle class of professionals and business people, mostly thriving behind the remaining walls of prejudice, and now a considerably increased group of skilled and union protected workers, the majority of Negroes are much poorer and have had less education and training than the average white Americans. They are consequently more vulnerable in the present situation where labor demand is, and must be, turning towards those who have been educated and trained.

They are also directly discriminated against, legally and illegally, when seeking a home. Negro slums are getting the more overcrowded and dilapidated for this reason. . . . All other acts of prejudice and discrimination tend to press the Negroes down economically and socially. . . . The reforms are slow to work themselves out in terms of substantial changes in the Negroes' living conditions.

High and rising unemployment among Negroes is, on the one hand, an aggravating cause, in many ways hampering the rise in status of the American Negroes. On the other hand, these inferior living conditions, including inadequate education and training, tend to make it more difficult for Negroes to get and hold the good jobs. The greatest danger threatening the gratifying upward trend in race relations in America stems from this vicious circle, operating in a situation of generally high and rising unemployment. . . .

But to the large number of Negro workers —more than 10 per cent of the labor force— who more than others are hit by unemployment when it is high and rising, and to the Puerto Ricans, the Mexicans, and other minority groups affected in the same way, must be added poor white people everywhere in America who will be pressed down, and by the vicious circle held down, in this substratum which is excluded from the prosperity of the nation at large and the progress of the American way of life.

#### POVERTY

The Bureau of the Census, several of the departments in Washington and of the state administrations, university institutions, and other research outfits have in recent years done a commendable job of laying bare the facts of American poverty and of the causal relations behind this poverty. . . .

The summary condensation below of the results of these various studies is derived from *Poverty and Deprivation in the U.S.*, published by the Conference on Economic Progress (Washington, 1962), which has taken them all into consideration and properly accounted for the methods used to arrive at the figures.

If poverty is defined as having to live on an annual income under $4,000 for multiple-person families and $2,000 for unattached individuals, 38 million Americans, or more than one fifth of the nation, were poor in 1960. In deprivation, above poverty but short of the requirements for what in America is now considered a modestly comfortable level of living—from $4,000 to $6,000 for families and from $2,000 to $3,000 for unattached individuals—were more than 39 million people, or again more than one fifth of the nation. Utter destitution, estimated to be the situation of people with less than half of the income representing the poverty line, was the destiny of more than 12½ million Americans, or nearly 7 per cent of the population in the United States.

The proportion of people in these different categories of deprivation, poverty, and destitution has been decreasing since the depression years, first rapidly and then slowly. The slowdown has become particularly marked during the last decade. The proportion of the destitute with incomes under half the level taken to be the poverty line has actually increased a little. . . .

Poverty is greater in the South. It is more than twice as common among the nonwhite population all over the country. More than three times as many nonwhites as whites have less than half of the income taken to demarcate the poverty line.

Poverty is also greater in agriculture. It there afflicts the small farmers, the small tenants, and the hired workers who make up the majority of rural people. About two thirds of the latter group earned less than $1,000 a year.

Much more frequently poverty hits families whose head is female, whether they have lost a husband and father or never had one. People over sixty-five years of age are particularly poor in America. Of those aged sixty-five and having a family, close to two thirds lived in poverty and nearly one third were destitute, according to the definitions given above. Indeed, one tenth of the families had to live on less than $1,000 a year which means utter destitution. The lonely elderly persons were even worse off. Four fifths lived in poverty and nearly half were destitute. The median income of families with heads aged sixty-five and over was under $3,000 and of unattached individuals only a little over $1,000. This age group is now increasing almost twice as fast as ten years ago.

Low income is closely related to the amount of schooling people have had. . . .

More than 40 per cent of the families whose heads were unemployed lived in poverty. They constituted a fourth of the total population living in poverty. The other three fourths had occupations for which we have invented the new term "underemployed" when analyzing the development problems in underdeveloped countries in order to characterize people who have been stuck in localities and jobs on a low level of productivity and, consequently, of earnings.

To the underemployed in this sense belong the larger part of the agricultural population of which the progressive, and prosperous, mainly large-scale farm operators, are a minority. In the cities they have low-paid jobs, often of a casual nature.

### INCREASED INEQUALITY IN THE MIDST OF GENERAL EQUALITY

It is perfectly possible for the majority of Americans to live, together with practically everybody they have primary contact with, in a situation of full and even overfull employment where there is brisk demand and competition for their labor, while they read in the newspapers that there is large and growing unemployment beneath them. That this can be so is the result of the nature of unemployment being to a large extent structural in character.

While this is happening at the bottom of American society it is perfectly possible that there is ever greater social mobility, liberty, and equality of opportunity and a generally rising economic and cultural level in majority America. More and more individuals and families may move further away from the neighborhood of the dividing line. Social welfare policies have, as I pointed out, been framed to give greater security especially for that middle group in the nation. And there might even be some successful passing of the poverty line by individuals coming from beneath it, which then gives a false assurance that America is still the free and open society of its cherished image and well established ideals.

*But as less and less work is required of the type the people in the urban and rural slums can offer, they will be increasingly isolated and exposed to unemployment, to underemployment, and to plain exploitation.* There is an ugly smell rising from the basement of the stately American mansion.

# THE SOVIET INCOME REVOLUTION

*Murray Yanowitch*

A number of studies of income distribution have suggested that income inequality in the

From *Slavic Review*, Vol. XXII, No. 4, December, 1963, pp. 683–697. Reprinted by permission.

United States showed some tendency to decline during the 1930s and the war years. Although the extent and timing of the decline may be in dispute among specialists in this area, and some recent studies suggest that no significant changes in income shares have occurred since 1944, the American Income Revolution has nonetheless been widely accepted and acclaimed.[1] All the more reason, it would seem, that studies of changes in income inequality in Soviet Russia should prove of great interest. If income inequality has been reduced in the world's major capitalist economy, what has been happening to income distribution in the Soviet Union?

Until recently the kind of income data required to answer this question have been unavailable. Some reliance, however, could be placed on official policy statements on wage structure. For almost thirty years, beginning in 1931, every major statement of Soviet wage policy was accompanied by a denunciation of "equalitarianism." Wage-leveling was identified as a petty bourgeois and utopian socialist policy; at times it was linked with even more ominous associations.[2] Since wage structure was centrally controlled, it was logical to assume that a government which was combating equalitarianism was pursuing a policy designed to increase income inequality. Reports of extremely high incomes for individual scientists, literary figures, and composers reinforced this impression.

The anomaly of a self-proclaimed socialist government promoting and extending income inequality while inequality was being reduced in the United States provided an intriguing contrast. Some scholars, apparently uninhibited by the paucity of data, concluded that income inequality in Soviet Russia far exceeded anything existing in the Western world.[3] The fact remains, however, that there was little upon which to base such judgments other than official Soviet statements of wage policy and a scattering of wage and salary rate data.

The situation has changed markedly since 1956 in several important respects. Beginning with the 20th Party Congress in 1956 and culminating with the program adopted by the 22nd Party Congress in 1961, the main emphasis in Soviet wage policy has been placed on a narrowing of the income gap between high- and low-paid personnel. The theme was first enunciated by Mikoyan at the 20th Party Congress;[4] it was implemented at the 21st Congress in 1959, at which time a program of increasing minimum wages from their prevailing level of 27–35 rubles to 50–60 rubles per month by 1965 was announced;[5] and it was reasserted at the 22nd Congress, where it was declared in the program that in the next twenty years "the disparity between high and comparatively low incomes must be steadily reduced."[6]

Since 1956 these policy declarations have been accompanied by the issuance of new wage and salary schedules and by the publication of some earnings data which permit us to establish recent trends in Soviet income structure. Projected changes in the incomes of various groups of the population also make it possible to determine what extremes in Soviet income differentials will look like in the future if the policies enunciated at the last three Party Congresses continue to be implemented.

Our concern here is with the money incomes of those classified as "workers and salaried personnel" (*rabochie i sluzhashchie*). Thus we shall not consider the impact on wage structure of recent income tax changes and the ending of compulsory bond purchases in 1958. The broad effect of the first of these measures, however, seems reasonably clear. The suspension of the program to eliminate all income taxes on wages and

[1] . . . An effective presentation of a dissenting view appears in Gabriel Kolko, *Wealth and Power in America* (New York, 1962). . . .

[2] Thus in А. Ляпин, *Труд при социализме* (Moscow, 1951), p. 60, it was identified as a policy of "Trotskyites, Zinovievites, Bukharinites and other enemies of the people. . . ."

[3] One such example is the sociologist S. M. Lipset in *Socialist Call,* Summer, 1961, p. 12. However, he cites Italy as an exception.

[4] *Правда*, Feb. 18, 1956.

[5] All ruble figures in this paper are given in terms of the new rubles introduced in January, 1961. The original figures here were 270–350 rubles and 500–600 rubles.

[6] *Program of the Communist Party of the Soviet Union Adopted by the 22nd Congress of the CPSU, October, 1961* (New York, 1961), p. 95; hereafter cited as *Party Program.*

salaries after taxes had been ended on incomes up to 60 rubles per month (and reduced on incomes between 61 and 70 rubles per month) has certainly operated to narrow income inequality. It is possible, however, that the ending of compulsory bond purchases has worked in the opposite direction. Nor will we consider the increasing portion of income which is scheduled for distribution in the form of free goods and services in the future, except to note that it will reinforce whatever trend toward equalization is observed in the distribution of money income. Further, our comments apply only to the non-agricultural sector of the population.[7]

## RECENT TRENDS IN SOVIET INCOME STRUCTURE

*Wage Workers.* It is now quite clear that the gap between the income of relatively high- and low-paid workers increased between the state of the anti-equalitarian campaign in the early 1930s and the holding of the 20th Party Congress in 1956. This can hardly occasion great surprise. What is perhaps of greater interest is the extent to which the trend toward greater income differences has been reversed since 1956 and how income inequality among workers in recent years compares with that prevailing in the past.

Trends in Soviet wage inequality over the last thirty years may be traced by observing changes in the ratio of the ninth to the first decile of the distribution of Soviet workers according to earnings and similarly the ratio of the third to the first quartile.[8] These are summary measures of wage dispersion, and it is in this sense that we shall refer to inequality here. They tell us nothing about the share of total income received by any percentage of the population.[9] But they are the best measures currently available for our purpose. We may refer to them henceforth (admittedly somewhat loosely) as the ratios of upper-to-lower tenth incomes (D9/D1) and upper-to-lower quarter

[7] Incomes of collective farmers are scheduled to rise more rapidly than those of workers (*ibid.*, p. 96).

[8] The ninth decile wage is the wage which was exceeded by the top 10 per cent of the workers; the first decile wage is the wage which the bottom 10 per cent failed to reach. The third and first quartiles may be defined similarly for the corresponding 25 per cent of workers. Changes in these ratios reflect not only changes in the relative wages of particular occupations but also changes in the relative importance of the various occupations. Hence, these ratios are more properly designated as measures of wage variation rather than of wage differentiation. See Abram Bergson, *The Structure of Soviet Wages* (Cambridge, Mass., 1946), p. 55.

[9] It is possible, reading from a Soviet chart, to derive rough estimates of the share of wage income received by different proportions of Soviet workers and on this basis to construct Lorenz curves of wage distribution for 1934, 1956, and 1959 (М. Можина, «Изменения в распределении промышленных рабочих СССР по размерам заработной платы», *Бюллетень научной информации, труд и заработная плата*, No. 10, 1961, p. 24).

The chart shows the percentage of workers on the vertical axis and mid-points of income classes on the horizontal axis, with the mid-points expressed as percentages of the median wage. It is our judgment, however, that the values that may be read from this chart are of dubious value for observing changes in the size distribution of Soviet wage incomes. Portions of the chart are barely distinguishable, and there is particular uncertainty about the low- and high-income extremes. The Lorenz curves that may be derived from this chart (at least in our reading of the values) appear to be essentially the same for 1934, 1956, and 1959. Whether this reflects the actual state of affairs or the roughness of the chart (or our reading of it), we prefer to leave for future study. We may note, however, that the income shares estimated from the chart for 1934 exhibit less inequality than was suggested by Bergson's study of Soviet wages in that year (Bergson, *op. cit.*, p. 123):

| | | | | | | | | | | |
|---|---|---|---|---|---|---|---|---|---|---|
| Cumulative percentage of workers | 10 | 20 | 30 | 40 | 50 | 60 | 70 | 80 | 90 | 100 |
| Cumulative percentage of wage bill (Bergson) | 3.4 | 8.7 | 15.0 | 22.3 | 30.5 | 39.9 | 50.5 | 62.7 | 77.7 | 100.0 |
| Cumulative percentage of wage bill (Soviet chart) | 4.8 | 10.2 | 17.5 | 25.1 | 34.0 | 44.2 | 55.6 | 68.8 | 82.0 | 100.0 |

For 1956 and 1959 the estimated shares of the wage bill differ altogether insignificantly from those read from the Soviet chart for 1934.

incomes (Q3/Q1) respectively. The results are shown below:[10]

| YEAR | *Decile Ratio* (D9/D1 IN PER CENT) | *Quartile Ratio* (Q3/Q1 IN PER CENT) |
|---|---|---|
| 1929 | 315 | 182 |
| 1934 | 317 | 182 |
| 1956 | 338 | 185 |
| 1959 | 328 | 184 |

The anti-equalitarian campaign was begun in the early 1930s, and its full impact would not yet have been apparent by 1934. Hence the figures show only a slight increase in wage inequality between 1929 and 1934 if the first of our measures is used, while no change is exhibited by the second measure. By 1956 however (before the decisions announced at the 20th Party Congress could be implemented), our indicators of wage inequality had risen by 21 percentage points as measured by the ratio of upper-to-lower tenth incomes, and 3 percentage points if the less sensitive ratio of upper-to-lower-quarter incomes is used. After 1956 there was a decline in dispersion, thereby reversing the earlier trend, but inequality remained greater in 1959 than it had been in the late 1920s and early 1930s.

What is particularly striking, however, is that almost one half of the increase in wage dispersion between 1934 and 1956 (as recorded by the more sensitive of these ratios) was wiped out in the brief period between the 20th and 21st Party Congresses (1956 to 1959).[11]

Where direct evidence exists of changes in wage dispersion since 1959, it points in the same direction as the decile and quartile ratios cited above—to a narrowing of wage inequality in recent years. Changes in wage structure at the *Elektrosila* electrical machinery plant between 1959 and 1960 are cited as typical of those in this industry as a whole. They are presented below:[12]

| YEAR | *Decile Ratio* (D9/D1 IN PER CENT) | *Quartile Ratio* (Q3/Q1 IN PER CENT) |
|---|---|---|
| June, 1959 | 228 | 159 |
| June, 1960 | 213 | 154 |

There is every reason to believe that the decline in income differences among workers observed since 1956 has continued to the present (1963) and that upper-to-lower income ratios today are not much higher (if at all) than they were some thirty years ago. This seems evident from the continuing implementation of three policies: (1) Wage-rate differentials between skilled and unskilled occupations are being reduced in newly issued wage scales. The ratios of extreme rates in wage scales issued in 1960 and 1961 have generally been in the neighborhood of 2 to 1 or 1.8 to 1, compared to the 2.8 to 1 and higher that was typical of earlier scales. Although these ratios exclude premiums, the reduction of basic wage-rate differentials suggests at least the direction of change in actual earnings differentials. (2) Minimum wages were raised to 40–45 rubles per month in 1962 compared to the 27–35 rubles established in 1957. This change narrowed not only occupational but also inter-industry wage differentials, thereby reinforcing a process that began even before 1956.[13] (3) The piece-rate system of wage

[10] Можина, *op. cit.*, pp. 21, 25. The decile and quartile ratios given here for 1934 are below those which may be derived from Bergson's study (*op. cit.*, p. 128). The Bergson data imply decile and quartile ratios of 374 and 194 respectively, thus suggesting greater wage dispersion in 1934 than that indicated by the figures presented here (317 for the decile ratio and 182 for the quartile ratio). The discrepancies may possibly be explained by differences in coverage and Bergson's need to rely on interpolation of the required values.

[11] It should be noted, however, that the peak in wage inequality probably occurred before 1956. Wage rate differentials had been reduced after the war. Most of the increase between 1934 and 1956 in the ratios shown above may reflect the widening of wage differentials prior to the war.

[12] А. Агеева and А. Тыклин, «Анализ сокращения различии в оплате труда низко- и высокооплачиваемых работников электротехнической промышленности,» *Бюллетень научной информации, труд и заработная плата*, No. 12, 1961, p. 32.

[13] Between 1950 and 1956 wages in the most highly paid sectors (coal, oil, steel) increased less than average earnings in industry as a whole (Можина, *op. cit.*, p. 24).

payment is gradually being replaced by time rates. This is clear from the data presented in Table 1.

Although the bulk of Soviet workers are still on some form of piece rates (about two-thirds in 1961 compared to three-fourths in 1959), there is clear recognition that the measurement of individual output is increasingly incompatible with new technology, particularly that associated with automation.[14] Soviet writers expect the number of piece workers to decline to 45 to 50 per cent of all industrial workers within a decade.[15] The progressive piece-rate system has all but disappeared, with only 1 per cent of the workers in industry being paid according to this method in 1961.

If these policies continue to be pursued throughout the 1960s (and the current Soviet literature on the subject suggests that they will be), by the end of the decade income differentials among workers may be less than those which prevailed before the attack on equalitarianism.

**Wage Workers and Salaried Personnel.** Another aspect of the changing Soviet income structure may be observed by asking what happened to the earnings of workers compared to those of other groups, in particular to the salaried personnel category. Salaried personnel in Soviet industry fall into two categories: (1) "engineering-technical personnel," ranging from foreman to plant director and including also technicians, engineers, and shop superintendents; (2) "employees," which corresponds roughly to our white-collar office and accounting personnel. The results of such a comparison are quite revealing and are indicated below.[16]

| *Year* | *Average Earnings of Engineering-Technical Personnel in Per Cent of Average Earnings of Workers* | *Average Earnings of Employees in Per Cent of Average Earnings of Workers* |
|---|---|---|
| 1932 | 263 | 150 |
| 1935 | 236 | 126 |
| 1940 | 210 | 109 |
| 1950 | 175 | 93 |
| 1955 | 165 | 88 |
| 1960 | 150 | |

These figures suggest a rather remarkable change in the Soviet income structure. While the average earnings of engineering-technical personnel exceeded those of workers by some two and one-half times in the early 1930s, their relative wage advantage over workers had fallen to 50 per cent by 1960. As for employees, their earnings fell below those of workers in the postwar period after having been 50 per cent above them in the early 1930s. The most striking aspect of this improvement in the relative income status of workers compared to salaried personnel is surely the narrowing of the average earnings gap between workers and engineering-technical personnel. This narrowing is apparent not only on an all-industry basis (the figures above) but also within those individual industries for which

[14] Г. Х. Гендлер, *Заработная плата и технический прогресс* (Moscow, 1961), p. 65.

[15] Е. И. Капустин, *Заработная плата в промышленности СССР и ее совершенствование* (Moscow, 1961), p. 98.

[16] А. Г. Аганбегян В. Ф. Майер, *Заработная плата в СССР* (Moscow, 1959), p. 202; ЦУНХУ, *Труд в СССР* (Moscow, 1936), p. 96; *Социалистический труд*, No. 10, 1961, p. 31. While the figures through 1955 clearly apply to earnings, including premiums, there may be some doubt as to the figure for 1960 cited in the latter source. The 1960 figure is referred to as "the relationship between average wages of workers and the average rate (*oklad*) of engineering-technical personnel." However, the same terminology is also used here for a 1932 figure which other sources make clear applies to earnings. In any case, the trend from 1932 to 1955 revealed in the figures above remains unaffected.

**TABLE 1 Distribution of Soviet Workers by Form of Wage Payment in Selected Industries, 1956 and 1961 (in Per Cent)**

| *Industry* | *1956* | | *1961* | |
|---|---|---|---|---|
| | *Piece Work* | *Time Work* | *Piece Work* | *Time Work* |
| Ferrous metallurgy | 70.9 | 29.1 | 60.1 | 39.9 |
| Coal | 59.1 | 40.9 | 48.9 | 51.1 |
| Oil extraction | 51.1 | 48.9 | 17.7 | 82.3 |
| Oil refining | 65.0 | 35.0 | 8.9 | 91.1 |
| Machine-building and metalworking | 74.2 | 25.8 | 57.3 | 42.7 |
| Chemical | 68.5 | 31.5 | 39.0 | 61.0 |
| Woodworking | 87.6 | 12.4 | 76.9 | 23.1 |
| Paper | 87.4 | 12.6 | 58.7 | 41.3 |
| Cement | 80.1 | 19.9 | 64.7 | 35.3 |
| Textiles | 84.8 | 15.2 | 68.4 | 31.6 |
| Food | 82.0 | 18.0 | 58.4 | 41.6 |
| Printing | 67.2 | 32.8 | 59.5 | 40.5 |
| Shoe | 85.6 | 14.4 | 82.9 | 17.1 |
| Glass and porcelain | 81.2 | 18.8 | 65.1 | 34.9 |

Sources: Г. Х. Гендлер, *Заработная плата и технический прогресс* (Moscow, 1961). p. 65; *Вестник статистики*, No. 6, 1962, pp. 94–96. The 1961 figures apply to March 31.

the appropriate wage data are available for the 1930s and 1950s (see Table 2). The narrowing of these differentials seems all the more significant when it is realized that it apparently applies to earnings, inclusive of premiums, rather than to basic wage rates. At least this is suggested by the terminology used (*zarabotnaia plata* rather than *oklady* or *stavki*).

Where the data for individual sectors can be extended to 1960, they point in the same direction. Thus in 1960 the ratio of engineering-technical earnings to workers' earnings stood at 1.83 in nonferrous metallurgy and 1.58 in the cement industry as compared to 2.06 and 1.76 respectively before the wage adjustments made in the late 1950s.[17]

Part of the explanation of this phenomenon undoubtedly lies in the changing occupational composition of the workers and engineering-technical personnel categories. Among workers the relative importance of the more skilled and therefore the most highly paid occupations within the group increased markedly after the 1930s. These were also the groups that gained most from the anti-equalitarian wage

[17] Капустин, *op. cit.*, p. 41.

**TABLE 2 Average Monthly Earnings of Engineering-Technical Personnel in Per Cent of Average Earnings of Workers, 1934 and 1956**

| *Industry* | *1934* | *1956* |
|---|---|---|
| Nonferrous ore mining | — | 240 |
| Iron ore mining | 294 | 170 |
| Coal mining | 301 | 160 |
| Logging | — | 150 |
| Machine-building | 222 | 150 |
| Cotton | 290 | 160 |
| Wool | 302 | 140 |
| Knitted goods | 246 | 135 |
| Fishing | — | 200 |
| Fruit production | — | 180 |
| Meat | 277 | 160 |
| Butter and dairy products | — | 130 |
| Electric power stations | 257 | 180 |

Sources: 1934 figures for knitted goods and meat apply to October, 1934, while for other sectors they are based on average monthly earnings for the whole year. Figures for 1934 were calculated from ЦУНХУ, *Труд в СССР* (Moscow, 1936); ЦУНХУ, *Заработная плата рабочих крупной промышленности в октябре 1934 г.* (Moscow, 1935). Figures for 1956 are from А. Г. Аганбегян and В. Ф. Майер, *Заработная плата в СССР* (Moscow, 1959), p. 202; А. Я. Аврух, *Себестоимость электрической и тепловой энергии* (Moscow, 1957), p. 88.

policy. Among engineering-technical personnel, on the other hand, comparatively low-paid occupations increased in importance more rapidly than highly paid ones.

But even independently of changes in occupational composition within the two groups, Soviet wage policy since at least the end of the war has operated to narrow the earnings gap between workers and engineering-technical personnel. Thus, wage increases granted at the end of 1946—which were designed partially to compensate relatively low-paid personnel for price increases attendant on derationing—benefited primarily wage workers and office employees. Similarly, the wage increases announced for workers' occupations as a group since 1956 have exceeded those granted to engineering-technical personnel. Where the opposite trend has appeared in individual plants it has been treated as a "negative feature" in conflict with current Soviet wage policy.[18] Further, salary differentials within the engineering-technical category are also being reduced. In 1958 salary-scale revisions in some sectors were reported to have reduced the ratio of plant directors' to foremen's rates from 4–5 to 1 to 3–3.5 to 1. Between 1959 and 1965 the difference between the earnings of plant directors and engineers, is scheduled to decline by 50 per cent.[19]

In some industries the narrowing of the wage differential between workers and engineering-technical personnel has also been accompanied by a considerable overlapping of incomes received by personnel in the two groups. Thus in 1956 the wages of approximately 30 per cent of the workers in some sectors of the coal and machine-building industries exceeded the average earnings of the engineering-technical category as a whole in these sectors.[20] Basic wage rates authorized in recently issued wage scales for the most skilled workers' occupations exceed those set for the lower categories of engineering personnel.

The overlapping of worker and engineering-technical incomes is also related to the marked inter-industry wage differentials which have continued to characterize Soviet wage structure. Thus in the mid-fifties the average earnings of workers in coal mining exceeded those of workers in the food industry by more than 100 per cent, in the textile industry by about 95 per cent, in logging operations by more than 60 per cent, and in machine-building by almost 50 per cent.[21] Judging by the regional data available for 1959 (for the Ukraine) similarly large inter-industry wage differentials are still in effect.[22] Juxtaposing these figures with those given in Table 2 on the ratios of engineering-technical to workers' earnings it is clear that the average wages of workers in coal mining exceeded the average earnings of engineering-technical personnel in the food, textile, and logging industries, and approached them in machine-building. Workers' average earnings in such highly paid sectors as steel and nonferrous metallurgy also exceeded those of engineering-technical personnel employed in some consumer goods sectors.

The material reviewed here, particularly on the narrowing of the earnings gap between workers and salaried personnel, suggests the strong possibility that inequality in the distribution of *wage and salary income combined* diminished between the early 1930s and the late 1950s. Although the available measures of income inequality are not really adequate, it does seem significant that the only two measures available both point in the direction of reduced inequality:

(1) The only serious Western study of Soviet income inequality, that by Abram Bergson, found that in 1934 the top 10 per cent of wage and salary recipients in industry received 24.3 per cent of the total wage bill, while the bottom 10 per cent received 3 per cent. This 1934 ratio of

[18] Агеева and Тыклин, *op. cit.*, p. 38.

[19] *Социалистический труд*, No. 11, 1958, p. 20; Аганбегян and Майер, *op. cit.*, p. 228.

[20] В. Е. Комаров, *Экономические основы подготовки специалистов для народного хозяйства* (Moscow, 1959), p. 156.

[21] Аганбегян and Майер, *op. cit.*, p. 187; Можина, *op. cit.*, p. 24.

[22] Thus the average earnings of coal miners in the Ukraine in 1959 were about 260 per cent of the earnings of workers in the food industry, 250 per cent of those in light industry, and 220 per cent of those in the forestry, paper, and woodworking industries (Капустин, *op. cit.*, p. 197).

approximately 8 to 1 between the average earnings of the highest and lowest paid 10 per cent of wage and salaried personnel combined may be compared with a ratio of 5.8 to 1 announced in recent Soviet publications for 1959.[23]

(2) Soviet wage studies have found that the ratio of the third to the first quartile of the earnings distribution of wage and salaried personnel combined declined slightly between 1946 and 1956.[24]

Trends in income structure in Soviet industry over the last three decades may be summarized briefly as follows. Wage inequality among workers tended to increase over most of the period between the early 1930s and the late 1950s. This reflected the implementation of an anti-equalitarian wage policy by means of widening occupational wage-rate differentials between skilled and unskilled workers and the extensive application of the piece-rate system. Wage inequality declined between 1956 and 1959 but remained greater in 1959 than it was in the early 1930s. The period since 1956 has been marked by a narrowing of skill differentials in wage rates, substantial increases in minimum wages, and the declining importance of the piece-rate system. These policies promise to reduce wage inequality among workers below the level prevailing in the early 1930s, if they have not done so already.

While wage inequality among workers was increasing, the income gap between workers and the bulk of engineering-technical personnel was declining. Workers also improved their income position relative to that of office personnel.

## SOVIET INCOME DIFFERENTIALS IN THE FUTURE

The new party program and the other documents of the 22nd Party Congress do not contain much in the way of precise quantitative material on planned changes in income structure. By 1970 the real incomes of "low paid" workers and employees are scheduled to approximately triple, while for all personnel they will be "almost doubled." These documents, however, frequently reaffirm the previously announced intention of further reducing income inequality. We may summarize some of the earlier announcements bearing on future trends in income inequality as below.

To complete the picture we may note one additional bit of information. The wages of those who earned more than 140 rubles per month in 1959 are to remain "basically unchanged" by 1965; the wages of those earning 60 to 140 rubles per month are to rise by an average of 20 to 25 per cent, while the average increase for those earnings below 60 rubles will be in the range of 45 to 60 per cent.[25]

In the West we have been accustomed to viewing marked changes in income structure as normally requiring a rather extended period of time. Considering the short period within which the Soviet program outlined above is to be achieved and the magnitude

[23] П. С. Мстиславский, *Народное потребление при социализме* (Moscow, 1961), p. 86. The data for 1934 are in Bergson, *op. cit.*, p. 123.

[24] Можина, *op. cit.*, p. 22.

[25] Мстиславский, *op. cit.*, pp. 85–86. The average wage figures above are estimated from data in С. П. Фигурнов, *Реальная заработная плата и подъем материального благосостояния трудящихся в СССР* (Moscow, 1960), p. 136.

| | *1959* | *1965* |
|---|---|---|
| Ratio of average wages of top 10 per cent of workers and salaried personnel to bottom 10 per cent | 5.8:1 | 3.8:1 |
| Ratio of average incomes of top 10 per cent of families to bottom 10 per cent (including money and non-money incomes) | 4.75:1 | 3:1 |
| Minimum wages (in rubles per month) | 27–35 | 50–60 |
| Average wages of workers and salaried personnel (in rubles per month) | 79 | 99 |

of the changes involved, the term Soviet "income revolution" does not seem like an exaggeration.[26]

However, even if the planned changes in income structure are actually realized, Soviet Russia will hardly approximate the vision of an equalitarian society. This is apparent if we observe how large the wage differentials which will separate the top from the bottom of the occupational ladder will be in 1965. Since we lack the necessary earnings data, reliance will have to be placed on basic salary rates (exclusive of bonuses and other supplementary income). To represent the upper extreme we may select the top rates of some of the highly paid occupations whose wages will remain essentially stable between 1959 and 1965. The bottom of the income ladder may be represented by occupations whose lowest rates were at or slightly above the prevailing minimum wage in 1959. The extremes in Soviet salary rates will look approximately as follows in the steel industry in 1965 as compared to 1959 (in rubles per month):[27]

| | *1959* | *1965* |
|---|---|---|
| Director of scientific research institute | 600 | 600 |
| Director of steel plant | 400 | 400 |
| Elevator operator, janitor, watchman | 35 | 60 |
| Typist, secretary | 41 | 60 |

Thus if the lowest 1959 rates increase to the extent implied by the minimum wage goal for 1965, while the top rates remain unchanged, the ratio of highest to lowest rates will still be 10:1 compared to 17:1 in 1959. Further, this ratio obviously understates the difference between extremes in actual money earnings as distinct from basic salary rates. The director of the steel plant is more likely to receive a bonus supplement than is the elevator operator or janitor, and the research institute director will probably receive royalties and additional pay for teaching at the local university. It is clear that whatever may be the share of monetary and non-monetary supplements in the incomes of the lowest paid occupations, differences between extremes in real incomes in Soviet society will remain considerable by any standards throughout the 1960s.

## THE NON-EQUALITARIAN REDUCTION OF INCOME INEQUALITY

How are we to explain the reduction in workers' wage differentials since 1956 and the planned reduction of income inequality in the future? First, it is clear that these phenomena cannot be explained by the growth of equalitarian sentiments among the Soviet leaders. Indeed, it is a curious feature of the current Soviet scene that in the midst of what is obviously a serious attempt to narrow income differentials, great pains are taken to disassociate this policy from any equalitarian taint. Khrushchev's report to the 22nd Party Congress and the party program make this distinction time and

[26] It is hazardous but tempting to compare Soviet income inequality with that prevailing in the United States. We may simply indicate what some highly provisional findings reveal. Among workers the ratio of the third to the first quartile (Q3/Q1) of a wage distribution covering about two-fifths of non-farm wage earners in the United States in 1956 was 1.37; Paul T. Homan, Albert G. Hart, and Arnold W. Sametz, *The Economic Order* (New York, 1958), p. 285. As noted above, the corresponding Soviet figures in recent years have been in the neighborhood of 1.85. Although there are serious questions concerning the comparability of the data, the direction in which these figures point is unmistakable—wage dispersion among workers is greater in Soviet Russia than in the United States. However, comparisons of income inequality for the whole population of the two countries point in the opposite direction. In the United States the share of money income received by the highest 10 per cent of spending units in recent years has been approximately thirty times that received by the lowest 10 per cent (U.S. Bureau of the Census, *Statistical Abstract of the United States, 1961*, p. 315). The Soviet ratio of incomes—money and non-money—of the top 10 per cent of families to the bottom 10 per cent (4.75:1) is, of course, not comparable to these United States figures. But it seems quite unlikely that the necessary adjustments to the Soviet figures would raise the Soviet ratio to the United States level. The chief adjustments would require inclusion of the farm population's income and elimination of all non-money incomes. The latter adjustment alone would raise the Soviet ratio to no more than 6:1 or 7:1 (Фигурнов *op. cit.*, p. 94).

[27] С. М. Левин and М. Н. Тимошполский, *Организация заработной платы в черной металлургии* (Moscow, 1959), pp. 194, 196–98.

again.[28] Thus for some thirty years now, beginning with Stalin's denunciation of anonymous equalitarians in 1931 and extending through periods of both increasing and decreasing wage inequality, equalitarianism has been a term of opprobrium in Soviet Russia. Why should this have been necessary in the past and why is this still the case? A brief examination of the shifting uses of this term casts a revealing light on the way in which both continuity and change may appear in Soviet policy-making.

When the attack on equalitarianism began in the early 1930s it was not immediately clear who or what was being attacked. There had been no widespread pressure—at least in print—for wage equalization from any section of the party or trade union leadership in the immediately preceding period. In any explicit discussions of equalitarianism that appeared in the more academic publications in the late 1920s, the main purpose was to distinguish it from what was viewed as the genuine socialist tradition.[29] It is true that in 1926 at the 7th Congress of Trade Unions (with Stalin and other party leaders present) a policy of reducing wage differentials had been adopted and M. P. Tomsky, the head of the Soviet trade unions at the time, referred to this as a matter of "elementary class justice." But this policy had not been carried very far by 1931 and there is no evidence that such statements were still being made. Who, then, were the equalitarians? Considering the vigor of the attack against them, one would expect that they represented an influential group of party or trade union leaders urging the immediate elimination or marked reduction of wage inequality. In this sense, the answer to the question, who were the equalitarians, must be that they were at least partly a myth.

Having decided on a policy of rapid industrialization, the Soviet leadership realized that this would require a similarly rapid change in the occupational composition of the industrial work force, in particular a sharp increase in the number of skilled workers. One instrument for achieving this goal was to be a rather prolonged policy of widening wage differentials between skilled and unskilled occupations. The attack on equalitarianism, then, was in reality less an attack on a specific group of opponents of party policy than it was a way of focusing attention on a crucial problem—the need to utilize monetary incentives to promote the development of scarce skills. But like any other major policy of the period it had to be pursued as a "struggle" against something, that is, against an anonymous, largely mythical group of wage-levelers.

To the extent that equalitarianism was not a myth but a real obstacle, it represented a general unawareness of this problem, an unawareness to which the socialist tradition had contributed. For the whole tradition of socialist thought, including its Marxian wing, had long been imbued with the vision of eliminating the income inequalities associated with capitalism. While there were differences within this tradition with respect to the timing and the extent of the increased equality expected under socialism, there was nothing in socialist thought to suggest that the new society would ever require a widening of income inequality among workers. Marx's concept of distribution in the first phase of the Communist society ("according to work performed") involved acceptance of income inequality. This inequality, however, reflected the defects of the old society from which the first phase of communism would emerge, not a feature which the new society should promote.

But if the Soviet leaders' attack on equalitarianism in the 1930s served a useful purpose, what function does the continued rejection of equalitarianism serve now that differences in income are being reduced? Erich Fromm has pointed to the ritualistic character of some Soviet statements, in which it becomes necessary to speak as an upholder of an old orthodoxy even while the latter is being rejected in practice. After thirty years it is possible that anti-equalitarianism has become such an orthodoxy. While this explanation may have some validity as applied to the statements of

[28] N. S. Khrushchev, *Report on the Program of the Communist Party of the Soviet Union* (New York, 1961), I, 130; II, 87–88; *Party Program* p. 93.

[29] В. Волгин, «Социализм и эгалитаризм,» *Вестник коммунистической академии*, XXIX (1928), 13–27.

lower-echelon officials and writers (among whom old habits of speech and thought seem particularly persistent) it seems to us too facile an explanation of the anti-equalitarian strictures voiced by Soviet leaders. Of all the Stalinist orthodoxies which are being abandoned why should this particular one be retained?

Another possibility is that the continuing criticism of equalitarianism is now directed against popular misconceptions of "distribution according to needs" and "Communist equality," both of which have been presented by Soviet leaders as the principles of income distribution in the future Soviet society. Thus some Soviet writers warn that these principles do not imply absolute equality of income for all or "equal shares" in the total product, conceptions which these writers link with equalitarianism.[30] But it is difficult to believe that much of the Soviet population envisions either the immediate or distant future in terms of "equal shares." Neither the Marxian tradition nor what we know of the Soviet people's aspirations point in this direction. If the warnings against equalitarianism were to be primarily aimed at such views they would be battling a largely nonexistent danger.

There is another explanation for these strictures which seems quite simple and which simultaneously focuses attention on the reasons for the policy of reducing income inequality. Income differentials are now being reduced largely because a substantial rise in the educational, and hence in the skill, level of new entrants into the labor force has made the wide differentials of early industrialization unnecessary. Not only are they unnecessary; in some economic sectors their retention would be clearly harmful. Although the typical new entrant into the labor force is probably capable of performing at least semiskilled work (if not immediately, then within a few months), there are still a considerable number of unskilled jobs that must be performed in Soviet industry. The reluctance of workers to accept such jobs when their training permits their employment in more skilled and therefore more remunerative work clearly makes reduced wage differentials for skill a desirable policy. The strange phenomenon (strange for Soviet industry) of a "shortage of unskilled labor" has been explicitly cited in Soviet discussions of labor and wage policy.[31] Where this is not a problem, the leveling of workers' skills and proficiency as a result of the broad extension of technical education is itself a factor which makes the reduction of income differentials appear advisable.

The relevance of all this to the continuing rejection of equalitarianism seems quite clear. The principal reasons for the policy of reducing income inequality are rooted in "objective factors," that is, in the changing relative scarcities of skilled and unskilled labor. They have little if anything to do with Tomsky's sentiments of "elementary class justice" (at least thus far). Equalitarianism, then, has come to signify a narrowing of income differentials that would go beyond the limits imposed by these "objective factors." Thus the Central Committee report to the 22nd Party Congress contrasts equalitarianism with the present policy of reducing wage differentials in conformity with the disappearance of the unskilled worker category. Looking ahead to the future when the principle of "distribution according to needs" will govern, the report emphasizes that attempts to introduce this principle prematurely "would be outright equalitarianism." Its introduction requires a much higher level of material abundance than presently exists and the transformation of work from a means of earning a livelihood to a "social calling, a moral duty" (or, in the more usual terminology, "the first necessity of life"). The point was made clearly in an article written more than a year before the latest Party Congress: "The first and foremost problem of the construction of Communism is not how to distribute justly but how to create an abundance of material values."[32]

While in the 1930s the strictures against

[30] С. П. Первушин, *Некоторые проблемы перехода от социализма к коммунизму* (Moscow, 1960), pp. 96–97.

[31] А. Каценелинбойген, «О редукции труда,» *Вопросы экономики*, No. 3, 1961, p. 57.

[32] М. Саков, «От каждого по способностям, каждому по потребностям,» *Политическое самообразование*, No. 8, 1960, p. 27.

equalitarianism were linked with a policy of increasing wage differentials for skill, today they serve to emphasize the limits within which the opposite policy may be pursued. In both the 1930s and 1960s, however, the primary concern is with increasing output, not with "how to distribute justly."

The latter question will come into its own when material abundance and changed attitudes toward work will have been achieved. When this occurs, the problem of equalitarianism will disappear and "Communist equality" in distribution will prevail, that is *equal access* by all to the goods and services required to satisfy rational human needs.

Whatever the possibility of realizing this vision of the future, it is clear that inequality in the distribution of income is currently being reduced. But this, of course, is only one form of inequality in Soviet society. It is not at all clear that inequality in the distribution of political power is moving in the same direction.

# Power Inequality

## THE NEW CLASS

*Milovan Djilas*

I.

Everything happened differently in the U.S.S.R. and other Communist countries from what the leaders—even such prominent ones as Lenin, Stalin, Trotsky, and Bukharin—anticipated. . . . The greatest illusion was that industrialization and collectivization in the U.S.S.R., and destruction of capitalist ownership, would result in a classless society. In 1936, when the new Constitution was promulgated, Stalin announced that the "exploiting class" had ceased to exist. The capitalist and other classes of ancient origin had in fact been destroyed but a new class, previously unknown to history, had been formed. . . .

This new class, the bureaucracy, or more accurately the political bureaucracy, has all the characteristics of earlier ones as well as some new characteristics of its own. Its origin had its special characteristics also, even though in essence it was similar to the beginnings of other classes.

Other classes, too, obtained their strength and power by the revolutionary path, destroying the political, social, and other orders they met in their way. However, almost without exception, these classes attained power *after* new economic patterns had taken shape in the old society. The case was the reverse with new classes in the Communist systems. It did not come to power to *complete* a new economic order but to *establish* its own and, in so doing, to establish its power over society.

In earlier epochs the coming to power of some class, some part of a class, or of some party, was the final event resulting from its formation and its development. The reverse was true in the U.S.S.R. There the new class was definitely formed after it attained power. Its consciousness had to develop before its economic and physical powers, because the class had not taken root in the life of the nation. This class viewed its role in relation to the world from an idealistic point of view. Its practical possibilities were not diminished by this. In spite of its illusions, it represented an objective tendency toward industrialization. Its practical bent emanated from this tendency. The promise of an ideal world increased the faith in the ranks of the new class and sowed illusions among the masses. At the same time it inspired gigantic physical undertakings.

Because this new class had not been formed as a part of the economic and social life before it came to power, it could only be created in an organization of a special type, distinguished by a special discipline based on identical philosophic and ideological views of its members. A unity of belief and iron discipline was necessary to overcome its weaknesses.

From *The New Class*, by Milovan Djilas, Frederick A. Praeger, 1965. Reprinted by permission.

The roots of the new class were implanted in a special party, of the Bolshevik type. . . . To be more precise, the initiators of the new class are not found in the party of the Bolshevik type as a whole but in that stratum of professional revolutionaries who made up its core even before it attained power. . . . The new ruling class has been gradually developing from this very narrow stratum of revolutionaries. These revolutionaries composed its core for a long period. Trotsky noted that in pre-revolutionary professional revolutionaries was the origin of the future Stalinist bureaucrat. What he did not detect was the beginning of a new class of owners and exploiters.

This is not to say that the new party and the new class are identical. The party, however, is the core of that class, and its base. It is very difficult, perhaps impossible, to define the limits of the new class and to identify its members. The new class may be said to be made up of those who have special privileges and economic preference because of the administrative monopoly they hold. . . .

In loose terms, as the new class becomes stronger and attains a more perceptible physiognomy, the role of the party diminishes. The core and the basis of the new class is created in the party and at its top, as well as in the state political organs. The once live, compact party, full of initiative, is disappearing to become transformed into the traditional oligarchy of the new class, irresistibly drawing into its ranks those who aspire to join the new class and repressing those who have any ideals.

The party makes the class, but the class grows as a result and uses the party as a basis. The class grows stronger, while the party grows weaker; this is the inescapable fate of every Communist party in power.

If it were not materially interested in production or if it did not have within itself the potentialities for the creation of a new class, no party could act in so morally and ideologically foolhardy a fashion, let alone stay in power for long. Stalin declared, after the end of the First Five-Year Plan: "If we had not created the apparatus, we would have failed!" He should have substituted "new class" for the word "apparatus," and everything would have been clearer.

It seems unusual that a political party could be the beginning of a new class. Parties are generally the product of classes and strata which have become intellectually and economically strong. However, if one grasps the actual conditions in pre-revolutionary Russia and in other countries in which Communism prevailed over national forces, it will be clear that a party of this type is the product of specific opportunities and that there is nothing unusual or accidental in this being so. Although the roots of Bolshevism reach far back into Russian history, the party is partly the product of the unique pattern of international relationships in which Russia found itself at the end of the nineteenth and the beginning of the twentieth century. Russia was no longer able to live in the modern world as an absolute monarchy, and Russia's capitalism was too weak and too dependent on the interests of foreign powers to make it possible to have an industrial revolution. This revolution could only be implemented by a new class, or by a change in the social order. As yet, there was no such class. . . .

**2.**

The social origin of the new class lies in the proletariat just as the aristocracy arose in a peasant society, and the bourgeoisie in a commercial and artisans' society. There are exceptions, depending on national conditions, but the proletariat in economically underdeveloped countries, being backward, constitutes the raw material from which the new class arises.

There are other reasons why the new class always acts as the champion of the working class. The new class is anti-capitalistic and, consequently, logically dependent upon the working strata. The new class is supported by the proletarian struggle and the traditional faith of the proletariat in a socialist, Communist society where there is no brutal exploitation. It is vitally important for the new class to assure a normal flow of production, hence it cannot ever lose its connection with the proletariat. Most important of all, the new class cannot achieve industrialization and consolidate its power without the help of the working class. On the other hand, the working class sees in expanded industry the salvation from its poverty and despair. Over a long period of time, the interests, ideas, faith, and hope of the new class, and of parts of the working class and of the poor peasants, coincide and unite Such mergers have occurred in the past among other widely different classes. Did not the bourgeoisie represent the peasantry in the struggle against the feudal lords?

The movement of the new class toward power comes as a result of the efforts of the proletariat and the poor. These are the masses upon which the party or the new class must lean and with which its interests are most closely allied. This is true until the new class finally establishes its power and authority. Over and above this, the new class is interested in the proletariat and the poor only to the extent necessary for developing production and for maintaining in subjugation the most aggressive and rebellious social forces.

The monoploy which the new class establishes in the name of the working class over the whole of society is, primarily, a monopoly over the working class itself. This monopoly is first intellectual, over the so-called *avant-garde* proletariat, and then over the whole proletariat. This is the biggest deception the class must accomplish, but it shows that the power and interests of the new class lie primarily in industry. Without industry the new class cannot consolidate its position or authority.

Former sons of the working class are the most steadfast members of the new class.... In this case a new exploiting and governing class is born from the exploited class.

### 3.

When Communist systems are being critically analyzed, it is considered that their fundamental distinction lies in the fact that a bureaucracy, organized in a special stratum, rules over the people. This is generally true. However, a more detailed analysis will show that only a special stratum of bureaucrats, those who are not administrative officials, make up the core of the governing bureaucracy, or, in my terminology, of the new class. This is actually a party or political bureaucracy. Other officials are only the apparatus under the control of the new class; the apparatus may be clumsy and slow but, no matter what, it must exist in every socialist society. . . .

It is important to note the fundamental differences between the political bureaucracies mentioned here and those which arise with every centralization in modern economy—especially centralizations that lead to collective forms of ownership such as monopolies, companies, and state ownership. The number of white-collar workers is constantly increasing in capitalist monopolies, and also in nationalized industries in the West. . . .

While such functionaries have much in common with Communist bureaucrats, especially as regards "esprit de corps," they are not identical. Although state and other bureaucrats in non-Communist systems form a special stratum, they do not exercise authority as the Communists do. Bureaucrats in a non-Communist state have political masters, usually elected, or owners over them, while Communists have neither masters nor owners over them. The bureaucrats in a non-Communist state are officials in modern capitalist economy, while the Communists are something different and new: a new class.

As in other owning classes, the proof that it is a special class lies in its ownership and its special relations to other classes. In the same way, the class to which a member belongs is indicated by the material and other privileges which ownership brings to him.

As defined by Roman law, property constitutes the use, enjoyment, and disposition of material goods. The Communist political bureaucracy uses, enjoys, and disposes of nationalized property.

If we assume that membership in this bureaucracy or new owning class is predicated on the use of privileges inherent in ownership—in this instance nationalized material goods—then membership in the new party class, or political bureaucracy, is reflected in a larger income in material goods and privileges than society should normally grant for such functions. In practice, the ownership privilege of the new class manifests itself as an exclusive right, as a party monopoly, for the political bureaucracy to distribute the national income, to set wages, direct economic development, and dispose of nationalized and other property. This is the way it appears to the ordinary man who considers the Communist functionary as being very rich and as a man who does not have to work....

To divest Communists of their ownership rights would be to abolish them as a class. To compel them to relinquish their other social powers, so that workers may participate in sharing the profits of their work—which capitalists have had to permit as a result of strikes and parliamentary action—would mean that Communists were being deprived of their monopoly over property, ideology, and government. This would be the beginning of democracy and freedom in Communism, the end of Communist monopolism and totalitarianism. Until this happens, there can be no indication that important, fundamental changes are taking place in Communist systems, at least not in the eyes of men who think seriously about social progress.

The ownership privileges of the new class and membership in that class are the privileges of *administration*. This privilege extends from state administration and the administration of economic enterprises to that of sports and humanitarian organizations. Political, party, or so-called "general leadership" is executed by the core. . . . Discrepancies between the pay of workers and party functionaries are extreme; this could not be hidden from persons visiting the U.S.S.R. or other Communist countries in the past few years.

Other systems, too, have their professional politicians. . . . However, there are fundamental differences between professional politicians in other systems and in the Communist system. In extreme cases, politicians in other systems use the government to secure privileges for themselves and their cohorts, or to favor the economic interests of one social stratum or another. The situation is different with the Communist system where the power and the government are identical with the use, enjoyment, and disposition of almost all the nation's goods. He who grabs power grabs privileges and indirectly grabs property. Consequently, in Communism, power or politics as a profession is the ideal of those who have the desire or the prospect of living as parasites at the expense of others.

Membership in the Communist Party before the Revolution meant sacrifice. Being a professional revolutionary was one of the highest honors. Now that the party has consolidated its power, party membership means that one belongs to a privileged class. And at the core of the party are the all-powerful exploiters and masters. . . .

**4.**

. . . Behind Lenin, who was all passion and thought, stands the dull, gray figure of Joseph Stalin, the symbol of the difficult, cruel, and unscrupulous ascent of the new class to its final power.

After Lenin and Stalin came what had to come; namely, mediocrity in the form of collective leadership. And also there came the apparently sincere, kind-hearted, non-intellectual "man of the people"—Nikita Khrushchev. The new class no longer needs the revolutionaries or dogmatists it once required; it is satisfied with simple personalities . . . whose every word reflects the average man. The new class itself is tired of dogmatic purges and training sessions. It would like to live quietly. It must protect itself even from its own authorized leader now that it has been adequately strengthened. . . . Without relinquishing anything it created under Stalin's leadership, the new class appears to be renouncing his authority for the past few years. But it is not really renouncing that authority—only Stalin's methods which, according to Khrushchev, hurt "good Communists."

Lenin's revolutionary epoch was replaced by Stalin's epoch, in which authority and ownership, and industrialization, were strengthened so that the much desired peaceful and good life of the new class could begin. Lenin's *revolutionary* Communism was replaced by Stalin's *dogmatic* Communism, which in turn was replaced by *non-dogmatic* Communism, a so-called collective leadership or a group of oligarchs.

These are the three phases of development of the new class in the U.S.S.R. or of Russian Communism (or of every other type of Communism in one manner or another).

The fate of Yugoslav Communism was to unify these three phases in the single personality of Tito, along with national and personal characteristics. . . . The road which Yugoslav Communism has traveled—attaining a revolution, copying Stalinism, then renouncing Stalinism and seeking its own form—is seen most fully in the personality of Tito. . . .

The heroic era of Communism is past. The epoch of its great leaders has ended. The epoch of practical men has set in. The new class has been created. It is at the height of its power and wealth, but it is without new ideas. It has nothing more to tell the people. The only thing that remains is for it to justify itself.

. . . . . . . . . . . . . . . . . . . . . . . . . . . . . . . . . .

**5.**

. . . Since the hold of the new class on economic life and on the social structure was fairly precarious, and since it was fated to arise within a specific party, it required the highest possible degree of organization, as well as a consistent effort to present a united, balanced, class-conscious front. This is why the new class is better organized and more highly class-conscious than any class in recorded history.

This proposition is true only if it is taken relatively; consciousness and organizational structure being taken in relation to the outside world and to other classes, powers, and social forces. No other class in history has been as cohesive and single-minded in defending itself and in controlling that which it holds—collective and monopolistic ownership and totalitarian authority.

On the other hand, the new class is also the most deluded and least conscious of itself. Every private capitalist or feudal lord was conscious of the fact that he belonged to a special discernible social category. He usually believed that this category was destined to make the human race happy, and that without this category chaos and general ruin would ensue. A Communist member of the new class also believes that, without his party, society would regress and founder. But he is not conscious of the fact that he belongs to a new ownership class, for he does not consider himself an owner and does not take into account the special privileges he enjoys. He thinks that he belongs to a group with prescribed ideas, aims, attitudes, and roles. That is all he sees. He cannot see that at the same time he belongs to a special social category: the *ownership* class.

Collective ownership, which acts to solidify the class, at the same time makes it unconscious of its class substance, and each one of the collective owners is deluded in that he thinks he uniquely belongs to a movement which would abolish classes in society.

A comparison of other characteristics of the new class with those of other ownership classes reveals many similarities and many differences. The new class is voracious and insatiable, just as the bourgeoisie was. But it does not have the virtues of frugality and economy that the bourgeoisie had. The new class is as exclusive as the aristocracy but without aristocracy's refinement and proud chivalry.

The new class also has advantages over other classes. Because it is more compact it is better prepared for greater sacrifices and heroic exploits. The individual is completely and totally subordinated to the whole; at least, the prevailing ideal calls for such subordination even when he is out seeking to better himself. The new class is strong enough to carry out material and other ventures that no other class was ever able to do. Since it possesses the nation's goods, the new class is in a position to devote itself religiously to the aims it has set and to direct all the forces of the people to the furtherance of these aims.

. . . . . . . . . . . . . . . . . . . . . . . . . . . . . . . . . .

In the new class, just as in other classes, some individuals constantly fall by the wayside while others go up the ladder. . . . The road to the top is theoretically open to all, just as every one of Napoleon's soldiers carried a marshal's baton in his knapsack. The only thing that is required to get on the road is sincere and complete loyalty to the party or to the new class. Open at the bottom, the new class becomes increasingly and relentlessly narrower at the top. Not only is the desire necessary for the climb; also necessary is the ability to understand and develop doctrines, firmness in struggles against antagonists, exceptional dexterity and cleverness in intra-party struggles, and talent in strengthening the class. Many present themselves, but few are chosen. Although more open in some respects than other classes, the new class is also more exclusive than other classes. Since one of the new class's most important features is monopoly of authority, this exclusiveness is strengthened by bureaucratic hierarchical prejudices.

Nowhere, at any time, has the road been as wide open to the devoted and the loyal as it is in the Communist system. But the ascent to the heights has never at any time been so difficult or required so much sacrifice and so many victims. On the one hand, Communism is open and kind to all; on the other hand, it is exclusive and intolerant even of its its own adherents.

**6.**

The fact that there is a new ownership class in Communist countries does not explain everything, but it is the most important key to understanding the changes which are periodically taking place in these countries, especially in the U.S.S.R. . . . All changes initiated by the Communist chiefs are dictated first of all by the interests and aspirations of the new class, which, like every social group, lives and reacts, defends itself and advances, with the aim of increasing its power. This does not mean, however, that such changes may not be important for the rest of the people as well. . . .

The Communist regime, in common with others, must take into account the mood and movement of the masses. Because of the exclusiveness of the Communist Party and the absence of free public opinion in its ranks, the regime cannot discern the real status of the masses. However, their dissatisfaction does penetrate the consciousness of the top leaders. In spite of its totalitarian management, the new class is not immune to every type of opposition.

Once in power, the Communists have no difficulty in settling their accounts with the bourgeoisie and large-estate owners. The historical development is hostile to them and their property and it is easy to arouse the masses against them. Seizing property from the bourgeoisie and the large-estate owners is quite easy; difficulties arise when seizure of small properties is involved. Having acquired power in the course of earlier expropriations, the Communists can do even this. Relations are rapidly clarified: there are no more old classes and old owners, society is "classless," or on the road to being so, and men have started to live in a new manner.

Under such conditions demands to return to the old pre-revolutionary relations seem unrealistic, if not ridiculous. Material and social bases no longer exist for the maintenance of such relations. The Communists meet such demands as if they were jests.

The new class is most sensitive to demands on the part of the people for a special kind of freedom, not for freedom in general or political freedom. It is especially sensitive to demands for freedom of thought and criticism, within the limits of present conditions and within the limits of "socialism"; not for demands for a return to previous social and ownership relations. This sensitivity originates from the class's special position.

. . . . . . . . . . . . . . . . . . . . . . . . . . . . . . . . . . .

Every real demand for freedom in Communism, the kind of demand that hits at the substance of Communism, boils down to a demand for bringing material and property relations into accord with what the law provides.

A demand for freedom—based on the position that capital goods produced by the nation can be managed more efficiently by society than by private monopoly or a private owner, and consequently should actually be in the hands or under control of society exercised through its freely elected representatives—would force the new class either to make concessions to other forces, or to take off the mask and admit its ruling and exploiting characteristics. . . .

This does not mean that the new class cannot make concessions to the people, even though it only considers its own interests. Workers' management, or decentralization, is a concession to the masses. Circumstances may drive the new class, no matter how monopolistic and totalitarian it may be, to retreat before the masses. In 1948, when the conflict broke out between Yugoslavia and the U.S.S.R., the Yugoslav leaders were forced to carry out certain reforms. But they stopped the process and even reversed it, as soon as they felt that they were in jeopardy. Something similar happened recently in other East European countries. . . .

The new class cannot avoid falling continuously into profound internal contradictions; for in spite of its historical origin it is not able to make its ownership lawful, and it cannot renounce ownership without undermining itself. Consequently, it is forced to try to justify its increasing authority, invoking abstract and unreal purposes.

This is a class whose power over men is the most complete known to history. For this reason it is a class with very limited views, views which are shaky because they are based on falsehoods. Closely knit, isolated, and in complete authority, the new class must unrealistically evaluate its own role and that of the people around it. . . .

Having achieved industrialization, the new class can now do nothing more than strengthen its brute force and pillage the people. It ceases to create. Its spiritual heritage is overtaken by darkness.

While the revolution can be considered an epochal accomplishment of the new class, its methods of rule fill some of the most shameful pages in history. Men will marvel at the grandiose ventures it accomplished and will be ashamed of the means it used.

When the new class leaves the historical scene—and this must happen—there will be less sorrow over its passing than there was for any other class before it. . . .

# FROM THE RULING CLASS TO THE POWER ELITE

*T. B. Bottomore*

The value of Marx's concept of the ruling class depends upon the truth of his general social theory. If that theory is not universally valid a ruling class may be conceived as originating from military power, or in modern times from the power of a political party, just as well as from the ownership of the means of production. It may still be maintained, however, that the consolidation of a ruling class requires the concentration of the various types of power—economic, military and political—and that, as a matter of fact, in most societies the formation of this class has begun with the acquisition of economic power. But this raises a more fundamental question about the idea of a ruling class. Is it the case that in every society other than the most simple and primitive this concentration of power occurs, that a ruling class is formed? It should be said at once that the different types of society conform in varying degrees with Marx's model of a society which is clearly divided between a ruling class and subject classes. The most favourable case is probably that of European feudalism, characterized by the rule of a warrior class[1] which had securely in its hands the ownership of land, military force, and political authority, and which received the ideological support of a powerful Church. But even here, a number of qualifications are necessary. The idea of a cohesive ruling class is contradicted by the decentralization of political power which was characteristic of feudal societies,[2] and at the stage when this decentralization was overcome—in the absolute monarchies—the European societies were no longer ruled, in a strict sense, by a warrior nobility. Nevertheless, the nobility of the *ancien régime* does come close to the ideal type of a ruling class.

Another case which fits Marx's model well in many respects is that of the *bourgeoisie* of early capitalism. The development of the *bourgeoisie* as an important social class can well be explained by economic changes, and its rise in the economic sphere was accompanied by the acquisition of other positions of power and prestige in society—in politics, administration, the armed forces and the educational system. This conquest

From *Elites and Society,* by T. B. Bottomore, © T. B. Bottomore 1964, Basic Books, Inc., Publishers, New York.

[1] Marc Bloch, *Feudal Society*, Vol. II, Book III, Chap. I.

[2] Marc Bloch, *op. cit.*

of power in the different spheres of society was a long and confused process, which had many local variations in the European countries, and Marx's model was an abstraction from the complex historical reality, bringing together the experiences of the revolution in France—the most violent ideological and political expression of the rise of a new class—and those of the industrial revolution in England. Nevertheless, the pattern of events does conform broadly with Marx's scheme; in England, the Reform Act of 1832 gave political power to the *bourgeoisie*, and it produced changes in the character of legislation even if it did not, for some considerable time, change the social composition of Parliament or cabinets[3]; the reform of the Civil Service after 1855 opened the way for upper middle class aspirants to the highest administrative posts[4]; and the development of public schools created new opportunities for children from the newly rich industrial and commercial families to be trained for elite positions. The *bourgeoisie* also gained powerful ideological support, according to Marx's account, from the political economists and the utilitarian philosophers.

Nevertheless, the *bourgeoisie* appears in several respects a less cohesive ruling class than the feudal nobility. It does not actually combine in the same persons military, political and economic power, and there arises the possibility of conflicts of interest between the different groups which *represent* (as Marx says) the *bourgeoisie*. Furthermore, capitalist society is more open and mobile than was feudal society, and in the ideological sphere especially, with the development of secular intellectual occupations, conflicting doctrines may arise. Marx expected that the polarization of the two principal classes—the *bourgeoisie* and industrial working class—would accompany the development of capitalism, and that the rule of the *bourgeoisie* would become more manifest and more onerous. But this did not happen in the advanced capitalist societies: the different spheres of power appear to have become more distinct, and the sources of power more numerous and varied; the opposition between the "two great classes" of Marx's theory has been modified by the growth of the new middle classes and by a much more complex differentiation of occupation and status; and political rule has become altogether more mild and less repressive. One important element in this development has been the introduction of universal adult suffrage, which produces, in principle, a separation between economic and political power. Marx himself considered that the attainment of universal suffrage would be a revolutionary step, and that it would transfer political power to the working class.[5] Thus, whereas the connexion between economic and political power can easily be established in the case of feudal society, or in the case of early capitalism with its limitation of political rights to property owners, it cannot be so easily established in the case of the modern capitalist democracies, and the notion of a distinct and settled ruling class becomes dubious and unclear. Marxist fundamentalists, in their attempts to preserve Marx's social theory intact, have been obliged to argue that even in political democracies the *bourgeoisie* always effectively rules through

[3] See W. L. Guttsman, *The British Political Elite*, Chap. 3, "The changing social structure of the British political elite: 1868–1955."

[4] See J. Donald Kingsley, *Representative Bureaucracy*, especially Chap. III, "Middle Class Reform: the Triumph of Plutocracy." Kingsley concludes that "the middle classes had by 1870 destroyed the *ancien régime* on almost every front, [but] the chief gains had been made by the upper ranks of those classes. In the House of Commons wealthy merchants, bankers, industrialists, were displacing the landlords and would begin before many years to replace them in the cabinet. In the Civil Service a somewhat comparable change had occurred. Entrance to the higher posts was no longer a matter of aristocratic influence. The key that now unlocked the door was a costly education which . . . gave to the new system a 'plutocratic character'" (p. 76).

[5] Karl Marx, "The Chartists", *New York Daily Tribune*, 25th August 1852. ". . . Universal Suffrage is the equivalent of political power for the working class of England, where the proletariat forms the large majority of the population, where, in a long, though underground civil war, it has gained a clear consciousness of its position as a class, and where even the rural districts know no longer any peasants, but only landlords, industrial capitalists (farmers) and hired labourers. The carrying of Universal Suffrage in England would, therefore, be a far more socialistic measure than anything which has been honoured with that name on the Continent. Its inevitable result, here, is *the political supremacy of the working class.*"

the indirect influence of wealth, but this is more easily asserted than demonstrated.

These, in brief, are some of the principal difficulties in Marx's conception of the ruling class. . . .

The concept of the "governing elite" or "political class" was proposed as an alternative, partly, . . . in order to demonstrate the impossibility of attaining a classless form of society, but also to meet the theoretical difficulties which we have just considered. The concept of a governing elite avoids, in particular, the difficulty of showing that a particular class, defined in terms of its economic position, does in fact dominate all the spheres of social life; but it does so only at the cost of abandoning any attempt to explain the phenomena to which it refers. The governing elite, according to Mosca and Pareto, comprises those who occupy the recognized positions of political power in a society. Thus, when we ask, who has power in a particular society, the reply is, those who have power, i.e. those who occupy the specified positions. This is scarcely illuminating; it does not tell us how these particular individuals come to occupy the positions of power. Or else it is misleading; if, for example, those who appear to have power in the formal system of government are in fact subject to the power of other individuals or groups outside this system. . . .

The difficulties in the concept of a governing elite can be seen most clearly in a recent work which shows the influence of Marx on one side and of Mosca and Pareto on the other—the late C. Wright Mills' *The Power Elite*. Mills explains his preference for the term "power elite" rather than "ruling class" by saying: " 'Ruling class' is a badly loaded phrase. 'Class' is an economic term; 'rule' a political one. The phrase 'ruling class,' thus contains the theory that an economic class rules politically. That short-cut theory may or may not at times be true, but we do not want to carry that one rather simple theory about in the terms that we use to define our problems; we wish to state the theories explicitly, using terms of more precise and unilateral meaning. Specifically, the phrase 'ruling class,' in its common political connotations, does not allow enough autonomy to the political order and its agents, and it says nothing about the military as such . . . We hold that such a simple view of 'economic determinism' must be elaborated by 'political determinism' and 'military determinism'; that the higher agents of each of these three domains now often have a noticeable degree of autonomy; and that only in the often intricate ways of coalition do they make up and carry through the most important decisions."[6]

Mills defines the power elite in much the same way as Pareto defined his "governing elite," for he says, "we may define the power elite in terms of the means of power—as those who occupy the command posts."[7] But the analysis which proceeds from this definition has a number of unsatisfactory features. In the first place, Mills distinguishes three major elites in the USA—the corporation heads, the political leaders and the military chiefs—and he is obliged to go on to inquire whether these three groups together form a single power elite, and if so, what it is that binds them together. One possible answer to these questions is to say that the three groups do form a single elite because they are representatives of an upper class, which has to be regarded, consequently, as a ruling class. But Mills, although he emphasizes that most of the members of these elites are in fact drawn from a socially recognized upper class, says initially that he will leave open the question of whether or not it is such a class which rules through the elites, and when he returns to the problem it is only to reject the Marxist idea of a ruling class in the brief passage cited above. In short, the question is never seriously discussed, and this is a curious failing in the particular case which Mills is examining, and in the context of the ideas which he is expressing. He has previously rejected the view that there is popular control of the power elite through voting or other means, and has emphasized the unity of the elite, as well as the homogeneity of its social origins—all of which points to the consolidation of a ruling class. The formulation which he actually gives is vague and

[6] *Op. cit.*, p. 277.
[7] *Op. cit.*, p. 23.

unconvincing: it is a reference to "the often uneasy coincidence of economic, military, and political power," a coincidence which he proposes to explain largely by thepressures of the international conflict in which America has been engaged.

These problems have frequently been raised in criticisms of Mosca and Pareto. Thus, Carl J. Friedrich observed that one of the most problematical parts of all elite doctrines is the assumption that the men of power do constitute a cohesive group: "In the light of the continuous change in the composition of the majority, it is not possible to say, under conditions such as prevail in a functioning democracy, that those who play some considerable part in government constitute a cohesive group."[8] This view of the elite in modern democracies has been widely held; it is stated boldly in the conclusions of a recent study of the upper strata of British society: ". . . the rulers are not at all close-knit or united. They are not so much in the centre of a solar system, as in a cluster of interlocking circles, each one largely preoccupied with its own professionalism and expertise, and touching others only at one edge . . . they are not a single Establishment but a ring of Establishments, with slender connexions. The frictions and balances between the different circles are the supreme safeguard of democracy. No one man can stand in the centre. for there is no centre."[9]

Mills rejects this fashionable liberal-minded doctrine, which he summarizes as follows: "Far from being omnipotent, the elites are thought to be so scattered as to lack any coherence as a historical force. . . . Those who occupy the formal places of authority are so checkmated—by other elites exerting pressure, or by the public as an electorate, or by constitutional codes—that although there may be upper classes, there is no ruling class; although there may be men of power, there is no power elite; although there may be a system of stratification, it has no effective top."[10] As we have seen, he insists that the three principal elites—economic, political and military—are, in fact, a cohesive group, and he supports his view by establishing the similarity of their social origins, the close personal and family relationships between those in the different elites, and the frequency of interchange of personnel between the three spheres. But since he resists the conclusion that the group is a ruling class he is unable to provide a convincing explanation, as distinct from description, of the solidarity of the power elite. Furthermore, by eliminating the idea of a ruling class, he also excludes that of classes in opposition; and so he arrives at an extremely pessimistic account of American society. The real themes of his book are, first, the transformation of a society in which numerous small and autonomous groups had an effective say in the making of political decisions, into a mass society in which the power elite decides all important issues and keeps the masses quiet by flattery, deception and entertainment; and secondly, the corruption of the power elite itself, which he attributes primarily to a state of affairs in which it is not accountable for its decisions to any organized public, and also to the dominant value of the acquisition of wealth. Mills' account of the historical changes, which does indeed bring to light some important features of modern politics—the growing political influence of military chiefs, for example—is pessimistic in the sense that it suggests no way out of the situation which it describes and condemns. Like Pareto and Mosca, Mills seems to be saying that if we look at modern societies without illusions we shall see that, however democratic their constitutions, they are in fact ruled by an elite; and to be adding, in a devastating fashion, that even in a society so favourably placed as was the USA at its origins—without a feudal system of ranks, with very considerable equality of economic and social condition among its citizens, and with a strongly democratic ideology—the force of events has produced a governing elite of unprecedented power and unaccountability. Where Mills differs from the other Machiavellians is in condemning a

[8] Carl J. Friedrich, *The New Image of the Common Man*, pp. 259–60.

[9] Anthony Sampson, *Anatomy of Britain*, p. 624.

[10] *Op. cit.*, pp. 16–17.

state of affairs which they either praised or, in a spirit of disillusionment, accepted.

The concepts of "ruling class" and "governing elite" are used in descriptions and explanations of political happenings, and their value must be judged by the extent to which they make possible reasonable answers to important questions about political systems. Do the rulers of society constitute a social group? Is it a cohesive or divided, an open or closed group? How are its members selected? What is the basis of their power? Is this power unrestricted or is it limited by that of other groups in society? Are there significant and regular differences between societies in these respects, and if so, how are they to be explained?

The two concepts are alike in emphasizing the division between rulers and ruled as one of the most important facts of social structure.[11] But they state the division in different ways: the concept of a "governing elite" contrasts the organized, ruling minority with the unorganized majority, or masses, while the concept of a "ruling class" contrasts the dominant class with subject classes, which may themselves be organized, or be creating organizations. From these different conceptions arise differences in the way of conceiving the relations between rulers and ruled. In the Marxist theory, which employs the concept of a ruling class, the conflict between classes becomes the principal force producing changes of social structure; but in the elite theories—in spite of the fact that Pareto praised highly Marx's conception of class struggle, which he described as "profoundly true,"[12]—the relations between the organized minority and the unorganized majority are necessarily represented as more passive, and the resulting problem of how to explain the rise and fall of ruling elites, if it is confronted at all, has to be dealt with either by postulating a recurrent decadence in the elite (Pareto) or by introducing the idea of the rise of new "social forces" among the masses (Mosca) which brings the theory close to Marxism.

A further difference between the two concepts lies in the extent to which they make possible explanations of the cohesion of the ruling minority. The "governing elite," defined as those who occupy the positions of command in a society, is merely assumed to be a cohesive group, unless other considerations, such as their membership of the wealthy class, or their aristocratic family origins are introduced (as they are consistently by Mosca, and occasionally by Pareto). But the "ruling class," defined as the class which owns the major instruments of economic production in a society, is shown to be a cohesive social group; first, because its members have definite economic interests in common, and, more importantly, because it is engaged permanently in a conflict with other classes in society, through which its self-awareness and solidarity are continually enhanced. Furthermore, this concept states in a precise form what is the basis of the minority's ruling position, namely its economic dominance, while the concept of the "governing elite" says little about the bases of the power which the elite possesses, except in so far as it incorporates elements from the Marxist theory of classes. In Mills' study of the "power elite," there is an attempt to explain the power position of the three principal elites taken separately—that of the business executives by the growth in size and complexity of business corporations; that of the military chiefs by the growing scale and expense of the weapons of war, determined by technology and the state of international conflict; and that of the national political leaders, in a somewhat less satisfactory way, by the decline of the legislature, of local politics and of voluntary organizations—but the unity of the power elite as a single group, and the basis of *its* power, are not explained. Why is there *one* power elite and not *three*?

The superiority of the concept of "ruling class" lies in its greater fertility and suggestiveness and in its value in the construction of theories. But I have pointed out earlier some of its defects, and it is now necessary to consider whether these can be overcome. The most important step in this

[11] "From the point of view of scientific research the real superiority of the concept of the ruling, or political, class ['political elite' in our terminology. TBB] lies in the fact that the varying structure of ruling classes has a preponderant importance in determining the political type, and also the level of civilization, of the different peoples". Mosca, *op. cit.*, p. 51.

[12] Pareto, *Les systèmes socialistes*, II, p. 405.

direction would be to give up the Marxist view of the concept as a description of a real phenomenon which is to be observed in all societies in the same general form, and to regard it instead as an "ideal type," in the sense which Max Weber gave to this term.[13] If we treat the concept in this way we can proceed to ask how closely the relationships in a particular society approach the ideal type of a ruling class and subject classes; and so employ the concept, properly, as a tool of thought and investigation. It is then possible to see clearly that the idea of a "ruling class" originated in the study of a particular historical situation—the end of feudalism and the beginnings of modern capitalism[14]—and to consider how far, and in what respects, other situations diverge from this ideal type, as a result of the absence or weakness of class formation, the influence of factors other than the ownership of property in the creation of classes, and the conflict between different forms of power.

There are two sorts of situation in which we can see especially plainly a divergence from the ideal type of a ruling class. One is that in which, although there is an "upper class"—that is to say, a clearly demarcated social group which has in its possession a large part of the property of society and receives a disproportionately large share of the national income, and which has created on the basis of these economic advantages a distinctive culture and way of life—this class does not enjoy undisputed or unrestricted political power, in the sense that it is able to maintain easily its property rights or to transmit them unimpaired from generation to generation. This kind of situation has been discerned by many observers particularly in the modern democracies, in which, as I noted earlier, there is a potential opposition between the ownership of wealth and productive resources by a small upper class, and the possession of political power, through the franchise, by the mass of the population. . . .

In order to determine whether in such a case there is a "ruling class" it is necessary first to examine the degree in which the upper class has been successful in perpetuating its ownership of property. We shall have to note, on one side, that in the democratic countries during the present century a considerable number of restrictions have been placed upon the use of private property, and that there has probably been some reduction in the inequalities of wealth and income, as a result of progressive taxation, and of the growth of publicly owned property and publicly administered social services. On the other side we must note that the decline in the proportion of private wealth owned by the upper class has been modest and very slow, and that the redistribution of income through taxation has not proceeded very far. The situation in Britain was very carefully examined by John Strachey,[15] who concluded that "up to 1939 there had been little or no redistribution of the national income in favour of the mass of the population, either through trade union pressure or budgetary changes. . . ."[16] In the following period, up to 1951, there was some redistribution of income which resulted in transferring some 10 per cent of the total

[13] An ideal type concept "brings together certain relationships and events of historical life into a complex which is conceived as an internally consistent system . . . this construction itself is like a *utopia* which has been arrived at by the analytical accentuation of certain elements of reality . . . it *is* no hypothesis but it offers guidance in the construction of hypotheses. It is not a *description* of reality but it aims to give unambiguous means of expression to such a description. . . . An ideal type is formed by the one-sided *accentuation* of one or more points of view and by the synthesis of a great many diffuse, discrete, more or less present and occasionally absent *concrete individual* phenomena, which are arranged according to those one-sidedly emphasized viewpoints into a unified *analytical* construct". Max Weber, *The Methodology of the Social Sciences*, p. 90.

[14] As Croce observed of the whole theory of historical materialism: "The materialistic view of history arose out of the need to account for a definite social phenomenon, not from an abstract inquiry into the factors of historical life". B. Croce, *Historical Materialism and the Economics of Karl Marx*, p. 17.

[15] John Strachey, *Contemporary Capitalism*, Chap. VIII, "The Real Development". Strachey draws upon a number of other studies, including Douglas Jay, *The Socialist Case;* and Dudley Seers, *The Levelling of Incomes since 1938* and *Has the Distribution of Income Become More Unequal?*

[16] *Op. cit.*, pp. 137–8.

national income from property owners to wage-earners, but this trend was probably reversed again after 1951.[17] Strachey concludes: "All this is evidence that capitalism has in fact an innate tendency to extreme and ever-growing inequality. For how otherwise could all these cumulatively equalitarian measures which the popular forces have succeeded in enacting over the past hundred years have done little more than hold the position constant? Is it not clear that, if the workings of the system had not been continuously modified, it would have produced just that ever sharper polarization which Marx diagnosed as its essential tendency?"[18] It is evidence, to put the matter in another way, that the upper class in Britain has been able to resist with considerable success the attacks upon its economic interests, and that in this sense of having the power to defend its interests it has maintained itself during the present century as a ruling class. The situation in the other democratic countries, with the exception of the Scandinavian countries, does not differ greatly from that in Britain; in all of them, right-wing governments have been in power during most of the present century and the redistribution of wealth and income has occurred slowly, if at all. One must be sceptical, therefore, of the view that the extension of voting rights to the mass of the population can establish at once—or has in fact established in the short period of time in which modern democracies have existed—popular rule, and eliminate the power of a ruling class. What seems to have taken place in the democratic countries up to the present time is not so much a reduction in the power of the upper class as a decline in the radicalism of the working class.

The second type of situation in which there is a divergence from the "ruling class—subject classes" model is that in which the ruling group is not a class in Marx's sense. One instance is provided by those societies in which a stratum of intellectuals or bureaucrats may be said to wield supreme power—in China under the rule of the *literati*, or in India under the rule of the Brahmins. Another instance is to be found in the present-day Communist countries where power is concentrated in the leaders of a political party. In these cases, however, we need to examine carefully how far the ruling stratum is clearly distinguishable from a ruling class. In India, the Brahmins during the ages when they were most powerful, were also substantial landowners, and they were closely allied with the landowning warrior castes in the imperial and feudal periods of India's history. On occasion, they themselves founded ruling or noble houses, and there seems to have been, at times, an amount of movement of individuals and families between the Brahmin and Kshatriya (warrior) castes, which the doctrines of caste exclusiveness expounded in the classical texts do not indicate.

Again, in China, the *literati* were recruited, in the feudal period, from the principal landowning families, and at other times they came in the main from wealthy families[19]; so that they were always closely linked with an upper class. There is, moreover, another important economic aspect of the rule of these groups of intellectuals and administrators to which Karl Wittfogel has drawn attention.[20] One of the principal instruments of production in China and India (and in a number of other ancient societies)[21] was the system of irrigation, and the *literati* and the Brahmins, without owning this property upon which agricultural production depended, still exercised a more or less complete control over its use. Consequently they possessed, in addition to their ownership of land, a vital economic power which, according to Wittfogel, was the principal support of their political dominance.

But notwithstanding these qualifications the distinction between social strata of this kind and ruling classes which base their power directly upon the legal ownership of property remains. The possession of the

[17] *Ibid.*, p. 146. More recently, Richard M. Titmuss, in his *Income Distribution and Social Change*, has undertaken the most thorough study yet made in Britain of the sources of information about the distribution of income. . . .

[18] Strachey, *op. cit.*, pp. 150–1.

[19] See T. B. Bottomore, *Elites and Society*, New York, Basic Books, 1964, p. 65. (C. S. H.)

[20] Karl Wittfogel, *Oriental Despotism*.

[21] See Julian H. Steward *et al.*, *Irrigation Civilizations: A Comparative Study*.

means of administration may be, as Max Weber argued, an alternative to the possession of means of economic production, as a basis of political power.[22] This distinction is perhaps more obvious in the case of the present-day Communist countries, in which there is no private ownership of the means of production, and in which the officials of the ruling party and the state control the economy. Wittfogel has attempted, in a very ingenious way, to assimilate this type of political power to the general category of "oriental despotism"[23] but I think the differences are too great—the existence of private ownership of land and other resources, and the intimate bonds between the officials and the property-owning classes in one case, and the specific characteristics of rule by a political party in the other[24]—for this attempt to be successful. The political system of the Communist countries seems to me to approach the pure type of a "power elite," that is, a group which, having come to power with the support or acquiescence of particular classes in the population, maintains itself in power chiefly by virtue of being an organized minority confronting the unorganized majority; whereas in the case of ancient China or India we have to deal with a system which combines the features of a ruling class and a power elite.

There is another element in the position of a ruling class, which has already been mentioned and which needs to be examined more fully in its bearing upon those situations in which the existence of such a class is doubtful. Since the power of a ruling class arises from its ownership of property, and since this property can easily be transmitted from generation to generation, the class has an enduring character. It is constituted by a group of families which remain as its component elements over long periods of time through the transmission of the family property. Its composition is not entirely immutable, for new families may enter it and old families may decline, but the greater part of its members continue from generation to generation. Only when there are rapid changes in the whole system of production and property ownership does the composition of the ruling class change significantly; and in that case we can say that one ruling class has been replaced by another. If, however, we were to find, in a particular society or type of society, that the movement of individuals and families between the different social levels was so continuous and so extensive that no group of families was able to maintain itself for any length of time in a situation of economic and political preeminence, then we should have to say that in such a society there was no ruling class. It is, in fact, this "circulation of elites" (in the terminology of the elite theorists) or "social mobility" (in the language of more recent sociological studies) that has been fixed upon by a number of writers as a second important characteristic of modern industrial societies—the first being universal suffrage—which must qualify severely, if it does not altogether exclude, the assertion that there is a ruling class in these societies. By this means we may arrive at the view, which was formulated by Karl Mannheim among others,[25] that the development of industrial societies can properly be depicted as a movement from a class system to a system of elites, from a social hierarchy based upon the inheritance of property to one based upon merit and achievement.

This confrontation between the concepts of "ruling class" and "political elite" shows, I think, that, while on one level they may be totally opposed, as elements in wide-ranging theories which interpret political life, and especially the future possibilities of political organization, in very different ways, on another level they may be seen as complementary concepts, which refer to different types of political system or to different aspects of the same political system. With their help we can attempt to distinguish between societies in which there is a ruling class, and at the same time elites which represent particular aspects of its interests; societies in which there is no ruling class, but a political elite which founds its power upon the control of the

[22] The characteristics of bureaucratic societies have been examined at length in a recent study: S. N. Eisenstadt, *The Political Systems of Empires.*

[23] Wittfogel, *op .cit.*

[24] See T. B. Bottomore, *op. cit.*, see pp. 77–80. (C. S. H.)

[25] See especially, *Man and Society,* Part II, Chap. II.

administration, or upon military force, rather than upon property ownership and inheritance; and societies in which there exists a multiplicity of elites among which no cohesive and enduring group of powerful individuals or families seems to be discoverable at all. In order to establish such a classification we need to examine more closely . . . the circulation of elites, the relations between elites and classes, and the ways in which new elites and new classes are formed.

# POWER IN THE LOCAL COMMUNITY

*Richard A. Schermerhorn*

. . . Social research on the power structures of local communities is somewhat more advanced than inquiry into the national patterns. Though not yet detailed enough to supply answers to many specific questions, these findings nevertheless suggest an outline the details of which can be specified locally. The following review will focus on four major themes: governmental versus non-governmental controls, patterns of power distribution, selection of issues for decision-making, and role images of leaders.

## GOVERNMENTAL VERSUS NON-GOVERNMENTAL CONTROLS IN THE COMMUNITY

In every town or city certain decisions are made outside the city council or mayor's office, others are referred to the government only when they have substantial support, and still others at least appear to be initiated and carried through by government personnel alone. It is hard to be sure that decisions of the last type are not the result of invisible community pressures.

Arthur Vidich and Joseph Bensman speak of the "minimal non-surrenderable functions of police control, street maintenance, water supply and elections" as areas where publicly visible decisions are absolutely required.[1] At the same time, many decisions appear to be made by extra-governmental means while the government plays the role of registering those that require political action to make them legal. At the informal or non-governmental level, leaders, cliques, and associations exercise power through networks of social groupings that form temporary alliances or, in other cases, more permanent coalitions. Some of these may include members of the city council or the mayor so that networks of communication are constantly kept open.

These informal clusters of power may have their source of legitimacy in the folkways, some of which may be unique to the community. As J. S. Coleman remarks, "the outcome of one dispute loads the dice in favor of a similar outcome the next time. Only a few such incidents may be necessary to fix the path of community disputes for fifty or a hundred years to come."[2] However, research is still needed to determine whether the sources of legitimacy are community-wide or whether they are restricted to limited groups whose prestige or coerciveness enables them to impose their views upon others. Further probes are also required to discover whether legitimacy in the community is restricted to highly limited spheres of decision-making. There probably is a good deal of variability from one community to another on such matters.

A pervasive value-system may reflect the national ethos and affect many communities. American individualism, for example, commands widespread attachment in the United States. One feature of individualism, the priority of informal over formal controls, forms the motif of freedom and laissez-faire in social life by tending to establish extra-governmental forms of activity as preferable to governmental action. As Robin Williams puts it, "a major implicit cultural premise



[1] Arthur J. Vidich and Joseph Bensman, *Small Town in Mass Society: Class, Power and Religion in a Rural Community*, p. 135 (Princeton, Princeton University Press, 1958).

[2] James S. Coleman, *Community Conflict*, p. 2 (Glencoe, Ill., The Free Press, 1957).

in the dominant valuation of freedom has been the equating of freedom with control by diffuse cultural structure rather than by a definite social organization. Thus it has seemed to make a great difference whether the individual receives a certain income or has a certain type of occupation as a result of impersonal, anonymous, diffuse competitive process as against being forced to accept that employment or remuneration by law or by the command of a visible social authority."[3]

In like fashion, individualism, growing out of the American experience of subduing the wilderness, exploiting the vast resources of a continent, and establishing new communities where none had been before, relegated the task of social coordination to the background of attention. Government often enough, became an afterthought, subordinate to the "real" concerns of men, which were largely economic. In many ways legitimacy for government became ceremonial and symbolic while business and agriculture attained a higher value priority.

Local communities reflect these individualistic values when they choose community leaders who are not political officials to make weighty decisions. Vidich and Bensman document this pattern for a rural village in upstate New York and they speak of the invisible government.[4] Floyd Hunter reports that in a large Southern city, a small number of influential citizens dominate community policy-making by acting in concert through informal business cliques while political leaders occupy lower echelons of power.[5] Norton Long, in a study of several metropolitan centers, maintains that when the press and broadcasters ask for leaders to solve crises, their demand is for private rather than official public leaders. In his judgment, when citizens posit the existence of such leaders, this action furnishes them with a kind of psychic security which fills the vacuum left by the absence of the more absolutistic rulers of the past. The mass media often credit such informal leaders with both running things and neglecting things; "the idols are both worshipped and beaten, at least verbally . . . This belief in part creates the role of top leadership and demands that it somehow be filled."[6] Vidich and Bensman comment similarly on a dominant leader behind the scenes in Springdale: "All groups and individuals over-estimate his authority, but by this very fact they increase his power since they act on the basis of their estimation."[7]

Research has established the fact that the top leaders in the informal structure are likely to be businessmen. Delbert Miller makes this point clear by comparing the nature of leadership in American and English communities. His study shows that business leaders form 67 per cent of the key influentials (those at the apex of the power structure) in Pacific City, 75 per cent in the Southern metropolis studied by Hunter, but only 25 per cent in a comparable English city. In the latter, professional persons in education, religion, civic organizations, and cooperatives, as well as prominent figures in trade unions and the Labor Party are abundantly represented; the English city has a more diversified group of leaders than is characteristic of the American communities studied.[8]

Although it is yet uncertain how widespread the pattern is, the American communities that have been carefully investigated show a decided preference for nongovernmental controls, private rather than official leaders, and business leaders rather than men from other occupations. These findings require independent verification for other communities and must be balanced by inquiry into the way power structures are organized.

[3] Robin M. Williams, Jr., *American Society, A Sociological Interpretation*, p. 419 (New York, A. A. Knopf, 1951).

[4] Vidich and Bensman, *op. cit.*, pp. 146ff.

[5] Floyd Hunter, *Community Power Structure, A Study of Decision-Makers*, pp. 62, 90ff. (Chapel Hill, N. C., University of North Carolina Press, 1953).

[6] Norton E. Long, "The Social Community as an Ecology of Games," *American Journal of Sociology* 64: 251–261, pp. 255–256 (November, 1958).

[7] Vidich and Bensman, *op. cit.*, p. 277.

[8] Delbert C. Miller, "Decision-Making Cliques in Community Power Structures: A Comparative Study of an American and an English City," *American Journal of Sociology* 64: 299–310 (November, 1958).

## PATTERNS OF POWER DISTRIBUTION

Is there a typical "shape"for the power structure in American communities? It has been common for students of the problem to think of such a pattern as a pyramid having a small oligarchy of highly influential leaders at the top, a larger group of lesser figures at middle levels, and numerous followers at the base. Hunter's study undoubtedly did much to disseminate this view since he pictured a group of financial and corporation executives in Regional City at the apex of power, with their decisions possessing great weight even though such men had no formal authority. Policy decisions were made in private sessions and passed down to the second echelon of power (professional and political leaders) where a larger group of subordinates mobilized public opinion on behalf of policies already adopted. Being assured of support from the top echelons, secondary leaders were usually quite successful in carrying out the plans already formulated. Although Hunter disclaims the use of the pyramidal pattern, students of his findings conclude that it is difficult to interpret his research conclusions in any other way.[9]

Subsequent studies have shown wide differences in community power distribution. Roland J. Pellegrin and Charles H. Coates report, for example, that the leaders of Bigtown, a Southern city of 200,000 population, spoke approvingly of Regional City (the scene of Hunter's research) where things were "done right" and a small compact group "controls civic affairs with a firm hand." The same Bigtown leaders were pessimistic about their own community, deploring its lack of unity, the conflict between business cliques, and the failure to carry out many plans of community development.[10] On the basis of Pellegrin and Coates's observations, Bigtown appeared to have not a pyramidal or hierarchical pattern but a series of elongated, finger-like structures extending downward from upper levels of power.

The studies of Robert Schulze, C. W. M. Hart, and James McKee reveal power configurations of even greater diversity. Schulze investigated an industrial suburb where major industrial plants had been absorbed by absentee-owned corporations. The managers of these plants maintained a strictly hands-off policy in local affairs, leaving their direction to men who were not economic dominants.[11] This neglect appeared to leave a unique power vacuum at the top where several large companies were involved. It seemed that local managers did not agree on this permissive policy beforehand but adopted it singly in response to national company directives separately issued. These different directives converged in the local community.

It is quite obvious that policies made outside the community narrow the range of decisions made within it, or, in extreme cases determine what will be done locally. Roland Warren, whose provisional study of this problem has opened up important avenues for exploration, shows the existence of various types of control from outside the community—informal control through culture patterns and formal control through governmental regulations at the state level affecting taxation and education, working conditions, and wage deductions. Frequently there are economic units that are parts of organizations, which set forth policies or regulations to govern operations of these units in each city or town. Finally there are national or international organizations, such as the Red Cross, American Legion, and the Roman Catholic Church, which, while allowing a certain leeway for local variations, often enough formulate broad programs and policies that are binding on their sub-units.[12] Vidich and Bensman provide specific examples of how larger organizations restrict community action in various ways.[13] Small towns and one-industry cities seem to

[9] Herbert Kaufman and Victor Jones, "The Mystery of Power," *Public Administration Review* 14: 205–212, p. 207 (Summer, 1954).

[10] Roland J. Pellegrin and Charles H. Coates, "Absentee-Owned Corporations and Community Power Structure," *American Journal of Sociology* 61: 413–419 (March, 1956).

[11] Robert O. Schulze, "Economic Dominants in Community Power Structure," *American Sociological Review* 23: 3–9, pp. 6–8 (February, 1958).

[12] Roland L. Warren, "Toward a Typology of Extra-Community Controls Limiting Local Community Autonomy," *Social Forces* 34: 338–341 (May, 1956).

[13] Vidich and Bensman, *op. cit.*, p. 113.

be particularly vulnerable in this respect.

The organizational drift from local to national scope has led to increased decision-making in central headquarters; this is true of both large-scale corporations and unions. Similarly the increase of federal functions and controls in government has progressively narrowed the choices of local officials and leaders. In some cases this development has led more citizens to vote in national elections than in local community contests,[14] because, perhaps, they realize the greater importance to them of the issues involved. At any rate it is now important to learn what decisions are left to the local community and to whom they are vitally significant. One thing seems certain and should be kept in mind: community decisions are only partly autonomous.

The apparent power vacuum at the top in Schulze's example of the community with absentee-owned corporations may be a consequence of the fact that the local community is no longer in a position to make decisions significantly affecting corporate interests. On the other hand, this situation may represent a power potential rather than a power vacuum. Corporations with local branches may decides not to throw their weight around in smaller communities, but these firms hold in reserve a weapon of great effectiveness, namely the ability to move any local plant to a different location. In towns where employment is mainly dependent on one or two large companies, a decision to relocate manufacturing units can disrupt the entire economic base of the community. Although such decisions depend on national and international market and supply conditions, they are related to local political factors also. Absentee-owned corporations pay a disproportionate share of taxes in small towns; as a result the local government refrains from changing the tax structure drastically upward for this would kill the goose that lays the golden egg. As long as this tax situation continues, corporations can afford to maintain the kind of hands-off policy noted by Schulze. But such abdication of power is conditional rather than fixed policy.

[14] V. O. Key, Jr., *Politics, Parties and Pressure Groups,* 4th ed., p. 627 (New York, Crowell, 1958).

Hart, in his study of Windsor, Ontario, presents quite a different power configuration from those sketched above. As he reports it, this community is dominated by four major groups: big business (Ford and Chrysler), the Roman Catholic Church, the unions, and finally the local business group including the Chamber of Commerce. So discrete and cohesive do these groups appear that Hart can find no trace of a general public. Its absence engenders conflicts that are naked and overt. Commenting on the lack of a power pyramid, Hart declares that it may not be clear who "runs the town," but at least "it is not the top management of Ford or Chrysler nor 'stooges' for those managements."[15] McKee, in a similar study, notes the central role of the CIO in Lorain, Ohio, and sees community power in terms of multiple groups combined differently on separate issues. He insists that the familiar pyramidal model seriously distorts many relationships in that city.[16]

Realistic analysis requires more than cross-sectional study of the local community; it must not neglect changes through time. For example, founder-owners of rapidly growing industries have often established family dominance of a corporation, which has gone hand in hand with almost monopolistic power in the local community. Robert and Helen Lynd documented this pattern in their second Middletown volume, showing that the "X family," which founded the local glass jar industry, extended its control into banking, real estate, retail business, education, recreation, religious institutions, charities, the press, and, to a considerable degree, local government.[17] Such dynastic control changes markedly as industry passes from family to managerial dominance. Any power shifts within industry bring in their train other shifts in community

[15] C. W. M. Hart, "Industrial Relations Research and Industry," *Canadian Journal of Economics and Political Science* 15: 53–73, pp. 59–60, 66, 68 (February, 1949).

[16] James B. McKee, "Status and Power in the Industrial Community: A Comment on Drucker's Thesis," *American Journal of Sociology* 58: 364–370, p. 369 (January, 1953).

[17] Robert S. Lynd and Helen M. Lynd, *Middletown in Transition, A Study in Cultural Conflicts,* Chapter 3 (New York, Harcourt, Brace & Co., 1937).

power as local familial controls are replaced by specialized management and as labor unions develop; further changes result when local plants are sold outright to absentee-owned corporations.

Consequently any attempt to assess the organization of power in the local community must take into account the stage of maturation of its industry. It is perhaps too early to agree with Daniel Bell that "by and large, the system of family control is finished."[18] For example, one reason that Hunter's Regional City reveals such a marked hierarchical power pattern seems to be that hereditary wealth dominates business activity in that Southern metropolis; at least twenty-five out of Hunter's top forty leaders were so assisted in gaining positions of economic prominence.[19] There may be important regional differences in this respect; Schulze hints that the prevalence of family control in the South seems to be greater than it is elsewhere.[20]

Studies of changing power configurations over time would also probably show an increasing prominence of formerly submerged groups in American community life. Arnold Rose, commenting on this historic shift in the power balance, says that "now a significant proportion of the lower classes is organized into labor unions and a significant proportion of ethnic minorities have organized into reform groups; and both are participating in political organizations. Thus both the lower classes and the ethnic minorities today have a significant measure of power."[21] This change should be investigated in its relation to industrial maturation in different types of cities.

Generalizations such as Peter Rossi's statement, "the less diversified the economic base of the community, the more clustered is the power,"[22] do not appear to be applicable to all types of American communities. As we have seen, this proposition neglects those cases where absentee-owned corporations abdicate their power or where the rapid growth of unions in other industrial towns broadens the base of power distribution patterns.

While a good many American communities are notably similar in preferring non-governmental to governmental controls, the plurality of power distribution in the wider societal area seems to preclude any uniform pattern. In some cases a commonly shared value system may impose a good deal of uniformity; in other situations the economic organization results in multiple power configurations for which as yet no adequate classification has been made. At the present stage of knowledge, social scientists are limited, for the most part, to searching out and reporting the unique power distribution in each community investigated. Yet structural similarities, as well as differences, are revealed in these community studies. This fact suggests that it may soon be possible to work out a typology of communities in terms of economic and social structure, including their functional relationships with the wider society. If this happens it will transcend the traditional distinctions of urban sociology which classifies communities into the broader and less useful categories of institutional cities, trading centers, metropolitan cities, and resort towns.[23] The use of local power patterns will be helpful to sharpen our analysis and furnish a new typology.

## THE SELECTION OF ISSUES

What issues are decided at what levels in American communities? George Belknap and Ralph Smuckler found in a Midwest city that the top leadership remains constant, whatever the issue, while lower echelon leaders change in accordance with the problem.[24] Miller, on the other hand, reports considerable fluidity among key

[18] Daniel Bell, "The Power Elite—Reconsidered," *American Journal of Sociology* 64: 238–250, p. 248 (November, 1958).

[19] Miller, *op. cit.*, p. 307.

[20] Schulze, *op. cit.*, p. 8.

[21] Arnold Rose, "Power Distribution in the Community Through Voluntary Association," *Problems in Social Psychology, An Interdisciplinary Inquiry*, J. E. Hulett and Ross Stagner, eds., p. 80 (Urbana, Ill., University of Illinois, 1952).

[22] Peter H. Rossi, "Community Decision-Making," *Administrative Science Quarterly* I: 415–443, p. 440 (March, 1957).

[23] Svend Riemer, *The Modern City*, pp. 41–44 (New York, Prentice-Hall, 1952).

[24] George Belknap and Ralph Smuckler, "Political Power Relations in a Mid-West City," *Public Opinion Quarterly* 20: 73–81, p. 81 (Spring, 1956).

influentials as issues change.[25] Research into the reasons for this conflicting evidence should uncover more basic factors affecting community issues. Hunter, for example, mentions the fact that many issues are bandied about by subleaders; in due time they emerge for top level policy consideration.[26] The initiation of issues and the decisions about them may occur at quite different levels in the power structure.

James Coleman has furnished a trenchant analysis of community issues when they become matters of controversy or conflict. He distinguishes between the initiation of conflict and its perpetuation. In the initiatory phase, three major areas of life provide what Coleman calls bases of response to controversial issues. The first is the economic area, where conflicts arise over items like taxes or the movement of a factory to town; the second is the area of authority, where disputes about such things as city-manager plans and proportional representation arise; the third area consists of cultural values or beliefs, as when disagreements arise over the educational philosophy of school superintendents or about desegregation. Coleman notes that conflicts over cultural values take place especially in cities where there is a rapid influx of inhabitants with different styles of life, suburban communities, and in Southern towns.[27]

Throughout his discussion, Coleman observes two additional bases of response in the perpetuation stage: attachments or identifications with individuals or groups already involved in the dispute ("psychological") and associational membership that limits word-of-mouth discussions by restricting communication to specific channels ("sociological"). Associational ties seem to have greater influence on middle and upper class persons than on those of lower status; personal attachments play a greater role in small towns than in larger ones. In both the initiatory and later stages of controversy, the national climate of opinion may be pivotal, as it was during the McCarthy era when labor unions took no stand on the issue because of divided opinion within the membership. Coleman also observes that people who are weakly identified with the community at large (found especially among the lower classes and newer migrants) are apt to overstep the bounds of legitimate methods more quickly when aroused.[28]

Coleman has advanced our general knowledge about the operation of controversial issues in the community; power analysis raises additional questions. What issues are kept out of the arena of public discussion and what problems are allowed to reach the attention of the community? Is there a mechanism for keeping sensitive issues away from the public, and is it used by the private leaders who already possess significant power? This problem is important because the selection of issues—at least public issues—precedes the making of decisions. Often the local newspaper plays a significant role by accenting or exaggerating some problems while minimizing others or eliminating them entirely. Not only does the average citizen perceive the issues as they are revealed in the organs of public opinion, he has a tendency to accept the assigned importance of the issues themselves. Value preferences of the editor or publisher (sometimes related to his clique position) may be a key to the community perception of issues as presented in his newspaper, and these may reflect the views of top-level leaders.

Community issues thus furnish an important lead to two significant questions: How do these issues serve as channels for the operation of power structures already firmly set in the community? How do they supply focal situations for change in the community power balance? Hunter and his associates suggest how this problem may be approached when they indicate that a new issue raises three questions in the minds of community leaders: (1) who is behind this thing? (2) how much is it going to cost? (3) what will it do to my business or my agency or my reputation?[29]

[25] Miller, *op. cit.*, pp. 306, 310..

[26] Hunter, *op. cit.*, p. 225.

[27] James S. Coleman, *Community Conflict*, pp. 6–7 (Glencoe, Ill., The Free Press, 1957).

[28] Coleman, *op. cit.*, pp. 13, 21.

[29] Floyd Hunter, Ruth Connor Schaffer and Cecil G. Sheps, *Community Organization, Action and Inaction*, p. 33 (Chapel Hill, N.C., University of North Carolina Press, 1956).

## ROLE IMAGES OF LEADERS

Public opinion, changeable and vacillating as it may be, has a definite bearing on the way in which power is exercised in the community. Community confidence in its leadership, both formal and informal, often determines what can or cannot be done by those who wield one type of authority or another. Assume for a moment that in a given community the role of private leaders has more legitimacy than that of public leaders in the local government. What happens when the public loses confidence in its private top leadership? Probably one of two things will occur: the public will raise its estimation of public authorities and demand that they do something or it will minimize the present mistakes of private leaders and laud them for what they have achieved for the community in the past. The issue will die down, and eventually the public will restore its belief in top leadership as a kind of prop for security feelings.

However there is not one public but many. Will people at different levels in the class structure have the same role images of their leaders? David Riesman and Nathan Glazer declare that "only the more disabused folk in the lower strata nourish the myth that there is an inner circle which knows how to manage them and to manage events."[30] Is this statement true or does it reflect certain assumptions about the class structure that are unproved?[31] Riesman and Glazer make their assertions confidently without the use of supporting evidence, so it is only natural for doubts to appear. At any rate, further research is definitely needed to determine how much difference there is in the way people at various socio-economic levels perceive both public and private authorities. This would furnish an invaluable clue to the way in which such leaders could or could not manipulate the masses.

On the other hand, the self-images of leaders have a great deal to do with the way they exercise their authority. Norton Long distinguishes the self-images of governmental and non-governmental leaders in the following way: "The politicians who hold the offices do not regard themselves as governors of the municipal territory but largely as mediators or players in a particular game that makes use of the other inhabitants." Informal leaders, on the other hand, are often "genuinely reluctant, fearful, and even morally shocked at their positions' becoming that of a recognized territorial government."[32] If this applies to all communities, we would have to conclude that even though power is desired, responsibility may not be. It seems likely that there is greater variability from one city to another on this issue than Long suggests. At any rate, a more thorough assessment of the way community power-holders view themselves will furnish a clue to the way they exercise their leadership.

Finally, how do community leaders view the public? Riesman and Glazer speak of upper-level leaders as feeling "mastered by vague events" and of how often they claim that public opinion will not "stand for" this or that policy; frequently such leaders "take refuge behind public opinion for their own inability to act."[33] Here again we may have an insight rather than the statement of a trend. But the issue has crucial significance; what are the images of the public held by dominant community leaders and what are the reciprocal role images of the leaders entertained by their followers? This sort of information can single out important factors in the climate of public opinion that have special relationship to the way different forms of power may be exercised.

In this final chapter we have reviewed enough of the literature on community power studies to give the reader a few salient points of reference which he can apply to his own city or town. It is hoped in this way to furnish not a mere intellectual exercise but a method of analysis that will help him to see the political process in sociological terms. In summary, some of the questions that may be found useful are: Who are the formal and informal leaders and what is their relationship to each other? What is the shape of the power structure? What is the stage of industrial maturity locally? What is

[30] David Riesman and Nathan Glazer, "Criteria for Political Apathy," *Studies in Leadership*, A. W. Gouldner, ed., p. 517 (New York, Harper & Bros., 1950).

[31] Leonard Reissman, *Class in American Society*, pp. 196–202 (Glencoe, Ill., The Free Press, 1959).

[32] Long, *op. cit.*, pp. 255, 259.

[33] Riesman and Glazer, *op. cit.*, p. 514.

the tradition of past decision? Who are the people most committed and least committed to the community as a focus of loyalty? What are the modes of formal and informal control? What is the role of the political party in joining the two? What types of decision depend chiefly on forces outside the community? How are issues selected for community decision and at what level? How do newspaper policies and the treatment of issues in the press affect the public? How much confidence is invested in both formal and informal leaders? How do members of the community at different socio-economic levels view the community leaders? How do the leaders see their own role and the role of the public?

Questions like these will perhaps reveal more than asking how many Democrats or how many Republicans there are in the city. At any rate, answers to such questions will help the reader to understand the enlargement of perspective, the excitement of exploration, and the satisfaction at reaching even tentative conclusions that motivate the social scientist in his study of power.

# Status Inequality

---

## WHAT SOCIAL CLASS IS IN AMERICA

*W. Lloyd Warner with Marchia Meeker and Kenneth Eells*

### THE AMERICAN DREAM AND SOCIAL CLASS

In the bright glow and warm presence of the American Dream all men are born free and equal. Everyone in the American Dream has the right, and often the duty, to try to succeed and to do his best to reach the top. Its two fundamental themes and propositions, that all of us are equal and that each of us has the right to the chance of reaching the top, are mutually contradictory, for if all men are equal there can be no top level to aim for, no bottom one to get away from; there can be no superior or inferior positions but only one common level into which all Americans are born and in which all of them will spend their lives. We all know such perfect equality of position and opportunity does not exist. All Americans are not born into families of equal position: some are born into a rich man's aristocracy on the Gold Coast; some into the solid comfort of Suburbia's middle classes; and others into a mean existence among the slum families living on the wrong side of the tracks. It is common knowledge that the sons and daughters of the Gold Coasts, the Main Lines, and Park Avenues of America are more likely to receive recognition for their efforts than the children of the slums. The distance these fortunate young people travel to achieve success is shorter, and the route up easier, than the long hard pull necessary for the ambitious children of the less fortunate middle class. Though everyone has the common right to succeed, it is not an equal "right". . . .

When some men learn that *all* the American Dream does not fit *all* that is true about the realities of our life, they denounce the Dream and deny the truth of *any* of it. Fortunately, most of us are wiser and better adjusted to social reality; we recognize that, though it is called a Dream and though some of it is false, by virtue of our firm belief in it we have made some of it true. Despite the presence of social hierarchies which place people at higher and lower levels in American communities, the principles of democracy do operate; the Christian dogma that all men are equal in the sight of God because He is our Father and we are His spiritual children, buttressed by the democratic faith in the equality of men and the insistence on their equal rights as citizens, is a powerful influence in the daily life of America.

. . . . . . . . . . . . . . . . . . . . . . . . . . . . . . . . . . . .

Most of us know from novels such as those of Sinclair Lewis of the Main Streets that run through all our towns and cities, populated by Babbitts, or, more explicitly stated, by "the substantial upper-middle class"; and by now, thanks to another group of novelists such as Erskine Caldwell, we know there is a low road, a Tobacco Road, that runs not only by the ramshackle houses of the poor whites of the South, but by the tarpaper shanties of the slums and river bottoms or Goat Hills of every town and city in the United States.

The "superior people" of Marquand's New England, "the North Shore crowd," divided into a top level of "old families" with a set of values and a way of life rated above those of the "new families," are matched by Philadelphia's "Main Line" families in Christopher Morley's *Kitty Foyle* and by similar groups in many other novels which report on the dominance of "the upper classes" in all regions of the United States. Reading them, together with similar novels reporting on Suburbia and Main Street for the middle classes and those on the Tobacco Roads and the city slums for the lower levels, gives one the understanding that throughout the towns and cities of America the inhabitants are divided into status levels which are ways of life with definite characteristics and values. . . .

Although well aware of social class, social scientists have been more concerned with their theories and with quarreling among themselves about what social class is than with studying its realities in the daily lives of the people. Until recently, they have lagged behind the novelists in investigating what our classes are, how they operate in our social life, and what effect they have on our individual lives. . . .

The researches on social class in the several regions of the United States make it possible to fill in much of the missing knowledge necessary to give Americans such explicit understanding of social class and to answer some of the important questions we raise about it when adjusting to the realities of our existence.

. . . . . . . . . . . . . . . . . . . . . . . . . . . . . . . . . . . . .

## THE STRUCTURAL IMPERATIVE—WHY WE HAVE A CLASS SYSTEM

. . . Just as students of comparative biology have demonstrated that the physical structure of the higher animals must have certain organs to survive, so students of social anthropology have shown that the social structures of the "higher," the more complex, societies must have rank orders to perform certain functions necessary for group survival.

When societies are complex and service large populations, they always possess some kind of status system which, by its own values, places people in higher or lower positions. Only the very simple hunting and gathering tribes, with very small populations and very simple social problems, are without systems of rank; but when a society is complex, when there are large numbers of individuals in it pursuing diverse and complex activities and functioning in a multiplicity of ways, individual positions and behaviors are evaluated and ranked.[1] This happens primarily because, to maintain itself, the society must co-ordinate the efforts of all its members into common enterprises necessary for the preservation of the group, and it must solidify and integrate all these enterprises into a working whole. In other words, as the division of labor increases and the social units become more numerous and diverse, the need for co-ordination and integration also increases and, when satisfied, enables the larger group to survive and develop.

Those who occupy co-ordinating positions acquire power and prestige. They do so because their actions partly control the behavior of the individuals who look to them for direction. Within this simple control there is simple power. Those who exercise such power either acquire prestige directly from it or have gained prestige from other sources sufficiently to be raised to a co-ordinating position. . . .

[1] L. T. Hobhouse, G. C. Wheeler, and M. Ginsberg, *The Material Culture and Social Institutions of the Simpler Peoples,* London: Chapman and Hall, 1915. This exhaustive study of hundreds of communities and societies of the world demonstrates how social stratification and rank are highly correlated with technological advancement and the increase in social complexity. See in particular pages 228–237.

The studies of other societies have demonstrated one other basic point: the more complex the technological and economic structure, the more complex the social structure; so that some argue (the Marxians and many classical economists) that technological advancement is the cause of social complexity and all class and status systems. It cannot be denied that economic and technological factors are important in the determination of class and status orders. We must not lose sight of the fact, however, that the social system, with its beliefs, values, and rules, which governs human behavior may well determine what kind of technology and what kind of economic institutions will survive or thrive in any given tribe or nation. In any case, social complexity is necessary for economic advancement. Furthermore, social complexity is a basic factor determining the presence or absence of class.

The Marxians have argued that the economic changes our society is undergoing always result in a class war in which "the proletariat" will be triumphant and out of which a "classless society" will result. The authors do not agree with them for several reasons. The principal reasons are: (1) the presence of a class order does not necessarily mean class conflict—the relations of the classes can be and often are amiable and peaceful; (2) classless societies (without differential status systems) are impossible where there is complexity for the reasons previously given. Russia's communistic system, supposedly designed to produce a pure equalitarian society, necessarily has citizens who are ranked above and below each other. Generals, there, outrank privates; commissars, the rank and file; and members of the Politburo, the ordinary comrade. Occupants of these higher ranks in Russia tend to associate together; those of the lower ranks form their own groups. Their children are trained according to the rank of their parents. This means that the younger generation learns these status differences, thereby strengthening status differences between levels and fostering the further development of social class in Communistic Russia.

All this has occurred despite the fact the Russians have removed the means of production from private hands and placed them under the control of the State ("the people"). The economic factor which by Marxian doctrine produced social classes is largely absent; yet social hierarchies and social classes are present for the reason that Russia is a complex society and needs them to survive. . . .

But let us return to the United States. We, too, have a complex, highly diverse society. We, too, possess an elaborate division of labor and a ramified technology. And we, too, possess a variety of rank orders built on the need of maintaining unity and cohesion in making our common enterprises successful. . . . Children are always born to their families' position. Through life they may increase or decrease their status. The family thereby strengthens and helps maintain our class order. Social status in America is somewhat like man's alimentary canal; he may not like the way it works and he may want to forget that certain parts of it are part of him, but he knows it is necessary for his very existence. So a status system, often an object of our disapproval, is present and necessary in our complex social world. . . .

## CLASS AMONG THE NEW ENGLAND YANKEES

Studies of communities in New England clearly demonstrate the presence of a well-defined social-class system.[2] At the top is an aristocracy of birth and wealth. This is the so-called "old family" class. The people of Yankee City say the families who belong to it have been in the community for a long time—for at least three generations and preferably many generations more than three. "Old family" means not only old to the community but old to the class. Present members of the class were born into it; the families into which they were born can trace their lineage through many generations participating in a way of life characteristic of the upper class back to a generation marking the lowly beginnings out of which their family came. Although the men of this level are occupied gainfully, usually as large merchants, financiers, or in the higher professions, the wealth of the family, inherited

[2] . . . New and poorly organized towns sometimes have class systems which have no old-family (upper-upper) class.

from the husband's or the wife's side, and often from both, has been in the family for a long time. Ideally it should stem from the sea trade when Yankee City's merchants and sea captains made large fortunes, built great Georgian houses on elm-lined Hill Street, and filled their houses and gardens with the proper symbols of their high position. They became the 400, the Brahmins, the Hill Streeters to whom others looked up; and they, well-mannered or not, looked down on the rest. They counted themselves, and were so counted, equals of similar levels in Salem, Boston, Providence, and other New England cities. Their sons and daughters married into the old families from these towns and at times, when family fortune was low or love was great, they married wealthy sons and daughters from the newly rich who occupied the class level below them. This was a happy event for the fathers and mothers of such fortunate young people in the lower half of the upper class, an event well publicized and sometimes not too discreetly bragged about by the parents of the lower-upper-class children, an occasion to be explained by the mothers from the old families in terms of the spiritual demands of romantic love and by their friends as "a good deal and a fair exchange all the way around for everyone concerned."

The new families, the lower level of the upper class, came up through the new industries—shoes, textiles, silverware—and finance. Their fathers were some of the men who established New England's trading and financial dominance throughout America. When New York's Wall Street rose to power, many of them transferred their activities to this new center of dominance. Except that they aspire to old-family status, if not for themselves then for their children, these men and their families have a design for living similar to the old-family group. But they are consciously aware that their money is too new and too recently earned to have the sacrosanct quality of wealth inherited from a long line of ancestors. They know, as do those about them, that, while a certain amount of wealth is necessary, birth and old family are what really matter. Each of them can cite critical cases to prove that particular individuals have no money at all, yet belong to the top class because they have the right lineage and right name. While they recognize the worth and importance of birth, they feel that somehow their family's achievements should be better rewarded than by a mere second place in relation to those who need do little more than be born and stay alive.

The presence of an old-family class in a community forces the newly rich to wait their turn if they aspire to "higher things." Meanwhile, they must learn how to act, fill their lives with good deeds, spend their money on approved philanthropy, and reduce their arrogance to manageable proportions.

The families of the upper and lower strata of the upper classes are organized into social cliques and exclusive clubs. The men gather fortnightly in dining clubs where they discuss matters that concern them. The women belong to small clubs or to the Garden Club and give their interest to subjects which symbolize their high status and evoke those sentiments necessary in each individual if the class is to maintain itself. Both sexes join philanthropic organizations whose good deeds are an asset to the community and an expression of the dominance and importance of the top class to those socially beneath them. They are the members of the Episcopalian and Unitarian and, occasionally, the Congregational and Presbyterian churches.

Below them are the members of the solid, highly respectable upper-middle class, the people who get things done and provide the active front in civic affairs for the classes above them. They aspire to the classes above and hope their good deeds, civic activities, and high moral principles will somehow be recognized far beyond the usual pat on the back and that they will be invited by those above them into the intimacies of upper-class cliques and exclusive clubs. Such recognition might increase their status and would be likely to make them members of the lower-upper group. The fact that this rarely happens seldom stops members of this level, once activated, from continuing to try. The men tend to be owners of stores and belong to the large proprietor and professional levels. Their incomes average less than those of the lower-upper class, this latter group having a larger income than any other group, including the old-family level.

These three strata, the two upper classes and the upper-middle, constitute the levels above the Common Man. There is a considerable distance socially between them and the mass of the people immediately below them. They comprise three of the six classes present in the community. Although in number of levels they constitute half the community, in population they have no more than a sixth, and sometimes less, of the Common Man's population. The three levels combined include approximately 13 per cent of the total population.

The lower-middle class, the top of the Common Man level, is composed of clerks and other white-collar workers, small tradesmen, and a fraction of skilled workers. Their small houses fill "the side streets" down from Hill Street, where the upper classes and some of the upper-middle live, and are noticeably absent from the better suburbs where the upper-middle concentrate. "Side Streeter" is a term often used by those above them to imply an inferior way of life and an inconsequential status. They have accumulated little property but are frequently home owners. Some of the more successful members of ethnic groups, such as the Italians, Irish, French-Canadians, have reached this level. Only a few members of these cultural minorities have gone beyond it; none of them has reached the old-family level.

. . . Ten per cent of the population belongs to the upper-middle class, and 28 per cent to the lower-middle level. The upper-lower is the most populous class, with 34 per cent, and the lower-lower has 25 per cent of all the people in the town. . . .

The upper-lower class, least differentiated from the adjacent levels and hardest to distinguish in the hierarchy, but clearly present, is composed of the "poor but honest workers" who more often than not are only semi-skilled or unskilled. Their relative place in the hierarchy of class is well portrayed by comparing them with the classes superior to them and with the lower-lower class beneath them in the category of how they spend their money.

A glance at the ranking of the proportion of the incomes of each class spent on ten items (including such things as rent and shelter, food, clothing, and education among others) shows, for example, that this class ranks second for the percentage of the money spent on food, the lower-lower class being first and the rank order of the other classes following lower-middle according to their place in the social hierarchy. The money spent on rent and shelter by upper-lower class is also second to the lower-lower's first, the other classes' rank order and position in the hierarchy being in exact correspondence. To give a bird's-eye view of the way this class spends its money, the rank of the upper-lower, for the percentage of its budget spent on a number of common and important items, has been placed in parentheses after every item in the list which follows: food (2), rent (2), clothing (4), automobiles (5), taxes (5), medical aid (5), education (4), and amusements (4–5). For the major items of expenditure the amount of money spent by this class out of its budget corresponds fairly closely with its place in the class hierarchy, second to the first of the lower-lower class for the major necessities of food and shelter, and ordinarily but not always, fourth or fifth to the classes above for the items that give an opportunity for cutting down the amounts spent on them. Their feelings about doing the right thing, of being respectable and rearing their children to do better than they have, coupled with the limitations of their income, are well reflected in how they select and reject what can be purchased on the American market.[3]

The lower-lower class, referred to as "Riverbrookers" or the "low-down Yankees who live in the clam flats," have a "bad reputation" among those who are socially above them. This evaluation includes beliefs that they are lazy, shiftless, and won't work, all opposites of the good middle-class virtues belonging to the essence of the Protestant ethic. They are thought to be improvident and unwilling or unable to save their money for a rainy day and, therefore, often dependent on the

[3] The evidence for the statements in this paragraph can be found in W. Lloyd Warner and Paul S. Lunt, *The Social Life of a Modern Community*, Vol. I, "Yankee City Series" (New Haven: Yale University Press, 1941), pp. 287–300.

philanthropy of the private or public agency and on poor relief. They are sometimes said to "live like animals" because it is believed that their sexual mores are not too exacting and that pre-marital intercourse, post-marital infidelity, and high rates of illegitimacy, sometimes too publicly mixed with incest, characterize their personal and family lives. It is certain that they deserve only part of this reputation. Research shows many of them guilty of no more than being poor and lacking in the desire to get ahead, this latter trait being common among those above them. For these reasons and others, this class is ranked in Yankee City below the level of the Common Man (lower-middle and upper-lower). For most of the indexes of status it ranks sixth and last.

## CLASS IN THE DEMOCRATIC MIDDLE WEST AND FAR WEST

Cities large and small in the states west of the Alleghenies sometimes have class systems which do not possess an old-family (upper-upper) class. The period of settlement has not always been sufficient for an old-family level, based on the security of birth and inherited wealth, to entrench itself. . . . The family, its name, and its lineage must have had time to become identified in the public mind as being above ordinary mortals.

While such identification is necessary for the emergence of an old-family (upper-upper) class and for its establishment, it is also necessary for the community to be large enough for the principles of exclusion to operate. For example, those in the old-family group must be sufficiently numerous for all the varieties of social participation to be possible without the use of new-family members; the family names must be old enough to be easily identified; and above all there should always be present young people of marriageable age to become mates of others of their own class and a sufficient number of children to allow mothers to select playmates and companions of their own class for their children.

When a community in the more recently settled regions of the United States is sufficiently large, when it has grown slowly and at an average rate, the chances are higher that it has an old-family class. If it lacks any one of these factors, including size, social and economic complexity, and steady and normal growth, the old-family class is not likely to develop. . . .

When the old-family group is present and its position is not recognized as superordinate to the new families, the two tend to be co-ordinate and view each other as equals. The old-family people adroitly let it be known that their riches are not material possessions alone but are old-family lineage; the new families display their wealth, accent their power, and prepare their children for the development of a future lineage by giving them the proper training at home and later sending them to the "right" schools and marrying them into the "right" families.

Such communities usually have a five-class pyramid, including an upper class, two middle, and two lower classes.[4]

Jonesville, located in the Middle West, approximately a hundred years old, is an example of a typical five-class community. The farmers around Jonesville use it as their market, and it is the seat of government for Abraham County. Its population of over 6,000 people is supported by servicing the needs of the farmers and by one large and a few small factories.

At the top of the status structure is an upper class commonly referred to as "the 400." It is composed of old-family and new-family segments. Neither can successfully claim superiority to the other. Below this level is an upper-middle class which functions like the same level in Yankee City and is composed of the same kind of people, the only difference being the recognition that the distance to the top is shorter for them and the time necessary to get there much less. The Common Man level, composed of lower-middle- and upper-lower-class people and the lower-lower level are replicas of the same classes in Yankee City.

The communities of the mountain states and Pacific Coast are new, and many of them have changed their economic form from mining to other enterprises; consequently, their class orders are similar to

[4] It is conceivable that in smaller communities there may be only three, or even two, classes present.

those found in the Middle West. The older and larger far western communities which have had a continuing, solid growth of population which has not destroyed the original group are likely to have the old-family level at the top with the other classes present; the newer and smaller communities and those disturbed by the destruction of their original status structure by large population gains are less likely to have an old-family class reigning above all others. San Francisco is a clear example of the old-family type; Los Angeles, of the more amorphous, less well-organized class structure.

## CLASS IN THE DEEP SOUTH

Studies in the Deep South demonstrate that, in the older regions where social changes until recently have been less rapid and less disturbing to the status order, most of the towns above a few thousand population have a six-class system in which an old-family elite is socially dominant.

For example, in a study of a Mississippi community, a market town for a cotton-growing region around it, Davis and the Gardners found a six-class system.[5] Perhaps the southern status order is best described by Chart I . . . which gives the names used by the people of the community for each class and succinctly tells how the members of each class regard themselves and the rest of the class order.

The people of the two upper classes make a clear distinction between an old aristocracy and an aristocracy which is not old. There is no doubt that the first is above the other; the upper-middle class views the two upper ones much as the upper classes do themselves but groups them in one level with two divisions, the older level above the other; the lower-middle class separates them but considers them co-ordinate; the bottom two classes, at a greater social distance than the others, group all the levels above the Common Man as "society" and one class. An examination of the terms used by the several classes for the other classes shows that similar principles are operating.

The status system of most communities in the South is further complicated by a color-caste system which orders and systematically controls the relations of those categorized as Negroes and whites. . . . Color-caste is a system of values and behavior which places all people who are thought to be white in a superior position and those who are thought of as black in an inferior status.

Characteristics of American Negroes vary from very dark hair and skin and Negroid features to blond hair, fair skin, and Caucasian features, yet all of them are placed in the "racial" category of Negro. The skin and physical features of American Caucasians vary from Nordic blond types to the dark, swarthy skin and Negroid features of some eastern Mediterranean stocks, yet all are classed as socially white despite the fact that a sizable proportion of Negroes are "whiter" in appearance than a goodly proportion of whites. The members of the two groups are severely punished by the formal and informal rules of our society if they intermarry, and when they break this rule of "caste endogamy," their children suffer the penalties of our caste-like system by being placed in the lower color caste. Furthermore, unlike class, the rules of this system forbid the members of the lower caste from climbing out of it. Their status and that of their children are fixed forever. This is true no matter how much money they have, how great the prestige and power they may accumulate, or how well they have acquired correct manners and proper behavior. There can be no social mobility out of the lower caste into the higher one. (There may, of course, be class mobility within the Negro or white caste.) The rigor of caste rules varies from region to region in the United States.[6]

The Mexicans, Spanish Americans, and

[5] Allison Davis, Burleigh B. Gardner, and Mary R. Gardner, *Deep South* (Chicago: University of Chicago Press, 1941). Also read: John Dollard, *Caste and Class in a Southern Town* (New Haven: Yale University Press, 1937); Mozell Hill, "The All-Negro Society in Oklahoma" (Unpublished Ph.D. dissertation, University of Chicago, 1936); Harry J. Walker, "Changes in Race Accommodation in a Southern Community" (Unpublished Ph.D. dissertation, University of Chicago, 1945).

[6] See St. Clair Drake and Horace R. Cayton, *Black Metropolis* (New York: Harcourt, Brace & Co., 1945), for studies of two contrasting caste orders; read the "Methodological Note" by Warner in *Black Metropolis* for an analysis of the difference between the two systems.

**CHART 1**

The Social Perspectives of the Social Classes*

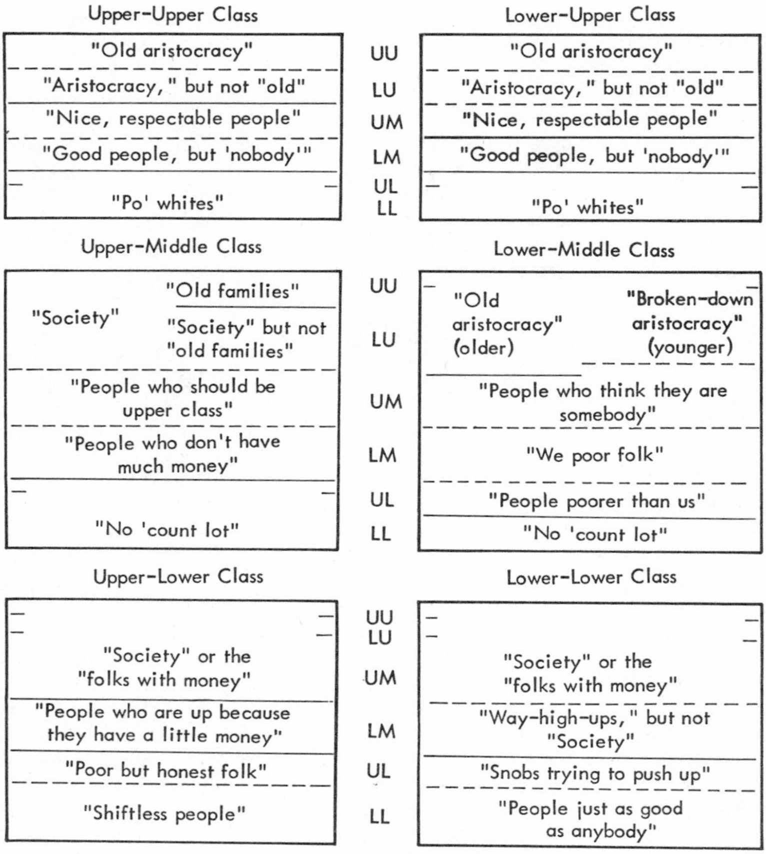

| | Upper-Upper Class | Lower-Upper Class | Upper-Middle Class | Lower-Middle Class | Upper-Lower Class | Lower-Lower Class |
|---|---|---|---|---|---|---|
| UU | "Old aristocracy" | "Old aristocracy" | "Society" — "Old families" | "Old aristocracy" (older) / "Broken-down aristocracy" (younger) | — | — |
| LU | "Aristocracy," but not "old" | "Aristocracy," but not "old" | "Society" — "Society" but not "old families" | "Old aristocracy" (older) / "Broken-down aristocracy" (younger) | — | — |
| UM | "Nice, respectable people" | "Nice, respectable people" | "People who should be upper class" | "People who think they are somebody" | "Society" or the "folks with money" | "Society" or the "folks with money" |
| LM | "Good people, but 'nobody'" | "Good people, but 'nobody'" | "People who don't have much money" | "We poor folk" | "People who are up because they have a little money" | "Way-high-ups," but not "Society" |
| UL | "Po' whites" | "Po' whites" | "No 'count lot" | "People poorer than us" | "Poor but honest folk" | "Snobs trying to push up" |
| LL | "Po' whites" | "Po' whites" | "No 'count lot" | "No 'count lot" | "Shiftless people" | "People just as good as anybody" |

* Allison Davis, Burleigh B. Gardner, and Mary R. Gardner, *Deep South* (Chicago: University of Chicago Press, 1941), p. 65.

Orientals occupy a somewhat different status from that of the Negro, but many of the characteristics of their social place in America are similar.[7]

The social-class and color-caste hypotheses, inductively established as working principles for understanding American society, were developed in the researches which were reported in the "Yankee City" volumes, *Deep South*, and *Caste and Class in a Southern Town*. . . .[8]

## THE GENERALITIES OF AMERICAN CLASS

It is now time to ask what are the basic characteristics of social status common to

[7] See W. Lloyd Warner and Leo Srole, *The Social Systems of American Ethnic Groups*, Vol. III, "Yankee City Series" (New Haven: Yale University Press, 1945). Chapter X discusses the similarities and differences and presents a table of predictability on their probable assimilation and gives the principles governing these phenomena.

[8] . . . For an early publication on color-caste, see W. Lloyd Warner, "American Caste and Class," *American Journal of Sociology*, XLII, No. 2 (September, 1936), 234–37, and "Formal Education and the Social Structure," *Journal of Educational Sociology*, IX (May, 1936), 524–531.

the communities of all regions in the United States and, once we have answered this question, to inqure what the variations are among the several systems. Economic factors are significant and important in determining the class position of any family or person, influencing the kind of behavior we find in any class, and contributing their share to the present form of our status system. But, while significant and necessary, the economic factors are not sufficient to predict where a particular family or individual will be or to explain completely the phenomena of social class. Something more than a large income is necessary for high social position. Money must be translated into socially approved behavior and possessions, and they in turn must be translated into intimate participation with, and acceptance by, members of a superior class....

To belong to a particular level in the social-class system of America means that a family or individual has gained acceptance as an equal by those who belong in the class. The behavior in this class and the participation of those in it must be rated by the rest of the community as being at a particular place in the social scale.

Although our democratic heritage makes us disapprove, our class order helps control a number of important functions. It unequally divides the highly and lowly valued things of our society among the several classes according to their rank. Our marriage rules conform to the rules of class, for the majority of marriages are between people of the same class. No class system, however, is so rigid that it completely prohibits marriages above and below one's own class. Furthermore, an open class system such as ours permits a person during his lifetime to move up or down from the level into which he was born. Vertical social mobility for individuals or families is characteristic of all class systems. . . . Although economic mobility is still important, it seems likely now that more people move to higher positions by education than by any other route. We have indicated before this that the mere possession of money is insufficient for gaining and keeping a higher social position. This is equally true of all other forms of mobility. In every case there must be social acceptance.

Class varies from community to community. The new city is less likely than an old one to have a well-organized class order; this is also true for cities whose growth has been rapid as compared with those which have not been disturbed by huge increases in population from other regions or countries or by the rapid displacement of old industries by new ones. The mill town's status hierarchy is more likely to follow the occupational hierarchy of the mill than the levels of evaluated participation found in market towns or those with diversified industries. Suburbs of large metropolises tend to respond to selective factors which reduce the number of classes to one or a very few. They do not represent or express all the cultural factors which make up the social pattern of an ordinary city.

Yet systematic studies . . . from coast to coast, in cities large and small and of many economic types, indicate that, despite the variations and diversity, class levels do exist and that they conform to a particular pattern of organization.

# SOCIAL STRATIFICATION OF THE JEWISH COMMUNITY IN A SMALL POLISH TOWN[1]

*Celia Stopnicka Heller*

Various bases for social stratification existed in Stoczek. The old biblical classification was still adhered to but served only

*American Journal of Sociology*, "Social Stratification of the Jewish Community in a Small Polish Town," by Celia Stopnicka Rosenthal, Vol. LIX, No. 1, July, 1953. Reprinted by permission of The University of Chicago Press, Chicago, Ill. Copyright 1953 by the University of Chicago.

[1] This paper is part of a study of a small-town Jewish community in central Poland in the period between the two world wars. The town is called Stoczek and is located fifty-five miles from

for religious purposes and at times tended to play havoc with the existing status pattern. According to the biblical classification, the Jews were divided into priests (*Cohanim*), Levites (*Leviim*), and Israelites (*Israelim*). The priests had the function of blessing the congregation on holidays. Before the blessing ceremony those members of the community who enjoyed the greatest prestige served the priests by pouring water over their hands. It often happened on holidays that the "beautiful Jews," men of highest status, poured water on the hands of some "plain Jews" who were priests.

The existing status pattern was based on classifications in terms of occupation, money, learning, and lineage. This was recognized by the culture, which evolved special terms to designate each category. It is the aim of the writer, however, to show that, no matter which of the above dimensions one uses, one will find the same people with slight variations on the same point of the social scale.

Occupationally, the community was divided into three groups. At the bottom of the scale were the "men of labor," wage laborers and craftsmen. Among the manual occupations there existed a hierarchy of preference extending from watchmakers down to such lowly occupations as barbers, porters, and shoemakers. Above the men of labor stood the "businessmen," who ranged from small storekeepers to owners of forests and mills. Although no statistics are available, it is safe to estimate that about 30 per cent of Jewish men were businessmen while about 69 per cent were workers. The third category, "learners," less than 1 per cent of the population, devoted all their time to learning, from which they derived no material benefit. No one looked down on them for not occupying themselves with making a living. On the contrary, they were treated with great respect. Usually the wife was the economic provider, and she was highly respected for being married to a man who devoted his life to learning. Parents-in-law often supported such a learner and his family.

Even though there was stigmatization of manual labor, an impoverished businessman who resorted to such labor was not looked down upon but pitied. It was assumed that no *balebatisher mensh,* man of middle-class respectability, would resort to manual labor unless he had no other alternative. On the other hand, a worker who became a businessman did not automatically gain in status but had to start living "respectably" in order to reach higher status.

The classification in terms of money presents a more complicated picture than that in terms of occupation. When former residents of Stoczek were asked to identify the source of prestige in their town, they invariably answered "not money." And yet, when they were asked to name the most highly esteemed people in Stoczek, they named those with much money, good lineage, great learning, or a combination of these. This apparent inconsistency becomes clear when one looks at the particular meaning ascribed to money in Stoczek.

In observing the people in Stoczek, one is impressed with their great desire to have money. This desire was expressed vividly in everyday conversation and in stock phrases. Even the poorest would start a sentence with "I should have as many millions as" and finish in a variety of ways, such as "the pairs of shoes I made" or "the number of chickens I sold." To an outsider it may have sounded strange that a man in rags who did not have enough money to buy bread spoke in terms of millions. In Stoczek it was the accepted way of talking and was never questioned or analyzed. Colorful terminology

---

Warsaw. In 1938 . . . the town's population was 4,000, out of which 2,500 comprised the Jewish community.

The paper is based on interviews with ten survivors on seven biograms received from Stoczek people now living in Israel. . . . Unfortunately, those interviewed do not constitute a representative sampling of the population, since so few survivors remain. Furthermore, the generalizations made are not based on direct observation of the community, but rather on recollection. Ideally, a study such as this should be made on the spot. . . . This, of course, is impossible as far as the Jewish communities in Poland are concerned, for they no longer exist. Apart from literary sources, the only way that their culture can be reconstructed is by interviewing persons who once lived in the small towns of Poland. This approach must, of course, be used with caution, since recollection is not identical with the facts of life as they once were. . . .

existed in reference to various gradations of wealth ranging from the very rich *magnates* and *gvirim*, through the rich *oishers*, to the poor *orime lait* and the very poor *kaptzunim*. . . .

Why was there such great emphasis on money in Stoczek? Did it represent the longing for food and material comforts of an impoverished community? It did represent that, but not that alone. As we shall see from the subsequent analysis, the material benefits of money, although recognized and enjoyed, were not its most significant ends. There were rich people who were envied for having money but who commanded no respect. By comparing the moneyed people who commanded respect with those who did not, we find one outstanding difference. Respected people used part of their money to do good deeds, *mitzvos*, for the needy. And, indeed, the common denominator of all good deeds was that they flowed from the haves to the have-nots.

The culturally favored response in the giving pattern was to the situation rather than to the individual. As one informant put it, "The man who did not look to see whether he would get his money back but rather whether the borrower needed it was considered to be good." Thus, one was required to help a person in need no matter who he was. This manner of help marked the donor as having a true "Jewish heart."

The point that was emphasized most in describing a man was his charitableness. "He is a man of great charity (*baal tzdokoh*)," was a description in itself which would bring a definite picture of the man to the listener's mind. In addition to charity, performing a *gmilus khesed,* act of loving kindness, that is, lending money to people in need without charging interest or demanding notes and securities, was considered a good deed. Aid to a sick person also ranked high as a good deed. The phrase "to save a Jewish soul" was used without additional elaboration. Well-to-do women sent the best food and delicacies to poor people who were sick and to destitute mothers who had just given birth. It was a good deed to visit the sick and people in mourning. The greater the social distance, the higher did the deed rank. Bringing peace to the community or to a divided family also ranked very high as a good deed, and a man who was known as a peacemaker earned much prestige in Stoczek. Moreover, an individual who did a good deed for an orphan received greater credit than if he had performed a similar deed for any other person in the community.

The one who performed good deeds for the needy overcame his initial human failing of not being able to project himself into the position of the needy. "The well-fed does not believe the hungry one," went the saying. His returns for doing good deeds were, therefore, very high. The belief was prevalent that, when a man died and was called before God to be judged, his good deeds came forth to testify for him. Men at funeral processions chanted, "Charity prevents death." Thus, using money to do good deeds meant storing up credit for the afterlife. However, one also received high earthly rewards in terms of honor and respect.

Although giving brought prestige, taking when in need was shameful. An event which vividly illustrates the shame connected with taking occurred when the city council voted a substantial sum of money for milk to be distributed in school to needy children. The neediest of Jewish children did not accept the milk, while Polish children stood in line for it, even if they were not from the most destitute families. This shame of taking is especially puzzling in view of the fact that the one who took afforded the giver the opportunity to do a good deed. Therefore, it might seem that giving and taking was a reciprocal relationship. Why, then, was shame felt? The fact is that the culture did not recognize the giving and taking pattern as a reciprocal relation. Rather, the act of giving was phrased as an unselfish deed which originated in the giver's being a man of mercy and good heart. Only when we remember this particular phrasing, do we come to understand the role of shame.

Because taking was so shameful, the ideal pattern for an individual who gave charity was to deposit the gift with the needy person without confronting him and without his knowing the source of help. On the one hand he thus showed that he did not give to gain prestige and, therefore, bore testimony to the culture's phrasing of giving. On the other hand, he spared the taker the shame of facing the giver. The ideal pattern is understandable when we recall that, although charity and good deeds bring a person benefits in his afterlife and assure him of honor in this world, individual motivation for doing good is supposed to be induced not by those rewards but by the person's "Jewish heart." Actually, however, very few acted in terms of the ideal pattern, preferring to reap the earthly benefits of prestige for their good deeds.

A mechanism was developed whereby the taker was spared the shame of confronting the giver, and yet the giver could have the satisfaction of being known as such. There were persons, often children of good families who went from house to house to collect money for specific needy people. This was considered a noble act which brought much admiration for both grown-ups and children who engaged in it.

Where neither of the above methods of giving was used, and the giver confronted the taker, the giver was expected to make the shame bearable by setting into motion the mechanism of "beautification." Beautification, the process of making the taker feel equal, was used to remove the shame of the have-nots. The feelings of shame were not only characteristic of the poor but also of those who lacked any of the things that the culture valued highly. Although the culture did not recognize that the lack of possessions which it held significant, such as parents, children, money, and health, was in itself shameful, nevertheless, people so deprived were considered more sensitive and more easily shamed.

One of the acts of beautification was to ask a needy stranger—a wanderer, beggar, or soldier who happened to be passing through the town—to a Sabbath or holiday meal. To beautify him, such a man was called a "guest" and was, indeed, treated like a very worthy guest of the family. He was given an honorable place at the table, served the choicest foods, asked to lead in the after-meal prayer, to sing a hymn, and invited to relate some news. Even the stylized conversation between the head of the house and the guest becomes meaningful when one understands the mechanism of shame and beautification. The guest did not start the conversation, for he was imbued with shame. He was constantly approached by the host, who, in addressing him, substituted the expression "a Jew" for "you." Thus, the head of the family would ask: "From where does a Jew hail?" "What is a Jew's name?" "Perhaps a Jew will sing a hymn?" In acting thus, it was as though the host were saying to the man: "You are poor; you cannot spend the holiday with your family, and you are, therefore, ashamed. But we are both Jews. I will make you forget your shame and make you feel like an equal."

To marry off an orphan or a girl from a very poor family ranked high as an act of beautification. A certain man in Stoczek attained the pinnacle of prestige by arranging a double wedding for his daughter and an orphaned girl. Since it was shameful for a bride-to-be not to have a trousseau, a person who supplied such a girl with a trousseau performed a good and beautifying deed. Adoption of an orphan also ranked high as an act of beautification. To make an orphan feel that he belonged and was not deprived, by providing him with parents and home, was indeed a *mitzva* ("good deed").

In order to understand the particular function of shame in the charity pattern, it is worth while to look at a situation in which shame did not exist. Professional beggars who came to Stoczek were insolent and arrogant. They seldom expressed thanks for the alms they received and often insulted the donor into giving more. The word *shnorer* ("beggar") was charged with much negative meaning and was used as an insult by both adults and children. The contempt and dislike of the beggar is explained by his behavior. The beggar discovered, and capitalized upon his discovery, that he was actually doing the donor a favor. He seemed to serve notice that he did not owe anyone thanks and honor for the donation given him, since he was thereby helping the donor reach salvation. Consequently, since the beggar did not feel shame, there was no need for the giver to exert himself in order to beautify him, and indeed he did not.

Yet, even these lowly outcasts, the beggars, were supposed to be imbued with the Jewish characteristic of shame during the

Sabbath and holidays. And, because it was assumed that they experienced shame on those days, the donor tried to beautify them. As was shown earlier, the beggar who was invited to a Sabbath or holiday meal was not referred to as a beggar but as a guest. Looking back on her memories of the beggar, the writer feels that during the Sabbath and holiday he abandoned his insolence and arrogance and conformed with the general pattern of behaving in a manner befitting one who receives charity. . . .

Just as a man who beautified a deprived person performed a good deed and was greatly respected for it, so the man who shamed such a person committed a sin and was looked upon with contempt. All members of the community were thought to be imbued with the Jewish susceptibility to shame, and it was, therefore, considered evil to do anything that would tend to shame another person. "One is not allowed to shame a human being," was the stock phrase. One was not supposed to point to a person's lowly occupation, state of deprivation, bad health, or misfits in the family, for that would produce shame. "As a child I had a friend from that family in which there was a *shmadke* (woman who changed her faith). My mother warned me that I should never mention the word 'convert' or anything similar in her presence so as not to hurt her," related one informant.

In both beautification and shaming it was presupposed that the act flowed from a man of higher status to a man of lower status. It was not conceivable that a man could beautify a person who stood higher than himself in the social scale. Such a man could afford honor but never beautify. The same was true of shaming. A man might be looked down upon by the community for being "insolent" to one of higher status but never for having "shamed" him.

Shame performed important functions in the culture of which the people in the community were not aware. On the one hand, it prevented people from asking for help, which the culture defined as highly dishonorable. This tended to perpetuate the belief that those who were able to help would move forward without being asked by the needy. Shame also averted refusal, which was painful for both the person who refused and the one who was refused. Furthermore, it tended to prevent abuses in taking, for one would not expose himself to the shame of taking unless he were in great need. There were, of course, deviants who asked for help without needing it and took advantage of the good hearts of others, but they were considered to be very lowly people. On the other hand, shame helped to set in motion the whole mechanism of beautification. By using beautification, the giver would emerge feeling like a giver and not as in the beggar situation, where the giver was made to feel that he was taking as much as giving. Furthermore, he received part of his reward immediately in the form of honor and thanks from the man to whom he gave rather than having to wait for his return until the afterlife.

The purpose of this detailed discussion of the giving-taking pattern is to show that wealth alone did not assure a person of status in the community. Wealth was a source of prestige only in so far as it enabled a man to contribute to the welfare of the community, to do good deeds, and to give charity. Consequently, money was greatly valued, since with it one could obtain status. As the sayings went: "The rich man has this world and the next world" and "With money you can buy *yikhus* (lineage) and *koved* (honor and respect)." The substance of these sayings is that, by doing good deeds, the rich man not only assured himself of honor but also secured a "seat in heaven" for himself.

Just as a man did not gain status by virtue merely of obtaining money, his status did not diminish if he lost his money. An impoverished man of high status was pitied for not being able to live in the manner befitting him, but he did not suffer in prestige. . . .

However, it must not be deduced that money was valued only in so far as it enabled a person to do good deeds. The role of money in enabling a person to eat well, dress well, and have pleasure in so doing was clearly recognized. But the man who used his money only to satisfy his physical needs was lacking in Jewishness. Such a man would be referred to as a pig and the Polish saying, "Maciek (popular Polish given name) made it; Maciek ate it," was applied to him.

Nevertheless, the mere possession of money, even when it was not used in the socially prescribed manner, gave one a sense of power. A wealthy man who did not use part of his money to do good deeds did not receive *koved,* and people spoke badly of him, but he was accorded deference even if this was spurious. The reason for such deference was tied to Jewish experience with the outside world. Money was the only Jewish value that non-Jews appreciated. Hence, men of wealth had more contact with city officials than the rest of the community. It was assumed that a man who had money and did not "behave the way a Jew should," that is to 'say, did not give charity, was low enough to cause trouble with the officials for anyone who did now show him deference. "It is better not to start with such a one," went the saying, and people tried to keep out of his way.

Having examined the meaning of money in Stoczek, we can turn to the problem of conspicuous consumption. People were very much afraid of other people's jealousy. It was pointed out endlessly that "you are not allowed to take out other people's eyes," that is, that one should avoid making others jealous. Thus, ostentation was discouraged from childhood on, and society called for private enjoyment of the items of consumption. Ostentation was condemned also because of the effect it had on strengthening the hostile attitudes of the Polish population. Despite conscious discouragement in terms of the above two factors, however, ostentatiousness tended to flourish. Evidently, conspicuous consumption must have exercised an important latent function, since it persisted despite all verbal attacks. The explanation lies in the meaning of money in Stoczek. Display of wealth served notice of two things: (1) the displayer was in a position to dispense favors and (2) he was powerful enough to deal with the outside world.

Since the value of money was unstable, it was expected that the person who had it would use it to obtain more lasting sources of status, such as learning and lineage. Thus the dictum was to educate one's sons and marry one's daughters into *yikhus* ("lineage").

We have previously discussed learning as part of the social stratification in terms of occupation. We now come to a discussion of learning as a separate basis of social stratification. Before describing the status that went with learning, however, it is necessary to clarify the nature of Jewish learning. Learning was not considered a process which stopped at any given time or point but was conceived to go on throughout one's life. "The Torah (learning, teaching, and doctrine) has no bottom," went the saying. This concept of learning as a continuous process is reflected in the terms applied to a learned man. He was never referred to as a "learned man" when one spoke of his absorption with Jewish learning. The expression "He is an educated man" applied to secular education. "He knows how to learn" and "He is a great learner" designated a man's standing in Jewish learning. The words *talmid khokhom* denoted a man of highest Jewish learning and not merely a "smart student."

Learning was considered so valuable that it needed no validation in terms of good deeds. To be sure, a man who shared his learning with others received additional prestige, but the fact alone that "he knew how to learn" assured him status. Thus, even if he did not share his learning or give charity, he was never "common" or a "pig," terms which referred to a man of wealth who did not share his wealth. It was quite conceivable that a man could have much wealth and yet not behave properly, but it was unimaginable that a man of learning could behave improperly. Learning was equated with refinement, and the term *aydele Yid* ("refined Jew") meant a learned man. The rich man, even if he were charitable and did good deeds but had no learning, did not reach his maximum status until he married his children into *yikhus.* The learner needed only to be greatly learned to reach highest status. Thus, the learner created his own *yikhus* and did not need ancestral support.

Just as learning did not need validation in terms of other things, so it was not supposed to be used as a means of obtaining material benefits. Learning was a goal in itself, and one pursued it with love and joy. Persons who devoted their spare time to learning and were known to sit up until late at night studying were talked about with reverence. "He cannot tear himself away from learning," went the saying. The learned man would often be turned to for advice and opinions on community and world affairs. Men used to come to a learner's house on Saturday afternoon so that he "should learn with them." With them, he posed questions, answered difficult questions, and interpreted the text. Children were sent to such a man to be tested in their learning. It was inconceivable that he would accept money as a reward, and no one dared to offer it to him. The learner's rewards were great respect and joy from the fulfillment of one of the most important commandments of Jewish law, teaching the people.

However, not only status went with learning but a sense of power as well. The learners felt so powerful that a case once occurred wherein a learned man opposed the rabbi on a certain issue. Only someone highly powerful, highly honored and esteemed, would dare to do so. This power is also borne out by the fact that the learners were not bound by the same pattern of behavior as the rest of the community. As we have seen, taking was shameful, and yet the learner could be supported without shame by his wife or even by strangers. Children and youths who went to out-of-town *yeshivas* (schools of higher learning) ate in other people's houses without feeling shame. There is a striking similarity between the learner at the top of the social pyramid and the beggar at the bottom, neither of whom was ashamed to take. It would be inconceivable of course for somone in the culture to compare the two, since they were on opposite sides of the social scale. However, this comparison helps to reinforce our hypothesis concerning the functions of shame. The learner was very much aware that by devoting himself to learning he was doing the community a great favor. He kept the heritage of the Torah alive. Similarly, the beggar knew that he was the actual giver and could, therefore, receive without shame.

There remains to be discussed, among the sources of status, that which was called in Stoczek *yikhus*. *Yikhus* was a very important concept and yet was so elusive that it is hard to define. A notable fact is that each person knew the other's *yikhus*. It was one of the first things to be established when two strangers talked to each other or when two people spoke about a third. *Yikhus* is pedigree, lineage in terms of learned, wealthy, and charitable ancestors, that is, in terms of ancestors of high status. However . . . each person considered himself to be a man of *yikhus,* although he might not have been recognized to be so by others. He merely traced back to some ancestor, no matter how far removed, who was learned or prosperous and generous and leaned on him for self-esteem. The people whom the whole community considered to be of great *yikhus* were those whose families traced themselves back to revered rabbis, greatly learned men, and very rich persons who were community-conscious and gave *tzdokoh*, justice, meaning charity.

*Yikhus,* like learning, was based on solid and permanent foundations. However, a man of *yikhus* had to live up to his position. If he was not learned and charitable, he did not receive honor and respect, although it was never forgotten that he came from a good family. In fact, he was looked upon as having squandered his inheritance.

We have now completed the analysis of status in Stoczek in terms of occupation, money, learning, and lineage. What we find is a convergence of status so that, for example, the workers, the poor, and the uneducated were likely to be the same people. The community divided itself into three classes. . . . At the top of the social pyramid in Stoczek were the beautiful Jews. It is interesting to note that beautiful Jew never referred to physical beauty but to endowment which the culture valued. To the class of beautiful Jews belonged people of great *yikhus,* much learning, and those who combined wealth with much charity giving. Occupationally, they were usually men of independent means or learners. The middle class were the *balebatim.* To them belonged the shopkeepers and traders who had some means and some learning. At the bottom of the scale were the plain Jews, workers and craftsmen, who had little learning, no *yikhus,* and little or no money.

However, there were exceptions, people who fitted into one category occupationally and into another in terms of money or learning. There were a few workmen in Stoczek who spent all their spare time learning and were known to "know how to learn a little." Thus, occupationally they were at the bottom of the scale, but they were in the center of the learning scale. Such men were talked about in the following manner: "He is a worker but he is a *balebatisher mensh* (man of middle-class respectability)." On the other hand, there were some wealthy men of no education. One man in town who was known for his wealth and charity was spoken of by the learners as barely knowing how to read the Hebrew prayers. He was nevertheless respected because he gave bountifully. Men of great wealth who neither were charitable nor knew "how to learn" were referred to in the lowest terms.

The chief role of the beautiful Jews was to devote themselves to the welfare of the community and to be at the community's disposal. The members of the community came to them for help and advice on family, business, and religious matters. People of high status did not receive any material advantage from playing their role of community-minded, learned, and charitable individuals. They derived honor and respect and a good name in the community. "A good name is better than money," went the saying. Honor was, indeed, conceived to be something distinct from material possessions. The Jews often employed the following Polish saying: "I do not possess money, but I have honor." *Koved* ("honor") lived on, even after a person died. The beautiful Jew was long remembered after his death, and, when one talked about his son, one always mentioned that the father "gave much charity" or that the father was "a great learner."

Class distinction in Stoczek was very definite, and the people below owed deference to the people above. A man who did not behave with proper respect toward the man above was known to be "insolent" and was looked down upon by the whole community. If a man of the lower class used obscene language in the presence of people of the upper class, and that occurred very rarely, he was talked about as a "fellow from the streets." The man of high status did not argue with a man from the lower class who behaved disrespectfully to him. It was below his dignity to do so. Although there was much contact between the classes, as when persons of higher status attended weddings, funerals, circumcisions, and *bar mitzvahs* of the poor, the relationship was never that of equality but that of the man higher up beautifying the man below. There were no friendships between adults of different classes. The culture held that men of higher status could not mix with men of lower status because in the end the people below would not remember "who you are and who they are," that is, would behave disrespectfully. Where attempts at social intercourse between individuals of unequal status ended with the person of lower status behaving disrespectfully, people quoted the Polish saying: "Do not mix with slops, and the pigs will not eat you."

There was strong condemnation of faking status, and a man who "pretended to be big" was spoken of with great contempt and derision. The cultural concept existed that one could not hide his social background, for sooner or later one's behavior would reveal it. To bear out this conception, two Polish proverbs were often quoted: "You can tell a gentleman by his boots" and "The awl slips out of the bag."

Since a man's true social standing was easily discernible, one was supposed never to boast about it. A person who bragged was characterized as "he blows from himself." One was not supposed to talk about the good deeds he performed, and people were very careful not to transgress in this matter. People of the upper class were also expected not to engage in gossip. A beautiful Jew who heard members of his family speaking of another, even if not in a derogatory manner, after admonished them with the following saying: "Our teachers say that one should not discuss another person, for even if one starts with good words, one finishes with evil ones." Neither did a beautiful Jew engage in "empty words," which embraced small talk as well as gossip. He was supposed to talk about worthy matters and, if he had nothing worthy to say, to remain silent. A beautiful Jew would not laugh excessively, since this was considered to be a sign of stupidity and merited the observation, "Why do you laugh so much? Is stupidity pushing you?"

The members of the upper class were expected more than others to live up to the ideal cultural ways prescribed for the whole community. A man who broke a vow would lose face, and particularly so if he were from the upper class. All men were supposed to act with justice, especially the beautiful Jews. Obscene language was never used by the upper class.

The culture recognized appropriate behavior in accordance with the class to which one belonged. Such fitting behavior was nurtured from childhood. A mother whose son or daughter did not behave properly admonished her child by saying, "It does not befit a child of so-and-so (here she mentioned the full name of the husband) to behave thus."

Membership in a class was, for the most part, hereditary. Theoretically, higher status could be achieved by every Jew. The two "elevators," to use Sorokin's terms, were money and learning. A boy from the lower class who was talented and ambitious could become a learner, and, if he had luck, he could become well to do. However, a man who rose from the lower class, unless he were a learner, was on shaky ground. Money alone did not bring prestige to an individual. In order to be eligible for prestige, a newly rich man had to begin to behave in a "respectable manner." But even if he gave charity and tried to behave respectably, every misstep, no matter how trivial, caused people to refer to his lowly origin. It was also implied in Stoczek that a man of the lower class who became wealthy grew bad in the process of attaining wealth. "Woe, oh, woe, when a beggar becomes a lord," was the often employed Polish saying. In contrast to the newly rich, the position of a learned man who came from the lower class was not different from that of other learned men. The fact that his father was a worker was mentioned only to point to his great personal worth, for in spite of such an obstacle he had risen to be a learner. It was inconceivable that he could behave in any other way than properly, since the culture equated learning with refinement.

There was actually little movement upward in the social scale. On the contrary, there was mass descent in terms of money and occupation. This descent, however, was not marked by loss of prestige. The wave of organized anti-Semitism and planned boycotting of Jewish stores made it almost impossible for a poor Jewish man to make good. Advancement in terms of learning was also hampered by great economic obstacles. It is true that a poor youth who was capable and devoted himself to learning could always be accepted in a *yeshiva* and did not have to starve. But a poor family could ill afford to relinquish the little money that a boy would bring in if he worked.

It was generally recognized that opportunities for advancement were meager. Although to be smart, *klig*, was highly valued in the culture, nevertheless, there was no attempt to correlate smartness with specific class, occupation, or status. Nowhere in the people's sayings or in their actions do we find an attempt to place wisdom in a certain class or claim that it is more prevalent in any group. It is inconceivable that a man who did not advance in Stoczek could have said of himself, "I guess I am stupid."

The social status of the Jew determined his seat in the synagogue. All seats were oriented to the east, for when a Jew prayed, he always faced east toward Jerusalem. The men of highest prestige occupied places nearest to the eastern wall. At the western wall sat the lower class, and in between the beautiful Jews and plain Jews sat the people from the middle class, the *balebatim*.

Status was also expressed in marriage. It happened occasionally that an impoverished good family made arrangements for a son to marry the daughter of a rich man who had risen from the lower class. This was considered a tragedy for the *yikhus* family and a highly significant event for the wealthy family. The community definitely thought the first to be the loser and the seond the gainer. This further bears out the generalization that the values of lineage and learning were placed far above that of money.

# OCCUPATIONAL PRESTIGE IN THE UNITED STATES, 1925–63

*Robert W. Hodge, Paul M. Siegel, and Peter H. Rossi*

The prestige hierarchy of occupations is perhaps the best studied aspect of the stratification systems of modern societies. Extensive empirical studies have been undertaken in a variety of nations, socialist and capitalist, developed and underdeveloped. Intensive analyses have been undertaken of results of particular studies searching for the existence of disparate prestige hierarchies held by subgroups within nations.[1] Despite rather extensive searches conducted by a variety of techniques, it appears that occupational-prestige hierarchies are similar from country to country and from subgroup to subgroup within a country. This stability reflects the fundamental but gross similarities among the occupational systems of modern nations. Furthermore, knowledge about occupations and relatively strong consensus on the relative positions of occupations are widely diffused throughout the populations involved.

The consensus within and among populations on the prestige positions of occupations leads one to expect that there will be considerable stability over time in the positions of particular occupations. Industrialization has proceeded to different points in the several countries whose prestige hierarchies have been studied without seriously affecting the relative positions of occupations in the countries involved. Cross-sectional comparisons between different countries at different stages of industrial evolution suggest that it would be erroneous to expect any considerable change in the *prestige* structure of a single country over time, even though that country might be experiencing appreciable changes in *occupational* structure. We can only expect to observe changes on the order of those previously found between two nations at different stages of economic development.

On the other hand, there are cogent reasons for expecting that changes in occupational structure will be reflected, at least ultimately, in corresponding changes in the prestige positions of occupations. The prestige position of an occupation is apparently a characteristic generated by the way in which the occupation is articulated into the division of labor, by the amount of power and influence implied in the activities of the occupation, by the characteristics of incumbents, and by the amount of resources which society places at the disposal of incumbents. (Other factors are undoubtedly at work, but these are the most obvious.) Hence, as occupations shift in these respects over time, corresponding adjustive shifts in prestige positions can be anticipated.

Considerable changes have occurred since 1947 in the occupational structure and labor force of the United States. The long-term trend in the growth of professional and scientific occupations persisted and was even accelerated during this period. Governmental and popular concern over the numbers and quality of our professional and technical manpower was expressed in a great expansion of our universities as well as in more attention being given lower levels of schooling. The proportion of the labor force devoted to agricultural pursuits declined along with unskilled and heavy labor components. This was also the period

Reprinted from the *American Journal of Sociology*, Vol. 70, November, 1964, by permission of the University of Chicago Press. 

[1] See, e.g., Kaare Svalastoga, *Prestige, Class and Mobility* (Copenhagen: Gyldendal, 1959), pp. 43–131; C. A. Moser and J. R. Hall, "The Social Grading of Occupations," in D. V. Glass (ed.), *Social Mobility in Britain* (London: Routledge Kegan Paul, 1954), pp. 29–50; and Albert J. Reiss, Jr., Otis Dudley Duncan, Paul K. Hatt, and C. C. North, *Occupations and Social Status* (New York: Free Press of Glencoe, 1961). The last mentioned volume contains the major analysis, the 1947 North-Hatt-NORC study of occupation prestige.

during which automation continued to expand, raising a serious question as to whether the American labor force could absorb both workers freed from jobs eliminated by technological progress and the large cohorts of postwar births now beginning to enter the labor force. Mention must be made of the stepped-up drive for equality on the part of Negroes, although we cannot tarry here to examine it. The question at issue is whether changes in the occupational structure have been reflected in shifts in the prestige of occupations between the two points in time.

On the basis of our empirical knowledge concerning the stability under a variety of conditions of the hierarchy of occupational prestige, we can support an expectation that there will be relatively few changes in the positions of occupations as we proceed from the 1947 to the 1963 study. On the basis of what seems to be a reasonable model of how these prestige positions have been generated, we expect somewhat more in the way of changes. Neither point of view produces very precise expectations for we need to know what is an acceptable level of stability (or change) either to conform to or to negate each expectation.

One further problem plagues interpretation of any comparisons such as this study envisages: Consider a set of occupational titles for which we have an aggregate prestige rating at two points in time; the difference between these ratings can be attributed either to a general increase in the amount of prestige in the occupational system or to an increase in the prestige of the aggregate of occupations in the set and a corresponding decrease in the prestige of some occupations not in the set. There is no conceivable way of choosing between these interpretations with the present data.

In view of the large number of professional occupations included in the NORC list, it may well be the case that in the aggregate the ninety occupations stood higher in the prestige hierarchy in 1963 than in 1947. If prestige is regarded as a "commodity" that behaves like the payoff in a "zero-sum" game, then, to be sure, what one set of occupations gains another must lose. But the NORC titles might get higher ratings in 1963 than 1947 because there is, all told, a greater amount of prestige in the system. If the latter is the case, the ninety NORC titles may get higher ratings and at the same time a smaller share of all prestige and a lower place in the total prestige hierarchy.[2]

These remarks are perhaps sufficient to alert the reader to the ambiguities which characterize the study of occupational prestige. Indeterminacies encountered in the study of a set of occupations are, of course, duplicated when the focus is upon a single occupation. It is for this reason that our focus is largely on the ordering of the ninety NORC occupational titles in two time periods and not upon changes in the prestige of particular occupations. All indications of changes in occupational prestige revealed here are of necessity relative to the set of ninety titles under consideration. These occupations exhaust our universe, and changes in their prestige are assumed to indicate restructuring of the relative prestige of the occupations under consideration.

## METHODS AND PROCEDURES

A small-scale replication of the 1947 study was undertaken in the spring of 1963. In order properly to compare the replication with the original, it was necessary to replicate the study using procedures as nearly identical as possible with those of the earlier study. . . .

Because of the stability of prestige positions of occupations from subgroup to subgroup in the 1947 study, it was felt that a relatively small national sample would be sufficient for the replication. In all a total of 651 interviews was collected according to quota sampling methods from a national sample of adults and youths.[3]

As in the 1947 study, occupational

[2] This point is perhaps more clearly illustrated with a more familiar commodity: money income in dollars. It is fairly easy to see how a group could receive a smaller proportion of all income over time, but at the same time have greater income because there is more income to spread between groups.

[3] Justification for our claim that 651 cases suffice to give a reliable intertemporal comparison can be derived from examination of sampling error estimates based on the assumption of a random sample. . . .

TABLE 1. Distributions of Prestige Ratings, United States, 1947 and 1963

| Occupation | March, 1947 | | | | | | | | June, 1963 | | | | | | | |
|---|---|---|---|---|---|---|---|---|---|---|---|---|---|---|---|---|
| | PER CENT | | | | | | | | PER CENT | | | | | | | |
| | Excel-lent* | Good | Aver-age | Below Aver-age | Poor | Don't Know† | NORC Score | Rank | Excel-lent‡ | Good | Aver-age | Below Aver-age | Poor | Don't Know§ | NORC Score | Rank |
| U.S. Supreme Court justice | 83 | 15 | 2 | ‖ | ‖ | 3 | 96 | 1 | 77 | 18 | 4 | 1 | 1 | 1 | 94 | 1 |
| Physician | 67 | 30 | 3 | ‖ | ‖ | 1 | 93 | 2.5 | 71 | 25 | 4 | ‖ | ‖ | 1 | 93 | 2 |
| Nuclear physicist | 48 | 39 | 11 | 1 | 1 | 51 | 86 | 18 | 70 | 23 | 5 | 1 | 1 | 10 | 92 | 3.5 |
| Scientist | 53 | 38 | 8 | 1 | ‖ | 7 | 89 | 8 | 68 | 27 | 5 | ‖ | ‖ | 2 | 92 | 3.5 |
| Government scientist | 51 | 41 | 7 | 1 | ‖ | 6 | 88 | 10.5 | 64 | 30 | 5 | ‖ | 1 | 2 | 91 | 5.5 |
| State governor | 71 | 25 | 4 | ‖ | ‖ | 1 | 93 | 2.5 | 64 | 30 | 5 | ‖ | 1 | 1 | 91 | 5.5 |
| Cabinet member in the federal government | 66 | 28 | 5 | 1 | ‖ | 6 | 92 | 4.5 | 61 | 32 | 6 | 1 | 1 | 2 | 90 | 8 |
| College professor | 53 | 40 | 7 | ‖ | ‖ | 1 | 89 | 8 | 59 | 35 | 5 | ‖ | ‖ | 1 | 90 | 8 |
| U.S. representative in Congress | 57 | 35 | 6 | 1 | 1 | 4 | 89 | 8 | 58 | 33 | 6 | 2 | ‖ | 2 | 90 | 8 |
| Chemist | 42 | 48 | 9 | 1 | ‖ | 7 | 86 | 18 | 54 | 38 | 8 | ‖ | ‖ | 3 | 89 | 11 |
| Lawyer | 44 | 45 | 9 | 1 | 1 | 1 | 86 | 18 | 53 | 38 | 8 | ‖ | ‖ | ‖ | 89 | 11 |
| Diplomat in the U.S. foreign service | 70 | 24 | 4 | 1 | 1 | 9 | 92 | 4.5 | 57 | 34 | 7 | 1 | 1 | 3 | 89 | 11 |
| Dentist | 42 | 48 | 9 | 1 | ‖ | ‖ | 86 | 18 | 47 | 47 | 6 | ‖ | ‖ | ‖ | 88 | 14 |
| Architect | 42 | 48 | 9 | 1 | ‖ | 6 | 86 | 18 | 47 | 45 | 6 | ‖ | ‖ | 2 | 88 | 14 |
| County judge | 47 | 43 | 9 | 1 | ‖ | 1 | 87 | 13 | 50 | 40 | 8 | 1 | ‖ | 1 | 88 | 14 |
| Psychologist | 38 | 49 | 12 | 1 | ‖ | 15 | 85 | 22 | 49 | 41 | 8 | 1 | ‖ | 6 | 87 | 17.5 |
| Minister | 52 | 35 | 11 | 1 | 1 | 1 | 87 | 13 | 53 | 33 | 13 | 1 | 1 | 1 | 87 | 17.5 |
| Member of a board of directors of a large corporation | 42 | 47 | 10 | 1 | ‖ | 5 | 86 | 18 | 42 | 51 | 6 | 1 | ‖ | 1 | 87 | 17.5 |
| Mayor of a large city | 57 | 36 | 6 | 1 | ‖ | 1 | 90 | 6 | 46 | 44 | 9 | 1 | 1 | ‖ | 87 | 17.5 |
| Priest | 51 | 34 | 11 | 2 | 2 | 6 | 86 | 18 | 52 | 33 | 12 | 2 | 1 | 6 | 86 | 21.5 |
| Head of a department in a state government | 47 | 44 | 8 | ‖ | 1 | 3 | 87 | 13 | 44 | 48 | 6 | 1 | 1 | 1 | 86 | 21.5 |
| Civil engineer | 33 | 55 | 11 | 1 | ‖ | 5 | 84 | 23 | 40 | 52 | 8 | ‖ | ‖ | 2 | 86 | 21.5 |
| Airline pilot | 35 | 48 | 15 | 1 | 1 | 3 | 83 | 24.5 | 41 | 48 | 11 | 1 | ‖ | 1 | 86 | 21.5 |
| Banker | 49 | 43 | 8 | ‖ | ‖ | 1 | 88 | 10.5 | 39 | 51 | 10 | 1 | ‖ | ‖ | 85 | 24.5 |
| Biologist | 29 | 51 | 18 | 1 | 1 | 16 | 81 | 29 | 38 | 50 | 11 | ‖ | ‖ | 6 | 85 | 24.5 |
| Sociologist | 31 | 51 | 16 | 1 | 1 | 23 | 82 | 26.5 | 35 | 48 | 15 | 1 | 1 | 10 | 83 | 26 |
| Instructor in public schools | 28 | 45 | 24 | 2 | 1 | 1 | 79 | 34 | 30 | 53 | 16 | 1 | ‖ | ‖ | 82 | 27.5 |
| Captain in the regular army | 28 | 49 | 19 | 2 | 2 | 2 | 80 | 31.5 | 28 | 55 | 16 | 2 | ‖ | 1 | 82 | 27.5 |
| Accountant for a large business | 25 | 57 | 17 | 1 | ‖ | 3 | 81 | 29 | 27 | 55 | 17 | 1 | ‖ | ‖ | 81 | 29.5 |
| Public school teacher | 26 | 45 | 24 | 3 | 2 | ‖ | 78 | 36 | 31 | 46 | 22 | 1 | ‖ | ‖ | 81 | 29.5 |

| | | | | | | | | | | | | | | | | |
|---|---|---|---|---|---|---|---|---|---|---|---|---|---|---|---|---|
| Owner of a factory that employs about 100 people | 30 | 51 | 17 | 1 | 1 | 2 | 82 | 26.5 | 28 | 49 | 19 | 2 | 1 | 1 | 80 | 31.5 |
| Building contractor | 21 | 55 | 23 | 1 | \|\| | 1 | 79 | 34 | 22 | 56 | 20 | 1 | \|\| | \|\| | 80 | 31.5 |
| Artist who paints pictures that are exhibited in galleries | 40 | 40 | 15 | 3 | 2 | 6 | 83 | 24.5 | 28 | 45 | 20 | 5 | 2 | 4 | 78 | 34.5 |
| Musician in a symphony orchestra | 31 | 46 | 19 | 3 | 1 | 5 | 81 | 29 | 25 | 45 | 25 | 3 | 1 | 3 | 78 | 34.5 |
| Author of novels | 32 | 44 | 19 | 3 | 2 | 9 | 80 | 31.5 | 26 | 46 | 22 | 4 | 2 | 5 | 78 | 34.5 |
| Economist | 25 | 48 | 24 | 2 | 1 | 22 | 79 | 34 | 20 | 53 | 24 | 2 | 1 | 12 | 78 | 34.5 |
| Official of an international labor union | 26 | 42 | 20 | 5 | 7 | 11 | 75 | 40.5 | 21 | 53 | 18 | 5 | 3 | 5 | 77 | 37 |
| Railroad engineer | 22 | 45 | 30 | 3 | \|\| | 1 | 77 | 37.5 | 19 | 47 | 30 | 3 | 1 | 1 | 76 | 39 |
| Electrician | 15 | 38 | 43 | 4 | \|\| | 1 | 73 | 45 | 18 | 45 | 34 | 2 | \|\| | \|\| | 76 | 39 |
| County agricultural agent | 17 | 53 | 28 | 2 | \|\| | 5 | 77 | 37.5 | 13 | 54 | 30 | 2 | 1 | 4 | 76 | 39 |
| Owner-operator of a printing shop | 13 | 48 | 36 | 3 | \|\| | 2 | 74 | 42.5 | 13 | 51 | 34 | 2 | \|\| | 2 | 75 | 41.5 |
| Trained machinist | 14 | 43 | 38 | 5 | \|\| | 2 | 73 | 45 | 15 | 50 | 32 | 4 | \|\| | \|\| | 75 | 41.5 |
| Farm owner and operator | 19 | 46 | 31 | 3 | 1 | 1 | 76 | 39 | 16 | 45 | 33 | 5 | \|\| | 1 | 74 | 44 |
| Undertaker | 14 | 43 | 36 | 5 | 2 | 2 | 72 | 47 | 16 | 46 | 33 | 3 | 2 | 3 | 74 | 44 |
| Welfare worker for a city government | 16 | 43 | 35 | 4 | 2 | 4 | 73 | 45 | 17 | 44 | 32 | 5 | 2 | 2 | 74 | 44 |
| Newspaper columnist | 13 | 51 | 32 | 3 | 1 | 5 | 74 | 42.5 | 10 | 49 | 38 | 3 | 1 | 1 | 73 | 46 |
| Policeman | 11 | 30 | 46 | 11 | 2 | 1 | 67 | 55 | 16 | 38 | 37 | 6 | 2 | \|\| | 72 | 47 |
| Reporter on a daily newspaper | 9 | 43 | 43 | 4 | 1 | 2 | 71 | 48 | 7 | 45 | 44 | 3 | 1 | 1 | 71 | 48 |
| Radio announcer | 17 | 45 | 35 | 3 | \|\| | 2 | 75 | 40.5 | 9 | 42 | 44 | 5 | 1 | 1 | 70 | 49.5 |
| Bookkeeper | 8 | 31 | 55 | 6 | \|\| | 1 | 68 | 51.5 | 9 | 40 | 45 | 5 | 1 | \|\| | 70 | 49.5 |
| Tenant farmer (one who owns livestock and machinery and manages the farm) | 10 | 37 | 40 | 11 | 2 | 1 | 68 | 51.5 | 11 | 37 | 42 | 8 | 3 | 1 | 69 | 51.5 |
| Insurance agent | 7 | 34 | 53 | 4 | 2 | 2 | 68 | 51.5 | 6 | 40 | 47 | 5 | 2 | \|\| | 69 | 51.5 |
| Carpenter | 5 | 28 | 56 | 10 | 1 | \|\| | 65 | 58 | 7 | 36 | 49 | 8 | 1 | \|\| | 68 | 53 |
| Manager of a small store in a city | 3 | 40 | 50 | 4 | 1 | 1 | 69 | 49 | 3 | 40 | 48 | 7 | 2 | \|\| | 67 | 54.5 |
| A local official of a labor union | 7 | 29 | 41 | 14 | 9 | 11 | 62 | 62 | 8 | 36 | 42 | 9 | 5 | 4 | 67 | 54.5 |
| Mail carrier | 8 | 26 | 54 | 10 | 2 | \|\| | 66 | 57 | 7 | 29 | 53 | 10 | 1 | \|\| | 66 | 57 |
| Railroad conductor | 8 | 30 | 52 | 9 | 1 | 1 | 67 | 55 | 6 | 33 | 48 | 10 | 3 | \|\| | 66 | 57 |
| Traveling salesman for a wholesale concern | 6 | 35 | 53 | 5 | 1 | 2 | 68 | 51.5 | 4 | 33 | 54 | 7 | 3 | 2 | 66 | 57 |
| Plumber | 5 | 24 | 55 | 14 | 2 | 1 | 63 | 59.5 | 6 | 29 | 54 | 9 | 2 | \|\| | 65 | 59 |
| Automobile repairman | 5 | 21 | 58 | 14 | 2 | \|\| | 63 | 59.5 | 5 | 25 | 56 | 12 | 2 | \|\| | 64 | 60 |
| Playground director | 7 | 33 | 48 | 10 | 2 | 4 | 67 | 55 | 6 | 29 | 46 | 15 | 4 | 3 | 63 | 62.5 |
| Barber | 3 | 17 | 56 | 20 | 4 | 1 | 59 | 66 | 4 | 25 | 56 | 13 | 2 | 1 | 63 | 62.5 |
| Machine operator in a factory | 4 | 20 | 53 | 20 | 3 | 2 | 60 | 64.5 | 6 | 24 | 51 | 15 | 4 | 1 | 63 | 62.5 |
| Owner-operator of a lunch stand | 4 | 24 | 55 | 14 | 3 | 1 | 62 | 62 | 4 | 25 | 57 | 11 | 3 | 1 | 63 | 62.5 |
| Corporal in the regular army | 5 | 21 | 48 | 20 | 6 | 3 | 60 | 64.5 | 6 | 25 | 47 | 15 | 6 | 2 | 62 | 65.5 |
| Garage mechanic | 4 | 21 | 57 | 17 | 1 | \|\| | 62 | 62 | 4 | 22 | 56 | 15 | 3 | \|\| | 62 | 65.5 |
| Truck driver | 2 | 11 | 49 | 29 | 9 | \|\| | 54 | 71 | 3 | 18 | 54 | 19 | 5 | \|\| | 59 | 67 |

TABLE 1. Distributions of Prestige Ratings, United States, 1947 and 1963 (continued)

| Occupation | March, 1947 | | | | | | | | June, 1963 | | | | | | | |
|---|---|---|---|---|---|---|---|---|---|---|---|---|---|---|---|---|
| | PER CENT | | | | | | | | PER CENT | | | | | | | |
| | Excellent* | Good | Average | Below Average | Poor | Don't Know† | NORC Score | Rank | Excellent‡ | Good | Average | Below Average | Poor | Don't Know§ | NORC Score | Rank |
| Fisherman who owns his own boat | 3 | 20 | 48 | 21 | 8 | 7 | 58 | 68 | 3 | 19 | 51 | 19 | 8 | 4 | 58 | 68 |
| Clerk in a store | 2 | 14 | 61 | 20 | 3 | ‖ | 58 | 68 | 1 | 14 | 56 | 22 | 6 | ‖ | 56 | 70 |
| Milk route man | 2 | 10 | 52 | 29 | 7 | 1 | 54 | 71 | 3 | 12 | 55 | 23 | 7 | 1 | 56 | 70 |
| Streetcar motorman | 3 | 16 | 55 | 21 | 5 | 2 | 58 | 68 | 3 | 16 | 46 | 27 | 8 | 2 | 56 | 70 |
| Lumberjack | 2 | 11 | 48 | 29 | 10 | 8 | 53 | 73 | 2 | 16 | 46 | 29 | 7 | 3 | 55 | 72.5 |
| Restaurant cook | 3 | 13 | 44 | 29 | 11 | 1 | 54 | 71 | 4 | 15 | 44 | 26 | 11 | ‖ | 55 | 72.5 |
| Singer in a nightclub | 3 | 13 | 43 | 23 | 18 | 6 | 52 | 74.5 | 3 | 16 | 43 | 24 | 14 | 3 | 54 | 74 |
| Filling station attendant | 1 | 9 | 48 | 34 | 8 | 1 | 52 | 74.5 | 2 | 11 | 41 | 34 | 11 | ‖ | 51 | 75 |
| Dockworker | 2 | 7 | 34 | 37 | 20 | 8 | 47 | 81.5 | 2 | 9 | 43 | 33 | 14 | 3 | 50 | 77.5 |
| Railroad section hand | 2 | 9 | 35 | 33 | 21 | 3 | 48 | 79.5 | 3 | 10 | 39 | 29 | 18 | 2 | 50 | 77.5 |
| Night watchman | 3 | 8 | 33 | 35 | 21 | 1 | 47 | 81.5 | 3 | 10 | 39 | 32 | 17 | 1 | 50 | 77.5 |
| Coal miner | 4 | 11 | 33 | 31 | 21 | 2 | 49 | 77.5 | 3 | 13 | 34 | 31 | 19 | 2 | 50 | 77.5 |
| Restaurant waiter | 2 | 8 | 37 | 36 | 17 | 1 | 48 | 79.5 | 2 | 8 | 42 | 32 | 16 | ‖ | 49 | 80.5 |
| Taxi driver | 2 | 8 | 38 | 35 | 17 | 1 | 49 | 77.5 | 2 | 8 | 39 | 31 | 18 | 1 | 49 | 80.5 |
| Farm hand | 3 | 12 | 35 | 31 | 19 | 1 | 50 | 76 | 3 | 12 | 31 | 32 | 22 | ‖ | 48 | 83 |
| Janitor | 1 | 7 | 30 | 37 | 25 | 1 | 44 | 85.5 | 1 | 9 | 35 | 35 | 19 | 1 | 48 | 83 |
| Bartender | 1 | 6 | 32 | 32 | 29 | 4 | 44 | 85.5 | 1 | 7 | 42 | 28 | 21 | 2 | 48 | 83 |
| Clothes presser in a laundry | 2 | 6 | 35 | 36 | 21 | 2 | 46 | 83 | 2 | 7 | 31 | 38 | 22 | 1 | 45 | 85 |
| Soda fountain clerk | 1 | 5 | 34 | 40 | 20 | 2 | 45 | 84 | ‖ | 5 | 30 | 44 | 20 | 1 | 44 | 86 |
| Sharecropper—one who owns no livestock or equipment and does not manage farm | 1 | 6 | 24 | 28 | 41 | 3 | 40 | 87 | 1 | 8 | 26 | 28 | 37 | 2 | 42 | 87 |
| Garbage collector | 1 | 4 | 16 | 26 | 53 | 2 | 35 | 88 | 2 | 5 | 21 | 32 | 41 | 1 | 39 | 88 |
| Street sweeper | 1 | 3 | 14 | 29 | 53 | 1 | 34 | 89 | 1 | 4 | 17 | 31 | 46 | 1 | 36 | 89 |
| Shoe shiner | 1 | 2 | 13 | 28 | 56 | 2 | 33 | 90 | ‖ | 3 | 15 | 30 | 51 | 2 | 34 | 90 |
| Average | 22 | 31 | 30 | 11 | 7 | 4 | 70 | ....... | 22 | 32 | 29 | 11 | 6 | 2 | 71 | ....... |

* Bases for the 1947 occupational ratings are 2,920 less "don't know" and not answered for each occupational title.

† Base is 2,920 in all cases.

‡ Bases for the 1963 occupational ratings are 651 less "don't know" and not answered for each occupational title.

§ Base is 651 in all cases.

‖ Less than 0.5 per cent.

Source of 1947 distributions: Albert J. Reiss, Jr., and others, *Occupations and Social Status* (New York: Free Press of Glencoe, 1963), Table ii-9.

ratings were elicited by asking respondents to judge an occupation as having *excellent, good, average, somewhat below average,* or *poor* standing (along with a "don't know" option) in response to the item: "For each job mentioned, please pick out the statement that best gives *your own personal opinion* of the *general standing* that such a job has."

One indicator of prestige position is the proportion of respondents (among those rating an occupation) giving either an "excellent" or a "good" response. Another measure which can be derived from a matrix of ratings by occupation requires weighting the various responses with arbitrary numerical values: We can assign an excellent rating a numerical value of 100, a good rating the value of 80, an average rating the value of 60, a somewhat below average rating the value of 40, and a poor rating the value of 20. Calculating the numerical average of these arbitrarily assigned values over all respondents rating the occupation yields the NORC prestige score. This latter measure has received rather widespread use despite arbitrariness in the numerical weights assigned to the five possible ratings.

The ratings and derived scores for each of the ninety occupations obtained in 1947 and in 1963 are shown in Table 1. We present the findings in such detail because of their intrinsic interest. However, the bulk of the analysis contained in this paper is more concerned with characteristics of the distributions of these ratings than with the positions of particular occupations.

## CONGRUITIES IN OCCUPATIONAL PRESTIGE: 1947–63

The major result of the 1963 restudy is dramatically summarized in the product-moment correlation coefficient of .99 between the scores in 1947 and the scores in 1963. The linear regression of the 1963 on the 1947 scores is given by

$$\mathbf{Y} = 0.97\,X + 2.98,$$

a result which indicates that there are very little regression toward the mean and a slight net upward shift in scores.[4] (Here and elsewhere in the text boldface symbols are used to represent regression estimates.)

The high over-all correlation in the total set of occupations is matched by high correlations within subsets of occupations. If we group occupations into professional occupations, other non-manual occupations, and manual occupations, as in Table 2, we can see that the regression lines within the three groups are quite similar.[5]

The very slight effect of grouping occupations is shown again in Figure 1, where the three within-group regression lines are plotted over the range of the 1947 NORC scores contained within each group. The three lines nearly coincide over the observed range of the NORC scores and do not appreciably depart from the line $Y = X$ (where the 1963 and the 1947 scores are equal).

The gross similarity between the 1947 and the 1963 NORC scores tends to overshadow some interesting small changes revealed by the data. Thus, in Figure 1 the regression line for blue-collar occupations lies above (and, in fact, parallels) the line $Y = X$. Consequently, one infers that all blue-collar occupations had slightly higher scores in 1963. For professionals and other white-collar workers, however, the picture is more complex, since the within-group regression lines for these two broad groupings cross over the line $Y = X$. Consequently, in the case of professionals, those particular occupations with the highest prestige scores in 1947 (largely scientific and free professional occupations) slightly increased their scores, whereas those professional occupations with relatively low prestige in 1947 (marginal professional occupations such as "singer in a nightclub") receive somewhat lower scores. Among "other white-collar occupations" the situation is reversed. That is, from the within-group regression line we see that the other white-collar occupations with highest prestige in 1947 (largely managerial and political occupations) tended on the average to decline slightly, whereas lower white-collar

[4] When the NORC scores are ranked, we find a Spearman rank-order correlation of .98 between the 1947 and 1963 ranks.

[5] The hypothesis that a common regression line fits all groups may be rejected at the 0.07 level of confidence, as indicated by the $F$-ratio resulting from an analysis of covariance.

occupations slightly increased in prestige.[6]

[6] There is a slight increase in the ability of the within-group regression lines to predict the direction of changes in scores between 1947 and 1963, as compared with the regression line for the total set. Correct predictions about the directions of change can be made by the over-all regression in 60.5 per cent of the cases and by the within-group regression lines in 62.8 per cent of them, an increase in efficiency of 5.8 per cent.

One other point is brought out sharply by Figure 1 and deserves mention. Since the within-occupational-group regression lines are plotted only for the range of 1947 scores observed within the group, one can easily see the appreciable overlap in scores between professional, other white-collar, and blue-collar occupations. Although these divisions are often employed by social

**TABLE 2 Regressions Within Subsets of Occupations**

| *Occupation Group* | *Regression Coefficient* | *Regression Constant* | *Correlation* |
|---|---|---|---|
| Total, all occupations (*n*=90) | 0.97 | 2.98 | .99 |
| Professional, including one title duplicated for validation purposes (*n*=33) | 1.05 | −3.61 | .96 |
| One non-manual occupation (*n*=21) | 0.92 | 5.85 | .98 |
| All manual occupations, including one craft occupation duplicated for validation purposes and two military titles (*n*=21) | 1.00 | 2.00 | .99 |
| Farm occupations (*n*=4); not computed | | | |

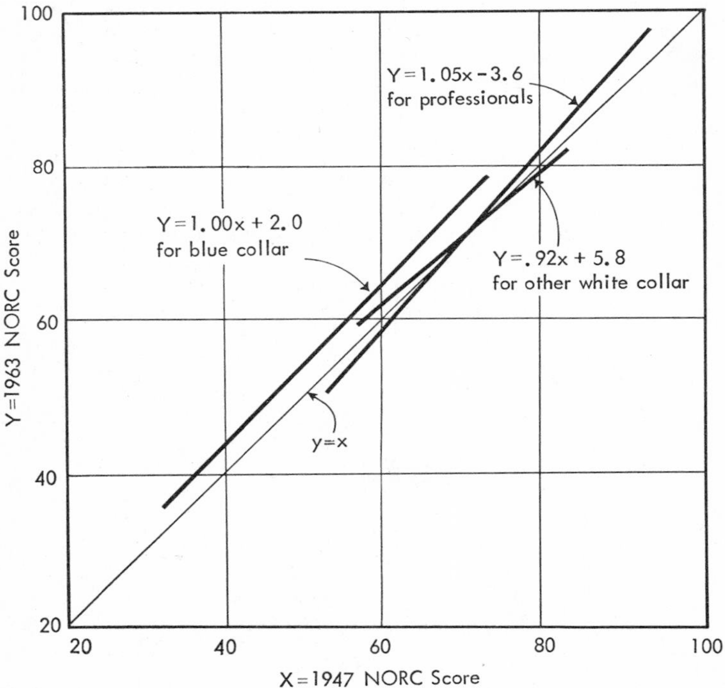


*Figure 1. Regressions of 1963 NORC score on 1947 NORC score within occupational groups.*

scientists as though they represented fundamental class barriers,[7] Figure 1 makes clear that no such barrier can be detected on the basis of occupational prestige. The cleavage between white-collar and blue-collar—if it exists at all—is based not so much upon matters of societal evaluation as perhaps upon the character of dress and work in the three groups.

All in all the preceding results indicate a striking similarity between the structure of the 1947 and the 1963 NORC scores. While we shall subsequently document a number of systematic shifts in the prestige of specific occupational groups, it is abundantly clear that these shifts are small and did not produce any substantial reordering of the relative prestige of the ninety occupations under consideration here.

There are several good reasons for this observed stability. First, relative differential educational requirements, monetary rewards, and even something as nebulous as the functional importance of occupations are not subject to rapid change in an industrial society.[8] Second, any dramatic shifts in the prestige structure of occupations would upset the dependency which is presumed to hold between the social evaluation of a job, its educational prerequisites, its rewards, and its importance to society. Finally, instabilities would further ambiguities or status inconsistencies if the prestige structure were subject to marked and rapid change. Indeed, the meaning of achievement, career, seniority, and occupational mobility would be fundamentally altered if occupational prestige were subject to large-scale changes. No small amount of intragenerational mobility between prestige classes would, for example, be induced solely by the changing structure of occupational prestige *even though individuals did not change their occupations over time.*

[7] This is, e.g., the major distinction employed in a recent comparative study of occupational mobility (Seymour Martin Lipset and Reinhard Bendix, *Social Mobility in Industrial Society* [Berkeley: University of California Press, 1959]).

[8] For a discussion of this point see Otis Dudley Duncan, "Properties and Characteristics of the Socio-economic Index," in Reiss *et al., op. cit.*, pp. 152–53. A correlation of .94 was found between an aggregate measure of the income of an occupation in 1940 and a similar indicator in 1950; a correlation of .97 was found between the proportion of high-school graduates in an occupation in 1940 and the same measure in 1950.

. . . . . . . . . . . . . . . . . . . . . . . . . . . . . . . . . . .

## OCCUPATIONAL PRESTIGE SINCE 1925

Since the appearance of George S. Counts' pioneering 1925 study of occupational prestige, a number of readings have been taken on the distribution of occupational prestige. These studies have utilized a variety of different measurement techniques and different types of samples of raters, college students being quite popular. However, there is evidence that the over-all structure of prestige is invariant under quite drastic changes in technique.[9] Furthermore, one of the major findings of the original 1947 NORC survey was that *all* segments of the population share essentially the same view of the prestige hierarchy and rate occupations in much the same way.[10] With these findings in mind, we may utilize selected prestige studies conducted since 1925 to ascertain whether any substantial changes in the prestige structure of occupations have occurred since that date.

A pre-World War II and post-Depression bench mark is provided by the investigations of Mapheus Smith, who provides the mean ratings of one hundred occupations as rated by college and high-school students in the academic years 1938–39, 1939–40, and 1940–41. The rating technique used by Smith differs considerably from that employed in the NORC study. Respondents were originally required to *rank* occupations according to how far an average incumbent would be seated from the guest of honor at a dinner honoring a celebrity and then to *rate* the occupations on a 100-point

[9] One study, e.g., requested respondents to sort seventy of the occupations in the NORC list into groups of *similar* occupations. The respondent was then asked to order the groups of similar occupations he had formed into social levels. Nevertheless, a rank-order correlation of .97 was found between scores derived from this study and scores obtained from the 1947 NORC study (see John D. Campbell, "Subjective Aspects of Occupational Status" [unpublished Ph.D. thesis, Harvard University, 1952], chap ii).

[10] Reiss *et al., op. cit.*, pp. 189–90.

scale of prestige (according to the rater's personal estimation).[11]

A pre-Depression bench mark of occupational prestige is provided by Counts' study, which provides rankings of forty-five occupations according to their "social standing." The data were collected from high-school students, high-school teachers, and college students.[12] Unlike the NORC and Smith studies, rankings rather than ratings were obtained by Counts. Counts provides rankings for six groups of respondents, and a continuous type variable can be derived by taking the average rank of an occupation over the six groups, weighting for the number of respondents in each group.

These four studies, then, provide an opportunity to examine occupational prestige since 1925. A fairly large number of titles are shared in common between each pair of studies, so that the number of titles utilized in any given comparison is larger than the total number of titles that have been rated in many prestige studies.[13]

Product-moment correlations between the prestige ratings of occupations common to each pair of studies are presented in Table 3, together with the number of matching titles. It is evident from the data presented in Table 3 that *there have been no substantial changes in occupational prestige in the United States since 1925.* The lowest correlation observed is .934, and this occurs between the 1963 NORC scores and the mean ranks derived from the 1925 study of Counts. In view of the high correlation between 1947 and 1963 NORC scores, it is not particularly surprising that high correlations are found between any pair of studies from adjacent points in time. That no substantial changes are observed over a span of approximately 40 years is a bit more surprising and is further evidence of constraints toward the stability of prestige hierarchies.

Slight though the variation in correlations in Table 3 may be, it is noteworthy that the observed variation is apparently a function of elapsed time. The longer the elapsed time between any two studies, the smaller tends to be the correlation between them. Although this point is readily apparent on inspection of Table 3, we can provide a convenient quantitative summary by correlating the squares of the correlations between the $i$th and $j$th time periods and the elapsed times between the $i$th and $j$th time period, yielding a coefficient of $-.85$, a value significantly different from zero at the 0.025 level despite the fact that only six observations are involved.

Small changes in occupational prestige can be obscured by the very high degree of intertemporal stability. Although the techniques used in the studies by NORC,

[11] Mapheus Smith, "An Empirical Scale of Prestige Status of Occupations," *American Sociological Review,* VIII (April, 1943), 185–92.

[12] George S. Counts, "The Social Status of Occupations: A Problem in Vocational Guidance," *School Review,* XXXIII (January, 1925), 16–27.

[13] See, e.g., the national studies cited by Alex Inkeles and Peter H. Rossi, "National Comparisons of Occupational Prestige," *American Journal of Sociology,* LXI (January, 1956), 329–39.

**TABLE 3 Correlations Between Occupational Prestige Ratings at Selected Time Periods, 1925–63***

| *Study and Time Period* | *C* | *S* | *X* | *Y* |
|---|---|---|---|---|
| C (Counts' mean ranks, 1925) | | .968 | .955 | .934 |
| S (Smith's mean ratings, *ca.* 1940) | 23 | | .982 | .971 |
| X (NORC scores, 1947) | 29 | 38 | | .990 |
| Y (NORC scores, 1963) | 29 | 38 | 90 | |

* Correlations placed above diagonal in Figure 1; no. of matching titles placed below diagonal.

Sources: George S. Counts, "The Social Status of Occupations: A Problem in Vocational Guidance," *School Review,* XXXIII (January, 1925), 20–21, Table 1; Mapheus Smith, "An Empirical Scale of Prestige Status of Occupations," *American Sociological Review,* VIII (April, 1943). 187–88, Table I; National Opinion Research Center, "Jobs and Occupations: A Popular Evaluation," *Opinion News,* IX (September 1, 1947), 3–13. See text for details.

Smith, and Counts make direct comparisons precarious, regression analysis permits us to follow changes in the prestige of nineteen occupations common to all studies over the span 1925–63. . . .

. . . There is little evidence of any particular pattern to the small changes in prestige observed between the studies and no evidence whatsoever of any substantial changes in the over-all structure of prestige.

The residuals from the three regression equations linking the four studies in a time sequence can be examined in another way. . . . Although the patterns of change indicated by these residuals are highly irregular and do not lend themselves to an over-all interpretation, changes observed for particular occupations invite speculation. For example, the residuals indicate that the prestige of physicians increased slightly between 1925–40 and 1940–47, but declined in the period 1947–63. Increases in the two initial periods might be attributed to concomitant progress in medical technology, while the medical profession's attitude toward Medicare and other public medical plans might account for the recent decline in the prestige of physicians. Some corroboration of this interpretation can be derived from unpublished tabulations from the 1947 study and its replication of ratings by age cohorts. While the reader familiar with previous reports of prestige ratings will recall that subgroup differences are small, shifts in the prestige rating of physicians by age cohorts—small though they are—tend to indicate that older persons, more likely to be affected by health plans, were responsible for the relative decline in the prestige of physicians. This interpretation remains, however, an *ad hoc* one and has little but plausibility to support it.

. . . . . . . . . . . . . . . . . . . . . . . . . . . . . . . . . . .

## CHANGES IN OCCUPATIONAL PRESTIGE, 1947–63

The major occupation groups of the Census are far from homogeneous, and the allocation of NORC titles to these groups tends to obscure a number of important differences in the patterns of change observed within various occupational situses. . . .

In order to surmount this difficulty and to highlight some of the systematic, if small, prestige changes that were taking place, a classification of NORC titles was expressly designed to illuminate the changes; its chief virtue is the economy of presentation which it facilitates. The groups used in the classification are given in the stub of Table 4 and the specific NORC titles allocated to each group are shown at the bottom of the table. Some titles are dubiously classified and the classification clearly employs several dimensions of occupational structure ranging from class of worker to the kinds of interpersonal contact most frequently encountered on the job.

Several important points emerge on consideration of the classification of NORC titles into occupational situses. . . . The free professions, including occupations like physician and civil engineer, increased in prestige, while cultural or communication-oriented professions, such as "musician in a symphony orchestra" and "radio announcer," declined in standing. Perhaps the most dramatic change is among the scientific occupations, which, with the single exception of "economist," enjoyed positive score differences. A second change . . . was the slight decrease in prestige experienced by political and governmental occupations. One major exception to the rule for other governmental titles was "policeman," which experienced an upswing in prestige. However, such a change is difficult to interpret since there are no other governmental titles of fairly low prestige. Whether it represents regression toward the mean or a genuine increment in respect for law-enforcement officers is difficult to say. The remaining situses in Table 4 are more loosely identified, and we are loath to place any interpretation upon the directions of change observed in them (with the exception of "artisans," largely a craft occupation). They may, however, provide useful guidelines for other researchers seeking to classify the NORC titles into more meaningful categories than those currently available. Taken as a whole, the classification is, however, more closely related to the score differences and the percentage change in score than are the major occupation groups. Correlation ratios of .50

**TABLE 4 Selected Measures of Prestige Change, 1947–63, by Occupational Situs***

| *Occupational Situs* | *No. of NORC Titles* | *Average Score Differences* | *Average Percentage Change* |
|---|---|---|---|
| Total, all occupations | 90 | +0.8 | +1.4 |
| Free professionals | 13 | +1.5 | +1.8 |
| Cultural/communication-oriented professions | 7 | −2.0 | −2.4 |
| Scientific professions | 8 | +2.6 | +3.1 |
| Political/government occupations | 10 | −0.7 | −0.6 |
| Big businessmen | 4 | −0.8 | −0.8 |
| Customer-oriented occupations | 11 | +0.1 | +0.4 |
| Artisans | 8 | +1.6 | +2.4 |
| Outdoor-oriented occupations | 10 | +1.7 | +3.2 |
| Dead-end occupations | 5 | +2.8 | +7.2 |
| All farm | 4 | −0.2 | 0.0 |
| Other | 10 | +1.0 | +1.5 |

* NORC titles are classified into occupational situses as follows:

*Free professionals:* physician, college professor, minister, architect, dentist, lawyer, priest, civil engineer, accountant for a large business, instructor in the public schools, public school teacher, undertaker, welfare worker for a city government.

*Cultural/communication-oriented professions:* artist who paints pictures that are exhibited in galleries, musician in a symphony orchestra, author of novels, radio announcer, newspaper columnist, reporter on a daily newspaper, singer in a nightclub.

*Scientific occupations:* scientist, government scientist, chemist, nuclear physicist, psychologist, sociologist, biologist, economist.

*Political/government occupations:* U.S. Supreme Court justice, state governor, cabinet member in the federal government, diplomat in the U.S. foreign service, mayor of a large city, U.S. representative in congress, county judge, head of a department in a state government, county agricultural agent, policeman.

*Big businessmen:* banker, member of the board of directors of a large corporation, owner of a factory that employs about 100 people, building contractor.

*Customer-oriented occupations* that require face to face contact with the public in the ordinary course of a day's work: manager of a small store in a city, railroad conductor, owner-operator of a lunch stand, barber, clerk in a store, streetcar motorman, taxi driver, restaurant waiter, soda fountain clerk, bartender, filling-station attendant.

*Artisans:* owner-operator of a printing shop, electrician, trained machinist, carpenter, automobile repairman, plumber, garage mechanic, restaurant cook.

*Outdoor-oriented occupations* in which an ordinary day's work is typically performed either outside or in an outdoors setting: airline pilot, mail carrier, railroad engineer, fisherman who owns his own boat, milk route man, truck driver, lumberjack, coal miner, railroad section hand, dock worker.

*Dead-end occupations* which have no possibilities of future advancement: night watchman, janitor, garbage collector, street sweeper, shoe shiner.

*All farm:* farm owner and operator, tenant farmer (one who owns livestock and machinery and manages the farm), farm hand, sharecropper (one who owns no livestock or equipment and does not manage farm).

*Other:* captain in the regular army, official of an international labor union, bookkeeper, insurance agent, traveling salesman for a wholesale concern, playground director, local official of a labor union, corporal in the regular army, machine operator in a factory, clothes presser in a laundry.

Some of the titles in the "other" category might be reclassified into the remaining categories at some expense in homogeneity; such a reclassification does not affect the results presented in this table.

and .51 were found between the classification and, respectively, the score differences and percentage changes in scores.

A few other changes not previously noted and still obscured by the classification of NORC titles into occupational situses should be mentioned. Among the more important of these are the increases in scores observed for "a local official of a labor union" and "official of an international labor union." That these titles should experience increasing prestige, despite the sensational government investigations into the conduct of labor officials during the past decade, is perhaps indicative of the extent to which unions have been assimilated by, and have themselves adopted a more accommodating attitude toward, the established order.

The two military titles in the NORC list, "captain in the regular army" and "corporal in the regular army," remained much the same in the two time periods. Similarly, the two occupations rated twice under slightly different titles for reliability purposes, "public school teacher" (instructor in the public schools) and "automobile repairman" (garage mechanic), received nearly identical ratings under both stimulus titles in the replication, as had been the case in 1947. The reader will notice in Table 1 that one- and two-point differences in NORC scores can be produced by simply rating the same occupation under slightly different titles. It seems likely, therefore, that changes of one or two points in the NORC score of an occupation could hardly be adequate for establishing a real change in prestige or even the direction of change in prestige (if any). The results for the duplicated titles indicate, therefore, that many of the observed changes in prestige scores discussed above are quite negligible and might possibly have been reversed if a slightly different phrasing of the occupational title had been employed.

One other point is worthy of mention before turning to a summary. Duncan has recently used regression techniques to extend the 1947 NORC scores to all occupations in the detailed classification of the U.S. Bureau of the Census. In the course of presenting his results, Duncan had occasion to discuss the temporal stability of his index and the implication that changes in occupational socioeconomic status might have for the validity of his results. On the basis of comparisons between aggregate education and income of occupations as observed in the 1940 and 1950 censuses, Duncan suggested that "changes—albeit minor ones for the most part—were indeed occurring in the socioeconomic status of occupations during the decade 1940–50," adding that "such evidence as we have suggests a rather high temporal stability of occupational prestige ratings, although the time periods concerned have not been lengthy ones."[14] Surely there is nothing in the present study to alter these conclusions (which, indeed, provide a fair summary of the results of this paper). As the 1960 Census data become available for detailed occupations it will, of course, be possible to revise Duncan's index on the basis of the present replication, but barring any dramatic shifts in the aggregate income and education of occupations over the period 1950–60, there is no reason to believe that such a revision would alter in any appreciable way the socioeconomic scores which Duncan assigned to occupations on the basis of the 1947 NORC study and the 1950 Census data.

## CONCLUSIONS

The theme of this paper has been accurately captured by an eminent pathologist who remarked of biochemical phenomena: "Universal instability of constituents seems to be compatible with a stability and even monotony of organized life."[15] Such is the picture one gleans of occupational structures from the present endeavor. Between 1947 and 1963 we are fully aware that many *individual* changes in occupation were under way as men advanced in their career lines, retired, or entered the labor force. Yet, despite the turnover of incumbents, occupational morphology, at least insofar as prestige is concerned, remained remarkably stable. To be sure, systematic patterns of change could be detected, but one would miss the import of this paper if one failed to recognize that

[14] Duncan, *loc. cit.*

[15] René Dubos, *The Dreams of Reason: Science and Utopias* (New York: Columbia University Press, 1961), p. 124.

these changes were minor relative to the over-all stability. The view developed here is that a stable system of occupational prestige provides a necessary foundation to which individuals may anchor their careers.

System maintenance is, however, only part of the story. Small, but nevertheless systematic, changes can be detected between 1947 and 1963. In some cases these changes appear to be attributable to increasing public knowledge of occupations, but it was suggested that any complete understanding of prestige shifts and their causes would require a time series pertaining to the standing of particular occupations. The present study is a step in that direction. Our purposes will be adequately accomplished if others are stimulated to make periodic readings of, as it were, the occupational weather.

# STATUS CONSISTENCY AND INCONSISTENCY

*Gerhard E. Lenski*

When one takes a multidimensional view of distributive systems he soon finds himself confronted with another interesting problem involving men's reactions to the unequal distribution of power and privilege. . . . This is the question of *men's reactions to the phenomenon of status inconsistency.*

The recognition of this problem is largely a modern development because unidimensional views of stratification had such a strong hold on men's minds until recently that the very existence of the problem passed almost unnoticed. Even the few who did note it, such as Cooley and Sorokin, gave it scant attention.

More recently, however, a body of theory and research has developed which suggests that pronounced status inconsistencies of certain kinds tend to be a source of stress and give rise to distinctive reactions which are not predictable simply from a knowledge of the rank of the individual in each of the respective status systems.[1] This theory is based on the postulate that individuals strive to maximize their satisfactions, even, if necessary, at the expense of others. This means that an individual with inconsistent statuses or ranks has a natural tendency to think of himself in terms of that status or rank which is highest, and to expect others to do the same. Meanwhile others, who come in contact with him have a vested interest in doing just the opposite, that is, in treating him in terms of his lowest status or rank.

One can see how this works, and the consequences of it, by imagining the interaction of a Negro doctor and a white laborer in a situation where neither the racial nor occupational status system alone is relevant. The former, motivated by self-interest, will strive to establish the relation on the basis of occupation (or perhaps education or wealth), while the latter, similarly motivated, will strive to establish the relationship on the basis of race. Since each regards his own point of view as right and proper, and since neither is likely to view the problem in a detached, analytical fashion, one, or both, are likely to be frustrated,



[1] Unfortunately, there is still no good summary of the relevant literature on this subject and no definitive treatment. Among others, the following have given special attention to the stress hypothesis: George Homans, "Status Among Clerical Workers," *Human Organization*, 12 (1953), pp. 5–10; Gerhard Lenski, "Status Crystallization: A Non-vertical Dimension of Social Status," and "Social Participation and Status Crystallization," *American Sociological Review*, 19 and 21 (1954 and 1956), pp. 405–413 and 458–464; Irving Goffman, "Status Consistency and Preference for Change in Power Distribution," *ibid.*, 22 (1957), pp. 275–281; A. Zaleznik *et al.*, *The Motivation, Productivity, and Satisfaction of Workers* (Cambridge, Mass.: Harvard University Press, 1958); Elton Jackson, "Status Consistency and Symptoms of Stress," *American Sociological Review*, 27 (1962), pp. 469–480. Methodological problems have been a source of difficulty in this area, but two recent papers point the way to their resolution. These are Lenski, "Comment," *Public Opinion Quarterly*, 28 (1964), pp. 326–330, and Elton Jackson and Peter Burke, "Status and Symptoms of Stress: Additive and Interaction Effects," *American Sociological Review*, 30 (1965), pp. 556–564.

and probably angered, by the experience.

The practice of "one-upmanship," as this pattern of action has sometimes been called, is so common in everyday life that most who indulge in it hardly give it any thought. The net effect, however, is to create considerable stress for many persons of inconsistent status. As a result, such persons are likely to find social interaction outside the bounds of the primary group (where others tend to be like themselves) somewhat less rewarding than does the average person. . . .

## CLASS AND STATUS CONSISTENCY

Considering the diversity of resources which affect the distribution of rewards in modern industrial societies, the question inevitably arises as to how they are interrelated. This, in turn, gives rise to questions of how discrepancies in an individual's statuses affect his actions, and how his actions affect the society of which he is a part. . . .

With respect to the first problem—the degree of relationship between dimensions—census data, as well as data from other sources, make it clear that the rank of individuals and families in one dimension is never a simple function of rank in another. Correlations between property holdings, political status, occupational status, educational status, status-group rank, age status, and sex status are never perfect, and usually are far from it.

One of the closest relationships is that between education and occupation, but studies in the United States have produced correlation coefficients no higher than .77, and in some instances as low as .30.[2] At the other extreme there are certain relationships where the correlation is almost .00. This is clearly the case in the relationship between age and sex, and also with respect to relations between the following pairs: sex status and property holdings; age and occupational status; and finally, both age and sex on the one hand and status-group rank and educational status on the other. Other relationships tend to fall in the middle range.

In a few rare instances, the correlations between resources are actually negative. This is true with respect to age and sex because women now outlive men. More important, it is true of age and educational status where the younger generation has more years of schooling than the older generation because of rising educational standards.

The low correlations between the various types of resources indicates that there are substantial numbers of persons who find themselves confronted with inconsistent statuses of every type. . . . On grounds of deductive logic a good case can be made for the hypothesis that discrepancies between major status dimensions can be a source of stress, first of all for the individuals affected and, through them, for the society of which they are a part. As yet there is only a limited amount of systematic research on this subject, but, such as it is, it tends to support the hypothesis. For example, data gathered in two sample surveys of Greater Detroit in the early 1950s showed that persons with discrepant statuses were more likely to support the Democratic Party and take liberal positions on issues than persons of consistent status.[3] This was especially true in cases where racial-ethnic status was inconsistent with occupational status, and was most pronounced when the inconsistencies were substantial. To a lesser degree, the same pattern prevailed when there were inconsistencies between occupational and educational statuses. In a study based on a

[2] The highest coefficient comes from Warner's study of "Jonesville." See W. I. Warner, *et al.*, *Social Class in America* (Chicago: Science Research, 1949), table 13, p. 172. Godfrey Hochbaum *et al.* report a correlation of .65 from Minneapolis, in "Socioeconomic Variables in a Large City," *American Journal of Sociology*, 61 (1955) p. 34. Robert Angell reports a figure of .39 for Detroit and .30 from Samuel Stouffer's national survey on communism and civil liberties, in "Preferences for Moral Norms in Three Problem Areas," *ibid.*, 67 (1962), pp. 651–652.

[3] For an earlier examination of one of these samples, using a not completely satisfactory methodology, see Gerhard Lenski, "Status Crystallization: A Non-vertical Dimension of Social Status," *American Sociological Review*, 19 (1954). For data on both samples using a better methodology, see Gerhard Lenski, "Comment," *Public Opinion Quarterly*, 28 (1964), especially tables 2 and 3. See also Werner S. Landecker, "Class Crystallization and Class Consciouness," *American Sociological Review*, 28 (1963), pp. 219–229, which analyzes the first of these samples from a different perspective but obtains essentially similar results.

national sample, similar results were obtained. Persons with discrepant statuses (involving occupation, education, and income) were more favorably disposed to changes in the distribution of power within American society than those with consistent statuses.[4]

The number of persons affected in this way by status discrepancies does not appear to be large, at least compared with the total population. More important than numbers, however, may be the fact that discrepant status brings into the ranks of the discontented, persons with many badly needed skills and other resources. In other words, such persons are singularly well equipped to provide the leadership and other resources which uneducated members of the working and nonpropertied classes are unable to provide for themselves. As noted previously, status discrepancy and the reactions it produces may well be a major source of the revolutionary leadership which Marx and Engels predicted (without explaining) would come from the ranks of the more privileged classes.

On the basis of limited studies like those cited above, one would hesitate to say that this hypothesis is much more than interesting speculation. However, there is also a considerable body of unsystematic evidence to support it. The role of ethnic and racial minorities in radical movements has long been noted, and it has also been observed that even the successful members of these minorities are attracted to such movements; in fact, they often provide much of the leadership.[5]

[4] Irwin Goffman, "Status Consistency and Preference for Change in Power Distribution," *American Sociological Review,* 22 (1957), pp. 275–281.

[5] See, for example, Robert Michels on the role of the Jews in the Socialist movement in Europe, *Political Parties: A Sociological Study of Oligarchical Tendencies in Modern Democracy,* translated by Eden and Cedar Paul (New York: Dover, 1959, first published 1915), pp. 258–262, or S. M. Lipset on the role of ethnic minorities in Canada's Socialist Party, in *Agrarian Socialism* (Berkeley, Calif.: University of California Press, 1950), p. 191. See also Stanislaw Ossowski, *Class Structure in the Social Consciousness,* translated by Sheila Patterson (New York: Free Press, 1963), p. 53, on the role of impoverished members of the Polish nobility in the early revolutionary movements in that country.

Obviously not all forms of status discrepancy generate political discontent. For example, one finds little of it among wealthy women or young members of the managerial class. One of the tasks for both theory and research in coming years is to specify the conditions under which this type of reaction occurs, and those under which some alternative reaction, or none at all, is more likely.

# Subjective Dimension of Inequality

---

## NON-EGALITARIAN CLASSLESSNESS—SIMILARITIES IN INTERPRETING MUTUALLY OPPOSED SYSTEMS

*Stanislaw Ossowski*

*We believe that further research and writing on social stratification must be prepared for inequality to resurge in many particular guises.*

N. N. FOOTE

This Chapter was written in 1953 and 1954. The comparison which it draws between the interpretation of the structure of United States society that is popular in certain American circles and the official interpretation of the structure of the Soviet

From *Class Structure in the Social Consciousness,* by Stanislaw Ossowski, 1963. Reprinted by permission of the Macmillan Company and also of Routledge & Kegan Paul Ltd.

Union is in general based on material available in 1953 at the latest. Thus it deals with the period in which the social structure of the Soviet Union was relatively stable and provided the model followed by the people's republics, particularly after 1948.

Our discussions do not therefore cover the changes that have occurred in the Soviet Union in recent years. . . . Nor do they cover the recent changes which have occurred in the United States. . . .

The subject-matter of this chapter has in my opinion a wider significance in that it provides an illustration of the way of conceiving the social structure which was outlined in the foregoing chapter; it also provides a particularly striking example of the application of a similar interpretation of social relationships in mutually opposed systems.

## THE PROBLEM OF CLASS CONSCIOUSNESS IN THE UNITED STATES

It is generally accepted, not without some grounds, that in the consciousness of the mass of the population the "class" aspect of one's own society plays a much smaller role in the United States than it does in the capitalist countries of Europe. Such factors as the absence of estate-traditions,[1] the long-drawn-out territorial expansion to the West, the turbulent development of the country's industry, the dizzy careers made by individuals, the opportunities for upward social mobility (so much greater than in Europe), the heterogeneous ethnic composition of the working class, and finally the Negro question—these are the circumstances which have repeatedly been cited as reasons for the differing social attitudes of the American and the European worker, and for the feeble development of the Communist and Socialist movement in the country where private capital is at its most powerful, industrial production greatest and the income-range widest.

This state of affairs is also reflected in American sociology. Except for a small number of sociologists whose attitudes are somewhat "un-American", American sociology has been isolated from Marxian problems and from Marxian methods of social analysis to a far greater degree than sociology in Western Europe. Just before the Second World War Robert Lynd accused American sociologists of avoiding the term "class" and the problems connected with it.[2] After the war, this charge was repeated by R. Centers.[3] The Swedish investigator of American social relationships, Gunnar Myrdal, though he drew attention elsewhere and in a different context to the recent interest shown in the problem of social class by the group of investigators led by Professor Lloyd Warner, also wrote in 1944: ". . . American sociology (which generally must be given the highest ranking in the world) is weak and undeveloped in regard to the problems of social stratification."[4]

Since these comments were made, studies of the class structure of American society have attained a leading place in the set of problems with which American sociology is concerned. . . . Today there is a growing body of field-research devoted to the class structure of the United States, and particularly of research which has as its common assumption recognition of the psychological criterion of social class, and has as its subject-matter people's opinions about the class-system in which they participate. This sort of approach to social structure is supported by the conviction that in social relationships the only things that matter are those which are immediately predominant in the consciousness of the participants.

As we already know, the American class structure is rather rarely interpreted otherwise than in terms of a scheme of gradation, whether we consider the statements of people representing various American milieux or the findings of field-researchers. Usually a synthetic gradation is involved: the synthesis is achieved in the social consciousness, whereas the theoretician

[1] In the legal sense of this term, passing over the *quasi*-estate culture of the Southern States.

[2] *Knowledge for What?* 1939: third edition, Princeton University Press, 1947, p. 227.

[3] "Perhaps no area of social and psychological research has been so neglected by American scientists as that of class conflict and class consciousness." *The Psychology of Social Class*, Princeton University Press, 1949, p. 8.

[4] *An American Dilemma*, New York, 1944, p. 670.

endeavours at best to define the role of the different elements in the synthesis.

## THE STRATIFICATION OF AMERICAN SOCIETY IN AMERICAN SOCIOLOGY

It is first and foremost within this framework—the scheme of gradation and the psychological criteria of class membership—that discussions of the actual stratification of American society or of its trends of development are carried out amongst American sociologists or political commentators. In discussions of the actual situation, differences of opinion are usually differences in assessing the degree to which certain features of the social structure should be regarded as characteristic of American society. In discussions concerned with trends of development, opposing standpoints clash with each other: destratification or restratification? polarization or the extension of the middle class? Does the class system become more rigid or do rigid class barriers gradually disappear?[5] Nevertheless these opposing standpoints are for the most part not formulated too sharply. In their article *Patterns of American Stratification as Reflected in Selected Social Science Literature*,[6] Paul Hatt and Virginia Ktsanes surveyed the different modes of conceiving the structure of American society found in the work of twenty American social scientists over a quarter-century (1924–1949). They were concerned firstly with the degree of the stratification and distances between classes; secondly with the amount of individual mobility; and thirdly with the emphasis on economic factors in class stratification.

Another subject of discussion in the United States is the importance of the middle class in the American social structure. Until recently it was generally held that the vast majority of people in the United States regard themselves as members of the middle class. This conviction was supported by the Gallup findings of 1939, by the *Fortune* survey and by Cantril's work in 1943.[7] These showed that between 79 and 88 per cent of the population of the areas included in the surveys regarded themselves as belonging to the middle class. Because a certain percentage of respondents did not answer the questions, the percentage of middle class members amongst those who had a definite opinion about their class affiliation was still higher. For instance, 88 per cent of the respondents in the Gallup Institute Poll described themselves as members of the middle class, while only 6 per cent admitted to membership of the upper or lower classes.

Later studies, including the work of Centers, showed that the percentage of persons admitting middle class membership varies according to the manner in which the questions are formulated. For instance, the figure decreases considerably if, instead of giving the respondent a choice between upper, middle and lower classes an open-ended question is asked. The figure decreases still more if the term "working class" is included amongst the possible answers. In the latter case, Centers got a response of 43 per cent for "middle class" and 51 per cent for "working class." In any event, even when these differences are taken into account, the percentage of respondents admitting middle class affiliation clashes sharply with the Marxian prediction of polarization in capitalist societies.

The differing opinions expressed by American writers about the social structure of the United States are concerned not only with the stratification as defined by people's attitudes but also about the objective economic relationships which condition this subjective stratification.[8] Despite all the reservations which I made in Chapter III with regard to the simplification of the American picture of social structure, one should not forget the lively American

[5] N. N. Foote, "Destratification and Restratification". *A.J.S.* Jan. 1953; A. B. Hollingshead: *Trends in Social Stratification A.S.R.* Dec. 1952; G. Sjoberg: *Are Social Classes in America Becoming More Rigid? A.S.R.* Dec. 1951.

[6] *A.S.R.* Dec. 1952.

[7] G. Gallup and S. F. Rae, *The Pulse of Democracy*, New York, 1940; "The People of the United States—a Self Portrait", *Fortune*, 1940; H. Cantril, "Identification with Social and Economic Class", *Journ. Abnorm. and Social Psychology*, 1943, cited from Centers, *The Psychology of Social Class*, Princeton University Press, 1949, pp. 30–31 and 237–40.

[8] Cf. J. J. Spenger, "Changes in Income Distribution and Social Stratification", *A.J.S.*, Nov. 1958.

interest in a simple economic gradation; that is to say, the classification of people according to their income-level and the distinction of various income-groups is a common phenomenon, while terms such as "five thousand dollar men" or "twenty-five thousand dollar men" have become everyday currency.

### THE CONCEPTION OF THE CLASSLESS SOCIETY IN THE UNITED STATES

In these American discussions of the social structure of the United States we may distinguish an extreme point of view. This is the "democratic optimism" that questions the whole reality of social classes in American society, thereby shifting the subject of discussion. Here we reach the model of social structure which in the last chapter I called the concept of a classless and inegalitarian society.

In an article published in 1952, G. H. Lenski contrasted two viewpoints held by different American sociologists. He noted that the American social classes on the one hand are regarded as statistical categories which can have only a heuristic significance,[9] on the other as social groups based on a psychological bond.[10] Supporters of the first approach claim that in America the social-status scale from top to bottom closely approximates to a continuum[11] and that the concept of class is alien to American society.

The view that the concept of class is alien to American society is based on the conviction that the social attitudes of the average American are formed by the traditional ideology—the so-called American Creed. Is it not true that there are no second or third class compartments in American trains in order that railway installations should not conflict with the principle that there are no classes within the bosom of the great American nation, as William Archer ironically observed at the beginning of this century. For an additional payment one can of course travel in a pullman compartment or a drawing-room, but these are not compartments of a different class. In America, Daumier could not have conceived his lithographs in which the classes on the railway-coaches became symbols of the social structure.

As Ralph Bunche once wrote,

> Every man in the street, white, black, red or yellow, knows that this is the land of the free, the "land of opportunity", the "cradle of liberty", the "home of democracy", that the American flag symbolises the "equality of all men" . . .[12]

One argument adduced to support the view that there are no distinct social classes in America is the way in which those sociologists who do not regard classes as a "heuristic concept" but consider the social-class system as a real phenomenon in the social consciousness fail to agree as to the number of classes which they differentiate. S. A. Hetzler wrote,

> The Usemovs and Tangent found three distinct social classes, Centers found four, Hollingshead found five and Warner found six. In view of these discrepancies it is quite important that we ascertain whether contemporary society consists of clearly delineated classes or of a composite of statuses and roles arranged loosely on a continuum.[13]

In the town of Danielson in Connecticut, where Lenski conducted his field-research he found that different people divided the population of Danielson into three, four, five, six and even seven social classes.[14] Lasswell, reporting his findings with regard to the social stratification in a small town in Southern California, stated that the number of social strata mentioned by respondents varied from one (i.e. from a negation of class differentiation) to seven, no one category obtaining more than 17 percent of the total response. He also pointed to the lack of uniform criteria of class affiliation.

[9] "American Social Class: Statistical Strata or Social Group", *A.J.S.* Sept. 1952. Elsewhere we find the same opposition expressed in different terms: namely, that of the "substantive" and "classificatory nature of class". P. Hatt, "Stratification in the Mass Society", *A.S.R.* April 1950.

[10] Cf. O. Cox: *Caste, Class and Race,* New York, 1948.

[11] G. C. Homans, *English Villagers of the XIIIth Century*, Harvard University Press, 1941.

[12] Myrdal, *op. cit.*, p. 4.

[13] "An Investigation of the Distinctiveness of Social Class", *A.S.R.* Oct., 1953, p. 494.

[14] G. Lenski, "Status Crystallization", *A.S.R.*, 1954, p. 143.

These were some of the findings on which he based his conclusion that social strata in Citrus City are not rigorously distinguished by the general population.[15]

The view that there are no classes in American society is frequently encountered in investigations carried out in various American milieux, even when the questionnaire mentions class divisions. "I don't believe in classes" is a statement expressed by quite a number of American citizens when asked about their class affiliation or inter-class relationships.

As one might have anticipated, this conviction is class-determined, statistically speaking. During an investigation carried out in four districts of Minneapolis, the question was put: "What social classes do you think there are in Minneapolis and which one of these classes are you in?" In the wealthiest district 19 per cent of respondents replied that there were no social classes at all, whereas only 6 per cent gave the same response in the poorest district.[16] In this type of enquiry it is, of course, difficult to determine how far one is dealing with the repetition of ideological formulae and at what point one is confronted with genuine convictions.

What is in the minds of those who talk of the "American belief in classlessness"[17] or the American "tradition that class divisions are un-American"?[18] What is in the minds of those American citizens who say that they "do not believe in classes"?

From the commentaries on such statements we may deduce that those Americans who believe or would like to believe that they live in a classless society have in mind the sort of "classlessness" which we have been considering. This involves an image of society which meets the following conditions:

1. The social and economic status of individuals is not determined by descent; the road to the highest positions is open to all, even though they may not have an equal start.[19]
2. The social-status scale is not broken by any distinct barriers which could transform the continuum-like status order into a gradation of different strata.
3. In accordance with the last condition no definite privileges are attached to the various segments of that scale, nor do any permanent conflicts of interest exist between higher and lower levels of social status.[20]
4. There is no separation or restriction in social contacts between strata.

Civic equality, which is a tenet of the American Creed, is supposed to be based precisely on such classlessness, and not on a levelling-out of social status or income. Each citizen has equal rights and in a certain sense equal opportunities to aspire to lower or higher positions. It is assumed that inequalities of economic or social status are determined not by class affiliation but by personal qualifications, but nobody denies the existence of these inequalities. The great range of achievements is in accordance with the demands of free competition.

Those who rejected this optimistic image of American society did not need to appeal to a Marxian line of argument. . . . At the beginning of this century, William Archer wrote that the lack of class divisions in American trains was just as much a fiction as the classlessness of American society. Forty years later McGuire wrote: "Social class is a reality of American social stratification if the primary data of contemporary

[15] T. E. Lasswell: "A Study of Social Stratification", *A.S.R.* June 1954, p. 313. A similar conclusion is suggested in a rather less obvious manner by some material on the attitudes of textile workers in Patterson, New Jersey (cf. J. G. Manis and B. N. Meltzer: "Attitudes of Textile Workers to Class Structure", *A.J.S.* June 1954).

[16] N. Gross: "Social Class Identification in the Urban Community", *A.S.R.*, August 1953, p. 402.

[17] G. Sjoberg, *op. cit.*, (see p. 115, n. 2).

[18] Centers, *op. cit.*, p. 8.

[19] Parsons maintains that an equal start is impossible in a society in which an "occupationally-differentiated industrial system and a significantly solidary kinship system" are combined. *The Social System*, Free Press, Glencoe, p. 161.

[20] "The bourgeoisie are not obviously set apart from the proletariat", wrote M. Rosenberg in a passage contrasting American and European relationships, "by virtue of owning a car. The differentiation is continuous rather than polar. One man owns a newer or better car than another but this will not induce a feeling of class consciousness in his slightly less fortunate fellow." "Perceptual Obstacles to Class Consciousness", *Social Forces*, Oct. 1953.

community studies are to have any meaning".[21] A little earlier Robert Lynd[22] had compared American society to an arena in which elephant and chickens have an equal chance to dance.

The characteristics of the various classes seen as distinct component elements of American society are to be found in the work of various field-researchers who did not confine themselves to questionnaires but followed Lynd's methods.[23] The characteristics of the poor white class in the Southern States as outlined by L. W. Doob remind one of the comparison between social classes and nations made by Disraeli and Engels.[24] Centers spoke of class solidarity and class interests. And in his reference to the great coal strike and President Truman's address to the American people on 24 May, 1946, he speculated whether the class struggle in the United States "had reached a stage where one could not help but wonder if men were not finding loyalty to a class a bigger and nobler thing than loyalty to a Government".[25]

## THE CONTRASTING BACKGROUND

Independently of the degree to which the conception of a classless society actually finds support in the social consciousness and of the sectors of American society in which this occurs, we should remember that in America this image of the social structure is set against the background of the caste-like relationships between white and black, and that this system of caste relationships is marked by characteristics which are a radical negation of all four conditions mentioned earlier. For caste membership and caste-bound social status are decided exclusively by descent; caste-membership is determined for life before a child is born, and the barrier dividing the two classes cannot in principle be crossed. Between white and coloured there is no intermediate status. In the United States, unlike South America, a light-coloured mulatto remains a Negro in his relations with the white caste. There is caste endogamy and social separation, and the Deep South has strictly enforced institutional separation between the castes. Finally, there are caste privileges, caste etiquette and caste discrimination, masked by the "Jim Crow" formula of "separate but equal" but fooling nobody.

This separation of the castes makes it easy to overlook the existence amongst the white population of exclusive clubs which are open only to individuals from the upper social brackets, or of such institutions as the *New York Social Register*. This is an annually-published list of the names of a few hundred distinguished individuals. . . .[26] Against a background in which caste membership is absolutely determined from birth, the influence of the parents' property and income-level on the class status of their children becomes less apparent, and the frequency with which class status is inherited less striking.

There is one further circumstance which helps Americans to feel this democratic optimism about the social structure of their own country. This is the old tradition of rejecting the class-divisions of Europe, a tradition which goes back as far as the eighteenth century. Americans see these class-divisions chiefly in terms of the relics of feudalism—estate distinctions, aristocratic exclusiveness, the privileges attached to descent from a good family.[27] America banned aristocratic titles in the dawn of its independence, and the good American citizen has been accustomed to compare his country with class-divided Europe, with its dukes, lords, counts and its primitive peasantry, whose representatives he could see in the East and South European immigrant districts of America's cities. And when the son or grandson of such an uneducated immigrant achieved high office in the United States, as a mayor, governor or the owner of a large business, this provided a forceful argument in favour of

[21] McGuire, "Social Stratification and Mobility Patterns", *A.S.R.*, April 1950.

[22] Lynd, *Knowledge for What?* 1939; 3rd ed., Princeton Univ. Press, 1947, p. 111.

[23] R. S. Lynd and H. M. Lynd: *Middletown*, New York, 1929; *Middletown in Transition*, New York, 1937.

[24] "Poor Whites: a Frustrated Class", Appendix to J. Dollard, *Caste and Class in a Southern Town*, ed. 1949, pp. 445–484.

[25] Centers: *op. cit.*, p. 7.

[26] G. Gorer, *The American People*, New York, 1948, p. 217.

[27] Cf. Myrdal, *op. cit.*, p. 670 and p. 1375.

the fundamental tenets of the American Creed.[28]

This dual background—that of the Negro caste and that of the European "old countries"—has made it easier for good Americans to see the system of social relationships within white society in the United States as a harmonious, dynamic and classless structure: harmonious in respect of the absence of class antagonism and polarising tendencies and also in respect of the number and prestige of the middle strata; dynamic in respect of the degree of mobility of individuals on the rungs of the social ladder.

In all these respects this image of social structure is opposed to the Marxian vision of the capitalist society, the vision of class antagonisms. Nor should we be misled by the use of the term "dynamic". The image of American society is dynamic in quite a different sense than is the Marxian theory of classes.

## THE PROBLEM OF CLASSLESSNESS IN SOVIET SOCIETY

Looking at the social structure of the United States with eyes accustomed to observe reality through the prism of the class struggle, an East European Marxist is bound to regard American modes of conceiving American social stratification, even those that lay stress on a class hierarchy and on relatively rigid class boundaries, as a sort of mystification aimed at masking the essential class conflicts. The American conception of a classless society must appear absurd to him, for it combines classlessness with capitalism.

Nevertheless, there is one reason why this American conception should not strike a Marxist as absurd. For this extreme, optimistic and democratic view of society, combining classlessness with the maintenance of great differences in the share in the national income, which is contained in a certain version of the American Creed, is by no means alien to the Soviet Union and the People's Democracies in relation to their own societies.

How did the Soviet society of the Stalinist period, described as being "the second stage of the development of the Soviet state, and which came after the victory of socialism and the transformation of the class structure",[29] appear from the viewpoint of the Communist Creed?

From the phrase just quoted about the transformation of the class structure, it would follow that the Soviet society of this period was not classless. And indeed, according to the Stalinist conception, classes do still exist in the Soviet Union, but they are "non-antagonistic classes", none of them being in a position to appropriate the labour of another class.[30] These classes are the workers and the *kolchoz* peasants—that is to say, the classes whose differentiation is based on the distinction between two forms of socialist property, state property and co-operative property. This differentiation remains in a certain correlation with the differentiation between town and country. The great Soviet Encyclopaedia also links the differentiation with the concept of the two sectors of socialist production. The intelligentsia is mentioned as a third component of Soviet society, but in accordance with Stalin's arguments it is not accorded the name of "class", but only of "stratum".[31]

Seen from the viewpoint of Marx and Lenin, "non-antagonistic classes" constitute a *contradictio in adiecto*. The authors of *Historical Materialism* appear to realize this; after citing Lenin's definition of class they write: "In this sense one can no longer call our society a class-society".

But the Stalinist conception of "non-antagonistic classes" breaks away from the concept of class found in Marx and Lenin in favour of a concept that is closer to Adam Smith's idea of classes (different

[28] "How always have men's hearts beat", wrote Woodrow Wilson in 1913, "as they saw the coast of America rise to their view. How it has always seemed to them that the dweller there would at last be rid of kings, of privileged classes, and of all those bonds which had kept men depressed and helpless". *The New Freedom*, New York, 1914.

[29] *Istoricheski materializm* (*Historical Materialism*), ed. Professor F. B. Konstantinov, Moscow, 1951, pp. 363–402.

[30] V. I. Lenin, "A Great Beginning" (1919), from *The Essentials of Lenin*, London, Lawrence & Wishart, 1947, Vol. II, p. 492.

[31] Cf. for instance, Konstantinov, *op. cit.*, p. 402

types of property, different sources of income). In relation to the basic concept of social class in Marxist doctrine the qualification "non-antagonistic" has a modifying and not a specifying function; but in relation to Adam Smith's concept of class it has a specifying function, because Smith acknowledged the existence of class antagonisms, although he did not deduce them from his definition of class.

The conception of "non-antagonistic classes" arose out of certain requirements of Soviet internal policy. The official recognition of the class of workers and the *kolchoz* peasantry as the only classes still existing in the Soviet Union, distinguished according to objective economic criteria, provided in advance a negative answer to the question whether privileged and underprivileged classes existed in the new social structure. The traditional meaning of the term "classless society" . . . was probably also involved. This associated the "classless society" with the Communist system, which is to be attained only in the future. But a spokesman for the ruling ideology, while acknowledging that classes still exist in Soviet society, will not call it a "class society" because of the term's old associations: for Soviet society is opposed to such class societies. Therefore it is stated that the fundamental class differences (*korennye klassovye razlicyiha*) have already been altogether overcome in the Soviet Union in consequence of the victory of Socialism.[32]

Quite apart from such terminological complications, the official Soviet image of contemporary Soviet society—an image which is part of the ideological training programme for the whole population—is of a society without class stratification, not only from the Marxist and Leninist viewpoints, but also from the viewpoint derived from the American criteria of the concept of class. In this society there is no exploitation of man by his fellow man, nor are there upper classes and lower classes in the sense in which we encountered them in the American scheme of gradation. The superiority of the working class in relation to the peasantry is, according to Soviet ideology, a superiority of merit and not of privileges. This class occupies the leading place on the common road to Communism and not a higher level in the social structure. The often repeated expression concerning the "moral and political unity of the Soviet nation" is also a certain way of asserting the classless character of Soviet society, particularly when we consider the Marxist traditions concerned with the ideological superstructure.

This society without class privileges and class antagonisms is not of course an egalitarian society. No Soviet Marxist will deny that the share of individual Soviet citizens in the national income differs considerably. The tendency to *uravnilovka* (equalization or levelling of wages) which characterised the early phase of Soviet society was condemned as incompatible with the principles of Socialism. In the Polish People's Republic, too, President Bierut more than once spoke publicly of progress "in the direction of putting an end to the so-called *uravnilovka*" and of the need for a further campaign against *uravnilovka,* since private ownership of the means of production had been abolished.

In the Soviet Union economic privileges and discriminations have, in accordance with Soviet doctrine, nothing in common with class divisions. Even large differences of income are not associated with any sort of relationships such as could transform the extensive social-status scale into a class hierarchy. Instead, the individual's place in the scale is determined by his merits.

The idea that a new privileged class may be created as a result of the increasing range of income-differentials is not considered at all. In this respect the Soviet theory of the social structure in the land of socialism differs fundamentally from American conceptions. In judging whether a society is a "class society" or not, an American is thinking of a gradation of classes based above all, though not exclusively, on income-differences. In the Soviet Union and the People's Democracies this scheme of class structure is not applied at all. Soviet ideology employs only two conceptions of class: the Marxian in relation to other

[32] T. Gubariew, *O priodolenii klassovykh razlichii v SSSR* ("About the overcoming of class differences in the U.S.S.R."), *Bolshevik,* 1951, No. 5, p. 19.

countries, and Adam Smith's conception—in a certain sense—in relation to its own society. The transition from the present socialist system to the classless society is to be accomplished not by a levelling-off of wages but by the abolition of the fundamental differences between towns and countryside and by the merging of the two sectors of the economy—state and *kolchoz*—into one production sector.[33] This conception is linked with the thesis that the present class system in the socialist state is horizontally and not vertically structured.

## SIMILARITIES AND DISSIMILARITIES

In contrast to the United States, where the American Creed and the conception of "classlessness" are the subject of analysis and dispute, no variants of the conception of Soviet society were as a rule to be found in Soviet publications before 1954. In comparison with the American optimistic view of American society, the Soviet conception of a harmonious and dynamic society, without antagonistic classes and without *uravnilovka,* was formulated in a more definite and radical manner. The similarities are however sufficiently apparent, despite the basic difference over the requirements for human cooperation: there the cult of private enterprise is stressed, here the subordination of individual activity to social planning on the widest scale.[34]

The Socialist principle "to each according to his merits" is in harmony with the tenets of the American Creed, which holds that each man is the master of his fate, and that a man's status is fixed by an order of merit.[35] The Socialist principle allows of the conclusion that there are unlimited opportunities for social advancement and social demotion; this is similar to the American concept of "vertical social mobility". The arguments directed against *uravnilovka* coincide with the arguments put forward on the other side of the Atlantic by those who justify the necessity for economic inequalities in a democratic society. "The maximisation of effort in an achievement-oriented society calls for considerable inequality"—wrote Spenger in 1953.[36] This sentence could equally well have been uttered by a statesman in the Soviet Union or the Peoples' Democracies. In the United States this "optimistic" conception of the system of relationships within the white population has as its background the old countries of Europe and the Negro caste situation within the country. In the Soviet case, the background consists of the relationships that prevailed in pre-revolutionary Russia, and of the capitalist world that today encircles the socialist countries. Stalin wrote,

> The feature that distinguishes Soviet society today from any capitalist society is that it no longer contains antagonistic, hostile classes; that the exploiting classes have been eliminated, while the workers, peasants and intellectuals, who make up Soviet society, live and work in friendly collaboration.[37]

Communist doctrine assumes that a necessary condition of the development towards a harmonious society—a society in which everyone has an equal start, and there are no antagonistic classes—is the abolition of the private ownership of the means of production. But the American Creed does not accept this assumption at all. On the contrary, it regards the system guaranteed by the American Constitution as the one that offers the most favourable conditions for achieving just this kind of society. These incompatible assumptions enable similar conceptions of social structure to be applied in countries with such widely varying economic systems.

In comparing the official conception of Soviet society with the most optimistic and

[33] See the *Great Soviet Encyclopaedia,* under the heading *Classes.*

[34] For the changes which have been taking place recently in this connexion in American society see W. Friedmann, "Changes in Property Relations," *Transactions of the Third Sociological Congress in Amsterdam,* vol. II, 1956.

[35] "... An order of merit in terms of which men differ with respect to their rights and duties". J. J. Spenger, "Changes in Income Distribution and Social Stratification", *A.J.S.*, November, 1953.

[36] *Ibid.*, p. 258.

[37] J. Stalin, "Report on the Work of the Central Committee to the Eighteenth Congress of the C.P.S.U. (B.)", delivered March 10, 1939, published in J. Stalin, *Problems of Leninism,* Moscow, Foreign Languages Publishing House, 1947, p. 621.

extreme American viewpoints, we should not forget that this similarity refers only to images of the present situation. For both on one side and on the other the trends of development are presented in quite a different manner. The American Creed does not envisage a more perfect system, although it foresees progress in some respects within the present system. The Communist Creed, on the contrary, holds that the socialist society of today is only a stage on the road to a communist society.

This transition to a communist society should, however, according to the prospects outlined by Stalin himself be achieved not by means of upheavals—as is to be expected of all transitions from one "formation" to another—but via "the continuous expansion and perfecting of socialist production on the basis of higher technique".[38] This means by way of evolution, in the same sort of way in which Americans who, while taking the "optimistic" view, do not yet regard the American society of today as a "classless society", visualize the further democratization of the United States.[39] When the future of their own society is concerned, the ruling groups in both the capitalist and the socialist countries always take an evolutionary attitude.

Meanwhile the evolutionary processes are not necessarily proceeding in the predicted direction. The difficulties with which Communist ideology has to cope in connexion with the changes which have taken place in the socialist society are no less than those which the American Creed has encountered in its collision with the American reality. In the United States it was easier to believe in classlessness amongst the white community before the end of the expanding Western frontier with the unlimited possibilities which it offered to enterprising individuals, before the disappearance of the "no-man's land", and before the great industrial concerns destroyed over large areas the free economic competition that is one of the tenets of the American Creed. And in the Soviet Union it was easier in 1918 to justify the ratios of the differential state wage scale ranging from 100 to 175 than it was in 1950 to justify the ratios of 1 to 40 which prevailed at that time.

## THE MARXIST ANALYSIS AS A WEAPON OF STRUGGLE

The application of the Marxian scheme of social structure exclusively to the capitalist societies is entirely justified from the viewpoint of the Marxian theoretical approach, since the Marxian analysis referred solely to the class-system prevailing in a social order where class antagonisms were the result of private ownership of the means of production. Neither Marx nor Engels undertook to analyse the structure of a society in which the means of production were nationalized, and indeed such a society did not exist anywhere at that time. Thus in the Soviet image of Soviet society there is no relinquishing of Marxian assumptions, despite the introduction of the non-Marxian concept of "non-antagonistic classes". It would, on the other hand, be possible to say that there has been a relinquishing of Marxian methods of sociological analysis.

Because of the propaganda functions of the social sciences, Marxian methods—and in general all sociological methods that threaten stereotypes and social fictions—are rarely found suitable from the viewpoint of the ruling or privileged groups for the analysis of their own society. On the other hand, they are a useful weapon against outside enemies.

So it is the Soviet Union's opponents in the United States or Western Europe who attempt to use these methods in relation to the Soviet Union. A particularly active part in this is played by Russian émigré intellectuals, who are better acquainted with Marxism and with Russia than are their Western colleagues. In place of the "non-antagonistic classes" arising from different types of socialist property, they try to detect the formation of a new class structure based on economic privileges and on the

[38] J. Stalin, *Economic Problems of Socialism in the U.S.S.R.*, Moscow, Foreign Languages Publishing House, 1952, p. 45.

[39] Cf. for instance this passage from C. Sjoberg: "Although it can hardly be denied that, measured by objective criteria, some kind of class system exists in the United States, historical changes in the social structure may well give substance to the American creed of 'classlessness.'" "Are Social Classes in America Becoming More Rigid?" *A.S.R.*, Dec. 1951, p. 783.

exploitation of the labour of others by a privileged class composed of institutionally-established groups: this exploitation being carried out not directly but by means of the state administration and the state treasury, as was done by the court aristocracy in France under the last Bourbons. Those who like to apply Marxian methods to Soviet society in the Stalinist period stress the wide range of wage-scales and the importance of such economic privileges as were not included in the total of monetary rewards. They try to emphasize the tendency to stabilize class differences, citing such features as the great reduction in death duties and the sliding scale for income tax introduced in 1943; the reintroduction of fees for secondary and higher education in 1940, which was confirmed by the amendment of the 121st article of the Stalinist constitution in 1947; the institutionalization of "class barriers" evidenced by the whole system of rights, subsidies, privileges and so on. In general, they attempt to apply the Marxian theory of the state to the Soviet state, and the Marxian theory of "opium for the masses" to the ideology propagated in the socialist states.

In the last two chapters I examined the conception of classlessness in the light of certain social tendencies, namely the tendencies to soften the "class" aspect of the social structure. It emerged that the concept of the classless non-egalitarian society—the concept, not the term—within the frame of differing theories of social class is used for the characterization of one's own society in the leading countries of both the socialist and the capitalist world. In one case this conception is part of the official ideology in which the mass of citizens are reared, while in the other it may rather be said to constitute an extreme expression of a trend which is characteristic of the civic training propagated in that country. In both countries the view of their own society is based on the assumption that even widely ranging shares in the national income are not sufficient to establish social stratification, nor do they necessarily cause either class antagonisms or other symptoms characteristic of a class structure. The differences in economic system prevailing in the two countries are responsible for the fact that this assumption is interpreted in one way on the Western side of the Atlantic and in a different manner in Eastern Europe.

The similarity between the two interpretations of a non-egalitarian social structure is linked with a wider question: that of the causal determination of the various important phenomena of social life which, despite appearances and despite the theoretical simplifications convenient for polemical purposes, do exist in each of the two contemporary opposing forms of economic system. The similarity is also linked with the following threefold problem: in what respects do the institutions and ideologies of the contemporary states which have nationalized the means of production and established a new political order constitute the opposite of the capitalist system; in what respects do they form a continuation of it; and in what respects are the new stages of this new system, now in the process of stabilization, accompanied by a revival of the institutions, relationships, psychological attitudes, and ideas of pre-socialist, socio-economic formations?

# SOCIAL CLASS, IDEOLOGY, AND VOTING PREFERENCE:

## An Analysis of the 1964 Presidential Election

*Gertrude Jaeger Selznick and Stephen Steinberg*

The pervasiveness of social class as a factor in voting behavior is a well-documented

This is a revised version of a paper read at the 1966 Annual Meeting of the American Sociological Association. The data for this analysis are derived from a larger study supported by the Anti-Defamation League. Printed by permission of the authors.

fact.[1] In every presidential election since 1936, when polling data first became available, blue-collar or working-class voters have voted for Democratic candidates in far greater proportions than have white-collar or middle-class voters. From one election to another the proportions have varied. Nevertheless, in every election social class has predicted voting preferences.[2]

The *fact* that social class predicts vote is well-established. The *concept* of social-class voting, however, goes beyond the bare empirical relation between class and vote to include the idea that there are social-class reasons for social-class voting. In other words, there is a theory of social-class voting, although it is rarely put to an empirical test. According to this theory, much voting is rather directly inspired by immediate social-class interests, as these are perceived by the voter. Workers who vote Democratic are presumed to be doing so to further their pocketbook interests, just as the more privileged vote Republican to further theirs.

Past research has also demonstrated that political beliefs or ideology predict vote. Stated simply, some people take their basic ideological convictions into account when deciding their vote. But the problem arises of how to distinguish between ideological and social-class voting. A pro-welfare stand on economic issues can and frequently does have its roots in the urgencies of economic disprivilege, but it can be grounded in political philosophy, belief, or ideology as well. Similarly, an anti-social welfare stand can have its roots in the prerogatives of privilege, but it too can be ideologically determined. Clearly, until social class, political ideology, and opinion on pocketbook issues are analyzed *simultaneously,* we cannot determine to what extent the relation between social class and vote is explained by social-class differences in ideology or by social-class differences in pocketbook concerns.[3]

These considerations are crucial for an understanding of social-class voting. It is one thing if workers vote Democratic because they are committed to both liberal political principles and a liberal economic policy. But it is another thing if they are conservative in their broad political outlook, but vote Democratic simply out of immediate economic self-interest. If this second possibility holds up in fact, then workers might in the future switch their political allegiance to a conservative or reactionary political party that makes an appeal—genuine or demagogic—to their economic interests.

This paper has two related purposes. First, it seeks a conceptual clarification of the concepts of social-class and ideological voting. Even though both have been discussed in past studies,[4] there has been little effort to assess the extent to which, and the conditions under which, each occurs. Secondly, this paper attempts a better understanding of the reasons for Goldwater's overwhelming defeat in the 1964 election. It is easy to show that both social-class and ideological agreement with Goldwater predict the Goldwater vote. If our reasoning is correct, however, this does not tell us whether the overwhelming vote against Goldwater stemmed primarily from ideological rejection of Goldwater's reactionary political philosophy, or merely from rejection of his stand on specific bread-and-butter issues of particular concern to workers.

From the outset it should be noted that

[1] See, for example, A. Campbell, G. Gurin, and W. E. Miller, *The Voter Decides*, Evanston, Ill.: Row, Peterson, 1954; A. Campbell, P. E. Converse, W. E. Miller, and D. E. Stokes, *The American Voter*, New York: Wiley, 1960; P. Lazarsfeld, B. Berelson, and H. Gaudet, *The People's Choice*, New York: Duell, Sloan and Pearce, 1944. For a summary and analysis of the results of many voting studies, see S. M. Lipset *Political Man*, New York: Doubleday, 1964, especially chap. 9.

[2] R. R. Alford, "The Role of Social Class in American Voting Behavior," *The Western Political Quarterly*, Vol. 16, No. 1, March, 1963, pp. 180–194.

[3] Numerous studies have demonstrated that voting is statistically related to social class, political ideology, and opinion on pocketbook issues. However, these variables are themselves interrelated. Little or no effort has been made to use multivariate analysis to factor out the ideological and the pocketbook elements in the social-class vote.

[4] Especially Philip Converse's essay in D. E. Apter, ed., *Ideology and Discontent*, New York: Free Press, 1964, chap. 8.

this study may have a basic limitation stemming from the peculiar character of the 1964 election. Both economic and ideological issues were particularly salient because of Goldwater's open attacks on social welfare programs and his outspoken advocacy of conservative principles. For this reason it is problematic to what extent the findings in this paper would apply to other elections, past or future. This, however, is a question that can be resolved only through replication.

## THE DATA

The data for this analysis are derived from a national survey conducted during the weeks preceding the 1964 election. The survey was not designated as an election study. In effect, this is a secondary analysis, subject to the usual limitations.

The sample is a modified probability sample of almost 2000 cases.[5]

Certain groups are excluded from the analysis, reducing the working sample to just under 1400 cases. Negro and Jewish respondents are omitted because their voting behavior was obviously predicated on special factors, and they voted for Johnson with virtual unanimity. Also omitted are respondents who said they definitely would not vote, as well as the 5 per cent who refused to indicate their voting intentions. Otherwise, the sample is representative of white voters in the last election.

## SOCIAL CLASS AND VOTE

In the 1964 election, as in other elections in the recent past, high social status is strongly associated with a tendency to vote Republican. Table 1 examines the Goldwater vote by occupation, education, and income. Compared to past elections, the Republican vote was sharply reduced at every occupational level. In 1964, people classified as managers, officials, and proprietors, or as farm managers or proprietors—the traditional backbone of Republican support—gave Goldwater at best half their votes. Among the lower occupations, in which the great bulk of the working force is found, support for Goldwater was at a virtually unprecedented low. He received just 39 per cent of the vote among clerical workers, and only a quarter of the vote among the four categories of manual workers.

Much the same picture emerges when the vote is inspected by education and income. Only those who finished college gave Goldwater a majority; among post-graduates the Goldwater vote decreases somewhat. The majority of Americans still have a high school education or less; yet below the college level Goldwater got less than a third of the votes. The relation between income and vote is less consistent, but in no income category did Goldwater receive a majority, except among that relative handful who earned $15,000 or more.

To facilitate analysis, education, income, and occupation are combined into an index of social class. Three criteria of social class were used: having four years of high school or more, a family income of $8000 or more, and a white-collar job. Persons with all three of these characteristics (19 per cent of the sample) are referred to as upper middle class. Persons with none of the three defining characteristics (31 per cent of the sample) are referred to as working class; the remaining 50 per cent are called middle class.

Using this index of social class, the figures in Table 2 document once again the systematic relation between social class and vote. The per cent voting for Goldwater ranges from 26 per cent in the working class to 47 per cent in the upper middle class, a spread of 21 percentage points. These figures confirm what was implicit in the magnitude of Goldwater's defeat and evident in Table 1. For the first time since 1936, when survey data first became

[5] The sample design and interviewing were conducted by the National Opinion Research Center. The sample combines probability and quota techniques. Comparisons with census materials indicate that it has a high degree of representativeness. Our prediction of the election result compared favorably with that of the final Gallup Poll. Gallup reported that 32 per cent of the electorate would vote for Goldwater, and that 7 per cent was undecided. In our survey 31 per cent definitely favored Goldwater and an additional 5 per cent were undecided. Both estimates were low; in the actual election Goldwater received 39 per cent of the vote.

**TABLE 1[a] Per Cent Voting for Goldwater by Occupation, Education, and Income (White Voters Only)**

| | | Per Cent for Goldwater | |
|---|---|---|---|
| OCCUPATION (OF THOSE PRESENTLY EMPLOYED) | | | |
| Sales workers | | 54% (74) | |
| Managers, officials, and proprietors | | 49 (97) | |
| Farm managers and proprietors | | 48 (83) | |
| Professionals | | 45 (85) | |
| Semiprofessionals | | 40 (52) | |
| Clerical | | 39 (131) | |
| Service workers | Manual workers | 30 (104) | 26% (431) |
| Craftsmen and foremen | | 29 (167) | |
| Operatives | | 24 (135) | |
| Laborers | | 8 (25) | |
| EDUCATION | | | |
| Grade School | | 28% (363) | |
| Some high school | | 29 (254) | |
| Finished high school | | 36 (449) | |
| Some college | | 44 (172) | |
| Finished college | | 56 (104) | |
| Postgraduate | | 47 (55) | |
| INCOME | | | |
| Less than $3000 | | 34% (245) | |
| $3000 to $4999 | | 35 (252) | |
| $5000 to $6999 | | 26 (261) | |
| $7000 to $9999 | | 37 (298) | |
| $10,000 to $14,999 | | 42 (233) | |
| $15,000 or more | | 53 (62) | |

[a] In this and subsequent tables, the number of cases is always less than the total of 1,397 in the working sample. This occurs because respondents occasionally failed to answer a question or because some responses could not be classified.

available, the Republican Party failed to win a clear-cut majority among the more privileged segments of our society. The proportion of the working class voting Democratic is also virtually unprecedented, and matches only the working-class vote for Truman in 1948.

**TABLE 2 Per Cent Voting for Goldwater by Social Class (White Voters Only)**

| *Social Class* | *Per Cent for Goldwater* |
|---|---|
| Working | 26% (405) |
| Middle | 37 (656) |
| Upper middle | 47 (253) |

Our task now is to analyze the basic relation between social class and vote in terms of both political ideology and opinion on concrete pocketbook issues.

## POLITICAL IDEOLOGY AND VOTE

When the interview schedule was written, no study of the election result was contemplated. However, five questions included in the interview can be said to tap ideological agreement with Goldwater. The items and the marginal distributions are presented in Table 3. The term *ideology* as it appears in the literature, has different and frequently highly specialized meanings. In this paper it is used simply to refer to rather general political beliefs, in contrast to opinion on concrete pocketbook issues. It is important to note that none of the items in Table 3 deals with a concrete policy issue of a bread-and-butter character.

**TABLE 3 Distribution of Responses on Items Measuring Ideological Agreement with Goldwater[a] (White Voters Only)**

| | |
|---|---|
| The Federal government is gradually taking away our basic freedoms. | |
| *Agree* | 47% |
| Disagree | 48 |
| Don't know | 5 |
| In the past 25 years this country has moved dangerously close to socialism. | |
| *Agree* | 45% |
| Disagree | 41 |
| Don't know | 14 |
| Which of the statements on this card comes closest to expressing how you feel about the state of morals in this country at the present time? | |
| *They are pretty bad, and getting worse* | 42% |
| They are pretty bad, but getting better | 13 |
| They are pretty good, but getting worse | 21 |
| They are pretty good, and getting better | 16 |
| Don't know, or the same as ever | 8 |
| How great a danger do you feel that American Communists are to this country at the present time—a very great danger, a great danger, some danger, hardly any danger, or no danger? | |
| *A very great danger* | 18% |
| *A great danger* | 23 |
| Some danger | 39 |
| Hardly any danger | 12 |
| No danger | 5 |
| Don't know | 3 |
| Do you feel the United States is losing power in the world or is it becoming more powerful? *If Losing Power:* How much does this disturb you—a great deal, somewhat, or very little? | |
| *Losing power and disturbed a great deal* | 15% |
| *Losing power and disturbed somewhat* | 10 |
| Losing power and disturbed very little | 5 |
| Becoming more powerful | 41 |
| Staying the same | 24 |
| Don't know | 5 |

[a] Responses in italics are considered in ideological agreement with Goldwater.

Goldwater repeated the traditional Republican charges that the Federal government is usurping individual freedoms and that the United States is drifting down the road to socialism. Agreement with Goldwater's position on these issues was widespread: almost half the voters agreed with each. With regard to the state of contemporary morals, an issue which Goldwater highlighted during the campaign, 42 per cent of the voters in our sample chose the statement that morals are pretty bad and getting worse. Almost the same proportion agreed with Goldwater's position concerning the threat of internal Communism; four out of ten said that Communists are a great or very great danger. Of the five issues examined, it is only on the issue of American power abroad that Goldwater received relatively little support. Just a quarter of the sample believed that the United States is losing power in the world and said that this disturbed them a great deal or somewhat.

These five items were combined into a cumulative index by assigning one point for every instance of agreement with Goldwater. Column A of Table 4 shows that the index powerfully predicts the Goldwater vote. (This in itself is a persuasive validation of the index.) Among those who agreed with Goldwater on none of the five issues, 6 per cent voted for him. Percentages steadily rise until, among those in complete agreement, 87 per cent voted for him. The distribution across the index can be seen in column B of Table 4. When the figures in column A are combined with those in

**TABLE 4 Per Cent Voting for Goldwater by Ideological Agreement (White Voters Only)**

| *Score on Index of Ideological Agreement* | *A* *Per Cent for Goldwater* | *B* *Per Cent of Total Sample* |
|---|---|---|
| 0 | 6% (265) | 19% |
| 1 | 18 (330) | 24 |
| 2 | 34 (295) | 21 |
| 3 | 56 (225) | 16 |
| 4 | 64 (180) | 13 |
| 5 | 87 (90) | 7 |
| Total | | 100% (1,385) |

column B, the arithmetic of Goldwater's defeat becomes clear. Only among those who agreed with Goldwater on three or more issues did the Republican vote reach a majority. But only a third of the sample—36 per cent—expressed this level of agreement. This leaves 64 per cent who agreed with Goldwater on no more than two issues, and here the Goldwater vote fell far short of a majority. It thus appears that, despite fairly high levels of agreement on individual items, Goldwater's political beliefs were *consistently* accepted by only a minority. This was true quite apart from his stand on pocketbook issues.

It has just been observed that both social class and political ideology are related to how people voted in the last election. One might expect, then, that social class is also related to ideology. This is not the case, however. As can be seen in Table 5, social class is only mildly related to agreement with Goldwater. Differences between the three class levels are small, whether measured by the proportions at each level of ideological agreement or by mean scores on the index, shown at the bottom of Table 5. At best there is an 11 percentage-point difference between the working and upper middle class when the percentages scoring 4 and 5 on the index are combined. This compares to a difference of 21 percentage points in the proportions who actually voted for Goldwater. In short, ideological agreement and disagreement with Goldwater were fairly equally distributed throughout the class structure, yet workers were much less likely to vote for him.[6]

Table 6 now examines social class and ideology simultaneously in their relation to vote. This table lends itself to two important conclusions. First, at extremes of ideological agreement, social class bears no relation to voting behavior. Among those who strongly disagreed with Goldwater (that is, had scores of 0 or 1 on the index) and among those who strongly agreed with him (score of 5), social class had virtually no effect on how people voted. This indicates that some people determined their vote on the basis of their ideological convictions, and did so regardless of their social class. Little or no tendency can be seen for the more privileged to vote Republican when they were in sharp ideological disagreement with Goldwater. Nor was there a pull toward the Democratic Party among those few working-class voters with very strong right-wing convictions.

The second conclusion to be drawn from Table 6 is that where opinion is not sharply polarized and is perhaps inconsistent, social class has a powerful influence. Among those who partially agreed with Goldwater, people were much less likely to vote

[6] Of the five items that comprise the index of ideological agreement, social class has no relation to two (decaying morals and the internal Communist danger), a weak relation to two (excessive Federal expansion and creeping socialism), and a fairly strong relation to one (loss of American power abroad). Where there is a relationship, workers were slightly less likely to be in agreement with Goldwater.

**TABLE 5 Ideological Agreement with Goldwater by Social Class (White Voters Only)**

| *Score on Index of Ideological Agreement* | *Social Class* | | | | | |
|---|---|---|---|---|---|---|
| | WORKING | | MIDDLE | | UPPER MIDDLE | |
| 0 | 20% | 45% | 18% | 44% | 20% | 37% |
| 1 | 25 | | 26 | | 17 | |
| 2 | 23 | 50 | 21 | 50 | 21 | 55 |
| 3 | 18 | | 15 | | 17 | |
| 4 | 9 | | 14 | | 17 | |
| 5 | 5 | | 6 | | 8 | |
| | (399) | | (648) | | (251) | |
| Mean Score | 1.97 | | 2.00 | | 2.12 | |

for him if they were working class. This was true whether individuals had a score of 2, 3, or 4. Taking partial agreers as a whole (bottom row, Table 6), 63 per cent of the upper middle class voted for him. In striking contrast, among the working class only half as many—32 per cent—did so. This is a difference of 31 percentage points. In other words, the impact of social class on voting is limited to those with inconsistent political philosophies, and here the impact is great. This finding makes good sense: When people have no clear-cut and consistent ideological grounds on which to form an opinion, they necessarily have to bring other considerations into play. Voting under these conditions becomes strongly influenced by social class.

## SOCIAL CLASS, POLITICAL IDEOLOGY, AND OPINION ON POCKETBOOK ISSUES

We have yet to determine whether there were distinctive social-class reasons for the

**TABLE 6 Per Cent Voting for Goldwater by Social Class and Ideological Agreement (White Voters Only)**

| *Social Class* | WORKING | MIDDLE | UPPER MIDDLE | PERCENTAGE DIFFERENCE |
|---|---|---|---|---|
| *Score on Index of Ideological Agreement* | *Per Cent for Goldwater* | | | |
| 0 (Strongly Disagree) | 6% | 5% | 8% | 2 |
| | (81) | (116) | (51) | |
| 1 (Strongly Disagree) | 16 | 19 | 19 | 3 |
| | (98) | (168) | (42) | |
| 2 (Partially Agree) | 24 | 37 | 42 | 18 |
| | (92) | (135) | (52) | |
| 3 (Partially Agree) | 40 | 56 | 76 | 36 |
| | (72) | (98) | (42) | |
| 4 (Partially Agree) | 38 | 68 | 75 | 37 |
| | (37) | (90) | (44) | |
| 5 Strongly Agree | 86 | 86 | 85 | −1 |
| | (21) | (42) | (20) | |
| 2–4 | 32% | 51% | 63% | |

social-class vote among partial agreers. It has just been observed that persons who were somewhat sympathetic with Goldwater's political ideology tended not to vote for him when they were working class. To what extent was their rejection of Goldwater a reaction to his anti-social welfare stand?

Respondents were asked whether or not they thought the Federal government should pass a law to provide medical care for the aged, a crude paraphrase of the Medicare program. As the bottom row of Table 7 shows, there is a direct relation between socioeconomic status and favoring Medicare: 84 per cent of those classified as working class approved of Medicare as compared to 53 per cent of the upper middle class. Despite this class difference, it should not be overlooked that even among the most privileged segment of the population considerable support for Federal programs exists, at least in the area of Medicare for the elderly.

The body of Table 7 shows, not surprisingly, that those who agreed more strongly with Goldwater were more likely to disapprove of Medicare. This was true at every class level. As with vote, however, the impact of social class on favoring Medicare is greatest among those who partially agreed with the Goldwater ideology. Among this group, fully 80 per cent of the working class favored Medicare, whereas only 40 per cent of the upper class did so.[7] This makes for a difference of 40 percentage points. Among strong agreers and strong disagreers, on the other hand, the percentage point differences are just 12 and 18, respectively. This again shows the small impact of social class where people have well-defined political convictions.

We can now turn to the final question: Does the impact of social class on opinions on Medicare help to explain why the working class tended to vote for Johnson even when they were in partial ideological agreement with Goldwater? Table 8 brings together all of the variables considered in the analysis. As observed before, social class has no impact on people who either disagreed or agreed strongly with Goldwater. The effect of social class is still confined to the partial agreers. It is also immediately apparent that people who

[7] Three-quarters of those in the working class favored Medicare even when they agreed that "the Federal government is gradually taking away our basic freedoms" or that "in the past twenty-five years this country has moved dangerously close to socialism." Even among those who indicated they strongly or somewhat approved of the John Birch Society, the overwhelming majority —89 per cent—approved of Medicare. Once again, this points to the tendency among workers to take a stand on pocketbook issues that is incongruent with their general political beliefs. Indeed, when their bread-and-butter interests are involved, political ideology seems to count for little.

**TABLE 7 Per Cent Who Favor Medicare by Ideological Agreement and Social Class (White Voters Only)**

| *Ideological Agreement with Goldwater* | WORKING | MIDDLE | UPPER MIDDLE | PERCENTAGE DIFFERENCE |
|---|---|---|---|---|
| | *% Favoring Medicare* | | | |
| Strongly disagree | 92% (179) | 84% (323) | 74% (93) | 18 |
| Partially agree | 80 (200) | 62 (323) | 40 (138) | 40 |
| Strongly agree | 57 (21) | 38 (42) | 45 (20) | 12 |
| Total | 84% (400) | 71% (649) | 53% (251) | 31 |

**TABLE 8 Per Cent Voting for Goldwater by Social Class, Ideological Agreement, and Opinion on Medicare (White Voters Only)**

| *Social Class* | WORKING | | | MIDDLE | | | UPPER MIDDLE | | |
|---|---|---|---|---|---|---|---|---|---|
| *Ideological Agreement* | STRONGLY DISAGREE | PARTIALLY AGREE | STRONGLY AGREE | STRONGLY DISAGREE | PARTIALLY AGREE | STRONGLY AGREE | STRONGLY DISAGREE | PARTIALLY AGREE | STRONGLY AGREE |
| | *Per Cent for Goldwater* | | | | | | | | |
| *Opinion on Medicare*[a] | | | | | | | | | |
| Favor Medicare | 10% (165) | 26% (159) | 75% (12) | 12% (239) | 38% (202) | 81% (16) | 6% (69) | 40% (55) | 78% (9) |
| Oppose Medicare | 36 (11) | 57 (35) | 100 (9) | 21 (38) | 75 (110) | 88 (25) | 35 (20) | 79 (80) | 91 (11) |
| Total | 12% (179) | 32% (201) | 86% (21) | 13% (284) | 51% (323) | 86% (42) | 13% (93) | 63% (138) | 85% (20) |

[a] The 39 white voters who had no opinion on Medicare are excluded.

favor Medicare were much less likely to vote for Goldwater no matter what their social class or the extent of their ideological agreement or disagreement. However, the key question is whether opinion on Medicare helps to explain the social-class vote among those who partially agreed with him. The answer is yes: Among those who expressed partial agreement, the effect of social class is now reduced. The original difference between the working class and the upper middle class was 31 percentage points among partial agreers. It is now 22 percentage points among those who are against Medicare and only 14 percentage points among those who favor Medicare. The original 12 percentage point difference between the middle and upper middle class is now reduced to 2 and 4 percentage points.

It is apparent that at every social-class level, many voters were in conflict between a fairly conservative political ideology and a pro-social-welfare orientation. When this was the case, the likelihood was that their social-welfare orientation would take precedence and they would vote Democratic. However, a social-welfare orientation was most prevalent among workers, and this helps to explain their overwhelming vote for Johnson, even when they were in partial ideological agreement with Goldwater.[8]

## CONCLUSIONS

What descriptive statements can be made concerning the reasons for Goldwater's crushing defeat? The data have shown that both social-class and ideological voting occurred on a wide scale in the 1964 election and together they account for the magnitude of Goldwater's defeat. About four out of ten voters at every class level agreed with Goldwater on no more than one of the five issues examined, and when this was the case only about 12 per cent voted for him. Most of these people also disagreed with Goldwater's position on social welfare, as represented by the Medicare issue. Hence, enough voters strongly disagreed with Goldwater on *both* economic and noneconomic issues to guarantee his defeat. Significantly, the upper class was just as likely as the lower classes to vote against Goldwater when they were in ideological disagreement with him.

However, about half at every class level were on the ideological fence. They agreed with Goldwater on 2, 3, or 4 of the 5 issues, and when this was the case, social-class voting was very marked. The working class tended overwhelmingly to vote for Johnson, the upper middle class to vote for Goldwater. This rather strongly suggests that the less privileged were voting their perceived economic interests, and this interpretation holds up in fact. Opinion on Medicare went a long way toward wiping out social-class differences. Thus although Goldwater's defeat was made inevitable by widespread disagreement with his political ideas, it was worsened when he failed to win the votes of potential ideological supporters because of his economic conservatism.

What are the implications of these data for some reactionary political movement in the future? On one side it can be said that large proportions of voters at every class level rejected Goldwater's political ideology as well as his economic conservatism. On the other side, it is significant that the social-welfare liberalism of large numbers of Johnson's voters was unsupported by a consistent set of liberal political beliefs. The danger of opportunistic voting, when it is accompanied by conservative ideological tendencies, is that such people are vulnerable to a reactionary movement, especially one that does not threaten their economic interests.

Finally, what general conclusions might

[8] It was thought that the remaining percentage point difference between the working and middle classes might be explained by the traditional loyalty of workers to the Democratic Party. Even though party identification powerfully predicted the Goldwater vote, particularly among partial agreers, it does not improve the interpretation of the relation between social class and vote.

Party identification has been given little attention here for two reasons. For one thing, like voting preference it is strongly predicted by political ideology and opinion on pocketbook issues. Secondly, our main concern has not been to explore all of the factors that enter into the voting decision, but to explain the *relation* between social class and vote. In this respect, party identification is not an important factor when political ideology and opinion on pocketbook issues are controlled.

be drawn about the nature and prevalence of ideological and social-class voting? It appears that, in the United States at the present time, social class has little relation to basic political ideology. Approval of social-welfare programs appears to be widespread, but it often occurs under an umbrella of at least verbal agreement on basic principles of a rather conservative character. Social class is significant, however, if only because it modifies the relation between political ideology and opinion on concrete issues. It determines to some extent whether people will draw policy conclusions congruent or incongruent with their basic political beliefs. In general, where political beliefs are consistent and strong, social class has little or no impact, and ideological voting occurs. On the other hand, among those with inconsistent or weak political beliefs, the impact of social class both on policy opinions and on voting is very strong.

# RELATIVE DEPRIVATION—ATTITUDES TO CLASS AND STATUS INEQUALITY IN ENGLAND

*W. G. Runciman*

## THE HISTORICAL BACKGROUND, 1918–1962

From this summary of the decades leading up to 1962, it is clear that the magnitude and frequency of relative deprivation has seldom been in close correlation with the facts of inequality of class. Each of the two world wars has set off a disturbance of reference groups and an upsurge of expectations. But after both of them, other influences have inhibited the mounting egalitarianism which had been aroused. After the First World War, the Depression and its apparent irremediableness prevented manual workers and their families from seeing it as feasible that they should demand comparable rewards to those for non-manual work. After the Second, relative deprivation was damped down by the achievement of some gradual amelioration of the class-situation of manual workers and the conviction that a greater redistribution was taking place than did in fact occur. If the account which I have given is correct, then we should expect the evidence of the 1962 survey to show that in terms of inequalities of class, the respondents least likely to express relative deprivation will be those at the top of the manual stratum; working class reference groups will not often be taken from the other side of the manual/non-manual line; and an awareness, or even disapproval, of the greater prosperity of others will be more frequent among middle-class people looking at working-class people than the other way round. There is not yet, however, any conclusion to be drawn as to whether a similar relationship will hold between inequality and relative deprivation of status. . . .

## REFERENCE GROUPS AND INEQUALITIES OF CLASS

The analysis of survey evidence on relative deprivation of class is in principle straightforward. If, for example, people are asked who (if anyone) they think of as better off than themselves, this information can then be related to the extent of their own wealth and the wealth of the comparative reference group which they have given. There are not the difficulties which bedevil even ordinal comparisons of status, and the actual discrepancy between inequality and relative deprivation can be expressed in quantitative terms. . . . I have used people's stated incomes (or, in the case of married women, their husband's income) rather than household income or sub-category of occupation, as my criterion. . . . The form of question used in the present survey was "Could you give me an idea roughly how much you (your husband) earn(s) each week after deductions?" . . . For the purpose of assessing relative deprivation . . . people's

**TABLE 1 Satisfaction with Own or Husband's Present Income; by Stated Income Within Occupational Stratum**

| | *Non-Manual* | | | *Manual* | | |
|---|---|---|---|---|---|---|
| | HIGH % | MEDIUM % | LOW % | HIGH % | MEDIUM % | LOW % |
| Yes | 63 | 50 | 56 | 72 | 57 | 47 |
| No | 37 | 50 | 41 | 27 | 41 | 51 |
| Don't know | 0 | 0 | 3 | 1 | 2 | 2 |
| Total | 100% | 100% | 100% | 100% | 100% | 100% |
| | (N = 160) | (N = 107) | (N = 75) | (N = 99) | (N = 278) | (N = 368) |

estimates of their incomes are if anything more important than their actual incomes. . . . In the subsequent discussion I shall refer simply to either "high," "medium" and "low" or "top," "middle" and "bottom" levels of income. . . .

The questions asked about income . . . confirm the expectations suggested by the earlier discussion. Not merely are comparative reference groups among manual workers and their wives so far restricted as to result in a marked discrepancy between relative deprivation and actual inequality; their retention of working-class standards of comparison means that manual workers and their wives are consistently less likely to feel relatively deprived than are non-manual workers and their wives who are earning the same (or at the top level probably a great deal more). Only among the poorest does this conclusion need to be qualified at all; and even here, it can only be said that manual workers and their wives are less often avowedly satisfied, not that they more often feel relatively deprived.

It is not surprising that at the top level of incomes the standards of non-manual workers should be very much higher. A wage that would satisfy a skilled artisan is unlikely to satisfy a managing director or a high court judge. But the relation between relative deprivation and inequality is more complex than can be inferred from this predictable contrast by itself. The survey not only confirms that the comparative reference groups of the two strata are different. It also confirms how many qualifications must be made to the suggestion that prosperity has made manual workers and their wives "middle-class". Those few who are in the top third of the overall income distribution are . . . likelier than the less prosperous manual respondents to have members of the non-manual stratum in mind. But even when they describe themselves as "middle-class" and have, therefore, in some sense a different reference group from almost all of those who describe themselves as "working-class", they are no more likely to see others as doing better. The influence of the reference group is strong only when they are asked whether they agree that manual workers are doing much better than white-collar; only then are those who think of themselves as "working-class" very much less likely to agree. Without some external stimulus powerful enough to dislodge the hold of traditional standards of comparison, the relative deprivations of manual workers, including even the most prosperous, will derive from very different reference group comparisons from those of non-manual workers and their families.

. . . . . . . . . . . . . . . . . . . . . . . . . . . . . . . . .

There is no way of ascertaining in detail from the survey just what influences underlie this restriction of comparisons. If the normal response to economic inequality is to make comparisons only to those closest to oneself rather than to those by contrast with whom one is most unequally placed, then these results need, perhaps, no explanation whatever. But since it is clear that this is not universally true, the question remains to what extent and for what reasons reference groups are so restricted. A glance over the social history of Britain since 1918 reveals some, at least, of the reasons why on matters of economic class—but not status—there has not been a cumulative spiral of aspiration and prosperity since the collapse of the militant radicalism which followed the First World War. But the principal interest of the 1962 survey lies not in demonstrating what influences are at work—this must rest on the historical evidence for the period before the survey was taken—but in revealing to what extent the reference groups of the less well placed are limited in scope, unspecifically defined, and mildly expressed. Several different forms of question were used to elucidate the reference group comparisons made, and each served only to reinforce the same impression. Both the magnitude and frequency of relative deprivation among manual workers and their wives are very much lower than would accord with the facts of economic inequality. The lack of "class-consciousness" which is sometimes attributed to the British working class is in this sense, at least, amply confirmed. . . .

Within the manual stratum, income does not affect the choice of reference groups in any consistent pattern. . . . None of the differences which are not uniform with income—where, that is, a higher percentage of those at the middle level give a particular reply than those at either the top or the bottom—are at all large. But if all the differences of 3% or over are looked at together, they seem to confirm the picture of this group as the "fraternalists" of the manual stratum, who do not aspire in any sense to rise out of the working class but who do not yet have what they now see as attainable for manual workers as such. Within the manual stratum, those at the middle level of incomes are likelier than those at either the top or the bottom to have the following characteristics or attitudes: to say that they want or need something not mentioned on either of the two lists of goods; to think that manual workers are not doing "much better" than white-collar workers; to be dissatisfied with their (or their husband's) present income on the grounds of being worth more pay; to think that manual workers ought to be doing as well as they are doing by comparison with white-collar workers; to want, if they do not have, a car, a refrigerator, ownership of a house, a spare room and foreign holiday travel; if assigning themselves to the "working class" to define this by reference to manual work; to belong to a trade union; to think that the state should provide unemployment pay at full rate without a means test for as long as a man is unemployed; and to support the Labour Party. Given the inadequacy of the figures for the distribution of incomes, these differences cannot be pressed too hard. But they furnish a marked contrast to those results which suggest that where inequalities of status are at issue relative deprivation is more frequent among manual workers and their wives at the top level of incomes, and that this relative deprivation is of an "egoistic" rather than a "fraternalistic" kind.[1] This, however, is to anticipate the argument. For the moment, the main conclusion to have emerged is the restricted and even illogical choice of comparative reference groups, particularly in the manual stratum, on matters of economic class.

## REFERENCE GROUPS AND INEQUALITIES OF STATUS

If my argument about inequalities of status is correct, then the questions in the survey which bear on it should disclose a very different pattern from those concerned with differences in income or resources. . . . The topics raised in the survey on inequalities of status are more ambiguous and less precise than those raised on inequalities of wealth or income. But if questions can be asked which it is legitimate to interpret as reflecting attitudes towards the hierarchy of status, as opposed to class or power, these can furnish at least some further evidence for or against the view that relative deprivation of status among the less well placed has been progressively increasing with the advance towards some greater measure of equality.

There are, however, two important differences from the discussion of class. The

[1] Egoistic is when one is dissatisfied with his present situation but not in a way that gives him a common cause with others like him. It designates one who feels deprived within his class but not on behalf of his class. Fraternalistic is a feeling of relative deprivation on behalf of the class of which one is a member. (C. S. H.) See Runciman, *op. cit.*, pp. 33–34.

first is that we are now considering "egoistic" as well as "fraternalistic" relative deprivations. I have argued that higher aspirations of status have been steadily spreading among manual workers and their families throughout the period since 1918; but these have in some ways been "egoistic" aspirations as much as a sense of relative deprivation on behalf of the working class as such, and they have been accompanied by a decline in the sort of intensely fraternalistic feelings characteristic of the traditional working-class militant. Such feelings are still common among some sections of the manual stratum, and particularly those workers who are socially isolated by the nature of their work and for whom an increase in prosperity may well exacerbate feelings of relative deprivation of social esteem. Miners and dockers should both be expected from any generalization about the spread of a wish on the part of manual workers to rise out of their status-group rather than with it. But the relative deprivation of status felt by manual workers and their families was probably less often and also less intensely fraternalistic in 1962 than in 1919. Even if this could be statistically demonstrated, it still would not mean that the manual workers of 1962 could properly be described as having "become middle-class". But as more and more manual workers and their families came to feel heightened aspirations of status, this tended to detach them from those whose more "traditional" working-class attitudes involved a relative deprivation of status—if any—only on behalf of all manual workers as such.

The second difference is that the questions asked with a view to elucidating feelings about status were mostly asked in terms of how respondents felt about the education and careers of their children (or hypothetical children). This is one of the most obvious ways in which changing aspirations of status are expressed, but it is a very different form of question from those used in asking about attitudes relevant to relative deprivation of class. Many people, when they are asked about their children, will express higher aspirations on their behalf than they would for themselves, and if the respondents in the survey had been asked what they hoped that their children would earn, they might have given a much more extravagant answer than they did when asked about the "proper" standard of living for "people like themselves". The questions about education, therefore, cannot be interpreted as strictly comparable to the questions about income. . . .

It should, however, be possible to show whether normative reference groups, as suggested by self-rated "class", have an influence on the attitudes of manual workers and their wives towards education and careers for their children. A manual worker may, of course, think of himself as "middle-class" and still feel that manual workers as such should be given better educational facilities by comparison with those enjoyed by the entrants into white-collar occupations. But for him to want higher education for his son implies a willingness that the son should rise out of the status group of his birth into another—a willingness which, as we have seen, was probably much less common a generation before.

In the same way, a manual worker's preference that his son should have a non-manual job, particularly if it is no better or even less well paid, can be plausibly interpreted as an attitude to status as much as to class. During the Depression, the attraction of a clerical job to working-class families was, as the Pilgram Trust investigators commented, its security more than anything else. After the Second World War, this was no longer so. There might be in the minds of some working-class parents a residual fear of unemployment which would lead them to prefer a white-collar occupation for their sons. Some also might be aware of just those reasons cited earlier why the ostensible equality between upper manual and lower non-manual earnings should not be taken to demonstrate a genuine equality in the class-situation of the two. But in an enquiry conducted in 1962 it is plausible to interpret a manual worker's preference for a non-manual job for his son as indicating a wish that the son should rise out of, rather than with, the status-group of manual workers. A preference that the son should take a manual job need not, of course, always mean an attitude of militant fraternalism;

it may mean an acceptance of the subordinate status of the manual worker, or a complete indifference to considerations of status, or even a conviction that the manual worker is not accorded any less prestige by society than the non-manual. In any such case, the person belongs to the category which was labelled Type A—the person who feels relatively deprived neither as a member of his group nor on behalf of it. But given the social structure of Britain in 1962, it seems safe to assume that the manual worker who would prefer his son to have a manual job does not do so because he regards it as enjoying higher status. He either does not resent the subordinate status attached to manual work, or, while feeling that manual work is accorded too little status, still does not want a son of his to achieve higher status by "abdicating" from the working class. If, on the other hand, he would prefer a non-manual job for his son, then this can be plausibly interpreted as some sense of relative deprivation of status of an "egoistic" kind.

The evidence which can be drawn from the survey about attitudes to inequalities of status is not entirely confined to the questions about education or career for a son. There have already been some implications to be drawn from the analysis of self-assigned "class", and in addition two further questions were introduced as having some possible implications for attitudes to status. The questions which must, however, bear the brunt of interpretation on this elusive topic are those about attitudes to a hypothetical son.

The actual extent of educational inequality, as opposed to the frequency of relative deprivation aroused by it, can be measured in terms of the proportion of each stratum leaving school at the minimum age, the proportion remaining in secondary school and the proportion going on to higher education. Of the manual respondents in the sample, only 9% had stayed on at school beyond whatever was the minimum statutory age at the time; of non-manual respondents, the proportion was 49%, of whom 22% had had some university or college education. The advance towards actual equality is reflected in the answers given by those respondents with children under 15 when they were asked at what age they expected their children to leave school. Of non-manual parents, only 7% said that they expected their children to leave at the minimum age, while the proportion among manual parents was 36%. The difference is still a large one; but the figure of 36%, even if it reflects some over-optimism among working-class parents, is still evidence of a radical change from the actual experience of the working-class parents in the sample. Furthermore, the proportion rises with income: over two-thirds of working-class parents at the top level of incomes expected at least one of their children to stay on beyond the minimum age. These figures not only provide ample confirmation that in this respect, at least, inequality of status between the manual and non-manual strata is very much less than it was, but suggest at the same time that the frequency of relative deprivation has been rising.

The survey also provides ample evidence for the extent to which the aspiration for higher education is shared by both strata. When asked the question, "Would you like any son of yours to have a university education?", 82% of manual respondents said "yes". . . . The figure for non-manual respondents is only 6% higher than the figure for manual. This question, however, is perhaps too loosely phrased to afford evidence of genuine aspirations; it may be a little too much like asking "would you like any son of yours to have a lucrative job?" in order to elucidate attitudes to inequalities of class. But the expectations of the working-class parents in the sample who have children under 15 furnish more tangible evidence of the extent to which educational aspirations have spread. Only at the top level of incomes do as many as half of the manual parents in the sample expect at least one of their children to have some form of education beyond school, and only a further half of these expect this further education to be at a university. But this reflects a large increase in the pre-war pattern not merely of hopes but of expectations of what is seen to be feasible. Furthermore, the replies show an effect made not only by income, but by self-rated "class". . . .

A better indicator, however, might be not what parents expect their children to achieve so much as whether they are prepared to contribute fees in order to help their children up the educational ladder. As on all these questions, it cannot be unerringly assumed that such a willingness implies an ambition of status for the children. . . . But the link between education and status is sufficiently close for it to be plausible to make some inferences about attitudes to status from attitudes about private education. . . .

The proportion of working-class parents with children who attended, or are expected to attend, a fee-paying school at any stage of their educational careers is, predictably, extremely small—6% (and only 8% even at the top level of incomes) as compared to 35% of non-manual parents. But a difference is made by self-rated "class" even among the handful of manual parents: 9% of those describing themselves as "middle-class" have children who either have attended, attend, or are expected to attend fee-paying schools, as against 5% of those describing themselves as "working-class". A similar difference is visible in the answers to the question "Do you have (or, would you like to have) private education for your children?" A number of people said that they did not know, which is obviously a reasonable response for those to whom the question was an entirely unreal one. These "Don't Knows" to some extent confuse the analysis of the answers by income and self-rating; but when both are held constant it is clear that both have an independent influence among manual respondents. The majority do not (or would not) want any form of private education for their children. But the proportion drops between the middle and top levels of income, whatever the "class" to which the respondents assign themselves, and at all three levels of income a clear difference is made by self-rating. The figures are shown in Table 2.

Self-rated "class" thus shows a clear influence on the answers to a question which can be plausibly linked to attitudes to inequality of status. Indeed, those manual workers and their wives who describe them selves as "middle-class" are if anything less likely to reject the idea of a private education for their children than non-manual workers and their wives at the bottom or middle levels of income. Only at the top level of incomes, where nearly half the non-manual respondents would either like or, if they are parents, already have a private education for their children is there a marked difference from the manual respondents. Once again, these figures cannot demonstrate by themselves that there has been a steady spread of status-aspirations among the manual stratum during the post-war period; perhaps just as many manual workers and their wives would have said in 1938 that they would, in principle, like a private education for their children. But this is on the face of it implausible, and the difference between the attitudes of older and younger manual respondents suggests, as we shall see, a considerable change in attitudes. Furthermore, the influence of self-rated "class" on attitudes to status (unlike attitudes to income) is so far confirmed.

Since, however, questions about education may be misleading as a guide to attitudes to inequality of status, two questions were asked about the job which people would prefer for a hypothetical son. The respondents were first of all asked if they

**TABLE 2 Proportion of Manual Respondents Who Do Not (Would Not) Want a Private Education for Their Children; by Self-Rated "Class" Within Income**

| *High* | | *Medium* | | *Low* | |
|---|---|---|---|---|---|
| SELF-RATED MIDDLE | SELF-RATED WORKING | SELF-RATED MIDDLE | SELF-RATED WORKING | SELF-RATED MIDDLE | SELF-RATED WORKING |
| 46% (N= 41) | 57% (N = 56) | 55% (N = 101) | 66% (N = 176) | 54% (N = 91) | 65% (N = 276) |

would prefer a manual or non-manual job, assuming that they had a son who was at the moment choosing a job; they were then presented with the hypothetical alternative of a job with higher pay but lower status—a factory foreman—or a job with lower pay but higher status—a schoolteacher. . . . Where the question is put in terms of an unqualified manual/non-manual choice of job, then there may be no warrant for inferring that a preference for a non-manual job is based on status rather than class. But where the choice is weighted against the non-manual job in terms of income, then it does seem legitimate to draw some inference about attitudes to the hierarchy of status.

When manual workers and their wives were asked "If a son of yours was actually choosing a job at the moment, would you rather he chose a manual or a non-manual job?", almost a quarter said that they didn't know, or that it would be up to him, or that they would have no personal preference in the matter; of the remainder, 32% said "manual" and 49% said "non-manual". When, however, they were asked "If he had the choice of a foreman's job at £20 a week or a schoolteacher's job at £15, which would *you* prefer him to choose?" the proportion of Don't Knows . . . would prefer the school teacher to the foreman than vice versa—41% as against 40%. Of the non-manual respondents, more than four times as many expressed a preference for a non-manual job as for a manual, and at the top level of incomes more than eight times as many. When the choice of foreman or schoolteacher was put to them, the proportion choosing the foreman rose to 25%, but this is still less than half as many as chose the schoolteacher.

These results are of sufficient interest to call for a slight digression. If I am right about the changes which occurred in Britain in the decades preceding the survey, then this was a period in which relative deprivation of status was rising in both magnitude and frequency as equality of status came closer to being achieved. This period, in other words, corresponds to the rising slope of the hypothetical curve depicted in Chapter Two—the point at which equality has not yet been so far attained that the frequency of relative deprivation starts once again to fall. What, therefore, would happen if equality of status were in fact to be achieved? We can safely assume that the status of the teacher was higher than that of the foreman by the standards of English society in 1962. This difference of status is clearly reflected in the preferences expressed by respondents when confronted with the choice for their sons. A generation or more earlier, however, fewer manual workers and their wives would have chosen the schoolmaster's job for their son, since there was then still less equality of status between the manual and non-manual strata, and the reference groups of the manual stratum were still more limited. Conversely, if equality of status were to progress still further, then the frequency of preference for the schoolteacher ought to fall once again. Since the status of the two is not yet equal, there is no way of testing this for Britain. . . .

It requires to be demonstrated, however, that there is a difference between older and younger manual workers and their wives. If it is true that there has been a marked change in the forty years preceding the survey, then we should expect to find that older manual workers are less likely to express a preference in favour of a non-manual job for their sons. But since there should also be an effect shown by self-rated "class", it is necessary to test the effect of both together in order to insure against an overlap. On the initial question about an unspecified choice between a manual and non-manual job for a son, it turns out that self-rating makes the difference rather than age. Age does, however, show an effect independent of self-rating, particularly among those who describe themselves as "working-class". Manual workers or their wives who are aged between 21 and 45 are more likely to choose a non-manual than a manual job for a son, even if they describe themselves as "working-class", and so are those over 45 who describe themselves as "middle-class". But those who are over 45 and also describe themselves as "working-class" are no more likely to express a preference for the non-manual than for the manual job. The figures are given in Table 3.

When the specific alternatives of schoolmaster and foreman are suggested, the

**TABLE 3 Choice for Son of Manual or Non-Manual Job; Manual Respondents by Age Within Self-Rated "Class"**

| | *Self-Rated Middle* | | *Self-Rated Working* | |
|---|---|---|---|---|
| | 21–45 % | 46 + % | 21–45 % | 46 + % |
| Manual | 26 | 28 | 33 | 36 |
| Non-manual | 51 | 57 | 45 | 36 |
| Don't know | 23 | 15 | 22 | 28 |
| Total | 100% (N = 125) | 100% (N = 178) | 100% (N = 254) | 100% (N = 356) |

pattern is slightly different. The effect of both self-rating and age is more marked: those of 45 or under, whatever their self-rated "class", are likelier to prefer the schoolteacher than the foreman, and so are those over 45 who describe themselves as "middle-class". But those who describe themselves as "working-class" and are over 45 are a good deal more likely to prefer the foreman than the schoolmaster. The figures are shown in Table 4.

This table provides clear evidence that first, there has been a significant change in attitudes to the hierarchy of status among manual workers and their wives, and second, these attitudes are influenced by normative reference groups as implied by self-rated "class". Indeed, the effect of self-rated "class" persists when either age or sex or education or income or father's occupation is held constant. It does not account for all the variation; each of these other attributes shows an independent effect, and sometimes quite a marked one. But the effect of self-rating is persistent and unmistakable, quite unlike its negligible effect on the questions related to inequalities of class. On questions of income it showed a distinct effect only where those describing themselves as "working-class" were found to be a good deal less likely to agree to the general suggestion that "manual workers are doing much better nowadays than white-collar workers"—a question on which the bearing of self-rated "class" seemed more closely analogous to its bearing on party choice than on direct perceptions of comparative reference groups who are seen to be better off. But on the question which of all those in the survey it is safest to interpret as indicating attitudes to status, self-rated "class", despite the diversity of meanings which underlies it, shows a strong independent effect.

A corollary of this is that some categories of manual workers and their wives who described themselves as "working-class" were a good deal more likely to prefer the foreman than the schoolteacher. When a working-class self-rating is combined with

**TABLE 4 Choice for Son of Foreman's Job at £20 a Week or Schoolteacher's at £15; Manual Respondents by Age Within Self-Rated "Class"**

| | *Self-Rated Middle* | | *Self-Rated Working* | |
|---|---|---|---|---|
| | 21–45 % | 46 + % | 21–45 % | 46 + % |
| Foreman | 24 | 40 | 33 | 49 |
| Schoolteacher | 61 | 47 | 47 | 28 |
| Don't know | 15 | 13 | 20 | 23 |
| Total | 100% (N = 125) | 100% (N = 178) | 100% (N = 254) | 100% (N = 356) |

either an age over 45, or a father who was in a manual job, or a stated income at the bottom of the three levels, then the person concerned is more likely to prefer the foreman than the schoolteacher. These categories, moreover, comprise a substantial proportion of the manual stratum, and it is they who explain why the preference for the schoolteacher among the manual respondents taken as a whole is so narrow as to be almost negligible. . . .

There are two categories of manual respondents among whom a middle-class self-rating shows a particularly strong effect. The first is women, and the second those at the top level of incomes. . . . On the choice of jobs for a son, women who are manual workers or are married to manual workers and describe themselves as "middle-class" are particularly likely to express a preference for the schoolteacher rather than the foreman. . . . But women in the manual stratum who describe themselves as "middle-class" are more than twice as likely to prefer the schoolteacher than to prefer the foreman. . . .

Self-rating also makes a particularly marked difference at the top level of income. Here, those manual workers and their wives who describe themselves as "working-class" are likelier by 12% to express a preference for the schoolteacher than a preference for the foreman—a difference which is the same, within a few per cent., as among those at the middle level of income, whether they describe themselves as "middle-" or "working-class". Among those at the top level who describe themselves as "middle-class", however, the difference is 49%. From the size of this difference, it would appear that manual workers who reach the top level of income will be likely to feel a fraternalistic relative deprivation of status only if they retain as their normative reference group the "working class" (whatever this may mean to them). If, on the other hand, they think of themselves as "middle-class" this will make them anxious to distinguish themselves in status from other manual workers. The two are for obvious reasons likely to be bound up together—a middle-class self-rating and a preference for a higher-status job for a son are presumably both manifestations of an attitude to the status hierarchy which, whatever its determinants, is different from that of the majority of those manual workers and their wives who prefer to call themselves "working-class". But it would seem that those who have reached the top level of income are not only more likely to describe themselves as "middle-class" but more likely, if they do, to have attitudes to the hierarchy of status which imply a divergence from the fraternalistic relative deprivations of status of the traditional proletarian.

. . . . . . . . . . . . . . . . . . . . . . . . . . . . . . . . . .

Self-rated "class" is a persistent correlate of attitudes to status, and the correlation—whether or not it can be properly described as a cause—is particularly marked among the richest manual workers and their wives. The correlation is not, perhaps, remarkable, once it has been shown that what manual workers and their wives mean by assigning themselves to the "middle class" can, despite the diversity of meanings, be generally interpreted as some sort of self-differentiation in terms of status. But there is a further conclusion to be drawn. Whereas the feelings of relative deprivation of class experienced by manual workers and their wives are a function of the comparisons which most readily present themselves to them, their relative deprivations of status are a function of normative as well as of comparative reference groups. It may be that if a question could be devised to show what comparative reference groups people choose when they have inequalities of status in mind, these would be found to correlate both with aspirations of status and with the choice of normative reference groups. But even if so, this would not alter the finding that the choice of self-assigned "class" has an effect on attitudes bearing on inequalities of status in a way that it does not on attitudes bearing on inequalities of class.

. . . . . . . . . . . . . . . . . . . . . . . . . . . . . . . . . .

It hardly needs saying that these questions do no more than touch on a few small facets of people's feelings about the inequalities in the social structure. It is possible not only that these are quite different on other topics which were not included in the questionnaire but also that within any one of the three dimensions of social inequality the same people may hold inconsistent or conflicting views. But it can, I think, be claimed on the evidence of the survey both that there is a clearly visible difference between attitudes to class and to status of the kind that the historical discussion suggested, and also that the influence of comparative and normative reference groups is demonstrably different in each case. It is in the light of these differences, therefore, that we must turn to the question how far the relative deprivations which English people were feeling in 1962 could be vindicated by appeal to social justice.

# CHANGES OF SOCIAL STRUCTURE IN SOCIAL CONSCIOUSNESS

*Stefan Nowak*

The objective transformations effected by a socialist revolution in the social structure of a capitalist or pre-capitalist country are well known both from the theoretical literature and empirical research, or as well from official data and political programs.[1] . . . Comparatively less is known about the subjective aspects of these historical processes, i.e., the psychological concomitants of the changes in the social structure, and of psychological correlates of the newly shaped social stratification . . . with which this article is concerned. It is based on a questionnaire survey carried out in 1961 by the Chair of Sociology I of Warsaw University and the Public Opinion Research Centre at the Polish Radio. The survey was conducted on a quota sample of a male urban population above 18 years old.[2]

. . . . . . . . . . . . . . . . . . . . . . . . . . . . . . . . . . . .

## FACTORS DETERMINING SOCIAL STATUS PERCEPTION

The first question of the questionnaire reads, "Is your position in society high or low as compared with that of other people in Poland?" The pre-categorized answers were classified on a seven-point scale, running from "very high" to "very low," and supplemented by the answer "hard to say."[3] The distribution of the answers is shown in Table 1.

Table 1 calls for a few remarks. The distribution of the subjective assessment of one's own social status approximates the shape of a normal curve biased "downward." But the largest percentage of answers falls into the "average" position. Furthermore, if it were possible to indicate some

*This is a slightly revised version of the article that appeared in the *Polish Sociological Bulletin*, Vol. 2, 1964. Reprinted by permission of the author.

[1] See e.g. W. Wesołowski, A. Sarapata, *Prestiż zawodów i stanowisk* (*The Prestige of Occupations and Jobs*), "Studia Socjologiczne" 1961, No. 2; A. Malewski, *Czynniki determinujące postawy egalitarne* (*Factors Determining Egalitarian Attitudes*) Mimeographed; S. Nowak, *Social Views of Warsaw Students*, "The Pol. Soc. Bull.", 1962, No. 3–4 (5–6); A. Sarapata, *Iustum Pretium.* "The Pol. Soc. Bull." 1963, No. 1 (7).

[2] The survey was conducted both on a rural and on an urban quota sample of male population, but I omit in this report the rural data. The variables taken into account were: age, educational category and occupation (manual, non-manual) for the urban sample and age, occupational group and size of the farm for the rural sample.

After having fixed necessary proportions for the sample I realized that it comprised only few representatives of persons with university education (upper stratum of "intelligentsia") so I decided to bias the sample by adding 270 persons belonging to this social group so that both descriptive generalizations and multivariate analysis would be possible for this group. The questionnaires and the punch cards of the "overrepresentation" were marked in a special way and some of the analyses were done for the representative sample (tables marked by "R") and some for the total biased sample and these are marked by "T".

[3] The interviewer's instructions did not make more precise the meaning of the concepts "position in society" and aspects of social stratification which should be taken into account in answering this question. On the contrary, they were told to limit to the minimum any suggestions on the content of the questions, relying entirely on the respondents' intuition. For the aim of that question was to get a kind of general feeling and general perception of one's social status.

kind of division classifying extreme groups, then I would be inclined to consider points 1 (very low) and 2 (low) as evaluations expressing the feeling of deprivation connected with one's own social status; while points 5 (better than average), 6 (high) and 7 (very high) would be classified as positive evaluations. Finally, evaluations 3 and 4 would be treated as "emotionally neutral" positions. Thus, 28 per cent of the polled sample would be counted in the category feeling deprivation because of their social status, about 12.5 per cent—a positive evaluation and 54 per cent—a neutral evaluation. It is interesting that only 6 per cent were unable to answer the above question concerning their social status. . . .

**TABLE 1 (R)**

| ***Is Your Position in Society High or Low as Compared with that of Other People in Poland?*** | % |
|---|---|
| 7. Very high | 0.5 |
| 6. High | 4.5 |
| 5. Higher than average | 7.4 |
| 4. Average | 39.6 |
| 3. Lower than average | 14.0 |
| 2. Low | 21.8 |
| 1. Very low | 6.0 |
| Hard to say | 6.2 |
| Arithmetic mean of scores from 1 (very low) to 7 (very high) for the total sample | 3.39 |

It was to be expected that differentiation by occupational groups would not be without significance here. And Table 2 shows this to be so. As can be seen, the occupational groups could be ordered on the basis of their "status evaluation". A number of additional conclusions flow from Table 2. First, in the category of unskilled workers more than half of the subjects expressed the feeling of deprivation connected with their social status, i.e., as evaluating their status as low or very low. At the same time, more than half of the creative intelligentsia and free professional group clearly belong to the privileged-feeling category, i.e., their evaluations being higher than average. As far as the skilled and non-manual workers are concerned, more than half of them fall into the intermediate, emotionally neutral category, while the decidedly dominant proportion of both groups define their status as average.

Both the percentage breakdown of the answers and the arithmetical mean of the corresponding scores seem to suggest still another conclusion: the distance dividing the skilled and non-manual workers is smaller than that separating these two from extreme groups.

Since our sample showed much educational differentiation, it would be reasonable to expect that the assessment of one's position in society would vary with education. The empirical findings, omitted here, proved this to be the case. The higher the

**TABLE 2 (R) Relationship Between the Perception of One's Social Status and Occupation (%)**

| *Status Perception*<br><br>OCCUPATIONAL CATEGORY* | *7. Very high and 6. high* | *5. Higher than average* | *4. Average* | *3. Lower than average* | *2. Low and 1. very low* | *1. Mean score* |
|---|---|---|---|---|---|---|
| Unskilled workers | 3.1 | 2.8 | 21.1 | 14.1 | 52.3 | 2.65 |
| Skilled workers | 2.7 | 4.2 | 42.8 | 14.9 | 30.2 | 3.25 |
| Non-manual workers | 7.1 | 11.9 | 46.0 | 14.0 | 15.0 | 3.78 |
| Creative intelligentsia and free professions | 24.3 | 25.7 | 31.4 | 7.1 | 7.2 | 4.53 |

* I omitted in Tables 6, 7, 8 the handicrafts group as too small. But I would like to add here that the mean score for handicraftsmen has been reckoned at 3.56, i.e., between skilled workers and non-manual workers.

**TABLE 3 (T) Relationship Between Negative Perception of One's Social Status and Both Occupation and Education (%)**

| *Occupational Category* | *Educational Category* | | | | | |
|---|---|---|---|---|---|---|
| | INCOMPLETE ELEMENTARY | ELEMENTARY | INCOMPLETE SECONDARY | SECONDARY | INCOMPLETE HIGHER | HIGHER |
| Unskilled workers | 69.8 | 62.8 | — | — | — | — |
| Skilled workers | 58.0 | 44.3 | 40.1 | 29.0 | — | — |
| Non-manual workers | — | 41.9 | 33.4 | 26.2 | 25.1 | 12.8 |
| Free professions and creative intelligentsia | — | — | — | — | — | 9.3 |

Note: The cells of the Table present the percentage of the following answers: very low + low + lower than average.

**TABLE 4 (T) Relationship Between the Perception of One's Status (Mean Scores) and Occupation, Education, and Income—Combined**

<table>
<tr><th rowspan="2">Occupation</th><th rowspan="2">Education</th><th colspan="4">Monthly Earnings</th></tr>
<tr><th>to 1100</th><th>1101–1800</th><th>1801–2900</th><th>above 2901</th></tr>
<tr><td>Unskilled workers</td><td>incomplete elementary</td><td>2.40</td><td>2.73</td><td colspan="2">2.75</td></tr>
<tr><td></td><td>elementary</td><td>2.49</td><td>2.72</td><td colspan="2">3.23</td></tr>
<tr><td>Skilled workers</td><td>incomplete elementary</td><td>2.39</td><td>2.34</td><td colspan="2">3.44</td></tr>
<tr><td></td><td>elementary</td><td>2.84</td><td>3.16</td><td>3.43</td><td>3.64</td></tr>
<tr><td></td><td>incomplete secondary</td><td colspan="2">3.12</td><td colspan="2">3.65</td></tr>
<tr><td></td><td>secondary</td><td colspan="2">3.44</td><td colspan="2">3.90</td></tr>
<tr><td>Non-manual workers</td><td>elementary</td><td colspan="2">3.44</td><td colspan="2">4.68</td></tr>
<tr><td></td><td>incomplete secondary</td><td>2.76</td><td>3.55</td><td colspan="2">4.19</td></tr>
<tr><td></td><td>secondary</td><td>3.31</td><td>3.58</td><td>3.90</td><td>4.35</td></tr>
<tr><td></td><td>incomplete higher</td><td colspan="2">3.81</td><td>3.98</td><td>5.00</td></tr>
<tr><td></td><td>higher</td><td colspan="2">3.81</td><td>4.30</td><td>4.76</td></tr>
<tr><td>Professions and creative intelligenstia</td><td>higher</td><td>3.40</td><td>4.22</td><td>4.53</td><td>5.10</td></tr>
</table>

* Note: Small categories are joined to the nearest category.

**TABLE 5 (R). Inter-generational Social Mobility of Urban Males in Poland***

| *Subject's Occupation* / *Father's Occupation* | | *A. Agricultural Labourer* | | *B. Farmer* | | *C. Unskilled Worker* | | *D. Worker (without qualification)* | | *E. Skilled Worker* | |
|---|---|---|---|---|---|---|---|---|---|---|---|
| | | NO. | % | NO. | % | NO. | % | NO. | % | NO. | % |
| 1. Unskilled worker | No. | 15 | 4.6 | 89 | 27.2 | 32 | 9.8 | 81 | 24.8 | 57 | 17.4 |
| | % | 37.5 | | 22.1 | | 26.4 | | 30.3 | | 14.8 | |
| 2. Skilled worker | No. | 19 | 2.3 | 164 | 20.0 | 61 | 7.5 | 118 | 14.4 | 233 | 28.5 |
| | % | 47.5 | — | 40.7 | — | 50.4 | — | 44.2 | — | 60.6 | — |
| 3. Handicraftsman | No. | — | — | 2 | 7.2 | — | — | 1 | 3.7 | 5 | 18.5 |
| | % | | | 0.5 | | | | 0.4 | | 1.3 | |
| 4. Non-manual worker without | No. | 6 | 1.0 | 127 | 21.5 | 25 | 4.2 | 59 | 10.0 | 81 | 13.7 |
| higher educ.** | % | 15.0 | | 31.5 | | 20.7 | | 22.1 | | 21.0 | |
| 5. Non-manual worker with | No. | | | 13 | 13.0 | 3 | 13.0 | 5 | 5.0 | 5 | 5.0 |
| higher educ. | % | — | — | 3.2 | | 2.5 | | 1.9 | | 1.3 | |
| 6. Others and no | No. | | | 8 | 22.9 | | | 3 | 8.9 | 4 | 11.4 |
| answer | % | — | — | 2.0 | | — | — | 1.1 | | 1.0 | |
| Total father's | No. | 40 | 2.1 | 403 | 21.2 | 121 | 6.4 | 267 | 14.3 | 385 | 20.3 |
| occupation | % | 100% | | 100% | | 100% | | 100% | | 100% | |

* The following sub-groups have been counted in the category "upwardly mobile": A.1, 2, 3, 4, 5: B. 1, 2, 3, 4, 5: C. 2, 3, 4, 5: D. 3, 4, 5: F. 4, 5: G. 4, 5: H. 5. This gives jointly 798 persons, or 42% of the sample.

education of our respondents, the more likely they were to perceive their social status as very high, high, or at least above average. The same direction of relationships was found when income was treated as the independent variable.

Hence the conclusion might be drawn that the perception of the rank of one's status depends on occupation as on education and material conditions. But the data in our survey indicating a strong relationship between the objective parameters of the social structure would caution against such a hasty conclusion. Under these circumstances, as is known, at least some of the correlations represented here might be spurious or might have to be explained by some intervening variable.

It may be suspected that differences in the perception of one's status by individual occupational groups may be "reduced" to the differences in income or education among them. Let us analyse this hypothesis.

Table 3 presents the dependence of the perception of one's own status on both occupation and education of our subjects. It shows that education and occupation determine status perception independently of each other, i.e., that within the framework of each occupational group there exists a separate definite interrelation between status perception and education. Table 3 suggests still another interesting conclusion: with education held constant, the interrelation is no less definite between status perception and occupation. Among individuals with incompleted elementary education one's status evaluation is as a rule lower among unskilled than among skilled workers. And even among those with completed higher education one's status evaluation is higher among the creative

| *F. Handicraftsman* | | *G. Merchant (store keeper)* | | *H. Non-Manual Worker Without High Educ.* | | *I. Nonman. Worker with Higher Educ. and Free Profession* | | *J. Capitalist and Landowner* | | *K. Other and No Answer* | | *Total Subjects' Occupation* | |
|---|---|---|---|---|---|---|---|---|---|---|---|---|---|
| NO. | % | NO. | % | NO. | % | NO. | % | NO. | % | NO. | % | NO. | % |
| 25 | 7.6 | 2 | 0.6 | 10 | 3.1 | 2 | 0.6 | — | — | 14 | 4.6 | 327 | 100% |
| 10.6 | | 3.9 | | 4.0 | | 2.4 | | | | 24.1 | | 17.2 | |
| 133 | 16.3 | 17 | 2.1 | 45 | 5.5 | 10 | 1.2 | — | — | 18 | 2.2 | 818 | 100% |
| 56.4 | — | 33.3 | — | 18.1 | — | 12.0 | — | — | — | 31.0 | — | 43.1 | |
| 12 | 44.4 | 4 | 14.8 | 1 | 3.7 | 1 | 3.7 | 1 | 3.7 | — | — | 27 | 100% |
| 5.1 | | 7.5 | | 0.4 | | 1.2 | | 25.0 | | | | 1.4 | |
| 52 | 8.8 | 21 | 3.6 | 157 | 26.6 | 40 | 6.8 | 3 | 0.5 | 13 | 3.2 | 590 | 100% |
| 22.0 | | 41.2 | | 63.1 | | 48.2 | | 75.0 | | 37.2 | | 31.1 | |
| 10.0 | 10.0 | 6 | 6.0 | 26 | 26.0 | 28 | 28.0 | | | 4 | 4.0 | 100 | 100% |
| 4.2 | | 11.8 | | 10.4 | | 33.8 | | — | — | 7.0 | | 5.3 | |
| 4 | | 1 | 2.9 | 10 | 28.9 | 2 | 5.8 | | | 3 | 8.9 | 35 | 100% |
| 1.1 | 11.4 | 2.0 | | 4.2 | | 2.4 | | — | — | 5.2 | — | 1.9 | |
| 236 | 12.4 | 51 | 2.7 | 249 | 13.1 | 83 | 4.4 | 4 | 0.2 | 58 | 3.1 | 189 | |
| 100% | | 100% | | 100% | | 100% | | 100% | | 100% | | 100% | |

** Respondents' occupations are categorized differently than in the previous tables. To obtain a category as close as possible to the category of the question on the father's occupation, the groups "non-manual workers" and "free professions" are combined, and then divided on the basis of completed higher education. Tables 5, 6, 7 data are calculated thus.

intelligentsia than among the non-manual workers category, although many of them undoubtedly occupy managerial positions in administration and in the economy. The same results were obtained when in multivariate analyses, first income and then occupation were each treated as independent variables.

Let us now see if we can grasp the interaction of all the three independent factors in determining the dependent variable (mean scores of social status perceptions). The necessary data are given in Table 4. They show that with any two of the independent variables held constant, the answers to the question on status perception are with clear regularity the function of the third variable.

The preceding paragraph hence may be summarised by the following conclusion: the perception of the rank of one's own social status in post-war Poland is independently determined by occupation, the economic situation and education; while these factors—which are in turn mutually interdependent—may either supplement or cancel the effects of each other.

## THE PROCESSES OF SOCIAL MOBILITY AND THEIR REFLECTION IN SOCIAL CONSCIOUSNESS

. . . It is a well known fact that a large scale process of social mobility has taken place in Poland as a result of the social transformations. This has nevertheless been accompanied by only a fragmentary knowledge of the more precise course of this process.[4] Let us analyse the course and chief trends of

[4] See e.g. M. Pohoski, *Migracje ze wsi do miast* (*Migrations from the Rural Areas to the Cities*), Warszawa 1963.

the inter-generational social mobility by studying the relationships between occupational category of our respondents, and the occupation of their fathers.[5] The corresponding data are presented by Table 5. . . .

Let us now examine the pattern of inter-group movement. Lack of space precludes any detailed analysis, we can only signalise some of the most important conclusions.

(1) First of all it confirms the stereotypic knowledge about the extended social mobility in postwar Poland, predominantly upward mobility. But if we assume for the present that the transition from rural unskilled to skilled labour, from manual to non-manual work and from clerks to "intelligentsia with a higher education" (as suggested by the notes to Table 5) represents the improvement of social status, then it must be said that 42 per cent of respondents hold higher positions than their fathers did at the same age.

The conclusion hence follows that under the above assumption 42 per cent of urban adult males must be reckoned in the category of "upwardly mobile."

(2) An analysis of the percentages in the vertical columns indicates that the parents' occupational status was not without its effect on that of their sons. Whereas an average of 23 per cent of the sons of workers attained non-manual occupations, 34 per cent of the sons of peasants who moved to the cities did so. (Of course, this percentage would be much lower if we counted the whole population of peasants' sons.) The proportion of non-manual workers among the sons of non-manual workers without higher education amounted to 73 per cent and to 82 per cent among those of the free professions and intelligentsia with higher education. . . . Let us analyse now how the above objective changes in social status reflect themselves in social consciousness. (See Table 6.)

The lower marginals of Table 6 disclose that 44 per cent evaluate their status as "higher", while 22 per cent, or half as many, consider their status to have worsened as compared to that of their parents. It should be also noted that the higher the actual position of the given group, the more frequent are the convictions about their social advancement.

The 44 per cent figure of total advancement is quite close to the 42 per cent calculated by me on the basis of Table 5.

Table 7 establishes a fairly high contingency between the objective mobility on the social ladder and its subjective perception. The greater the distance between the occupations of father and son, the greater the chance of the corresponding change being reflected in the subject's evaluation—

[5] The wording of an open-ended question concerning fathers' occupation was as follows: "What was the occupation of your father when he was at your actual age?" The answers were coded in the way presented in Table 5.

**TABLE 6 (T) Relationship Between the Occupation and Perception of the Respondent's Own Social Mobility***

| *Occupational Groups* | *Is Your Present Social Status Higher or Lower than That of your Father at the Same Age?* | | | | |
|---|---|---|---|---|---|
| | MUCH HIGHER | HIGHER | ABOUT THE SAME | LOWER | MUCH LOWER |
| Unskilled workers | 2.1 | 21.4 | 11.3 | 20.2 | 5.5 |
| Skilled workers | 5.4 | 33.0 | 33.4 | 17.7 | 4.3 |
| Non-manual workers | 13.3 | 42.3 | 19.2 | 16.7 | 4.7 |
| Creative intelligentsia | 15.9 | 40.3 | 20.1 | 14.4 | 5.7 |
| Total sample | 8.8 | 35.1 | 23.6 | 17.3 | 4.9 |

* The percentages do not add up horizontally to 100 because the "no answer" percentages are omitted. (C. S. H.)

## TABLE 7 (R). Relationship Between Intergenerational Social Mobility and its Evaluation by the Respondent

| Father's Occupation | Respondent's Occupation | Number of Persons in Given Group* | Is Your Present Status in the Society Higher or Lower than That of Your Father at the Same Age? | | | | | | Evaluation of Status Changes in General | | |
|---|---|---|---|---|---|---|---|---|---|---|---|
| | | | MUCH HIGHER | HIGHER | ABOUT THE SAME | LOWER | MUCH LOWER | HARD TO SAY | HIGHER | LOWER | DIFFERENCE HIGHER-LOWER |
| 1 | 2 | 3 | 4 | 5 | 6 | 7 | 8 | 9 | 10 | 11 | 12 |
| A. Agricultural laborer | 1. unskilled worker | 15 | 6.7 | 6.7 | 40.0 | 20.0 | — | 26.7 | 17.4 | 20.0 | −2.6 |
| | 2. skilled worker | 19 | 10.5 | 52.6 | 15.8 | 15.8 | 5.3 | — | 63.1 | 21.3 | +41.8 |
| B. Farmer | 1. unskilled worker | 89 | 1.1 | 28.1 | 37.1 | 16.9 | 5.6 | 11.2 | 29.2 | 22.5 | +6.7 |
| | 2. skilled worker | 164 | 5.5 | 43.3 | 28.0 | 12.2 | 3.7 | 7.9 | 48.8 | 15.9 | +32.9 |
| | 4. non-manual worker** | 127 | 15.0 | 50.4 | 12.6 | 13.4 | 1.6 | 7.1 | 65.4 | 15.0 | +50.4 |
| | 5. non-manual worker with higher educ. and free profession | 13 | 38.5 | 53.8 | — | — | — | 7.1 | 92.3 | — | +92.3 |
| C. Unskilled worker | 1. unskilled worker | 32 | 3.1 | 28.1 | 43.8 | 9.4 | 3.1 | 9.4 | 31.2 | 12.5 | +18.7 |
| | 2. skilled worker | 61 | 8.2 | 50.8 | 27.9 | 8.2 | — | 3.3 | 59.0 | 8.2 | +50.8 |
| | 4. non-manual worker | 25 | 32.0 | 40.0 | 20.0 | 2.0 | — | — | 72.0 | 2.0 | +70.0 |
| D. Worker without qualification | 1. unskilled worker | 81 | — | 17.3 | 60.5 | 14.8 | 3.7 | 3.7 | 17.3 | 18.5 | −1.2 |
| | 2. skilled worker | 118 | 5.9 | 33.1 | 38.1 | 16.1 | 2.5 | 4.2 | 39.0 | 18.6 | +20.4 |
| | 4. non-manual worker | 59 | 16.9 | 54.2 | 8.5 | 8.5 | 3.4 | 8.5 | 71.1 | 11.9 | +59.2 |
| E. Skilled worker | 1. unskilled worker | 57 | 5.3 | 17.5 | 35.1 | 24.6 | 10.5 | 7.0 | 22.8 | 35.1 | −12.3 |
| | 2. skilled worker | 23.3 | 5.6 | 31.3 | 36.1 | 16.3 | 3.4 | 7.3 | 36.9 | 19.7 | +17.2 |
| | 4. non-manual worker | 81 | 11.1 | 50.6 | 14.8 | 11.1 | 6.2 | 6.2 | 61.7 | 17.3 | +44.4 |
| F. Handicraftsman | 1. unskilled worker | 25 | 4.0 | 24.0 | 28.0 | 40.0 | 4.0 | — | 28.0 | 44.0 | −16.0 |
| | 2. skilled worker | 133 | 4.5 | 21.8 | 42.1 | 21.1 | 5.3 | 4.5 | 26.3 | 26.4 | −0.1 |
| | 3. handicraftsman | 12 | 25.0 | 16.7 | 25.0 | 25.0 | 8.3 | — | 41.7 | 33.3 | +8.4 |
| | 4. non-manual worker | 52 | 13.5 | 42.3 | 15.4 | 13.5 | 9.6 | 5.8 | 55.8 | 23.1 | +32.7 |
| | 5. non-manual worker with higher educ. and free profession | 10 | 30.0 | 60.0 | — | 10.0 | — | — | 90.0 | 10 | +80.0 |
| G. Merchant | 2. skilled worker | 17 | — | 5.9 | 47.1 | 41.2 | 5.9 | — | 5.9 | 47.1 | −41.2 |
| | 4. non-manual worker | 21 | 14.3 | 38.1 | 23.8 | 9.5 | 9.5 | 4.8 | 52.4 | 19.0 | +33.4 |
| H. Non-manual worker without higher education | 1. unskilled worker | 10 | — | 20.0 | 30.0 | 40.0 | 10.0 | — | 20.0 | 50.0 | −30.0 |
| | 2. skilled worker | 45 | 4.4 | 26.7 | 22.0 | 33.3 | 8.9 | 4.4 | 31.1 | 42.2 | −11.1 |
| | 4. non-manual worker | 157 | 3.8 | 29.9 | 31.2 | 24.8 | 6.4 | 3.8 | 33.7 | 31.2 | +2.5 |
| | 5. non-manual worker with higher educ. and free profession | 26 | 7.2 | 42.3 | 23.1 | 19.2 | 3.8 | 3.8 | 49.5 | 23.0 | +26.5 |
| I. Non-manual worker with higher educ. and free profession | 2. skilled worker | 10 | — | — | 20.0 | 30.0 | 40.0 | 10.0 | — | 70.0 | −70.0 |
| | 4. non-manual worker | 40 | 5.0 | 10.0 | 20.0 | 52.5 | 10.0 | 2.5 | 15.0 | 62.5 | −47.5 |
| | 5. non-manual worker with higher educ. and free profession | 28 | 3.6 | 17.9 | 42.9 | 25.0 | 14.3 | — | 21.5 | 39.3 | −17.8 |

* We omitted the groups below 10 persons in number.
** Category "non-manual worker" refers to non-manual workers without higher education.

**TABLE 8 (R) Conviction of Advancement and Downgrading According to Father's and Son's Occupation (%)**

| | *Father's Occupation* | *Son's Occupation* | *Conviction of Advance-ment* | *Conviction of Down-grading* | *Difference* |
|---|---|---|---|---|---|
| C. 1 | Unskilled worker | unskilled worker | 31.2 | 12.5 | +18.7 |
| D. 2 | Skilled worker | skilled worker | 39.0 | 18.6 | +20.4 |
| F. 3 | Handicraftsman | handicraftsman | 41.7 | 33.3 | +8.4 |
| H. 4 | Non-manual worker | non-manual worker | 33.7 | 31.2 | +2.5 |
| I. 5 | Free profession and intelligentsia with higher education | free profession and intelligentsia with higher education | 21.5 | 39.3 | −11.8 |

in the form of a dominant conviction of advancement or downgrading. Nevertheless, the correlation between the objective mobility, as signified by Table 5, and the conviction that the subject's social status is higher or lower than his father's, was by no means a perfect one. Let us consider some of the deviations from it.

There is first of all the fact that the feeling of advancement was by no means dominant in all the groups characterized as "upwardly mobile" in Table 5.

An analysis of the last column of Table 7 shows that the sons of agricultural labourers or peasants being now unskilled workers were by no means convinced in majority that their status was higher than that of their parents. It hence follows that on a mass scale migrants from rural to urban areas have advanced socially only when they attain at least the position of skilled workers.

Secondly, among some of the groups we did not count in the socially advanced category, e.g., in which the father and son have the same occupation, there is a dominant conviction of social advancement. This question deserves a little more attention.

An analysis of the rows, with a convergence of father and son occupations, gives the figures shown in Table 8.

Reflected in these figures, in my opinion, are what may be called the advancement or downgrading of entire social groups. Thus workers—sons of workers locating their own and their parents' positions on the background of the corresponding social structures—evaluate their status as higher though they belong to "the same" occupational category. They thereby also express

**TABLE 9 (T) Perception of Changes in Social Structure by Occupational Group**

| *Social-Occupational Groups* | *Are Social Distinctions Between People of Different Groups in Poland Generally Greater or Smaller Today than Before the War?** | | | | |
|---|---|---|---|---|---|
| | MUCH SMALLER | A LITTLE SMALLER | ABOUT THE SAME | A LITTLE GREATER | MUCH GREATER |
| Unskilled workers | 22.3 | 29.2 | 13.5 | 7.6 | 7.3 |
| Skilled workers | 28.2 | 29.6 | 13.9 | 5.7 | 7.3 |
| Non-manual workers | 37.9 | 31.2 | 10.8 | 4.3 | 5.2 |
| Creative intelligentsia and free professions | 30.9 | 36.0 | 16.0 | 2.2 | 3.6 |
| Total sample | 29.2 | 30.3 | 13.2 | 3.8 | 7.0* |

* 14.1% of respondents answered: "hard to say." Most of them belonged to the younger age groups.

indirectly the conviction that the over-all position of the working class in the social structure has improved. It's significant that the handicraftsmen arrive at a similar conclusion, although perhaps in a more controversial manner. Among non-manual workers without higher education the percentage convinced of their advancement is just a little above those convinced of the opposite. Whereas those whose fathers before the war were in the free professions and intelligentsia with higher education category definitely evaluate their own status as worse, although they belong to the same category. They thereby express the conviction that the status of this group as a whole grew worse because of the changes in the social structure.

## EVALUATION OF SOCIAL DISTANCE AND THE PERCEPTION OF DIFFERENTIATION IN THE SOCIAL STRUCTURE

Let us see now to what degree the transformations in the social structure of postwar Poland are reflected in the social consciousness.

According to the lower marginals of Table 9 the conviction is dominant that the changes effected a lessening of social differences. But the answers to this question are not independent of the respondents' social position. As the data indicate, there is a definite tendency to the growth of optimism with regards to the egalitarian character of the changes, with the rise in the respondents' social status. As many as 38 per cent of non-manual workers and only 22 per cent of unskilled workers are convinced that social differences are much smaller today. It is worth noting that a certain decline of optimism (as compared with non-manual workers) in the evaluation of the egalitarian processes of the social structure is again observable among the creative intelligentsia and in the free professions.

The prevailing social structure is nevertheless regarded as marked by a fairly strong system of differentiation. In answer to the question what divides people in Poland, we obtained an interesting number of factors of division in the social structure. The relative data are presented in the first columns of Table 10.

The answers indicate that economic differentiation is regarded as the factor that divides people most. It is interesting that the factors which could be described as highly personal, such as political attitude or religious views, are considered weaker bases of social division than education or occupation, so clearly connected with social stratification. Also worthy of notice

**TABLE 10 (R) Perceived Factors of Social Division and Social Animosity (%)**

| *Basis of Differentiation* | WHICH IN YOUR OPINION DIVIDES PEOPLE IN OUR SOCIETY? | | WHICH OF THE LISTED DIFFERENCES ARE IN YOUR OPINION THE CAUSE OF ANIMOSITY IN OUR SOCIETY? |
|---|---|---|---|
| | Very strongly | Rather strongly | |
| Differences in earnings or wealth | 45.7 | 36.0 | 71.5 |
| Differences in education | 26.1 | 45.0 | 45.5 |
| Differences between managerial and non-managerial positions | 25.0 | 33.1 | 41.8 |
| Division into manual and non-manual workers | 15.9 | 41.1 | 35.4 |
| Differences in manner of behaving in company | 16.7 | 39.8 | 28.0 |
| Differences in religious outlook | 21.3 | 26.9 | 41.3 |
| Differences of political views | 13.8 | 27.4 | 43.6 |
| Division between city and country | 10.9 | 33.3 | 30.2 |
| Differences of social origin | 6.4 | 16.2 | 16.7 |

**TABLE 11 (R) Typology of Ways of Perceiving Social Animosity Along Different Dimensions of Social Stratification**[6]

| *Basis of Differentiation* | BELIEVING THAT EITHER ALL OR AT LEAST MAJORITY OF THE GIVEN CATEGORY FEELS ANIMOSITY | | | |
|---|---|---|---|---|
| | "At the top" as well as "at the bottom" | Only "at the top" | Only "at the bottom" | Neither "at the top" nor "at the bottom" |
| Education | 19.8 | 18.1 | 18.9 | 31.4 |
| Manual and non-manual work | 17.9 | 11.8 | 22.7 | 38.2 |
| Subordinates—authorities | 21.6 | 10.1 | 19.8 | 34.3 |
| Income | 20.5 | 3.7 | 47.6 | 12.4 |
| High or low positions | 23.5 | 13.6 | 20.1 | 24.9 |
| Country—city | 19.8 | 11.0 | 13.4 | 41.0 |

is the fact that social origin is basically regarded as an entirely indifferent factor of social division.

Answers to the question as to which dividing factors cause social animosity are given in the last column of the same Table 10.

Let us now consider the rank order of different factors. Examining the columns of Table 10 we see that differences in earnings are clearly and uniformly given priority. Education is second in importance, while differences in social origin are definitely in the last place in both rank orders. It must be considered however that differences in religious or political views—among the lowest places as factors of social division—occupy considerably higher positions as factors of animosity among people.

The question on the source of animosity between people is to be found also at the end of the questionnaire, but in a different form. We asked for instance, if the educated dislike the uneducated and if the uneducated dislike the educated, if the high earners dislike the low paid, and vice versa, etc. This enabled us to study not only what, according to our respondents, were the sources, but also the social location and the directions of social animosity.

On the basis of these answers we were able then to classify our respondents as to whether (within the given dimension of social stratification such as education for instance) they feel animosity to come only "from the top" (from the educated for the uneducated) or only "from the bottom" (from the uneducated for the educated) or from both at once, or if they are convinced that there is no conflict along the given stratification dimension. As a result we made the following typology of the manners of perceiving tension in the social structure by different occupational groups.

Table 11 shows certain interesting regularities. We first of all ascertain that the most numerous category consider the social system to be free of tension on both sides of the lines of social division. The next category sees the mutual animosity on both sides of mentioned lines of differentiation. We see furthermore that on all dimensions animosity is perceived more frequently as coming "from the bottom" than "from the top." This difference is most pronounced in dimension of income, 3.7 and 47.6, respectively. Hence when tension of a one directional character is perceived in our sample the tendency is to locate it more frequently in the lower social strata.

It could be expected that the attitude toward the social structure and toward the sources of tension within it would be

[6] The question, as it appeared in the Polish version of the article, read, "In your opinion which people in our country feel animosity? (a) educated toward uneducated: almost all, majority, minority, nobody or almost nobody, difficult to say. (b) uneducated toward educated: almost all, majority, minority, nobody or almost nobody, difficult to say." See Stefan Nowak, *Psychologiczne Aspekty Przemian Struktury Spolecznej, Studja Socjologiczne,* Vol. 2, No. 21, 1966, p. 101. (C. S. H.)

TABLE 12 (T) **Perception of Sources of Division in Society by Respondents' Occupation**

| *Occupational Groups* | WHAT IN YOUR OPINION DIVIDES PEOPLE IN OUR SOCIETY? (% OF ANSWERS "VERY STRONGLY") | | | | | |
|---|---|---|---|---|---|---|
| | Education | Income | Political views | Kind of behaviour | Manual and non-manual work | Managerial and non-managerial position |
| Unskilled workers | 34.2 | 54.1 | 18.3 | 16.8 | 23.3 | 32.1 |
| Skilled workers | 27.2 | 45.7 | 19.6 | 15.0 | 18.5 | 25.2 |
| Non-manual workers | 19.4 | 35.6 | 20.2 | 17.1 | 11.2 | 19.7 |
| Creative intelligentsia and free professions | 23.7 | 46.8 | 28.1 | 23.7 | 6.5 | 20.1 |

TABLE 13 **How Different Occupational Categories Perceive the Patterns of Social Tension Along the Different Dimensions of Social Stratification (% Who Think Almost All or at Least a Majority Feel Dislikes)**

| *Occupation* | EDUCATION | | | | MANUAL—NON-MANUAL | | | | MANAGERIAL—NON-MANAGERIAL | | | | INCOME | | | | DIFFERENCE OF POSITIONS | | | |
|---|---|---|---|---|---|---|---|---|---|---|---|---|---|---|---|---|---|---|---|---|
| | 1* | 2 | 3 | 4 | 1 | 2 | 3 | 4 | 1 | 2 | 3 | 4 | 1 | 2 | 3 | 4 | 1 | 2 | 3 | 4 |
| 3. Unskilled workers | 21.4 | 22.6 | 13.8 | 25.7 | 20.7 | 20.5 | 15.0 | 32.1 | 22.3 | 12.2 | 15.3 | 28.7 | 25.1 | 6.9 | 38.2 | 9.5 | 22.9 | 16.8 | 17.7 | 16.6 |
| 4. Skilled workers | 20.2 | 22.8 | 13.0 | 31.3 | 22.4 | 13.9 | 16.8 | 36.8 | 22.4 | 11.0 | 16.7 | 35.8 | 22.2 | 3.9 | 44.4 | 14.3 | 23.6 | 13.8 | 17.6 | 26.5 |
| 5. Non-manual workers | 16.2 | 10.3 | 29.6 | 35.3 | 11.7 | 5.2 | 35.9 | 39.4 | 17.6 | 7.5 | 26.9 | 36.4 | 16.0 | 3.2 | 58.3 | 11.6 | 20.5 | 11.3 | 27.4 | 27.1 |
| 6. Creative intelligentsia and free professions | 12.9 | 7.2 | 43.2 | 28.8 | 9.4 | 2.2 | 39.6 | 40.4 | 17.3 | 6.5 | 36.7 | 28.8 | 20.1 | 0.7 | 60.4 | 7.9 | 20.9 | 5.0 | 25.3 | 23.0 |

* 1—at the top as well as at the bottom; 2—only at the top; 3—only at the bottom; 4—neither at the top nor at the bottom.

dependent on the place one occupies in the social system. That this is so is shown by the data in Table 12, in which the bases of social division are related to respondents' occupations.

What conclusions are suggested by Table 12? We observe first of all a definite tendency that the higher the respondents' social position the more rarely are they convinced that certain social differences create divisions among the people in Poland. This pertains to earnings, education, to the distinction between manual and non-manual labour, importance of positions or posts held, etc. But it must be noted that in 3 out of 4 cases the creative intelligentsia is more frequently convinced than are the non-manual workers that given differentiations definitely create divisions among people in Polish society.

The creative intelligentsia also seems to attach much greater importance than any other occupational group to . . . other sources of social distinction: differences in political views and in kind of behaviour ("good manners").

There is an interesting correlation between the perception and localization of social animosity and the respondent's social position. Two different and complementary tendencies seen from Table 13 are to be noted here:

1. The higher is the social position, the greater the chance that the respondent will regard the structure as a non-conflicting one in both directions. And the converse: the lower the social position—the greater the chance of his perceiving mutual animosity between the groups.
2. The higher the respondent's position the greater the tendency to see the animosity as coming from the bottom. The lower the position—the greater is the tendency to see it as coming from the top, regardless of what line of dichotomic division is taken into account.

The first of the mentioned mechanisms is well known from other researches on psychological aspects of social stratification in different countries.

The cause of the latter mechanism might be seen perhaps in the fact that in Poland, owing to the widespread socialist patterns of egalitarian ideology and of harmonious images of the social structure, inter-group tensions are inhibited. Instead of being expressed in the direct answers they may occur rather in a "projective" form.

The combined action of the two mechanisms gives us a system of relationships in which a high social position increases the chances either to see the source of antagonism in the lower social strata, or to regard the structure as a whole as being harmonious. Conversely, the members of the lower social strata are inclined either to see animosity as coming only from those on top, or to perceive the structure as a conflicting one along the given dimension.

Let us now analyse another item of our questionnaire, namely, the demands for the egalitarianization of the social structure in the future.

We see from the lower marginals of Table 14 that over 80 per cent of the respondents demand the increase of equality in our social structure and almost half of them demand the complete abolition of all social differentiation. It's interesting that here too there is a relationship with the respondents' occupational status. As many as 53 per cent of skilled workers demand complete equality in that social structure as compared to 38 per cent of the creative intelligentsia.

## CONCLUSIONS

Let us briefly summarize the main conclusions of the above preliminary analysis of the data of our survey. The social structure of the post-war Poland is characterized by a fairly large amount of upward social mobility with fairly high opportunities for social advancement. Both the inter-generational mobility and the advancement opportunities are fairly correctly "reflected" by social consciousness and there is a visible correlation between the changing of one's social position and its perception. At the same time a conviction prevails that there has been a reduction of social distance between the various social groups.

On the other hand, despite the sharp perception of all these social transformations, in the people's consciousness the egalitarian process is by no means regarded as completed. There are first of all clearly

**TABLE 14 Egalitarian Postulates for the Future as Related to Occupation**

| *Occupational Category* | WOULD YOU WANT TO SEE IN THE FUTURE THE SOCIAL DIFFERENCES IN POLAND? | | | |
|---|---|---|---|---|
| | Entirely disappear | Diminish | Remain unchanged | Increase |
| Unskilled workers | 44.0 | 38.2 | 4.0 | 3.7 |
| Skilled workers | 52.7 | 36.9 | 2.8 | 2.8 |
| Non-manual workers | 48.0 | 41.2 | 3.2 | 2.2 |
| Free professions and creative intelligentsia | 38.1 | 43.2 | 3.6 | 7.2 |
| Total sample (R) | 45.5 | 38.0 | 3. | 2.8 |

differentiated feelings regarding social status, strongly correlated with one's occupation, income and education. At the same time a number of factors are still identified as sources of social division and tension in the social structure—with the economic differences in the first place among them. The perception of social differentiation combined with the acceptance of egalitarian ideals leads to the demand for the further reduction of, and, with almost half of the people, for the complete abolition of all social differences in the social structure.

The studied population seems to be influenced by two mechanisms shaping the image of the existing structure and the demand for the extension of social equality. On the one hand, the population as a whole is under the strong influence of the egalitarian ideals of socialism with the demand for transformation of the social structure in the direction of the abolition of social differences. On the other hand, the well known sociological mechanisms continue to operate and they cause a decrease in the attractiveness of egalitarian ideals with the increase of social and economic position, while the egalitarian demands increase, as they are linked with hopes that they will lead to the improvement of social position. The interaction of both these mechanisms—interest group determinant of social consciousness and pressure of egalitarian ideals of socialist ideology—was presented above.

# PART IV
# Consequences of Stratification: Differential Life Chances and Ways of Life

In a complex society there is hardly an area of social life in which some aspects do not differ with social stratum. This is acknowledged in the methodological procedure of empirical sociological studies, almost automatic today, of statistically controlling the *class factor,* irrespective of the subject of study. Of all the variables that the sociologist employs in his analysis, few are as predictive as socioeconomic status. The vast number of specific areas, patterns, and nuances of behavior that vary with social stratum could perhaps be best subsumed under the concepts of *life chances* and *ways of life*. The first is easily recognized as derived from Max Weber. The second is a revision of Weber's *styles of life*. The word *style*, it seems to me, may not convey the breadth of the meaning of the concept because it carries the connotation of form, of manner of expression, rather than the substance of life. Way of life conveys an image of the total nature of social existence—including the general orientation to basic universal human problems, the goals and values, and the social organization—as well as its modes of expression.

To begin with life chances, the possibilities throughout one's life cycle, from the chance to stay alive during the first year after birth, through the school years—the chance to attend a scholastically adequate primary school, to finish high school, to go to college—to the chance of reaching a ripe old age, all are to some extent determined by the stratum to which one is born. The first selection in this Part deals with the basic chance to stay alive. In his "Social Class, Life Expectancy and Overall Mortality," Aaron Antonovsky surveys the statistical data of thirty studies ranging through the centuries and different Western nations. On the basis of this extensive survey he arrives at the general hypothesis—presented at the end of his article—that when mortality rates are very high or very low in a society, class differences tend to be small. As he expresses it, "when men are quite helpless before the threat of death or when men have made great achievements in dealing with this threat, life chances will tend to be equitably distributed." But when the achievements are only moderate, the class differences are substantial.

As for the data that suggested this conclusion, those *prior* to the nineteenth century are rather limited. They seem to indicate, however, that life expectancy, which was quite short in comparison with today's, did not differ with social stratum. The less-limited nineteenth-century data reveal a tendency toward the widening of class differences in mortality. This was probably the result of the rapid increase in the life expectancy of the middle and upper strata while that of the lower strata remained low. Toward the latter half of that century the class differences began to decrease, and by now they are narrow as compared to the past. But in the last three decades the trend toward the closing of the class gap "has been checked, if not halted." The large difference that exists is between the lowest level of the working class (Warner's lower lower) and the rest of the population.

Antonovsky poses the problem of forecasting future trends, always a delicate issue in sociology. He does not, however, go beyond stating (and, in light of present knowledge, he could not validly do so) the various logical possibilities of what might occur in the future: the narrow gap might remain; it might completely disappear; or it might widen. In a sense, the inability to foretell future trends in this area resembles very much the situation of class differentials in the fertility of Western countries. As national birth rates went down, class differentials in fertility were increased. But the trend that followed during the first decades of the twentieth century was one of a narrowing in the degree of inverse correlation between fertility and class. As for predicting the future trend, two alternative views are vying with each other: There are those who anticipate a complete disappearance of class differentials and those who predict the ultimate emergence of a positive correlation between fertility and status.[1] But then it would seem far harder still to forecast the future of differential class fertility than of mortality. Class variations in mortality, after all, depend primarily on access to public health and medicine. In fertility, family size preferences must be taken into account. The latter are surely more variable and uncertain than the former.

In moving from life chances to a discussion of our readings about the ways of life of different strata, it is important to state at the outset that two competing hypotheses run through the vast sociological literature on this subject. Ralph H. Turner labels them the *culture variation* and the *subculture* hypotheses. The first holds that there is a uniform system of values, common to all classes, and that class differences consist mainly of variations of these values, differential commitment to them, and differential rates of deviation from them. In contrast, the assumption behind the subculture approach is that each class is to some extent a "self-contained universe, developing a distinctive set of values which guides its members' way of life." And, although these class subcultures "are constrained by the necessity to maintain working relations with other classes within a general national framework," they are nevertheless fundamentally different from each other, even contradictory in many respects.[2]

For analytic purposes, these two positions can be stated as if they were mutually

[1] Dennis H. Wrong, "Trends in Class Fertility in Western Nations," *The Canadian Journal of Economics and Political Science,* Vol. XXIV, No. 2, May, 1958, pp. 216–229.

[2] Ralph H. Turner, *The Social Context of Ambition,* San Francisco: Chandler Publishing Company, 1964, pp. 9–10.

exclusive, but in reality they are not. As a matter of fact, the major exponents of each do not deny the other but rather give less importance to the other position. Those who stress the common value system, foremost among whom is Parsons, also recognize the existence of "secondary or subsidiary or variant value patterns."[3] On the other hand, those who stress that different values are held by different classes do not deny that a common core of values also exists. Thus, the disagreement is mainly over the relative importance of common values or different class values in a society. Nevertheless, attempts have been made to reconcile these views as if they were inherently contradictory. Among those attempting reconciliation, Hyman Rodman devised the concept of "lower-class value stretch" as a way of resolving the "contraditions, or apparent contradictions"[4] between the preceding two positions. The concept refers to a supposed lower commitment of the lower classes to the general values of society—they accept and even look with favor on certain deviations from these values—and a wider range of specific values. Its validity, it seems, could be questioned on the basis, among other things, of Sutherland's material on "white-collar" crime. He demonstrated vast areas of criminal behavior of persons not in the lowest strata.[5] All strata seem to accept certain deviations but those deviations accepted in one may not be accepted in another.

Herbert Gans, as will become evident to the reader, clearly leans heavily toward the subculture hypothesis. In our selection from his *Urban Villagers,* he addresses himself to the main class subcultures in contemporary America. His descriptions are based on the voluminous literature that exists on this subject, as well as on his own observations. Because his is a concise presentation that manages to capture the essence of each subculture, it can serve as a frame in which to place the remaining selections in this part of the book. Alas, what is lacking in his pages is a description of the upper-class subculture. Perhaps this reflects the comparatively meager knowledge that we have of it, for the upper class is not easily accessible for sociological study.[6] Still, what we do know suggests that, although it is at the opposite side of the social hierarchy, its subculture has a number of similarities with that of the lower class. For example, the family structure of each has certain

[3] Talcott Parsons, *The Social System,* New York: Free Press, 1964, p. 169.

[4] Hyman Rodman, "The Lower-Class Value Stretch," *Social Forces,* Vol. 42, December, 1963, pp. 205–215.

[5] Yes, criminal statistics consistently show that crime varies inversely with social class. But despite the challenge by Sutherland, over three decades ago, that official statistics are not a valid measure, sociological analysis to this very day proceeds largely as if they were. Sutherland challenged the conventional concept of crime, which is the taking-off point of the theories of crime. The theories are incorrect because their concept of crime is insufficient, a reflection of the popular notion of it, which omits white-collar crime. Basically white-collar crime does not differ from the crime of the lower strata: both are violations of the criminal laws. They differ mainly in the implementation of the criminal laws that apply to them, Sutherland argues. The upper class has greater influence in administering them in their own interests.

Once the concept of crime is clarified to include white-collar crime, it puts into question the presumptive high association between low socioeconomic status and crime. And yet today—so many years after Sutherland gave us this conceptual clarification—we still do not know the comparative rate of criminality (*including white-collar crime*) among the various classes. Thus we cannot say with confidence more than could be deduced from the Sutherland essay: the *type* of criminal behavior varies with social class. Whether the total amount differs with class is still an unanswered question. And this, I am convinced, could be extended to deviant behavior in general. See Edwin H. Sutherland, *White Collar Crime*, New York: Holt, Rinehart and Winston, 1949; Gildert Geis, ed., *White-Collar Criminal,* New York: Atherton Press, 1968.

[6] For some insight into the upper-class subculture, see Digby Baltzell, *Philadelphia Gentlemen,* Glencoe, Illinois: Free Press, 1958, and his *Protestant Establishment,* New York: Vintage Books, 1964. Also see August B. Hollingshead and Frederick C. Redlich, *Social Class and Mental Illness*, New York: John Wiley & Sons, Inc., 1958.

*extended-family* features, in contrast to the isolated nuclear type of the middle classes. The function of extension in each is, however, different: in the upper class it serves mainly to perpetuate advantages; in the lower, it serves as a mechanism of mutual aid. Another example is that both lack emphasis on upward mobility, so characteristic of the middle-class subculture. Upper-class people are already on top, whereas the lower class tends to view social advancement as beyond them.

Gans, however, talks of two subcultures in the lower strata. He separates sharply working-class subculture from the lower-class one (corresponding to Warner's lower-lower and to Myrdal's underclass), as well as from the middle-class subculture. But the fourth subculture that he describes, what he terms *professional upper-middle class,* he considers a "variant of the middle class." In addition to the basic description of each, we find an answer to an implicit question: Why these different subcultures? And this is especially important because many sociologists begin with subculture—usually in the narrow sense of values—as a given and explain specific differential class behavior in terms of it. In some of these treatments the differential class values appear as the prime movers, and one gets no indication of where they come from or why they exist. Gans explains the differential class subcultures as *responses* that have developed to a common life situation in which people of a given stratum find themselves. He expresses it, however, a bit differently: they are responses to "the opportunities and deprivations that they encounter"—the occupational opportunities of males being especially crucial.

The author carries his analysis beyond the explanation of the "why" of differential class subculture into what he terms the *evaluation* of the working-class and lower-class subcultures. He sees the first as "a generally satisfactory way of adapting to the opportunities which society has made available" but also points to some negative features. But the net effect of the lower-class subculture he evaluates as negative, as pathological. One could rephrase his presentation in more neutral terms—but in what some might consider the usual functional parlance—by considering the positive and negative consequences of each of these subcultures for its participants.

Gans points to the negative consequences of the *female-based family*, which is so prevalent in the lower class. Its socialization of male children is particularly inadequate: it produces people who can only work at unskilled jobs and these are becoming scarce. Subsequently to the Gans presentation, it has been shown that such families are on the rise in the United States.[7] It has also been argued that certain trends of modernization and reduction of family economic roles lead to an increase in *matrifocality*.[8] More recently, on the basis of a study of families in public housing, Helen Icken Safa advanced the hypothesis that the modern welfare state provides one more condition that weakens the economic role of the man in the lower-class household:

> It is impossible to isolate any single factor of matrifocality—be it economic insecurity, the physical division of labor, or the modern welfare state. Any of these factors will hamper the man in his role as economic provider while the woman's role in caring for the household and children is left intact. Thus, whenever these factors operate, and

[7] Helen Icken Safa, "The Female-Based Household in Public Housing: A Case Study in Puerto Rico," *Human Organization,* Vol. 24, Summer, 1965, p. 135.

[8] Peter Kunstadter, "A Survey of Consanguine or Matrifocal Family," *American Anthropologist,* Vol. 65, No. 1, 1963, p. 64.

whenever the man is dependent largely on his economic role to maintain his position in the household, then matrifocal families are likely to develop.[9]

These studies suggest then that modern industrial society is working at a cross-purpose in this sphere. On the one hand, modernization and the welfare state lead to an increase in female-based households; on the other, it requires fewer of the type of males bred in such households, whose socialization makes them mostly fit for unskilled jobs that are diminishing. The implication is that a family structure is spreading in the lower class whose negative consequences for society as a whole may even outweigh such consequences for the lower-class individual.

A deeper insight into some negative consequences of the working-class subculture, as distinct from that of the lower class, is obtained from our next reading: "Blue-Collar Marriage—Barriers to Marital Communication" by Mirra Komarovsky. It is based on a study of fifty-eight marriages, using the case-study method, in a community of 50,000, with a heavy working-class population, which the author calls Glenton. These marriages are of people whom she designates the "stable blue-collar class" and that corresponds to Gans' working class, *not* his lower class. As Komarovsky explains in the book from which the selection here is taken, she set out to study the married life of what was intended to be a homogenous group of blue-collar workers: all husbands currently employed, native-born of native parents, not over forty years of age, with high school education or less, and parents of at least one child. But this restricted sample turned out to be not so homogenous with respect to the characteristics of their marriages. As the reader will gather from the selection, and it is true of most of the aspects of marriage studied by the author, the variation follows the level of education. (The major contrast appears between high school graduates and those who had not completed high school.) But, as she emphasizes, they are variations within the same subculture. The differences found between educational categories are "of degree, with considerable overlapping among them."[10]

Our selection from Komarovsky's book focuses on the socially structured barriers to communication between husbands and wives that are rooted in the working-class subculture. Very few shared interests are found between spouses. She traces back the sharp separation of male and female interests to the emphasis on male-female differences in early home socialization.[11] In addition, the home socialization results in a "trained incapacity to share," says the author. The subculture stresses the nonverbosity and reserve of men as distinct from the characteristics of women. Another factor, according to Kamarovsky, is "the impoverishment of the quality of life" among blue-collar people that severely limits their interests. It narrows the overlapping interests between husband and wife and also stunts personal development. There may be little or nothing to communicate. This, as the reader will gather, is quite different from the evaluation of the working-class subculture by Gans and resembles more his view of lower-class life. However,

[9] Safa, *op. cit.*, p. 139.

[10] Mirra Komarovsky, *Blue-Collar Marriage*, New York: Vintage Books, 1967, pp. 20–22.

[11] Relevant here is the subsequent analysis of working-class home socialization as failing to give individuals experience in role distance. See Julienne Ford, Douglas Young and Steven Box, "Functional Autonomy, Role Distance and Social Class," *British Journal of Sociology*, Vol. 18, December, 1967, pp. 370–381; for a thorough analysis of the findings of empirical studies in the United States over a 25-year period of social-class differences in child rearing, see Urie Bronfenbrenner, "Socialization and Social Class Through Time and Space," in E. E. Maccoby, T. M. Newcomb, and E. L. Hartley, eds., *Readings in Social Psychology*, New York: Henry Holt and Co., 1958, pp. 400–425.

we also get in the Komarovsky presentation a glimpse of some positive consequences of the working-class subculture. They are brought out indirectly when the author turns her attention to those couples in her sample whose communication is quite satisfying to each partner and who, nevertheless, in their values and behavior adhere to the working-class subculture. Despite the vulnerabilities inherent in that culture, these marriages function well because they benefit from *special supports* that are also rooted in the working-class subculture. These are the availability of close relatives and friends who fulfill for both, but primarily for the wife, functions lacking in marriage.

The crucial tie between family and stratification comes through not only in the readings by Gans and Kamarovsky but also in many of the theoretical and empirical articles throughout the book. What makes Kent Geiger's article, especially written for this volume, so pungent is that it deals with this family tie in the Soviet Union, a society that once made a determined effort to abolish it. First of all, in the Soviet Union, as elsewhere, there are the obvious differential chances and advantages that are automatically transmitted to children, because they live together with their parents, that can be subsumed under standard of living. The differences in such areas as housing and consumer goods and services may in a sense be sharper than in Western democracies because of the greater shortages of these goods in the Soviet Union.

Apart from the pronounced differences in the standard of living, there is the widespread pattern, discussed by Geiger, of persons in higher positions obtaining special access to opportunities and services for themselves and their families.[12] And even in the Soviet Union differential home socialization of the different strata plays an important part, despite the fact that socialization by agencies other than the family is unquestionably stronger there than in Western countries. The government, youth organizations, mass media, and so on, make a consistent effort to instill official values and approved modes of behavior in the entire population, irrespective of socioeconomic position. Nevertheless, we learn from the evidence presented by Geiger that such behavior varies from stratum to stratum. Take, for example, religious behavior in the Soviet Union, which is branded as a "survival" perpetuated by the family. There is a marked inverse relationship between religious practice and social stratum or what Geiger refers to as "social level." Parenthetically, this represents an opposite relation to that which exists in the United States. Numerous studies reveal a strong positive relationship between church participation and social class in America.[13] But then religious observance represents normative behavior in America and deviant behavior in the Soviet Union.

If religious and other behavior that is in conflict with the societal norms varies inversely with social position in the Soviet Union, the opposite seems to hold true for certain kinds of normatively approved behavior. Geiger tells us that evidence points to political conformity varying directly with *social level.* Also, the proportion

[12] For additional corroboration, see the impressive evidence on the advantages of Soviet children from the upper strata over their working-class competitors in seeking managerial positions assembled by David Granick, *The Red Executive,* Garden City: Doubleday Company, 1960, chap. 3. Also see Janina Markiewicz–Lagneau, "Les Problèmes de Mobilité Sociale en U.R.S.S.," *Cahiers du Monde Russe et Soviétique,* Vol. 7, No. 2, 1966, pp. 160–188.

[13] Eric Goode, "Social Class and Church Participation," *American Journal of Sociology,* Vol. 72, July, 1966, pp. 102–111; N. J. Demerath, III, *Social Class in American Protestantism,* Chicago: Rand McNally and Co., 1965.

of youngsters who graduate from high school and attend a university varies directly. There is, moreover, a positive association between parental societal status and the educational and occupational aspirations of youth, quite similar to the pattern found in the United States.

Some light is thrown on American class differences in educational and occupational aspiration by Mizruchi. In the selection here from his book, *Success and Opportunity,* he concentrates on the values of different classes, specifically values related to the American notion of success. The author set before himself the larger task of testing Merton's theory of anomie: that the social structure exercises pressure on lower-class individuals to engage in nonconforming behavior. To summarize Merton's well-known thesis: the goals of success are held out as legitimate objectives for all in the United States while the acceptable means of reaching these goals are largely unavailable to people in the lower classes. This results in a tendency in these classes toward practices that deviate from institutional norms.[14]

Some time ago Herbert H. Hyman questioned whether the goals of success have been uniformly assimilated in the American population.[15] Responding to this, Merton stated that ". . . among the problems calling for further research [is] the following: the extent to which Americans in different social strata have in fact assimilated the same culturally induced goals and values."[16] Mizruchi's work represents such research and it proceeds very much along the lines set by Herbert Hyman in his pioneering essay, "The Value System of Different Classes." The basic questions, quite similar to Hyman's, to which Mizruchi's empirical study addressed itself were: "What is the distribution of success values among the social classes?" "To what extent do members of different classes hold other values that aid or hinder them in their efforts to achieve success?" "To what extent do these members believe that opportunities for getting ahead are available to them?"

One of his findings is that education is more highly valued as an end in itself in the middle than in the lower strata. His contention is that the greater importance given to education as an end value by the middle classes provides them with greater opportunities for advancement.

If ability and formal education have long vied for first place as a means for advancement in American society, the latter has by now gained its victory. One must keep in mind that achievement in many positions that rank high in occupational status actually requires formal education. Occupational achievement is positively correlated with both amount and quality of education. In the words of Parsons, ". . . in our society experience in the course of formal education is to be regarded as a series of apprenticeships for adult occupational roles."[17]

That this kind of experience differs considerably with social class has been amply demonstrated by numerous empirical studies conducted in the last twenty years.[18] They consistently show a positive correlation between social class and academic achievement. Lower-class children tend to be poorer in school performance (in terms of grades, failures, and scholastic awards) and much higher in

[14] Robert K. Merton, "Social Structure and Anomie," in *Social Theory and Social Structure,* Glencoe, Illinois: Free Press, 1957, pp. 131–160.

[15] Herbert H. Hyman, "The Value System of Different Classes: A Social Psychological Contribution to the Analysis of Stratification," in Reinhard Bendix and Seymour Martin Lipset, eds., *Class, Status, and Power,* Glencoe, Illinois: Free Press, 1953, pp. 426–442.

[16] Merton, "Continuities in the Theory of Social Structure and Anomie," in *op. cit.,* p. 170.

[17] Parsons, *op. cit.,* p. 240.

[18] For a summary of their findings, see Robert E. Herriott and Nancy Hoyt St. John, *Social Class and the Urban School,* New York: John Wiley and Sons, Inc., 1966, pp. 4–12, 22–25, 203–211.

early withdrawal from high school (dropouts). In the newer studies the focus has shifted from that on the social class of the individual child to a focus on the social class composition of the school and its effects on learning. The essence of these effects is well captured in one sentence by Bernard Barber, "The public schools, then, do train a small number of their students for social mobility, but most of their students they train to keep pretty much the same class position as their parents have."[19]

Thus working-class children land overwhelmingly in working-class occupations as adults. How these people generally feel about their work comes through vividly in the Komarovsky selection discussed earlier. Her description of their disdain and boredom reads very much like the one by Harvey Swados, who, in "The Myth of the Happy Worker," exposed the worker's attitude toward his work as generally "compounded of hatred, shame, and resignation."[20] Considering that their kind of work produces feelings of powerlessness, meaninglessness, and self-estrangement—as contrasted with the self-actualization of "creative" work—it is not surprising that working-class people tend to view work simply as a means of getting things that one needs or desires and not as a virtue in itself.

[19] Bernard Barber, *Social Stratification,* New York: Harcourt, Brace and Company, 1957, p. 257.
[20] Maurice R. Stein, Arthur J. Vidich, and David M. White, eds., *Identity and Anxiety,* Glencoe, Illinois: Free Press, 1960, pp. 198–204.

# SOCIAL CLASS, LIFE EXPECTANCY AND OVER-ALL MORTALITY*

*Aaron Antonovsky*

. . . recalling what happened when an "unsinkable" trans-Atlantic luxury liner, the *Titanic*, rammed an iceberg on her maiden voyage in 1912 . . . The official casualty lists showed that only 4 first class female passengers (3 voluntarily chose to stay on the ship) of a total of 143 were lost. Among the second class passengers, 15 of 93 females drowned; and among the third class, 81 of 179 female passengers went down with the ship.[1]

Death is the final lot of all living beings. But, as the tragic experience of the *Titanic* passengers dramatically illustrates, the time at which one dies is related to one's class. The intent of this paper is to examine the evidence which bears upon the closeness of this relationship, ranging as far back as the data will allow. It will first focus on the question of life expectancy at birth, and subsequently turn to that of overall mortality.

## STUDIES OF LIFE EXPECTANCY

The average infant born today in the Western world can look forward, barring unforeseen events and radical changes in present trends, to a life span of about 70 years. That this has not always been the case for the human infant—and still is not for by far most infants born today—is well known. Whatever the situation prior to the era of recorded history, for the greater part of this era, that is, until the nineteenth century, most men lived out less than half their Biblical span of years.

In what is probably the first study of a total population, Halley, using data for the city of Breslau, Germany, for 1687 to 1691, calculated an average life expectancy at birth of 33.5 years.[2] Henry's estimate for the expectation of life of Parisian children born at the beginning of the eighteenth century was 23.5 years.[3] Half a century later, in the Vienna of 1752 to 1755, of every 1,000 infants born alive, only 590 survived their first year, 413 their fifth year, and 359 their fifteenth year.[4] . . .

Ansell found a life expectation at birth for the total British population in 1874 of about 43 years.[5] At about the same time, the reported figures for Italy were somewhat lower: 35 years (1871 to 1880); 36.2 years for males, 35.65 years for females (1881–1882).[6]

Whatever the discrepancies and unreliabilities of these various sets of data, they consistently paint a picture of the Western world up to recent centuries which is quite similar to that of the world of presently "developing" societies until the last decade or two. Moreover, in the period of recorded history prior to the eighteenth century, no sizable increment had been added to the average life span. But if, from Greco-Roman times through the eighteenth or perhaps even the nineteenth century, the mythical "average" infant could anticipate living some 20 to 30 years, does any evidence indicate that dramatic class differences existed? Though the evidence

From The Milbank Memorial Fund *Quarterly*, Vol. XLV, No. 2, April, 1967. Reprinted by permission of the Millbank Memorial Fund.

[1] Hollingshead, August B. and Redlich, Frederick C., *Social Class and Mental Illness*, New York, John Wiley & Sons, Inc., 1958, p. 6, citing Lord, Walter, *A Night to Remember*, New York, Henry Holt, 1955, p. 107.

[2] Cited in Dublin, Louis I., Lotka, Alfred J. and Spiegelman, Mortimer, *Length of Life*, revised edition, New York, Ronald Press, 1949, pp. 34, 30–43. The book as a whole is one of the most detailed treatments of the subject of life expectancy.

[3] Henry, Louis, The Population of France in the 18th Century, *in* Glass, David V. and Eversley, D. E. C. (Editors), *Population in History*, London, Edward Arnold, 1965, p. 444.

[4] Peller, Sigismund, Births and Deaths Among Europe's Ruling Families Since 1500, *in* Glass and Eversley, *op. cit.*, p. 94.

[5] Ansell, C., Vital Statistics of Families in the Upper and Professional Classes, *Journal of the Royal Statistical Society*, 37, 464, 1874, cited *in* Titmuss, Richard, *Birth, Poverty and Wealth*, London, Hamish Hamilton Medical Books, 1943, p. 19.

[6] Cipolla, Carlo M., Four Centuries of Italian Demographic Development, *in* Glass and Eversley, *op. cit.*, pp. 578, 582.

is perforce limited, the answer would seem to be no.[7]

. . . . . . . . . . . . . . . . . . . . . . . . . . . . . . . . . . . .

In other words, given a society which, though it manages to survive, does so at or near what might be called a rock-bottom level of life expectancy, one is not likely to find great differences among the strata of that society.

The data suggest the possibility that the trend in the nineteenth century, and perhaps even earlier, was toward a substantial widening of class differences. No report is available comparing the life expectancies of social strata of the population prior to the nineteenth century.

Can any conclusion be drawn from these data,[8] most of which are admittedly tenuous and not overly reliable? A crude picture . . . could be inferred which indicates the following. The bulk of recorded history was one of high birth and high death rates, which offset each other and led to at most a very small increase in population. During the first 16 centuries of the Christian era, world population increased from about one-quarter to one-half billion people, an annual growth rate of about .005 per cent. Conceivably, throughout this period, no substantial differentials in life expectancy could be found among different social strata of the population. From 1650 to 1850 world population again doubled, most of the increase being in the Western world, representing an average annual increase of .05 per cent. These two centuries would seem to mark the emergence of an increasing class gap in life expectancy, starting slowly but gathering increasing momentum and reaching its peak about the time Malthus made his observations. On the one hand, the life expectancy of the middle and upper strata of the population increased at a rapid rate. On the other, the lowest strata's life expectancy may have increased much more slowly or, conceivably, even declined as an industrial proletariat emerged. At some time during the nineteenth century, probably in the latter half, this trend was reversed, and the class gap began to diminish. This is reflected in the doubling of the world's population, again mostly in the West, this time in the 80 years from 1850 to 1930. In recent decades, the class gap has narrowed to what may be the smallest differential in history, but evidence of a linear gradient remains, with a considerable differential, given man's life span.

This supposition—not claimed to be more than that—seems to be of more than historical interest. It is, for two important reasons, most germane to the concern of this paper. In the first place, the scientist, no less than the lay person, often seems, in considering the question of the relationship between class and health, to be beset by a nineteenth century notion of perpetual progress. Ideologically committed, in this area, to the desirability of the disappearance of the class gap, he tends to assume, with or without data, that the historical picture is unilinear; the history of mankind, in his view, shows steady progress in this respect. The realization that this may well be an inaccurate image, that the relationship is

[7] Dublin, Lotka and Spiegelman, *op. cit.*, pp. 31–32; Peller, *op. cit.*, p. 95.

[8] Pages reviewing the data are omitted. The studies containing the data are listed here (C. S. H.). Villerme, Louis R., *Tableau de L'état Physique et Moral des Ouvriers*, Vol. 2, Paris, Jules Renouard et Cie., 1840, pp. 251, 376–385; Farren, *Observations on the Mortality Among the Members of the British Peerage*, cited *in* Titmuss, *op. cit.*, p. 17; Morris, Jeremy N., *Uses of Epidemiology*, second edition, Edinburgh and London, E. and S. Livingstone, 1964, pp. 161–162; Titmuss, *op. cit.*, p. 18; Bailey, A. H. and Day, A., On the Rate of Mortality Prevailing Amongst the Families of the Peerage During the 19th Century, *Journal of the Institute of Actuaries*, 9, 305, cited in Collins, Selwyn D., *Economic Status and Health*, Washington, United States Government Printing Office, 1927, p. 14; Farr, William, *Vital Statistics. A Memorial Volume of Selections from the Reports and Writings of William Farr*, Humphreys, N. A. (Editor), London, The Sanitary Institute, 1885, pp. 393–394, also cited *in* Titmuss, *op. cit.*, pp. 17–18; Ansell, C., cited *in* Titmuss, *op. cit.*, p. 19; Mayer, Albert J. and Hauser, Philip, Class Differentiations in Expectation of Life at Birth, *in* Bendix, Reinhard and Lipset, Seymour M. (Editors), *Class, Status and Power*, Glencoe, Illinois, Free Press, 1953, pp. 281–284; Tietze, Christopher, Life Tables for Social Classes in England, Milbank Memorial Fund *Quarterly*, 21, 182–187, April, 1943; Yeracaris, Constantine A., Differential Mortality, General and Cause-Specific, in Buffalo, 1939–41, *Journal of the American Statistical Association*, 50, 1235–1247, December, 1955; Tayback, Matthew, The Relationship of Socioeconomic Status and Expectation of Life, *Baltimore Health News*, 34, 139–144, April, 1957.

more complex, suggests a more cautious orientation. Such an orientation would suggest various possibilities: a narrowing gap being transformed into one which is widening; differing positions, on any given index of health, of different strata of the population at various times.

The second reason for stressing the possibility of a curvilinear relationship between class and life expectancy over time is that such a relationship may help in forming an adequate idea of the relationship between class and health, and, more broadly, an adequate theory of disease. Once the search begins for explanations of why, in a given period, one stratum seems to be making more health progress than another, and less so in another period, factors are uncovered which must be integrated into a theory of disease.

Thus, for example, McKeown and Brown, arguing that the increase in the population of England in the eighteenth century was overwhelmingly due to the decline in mortality, attribute that decline to improvements in the environment (housing, water supply, refuse disposal, nutrition) rather than to any advances in medical care.[9] Supposedly, such improvements first appeared in the upper strata of society, and only slowly percolated downward. This would explain the increasing class differences in life expectancy. Once the environmental sanitation gap began to narrow, some reversal in the trend could be expected which, however, might soon be offset by other factors; e.g., the malnutrition of poverty. The point is that a very careful collection of data over time and the search for ups and downs may serve to pinpoint the various factors, and their modes of interaction, which influence overall mortality or the course of any specific disease.

## CLASS DIFFERENCES IN MORTALITY BEFORE WORLD WAR II

Twentieth century investigators have by and large focused on class differences in mortality rates. Chapin's study of Providence, Rhode Island, probably provides the earliest relevant information. Using census and tax records of 1865, he located all but about 200 of the 2,000 taxpayers, covering a total of 10,515 individuals. Every deceased person in that year was assigned to either the taxpayer or non-taxpayer group. Chapin then calculated the death rates per thousand in each group. The crude annual death rate of the latter (24.8 per 1,000 living) was more than double that of the taxpayers (10.8). This disparity is found in all but the five- to nine-years age cohort, and is greatest in the productive years (30 to 49) and in the 70 and over cohort. Since the non-taxpayer group includes more than 80 per cent of the population, had Chapin been able to make a finer class breakdown he presumably would have found even greater differences between the top and bottom strata. . . .

The earliest data presented by Collins refer to Danish mortality rates from 1865 to 1874, the 1870 census having been used to obtain denominator information.[10] Individuals were assigned to high, middle or poor classes on the basis of the head of household's occupation. . . . The age-adjusted mean annual death rates, by sex, of the population aged 20 and over in Copenhagen and in other towns . . . the data show that class differences are greater in Copenhagen than in provincial towns, and greater among males than among females. More significantly, although the rates show primarily an inverse class gradient, the differences between the high and middle classes are relatively small compared to the gap between them and the poor class. . . .

The first of many ecological studies was Rowntree's well-known survey of York, England, in 1899.[11] Rowntree divided the wage-earner areas of the city of York into three levels. The overall death rates per thousand persons (not age-standardized) he reports for 1899 are: highest, 13.5; middle, 20.7; poorest, 27.8 (ratios of 100:153:206). In this case, unlike the earlier Danish data, the inverse gradient is quite regular.

[9] McKeown, Thomas and Brown, R. G., Medical Evidence Related to English Population Changes in the Eighteenth Century, *Population Studies*, 9, 119–241, 1955 (reprinted *in* Glass and Eversley, *op. cit.*, pp. 285–307).

[10] Collins, *op. cit.*, p. 13.

[11] Rowntree, Seebohm B., *Poverty and Progress: A Second Social Survey of York*, London, Longmans, Green & Co., 1941, p. 296.

In a paper focusing on later data, Britten calculates overall death rates for 1900 in the nine states and the District of Columbia, which then comprised the death registration area.[12] He compared white-collar rates to those for the "laboring and servant" class in three age groups. Taking the white-collar death rate as 100, the ratios for the lower class group were: for ages 15–24, 151; for ages 25–44, 165; and for ages 45–64, 159.

As a prologue to her analysis of 1950 death rates, Guralnick presents, without analysis, the full set of data upon which Britten evidently based his calculations, as well as similar date for 1890.[13] . . . The most striking fact about these data is the very sizable difference, at all ages, between the "laboring and servant" class and all other groups. In both 1890 and 1900, the ratio of this class is highest in ages 25–44 and 45–64, somewhat lower at ages 15–24, and lowest—though still relatively high—in the 65 and over category. An interesting pattern is shown by the clerical and official group: in the youngest age category its ratio is quite high, in 1900 approaching that of the lowest class; in each successive age category its ratio goes down, so that in the 65 and over category it has by far the lowest mortality rate. . . .

Huber[14] examined occupational mortality in France for 1907–1908, calculating death rates on the basis of the 1906 census. His figures are primarily for individual occupations, but he does give age-specific death rates for four broad groups. . . . Managers and officials consistently show the lowest rates. Clerical workers have, at ages 25–34, the highest rates, but thereafter craftsmen and kindred workers have higher rates. The rates of these two groups are, throughout, closer to each other than to those of the managerial group. Class differentials are greatest at ages 45–54. Private household workers, presumably a low status group, have relatively low rates. Since the data refer only to males, who presumably served primarily in well-to-do households, such rates need not be inexplicable. . . .

In a relatively early review of morbidity and mortality data, Sydenstricker, one of the pioneers in the field, cites Bruno's study of 22,600 deaths among 1.3 million wage-earners in 1915–1916, with life insurance in 12 American companies, showing a clear inverse occupational gradient.[15] The death rates per 1,000 policyholders were: professional and semiprofessionals, 3.3; skilled workmen, 3.7; semiskilled workmen, 4.5; unskilled workmen, 4.8. Using the rate of the professional class as 100, the ratios of the other three were 112, 136 and 145.

. . . . . . . . . . . . . . . . . . . . . . . . . . . . . . . . . .

Whitney's study using 1930 data was the first large-scale American study following the pattern which had been set by the British Registrar General.[16] Death certificate data were obtained from ten states: Alabama, Connecticut, Illinois, Kansas, Massachusetts, Minnesota, New Jersey, New York, Ohio and Wisconsin. These states contained 39 per cent of the gainfully employed. The census was used to obtain denominator information. Analysis was limited to males aged 15 to 64, in an attempt to limit the unreliability introduced by retirement. Age-standardized data are presented within the social-economic classification developed by Edwards and used standardly by the United States Census.

As can be seen in Table 1, mortality rates vary inversely with class in the total age group of 15–64. Only the proprietor group is out of line. If retail dealers, whose rate is 8.4, are excluded from this category, the

[12] Britten, Rollo H., Mortality Rates by Occupational Class in the U.S., *Public Health Reports*, 49, 1102, September, 1934.

[13] Guralnick, Lillian, Mortality by Occupation and Industry Among Men 20 to 64 Years of Age, U.S., 1950, *Vital Statistics, Special Reports*, 53, 56, Sepember, 1962.

[14] Huber, Michel, *Bulletin Statistique General de la France*, fasc IV, 1912, quoted *in* Daric, Jean, Mortality, Occupation, and Socio-Economic Status, *Vital Statistics, Special Reports*, 33, 175–187, September, 1951.

[15] Bruno, Frank J., Illness and Dependency, *Miscellaneous Contributions*, No. 9, The Committee on the Costs of Medical Care, Washington, 1931, cited *in* Sydenstricker, Edgar, *Health and Environment*, New York, McGraw-Hill Book Company, 1933, p. 94.

[16] Whitney, Jessamine S., *Death Rates by Occupation, Based on Data of the U.S. Census Bureau*, 1930, New York, National Tuberculosis Association, 1934, pp. 17, 32.

**TABLE 1 Annual Death Rates per 1,000 Gainfully Occupied Males, Aged 15 to 64 Years (Age-Standardized) by Age Groups According to Socioeconomic Class, 1930**[17]

| Socioeconomic Class | Age Groups* | | | | | | | |
|---|---|---|---|---|---|---|---|---|
| | 15–64 | | 15–24 | | 25–44 | | 45–64 | |
| | Rate | Ratio** | Rate | Ratio | Rate | Ratio | Rate | Ratio |
| All gainfully employed males | 9.1 | 100 | 3.2 | 100 | 5.5 | 100 | 17.9 | 100 |
| Professional men | 6.7 | 74 | 2.3 | 72 | 3.5 | 64 | 16.2 | 90 |
| Proprietors, managers and officials | 7.9 | 87 | 3.1 | 97 | 4.2 | 76 | 15.8 | 88 |
| Clerks and kindred workers | 7.8 | 86 | 2.3 | 72 | 4.1 | 74 | 16.5 | 92 |
| Skilled workers and foremen | 8.3 | 91 | 3.0 | 94 | 4.9 | 89 | 17.1 | 96 |
| Semiskilled workers | 10.1 | 111 | 3.2 | 100 | 6.1 | 111 | 20.8 | 116 |
| Unskilled workers | 14.5 | 159 | 4.7 | 147 | 9.6 | 174 | 24.8 | 138 |

* The age-standardized figures for the age group 15–64 are based on the 53 occupational groups with 500 or more deaths (Whitney, Table 8, p. 32). These cover 79 per cent of the gainfully employed. This set of data was selected as more reliable than the figures for all deaths, given by Whitney in Table 1, p. 17. The trends in the two sets of data are very similar. The age-specific data are only available in Whitney's Table 1, and cover the entire surveyed population.

** Rate for all gainfully employed males = 100.

rate would be 7.0, making a linear relationship. The curve, however, is not smooth, as can be seen clearly from the ratios presented in the table. The largest difference is found between unskilled and semiskilled workers, with a sizable difference between the latter and skilled workers. Beyond this level the differences, although existent, are relatively small.

The same general pattern appears in each of the three age-specific sets of data. The spread, however, is greatest in the 25–44 age group and least in the oldest group. In the latter, differences among the four occupational categories from skilled workers and up are almost nonexistent. This study indicates, then, that class is most intimately related to mortality rates among the unskilled and, secondarily among the semiskilled workers, and during middle age.[17]

Sheps and Watkins[18] sought to overcome the weakness of ecological studies by utilizing information obtained in careful sociological study which grouped areas in New Haven, Connecticut, into "natural areas." The boundary lines of these areas were such that information about census tracts could be used for purposes of setting denominators and standardizing for age. . . . The seven areas were ranked from best to worst, based on a composite of factors including rental, delinquency rates, social standing and financial dependency. All data were age-adjusted.

Taking the average annual death rate over the five-year period of the best area (8.0 per 1,000 persons) as 100, the ratios of the other six areas, going down the socio-economic scale, were: 111, 110, 128, 136, 145, 148. Other than the fact that the rates for the second and third highest areas are almost identical, a clear inverse linear relationship is found. When the authors combined the seven areas into three, the range was substantially narrowed (100:114:134). The strongest relationship between mortality rates and economic level were found at ages 0–5 and 25–64.

[17] Whitney's data are quoted and discussed by Britten, *op. cit.*, and Guralnick, *op. cit.*

[18] Sheps, Cecil and Watkins, J. H., Mortality in the Socio-Economic Districts of New Haven, *Yale Journal of Biology and Medicine*, 20, 51–80, October, 1947

## WORLD WAR II TO THE PRESENT

Mortality rates in the Netherlands are among the lowest in the world. In this context, determination of social class differences becomes of particular interest. DeWolff and Meerdink[19] studied the mortality rates of gainfully employed males, aged 15–64 in Amsterdam in 1947–1952, using the 1947 census to provide denominator information. . . . The difference between the most favored group and the workers (117:100) barely reaches statistical significance. In contrast to the findings of all other studies, unskilled workers do not differ from skilled workers. Only the clerical group is relatively high (though a death rate of 5.1 is, as such, quite low). The authors suggest two reasons for this rate. First, the clerical workers do not reach the standards of physical fitness required to obtain civil service employment, which would have placed them in the top level. Second, many are probably children of manual workers and are not sufficiently fit to work.

By the 1950s, the number of studies of socioeconomic mortality differentials had increased considerably. . . . Tayback[20] divided Baltimore's 168 census tracts on the basis of the 1950 median tract rentals, grouping them into equal-sized population quintiles. . . . In overall terms, a clear inverse class gradient is seen, the male slope being somewhat steeper than the female slope, with very few figures being out of line. The gap tends to be quite large in the younger age groups, where the death rate is low. Class differences in middle age (35–54) are very sizable. At this age, the major differences seem to be at the top and bottom, between the highest and next-highest and between the lowest and second-lowest economic levels. Differences remain considerable at ages 55–64, but tend to become much smaller thereafter.

Ellis conducted a very similar study in Houston.[21] The index used to rank census tracts was a modification of the index of social rank developed by Shevky and Williams, which utilizes measures of education, occupation and median family income. Tracts were grouped into quintiles, each of which contained 12 or 13 tracts. . . . Although class differentials do appear, they differ from those in other studies. The range of differences is smaller, though still substantial. The two top groups of tracts, for males, and the three top, for females, are quite similar in their death rates. Most puzzling, perhaps, is the fact that males in the lowest tract level have a lower rate than do those in the adjacent level. Ellis suggests as a possible explanation the availability of free medical treatment for the lowest group. Group 4, not having such an advantage but having a limited income, may utilize funds for the females, who do have a lower rate than the females in group 5, whereas the males go on working and refrain from using such funds for themselves. . . .

Stockwell, whose concern was methodological as well as substantive, presents data exactly parallel to the above. . . . He also used a modified form of the Shevky-Williams index, studied deaths in 1949–1951, and included about one-fifth of the number of tracts in each socioeconomic level. Stockwell's data pertain to Providence and Hartford. The class differentials in these two cities are quite similar to those in Houston. In Providence, little difference is found among the top three levels of males or the top two levels of females. Hartford females do not differ among all five strata; levels 2 and 3 and levels 4 and 5 have almost identical rates.

Stockwell proceeded to compute rank order correlation coefficients between the census tracts in each city ranked by age-sex-standardized death rates and each of eight socioeconomic variables (occupation, two education variables, two income variables,

[19] DeWolff, P. and Meerdink, J., Mortality Rates in Amsterdam According to Profession, *Proceedings of the World Population Conference*, 1954, Vol. I, New York, United Nations (E/Conf. 13/413), pp. 53–55.

[20] Tayback, *op. cit.*, p. 142.

[21] Ellis, John M., Socio-Economic Differentials in Mortality from Chronic Diseases, *Social Problems*, 5, 30–36, July, 1957. Reprinted in expanded form in Jaco, E. Gartly (Editor), *Patients, Physicians and Illness*, Glencoe, Illinois, Free Press, 1958, p. 32.

two rent variables, crowding). In all cases, the correlation coefficients were significant.[22]

Since the British Registrar General system of social classification is the richest source of data on mortality differences over time among different socioeconomic levels, a number of attempts have been made to construct a comparable ranking in the United States. Breslow and Buell,[23] using the 1950 census for denominator data, classified all deaths of California males, aged 20–64, from 1949 to 1951, in one of five occupational classes. . . .

For the entire age group, a rough inverse gradient is seen between class and mortality. . . .

A more ambitious attempt along the same lines was conducted by Guralnick, who analyzed all male deaths in age group 20 to 64 in the United States in 1950.[24] In view of the fact that one primary purpose was to compare the United States data with the British, Guralnick collapsed classes II to IV to make this intermediate group comparable in the two countries. . . . For the entire age group, the picture is quite similar to that presented in the California study: a linear inverse gradient, with the intermediate occupational level being closer to class I, and the major gap occurring between class V and the intermediate group. Another publication by Guralnick,[25] in which standard mortality ratios are given separately for the five classes, presents figures almost identical with the California figures. The standardized mortality ratios for all United States males aged 20–64, in 1950, from class I to class V, are: 83, 84, 96, 97, 120. These ratios are for whites only, except for class I, which contains a few nonwhites. Once again classes I and II do not differ, nor do classes III and IV.

Examination of the age-specific rates . . . shows the largest class gap to lie in the 25 to 44 age group, with classes II to IV being closer to class I than to class V. A considerable gap remains at ages 45–54, but it is substantially narrowed by ages 55–64.

Guralnick also analyzed the same 1950 data along more traditional American lines, using the occupational classification developed by Edwards for the United States Census.[26] This scheme seeks to rank occupations by socioeconomic levels. The standardized mortality ratios presented in Table 2, for white males aged 25–59, shows an inverse gradient, but one which does not distinguish among all of the eight occupational groups. The lowest ratios are found among the top three groups; they are followed closely by sales, skilled and semiskilled workers, whose ratios are identical. Service workers fare substantially poorer, and, finally, laborers have a considerably higher mortality ratio.

This pattern does not hold in all age groups. Prior to age 30, only the roughest

[22] Stockwell, Edward G., *Socio-Economic Mortality Differentials in Hartford, Conn. and Providence, R. I.: A Methodological Critique,* unpublished doctoral dissertation, Brown University, 1960. Relevant papers published by Stockwell based on his dissertation include: ——, A Critical Examination of the Relationship Between Socioeconomic Status and Mortality, *American Journal of Public Health*, 53, 956–964, June, 1963; ——, Socioeconomic Status and Mortality, *Connecticut Health Bulletin*, 77, 10–13, December, 1963.

Stockwell investigated the difference made in the analysis of socioeconomic mortality data when different indices of class are used. He notes that the precise conclusions one draws will "vary considerably with the methodological conditions characterizing a particular study," however the overall patterns are sufficiently similar so that, for present purposes, it is adequate to refer to only one or two of his measures. Since many studies reported in the present paper used median rental, however, it is important to note that Stockwell's data indicate that, of all eight variables, this is the poorest predictor of mortality rates.

[23] Breslow, Lester and Buell, Philip, Mortality from Coronary Heart Disease and Physical Activity of Work in California, *Journal of Chronic Diseases*, 11, 421–44, April, 1960.

[24] Guralnick, Lillian, Socioeconomic Differences in Mortality by Cause of Death: United States, 1950 and England and Wales, 1949–1953, *in International Population Conference, Ottawa,* 1963, *op. cit.*, p. 298.

[25] ——, Mortality by Occupation Level and Cause of Death Among Men 20 to 64 Years of Age, U.S., 1950, *Vital Statistics, Special Reports,* 53, 452–481, September, 1963. For an earlier paper reporting provisional death rates in the same population by the five classes and seven age categories, *see* Moriyama, Iwao M. and Guralnick, Lillian, Occupational and Social Class Differences in Mortality, *in Trends and Differentials in Mortality*, New York, Milbank Memorial Fund, 1956, p. 66.

**TABLE 2 Annual Death Rates per 1,000, and Ratios, White Males, by Age and Major Occupation Group, United States, 1950[26]**

| | | Age Group | | | | | | | | | | | | | |
|---|---|---|---|---|---|---|---|---|---|---|---|---|---|---|---|
| | 25–29 | 20–24 | | 25–29 | | 30–34 | | 35–44 | | 45–54 | | 55–59 | | 60–64 | |
| MAJOR OCCUPATION GROUP | SMR** | X | Y* | X | Y | X | Y | X | Y | X | Y | X | Y | X | Y |
| All occupations | 93 | 1.7 | 100 | 1.6 | 100 | 2.0 | 100 | 3.9 | 100 | 10.1 | 100 | 19.4 | 100 | 28.8 | 100 |
| Professional, technical, kindred | 82 | 1.2 | 73 | 1.2 | 70 | 1.5 | 76 | 3.2 | 81 | 9.4 | 93 | 18.9 | 98 | 29.2 | 101 |
| Managers, officials, proprietors, nonfarm | 85 | 1.5 | 86 | 1.3 | 79 | 1.5 | 76 | 3.3 | 85 | 9.5 | 94 | 18.9 | 98 | 28.9 | 100 |
| Clerical, kindred | 83 | 0.9 | 54 | 1.3 | 78 | 1.5 | 76 | 3.3 | 86 | 9.6 | 95 | 18.2 | 94 | 26.9 | 93 |
| Sales | 94 | 1.1 | 62 | 1.1 | 66 | 1.7 | 82 | 3.6 | 94 | 11.0 | 109 | 21.7 | 112 | 31.8 | 110 |
| Craftsmen, foremen, kindred | 94 | 1.8 | 103 | 1.6 | 97 | 2.0 | 99 | 4.0 | 102 | 10.1 | 100 | 20.8 | 107 | 32.1 | 111 |
| Operatives, kindred | 94 | 1.8 | 106 | 1.8 | 108 | 2.2 | 107 | 4.1 | 106 | 10.3 | 102 | 19.4 | 100 | 28.6 | 99 |
| Service, except private household | 116 | 1.2 | 72 | 1.6 | 98 | 2.4 | 117 | 5.1 | 133 | 13.8 | 136 | 22.4 | 116 | 29.2 | 101 |
| Laborers, except farm and mine | 131 | 2.6 | 149 | 2.8 | 171 | 3.6 | 178 | 6.5 | 167 | 14.5 | 144 | 23.8 | 123 | 34.9 | 121 |

* X = death rate per 1,000. Y = ratio, computed on the basis of rate for all occupations in each age category = 100.

** Standardized mortality ratios are computed on the basis of the entire population. Since nonwhite are excluded in this table, SMRs can fall below 100.

[26] Guralnick, Lillian, Mortality by Occupation and Industry Among Men 20 to 64 Years of Age, U.S., 1950, *Vital Statistics, Special Reports,* 53, 59, 61, 84–86, September, 1962.

gradient appears, though laborers fare markedly worst. A clear gradient appears in the 30–34 groups, which is maintained in the next ten year cohort. In both cases, the ratios of the top three occupational groups are nearly identical. This pattern holds in ages 45–54 and 55–59 in part. Three mortality levels can be distinguished in these groups, which do not conform to the socioeconomic ranking: non-manual workers except sales workers; sales, skilled and semiskilled workers; and service and unskilled workers. In the oldest age category only laborers continue to differ from all other groups.

. . . . . . . . . . . . . . . . . . . . . . . . . . . . . . . . . .

Hansluwka's review of Austrian mortality data[27] begins with reference to a number of early studies which were based upon workers covered by social insurance, reflecting only a very small part of the population. He does, however, present data for the entire employed population for 1951–1953. . . . For the very gross categories of "middle and upper class" and "working class" occupations, few sizable differences emerge, though the latter's rates are higher. At ages 14–17, the former's rate is appreciably higher. At ages 60–64, however, the working class has a much higher death rate. Hansluwka also presents a bar chart showing mortality in Vienna in 1951–1953. The city's 23 districts were classified on the percentage of workers of the labor force in each district and grouped into four categories. The data, he concludes, show "a clearcut pattern of social grading of mortality."

A problem which has consistently bedeviled those who seek to study socioeconomic differentials on mortality by use of death certificates and census records is the frequent noncomparability of data in the two sources, which leads to overestimation of the denominator in some occupations and underestimation in others, or difficulty in making any calculations. The nature of the problem has been explored, theoretically and empirically, by several writers.[28] Among these, Kitagawa and Hauser have sought to overcome the difficulties by individual matching of 340,000 death certificates from deaths occurring in the United States from May through August, 1960, with census information recorded for these individuals in the 1960 census. In addition, personal interviews were conducted with individuals knowledgeable about 94 per cent of a sample of 9,500 of the decedents.

A preliminary analysis of the data using education and family income for white persons has been reported, though not yet published.[29] Consideration of the education variable, which is broken down into four levels of completed education by persons 25 and older, shows an inverse gradient of mortality rates by amount of education for both sexes in ages 25 to 64. Interestingly enough, this gradient disappears for males 65 and over, but remains quite strong for females of this age.

The latest mortality study available is Tsuchiya's presentation of standardized mortality ratios for an occupational industrial categorization of Japanese males, age 15 and over, in 1962.[30] No clear occupational gradient emerges from the data. The ratios, ranked from low to high, are: "management," 58; "clerks," 67; "mechanics and simple," 88; "sales," 89; "professional and technical," 92; "transporting and communicating," 135.

[27] Hansluwka, Harold, Social and Economic Factors in Mortality in Austria, *in International Population Conference, Ottawa,* 1963, *op. cit.*, pp. 315–344.

[28] Buechley, Robert, Dunn, John E. Jr., Linden, George and Breslow, Lester, Death Certificate Statement of Occupation: Its Usefulness in Comparing Mortalities, *Public Health Reports*, 71, 1105–1111, November, 1956; Kitagawa, Evelyn M. and Hauser, Philip M., Methods Used in a Current Study of Social and Economic Differentials in Mortality, *in Emerging Techniques of Population Research*, New York, Milbank Memorial Fund, pp. 250–266; and ——, Social and Economic Differentials in Mortality in the U.S., 1960: A Report on Methods, *in International Population Conference, Ottawa,* 1963, *op. cit.*, pp. 355–367.

[29] Kitagawa, Evelyn M. and Hauser, Philip M., Social and Economic Differentials in Mortality, United States, 1960. Paper presented at the 1966 annual meeting of the Population Association of America.

[30] Tsuchiya, Kenzaburo, The Relation of Occupation to Cancer, Especially Cancer of the Lung, *Cancer*, 18, 136–144, February, 1965.

## CLASS MORTALITY DIFFERENTIALS IN ENGLAND AND WALES

Since William Farr initiated the systematic study of occupational mortality statistics in 1851, the decennial reports of the British Registrar General for England and Wales have served as the outstanding source of information on the relationship of social class and mortality. For many years, the focus was on differential mortality risks of specific occupations. In the analysis of the 1910–1912 data, the various occupations were, for the first time, grouped together into five social classes. . . .

In 1930–1932 a further step was taken in moving from a concern with occupational hazards toward one with comparison of mortality risks of people sharing a given social environment: the mortality of married women classified according to husband's occupation was introduced as a systematic part of the data analysis. Since this time, despite reclassification of various occupations, the five-class scheme of the Registrar General has been maintained.[31]

. . . . . . . . . . . . . . . . . . . . . . . . . . . . . . . . . . .

The five social classes are described as follows (the proportion of occupied and retired men aged 15 and over in 1951 is given in brackets);

**Class I.** Higher administrative and professional occupations and business directorships (3.3 per cent).

**Class II.** Other administrative, professional and managerial, and shopkeepers: persons responsible for initiating policy and others without this responsibility, but with some responsibility over others (15 per cent).

**Class III.** Clerical workers, shop assistants, personal service, foremen, skilled workers: skilled workers with a special name, special responsibility and adaptability (52.7 per cent).

**Class IV.** Semiskilled workers: persons who are doing manual work which needs no great skill or training but who are doing it habitually and in association with a particular industry (16.2 per cent).

**Class V.** Unskilled workers: laborers, cleaners and other lowly occupations (12.8 per cent). . . .

Farmers and farm managers are included in class II and agricultural workers in class IV. Also, class III, which includes more than half the population, is composed of both manual and non-manual workers.

From the great amount and variety of data available in the reports of the Registrar General and papers based on these reports, those that seem to be the most important have been selected for present purposes. These are presented in Table 3. Collins' analysis of the 1910–1912 data for occupied and retired males aged 15 and over, which refers to classes I, III and V and excludes textile workers, miners and agricultural laborers, shows a regular inverse gradient, with the largest gap being between class III and class V.[32] Stevenson's figures for the same period,[33] which also exclude the same three occupational categories, but refer to males aged 25–64 in the five social classes, show a similar gradient. The ratios for classes II, III and IV, however, are nearly identical, and not very much higher than for class I. Stevenson argued that about ten per cent of the laborers on the census are misclassified as class IV rather than class V, which tends to lower the rates for the former and increase those for the latter. Changing the denominators to this extent would, he notes, produce a smoother gradient, as

[31] . . . Registrar General's *Decennial Supplement, England and Wales, 1951, Occupational Mortality,* Part II, Vol. 1, *Commentary,* London, Her Majesty's Stationery Office, 1958, pp. 12–13. This system of classification is also described *in* Logan, W. P. D., Social Class Variations in Mortality, *in Proceedings of the World Population Conference, op. cit.*, pp. 185–188; and Brockington, Fraser C., *The Health of the Community*, third edition, London, J. & A. Churchill Ltd., 1965, pp. 325–334. The percentage distribution of the social classes is taken from Logan, p. 201. For further discussions of the antedecents and development of the Registrar General system of classification, *see* Greenwood, Major, *Medical Statistics from Graunt to Farr,* Cambridge, University Press, 1948; and ——, Occupational and Economic Factors of Mortality, *British Medical Journal*, 1, 862–866, April, 1939.

[32] Collins, *op. cit.*, p. 15.

[33] Stevenson, T. H. C., The Social Distribution of Mortality from Different Causes in England and Wales, 1910–1912, *Biometrika*, 15, 384–388, 1923; Logan, *op. cit.*, p. 204. Logan's paper was also published, with variations, under the same title, *in British Journal of Preventive and Social Medicine*, 8, 128–137, July, 1954, and *in Public Health Reports*, 69, 1217–1223, December, 1954.

**TABLE 3 Standardized Death Rates per 1,000 and Standardized Mortality Ratios, England and Wales, for Selected Age–Sex Groups and Time Periods, by Social Class**

| *Time Period* | *I* | *II* | *III* | *IV* | *V* | *Population Group* |
|---|---|---|---|---|---|---|
| 1910–12 | | | | | | |
| Death rate per 1,000 | 12.0 | — | 13.6 | — | 18.7 | Occupied and retired males, age 15+, excludes textile workers, miners, agricultural laborers |
| Ratio (I = 100) | 100 | — | 114 | — | 156 | |
| Standardized mortality ratio | 88 | 94 | 96 | 93 | 142 | Males, age 25–64, excludes textile, miners, agricultural laborers |
| Standardized mortality ratio | 88 | 94 | 96 | 107 | 128 | As immediately above, modified by Stevenson |
| 1921–23 | | | | | | |
| Death rate per 1,000 | 7.4 | 8.6 | 8.7 | 9.2 | 11.5 | Males |
| Ratio (I = 100) | 100 | 116 | 117 | 124 | 155 | |
| Standardized mortality ratio | 82 | 94 | 95 | 101 | 125 | Males, 20–64 |
| 1930–32 | | | | | | |
| Standardized mortality ratio | 90 | 94 | 97 | 102 | 111 | Males, 20–64 |
| | 81 | 89 | 99 | 103 | 113 | Married women, 20–64 |
| 1949–53 | | | | | | |
| Standardized mortality ratio | 98 | 86 | 101 | 94 | 118 | Males, 20–64 |
| | 96 | 88 | 101 | 104 | 110 | Married women, 20–64 |
| | 100 | 90 | 101 | 104 | 118 | Occupied males, 20–64, adjusted to control for occupational changes since 1930–32 |
| Death rate per 1,000 | 6.6 | | 6.4 | | 9.5 | Males, 20–64, excludes agricultural workers |
| Ratio (I = 100) | 100 | | 97 | | 144 | |

shown in Table 3. Collins also took the 1900–1902 and 1890–1892 data for 100 specific occupations and classified them as they had been classified in 1910, adjusting the death rates for age. . . . Collins proceeded to analyze the age-specific rates, which show that class differentials were largest in the 25–54 age groups. This is supported by Stevenson's analysis.

A similar picture emerges from the data for 1921–1923, despite the significant changes in classification. The gap between classes I and II is somewhat greater than in the previous decade. Classes II and III have near-identical ratios and class IV a somewhat higher ratio, while class V is still widely distinct from the others. Britten's analysis[34] of the age-specific rates compares class I to class III and class III to class V. For the former comparison, the greatest gap is at ages 16–19, and declines with regularity at each succeeding age. The pattern of the class V : III ratio, however, is different. Here the greatest gap is at ages 35–44 and, though a bit less so, at 45–54.

By 1930, class differentials, though now presenting a regular inverse gradient, had narrowed, with standardized mortality ratios of 90 for class I and 111 for class V, for males, aged 20–64. The innovation introduced in the data analysis for these years

[34] Britten, Rollo H., Occupational Mortality Among Males in England and Wales, 1921–1923, *Public Health Reports*, 43, 1570, June, 1928.

shows that general socioeconomic differences rather than specific occupational hazards were crucial in the relationship between class and mortality. This is seen in the data for married women classified by husband's occupation, in which the gradient is somewhat more steep than for the males.

The latest available data, for 1949–1953, show a rather different picture than that of previous decades. Class V still has a substantially higher ratio than the other classes; for the males, it is even higher than in 1930. Class II, however, now has the lowest ratio, followed by classes IV, I and III, in that order. For married women, the inverse gradient persists, except that here too, as among the males, class II has a lower ratio than class I. The relatively low ratio of class IV may well be an artifact of classificational changes from one social class to another. Adjustment of the data for occupied males to take account of these changes "has had the important effect of raising the SMR of Social Class IV from 94, where it was second lowest, to 104, where it occupies the second highest position, as it did in 1921–1923 and 1930–1932."[35] Guralnick's analysis of the British data,[36] excluding all gainfully employed in agriculture, and collapsing classes II–IV, shows that this latter group had a very slightly lower death rate than class I, while class V remains very much higher.

Moriyama and Guralnick,[37] in their attempt to compare data for males from the United States and England and Wales, present age-specific ratios for the latter combining the three middle classes and excluding all engaged in agriculture, for 1950 only. For most age groups, little difference is seen between class I and classes II–IV; this is particularly true from age 45 upwards. Class V has consistently higher rates; but whereas this is the case to a moderate degree at ages 20–24, the differential increases thereafter, reaching a peak at ages 35–44, after which it declines again and nearly disappears at ages 60–64. (The respective ratios of the three class groups I, II–IV and V, taking the rate of all occupations as 100, are: at ages 20–24, 102, 94, 122; at ages 25–34, 90, 95, 138; at ages 35–44, 83, 96, 143; at ages 45–54, 98, 97, 129; at ages 55–59, 99, 99, 115; and at ages 60–64, 100, 101, 106.)

Viewing the data for England and Wales in overall terms, class differentials in mortality in the twentieth century both have and have not declined. On the one hand, the differentials between the middle levels (among whom mortality rates differed little even in the earlier years) and class I have more or less disappeared. On the other hand, class V is still strikingly worse off than the rest of the population. Though indications are that its relative position improved in the earlier decades of the century, this does not seem to be the case between 1930 and 1950.

## CONCLUSIONS

This statistical examination clearly provides no basis to reject the inference drawn from the figures of the *Titanic* disaster. Despite the multiplicity of methods and indices used in the 30-odd studies cited, and despite the variegated populations surveyed, the inescapable conclusion is that class influences one's chance of staying alive. Almost without exception, the evidence shows that classes differ in mortality rates. Only three such exceptions were found, indicating no or almost no class difference. Altenderfer, comparing 1939–1940 mortality rates of 92 United States cities classified into three mean income groups, shows a relatively small difference among them. Szabady, comparing nonagricultural manual and non-manual workers in Hungary in 1959–1960, shows the same. In both cases, the classification is so gross as to minimize differences which a finer analysis might reveal. Only DeWolff and Meerdink's study in Amsterdam in 1947–1952 can legitimately be regarded as strongly contradictory of the link between class and mortality. Their data, however, must be seen in the context of a population which has just about the lowest death rate ever recorded. This is not to dismiss the importance of their findings. On the contrary, it suggests the extremely important hypothesis that as the overall death rate of a population is

[35] Registrar General, *op. cit.*, p. 20.
[36] Guralnick, *op. cit.* (International Population Conference), p. 298.
[37] Moriyama and Guralnick, *op. cit.*, p. 69.

lowered, class differentials may similarly decline.

This hypothesis finds support in an overall trend reflected in the studies reported. In the earlier studies, the differential between the mortality rates of extreme class groups is about a 2:1 ratio, but later studies show a narrowing of this differential, so that by the 1940s, a 1.4:1 or 1.3:1 ratio is much more typical. As can be seen from studying the death rates, three years witnessed a progressive decline in the overall death rate. At the same time, a cautionary note must be exercised. Despite an undoubted overall decline in mortality in the past three decades, the trend in the earlier decades of the century toward the closing of the class gap has been checked, if not halted.

This indication focuses on the differences between mortality rates of the lowest class and other classes. A more accurate picture of the overall pattern would be to suggest that what has happened is a blurring, if not a disappearance, of a clear class gradient, while class differences remain. On the basis of the existent data—using, for the sake of convenience, a five-fold class distinction, this being the most popular—it is difficult to conclude whether classes I to IV now no longer differ in their mortality rates, or whether classes I and II have the lowest rates, and III and IV have higher rates, though not necessarily substantially so. What seems to be beyond question is that, whatever the index used and whatever the number of classes considered, almost always a lowest class appears with substantially higher mortality rates. Moreover, the differential between it and other classes evidently has not diminished over recent decades.

At this point discussion of the complex question of explanations for such patterns would not be appropriate. A possibility could be suggested, however. The truly magnificent triumphs over infectious diseases have been crucial in both narrowing the overall class differentials and in nearly eliminating differentials among all but the lowest class. In recent decades, however, access to good medical care, preventive medical action, health knowledge, and limitation of delay in seeking treatment have become increasingly important in combating mortality, as chronic diseases have become the chief health enemy in the developed world. In these areas, lower class people may well be at a disadvantage. As such factors become more and more important, as the historical supposition presented in the first pages of this paper suggests, increasing class differentiation may occur. This approach does not necessarily preclude consideration of genetic selection and what has commonly come to be called "the drift hypothesis."

The data reviewed lead to a further conclusion. With amazing consistency, the class differentials are largest in the middle years of life. This is no less true in the latest than in the earliest studies. Over and over again, the greatest gap is found in young and middle adulthood. The predominant pattern characterizing class differentials by age is that in which class differences are moderately high in the younger ages, rise to a peak at ages 30 to 44, begin to decline at that point and tend to disappear beyond age 65. Where a given set of data varies from this pattern, it is in one of two directions: in the former cases, class differentials are lowest in the younger and older groups; in the latter, the decline in class differentials only begins in late middle age.

This pattern of greatest class differences in middle adulthood may be linked to the two historical suppositions which have heretofore been presented. To hypothesize in more general terms, when mortality rates are extremely high or extremely low, class differences will tend to be small. In other words, when men are quite helpless before the threat of death, or when men have made great achievements in dealing with this threat, life chances will tend to be equitably distributed. On the other hand, when moderate progress is being made in dealing with this threat, differential consequences are to be expected. The crucial idea that may be involved here is that of preventable deaths, at any given level of knowledge, technique and social organization Where and/or when such deaths are concentrated, class differentials will be greatest, unless appropriate social action is taken This differential is not inevitable.

Much more, of course, could be said in summary, with reference to both substantive and methodological issues Needless to say, consideration of patterns of class differences by cause of death is essential for a full understanding of this relationship But this would have extended the paper into a book.

# CLASS SUBCULTURES IN AMERICAN SOCIETY

*Herbert J. Gans*

The voluminous literature of class studies in America and elsewhere and the considerable similarity of the classes all over the industrialized world have made it possible to begin a delineation of the principal class subcultures. While I shall not attempt this task here, I do want to suggest what seem to me to be some of the major "focal concerns"[1] of four of the subcultures: working class, lower class, middle class, and professional upper-middle class. These brief outlines are based on observations made in the West End[2] and elsewhere, and on the research literature. For the most part, they describe the subcultures in America and in one period of the life cycle: that of the family which is rearing children.

Perhaps the most important—or at least the most visible—difference between the classes is one of family structure. *The working-class subculture* is distinguished by the dominant role of the family circle. Its way of life is based on social relationship amidst relatives. The working class views the world from the family circle, and considers everything outside it as either a means to its maintenance or to its destruction. But while the outside world is to be used for the benefit of this circle, it is faced with detachment and even hostility in most other respects. Whenever feasible, then, work is sought within establishments connected to the family circle. When this is not possible—and it rarely is—work is primarily a means of obtaining income to maintain life amidst a considerable degree of poverty, and, thereafter, a means of maximizing the pleasures of life within the family circle. The work itself may be skilled or unskilled; it can take place in the factory or in the office—the type of collar is not important. What does matter is that identification with work, work success, and job advancement—while not absolutely rejected—are of secondary priority to the life that goes on within the family circle. The purpose of education is to learn techniques necessary to obtain the most lucrative type of work. Thus the central theme of American, and all Western, education—that the student is an individual who should use his schooling to detach himself from ascribed relationships like the family circle in order to maximize his personal development and achievement in work, play, and other spheres of life—is ignored or openly rejected.

The specific characteristics of the family circle may differ widely—from the collateral peer group form of the West Enders, to the hierarchical type of the Irish, or to the classic three-generation extended family. Friends may also be included in the circle, as in the West Enders' peer group society. What matters most—and distinguishes this subculture from others—is that there be a family circle which is wider than the nuclear family, and that all of the opportunities, temptations, and pressures of the larger society be evaluated in terms of how they affect the ongoing way of life that has been built around this circle.

The *lower-class subculture* is distinguished by the female-based family and the marginal male. Although a family circle may also exist, it includes only female relatives. The

Reprinted with permission of The Macmillan Company from *The Urban Villagers*, by Herbert T. Gans. © The Free Press of Glencoe, a Division of The Macmillan Company, 1962.

[1] I borrow this term from Walter Miller, who uses it as a substitute for the anthropological concept of value in his study of lower-class culture. See "Lower Class Culture as a Generating Milieu of Gang Delinquency," *Journal of Social Issues*, Vol. 14, 1958, p. 7. I use it to refer to behavior as much as to attitude, and to phenomena of social structure as well as culture.

[2] The Boston Italian-American community that is the main subject of the book from which this selection is taken. (C. S. H.)

male, whether husband or lover, is physically present only part of the time, and is recognized neither as a stable nor dominant member of the household. He is a sexual partner, and he is asked to provide economic support. But he participates only minimally in the exchange of affection and emotional support, and has little to do with the rearing of children. Should he serve as a model for the male children, he does so largely in a negative sense. That is, the women use him as an example of what a man should not be.

The female-based family must be distinguished, however, from one in which the woman is dominant, for example, the English working-class family. Although this family may indeed revolve around the "Mum," she does not reject the husband. Not only is he a member of the family, but he is also a participant—and a positive model—in child-rearing.

In the lower class, the segregation of the sexes—only partial in the working class—is complete. The woman tries to develop a stable routine in the midst of poverty and deprivation; the action-seeking man upsets it. In order to have any male relationships, however, the woman must participate to some extent in his episodic life style. On rare occasions, she may even pursue it herself. Even then, however, she will try to encourage her children to seek a routine way of life. Thus the woman is much closer to working-class culture, at least in her aspirations, although she is not often successful in achieving them.

For lower-class men, life is almost totally unpredictable. If they have sought stability at all, it has slipped from their grasp so quickly, often, and consistently that they no longer pursue it. From childhood on, their only real gratifications come from action-seeking, but even these are few and short-lived. Relationships with women are of brief duration, and some men remain single all their lives. Work, like all other relationships with the outside world, is transitory. Indeed, there can be no identification with work at all. Usually, the lower-class individual gravitates from one job to another with little hope or interest of keeping a job for any length of time. His hostility to the outside world therefore is quite intense, and its attempts to interfere with the episodic quality of his life are fought. Education is rejected by the male, for all of its aims are diametrically opposed to action-seeking.

The *middle-class subculture* is built around the nuclear family and its desire to make its way in the larger society. Although the family circle may exist, it plays only a secondary role in middle-class life. Contact with close relatives is maintained, but even they participate in a subordinate role. Individuals derive most of their social and emotional gratifications from the nuclear family itself. One of the most important of these is child-rearing. Consequently, the middle-class family is much more child-centered than the working-class one and spends more of its spare time together. Outside social life takes place with friends who share similar interests. The nuclear family depends on its friends—as well as on some caretaking institutions—for help and support. Relatives may also help, especially in emergencies.

The middle class does not make the distinction between the family and the outside world. In fact, it does not even see an outside world, but only a larger society, which it believes to support its aims, and in which the family participates. The nuclear family makes it way in the larger society mainly through the career of its breadwinner. Thus work is not merely a job that maximizes income, but a series of related jobs or job advances which provide the breadwinner with higher income, greater responsibility, and, if possible, greater job satisfaction. In turn his career enhances the way of life of the rest of the family, through increases in status and in the standard of living.

Education is viewed, and used, as an important method for achieving these goals. The purpose of education is to provide the skills needed for the man's career and for the woman's role as a mother. In and out of school, it is also used to develop the skills necessary to the maintenance and increase of status, the proper use of leisure time, and the occasional participation in community activities. Thus, much of the central theme of education is accepted. But the idea that education is an end in itself, and should be used to maximize individual development of the person, receives only lip service.

The subculture I have described here is a

basic middle-class one; a more detailed analysis would distinguish between what is currently called the middle-middle class and the lower-middle class. The upper-middle-class subculture is also a variant of the basic middle-class culture. There are at least two such subcultures, the managerial and the professional. Since I shall be concerned with the latter in subsequent sections of this chapter and the next, it is of primary interest here.

The *professional upper-middle-class culture* is also organized around the nuclear family, but places greater emphasis on the independent functioning of its individual members. Whereas the middle-class family is a companionship unit in which individuals exist most intensely in their relationships with each other, the upper-middle-class family is a companionship unit in which individuals seeking to maximize their own development as persons come together on the basis of common interests. For this subculture, life is, to a considerable extent, a striving for individual development and self-expression, and these strivings pervade many of its relationships with the larger society.

Therefore, work is not simply a means for achieving the well-being of the nuclear family, but also an opportunity for individual achievement and social service. Although the career, income, status, and job responsibility are important, job satisfaction is even more important, although it is not always found. Indeed, professional work satisfaction is a focal concern not only for the breadwinner, but often for the woman as well. If she is not interested in a profession, she develops an alternative but equally intense interest in motherhood, or in community activity. Child-rearing, moreover, gives the woman an opportunity not only to maximize her own individual achievements as a mother, but to develop in her children the same striving for self-development. As a result, the professional upper-middle-class family is not child-centered, but adult-directed. As education is the primary tool for a life of individual achievement, the professional upper-middle-class person not only goes to school longer than anyone else in society, but he also accepts its central theme more fully than do the rest of the middle class.

This concern with individual achievement and education further enables and encourages the members of this subculture to be deliberate and self-conscious about their choices. They are a little more understanding of the actions of others than the members of less educated strata. Their ability to participate in the larger society, plus their high social and economic status, also gives them somewhat greater control over their fate than other people, and makes the environment more predictable This in turn facilitates the practice of self-consciousness, empathy, and abstraction or generalization.

The possession of these skills distinguishes the upper-middle class from the rest of the middle class, and even more so from the working and lower classes. For the latter not only live in a less predictable environment, but they are also detached from the outside world, which increases their feeling that it, and, indeed, all of life, is unpredictable. In turn this feeling encourages a pervasive fatalism that pre-empts the optimism or pessimism of which the other classes are capable. The fatalism of the working and lower classes, as well as their lack of education and interest in personal development and object goals, minimizes introspection, self-consciousness, and empathy for the behavior of others.

## CLASS: OPPORTUNITY AND RESPONSE

The subcultures which I have described are *responses* that people make to the *opportunities* and the *deprivations* that they encounter. More specifically, each subculture is an organized set of related responses that has developed out of people's efforts to cope with the opportunities, incentives, and rewards, as well as the deprivations, prohibitions, and pressures which the natural environment and society—that complex of coexisting and competing subcultures—offer to them. The responses which make up a subculture are compounded out of what people have retained of parental, that is, traditional responses, the skills and attitudes they have learned as children, and the innovations they have developed for themselves in their own encounters with opportunity and deprivation.

These responses cannot develop in a vacuum. Over the long range, they can be seen as functions of the resources which a society has available, and of the opportunities which it can offer. In each of the subcultures life is thus geared to the availability of specific qualitative types and quantities of income, education, and occupational opportunities. Although I have used occupational labels to distinguish between the major subcultures,[3] a man's job does not necessarily determine in which of these he shall be placed. In the long run, however, the existence of a specific subculture is closely related to the availability of occupational opportunities. For example, the functioning of the family circle and the routine-seeking way of life in the working class depend on the availability of stable employment for the man. The lower-class female-based family is a response to, or a method of coping with, the lack of stable male employment. The goals of middle- and upper-middle-class culture depend on the availability of sufficient income to finance the education that is necessary for a career, and on the availability of job opportunities that will allow middle-class individuals to find the type of job satisfaction for which they are striving.

When these opportunity factors are lacking, the cultural responses made by people are frustrated. Should opportunities be deficient over a long enough period, downward mobility results. Should they disappear entirely, the subculture will be apt to disintegrate eventually. For example, working-class culture can function for a time in a period of unemployment, but if no substitute sources of stability are made available, people initially resort to protest. Eventually, the family circle begins to break up under the strain, and its members adopt many if not all of the responses identified with the lower-class subculture.

[3] It is relevant to note that the words I have used to label the class subcultures are somewhat misleading. For example, I describe the middle class not as a group in the middle of the economic and power structure, but as a subculture focally concerned with the nuclear family. Likewise, the working class obviously works no more or less than any other group. Only the lower-class label fits well, since this subculture is in so many ways a response to the deprivations to which it is exposed.

Similar reactions take place in the other subcultures, although the ways in which they are expressed may differ. If job opportunities are lacking so as to frustrate the career desires of the middle class, or the professional desires of the upper-middle class, one reaction is to transfer aspirations elsewhere, for example, into non-work pursuits. Since upper-middle-class people are able and willing to act in the larger society, they may also develop social and political protest movements in order to create these opportunities, or to change society. Bourgeois socialist movements in America, taking their lead from the Marxist aim to "humanize" work so that it will provide quasi-professional job satisfaction to all people, are examples of such a reaction. Although downward mobility in the working class results in the adoption of lower-class responses, middle-class downward mobility does not bring about a working-class response. People may depend more on relatives as adversity strikes, but other differences between middle- and working-class subcultures remain in effect.

. . . . . . . . . . . . . . . . . . . . . . . . . . . . . . . . . .

## THE EVALUATION OF WORKING- AND LOWER-CLASS SUBCULTURES

It should be evident from the description of the West Enders in the previous chapters that I believe the working-class subculture to be a generally satisfactory way of adapting to the opportunities which society has made available. Even so, it does have a number of negative features that constitute disadvantages both to working-class people and to the larger society.

One of these is the inability to participate in formal organizations and in general community activity. Although the lack of interest in voluntary associations is relatively unimportant, the inability to organize per se deprives working-class people of a method of political representation that is very important in a pluralistic society. Generally less well represented in the political arena than the economically more powerful, and socially more skillful groups, they are thus hampered in expressing their point of view, and in defending their interests. Consequently, they delegate the political representation function to others, yet only at some cost. Urban political machines and labor unions defend their interests, but the leadership of these organizations is not always fully representative. Moreover, when these agencies are not responsive, working-class people may turn to authoritarian and occasionally violent forms of protest—more out of desperation than choice. But such solutions are not always desirable or effective.

A related drawback is the general inability to understand bureaucratic behavior and object-orientation. This encourages the development of a conspiracy theory to explain the outside world, and breeds suspicions that are frequently inaccurate. As a result, the already existing gap between the working class and the larger society is widened.

Much of the time, the working class can protect itself from real or imagined injury by minimizing its dependence on the larger society. But this solution, which may work in prosperous times and in periods of social stability, is not always effective. In depressions, emergencies, and periods of rapid social change, however, the many indirect relationships to the larger society become apparent, mainly as they are being interrupted or altered. It is at these times that normal methods of class conflict over the distribution of opportunities go awry, and the gap between the working class and the larger society—notably the government—threatens to become harmful to both. The former is hurt by its inability to understand and deal with the changes that are taking place; the latter, by its inability to develop methods to solve the resulting problems even when it wants to do so. This state of affairs was illustrated only too well by the redevelopment of the West End. . . . The West Enders could not defend their interests, and the redevelopment agency was unable to understand their needs. Similarly, as automation and other technological changes alter the labor market, and reduce the need for semiskilled and unskilled workers, the working-class subculture's detachment from the larger society hampers the adjustment to changing conditions. Fortunately, the belief in education as a means to occupational success has allowed many working-class people to train themselves for the new job types that are now needed, and the problem is not as severe as it is in the lower class.

Another disadvantage of the working-class subculture is its rejection of certain types of caretakers, especially those whose services cannot be provided by the family circle. I am thinking here especially of the unwillingness to use medical specialists and psychotherapists. Although such caretakers may treat their clients as if they were middle class—which explains why they are so often rejected even when cost is no problem—the health goals which they further are sought by the working class as much as by any other. The family circle does provide a considerable amount of advice and emotional support to its members, but not always of the right kind. Indeed, some forms of care cannot be given by laymen, especially if the latter share the patient's mistaken beliefs. In dealing with mental illness, for example, the aid given by the family circle can even be harmful.

Finally, the emphasis on group life, the low value placed on privacy, and the general conservatism of the working-class culture all penalize those who deviate. For most people, this is no problem. Those who deviate by being mobile, for instance, are able to leave. But for people who are not mobile and who are different without wanting to be—such as those with neuroses that detach them from the group—the sanctions against deviance are harsh.

More intensive research of the dominant cultural patterns would undoubtedly indicate other patterns with deleterious consequences. For example, the impulsive child-rearing methods may have undesirable effects for some children who, for one reason or another, do not learn to cope with them. Only a highly detailed and longitudinal study of the subculture, however, will be able to unearth such patterns.

My limited observations suggest that, on the whole, the advantages of working-class subculture do outweigh the disadvantages. The latter are real, and ought to be removed, but they are not overwhelming. Thus, given our present knowledge, there is no justification for planning and caretaking programs which try to do away with the working-class subculture. John Seeley has suggested why it should not be done away with in his description of a Polish working-class group with whom he once lived:

> . . . no society I have lived in before or since seemed to me to present so many of its members . . . so many possibilities and actualities of fulfillment of a number at least of basic human demands: for an outlet for aggressiveness, for adventure, for a sense of effectiveness, for deep feelings of belonging without undue sacrifice of uniqueness or identity, for sex satisfaction, for strong if not fierce loyalties, for a sense of independence from the pervasive omnicompetent, omniscient authority-in-general which at that time still overwhelmed to a greater degree the middle-class child. . . . These things had their prices, of course—not all values can be simultaneously maximized. But few of the inhabitants whom I reciprocally took "slumming" into middle-class life understood it or, where they did, were at all envious of it. And, be it asserted, this was not a matter of "ignorance" or incapacity to "appreciate finer things," but an inability to see one moderately coherent and sense-making satisfaction-system which they didn't know as preferable to the quite coherent and sense-making satisfaction-system they did know.[4]

Although his evaluation puts the case a little more enthusiastically than I might, it says very well that working-class culture is a positive response to the opportunities and deprivations which it encounters.

This is not true, however, of the lower-class subculture. Like all other cultures, it too tries to cope with the existing opportunities and deprivations, and to make life as bearable as possible. That it fails to succeed is largely the result of the intense deprivations with which it is saddled. Moreover, the response to these deprivations has consequences which make it difficult for lower-class people to accept opportunities for improvement if and when they are available.

Although lower-class culture has innumerable problems, perhaps the basic one is occupational. It seems to produce people who can work only in unskilled jobs. These jobs, however, are becoming more and more scarce, and they may virtually disappear in the not so distant future—surely to no one's sorrow. But while lower-class women have developed working-class or quasi-working-class aspirations, the female-based family seems to raise men who find it difficult to develop the skills and the motivations that are necessary for obtaining and holding the jobs that will be available. In addition, these men are ambivalent about themselves and their role in society, and thus have considerable problems in achieving some sort of personal stability even when they want it, and even when they have gained some measure of economic stability. At present, then, lower-class culture breeds men who find it increasingly difficult to survive in modern society, and who, in a more automated future, will be unable to do so.

Lower-class women seem to be able to achieve some measure of stability—however problem-laden it may be—within and through the family. Even so, they are content neither with the subculture, nor with the female-based family, and try to see that their children escape it. This in itself suggests a major difference between the lower class and the other subcultures. The people within other subcultures are by and large satisfied with them and pass them on much more willingly to their children, at least to the extent that culture is ever transmitted deliberately. Lower-class women may not often succeed in raising their children to reject the culture they live in, but the mere fact that they try illustrates the absolute qualitative difference between the lower-class subculture and all the others.

There are more persuasive illustrations of this difference. Many lower-class children grow up in homes ravaged by alcoholism, drug addiction, and mental illness, and the subculture that they inherit is overlaid with pathology, for besides the comparatively more functional elements of lower-class subculture, there are many that are the result of pathological conditions, such as being raised by mentally ill parents. For example, many of the focal concerns of lower-class culture described by Walter Miller are useful methods of coping with the environment,[5] but there are some forms

[4] John R. Seeley, "The Slum: Its Nature, Use and Users," *Journal of the American Institute of Planners*, Vol. 25, 1959, pp. 7–14, at p. 10.

[5] "Lower Class Culture as a Generating Milieu of Gang Delinquency," *Journal of Social Issues*, Vol. 14, No. 3, 1958, pp. 5–19.

of action-seeking that reflect desperation more than adaptation. The episodes of riotous pleasure do not make up for the depression and self-destruction that accompany them. Significantly, the lower class not only has higher rates of mental illness than the others, but these rates are considerably higher than those of the working class.[6] Indeed, the difference in rates between these two classes is so great as to suggest that many elements of lower-class life are not merely culturally different from other ways of life, but that they are in fact pathological.

. . . . . . . . . . . . . . . . . . . . . . . . . . . . . . . . .

# BLUE-COLLAR MARRIAGE —BARRIERS TO MARITAL COMMUNICATION

## *Mirra Komarovsky*

One of every three marriages in this study falls short of the prevailing American ideal of psychological intimacy between married partners. These reserved couples are examined in order to discover the barriers to communication. The emphasis upon barriers unfortunately reinforces the common assumption that high rapport in marriage is natural and requires no explanation. The ability of two individuals to share fully their inner lives is no more natural, however, than their failure to do so. Rapport and the breakdown of interaction are two facets of the same riddle, the solution of which ultimately requires a comparison of both kinds of relationships. But barriers to communication are more visible than conditions which facilitate it.

Socially structured barriers, those rooted in shared values and conditions of life, will be considered. . . .

### SHARP DIFFERENTIATION IN THE INTERESTS OF THE SEXES

Husbands and wives need not share identical mental worlds to understand one another, but their two separate worlds must be in contact at some points. This overlapping of interests is so narrow for a number of Glenton[1] couples that neither partner can serve as a satisfactory audience for the other. . . .

The upbringing of working-class children undoubtedly contributes to this separation of the sexes. Working-class parents make sharper distinctions than do the middle classes between the social roles of boys and girls. One investigator concludes that "middle-class mothers' conceptions of what is desirable for boys are much the same as their conceptions of what is desirable for girls. But working-class mothers make a clear distinction between the sexes. . . ."[2]

In another inquiry, working-class boys and girls were found to be aware of sex roles earlier and more clearly than both boys and girls of the middle-class group, as indicated by the recognition of "appropriate" toys and behavior.[3] Whatever the role of their upbringing, the gulf between the sexes does exist. The following excerpts from the interviews illustrate a variety of reactions to this situation—the boredom of the wives, the contempt and exasperation of the husbands, the resignation of some and the yearnings of others.

A 23-year-old husband, a grammar school graduate, married three years, declared:



[6] August B. Hollingshead and Fredrick C. Redlich, *Social Class and Mental Illness*, New York: Wiley, 1958, Chap. 7. The authors also note that male rates in the lower class (Class V) are higher than female ones, a disparity not prevalent in other classes. *Ibid.*, p. 200.

[1] Fictitious name of a community of fifty thousand, heavily working class, located five miles from a city of about half a million and less than twenty miles from a metropolis. (C. S. H.)

[2] Melvin L. Kohn, "Social Class and Parental Authority," *American Sociological Review*, Vol. 24, June, 1959, p. 365.

[3] Meyer Rabban, "Sex-Role Identification in Young Children in Two Diverse Social Groups," Genetic Psychological Monograph, Vol. 42, August, 1950, pp. 140–141.

"What is it about women that they want to talk about things when there is really nothing to talk about? Why do they have to hash it over? They talk about screwy things. Keep quacking, like beating a dead horse." He and his buddies agreed that "it seems to be this way all around."

. . . . . . . . . . . . . . . . . . . . . . . . . . . . . . . . .

Similar dissatisfactions were expressed by a wife who was trying to explain why talking with girl friends frequently proved more satisfying than conversations with her husband. When she once told her husband about a young woman in the community who had an illegitimate baby, he ended the discussion with: "It happens all the time." But with her girl friends she can talk over such matters in detail. (Does the girl really want to give up her baby? Should she? Would she marry the father of her baby if he asked her to? And so on.)

This pattern was detected in case after case.

. . . . . . . . . . . . . . . . . . . . . . . . . . . . . . . . .

Generally, having neither competence nor interest in the mate's topic of conversation, each complains that the other "goes on and on about boring things" in unnecessary detail. One of the conditions causing this gulf between the interests of husbands and wives is the exclusion of the wives from their husband's world of work.

### THE WIFE AND HER HUSBAND'S JOB

There is scarcely a couple among these Glenton families who does not occasionally discuss the husband's job or his occupational plans. But these matters head the list of topics which the husbands admittedly disclose least to their wives. The interviews reveal several grounds for this reserve.

***The Monotonous Nature of the job.*** This is one reason for limited conversation. "There is nothing to elaborate about my job," said a 36-year-old steeplejack, "I just mix paint all day and put it on. It is monotonous." The men frequently note that if something humorous or unexpected takes place during their work day, they are apt to tell their wives about it. . . .

A 33-year-old hand truckman's testimony is characteristic "I'm glad enough to be away from there. When I get away from the plant, I'd rather just let that rest till the next day. After all, it's no great fun; it's just something I got to make a living by. That's all." When asked "Does your wife take an interest in your job?" another husband replied: "I don't take much interest in it myself so I wouldn't expect her to if I couldn't."

***The Job Is Usually Felt to Be Too Technical for Woman.*** Every husband was asked whether his wife understood the problems he encountered during his working day. Although a few of the husbands claimed that anyone, including their wives could easily understand their work, the great majority, many of whom held semi-skilled jobs of low technical level, agreed with the man who said, "She'd have to work alongside of me to understand. I don't expect her to." They often felt that only a man in the same line of work could comprehend the technical problems, the irritations, and the satisfactions of the daily routine. The social relationships on the job were seldom discussed at home and social contacts with co-workers were extremely rare. . . .

***Talk About the Job Carries the Connotation, for the Husband, of "Griping," Which Is Thought to Be Unmanly.*** Our repeated question, "Can you talk to your wife about your job?" brought forth an unmistakable expression of a value: "I don't believe in bringing my job home." To talk about the job meant to "gripe about it." A 40-year-old sash fitter said apologetically, "Sometimes things go wrong and you come home and you got to get it out of your system and you can't help it if it spills over a little bit." A 23-year-old sanitation worker, in answer to the question about talk (a question which made no reference whatsoever to complaints), said, "Yes, I guess I do blow my stack sometimes: I try not to, but sometimes it sort of busts out of me."

The wives also tend to equate talk about the job with "griping." The item "tells wife about what happens on the job" was included in the schedule of "What makes a good husband?" Only 18 per cent of the women rated it as an important quality. And even this minority endorses conversation about the husband's work because of its presumed mental health function—"Let him talk if he has to get it off his chest." A more prevalent attitude is expressed by another woman who said, "When the hours is done, that is the end." In fact, the only women who complain that their husbands do not tell them enough about the job are a few unhappy wives for whom this silence seems to be another manifestation of the general withdrawal of the husbands.[4]

However self-critical their attitude towards "griping" about the job, we estimate about one-fifth of the husbands wished nevertheless that their wives were more interested in their work problems. On occasions when they wanted to share their work experiences they found their wives preoccupied with the children or uninterested.

***Work and Home Should Be Kept Separate.*** The great majority of the wives, some 80 per cent, have no social contact with their husband's work-mates. The friendships husbands may form on the job do not include their wives. Indeed, in more than one-half of the cases the wives either never met their husbands' co-workers or saw them only once or twice when the latter delivered messages to, or called for, the husbands. In about 30 per cent of the cases, the wife did meet one or more fellow workers at some social gathering, a Christmas party or an outing. And in the remaining one-fifth of the cases, wives had more frequent contacts with co-workers. In several instances co-workers were relatives of the couple.

The feeling that work-mates do not belong in one's home was expressed by a 32-year-old painter: "It isn't nice to bring work people home. Homes are not for that. At home you raise children and relax. If you have friends from work, you're going to talk things over with them, and not want to have to hear babies crying or to go out shopping. When you're home you want to ease up and not have to keep on your toes." The idea that the home is too "pure" for masculine comradery was also expressed by several men who noted that the talk among the fellows at work is too rough and vulgar for women. Thus a 38-year-old cable layer said to us, "Nah, they ain't got no call to come on home with me, what would they do there? We might feel like having a drink, or raising a ruckus, and you ought not to do that at home. It is a lot better in the tavern, or the dog-wagon or hanging around the street someplace."

***Some Husbands Opt for Reciprocal Reticence.*** Instead of mutual sharing of daily experiences, some husbands recommend reserve. Thus a 31-year-old truck driver declared: "It don't do no good to go home and belly-ache to your wife. If you don't want to know about what happens with the washing and with the neighbors' kids, you shouldn't ought to tell her about what goes on at the plant either." And another husband: "The only things we don't tell each other are things the other don't want to hear. She don't want to know what I did in the warehouse and I don't want to know if the baby is sick, so long as it ain't really sick." . . .

The working-class situation stands in sharp contrast to the frequently reported involvement of the "corporation wife" in her husband's career.[5] The daily assessment of office politics, the prudent entertaining of superiors and associates and the resulting feeling of personal participation in a husband's career are all lacking here. If the workingman, in contrast to the corporation careerist, misses the opportunity to share his world of work, he enjoys a greater immunity from his wife's scrutiny of his daily performance. In any case, for better or worse, the husband's job is not an area of active common interest for the large majority of our couples.

In all social classes, to be sure, the sexes are bound to have some separate interests because their social roles differ. Neither husband nor wife can be expected to be interested in the purely technical aspects of the other's daily tasks. A woman friend, confronted with similar problems, will

[4] The wives, as well as the husbands, were questioned about the job as a topic of conversation. This served as a safeguard against the possibility that husbands minimized the extent of their talk because, in their own minds, this was "griping."

[5] See, e.g., William H. Whyte, Jr., "The Corporation and the Wife," *Fortune*, Vol. 44, October, 1951, 86 ff; and "The Wives of Management," *Fortune*, Vol. 44, November, 1951, 109 ff.

naturally have a more lively interest than the husband in the baby's diet, a new recipe or a bargain. Similarly, a fellow worker will be more competent than one's wife to discuss the technical problems of the job. Insofar as the husband is drawn into the domestic sphere or the wife gets involved in her husband's career, their interests converge. Neither of these conditions obtained for most of Glenton's families.

Men and women, however, may have their separate tasks and still share common interests in the psychological problems of child rearing, in their personalities, in social life and aspirations for the future. But it is only a slight exaggeration to say that for many of Glenton families life contains little else apart from the immediate daily tasks. The impoverishment of life and of personality curtails the development of shared interests.

### THE IMPOVERISHMENT OF LIFE

Writers concerned with the meagerness of marital communication sometimes imply that it would flow abundantly were we only able to open the floodgates. However, the impoverishment of the quality of life not only narrows the overlapping of interests and consequent sharing of experiences, but also stunts personal development. There may be little or nothing to communicate. Speaking of television, for example, typical comments by the respondents were: "We both see it, why talk about it," and "What's there to talk about other than to say it's good or bad." In more general terms, one woman put it this way: "We tell each other things, but I don't know as how we talk about them. He'll tell me or I'll tell him something has happened, but there ain't nothing much to say. . . ."

If external life is restricted for these families, so is their inner world. For example, the meagerness of joint social life deprives the couples of conversation about mutual friends, gossip, planning of social affairs and "party post-mortems." Over one-third of these couples either never visit with another couple apart from relatives or do so only very infrequently, a few times a year on some special occasion of an anniversary or a New Year's celebration. Low level of interest in reading, in current events and in cultural subjects has a similar impoverishing effect.

Couples who are exposed to the middle-class values of companionship, but whose mode of life does not stimulate common interests, are sometimes acutely aware of this discrepancy. They know that husbands and wives are supposed to talk with one another, but they do not have anything to say. Characteristically, one young husband, a high school graduate, said: "I wish we had more things to talk about, but when I try to think of something I don't know anything to talk to her about. I wish we could get out and see the shows or something like that." And another man expressed a similar dissatisfaction: "If my wife and I had a little more education maybe we'd have what you call it—more interests? Maybe we could come together better, maybe life would be more interesting for us."

The barriers to communication described so far derive from the meager content of common interests. Deficient skills of communication, especially on the part of the less-educated husbands, also hinder the sharing of experiences.

### THE TRAINED INCAPACITY TO SHARE

The phrase "trained incapacity to share" aims to convey a certain view about the men's inarticulateness. The ideal of masculinity into which they were socialized inhibits expressiveness both directly, with its emphasis on reserve, and indirectly, by identifying personal interchange with the feminine role. Childhood and adolescence, spent in an environment in which feelings were not named, discussed or explained, strengthened these inhibitions. In adulthood they extend beyond culturally demanded reticence—the inhibitions are now experienced not only as "I shouldn't," but as "I cannot." In explaining instances of reserve in marriage many more husbands than wives say: "It is hard to talk about such things." . . .

I used to try to ask him when we were first married, said a 26-year-old woman about her husband, why he gets into those real flippy moods, but he used to say nothing was wrong, and asking seemed to make him worse. The more I tried, the worse he'd get. So I found out that if you just don't bother him, it wears off. Another young woman described her husband: Sometimes he could get real black and quiet and you'd just better keep out of his way and not say anything.

The wives endorse the therapeutic value of talk more frequently than the husbands. Thus a 30-year-old woman:

> Lots of people say it's not good to go around shooting off your lips about what's eating them, but I think the good thing is to talk it out and get it out of your system. But I have to leave him alone because if I try to get him to talk he'll get really sore, or he'll go off the deep end and walk out of here. Or maybe he'd tell me something else, lying like, just so I wouldn't get at the thing that makes him sore. He is strictly hands-off if something hurts him. . . . It makes it rough . . . not knowing what's eating him hurts you worse than it hurts him.

. . . These comments are not exceptional. Twenty-six per cent of the wives, but only 9 per cent of the husbands, in answer to questions about dissatisfactions with communication, complain that their mate "does not reveal worries." The responses to the projective story about the husband who doesn't talk enough . . . convey the same idea. Although the story contained no reference whatsoever to worry, 11 per cent of the respondents agreed: "He might not want to talk because something is wrong." Of 23 qualities of a good husband, the women ranked "speaks his mind when something is worrying him" as the second most important quality. These rankings reflect current deprivations—not merely ideals. The wives value the trait of speaking out precisely because they miss it in their husbands.

The ideal of masculinity accepted by the men is certainly one factor in their meager disclosure of stressful feelings. To gripe about the job .carries the connotation of weakness. A strong man bears his troubles in silence and does not "dump his load on the family"; he does not ask for solace and reassurance. Indeed, an adult male does not even experience hurt, much less admit it. "When I don't feel good," said one husband, "I light out and don't dump my load on them." Speaking of his wife, a 40-year-old carpenter (with eight years of school) described the masculine norm quite explicitly: "Sure she gets hurt. Men are supposed to be braver than women, but women is bound to get hurt, it's in their nature, ain't it?"

The strength of such norms is demonstrated in the section of the interview dealing with feelings of hurt and of anger. When asked for sources of hurt feelings, almost twice as many men as women expressed disapproval of the very experience of hurt in an adult: "After a man gets on his feet, he shouldn't be hurt deeply about anything"; "You ought to outgrow it." More men than women say, "Nothing can hurt me anymore," or "Don't know what could reach me anymore." They generally add that at some earlier time—in childhood, "before the army," "before marriage," their feelings were hurt. Among the less-educated, 30 per cent of the men, but only 15 per cent of the women, denied completely that they experienced hurt at present. The sexes, however, report the experience of anger with nearly identical frequency: only 5 per cent of the women and 8 per cent of the men maintain that they are never angry.

It may be argued that the men experience hurt feelings less frequently (thus not merely concealing such feelings) than the allegedly more sensitive females. But the testimony of the high school graduates weakens this argument because the difference by sex in the reporting of hurt feelings narrows: 12 per cent of women and 17 per cent of the men in this educational category deny feelings of hurt. The high school men may have a less rigid norm of masculinity and be more willing to admit being hurt than the less-educated men. Consistent with this idea is the similarity between the two groups of men in their admission of anger: only 8 per cent of the less-educated and only 6 per cent of the high school graduates denied the experience of anger. Unlike the experience of hurt, anger does not carry the connotation of weakness to the less-educated men.

Socialized to identify the expression of certain emotions with a lack of masculinity, the men inhibit self-disclosure. Lack of education plays an independent role in limiting the capacity to identify, interpret and express feelings. . . . Of the four subgroups (high school and less-educated husbands and wives) the less-educated husbands are consistently the most withdrawn. They reveal less of themselves to their wives, are less inclined to find relief by openly expressing emotion, and tend to react to marriage conflict by withdrawal. Of all the aids in overcoming emotional stress listed by the uneducated husbands, only 28 per cent involve interaction with others, as against 42 per cent of such aids for the less-educated wives. These men seek relief in action rather than in talk.

The reticence of the less-educated husbands is also apparent in the relative scantiness of their replies to the section of the interview on self, personality and psychological relationships. The questions called for sources of feelings of hurt, happiness, worry, self-satisfaction and guilt, and for assessments of one's strong points and shortcomings. The less-educated husband lists fewer items per person than any of the other respondents. For example, in describing his strong and weak traits, he lists 5.4 fewer traits than does the less-educated woman. But among the high school graduates the sex difference is narrowed to only 2.1 items in favor of women. The inhibitions of the less-educated men are further revealed by the fact that, of all the four subgroups, the less-educated husbands are the only ones who list fewer items about their own personality than about the personality of their mates.

. . . . . . . . . . . . . . . . . . . . . . . . . . . . . . . . . .

## THE EDUCATIONAL FACTOR IN COMMUNICATION

The foregoing pages have dealt with socially structured . . . barriers to marital communication. We have seen that communication between husbands and wives is hindered by certain traditional values. Having embraced these values, some men contemptuously relegate conversation about persons to "old women's gossip," and attribute self-disclosure of painful emotions to lack of self-sufficiency. Question: "Do you talk to your wife about this?" Answer: "Yes, once in a while I might *cry on her shoulder*" (emphasis ours), they admit shamefacedly. The separation between the masculine and the feminine spheres of interest also thwarts communication. The humdrum or the technical nature of the man's job makes it of little interest to the wife. The husband wants some "peace and quiet" upon his return home. . . .

The above analysis helps to account for the fuller self-disclosure of the high school graduates. Better education and associated social conditions help to lower a number of the barriers. Role differentiation in marriage is not so sharp among the better-educated as among the less-educated families. The high school fathers are somewhat more active in child care. And there is more discussion of the husband's job: of 18 high school graduates, 39 per cent and of 40 less-educated men, only 15 per cent discuss their jobs with their wives "quite a lot."[6] In the former group, an overlap in activities promotes communication by supplying a common content of experience. The high school graduates also exceed the less-educated in the extent of shared leisure-time activities. . . . Furthermore, the better-educated husbands admit feelings of hurt and describe their personalities in fuller detail than the less-educated men. Economic failure of the husband affects adversely the freedom of communication, and there are more such failures among the less-educated men. . . . The high school wives have more power in marriage in comparison with the less-educated women. . . . It is our impression that enjoying this power they are able to control the relationship more effectively and to give expression to their interest in sharing experiences. Finally, the high school graduates have relatively fewer very unhappy marriages in which marital conflict leads to a breakdown of communication. All such circumstances combine to raise the level of self-disclosure to mate among the high school graduates.

It should be stressed, however, that higher education by no means guarantees effective marital communication. To be sure, the marital dialogue of the high school graduates is, on the whole, fuller than that of the

[6] Robert O. Blood, Jr., and Donald M. Wolfe, however, found that low blue-collar husbands were more likely than high blue-collar husbands to report happenings on the job to their wives. *Husbands and Wives*, Glencoe, Illinois: Free Press, 1960, p. 168.

less-educated couples, but the overlap between the self-disclosure ratings of the two educational groups is substantial. Some better-educated couples are characterized by moderate or meager self-disclosure for a variety of psychological reasons. Conversely many less-educated couples enjoy deep and close relationships. Some of the latter are the poorly educated, who, apart from their few years of formal schooling, resemble the high school graduates in their values and mode of life. Some less-educated respondents, for example, expressed "middle-class" values on the projective stories.

More interesting, because more revealing of new insights, are the less-educated couples who enjoy satisfying communication and at the same time hold values and display the mode of life typical of the less-educated in general. We shall examine such a case.

### EXISTENCE OF CLOSE, HAPPY MARRIAGES AMONG THE LESS-EDUCATED

Mr. and Mrs. King are both 26, married for eight years and expecting their fourth child. Both had ten years of schooling. They share few general interests and spend much of their leisure separately. They express many working-class norms of marriage. Do cases of this kind imply that social factors are, after all, unimportant—that perhaps "love" does conquer all?

The clue to the paternal role played by Mr. K. in this marital relationship was provided by his wife, who, the youngest of six siblings, found her marital role congenial.

> He is no older than I am but he sure knows how to handle me if I get a head of steam on, said Mrs. K. He can steady me sometimes by just looking at me in a very nice way with his real blue eyes. She described an argument about making the boy eat his breakfast. Her husband slammed his hand on the table and told her not to discuss it in front of the children. That made me mad enough to cry. So she got up and started washing up, slamming dishes and pots around. Well, he came over and put his arm around me and he made me hold still and just looked at me and he said he had to go out and he hoped I'd be over this when he came back. So then I began to cry and he kissed me a little and left. All of a sudden I started to laugh at myself crying into the dishpan.

The K.'s gave typical working-class responses on the test stories. Their interests are sex-linked, and each (especially the wife) is deeply involved in their respective relationships with same-sex groups.

Both Mr. and Mr. K. felt that the wife who wanted her husband to give up evenings with his male friends was unreasonable and so was the husband who resented his wife's intimacy with her mother. The husband who comes home and does not talk to his wife should be left in peace by his "selfish" wife. . . .

Mrs. K. is the youngest of six children and Mr. K. has five siblings—the parents of each are living in the same community and none of the siblings is far away. The extraordinary closeness of family and in-law relations is a fact of great significance in the life of this couple. Economically, emotionally, recreationally—their daily lives are interwoven with the lives of their parents and siblings.

Mr. and Mrs. K. described a typical working-class division of interests. They talk little of his job. He discusses politics, sports and hobbies with men because she is not interested in these subjects. Mrs. K. on her side described most eloquently how "women should stick together and men should stay by themselves because they don't understand some things." She is in constant and intimate communication with mother, sisters, sisters-in-law and girl friends. Although she is shy and modest about sex, this subject is also discussed among the girls.

Mrs. K. gives the impression that she is more at ease in her female world. Her great respect for her husband and the desire to please him makes her cautious: "If he is feeling dopey I don't want to talk to him because he might get mad at me and I'd feel terrible."

Many an evening a week, Mr. K. goes out for a walk, to see his brother or to the tavern. He often does not tell his wife where he is going or when he expects to return.

Mr. K. does not help with housework or the care of children. Though sometimes he "sticks around" and wipes the dishes and baby-sits if Mrs. K. has something special she wants to do, the task allocation is traditional. Mr. K. is a devoted father. He can "make them mind him better" than their mother, but child care and discipline is Mrs. K.'s responsibility.

Mr. K. describes the typical male difficulty in expressing unhappy emotions and tends to withdraw when he is depressed. Mrs. K. said that she is not quite sure how her husband overcomes his bad moods: "He never bawls me out and he doesn't talk to me." Perhaps, "when he goes out he talks things over with his brother. I used to ask him why he was 'flippy' but it seemed to make him worse. . . . So I found out if you just don't bother him it wears off."

Mr. K. dislikes his job, despite its adequate pay, but does not reveal the full extent of his unhappiness so as not to worry his wife. He feels depressed at times, does not always understand the reason for these moods, and does not discuss them with his wife. She wishes that he did: "It would make it a lot easier for me if he'd explain why he felt the way he did sometimes when he comes home. I'd know if I had to shut up or if I could go on. This way I keep wondering what's the matter with him."

Despite many features which might be expected to estrange the couple, the marriage is close and deeply satisfying to both.

The personality needs of each are fulfilled at the emotional core of the marriage. Sex relations are satisfactory also.

Mrs. K., as the baby of the family, was always teased affectionately and is still easily hurt. "They sometimes called me a dumb Dora—it's on account of I can't talk sometimes. He bawls me out for minding what the others say and he says I'm not so dumb." Her husband gives her a combination of support, protection and appreciation which makes her say fervently, "Oh, he's the most!" He always compliments her when she cooks an especially good meal. His praise matters, she said, because unlike the in-laws who praise out of politeness, he doesn't say things he doesn't mean. He is the stronger of the two; she tries to please him and he rewards her adequately: "Whenever she's done a good job, I tell her so."

In his interview Mr. K. said: "I don't know if she'd tell you because she's kind of bashful but she's real good in bed. . . . I think you might call it ideal: a woman who is bashful and keeps to herself with everybody else and who's better than anybody with you." . . .

Mr. K. is, in turn, fulfilled in marriage. He had a vulnerable spot of his own. He never cared for school and his brothers used to "ride him about being a dummy." His "wonderful mother" would tell them to lay off him. Now he enjoys the deep respect of his wife—"I am the skipper of this marriage." She often tells him how very patient he is. His wife sums up this aspect of their marriage with deep insight: "He ain't stuck on himself at all. Him and me is a little bit alike that way. We have to tell each other not to mind things and that we're better than we think we are. Only he bawls me out more than I do him because he's a man." And Mr. K.: "When I got something to say she listens. She didn't sit there and wish I'd stop or be thinking about something else. Sometimes she'll be talking about the babies that aren't my work, but I listen to her."

Both Mr. and Mrs. K. have patience and capacity to get along with people. Mrs. K. said that both have good dispositions. One of his brothers was teasing them and said, "There goes the patient couple." Mr. K. said in discussing her moods, "She is too nice to get furious, but she gets upset."

To return to the question posed at the outset of this analysis: do occasional marriages like this one indicate that the lower-class norms of marriage—segregation of interests along sex lines, reticence, and separate leisure-time pastimes—do not impair communication after all?

For one thing, a marriage which is so deeply satisfying can apparently affect behavior even in the absence of certain norms. The gratification derived from the relationship leads to mutual concern—"It isn't that I'm that much interested in the neighbors, I am interested in her," explains Mr. K. in describing their conversations. It appears also that the content of shared experiences must be distinguished from the scope of sharing. The sense of closeness is apparently compatible with a very specialized pattern of sharing: *what* specifically is shared may be more important for the feeling of intimacy than *how much* of one's life is shared.

But if "love" does offset the potentially estranging social factors, it isn't love alone that does it. These factors do create typical vulnerabilities. To maintain its happy equilibrium this type of marriage requires some special supports.

The equilibrium of this marriage is maintained by the shared ability of close relatives and friends who fulfill for both, but especially for the wife, functions lacking in marriage. "No [Mr. K.] don't give a hoot," said Mrs. K. about many things which are very important to her, and about which no man, she added, could be expected to care. If Mrs. K. were isolated or, like some of the other women in Glenton, not on good terms with her relatives and in-laws, and had to depend upon her husband to be her audience, the marriage probably would be strained. As it is Mr. K. is somewhat irritated by his wife's "gossip." Mr. K., in turn, spends much of his lesiure in masculine company and his wife suspects that, in his "flippy moods," his brother is more of a help to him that she is.

Mrs. K.'s deep involvement with her mother and sister is tolerated by her husband partly because he likes his in-laws and they like him. Mr. K. was asked, "Do women have more need than men for heart-to-heart talk?" and he replied, "Well my wife sure in hell does and that's for sure. I could go for a month without talking to anybody but she's gotta talk to them just about every day." It is easy to imagine how this mild irritation would be aggravated were his relations with his in-laws less satisfactory or his position in marriage less secure.

Moreover, satisfactory economic conditions and common economic aspirations add to the assets of the marriage. The K.'s have recently purchased a house with some help from their families, but also as a result of joint planning and effort. "I feel real happy and real proud," said Mrs. K., "I had a lot to do with it, working between having babies and living cheaply and saving up." Their satisfaction in this accomplishment was revealed when in answer to a question, "When did Mr. K. last tell you he loved you?" Mrs. K. replied, "He don't do it regular like a school kid but a couple of nights ago we were watching T.V. and the kids had gone to bed. We were feeling kind of good about the house and he just up and said he loved me."

The case of Mr. and Mrs. K. illustrates how close and satisfying marriage can be despite a very specialized pattern of sharing. Even within the strictly personal sphere (her hurts, enthusiasm and problems) Mrs. K. makes a sharp distinction between what is appropriate to share with her husband, on the one hand, and with her girl friends and female relatives, on the other. Deeply satisfied in their emotional needs, Mr. and Mrs. K. live large segments of their lives apart from one another.

This chapter has specified social . . . factors that tend to limit the sharing of experiences with the spouse. Being more prevalent among the less-educated than among the high school graduates, many of these factors account for the relatively meager self-disclosure of the poorly educated respondents. The final case study advances the analysis further. The close and happy marriage of the poorly educated Kings reveals some conditions offsetting the estranging factors. Deep psychic congeniality, for instance, can create mutual concern even in the absence of the social norm of companionship. This case demonstrates still another fact—that satisfaction with communication and a sense of closeness do not, apparently, require that the totality of one's experiences be shared with the mate. Such emotions may co-exist with a very specialized pattern of sharing. But we have indicated some other factors as, for example, availability of congenial relatives and friends and satisfactory economic conditions, which, apart from emotional complementarity, support this type of marriage.

# SOCIAL CLASS DIFFERENCES IN FAMILY LIFE IN THE USSR*

*H. Kent Geiger*

Many of a society's most poignant discrepancies between its ideology and social

*Printed by permission of the author.

reality come to a head in the question of stratification. This is especially the case in the USSR, where the old order was overthrown in the name of the oppressed and where the building of a classless society is held as a national goal. In this and in related issues Soviet society exhibits some relatively unique features of great interest. The various groups and strata in the Soviet population have suffered or prospered in ways not commonly found in the history of other societies. There has been sustained intervention and control exerted by political authority over the structures and processes allowed more spontaneous development in other lands. Special attention has been accorded to the upgrading of women, but success in bringing them full equality with men cannot as yet be granted. And so on.

Many of the characteristics of Soviet social stratification are germane to our topic, social level differences in family patterns, but two are of particular consequence. It is widely recognized that the Soviet population is quite stratified, but the precise nature and extent of differentiation is little known, and least of all perhaps in respect to family life. In Part I, a number of the most important of these differences are identified. In Part II, I discuss the relevance in family life of dimensional inconsistency or, more precisely, inconsistency in the distribution of status elements. This is the tendency for the political, economic and social dimensions or orders of the Soviet system of stratification to be less highly correlated than in other societies.

## THE NATURE AND EXTENT OF STATUS DIFFERENTIATION

***The Standard and Style of Living.*** Comprehensive data describing the income or property of different categories of the population have not been published, but Soviet sociologists have in the recent past contributed statistical information for selected areas and groups which is well worth our attention. Some important aspects of the living standard and style of life are presented in Table 1, for the population of Terpenie, a Ukrainian village. When the families studied are grouped by occupational type and level of heads of households, such indicators of living standard as masonry rather than log construction of walls, wood rather than dirt floors and number of cows owned per family (considerably less than one) suggest the important items and range of variation found in Soviet villages.

In one respect, at least, the rural family does not fare poorly in relation to the urban family. In Terpenie housing is primitive but most families in the village can boast of three separate rooms. In Soviet cities the ordinary family must live in a single room and share a kitchen with others.[1] The elite, of course, generally enjoy several rooms in a well-heated and furnished flat, and may even have the luxury of hot and cold running water and a private bath. Another feature of the family life of the Soviet urban elite is that many own country houses or *dachas* to which they can retire for vacations and week-ends. While typically small and simple, these are much cherished, and probably serve as important status symbols as well as a source of restorative escape from the city.

Table 2 shows differences among officials, employees and workers in enterprises of the Leningrad machine-building industry for a recent year. The differences in monthly pay at different job levels seem quite small, although the top category includes directors of "shops" and "departments" as well as enterprises, which doubtless considerably depresses the average pay for the group. Such an interpretation is supported by the fact that the variation for entries in that category is considerably larger than for the other categories. In general, Soviet factory directors, scientists, artists, etc., enjoy a standard of living which is low compared with similar elites in Western democratic societies but noticeably higher than their own less distinguished fellow citizens.

In the USSR the members of families must not only engage in a struggle for income but often must search vigorously for effective and enjoyable ways to spend it.

[1] At the end of 1961 urban housing conditions were comparable to those of 1926. Per capita living space at that time was only about a third of the amount available to the population of the USA. See Timothy Sosnovy, "The Soviet City," pp. 321–45 in Joint Economic Committee of the U.S. Congress, 87th Session, *Dimensions of Soviet Economic Power*, Washington, D.C., 1962.

**TABLE 1 Representative Status Characteristic. Differences by Type of Labor of Household Head, Village of Terpenie, Uk. SSR, 1964**

| *Type of Labor* | *Per Cent of Houses with Masonry Walls* | *Per Cent of Houses with Wooden Floors* | *Cows per Hundred Families* | *Average No. of Years of Education* | *Per Cent of Houses with Religious Icons* |
|---|---|---|---|---|---|
| | **(1)** | **(2)** | **(3)** | **(4)** | **(5)** |
| Skilled non-manual | 75 | 100 | 75 | 12 | 7 |
| Other non-manual | 20 | 100 | 20 | 9 | 24 |
| Skilled manual | 37 | 86 | 33 | 7 | 34 |
| Other manual | 16 | 70 | 31 | 4 | 57 |

Source: Iu. V. Arutiunian, "The Social Structure of the Rural Population," *CDSP* 18.25:20–25, trans. from *Voprosy Filosofii*, No. 5, 1966, pp. 51–61.

The figures are adapted from Tables 3 and 4 and from the text. The first three columns refer only to kolkhoz families (N = 161). Columns (4) and (5) refer to the families of workers employed in state institutions and enterprises (N = 189) as well as those of the collective farmers in the village. Figures were rounded to the nearest even number.

The notorious weakness of retail distribution compounds the already short aggregate supply of consumer goods and services, so that the "opportunity to spend" has become itself an important component in the Soviet living standard. This is one reason why many people are so eager to leave the countryside to live in the city.

Residential location is extraordinarily important as a determinant of status in the USSR. Three distinctions are commonly made, probably of about equal importance. Siberia, the Far North and Central Asia contrast with the preferred European areas; the countryside contrasts with settled urban areas; and smaller, "provincial" towns and cities contrast with the central metropolitan areas, especially Moscow, Leningrad, and Kiev. The former in each of the paired categories suffers from more primitive conditions of life, greater scarcity of cultural, educational and recreational facilities, more inaccessibility, greater extremes of climate and topology, and so on. Those who reside in such areas suffer a corresponding status degradation.

The Soviet Government has in the past gone quite far in designating certain retail stores as special access or "closed distribution" institutions, thus reserving the chance to buy items desired but in short supply as a privilege. Other such services and privileges are at times reserved for the elite—dispensation from having to stand in line, allocation of a special lane on broad thoroughfares for the use of officials' cars, and so on.[2]

Typically Soviet are the state-operated public dining facilities and recreational or "cultural" clubs. The evidence suggests that eating outside the home in cafeterias and restaurants is positively associated with social level, and that the use of clubs is inversely associated with it. For example, one study reported from Leningrad that 25 per cent of the young people from worker family backgrounds but only 2 per cent of those from intelligentsia families visited a club during the preceding year.[3]

Certain patterns of public facility use are differentiated by social level for special reasons or involve distinctive implications. Placing a young child in a public institution such as an infants home for temporary care on a voluntary basis would seem to increase on higher social levels, because of the need for long trips connected with the job, field work to gain the practical experience required for a higher degree, and the like. But the surrender of a young child by its parent or parents on a permanent basis is more frequent on lower social levels. Much

[2] Joseph Novak, *The Future Is Ours, Comrade: Conversations with the Russians*, New York: Doubleday, 1960, pp. 38–39.

[3] A. G. Kharchev, "A Sociologist's Notes: A Free Evening," *CDSP* 17.46: 14–15, trans. from *Nedelia*, No. 42, Oct. 10–16, 1965, pp. 8–9.

**TABLE 2 Selected Status Characteristics at Different Levels of Job Skill in Enterprises of the Machine-Building Industry, Leningrad, 1965**

| *Occupational Group* | *Monthly Pay in Rubles* | *Years of Education* | *Per Cent Members of Party or YCL* | *Per Cent Participating in Public Activity* | *Per Cent Fully Satisfied with Occupation* | *N* |
|---|---|---|---|---|---|---|
| | (1) | (2) | (3) | (4) | (5) | |
| Directors and organizers | 173 | 14 | 61 | 84 | n.a. | (92) |
| Technical and scientific | 127 | 14 | 40 | 70 | 63 | (135) |
| Skilled non-manual | 110 | 12 | 43 | 82 | n.a. | (287) |
| Semi-professional | 129 | 9 | 38 | 79 | 80 | (67) |
| Skilled manual workers | 120 | 8 | 37 | 61 | n.a. | (1002) |
| Semi-skilled non-manual | 84 | 9 | 27 | 55 | n.a. | (353) |
| Semi-skilled manual | 107 | 8 | 39 | 54 | 61 | (837) |
| Unskilled manual | 98 | 6 | 14 | 35 | 25 | (115) |

Source: O. I. Shkaratan, "Social Differentiation in the Soviet Working Class," *CDSP* 19.12:3–8, trans. from *Voprosy Filosofi*, No. 1, 1967, pp. 28–39. This is an adaptation of Table 2 . . . and information reported in the text. Figures are rounded to the nearest even number.

the same has been true of attendance at Soviet boarding schools. Since the time when these institutions originated in 1956, they have been populated mainly by so-called "difficult children" or by children whose families did not adequately look after them. The tendency to use the boarding school like a corrective institution has brought them low esteem among the population at large and caused them to be widely considered a failure.[4]

Soviet sociological research has always paid a lot of attention to patterns of time usage, and studies almost always reveal that the higher status urban occupational groups work longer hours than do members of the working class.[5] We do not always know how to relate such knowledge to the comparative standard of living, since the variation by social level of relevant preferences is not entirely clear. Thus, higher status persons typically also display a substantially higher level of job satisfaction. See Table 2 for one example. Consequently, we do not know which group is better off; most probably this is an area where value consensus is lacking, and length of working day is not a decisive differentiating factor in respect to welfare.

How do the members of Soviet families spend their free time? In 1965 a representative national sample of 2730 urban adults was polled by the Public Opinion Institute of *Komsomolskaia Pravda*, the Soviet youth newspaper. Respondents were asked to describe their activities in terms familiar to Western survey researchers. The results suggest, among other things, that the Soviet urban population is highly literate. Eighty-two per cent of the sample reportedly read a newspaper each day, 71 per cent listen to the radio, 70 per cent read books at least several times a week, and 38 per cent watch a television program several times a week.

Of some 24 different activities investigated, there were sizable social group differences (more than 10 per cent between the high category, "intelligentsia," and the low category, "workers") for eight of them. These are gathered under three more general rubrics supplied by the present writer in Table 3. The most striking difference between intelligentsia and worker respondents concerned an activity rather uniquely Soviet, attending to one's "political education." Although it is not made clear precisely what this means, reading Marx, Engels, Lenin, studying the history and program of the CPSU, etc., would probably qualify, as would attendance at lectures on political affairs. The social group difference confirms the important fact that political conformity varies directly with social level.

Other patterns of educational activity also reveal social group differences. Self-directed study is more common for intelligentsia families, whereas in the working-class family, study during the hours free from work is more likely to be formal in nature, outside of the home, as would be the case for instruction in night school. The inverse association between social level and formal instruction joins other evidence suggesting that education in the working-class is strongly vocational.

In the case of friendly visiting and attending "social functions" the worker adults are more active. The differences are sufficiently large to be significant and this is an important result, for it contradicts the pattern usually found in the United States. Perhaps it is connected with the fact that the traditional Russian national character appears to be highly loaded on the traits of gregariousness and affiliation,[6] and that the higher social levels are constrained to sacrifice this source of pleasure in order to maintain their positions. An interpretation

[4] For a revealing discussion, see Boris Izyumski, "Reflections on Boarding Schools: Just Like Home," *CDSP* 18.46:31–2, trans. from *Pravda*, Nov. 13, 1966, p. 3.

[5] The best evidence found is in *Komsomolskaia Pravda* for February 24–26, 1966. Table 1 on p. 3 of the Feb. 24 issue gives a breakdown of the length of the working day in the national sample for four different categories of urban occupational positions. Thirty-nine per cent of the professional intelligentsia and 17 per cent of the technical intelligentsia work nine hours or more per day, but only 12 per cent of the lower-status "employee" and 6 per cent of the "worker" categories work that long.

[6] For more detail see Alex Inkeles, *et al.*, "Modal Personality and Adjustment to the Soviet Socio-Political System," *Human Relations* 11:3–22, 1958, especially "Social Class Differentiation," pp. 17–19.

**TABLE 3 Major Social Group Differences in Use of Free Time: Percentages of Soviet Urban Adults Engaging in Different Activities, National Sample, 1965**

| | *Educational* | | |
|---|---|---|---|
| SOCIAL GROUP | POLITICAL STUDY SEVERAL TIMES WEEKLY | SELF-DIRECTED STUDY SEVERAL TIMES WEEKLY | NIGHT SCHOOL AND CORRESPONDENCE STUDY DAILY |
| Intelligentsia | 67 (347) | 53 | 18 |
| Employees | 56 (516) | 37 | 25 |
| Workers | 38 (1092) | 38 | 30 |
| | *Friendly Social* | | |
| | VISITING AND ENTERTAINING SEVERAL TIMES A MONTH | | ATTENDING PARTIES, DANCES SEVERAL TIMES A MONTH |
| Intelligentsia | 57 | | 12 |
| Employees | 62 | | 19 |
| Workers | 68 | | 29 |
| | *High Culture* | | |
| | READ MAGAZINES SEVERAL TIMES A MONTH | ATTEND THE THEATER SEVERAL TIMES A YEAR | ATTEND SYMPHONIC CONCERTS, LITERARY RECITALS SEVERAL TIMES A YEAR |
| Intelligentsia | 87 | 55 | 34 |
| Employees | 86 | 44 | 18 |
| Workers | 67 | 39 | 13 |

Source: Adapted from information published by Boris A. Grushin in three articles in *Komsomolskaia Pravda,* February 24–26, 1966. The cross-tabular data are presented separately for two groups of the intelligentsia, the "technical intelligentsia" and the "professional" or "intelligentsia not engaged in material production (teachers, physicians, scientific workers, etc.)." I collapsed them into a single category and recomputed the percentages to provide a simpler comparison by status level of the three major urban occupational groups.

of this nature would be buttressed were we to find that the direction of the social level differences is reversed in response to the question: "How would you *like to spend* your free time?" for this would suggest the presence of pertinent dissatisfaction on the part of persons occupying higher social levels. While this does turn out to be the case for responses indicating a desire to spend free time visiting, the difference, which favors the intelligentsia, is only about one per cent in magnitude.[7]

The final difference shown in use of free time, concerning patterns labeled "high culture," reading magazines and attending theater, concerts, etc., are all strongly associated with the economic resources and educational training of persons in families on each social level.

The members of Soviet families do not all enjoy the same opportunities to strive for welfare and happiness. While children from families on all social levels seem to share high occupational aspirations, the fact is that the achievement of such aspirations is much more likely on the part of children who have a good start in life in the sense of coming from families from higher-ranking social levels. Recently in the city of Gorky 80 per cent of the children in the lower grades of school were of worker background and 20 per cent were children of members of the Soviet intelligentsia. As a result of the typical school drop-out pattern, most pronounced in the working class, the ratio was reversed among those graduating

[7] Table 7, p. 3, in *Komsomolskaia Pravda*, Feb. 26, 1966.

from secondary school, leading to what a Soviet commentator terms "inadequate social mobility."[8] See also Table 4 and accompanying comment below.

***Patterns of Deviance and Conformity.*** The Soviet regime is committed to a thorough reconstruction of society by planned, occasionally forcible, intervention in social affairs. The family, however, is not a public institution. As a legally defined private grouping, it is minimally eligible for control by political authority. This fact has always been viewed by the Communist Party as somewhat of a defect, because the family harbors many of the patterns labeled "survivals" in the Soviet lexicon. Thus, "It is hardest of all to eliminate the survivals of harmful ways and hoary traditions in the sphere of family and everyday life. But it is very important for society that this sphere develop in step with the general progress."[9]

Soviet writers have been generous in their charges that the family breeds deviant behavior and have written at length about it. But they have been very reluctant explicitly to identify by social level the location or frequency of particular types of these undesired patterns. It will be our purpose here to make such an effort and to sample in the realm of social conformity as well.

Five important types of deviance seem to be inversely associated with social level: crime and delinquency, drunkenness, petty theft of public property, illegitimacy and religious activity. Research design and techniques of analysis and reporting leave a lot to be desired, but Soviet accounts of criminal behavior and drinking bouts, and the relevant though sparse statistics generally indicate that the participants are of low status. Drinking vodka on social occasions plays an important role in the Russian peasant tradition, and it must be reckoned as one of the main current diversions of men in these and worker families.[10]

I make special note of petty theft of state property and of illegitimacy because both are linked in much the same way to the problem of families with few resources. Poverty has led in each case to a semi-institutionalized pattern. A letter to *Izvestiia* from a young worker who objects to the pattern expresses the idea: "If you borrow a few kopecks from someone, woe be to you if you don't return every last kopeck. But we can steal from the state, can't we? One day I saw a mechanic wrapping up some pieces of pipe to take them home. I said to him: 'Why do you steal things from the plant?' He stared at me as if I had fallen from the moon. . . . Today pieces of pipe, tomorrow paint, next, who knows? The result is that our public property is pilfered without a thought."[11]

Illegitimacy has been tremendously inflated as a result of Soviet divorce policy. From 1944 until 1965 the law placed major obstacles in the path of those seeking divorce. Great numbers of unhappy unions were simply dissolved without legal recourse. Often the partners subsequently entered into new relationships which could not be registered as legal marriages because of the law prohibiting bigamy. Children born to persons in such families were technically illegitimate, and on occasion so identified publicly. There are disproportionate numbers of such children in the lower levels of the status system.

The Soviet population maintains religious interests, but in strong inverse association with social level. For example, the

[8] Vladimir Kantorovich, "Reflections on What Has Been Read: A Science Kindred to Us," *CDSP* 18.26:14–16, trans. from *Literaturnaia Gazeta*, May 5, 1966, pp. 1–2 and May 14, 1966, pp. 1–2.

[9] F. Konstantinov and V. Kelle, "Historical Materialism—Marxist Sociology," *CDSP* 17.8: 3–9, trans. from *Kommunist*, No. 1, 1965, pp. 9–23.

[10] For a sampling of the kind of evidence from which these generalizations are drawn see D. M. Aptekman, "Causes of the Vitality of the Ceremony of Baptism Under Modern Conditions," *Soviet Sociology* 4.2:10–16, 1965, trans. from *Voprosy Filosofii*, No. 3, 1965; G. M. Minkovski, "Problems of Criminology: Some Causes of Juvenile Delinquency in the USSR and Measures to Prevent It," *CDSP* 18.30:9–13, trans. from *Sovetskoe Gosudarstvo i Pravo*, May, 1966, pp. 84–93; K. Kostenko, "On False Manliness and an Indifferent Province Committee," *CDSP* 6.29:6–7, trans. from *Komsomolskaia Pravda*, July 17, 1954, p. 2.

[11] Yu. Feofanov, "Reflections on Letters: Are You Holding Out Your Hand to Him?" *CDSP* 18.46:24–25, trans. from *Izvestiia*, Nov. 18, 1966, p. 6.

lower the social level the more likely is the Soviet parent to baptize his child.[12] Similarly, as Table 1 reveals, the lower the social level the more likely is the family to display holy icons.

Some survivals are directly correlated with social level. Divorce, a mild form of deviance since the mid-thirties, has in its legally constituted form almost certainly been distributed in positive association with social level simply because it has been expensive. How much of the association has been due to capacity to pay as opposed to the absence of traditional prejudice against divorce, still strong among the peasants, is not known.

A pattern of deviance peculiar to more affluent circles in cities has been exceptionally disturbing to the Soviet leaders. It is a complex of dissidence among the youth, probably the closest Soviet version to a rebellious youth culture. Some young persons refuse to follow the standards of behavior prescribed for a patriotic member of the Young Communist League. They refuse to work, cultivate personal appearance, seek out objects and styles of art, music, conversation, and clothing originating abroad, search for adventure and fun, fail to volunteer for recommended civic activities, and assume skeptical, disrespectful attitudes toward the Communist Party, older persons and much of the established Soviet way of life. They are variously identified and pilloried in the USSR as "stylists," "social parasites" or "nihilists."[13]

Another mode of deviant behavior derives from efforts made by upper level persons to obtain scarce goods, services and opportunities. The Soviet press has many complaints about collusion, nepotism, mutual protection and, above all, bribery, by which people seek to protect and enhance their economic and social interests in a society of perennial shortages. This is treated below under Part II.

Patterns of social conformity tend also to vary by social level. The bulk of virtuous patterns are manifested increasingly or predominantly in individuals and families of the higher-ranking social levels. Some of the most important are displayed in Tables 1 and 2. Completing a large number of years of formal education, taking a positive attitude toward work (shown here in the form of job satisfaction), participating in public activity, being a member of the Communist Party or YCL. are all patterns associated positively with social level. Others are easy to name or hypothesize. For instance, the general link between social level and political loyalty or ideological orthodoxy is manifested in the greater likelihood of the portrait of Marx, Lenin and the current First Secretary of the CPSU to be found in the home.

One of the few ways in which conformity varies inversely with social level is found in the production of children. I take "conformity" in this case to refer exclusively to the standards expressed by the party and state. In the official view there is a certain value in the production of children, and there are indeed more children per family in peasant than worker families, more in the latter than in intelligentsia families, and the inverse relation with social level holds for both urban and rural populations separately.[14] Because of government fertility policy, the lower the social level the more likely is the Soviet mother to merit special rewards for such conformity, to earn an honorary title ("Mother Heroine," etc.), receive a medal, and gain substantial monetary support for the many children she has borne.

***Family Roles.*** Patterns of social conformity in the larger society constitute a proper starting point for the characterization of class differences in family roles. Responsible and efficient discharge of occupational, political, school, etc., duties tend to vary in direct association with the social level of the incumbent's family. The same is true in respect to most behavior

[12] See, for one report, p. 31 in V. B. Olshanski, "The Individual and Social Values," *Soviet Sociology*, 5.2:11–45, 1966, trans. from *Sotsiologiia v SSSR*, Vol. 1, Moscow, 1965, pp. 471–530.

[13] Of the many items published on this subject, one of the most absorbing is Lev Kassil, "Youth and the Young Without Youth (A Writer's Notes)," *CDSP* 9.27:12–14, trans. from *Literaturnaia Gazeta*, May 25, 1957, p. 2.

[14] Data on fertility and on family size resulting from a 1960 study of 37,000 families and 54,500 women over 17 are presented in A. Vostrikova, "Nekotorye dannye o rozhdaemosti v SSSR," *Vestnik Statistiki*, No. 12, 1962, pp. 42–46.

and attitudes displayed within the family. Thus, though higher level parents have fewer children, they or delegated relatives or servants spend more time with them and attend to their needs more carefully than parents on lower social levels.[15]

Soviet researchers note an important trend in family life, namely, increasing emphasis on achievement rather than ascription as a standard for status determination inside the family. In one report on the contemporary Turkmen worker family it is stated that "the position of each adult member of the family, regardless of age and sex, is determined by the work record on the job, and the moral qualities manifested in family and public life."[16] There has been a phenomenal rise in the number and level of opportunities in the larger social system made available to Soviet women in the years since the Revolution. There is good evidence that they have responded vigorously to these, and that their rise in general status is paralleled by an increase in their status inside the family.

Since there is a tendency for old and new ways of life on the one side to correspond with lower and higher social levels on the other, achievement as a basis for status recruitment to particular roles inside the family probably increases with higher social standing. Thus, the rate of intermarriage between persons of different ethnic background, a rough index of the lack of importance of this particular ascriptive factor, varies directly with social level, just as it finds more favor in the eyes of youth than amongst their elders.[17] Similarly, holding to the principle of sex equality or, perhaps more accurately, opposition to social inequality based on sex varies directly with social level. The patriarchal tradition still enjoys some esteem among the peasantry and even more among the less assimilated Muslim portions of the population.

There is some variation by social level in the modes of feeling and styles of expressing emotion. Sentiments of hostility and anger appear more openly in lower level family life. Indeed, men who beat or assault their wives are not infrequently exposed in the daily press, and it seems that such scandals take place most frequently in peasant or working-class families. In contrast, open displays of tenderness or love tend to be subject to a norm of "masculine restraint" (*muzhskaia sderzhannost*) by which men are reluctant to reveal such feelings. I would assign more prominence to such a norm and accompanying behavior in lower level families. Correspondingly, the lower the level the less importance is attached to love as an experience; peasants, for instance, are said to choose marital partners in an impersonal way, without anticipation of a love relationship to aid in the selection.[18]

The picture of Soviet family life would not be complete without reference to interpersonal conflict. There is more conflict in the peasant families which retain features of the traditional way of life. Such conflict focuses on the problem of authority and differences in outlook between the older and younger generations. The young people frequently demand more say in the conduct of family life and their own affairs than their parents are willing to grant, and fail to share some of their parents' orientations, most notably their religious and political values.

## II. REFLECTIONS OF INCONSISTENCY IN THE DISTRIBUTION OF STATUS ELEMENTS

I noted earlier the pronounced inconsistency in the way social honor, economic

[15] H. Kent Geiger, "The Soviet Family," in M. F. Nimkoff (ed.), *Comparative Family Systems*, Boston: Houghton-Mifflin Co., 1965, pp. 301–328.

[16] Shikhberdy Annaklychev, "The Life of the Oil Workers of Nebit-Dag and Kum-Dag (Part IV)," *Soviet Sociology*, 4.2:34–57, 1965, trans. from the Russian edition of 1961, published in Ashkhabad, TSSR.

[17] A review and discussion of Soviet studies may be found in A. G. Kharchev, *Brak i semia v SSSR*, Moscow, 1964, pp. 192–196. The main thesis argued is that the Soviet social order has decreased racial and ethnic prejudice and that intermarriage rates have gone up. Data on marriages and divorces registered for different years and different places also suggest that the non-Slavic partner is more likely to be male than female, but that when the non-Slavic partner is female, she is apt to be of the intelligentsia (p. 193).

[18] A village-community study quotes a young collective farmer: "We don't look for a great friendship. You like the girl, so you marry her." P. I. Kushner (ed.), *Selo Viriatino v proshlom i nastoiashchem*, Akad. Nauk SSSR, Trudy Instituta Etnog. imeni Miklukho-Maklaia, Novaia Seriia, Tom 41, Moscow, 1958, p. 226.

reward and political power are distributed in the Soviet system of social stratification. The fact is that there is a lot of *social* equality in the USSR which coexists in uneasy relation with a good amount of *economic* inequality. Effective performance in work is expressed in the functional or incentive reward system chiefly in the form of differentiated wage and salary levels, but also in terms of differentials in occupational prestige which are quite similar to those found in Western societies. Continuing devotion to equalitarianism by the ruling regime is expressed in the realm of the modest but widely available rewards provided by recreational and cultural facilities, opportunity for education and social mobility, accessible medical care, and the strongly fostered ideology of the dignity of labor and other aspects of what is sometimes referred to as Soviet humanism. In political life the degree of inequality is greatest. This is probably the best-known feature of Soviet society, a phenomenon reaching its most extreme form during the Stalin era, but which is still of paramount significance in Soviet society today.

In brief, then, Soviet society offers an unusual amount of social equality, a degree of economic differentiation quite ordinary or typical in modern societies, and an extraordinary level of political inequality. Taken together these facts are termed inconsistency in the distribution of status elements (or "distributive" or "dimensional" inconsistency) to refer to a property of the Soviet system of stratification as a whole. In reference to the individual citizen and his family they suggest widespread status inconsistency.

How is this situation reflected at different status levels of Soviet family life? The discrepancy between social equality and economic inequality is experienced in the upper level family as lack of opportunity for appropriate status display, and produces corresponding efforts in that direction. These are not considered legitimate channels for initiative, and from time to time the press prints exposés of persons manifesting such unworthy sentiments. A certain high ranking Soviet officer, for example, was reported as quite indignant, unable to reconcile himself, with the thought that he, a lieutenant colonel, had to live ". . . under the same roof with a former sergeant, now an ordinary worker."[19] A professor and his wife also revealed themselves to be snobs. They displayed coats-of-arms and diplomas in their home to call attention to their social importance, and were also brought to account for their frantic effort to discredit the wife of their son. She was of low social origin, the daughter of a miner, and they were opposed to the marriage.[20]

A more serious problem stems from the temptation for higher status persons to use their money unscrupulously, in effect to reduce social equality in consumption and the provision of equal opportunity. If they succumb, the sharpest resentment is aroused in regime and people when parents seek to guarantee access for their children to the limited places available for study in institutions of higher learning by bribing educational administrators.[21]

Families on lower social levels are faced with quite a different situation. Confronted by an immense gap between their economic ranking on the one side and the doctrine of social equality on the other, they commonly react in either or both of two ways. One involves selective cognitive stress on formal social equality irrespective of occupational differentiation. This tendency typically involves the denial of differences in occupational prestige, is officially encouraged, and receives suitable publicity from time to time. For instance, when N. Vikhrov told his former school teacher that he had become a mechanic, she expressed regret: "You had such talent. You could have become an engineer." Similar

[19] "Sovetskaia semia," *Pravda Ukrainy*, Sept. 16, 1959, p. 4.

[20] L. Likhodeyev, "Social Notes" (feuilleton), *CDSP*, 13.32:25–26, trans. from *Literaturnaia Gazeta*, July 1, 1961, p. 2.

[21] On April 19, 1958, N. S. Khrushchev was quoted in *Pravda* as follows: ". . . it sometimes happens that a person is admitted to a higher educational establishment not because he is well prepared, but because he has an influential papa and mama who can help him to get in." For further discussion of the problem, see "Entrance Requirements, Supply and Selection of Applicants in Soviet Higher Education," pp. 242–274 in Nicholas DeWitt, *Educational and Professional Manpower in the USSR*, Washington, D.C.: National Science Foundation, 1961.

sentiments are reported by him to be held by others. Vikhrov is critical of them. He asks, "Why doesn't a grandmother say proudly, 'My son drives a truck'?" Further, he queries, with apparent naiveté, "It is understandable that a person with a diploma has a higher position in any work collective, but will a good, highly skilled worker really enjoy any less respect?"[22]

A more common lower class reaction, we may suppose, though not necessarily always dislodging the first, goes in the contrary direction. It is to acknowledge the gap between the two status dimensions, find it distressing, consciously depreciate the significance of "social equality," and aspire strongly to occupational mobility. As we shall see, the strength of the aspiration does not guarantee the success of the enterprise, but the reflection within the family consists essentially in the appearance of articles of faith asserting that a good husband is one who constantly improves his occupational qualifications, perhaps by going to night school, that a good parent is one who ensures the successful education of his children, and that a good child is one who does well in school.

Some support for this interpretation is given by Table 4, where the aspirations for higher education and the actual fates of a 10 per cent sample of secondary school graduates for the year 1963, Novosibirsk Region, are compared for different social levels. The per cent wishing to continue studying past secondary school (column 1) is impressively high on all levels, suggesting, if we grant that the link between educational achievement and occupational mobility is well known, how eagerly sought after the latter must be.

Another story is told by the positive association between social level and actual achievement. A follow-up survey at a later date to see how many actually continued their studies established the association seen in column 2 of the table. I subtracted the figures in column 2 from those in column 1 to produce a measure of discrepancy between aspiration and achievement for each social group.

As the Soviet reporter notes, ". . . the

[22] N. Vikhrov, "Looking into the Mail: What Does 'Getting on in the World' Mean?" *CDSP* 18.12:19, abst. from *Komsomolskaia Pravda*, Dec. 21, 1965, p. 2.

**TABLE 4 Secondary School Graduates' Desire to Continue Formal Education and Actual Outcome by Social Group of Parental Family, Novosibirsk Region, 1963**

| *Social Group of Parental Family* | *Per Cent Wishing to Continue Full-time Study* | *Per Cent Actually Continuing Full-time Study* | *Discrepancy* |
|---|---|---|---|
| | (1) | (2) | (3) |
| Urban non-manual | 93 | 82 | 11 |
| Rural non-manual | 76 | 58 | 18 |
| Non-agricultural manual | 80 | 55 | 25 |
| Agricultural manual | 76 | 10 | 66 |
| Entire sample | 83 | 61 | 22 |

Source: V. N. Shubkin, "Youth Starts Out in Life," *Soviet Sociology*, 4.3:3–15, 1966, also in *CDSP*, 17.30:3–9, trans. from *Voprosy Filosofii*, No. 5, 1965, pp. 57–70.

This is an adaptation of the original data. It excludes all respondents who envisaged combining work and study, excludes the residual social group category "others" and presents a single mean percentage figure for the three categories of non-agricultural manual workers—industry and construction, transport and communication, and service—analyzed separately in the original table. Social group is judged by father's occupation, or mother's if there was no father. The total and subgroup sample sizes are not revealed. However, a previous publication dealing with the same study indicates that the 10 per cent sample of eight year school 1963 graduates is "around 9,000," and that in autumn of the same year the researchers gathered information about the actual fate of "several thousand of the graduates we had studied." (Page 18 in V. N. Shubkin, "Vybor professii v usloviakh kommunisticheskogo stroitelstva," *Voprosi Filosofii*, No. 8, 1964.)

paths through life taken by young people from various social groups show significant divergences."[23] We might add that the really massive discrepancy, which we can also provisionally interpret as a measure of frustration, is that for the "agricultural manual" group—Soviet peasants working as collective and state farmers. In their high hopes and disadvantaged chances in life, these parts of the Soviet population seem to be suffering the fate of lower class and less developed people throughout the world, immersion in a tide of rapidly rising ex-expectations unaccompanied by equivalent increases in opportunity.

One also finds in the Soviet scene an unusual discordance between the distribution of economic rewards and the distribution of political power. Soviet society, far from democratic, concentrates power in the top hierarchy. The local area is often a replica of the national picture: a few officials of the party and government enjoy extraordinary power.

The chief reflection of this in high level circles arises out of the chance for officials to abuse power in order to achieve personal or family goals. Family loyalty continues to be strong, opportunities for consumption not always responsive to the ruble, and Soviet politicians are subject to wishes and demands for special favors emanating from their wives and own dear children. The case of Sergei, a high party official, is most instructive. In the course of a short period, his wife or his mother made the following specific "requests" of him: (1) speak to the director of the agricultural experimental station about buying some currants, bigger, firmer, available in thick clusters and cheaper than those bought through the usual channels; (2) telephone the manager of a store about the purchase of a wool blouse for his wife, to avoid the "frightful waiting-in-line"; (3) telephone the director of the theatre for the favor of seats without previous purchase of tickets; (4) arrange an exception to the hospital rule so his wife could stay there with their sick daughter. Some of these requests were granted by Sergei; others were refused, but elicited vigorous reproaches from his wife: "I am not inciting you to crime, after all!" or "You're no father, you're a walking moral code! Prude!" How, wonders this would-be model Communist, can he explain to his wife that ". . . a high official has less of a moral right than anyone else to use his official position, even in trivial matters?"[24]

How is the situation seen at the other end of the status continuum? For an answer, we turn to a case . . . of an influential father who went even further in exploiting his political position. He made a mockery of the notion of social equality by rescuing his hoodlum son from the constituted processes of Soviet justice. A drunken brawl during the summer of 1966 in the town of Iglino, Bashkir ASSR, was broken up by a militiaman. One of the participants, Fakhretdinov, was the son of an important local official. The father turned up at the station house, had his son released from custody, and the case was never brought to trial. When the affair became known to the townspeople, among other developments there was a letter sent to *Izvestiia*:

> Everything is allowed to someone like Renat Fakhretdinov, for he is the son of the chairman of the district executive committee! He'll get away with everything, he can do anything, his daddy will fix it all up. But if he were the son of a worker, he would catch it quickly enough.[25]

Abuse of power produces resentment, antagonism and apathy at the bottom levels of society. While there has been curtailment of such abuse at the national level since the demise of Stalin, we cannot be certain of similar adjustments on the local scene nor that highly concentrated power will not be again abused in the future. Whether still largely present or only fresh in memory, it seems quite likely that such exploitation plays a significant role in the lives of Soviet working-class and peasant families as targets of recrimination and hostility.

On all levels of Soviet society there is

[23] V. N. Shubkin, "Youth Starts Out in Life," *Soviet Sociology* 4.3:3–15, 1966; also in *CDSP* 17.30:3–9; trans. from *Voprosy Filosofii*, No. 5, 1965, pp. 57–70.

[24] A. Volkov, "Incorruptible Conscience" (short story), *CDSP* 14.3:30–31, trans. from *Izvestiia*, Jan. 16, 1962, p. 4.

[25] F. Chernetski, "Kreslo ne pomoglo," , Aug. 20, 1966, p. 3.

some consciousness of the contradiction between the social and the political dimensions of stratification, between what I have termed unusual social equality and extraordinary political inequality. Alongside it one finds a standard tendency for cognitive separation of peoples' images of Soviet social structure into two parts. One stresses the social equality side of things—interpersonal and intergroup harmony, equality, cooperative labor and service to society—and is a fully legitimate image, fit for open admission and public display. The other part focuses squarely on the dimension of unequal power. It sees Soviet society as divided into "we" and "they." Which groupings qualify as "we" and which are lodged in the other category depends upon the political level of the viewer, but in any case, this is not a legitimate image. It is not usually revealed publicly, but like other sensitive issues in Soviet life it does attract some attention in discussion within the family.

. . . . . . . . . . . . . . . . . . . . . . . . . . . . . . . . . . .

# SOCIAL CLASS AND SUCCESS

## *Ephraim H. Mizruchi*

Our specific task . . . is to launch our exploration of Merton's hypothesis that differential access to the various means of achieving success in American society leads to greater anomie in the lower classes compared to the relatively high classes.

. . . . . . . . . . . . . . . . . . . . . . . . . . . . . . . . . . .

Merton's study is primarily concerned with types of individual reactions to anomie, particularly deviant reactions. . . .[1]

Merton's theory consists of two approaches. On one hand, there is the discrepancy between aspiration and achievement; on the other, attempts to cope with this situation among different segments of the social structure. The notion of discrepancy is derived from Durkheim's theory that widespread aspiration for what is unattainable reflects anomie in the social structure. The typology of reactions to structured strain is Merton's own theoretical formulation. Srole, Bell, Hyman, and the other writers . . . are in reality attempting to test Durkheim's theory as Merton has applied it to American society, rather than Merton's theory of individual reactions. Our own study may also be placed in the category of assessments of the Durkheimian theory within the Mertonian framework. . . .

### SUCCESS VALUES

Our major concern in this work is to test hypotheses systematically by utilizing empirical data gathered for that specific purpose. . . . Questions "concerning the objectivity of values [or] . . . their quality of absoluteness or lack of it," as Williams points out (1960, p. 402),[2] need not concern us here. . . . From our point of view, then, a value is *z* group's conception of the desirable (Williams, 1960, p. 402). The specific nature of the value-referent, although we will make extensive references to it, is not crucial to the test of our hypotheses. In our analysis, we use care in distinguishing between what are often referred to as values—the reified referents of the process of valuation—and the underlying conception that influence our judgments of these values.

Reprinted from *Success and Opportunity*, New York: Free Press, 1964.

[1] Writers who have dealt with this aspect of Merton's theory are, to name only a few, Robert Dubin, "Deviant Behavior and Social Structure," *American Sociological Review*, 24 (April, 1959), pp. 147–164; Richard A. Cloward, "Illegitimate Means, Anomie, and Deviant Behavior," *American Sociological Review*, 24 (April, 1959), pp. 164–176; Albert K. Cohen, "The Study of Social Disorganization and Deviant Behavior," in Robert K. Merton *et al.*, *Sociology Today* (New York: Basic Books, Inc., 1959), pp. 461–484; and Talcott Parsons, *The Social System* (New York: The Free Press of Glencoe, 1951), Chapter 7.

[2] Robin H. Williams, Jr., *American Society*, New York: Alfred A. Knopf, 1960. (C. S. H.)

It is only in the latter case that we are truly dealing with values. . . .

The specific values, indices of which we are attempting to analyze, are those associated with the American notion of "success."

. . . . . . . . . . . . . . . . . . . . . . . . . . . . . . . . . . .

Although there are several possible ways of approaching the study of values empirically, we use only one, an indirect approach to verbal value responses. We have asked a series of questions designed to elicit descriptions of behavior and possessions that reflect basic value systems. Although we are attempting to tap as broad a range of values as possible, we do not attempt to describe a total value system or even a sub-system. . . .

We begin our empirical analysis by examining the distribution among the several social classes of selected values pertinent to our problem. . . .

An attempt will be made here to answer the following questions: What is the distribution of success values among the classes? To what extent do members hold values that aid or hinder them in their efforts to achieve success? To what extend do members believe that opportunities of getting ahead are available to them?[3]

. . . . . . . . . . . . . . . . . . . . . . . . . . . . . . . . . . .

## SOCIAL CLASS AND "GETTING AHEAD"

In Merton's essay, "Continuities in Social Structure and Anomie," he attempts to evaluate several studies designed to test his hypothesis. In commenting on Hyman's findings that differences *do* exist among classes, in terms of values related to success in American society, he makes the following statement:

The survey data available to Hyman do not discriminate between the *degrees* of commitment to the goal but indicate only the relative *frequency* with which individuals in the samples drawn from the several social strata express some unknown degree of acceptance of the success goal and of related values . . . it appears that subsequent inquiry might be usefully directed toward studying the intensity as well as the extent to which these values are held in diverse groups, social strata, and communities. (1957, p. 171).

In order to test the Merton hypothesis, we selected what seemed a well designed question to elicit the kind of response necessary for adequate assessment of the distribution of success values in American society. Morris Rosenberg has used a measure of the degree of importance placed upon striving for success in American society.[4] . . .

Rosenberg's question is phrased, "How important to you, personally, is it to get ahead in life?" Of the 226 respondents to Rosenberg's question in our survey, 174 (77%) answered that "getting ahead" is important, while only fifty-two replied that "getting ahead" is unimportant to them. Rosenberg found that 88% of his respondents thought "getting ahead" was important (1957, p. 159). His subjects were, however, college students, whom we should expect to be more involved in striving for success than our respondents, many of whom have already achieved some of their life goals.

Not only do *most* of our respondents feel that getting ahead is important, but our data indicates that it is slightly more important to the lower-class segments of the population.[5] The lower-class respondents

[3] Data were gathered in 1958 in a small upstate New York town (population about 16,000).

[4] Morris Rosenberg, *Occupations and Values* (New York: The Free Press of Glencoe, 1957); Robin M. Williams, Jr., ed. *Friendship and Social Values in a Suburban Community* (Eugene: Dept. of Sociology, U. of Oregon, 1956, Mimeographed); and Rose K. Goldsen, Morris Rosenberg, Robin M. Williams, Jr., and Edward Suchman, *What College Students Think* (New York: Van Nostrand, 1959). I should like to thank Professor Robin M. Williams, Jr., for permission to use questions that he has developed in connection with his research on values and for a number of important suggestions about the kinds of problem associated with research on the relationship between aspiration for success and anomie.

[5] Chi-square = 4.7, 2 degrees of freedom, P = .10. Although we are suggesting an arbitrary limit to acceptance or rejection of a probability statement as support for a particular finding, we want to avoid holding ourselves to any limit. We shall be content if the reader interprets the findings as they are presented, using his own judgment of whether or not they appear *theoretically* significant.

show a greater "degree of commitment," in Merton's terminology, as well as greater frequency of acceptance of success goals.

These data, if taken alone, might provide additional support for the findings of Srole and others that anomie is greater in the relatively low classes. It could then be argued that, since success is apparently more important to lower-class respondents and since anomie is already known to be higher among the lower classes, the greater degree of importance placed on success is a cause of anomie. In order to make a more complete assessment of the theory, however, it is necessary to relate anomie to class when acceptance of success goals is constant among all classes. . . .

## SOCIAL CLASS, SUCCESS, AND RELATED VALUES

Our second question about the relationship between social class and values is, To what extent do members of the different classes have values what aid or inhibit them in their efforts to achieve success? What is success from the point of view of the respondent, how is it attained, and what part does his conception of success and its corollary values play in his opportunities for achievement? . . .

***Social Class and Success Symbols.*** One method of exploring Americans' conception of the nature of success is to analyze the importance attributed to the symbols they associate with it. In an effort to uncover these symbols, we asked, "Could you list, in order of importance, those things which you believe to be signs of success in our society?" Six possible responses were read by the interviewer, and the respondent stated an order of preference. The six elements were based on a code taken from open-ended replies to the same question in an earlier study. It is sufficient for our purposes to present only the first choices. The class categories, from the highest (I) to the lowest (V), are taken from Hollingshead's Two-Factor Index of Social Position. . . . The basis for our classification is occupational and educational attainment of the male head of the household in which the respondent resides.

As Table 1 indicates, there are several tendencies associated with the selection of success symbols among our respondents. The symbols rated first in importance by the greatest proportion of our sample (31%), was home ownership. "Having a good education" was ranked most important by 29% and "having a good, steady job" by 23%. When we review the distribution by class, we notice certain trends. Home ownership tends to be selected more frequently as class declines. There is also a slight similar tendency in selection of job security. Education, however, tends to be selected more frequently as we ascend the class structure.

A closer examination of the data suggests that these relationships are not simply the

**TABLE 1 Class and Most Important Symbol of Success as Selected by Respondent (in Percentages)**

| | *Class* | | | | | *Total* | |
|---|---|---|---|---|---|---|---|
| | I | II | III | IV | V | PER CENT | N |
| Education | 61 | 37 | 30 | 26 | 21 | 29 | 63 |
| Many friends | 0 | 10 | 17 | 5 | 3 | 7 | 16 |
| Prestige | 8 | 10 | 4 | 6 | 5 | 6 | 13 |
| Job security | 15 | 21 | 17 | 27 | 24 | 23 | 51 |
| Home ownership | 8 | 16 | 32 | 31 | 41 | 31 | 70 |
| Money | 8 | 6 | 0 | 5 | 6 | 4 | 10 |
| Totals | 100 | 100 | 100 | 100 | 100 | 100 | 223 |
| N | (13) | (19) | (47) | (81) | (63) | | |

Chi-square = 12.6, 3 d.f., P = .01.

result of chance. By grouping job security, home ownership, and money into a category designated "material-economic symbols," as contrasted with "non-material-economic symbols," we find that class and category of success symbol are associated. A chi-square analysis yields a probability of .01, a much greater concentration of "material-economic" responses in the lower classes than we would expect by chance alone. It is clear, then, that symbols of the attainment of success are different for respondents in the several classes.

There are at least three possible interpretations of this finding that are worthy of consideration. First, the data may reflect the degree of awareness, that is, the limited range of experience, among the lower classes, of certain symbols and their referents. This reflection is analogous to the oft-noted suggestion that those at the bottom of the class structure know very little about those at the top. This observation is particularly true of life styles, tastes, and other class-related symbolic behavior. The symbols of success in the lower classes are limited, then, to the attainments they have had opportunities to see, particularly the most conspicuous. These goals are concrete and easily identified.[6]

A second possible interpretation is that people value most what they have least. On the lower levels, therefore, people still strive for the basic necessities, and only after attaining them do they seek other goals (*cf.* Inkeles, 1960).[7] The process of attainment in a society in which products are constantly being introduced and improved and goals are frequently reformulated—a society that tends toward a great deal of anomie in its sub-systems—involves reaching goals and then seeking still other goals, endlessly. This process has been called the "escalator process." The mass media of communication, children and neighbors, and a host of other influentials encourage people to continue accumulating and trading in the old model for the new. In the middle classes, goals have shifted beyond the material, which presumably anyone can attain, to more intangible goals.

Finally, and this explanation provides a broad enough framework for incorporation of our first two, there are elements—reflected in their choices of symbols—of Williams's distinction between "achievement" and "success." He has written:

> Whereas achievement refers to valued accomplishments, success lays the emphasis upon rewards. Amoral success-striving may not have gone to the lengths suggested by some observers, but the important point is that once success goals are divorced from the ultimate values of society, the way is opened for a corrosion of regulative norms. In the United States, the available evidence suggests that . . . the success pattern is still linked to achievement, achievement is still associated with work, and work is still invested with an almost organic complex of ethical values. Thus, success is still not a primary criterion of value in its own right, but rather a derivative reward *for* active, instrumental performance (1960, p. 419).

. . . The lower-class symbols are clearly *success* symbols as contrasted with the middle-class *achievement* symbols.[8] Occupational pursuits in the lower-class groups, for example, are much less likely to lead to achievement. Even the skilled technician has difficulty thinking of his work in such terms, as does the clerk in the same class category (Class IV). In contrast, the engineer, the scientist, or the small business owner who constantly speaks of "building" his business demonstrates a broader dimension of aspiration. It is not until the minimal *success* symbols have been attained that *achievement* becomes a goal in contemporary American society. In this respect, the lower classes do not suffer from structured

[6] James Beshers has suggested that secrecy about symbols is a means of maintaining a status group intact and keeping lower status groups in subordinate positions. See *Urban Social Structure* (New York: The Free Press of Glencoe, 1961). Note also that this suggestion explains why socially mobile groups grasp the symbols that are most concrete and conspicuous, those that they recognize as associated with higher status, only to find that they are not the symbols that count.

[7] Alex Inkeles, "Personality and Social Structure," in Merton, *et al.*, ed., *Sociology Today*, New York: Basic Books, Inc., 1959. (C. S. H.)

[8] Robert and Helen Lynd have made a similar observation, pointing out that the lower classes are concerned in their jobs with *things* while the middle classes are concerned with *people*, *Middletown*, New York: Harcourt, Brace & World, Inc., 1929, p. 22.

strain so much as those in the higher classes. There is comparatively little struggle for abstract goals, which are difficult to attain, among those in the lower classes. Their problem is the attainment of goals that are inherently more limited. The middle-class American, however, does seek goals that are more difficult to attain—though he often does manage to attain them—and struggles also with questions about the relative legitimacy of his *success* or lack of *success*, as contrasted with *achievement*. It is on the higher-class levels that we observe the consequences of structured strain of a particular type. For certain occupational groups, particularly the intellectuals, the gap between success and achievement is wide. While many have achieved some degree of prominence in their occupational spheres, they have often not been rewarded with adequate symbols of success. From this group come many of the intellectual-political critics of industrial societies.[9] Furthermore, there is a tendency toward the converse as well. The groups that have attained *success* without having *achieved* tend to look upon themselves and be looked upon by others as not quite legitimate. Americans are reluctant to give power to those who have not earned their wealth—a prototype is the speculator who seeks control of a long established business enterprise—and they accord less status honor to the attainers of success alone than to those whose success is the result of their own achievements. . . .

***Characteristics Associated with Success.*** In addition to asking more abstract questions about "getting ahead" and "signs of success," we attempted to reach much more concrete levels of perceived success. One type of question was designed to project the respondent momentarily into his community setting, in order to describe a particular phenomenon (an element of this approach was embodied in our question on signs of success). One concrete example is the question, "If you were asked to describe a successful person in your community how would you do it?" Response categories to this question were precoded in order to classify the characteristics stressed. The question was, however, open-ended, and the coding was done after the interview was completed. . . .

Our data were grouped to combine cells in which there were very few cases into broader, yet meaningful categories. Most of our respondents stressed characteristics of success that fell into the prestige-recognition category. Of the 179 respondents, eighty-eight (49%) stressed factors associated with "good" reputation in the community. Sixty-two (35%) emphasized those associated with the accumulation of material goods and security. Only 16% described success in terms of factors associated with family welfare or personal happiness. A chi-square analysis of these results yields a value significant at the .05 level of probability. There is a marked difference in perceptions of success among the several classes, the lower classes stressing material symbols.

These data are consistent with those presented earlier and suggest that both sets reflect underlying value systems that influence the choice of value-referents. The data, as a result, support our distinction between success and achievement, as a reflection of different value configurations among the classes.

***The Differential Significance of Money and Security.*** Since the foregoing analyses have suggested that money and security are preferences that characterized the responses of the lower-class subjects and since the several studies of social class and anomie have shown that anomie has a greater impact on these classes, we shall investigate the relationship between money and security, on one hand, and social class, on the other. In analyzing two types of response, we may be able to assess the relative valuation associated with each among the several social classes.

[9] That this criticism represents structured strain is supported by our findings, reported later, that only the college- and high school-educated tend to be anomic when their incomes are below $5000 a year (P=.001 and P .03, respectively). It has often been suggested that the late President Franklin D. Roosevelt organized groups of artists, writers, and scholars into workshops during the depression of the 1930s to avert organized criticism of the system by this influential and potentially radical segment of the population. This insight was suggested to the writer some years ago by Professor St. Clair Drake.

Hyman reports some findings of a 1942 Roper survey based on a national sample of high school students, who were asked "to express their preference for one of three types of job: a low-income but secure job, a job with good pay but with an even risk of losing it, or a job with extremely high income and great risk" (1953, p. 433). According to Hyman, "The poor youth cannot accept the risk involved in becoming less poor" (*op. cit.*). Another sample taken by Roper in 1947 is reported by Hyman and provides data on adult responses to this question, reflecting a similar class pattern. "Thus, for example, a low income but secure job is chosen by 60% of factory workers but only by 26% of professional and executive persons. In 1949, a question presenting a similar choice situation between a secure job and a risky but promising career in one's own business yielded parallel results" (*op. cit.*, p. 434). . . . Roper's findings do suggest that security is of more concern to lower-class respondents than is money.

Our own interest is in the relative significance of money as a goal, compared to security, since our over-all findings suggest that both are more highly valued in the lower classes than they are in the middle classes. The same question Hyman asked was used in our study.

Of the 222 respondents to this question, 145 (63%) indicated that their choice of occupation would be one that pays only a low income but is secure. Only thirty-three (16%) would choose jobs that pay extremely high salaries to the successful, with a high risk of dismissal for the unsuccessful. A chi-square analysis of the association between social class and occupational choice yields a value with a probability of .001. Our data clearly indicate that the segments of the population for whom security is more important are the Class IV and V respondents, which is consistent with our other findings. These data also clarify the *specific* values that seem most important to lower-class respondents and help to support our explanation for the absence of emphasis upon *achievement* in the lower classes. *Security* has been isolated as a major concern of lower-class respondents. . . .

***Education as a Value.*** Because education has been found to be a relatively important symbol of underlying values and because it plays a major role in opportunity for advancement, we attempted to take a closer look at the part education plays in the evaluative perceptions of our respondents. Hyman has devoted a large part of his analysis to the value placed on formal education. As he points out, the degree to which education is valued is a significant factor in differential opportunities to achieve success. He suggests that:

> Part of the ideology of American life is that important positions are not simply inherited by virtue of the wealth of one's parents, but can be achieved. Such achievement, however, requires for many types of important positions considerable formal education. One cannot, for example, become a physician or a lawyer or an engineer without advanced education. Consequently, insofar as the lower classes placed less value on higher education, this would constitute an aspect of a larger value system which would work detrimental to their advancement (1953, p. 429).

Hyman proceeds to show that there is differential preference among the classes for college education, increasing with higher class position. Even though our own data support Hyman's findings and generalizations, we should approach his interpretation with some caution. The use of indices of "preference for college education" as a means of assessing educational values seems to the writer to involve a middle-class bias on the part of the investigator. We believe that success in a lower-class position can be achieved with high school education alone. The skilled technician and the shop foreman, for example, have certainly attained modest degrees of success in an objective sense, and college education for them seems superfluous if not completely meaningless. For those of the middle classes whose aspirations include professional achievement, however, college education may be much more meaningful.

We are dealing here with *means-values* rather than with *ends-values*. College education is being viewed as a means toward other ends, one of several alternative means for achieving "success." Our earlier findings, however, suggest that education is more highly valued by the middle classes as an *end-value* than it is by the lower classes. We hypothesize that the greater importance of education as an *end-value* for the middle classes provides them with greater opportunities for advancement *because* they view it as an *end-value*. As Hyman suggested, the nature of the value systems themselves limits or expands opportunities for success.

Values can have consequences that are either compatible or incompatible with the objectives of the actors in a social system, and these consequences may or may not be known to actors or to group members generally. There may, in fact, be latent, i.e., unrecognized, consequences of values for particular groups. Education's role as an *end-value* for the middle classes for example has the latent consequence of providing relatively greater chances of attaining both success and achievement goals, while for the lower classes the *lack* of education as an important *end-value* has the latent consequence of limiting chances for reaching goals in skilled, commercial, or professional occupations.

We should, then, expect to find that education itself is evaluated differently among the several classes. In order to test this hypothesis, our respondents were asked the following question taken from Williams (1956, Appendix I, p. 11), "Here are some reasons different people have given for wanting to have their children finish a certain amount of education. Which one of these would you say is most important?" The responses were grouped into two categories: instrumental perception of education and noninstrumental perception of education.

Our findings are reported in Table 2.

There is a marked tendency for instrumental perception of education to increase inversely to social class. . . . Our middle class respondents, then, tend to see education, not only as a means of achieving a better job or income, but also as a source of personal satisfaction. We should guess that our lower-class respondents tend to view education as somethng that would have helped them in adulthood had they pursued it in childhood and adolescence. While they see it as a means to success, they do not evaluate it so highly as other symbols (see Table 1). Floud and his colleagues, in a study entitled *Social Class and Educational Opportunity*, also noted the lower evaluation of education among working-class parents in England (1957, p. 81).[10]

Our lower-class respondents are caught in a situation analogous to Merton's conception of anomie on the social structural level. In the rational or *cognitive* sphere, education is viewed realistically by the lower classes as a means for the attainment of success. In the nonrational evaluative sphere, education is not highly valued. There is thus a disparity between the cognitive and evaluative dimensions that fosters a greater tendency to limited achievement in the lower classes. This disparity reflects strain between the subcultural system and the requirements of the lower-class social structure, an additional source of structured strain.

[10] J. E. Floud, A. H. Halsey, and F. M. Martin, *Social Class and Educational Opportunity*, London: William Heinemann, 1957. (C. S. H.)

**TABLE 2 Class and Instrumental and Noninstrumental Perception of Education (in Percentages)**

| | *Class* | | | | | *Totals* | |
|---|---|---|---|---|---|---|---|
| | I | II | III | IV | V | PER CENT | N |
| Noninstrumental | 91 | 72 | 55 | 46 | 44 | 52 | 107 |
| Instrumental | 9 | 28 | 45 | 54 | 56 | 48 | 98 |
| Totals | 100 | 100 | 100 | 100 | 100 | 100 | 205 |
| N | (11) | (18) | (47) | (68) | (61) | | |

Chi-square = 11.5, 3 d.f., P = .01.

Bronfenbrenner has made a similar observation:

> Perhaps this very desperation, enhanced by early exposure to impulse and aggression, leads working-class parents to pursue new goals with old techniques of discipline. While accepting middle-class levels of aspiration he has not yet internalized sufficiently the modes of response which makes these standards readily available for himself or his children. He has still to learn to wait, to explain, and to give and withhold his affection as the reward and price of performance (1958, p. 423).[11]

It should be noted, however, that our data do not totally support Bronfenbrenner's assumption that the "levels of aspiration" are identical with those of the middle class.

In answer to our second question—To what extent do members of the several classes hold values that aid or hinder them in their efforts to attain success in American society?—we must conclude that, although our lower-class respondents are aware of the utility of education as a means for getting ahead, that they do not view it as a high *end-value* does limit their chances for even modest advancement. We must agree with Hyman that the lower-class population does thus share a self-imposed tendency to nonachievement of success goals.

## SOCIAL CLASS AND PERCEIVED OPPORTUNITY

We have so far attempted to answer the first two of our three questions about class distribution of success values and the relationship between certain values and their roles in the process of striving for success. The third question is, To what extent do members of the various classes believe that opportunities for getting ahead are available to them? We turn again to Hyman for suggestions on what we may expect to learn from our data. In interpreting Roper's data, Hyman indicates that the lower classes believe that economic opportunities are limited for them in comparison to opportunities for higher classes (1953, p. 437). He also suggests that there are class differences in perceptions of the most important factors in job advancement. We should expect that such perceptions are an important factor in the study of effects of social structural anomie on group participants.

We asked three questions about perception of opportunities for success. . . . Specifically, the questions deal with perceptions of universalistic or particularistic criteria for advancement; implicit acceptance of the success ideology and the opportunities of the striver; perception of the respondent's own chances of getting ahead as indicator of a class determined reaction; and the discrepancy between sought and achieved occupational rank.

***Ability as a Factor in Success.*** In order to gauge perception of the degree to which legitimate striving will be rewarded, we asked, "Do you feel that a person with ability has a good chance of achieving success in our society, or do you feel that ablity has little to do with it?" Of the 224 subjects who responded, only fourteen replied that ability had little to do with it. . . . It appears, then, that the American dream of equal opportunity for all who have ability remains a potent ideological force in American society.

We use the term "ideological" with a clear understanding of its implications. We believe that, since objective conditions demonstrate that success is limited for those born into lower-class families and since the vast majority of lower-class respondents in our study still believe that ability is a major factor in advancement toward success, there is a disparity between the cognitive and evaluative dimensions of class perception. It should be clear from their perspective that ability *is not* a major factor in achieving success in our society unless they are willing to admit that they, as members of the lower classes, are people of low abilities. One way to close the gap between objective social circumstances and the group's limited capacity to deal with them is through ideology, that is, a set of beliefs and sentiments that will provide the group with goals, realistic or not, to give life meaning. In the American ideology of

[11] Urie Bronfenbrenner, "Socialization and Social Class Through Time and Space," in Eleanor Maccoby, T. M. Newcomb, and E. L. Hartley, eds., *Readings in Social Psychology*, New York: Henry Holt and Company, 1958, 3rd edition, pp. 400–425. (C. S. H.)

success, if one remains faithful to his task, continues to strive and to hope, he too will be rewarded by advancement. We hold that the ideology provides support only as long as objective conditions do not cause too great a gap between aspirations and opportunities for achievement. As the gap widens, the supportive potential of the ideology lessens. This factor is one of several that may explain our observation that average anomia decreases with age, climbing sharply upward only after age 55.[12]

***Perceived Chances of Getting Ahead.*** Our second finding supports this interpretation. As our data show, there is a class differential in the respondents' perceptions of their own chances of getting ahead. As class declines, we note an increase in responses that reflect awareness and expectations of limited success even though the over-all distribution of responses is relatively even. Fifty-three per cent saw their chances as excellent or fair, compared to 47% who saw them as limited or almost nonexistent. The data provide a sharper picture when we combine Classes I and II, our smallest groups. Then we find 83% giving responses of "excellent" or "fair" and 17% giving less hopeful replies. A chi-square analysis yields a probability of less than .01.

It can be concluded, from this finding, that the lower classes in our sample tend to see their objective chances of success as limited. How does this result fit with our finding that most respondents in the same class had, only moments before in the interview, replied that a person with ability has a good chance of achieving success? We should expect from these two replies that those on the lowest rungs of the social-class ladder believe themselves lacking the *ability* to get ahead. Yet these data may also be interpreted as providing support for our suggestion that the disparity between *cognitive* perception and *evaluative* perception—another instance of socially structured strain—creates a vacuum that is filled by the ideology of success.

[12] A class-controlled analysis indicates that, for lower-class groups, the curve rises after age 60, while, for the middle classes, the rise begins after age 55.

Merton is correct in pointing out that the system is not threatened by the failure of particular individuals to achieve their aspirations. The system, as our data show, is not put to the test. Instead, the individual continues to hope for eventual reaping of rewards, or he turns the blame for failure upon himself. If we compare those in the lower classes who feel their chances are fair or excellent to those in the lower classes who feel their chances are limited, anomia scores reflecting structured strain will be higher for the latter. On one hand, using perception of limited opportunities as an index to the malfunctioning of the success ideology, we should expect anomia to increase with the decrease in expectation of success. On the other, we should expect this relationship to be stronger in the lower classes because they are more likely to see their chances as limited. A controlled analysis suggests that this expectation is not borne out. Anomia is associated with perception of limited expectations for the *middle* classes only! How do we explain this unexpected finding?

We begin by noting that the middle-class respondents are more involved in the competitive struggle for success. They affirm the American dream, and, while their chances of attaining success or achievement, are greater, their chances of failure are greater too. Those in the lower classes do not have far to fall if they fail. The lower-class respondent, furthermore, sees about him others whose opportunities are circumscribed, and rationalization comes more easily under these circumstances. By contrast, the middle-class *milieu* is one of success and continuous striving. Among those who have had access to education and job opportunities, what excuses can be offered for failure? Our preliminary results, which indicate that income and anomia are significantly associated only for those respondents who have gone to high school and college, provide further support for this hypothesis. The college educated respondents who earned less than $5000 a year were more likely to become anomic than were members of any other educational group. . . .

***Social Class and Aspiration for Achievement.*** The third general question we set out to answer in this chapter was, what is the relationship of disparity between aspiration and achievement to social class? Although this question is, in reality, a test of the Durkheim-Merton hypothesis, since such a disparity may be viewed as an index to anomie, we are treating it here in the limited context of the relationship between social class and social values.

In an effort to develop a measure of structured strain independent of Srole's anomia scale, we decided to combine two separate items into what is, for the time being, a crude index to the disparity between the respondent's past occupational preference and his current occupational rank. Both elements were ranked according to the Hollingshead scale of occupations, a part of his index of social position. We asked, "Do you wish you had gotten into another line of work when you were younger?" The respondents who replied "yes" were then asked to describe the occupation to which they had formerly aspired. Since some of the respondents selected occupations different from their own on a horizontal plane—occupations with the same rank—we excluded them from our analysis It is on the vertical plane that we should expect the effects of anomie to manifest themselves, since disparity in occupational level is our major concern.

Our findings are reported in Table 3. . . . The distribution of low disparity declines from Classes I, II, and III to Class V, and that for high disparity ascends comparably.[13] . . . Our findings, then, indicate specifically that there is a greater gap between earlier occupational aspiration and occupational achievement in the lowest class (V) and, more generally, that the Durkheim-Merton hypothesis is supported. . . .

## SUMMARY

Our problem in this chapter has been to explore the distribution of success values among the several social classes as reflected in responses to questions dealing with the importance of getting ahead; symbols of success; perceived characteristics of successful people; the selection of occupations in terms of security and monetary compensation; and the quality of educational preferences. In addition, related questions were asked on the role that ability plays in achieving success and on differential perceptions of opportunities for advancement.

Several sociologically interesting themes are evident. The importance of getting ahead is stressed, not only by most of our respondents throughout the class structure, but most heavily by the lower classes. This finding is true for both the extent and intensity of belief in getting ahead and therefore satisfies Merton's criterion for an "adequate" test of his theory. This index to the importance of success clearly lends support to Merton, Srole, Bell, and others

[13] "High disparity" means that three or more rank levels separated the aspired and achieved; "moderate," two levels; and "low," one level.

**TABLE 3 Class and Disparity Between Earlier Occupational Aspiration and Achievement (in Percentage)**

| | *Class* | | | *Totals* | |
|---|---|---|---|---|---|
| DISPARITY | I, II, III | IV | V | PER CENT | N |
| Low | 44 | 35 | 18 | 31 | 26 |
| Moderate | 25 | 32 | 15 | 26 | 21 |
| High | 31 | 33 | 67 | 43 | 36 |
| Totals | 100 | 100 | 100 | 100 | 83 |
| N | (16) | (40) | (27) | | |

Chi-square = 9.3, 4 d.f., P = 0.06.

who have assumed that Americans share similar life goals. We can report, then, at this stage of our analysis, that there is evidence to support the Durkheim-Merton hypothesis.

We have also found that, by using Williams's distinction between "success and "achievement," we obtain a clearer understanding of the nature of values and greater insights into the differential aspects of striving for success in the several classes. The distinction leads us, for example, to explore and to explain middle-class anomie.

Our data, at the same time, indicate that the idea of limited opportunity for the attainment of life goals is more complicated than Merton recognized. The tendency for the lower classes to select material symbols and preferences supports Hyman's suggestion that those objects and activities they rank highest are those that contribute least to the attainment of success. There is, as Hyman has noted, a self-imposed tendency to anomie in the lower classes thanks to low evaluation of the cultural mechanisms—objects and activities—instrumental in the attainment of success. This low evaluation is particularly true of education. In the middle classes, where education is valued more highly, the pursuit of learning, no matter how minimal or superficial, furnishes by-products that become assets in later life. We have suggested that when the question of future achievement is assessed cognitively, the middle-class adolescent, for example, has already developed many of the social and intellectual skills necessary to movement up the ladder of success. For the lower-class respondent, it is often too late. Although he can recognize education and its concomitants as instruments for the climb, there is little he can do to recapture his formative years. The lower classes, as a result, are "boxed in" by the consequences of a kind of structured strain, the discrepancy between their evaluative and cognitive perceptions of education.

This process, combined with the limitations imposed by the social structure and, more specifically, by the objective requirements for occupational advancement, leads to a cyclical phenomenon analogous to a self-fulfilling prophecy (Merton, 1957, pp. 421–38). Lack of education blocks advancement and opportunities to move out of the lower-class *milieu*. Furthermore, lack of opportunity to incorporate middle-class values reinforces the tendency to seek more available means for getting ahead. "To him that hath shall be given."

We have implied that the lower-class situation is very much like that of the minority group. The nature of the values that characterize the lower classes by themselves explain much of the failure to advance from those classes.

We generalize that the belief that a man with ability can get ahead in American society is uniformly held throughout the class structure. The American dream remains intact, in spite of the objective social conditions of the lower-class milieu. Nevertheless, a number of respondents see their own chances of getting ahead as limited. Purely rational self-analysis might be expected to lead to a corresponding belief that such limited chances are owing to low ability. The success ideology, which effectively fills the gap between the cognitive and evaluative spheres, however, provides solace and hope that sooner or later success will be won as a just reward for legitimate striving. That this ideology protects the social order from disruptive criticism has been demonstrated by Merton. We add that this particular ideology fills the gap between the objective conditions of the "working class," as Marx described them, and their lack of a revolutionary orientation. Marx assumed that the working class would eventually become aware of its condition and would overthrow the "capitalist" classes.

. . . Marx failed to take account of alternative ideologies in his analysis. The success theme is such an alternative. Our view is that lack of class identification is not in itself what is responsible for so-called "working-class apathy" but the specific quality of the American dream itself. As Merton has noted, the American who believes he has equal opportunity for advancement has only himself to blame if he fails to succeed. Our findings support this suggestion.

Finally, we assessed the disparity between earlier occupational aspiration and current achievement and found it greatest among the lower classes. This finding provides a test of the Durkheim-Merton theory and lends it at least initial support.

In sum, we have managed to isolate four sources of structured strain in the social-class system of the small city from which our data are taken.[14] One was suggested by Merton and may be designated "external" to particular classes. He focused on the limits imposed upon the lower classes by the middle classes, which place obstacles in the path of those attempting to attain culturally prescribed goals. Three sources that are reflected in our data arise from class value systems themselves and may be described as "internal." Our choice of these terms is based on the extent to which groups other than those acting to achieve a particular goal are a primary source of strain (external) and on factors within the group that are primary sources of strain (internal).

Of the internal sources, there is first the disparity between the success ideology, particularly the belief that all can achieve success, and the objective conditions of American life, which limit achievement and success to relatively few at each level of the class structure. For example, only a few signers can join the Metropolitan Opera Company, even though there may be many who are capable. Second, there is a disparity between the lower-class value system and the requirements for attainment of success in American society. The values themselves tend to circumscribe opportunities among the lower classes. Finally, there is the distinction between achievement and success.

Whether or not these observations clarify processes at work in other communities can be determined only by systematic observation. It is our view that they represent significant focal points for the study of social structure and anomie in American society.

[14] See Leon Festinger, *A Theory of Cognitive Dissonance* (New York: Harper & Row, Publishers, 1957) for a discussion that offers a possible method of integrating the social psychological and sociological approaches to structured strain.

# PART V
# Social Mobility

---

Throughout this book we have encountered references to the concept of social mobility and numerous assertions about its manifestations. Where it figured most prominently was in Part II, major types of stratification systems. There we discovered that the norms concerning mobility, as well as the amount of actual mobility, are integral features of different types of stratification systems. (Recall that, although the norms of given systems call for it, in fact no society is completely open or completely closed.) Now, however, the focus is on social mobility.

The first selection here is from Pitirim Sorokin's pioneer work, *Social Mobility,* which appeared in 1927 and which marks the beginning of the systematic sociological study of this subject. For a while it was not given the deserved recognition by sociologists, but it is now being rediscovered and hailed as a work unequaled among the many on the topic of social mobility that have appeared since it was published. (It is no exaggeration to say that no area of social stratification has received more attention in the last two decades, judging by the quantity of studies, than has that of social mobility.)

Our selection from Sorokin's book contains the well-known terms he coined and their definitions: *vertical mobility* and *horizontal mobility.* It is important to note that Sorokin defines social mobility as the transition from one *social position* to another, but when he turns to the preceding two concepts, referring to types of mobility, he tends to abandon *position* in defining them. Instead he defines each as a certain kind of movement from group to group or stratum to stratum. I think that it is preferable to define horizontal and vertical mobility also in terms of the more basic element of position. This, besides making the definitions more consistent with one another, would perhaps open the door to the study of intraclass vertical mobility, which has been much neglected. Thus, I would suggest that we slightly modify the Sorokin definitions to read: (1) horizontal mobility—the transition of an individual from one social position to another of the same rank and (2) vertical mobility—transition of an individual from one social position to another of different rank, or the change of the same position from one rank to another.

Perhaps the latter part of the definition of vertical mobility that I spelled out needs some elaboration. What is meant is that an individual may experience social mobility while remaining in the same position if that position changes in rank from one time to another. For example, if, as we have learned from our previous readings, scientists rank higher today than they did twenty years ago, then the individual scientist of twenty years ago who is still practicing his profession has experienced social mobility even if he has not changed positions. The case falls within the category of social mobility because a change has taken place in the ranking of the same position.

The preceding formulation again has its origin, as the reader will soon discover, in Sorokin's conceptualization and simply translates his ideas, substituting the more basic element of position. I have in mind Sorokin's idea that vertical mobility, in addition to the movement of individuals, also refers to the change in the rank of a group or stratum. He utilizes it in his discussion of the two types of vertical mobility, which he terms *ascending* and *descending,* but which are better known today as *upward* and *downward.* One of his historical examples of the first type is the Brahmin caste in India, whose rank supposedly was not always as high as it has been in the last two thousand years.

Subsequent to Sorokin's work, J. H. Hutton, in his book *Caste in India* demonstrated that the characteristic form of mobility in India was not individual movement, but the collective splitting off by subcastes. He referred to this as the "fissiparous tendencies in Indian castes,"[1] and described its process. It involves the subcaste's establishing a claim to superiority, changing its name, and in the final step denying any connection with the caste of origin.

Other concepts employed by Sorokin have proved useful in the study of social mobility. Take, for example, his formulation concerning the factors that bring about mobility, presented in summary form at the end of the selection here. There is the general tendency for individuals in high positions to seek to transfer their priviliges to their offspring and kin. But there are also "permanent and universal" factors that counteract this trend and bring about mobility. He locates three such factors: the demographic, "change of environment," and "dissimilarity of parents and children." The last we are only rediscovering lately in our concern about the insufficient supply of talent. The first two figure prominently in contemporary discussions on the subject of social mobility, the second being termed now either as factors of technological change or structural factors. In regard to the demographic factors, his analysis of statistics and historical materials (not included in our selections) lead him to the conclusion that the rate of reproduction of the higher strata is often less than that of the lower ones. Thus vacant top positions have to be filled by people from below. As for the second type, on the basis of extensive historical material (omitted from our selection), he concludes that social change facilitates social mobility.

Regrettably, modern analysis has not gone far beyond the accomplishments of Sorokin. The most important attempt to *measure* the effect of technological change on mobility was made by Kahl.[2] Comparing data in the United States on the occupational distribution in 1920 and 1950, he equated the interperiod change with intergenerational mobility (changes in the occupational standing of sons relative to their fathers). He then proceeded to calculate how much of this change was the result of the four factors he isolated: technological, reproductive, immigration and "individual mobility." (The last is a rather vague concept, explained by

[1] J. H. Hutton, *Caste in India,* Cambridge: The University Press, 1946, especially pp. 41–61, 97–100.

[2] Joseph A. Kahl, *The American Class Structure,* New York: Holt, Rinehart and Winston, 1961, pp. 251–272.

the author thus: "Some people slip down and make room for others to move up."[3]) He concluded that about 7 per cent of the labor force had to be mobile in order to compensate for differential fertility. According to his calculations, about one-third of all cases of intergenerational mobility were the result of technological change. Except for reproductive mobility, the rest largely represented "individual mobility." He found that only about 1 per cent of the native-born men were upgraded by immigration and concluded that in the generation preceding 1950 the effect of immigration on the mobility of the native born was almost nil.[4]

Kahl's findings were subsequently reexamined by experts who questioned their validity. Duncan characterized Kahl's statistical procedures as "ingenious uses of defective materials," but his main attack was on Kahl's conceptual framework. Kahl's estimate was based on the assumption that over a thirty-year period there is a complete replacement of fathers by their sons, when in fact, says Duncan, there is considerable overlap. Still, Duncan's article contains the following statement, which in a way praises Kahl's work: "Although . . . Kahl's effort was a failure—and for fundamental reasons, not merely because of flaws in the data available to him—it falls into the class of honorable failures which needed to be made in order to force a re-examination of the problem."[5] And so, notwithstanding Kahl's effort, other experts too were forced to conclude that the importance of technological change in the mobility process is largely unknown.[6]

If one compares the conclusions about the positive and negative consequences of mobility found in Sorokin[7] and the present state of knowledge concerning this subject, he is again likely to find only small advances, for they are still scanty and impressionistic.[8] To the limited degree that hypotheses on this subject have been tested, they bear out Sorokin's statements. For instance, a panel-design research on lower-class youth entering a high-status university was used to test three competing hypotheses of the personal and social consequences of upward mobility, including one by Sorokin. Their evidence supported what the authors term the *dissociative hypothesis* formulated by Sorokin. In describing the negative psychological consequences, Sorokin asserted that social mobility "diminishes intimacy and increases psychosocial isolation and loneliness."[9] The authors demonstrate that their data bear out the hypothesis that upward mobility is a disruptive social experience that produces rootlessness in and lack of effective social support for the individual.[10]

In light of this discussion, the following remarks by Smelser and Lipset, made in 1966, concerning Sorokin's *Social Mobility* and the state of contemporary knowledge on this subject assume special significance:

[3] *Ibid.*, p. 253.

[4] For a discussion of how immigration can be a factor in both upward and downward mobility, see Elbridge Sibley, "Some Demographic Clues to Stratification," *American Sociological Review*, Vol. 7, 1942, pp. 322–330.

[5] Otis Dudley Duncan, "Methodological Issues in the Analysis of Social Mobility," in Neil J. Smelser and S. M. Lipset, eds., *Social Structure and Mobility in Economic Development*, Chicago: Aldine Press, 1966, pp. 54–55.

[6] Kaare Svalastoga, *Social Differentiation*, New York: David McKay Co., 1965, p. 142. Also see pp. 105–143.

[7] Pitirim A. Sorokin, *Social and Cultural Mobility*, New York: Free Press, 1959, pp. 508–545.

[8] Melvin M. Tumin, "Some Unapplauded Consequences of Social Mobility in a Mass Society," *Social Forces*, Vol. 36, October, 1957, p. 32; Svalastoga, *op. cit.*, p. 143.

[9] Sorokin, *op. cit.*, pp. 522–526.

[10] Robert A. Ellis and W. Clayton Lane, "Social Mobility and Social Isolation: A Test of Sorokin's Dissociative Hypothesis," *American Sociological Review*, Vol. 32, April, 1967, pp. 237–253.

This work first published in 1927, which is rarely cited today, is not only a rich source of comparative data, but contains highly sophisticated analyses of both causes and consequences of social mobility. Much of the recent work in this field touches precisely on the issues Sorokin dealt with, and often "rediscovers" processes he specified. Unlike some of the more recent writers, Sorokin recognized the difficulties involved in trying to be overprecise in comparative research, and did not draw precise conclusions from what was and is only roughly comparable data.[11]

The last sentence is particularly noteworthy because Lipset himself was involved in studies of comparative mobility in industrial societies.[12]

Subsequently a number of critics have pointed to errors—resulting from methodological difficulties—in the international comparisons of intergenerational occupational mobility from which international similarities or differences were inferred. One such critic, Harold L. Wilensky, terms the errors "grievous" and claims that the categories compared in these studies are "both heterogenous and non-comparable." According to him, the samples are also noncomparable because they are of populations that differ substantially in age distribution and therefore will result in a large sampling error. And last but not least, the data-gathering efficiency varies from country to country. Thus he urges more caution than is being manifested in discussing comparative mobility rates.[13]

Fully conscious of these recent criticisms, we have nevertheless reprinted a portion of S. M. Miller's influential *Comparative Social Mobility*, convinced that it is a cautious work and among the best done in this field. But his study, like most empirical studies to date, is confined to intergenerational mobility.

He found that in fewer than one-third of the nations studied did upward mobility exceed downward mobility. Thus, downward rather than upward movement is the more compelling fact about mobility in industrialized societies. (Studies that have appeared subsequent to Miller's book show that, contrary to the general impression, there is also extensive downward mobility in emerging industrializing societies.)[14] In examining both types in the seventeen nations studied, Miller found that high rates of upward mobility may be associated with either low or high rates of downward mobility. He considers this varied connection between upward and downward mobility the most important new finding of his study. But others have found therein additional important contributions. Kaare Svalastoga, a well-known student of mobility, asserts that Miller presents "the most important collection of mobility tables available at present."[15] Moreover, he says that one of the most striking analytic contributions is Miller's deliberate emphasis on the distance of mobility in contrast to its neglect hitherto in the studies of rates of mobility.

[11] Smelser and Lipset, *op. cit.*, p. 47, footnote 93.

[12] See, for example, S. M. Lipset and Reinhard Bendix, *Social Mobility in Industrial Society*, Berkeley: University of California Press, 1959, chap. 2, pp. 22–76; also S. M. Lipset and H. L. Zetterberg, "A Theory of Social Mobility," *Transactions of the Third World Congress of Sociology*, Vol. II, 1956, pp. 155–177.

[13] Harold L. Wilensky, "Measures and Effects of Social Mobility," in Smelser and Lipset, *op. cit.*, pp. 98–105.

[14] Smelser and Lipset, "Social Structure, Mobility and Development," in *Social Structure and Economic Development, op. cit.*, pp. 45–50. It is noteworthy that again we encounter a finding consistent with Sorokin's formulation. In his book, Sorokin presented considerable evidence from various studies in the late nineteenth and early twentieth centuries demonstrating that a considerable proportion of the manual force in then industrially developing Europe were sons of middle-class and even elite fathers. See Sorokin, *op. cit.*, p. 435–449.

[15] Svalastoga, *op. cit.*, p. 123.

It should be mentioned that the concept of *distance of mobility* is found in the Sorokin reading under the term *intensiveness*. He defined it as "the vertical social distance . . . crossed by an individual in his upward or downward movement in a definite period of time." Sorokin made clear that in order to have a measure of over-all mobility in a society, one would have to devise an index that would combine "intensiveness"—that is, distance—with the "generality of the vertical mobility." (By generality he meant the number or proportion of individuals who have moved up or down.)

Although Miller has not devised such an index, he does succeed in projecting a picture of over-all mobility by presenting in tabular form the *national profiles*, which include measures of both aspects. (See his Table 8.) It is worthwhile to note how similar the profiles of the United States and the USSR are. Both show a general pattern of upward mobility with limited downward mobility.

Now Miller arrived at his profile of mobility in the United States on the basis of two sets of data: USA I refers to the white male 1946 data of Richard Centers; USA II to the Survey Research Center's 1956 data for white and Negro males. From our next selection by Peter M. Blau and Otis Dudley Duncan, which utilized 1962 data, we gather that the mobility profile has not changed much. As the authors point out in their book based on the same data, in 1962 there was no immediate cause for concern that the American occupational structure was becoming more rigid. On the contrary, there seemed to be more upward and less downward mobility in 1962 than earlier. At the end of their book the authors convincingly argue that higher rates of upward mobility do not intrinsically signify fairness in allocation of rewards. There is nevertheless, as they point out, a fundamental difference between a stratification system with high mobility and one with low mobility. The first perpetuates a structure of differential positions but not their inheritance, the latter perpetuates both.[16]

The reprinted article by Blau and Duncan is the preliminary report of the findings of the 1962 survey. (These were later elaborated upon in their book, discussed above.) Note, this was the first comprehensively designed inquiry into social mobility in the United States; the sample consisted of 20,700 men. The findings presented in the article deal with education, ethnic background, community size, migration and parental family as factors in occupational mobility.

The next reading on "Sponsored and Contest Mobility and the School System" by Ralph H. Turner turns our attention from the extent of mobility to that of *modes* of mobility. That education in advanced industrial society is the predominant channel of upward mobility is a well-documented proposition.[17] This statement in no way contradicts what was said in the introduction to the preceding section about the educational system in its relation to the social stratification system being mainly a mechanism whereby social-class positions are stabilized across the generations. (Numerous studies show that the higher one's class, the more and better the education he receives.) The educational system nevertheless also serves as a

[16] Peter M. Blau and Otis Dudley Duncan, *The American Occupational Structure*, New York: John Wiley, 1967, pp. 424–441.

[17] One of the latest studies bearing it out is that by Thomas Fox and S. M. Miller, "Economic, Political, and Social Determinants of Mobility. An International Cross-Sectional Analysis," *Acta Sociologica* 9, 1966, pp. 76–93. Another is Otis Dudley Duncan and Robert W. Hodge, "Education and Occupational Mobility: A Regression Analysis," *American Journal of Sociology*, Vol. 68, 1963, pp. 629–644. For an article casting some doubt on it, see Arnold Anderson, "A Sceptical's Note on the Relation of Vertical Mobility to Education," *American Journal of Sociology*, Vol. 66, 1961, pp. 560–570.

mechanism of social mobility. Many studies have been conducted on the ways given school systems facilitate or impede such mobility. But Turner adds a new dimension by raising the problem of varying societal norms concerning the accepted mode of upward mobility, which he considers a crucial factor in shaping the school system.

Specifically, the author contrasts the English norm of *sponsored mobility* with the American norm of *contest mobility*. The English norm requires that the existing elite grant elite status to those not born to it but nevertheless deserving it. Under the American norm, elite status should be, and is thought to be, the prize in an open contest. Consistent with this, in America the final award tends to be delayed as long as is practicable and an effort is made to keep lagging contestants in the race until the climax in order to insure the fairness of the race. On the other hand, in England the recruits are chosen early, to control their proper training for elite status. The varied norms of the two countries account then to a large extent, according to Turner, for the divergence between the English and American systems of social control and education. He shows how the logic of each affects the secondary school system, the kind of value placed on education, the content of education, and the system of examinations—all of which differ in the United States and in England.

It seems to me that despite the lack of systematic study of the phenomenon, it is not incorrect to say that much *noninstitutionalized* sponsored mobility has long been present in the United States. Although the ideology does not take cognizance of it, there is considerable awareness in this country of the importance of "contacts" in moving up the social ladder. The lower strata are especially conscious of the prevalence of this mechanism, as exemplified in their often used expression "It's not what you know; it's who you know." But then there is good reason to think that this sort of sponsorship was not included by Turner in the concept of sponsored mobility. However, even if we focus on the *institutionalized* form that his concept stands for, it appears that America is now leaping in the direction of sponsored mobility, at least on the university level: Witness the great expansion of scholarships and fellowships.

Turner visualized that his scheme could be applied to further comparisons between other countries. A systematic comparison between England and the USSR could reveal the latter outdoing the former in the pattern of institutionalized sponsored mobility. As Turner explains, the governing objective of this mode of mobility is the best utilization of talents in society, "by sorting persons into their proper niches," whereas that of contest mobility "is to give elite status to those who earn it." To express it in another way, the main manifest goal of the first is collective and of the second individualistic. The theme of utilization of talents in the interest of society is much stronger in the Soviet Union and other Soviet-type societies than in England. It has been shown that most Soviet citizens who occupy the top of the social pyramid are there because the party has facilitated their rise, stage by stage, to a position of distinction and leadership. This holds true for scholars, scientists, and artists, as well as government officials and industrial managers.[18] Talent is sought out early and cultivated by special schooling.

As is suggested by Turner, the emphasis on ambition and on motivation goes hand in hand with contest mobility, whereas emphasis on intelligence or ability is more characteristic of sponsored mobility. Thus Turner also touches on the subjective factors in mobility, which is the main concern of the next selection from the

[18] Frederic C. Barghoorn, *Politics in the USSR*, Boston: Little Brown, 1966, pp. 184–185.

much acclaimed book *Social Mobility in Industrial Society,* by S. M. Lipset and Reinhard Bendix. One cannot help but wonder whether the usual designations of such factors as *subjective* or *psychological* are adequate; some explanation of what is meant by these terms is therefore in order. Earlier in this discussion we spoke about technological or structural factors in mobility. These concern the rise or fall of certain positions and the expansion or shrinkage of positions. In a sense they are the objective conditions for mobility. When turning to subjective factors, the central question is, Why, given the same structural conditions, are some individuals mobile while others who originated in the same stratum are not? Put differently, and more specifically, if there is room at the top of the social hierarchy for people below to move into, who among them is most likely to do so?

Now, provided there is room, achievement is dependent on at least two kinds of factors: (1) that one have the motivation to move up and (2) that one have the necessary resources, such as ability and "know-how" for reaching the goals. We have already gathered from previous selections that the goals and means of mobility are differentially distributed among the social strata. In the reading by Lipset and Bendix we encounter additional empirical materials on this theme.[19] What is new for us is the well-documented discussion found therein of the *intra-stratum* variation of these subjective factors in its relation to mobility. The authors pulled together in a concise presentation the extensive materials that bear upon this subject. They have organized the materials differently, but hopefully it will be convenient to think of them as contributions to the knowledge of the motivation and means for mobility.

The authors begin with the *means*, insofar as they start with the discussion of intelligence. But let me first make a few comments about achievement motivation, because it logically precedes the means. Also, recent evidence indicates that motivation affects the utilization of the means of mobility. For example, Jackson and Marsden have shown the great importance of motivation in determining the academic success of British working-class youth.[20] We find at the end of the Lipset and Bendix presentation a discussion of the achievement motivation of children of the same social class, being related to early home socialization. Those working-class parents whose reference group is middle class are likely to socialize their children in middle-class values. Working-class boys' anticipatory socialization in such values may, on the other hand, take place when those boys associate with middle-class peers, as studies conducted after the publication of the Lipset and Bendix book suggest. Thus, for example, one study shows that working-class boys with high aspirations interact more with boys higher in status than do those with low aspirations.[21] Another study found that such boys were more similar to ambitious middle-class boys than to working-class boys with low aspirations in their tendency to be members of organizations and clubs as well as in naming only middle-class boys as friends.[22]

[19] For a concise treatment of materials that have appared since—that, as the author makes explicit, follows the framework of the Lipset and Bendix presentation—see Harry Crockett, "Psychological Origins of Mobility," in Smelser and Lipset, *op. cit.*, pp. 291–309.

[20] Brian Jackson and Dennis Marsden, *Education and the Working Class: Some General Themes Raised by the Study of 88 Working-Class Children in a Northern Industrial City,* New York: Monthly Review Press, 1962.

[21] Gerald D. Bell, "Processes in the Formation of Adolescents' Aspiration," *Social Forces,* Vol. 42, December, 1963, pp. 179–186.

[22] Richard L. Simpson, "Anticipatory Socialization and Social Mobility," *American Sociological Review,* Vol. 27, August, 1962, pp. 517–522.

In proceeding to a few remarks concerning intelligence as a factor in upward mobility, attention should be drawn to the fact that the findings presented under this heading in the Lipset and Bendix selection are largely about variations in IQ distribution. And, as the authors mention at one point, the evidence from the study of IQ distributions does not allow any definite conclusions about the effect of intelligence on social mobility because of the difficulties of separating in the IQ measure, native intelligence from the effects of differential class socialization. Still, I would say, the kind of ability that goes into scoring well on an IQ test may be an even greater asset to upward mobility in the United States than native intelligence. This is precisely so, because, as has been widely shown, the IQ test does not measure intelligence alone but a good deal of obviously acquired knowledge and skill and special abilities distinct from intelligence.[23] Further support for this contention can be gained from Anastasi's demonstration that the criterion used in validating intelligence tests "has nearly always been success in our social system."[24]

In light of this, the evidence presented in the Lipset and Bendix reading that intraclass variation in IQ is greater than interclass variation assumes special significance. The high IQ's of some working-class youngsters could be considered indicators that they have acquired certain skills conducive to advancement. True, social class is a greater determinant than IQ of motivation to go to college, as is amply demonstrated in the reading by Lipset and Bendix. Nevertheless, if one focuses on the data they present about working-class boys, he will find that a larger proportion of those who rank high in IQ plan to go to college than those who rank low. And, if working-class boys manage to get into college, their educational achievement does not differ from students from other class backgrounds.

Now, given the same high IQ's, those working-class boys whose parents have more education are more likely to land in college than those who do not. Thus, apart from IQ, parents' influence is an important factor in securing the additional means for advancement that college education represents. Another important factor is size of family. The consistent finding of many studies is that better-educated and upwardly mobile children of the lower classes tend to be from small families. Lipset and Bendix also outline additional factors in the intraclass distribution of means of mobility.

In reading about the subjective factors in social mobility it is important to bear in mind that usually a number of these factors are operating simultaneously and that their effects on a given individual may either cancel out or reinforce each other. Thus individuals in the same class, given the same opportunities, still vary considerably in mobility achievement.

[23] Raymond B. Cattell, "A Culture-Free Intelligence Test," *Journal of Educational Psychology*, March 31, 1940, p. 162; Susan S. Stodolsky and Gerald Lesser, "Learning Patterns in the Disadvantaged," *Harvard Educational Review*, Vol. 37, Fall, 1967, pp. 546–593.

[24] She shows that "Scores on the test are correlated with school achievement or perhaps with some more general measure of success in our society. If such correlations are high, it is concluded that the test is a good measure of 'intelligence.'" See: Ann Anastasi, *Differential Psychology*, 3rd ed., New York: The Macmillan Company, 1958, pp. 566–567.

# SOCIAL MOBILITY*

*Pitirim A. Sorokin*

## CONCEPTION OF SOCIAL MOBILITY AND ITS FORMS

By social mobility is understood any transition of an individual or social object or value—anything that has been created or modified by human activity—from one social position to another. There are two principal types of social mobility, *horizontal* and *vertical*. By horizontal social mobility or shifting, is meant the transition of an individual or social object from one social group to another situated on the same level. Transitions of individuals, as from the Baptist to the Methodist religious group, from one citizenship to another, from one family (as a husband or wife) to another by divorce and remarriage, from one factory to another in the same occupational status, are all instances of social mobility. So too are transitions of social objects, the radio, automobile, fashion, Communism, Darwin's theory, within the same social stratum, as from Iowa to California, or from any one place to another. In all these cases, "shifting" may take place without any noticeable change of the social position of an individual or social object in the vertical direction. By *vertical* social mobility is meant the relations involved in a transition of an individual (or a social object) from one social stratum to another. According to the direction of the transition there are two types of vertical social mobility: *ascending* and *descending*, or *social climbing* and *social sinking*. According to the nature of the stratification, there are ascending and descending currents of economic, political, and occupational mobility, not to mention other less important types. The ascending currents exist in two principal forms: as an *infiltration* of the individuals of a lower stratum into an existing higher one; and as a *creation of a new group by such individuals, and the insertion of such a group into a higher stratum instead of, or side by side with, the existing groups of this stratum.* Correspondingly, the descending current has also two principal forms: the first consists in a dropping of individuals from a higher social position into an existing lower one, without a degradation or disintegration of the higher group to which they belonged; the second is manifested in a *degradation of a social group as a whole, in an abasement of its rank among other groups, or in its disintegration as a social unit.* The first case of "sinking" reminds one of an individual falling from a ship; the second of the sinking of the ship itself with all on board, or of the ship as a wreck breaking itself to pieces.

The cases of individual infiltration into an existing higher stratum or of individuals dropping from a higher social layer into a lower one are relatively common and comprehensible. They need no explanation. The second form of social ascending and descending, the rise and fall of groups, must be considered more carefully.

The following historical examples may serve to illustrate. The historians of India's caste-society tell us that the caste of the Brahmins did not always hold the position of indisputable superiority which it has held during the last two thousand years. In the remote past, the caste of the warriors and rulers, or the caste of the Kshatriyas, seems to have been not inferior to the caste of the Brahmins; and it appears that only after a long struggle did the latter become the highest caste.[1] If this hypothesis be true, then this elevation of the rank of the Brahmin caste as a whole through the ranks of other castes is an example of the second type of social ascent. The group as a whole being elevated, all its members, *in corpore,* through this very fact, are elevated also. Before the recognition of the Christian religion by Constantine the Great, the position of a Christian Bishop, or the Christian clergy,

Reprinted with permission of The Macmillan Company from *Social and Cultural Mobility* by Pitirim A. Sorokin. 

[1] See Bouglé, C., "Remarques sur le régime des castes," pp. 53 *et seq.; The Cambridge History of India*, pp. 92 *et seq.*

was not a high one among other social ranks of Roman society. In the next few centuries the Christian Church, as a whole, experienced an enormous elevation of social position and rank. Through this wholesale elevation of the Christian Church, the members of the clergy, and especially the high Church dignitaries, were elevated to the highest ranks of medieval society.[2]

. . . . . . . . . . . . . . . . . . . . . . . . . . . . . . . . .

The situation is summed up in the following scheme.

### INTENSIVENESS OR VELOCITY AND GENERALITY OF VERTICAL SOCIAL MOBILITY

From the quantitative point of view, a further distinction must be made between the intensiveness and the generality of the vertical mobility. By its *intensiveness* is meant the vertical social distance, or the number of strata—economic or occupational or political—crossed by an individual in his upward or downward movement in a definite period of time. If, for instance, one individual in one year climbed from the position of a man with a yearly income of $500 to a position with an income of $50,000, while another man in the same period succeeded in increasing his income only from $500 to $1,000, in the first case the intensiveness of the economic climbing would be fifty times greater than in the second case. For a corresponding change, the intensiveness of the vertical mobility may be measured in the same way in the field of the political and occupational stratifications. By *the generality of the vertical mobility,* is meant the number of individuals who have changed their social position in the vertical direction in a definite period of time. The absolute number of such individuals gives the *absolute generality* of the vertical mobility in a given population; the proportion of such individuals to the total number of a given population gives *the relative generality of the vertical mobility.*

Finally, combining the data of intensiveness and relative generality of the vertical mobility in a definite field (*e.g.,* in the economic), *the aggregate index of the vertical economic mobility of a given society* may be obtained. In this way a comparison of one society with another, or of the same society at different periods may be made, to find in which of them, or at what period, the aggregate mobility is greater. The same may be said about the aggregate index

[2] See Guizot, F., *The History of Civilization,* Vol. I, pp. 50–54, New York, 1874.

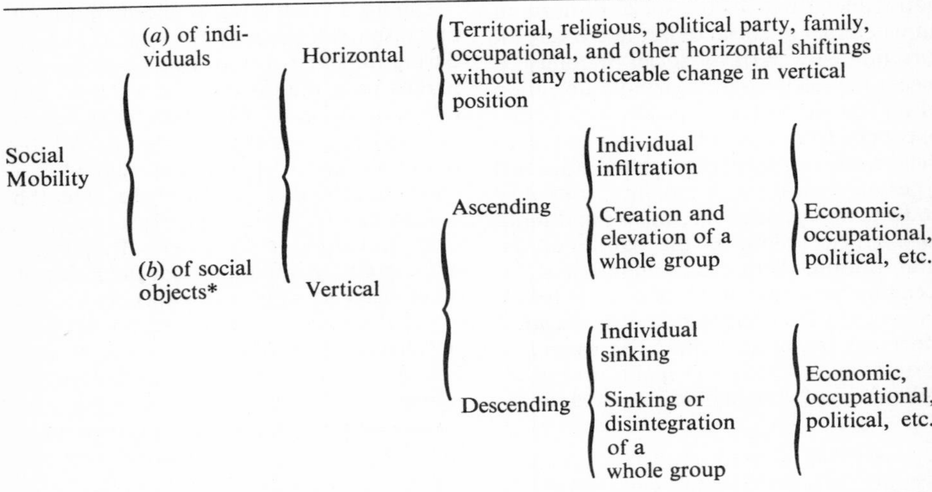


* The mobility of social objects and values and the horizontal mobility, in spite of the great importance of the problem, is not an object of this study.

of the political and occupational vertical mobility.

## IMMOBILE AND MOBILE TYPES OF STRATIFIED SOCIETIES

On the basis of the above, it is easy to see that a social stratification of the same height and profile may have a different inner structure caused by the difference in the intensiveness and generality of the (horizontal and) vertical social mobility. Theoretically, there may be a stratified society in which the vertical social mobility is nil. This means that within it there is no ascending or descending, no circulation of its members; that every individual is forever attached to the social stratum in which he was born; that the membranes or hymens which separate one stratum from another are absolutely impenetrable, and do not have any "holes" through which, nor any stairs and elevators with which, the dwellers of the different strata may pass from one floor to another. *Such a type of stratification may be styled as absolutely closed, rigid, impenetrable, or immobile.* The opposite theoretical type of the inner structure of the stratification of the same height and profile is that in which the vertical mobility is very intensive and general; here the membranes between the strata are very thin and have the largest holes to pass from one floor to another. Therefore, though the social building is as stratified as the immobile one, nevertheless, the dwellers of its different strata are continually changing; they do not stay a very long time in the same "social story," and with the help of the largest staircases and elevators are *en masse* moving "up and down." *Such a type of social stratification may be styled open, plastic, penetrable, or mobile.* Between these two extreme types there may be many middle or intermediary types of stratification.

. . . . . . . . . . . . . . . . . . . . . . . . . . . . . . . . . .

## GENERAL PRINCIPLES OF VERTICAL MOBILITY

1. *First Proposition.—There has scarcely been any society whose strata were absolutely closed, or in which vertical mobility in its three forms—economic, political and occupational—was not present.* . . . The nearest approach to an absolutely rigid society, without any vertical mobility, is the so-called caste-society. Its most conspicuous type exists in India. Here, indeed, vertical social mobility is very weak. But even here it has not been absolutely absent. Historical records show that in the past, when the caste-system had already been developed, it did happen that members of the highest Brahmin caste, or the king and his family, were overthrown or cast out for crimes. . . . On the other hand, the outcasts, after a suitable repentance, might be reinstated, or individuals born in a lower social stratum might succeed in entering the Brahmin caste, the top of the social cone of India.

. . . . . . . . . . . . . . . . . . . . . . . . . . . . . . . . . .

. . . It is evident, therefore, that, in spite on the fact that the caste-society of India is apparently the most conspicuous example of the most impenetrable and rigidly stratified body, nevertheless, even within it, the weak and slow currents of vertical mobility have been constantly present. If such is the case with the India caste-society, it is clear that in all other social bodies vertical mobility, to this or that degree, must obviously be present. This statement is warranted by the facts. The histories of Greece, Rome, Egypt, China, Medieval Europe, and so on show the existence of a vertical mobility much more intensive than that of the Indian caste-society. The absolutely rigid society is a myth which has never been realized in history.

2. *The Second Proposition.—There has never existed a society in which vertical social mobility has been absolutely free and the transition from one social stratum to another has had no resistance.* This proposition is a mere corollary to the premises established above, that every organized society is a stratified body. If vertical mobility were absolutely free, in the resultant society there would be no strata. It would remind us of a building having no floors separating one story from another. But all societies have been stratified. This means that within them there has been a kind of "sieve" which has sifted the individuals, allowing some to go up, keeping others in the lower strata, and contrariwise.

Only in periods of anarchy and great

disorder, when the entire social structure is broken and where the social strata are considerably demolished, do we have anything reminding us of a chaotic and disorganized vertical mobility *en masse*.[3] But even in such periods, there are some hindrances to unlimited social mobility, partly in the form of the remnants of the "sieve" of the old régime, partly in the form of a rapidly growing "new sieve." After a short period, if such an anarchic society does not perish in anarchy, a modified "sieve" rapidly takes the place of the old one and, incidentally, becomes as tight as its predecessor. . . .

3. *The Third Proposition.—The intensiveness, as well as the generality of the vertical social mobility, varies from society to society (fluctuation of mobility in space).*

. . . . . . . . . . . . . . . . . . . . . . . . . . . . . . . . . . .

4. *The Fourth Proposition.—The intensiveness and the generality of the vertical mobility—the economic, the political and the occupational—fluctuate in the same society at different times.* In the course of the history of a whole country, as well as of any social group, there are periods when the vertical mobility increases from the quantitative as well as from the qualitative viewpoint, and there are the periods when it decreases. . . .

Though accurate statistical material to prove this proposition is very scarce and fragmentary, nevertheless, it seems to me that these data, together with different forms of historical testimony, are enough to make the proposition safe.

The first series of corroborations is given by the great social upheavals and revolutions which have occurred at least once in the history of every society. It is certain that in the periods of such upheavals vertical social mobility in its intensiveness and generality is far greater than in periods of order and peace. Since, in the history of all countries, periods of upheaval have taken place, this means that the intensiveness and generality of the vertical mobility in every country has oscillated also. Here are a few examples. . . .

. . . . . . . . . . . . . . . . . . . . . . . . . . . . . . . . . . .

The conquest by the Aryans of the native population of Ancient India; by the Dorians, of the earlier population of Greece; by the Spartans, of Messenia; by the Romans of their "predia"; by the Spaniards of the native population of America and so on, have involved similar great depressions of the previous highest strata and the creation of a new nobility out of the people who had often been before very low. Even when a war is concluded without conquest or subjugation, it nevertheless calls forth similar results because of a great loss of the higher strata—especially political and military aristocracy—and because of the financial bankruptcy of some of the rich people and the enrichment of skillful swindlers from the new people. The "vacuum" in the nobility caused by the losses has to be filled, and this leads to a more intensive promotion of the new people to the higher positions.

For the same reason in such periods there is a greater occupational shifting, and, hence, a greater occupational mobility, than in a more normal time. The above considerations show the existence of a rhythm of static and dynamic periods in the vertical mobility within the same society at different periods.

. . . . . . . . . . . . . . . . . . . . . . . . . . . . . . . . . . .

5. *The Fifth Proposition.—As far as the corresponding historical and other materials permit seeing, in the field of vertical mobility, in its three fundamental forms, there seems to be no definite perpetual trend toward either an increase or a decrease of the intensiveness and generality of mobility. This is proposed as valid for the history of a country, for that of a large social body, and, finally, for the history of mankind.* Thus, in the field of vertical mobility, the same conclusion of "trendless" change is reached which was met with in the field of social stratification.

In these dynamic times, with the triumph of the electoral system, with the industrial revolution, and especially a revolution in transportation, this proposition may appear strange and improbable. The dynamism of our epoch stimulates the belief that history has tended and will tend in the future toward a perpetual and "eternal" increase of vertical mobility. There is no need to say that many social thinkers have such an opinion. And yet, if its bases and reasons

[3] See Sorokin, P., *Sociology of Revolution*, Philadelphia, 1925, Pt. III.

are investigated it may be seen that they are far from convincing.*

## THE CHANNELS OF VERTICAL CIRCULATION

Since vertical mobility actually functions to some degree in any society, there must be in the "membranes" between the strata "holes," "staircases," "elevators," or "channels" which permit individuals to move up and down, from stratum to stratum. The problem to be discussed now is: What are these channels of social circulation?

***Various Social Institutions Perform This Function.***—Among them there are few especially important from our standpoint. Of these few, which may be in different societies or in the same society, at different periods, one or two are particularly characteristic for a given type of society. The most important institutions of this kind have been: army, church, school, political, economic, and professional organizations.

. . . . . . . . . . . . . . . . . . . . . . . . . . . . . . . . . .

Of other channels of vertical circulation may be mentioned the family and marriage with a person of another social stratum. Such a marriage usually leads one of the parties either to social promotion or degradation. In this way some people have made their careers; some others have ruined them. In the past, a marriage to a slave or a member of the lower caste led to the degradation of a higher party and his offspring. . . .

At the present moment in our democratic societies, we see a mutual "gravitation" of rich brides and of the poor but titled bridegrooms. In this way both parties try: one to get a financial basis for keeping his titled position on a necessary level, the other to get a social promotion through money.

Besides these channels there undoubtedly are many others, but they seem to be not so important as the preceding ones. These have always been the most common and convenient elevators which have carried up and down the streams of people "traveling" in the vertical plane. Those who, like farmers and manual workers, have not tried to enter one of these elevators, have been doomed to stay in the lower strata, having very little chance either to go up or down. Playing in all periods to this or that degree the rôle of channels, each of the above institutions has played an especially important part in a definite society in a certain period. The army plays a great rôle in a period of war and social disturbances; a moderate one in a period of peace. The Church had a great importance in the Middle Ages and has a less one at the present time. Money making and political activity have great significance now and had less a few centuries ago.

Varying in their concrete forms and in their size, the channels of vertical circulation exist in any stratified society, and are as necessary as channels for blood circulation in the body.

. . . . . . . . . . . . . . . . . . . . . . . . . . . . . . . .

## THE FACTORS OF VERTICAL CIRCULATION

### PRIMARY PERMANENT FACTORS

Since vertical circulation in some degree exists in every society it follows that among its factors, besides local, temporary, and specific conditions, there must be conditions which operate in all societies, in all periods. Correspondingly, the factors of vertical circulation may be divided into: (*a*) primary or general, and (*b*) secondary, or local and temporary, which facilitate or hinder mobility.

Among the primary factors are: (1) demographic factors. . . ; (2) dissimilarity of parents and children; (3) change of environment, especially of the anthropo-social environment; (4) defective social distribution of individuals within social layers.

### DEMOGRAPHIC FACTORS OF VERTICAL CIRCULATION

Under this heading are meant all forces which call forth sterility, lower differential

* Many pages of historical facts which run counter to the reasons for assuming a perpetual trend follow this statement in Sorokin's book. C. S. H.

birth rate, or higher mortality of the upper classes. In the course of time they cause either an extinction of the aristocratic families, or a decrease of their proportion in the total increased population of a society. In both cases such a situation creates a kind of "social vacuum" within the upper strata. As the performance of the functions carried on by the upper strata continues to be necessary, and as the corresponding people cannot be recruited any longer from a diminishing upper population, it is natural that this "vacuum" must be filled by the climbers from the lower strata. Such in essence is this factor of vertical circulation.

It is not certain that the fecundity of the upper strata is always and everywhere lower than that of the lower strata. But it is possible to say that such a phenomenon has taken place within many societies and at different periods. Besides, it seems possible to contend that in some way, not exactly known to us, almost any aristocratic family sooner or later dies out either biologically or socially, in the sense that its descendants cease to be noticeable as the continuators of a given aristocratic family.

. . . . . . . . . . . . . . . . . . . . . . . . . . . . . . . . . .

If the figures are reliable, they show that within the royal families, fertility and sterility fluctuate considerably in time, and from dynasty to dynasty. Several other studies show similar oscillations. It follows from this that the difference between the fertility of the upper and the lower strata may fluctuate. It seems to be probable, nevertheless, that the lower fertility of the upper strata is, if not a permanent phenomenon, at least common for many societies and many periods.[4] . . .

Although, as we have seen, the mortality of the lower classes has been considerably higher than that of the upper strata, nevertheless, it does not compensate for the lower rate of increase of population of the upper strata. Some previously given data show this. The indicated sources give many additional corroborations of this statement. *In spite of lower mortality the members of the higher strata, owing to their lower fertility, increase often less rapidly than the members of the lower ones.*

To the factor of lower fertility must be added that of a *high death rate by violence* which takes place in regard to some groups of aristocracy (royal, executive, and military), and which leads to the extinction of many aristocratic families, and, through that, creates a "social vacuum." Here are some illustrations of the statement.[5]

. . . . . . . . . . . . . . . . . . . . . . . . . . . . . . . . . .

The above sufficiently corroborates the statement concerning the demographic factors of social circulation. Whatever may be the concrete causes . . . these demographic conditions make social mobility necessary and inevitable. *And the greater the difference in the number of surviving children of the upper and the lower strata, the more intensive the vertical circulation caused by this factor will be.* . . . As this difference varies from time to time, it follows that, in the past, the periods of increase of the difference should have been the periods of an intensification of the vertical circulation, providing this factor were not checked by opposite factors.

## DISSIMILARITY OF PARENTS AND CHILDREN AS A FACTOR OF VERTICAL CIRCULATION

Since the publication of the works of Francis Galton, especially of his *Hereditary Genius*, it has become customary to think that talented parents beget talented children, while stupid parents beget stupid children. The reason for this is seen in the factor of heredity. At the present moment, there seems to be no doubt that this rule is, in many cases, true. But is it a rule which is universal and does it not know any exceptions? It seems not. We certainly know many cases where the children of prominent parents happened to be below normal, and the children of quite average parents quite prominent. Dr. A. Marro rightly says

> While one has seen children inheriting from their parents qualities by which parents have

[4] The exceptions to this rule seem to exist principally in polygamous societies where the chances for procreation of the upper classes are greater than in monogamic groups.

[5] Sorokin, P., "The Monarchs and Rulers," *Journal of Social Forces*, March 1926.

become eminent, other children, on the contrary, do not correspond at all to this expectation. One is painfully surprised to see the sons of Hippocrates quite stupid, and one is struck with astonishment in noting that from the race of Socrates and Aristotle there has not arisen the least spark of science, that Charles V, Peter the Great, and Napoleon I had only foolish sons.[6]

A similar admission is made by Francis Galton himself. "It has often been remarked that the men who have attained pinnacles of celebrity failed to leave worthy successors," says Galton.[7] It is possible to give hundreds of historical cases of this kind. . . . On the other hand, it is possible to indicate hundreds of historical cases where the children of quite average parents have turned out to be eminent men of genius: Shakespeare, Beethoven, Schubert, Faraday, Pasteur, Lincoln, and the greater part of the self-made men, achievers and climbers—these supply examples of this fact.

Whatever may be the causes of this phenomenon, the fact of the dissimilarity of the parents and the children in many cases is beyond doubt. And, it seems to me, the number of such cases is not so small as was formerly believed. . . . Meanwhile, the opposite is to be found in almost every study of heredity. I do not know a single investigation of such cases where the correlation between the qualities of the parents and the children would be perfect. In the best cases, even in such comparatively simple traits as stature, pigmentation, the color of hair or eyes, not to mention other traits, the correlation happens to be approximately 0.5.[8] In regard to other traits it was much lower. Similarly, there scarcely may be found any study of this kind which would not indicate the fact of "overlapping." The presence of overlappings and the indicated difference between the theoretically perfect and the actual coefficient of correlation are found in all statistical studies of heredity. This means that *the fact of dissimilarity of parents and children is also permanent and universal.*[9]

. . . . . . . . . . . . . . . . . . . . . . . . . . . . . . . . . . . .

*A common result of dissimilarity between fathers and children is the discrepancy between the social position of individuals and their inner and acquired qualities, necessary for a successful performance of the functions of the position.* If a father is quite fitted for his position, his dissimilar son may be unsuitable for it. And the greater the dissimilarity, the more necessary becomes a voluntary or a compulsory vertical shifting of individuals.

The shifting of individuals is carried on in three principal ways. In the first place, *through the preventive shifting of individuals, performed through the machinery of social testing and selection of the individuals.* Its essence consists in the fact that the children, before obtaining their social position, are tested and are either barred or promoted, according to the results of the test. The stupid children from a family of high social standing cannot pass through school and be graduated (the cases of misuse are not interesting for us now). The profligate persons could not pass the test of the medieval Church, as a rule. The same may be said about an occupational test. As a result, in spite of their birth in a high stratum, many failures of this kind may be prevented from obtaining a high position. In this way many would-be successors to a throne have been eliminated; many would-be heads of industrial corporations have been put aside from a responsible position. Many sons of prominent scholars are barred from graduation or the position of a professor. Many candidates are beaten in elections. Many sons of high officials have been excluded from responsible official ranks. In brief, in any society there are many sieves which perform this eliminating function. It is true that in this way only a part—and sometimes a small one—of the unsuitable individuals are sifted and barred or promoted. But this part is enough to produce a strong or weak stream of vertical circulation.

In the second place, *there is a repressive way of shifting of individuals from the social*

[6] See Marro, A., "The Influence of the Age of the Parents upon the Psychophysical Character of Children," *Problems of Eugenics*, p. 119.

[7] Galton, Francis and Schuster, E., *Noteworthy Families*, p. xv, London, 1906.

[8] See Pearson, Karl, *The Scope and Importance to the State of the Science of National Eugenics* pp. 27–29, London, 1909.

[9] Cf. Conklin, E. G., *The Direction of Human Evolution*, pp. 128 *et seq.*, New York, 1922.

*stratum in which they have been born. It is performed through a repressive social pressure.* Their unsuitableness for the position leads to a failure in the fulfillment of duties. A poor performance calls forth either dismissal or degradation of such a person; or, if a man is a manager of his own business, his poor management causes its failure; the business is ruined, the man himself is put down. If the man is an executive of a church, a school, an army, or an empire, his failure leads to disorganization of the institution. Owing to the disorganization many people begin to suffer. Suffering urges them to get rid of such a leader. This creates a social pressure which often puts down the leader and promotes a lower-born person. In this way many failures from the upper strata have been put down, and many "risers" from the lower classes promoted.

In the third place, *individuals being placed by their birth in a position for which they are unsuited, become dissatisfied and begin to try to change it in the way which is dictated by their "natural proclivities."* An inborn ruler or a great thinker, born from slave parents, tries to obtain a position which permits an adequate expression. For many an inborn slave, born in the position of a ruler, power is a burden; such persons try to get rid of it or hold the power only nominally in the form of "reigning without ruling," or, at least, do not hold steadfastly to their position and easily give way to anybody who craves it. . . .

## CHANGE OF ENVIRONMENT, AND ESPECIALLY OF THE ANTHROPO-SOCIAL ENVIRONMENT AS A FACTOR OF VERTICAL CIRCULATION

An individual or a group may be unfit for the successful performance of their social functions not only through their own fault but because of the change of the environment in which they act. A man with the specific talent for strategy may climb up very rapidly in time of war, and may not promote himself in time of peace. A fine artisan may rise in a society with a system of handicraft industry, and he may not have any chance in a society of machine production. A purely physical force often has been the cause of leadership in primitive societies, but it has much less importance in present society. An exclusive honesty and asceticism led to a social rise in the Middle Ages, and the same qualities are likely often to ruin a man under existing conditions. . . . Any considerable change of it [of social environment] results in a social redistribution of individuals: those who, through the change, are put in a favorable position begin to rise or continue to hold their high positions; those who cannot or do not wish to adapt themselves to the change, are likely to go down.

*As the social environment of human beings is always changing, and the rate of change is especially intensive now, this means that within social life there is a permanent factor of vertical circulation.* It incessantly operates within a society and incessantly produces social redistribution of its members. Any invention, any change in the methods of production, in *mores,* beliefs, standards, literary and dress fashions, in science and arts, in the means of transportation—in brief, in any field of social life—may ruin one group of individuals, and promote another. . . . Some changes may be favorable for the promotion of honest men, some for dishonest; some for the ascetic, some others for the licentious; some for the conservative temperament, some others for the progressive. In short, the variety of changes of environment have caused a promotion of the most different types of human beings. Through this factor, whole social layers, fitted for their positions under certain conditions, may become quite unfitted under other ones, and *vice versa.*

A few historical examples are sufficient to illustrate this.

A change of social environment, which led to the legalization of the Christian Church by Constantine the Great, caused a social promotion of the Christians, who before had been persecuted, and a sinking of the non-Christians, who before had been promoted. An increased rôle of money since the thirteenth and fourteenth centuries in England called forth a social rise of the money-making class, and facilitated social sinking of the landed aristocracy. . . . *All factors which facilitate change are factors facilitating vertical social shifting, and vice versa.*

### DEFECTIVE SOCIAL DISTRIBUTION OF INDIVIDUALS AND THE LAG IN SHIFTING AS A CAUSE OF THE EXTRAORDINARY VERTICAL CIRCULATIONS

Though the previous three factors of social circulation operate permanently, nevertheless, their work has been, it seems, not so intensive, nor so perfect qualitatively, in many cases, as it should be. From a quantitative viewpoint, its almost permanent defect has consisted in that only a part, and sometimes an insignificant part, of the "non-suitable" individuals have been shifted in time, while another part—and often the majority—of the non-suitable men have been left in positions for which they have not been fitted.

The institute of juridical or factual inheritance of social position, into which the individuals have been born, has always hindered timely and proper shifting of all non-suitable individuals to places corresponding to their innate and acquired qualities. It is certain that even in the United States, among present dwellers in the economic, occupational, or political strata, there is a considerable proportion of unsuitable individuals. It is not a very rare picture to see a mediocre man placed above a man of ability, and an incapable person giving orders to a more capable one. Such discrepancy between the social position of individuals and their physical and mental qualities has been shown above in the part devoted to the study of the population of the different strata. Though there is a correlation between social status and many physical and mental qualities of the social classes; yet, in regard to the physical and other traits everywhere, the fact of overlapping has been met. The characteristics of the upper strata are not common to all their members, and at the same time are found among the members of the lower classes. And, contrariwise, the traits typical for the majority of the lower classes are found also among a part of the upper classes. This is an evident manifestation of defectiveness in the social distribution of individuals or that of the existence of a lag.

Even in the most mobile society the membranes which separate one stratum from another are not so permeable as to permit an infiltration of all capable "newcomers," or an ousting of all "unsuitable" dwellers born within a stratum. The testing, selecting, and distributing agencies shift only a part of the unsuitable persons. Another part, owing to various causes, continues to stay where it was born. *In brief, one of the permanent defects of any society is a lag in the distribution of its members according to their qualities, and an existence within each social stratum of individuals not suited to their social position.* Such is the defect from a quantitative point of view.

From the *qualitative standpoint,* an almost permanent defect of social distribution of individuals has consisted in a looseness of correspondence between the type of the people desirable for each stratum at a certain period and the type of people who have really been selected for each stratum by the machinery of social distribution of individuals. . . .[10]

Besides these permanent factors of vertical circulation of individuals there are many other secondary conditions which may facilitate or hinder vertical mobility. . . .

# COMPARATIVE SOCIAL MOBILITY

*S. H. Miller*

### THE ADVANTAGES OF A CROSS-NATIONAL APPROACH

A cross-national, comparative approach to social mobility can contribute effectively to our understanding of society. A study of mobility in a particular nation, by itself, cannot reveal whether a rate of mobility is high or low. . . . With comparative data, it becomes possible to assert that the highest rate of mobility that has been attained in a

From "Comparative Social Mobility," by S. M. Miller, *Current Sociology,* Vol. IX, No. 1. Reprinted by permission.

[10] See Sorokin, P., *The Sociology of Revolution,* Pts. III and V.

given type of economic and social order is of a particular level, which may be deemed as one of the benchmarks of mobility. It may be used, then, in viewing rates of mobility in a society of similar or different characteristics.

More important, perhaps, is the possibility that comparative mobility analysis can lead to an isolation of the significant variables affecting mobility. The comparative method *approximates* an experimental method. Does a particular form and level of economic activity produce higher mobility than another? Are there significant differences in rates of mobility in nations of similar economic development so that non-economic factors must be introduced to explain them? The possibility then emerges after the variables are isolated of developing a general theory of mobility.

A comparative approach can also be important in analyzing the consequences of mobility. Where rates of mobility are similar, do similar attitudinal complexes emerge or do additional cultural factors intrude? . . .

Finally, comparative studies clarify the kind of data which are most useful for analysis and turn us back to the initial issue in the study of mobility, the collection of quality data.

### COMPARATIVE DANGERS

In the previous section, we have reviewed some difficulties involved in studying social mobility. These difficulties are compounded in comparative analysis for the results of rather disparate investigations have to be molded into a form permitting them to be compared with one another. Distortion is inevitable. One must operate with the hazardous assumption that the distortion does not destroy the product. . . .

### BASIC DATA

This monograph does not represent primary research. It is an effort to utilize available primary studies for the 18 nations where data are available.

The unit of the comparisons is basically though not exclusively the nation. . . . For four nations, data are reported on a city (in the case of Belgium, two towns); following the suggestion of the Sub-Committee on Social Stratification and Mobility of the ISA, I have included these data because of the possibility that they may be representative to some degree of the national facts, as discussed in Section I. In a fifth nation, we have also deviated from the practice of a national representative sample: for the Soviet Union the only available mobility information for the nation as a whole is the emigré study of the Russian Research Center of Harvard University. National samples and a Hungarian census are employed in the other 13 nations.

. . . . . . . . . . . . . . . . . . . . . . . . . . . . . . . . . .

Only two-step intergenerational (father-son) mobility is studied.

The time of the studies varies, although all are post-World War II studies with the exception of the report on the USSR. This report is as of 1940; the other reports range from 1946 to the middle fifties. Thus, there is no exact comparability in time.

. . . . . . . . . . . . . . . . . . . . . . . . . . . . . . . . . .

### TYPES OF COMPARISONS

Despite all the difficulties with the manual/non-manual classification, it was decided to concentrate on comparisons of this sort. The lively interest in mobility still largely centers on crossing from manual to non-manual work even if the line between them is wavy and changing. Downward movement of the non-manuals as well as upward movement of the manual received special attention.

. . . . . . . . . . . . . . . . . . . . . . . . . . . . . . . . . .

### THEIR FATHERS' SONS

The comparisons offered in this section are only a few of the many possibilities. . . . No one rate can be said to express *the* rate of mobility of a nation. Rather, it is perhaps most accurate to say—"Nation A has a higher rate of mobility *of this type* than does Nation B; Nation B has a higher rate *of this type*."

### MANUAL TO NON-MANUAL

In many studies, urban workers are included with farm workers and cannot be separated out. This mixed category we have termed "manual" to distinguish it from

**TABLE 1 Non-Manual Sons of Manual and Working-Class Fathers**

| | *(1) Manual into Non-Manual* | *(2) Working Classes into Non-Manual* |
|---|---|---|
| I. NATIONAL DATA | % | % |
| Denmark | 24.1 | * |
| Finland | 11 | * |
| France I | 30.1 | 34.9 |
| France II | 29.6 | 32.9 |
| Great Britain | 24.8 | * |
| Hungary | 14.5 | 21.8 |
| Italy | 8.5 | * |
| Japan | 23.7 | * |
| Netherlands | 19.6 | * |
| Norway | 23.2 | 25.8 |
| Puerto Rico | 14.3 | 18.7 |
| Sweden | 25.5 | 29.3 |
| USA I | 28.8 | * |
| USA II | 28.7 | * |
| West Germany | 20.0 | 21.2 |
| II. URBAN DATA | | |
| Australia (Melbourne) | 24.1 | * |
| Belgium I (St–Martens–Latem) | 5.7 | 6.4 |
| Belgium II (Mont–Saint–Guibert) | 30.9 | * |
| Brazil (São Paulo) | 29.4 | * |
| India (Poona) | 27.3 | * |
| III. SPECIAL DATA | | |
| USSR (emigrés) | * | 34.9 |

* Unavailable.

the "working classes," which exclude farm workers and purport to represent those non-agricultural employees who work with their "hands." In Table 1 data are reported of the upward mobility of sons of fathers in the "manual" and in the "working-class" category.

Upward mobility for these two groups is defined as crossing into non-manual work, which includes all white-collar work, whether as employees, independent practitioners, and the self-employed in business.[1] Independent farmers are not included so that some upward movement of the manuals is excluded since movement into independent farming status is upward mobility for all who originate in farm-laboring families, and for some whose fathers were working men. . . . The mobility within the manual strata (e.g. from unskilled to skilled or semi-skilled) is ignored; obscured as well is the lack of consistency in rates within the classification—skilled, for example, having higher upward rates than farm workers or unskilled.

Column (1) shows that in France about 30% of the sons of manual fathers ended up in non-manual occupations. Among the nations, this is the highest rate, while the lowest rate for nations is Italy's 8.5%. The range, then, is considerable. Almost as many nations have rates under 20% as have rates over 20%, although if we include the city data, there is an increase in the number of nations in the over 20% group. Italy, Finland, Hungary, Puerto Rico and Belgium I lag behind all the others in having rates below 15%. Thus, about one quarter of the nations are distinctly low.

[1] In some nations, artisans who are self-employed are classified as workers and were not reclassifiable because of coding procedures.

The differences among the high rate nations—France, USA, Belgium II, Brazil (São Paulo), India (Poona)—are minor, so that we have a group of nations with a decidedly higher rate than the rest.

### WORKING CLASSES INTO NON-MANUAL

Column (2) of Table 1 presents the data on working-class mobility into non-manual occupations for the smaller number of nations where data are unavailable for the more traditional occupations of skilled, semi-skilled and unskilled non-agricultural labor.

The comparison between Columns (1) and (2) is instructive: in all cases, working-class mobility is greater than manual. . . . These findings are not surprising since it is well known that it is more difficult to enter white-collar work from a rural background than from urban origins. The order of differences suggests that if we add 3%–4% to figures for manual mobility into non-manual work, we shall not be far off the actual working-class upward mobility. . . .

What can be concluded about overall upward mobility from manual and working-class occupations?

1. The United States does not have the highest upward mobility rate out of manual/working-class occupations. France, the Soviet Union and the United States are rather similar.

2. There is a fair clustering of nations—9 of the 18 nations (Belgium counted only once despite the two discrepant reports) range between 24% and 31% in the manual analysis and 4 of 8 between 24% and 35% in the working-class tabulation.

3. Several nations have distinctly lower rates of mobility than other nations for which data are available. These are Finland, Italy, Hungary (for the manual category only), Puerto Rico (for the manual category only) and Belgium I.

4. Whether industrial nations can be considered to have a similar rate of movement of manual/working class into non-manual depends upon the criterion employed and whether one wishes to emphasize similarity or diversity. The Soviet Union and French working-class figures are almost twice that of Puerto Rico, but the latter is not highly industrialized. If we exclude Puerto Rico, Hungary and Belgium I from the working-class comparisons, we have a range from 21.2 (West Germany) to the 35% of USSR and France I. The manual range, excluding Italy, Finland, Belgium I, Puerto Rico and Hungary, is from 19.6% (Netherlands, probably too high a figure for this nation) to 30+ % (France I, Belgium II). . . .

### NON-MANUAL TO MANUAL

We assume for purposes of Table 2 that movement into manual work is downward mobility for all who originate in non-manual occupations. This assumption is especially dubious at the crossing over from lower-level non-manual to skilled manual work. . .

The willingness to discuss movement of non-manuals into manual and working-class occupations arises from the great concern with the presumably political implications of this movement. The economic differentials involved in such movement may indeed be slim and often may involve an income gain, but even those most aware of these discrepancies have an interest in this kind of movement.

The most startling element in Table 2 is the fact that in three nations more than 40% of sons of non-manual families end up in manual occupations. . . . Certainly, the differential economic and social effects of manual/non-manual may differ widely from nation to nation, but earlier estimates have not prepared us for such a drastic change in social fortunes. The relation of the drop from non-manual into manual occupations to concern with social status is a question that immediately arises: is it true that the easier the drop, the more the concern with status and social distance?

Almost equally striking is the range between the USSR's 15% and the highs of Great Britain, Netherlands and Puerto Rico. (The two Belgian studies, which differed markedly on up mobility, show great similarity in downward mobility.) There is no particular clustering: the three categories of under 25%, between 25% and 35%, and over 35% have fairly equal numbers of nations. While 12 nations are under 30% and six above, three of the former hover about the 30% mark.

**TABLE 2 Manual Working-Class Sons of Non-Manual Fathers**

| | (1) Non-Manual into Manual | (2) Non-Manual into Working Classes |
|---|---|---|
| I. NATIONAL DATA | % | % |
| Denmark | 36.8 | * |
| Finland | 24.0 | * |
| France I | 20.5 | 18.2 |
| France II | 26.9 | 25.9 |
| Great Britain | 42.1 | * |
| Hungary | 27.5 | 25.8 |
| Italy | 34.4 | * |
| Japan | 29.7 | * |
| Netherlands | 43.2 | * |
| Norway | 28.6 | 27.9 |
| Puerto Rico | 42.7 | 35.6 |
| Sweden | 27.7 | 25.7 |
| USA I | 19.7 | 18.6 |
| USA II | 22.6 | * |
| West Germany | 29.0 | 28.2 |
| II. URBAN DATA | | |
| Australia (Melbourne) | 37.1 | * |
| Belgium I (St–Martens–Latem) | 8.9 | 7.1 |
| Belgium II (Mont–Saint–Guibert) | 3.4 | * |
| Brazil (São Paulo) | 18.5 | * |
| India (Poona) | 26.9 | * |
| III. SPECIAL DATA | | |
| USSR (emigrés) | 15.0 | 12.8 |

* Unavailable.

## NON-MANUAL INTO WORKING CLASSES

Only in the case of Puerto Rico does restriction to non-agricultural "hands" employment make a sizable difference (7.1%). In the other nations, the restriction in analyzing downward movement involves 2.3% or less. Non-manual downward movement is largely into industrial occupations rather than farm labor.

The Soviet Union has the extremely low rate of one of eight sons of non-manual origin terminating in working-class occupations. The USA and France (an average of the two figures) hover about the figure of one of five non-manual sons, while for Norway and Sweden, one of four non-manual sons have working-class occupations.

While we do not show the data here, a substantial part of the non-manual into working-class and manual employment is into the skilled labor category. And the overwhelming rate of all non-manual movement into manual is from the lower end of the non-manual category (e.g., clerks). Nonetheless, the size of "downward" movement raises a number of questions: among others are the purposes and practices of educational systems, the forces producing fluidity in society, the character of reactions to downward mobility in societies where it is frequent and where it is infrequent.

## A TYPOLOGY OF MANUAL/NON-MANUAL MOVEMENT

Bringing together rates of movement of manual into non-manual and non-manual into manual movement . . . permits some very interesting comparisons. (See

Tables 1 and 2. C. S. H.) . . . The manual category is used so that all the nations can be included in the analysis. The USSR (emigrés) figure for upward mobility is, however, for the working classes.

In only 5 of 17 nations (omitting Belgium where the two studies are inconsistent), does up-mobility exceed down-mobility. These 5 nations [France, USA, Brazil (São Paulo), India (Poona), and USSR (emigrés)] are all characterized by relatively high up-mobility, but in not all nations with high up-mobility does this latter rate exceed the downward movement of non-manuals into manual strata. *Downward movement is a more compelling fact about mobility than upward!* In Italy, Puerto Rico, Netherlands, Finland, and, to a lesser extent, Hungary and Great Britain, the downward rate is considerably in excess of the upward. (The Dutch rate is probably high because of the coding problems of the data.)

Perhaps the most interesting aspect of manual movement into non-manual occupations and non-manual movement into manual occupations is their complexity. Some nations are high on one, low or middle on another; others have a different pattern. A fourfold table makes possible the setting up of types or patterns of movement. If we dichotomize movement as high (over 24%) or low (24% or less), we have these four types of patterns. . . .

Cell A represents a nation with high upward and downward mobility; Cell C, one with low rates of movement of non-manuals into manual occupations and high rates of manual movement into non-manual activity.

Below are grouped all the nations under the patterns which typify them:

A. *High Downward Non-Manual, High Upward Manual* (+ +): Denmark, France II, Great Britain, Sweden, Australia (Melbourne), India (Poona)

B. *High Downward Non-Manual, Low Upward Manual* (+ −): Hungary, Italy,

**TABLE 3 Inequality of Opportunity**

| | *(1)* *Non-Manual into Non-Manual (Stability)* | (2) *Manual into Non-Manual* | (3) *Index of Inequality* $\frac{(1)}{(2)}$ |
|---|---|---|---|
| | % | % | % |
| Australia (Melbourne) | 62.9 | 24.1 | 261 |
| Belgium I (St–Martens–Latem) | 91.1 | 5.7 | 1,598 |
| Belgium II (Mont–Saint–Guibert) | 96.6 | 30.9 | 313 |
| Brazil (São Paulo) | 81.5 | 29.4 | 277 |
| Denmark | 63.2 | 24.1 | 262 |
| Finland | 76.0 | 11.0 | 691 |
| France I | 79.5 | 30.1 | 264 |
| France II | 73.1 | 29.6 | 247 |
| Great Britain | 57.9 | 24.8 | 234 |
| Hungary | 72.5 | 14.5 | 500 |
| India (Poona) | 73.1 | 27.3 | 268 |
| Italy | 63.5 | 8.5 | 747 |
| Japan | 70.3 | 23.7 | 297 |
| Netherlands | 56.8 | 19.6 | 290 |
| Norway | 71.4 | 23.2 | 308 |
| Puerto Rico | 57.3 | 14.3 | 401 |
| Sweden | 72.3 | 25.5 | 284 |
| USA I | 80.3 | 28.8 | 279 |
| USA II | 77.4 | 28.7 | 270 |
| USSR (emigrés) | 85.0 | 34.9 | 244 |
| West Germany | 71.0 | 20.0 | 355 |

Japan, Netherlands, Norway, Puerto Rico, West Germany

**C.** *Low Downward Non-Manual, High Upward Manual* (− +): France I, USA I and II, Belgium II (Mont–Saint–Guibert), Brazil (São Paulo), USSR (emigrés)

**D.** *Low Downward Non-Manual, Low Upward Manual* (− −): Finland, Belgium I (St–Martens–Latem)

. . . The four patterns of mobility outlined here strongly suggest that rather than omnibus statements on gross similarities or differences in some overall rate of mobility, we need to develop explanations of *each* of these four different patterns in terms of their causes, processes and consequences.

To sum up, asymmetry exists among the mobility indicators: high rates of up-mobility may be associated with low or high rates of down-mobility. High rates of down-mobility may be associated with high or low rates of up-mobility. To describe the rate of upward mobility in a nation does not automatically give us an estimate of down-mobility. *The varied connections of upward and downward mobility form the most important new element in the present report.*

## INEQUALITY OF OPPORTUNITY

In Table 3, the ability of non-manual sons to stay in the non-manual levels is compared with the ability of manual sons to move into these levels. The figures of column (3) are an index of inequality since they reflect the relative advantage of non-manual sons over manual sons in having non-manual positions.

. . . In no nation is the advantage of middle-class sons less than two to one (Great Britain: 234%). The most common advantage is between two and a half to one and three to one. The closeness of Denmark, France, Great Britain, Sweden, USA and USSR (emigrés) is particularly striking.

## WORKING CLASSES AND MANUAL INTO THE ELITES*

In the preceding sections, there has been no concern with the height (or distance) of the mobility. The question has been: How much change of any extent has occurred? In light of the controversy concerning the advisability of considering all mobility into non-manual ranks as upward mobility for workers, it is particularly desirable to investigate mobility into the highest reaches of society.

Table 4 organizes the available data. . . .

1. As with movement into non-manual occupations, working-class mobility is higher into the elites than is manual mobility since the former excludes the farm workers with their low rates of entrance into the higher reaches of society. . . .

2. Movement into Elite I from the manual strata shows a small range from 0 in Italy to 3.9% in Japan. It *is* striking, however, that Britain has an extremely low movement from manual into elite occupations for its Elite I size; Britain's manual → elite movement is much lower than Sweden's and the Netherlands', although all three nations have the same elite size. Interesting also is the fact that Japan has a slightly higher rate than the USA.

3. Movement into Elite II shows a slightly greater range than does movement into Elite I. Puerto Rico is highest and the Netherlands has the second highest rate, but this may be at least partly attributable to our classification problems with that nation.

4. The bringing together of Elite I and II movement gives a very sizable range: from the Soviet Union (emigrés) figure of 14.5% to the low reports for West Germany, Italy and France II and Belgium I (St–Martens–Latem) and India (Poona). (France I is quite a bit higher.) The Soviet Union has a very large Elite I and II; Denmark, which follows Puerto Rico in movement, has a small Elite I and II. . . .

No clear-cut relationship exists between the rates for manual into non-manual movement, and for manual into elite mobility. The USSR (emigrés) and the USA have relatively high rates on both, but the USA (Elite I and II) is not so different from nations . . . with their smaller elites. In . . . the USA (Elite I), with its high manual into non-manual rate, is no higher than countries with low rates for such movement. Similarly, France (Elite I and II), another

* The author distinguishes two elites: Elite I—occupations "with the highest standing," and Elite II "with somewhat less standing but of distinctly higher standing than the other occupational groupings." (C. S. H.)

**TABLE 4 Working Classes and Manual into Elite I and II**

| | (1) *Working Classes into Elite I* | (2) *Manual into Elite I* | (3) *Working Classes into Elite II* | (4) *Manual into Elite II* | (5) *Working Classes into Elite I and II* | (6) *Manual into Elite I and II* | (7) *Size of Elite I* | (8) *Size of Elite II* | (9) *Size of Elite I and II* |
|---|---|---|---|---|---|---|---|---|---|
| I. NATIONAL | % | % | % | % | % | % | % | % | % |
| Denmark | * | * | * | * | * | 1.1 | * | * | 3.3 |
| France I | 1.9 | 1.4 | 2.3 | 2.2 | 4.2 | 3.5 | 3.9 | 4.6 | 8.5 |
| France II | * | * | * | * | 2.0 | 1.6 | * | * | 6.1 |
| Great Britain | * | 0.6 | * | 1.7 | * | 2.2 | 2.9 | 4.6 | 7.5 |
| Italy | * | 0.0 | * | 1.5 | * | 1.5 | 0.9 | 5.7 | 6.6 |
| Japan | * | 3.9 | * | 3.1 | * | 7.0 | 7.1 | 4.6 | 11.7 |
| Netherlands | * | 1.2 | * | 5.5 | * | 6.6 | 2.9 | 8.2 | 11.1 |
| Puerto Rico | 2.6 | 1.5 | 8.9 | 7.1 | 11.4 | 8.6 | 2.7 | 11.0 | 13.8 |
| Sweden | 2.3 | 1.8 | 2.1 | 1.7 | 4.4 | 3.5 | 2.9 | 3.8 | 6.7 |
| USA I | * | 3.4 | * | 4.5 | * | 7.8 | 7.4 | 8.6 | 16.0 |
| West Germany | * | * | * | * | 1.6 | 1.5 | * | * | 4.6 |
| II. URBAN | | | | | | | | | |
| Belgium I (St–Martens–Latem) | * | * | * | * | 0.0 | 0.0 | * | * | 2.3 |
| Brazil (São Paulo) | * | 1.0 | * | 4.3 | * | 5.3 | 6.8 | 10.2 | 17.1 |
| India (Poona) | * | 0.7 | * | 0.8 | * | 1.4 | 1.7 | 2.4 | 4.1 |
| III. SPECIAL DATA | | | | | | | | | |
| USSR (emigrés) | * | * | * | * | 14.5 | * | * | * | 20.7 |

* Unavailable.

nation with a high rate for manual into non-manual movement, is no higher (and on the basis of France II data, lower) on manual into elite motion than nations with low rates of manual into non-manual when elite size is held constant.

These data support again the notion of asymmetry of mobility, for from one indicator of mobility (in this case manual into non-manual) we cannot indicate movement along another indicator (manual into elite).

Excluding the USSR data, what can be concluded about Elite I and II mobility of the manual strata when we disregard elite size?

1. No nation has considerable movement into the upper levels. Only a small part of the manual strata are able to obtain such positions.[2]

[2] This "small part" can be a large percentage of all those in the elite because of the disparity in size of the elite and manual strata. But from the point of view of the manuals . . . only a relatively few have made the big leap.

2. Nations with high overall upward movement (e.g., France) may not have, for the manual strata, high rates of access to the top positions.
3. The range is from less than 2% in 5 nations to almost 8% (USA) and 8.6% in Puerto Rico. It is possible to state that (*a*) the highest nation has five times the rate of upward movement into Elite I and II occupations that the lowest nation has, or that (*b*) the span between the highest and lowest nations is only 7 percentage points. Nonetheless, the differences may be important. I am particularly impressed by the fact that five nations have rates of movement into Elite I and II that are under 2.5% while the other rates are fairly well strung out.
4. The USA has a comparatively high rate for only Puerto Rico and the USSR (emigrés) exceed it. But Japan and the Netherlands, with considerably smaller

**TABLE 5 Mobility of Manual Strata into Elite I and II Combined and into Non-Manual Strata**

| *Size of Elite I and II* | *(1)* *Manual into Elite I and II* | *(2)* *Manual into Non-Manual* | *(3)* *Elite I and II Mobility as Percentage of Non-Manual Mobility* $\frac{(1)}{(2)}$ |
|---|---|---|---|
| A. UNDER 4.6% | % | % | % |
| Denmark | 1.1 | 24.1 | 4.6 |
| West Germany | 1.5 | 20.0 | 7.5 |
| Belgium I (St–Martens–Latem) | 0.0 | 5.7 | 0.0 |
| India (Poona) | 1.4 | 27.3 | 5.1 |
| B. 6%–8.5% | | | |
| France I | 3.5 | 30.1 | 11.6 |
| France II | 1.6 | 29.6 | 5.4 |
| Great Britain | 2.2 | 24.8 | 8.9 |
| Italy | 1.5 | 8.5 | 17.7 |
| Sweden | 3.5 | 25.5 | 13.7 |
| C. 10%–15% | | | |
| Japan | 7.0 | 23.7 | 29.5 |
| Netherlands | 6.6 | 19.6 | 33.7 |
| Puerto Rico | 8.6 | 14.3 | 60.1 |
| D. OVER 15% | | | |
| Brazil (São Paulo) | 5.3 | 29.4 | 18.0 |
| USA I | 7.8 | 28.8 | 27.1 |
| USSR (emigrés) | 14.5[1] | 34.9 | 41.5 |

[1] This is a figure for the working classes, and therefore overstates manual movement into the elites.

percentages in Elites I and II, do not have much lower rates.

When the data for the Soviet Union (emigrés) are entered into the analysis, the differences are much greater and raise questions about (*a*) the similarity of rates in industrial nations, and (*b*) the validity of an explanation of mobility rates in terms of level of industrial development alone.

## MANUAL INTO ELITE AND NON-MANUAL

. . . Another type of comparison which may influence attitudes toward the social structure is the ratio of the number of individuals who rise out of the working-class/manual strata to those from the strata who move into the top-level positions. What are the chances of long-distance mobility, if there is *any* upward mobility at all? Table 5 presents these figures.

The high Puerto Rican figure is, of course, the most surprising for 6 out of 10 of the manual sons who end up in the non-manual strata move into the top brackets. The size of the overall manual to non-manual movement does not appear to be closely connected to the ratio computed. It does appear, though, that the size of elites affects the ratio of elites to non-manual movement, for categories C and D are uniformly higher than the two smaller elite categories. The

**TABLE 6 Movement into Elites from Various Strata**

| *Size of Elite* | *(1) Middle Classes* | *(2) Working Classes* | *(3) Manual Classes* | *(4) Independent Farmer* | *(5) Farm Worker* | *(6) (1)/(2)* | *(7) (1)/(3)* |
|---|---|---|---|---|---|---|---|
| 2.5%–4.6% | % | % | % | % | % | % | % |
| Denmark (Elite I and II) | 4.6 | * | 1.1 | * | * | * | 418 |
| France I (Elite I) | 5.1 | 1.9 | 1.4 | 0.8 | 0.0 | 268 | 364 |
| Great Britain (Elite I) | 2.5 | * | 0.6 | * | * | * | 417 |
| India (Poona) (Elite I and II) | 6.2 | * | 1.4 | * | * | * | 443 |
| Netherlands (Elite I) | 2.6 | * | 1.2 | * | * | * | 217 |
| Puerto Rico (Elite I) | 6.1 | 2.6 | 1.5 | 2.0 | 0.9 | 235 | 407 |
| Sweden (Elite I) | 7.9 | 2.3 | 1.8 | 1.1 | 0.4 | 344 | 439 |
| West Germany (Elite I and II) | 8.3 | 1.6 | 1.5 | 2.1 | 0.6 | 519 | 553 |
| 6%–8.5% | | | | | | | |
| Brazil (São Paulo) (Elite I) | 5.4 | * | 1.0 | * | * | * | 540 |
| France I (Elite I and II) | 12.3 | 4.2 | 3.5 | 1.9 | 2.0 | 293 | 351 |
| France II (Elite I and II) | 10.5 | 2.0 | 1.6 | 1.7 | 0.4 | 525 | 656 |
| Great Britain (Elite I and II) | 8.6 | * | 2.2 | * | * | * | 391 |
| Italy (Elite I) | 7.5 | * | 1.7 | * | * | * | 500 |
| Japan (Elite I) | 8.3 | * | 3.9 | * | * | * | 213 |
| Sweden (Elite I and II) | 18.1 | 4.4 | 3.5 | 2.6 | 1.0 | 411 | 517 |
| USA I (Elite I) | 9.5 | * | 3.4 | * | * | * | 279 |
| 10%–15% | | | | | | | |
| Japan (Elite I and II) | 15.1 | * | 7.0 | * | * | * | 216 |
| Netherlands (Elite I and II) | 11.6 | * | 6.6 | * | * | * | 176 |
| Puerto Rico (Elite I and II) | 23.2 | 11.4 | 8.6 | 13.1 | 7.1 | 204 | 270 |
| OVER 15% | | | | | | | |
| Brazil (São Paulo) (Elite I and II) | 18.5 | * | 5.3 | * | * | * | 349 |
| USA I (Elite I and II) | 19.8 | * | 7.8 | * | * | * | 254 |
| USSR (emigrés) (Elite I and II) | 42.3 | 14.5 | * | 7.9 | * | 292 | * |

* Unavailable.

difference between USA I and USSR (emigrés) and Puerto Rico is intriguing; the high Dutch rate is also a surprise.

. . . Our concern so far has been with manual and working-class strata except for a brief examination of the downward movement of non-manual strata. Now, we turn to a closer examination of the largest part of the non-manual strata, the middle classes. . . .

## MIDDLE CLASSES INTO ELITES

Table 6 continues the analysis of middle-class movement into the elites; in it nations are grouped by size of elite, as in some earlier tables, and data on similar working-class and manual mobility are also reported for comparative purposes.[3]

Column (1) shows that the middle-class movement into the elites is affected by the size of the elites, as one would expect. While there is some overlap among the four size groups into which elites are classified, there seems to be a fair break between them in percentage moving into elites. Group A, those elites under 4.6%, shows a range from Britain's 2.5% (for Elite I) to West Germany's 8.3% (for Elite I and II). In Group B, a greater range exists between the 5.4% of the middle classes of Brazil (São Paulo) which moves into the elites (Elite I) to the 18.1% for the middle classes of Sweden (Elite I and II). The Swedish figure is very high, clearly higher than similar figures for its size elite and overlapping with those of nations with larger elites. France (Elite I and II) has a higher rate than the USA (Elite I). Britain (Elite I and II) is not very different from the United States, although for the smaller-size elites it was indeed low. In Group C, the high rate of Puerto Rico is pronounced. Group D produces the most interesting result—the extremely high figure for the Soviet Union (emigrés). Four of ten middle-class sons enter the elite according to the Harvard study. No other nation is near; the USA is closest with two of ten sons making this jump. As Table 7 shows even more sharply, the greatest opportunities for the middle-class sons are in the Soviet Union, the least in Denmark. (The

[3] A more complete analysis would also adjust for different sizes of the middle classes.

**TABLE 7 Upward and Downward Movement of Middle-Class Strata**

| | (1) *Into Working Classes* | (2) *Into Manual* | (3) *Into Elite I and II* | (4) *Into Independent Farmer* | (5) (1)/(3) | (6) (2)/(3) | (7) (2)+(3) |
|---|---|---|---|---|---|---|---|
| | % | % | % | % | % | % | % |
| Belgium I (St–Martens–Latem) | 7.9 | 9.9 | 7.2 | * | 110 | 138 | 17.1 |
| Belgium II (Mont–Saint–Guibert) | * | 3.4 | * | 0.9 | * | * | 3.4 |
| Brazil (São Paulo) | * | 24.1 | 18.5 | * | * | 130 | 42.6 |
| Denmark | * | 38.2 | 4.6 | * | * | 830 | 42.8 |
| France I | 20.1 | 22.8 | 12.3 | 6.2 | 163 | 185 | 35.1 |
| France II | 28.9 | 29.8 | 10.5 | 4.0 | 275 | 284 | 40.3 |
| Great Britain | * | 48.8 | 8.6 | * | * | 567 | 57.4 |
| India (Poona) | * | 28.1 | 6.2 | * | * | 453 | 34.3 |
| Italy | * | 32.5 | 7.5 | * | * | 433 | 40.0 |
| Japan | * | 31.6 | 15.1 | * | * | 209 | 46.7 |
| Netherlands | * | 49.2 | 11.6 | * | * | 424 | 60.8 |
| Puerto Rico | 40.2 | 45.1 | 23.2 | 6.1 | 173 | 194 | 68.3 |
| Sweden | 29.7 | 32.3 | 18.1 | 5.2 | 164 | 179 | 50.4 |
| USA I | 19.8 | 20.7 | 19.8 | 4.1 | 100 | 105 | 40.5 |
| USSR (emigrés) | 12.6 | 13.5 | 42.3 | * | 30 | 32 | 55.8 |
| West Germany | 29.6 | 30.5 | 8.3 | 2.0 | 357 | 368 | 38.8 |

* Unavailable.

Danish figure would be increased if elite size were in the same range as Britain.)

Columns (6) and (7) compare the rates of advance into the elites for the middle-class sons with those for the working-class and manual sons. The greatest comparative advantage of the middle-class sons is in France II (Elite I and II), but France I shows a much lower figure. West Germany has the next greatest advantage of middle-class sons. The USSR (emigrés) figure is not high on this index because manual sons also have a particularly good chance to rise into the elites. As a result the relative advantage of middle-class sons is not much different in USA I and in USSR (emigrés).

## MIDDLE CLASSES: OUTFLOW

Table 7 provides a broad view of the outflow from the middle classes. Columns (1)–(4) show that the percentages of movement out of the middle classes range widely among the 16 studies reported. From the point of view of stability of position, the Belgium I (St–Martens–Latem) report indicates that over 90% of the middle-class sons remain in their class; in Puerto Rico, at the other extreme, only a quarter are immobile. The next lowest stability figure is for India (Poona), where 66% of the sons are stable, and this is probably a better figure than either Belgium figure to indicate the maximum stability which exists. Five nations—Great Britain, Netherlands, Puerto Rico, Sweden, USSR (emigrés)—are characterized by less than 45% stability for their middle-class sons. Overall middle-class sons are the most mobile group of the class structure.

The insecure hold of the middle classes is sharply evidenced by the comparison of column (2), the movement into the manual class, with column (3). the movement into Elite I and II, which is made in column (6). In only one nation—the USSR (emigrés)—do we find that the middle-class son, when he is mobile, has a better chance of terminating in the elites than in the manual strata. In Denmark, the chances are eight to one, that he will be downwardly mobile; in Britain, five and a half to one. In Japan the chances are two to one for downward mobility, while in the USA upward and downward movement are equally likely. There does not seem to be any apparent relationship between the degree of stability of a nation and the likelihood of upward or downward movement of its middle-class sons; Germany with a rather stable middle class has a fairly high rate of downward relative to upward movement, while the Netherlands with an unstable middle class does not have a much greater possibility of downward movement for its middle-class sons. Small movement out of the middle class does not increase the chances of upward or downward movement.

A closer examination of columns (2) and (3) reveals that the range of movement into the manual strata is greater than the range for movement into the elites. In Britain, Netherlands and Puerto Rico, the middle-class son is as likely to move into manual occupations as to advance into the elites, to maintain a position in the middle classes or to assume an independent farming position.[4] The USA I and USSR (emigrés) offer the best chances, ignoring Belgium, for middle-class sons not to fall into manual strata. While, in general, a high rate of downward mobility means that the latter is likely to far exceed upward mobility out of the middle classes, this is not uniformly true, e.g. Puerto Rico. High downward movement can be associated with high upward mobility.

The rate of upward mobility for the middle classes is most striking for the USSR (emigrés) where over 40% of middle-class sons move up. Even deflating this figure quite a bit, as it probably deserves, would still give the USSR a high upward figure. Puerto Rico, the USA, Brazil (São Paulo) and Sweden come next in providing opportunities for the middle-class son. The high Swedish figure is in contrast with the low Danish figure; while the two nations were close in regard to non-manual movement of manual sons, here they are quite different.

[4] Since the "middle classes" is a broad category, we are ignoring what may be considerable mobility within the middle classes—movement of the sons of lower-level middle-class fathers to higher-level positions and the reverse movement, neither of which is captured by our wide categories. This is the same phenomenon as we had earlier with the manual and working-class strata which also represent broad groupings in which considerable and important internal motion can occur.

In general, though, there does appear to be a slight relation between upward movement of manual sons (Table 1) and upward movement of middle-class sons.

The movement into independent farming is not insignificant when compared with movement into the elites of the middle-class sons. The movement into the farm worker category—column (2) minus column (1)—is small except in Puerto Rico, where it is almost as great as the movement into independent farming. Overall, agriculture does not become the terminus of a great many middle-class sons.[5]

[5] Since in some nations, independent farmers are not separately categorized, but are included in the middle classes or, less frequently, the manual strata, it is not possible to portray the movement into the farmer position for all nations.

**TABLE 8 National Profiles**

| | (1) *Manual into Non-Manual* | (2) *Non-Manual into Manual* | (3) *Manual into Elite I and II* | (4) *Middle Classes into Elite I and II* | (5) *Total Movement Out of Elite I and II* | (6) *Middle Classes Downward to Upward Movement* | (7) *Elite I and II into Manual* | (8) *Index of Association* |
|---|---|---|---|---|---|---|---|---|
| Australia (Melbourne) | H | H | * | * | * | * | * | I |
| Belgium I (St–Martens–Latem) | L | L | L | L | L | L | L | H |
| } Belgium I and II | L | L | L | L | L | L | L | H |
| Belgium II (Mont–Saint–Guibert) | H | L | * | * | * | * | * | I |
| Brazil (São Paulo) | H | L | H | H | L | L | L | L |
| Denmark | H | H | L | L | H | H | L | I |
| Finland | L | H | * | * | * | * | * | H |
| France I (Bresard) | H | L | L | L | H | L | L | H |
| } France I and II | H | L | L | L | L | L | L | H |
| France II (Desabie) | H | H | L | L | L | H | L | H |
| Great Britain | H | H | L | L | H | H | H | L |
| Hungary | L | H | * | * | * | * | * | H |
| India (Poona) | H | H | L | L | L | H | L | L |
| Italy | L | H | L | L | H | H | H | I |
| Japan | L | H | H | H | H | L | H | I |
| Netherlands | L | H | H | L | L | H | H | I |
| Norway | L | H | * | * | * | * | * | H |
| Puerto Rico | L | H | H | H | H | L | H | I |
| Sweden | H | H | L | H | L | L | L | I |
| USA I (Centers) | H | L | H | H | L | L | L | L |
| } USA I and II | H | L | H | H | L | L | L | L |
| USA II (SRC) | H | L | * | * | * | * | * | L |
| USSR (emigrés) | H | L | H | H | L | L | H | L |
| West Germany | L | H | L | L | L | H | L | H |
| | under 24—L<br>over 24—H | under 24—L<br>over 24—H | under 3.6—L<br>over 3.6—H | under 15.1—L<br>over 15.1—H | under 50% outflow—L<br>over 50% outflow—H | under 250%—L<br>over 250%—H | under 15.8%—L<br>over 15.8%—H | High<br>Low<br>Inconsistent |

* Unavailable.

## INTERPRETATIONS AND CONCLUSIONS

### NATIONAL PROFILES

The data presented . . . have been complex and variegated; the only attempts at synthesis have been the two sets of typologies (relating rates of manual movement into non-manual levels with non-manual movement into manual and exit from the elites with entrance into the elites). A further attempt at synthesis has been made in Table 8 which brings into one table some of the more important indices which have been employed in the study. By looking across the rows, we obtain a brief profile of each nation.

The table shows, for example, that Great Britain has high up-mobility of the manual, high down-mobility of the non-manual, low long-range up-mobility of the manual, low long-range up-mobility of the non-manual, high movement out of the elites, high down-mobility of the middle classes (relative to the up-mobility of the same strata), high long-run down-mobility of elites and low indices of association for the various strata. It is possible from such information to develop new indices of total movement, of consistency of direction of movement, of distance of mobility by combining two or more columns.

What is particularly noteworthy is the close parallel of findings for USA, USSR (emigrés) and Brazil (São Paulo). The only divergence among them is in regard to column (7), Elite I and II into manual (the low of the USA is very close to the breaking point). This summary strengthens the earlier references to the similarities of movement in the USA and USSR (emigrés). It is an interesting pattern of high upward short and long distance manual mobility; high upward mobility of the middle classes and relatively low downward movement; low downward motion of the non-manual and the elites; low occupational inheritance with variation among the three in extent of long-range downward mobility of the elites. It is thus a general pattern of upward mobility with limited downward mobility.

Great Britain and India (Poona) have a somewhat similar pattern: high rates of movement, but with downward and limited upward movement much more pronounced than in the previous type.

Less clear as a group are Italy, Japan, the Netherlands and Puerto Rico. The dominant tendency seems to be downward mobility, although in Japan and Puerto Rico access to the elites is relatively high.

It is important to reassert the earlier warnings about the mixed quality of the data. Presenting materials in tabular form tends to "harden" them; the fact that numbers can be used obscures the weak procedures leading to the production of these numbers. I am acutely aware of the coercive manipulations of data which have necessarily occurred in this report and hope that all the comparisons here, as in other international analyses, will be viewed as "suggestive" of trends, rather than adequate descriptions of nations. Inevitably, we must build on shaky foundations, but awareness of the infirmities is important to the construction of a healthy structure.

These profiles, the culmination of the data of this report, must be taken as no more than suggestive of possibilities.

### IMPLICATIONS OF THE DATA

***Asymmetry.*** The point of departure of the monograph has been strongly supported by the data. Mobility is not a symmetrical phenomenon—perhaps better put, at least our knowledge at this time does not reveal its symmetry. A nation can be high in one measure of mobility and low in another. The patterns just suggested should not be assumed to have a definitive character. The profiles and typologies of this report are only limited ways of organizing the data.

The connections between mobility of one kind and mobility of another kind are unclear. We must, therefore, in making comparisons, specify the measure on which the comparison is based. *The* measure of mobility does not exist, only many measures tapping different dimensions of mobility which do not as yet at least form a smooth pyramid.

***The Clear Result.*** The most striking result of the comparisons is that on both the simple comparison of working classes into non-manual and manual into elite strata, the Soviet Union (emigrés) has the highest rates. (France I has a similar working class into non-manual rate.) These rates are probably high, but even if reduced would probably still show the Soviet Union at the top of these comparisons. On the other hand, the Soviet Union had a rather low rate of downward movement out of the non-manual categories generally, and out of the elite strata specifically. Thus, the upward manual movement is not due to the decline of the middle classes and the elite, but to the expansion of these strata.

The United States has a high rate of manual movement into non-manual occupations, but not one that is distinctively higher than that of France or USSR (emigrés). On the other hand, it is distinctively higher in the manual movement into the elite strata than all nations other than the Soviet Union (emigrés).

***Comparison with Lipset–Bendix–Zetterberg.*** Because of the forthright contentions of Lipset–Bendix–Zetterberg[6] in analyzing social mobility rates, there will be interest in comparing the results of the present analysis with theirs. In regard to their basic points, the scoreboard seems to be as follows:

(*a*) The United States is not distinctively higher on movement into non-manual from manual levels than are some industrial nations. On this account, Lipset and his colleagues are supported.

(*b*) The United States has a higher rate of movement into the elite strata from the manual strata than do all other nations except the Soviet Union (emigrés). This result does not support the L–B–Z thesis of the non-exceptionality of the United States which is based on one main type of measure, movement from manual into non-manual.

(*c*) The Lipset *et al.* thesis is that the rates of mobility are similar in industrialized nations. (1) The rates of manual into non-manual occupations seem to be the closest together, if we disregard the low Italian and Finnish figures and the high Soviet one. Even so, the range is not narrow, from 14+ % in Hungary and Puerto Rico to 30% in France. If we disregard the former two as not very industrialized, the lower limit is about 20% in the Netherlands and West Germany. (2) The rates of non-manual into manual occupations show a spread between the under 20% of USA I and USSR (emigrés) on the one hand and the more than 30% of several nations. (3) The rates of movement of manual strata into the elite strata reveal a considerable range as well. (4) The rates of movement out of elite strata are widely varying.

It is difficult to summarize these findings. If we ignore nations at the extremes like the Soviet Union and Italy because of sampling and allied problems, we can see some convergence in rates of manual movement into non-manual. But if these nations had not appeared at the extremes, would we have been so ready to ignore them?

There probably is more convergence in rates than most people had believed. But that does not mean that the actual convergence is overwhelming; if we were able to approach the data without the background of decades of speculation, we would probably be concerned with the variation in the rates. Even if we were to accept the L–B–Z thesis of the similarity of rates, at some stage of analysis we have to turn attention to the reasons for the kind of divergences that have occurred. Here a great lack exists.

## AN UNDERDEVELOPED AREA: DOWNWARD MOBILITY

As I have argued elsewhere, the concern with upward mobility has obscured the importance and amount of downward mobility. In the present study, it is striking how high the rate of movement from non-manual to manual is, and from elite strata to all other strata. A whole host of basic social issues arise, especially concerning the nature of education, which are not directly germane to the narrow focus of this monograph. But one aspect of this downward mobility is.

It may well be that downward mobility is a better indicator of fluidity in a society than is upward mobility.[7] The latter type of movement is a product of fluidity and opportunity, changes in the occupational

[6] Lipset, S. M., Bendix, R., *Social Mobility in Industrial Society*. Berkeley, University of California, 1959 : 301 pp.

[7] We use fluidity in the sense of the ease of movement from stratum to stratum in society that is not due to changes in the occupational structure.

distribution, as well as of demographic changes. Downward mobility is also a product of these factors, but here social fluidity is more important. In any case, a society which is dropping sons born in advantaged strata out of these strata has more openness than one which brings up talented manual sons but safeguards the privileges of the already advantaged.

Utilizing downward mobility as an indicator, then, the USSR, high on other indicators of mobility, does not show much movement. In many other nations, the down rate is much higher, e.g., France and Great Britain. The USSR may have more upward mobility, but not necessarily more fluidity in the social structure.

The psychological and social aspects of downward mobility are unclear. A society may have high downward mobility, high upward mobility and still lack a strong egalitarian ideology and even structural supports for facilitating up and down movement. The statement of rates does not exhaust the complicated relationships between mobility, ideology, structure and behavior. As Feldman[8] has indicated in his thoughtful analysis of Lipset and Bendix, there are many types of relations between ideology and rates to consider.

## THE MEASURE OF MOBILITY

In interpreting results, it is not only important to be aware of the different measures of mobility and the varying quality of the data, but also of the basic definition of mobility which is involved. . . . the sociological study of mobility has been largely restricted to investigation of occupational mobility and to the prestige dimension of occupational mobility. Therefore, our comparisons of national rates of mobility are about this one slice of mobility. As Arnold Rose has indicated, if we were to study other aspects, such as political power of great masses of the citizenry or the degree of egalitarianism and social distance which prevails, then other results might be produced.[9] Rose feels, for example, that nations which have already achieved high industrialization, e.g., the United States, are inevitably going to have lower rates of occupational mobility than nations at a lower stage of industrialization which necessarily have to upgrade many in order to fit them into the new technological demands of the economic structure. One way of meeting this problem would be to subtract the mobility due to changing occupational opportunities from the overall rates of mobility; where this has not been done, it is important to recognize that measures of mobility such as those reported in the present monograph, except for the index of association, are refractions to a considerable extent, although certainly not exclusively, of the occupational structure, a product of a stage of industrialization.

The measure of mobility affects the rate. The emphasis on occupational mobility may lower the rate of the already high industrial achievers relative to those nations striving to reach these levels. This point of Rose's is not an argument against using occupational data, but against using them as the sole dimension of mobility.

[8] Feldman, A. S. "Economic Development and Social Mobility," *Economic Development and Cultural Change*. 8 (3), April, 1960: 311–321.

[9] Arnold M. Rose, "Social Mobility and Social Values," unpublished manuscript.

# OCCUPATIONAL MOBILITY IN THE UNITED STATES

*Peter M. Blau*
*and Otis Dudley Duncan*

This is a preliminary report from a study of occupational mobility in the United States. The objectives of the study are to describe the patterns of social mobility in some detail, to estimate the influence of various factors on occupational life chances, and to ascertain a few consequences of

Original title: "Some Preliminary Findings on Social Stratification in the United States." Reprinted from *Acta Sociologica*, Vol. 9, fasc. 1–2, 1965, by permission.

socio-economic status and mobility, such as their implications for fertility. The present paper reports selected findings pertaining to factors affecting occupational achievement and the chances to move away from one's social origins. In particular, we shall examine the significance for occupational attainment of education, ethnic background, community size, migration, and parental family.

In addition to presenting preliminary substantive findings from our research, this paper also provides an opportunity for illustrating the analytical procedures we have used. The analysis relies to a large extent on the regression approach. Two major advantages of this approach which prompted our decision to adopt it are that it is a very efficient method of large-scale data reduction and that it permits, consequently, the simultaneous examination of the interrelations of fairly large numbers of variables, especially if computers are used. Contingency tables containing half a dozen or more variables and many hundreds of cells are too complex to be analyzed by inspection, whereas the regression method permits the analysis of these interrelations. To be sure, a limitation of regression analysis is that it makes restrictive assumptions about linearity and the absence of interaction effects, but the assumptions can be taken into account and hence removed in more complex analytical models. Simpler methods we use, such as comparisons of mean scores of occupational status, are complemented by regression analysis to determine not only the gross effects of various factors on socio-economic status but also the net effects with other variables held constant.

## RESEARCH PROCEDURES

The data for this research were collected by the U.S. Bureau of the Census in March, 1962, partly in the course of its regular "Current Population Survey" interview, and partly in a supplementary self-administered questionnaire specifically designed for the purpose of our research. The sample of 20,700 American men between the ages of 20 and 65 represents the 45 million men in this age group who are in the "civilian noninstitutional population," that is, who are neither in the Armed Forces nor in institutions. A subsample of those respondents who failed initially to return the supplementary questionnaire by mail was interviewed and appropriately weighted to make the sample highly representative. The present analysis, however, is confined to men whose fathers were *not* in farming occupations, which excludes a quarter of the total group. (In brief, the data derive from a representative sample of the 33 million American men with nonfarm backgrounds between 20 and 65 years old who are not in military service and do not live in institutions.[1])

Respondent's occupation and that of his father when the respondent was 16 years old were transformed into SES (socioeconomic status) scores. The score, which ranges from 0 to 96, is based on the proportion of men in a specific occupation ("detailed occupational classification") who were, at least, high school graduates and the proportion reporting an income of over $3,500 in 1949, making adjustments for differences in age distribution between occupations.[2] The multiple correlation between these two predictors—the education and the income of the men in an occupation—and the N.O.R.C. prestige rating[3] for the 45 occupations that could be matched is +.91, and the regression equation that expresses this multiple correlation is used to determine the SES scores for all 446 detailed occupations. Respondent's education was transformed into an arbitrary score ranging from 0 to 8 which takes into account the special significance graduation from a

[1] All frequencies in the original tables, from which the analytical tables presented in this report are derived, refer to the estimated actual population in the United States in the given categories, reported in 1000's. The sampling ratio is, on the average, 1:2,173. To obtain the approximate numbers of actual cases from whom data were collected, therefore, the numbers reported in 1000's should be divided by 2.2.

[2] See Otis Dudley Duncan, *A Socio-Economic Index for All Occupations* in Albert J. Reiss, Jr., Occupations and Social Status, New York: Free Press, 1961. (This score was derived from the 1950 U.S. Census of Population, not from our sample.)

[3] National Opinion Research Center, *Jobs and Occupations*, Opinion News, Vol. 9 (1947), pp. 3–13.

given school level has.[4] Whereas socio-economic status and education are assumed to be continuous quantitative variables, no such assumption is made concerning the other factors used in the analysis, which are treated as qualitative attributes in terms of which individuals are classified into discrete categories.

To convey the meaning of the SES scores, the average scores of the conventional major groups of nonfarm occupations are presented below:

| | |
|---|---|
| Professionals and technicians | 75 |
| Managers, proprietors, and officials | 57 |
| Sales and clerical occupations | 47 |
| Skilled workers and foremen | 31 |
| Semiskilled workers | 18 |
| Unskilled workers | 7 |

The average difference between two adjacent categories is 13.6. Hence, the finding that an attribute affects the SES score by four or five points implies that, on the average, one third of the men with this attribute are one full step higher in this rank order (for example, are skilled rather than semiskilled workers) than those without this attribute. Fairly small differences in score are, therefore, of substantive significance, and given our large number of cases such small differences also are statistically significant.

## EDUCATION AND ETHNIC BACKGROUND

The over-all correlation between father's and son's occupational status is +.38. This indicates that there is much occupational mobility in the United States; only one seventh of the variance in socio-economic status is attributable to the influence of father's socio-economic status. Nevertheless, this amount of mobility does not seem to be excessive compared to that in other Western countries. To make some rough comparisons, we computed the coefficient of association derived by Carlsson from the index earlier employed by Glass and Rogoff to measure occupational inheritance.[5] Since the Swedish data, which otherwise are most comparable with ours, include persons of farm origins, we did so too in these computations. (The correlation coefficient for the total U.S. population, including men with farm background, is +.42.) Using ten categories of SES scores, this measure of inheritance is 1.51, and using ten occupational categories,[6] as required to make it comparable to the Swedish data, it is 1.95. The same measure applied to the Swedish data divided into ten occupational categories is 1.89 or 2.28, depending on the method used,[7] which implies that there is about as much occupational inheritance in the United States as in Sweden. One of our former associates, R. W. Hodge, has computed age-specific father-son correlations from the British data, using an arbitrary scoring of prestige categories. He finds coefficients varying between .44 and .50 over five age groups. This suggests a slightly higher degree of association between son's and father's status in Britain than in America, although lack of comparability in study design makes one loath to stress this conclusion. Svalastoga's correlations for Denmark are of the same order of magnitude.[8]

To examine the relative importance of social origins and of education for occupational attainments, the (nonfarm background) sample is first divided into five cohorts, providing a control for age (20–24, 25–34, 35–44, 45–54, 55–64). The multiple correlation of education and father's socio-economic status on son's SES increases from +.51 for the youngest group to +.66 for those 25–34 years old and then decreases again to +.59 for the oldest group (Table 1, row 1). This nonmonotonic relationship with age suggests that the influences of social background and of education on a man's career extend beyond its early phases

[4] Education is scored by the following system, which takes into account the special significance of graduation from one of the three main levels of schooling: 0 No School; 1 Elementary, 1 to 4 years; 2 Elementary, 5 to 7 years; 3 Elementary, 8 years; 4 High school, 1 to 3 years; 5 High school, 4 years; 6 College, 1 to 3 years; 7 College, 4 years; 8 Graduate school, 1 year or more.

[5] Gösta Carlsson, *Social Mobility and Class Structure*, Lund: Gleerup, 1958, pp. 74–75.

[6] The ten occupational categories are the six previously reported in the text, except that clerical and sales occupations are divided, service occupations are separately shown, and two categories of farm occupations are added, farmers and farm managers, and farm laborers.

[7] *Ibid.*, p. 114.

[8] Kaare Svalastoga, Prestige, Class and Mobility, Copenhagen: Glydendal, 1950, p. 351.

**TABLE 1 Correlation Analysis: Respondent's Occupational SES on Education and Father's SES, for American Men with Nonfarm Backgrounds, Age 20 to 64, 1962**

| *Item* | *20–24 Years* | *25–34 Years* | *35–44 Years* | *45–54 Years* | *55–64 Years* |
|---|---|---|---|---|---|
| 1. Multiple correlations (SES on education and father's SES) | .51 | .66 | .65 | .61 | .59 |
| a. *Beta* coefficient, education | .46 | .61 | .57 | .53 | .52 |
| b. *Beta* coefficient, father's SES | .09 | .12 | .15 | .16 | .13 |
| 2. Zero order correlation, SES and father's SES | .29 | .37 | .40 | .38 | .34 |
| Components* | | | | | |
| a. Independent of education | .09 | .12 | .15 | .16 | .13 |
| b. Mediated through education | .20 | .25 | .25 | .22 | .21 |

* For method of calculation, see O. D. Duncan and R. W. Hodge, "Education and Occupational Mobility: A Regression Analysis," *American Journal of Sociology*, 68 (May, 1963), 629–44.

and become increasingly pronounced for some years but that the significance of these factors eventually declines as they recede in time. An alternative explanation of this finding is that the influence of education has become increasingly important since the beginning of this century although a decline may now be under way. There has probably been little change in the significance of father's occupational SES for that of his son in this century.[9] The *beta* coefficients indicate that the net influence of education is at a maximum at about age thirty and then decreases, whereas that of father's SES continues to increase until about age fifty (rows 1a and 1b). Taking these partial regression coefficients in standard form (*beta* coefficients) as indications of the relative significance of the two antecedents, the data also show that the impact on occupational status of education independent of social origin is considerably greater than that of social origin independent of education.[10]

[9] Although we plan to investigate the problem of estimating time trends more thoroughly in the future, a re-analysis of Rogoff's data for the city of Indianapolis by Duncan indicates that there is no change in the father-son correlation between 1910 and 1940.

[10] Since the index used to score the status of an occupation is based on the amount of education and the amount of income that prevailed in the occupation, it is necessarily related to education to some degree. Experimentation, with an alternative index of occupational SES, not based explicitly on education levels, however, shows that the results are not dependent on the specific form of SES index used here.

This finding implies that the influence of father's socio-economic status on son's status is largely mediated in the United States by education. A man's chances of occupational advancement depend on his education (zero-order correlation, +.61), which, in turn, depends to a considerable degree on the socio-economic status of his father (+.41). These relationships can be further clarified by restating them in a slightly different way. Instead of asking how SES is affected by education and by father's SES separately, as we did above, we take now the (zero-order) correlation between father's and son's SES (Table 1, row 2) and ask to which extent this influence of father's SES on son's status is mediated through education (row 2b) and to which extent it is independent of education and thus due to other factors (row 2a). It is apparent from the data that education is the major means by which fathers affect the occupational chances of their sons. It should not be ignored, however, that social origins also have a definite effect on occupational opportunities that has nothing to do with educational qualifications. . . .

. . . . . . . . . . . . . . . . . . . . . . . . . . . . . . . . . .

Negroes have, of course, far less educational opportunity than whites in the United States. Whereas 18 per cent of the native whites have no more than eight years of schooling, fully 37 per cent of the nonwhites do.[11] The education of the second-generation Americans hardly differs from that of other native whites (21 per cent), but the foreign born are nearly as poorly educated as the Negroes, with 35 per cent not having gone beyond the eight years of elementary school. It is interesting that age affects educational attainment to an even greater extent than race. Among the native whites with native parents, only 8 per cent of the men 20–24 years old have no more than eight years of schooling, as compared with 39 per cent of those 55–64 years old. Among the Negroes, similarly, 22 per cent of the youngest age cohort in contrast to 70 per cent of the oldest one have not gone beyond elementary school. Discrimination notwithstanding, young Negroes in today's nonfarm population are better educated than old whites. Negroes, nevertheless, continue to suffer serious educational handicaps and these are, moreover, not the only handicaps that impede their occupational opportunities.

To ascertain the impact of various attributes, such as ethnic background, on occupational chances, the following procedure is used. The mean SES score for each age cohort is determined, and so are the deviations from this mean in various subgroups under consideration. Differences between these deviations from the mean indicate the gross effect of the attribute on SES, for example, the gross effect of being a Negro rather than a white with a given education on occupational status. The net effects the same attribute has on SES when father's SES is held constant are derived from a regression equation.[12] These net effects can be considered approximate indications of occupational mobility in the sense that they refer to average occupational achievements of groups whose point of social origin has been standardized. An interesting over-all finding that emerges from our analysis is that controlling for father's occupation reduces the influence of various attributes but hardly ever alters the patterns of influence observed. In other words, the same factors that are associated with differential occupational status are also associated with differential achievements independent of level of origin.

Even when education is held constant, the occupational status of Negroes is far inferior to that of whites in the United States. Twenty independent comparisons between native whites of native parentage and nonwhites can be made in Table 2 (four educational groups in each of the five age cohorts). In all twenty, the score of whites is higher, and the average difference is 12.1, nearly a full step in the rank order of major occupational classes. This is a clear indication of the serious discrimination Negroes with the same educational qualifications as whites suffer in the employment market.[13] Moreover, controlling for father's occupation does not wipe out this difference. All twenty net effects favor the whites, an average of 10.2, notwithstanding the fact that Negroes, due to past discrimination, have much lower social origins than whites. In sum, Negroes are handicapped by having less education and by having lower social origins than whites. But even if these handicaps are controlled statistically—asking, in effect, what the chances of Negroes would be if they had the same education and social origins as whites—the occupational attainments of Negroes are still considerably inferior to those of whites.

[11] Our data actually refer to "nonwhites" but 92 per cent of all nonwhites in the United States are Negroes.

[12] For an explanation of the statistical model used, see Otis Dudley Duncan, *Farm Background and Differential Fertility,* paper presented to the Population Association of America at its June 1964 annual meeting. For a published discussion, see T. P. Hill, *An Analysis of the Distribution of Wages and Salaries in Great Britain,* Econometrics, Vol. 27 (July, 1959), pp. 355–381.

[13] It should be noted that some of the difference between Negroes and whites, though hardly all of it, may be due to the fact that holding constant the amount of education for the two groups does actually not hold constant their educational qualifications, since many of the schools to which Negroes go are inferior to those whites attend. Moreover, our broad categories do not even hold the amount of education fully constant, since, given the lower educational attainments of Negroes, there are undoubtedly fewer Negroes than whites near the upper end of the distribution within each category; for example, within the category, "one year of college or more," the proportion of college graduates is slightly smaller for Negroes than for whites.

**TABLE 2 Ethnic Background, Education, and Occupational SES of American Men with Nonfarm Background, Age 20 to 64**

| *Ethnicity by Education* | *20–24 Years* | *25–34 Years* | *35–44 Years* | *45–54 Years* | *55–64 Years* |
|---|---|---|---|---|---|
| GRAND MEAN, ALL GROUPS | 31.5 | 41.0 | 42.6 | 40.1 | 40.0 |
| | | | *Gross Effects* | | |
| Native white, native parentage | | | | | |
| 8 years of schooling or less | −12.9 | −18.1 | −18.7 | −13.8 | −10.6 |
| 9 to 11 years of schooling | − 8.7 | −13.6 | −11.1 | −5.6 | 0.3 |
| High school graduate | 0.2 | −3.1 | 1.7 | 3.0 | 8.0 |
| 1 year of college or more | 8.3 | 20.1 | 22.2 | 19.3 | 20.9 |
| Native white, foreign parentage | | | | | |
| 8 years of schooling or less | −12.9* | −18.0 | −18.1 | −14.6 | −9.0 |
| 9 to 11 years of schooling | 2.5* | −11.6 | −14.3 | −6.6 | −0.9 |
| High school graduate | 4.7 | −3.0 | −0.8 | 6.4 | 6.7 |
| 1 year of college or more | 12.3 | 21.2 | 20.3 | 24.1 | 21.2 |
| Foreign-born white | | | | | |
| 8 years of schooling or less | −12.9* | −15.5* | −19.4 | −13.8 | −10.8 |
| 9 to 11 years of schooling | 0.3* | −9.6* | −12.8* | −3.0 | 1.5 |
| High school graduate | 1.1* | −13.2* | 3.8 | −2.9 | 4.9 |
| 1 year of college or more | 5.4* | 19.3 | 12.9 | 17.0 | 19.6 |
| Nonwhite | | | | | |
| 8 years of schooling or less | −20.3 | −25.3 | −23.8 | −21.0 | −19.5 |
| 9 to 11 years of schooling | −13.5 | −23.4 | −20.9 | −17.7 | −20.6 |
| High school graduate | −7.5 | −19.0 | −18.3 | −18.3 | −2.8* |
| 1 year of college or more | −1.4* | 9.7 | 5.4 | −3.9* | 8.1* |
| | | | *Net Effects*** | | |
| Native white, native parentage | | | | | |
| 8 years of schooling or less | −12.0 | −16.8 | −16.8 | −12.1 | −9.4 |
| 9 to 11 years of schooling | −8.0 | −12.9 | −10.4 | −5.6 | (−)0.0 |
| High school graduate | 0.1 | −3.0 | 1.3 | 2.4 | 6.4 |
| 1 year of college or more | 7.6 | 18.6 | 18.9 | 16.3 | 18.9 |
| Native white, foreign parentage | | | | | |
| 8 years of schooling or less | −12.2* | −17.2 | −15.8 | −12.8 | −8.0 |
| 9 to 11 years of schooling | 2.9* | −10.2 | −12.8 | −5.2 | −0.7 |
| High school graduate | 4.8 | −2.6 | −0.2 | 6.3 | 6.3 |
| 1 year of college or more | 11.6 | 20.2 | 20.2 | 21.7 | 20.0 |
| Foreign-born white | | | | | |
| 8 years of schooling or less | −12.4* | 14.8* | −17.9 | −12.1 | −10.0 |
| 9 to 11 years of schooling | 0.5* | −10.6* | −13.2* | −1.7* | 1.7 |
| High school graduate | 0.7* | −13.4* | 3.8 | −2.6 | 3.7 |
| 1 year of college or more | 4.8* | 17.5 | 12.2 | 15.0 | 18.3 |
| Nonwhite | | | | | |
| 8 years of schooling or less | −18.8 | −23.8 | −20.6 | −18.3 | −17.5 |
| 9 to 11 years of schooling | −12.1 | −21.7 | −17.9 | −15.4 | −19.4 |
| High school graduate | −6.2 | −17.8 | −16.5 | −16.2 | −4.9* |
| 1 year of college or more | −0.5* | 10.0 | 6.8 | −1.7* | 12.5* |

* The cell frequency on which this value is based is less than 100.
** Father's occupational SES held constant.

Foreign-born Americans and their children, the second-generation Americans, in sharp contrast to Negroes, do not differ in occupational attainments from the native whites of native parentage on the same educational levels. The twenty comparisons of gross effects between native whites of native parentage and native whites of foreign parentage are inconsistent (averaging −1.1), and so are the twenty comparisons between the former and the foreign born (averaging 0.8). The various white ethnic groups in the United States apparently achieve occupational positions commensurate with their education. Whatever occupational discrimination may exist against some of these ethnic groups must be compensated for by other factors since it does not find expression in their over-all occupational chances.

Another perspective on the disadvantaged situation of the American Negro can be gained by examining the rewards he obtains for given educational investments compared to those a white person obtains. The average difference for the five age groups between native whites of native parentage who have some college education and those who have only an elementary school education is 33.0, whereas the corresponding average difference for Negroes is 25.6. In other words, roughly the same amount of educational investment has one and one third times as much payoff for a white man as for a Negro. The fact that Negroes obtain comparatively little reward for their educational investments, which robs them of incentives to incur these costs, might help explain why Negroes often manifest only weak motivation to pursue their education. The early school leaving that results from this lack of motivation further intensifies the disadvantaged position of the Negro in the labor market.

## CITY SIZE AND MIGRATION

The discussion of the relationships between size of place, migration, and occupational opportunities will concentrate upon the urban areas, since the present analysis is confined to men whose fathers were not in farming occupations. Although data for nonfarm rural areas will be presented too, these must be interpreted with great caution, inasmuch as all the sons of farmers living in these areas are excluded from consideration.[14] It should also be remembered that the large number of migrants from farms to cities is not reflected in the data that are now being analyzed.

The findings on size of community reveal few surprises. Table 3 presents the deviations from the mean socio-economic score in each age cohort by city size and by location in the central city or its suburban fringe. People who live in the urban fringe of cities have somewhat higher socio-economic status than those who live in the central cities, and this difference persists if their father's SES is controlled. Of the 15 possible comparisons (three city sizes by five age cohorts), 14 of the gross differences favor the fringe over the central city, an average of 4.1 points, and 12 of the net differences do so, an average of 2.7. The socio-economic status of men who live in suburbs is directly related to the size of the central city, at least for younger men, but the status of the inhabitants of the central cities is not monotonically related to city size.

Within the central city, socio-economic status is highest in cities with between one quarter and one million inhabitants It is somewhat lower in the largest cities of over one million (an average difference of 3.3 points from the former), as well as in the medium cities with 50,000 to 250,000 inhabitants (2.5) and in the small towns with 2,500 to 50,000 inhabitants (2.1). The average socio-economic status in the smallest American towns, however, is still higher than that in rural areas even when farm workers and their sons are excluded from the comparison (2.8). All these differences persist in slightly attenuated form when social origins are controlled, as the net effects in Table 3 show. In short, occupational opportunities are poorest in rural areas and best in fairly large cities, and they differ little on the average in the very large

[14] Since the criterion of nonfarm background is whether a man designated his father's occupation as being in farming, not whether he lives on a farm, there are a few farm residents in this nonfarm population. Wherever possible, these have been excluded from this analysis, but this was not possible in all cases. However, the numbers involved are so small that it is unlikely that these farm residents affect the results substantially.

**TABLE 3 Size of Place and Occupational SES of American Men with Nonfarm Background, Age 20 to 64**

| *Size of Place* | *20–24 Years* | | *25–34 Years* | | *35–44 Years* | | *45–54 Years* | | *55–64 Years* | |
|---|---|---|---|---|---|---|---|---|---|---|
| | *Central City* | *Urban Fringe* | *Central City* | *Urban Fringe* | *Central City* | *Urban Fringe* | *Central City* | *Urban Fringe* | *Central City* | *Urban Fringe* |
| Grand Mean, All Places | 31.5 | | 41.0 | | 42.6 | | 40.1 | | 40.0 | |
| | | | | | *Gross Effects* | | | | | |
| Very large city (over 1 million) | 1.8 | 4.3 | −2.2 | 6.4 | −3.7 | 5.7 | −3.5 | 4.8 | −0.5 | 3.4 |
| Large city (¼–1 million) | 1.1 | 0.0 | 2.7 | 5.6 | 1.2 | 5.4 | 3.4 | 5.8 | 0.2 | 4.0 |
| Medium city (50,000–250,000) | −1.6 | −1.0 | −1.7 | 2.0 | −1.5 | 3.0 | −1.3 | 5.7 | 2.3 | 3.4 |
| Small town (2,500–50,000) | 0.0 | | −1.4 | | −0.8 | | 0.6 | | −0.5 | |
| Rural area (under 2,500) | −3.3 | | −2.8 | | −2.4 | | −4.1 | | −3.4 | |
| | | | | | *Net Effects* | | | | | |
| Very large city | 1.9 | 2.6 | −2.0 | 5.1 | −2.6 | 4.5 | −2.4 | 3.4 | −0.1 | 3.3 |
| Large city | 0.5 | −1.1 | 2.0 | 3.3 | 1.1 | 4.0 | 3.2 | 5.9 | 0.1 | 3.1 |
| Medium city | −1.4 | 0.3 | −0.4 | −0.6 | −1.8 | 1.4 | −1.0 | 4.2 | 1.8 | 0.7 |
| Small town | 0.2 | | −0.2 | | −0.9 | | 0.2 | | −0.8 | |
| Rural area | −2.1 | | 2.2 | | −1.6 | | −3.3 | | −2.6 | |

Note: No cell frequency is less than 100 and only one—fringe of medium cities for youngest age cohort—is less than 200.

cities and those that are medium or small.

The question arises whether this pattern of differences is the result of migration. The answer appears to be that although migration plays a role the basic pattern has not been produced by it. . . . The socio-economic status of the nonmigrants—the men who reached adolescence in the same community where they live now—reveals a pattern similar to that previously encountered for the total population.* For all five age groups of nonmigrants . . . average SES is higher in cities of at least medium size than in small towns (an average difference of 5.2), and it is higher in small towns than in rural areas (3.6), and the same is true for the net differences when father's SES is held constant (4.4 and 2.6). Since all cities with more than 50,000 inhabitants were combined for this analysis, as were the central cities and their urban fringe, it is not possible to determine whether all specific differences observed in the total populations are reflected in parallel differences among nonmigrants. But the evidence does show that the over-all pattern is the same and that migration cannot account for the status differences between fairly large cities and small ones and between the latter and rural regions.

The socio-economic status of urban migrants is clearly superior to that of nonmigrants, though rural migrants are not superior to nonmigrants. In order to isolate the significance of migration as such from that of either living now or having lived previously in a certain environment, nonmigrants will be compared with only those migrants who reside at present in communities of the same size and who also lived as adolescents in communities of about the same size, that is, with those migrants who moved from as well as into communities of approximately the same size. . . . In all ten comparisons of urban nonmigrants with

* We have omitted from the original text the table on which this conclusion is based and from which the following figures are taken. (C. S. H.)

migrants who came from and are now in the same environment (two city sizes for five age cohorts), the socio-economic status of the migrants is superior, an average of 7.0 (net of father's SES, 5.4). The five comparisons between nonfarm rural migrants and nonmigrants yield no consistent results —two going in one and three in the other direction—and the average difference is very small (0.6; net, 1.3). Migrants within urban areas, then, tend to occupy superior occupational positions and enjoy higher achievements relative to their social origins than their nonmigrant counterparts, but there are no corresponding differences between the migrants within rural areas and the nonmigrants in these areas. These differences cannot be primarily due to the fact that migrants frequently move from smaller to larger communities where occupational opportunities are superior, because the influence of city size has been roughly controlled in this analysis. The inference therefore is that intra-urban migration is selective of men predisposed to occupational success, whereas this is not the case for intra-rural migration.

We turn now to examine the significance of the change in environment migration produces, which is the very factor we attempted to control in the preceding analysis of the significance of migration itself. What are the implications of the migrant's area of destination for his occupational chances? Regardless of geographical origins, men who move into urban areas tend to achieve higher socio-economic status than those who move into rural areas. Most pronounced is the difference between migrants to small cities and those to rural regions, with nine of ten comparisons indicating a higher SES for the men who moved to small cities, the average difference being 4.2 (and 3.5 if father's SES is held constant).[15] This difference parallels that between nonmigrants in small cities and rural areas. When cities over 50,000 are compared with smaller ones, however, the findings assume quite another pattern. Here point of origin makes a difference, and the situation of migrants differs from that of nonmigrants in the same type of place. Whereas nonmigrants tend to achieve *higher* occupational status in the relatively larger cities than in small ones, the status of migrants from rural areas does not differer consistently in the two localities, and migrants from other urban areas achieve lower status in the larger than in the small cities. . . . The SES of nonmigrants is *higher* in the larger than in the smaller cities in five instances out of five, the average difference being +5.2 (net, +4.4), but the SES of migrants from urban areas (rows 2 and 3) is *lower* in the larger than in the smaller cities in nine cases out of ten, the average difference being −2.3 (net, −2.0).

It seems paradoxical that the occupational chances of urban migrants are worse, and those of rural migrants are no better, in larger cities than in smaller ones, while the occupational opportunities of the natives are better in the larger than in the smaller cities. It must be remembered that the urban migrants to larger cities are somewhat superior in socio-economic status to the nonmigrants there, but their superiority is not as great as that of migrants over nonmigrants in small cities. One possible explanation of these findings is that the migrants to larger cities constitute a more heterogeneous group than those to smaller towns, including not only disproportionate numbers with good occupational qualifications but also very many with extremely poor qualifications. Thus the migrants who stream into the large Northern cities from the South can frequently only obtain the least desirable occupational positions, and these migrants take the place at the bottom of the industrial hierarchy that was once occupied by the recent immigrants from Europe. Another reason for the lesser superiority of migrants over nonmigrants in larger cities might be that being raised in large cities gives the natives an advantage in the struggle for occupational success that compensates for some of the other advantages the migrants have. The comparison of men reared in places of different size supports this interpretation.

[15] Since only one value for migrants from the two urban to rural areas is given, the unweighted average of the two values for the migrants to small towns from large cities and those from small towns was used in computing the differences. In case of the youngest age group, for instance, 1.9 was subtracted from 5.4 (the average of 5.8 and 5.0).

Migrants who lived in larger cities when they were 16 years old tend to be superior in socio-economic status to those raised in smaller cities, and the latter tend to be superior to those who grew up in rural areas. . . . Of ten comparisons between migrants coming from larger and those coming from smaller cities, nine show that the former have a higher SES, the average difference being 4.0 (net, 2.9), and of 15 comparisons between migrants raised in small cities and those raised in rural areas, 14 show that the former have higher SES, the average difference being 8.6 (net, 5.5). The same difference is reflected in the finding that the SES of nonmigrants is directly related to the size of their present community, since in the case of nonmigrants the present community is, of course, identical with the place where they lived at age 16. Whether a man is a migrant or not, therefore, and regardless of the size of the community where he now works, the larger the community where he grew up, the better are his chances to achieve occupational success and to move up from the status of his father.

Since growing up in a large city is an occupational advantage, and so is being a migrant to a small city, the highest occupational status is achieved by migrants from larger to small cities, whose status is, on the average, 9.1 points above the mean (net, 7.1 points). One might speculate why men raised in large cities have greater chances of success in their careers. The advantage of the urban over the rural environment is undoubtedly in large part due to the superior educational facilities in the former, but it is questionable whether the superiority of the large-city environment over that in small cities can be attributed to differences in the educational system. It may be that at least part of this superiority is due to the greater sophistication about the labor market and occupational life generally that boys growing up in large cities tend to acquire.

## PARENTAL FAMILY

A man's occupational chances are strongly affected by the size of his parents' family. The socio-economic status of men with three or fewer siblings is considerably superior to that of men with four or more siblings. The data in Table 4 permit 20 independent comparisons between men from small and from large families (excluding only children). All 20 indicate that the SES of men from smaller families is superior, the average difference being 8.0. Some of this difference is due to the fact that poorer couples tend to have larger families rather than to the influence of family size on the occupational chances of sons. But even if the former factor is controlled by holding father's socio-economic status constant, the socio-economic status of men from smaller families continues to be higher than that of men from larger families in all 20 comparisons, an average of 5.2 points. This net effect shows that a man's chances of occupational success are impeded by many siblings. Although in strictly economic terms only children must have an advantage over others, since they do not have to share their parents' financial resources with anybody, this economic advantage is not reflected in their careers. Only children do not achieve higher occupational positions than those from small families; the differences between the two groups are inconsistent, and the average approximates zero.

Sibling position as well as number of siblings influences occupational attainments. There are no consistent differences between oldest and youngest children, but the SES of both tends to be superior to that of middle children. Ten independent comparisons can be made between oldest children and middle children with an older brother (two sizes for five age cohorts). Eight of these indicate that the oldest child has a higher status, one that the middle child has, and one reveals no difference. The average difference is 3.7, which is reduced to 2.7 if father's SES is controlled. When youngest children are compared to middle children with an older brother, the youngest are seen to have superior SES in all ten cases, the average difference being 4.3, and this difference persists if father's SES is controlled (net, 4.0). (Comparisons with middle children without an older brother yield essentially the same results.) Both oldest and youngest children gain advantages from their positions compared to middle children, but perhaps for

**TABLE 4 Parental Family and Occupational SES of American Men with Nonfarm Background, Age 20 to 64**

| *Sibling Position and Number of Siblings* | 20–24 Years | 25–34 Years | 35–44 Years | 45–54 Years | 55–64 Years |
|---|---|---|---|---|---|
| Grand Mean | 31.5 | 41.0 | 42.6 | 40.1 | 40.0 |
| | | | *Gross Effects* | | |
| 1. Only child, no siblings | 5.1 | 6.0 | 4.1 | 7.0 | 3.0 |
| 2. Oldest, 1 to 3 siblings | 3.6 | 6.4 | 6.1 | 4.7 | 7.0 |
| 3. Oldest, 4 or more siblings | −2.1 | −6.0 | −6.0 | −4.8 | −0.3 |
| 4. Youngest, 1 to 3 siblings | 5.3 | 3.6 | 6.5 | 5.3 | 5.6 |
| 5. Youngest, 4 or more siblings | −2.3 | −2.4 | −2.5 | −2.3 | −1.6 |
| 6. Middle, 2–3 s's, no older brother | −2.1 | 0.6 | 4.7 | 0.3 | 10.2 |
| 7. Middle, 2–3 s's, older brother | −2.3 | −0.8 | 3.7 | 1.5 | −0.1 |
| 8. Middle, 4+ s's, no older brother | −7.3 | −4.3 | −8.2 | −4.8 | −5.4 |
| 9. Middle, 4+ s's, older brother | −6.3 | −7.6 | −7.5 | −3.6 | −5.1 |
| | | | *Net Effects** | | |
| 1. Only child, no siblings | 3.8 | 3.9 | 2.9 | 4.2 | 3.0 |
| 2. Oldest, 1 to 3 siblings | 2.6 | 4.0 | 4.2 | 2.6 | 4.4 |
| 3. Oldest, 4 or more siblings | −1.8 | −4.5 | −4.0 | −3.1 | 0.8 |
| 4. Youngest, 1 to 3 siblings | 4.4 | 2.3 | 4.0 | 3.5 | 4.6 |
| 5. Youngest, 4 or more siblings | 0.1 | −0.4 | 0.7 | −0.6 | −0.2 |
| 6. Middle, 2–3 s's, no older brother | −3.0 | −0.1 | 3.8 | 0.3 | 8.4 |
| 7. Middle, 2–3 s's, older brother | −2.3 | −0.5 | 1.9 | 1.1 | −0.7 |
| 8. Middle, 4+ s's, no older brother | −5.6 | −2.6 | −7.1 | −4.6 | −3.8 |
| 9. Middle, 4+ s's older brother | −4.5 | −5.1 | −5.3 | −1.9 | −4.5 |
| | | | *Residual Effects*** | | |
| 1. Only child, no siblings | 1.5 | −1.2 | −1.3 | 0.5 | −0.9 |
| 2. Oldest, 1 to 3 siblings | 1.0 | 1.0 | 1.4 | 0.5 | 1.3 |
| 3. Oldest, 4 or more siblings | 0.3 | −0.3 | 0.2 | −0.8 | 1.7 |
| 4. Youngest, 1 to 3 siblings | 2.4 | −0.3 | 0.6 | 0.6 | 1.4 |
| 5. Youngest, 4 or more siblings | 0.3 | 0.9 | 2.4 | −2.5 | 0.5 |
| 6. Middle, 2–3 s's, no older brother | −2.7 | 0.5 | 2.0 | −1.0 | 6.5 |
| 7. Middle, 2–3 s's, older brother | −3.4 | −0.8 | 1.8 | 1.5 | −1.2 |
| 8. Middle, 4+ s's, no older brother | −3.3 | 0.5 | −3.2 | −0.2 | −1.1 |
| 9. Middle, 4+ s's, older brother | −1.0 | 0.0 | −1.7 | 0.2 | −1.7 |

Note: No cell frequency is less than 100 and only one—youngest in large families for cohort 20–24 years—is less than 200.

* Father's occupational SES held constant.

** First job, education, father's occupational SES, ethnic classification, region and place of birth and residence, and geographic mobility held constant.

different reasons. The fact that the occupational advantages of oldest children depend in part on the socio-economic status of their fathers while those of youngest children do not suggest that the latter are due to socio-psychological rather than economic factors. It maybe that the occupational success of youngest children is primarily due to the greater social and emotional support they receive in their families rather than to the fact that their education pre-empts the economic resources of their parents.

Middle children with and without an older brother have been separated in order to examine the implications of having an older brother for occupational chances. The significance of an older brother for careers appears to be slight and confined to small families. Four of the five comparisons in small families (Table 4, rows 6 and 7) indicate that middle children without an older brother have higher SES than those with one, with an average difference of +2.3, but four of the five comparisons in large families go in the opposite direction and the average difference is zero. If father's SES is controlled, the difference in small families is +2.0 and that in large ones is −0.5. Having no older brother is a slight advantage for middle children in small families but not in large ones.

The bottom third of Table 4 presents the residual effects of size of parental family and sibling position when not only father's SES but also a number of other factors are controlled, namely, respondent's education, his first job, his ethnic background, the region where he was born and where he lives at present, the size of his place of birth and of his present community, and migration status. It is evident from the table that the residual effects of parental family on socio-economic status that remain after all these conditions have been held constant are small. This does not mean, however, that the effects of number of siblings and sibling position previously observed were spurious, because the factors that are now being controlled are not independent of a man's parental family. Some of these control factors are directly determined by the family into which a man is born, such as his ethnic affiliation and the area where he grows up, and others are strongly affected by the size of his family and his position in it, such as his education and his first job. The reduction in effects produced by the introduction of these controls indicates, by and large, the degree to which the initial effects of parental family were mediated by various social and economic conditions, for example, the training and experience a man obtained and the opportunities existing in the area where he was raised. If the initial (gross) effects are little reduced by introducing the controls, it suggests that they are not primarily due to the economic advantages children gain from their families, directly or indirectly, but to other, socio-psychological forces in the family.

Whereas the gross effects on SES of sibling position are considerably smaller than those of sib size, the former persist to a greater degree than the latter when economic conditions are controlled. Instituting these controls reduces the impact of family size on SES very much, it reduces the influence of sibling position a great deal, though not as much, and it reduces the interaction effect of having no older brother in small families hardly at all. The average gross difference in SES between men from small and from large families of 8.0 points is reduced to a residual average difference of merely 1.1 points in Table 4. In contrast to this decrease to one seventh of the original difference, instituting controls decreases the effects of sibling position on SES considerably less, only to about one third of their original size, from 4.3 to 1.3 for youngest (vs. middle) and from 3.7 to 1.3 for oldest (vs. middle) children. The case is more extreme for the interaction effect of having no older brother and family size on SES. The gross differences in SES between middle children with no older brother and those with an older brother are +2.3 in small families and 0.0 in large ones, and the residual differences are +1.5 in small and −0.6 in large families. Hence, the difference between these differences, which indicates the interaction effect, is virtually not affected by introducing controls, being 2.3 originally and still 2.1 for the residuals. Although the residual effects are very small, the reduction in gross differences effected by introducing controls varies so greatly that we are tempted to hazard some interpretations based on these variations.

The superior occupational achievements of children from small families are largely accounted for by the better economic conditions in which they find themselves compared to children from large families. The superior occupational achievements of oldest and youngest children relative to those of middle children, on the other hand, seem to be due to a combination of economic and psychological factors. The distinctive position the oldest and the youngest child occupy in the family may not only have the result that parents devote disproportionate resources to their training but also make it likely that these children receive more social and emotional support from other members of the family than do middle children. (Since the residual effects for oldest and for youngest child do not differ, we had to modify here an interpretation advanced earlier that distinguished the situation of the youngest from that of the oldest.)

The occupational advantages middle children with older brothers have in small families but not in large ones are apparently not due to economic factors. A possible explanation of this interaction effect is that an older brother is more likely to be the oldest child in a small than in a large family, and oldest children occupy, as we have seen, privileged positions, which means that not having a brother who is an oldest child is an advantage. One might also speculate whether older sisters are protective and supportive of younger brothers and thereby strengthen their potential for subsequent occupational success. If older sisters actually have such a beneficial influence on their younger brothers, it would explain the observed interaction effect, because the middle child without an older brother necessarily has an older sister, and the middle child with an older brother in a small family is unlikely to have also an older sister but in a large family he is likely to have also an older sister.

## CONCLUSIONS

We have illustrated our procedures as well as some preliminary findings from our research in this paper. The complexity of the analysis required when several factors influence occupational success has undoubtedly become evident. Since the condensed discussion may well have been difficult to follow at various points, it might be useful to summarize in conclusion the main substantive findings.

There is much intergenerational occupational mobility in the United States, though probably not much more than in other Western countries such as Sweden and Britain. The correlation between father's and son's SES is +.38. The influence of father's on son's status is largely mediated through education, in apparent contrast to the situation in some other countries, but socio-economic origins also influence career chances independent of education.

It hardly comes as a surprise that racial discrimination in the United States is reflected in the Negro's inferior chances of occupational success, although the extent to which Negroes with the same amount of education as whites remain behind in the struggle for desirable occupations is striking. Negroes receive much less occupational return for their educational investments than whites do, and their consequent lesser incentive to acquire an education further disadvantages them in the labor market. What may be surprising, however, is that white ethnic minorities, on the average, appear to have as good occupational chances as the majority group. At least, the occupational achievements of foreign-born and second-generation Americans are no worse than those of native whites of native parentage with the same amount of education.

Urban migrants are more likely to occupy desirable occupational positions and to have moved up from the socio-economic status of their fathers than nonmigrants. Migration to urban areas brings occupational success more often than migration to rural areas (for the nonfarm population here under consideration), and migration from urban areas to small cities is particularly advantageous. The larger the place where a migrant grew up, the greater are the chances of his occupational success, regardless of the type of place where he ends up working. Indeed, for nonmigrants as well as migrants, there is a direct correlation between the size of the place where a man was reared and his occupational achievement.

Size of parental family and sibling position affect careers. The occupational attainments of men with many siblings, with whom they had to share parental resources, are inferior to those of men with few siblings, but only children do not achieve higher socio-economic positions than men from small families. Oldest and youngest children tend to have more successful careers than middle ones. In small families, though not in large ones, finally, having no older brothers appears to give a middle child a slight advantage in the struggle for occupational success, which suggests that older sisters improve future life chances.

# SPONSORED AND CONTEST MOBILITY AND THE SCHOOL SYSTEM[1]

*Ralph H. Turner*

This paper suggests a framework for relating certain differences between American and English systems of education to the prevailing norms of upward mobility in each country. Others have noted the tendency of educational systems to support prevailing schemes of stratification, but this discussion concerns specifically the manner in which the *accepted mode of upward mobility* shapes the school system directly and indirectly through its effects on the values which implement social control.

Two ideal-typical normative patterns of upward mobility are described and their ramifications in the general patterns of stratification and social control are suggested. In addition to showing relationships among a number of differences between American and English schooling, the ideal-types have broader implications than those developed in this paper: they suggest a major dimension of stratification which might be profitably incorporated into a variety of studies in social class; and they readily can be applied in further comparisons between other countries.

## THE NATURE OF ORGANIZING NORMS

Many investigators have concerned themselves with rates of upward mobility in specific countries or internationally,[2] and with the manner in which school systems facilitate or impede such mobility.[3] But preoccupation with the *extent* of mobility has precluded equal attention to the predominant *modes* of mobility. The central assumption underlying this paper is that within a formally open class system that provides for mass education the organizing folk norm which defines the accepted mode of upward mobility is a crucial factor in shaping the school system, and may be even more crucial than the extent of upward mobility. In England and the United States there appear to be different organizing folk norms, here termed *sponsored mobility* and *contest mobility,* respectively. *Contest* mobility is a system in which elite[4] status is the prize in an open contest and is taken by the aspirants' own efforts. While the "contest" is governed by some rules of fair play, the contestants have wide latitude in the strategies they may employ. Since the "prize" of successful upward mobility is not in the hands of an established elite to give out, the latter can not determine who shall attain it and who shall not. Under *sponsored* mobility elite recruits are chosen by the established elite or their agents, and elite status is *given* on the basis of some criterion of supposed merit and cannot be *taken* by any amount of effort or strategy. Upward mobility is like entry into a private club where each candidate must be "sponsored" by one or more of the members. Ultimately the members grant or deny upward mobility on the basis of whether they judge the

From the *American Sociological Review*, Vol. 25, No. 6, December, 1960. Copyright 1960 by the American Sociological Association. Reprinted by permission.

[1] . . . Special indebtedness should be expressed to Jean Floud and Hilde Himmelweit for helping to acquaint the author with the English school system.

[2] A comprehensive summary of such studies appears in Seymour M. Lipset and Reinhard Bendix, *Social Mobility in Industrial Society*, Berkeley and Los Angeles: University of California Press, 1959.

[3] *Cf.* C. A. Anderson, "The Social Status of University Students in Relation to Type of Economy: An International Comparison," *Transactions of the Third World Congress of Sociology*, London, 1956, Vol. V, pp. 51–63; J. E. Floud, *Social Class and Educational Opportunity*, London: Heinemann, 1956; W. L. Warner, R. J. Havighurst, and M. B. Loeb, *Who Shall Be Educated?* New York: Harper, 1944.

[4] Reference is made throughout the paper to "elite" and "masses." The generalizations, however, are intended to apply throughout the stratification continuum to relations between members of a given class and the class or classes above it. Statements about mobility are intended in general to apply to mobility from manual to middle-class levels, lower-middle to upper-middle class, and so on, as well as into the strictly elite groups. The simplified expressions avoid the repeated use of cumbersome and involved statements which might otherwise be required.

candidate to have those qualities they wish to see in fellow members.

Before elaborating this distinction, it should be noted that these systems of mobility are ideal types designed to clarify observed differences in the predominantly similar English and American systems of stratification and education. But as organizing norms these principles are assumed to be present at least implicitly in people's thinking, guiding their judgments of what is appropriate on many specific matters. Such organizing norms do not correspond perfectly with the objective characteristics of the societies in which they exist, nor are they completely independent of them. From the complex interplay of social and economic conditions and ideologies people in a society develop a highly simplified conception of the way in which events take place. This conception of the "natural" is translated into a norm—the "natural" becomes what "ought" to be—and in turn imposes a strain toward consistency upon relevant aspects of the society. Thus the norm acts back upon the objective conditions to which it refers and has ramifying effects upon directly and indirectly related features of the society.[5] . . .

Two final qualifications concerning the scope of this paper: First, the organizing folk norm of upward mobility affects the school system because one of the latter's functions is the facilitation of mobility. Since this is only one of several social functions of the school, and not the most important function in the societies under examination, only a very partial accounting of the whole set of forces making for similarities and differences in the school systems of United States and England is possible here. Only those differences which directly or indirectly reflect the performance of the mobility function are noted. Second, the concern of this paper is with the current dynamics of the situation in the two countries rather than with their historical development.

## DISTINCTIONS BETWEEN THE TWO NORMS

Contest mobility is like a sporting event in which many compete for a few recognized prizes. The contest is judged to be fair only if all the players compete on an equal footing. Victory must be won solely by one's own efforts. The most satisfactory outcome is not necessarily a victory of the most able, but of the most deserving. The tortoise who defeats the hare is a folk-prototype of the deserving sportsman. . . . Applied to mobility, the contest norm means that victory by a person of moderate intelligence accomplished through the use of common sense, craft, enterprise, daring, and successful risk-taking[6] is more appreciated than victory by the most intelligent or the best educated.

Sponsored mobility, in contrast, rejects the pattern of the contest and favors a controlled selection process. In this process the elite or their agents, deemed to be best qualified to judge merit, choose individuals for elite status who have the appropriate qualities. Individuals do not win or seize elite status; mobility is rather a process of sponsored induction into the elite.

Pareto had this sort of mobility in mind when he suggested that a governing class might dispose of persons potentially dangerous to it by admitting them to elite membership, provided that the recruits change character by adopting elite attitudes and interests.[7] Danger to the ruling class would seldom be the major criterion for choice of

[5] The normative element in an organizing norm goes beyond Max Weber's *ideal type*, conveying more of the sense of Durkheim's *collective representation; cf.* Ralph H. Turner, "The Normative Coherence of Folk Concepts," *Research Studies of the State College of Washington*, 25 (1957), pp. 127–136. Charles Wagley has developed a similar concept which he calls "ideal pattern" in his as yet unpublished work on Brazilian kinship. See also Howard Becker, "Constructive Typology in the Social Sciences," *American Sociological Review*, 5 (February, 1940), pp. 40–55.

[6] Geoffrey Gorer remarks on the favorable evaluation of the successful gamble in American culture: "Gambling is also a respected and important component in many business ventures. Conspicuous improvement in a man's financial position is generally attributed to a lucky combination of industry, skill, and gambling, though the successful gambler prefers to refer to his gambling as 'vision.'" *The American People*, New York: Norton, 1948, p. 178.

[7] Vilfredo Pareto, *The Mind and Society*, New York: Harcourt, Brace, 1935, Vol. 4, p. 1796.

elite recruits. But Pareto assumed that the established elite would select whom they wished to enter their ranks and would inculcate the attitudes and interests of the established elite in the recruits.

The governing objective of contest mobility is to give elite status to those who earn it, while the goal of sponsored mobility is to make the best use of the talents in society by sorting persons into their proper niches. In different societies the conditions of competitive struggle may reward quite different attributes, and sponsored mobility may select individuals on the basis of such diverse qualities as intelligence or visionary capability, but the difference in principle remains the same. . . .

Under the contest system society at large establishes and interprets the criteria of elite status. If one wishes to have his status recognized he must display certain credentials which identify his class to those about him. The credentials must be highly visible and require no special skill for their assessment, since credentials are presented to the masses. Material possession and mass popularity are altogether appropriate credentials in this respect, and any special skill which produces a tangible product and which can easily be assessed by the untrained will do. The nature of sponsored mobility precludes these procedures, but assigns to credentials instead the function of identifying elite members to one another. Accordingly, the ideal credentials are special skills that require the trained discrimination of the elite for their recognition. In this case, intellectual, literary, or artistic excellencies, which can be appraised only by those trained to appreciate them, are fully suitable credentials. Concentration on such skills lessens the likelihood that an interloper will succeed in claiming the right to elite membership on grounds of the popular evaluation of his competence.

In the sporting event there is special admiration for the slow starter who makes a dramatic finish, and many of the rules are designed to insure that the race should not be declared over until it has run its full course. Contest mobility incorporates this disapproval of premature judgments and of anything that gives special advantage to those who are ahead at any point in the race. Under sponsored mobility, fairly early selection of only the number of persons necessary to fill anticipated vacancies in the elite is desirable. Early selection allows time to prepare the recruits for their elite position. Aptitudes, inherent capacities, and spiritual gifts can be assessed fairly early in life by techniques ranging from divination to the most sophisticated psychological test, and the more naive the subjects at the time of selection the less likely are their talents to be blurred by differential learning or conspiracy to defeat the test. Since elitists take the initiative in training recruits, they are more interested in the latters' capabilities than in what they will do with them on their own. and they are concerned that no one else should first have an opportunity to train the recruits' talents in the wrong direction. Contest mobility tends to delay the final award as long as practicable to permit a fair race; sponsored mobility tends to place the time of recruitment as early in life as practicable to insure control over selection and training.

Systems of sponsored mobility develop most readily in societies with but a single elite or with a recognized elite hierarchy. When mutiple elites compete among themselves the mobility process tends to take the contest pattern, since no group is able to command control of recruitment. Sponsored mobility further depends upon a social structure that fosters monopoly of elite credentials. Lack of such monopoly undercuts sponsorship and control of the recruitment process. Monopoly of credentials in turn is typically a product of societies with well entrenched traditional aristocracies employing such credentials as family line and bestowable title which are intrinsically subject to monopoly, or of societies organized on large-scale bureaucratic lines permitting centralized control of upward social movement.

English society has been described as the juxtaposition of two systems of stratification, the urban industrial class system and the surviving aristocratic system. While the sponsored mobility pattern reflects the logic of the latter, our impression is that it pervades popular thinking rather than merely coexisting with the logic of industrial stratification. Patterns imported into an established culture tend to be reshaped, as they are assimilated, into consistency with the established culture. Thus it may be that changes in stratification associated with industrialization have led to alterations in the rates, the specific means, and the rules of mobility, but that these changes have been guided by the but lightly challenged organizing norm of sponsored mobility.

## SOCIAL CONTROL AND THE TWO NORMS

Every society must cope with the problem of maintaining loyalty to its social system and does so in part through norms and values, only some of which vary by class position. Norms and values especially prevalent within a given class must direct behavior into channels that support the total system, while those that transcend strata must support the general class differential. The way in which upward mobility takes place determines in part the kinds of norms and values that serve the indicated purposes of social control in each class and throughout the society.

The most conspicuous control problem is that of ensuring loyalty in the disadvantaged classes toward a system in which their members receive less than a proportional share of society's goods. In a system of contest mobility this is accomplished by a combination of futuristic orientation, the norm of ambition, and a general sense of fellowship with the elite. Each individual is encouraged to think of himself as competing for an elite position so that loyalty to the system and conventional attitudes are cultivated in the process of preparation for this possibility. It is essential that this futuristic orientation be kept alive by delaying a sense of final irreparable failure to reach elite status until attitudes are well established. By thinking of himself in the successful future the elite aspirant forms considerable identification with elitists, and evidence that they are merely ordinary human beings like himself helps to reinforce this identification as well as to keep alive the conviction that he himself may someday succeed in like manner. To forestall rebellion among the disadvantaged majority, then, a contest system must avoid absolute points of selection for mobility and immobility and must delay clear recognition of the realities of the situation until the individual is too committed to the system to change radically. A futuristic orientation cannot, of course, be inculcated successfully in all members of lower strata, but sufficient internalization of a norm of ambition tends to leave the unambitious as individual deviants and to forestall the latters' formation of a genuine subcultural group able to offer collective threat to the established system. Where this kind of control system operates rather effectively it is notable that organized or gang deviancy is more likely to take the form of an attack upon the conventional or moral order rather than upon the class system itself. Thus the United States has its "beatniks"[8] who repudiate ambition and most worldly values and its delinquent and criminal gangs who try to evade the limitations imposed by conventional means[9] but very few active revolutionaries.

These social controls are inappropriate in a system of sponsorship since the elite recruits are chosen from above. The principal threat to the system would lie in the existence of a strong group the members of whom sought to *take* elite positions themselves. Control under this sytem is maintained by training the "masses" to regard themselves as relatively incompetent to manage society, by restricting access to the skills and manners of the elite, and by cultivating belief in the superior competence of the elite. The earlier that selection of the elite recruits is made the sooner others can be taught to accept their inferiority and to make "realistic" rather than fantasy plans. Early selection prevents raising the hopes of large numbers of people who might otherwise become the discontented leaders of a class challenging the sovereignty of the established elite. If it is assumed that the difference in competence between masses and elite is seldom so great as to support the usual differences in the advantages accruing to each,[10] then the differences must

[8] See, e.g., Lawrence Lipton, *The Holy Barbarians*, New York: Messner, 1959.

[9] *Cf.* Albert K. Cohen, *Delinquent Boys: The Culture of the Gang*, Glencoe, Ill.: Free Press, 1955.

[10] D. V. Glass, editor, *Social Mobility in Britain*, Glencoe, Ill.: Pree Press, 1954, pp. 144–145, reports studies showing only small variations in intelligence between occupational levels.

be artificially augmented by discouraging acquisition of elite skills by the masses. Thus a sense of mystery about the elite is a common device for supporting in the masses the illusion of a much greater hiatus of competence than in fact exists.

While elitists are unlikely to reject a system that benefits them, they must still be restrained from taking such advantage of their favorable situation as to jeopardize the entire elite. Under the sponsorship system the elite recruits—who are selected early, freed from the strain of competitive struggle, and kept under close supervision—may be thoroughly indoctrinated in elite culture. A norm of paternalism toward inferiors may be inculcated, a heightened sensitivity to the good opinion of fellow elitists and elite recruits may be cultivated, and the appreciation of the more complex forms of aesthetic, literary, intellectual, and sporting activities may be taught. Norms of courtesy and altruism easily can be maintained under sponsorship since elite recruits are not required to compete for their standing and since the elite may deny high standing to those who strive for position by "unseemly" methods. The system of sponsorship provides an almost perfect setting for the development of an elite culture characterized by a sense of responsibility for "inferiors" and for preservation of the "finer things" of life.

Elite control in the contest system is more difficult since there is no controlled induction and apprenticeship. The principal regulation seems to lie in the insecurity of elite position. In a sense there is no "final arrival" because each person may be displaced by newcomers throughout his life. The limited control of high standing from above prevents the clear delimitation of levels in the class system, so that success itself becomes relative: each success, rather than an accomplishment, serves to qualify the participant for competition at the next higher level.[11] The restraints upon the behavior of a person of high standing, therefore, are principally those applicable to a contestant who must not risk the "ganging up" of other contestants, and who must pay some attention to the masses who are frequently in a position to impose penalties upon him. But any special norm of paternalism is hard to establish since there is no dependable procedure for examining the means by which one achieves elite credentials. While mass esteem is an effective brake upon over-exploitation of position, it rewards scrupulously ethical and altruistic behavior much less than evidence of fellow-feeling with the masses themselves. . . .

Certain of the general values and norms of any society reflect emulation of elite values by the masses. Under sponsored mobility, a good deal of the protective attitudes toward and interest in classical subjects percolates to the masses. Under contest mobility, however, there is not the same degree of homogeneity of moral, aesthetic, and intellectual values to be emulated, so that the conspicuous attribute of the elite is its high level of material consumption—emulation itself follows this course. There is neither effective incentive nor punishment for the elitist who fails to interest himself in promoting the arts or literary excellence, or who continues to maintain the vulgar manners and mode of speech of his class origin. The elite has relatively less power to punish or reward a man for his adoption or disregard of any special elite culture. The great importance of accent and of grammatical excellence in the attainment of high status in England as contrasted with the twangs and drawls and grammatical ineptitude among American elites is the most striking example of this difference. . . .

This is not to imply that there are no groups in a "contest" society devoted to the protection and fostering of high standards in music, literature, and intellectual pursuits, but that such standards lack the support of the class system which is frequently found when sponsored mobility prevails. . . .

## FORMAL EDUCATION

Returning to the conception of an organizing ideal norm, we assume that to the extent to which one such norm of upward mobility is prevalent in a society there are constant strains to shape the educational system into conformity with that norm.

[11] Gorer, *op. cit.*, pp. 172–187.

These strains operate in two fashions: directly by blinding people to alternatives and coloring their judgments of successful and unsuccessful solutions to recurring educational problems; indirectly, through the functional interrelationships between school systems and the class structure, systems of social control, and other features of the social structure which are neglected in this paper.

The most obvious application of the distinction between sponsored and contest mobility norms affords a partial explanation for the different policies of student selection in the English and American secondary schools. Although American high school students follow different courses of study and a few attend specialized schools, a major educational preoccupation has been to avoid any sharp social separation between the superior and inferior students and to keep the channels of movement between courses of study as open as possible. Recent criticisms of the way in which superior students may be thereby held back in their development usually are nevertheless qualified by the insistence that these students must not be withdrawn from the mainstream of student life.[12] Such segregation offends the sense of fairness implicit in the contest norm and also arouses the fear that the elite and future elite will lose their sense of fellowship with the masses. Perhaps the most important point, however, is that schooling is presented as an opportunity, and making use of it depends primarily on the student's own initiative and enterprise.

The English system has undergone a succession of liberalizing changes during this century, but all of them have retained the attempt to sort out early in the educational program the promising from the unpromising so that the former may be segregated and given a special form of training to fit them for higher standing in their adult years. Under the Education Act of 1944, a minority of students has been selected each year by means of a battery of examinations popularly known as "eleven plus," supplemented in varying degrees by grade school records and personal interviews, for admission to grammar schools.[13] The remaining students attend secondary modern or technical schools in which the opportunities to prepare for college or to train for the more prestigeful occupations are minimal. The grammar schools supply what by comparative standards is a high quality of college preparatory education. Of course, such a scheme embodies the logic of sponsorship, with early selection of those destined for middle-class and higher-status occupations, and specialized training to prepare each group for its destined class position. This plan facilitates considerable mobility, and recent research reveals surprisingly little bias against children from manual laboring-class families in the selection for grammar school, when related to measured intelligence.[14] It is altogether possible that adequate comparative study would show a closer correlation of school success with measured intelligence and a lesser correlation between school success and family background in England than in the United States. While selection of superior students for mobility opportunity is probably more efficient under such a system, the obstacles for persons not to be selected of "making the grade" on the basis of their own initiative or enterprise are probably correspondingly greater. . . .

This well-known difference between the British sorting at an early age of students into grammar and modern schools and the American comprehensive high school and junior college is the clearest application of the distinction under discussion. But the organizing norms penetrate more deeply into the school systems than is initially apparent. The most telling observation regarding the direct normative operation of these principles would be evidence to support the author's impression that major

[12] See, e.g., *Los Angeles Times*, May 4, 1959, Part I, p. 24.

[13] The nature and operation of the "eleven plus" system are fully reviewed in a report by a committee of the British Psychological Society and in a report of extensive research into the adequacy of selection methods. See P. E. Vernon, editor, *Secondary School Selection: A British Psychological Inquiry*, London: Methuen, 1957; and Alfred Yates and D. A. Pidgeon, *Admission to Grammar Schools*, London: Newnes Educational Publishing Co., 1957.

[14] J. E. Floud, A. H. Halsey, and F. M. Martin, *Social Class and Educational Opportunity*, London: Heinemann, 1956.

critics of educational procedures within each country do not usually transcend the logic of their respective mobility norms. Thus the British debate about the best method for getting people sorted according to ability, without proposing that elite station should be open to whosoever can ascend to it. Although fear of "sputnik" in the United States introduced a flurry of suggestions for sponsored mobility schemes, the long-standing concern of school critics has been the failure to motivate students adequately. Preoccupation with motivation appears to be an intellectual application of the folk idea that people should *win* their station in society by personal enterprise.

The functional operation of a strain toward consistency with the organizing norms of upward mobility may be illustrated by several other features of the school systems in the two countries. First, the value placed upon education itself differs under the two norms. Under sponsored mobility, schooling is valued for its cultivation of elite culture, and those forms of schooling directed toward such cultivation are more highly valued than others. Education of the non-elite is difficult to justify clearly and tends to be half-hearted, while maximum educational resources are concentrated on "those who can benefit most from them"—in practice, this means those who can learn the elite culture. The secondary modern schools in England have regularly suffered from less adequate financial provision, a higher student-teacher ratio, fewer well trained teachers, and a general lack of prestige in comparison with the grammar schools.[15]

Under contest mobility in the United States, education is valued as a means of getting ahead, but the contents of education are not highly valued in their own right. Over a century ago Tocqueville commented on the absence of an hereditary class "by which the labors of the intellect are held in honor." He remarked that consequently a "middling standard is fixed in America for human knowledge."[16] And there persists in some measure the suspicion of the educated man as one who may have gotten ahead without really earning his position. . . .

Second, the logic of preparation for a contest prevails in United States schools, and emphasizes keeping everyone in the running until the final stages. In primary and secondary schools the assumption tends to be made that those who are learning satisfactorily need little special attention while the less successful require help to be sure that they remain in the contest and may compete for the final stakes. As recently as December, 1958, a nationwide Gallup Poll gave evidence that this attitude had not been radically altered by the international situation. When asked whether or not teachers should devote extra time to the bright students, 26 per cent of the respondents replied "yes" and 67 per cent, "no." But the responses changed to 86 per cent "yes" and only nine per cent "no" when the question was asked concerning "slow students."[17]

In western states the junior college offers many students a "second chance" to qualify for university, and all state universities have some provision for substandard high school students to earn admission.

The university itself is run like the true contest: standards are set competitively, students are forced to pass a series of trials each semester, and only a minority of the entrants achieve the prize of graduation. This pattern contrasts sharply with the English system in which selection is supposed to be relatively complete before entrance to university, and students may be subject to no testing whatsoever for the first year or more of university study. Although university completion rates have not been estimated accurately in either country, some figures are indicative of the contrast. In American institutions of higher learning in 1957–1958, the ratio of bachelor's and first-professional degrees to the number of

[15] Less adequate financial provision and a higher student-teacher ratio are mentioned as obstacles to parity of secondary modern schools with grammar schools in *The Times Educational Supplement*, February 22, 1947, p. 241. On difficulties in achieving prestige comparable with grammar schools, see G. Baron, "Secondary Education in Britain: Some Present-Day Trends," *Teachers College Record*, 57 (January, 1956), pp. 211–221; and O. Banks, *Parity and Prestige in English Secondary Education*, London: Routledge and Kegan Paul, 1955. See also Vernon, *op. cit.*, pp. 19–22.

[16] Alexis de Tocqueville, *Democracy in America*, New York: Knopf, 1045, Vol. I, p. 52.

[17] Reported in the *Los Angeles Times*, December 17, 1958, Part I, p. 16.

first-time degree-credit enrollments in the fall four years earlier was reported to be .610 for men and .488 for women.[18] The indicated 39 and 51 per cent drop-out rates are probably underestimates because transfers from two-year junior colleges swell the number of degrees without being included in first-time enrollments. In England, a study of the careers of individual students reports that in University College, London, almost 82 per cent of entering students between 1948 and 1951 eventually graduated with a degree. A similar study a few years earlier at the University of Liverpool shows a comparative figure of almost 87 per cent.[19] Under contest mobility, the object is to train as many as possible in the skills necessary for elite status so as to give everyone a chance to maintain competition at the highest pitch. Under sponsored mobility, the objective is to indoctrinate elite culture in only those presumably who will enter the elite, lest there grow a dangerous number of "angry young men" who have elite skills without elite station.

Third, systems of mobility significantly affect educational content. Induction into elite culture under sponsored mobility is consistent with an emphasis on school *esprit de corps* which is employed to cultivate norms of intra-class loyalty and elite tastes and manners. Similarly, formal schooling built about highly specialized study in fields wholly of intellectual or aesthetic concern and of no "practical" value serves the purpose of elite culture. Under contest mobility in the United States, in spite of frequent faculty endorsement of "liberal education," schooling tends to be evaluated in terms of its practical benefits and to become, beyond the elementary level, chiefly vocational. Education does not so much provide what is good in itself as those skills, especially vocational skills, presumed to be necessary in the competition for the real prizes of life.

These contrasts are reflected in the different national attitudes toward university students who are gainfully employed while in school. More students in the United States than in Britain are employed part-time, and relatively fewer of the American students receive subsidies towards subsistence and living expenses. The most generous programs of state aid in the United States, except those applying to veterans and other special groups, do not normally cover expenses other than tuition and institutional fees. British maintenance grants are designed to cover full living expenses, taking into account parental ability to pay.[20] Under sponsored mobility, gainful employment serves no apprenticeship or testing function, and is thought merely to prevent students from gaining the full benefit of their schooling. L. J. Parry speaks of the general opposition to student employment and asserts that English university authorities almost unanimously hold that ". . . if a person must work for financial reasons, he should never spend more than four weeks on such work during the whole year."[21]

Under contest mobility, success in school work is not viewed as a sufficient test of practical merit, but must be supplemented by a test in the world of practical affairs. . . . By "working his way through school" the enterprising student "earns" his education in the fullest sense, keeps in touch with the practical world, and gains an apprenticeship into vocational life. Students are often urged to seek part-time employment, even when there is no financial need, and in some instances schools include paid employment as a requirement for graduation. As one observer describes the typical American view, a student willing to work part-time is a "better bet" than "the equally bright student who receives all of his financial support from others."[22]

Finally, training in "social adjustment" is peculiar to the system of contest mobility.

[18] U.S. Department of Health, Education, and Welfare, Office of Education, *Earned Degrees Conferred by Higher Education Institutions, 1957–1958*, Washington, D.C.: Government Printing Office, 1959, p. 3.

[19] Nicholas Malleson, "Student Performance at University College, London, 1948–1951," *Universities Quarterly*, 12 (May, 1958), pp. 288–319.

[20] See, e.g., C. A. Quattlebaum, *Federal Aid to Students for Higher Education*, Washington, D.C.: Government Printing Office, 1956; and "Grants to Students: University and Training Colleges," *The Times Educational Supplement*, May 6, 1955, p. 446.

[21] "Students' Expenses," *The Times Educational Supplement*, May 6, 1955, p. 447.

[22] R. H. Eckelberry, "College Jobs for College Students," *Journal of Higher Education*, 27 (March 1956), p. 174.

The reason for this emphasis is clear when it is understood that adjustment training presumably prepares students to cope with situations for which there are no rules of intercourse or for which the rules are unknown, but in which the good opinions of others cannot be wholly ignored. Under sponsored mobility, elite recruits are inducted into a homogeneous stratum within which there is consensus regarding the rules, and within which they succeed socially by mastering these rules. Under contest mobility, the elite aspirant must relate himself both to the established elite and to the masses, who follow different rules, and the elite itself is not sufficiently homogeneous to evolve consensual rules of intercourse. Furthermore, in the contest the rules may vary according to the background of the competitor, so that each aspirant must successfully deal with persons playing the game with slightly different rules. Consequently, adjustment training is increasingly considered to be one of the important skills imparted by the school system.[23] That the emphasis on such training has had genuine popular support is indicated by a 1945 *Fortune* poll in which a national sample of adults was asked to select the one or two things that would be very important for a son of theirs to get out of college. Over 87 per cent chose "Ability to get along with and understand people;" and this answer was the second most frequently chosen as the *very* most important thing to get out of college.[24] In this respect, British education may provide better preparation for participation in an orderly and controlled world, while American education may prepare students more adequately for a less ordered situation. The reputedly superior ability of "Yankees" to get things done seems to imply such ability.

To this point the discussion has centered on the tax-supported school systems in both countries, but the different place and emphasis of the privately supported secondary schools can also be related to the distinction between sponsored and contest mobility. Since private secondary schools in both countries are principally vehicles for transmitting the marks of high family status, their mobility function is quite tangential. Under contest mobility, the private schools presumably should have little or no mobility function. On the other hand, if there is to be mobility in a sponsored system, the privately controlled school populated largely with the children of elite parents would be the ideal device through which to induct selectees from lower levels into elite status. By means of a scholarship program, promising members of lesser classes could be chosen early for recruitment. The English "public" schools, in fact, have incorporated into their charters provisions to insure that a few boys from lesser classes will enter each year. Getting one's child into a "public" school, or even into one of the less prestigeful private schools, assumes an importance in England relatively unknown in the United States. If the children cannot win scholarships the parents often make extreme financial sacrifices in order to pay the cost of this relatively exclusive education.[25]

How much of a role private secondary schools have played in mobility in either country is difficult to determine. American studies of social mobility usually omit information on private *versus* tax-supported secondary school attendance, and English studies showing the advantage of "public" school attendance generally fail to distinguish between the mobile and the nonmobile in this respect. However, during the nineteenth century the English "public" schools were used by *nouveaux riches* members of the manufacturing classes to enable their sons to achieve unqualified elite status.[26] In one sense, the rise of the manufacturing classes through free enterprise introduced a large measure of contest mobility which threatened to destroy the traditional sponsorship system. But by using the "public"

[23] Adjustment training is not a necessary accompaniment of contest mobility. The shift during the last half century toward the increased importance of social acceptability as an elite credential has brought such training into correspondingly greater prominence.

[24] Reported in Hadley Cantril, editor, *Public Opinion 1935–1946*, Princeton: Princeton University Press, 1951, p. 186.

[25] For one account of the place of "public" schools in the English educational system, see Dennis Brogan, *The English People*, New York: Knopf, 1943, pp. 18–56.

[26] A. H. Halsey of Birmingham University has called my attention to the importance of this fact.

schools in this fashion they bowed to the legitimacy of the traditional system—an implicit acknowledgement that upward mobility was not complete without sponsored induction. Dennis Brogan speaks of the task of the "public" schools in the nineteenth century as "the job of marrying the old English social order to the new."[27]

With respect to mobility, the parallel between the tax-supported grammar school and the "public" schools in England is of interest. The former in important respects have been patterned after the latter, adopting their view of mobility but making it a much larger part of their total function. Generally the grammar schools are the vehicle for sponsored mobility throughout the middle ranges of the class system, modeled after the pattern of the "public" schools which remain the agencies for sponsored mobility into the elite.

. . . . . . . . . . . . . . . . . . . . . . . . . . . . . . . . .

### CONCLUSION: SUGGESTIONS FOR RESEARCH

The foregoing discussion is broadly impressionistic and speculative, reflecting more the general impression of an observer of both countries than a systematic exploration of data. Relevant data of a variety of sorts are cited above, but their use is more illustrative than demonstrative. However, several lines of research are suggested by this tentative analysis. One of these is an exploration of different channels of mobility in both England and the United States in an attempt to discover the extent to which mobility corresponds to the mobility types. Recruitment to the Catholic priesthood, for example, probably strictly follows a sponsorship norm regardless of the dominant contest norm in the United States.

The effect of changes in the major avenues of upward mobility upon the dominant norms requires investigation. The increasing importance of promotion through corporation hierarchies and the declining importance of the entrepreneurial path of upward mobility undoubtedly compromise the ideal pattern of contest mobility. The growing insistence that higher education is a prerequisite to more and more occupations is a similar modification. Yet, there is little evidence of a tendency to follow the logic of sponsorship beyond the bureaucratic selection process. The prospect of a surplus of college-educated persons in relation to jobs requiring college education may tend to restore the contest situation at a higher level, and the further possibility that completion of higher education may be more determined by motivational factors than by capacity suggests that the contest pattern continues within the school.

In England, on the other hand, two developments may weaken the sponsorship system. One is positive response to popular demand to allow more children to secure the grammar school type of training, particularly by including such a program in the secondary modern schools. The other is introduction of the comprehensive secondary school, relatively uncommon at present but a major plank in the labor party's education platform. It remains to be determined whether the comprehensive school in England will take a distinctive form and serve a distinctive function, which preserves the pattern of sponsorship, or will approximate the present American system. . . .

[27] *Op. cit.*, pp. 24–25.

# PSYCHOLOGICAL FACTORS IN SOCIAL MOBILITY: INTELLIGENCE AND MOTIVATION

*Seymour Martin Lipset and Reinhard Bendix*

In the preceding chapter we have demonstrated how structural analysis may help account for varying propensities for mobility. In this chapter, however, we shall deal with those basically psychological approaches which stress the effect of variations in ability and achievement motivation.

From Seymour Martin Lipset and Reinhard Bendix, *Social Mobility in Industrial Society*, University of California Press, 1962. Reprinted by permission.

Often unable to find structural determinants of deviation from group norms, many students of social mobility have dismissed or ignored the latter type of research, which, because it deals with individual differences, is presumed to be outside their legitimate sphere of interest.

## THE ROLE OF INTELLIGENCE

Intelligence, as measured by various pen-and-paper intelligence-quotient examinations, has relevance for social mobility because, as we have seen, educational achievement is the main source of occupational achievement in a bureaucratized industrial society. . . . It may be expected that educational achievement will vary with intelligence, and that continuation in the educational system will depend, therefore, upon "above average" intelligence, especially when the student has a low-status background. However, students with middle- or upper-class backgrounds frequently continue in school despite their lack of scholastic aptitude.

It has proved exceedingly difficult to go much beyond this general conclusion, because the part played by "native ability" cannot be readily differentiated from that played by various environmental factors. For example, educational achievement not only depends upon intelligence and the financial resources of the family, but also upon a strong motivation to succeed in the school system. Students who come from well-to-do families will identify quite closely with the prevailing values of the school culture, partly because of parental urging and partly because parents, students, and teachers share the same middle-class values, and such sharing facilitates teacher-student communication. Students who come from lower-class families do not possess this cultural advantage and the question is, therefore, how they may overcome this handicap, provided that they have high intelligence[1]. . . .

Yet it is possible to show the general character of the interrelationship between parental social class, intelligence, and orientation towards educational achievement. Boston high school students were asked to indicate whether or not they expected to go to college, and their answers to this question were then related to their fathers' occupations and their own I.Q.'s. . . . These data suggest that, although intelligence is important, parental social status provides more motivation for high school students to attend a university.[2] Most sons of high-status families declare their intention to go to college, and thus appear motivated—even those whose intelligence is quite low. On the other hand, only 29 per cent of the sons of unskilled and semi-skilled workers and 40 per cent of skilled workers' sons who ranked in the highest fifth on the intelligence test were planning to go to college. It is rather among those whose fathers are in the middle range of the class structure that intelligence appears to be particularly important as a factor affecting the intention of going to college.

But intention is one thing, action another. When one compares parental background, motivation, and I.Q., with the actual enrollment in college, it appears that intelligence does not necessarily determine who, among those motivated to do so, will actually go to college. Data from a study of the Cleveland area indicate that parental social class is much more significant than I.Q., although the latter seems to have some slight significance. However, after adolescents get into college their educational achievement does not seem to be affected

[1] . . . Studies of intelligence tests reveal the influence of social bias. Allison Davis reports that by changing the vocabulary of test questions while retaining the logical operations which the question is supposed to test, the class differential in performance could be markedly reduced. See his "Education for the Conservation of Human Resources," *Progressive Education*, 27 (1950):221–224.

[2] Another study of the problem is William H. Sewell, *et al.*, "Social Status and Educational and Occupational Aspiration," *American Sociological Review*, 22 (1957):67–73. They found that in Wisconsin, the educational aspirations of high school seniors whose fathers' occupations were in the lower three quintiles in occupational prestige were about the same, while the top two quintiles were more highly motivated. On the other hand, both educational aspirations and aspirations for professional positions were directly and strongly related to intelligence quotients. The considerable difference between Sewell's and Kahl's results may be due to the fact that the Wisconsin study tested high school seniors, so that many with low aspirations may have been eliminated, while the Kahl study tested students earlier in high school. . . .

by their family background. The records of different colleges show, according to the Commission on Human Resources and Advanced Training, that, "after students get to college . . . the influence of socio-economic differences disappears almost entirely. When college entrants are classified by the occupations of their fathers the percentages getting degrees are fairly constant . . . unless [the father] be a farmer."[3]

In contemporary Britain, where a great emphasis is placed on intelligence-testing, I.Q. is a prime determinant of educational achievement, and presumably of consequent social mobility. At age 10 or 11, all students in state schools are divided into two groups: one, those who are admitted to "grammar school," which prepares students for higher-status occupations and continuation in the school system as far as the university, and the other, those who will continue in schools designed to prepare them for lesser pursuits. A recent study of admission to these various schools reports that admission to the grammar schools is so highly correlated with I.Q. that, when intelligence of students is held constant, there is no difference in the proportion admitted from the different social classes.[4] That is, the intelligent child from a middle-class family has the same opportunity of continuing on in grammar school as an equally intelligent working-class youth. Similar findings were reported in an earlier study, which indicated "very little overlap" in intelligence level between grammar and other schools.[5] There were few students not in grammar schools who were intelligent enough to qualify for it.

This is not to suggest that the classes have equal representation in English higher education. In fact sons of manual workers accounted for only 26 per cent of English males admitted to universities in 1955–56 although manual workers made up 72 per cent of the population at large.[6] This discrepancy can be accounted for only in part by the fact that both intelligence and achievement aspirations are differentially distributed among the social strata.

. . . . . . . . . . . . . . . . . . . . . . . . . . . . . . . . . .

The evidence does not permit any definite conclusion about the precise effect of intelligence as a factor in social mobility, largely because of the difficulties in isolating "native intelligence" from the effects of

[3] Dael Wolfe, *America's Resources of Specialized Talent* (New York: Harper's, 1954), pp. 160–161.

[4] Jean Floud, *et al., Social Class and Educational Opportunity* (London: Heinemann, 1956), pp. 42–61. T. H. Marshall has described in somewhat greater detail how the English educational system attempts to eliminate social class discrimination by segregating pupils on the basis of performance in intelligence tests: "Equality of opportunity is offered to all children entering the primary schools, but at an early age they are usually divided into three streams—the best, the average and the backward. Already opportunity is becoming unequal, and the children's range of chances limited. About the age of eleven they are tested again, probably by a team of teachers, examiners and psychologists. None of these is infallible, but perhaps sometimes three wrongs may make a right. Classification follows for distribution into the three types of secondary school. Opportunity becomes still more unequal, and the chance of further education has already been limited to a select few. Some of these, after being tested again, will go on to receive it. In the end the jumble of mixed seed originally put into the machine emerges in neatly labelled packets ready to be sown in the appropriate gardens.

"I have deliberately couched this description in the language of cynicism in order to bring out the point that, however genuine may be the desire of the educational authorities to offer enough variety to satisfy all individual needs, they must, in a mass service of this kind, proceed by repeated classification into groups, and this is followed at each stage by assimilation within each group and differentiation between groups. That is precisely the way in which social classes in a fluid society have always taken shape. Differences within each class are ignored as irrelevant; differences between classes are given exaggerated significance. Thus qualities which are in reality strung out along a continuous scale are made to create a hierarchy of groups, each with its special character and status. The main features of the system are inevitable, and its advantages, in particular the elimination of inherited privilege, far outweigh its incidental defects. The latter can be attacked and kept within bounds by giving as much opportunity as possible for second thoughts about classification, both in the educational system itself and in afterlife." T. H. Marshall, *Citizenship and Social Class* (Cambridge: Cambridge University Press, 1950), pp. 66–67.

[5] H. T. Himmelweit, A. H. Halsey, and A. N. Oppenheim, "The View of Adolescents on Some Aspects of the Social Class Structure," *British Journal of Sociology*, 3 (1952): 149 n.

[6] R. K. Kelsall, *Report on an Inquiry into Applications for Admission to Universities* (London: Association of Universities of the British Commonwealth, 1957), p. 9.

social class and educational environment. There can be no doubt, however, that the discrepancy between the distribution of intelligence in a given generation of youth and the distribution of social positions in the parental generation is a major dynamic factor affecting mobility in all societies in which educational achievement or other qualities associated with intelligence play an important role in status placement. That is to say, the correlation between high family status and the intelligence level of children, although strong,[7] is still compatible with the fact that a considerable number of lower-class youth have high I.Q.'s. According to Himmelweit, "previous research has shown that, except for the extremes of the occupational ladder, variations in I.Q. *within* occupation groups are generally greater than those *between* the groups. Very large occupational groups like those to which semiskilled and unskilled manual workers belong should, therefore, contain a larger absolute number of individuals of the requisite ability than some of the numerically much smaller middle-class occupational groups, despite the higher average intelligence level to be found among the latter."[8] Whatever the distribution of intelligence by class among the youth of a country may be it remains true that considerable upward and downward mobility will result from the discrepancies involved when children of lower-class parents are high in intelligence, and offspring of middle-class families are low.

## DIFFERENTIAL MOTIVATION

Studies of the influence of social background and intelligence on social mobility must deal with two related phenomena: the structure of opportunities to which the individuals are exposed, and their capacity to take advantage of these opportunities. Capacity consists of motivation or drive as much as it consists of intelligence. In a middle-class society the "bohemian" is, among other things, a person who has the intelligence but lacks the motivation to achieve. . . .

There can be little doubt, for example, that directly urging children to achieve plays a determining role. In the Boston area, among boys from the lower middle class and the skilled working class who had I.Q.'s in the top quintile, urging by the family to get further education for the sake of occupational advancement clearly differentiated those who intended to go to college from those who did not.[9] In England the same relationship was found between parental attitude and the admission of working-class children to grammar (preuniversity) schools, with the reservation that the parents' attitudes make the difference only among those who have real opportunities,[10] that is, live in a good working-class district. (Among those sons of workers who lived in slum areas, it was found that the income level of a working-class family made more difference in gaining admission to grammar school than did parental attitudes.)

[7] A comprehensive summary of the literature and bibliography on the relation of intelligence to the variable "socioeconomic status," as well as to the variables "size of family and order of birth," is found in Jean Sutter, "La Valeur de l'intelligence suivant le milieu: état présent des connaissances," *in* Institut National d'études Démographiques, *Le Niveau intellectuel des enfants d'âge scolaire*, No. 13 (Paris: Presses Universitaires de France, 1950), pp. 41–62.

[8] H. T. Himmelweit, "Social Status and Secondary Education Since the 1944 Act: Some Data for London," *in* D. W. Glass, ed., *Social Mobility in Britain* (Routledge and Kegan Paul, 1954), p. 145 (emphasis in original). Similar conclusions have been recently presented in an analysis of a mathematical genetic model of the distribution of high intelligence. Even when high intelligence is assumed to be completely inherited and of greater frequency in the high social stratum, it will exist in greater absolute numbers in the lower orders. A. H. Halsey, "Genetics, Social Structure and Intelligence," *The British Journal of Sociology*, 9 (1958): 15–28.

[9] J. A. Kahl, "Educational and Occupationa Aspirations . . .," pp. 186–203. This has also been confirmed by Elizabeth Cohen's study of working-class boys which found that "parents of mobile sons reported more deliberate encouragement of upward mobility through educational channels, starting in the boy's childhood," and that "parents of mobile sons were more likely to have a middle-class occupational aspiration for their sons." However, a surprising finding of this research was that there were no differences between parents of mobile and nonmobile sons in their concern with their children's high school performance. Elizabeth G. Cohen, *Parental Factors in Educational Mobility* (Unpublished Ph.D. dissertation, Harvard University, 1958), pp. 136–137.

[10] Jean E. Floud, *et al.*, *Social Class . . .*, pp. 93–95, 107–108.

One would expect that the higher the education of the parents, the more likely they would be to instill motivation for upward movement in their children. This is confirmed by a number of studies. In the Boston area, approximately 40 per cent of working-class high school pupils with high I.Q.'s whose fathers graduated from high school went on to college, compared to only 25 per cent of those high-I.Q. students whose fathers had less education.[11] In Denmark, if fathers in lower strata have more education than the class mean, their sons are likely to be upwardly mobile. Similarly, in England, working-class children who reach the grammar school are likely to have parents whose education is higher than the average for their class. A report on Belgian studies states that the cultural level of lower-status families, rather than their material situation, determines the tendency toward upward mobility.[12]

One would expect further that parents who are themselves downward mobile would attempt to compensate by encouraging their children to rise. Elizabeth Cohen confirmed this relationship in her study of 100 working-class high school boys. She matched the boys by I.Q., ethnicity, and school, into two groups of 50 boys who were going to college, and 50 who were not. Of those fathers who had been downward mobile, 64 per cent had sons planning college compared to only 45 per cent of the sons of stationary fathers. Downward mobility of the mother proved to be even more highly associated with a son's mobility potential.[13] . . .

Increased amounts of stimulation for achievement may also result from especially early and long-continued association with adults and their values, rather than with other children.[14] This may help explain the findings that the most successful persons in many fields occupied sibling positions which intensified their relations with their parents and weakened those with other children. The more successful among Methodist ministers,[15] top scientists,[16] and a sample of extremely gifted children in New York,[17] were all more likely to be only children, oldest children, or children with longer than average distance between themselves and the next older child, than could be explained by chance.[18] Studies of the determinants of intelligence-test scores consistently show

[11] Samuel Stouffer, "First Rough Draft of Summary Report on Some Statistics Collected in the Harvard Mobility Study" (Unpublished manuscript, Harvard University, 1958).

[12] K. Svalastoga, "An Empirical Analysis of Intrasocietary Mobility Determinants" (Working Paper Nine submitted to the Fourth Working Conference on Social Stratification and Social Mobility, International Sociological Association, December, 1957); J. E. Floud, F. M. Martin, and A. H. Halsey, "Educational Opportunity and Social Selection in England," in *Transactions of the Second World Congress of Sociology*, Vol. II, pp. 194–208; Paul Minon, "Choix d'une profession et mobilité sociale," *ibid.*, pp. 209–213.

[13] Elizabeth G. Cohen, *Parental Factors in Educational Mobility*, pp. 67–70.

[14] This does not imply, of course, that the attitudes of peer groups may not in some situations stimulate mobility aspirations. The lower-class youth of "Elmtown" whose sociometric choices showed high educational expectations were much more likely to attend college. R. J. Havighurst and R. R. Rodgers, "The Role of Motivation in Attendance at Post-High-School Educational Institutions," *in* Byron S. Hollinshead, *Who Should Go to College?* (New York: Columbia University Press, 1952), pp. 135–165.

[15] Phillip J. Allen, "Childhood Backgrounds of Success in a Profession," *American Sociological Review*, 20 (1955): 186–190.

[16] Anne Roe, *The Making of a Scientist* (New York: Dodd-Mead, 1953), pp. 70–74; and Francis Bello, "The Young Scientists," *Fortune*, June, 1954, pp. 142–148 ff.

[17] Paul M. Sheldon, "The Families of Highly Gifted Children," *Marriage and Family Living*, 16 (1954): 59 ff.

[18] The Scottish Intelligence Survey showed that in each size of family the *first-born* and the *last-born* had higher I.Q. scores than middle-born siblings. A plausible explanation is that both the oldest child and the "baby of the family" receive disproportionate amounts of parental attention. Sir Godfrey Thomson, "Intelligence and Fertility: The Scottish 1947 Survey," *The Eugenics Review*, 41 (1950): 168. Similarly, a British study found that a working-class boy had a greater chance of entering an upper school if he were an elder or eldest child. See A. H. Halsey and L. Gardner, "Selection for Secondary Education and Achievement in Four Grammar Schools," *British Journal of Sociology*, 4 (1953): 60–75, cited in Floud, Martin, and Halsey, "Educational Opportunity . . .," p. 208. More evidence that the middle sibling position is a handicap comes from the Harvard mobility study, which found that with occupation and size of family held constant, middle children are considerably less likely to go to college. See S. Stouffer, "First Rough Draft. . .," p. 21.

that those from larger families do less well than children from small families.[19] Both the study of scientists and the study of gifted children show that the families of those who become exceptional have kept them isolated from other children,[20] and Robert E. L. Faris found that isolation in childhood was a very common experience of the "geniuses" he studied.[21] Available evidence also indicates that the degree of adult contact may be the most important single factor in linguistic development.[22] One might summarize the implications of these studies for social mobility by saying that all factors which intensify the involvement of a child with his parents or other adults, and reduce his involvement with other children, increase the likelihood that he will be upwardly mobile.

These findings which indicate a relationship between "isolation from contact with other children" and upward mobility tie in with the historic association between social advancement and a small family of orientation: restricted fertility has recently been discussed as a factor in the long-term process which enabled certain French bourgeois families to enter the nobility in the *ancien régime*.[23]

Modern studies of social mobility from six Western European countries—England, France, Belgium, Denmark, Sweden, and Italy—all indicate that the upwardly mobile and better-educated children from lower-status groups are likely to come from small families.[24] Evidence from Italy and England suggests that a restricted family may be an important factor in enabling children of the upper classes to *maintain* the high position of their parents: children of large families in the upper strata are more likely to be downwardly mobile.[25]

A striking illustration of the relationship between mobility and restricted family size is found in a Swedish study. Using matriculation in secondary schools as an indicator of probable mobility, Moberg found that the educationally successful sons of craftsmen, workers, and minor officials came from smaller families and had fewer children themselves than the matriculated sons of higher-status and better-educated families: it would seem, from his study, that in order to rise, lower-class families must be even smaller than upper-strata families.[26]

It can be argued that "small family" is simply a spurious variable which "intervenes" between the motivation and education of the parents and the motivation and education of the offspring: that it is the better-educated and mobility-motivated parents from the lower strata who tend to restrict the number of their children, and that these are also the parents who motivate their children to advance and would do so whatever the size of their family. Although there is an element of truth in this, research data indicate that the size of family itself has

[19] See J. Nisbet, *Family Environment* (London: Eugenics Society, 1953), for a review of the relevant literature.

[20] Anne Roe, *The Making of a Scientist*, pp. 88–93 and Paul Sheldon, "The Families of Highly Gifted Children," pp. 59–60.

[21] R. E. L. Faris, "Sociological Causes of Genius," *American Sociological Review*, 15 (1950): 689–699.

[22] Anne Anastasi and John P. Foley, Jr., *Differential Psychology*, rev. ed. (New York: Macmillan, 1949), p. 338 f.

[23] J. G. C. Blacker, "Social Ambitions of the Bourgeoisie in 18th Century France and Their Relation to Family Limitation," *Population Studies*, 11 (1957): 46–63. In twentieth century America also, mobile entrants into the upper class have fewer children than the old-family sector of the social elite. See E. Digby Baltzell, "Social Mobility and Fertility Within an Elite Group," *The Milbank Memorial Fund Quarterly*, 31 (1953): 411–420.

[24] Floud, Martin, and Halsey, "Educational Opportunity . . ."; Marcel Bresard, "Mobilité sociale et dimension de la famille," *Population*, 5 (1950): 533–566; Alain Girard, "Mobilité sociale et dimension de la famille," *Population*, 6 (1951): 103–124; Paul Minon, "Choix d'une profession et mobilité sociale"; K. Svalastoga, "An Empirical Analysis of Intrasocietary Mobility Determinants"; Sven Moberg, "Marital Status and Family Size Among Matriculated Persons in Sweden," *Population Studies*, 4 (1950): 115–127; and Alessandro Lehner, "Mobilité sociale par rapport à la dimension de la famille," *Proceedings of the World Population Conference, 1954* (New York: United Nations, 1954), pp. 911–931.

[25] A. Lehner, "Mobilité sociale . . ." In England upper-middle-class parents have been severely limiting their family size in order to afford public school education for their sons. *Royal Commission on Population* (London: His Majesty's Stationery Office), p. 145, cited in E. Digby Baltzell, *Philadelphia Gentlemen* (Glencoe: The Free Press, 1958), p. 318,

[26] S. Moberg, "Marital status . . ."

a number of dynamic consequences which affect social mobility, and should therefore be considered as an "independent variable."

The first consequence is obvious and corresponds to the conscious, manifest intent of parents who restrict fertility. For people of limited income, the fewer the children the better they can be fed, clothed, and educated. Thus one of the French studies found that although size of family had no effect on the ability of wealthy parents to provide higher education for their children, only those in "modest" circumstances who restricted the size of their families could afford secondary education for their children.[27] Two other French studies also show an inverse relationship between size of family and length of education for children of low-status parentage, but indicate that size of family bears no relationship to continuation in school for those with a high-status background.[28] . . .

A second consequence of a small family is perhaps more unintended and latent. Interaction in the smaller family unit, by increasing the involvement of the children with adults, seems to lead to higher intelligence and greater motivation, which, in turn, means greater likelihood of educational and occupational success. In addition to the evidence for this presented earlier, the findings of two national surveys are striking.

Although the Scottish Intelligence Survey found the usual associations between (1) high-status occupation and high intelligence-test scores, (2) high-status occupation and small family size, and (3) high intelligence-test scores and small family size, the finding that is significant in the present context is that *within each occupational class, the children from smaller families consistently had higher intelligence test scores.*[29]

Similarly, a French national survey found that performance on intelligence tests varies with rural-urban residence, father's occupation, and size of family. But, except for the children of professionals, there was an inverse relationship between size of family and test performance within each occupational group (residence held constant).[30]

These research findings on the relation of restricted fertility to possibilities for social advancement agree with modern population theory and research, which in recent years has given increasing consideration to the desire for upward mobility as one of the significant factors in the secular trend toward smaller family size.[31]

The recent efforts of sociologists to locate the sources of motivation towards achievement in the cultural values of different groups, and to explain which individuals secure high status by being urged toward education, hard work, proper dress, etc., have been paralleled by the work of psychologists who have sought to find in personality the sources of varying motivations to achieve. The work of David McClelland and his associates has been particularly important in this area. They have developed a number of projective and content analysis techniques that make it possible to analyze the strength of the "need for achievement." The core of this method is a coding of fictional and fantasy materials according to criteria which are measures of the extent to which the described action is interpreted by the respondent as an attempt to "achieve," either relative to some standard or to some other person.[32] Once the strength

[27] A. Girard, "Mobilité sociale . . ."

[28] M. Bresard, "Mobilité sociale . . .," p. 554, and data in table 9.4.

[29] James Maxwell, "Intelligence, Fertility and the Future: A Report on the 1947 Scottish Mental Survey," *Proceedings of the World Population Conference, 1954* (New York: United Nations, 1954), p. 738.

[30] Institut National d'études Démographiques, *Le Niveau intellectuel* . . ., pp. 187–193. Thus while the overall performance of the children of white-collar workers in a given age group is six to eight points higher than that of the children of manual workers, an "only" child from a working-class family tends to have a score equal to or a little higher than that of children from large white-collar families (three or four children).

[31] See Charles F. Westoff, "The Changing Focus of Differential Fertility Research: The Social Mobility Hypothesis," *Milbank Memorial Fund Quarterly*, 31 (1953): 24–38. John F. Kantner and Clyde V. Kiser, "The Interrelation of Fertility, Fertility Planning and Inter-Generational Social Mobility: Social and Psychological Factors Affecting Fertility," *Milbank Memorial Fund Quarterly*, 32 (1954): 76–78; Jerzy Berent, "Fertility and Social Mobility," *Population Studies*, 5 (1952): 244–260. . . .

[32] An exposition of the techniques of this method and some validating materials, along with some preliminary empirical results, are presented in David C. McClelland, *et al.*, *The Achievement Motive* (New York: Appleton-Century-Crofts, 1953).

of the motivation to achieve is measured, it may be related to such other variables as religious affiliation, family structure, child-rearing practices of various cultures, and so on.[33]

There is evidence that this achievement motive is a true personality component that stems in large part from early childhood experiences, much like the propensity to anxiety.[34] Early training for independence is related to high achievement motivation; that is, children who are weaned earlier, who are treated as independent individuals earlier, who are forced to take care of many personal functions at an early age, are much more likely to have an orientation to high achievement than those who are protected in this early period. Early training for independence is, moreover, much more characteristic of middle-class than working-class families. We would therefore expect that middle-class children would possess higher achievement motivation than working-class children and that this fairly common-sense notion could be substantiated by empirical research. This has been done by one of McClelland's associates who found that 83 per cent of New Haven high school boys from the two highest social classes scored high on an achievement scale compared to only 32 per cent of the boys from the three lowest strata.[35]

The few empirical findings which are available not only substantiate the notion that the middle class is more oriented to achievement than the lower class, but also that it is superior to the *upper class* in these traits of drive and ambition. Charles McArthur's study of the personality characteristics of upper- and middle-class men at Harvard shows that the latter are much more likely to be work oriented and to reject both strong family ties in general and in particular their father, whom they desire to surpass in status.[36] . . . Two other studies by Rosen also found that the "need achievement" scores of middle-class respondents are higher than those of the upper class though the differences in each study are very small.[37] According to McArthur these findings on achievement motivation help explain why at elite colleges such as Harvard "public school boys consistently achieve higher grades than do boys with a private school background." A number of investigations agree that "intelligence held constant, college grades showed a constant inverse relation to economic advantage." The scions of the upper class at private schools and Harvard get a "gentleman's C" and are presumably gentlemen first and achievers second in later life, while those from middle-class families are more likely to "make an A," worry about marks, take a pretechnical major, and presumably put

[33] M. Winterbottom, "The Sources of Achievement Motivation in Mother's Attitudes Toward Independence Training," *in* McClelland, *et al.*, *The Achievement Motive*, pp. 297–304; D. C. McClelland and G. A. Friedman, "A Cross Cultural Study of the Relationship between Child-training Practices and Achievement Motivation Appearing in Folk Tales," *in* G. Swanson, *et al.*, eds., *Readings in Social Psychology* (New York: Henry Holt, 1952), pp. 243–249; and McClelland, *et al.*, "Religious and Other Sources of Parental Attitudes Toward Independence Training," *in* McClelland, ed., *Studies in Motivation* (New York: Appleton-Century-Crofts, 1955), pp. 389–397.

[34] Havighurst found that upwardly mobile persons do not find relaxation in leisure-time pursuits but "play" in much the same striving, energetic manner in which they approach work and other areas of life. Robert J. Havighurst, "The Leisure Activities of the Middle-Aged," *American Journal of Sociology*, 63 (1957): 158.

[35] Bernard C. Rosen, "The Achievement Syndrome: A Psychocultural Dimension of Social Stratification," *American Sociological Review*, 21 (1956): 206. The most comprehensive summary of the results of the many psychological studies of socialization during the past twenty-five years concludes: "Though more tolerant of expressed impulses and desires, the middle class parent . . . has higher expectations for the child. The middle class youngster is expected to learn to take care of himself earlier, to accept more responsibilities about the home, and—above all—to progress further in school." Urie Bronfenbrenner, "Socialization and Social Class Through Time and Space," *in* E. E. Maccoby, *et al.*, eds., *Readings in Social Psychology* (New York: Henry Holt, 1958), p. 424.

[36] Charles McArthur, "Personality Differences Between Middle and Upper Classes," *The Journal of Abnormal and Social Psychology*, 50 (1955): 247–258.

[37] B. Rosen, "The Achievement Syndrome . . ." p. 206; and David C. McClelland, "Community Development and the Nature of Human Motivation; Some Implications of Recent Research," (Unpublished manuscript, 1957), table 1.

achievement first after leaving Harvard.[38] Perhaps this superiority in achievement and drive of a rising middle class over established elites is endemic in stratified societies which are economically progressive. In his analysis of the repeated rise of "new men" into the leading positions in the economy from the Middle Ages down to the nineteenth century, Henri Pirenne has pointed to the fact that descendants of the new rich always lose interest in achievement, and ultimately "withdraw from the struggle. . . . In their place arise new men, courageous and enterprising."[39] Thus class differences in personality must be considered a factor in the perennial "circulation of the elites."

Unfortunately, granted the exciting implications for social analysis suggested by the work of these psychologists, they have not yet provided us with actual evidence that high achievement motivation is actually related to occupational success.

There is no evidence that motivation (of the sort measured by the techniques mentioned above) results in higher occupational achievement among those with equal opportunity. We do not know whether those who have achieved the transition from a working-class background into the middle class have stronger motivations than those who only maintain the positions of their families. We also do not know whether motivation for achievement which cannot be fulfilled by a high-status occupation can be easily satisfied, for example, by athletic achievement, or by doing a good job at a lower level.

However there is evidence that achievement *motivation* is related to concrete achievement *behavior* among students. Rosen in his study of New Haven high school boys found that within both upper and lower social strata, boys with high achievement motivation scores received high grades and boys with low achievement scores received low grades.[40] . . .

The process of social mobility requires, beyond the motivation to achieve, the capacity to leave behind an early environment and to adapt to a new one.[41] This capacity to form social relationships at a higher level and to give up those at a lower level is probably related to personality. Thus, the socially mobile among business leaders show an unusual capacity to break away from those who are liabilities and form relationships with those who can help them.[42] The childhood experiences of lower-status men who later become business leaders often show a pattern of strong mothers and weak fathers, and an emotionally unsatisfying

[38] Charles McArthur, "Personalities of Public and Private School Boys," *Harvard Educational Review*, 24 (1954): 256–261; quote about intelligence is taken by McArthur from A. B. Crawford, *Incentives to Study* (New Haven: Yale University Press, 1929).

[39] Henri Pirenne, "Stages in the Social History of Capitalism," *in* R. Bendix and S. M. Lipset, eds., *Class, Status and Power* (Glencoe: The Free Press, 1953), p. 502. The entire article is pertinent.

[40] Bernard C. Rosen, "The Achievement Syndrome . . .," p. 210. The most recent knowledge available on how achievement motivation is related to differential behavior has been summarized by McClelland: "The 'highs' work harder at laboratory tasks, learn faster, do somewhat better school work in high school even with IQ partialled out, and seem to do their best work when it counts for their record and not when other special incentives are introduced such as pressure from the outside to do well, money prizes, or time off from work. They are more resistant to social pressure, choose experts over friends as work partners, and tend to be more active in college or community activities, like risky occupations, perform better under longer odds, and choose moderate risks over either safe or speculative ones." David C. McClelland, "Community Development . . .," pp. 4–5. This paper contains the references which document each of the above listed findings. See also David C. McClelland, *et al.*, *Talent and Society* (Princeton: Van Nostrand, 1958).

[41] See W. Lloyd Warner and James C. Abegglen, *Big Business Leaders in America* (New York: Harper, 1955), pp. 59–64; W. Foote Whyte, *Street Corner Society*, pp. 94–108; and Peter M. Blau, "Social Mobility and Interpersonal Relations," *American Sociological Review*, 21 (1956): 290–295.

[42] A study which contrasted the socialization patterns in Jewish- and Italian-American families found that certain beliefs, values, and personality traits conducive to high achievement and upward mobility were inculcated in Jewish, but not in Italian families. These included: "a belief that the world is orderly and amenable to rational mastery, and that therefore, a person can and should make plans which will control his destiny; . . . a willingness to leave home to make one's way in life; . . . and a preference for individualistic rather than collective credit for work done." Fred L. Strodtbeck, "Family Interaction, Values, and Achievement," *in* Marshall Sklare, ed., *The Jews: Social Patterns of an American Group* (Glencoe: The Free Press, 1958), pp. 162–163.

family life.[43] If it is assumed that a situation in which the mother has higher social status than the father is likely to result in this pattern of intrafamily relations, then families in which the mother had a higher occupational status than the father before marriage should result in higher social mobility. Two interesting British studies support this hypothesis. The study cited above . . . found that "the mothers of successful [in getting into the highly selective grammar school at the age of 10–11] working class children moreover had frequently followed an occupation 'superior' to that of their husbands."[44] A second study reports that working-class parents are more likely to prefer grammr school education for their children when the mother's occupation, before marriage to a manual worker, was nonmanual rather than manual.[45] A similar pattern has been observed in America by Allison Davis, who writes that "many parents who push children toward social mobility are members of mixed-class marriages. . . . A lower-middle class woman who marries a man from the upper part of the working class usually begins to try and recoup her original social class status either by reforming and elevating her husband's behavior to meet lower-middle class standards or by seeking to train and propel her children toward the status she once had."[46]

The characteristic family experiences in childhood of the upward mobile and his typical personality structure remain still a relatively unexplored area. The contrast among the findings of the studies on these subjects is striking. Douvan and Adelson, who investigated the occupational aspirations of 1,000 high school boys, found that those whose aspirations were upward tended to come from warm, permissive family *milieux* which encouraged the development of achievement and autonomy and of realistic attitudes toward parents and the self. The upward-aspiring boys were more likely to share leisure activities with parents than the boys without higher aspirations.[47] On the other hand, a number of studies of which the one of business leaders by Warner and Abegglen is the most comprehensive, found that the upwardly mobile tended to be escaping from an impoverished home pervaded by a "spiritually bleak and physically depressed family atmosphere," in which quite often the father was an inadequate and unreliable figure. Although these men also show strong traits of independence, they are characterized by an inability to form intimate relations and are consequently often socially isolated men.[48]

Warner and Abegglen's negative picture of family environment and personality structure is supported by a number of more limited studies. . . .

Mental illness rates would seem to provide additional data for the notion that the upwardly mobile tend to be deprived psychodynamically. People who are upward mobile, but *not* those who are downward mobile or geographically mobile, have higher rates of mental disorder than those who are stationary.[49] This suggests that it is not the anomic situation associated with mobility that is responsible for the greater vulnerability, because one would expect downward mobility to be at least as threatening to psychic equilibrium as upward mobility. It is therefore probable that a particular type of ego structure which results from a characteristic family environment is both favorable for upward mobility

[43] Warner and Abegglen, *Big Business Leaders . . .*, pp. 64–107.

[44] Floud, *et al.*, *Social Class . . .*

[45] F. M. Martin, "An Inquiry into Parents' Preferences in Secondary Education," *in* D. V. Glass, ed., *Social Mobility in Britain*, p. 169.

[46] Allison Davis, "Personality and Social Mobility," *The School Review*, 65 (1957): 137. American data which give empirical support to this hypothesis are provided by Cohen, who found that 80 per cent of the boys whose fathers were manual workers, but whose mothers had white-collar family backgrounds were going to college, compared to only 42 per cent of those working-class boys whose mother's background too was working class. E. G. Cohen, *Parental Factors in Educational Mobility*, p. 70.

[47] Elizabeth Douvan and Joseph Adelson, "The Psychodynamics of Social Mobility in Adolescent Boys," *The Journal of Abnormal and Social Psychology*, 56 (1958): 31–44.

[48] Warner and Abegglen, *Big Business Leaders . . .*, pp. 59–83.

[49] A. B. Hollingshead, R. Ellis, and E. Kirby, "Social Mobility and Mental Illness," *American Sociological Review*, 19 (1954): 577–584 and A. B. Hollingshead and F. C. Redlich, "Schizophrenia and Social Structure," *American Journal of Psychiatry*, 110 (1954): 695–701.

and vulnerable to mental illness.[50] The various researches in this area all suggest that the downward mobile have been overprotected and loved as young children, and hence are perhaps better able to cope with stress. They also have much less of a need for achievement and therefore should feel less frustrated by failure.

It seems quite likely that the personality determinants and consequences of upward mobility would differ according to the extent and character of the mobility process. Perhaps it is *extreme mobility,* especially mobility into and within elites such as the professions and the higher positions in business, that attracts personality configurations which are a result of childhood deprivation.

. . . . . . . . . . . . . . . . . . . . . . . . . . . . . . . . .

These studies suggest that upward mobility selects people who are distinctive in psychodynamic terms. They also indicate that a crucial variable in the motivation for social mobility is the structure of the family, perhaps independently of direct urging toward social mobility.

The relations between motivation for achievement deriving from personality structure and motivation deriving directly from the social structure remain to be investigated, but recent explorations in psychology constitute the most promising line of research yet developed to supplement the sociological analysis of the relation of mobility to structural factors such as class or ethnic background. Such studies may enable us to specify how different positions in the social structure may affect family behavior, and child-rearing practices in particular.

. . . . . . . . . . . . . . . . . . . . . . . . . . . . . . . . .

On a theoretical level, perhaps the most interesting effort to bridge the gap between psychological and sociological research may be found in the "reference-group theory," particularly as it has been systematized by Robert K. Merton and Alice S. Rossi.[51] . . . To use a group as a normative reference group, on the other hand, is to take over its norms, to emulate its members. . . . Reference-group theory suggests that the potentially upward mobile usually reveal *anticipatory socialization,* that is, they absorb the norms and behavior traits of higher strata long before they have actually changed their social position. As Merton and Rossi have put it, such people "conform" to the norms of groups of which they are not yet members, thus becoming "nonconformists" within their group of origin.

It should be noted, however, that although conformity to the standards of a group with higher status undoubtedly facilitates upward mobility, such conformity is not always a product of an orientation toward the higher-status group as a reference group, a possibility that is ignored in much of the writing on reference-group theory and mobility. Thus, lower-class individuals who exhibit good work habits, cleanliness, concern for personal appearance, and generally follow the established rules of "middle-class morality" are much more likely to move up in the social structure than those who reject these norms. The motivation to behave in this fashion may, however, have little or nothing to do with having a middle-class reference group, but may, for example, have developed out of the inner dynamics of a religious belief. Thus, ascetic sects which have arisen among the lower classes in various Protestant countries often insist that their members conform strictly to Christian principles, which, from another perspective means conformity to middle-class standards. Similarly, the upward mobility of Japanese-Americans has been explained in terms of a "significant compatibility . . . between the value systems

[50] Some of the case-study materials on the adjustment of families to the Depression suggest that those families whose members were motivated to be socially mobile were more rigid in their reponse than were families less concerned with economic success. See Ruth S. Cavan and Catherine H. Ranck, *The Family and the Depression* (Chicago: University of Chicago Press, 1938), p. 90; Mirra Komarovsky, *The Unemployed Man and His Family* (New York: Dryden Press, 1940), pp. 78–83, 116–122: and Robert Angell, *The Family Meets the Depression* (New York: Scribners, 1936), pp. 17–18, 192–193.

[51] See esp. Robert K. Merton and Alice S. Rossi, "Contributions to the Theory of Reference Group Behavior," *in* R. K. Merton, *Social Theory and Social Structure*, rev. ed. (Glencoe: The Free Press, 1957), pp. 225–280, and R. K. Merton, "Continuities in the Theory of Reference Groups and Social Structure," *ibid.*, pp. 281–386.

found in the culture of Japan and the value systems found in American middle class culture" rather than in terms of a conscious orientation of lower-status Japanese-Americans to the middle class as a reference group.[52] The study of anticipatory socialization should, therefore, always try to differentiate between that behavior which is manifestly anticipatory and that which is directed towards a different goal, even though both may serve the same function—that of preparing individuals to succeed in new roles.

[52] W. Caudill and G. DeVos, "Achievement, Culture, and Personality . . .," p. 1107.

Both reference-group theory and the data on role conformity, anticipatory socialization, and reference-group behavior suggest that by merging the sociological and psychological approaches to the study of social mobility we may be able to advance the study of the mechanisms by which individuals and groups reach their positions in the stratification structure.

# PART VI
# Ethnicity, Race, and Class

Ethnicity and class constitute two major and connected features of a number of contemporary societies. It is therefore important to know the relationship between them. But as yet no over-all sociological theory has been formulated to explain the connection between them in general. What we do have is a series of recent studies about ethnicity and class in given societies. And these show that the relationship is complex and varies sharply from continent to continent and society to society.

We are using the term *ethnic* group in its *broad* meaning of any group of people defined by or singled out because of race, religion, national origin, or a combination of these. Our first reading, however, is primarily concerned with one kind of ethnic differentiation—the racial one—and its relevance to class in Latin America. It will serve as a frame of comparison for the subsequent readings on race and class in the United States.

Despite certain common historical experiences—of European expansion, colonization, and *slavery*—the relationship between race and class in Latin America is fundamentally different from that in the United States, as is made explicit by Julian Pitt-Rivers in his "Race, Color, and Class in Central America and the Andes." It could be said that in Latin America class is a more important determinant of social position than race. Given, for instance, two people with the same racial characteristics, one might be considered white and the other colored, depending on the class to which they belong. In contrast to the United States, with its color bar dividing people into two categories, white and Negro, "color" in Latin America is a matter of degree and class. Class differences are often referred to in Latin America in idioms of race. The reason is the historical association between class and race there. The upper classes were white, the lower Negro or Indian. But the point is that individuals with Negroid or Indian physical features are found in the upper classes. Their standing is secured by other criteria of class, which outweigh the criterion of race. Color in Latin America, in the words of the author, "is an ingredient, not a determinant of class," and can be therefore traded for other ingredients, such as money or power. It is quite common to trade these things in marriage so that an impoverished white person will marry a rich person with Negroid or Indian features.

Pitt-Rivers suggests that the phenotypical association of class (correlation between class and physical appearance) is increasing rather than diminishing in Latin America.[1] He ties this to recent demographic trends. On the one hand, the rural migration to cities means the absorption of people with Indian features into the urban lower classes. On the other, European immigrants are being absorbed into the upper classes. In contrast to the local community where everyone knows everyone's standing and background, color is gaining as a symbolic indicator of status in the big impersonal cities while clothing, speech, and manners are losing ground.

Color in both rural and urban areas of the United States has traditionally been the symbol of caste, not class. Although Negroes belong to different classes, whites react to them more in terms of race than in terms of class membership. But before proceeding to discuss the readings on race and class in the United States, we shall place them in the perspective of the general orientation of sociological studies in this field.

In casually surveying the theoretical discussions and empirical studies that touch on the relationship between class and ethnicity in the United States, one arrives at the conclusion that they center around the following three related questions: (1) What is the relationship between membership in a given ethnic group and the position in the total system of social stratification? (2) What is the class distribution of a given ethnic group and how does it compare with that of the majority population? (3) When the behavior of a given ethnic group differs from that of the majority, to what extent are these differences the result of the differential class distribution of the ethnic group as compared with the majority population?

A concept that connects these questions and may connect our selections is that of *ethclass,* formulated by Milton Gordon.[2] The term refers to the *subsociety* created by the *intersection* of ethnic group and class. By specifying that the ethclass is a subsociety, he gives notice that it is a "... functioning unity which has an integrated impact on the participating individual." Thus, he cites such examples of ethclasses as upper-middle-class white Protestant or lower-middle-class Irish or upper-lower-class Negro. In these ethclasses people tend to concentrate their primary social relationships. As Gordon expresses it, with a person of the same social class but of a different ethnic group "one shares behavioral similarities but not a sense of peoplehood." With those of the same ethnic group but of different social class, one shares the sense of peoplehood but not behavioral similarities. "The only group which meets both of these criteria are people of the same ethnic group *and* same social class."[3] In this last group one feels at home, one interacts with ease. This concrete structure of the ethclass is then the result of the combination of two factors, class and ethnicity, which analytically can be and often are separated, as we shall see in the forthcoming readings.

The consistent note that emerges from studies dealing with race and class in the United States is that the greatest differences in behavior between the races are found in the lower classes. Much discussion, for example, revolves around the

[1] For a systematic exploration and statistical treatment of the association between class and phenotype in the West Indies, see M. G. Smith, *Stratification in Grenada,* Berkeley: University of California Press, 1965, pp. 158–174. On class and ethnicity in Mexico, see: Rodolfo Stavenhagen, "Classes, Colonialism, and Acculturation," in Joseph A. Kahl, ed., *Comparative Perspectives on Stratification,* Boston: Little, Brown and Company, 1968, pp. 31–63.

[2] Milton M. Gordon, *Assimilation in American Life,* New York: Oxford University Press, 1964, pp. 46–54.

[3] *Ibid.,* p. 53.

great instability of the lower-class Negro family. The frequent explanation is the historically based matriarchal tradition that exists in the Negro family.[4] But, as G. Franklin Edwards points out convincingly in the reprinted article "The Negro American—Community and Class Realities: The Ordeal of Change," the instability of the Negro family is only partly explained by the tradition (dating back to slavery) under which the father-child ties of Negroes were not honored. Its continuation is tied to today's socioeconomic conditions, which limit the possibility of the standard American family form replacing the matrifocal one so prominent among Negroes, who are still overwhelmingly lower class. And the same factors are operating here to which Gunnar Myrdal pointed as the causes of social disorganization in the underclass: the unemployment and underemployment of Negro males.[5] Edwards points out the important study by Hylan Lewis that presents evidence of the Negro male's concern about his responsibility to the family. One concludes from this study that, in the words of Edwards, the behavior of these absent fathers "is a practical response to untoward circumstances which undermine the well intentioned, but often unattainable goals" of fulfilling family responsibilities. Similarly, many other differences in the behavior patterns of lower-class Negroes and whites are not only the legacy of slavery but also the fruit of discrimination.

Another consistency in the sociological studies of race and class in the United States are the findings concerning the similarity between the patterns of behavior of the Negro middle class and the white middle class. However, the Negro middle class is proportionally very much smaller than the white middle class. This, Edwards shows, is tied to the fact that social mobility among Negroes until recently was primarily determined by the needs of the Negro community rather than the general conditions in the country. Thus Negro professionals were largely professionals serving Negroes, Negro businessmen largely selling to Negroes, and so on.

Subsequently this type of mobility has been analyzed as a "mobility trap" by Norbert F. Wiley. This concept refers to the structural condition in which the means for moving up within the ethnic group are contrary to those for moving up within the dominant social structure. There are certain opportunities for mobility within the ethnic group (as exemplified by the preceding discussion of Negro businessmen). However, they may constitute mobility traps as far as mobility within the dominant social structure is concerned. The underlying metaphor in this formulation is that of climbing a tree rather than that of climbing a ladder, the metaphor so widely employed in mobility studies. Thus a person who has moved up within a given ethnic group may be visualized as on top of an isolated limb. If he wants to move up in the dominant structure (climb the trunk), he faces the problem of how to get off the limb. And the possibility of accomplishing this varies with ethnic group. As the author puts it, for Negroes it is almost impossible and, one could add, for Mexican Americans it is quite difficult.[6]

[4] For example, Richard Bloom, Martin Whiteman, and Martin Deutsch, "Race and Social Class as Separate Factors Related to Social Environment," *American Journal of Sociology,* January, 1965, p. 472.

[5] For the effects of unemployment on family stability, see the studies of the depression: Bohdan Zawadzki and P. F. Lazarsfeld, "The Psychological Consequences of Unemployment," *Journal of Social Psychology,* Vol. VI, 1935, pp. 225–251, and Marie Lazarsfeld Jahoda and Hans Zeisel, *Die Arbeitslosen von Marienthal,* Leipzig: Verlag von S. Hirzel, 1933. See also E. W. Bakke, *The Unemployed Man,* New York: E. P. Dutton & Co., 1934; and E. W. Bakke, ed., *The Unemployed Worker,* New Haven: Yale University Press, 1940.

[6] Norbert F. Wiley, "The Ethnic Mobility Trap and Stratification Theory," *Social Problems,* Vol. 15, Fall, 1967, pp. 147–159.

One must point out that the smallness of the Negro middle class, contrary to prejudiced views, cannot be explained in terms of lack of ambition.[7] The high educational aspirations of Negroes deserve special attention because, as we recall from the preceding part of our book, education proves to be less profitable for them than for whites. The same amount of education yields considerably less return in the form of occupational status or income to Negroes than to whites. (See pp. 340–352 in this volume).

If indeed the situation is that suggested from the Bloom, Whiteman, and Deutsch study, that mobility aspirations of Negroes do not vary substantially with class, then they are now displaying a characteristic present in those ethnic groups that have advanced fairly rapidly, notably the Jews. The chief obstacle then for Negroes, as far as taking advantage of existing opportunities for advancement is concerned, is not lack of ambition but the problem of inadequate education, as is described by Edwards.

In contrast to the ethnic groups that have advanced rapidly, Celia S. Heller argues, those that have shown small intergenerational advancement display substantial class variation in characteristics conducive to mobility, such as in stress on education, in IQ scores, or in occupational aspirations. The group she concentrates on is America's "forgotten" minority, its third largest: the Mexican Americans.[8] The latest analyzed data show that of all sizable "cultural" minorities (national origin) in the United States, this is the only one that fails to show a substantial intergenerational rise in socioeconomic status. The author explains that the traditional values of this ethnic group, which do not vary with class—honor, respect, family obligation, manliness—are not conducive to early stages of upward mobility. And those qualities that foster upward mobility, such as stress on mental effort and education, differ inversely with social class among the Mexican Americans.

Our last selection by E. Digby Baltzell deals with members of an ethnic group who positionally have succeeded in climbing the trunk to the very top but who, to continue with Wiley's terminology, suffer from reputational inconsistency. It also can be related to the Heller article, for if her essay deals with the problems of ethnic groups in the early stage of advancement (from working-class to middle-class position), the focus of Baltzell's study is on the last stage: members of an ethnic group being allowed to move into the national upper prestige stratum, which is actually nothing but an ethclass—white Protestant—to use Gordon's concept.

The latter problems by and large are those of third-generation and the former of second-generation Americans. But as we gather from the Heller article, third-generation Mexican Americans are showing the manifestations that other ethnic groups displayed in the second generation. Also the Negroes, who are among the oldest American groups, are facing many of the problems that other ethnic groups were confronted with in the second generation.

The key concepts in our reprinted pages from E. Digby Baltzell's "The Protestant

[7] Bloom, Whiteman, and Deutsch, *op. cit.*, pp. 471–476. Also, James S. Coleman, ed., *Equality of Educational Opportunity,* Washington, D.C.: U.S. Government Printing Office, 1966, pp. 278–281. For other evidence showing that the achievement values and educational aspirations of Negroes are high, being comparable to those of Jews, Greeks, and white Protestants, and higher than those of other ethnic groups, such as Italians, see Bernard C. Rosen, "Race, Ethnicity, and the Achievement Syndrome," *American Sociological Review,* Vol. 24, February, 1959, pp. 47–60.

[8] For a brief account of the history and geographic distribution of this minority, see Celia S. Heller, *Mexican American Youth: Forgotten Youth at the Crossroads,* Random House, 1966, pp. 3–21.

Establishment—Aristocracy and Caste in America," as well as in the book as a whole, are the three named in the title plus *elite* and *upper class* (Baltzell does not make use of the term *ethclass*, and in contrast to Gordon, he, like Heller, employs the term *ethnic* in the narrow sense of national origin). He alternately refers to the elite as individuals in top *functional* positions or individuals at the top of the power hierarchy. The upper class in his usage is the group of families at the top of the social-status hierarchy, analogous to Warner's upper-upper. By *establishment* he means the leaders within the elite. Baltzell tells us that during the first decades of our century the *WASP* upper class was in control of the elite. But since then some families from more recent ethnic groups have reached top economic and political positions. In the elite, says Baltzell, class replaces religion, national origin, and even race as the independent variable in social relationships. But here Baltzell seems to use class in a different sense than is usual in his work. Perhaps one could get a better sense of what he means by restating that in the elite *eliteship* replaces *ethnicity* as the important independent variable in primary relationships. The elite reside near one another, marry one another, and so forth, irrespective of national or religious origin. To use Milton Gordon's terminology, the *participational identification* of those people is not the ethclass but the elite. Now, the picture we get from Baltzell's description is that the WASP members of the elite are within the class system, being members of the upper class, but the others are marginal, outside the class system. The latter have either left or never belonged to the ethclass for which they qualify—Jewish upper class, Irish upper class, and so on. But the door is closed to the nationwide upper class that clings to the tradition of being "an Anglo Saxon caste." The author maintains that the WASP establishment has been forced to share its power, but it continues to hoard its social prestige. He sees two opposite tendencies at work in the WASP establishment and WASP upper class: one is toward closure, which he terms *caste*; and the other toward openness to the most prominent and polished families of the nation, regardless of ethnic origin, which he designates as a tendency toward *aristocracy*.

The policies of country club admission committees, Baltzell tells us, are one of the main ways of maintaining the upper class as a caste. And he seems to plead with these clubs to assume "the aristocratic role as leaders of assimilating association" and for the upper class "to regenerate its original ideals of equality of opportunity." Of course, equality of opportunity means something else here than equality of opportunity for the Mexican Americans and Negroes in the initial stage of ethnic mobility. For the latter it means equal opportunity for an education and a job, for the former it is the opportunity to join a WASP country club. Digby Baltzell presents the theme of the American Dilemma in the upper-class key. Although interesting sociologically, it is rather trivial and hardly as moving as the same theme in the lower-class key, except to the top climbers themselves.

# RACE, COLOR, AND CLASS IN CENTRAL AMERICA AND THE ANDES

*Julian Pitt-Rivers*

Among its many *fiestas,* the Hispanic world celebrates one with the name of "El día de la raza" (which is what is called Columbus Day in the United States). Why it should be so called remains something of an enigma. . . .

Quite apart from the mysteries surrounding The Day of the Race, the concept of *race* itself is unclear in Latin America. My concern here is not with what anthropologists mean by *race,* but only with what the people of Latin America think the word means when they encounter it in their daily speech. By minimal definition, it refers to a group of people who are felt to be somehow similar in their essential nature. . . .

The word *race* is, of course, also used to mark differences of ethnic identity within the nation. Sometimes awareness of any implication of heredity is so slight that a man can think of himself as belonging to a race different from that of his parents. The word clearly owes little to physical anthropology but refers, however it may be defined, to the ways in which people are classified in daily life. What are called race relations are, in fact, always questions of social structure.

. . . . . . . . . . . . . . . . . . . . . . . . . . . . . . . . .

A study that straddles the frontiers of established disciplines requires consideration from . . . varied viewpoints. It must above all achieve a synthesis of the cultural and the social aspects. . . . The preliminary condition of such an enterprise is a clear description of the systems of ethnic classification at the local level and a recognition of their social significance. Charles Wagley was making this point when he coined the phrase "social race."[1] He went on to point to the importance of knowing how the terminology varies, for this matter is filled with confusion. Not only do the words used vary from area to area and from class to class, but the conceptions to which they correspond also change, and the criteria on which the system of classification is based vary in relevance. It is difficult to say what is an Indian,[2] but it is scarcely easier to say what is a Negro.

Terminological inconsistencies complicate from the outset discussion of race relations in Latin America. Indeed, there is not even agreement as to whether or not a "problem" of race relations exists in Latin America. The nationals of these countries often deny the existence of racial discrimination. They claim from this fact a virtue that makes them, despite their supposed economic and technological underdevelopment, the moral superiors of their northern neighbor, whose "inhumanity" toward colored people they deplore. Moreover, this opinion is held not only by Latin Americans themselves, but by outside observers, the most eminent of whom is Professor Arnold Toynbee, who speaks of the Latin American's freedom from race prejudice.[3]

This point of view, in many cases a way of expressing criticism of the United States,

From *Daedalus,* "Race, Color, and Class in Central America and the Andes," by Julian Pitt-Rivers, Spring, 1967. Reprinted by permission of the author, the publisher, and the American Academy of Arts and Sciences.

[1] Charles Wagley, "On the Concept of Social Race in the Americas," *Actas del 33 Congreso Internacional de Americanistas* (San José, 1959). Reprinted in Dwight B. Heath and Richard N. Adams, eds., *Contemporary Cultures and Societies of Latin America* (New York, 1965).

[2] Woodrow Borah, "Race and Class in Mexico," *Pacific Historical Review,* Vol. 23, No. 4 (November, 1954); Julian Pitt-Rivers, "Who Are the Indians," *Encounter* (September, 1965).

[3] "In Latin America happily this racial distinction is not important and this is very much to Latin America's credit." Arnold Toynbee, *The Economy of the Western Hemisphere* (Oxford, 1962), p. 4. "Here is a country [Mexico] whose population is racially diversified yet is socially and culturally united. . . . I can only hope that the Latin American and Islamic freedom from race prejudice is the 'wave of the future.' " Arnold Toynbee, "The Racial Solution," *Encounter* (September, 1965), p. 31.

is also held by many patriotic American citizens, including especially some who are "colored" and whose testimony, if first-hand, might be thought to suffice.[4] Nevertheless, it is not by any means held universally and is sometimes regarded as a myth. Certain critics, both national and foreign, maintain that race is as important in Latin as in North America, once it is admitted that in addition to differences in the form discrimination takes, there is a major difference: The race that is penalized is the Indian rather than the Negro. Neither of these points of view appears correct.[5] Both are confused as to the nature of the question. Yet by examining the observations upon which they are based and how they have come to hold sway, one can understand better the role ethnic distinctiveness plays in ordering the society of Latin America.

"Segregation" as it is found in the United States does not exist in Latin America. "Color" in the North American sense is not the basis of a classification into two statuses to which differential rights attach. Segregated schools, public facilities, transport, or restaurants do not exist in Latin America. The Negro is not formally distinguished at any point. While many institutions are devoted specifically to the Indians, the definition of Indian in this regard is not based on physical criteria. Moreover, neither color nor phenotype has sufficed in the past to debar men from prominence in the national life, as the long list of Negroid or Indian-looking men of eminence in Latin American history shows.[6]

Intermarriage is not regarded with horror. Among the upper classes and in many places among the population generally, it is, however, considered denigrating to marry someone much darker than oneself. This is so, for example, in Barranquilla, Colombia, where the greater part of the population is more or less Negroid. The idea of physical contact with darker races is nowhere considered shocking, nor is it regarded as polluting by the whites. Dark-skinned people are thought to be more sensual and therefore more desirable sexually. This is not the expression of a neurotic fear of sexual insufficiency but an accepted and openly stated commonplace. Pale-skinned people of both sexes are thought to be more frigid and proud, and less warmhearted. Mistresses tend, consequently, to be more swarthy than wives, whose pale skin indicates social superiority.

The immense majority of the population from Mexico to Bolivia are well aware of their mixed ancestry. "A touch of the tarbrush" can, therefore, never mean total social disqualification. "We are all half-castes," Mexicans commonly remark, pointing to their forearm to show the color of their skin. Still, they sometimes go on to stress that only a small percentage of their blood is Indian. National unity demands that to be truly Mexican they must have some Indian blood, but social aspirations require that they should not have too much. Color is a matter of degree, not the basis of a division into black and white.

In consequence, physical characteristics cannot be said to be socially insignificant; their significance is only different. Physical traits never account for more than part of the image that individuals present. These images are perceived in terms of what they can be contrasted with; there is no color problem where the population is homogeneous in color, whatever that color may be. Social distinctions must then be made according to other criteria. From one place to another, in greater or lesser degree, physical traits are qualified by cultural and economic indicators in order to produce that total image which accords a social identity. . . .

In Barranquilla, Colombia, color is qualified by other social factors, and the term *Negro* confined to the slum-dwellers of the city. In the modern housing developments where no one is to be seen who would not

[4] For example. Robert S. Browne, *Race Relations in International Affairs* (Washington, 1961), p. 22: "South and Central America have in some places developed veritable interracial societies." The qualification is vital.

[5] Juan Comas reviews some of the more scholarly versions of the two views in "Relaciones inter-raciales en America Latina, 1940–60," *Cuadernos del Instituto de Historia, serie antropologica*, No. 12 (Mexico, 1961).

[6] Paez, Morelos, and Alamán looked Negroid; Porfirio, Díaz, Juarez, and Melgarejo looked Indian. This can be verified from contemporary evidence. In modern popular literature and school-books they are sometimes quite literally "white-washed."

qualify as a Negro in the United States, one may be told: "Only white people live here." The definition of *Negro* varies from place to place and, of course, from class to class. A man may be defined as Negro in one place, but simply as *moreno, trigueño, canela,* or even white in another. A man who would be considered Negro in the United States might, by traveling to Mexico, become *moreno* or *prieto*, then *canela* or *trigueño* in Panamá, and end up in Barranquilla white. The definition of *Indian* presents a comparable problem once the word no longer refers to a member of an Indian community. Different places and classes use different criteria.

Skin color is merely one of the indices among physical traits that contribute to a person's total image. It is not necessarily more significant than hair type or shape of eye. The relative evaluation of different physical traits varies. . . .

The system of classification makes what it will of the objective reality of the phenotype. The forces of the social structure utilize the raw material of phenotypical distinctions, building out of it the social statuses into which people are classified.

It has sometimes been said that the difference between Anglo and Latin America is that in the former anyone who has a drop of Negro blood is a Negro, whereas in the latter anyone who has white blood is a white.[7] The first statement is approximately true, but the second is emphatically not so. The concept of "blood" is fundamentally different in the two and has, in the past, varied from one century to another.

In Latin America, a person with non-white physical traits may be classed as white socially. A trace of European physique is, however, quite insufficient in itself to class a person as white. Although Indians with pale skin and European traits or gray hair may be found sporadically throughout Latin America, they are considered to be no less Indian on this account. In any market in the Andes one or two can usually be seen, and the *indio gringo* "(fair-skinned" or "blond" Indian) is a recognized type in parts of northern Peru. There is nothing anomalous in this description. "Indian" is not, in the first place, a physical type but a social status. The Indian is distinguished not by genetic inheritance but by birth in, and therefore membership of, an Indian community and by possession of that community's culture. This is all that is needed for the definition of an Indian, though Indians normally look "Indian." The word *Indian* has, therefore, come to mean "of Indian descent"; it is used of persons who no longer occupy Indian status, but whose physical resemblance to the Indians implies descent from them. Since Indians are the "lowest" or least "civilized" element of the population, the word in this sense means "low class." It can also be used to mean "savage," or "uncivilized," or "bad" in a purely figurative way—equivalent, say, to that of *canaille* in French. *Negro,* on the other hand, denotes a physical type that commonly carries with it the general implication of low class, but culture is usually quite subsidiary to the definition.[8]

Racial status in the United States, defined in terms of "blood" and identified purely by physical appearance, divides the population into two halves within which two parallel systems of class differentiation are recognized. In Latin America, appearance is merely one indicator of social position. It is never sufficient in itself to determine how an individual should be classed. The discrimination imposed on the basis of "color" in the United States has sometimes been called a "caste" system and has been contrasted with class systems. This distinction is impossible in Latin America where color is an ingredient of total social position, not the criterion for distinguishing two racial "castes." A policy of segregation on the basis of color would, therefore, be not merely repugnant to Latin Americans but literally impossible.

Even in Panamá where the bulk of the urban population is Negro and the "oligarchy," as the traditional upper class is called, entirely European, the notion of segregation is repulsive. A member of the Panamanian upper class concluded a bitter

[7] See. for example, Albert Sireau, *Terre d'angoisse et d'espérance* (Paris, 1959), p. 22.

[8] The situation in Panamá, referred to above, is exceptional. It derives from the influx of a large number of persons of different language and culture. Some slight difference in style of speech is attributed to Negroes in certain regions.

criticism of discrimination in the United States with the remark: "After all, it's a matter of luck whether one is born black or white." It remained to be added, of course, that in Panamá it is nevertheless bad luck to be born black and good luck to be born white.

At the time of the race riots in Oxford, Mississippi, Hector Velarde, a distinguished critic, took the occasion to deplore racial discrimination in the United States in an article in a Peruvian newspaper. Why can the North Americans not learn from us the virtue of racial tolerance? he asked. He went on to illustrate his argument with the usage of the word *negrita* as a term of affection. *Negrita de mi alma* was an expression used toward a sweetheart, he said. Indeed he did not exaggerate, for *negrita* and *negra* are both forms of address that imply a certain intimacy or informality (as a diminutive the former carries the implication of a potential sexual interest the latter lacks). Velarde did not mention the Indians (who are very much more numerous in Peru than the Negroes). If he had, it would not have helped his thesis since *Indian* is never used in an equivalent fashion, though *cholo* ("civilized Indian") and *zambo* ("half-caste") are both used as terms of affection among comrades.[9]

The implication of racial equality that he drew from his examples invites precision. Such terms do not find their way into such a context because they are flattering in formal usage, but precisely because they are not. Intimacy is opposed to respect; because these terms are disrespectful, they are used to establish or stress a relationship in which no respect is due. The word *nigger* is used in this way among Negroes in the United States, but only among Negroes. Color has, in fact, the same kind of class connotation in the Negro community as in Latin America. Pale-skinned means upper class. Hence *nigger,* in this context dark-skinned or lower class, implies a relationship that is free of the obligation of mutual respect. Velarde's example, consequently, shows that color is an indicator of class, not a criterion of caste.

[9] The same is true in Ecuador. N. E. Whitten, *Class, Kinship and Power in an Ecuadorian Town* (Stanford, 1965), p. 91.

Those who find no racial discrimination in Latin America take the United States as their model. They point out, correctly, that there is no color bar and that race riots do not occur. (Indian risings are a matter they do not consider.) On the other hand, those who do find racial discrimination in Latin America are concerned with the fact that there exist high degrees of social differentiation that are habitually associated with physical traits and frequently expressed in the idiom of "race." They justify their view by the racial overtones given to social distinctions. In Latin America, these critics are commonly persons of left-wing sympathy who see racial discrimination as a bulwark of class distinction and, evading all nuances, they equate the two. . . . Because there is no color bar but rather a color scale that contributes only partially to the definition of status, they are pushed to an implied definition of race that is worthy of Gobineau. They speak of "racial hypocrisy" to explain why certain people claim a "racial" status to which their phenotype would not entitle them if "race" were really a matter of genes. This "false race-consciousness" is false only by the standards of a theory that would obliterate the historical evolution of the past four hundred years. History may validate these theorists if the Chinese interpretation of Marxist-Leninism acquires authority, and the class struggle, transposed to the international plane, becomes a matter of race.

The contrary opinion is usually held by persons of right-wing views. They regard class distinctions as either unobjectionable, insignificant, or at least inevitable. Once they can cite examples of people of upper-class status who show marked traces of non-European descent, they are satisfied that there is no racial discrimination in their country. (This conviction accords with the liberality of their nature and the official creed of their nation.) They are content that there is no problem if there is no "discrimination" as in the United States.

In the first case, the distinctiveness of class and color must be denied; in the second, the association between the two. The first theory ignores the individual instance; only the statistical aspect counts. The exception is evaded lest it disprove the rule. The second theory takes as significant only the chosen individual instance, overlooking the existence of a statistical norm. Indeed, no one is boycotted on account of his phenotype if his class standing is secured by the other criteria that define high status. In such a case, infrequent as it may be in Panamá, color may properly be said to be a matter of luck in the sense that it is a contingency that carries little of the weight of social definition. Economic power, culture, and community are what count.

The disapproval that Latin American visitors to the United States feel of the segregation they find there is not unconnected with the disrespectful attitude they are likely to inspire as Spanish speakers. They know that as Hispanics they are judged socially inferior in many places. Visitors from the United States, on the other hand, are often highly critical of the treatment the Indians of Latin America receive. This strikes them as much more reprehensible than the treatment of the Negroes in their own country, who have indeed much greater opportunities to improve their economic position and who, as domestic servants, are treated with more courtesy and consideration by their employers than the Indians of Latin America —a fact not unconnected with the shortage of domestic servants in the United States. Moreover, the treatment of Indians appears all the less justifiable to these visitors because Indians are not the object of discrimination throughout the greater part of North America.

Thus, comfortably blinkered by the assumptions of their own culture, each nation sees the mote in the other's eye.

In the United States one does sometimes find strong sentiments of hostility toward Indians in areas surrounding their communities; the same is sometimes true in Latin America of the Negroes (however they happen to be defined there). If Indians are not generally subject to discrimination in the United States nor Negroes in Latin America, it is in the first place due to their numerical weakness. In both countries, they pose local, not national, problems. There is roughly one Indian to fifty Negroes in the United States; in Latin America, the inverse disproportion would be greater even if one were to include only those recognized as Negro. Such a comparison can be taken no further than this, however, since the nature of social distinctions is different in the two lands.

The Indian's predicament in Latin America can be likened to that of the Negro in the United States in only one way: Both provide a major national problem at the present time. There the resemblance stops. Not only is the nature of race relations fundamentally different in the societies that evolved from the English and Spanish colonies, but Indians and Negroes are different in their physical appearance and cultural origins. They are different above all in their place within the structure of the two societies, and have been so from the very beginning of colonial times. The Indians were the original inhabitants of the land; their incorporation or their refusal to be incorporated into colonial society hinged on the existence of Indian communities with a separate culture and a separate identity. The Negroes came in servile status and were marketed as chattel to the industrialized producers of sugar and metals. Cut off from their fellows, they soon lost their language and their original culture and became an integral part of colonial society.[10]

The Negro's status was within colonial society. The Indian's was not. To the extent that the Indian abandoned his Indian community and changed his culture, he lost his Indian identity. While the status of Negro refers to phenotype and attaches to individuals, Indian status refers to culture and attaches to a collectivity. One might speak of individual versus collective status, with all that these imply in terms of social structure. Consequently, while phenotypical differences are irrelevant to the definition of the Indian—hence the *indio gringo*—they

[10] This loss of language and culture does not hold for parts of the West Indies and Brazil. Aguirre Beltran maintains that elements of African culture have survived in Mexico. This is true in the case of certain details of material culture and musical style, though it might be more exact to call these Caribbean rather than African. In any case, they have long since ceased to be recognized as such. See, Aguirre Beltran, *Gonzalo: La Poblacion Negra de Mexico, 1519–1810* (Mexico, 1946), p. 96.

have importance in according an individual status once he becomes "civilized." They establish a presumption as to descent, and this is an ingredient of class status. Paradoxically, the genetic background is important only in social distinctions between persons who are recognized as belonging to the same "non-Indian" race; not in the distinction between them and the Indians. "Race" is a matter of culture and community, not of genes, though class is connected with genes.

The problems of race relations in North America and Latin America are, therefore, fundamentally different. One concerns the assimilation of all ethnic groups into a single society; the other, the status distinction between persons who have been assimilated for hundreds of years but who are still distinguished socially by their appearance. The two are comparable only at the highest level of abstraction. One may wonder, therefore, whether the word *caste,* which is so often used in reference to the status distinction between Indians and *mestizos* (or *ladinos*) in Latin American society is not something of a misnomer. It carries quite different implications in Latin as opposed to North America. It would appear that it comes into the sociological literature about Latin America on the basis of several different and all equally false assumptions which will be dealt with elsewhere.

While the value of color is somewhat similar within the Negro community of the United States and the Hispanic section of Latin America, the Negro community is separated by a *caste* distinction from a socially superior element defined by phenotype; the Hispanic population of Latin America is distinguished by language and customs, beliefs and values and habitat from an element it regards as inferior, which does not participate in the same social system and, for the most part, far from wishing to be integrated into it, desires only to be rid of the *mestizos* physically. For this reason, the aims of Indian rebellions are the opposite of the aims of race riots. The former would like to separate once and for all the two ethnic elements; the latter are inspired by the resentment at the existence of a separation. Indians rebel to drive the intruders out of the countryside; Negroes riot in towns when they are not accorded full civic privileges.

The ethnic statuses of modern Latin America vary in number from the simple division into Indian and *mestizo* found in Mexico north of the Isthmus to the four tiers of highland Peru which include *cholos* and *blancos:* (*indio, cholo, mestizo, blanco*). These "social races" have much in common with the class distinctions of stratified societies. Woodrow Borah has even maintained that the ethnic distinction in Mexico is no more in essence than a matter of social class. This view raises a further problem in those areas where a regional ethnic consciousness emerges, for example among the Tlascalans, Isthmus Zapotecs, and the wealthy, educated Indians of Quetzaltenango in Guatemala.

Admitting that the class structure of Latin America carries ethnic overtones, how is this structure affected by class differences being thought about largely in the idiom of "race"? Such a view implies that classes are different in their essential nature. If the concept of "social race" teaches us to think about race in terms of social structure, we should also have a concept of "ethnic class" to remind us that class systems no longer function in the same way once class has phenotypical associations. Processes of selection come into operation that cannot exist in a homogeneous population however it is stratified.

This observation leads to a conclusion that does not altogether accord with that of Professor Wagley[11] who states: "At least, theoretically, it is only a question of time until such populations may be entirely classed as mestizo by social race and social differentiation will be entirely in terms of socioeconomic classes."[12]

In terms of his thesis continued racial intermixture produces in Latin America, unlike North America, a blurring of the

[11] If I disagree with Professor Wagley ultimately with regard to the prospects of the future (about which wise anthropologists refrain from speculating), I do not wish to obscure my debt to Professor Wagley's thinking on this subject nor to deny homage to his admirable essay. But I would not write about this subject at all if I did not think there remains something more to be said.

[12] Wagley, "On the Concept of Social Race in the Americas," p. 540.

distinctions among different "social races." This would be true enough, if time could be trusted to produce phenotypical homogeneity, but it ceases to be so once one introduces the notion of selection into the theory. The absence of a bar on intermarriage does not necessarily produce homogeneity.

Distinctions of status are not always exhibited in the same ways. The castes of India are held apart by prohibitions on physical contact and commensality, and by endogamy. Feudal Europe accorded no importance to the first two and little to the third. The division of labor implied by any social distinction can bring people into either direct co-operation or segregation, depending upon the range of their ties and the basis of their "complementarity." If their status difference is assured in one way, it may prove indifferent to any other basis of distinction. For this reason the intimacy to which servants were admitted by their masters was greater in an earlier age when social distinctions were more clear-cut.

Physical differences can never be obliterated, but whether they, rather than cultural or social differences, are regarded as significant is a matter each social system decides for itself. It is for this reason that the value accorded to physical appearance varies so greatly from place to place and class to class in Latin America. But the significance of phenotype also varies greatly according to context. Political or commercial alliances are not the same as alliances through marriage. Their products are of a different order. Profits are colorless, children are not. Hence, phenotype may not matter in commercial dealings, but it is never more important than in marriage.

In Latin America today the grandchildren of a rich man who looks Indian or Negroid always appear much more European than he is himself. Color is an ingredient, not a determinant of class. It can, therefore, be traded for the other ingredients. It is not something that can be altered in the individual's life, but it is something that can be put right in the next generation. For this reason, the wives of the well-to-do tend to look more European than their husbands. In the lower classes, paler children are sometimes favored at the expense of their more swarthy siblings; their potential for social mobility is greater.

Individual motivations are ordered to produce conformity with an ideal image of ethnic class. This tends to reinforce the original image. Moreover, demographical factors reinforce this conformity in other ways—through the immigration of Europeans into Latin America and the existence of a pool of unassimilated Indians on the land. Indians are constantly abandoning their Indian identity and becoming integrated into the nation. This process is not unconnected with the current flight to the cities, for you lose Indian status once you settle in the city.[13] The result is a continual influx of persons of mainly Indian physique into the proletariat. At the same time, the immigration of Europeans into these countries has been very considerable in the last two decades, and these Europeans have almost all been absorbed into the upper classes. For demographic reasons, the correlation between class and color is increasing rather than diminishing.

Moreover, the significance of this correlation is also increasing under modern conditions. (It would be rash to say that it will go on increasing in the future, for the structure itself may well change to offset this effect.) The expansion of the open society at the expense of the local community changes the criteria whereby people are defined socially. Where known descent establishes status, color may carry little of the weight of social definition, but the descent must be known. It must be known whose child you are if you are to inherit the status of your father. If you have exchanged your local community for the big city, your descent becomes a matter of conjecture; you can no longer be respected because of your birth despite your Indian features. If you look Indian, it will be concluded that you were born of Indian parents. Thus, in the open society, appearance takes over the function of descent in allocating social status. In a world in flux, the fact that appearance cannot be dissimulated recommends it

[13] Only exceptionally, as in the Isthmus of Tehuantepec or Quetzaltenango, can a man become integrated while retaining an Indian (or is it a pseudo-Indian?) identity. Then region replaces community as the defining unit.

above all other indicators. Clothing, speech, and culture are losing force as indicators of status in the context of expanding cities, but color is becoming ever more crucial.

Although these same conditions might create an increase in social mobility that would tend to reduce the phenotypical correlation of class, it appears that the opposite is happening today. If the classification into social races is losing its precision, the ethnic aspect of class is coming to have increased importance. The social structure is changing and with it the criteria of social classification. Under modern industrial conditions, much of Latin America is moving from the systems of social race that flourished in the communities of yesterday to a system of ethnic class adapted to the requirements of the open society of tomorrow.

# THE NEGRO AMERICAN—COMMUNITY AND CLASS REALITIES: THE ORDEAL OF CHANGE

## *G. Franklin Edwards*

One of the paradoxes of American life is that though the Negro is an old-line American he is not yet fully American. His presence in this country antedates that of most immigrant groups, but his career and community life are greatly different from those of immigrants from northern and southern Europe. In terms of the basic socialization processes and the community contexts in which they occur, differences between the Negro and these immigrant groups, including the most recent large-scale arrivals, the Puerto Ricans, are apparent.

Immigrant groups from Europe have followed a somewhat typical process as they moved into the main stream of American life. Most members of these groups entered the work force at the bottom of the economic ladder, as small farmers and as unskilled, semiskilled, and service workers. They lived initially among fellow immigrants in small village communities or in poorer city neighborhoods in which communal institutions helped cushion the cultural shock induced by the differences between life in their countries of origin and life in the United States. Family, church, the foreign language press, and mutual aid organizations helped in the adjustment process. Members of the second and succeeding generations acquired increasing amounts of education and the skills necessary to take advantage of available opportunities; eventually the Americanization process was fairly complete. . . .

In contrast to the pattern of immigrant groups, the Negro has remained socially and morally isolated from the American society. At no time in the almost three and a half centuries of his history in this country has he been "counted in." His caste-like position is owing more to restraints from without than to any centripetal force serving to keep him separated from other groups. He has lived, according to E. Franklin Frazier's characterization, as "a nation within a nation."[1] Robin Williams recently has referred to the general Negro community as "a world in the shadow,"[2] and James Silver, in describing an extreme instance of a local community's exclusion of Negroes, has referred to the "closed society."[3]

One basic difference between the Negro and these immigrant groups is that the former served for nearly two centuries as slaves. Although succeeding generations of Negroes acquired increased amounts of education after the Emancipation, access to opportunities commensurate with formal training often was denied because of color. The failure to learn certain basic skills to

*Daedalus*, "Community and Class Realities: The Ordeal of Change," by G. Franklin Edwards, Winter, 1966. Reprinted by permission of the author, the publisher, and the American Academy of Arts and Sciences.

[1] E. Franklin Frazier, *Black Bourgeoisie* (New York, 1957), p. 15.

[2] Robin M. Williams, Jr., *Strangers Next Door* (New York, 1964), p. 252.

[3] James W. Silver, *Mississippi: The Closed Society* (New York, 1963), p. 164.

qualify for jobs in the world of work placed serious limitations upon the horizontal and social mobility experienced by members of the group. As a matter of fact, the social mobility of Negroes up to the present has been determined more by conditions within the Negro community than by those of the broader society. The number and distribution of Negroes within the professions, for example, have been related more directly to the needs of the Negro community for certain types of services than to the demands of the broader society.[4] It is for this reason that clergymen and teachers, functionaries required by the segregated Negro community, have represented at least one-half of all Negro professional persons at any given period.

The segregation of Negroes from the main stream of American life has produced institutional patterns and behavior which have a bearing upon contemporary efforts to eliminate inequalities between the two major racial groups. The behaviors are expressed as deviations of Negroes from many normative patterns of American life and suggest something of the magnitude of the differentials which must be dealt with if reconciliation, rather than further alienation, is to be achieved.

The contrasts in background experiences between the Negro and immigrant groups raise the fundamental question of whether, given the promise of recent changes, the Negro will now be integrated into American society in much the same manner as have these other groups. Any strict analogy between the future course of the Negro's relationship to American society and the processes which occurred in the experiences of immigrant groups, however, is subject to serious limitations and error.

The long history of oppression has profoundly affected the Negro's self-esteem. The fears, suspicions and feelings of inadequacy generated in the Negro by his subordinate status are not duplicated in the experiences of immigrant groups. Moreover, color and other physical traits distinguish the Negro sharply from other groups in the society. In the past these characteristics were taken as physical stigmata which reinforced negative attitudes toward the Negro. Sharp physical differences were not present to complicate the relationships of immigrants to American society, although differences in this regard can be observed between the northern Europeans, on the one hand, and southern Europeans and Orientals, on the other. . . .

It should be observed that significant advancement in the status of the Negro comes at a time when economic conditions are quite different from those faced by immigrant groups. The great influx of immigrants came at a time when there was a market for agricultural labor and unskilled work and mobility through these avenues was still possible. The Negro today has been displaced from the farm and must now compete for work in an urban market which requires a somewhat higher degree of education and technical skill than was the case a half century ago. Given the present educational and occupational inadequacies of a large segment of the Negro population, the task of overcoming these deficiencies is formidable.

While it is clear that further changes in the status of the Negro will occur in the years ahead, moving the Negro nearer to equality with other Americans, the processes by which this will be achieved are certain to be difficult and tortuous. The remainder of this essay is an elaboration of this viewpoint.

Foremost among the indicators of the social isolation of Negroes is the Negro ghetto. It represents at once the restrictions placed upon the living space of the Negro minority and, as Kenneth Clark recently has pointed out, a way of life with a peculiar institutional patterning and psychological consequences.[5] Unlike most immigrant ghettos, which show a tendency to break up, the Negro ghetto, especially in Northern cities, has become more dense. . . .

The growing awareness of the limitations of life in the ghetto, as a result of the influence of mass media, increased physical mobility, and better education, has played a vital part in precipitating the "Negro Revolution." The mass demonstrations for equality of treatment in places of public

[4] G. Franklin Edwards, *The Negro Professional Class* (Chicago, 1959), pp. 23–26.

[5] Kenneth Clark, *Dark Ghetto* (New York, 1965), pp. 63–80.

accommodations, for access to better quality schools, for equal employment opportunities and voting rights are thought of as efforts by Negroes to achieve first-class citizenship. In another sense, they are efforts to overcome the barriers which have isolated Negroes from aspects of American life.

The difficulty of overcoming the problems created by the physical fact of the ghetto is indicated by attempts to improve the quality of education of schools in slum areas. In our large metropolitan cities, because of the segregation in housing and the traditional neighborhood concept of school attendance, a disproportionate number of schools, particularly at the elementary level, becomes predominantly Negro or predominantly white, with the Negro schools being inferior. Opposing theories for dealing with this situation, generally regarded as undesirable, have generated serious community conflicts. There are those who feel that the efforts should be concentrated upon improving the quality of education in these depressed areas by larger allocations for plant improvement, remedial work, new curricula, and better trained teachers. Other students of the problem contend that substantial improvement of slum schools cannot be achieved until such schools lose their predominantly Negro or predominantly white character. It becomes necessary in the thinking of the protagonists of this latter view to develop methods for overcoming racial imbalances in the schools. While a variety of techniques have been proposed, each has generated rather serious opposition. It is patent that this problem, one of the serious concerns of the leaders of the Negro Revolution largely because it is tied to segregation in housing, will not be easily solved.

. . . The ghetto has not only restricted the interaction of Negroes with other members of the society, and hence symbolized the isolation under which Negroes have lived; but it has also been a primary force in the generation and persistence of atypical institutional patterns which are viewed as dysfunctional in any effort at reconciliation. Doubtless the foremost of these institutions is the Negro family which, because of historical circumstances connected with slavery and the isolated conditions under which Negroes have lived in both urban and rural areas, is characterized by rather significant variations from the dominant American family pattern. It is not so much the differences *per se,* or any mere deviation of Negro family characteristics from those of white middle-class families, but the variations in structural and interactional features known to be desirable in family living which become causes of concern.

The most salient feature of Negro family life which captures the attention of those concerned with integration of Negroes into American life is the degree of disorganization represented by structural breakdown. In only three-quarters of all Negro families, as compared with approximately nine-tenths of all white families, were both spouses present. One Negro family in five (21 per cent) was headed by a female and 5 per cent had only the male head present. Thus one Negro family in four, as compared with one white family in ten, was headed by a single parent. This differential in the percentage of families headed by one parent accounts in part for the fact that in 1960 only one-third of Negro children under eighteen years of age, as compared with one in ten white children of comparable age, lived in families in which only one parent was present.

The assumption underlying the desirability of family unity—the presence of both spouses—is that on balance the economic, social, and affectual roles may be best discharged when both mates are present in the home. Divorce, desertion, and separation follow the generation and expression of tensions which, even before rupture occurs, reduce the effectiveness with which the mates can discharge the duties and obligations of family life, as well as deny the satisfactions derived from the intimate sharing of experiences and attainments of goals. In essence, the organized and unified family becomes at once a matrix for the personal satisfaction of the marital partners and for the protection, proper socialization, and well-being of their children. This is not to deny that the basic goals of family life, regarding child-rearing and other functions, may not be achieved by the single-parent family. Given the complexities of modern urban life and the established normative values around which the modern family is organized, however, the discharge of family functions may best be achieved when the family is unified.

In analyzing the statistics on the Negro family one becomes aware that the instability of the Negro family unit is greater than is represented by statistics on the percentages of males and females enumerated as widowed or divorced. In 1960, 15 per cent of all Negro males and 20 per cent of all Negro females, though enumerated by the Census as married, were living apart from their mates. The percentage of Negro males separated from their mates is four times as large as the comparable percentage for white males, and for Negro females four and one-half times as large as for white females.

The instability of Negro family life is explained only in part by the historical conditioning of attitudes toward family life, beginning with slavery, when strong family ties were not encouraged and Negroes, as Elkins has suggested, were made dependent upon whites.[6] The phenomenon arises also from forces of contemporary American life which place limits upon the possibility of successful family organization. These are reflected in the statistics on characteristics of the heads of Negro families.

As reported by the last Census, approximately one-half, 48.5 per cent, of the heads of nonwhite (mainly Negro) families had not finished elementary school. Even in urban areas where access to educational opportunities is somewhat greater and school-attendance laws somewhat better enforced than in rural farm and nonfarm areas, two out of five nonwhite family heads failed to reach the last year of elementary school. Of nonwhite heads living in rural nonfarm and rural farm areas, 70 and 80 per cent, respectively, had failed to attain this level of schooling.[7] The low level of educational achievement for such a large proportion of nonwhite family heads has obvious implications for the cultural life to which the Negro child is exposed in the home and doubtless for the type of motivation the child receives for achievement in school. It also is related to the labor-force participation and income of nonwhites.

In an economy in which automation is rapidly introducing changes in the demand for certain types of labor, the heads of nonwhite families were disproportionately represented in those occupational categories in which fewer workers are required and monetary returns are small. Only 13 per cent of all nonwhite family heads, as compared with 40 per cent of white heads, were in professional, managerial, and clerical occupations for which labor demands are increasing. One in five white heads, but only one in ten among nonwhite, was a skilled worker. Thus, one in four nonwhite heads, as compared with three in five white, were white-collar and skilled workers.[8] The heavier identification with semiskilled and unskilled work accounts in part for the nonwhite employment rate being twice as large as the comparable rate of whites and for greater underemployment among nonwhites.

The type of job and both underemployment and unemployment influence the relatively low income of nonwhite family heads. The median nonwhite family income of $3,465 in 1963 was only approximately 53 per cent of the white family income of $6,548. More than two-fifths of all nonwhite families (41 per cent) earned less than $3,000 in 1963, which placed them at the poverty level, and only one in twenty earned $10,000 or more in the same year.[9] It is significant to note, in line with our previous discussion regarding the desirability of family closure—both parents in the home—that in 1959 families in which both husband and wife were present in the home had a median income of $3,633 as compared with a median of $1,734 for families having a female head.[10]

[6] Stanley Elkins, *Slavery* (Chicago, 1959), pp. 115–133.

[7] The statistics in this section are taken from G. Franklin Edwards, "Marriage and Family Life Among Negroes," *The Journal of Negro Education*, Vol. 32 (Fall 1963), pp. 451–465.

[8] *Ibid.*, p. 463.

[9] Current Population Reports, "Income of Families and Persons in the United States: 1963," Series P-60, No. 43 (Washington, D.C., 1964), Table 1, p. 21.

[10] *U.S. Census of Population: 1960, U.S. Summary,* Detailed Characteristics, Final Report PC(1)-ID (Washington, D.C., 1963), Tables 224 and 225, pp. 594–603.

The problems of the Negro family, then, in terms of its instability and the associated phenomena of crime, delinquency, school dropouts, high morbidity and mortality are related to a complex of interwoven factors, of which level of educational attainment and income are important components. . . .

A definitive study by Hylan Lewis of child-rearing practices among low-income Negro families in the District of Columbia reveals that there is, indeed, still much to be learned about the operating dynamics and underlying causes of disorganization among such units.[11] What often is accepted as knowledge about these families is in fact mythology. It is noted, in the first instance, that these families are not homogeneous as regards their organization, functioning, and ambitions for their children. In many of them considerable strength is to be noted, but the exigencies of daily living often deny the achievement of the parents' most ambitious plans. Though parents set training and discipline goals for their children, these are often undermined by influences beyond their power, and the actual control over their children may be lost as early as the fifth or sixth year.

Investigation reveals that many of these parents, particularly the mothers, are warm, human, and concerned individuals who, despite deprivation and trouble, are persistent in their desires to have their children become respectable and productive citizens and in their willingness to sacrifice for them. The picture contrasts with the common belief that in an overwhelming majority of low-income families parents reject their children and are hostile to them.

Lewis' study raises questions regarding assigned reasons for alleged male irresponsibility toward family obligations and the degree of family concern with pregnancy out of wedlock and illegitimate births. There does appear to be a greater degree of concern by the male regarding his responsibilities and by family members regarding the sexual behavior of their offspring than is commonly recognized. What in fact emerges is that the behavior of these lower-income families is a practical response to untoward circumstances which undermine the well-intentioned, but often unattainable, goals of these units.

The major problems of the Negro family are experienced in urban areas where more than 70 per cent of such families now live. There has been a heavy migration during the past twenty-five years from farms and small towns to large metropolitan areas. The limited extent to which many of these families can cope with the demands of urban life, given the low educational level and obsolescent skills of the adults, raises serious questions for the American society as well as for the families themselves. The War on Poverty, youth opportunity programs, Medicare and other changes in our social security program are certain to exercise some influences in ameliorating existing conditions. But the deep-seated nature of many of those conditions and the personality damage they have produced, as expressed in feelings of powerlessness, hopelessness, and forms of anti-social conduct, give rise to the prediction that no easy solution to problems of the Negro family may be found. This is especially true of those "hard core" or multi-problem families in many of which at least two generations have been dependent on public assistance programs. Present efforts to focus upon the young, as evidenced in Project Head Start and programs for youth, on the assumption that this population is most amenable to change, are based upon sound theory. There remains, however, the complex problem of improving the skills and enhancing the self-esteem of the adult members whose personalities are crystallized and whose levels of expectation have been shaped under an entirely different set of conditions. What is apparent is that the problems of the Negro family are intimately tied to those of the larger community.

The elimination of many of these difficulties depends upon a commitment to invest a great deal more of our resources in improving educational and social services, including more effective family limitation programs.

. . . . . . . . . . . . . . . . . . . . . . . . . . . . . . . . .

[11] Lewis' study, conducted over a period of five years, is now being prepared for publication. The references in this paper were taken from various reports which the investigator made available to the writer.

The disabilities of the Negro family discussed in the preceding paragraphs are most characteristic of low-income units. Not all Negro families are affected by inadequate income, education, and employment opportunities, and many of them do not lack strong family traditions. There is a considerable differentiation within the Negro community in terms of status groups and social classes.

E. Franklin Frazier observed that as late as World War I the Negro middle class was composed "principally of teachers, doctors, preachers, trusted persons in personal service, government employees, and a few business men."[12] He stated further that:

> This group was distinguished from the rest of the Negro population not so much by economic factors as by social factors. Family affiliation and education to a less degree were as important as income. Moreover, while it exhibited many middle-class features such as its emphasis on morality, it also possessed characteristics of an upper class or aristocracy.[13]

The urbanization of the Negro population, beginning with World War I and continuing to the present, resulted in the formation of large ghettos in Northern and Southern cities and provided the condition for greater occupational differentiation within the Negro community. The differentiation was more pronounced in Northern communities where Negroes had a substantially greater opportunity to enter clerical and technical occupations than was true in Southern cities, and where the large population base provided economic support for a sizable corps of professional functionaries. Education and income became more important than social distinctions in determining class membership.

The Negro middle class today includes a still relatively small, but expanding, number of persons. If occupation is used as a criterion for determining membership and those in professional and technical, clerical, sales, and skilled occupations are included, only approximately 26 per cent of all nonwhite workers belong to the middle class. White workers in these above-mentioned categories represent 64 per cent of all whites in the labor force.[14] The contrast between the two occupational structures is further indicated by the fact that the percentage of white workers, taken as a proportion of all white workers, is twice as large as the comparable percentage of nonwhite workers in professional and kindred occupations, and in clerical and skilled work; four times as large in managerial occupations; and three times as large in the sales category.

In none of the specific occupational categories associated with the middle class did nonwhite male workers achieve parity with white males in median income. The nearest approximation to parity in 1959 was in clerical and kindred occupations in which the nonwhite male median earnings of $4,072 was approximately 85 per cent of the white male median of $4,785. In none of the other categories did nonwhite male workers receive so much as 70 per cent of the median income of white males in the category.[15]

The expansion of the Negro middle class has been most marked by accretion of persons in professional, technical, clerical, and sales occupations. This expansion by approximately 300,000 persons since 1940 has been influenced in part by government policy which prohibits those business firms holding contracts with the federal government from discriminating against workers on the basis of race, religion, creed, or national origin. In engineering, architecture, and the natural sciences, occupations oriented to the wider world of work rather than to the Negro community, the increases among Negroes, though small in absolute numbers, have been rather dramatic. Between 1950 and 1960, there was a three-fold increase in the number of Negro engineers. The number of Negro architects increased by 72 per cent, and the number of natural scientists by 77 per cent.[16] This expansion

[12] E. Franklin Frazier, "The New Negro," in *The New Negro Thirty Years Afterward* (Washington, D.C., 1955), p. 26.

[13] *Ibid.*

[14] Computed from U.S. Bureau of the Census, *U.S. Census of Population: 1960, U.S. Summary,* Detailed Characteristics, Final Report PC (1)-ID, Table 208.

[15] *Ibid.*

[16] Computed from *U.S. Census of Population: 1940,* Vol. II, *Characteristics of the Population,* Part 1, *U.S. Summary,* Table 128, p. 278; and *U.S. Census of Population: 1960,* Vol. I, *Characteristics of the Population,* Part 1, *U.S. Summary,* Table 205, p. 544.

comes at the end of a half century in which Negroes could hardly expect to earn a living in these fields and thus were not encouraged to prepare for entering them.

The number of Negroes in medicine, dentistry, and law, whose services traditionally have been oriented to the Negro community, has begun to increase rather significantly. During the 1950's, physicians increased by 14 per cent, dentists by 31 per cent, and lawyers by 43 per cent.[17] More substantial fellowship and scholarship aid, ability to pay for professional education, as well as the opening of the segregated professional schools in the Southern states, have contributed to this result.

It is not only the increase in number of these professionals which deserves attention; the improved opportunities for advanced training and learning experiences are also of importance. On the basis of increased opportunities for internships and residency training, the number of Negro physicians who became diplomates of medical specialty boards increased from 92 in 1947 to 377 in 1959.[18] Negro physicians, lawyers, and dentists are admitted today to membership in local societies of national professional organizations in larger numbers and enjoy the privileges these societies provide for continued professional growth.

It should be remembered, however, that these gains, while significant in terms of what has occurred in Negro life heretofore, are relatively small. The ratios of the actual to expected numbers of Negroes in middle-class occupations, as measured by the total labor force distribution, are extremely small.[19]

The differences between Negro and white community life cannot be measured solely by variations in income, occupation, education, and other objective indicators. In assessing the differences, it is important to recognize that the Negro class structure and institutions have emerged in response to segregation and represent adjustments to the isolation under which Negroes have lived. The meaning of relationships within the community and the values placed upon them must be considered.

Frazier has observed, for example, that in the absence of a true upper class based upon old family ties and wealth, the Negro middle class simulates the behavior of the white upper class without possessing the fundamental bases upon which such behavior rests.[20] Moreover, segregation has provided a monopoly for many Negroes in business and the professions and has introduced, in many cases, differential standards of performance. This has important consequences for any consideration of desegregation, for those who enjoy a vested interest in the segregated community are not likely to welcome competition from the broader community. The Negro church represents an extreme instance of vested interest in the Negro community and, at the same time, is the most important institution giving expression to the Negro masses. For this reason no degree of acceptance of Negroes by white churches is likely to bring about the dissolution of Negro churches.[21]

The Negro community doubtless will be the source of social life of Negroes for some time into the future. Sororities, fraternities, clubs, and other organizations will continue to serve a meaningful function. The acceptance by whites of Negroes as fellow workers often bears little relationship to their willingness to share social experiences with them outside the plant or office or to have them as neighbors.

The importance of the Negro community as a source of social life is indicated by the fact that, though the majority of the members of a Negro professional society felt that its members should identify with the local chapter of the national organization representing the profession when the opportunity became available, one-quarter had some reservation about joining and another

[17] *Ibid.*

[18] From data supplied the writer by W. Montague Cobb, M.D., editor of the *Journal of the National Medical Association.*

[19] Ratios for many of these occupations are supplied in Leonard Broom and Norval Glenn, *Transformation of the Negro American* (New York, 1965), Table 5, pp. 112–113.

[20] This is the thesis of E. Franklin Frazier, *Black Bourgeoisie* (Chicago, 1957). See, especially, pp. 195–212. See, also, Frazier, "Human, All too Human," *Survey Graphic:* twelfth Calling America Number (January 1947), pp. 74–75, 99–100.

[21] E. Franklin Frazier, "Desegregation as a Social Process," in Arnold Rose (ed.), *Human Behavior and Social Processes* (Boston, 1962), p. 619.

5 per cent were opposed to joining. The underlying reasons for reservations to becoming members of the formerly white organization were that, though Negroes may be accepted as professional colleagues, they would not be treated as social equals and that opportunities for leadership roles would be lost if the Negro association were dissolved.[22] What is patently indicated is that most members thought they should have the *right* to membership in the local chapter of the national organization, but they should retain their own association for social and professional reasons.

Despite the effort to conserve the conceived advantages of the Negro community, the larger social forces are introducing changes. Already the small Negro entrepreneurial group is threatened by these forces. Speaking to a group of Negro businessmen in Detroit, the Assistant Secretary of Commerce for Economic Affairs referred to the disappearance of the monopoly Negroes formerly held in certain businesses.[23] The impact of desegregation is being felt, he said, in the Negro market, for, as the income of Negro consumers expands, white businessmen become more conscious of the Negro's purchasing power. To this end they have added a cadre of professional Negro salesmen to their payrolls for the specific purpose of developing the Negro market. The success of this undertaking is indicated by the fact that many of the employed Negroes have risen to top executive posts in these organizations. Moreover, Negroes have begun to buy in increasing amounts from shopping centers serving the Negro community and have begun to patronize places of public accommodations other than those traditionally operated by Negroes. This change in consumer behavior represents a steady and gradual erosion of the position of the Negro businessman. The cruelest blow of all, the Assistant Secretary stated, is that "the large life insurance companies serving the market at large are bidding away Negro life insurance salesmen at an increasing rate."[24] These and other changes are certain to influence the structure of the Negro community.

## THE ORDEAL OF CHANGE

From observing current developments in race relations and the operation of the larger social forces in our society, it is evident that several basic conditions operate to influence the pattern and pace at which change is occurring. These provide some insight into what may be expected in the future in regard to the general status of the Negro minority; they document the theory of slow and gradual change for some time to come in most areas and somewhat more rapid change in others.

A first consideration, not prominently mentioned heretofore, is the opposition to change by segments of the white community. Beginning with the school desegregation decision, there has been a mobilization of white community efforts to prevent the attainment of desegregation in many aspects of community life. This opposition has taken a variety of forms: the closing of schools, violence visited upon Negroes, intimidation of Negroes and threats to their job security, the rise of some hate groups—such as Citizens' Councils and Night Riders—and the strengthening of others—such as the Ku Klux Klan—the resurrection of racial ideologies having the purpose of establishing the inferiority of the Negro, and a variety of other techniques designed to slow the desegregation process.[25]

What is important in this connection is that many of the organizations connected with the opposition have had the support, if not the leadership, of prominent persons in the power structure; many governors, mayors, legislators, and prominent businessmen have all given support to the resistance efforts, owing to political and economic expediency, if not to personal sentiment.

[22] Martha Coffee, "A Study of a Professional Association and Racial Integration," unpublished Master's Thesis, Department of Sociology, Howard University, Washington, D.C., 1953.

[23] "Desegregation and the Negro Middle Class," remarks of Dr. Andrew F. Brimmer, Assistant Secretary of Commerce for Economic Affairs, Detroit, Michigan, July 16, 1965.

[24] *Ibid.*

[25] A good discussion of these hate groups is given in James W. Vander Zanden, *Race Relations in Transition: The Segregation Crisis in the South* (New York, 1965), pp. 25–54. See, also, Arnold Forster and Benjamin Epstein, *Report on the Ku Klux Klan* (New York, 1965).

Moreover, persons with some claim to scientific respectability in the academic community have contributed to the questioning of whether differentials between Negroes and whites stem from the former's disadvantaged community life or from the Negro's innate biological inferiority.[26] . . .

A second important force affecting change is inherent in the nature of the phenomenon itself, especially the contribution made by the accumulated disabilities of the Negro family, and in individuals in terms of inadequate education, job skills, housing, patterns of dependency, and low self-esteem. The advancement toward a more equalitarian society depends upon how fully these disabilities can be overcome or eliminated. Any analysis must consider the generational problem, for the extent to which the education and job skills of many adult family heads—those over forty-five, for example—can be improved is problematic.

A stronger basis of hope rests with the generation which begins school under improved educational conditions and whose levels of aspiration will be shaped by a social context which varies considerably from that of the past half century, and may be expected to vary even more in the future. But even under the most favorable circumstances, the improvement of educational qualifications of Negroes to a position of parity with those of whites, an essential factor for job equality, may not be easily achieved. One prominent sociologist on the basis of statistical calculations concluded:

> Whatever the future may hold with respect to the on-coming cohorts of young Negroes, the performance to date, together with the postulate that educational attainment is a "background" characteristic [for employment], enables us to make a most important prediction: the disparity between white and nonwhite levels of education attainment in the general population can hardly disappear in less than three-quarters of a century. Even if Negroes in their teens were to begin immediately to match the educational attainment of white children, with this equalization persisting indefinitely, we shall have to wait fifty years for the last of the cohorts manifesting race differentials to reach retirement age.[27]

The achievement of educational and occupational equality is far more difficult to attain than equal treatment in public accommodations. Many civil rights leaders recognize this and, now that the public accommodations struggle has been successful, consider that the movement has entered a new and much tougher phase. . . .

The most significant influence in determining the pattern and pace of race relations changes is the federal government. The early court decisions, particularly in the area of public accommodations, orders by the executive, and recent legislation by the Congress have had salutary effects in altering disability-producing conditions. With more rigorous enforcement, they are likely to have an even more important influence in the future. The Civil Rights Act of 1964 provides a wedge for undermining, or at least neutralizing, much of the support for denying the constitutional rights of Negroes. . . . This result, along with the greater political consciousness of Negroes throughout the country, is certain to improve the power position of the group and result in the election of large numbers of Negroes to public office.[28]

The change in the position of the government in respect to the status of Negroes results from the altered position of this country in world affairs since the end of World War II and to a substantial shift in public opinion regarding the position of the Negro during that period. It is important, therefore, to view contemporary changes as a part of broader social movements toward improved welfare for the disadvantaged within the country and in the world. These broad forces tend to override resistances, but they are subject to

[26] See the following: Wesley C. George, *The Biology of the Race Problem* (A report prepared by commission of the Governor of Alabama, 1962); and Dwight J. Ingle, "Racial Differences and the Future," *Science*, Vol. 146 (October 16, 1964), pp. 375–379.

[27] Otis Dudley Duncan, "Population Trends, Mobility and Social Change," a paper prepared for the Seminar on Dimensions of American Society, Committee on Social Studies, American Association of Colleges for Teacher Education, p. 52. (Quoted with the permission of the author.)

[28] For a list of the growing number of Negro office holders, see Harold F. Gosnell and Robert E. Martin, "The Negro as Voter and Office Holder," *Journal of Negro Education*, Vol. 32 (Fall 1963), pp. 415–425.

challenges and counter pressures. If viewed in this broad perspective, it is clear that more significant changes which will bring the Negro greater opportunities for participation in our society lie ahead. When, in fact, basic equalities will be achieved cannot be predicted.

# CLASS AS AN EXPLANATION OF ETHNIC DIFFERENCES IN UPWARD MOBILITY

## THE CASE OF MEXICAN AMERICANS

*Celia Stopnicka Heller*

**The aim of this paper** is to challenge the indiscriminate use of *class* as an explanation of ethnic differences in mobility behavior. The fact that some differences—such as in mobility aspirations—between a given ethnic group and the majority population can be *statistically* accounted for by class is often interpreted to mean that class adequately explains these differences. Our contention is that such an interpretation is both unwarranted and incorrect.

Although the usual procedure involved in the explanation we are questioning is well known, it seems appropriate, for the sake of clarity, to begin by briefly summarizing it. The first step in this procedure is to compare the occupational, educational, material, or other mobility aspirations of a given ethnic group, in which the researcher is interested, with that of the majority population. When substantial differences are discovered, the factor of class is statistically controlled. If the differences disappear when class is controlled, the relation between ethnicity and aspirations is adjudged to be spurious and class is treated as the explanatory factor. If, on the other hand, the differences do not disappear but shrink, class is considered an important factor and the remaining differences are treated as being the result of the *ethnic* factor (unique characteristics of the group studied).

The procedure initially followed in our study of aspirations and the means of mobility of Mexican American youth was the same in manner. The quantitative data consisted of answers to a questionnaire administered in 1955 by Ralph H. Turner to seniors in ten Los Angeles high schools. These were chosen as a representative sample of the metropolitan area. Of the entire sample of male students, 165, or 12 per cent, turned out to be Mexican American.[1]

In comparing the answers of the Mexican Americans and the white non-Mexican boys, referred to as Anglo Americans, we found substantial differences in their occupational and educational expectations, and also in their IQ scores. (See Tables 1 and 2.) Over twice as many Anglo Americans as Mexican Americans expected to enter a *profession* (36.8 and 15.4 per cent, respectively) and, conversely, the proportion of Mexican Americans who chose *skilled labor* was almost twice that of Anglo Americans (41.3 and 22.4 per cent, respectively). The answers to the question concerning educational expectation were similarly patterned.[2] More than twice as many Mexican Americans did not expect to go beyond high school. At the opposite end of the educational scale, the proportion of Mexican Americans who anticipated graduating from college or better was only one-third that of Anglo-Americans.

As for IQ scores, the differences were still larger. The average score of the Mexican American male high school seniors was 90.5 as compared with 103.3 of the Anglo Americans. Almost half of the Mexican American students were below average in

This is a slightly revised version of the article that appeared in the *International Migration Review,* Vol. II, Fall, 1967. Reprinted by permission of the author.

[1] Celia Stopnicka Heller, "Ambitions of Mexican-American Youth—Goals and Means of Mobility of High School Seniors," unpublished Ph.D. dissertation, Columbia University, 1963.

[2] Table is omitted.

IQ, in contrast to 13 per cent of the Anglo Americans. Only 6 per cent of them, but 30 per cent of the Anglo Americans, fell into the "bright" and "superior" categories. (See Table 2).

Following the commonly used techniques, we controlled statistically the class factor and concluded—in accordance with the prevalent interpretation we are now disputing—that class largely explains the differences in occupational and educational expectations but does not explain IQ differences. In other words, we maintained that the fact of being Mexican American has little explanatory power, but the fact of being lower-class has much explanatory power for the understanding of the lower mobility aspirations of Mexican American youths. This conclusion was based on the findings that when class was statistically held constant, the differences in occupational and educational expectations were small, but the differences in IQ scores remained large. (See Tables 1 and 2.)

However, at this point, it must be admitted that our explanation was faulty. We were not justified in inferring that the relationship between mobility aspiration and Mexican American ethnicity is largely a spurious one. The problem of ethnic differences in mobility is not solved by holding the class factor constant, because the very class structure of the ethnic group is part of the *intrinsic* problem. In other words, *the class distribution of a given ethnic group, whether it differs from or resembles that of the majority population, must be accounted for.*

Because recent immigrants, as a whole, irrespective of country of origin, concentrate at the bottom of the socioeconomic ladder,[3] to make the leap that would enable them to approximate the class distribution of the majority population (let alone improve on it), they must at some point in their history exceed the aspirations of the majority population of the same class. If they simply advanced to the same degree as lower-class individuals in the majority group, the gap between their class distribution and that of the majority population would continue. And yet we know that there is more than one ethnic group which has not only approximated the class composition of the majority population but exceeded it.[4]

Among many ethnic groups, the process of moving toward the occupational structure of the majority population begins with the second generation; among some it begins later;[5] and among a few, such as Jews and Japanese, it begins in the first generation.[6] Although the occupational aspirations of these last groups undoubtedly varied with class in their countries of origin, transplanted to a relatively mobile society they responded to the promises of that society irrespective of the class they occupied in their country of origin or at the beginning of their stay here. There are indications that among these ethnic groups, in contrast to nonethnic Americans, mobility aspirations do not differ significantly with class.[7]

Similarly, class is not an adequate explanation if one proceeds to an analysis of the educational expectations of Mexican American youth. According to the class explanation, the lower educational expectations of Mexican Americans simply reflect their lower-class background. The general proposition from which it follows is the one

[3] Oscar Handlin, "Historical Perspectives of the American Ethnic Group," *Daedalus*, Spring, 1961, p. 228.

[4] Bernard Rosen, "Race, Ethnicity, and the Achievement Syndrome," *American Sociological Review*, Vol. 24, February, 1959, p. 47.

[5] E. P. Hutchinson, *Immigrants and Their Children, 1850–1950*, New York: John Wiley & Sons, 1956.

[6] Harry J. Crockett, "The Achievement Motive and Differential Occupational Mobility in the United States," *American Sociological Review*, Vol. 27, April, 1962, pp. 191–205.

[7] See Nathan Glazer, "Social Characteristics of American Jews, 1654–1954," in Morris Fine, ed., *American Jewish Year Book*. (Philadelphia: Jewish Publication Society of America, 1955), pp. 32–33.

Perhaps the following finding by McClelland also suggests the above. In comparing the "need" for achievement among four ethnic groups in the United States—French, Canadian, Italian, Greek and Jewish—he concludes that "the Jews are the only group . . . which do not show a drop in average *n* Achievement level for the lower socioeconomic classes." The only reservation is that by McClelland's admission, the "need" for achievement is not necessarily correlated with occupational aspirations. See: David C. McClelland, *The Achieving Society*, New York: D. Van Nostrand Co., 1961, p. 362.

**TABLE 1 Occupational Expectations of Male High School Seniors in the Los Angeles Metropolitan Area, 1955 (in percentages)**

| *Occupational Category* | ENTIRE SAMPLE | | | OF WORKING-CLASS BACKGROUND (BREADWINNER'S OCCUPATION: MANUAL) | |
|---|---|---|---|---|---|
| | Anglo American | Mexican American | Standardized Anglo American * | Mexican American | Anglo American |
| 1. Unskilled labor | .4 | 1.8 | 1.3 | 1.9 | .7 |
| 2. Semi-skilled labor | 1.3 | 1.8 | 3.6 | .0 | 2.3 |
| 3. **Skilled labor** | **22.4** | **41.3** | **34.1** | **42.1** | **33.3** |
| 4. Clerical & Sales Clerks | 3.1 | 3.1 | 2.5 | 2.8 | 3.4 |
| 5. Small business owners—managers & salesmen | 11.7 | 13.0 | 12.3 | 11.2 | 10.5 |
| 6. Semi-professionals | 17.9 | 19.8 | 16.5 | 21.5 | 19.4 |
| 7. Business agents & managers | 3.1 | 3.7 | 2.6 | 3.7 | 3.2 |
| 8. Large business owners & officials | 3.3 | .0 | 1.1 | .0 | .9 |
| 9. **Professionals** | **36.8** | **15.4** | **26.0** | **16.8** | **26.4** |
| Total | 100.0% | 99.9% | 100.0% | 100.0% | 100.1% |
| Total Number | (1057) | (165) | | (107) | (443) |
| No answer & unclassifiable | (10) | (3) | | (0) | (4) |
| Chi square (last two columns)** | | | | $\chi^2 = 3.27$ Not significant at .30 level | |

* These are calculated Anglo-American rates if the Anglo–Americans had the same occupational background as the Mexican Americans.
**For the chi square test the categories were thus combined: (1, 2, 3), (4, 5, 7, 8).

**TABLE 2 I.Q. Scores of Male High School Seniors (in percentages)**

| *IQ Class Interval* | *Verbal Characterization*[a] | TOTAL SAMPLE | | OF WORKING-CLASS BACKGROUND[b] | |
|---|---|---|---|---|---|
| | | Mexican American | Anglo American | Mexican American | Anglo American |
| 1. Below 80 | Borderline | 19.6 | 3.6 | 15.1 | 4.1 |
| 2. 80–90 | Dull | 28.2 | 9.7 | 21.7 | 12.6 |
| 3. 90–99 | Average | 26.4 | 22.8 | 31.1 | 27.9 |
| 4. 100–109 | Average | 20.2 | 33.8 | 26.4 | 35.0 |
| 5. 110–119 | Bright | 4.3 | 20.5 | 4.7 | 16.5 |
| 6. 120–129 | Superior | 1.2 | 7.7 | .9 | 3.4 |
| 7. 130 and over | Very superior | .0 | 1.8 | .0 | .5 |
| Total | | 99.9% | 99.9% | 99.9% | 100.0% |
| Total Number | | (165) | (1057) | (107) | (443) |
| No scores available | | (2) | (37) | (1) | (6) |
| Mean IQ | | 90.45 | 103.31 | 92.80 | 100.43 |
| Standard deviation | | 12.94 | 12.68 | 12.39 | 11.53 |
| Chi square | | | | $\chi^2 = 65.83$[c] Significant at .001 level | |

[a] Used by educators.
[b] Breadwinner's occupation is manual.
[c] Categories 5–7 were combined.

stated by Lipset and Bendix that "the higher the education of the parents, the more likely they would be to instill motivation for upward movement in their children.[8] Its specific reading would be: The parents of Mexican American students, being less educated than the Anglo American parents, are less likely to influence their children to obtain a higher education. And yet the argument is not entirely convincing. The confirmation of the Lipset and Bendix proposition, it could be said, comes from the empirical studies of non-ethnic youth.[9] *Parents' educational achievement and parents' influence on their children's educational motivation is not a necessary, although often found, equation.* The two cases in point are the American Jews and Japanese Americans.

The educational ambition and striving of the children of poor and uneducated Jewish immigrants have become proverbial and well documented. But why is this so? We know that in the traditional Jewish culture, sacred education was stressed as the channel of mobility open to all Jews: poor and rich, of educated and uneducated parents. The immigrants transferred their aspirations for their sons from religious to secular education.[10] They influenced their children to want an education and helped them secure it.

Much less is known about the mainspring of the Japanese Americans' stress on education, although it is easily observed that in terms of educational ambition and achievement they resemble the Jews. The Japanese immigration to the United States was also largely a lower-class immigration, even if in contrast to the Jewish one, it was mostly composed of peasants. These lower-class immigrants put great emphasis on education and influenced their children in that direction.[11] Thus, already in 1940, the educational level of the Nisei was 12.2 median years of school completed, as compared with 10.1 years for American-born white children in the Pacific coast states.[12]

In extreme contrast to the Jewish and Japanese stand the Mexican immigrants, whose cultural heritage—like that of some other immigrant groups, such as the Italian and Polish—did not contain the goal of education for all irrespective of social class. But their relative failure to aspire or influence their children to aspire or achieve higher education must *not* be considered indicative of a low value placed on education, as some writers have argued in studying lower socioeconomic groups of the majority population.[13] Long ago, when studying the immigrants in the United States, Robert E. Park stated that "even the Polish peasant . . . appreciates learning though not for his class."[14] Somehow, the Mexican Americans have long held on to the belief that formal education was useless for *them* and did not get them anywhere.[15] They viewed it as leading their children not toward mobility, but toward frustration and humiliation. To help their children avoid the latter, parents pointed to those Mexican Americans who received an education and yet did not hold a job appropriate to it.[16]

Finally, we should like to examine class as an explanation of ethnic differences in IQ. Although IQ scores are not adequate measures of innate capacity,[17] they do depict the reality of differing socially and culturally structured capacities, that is,

[8] S. M. Lipset and Reinhard Bendix, *Social Mobility in Industrial Society*, Berkeley: University of California Press, 1962, p. 237.

[9] *Ibid.*

[10] Jackson Toby, "Educational Maladjustment As a Predisposing Factor in Criminal Careers: A Comparative Study of Ethnic Groups," unpublished Ph.D. dissertation, Harvard University, 1950, p. 159.

[11] R. A. Schermerhorn, *These Our People*, Boston: D. C. Heath and Company, 1949, p. 214.

[12] William Caudill and George De Vos, "Achievement, Culture and Personality: The Case of Japanese Americans," *American Anthropologist*, Vol. 58, 1956, p. 1124.

[13] Herbert H. Hyman, "The Value System of Different Classes: A Social Psychological Contribution to the Analysis of Stratification," in Reinhold Bendix and S. M. Lipset, eds., *Class, Status and Power*, Glencoe, Illinois: Free Press, 1953, p. 429.

[14] Robert E. Park and Herbert A. Miller, *Old World Traits Transplanted*, New York, 1921, p. 268.

[15] Ruth Tuck, *Not With The Fist*, New York: Harcourt, Brace & Co., 1946, pp. 189–190. Florence R. Kluckhohn and Fred Strodtbeck, *Variations in Value Orientations*, New York: Row, Peterson Co., 1961, p. 248. Celia Stopnicka Heller, "Ambitions of Mexican-American Youth: Goals and Means of Mobility of High School Seniors," unpublished Ph.D. dissertation, Columbia University, 1963, pp. 167–171.

[16] Tuck, *ibid.*, p. 248.

[17] Otto Klineberg, *Social Psychology*, rev. ed., New York: Henry Holt & Co., 1954, pp. 304–312.

capacities for advancement in *our* society. As Anastasi demonstrates, "The criterion employed in validating intelligence tests has nearly always been success in our social system."[18]

Again, class is not an adequate explanation because, first of all, *IQ does not necessarily vary with class*. It is true that it varies with class in many collectivities that have been studied, but some empirical data support the above assertion that such variation is neither universal nor a necessary consequence of social stratification. An interesting study, conducted in London, showed that among the Jews there, IQ did not differ with class. According to this study, the average IQ of non-Jews dropped as the occupational index of parents fell, but the IQ of Jews remained on about the same level.[19]

Even if empirical studies were to prove that some Jewish communities are the only ones among whom the preceding is true, the analysis of this deviant case holds the promise of yielding important clues to further our knowledge about social mobility. It suggests, for example, that in as far as a culture emphasizes intellectual pursuits for all classes as an end in itself, it equips the members of the lower classes with a powerful means for potential mobility. In a relatively nonmobile society such people are more likely to escape through the rigid boundaries of class. Even when bred in a closed system, they are at an advantage when they move to an open society. In contrast to them, lower-class people formed in cultures where intellectual pursuits are expected of the upper class only, are not as well fit to seize the opportunities for advancement when they find themselves in a relatively open society. The Jews seem to represent an extreme case of the first and the Mexican Americans an extreme case of the latter.

In all complex cultures there are certain traits that are considered appropriate for all irrespective of social position and other traits that are class bound. However, the traits that do not vary with class in one culture may be the very ones that differ with class in another. In the case of Mexicans, honor, respect, family obligation, and manliness are some of the elements that are deemed important for all. But these are not the values that are very conducive to mobility; on the contrary, they are obstacles in the initial stages of social advancement, however praiseworthy on other grounds. And, in contrast to the Jews, Mexicans consider those qualities that are especially suited to mobility—intellect and education—to be the domain of the upper classes.

But if some ethnic groups start sooner and proceed faster to catch up with the socioeconomic positions of the population at large and a few even exceed it,[20] all ethnic

[18] Anastasi shows that "Scores on the test are correlated with school achievement or perhaps with some more general measure of success in our society. If such correlations are high, it is concluded that the test is a good measure of 'intelligence'": (See Anne Anastasi, *Differential Psychology*, 3rd ed., New York: The Macmillan Co., 1958, pp. 566–567.)

[19] As reported in Toby, *op. cit.*, p. 204. Parenthetically, the preceding fits rather well the folk beliefs of the Jews in Eastern Europe. They did not tend to think that "smartness" or talent varied with class among Jews, although they recognized that it differed with class among Gentiles. Nowhere in the people's sayings or their behavior do we find an attempt to place intelligence in a certain class of Jews or claim that it is more prevalent there. See Celia Stopnicka Heller, "Social Stratification of the Jewish Community in a Small Polish Town," *American Journal of Sociology*, Vol. 59, July, 1953, p. 10. (Reprinted in this volume, pp. 183–191, C.S.H.)

[20] It is often suggested that the rapid advancement of Jews is largely due to their urban heritage as compared with the rural background of other ethnic groups. (See Lipset and Bendix, *op. cit.*, p. 223.) Another explanation is that Jews more than any other groups were engaged for generations in middle-class occupations. (See Glazer, "Social Characteristics of American Jews," *op. cit.*, p. 30.) Although the factual basis of the latter could be seriously questioned, because the East European immigration to the United States was largely a lower-class immigration, or, if one prefers, an immigration of extremely impoverished sectors of the population, it might suffice to show that neither of the preceding factors are the necessary ingredients of rapid advancement. It should be recalled that the Japanese in the United States were not originally of the urban middle class but of peasant origin, and yet they displayed a similar pattern of mobility to that of Jews. By 1960 the Japanese ranked higher than whites in both occupational and educational status but their income level was lower. (See: Calvin F. Schmid and Charles E. Nobbe, "Socioeconomic Differentials Among Nonwhite Races," *American Sociological Review*, Vol. 30, December, 1965, pp. 909–922; Also, Caudill and De Vos, *op. cit.*, pp. 1102–1126).

groups have eventually responded to the American ideology of advancement. Until now, the only exception appears to be that of the Mexican Americans. On the basis of his careful analysis of 1950 census data, Donald J. Bogue concludes that the Mexican Americans constitute "*. . . the only ethnic group for which a comparison of the characteristics of the first and second generation fails to show a substantial intergenerational rise in socio-economic status*" (italics supplied).[21]

However, our data seem to suggest that the Mexican Americans are now entering, to borrow Walt W. Rostow's term, the "take off stage" of mobility. We arrive at this new "trend" among Mexican Americans not through holding class statistically constant, but by comparing the sons with the fathers. It can now be said, on the basis of our findings, that there is a portion of Mexican American youth who, if they could fulfill their aspirations and expectations, would substantially exceed their parental generation in occupational, educational, and in self-employment status. Specifically, only 4 per cent of the Mexican American boys expect to be doing unskilled or semiskilled labor, whereas 42 per cent of them come from such backgrounds. Conversely, 35 per cent of them aspire to semiprofessional or professional occupations, whereas only 2 per cent of their fathers are in these occupations.

As for education, only 5 per cent come from homes where the breadwinner attended college, but 44 per cent of them expect to do so. Eighty-seven per cent of their fathers had no education beyond high school, but only 31 per cent of them foresee not continuing their schooling.

Again, in the comparison of independent-employee status, 41 per cent of them think that they will have their own business or practice, whereas only 13 per cent of them are from homes where the breadwinner works for himself or owns a business. Also distinctive is that, unlike the Anglo Americans, the proportion of Mexican Americans who expect to be employed, is smaller than the proportion of those whose fathers are employees.

[21] Donald J. Bogue, *The Population of the United States*, Glencoe: The Free Press, 1959, p. 372.

If, as Turner argues, the comparable distributions of the Anglo Americans indicate that the movement from an employee to independent status is not regarded by the majority youth as upward movement,[22] then those of the Mexican Americans indicate a contrasting attitude. A shift from employee to independent status seems to mean to them what it has traditionally meant in America: going up in the world. In a sense, the Mexican Americans may only now be taking hold of the pattern that the majority population is already abandoning. Possibly, these third- and fourth-generation Americans of Mexican descent are showing the pattern that some ethnic groups, such as Jews, showed in the first generation. The mobility path of many immigrant Jews was to leave the factory and establish a small business.[23]

In terms of independent-employee status, as well as in terms of occupation and education, we see then that our sample of Mexican American boys does not expect to conform to the Mexican American pattern of no intergenerational difference in socioeconomic status. As a matter of fact, if we use the approach of *relative* mobility aspirations, the Mexican American boys seem quite mobility oriented.[24]

The analysis of relative mobility aspirations points to a change in the achievement orientation of Mexican Americans. We could not have detected this new trend by holding class statistically constant because the preceding technique, contrary to the prevalent interpretation of the results it yields, tells us no more than how the pattern of class variation (in the behavior under consideration) of a given ethnic group compares with the majority group *at one specific time* (the time of study). This is insufficient for understanding ethnic differences in mobility aspirations and achievement. For

[22] Ralph H. Turner, *The Social Context of Ambition*, San Francisco: Chandler Publishing Company, 1964, pp. 39, 180, 199.

[23] Fred L. Strodtbeck, "Jewish and Italian Immigration and Subsequent Status Mobility," in McClelland, *op. cit.*, p. 263.

[24] LaMar T. Empey, "Social Class and Occupational Aspiration: A Comparison of Absolute and Relative Measurement," *American Sociological Review*, Vol. 21, December, 1956, pp. 703–709.

that it is necessary to know whether the traits important in upward mobility are class bound in the original culture of the studied ethnic group. Furthermore, one must locate the class variable in the ethnic group's span of time in the United States, not merely at the time of study.

Mexican Americans, similarly to some other ethnic groups—such as Italian Americans, Polish Americans, and so forth—come from a culture where those traits that are especially suited to mobility are restricted to the upper classes. But in addition, the rate of acculturation of Mexican Americans has been slower than that of most of these groups. Mexican Americans have moved rather slowly out of the culture of the immigrants. In the strength of the traditional culture, they resemble more ethnic minorities in Europe than those in the United States. This is in part due to the fact that Mexican American history in this country began with the American conquest of territories in which Mexicans lived. The twentieth-century Mexican immigrants who came to the United States found here an indigenous Spanish-speaking population of long standing. They did not found immigrant colonies so much as move in with relatives.

Also contributing to cultural persistence and limited acculturation is the proximity to Mexico. The Mexican American population is largely concentrated in border states. There is continuous movement back and forth across the border. New immigrants are constantly added to the community; old immigrants, as well as their American born children, grandchildren, and great-grandchildren, "visit with relatives" in Mexico for short or long periods.[25] These then are the special factors that may account for the *apparent* uniqueness of the Mexican American group as compared with other ethnic groups (in the sense of no significant intergenerational advancement).

In conclusion, the analysis of relative mobility aspirations suggests a change in the Mexican American group showing it not to be the exception to the ethnic pattern in the United States. The process of responding to the American ideology of advancement observed in all other ethnic groups is similarly reenacted here, although it took a few more generations to initiate it. This change could not have been detected through the technique of statistically controlling the class factor.

[25] Carey McWilliams, *North from Mexico—The Spanish-Speaking People of the United States*, Philadelphia: Lippincott, 1949; Celia S. Heller, "Origin and Background," in *Mexican American Youth: Forgotten Youth at the Crossroads*, New York: Random House, 1966 pp. 9–26.

# THE PROTESTANT ESTABLISHMENT—ARISTOCRACY AND CASTE IN AMERICA

*E. Digby Baltzell*

## THE IMMIGRANTS' PROGRESS AND THE THEORY OF THE ESTABLISHMENT

Several years ago an Englishman, visiting America for the first time, remarked to an editor of *Harper's* magazine that nobody had prepared him for his quick discovery that this was not an Anglo-Saxon nation.[1] Although he had long been aware of our multinational, racial and religious origins in the abstract, he simply had not visualized the heterogeneity of our population in general, nor the heterogeneity of the persons of talent and ability in leadership positions. Hollywood, of course, portrays America to people all over the world. Yet the personalities of our screen stars, well-publicized representatives of the American rags-to-riches dream, had done little to dissuade him of our over-all Protestant and Anglo-Saxon ancestry. A brief look at the



[1] *Harper's*, March, 1955, p. 81.

original names of some of our more famous, pseudo-Anglo-Saxon, Hollywood heroes was indeed a revelation. . . . Just as the original names of these famous stars suggest the ethnic diversity of talent in modern America, so their assumed names attest to the Anglo-Saxon ideal which still persists in our culture. For, in spite of the fact that some forty million immigrants of diverse religious and ethnic origins came to America in the course of the nineteenth and early twentieth centuries, we were a predominantly Anglo-Saxon–Protestant people for almost the first two-thirds of our history. Thus our earliest cultural traditions—in language and literature as well as in our legal, political and religious institutions—were modeled on those of seventeenth- and eighteenth-century England. And, above all, our upper class has always been overwhelmingly Anglo-Saxon and Protestant in both origins and values. The "Sixty Families" or the "Four Hundred," the "Rich and the Well-Born," the "Harvard Man," the "Senator," the "Diplomat," the "Socialite," and the "Man of Distinction in the Executive Suite" are all continuing symbols of this Anglo-American ideal which the Hollywood stars, regardless of their own ethnic origins, have tended to perpetuate. The uncomfortable paradox of American society in the twentieth century is that it has tried to combine the democratic ideal of equality of opportunity in an ethnically diverse society with the persistent and conservative traditions of an Anglo-Saxon caste ideal at the top.

. . . As we have seen, the WASP upper class remained more or less in control of the American elite throughout the first three decades of this century.[2] This was perhaps inevitable, and, as it served to maintain a continuity of tradition at the level of leadership, it was a healthy thing for society as a whole. In the meantime, however, new ethnic families were gradually establishing themselves on the ladder of economic, political and social mobility. By and large this was a three-generational process.

. . . . . . . . . . . . . . . . . . . . . . . . . . . . . . . .

## THE ELITE AND THE MARGINAL MAN

Winston Churchill once said that in any hierarchical situation there is all the difference in the world between the number one man and number two, three, four and the rest. Thus, while most Americans, . . . are living and moving up the class hierarchy within each of our larger religious communities, there exists today an important qualitative difference in the nature of social relationships at the very top levels of society. In other words, while there are upper-, middle- and lower-class levels *within the Protestant, Catholic and Jewish communities,* there are Protestants, Catholics and Jews *within the elite*. To put it another way, class tends to replace religion (and even ethnicity and race) as the independent variable in social relationships at the highest levels of our society (see Diagram I).

And this difference as between the elite and the rest of society is more pronounced in the third, as against the first and second generations. Whereas, for instance, Mayor John Francis Fitzgerald was an "FIF" (First Irish Family) within the Boston Catholic community, his son-in-law became a member of the national elite, both as a multimillionaire businessman and Ambassador to the Court of St. James. While the second generation was still emotionally rooted in a *marginal culture,* the third generation was still emotionally rooted in a *marginal man*. This same marginality, as has been shown above, characterized the lives of Baruch, La Guardia and Weinberg, because of their elite positions. While Weinberg, for instance, was very naturally led into such intimate relationships as cruising in Maine with Charles Dickey because of their common elite positions at Goldman-Sachs and J. P. Morgan respectively, the majority of Jewish employees at Goldman-Sachs, even at quite high levels, led their private lives entirely within Jewish communities (and probably had not even met their gentile counterparts at the Morgan

[2] In the words of the author, "The elite concept has no evaluative connotations such as the 'best' but refers solely to those *individuals* who have succeeded in rising to the top positions in any society. The democratic process means then that the *elite is open* and is based on the American ideal of equality of opportunity." See *The Protestant Establishment*, New York: Random House, 1964, p. 7. (C. S. H.)

***Diagram 1***

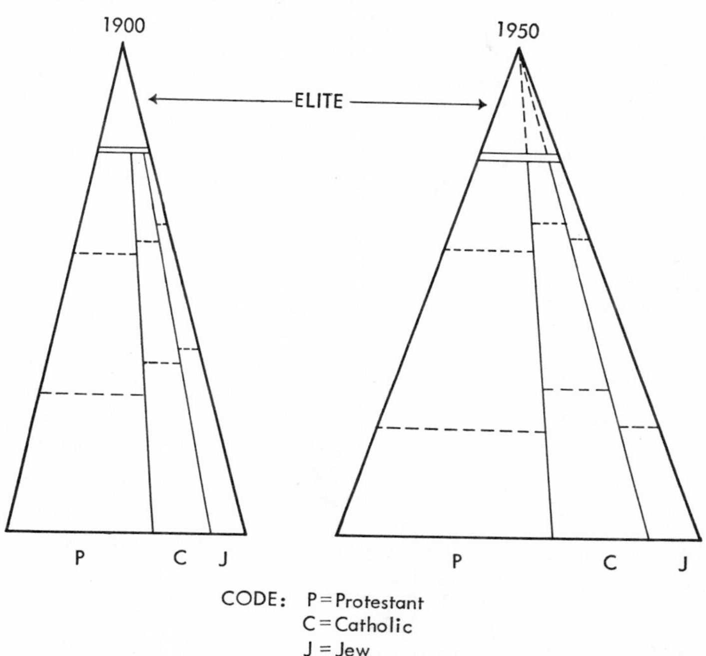


firm). And similarly, part of the tragedy of La Guardia's life was that, though he had led a rich and convivial social life among his artistic and professional friends of Italian and Jewish extraction while he was a rising young lawyer in Greenwich Village, when he went to Washington, and later when he became Mayor of New York, he was forced by his functional position of leadership either to lead a social life within the elite or to have no social life at all.

The functional necessity that elite members associate with each other regardless of background or religion (or race, as the complications in the lives of such eminent Americans as Ralph Bunche or Marian Anderson attest to) is paralleled in many other areas of life. In residential patterns, for instance, the lower-class Jew will live within an entirely Jewish neighborhood, the middle-class Jew in a predominantly, but not wholly, Jewish suburb, while the elite Jew will more likely be found in an almost predominantly gentile neighborhood.

. . . . . . . . . . . . . . . . . . . . . . . . . . . . . . . . . .

This elite pattern also extends to the socialization of children at school and at college. While public schools are largely neighborhood schools, and thus often ethnically homogeneous, the best private schools cater to a class clientele from all parts of the city and its suburbs, and increasingly tend to include a small nucleus of children from elite Jewish families. The boarding school is, of course, even a more powerful class-assimilating atmosphere for the minority of Jewish youths who go there from wealthy and prominent families. Similarly, the sons of the elite will be living in a far more class-bound atmosphere at Harvard than at the College of the City of New York.

Finally, of course, the class-limited way of life at the top is naturally reflected in the frequency of intermarriages and religious conversions. Thus Baruch, La Guardia and Schiff all married gentiles. . . .

. . . . . . . . . . . . . . . . . . . . . . . . . . . . . . . . . . . .

The theory of the triple melting pot, then, must be modified at the elite level in order to take into account the overwhelming factor of class. While in the third generation and at most class levels there is a return to ethnic and religious roots, centered in the suburban synagogue and church, there is a reversal of this trend today at the top levels of national leadership. And the pinch of prejudice will increasingly be felt as more and more non-Anglo-Saxon Protestants rise to this level of society. At the same time, it should be emphasized that this importance of class makes the theory of the persistence of the Anglo-Saxon Ideal—which many sociologists have seen as an important modifying factor in the melting-pot theory—even

*Diagram II*

The Establishment and
the Triple Melting Pot

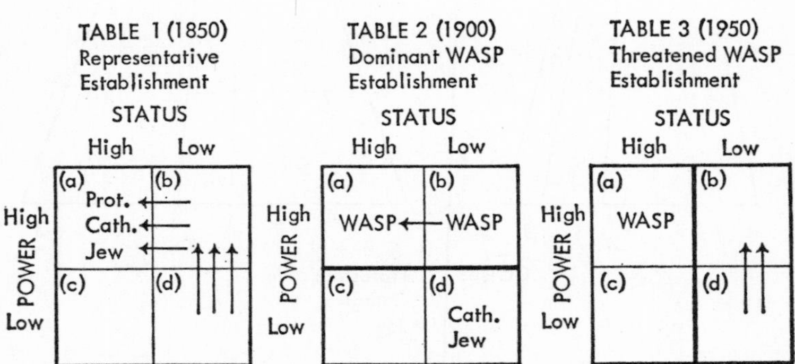


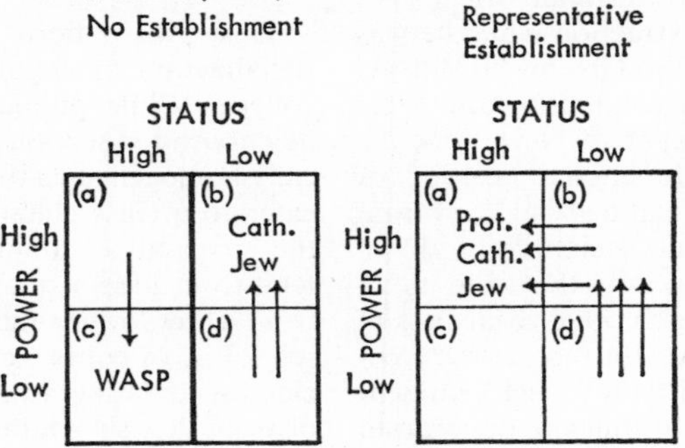


KEY CONCEPTS: Elite: Boxes (a) and (b) (High Functional Power)
Upper Class: Boxes (a) and (c) (High Social Status)
Establishment: Box (a) (Power, Status and Authority)
WASP: White-Anglo-Saxon-Protestant
Caste: Status without Authority (Box (c))
Aristocracy: Status with Authority (Box (a)).

more important at the elite level than at other social-class levels. This is of course because the nation's leadership is still dominated by members of the WASP upper class, the primary source and carrier of this ideal.

. . . . . . . . . . . . . . . . . . . . . . . . . . . . . . . . . . . .

. . . While the social organization of the triple melting pot serves quite effectively in assimilating the descendants of the more recent immigrants into most levels of our pluralistic society, there is, at the same time, constant pressure at the top levels of leadership today, which is increasingly composed of hyphenated-Americans of the third generation, to assimilate *all* talented and powerful men, regardless of their origins or religious convictions, into the main stream of traditional authority by ultimately rewarding them with the dignity, security and family honor implied and nourished by membership in an establishment.

## THE TRIPLE MELTING POT AND THE THEORY OF THE ESTABLISHMENT

In order to sharpen and elaborate the theory of the establishment, I have attempted to conceptualize, in a series of logical models shown in Diagram II, the past and possible future relationships between the three main ethnic-religious groupings in American society and the two variables of stratification: *social power* (position and power in the functional hierarchy of politics, business, religion, art, etc.) and *social status* (family position and prestige in the social-class hierarchy). Diagram II, in other words, conceptualizes the logically possible relationships between Protestants (WASPs), Catholics and Jews and the social organization of leadership. The *elite* concept, then, refers to those *individuals* at the top of the social power hierarchy (Diagram II, Box a and b); the *upper-class* concept refers to those *families* at the top of the social-status hierarchy (Box a and c): and the *establishment* refers to those leaders within the elite whose families also belong, or are in the process of belonging, to the upper class (Box a).

All social organizations are, of course, hierarchical. For social action depends on the differential distribution of power as between classes and individuals. The essential problem of social order, in turn, depends not on the *elimination* but the *legitimation* of social power. For power which is not legitimized (Box b) tends to be either coercive or manipulative. Freedom, on the other hand, depends not in doing what one wants but on wanting to do what one ought because of one's faith in long-established authority. An establishment (Box a), then, is composed of families who carry traditional authority deriving from the past, and present, power of their members. Both Franklin Roosevelt and Fiorello La Guardia, for instance, had power because of their personal qualities and functional positions. The Roosevelt family, however, possessed the kind of established authority which was denied the family of La Guardia.

This is not to say that all leaders in a changing society should be members of the establishment (Box a). They definitely should not. For new men (Box b) are always needed in every generation. The trouble comes when whole classes of new men, because of the accidents of ancestry, are denied the opportunity of translating their power and talent into some sort of family authority. But caste[3] not only denies the families of new men access to established authority; caste also weakens established authority itself because it tends to alienate its supposed beneficiaries by emphasizing their *rights* to privilege (Box c) rather than their *duties* to lead (Box a). Both the Roosevelt family's continual assumption of leadership *and* the continuous assimilation of men like La Guardia and Weinberg into the ranks of the upper class tend to strengthen the establishment's authority. On the other

[3] The author explains thus what he means by caste: "When, in any society, there is an upper class which protects its privileges and prestige but *does not continue* (1) to contribute leadership or (2) to assimilate new elite members, primarily because of their *racial or ethnic origins*, I shall refer to the process of *caste*. If an upper class degenerates into a caste, moreover, the traditional authority of an establishment is in grave danger of disintegrating, while society becomes a field for careerists seeking success and affluence. The caste process is the very antithesis of the aristocratic process and inevitably, in the long run if not immediately, leads to the decline of *authority* and a crisis in leadership." See *The Protestant Establishment, ibid.* p. 8. (C. S. H.)

hand, both when the established fail to lead and when leaders fail to become established, authority is in grave danger of degenerating into authoritarianism, and an organic social order becomes an atomized horde of fearful, alienated and manipulated individuals. The most difficult and delicate problem faced by democratic societies is that of balancing the liberal need for the continuous circulation of individual elites (Box b) with the conservative need for maintaining a continuity of family authority (Box a).

It is the theory of the establishment, then, that the processes of history may be conveniently conceptualized in terms of classes of men and their families circulating counterclockwise on the logical model outlined in Diagram II. When the cycle is complete, and is working without the corruptions of caste, the accomplishments and power of individual leaders are translated into family prestige and the continuity of established authority is maintained. From this point of view American leadership has gone through three more or less distinct periods.

In the first period, from the nation's founding and roughly through the first half of the nineteenth century, positions in the establishment were open to all white men, regardless of ethnic origin (Diagram II, Table 1). Thus, although there was a great deal of anti-Catholicism and fear of "Popery," individual Catholics were assimilated into the upper class on the basis of achievement and manners. The famous anti-Catholic riots in Philadelphia during the 1840s were really anti-Irish, and there was little or no antipathy toward middle-class German Catholics and certainly none toward the few distinguished Catholics who belonged to the upper class. At this time many leading families of Irish and Catholic origins became converts and passed on to their descendants solidly established positions in the Eastern Seaboard upper class. This was the case, for example, for such leading members of the Protestant establishment in Philadelphia as the Drexels of banking eminence (originally Austrian Catholics). . . . And this same pattern of accepting men on their merits and manners and assimilating their families into the establishment was followed, as we have seen, in the case of the Jews. The power of aristocratic assimilation[4] which existed at this time, for example, was implied in a recently published history of the Philadelphia Assemblies—annual balls, attendance at which still marks a family's inclusion within the innermost circles of Philadelphia's upper class and which have been held continuously since George Washington was one's dancing partner. Thus the author of this history was proud to write that "there are on the Subscribers' List of the Assemblies today, families of the following racial strains: English, Welsh, Irish, French, German, Dutch, Swiss, Italian, Spanish, Portuguese, Swedish, and Polish."[5] (What he meant was that the impeccable WASP establishment in the city of Philadelphia was composed of families whose ancestors included Spanish, Portuguese, German and Polish Jews, Irish, French and Italian Catholics, as well as Protestants from all these nations and dominated by those from the British Isles.) In this first historical period, then, the American establishment, though rooted in a mercantile upper class which was exclusive, proud, uniform in manners and certainly less patronizingly democratic in its treatment of the rest of the population than is the case today, was nevertheless still representative of the ethnic and religious composition of the white population.

But all this was to change after the Civil War, when the ethnic composition of

[4] The author explains thus what he means by aristocratic assimilation: "By an aristocracy I mean (1) a *community of upper-class families* whose members are born to positions of high prestige and assured dignity because their ancestors have been leaders (elite members) for one generation or more; (2) that these families are carriers of a set of traditional values which command *authority* because they represent the aspirations of both the elite and the rest of the population; and (3) that this class continues to justify its authority (a) by contributing its share of contemporary leaders and (b) by continuing to assimilate, in each generation, the families of new members of the elite. As with the elite concept, I do not conceive of the aristocracy as the 'best' or the 'fittest' in the sense of the term 'natural aristocracy' as used by Jefferson. The aristocratic process means that the *upper class is open*." See *The Protestant Esatblishment, ibid.*, pp. 7–8. (C. S. H.)

[5] Joseph P. Sims, *The Philadelphia Assemblies, 1748–1948*, privately printed, p. 8.

American society was radically altered by the new immigration. This second historical period, which reached its peak somewhere between 1900 and the First World War, was marked by an associationally exclusive establishment of White–Anglo-Saxon–Protestants who dominated the leadership of the nation. . . . The WASP establishment during this period was still representative of the elite, even though it was increasingly less representative of the population as a whole (Diagram II, Table 2). For this reason the establishment still possessed authority. In other words, it is not necessary, in the short run at least, that an upper class be representative of the whole people. In fact upper-class families are not recruited from the population at all but only from its leadership. The elite, on the other hand, must in the long run reflect and draw on the pool of national talent which inevitably resides in all classes. This is especially true where the people are literate and where a considerable majority have an opportunity for education. As of 1900, there was an authoritative establishment even though there was a more or less closed caste line drawn at the elite level which excluded those hyphenated-Americans of the Catholic and Jewish communities.

The significant difference in the structure of leadership in America in the third, as against the second, historical period is the fact that the caste line is now drawn in a status rather than a power sense, or, as it were, right down the middle of the elite (Diagram II, Table 3). In other words, our open class system has continued to work quite well and has produced a more or less ethnically representative elite. Our status system, on the other hand, has failed to keep pace. The WASP establishment has been forced to share its power while at the same time continuing to hoard its social privileges. In a very important sense, we now have in America, at the elite level of leadership, a *caste-ridden, open-class* society. And the consequent pressure upon the upper class to open its doors to the most talented and polished descendants of the newer immigrants has increased tremendously. . . .

At this time it is hard to see how the dynamic tension between the pressures of caste exclusion and of aristocratic assimilation which is now characteristic of the nation's leadership will finally be resolved. Today the situation is an ambivalent one. In the long run, there are two logically possible alternatives: either the WASP establishment will eventually develop into a closed caste, protecting its way of life and privileges while gradually abdicating from its position of leadership (Diagram II, Table 4), or a new aristocracy will emerge with the energy and ability to absorb the most prominent and polished families in the nation, regardless of their ethnic origins or religious convictions (Table 5). These strictly logical alternatives are, of course, only polar tendencies, and reality will fall somewhere in between.

## CASTE AND THE CLUB

Lacking the communal solidarity which older social structures have inherited from their feudal pasts, American society has always been faced with the dangerous consequences of extreme individualism. Atomized individualism always tends to degenerate into anarchy on the one hand, and more or less extreme forms of centralization on the other. Yet fortunately, up till now, we have avoided both these two extremes through our traditional ability to create a host of mutually excluding, yet interlocking, voluntary associations. "Wherever at the head of some new undertaking," wrote Tocqueville over a hundred years ago, "you see the government in France, or a man of rank in England, in the United States you will be sure to find an association." . . .

At the upper-class level in America, moreover, the club (a private voluntary association) lies at the very core of the social organization of the accesses to power and authority. . . . It is the anachronistic admissions policies of the leading upper-class clubs in America today . . . which lie at the very basis of the decline of upper-class authority, and the resulting confusion in communal and national leadership. The authority structure in this country is indeed in trouble, for instance, when a member of the oldest country club in the nation was able to say, not long before President Kennedy was killed, that he was proud of the fact that his club's admissions policies had not yet descended to the level of accepting any member of the nation's First Family. The absurdity of the statement is more understandable, however, when one takes into account the fact that the vast majority of the distinguished doctors, lawyers and business executives and their families who reside in the Boston suburb where the country club is located (and where John F. Kennedy was born) are categorically unacceptable for membership because of their ethnic origins.

. . . What Henry James found to be one of the uniquely characteristic American institutions was born with the founding of The Country Club, at Brookline, Massachusetts, in 1882. . . .

The boom in suburban clubs since the war has come about for several reasons. Of most importance is the fact that the policies of country-club admissions committees are one of the main ways of perpetuating caste divisions in an age when both the suburbs and elite leadership positions have been greatly democratized. From the time The Country Club, in Brookline, was founded until roughly up to the end of the Second War, the American upper-class suburb was almost entirely the monopoly of Anglo-Saxon Protestants. Country-club membership, then, was largely a reflection of community composition. As the upper classes still lived in large houses with spacious rooms and plenty of servants, moreover, the club was primarily a functional association used for the single purpose of sport (mainly golf, as private tennis courts and swimming pools were the rule).

On the other hand, the country club of today has become a veritable community. Space is at a premium even in the sixty- and seventy-thousand-dollar executive housing developments, while servants are scarce and overdemanding if not unobtainable. Consequently leisure-time and sporting activities have moved to the country club, where restaurants and bars do a thriving business (dues of course can often be written off as a business expense in these days when business and leisure so often interlock). But more than the economic factor is involved. Even the most exclusive suburbs are now no longer the monopoly of Anglo-Saxons, and the club serves to protect one's ethnic purity in increasing heterogeneous neighborhoods. This is especially true as far as elite Jews are concerned, for middle-class Jews are still most likely to settle in predominantly Jewish suburbs. It is the most talented and successful Jewish leaders in the community who of necessity deal on close social terms with gentiles in countless civic and charitable activities, who are also most likely to live in predominantly gentile upper-class neighborhoods. At the same time, as one Jewish civic leader reported: "They'll call on me to lead their Community Chest campaign or help on the Red Cross. But when it comes to the country club, I'm not good enough for them." Catholics are also moving to the suburbs in large numbers. Thus a Democratic political leader who was worried about affluent and suburbanized Catholics deserting to the Republican Party told Theodore H. White during the last Presidential campaign: "These guys whose grandfathers used to want to be captain of the ward now all want to be president of the country club."[6]

In response to the new suburban heterogeneity as well as to the caste values of the old-stock Protestants who got there first, minority country clubs have multiplied since the war and are now preserving the triple melting pot in the elite suburbs.

. . . . . . . . . . . . . . . . . . . . . . . . . . . . . . . . . . .

## THE CLUB AND THE CORPORATE ELITE: THE TAIL THAT WAGS THE DOG

At noon every day in the week, the men at the top of the executive suites in the city of Pittsburgh gather for lunch in a great brownstone pile which has housed the Duquesne Club since 1889. As one old-timer at the club remarked: "The way to tell if a fellow's getting along in any Pittsburgh company is to see if he's yet a member of the Duquesne. As soon as his name goes up for membership, you know he ought to be watched. He's a comer."[7] . . .

The Duquesne Club lies at the very core of the associational organization of

[6] Theodore White, *The Making of the President, 1960*. New York: Atheneum Press, 1962, p. 240.

[7] Osborn Eliott, *Men at the Top*. New York: Harper & Brothers, 1959, p. 164.

leadership in Pittsburgh. In fact, it has been argued by the club's management in the federal courts that income from dues should not be taxable because it is a business organization.

. . . . . . . . . . . . . . . . . . . . . . . . . . . . . . . . . .

Here indeed is a distinctly American institution where close primary relationships are forged between top management men who have the power of decision over transcommunal corporate activities which affect the lives of men and women all over the world, from the Atlantic to the Pacific, from the Monongahela to the Amazon. It is, too, a kind of associational aristocracy-by-ballot which is ideally suited to a dynamic and democratic society's continual need to assimilate new men of talent and power into the top levels of established leadership.

But at the same time this aristocratic function fails, at clubs like the Duquesne, to reach out beyond the boundaries of nominal-Christian affiliations. In the long run, these caste boundaries will inevitably create embarrassing situations which will be downright dysfunctional to the organization and recruitment of leadership. Even today there is in Pittsburgh an executive at the very top level of leadership in one of the nation's major corporations who has never been taken into the Duquesne because of his Jewish origins (even though he has never been associated in any way with the city's Jewish community).

. . . . . . . . . . . . . . . . . . . . . . . . . . . . . . . . . .

It is not, of course, that the values of the gentile gentlemen who dominate the admissions policies of the Duquesne are out of the ordinary. On the contrary, they mirror the mores of most of the leading metropolitan men's clubs in the nation. In city after city, the admissions policies of the top clubs are increasingly causing our national corporations to bar some of their best-qualified men from top leadership positions. . . .

One wonders how the younger generation of potential executives now coming out of the leading universities and the graduate schools of business will fit into this pattern of caste exclusion at clubs like the Duquesne. Most of them will, of course, go along with the conventional mores. Or they will choose careers elsewhere; which many sons of present business leaders will surely do for this very reason. And they will presumably be the kind of men who prefer a world where convictions count. A world, for example, where men like Angier Biddle Duke are not afraid to resign from organizations whose policies they consider dysfunctional to the nation's leadership. . . . Perhaps the main point at issue here, is the fact that not only are caste policies dysfunctional as far as the associational organization of leadership within the business community itself is concerned; these policies are also dysfunctional in that they will, in the future, alienate more and more young men of talent and principle from seeking careers in the business world. . . .

## THE CLUB AND THE RUMBLINGS OF REVOLT

Although policies of caste exclusion still characterize the vast majority of metropolitan men's clubs in America, there are signs of change, even though the bastions of the business establishment still lag behind.

. . . . . . . . . . . . . . . . . . . . . . . . . . . . . . . . . .

. . . Also in accord with our thesis, Amory sees the decline in New York's club life as partly a result of the younger generation's *disenchantment with anti-Semitism*. . . . On the other hand, Amory finds that the most successful social clubs in New York in the 1960s—the Century, the Cosmopolitan, the River, and the Regency, as well as the socio-theatrical and literary clubs like the Lotos, the Players and the Coffee House—all have members who also happen to be of Jewish origins. But above all, the college clubs have been the most successful in the city. Once citadels of snobbery . . . these clubs are now the most useful in the city because, as one member of the Harvard and Century clubs, who recently resigned from the Union after almost a quarter of a century's membership, put it recently: "I want a club where I can take a couple of friends without producing a birth certificate, a marriage license and a blood test." [8] . . . But in spite of the acceptance of change

[8] Cleveland Amory, *Who Killed Society?* New York: Harper & Brothers, 1960, p. 227.

which marks the policies at the Harvard and Century clubs, such eminent clubs as the Union, Knickerbocker and the Links are still dominated by the society and bourgeois ideals of caste exclusion.

The differential response to the social changes of our era are reflected in the club system in New York; indeed they reflect the conflicting social forces which lie at the very heart of our whole social system. Sometimes apparently unrelated sociological facts . . . have a way of hanging together to form a pattern. Thus the nature of American leadership at any given time is partly a reflection of its leaders' attitudes toward clubs. . . . But by far the most important clue to the difference between the Democratic and Republican leadership in America today is to be found by examining the membership and admission policies of the Links and Century clubs in New York City. . . . Although the Knickerbocker and Union clubs have long been strongholds of the Protestant Anglo-Saxon business establishment in America, centered in the family firm and Wall Street investment banking houses, the Links Club, since the war, has become the New York *rendezvous* of the national corporate establishment. It is of symbolic interest that the Links was founded in 1921, not as a purely business club, but rather "to promote and conserve throughout the U.S. the best interests and true spirit of the game of golf." Its out-of-town membership is almost entirely business and includes such eminent members as a Crocker from San Francisco, a Pillsbury from Minneapolis, a Ford from Detroit, a Field from Chicago, a Humphrey from Cleveland, a Mellon from Pittsburgh, a du Pont from Wilmington, a Pew from Philadelphia, and a Cabot from Boston. Of course its membership does not include such eminent and public-spirited business leaders as Sidney Weinberg or Meyer Kestnbaum, even though they may be intimate friends of many members. No Jews, and few if any professors or Democrats, belong to the Links.

The Century Association is far older than the Links and was founded for very different purposes by a group of artists and authors, in 1847. But "authors and artists cannot stand apart from the practical world," wrote the founders. . . . And so they invited into their club "gentlemen of any occupation provided their breadth of interest and moral qualities and imagination make them sympathetic, stimulating and congenial companions to the society of authors and artists."[9] This tone set by the founders has stood the test of time. At the Century today, one meets artists, professors, college presidents and distinguished men of affairs from both business and politics. As artists are not likely to be awed by a man's origins, there are Jews among the membership. . . .

In the middle of the twentieth century, then, the contrasting membership and admissions policies at the Links and Century clubs are arresting examples of the forces of caste, on the one hand, and aristocracy, on the other. On the whole, while the Links represents the authority of the business-Republic establishment, the Century's membership reflects the cultural and political leadership of the nation and is far more receptive to the ideals of the Democratic Party. The club affiliations of the Rockefeller family are of interest here. The family is of course Republican, and Nelson is one of the most eminent members of the party. . . . Nelson lists membership in the aristocratic Century rather than the caste-bound Links. For perhaps Nelson Rockefeller, whose family symbolizes the very essence of established communal authority in this country, may eventually be able to lead his party to a new position of established political authority. But, as the eight Eisenhower years so amply demonstrated, this transformation will not be produced by any single victory or series of victories at the polls; it will not be done through campaign oratory and platforms professing the ideals of civil liberty; it will not be done by putting forth minority candidates for office or by appointing Catholics or Jews to important governmental positions; it will, in the long run, be accomplished only when the established communal leaders who dominate the Republican Party in city after city assimilate within their ranks the most distinguished and talented men in their respective communities, regardless of their ethnic or religious origins. This will not be done until, among other things, the admissions

[9] *Ibid.*, p. 215.

committees of the leading metropolitan men's clubs, in the style of the Century rather than the Links, take seriously their aristocratic role as leaders of assimilating associations in the communal organization of power. Or, as Richard Nixon put it after his recent defeat, until the Republicans "quit being an exclusive social club."

What is needed, then, is a sociological, rather than a political, revolution within the ranks of the establishment. And this revolution, in accord with the Whig tradition in England rather than the radical tradition in France, needs only to regenerate its original ideals of equality of opportunity. . . .

# PART VII
# Change in Stratification Systems

Social change has for some time been the neglected branch of sociology, a fact generally recognized and deplored in the discipline. As T. H. Marshall assessed it, in no field of study is this neglect more evident than in that of social stratification. Students of stratification not only fail to pay attention to the "dynamic forces" but "often deliberately eliminate these dynamic forces in an endeavor to discover the essence of the present system, viewed in its own right as a system."[1]

Approached from this perspective, all our readings in this section have the distinction of focusing on change. The first is on the "Interaction Between Industrial and Pre-Industrial Stratification Systems," by Bert F. Hoselitz. He distinguishes four different patterns of change that have followed the introduction of Western economic and political elements into relatively stable tradition-oriented societies. His analysis, however, concentrates on only one of these patterns: some form of slow integration of the new elements with the old ones. As examples of societies where it is taking place, he mentions Indonesia, India, and Pakistan. The most important fact here, according to the author, is that industrialization leads to urbanization. The industrially employed labor force is concentrated in cities and at the beginning there is a deep gulf between them and the rest of the population, much larger in number, who continue to be employed in agriculture. However, as economic change proceeds, the rural and urban sectors become increasingly interdependent. The stratification system that evolves first in the urban areas and then spreads to the country at large, tends to resemble that of Western societies. Thus he see this type of stratification—associated with economic growth—compatible with different types of original cultures in the societies prior to industrialization. He predicts that in many countries of Asia and Africa, differing in their cultures, similar systems of stratification will develop in the next few decades.

In a sense, the picture of change in Peru drawn by David Chaplin in our second

[1] T. H. Marshall, "Changes in Social Stratification in the Twentieth Century," in *Class, Citizenship and Social Development*, Garden City, Doubleday, 1964, p. 124.

selection has many points in common with those made by Hoselitz, and yet it does not completely fit into Hoselitz' scheme. The focus is also on urbanization, but Chaplin shows that in Peru urbanization largely precedes rather than follows industrialization. To put it plainly, Peru is more urbanized than industrialized. In that country, marked by a rigid class structure with persisting feudal features and low economic development, some changes have been taking place ahead of industrialization. They are being brought about by urbanization based on foreign trade rather than domestic industrial development. Thus in Peru—as well as in some other countries in Latin America,[2] and perhaps in other parts of the world such as the Near East—we witness effects on the existing stratification system of urbanization ahead of industrialization. One would therefore suppose that Chaplin's analysis of Peru is applicable to some extent to all such countries.

Especially noteworthy is Chaplin's hypothesis that urbanization in Peru, and in Latin America in general, unlike that which occurred in Europe, is having a negative effect on urban lower-class protest, leading to *deradicalization*, that is, the stifling of radicalism in that class. The radicals are the university students of "modest" socioeconomic background who suffer from status deprivation. But once they complete their university training they are easily coopted. One might add that the cooptation of lower-class leaders is a common and perfected procedure in Latin America. It appeared to this writer, while studying stratification in Colombia, South America, from 1953–1956, as if at times the oligarchy were consciously following Pareto's prescription of how a ruling class is to maintain itself in power.[3] That it might not be as successful in the future, nevertheless, is suggested by the case of Cuba. The potential followers of revolutionary leaders in Peru, as in Cuba, according to Chaplin, are the landless peasants. Here he seems in accord with Raymond Aron's generalization that "wherever feudal hierarchies survive and wherever great landowners cultivate, more or less carelessly, the land on which the farmers and agricultural workers labour, propaganda for a classless society will find large numbers of followers."[4] That it has not found them in large numbers among the peasants of Peru is because many of them are Indians who are still nonparticipants in the larger Peruvian society. The Indians in Peru, who comprise about one-third of the total population, fit into one of the four aforementioned patterns outlined by Hoselitz: the pattern of the indigeneous group remaining for a long time a separate entity.

Another possible pattern resulting from the introduction of Western elements into the tradition-oriented societies named by Hoselitz is that of complete reorientation along Western lines. He considers the transformation of Japan in the last hundred years the best example of this pattern.

Perhaps the other case of modernization that could match Japan in its rapidity is that of Isreal. But apart from this, the selection from Eisenstadt's book *Israeli Society* is impressive because it represents the unique case of the study by a sociologist of the inception of a stratification system in a total society. Here is a study

[2] For a general understanding of stratification in Latin America see Ralph L. Beals, "Social Stratification in Latin America," *American Journal of Sociology*, No. 58, 1953, pp. 327–339.

[3] On cooptation of rising leaders by the dominant political party of Mexico, see Claudio Stern and Joseph A. Kahl, "Stratification Since the Revolution," in Joseph A. Kahl, ed., *Comparative Perspectives on Stratification*, Boston: Little, Brown and Company, 1968, p. 27. One lites and development in Latin America, see Seymour Martin Lipset and Aldo Solari, eds., *Elites in Latln America*, New York: Oxford University Press, 1967.

[4] Raymond Aron, "Social Structure and the Ruling Class," *British Journal of Sociology*, Vol. I, March, 1950, p. 86.

of a stratification system emerging in a society whose founders were dedicated to the creation of a classless society. It has then some resemblance to the case of Russia where the founders of the new Soviet regime were committed to the ideology of a classless society. But it differs in other important respects, as will become clear. From a sociological point of view, perhaps the most important difference is that in postrevolutionary Russia the tendency toward equilibrium, as formulated by Pareto, set in: gradually old patterns, or certain aspects of them, returned. But in Israel the stratification system was and is emerging simultaneously with the emerging of a society. Here we find a new society and a new stratification system in the making. Eisenstadt outlines for us the multiple tendencies that are at play, some contradictory to one another and some reinforcing each other. He traces their origin and development through the three periods of the new society: during the *Old Yishuv*, the original pioneer settlement prior to Palestine's becoming an English mandate; during the mandatory period; and in the present period, after the achievement of statehood. To give a simplified characterization of those periods—the specifics of which can be found in the selection—the first was a period of relative social equality; the second of the beginning of the structuring of inequality; and the third of a growing system of social inequality. Although some trends contradictory to the pioneering ideology have become especially strong during statehood—with its unified political framework, increasing economic development, and influx of Jewish immigrants from the Orient—nevertheless the ideology of pioneering, of service to the nation, has put its stamp on the emerging stratification system. One of the contradictory trends, which the author considers especially important and to which he gives considerable attention, is the growing importance of political power as a criterion of evaluation and as an avenue of access to high economic position.

A similarity may be observed here between the situation of the lowest socioeconomic groups in Israel and what Myrdal designated as the underclass in the United States. As Eisenstadt describes them, they are in a sense marginal within the society. There is also a similarity in their composition: in the United States an overrepresentation of Negroes, Mexican Americans and Puerto Ricans, and in Israel of Oriental Jews in the lowest socioeconomic levels.

In the next selection in this part of our book the complex problem of the nature of stratification in industrial society is succinctly discussed by John Goldthorpe. In his essay a poignant critique of the much-accepted view of industrial development as the prime determinant of the pattern of change in the stratification systems of advanced, or what he terms mature, industrial societies is found. This idea is part of a conception of "the standardizing effects upon social structures of the exigencies of modern technology and of an advanced economy."[5] These factors supposedly cancel out the effects of other factors that vary from one society to another—such as the national culture or the political system—and press for an essential similarity in the stratification systems of advanced industrial societies. By the time the reader turns to Goldthorpe's essay he will have already come across this conception in a number of our selections, most recently in the Hoselitz article just discussed. Clearly, Hoselitz adhers to this conception. But one of the first, and perhaps the most explicit sociological expositions of this thesis on stratification in advanced industrial society is found in Theodor Geiger's *Die Klassengeselschaft*

[5] A later rendition of this thesis is found in John Kenneth Galbraith, *The New Industrial State*, Boston: Houghton Mifflin, 1967.

*im Schmelztiegel*, to which Goldthorpe does not refer. The reader who recalls its main arguments from the selection reprinted in Part II of this book will now have the chance to judge whether it withstands the empirical evidence marshaled by Goldthorpe against later versions of the same thesis.

Goldthorpe breaks down the thesis into three parts and proceeds to show how each is not in accord with empirical data from Western societies. The data he refers to—on distribution of income and wealth, on status inconsistency, and on social mobility—will be familiar to the reader who has studied the earlier selections. What he will find new here is the use Goldthorpe makes of them to test hypotheses concerning changes of stratification systems in advanced industrial societies.

Having shaken the thesis by pointing to the numerous empirical findings at odds with it, he moves on to what he considers more fundamental theoretical criticisms. He arrives at these through examining stratification in the Soviet Union and comparing it with stratification in the West. Although there are similarities between them, Goldthorpe, in contrast to Theodor Geiger, insists that they are of a *phenotypical kind*, that is in appearance only. *Genotypically*, that is in essence, they differ sharply. He makes the point that in the West economic forces constitute the crucial stratifying agency. In the Soviet Union, the system of stratification is subject to political regulation. As he expresses it, the Soviet stratification system is characterized by an important element of deliberateness that sets it apart from the Western system.

It might be appropriate to add here that Goldthorpe's analysis resembles Raymond Aron's formulation. According to the latter "the fundamental difference between a society of the Soviet type and one of the Western type is that the former has a unified *elite* and the latter a divided elite."[6] In the hands of the first are concentrated both political and economic powers, which are absolute and unbounded. They have infinitely more power than the rulers in Western democracies. The main point of Goldthorpe's detailed discussion, as well as of Aron's, is that essentially different systems of stratification exist in Soviet and Western types of societies, although both are in a state of advanced industrialization.

The thesis of essentially different stratification systems in contemporary socialist and capitalist societies is central in our next selection. "Strata and Strata Interests in Socialist Society," a paper delivered at the Sixth World Congress of Sociology by the Polish sociologist Wlodzimierz Wesolowski. However, his argument rests on other grounds than those of Goldthorpe or Aron. Although it deviates from the "official" line on stratification (which is pronounced with boring repetition by Soviet "sociologists" at international meetings) and in this sense is "revisionist," it nevertheless begins with the same assumption. Wesolowski assumes that the classic Marxist criterion of relation to the means of production ceases to play an important part in socialist society because private ownership of the means of production is largely abolished. The author completely disregards the question of who controls the means of production (recall the selections by Theodor Geiger and Djilas). Thus he sees socialism as representing the eventual equalization in relation to the means of production and therefore as a classless society. (But we could add, only as far as formal ownership is concerned; not as far as control over it is concerned.) And his analysis of stratification in socialist society largely ignores

[6] Aron, *op. cit.*, p. 10.

the unequal distribution of power while concentrating on income, education, and prestige inequality. This is especially noteworthy in light of the fact that in an earlier article devoted to the criticism of the functional theory of stratification, he gave much attention on theoretical grounds to inequality in authority and concluded that it is characteristic of all stratified societies. (See pp. 503–511 in this volume.) But when he deals specifically with stratification in socialist society—what he said about Davis and Moore could be said about him—he is "inclined to relegate authority to the background."

Wesolowski analyzes the process of change in the stratification system of socialist society. Even though socialist society succeeds in abolishing the capitalist class, it nevertheless inherits from the capitalist system the *class* of small farmers and the *stratum* of intelligentsia, white-collar workers and professionals. (The first in the "official Marxist" conception is a class because its distinguishing characteristic lies in its relation to the means of production. But this is not the case of the latter and that is why it is termed a stratum whose distinguishing characteristic is nonmanual labor.)

The process of transformation in the class structure inherited from capitalism, according to Wesolowski, varies in speed from one socialist society to another but always proceeds in two directions: (1) equalization of the relation to means of production—small farmers are at first tolerated but eventually eliminated or, as the author expresses it, changed into "employees of the state" and (2) income, prestige, and opportunity cease to be determined by the relation to the means of production.

What is not to be overlooked in Wesolowski's article is the attention he pays to conflicting interests in socialist society. This represents a marked departure from the official Marxist line, which holds that once private ownership of the means of production is abolished, antagonistic interests disappear. But Wesolowski is careful to trace his concept of *contradiction of interests* in socialist society to Marx's writings. (This is a common procedure among scientists in socialist countries who depart from the official line; it takes more exaggerated forms in the Soviet Union than in Poland.) Marx, Wesolowski explains, spoke not only about the opposite interests between classes but also among workers competing for the same jobs. The author argues that socialist society to this very day is marked by a scarcity of generally desired goods or values and "their distribution is by necessity such that any increase of the share of one group is bound to bring cuts in the share of another group." Therein lie the roots of opposite interests in socialist society.

The author does not confine himself to the analysis of the objective side of the contradiction of interests but moves on to an analysis of the subjective perception of these interests as conflicting or not, depending on one's location in the social structure. The wide acceptance of the formula "to each according to his work" as just, he argues, works in the direction of diminishing the awareness of the opposite interests that exist in socialist society. But when there are departures from this formula, even when these are in accordance with other socialist principles, they result in such awareness, especially among the lowest income groups.

As we read Wesolowski's exposition we cannot help but note numerous similarities between stratification in contemporary socialist and capitalist societies. The author himself does not seem to be able to escape them, but he insists in the footnotes that they are only phenotypical similarities. In this sense his position resembles that of Goldthorpe.

Despite the thorough analysis by Goldthorpe and Wesolowski, the question of the similarity and difference between the Soviet type and the Western type of stratification is not yet answered conclusively. Thus our last two selections devoted to change connect rather well with the readings that follow them in the final part of the book, "Unresolved Issues in Stratification Theory."

# INTERACTION BETWEEN INDUSTRIAL AND PRE-INDUSTRIAL STRATIFICATION SYSTEMS

*Bert F. Hoselitz*

A common aspect of economic development, in societies that already have experienced it as well as those engaged in bringing it about, is the increase of the secondary and tertiary sectors in the economy. Although technical and other improvements of agriculture are being considered or carried out in all these societies, the major socioeconomic change with which development is usually associated is the change from technically simple production methods. With this change is associated an increase in the numbers of highly educated people and skilled and specialized workers, and an absolute or proportional decline of the rural, especially the small village population, as towns and urban areas grow.

I offer this crude description of economic advancement here, not in an attempt to describe economic development as a process, but to suggest the very general characteristics of change in economic practices, in residential patterns, and in the nature of economically and socially interacting groups, which are usually associated with economic development. In some countries these changes have been relatively rapid, in others slow, and in others they are just beginning. My purpose is to describe in rather general terms the characteristics of societies in which certain parts are still strongly influenced by the "old-fashioned" conditions of social structure and in which other parts, especially the industrialized urban sectors, have accepted or been forced into new forms of social organization and new relations between persons belonging to different and possibly new social classes.

From Neil J. Smelser and Seymour Martin Lipset, eds., *Social Structure and Mobility in Economic Development*. Reprinted by permission of the Aldine Publishing Company.

## DUALISM AND ECONOMIC DEVELOPMENT

In his doctoral dissertation, presented in 1910, J. H. Boeke set forth a theory of social and economic development founded on the concept of "dualism," and the present analysis is strongly influenced by his work. Boeke's extensive reading and research on Dutch practices and policies in Indonesia brought him to the conclusion that social and economic conditions and life patterns in Indonesia, and possibly in other tropical Asian territories, were so different from those prevailing in Europe that theories concerned with Western social and economic growth and development were an inadequate and unrealistic basis for interpreting socioeconomic relations in the less industrialized, economically non-rationalized societies of tropical Asia.[1] . . .

A very informative statement of the views supporting and objecting to Boeke's ideas was published recently,[2] and some economists have published a series of essays rather critical of dualism, even rebutting Boeke's views, although an anthropologically-inclined sociologist and a few economists concerned with some of the more interesting countries experiencing economic change and growth have adopted certain aspects of dualism.[3] . . .

[1] Julius H. Boeke, *Dualistische Economie* (Leiden: S. C. van Doesburgh, 1930); *Oriental Economics* (New York: Institute of Pacific Relations, 1947).

[2] See the "Introduction" (writer's name not indicated) to *Indonesian Economics: The Concept of Dualism in Theory and Policy,* Vol. 6 of *Selected Studies on Indonesia,* by Dutch Scholars (The Hague: W. van Hoeve, 1961), esp. pp. 30–64.

[3] Among the opposing essays are Benjamin H. Higgins, "The 'Dualistic Theory' of Underdeveloped Areas," *Economic Development and Cultural Change,* 4 (1956), pp. 99–115, and Yoichi Itagaki, "Some Notes on the Controversy Concerning Boeke's 'Dualistic Theory'; Implications for the Theory of Economic Development in Underdeveloped Countries," *Hitotsubashi Journal of Economics,* 1 (October, 1960), pp. 13–28. For a more positive treatment of dualism, see John H. Rex, "The Plural Society in Sociological Theory," *British Journal of Sociology,* 10 (June, 1959), pp. 114–124, and William J. Barber, *The Economy of British Central Africa* (Stanford: Stanford University Press, 1961), *passim.*

. . . Whereas Boeke argued that the imposition of Western social, economic and political elements on non-Western societies would produce a structure permanently bifurcated into Western and non-Western systems, Nash insists that introducing Western social and economic conditions is likely to produce a plural system, subject to change and evolution, and that the more highly developed and the more traditional parts of the society may be interrelated to different degrees in different tropical countries.[4] Since this criticism seems valid, I shall apply it in the following discussion of different patterns of economic growth and political change.

First, I shall outline the general changes that may take place under the impact of various Western economic and political institutions in underdeveloped societies. Let us assume that the societies not yet exposed to foreign technical or economic procedures are relatively well integrated and functionally not highly differentiated, and that they can maintain themselves in their social and economic environment, in which some long-range changes may go on. These societies may appear to many foreign observers to be stable and essentially unchanging. Political activities tend to be hierarchical and probably not democratic in the modern sense. Minor disturbances can be handled without upsetting the social and economic equilibrium and without altering the nature of the society. . . .

The imposition of Western institutions on a relatively stable, strongly tradition-oriented society may destroy the economically simpler society completely, and though its people may survive, they are either integrated with the more advanced population or maintained on a welfare basis. An example of this pattern of change is the destruction, absorption, or socio-economic subjection of the American Indians during the settlement of the United States. Although quite a few Indian communities still exist on United States territory, their independent economic activity has ceased and their social and political systems have been destroyed. A number of Indians have been assimilated to some extent, but only those who settled in white American areas and completely gave up their associations with other members of the original societies.

A second pattern is the adoption of completely new forms of economic, social, and political organization. Although these non-Western social systems may have been relatively well developed, they become completely reoriented. The transformation of Japan in the last hundred years is perhaps the best example, but the same pattern has also occurred in geographically more limited areas such as Singapore and Hong Kong. There, colonial organization was politically limited by the boundaries between these urban populations and the much more stable populations in surrounding areas. The Japanese case is different, for here a large society adopted new methods of production —and as a result altered its political structure and social organization to produce a new social system. The latter cannot be said to exhibit dualism, for it is an integrated form of socioeconomic organization basically different from the form that existed before the major innovations took place.

In addition to complete destruction of the non-Western society and its complete reorganization, two other possibilities are substantively of greater significance and more closely related to the problem of dualism. One is the situation where an indigenous tribal or related group remains for a long time a self-centered, separate entity. For example, Barber argues that the Barotse tribe of Northern Rhodesia has remained socially and economically isolated and has scarcely interacted in any way with the remainder of the country.[5] Other instances of this type are known, though it is questionable how long these isolated communities can persist. The Indian societies in South America that survived Spanish colonialization belong in this class. Similarly, a number of separate tribal groups in India led a life of their own during all or most of the British colonial rule and did

[4] This is a somewhat modified presentation of ideas expressed by Manning Nash in "Southeast Asian Society—Dual or Multiple," *Journal of Asian Studies*, Vol. XXIII, No. 3, pp. 420–422.

[5] See Barber, *op. cit.*, pp. 20 and 44.

not interact with the part of the society that was under Western domination. Similar situations may exist in some Indonesian islands and elsewhere, and in some parts of Africa separate tribal groups have only minimal contact with non-tribal populations.

These situations are probably not permanent, and changes occurring in the surrounding areas will eventually bring about some form of change in the relatively isolated groups. They may become integrated with the surrounding populations; this appears to be an important and powerful development in many parts of the world. Until a few years ago, for example, portions of Tibet formed a self-sustained, economically integrated social and political entity, whose connections with both the Indians and the Chinese were very limited. The Chinese invasion of Tibet altered this situation, and within the next few years the Tibetans will either be exterminated, essentially, or integrated with the Chinese people. Similar developments will probably take place in Africa and Asia, where independent and relatively isolated tribal groups still exist. In the Amazonian areas of Brazil a few very small, extremely isolated tribal communities still exist: they will be exterminated, completely subordinated like North American Indians, or incorporated in the wider Brazilian society. Similar patterns are likely to occur among Canadian and Alaskan Eskimos.

These are, in some ways, the most important and genuine examples of dualism, but modern communication methods, rising political aspirations, and the tendency toward unified political and social communities even among African and other still undeveloped societies, create conditions under which isolated communities can last only a relatively short time. At present, however, a good many such communities do exist, and research on them and their peculiarities during the past may be of some interest.

Finally I come to the fourth case, some form of integration of the more with the less westernized portions of a colonial area. Indonesia, India, Pakistan and many other areas in tropical Asia and Africa represent this situation. . . .

## INTERACTION BETWEEN INDUSTRIAL AND PRE-INDUSTRIAL STRATIFICATION SYSTEMS

In countries that have recently become independent and established new socio-political systems, the most significant social phenomenon is not dualism, but the fact that industrialization has created an urban, industrially employed labor force, superimposed on or coordinated with a larger number of agricultural workers and producers. In many of these countries, particularly in Africa and Asia, by far the largest proportion of the economically active population—between 60 and 80 per cent or even more—is still in agriculture. Industries, as well as various services, are usually located in urban areas; hence agriculturalists differ substantially from persons in secondary and tertiary occupations, not only in terms of occupational activity but often in terms of the locality where it is carried out.

Where old cultures are well established, however—as, for example, in India—local differentiation between farming and other forms of productive activity is less important than it is in some of the African and Southeast Asian countries where persons in non-agricultural occupations are often foreigners or members of a linguistically or "nationally" distinct group. Examples are the Chinese in various Southeast Asian countries, the Lebanese and Syrians in parts of Africa, and the Indians in various parts of East Africa. Many of these people are in service and trade occupations, but to some extent modern industrial development has brought them into commercial activities as well. Thus, differences between urban and rural populations, between native and originally foreign persons, and between industrially and agriculturally occupied persons have tended to produce different processes of adjustment and change in different areas. Where important and apparently insuperable conflicts arose between two or more sections of the population, dualism or pluralism was discovered. But a more careful analysis of these changes shows that such contrasts and conflicts may not be insuperable and that gradual, if slow, adjustment is possible and even probable.

Manning Nash has written a detailed description of the introduction of industrial production methods in a peasant society: Cantel, in Guatemala.[6] Cantel is a small Indian community, originally based entirely on agriculture, whose relations with other communities and other social groups clearly exhibited traditions prevalent among Central American Indians. Though the different native communities in Guatemala possessed a variety of dialects, costumes, saints, and sacred ceremonies, their interrelations within a village and between villages created a culturally and sociologically stable system, changing little. Then a textile factory was set up in one community. The factory employed Indians from the neighborhood, some of whom had previously not earned money income, few of whom had lived close to the factory, and none of whom had been engaged in an economic activity requiring regular working hours, specific behavior at the work place, or other related forms of behavior.

Nash describes the whole process of change in the article cited and in a book dealing with the same problem; I shall not repeat this here, but I want to stress one point that he discusses, having to do with social relations in Cantel after the factory had been present for about 30 years. Nash discusses differences between the factory workers and those who remained traditional agricultural operators in Cantel and the surrounding area. Changes in industrial workers' houses and their furnishings have been minimal; similarly, foods and cooking arrangements have changed little. Above all, family relations have remained essentially identical. The factory workers share with the remaining peasants the same religious beliefs and practices and enjoy the same festivities. The closeness of personal relations in a number of important social areas is summed up by Nash as follows:

> Unquestioning acceptance of folk ideas of reality is part of everyone's life, irrespective of his occupational role. In Cantel this includes acceptance of folk remedies, origin myths, modes of cure, and the belief that foods and persons are "hot" and "cold," that smoke from the candles carried one's prayer to heaven, that the sacrifice of a sheep keeps death from a household, and that an eclipse is a battle between good and evil. What is apparent in this matter of world view is the extent to which spheres of rationality and irrationality coincide among factory and non-factory workers.[7]

Yet, to some extent certain social differences did develop in Cantel, among them the new friendship clubs for factory workers —which previously did not exist at all—a sports club composed of bicycle riders and basketball players (sports introduced from more advanced societies), and labor union activity introduced by organizers from the outside.

In personal relations, in belief systems, in the more intimate behavior patterns, then, change has been negligible or nonexistent. Now, anyone looking at various developing countries in Asia and Africa will also have found that in many regions, personal, familial and other basic life patterns have changed least. Such changes as have occurred have involved new social groupings produced by the new work situation, new political associations arising at least in part from the formation of new states or other new political entities, and new patterns of economic behavior resulting primarily from new and especially industrial methods of production rather than from altered social or cultural conditions.

In general, I think one can argue that the significant differences and patterns of change attributable to the introduction of new productive activities principally reflect changes in economic conditions, together with individual propensities to enter new and previously nonexistent social groups, rather than changes in attitudes or in family structure. It must be emphasized, however, that industrialization took place in Cantel only on a very limited scale. The factory was set up in a rural community, and though the population increased a bit and several new houses were constructed near the factory, and though other changes took place within the community, including the availability, to workers, of new and improved commodities that the peasants were too poor to buy, basic personal and even socio-cultural conditions altered not at all,

[6] This discussion is based on Manning Nash, "Introducing Industry in Peasant Societies," *Science*, 130 (November 27, 1959), pp. 1456–1462.

[7] *Ibid.*, p. 1460.

or at most only very little. Dualism is absent from Cantel, because the new economic activities were fully integrated into the peasant community.

Now, industrialization often involves productive entities much larger than a small textile firm, and it usually occurs primarily in urban rather than in rural areas. Consequently, persons who enter the industrial enterprises leave their original place of work, move to an urban center, and lose contact with many members of their families and others with whom they have traditionally associated. As observers of Indian or Indonesian cities have often reported, however, members of a given group (whether it is based on a common language, on caste, or on village of origin) try to associate with others from the same group and to maintain close relations with them. Moreover, urban residents in these countries, and in other newly industrializing nations in which urban areas have grown quickly and relatively recently, often return to the villages whence they came, when their urban employment ends. For example, in a survey of migration into and out of major urban centers in India, S. N. Agarwala found that in the older age groups emigration considerably exceeds immigration, an indication that these older people return to the villages or small towns from which they originally came.[8]

This implies that urbanization is an important factor in changes in social structure in the newly developing countries. For, although urban residents from similar social and geographical areas try to establish relations similar to those in the villages, these groups are often small, and in many instances associations of this type are impossible. Workers moving to urban areas in which industrial employment is available often come without their families, and inter-action among temporarily single men differs substantially from interaction among rural families in Asian and African countries.

Hence the increasing settlement of workers in cities, and the urban concentration of industrial establishments and related services are important factors in breaking up existing social relations and creating new forms of social interaction and social stratification. In short, alteration in stratification systems depends on the growth and increasing urban concentration of the population of developing countries.

Little research has been done on the changing stratification patterns in urban areas of developing Asian and African countries, partly because in many urban areas immigrant workers are still highly mobile. But studies of Indian cities,[9] for example, suggest that stratification in the urban areas of some developing countries generally resembles that of Western countries. Hence, the notion of "dualism" is mainly based on the observation that stratification in agricultural areas has changed little whereas in urban areas it has taken on many Western features. Changes in urban areas have been only partial, however, and without doubt have begun to affect rural areas in some parts of the world, though empirical knowledge on this is still very limited.

An additional problem involves the entry of foreign people, not through colonization, but through the immigration of ordinary people from other Asian or African societies at a similar level of development. The migration of Chinese into parts of South and Southeast Asia, the migration of Indians to parts of Africa and Southeast Asia, and that of various Middle Easterners to many parts of the world are examples. Where these immigrations involved large groups of foreigners, they usually concentrated on certain specialized economic activities, created their own residential centers in urban areas, and in general continued the social relations characteristic of their native countries.

But in a number of areas, as time goes on, changes have been taking place which are likely to increase interaction between the native inhabitants and the immigrants. European colonial powers did not interfere

[8] See S. N. Agarwala, "A Method for Estimating Decade Internal Migration in Cities in India from Indian Census Data"' *Indian Economic Review,* 4 (February, 1958), p. 71.

[9] See for example, S. N. Sen, *The City of Calcutta* (Calcutta: Bookland, n.d.—ca. 1960), and C. W. Ranson, *A City in Transition: Studies in the Social Life of Madras* (Madras: The Christian Literature Society of India, 1938).

with or impose special rules on "colored" immigrants from Asian or African countries, but when these developing countries became politically independent, and political power was transferred to the natives, it became important to integrate these foreigners with the domestic social structure. Full integration cannot easily be achieved, and in the process the ethnically and linguistically distinct immigrants must choose whether to return to their home countries or to find a place in the social and economic life of the dominant and politically more powerful native population.

I do not regard the previous situation, which is now being altered everywhere in newly independent countries, as dualism. To be sure, substantial differences in personal associations and in stratification systems have divided immigrants from natives. But with one or two exceptions—Malaya being the principal one—the total number of foreign immigrants was too small to permit economic and political independence from the domestic majority. And with political independence and indigenous political leadership, any apparent elements of dualism in the relations between ethnic minorities and domestic majorities will gradually disappear.

In the United States, the gradual integration and "Americanization" of persons with very different linguistic and national origins, in the pre-World War I and pre-World War II periods, is clearly an instance of this tendency to form a national unity. And although the United States is still "dualistic" with respect to different racial groups, current policies are designed to bring about closer integration and ultimately, perhaps, a complete eradication of various forms of dualism or "segregation."

The process of integrating ethnic groups does tend to produce a system of social stratification in which some difficulties and inconsistencies are inevitable. In many instances the ethnic minorities occupy positions in specialized secondary production, or in commercial activities, and therefore enjoy an income level higher than that of most of the indigenous population. For example, the income of the few thousand Indians who live in Nyasaland was estimated to be, on the average, 15 to 20 times higher than that of the indigenous Nyasas, and though the income differences may be smaller in Thailand between Chinese and Thais, or in Indonesia between Chinese and Indonesians, they still create an obstacle to the social and economic integration of the ethnic minorities. But as these countries achieve political independence, and take moderately successful steps toward modernization, economic growth will improve the social and economic positions of the indigenous people. More than any other factor, this tends to make possible the integration of foreign ethnic minorities into the social structure of newly developing countries. Some phases of the integration of ethnic minorities may be complex and difficult, however, leading to violence or other forms of serious social conflict. But in the long run ethnic "dualism" will disappear, as a structurally more simplified and better integrated society emerges.

## CONCLUSION

Among the major issues I have raised, in connection with dualism as a feature of social stratification in societies containing both industrialized and non-industrialized sectors, one of the most important is the problem of social mobility, both between agricultural and industrial sectors and within each of them. As economic change of various kinds takes place in developing economies, the rural and urban, or agricultural and industrial sectors tend to become increasingly interdependent. With the growth of international commerce and the rise of internal markets, assisted by the extension of roads and railways, the old self-sufficiency of the village has been progressively worn down; the rigidity of the old village division of labor has softened; the old social barriers to economic mobility are slowly yielding, and in most villages—at least in most parts of Asia and probably within the next few years also in Africa—cash is replacing barter. At the same time the expansion of towns and the diversification of employment opportunities, the rise of new trades and the somewhat more limited decline of old ones, have been breaking down the formerly rather complete control exercised by the family, though in many developing countries the family is still a strong force. The spread of education, which has been very substantial in many developing countries, is working in the same direction. India, in particular, epitomizes these developments in many ways. There political independence, the formation of indigenous political movements, the formal abolition of large landed estates and the alleged and, in some cases genuine, increase of tenants' rights, have broadened village horizons. The substitution of a new social order for the old one has become concretely associated with more modern patterns of economic and social organization.[10]

In other words, the forms of social stratification characteristic of urban industrial and tertiary occupations have to some extent affected economic and related social patterns in the rural areas of developing countries. In some of the more isolated areas this change has not yet taken place, but with the growth of communication and transport systems the size and importance of these regions will decline. This is especially true in Asia, but it is beginning in Africa and will probably continue on both continents at a rapidly increasing rate.

Thus we may say that dualism either did not exist in the newly developing countries of Asia and Africa, or, where it did exist in some form, it is disappearing. For the changing social and economic conditions in these countries are making individuals in different productive activities more interdependent, and the major bases of social differentiation are increasingly confined to the more intimate spheres, to family relations, religious beliefs, and primary groups whose identity and composition have a long-standing and well-established significance. Changes in social structure are closely based, in my opinion, on changes in the nature and conditions of economic growth, and on the whole the basic processes of economic growth are very similar in all newly developing countries. What varies among these peoples are certain cultural conditions, most of which are inherited from a long past. Though in its intermediate phases the type of stratification associated with economic growth may appear to be dualistic, it is also compatible with quite different cultural conditions, and in the next few decades systems of stratification in different Asian and African countries should become increasingly similar.

[10] On India, and for other related aspects as well, see UNESCO, *Social Change and Economic Development* (Paris: UNESCO, 1963), esp. pp. 90–99, 110–118, and 157–163.

# PERUVIAN STRATIFICATION AND MOBILITY—REVOLUTIONARY AND DEVELOPMENTAL POTENTIAL

*David Chaplin*

While Peru's economic development is highly influenced by its resource endowment and the price structure of its exports, the style of industrialization will be determined in large part by the type and amount of social mobility its class structure permits. Although similar ethnically to Guatemala and Bolivia, Peru has so far (1967) managed to forestall a basic social revolution and has developed under one of the most private "free enterprise" regimes in Latin America. It should therefore be interesting to examine the type of class structure and social mobility which underlies this stage of development.

In terms of a model of the process of industrialization, I shall emphasize the distinctive features of the transitional stage. It seems that a folk-urban, traditional-modern dichotomy—or even a transitional type which is merely "half way" between these extremes—is not adequate. There are features of the class structure which are apparently peculiar to the transitional stage, such as the multiple "full-time" occupations of the middle class. This stage is not merely a mixture of "the old and the new." It may turn out on reanalysis that some of these features are not limited to the currently underdeveloped countries into which

Printed by permission of the author.

industrialization has been introduced from the outside, but will be found to have existed also in the "Western case" of spontaneous development.

In addition to the above perspectives, the question of downward mobility, which has been neglected in many studies of social mobility,[1] is particularly interesting in Peru. Fox and Miller suggest that the amount of downward mobility in a society is the best measure of its openness.[2] In the case of the United States it could be argued, contrary to its avowed universalism, that its economic development has been such as to allow considerable upward mobility *as well as* considerable upper-class continuity since so much room is being created at the top. . . . Fox and Miller note, for instance, that in comparing the United States, Great Britain, the Netherlands and Japan, "the ability of sons of elite fathers to inherit their father's socio-economic status is greatest in the United States, 24 per cent greater than in Great Britain. . . . The United States has high inheritance [of elite positions] *and* high accessibility."[3]

It may be the case in Peru that, cultural particularism notwithstanding, there is both low internal accessibility *and* relatively low inheritance, the latter arising from high elite fertility, inheritance laws calling for an equal division of property—as well as a small but socially significant foreign immigration moving "in at the top."

## PERUVIAN SOCIAL STRUCTURE

Before discussing mobility an attempt will be made to describe Peru's class structure. Its most outstanding feature is its large Indian population. An "Indian" is someone who speaks little or no Spanish, wears Indian garb and sandals or walks barefoot and chews coca (cocaine) leaves. By this cultural definition, they are probably not over a third of the population.

Historically, the Indians were a subordinate "caste" majority, so the process by which they have decreased in relative importance is one of the most significant types of social mobility in Peru. Even after independence the Indians continued to be treated as a separate group with special burdens (tithing for support of the Church until 1854) and few privileges. In fact, most historians agree that their condition worsened markedly after the somewhat restraining hand of the Crown was eliminated in 1821. On the other hand, since a majority of Peruvians today are racially mestizo (Indian and White mixture), a strict caste endogamy has obviously not been maintained.

Paralleling this division between the Indian and non-Indian is the rural-urban difference in class structure. Although some observers feel class to be an urban phenomenon in developing societies, Peru's highland Indians are not an egalitarian subsistence "hunting and gathering" folk culture. Most of them are inside or near large plantations. They have also acquired a strong Western sense of private property, indigenist ideologists notwithstanding.

In cities of the importance of departmental capitals the upper stratum consists of a light-skinned class based on land, profession, governmental office and commerce in rural departments and finance, commerce, land and government in Lima. There is a sharp break between Lima (1,500,000 in 1961), and the rest of Peru's towns (Arequipa, the next largest, is only one-tenth as large).

The major split in Peru's "oligarchy" is found between the inefficient feudal *latifundistas* in the mountains (*gamonales*) and the modern export-oriented cotton and sugar plantation owners along the coast. The former group is still dominant only in local affairs while the national "power elite" is made up largely of coastal plantation owners. This oligarchy, Bourricaud feels, is not a true elite or ruling class but a monopolistic collection of "clans" which is based on the neutralization of the middle classes and "shoving aside" the "forgotten" lower classes.[4] Unfortunately the use of bearer stock (*acciones al portador*) and the secretive nature of Peruvian business

[1] Thomas Fox and S. M. Miller, "Occupational Stratification and Mobility: Intra-Country Variations," in *Studies in Comparative International Development*, Vol. I, No. 1, 1965, p. 1.

[2] *Ibid.*, p. 3.

[3] *Ibid.*, p. 8.

[4] See François Bourricaud, "Structure and Function of the Peruvian Oligarchy," *Studies in Comparative International Development*, Vol. II, No. 2, 1966.

**TABLE 1 1961 Socio-Economic Status Structure**[5]

| | *Total Peru* | *Lima* | *Callao* | *Ayacucho* | *Loreto* | *Pasco* |
|---|---|---|---|---|---|---|
| | % | % | % | % | % | % |
| I. Upper class (administrative) | 1.5 | 3.5 | 3.2 | .3 | 1.5 | 1.8 |
| II. Upper middle class (professional, technical) | 3.5 | 6.3 | 4.4 | 2.1 | 3.5 | 3.0 |
| III. Middle class (office employees) | 4.5 | 11.0 | 13.9 | .8 | 2.5 | 3.0 |
| IV. Lower middle class (salesmen, clerks, etc.) | 7.6 | 12.3 | 10.6 | 4.9 | 7.4 | 5.2 |
| V. Upper lower class (miners, artisans, chauffeurs, factory workers) | 19.7 | 30.6 | 37.4 | 8.3 | 11.5 | 28.5 |
| VI. Lower lower class (peasants, domestic servants) | 63.2 | 36.3 | 30.5 | 83.6 | 73.6 | 58.5 |
| | 100.0 | 100.0 | 100.0 | 100.0 | 100.0 | 100.0 |

[5] *Censo Nacional de Población, Dirección Nacional de Estadística y Censos,* Vol. I, Tomo IV, Tables 8 and 18, Lima, 1966.

life make a more detailed or reliable evaluation of upper-class economic behavior very difficult. It is fairly clear, however, that Peru's national upper class does have the following characteristics: It is overwhelmingly based in Lima, quite open to infiltration by financially successful European or North American entrepreneurs, and quite disunited by familial, commercial and political competition.

Turning to the 1961 census, there is some "objective" data available on class strata. If we type the eleven explicit occupational categories provided by the census by their median income, the following socio-economic status type strata can be delimited:

For the country as a whole this distribution fits the pattern expected in underdeveloped countries with only 1.5 per cent in the upper class and 15.6 in the middle. The most urban and industrial departments, Lima (86 per cent urban) and Callao (96 per cent urban—Lima's nearby port city), have predictably the largest middle classes. Ayacucho is a prototypical Indian sierra department with a very large lower class and a disproportionately large upper middle class made up predominantly of government officials in the departmental and provincial capitals. The upper and middle classes listed in Loreto (Peru's largest department, consisting of sparsely populated jungle) live largely in one town—the capital at Iquitos. Pasco is the sierra department with the heaviest concentration of modern mining operations. . . .

In terms of the occupational structure (see Table 2), Peru's distinctive features are (1) An excessive tertiary sector composed of both government workers and lawyers as well as surplus "primitive" services such as domestic servants, street vendors, etc. (2) A proliferation of multiple full-time type occupation-holding (not visible in the following Table) most striking in those modern middle-class positions in which such behavior would be judged as diluting professional specialization if not involving actual conflicts of interest. (3) A retarded development of industrial, especially manufacturing jobs. In this category we also find a "premature" exclusion of women owing to their higher cost due to the selective enforcement of labor and welfare laws in this industrial sector.

. . . One of the peculiarities of Peruvian social structure has been that the manual–non-manual gap, already very wide traditionally, was increased in the labor laws passed between 1920 and 1960. In general,

**TABLE 2 The Peruvian Labor Force[6] 1940–1961**

| | *The % Male* | | *Total* | | | | |
|---|---|---|---|---|---|---|---|
| | 1940 % | 1961 % | 1940 % | 1961 % | | 1940 % | 1961 % |
| 1. Agriculture | 68.5 | 86.2 | 62.4 | 49.7 | Primary sector | 64.4 | 51.8 |
| 2. Extractive | 97.3 | 97.3 | 1.8 | 2.2 | | | |
| 3. Manufacturing | 43.5 | 71.8 | 15.4 | 13.1 | Secondary | 17.2 | 16.6 |
| 4. Construction | 98.0 | 99.0 | 1.9 | 3.3 | | | |
| 5. Commerce | 67.8 | 72.1 | 4.6 | 9.1 | Tertiary | 16.8 | 27.2 |
| 6. Transportation & communication | 95.3 | 95.1 | 2.1 | 3.0 | | | |
| 7. Services | 50.9 | 50.8 | 10.2 | 15.2 | | | |
| 8. Other | 80.1 | 78.4 | 1.6 | 4.4 | | 1.6 | 4.4 |
| % Male of all economically active | 64.6 | 78.2 | 100.0 | 100.0 | | 100.0 | 100.0 |

[6] *Censo Nacional de Población y Ocupación,* Vol. I, 1940, *Dirección Nacional de Estadística,* Lima, 1944, pp. 360, 606–607, and 669. *Sexto Censo Nacional de Población—Resultados Finales de Primera Prioridad, 1961, Dirección Nacional de Estadística y Censos,* Lima, March, 1964, p. 230, Table 11.

the benefits of *empleados* (white-collar workers) were twice as good as those of *obreros* (blue-collar workers). In the early 1960s the *obreros'* benefits were pulled up to the level of the *empleados* except for the sharp distinction still maintained in medical facilities. The *obrero* labor and welfare laws are, however, enforced only for a small segment of the labor force, namely the organized workers in the Lima-Callao area and the few provincial centers of industry.

In the white-collar sector there are two major categories in the 1961 census, governmental and private employees. The most striking feature of this white-collar sector is the relative size of government employment. For the country as a whole, the ratio of white-collar workers who worked for the government to those working for private employers was .65. This varied, from a low of .48 in the department of Lima (in which the capital is over 80 per cent of the population) to a high of 3.9 in the jungle department of Amazonas. Thus while both government power and personnel are highly centralized in Lima, commerce and industry are even more concentrated there. Within provincial towns then, government workers are relatively more numerous than in the capital.

The difference between these two types of white-collar occupations is also revealed in this comparison of their income distribution. The private employees span a much wider range of income levels by including more highly paid as well as poorly paid workers than those in government.[7] . . .

The main problem in interpreting this comparison between government and private *empleados* is that the larger the town the more likely government workers are to also have one or more non-governmental jobs. So while the official report (undoubtedly underestimating the income of private employees) presumably avoids double counting, it can not give an accurate picture of the total income of government employees either.[8]

Another way of approaching the question of occupational differentials is to examine the gap between the urban *empleado* and *obrero* income and the per cent urban by

[7] *Censo Nacional de Población,* Vol. I, Tomo IV, Table 115, *Dirección Nacional de Estadística,* Lima, 1966.

[8] An additional problem in Peru is the institution of *acciones al portador* or bearer stock through which the ownership, and hence dividend recipients, of "anonymous societies" remain unknown.

departments. There is a strong negative correlation between the size of this gap and the per cent urban—that is, the more rural an area the greater the distance is between these groups within local towns. In Lima and Callao, therefore, we find a minimal difference in median monthly income of 450 shill between urban *empleados* and *obreros*, whereas in the isolated sierra department of Ayacucho this difference (even at a lower absolute level of income for both) is greatest—at 1150 shill. (Ayacucho also has the fourth highest ratio of government to private *empleados* in the country: 2.7.)

Turning to the Peruvian middle class, we find a dearth of empirical studies. The most distinctive feature of this stratum has already been described—namely multiple occupation-holding. The "ideal" combination of occupations would be a university professorship for prestige, a government position for power and prestige, and various private jobs related to the governmental post for income. It is partly through the latter activities that a European type of bourgeois consciousness is diluted. As Bourricaud observed, "the middle class has not evolved an original value system . . . vis-a-vis the oligarchs. . . . The characteristic trait of [the] Peruvian middle class—whether . . . old or new . . . is that it is a *dependent* group." This dependence arises from the fact that "this country has no bureaucracy in the Weberian sense" nor has it produced a nineteenth-century type of entrepreneur. The few successful men of this type were generally foreigners who "were bought out by the oligarchy, enjoying a rapid absorption into the traditional ruling class."[9]

This blurring of occupational identity could be interpreted as illustrating the point that in this transitional phase of industrial development, in the middle and upper classes, occupations are perhaps least relevant to a man's over-all status. I am assuming, perhaps incorrectly, that there was a somewhat greater tendency for the very small (but certainly existent) colonial and nineteenth-century middle class to have one major occupation as is still more the case in small towns. Today, the expansion of the "infrastructure" beyond the supply of qualified personnel, and the depressing effect of inflation—cause middle-class professionals to take on as many sources of income as possible even if they are all full-time type occupations whose various commitments they could not properly meet. . . . Multiple occupations are linked with a leisure-oriented basis for social status. It is the middle-class man's style of consumption rather than production which determines his prestige.[10] Such an ephemeral basis for status naturally leads to a high degree of social instability and anxiety. One aspect of this behavior is the abuse of the title Doctor, or Engineer, for almost anyone with a university level education.

Peru's middle classes are different from Western also in being made up largely of employees of the government or large foreign firms. The independent businessman is relatively rare and usually foreign in origin (even if Peruvian in nationality as in the case of the Chinese).

A central factor in the situation of such a salaried class is inflation. MacLean y Estenos places the first proletarianization of the lower middle class during the inflation of World War I.[11] It would be extremely difficult to pinpoint when the better paid factory workers surpassed the income of the lower white-collar workers, but this "modern" phenomenon had occurred at least by 1958.[12] This latter shift was not primarily a matter of a relative decline in white-collar wages, but rather the substantial gains in welfare benefits as well as wages enjoyed by

[9] Bourricaud, *op. cit.*, p. 27. MacLean y Estenos suggests that the absence of independent guilds (the Indians were used for artisan work, or such goods were imported) is one factor accounting for the non-bourgeois character of Peru's middle class. Robert MacLean y Estenos, *Sociología Peruana*, Lima, 1942, p. 118. We could add the absence of a "free city" tradition. Lima has always been dominant over Peru but until recently subservient to a landowning plutocracy.

[10] François Bourricaud, "Algunas características originales de la cultura mestiza en el Peru contemporaneo," *Revista del Museo Nacional*, Tomo XXIII, 1954, p. 165.

[11] MacLean y Estenos, *op. cit.*, p. 118.

[12] David Chaplin, "Industrialization and the Distribution of Wealth in Peru," *Studies in Comparative International Development*, Vol. III, No. 3, 1967–1968, p. 58.

the privileged sector of Lima's organized factory workers.

The urban lower class has been studied primarily in Lima. Its most outstanding characteristic is its failure to radicalize. The urban proletariat has looked (successfully) more to paternalistic military dictators than middle-class revolutionary leaders. In Peru's case the famous Aprista party (one of the earliest significant non-Communist radical parties after the Mexican revolution) must also share the credit or blame for this situation since it has used its lower-class base largely to benefit its middle-class leadership. It is closely linked to the textile federation, the earliest major urban industrial union, but even so, most of the considerable benefits enjoyed by these workers were enacted by the military dictators, Benavides (1933–1939) and Odría (1948–1956), rather than by more democratic regimes.

It seems that urbanization in Latin America, unlike the case of the West, dilutes lower-class protest so effectively that a deradicalization (or stifling of radicalization) could be said to be occurring.[13] An explanation for this "deviant" transitional phenomenon could be that: (1) As in other Latin American countries, the small group of highly organized urban factory workers (the only group which could effectively protest) are relatively well taken care of by the selective enforcement of very advanced labor and welfare benefits. This can be done because factory owners are not yet a major sector of the national elite. They are also largely foreign in Peru. In addition, Peru's factories are more capital intensive and protected than were England's at a comparable level of economic development, hence they can afford to pay higher wages. (2) This industrial sector is still very small and, thanks to its relative capital intensity, it is not likely to ever be as large a per cent of the national labor force as was the case in Western development. The great lead of the tertiary sector is not likely to be reversed. (3) Although 70 per cent of Peru's industrial establishments are located in the Lima-Callao area, they are overshadowed by the size and complexity of this metropolis.[14] Moreover, the median size of employment per manufacturing establishment is under 300. The few mining towns in Peru, however, do reveal the same pattern of polarized intense labor-management conflict that Kerr and Seigel noted for Western countries.[15] (4) The mass of Lima's lower class has its political and economic leverage diluted by the enormous influx of increasingly "Indian" migrants. Most slum dwellers try to handle their problems in an individualistic manner since they seem to be unable to develop effective voluntary associations. (Many are created but few accomplish anything.)

## NINETEENTH-CENTURY SOCIAL MOBILITY

Contrary to the stereotyped view, the nineteenth century was not a period of "feudalistic" stability but one of turbulent change even in rural areas. Factors increasing the level of elite change in Peru during this period are (1) The abolition of primogeniture and entail. Landed estates were divided up equally among all children—of both sexes, legitimate and illegitimate. One must also remember that fertility in Peru at this time undoubtedly varied directly rather than inversely with wealth. Most of the poor died before adolescence and so could barely reproduce themselves. Thus there existed a demographic pressure for downward mobility for some of the descendants of wealthy families. (2) With a custom of dowries together with the chance sex ratio among children—the wrong mixture of children and marriages could ruin a family. In fact, one could say that only

[13] Ratinoff, in his survey of middle-class ideology in Latin America, sees several stages to this deradicalization. At first, the rising middle class is in favor of limits on individual freedoms—especially property rights since they are interested in undercutting the power of the plutocratic elite. Later when their position is more established they favor a return to individual property rights. Luis Ratinoff, *La clase media en América Latina, Revista Paraguaya de Sociología, Año* 2, No. 4, *Set.–Dic.* 1965, pp. 16–18.

[14] *Censo de Manufactura—1963, Dirección Nacional de Estadística y Censos,* Lima, 1965, p. v.

[15] Clark Kerr and Abraham Siegel, "The Interindustry Propensity to Strike—An International Comparison," chap. 14 in Arthur Kornhauser, *et al., Industrial Conflict,* New York: McGraw-Hill, 1954.

an extraordinarily adroit and lucky family could preserve their status in rural Peru generation after generation.[16]

It should also be noted that Peru's nineteenth-century plutocratic families did not maintain any sense of "racial" or ethnic purity with respect to the few European or North American migrants who came to Peru during this period. Like the sixteenth–seventeenth-century British landed aristocracy they were only too happy to effect ties to an entrepreneurial group.[17] From a period of extreme provincial isolation when even the elite in Lima could cherish a sense of being the center of a universe, the devaluation of Peru's culture has grown to a national disease. As a result, Peru's elite is denationalized by various foreign cultures of orientation—often not shared even within the same family. The committed nationalists are then only a segment of the middle class—and, of course, the politicians, since the largely disenfranchised Indians are not yet part of Peru's "civic culture."

## TWENTIETH-CENTURY SOCIAL MOBILITY

The major change in social stratification in Peru's provincial towns has been the exodus of the original creole landed "aristocracy."[18] There has always been a pattern of absenteeism, but before the turn of the twentieth century it usually took the form of having a town house in the provincial or departmental capital so that frequent and prolonged visits to the plantation could be made. Thereafter a redefinition of an acceptable level of physical comfort and style, together with the eroding effect of Indian unrest, caused these provincial elites to abandon their landholdings to managers while they fled to Lima. Such a move usually meant a downgrading to upper middle clas at best since the Lima pyramid towers above that of all other cities. In a similar manner, movement out of Lima makes relative upward mobility possible although acceptance by provincial society would be slower. Subsequently even an upper-middle-class status in Lima may be difficult to maintain since absentee-managed highland plantations are likely to yield declining revenues—especially today in the face of Indian invasions and the threat of land reform. As a result, unless such ex-provincial elite families can rise to the challenge of developing a new urban economic base they are likely to slip still further.

The most striking effect of the heavy waves of rural migration to Lima has been the ruralization of sections of the city. At the same time Peru's upper class, located overwhelmingly in Lima, becomes more cosmopolitan in its outlook—thus there is less of a shared culture in Lima today than 50 years ago due not only to the increase in the absolute size of the population but more crucially to these divergent influences.

Another current of migration also of growing significance since 1940 has been the increasing number of middle-class Peruvians educated abroad. Education in general is the most important means of upward mobility (a good professional education can, of course, also cushion the fall of the son of an ex-provincial "aristocrat"). As the national universities are increasingly democratized the prestige value of their degrees declines and hence a foreign education becomes even more desirable aside from its usually much greater functional utility. Before World War II the majority of Peruvians studying abroad were upper class. With the closing off of Europe during the Second World War and the growing importance of the United States in the Peruvian economy, the predominant locale of the foreign educated changed. The surplus demand in North American universities meant that no longer could scions of the best families count on getting into the elite foreign universities. Their places were increasingly likely to be taken by more talented and ambitious middle-class Peruvians.

The initial expectation of the North

[16] Lenski has also noted a high level of agrarian elite turnover in studies on medieval Europe. See Gerhard E. Lenski, *Power and Privilege*, New York: McGraw-Hill, 1966, p. 239.

[17] Lawrence Stone. "Marriage Among the English Nobility in the Sixteenth and Seventeenth Centuries," *Comparative Studies in Society and History*, Vol. III, No. 2, January, 1961, pp. 182–206.

[18] Gabriel Escobar M., *La estructura política rural del departamento de Puno*, Published doctoral thesis in Anthropology, Universidad Nacional de San Antonio Abad del Cuzco, Cuzco, December, 1961.

American foundations paying for the education of this new group was that they would "of course" return to their countries where the need for their talents was so great. The actual outcome is now described as the problem of the Brain Drain (inadequately compensated for by the importation of short-term foreign "experts"). The problem for the foreign schools is that if they selected Peruvian students only on the basis of ability they could be turning out some graduates of such modest social background that the gap between the position they were trained for and the one they could hope to obtain would be unbearable—and so they would return to "their" foreign country or become revolutionaries. Even where "excessive" social mobility is not involved, a prolonged period of training in the "West" tends to have the following disadvantages: (1) The student may unlearn the *criollo* (creole, or in this context, "operator") approach to career success and instead come to expect to win a position on merit alone. He thus is psychologically unprepared to play the game—as it still must be played in Peru.[19] (2) He may also simply lose touch with his clique or patron.

A related matter for those not working primarily for the government is whether they seek employment with a national or foreign-owned firm. Each has obstacles to advancement. The national firm is normally a family enterprise in which the best positions will go to relatives. The foreign firm for its part often reserves the top positions for its own countrymen. However, in the latter case there are two countervailing factors. The average total size and relative proportion of higher level positions are larger in foreign firms. They are also, at least, true corporations and not family enterprises. Moreover, they can be pressured by the government into "nationalizing" their personnel up to the highest local level. Some of those top positions, however, are also particularistic in a "functional" way. Each foreign firm needs a protective wall of local influentials whose only talent need be personal ties to the ruling oligarchy. These positions are therefore not open to talented "upstarts."

## LOWER-CLASS MOBILITY

Lower-class rural mobility occurs mainly through migration to cities precipitated by available education and transportation routes. Culturally, it is described as the process of *cholificación*—of Indians becoming *cholos*.[20] *Cholos* are viewed as the next higher stratum to Indians (followed by mestizos and then creoles). However, they are also in a different situs since Indian communities have their own internal stratification system based on wealth, age and political office. Their distinguishing traits are bilingualism and an aggressive self-reliant relationship to the dominant mestizo and creole classes. They have sloughed off the deference and inferiority complex of the Indians without compromising their aggressions through the adoption of middle-class aspirations. As a marginal category, they lack stable reference groups and so live a disorganized existence. They are, however, the most dynamic element in the sierra even if this involves taking advantage of the Indian.

In the 1920s a series of Indian revolts against further encroachment on their lands by plantation owners in the southern sierra brought about an "Indigenous Community" reform law. It was designed to protect the surviving *ayllus* (traditional Indian communities created by the colonial *reducciones*) from further expropriation. In principle, this seemed to promise a United States-type reservation system which could slow down the acculturation of the Indian, thus keeping him out of national life. In fact, the results were quite different. (The traditional subsistence plantation with its "attached" Indians is actually the most effective isolating institution.) Since taking advantage of this law required the employment of a lawyer

[19] See Anthony Leeds, "Brazilian Careers and Social Structure: an Evolutionary Model and Case History," *American Anthropologist*, Vol. 66, No. 6, Part 1, December, 1964, for an excellent description of the operation of this same prebendary *patronazgo* (patronage) system in Brazil. Ratinoff generalizes Leeds' findings to all of Latin America (Luis Ratinoff, *La clase media en América Latina, Revista Paraguaya de Sociología, Año* 2, No. 4, *Set.–Dic.* 1965).

[20] Gabriel Escobar M., *El mestizaje en la región andina: el caso del Peru, Revista de Indias,* Nos. 95 and 96, *Enero–Junio*, Madrid, 1964, pp. 197–220.

and a direct relationship with the Ministry of Labor and Indian Affairs in Lima, the registered communities were actually projected into greater participation in national life. A related factor accelerating acculturation is that although some Peruvian intellectuals and folklorists idealize the Indian (primarily the defunct Incaic civilization) the contemporary Indian is generally despised for his "dirty uncultivated" habits.

Mobility within Indian communities occurs largely through the lavish patronizing of fiestas and election to local political office. But even this internal mobility requires participation in the national economy to raise the necessary money.

## DISTRIBUTION OF INCOME AND WEALTH

For the middle third of the twentieth century some data is available on changes in the distribution of wealth and income.[21] All of the available sources suggest that while a small proportion of the organized urban industrial labor force is gaining both relatively and absolutely, the over-all distribution of wealth and income has become increasingly unequal both by class and region. The reasons for this are

1. Movement into the market economy of the relatively larger, elite-owned resources previously possessed but not evaluated in commercial market terms. The extension of commercialism also means that real estate is exchanged for money rather than primarily as familial inheritance or bridal dowries. Hence the possibility for a more rational concentration of holdings.
2. Since only the upper class can save significantly, commercialization increases the economic opportunities of those already on top.
3. There is an increasing gap between the urban and rural world resulting from the concentration of industrialization in the largest cities—in Peru's case almost exclusively in Lima—since increases in per capita productivity come more rapidly in the urban industrial sector.
4. Excessive population growth decreases the level of living of the mass of landless peons thus widening the gap even if the wealth of the elite remains stable.
5. The usual inflation which undercuts the position of the majority group of employees in favor of the owners of land and other flexible price assets.

[21] See Chaplin, *op. cit.*

## AGRARIAN REFORM

In this connection the question of the aims and the probable consequences of land reform should be raised. They are (1) Social justice through a redistribution of wealth; and (2) increased food production for Peru's booming population. A not so explicit goal is the creation of a conservative petit bourgeois peasantry to offset the danger of a revolutionary landless proletariat. (I am speaking of the type of "bourgeois-reformist" land reform as it is generally defined in Latin America—not of Soviet-type collectives or state farms.) Of course there are still some obtuse die-hards who view this program as itself revolutionary because it will require the expropriation of the notoriously inefficient (but also economically unpromising) mountain *latifundia.* Actually land reform is sophisticated conservatism in the same sense as is birth control for the masses. Communists do, or should from their own perspective, see it as a bourgeois trick to repeat the unintended effect of the early Soviet (which created the ultra-conservative Kulaks) or the Napoleonic land reforms.[22] Nevertheless, they must pay it lip service since land reform has become an article of faith with most Latin American progressives.

As to its practical consequences for changing the social structure, we can perhaps turn to Bolivia. There the old class of landlords was indeed destroyed in the 1952 revolution and a new rural political base developed with which the government could offset the persistently rebellious mine union and its militia. (A comparable goal was achieved in Venezuela.) The same type of minimal immediate improvement in economic condition could be accomplished in

[22] Karl Marx, *The Eighteenth Brumaire of Louis Bonaparte,* George Allen and Unwin, London, 1943, pp. 135–137. Marx also observed that the benefits to the peasantry of such a division of land had to be transitory—enough to buy support and time for one regime but subsequently equally great poverty would result.

Peru in spite of the extremely conservative and laggard nature of their law and program. (In Peru no redistribution of wealth is contemplated since the landlords would be well compensated by government bonds with extraordinary financial support.) On the other hand, it seems unlikely that the ultimate development of land redistribution in Peru will be much structured by this law since most of the division of land so far has been a legalization of the many land invasions outside the law. Moreover, it seems very unlikely that, were the Indians to default on their mortgage payments, the government would forcibly eject them en masse.

In the long run, even an immediately successful land reform program can not avoid the inevitable reconcentration of land which seems to occur in any industrialized society, Communist or capitalist—only a system of uneconomic subsidies (such as those of the United States, which Peru could not afford) could maintain an agricultural sector of independent farm families. This reconcentration will be hastened by the desperate need for more food for the production of which there is not enough time or personnel to painfully retrain the mass of Peruvian Indians. Moreover, it seems likely that one of the consequences of land reform would be an increase in peasant fertility thus wiping out, in a generation, the gain in food production and increase in land holdings to lots of minimal scale efficiency which land reform provides initially. In traditional communities, an Indian does not establish his own family until he can acquire land. A land shortage thus results in postponed marriages and/or emigration. The sudden provision of more land for all would lower the age at marriage and probably increase the per cent married, thereby increasing the size of completed families in such a "non-contracepting" population.

Land reform, then, can be viewed as a short-term stop-gap and a politically unavoidable effort to buy time (against a Communist revolution—and/or regression to chaos) which can only work if parallel efforts are made in the urban industrial sector in which most of the subsequent generations will be living.

## EDUCATION

The primary avenue to social mobility in Peru is formal education. In this respect Peru is not following the pattern of Western industrialization but is rather "prematurely" up to date. Unlike the United States in the nineteenth century (and this source has been much exaggerated) there are very few Peruvians who have risen primarily through business activities. As mentioned above, entrepreneurs in Peru have been overwhelmingly of foreign extraction.

Education thus has to bear an especially heavy burden of ambition which it creates or aggravates only to then frustrate due to either its nonfunctional or poor quality or to the many obstacles to merit mentioned above. It is for this reason that the primary source of revolutionary ferment is in the universities rather than the factories. Rebel leaders are those who suffer the widest gap between their aspirations and achievements, rather than those at the most deprived level of existence or in "classic" proletarian situations.

This radicalizing effect of higher education may, in part, account for the decision of the Peruvian government to reopen or establish universities in provincial towns rather than merely adding more in Lima. The expectation may have been that either such unsophisticated locales would restrain radicalization—or that it could be more easily contained—and the accessibility of the national government to intimidation by student unrest reduced. Only the latter goal could be said to have been partially accomplished. From the start, in the late 1950s, the program of establishing additional provincial universities has been plagued with staffing problems. Most educated Peruvians want to move to or stay in Lima. Only those lacking either influential connections, talent or those imbued with considerable idealism (often revolutionary) would have to or care to teach outside of Lima. As a consequence, students at provincial universities tend to be exposed to more radical faculty influence than in Lima.

This radicalization of the university educated tends, however, to be a transitory phenomenon for the individual even if it increases for the country as a whole due to the larger proportion in school. The radicalization of the university student is a feature of the middle years of his studies and tends to disappear, except perhaps in private conversation, as he comes to terms with careerist pressures. There is, as Theisenhusen notes, "an unseemly willingness of the liberal-minded university-trained in Latin America to be co-opted by the establishment."[23]

Primary and secondary education in Peru remain highly class stratified and hence reinforce the current class structure, except at the bottom. . . . The government-run schools (with a few exceptions in Lima) are for the lower class. Middle- and upper-class children attend private schools. All primary and secondary students wear official uniforms which differ by school and hence bear explicit class stigma.

## THE MILITARY AND THE CHURCH

There are two other major institutions which also offer increasing opportunities for lower-class mobility—the armed forces and the Church. The former has its internal stratification system with the navy being the most elite, followed closely by the air force and then the army. The Guardia Civil apparently suffers a much lower status, drawing its officer corps from the *cholo* class, while the army officers are largely *mestizo* and the navy and air force largely white and upper middle class. One could interpret these differences both as a matter of the differential pressure for practical performance (the navy is largely decorative while the Guardia Civil—as a sort of "state police" in the United States sense—is constantly employed), or attempt to explain them in terms of different foreign cultures of orientation since the air force and navy are largely United States-trained, while the army, until 1939, was French trained. In any case, the army and Guardia Civil do offer the possibility for career mobility to thousands of lower-class males—much more so than the civilian government services.

Such "social democracy" has no necessary tie to a preference for parliamentary democracy. In fact, the military ethos of discipline and disdain for "politicians" leads, at best, to a technocratic professionalism at the higher levels while at the lower ranks it serves to so alienate the Indian recruit from his people that he will willingly kill them if necessary. The army's system of training and assignments effectively turns Indians into *cholos* who tend to despise "their people."

The Catholic clergy also offers an increasing opportunity for lower-class mobility due to the decline in the attractiveness of this profession for the middle and upper class. Today, although the highest positions in the Peruvian hierarchy are still held largely by upper-class priests (with Peruvian congressional and presidential approval), this group has few successors among the coming generation. The clergy, in general, has shrunk due to the decline in recruits and also "darkened" as it declined—that is, a larger proportion of the declining numbers of entrants are lower class in origin.

## CONCLUSION AND FURTHER SPECULATION

In concluding this discussion it should be reiterated that more solid evidence is needed for most of the foregoing assertions. While all are based on field observations, few are buttressed by systematic empirical investigations. There is, however, some concrete evidence that the distribution of wealth and of income is becoming even more unequal than it was some 50 years ago. The crucial exception to this is a small elite segment of urban manufacturing workers whose income has risen relatively as well as absolutely since 1940.

In terms of economic development, the small but strategic flow of foreign migrants to Peru could be said to have the following alternative consequences: (1) a replacement for Peruvians lost through the brain drain; (2) an obstacle to upward mobility within Peru; (3) dynamic entrepreneurship in the form of creating their own—as well as other—positions for Peruvians, rather than blocking internal mobility. (Peruvian writers tend to view foreigners at least as an obstacle if not as outright exploiters of national resources and manpower.) The major obstacle to the entrepreneurship role is the high degree of acceptance of "elite

[23] William C. Theisenhusen, "How Big Is the Brain Drain?" Land Tenure Center Paper No. 29, University of Wisconsin, Madison, January, 1967, pp. 20–22.

strangers" by Peru's established elite. Such absorption tends to dilute the dynamic function of at least the next generation.

Over all, it seems probable that, in spite of Peru's low level of economic development and supposedly rigid social structure, there may be a rather high level of social mobility down as well as up. The significant size of the educational system, the military and the Church provide various channels of upward mobility while inheritance practices, inflation, high upper-class fertility and other factors foster a high rate of downward mobility.

It is hoped that this discussion also contributes toward a model, or at least models, of the transitional stage as not merely derivable from a traditional and modern era. At the present level of abstraction, we would have to include such factors as: (1) whether a country had ever been a colony —and if so, whether freed before or after the first Industrial Revolution; (2) its economic structure; (3) whether a revolutionary, traditionalist or "reform-mongering" regime was in power.

Some of the general features of the current transitional stage seem to be (1) the "advantage" of a late start—which, depending on one's evaluation, might include a relatively wide franchise and very ample (but selectively enforced) labor and welfare legislation; (2) urbanization and population growth ahead of local industrialization; and (3) multiple occupation-holding.

In terms of revolutionary potential, Peru's most subjectively deprived category is its nationally educated university students. They are the major exception to the peculiarly deradicalizing effect urbanization has had on Peru's class conflict. This phenomenon illustrates the central point that Peru is far more urbanized than industrialized, since its level of urbanization is based on foreign trade rather than domestic industrial development or an adequate internal hinterland.

At present the most "promising" mass base for the student middle-class revolutionary leadership is the landless peasantry. The acceptance by this leadership of the petit bourgeois type of land reform program popular in Latin America as a necessary intervening stage threatens to deprive them of the continued support of the small number of peasants they have been able to attract.

At this over-urbanized stage, the potential protest of the industrial proletariat has been "bought off" or deflected. However, the relatively high wages and fringe benefits required for this situation have already raised the prices of Peru's manufactured goods so far above the level of comparable imports that a productivity showdown has only been postponed. Some future government will have to reorganize Peru's industrial system. The resultant labor reaction could be exploited by either a rightist or a leftist party.

# THE EMERGING PATTERN OF ISRAELI STRATIFICATION

*S. N. Eisenstadt*

## 1 SOCIAL ORGANIZATION AND STRATIFICATION IN THE YISHUV[1]

***Introduction—The Problem and the Setting.*** . . . We have seen that one of the major aims of Zionist ideology was to create a new type of modern society—one in which some of the pitfalls of other societies would be avoided. As it developed, however, more and more problems similar to those of other modern societies became apparent and varied social groups and organizations, with different styles of life, values, and traditions emerged. The activities which crystallized from them had to be evaluated —in terms of the major social rewards— money, power, and prestige. Israeli society —as any other—was therefore faced with

From *Israeli Society*, by S. N. Eisenstadt, Basic Books, Inc., Publishers, New York.

[1] This refers to the Jewish community in Israel, formerly Palestine, from its beginnings in the late 1880s. (C. S. H.)

the problems of organizing different social positions, and the allocations of people into these positions. . . .

In one important aspect the development of the Yishuv differed from normal, peasant or traditional societies, and even from most colonizing societies: in the initial stages of development ecological units and basic ascriptive solidarities such as kinship groups, territorial or class divisions, etc., did not constitute the most important or binding factor from which the more specific groups developed and crystallized.

Initially, the basic groups within the Yishuv were the various pioneering groups and sects. Some ecological groups of the older Yishuv existed throughout the initial period, and most new ones—whether agricultural settlements or new urban quarters—were, at first, offshoots of these sects and did not develop any strong traditions or symbols of identification of their own.

Moreover, the special nature of the migratory movement to Palestine implied that no strong ascriptive solidarities such as kinship or ethnic groups or social strata developed initially. It was only much later that such different collectivities—sometimes of a rather special type—developed, and ecological settings as well as ascriptive solidarities acquired some autonomy and tradition of their own. But even these were greatly influenced by the characteristics of the sects from which they stemmed and the most important of which was perhaps that these sects and groups were orientated towards complex social, economic, political, and cultural activities which soon outstripped their concrete needs. . . .

From these beginnings, the social structure of the Yishuv developed in two "ideal-type" directions which, though greatly differing, had some common characteristics.

One can be seen in the rural and urban settlements of the first aliya,[2] and in what came to be called the "private" sector of the Yishuv. The second trend developed from within the more sectarian groups which comprised the "workers'" camp. In between these two several meeting points existed in various cultural, educational, and even professional activities.

. . . . . . . . . . . . . . . . . . . . . . . . . . . . . . . .

***The Structure of the Major Roles. . . .*** Initial Zionist ideology, common to a large extent to the different branches of the Zionist movement, envisaged the full development of all occupational, economic, social, cultural, and political functions, as being permeated by a spirit of national identification and social justice and equality.

In this image the only real role was that of the pioneer with its basic dedication to national goals and pioneering movements.

More autonomous demands of such functions—their claim for prestige, for technical competence, or for intrinsic achievement and performance were very often looked down on as infringing on the purity of the pioneering role. In more ideological formulations this lack of emphasis on any concrete task was seen as a manifestation of the lack of "human self-alienation," characteristic of so many modern, and especially capitalist, societies. In the more realistic-political terms which developed during the third aliya, such demands for the autonomy of different functions were considered as weakening political ardour and identification with the various sects and parties of the workers' sector.

Ideological orientations against such tendencies were also greatly reinforced by the fear of "premature normalization"—as in the case of the first aliya.

This fear of premature normalization coupled with strong ideological orientations was seen most clearly in one of the most vital roles of the period—that of the agriculturist which crystallized as early as the first aliya, matured in the period of the second aliya[3] and fully developed in the mandatory period.

The most important characteristic of this "peasant" role was the de-emphasizing of occupational and "traditional" aspects of peasant life, at the expense of the more élitist conception of agricultural work as the main symbolic expression of pioneering.

[2] The first wave of immigration to Palestine, 1882–1903. It consisted of 20–30,000 immigrants. See S. N. Eisenstadt, *Israeli Society*, New York: Basic Books, 1967, pp. 23–24.(C. S. H.)

[3] Second wave of immigration, 1904–1914. It consisted of 35–40,000 immigrants. *Ibid.* (C.S.H.)

Later, during the third aliya,[4] these élitist orientations were consolidated in the various kibbutz movements,[5] which placed greater importance on ideological orthodoxy than on agricultural activities or a rural way of life.

Although the moshavim[6] established during the third aliya placed greater emphasis on agricultural activities and family life, these tendencies were yet part of a socio-political movement and ideology.

A similar, though perhaps less intensive, tendency developed within the cultural and educational sectors, in which the role of the teacher was defined and developed so as to include the cultural ingredient in the general image of the pioneer.

***Evaluation of Roles.*** Closely related to the definition of different roles was their evaluation and the status levels that developed in the various sectors of the Yishuv.

The criteria of evaluation in the private sector were in many ways the "usual" criteria of economic and professional competence with somewhat stronger emphasis being placed on family status by economic standing and family lineage. But even within this sector strong emphasis was placed on national goals and service, although several of the basic assumptions of the pioneer group were rejected.

The situation was necessarily different in the pioneer groups and in the workers' sector. There, the basic criterion of status evaluation was devotion to pioneering-collective tasks with prestige in the eyes of the community the main reward. It was assumed that material rewards—and especially *differential economic* (and even prestige and power) rewards—were not only unimportant but even dangerous and potentially disruptive to the solidarity of the pioneering group.

These evaluations of activities in the workers' groups and in the first settlements were, in their pure form, much more adapted to the small avant-garde élite groups than to wider and functionally differentiated settings. Hence it is no accident that the fullest manifestation of these criteria of evaluation was to be found in the collective settlements. Because of this, the maintenance of these criteria by the élite groups was greatly dependent on the minimizing of the occupational and status aspects of their peasant orientations and on the stress of the élitist orientations to the settlement and the movement. Within these groups such criteria and rewards could be upheld in all their purity...

***The Image of Society.*** These variations in social stratification were closely related to the image of a society developed by these groups and derived from their basic ideology. . . .

The views as expressed there are mainly concerned with a "classless" society, composed of different groups and movements, and bound by common aspirations and activities, in which there is but little division of labor and small difference in wealth. However, these images were purely ideological and utopian, and bore few connexions to existing society.

It is significant that neither in the basic ideologies nor in this embryonic image of society was there any reference to the problems of distribution of power, or of power as a basis for social status. This omission was due to the limited scope of the settlements and groups, to the strong utopian elements of their ideology and to the fact that the main resources of most groups came from outside the Yishuv. This fact had many important repercussions on the developing social organization and stratification.

***Interrelations Between the Scale of Collectivities, Role Structure and Criteria of Status.*** The three major aspects of social organization—the nature of collectivities, the definition of roles, and the criterion of status, tended to complement each other in controlling incipient social differences.

This was due to various factors: One was the relatively small degree of differentiation

[4] Third wave of immigration, 1919–1923. It consisted of 35,000 immigrants. *Ibid.* (C.S.H.)

[5] *Kibbutz:* an agricultural collective founded on the principle "from each according to his ability to each according to his need." (C.S.H.)

[6] Plural form of *moshav:* an agricultural cooperative, the land of which is divided into equal farmsteads, each of which is worked by a family. For a comparative analysis of the kibbutz and moshav and the bearing that these organizations have on stratification theory, see Richard D. Schwartz, "Functional Alternatives to Inequality," *American Sociological Review*, Vol. 20, August, 1955, pp. 424–430. (C.S.H.)

in the Yishuv's social structure, a tendency which was reinforced by the fact that the Yishuv was at that time composed of many small "parallel" settlements and organizations, allowing little occupational or economic differentiation to develop. Little specialization took place among the many similarly composed yet different groups, and even the activities of the professional and cultural bodies were not geared to any specific needs but rather to those of a "future" society. Only gradually a more concrete interrelationship between the various groups developed and with it a growing change in tasks.

The second major reason for the limited differences was rooted in the ideology of the pioneering group.

Historically, these two conditions were closely connected. However, each was more strongly operative in one sector than in another and hence their development varied between the sectors and probably influenced later developments in the Yishuv's social structure.

These initial tendencies left their imprint in several crucial areas. The first important characteristic, common to the Yishuv as well as to many other colonizing countries, was the absence of an aristocracy. This was due not only to lack of special family tradition but also to the fact that much of the land, and the available capital, was vested in public hands, often abroad. The second characteristic was the concentration of wealth in various public bodies and organizations. Thirdly, the strong egalitarian emphasis in the social structure of the Yishuv became apparent even at this stage, and fourthly, side by side with the strong egalitarianism, there was also the emphasis on the élite inherent in the image of the pioneer. This combination had many interesting repercussions on the social structure and organization of the Yishuv.

***Growing Differentiation in the Mandatory Period—Competition Between the Sectors. Patterns of Voluntary Associations.*** With the mandatory period the relatively homogeneous social structure became more complex and diversified, and distinct from older types of homogeneous sects and small, "under-developed" ecological communities.

With the growing expansion of the Yishuv's economy, many new occupational activities—industrial, professional, and clerical—developed. These were connected with the growth of more diversified ecological settings, with the many new types of organizations and groups, and with the growing interdependence of the different sectors of the Yishuv. The growth of autonomous functions and specialized groups as well as the growing importance of monetary and economic rewards also influenced this development.

These developments created new tendencies in the distribution of wealth and power, giving rise to growing differences between economic groups and between the incipient occupational groups.

Concomitantly, ascriptive solidarities began to develop in the private sector, based on kinship, and ecological and occupational traditions, with more widespread emphasis on criteria of economic status, occupational achievements, and differential remuneration.

Within the workers' sector these developments constituted a challenge to the basic ideological pioneering premises. . . .

***Patterns of Institutionalization of Ideology.*** The challenges of growing social differences were taken up by the leaders of the working sector in several ways . . . ideology became institutionalized partly through the selection of élites, and partly through affiliation by the élites with the pioneering groups as well as by allocating symbolic élite status to the settlements. . . .

. . . . . . . . . . . . . . . . . . . . . . . . . . . . . . . . .

Ideologically, many attempts were made to define the industrial workers as individual or group pioneers whose duties and image did not differ greatly from those of the older pioneer type. . . .

The worker's function was defined more and more in collective terms of social and political identification and, even less than in the case of the agricultural pioneer, in terms of occupational or technical contribution.

***Criteria of Allocation and Organizations in the Workers' Sectors.*** Attempts to institutionalize the pioneering ideology brought to light some of the structural implications and potential contradictions inherent in this ideology.

Access to different functions and resulting rewards became important at that time.

Although official formulation of the pioneering ideology emphasized the importance of free access by all to the pioneering tasks, strong selectivism was in fact practised within it. This was stressed by the importance placed on membership in the various collective organizations and was inherent in the nature of élitist orientation. With the growing problem of adapting the ideology to the developing social structure, this became even more general, applying to the allocation of rewards, the organizational patterns within the movements, and the different ways of life in the workers' sectors. Such ways were based on membership of different élitist groups and movements centred in the communal settlements, the youth movements, and the workers' quarters in the cities, but showed few autonomous class or strata orientations.

Leaders of the workers' sector aimed at maintaining the older homogeneity of status criteria. Membership in these associations became an important means of access to different positions, and resources.

***The Social Structure at the End of the Mandate—Social Differentiation and Ideology.*** By the end of the mandatory period, social organization and stratification in the Yishuv was already much more complicated than in the incipient stages of its development. A greater variety of collective bodies existed, as did ecological groups, functional organizations, voluntary associations, broad movement organizations, and fraternities, as well as various types of latent ascriptive solidarities—and the differences between urban and rural settings continuously increased.

However, gradually a greater number of more specific occupational, political, and cultural functions and functional groups emerged which, although as yet embedded in the collective and ideological definitions of the pioneering image, acquired growing autonomy and began to cut across their initial collective sectors. As a result of these developments the differences in standards and ways of life between groups grew.

Most of these differences were still small compared to those in other modern countries, but nevertheless "lower-class" areas or even slums developed as, for instance, in the Hatigvah quarter of Tel Aviv. These were mostly composed of groups from a lower class and educational background with little pioneering orientation.

Adherence to the sects of the official pioneering ideology as the major framework to all social developments, and the continuous expansion of the social structure, prevented these inequalities and incipient social problems from being fully perceived; one by-product was the slow, and initially inadequate, development and recognition of social work. . . .

. . . . . . . . . . . . . . . . . . . . . . . . . . . . . . . . . .

Moreover, the attempts made by leaders of the workers' groups to institutionalize the ideology gave rise to new tensions and problems, as well as to many paradoxical and unintended consequences.

Among these was the growing and yet not fully-recognized importance of power and power positions in the system of social organization and stratification.

Few clear norms therefore emerged to deal with the distribution or regulation of power. Most economic and organizational frameworks constituted important power positions, and the gradual transition of the Yishuv from a series of groups connected mostly by "mechanical" solidarity and ideological orientation, to a more differentiated social structure, necessarily enhanced the power positions and value of all these groups and enterprises. The growing importance of power positions was only partly offset by the "federative" nature of the expanded social structure, and by continuous preoccupation with the implementation of collective goals. This naturally changed with the establishment of the State.

## 2
## SOCIAL ORGANIZATION AND STRATIFICATION IN THE STATE OF ISRAEL—EMERGING TRENDS

***The Establishment of the State—Major Changes in Social Organization.*** With the establishment of the State of Israel, the trends, tensions, and problems of social organization and stratification described in the preceding section were thrown into greater relief. In many ways national independence proved to be a turning point in development and crystallization, highlighting several factors of crucial importance:

1. The first was the growing unification of different sectors with their often separate "systems" of stratification and social organization. This was accompanied by a weakening of relative autarchy and the dissolution of the "federative" nature of relations between the sectors.

   This unification was caused by the establishment of a central political framework and by the growing importance of political considerations and criteria in the allocation of "material" and prestige rewards.[7]
2. The second major development which influenced social organization was the great influx of new manpower in the form of new immigrants, with their special social, cultural, and educational backgrounds and with their specific motivations for immigration. . . . This influx created great problems in terms of pressures on various resources, the extent of mobility open to these groups, and in tendencies to maintain or develop their own styles of life and traditions.
3. This process of absorption was closely connected with continuous economic development and social and economic differentiation. The very establishment of the state with its administrative and political frameworks created new occupational and prestige positions, which were enhanced by the expansion in the economic structure, giving rise to new occupational roles, organizations, and patterns of mobility. Equally, new problems of differential mobility with regard to both old and new immigrants emerged.
4. The fourth major development was the growing importance of political power as a social reward, a criterion of social status and position, and as a means of access to major occupational and economic positions.
5. This development also brought out important changes in value-orientations among the different sectors, the most important of these being a weakening in the "forward-looking" outlook and, instead, a growing emphasis on the present as an important dimension of social action. Growing emphasis was therefore placed on a wider spectrum of rewards and on the struggle and competition for these rewards. . . .
6. All these trends necessarily sharpened the conflict between the official pioneering ideology and the developing social reality. The establishment of the state brought the bearers of the pioneering-socialist ideology to power but, at the same time, a new reality resulted from their own policies and their change into a ruling élite.

***Growing Differentiation of Roles and Organization.*** . . . The most general trend in this period was a growing change from the predominant pattern (whereby various functions of society were performed by the same people in a given group) through a process of gradual emphasis on separate tasks which crystallized into distinctive roles and organizations.

Many new industrial enterprises developed, bringing with them a growing managerial and professional class and increased differentiation between technical, skilled, and semi-skilled jobs. In addition, the army and the civil service provide conspicuous examples of entirely new or previously underdeveloped functions.

Similar developments took place in other spheres. In the field of public services banking was greatly expanded and new sectors, such as a growing hotel trade, evolved. Continuous expansion also took place in the older professions, such as law, medicine, and teaching, while engineering and architecture which had not developed much in the previous period, grew very rapidly. Relatively "underdeveloped" professions such as social work also gained in importance. Moreover, there was a continuous inclination towards professionalization in

[7] The growth in importance of overall political considerations in the allocations of material rewards was most clearly shown in the fact that major problems of wage policy and differences as well as labor conditions were decided by the central political authorities on a more or less country-wide basis, thus becoming a focal point in the central political struggle.

many new occupations. This showed itself in a growing emphasis on formal educational standards for the attainment of occupational grades in the civil service, in the army, and in business, as well as in the growing tendency of such groups to organize themselves in relatively autonomous professional organizations.

Closely connected with this was the development of new forms of large, bureaucratic administrative and economic organizations—a tendency which could also be found in agriculture. . . .

. . . . . . . . . . . . . . . . . . . . . . . . . . . . . . . . .

However, the most important structural result of this growing occupational differentiation was perhaps that it created a situation of irreversibility of occupational roles. Unlike the original pioneer-ideology which assumed that a person can easily shift his occupational role according to collective demands, the economic development after the establishment of the State caused commitment to an occupational role to become more set.

People could and did retrain, but the time spent and the specialized demands of most jobs were such that the possibilities of continuous shifts in occupation by adults became more difficult.

This growing occupational specialization constituted the most important breakthrough to economic modernization in Israel.

However, all these changes and trends to differentiation did take place within the framework of a relatively small-scale society. Although the population of this society has, since the establishment of the state, been almost quadrupled—yet its absolute numbers were yet relatively small in terms of comparison with other modern facilities.

This fact had . . . many repercussions on the very direction of these processes of differentiation, on their structural repercussion and on the relations between the élite and the broader groups of the population. . . .

. . . . . . . . . . . . . . . . . . . . . . . . . . . . . . . . .

***Trends in Crystallization of Status.*** The continued impact of the various social, economic, and occupational differences and the policies evolved by the élite, produced some lasting, if unexpected, tendencies in the Israeli social organization.

The most obvious change was in the manifestations of different styles of life and in the ways in which accessibility to basic resources became organized. . . .

Perhaps the most important general development here was the weakening of the "movement" style of life. The growing emphasis on common standards of consumption diminished the differences between private and collective sectors, but accentuated the differences between occupational, economic, and ethnic groups and strata.

This gave rise to a blurring of differences between the major formal or semi-formal sectors in the Yishuv, and affected all sections of the population.

At the same time relations between the different sectors accentuated the stress on power and greatly increased in importance as a basic element in the system of stratification. This was part of the wider process of proliferation of the various centres of power in Israeli society, rooted in the establishment of the State, in the diversification of administrative-bureaucratic agencies, and in the growing importance of political positions within the social organization. . . .

This weakening of the élitist and movement orientations, intensified the problems of access to various positions and resources —partly because this development went against the egalitarian assumptions of the élites and partly because the process of differentiation itself was apt to weaken the control by the élite over access to major positions and resources.

The most important transformation in stratification developed around economic differentiation and the diverse styles of living. . . .

While the growing importance of consumption as a criterion of status strengthened the class or stratum in the social stratification at the expense of the older élite movement ideologies, yet within it new trends, specific to the Israeli scene, developed.

***Trends in Class Crystallization.*** An analysis of the trend of occupational, positional, and income differentials may well be the best approach to these developments.

In order to analyse the specific characteristics of Israeli society, it is not enough to indicate general trends—rather it is essential to analyse the constellations and coalescence between criteria of status, education, occupation and income—as they developed.

Some peculiar characteristics emerged, closely related to some of the aspects of social mobility analysed above.

The data in Table 35 give a preliminary view of this problem.[8]

Analysis shows a high discrepancy between the different scales, and the lower grades, especially people at the lowest educational level, emerge with a fair chance of achieving a relatively high-level income.

Thus, whereas 51.1 per cent of all Israelis belong to the lowest educational grade, only 33.2 per cent belong to the lowest income level. Unlike the United States of America where we find a high correspondence between occupational prestige and income in the *upper grades* of the two scales, in Israel the trend seems to be the opposite.

[8] Bar-Yosef, R. and Padan, D.: "The Oriental Communities in the Class Structure of Israel," *Molad*, Vol. XXII, Nov. 1964, pp. 195–6.

The upper grades show a marked discrepancy between occupational prestige and income: 10.5 per cent of Israelis are in the higher occupational prestige grade but only 3.9 per cent are counted in the highest income level.

This means that when distributing the population on an income scale, the slant is toward the lower grades, whereas in the *occupational scale* this distribution points toward the *upper* ones.

As most of the statistical data are more reliable with regard to wage-earners than to self-employed, these findings and implications have, to be corrected accordingly, even though exact data for a full correlation are not yet available. . . . It is possible that this indicates a discrepancy between income and occupational prestige in the higher levels which may be somewhat smaller than assumed, especially with regard to non-professional occupations in the private or semi-public sectors.

However, whatever the extent of these cleavages, the class system in Israel tends towards a strong emphasis on the lower middle and middle class, a fact which is also borne out by the preliminary data on mobility. . . .

An interesting paradox of this is the fact

**TABLE 35 Status Crystallization (Percentage of Population) in Isreal**

| | *Income* | *Occupation* | *Education* |
|---|---|---|---|
| High | 3.9 | 10.5 | 12.2 |
| Upper middle | 19.5 | 34.0 | 35.1 |
| Lower middle | 43.4 | 24.7 | — |
| Low | 33.2 | 25.5 | 51.1* |

* The following criteria were used to characterize the class scale:—

Education: Low = no schooling—elementary education
Middle = high school
High = University or its equivalent of after high school education

Occupation: Low = unskilled manual work services
Lower Middle = skilled workers, semi-skilled workers, minor clerical positions and minor business and sales groups
Higher Middle = white collar employees in middle range positions
High = business men, self-employed and employed professionals, highest managerial grade

Income: the grade frontiers are based mostly on the socially accepted evaluation of low, middle, and high income:
Low = 1,000–1,999 IL
Lower Middle = 2,000–3,999 IL
High = 7,500–10,000 + IL

Source: R. Bar-Yosef and D. Padan, *op. cit.*

that the economic situation of the lower groups is very low indeed and that they form a marginal group within the society.

Even more important, the relative percentage of these lower groups has not decreased, despite the heavy emphasis of official social policies on minimizing inequality. Some of these policies, such as the lack of full-scale health insurance, as well as the importance of political pressures in their implementation, may well tend to reinforce and perpetuate this situation.

On the other end of the scale, the various middle classes greatly stressed differential symbolic consumption, and encouraged the continuous growth of a small, but continuously expanding, "upper" class of millionaires or very affluent groups of industrialists, bankers, foreign investors, and some professionals.

It was also partially legitimized by the general emphasis on conspicuous consumption and by the participation of many public figures and officials in such consumption. . . . This, in its turn, greatly influenced the direction of the processes of mobility in Israeli society.

This overall trend towards middle-class crystallization becomes even more evident in the self-evaluation of Israelis in terms of status and class criteria. One preliminary research[9] has shown that, in spite of the fact that Israel is known for strong ideological and political orientation towards labor movements, and although the USA is regarded as the stronghold of capitalism the data on class identification in the two countries show a reverse picture. Interestingly enough even a third of the members of socialist collective settlements (kibbutzim) considered themselves as belonging to the middle class.

Another research[10] which used a somewhat different questionnaire indicates what at first glance may seem to be different results, but are basically rather similar ones. This research used the following status categories, derived to some extent from the "pioneering" ideology: (1) Middle class; (2) Working intelligentsia; (3) Labour class; (4) Working class.

It was found that self-identification with one of these class-categories is closely connected with objective occupational status and educational attainment. Fifty per cent of the non-matriculated wage-earners who were investigated identified with "working class" and less than 20 per cent with "middle class." Fifty-one per cent of the non-matriculated and 62 per cent of the matriculated self-employed identified with "middle-class"; while 50 per cent of the matriculated wage-earners categorized themselves as "working-intelligentsia," an additional 22 per cent as middle-class and only 10 per cent as "working-class."

Thus here also there seems to be a strong emphasis on the "middle" strata—even if defined by somewhat different categories—than on the "truly" proletarian or "low" ones.

All these data indicate an interesting trend of development of the Israeli status system. They do indeed indicate that occupation has become an important, even if not a single, determinant of socio-economic status in Israel. During the pre-state period the objective process of downward intergenerational mobility was recognized and idealized ("proletarization," "normalization of the occupational pyramid"). Formal education was devaluated and the stereotype of the "cultured worker" fostered by the "halutzic sector" enhanced the self-image of the "class-conscious worker" (at least so we are told). Remnants of this idealization are probably still operating today. Yet no doubt there exists today a greater variety of significant status components than in the past competing with "class," occupation, and ideology as potential foci of identification and solidarity. . . .

The plurality of status components and the relative absence of congruity between the various criteria prevents the emergence of a status-consciousness based upon the primacy of a single deprecatory factor even of the most basic kind. Through increasing the salience of status-enhancing factors low-status individuals are enabled to form a

[9] A. Antonovsky: "Social and Political Attitudes in Israel," *Allot*, June–July, 1963.

[10] Adapted from fieldwork for: A. Zloczower: *Mobility Patterns and Status Conceptions in an Urban Israeli Setting*. Ph.D. Thesis, The Hebrew University of Jerusalem, 1966.

relatively favourably status-image for themselves. . . .

## NEW STATUS CRYSTALLIZATION: OCCUPATIONAL, ETHNIC, POLITICAL, AND RELIGIOUS AFFILIATIONS

These crystallizations of "middle class" orientations indicate the growing importance of occupational criteria in evaluation of status. But in spite of this, there also developed growing differences in hierarchies of prestige according to various non-professional criteria, among the most important of which were religion and ethnic background. . . .

## THE ETHNIC ELEMENT IN THE TRANSFORMATION OF TRADITIONAL STRUCTURES

Due to the basic characteristics of the various immigrant groups and because of the initial conditions of absorption . . . some of the major "ethnic" groups tended to concentrate, at least temporarily, in special clusters.

Although these groups maintained some of their traditions and ways of life, they were naturally strongly affected by the impact of the absorbing society—the educational system, the army, and economic and occupational pressures.

These clusters were indicative of the common "fate" of the different immigrant groups in the process of absorption.

In this context the extent of coalescence between economic "class" and "ethnic" criterion, achieved a special importance. . . .

Ethnic background and identity were most strongly articulated among the oriental, but, to a smaller degree, also among some European groups—and became an important new factor in the pattern of social organization. Effects were also felt in the re-crystallization of the avenues of access to different occupational and political positions and to economic and political resources.

The development by the oriental immigrants of specific subcultures within the Israeli system of stratification is indicated by several different reinforcing trends and is closely related to the continuous coalescence—especially within oriental groups—of low occupational, educational, and economic status.

Among oriental groups the less differentiated images of society seem to be more prevalent. Similarly, they evince patterns of mobility aspiration, which emphasize larger incomes rather than the attainment of advance education. This is related to findings that, at the same level of income, the oriental group tends to invest less in education and more in direct consumption. The continuous educational backwardness of many of these groups . . . is, of course, closely related to this.

The crystallization of the specific ethnic element as distinct and divisive, also becomes apparent in the data on intermarriage between groups of different origin. These show that in 86 per cent of all marriages performed in 1959, partners were of similar ethnic origin, whereas in only 14 per cent were their origins "mixed." . . .

We see thus that the ethnic and especially the oriental element could crystallize as a specific new ascriptive element in the Israeli social structure, a development which constitutes one of the most important within Israeli society and a challenge to it. In addition, the ethnic factor also caused new cleavages and tensions in the social and political fields.

Closely connected with these developments were the many attempts made to change the negative relationship between ethnic background and access to occupational and educational positions. One attempt was a demand for more help in acquiring the resources (especially education) necessary for the achievement of various positions and occupations.

The other attempt made was to increase demands for more direct access to such positions by virtue of belonging to a given ethnic group.

These directions combined through the political organizations of various ethnic groups and reinforced several broader tendencies of crystallization of status in Israeli society.

## POLITICS AND POWER IN THE CRYSTALLIZATION OF STRATA AND STATUS

A similar picture emerges with regard to the second new criterion of status—the political-administrative one.

Of the many organizations which, increasingly, affected the life of the Israeli citizen, the most important, encompassing almost every sphere of life, was the Histadrut. This organization controlled areas of work (and until lately also access to work through the various labour exchanges), health services (through *Kupat Cholim*), and a large part of the access to housing and other basic necessities.

The various government departments and agencies constituted another important conglomeration of organizations dominating the access to basic areas and facilities. For many of the new immigrants the Jewish Agency and the different parties constituted the all-important sources of allocation of resources and goods. These various organizations often competed among themselves and had to take recourse to the central political and administrative organs of the State to develop some *modus vivendi*. This greatly increased the importance of power in the context of social organization—as a criterion of status, as a resource, and as a focus of conflict within the social structure.

Many of the élite policies tried to enhance the value of power and the prestige of political position and their control over access to resources. The growth of large-scale economic organizations in both private and public sectors, encouraged by the Government's economic and tax policies, reinforced the importance of political and organizational criteria in the state system.

Seen from the political and administrative criteria of stratification, the Israeli population divides according to differences in access to the various facilities, and according to the channels through which such access is organized.

Since the various political groups largely control access to major facilities, membership in one of them may be virtually essential. While it is relatively easy to evaluate different groups according to relative standard of living, wealth, and education, the picture becomes more complicated with additional criteria. In many cases the lack of affiliation to any collective, party, or bureaucratic organization, is a sign of the lowest possible status group. Among many groups of new immigrants, however, while access to collective agencies certainly mitigates low status, a too exclusive dependence on only one organization, may freeze different groups of the population at a relatively low occupational level.

There is no doubt for example that a very large percentage of those who are not members of any Sick Fund belong to the lowest strata of the population for whom the attainment of full rights in the *Kupat Cholim* of the Histadrut would mean a very great advance.

As in many other welfare societies, social services in Israel tend to discriminate in favour of the more powerful or rich, so that the lower rungs who have neither additional income nor the pull of membership in other organizations, receive only minimal attention which may well minimize their possibilities of advancement. Therefore the access to a number of more active organizations may be of crucial importance for the achievement of higher mobility.

On the other hand, especially among the higher occupational groups, constant recourse to such organizations becomes a constricting factor which may impede the possibility of further social mobility and participation.

Among these groups, especially among the professional ones, more autonomous hierarchies of prestige emerged, and with them important tensions and cleavages in reaction to restrictions imposed by political and administrative bodies. . . .

The first cleavage appeared between the salaried and self-employed sectors, and was particularly pronounced among the upper and middle groups. The second cleavage seems to be developing within the salaried professionals, between those employed in sectors (like government service) where official wage policy is more or less maintained, and those private sectors and government companies where this is not the case. These cleavages explain the growing conflicts and tensions between professionals and non-professionals in the public service.

These tensions produced two broad tendencies of structural crystallizations of great importance for the merging patterns of stratification in Israel. The first such tendency found expression in growing occupational and social differentiations, in multiplication of avenues of mobility, and in heterogeneous points of prestige and status.

The second tendency developed in the direction of growing concentration on and restriction of access to resources, positions, and prestige, affecting members of various, either new political, or ethnic (or religious) organizations.

Thus, within the professional groups, attempts were made to break the monopoly of the Histadrut, while at the same time new ascriptive groups were organized which could become a second Histadrut, assuring members of various benefits.

. . . . . . . . . . . . . . . . . . . . . . . . . . . . . . . . .

## ECOLOGICAL PATTERNS OF STRATIFICATION

It may be worthwhile to describe briefly some of the major social organizations that crystallized in different ecological settings.

As a result of factors analysed above, different social patterns and groupings are in constant development. The strong movement patterns as seen in the kibbutz and the moshav are at one extreme, with new immigrant settlements—especially the moshavim—constituting a special sub-category within this framework. These patterns are mostly characterized by a more positive attitude to agriculture, by growing interests in urban patterns of life, and by more organized leisure activities, interwoven within different patterns and traditions. In the non-movement rural sectors and in the older moshavot, a wealthy suburban peasant type developed with close family tradition, connected with economic and occupational orientations, around which the new semi-urban immigrant groups tended to settle.

However the most varied development took place in the various urban centres of Jerusalem, Tel Aviv, and Haifa.

It is here that the different occupational, professional, and economic groups changed and crystallized most dramatically. Here also many of the religious groups are concentrated, and the most conspicuous "ethnic" problem areas developed.

. . . . . . . . . . . . . . . . . . . . . . . . . . . . . . . . .

An entirely new pattern of social organization in which some of the "new trends" have crystallized can be found in the various development towns and areas, such as Beersheba, and the much less urbanized development areas, such as Kiryat Shmona and Kiryat Gat.

Within these frameworks the criterion of occupation and origin—as well as the length of stay in the country is gaining increasing importance, and different groups and strata tend to crystallize according to occupation, education, ethnic origin, etc.

While many variations exist in the development areas, the following survey[11] of one of these medium-sized towns may give an indication of some of the emerging trends in the development areas.

The town under study was established as the result of a twofold policy: development of arid areas and settlement of the numerous immigrants who entered Israel in the 'fifties. The construction of the town was part of a plan which included the establishment of agricultural settlements. An industry based on agriculture was to be set up, and the town was also intended to serve as an administrative, commercial, and cultural centre.

The first settlers were new immigrants from North Africa who came to the town directly from the port. Within a few years more North African immigrants followed, mainly from Morocco, as well as some immigrants from Egypt, Eastern Europe (mainly from Poland and Romania), and a small group from English-speaking countries.

From the beginning these groups were joined by veteran citizens who came from all parts of the country, and at the time the study was undertaken, the population of the town was about 10,000.

The main criteria of social differentiation in the town are length of stay in the country and ethnic origin. Ethnic origin also determines affiliation to different communities with their own cultural and religious traditions: the Ashkenazi community which includes mainly European Jews, and the Sephardic community which includes Jews of Spanish descent and oriental Jews. The

[11] This is based on: E. Cohen, L. Shamgar and Y. Levy. Research Report: *Absorption of Immigrants in a Development Town.* The Hebrew University, Department of Sociology, 1962.

differentiation among these various groups embraces all spheres of life, including politics.

At first the old settlers filled all the central roles in the occupational sphere. They were sent to the town in order to function as an administrative and cultural élite, to teach, to instruct, and to build up the municipal and public institutions. Their occupational concentration, relatively high standard of living, and common culture and way of life, made them into a rather closed social stratum in which members enjoy high social status.

This strata contains the senior officials in the municipal institutions and in government service, such as social welfare and health, as well as the first political party officials sent there as the population grew. In this way the veterans were at the head of the political organization from the very beginning.

In contrast to the veterans, the new immigrants generally lack economic resources and means of obtaining employment, and are dependent on various governmental and municipal agencies for such basic needs as housing and work.

After the first difficult period of adaptation, differences among the several groups of new immigrants became apparent, mainly in their economic situation and way of life.

Highest average incomes and occupational positions are held by the immigrants from English-speaking countries, who form a small group. They live in the best part of the town, together with many veterans and some prosperous immigrants from Eastern Europe. They are active mainly in the economic field, whereas in public-political life their impact is hardly felt. In general, the situation of the East European immigrants is less good, particularly as regards the many elderly persons who have difficulties in getting re-established. . . .

Due to their higher level of education and professional training, and because of their cultural closeness to the Old Yishuv, as well as their personal ties with the old settlers, the European and Anglo-Saxon immigrants have access to many avenues of individual social mobility.

The situation of the oriental immigrants who lack the above mentioned characteristics is much harder. Among the Egyptian immigrants there is a small nucleus of persons whose educational and professional formation is European. They occupy relatively good positions and form an élite at the centre of their group.

The North African immigrants who constitute half the town's population are the most backward of all newcomers and form the greater part of unemployed and relief workers. The average income of a Moroccan family is often inadequate even for minimum food requirements. Their level of formal education is usually very low. Most Moroccan families are large and a considerable number of them are under the care of governmental social welfare. Many of these immigrants live in the oldest housing quarters which are now near-slum areas. The older Moroccan immigrants are traditionalists and the synagogue to them is a social institution of prime importance. However, they lack central traditional—or other—leadership, and they are socially divided into a number of rival groups.

The study has shown that the various ethnic groups, and the veteran residents, form distinct social units with major social ties. Nevertheless these groups are not homogeneous from the point of view of stratification, and within each group economic and educational differences exist. Indications show that different ethnic groups, of a relatively high economic or educational level, tend to tie up in "status-groups" which cut across ethnic barriers and create new social units whose bases are economic and cultural. However, they do not, normally, cut across the boundaries between the two community formations: the Ashkenazim and the orientals.

Thus economic and cultural criteria gradually assumed increased importance in the more developed groups of the population, which, in turn, led to greater emphasis on divisions among the communal groups.

Naturally, the organizational settings of the various development towns differ in many details, especially in those towns where the original political or administrative élite was composed of "oriental" settlers who received the newcomers, among them also European groups. But nonetheless, the crystallization of status and ethnic groups with concomitant ethnic tensions was of equal importance.

***The Importance of Ascriptive and Power Elements.*** It is interesting to see to what extent the new patterns of "strata" crystallization and the growing importance of power and ascriptive criteria, influenced the perception of the social structure.

Several recent research projects arrived at the conclusion that, in modern industrial societies, most stratification images can be classified into one or two types, or into a combination of the two. These two types are: (a) The hierarchic image, in which society is seen as a composition of usually three groups forming an "open-class" system. These groups differ in their functions and in their way of life, but together they are conceived as constituting a relatively harmonious social entity with few overall conflicts. . . . (b) The power image, in which society is seen as a dichotomy of two sharply distinguished classes.

Some studies undertaken in Israel[12] substantiated these findings and have shown that here, as in most other societies, the more hierarchic image is characteristic of the higher social groups, while the second is typical of the lower. But some specific characteristics seem to emerge.

The survey mentioned above showed that the most common images of social structure among the dwellers of our development town were found to be the following: (1) A non-hierarchical, multi-group image, in which the groups differ in the ethnic origin of their members (18.1 per cent of the total answers). According to this conception, the community is made up of a number of ethnic groups of equal status and without conflict. No possibility of mobility between them exists since the distinguishing criterion is ascriptive and one simply "belongs" to the group. As these groups have equal status, this image was named "the egalitarian image." (2) A hierarchical, multi-class image, in which classes differentiate according to economic criteria (12.8 per cent of the total answers). According to this conception, the community is a hierarchy of economic groups, mostly occupational, income-bracket groups. The distinction between them is not as clear-cut as in the previous image, for, together, they constitute an organic entity without contrasts or appreciable discrepancies. Since the distinguishing criterion is one of economic achievement and the groups form a hierarchy, mobility from one group to another is possible. (3) A hierarchical, two-class image in which distinction is made along the lines of economic criteria (17 per cent of the total answers). According to this conception the community is made up of two groups whose economic situations differ sharply. The existence of social conflict is inherent in this image. Thus, free movement between the two classes is more limited than in the previous image, although the distinguishing criterion is one of economic achievement. Here the differential *economic power* status of the groups is emphasized. (4) A hierarchical, two-group image, in which the groups are differentiated by the criterion of origin (26.9 per cent of the total answers). With this approach, the community is also made up of two groups, but these are distinguished either by length of stay in the country or by ethnic origin and communal affiliation (veteran-new immigrant; Ashkenazi-oriental). The groups constitute a dichotomy, and there is a conflict of interests between them. As the distinguishing criterion is ascriptive, there is no possibility of mobility between the groups; and this image may be labelled as the "caste image."

The project concludes that the egalitarian image which is non-hierarchic, is characteristic of those of higher status. The extent of hierarchization increases as status decreases, and, among those of lowest status, we find the "caste" image, which is extremely hierarchical by nature. The usual two images—"the hierarchic image" and "the power image," are therefore placed between the two new images which were encountered in our research; they are characteristic of the groups which occupy the highest and the lowest positions in the social structure of the town. It is also interesting to note that both groups have ascriptive bases of valuation, while the common base of the two intermediary groups is achievement.

These findings are based mostly on

[12] E. Cohen, L. Shamgar, Y. Levy, *op. cit.*, 1962.

material gleaned from development areas and necessarily reflect some of the specific problems of these areas. Tentative comparison between the stratification images of the town and of the whole country shows that, on the national level, both the "conflicting" images (the "power" and the "caste" images) and the ascriptive images (equality and caste) were stressed to a smaller, but not insignificant, degree.

The picture of Israeli society as perceived by some groups, differs greatly from the more official ideological view of a "classless" working society—the ideological image of the élite.

Our picture indicates not only the emergence of growing differences between various groups but also the growing importance of several new elements of power and ascription, both in the actual processes of crystallization of social stratification and in the perception of the social structure.

# SOCIAL STRATIFICATION IN INDUSTRIAL SOCIETY

*John H. Goldthorpe*

For a decade or so now, a growing interest has been apparent, chiefly among American sociologists, in the pattern of long-term social change within relatively mature industrial societies. This interest appears to derive from two main sources.

In the first place, it can be seen as resulting from broadly based studies of the sociology of industrialization, concentrating originally on the underdeveloped or developing countries of the world. For example, work conducted as part of the Inter-University Study of Labour Problems in Economic Development led up to the theoretical statement on the "logic" of industrialism attempted by Clark Kerr and his associates in their book, *Industrialism and Industrial Man.*[1] Secondly, this interest has undoubtedly been stimulated by the revival in comparative studies of social structure and social processes in economically advanced countries. Important here, for example, has been the work of Professor Lipset and a number of other members of the Berkeley campus of the University of California; and even more so, perhaps, studies which have chiefly involved comparisons between Western and Communist societies, such as those produced in connection with the Harvard Project on the Soviet Social System by Professor Inkeles and his colleagues.[2]

However, it is notable that in spite of possibly different origins, current American interpretations of the development of industrial societies often reveal marked similarities. Basically, it may be said, they tend to be alike in stressing the standardizing effects upon social structures of the exigencies of modern technology and of an advanced economy. These factors which make for uniformity in industrial societies are seen as largely overriding other factors which may make for possible diversity, such as different national cultures or different political systems. Thus, the overall pattern of development which is suggested is one in which, once countries enter into the advanced stages of industrialization, they tend to become increasingly comparable in their major institutional arrangements and in their social systems generally. In brief, a *convergent* pattern of development is hypothesized.

Kerr and his associates have been the most explicit in this connection—and also in the matter of specifying the type of society on which the process of convergence is focussed. In their conception, "the road ahead" for all advanced societies leads in the direction of what they call "pluralistic" industrialism. By this they mean a form of industrial society in which the distribution

From *The Development of Industrial Society,* Paul Halmos, ed., the *Sociological Review,* Monograph No. 8, 1964. Reprinted by permission of the *Sociological Review* and the Sociological Review Monographs.

[1] Clark Kerr, J. T. Dunlop, F. H. Harbison and C. A. Myers, *Industrialism and Industrial Man,* 1960.

[2] See, e.g., Raymond A. Bauer, Alex Inkeles and Clyde Kluckhohn, *How the Soviet System Works,* 1956; Inkeles and Bauer, *The Soviet Citizen,* 1959.

of power is neither "atomistic" nor "monistic", nor yet radically disputed by warring classes; but rather a social order in which an "omnipresent State" regulates competition and conflict between a multiplicity of interest groups on the basis of an accepted "web of rules," and at the same time provides the means through which a degree of democratic control can be exercised over the working of the economy and over other key social processes such as the provision of welfare and public services, education and so on.[3] Other theorists have usually been a good deal more guarded than this in their formulations; but it would nonetheless be fair to say that, in the main, they have adopted views which have been broadly consistent with the Kerr thesis. In general, the "logic" of industrialism has been regarded as powerfully encouraging, even if not compelling, the emergence of a new type of society from out of former "class" and "mass" societies alike.

Clearly, then, a central theme in the interpretations in question concerns the development in advanced societies of systems of social stratification. And it is perhaps indicative of the importance of this theme that it has on several occasions been singled out for special discussion. In this paper[4] my main purpose will be to consider this particular aspect of current theories of industrialism and, further, to raise certain doubts and objections which seem to me to be of a serious kind and to have negative implications for these theories *in toto*. But at the outset I should say that I in no way intend to criticize the *kind* of sociological endeavour which is here represented. On the contrary, we are, I believe, much indebted to the authors of these theories for showing us a way to escape from the cramped quarters of trivialized empiricism without falling victim to highly speculative building with "empty boxes."

The arguments concerning the development of social stratification which form a core element in American interpretations of industrialism can be usefully stated under three main heads: differentiation, consistency and mobility.[5] To begin with, I would like to consider these three sets of arguments in turn.

## DIFFERENTIATION

In regard to differentiation, the major proposition that is put forward is that, in course of industrial advance, there is a decrease in the degree of differentiation in all stratification subsystems or orders. In other words, to follow Inkeles' formulation: "a process of relative homogenization takes place, reducing the gap or range separating the top and bottom of the scale"—in income and wealth, in status formal and informal, and in political power.[6] As a result of this process, a marked increase occurs within each stratification order in the proportion of the total population falling into the middle ranges of the distribution. The "shape" of the stratification hierarchy thus ceases to be pyramidal and approximates, rather, to that of a pentagon or even of a diamond.

This trend is related to the "logic" of industrialism in several different ways. But, primarily, the connection is seen as being through the changing division of labour. An advancing technology and economy continually repattern the occupational structure, and in ways which progressively increase the number of higher level occupational rôles; that is to say, rôles requiring relatively high standards of education and training and at the same time commanding relatively high economic rewards

[3] Kerr, *et al., op cit.,* Chs. 1, 2 and 10 especially.

[4] I am indebted to my friend M. Alfred Willener for his criticisms of an earlier draft of this paper and also to colleagues in the Faculty of Economics and Politics of the University of Cambridge who have discussed many specific points with me.

[5] The following exposition is derived from Kerr, *et al., op. cit.*; Inkeles, "Social Stratification in the Modernization of Russia" in Cyril E. Black (ed.), *The Transformation of Russian Society,* 1960; and W. E. Moore (ed.), *Industrialisation and Society,* 1963, pp. 318–322, 353–359 especially. It is, however, important to note the very marked differences in tone and style between these contributions. Kerr and his colleagues are most dogmatic and "prophetic", but also the most diffuse in their arguments; Inkeles, on the other hand, is the most explicit yet is clearly writing, as he says, "not to settle a point but to open a discussion"; while Moore, aiming at the summing-up of a body of research data, puts forward by far the most cautious and qualified statements.

[6] *Loc. cit.,* p. 341. Cf. Kerr *et al., op. cit.,* pp. 286–294. . . .

and social status. Thus, the middle of the stratification hierarchy becomes considerably expanded.

So far as Western societies are concerned, a further factor in this homogenizing process is also recognized in the growing intervention of the state in economic affairs; particularly in governmental policies which lead to the redistribution and control of economic power. For example, it is observed that policies of progressive taxation and of social welfare in various ways modify for the benefit of the less privileged the division of income and balance of social advantage which would have resulted from the free operation of market mechanisms. However, in this case great stress is placed on the close relationship that exists between this expansion in the regulatory functions of government and the direct requirements of the industrialization process. The state, it is argued, *must* be the key regulatory organization in any advanced society: the complexity of its technology and economy demand this. At minimum, the state must be responsible for the general rate of economic progress, and thus ultimately, for the overall allocation of resources between uses and individuals, for the quality of the national labour force, for the economic and social security of individuals and so on.[7]

In other words, even where greater social equality results directly from the purposive action of governments, the tendency is to see behind this action not a particular complex of socio-political beliefs, values or interests but rather the inherent compulsions of "industrialism" itself.[8]

. . . Furthermore, one should note, a similar viewpoint is taken in arguing that greater equality in political power—in the form of a pluralistic system—will tend to emerge in societies which now have totalitarian (or autocratic) regimes. In the first place, it is held, the production technology of an industrial society is such that any regime must become increasingly interested in the consent of the mass of the labour force; for the efficient use of this technology requires responsible initiative and freely given co-operation on the part of those who operate it. Secondly, the growing complexity of technical problems arising in the process of government itself necessitates the greater involvement in decision-making of experts and professionals, and in this way the latter come to acquire some independent authority. Thus, a monolithic structure gives way to one in which there are a number of "strategic" elites and of different foci of power. In brief, industrialism is regarded as being ultimately inimical to any form of monistic political order.[9]

## CONSISTENCY

In this respect, the central argument is that as societies become increasingly industrial, there is a growing tendency within the stratification system towards what Inkeles terms "equilibration"; that is, a tendency for the relative position of an individual or group in any one stratification order to be the same as, or similar to, their position in other orders.[10] In traditional societies, it is observed, inconsistencies in the stratification system may have been contrary to the prevailing ideology but were nonetheless frequent because of the rigidity of the levels

[7] Cf. Kerr, *et al., op. cit.*, pp. 31, 40–41, 273–274, 290–292; Moore, *op. cit.*, pp. 357–359.

[8] For a discussion of the strengths and weaknesses of attempts to apply this approach to the explanation of the development of social policy in 19th century England, see John H. Goldthorpe, "Le développement de la politique sociale en Angleterre de 1800 à 1914", *Sociologie du Travail*, No. 2, 1963. (English version . . . in *Transactions of the Vth World Congress of Sociology*, Vol. IV, 1964).

[9] Cf. Kerr *et al., op. cit.*, pp. 274–276, 288–290; Inkeles, p. 346. As earlier noted, Moore diverges here. He notes (p. 359) the empirical probability of increased political participation as societies become industrial, but argues that so far there is no evidence of a *necessary* incompatibility between industrialism and totalitarianism.

[10] Inkeles' "equilibration" (following E. Benoit-Smullyan, "Status Types and Status Interrelations", *Am. Soc. Rev.*, Vol. 9, 1944) thus largely corresponds to what Lenski and Landecker have referred to as "crystallization" and Adams and Homans as "congruence". See Gerhard E. Lenski, "Status Crystallization: a Non-Vertical Dimension of Social Status", *Am. Soc. Rev.*, Vol. 19, 1954; Werner S. Landecker, "Class Crystallization and Class Consciousness", *Am. Soc. Rev.*, Vol. 28, 1963; Stuart Adams, "Social Climate and Productivity in Small Military Groups", *Am. Soc. Rev.*, Vol. 19, 1954; G. C. Homans, "Status Congruence" in *Sentiments and Activities*, 1962. Moore refers simply to "consistency" or "coalescence".

within the different subsystems and the relatively low degree of interaction between them. For example, a merchant might become extremely wealthy yet be debarred from "noble" status; in fact, legally, he could be of peasant status and might be treated as such in certain circumstances in spite of his wealth. In industrial societies, by contrast, there are far fewer difficulties in the way of "adjustments" which serve to bring the position of individuals and groups more or less into line from one stratification order to another. Moreover, there is also a shift away from the relative diversity of the bases of stratification which is characteristic of traditional society. With industrialism, the occupational structure takes on overwhelming primacy in this respect. The occupational rôle of the individual is in general in close correlation with most other of his attributes which are relevant to his position in the stratification hierarchy as a whole: his economic situation, his educational level, his prestige in the local community and so on.[11]

In the same way as the trend towards greater equality, the trend towards greater consistency in stratification systems is also treated as an integral part of the industrialization process and as being directly linked to technological and economic advance. In industrial society, it is argued, the distribution of both economic rewards and prestige must come into a close relationship with occupational performance since this type of society in fact presupposes an overriding emphasis upon achievement, as opposed to ascription, as the basis of social position—and specifically upon achievement in the sphere of production. At the same time, though, as a result of technological progress, occupational achievement becomes increasingly dependent upon education, and in this way closer ties are formed between economic standing on the one hand and life-styles and subculture on the other. The ignorant and vulgar tycoon and the poor scholar are seen alike as figures of declining importance. In other words, the argument is that inevitably in modern societies, the various determinants of an individual's placing in the overall stratification hierarchy come to form a tight nexus; and that in this nexus occupation can be regarded as the central element—providing as it does the main link between the "objective" and "subjective" aspects of social inequality.

Implicit, then, in this interpretation is the view that in industrial societies stratification systems tend to become relatively highly integrated, in the sense that specifically class differences (i.e. those stemming from inequalities in the economic order) are generally paralleled by status differences (i.e. those based on inequalities in social evaluation); and, thus, that changes in the pattern of the former will automatically result in changes in the pattern of the latter. For example, Kerr and his associates see the growth of "middle incomes" as making for a "middle class society"; that is, a society in which middle class values are widely accepted, both among manual workers and elite groups, and in which the bulk of the population share in "middle class" status.[12]

## MOBILITY

In regard to mobility, the central proposition that is made is one which complements the previous arguments concerning differentiation and consistency. It is that once societies have reached a certain level of industrialization, their overall rates of social mobility tend to become relatively high—higher that is, than is typical in pre-industrial or traditional societies. The increasing number of intermediate positions in the stratification hierarchy widens the opportunity for movement upward from the lower levels, while the emphasis upon occupational achievement rather than on the ascription of social positions means that intergenerationally the talented will tend to rise at the expense of those whose talent is unequal to their birth. In this respect, the educational system is seen as the crucial allocative mechanism, sieving ability and matching capacity to the demands and responsibilities of occupational rôles.[13]

In other words, then, industrial society

[11] Cf. Kerr *et al., op. cit.,* pp. 272–273, 284, 292–293; Inkeles, *op. cit.,* pp. 341–342; Moore, *op. cit.,* pp. 356–357.

[12] Kerr, *et al., op. cit.,* pp. 272–273, 286.

[13] Cf. *ibid.,* pp. 35–37; Moore, *op. cit.,* pp. 319–321, 343–344.

is regarded as being essentially "open" and "meritocratic". And once more, one should note, the interpretation derives from a conception of the structural and functional imperatives of this type of social order. . . .

In this approach, thus, there is little room for consideration of institutional variations or of value differences between industrial societies which might be associated with *differing* patterns of mobility. It is taken that the overall similarities in this respect are, or at any rate are certainly becoming, the feature of major significance.

. . . I would now like to turn to what I have to say by way of criticism of these arguments and, to begin with, I would like to comment on each of the three themes on which I based the foregoing exposition. My main purpose here will be to indicate that the views which I have outlined are not always in entire accord with empirical data, and in this connection I shall refer primarily to the industrial societies of the West. . . .

On the question of reduced differentiation—or greater equality—in stratification systems, my remarks at this stage will be largely confined to the economic order. This is because it is chiefly in this regard that we have data which will permit, at least in principle, some test of the arguments involved; that is, data on the distributions of income and wealth.[14]

At the outset it may be said that, although the evidence is often very patchy, a broad trend towards greater economic equality *does* seem to be discernible in the case of all those societies which have so far progressed from a traditional to an industrial form. Myths of "golden ages" of economic equality in pre-industrial times are now little heeded, and, as a rough generalization, it would, I think, be widely accepted that the poorer the society, the greater the "skew" one may expect in its distributions of income and wealth alike.[15] With this view I would not wish to quarrel—provided that it is taken merely as a formula summing up historical experience, and as one which is subject to exceptions. But there are no grounds at all, in my view, for regarding the regularity in question as manifesting the operation of some process inherent in industrialism—of some general economic law—which will necessarily persist in the future and ensure a continuing egalitarian trend. Rather, the possibility must be left quite open that where such a trend exists, it may at some point be checked—and at a point, moreover, at which considerable economic *in*equality remains. In fact, in my assessment, the relevant data suggest that such a check may already be occurring in some of the more advanced societies of the West; or, at any rate, I would say that on present evidence *this* conclusion is indicated as much as any other.

For the distributions of income and wealth alike, it is true that figures exist to show a movement towards greater equality in most western industrial societies over the years for which adequate time-series are available; that is, from the late inter-war or early post-war period onwards.[16] However, it is now becoming increasingly clear that these figures, which are largely based on tax returns, are not always to be taken at their face value. And, in general, their defects appear to be such that they tend on balance to underestimate the income and wealth which accrue to the economically more favoured groups and in this and other ways to give a somewhat exaggerated idea of the degree of "levelling" that has taken place. In fact, for some western societies at least, there are now grounds for believing

[14] It should be acknowledged, however, that for the West, at least, there is clear evidence on one other important point; that is, on the reduction, indeed virtual elimination, of *formal* inequalities of status. This has been the concomitant of the growth of "citizenship" through which all members of national communities have been granted equal civil, political and social rights. Cf. T. H. Marshall, "Citizenship and Social Class" in *Sociology at the Crossroads,* 1963.

[15] Cf. United Nations, *Preliminary Report on the World Social Situation,* 1952, pp. 132–134; and *Report on the World Social Situation,* 1961, pp. 58–61.

[16] See, e.g., United Nations, *Economic Survey of Europe in 1956,* 1957, Ch. VII; R. M. Solow, "Income Inequality since the War" in Ralph E. Freeman (ed.), *Postwar Economic Trends in the United States,* 1960. Recent studies relating specifically to Great Britain are H. F. Lydall, "The Long-term Trend in the Size Distribution of Income", *Journ. Royal Stat. Soc.,* Vol. 122, Part I, 1959, and H. F. Lydall and D. C. Tipping, "The Distribution of Personal Wealth in Britain", *Oxford Inst. Stat. Bull.,* Vol. 23, 1961.

that during the last twenty years or so, overall economic inequality has in reality declined only very little, if at all. And particularly so far as wealth is concerned, it is likely that such changes as have occurred have been virtually negligible in their implications for social stratification.[17] Such conclusions have been suggested for the United Kingdom, for example, in Professor Titmuss' recent study, *Income Distribution and Social Change*.[18] . . .

A similar point of view is maintained, with reference to the United States, in Gabriel Kolko's somewhat neglected book, *Wealth and Power in America*. . . . Kolko supplements material from official sources with generally more reliable survey data, and on this basis suggests that over as long a period as 1910 to 1959 there has been no significant *general* trend in the United States towards greater income equality.[19]

Kolko's study prompts one to note the often overlooked point that simply because there may be some levelling of incomes going on in *certain ranges* of the total income distribution, this does not necessarily mean that *overall* equality is increasing; for in other ranges inegalitarian trends may simultaneously be operating. For example, there may be a tendency towards greater equality in that the number of middle-range incomes is growing; but at the same time the position of the lower income groups, relative to the upper and middle groups alike, may be worsening.

In fact, it seems more than possible that a pattern of change of this kind is now going on in the United States. This is indicated by a good deal of recent investigation, apart from that of Kolko, and particularly by the growing volume of work on the extent of poverty. Gunnar Myrdal, for example, has argued in his book, *Challenge to Affluence*, that while many Americans in the intermediate social strata may well be benefiting from a levelling upwards of living standards, at the base of the stratification hierarchy there is increasing inequality, manifested in the emergence of an "underclass" of unemployed and unemployable persons and families. In other words, the middle ranks of the income distribution may be swelling, but the gap between the bottom and the higher levels is, if anything, tending to widen.[20]

Moreover, what is also significant in Myrdal's study for present purposes is the way in which he brings out the *political* aspects of the problem. Myrdal observes that structural unemployment, resulting from technological innovation in industry, is a basic, and increasingly serious, cause of poverty in America, whereas in a country like Sweden, in which technological advance is also proceeding rapidly, full employment has been steadily maintained. Again, he notes the relative failure of the United States, compared with most western European countries, to stabilize aggregate demand in its economy on a high and rising level.[21] The explanation of these differences, Myrdal then argues, while not of course entirely political, must nonetheless be regarded as

[17] Chiefly, this is because much levelling which appears to have gone on at the top of the distribution has in fact taken place simply *within* families—particularly between parents and children and generally as a means of avoiding taxation. E.g., Lydall and Tipping (*op. cit.*) note the "growing tendency for owners of large properties to distribute their assets amongst the members of their families well in advance of death" (p. 85). However, it is, of course, the family, not the individual, that must be regarded as the basic unit of stratification.

[18] See, e.g., the critical review of Titmuss' book by A. R. Prest, and Titmuss' reply, in *British Tax Review*, March–April, 1963. *Income Distribution and Social Change*, 1962, p. 198. In this connection it should also be remembered that certain major developments which have made for greater equality in incomes in the recent past are of a non-repeatable kind—notably, the ending of large scale unemployment and the considerable expansion in the number of working class wives in gainful employment.

[19] *Wealth and Power in America*, 1962, Ch. 1. The data in question refer to pre-tax incomes, but Kolko is prepared to argue (Ch. 2) that "Taxation has not mitigated the fundamentally unequal distribution of income. . . ."

[20] *Challenge to Affluence*, 1963, Ch. 3. The data assembled by the Conference on Economic Progress, *Poverty and Deprivation in the United States*, 1962, suggest that there was real improvement in the income position of low-income groups during World War II but that since then the economy has not greatly enhanced the living standards of the low-income population. In regard to the distribution of wealth, Robert J. Lampman, *The Share of Top Wealth-Holders in National Wealth*, 1962, has produced data to show that the share of personal sector wealth held by the wealthiest 1% of adults in the USA has steadily increased from 1949 to 1956.

[21] Myrdal, *ibid.*, pp. 13–15, 27–30.

being significantly so. In particular, he stresses the inadequate achievement of government in America in long-range economic planning, in redistributional reforms, and in the provision of public services and advanced social welfare schemes. And the sources of this governmental inadequacy he traces back to certain basic American socio-political dispositions and also to a relative lack of "democratic balance" in the institutional infrastructure of the American policy. On the one hand, Myrdal claims, there is among the powerful business community and within government itself a reluctance to take the long view and to envisage more central direction and control of the economy; also "a serious and irrational bias against public investment and consumption." On the other hand, among the lower strata of American society there is an unusual degree of political apathy and passivity which is most clearly seen in the general failure of the poorer sections of the population to organize themselves effectively and to press for the fundamental social reforms that would be in their interest. In this way an imbalance in organized power is brought about within the "plural society" which makes the need for initiative on the part of government all the more pressing—at the same time as it seems to paralyse this.[22]

If, then, Myrdal's analysis has any general validity—and it has yet, I think, to be seriously disputed—it follows that we should look somewhat doubtfully on arguments about a new equality which "has nothing to do with ideology" but which is the direct outcome of technological and economic advance. Such new equality there may be for some. But for those at the base of stratification hierarchies at least—how "equal" they are likely to become seems to have a good deal to do with ideology, or at any rate with purposive social action, or lack of this, stemming from specific social values and political creeds as well as from interests.[23] And differences between some industrial societies in these respects may well be giving rise to divergent, rather than convergent, patterns of change in their stratification systems.

On the second set of arguments—those concerning growing consistency between different stratification orders—I shall have relatively little to say for the good reason that there is little empirical data which directly bears on the crucial issue here; that is, the issue of whether there really is a *continuing* increase in the degree of integration of the stratification systems of *advanced* societies. About the long-term historical trend, one would not wish to argue; but again it is a question of whether such a trend is a reliable guide to the present and the future.

My main comment is that such evidence as does appear relevant to this issue indicates that in some industrial societies, at least, on-going economic progress is resulting in stratification systems becoming, if anything, somewhat *less* well integrated in certain respects. This evidence refers to what has become known as the "new working class." It suggests that the appreciable gains in income and in general living standards recently achieved by certain sections of the manual labour force have not for the most part been accompanied by changes in their life-styles of such a kind that their *status* position has been enhanced commensurately with their *economic* position. In other words, there is evidence of cultural and, in particular, of "social" barriers still widely existing between "working class" and "middle class" even in cases where immediate material differences have now disappeared.[24] Thus it seems that,

[22] *Ibid.*, chs. 4, 6 and 7. A basically similar view is presented in Michael Harrington, *The Other America,* 1962. On the organizational, and thus political, weakness of the poor, see pp. 13–17; on the past failure and present responsibility of the Federal Government, pp. 163–170. Cf. also Stephen W. Rousseas and James Farganis, "American Politics and the End of Ideology", *Brit. Journ. Soc.,* Vol. XIV, No. 4, 1963.

[23] Cf. Harrington's emphasis on the fact that "If there is to be a way out (of poverty) it will come from human action, from political change, not from automatic processes" (p. 162). . . .

[24] See, e.g., for Great Britain, John H. Goldthorpe and David Lockwood, "Affluence and the British Class Structure," *Soc. Rev.,* Vol. II, No. 2, 1963; for the USA, Bennet Berger, *Working Class Suburb: a Study of Auto Workers in Suburbia,* 1960; for France, A. Andrieux and J. Lignon, *L'Ouvrier D'Aujourd'hui,* 1960. In all these contributions a common emphasis is that on the growing *disparity* between the situation of the manual worker as *producer* and *consumer*.

contrary to the expectations of Kerr and his associates, "middle incomes" have not resulted, as yet at least, in the generalization of "middle class" ways of life or of "middle class" status.

Moreover, there are grounds for believing that notable discrepancies in stratification will persist in industrial societies. As Kerr himself recognizes, there will still exist in the foreseeable future in such societies a division between "managers" and "managed"—between those who are in some way associated with the exercise of authority in productive and administrative organizations and those who are not. And this division, one would suggest, will remain associated with differences in prestige as well as in power, while at the same time managers and managed overlap to some extent in terms of living standards. One would agree that in an economically advanced society a broad stratum of workers, performing skilled or, one would add, particularly arduous or irksome jobs, are likely to earn middle-range incomes. But there are no grounds for automatically assuming that they will thereby become socially accepted and assimilated into even the lower levels of what Renner has usefully termed the "service class".[25] After all, it must be recognized that groups which have some serious basis for claiming superior status generally take advantage of this. And further, it should be borne in mind that, increasingly, the members of this "service class" will be selected through their educational attainments rather than being recruited from the rank and file. Thus, if anything, they are likely to become more set apart from the latter in terms of culture and life-styles than they are at present.

In sum, one might suggest that the "increasing consistency" argument is flawed because it fails to take into account first, that occupational rôles with similar economic rewards may in some instances be quite differently related to the exercise of authority; and secondly, that relatively high income may serve as recompense for work of otherwise high "disutility" to the operative as well as for work involving expertise and responsibility.

Lastly, then, we come to the matter of social mobility. In this case, the first question which arises is that of whether it is in fact valid to regard industrial societies as having regularly higher rates of mobility than pre-industrial societies. Several writers, one should note, have recently argued that this view should not be too readily taken and have produced evidence to suggest that certain pre-industrial societies were far less rigidly stratified than seems generally to have been supposed.[26] Nevertheless, I would not wish to argue here against the more orthodox view, except to make the point that an increased rate of *inter*generational mobility in advanced societies is likely to be associated with some limitation of *intra*-generational or "career" mobility. To the extent that education becomes a key determinant of occupational achievement, the chances of "getting ahead" for those who start in a lowly position are inevitably diminished. This fact is most clearly demonstrated in recent studies of the recruitment of industrial managers. These show that as the educational standards of managers have risen, the likelihood of shop floor workers being promoted above supervisory level has been reduced.[27] Furthermore, in an advanced society, increasingly dominated by large scale organizations, the possibilities for the "little man" of starting up a successful business of his own also tend to be more limited than they were at an earlier phase in the industrialization process. Thus, for that large proportion of the population at least, with rank-and-file jobs and "ordinary" educational qualifications, industrial society appears to be growing significantly *less* "open" than it once was.

However, other, and perhaps more basic,

[25] Karl Renner, *Wandlungen der modernen Gesellschaft; zwei Abhandlungen über die Probleme der Nachkriegzeit,* 1953.

[26] See, e.g., for China, Robert M. Marsh, *The Mandarins: the Circulation of Elites in China, 1600–1900,* 1961, and "Values, Demand and Social Mobility," *Am. Soc. Rev.,* Vol. 28, 1963, also, Ping-ti Ho, *The Ladder of Success in Imperial China: Aspects of Social Mobility, 1368–1911,* 1963.

[27] For Great Britain, see Acton Society Trust, *Management Succession,* 1965, and R. V. Clements, *Managers: a study of their careers in industry,* 1958. For the USA, see W. Lloyd Warner and James C. Abegglen, *Occupational Mobility in American Business and Industry,* 1955.

issues arise from the arguments concerning mobility which I earlier outlined; in particular issues relating to the determinants of mobility patterns and rates. What are the grounds, one might ask, for believing that in advanced societies the crucial factor here is the occupational distribution, and thus that from one such society to another social mobility will tend to be much the same? Support for this view can be found in the well-known Lipset and Zetterberg study which led, in fact, to the conclusion that Western industrial societies have broadly similar rates of intergenerational mobility, and which produced no evidence to suggest that factors other than the "standardizing" one of the occupational structure were of major significance.[28] Their data, the authors claim, give no backing for the idea that differences in social ideologies, religious beliefs or other aspects of national cultures exercise a decisive influence on mobility. But it has to be noted that, as Lipset and Zetterberg themselves make quite clear, their findings in this respect refer only to "mass" mobility; that is, simply to movements across the manual–nonmanual line. And indeed they point out that the investigation of some aspects of "élite" mobility —for example, the recruitment of higher civil servants—has indicated some important national variations.[29]

Moreover, we have more recently the outstanding study of comparative social mobility made by Professor S. M. Miller.[30] This covers a still greater amount of data than Lipset and Zetterberg's work and demonstrates fairly conclusively that when *range* as well as frequency of mobility is taken into consideration, industrial societies do reveal quite sizeable differences in their mobility patterns. Such differences tend to be most evident in the case of long-range mobility. This is generally low—another reason for querying just how "open" and "meritocratic" industrial societies have so far become—but certain countries, the USA and USSR, for example, appear to have attained quite significantly higher rates of "élite" mobility than do others, such as many in western Europe. Further, though, Miller shows that countries with low long-range mobility may still have relatively high short-range mobility—as, for instance, does Great Britain: there is no correlation between rates of mobility of differing distance. Thus, industrial societies have quite various "mobility profiles"; the overall similarity indicated by the study of "mass" mobility turns out to be somewhat spurious.

On this basis, then, Miller is able to argue very strongly that patterns of social mobility in advanced societies cannot be understood *simply* in terms of occupational structure[31] —or, one would add, in terms of any "inherent" features of industrialism. Their diversity precludes this. It appears necessary rather, to consider also the effects on mobility of other, and more variable, aspects of social structure—educational institutions, for example, and their articulation with the stratification hierarchy itself—and further, possibly, *pace* Lipset and Zetterberg, the part played by cultural values.[32] As Miller points out, what is perhaps most surprising about his data is the *lack* of convergence in mobility patterns that is indicated between societies at broadly comparable levels of economic development. The "logic" of industrialism, it appears, is often confused by "extraneous" factors.

These, then, are some of the objections that may be made on empirical grounds to the hypotheses concerning changes in stratification systems which I previously outlined. . . . In conclusion of this paper, I would like to make a more basic objection which relates to the theoretical position underlying these arguments. Specifically, I would like to question the idea that the stratification systems of all industrial societies are *ipso facto* of the same generic type, and thus that they may in principle be

[28] See S. M. Lipset and Hans L. Zetterberg, "A Theory of Social Mobility," *Transactions of the Third World Congress of Sociology,* 1956, Vol. III, pp. 155–177, and Ch. II, "Social Mobility in Industrial Society" in S. M. Lipset and R. Bendix, *Social Mobility in Industrial Society,* 1959.

[29] *Ibid.,* pp. 38–42.

[30] S. M. Miller, "Comparative Social Mobility," *Current Sociology,* Vol. IX, No. 1, 1960.

[31] *Ibid.,* pp. 22–23, 57–58.

[32] As an example of the kind of study which would seem particularly relevant and valuable, see Ralph H. Turner, "Modes of Social Ascent through Education: Sponsored and Contest Mobility" . . . [reprinted in this book].

expected to follow convergent or parallel lines of development. Against this view, I would like to suggest that social stratification in the advanced societies of the Communist world—or at any rate in the USSR and its closer satellites—is *not* of the same generic type as in the West and that, because of this, the hypotheses earlier discussed cannot in this case really apply.

Soviet society is, of course, stratified; and, furthermore, it is true that in spite of the absence of private property in production, it appears to be stratified on an often similar pattern to the capitalist or post-capitalist societies of the West. For example, to a large degree there is apparent similarity in the connections between occupational rôle, economic rewards and social prestige, in the part played by education in determining occupational level, in the operation of an informal status system, and so on. But, I would argue, this similarity is only of a phenotypical kind: genotypically, stratification in Soviet society is significantly different from stratification in the West.

Primarily, it may be said, this difference derives from the simple fact that in Soviet society the economy operates within a "monistic", or totalitarian, political order and is, in principle at least, totally planned, whereas in advanced Western societies political power is significantly less concentrated and the economy is planned in a far less centralized and detailed way. From this it results that in the West economic, and specifically market, forces act as the crucial stratifying agency within society. They are, one could say, the major source of social inequality. And consequently, the *class* situation of individuals and groups, understood in terms of their economic power and resources, tends to be the most important single determinant of their general life-chances. This is why we can usefully speak of Western industrial society as being "class" stratified. However, in the case of Soviet society, market forces cannot be held to play a comparable rôle in the stratification process. These forces operate, of course, and differences in economic power and resources between individuals and groups have, as in the West, far-reaching social and human consequences. But, one would argue, to a significantly greater extent than in the West, stratification in Soviet society is subjected to *political* regulation; market forces are not permitted to have the primacy or the degree of autonomy in this respect that they have even in a "managed" capitalist society. Undoubtedly, the functional requirements of the economy exert pressures upon the system of stratification, and these pressures may in some cases prove to be imperative. But the nature of the political order means that far more than with Western democracy, the pattern of social inequality can be shaped through the purposive action of the ruling party, and still more so, of course, the "life-fates" of particular persons.[33]

For example, during the years of Stalin's rule, economic inequality in the USSR generally increased.[34] . . . By the end of the war decade, these developments had led to a degree of inequality in Soviet society which, in the view of many commentators, was greater than that which was generally to be found in the industrial societies of the West.[35] However, in more recent years it has become clear that contrary to most expectations, this inegalitarian trend in the USSR has been checked and, moreover, that in certain respects at least it has even been reversed. Minimum wages in industry have been increased several times since the late 1950s and the incomes of the *kolkhozy* have for the most part risen quite considerably. This latter development has had the effect of closing somewhat the income gap between industrial and agricultural workers and has also been associated with a reduction in differentials in the earnings of the *kolkhoz* peasants themselves. At the same time, there is evidence of limitations being placed on the more excessive salaries of higher officials and of more stringent measures being taken against the abuse of

[33] Also relevant here, of course, is a further distinctive feature of a totalitarian political system —the absence of the "rule of law".

[34] Probably the best analysis in this respect is that provided by Barrington Moore, Jr., *Soviet Politics—the Dilemma of Power,* 1950.

[35] See, e.g., Alex Inkeles, "Social Stratification and Mobility in the Soviet Union: 1940–1950," *Am. Soc. Rev.,* Vol. 15, 1950. This paper contains an excellent factual account of the ways through which both economic and status inequality were increased during the Stalin era.

privileges. Finally, tax changes in the past few years have tended to favour the poorer against the richer groups, and various kinds of welfare provision have been substantially improved. In these ways, then, economic differences between the manual and non-manual categories overall have almost certainly been reduced to some extent, as well as differences within these categories.[36]

Now these changes can, of course, be rightly regarded as being in some degree economically conditioned. Clearly, for instance, the increased differentiation in wages and salaries in the Stalin era must in part be understood in terms of the exigencies and consequences of rapid industrialization. But, I would argue, there can be little question that at the same time these changes were the outcome of political decisions—of choices made between realistic alternatives—and, furthermore, that frequently they were brought about with political as well as with specifically economic ends in view. Stalin, it is true, wanted rapid industrialization: but he had the further political objective that this process should be carried through under his own absolute control. Thus, this entailed not only depriving a large section of the population of material returns from their labour in order to achieve maximum expansion of industrial capacity, but also the building-up of a group of exceptionally favoured administrators and managers who would be highly motivated to retain their enviable positions through loyalty to Stalin and through high level performance. To this latter end, in fact, appropriate status as well as economic inequalities were also developed. For example, during and after the war years, formal titles, uniforms and insignia of rank were introduced into various branches of industry and the governmental bureaucracy. Moreover, the wide social distance which was in this way created between the top and bottom of the stratification hierarchy had the manifest function of insulating the "élite" from the masses and from their needs and wishes. And thus, as Professor Feldmesser has pointed out, those in high positions were helped to learn "that success was to be had by winning the favour not of those below them but of those above them, which was exactly what Stalin wanted them to learn."[37]

Similarly, the more recent moves towards reducing inequalities have again fairly evident political aims, even though, in some cases, they may also have been economically required.[38] On the one hand, it seems clear that the present Soviet leadership is working toward a future Communist society which will be characterized by a high level of social welfare, and indeed eventually by private affluence, while still remaining under the undisputed dominance of the Party. In other words, the creation of the "good life" for all appears destined to become one of the régime's most important sources of legitimacy. In fact, as Professor Shapiro has noted, the 1961 Programme of the CPSU makes this more or less explicit. The Programme, he writes,

> enunciates squarely the concrete fact that party rule has come to stay. It calls upon the Soviet citizen to recognize and accept this fact, and to abandon the illusion that in this respect, things are going to change. In return, it promises him great material benefits and prosperity.[39]

On the other hand, the security of the régime also requires that the bureaucratic and managerial "élite" does not become so well established as to gain some measure

[36] For a general discussion of these changes, see Robert A. Feldmesser, "Towards the Classless Society?". Also Alec Nove, "Is the Soviet Union a Welfare State?", both in Alex Inkeles and Kent Geiger (eds.), *Soviet Society,* 1961.

[37] *Ibid.,* p. 579. This political subordination of members of the "élite", concomitant with their economic and status elevation, is the reason for using inverted commas [quotes]. As Feldmesser notes, the "élite" created by Stalin is surely distinctive by virtue of its general lack of autonomy.

[38] As, e.g., in the case of the increase in peasant incomes which was essential if genuine incentives to improve production were to be offered in agriculture. Cf. Seweryn Bialer, "But Some Are More Equal than Others," *Problems of Communism,* Vol. IX, No. 2, 1960.

[39] Leonard Shapiro, "From Utopia towards Realism" in Shapiro (ed.), *The USSR and the Future: an Analysis of the New Program of the CPSU,* 1963. See also in this volume Erik Boettcher, "Soviet Social Policy in Theory and Practice". The text of the Programme itself is printed as an Appendix; note, in particular, Part Two, Sections II, III, V and VII.

of independence from the Party chiefs. Thus, Krushchev has been concerned to show the members of this group that they remain the creatures of the Party and that their privileges are not permanent but still rest upon their obedience and service to the Party. Those whom Djilas has referred to as the "new class" in Communist society[40] cannot in fact be allowed by the Party leadership to become a class—in the sense of a collectivity which is capable of maintaining its position in society (and that of its children) through its own social power, and which possesses some degree of group consciousness and cohesion. For the emergence of such a class would constitute a serious threat to the Party's totalitarian rule, different only in degree from the threat that would be posed by the emergence of an independent trade union, professional body or political organization. It is awareness of this danger, one would suggest, which chiefly lies behind the recent attacks —verbal as well as material—which have been made upon higher officialdom and the top industrial personnel. For apart from the curtailment of economic rewards in some cases, it is interesting to note that the quasi-military status distinctions of the war decade have now been largely abolished and that the Party has actually encouraged rank-and-file employees in industry and agriculture to expose inadequacy and inefficiency on the part of their superiors.[41] Furthermore, there has been some weeding out of superfluous posts, and demotions appear to have become much more common.[42] Finally, though, it is probably Krushchev's educational reforms which have been of greatest significance. These were carried through at a time when pressure on the institutions of secondary and higher education was reaching a peak; yet they were designed to make access to these institutions less dependent than previously upon economic resources and the new rules for competitive entry which were introduced seem, if anything, to shift the balance of "social" advantage away from the children of the "élite" and towards candidates from worker or peasant families. As Feldmesser notes, if a "new class"—a "state bourgeoisie"—were in fact in existence in the USSR, then exactly the reverse of this might have been expected; that is, a move to make access to these scarce facilities *more*, rather than less, dependent upon the ability to pay.[43]

It is then not too much to say that in Soviet society hierarchical differentiation is an instrument of the régime. To a significant degree stratification is *organized* in order to suit the political needs of the régime; and, as these needs change, so too may the particular structure of inequality. In other words, the Soviet system of stratification is characterized by an important element of "deliberateness", and it is this which basically distinguishes it from the Western system, in spite of the many apparent similarities. In the industrial societies of the West, one could say, the action of the state sets limits to the extent of social inequalities which derive basically from the operation of a market economy: in Soviet society the pattern of inequality also results in part from "market" forces, but in this case these are subordinated to political control up to the limits set by the requirements of the industrial system.[44] For this reason, one may conclude, Soviet society is not, in the same way as Western society, *class* stratified. As Raymond Aron has observed, class stratification and a monistic political system are to be regarded as incompatibles.[45]

If, then, the foregoing analysis is accepted, it follows that the arguments I earlier outlined on the development of stratification systems can have no general validity. Their underlying rationale, in terms of the exigencies of an advanced industrial technology and economy, is destroyed. The experience of Soviet society can be taken as

[40] Milovan Djilas, *The New Class,* New York: Frederick A. Praeger, 1957.

[41] Feldmesser, *op. cit.,* pp. 573–575.

[42] Bialer, *op. cit.,* pp. 576–578.

[43] Feldmesser, *op. cit.,* pp. 576–578.

[44] This assessment is consistent with the more general interpretations of the Soviet social system advanced by writers such as Brzezinski and Daniel Bell, in some opposition to the interpretation of Inkeles and his associates. . . . Zbigniew K. Brzezinski, *Ideology and Power in Soviet Politics,* 1962, p. 31. Daniel Bell, "Ten Theories in Search of Reality: the Prediction of Soviet Behaviour" in *The End of Ideology,* New York: Collier Books, 1961, pp. 340–341.

[45] See his "Social Structure and the Ruling Class," *Brit. Journ. Soc.,* Vol. I, 1950.

indicating that the structural and functional imperatives of an industrial order are not so stringent as to prevent quite wide variations in patterns of social stratification, nor to prohibit the systematic manipulation of social inequalities by a régime commanding modern administrative resources and under no contraints from an organized opposition or the rule of law.

The crucial point, in fact, at which the rationale breaks down is in the supposition that industrialism and totalitarianism cannot "in the long run" co-exist; that is, in the idea that with industrial advance a progressive diffusion of political power must of necessity occur. Were this idea valid, then it would become difficult to maintain the claim that differences between the stratification systems of the Western and Communist worlds are of a generic kind. However, it may be said that no serious grounds exist for believing that within Soviet society any such diffusion of power is taking place, or, at least, not so far as the key decision-making processes are concerned.[46] The régime may be compelled to give more consideration to the effect of its decisions on popular morale and to rely increasingly on the expertise of scientists, technicians and professionals of various kinds; it may also find it desirable to decentralize administration and to encourage a high degree of participation in the conduct of public affairs at a local level. But the important point is that all these things can be done, and in recent years *have* been done, without the Party leadership in any way yielding up its position of ultimate authority and control. Indeed, it is far more arguable that since the end of the period of "collective" rule, the power of the Party leadership has become still more absolute and unrivalled. This situation, one would suggest, has been brought about as a result of Krushchev's success in reducing the power and independence, relative to the Party machine, of the other major bureaucratic structures within Soviet society—those of the political police, of the military and of government and industry. In some cases, it might be noted, the changes involved here can be seen as aspects of "destalinization"—for example, the mitigation of the terror or the dissolution of a large part of the central state apparatus. Yet at the same time these changes have had the effect of accentuating still further the totalitarian nature of Party rule. As Bialer points out:

> The party bureaucracy is at present the only remaining apparatus which is centralized in its organization, which operates at all levels of the society, and which "specializes" in every sphere of societal activity. In its functions of communicating, controlling and to an ever greater degree directly organizing the tasks set forth by the leadership, it influences the operation of the other bureaucratic apparatuses, but is not in turn subject to any outside interference. It is subordinate only to the top leadership and to its own hierarchical line of authority.[47]

. . . What one would wish to stress, then, is that if such views as these are sound (as I believe they are), it becomes difficult to see how one can formulate *any* general and comprehensive propositions concerning stratification change as part of a "logic" of industrial development. For the essential assumption involved in such propositions—that of some necessary "primacy" of the economic system over the political—is no longer a reliable one. It has to be recognized, rather, that stratification systems are not to be understood as mere "reflections" of a certain level of technology and industrial organization but are shaped by a range of other factors, important among which may be that of purposive political action; and further, that the importance of this latter factor in societies in which political power is highly concentrated is such as to create a distinctive type of stratification which is

[46] For recent discussion of the issue of the compatibility of industrialism and totalitarianism from both empirical and theoretical points of view, see Brzezinski, *op. cit.*, Chs. I and III, and R. Aron (ed.), *World Technology and Human Destiny*, 1963.

[47] Bialer, *op. cit.*, pp. 48–49. In addition to Bialer's paper, see also on the strengthening of Party rule under Krushchev, Brzezinski, *op. cit.*, Ch. III, and Edward Crankshaw, *Krushchev's Russia*, 1957, pp. 69, 76–79. Crankshaw shows how this process is in no way inconsistent with the widening of opportunities for popular participation in administrative work at a local level via the "public organizations". See pp. 94–98.

difficult even to discuss in terms of concepts developed in a Western, capitalist context.[48]

# STRATA AND STRATA INTEREST IN SOCIALIST SOCIETY

## TOWARD A NEW THEORETICAL APPROACH

*Wlodzimierz Wesolowski*

### INTRODUCTION

The question of the class structure of socialist society is the subject of lively discussion among Polish sociologists and economists. Apart from the findings of empirical research on particular classes and strata conceived in the traditional fashion as the working class, the stratum of intelligentsia, and the class of small peasants, several articles recently appeared with new theoretical propositions regarding the class structure of socialist society.[1] In their interest in these problems Polish scientists are by no means alone. A similar trend can be noted in other socialist countries.[2]

The present paper is intended as a contribution to the current discussion. This discussion is steadily widening in scope and hence it seems worthwhile to present some of its problems to the wider circles of experts working in the field of social stratification. The ideas outlined below constitute a preliminary inquiry rather than a definite solution.

In the current discussion in Poland the economist Bronislaw Minc has advanced the most original and at the same time controversial conception. Lack of space prevents a full exposition of that conception. It is nevertheless necessary to mention it at least briefly since I advance a clearly varying proposition. Both our conceptions are based on general Marxist sociological principles. But they propose different concrete theoretical solutions.

Minc proposes[3] to distinguish in socialist society, where socialist construction has been completed, where there are no longer any private factories, nor the private ownership of the means of production, two social classes: a class of workers of the State sector and a class of workers of the cooperative sector. His point of departure is the assumption that a socialist society retains the "relation to the means of production" as

Paper delivered at Sixth World Congress of Sociology, Evian, France, September 1966. Printed by permission of the author.

[48] As Feldmesser has indicated, the argument that Soviet society is not "class" stratified in the manner of Western industrial societies can also be supported from the "subjective" point of view. See his paper, "Social Classes and the Political Structure" in Black (ed.), *op. cit.*, pp. 235–252. The available evidence suggests that Soviet citizens exhibit a relatively low level of class consciousness in the sense that their class situation is not of fundamental importance in patterning their dominant modes of thought and action. Members of different social strata in Soviet society seem more alike in their social ideologies and attitudes than their counterparts in the West, while the feature of the social structure which is most strongly reflected in their social consciousness at all levels is that of the division between "Party people" and "non-Party people". On this latter point see Inkeles and Bauer, *op. cit.*, Ch. XIII.

[1] Cf. Bronislaw Mino, *Klasy i warstwy w społeczeństwie socjalistycznym,* "Classes and Strata in Socialist Society," *Polityka,* Nos. 39, 42, 46, 1961; J. Wiatr, *Uwarstwienie społeczne a tendencje egalitarne,* "Social Stratification and Egalitarian Tendencies," *Kultura i Społeczeństwo,* No. 2, 1962; B. Gałęski, *Niektóre problemy struktury społecznej w świetle badań wiejskich,* "Some Problems of Social Structure in the Light of Investigations of the Rural Communities," *Studia Socjologiczne,* No. 1, 1963; Bronislaw Mino, *O rozwarstwieniu społeczeństwa socjalistycznego,* "Social Stratification in Socialist Society," *Kultura i Społeczeństwo,* No. 3, 1963; W. Wesolowski, *Proces zanikania rożnic klasowych,* "Process of Disappearing of Class Differences," *Studia Socjologiczne,* No. 2, 1964; S. Widerszpil, *Interpretacja przemian struktury społecznej w Polsce Ludowej,* "An Interpretation of Changes of Social Structure in People's Poland," *Nowe Drogi,* No. 1, 1963.

[2] Cf. P. N. Fiedosijew, ed., *Ot socjalizma k komunizmu,* "From Socialism to Communism," Moscow 1962; *Socjologija w SSSR,* "Sociology in the Soviet Union," Vol. I, Moscow 1965; *Socjologija* Nos. 1–2, 1966, Beograd, special issue of the Yugoslav sociological journal devoted to the problems of "Socialism and the Changes in Class Structure."

[3] Cf. Minc, *Klasy i warstwy w społeczeństwie socjalistycznym, op. cit.*

the criterion of class differentiation, since two different economic sectors continue to exist. One is the State sector in which the means of production are the general property of the nation; the second is the cooperative sector in which the means of production are owned by a smaller group, members of a given cooperative.

According to Mino, two manual workers, turners, for example, will be considered to belong to two different classes only on the basis that one works for the government and the other in a cooperative enterprise. Analogically, the class affiliation of two engineers or two directors would be determined by the fact that they are employed in two different economic sectors. . . .

Sociologists cannot accept these propositions since they are too formalistic. The crucial argument against them is that under the socialist economic system the social consequences of being employed in the State or in the cooperative sector are not important enough to be regarded as a basis for social differentiation. Sectors do not determine in any significant extent the distribution of crucial stratificational variables or, in other words, the distribution of the important social status characteristics such as income, life chances, power, prestige, and so on.

Through the theory of the two classes, based on the two sectors of economy, Mino wants to stress the lasting role of the "relation to the means of production" in the socialist society and in this way to retain the classical Marxist criterion of classes as valid for that type of society. This author believes, on the contrary, that the new social situation resulting from the "socialized" economic system demands a new theoretical approach. It is unwarranted to stress so heavily the classical criterion, while its role is gradually diminishing and some other factors enter in its place.

## THE MARXIAN CLASS THEORY AND SOCIALIST SOCIETY

The Marxian theory of class structure stipulates first of all the existence of two mutually antagonistic groups involved in the process of production. These are so-called basic classes. They differ from each other by their relations to the means of production. One of these classes owns them; the other is deprived of them although it operates them. This relation determines the character of the first as an exploiting, and of the second as an exploited class.

The objective conflict of interests is rooted in the antagonistic positions of the two classes, and a different consciousness arises on the foundation of these antithetic social positions. The emergence of the class struggle demonstrates the existence of such classes.

This brief summary leads to what has become a commonplace, that proletarian revolution abolishes the thus conceived class structure. Socialization of the capitalist owned means of production means the liquidation of one of the elements of the antagonistic capital-labor relations. And with this disappears the fundamental class relation typical for capitalist society. Without their opposite pole the workers cease being a class in the old sense of the term. For there has ceased to exist the basic characteristic constituting them as a class in capitalist society: exploitation by the owners of the means of production. In the Marxist sense, they are no longer an *actual class,* but rather a *former class.*

The above statement is deliberately simplified to underscore the fundamental difference. When the workers free themselves from their "Siamese Twin" they lose the principal characteristic of their social position but they are not thereby automatically deprived of other characteristics. These other traits make it advisable to continue to call them the workers, although not the class in Marx's sense of that term. Perhaps it would be convenient to call them stratum of workers. The workers continue to be linked with a certain type of production, industrial production, and a specific type of labor, manual labor. They are characterized by certain social and cultural traits. In other words, the workers occupy a given place in the social division of labor; they have a definite type of income, education, way of life, political attitude, and a number of other important social characteristics or attributes.

Involved here is one of the important, though not always clearly perceived, characteristic traits of the Marxian theory of classes. In that theory one characteristic and one social relation connected with it—the monopoly of the means of production on one side and deprivation of them on the other—are regarded as the bases of the complex structure of class characteristics.

The class characteristics create a sort of specific hierarchy and causal chain of interrelations. There is a constellation of characteristics on the side of the capitalists and a different one on the workers' side. Ownership of the means of production puts the capitalist in control of the production process and gives a privileged position in the division of income derived from production. The worker carries out orders in the course of the production process and suffers discrimination in the division of income derived from production. From the combination of these elements flow further characteristics of the social position of capitalists and workers. These may be defined as unequal opportunities to attain and benefit from various values, such as education, health, enjoyment of cultural assets. On the basis of all these characteristics of the social position there take shape different ways of life, a different consciousness and dissimilar political attitudes.

It is true that some of these attributes were heavily stressed by Marx, while others were merely mentioned. In writings of many later Marxists some of these attributes were overlooked. But they were present in Marx's deliberations.

It should be noted in addition that the causal relations are not like a uniform linear chain. For instance, the relation to the means of production shapes class consciousness by determining the income level and status in the social organization of the labor process. The magnitude of income reacts on class consciousness by the opportunities it offers and by social prestige. There is furthermore an interaction between some characteristics.[4]

. . . . . . . . . . . . . . . . . . . . . . . . . . . . . . .

. . . The following facts are important for our treatment of the question of transformation in the class structure of socialist society: (1) the abolition of the capitalist production relations eliminates the fundamental connections and basic characteristics distinguishing the workers in capitalist society, setting in motion the means of production belonging to another class, but (2) all the other characteristics of their social position do not automatically disappear as a result. While free or cut out from the previously determining characteristic, namely relation to the means of production, these other attributes of workers are retained. They continue to fulfill their differentiating role, no longer in relation to the capitalists, but to other groups or strata.[5]

Capitalist society is composed not only of basic classes: capitalists and workers but also of some other classes and strata. These strata are "inherited" by socialist society. Usually they are conceived by Marxists as the *stratum of intelligentsia*, understood as the broad group of white-collar workers, and the small commodity agricultural producers, farmers.

Those other strata also have definite characteristics of social position, similar to those included in our schemes. The characteristics of intelligentsia are peculiar in that they do not comprise any "relation to

---

[4] The above enumeration of class characteristics of social position reveals that the difference between Marxists and non-Marxist students of social stratification is not so much in their choice of the set of characteristics as in their perspectives in approaching that set of characteristics. The Marxist approach could be called deterministic, the non-Marxist approach, operational. Marxists look at the whole structure of status characteristics from the bottom up. Most of the non-Marxists divide all inhabitants of a given community into *prestige classes,* being less interested in the underlying structure of other characteristics. Of course, there are other differences between the two approaches, but it is worthwhile to see also similarities. This point was further elaborated in the present author's introduction to the Polish edition of C. W. Mills' *White Collar, cf. Białe kołnierzyki: Amerykańskie klasy średnie,* Warsaw, 1965.

[5] The current tendency in capitalist countries is for the government to exert its influence on some of the status characteristics of the working class by introducing social legislation, giving grants, fixing minimum wages, and so on. As a result, the direct dependence of some of the status characteristics on the relation of the given social group to the means of production is weakened, though the two basic classes, capitalists and workers, continue to differ sharply in their status characteristics which in the last analysis depend on the relation to the means of production.

the means of production" which would put this stratum in antagonism to any other class. Marxists therefore insist on calling the intelligentsia a stratum, rather than a class. What distinguishes the white-collar workers as a stratum are: type of occupation (nonmanual labor), income (usually defined as medium, that is somewhere between the income of capitalists and that of the laborers), opportunities, way of life, prestige, and so on.

The peculiar characteristics of the farmers as small-scale agricultural producers consist in the specific nature of their means of production and their relations to those means of production. In capitalist society, the farmers, similar to the white-collar workers, have no direct polar relationship to any other class, unlike the laborers and capitalists. The farmers are owners of their means of production but they employ their own labor to use them. As in the case of the laborers or capitalists, the above characteristic of the farmers determines a number of other characteristics of their social position. . . .

Thus the small-commodity agricultural producer—like the worker and the representative of the intelligentsia—is characterized by a certain syndrome of traits. With respect to individual characteristics, his position may be compared to that of the worker or white-collar in the proportion of manual and mental labor, size of income, and so on.

The transformation of the class of small-commodity producers under socialism takes the direction of turning its members into employees of the socialized sector. The aim of the socioeconomic policy of the State is to make their relation to the means of production conform to that of laborers and white-collar workers. This means a desire to eliminate their relation to the means of production as a characteristic distinguishing this group from others. This is accompanied by the desire to deprive this characteristic of its role of decisive determinant of the social position and psychological attributes specific to that group.

This process may be of shorter or longer duration and it may also take different forms. We shall leave that question aside. It may be said, however, that the transformations in the class structure inherited from capitalism evolve towards: (a) equalization of the relation to the means of production of the former small-commodity producers, the workers and intelligentsia, (b) complete deprivation of the relation to the means of production of its decisive role in determining other status characteristics, income, prestige, opportunity, and so on. *From here on the relation to the means of production is uniform for all citizens. And if there appear differences in income, character of labor, prestige, opportunity, political attitude, it is not this relation which determines them.*

## PROCESS OF DISINTEGRATION OF CLASS CHARACTERISTICS

The following conclusion is suggested by the above: the evolution of the class structure in socialist society consists of the gradual evening out of the relation of different groups of the population to the means of production. Parallel with that occurs a gradual diminution of the role of that relation as a determinant of other status characteristics and of the content of social consciousness.

Hence the role of differentiating characteristics of society is assumed to an ever-growing degree by such status characteristics as: the nature of labor, income, education, prestige, and so forth.[6] These characteristics, removed from the determining influence of the relation to the means of production, retain an autonomous existence under socialism. Thus, although classes, in Marx's sense of that term, disappear in a developed socialist society, there remain social differentiations which may be called social stratification.

This stratification may be conceived in a dual manner. The first conception refers to income, occupational or prestige stratifications along its various dimensions. This is a fairly simple theoretical concept which

[6] Until now we used the terms *class characteristics* or *class attributes*. From here on we will use rather the term *status characteristics* or *status attributes* since the *relation to the means of production* ceases to play any important role in our deliberations. The characteristics of social position from the upper layers of our schemes are usually associated with the term *status* or *social status*.

lends itself easily to research. It would involve the application of a simplified concept of multidimensional stratification to an investigation of socialist society. Each characteristic would then constitute a separate research subject and its intensity would be a criterion for distinguishing the individual stratification levels.

The second concept is more complex, but it therefore enables a better grasp of social processes and structures. It is the multidimensional approach proper.

It should be recalled here that for Marx classes differ in respect to a number of related characteristics. The bourgeoisie enjoys a high income, high education level and high prestige. The workers have low incomes, a low educational level and low prestige. The petty bourgeoisie have a medium income, enjoy medium prestige and their educational level is above that of the workers and below that of the bourgeoisie. This class concept appeared not only in Marx but in a number of non-Marxist theoreticians.

There hence arises the exceptionally important question: To what extent is there a congruence of certain characteristics among the strata of a socialist country? Is there a correspondence, for instance, between income on the one hand and education and prestige on the other? Is it the problem of status crystallization, in Lenski's terms?[7]

The processes of revolutionary transformation effect a certain disintegration or *decomposition* of status characteristics. The given character of labor, size of income, level of education, and degree of prestige tends to disintegrate. There are groups with low education and high incomes, or with high incomes and low prestige, and so on. This is brought about by the changes in the economic system and in ideology. Many evidences of these disintegration processes are to be found in Poland. The theoretical significance of them is overlooked by sociologists and economists.

[7] G. Lenski, "Status Crystallization: A Non-Vertical Dimension of Social Status," *The American Sociological Review,* No. 4, 1954. See also, L. Broom, "Social Differentiation and Stratification," in R. K. Merton, L. Broom, L. S. Cottrell, Jr., eds., *Sociology Today,* New York, 1959.

The processes of disintegration of status characteristics intermingle with the processes of evening out some differences. Some decompositions may be considered as the processes leading to equalization. If for instance an unskilled laborer earns as much as a doctor, this may be considered an equalization of their social position in respect to one area of difference, income, while the difference in another area, education, is retained. The same applies to the equalization of the earnings of a turner and an engineer, for example. But other processes are also taking place when a turner earns more than an engineer, or a miner enjoys a greater prestige than a lawyer; the disintegration of status characteristics exceeds the bounds of the equalization of levels and leads to a deeper or more distant dislocation. Certain groups begin to differ one from another as being in a reverse relation with respect to certain attributes than was the case in the previous socio-economic system.

The disintegration of social-status characteristics may hence assume two forms. One is the equalization of the levels of some characteristics pertaining to some particular former classes or strata. The second is the case of one class leaping ahead of another in relation to some of these characteristics.

By way of example we present below some empirical material on the disintegration of three status characteristics in contemporary Poland. These are the nature of labor, size of income, and degree of prestige.

In interwar Poland virtually every white-collar worker earned more than manual workers. The average wage of a white-collar worker was more than double that of a manual worker. Table 1 presents the comparative income structure of the two groups today.[8]

True, the table shows a higher percentage of manual workers among the lowest paid and a higher percentage of white-collar workers among the highest paid. Nevertheless, two other phenomena indicated in the table are no less important. Thus a high percentage of manual and nonmanual workers earns the same amount, from 1200 to 2000 zlotys a month. This speaks for income

[8] *Poland in Figures 1944–1964,* Warsaw, 1965, p. 104.

**TABLE 1 Gross Monthly Earnings of Employees by Income Groups in 1963**

| *Income Group* | *Manual Workers, Per cent* | *Nonmanual Workers, Per cent* |
|---|---|---|
| 701–800 | 10.7 | 1.3 |
| 801–1000 | 7.2 | 5.4 |
| 1001–1200 | 8.7 | 9.1 |
| 1201–1500 | 15.6 | 17.1 |
| 1501–2000 | 24.7 | 26.3 |
| 2001–2500 | 15.9 | 16.3 |
| 2501–3000 | 8.5 | 10.4 |
| Over 3000 | 8.7 | 14.1 |
| | 100.0 | 100.0 |

equalization. Then there is a large number of workers who earn more than white-collar workers. Of manual workers 33.1 per cent earn more than 2000 zlotys, while 59.2 per cent of nonmanual workers earn less. Here we enter the trail of the disintegration of two characteristics: nature of labor and size of income.

An investigation of occupational prestige in Poland today suggests the disintegration of another pair of characteristics: the nature of labor and social prestige. It indicates that some manual occupations enjoy greater prestige than some nonmanual vocations. Thus skilled workers occupy a higher place in the prestige hierarchy than do clerks and similar categories of white-collar employees. In contrast a sociologist wrote about the corresponding prewar situation: "Perhaps nowhere is the social gulf so glaring as in Poland between nonmanual work—even of the most subordinate kind—and manual work, no matter how constructive."[9]

Also evident is a partial separation of income and prestige. For instance, earnings in the teaching and nursing professions are relatively low today. A school teacher earns from 1500 to 2000 zlotys monthly and a nurse about 1500. But they occupy a higher place on the prestige ladder than does the turner with three to four thousand zlotys or the private merchant whose income is still higher.

Members of the society are of course aware of this disintegration process. In the above cited investigations the respondents were asked to evaluate the same two occupations according to the criteria of material benefit and prestige. The hierarchies of the two did not correspond. Each occupation occupied one place on the income scale and another on the prestige scale. In contracted form this is shown in Table 2.

It should also be noted here that a certain decomposition of status characteristics of some categories of manual and nonmanual workers is also to be noted in some contemporary capitalist societies. But its range is much smaller than in the socialist societies.

## CONTRADICTION OF INTERESTS IN SOCIALIST SOCIETY

The problem of interests, and especially of contradictions of interests plays an important role in Marx's theory of social structure. Discussing the changes in class structure in the socialist society we shall focus on the sphere of social interests. The problems involved here are of extreme complexity. Until now they were rarely and rather incidentally studied by Marxist scholars. . . .

At the very beginning some distinctive features of the capitalist versus the socialist society should be pointed out. This might help to understand some peculiarities of the socialist society.

According to Marx, the capitalist mode of production is characterized by the presence of two social classes of which one appropriates the results of the labor of the other. The capitalist class seizes the *surplus value* produced by the workers. This kind of class relation is connected with the distribution of goods according to "the ownership principle of distribution." When this principle is in operation a person need not be working to take part in the distribution of economic goods, or even to enjoy privileges in this distribution.

The ownership principle of distribution ceases to operate with the abolition of the capitalist ownership of the means of

[9] W. Wesołowski and A. Sarapata, *Hierarchia zawodów i stanowisk,* "Hierarchies of Occupations and Positions," *Studia Socjologiczne,* No. 2, 1961, p. 101.

**TABLE 2 Evaluation of Occupational Groups According to Material Rewards and Social Prestige[10]**

| *Occupational Group* | MATERIAL REWARD | | PRESTIGE | |
|---|---|---|---|---|
| | Rank | Score | Score | Rank |
| Private entrepreneurs | 1 | 1.81 | 2.81 | 3 |
| Professionals | 2 | 2.35 | 1.74 | 1 |
| Skilled workers | 3 | 2.40 | 2.33 | 2 |
| White-collar | 4 | 3.30 | 3.17 | 4 |
| Unskilled workers | 5 | 4.12 | 4.06 | 5 |

[10] *Ibid.*, p. 104. In this table all nonmanual workers, called in the present paper intelligentsia and white collar, are divided into two groups: professionals and white collar. The reason for this division is that university professors, physicians, engineers, lawyers are evidently on different layers of the hierarchy than nurses, bookkeepers, office department directors, etc. (See Table 1.)

production. This also means an end to the contradiction of class interests characteristic of capitalist society, that is between the class of capitalists and the working class.

In socialist society, the place of the ownership principle is taken by the principle of distribution according to work. Thus an individual's share in the social product is determined by the quality and quantity of work done by that individual. This principle is not entirely new. In capitalist society it applies to people without capital, that is to say, to people who live from their own labor. With the abolition of the interest rate on capital in socialism the principle of distribution according to work acquires universal validity. In socialist society there is only one criterion of an individual's share in the social product: the amount and quality of the work done by him.[11]

Let us examine some questions connected with the application of the formula "to each according to his work." The problems of social stratification are related to that part of the formula which postulates wages as a function of the quality of labor, that is a function of the level of skill and education required for the performance of a given job. There is a marked difference in that level between, for example, the unskilled laborer and the university professor.

It is necessary to clarify what situation we have in mind as creating the "contradiction of interest." It should be recalled that Marx had a very broad concept of the contradiction of interests. He wrote about contradictions of interests between classes as well as between two workers competing for the same job. Following his approach, this author is inclined to look for a contradiction of interests wherever there is a scarcity of generally desired goods, or broader values, and their distribution is by necessity such that any increase of the share of one group is bound to bring cuts in the share of another group.

## TWO TYPES OF CONTRADICTION RESULTING FROM THE UNEVEN DISTRIBUTION OF GOODS

If we consider the formula "to each according to his work" and the proposed definition of the contradiction of interests we come to the conclusion that the uneven distribution of goods among the socio-occupational groups, or strata, may take two forms. The first occurs when the uneven distribution of goods is conditioned by the operation of the principle "to each according to his work." The second, when the uneven distribution is due to other factors than the operation of this principle, or to inadequacies in the application of this principle. In either case we face an objective

[11] In this paper the question of the unity of interests in a socialist society is omitted. This important problem has been discussed in the present author's *Klasy, Warstwy i Władza,* "Classes, Strata and Power," Warsaw, 1966, chap. 4. The need for relativism in the treatment of "interests" is discussed in W. Wesolowski, "Ruling Class and Power Elite," *The Polish Sociological Bulletin*, No. 1, 1965.

contradiction of interests. And yet there is a significant difference between these two situations.

The principle "to each according to his work" is regarded as the basic principle of distribution in socialist society, but it is not always strictly implemented. In the first place because economists have failed so far to develop precise measures of labor quality that would account for the level of skills involved and some other factors which should be taken into account, for example, the degree of responsibility and risk, existing measures are largely intuitive. As long as precise measures are not available, it is extremely difficult to tell to what extent the wage of, for instance, a loader and a nurse, or a public servant and a factory manager, or a turner and a university professor, and in general, the whole system of wages, conforms to the principle "to each according to his work."

Two problems have to be considered here. One is connected with the extent to which the objective contradiction of interests is compatible with the socialist system. It could be said that a departure from the socialist principle of distribution may result in the "overpayment" of one and "underpayment" of others due to their particular work. As a result, the socialist contradictions of interests could grow into something like antagonistic contradictions, for the overpayment or underpayment may be viewed as a peculiar form of the exploitations of some people by other people (in conditions of the social ownership of means of production).

On the other hand, there is the psychological aspect of interest contradictions in socialism. The employees in Poland, for instance, are sensitive not so much to inequalities in wages as to the relative level of wages paid to people in different occupations. There is a general feeling that a just and equitable pay is the one which conforms to the principle "to each according to his work." People are on their watch lest somebody else gets their "sawbuck." These findings suggest that overpayment-underpayment practices may result not only in a quasiexploitation but also in augmentation of discontent. It seems that the objective contradiction of interests involved in the uneven distribution of goods in conformity with the principle "to each according to his work" itself does not evoke such strong conflict-generating tendencies.

The term *contradiction of interests* is used here to denote an objective state of affairs. The term *conflict of interests* is conceived as reflecting the subjective interpretation of a state of affairs as being the subject's interests. These being two different phenomena, the need was felt for two different terms.

***Limitations on the Principle "To Each According to His Work."*** We shall now turn to some additional factors influencing the system of wages. The principle "to each according to his work" fails to be applied with consistency not only because of the lack of precise measurements. There are some other formulas that are considered part of the socialist credo and hence translated into practical policies.

Thus, we may have overpayments and underpayments compatible with the principles of socialism in spite of the discordance with the cardinal formula of remuneration.

One such departure from the formula is the overpayment of less skilled laborers and underpayment of highly skilled workers. Both minimum wages and limitations on extra-high wages are in all likelihood departures from the principle "to each according to his work." And both these phenomena seem to exist in socialist society.[12]

The second departure consists in giving advantages to workers employed at big investment projects located far from the existing urban and industrial centers. . . . The comparatively higher wages for workers employed in those conditions should be seen as a kind of compensation for the unfavorable working and living conditions he had agreed to accept. Such a wage may be viewed as a normal wage multiplied by a factor that accounts for the additional social and psychological costs incurred by the worker. In contrast with the purely *economic* wage, this kind of payment has

[12] Z. Morecka, *Placa w gospodarce socjalistycznej,* "Wage in a Socialist Economy," in O. Lange, ed., *Zagadnienia ekonomii politycznej socjalizmu,* 1960.

been termed *socioeconomic wage.*[13] In addition to labor as such, this wage accounts for a number of deprivations suffered by the worker.

We have defined some of the departures from the principle "to each according to his work" which are due to the operation of other principles which are also consistent with the ideas of socialism. But the mechanics of social life being today a highly complex affair, there is no room in everyday life for the man in the street to follow it in all details. There is a tendency for people to assume standards of judgment based on plain facts and simplified formulas that catch their imagination and suit their sense of morality. And for that reason it seems that any departure from the formula "to each according to his work," whether fully justifiable on social and economic grounds, or caused by unwarranted and inequitable privileges, or else generated by lack of objective measures of quality of labor—all these appear to lead to one and the same result: a deepening of the awareness of conflicts of interests in socialist society. Of course it is a matter for future empirical studies to decide to what extent awareness of conflict is generated by the very objective contradiction of interests involved in the operation of the socialist distribution principle "to each according to his work," on the one hand, and by departures from this principle, on the other. Difficult as they are, such studies would prove very revealing.

Certain other hypotheses deserve to be tested empirically. For instance, there are probably two factors that either generate, or simply aggravate, the awareness of conflict. One could be defined as the burden of the past and the other as anticipation of the future.

The burden of the past is felt among members of those groups that received higher wages in the past, in the capitalist system. These people keep asking, "Why does a laborer get so much, and why does a physician get so little?" Conversely, members of the previously handicapped groups tend to anticipate the future, that is, the principle "to each according to his needs," postulated for communism, by asking, "Why does the charwoman get so little and the manager so much?"

Moreover, there seems to be a natural tendency toward conflict awareness among members of extreme income groups. Consequently, even in the socialist system some people, especially those earning little, tend to speak of the rich and the poor, of the privileged and the plain folks. This is understandable if we consider the relativism of human judgment with respect to one's own economic position.

***Interest Contradiction and the State.*** In the socialist society the uneven distribution of goods in high demand is mediated by the mechanism of government decisions. The general system of wages is determined by the government, as is the income of the individual citizen. Contradictions of interest may occur here on two planes: one is the plane of contradictions between groups with different incomes, the other is the plane existing between these groups and the *general regulator* represented by the government, in a wide sense of the word.

Objective contradictions between the interests of groups who share in different degrees in the national product exist irrespective of the mechanism of distribution. When this mechanism is the market, the government also acts as regulating factor by maintaining market relations, or by direct intervention in market relations, for example, by fixing a wage minimum, or interfering with collective agreements. Such is the situation in present-day capitalism.

In the socialist system, the government acquires the role of direct regulator. This accounts for a peculiar psychological situation. People with discrepant incomes tend to blame the government, as the regulator of their income, rather than the better-off groups. This tendency is much less common and much less explicit in the capitalist system. There, interest contradictions are chiefly conceived as contradictions between different social groups. This difference between the two systems is of tremendous importance for any discussion of conflicts of interests.

Equipped with the concepts of overpayment and underpayment, as well as the

[13] Z. Morecka, *Płaca ekonomiczna czy socjo-ekonomiczna,* "Economic or Socio-Economic Wage?" *Życie Gospodarcze,* Nos. 8, 9, 1958.

distinction between objective interest contradictions and subjectively felt conflicts, we can now attempt to delve deeper into the theoretical complexities of the situation created by the direct regulatory function of the State. Let us consider a number of possibilities.

In determining the system of wages, the government may be acting in one of the following ways: (1) respecting fully the principle "to each according to his work," (2) applying this principle with certain departures in favor of the highly skilled, (3) applying this principle with departures in favor of unskilled strata. Considering the marked discrepancies in the systems of wages of the various socialist countries, those three alternatives are likely to exist in reality.

In the first example, the government acts as a just and impartial regulator of wages. The better skilled workers are assigned higher wages, in line with the socialist principle of remuneration. But the contradiction of interest arising in this case between different social and occupational groups, or strata, is a direct result of government policies. This alone may give rise to an awareness of conflict on the part of the lower-paid people, and their feelings will be directed against the state (government). There is an objective contradiction between the interests of different social and occupational groups, but at the same time there is also the awareness of conflict on the part of the lower-paid people directed against the government. We are facing here a *transfer* of conflict awareness against the *general regulator*. Evidently, this type of intergroup contradiction of interests is unavoidable in socialism.

The situations described under (2) and (3) are of a different nature. Here the government overpays some and underpays other social and occupational groups, or entire strata. This may well enhance the satisfaction of some but will also aggravate the awareness of conflict among some others. The conflict-generating tendencies are born from the "partiality" of the government; the resultant contradictions transgress the framework of the socialist system of remuneration. The awareness of conflict among the people is heightened in view of such bias, the more so when the underpayment concerns the unskilled, and hence, less well-off people. The reverse occurs perhaps more frequently in practice. In Poland, for example, if any group is overpaid. it is the less-skilled group. For society as a whole this appears to result in a reduction of the awareness of the conflict.

Finally, one more possibility is given in the situation in which the group responsible for fixing the wage system, meaning the political leaders of the country at large, is overpaid. Whereas in the previous examples the leaders as a group did not stand in a nonsocialist contradiction of interests to the, or some, other groups, the latter example provides for precisely such a contradiction. This is a fertile ground for a sharp rise in awareness of conflict.

The situations listed above are purely theoretical. They derive from a specific, broadly conceived interpretation of interest contradictions and from the conception of overpayment and underpayment. In order to employ those conceptions in empirical research we must first determine objective measures of the social value of different types of labor. These measures will have to account for not only the purely economic value of labor but also for some other factors of a socioeconomic nature. Though it might not be easy to determine such measures, one cannot think of any other way of effectively studying the objective interest contradictions existing in socialism. . . .

***Contradictions of Interests Concerning Noneconomic Goods.*** Besides an uneven distribution of income, we also find in socialist society an uneven distribution of various other values. The distribution of income involves the distribution of some other goods, owing to the partial convertibility of those values. In a situation where a wide range of noneconomic values, for example, cultural, can be obtained for money in the market, the acquisition of other goods is determined by the distribution of income. We may therefore feel justified to focus our attention on the distribution of income. Being fully characteristic of capitalist society, the above conditions apply to a marked degree to socialist society also. But a peculiar feature of the latter is the weakened interrelation between size of income and participation in other values. In effect, the noneconomic goods distributed through separate channels are subject to extremely important contradictions of interests. Among those values are education, some goods in the sphere of so-called cultural consumption, for example, holidays at reduced rates, health benefits, and many others.

Take for example education. . . . In any industrial society, the individual level of education is a major component of professional qualifications, and the latter form the foundation of the individual's general status. In capitalist society, however, this interdependence does scarcely apply to members of the capitalist class. Their status and opportunities are chiefly determined by the amount of capital at their disposal, rather than by their education. Education represents here only an additional bonus enabling the capitalist to take up some occupation.

In socialist society, the situation of any individual is largely determined by his occupational status, and the latter depends very much on his education and the skills ensuing from that education. . . . And since there is a direct link between occupation and both income and social prestige, education amounts to an important instrument for obtaining various other values.

We have just referred to the intragenerational instrumental role of education, but there is also an intergenerational one. . . . Education is the chief instrument serving to define the future occupational position of a young man on his entering adult social life.

It should be borne in mind that in those societies where school education is not free, the level of education acquired by a young person depends largely on the income of his parents; his future income is in turn determined by his education. As a result of that mechanism, the status is subject to a *hereditary* tendency. In the above general model, no consideration is given to modifications resulting from the system of scholarships and grants for gifted children from poor homes.

In socialist society, where education at all levels is free, the interrelation between the parents' income and the educational opportunities of their children is greatly reduced, although the education acquired by an individual is a major determinant of his future income and social status. This reflects the reduced intergenerational instrumental role of income and the increased intergenerational instrumental role of education in socialist society.

But there is as yet no abundance of secondary and higher schools in the socialist countries. Consequently there is ground for interest contradictions between social strata as regards the criteria of admission to educational institutions at secondary and higher levels. This contradiction applies to the operation of channels through which education, an instrumental and "autonomous" factor with regard to income, is distributed.

The peculiar social conditions underlying that contradiction are connected with the discrepancies in the general intellectual development of children from workers and peasant homes on one hand and the children of the intelligentsia. This is highlighted during entrance examinations at universities and colleges, but also during similar examinations at secondary schools.

The differentiated cultural conditions in individual homes account for differentials in the initial achievements of children from different social strata. In view of this, the workers and farmers favor the preferential system of school admission, under which their children are granted additional counts for social background. This system works toward reducing the chances of admission of the children of the intelligentsia. Hence the educated people are in favor of a system of selection based on the outcomes of purely competitive examinations. The latter system tends to reduce the chances of admission of children from workers' and farmers' homes, of course.

In conditions of free education, the lack of equilibrium between the supply of educational facilities and the demand for education is the source of contradictions of interests concerning the principles of selection.

***The Cumulative and Noncumulative Distribution of Values.*** The distribution of values in capitalist society is largely cumulative:

high income, great political influence, high education, and high prestige are vested in some persons, while other persons suffer from inadequacies in those respects. Thus there is a high congruence of status characteristics in capitalist society, especially when we consider the two basic classes in the Marxist sense.

In socialist society we observe a decomposition of characteristics of social status as resulting from the noncumulative distribution of generally desired values. Income, education, political influence, and prestige are distributed more or less independently from one another. The effect of this phenomenon on the sphere of interests is enormous.

Two general hypotheses may be advanced in this connection: (1) the cumulative distribution of values and, as its result, the congruence of status characteristics both favor the development of fairly well-defined social strata or classes. (2) The same phenomena result in an aggravation of objective interest contradictions between the groups (strata), by creating parallel and correlated spheres of social inequalities.

Those two hypotheses lead us to another general proposition: Both the objective contradictions of interests and the subjective awareness of conflicts of interests tend to decrease in socialist society when compared with capitalist society.

## TWO TENDENCIES

We have stressed the decomposition of status characteristics in socialist society because of the relative novelty of this phenomenon, often neglected or overlooked by sociologists. It would be wrong, however, to forget the existing congruences of characteristics. The latter may be either a heritage of the past, or may result from the socialist mechanisms of distribution. In fact, there is good reason to search for the sources of congruence in status characteristics.

The principle "to each according to his work" operates toward synchronizing at least some of the status characteristics.

It may be assumed that certain severe decompositions observed in Poland were caused, among other things, by disregard for this principle under the pressure of an egalitarian ideology and of economic necessities, for example, manpower shortages in certain occupations.

The principle "to each according to his work" contributes to the synchronization of status characteristics because it regulates income according to the *quality* of work and hence according to education and the ensuing professional skills. Formal, that is, school, education is of decisive influence on professional qualifications in highly developed industrial societies. Adherence to the principle "to each according to his work" tends to increase the congruence between education and income. There is a similar tendency toward congruence between position, in power or management structures, and income. The same synchronizing tendency is reinforced by the dependence of prestige on education.

At the same time an opposite tendency is at work. Certain decomposition tendencies are aroused by those deliberate departures from the principle "to each according to his work" that are aimed at raising the income of the least-skilled people. The result is a discrepancy between skills, for example, low, and income, for example, medium. Similar effects are produced by departures from the principle such as wage limitations for highly skilled people.

Generally speaking, the scale of skills seems to be greater than the scale of income. Thus, a leveling out of income to a middle position results in certain decompositions of status characteristics. These are decompositions in the form of leveling out rather than in the form of leaping ahead. A rise occurs in one status characteristic of a social and occupational group or a whole stratum, while all other characteristics remain unchanged. Such decompositions are probably the most common.

It is easier to observe such a partial decomposition of status characteristics against the background of a wide range of status characteristics. Take prestige, for example.

There are groups of highly skilled people in Poland who enjoy great prestige but get only medium pay, for example, physicians, or junior research workers. There are occupations that require medium qualifications, ensure low income, and enjoy medium prestige, for example, nurses. In the first case the skill and prestige are uniformly high, while income is lowered toward the middle of the scale. In the latter case, qualifications and prestige are the same (medium), and again income lags behind. Both cases exemplify a partial decomposition of status characteristics, and both demonstrate a higher congruence of prestige and qualifications than prestige and income. There is also some indication in both cases for an autonomization of prestige in relation to other status characteristics.[14]

Thus in socialist society we find two opposite tendencies in the realm of the distribution of values representing important status characteristics—education, income, and social prestige. Either tendency is connected with different socialist principles. One tendency, the congruence of status characteristics, is connected with the principle "to each according to his work." The other tendency is associated with egalitarian ideals and leads to a decomposition, at least partial, of status characteristics. . . .

[14] The nature of social prestige seems to be changing gradually in socialist society over what it was in a capitalist society. Hence it is subject to greater autonomization in relation to certain objective status characteristics, income, power, and so on. The present paper leaves no room for any wider discussion of that problem.

# PART VIII
# Unresolved Issues in Stratification Theory

The great unanswered questions, the unsettled issues in stratification theory are in many ways the most intriguing ones. In studying them, what we know and what we do not know about structured social inequality come to a most intellectually exciting confluence. Our readings concern two types of unresolved issues. The first four center around the problem of the nature of stratification in general. Here these questions loom large: Why is stratification universal—or more accurately—nearly universal? Is stratification necessary for society? Is it the usual consequence of or a necessary condition for society's existence? The last three readings here deal with a different kind of issue. They struggle to grasp the outline of the new system of structured inequality that is now shaping in advanced industrial society.

We know that two opposed theoretical models for interpreting social phenomena are used in contemporary sociology: the structural-functional and the conflict models. The field of stratification is no exception. Here also these two antithetical theories have vied with each other for years as explanations of stratification. The most recent manifestation is the recognition that each of them contains a measure of validity. And it takes two forms: (1) the assertion that each theory is suited to a different set of empirical phenomena and problems and (2) the assertion that a theory representing a synthesis of the functional and conflict theories is needed, is possible, and, sometimes, has already been at least partially achieved.

The controversy between functional and conflict interpretations has been fought on two fronts. To simplify it, one is the intellectual battle over the problem of what stratification is, and the other concerns the reason why stratification exists. In the first, the functionalists were led so to speak by Parsons; in the second by Davis and Moore. To begin with the first, the functionalists take the position that stratification is integrative because it results from common values; the conflict theorists maintain that conflict is endemic to it because it results from coercion. The exponents of or adherents to the *integrative* theory emphasize the common values that bind the different strata; those of the *conflict* theory emphasize the divergent interests that divide them. Whereas the former see consensus as the basis of social unity, the latter see unity achieved by coercion.

We have already encountered in our previous readings the emphasis on the integrative function of stratification, especially in Warner. But, as expressed by Dahrendorf in our first selection, the most eminent sociological theorist of integration is Talcott Parsons. And Dahrendorf gives us a rendition of Parsons' theory.[1] Dahrendorf's writing preceded and therefore made no mention of M. G. Smith's test of Parsons' assumption that a common value system is the indispensable basis of all society. In reading Dahrendorf's discussion of Parsons' theory, we should bear in mind the results of Smith's study of Grenada in the British Caribbean. Smith was guided by J. S. Furnivall's theory of plural society, which explicitly denied that such overarching systems of common values are found in plural societies. Smith's analysis revealed a substantial divergence of values among the Grenadian society. In his words,

> At one extreme, among the highest-ranking Westernized Creole "whites," we find an undiluted ascriptive orientation with solidary particularistic stress; at the other, in the dark, low-ranking elite levels above the folk, the prevailing set of values is individualistic and achievement-oriented. These two value sets challenge and clash with each other. *Their coexistence at different levels of the elite hierarchy represents dissensus rather than the prevalence of common system of values*[2] (italics supplied).

Thus, the empirical facts, as studied by Smith, seem at odds with Parsons' theory, which postulates that a common value system is "a *condition* of the stability of social systems" (italics supplied).[3]

Dahrendorf's essay may also be read as a compact presentation of conflict theory or what he calls coercion theory. This is an important contribution in itself, for, as has been stated by the Danish sociologist Kaare Svalastoga, ". . . the conflict centered theories have nowhere received a level of elaboration comparable to functional theory."[4] Dahrendorf reduces the conflict theory to its basic tenets. One of these is that "every society is based on the coercion of some of its members by others." The differential distribution of authority is the determining factor of systematic social conflicts. He proceeds to develop this idea further by pointing to social organizations as the *locus* of conflict: "they generate conflict of interests and become the birthplace of conflict groups."

According to Dahrendorf each theory—integration and conflict—is suitable for only one "face" of society but society is Janus-headed and has two faces. Thus he views these theories as complementary rather than mutually exclusive. He does raise the issue of a *unified* theory, which would explain both the integration and conflict inherent in society. But, as far as he is concerned, there is no such theory today and, moreover, its feasibility in the future is questionable.

[1] For the first statement of this theory, see "An Analytical Approach to the Theory of Social Stratification," in *Essays in Sociological Theory,* Glencoe, Ill.: Free Press, 1954, pp. 69–88. Parsons presented later a revised version of his stratification theory. See Talcott Parsons, "A Revised Analytical Approach to the Theory of Social Stratification," in Reinhold Bendix and Seymour Martin Lipset, eds., *Class, Status and Power,* Glencoe, Ill.: Free Press, 1953, pp. 92–128.

[2] M. G. Smith, *Stratification in Grenada,* Berkeley: University of California Press, 1965, p. 253.

[3] Parsons, "A Revised Analytical Approach to the Theory of Social Stratification," *op. cit.,* p. 93.

[4] Kaare Svalastoga, *Social Differentiation,* New York: David McKay Company, 1965, p. 4.

Others seem more optimistic about theoretical synthesis. In his book, *Power and Privilege,* Gerhard Lenski makes the claim that his theory represents such a synthesis. (But some critics say that he failed to achieve this goal.)[5] Lenski asserts that the reason why theorists of the two opposing schools have gotten into so many impasses is that "both parties have asked the same wrong question or utilized the same faulty concepts."[6] And he sees himself lifting stratification theory from the impasses and moving it toward a synthesis by a process of reformulating problems and concepts. Lockwood, on the other hand, ascribes the achievement of synthesis to Marxian theory.[7] He charges that the contemporary conflict theorist cannot answer why some conflict results in change, and other conflict, equally endemic and intense in a social system, does not lead to change. But the answer is implicit in Marx's thought, for there we find a distinction between *the propensity* to class antagonism and the *dynamics* of class antagonism. According to Lockwood, Marx saw the *tendency* toward conflict as resulting from the character of production relationships. (This Lockwood designates as the *social integration aspect.*) But Marx saw dynamics of change as related to the growing contradictions in the economic system. (Lockwood labels this aspect *system integration.*) Thus structural contradictions are central to Marx's theory of change.

And it is most important that Marx's idea of a contradiction between the material conditions of production and the productive institutions of the economic system should not be ignored by sociologists. Lockwood assures the sociologists that if they were to use Marx's idea of a *functional incompatibility* between the dominant institutional order and the material base of a social system, they would *not* necessarily have to adopt Marx's conclusion that this inevitably leads to the breakdown of a system and its replacement by another.

The reading that follows the Dahrendorf selection is the much discussed article "Some Principles of Stratification," by Kingsley Davis and Wilbert E. Moore. The controversy generated by it is one of the most enduring disputes in current sociology. The authors present a functional theory of why stratification exists. They contend that social stratification—which they equate with the unequal distribution of rewards—is functionally necessary and that is why it is a universal and permanent feature of society. The main functional necessity, they say, which explains the universality of stratification "is precisely the requirement faced by any society of placing and motivating individuals in the social structure." Throughout the reprinted article they develop the theme that stratification is an "unconsciously evolved device by which societies insure that the most important positions are conscientiously filled by the most qualified persons" (p. 497).

Future historians and sociologists of knowledge might see this functional theory as a rationalization of social inequality existing in advanced industrial society. This suggests itself as plausible when we read R. H. Tawney's interpretation of the ideological significance of the functional theory that prevailed in the Middle ages.

The facts of class status and inequality were rationalized in the Middle Ages by a functional theory, as the facts of competition were rationalized in the eighteenth by

[5] For example, Seymour M. Lipset's criticism at the "Author Meets the Critic" session at the annual meeting of the Eastern Sociological Society, New York, N.Y., on April 16, 1967.

[6] Gerhard Lenski, *Power and Privilege,* New York: McGraw-Hill Book Co., 1966. The quote is from p. 20.

[7] David Lockwood, "Social Integration and System Integration," in *Explorations in Social Change,* George K. Zolischan and Walter Hirsch, eds., New York: Houghton Mifflin, 1964, pp. 244–257.

the theory of economic harmonies. . . . Society, like the human body, is an organism composed of different members. Each member has its own function; prayer, or defence, or merchandise, or tilling the soil. Each must receive the means suited to the station, and must claim no more. . . . Between classes there must be inequality; for otherwise a class cannot perform its function . . . .[8]

For more than twenty years since its appearance, the Davis-Moore theory has been extensively criticized, sometimes on grounds of ideological bias but more often on grounds of lacks in the validity of its concepts and propositions. For example, Foote and Hatt questioned whether stratification would continue in "massified" societies such as the one in the United States.[9] Buckley found fault with Davis' and Moore's neglect of the family as a determinant of status, contending that ". . . positions are determined on the whole by social inheritance, and only secondarily by . . . performance." He also criticized their use of the term *social stratification*, charging that they confused it with social differentiation.[10] In reply to Buckley, Davis reiterated that he and Moore applied the term *social stratification* ". . . to the system of unequal rewards attached to different positions in society. It is the existence of such unequal reward systems that the theory tries to explain."[11]

On the other hand, Dennis Wrong in an article that appeared about fifteen years after the Davis and Moore essay, surveying the criticisms directed at it, concluded that the critics succeeded only in showing that there are many things about stratification that are not explained by the Davis and Moore theory but that "they have not succeeded in seriously denting the central argument that unequal rewards are necessary in any societies with a division of labor extending much beyond difference in age and sex."[12] He explains that Davis and Moore are only committed to the view that there must be unequal rewards. How unequal these rewards need to be—the subject of some of the critics of their theory—is another question and a question to which Davis and Moore did not address themselves. Their theory, says Wrong, does not deny that the distribution of rewards in a given society may be way in excess of the "minimum inequalities necessary to maintain a complex division of labor."[13]

Of the many discussions of the Davis and Moore theory, the one by Wesolowski reprinted here is among the latest and seems to me to have succeeded where Dennis Wrong claims the earlier ones have failed, that is, in denting the central argument. This is not to say that this is the only one that has succeeded. Quite germane, for example, is a note by Huaco. We are referring to his criticism *on logical grounds* of the Davis-Moore theory and especially of its proposition that those positions convey the best rewards which have the greatest functional importance for society. Huaco argues that in the present state of social science we have no scientifically adequate empirical evidence as to which roles make the greater contribution to the

[8] R. H. Tawney, *Religion and the Rise of Capitalism*, Harmondsworth, England: Pelican Books, 1938, p. 37, as quoted in Barber, *op. cit.*, p. 201.

[9] Nelson N. Foote and Paul K. Hatt, "Social Mobility and Economic Advancement," *American Economic Review*, Vol. XLIII, May, 1953, pp. 387–394.

[10] Walter Buckley, "Social Stratification and Social Differentiation," *American Sociological Review*, Vol. 23, August, 1958, pp. 369–375.

[11] Kingsley Davis, "The Abominable Heresy: A Reply to Dr. Buckley," *American Sociological Review*, Vol. 24, 1959, p. 82.

[12] Dennis Wrong, "The Functional Theory of Stratification: Some Neglected Considerations," *American Sociological Review*, Vol. 24, December, 1959, p. 773.

[13] *Ibid.*, pp. 774–776.

survival of a given society. Thus the concept of unequal functional importance "is a complete unknown; and as it stands, it cannot serve as a legitimate explanation for 'unequal rewards,'" for it is a rule of logic that you cannot explain one unknown by another unknown.[14] In the same issue of the *American Sociological Review* in which this note appeared, another important contribution is found by Arthur Stinchcombe. He points out that the Davis-Moore theory, despite all the attention it has received, has "stimulated remarkably few studies." He therefore sets before himself the task of outlining some empirical implications of the theory, convinced that, like other scientific theories, it contains implications which can be demonstrated to be either true or false. "Deciding whether they are true or false," he says, "is not a theoretical or ideological matter, but an empirical one." And this decision therefore awaits empirical testing.[15]

The article by Wlodzimierz Wesolowski deserves attention not only because of its exceptional clarity and logical rigor, but also because it represents a reaction to the functional theory by a sociologist from Poland, a "socialist" society. He reduces the theory to three main propositions, each of which he examines critically. Contrary to Davis and Moore's claim that theirs is a theory of stratification in general, Wesolowski convincingly demonstrates that it is only a theory of the stratification of systems that rely principally on achievement rather than on ascription in filling positions. But even if limited to such systems, he charges, the theory contains erroneous assumptions about human nature, patterns of society, and structure of values. Concerning the last, Davis and Moore see as the main goals material advantages and prestige. But it is possible, argues Wesolowski, to have a society where other goals, such as education and authority, are ultimate. In such a society positions calling for education and training, as well as positions of authority, would be filled not because of their material advantages but because of their intrinsic attributes—skill, knowledge and power—which could be sufficiently attractive. Those latter values, which in the Davis-Moore theory are treated as intermediate values, may appear as terminal values. (Although Wesolowski's point is well taken, one may wonder whether a stratification system that recruited into positions of power solely people who enjoy power would not prove more oppressive and rigid than the systems where material rewards attract people into such positions. But, of course, this does not damage his thesis.)

Wesolowski further criticizes the Davis-Moore theory for concentrating on material advantages and prestige and neglecting authority, the more important element of stratification from a functional point of view. Moreover, he attempts to demonstrate that if there is any functional necessity for stratification, it is the necessity of unequal authority rather than of unequal material goods or prestige. Hierarchies of authority are inevitable in large social structures. There is a great similarity between this conclusion and Dahrendorf's thoughts on inequality. Dahrendorf maintains that inequality in power and authority inevitably accompanies social organization. There are those who have the right to control the action of others and issue commands and others who are controlled and have to obey. What makes Wesolowski's conclusion especially noteworthy is that its implications are not in line with the Soviet conception of nonantagonistic classes in Soviet-type

[14] George A. Huaco, "A Logical Analysis of the Davis-Moore Theory of Stratification," *American Sociological Review,* Vol. 28, October, 1963, pp. 801–803.

[15] Arthur L. Stinchcombe, "Some Empirical Consequences of the Davis-Moore Theory," *American Sociological Review,* 28, October 1963, pp. 805–808.

societies. If there is inequality in authority in such societies, there is also potential conflict.[16]

Missing in Wesolowski's criticism of the Davis-Moore theory is a challenge to their assertion that stratification is universal. And yet for some time anthropologists have been saying that this is not the case, that stratification is a feature of some but not all societies. Gunnar Landtman, for instance, in the book he published in 1938, proclaimed as a fact "that a condition of almost complete equality reigns among peoples in the lowest degrees of culture.[17] One of the latest anthropological essays on this subject cites various concrete examples of unstratified societies in East Africa and Australia. Its author, M. G. Smith, also addresses himself to the fascinating question of why so many sociologists proceed on the assumption that stratification is universal when social anthropologists are denying it. He suggests that sociologists see in inequality the proof that stratification exists. Anthropologists, on the other hand, first ask what form inequality takes and what its degree and scale are before they decide that stratification is present in a given society. In the view of the latter, Smith says "the principles by which observable inequalities are institutionalized are the critical data." Thus, according to Smith, inequality in a given society does not per se mean that it is stratified, but institutionalized inequality in the access to favored positions is "decisive for societal classification as stratified."[18]

If sociologists tended in the past to equate inequality with stratification, then it is no longer true of some, as is reflected in the two readings by Moore and Wrong that follow Wesolowski's. The reprinted selection by Wilbert Moore represents the last step in the last round of the Tumin-Moore debate, which appeared at the end of the second decade of the theoretical controversy generated by the Davis and Moore essay. It is worthwile to recall that Tumin was one of the first to challenge the Davis-Moore theory. In his initial criticism of that theory he objected, among other things, to its assumption of a scarcity of trained and talented personnel. He asserted that, contrary to what the theory postulates, stratification interferes with rather than facilitates the selection of talented people.[19] He thus directed himself to some of the dysfunctions of stratification. In addition, he challenged the Davis-Moore assumptions concerning human motivation:

A generalized theory of social stratification must recognize that the prevailing system of inducements and rewards is only one of many variants in the whole range of possible systems of motivation which, at least theoretically, are capable of working in human society.[20]

[16] Various empirical studies conducted in these countries show that social conflict did not cease with state ownership of the means of production. However, the term social conflict is used only by some Polish sociologists. Sociologists in other socialist countries use such guarded terms as *problem of technological and social progress* or *functional differentiation of socialist society* when discussing problems of conflict in their own societies. See Gabor Kiss, *Gibt es eine Marxistische Soziologie*, Köln: Westdeutscher Verlag, 1960, pp. 43–60. As we saw in the other article by Wesolowski in a preceding part of this book (which the author presented subsequently to the one we are now discussing), he did address himself to conflict in interests in socialist countries but, significantly, left out of it the dimension of power. See pp. 465–477 in this volume.

[17] Gunnar Landtman, *The Origin of the Inequality of the Social Classes*, London: Kegan Paul, Trench Trubner and Co., 1938, p. 3.

[18] Michael G. Smith, "Pre-Industrial Stratification Systems," in Neil J. Smelser and S. M. Lipset, eds., *Social Structure and Mobility in Economic Development*, Chicago: Aldine Press, 1966, pp. 141–176. Direct quotes from p. 149.

[19] Melvin Tumin, "Some Principles of Stratification: A Critical Analysis," *American Sociological Review*, Vol. 18, August, 1953, pp. 387–394.

[20] *Ibid.*, p. 388.

The last round of the debate appeared in the February, 1963 issue of the *American Sociological Review*. In it is found the article by Wilbert Moore, "But Some Are More Equal than Others," in which he summarized the criticisms raised by sociologists, with special attention to those of Tumin, accepting some and rejecting others. He conceded to the critics that the functional theory of stratification neglected dysfunctions of stratification. Also, he made it clear that he considered his and Davis' equating of social stratification with unequal rewards unfortunate, thus expressing some sympathy for Buckley's criticism on this point. But he did not find the critics persuasive on the possibility of eliminating inequality. He therefore reiterates the original contention that functional differentiations of positions "will inevitably entail unequal rewards" and adds to it that "differences in performance must be expected to be and will be differentially valued."[21] Moore maintains then that social inequality is "an essential feature of social systems."[22] The implication of Moore's argument seems to be, although he does not express it thus, that stratification may not be necessary but that inequality is. (As noted here, he no longer considers stratification synonymous with unequal rewards.)

The article by Moore was followed in the same issue of the *Review* by Melvin Tumin's "On Social Inequality." In it Tumin expressed the conviction that the difficulty in the past exchanges with Moore arose partially from the ambiguity of the term social inequality. He proceeds therefore to specify five forms of inequality, no known society being without some or all of these: (1) role differentiation; (2) ranking in accordance with the intrinsic attributes of a role; (3) ranking in terms of approximation to social values and norms; (4) ranking according to functional contribution; and (5) diffusion and transfer of "differentials in property, power, and prestige."[23] His contention is that any of these can become subject to stratification, and some are more likely to than others, but *none must become stratified in order that society survive.* According to him, little can be learned about existing stratification, or about existing society in general, by focusing on what is necessary for minimum social survival. He insists that most existing stratification ". . . enjoys little or no consensus, has little to do with social integration, and is probably seriously dysfunctional for social productivity."[24]

Tumin finishes on a moral note in behalf of equality, the logic of which is easily dented, and this is accomplished by Moore in the reprinted rejoinder, which we have titled "The Tumin–Moore Polemics—Remaining Points of Disagreement." Still, Moore gives recognition to the main accomplishment of the Tumin article: It has reduced substantially the previous area of disagreement between them by addressing itself to the general issues of inequality. Moore specifies the points on which there is no longer disagreement and moves on to the ones on which they are still divided. He takes special issue with Tumin's contention that most social differentiation does not involve invidious valuation, asserting that "it is not at all established that functional differentiation and unequal valuation are independently variable."

Moore ends his rejoinder by pointing out that the exchange between him and Tumin has not touched on some important issues relevant to stratification. Foremost among them is whether class continues to be a useful explanatory concept.

[21] Wilbert E. Moore, "But Some Are More Equal than Others," *American Sociological Review*, Vol. 28, February, 1963, pp. 13–18.

[22] *Ibid.*, p. 14.

[23] Melvin Tumin, "On Social Inequality," *American Sociological Review*, Vol. 28, February, 1963, pp. 19–26.

[24] *Ibid.*, p. 25.

This is precisely the central question in the last three essays in this section, and the authors take opposite positions on it. Dennis Wrong in his "Social Inequality Without Social Stratification" allies himself with the view—which he tells us is rejected by the majority of American sociologists—that the concept of social class is becoming irrelevant to the understanding of advanced industrial society because social classes have disappeared or are disappearing therefrom. In a sense, Suzanne Keller's argument—in the selection that follows Wrong's—that elites may exist independently of a ruling class is related to Wrong's argument that inequality may exist apart from a class system. To the contrary, Bottomore, in the excerpt from his *Classes in Modern Society,* puts forth the view that the concept of class, and specifically ruling class and working class, has not lost all its meaning, but that the manifestations of class in advanced industrial society are different from what they were in the earlier stages of industrial society.

In the essay prepared especially for this volume, which she based on her book *Beyond the Ruling Class,* Keller maintains that the concept of ruling class does not fit the realities of today's emerging stratification system. Modern society is characterized by a proliferation of elite groups.[25] The ones she concentrates her attention on are what she labels *strategic elites.* They are distinguished from the rest of the elites in that their "judgments, decisions and actions have determinable consequences for all or most members of society." She argues that they are not ruling classes but the *structural alternatives* to them. In addition to the difference in internal organization, they are marked by greater functional specialization than the ruling classes that preceded them. Another distinguishing feature is that they are recruited on the basis of proven capacity to perform. In this respect Keller's strategic elites bear some resemblance to Michael Young's meritocracy, which is discussed by Dennis Wrong in the essay preceding Keller's.

Dennis Wrong is convinced that the now-emerging social structure can be best understood by abandoning the concept of social class and by concentrating on the sociology of equality and inequality. He makes it clear that although he does contend that contemporary industrial society is classless he is not implying that it represents a trend toward general equality. The keen observation by Bernard Barber might fit here: In *styles of life* the trend has been and is toward the pattern of *gross equality* and *subtle inequality.*[26] But Wrong points to the "considerable institutionalized social inequalities" and asserts that the absence of social classes may hide them more effectively than does a class society. He also outlines other major differences between class societies and what he considers the modern classless societies. In the process, he reviews and rejects the arguments of those theorists, notably Dahrendorf, who hold that the concept of class should be retained. He labels Dahrendorf's conception of class "the most quixotic effort" in recent sociological writings to hold on to the concept of class. Subsequent to Wrong's article, another major effort has been made, this time by Lenski, to uphold the continuing usefulness of the concept of class, and one cannot help but wonder whether Wrong would apply the same label to it. As did Dahrendorf, Lenski contends that a single individual may simultaneously be a member of several

[25] For an analysis of the conflict between the underlying egalitarian assumptions of the modern welfare state and the use of an elite of trained personnel, see Piet Thoenes, *The Élite in the Welfare State,* New York: Free Press, 1966.

[26] Bernard Barber, "Social Stratification Structure and Trends of Social Mobility in Western Society," in Talcott Parsons, ed., *American Society*, New York: Basic Books, 1968, p. 192.

different classes. But the reasons are different. According to Dahrendorf there are as many class systems in a modern society as there are functional hierarchies of power in it. To Lenski there are a number of class systems in a society, a class system being a hierarchy of classes ranked in terms of a single criterion, such as occupation, property, ethnicity, education, *sex and age*. Thus he refers to a "sexual class system" and "age class system" as well as to occupational, educational, and power class systems.[27]

In light of these curious attempts at redefinitions of class, Bottomore's use of class represents continuity in the meaning of the concept. It is reflected, for example, in his analysis of the working class in modern industrial society as exercising an independent force in political life, despite the fact that it has in many respects not followed the course that Marx and the early Marxists expected it to follow. Very thought provoking is Bottomore's warning against accepting the view of relative peace in industrial society. He thinks it not only possible but likely that there will be new discontent as the disadvantaged become aware that there is no general trend toward greater economic equality and that "there are very powerful movements which tend to produce a more unequal distribution of income and wealth whenever the industrial and political pressure of the working class is relaxed." More important yet than this in generating discontent, according to Bottomore, is the growing discrepancy between conditions of work and conditions of leisure for the working class. There is an increasing freedom of choice and independence of action outside the workplace, but work is still characterized by "constraint, strict subordination, lack of responsibility, absence of means of self-expression."[28] Note, these formulations by Bottomore were made in 1965. Subsequent events—such as the 1968 General Strike in France and the Poor People's Campaign in the United States—dramatically bore out his thesis and gave a note of obsolescence to the opposite thesis of the affluent society and *embourgeoisement* of the working class.

In a way similar to Dennis Wrong's, but on different grounds, Bottomore finishes with a criticism of recent sociological studies. Wrong criticizes them for holding to the concept of class, which he considers obsolete. Bottomore critizes them for the lack of a "historical sense" in their treatment of contemporary social classes. He considers the historical analysis of the changing class structure "one of the most important unfulfilled tasks of sociology today."

Implicit in the last two articles is the general problem of a lack of a basic, standardized vocabulary in the field of stratification studies. Although it is characteristic of sociology in general the malady is especially pronounced here. It is superfluous to spell it out at this time, for the reader is by now well acquainted with it—having been subjected in the readings to the various explicit or implicit meanings of such terms as class, status, stratification, class consciousness, and so on. Perhaps what should be stated is that much energy in the sociological controversies is spent in argument over words. And yet there is no immediate solution in sight for this Tower of Babel. It seems that the best one can do at this stage of our science is to make explicit what he means by a given term when employing it in a manner consequential to the exposition of a thesis, but one must admit that this is a cumbersome procedure, easier to preach than to practice.

[27] Lenski, *op. cit.*, p. 80.

[28] We might add to Bottomore's list of present sources of discontent, the lack of a "humane and informed administration of social service." See: Richard M. Titmuss, "Goals of Today's Welfare State," in Joseph A. Kahl, ed., *Comparative Perspective on Stratification*, Boston: Little, Brown and Company, 1968, p. 90.

# SOCIAL STRUCTURE, GROUP INTERESTS, AND CONFLICT GROUPS

*Ralf Dahrendorf*

## INTEGRATION AND VALUES VERSUS COERCION AND INTERESTS: THE TWO FACES OF SOCIETY

Throughout the history of Western political thought, two views of society have stood in conflict. Both these views are intended to explain what has been, and will probably continue to be, the most puzzling problem of social philosophy: how is it that human societies cohere? There is one large and distinguished school of thought according to which social order results from a general agreement of values, a *consensus omnium* or *volonté générale* which outweighs all possible or actual differences of opinion and interest. There is another equally distinguished school of thought which holds that coherence and order in society are founded on force and constraint, on the domination of some and the subjection of others. To be sure, these views are not at all points mutually exclusive. The Utopian (as we shall call those who insist on coherence by consensus) does not deny the existence of differences of interest; nor does the Rationalist (who believes in coherence by constraint and domination) ignore such agreements of value as are required for the very establishment of force. But Utopian and Rationalist alike advance claims of primacy for their respective standpoints. . . .

Conflicting philosophical positions must inevitably, it seems to me, reappear constantly in theories of science. Even if this should not generally be the case, I would claim that the philosophical alternative of a Utopian or a Rational solution of the problem of order pervades modern sociological thinking even in its remotest manifestations. Here, as elsewhere, philosophical positions do not enter into scientific theories unchanged. Here, as elsewhere, they pass through the filter of logical supposition before they become relevant for testable explanations of problems of experience. The sociological Utopian does not claim that order *is based on* a general consensus of values, but that it *can be conceived of in terms of* such consensus, and that, if it is conceived of in these terms, certain propositions follow which are subject to the test of specific observations. Analogously, for the sociological Rationalist the assumption of the coercive nature of social order is a heuristic principle rather than a judgment of fact. But this obvious reservation does not prevent the Utopians and the Rationalists of sociology from engaging in disputes which are hardly less intense (if often rather less imaginative and ingenious) than those of their philsophical antecedents. The subject matter of our concern in this study demands that we take a stand with respect to this dispute. . . . Generally speaking, it seems to me that two (meta-)theories can and must be distinguished in contemporary sociology. One of these, the *integration theory of society,* conceives of social structure in terms of a functionally integrated system held in equilibrium by certain patterned and recurrent processes. The other one, the *coercion theory of society,* views social structure as a form of organization held together by force and constraint and reaching continuously beyond itself in the sense of producing within itself the forces that maintain it in an unending process of change. Like their philosophical counterparts, these theories are mutually exclusive. . . .

In recent years, the integration theory of society has clearly dominated sociological thinking. In my opinion, this prevalence of one partial view has had many unfortunate consequences. However, it has also had at least one agreeable consequence, in that the very onesidedness of this theory gave rise to critical objections which enable us today to put this theory in its proper place. Such objections have been stimulated with increasing frequency by the works of the most

Reprinted from *Class and Class Conflict in Industrial Society* by Ralf Dahrendorf with permission of the publishers, Stanford University Press. 

eminent sociological theorist of integration, Talcott Parsons. It is not necessary here to attempt a comprehensive exposition of Parsons' position; nor do we have to survey the sizable literature concerned with a critical appraisal of this position. . . . There is one objection to Parsons' position, however, which we have to examine if we are to make a systematic presentation of a theory of group conflict. In a remarkable essay, D. Lockwood claims "that Parsons' array of concepts is heavily weighted by assumptions and categories which relate to the role of *normative* elements in social action, and especially to the processes whereby motives are structured normatively to ensure social stability. On the other hand, what may be called the *substratum* of social action, especially as it conditions interests which are productive of social conflict and instability, tends to be ignored as a general determinant of the dynamics of social systems."[1] . . . Lockwood's claim touches on the core of our problem of the two faces of society. . . .

It is certainly true that the work of Parsons displays a conspicuous bias in favor of analysis in terms of values and norms. It is equally true that many of those who have been concerned with problems of conflict rather than of stability have tended to emphasize not the normative but the institutional aspects of social structure. The work of Marx is a case in point. Probably, this difference in emphasis is no accident. It is nevertheless as such irrelevant to an understanding of or adoption of the alternative images of society which pervade political thought and sociological theory. The alternative between "normative elements in social action" and a factual "substratum of social action," which Lockwood takes over from the work of Renner, in fact indicates two levels of the analysis of social structure which are in no way contradictory. There is no theoretical reason why Talcott Parsons should not have supplemented (as indeed he occasionally does) his analysis of normative integration by an analysis of the integration of social systems in terms of their institutional substratum. However we look at social structure, it always presents itself as composed of a moral and a factual, a normative and an institutional, level or, in the doubtful terms of Marx, a superstructure and a substratum. The investigator is free to choose which of these levels he wants to emphasize more strongly—although he may be well-advised, in the interest of clarity as well as of comprehensiveness of his analysis, not to stress one of these levels to the exclusion of the other.

At the same time, there is an important element of genuine critique in Lockwood's objection to Parsons. When Lockwood contrasts stability and instability, integration and conflict, equilibrium and disequilibrium, values and interests, he puts his finger on a real alternative of thought, and one of which Parsons has apparently not been sufficiently aware. For of two equivalent models of society, Parsons has throughout his work recognized only one, the Utopian or integration theory of society. His "array of concepts" is therefore incapable of coping with those problems with which Lockwood is concerned in his critical essay, and which constitute the subject matter of the present study.

For purposes of exposition it seems useful to reduce each of the two faces of society to a small number of basic tenets, even if this involves some degree of oversimplification as well as overstatement. The integration theory of society, as displayed by the work of Parsons and other structural-functionalists, is founded on a number of assumptions of the following type:

1. Every society is a relatively persistent, stable structure of elements.
2. Every society is a well-integrated structure of elements.
3. Every element in a society has a function, i.e., renders a contribution to its maintenance as a system.
4. Every functioning social structure is based on a consensus of values among its members.

. . . However, it is abundantly clear that the integration approach to social analysis does not enable us to comprehend all problems of social reality. . . . On the 17th

[1] David Lockwood, "Some Remarks on 'The Social System,'" *British Journal of Sociology*, Vol. VII, No. 2, 1956, p. 136.

of June, 1953, the building workers of East Berlin put down their tools and went on a strike that soon led to a generalized revolt against the Communist regime of East Germany. Why? . . . Evidently, the uprising of the 17th of June is neither due to nor productive of integration in East German society. It documents and produces not stability, but instability. It contributes to the disruption, not the maintenance, of the existing system. It testifies to dissensus rather than consensus. The integration model tells us little more than that there are certain "strains" in the "system." In fact, in order to cope with problems of this kind we have to replace the integration theory of society by a different and, in many ways, contradictory model.

What I have called the coercion theory of society can also be reduced to a small number of basic tenets, although here again these assumptions oversimplify and overstate the case:

1. Every society is at every point subject to processes of change; social change is ubiquitous.
2. Every society displays at every point dissensus and conflict; social conflict is ubiquitous.
3. Every element in a society renders a contribution to its disintegration and change.
4. Every society is based on the coercion of some of its members by others.

If we return to the problem of the German workers' strike, it will become clear that this latter model enables us to deal rather more satisfactorily with its causes and consequences. The revolt of the building workers and their fellows in other industries can be explained in terms of coercion.[2] The revolting groups are engaged in a conflict which "functions" as an agent of change by disintegration. A ubiquitous phenomenon is expressed, in this case, in an exceptionally intense and violent way, and further explanation will have to account for this violence on the basis of the acceptance of conflict and change as universal features of social life. I need hardly add that, like the integration model, the coercion theory of society constitutes but a set of assumptions for purposes of scientific analysis and implies no claim for philosophical validity—although, like its counterpart, this model also provides a coherent image of social organization.

Now, I would claim that, in a sociological context, neither of these models can be conceived as exclusively valid or applicable. They constitute complementary, rather than alternative, aspects of the structure of total societies as well as of every element of this structure. We have to choose between them only for the explanation of specific problems; but in the conceptual arsenal of sociological analysis they exist side by side. Whatever criticism one may have of the advocates of one or the other of these models can therefore be directed only against claims for the exclusive validity of either.[3] Strictly speaking, both models are "valid" or, rather, useful and necessary for sociological analysis. We cannot conceive of society unless we realize the dialectics of stability and change, integration and conflict, function and motive force, consensus and coercion. In the context of this study, I regard this point as demonstrated by the analysis of the exemplary problems sketched above.

It is perhaps worth emphasizing that the thesis of the two faces of social structure does not require a complete, or even partial, revision of the conceptual apparatus that by now has become more or less generally accepted by sociologists in all countries. Categories like role, institution, norm, structure, even function are as useful in terms of the coercion model as they are for the analysis of social integration. In fact, the dichotomy of aspects can be carried through all levels of sociological analysis; that is, it can be shown that, like social

[2] For purposes of clarity, I have deliberately chosen an example from a totalitarian state. But coercion is meant here in a very general sense, and the coercion model is applicable to all societies, independent of their specific political structure.

[3] This, it seems to me, is the only—if fundamental—legitimate criticism that can be raised against Parsons' work on this general level. In *The Social System,* Parsons repeatedly advances, for the integration theory of society, a claim that it is the nucleus of "the general" sociological theory—a claim which I regard as utterly unjustified. It is Lockwood's main concern also, in the essay quoted above, to reject this claim to universal validity.

structure itself, the notions of role and institution, integration and function, norm and substratum have two faces which may be expressed by two terms, but which may also in many cases be indicated by an extension of concepts already in use. . . . The notions of interest and value indeed seem to describe very well the two faces of the normative superstructure of society: what appears as a consensus of values on the basis of the integration theory can be regarded as a conflict of interests in terms of the coercion theory. Similarly, what appears on the level of the factual substratum as integration from the point of view of the former model presents itself as coercion or constraint from the point of view of the latter. . . .

While logically feasible,[4] the solution of the dilemma of political thought which we have offered here for the more restricted field of sociological analysis nevertheless raises a number of serious problems. It is evidently virtually impossible to think of society in terms of either model without positing its opposite number at the same time. There can be no conflict, unless this conflict occurs within a context of meaning, i.e., some kind of coherent "system." No conflict is conceivable between French housewives and Chilean chess players, because these groups are not united by, or perhaps "integrated into," a common frame of reference. Analogously, the notion of integration makes little sense unless it presupposes the existence of different elements that are integrated. . . .

Inevitably, the question will be raised, also, whether a unified theory of society that includes the tenets of both the integration and the coercion models of society is not at least conceivable—for as to its desirability there can be little doubt. Is there, or can there be, a general point of view that synthesizes the unsolved dialectics of integration and coercion? So far as I can see, there is no such general model; as to its possibility, I have to reserve judgment. It seems at least conceivable that unification of theory is not feasible at a point which has puzzled thinkers ever since the beginning of Western philosophy.

For the explanation of the formation of conflict groups out of conditions of social structure, we shall employ a model that emphasizes the ugly face of society. In the following sections of this chapter I shall try to show how, on the assumption of the coercive nature of social structure, relations of authority become productive of clashes of role interest which under certain conditions lead to the formation of organized antagonistic groups within limited social organizations as well as within total societies. . . .

## POWER AND AUTHORITY

From the point of view of the integration theory of social structure, units of social analysis ("social systems") are essentially voluntary associations of people who share certain values and set up institutions in order to ensure the smooth functioning of cooperation. From the point of view of coercion theory, however, the units of social analysis present an altogether different picture. Here, it is not voluntary cooperation or general consensus but enforced constraint that makes social organizations cohere. In institutional terms, this means that in every social organization some positions are entrusted with a right to exercise control over other positions in order to ensure effective coercion; it means, in other words, that there is a differential distribution of power and authority. One of the central theses of this study consists in the assumption that this differential distribution of authority invariably becomes the determining factor of systematic social conflicts of a type that is germane to class conflicts in the traditional (Marxian) sense of this term. The structural origin of such group conflicts must be sought in the arrangement of social roles endowed with expectations of domination or subjection. Wherever there are such roles, group conflicts of the type in question are to be expected. Differentiation of groups engaged in such conflicts follows the lines of differentiation of roles that are relevant

[4] As is demonstrated most clearly by the fact that a similar situation can be encountered in physics with respect to the theory of light. Here, too, there are two seemingly incompatible theories which nevertheless exist side by side, and each of which has its proper realm of empirical phenomena: the wave theory and the quantum theory of light.

from the point of view of the exercise of authority. Identification of variously equipped authority roles is the first task of conflict analysis;[5] conceptually and empirically all further steps of analysis follow from the investigation of distributions of power and authority.

. . . So far as the terms "power" and "authority" and their distinction are concerned, I shall follow in this study the useful and well-considered definitions of Max Weber. . . . We say—as does Max Weber—that while power is merely a factual relation, authority is a legitimate relation of domination and subjection. In this sense, authority can be described as legitimate power.

In the present study we are concerned exclusively with relations of authority, for these alone are part of social structure and therefore permit the systematic derivation of group conflicts from the organization of total societies and associations within them. The significance of such group conflicts rests with the fact that they are not the product of structurally fortuitous relations of power but come forth wherever authority is exercised—and that means in all societies under all historical conditions. (1) Authority relations are always relations of super- and subordination. (2) Where there are authority relations, the superordinate element is socially expected to control, by orders and commands, warnings and prohibitions, the behavior of the subordinate element. (3) Such expectations attach to relatively permanent social positions rather than to the character of individuals; they are in this sense legitimate. (4) By virtue of this fact, they always involve specification of the persons subject to control and of the spheres within which control is permissible.[6] Authority, as distinct from power, is never a relation of generalized control over others. (5) Authority being a legitimate relation, noncompliance with authoritative commands can be sanctioned; it is indeed one of the functions of the legal system (and of course of quasi-legal customs and norms) to support the effective exercise of legitimate authority.

Alongside the term "authority," we shall employ (and have employed) in this study the terms "domination" and "subjection." . . .

It seems desirable for purposes of conflict analysis to specify the relevant unit of social organization in analogy to the concept of social system in the analysis of integration. To speak of specification here is perhaps misleading. "Social system" is a very general concept applicable to all types of organization; and we shall want to employ an equally general concept which differs from that of social system by emphasizing a different aspect of the same organizations. It seems to me that Max Weber's category "imperatively coordinated association" (*Herrschaftsverband*) serves this purpose despite its clumsiness.[7] . . . In looking at social organizations not in terms of their integration and coherence but from the point of view of their structure of coercion and constraint, we regard them as (imperatively coordinated) associations rather than as social systems. Because social organizations are also associations, they generate conflicts of interest and become the birthplace of conflict groups.

I have assumed in the preceding remarks that authority is a characteristic of social organizations as general as society itself.

[5] To facilitate communication, I shall employ in this study a number of abbreviations. These must not however be misunderstood. Thus, "conflict analysis" in this context stands for "analysis of group conflicts of the class type, class being understood in the traditional sense." At no point do I want to imply a claim for a generalized theory of social conflict.

[6] This element of the definition of authority is crucial. It implies that the manager who tries to control people outside his firm, or the private lives of people inside his firm, trespasses the borderline between authority and power. Although he has authority over people in his firm, his control assumes the form of power as soon as it goes beyond the specified persons and spheres of legitimate control. This type of trespassing is of course frequent in every authority relation; and an empirical phenomenon well worth investigating is to what extent the fusion of authority and power tends to intensify group conflicts.

[7] Parsons, in his translation of Weber's *Wirtschaft und Gesellschaft,* suggests "imperatively coordinated group." Any translation of Weber's term is bound to be somewhat awkward, but it seems to me that the word "group" in Parsons' translation is false. Weber uses *Verband,* e.g., to describe the state, or a church—units of organization which can hardly be called "groups." "Association" is probably as precise an English equivalent of *Verband* as is likely to be found.

Despite the assertion of Renner—and other modern sociologists—that in some contemporary societies the exercise of authority has been eliminated and replaced by the more anonymous "rule of the law" or other nonauthoritative relations, I should indeed maintain that authority is a universal element of social structure. It is in this sense more general than, for example, property, or even status. . . . Authority relations exist wherever there are people whose actions are subject to legitimate and sanctioned prescriptions that originate outside them but within social structure. This formulation, by leaving open who exercises what kind of authority, leaves little doubt as to the omnipresence of some kind of authority somehow exercised. For it is evident that there are many forms and types of authority in historical societies. There are differences of a considerable order of magnitude between the relations of the citizen of classical Athens and his slaves, the feudal landlord and his villeins and serfs, the nineteenth-century capitalist and his workers, the secretary of a totalitarian state party and its members, the appointed manager of a modern enterprise and its employees, or the elected prime minister of a democratic country and the electorate. No attempt will be made in this study to develop a typology of authority. But it is assumed throughout that the existence of domination and subjection is a common feature of all possible types of authority and, indeed, of all possible types of association and organization. . . .

It is certainly true that for many purposes of analysis, power or—as I should prefer to say—authority, both realizes and symbolizes the functional integration of social systems. To use a pertinent illustration: in many contexts, the elected president or prime minister of democratic countries represents his country as a whole; his position expresses therefore the unity and integration of a nation. In other contexts, however, the chief of government is but the representative of the majority party, and therefore exponent of sectional interests. I suggest that as in the position of the prime minister neither of these elements is primary or secondary, thus neither the integrative nor the disruptive aspect of authority in social analysis is primary or secondary. Like all other elements of social structure, authority has two faces—those, so to speak, of Mills and of Parsons—and on the highest level of abstraction it is illegitimate to emphasize either of these to the exclusion of the other. Authority is certainly not *only* productive of conflict; but neither is it *only* (or even primarily) "a facility for the performance of function in and on behalf of the society as a sytem." If we are concentrating in this study on what Parsons would call the "negative functions" of authority, we do so because this aspect is more appropriate and useful for the analysis of structurally generated systematic social conflicts.

In referring to the ugly face of authority as a "zero-sum" concept, Parsons brings out one further aspect of this category which is essential for our considerations. By zero-sum, Parsons evidently means that from the point of view of the disruptive "functions" of authority there are two groups or aggregates of persons, of which one possesses authority to the extent to which the other one is deprived of it. This implies—for us, if not for Parsons—that in terms of the coercion theory of society we can always observe a dichotomy of positions in imperatively coordinated associations with respect to the distribution of authority. Parsons, in his critique of Mills, compares the distribution of authority to the distribution of wealth. It seems to me that this comparison is misleading. However unequally wealth may be distributed, there always is a continuum of possession ranging from the lowest to the highest rank. Wealth is not and cannot be conceived as a zero-sum concept. With respect to authority, however, a clear line can at least in theory be drawn between those who participate in its exercise in given associations and those who are subject to the authoritative commands of others. Our analysis of modern societies in later chapters will show that empirically it is not always easy to identify the border line between domination and subjection. Authority has not remained unaffected by the modern process of division of labor. But even here, groups or aggregates can be identified which do not participate in the exercise of authority other than by complying with given commands or prohibitions. Contrary to all criteria of social stratification, authority does not permit the construction of a scale. So-called hierarchies of authority (as displayed, for example, in organization charts) are in fact hierarchies of the "plus-side" of authority, i.e., of the differentiation of domination; but there is, in every association, also a "minus-side" consisting of those who are subjected to authority rather than participate in its exercise.

In two respects this analysis has to be specified, if not supplemented. First, for the individual incumbent of roles, domination in one association does not necessarily involve domination in all others to which he belongs, and subjection, conversely, in one association does not mean subjection in all. The dichotomy of positions of authority holds for specific associations only. In a democratic state, there are both mere voters and incumbents of positions of authority such as cabinet ministers, representatives, and higher civil servants. But this does not mean that the "mere voter" cannot be incumbent of a position of authority in a different context, say, in an industrial enterprise; conversely, a cabinet minister may be, in his church, a mere member, i.e., subject to the authority of others. Although empirically a certain correlation of the authority positions of individuals in different associations seems likely, it is by no means general and is in any case a matter of specific empirical conditions. It is at least possible, if not probable, that if individuals in a given society are ranked according to the sum total of their authority positions in all associations, the resulting pattern will not be a dichotomy but rather like scales of stratification according to income or prestige. For this reason it is necessary to emphasize that in the sociological analysis of group conflict the unit of analysis is always a specific association and the dichotomy of positions within it.

As with respect to the set of roles associated with an individual, total societies, also, do not usually present an unambiguously dichotomic authority structure. There are a large number of imperatively coordinated associations in any given society. Within every one of them we can distinguish the aggregates of those who dominate and those who are subjected. But since domination in industry does not necessarily involve domination in the state, or a church, or other associations, total societies can present the picture of a plurality of competing dominant (and, conversely, subjected) aggregates. This, again, is a problem for the analysis of specific historical societies and must not be confounded with the clearer lines of differentiation within any one association. Within the latter, the distribution of authority always sums up to zero, i.e, there always is a division involving domination and subjection.

I need hardly emphasize that from the point of view of "settling" the concepts of power and authority, the preceding discussion has raised more problems than it has solved. I believe, however, that for the purposes of this study, and of a sociological theory of conflict, little needs to be added to what has been stated here. In order somewhat to substantiate this perhaps rather bold assertion, it seems useful to recapitulate briefly the heuristic purpose and logical status of the considerations of this section.

I have introduced, as a structural determinant of conflict groups, the category of authority as exercised in imperatively coordinated associations. While agreeing with Marx that source and level of income—even socioeconomic status—cannot usefully be conceived as determinants of conflict groups, I have added to this list of erroneous approaches Marx's own in terms of property in the means of production. Authority is both a more general and a more significant social relation. The former has been shown in our critique of Marx; the latter will have to be demonstrated by subsequent considerations and analyses. The concept of authority is used, in this context, in a specific sense. It is differentiated from power by what may roughly be referred to as the element of legitimacy; and it has to be understood throughout in the restricted sense of authority as distributed and exercised in imperatively coordinated associations. While its "disruptive" or conflict-generating consequences are not the only aspect of authority, they are the one relevant in terms of the coercion model of society. Within the frame of reference of this model, (1) the distribution of authority in associations is the ultimate "cause" of the formation of conflict groups, and (2), being dichotomous, it is, in any given association, the cause of the formation of two, and only two, conflict groups.

The first of these statements is logically an assumption, since it underlies scientific theories. It cannot as such be tested by observation; its validity is proven, rather, by its usefulness for purposes of explanation. We shall derive from this assumption certain more specific hypotheses which, if refuted, would take the assumption with them into the waster-paper basket of scientific theories. We assume in this sense that if we manage to identify the incumbents of positions of domination and subjection in any given association, we have identified the contenders of one significant type of conflicts—conflicts which occur in this association at all times.

As to the second statement, the one concerned with the dichotomy of authority positions in imperatively coordinated associations, it is not, I suggest, either an assumption or an empirical hypothesis, but an analytical statement. It follows from and is implicit in the very concept of authority that within specified contexts some have authority and others not. If either nobody or everybody had authority, the concept would lose its meaning. Authority implies both domination and subjection, and it therefore implies the existence of two distinct sets of positions or persons. This is not to say, of course, that there is no difference between those who have a great deal and those who have merely a little authority. Among the positions of domination there may be, and often is, considerable differentiation. But such differentiation, while important for empirical analysis, leaves unaffected the existence of a border line somewhere between those who have whatever little authority and the "outs." Strictly speaking, an analytical statement which states that there is a dichotomy of authority positions is tautological; but as this example shows, there are tautologies which are worth stating. . . .

## LATENT AND MANIFEST INTERESTS

The analytical process of conflict group formation can be described in terms of a model. Throughout, the categories employed in this model will be used in terms of the coercion theory of social structure. With this restriction in mind, the thesis that conflict groups are based on the dichotomous distribution of authority in imperatively coordinated associations can be conceived of as the basic assumption of the model. To this assumption we now add the proposition that differentially equipped authority positions in associations involve, for their incumbents, conflicting interests. The occupants of positions of domination and the occupants of positions of subjection hold, by virtue of these positions, certain interests which are contradictory in substance and direction.

. . . . . . . . . . . . . . . . . . . . . . . . . . . . . . . . . . . .

For purposes of the sociological analysis of conflict groups and group conflicts, it is necessary to assume certain structurally generated orientations of the actions of incumbents of defined positions. By analogy to conscious ("subjective") orientations of action, it appears justifiable to describe these as "interests." It has to be emphasized, however, that by so doing no assumption is implied about the substance of these interests or the consciousness and articulate orientation of the occupants of the positions in question.[8] The assumption of "objective" interests associated with social positions has no psychological implications or ramifications; it belongs to the level of sociological analysis proper.

## CLASSES OR CONFLICT GROUPS?

. . . In my opinion, the problem of the applicability of the concept of class is a purely terminological problem. In positive terms, this means that it is in part a matter of arbitrary decision, and in part a matter of convenience. Logically, there is no reason why we should not call quasi-groups and interest groups classes or anything else. Pragmatically, of course, the usage and history of words has to be considered; it is unwise to provoke misunderstandings by choosing words which carry associations that are not intended.

. . . . . . . . . . . . . . . . . . . . . . . . . . . . . . . . . . . .

[8] This statement will be qualified below by the distinction of "latent" and "manifest interests." Strictly speaking, it holds for latent interests only.

It is hard to weigh the "pros and cons" . . . entirely rationally; an element of personal preference will probably enter into any decision. Without trying to argue for this decision at any length, I will therefore state immediately that in my opinion the case in favor of retaining the concept of class is still sufficiently strong to warrant its application to even the most advanced industrial societies. This decision does involve, of course, a polemical stand against all those who "falsify" the term "class" by applying it to what should properly be called social strata. It also involves considerable extensions of the concept as it was used by Marx as well as by all Marxists and Marxians. But it emphasizes that in class analysis we are concerned (*a*) with systematic social conflicts and their structural origin, and (*b*) with but one specific type of such conflicts.

In terms of our model, the term "class" signifies conflict groups that are generated by the differential distribution of authority in imperatively coordinated associations. This definition implies no assumption as to the looseness or rigidity of their coherence, the presence or absence of a common culture or ideology (beyond specific interests) among their members, and the intensity or lack of intensity of their engagement in social conflicts. . . .

# SOME PRINCIPLES OF STRATIFICATION

*Kingsley Davis and Wilbert E. Moore*

In a previous paper some concepts for handling the phenomena of social inequality were presented.[1] In the present paper a further step in stratification theory is undertaken—an attempt to show the relationship between stratification and the rest of the social order.[2] Starting from the proposition that no society is "classless," or unstratified, an effort is made to explain, in functional terms, the universal necessity which calls forth stratification in any social system. Next, an attempt is made to explain the roughly uniform distribution of prestige as between the major types of positions in every society. Since, however, there occur between one society and another great differences in the degree and kind of stratification, some attention is also given to the varieties of social inequality and the variable factors that give rise to them.

Clearly, the present task requires two different lines of analysis—one to understand the universal, the other to understand the variable features of stratification. Naturally each line of inquiry aids the other and is indispensable, and in the treatment that follows the two will be interwoven, although, because of space limitations, the emphasis will be on the universals.

Throughout, it will be necessary to keep in mind one thing—namely, that the discussion relates to the system of positions, not to the individuals occupying those positions. It is one thing to ask why different positions carry different degrees of prestige, and quite another to ask how certain individuals get into those positions. Although, as the argument will try to show, both questions are related, it is essential to keep them separate in our thinking. Most of the literature on stratification has tried to answer the second question (particularly with regard to the ease or difficulty of mobility between strata) without tackling the first. The first question, however, is logically prior and, in the case of any particular individual or group, factually prior.

*American Sociological Review,* "Some Principles of Stratification," by Kingsley Davis and Wilbert E. Moore, Vol. 10, April, 1945. Reprinted by permission.

[1] Kingsley Davis, "A Conceptual Analysis of Stratification," *American Sociological Review.* 7: 309–321, June, 1942.

[2] The writers regret (and beg indulgence) that the present essay, a condensation of a longer study, covers so much in such short space that adequate evidence and qualification cannot be given and that as a result what is actually very tentative is presented in an unfortunately dogmatic manner.

## THE FUNCTIONAL NECESSITY OF STRATIFICATION

Curiously, however, the main functional necessity explaining the universal presence of stratification is precisely the requirement faced by any society of placing and motivating individuals in the social structure. As a functioning mechanism a society must somehow distribute its members in social positions and induce them to perform the duties of these positions. It must thus concern itself with motivation at two different levels: to instill in the proper individuals the desire to fill certain positions, and, once in these positions, the desire to perform the duties attached to them. Even though the social order may be relatively static in form, there is a continuous process of metabolism as new individuals are born into it, shift with age, and die off. Their absorption into the positional system must somehow be arranged and motivated. This is true whether the system is competitive or non-competitive. A competitive system gives greater importance to the motivation to achieve positions, whereas a non-competitive system gives perhaps greater importance to the motivation to perform the duties of the positions; but in any system both types of motivation are required.

If the duties associated with the various positions were all equally pleasant to the human organism, all equally important to societal survival, and all equally in need of the same ability or talent, it would make no difference who got into which positions, and the problem of social placement would be greatly reduced. But actually it does make a great deal of difference who gets into which positions, not only because some positions are inherently more agreeable than others, but also because some require special talents or training and some are functionally more important than others. Also, it is essential that the duties of the positions be performed with the diligence that their importance requires. Inevitably, then, a society must have, first, some kind of rewards that it can use as inducements, and, second, some way of distributing these rewards differentially according to positions. The rewards and their distribution become a part of the social order, and thus give rise to stratification.

One may ask what kind of rewards a society has at its disposal in distributing its personnel and securing essential services. It has, first of all, the things that contribute to sustenance and comfort. It has, second, the things that contribute to humor and diversion. And it has, finally, the things that contribute to self respect and ego expansion. The last, because of the peculiarly social character of the self, is largely a function of the opinion of others, but it nonetheless ranks in importance with the first two. In any social system all three kinds of rewards must be dispensed differentially according to positions.

In a sense the rewards are "built into" the position. They consist in the "rights" associated with the position, plus what may be called its accompaniments or perquisites. Often the rights, and sometimes the accompaniments, are functionally related to the duties of the position. (Rights as viewed by the incumbent are usually duties as viewed by other members of the community.) However, there may be a host of subsidiary rights and perquisites that are not essential to the function of the position and have only an indirect and symbolic connection with its duties, but which still may be of considerable importance in inducing people to seek the positions and fulfill the essential duties.

If the rights and perquisites of different positions in a society must be unequal, then the society must be stratified, because that is precisely what stratification means. Social inequality is thus an unconsciously evolved device by which societies insure that the most important positions are conscientiously filled by the most qualified persons. Hence every society, no matter how simple or complex, must differentiate persons in terms of both prestige and esteem, and must therefore possess a certain amount of institutionalized inequality.

It does not follow that the amount or type of inequality need be the same in all societies. This is largely a function of factors that will be discussed presently.

## THE TWO DETERMINANTS OF POSITIONAL RANK

Granting the general function that inequality subserves, one can specify the two factors that determine the relative rank of different positions. In general those positions convey the best reward, and hence have the highest rank, which (a) have the greatest importance for the society and (b) require the greatest training or talent. The first factor concerns function and is a matter of relative significance; the second concerns means and is a matter of scarcity.

***Differential Functional Importance.*** Actually a society does not need to reward positions in proportion to their functional importance. It merely needs to give sufficient reward to them to insure that they will be filled competently. In other words, it must see that less essential positions do not compete successfully with more essential ones. If a position is easily filled, it need not be heavily rewarded, even though important. On the other hand, if it is important but hard to fill, the reward must be high enough to get it filled anyway. Functional importance is therefore a necessary but not a sufficient cause of high rank being assigned to a position.[3]

***Differential Scarcity of Personnel.*** Practically all positions, no matter how acquired, require some form of skill or capacity for performance. This is implicit in the very notion of position, which implies that the incumbent must, by virtue of his incumbency, accomplish certain things.

There are, ultimately, only two ways in which a person's qualifications come about: through inherent capacity or through training. Obviously, in concrete activities both are always necessary, but from a practical standpoint the scarcity may lie primarily in one or the other, as well as in both. Some positions require innate talents of such high degree that the persons who fill them are bound to be rare. In many cases, however, talent is fairly abundant in the population but the training process is so long, costly, and elaborate that relatively few can qualify. Modern medicine, for example, is within the mental capacity of most individuals, but a medical education is so burdensome and expensive that virtually none would undertake it if the position of the M.D. did not carry a reward commensurate with the sacrifice.

If the talents required for a position are abundant and the training easy, the method of acquiring the position may have little to do with its duties. There may be, in fact, a virtually accidental relationship. But if the skills required are scarce by reason of the rarity of talent or the costliness of training, the position, if functionally important, must have an attractive power that will draw the necessary skills in competition with other positions. This means, in effect, that the position must be high in the social scale—must command great prestige, high salary, ample leisure, and the like.

***How Variations Are to Be Understood.*** In so far as there is a difference between one system of stratification and another, it is attributable to whatever factors affect the two determinants of differential reward—namely, functional importance and scarcity of personnel. Positions important in one society may not be important in another, because the conditions faced by the societies, or their degree of internal development, may be different. The same conditions, in turn, may affect the question of scarcity; for in some societies the stage of development, or the external situation, may wholly obviate the necessity of certain kinds of skill or talent. Any particular system of stratification, then, can be understood as a product of the special conditions affecting the two aforementioned grounds of differential reward.

[3] Unfortunately, functional importance is difficult to establish. To use the position's prestige to establish it, as is often unconsciously done, constitutes circular reasoning from our point of view. There are, however, two independent clues: (a) the degree to which a position is functionally unique, there being no other positions that can perform the same function satisfactorily; (b) the degree to which other positions are dependent on the one in question. Both clues are best exemplified in organized systems of positions built around one major function. Thus, in most complex societies the religious, political, economic, and educational functions are handled by distinct structures not easily interchangeable. In addition, each structure possesses many different positions, some clearly dependent on, if not subordinate to, others. In sum, when an institutional nucleus becomes differentiated around one main function, and at the same time organizes a large portion of the population into its relationships, the *key* positions in it are of the highest functional importance. The absence of such specialization does not prove functional unimportance, for the whole society may be relatively unspecialized; but it is safe to assume that the more important functions receive the first and clearest structural differentiation.

## MAJOR SOCIETAL FUNCTIONS AND STRATIFICATION

***Religion.*** The reason why religion is necessary is apparently to be found in the fact that human society achieves its unity primarily through the possession by its members of certain ultimate values and ends in common. Although these values and ends are subjective, they influence behavior, and their integration enables the society to operate as a system. Derived neither from inherited nor from external nature, they have evolved as a part of culture by communication and moral pressure. They must, however, appear to the members of the society to have some reality, and it is the role of religious belief and ritual to supply and reinforce this appearance of reality. Through belief and ritual the common ends and values are connected with an imaginary world symbolized by concrete sacred objects, which world in turn is related in a meaningful way to the facts and trials of the individual's life. Through the worship of the sacred objects and the beings they symbolize, and the acceptance of supernatural prescriptions that are at the same time codes of behavior, a powerful control over human conduct is exercised, guiding it along lines sustaining the institutional structure and conforming to the ultimate ends and values.

If this conception of the role of religion is true, one can understand why in every known society the religious activities tend to be under the charge of particular persons, who tend thereby to enjoy greater rewards than the ordinary societal member. Certain of the rewards and special privileges may attach to only the highest religious functionaries, but others usually apply, if such exists, to the entire sacerdotal class.

Moreover, there is a peculiar relation between the duties of the religious official and the special privileges he enjoys. If the supernatural world governs the destinies of men more ultimately than does the real world, its earthly representative, the person through whom one may communicate with the supernatural, must be a powerful individual. He is a keeper of sacred tradition, a skilled performer of the ritual, and an interpreter of lore and myth. He is in such close contact with the gods that he is viewed as possessing some of their characteristics. He is, in short, a bit sacred, and hence free from some of the more vulgar necessities and controls.

It is no accident, therefore, that religious functionaries have been associated with the very highest positions of power, as in theocratic regimes. Indeed, looking at it from this point of view, one may wonder why it is that they do not get *entire* control over their societies. The factors that prevent this are worthy of note.

In the first place, the amount of technical competence necessary for the performance of religious duties is small. Scientific or artistic capacity is not required. Anyone can set himself up as enjoying an intimate relation with deities, and nobody can successfully dispute him. Therefore, the factor of scarcity of personnnel does not operate in the technical sense.

One may assert, on the other hand, that religious ritual is often elaborate and religious lore abstruse, and that priestly ministrations require tact, if not intelligence. This is true, but the technical requirements of the profession are for the most part adventitious, not related to the end in the same way that science is related to air travel. The priest can never be free from competition, since the criteria of whether or not one has genuine contact with the supernatural are never strictly clear. It is this competition that debases the priestly position below what might be expected at first glance. That is why priestly prestige is highest in those societies where membership in the profession is rigidly controlled by the priestly guild itself. That is why, in part at least, elaborate devices are utilized to stress the identification of the person with his office—spectacular costume, abnormal conduct, special diet, segregated residence, celibacy, conspicuous leisure, and the like. In fact, the priest is always in danger of becoming somewhat discredited—as happens in a secularized society—because in a world of stubborn fact, ritual and sacred knowledge alone will not grow crops or build houses. Furthermore, unless he is protected by a professional guild, the priest's identification with the supernatural tends to preclude his acquisition of abundant wordly goods.

As between one society and another it seems that the highest general position awarded the priest occurs in the medieval type of social order. Here there is enough economic production to afford a surplus, which can be used to support a numerous and highly organized priesthood; and yet the populace is unlettered and therefore credulous to a high degree. Perhaps the most extreme example is to be found in the Buddhism of Tibet, but others are encountered in the Catholicism of feudal Europe, the Inca regime of Peru, the Brahminism of India, and the Mayan priesthood of Yucatan. On the other hand, if the society is so crude as to have no surplus and little differentiation, so that every priest must be also a cultivator or hunter, the separation of the priestly status from the others has hardly gone far enough for priestly prestige to mean much. When the priest actually has high prestige under these circumstances, it is because he also performs other important functions (usually political and medical).

In an extremely advanced society built on scientific technology, the priesthood tends to lose status, because sacred tradition and supernaturalism drop into the background. The ultimate values and common ends of the society tend to be expressed in less anthropomorphic ways, by officials who occupy fundamentally political, economic, or educational rather than religious positions. Nevertheless, it is easily possible for intellectuals to exaggerate the degree to which priesthood in a presumably secular milieu has lost prestige. When the matter is closely examined the urban proletariat, as well as the rural citizenry, proves to be surprisingly god-fearing and priest-ridden. No society has become so completely secularized as to liquidate entirely the belief in transcendental ends and supernatural entities. Even in a secularized society some system must exist for the integration of ultimate values, for their ritualistic expression, and for the emotional adjustments required by disappointment, death, and disaster.

***Government.*** Like religion, government plays a unique and indispensable part in society, But in contrast to religion, which provides integration in terms of sentiments, belief, and rituals, it organizes the society in terms of law and authority. Furthermore, it orients the society to the actual rather than the unseen world.

The main functions of government are, internally, the ultimate enforcement of norms, the final arbitration of conflicting interests, and the overall planning and direction of society; and externally, the handling of war and diplomacy. To carry out these functions it acts as the agent of the entire people, enjoys a monopoly of force, and controls all individuals within its territory.

Political action, by definition, implies authority. An official can command because he has authority, and the citizen must obey because he is subject to that authority. For this reason stratification is inherent in the nature of political relationships.

So clear is the power embodied in political position that political inequality is sometimes thought to comprise all inequality. But it can be shown that there are other bases of stratification, that the following controls operate in practice to keep political power from becoming complete: (a) The fact that the actual holders of political office, and especially those determining top policy must necessarily be few in number compared to the total population. (b) The fact that the rulers represent the interest of the group rather than of themselves, and are therefore restricted in their behavior by rules and mores designed to enforce this limitation of interest. (c) The fact that the holder of political office has his authority by virtue of his office and nothing else, and therefore any special knowledge, talent, or capacity he may claim is purely incidental, so that he often has to depend upon others for technical assistance.

In view of these limiting factors, it is not strange that the rulers often have less power and prestige than a literal enumeration of their formal rights would lead one to expect.

***Wealth, Property, and Labor.*** Every position that secures for its incumbent a livelihood is, by definition, economically rewarded. For this reason there is an economic aspect to those positions (e.g., political and religious) the main function of which is not economic. It therefore becomes convenient for the society to use unequal economic returns as a principal means of controlling the entrance of persons into positions and stimulating the performance of their duties. The amount of the economic return therefore becomes one of the main indices of social status.

It should be stressed, however, that a position does not bring power and prestige *because* it draws a high income. Rather, it draws a high income because it is functionally important and the available personnel is for one reason or another scarce. It is therefore superficial and erroneous to regard high income as the cause of a man's power and prestige, just as it is erroneous to think that a man's fever is the cause of his disease.[4]

The economic source of power and prestige is not income primarily, but the ownership of capital goods (including patents, good will, and professional reputation). Such ownership should be distinguished from the possession of consumers' goods, which is an index rather than a cause of social standing. In other words, the ownership of producers' goods is, properly speaking, a source of income like other positions, the income itself remaining an index. Even in situations where social values are widely commercialized and earnings are the readiest method of judging social position, income does not confer prestige on a position so much as it induces people to compete for the position. It is true that a man who has a high income as a result of one position may find this money helpful in climbing into another position as well, but this again reflects the effect of his initial, economically advantageous status, which exercises its influence through the medium of money.

In a system of private property in productive enterprise, an income above what an individual spends can give rise to possession of capital wealth. Presumably such possession is a reward for the proper management of one's finances originally and of the productive enterprise later. But as social differentiation becomes highly advanced and yet the institution of inheritance persists, the phenomenon of pure ownership, and reward for pure ownership, emerges. In such a case it is difficult to prove that the position is functionally important or that the scarcity involved is anything other than extrinsic and accidental. It is for this reason, doubtless, that the institution of private property in productive goods becomes more subject to criticism as social development proceeds toward industrialization. It is only this pure, that is, strictly legal and functionless ownership, however, that is open to attack; for some form of active ownership, whether private or public, is indispensable.

One kind of ownership of production goods consists in rights over the labor of others. The most extremely concentrated and exclusive of such rights are found in slavery, but the essential principle remains in serfdom, peonage, encomienda, and indenture. Naturally this kind of ownership has the greatest significance for stratification, because it necessarily entails an unequal relationship.

But property in capital goods inevitably introduces a compulsive element even into the nominally free contractual relationship. Indeed, in some respects the authority of the contractual employer is greater than that of the feudal landlord, inasmuch as the latter is more limited by traditional reciprocities. Even the classical economics recognized that competitors would fare unequally, but it did not pursue this fact to its necessary conclusion that, however it might be acquired, unequal control of goods and services must give unequal advantage to the parties to a contract.

***Technical Knowledge.*** The function of finding means to single goals, without any concern with the choice between goals, is the exclusively technical sphere. The explanation of why positions requiring great technical skill receive fairly high rewards is easy to see, for it is the simplest case of the rewards being so distributed as to draw talent and motivate training. Why they seldom if ever receive the highest rewards is also clear: the importance of technical knowledge from a societal point of view is never so great as the integration of goals, which takes place on the religious, political, and economic levels. Since the technological level is concerned solely with means, a purely technical position must ultimately be subordinate to other positions that are religious, political, or economic in character.

[4] The symbolic rather than intrinsic role of income in social stratification has been succinctly summarized by Talcott Parsons, "An Analytical Approach to the Theory of Social Stratification," *American Journal of Sociology*. 45:841–862, May, 1940.

Nevertheless, the distinction between expert and layman in any social order is fundamental, and cannot be entirely reduced to other terms. Methods of recruitment, as well as of reward, sometimes lead to the erroneous interpretation that technical positions are economically determined. Actually, however, the acquisition of knowledge and skill cannot be accomplished by purchase, although the opportunity to learn may be. The control of the avenues of training may inhere as a sort of property right in certain families or classes, giving them power and prestige in consequence. Such a situation adds an artificial scarcity to the natural scarcity of skills and talents. On the other hand, it is possible for an opposite situation to arise. The rewards of technical position may be so great that a condition of excess supply is created, leading to at least temporary devaluation of the rewards. Thus "unemployment in the learned professions" may result in a debasement of the prestige of those positions. Such adjustments and readjustments are constantly occurring in changing societies; and it is always well to bear in mind that the efficiency of a stratified structure may be affected by the modes of recruitment for positions. The social order itself, however, sets limits to the inflation or deflation of the prestige of experts: an over-supply tends to debase the rewards and discourage recruitment or produce revolution, whereas an under-supply tends to increase the rewards or weaken the society in competition with other societies.

Particular systems of stratification show a wide range with respect to the exact position of technically competent persons. This range is perhaps most evident in the degree of specialization. Extreme division of labor tends to create many specialists without high prestige since the training is short and the required native capacity relatively small. On the other hand it also tends to accentuate the high position of the true experts—scientists, engineers, and administrators—by increasing their authority relative to other functionally important positions. But the idea of a technocratic social order or a government or priesthood of engineers or social scientists neglects the limitations of knowledge and skills as a basic for performing special functions. To the extent that the social structure is truly specialized the prestige of the technical person must also be circumscribed.

## VARIATION IN STRATIFIED SYSTEMS

The generalized principles of stratification here suggested form a necessary preliminary to a consideration of types of stratified systems, because it is in terms of these principles that the types must be described. This can be seen by trying to delineate types according to certain modes of variation. For instance, some of the most important modes (together with the polar types in terms of them) seem to be as follows:

***(a) The Degree of Specialization.*** The degree of specialization affects the fineness and multiplicity of the gradations in power and prestige. It also influences the extent to which particular functions may be emphasized in the invidious system, since a given function cannot receive much emphasis in the hierarchy until it has achieved structural separation from the other functions. Finally, the amount of specialization influences the bases of selection. Polar types: *Specialized, Unspecialized.*

***(b) The Nature of the Functional Emphasis.*** In general when emphasis is put on sacred matters, a rigidity is introduced that tends to limit specialization and hence the development of technology. In addition, a brake is placed on social mobility, and on the development of bureaucracy. When the preoccupation with the sacred is withdrawn, leaving greater scope for purely secular preoccupations, a great development, and rise in status, of economic and technological positions seemingly takes place. Curiously, a concomitant rise in political position is not likely, because it has usually been allied with the religious and stands to gain little by the decline of the latter. It is also possible for a society to emphasize family functions—as in relatively undifferentiated societies where high mortality requires high fertility and kinship forms the main basis of social organization. Main types: *Familistic, Authoritarian* (*Theocratic* or sacred, and *Totalitarian* or secular), *Capitalistic.*

***(c) The Magnitude of Invidious Differences.*** What may be called the amount of social distance between positions, taking into account the entire scale, is something that should lend itself to quantitative measurement. Considerable differences apparently exist between different societies in this regard, and also between parts of the same society. Polar types: *Equalitarian, Inequalitarian.*

***(d) The Degree of Opportunity.*** The familiar question of the amount of mobility is different from the question of the comparative equality or inequality of rewards posed above, because the two criteria may vary independently up to a point. For instance, the tremendous divergences in monetary income in the United States are far greater than those found in primitive societies, yet the equality of opportunity to move from one rung to the other in the social scale may also be greater in the United States than in a hereditary tribal kingdom. Polar types: *Mobile* (open), *Immobile,* (closed).

***(e) The Degree of Stratum Solidarity.*** Again, the degree of "class solidarity" (or the presence of specific organizations to promote class interests) may vary to some extent independently of the other criteria, and hence is an important principle in classifying systems of stratification. Polar types: *Class organized, Class unorganized.*

### EXTERNAL CONDITIONS

What state any particular system of stratification is in with reference to each of these modes of variation depends on two things: (1) its state with reference to the other ranges of variation, and (2) the conditions outside the system of stratification which nevertheless influence that system. Among the latter are the following:

***(a) The Stage of Cultural Development.*** As the cultural heritage grows, increased specialization becomes necessary, which in turn contributes to the enhancement of mobility, a decline of stratum solidarity, and a change of functional emphasis.

***(b) Situation with Respect to Other Societies.*** The presence or absence of open conflict with other societies, of free trade relations or cultural diffusion, all influence the class structure to some extent. A chronic state of warfare tends to place emphasis upon the military functions, especially when the opponents are more or less equal. Free trade, on the other hand, strengthens the hand of the trader at the expense of the warrior and priest. Free movement of ideas generally has an equalitarian effect. Migration and conquest create special circumstances.

***(c) Size of the Society.*** A small society limits the degree to which functional specialization can go, the degree of segregation of different strata, and the magnitude of inequality.

### COMPOSITE TYPES

Much of the literature on stratification has attempted to classify concrete systems into a certain number of types. This task is deceptively simple, however, and should come at the end of an analysis of elements and principles, rather than at the beginning. If the preceding discussion has any validity it indicates that there are a number of modes of variation between different systems, and that any one system is a composite of the society's status with reference to all these modes of variation. The danger of trying to classify whole societies under such rubrics as *caste, feudal,* or *open class* is that one or two criteria are selected and others ignored, the result being an unsatisfactory solution to the problem posed. The present discussion has been offered as a possible approach to the more systematic classification of composite types.

# SOME NOTES ON THE FUNCTIONAL THEORY OF STRATIFICATION

*Wlodzimierz Wesolowski*

One might be tempted to find many reasons for the length and pertinacity of discussion aroused by the articles of K. Davis and W. Moore. No doubt one reason would be the

Reprinted from *The Polish Sociological Bulletin,* No. 3–4 (5–6), (1962), pp. 28–38, by permission of the author and the publisher.

abbreviated and abstract form in which the theory is presented, making it subject to various interpretations, as well as the "ideological overtone" attached to it. In my view, however, the most important reason for the length of discussion is the importance of the problem itself.

In the form in which it was presented in the *American Sociological Review*,[1] the theory would seem to contain three main assertions:

1. Social stratification (uneven distribution of material rewards and of prestige) is functionally necessary and is therefore a universal and permanent feature of society;
2. Stratification is functionally necessary because every society needs a mechanism inducing people to occupy positions which are socially important and require training; material rewards and prestige act as stimuli towards the occupation of such positions;
3. The existence of the above mechanism ensures that "the most important positions are conscientiously filled by the most qualified persons" ("the most qualified" here means: the ablest and best trained).

During the discussion following the articles,[2] and even earlier (in K. Davis' book, *Human Society*), the third assertion, suggesting the "perfection" of this social mechanism of selection, was withdrawn by the authors owing to its blatant inconsistency with many sociological facts. Attention was drawn to the fact that the occurrence of cases where (1) status is ascribed, (2) status is "prepared" by the position and efforts of the parents, and (3) the status and career of the individual are influenced by various group and clique determinants, means that (a) not all those who have equal ability have equal opportunity to acquire training, (b) not all those who are equal in training have equal opportunity to occupy positions bringing high prestige and income. For these reasons I shall not deal with the third assertion.[3] I should like, however, to make some comment on the first two assertions, which seem to me the core of the theory.

These assertions are concerned not so much with the system of selection, as with the system of motivation. When the third assertion is rejected, the theory asserts only that if positions which are important and require training are to be filled, then they must provide greater prestige and higher income; otherwise no-one would bother to train himself to fill them. Nevertheless, the theory does not say that everyone occupies a position suitable to his talents and, his training. There are some people who, although capable, had no chance to acquire a training. There are others, who, although trained, had no opportunity to gain high positions. But the very fact that there is differentiation of prestige and differentiation of income nevertheless acts as a stimulus encouraging people to make the effort to win a higher position.

The central point of the theory, then, is the hypothesis concerning motivation. According to this hypothesis, the striving for high income and high prestige is an indispensable and principal motive which drives people to make the effort to occupy positions which are important and require training. It is this assertion which will be the subject of our comment. Before we come to

[1] K. Davis, "A Conceptual Analysis of Stratification," *American Sociological Review*, Vol. 7, 1942, No. 3; K. Davis and W. Moore, "Some Principles of Stratification," *American Sociological Review*, Vol. 10, 1945, No. 2.

[2] M. M. Tumin, "Some Principles of Stratification: A Critical Analysis," *American Sociological Review*, Vol. 18, 1953, No. 4; K. Davis and W. Moore, "Reply and Comment," *American Sociological Review*, Vol. 18, 1953, No. 4; M. M. Tumin, "Reply to K. Davis," *American Sociological Review*, Vol. 18, 1953, No. 6. Among the large number of contributions to the discussion, the following should be especially noted: W. Buckley, "Social Stratification and the Functional Theory of Social Differentiation," *American Sociological Review*, Vol. 23, 1958, No. 3; D. H. Wrong, "The Functional Theory of Stratification: Some Neglected Considerations," *American Sociological Review*, Vol. 24, 1959, No. 6. The theory is also discussed in the following books: J. F. Cuber and W. F. Kenkel, *Social Stratification in the United States*, New York, 1954; J. A. Kahl, *The American Class Structure*, New York, 1957; M. M. Gordon, *Social Class in American Society*, North Carolina 1958; L. Reissman, *Class in American Society*, Glencoe 1959.

[3] The present author discusses this at greater length in an article: "Davis' and Moore's Functional Theory of Stratification," *Studia Socjologiczne*, 1962, No. 4.

this, however, a certain concept which is used in the theory calls for explanation. This is the concept of "importance" of position.

*"Importance" of position.* According to this theory, greater prestige and greater material rewards give positions which have greater importance for society and require greater training or talent. It is more or less clear what the authors mean by "training or talent." In this article I will take training into account and by it I will mean education (general and specific) which in modern industrial society is the chief means of attaining basic knowledge and skill required for most highly valued jobs (e.g., doctor, lawyer, engineer).[4] It is less clear, however, what should be regarded as making importance of position. Here we are left to our own suppositions and interpretation.

The authors write: "Unfortunately, functional importance is difficult to establish. To use the position's prestige to establish it, as is often unconsciously done, constitutes circular reasoning from our point of view. There are, however, two independent clues: (a) the degree to which a position is functionally unique, there being no other positions that can perform the same function satisfactorily; (b) the degree to which other positions are dependent on the one in question. Both clues are best exemplified in organized systems of positions built round one major function. Thus, in most complex societies the religious, political, economic, and educational functions are handled by distinct structures not easily interchangeable. In addition, each structure possesses many different positions, some clearly dependent on, if not subordinate to, others. In sum, when an institutional nucleus becomes differentiated around one main function, and at the same time organizes a large portion of the population into its relationships, the key positions in it are of the highest functional importance."[5]

Let us examine these assertions.

As "functionally unique" (see point *a* above) one can regard those positions that call for specific training. The "specific" character of this training and talent may consist in its "quality" or "quantity." The training of a doctor and of an engineer are qualitatively different and yet quantitatively similar (high educational level). Likewise, the training of a fitter in a factory and that of a nurse are qualitatively different, yet quantitatively similar.

The engineer cannot be replaced in his duties by the doctor; neither can the fitter be replaced by the nurse. Owing to their different "qualitative" training, both the doctor and engineer are equally "irreplaceable." Likewise with the fitter and the nurse. On the "horizontal" plane, therefore, it would be difficult to find differences in extent of "irreplaceability" between the various occupations. Such differences can only be found in the "vertical" plane. The doctor is more irreplaceable than the nurse because he can carry out the nurse's duties (although less efficiently), but the nurse cannot carry out the doctor's duties. Similarly, it would be easier for the engineer to carry out the duties of the fitter, than for the fitter to carry out the duties of the engineer; and easier for the manager to carry out the clerk's duties than the clerk to carry out the duties of the manager. Thus those occupational positions which call for higher specialized training (in industrial societies it means chiefly higher education) are more "irreplaceable." Thus the first clue indicating the "functional importance" of a position does not seem to contribute any new element to the theory, since the role of training is mentioned as the first determinant of the height of position (besides "functional importance" as the second determinant).

But the second clue indicating "functional

[4] Attention given here to the training and not to the talent seems to me in accordance with the main features of the theory under discussion since it is dealing with the mechanism of motivation to attain the positions that require training. This attention is also justified by the author's assertions that: (*a*) gaining the doctor's training is in capacity of anyone with average talent (the same is probably true about lawyer, engineer and many other occupations); (*b*) in cases of many occupations talents are fairly abundant in the population, but only training is long and costly. One can add also that even the artistic occupations in which inborn talents play a greater role, demand today not only talents but training.

[5] K. Davis and W. Moore, "Some Principles of Stratification," *American Sociological Review*, Vol. 10, 1945, No. 2, p. 243, footnote 3.

importance" (mentioned in point *b*) does seem to introduce a new element. Explanations given by Davis and Moore suggest that the second factor determining the functional importance of position is authority. For—according to them—those positions are important, which other positions are subordinate to, or which they depend on; formulated differently, they are "key positions." Examples given by the authors point to the highest positions in hierarchic structures of social institutions.[6]

The above analysis leads us to the conclusion that, according to this theory, unequal distribution of material advantages and prestige is needed to make people train for positions requiring higher occupational skills and, perhaps, positions of high occupational skill and of authority. A good example of the first position is the position of a medical doctor; examples of the second would be the position of a business executive or of a general.

***The Mechanism of Motivation.*** The authors regard their theory as being universally applicable to all known societies throughout history. But this is a view which is easy to disprove. It is very doubtful, for example, if ever differences of prestige and differences of income were "functionally necessary" for the filling of positions in stabilized societies where statuses were ascribed. And it should be remembered that societies of this type have been predominant throughout by far the greater part of history.

But the theory does seem to grasp the essential connections which occur in societies where statuses are achieved. This would appear to be the reason for the great liveliness of discussion on the articles by Davis and Moore. For modern industrial societies—both capitalist and socialist—are societies with achieved statuses. And in these societies are to be found many facts confirming the existence of the motivational mechanism described by the authors of this theory. The question arises, therefore, whether the theory holds good for all industrial societies where there is far-reaching division of labour and where statuses are attainable.

In Davis' and Moore's theory, it is this problem which is of the greatest interest. It seems possible, however, that a number of weighty theoretical arguments, as well as certain factual data, can be brought up against the theory.

## SOME GENERAL ARGUMENTS

The main theoretical argument against Davis' and Moore's conception is that their theory contains three erroneous assumptions. These are concerned with (*a*) the human nature, (*b*) the pattern of society, (*c*) the structure of values.

It has already been pointed out that in many respects Davis' and Moore's theory recalls the classical theory of political economy, for example its implicitly assumed conception of unchanging "human nature." According to Davis and Moore, human nature is characterized, on the one hand by a drive towards personal advantages, and on the other by laziness. In a society where human nature is such, then stratification (the unequal distribution of material rewards and prestige) is an unavoidable necessity if important positions requiring training are to be filled properly. It must be said, however, that whereas such a concept of human nature has not yet completely disappeared from the economic text-books, it does not occur at all in modern text-books of sociology, psychology, or cultural anthropology. In fact is may be said that the psychological content of Davis' and Moore's theory is inconsistent with modern theory of social psychology.

Here is what T. Newcomb says on this very subject: "Many motives which we, as members of our own society, think of as being part of human nature, are by no means dependable the world over. Motives of wanting prestige, wanting to be free from

[6] Authority is a kind of power—"institutionalized" power. Authority belongs to a person who as a result of his position in some institutional structure has the right to issue orders to other people who also occupy a position in that structure. These orders are carried out because of the customs or laws concerning the functioning of the structure as a whole. In any modern organization (industrial or political), the hierarchy of positions is the simplest example of the hierarchical system of positions in which authority, as here understood, is to be found. See R. Bierstedt, "An Analysis of Social Power," *American Sociological Review,* Vol. 15, 1950, No. 6.

the dominance of authority of others, jealousy in love relationships as well as motives of acquiring property, seem utterly natural to us. They are, in fact, fairly dependable in large sections of American society. Their dependability rests, however, upon the dependability of the cultural conditions under which they are acquired. They may, perhaps, be said to represent 'contemporary middle-class American nature,' but they do not correspond to anything dependable in human nature" (dependable = universal).[7]

The statement that the motives of people's behaviour depend on the type of culture in which they were brought up and in which they live is today universally accepted by sociologists, social anthropologists, and social psychologists. The same is true of the thesis that motives of behaviour are affected by two essential elements in any culture—the system of values and the objective living conditions.[8]

It can be said that each culture has its own specific values. But it is possible to hold a less extreme view, that certain cultures have similar, or even identical, sets of accepted values, but that these cultures differ from each other in the importance they attach to the various values. In other words, they differ as to the position of the various values in the structure of values as a whole. Both in the first and in the second case it is at least theoretically possible to have a culture in which the motive of personal material advantage and prestige is not one of the fundamental motives of human behaviour, not one of the fundamental motives underlying choice of occupation and job training (or, as a result, choice of social position).

I should like to put forward the hypothesis that in industrial societies which differ in their social organization (e.g., capitalist societies and socialist societies), it is possible that at least the inner structure of their system of values differs. The difference in this structure may consist not only of the different "weight" given to the diverse values in their whole system, but perhaps in the different "character" of the separate values.

Some values may be recognized as desirable because they themselves represent something desired; others may be recognized because they are a good means of attaining some other values. According to Davis and Moore, in the motivation of individuals education (knowledge, skill) and authority occur as values which are means of attaining the other values, material reward and prestige. In my opinion, the relationship between the values education and authority, and material reward and prestige, may be different. I also think that the striving for education or the striving for authority may be the chief motives of human behavior. Generally speaking, there is not any fixed constellation of values in their division between values-means and values-ends: there is not any universally pursued end-value either.

In Davis' and Moore's theory not only is it assumed that the motivation of the human individual is unchanging. It also assumes a certain unchanging "pattern" of society, or at least it assumes that some of the characteristics of that society are universal and permanent (this pattern again reminds us of classical political economy). If the authors assert that unequal distribution of material goods and of prestige must exist because otherwise people would not take the trouble to prepare for positions requiring training, then they assume that the acquisition of training is a matter of individual choice and effort, and that the acquisition of training also demands a certain amount of sacrifice. They also assume an insufficiency of products, the unequal distribution of these products according to position, and an insufficiency of trained personnel.

But other patterns of industrial societies are also possible. This may be illustrated by certain trends in the socialist countries or the *kibbutz* in Israel, although certain tendencies towards change can also be observed in contemporary capitalist societies. Trends towards the planned training and employment of qualified cadres, or towards the award of scholarships which relieve parents of the cost of educating their

[7] T. M. Newcomb, *Social Psychology*, New York, 1950, p. 137.

[8] Cf. J. W. Atkinson (Ed.), *Motives in Fantasy, Action and Society. A Method of Assessment and Study*. Part V. "Motivation and Society."

children, are becoming more and more marked in the modern world, especially in the socialist countries, but in the capitalist countries as well.

## MATERIAL ADVANTAGES

The values which drive people to acquire a training are material advantage and prestige. Both occur together in Davis' and Moore's theory. But they are separate values. They should therefore be examined separately. Let us first deal with material advantages.

Let us assume the existence of a society with the following attributes: (*a*) income differences are small, and the basic needs of most families are met; (*b*) education is assured without any sacrifice either on the part of the parent or of the child; the level of education of the community as a whole is relatively high; (*c*) the dominant ideas in the system of values are equality, social service, education and full development of personality.

In such a society, even where certain differences of income exist according to qualifications, it is possible that material advantages are not the main stimulus to education and training. Although the differences in material advantages exist, they may not result in significant differences in the standard of living. The system of values may not attach much importance to these differences, whereas the desire for full development of personality, and awakened interest in learning may make the desire to acquire education suiting the person's talents the principal motive for acquiring training. Education (knowledge, skill) which in Davis' and Moore's theory are values that are a means to an end, may in themselves become ends.

Certain elements in the situation described above are to be found in some contemporary societies. For example, in Poland (and similarly in Norway) there has been a distinct curtailment of the range of income. In Poland free education is open to all. At the same time, in propaganda more and more emphasis is being placed on education. Education, as some researches show, is very high on the scale of values accepted by the people for our country. Egalitarianism also has wide support—both in the sphere of postulates and in everyday behaviour.[9]

Like education, "authority" may appear as a value in itself and not as a means to an end. We assumed that, in Davis' and Moore's theory, material advantage and prestige are regarded as rewards for those who occupy positions of authority. But authority itself may be such a reward. Max Weber and Harold Lasswell wrote of this convincingly. In this connection it is worth noting that in industrial societies planning, and the general organizing of society, is becoming more common. In such a situation positions of authority provide an immense opportunity for the individual to express his own personality, his talents and ideas, quite apart from the opportunity such an individual has of satisfying his thirst for power, his desire to direct others.

Examples may be given illustrating the high value placed on authority by many people, even if it is not accompanied by material advantage or prestige. In present day conditions in Poland the factory foreman would seem to provide a good example. Neither in earnings nor in prestige is he superior to those under his authority. But the very fact that a foreman does have people under him is one of the assets of such a position, even although in other respects it does not stand very high.

Thus it seems quite possible to have an industrial society in which the differentiation of material advantages is not a "functional necessity." Positions calling for education and training, as well as positions of authority, may be filled not because they offer material advantages, but because their

[9] Cf. W. Wesołowski and A. Sarapata, "Hierarchia zawodów i stanowisk" ["Hierarchy of Jobs and Occupations"], *Studia Socjologiczne* 1961, No. 2. In recent research carried out in Łódź by Dr. A. Sarapata, 50% of the respondents replied "No" when asked if some occupations were more important than others—which should be regarded as a sign of an egalitarian attitude. In a new survey carried out by the present author on a sample of the rural population throughout Poland, the respondents were asked what should be the difference between incomes. About 65% declared that differences of income should be small. When asked who should earn more than the others, the majority of the respondents said "people whose work is the hardest."

principal attributes—skill, knowledge and power—prove to be sufficiently attractive. Those values, which in Davis' and Moore's theory are treated as intermediate values, may appear as end-values.

## PRESTIGE

As in the case when we analysed income differentiation, likewise in the case of prestige differentiation must we distinguish between: (*a*) the very existence of such differentiation, and (*b*) the role it fulfils as a stimulus for the occupation of "important positions requiring training." From the empirical point of view, such a differentiation may turn out to be extremely difficult; from the point of view of analysis, however, it is extremely important.

If differences of prestige were to be eliminated entirely, then we would have to have such a system of values in which "equality" would be a value completely outweighing all the other values (probably this would also necessitate the complete disappearance of differences in income, education, power and other social attributes). Even if we take it that egalitarian values are growing in favour and that more practical steps are being taken towards ensuring objective equality between people one can hardly imagine that a world without differences of prestige is imminent.

Yet the very fact that differences of prestige exist does not mean that Davis and Moore are right. For their theory states that prestige must occur as one of the main motives leading people to prepare for and fill social positions. Thus their theory would not hold true where education and authority were end-values, sufficiently strong to induce people to occupy certain positions in society. Differences in prestige connected with these positions would then cease to be "functionally necessary."

It is true that then there would be certain difficulties of interpretation.

If we accept the view that a desire for education (knowledge, skill) and a desire for authority act as motives for the occupation of important positions requiring training, then we must accept that education and authority are important values. And it would be difficult to imagine differences of education and differences of authority disappearing completely. In this situation, on the basis of differences of education and authority, there may arise different estimates as to the prestige of positions which have varying elements of skill and power.

The question therefore arises: should prestige differentiation then be treated as an epiphenomenon incapable of acting as principal stimulus, or should it be treated as an important stimulus giving rise to the desire to occupy positions which despite everything have greater prestige?

It is impossible at present to give an answer to this question. The whole situation is hypothetical. If ever such a situation were to exist, this question could be settled by means of research on the strength of various motives on the choice of social positions.[10]

## THE FUNCTIONAL ASPECT OF POWER AND STRATIFICATION

Material advantage and prestige are the two elements of stratification on which Davis and Moore concentrate their attention. They are inclined to relegate authority to the background. But from the functional point of view authority may be regarded as an important stratificatory element—perhaps even more fundamental than material advantage or prestige.

The "functionalism" of Davis' and Moore's theory consists mainly in the fact that it places stratification in the group of phenomena which in "functional analysis" are called "functional requirements," or "functional prerequisites" of every society.

There is no divergence of views that biological reproduction, the production of consumer goods, the socialization of the younger generation (together with indoctrination in some system of values), and social organization are functional prerequisites. The functionalists, however, tend to add to the number of these prerequisites.

[10] In our discussion we have avoided the question of divergence of motives of human behaviour, since this is a separate and extensive subject. It may only be mentioned that the values accepted in present-day societies are very varied and rather "autonomous" and in consequence there is a great variety of motive in choice of education and career. When a sufficiently high standard of living would be assured, this variety might be much more marked.

Because of the tendency to expand the "functional requirements" of any social system and in this way to attribute universality and permanence to the various elements of social life, the idea of these "functional requirements" has been fairly severely criticized. There has been a suggestion that "functional alternatives" should be sought and studied, that is, phenomena which may occur as the equivalents of other phenomena.[11]* Davis and Moore may be criticized because they declare stratification is universal by including it among the "functional prerequisites" of social life, and do not take into account the possibility that other phenomena may occur in its place, in the form of functional alternatives (e.g., such a system of values as would cause people to train and to fill positions of skill or authority without reckoning on future material advantages or prestige).

It is worth noting, however, that among the functional prerequisites of social life it would be difficult not to take social organization into account. Social life is group life. And group life involves the inner structuralization of the group. This structuralization consists among other things in the emergence of positions of command and subordination (as well as of "intermediate" positions at further stages of development). In such a structure, authority is unevenly distributed. For as soon as the positions of authority are filled, those who occupy the positions have the right (and duty) to give orders, while the others have the duty to obey them.

The inevitable occurrence of power relations of this kind in every complex social structure was long ago pointed out by social thinkers of very divergent theoretical orientations (quite independently of how they differed as to how positions of authority are, or should be, filled, or in whose interest authority is wielded, or what connection exists between the distribution of authority and the distribution of other values which occur as factors stratifying society, etc.). Engels, for example, who said that in a communist system the State as a weapon of class domination would wither away nevertheless declared that it would be impossible to think of any great modern industrial enterprise or of the organization of the future communist society without authority—or superiority-subordination relationships.[12] Mosca wrote, "There can be no human organization without rankings and subordination. Any sort of hierarchy necessarily requires that some should command and others obey."[13] M. Weber gave a number of reasons for the necessity of a functional division of authority in large administrative and political structures.[14] W. L. Warner is a contemporary author who explains in a brief form but explicitly the functional inevitability of stratification, pointing out that positions of authority are bound to occur.[15]

Davis and Moore seem to perceive the functional inevitability and stratifying role of authority relationships. Remarks on that are to be found in their considerations on "major societal functions" and the institutions fulfilling these functions. For example when they discuss "government" they say that "stratification is inherent in the nature of political relationships."[16] Yet they make no use of such a kind of observations in the construction of their theory. Neither do they explain how such statements are to be connected with the main propositions of their theory. Meanwhile it seems that these observations may lead us to quite a different explanation of the "functional inevitability" of stratification. This explanation may be as follows: The existence of great social structures creates social hierarchies built on authority. Thus if we are to take stratification to mean the

[11] Cf. R. K. Merton, "A Paradigm for Functional Analysis in Sociology," in *Social Theory and Social Structure,* Glencoe 1949.

* For an empirical study on this subject, see Richard D. Schwartz, "Functional Alternatives to Inequality," *American Sociological Review,* Vol. 20, August, 1955, pp. 424–430. (C. S. H.)

[12] F. Engels, "O zasadzie autorytetu" ["On the Principle of Authority"] in: K. Marx and F. Engels, *Dziela Wybrane* [*Selected Works*], Vol. I, Warszawa 1949.

[13] G. Mosca, *The Ruling Class,* New York 1939, p. 397.

[14] Cf. H. H. Gerth and C. W. Mills, *From Max Weber: Essays in Sociology,* New York 1958.

[15] W. L. Warner, M. Meeker and K. Eels, *Social Classes in America,* Chicago 1949, p. 8.

[16] Davis and Moore, *op. cit.,* p. 245.

occurrence of social positions among which there is an unequal distribution of some value, then it can be said that in the given structures there are positions among which the value which we call authority is unevenly distributed; in such cases, then, there is stratification along the dimension of authority.

In consequence it may be said that if there is any functional necessity for stratification, it is the necessity of stratification according to the criterium of authority and not according to the criterion of material advantage or prestige. Nor does the necessity of stratification derive from the need to induce people for the acquirement of qualifications, but from the very fact that humans live collectively.

# THE TUMIN–MOORE POLEMICS–REMAINING POINTS OF DISAGREEMENT [1]

*Wilbert E. Moore*

The opportunity for this further exchange has served both to reduce radically the previous area of disagreement and—because Tumin has addressed himself to the general issues of inequality creatively and not just defensively—to open up some new issues worthy of theoretical and empirical attention. Let me note some of the major points of agreement. (These represent a substantial modification of "original" positions on both sides of the controversy.)

It is agreed that performances will be differentially evaluated in terms of approximations to social values and normatively defined standards of conduct.

From the *American Sociological Review,* Vol. 28, February, 1963. Reprinted by permission.

[1] Title supplied. Appeared originally as "Rejoinder."

It is agreed that some social differentiation entails "intrinsic" inequality of position.

It is agreed that the relationship between such ubiquitous "inequalities" on the one hand and "stratification" as generalized and ranked social categories on the other is subject to investigation but by no means definitionally the same. Thus, one may theoretically imagine and, here and there, empirically encounter social differentiation with unequal rewards without this becoming a component of a "generalized" social status. Put the other way around, what Tumin calls the "diffusion" of inequality and its self-reinforcement have no intrinsic and necessary relationship to differential valuation of performance or differential valuation of functional positions.

It seems also to be agreed that the "utilization of human potential" is sub-optimal in all known social systems, and that in all known social systems the institutionalization of existing differentials is incomplete and subject to dynamic tensions. The implications of these dysfunctions and dynamic properties of unequal valuations seem still in dispute. I see no reason to suppose that the predictive inference to be drawn from them is a tendency to greater equality of position and reward.

Now what remains in useful contention? The first debatable issue, I suggest, revolves around Tumin's "minimal" estimate of the relevance of inequality. Let me start with his assertion of "the fact that in all societies the largest number of socially differentiated roles and social types do not involve differential evaluation and reward." Now if this allegation refers to evaluation of *performance* it is not only contradictory to the clearly stated concession on this point, but, more to the scientific point, it is overwhelmingly contravened by the evidence. If *positional* differentiation is the basis of the allegation, the matter is in principle subject to mensuration but none is in fact at hand. In the present state of knowledge, I suggest that the formulation is a non-fact. And although I shall note below that I dislike Tumin's extreme relativism concerning societies and cultures, I suggest here that any measurement of positions differentially evaluated or not would be highly relative to the degree of coalescence and consistency in status categories in one or another system of social "stratification." Thus the allegation appears patently false in a traditional "caste" system and probably in a totalitarian system of bureaucratic positions, as, say, in the Soviet Union.

I have spent some precious space on this point because Tumin reiterates twice more the assertion that most differentiation does not involve invidious valuation, but in the modified context of "stratification," narrowly speaking. I think it *is* agreed that functionally specific inequalities *may* not be generalized into a singular status or aggregates of such statuses into a stratum, but it is not at all established that functional differentiation and unequal valuation are independently variable.

The general position Tumin has espoused in his latest statement is debatable in several respects that warrant specification. He has adopted an extremely relativistic view of cultural values and social institutions that seems to me empirically unwarranted and theoretically doubtful. Without using the Sumnerian phrase, "the mores can make anything right," that is the position he has taken. As I read the evidence, the evaluation of functionally differentiated positions is by no means as randomly variable as his discussion asserts or implies. I suggest that behavior relevant to the maintenance of order, the provision of economic support, the protection of the society, and the exemplifications of religious and esthetic values *always* involves differential positional as well as merely personal valuation. Tumin's cultural relativism and his notion that anything is possible through socialization represent a kind of denial of orderly and reliable generalizations about human societies. I do not think this denial is immoral; it is just wrong.

Although Tumin asserts that scarce personnel can be motivated to take up functionally critical tasks without differential rewards, "or at least with much less and much less enduring forms of such invidious distinctions," there is surely no evidence for the bald assertion, without the modification, which he reiterates in subsequent paragraphs. I spoke of improbable "martyrdom" in the performance of exceptional tasks without unequal recognition and I still have no reason to retreat from my critical positions.

Tumin links an extreme cultural relativism and extensive randomness of cultural components with an extreme bio-social determinism within a *given* system. His final moral argument in behalf of rather extensive equality is to the effect that there is little social justice in rewarding differential talent (and performance?) which derives either from hereditary accident or the character of socialization that is imposed by the very system that allocates rewards. But here he uses a tell-tale, saving phrase, "assuming equal conscientiousness." Surely by now our understanding of the complex interplay between the individual and the social order does not permit so deterministic a view of human motivation or so easy a dismissal of the importance of purpose in human behavior. Though it is extremely unlikely that any social system will be able to overlook the consequences of the accident of birth in either the biological or sociological sense, since differential placement will likely take such consequences into account, there surely remains some interstitial area of human effort, or purpose, or conscientiousness that cannot be readily reduced to the influence of human heredity or the social environment. Though it is clearly the business of the sociologist to seek out the social sources and correlates of patterned human behavior, I do not think the evidence warrants the comfortable and individual guilt-absolving or excellence-degrading view that society is all and the complexities of individual motivation a purely dependent variable. Perhaps this difference of view only confirms the notion that assumptions regarding human nature underlie most if not all structural propositions of substantial generality.

Tumin and I have both been guilty, in these short statements, of anthropomorphizing "society." Such ellipsis is normally harmless, but I do want to dissent on one point. When Tumin stipulates as a condition for the "functional theory" of social inequality that the society be "rational," I suggest two modifications. The first is the evolutionary, "survival" test which Tumin has earlier doubted but not destroyed. The second point is that the denial of rationalism in a social decision-making is untenable, since it conspicuously exists as a norm in all contemporary societies, and, now and then, as a practice.

The protagonists in the current renewal of an enduring controversy are scarcely the designated spokesmen for recognizable clienteles. And lest it be thought that the issues relevant to stratification are all resolved or clarified, it should be noted that the whole concept of "class" as an explanatory variable has been barely touched in this exchange. Tumin in his suggested desiderata for the next steps in analysis of social inequality happily does not use the term "class"—which unfortunately our neighboring social scientists think is one of our most useful analytic tools—and his way of putting the questions does not presuppose that conceptual category. Can we get anyone to join the joyful march to sensible investigation?

# SOCIAL INEQUALITY WITHOUT SOCIAL STRATIFICATION

*Dennis H. Wrong*

Recently, several sociologists have, notwithstanding the increased preoccupation of their colleagues with the subject of class, argued that the concept of social class is becoming more and more irrelevant to understanding advanced industrial societies.[1] They have largely confined their remarks to the United States. Several European writers, however, have made similar suggestions with respect to the major countries of Western Europe, though rather more tentatively since much that has already become a reality in America remains a trend on the other side of the Atlantic.[2] On the whole, the claim that social classes have disappeared or are disappearing has been rejected by the majority of American sociologists. For the most part their rejection has been based on little more than a preference for different definitions of class and has been offered good-humoredly as if the matter were merely a trivial issue of terminology. Yet, as so often in sociology, definitions defended on pragmatic or operational grounds turn out on closer examination to obscure full recognition of the contrast between past and present and of the new possibilities latent in contemporary social reality.

Sociologists who argue that social class is no longer a useful concept take what has been called a "realist" position regarding the existence of classes. They are committed, that is, to the view that, in the words of one of them, social classes "are groups possessed both of real and vital common economic interests and of a group-consciousness of their general position in the social scale."[3] Their contention that social classes are disappearing in industrial societies rests on the failure to locate such groups. The opposing "nominalist" point of view regards classes as a useful classificatory concept for grouping together for purposes of analysis individuals who possess certain attributes in common, whether or not they feel any unity or are even aware of having something in common with their fellow class members. The sociologist, in effect, creates the "class structures" he describes, which are no more than a means of organizing his data on variations in human behavior. He may find several different class systems or pyramids of

This is a revised version of a paper presented to the annual meeting of the American Sociological Association in Los Angeles, August, 1963, and published in the *Canadian Review of Sociology and Anthropology*, Vol. 1. Reprinted by permission.

[1] Arnold M. Rose, "The Concept of Class and American Sociology," *Social Research*, XXV, Spring, 1958, 53–69; Robert A. Nisbet, "The Decline and Fall of Social Class," *Pacific Sociological Review, II*, Spring, 1959, 11–17; Wilbert E. Moore, "But Some Are More Equal Than Others," *American Sociological Review*, XXVIII, February, 1963, 14–15.

[2] T. H. Marshall, "General Survey of Changes in Social Stratification in the Twentieth Century," *Transactions of the Third World Congress of Sociology*, International Sociological Association, 1956, III, 1–17; George Lichtheim, *The New Europe: Today and Tomorrow* (New York, 1963), 198–215.

[3] Marshall, *ibid.*, 15.

stratification within a society, none of which are perceived or experienced as collective realities, as real social groups, by their members.

A denial of the existence of social classes as defined by the "realist" perspective, however, in no way implies a trend towards general equality or social uniformity. Inequalities in the distribution of income, the invidious ranking of occupations with respect to prestige or status, and functional hierarchies of power and authority may remain solidly established in the absence of social classes. Individuals or social roles may be ranked with respect to varying income, status or power, as is commonly done by sociological researchers, but the categories or percentiles into which individuals or roles are grouped are not social classes in the realist sense unless there is independent evidence that their members are internally cohesive and see themselves as a distinct collectivity with *common* rather than merely *like* goals, interests and values.

The so-called "realist versus nominalist" dispute over the kind of objective reality that should be ascribed to social classes has long been a standard theoretical and methodological issue in discussions of social stratification. Yet it has not always been acknowledged that all of the major nineteenth- and twentieth-century theorists of class were unmistakably "realists," regardless of whether they thought classes were based on economic interests, shared values, or common access to social power.

To Marx, a class was not fully formed until it had ceased to be merely a potential membership-group (*Klasse an sich*) and had achieved a solidarity based on awareness of the common interests of its members in opposition to those of another class (*Klasse für sich*).

Joseph Schumpeter wrote: "Class is something more than an aggregation of class members. . . . A class is aware of its identity as a whole, sublimates itself as such, has its own peculiar life and characteristic 'spirit.'"[4]

Max Weber is frequently cited by American sociologists in support of the contention that stratification in modern societies involves at least three partially independent hierarchies, one of wealth, one of prestige, and one of power. He is also often invoked to justify the treatment of status rankings of occupations as synonymous with "class structure." Weber is the source of the "wealth–status-power" triad so favored by contemporary sociologists, but he was clearly concerned with identifying relatively cohesive groups differentiated with respect to these three bases of stratification and did not consider each as forming a continuous scale on which individuals or positions could be located. Thus, defining "class," like Marx, in strictly economic terms, he saw classes as "possible, and frequent, bases for communal action," although he was less certain than Marx that aggregates of people sharing like interests would become aware of their common interests and resort to "communal action" to advance them. Commonly regarded as the first modern social theorist to stress the importance of status, Weber was chiefly concerned to describe "status groups" or *Stände*—a term that clearly designates self-conscious collectivities. With reference to power, he used the less fortunate term "party," which nevertheless is unambiguous in connoting a collective entity rather than an attribute with respect to which individuals or roles vary continuously.

Finally, W. Lloyd Warner has always insisted that the six social classes he discovered in Newburyport, Massachusetts, were ultimately derived from "the way in which people in American communities actually classify themselves," although his critics have repeatedly challenged the validity of this claim after re-analyzing Warner's own data.

I doubt that any of these men would have devoted so much time and effort to the study of class had they thought it a matter of indifference whether classes "really" existed in the experience of their members or were no more than artifacts constructed by the sociologist as a means of ordering and summarizing his observations. The grouping together by the sociologist of individuals sharing a common position with respect to several distinct variables is a thoroughly legitimate and useful procedure in certain kinds of empirical research. But to call the

[4] Joseph A. Schumpeter, *Imperialism and Social Classes* (New York, 1955), 107.

resultant groupings "social classes" is to risk confusion with the quite different meaning of class in the writings of the leading theorists of stratification. Researchers who use such terms as "socioeconomic group" or "level" at least implicitly recognize the distinction. But there are others who persist in referring to combined measures of occupation, income, or education as "indexes" of social class, although the entity these measures allegedly indicate appears to have no independent reality and "class" becomes no more than a shorthand expression for the ensemble of the very variables that have been combined to form the index.[5]

Critics of the realist conception of social classes have attributed to it the necessary implication that members of a society must be fully aware of the class system and that its nature can therefore be determined by a simple opinion poll.[6] Surely, this is a specious argument. To assert that social controls and expectancies are present in the minds and sentiments of the people whose conduct they influence is not to maintain that these people can readily put them into words. Consider social norms in primary groups, which are clearly operative influences on behavior; those who conform to them are not always able to provide a coherent account of the codes that guide and restrain them in their day-to-day interactions with others.[7] The kind of awareness-in-behavior that frequently characterizes social class relations may involve still less self-consciousness since classes (except in small isolated local communities) are not even potential primary groups; hence the frequent use of the term "quasi-group" to describe them.

The existence of classes, however, is a matter of degree depending upon the extent to which their members are conscious of their unity and of the boundaries separating them from other classes.[8] But recognition of this does not invalidate the realist position. All the theorists previously mentioned, with the exception of the ahistorical Warner, dealt at length with what Schumpeter called *class formation* and saw it as a process frequently falling short of the eventual emergence of fully developed classes. All of them attempted to specify the conditions under which aggregates of similarly situated individuals acquire cohesion and begin to behave as if they constitute at least a fictive membership-group. Nor does the existence of individuals or families whose position is marginal within the class structure pose special theoretical difficulties, for this is an inevitable result of inter-class mobility, which is also a temporal process of uncertain outcome.

Finally, if the existence of a class system implies *some* stratification, it is also possible for particular classes—most frequently new and rising classes—to exist which do not fit into an orderly hierarchical system.[9] Thus if we regard social stratification as a stratification of groups, classes may be formed in partial independence of stratification. But,

[5] Marshal, *op. cit.*, 5–6; Rose, *op. cit.*, 65–69.

[6] See, for example, Bernard Barber, *Social Stratification* (New York, 1957), 76–7; Nelson N. Foote, Walter Goldschmidt, Richard Morris, Melvin Seeman and Joseph Shister, "Alternative Assumptions in Stratification Research," *Transactions of the Second World Congress of Sociology*, International Sociological Association, 1953, II, 386–7.

[7] William F. Whyte reports that his main informant, Doc, remarked to him: "Now when I do something, I have to think what Bill Whyte would want to know about it and how I can explain it. ... Before I used to do these things by instinct." *Street Corner Society* (Chicago, 1943), 10.

Many of the simplifications to which sociologists are prone in discussing the question of the degree to which people are aware of the determinants of their own behavior result from a failure to take into account Ryle's distinction between "knowing how" and "knowing that." See Gilbert Ryle, *The Concept of Mind* (New York, 1949), 25–61.

[8] As Andreas Miller has written: "A social class is a real group, set aside from its social environment by natural boundaries. ... In a classless society one can speak of differences in social status. It would, however, be of no value to look for a class-system in a society without differences in social status. ... An adequate conception of the class-system can only be reached by answering the question whether the community investigated is divided into strata by clear boundaries, what is their number, location, and strength." "The Problem of Class Boundaries and Its Significance for Research into Class Structure," *Transactions of the Second World Congress of Sociology*, 1953, II, 343, 348–9.

[9] Stanislaw Ossowski, "Old Notions and New Problems: Interpretations of Social Structure in Modern Society," *Transactions of the Third World Congress of Sociology*, 1956, III, 18–25.

more important, inequalities in the distribution of income, prestige, and power may exist in complete independence of it.

So far, my emphasis has been primarily definitional and I have done no more than insist on a number of distinctions that are widely recognized in principle, although often ignored in research practice. Applied to contemporary industrial societies, however, these distinctions are acquiring new relevance, for modern societies are unmistakably moving in the direction of maintaining considerable institutionalized inequality in the absence of a class system, a condition that the Polish sociologist, Stanislaw Ossowski, has characterized as "non-egalitarian classlessness."[10] This condition has not yet been fully achieved even in the United States, much less in Western Europe. But the steady approach toward it increasingly transforms social classes into "ghost" communities preserving a fitful and wavering identity rooted in historical memories, similar to that ascribed by Nathan Glazer to the "ghost nations" of third-generation American immigrants which continue to play a minor role in American politics.[11]

Since so many American sociologists have failed to see any significance in the disappearance of social classes in view of the survival of pronounced status inequalities, I shall briefly suggest several differences between societies where classes to some degree are present and societies where social inequality is relatively detached from stratification.

1. Income, educational and status mobility are experienced differently in the two societies. The person who moves upward (or downward) in a classless society does not encounter a class boundary in addition to the career obstacles he has to overcome in order to rise. Surely, it is the relative absence of classes in American society, whatever the historical causes for this absence, that accounts for the general belief that mobility is greater in the United States than in Europe, a belief that Lipset and Bendix have shown to be unfounded.[12] Quite minor improvements in status or income are more readily perceived as mobility where no class boundary has to be crossed or confronted. There have been no real counterparts in the United States to the British "angry young men": persons of provincial and working-class origin who rise through educational or occupational attainment but become embittered on experiencing real or imagined exclusion when they try to cross a class line. The closest American equivalent is the experience of upwardly mobile Negroes and members of ethnic or religious minorities. The fact that occupational status rankings are similar in America and Britain, and indeed in all advanced industrial societies,[13] merely underlines the difference between these rankings and a social class system.

2. More important, a distinction between stratification and social inequality aids us in understanding the political sociology of modern industrial societies. The distinction holds, it should be noted, regardless of whether economic interest or style-of-life is considered the essential basis of class. The latter—the "Marx vs. Warner" issue—is a separate definitional problem. However, last-ditch defenders of the relevance of the class concept, such as Rudolph Heberle in a recent paper,[14] fall back on the Marxist view of classes as interest-groups divided by ownership or non-ownership of the means of production. They plausibly argue that, although classes separated by sharp status and associational boundaries have been largely supplanted by a continuous hierarchy of status, conflicts of interest have by no means disappeared and the major opposing groups continue to think and act in concert politically, at the very least in their voting behavior. The prediction of American Marxists in the 1930s that national cleavages of economic interest would increasingly

[10] Stanislaw Ossowski, *Class Structure in the Social Consciousness* (New York, 1963), 100–18.

[11] Nathan Glazer, "Ethnic Groups in America: From National Culture to Ideology," in Morroe Berger, Charles H. Page and Theodore Abel, editors, *Freedom and Control in Modern Society* (New York, 1954), 172–3.

[12] Seymour Martin Lipset and Reinhard Bendix, *Social Mobility in Industrial Society* (Berkley, 1959), 11–75.

[13] Alex Inkeles and Peter H. Rossi, "National Comparisons of Occupational Prestige," *American Journal of Sociology*, LXI, January, 1956, 329–39.

[14] Rudolph Heberle, "Recovery of Class Theory," *Pacific Sociological Review*, II, Spring, 1959, 18–28.

supersede regional and ethnic divisions as the main basis of political alignment has on the whole been borne out.

But a second part of the prediction was that more tightly drawn class lines would result in an intensification of the political class struggle between Left and Right. The opposite has occurred: "class" has become a more important determinant of voting at the same time that the bitterness of class struggle has unmistakably abated.[15] While it may, therefore, be formally correct to insist that the term "class" in the Marxist sense is still applicable where society-wide conflicts of interest find political expression, it is surely more relevant to the understanding of modern politics to recognize that today economic interest-groups and the political associations based on them do not, in T. H. Marshall's words, "permeate the whole lives of their members, as social classes do, nor are they always in action, and at times the constituent sub-groups may be more important than the largest aggregates."[16]

Ralf Dahrendorf attributes the obsolescence of the Marxist two-class sytem to what he aptly calls the "institutional isolation of industry" in modern society. But he tries to preserve the emphasis on conflict and change in Marxist class theory by redefining classes as the result of tension between power-holders and their subordinates, arguing that the division between owners and non-owners of property, and even conflicts of economic interest in general are merely special cases of this more fundamental phenomenon.[17] Dahrendorf does not hesitate to conclude that there are as many class systems in a modern society as there are functional hierarchies of power and that a single individual may therefore simultaneously be a member of several different classes if he belongs to several associations each with its own structure of authority. In effect, Dahrendorf makes three main contentions: that social conflict is generated by differences in power; that classes are conflict-groups; and that all conflict-groups are classes. He may be right on the first two points (I am inclined to think that he is), but the third assertion surely represents the most quixotic effort to uphold the continuing usefulness of the concept of class in recent sociological writing.[18] Moreover, it would seem to be of no use at all in understanding the major political divisions in modern societies, although this has been precisely the most valuable feature of class theories which take their point of departure from Marx. Yet notwithstanding the inadequacies of his own class theory, Dahrendorf shows a far more acute grasp of the many differences between stratified and non-egalitarian classless societies than most American sociologists.

3. The absence of classes also helps account for the invisibility of poverty in the United States, to which several writers have recently called attention. The poor are composed of a number of categories of persons with particular demographic characteristics whose economic plight is no longer clearly linked to what Marx or Weber would consider a "class situation."[19] Both in status and in economic terms, only the American Negroes come close to constituting a definable and cohesive deprived group, with the possible exception of tenant farmers and

[15] Seymour Martin Lipset, *Political Man* (New York, 1960), especially chapters IX and XIII.

[16] Marshall, *op. cit.*, 13.

[17] Ralf Dahrendorf, *Class and Class Conflict in Industrial Society* (Stanford, Calif., 1959), especially Part Two.

[18] Both Kurt B. Mayer and Lewis A. Coser have similarly criticized Dahrendorf's thesis in reviews of his book. See Mayer's review of the German edition, *American Sociological Review*, XXIII, October, 1958, 592–3, and of the English edition, *ibid.*, XXV, April, 1960, 288; and Coser, *American Journal of Sociology*, LXV, March, 1960, 520–1.

[19] An exhaustive study of poverty in the United States by Oscar Ornati indicates that the following were "poverty-linked characteristics" in 1960: Non-white, Female head of household, Age 65 and over, Age 14–24 head of household. Rural Farm, Residence in South, Non-wage earner, Part-time wage earner, More than Six Children under 18, Education less than 8 years. None of the groups defined by these characteristics, with the possible exception of Rural Farm, represents a socioeconomic class. Ornati, *Poverty in an Affluent Society*, Preliminary Draft, New York: The New School for Social Research and The Twentieth Century Fund (Mimeographed), chapter 5. For a discussion of the non-class nature of contemporary American poverty see Henry M. Pachter, "The Income Revolution," *Dissent*, IV, Summer, 1957, 315–18.

laborers in certain sectors of the agricultural economy. There is indeed some justification for calling Negroes *the* American lower class.[20]

The emerging social structure of post-bourgeois industrial society can best be understood if, except for secondary purposes and for historical analysis, we abandon the concept of social class and redefine much of the work done under this label as a contribution to the sociology of equality and inequality. But American sociologists have been unwilling to make this necessary redefinition, in part for ideological reasons.

Celebrations of the United States have traditionally affirmed its "classlessness" and extolled at the same time the equality of opportunity to attain unequal rewards it allegedly provides. In challenging the reality of the latter, sociologists have been unwilling to concede any truth to the claim of classlessness lest they should appear to be denying the facts of inequality and barriers to opportunity. A spirit of liberal muckraking still pervades much American sociological writing on stratification whether the writer's intent is to deplore or, like W. Lloyd Warner to counsel adjustment to the "brute facts" of inequality that are concealed or minimized by the official egalitarian ideology. The result has been that sociologists have perpetuated the very confusion of classlessness with equality that the official ideology makes.

American sociologists have failed to see that the absence of classes may both in ideology and in social fact *more* effectively conceal existing inequalities than a social structure clearly divided into recognizable classes. The invisibility of poverty in the United States, already referred to, suggests such a conclusion, as does the fact that income distribution has become more unequal in the past decade,[21] the very decade of the "affluent society," which has witnessed so much individual and collective mobility, the mass diffusion of formerly restricted status symbols, and the breakdown of long-standing ethnic, religious, and even racial barriers to opportunity.

In distinguishing conceptually between stratification and inequality and noting some of the consequences of their increasing factual separation in contemporary society, I have avoided direct discussion of mobility and equality of opportunity. Many writers who have insisted as I have that stratification involves a hierarchy of groups rather than of positions or of individuals possessing unequal amounts of income, prestige, and power, have gone on to argue that stratified groups, or social classes, must necessarily be hereditary.[22] By transmitting the unequal privileges of one generation to the next through the family, classes thus inevitably prevent the full institutionalization of equality of opportunity.

The class systems of the past have undeniably been hereditary, though permitting sufficient mobility to justify distinguishing them from *caste* systems. But need this be so in the future? Historically, biological continuity has been the major means of preserving the internal solidarity and the distinctive ethos of classes from generation to generation, but is it necessarily the only possible means? George Orwell wrote: "The essence of oligarchical rule is not father-to-son inheritance, but the persistence of a certain world-view and a certain way of life imposed by the dead upon the living. A ruling group is a ruling group so long as it can nominate its successors. Who wields power is not important, provided that the hierarchical structure remains always the same."[23] Orwell was writing of political elites, but his point that permanence of structure need not depend on biological continuity may well have a broader relevance. Hereditary social classes may not be succeeded by non-egalitarian classlessness but by new classes whose members are not recruited by

[20] Rose, *op. cit.*, 64.

[21] I am indebted to Oscar Ornati for having shown me the data from a later section of his study, *Poverty in an Affluent Society*, indicating this to be unmistakably the case.

[22] See especially Walter Buckley, "Social Stratification and the Functional Theory of Social Differentiation," *American Sociological Review*, XXIII, August, 1958, 369–75; and Kurt B. Mayer, "The Changing Shape of the American Class Structure," *Social Research*, XXX, Winter, 1963, 458–68.

[23] *Nineteen Eighty-Four* (New York, 1949), 370–1.

the intergenerational transmission of privileges through the family and whose cohesion does not depend on familial socialization.

Equality of opportunity could literally be achieved in full only by a method of allocating individuals to social positions that was strictly random, such as drawing lots. In contrasting equal opportunity with the inheritance of social position, however, sociologists obviously mean by the former the allocation of individuals to positions according to the single criterion of demonstrated ability to carry out the position's requirements. They have usually assumed that equality of opportunity thus defined is not only morally superior to any hereditary principle but would also prove to be more humanly tolerable, eliminating the social gulf that has existed between hereditary social classes and removing the envy and sense of injustice of low-status individuals who feel deprived of social rewards only by the accident of birth.

There is some evidence that the absence of clear-cut class lines in the United States and the prevailing "democracy of manners" make it easier for low-status individuals to tolerate hereditary inequalities provided they continue to believe that at least *some* opportunity to rise is available to them and their children.[24] But the most devastating attack on the belief that an inegalitarian order combined with full equal opportunity would reduce social conflict has been made by the English sociologist, Michael Young, in his brilliant sociological satire *The Rise of the Meritocracy: 1870–2033.*[25] . . .

Young's book is cast in the form of an historical interpretation written by a sociologist in the year 2033. His meritocratic social order is located in England, rather than "nowhere," and its evolution under the pressure of social forces powerfully at work in today's world is fully described. . . . The meritocracy is the result of three forces: the attack by socialists on all hereditary privileges, the pace of international economic competition requiring Britain to maintain high rates of economic growth,[26] and improvements in intelligence testing which have made it possible to reorganize the school system so that students can be segregated by intelligence at progressively earlier ages and trained for their eventual positions in the social order. The testing centers and the school system thus have become the vehicles for selecting the ruling elite of meritocrats. Possessing a monopoly of ability, the meritocracy easily prevails in conflicts of interest with the lower strata, who are completely bereft of leadership since all their potential leaders have been elevated into the meritocracy, and who must live with the knowledge that they have been scientifically proven to be inferior in ability to their rulers. The family, however, has survived in its present form and, echoing the functional theory of inequality, Young sees this as the Achilles heel of the regime. The meritocratic parents of inferior children and women, whose occupational skills suffer as a result of their withdrawal to bear and raise children, become infected with a discontent that eventually leads to revolution.

In Young's account the meritocracy clearly constitutes a unified ruling group, sharing common interests and a similar style of life, even though it is not recruited by heredity. And the same is true to a lesser degree of the "technicians"—the regime's euphemism for the industrial working class. Rather than defining class and stratification by the hereditary principle and calling the meritocracy a "classless" or unstratified society, it is surely more reasonable to see it as a new form of class society.

Yet one must raise some doubts about the general relevance of Young's meritocracy to contemporary trends in advanced industrial societies. One might question, to begin with, his assumption that the family will remain cohesive and unchanged when so much else has been transformed. More important, the very plausibility of Young's account

[24] Robert E. Lane, *Political Ideology: Why the American Common Man Believes What He Does* (New York, 1962), 57–81.

[25] London, 1958, *passim.*

[26] Several writers have recently argued that the maintenance of high rates of economic growth sets severe limits to the achievement of greater equality of condition as distinct from equality of opportunity. See George Lichtheim, *The New Europe,* New York: Frederick A. Praeger, 1963, 188–9; also C. A. R. Crosland, *The Conservative Enemy* (New York, Schocken Books, 1962), 29–34.

depends heavily on the roots of the meritocracy in English history with its characteristic "inevitability of gradualness." Thus Young sees the sharpness of class lines and the steepness of the status hierarchy that have existed in English society from feudalism to the present day as surviving even when birth has been entirely supplanted by merit as the basis of status. While the independence of stratification in general from the particular form of stratification by hereditary social classes is thus brilliantly suggested, one is forced to wonder whether a meritocracy would have the same consequences in an industrial society that lacked the pervasive continuities of English history—in, say, the United States.

I know of only one even sketchy account of a possible American meritocracy. It is provided, not by a sociologist, but by a lawyer and unsuccessful politician, Stimson Bullitt, in his perceptive little book *To Be a Politician.*[27] Bullitt envisages an American meritocratic order as being far more stable and less riven by class conflict than Young's Britain. He writes:

> The free flow up and down and the narrow range of variations in revealed ability among members of the great majority will make class differences less sharp. Also, the classes will be equally well fed and in most ways equally free; people on different levels of talent will be closer in many ways than were the social classes of the past. All people will have greater understanding, and therefore sympathy, for persons on other levels of talent than used to be the case between classes whose members lived like different species. (177–8.)

While Bullitt attributes the absence of class tensions in a meritocratic United States in part to general prosperity and a high degree of material equality, conditions which are absent in Young's less economically self-sufficient England—the traditional classlessness of American society clearly leads him to anticipate an American meritocracy that would resemble a continuous hierarchy of unequal positions rather than Young's more stratified order.

Will the decline of hereditary social classes and the trend toward meritocracy eventuate in non-egalitarian classlessness or in a new class society allocating individuals by specialized abilities rather than by birth? What will be the peculiar discontents of each order? What form will the ancient dream of an egalitarian society, equally frustrated by both, take under these conditons? These are likely to be the questions, only dimly adumbrated in our present imperfectly affluent society, with which future sociologists of inequality will concern themselves. We are not likely to make much progress in answering them if we cling to a conceptual apparatus that does not distinguish between stratification and inequality or between stratification in general and the particular form it has taken in the hereditary class societies of the past.

[27] (New York, Doubleday Anchor Books, 1961), 162–93.

# BEYOND THE RULING CLASS—STRATEGIC ELITES

*Suzanne Keller*

Influential minorities exist in all organized societies. Whether a community is small or large, rich or poor, simple or complex, it always sets some of its members apart as very important, very powerful, or very prominent. The notion of a stratum elevated above the mass of men may prompt approval, indifference, or despair, but regardless of how men feel about it, the fact remains that their lives, fortunes, and fate are and have long been dependent on what a small number of men in high places think and do.

The reasons for the ubiquity and persistence of such leading minorities are not easy to fathom, being rooted in complex needs for social leadership in simple and more advanced societies. Wherever we find large-scale multipurpose organizations

This selection was especially prepared for this volume. Part of it is drawn by the author from her book, *Beyond the Ruling Class,* 1963. Reprinted by permission from Random House, Inc.

called societies, sustained by such leadership groups, we may anticipate the presence of such leadership groups. And just as individual leaders of small primary groups have been shown to embody the salient characteristics and aims of their followers, so the leadership of a society will likewise exhibit that society's characteristic traits, ideals, and purposes, and will vary in structure, style, and stance as these do.

Modern industrial societies may thus be expected to possess leadership groups appropriate to their structure and purposes. Mass democracy, social mobility, and technological diversity notwithstanding, socially significant elites are no less essential in these societies than in feudal, classical, or primitive ones. In fact, in certain respects, their significance is actually growing as one of the striking trends of our time is not, as many would have supposed, toward a decline of elite groups, but toward their proliferation, greater variety, and more extensive, though highly specialized, powers. The very fact of social, technical, and economic differentiation makes imperative the emergence of unifying and coordinating elements which these elites, as guardians and creators of common purpose and as managers of collective aims and ambitions, exemplify.

Elites are therefore fundamental to social continuity and social order in any differentiated aggregate, from delinquent gangs, to socialist political parties, to pluralist societies. And everywhere, their rule is rather similar even if their specific characteristics, tactics, and tastes vary with time, place, and circumstances. Essentially, they are expected to keep their establishments in working order, confronting and surpassing the minor and major crises that occur by giving a sense of purpose and direction to the totality. How they do so and how successful they are affect for good or ill the destinies of men and of nations.

This brings us to the question of which elites to study, and this depends on how they are defined. In noting that all elites are important in some social and psychological context, we must not fall into the error of attributing equal social importance to all. Those elites having major and sweeping social significance must somehow be distinguished from the rest. There is in effect a hierarchy among elites with some—beauty queens, criminal masterminds, champion bridge players, and master chefs—holding top rank in specific pyramids of talent or power but lacking a sustained general social impact. Other elites—leading generals, scientists, and statesmen—do have such an impact, as their judgments, decisions, and actions have determinable consequences for all or most members of society. These we designate as the *strategic* elites thereby distinguishing them from segmental elites. Strategic elites, in our view, comprise not only political, economic, and military leaders, but also normal, cultural, and recreational ones. Whether or not an elite is counted as strategic depends not so much on its particular activities than on its scope, impact, and society-wide influence.

The social significance of an elite cannot be discerned by examining either the intrinsic nature of activities, or the intrinsic motives and desires of its actual and potential members. It is thus misleading to make the subjective desires of individuals for wealth, fame, or power account for the existence of elite positions that provide such rewards. For this confuses the role of an elite in the life of society with individual reasons and justifications for wanting to participate in that role. The objective responsibilities of elites and the subjective rewards of their members are distinct dimensions that cannot be inferred from one another. For example, an individual may understandably aspire to a leading position in the world of big business in order to amass a personal fortune, but from this one can hardly conclude that the major social task of the business elite is the private accumulation of wealth. Even if this were the principal preoccupation of an individual member, it would not describe their collective responsibilities of directing the economic affairs of society in accord with prevailing standards and values. In any case, objective function and subjective reward must be considered apart if they are to aid our understanding of the system of values underlying the preeminence of given elites.

***Elites as a Special Form of Societal Leadership.*** Strategic elites have both novel and familiar aspects, reflecting their kinship with older social forms from which they sprang as well as the new forces at work in a complex and changing world. The ruins of many extinct civilizations and the pasts of living ones are replete with a family of institutions with whom these elites are frequently confused—ruling castes, aristocracies, high estates, and ruling classes. Close scrutiny suggests that strategic elites are a crystallization, an outgrowth, a further development of these precursors, and may be viewed as structural alternatives to them, representing a more specialized form of social leadership. In this sense, of course, strategic elites are as old as the first organized human societies, with their leading minorities of priests, elders, warrior kings, or legendary sages and heroes—agents for and symbols of the common life. The new features stem from changed patterns of selection and reward as well as the changed demands made on them.

### STRATEGIC ELITES AND RULING CLASSES

To help clarify this point let us contrast two of the five principal types of social leadership groups—that of a ruling caste and that of a ruling class. A ruling caste comprises a homogeneous stratum expected to perform the most important social tasks and recruit its personnel through biological reproduction. Ranking highest in prestige, it is set apart from the rest of society by religion, kinship, language, residence, economic standing, and occupational activities. Social control is enforced by religious ritual rather than by a centralized body of law, and the state is either nonexistent or plays a minor role in the life of society. Individuals enter the ruling caste through birth and leave it through death. The chief characteristics of caste systems—their rigidity and permanence—can be traced to how the ruling caste is recruited and maintained.

Social leadership concentrated in a ruling class also exhibits the presence of a single stratum in charge of various key social functions. However, it is recruited in a variety of ways and although heredity continues to provide access to this class it no longer constitutes the chief justification for such access. Lineage makes way for property and wealth, whether ascribed or achieved. The members of a ruling class share not only their functional positions but also more general habits and culture.

Social leadership exercised by strategic elites differs from each of these. For one thing, several social strata may supply personnel to the leading social positions. Merit, regardless of other attributes—sex, race, class, religion, or even age—is the predominant justification for attaining elite positions, thus destroying the notion of all-round excellence or over-all superiority.

Selection on the basis of individual competence implies dismissal for incompetence, and this principle links these modern elites to the primitive institution of chiefship, where the chief—be he priest, king, or warrior—may be killed if he fails to bring about the desired end: peace, the harvest, or health. Thus strategic elites are marked by functional specialization and recruitment on the basis of proven capacity to perform their specialized roles. Along with the specialization, diversity, and impermanence of elites, new problems arise—those of cohesion and unity, morale, balance, and a new type of interdependence at the top, now requiring the cooperation of several interdependent strategic elites. No single elite can outrank all others because no one elite knows enough about the specialized work of all others. In sum, strategic elites differ from ruling classes and castes in their manner of recruitment, internal organization, and degree of specialization. Strategic elites, in some form, exist in every organized human society; ruling classes do not and need not. And although strategic elites have emerged from ruling classes and castes, they cannot be equated with them. As modern equivalents of these earlier historic forms, they also have their unique aspects, which must be assessed and appraised in their own right.

### STRATEGIC ELITES AND SOCIAL CLASSES

Elites have often been discussed as if they were interchangeable with social classes. But although the two are related they are by no means identical. The origin of strategic elites (as of all top leadership groups) lies in the heterogeneity of the community—as regards age, sex, ethnicity, skills, strength, and the like. The origin of social classes lies in the social division of labor and the hierarchy of values associated with it.

Both phenomena increase as social differentiation increases. Even without attributing to primitive societies a perfect harmony and homogeneity, it is evident that their relatively small degree of differentiation separates them sharply from the occupationally and technologically more advanced communities. And it is this internal differentiation that permits the rise of strategic elites—where it is slight, elites are few in number and comprehensive in scope; where it is extensive, elites are many and specialized. The tremendous variety of cultures and social structures should not obscure a fundamental similarity in the patterns with which societies have responded to the facts of growth and diversity. At one point in time, we find neither social classes nor an extensive social differentiation, but we do find strategic elites in the form of single chiefs, groups of elders, or high priests performing their functions sporadically and on a temporary basis. At some later time, perhaps a hundred years, or a thousand, or only a few decades, the population increased, a variety of occupations emerged, social classes arose, and the minorities in charge of social leadership became more numerous, more extensive, and more enduring. The organized boundaries of society no longer coincided with its numerical boundaries and in that sense, society became separate from the total membership, as well as longer-lived. Once a certain degree of social differentiation was reached, the emergence of a societal center, a core, a fulcrum, existing apart from and above the community, sacred and exalted, was mandatory. This core symbolized at once the most precarious and the most exalted aspects of organized collective life.

Strategic elites and social classes must therefore be considered as twin-born but not identical. Their development, although related in complicated ways, is not interchangeable. Just as there is a close association between social classes and the existence of a state, but each is a separate consequence of a series of social developments, so elites and classes are independent social occurrences. The subdivision of a population into occupations, castes, guilds, or classes is paralleled by its unification around a symbolic center. The shape of this center is determined by the complexity and variety of the whole—the more varied and complex the one, the more varied and complex the other.

There is one way, however, in which strategic elites have been historically dependent on particular aspects of the social class structures of their societies—via their recruitment and selection. As long as these elites were principally recruited from a small exclusive circle tied by economic position and kinship—that is, from an upper class—it was difficult, if not impossible, to distinguish between the strategic elites and the class that supplied most of their membership. This was even truer if class background rather than social functions was used to justify the holding of strategic elite positions in society. This confusion between the characteristics of functioning leadership groups and the characteristics of the reservoir from which they were drawn arose from the historic fusion of function, attributes, and rewards. An aristocrat, for example, was a leading politician, born of an ancient and noble family, who became merged with his mode of recruitment (kinship and lineage) and his manner of reward (wealth and an elegant style of life). If most politicians were indeed to the manor born, it might readily be assumed that noble birth was indispensable for the exercise of political leadership. As long as these elements were fused, in fact, they were not analytically distinguished. Thus, in the past, strategic elites had two sources of social superiority. One derived from their crucial role in preserving and furthering key social values and goals, the other from their traditional modes of recruitment. In the popular mind, social class and elite rankings were readily confused as the high status of the one reflected on that of the other.

In this age of specialization, demands for specialized excellence have altered the class-linked recruitment patterns of the past and with them some of our traditional assumptions about their indispensability. This is not to say that social class has ceased to play a significant role in recruitment, selection, and opportunity for access to elite positions in society, but only that its role has become attenuated. High social-class position is no longer a formal prerequisite for the attainment of elite positions or for the performance of elite functions. The study of strategic elites must therefore endeavor to keep three factors separate and distinct. The first refers to the duties, responsibilities, and tasks of these elites, the second to their manner of recruitment. If they reproduce themselves, then society is managed by one or more ruling castes; if they are drawn only from the rich and propertied, then the society has a ruling class; if incumbents must demonstrate proven abilities, in specialized spheres, then we have strategic elites in modern dress. The third factor refers to the manner of rewarding these elites for adequate performance. In some instances they get more of the desirable things of life, in others less.

In sum, although the emergence of social classes divides a society, the development of its symbolic center, manned by strategic elites, integrates and reunifies it once more. In this way a society can act in concert even though its various parts are not identical or coequal. With this two-fold development, new and perplexing questions arise: Who is to participate in this center? How large should this group be? How long should given individuals participate? How should they be rewarded? The fate of many societies, including our own, has hung on the ways in which these questions have been answered.

## CLASSES IN MODERN SOCIETY

*T. B. Bottomore*

The egalitarian movement which came to life in socialist clubs, trade unions, cooperative ventures and utopian communities grew stronger throughout the nineteenth century as capitalism developed. In the course of time this movement has taken many different forms—struggles for women's rights and against racial discrimination, and most recently the efforts to close the gap between rich and poor nations—but its driving force has remained the opposition to the hierarchy of social classes. The class system of the capitalist societies is seen as the very fount of inequality, from which arise the chief impediments to individual achievement and enjoyment, the major conflicts within and between nations, and the political dominance of privileged minorities.



In this movement Marx's analysis of capitalist society acquired—directly or indirectly—a large influence. . . .

The appeal of Marx's theory is twofold: it provides a clear and inspiring formulation of the aspirations of the working class, and at the same time it offers an explanation of the development of forms of society and government, and especially of the rise of the modern labour movement itself. There are not lacking, in the present age, governments which are quite plainly the instruments of rule by an upper class, as in those economically backward countries where the landowners dominate an uneducated, unorganized and dispirited peasantry. When Marx undertook his studies the class character of governments was just as apparent in the European countries which had embarked upon industrialization. During much of the nineteenth century only property-owners in these societies enjoyed full political rights; and it was scarcely an exaggeration to conceive the government as "a committee for managing the common affairs of the *bourgeoisie* as a whole." In many European countries it was only during the first two decades of the twentieth century that universal suffrage was finally established. . . .

The existence of large working-class parties has become a normal feature of the democratic capitalist countries, and this is one of the principal circumstances (another being the political system in the Soviet societies) which raise new problems concerning the relationship between class and politics. In a political system of this kind can the owners of property be regarded any longer as a permanent ruling class? Is the working class still a radical, revolutionary force which seeks to bring about an egalitarian society? Are the relations between classes in the political sphere still the same as they were in the nineteenth-century societies with their restricted franchise? Have new political divisions emerged alongside, or in the place of, those between classes; or have political conflicts lost some of the urgency and importance which they acquired in the period which saw the rise and growth of the labour movement? These questions lie at the heart of present controversies about the changing class structure of industrial societies.

It has become common, for example, to remark upon the great complexity of government in modern societies, and upon the influence which is exerted by the diverse interest groups which are consulted in the course of policy-making; and then to argue that where power is divided among many different groups, whose interests do not always coincide, the notion of a "ruling class" has lost all meaning. But if power is really so widely dispersed, how are we to account for the fact that the owners of property—the upper class in Marx's sense—still predominate so remarkably in government and administration, and in other elite positions; or that there has been so little redistribution of wealth and income, in spite of the strenuous and sustained effort of the labour movement to bring it about? Is it not reasonable to conclude, from the evidence provided in the last chapter, that notwithstanding political democracy, and despite the limited conflicts of interest which occur between elite groups in different spheres, the upper class in the capitalist societies is still a distinctive and largely self-perpetuating social group, and still occupies the vital positions of power? Its power may be less commanding, and it is certainly less arrogantly exercised, than in an earlier period, because it encounters an organized opposition and the test of elections, and because other classes have gained a limited access to the elites; but the power which it has retained enables it to defend successfully its most important economic interests.

There are other difficulties with the concept of a "ruling class," but I have examined them at length elsewhere[1] and I shall not consider them further in the present context. It is in any case the changes in the condition of the working class, and especially in its political role, which have most impressed students of class structure in the postwar period. The "new working class," it is claimed, is economically prosperous and aspires to middle-class standards of living:[2] and in consequence it has become less class conscious and less radical in politics. How far are these political inferences warranted? Class consciousness, in a broad sense, may be regarded as one form of the "consciousness of kind" which develops in all enduring social groups; for example, the consciousness of belonging to a particular nation. In this sense, the emergence of class consciousness, the increasing use of the term "class" to describe an individual's position in society, is itself a sign that new social groups have come into existence.[3] But in Marx's usage, which has had a profound influence both upon sociological theories and upon political doctrines, "class consciousness" involves something more than this; namely, the gradual formation of distinctive ideologies and political organizations which have as their object the promotion of particular class interests in a general conflict between classes.

The growing class consciousness of the working class was represented by Marx as showing these characteristics in an exceptional degree; for it was expressed in ideologies and political movements which strongly emphasized the conflict of economic interest between capitalists and workers, and which proposed radical social changes in order to end the system of society based upon classes. The working class was, therefore, a revolutionary element in society; more revolutionary indeed than any earlier oppressed classes, since it aimed consciously at abolishing the whole class system. . . .

[1] See my *Elites and Society* (New York, 1965), Chapter 2. (Reprinted in this volume, pp. 160–168, C. S. H.)

[2] See *ibid.*, pp. 28–31.

[3] There is a good account by Asa Briggs, "The Language of 'Class' in Early Nineteenth Century England" in Asa Briggs and John Saville (eds.), *Essays in Labour History* (New York, 1960).

This conception of the working class, as the animator of a revolutionary movement which is to establish a classless society, appears to many sociologists to be highly questionable in the light of recent investigations. It is not that the prevalence of class consciousness in a broad sense, or the association between class membership and political affiliation, is generally denied. Social surveys have shown plainly that most people are familiar with the class structure of their society, and are aware of their own position within it. Equally, it has been shown that class membership is still the strongest single influence upon a person's social and political attitudes; and that the major political parties in most countries represent pre-eminently class interests. What is brought into question by recent studies is the view that the working class, in the advanced industrial countries, is striving to bring about a revolutionary transformation of society, rather than piecemeal reforms within the existing social structure; or that there is a total incompatibility and opposition between the doctrines and objectives of political parties which draw their main support from different classes. In Marx's theory the working class was revolutionary in two senses: first, that it aimed, or would aim, to produce the most comprehensive and fundamental change in social institutions that had ever been accomplished in the history of mankind, and secondly, that it would do so in the course of a sustained conflict with the *bourgeoisie* which was likely to culminate in a violent struggle for power. The nascent working class of the mid-nineteenth century fitted reasonably well into this scheme, which was constructed largely out of the experiences of the French Revolution. The "new working class" of the mid-twentieth century, it is argued, fits badly.

Studies of industrial workers during the past decade agree broadly in finding that there has been a decline in their attachment to collective ends, and so also in their enthusiasm for action as a class in order to establish a new social order. F. Zweig, in his study of workers in four modern enterprises, observes that "when speaking about classes a man would seem to be thinking primarily about himself, about the individual aspect of the problem, and not about the social situation or the social structure,"[4] and he goes on to say that although two-thirds of the workers he interviewed placed themselves in the working class, this recognition of their *class identity* was not accompanied by any strong feelings of *class allegiance*. A study of French workers[5] arrives at very similar conclusions. The authors distinguish three types of reaction among factory workers to their situation in the economy and in society: (1) evasion (the attempt to escape from industrial work either by rising to a higher position within the firm or by setting up in business on one's own account); (2) resignation (a dull and resentful acceptance of industrial work as an inescapable fate); and (3) revolt (opposition and resistance to the capitalist organization of industry). Of these three types, the second is by far the most common, while the third is the least so; and even the 9 per cent of workers in this category, who believe that they can improve their situation by collective action, no longer believe that any future society will be able to alter fundamentally the subordinate position of the worker in the factory. The authors summarize their results by saying that although the workers they studied still have a group consciousness (i.e., they regard themselves as "workers," clearly distinguished from other groups in the population), they no longer have any collective aims. The present-day workers is "a man who is cut off from working-class traditions and who possesses no general principles, no world-view, which might give a direction to his life."[6] This conclusion, they observe, agrees entirely with those reached in a number of studies in Germany, by Popitz, Bednarik and others. Popitz and his collaborators, in their study of workers in the Ruhr steel industry,[7] show that there is a strong working-class consciousness, which is built around the distinction between manual workers and those who plan, direct and command work;

[4] F. Zweig, *The Worker in an Affluent Society* (New York, 1961), p. 134.

[5] A. Andrieux and J. Lignon, *L'Ouvrier d'aujourd'hui* (Paris, 1960).

[6] *Ibid.*, p. 189.

[7] H. Popitz, H. P. Bahrdt, E. A. Jüres, H. Kesting, *Das Gesellschaftsbild des Arbeiters* (Tübingen, 1957).

but those who still think in Marxist terms of the victory of the working class and the attainment of a classless society are a small minority. Similarly, Bednarik concludes his essay on the young worker of today by saying that "society has ceased to be an ideal for the working class," and that the worker "tends more and more to withdraw into private life."[8]

Several of these ideas are brought together by Goldthorpe and Lockwood, in their analysis of the notion of *embourgeoisement*,[9,*] where it is suggested that there has been, in the Western industrial countries, a convergence between the "new middle class" and the "new working class," leading to a distinctive view of society which diverges both from the radical individualism of the old middle classes and from the comprehensive collectivism of the old working class. In this new social perspective collectivism is widely accepted as a means (and this accounts for the spread of trade unionism among white-collar workers), but no longer as an end (which accounts for the weakening of class allegiance among workers). Goldthorpe and Lockwood use the terms "instrumental collectivism" and "family centredness" to describe the complex of beliefs and attitudes in this conception of society. The second term refers to the phenomenon which other writers have described as a withdrawal into private life, and which is revealed by the individual worker's predominant concern with his family's standard of living, his own prospects of advancement, the education of his children and their opportunities to enter superior occupations.

The second feature of the working class as a revolutionary force, namely its involvement in violent class struggles, can be discussed more briefly. In all the advanced industrial countries the violence of class conflict has greatly diminished over the past few decades, and the working-class parties which still regard their aims as likely to be achieved by the use of force are few in number and insignificant. The change from the conditions at the end of the nineteenth century has been produced by several factors, among which we may single out the development of political democracy, the more effective power of modern governments, aided by the great advances in military technology, in administration and in communication, and the changes in the nature of working-class aims as well as in the relations between classes. . . .

Changes in the relations between classes in the capitalist societies have accompanied the changes in the character of the major social classes, influencing and being influenced by the latter. In so far as social mobility has increased, and the middle class has grown in numbers, the image of society as divided between two great contending classes has become blurred by the superimposition of another image, in which society appears as an indefinite and changing hierarchy of status positions, which merge into each other, and between which individuals and families are able to move with much greater facility than in the past. In addition, the everyday economic struggle between workers and employers has been regulated more and more by the state, through the creation of new social institutions for negotiation, arbitration and joint consultation. It is this situation which leads Ralf Dahrendorf, in his *Class and Class Conflict in Industrial Society,* to write of "post-capitalist societies" in which industrial conflicts have been institutionalized and thereby insulated from the sphere of politics; and although this is an exaggeration, inasmuch as political conflicts are still very largely about class interests, and are widely recognized as such, it contains an element of truth in so far as it points to the emergence of political issues which are in some measure detached from questions of class interest. There is unquestionably some common ground between the main political parties in the Western industrial countries; and the development of science and technology, economic growth and rising levels of living, urban congestion and crime, are among the issues which

[8] K. Bednarik, *Der junge Arbeiter von heute—ein neuer Typ* (1953), pp. 138–9, 141.

[9] John H. Goldthorpe and David Lockwood, "Affluence and the British Class Structure," *Sociological Review,* XI (2), July, 1963.

* For a subsequent specification of this notion, see Garvin MacKenzie, "The Economic Dimensions of Embourgeoisement," *The British Journal of Sociology,* Vol. XVIII, March, 1967, pp. 29–45. C. S. H.)

have to be dealt with politically along much the same lines in *all* the industrial countries.

The social changes which have produced the "new working class," as well as a political climate in which violent confrontations between the classes are rare, have been interpreted by some sociologists as a crucial phase in a process which is leading to the complete assimilation of the working class into existing society, as a beginning of the "end of ideology" in the precise sense of the decline of socialist doctrines which offer a radical criticism of present-day society and the hope of an alternative form of society. But this interpretation goes beyond the facts which have been discovered by sociological research. It relies, for instance, upon a tacit comparison between the present state of working-class consciousness and its state in some vaguely located and imperfectly known past age, which is seen as a time of heroic resolution and militancy. Against this it should be observed that in the past few decades, in the very period in which the working class is supposed to have become more middle class in its outlook, the support for socialist parties in Europe has been maintained or has substantially increased. It may be objected that this support has been gained by the progressive elimination of distinctively socialist ideas from the programmes of such parties. But this too is doubtful. The language of socialism has changed over the past century, in ways which it would be rewarding to study more closely, but the ends of the labour movement—collectivism and social equality—have not been abandoned or even seriously questioned.

The picture of working-class apathy and lack of enthusiasm for collective ends which is given by the studies mentioned earlier has to be seen, therefore, as a portrait taken at one moment of time and not as the final episode of a serial film. Even as a momentary picture it may not do justice to all the features of the situation. Serge Mallet, in his study of the "new working class" suggests that because the worker as a producer is still dominated and constrained, while as a consumer he experiences a new freedom and independence, it is in relation to the working environment that class consciousness is most vigorously expressed;[10] and this is apparent, he thinks, in the changing nature of trade-union demands in the modern sectors of industry, which are concerned increasingly with shorter hours of work, longer holidays, and greater control over the policies of management. These demands reflect the desire of the "new working class" to alter radically its position in the system of production, in a sense which is close to the ideas of classical socialist thought. The same aspirations, it may be added, find expression in the widening discussion of various forms of producers' co-operation, which has been inspired very largely by the progress of workers' self-management in Yugoslavia.

There are several other influences at work in the Western industrial societies which sustain the ideological controversies over the future form of society, and which lend support, in particular, to the socialist doctrines of the working class. One of the most important is the extension, and the more general acceptance, of public ownership of industry, public management of the economy, and public provision of a wide range of social and cultural services. The contrast between "private opulence" and "public squalor," to which J. K. Galbraith has pointed, has awakened many people to the fact that in modern societies many of the most valuable private amenities can only be got or preserved through public action. Individuals may be prosperous enough to provide adequately for their personal needs in food, housing, transport, and some kinds of entertainment, but they cannot individually assure what is needed for full enjoyment in the way of roads, facilities for sport and recreation, good working conditions, or a congenial and attractive urban environment. The unrestricted pursuit of

[10] This appears very clearly in the comments of workers reported in the study by Andrieux and Lignon (op. cit.). They mention frequently and bitterly the different in the treatment which they receive from other people according to whether they are recognized as workers (in the factory, travelling to work) or as citizens (in leisure time). One worker summed it up by saying that as a worker he was pushed around, but ". . . when I am out in my car and stop to ask for directions the policeman comes up touching his cap because he thinks he is dealing with a gentleman" (pp. 31–32).

private wealth and private enjoyment leads, indeed, to the impoverishment of these vital public services.

In the economic sphere the growth in the size of firms in major branches of industry, and the approach to monopolistic control in some sectors, has reduced the difference between the operations of publicly owned and privately owned enterprises; and if there is, at the present time, no great public excitement over the issue of "nationalization" of industry, this is in part because it is taken for granted that a change of ownership would not affect the economic performance of the industry. In part, also, it is due to recognition of the fact that the economy as a whole, in a modern society, must anyway be increasingly regulated and directed by the political authorities if a consistently high rate of growth is to be achieved, through the systematic application of science to production. Today the entrepreneur has become much less important; while the trained manager (who can perfectly well be a public servant) and the scientist have become much more important.

The increasing provision of social services by the state, which in recent times has been largely brought about by the pressure of the labour movement, has also fortified the socialist conception of a more equal, more collectivist society. Social legislation in the Welfare State may not be preponderantly egalitarian, either in intention or in effect,[11] but as it is extended and comes eventually to include an "incomes policy" so it approaches the conditions in which, as a German social scientist has observed, the task of social policy is to determine the order of priority of claims against the national product.[12] And these are conditions which would accord most fully with the institutions of a classless society.

This discussion of classes and ideologies in the Western societies, if it suggests that the working class may still be considered an independent force in political life, and one which still aims to bring about radical changes in the social structure, also indicates that the development of the working class has diverged in many respects from the course which Marx and the early Marxists expected it to follow. Marx's theory dealt, necessarily, with the first stages in the formation of the working class, and it proposed broad hypotheses rather than settled conclusions based upon intensive research. The Marxist sociologists—in any case few in number—have not greatly advanced the empirical study of social classes. Often they have seemed to be writing about an imaginary society, in which a pure class struggle continues inexorably, unsullied by such events of practical life as the advent of political democracy, the extension of welfare services, the growth of national income, or the increasing governmental regulation of the economy. . . .

Neither Marx not his followers examined sufficiently the strengths and weaknesses of the major social classes in capitalist society, many of which, indeed, have only become apparent through the experiences of the past fifty or sixty years. Marx insisted that the ruling ideas in any society are the ideas of the ruling class. But he did not seriously consider how important the ideas themselves might be in sustaining that rule, or how difficult it would be for the working class to oppose them with its own ideas.[13] Doubtless he thought that his own social theory would have a great effect (as it has), and he also counted upon the economic failure of capitalism—the ever-worsening crises—to discredit bourgeois ideas. In fact, bourgeois ideas have only been discredited, for brief periods, in those societies which have suffered defeat in war, and it is in such circumstances that the major revolutions of the twentieth century have occurred. Otherwise it is true to say that the working class in all countries has continued to be profoundly influenced by the dominant ideas of capitalist society; for example, by nationalism and imperialism, by the competitive,

[11] For a discussion of this point see T. H. Marshall, *Social Policy* (New York, 1965), Chapter 13, "Retrospect and Prospect."

[12] Quoted by T. H. Marshall, *Social Policy*, p. 183.

[13] Among later Marxists, Gramsci was the only one who gave much serious attention to these questions, and I should think that he was influenced in this direction by the work of his compatriot Mosca, who had introduced the term "political formula" to describe the body of doctrine which every ruling class, in his view, has to develop and to get accepted by the rest of society if it is to retain power.

acquisitive and possessive conceptions of human nature and social relations, and in recent times by a view of the overriding purpose of society as being the creation of ever greater material wealth. The attempts to combat these ideas reveal the immense difficulties involved in doing so. The ideal of working-class internationalism, in opposition to national rivalries and war between nations, has never been realized in more than a fragmentary form, in the face of differences of language and culture, and the manifold problems of establishing international associations at any level. On the other side, the idea of competition and of activity as mainly acquisitive easily becomes acceptable when it is associated with equality of opportunity—real or supposed—for which the working class itself has striven; while the idea of uninterrupted economic growth must clearly appeal, with reason, to those who are struggling to escape from cramping poverty.

Yet in spite of these difficulties, egalitarian and collectivist ideas have spread widely during this century. . . . The question now is whether these ideas have lost their vigour and have begun to recede, or whether they are still active and effective. A number of sociologists, as we have seen, observe a decline in the enthusiasm of the working class for collective ends, a loss of interest in any social mission, and the gradual erosion of a distinctive working-class culture. A few, among them S. M. Lipset, regard the combination of political democracy and high levels of living as the final achievement of the "good society," and thus as the terminal point of the labour movement: "democracy is not only or even primarily a means through which different groups can attain their ends or seek the good society; it is the good society itself in operation."[14] Lipset concedes that there is still a class struggle of sorts in the capitalist countries, but he sees it as being concerned only with the distribution of income, not with any profound changes in the social structure or culture; and he assumes that there is a constant trend towards greater equality of income which is turning the struggle into a process of limited bargaining between interest groups, while denuding it of all ideological or political significance.

There are several reasons to be cautious about accepting this view that the relative peace on the ideological front, and the apparent decline in the vigour of working-class social ideals, have become permanent features of the capitalist societies; that the final form of industrial society has been reached. First, it is likely that there will be growing discontent as it becomes evident that there is no general trend towards greater economic equality, and that, on the contrary, there are very powerful movements which tend to produce a more unequal distribution of income and wealth whenever the industrial and political pressure of the working class is relaxed. . . .

A second consideration, which seems to me still more important, is that there is a growing discrepancy between the condition of the working class at work and in leisure time. Security of employment and rising levels of living have brought greater freedom of choice and independence of action for industrial workers outside the workplace, and younger workers in particular have taken advantage of their new opportunities. But one result of this is that the contrast between work and leisure has become more intense: at work there is still constraint, strict subordination, lack of responsibility, absence of means for self-expression. All the studies of the modern working class which I reviewed earlier bring out clearly that workers are profoundly aware of this division in their lives, and that they have a deep hatred of the present system of industrial work. They would undoubtedly recognize their condition in Marx's observation that a worker "does not fulfil himself in his work but denies himself, has a feeling of misery rather than well-being, does not develop freely his mental and physical powers but is physically exhausted and mentally debased," that "his work is not voluntary but imposed, *forced labour*," and that he "feels himself at home only in his leisure time."[15]

It is hard to believe that such a division can continue unchanged, but it may be overcome or mitigated in several different ways.

[14] S. M. Lipset, *Political Man* (New York, 1960), p. 403.

[15] Karl Marx, *Economic and Philosophical Manuscripts* (1844).

Sustained economic growth may result in such a reduction of working hours and expansion of leisure time that the hierarchical and authoritarian structure of industry comes to play a negligible part in the individual's personal and social life, and is no longer a matter for concern. Or, on the other hand, there may be renewed efforts to introduce into the sphere of economic production some of the freedom and independence which exist in leisure time, and these efforts may be helped by changes in the character of production itself, as it becomes increasingly a scientific activity—using both the natural and the social sciences—which needs the services of highly educated and responsible individuals to carry it on. Most probably, there will be some combination of these two movements; but in so far as the second one takes place at all it will be through the action of working-class organizations seeking to control the labor process, which still appears, as it did to Marx, as the fundamental activity in every social system.

The rise of the working class in modern societies has been a more protracted affair than Marx supposed, and it has only rarely approached that state of decisive struggle with the *bourgeoisie* which he expected. In the future a similar gradual development appears most likely, but the end may still be Marx's ideal society, a classless society. Indeed, it is only now, when the tremendous development of the sciences has created the possibility of truly wealthy societies—but for the uncertainties of population growth and nuclear warfare—that the economic foundations of a classless society can be regarded as assured. What kinds of inequality would remain in the absence of social classes, and in conditions where individuals had independence and responsibility both at work and in leisure, can only be conjectured. There would doubtless be some differences in the prestige of occupations, in incomes, and in the social position of individuals, but there is no reason to suppose that these would be very large, or that they would be incompatible with an awareness of basic human equality and community.

The principal fault in many recent studies of social classes has been that they lack an historical sense. Like the economists of whom Marx said that they believed there had been history, because feudalism had disappeared, but there was no longer any history, because capitalism was a natural and eternal social order, some sociologists have accepted that there was an historical development of classes and of class conflicts in the early period of industrial capitalism, but that this has ceased in the fully evolved industrial societies in which the working class has escaped from poverty and has attained industrial and political citizenship. But this assumption is made without any real study of the evolution of social classes in recent times, or of the social movements at the present time which reveal the possibilities of future social change. An historical analysis of the changing class structure in modern societies, such as I have merely outlined here, remains one of the most important unfulfilled tasks of sociology today.

# NAME INDEX


Abegglen, James C., 370, 371, 459
Adams, Stuart, 454
Adelson, Joseph, 371
Alford, R. R., 217
Allen, Philip J., 366
Amory, Cleveland, 411
Anastasi, Ann, 316, 367, 401*n.*
Anderson, Arnold, 313
Anderson, C. A., 353
Andreski, Stanislav, 109
Andrieux, A., 458, 526, 528
Angell, Robert, 205, 372
Annaklychev, Shikhberdy, 292
Ansell, C., 257
Antonovsky, Aaron, 249, 257–70, 446
Appel, C., 86
Aptekman, D. M., 290
Archer, William, 210
Aristotle, 2, 9, 65
Aron, Raymond, 59*n.*, 416, 418, 463, 464
Arutiunian, V., 286
Atkinson, E. T., 80
Atkinson, J. W., 507
Awad, Mohamed, 51

Bahrdt, H. P., 526
Bailey, A. H., 258
Bailey, F. C., 75, 76, 79
Bakke, E. W., 377
Baltzell, Digby, 251, 367, 378–79, 403–13
Banks, O., 359
Barber, Bernard, 1, 58, 126, 256, 486, 515
Barber, William J., 421, 422
Barghoorn Frederic C., 314
Baron, G., 359
Barrow, R. H., 66
Bar-Yosef, R., 445
Bastide, Roger, 73
Bauer, Raymond, 130, 452, 465
Beals, Ralph L., 416*n.*
Becker, Howard, 355
Bednarik, K., 526, 527
Belknap, George, 172
Bell, Daniel, 172
Bell, Gerald D., 315
Bello, Francis, 366
Beltran, Aguiree, 384
Bendix, Reinhard, 1, 2, 7, 58, 124, 199, 315–16, 339, 353 362–73, 400, 401*n.*, 516
Benoit, F., 89
Benoit-Smullyan, E., 454
Bensman, Joseph, 117–18, 168, 169, 170
Berelson, B., 217
Berent, Jerzy, 368
Bergel, Egon E., 51
Berger, Bennet, 458
Bergson, Abram, 145, 146, 149, 150
Berreman, Gerald D., 56–57, 74–81
Beshers, James, 299
Bialer, Seweryn, 462, 463, 464
Bierstedt, Robert, 506
Black, Cyril E., 453
Blacker, J. G. C., 367
Blau, Peter M., 313, 341–52, 370
Bloch, Marc, 57–59, 81–91, 160
Blood, Robert O., 281
Bloom, Richard, 377, 378
Boeke, Julius H., 421
Boettcher, Erik, 462
Bogue, Donald J., 402
Borah, Woodrow, 380
Bose, N. K., 76
Bottomore, T. B., 12, 51, 59, 108, 113–14, 160–68, 487, 524–31
Bouglé, C., 317
Bourricaud, François, 429, 431
Box, Steven, 253
Breslow, Lester, 263, 265
Briggs, Asa, 525
Brimmer, Andrew F., 394
Britten, Rollo H., 260, 267
Brockington, Fraser C., 266
Brogan, Dennis, 361
Bronfenbrenner, Urie, 253, 302, 369*n.*
Broom, Leonard, 393, 469
Brown, R. G., 259
Bruno, Frank J., 260
Brzezinski, Zbigniew K., 463, 464
Buckland, W. W., 66, 67
Buckley, Walter, 482, 504, 518
Buechley, Robert, 265
Buell, Philip, 263

Bukharin, Nikolai, 154
Bullitt, Stimson, 520
Bunche, Ralph, 209
Burke, Peter, 204
Burnham, James, 11, 60, 96, 99, 100
Burns, Arthur F., 133

Campbell, A., 217
Campbell, John D., 199
Cantril, Hadley, 208, 361
Carlsson, Gösta, 342
Castro, Fidel, 109*n.*
Cattell, Raymond, 316
Catterall, Helen T., 66, 67
Caudill, W., 373, 400, 401*n.*
Cavan, Ruth S., 372
Cayton, Horace R., 181
Centers, Richard, 125–27, 129, 207, 208, 210, 211, 313
Chambliss, William J., 122
Chaplin, David, 415–16, 427–38
Chapman, Janet G., 110
Chapple, E. D., 74
Chernetski, F., 295
Chinoy, Ely, 9
Churchill, Winston, 404
Cipolla, Carlo M., 257
Clark, Kenneth, 388
Clements, R. V., 459
Cloward, Richard A., 296
Coates, Charles H., 170
Coffee, Martha, 394
Cohen, Albert K., 296, 356
Cohen, E., 449, 451
Cohen, Elizabeth G., 365*n.*, 366, 371*n.*
Cohn, B. S., 79, 80
Coleman, James S, 168, 173, 378
Collins, Selwyn D., 258, 259
Comas, Juan, 73, 381*n.*
Comte, Auguste, 1
Conklin, E. G., 323
Converse, P. E., 217
Cooley, Charles H., 1, 204
Coon, C. S., 74, 75
Coser, Lewis A., 517
Coulborn, Rushton, 57
Counts, George S., 118, 199, 200
Cox, Oliver C., 74, 75, 209
Crankshaw, Edward, 464
Crawford, A. B., 370
Croce, B., 165*n.*
Crockett, Harry J., 315, 397
Crosland, C. A. R., 519
Cuber, J. F., 504

Dahrendorf, Ralf, 2, 7, 8, 59, 96, 112–13, 480, 483–84, 486–96, 517, 527
Darick, Jean, 260
Davis, Allison, 74, 181, 363*n.*, 371
Davis, David Brion, 53, 54, 55
Davis, James A., 132
Davis, Kingsley, 53, 69, 74, 419, 479, 481–84, 496–503, 504–11
Day, A., 258
Degler, Carl N., 68
Deutsch, Martin, 377, 378
De Vos, George, 57*n.*, 373, 400, 401*n.*
De Witt, Nicholas, 293
De Wolff, P., 262
Disraeli, Benjamin, 211
Djilas, Milovan, 110–11, 113–14, 154–60, 418, 463
Dollard, John, 56, 74, 77, 211
Donoghue, J. D., 74
Doob, L. W., 211
Dornhoff, G. William, 114
Douglas, William O., 138
Douvan, Elizabeth, 371
Drake, St. Clair, 181, 300*n.*
Dube, S. C., 75
Dubin, Robert, 296
Dublin, Louis I., 257, 258
Dubois, René, 203
Duncan, O. D., 115, 120, 192, 199, 203, 311, 313, 341–52, 395
Dunlop, J. T., 452
Dunn, John E., 265
Durkheim, Emile, 106, 295, 305, 306, 307, 354

Eckelberry, R. H., 360
Edwards, G. Franklin, 377, 387–96
Eells, Kenneth, 115, 175–83
Eisenstadt, S. N., 167, 416–17, 438–52
Elkins, Stanley, 63, 64, 65, 66*n.*, 69, 71, 72
Ellis, John M., 262
Ellis, Robert A., 311, 371
Empey, La Mar T., 402
Engels, Friedrich, 8, 14–22, 23, 24*n.*, 211, 510
Epstein, Benjamin, 394
Escobar, Gabriel M., 433, 434

Farganis, James, 458
Faris, Robert E. L., 367
Farr, William, 258
Feldman, A. S., 340
Feldmesser, Robert A., 462, 463, 465*n.*
Feofanov, Y., 290
Festinger, Leon, 306
Fiedosijew, P. N., 465
Finley, M. J., 52–53, 65, 72*n.*
Fitzwilliams, Jeanette, 133, 134
Florentius, 53
Floud, Jean E., 302, 353, 358, 364, 365, 366, 367, 371
Foley, John P., 367
Foote, Nelson N., 208, 482, 515

Ford, Julienne, 253
Fox, Thomas, 313, 428
Franklin, John Hope, 68, 72
Frazier, E. Franklin, 387, 393
Freeman, Ralph E., 456
Freyre, Gilberto, 73
Friedman, G. A., 369
Friedmann, W., 214
Friedrich, Carl J., 163
Fromm, Erich, 152
Furnivall, J. S., 480

Galbraith, John K., 60, 417*n.*, 528
Galeski, B., 465
Gallagher, Buell G., 74, 77
Gallup, G., 208
Galton, Francis, 323
Gans, Herbert J., 254, 270–76
Gardner, Burleigh B., 181
Gardner, L., 366
Gaudet, H., 217
Geiger, Kent, 254–55, 284–96
Geiger, Theodor, 3, 59–60, 91–104, 110, 128, 417, 418
Geis, Gilbert, 251
Genovese, Eugene D., 54
George, Wesley C., 395
Gerth, Hans H., 7, 24
Ginsberg, M., 176
Girard, Alain, 367, 368
Glass, D. V., 192, 342, 356
Glazer, Nathan, 174, 397, 401*n.*, 516
Glenn, Norval, 393
Gobineau, Arthur de, 383
Goffman, Irving, 204, 206
Goldschmidt, Walter, 515
Goldsen, Rose, 297
Goldthorpe, John H., 128, 417–18, 452–64, 527
Goode, Erich, 254
Gordon, Milton M., 115, 376, 379, 504
Gorer, Geoffrey, 211, 354
Gosnell, Harold F., 395
Granick, David, 254
Greenwood, Major, 266
Gross, Neal, 126, 210
Grushin, Boris A., 289
Gubariew, T., 213
Guizot, F., 318
Guralnick, Lillian, 260, 263, 268
Gurin, G., 217
Guttsman, W. L., 161

Hall, Douglas, 70
Hall, J. R., 192
Haller, Archibald, 119
Halsey, A. H., 302, 358, 361*n.*, 364, 365, 366, 367
Hamilton, Alexander, 9
Hammond, Harley Ross, 73
Handlin, Mary, 68
Handlin, Oscar, 68, 397
Hansluwka, Harold, 265
Harbison, F. H., 452
Harrington, Michael, 458
Hart, Albert G., 151*n.*
Hart, C. W. M., 171
Hatt, Paul K., 120, 192, 208, 209, 482
Hauser, Philip, 258, 265
Havighurst, R. J. 353, 366*n.*, 369*n.*
Heberle, Rudolph, 516
Heller, Celia Stopnicka, 116, 183–91, 378, 378n., 379, 396-403
Henry, Louis, 257
Herriott, Robert E., 255
Hertz, Alexander, 131
Hetzler, S. A., 209
Higgins, Benjamin H., 421
Hill, T. P., 344
Himmelweit, Hilde T., 353, 364, 365
Ho, Ping-ti, 459
Hobhouse, L. T., 176
Hochbaum, Godfrey, 205
Hodge, Robert W., 119–20, 192–204, 313, 342, 343
Hodges, Harold M., 115
Hofstadter, Richard, 63
Hollingshead, August B., 208, 251, 257, 276, 371
Homan, Paul T., 151*n.*
Homans, George C., 5, 204, 209, 454
Hoselitz, Bert F., 415, 416, 421–27
Huaco, George A., 482–83
Huber, Michel, 260
Hunter, Floyd, 111, 169, 170, 173
Hutchinson, E. P., 397
Hutton, J. H., 310
Hyman, Herbert H., 129, 255, 301, 302, 303, 306, 400

Inkeles, Alex, 109, 118, 130, 288, 299, 452, 453, 454, 455, 461*n.*, 465, 516
Ingle, Dwight J., 395
Isaacs, Harold C., 56
Isnard, M. Z., 89
Itagaki, Yoichi, 421
Izyumski, Boris, 288

Jackson, Brian, 314
Jackson, Elton, 204
Jahoda, Marie Lazarsfeld, 377
Jay, Douglas, 165
Johnson, C. S., 74, 75
Jones, Victor, 170
Jordan, Winthrop D., 67, 68
Jüres, E. A., 526

Kadushin, Charles, 117

Kahl, Joseph A., 1, 127, 132, 310–11, 363*n.*, 365, 376, 416, 504
Kantner, John F., 368
Kantorovich, Vladimir, 290
Kassil, Lev, 291
Kaufman, Herbert, 170
Keller, Suzanne, 112, 486, 520–24
Kelly, K. Dennis, 122
Kelsall, R. K., 364
Kenkel, F. W., 122, 504
Kerr, Clark, 432, 452, 453, 454, 455, 459
Kesting, H., 526
Key, V. O., 171
Kharchev, A. G., 286, 292
Khrushchev, N. S., 152, 157, 464*n.*
Kingsley, J. Donald, 161
Kirby, E., 371
Kiser, Clyde V., 368
Kiss, Gabor, 484*n.*
Kitagawa, Evelyn M., 265
Klein, Herbert S., 54, 56
Kleinberg, Otto, 400
Kluckhohn, Clyde, 452
Kluckhohn, Florence E., 400
Kohn, Melvin L., 276
Kolabinska, 35*n.*, 37*n.*
Kolko, Gabriel, 144, 457
Komarovsky, Mirra, 253–54, 256, 276–84, 372
Konstantinov, F. B., 212, 290
Kornhauser, Arthur, 127
Kornhauser, Ruth, 115
Kornhauser, William, 114
Kostenko, K., 290
Ktsanes, Virginia, 208
Kunstadter, Peter, 252
Kushner, P. I., 292

Lampman, Robert J., 457*n.*
Landecker, Warner, 121–22, 205, 454
Landtman, Gunnar, 484
Lane, Robert E., 519
Lane, W. Clayton, 311
Lasswell, T. E., 209, 210
Lazarsfeld, P., 217, 377
Leach, E. R., 75
Leeds, Anthony, 434
Legett, John C., 128
Lenin, V. I., 154, 157, 212
Lenski, Gerhard E., 2, 114–15, 121–23, 204–207, 209, 433, 454, 469, 481, 486-87
Lesser, Gerald, 316
Levy, Y., 449, 451
Lewis, David M., 119
Lewis, Hylan, 108, 377, 391
Lewis, Oscar, 75
Leyburn, James, 73*n.*
Lichtheim, George, 513, 519
Lignon, J., 458, 526, 528
Likhodeyev, L., 293
Linden, George, 265
Lipset, Seymour Martin, 1, 2, 7, 58, 124, 144, 199, 206, 217, 312*n.*, 315–16, 339, 353, 362–73, 400, 401*n.*, 416, 452, 460, 516, 517, 530
Lipton, Lawrence, 356
Livingston, Arthur, 11, 34, 35*n.*, 36*n.*
Lockwood, David, 128, 458, 481, 489, 527
Loeb, M. B., 353
Long, Norton E., 169
Lord, Walter, 257
Lotka, Alfred J., 257, 258
Lull, Raimon, 87
Lundberg, G. A., 1
Lunt, Paul, 179
Lydall, H. F., 456, 457
Lynd, Helen M., 111, 171, 211, 299
Lynd, Robert, 111, 171, 207, 211, 299

McArthur, Charles, 369, 370
McClelland, David C., 368*n.*, 370*n.*, 397
McGuire, Carson, 211
McKee, James B., 171
MacKenzie, Garvin, 527
McKeown, Thomas, 259
MacLean, Robert, 431
McWilliams, Carey, 403
Mahar, Pauline M., 78
Majumdar, D. N., 80
Malaspina, Albert de, 86
Malewski, Andrzej, 122–23, 235
Malleson, Nicholas, 360
Mallet, Serge, 528
Manis, J. G., 210
Mannheim, Karl, 167
Mardsen, Dennis, 315
Markiewicz-Lagneau, Janina, 254
Marriott, McKim, 75, 79
Marro, A., 323
Marsh, Robert M., 459
Marshall, T. H., 59, 364*n.*, 415, 456*n.*, 513, 515, 517, 529
Martin, F. M., 302, 358, 366, 367, 371
Martin, Robert E., 395
Marx, Karl, 1, 3, 7–10, 14–24, 59–60, 97, 91–105, 107, 113, 115–16, 125, 128, 134, 152, 160–62, 164, 166, 212, 306, 419, 435*n.*, 466, 471, 481, 487, 489, 494, 496, 514, 517, 524–26, 529, 530–31
Matza, David, 108
Maxwell, James, 368
Mayer, Albert J., 258
Mayer, Kurt B., 1, 4, 51, 58, 59, 115, 117, 317, 518
Meeker, Marchia, 115, 175–83
Meerdink, J., 262
Meltzer, B. N., 210

Merton, Robert K., 255, 296, 297, 298, 304, 305, 306, 307, 372, 510
Michels, Robert, 206
Miller, Andreas, 515*n.*
Miller, Delbert C., 169, 172, 173
Miller, Herman P., 106–107, 133–38
Miller, S. M., 108, 312–13, 325–40, 428, 460
Miller, W. E., 217
Miller, Walter, 270, 275
Mills, C. Wright, 7, 24, 112–13, 114, 162–64, 467*n.*, 493
Minc, Bronislaw, 465, 466
Minkovski, G. M., 290
Minon, Paul, 366, 367
Mintz, Sidney W., 71, 73
Mizruchi, Ephraim H., 255, 296–307
Moberg, Sven, 367
Moore, Barrington, Jr., 461
Moore, Wilbert E., 53, 56, 63, 67, 69, 70, 72, 419, 453, 454, 455, 479, 481–85, 496–503, 504–13
Morecka, Z., 472, 473
Moriyama, Iwao M., 263, 268
Morris, Jeremy N., 258
Morris, Richard, 515
Mosca, Gaetano, 11–12, 60–61, 113, 162, 163, 164, 510, 529
Moser, C. A., 192
Myers, C. A., 452
Myrdal, Gunnar, 74, 107–108, 138–43, 207, 209, 211, 377, 417, 457, 458

Nadel, S. F., 74, 76, 77*n.*
Nash, Manning, 422, 423, 424
Newcomb, T. M., 506–507
Nieboer, H. J., 63
Niehoff, Arthur, 76
Nietzsche, Friedrich, 30, 53
Nisbet, J., 367
Nisbet, Robert A., 513
Nobbe, Charles E., 401*n.*
Noguiera, Oracy, 73
North, C. C., 120, 192
Novak, Joseph, 286
Nove, Alec, 462
Nowak, Stefan, 125, 130–32, 235–47

Olshanski, V. B., 291
Opler, M. E., 75
Oppenheim, A. N., 364
Ornati, Oscar, 517*n.*, 518
Orwell, George, 518
Osborn, Eliott, 410
Ossowski, Stanislaw, 2, 7, 9, 59*n.*, 124–25, 131, 206, 207–16, 515, 516

Pachter, Henry M., 517
Padan, D., 445
Pareto, Vilfredo, 1, 3, 5, 11–12, 34–39, 113, 129, 137, 162, 163, 164, 354, 355, 417
Park, Robert E., 400
Parry, L. J., 360
Parsons, Talcott, 69, 112, 124*n.*, 210, 251, 255, 296, 479, 480, 489, 490, 491, 493, 501*n.*
Pearson, Karl, 323
Pellegrin, Roland J., 170
Peller, Sigismund, 257
Pfautz, Harold P., 115
Philips, Ulrich B., 64
Pidgeon, D. A., 358
Pirenne, Henri, 370
Pitt-Rivers, Julian, 375–76, 380–87
Plato, 2
Popitz, H., 526
Potter, David M., 72
Prest, A. R., 457

Quattlebaum, C. A., 360
Quill, Michael, 137

Rabban, Meyer, 276
Rae, S. F., 208
Ranck, Catherine, 372
Ranson, C. W., 426
Ratinoff, Luis, 432, 434
Redlich, Frederick C., 251, 257, 276, 371
Reiss, Albert J., 192, 341
Reissman, Leonard, 174, 504
Renner, Karl, 459, 489, 493
Rex, John H., 421
Reimer, Svend, 172
Riesman, David, 114, 174
Rodgers, R. R., 366*n.*
Rodman, Hyman, 251
Roe, Anne, 366, 367
Rogoff, Natalie, 342
Roosevelt, Franklin D., 300*n.*
Rose, Arnold M., 114, 172, 340, 393, 513, 515
Rosen, Bernard C., 369, 370, 378, 397
Rosenberg, Morris, 210, 297
Rosenthal, Celia Stopnicka, 183, 401*n.* *see also* Heller, Celia Stopnicka
Rossi, Alice S., 372
Rossi, Peter, 111, 118, 119–20, 172, 192–204, 516
Rousseas, Stephen W., 458
Runciman, W. G., 121, 128–29, 226–34
Ryle, Gilbert, 515*n.*

Safa, Helen Icken, 252
St. John, Nancy Hoyt, 255
Saint-Simon, Claude Henri, 1
Sametz, Arnold W., 151
Sampson, Anthony, 163
Samuelson, Paul, 133

Sarapata, Adam, 130, 234, 470, 508
Saville, John, 525
Schaffer, Ruth Connor, 173
Schermerhorn, Richard A., 111–12, 168–75, 400
Schlessinger, Arthur, 9
Schmid, Calvin F., 401*n.*
Schulze, Robert O., 170, 171, 172
Schumpeter, Joseph, 1, 12–13, 39–50, 514
Schuster, E., 323
Schwartz, Richard D., 440*n.*, 510
Seebohm, Rowntree B., 259
Seeley, John, 275
Seeman, Melvin, 515
Seers, Dudley, 165
Sellers, Charles, 69
Selznick, Gertrude Jaeger, 127–28, 216–26
Sen, S. N., 426
Sewell, William H., 363*n.*
Shamgar, L., 449, 451
Shapiro, Leonard, 462
Sheldon, Paul M., 366
Sheps, Cecil G., 261
Sherrard, O. A., 73
Shister, Joseph, 515
Shubkin, V. N., 294, 295
Sibley, Elbridge, 311
Siegel, Abraham, 432
Siegel, Paul M., 119–20, 192–204
Silver, James W., 387
Simpson, G. E., 74, 75
Simpson, Richard L., 315
Sims, Joseph P., 408
Singh, Kailash K., 78
Singh, R. D., 75
Sio, Arnold A., 53–55, 63–73
Sireau, Albert, 382
Sjoberg, G., 208, 210, 215
Sklare, Marshall, 370
Smelser, Neil J., 69, 312*n.*
Smith, Adam, 212
Smith, Marpheus, 199, 200
Smith, Michael G., 63, 376*n.*, 480, 484
Smuckler, Ralph, 172
Solari, Aldo, 416
Solzhenitsyn, Alexander, 108
Sorokin, Pitirim, 8, 204, 309–12, 317–25
Sosnovy, Timothy, 285
Spencer, Herbert, 1
Spenger, J. J., 208, 214
Spiegelman, Mortimer, 257, 258
Spinard, William, 112
Srinivas, M. N., 75, 76, 78
Srole, Leo, 182
Stalin, Joseph V., 154, 157, 214, 215
Stampp, Kenneth, 63, 64, 65, 66*n.*, 69, 72, 74
Stavenhagen, Rodolfo, 376*n.*
Stein, Maurice R., 256
Steinberg, Stephen, 127–28, 216–26
Stern, Claudio, 416
Stevenson, T. H. C., 266
Steward, Julian H., 166
Stinchcombe, Arthur L., 483
Stockwell, Edward G., 263
Stodolsky, Susan S., 316
Stokes, D. E., 217
Stone, Lawrence, 433
Stouffer, Samuel, 205, 366
Strachey, John, 165, 166
Strayer, Joseph R., 57
Strodtbeck, Fred L., 370, 400, 402
Sumner, William Graham, 1
Sulzberger, C. L., 51
Sutherland, Edwin H., 251
Svalastoga, Kare, 192, 311, 312, 342, 366, 367, 480
Swados, Harvey, 256
Szczepanski, Jan, 131

Tannenbaum, Frank, 53, 63, 64, 65, 66*n.*, 69, 71
Tawney, R. H., 481–82
Tayback, Matthew, 258, 262
Theisenhusen, William C., 437
Thoenes, Piet, 486*n.*
Thomas, Murray, 118
Thomas, P., 87
Thompson, E. P., 93*n.*
Thomson, Godfrey, 366*n.*
Thorpe, Earle E., 64
Tietze, Christopher, 258
Tipping, D. C., 456, 457
Titmuss, Richard M., 106, 166, 257, 258, 457, 487
Tito, J. B., 158
Toby, Jackson, 400, 401
Tocqueville, Alexis de, 359
Toennies, Ferdinand, 58
Tomsky, M. P., 152, 153
Toynbee, Arnold, 67, 107, 380*n.*
Treiman, Donald J., 119
Trotsky, L., 154
Tsuchiya, Kenzaburo, 265
Tuck, Ruth, 400
Tumin, Melvin, 74, 311, 484–85, 504, 511–13
Turner, Ralph H., 251, 313–14, 353–62, 396, 402, 460*n.*

Varma, Baidya Nath, 56
Veblen, Thorstein, 107, 116, 134
Vernon, P. E., 358
Vico, Giambattista, 121
Vidich, Arthur J., 168, 169, 170, 256
Vikhrov, N., 294
Villermer, Louis R., 258
Volkov, A., 295
Voltaire, F. M., 90
Vostrikova, A., 291

Wagatsuma, Hiroshi, 57*n*.
Wagley, Charles, 73, 354, 380, 385*n*.
Walker, Harry J., 181
Ward, Lester F., 1
Warner, Lloyd, 74, 115–16, 117, 175–83, 205, 207, 353, 370, 371, 379, 459, 480, 510, 514
Watkins, J. H., 261
Weber, Max, 1, 3, 7, 9–11, 24–34, 52*n*., 57, 105, 115, 165, 167, 354, 492, 510, 514
Wesolowski, Wlodzimierz, 125, 235, 418–19, 465–76, 482–84, 503–11
Westermann, William L., 65, 66, 67, 68, 69, 71
Westoff, Charles F., 368
Wheeler, G. C., 176
White, Theodore, 410
Whiteman, Martin, 377, 378
Whitney, Jessamine S., 260
Whitten, N. E., 383
Whyte, William Foote, 370, 515
Whyte, William H., Jr., 278
Widerszpil, S., 465
Wilbur, Martin, 71
Wilensky, Harold L., 312
Wiley, Norbert, 123, 377
Willener, M. Alfred, 453*n*.
Williams, Robin M., 56, 70, 168, 169, 296, 297, 387
Wilson, Woodrow, 212
Winterbottom, M., 369
Wittfogel, Karl, 166, 167
Wolfe, Dael, 364
Wolfe, Donald M., 281
Wolfinger, Raymond E., 112
Woodward, C. Vann, 71*n*.
Wrong, Dennis H., 250, 482, 486, 504, 513–20

Yanowitch, Murray, 108–10, 143–54
Yates, Alfred, 358
Yeracaris, Constantine A., 258
Yinger, J. M., 74, 75
Young, Douglas, 253
Young, Michael, 486, 519–20

Zaleznick, A., 204
Zanden, James W. Vander, 394
Zawadzki, Bohdan, 377
Zeisel, Hans, 377
Zeitlin, Maurice, 128
Zetterberg, Hans L., 339
Zloczower, A., 446
Znaniecki, Florian, 124
Zweig, F., 526

# SUBJECT INDEX


Achievement, 52, 61
  motivation, 314–15, 360–73, 396–403
    and home socialization, 369, 369*n.*
    and occupational success, 370
  need for, 368–69
  occupational, and family size, 349–52
    and sibling position, 349–52, 350*t.*
Achievement aspiration, class variation in, 230–31, 255, 294, 294*t.*, 305–306, 315, 363
  Negro, 378
Africa, social change in, 420–27
Agrarian reform, 435–36
American Dream, The, 175
Anomie, theory of, 255, 256
  test of, 296–307
Anticipatory socialization, 315, 372–73
Aristocracy, 36–39, 41–44
  in U.S., 177, 181, 379, 403–13
  *see also* Nobility
Ascription, 52, 56–57, 61
Asia, social change in, 420–27
Aspiration, and achievement, discrepancy between, 293–94, 296, 305*t.*
  egoistic *vs.* fraternalistic, 228–30
Austria, class and mortality, 265
Automation, unemployment and, 137–38

Blue-collar marriage, 253–54, 276–84
Bolivia, social change in, 435
Bourgeoisie, 8, 14*n.*, 14–20, 160–61
Bureaucracy, in capitalist society, 101–102, 156
  in socialist society, 100–101, 156–57
  in Soviet Union, 154–56, 462–64

Capitalist society, industrial society and, 59
  stratification in, 8–9, 14–16, 97–101, 467–68, 527–28
Caste, 29–31, 56–57, 74–81
  club and, 379, 409–13
  defined, 56, 74
  ethnicity and, 29–31, 404–409
  in India, 56, 74–78, 310, 317, 319
  India and U.S. compared, 56, 74–81
  Latin America and U.S. compared, 384
  race and, 55–56, 67–68, 80–81, 181–82
  sexual gain in, 77
  social mobility and, 37, 310, 319
  in U.S., 55, 56, 181, 211, 404–409
Change, in income distribution, in U.S., 136–38
    in Soviet Union, 143–54
  in occupational structure of U.S., 192–93
  in stratification, 14–18, 235, 235*n.*, 320, 415–77, 513–31
    patterns of developing nations, 415, 422–27
    perception of, 130–31, 243–44
    role of landless peasants, 416, 434–35
China, *literati* in, 166
Circulation of elites, 11–12, 34–39, 354–56
Class
  dichotomous conceptions, 8–9
  ethnicity and, 375–413, 447, 449–51
    mobility trap, 377–78
  as explanation of ethnic differences, 378, 396–403
  function and rank of, 49–50
  Marx's concepts, 8–10, 14–24, 125
  modern concepts, 486–87, 495–96, 514–15
  in modern society, 91–103, 486–87, 513–20, 522–31
  objective, 9, 105–23, 125, 133–206
  as rank, 115
  strategic elites and, 522–24
  as stratum, 8, 12
  subjective, 9, 123–32, 206–47
  Weber's concept, 10, 25–27
  *see also* Stratification
Class action, *see* Class consciousness
Class conflict, 14–24, 26–28, 38–39, 59, 75, 78–79, 93–96, 491–95, 517, 527
  avoidance of, 356–57
  institutionalization of, 60, 96, 527–28
  perception of, 244–46, 451–52
  in socialist society, 160, 212–13, 215–16, 244–46, 295–96
Class consciousness, 9, 19, 26, 91–92, 140, 158, 514–15
  in Britain, 128–29, 228–29, 234–35

Class consciousness *(Cont'd)*
identification, 125–26, 129, 233–34, 446
in Israel, 446, 451–52
organization, 19, 26–27, 141, 158, 172
perception of inequality, 130, 131–33, 226–47, 295–96, 419, 451–52, 472
in Poland, 130–32, 235–47, 472
politico-economic orientation, 122, 126–28, 217, 219–25, 220*t.*, 222*t.*, 223*t.*, 526–27
in Soviet Union, 130, 130*n.*, 295–96
in U.S., 124, 126–29, 207–208, 221, 233–34, 525
*see also* Ideology, Relative deprivation, Voting behavior
Class for itself, 9, 23, 514
*see also* Class consciousness
Class interests, 22, 23, 26–27, 78, 127, 159, 217, 223, 223*t.*, 224*t.*, 470–71, 495
Class situation, 25–26
Class structure,
change in, 39, 419, 467–68
and income, 95–96
open-closed, 37, 52, 56–57, 58, 61, 183, 313, 319–20
*see also* Stratification
Class struggle, *see* Class conflict
Class subcultures, 250–54, 270–76, 278–51, 288–96
*see also* Way of life
Classless society, American conception, 209–12, 518
American and Soviet conceptions compared, 213–15
Marx's conception, 24
nonegalitarian conceptions, 206–16, 513–20
possibility of, 162
propaganda for, 416
Soviet conception, 154, 212–14, 284, 417
Zionist conception, 416, 440
Clubs, upper class, 29, 211, 379, 409–13
Coercion theory, 488–90
*see also* Conflict theory
College attendance, class variation in, 316, 363–64, 366
*Communist Manifesto, The,* 8–9, 14–21
Community power, 111–12, 168–75
decision making, 111–12, 172
governmental *vs.* nongovernmental, 168–69
leaders, 174–75
types of structure, 111
Community stratification, 115–17, 177–91
Conflict theory, assumptions and tenets of, 479–80, 490, 491–96
of Marx, 14–24
radical tradition and, 2–3
Conspicuous consumption, 116, 188
Cooptation, 416, 437

Crime, class variation in, 251, 251*n.*
white-collar, 251, 251*n.*
Cuba, social change in, 109*n.*, 416
Culture, *see* Class subcultures

Developing nations, occupational ranking in, 118–19
stratification in, 415–52
Deviancy, class differences in, 254–55, 290–91
Discrimination, in clubs, 409–13
racial, in Latin America, 380–81
in U.S., 68, 344
consequences of, 377, 388, 409–13
Divorce, class differences in, 290–91
Dropouts, class variation, in Soviet Union, 289–90
in U.S., 256, 363
Dualism, 421–23

Economic inequality, 105–10, 133–38, 143–54, 440, 445, 456–58, 461–62, 471–76
function of, 500–501
perception of, 129, 243, 243*t.*, 440, 472
*see also* Income distribution, Property, Wealth distribution
Education, attitudes toward, class variation in, 270–72
Japanese-American, 400
Jewish, 116–17, 188–89, 400
Mexican American, 400
as a factor in social mobility, 140, 342–44, 378, 433–34, 436–37
as a means, 255, 363, 475
as a value, 116–17, 188–89, 255, 301–303, 378
Educational achievement, class and, 254–56, 286*t.*, 288–90, 360–61, 363–64, 366–70, 445–47, 475
social origin and, 342–43
Educational aspiration, class variation in, 255, 294, 294*t.*, 363
Egalitarian attitudes, growth of, 524, 530
international comparisons, 131–32
in Israel, 439, 440, 451
in Poland, 131, 246–47
in Soviet Union, 293
in U.S., 209–11
Elite, circulation of, 11–12, 34–39, 354–56
defined, 34–35, 35*n.*
governing, 11–12, 35, 113, 162–64, 518–19, 521
in industrial society, 167, 486, 518–19, 521–24
ruling class and, 11–12, 113–14, 162–68, 486, 522
strategic, 486, 520–24
defined, 521
in U.S., 112–14, 162–64, 379, 404–409

*Embourgeoisement,* of working class, 91, 128, 227, 525–27
Endogamy, 56–57
England, *see* Great Britain
Estates, 58
Ethclass, concept of, 376
Ethnic differences, 378
  class explanation of, 378, 396–403
Ethnic group, concept of, 375
Ethnic mobility, 370*n.,* 372–73, 378, 396–403, 403–13, 425–27
Ethnicity, class and, 375–413
  in Israel, 447, 449–51
  in Latin America, 385–87
  mobility trap, 377
  unemployment and, 141–42
  in U.S., 375–77, 396–413

Family, in capitalist society, 16
  and class
    in Soviet Union, 254, 284–96
    in U.S., 177–78, 183, 251–54
  class variation of, 250–55, 270–72, 284–96
  in feudal society, 85–86
  matrifocality in, 252–53
  Negro, 377, 389
  role in Soviet Union, 291–92
  sibling position and social mobility, 349–52, 350*t.,* 366
  size and children's I.Q., 366–67
  size and mobility, 349–52, 367–68
  structure and social mobility, 370–71, 370*n.,* 372
Fascism, class and, 60
Fertility, class differentials in, 250, 291
Feudalism, 15–16, 22–23, 41–49, 57–59, 81–91, 160
  concept of, 89–91
  in China, 166
  in France, 82–89
  in Germany, 41–49
  and hierarchy, 58–59, 90–91
  and law, 58, 87–89
  social mobility in, 317–18
  *see also* Stratification, feudal
France, feudalism in, 82–89
  rise of bourgeoisie, 161
  social mobility in, 327
Functionalist theory, assumptions and tenets of, 479–82, 491, 495–503, 504–505
    motivation hypothesis, 504, 506
  critique of, 482–84, 489–90, 503–13
    conservative bias, 2–3, 481–82
  of Davis and Moore, 496–513
  of Schumpeter, 12–13, 40–50
  test on slavery, 52–53
  of Warner, 115, 176–77

Germany, rise and fall of aristocracy, 41–44
Goldwater, Barry, defeat of, 127–28, 216–26
Great Britain, attitudes toward class and status inequality, 226–35
  class and mortality in, 259–70, 267*t.*
  educational aspiration in, 230–31
  the Establishment in, 163
  rise of bourgeoisie, 161
  secondary school and mobility in, 358–62
  sponsored mobility in, 314, 355–62
  stratification system in, 355–56
    economic inequality, 106, 165–66
    underclass, 108
Guatemala, social change in, 423–25

Hierarchy, class and, 515–16
  feudalism and, 58–59
Horizontal mobility, concept, of 309

Ideology, American, 136–38, 175
  and American sociology, 124, 207–208, 518
  class and, 21–22, 104, 127–28, 221, 222*t.,* 222–26, 306, 417
    Israeli, 438–52
    American and Soviet compared, 124, 206–16
  definition of situation and, 123–24, 124*n.*
  end of, 528
  institutionalization of, 441
  and Soviet sociology, 124–25
Illegitimacy, class and, 290
Income, class structure and, 95–96, 213, 469–70
  Negro-white differentials in, 135, 135*t.*
Income distribution, 106–10
  change in, 136, 144–51
  in Israel, 445, 445*n.,* 445*t.*
  in Peru, 435
  in Poland, 469–70
  in Soviet Union, 108–10, 143–54
  stability of, 137
  in U.S., 106–108, 133*t.,* 133-38, 134*t.*
Income expenditure and class, 179
India, Brahmins in, 166, 317
  caste in, 54, 74–78, 310, 319
  change in stratification of, 427
Indians, in Latin America, 381–82, 384–87, 416, 428, 434–35
    compared with Negroes in U.S., 384
Industrial society, capitalist and, 59–60
  class in, 91–103, 486–87, 513–20, 522–31
  class conflict in, 519–20, 527
  economic inequality in, 456-58
  elites in, 167, 486, 518–19, 521–24
  meritocracy in, 486, 519–20
  occupational ranking in, 118
  pluralistic, 452–53
  power inequality in, 461–64, 525
  social differentiation in, 453–54, 523

Industrial society *(Cont'd)*
social mobility in, 339, 455–56, 516
status consistency in, 454–55, 458–59, 469–70, 475–77
stratification in, 452–65, 479, 486–87, 513–31
capitalist and socialist compared, 97–104, 418, 461–65, 465–68, 470–71, 475–77
Industrialization, differentiation and, 453–54
and social mobility, 455–56, 459–60
and status consistency, 454–55, 458–59
and stratification, 97–104, 417, 421–27, 453–54, 464–65
and urbanization, 415–16, 424–25, 432
Inequality, *see* Social inequality
Inheritance of position, 56, 67–68, 191, 211, 289, 518–19
Integration theory, 115–16, 176, 488–90
*see also* Functionalist theory
Intelligence, ability and social mobility, 314–15, 316, 363–65
I.Q. scores
intra- *vs.* interclass variation, 316, 400–401
of Mexican American students, 396–97
Israel, class identification, 446
egalitarianism in, 438–39
emerging pattern of stratification, 438–52
crucial factors in, 443
ethnicity and class in, 447, 449–51
ideology and class in, 438–52
income distribution, 445, 445*n.*, 445*t.*
occupation, education, and income, 445*n.*, 445*t.*, 445–47
perception of inequality, 451–52

Japan, class and mortality in, 265
social change in, 416, 422
Japanese-Americans, education among, 400
Jews, biblical stratification of, 184
I.Q. and class among, 401, 401*n.*
in Israel, 438–52
in Poland, 116–17, 183–91
social mobility among, 191, 405
in socialist movements, 206*n.*
traditional values of, 184–91
stress on education, 116–17, 188–89, 400
in U.S., 400–401, 401*n.*, 404–405, 409

Latin America, agrarian reform in, 435–36
cooptation in, 416, 437
deradicalization of lower class, 416, 432
ethnicity and class in, 385–87
Indians in, 381–82, 384–87, 416, 428, 434–35
race and class in, 375–76, 380–87
slavery in, 53–54, 63, 73
social change in, 416, 423–25
urbanization in, 416
*also see* Bolivia, Cuba, Peru
Life chances, 5, 249–50, 254, 257–70
Life expectancy, class and, 249, 257–59
studies of, 257*n.*, 258*n.*, 259*n.*
Lower class, *see* Working class, Underclass
*Lumpenproletariat,* 20, 108
*see also* Underclass

Machiavellians, 11–12, 34–39, 162–63
Managerial revolution, 60, 96–97
Manumission, 55, 70
Marriage, barriers to communication in, 253–54, 276–84
as a channel of mobility, 321
in feudal society, 85–86
Marxism, appeal of, 524
class theory, 7–9, 14–24, 57, 59, 111
concept of ruling class in, 160–62, 164–65
and contemporary socialist society, 102–104, 418, 466–68
critique of, 56–60, 91–104, 115, 160–62, 164–65, 176–77, 215–16, 306, 529–31
synthesis of conflict and integration concepts in, 481
Matrifocality, 252–53, 389–91
Meritocracy, 486, 519–20
Methodological techniques and problems of, constructing class indexes, 218, 132
forecasting trends, 250
international comparisons, 119, 312, 314, 340
measuring class identification, 125–26
measuring political attitudes, 220–21
occupational ranking, 193, 197
regression approach, 341
studying social mobility, 310–11, 312, 314, 340–42
Mexican American, 396–403
change in mobility pattern of, 403
class differentials in traits, 378, 401
educational aspirations, 397, 398, 402
I.Q. scores of high school students, 396–97, 399*t.*
intergenerational advancement, 378, 402–403
occupational aspirations, 396, 398*t.*, 402
Middle class, lower, 179
upper, 178–79
new, 59–60, 92–96, 161–62
old, 59–60, 92–96
in Peru, 431–32
relative deprivation among, 226–35
similarity between Negro and white, 377
subculture, 252, 271–72
Mobility trap, concept of, 377–78
Mortality, class and, 259–70, 261*t.*, 264*t.*
Motivation, achievement and, 314–15, 365–73, 504, 506, 512

Nazism, class and, 60
Negroes, in Latin America, 382–83
  in U.S., change in status and situation, 394–96
    class among, 392–93
    community life of, 393–94
    compared to immigrant groups, 387–88, 517–18
    discrimination against, 68
    education of, 343–46, 344*n.*, 345*t.*, 378, 389
    family structure of, 377, 389–91
    ghettos, 388–89
    income inequality of, 135, 135*t.*, 390, 391
    middle class of, 377, 378, 382–83
    occupational inequality of, 344
    social mobility of, 377, 378, 388
    unemployment, 141–42
  *see also* Slavery
Netherlands, class and mortality, 252
*New Class, The* (Djilas), 110–11, 154–60
Nobility, and the bourgeoisie, 48, 58
  defined, 81–82
  in Germany, 41–49
  warrior function of, 82–84
*Non-antagonistic classes,* Soviet conception, 212–13
Novels, social stratification in, 176

Occupational groups, 32
  income differentials of, 135–36, 136*n.*, 147–50, 445, 445*n.*, 469–70
Occupational ranking, 118–19, 184
  change in, 193, 197–99, 201–203, 202*t.*
  in developing nations, 118–19
  international comparisons of, 118–19
  in Poland, 470
  stability in, 119–20, 193, 197–99, 203–204
  in U.S., 119–20, 192–204
Occupational structure, changes in, 192–93, 469–70
Opportunity, and achievement, 316
  class subculture as repsonse to, 272–73
  class variation in perception of, 303–304
  equality of, 518–19
  inequality in, 254, 272–73, 289–96, 379

Pareto's Law, 137
Pariah people, 30
Party, class, status, 33–34
Patrimonialization, 44–49
  defined, 44
Peru, class structure, 428–32
  Indians in, 416, 428, 434–35
  lower class in, 432, 434–35
  stratification and mobility in, 427–38
Poland, change in class structure of, 235, 235*n.*, 469–70
  class consciousness in, 235–47
  liberalization in, 125
  perception of inequality in, 130–32, 235–47, 472
  relative deprivation in, 130
  social mobility in, 239–43
  status consistency in, 469–70
  stratification of a Jewish community in, 116–17, 183–91
Poverty in U.S., 142–43
  invisibility of, 517–18
Postcapitalist society, 59–61
  *see also* Industrial society
Power, 10–11, 60–61, 82, 97
  authority and, 491–95
  Communist, 110, 113–14, 154–60, 166
  defined, 24
  economic, 24, 161–62, 454
  functional aspect of, 509–11
  legitimation and, 24
  Marx's concept, 9, 161–62
  Pareto's dichotomous conception, 11, 162–64
  political, 101–103, 161–62, 166–67, 295–96, 447–49, 454
  status and, 24, 116, 295–96
  of veto groups, 114
  Weber's concept, 10–11, 24–25, 166–67
  zero-sum concept of, 112, 493–94
  *see also* Community power
Power elite, 11–12, 112–14, 162–68
  compared to ruling class, 113–14, 162–68
*Power Elite, The* (Mills), 112–14, 162–64
Power inequality, 110–14, 154–60
  in socialist society, 154–60, 166, 461–64
  in Soviet Union, 154–60, 295–96, 462–64
  in U.S., 111–14, 162–63, 170–72
    role of clubs in, 409–13
Proletariat, 8, 18–20
  *see also* Working class
Property, class and, 25–26, 156–57, 184–85, 470–71
  concept of, 97–99
  ownership and control of, 60, 82, 97–104, 110–11, 113, 156–57, 167, 418–19, 470–71, 529
  slaves as, 63–65, 69–73
*Protestant Establishment, The* (Baltzell), 378–79, 403–13

Race, and caste, 55–56, 67–68, 80–81, 181–82, 376
  and class, in Latin America, 375–76, 380–87
    in U.S., 376–77, 387–96
  Latin American conception of, 380
  U.S. vs. Latin American conception of, 375, 380–87
  *see also* Slavery

Rank, positional, determinants of, 497-98, 505–506, 511–12
function and, 49–50, 52–53, 176
*see also* occupational ranking
Reference group, and economic inequality, 226–28
and relative deprivation, 128–29, 226–28, 233, 233*t.*
and status inequality, 228–35
Relative deprivation, in Britain, 226–35
concept of, 128–29
economic, 106, 134, 226–28
status, 229–35
in Poland, 130, 236, 236*t.*
Religion, and class, 191, 254, 254*n.*, 290–91, 372
role of, 499–500
and class, 191, 254, 254*n.*, 290–91, 372
Revolution and stratification, 38, 320
Ruling class, 9, 11–12, 21–22, 37, 82, 160–64
decline and fall of, 12, 20–21, 38–40, 43–44, 50, 111, 160, 320
in modern society, 525
rise of, 12, 41–43, 110–11, 154–56, 317–18, 320
in Soviet Union, 154–60
*see also* Elite, Power elite
Ruling ideas, 21–22
Russia, *see* Soviet Union

School system, American and English compared, 353–62
and class structure, 256, 405
as mechanism for social mobility, 140, 313–14
perpetuation of inequality by, 313
sponsored and contest mobility and, 353–62
Skilled and unskilled workers, 135–36, 152, 153
Slavery, 51, 52–56, 63–73
defined, 63
functional theory and, 56–57
laws of, 63, 69–73
property and, 64–65, 69–72
race and, 55–56, 65, 67–68, 72–73
U.S., compared with ancient, 53–55, 63, 65–72
U.S., compared with Latin American, 53–54, 63–73
Social change, 320, 415–16, 420–27, 435, 452
and dualism, 421–23
and social mobility, 310, 320
Social differentiation, compared with an stratification, 3–4, 485, 511–12, 523
and industrialization, 443–44, 453–54
Social equality, *see* Egalitarian attitudes
Social inequality, basic forms of, 485, 511
Greek thought on, 2
Hebrew prophets' views of, 2
hierarchy and, 58–59, 515–20
institutionalization of, 52, 57, 58, 76, 515–16
major perspectives on, 2, 105
perception of, 130–33, 226–47, 295–96, 419, 451–52, 472
without stratification, 486, 512–20
*see also* Economic inequality, Power inequality, Status inequality, stratification
Social justice, 129–30, 235
Social mobility, absence of a perpetual trend in, 320–21
in caste society, 37, 310, 319
channels of, 313–14, 321, 361–62
city size, migration, and, 346–49, 347*t.*
defined, 5, 309–10, 317
determinants of, 310–11, 321–25
demographic, 321–22, 349–52, 366–68
education, 342–44
ethnic background, 344–46, 345*t.*, 372–73
in developing nations, 339–40
distance of, 312, 318, 331–37, 332*t.*, 333*t.*, 334*t.*
ethnic differences in, 377–78, 388, 396–403
factors in, ability and intelligence, 316, 363–65
motivation, 314–15, 365–73, 378, 401
psychological, 315, 363–73
subjective, defined, 315
general propositions about, 319–21
in industrial society, 339, 455–56, 516
intergenerational, 312, 326–52
international comparisons, 325–41, 327*t.*, 329*t.*, 342, 367
means of, 315–16, 363–72, 433–34, 436–37
modes of, sponsored and contest, 313–14, 353–62
and mental illness, 371–72
methodological techniques and problems, 310–12, 314, 340–42
national profiles of, 313, 333*t.*, 338
Pareto's conception, 11–12, 36–39
in Peru, 432–35
in Poland, 130, 239, 241*t.*, 242, 242*t.*, 243, 246–47
positive and negative consequences of, 311
and social control, 356–57
in socialist society, 158–59
in Soviet Union, 289–90
in U.S., 339, 340–52
upward vs. downward, 312, 312*n.*, 317, 339–40
Social race, concept of, 380
Social stratification, *see* Stratification
Socialist society, class consciousness in, 158, 419

classes and strata in, 99–104, 177, 284, 418–19, 465–77
conflicting interests in, 419, 470–76
and the state, 473–76
and freedom, 159–60
power inequality in, 154–60, 166, 461–64
status privileges in, 286
uneven distribution of goods, 471–76
*see also* Poland, Soviet Union
Socialization at home, achievement motivation and, 369, 369*n.*
class differences in, 254
lower class, 252–53, 276, 315
and reference group, 315, 372
Soviet Union, class and family in, 284–96
class differences in
values, 291–92
deviant behavior, 290–91
in education, 254, 286, 286*t.*, 287*t.*, 288–90
in use of free time, 288–89, 289*t.*
class structure in, 154–60, 167
political bureaucracy, 154–56
underclass, 108
economic inequality in, 108, 109–10, 143–54, 285–86, 293, 461–62
wage policy, 144–54
egalitarianism in, 110, 144, 151–54, 293
power inequality, 154–60, 295–96, 462–64
social mobility in, 289–90
sponsored, 315
status inequality, 285–91, 295–96
subjective class in, 130, 130*n.*, 295–96
Status (honor and prestige), American pattern, 29, 177–83
concept of, 10, 25, 28–29, 115
economic position and, 10, 28–29, 31–33, 128, 185-88, 470, 476–77
in feudalism, 82
pattern of Polish Jews, 184–91
privileges, 31, 286, 295–96
sources of, 116–17, 120, 183, 184–89
symbols of, 116, 376
Status (position), ascription-achievement, 52
Status communities, 117*n.*, 117–18, 410
Status consistency and inconsistency, conceptualization, 121–22
consequences of, 122–23, 204–206, 293–96
in industrial society, 454–55, 458–59, 469–70, 475–77
in socialist society, 469–70, 475–77
in Israel, 444–46, 445*n.*, 445*t.*
in Soviet Union, 293–96
in U.S., 205–206
Status crystallization, *see* Status consistency and inconsistency
Status group, caste and, 29–31, 57
compared with class, 10, 28–29, 31–33
occupational groups as, 32
Status inequality, 114–23, 175–206
in Great Britain, 228–35
in a Jewish community, 184–91
in Poland, 235–47, 472
perception of and attitudes toward, 128–33, 228–39, 231*t.*, 233*t.*, 236*t.*, 237*t.*
in Socialist society, 130
in Soviet Union, 285–91
in U.S., 177–83, 408–13
Strata, *see* Class, Stratification
Stratification, in caste society, 56–57, 74–81
change in, 5, 8, 13, 14–18, 24, 39–50, 235, 235*n.*, 320, 415–77, 513–31
concept of, 4
question of necessity of, 2, 4, 167–77, 497
question of universality of, 4, 319, 520–21
complexity and, 4, 176–77
consequences of, 249–307
in developing nations, 415–52
dimensions of, objective, 105–23
subjective, 123–32
ethnicity and, 5, 29–31, 375–413, 447, 449–51
in feudal society, 13, 14–16, 57–59, 81–91
indexes of, 132
in industrial society, 5, 59–60, 92–104, 417–18, 452–65, 479, 513–31
capitalist, 8–9, 14–16, 97–101, 467–68, 527–28
capitalist and socialist compared, 97–104, 418, 461–65, 465–68, 470–71, 475–77
socialist, 99–104, 177, 284, 418–19, 461–63, 465–77
in Israel, 438–52
in a Jewish community, 116–17, 183–91
major functions of, 499–502
principles of, 496–503
in Peru, 427–38
in slave society, 51–56
in Soviet Union, 461*n.*, 461–63
study of, 1, 487, 514–15, 531
theories of, classic tradition, 7–50
modern, 486, 514–15
unresolved issues in, 479–531
in U.S., 1, 175–83
regional differences, 177–83
*see also* Class, Social inequality
Stratification systems, 51–103
change in, 415–77
ideal types, 51–52, 56–57, 58, 60–61, 74, 503
interaction between industrial and preindustrial, 415, 421–27
open-closed, 37, 52, 56-58, 61, 183, 313, 319–20
perception of change in, 130–31, 243–44

Style of life, 29–30, 179, 249, 285, 486
  *see also* Way of life
Subculture, *see* Class subcultures
Success, class and, 296–307
    variation, in perception of, 300
  in symbols of, 298–300
  *vs.* achievement, 299–300, 306
  *see also* Achievement
Synthesis of functionalist and conflict theories, 3, 480–81, 490–91

Triple melting pot, 406–409

Underclass, 107–108, 417
  in Soviet Union, 108
  subculture of, 270–71, 273–76
  in U.S., 138–43
Unemployment, 107–108, 137–38
  cures of, 140, 141
  consequences of, 140
  vicious circle of, 140–41
  in U.S., 137–38, 138–42
Urbanization and industrialization, **415–16**, 424–25
United States, class in, 175–83
    ethnicity and, 357–77, 396–413
    mortality and, 260–70, 261*t*.
    race and, 376–77, 387–96
    success and, 296–307
    subcultures and, 270–76
  community power in, 168–74
  elite in, 112–14, 162–64, 379, 404–409
  economic inequality in, 106–108, **133–38**, 143
    occupational structure, 192–93
  family in, 276–84
  poverty in, 142–43
  power inequality, 111–14, 162–63, 170–72
    role of clubs, 409–13
  Protestant Establishment in, 378-79, 403-13
  social mobility, occupational, 340–52
    school and, 358–62
    sponsored and contest, 315, 353–54, 358–62
  unemployment in, 137–38, 138–43
  voting behavior in, 127–28, 216–26
Upper class, clubs, 29, 379, 409–13
  in Jewish community, 190
  lower-upper, 178
  in Peru, 428–29
  in socialist society, 110–11, 154–60
  subculture, 251–52, 404–13
  in U.S., 177, 181, 379, 404–13
  upper-upper, 178

Value stretch, 251
Values, 507, 512
  class variation of, 191, 250–51, 291–92, 357, 378, 401–403
  of education, 116–17, 188–89, 255, 301–303
  egalitarian, 131–32, 246–47, 293
  in feudal society, 22, 83–86
  in industrial society, 507–509
  Jewish traditional, 184–91
  of success, class variation, 255, 296–305, 368–69
  working class, 277–81, 305–306
Vertical mobility, 309–10
  *see also* Social mobility
Voting behavior, class and, 216–26, **219*t*.**, 222*t*.
  ideology and, 216–26, 221*t*., 222*t*., 224*t*.

Wages, *see* Income distribution
Wales, class and mortality in, 266–68
Way of life, 5, 249
  class and culture variation hypothesis, 250–51
  class subculture hypothesis, 250–51
  class variation in, 179, 190–91, 250–54, 270–307
  of nobility, 84–86
  of unemployed, 140
  *see also* Style of life
Wealth distribution, 106, 116, 435
Welfare state, 60, 253, 529
Working class, attitudes and values of, 277–81, 305–306
    manliness, 277–78
    work, 140, 256, 530–31
  consciousness, 128–29, 525–29
  deradicalization and *embourgeoisement* of, 91, 128, 227, 416, 432, 525–31
  family, 252–53, 270–71
    marriage, 253–54, 276–84
    sex differentiation, 276–81
  impoverishment of life in, 279
  lower-lower, 179–80, 252–53, 270–71, 273–76
  in Peru, 432, 434–35
  racial differences in behavior, 376–77
  reference groups of, 228–35, 315
  relative deprivation among, 130, 226–35
  in Soviet Union, 284–96
  subculture, 252–54, 270–71, 273–76
  upper-lower, 179
  voting behavior of, 218–19, 222*t*., 222–26
  *see also* Proletariat, Underclass

Yankee City, 115, 116, 177–81
Yugoslavia, ruling class in, 157–58, 159–60

Focusing on change, this excellent text
reflects a [illegible] rati[illegible] ntation [illegible]
[illegible] dif[illegible]

**Combined** with the resources you have trusted throughout the years to provide you with the best business resources available:

- ***In the News***—New current events articles are added throughout the year. Each article is summarized by our teams of experts, and fully supported by exercises, activities, and instructor materials.
- ***Online Study Guide***—Three quizzes are linked to each text chapter and include "hints" for each question. Each quiz is graded immediately upon submission, provides immediate feedback on each given answer, and enables students to e-mail results to the instructor.
- ***Research Area***—Your own personal resource library includes tutorials, descriptive links to virtual libraries, and a wealth of search engines and resources.
- ***Internet Resources***—These provide discipline-specific sites, including preview information that allows you to review site information before you view the site, ensuring you visit the best available business resources found by our learning community.

## For the professor

- ***Teaching Resources*** provide material contributed by professors throughout the world—including teaching tips, techniques, academic papers, and sample syllabi—and Talk to the Team,a moderated faculty chat room.
- ***Online Faculty Support*** includes downloadable supplements, additional cases, articles, links, and suggested answers to Current Events Activities.
- ***What's New*** gives you one-click access to all newly posted PHLIP resources.

## For the student

- ***Talk to the Tutor*** schedules virtual office hours that allow students to post questions from any supported discipline and receive responses from the dedicated PHLIP/CW faculty team.
- ***Writing Resource Center*** provides an online writing center that supplies links to online directories, thesauruses, writing tutors, style and grammar guides, and additional tools.
- ***Career Center*** helps students access career information, view sample résumés, even apply for jobs online.
- ***Study Tips*** provides an area where students can learn to develop better study skills.

***ONLINE LEARNING SOLUTIONS***— Prentice Hall offers online solutions in Blackboard, Course Compass, and WebCT. Standard courses (free with new text purchase) include these course management features:

- Online Testing
- Course Management and Page Tracking
- Gradebook
- Course Information
- Multiple-Section Chat Rooms
- Bulletin Board Conferencing
- Syllabus and Calendar Functions
- E-mail Capability

**www.prenhall.com/keown**

**BAII PLUS Rebate Terms and Conditions**

This offer is valid only for BAII PLUS purchases between January 1, 2001 and May 1, 2003. All claims must be postmarked by July 31, 2003. Allow 8 to 10 weeks for processing. All purchases must be made in the U.S. or Canada. Rebates will be sent only to addresses in the U.S. and Canada and paid in U.S. dollars. Not redeemable at any store. Send this completed form along with the retail or on-line receipt (original or copy) and the UPC bar code to the address indicated. This original mail-in certificate must accompany your request and may not be duplicated or reproduced. Offer valid only as stated on this form. Offer void where prohibited, taxed, licensed, or restricted. Limit one rebate per household or address. Texas Instruments reserves the right to discontinue this program at any time and without notice.

AD067.99



Yes! I Want $5 Back On My Purchase of the BAII PLUS.

# FINANCIAL MANAGEMENT: PRINCIPLES AND APPLICATIONS

NINTH EDITION

# FINANCIAL MANAGEMENT: PRINCIPLES AND APPLICATIONS

**ARTHUR J. KEOWN**
Virginia Polytechnic Institute and State University
R.B. Pamplin Professor of Finance

**JOHN D. MARTIN**
Baylor University
Carr P. Collins Chair in Finance

**J. WILLIAM PETTY**
Baylor University
Professor of Finance
W. W. Caruth Chair in Entrepreneurship

**DAVID F. SCOTT, JR.**
University of Central Florida
Holder, Phillips-Schenck Chair in American Private Enterprise
Executive Director, Dr. Phillips Institute for the Study of American Business Activity
Professor of Finance

Prentice Hall, Upper Saddle River, New Jersey 07458

**Library of Congress Cataloging-in-Publication Data**

Financial management: principles and applications/Arthur Keown.—9th ed.

p.cm.

Rev. ed. of: Basic financial management. 7th ed. c1996.

Includes bibliographical references and indexes.

ISBN 0-13-033362-X

1. Business enterprises—Finance. 2. Corporations—Finance. I. Keown, Arthur J. II. Basic financial management.

HG4026 .B318 2001

658.15—dc21

2001021391

**AVP/Executive Editor:** Mickey Cox
**Editor-in-Chief:** PJ Boardman
**Managing Editor (Editorial):** Gladys Soto
**Assistant Editor:** Cheryl Clayton
**Editorial Assistant:** Melanie Olsen
**Media Project Manager:** Bill Minick
**Marketing Manager:** Joshua P. McClary
**Marketing Assistant:** Christopher Bath
**Managing Editor (Production):** Cynthia Regan
**Production Editor:** Carol Samet
**Production Assistant:** Diane Falcone
**Permissions Coordinator:** Suzanne Grappi
**Associate Director, Manufacturing:** Vinnie Scelta
**Production Manager:** Arnold Vila
**Manufacturing Buyer:** Diane Peirano
**Design Manager:** Patricia Smythe
**Senior Designer:** Janet Slowik
**Interior Design:** Craig Ramsdell
**Cover Design:** Janet Slowik
**Composition:** Carlisle Communications, Ltd.
**Full-Service Project Management:** Carlisle Communications, Ltd.
**Printer/Binder:** R.R. Donnelley & Sons Company

Credits and acknowledgments borrowed from other sources and reproduced, with permission, in this textbook appear on appropriate page within text. Photos courtesy of Harley-Davidson, Inc.

10 9 8 7 6 5 4 3 2
ISBN 0-13-33362-x

The ninth edition of Financial Management: Principles and Applications is dedicated to our families—the ones who love us the most.

*Barb, Emily, and Artie*
Arthur J. Keown

*Sally, Dave and Mel, and Jess*
John D. Martin

*To the future of four wonderful grandchildren: Ashley, Cameron, John, and MacKenzie.*
J. William Petty

*To my dear late wife Peggy. Thank you for 36 marvelous, irreplaceable years.*
David F. Scott, Jr.

# BRIEF CONTENTS

Preface xvii

**PART 1: THE SCOPE AND ENVIRONMENT OF FINANCIAL MANAGEMENT**

Chapter 1
An Introduction to Financial Management 1

Chapter 2
Understanding Financial Statements, Taxes, and Cash Flows 27

Chapter 3
Evaluating a Firm's Financial Performance 62

Chapter 4
Financial Forecasting, Planning, and Budgeting 99

**PART 2: VALUATION OF FINANCIAL ASSETS**

Chapter 5
The Time Value of Money 127

Chapter 6
Risk and Rates of Return 168

Chapter 7
Valuation and Characteristics of Bonds 211

Chapter 8
Stock Valuation 241

**PART 3: INVESTMENT IN LONG-TERM ASSETS**

Chapter 9
Capital-Budgeting Decision Criteria 271

Chapter 10
Cash Flows and Other Topics in Capital Budgeting 309

Chapter 11
Capital Budgeting and Risk Analysis 349

Chapter 12
Cost of Capital 381

Chapter 13
Managing for Shareholder Value 410

## PART 4: CAPITAL STRUCTURE AND DIVIDEND POLICY

Chapter 14
Raising Capital in the Financial Markets 439

Chapter 15
Analysis and Impact of Leverage 468

Chapter 16
Planning the Firm's Financing Mix 513

Chapter 17
Dividend Policy and Internal Financing 567

## PART 5: WORKING-CAPITAL MANAGEMENT AND SPECIAL TOPICS IN FINANCE

Chapter 18
Working-Capital Management and Short-Term Financing 606

Chapter 19
Cash and Marketable Securities Management 634

Chapter 20
Accounts Receivable and Inventory Management 665

## PART 6: SPECIAL TOPICS IN FINANCE

Chapter 21
Risk Management 698

Chapter 22
International Business Finance 732

Chapter 23
Corporate Restructuring: Combinations and Divestitures 23-1

Chapter 24
Term Loans and Leases 24-1

Appendices A-1
Glossary G-1
Index I-1

# CONTENTS

Preface xvii

## PART 1: THE SCOPE AND ENVIRONMENT OF FINANCIAL MANAGEMENT

### CHAPTER 1
### An Introduction to Financial Management 1

What Is Finance? 2

Goal of the Firm 3

Legal Forms of Business Organization 4

Ten Principles That Form the Basics of Financial Management 10

**Principle 1:** The Risk-Return Trade-Off—We won't take on additional risk unless we expect to be compensated with additional return 11

**Principle 2:** The Time Value of Money—A dollar received today is worth more than a dollar received in the future 12

**Principle 3:** Cash—Not Profits—Is King 12

**Principle 4:** Incremental Cash Flows—It's only what changes that counts 13

**Principle 5:**The Curse of Competitive Markets—Why it's hard to find exceptionally profitable projects 13

**Principle 6:** Efficient Capital Markets—The markets are quick and the prices are right 14

**Principle 7:** The Agency Problem—Managers won't work for owners unless it's in their best interest 15

**Principle 8:** Taxes Bias Business Decisions 16

**Principle 9:** All Risk Is Not Equal—Some risk can be diversified away, and some cannot 16

**Principle 10:** Ethical behavior is doing the right thing, and ethical dilemmas are everywhere in finance 18

Overview of the Text 19

Finance and the Multinational Firm: The New Role 21

How Financial Managers Use This Material 22

Summary 22

### CHAPTER 2
### Understanding Financial Statements, Taxes, and Cash Flows 27

The Income Statement: Measuring a Company's Profits 28

The Balance Sheet: Measuring a Firm's Book Value 30

Computing a Company's Taxes 36

Measuring Free Cash Flows 39

Financial Statements and International Finance 44

How Financial Managers Use This Material 44
Summary 45

CHAPTER 3
Evaluating a Firm's Financial Performance 62
Financial Ration Analysis 63
The DuPont Analysis: An Integrative Approach to Ratio Analysis 77
Summary 81

CHAPTER 4
Financial Forecasting, Planning, and Budgeting 99
Financial Forecasting 100
Limitations of the Percent of Sales Forecast Method 106
The Sustainable Rate of Growth 108
Financial Planning and Budgeting 109
How Financial Managers Use This Material 112
Summary 113

PART 2: VALUATION OF FINANCIAL ASSETS

CHAPTER 5
The Time Value of Money 127
Compound Interest and Future Value 128
Compound Interest with Nonannual Periods 136
Present Value 137
Annuities—A Level Stream 140
Annuities Due 147
Present Value of Complex Stream 150
Perpetuities and Infinite Annuities 153
Making Interest Rates Comparable 153
The Multinational Firm: The Time Value of Money 154
How Financial Managers Use This Material 155
Summary 155

CHAPTER 6
Risk and Rates of Return 168
Rates of Return in the Financial Markets 169
The Effects of Inflation on Rates of Return and the Fisher Effect 171
The Term Structure of Interest Rates 172
Expected Return 174
Risk 175
Risk and Diversification 179
Measuring Market Risk 182
Measuring a Portfolio's Beta 188
The Investor's Required Rate of Return 190

How Financial Managers Use This Material 193
Summary 194

CHAPTER 7
Valuation and Characteristics of Bonds 211

Types of Bonds 212
Terminology and Characteristics of Bonds 215
Definitions of Value 218
Determinants of Value 220
Valuation: The Basic Process 222
Bond Valuation 223
The Bondholder's Expected Rate of Return (Yield to Maturity) 226
Bond Valuation: Five Important Relationships 228
How Financial Managers Use This Material 234
Summary 234

CHAPTER 8
Stock Valuation 241

Features and Types of Preferred Stock 242
Valuing Preferred Stock 245
Characteristics of Common Stock 247
Valuing Common Stock 252
Stockholder's Expected Rate of Return 258
How Financial Managers Use This Material 260
Summary 260

PART 3: INVESTMENT IN LONG-TERM ASSETS

CHAPTER 9
Capital-Budgeting Decision Criteria 271

Finding Profitable Projects 272
Payback Period 274
Net Present Value 277
Profitability Index (Benefit/Cost Ratio) 280
Internal Rate of Return 281
Ethics in Capital Budgeting 294
A Glance at Actual Capital-Budgeting Practices 295
How Financial Managers Use This Material 297
Summary 298

CHAPTER 10
Cash Flows and Other Topics in Capital Budgeting 309

Guidelines for Capital Budgeting 310
An Overview of the Calculations of a Project's Free Cash Flows 314
Complications in Capital Budgeting: Capital Rationing and Mutually Exclusive Projects 324

The Multinational Firm: International Complications in Calculating Expected Free Cash Flows 332

How Financial Managers Use This Material 333

Summary 334

**CHAPTER 11**
**Capital Budgeting and Risk Analysis 349**

Risk and the Investment Decision 350

Methods for Incorporating Risk into Capital Budgeting 354

Other Approaches to Evaluating Risk in Capital Budgeting 361

The Multinational Firm: Capital Budgeting and Risk 367

How Financial Managers Use This Material 368

Summary 368

**CHAPTER 12**
**Cost of Capital 381**

The Cost of Capital: Key Definitions and Concepts 382

Determining Individual Costs of Capital 383

The Weighted Average Cost of Capital 390

Cost of Capital in Practice: Briggs & Stratton 394

Calculating Divisional Costs of Capital: PepsiCo, Inc. 396

Using a Firm's Cost of Capital to Evaluate New Capital Investments 397

How Financial Managers Use This Material 401

Summary 401

**CHAPTER 13**
**Managing for Shareholder Value 410**

Who Are the Top Creators of Shareholder Value? 412

Business Valuation—The Key to Creating Shareholder Value 414

Value Drivers 419

Economic Value Added *(EVA)*® 421

Paying for Performance 424

How Financial Managers Use This Material 429

Summary 430

## PART 4: CAPITAL STRUCTURE AND DIVIDEND POLICY

**CHAPTER 14**
**Raising Capital in the Financial Markets 439**

The Financial Manager, Internal and External Funds, and Flexibility 442

The Mix of Corporate Securities Sold in the Capital Market 445

Why Financial Markets Exist 445

Financing of Business: The Movement of Funds Through the Economy 448

Components of the U.S. Financial Market System 451

The Investment Banker 456

More on Private Placements: The Debt Side 460

Flotation Costs 461

Regulation 462

The Multinational Firm: Efficient Financial Markets and Intercountry Risk 464

How Financial Managers Use This Material 465

Summary 465

**CHAPTER 15**
**Analysis and Impact of Leverage 468**

Business and Financial Risk 469

Break-Even Analysis 472

Operating Leverage 482

Financial Leverage 486

Combination of Operating and Financial Leverage 490

The Multinational Firm: Business Risk and Global Sales 493

How Financial Managers Use This Material 495

Summary 495

**CHAPTER 16**
**Planning the Firm's Financing Mix 513**

Key Terms and Getting Started 514

A Glance at Capital Structure Theory 516

Basic Tools of Capital Structure Management 530

The Multinational Firm: Beware of Currency Risk 542

How Financial Managers Use This Material 542

Summary 550

**CHAPTER 17**
**Dividend Policy and Internal Financing 567**

Dividend Payment Versus Profit Retention 569

Does Dividend Policy Affect Stock Price? 570

The Dividend Decision in Practice 584

Dividend Payment Procedures 587

Stock Dividends and Stock Splits 588

Stock Repurchases 590

The Multinational Firm: The Case of Low Dividend Payments—So Where Do We Invest? 594

How Financial Managers Use This Material 595

Summary 596

## PART 5: WORKING-CAPITAL MANAGEMENT AND SPECIAL TOPICS IN FINANCE

**CHAPTER 18**
**Working-Capital Management and Short-Term Financing 606**

Managing Current Assets and Liabilities 607

Financing Working Capital with Current Liabilities 609

Appropriate Level of Working Capital 610

Hedging Principles 610
Cash Conversion Cycle 612
Estimation of the Cost of Short-Term Credit 614
Sources of Short-Term Credit 616
Multinational Working-Capital Management 623
How Financial Managers Use This Material 624
Summary 624

CHAPTER 19
Cash and Marketable Securities Management 634

What Are Liquid Assets? 635
Why a Company Holds Cash 635
Cash-Management Objectives and Decisions 638
Collection and Disbursement Procedures 639
Composition of Marketable Securities Portfolio 645
The Multinational Firm: The Use of Cash and Marketable Securities 652
How Financial Managers Use This Material 652
Summary 653

CHAPTER 20
Accounts Receivable and Inventory Management 665

Accounts Receivable Management 667
Inventory Management 676
TQM and Inventory-Purchasing Management: The New Supplier Relationships 684
How Financial Managers Use This Material 687
Summary 688

PART 6: SPECIAL TOPICS IN FINANCE

CHAPTER 21
Risk Management 698

Futures 699
Options 706
Currency Swaps 717
The Multinational Firm and Risk Management 718
How Financial Managers Use This Material 719
Summary 719

CHAPTER 22
International Business Finance 732

The Globalization of Product and Financial Matters 733
Exchange Rates 734
Interest-Rate Parity Theory 745
Purchasing Power Parity Theory 745
Exposure to Exchange Rate Risk 747

Multinational Working-Capital Management 751
International Financing and Capital-Structure Decisions 753
Direct Foreign Investment 755
How Financial Managers Use This Material 756
Summary 757

CHAPTER 23
Corporate Restructuring: Combinations and Divestitures 23-1

Why Mergers Might Create Wealth 23-3
Determination of a Firm's Value 23-6
Divestitures 23-14
How Financial Managers Use This Material 23-15
Summary 23-15

CHAPTER 24
Term Loans and Leases 24-1

Term Loans 24-2
Loan Payment Calculation 24-4
Leases 24-5
The Economics of Leasing Versus Purchasing 24-15
How Financial Managers Use This Material 24-19
Summary 24-19

Appendices A-1
Glossary G-1
Index I-1

# PREFACE

In many ways, Harley-Davidson is the American experience. Its beginnings date back to 1903 and the Industrial Revolution in America, and it survived two world wars, the Great Depression, and competition from countless competitors from both home and abroad. Then, in 1985, Harley-Davidson came close to becoming a part of history as it teetered on the verge of bankruptcy. However, since then, Harley-Davidson reinvented itself, becoming one of the most successful companies in America and, as President Reagan once proclaimed, "an American success story."

In many ways, the evolution of Harley-Davidson illustrates the enormous challenges faced by any company in today's world—surviving and prospering in a business world involves a continuous series of challenges. In this text, we focus on how the firm can create wealth for its shareholders. How did Harley-Davidson do? Between 1986, when Harley-Davidson returned to public ownership with a successful stock offering, and 1999, Harley's stock price rose approximately 100-fold. And how was all of this done? Through outstanding financial management. Harley-Davidson management made good decisions. That's what we're going to look at in this book. We'll look at what it takes to turn Harley-Davidson or any other company around, and what it takes to keep a company like Harley-Davidson alive and well.

## OUR APPROACH TO FINANCIAL MANAGEMENT

The first-time student of finance will find that corporate finance builds upon both accounting and economics. Economics provides much of the theory that underlies our techniques, whereas accounting provides the input or data on which decision making is based. Unfortunately, it is all too easy for students to lose sight of the logic that drives finance and to focus instead on memorizing formulas and procedures. As a result, students have a difficult time understanding the interrelationships between the topics covered. Moreover, later in life when the problems encountered do not fit neatly into the textbook presentation, the student may have problems abstracting from what was learned. To overcome this problem, the opening chapter presents 10 basic principles of finance that are woven throughout the book. What results is a text tightly bound around these guiding principles. In essence, the student is presented with a cohesive, interrelated subject from which future, as yet unknown, problems can be approached.

Teaching an introductory finance class while faced with an ever-expanding discipline puts additional pressures on the instructor. What to cover, what to omit, and how to do this while maintaining a cohesive presentation are inescapable questions. In dealing with these questions, we have attempted to present the chapters in a stand-alone fashion so that they could be easily rearranged to fit almost any desired course structure and course length. Because the principles are woven into every chapter, the presentation of the text remains tight regardless of whether or not the chapters are rearranged. Again, our goal is to provide an enduring understanding of the basic tools and fundamental principles upon which finance is based. This foundation will give a student beginning his or her studies in finance a strong base on which to build future studies and give the student who will take only one finance class a lasting understanding of the basics of finance.

Although historical circumstances continue to serve as the driving force behind the development and practice of finance, the underlying principles that guide our discipline remain the same. These principles are presented in an intuitively appealing manner in Chapter 1 and thereafter are tied to all that follows. With a focus upon the big picture, we provide an introduction to financial decision making rooted in current financial theory and in the current state of world economic conditions. This focus can be seen in a number of ways, perhaps most obvious being the attention paid both to valuation and to the capital markets and their influence on corporate financial decisions. What results is an introductory treatment of a discipline rather than the treatment of a series of isolated finance problems. The goal of this text is to go beyond teaching the tools of a discipline or a trade, and help students gain a complete understanding of the subject. This will give them the ability to apply what he or she has learned to new and yet unforeseen problems—in short, to educate students in finance.

## A TOTAL LEARNING PACKAGE

*Financial Management* is not simply another introductory finance text. It is a total learning package and reflects the vitality and ever-expanding nature of the discipline. Finance has grown too complex not to teach with an eye on the big picture, focusing on the interrelationships between the materials that are covered. Listed below are some of the distinctive pedagogical features that assist the student in understanding how concepts in finance link to the big picture of finance.

### Learning Aids in the Text

TEN PRINCIPLES OF FINANCE The fundamental principles that drive the practice of corporate finance are presented in the form of 10 principles. These principles first appear in Chapter 1 and thereafter appear in in-text inserts called "Relate to the Big Picture." These inserts serve to refocus the student's attention on the underlying principles behind what is being done. In effect, they serve to keep the student from becoming so wrapped up in specific calculations that the interrelationships and overall scheme is lost.

INTEGRATIVE END-OF-CHAPTER PROBLEMS An Integrative Problem is provided at the end of each chapter and covers all the major topics included in that chapter. This comprehensive problem can be used as a lecture or review tool by the professor. To aid the instructor in presenting this material, the solution is provided to the instructor in Microsoft PowerPoint format. For students, the integrative end-of-chapter problems provide an opportunity to apply all the concepts presented within the chapter in a realistic setting, thereby strengthening their understanding of the material.

FINANCE MATTERS Strong emphasis is also placed upon practice, where practice is used to demonstrate both the relevance of the topics discussed and the implementation of theory. Moreover, to add life to the discussion, "Finance Matters" boxed inserts are provided throughout the text. These boxes are largely taken from the popular press with analysis and implications provided following each box. In this way, the subject matter comes to life with added relevance to the student.

HARLEY-DAVIDSON CHAPTER INTRODUCTIONS Each chapter opens with an introductory example that involves Harley-Davidson and sets the stage for what is to follow. In this way, the student can easily understand the relevance, use, and importance of the material to be presented. Moreover, by focusing on the challenges facing a single company, the student can better understand the interrelationships between the different financial topics that are presented.

**UNIQUE TREATMENT OF MANAGERIAL COMPENSATION AND MANAGING FOR SHAREHOLDER VALUE** An important addition to the ninth edition of *Financial Management* is an entire chapter on managing for shareholder value. In the new Chapter 13, entitled Managing for Shareholder Value, we focus on the use of economic value added, or *EVA*®, to measure firm and divisional performance. This measure of performance has been found to be an effective tool for managing for shareholder value by a large number of firms both in the United States and abroad. In fact, even the U.S. Postal Service has implemented a variant of the model to better control its internal operations.

Traditionally, the finance profession has had little to say about performance appraisal of the firm beyond a cursory discussion of financial ratios. In this new chapter we discuss value creation first in terms of how the market accords value to the firm in the context of market value added. Next we connect value creation to the individual contributions that the firm makes year-to-year in the form of *EVA*®. But measuring value creation is not enough. The proponents of shareholder value creation point out, quite appropriately, that to assure the continued focus of the firm's employees on value creation, the firm must reward them for doing the things that lead to value creation. Thus, the second half of this new chapter focuses on managerial compensation. This is the first corporate finance text to undertake a synthesis of both the measurement (*EVA*®) and reward (compensation) systems that are commonplace among the top value creators in corporate America.

**INTERNATIONAL FINANCIAL MANAGEMENT** In view of the continued globalization of world markets, we have integrated examples of international finance throughout the text. In addition, at the close of most chapters a new section has been added dealing with how the material in that chapter relates to the multinational firm. Finally, recognizing the fact that many of us approach the teaching of international finance in different ways, a separate chapter on international financial management is also provided.

**CHAPTER LEARNING OBJECTIVES AND KEY TERMS** Each chapter begins by setting out the learning objectives for that chapter, and setting in mind what that chapter will enable the student to do. In addition, at the end of each chapter, key terms and their locations in the text are identified, making for an easy review for the student.

**FINANCIAL SPREADSHEETS AND CALCULATORS** The use of financial spreadsheets and calculators has been integrated throughout this text. This provides the student with access to both methods of problem solving and introduces the advantages of each. In addition, we provide the student with hints and strategies for the use of financial spreadsheets directly in the text, while providing an appendix in the back of the book that guides them through the use of a financial calculator.

**EXPANDED USE OF REAL-WORLD EXAMPLES OTHER THAN HARLEY-DAVIDSON** In addition to the focus on Harley-Davidson, we have greatly expanded the illustrative use of examples of problems facing other real-world firms. This adds to student interest both by showing the relevance of the subjects covered and by providing an exciting framework within which to discuss financial concepts.

**HOW FINANCIAL MANAGERS USE THIS MATERIAL** Each chapter closes with a section entitled "How Financial Managers Use This Material." This section ties the material presented in the chapter both to the student's future job setting and to real-world companies, thereby enhancing the student's interest and displaying the relevance of the material covered.

FUNCTIONAL INTEGRATION TO BUSINESS Where appropriate, we have pointed out the relevance of the material covered to those students who are not finance majors—information technology, accounting, marketing, and management majors. In this way, students who are not finance majors are brought into the subject matter.

## NEW TO THIS EDITION

In addition to an updating and streamlining of the material, the following list includes the major additions that are new to *Financial Management:*

- The use of free cash flows has been integrated and emphasized throughout the text.
- A new Chapter 13, titled, "Managing for Shareholder Value," has been added. This chapter addresses issues of measurement and rewards designed to create shareholder value; that is, *EVA*.
- Chapter 1 has been revised with a new section that provides a flow of funds overview at end of chapter. In addition, the discussion of taxes has been moved to Chapter 2.
- The discussion of financial statements in Chapter 2 was tightened and shortened, while taxes were added. In addition, the discussion of an accounting cash-flow statement was replaced with measuring free cash flows.
- The discussion of the cash budget previously in Chapter 4 was moved to the working capital chapter. In addition, the chapter was refocused on forecasting firm/project free cash flow.
- Chapter 6 now includes an introduction to interest rates, including the Fisher model of determinants of risk-free rates, term structure effects, default risk premiums, and market risk premiums.
- Chapters 7 and 8 were updated to include more timely examples.
- Chapter 10 now focuses its discussion around project expansion decision and use of free cash-flow valuation as opposed to the replacement decision.
- Chapter 11 now includes a discussion of real options and their role in the capital-budgeting decision.
- Much of Chapter 14, "Raising Capital in the Financial Markets," actually came from Chapter 2 in the previous edition. In addition, this chapter now contains a discussion of private equity and debt markets.
- Chapter 17, "Dividend Policy and Internal Financing," now addresses the trend toward share repurchase as preferred method of cash distribution to stockholders.
- Chapter 18, "Working-Capital Management and Short-Term Financing," now contains the discussion of the cash budget, which previously appeared in the financial forecasting chapter. In addition, the discussion has been streamlined.
- In addition, Chapters 23 and 24 are now available on the Internet.

As a final, but important, comment to the teacher, we know how frustrating errors in a textbook or instructor's manual can be. Thus, we have worked diligently to provide you with as error-free a book as possible. Not only did we check and recheck the answers ourselves, but Prentice Hall hired faculty members at other universities to check the accuracy of the problem solutions. We therefore make the following offer to users of *Financial Management.*

Any professor or student identifying an error of substance (e.g., an incorrect number in an example or problem) in *Financial Management,* in the text, that has not been previously reported to the authors, will receive a $10 reward. If a series of related errors occurs resulting from an original error, the reward will be limited to a maximum of $20 for the group of errors. Please report any errors to Art Keown at the following address:

**Art Keown**
Department of Finance
Virginia Tech
Blacksburg, VA 24061

## LEARNING AIDS SUPPLEMENTAL TO THE TEXT

*Financial Management* integrates the most advanced technology available to assist the student and the instructor. Not only does it make their financial management come alive with the most current information, but also enhances a total understanding of all tools and concepts necessary in mastering the course.

### The Support Package

STUDENT STUDY GUIDE Written by the authors, the Study Guide contains several innovative features to help the student of *Financial Management.* Each chapter begins with an overview of the key points, which can serve both as a preview and quick survey of the chapter content, and as a review. There are problems (with detailed solutions) and self-tests that can be used to aid in the preparation of outside assignments and to study for examinations. The problems are keyed to the end-of-chapter problems in the text in order to provide direct and meaningful student aid. Multiple-choice and true/false questions are also included to provide a self-test over the descriptive chapter material.

INSTRUCTOR'S MANUAL WITH SOLUTIONS The Instructor's Manual, prepared by the authors, contains these four key elements for each chapter:

1. A chapter orientation, which offers the instructor a simple statement of the authors' intent for the chapter, and a useful point of departure for in-class lecture;
2. A chapter outline for easy reference to key issues;
3. Answers to all end-of-chapter questions in the test;
4. A second set of alternative problems with answers.

TEST BANK The Test Bank, revised for this edition by Philip T. Thames of California State University, Long Beach, provides multiple-choice, true/false, and short-answer questions with complete and detailed answers.

PRENTICE HALL TEST MANAGER The Test Bank is designed for use with the Prentice Hall Test Manager, a computerized package that allows instructors to custom design, save, and generate classroom tests. The test program (in Windows format) permits instructors to edit, add, or delete questions from the test bank; edit existing graphics and create new graphics; analyze test results; and organize a database of tests and student results.

POWERPOINT PRESENTATION Lecture notes have been prepared by Professor Anthony Byrd of the University of Central Florida. These electronic slides exhibit full-color presentations of chapter overviews and examples coordinated with Financial Management, Ninth Edition. The PowerPoint slides are available from the Prentice Hall Web site www.prenhall.com/keown

**SPREADSHEET TEMPLATES AND SOLUTIONS** In addition to the solutions being provided in the Instructor's Manual, the authors have also developed Spreadsheet Solutions for virtually all of the end-of-chapter problems. These solutions have been prepared in Excel. The user can change the assumptions in the problem and thereby generate new solutions. Student templates consist of select end of chapter problems that are meant to be worked out off our website. (Available to download at www.prenhall.com/keown).

**SPREADSHEET MODELING IN CORPORATE FINANCE EDITION TO ACCOMPANY FINANCIAL MANAGEMENT, NINTH EDITION** Comes as a book and browser-accessed CD-ROM that teaches students how to build financial models in Excel. Created by Craig W. Holden, Indiana University.

**NEWSPAPER SUBSCRIPTIONS**

- ***The Financial Times,*** 15-week student subscription for a nominal fee! Adopting Professors will receive a 1-year subscription free!
- ***The Wall Street Journal*** **Print and Interactive Editions,** 10-week subscription to *The Wall Street Journal* print edition and *The Wall Street Journal* Interactive Edition for a nominal fee. Adopting professors will receive a free-1-year subscription of both the print and interactive version.

## Welcome to myPHLIP

Your personal guide to the free on-line resources for your book

Featuring one click access to all of the new resources created by our award-winning team of educators, myPHLIP provides a **personalized view** of the great new resources available:

*New* **myPHLIP pages**—Your personal access page unites all your myPHLIP texts.
*New* **Notes**—Add personal notes to our resources for personal reminders and references.
*New* **Messages**—Instructors can send messages to individual students, or all students linked to your course.
*New* **Student Resources**—Add premium PHLIP resources for your students to view and download (such as our PowerPoint slides, videos, and spreadsheets).
*New* **Syllabus Tool**—Improved new on-line syllabus tools help you add your own personal syllabus to our site in minutes.
*New* **Business Headlines**—Provide links to articles in today's business news.
*New* **Search**—Search all PHLIP resources for relevant articles and exercises.
*New* **Instructor Manual**—myPHLIP Instructor Manual provides tips and suggestions from our PHLIP faculty for integrating PHLIP resources into your course.

Combined with the resources you have trusted throughout the years to provide you with the best business resources available:

- ✓ **In the News**—New current events articles are added throughout the year. Each article is summarized by our teams of expert professors and fully supported by exercises, activities, and instructor materials.
- ✓ **On-Line Study Guide**—Results from the automatically graded questions for every chapter provide immediate feedback for students that can be e-mailed to the instructor.
- ✓ **Research Area**—Your own personal resource library includes tutorials, descriptive links to virtual libraries, and a wealth of search engines and resources.

**For the Professor**

✓ **Teaching Resources** include resources contributed by professors throughout the world, including teaching tips, techniques, academic papers, sample syllabi, and **Talk to the Team,** a moderated faculty chat room.

✓ **On-line faculty support** including downloadable supplements, additional cases, articles, links, and suggested answers to Current Events Activities.

✓ **What's New** gives you one click access to all newly posted PHLIP resources.

✓ **Internet Resources** provide discipline-specific sites, including preview information that allows you to review site information before you view the site, ensuring you visit the best available business resources found by our learning community.

**For the Student**

✓ **Talk to the Tutor** Virtual office hours allow students to post questions from any supported discipline and receive responses from the dedicated PHLIP/CW faculty team.

✓ **Writing Resource Center** On-line writing center provides links to on-line directories, thesauruses, writing tutors, style and grammar guides, and additional tools.

✓ **Career Center** Helps access career information, view sample resumes, even apply for jobs on-line.

✓ **Study Tips** An area for students to learn to develop better study skills.

WEBCT Prentice Hall provides the content and enhanced features to help instructors create a complete online course. These courses include the following content:

- Online study guide
- Test questions
- Lecture notes created by economics professors to support each chapter of the book
- Video clips with a summary of the key points of each chapter
- PowerPoints

*Please visit our web site at:*

www.prenhall.com/webct

BLACKBOARD Blackboard features all the content listed above, plus:

- Course Management Tools that include progress tracking, class and student management, grade book, communication, assignments, and reporting tools.
- Communication Tools that include the Virtual Classroom (chat rooms, whiteboard slides), document sharing, and bulletin boards.
- Design Tools and pre-set designs that help you customize your course.

*Please visit our web site at:*

www.prenhall.com/blackboard

COURSECOMPASS CourseCompass™ is a dynamic, interactive online course management tool powered by Blackboard. This exciting product allows you to teach with market-leading Pearson Education content in an easy-to-use customizable format

*Please visit our web site at:*

www.coursecompass.com

*For the latest information on our Finance titles and other economics resources, please visit:*

www.prenhall.com

## ACKNOWLEDGMENTS

We gratefully acknowledge the assistance, support, and encouragement of those individuals who have contributed to *Financial Management.* Specifically, we wish to recognize the very helpful insights provided by many of our colleagues. For their careful comments and helpful reviews of this edition of the text, we are indebted to:

Balasundram Maniam, Sam Houston State University
Edward Stendardi, St. John Fisher College
Stephen M. Horan, St. Bonaventure University
Michael W. Carter, University of Arkansas - Fayetteville
Ted R. Pilger, Southern Illinois University
Robert Kleiman, Oakland University
Glenn L. Stevens, Franklin and Marshall College

We would also like to thank those who have provided helpful insights in past editions. For their comments and reviews, we would like to thank:

Kamal Abouzeid, V. T. Alaganan, Michael T. Alderson, Dwight C. Anderson, Nasser Arshadi, Sung C. Bea, Gary Benesh, Laura Berk, Sam G. Berry, Randy Billingsley, Eric Blazer, Laurence E. Blouse, Russell P. Boisjoly, Robert Boldin, Michael Bond, Waldo L. Born, Virgil L. Brewer, Jozelle Brister, Paul Burzik, John Byrd, Theodore F. Byrley, Michael W. Carter, Don M. Chance, Perikolam Raman Chandy, K. C. Chen, Santosh Choudhury, Jeffrey S. Christensen, M. C. Chung, Albert H. Clark, David W. Cole, Steven M. Dawson, Yashwant S. Dhatt, Bernard C. Dill, Mark Dorfman, John W. Ellis, Suzanne Erickson, Marjorie Evert, Slim Feriani, Greg Filbeck, Sidney R. Finkel, Fredrick G. Floss, James Forjan, Lyn Fraser, John Glister, Sharon S. Graham, Jack Griggs, Nancy Lee Halford, Ken Halsey, James D. Harris, William R. Henry, Dr. Linda C. Hittle, Stephen M. Horan, Keith Howe, Charles R. Idol, Vahan Janjigian, Nancy Jay, Jeff Jenkins, William Jens, Steve A. Johnson, Ravi Kamath, Rajiv Karla, Djavad Kashefinejad, Terry Keele, James D. Keys, David R. Klock, Reinhold P. Lamb, Larry Lang, George B. F. Lanigan, William R. Lasher, Howard C. Launstein, David E. Letourneau, Leonard T. Long, Richard MacMinn, Judy E. Maese, Abbas Mamoozadeh, Terry S. Maness, Surendra K. Mansinghka, Michael G. McMillian, Iqbal A. Memon, James A. Miller, Naval Modani, Eric J. Moon, Scott Moore, M. P. Narayan, Willliam E. O'Connell Jr., Shalini Perumpral, Jeffrey H. Peterson, Mario Picconi, John M. Pinkerton, John Primus, Jane B. Romal, Stuart Rosenstein, Ivan C. Roten, Marjorie A. Rubash, Jack H. Rubens, Todd Schank, Peter A. Sharp, Jackie Shu, Michael Solt, Raymond F. Spudeck, Suresh Srivastava, Joseph Stanford, Edward J. Stendardi, Donald L. Stevens, David Suk, Elizabeth Sun, L. E. Sweeney, Philip R. Swensen, R. Bruce Swensen, Amir Tavakkol, Lee Tenpao, John G. Thatcher, Gary L. Trennepohl, Ronald Tsang, Paul A. Vanderheiden, K. G. Viswananthan, Al Webster, Patricia Webster, Herbert Weintraub, Kenneth L. Westby, Sandra Williams, Lawrence C. Wolken, Bob G. Wood Jr., Kevin Woods, Steve B. Wyatt, Wold Zemedkun, Marc Zenner.

We also thank our friends at Prentice Hall. They are a great group of folks. We offer our personal expression of appreciation to the two editors on this project, Maureen Riopelle who worked on the early parts of the revision and was instrumental in the decision to rework the book around Harley-Davidson, and Mickey Cox who stepped in at a critical moment and provided the leadership and direction to bring this project to a very successful completion. They are the best. We would also like to thank Cheryl Clayton for her administrative deftness. She continuously offered insights and direction, often serving as a sounding board for revisions and new ideas. We would also like to extend our thanks to Gladys Soto, who not only played a major role in this revision, but also did it while having a child. Welcome aboard Desmond! Your mom did a superb job, along with being a wonderful person and a true friend. Melanie Olsen also deserves credit and thanks for providing superb coordinating skills. With Melanie watching over us, there was no way the ball could be dropped. To Holly Jo Brown, our thanks for watching over us; she did a great job. Our thanks also go to Josh McClary for his marketing prowess. Josh has an amazing understanding of the market, coupled with an intuitive understanding of what the market is looking for. Lauren Tarino also gets our thanks for her marketing efforts, another one of the good people at PH. We also want to thank Bill Minick, media project manager, for his tireless efforts in providing and maintaining great media products. To Carol Samet, the production editor, we express a very special thank you for seeing the book through a very complex production process and keeping it all on schedule while maintaining extremely high quality. On top of all of this, Carol is just a great person—thanks Carol.

As a final word, we express our sincere thanks to those using *Financial Management* in the classroom. We thank you for making us a part of your team. Always feel free to give any of us a call or contact us through the Internet when you have questions or needs.

A.J.K.
J.D.M.
J. W. P.
D. F. S.

# AN INTRODUCTION TO FINANCIAL MANAGEMENT

In 1985, Harley-Davidson teetered only hours away from bankruptcy as one of Harley's largest lenders, Citicorp Industrial Credit, was considering bailing out on its loan. Since its beginning in 1903, the company survived two world wars, the great depression, and competition from countless competitors, but by the early 1980s, Harley had become known for questionable reliability and leaving oil stains on people's driveways. It looked for a while like the future was set, and Harley wouldn't be there. It looked like the future of motorcycles in America would feature only Japanese names like Honda, Yamaha, Kawasaki, and Suzuki. But none of that happened, and today Harley-Davidson stands, as President Reagan once proclaimed, as "an American success story." ● For a company in today's world, surviving one scare is not enough—Today the business world involves a continuous series of challenges. As for Harley, it was a major accomplishment to make it through the 1980s, allowing it to face another challenge in the 1990s: a market that looked like it might disappear within a few years. How did Harley do against what looked like a shrinking market? It increased its motorcycle shipments from just over 60,000 in 1990 to over 200,000 in 2000! How have the shareholders done? Between 1986, when Harley-Davidson returned to public ownership with a successful stock offering, and 1999, Harley's stock price rose approximately 100-fold. How did Harley-Davidson, a company whose name grown men and women have tattooed on their arms and elsewhere, a company that

## LEARNING OBJECTIVES

After reading this chapter, you should be able to

1. Describe what the subject of financial management is about.
2. Explain the goal of the firm.
3. Compare the various legal forms of business and explain why the corporate form of business is the most logical choice for a firm that is large or growing.
4. Explain the 10 principles that form the basics of financial management.
5. Explain what has led to the era of the multinational corporation.

conjures up images of burly bad boys and Easy Rider hippies in black leather jackets riding down the road, pull off one of the biggest business turnarounds of all time? Harley made good decisions. That's what we're going to look at in this book. We'll look at what it takes to turn Harley or any other company around. We'll look at how a company goes about making decisions to introduce new product lines. For example, in 2000, Harley-Davidson introduced the "Buell Blast," a low-cost, lightweight bike aimed at bringing new riders into the sport. How did it make this decision? We'll also follow Harley-Davidson throughout this book, examining how its experience fits in with the topics we are examining. In doing so, we will see that there are countless interactions among finance, marketing, management, and accounting. Because finance deals with decision making, it takes on importance, regardless of your major. Moreover, the tools, techniques, and understanding you will gain from finance will not only help you in your business career, but will also help you make educated personal investment decisions in the future.

In this chapter, we will lay a foundation for the entire book. We will explain what finance is, and then we will explain the key goal that guides financial decision making: maximization of shareholder wealth. We will examine the legal environment of financial decisions. Then, we will describe the golden thread that ties everything together: the 10 basic principles of finance. Finally, we will look at the importance of looking beyond our geographic boundaries.

## WHAT IS FINANCE?

OBJECTIVE 1 

Financial management is concerned with the maintenance and creation of economic value or wealth. Consequently, this course focuses on decision making with an eye toward creating wealth. As such, we will deal with financial decisions such as when to introduce a new product, when to invest in new assets, when to replace existing assets, when to borrow from banks, when to issue stocks or bonds, when to extend credit to a customer, and how much cash to maintain.

To illustrate, consider two firms, Merck and General Motors (GM). At the end of 1998, the total market value of Merck, a large pharmaceutical company, was \$153 billion. Over the life of the business, Merck's investors had invested about \$30 billion in the business. In other words, management created \$123 billion in additional wealth for the shareholders. GM, on the other hand, was valued at \$67 billion at the end of 1998; but over the years, GM's investors had actually invested \$85 billion—a loss in value of \$17 billion. Therefore, Merck created wealth for its shareholders, while GM lost shareholder wealth.

In introducing decision-making techniques, we will emphasize the logic behind those techniques, thereby ensuring that we do not lose sight of the concepts when dealing with the calculations. To the first-time student of finance, this may sound a bit overwhelming. However, as we will see, the techniques and tools introduced in this text are all motivated by 10 underlying principles or axioms that will guide us through the decision-making process.

## GOAL OF THE FIRM

We believe that the preferable goal of the firm should be *maximization of shareholder wealth,* by which we mean maximization of the price of the existing common stock. Not only will this goal be in the best interest of the shareholders, but it will also provide the most benefits to society. This will come about as scarce resources are directed to their most productive use by businesses competing to create wealth.

To better understand this goal, we will first discuss profit maximization as a possible goal for the firm. Then we will compare it to maximization of shareholder wealth to see why, in financial management, the latter is the more appropriate goal for the firm.

### Profit Maximization

In microeconomics courses, profit maximization is frequently given as the goal of the firm. Profit maximization stresses the efficient use of capital resources, but it is not specific with respect to the time frame over which profits are to be measured. Do we maximize profits over the current year, or do we maximize profits over some longer period? A financial manager could easily increase current profits by eliminating research and development expenditures and cutting down on routine maintenance. In the short run, this might result in increased profits, but this clearly is not in the best long-run interests of the firm. If we are to base financial decisions on a goal, that goal must be precise, not allow for misinterpretation, and deal with all the complexities of the real world.

In microeconomics, profit maximization functions largely as a theoretical goal, with economists using it to prove how firms behave rationally to increase profit. Unfortunately, it ignores many real-world complexities that financial managers must address in their decisions. In the more applied discipline of financial management, firms must deal every day with two major factors not considered by the goal of profit maximization: uncertainty and timing.

Microeconomics courses ignore uncertainty and risk to present theory more easily. Projects and investment alternatives are compared by examining their expected values or weighted average profits. Whether one project is riskier than another does not enter into these calculations; economists do discuss risk, but only tangentially.[1] In reality, projects differ a great deal with respect to risk characteristics, and to disregard these differences in the practice of financial management can result in incorrect decisions. As we will discover later in this chapter, there is a very definite relationship between risk and expected return—that is, investors demand a higher expected return for taking on added risk—and to ignore this relationship would lead to improper decisions.

Another problem with the goal of profit maximization is that it ignores the timing of the project's returns. If this goal is only concerned with this year's profits, we know it inappropriately ignores profit in future years. If we interpret it to maximize the average of future profits, it is also incorrect. Inasmuch as investment opportunities are available for money in hand, we are not indifferent to the timing of the returns. Given equivalent cash flows from profits, we want those cash flows sooner rather than later. Thus the real-world factors of uncertainty and timing force us to look beyond a simple goal of profit maximization as a decision criterion.

[1]See, for example, Robert S. Pindyck and Daniel Rubenfield. *Microeconomics,* 2d ed. (New York: Macmillan, 1992), 244–46.

Finally, and possibly most important, accounting profits fail to recognize one of the most important costs of doing business. When we calculate accounting profits, we consider interest expense as a cost of borrowing money, but we ignore the cost of the funds provided by the firm's shareholders (owners). If a company could earn 8 percent on a new investment, that would surely increase the firm's profits. However, what if the firm's shareholders could earn 12 percent with that same money in another investment of similar risk? Should the company's managers accept the investment because it will increase the firm's profits? Not if they want to act in the best interest of the firm's owners (shareholders). Now look at what happened with Burlington Northern.

Burlington Northern is a perfect example of erroneous thinking. In 1980, Richard Bressler was appointed as Chief Executive Officer (CEO) of the company. Bressler, unlike his predecessor, was not a "railroad man." He was an "outsider" who was hired for the express purpose of improving the value of the shareholders' stock. The reason for the change was that Burlington Northern had been earning about 4 percent on the shareholders' equity, when Certificates of Deposit (CDs) with no risk were paying 6 percent. Management was certainly increasing the firm's profits, but they were destroying shareholder wealth by investing in railroad lines that were not even earning a rate of return equal to that paid on government securities. We will turn now to an examination of a more robust goal for the firm: maximization of shareholder wealth.

### Maximization of Shareholder Wealth

In formulating the goal of maximization of shareholder wealth, we are doing nothing more than modifying the goal of profit maximization to deal with the complexities of the operating environment. We have chosen maximization of shareholder wealth—that is, maximization of the market value of the existing shareholders' common stock—because the effects of all financial decisions are thereby included. Investors react to poor investment or dividend decisions by causing the total value of the firm's stock to fall, and they react to good decisions by pushing up the price of the stock. In effect, under this goal, good decisions are those that create wealth for the shareholder.

Obviously, there are some serious practical problems in implementing this goal and in using changes in the firm's stock to evaluate financial decisions. We know the price of a firm's stock fluctuates, often for no apparent reason. However, over the long run, price equals value. We will keep this long-run balancing in mind and focus on the effect that our decision *should* have on the stock price if everything else were held constant. The market price of the firm's stock reflects the value of the firm as seen by its owners and takes into account the complexities and complications of the real-world risk. As we follow this goal throughout our discussions, we must keep in mind that the shareholders are the legal owners of the firm.

#### CONCEPT CHECK

1. What are the problems with the goal of profit maximization?
2. What is the goal of the firm?

## LEGAL FORMS OF BUSINESS ORGANIZATION

OBJECTIVE 3 

In the chapters ahead, we will focus on financial decisions for corporations. Although the corporation is not the only legal form of business available, it is the most logical choice for a firm that is large or growing. It is also the dominant business form in terms of sales in this country. In this section, we will explain why this is so. This will in turn allow us to simplify the remainder of the text, as we will assume that the proper tax code to follow is the corporate tax code, rather than examine different tax codes for different legal forms of businesses. Keep in mind that our primary purpose is to develop an understanding of the logic of financial decision making. Taxes will become important only when they affect our decisions, and our discussion of the choice of the legal form of the business is directed at understanding why we will limit our discussion of taxes to the corporate form.

Legal forms of business organization are diverse and numerous. However, there are three categories: the sole proprietorship, the partnership, and the corporation. To understand the basic differences between each form, we need to define each form and understand its advantages and disadvantages. As we will see, as the firm grows, the advantages of the corporation begin to dominate. As a result, most large firms take on the corporate form.

## Sole Proprietorship

The **sole proprietorship** is a business owned by a single individual. The owner maintains title to the assets and is personally responsible, generally without limitation, for the liabilities incurred. The proprietor is entitled to the profits from the business but must also absorb any losses. This form of business is initiated by the mere act of beginning the business operations. Typically, no legal requirement must be met in starting the operation, particularly if the proprietor is conducting the business in his or her own name. If a special name is used, an assumed-name certificate should be filed, requiring a small registration fee. Termination occurs on the owner's death or by the owner's choice. Briefly stated, the sole proprietorship is, for all practical purposes, the absence of any formal *legal* business structure.

**Sole proprietorship**
A business owned by a single individual.

## Partnership

The primary difference between a **partnership** and a sole proprietorship is that the partnership has more than one owner. A partnership is an association of two or more persons coming together as co-owners for the purpose of operating a business for profit. Partnerships fall into two types: (1) general partnerships and (2) limited partnerships.

**Partnership**
An association of two or more individuals joining together as co-owners to operate a business for profit.

GENERAL PARTNERSHIP In a general partnership, each partner is fully responsible for the liabilities incurred by the partnership. Thus, any partner's faulty conduct even having the appearance of relating to the firm's business renders the remaining partners liable as well. The relationship among partners is dictated entirely by the partnership agreement, which may be an oral commitment or a formal document.

LIMITED PARTNERSHIP In addition to the general partnership, in which all partners are jointly liable without limitation, many states provide for a limited partnership. The state statutes permit one or more of the partners to have limited liability, restricted to the amount of capital invested in the partnership. Several conditions must be met to qualify as a limited partner. First, at least one general partner must remain in the association for whom the privilege of limited liability does not apply. Second, the names of the limited partners may not appear in the name of the firm. Third, the limited partners may not participate in the management of the business. If one of these restrictions is violated, all partners forfeit their right to limited liability. In essence, the intent of the statutes creating the limited partnership is to provide limited liability for a person whose interest in the partnership is purely as an investor. That individual may not assume a management function within the organization.

FINANCE $ MATTERS

## Milton Friedman on the Social Responsibility of Corporations

There is a difference between acting in a socially responsible way and acting ethically. Milton Friedman does a good job of stating the argument that corporations do not have "social responsibility." This view is far from universally held. The purpose of the following is to make you think about this issue.

In a free-enterprise, private-property system, a corporate executive is an employee of the owners of the business. He has direct responsibility to his employers. That responsibility is to conduct the business in accordance with their desires, which generally will be to make as much money as possible while conforming to the basic rules of the society, both those embodied in law and those embodied in ethical custom.

Of course, the corporate executive is also a person in his own right. As a person, he may have many other responsibilities that he recognizes or assumes voluntarily—to his family, his conscience, his feelings of charity, his church, his clubs, his city, his country. He may feel impelled by these responsibilities to devote part of his income to causes he regards as worthy, to refuse to work for particular corporations, even to leave his job, for example, to join his country's armed forces. If we wish, we may refer to some of these responsibilities as "social responsibilities." But in these respects he is acting as a principal, not an agent; he is spending his own money or time or energy, not the money of his employers or the time or energy he has contracted to devote to their purposes. If these are "social responsibilities," they are the social responsibilities of individuals, not of business.

What does it really mean to say that the corporate executive has a "social responsibility" in his capacity as a businessman? If this statement is not pure rhetoric, it must mean that he is to act in some way that is not in the interest of his employers. For example, that he is to refrain from increasing the price of the product in order to contribute to the social objective of preventing inflation, even though a price increase would be in the best interests of the corporation. Or that he is to make expenditures on reducing pollution beyond the amount that is in the best interests of the corporation or that is required by law in order to contribute to the social objective of improving the environment. Or that, at the expense of corporate profits, he is to hire "hard-core" unemployed instead of better-qualified available workmen to contribute to the social objective of reducing poverty.

In each of these cases, the corporate executive would be spending someone else's money for a general social interest. Insofar as his actions with his "social responsibility" reduce returns to stockholders, he is spending their money. Insofar as his actions raise the price to customers, he is spending the customer's money. Insofar as his actions lower the wages of some employees, he is spending their money.

The stockholders or the customers or the employees could separately spend their own money on the particular actions if they wished to do so. The executive is exercising a distinct "social responsibility," rather than serving as an agent of the stockholders or the customers or the employees, only if he spends the money in a different way than they would have spent it.

But if he does this, he is in effect imposing taxes, on the one hand, and deciding how the tax proceeds shall be spent, on the other.

Source: From Milton Friedman, "The Social Responsibility of Business Is to Increase Its Profits," *The New York Times Magazine* (September 13, 1970), 33, 122–126. 

## Corporation

**Corporation**
An entity that *legally* functions separate and apart from its owners.

The **corporation** has been a significant factor in the economic development of the United States. As early as 1819, Chief Justice John Marshall set forth the legal definition of a corporation as "an artificial being, invisible, intangible, and existing only in the contemplation of law."[2] This entity *legally* functions separate and apart from its owners. As such, the corporation can individually sue and be sued, and purchase, sell, or own property; and its personnel are subject to criminal punishment for crimes. However, despite this legal separation, the corporation is composed of owners who dictate its direction and policies. The owners elect a board of directors, whose members in turn select individuals to serve as corporate officers, including president, vice president, secretary, and treasurer. Ownership is reflected in common stock certificates, designating the number of shares owned by its holder. The number of shares owned relative to the total number of shares outstanding

[2]*The Trustees of Dartmouth College* v. *Woodward,* 4 Wheaton 636 (1819).

determines the stockholder's proportionate ownership in the business. Because the shares are transferable, ownership in a corporation may be changed by a shareholder simply remitting the shares to a new shareholder. The investor's liability is confined to the amount of the investment in the company, thereby preventing creditors from confiscating stockholders' personal assets in settlement of unresolved claims. This is an extremely important advantage of a corporation. After all, would you be willing to invest in General Electric if you would be liable in the event that one of their airplane engines malfunctions and people die in a crash? Finally, the life of a corporation is not dependent on the status of the investors. The death or withdrawal of an investor does not affect the continuity of the corporation. The management continues to run the corporation when stock is sold or when it is passed on through inheritance.

## Comparison of Organizational Forms

Owners of new businesses have some important decisions to make in choosing an organizational form. Whereas each business form seems to have some advantages over the others, we will see that, as the firm grows and needs access to the capital markets to raise funds, the advantages of the corporation begin to dominate.

Large and growing firms choose the corporate form for one reason: ease in raising capital. Because of the limited liability, the ease of transferring ownership through the sale of common shares, and the flexibility in dividing the shares, the corporation is the ideal business entity in terms of attracting new capital. In contrast, the unlimited liabilities of the sole proprietorship and the general partnership are deterrents to raising equity capital. Between the extremes, the limited partnership does provide limited liability for limited partners, which has a tendency to attract wealthy investors. However, the impracticality of having a large number of partners and the restricted marketability of an interest in a partnership prevent this form of organization from competing effectively with the corporation. Therefore, when developing our decision models, we will assume that we are dealing with the corporate form. The taxes incorporated in these models will deal only with the corporate tax codes. Because our goal is to develop an understanding of the management, measurement, and creation of wealth, and not to become tax experts, in the following chapter we will only focus on those characteristics of the corporate tax code that will affect our financial decisions.

## The Role of the Financial Manager in a Corporation

Although a firm can assume many different organizational structures, Figure 1-1 presents a typical representation of how the finance area fits into a corporation. The Vice President for Finance, also called the Chief Financial Officer (CFO), serves under the corporation's Chief Executive Officer (CEO) and is responsible for overseeing financial planning, corporate strategic planning, and controlling the firm's cash flow. Typically, a Treasurer and Controller serve under the CFO. In a smaller firm, the same person may fill both roles, with just one office handling all the duties. The Treasurer generally handles the firm's financial activities, including cash and credit management, making capital expenditure decisions, raising funds, financial planning, and managing any foreign currency received by the firm. The Controller is responsible for managing the firm's accounting duties, including producing financial statements, cost accounting, paying taxes, and gathering and monitoring the data necessary to oversee the firm's financial well-being. In this class, we focus on the duties generally associated with the Treasurer and on how investment decisions are made.

**FIGURE 1-1**
How the Finance Area Fits into a Corporation

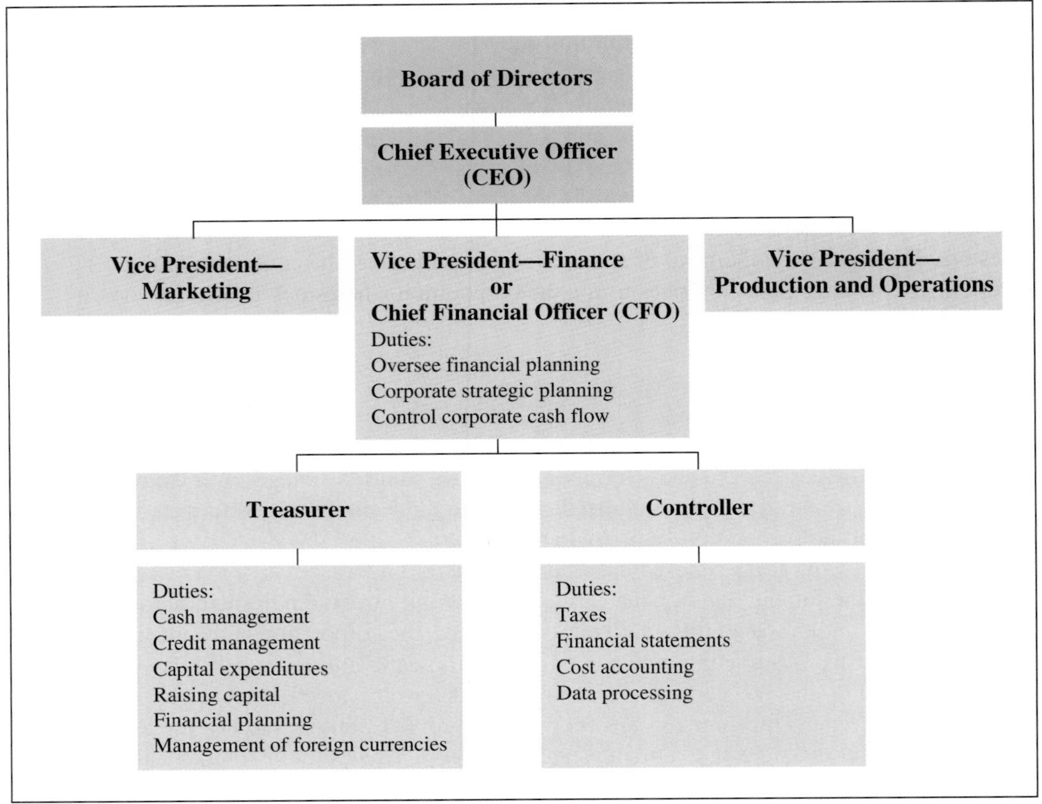


**CONCEPT CHECK**

1. What are the primary differences among a sole proprietorship, a partnership, and a corporation?
2. Explain why large and growing firms tend to choose the corporate form.
3. What are the duties of the Corporate Treasurer? Of the Corporate Controller?

## The Corporation and the Financial Markets: The Interaction

Without question, the ease of raising capital is the major reason for the popularity of the corporate form. While we will look at the process of raising capital in some detail in Chapter 14, let's spend a moment looking at the flow of capital through the financial markets among the corporation, individuals, and the government.

Figure 1-2 examines these flows. (1) Initially, the corporation raises funds in the financial markets by selling securities. The corporation receives cash in return for securities—stocks and debt. (2) The corporation then invests this cash in return-generating assets—new projects for example—and (3) the cash flow from those assets is then either reinvested

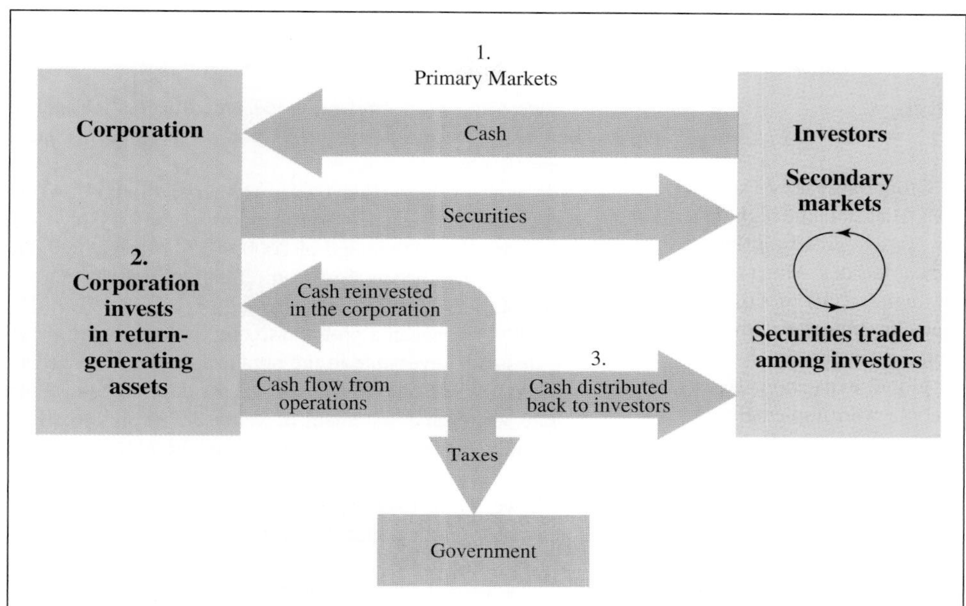


**FIGURE 1-2**
The Corporation and the Financial Markets: The Interaction
1. Initially, the corporation raises funds in the financial markets by selling securities—stocks and bonds. 2. The corporation then invests this cash in return-generating assets—new projects—and 3. the cash flow from those assets is either reinvested in the corporation, given back to the investors, or paid to the government in the form of taxes.

in the corporation; given back to the investors in the form of dividends or interest payments, or used to repurchase stock, which should cause the stock price to rise; or given to the government in the form of tax payments.

One distinction that is important to understand is the difference between primary and secondary markets. Again, we will reexamine raising capital and the difference between primary and secondary markets in some detail in Chapter 14. To begin with, a securities market is simply a place where you can buy or sell securities. These markets can take the form of anything from an actual building on Wall Street in New York City to an electronic hookup among security dealers all over the world. Securities markets are divided into primary and secondary markets. Let's take a look at what these terms mean.

A **primary market** is a market in which new, as opposed to previously issued, securities are traded. This is the only time that the issuing firm actually receives money for its stock. For example, if Nike issues a new batch of stock, this issue would be considered a primary market transaction. In this case, Nike would issue new shares of stock and receive money from investors. Actually, there are two different types of offerings in the primary markets: initial public offerings and seasoned new issues or primary offerings. An **initial public offering (IPO)** is the first time the company's stock is sold to the general public, whereas a **seasoned new issue** refers to stock offerings by companies that already have common stock traded in the secondary market. Once the newly issued stock is in the public's hands, it then begins trading in the **secondary market.** Securities that have previously been issued and bought are traded in the secondary market. For example, if you bought 100 shares of stock in an IPO and then wanted to resell them, you would be reselling them in the secondary markets. The proceeds from the sale of a share of IBM stock in the secondary market go to the previous owner of the stock, not to IBM. That is because the only time IBM ever receives money from the sale of one of its securities is in the primary markets.

**Primary market**
A market in which new, as opposed to previously issued, securities are traded.

**Initial public offering (IPO)**
The first time the company's stock is sold to the public.

**Seasoned new issue**
Stock offerings by companies that already have common stock traded.

**Secondary market**
The market in which stock previously issued by the firm trades.

ROAD RULES

## A FOCUS ON HARLEY-DAVIDSON

ROAD RULES

### An Interview with Jeff Bleustein, Harley-Davidson's CEO

Jeff Bleustein is the Chief Executive Officer at Harley-Davidson Company, Inc. In our interview with Mr. Bleustein, he highlighted a number of milestones that he believes have greatly influenced the company's success over the past two decades. Much of what he had to say related directly to the main topics of this book. Specifically, he talked about the company's strategies in the areas of investment decisions, working-capital management, financing decisions, marketing strategies, and global expansion. He also emphasized the importance of the people who implement these decisions. He insists that there is more to business than crunching the numbers; it is people that make the difference. Mr. Bleustein's remarks can be summarized as follows:

- In 1981, the management of Harley-Davidson bought the company from its parent company, AMF, in a leveraged buy-out. The extremely high level of debt incurred to finance the purchase placed the company in a very frail financial condition. The downturn in the economy, combined with the debt load, created a powerful incentive to improve operations to conserve cash. To add to the problems, the firm's principal lender, Citibank, announced in 1985 that it wanted out of its creditor position for the firm. Last-minute refinancing was arranged on December 31, 1985 to save the company from bankruptcy. Then, within a few short months the company's financial picture had improved to the point where we were able to take the company public in an initial public offering.
- During the past two decades, the company has made significant capital investments in new product lines, such as the Evolution engine, the Softail motorcycle, and most recently, the Twin Cam 88 engine, one of our current engine designs. Also, in 1998 we invested in new manufacturing facilities in Kansas City, Missouri, and Menominee Falls, Wisconsin.
- To improve the firm's management of its working capital, we introduced the use of just-in-time inventory control. We called our program MAN, which stands for Materials As Needed. This program allowed us to remove $51 million from our work-in-process inventory and provided much-needed capital to support our operations while we paid down on the firm's large amounts of debt.
- In 1983, we established our Harley Owner's Group (HOG) to encourage our customers to use their bikes and stay involved with the company. At the end of 2000, we had nearly 600,000 members. We also began a program of carefully managing the licensing of the Harley-Davidson name.
- In the 1980s, we began a program to empower our employees. We needed to let everyone in the organization know what was expected of him or her, which led us to the development of our corporate vision and statement of values.[1] I strongly believe that the only sustainable corporate advantage a company can have is its people.
- In 1994, we began fostering a partnership with our unions to enable them to participate fully in the business. Today our two unions participate fully with the firm's management in a wide range of decision making, including the firm's strategies.
- We also initiated our circle organization, which involves the use of a team structure at our vice president level of management to make the decisions. As a result, we eliminated a whole layer from top management.
- Beginning in the 1990s, we entered into a serious effort to globalize the company. We established a management team in Europe, and over time we acquired our independent distributors in major markets, such as the Benelufx, and Italy.

All of these decisions have significant financial implications that are tied to our study of finance. Specifically, they reflect financing choices, investment decisions, and working-capital management. So, we invite you to join us in our study of finance and, in the process, learn about a company that has accomplished in real terms what few others have been able to do.

[1]Harley-Davidson Motor Company's mission statement is, "We fulfill dreams through the experiences of motorcycling by providing to motorcyclists and the general public an expanding line of motorcycles, branded products and services in selected market segments. The firm's value statement is expressed as, 'Tell the truth, be fair, keep your promises, respect the individual, and encourage intellectual curiosity.' "

## TEN PRINCIPLES THAT FORM THE BASICS OF FINANCIAL MANAGEMENT

OBJECTIVE 4 

We will now look at the *finance* foundations that lie behind the decisions made by financial managers. To the first-time student of finance, the subject matter may seem like a collection of unrelated decision rules. This could not be further from the truth. In fact, our decision rules, and the logic that underlies them, spring from 10 simple principles that do not require knowledge of finance to understand. *However, while it is not necessary to understand finance in order to understand these principles, it is necessary to understand these principles in order to understand finance.* Keep in mind that although these principles may at first appear simple or even trivial, they will provide the driving force behind all that follows. These principles will weave together concepts and techniques presented in this text, thereby allowing us to focus on the logic underlying the practice of financial management. In order to make the learning process easier for you as a student, we will keep returning to these principles throughout the book in the form of "Relate to the Big Picture" boxes—tying the material together and letting you sort the "forest from the trees."

**PRINCIPLE 1** **The Risk-Return Trade-Off—We won't take on additional risk unless we expect to be compensated with additional return**

At some point, we have all saved some money. Why have we done this? The answer is simple: to expand our future consumption opportunities—for example, save for a house, a car, or retirement. We are able to invest those savings and earn a return on our dollars because some people would rather forgo future consumption opportunities to consume more now—maybe they're borrowing money to open a new business or a company is borrowing money to build a new plant. Assuming there are a lot of different people that would like to use our savings, how do we decide where to put our money?

First, investors demand a minimum return for delaying consumption that must be greater than the anticipated rate of inflation. If they didn't receive enough to compensate for anticipated inflation, investors would purchase whatever goods they desired ahead of time or invest in assets that were subject to inflation and earn the rate of inflation on those assets. There isn't much incentive to postpone consumption if your savings are going to decline in terms of purchasing power.

Investment alternatives have different amounts of risk and expected returns. Investors sometimes choose to put their money in risky investments because these investments offer higher expected returns. The more risk an investment has, the higher will be its expected return. This relationship between risk and expected return is shown in Figure 1-3.

Notice that we keep referring to *expected* return rather than *actual* return. We may have expectations of what the returns from investing will be, but we can't peer into the future and see what those returns are actually going to be. If investors could see into the future, no one would have invested money in the software maker Citrix, whose stock dropped 46 percent on June 13, 2000. Citrix's stock dropped when it announced that unexpected problems in its

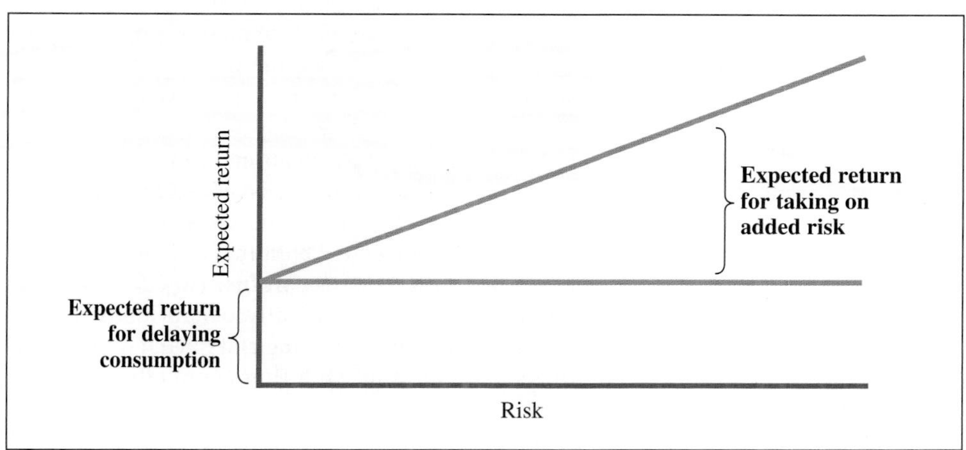


**FIGURE 1-3**
The Risk-Return Relationship

sales channels would cause second-quarter profits to be about half what Wall Street expected. Until after the fact, you are never sure what the return on an investment will be. That is why General Motors bonds pay more interest than U.S. Treasury bonds of the same maturity. The additional interest convinces some investors to take on the added risk of purchasing a General Motors bond.

This risk-return relationship will be a key concept as we value stocks, bonds, and proposed new projects throughout this text. We will also spend some time determining how to measure risk. Interestingly, much of the work for which the 1990 Nobel Prize for Economics was awarded centered on the graph in Figure 1-3 and how to measure risk. Both the graph and the risk-return relationship it depicts will reappear often in this text.

## PRINCIPLE 2 The Time Value of Money—A dollar received today is worth more than a dollar received in the future

A fundamental concept in finance is that money has a time value associated with it: A dollar received today is worth more than a dollar received a year from now. Because we can earn interest on money received today, it is better to receive money earlier rather than later. In your economics courses, this concept of the time value of money is referred to as the opportunity cost of passing up the earning potential of a dollar today.

In this text, we focus on the creation and measurement of wealth. To measure wealth or value, we will use the concept of the time value of money to bring the future benefits and costs of a project back to the present. Then, if the benefits outweigh the costs, the project creates wealth and should be accepted; if the costs outweigh the benefits, the project does not create wealth and should be rejected. Without recognizing the existence of the time value of money, it is impossible to evaluate projects with future benefits and costs in a meaningful way.

To bring future benefits and costs of a project back to the present, we must assume a specific opportunity cost of money, or interest rate. Exactly what interest rate to use is determined by **Principle 1: The Risk-Return Trade-Off,** which states investors demand higher returns for taking on more risky projects. Thus, when we determine the present value of future benefits and costs, we take into account that investors demand a higher return for taking on added risk.

## PRINCIPLE 3 Cash—Not Profits—Is King

In measuring wealth or value, we will use cash flows, not accounting profits, as our measurement tool. That is, we will be concerned with when the money hits our hand, when we can invest it and start earning interest on it, and when we can give it back to the shareholders in the form of dividends. Remember, it is the cash flows, not profits, that are actually received by the firm and can be reinvested. Accounting profits, on the other hand, appear when they are earned rather than when the money is actually in hand. As a result, a firm's cash flows and accounting profits may not be the same. For example, a capital expense, such as the purchase of new equipment or a building, is depreciated over several years, with the annual depreciation subtracted from profits. However, the cash flow, or actual dollars, associated with this expense generally occurs immediately. Therefore cash inflows and outflows involve the actual receiving and payout of money—when the money hits or leaves your hands. As a result, cash flows correctly reflect the timing of the benefits and costs.

## PRINCIPLE 4 Incremental Cash Flows—It's only what changes that counts

In 2000, Post, the maker of Cocoa Pebbles and Fruity Pebbles, introduced Cinna Crunch Pebbles, "Cinnamon sweet taste that goes crunch." There is no doubt that Cinna Crunch Pebbles competed directly with Post's other cereals and, in particular, its Pebbles products. Certainly some of the sales dollars that ended up with Cinna Crunch Pebbles would have been spent on other Pebbles and Post products if Cinna Crunch Pebbles had not been available. Although Post was targeting younger consumers with this sweetened cereal, there is no question that Post sales bit into—actually cannibalized—sales from Pebbles and other Post lines. Realistically, there's only so much cereal anyone can eat. The *difference* between revenues Post generated after introducing Cinna Crunch Pebbles versus simply maintaining its existing line of cereals is the incremental cash flows. This difference reflects the true impact of the decision.

In making business decisions, we are concerned with the results of those decisions: What happens if we say yes versus what happens if we say no? **Principle 3** states that we should use cash flows to measure the benefits that accrue from taking on a new project. We are now fine tuning our evaluation process so that we only consider *incremental* cash flows. The incremental cash flow is the difference between the cash flows if the project is taken on versus what they will be if the project is not taken on.

What is important is that we *think* incrementally. Our guiding rule in deciding whether a cash flow is incremental is to look at the company with and without the new product. In fact, we will take this incremental concept beyond cash flows and look at all consequences from all decisions on an incremental basis.

## PRINCIPLE 5 The Curse of Competitive Markets—Why it's hard to find exceptionally profitable projects

Our job as financial managers is to create wealth. Therefore, we will look closely at the mechanics of valuation and decision making. We will focus on estimating cash flows, determining what the investment earns, and valuing assets and new projects. But it will be easy to get caught up in the mechanics of valuation and lose sight of the process of creating wealth. Why is it so hard to find projects and investments that are exceptionally profitable? Where do profitable projects come from? The answers to these questions tell us a lot about how competitive markets operate and where to look for profitable projects.

In reality, it is much easier evaluating profitable projects than finding them. If an industry is generating large profits, new entrants are usually attracted. The additional competition and added capacity can result in profits being driven down to the required rate of return. Conversely, if an industry is returning profits below the required rate of return, then some participants in the market drop out, reducing capacity and competition. In turn, prices are driven back up. This is precisely what happened in the VCR video rental market in the mid-1980s. This market developed suddenly with the opportunity for extremely large profits. Because there were no barriers to entry, the market quickly was flooded with new entries. By 1987, the competition and price cutting produced losses for many firms in the industry, forcing them to flee the market. As the competition lessened with firms moving out of the video rental industry, profits again rose to the point where the required rate of return could be earned on invested capital.

In competitive markets, extremely large profits simply cannot exist for very long. Given that somewhat bleak scenario, how can we find good projects—that is, projects that return

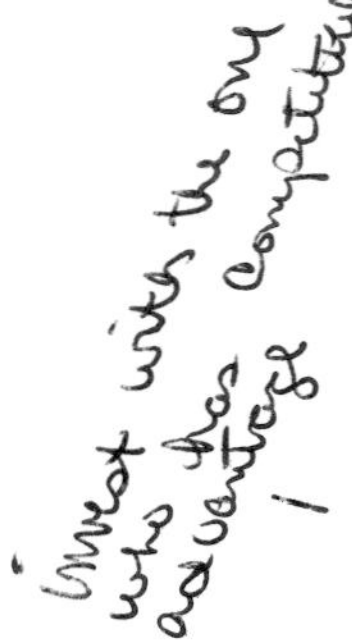

more than their expected rate of return given their risk level (remember Principle 1). Although competition makes them difficult to find, we have to invest in markets that are not perfectly competitive. The two most common ways of making markets less competitive are to differentiate the product in some key way or to achieve a cost advantage over competitors.

Product differentiation insulates a product from competition, thereby allowing a company to charge a premium price. If products are differentiated, consumer choice is no longer made by price alone. For example, many people are willing to pay a premium for Starbucks coffee. They simply want Starbucks and price is not important. In the pharmaceutical industry, patents create competitive barriers. Schering-Plough's Claritin, an allergy relief medicine, and Hoffman-La Roche's Valium, a tranquilizer, are protected from direct competition by patents.

Service and quality are also used to differentiate products. For example, Levi's has long prided itself on the quality of its jeans. As a result, it has been able to maintain its market share. Similarly, much of Toyota and Honda's brand loyalty is based on quality. Service can also create product differentiation, as shown by McDonald's fast service, cleanliness, and consistency of product that brings customers back.

Whether product differentiation occurs because of advertising, patents, service, or quality, the more the product is differentiated from competing products, the less competition it will face and the greater the possibility of large profits.

Economies of scale and the ability to produce at a cost below competition can effectively deter new entrants to the market and thereby reduce competition. Wal-Mart is one such case. For Wal-Mart, the fixed costs are largely independent of the store's size. For example, inventory costs, advertising expenses, and managerial salaries are essentially the same regardless of annual sales. Therefore, the more sales that can be built up, the lower the per-sale dollar cost of inventory, advertising, and management. Restocking from warehouses also becomes more efficient as delivery trucks can be used to full potential.

Regardless of how the cost advantage is created—by economies of scale, proprietary technology, or monopolistic control of raw materials—the cost advantage deters new market entrants while allowing production at below industry cost. This cost advantage has the potential of creating large profits.

The key to locating profitable investment projects is to first understand how and where they exist in competitive markets. Then the corporate philosophy must be aimed at creating or taking advantage of some imperfection in these markets, either through product differentiation or creation of a cost advantage, rather than looking to new markets or industries that appear to provide large profits. Any perfectly competitive industry that looks too good to be true won't be for long. It is necessary to understand this to know where to look for good projects and to accurately measure the project's cash flows. We can do this better if we recognize how wealth is created and how difficult it is to create it.

## PRINCIPLE 6 Efficient Capital Markets—The markets are quick and the prices are right

Our goal as financial managers is the maximization of shareholder wealth. How do we measure shareholder wealth? It is the value of the shares that the shareholders hold. To understand what causes stocks to change in price, as well as how securities such as bonds and stocks are valued or priced in the financial markets, it is necessary to have an understanding of the concept of **efficient markets.**

**Efficient market**
A market in which the values of all assets and securities at any instant in time fully reflect all available public information.

Whether a market is efficient or not has to do with the speed with which information is impounded into security prices. An efficient market is characterized by a large number of profit-driven individuals who act independently. In addition, new information regarding securities arrives in the market in a random manner. Given this setting, investors adjust to new information immediately and buy and sell the security until they feel the market price correctly reflects the new information. Under the efficient market hypothesis, information is reflected in security prices with such speed that there are no opportunities for investors to profit from publicly available information. Investors competing for profits ensure that security prices appropriately reflect the expected earnings and risks involved and thus the true value of the firm.

What are the implications of efficient markets for us? First, the price is right. Stock prices reflect all publicly available information regarding the value of the company. This means we can implement our goal of maximization of shareholder wealth by focusing on the effect each decision *should* have on the stock price if everything else were held constant. That is, over time good decisions will result in higher stock prices and bad ones, lower stock prices. Second, earnings manipulations through accounting changes will not result in price changes. Stock splits and other changes in accounting methods that do not affect cash flows are not reflected in prices. Market prices reflect expected cash flows available to shareholders. Thus, our preoccupation with cash flows to measure the timing of the benefits is justified.

As we will see, it is indeed reassuring that prices reflect value. It allows us to look at prices and see value reflected in them. While it may make investing a bit less exciting, it makes corporate finance much less uncertain.

## PRINCIPLE 7 The Agency Problem—Managers won't work for owners unless it's in their best interest

Although the goal of the firm is the maximization of shareholder wealth, in reality, the agency problem may interfere with the implementation of this goal. The **agency problem** results from the separation of management and the ownership of the firm. For example, a large firm may be run by professional managers who have little or no ownership in the firm. Because of this separation of the decision makers and owners, managers may make decisions that are not in line with the goal of maximization of shareholder wealth. They may approach work less energetically and attempt to benefit themselves in terms of salary and perquisites at the expense of shareholders.

**Agency problem**
Problem resulting from conflicts of interest between the manager (the stockholder's agent) and the stockholders.

To begin with, an agent is someone who is given the authority to act on behalf of another, referred to as the principal. In the corporate setting, the shareholders are the principals, because they are the actual owners of the firm. The Board of Directors, the CEO, the corporate executives, and all others with decision-making power are agents of the shareholders. Unfortunately, the Board of Directors, the CEO, and the other corporate executives don't always do what's in the best interest of the shareholders. Instead, they act many times in their own best interest. Not only might they benefit themselves in terms of salary and perquisites, but they might also avoid any projects that have risk associated with them—even if they're great projects with huge potential returns and a small chance of failure. Why is this so? Because if the project doesn't turn out, these agents of the shareholders may lose their jobs.

The costs associated with the agency problem are difficult to measure, but occasionally we see the problem's effect in the marketplace. For example, if the market feels management of a firm is damaging shareholder wealth, we might see a positive reaction in stock price to the removal of that management. In 1989, on the day following the death of John Dorrance, Jr., chairman of Campbell Soup, Campbell's stock price rose about 15 percent. Some investors felt that Campbell's relatively small growth in earnings might be improved with the departure of Dorrance. There was also speculation that Dorrance was the major obstacle to a possible positive reorganization.

If the management of the firm works for the owners, who are the shareholders, why doesn't the management get fired if it doesn't act in the shareholders' best interest? *In theory,* the shareholders pick the corporate board of directors and the board of directors in turn picks the management. Unfortunately, *in reality* the system frequently works the other way around. Management selects the board of director nominees and then distributes the ballots. In effect, shareholders are offered a slate of nominees selected by the management. The end result is management effectively selects the directors, who then may have more allegiance to managers than to shareholders. This in turn sets up the potential for agency problems with the board of directors not monitoring managers on behalf of the shareholders as they should.

We will spend considerable time monitoring managers and trying to align their interests with shareholders. Managers can be monitored by auditing financial statements and managers' compensation packages. The interests of managers and shareholders can be aligned by establishing management stock options, bonuses, and perquisites that are directly tied to how closely their decisions coincide with the interest of shareholders. The agency problem will persist unless an incentive structure is set up that aligns the interests of managers and shareholders. In other words, what's good for shareholders must also be good for managers. If that is not the case, managers will make decisions in their best interests rather than maximizing shareholder wealth.

## PRINCIPLE 8 Taxes Bias Business Decisions

Hardly any decision is made by the financial manager without considering the impact of taxes. When we introduced **Principle 4,** we said that only incremental cash flows should be considered in the evaluation process. More specifically, the cash flows we will consider will be *after-tax incremental cash flows to the firm as a whole.*

When we evaluate new projects, we will see income taxes playing a significant role. When the company is analyzing the possible acquisition of a plant or equipment, the returns from the investment should be measured on an after-tax basis. Otherwise, the company will not truly be evaluating the true incremental cash flows generated by the project.

The government also realizes taxes can bias business decisions and uses taxes to encourage spending in certain ways. If the government wanted to encourage spending on research and development projects it might offer an *investment tax credit* for such investments. This would have the effect of reducing taxes on research and development projects, which would in turn increase the after-tax cash flows from those projects. The increased cash flow would turn some otherwise unprofitable research and development projects into profitable projects. In effect, the government can use taxes as a tool to direct business investment to research and development projects, to the inner cities, and to projects that create jobs.

## PRINCIPLE 9 All Risk Is Not Equal—Some risk can be diversified away, and some cannot

Much of finance centers around **Principle 1: The Risk-Return Trade-Off.** But before we can fully use **Principle 1,** we must decide how to measure risk. As we will see, risk is difficult to measure. **Principle 9** introduces you to the process of diversification and demonstrates how it can reduce risk. We will also provide you with an understanding of how diversification makes it difficult to measure a project's or an asset's risk.

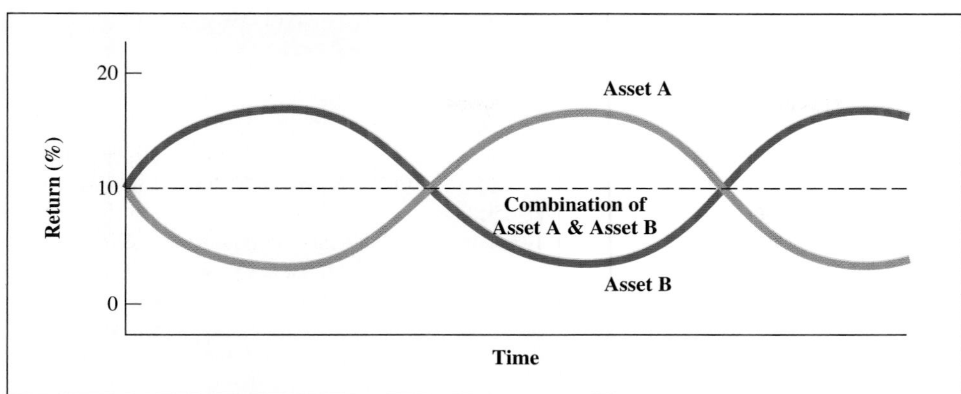


**FIGURE 1-4**
Reducing Risk Through Diversification

You are probably already familiar with the concept of diversification. There is an old saying, "don't put all of your eggs in one basket." Diversification allows good and bad events or observations to cancel each other out, thereby reducing total variability without affecting expected return.

To see how diversification complicates the measurement of risk, let us look at the difficulty Louisiana Gas has in determining the level of risk associated with a new natural gas well drilling project. Each year, Louisiana Gas might drill several hundred wells, with each well having only a 1 in 10 chance of success. If the well produces, the profits are quite large, but if it comes up dry, the investment is lost. Thus, with a 90 percent chance of losing everything, we would view the project as being extremely risky. However, if Louisiana Gas each year drills 2,000 wells, all with a 10 percent, independent chance of success, then they would typically have 200 successful wells. Moreover, a bad year may result in only 190 successful wells, and a good year may result in 210 successful wells. If we look at all the wells together, the extreme good and bad results tend to cancel each other out and the well drilling projects taken together do not appear to have much risk or variability of possible outcome.

The amount of risk in a gas well project depends upon our perspective. Looking at the well standing alone, it looks like a lot; however, if we consider the risk that each well contributes to the overall firm risk, it is quite small. This is because much of the risk associated with each individual well is diversified away within the firm. The point is: We can't look at a project in isolation. Later, we will see that some of this risk can be further diversified away within the shareholder's portfolio.

Perhaps the easiest way to understand the concept of diversification is to look at it graphically. Consider what happens when we combine two projects, as depicted in Figure 1-4. In this case, the cash flows from these projects move in opposite directions, and when they are combined, the variability of their combination is totally eliminated. Notice that the return has not changed—each individual project's and their combination's return averages 10 percent. In this case, the extreme good and bad observations cancel each other out. The degree to which the total risk is reduced is a function of how the two sets of cash flows or returns move together.

As we will see for most projects and assets, some risk can be eliminated through diversification, whereas some risk cannot. This will become an important distinction later in our studies. *For now, we should realize that the process of diversification can reduce risk, and as a result, measuring a project's or an asset's risk is very difficult.* A project's risk changes depending on whether you measure it standing alone or together with other projects the company may take on.

**FINANCE $ MATTERS**

## Is It Wrong to Tell a Lie?

In a February 1996 article in the *Journal of Business Ethics,* 400 people were asked to play the role of a fictional executive named Todd Fogler, who is faced with an ethical decision. The authors found that 47 percent of the top executives, 41 percent of the controllers, and 76 percent of the graduate-level business students they studied were willing to commit fraud by understating write-offs that cut into their companies' profits. When you hear about a study like this, the initial reaction of many students is that such ethical dilemmas are only the concerns of the top executives. They aren't—they are everywhere, and they are faced by everyone.

A teacher might not be able to change ethical standards in a college classroom, but he or she can teach students how to analyze questions so that they can bring to bear whatever ethical standards they have when they make decisions.

If you haven't already done so, there is no better time than now to develop a rule or set of rules against which you can measure the "rightness" or "wrongness" of your decisions and actions. It may be nothing more provocative than "Do unto others as you would have them do unto you." Or it may be a question or set of questions that you consistently ask: How would I feel about explaining to my parents or children what I did? How would I feel if the action I took were described, in detail, on the front page of my local newspaper? Have I avoided even the appearance of a conflict of interest in my decision? Would my action infringe on the liberty or constitutional rights of others?

Let's begin our look at ethical dilemmas in finance by asking this question: Is it wrong to tell a lie?

One of the roles of the financial manager is to transmit financial information to people outside the company. Occasionally, the facts that the financial manager must transmit and explain aren't particularly flattering to the firm. This presents the dilemma of whether it is unethical to tell a lie.

For example, at the annual stockholders' meeting, a senior financial manager is reviewing her company's financial performance for the previous year. The news is not good. Sales dropped 30 percent, and profits were down 50 percent. A stockholder asks the manager, "What caused this drastic decline and has it been corrected?" The manager knows that the primary cause of the decline was a series of poor top-management decisions made over the past several years, but she also knows that's not what her colleagues want her to say. Furthermore, she personally believes the decline is far from over, but she recognizes that's not what the stockholders want to hear.

Should this financial manager lie? Is lying always wrong, or is it acceptable under certain circumstances? What, if any, would those circumstances be? What do you think?



**PRINCIPLE 10** **Ethical behavior is doing the right thing, and ethical dilemmas are everywhere in finance**

Ethics, or rather a lack of ethics, in finance is a recurring theme in the news. During the late 1980s and early 1990s, the fall of Ivan Boesky and Drexel, Burnham, Lambert, and the near collapse of Salomon Brothers seemed to make continuous headlines. Meanwhile, the movie *Wall Street* was a hit at the box office and the book *Liar's Poker,* by Michael Lewis, chronicling unethical behavior in the bond markets, became a best seller. As the lessons of Salomon Brothers and Drexel, Burnham, Lambert illustrate, ethical errors are not forgiven in the business world. Not only is acting in an ethical manner morally correct, it is congruent with our goal of maximization of shareholder wealth.

Ethical behavior means "doing the right thing." A difficulty arises, however, in attempting to define "doing the right thing." The problem is that each of us has his or her own set of values, which forms the basis for our personal judgments about what is the right thing to do. However, every society adopts a set of rules or laws that prescribe what it believes to be "doing the right thing." In a sense, we can think of laws as a set of rules that reflect the values of the society as a whole, as they have evolved. For purposes of this text, we recognize that individuals have a right to disagree about what constitutes "doing the right thing," and we will seldom venture beyond the basic notion that ethical conduct involves abiding by society's rules. However, we will point out some of the ethical dilemmas that have arisen in recent years with regard to the practice of financial management. So as we embark on our study of finance and encounter ethical dilemmas, we encourage you to consider the issues and form your own opinions.

Many students ask, "Is ethics really relevant?" This is a good question and deserves an answer. First, although business errors can be forgiven, ethical errors tend to end careers and terminate future opportunities. Why? Because *unethical behavior eliminates trust, and without trust, businesses cannot interact.* Second, *the most damaging event a business can experience is a loss of the public's confidence in its ethical standards.* In finance, we have seen several recent examples of such events. It was the ethical scandals involving insider trading at Drexel, Burnham, Lambert that brought down that firm. In 1991, the ethical scandals involving attempts by Salomon Brothers to corner the Treasury bill market led to the removal of its top executives and nearly put the company out of business.

Beyond the question of ethics is the question of social responsibility. In general, corporate social responsibility means that a corporation has responsibilities to society beyond the maximization of shareholder wealth. It asserts that a corporation answers to a broader constituency than shareholders alone. As with most debates that center on ethical and moral questions, there is no definitive answer. One opinion is that because financial managers are employees of the corporation, and the corporation is owned by the shareholders, the financial managers should run the corporation in such a way that shareholder wealth is maximized and then allow the shareholders to decide if they would like to fulfill a sense of social responsibility by passing on any of the profits to deserving causes. Very few corporations consistently act in this way. For example, Bristol-Myers Squibb Co. gives away heart medication to those who cannot pay for it. This decision to give away heart medication came in the wake of an American Heart Association report showing that many of the nation's working poor face severe health risks because they cannot afford heart drugs. Clearly, Bristol-Myers Squibb felt it had a social responsibility to provide this medicine to the poor at no cost.

How do you feel about this decision?

### A Final Note on the Principles

Hopefully, these principles are as much statements of common sense as they are theoretical statements. These principles provide the logic behind what is to follow. We will build on them and attempt to draw out their implications for decision making. As we continue, try to keep in mind that although the topics being treated may change from chapter to chapter, the logic driving our treatment of them is constant and is rooted in these 10 principles.

**CONCEPT CHECK**

1. According to Principle 1, how do investors decide where to invest their money?
2. Why is it so hard to find extremely profitable projects?
3. Why is ethics relevant?

## OVERVIEW OF THE TEXT

In this text, we will focus on the maintenance and creation of wealth. Although this will involve attention to decision-making techniques, we will emphasize the logic behind those techniques to ensure that you do not lose sight of the concepts driving finance and the creation of wealth. The text begins by discussing the goal of maximization of shareholder wealth, a goal that is to be used in financial decision making, and presents the legal and tax environment in which these decisions are to be made. Since this environment sets the

FINANCE MATTERS

## The Wall Street Journal Workplace-Ethics Quiz

Without question, when you enter the workforce you will be faced with a number of ethical dilemmas that you have never considered. The spread of technology into the workplace has raised a variety of new ethical questions, and many old ones still linger. The following is a quiz dealing with ethical questions that will both give you some questions to think about, and also allow you to compare your answers with those of other Americans surveyed.

**Office Technology**

1. Is it wrong to use company e-mail for personal reasons?
   Yes No
2. Is it wrong to play computer games on office equipment during the workday?
   Yes No
3. Is it unethical to blame an error you made on a technological glitch?
   Yes No

**Gifts and Entertainment**

4. Is a $50 gift to a boss unacceptable?
   Yes No
5. Is a $50 gift from the boss unacceptable?
   Yes No
6. Of gifts from suppliers: Is it OK to take a $200 pair of football tickets?
   Yes No
7. Is it OK to take a $100 holiday food basket?
   Yes No
8. Can you accept a $75 prize won at a raffle at a supplier's conference?
   Yes No

**Truth and Lies**

9. Due to on-the-job pressure, have you ever abused or lied about sick days?
   Yes No
10. Due to on-the-job pressure, have you ever taken credit for someone else's work or idea?
    Yes No

**Ethics-Quiz Answers**

1. 34% said personal e-mail on company computers is wrong
2. 49% said playing computer games at work is wrong
3. 61% said it's unethical to blame your error on technology
4. 35% said a $50 gift to the boss is unacceptable
5. 12% said a $50 gift from the boss is unacceptable
6. 70% said it's unacceptable to take the $200 football tickets
7. 35% said it's unacceptable to take the $100 food basket
8. 40% said it's unacceptable to take the $75 raffle prize
9. 11% reported they lie about sick days
10. 4% reported they take credit for the work or ideas of others

Sources: Ethics Officer Association, Belmont, Mass.; Ethical Leadership Group, Wilmette, Ill.; surveys sampled a cross-section of workers at large companies and nationwide

Source: *The Wall Street Journal,* October 21, 1999, page B1 

ground rules, it is necessary to understand it before decision rules can be formulated. The 10 guiding principles that provide the underpinnings for what is to follow are then presented. Chapters 2 through 4 introduce the basic financial tools the financial manager uses to maintain control over the firm and its operations. These tools enable the financial manager to locate potential problem areas and plan for the future.

Chapter 5 explores how the firm and its assets are valued. It begins with an examination of the mathematics of finance and the concept of the time value of money. An understanding of this topic allows us to compare benefits and costs that occur in different time periods. We move on in Chapter 6 to develop an understanding of the meaning and measurement of risk. Valuation of fixed income securities is examined in Chapter 7, and Chapter 8 looks at valuation models that attempt to explain how different financial decisions affect the firm's stock price.

Using the valuation principles just developed, Chapter 9 discusses the capital-budgeting decision, which involves the financial evaluation of investment proposals in fixed assets. We then examine the measurement of cash flows in Chapter 10, and introduce methods to incorporate risk in the analysis in Chapter 11. In Chapter 12, we will examine the financing of a firm's chosen projects, looking at what costs are associated with alternative ways of raising new funds. Then, in Chapter 13, we look at managing the firm for shareholder value.

Chapter 14 examines the financial markets and the act of raising funds. Chapter 15 examines the firm's capital structure along with the impact of leverage on returns to the enterprise. Once these relationships between leverage and valuation are developed, we move on to the process of planning the firm's financing mix in Chapter 16. This is followed in Chapter 17 with a discussion of the determination of the dividend-retained earnings decision.

Chapters 18 through 20 deal with working-capital management, the management of current assets. We will discuss methods for determining the appropriate investment in cash, marketable securities, inventory, and accounts receivable, as well as the risks associated with these investments and the control of these risks.

Chapter 21 presents discussion of the use of futures, options, and swaps by financial managers to reduce risk. The final chapter in the text, Chapter 22, deals with international financial management, focusing on how financial decisions are affected by the international environment. In addition, Chapter 23, an introduction to corporate restructuring including mergers, spinoffs, and leveraged buyouts, is provided on the Internet. Similarly, Chapter 24, Loans and Leases, is also provided on the Internet.

## FINANCE AND THE MULTINATIONAL FIRM: THE NEW ROLE

In the search for profits, U.S. corporations have been forced to look beyond our country's borders. This movement has been spurred on by the collapse of communism and the acceptance of the free market system in Third World countries. All of this has taken place at a time when information technology has experienced a revolution brought on by the personal computer (PC). Concurrently, the United States went through an unprecedented period of deregulation of industries. These changes resulted in the opening of new international markets, and U.S. firms experienced a period of price competition here at home that made it imperative that businesses look across borders for investment opportunities. The end result is that many U.S. companies, including General Electric, IBM, Walt Disney, American Express, and General Motors, have restructured their operations in order to expand internationally. However, not only do U.S. firms have a freer access to international markets, but also foreign firms have an easier job of entering the U.S. markets and competing with U.S. firms on their own turf.

The bottom line is that what you think of as a U.S. firm may be much more of a multinational firm than you would expect. For example, Coca-Cola earns over 80 percent of its profits from overseas sales. Moreover, Coca-Cola earns more money from its sales in Japan than it does from all its domestic sales, and this is not uncommon. In fact, Dow Chemical, Colgate-Palmolive, 3M, Compaq, Hewlett-Packard, and Gillette make over half their sales overseas and earn over half of their profits from international sales. In addition to U.S. firms venturing abroad, foreign firms have also made their mark in the United States. You need only look to the auto industry to see what changes the entrance of Toyota, Honda, Nissan, BMW, and other foreign car manufacturers have made in the auto industry. In addition, foreigners have bought and now own such companies as Brooks Brothers, RCA, Pillsbury, A&P, 20th Century Fox, Columbia Pictures, and Firestone Tire & Rubber. Consequently, even if we wanted to, we couldn't keep all our attention focused on the United States, and even more important, we wouldn't want to ignore the opportunities that are available across international borders.

**CONCEPT CHECK**

1. What has brought on the era of the multinational corporation?
2. Has looking beyond U.S. borders been a profitable experience for U.S. corporations?

## HOW FINANCIAL MANAGERS USE THIS MATERIAL

As the chapter title states, this chapter provides you with an introduction to financial management. The principles presented in this chapter provide you with some clues as to the types of questions that will be dealt with by financial managers. As you will find out over the course of your studies, financial questions abound. In late 2000, headlines in *The Wall Street Journal* were full of financial decisions, including PepsiCo's decision, nearly 1 month after breaking off talks to acquire Quaker Oats Co. because of disagreements over price, to give it another try and open up discussions to acquire the maker of Gatorade and Cap'n Crunch for $14.3 billion in stock, and the leveraged buyout of the largest U.S. meat producer, IBP Inc., for $3.7 billion. In addition, making the news was the announcement that it was to the dog pound for the Sock Puppet. The canine mascot for Pets.com was put up for sale, along with the pet supply Web site's other assets, after the company announced it was shutting down. But financial questions and decisions also appeared in the headlines in the sports section when the New York Yankees signed the Orioles' Mike Mussina to an $88 million contract and Virginia Tech kept its head football coach Frank Beamer from defecting to North Carolina by upping his annual salary to in excess of $1 million.

What do all of these financial decisions have in common? They are all based on the 10 principles presented in this chapter, and they all deal with decision making. They are all financial decisions, because the focus of finance is how to raise and spend or invest money. Your goal as a financial manager is to manage the firm in such a way that shareholder wealth is maximized. As you will see, there are few, if any, major decisions that a manager makes that don't have financial implications.

## SUMMARY

OBJECTIVE 1 

OBJECTIVE 2 

OBJECTIVE 3 

This chapter outlines a framework for the maintenance and creation of wealth. In introducing decision-making techniques aimed at creating wealth, we will emphasize the logic behind those techniques. This chapter begins with an examination of the goal of the firm. The commonly accepted goal of profit maximization is contrasted with the more complete goal of maximization of shareholder wealth. Because it deals well with uncertainty and time in a real-world environment, the goal of maximization of shareholder wealth is found to be the proper goal for the firm.

The sole proprietorship is a business operation owned and managed by a single individual. Initiating this form of business is simple and generally does not involve any substantial organizational costs. The proprietor has complete control of the firm, but must be willing to assume full responsibility for its outcomes.

The general partnership, which is simply a coming together of two or more individuals, is similar to the sole proprietorship. The limited partnership is another form of partnership sanctioned by states to permit all but one of the partners to have limited liability if this is agreeable to all partners.

The corporation increases the flow of capital from public investors to the business community. Although larger organizational costs and regulations are imposed on this legal entity, the corporation is more conducive to raising large amounts of capital. Limited liability, continuity of life, and ease of transfer in ownership, which increase the marketability of the investment, have contributed greatly in attracting large numbers of investors to the corporate environment. The formal control of the corporation is vested in the parties who own the greatest number of shares. However, day-to-day operations are managed by the corporate officers, who theoretically serve on behalf of the common stockholders.

This chapter closes with an examination of the 10 principles on which finance is built that motivate the techniques and tools introduced in this text:

| | |
|---|---|
| **PRINCIPLE 1** | **The Risk-Return Trade-Off—We won't take on additional risk unless we expect to be compensated with additional return** |
| **PRINCIPLE 2** | **The Time Value of Money—A dollar received today is worth more than a dollar received in the future** |
| **PRINCIPLE 3** | **Cash—Not Profits—Is King** |
| **PRINCIPLE 4** | **Incremental Cash Flows—It's only what changes that counts** |
| **PRINCIPLE 5** | **The Curse of Competitive Markets—Why it's hard to find exceptionally profitable projects** |
| **PRINCIPLE 6** | **Efficient Capital Markets—The markets are quick and the prices are right** |
| **PRINCIPLE 7** | **The Agency Problem—Managers won't work for owners unless it's in their best interest** |
| **PRINCIPLE 8** | **Taxes Bias Business Decisions** |
| **PRINCIPLE 9** | **All Risk Is Not Equal—Some risk can be diversified away, and some cannot** |
| **PRINCIPLE 10** | **Ethical behavior is doing the right thing, and ethical dilemmas are everywhere in finance** |

With the collapse of communism and the acceptance of the free market system in Third World countries, U.S. firms have been spurred on to look beyond our own boundaries for new business. The end result has been that it is not uncommon for major U.S. companies to earn over half their income from sales abroad.

## KEY TERMS

**Agency problem, 15**
**Corporation, 6**
**Efficient market, 14**
**Initial public offering, 9**
**Partnership, 5**
**Primary market, 9**
**Seasoned new issue, 9**
**Secondary market, 9**
**Sole proprietorship, 5**

my**PHLIP**

Go To:
http://www.prenhall.com/keown
for downloads and current events associated with this chapter

## STUDY QUESTIONS

**1-1.** What are some of the problems involved in the use of profit maximization as the goal of the firm? How does the goal of maximization of shareholder wealth deal with those problems?

**1-2.** Compare and contrast the goals of profit maximization and maximization of shareholder wealth.

**1-3.** Firms often involve themselves in projects that do not result directly in profits; for example, IBM and Mobil Oil frequently support public television broadcasts. Do these projects contradict the goal of maximization of shareholder wealth? Why or why not?

**1-4.** What is the relationship between financial decision making and risk and return? Would all financial managers view risk-return trade-offs similarly?

**1-5.** Define (a) sole proprietorship, (b) partnership, and (c) corporation.

**1-6.** Identify the primary characteristics of each form of legal organization.

**1-7.** Using the following criteria, specify the legal form of business that is favored: (a) organizational requirements and costs, (b) liability of the owners, (c) continuity of business, (d) transferability of ownership, (e) management control and regulations, (f) ability to raise capital, and (g) income taxes.

## INTEGRATIVE PROBLEM

The final stage in the interview process for an Assistant Financial Analyst at Caledonia Products involves a test of your understanding of basic financial concepts. You are given the following memorandum and asked to respond to the questions. Whether or not you are offered a position at Caledonia will depend on the accuracy of your response.

To: Applicants for the position of Financial Analyst

From: Mr. V. Morrison, CEO, Caledonia Products

Re: A test of your understanding of basic financial concepts and of the Corporate Tax Code

Please respond to the following questions:

1. What are the differences between the goals of profit maximization and maximization of shareholder wealth? Which goal do you think is more appropriate?
2. What does the risk-return trade-off mean?
3. Why are we interested in cash flows rather than accounting profits in determining the value of an asset?
4. What is an efficient market and what are the implications of efficient markets for us?
5. What is the cause of the agency problem and how do we try to solve it?
6. What do ethics and ethical behavior have to do with finance?
7. Define (a) sole proprietorship, (b) partnership, and (c) corporation.

## CASE PROBLEM

### Living and Dying with Asbestos

What happens when you find your most profitable product is dangerous—an ethical dilemma for the financial manager.

Much of what we deal with in financial management centers around the evaluation of projects—when they should be accepted and when they should be terminated. As new information surfaces regarding the future profitability of a project, the firm always has the choice of terminating that project. When this new information raises the question of whether or not it is ethical to produce a profitable project, the decision becomes more difficult. Many times, ethical dilemmas pit profits versus ethics. These decisions become even more difficult when continuing to produce the product is within the law.

Asbestos is a fibrous mineral used for fireproofing, electrical insulation, building materials, brake linings, and chemical filters. If you are exposed long enough to asbestos particles—usually 10 or more years—you can develop a chronic lung inflammation called asbestosis, which makes breathing difficult and infection easy. Also linked to asbestos exposure is mesethelioma, a cancer of the chest lining. This disease sometimes doesn't develop until 40 years after the first exposure. Although the first major scientific conference on the dangers of asbestos was not held until 1964, the asbestos industry knew of the dangers of asbestos 60 years ago.

As early as 1932, the British documented the occupational hazards of asbestos dust inhalation.[a] Indeed, on September 25, 1935, the editors of the trade journal *Asbestos* wrote to Sumner Simpson, president of Raybestos-Manhattan, a leading asbestos company, asking permission to publish an article on the dangers of asbestos. Simpson refused and later praised the magazine for not

[a]See Samuel S. Epstein, "The Asbestos 'Pentagon Papers,' " in Mark Green and Robert Massie, Jr., eds., *The Big Business Reader: Essays on Corporate America* (New York: Pilgrim Press, 1980) 154–65. This article is the primary source of the facts and quotations reported here.

printing the article. In a letter to Vandivar Brown, secretary of Johns-Manville, another asbestos manufacturer, Simpson observed: "The less said about asbestos the better off we are." Brown agreed, adding that any article on asbestosis should reflect American, not English, data.

In fact, American data were available, and Brown, as one of the editors of the journal, knew it. Working on behalf of Raybestos-Manhattan and Johns-Manville and their insurance carrier, Metropolitan Life Insurance Company, Anthony Lanza had conducted research between 1929 and 1931 on 126 workers with 3 or more years of asbestos exposure. But Brown and others were not pleased with the paper Lanza submitted to them for editorial review. Lanza, said Brown, had failed to portray asbestosis as milder than silicosis, a lung disease caused by long-term inhalation of silica dust and resulting in chronic shortness of breath. Under the then-pending Workmen's Compensation law, silicosis was categorized as a compensable disease. If asbestosis was worse than silicosis or indistinguishable from it, then it too would have to be covered. Apparently Brown didn't want this and thus requested that Lanza depict asbestosis as less serious than silicosis. Lanza complied and also omitted from his published report the fact that more than half the workers examined—67 of 126—were suffering from asbestosis.

Meanwhile, Sumner Simpson was writing F. H. Schulter, president of Thermoid Rubber Company, to suggest that several manufacturers sponsor further asbestos experiments. The sponsors, said Simpson, could exercise oversight prerogatives; they "could determine from time to time after the findings are made whether they wish any publication or not." Added Simpson: "It would be a good idea to distribute the information to the medical fraternity, providing it is of the right type and would not injure our companies." Lest there should be any question about the arbiter of publication, Brown wrote to officials at the laboratory conducting the tests:

> It is our further understanding that the results obtained will be considered the property of those who are advancing the required funds, who will determine whether, to what extent and in what manner they shall be made public. In the event it is deemed desirable that the results be made public, the manuscript of your study will be submitted to us for approval prior to publication.

Industry officials were concerned with more than controlling information flow. They also sought to deny workers early evidence of their asbestosis. Dr. Kenneth Smith, medical director of a Johns-Manville plant in Canada, explained why seven workers he found to have asbestosis should not be informed of their disease:

> It must be remembered that although these men have the X-ray evidence of asbestosis, they are working today and definitely are not disabled from asbestosis. They have not been told of this diagnosis, for it is felt that as long as the man feels well, is happy at home and at work, and his physical condition remains good, nothing should be said. When he becomes disabled and sick, then the diagnosis should be made and the claim submitted *by the Company.* The fibrosis of this disease is irreversible and permanent so that eventually compensation will be paid to each of these men. But as long as the man is not disabled, it is felt that he should not be told of his condition so that he can live and work in peace and the Company can benefit by his many years of experience. Should the man be told of his condition today there is a very definite possibility that he would become mentally and physically ill, simply through the knowledge that he has asbestosis.

When lawsuits filed by asbestos workers who had developed cancer reached the industry in the 1950s, Dr. Smith suggested that the industry retain the Industrial Health Foundation to conduct a cancer study that would, in effect, squelch the asbestos-cancer connection. The asbestos companies refused, claiming that such a study would only bring further unfavorable publicity to the industry, and that there wasn't enough evidence linking asbestos and cancer industry-wide to warrant it.

Shortly before his death in 1977, Dr. Smith was asked whether he had ever recommended to Johns-Manville officials that warning labels be placed on insulation products containing asbestos. He provided the following testimony:

> The reasons why the caution labels were not implemented immediately, it was a business decision as far as I could understand. Here was a recommendation, the corporation is in business to make, to provide jobs for people and make money for stockholders and they had to take into consideration the effects of everything they did, and if the application of a caution label identifying a product as hazardous would cut out sales, there would be serious financial implications. And the powers that be had to make some effort to judge the necessity of the label vs. the consequences of placing the label on the product.

Dr. Smith's testimony and related documents have figured prominently in hundreds of asbestos-related lawsuits, totaling more than $1 billion. In March 1981, a settlement was reached in nine separate lawsuits brought by 680 New Jersey asbestos workers at a Raybestos-Manhattan plant. Several asbestos manufacturers, as well as Metropolitan Life Insurance, were named as defendants. Under the terms of the settlement, the workers affected will share in a $9.4 million court-administered compensation fund. Each worker will be paid compensation according to the length of exposure to asbestos and the severity of the disease contracted.

By 1982, an average of 500 new asbestos cases were being filed each month against Manville (as Johns-Manville was now called), and the company was losing more than half the cases that went to trial. In 10 separate cases, juries had also awarded punitive damages, averaging $616,000 a case. By August, 20,000 claims had been filed against the company, and Manville filed for bankruptcy in federal court. This action froze the lawsuits in their place and forced asbestos victims to stand in line with other Manville creditors. After more than 3 years of legal haggling, Manville's reorganization plan was finally approved by the bankruptcy court. The agreement set up a trust fund valued at approximately $2.5 billion to pay Manville's asbestos claimants. To fund the trust, shareholders were required to surrender half the value of their stock, and the company had to give up much of its projected earnings over the next 25 years.[b]

Note: Adapted by permission: William Shaw and Vincent Barry, "Living and Dying with Asbestos," *Moral Issues in Business,* 6th ed., 224–27. © 1995 by Wadsworth, Inc.

[b]See Robert Mokhiber, *Corporate Crime and Violence* (San Francisco: Sierra Club Books, 1988), 285–86; and Arthur Sharplin, "Manville Lives on as Victims Continue to Die," *Business and Society Review 65* (Spring 1988): 27–28.

Claims, however, soon overwhelmed the trust, which ran out of money in 1990. With many victims still waiting for payment, federal Judge Jack B. Weinstein ordered the trust to restructure its payments and renegotiate Manville's contributions to the fund. As a result, the most seriously ill victims will now be paid first, but average payments to victims have been lowered significantly, from $145,000 to $43,000. Meanwhile, the trust's stake in Manville has been increased to 80 percent, and Manville has been required to pay $300 million to it in additional dividends.[c]

## QUESTIONS

1. Should the asbestos companies be held morally responsible in the sense of being capable of making a moral decision about the ill effects of asbestos exposure? Or does it make sense to consider only the principal people involved as morally responsible—for example, Simpson and Brown?
2. Simpson and Brown presumably acted in what they thought were the best profit interests of their companies. Nothing they did was illegal. On what grounds, if any, are their actions open to criticism?
3. Suppose that Simpson and Brown reasoned this way: "While it may be in our firms' short-term interests to suppress data about the ill effects of asbestos exposure, in the long run it may ruin our companies. We could be sued for millions, and the reputation of the entire industry could be destroyed. So we should reveal the true results of the asbestos-exposure research and let the chips fall where they may." Would that be appropriate?
4. If you were a stockholder in Raybestos-Manhattan or Johns-Manville, would you approve of Simpson and Brown's conduct? If not, why not?
5. "Hands of government" proponents would say that it is the responsibility of government, not the asbestos industry, to ensure health and safety with respect to asbestos. In the absence of appropriate government regulations, asbestos manufacturers have no responsibility other than to operate efficiently. Do you agree?
6. Does Dr. Smith's explanation for concealing from workers the nature of their health problems illustrate how adherence to industry and corporate goals can militate against individual moral behavior? Or do you think Dr. Smith did all he was morally obliged to do as an employee of an asbestos firm? What about Lanza's suppression of data in his report?
7. It has been shown that spouses of asbestos workers can develop lung damage and cancer simply by breathing the fibers carried home on work clothes and that people living near asbestos plants experience higher rates of cancer than the general population does. Would it be possible to assign responsibility for these effects to individual members of asbestos companies? Should the companies themselves be held responsible?

[c]"Asbestos Claims to Be Reduced Under New Plan," *The Wall Street Journal* (November 20, 1990): A4; and "MacNeil-Lehrer Newshour," December 18, 1990.

# UNDERSTANDING FINANCIAL STATEMENTS, TAXES, AND CASH FLOWS

The announcement of its profits is a significant event for a firm. For publicly traded firms, this event occurs on a quarterly basis—much too often to suit many managers—when they have to report their earnings to their shareholders. Take Harley-Davidson, Inc., for instance. On July 11, 2000, the firm announced that its net income had increased 32 percent for the second quarter of 2000 to $90.6 million, compared to $68.6 million in the year-earlier period. In the meantime, revenues grew 24 percent to $755 million. As part of the announcement, the management also reported that the firm's gross profit margin (gross profits divided by sales) had declined to 34.1 percent from 35 percent the year earlier. Such a small decrease may seem insignificant, but adds up when we are talking about annual sales of $2 or $3 billion. Management attributed the decline in the company's gross profit margin to weakening European currencies and a higher mix of lower-margin product lines. ● What has happened to Harley-Davidson's profits since June 2000? Find out at the firm's Web page at www.harley-davidson.com. (When you get to the homepage, click on "Investor Relations" to find the company's latest financial information.)

Adapted from Dow Jones Business News, (Copyright © 2000, Dow Jones & Company, Inc.), July 11, 2000.

**LEARNING OBJECTIVES**

After reading this chapter, you should be able to

1. Compute a company's profits as reflected by an income statement.
2. Determine a firm's accounting book value, as presented in a balance sheet.
3. Compute a company's taxes.
4. Measure a company's free cash flows, both from an operating perspective and a financing perspective.
5. Explain the difficulty in comparing financial statements of U.S. firms and foreign companies.

**CHAPTER PREVIEW**

In this chapter, we view the world of finance primarily as an accountant sees it. To begin, we review the two basic financial statements that are used to understand how a firm is doing financially—the income statement, or what is sometimes called the profit and loss statement, and the balance sheet. We also spend a significant amount of time coming to understand how to measure and interpret a company's cash flows. No skill is more important in our study of finance than being able to calculate a firm's or a project's cash flows. Cash flow is a *very* significant issue for a company and is critical in our understanding of financial management. It will be discussed over and over in the chapters to follow. Thus, it is essential that we begin early to develop a good understanding of cash flows.

**RELATE TO THE BIG PICTURE**

Two principles are especially important in this chapter: **Principle 3** tells us that **Cash—Not Profits—Is King.** In many respects, cash is more important than profits. Thus, in this chapter, considerable time is devoted to learning how to measure cash flows. Second, **Principle 7** warns us there may be conflict between management and owners, especially in large firms where managers and owners have different incentives. That is, **Managers Won't Work for the Owners Unless It's In Their Best Interest to Do So.** Although the management is an agent of the owners, experience suggests that managers do not always act in the best interest of the owners. The incentives for the managers are, at times, different from those of owners. Thus, the firm's common stockholders, as well as other providers of capital (such as bankers), have a need for information that can be used to monitor the managers' actions. Because the owners of large companies do not have access to internal information about the firm's operations, they must rely on public information from any and all sources. One of the main sources of such information is the company's financial statements that are provided by the firm's accountants. Although this information is by no means perfect, it is an important source used by outsiders to assess a company's activities. In this chapter, we learn how to use data from the firm's public financial statements to monitor management's actions.

Let's begin our study by looking at the basic financial statements that are a primary source of information about a firm's financial performance. Only by understanding the makeup of these statements can we have any hope of learning about business, much less finance.

## THE INCOME STATEMENT: MEASURING A COMPANY'S PROFITS

OBJECTIVE 1 

**Income statement**
The statement of profit or loss for the period, comprised of net revenues less expenses for the period.

An **income statement,** or *profit and loss statement,* measures the amount of profits generated by a firm over a given time period. In its most basic form, an income statement can be expressed as follows:

$$\text{sales} - \text{expenses} = \text{profits}$$

The income statement answers the question, "How profitable is the business?" In providing this answer, the income statement reports financial information related to five broad areas of business activity:

1. Revenue (sales)—money derived from selling the company's product or service
2. Cost of goods sold—the cost of producing or acquiring the goods or services to be sold
3. Operating expenses—expenses related to (a) marketing and distributing the product or service, and (b) administering the business

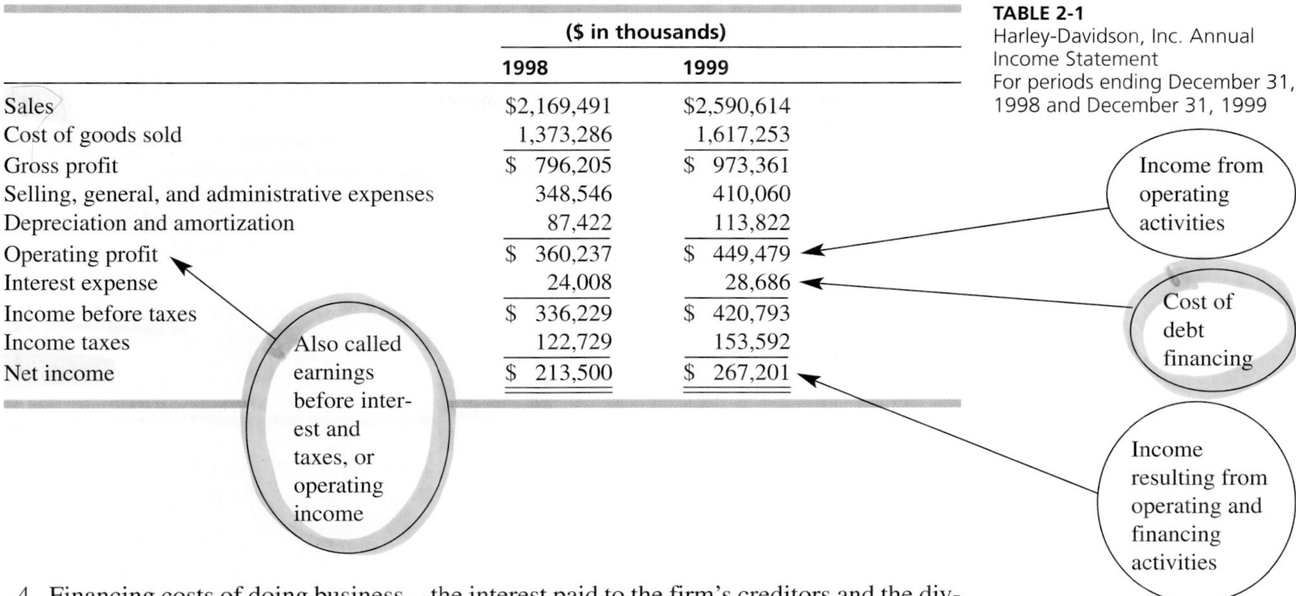


| | ($ in thousands) | |
|---|---|---|
| | 1998 | 1999 |
| Sales | $2,169,491 | $2,590,614 |
| Cost of goods sold | 1,373,286 | 1,617,253 |
| Gross profit | $ 796,205 | $ 973,361 |
| Selling, general, and administrative expenses | 348,546 | 410,060 |
| Depreciation and amortization | 87,422 | 113,822 |
| Operating profit | $ 360,237 | $ 449,479 |
| Interest expense | 24,008 | 28,686 |
| Income before taxes | $ 336,229 | $ 420,793 |
| Income taxes | 122,729 | 153,592 |
| Net income | $ 213,500 | $ 267,201 |

**TABLE 2-1**
Harley-Davidson, Inc. Annual Income Statement
For periods ending December 31, 1998 and December 31, 1999

4. Financing costs of doing business—the interest paid to the firm's creditors and the dividends paid to preferred stockholders (but not dividends paid to common stockholders)
5. Tax expenses—the amount of taxes owed based on a firm's taxable income

All of these "income statement activities" are illustrated in Table 2-1, where we present the annual income statement for Harley-Davidson, Inc. Looking at the firm's income statement, we see that for 1999:

1. Sales or revenues—determined by the amount of product sold times the price per unit—were more than $2.59 billion for the year.
2. The firm's cost of producing or acquiring its product was $1.62 billion.
3. Harley-Davidson spent $410 million in selling and administration expenses, and had approximately $113.8 million in depreciation expense.
4. Given these results, the firm had **operating income,** or **earnings before interest and taxes (EBIT),** of $449.5 million.
5. The firm paid $28.7 million in **interest expense,** which is determined by the amount of Harley-Davidson debt and the interest rate paid on the debt.
6. Harley-Davidson paid $153.6 million in taxes, which was approximately 36 percent of the company's **earnings before taxes.**
7. Finally, the **net income** available to Harley-Davidson's owners was equal to $267.2 million. This income may be distributed to the company's owners or reinvested in the company, provided, of course, there is cash available to do so.

**Operating income (earnings before interest and taxes)**
Profit from sales minus total operating expenses.

**Interest expense**
Interest paid on a firm's outstanding debt. A firm's interest expense is tax deductible.

**Earnings before taxes**
Operating income minus interest expense.

**Net income**
A figure representing the firm's profit or loss for the period. It also represents the earnings available to the firm's common and preferred stockholders.

What conclusion can we draw from Harley-Davidson's income statement? Well, for one thing, we learn that for every $1 in sales, Harley-Davidson earned about 38¢ in gross profits ($973,361 gross profits ÷ $2,590,614 sales), 17¢ in operating profits ($449,479 operating profits ÷ $2,590,614 sales), and 10¢ in net income ($267,201 net income ÷ $2,590,614 sales). To determine if these results are good, we must estimate if these profit-to-sales ratios are high enough that shareholder value is being created. We might also gain some insight if we could see how Harley-Davidson's performance compares against that of its competition—more about this in Chapter 3. For the time being, simply remember that the profit-to-sales relationships are important in assessing a firm's performance.

Three additional issues are important in understanding the information contained in an income statement:

1. Operating income (earnings before interest and taxes) is not affected by how the firm is financed, whether with debt or equity. Operating income is the firm's profits from all of its assets, regardless of whether the assets are financed from debt or stock. Understanding this fact is essential when we later want to evaluate management's performance at creating profits from the firm's assets. Just remember that operating income is affected only by management's investment decisions, and not by how the firm is financed.
2. Notice that interest expense is subtracted from income before computing the firm's tax liability, which is not true for dividends paid. In other words, interest is a tax-deductible expense; that is, for every dollar a company spends on interest, its tax expense is reduced proportionately. For example, if a firm's tax rate is 30 percent, $1 paid in interest reduces taxes by 30¢, which means that the after-tax cost of the debt is only 70¢ ($1.00 − $0.30).
3. As we shall see later, the fact that a firm has a positive net income does not necessarily mean it has any cash—possibly a surprising result to us, but one that we will come to understand.

**CONCEPT CHECK**

1. What does the income statement tell us? Why must we be careful when interpreting the income statement?
2. What is the basic relationship that we see in the income statement?
3. How is operating income different from net income as both relate to the five "business activities" reported in the income statement?

## THE BALANCE SHEET: MEASURING A FIRM'S BOOK VALUE

OBJECTIVE 2 

**Balance sheet**
A statement of financial position at a particular date. The form of the statement follows the balance sheet equation: total assets = total liabilities + owners' equity.

Whereas the income statement reports the results from operating the business for a period of time, such as a year, the **balance sheet** provides a snapshot of the firm's financial position at a specific point in time, presenting its asset holdings, liabilities, and owner-supplied capital. In its simplest form, a balance sheet follows this formula:

total assets = outstanding debt + shareholders' equity

Assets represent the resources owned by the firm, whereas the liabilities and shareholders' equity indicate how those resources are financed.

Figure 2-1 presents the basic components of a balance sheet. On the left side of Figure 2-1, the firm's assets are listed according to their type; on the right side, we see a listing of the different sources of financing a company could use to finance its assets.

### Types of Assets

As shown in Figure 2-1, a company's assets fall into three categories: (1) current assets, (2) fixed assets, and (3) other assets. Assets on a balance sheet are listed in the order of the length of time necessary to convert them into cash in the ordinary course of business. Current assets, excluding cash itself, are expected to be converted into cash within 12 months, with accounts receivable not taking as long to convert to cash as inventories. Fixed assets, such as equipment, are used over a number of years, and as such will not be converted into cash within the normal operating cycle of business.

CURRENT ASSETS **Current assets,** or **gross working capital,** as it is sometimes called, comprise those assets that are relatively liquid; that is, those that are expected to be converted into cash within a year. Current assets primarily include cash, accounts receivable, inventories, and prepaid expenses.

**Current assets (gross working capital)** Current assets consist primarily of cash, marketable securities, accounts receivable, inventories, and prepaid expenses.

- **Cash.** Every firm must have cash for current business operations. A reservoir of cash is needed because of the unequal flow of funds into (cash receipts) and out of (cash expenditures) the business. The amount of the cash balance is determined not only by the volume of sales, but also by the predictability of cash receipts and cash payments.
- **Accounts receivable.** The firm's **accounts receivable** consists of payments due from its customers who buy on credit.

**Accounts receivable** A promise to receive cash from customers who purchased goods from the firm on credit.

**FIGURE 2-1**
The Balance Sheet: An Overview

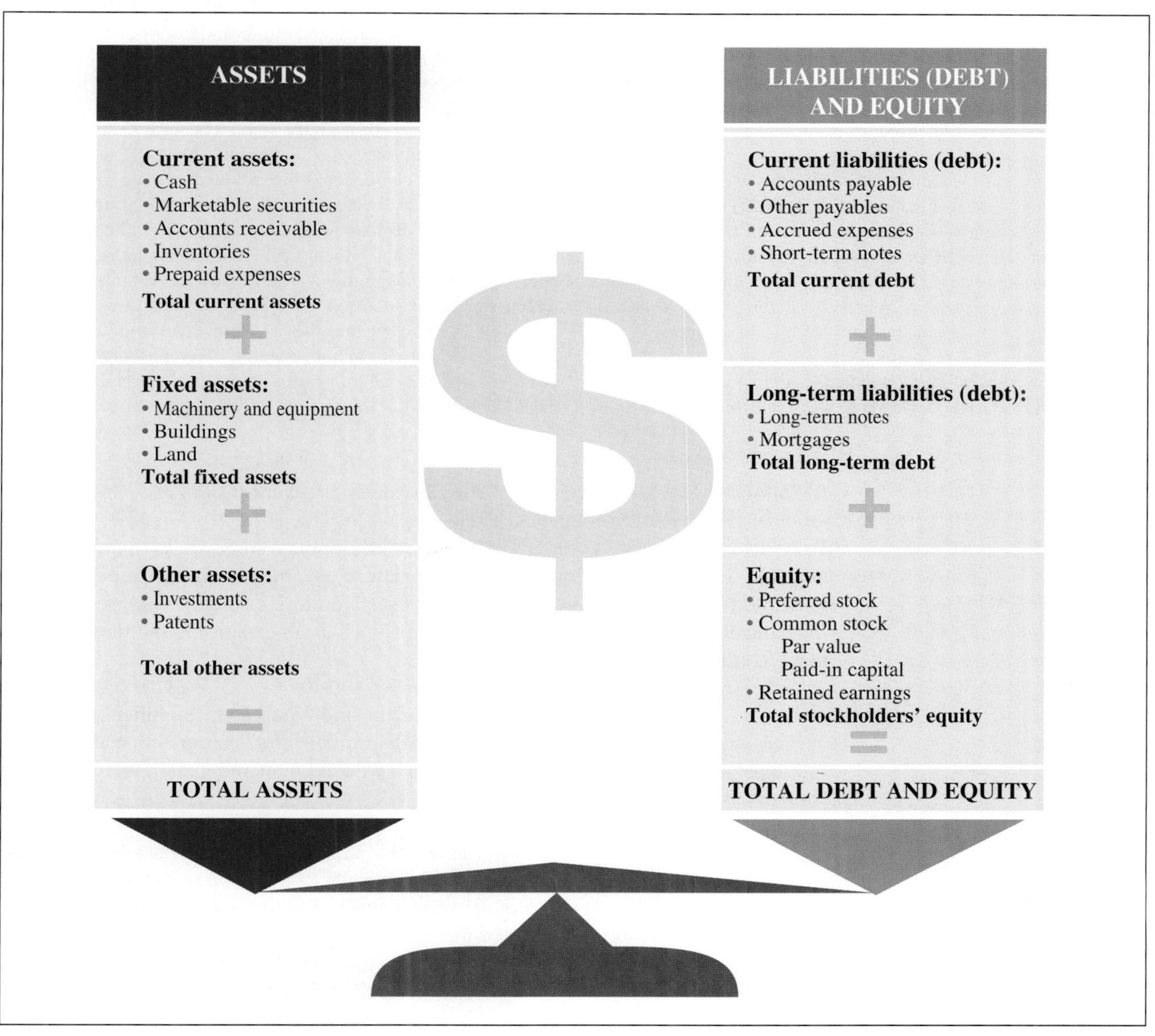

ROAD RULES

A FOCUS ON HARLEY-DAVIDSON

ROAD RULES

### The Path to CFO at Harley-Davidson: An Interview with Jim Ziemer

For as long as I can remember, I wanted to work at Harley-Davidson. Growing up just three blocks from the plant, I used to watch the test riders who sometimes ate lunch in my neighbor's yard and think "Wouldn't it be great to be paid to ride a motorcycle?"

I rode my first motorcycle, an M-50 Harley, when I was 15 years old. When I was 19, my wish came true; I went to work for the firm as a union employee, operating the elevator used to move parts from floor to floor. They'd punch the sheet metal on the first floor for the tanks and fenders and I'd take it up to the sixth floor where they painted it. I would take tube steel up to the 5th floor where it was bent and welded into frames. Then the bike flowed downward to the first floor for the final assembly. It was really great watching all the components of manufacturing come together into a beautiful motorcycle.

In the meantime, I entered the University of Wisconsin, Milwaukee, to study accounting. Actually, this was a bit of a fluke. When I started college I had no idea of what I wanted to be. I started in the school of engineering, but soon transferred to the school of science, with an interest in physics, and eventually ended up in chemistry. However, my work and studies were abruptly interrupted when I received a letter from Uncle Sam requesting my services in the army. While in the army, I took some accounting and economics courses, and when I got out, I thought, "The quickest way to graduate is to major in accounting." So I returned to Harley-Davidson to work full-time and finish my accounting degree. In my new job, I worked as a timekeeper, which helped me become familiar with all the operations within the plant. It was interesting to watch the gears being cut and the crankcases being machined, and in the process learning all about the inside components of an engine.

Then I got a job in the engineering department. With a limited background in engineering and an interest in accounting, I was put in charge of project management. After graduating, I had a number of jobs, ending up in financial planning, which allowed me to see what happened in the firm as a whole. From there, I worked as the controller in parts and accessories, which meant getting involved in sales and marketing and shipping and receiving.

In 1981, management bought the company from AMF (a conglomerate) through a management buyout, which meant the firm took on a lot of debt. Shortly thereafter, interest rates climbed to 20 percent; it was not a pretty sight. The firm went through a major downsizing that led to laying off about 40 percent of our employees. As a consequence, everybody ended up doing several jobs, and I became director of all the firm's accounting.

In 1986, we decided to take the company public through the initial public offering, which would allow us to get rid of a lot of debt. This was happening when I was working on my MBA, which was great situation for my master's studies. Finally, in February 1987, I became the vice president and controller at Harley-Davidson. I remember feeling very fortunate; I was 37 years old and the controller of what I thought was a great company. We had a lot of things to prove yet, but we were on our way.

**Inventory**
Raw materials, work in progress, and finished goods held by the firm for eventual sale.

**Prepaid expenses**
Expenses that have been paid in advance. These assets are recorded on the balance sheet and expensed on the income statement as they are used.

**Fixed assets**
Assets comprising equipment, buildings, and land.

**Other assets**
Assets not included in current assets or fixed assets.

**Accounting book value**
The value of an asset as shown on a firm's balance sheet. It represents the historical cost of the asset rather than its current market value or replacement cost.

- **Inventories. Inventory** consists of the raw materials, work-in-progress, and the final products held by a firm for eventual sale.
- **Prepaid expenses.** A company often needs to prepay some of its expenses. For example, insurance premiums may be due before coverage begins, or rent may have to be paid in advance. Thus, **prepaid expenses** are those cash payments recorded on the balance sheet as current assets and then shown as an expense in the income statement as they are used.

FIXED ASSETS **Fixed assets** include machinery and equipment, buildings, and land. Some businesses are more capital-intensive than others; for example, a manufacturer would typically be more capital-intensive than a wholesale operation and, therefore, have more fixed assets.

OTHER ASSETS **Other assets** are all assets that are not current assets or fixed assets, including for example, intangible assets such as patents, copyrights, and goodwill.

In reporting the dollar amounts of the various types of assets just described, the conventional practice is to report the value of the assets and liabilities on a historical cost basis. Thus, the balance sheet is not intended to represent the current market value of the company, but rather reports the historical transactions recorded at their cost, or what we call a firm's **accounting book value.** Determining a fair value of the business is a different matter.

## Types of Financing

We now turn to the right side of the balance sheet in Figure 2-1, labeled "Liabilities (Debt) and Equity," which indicates how the firm finances its assets. Financing comes from two main sources: debt (liabilities) and equity. **Debt** is money that has been borrowed and must be repaid at some predetermined date. **Equity,** on the other hand, represents the shareholders' investment in the company.

DEBT CAPITAL **Debt capital** is financing provided by a creditor. As shown in Figure 2-1, it is divided into (1) current, or short-term, debt and (2) long-term debt. **Current debt,** or short-term liabilities, includes borrowed money that must be repaid within the next 12 months. Sources of current debt include the following:

- **Accounts payable** represents credit extended by suppliers to a firm when it purchases inventories. The purchasing firm may have 30 or 60 days before paying for inventory that has been purchased. This form of credit extension is also called trade credit.
- **Other payables** include interest payable and income taxes payable that are owed and will come due within the year.
- **Accrued expenses** are short-term liabilities that have been incurred in the firm's operations, but not yet paid. For example, employees perform work that may not be paid for until the following week or month, which are recorded as accrued wages.
- **Short-term notes** represent amounts borrowed from a bank or other lending source that are due and payable within 12 months.

LONG-TERM DEBT **Long-term debt** includes loans from banks or other sources that lend money for longer than 12 months. For example, a firm might borrow money for 5 years to buy equipment, or for as long as 25 to 30 years to purchase real estate, such as a warehouse or an office building.

EQUITY Equity includes the shareholders' investment—both preferred stockholders and common stockholders—in the firm.

- **Preferred stockholders** receive a dividend that is fixed in amount. In the event of liquidation of the firm, these stockholders are paid after the firm's creditors, but before the common stockholders.
- **Common stockholders** are the residual owners of a business. They receive whatever is left over—good or bad—after the creditors and preferred stockholders are paid. The amount of a firm's common equity as reported in the balance sheet is equal to (1) the amount the company received from selling stock to investors plus (2) the firm's retained earnings. The amount the firm receives from selling stock is recorded in the common equity section in the accounts of **par value and paid-in capital.** These amounts may be offset by any stock that has been repurchased by the company, which is typically shown as **treasury stock. Retained earnings** is the cumulative total of all the net income over the firm's life less the common stock dividends that have been paid over the years. Thus, the common equity capital consists of the following:

$$\begin{aligned}\text{common equity} &= \text{common stock issued (less repurchases)}\\ &+ \text{cumulative net income over the firm's life}\\ &- \text{total dividends paid over the firm's life}\end{aligned}$$

which is shown in the balance sheet as:

$$\begin{aligned}\text{common equity} &= \text{common stock (par value + paid-in capital)}\\ &+ \text{retained earnings}\end{aligned}$$

**Debt**
Consists of such sources as credit extended by suppliers or a loan from a bank.

**Equity**
Stockholders' investment in the firm and the cumulative profits retained in the business up to the date of the balance sheet.

**Debt capital**
Funds provided to the firm by a creditor.

**Current debt**
Debt due to be paid within 1 year.

**Accounts payable**
Liability of the firm for goods purchased from suppliers on credit.

**Other payables**
Interest payable and income taxes payable that are to be paid within 1 year.

**Accrued expenses**
Expenses that have been incurred but not yet paid in cash.

**Short-term notes**
Amounts borrowed from a creditor that are due within 1 year.

**Long-term debt**
Loans from banks or other sources that lend money for longer than 12 months.

**Preferred stockholders**
Investors who own the firm's preferred stock.

**Common stockholders**
Investors who own the firm's common stock. Common stockholders are the owners of the firm.

**Par value and paid-in capital**
The amount the firm receives from selling stock to investors.

**Treasury stock**
The firm's stock that has been issued and reacquired by the firm.

**Retained earnings**
The cumulative earnings that have been retained and reinvested in the firm over its life (cumulative earnings − cumulative dividends).

**FINANCE MATTERS**

## Ethics

Sunbeam Corporation is considered by consumers to be a manufacturer of quality electronic appliances and camping equipment. However, to investors, Sunbeam has joined the ranks of companies such as Rite Aid, Phar-Mor, Oxford Health Plans, CUC International (now part of Cendant Corp.), and MicroStrategies that violated accounting rules in an attempt to increase stock price and shareholder wealth. Under the leadership of CEO Al Dunlap, known as "Chainsaw Al" for his ruthless leadership style, the firm's management used deceptive financial reporting information to create an illusion of a firm that had growing revenues and earnings. In fact, the hearty sales of electric blankets in the summer and barbecue grills in the fall were fictitious. When auditors Deloitte & Touche and Arthur Anderson reviewed Sunbeam's books in the fall of 1998, the company's recorded profits of $109.4 million in 1997 were in reality only $38.7 million. One analyst writing in *The Wall Street Journal* estimated the fraud cases involving Sunbeam, CUC, and Oxford resulted in losses to shareholders of $34 billion as the firms' stock prices plunged.

Rite Aid has a similar story. In July 2000, Rite Aid restated its financial statements and corrected $1 billion in overstated profits from the previous 2 years. For the fiscal year ended February 2000, the firm reported a net loss of $1.14 billion. While the SEC and the U.S. Attorney's Office investigate these irregularities, shareholders have filed a class-action suit against the firm's management and its accounting firm, KPMG, to recover losses from the decrease in stock price from $24 in mid-1999 to $5 in August 2000.

The Big Five accounting firms report that in 1999, 108 of the 205 private class-action lawsuits have been because of accounting irregularities. In the report, "Fraudulent Financial Reporting: 1987–1997," audit committees and company boards were found to be weak. Audit committees met infrequently while boards of directors consisted of insiders and others closely connected to the firm.

Boards of directors and shareholders who expect management to increase the stock price at any cost often set aggressive goals for the firm's executives. CEOs like Al Dunlap are often so domineering that management fears not meeting company goals. In this type of environment, chief financial officers and comptrollers are often pressured to overlook accounting irregularities that report less than accurate information on financial transactions.

What Sunbeam and other firms have discovered is that improper reporting of financial data has a far deeper impact than just declining stock price. Once investors discover intentional erroneous reporting of revenues and earnings, the firm's reputation is damaged irreparably. Even if the stock price increases, shareholders and analysts will wonder if the data supporting the price is fact or fiction.

Source: Paul Sweeney, "Accounting Fraud, Learning from the Wrongs," *Financial Executive,* September/October 2000, pp. 18–22.

## The Harley-Davidson, Inc. Balance Sheet

Balance sheets for Harley-Davidson, Inc. are presented in Table 2-2 for both December 31, 1998, and December 31, 1999, along with the changes in each account during the year. By referring to the two balance sheets, we can see the financial position of the firm both at the beginning and end of 1999. Furthermore, by examining the two balance sheets, along with the income statement for 1999, we will have a more complete picture of the firm's operations. We are then able to see what Harley-Davidson looked like at the beginning of 1999 (balance sheet on December 31, 1998), what happened during the year (income statement for 1999), and the final outcome at the end of the year (balance sheet on December 31, 1999).

The firm's investment in assets increased $191.9 million over the year, with most of the growth in accounts receivable and fixed assets. The increase in the firm's assets in turn required additional financing. Looking at the debt and equity parts of the balance sheet, we see that management used three sources of money to finance the growth:

1. A $237.0 million increase in retained earnings, which is the result of retaining a portion of the firm's net income, rather than paying it out in dividends.
2. Borrowing $39.1 million in additional short-term debt (current liabilities).
3. Borrowing $11.1 million in additional long-term debt.

We also observe that the firm's common stock was reduced by $105.8 million. This is due to a repurchase of outstanding shares of stock by Harley-Davidson.

**TABLE 2-2**
Harley-Davidson, Inc.
Balance Sheet

As of December 31, 1998 and December 31, 1999

| | ($ in thousands) | | |
|---|---|---|---|
| **ASSETS** | **1998** | **1999** | **Change** |
| Cash | $ 165,170 | $ 183,415 | $ 18,245 |
| Accounts receivable | 473,758 | 542,659 | $ 68,901 |
| Inventories | 155,616 | 168,616 | $ 13,000 |
| Other current assets | 50,419 | 54,304 | $ 3,885 |
| Total current assets | $ 844,963 | $ 948,994 | $ 104,031 |
| Gross plant, property, and equipment | $1,076,381 | $1,244,185 | $ 167,804 |
| Accumulated depreciation | 448,622 | 562,444 | $ 113,822 |
| Net plant, property, and equipment | $ 627,759 | $ 681,741 | $ 53,982 |
| Other assets | 447,487 | 481,342 | $ 33,855 |
| Total assets | $1,920,209 | $2,112,077 | $ 191,868 |
| **LIABILITIES** | | | |
| Accounts payable and accruals | $ 245,584 | $ 256,086 | $ 10,502 |
| Short-term debt | 222,931 | 262,068 | $ 39,137 |
| Total current liabilities | $ 468,515 | $ 518,154 | $ 49,639 |
| Long-term debt | 421,783 | 432,843 | $ 11,060 |
| Total liabilities | $ 890,298 | $ 950,997 | $ 60,699 |
| **EQUITY** | | | |
| Common stock (par + paid-in capital) | $ 155,612 | $ 49,771 | $(105,841) |
| Retained earnings | 874,299 | 1,111,309 | $ 237,010 |
| Total equity | $1,029,911 | $1,161,080 | $ 131,169 |
| Total liabilities and equity | $1,920,209 | $2,112,077 | $ 191,868 |

Note that when we are examining the changes in the balance sheet from one year to the next, as we just did with Harley-Davidson, Inc., we are gaining an understanding of where money came from and how it was used. For Harley-Davidson, we see that the firm's cash was invested in more assets and to repurchase common stock. Where did the money come from? A significant portion came from retaining a part of the firm's profits ($237.0 million). A lesser amount came from additional short-term borrowing ($39.1 million) and long-term debt ($11.1 million). Knowing this information is helpful in better understanding Harley-Davidson's finances. In fact, it is such an important matter that we will return to this issue later in the chapter.

To continue our discussion of Harley-Davidson's financial position, as reflected by its balance sheet, we have graphed the major types of assets and debt and equity in Figure 2-2, as of December 31, 1999. In looking at this graph, we see that for every dollar of assets, there must be a dollar of financing. There can be no exception. If we grow the firm's assets, we had best be prepared to find additional financing. Harley-Davidson has $2,112 million in total assets, which represents all of the investments made by creditors and stockholders in the firm.

**Net working capital**
The difference between the firm's current assets and its current liabilities. When the term *working capital* is used, it is frequently intended to mean net working capital.

NET WORKING CAPITAL Earlier we said that the term *current assets* is also called *gross working capital.* We can now define **net working capital** as current assets less current liabilities (current assets − current liabilities). Thus, net working capital compares the amount of current assets (assets that should convert into cash within the next 12 months) to the current liabilities (debt that will be due within 12 months). As shown in

**FIGURE 2-2**
Harley-Davidson Balance Sheet

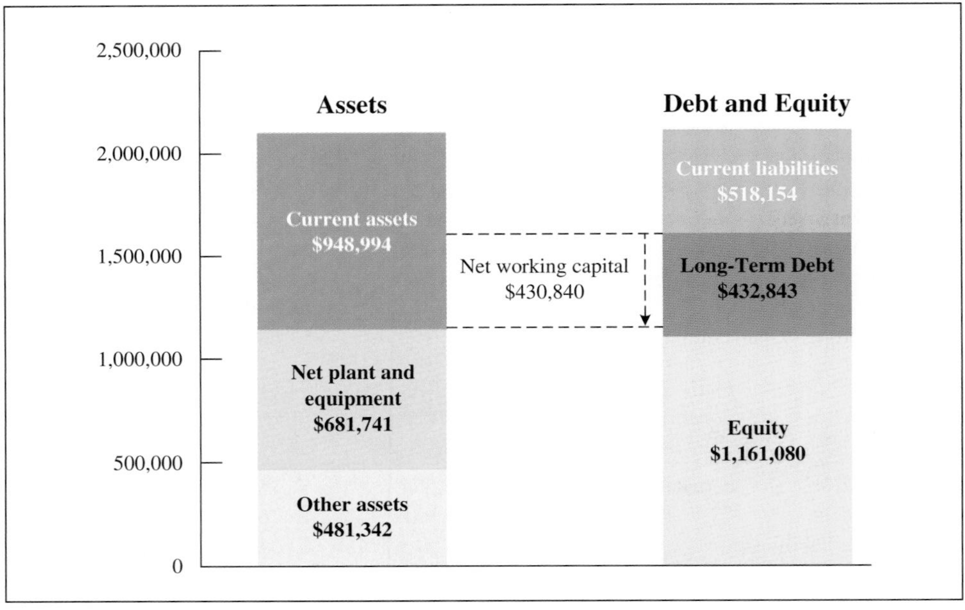


Figure 2-2, Harley-Davidson's net working capital is $430.8 million ($948.9 million current assets − $518.1 million current liabilities). A firm's net working capital is of particular importance to lenders who want to know if a company has adequate liquidity. **Liquidity** is the speed and ease at which an asset can be converted into cash. The more current assets that a firm has relative to its current liabilities, the greater the firm's liquidity. If you loan a company some money, you would want to know that it has adequate liquidity to be able to repay the loan.

**Liquidity**
The ability of a firm to pay its bills on time, and how quickly a firm converts its liquid assets (accounts receivables and inventories) into cash.

### Debt/Equity Mix

We can also see that by the end of 1999, Harley-Davidson was financing its assets about 45 percent from debt and 55 percent from equity. The debt-equity relationship is an important one to lenders and investors, as we will see on numerous occasions in our studies.

We next want to look briefly at one of the largest expenses a company encounters—taxes.

**CONCEPT CHECK**

1. Regarding the time frame reported, how is the balance sheet different from the income statement?
2. State the basic balance sheet formula and its meaning.
3. What is the definition of a firm's "accounting book value"?
4. What are the two principal sources of financing? What do these sources consist of?

## COMPUTING A COMPANY'S TAXES

Taxes are a critical factor in making many financial decisions. The tax rules can be extremely complex, requiring a lot of specialized expertise to understand them. However, for our purposes, we just need to understand how taxes are computed.

FINANCE MATTERS

### Who Can We Trust If Not Management?

On some rare occasions, management provides inaccurate accounting information to investors, even sometimes with the intent to mislead. While no judgment regarding fraud had been reached at the time we revised *Financial Management,* the management of the third-largest drugstore chain in the United States, Rite Aid, acknowledged that the firm's profits in 1998 and 1999 were not profits at all, but losses—and big ones. The drugstore chain had reportedly overstated its profits by more than $1 billion. Management also reported a net loss of $1.14 billion for the fiscal year ended in February 2000.

The restatement of profits forced the resignation of the founder's son as the CEO and caused the stock price to fall by more than 80 percent.

The Securities and Exchange Commission and the U.S. Attorney's Office were investigating the firm. Management had turned over the results of its own legal and accounting probes to the government agencies. Robert Miller, the firm's new chairman of the board and its Chief Executive Officer, said that Rite Aid would "cooperate fully" with the investigations.

The firm's losses reduced its retained earnings to the point that the outstanding debt was 15 times larger than the amount of equity on the balance sheet. The firm's annual interest expenses were more than the firm's profits. However, Miller predicted that future cash flow, combined with available borrowing power, would be sufficient to service the firm's debt and meet its operating expenses. In a presentation to security analysts, Miller said that the firm's operating problems had been resolved and that "we expect a dramatic improvement in sales" and positive earnings before interest, taxes, depreciation, and amortization next year (2001).

Based on his analysis of the situation, Paul Brown, an accounting professor at New York University, said, "They employed just about every accounting trick out there." For instance, Rite Aid's management had reported expenses as assets and had retroactively increased the useful lives of selected fixed assets, lowering depreciation expense and artificially boosting reported income. Adjustments in a category called "inventory and cost of goods sold" involved some $500 million in misstatement of income, such as recording credits from vendors that had not been earned.

The lesson learned: Even very large, reputable firms can make some really big mistakes and then try to cover them up by using misleading accounting methods. When this happens, there is a loss of trust that cannot be overcome, typically leading to the firing of management. We can be thankful, however, that we live in a country where these instances are the exception. Even so, it can be very costly to investors when it does happen.

Adapted from: Devon Spurgeon, "Rite Aid Overstated Profit for '98, '99; Posts Fiscal 2000 Loss of $1.1 Billion," *The Wall Street Journal,* July 12, 2000, p. A3.

To begin, we should ask, "Who is a taxpayer?" For the most part, there are three basic types of taxable business entities: sole proprietors, partnerships, and corporations. Sole proprietors report their income in their personal tax returns and pay the taxes owed. Partnerships report income from the partnership but do not pay taxes. Each partner reports his or her portion of the income and pays the corresponding taxes. The corporation, as a separate legal entity, reports its income and pays any taxes related to these profits. The owners (stockholders) of the corporation do not report these earnings in their personal tax returns, except when all or a part of the profits are distributed in the form of dividends. Because most firms of any size are corporations, we will restrict our discussion to corporate taxes.

## Computing Taxable Income

The taxable income for a corporation is based on the gross income from all sources less any tax-deductible expenses. *Gross income* equals the firm's dollar sales from its product less the cost of producing or acquiring the product. Tax-deductible expenses include any operating expenses, such as marketing expenses, administrative expenses, and depreciation expense. Also, interest expense paid on the firm's outstanding debt is a tax-deductible expense. However, dividends paid to the firm's stockholders are *not* deductible expenses, but rather distributions of income.

When computing depreciation for tax purposes, companies use the *modified accelerated cost recovery system;* however, to avoid unnecessary complexity, we will generally

**TABLE 2-3**
J&S Corporation Taxable Income

| | | |
|---|---|---|
| Sales | | $50,000,000 |
| Cost of goods sold | | (23,000,000) |
| Gross profit | | $27,000,000 |
| Operating expenses | | |
| Administrative expenses | $4,000,000 | |
| Depreciation expenses | 1,500,000 | |
| Marketing expenses | 4,500,000 | |
| Total operating expenses | | (10,000,000) |
| Operating income (earnings before interest and taxes) | | $17,000,000 |
| Interest expense | | (1,000,000) |
| Taxable income | | $16,000,000 |

NOTE: Dividends paid to common stockholders ($1,000,000) are not tax-deductible.

**TABLE 2-4**
Corporate Tax Rates

| Rates | Income Levels |
|---|---|
| 15% | $0–$50,000 |
| 25% | $50,001–$75,000 |
| 34% | $75,001–$100,000 |
| 39% | $100,001–$335,000 |
| 34% | $335,001–$10,000,000 |
| 35% | $10,000,001–$15,000,000 |
| 38% | $15,000,001–$18,333,333 |
| 35% | Over $18,333,333 |

use straight-line depreciation in our study. For instance, if a firm purchases a fixed asset for $12,000 that has a 5-year expected life and a $2,000 anticipated salvage value at the end of that period, straight-line depreciation would be $2,400 per year ($12,000 ÷ 5 years = $2,400). Although there is a $2,000 salvage value, this value is disregarded in computing annual depreciation expense for tax purposes.

To demonstrate how to compute a corporation's taxable income, consider the J&S Corporation, a manufacturer of home accessories. The firm, originally established by Kelly Stites, had sales of $50 million for the year. The cost of producing the accessories totaled $23 million. Operating expenses were $10 million. The corporation has $12.5 million in debt outstanding with an 8 percent interest rate, which has resulted in $1 million in interest expense ($12,500,000 × .08 = $1,000,000). Management paid $1 million in dividends to the firm's common stockholders. The taxable income for the J&S Corporation would be $16 million, as shown in Table 2-3.

**COMPUTING THE TAXES OWED** The taxes to be paid by a corporation on its taxable income are based on the corporate tax rate structure. The specific rates effective for the corporation, as of 2000, are given in Table 2-4. If you wonder about the economic rationale for the rates, don't waste your time. There is none. Politicians, not economists, determine the rates.

Based on the tax rates, J&S Corporation's tax liability would be $5,530,000, as computed in Table 2-5.

**Marginal tax rate**
The tax rate that would be applied to the next dollar of income.

The tax rates in Table 2-4 are defined as the **marginal tax rates,** or rates applicable to the next dollar of income. For instance, if a firm has earnings of $60,000 and is contemplating an investment that would yield $10,000 in additional profits, the tax rate to be used in calculating the taxes on this added income is the 25 percent marginal tax rate. However, if the corporation already expects $20 million without the new investment, the extra

**TABLE 2-5**
Tax Calculations for J&S Corporation

| Earnings | × | Marginal Tax Rate | = | Taxes |
|---|---|---|---|---|
| $50,000 | × | 15% | = | $ 7,500 |
| $75,000–$50,000 | × | 25% | = | 6,250 |
| $100,000–$75,000 | × | 34% | = | 8,500 |
| $335,000–$100,000 | × | 39% | = | 91,650 |
| $10,000,000–$335,000 | × | 34% | = | 3,286,100 |
| $15,000,000–$10,000,000 | × | 35% | = | 1,750,000 |
| $16,000,000–$15,000,000 | × | 38% | = | 380,000 |
| Total tax liability | | | | $5,530,000 |

$10,000 in earnings would be taxed at 35 percent, the marginal tax rate at the $20 million level of income.

For the J&S Corporation, with a taxable income of $16 million, its marginal tax rate is 38 percent; that is, any additional income from new investments will be taxed at a rate of 38 percent—at least until taxable income exceeds $18,333,333. Then the marginal tax rate would decline to 35 percent. Note, however, that while J&S Corporation has a 38 percent *marginal* tax rate, its **average tax rate**—taxes owed relative to the firm's total income—is 34.6 percent ($5,530,000 ÷ $16,000,000).

**Average tax rate**
Taxes owed by the firm divided by the firm's taxable income.

For financial decision making, it is the *marginal tax rate,* rather than the *average tax rate,* that matters because it is the marginal rate that is applied to any additional earnings resulting from a decision. Thus, when making financial decisions involving taxes, *always* use the marginal tax rate in your calculations and *not* the average tax rate. We cannot overemphasize the importance of remembering the preceding statement, which is a specific application of **Principle 4—It's Only What Changes That Counts.** We should always analyze decisions at the margin.

The tax rate structure used in computing the J&S Corporation's taxes assumes that the income occurs in the United States. Given the globalization of the economy, it may well be that some of the income originates in a foreign country. If so, the tax rates, and the method of taxing the firm, frequently vary. International tax rates can vary substantially and the job of the financial manager is to minimize the firm's taxes by reporting as much income as possible in the low tax-rate countries and as little as possible in the high tax-rate countries. Of course, other factors, such as political risk, may discourage efforts to minimize taxes across national borders.

**CONCEPT CHECK**

1. Distinguish among sole proprietors, partnerships, and corporations in terms of how they are taxed.
2. What is the difference between marginal tax rates and average tax rates?
3. Why do we use marginal tax rates, rather than average tax rates, when making financial decisions?
4. What should be the firm's goal when it comes to international taxes?

## MEASURING FREE CASH FLOWS

While an income statement measures a company's profits, profits are not the same as cash flows; profits are calculated on an *accrual* basis rather than a *cash* basis. Accrual-basis accounting records income when it is earned, whether or not the income has been received in cash, and records expenses when they are incurred, even if money has not actually been paid out. For example, sales reported in the income statement include both cash sales and credit sales. Therefore, sales for a given year do not correspond exactly to the actual cash collected from sales. Similarly, a firm must purchase inventory, but some of the purchases are financed by credit rather than by immediate cash payment. Also, under the accrual system, the purchase of equipment that will last for more than 1 year is not shown as an expense in the income statement. Instead, the amount is recorded as an asset and then depreciated over its useful life. An annual depreciation expense (this is not a cash flow) is recorded as a way to match the use of the asset with sales generated from its service. We could give more examples to show why profits differ from cash flows, but the point should be clear: *Profits and cash flows are not the same thing.* Failure to understand and recognize this important fact could cause some real problems.

In measuring cash flows, we could use the conventional accountant's presentation called a *statement of cash flows.* However, we are more interested in considering cash flows from the perspective of the firm's investors, rather than from an accounting view. So, what follows is similar to a conventional cash flow statement presented as part of a company's financial statements, but "not exactly."

We can think of a firm as a block of assets that produce cash flow, which can be either positive or negative. Once the firm has paid all its operating expenses and made all its investments, the remaining cash flows are free to distribute to the firm's creditors and shareholders—thus, the term **free cash flows.** If on the other hand, the free cash flows are negative, the creditors and investors are the ones who make up the shortfall—someone has to do it. Thus, the cash flows that are generated through a firm's operations and investments in assets equal its cash flows paid to—or received from—the company's investors (both creditors and stockholders). They have to be equal; that is:

**Free cash flows**
Amount of cash available from operations after paying for investments in net operating working capital and fixed assets. This cash is available to distribute to the firm's creditors and owners.

$$\text{Firm's operating free cash flows} = \text{Firm's financing free cash flows}$$

So, we can either calculate a firm's free cash flows from an operating perspective or from a financing perspective. Either way, we will get the same answer. However, the two calculations give us different perspectives about the firm's cash flows. So, let's look at each approach for measuring a company's cash flows.

## Calculating Free Cash Flows: An Operating Perspective

A firm's free cash flows, viewed from an *operating perspective,* are the after-tax cash flows generated from operating the business less the firm's investments in assets; that is:

$$\text{free cash flows} = \begin{matrix}\text{after-tax operating}\\\text{cash flows}\end{matrix} - \begin{matrix}\text{investment}\\\text{in assets}\end{matrix}$$

where the investment in assets may be expressed as follows:

$$\text{investment in assets} = \begin{matrix}\text{change in net operating}\\\text{working capital}\end{matrix} + \begin{matrix}\text{change in}\\\text{fixed assets}\\\text{and other assets}\end{matrix}$$

Thus, the procedure for computing a firm's free cash flows on an operating basis involves three steps:

1. Convert the income statement from an accrual basis to a cash basis (compute after-tax cash flows from operations).
2. Calculate the investment in *net* operating working capital.
3. Compute investments made in fixed assets and other assets (investment activities).

For the first step, we compute after-tax cash flows from operations as follows:

| | **Operating income (earnings before interest and taxes)** |
|---|---|
| + | depreciation |
| = | earnings before interest, taxes, depreciation, and amortization (EBITDA) |
| − | cash tax payments |
| = | after-tax cash flows from operations |

In the preceding calculation, we determine **earnings before interest, taxes, depreciation, and amortization (EBITDA)** by adding back depreciation to operating income because depreciation is not a cash expense. We then subtract taxes to get the cash flows on an after-tax basis.

**Earnings before interest, taxes, depreciation, and amortization (EBITDA)** Operating income plus depreciation and amortization expenses.

Let's return to Harley-Davidson, Inc., to illustrate how to compute a firm's after-tax cash flows from operations. Using Harley-Davidson's income statement in Table 2-1, we find that the firm's after-tax cash flow from operations is $409,709,000.

| | |
|---|---|
| Operating income (EBIT) | $449,479,000 |
| Plus depreciation and amortization | 113,822,000 |
| Earnings before interest, tax, depreciation, and amortization (EBITDA) | $563,301,000 |
| Less tax expense | 153,592,000 |
| After-tax cash flows from operations | $409,709,000 |

For the second step, the increase in net operating working capital is equal to the:

$$\begin{bmatrix}\text{change in}\\ \text{current assets}\end{bmatrix} - \begin{bmatrix}\text{change in noninterest-bearing}\\ \text{current liabilities}\end{bmatrix}$$

Earlier, we said that *net working capital* is equal to current assets minus current, or short-term, debt. However, in computing free cash flows, we only consider the **noninterest-bearing current liabilities** incurred in the normal day-to-day operating activities of buying and selling the firm's goods, such as accounts payable and accrued wages. Any interest-bearing debt (that is, where you explicitly pay interest for the use of the money) will be included in computing free cash flows from a financing perspective because borrowing money is a financing activity.

**Noninterest-bearing current liabilities** Current liabilities other than short-term debt.

For Harley-Davidson, the increase in net operating working capital is found by looking at the firm's balance sheets in Table 2-2 and computing the following:

$$\begin{bmatrix}\text{change in}\\ \text{current assets}\end{bmatrix} - \begin{bmatrix}\text{change in noninterest-bearing}\\ \text{current liabilities}\end{bmatrix}$$

$$= \$104{,}031{,}000 - \$10{,}502{,}000 = \$93{,}529{,}000$$

where the noninterest-bearing current liabilities are the firm's accounts payable and accruals.

The final step involves computing the change in *gross* fixed assets (not *net* fixed assets) and any other balance sheet assets that are not already considered. For Harley-Davidson, that includes the change in gross fixed assets and other assets, which equals $201,659,000:

| | |
|---|---|
| Increase in gross fixed assets | $167,804,000 |
| Increase in other assets | 33,855,000 |
| Total increase in long-term assets | $201,659,000 |

We can now compute Harley-Davidson's free cash flows from an operating perspective as follows:

| | |
|---|---|
| After-tax cash flow operations | $409,709,000 |
| Less: | |
| Investment in net operating working capital | 93,529,000 |
| Investment in long-term assets | 201,659,000 |
| Free cash flows (operating perspective) | $114,521,000 |

Given the preceding computations, we see that the firm's free cash flows are positive in the amount of $114,521,000. The firm's operations generated $409,709,000; however, part of this amount was consumed by the increases in net operating working capital ($93,529,000) and the investments in long-term assets ($201,659,000). Question: Where did Harley-Davidson's $114,521,000 in free cash flows go? Answer: To the investors. Let's compute the free cash flows from a financing perspective to confirm that the investors received the money.

## Calculating Free Cash Flows: A Financing Perspective

We will now compute free cash flows from a financing perspective, which are equal to the cash flows paid to or received from the investors. We can compute this amount as follows:

Interest received by the firm's creditors
- − change in debt principal
- − dividends paid to stockholders
- − change in stock

= financing free cash flows

Thus, to compute free cash flows from a financing perspective, we do the following:

1. Compute the interest paid to creditors.
2. Determine if the company repaid any debt principal to the creditors (creditors receive cash) or increased debt principal (creditors provide cash to the firm). This amount is found by computing the change in debt principal.
3. Ascertain if any dividends were paid to (received by) the stockholders.
4. Determine if any new stock was issued (investors provide cash to the firm) or if the firm repurchased stock from investors (investors receive cash from the firm). Here we take the change in the par value and paid-in capital for any stock issued and the change in treasury stock (stock that has been repurchased).

To conclude, free cash flows from a financing perspective are simply the net cash flows received by the firm's investors, or if negative, the cash flows that the investors are paying into the firm. In the latter situation in which the investors are putting money into the firm, it is because the firm's operating free cash flows are negative, thereby requiring an infusion of capital by the investors.

FINANCE MATTERS

## Earnings or Cash: Which Is Better?

A number of stock analysts at investment houses such as J. P. Morgan and Goldman Sachs are converting from using earnings to cash flows when valuing stocks.

Cash-flow valuations were favored by many of the "raiders" in the 1980s who wanted to see how much debt companies could suffer and still survive. But today's stock analysts are coming around to cash flow because they say it ignores accounting tricks and thus shows the true economic health of companies.

"The reported profits number is now considered an accounting fiction," says Michael Mayo, a bank analyst at First Boston. Cash-flow valuations are now in vogue in the cable, high-tech, Internet, pharmaceutical, and financial-services sectors.

Some analysts argue that cash flow may better estimate companies' true growth rates. For example, in 1999, analysts projected that Citigroup, Inc. and Wells Fargo & Co. would report above-average future earnings growth, partly due to events stemming from mergers. Mr. Mayo contended that these events could "potentially inflate the banks' future reported earnings, relative to cash flow." He warned that investors might overlook that the banks are not creating as much value as reported profits suggest.

Analysts say that when cash flow is lower than reported earnings, it is a sign that profits are coming from items other than cash—including possible accounting tricks. For example, before it restated its 1997 numbers due to alleged accounting irregularities, Sunbeam Corp. reported $109 million in net profits for 1997. But, at the same time, Sunbeam reported $8 million in net outflows of cash for the year, which suggests that reported earnings may have come instead from possible accounting manipulations.

There is an even more impressive indication from anecdotal evidence that cash flow is coming to have greater importance in the views of analysts. According to a study by Rick Escherich, a managing director in J. P. Morgan M&A group, 72 percent of 178 investment bankers surveyed publish a cash-flow earnings multiple. Escherich commented, "Fifteen years ago, there was very little emphasis on cash flow."

Source: Elizabeth MacDonald, "Analysts Increasingly Look To Cash Flow Over Earnings," *The Wall Street Journal*, April 1, 1999, p. C2.

For Harley-Davidson, we see that the investors did in fact receive $114,521,000, as we had expected. Relying on the data from the firm's financial statements in Tables 2-1 and 2-2, we can compute the free cash flows from a financing perspective as follows:

| | |
|---|---|
| Interest received by (paid to) creditors | $28,686,000 |
| Minus change in interest-bearing debt (short-term notes and long-term debt) | 50,197,000 |
| Minus dividends to stockholders | (30,191,000) |
| Minus change in common stock | (105,841,000) |
| Free cash flows (financing perspective) | $114,521,000 |

Thus, Harley-Davidson's investors received more money from the company than they invested. In fact, they received $114,521,000—the exact amount of the firm's free cash flows from an operating perspective.

## Harley-Davidson, Inc.: What Have We Learned?

Based on our review of Harley-Davidson, Inc.'s financial statements, we can now draw some conclusions. To this point, we have learned that:

- For every dollar of sales, Harley-Davidson earns 38¢ in gross profits, 17¢ in operating income, and 10¢ in net income.
- Most of the firm's investments are in current assets and in fixed assets.
- The firm finances its assets using about 45 percent debt and 55 percent equity.
- Harley-Davidson has positive free cash flows because it generates positive cash flows from operations, which are then used in part to finance the company's growth. The firm has not generated these positive cash flows from selling its assets (downsizing).

- The company invested primarily in fixed assets, with a lesser amount going to increasing working capital.
- Owners of the firm received $136,032,000 in the form of dividends and stock repurchase. The firm's creditors provided $21,511,000 in net additional financing.

**CONCEPT CHECK**

1. Why can an income statement not provide a measurement of a firm's cash flows?
2. What is the relationship between a firm's operating and financing free cash flows?
3. When computing a firm's operating free cash flows, why is it necessary to adjust operating income for increases (decreases) in net operating working capital and fixed assets?
4. What impact do positive or negative operating cash flows have on financing cash flows?

## FINANCIAL STATEMENTS AND INTERNATIONAL FINANCE

OBJECTIVE 5 

Many countries have different guidelines for firms to use in preparing financial statements. In other words, $1 of earnings in the United States is not the same as 1.84 German marks (the equivalent of a U.S. dollar based on the exchange rate). The two countries simply have different Generally Accepted Accounting Principles. In fact, the differences in accounting practices are significant enough that a firm reporting according to German standards could have $100 million in profits, but in the United States, that same company might report a loss. Just imagine what this does for an investor trying to interpret financial statements across different country boundaries.

As a result of this situation, the International Accounting Standards Committee (IASC), a private body supported by the worldwide accounting profession, is trying to develop international financial-reporting standards that will minimize the problem. The need for international standards became increasingly urgent as a result of the 1997 Asian crisis, which called attention to the perils of lax accounting in many Asian countries. In spite of the work to standardize accounting practices around the world, the U.S. accounting profession has rejected efforts toward international standards. On the other hand, the U.S. Congress, and the New York Stock Exchange, which wants to see more foreign companies list their stocks on the exchange, have encouraged the Securities and Exchange Commission (SEC) to accept the new international standards. Even so, the SEC has instead insisted that foreign companies seeking to list their shares in the United States must follow U.S. accounting standards, as developed by the Financial Accounting Standards Board (FASB).

Despite the push for acceptable uniform standards, this issue will not resolve itself quickly. Only time will tell what will happen.

## HOW FINANCIAL MANAGERS USE THIS MATERIAL

In this chapter, we have explained the contents of key financial statements—the income statement and the balance sheet. In addition, we have spent considerable time coming to understand cash flows from a finance perspective. Accounting data is the basis for so much that is done in finance. It is used in almost every aspect of financial management, either directly or indirectly. In a firm of any significant size, the data is used both to evaluate historical performance and to project future expectations. Managers are increasingly evaluated and compensated based on their firm's performance, and performance is measured in terms of *financial* performance, usually in terms of profitability. For many executives, up to half of their compensation is tied to performance incentives, frequently to increasing company earnings.

Not only do the financial managers use the data, but financial analysts and lenders rely on the firm's financial information to advise investors and to make loans. Lenders, for example, often require that the firm's earnings before interest, taxes, depreciation, and amortization (EBITDA) cannot fall below a given minimum, usually stated in terms of a ratio of EBITDA to interest and debt principal requirements. Or, they may say that the firm's equity cannot be less than some minimum amount.

Let there be no question, managers throughout an organization rely heavily on financial statements. Failure to understand this information would almost certainly prove fatal to the firm and to the careers of most managers.

## SUMMARY

A firm's profits may be viewed as follows:

gross profit = sales − cost of goods sold

earnings before interest and tax (operating profits) = sales − cost of goods sold − operating expenses

net profits (net income) = sales − cost of goods sold − operating expenses − interest expense − taxes − preferred stock dividends

Five activities that drive a company's profits:

1. Revenue derived from selling the company's product or service
2. Cost of producing or acquiring the goods or services to be sold
3. Operating expenses related to (a) marketing and distributing the product or service to the customer and (b) administering the business
4. Financing costs of doing business—namely, the interest paid to the firm's creditors
5. Payment of taxes

The balance sheet presents a company's assets, liabilities, and equity as of a specific date. Total assets must equal debt plus equity. Assets include current assets, fixed assets, and other assets. Debt includes short-term and long-term debt. Equity includes preferred stock, common stock, and retained earnings. All of the numbers in a balance sheet are based on historical costs. As such, they are considered to equal the firm's accounting book value, as opposed to its market value.

For the most part, a company's taxes are determined by multiplying the applicable tax rate times the firm's earnings after all expenses have been paid, including interest expense, but not dividend payments.

Free cash flow is the cash that is distributed to or received from the firm's investors. Free cash flow can be computed from an operating perspective or a financing perspective. In either case, they will be equal; that is:

| Free cash flow from: | | |
|---|---|---|
| **Operating perspective** | | **Financing perspective** |
| Earnings before interest, taxes, and depreciation (EBITDA)<br>− additional investments in assets | = | Interest and dividend payments<br>+ decreases in debt and stock or<br>− increases in debt and stock |

OBJECTIVE 5 

Foreign firms often follow accounting practices that differ significantly from the Generally Accepted Accounting Principles used by U.S. firms. The reporting differences may provide financial results that are misleading or misinterpreted. Attempts to implement international financial reporting standards have not been embraced by the U.S. accounting profession and the SEC. Therefore, investors viewing financial statements of foreign-based firms must view the data with caution.

## KEY TERMS

myPHLIP

Go To: http://www.prenhall.com/keown for downloads and current events associated with this chapter

**Accounting book value, 32**
**Accounts payable, 33**
**Accounts receivable, 31**
**Accrued expenses, 33**
**Average tax rate, 39**
**Balance sheet, 30**
**Common stockholders, 33**
**Current debt, 33**
**Current assets (gross working capital), 31**
**Debt, 33**
**Debt capital, 33**
**Earnings before interest, taxes, depreciation, and amortization (EBITDA), 41**
**Earnings before taxes, 29**
**Equity, 33**
**Fixed assets, 32**
**Free cash flows, 40**
**Income statement, 28**
**Interest expense, 29**
**Inventory, 32**
**Liquidity, 36**
**Long-term debt, 33**
**Marginal tax rate, 38**
**Net income, 29**
**Net working capital, 35**
**Noninterest-bearing current liabilities, 41**
**Operating income (earnings before interest and taxes, or EBIT), 29**
**Other assets, 32**
**Other payables, 33**
**Par value and paid-in capital, 33**
**Preferred stockholders, 33**
**Prepaid expenses, 32**
**Retained earnings, 33**
**Short-term notes, 33**
**Treasury stock, 33**

## STUDY QUESTIONS

**2-1.** A company's financial statements consist of the balance sheet, income statement, and statement of cash flows.

**a.** Describe the nature of the balance sheet and the income statement.

**b.** Why have we not used the conventional statement of cash flows in our presentation, computing instead what we call free cash flows?

**2-2.** What are the differences among gross profits, operating profits, and net income?

**2-3.** What is the difference between dividends and interest expense?

**2-4.** Why is it that the common equity section in the balance sheet changes from year to year regardless of whether new shares are bought or sold?

**2-5.** What is net working capital? How is it different from gross working capital? What is the difference between interest-bearing debt and noninterest-bearing debt?

**2-6.** Discuss the reasons why one firm could have positive cash flows and be headed for financial trouble, while another firm with negative cash flows could actually be in a good financial position.

**2-7.** Why is the examination of only the balance sheet and income statement not adequate in evaluating a firm?

**2-8.** Why do a firm's free cash flows from an operating perspective have to equal its free cash flows from a financing perspective?

## SELF-TEST PROBLEMS

**ST-1.** (*Review of financial statements*) Prepare a balance sheet and income statement for the Wood Corporation, given the following information:

| | |
|---|---|
| Accumulated depreciation | $38,000 |
| Long-term debt | ?? |
| Inventory | 5,000 |
| General and administrative expenses | 1,000 |
| Interest expense | 1,200 |
| Common stock | 50,000 |
| Cost of goods sold | 6,000 |
| Short-term notes | 750 |
| Depreciation expense | 600 |
| Sales | 13,000 |
| Accounts receivable | 10,000 |
| Accounts payable | 5,000 |
| Buildings and equipment | 120,000 |
| Cash | 11,000 |
| Taxes | 1,300 |
| Retained earnings | 10,250 |

**ST-2.** (*Corporate income tax*) Sales for Davies, Inc. during the past year amounted to $4 million. The firm supplies statistical information to engineering companies. Gross profits totaled $1 million, and operating and depreciation expenses were $500,000 and $350,000, respectively. Compute the corporation's tax liability.

**ST-3.** (*Measuring cash flows*) Given the following information for Neff Industries, compute the firm's free cash flows for the year 2001, first from an operating perspective and then from a financing perspective. What do you learn about the firm from these computations?

Neff Industries Balance Sheet
For December 31, 2000, and December 31, 2001

| | 2000 | 2001 |
|---|---|---|
| Cash | $ 9,000 | $ 500 |
| Accounts receivable | 12,500 | 16,000 |
| Inventories | 29,000 | 45,500 |
| Total current assets | $ 50,500 | $ 62,000 |
| Land | 20,000 | 26,000 |
| Buildings and equipment | 70,000 | 100,000 |
| Less: allowance for depreciation | 28,000 | 38,000 |
| Total fixed assets | $ 62,000 | $ 88,000 |
| Total assets | $112,500 | $150,000 |
| Accounts payable | $ 10,500 | $ 22,000 |
| Bank notes | 17,000 | 47,000 |
| Total current liabilities | $ 27,500 | $ 69,000 |
| Long-term debt | 28,750 | 22,950 |
| Common stock | 31,500 | 31,500 |
| Retained earnings | 24,750 | 26,550 |
| Total liabilities & equity | $112,500 | $150,000 |

Neff Industries Income Statement
For the Years Ended December 31, 2000, and December 31, 2001

| | 2000 | 2001 |
|---|---|---|
| Sales | $125,000 | $160,000 |
| Cost of goods sold | 75,000 | 96,000 |
| Gross profit | $ 50,000 | $ 64,000 |
| Operating expense | | |
| Fixed cash operating expense | 21,000 | 21,000 |
| Variable operating expense | 12,500 | 16,000 |
| Depreciation | 4,500 | 10,000 |
| Total operating expense | 38,000 | 47,000 |
| Earnings before interest and taxes | $ 12,000 | $ 17,000 |
| Interest | 3,000 | 6,100 |
| Earnings before taxes | $ 9,000 | $ 10,900 |
| Taxes | 4,500 | 5,450 |
| Net income | $ 4,500 | $ 5,450 |

## STUDY PROBLEMS (SET A)

**2-1A.** (*Review of financial statements*) Prepare a balance sheet and income statement as of December 31, 2001, for Belmond, Inc., from the following information.

| | |
|---|---|
| Inventory | $ 6,500 |
| General and administrative expenses | 850 |
| Common stock | 45,000 |
| Cash | 16,550 |
| Operating expenses | 1,350 |
| Notes payable | 600 |
| Interest expense | 900 |
| Depreciation expense | 500 |
| Net sales | 12,800 |
| Accounts receivable | 9,600 |
| Accounts payable | 4,800 |
| Long-term debt | 55,000 |
| Cost of goods sold | 5,750 |
| Buildings and equipment | 122,000 |
| Accumulated depreciation | 34,000 |
| Taxes | 1,440 |
| Retained earnings | ? |

**2-2A.** (*Review of financial statements*) Prepare a balance sheet and income statement as of December 31, 2001, for the Sharpe Mfg. Co. from the following information.

| | |
|---|---|
| Accounts receivable | $120,000 |
| Machinery and equipment | 700,000 |
| Accumulated depreciation | 236,000 |
| Notes payable | 100,000 |
| Net sales | 800,000 |
| Inventory | 110,000 |
| Accounts payable | 90,000 |
| Long-term debt | 160,000 |
| Cost of goods sold | 500,000 |
| Operating expenses | 280,000 |
| Common stock | 320,000 |

(*continued*)

| | |
|---|---|
| Cash | 96,000 |
| Retained earnings—prior year | ? |
| Retained earnings—current year | ? |

**2-3A.** (*Corporate income tax*) Delaney, Inc. sells minicomputers. During the past year, the company's sales were $4 million. The cost of its merchandise sold came to $2 million, cash operating expenses were $400,000, depreciation expense was $100,000, and the firm paid $150,000 in interest on bank loans. Also, the corporation paid $25,000 in the form of dividends to its own common stockholders. Calculate the corporation's tax liability.

**2-4A.** (*Corporate income tax*) Potts, Inc. had sales of $6 million during the past year. The cost of goods sold amounted to $3 million. Operating expenses totaled $2.6 million and interest expense was $30,000. Determine the firm's tax liability.

**2-5A.** (*Measuring cash flows*) Calculate the free cash flows for Pamplin, Inc., for the year ended December 31, 2001, both from an operating and a financing perspective. Interpret your results.

Pamplin, Inc., Balance Sheet at 12/31/00 and 12/31/01

| Assets | | |
|---|---|---|
| | **2000** | **2001** |
| Cash | $ 200 | $ 150 |
| Accounts receivable | 450 | 425 |
| Inventory | 550 | 625 |
| Current assets | 1,200 | 1,200 |
| Plant and equipment | 2,200 | 2,600 |
| Less: accumulated depreciation | (1,000) | (1,200) |
| Net plant and equipment | 1,200 | 1,400 |
| Total assets | $2,400 | $2,600 |

| Liabilities and Owners' Equity | | |
|---|---|---|
| | **2000** | **2001** |
| Accounts payable | $ 200 | $ 150 |
| Notes payable—current (9%) | 0 | 150 |
| Current liabilities | $ 200 | $ 300 |
| Long-term debt | 600 | 600 |
| Owners' equity | | |
| Common stock | $ 300 | $ 300 |
| Paid-in capital | 600 | 600 |
| Retained earnings | 700 | 800 |
| Total owners' equity | $1,600 | $1,700 |
| Total liabilities and owners' equity | $2,400 | $2,600 |

Pamplin, Inc. Income Statement
for years ending 12/31/00 and 12/31/01 ($ in thousands)

| | **2000** | **2001** |
|---|---|---|
| Sales | $1,200 | $1,450 |
| Cost of goods sold | 700 | 850 |
| Gross profit | $ 500 | $ 600 |
| Operating expenses | 30 | 40 |
| Depreciation | 220 | 200 |
| Net operating income | $ 250 | $ 360 |
| Interest expense | 50 | 60 |
| Net income before taxes | $ 200 | $ 300 |
| Taxes (40%) | 80 | 120 |
| Net income | $ 120 | $ 180 |

**2-6A.** (*Measuring cash flows*) Calculate the free cash flows for T. P. Jarmon Company for the year ended December 31, 2001, both from an operating and a financing perspective. Interpret your results.

T. P. Jarmon Company Balance Sheets
at 12/31/00 and 12/31/01

| Assets | 2000 | 2001 |
|---|---|---|
| Cash | $ 15,000 | $ 14,000 |
| Marketable securities | 6,000 | 6,200 |
| Accounts receivable | 42,000 | 33,000 |
| Inventory | 51,000 | 84,000 |
| Prepaid rent | 1,200 | 1,100 |
| Total current assets | $115,200 | $138,300 |
| Net plant and equipment | 286,000 | 270,000 |
| Total assets | $401,200 | $408,300 |

| Liabilities and Equity | 2000 | 2001 |
|---|---|---|
| Accounts payable | $ 48,000 | $ 57,000 |
| Notes payable | 15,000 | 13,000 |
| Accruals | 6,000 | 5,000 |
| Total current liabilities | $ 69,000 | $ 75,000 |
| Long-term debt | $160,000 | $150,000 |
| Common stockholders' equity | $172,200 | $183,300 |
| Total liabilities and equity | $401,200 | $408,300 |

T. P. Jarmon Company Income Statement
For the Year Ended 12/31/01

| | | |
|---|---|---|
| Sales | | $600,000 |
| Less: cost of goods sold | | 460,000 |
| Gross profits | | $140,000 |
| Less: expenses | | |
| General and administrative | $30,000 | |
| Interest | 10,000 | |
| Depreciation | 30,000 | |
| Total operating expenses | | $70,000 |
| Earnings before taxes | | $70,000 |
| Less: taxes | | 27,100 |
| Net income | | $42,900 |
| Net income | | $42,900 |
| Less: cash dividends | | 31,800 |
| To retained earnings | | $11,100 |

**2-7A.** (*Measuring cash flows*) Calculate the free cash flows for Abrams Manufacturing Company for the year ended December 31, 2001, both from an operating and a financing perspective. Interpret your results.

Abrams Manufacturing Balance Sheets
at 12/31/2000 and 12/31/2001

| | 2000 | 2001 |
|---|---|---|
| Cash | $ 89,000 | $100,000 |
| Accounts receivable | 64,000 | 70,000 |
| Inventory | 112,000 | 100,000 |
| Prepaid expenses | 10,000 | 10,000 |

(*continued*)

| | 2000 | 2001 |
|---|---|---|
| Plant and equipment | 238,000 | 311,000 |
| Accumulated depreciation | (40,000) | (66,000) |
| Total | $473,000 | $525,000 |
| Accounts payable | $ 85,000 | $ 90,000 |
| Accrued liabilities | 68,000 | 63,000 |
| Mortgage payable | 70,000 | 0 |
| Preferred stock | 0 | 120,000 |
| Common stock | 205,000 | 205,000 |
| Retained earnings | 45,000 | 47,000 |
| Total liabilities & equity | $473,000 | $525,000 |

Abram's Manufacturing Company Income Statement
For the Year Ended 12/31/01

| | |
|---|---|
| Sales | $184,000 |
| Cost of sales | 60,000 |
| Gross profit | 124,000 |
| Selling, general, and administrative expenses | 44,000 |
| Depreciation expense | 26,000 |
| Operating income | $ 54,000 |
| Interest expense | 4,000 |
| Taxes | 16,000 |
| Preferred stock dividends | 10,000 |
| Net income | $ 24,000 |

*Additional information:*
The firm paid $22,000 in common stock dividends during 2001.

**2-8A.** (*Analyzing free cash flows*) Following you will find our computation of the free cash flows for Starbucks. Interpret the information in terms of where cash came from and where it was used.

**Starbucks 1999 Free Cash Flows ($ in thousands)**

| | | |
|---|---|---|
| **CASH FLOWS FROM AN OPERATING PERSPECTIVE:** | | |
| After-tax cash flows from operations: | | |
| Operating income | $156,711 | |
| Depreciation | 97,797 | |
| Earnings before interest, tax, depreciation | | $254,508 |
| Tax expense | $ 62,333 | |
| Less change in income tax payable | (7,600) | |
| Less change in deferred taxes | (13,903) | |
| Cash taxes | | 40,830 |
| After-tax cash flows from operations | | $213,678 |
| Other income (losses) | | 10,532 |
| | | $224,210 |
| Change in net operating working capital: | | |
| Change in cash | $ (5,751) | |
| Change in accounts receivable | (3,326) | |
| Change in inventories | 37,768 | |
| Change in other current assets | 20,529 | |
| Change in current assets | | $ 49,220 |
| Change in accounts payable | $ 1,662 | |
| Change in accrued expenses | 32,283 | |
| Change in noninterest-bearing current debt | | 33,945 |
| Change in net operating working capital | | $ 15,275 |

(continued)

| | | |
|---|---|---|
| Change in fixed assets and other assets: | | |
| Purchase of fixed assets | $257,292 | |
| Change in investments | 43,334 | |
| Change in other assets | 7,710 | |
| Net cash used for investments | | $308,336 |
| Operating free cash flows | | $ (99,401) |
| **CASH FLOWS FROM A FINANCING PERSPECTIVE:** | | |
| Interest expense | | $ — |
| Less increase in long-term debt | | (7,018) |
| Less increase in short-term debt | | (30,577) |
| Plus dividends | | — |
| Less increase in common stock | | (61,806) |
| Financing free cash flows | | $ (99,401) |

**2-9A.** (*Analyzing free cash flows*) Following you will find our computation of the free cash flows for Amazon.com. Interpret the information in terms of where cash came from and where it was used.

| **FREE CASH FLOWS FROM AN OPERATING PERSPECTIVE: ($ IN THOUSANDS)** | | |
|---|---|---|
| After-tax cash flows from operations: | | |
| Operating income | $ (597,683) | |
| Depreciation | 251,500 | |
| Earnings before interest, tax, depreciation | | $ (346,183) |
| Taxes | | — |
| After-tax cash flows from operations | | $ (346,183) |
| Other income (losses) | | (104,388) |
| | | $ (450,571) |
| Change in net operating working capital: | | |
| Change in cash | $ 332,743 | |
| Change in inventories | 191,145 | |
| Change in other current assets | 64,036 | |
| Change in current assets | | $ 587,924 |
| Change in accounts payable | | 349,753 |
| Change in net operating working capital | | $ 238,171 |
| Change in fixed assets and other assets: | | |
| Purchase of fixed assets | $ 472,768 | |
| Change in investments | 1,101,606 | |
| Change in other assets | (154,261) | |
| Net cash used for investments | | $ 1,420,113 |
| Operating free cash flows | | $ (2,108,855) |
| **FREE CASH FLOWS FROM A FINANCING PERSPECTIVE:** | | |
| Interest expense | | $87,966 |
| Less increase in long-term debt | | (1,118,198) |
| Less increase in short-term debt | | (13,638) |
| Less increase in other current liabilities | | (213,969) |
| Less increase in common stock | | (851,016) |
| Financing free cash flows | | $ (2,108,855) |

## INTEGRATIVE PROBLEM

The following financial statements are for Briggs & Stratton, which primarily makes small gasoline engines, many of which are used in lawn mowers. Assume that you would be meeting with Jim Breen, the firm's controller. Based on the financials and the free cash computations, what would you tell Breen about his firm? What questions would you have for him?

Briggs & Stratton Financials ($ in thousands)

| | 1998 | 1999 |
|---|---|---|
| **ASSETS** | | |
| Cash and equivalents | $ 84,527 | $ 60,806 |
| Accounts receivable | 136,629 | 194,096 |
| Inventories | 107,876 | 137,448 |
| Prepaid expenses | 21,727 | 32,413 |
| Other current assets | 31,287 | 34,383 |
| Total current assets | $382,046 | $459,146 |
| Gross property, plant, and equipment | 812,428 | 874,301 |
| Accumulated depreciation | 420,501 | 469,847 |
| Net property, plant, and equipment | $391,927 | $404,454 |
| Investments | — | 2,730 |
| Other assets | 19,436 | 9,555 |
| TOTAL ASSETS | $793,409 | $875,885 |
| **LIABILITIES** | | |
| Short-term debt | $ 15,000 | $ 15,000 |
| Notes payable | 19,036 | 18,159 |
| Accounts payable | 76,915 | 117,757 |
| Taxes payable | 10,529 | 11,901 |
| Accrued expenses | 101,465 | 119,685 |
| Total current liabilities | $222,945 | $282,502 |
| Long-term debt | 128,102 | 113,307 |
| Other liabilities | 125,874 | 114,166 |
| TOTAL LIABILITIES | $476,921 | $509,975 |
| **EQUITY** | | |
| Common stock | $ 289 | $ 289 |
| Paid-in capital | 37,776 | 37,422 |
| Retained earnings | 531,695 | 611,075 |
| Less: treasury stock | 253,272 | 282,876 |
| TOTAL EQUITY | $316,488 | $365,910 |
| TOTAL LIABILITIES AND EQUITY | $793,409 | $875,885 |

BRIGGS & STRATTON

| **Reconciliation of Retained Earnings ($ in thousands)** | |
|---|---|
| Retained earnings, December 31, 1998 | $531,695 |
| 1999 net income | 106,101 |
| Dividends paid | 26,912 |
| Other gains | 191 |
| Retained earnings, December 31, 1999 | $611,075 |

BRIGGS & STRATTON INCOME STATEMENT ($ IN THOUSANDS)

| | 1998 | 1999 |
|---|---|---|
| Sales | $1,327,610 | $1,501,726 |
| Cost of goods sold | 1,025,425 | 1,147,025 |
| Gross profit | $ 302,185 | $ 354,701 |
| Selling, general, and administrative expense | 129,986 | 125,219 |
| Depreciation | 47,511 | 49,346 |
| Operating profit | $ 124,688 | $ 180,136 |

*(continued)*

| | 1998 | 1999 |
|---|---|---|
| Interest expense | 19,352 | 17,024 |
| Nonoperating income (expense) | 7,809 | 6,659 |
| Income before taxes | $ 113,145 | $ 169,771 |
| Provision for income taxes | 42,500 | 63,670 |
| Net income | $ 70,645 | $ 106,101 |

BRIGGS & STRATTON 1999 FREE CASH FLOWS ($ IN THOUSANDS)

| | | |
|---|---|---|
| **CASH FLOWS FROM AN OPERATING PERSPECTIVE:** | | |
| After-tax cash flows from operations: | | |
| Operating income | $180,136 | |
| Depreciation | 49,346 | |
| Earnings before interest, tax, depreciation | | $229,482 |
| Tax expense | $ 63,670 | |
| Less change in income tax payable | (1,372) | |
| Cash taxes | | $ 62,298 |
| After-tax cash flows from operations | | $167,184 |
| Other income (losses) | | 6,850 |
| | | $174,034 |
| Change in net operating working capital: | | |
| Change in cash | $(23,721) | |
| Change in accounts receivable | 57,467 | |
| Change in inventories | 29,572 | |
| Change in prepaid expenses | 10,686 | |
| Change in other current assets | 3,096 | |
| Change in current assets | | $ 77,100 |
| Change in accounts payable | $ 40,842 | |
| Change in accrued expenses | 18,220 | |
| Change in noninterest-bearing current debt | | $ 59,062 |
| Change in net operating working capital | | $ 18,038 |
| Change in fixed assets and other assets: | | |
| Purchase of fixed assets | $ 61,873 | |
| Change in investments | 2,730 | |
| Change in other assets | (9,881) | |
| Net cash used for investments | | $ 54,722 |
| Operating free cash flows | | $101,274 |
| **CASH FLOWS FROM A FINANCING PERSPECTIVE:** | | |
| Interest expense | | $ 17,024 |
| Plus decrease in long-term debt | | 14,795 |
| Plus decrease in other liabilities | | 11,708 |
| Plus decrease in notes payable | | 877 |
| Plus dividends | | 26,912 |
| Plus decrease in common stock | | 29,958 |
| Financing free cash flows | | $101,274 |

## STUDY PROBLEMS (SET B)

**2-1B.** (*Review of financial statements*) Prepare a balance sheet and income statement as of December 31, 2001 for the Warner Company from the following list of items.

| | |
|---|---|
| Depreciation | $ 66,000 |
| Cash | 225,000 |
| Long-term debt | 334,000 |
| Sales | 573,000 |
| Accounts payable | 102,000 |
| General and administrative expenses | 79,000 |
| Buildings and equipment | 895,000 |
| Notes payable | 75,000 |
| Accounts receivable | 153,000 |
| Interest expense | 4,750 |
| Accrued expenses | 7,900 |
| Common stock | 289,000 |
| Cost of goods sold | 297,000 |
| Inventory | 99,300 |
| Taxes | 50,500 |
| Accumulated depreciation | 263,000 |
| Prepaid expenses | 14,500 |
| Taxes payable | 53,000 |
| Retained earnings | 262,900 |

**2-2B.** (*Review of financial statements*) Prepare a balance sheet and income statement as of December 31, 2001, for the Sabine Mfg. Co. from the following list of items. Ignore income taxes and interest expense.

| | |
|---|---|
| Accounts receivable | $150,000 |
| Machinery and equipment | 700,000 |
| Accumulated depreciation | 236,000 |
| Notes payable—current | 90,000 |
| Net sales | 900,000 |
| Inventory | 110,000 |
| Accounts payable | 90,000 |
| Long-term debt | 160,000 |
| Cost of goods sold | 550,000 |
| Operating expenses | 280,000 |
| Common stock | 320,000 |
| Cash | 90,000 |
| Retained earnings—prior year | ? |
| Retained earnings—current year | ? |

**2-3B.** (*Corporate income tax*) Cook, Inc., sells minicomputers. During the past year, the company's sales were $3.5 million. The cost of its merchandise sold came to $2 million, and cash operating expenses were $500,000; depreciation expense was $100,000, and the firm paid $165,000 in interest on bank loans. Also, the corporation paid $25,000 in dividends to its own common stockholders. Calculate the corporation's tax liability.

**2-4B.** (*Corporate income tax*) Rose, Inc. had sales of $7 million during the past year. The cost of goods sold amounted to $4 million. Operating expenses totaled $2.6 million and interest expense was $40,000. Determine the firm's tax liability.

**2-5B.** (*Measuring cash flows*) Calculate the free cash flows for the J. B. Chavez Corporation for the year ended December 31, 2001, both from an operating and a financing perspective. Interpret your results.

J. B. Chavez Corporation, Balance Sheet
at 12/31/00 and 12/31/01 ($000)

| Assets | 12/31/00 | 12/31/01 |
|---|---|---|
| Cash | $ 225 | $ 175 |
| Accounts receivable | 450 | 430 |
| Inventory | 575 | 625 |
| Current assets | $1,250 | $1,230 |
| Plant and equipment | $2,200 | $2,500 |
| Less: accumulated depreciation | (1,000) | (1,200) |
| Net plant and equipment | $1,200 | $1,300 |
| Total assets | $2,450 | $2,530 |

| Liabilities and Owners' Equity | 12/31/00 | 12/31/01 |
|---|---|---|
| Accounts payable | $ 250 | $ 115 |
| Notes payable—current (9%) | 0 | 115 |
| Current liabilities | $ 250 | $ 230 |
| Bonds | $ 600 | $ 600 |
| Owners' equity | | |
| Common stock | $ 300 | $ 300 |
| Paid-in capital | 600 | 600 |
| Retained earnings | 700 | 800 |
| Total owners' equity | $1,600 | $1,700 |
| Total liabilities and owners' equity | $2,450 | $2,530 |

J. B. Chavez Corporation, Income Statement
for the years ending 12/31/00 and 12/31/01 ($000)

| | | 2000 | | 2001 |
|---|---|---|---|---|
| Sales | | $1,250 | | $1,450 |
| Cost of goods sold | | 700 | | 875 |
| Gross profit | | $ 550 | | $ 575 |
| Operating expenses | 30 | | 45 | |
| Depreciation | 220 | | 200 | |
| Net operating income | | $ 300 | | $ 330 |
| Interest expense | | 50 | | 60 |
| Net income before taxes | | $ 250 | | $ 270 |
| Taxes (40)%) | | 100 | | 108 |
| Net income | | $ 150 | | $ 162 |

**2-6B.** (*Measuring cash flows*) Calculate the free cash flows for RPI, Inc., for the year ended December 31, 2001, both from an operating and a financing perspective. Interpret your results.

RPI, Inc., Balance Sheets
for 12/31/00 and 12/31/01

| Assets | 2000 | 2001 |
|---|---|---|
| Cash | $ 16,000 | $ 17,000 |
| Marketable securities | 7,000 | 7,200 |
| Accounts receivable | 42,000 | 38,000 |
| Inventory | 50,000 | 93,000 |
| Prepaid rent | 1,200 | 1,100 |
| Total current assets | $116,200 | $156,300 |
| Net plant and equipment | 286,000 | 290,000 |
| Total assets | $402,200 | $446,300 |

| Liabilities and Stockholders' Equity | 2000 | 2001 |
|---|---|---|
| Accounts payable | $ 48,000 | $ 55,000 |
| Notes payable | 16,000 | 13,000 |
| Accruals | 6,000 | 5,000 |
| Total current liabilities | $ 70,000 | $ 73,000 |
| Long-term debt | $160,000 | $150,000 |
| Common stockholders' equity | $172,200 | $223,300 |
| Total liabilities and equity | $402,200 | $446,300 |

RPI, Inc., Income Statement
For the Year Ended 12/31/01

| | | |
|---|---|---|
| Sales | | $700,000 |
| Less: cost of goods sold | | 500,000 |
| Gross profits | | $200,000 |
| Less: operating and interest expenses | | |
| General and administrative | $50,000 | |
| Interest | 10,000 | |
| Depreciation | 30,000 | |
| Total expenses | | $ 90,000 |
| Profit before taxes | | $110,000 |
| Less: taxes | | 27,100 |
| Net income available to common stockholders | | $ 82,900 |
| Less: cash dividends | | 31,800 |
| Change in retained earnings | | $ 51,100 |

**2-7B.** (*Measuring cash flows*) Calculate the free cash flows for the Cameron Company for the year ended December 31, 2001, both from an operating and a financing perspective. Interpret your results.

Comparative Balance Sheets for December 31, 2000, and December 31, 2001, for the Cameron Company

| | 2000 | 2001 |
|---|---|---|
| Cash | $ 89,000 | $ 70,000 |
| Accounts receivable | 64,000 | 70,000 |
| Inventory | 102,000 | 80,000 |
| Prepaid expenses | 10,000 | 10,000 |
| Total current assets | $265,000 | $230,000 |
| Plant and equipment | $238,000 | $301,000 |
| Accumulated depreciation | (40,000) | (66,000) |
| Total assets | $463,000 | $465,000 |
| Accounts payable | $ 85,000 | $ 80,000 |
| Accrued liabilities | 68,000 | 63,000 |
| Total current liabilities | $153,000 | $143,000 |
| Mortgage payable | 60,000 | 0 |
| Preferred stock | 0 | 70,000 |
| Common stock | 205,000 | 205,000 |
| Retained earnings | 45,000 | 47,000 |
| Total debt and equity | $463,000 | $465,000 |

Cameron's 2001 income statement is as follows:

| | |
|---|---|
| Sales | $204,000 |
| Cost of sales | 84,000 |
| Gross profit | $120,000 |
| Selling, general, and administrative expenses | 17,000 |
| Depreciation expense | 26,000 |
| Operating income | $ 77,000 |
| Interest expense | 5,000 |
| Taxes | 30,000 |
| Preferred stock dividends | 8,000 |
| Net income | $ 34,000 |

*Additional information:*
The firm paid $32,000 in common stock dividends during 2001.

**2-8B.** (*Analyzing free cash flows*) Following you will find our computation of the free cash flows for Ben & Jerry's Ice Cream. Interpret the information in terms of where cash came from and where it was used.

BEN & JERRY'S FREE CASH FLOWS ($ IN THOUSANDS)

| **CASH FLOWS FROM AN OPERATING PERSPECTIVE:** | | |
|---|---|---|
| After-tax cash flows from operations: | | |
| Operating income | $13,129 | |
| Depreciation | 9,202 | |
| Earnings before interest, tax, depreciation | | $22,331 |
| Tax expense | $ 1,823 | |
| Less change in income tax payable | 1,215 | |
| Less change in deferred taxes | (4,174) | |
| Cash taxes | | $ 4,782 |
| After-tax cash flows from operations | | 17,549 |
| Other income (losses) | | (6,596) |
| | | $10,953 |

*(continued)*

| | | |
|---|---|---|
| Change in net operating working capital: | | |
| Change in cash | $ (638) | |
| Change in accounts receivable | 7,495 | |
| Change in inventories | 847 | |
| Change in other current assets | (2,666) | |
| Change in current assets | | $ 5,038 |
| Change in accounts payable | $ 5,456 | |
| Change in accrued expenses | 517 | |
| Change in noninterest-bearing current debt | | $ 5,973 |
| Change in net operating working capital | | $ (935) |
| Change in fixed assets and other assets: | | |
| Purchase of fixed assets | $ (757) | |
| Change in investments | (103) | |
| Change in other assets | 3,060 | |
| Net cash used for investments | | $ 2,200 |
| Operating free cash flows | | $ 9,688 |
| **CASH FLOWS FROM A FINANCING PERSPECTIVE:** | | |
| Interest expense | | $ 1,634 |
| Plus decrease in long-term debt | | 3,822 |
| Less increase in short-term debt | | (361) |
| Plus dividends | | — |
| Plus decrease in common stock | | 4,593 |
| Financing free cash flows | | $ 9,688 |

**2-9B.** (*Analyzing free cash flows*) Following you will find our computation of the free cash flows for iVillage. Interpret the information in terms of where cash came from and where it was used.

iVILLAGE CASH FLOWS ($ IN THOUSANDS)

| | | |
|---|---|---|
| **CASH FLOWS FROM AN OPERATING PERSPECTIVE:** | | |
| After-tax cash flows from operations: | | |
| Operating income | $ (97,324) | |
| Depreciation | 29,312 | |
| Earnings before interest, tax, depreciation | | $ (68,012) |
| Cash taxes | | — |
| After-tax cash flows from operations | | (68,012) |
| Other income (losses) | | 4,323 |
| | | $ (63,689) |
| Change in net operating working capital: | | |
| Change in cash | $ 76,680 | |
| Change in accounts receivable | 3,472 | |
| Change in inventories | 2,332 | |
| Change in other current assets | 2,478 | |
| Change in current assets | | $ 84,962 |
| Change in accounts payable | $ 4,657 | |
| Change in noninterest-bearing current debt | | 4,657 |
| Change in net operating working capital | | $ 80,305 |
| Change in fixed assets and other assets: | | |
| Purchase of fixed assets | $ 31,971 | |
| Change in investments | 178,108 | |
| Change in other assets | 250 | |
| Net cash used for investments | | $ 210,329 |
| Operating free cash flows | | $ (354,323) |

(*continued*)

| **CASH FLOWS FROM A FINANCING PERSPECTIVE:** | |
|---|---|
| Interest expense | $ — |
| Dividends | 23,612 |
| Plus decrease in short-term debt | 137 |
| Less increase in other current liabilities | (9,609) |
| Less increase in common stock | (368,463) |
| Financing free cash flows | $ (354,323) |

## SELF-TEST SOLUTIONS

**ST-1.**

| **INCOME STATEMENT:** | |
|---|---|
| Sales | $ 13,000 |
| Cost of goods sold | 6,000 |
| Gross profits | $ 7,000 |
| Depreciation expense | 600 |
| General and administrative expenses | 1,000 |
| Operating expenses | $ 1,600 |
| Operating income | $ 5,400 |
| Interest expense | 1,200 |
| Earnings before taxes | $ 4,200 |
| Taxes | 1,300 |
| Net income | $ 2,900 |
| **BALANCE SHEET:** | |
| Cash | $ 11,000 |
| Accounts receivable | 10,000 |
| Inventory | 5,000 |
| Total current assets | $ 26,000 |
| Buildings and equipment | 120,000 |
| Accumulated depreciation | 38,000 |
| Net buildings and equipment | 82,000 |
| Total assets | $108,000 |
| Accounts payable | $ 5,000 |
| Short-term notes | 750 |
| Current liabilities | $ 5,750 |
| Long-term debt | $ 42,000 |
| Total debt | $ 47,750 |
| Common stock | 50,000 |
| Retained earnings | 10,250 |
| Total debt and equity | $108,000 |

**ST-2.**

| | |
|---|---|
| Gross profits | $1,000,000 |
| Operating expenses | 500,000 |
| Depreciation | 350,000 |
| Taxable income | $ 150,000 |

| Earnings | × | Marginal tax rate | = | Taxes |
|---|---|---|---|---|
| $50,000 | × | 0.15 | = | $7,500 |
| $75,000–$50,000 | × | 0.25 | = | 6,250 |
| $100,000–$75,000 | × | 0.34 | = | 8,500 |
| $150,000–$100,000 | × | 0.39 | = | 19,500 |
| | | | | $41,750 |

**ST-3.**

Neff Industries Free Cash Flows
For the Year Ended December 31, 2001

| | |
|---|---|
| **FREE CASH FLOWS: OPERATING PERSPECTIVE** | |
| Operating income | $ 17,000 |
| Plus depreciation expense | 10,000 |
| Less tax expense | (5,450) |
| Less change in income tax payable | 0 |
| After-tax cash flows from operations | $ 21,550 |
| Change in net operating working capital | |
| Change in cash | $ (8,500) |
| Change in accounts receivable | 3,500 |
| Change in inventories | 16,500 |
| Change in accounts payable | (11,500) |
| Change in net operating working capital | $ 0 |
| Change in fixed assets and land | |
| Purchase of buildings and equipment | $ 30,000 |
| Purchase of land | 6,000 |
| Change in fixed assets and land | $ 36,000 |
| Free cash flows (operating perspective) | $ (14,450) |
| **FREE CASH FLOWS: FINANCING PERSPECTIVE** | |
| Increase in short-term notes | $ (30,000) |
| Decrease in long-term notes | 5,800 |
| Dividends | 3,650 |
| Interest expense | 6,100 |
| Free cash flows (financing perspective) | $ (14,450) |

# EVALUATING A FIRM'S FINANCIAL PERFORMANCE

In the 1999 Harley-Davidson Annual Report, Jeffrey Bleustein, the firm's Chief Executive Officer, begins his letter to shareholders by explaining that management's passion is captured in the opening words of the firm's Mission Statement, "We fulfill dreams . . ." He continues, "In what follows [in the Annual Report], we hope to show you not only how Harley-Davidson inspires, cultivates and shares the dream of

motorcycling with our customers, but also how we go about fulfilling the dreams of all our stakeholders." ● When Bleustein describes the firm's activities in "fulfilling dreams," he talks about investing heavily in expanding production in order to deliver the dream of motorcycle ownership to more riders, extensive redesign of product lines, and the continued growth of the Buell motorcycle line. He explains that in 1999, Harley-Davidson captured over 50 percent of the U.S. market share. Bleustein concludes, "Focusing on the current needs of our stakeholders assures the health of our business today. Anticipating, investing in and fulfilling the dreams of our stakeholders will assure sustainable growth for the future." ● In this chapter, we want to learn how to evaluate what Bleustein calls the "health" of a company, as viewed from a financial perspective.

**LEARNING OBJECTIVES**

After reading this chapter, you should be able to

1. Calculate a comprehensive set of financial ratios and use them to evaluate the financial health of a company.
2. Apply the DuPont analysis in evaluating a firm's performance.
3. Explain the limitations of ratio analysis.

This chapter is a natural extension of Chapter 2. In this chapter, we restate financial statements in relative terms to gain a more complete understanding about a firm's financial performance. Specifically, we look at key financial relationships in the form of ratios. The specific relationships we consider are:

- The risk that a firm will not have the needed cash to meet debt payments as they come due
- Whether management is generating an attractive rate of return on the capital that has been intrusted to them
- How management chooses to finance the company
- Whether the stockholders are receiving an acceptable rate of return on their investment

**RELATE TO THE BIG PICTURE**

As in Chapter 2, when we talked about financial statements, **Principle 7** continues to be a primary rationale for wanting to evaluate a company's financial performance. As stated in **Principle 7, managers won't work for the owners unless it's in their best interest to do so.** Thus, the firm's common stockholders have a need for information that can be used to monitor the managers' actions. Interpreting the firm's financial statements through the use of financial ratios is a key source of information that can be used in this monitoring.

**Principle 5** is also relevant in evaluating a firm's financial performance. This principle tells us that **competitive markets make it hard to find exceptionally profitable investments.** By *exceptional,* we mean investments that earn rates of return that exceed the opportunity cost of the money invested. Thus, the notion of a rate of return is a primary issue in knowing whether management is creating value. Although far from perfect, certain financial ratios can help us better know if management is finding exceptional investments, or if the investments are in fact just the opposite—exceptionally bad.

Finally, **Principle 1** is at work in this chapter; that is, **The Risk-Return Trade-Off—We won't take on additional risk unless we expect to be compensated with additional return.** As we will see, how management chooses to finance the business will affect the company's risk, and, as a result, the stockholders' rate of return on their investment.

## FINANCIAL RATIO ANALYSIS

In Chapter 2, we examined financial statements in absolute dollar terms for the purpose of coming to understand a firm's financial position. We chose to use the financial statements for Harley-Davidson to illustrate the format and content of the statements and to demonstrate an important financial measurement—free cash flows. We next want to restate the accounting data in relative terms, or what we call financial ratios. **Financial ratios** help us identify some of the financial strengths and weaknesses of a company. The ratios give us two ways of making meaningful comparisons of a firm's financial data: (1) We can examine the ratios across time (say, for the last 5 years) to identify any trends; and (2) We can compare the firm's ratios with those of other firms. In short, such a financial analysis will allow us to see if Harley-Davidson is as good as management claims it to be. After all, we need to decide that for ourselves, and not just take the word of Harley-Davidson's management.

**Financial ratios**
Restating the accounting data in relative terms to identify some of the financial strengths and weaknesses of a company.

**TABLE 3-1**
Harley-Davidson 1999 Income Statement ($000)

| | |
|---|---|
| Sales | $2,590,614 |
| Cost of goods sold | 1,617,253 |
| Gross profit | $ 973,361 |
| Selling, general, and administrative expenses | 410,060 |
| Depreciation and amortization | 113,822 |
| Operating profit | $ 449,479 |
| Interest expense | 28,686 |
| Income before taxes | $ 420,793 |
| Income taxes | 153,592 |
| Net income | $ 267,201 |

Mathematically, a financial ratio is nothing more than a ratio whose numerator and denominator are comprised of financial data. Sounds simple? Well, in concept it is. The objective in using a ratio when analyzing financial information is simply to standardize the information being analyzed so that comparisons can be made between ratios of different firms or possibly the same firm at different points in time. So try to keep this in mind as you read through the discussion of financial ratios. All we are doing is trying to standardize financial data so that we can make comparisons with industry norms or other standards.

In making a comparison of our firm with other companies, we could select a peer group of companies, or we could use industry norms published by firms such as Dun & Bradstreet, Robert Morris Associates, Standard & Poor's, and Prentice Hall. Dun & Bradstreet, for instance, annually publishes a set of 14 key ratios for each of 125 lines of business. Robert Morris Associates, the association of bank loan and credit officers, publishes a set of 16 key ratios for more than 350 lines of business. In both cases, the ratios are classified by industry and by firm size to provide the basis for more meaningful comparisons.

In learning about ratios, we could simply study the different types or categories of ratios, or we could use ratios to answer some important questions about a firm's operations. We prefer the latter approach and choose the following four questions as a map in using financial ratios:

1. How liquid is the firm?
2. Is management generating adequate operating profits on the firm's assets?
3. How is the firm financing its assets?
4. Are the owners (stockholders) receiving an adequate return on their investment?

Let's look at each of these questions in turn. In doing so, let's use Harley-Davidson to illustrate the use of ratios in answering these questions. For ease of reference, we again show the Harley-Davidson financial statements in Table 3-1 and Table 3-2.

## Question 1: How Liquid Is the Firm?

There are two ways to approach the liquidity question. First, we can look at the firm's assets that are relatively liquid in nature and compare them to the amount of the debt coming due in the near term.[1] Second, we can look at how quickly the firm's liquid assets—namely, accounts receivable and inventories—are being converted into cash.

[1]This approach has long been used in the finance community; however, it really measures solvency, not liquidity. A firm is solvent when its assets exceed its liabilities, which is in essence what we will be measuring by this approach. For an in-depth discussion of this issue, see Chapter 2 of Terry S. Maness and John T. Zietlow, *Short-Term Financial Management* (New York: Dryden Press, 1997).

**TABLE 3-2**
Harley-Davidson 1999 Balance Sheet ($000)

| **Assets** | |
|---|---|
| Cash | $ 183,415 |
| Accounts receivable | 542,659 |
| Inventories | 168,616 |
| Other current assets | 54,304 |
| Total current assets | $ 948,994 |
| Gross plant, property, and equipment | $1,244,185 |
| Accumulated depreciation | (562,444) |
| Net plant, property, and equipment | $ 681,741 |
| Other assets | 481,342 |
| Total assets | $2,112,077 |
| **Liabilities and Equity** | |
| **LIABILITIES** | |
| Accounts payable and accruals | $ 256,086 |
| Short-term debt | 262,068 |
| Total current liabilities | $ 518,154 |
| Long-term debt | 432,843 |
| Total liabilities | $ 950,997 |
| **EQUITY** | |
| Common stock | |
| Par value and paid-in capital | $ 49,771 |
| Retained earnings | 1,111,309 |
| Total equity | $1,161,080 |
| Total liabilities and equity | $2,112,077 |

MEASURING LIQUIDITY: APPROACH 1. The first approach compares cash and the assets that should be converted into cash within the year with the debt (liabilities) that is coming due and payable within the year. The assets here are the *current assets,* and the debt is the *current liabilities* in the balance sheet. Thus we could use the following measure, called the **current ratio,** to estimate a company's relative liquidity:

**Current ratio**
Current ratio indicates a firm's liquidity, as measured by its liquid assets (current assets) relative to its liquid debt (short-term or current liabilities).

$$\text{current ratio} = \frac{\text{current assets}}{\text{current liabilities}} \qquad \textbf{(3-1)}$$

Furthermore, remembering that the three primary current assets include (1) cash, (2) accounts receivable, and (3) inventories, we could make our measure of liquidity more restrictive by *excluding inventories,* the least liquid of the current assets, in the numerator. This revised ratio is called the **acid-test** (or **quick**) **ratio,** and is calculated as follows:

**Acid-test (quick) ratio**
Acid-test ratio indicates a firm's liquidity, as measured by its liquid assets, excluding inventories, relative to its current liabilities.

$$\text{acid-test ratio} = \frac{\text{current assets} - \text{inventories}}{\text{current liabilities}} \qquad \textbf{(3-2)}$$

To demonstrate how to compute the current ratio and acid-test ratio, we will use the 1999 balance sheet for Harley-Davidson (refer to Table 3-2). To have a standard for comparison, we could use industry norms published by Dun and Bradstreet or any of the other sources mentioned earlier. However, we chose instead to calculate the average ratios for a

ROAD RULES

A FOCUS ON HARLEY-DAVIDSON

ROAD RULES

### Words of Advice from Harley-Davidson Inc.'s CEO

We asked Jeff Bleustein, Harley-Davidson CEO, what advice he would offer students contemplating a career in business, and this is what he told us:

- *Understand that not all businesses are the same.* What works in one environment may not work in another. So, dedicate yourself to your study of fundamentals. In their applications, however, be flexible and open to the differences in company and industry environments that you might encounter.
- *Be bold and willing to experiment with something different.* This advice is as meaningful for individuals as it is for companies. Great companies are those that focus on an area, a product, or a set of competencies and then excel at it. If you always follow others you are going to be a mediocre company. Greatness comes from being willing to step out and be uniquely better than the competition.

group of similar firms or what could be called a *peer group.* The 1999 results for these first two ratios are as follows:

| **Harley-Davidson** | **Peer-Group Average** |
|---|---|
| $\text{current ratio} = \dfrac{\text{current assets}}{\text{current liabilities}}$ | |
| $= \dfrac{\$949\text{M}}{\$518\text{M}} = 1.83$ | 1.50 |
| $\text{acid-test ratio} = \dfrac{\text{current assets} - \text{inventories}}{\text{current liabilities}}$ | |
| $= \dfrac{\$949\text{M} - 169\text{M}}{\$518\text{M}} = 1.51$ | 1.06 |

So, in terms of the current ratio and acid-test ratio, Harley-Davidson is more liquid than the average peer-group firm. Harley-Davidson has \$1.83 in current assets for every \$1 in current liabilities (debt), compared to \$1.50 for comparable firms, and \$1.51 in current assets less inventories per \$1 of current debt, compared to \$1.06 for the peer group. Thus, Harley-Davidson has more liquid assets relative to its short-term debt, an indication that the firm has greater ability to meet its maturing obligations.

MEASURING LIQUIDITY: APPROACH 2. The second view of liquidity examines the firm's ability to convert accounts receivable and inventory into cash on a timely basis. The conversion of accounts receivable into cash may be measured by computing how long it takes to collect the firm's receivables; that is, how many days of sales are outstanding in the form of accounts receivable? We can answer this question by computing the **average collection period:**

**Average collection period**
Average collection period indicates how rapidly a firm is collecting its credit, as measured by the average number of days it takes to collect its accounts receivable.

$$\text{average collection period} = \frac{\text{accounts receivable}}{\text{daily credit sales}} \qquad \textbf{(3-3)}$$

If we assume all Harley-Davidson 1999 sales (\$2,591 million in Table 3-1) to be credit sales, as opposed to some cash sales, then the firm's average collection period is 76.5 days, compared to a peer-group norm of 75 days:

| **Harley-Davidson** | **Peer-Group Average** |
|---|---|
| $\text{average collection period} = \dfrac{\text{accounts receivable}}{\text{daily credit sales}}$ | |
| $= \dfrac{\$543\text{M}}{\$2{,}591\text{M} \div 365} = 76.5$ | 75 days |

Thus, Harley-Davidson takes just a little longer to collect its receivables as the average firm in the comparison group—76.5 days compared to 75 days for the industry.

We could have reached the same conclusion by measuring how many times accounts receivable are "rolled over" during a year, or the **accounts receivable turnover ratio.** For instance, Harley-Davidson turns its receivables over 4.77 times a year.[2]

**Accounts receivable turnover ratio**
Accounts receivable turnover ratio indicates how rapidly the firm is collecting its credit, as measured by the number of times its accounts receivable are collected or "rolled over" during the year.

| **Harley-Davidson** | **Peer-Group Average** | |
|---|---|---|
| $\text{accounts receivable turnover} = \dfrac{\text{credit sales}}{\text{accounts receivable}}$ | | **(3-4)** |
| $= \dfrac{\$2{,}591\text{M}}{\$543\text{M}} = 4.77 \text{ times/year}$ | 4.87 times/year | |

Whether we use the average collection period or the accounts receivable turnover ratio, the conclusion is the same. Harley-Davidson is ever so slightly slower at collecting its receivables than competing firms, but probably not enough that management would even worry about it.[3]

As a general rule, management would want to collect receivables sooner rather than later—that is, reduce collection period and increase turnover ratios. However, it may be that a company's management would intentionally extend longer credit terms as a policy for reasons it deems justifiable. Alternatively, slower collection could mean that management is simply not being as careful at enforcing its collection policies. In other words, it may not be managing receivables effectively.

We now want to know the same thing for inventories that we just determined for accounts receivable: How many times are we turning over inventories during the year? In this manner, we gain some insight into the liquidity of inventories. The **inventory turnover ratio** is calculated as follows:

**Inventory turnover ratio**
Inventory turnover indicates the relative liquidity of inventories, as measured by the number of times a firm's inventories are replaced during the year.

$$\text{inventory turnover} = \frac{\text{cost of goods sold}}{\text{inventory}} \qquad \textbf{(3-5)}$$

Note that sales in this ratio is replaced by cost of goods sold. Since the inventory (the denominator) is measured at cost, we want to use a cost-based measure of sales in the numerator. Otherwise, our answer would vary from one firm to the next solely due to differences in how each firm marks up its sales over costs.[4]

[2]We could also measure the accounts receivable turnover by dividing 365 days by the average collection period: 365/76.5 = 4.77

[3]Although it will not be discussed here, we could also evaluate how effectively management is managing accounts receivable by aging the firm's receivables. For example, we could calculate how many of the accounts are 0 to 30 days old, 30 to 60 days old, and over 60 days old.

[4]Whereas our logic may be correct to use cost of goods sold in the numerator, practicality may dictate that we use sales instead. Some suppliers of peer-group norm data use sales in the numerator. Thus for consistency in our comparisons, we too may need to use sales.

Given that Harley-Davidson's cost of goods sold was $1,617 million (Table 3-1) and its inventory was $169 million (Table 3-2), the firm's 1999 inventory turnover, along with the peer-group average, is as follows:

| **Harley-Davidson** | **Peer-Group Average** |
|---|---|
| $\text{inventory turnover} = \dfrac{\text{cost of goods sold}}{\text{inventory}}$ | |
| $= \dfrac{\$1{,}617M}{\$169M} = 9.57 \text{ times/year}$ | 5.78 times/year |

Given the preceding results, we can conclude that Harley-Davidson is clearly excellent in its management of inventory, turning its inventory over 9.57 times per year compared to 5.78 times for the peer group. In other words, Harley-Davidson sells its inventory in 38.1 days on average (365 days ÷ 9.57 times), whereas the average firm takes 63.1 days (365 ÷ 5.78 times).

To conclude, when it comes to Harley-Davidson's liquidity, we see that the firm has high current and acid-test ratios, indicating the firm has sufficient liquid assets to cover liabilities coming due in the next 12 months. However, the firm takes slightly longer to collect its accounts receivable (77 days) than its peer group (75 days). But, Harley-Davidson turns its inventory over nine times per year, indicating that this asset is very liquid.

In summary, a firm's liquidity—its ability to meet maturing debt obligations (short-term debt) and the ability to convert accounts receivables and inventories into cash on a timely basis—represents an important dimension to managers, lenders, and investors. The less liquid the firm, the greater the chance that the firm will be unable to pay creditors when payments are due.

## Question 2: Is Management Generating Adequate Operating Profits on the Firm's Assets?

We now begin a different line of thinking that will carry us through all the remaining questions. At this point, we want to know if the profits are sufficient relative to the assets being invested. The question is similar to a question one might ask about the interest being earned on a savings account at the bank. When you invest $1,000 in a savings account and receive $40 in interest during the year, you are earning a 4 percent return on your investment ($40 ÷ $1,000 = .04 = 4%). With respect to Harley-Davidson, we want to know something similar: the rate of return that management is earning on the firm's assets.

**Operating income return on investment**
Operating income return on investment indicates the effectiveness of management at generating operating profits on the firm's assets, as measured by operating profits relative to the total assets.

In answering this question, we have several choices as to how we measure profits: gross profits, operating profits, or net income. Gross profits would not be an acceptable choice because it does not include some important information, such as the cost of marketing and distributing the firm's product. Thus we should choose between operating profits and net income. For our purposes, we prefer to use operating profits, because this measure of firm profits is calculated before the costs of the company's financing policies have been deducted. Because financing is explicitly considered in our next question, we want to isolate only the operating aspects of the company's profits at this point. In this way, we are able to compare the profitability of firms with different debt-to-equity mixes. Therefore, to examine the level of operating profits relative to the assets, we would use the **operating income return on investment** (OIROI):

$$\text{operating income return on investment} = \frac{\text{operating income}}{\text{total assets}} \tag{3-6}$$

The operating income return on investment for Harley-Davidson (based on the financial data in Table 3-1 and Table 3-2), and the corresponding peer-group norm, are shown below:

| **Harley-Davidson** | **Peer-Group Average** |
|---|---|
| $\text{operating income return on investment} = \dfrac{\text{operating income}}{\text{total assets}}$ | |
| $= \dfrac{\$449M}{\$2{,}112M} = .213 = 21.3\%$ | 9.8% |

Hence we see that Harley-Davidson is earning over twice the return on investment of the average firm in the peer group. Management is generating significantly more income on $1 of assets than similar firms.[5]

If we were the managers of Harley-Davidson, we should not be satisfied with merely knowing that we are earning more than a competitive return on the firm's assets. We would also want to know why we are above average. To understand this issue, we may separate the operating income return on investment, OIROI, into two important pieces: the operating profit margin and the total asset turnover. The firm's OIROI is a multiple of these two ratios and may be shown algebraically as follows:

$$\text{OIROI} = \left(\begin{array}{c}\text{operating}\\ \text{profit margin}\end{array}\right) \times \left(\begin{array}{c}\text{total asset}\\ \text{turnover}\end{array}\right) \tag{3-7a}$$

or more completely,

$$\text{OIROI} = \frac{\text{operating income}}{\text{sales}} \times \frac{\text{sales}}{\text{total assets}} \tag{3-7b}$$

OIROI: COMPONENT 1. The first component of the OIROI, the **operating profit margin,** is an extremely important variable in understanding a company's operating profitability. It is important that we know exactly what drives this ratio. In coming to understand the ratio, think about the makeup of the ratio, which may be expressed as follows:

**Operating profit margin**
Operating profit margin indicates management's effectiveness in managing the firm's income statement, as measured by operating profits relative to sales.

$$\begin{array}{c}\text{operating}\\ \text{profit margin}\end{array} = \frac{\text{operating income}}{\text{sales}}$$

$$= \frac{\begin{array}{c}\text{total}\\ \text{sales}\end{array} - \begin{array}{c}\text{cost of}\\ \text{goods sold}\end{array} - \begin{array}{c}\text{general and}\\ \text{administrative}\\ \text{expenses}\end{array} - \begin{array}{c}\text{marketing}\\ \text{expenses}\end{array}}{\text{sales}}$$

Because total sales equals the number of units sold times the sales price per unit, and the cost of goods sold equals the number of units sold times the cost of goods sold per unit, we may conclude that the driving forces of the operating profit margin are the following:

1. The number of units of product sold[6]
2. The average selling price for each product unit

[5]The **return on assets** (ROA) is often used as an indicator of a firm's profitability and is measured as follows: return on assets = net income ÷ total assets.

We choose not to use this ratio because *net income* is influenced both by operating decisions and how the firm is financed. We want to restrict our attention only to operating activities; financing is considered later in questions 3 and 4. Nevertheless, sometimes the peer-group norm for operating income return on investment is not available. Instead, return on assets is provided. If so, we have no option but to use the return on assets for measuring the firm's profitability.

**Return on assets**
Return on assets determines the amount of net income produced on a firm's assets by relating net income to total assets.

[6]The number of units affects the operating profit margin only if some of the firm's costs and expenses are fixed. If a company's expenses are all variable in nature, then the ratio would not change as the number of units sold increases or decreases, because the numerator and the denominator would change at the same rate.

3. The cost of manufacturing or acquiring the firm's product
4. The ability to control general and administrative expenses
5. The ability to control expenses in marketing and distributing the firm's product

These influences are also apparent simply by looking at the income statement and thinking about what is involved in determining the firm's operating profits or income.[7] For Harley-Davidson and its peer group, the operating profit margins are 17.3 percent and 8.3 percent, respectively, determined as follows:

| **Harley-Davidson** | **Peer-Group Average** |
|---|---|
| $\text{operating profit margin} = \dfrac{\text{operating income}}{\text{sales}}$ | |
| $= \dfrac{\$449\text{M}}{\$2{,}591\text{M}} = .173 = 17.3\%$ | 8.3% |

Based on these findings, we may conclude that Harley-Davidson is far more than competitive when it comes to keeping costs and expenses in line relative to sales, as is reflected by the operating profit margin. In other words, management is extremely effective in managing the five driving forces of the operating profit margin listed previously. In terms of its high operating profit margin, Harley-Davidson has no equal.

**Total asset turnover**
Total asset turnover indicates management's effectiveness at managing a firm balance sheet—its assets—as indicated by the amount of sales generated per 1 dollar of assets.

OIROI: COMPONENT 2. As shown in Equation (3.7a), the **total asset turnover** is the second component of the operating income return on investment. The total asset turnover measures the dollar sales per one dollar of assets. The ratio is calculated as follows:

$$\text{total asset turnover} = \frac{\text{sales}}{\text{total assets}} \qquad \textbf{(3-8)}$$

This ratio indicates how efficiently a firm is using its assets in generating sales. For instance, if Company A can generate \$3 in sales with \$1 in assets, compared to \$2 in sales per asset dollar for Company B, we may say that Company A is using its assets more efficiently in generating sales, which is a major determinant in the firm's operating income return on investment.

Returning to Harley-Davidson, the firm's total asset turnover is calculated as follows:

| **Harley-Davidson** | **Peer-Group Average** |
|---|---|
| $\text{total asset turnover} = \dfrac{\text{sales}}{\text{total assets}}$ | |
| $= \dfrac{\$2{,}591\text{M}}{\$2{,}112\text{M}} = 1.23$ | 1.18 |

Based on the forgoing results, we see that Harley-Davidson generates about \$1.23 in sales per dollar of assets, whereas the competition on average produces \$1.18 from every dollar in assets. That is, Harley-Davidson is using its assets more efficiently than the average firm in its peer group.

While we have concluded that Harley-Davidson utilizes its assets more efficiently than does its peer group, it is also good to see what drives its superior performance. To deter-

**Net profit margin**
Net profit margin measures the net income of a firm as a percent of sales.

[7]We could have used the **net profit margin,** rather than the operating profit margin, which is measured as follows: net profit margin = net income ÷ sales.

The net profit margin measures the amount of net income per \$1 of sales. However, because net income includes both operating expenses and interest expense, this ratio is influenced both by operating activities and financing activities. We prefer to defer the effect of financing decisions until questions 3 and 4, which follow shortly.

mine the factors responsible for Harley-Davidson's performance, we examine the turnover ratios for the primary assets held by the firm—accounts receivables, inventories, and fixed assets. We have already calculated these ratios for accounts receivables and inventories, which are repeated as follows:

**Harley-Davidson** **Peer-Group Average**

*Accounts receivable turnover:*

$$\frac{\text{credit sales}}{\text{accounts receivable}} = \frac{\$2{,}591\text{M}}{\$543\text{M}} = 4.77 \qquad 4.87$$

*Inventory turnover:*

$$\frac{\text{cost of goods sold}}{\text{inventory}} = \frac{\$1{,}617\text{M}}{\$169\text{M}} = 9.57 \qquad 5.78$$

We next calculate a firm's fixed assets turnover ratio as follows:

$$\text{fixed assets turnover} = \frac{\text{sales}}{\text{fixed assets}} \tag{3-9}$$

**Harley-Davidson** **Peer-Group Average**

$$\frac{\text{sales}}{\text{net fixed assets}} = \frac{\$2{,}591\text{M}}{\$682\text{M}} = 3.80 \qquad 4.26$$

Given these turnover ratios, we can say that, in general, Harley-Davidson manages its assets efficiently—but some better than others. Management is particularly good at managing the firm's inventories, pretty typical at its collection of accounts receivables, but somewhat below average at utilizing the firm's fixed assets.

To summarize, a firm's operating income return on investment (OIROI) is a function of two elements, the operating profit margin and the firm's total asset turnover. For Harley-Davidson, the OIROI was determined as follows:

$$\text{OIROI}_{\text{HD}} = .173 \times 1.23 = .213 = 21.3\%$$

and for the peer group, this same ratio is

$$\text{OIROI}_{\text{pg}} = .083 \times 1.18 = .098 = 9.8\%$$

Based on these findings, we can say with complete confidence that Harley-Davidson is a superstar at managing its income statement, keeping its cost of goods and operating expenses extremely low relative to its sales (as indicated by its high operating profit margin). In terms of managing assets, the firm has much less inventory per dollar of sales than competing firms, which is good. However, the company is not as efficient when it comes to managing its fixed assets—that is, it has more invested in fixed assets per dollar of sales than is true for the average firm in the peer group.

## Question 3: How Is the Firm Financing Its Assets?

We now turn for the moment to the matter of how the firm is financed. We shall return to the firm's profitability shortly. The basic issue is the use of debt versus equity: Do we finance the assets more by debt or equity? In answering this question, we will use two ratios. Many more could be used. First, we simply ask what percentage of the firm's assets are financed by debt, including *both* short-term and long-term debt, realizing the

**Debt ratio**
Debt ratio indicates how much debt is used to finance a firm's assets.

remaining percentage must be financed by equity. We would compute the **debt ratio** as follows:[8]

$$\text{debt ratio} = \frac{\text{total debt}}{\text{total assets}} \tag{3-10}$$

For Harley-Davidson, debt as a percentage of total assets is 45 percent (taken from Harley-Davidson's balance sheet in Table 3-2) compared to a peer-group norm of 58 percent. The computation is as follows:

| **Harley-Davidson** | **Peer-Group Average** |
|---|---|
| $\text{debt ratio} = \frac{\text{total debt}}{\text{total assets}}$ | |
| $= \frac{\$951M}{\$2,112M} = .45 = 45\%$ | 58% |

Thus Harley-Davidson uses significantly less debt than the average firm in the peer group.

We should note that companies in general finance about 40 percent of their assets with debt and 60 percent in equity. Firms with more real assets, such as land and buildings (as with Harley-Davidson), are able to finance more of their assets with debt. High-technology firms where the assets are "soft," such as research and development, are less able to acquire debt financing. Thus, the amount of debt a firm uses depends on its proven income record and the availability of assets that can be used as collateral for the loan—and how much risk management is willing to assume.

Our second perspective regarding the firm's financing decisions comes by looking at the income statement. When we borrow money, there is a minimum requirement that the firm pay the interest on the debt. Thus, it is informative to compare the amount of operating income that is available to service the interest with the amount of interest that is to be paid. Stated as a ratio, we compute the number of times we are earning our interest. Thus a **times interest earned** ratio is commonly used when examining the firm's debt position and is computed in the following manner:

**Times interest earned**
Times interest earned indicates a firm's ability to cover its interest expense, as measured by its earnings before interest and taxes relative to the interest expense.

$$\text{times interest earned} = \frac{\text{operating income}}{\text{interest expense}} \tag{3-11}$$

Based on the income statement for Harley-Davidson (Table 3-1), the firm's times interest earned is 15.48, computed as follows:

| **Harley-Davidson** | **Peer-Group Average** |
|---|---|
| $\text{times interest earned} = \frac{\text{operating income}}{\text{interest expense}}$ | |
| $= \frac{\$449M}{\$29M} = 15.48$ | 3.93 |

Thus Harley-Davidson is well able to service its interest expense without any difficulty. In fact, the firm's operating income could fall to as little as one-fifteenth (1/15.48) its current level and still have the income to pay the required interest. We should remember, however, that interest is not paid with income but with cash, and that the firm may be

[8]We will often see the relationship stated in terms of debt to equity, or the debt-equity ratio, rather than debt to total assets. We come to the same conclusion with either ratio.

required to repay some of the debt principal as well as the interest. Thus, the times interest earned is only a crude measure of the firm's capacity to service its debt. Nevertheless, it does give us a general indication of a company's debt capacity.

## Question 4: Are the Owners (Stockholders) Receiving an Adequate Return on Their Investment?

Our one remaining question looks at the accounting return on the common stockholders' investment or **return on common equity;** that is, we want to know if the earnings available to the firm's owners or common equity investors are attractive when compared to the returns of owners of companies in the peer group.

**Return on common equity** Return on common equity indicates the accounting rate of return on the stockholders' investment, as measured by net income relative to common equity.

We measure the return to the owners as follows:

$$\text{return on common equity} = \frac{\text{net income}}{\text{common equity including par, paid-in capital and retained earnings}} \quad \textbf{(3-12)}$$

The return on common equity for Harley-Davidson and the peer group are 23 percent and 12 percent, respectively:

| **Harley-Davidson** | **Peer-Group Average** |
|---|---|
| $\text{return on common equity} = \frac{\text{net income}}{\text{common equity}}$ | |
| $\frac{\$267M}{\$1{,}161M} = .23 = 23\%$ | 12% |

Clearly, the owners of Harley-Davidson are receiving a return on their investment that is very attractive when compared to what owners involved with competing businesses receive. To understand the reasons, we need to draw on what we have already learned, namely that:

1. Harley-Davidson is far more profitable in its operations than its competitors. (Remember, the operating income return on investment, OIROI, was 21.3 percent for Harley-Davidson compared to 9.8 percent for the competition.) Thus, we could expect that Harley-Davidson would have a higher return on common equity.
2. Harley-Davidson uses considerably less debt (more equity) financing than does the average firm in the peer group. As we will see shortly, the more debt a firm uses, the higher its return on equity will be, provided that the firm is earning a return on investment greater than its cost of debt. Thus, given its low debt ratio, Harley-Davidson's higher return for its shareholders has been achieved totally by generating greater profits on the firm's assets, and not through the use of debt financing. Harley-Davidson could further increase its return to the owners by utilizing more debt; however, the more debt a firm uses, the greater the company's financial risk, which translates to more risk to the shareholders as well.

To help us understand the forgoing conclusion about the use of debt and its effect on shareholder return, consider the following example.

Firms A and B are identical in size, both having \$1,000 in total assets and both having an operating income return on investment of 14 percent. However, they are different in one respect: Firm A uses no debt, but Firm B finances 60 percent of its investments with debt at an interest cost of 10 percent. For the sake of simplicity, we will assume there are no income taxes. The financial statements for the two companies would be as follows:

| | Firm A | Firm B |
|---|---|---|
| Total assets | $1,000 | $1,000 |
| Debt (10% interest rate) | $ 0 | $ 600 |
| Equity | 1,000 | 400 |
| Total | $1,000 | $1,000 |
| Operating income (OIROI = 14%) | $ 140 | $ 140 |
| Interest expense (10%) | 0 | 60 |
| Net profit | $ 140 | $ 80 |

Computing the return on common equity for both companies, we see that Firm B has a much more attractive return to its owners, 20 percent compared to Firm A's 14 percent:

$$\text{return on equity} = \frac{\text{net income}}{\text{common equity}}$$

$$\text{Firm A:} = \frac{\$140}{\$1{,}000} = .14 = 14\% \qquad \text{Firm B:} \frac{\$80}{\$400} = .20 = 20\%$$

Why the difference? Firm B is earning 14 percent on its investments, but is only having to pay 10 percent for its borrowed money. The difference between the return on the firm's investments and the interest rate, 14 percent less the 10 percent, goes to the owners, thus boosting Firm B's return on equity above that of Firm A. We are seeing the favorable results of debt at work, where we borrow at 10 percent and invest at 14 percent. The result is an increase in the return on equity.

If debt enhances the owners' returns, why would we not use lots of it all the time? We may continue our example to find the answer. Assume now that the economy falls into a deep recession, business declines sharply, and Firms A and B only earn a 6 percent operating income return on investment. Let's recompute the return on common equity now.

| | Firm A | Firm B |
|---|---|---|
| Operating income (OIROI = 6%) | $60 | $60 |
| Interest expense | 0 | 60 |
| Net profit | $60 | $ 0 |
| Return on equity: | Firm A: $\frac{\$60}{\$1{,}000} = .06 = 6\%$ | Firm B: $\frac{\$0}{\$400} = .00 = 0\%$ |

Now the use of debt has a negative influence on the return on equity, with Firm B earning less than Firm A for its owners. This results from the fact that now Firm B earns less than the interest rate of 10 percent; consequently, the equity investors have to make up the difference. Thus, using debt is a two-edged sword; when times are good, debt financing can make them very, very good, but when times are bad, debt financing makes them very, very bad. Thus, financing with debt can potentially enhance the returns of the equity investors, but it also increases the uncertainty or risk for the owners.

Let's review what we have learned about the use of financial ratios in evaluating a company's financial position. We have presented the financial ratios calculated for Harley-Davidson in Table 3-3. The ratios are grouped by the issue being addressed: liquidity, oper-

**TABLE 3-3**
Harley-Davidson's Financial Ratio Analysis

| Financial Ratios | Harley-Davidson | Industry Average |
|---|---|---|
| **1. FIRM LIQUIDITY** | | |
| Current ratio $= \frac{\text{current assets}}{\text{current liabilities}}$ | $\frac{949\text{M}}{518\text{M}} = 1.83$ | 1.50 |
| Acid-test ratio $= \frac{\text{current assets} - \text{inventories}}{\text{current liabilities}}$ | $\frac{949\text{M} - 169\text{M}}{518\text{M}} = 1.51$ | 1.06 |
| Average collection period $= \frac{\text{accounts receivable}}{\text{daily credit sales}}$ | $\frac{543\text{M}}{2{,}591\text{M} \div 365} = 76.5$ | 75 |
| Accounts receivable turnover $= \frac{\text{credit sales}}{\text{accounts receivable}}$ | $\frac{2{,}591\text{M}}{543\text{M}} = 4.77$ | 4.87 |
| Inventory turnover $= \frac{\text{cost of goods sold}}{\text{inventory}}$ | $\frac{1{,}617\text{M}}{169\text{M}} = 9.57$ | 5.78 |
| **2. OPERATING PROFITABILITY** | | |
| Operating income return on investment $= \frac{\text{operating income}}{\text{total assets}}$ | $\frac{449\text{M}}{2{,}112\text{M}} = 21.3\%$ | 9.8% |
| Operating profit margin $= \frac{\text{operating income}}{\text{sales}}$ | $\frac{449\text{M}}{2{,}591\text{M}} = 17.3\%$ | 8.3% |
| Total asset turnover $= \frac{\text{sales}}{\text{total assets}}$ | $\frac{2{,}591\text{M}}{2{,}112\text{M}} = 1.23$ | 1.18 |
| Accounts receivable turnover $= \frac{\text{sales}}{\text{accounts receivable}}$ | $\frac{2{,}591\text{M}}{543\text{M}} = 4.77$ | 4.87 |
| Inventory turnover $= \frac{\text{cost of goods sold}}{\text{inventory}}$ | $\frac{1{,}617\text{M}}{169\text{M}} = 9.57$ | 5.78 |
| Fixed assets turnover $= \frac{\text{sales}}{\text{net fixed assets}}$ | $\frac{2{,}591\text{M}}{682\text{M}} = 3.80$ | 4.26 |
| **3. FINANCING DECISIONS** | | |
| Debt ratio $= \frac{\text{total debt}}{\text{total assets}}$ | $\frac{951\text{M}}{2{,}112\text{M}} = 45\%$ | 58% |
| Times interest earned $= \frac{\text{operating income}}{\text{interest expense}}$ | $\frac{449\text{M}}{29\text{M}} = 15.48$ | 3.93% |
| **4. RETURN ON EQUITY** | | |
| Return on equity $= \frac{\text{net income}}{\text{common equity}}$ | $\frac{267\text{M}}{1{,}161\text{M}} = 23\%$ | 12% |

**TABLE 3-4**
Harley-Davidson Ratio Analysis 1995–1999

| | 1995 | 1996 | 1997 | 1998 | 1999 |
|---|---|---|---|---|---|
| **FIRM LIQUIDITY** | | | | | |
| Current ratio | 1.45 | 1.63 | 1.95 | 1.80 | 1.83 |
| Acid-test ratio | 1.08 | 1.24 | 1.62 | 1.47 | 1.51 |
| Accounts receivable turnover | 10.09 | 11.16 | 4.62 | 4.58 | 4.77 |
| Inventory turnover | 10.62 | 9.96 | 9.67 | 8.82 | 9.59 |
| **OPERATING PROFITABILITY** | | | | | |
| Operating income return on investment | 18.1% | 18.3% | 18.0% | 18.8% | 21.3% |
| Operating profit margin | 13.4% | 15.3% | 15.7% | 16.6% | 17.4% |
| Total asset turnover | 1.35 | 1.20 | 1.14 | 1.13 | 1.23 |
| Accounts receivable turnover | 10.09 | 11.16 | 4.62 | 4.58 | 4.77 |
| Inventory turnover | 10.62 | 9.96 | 9.67 | 8.82 | 9.59 |
| Fixed assets turnover | 4.75 | 3.85 | 3.46 | 3.46 | 3.80 |
| **FINANCING DECISIONS** | | | | | |
| Debt ratio | 0.51 | 0.50 | 0.48 | 0.46 | 0.45 |
| Times interest earned | 18.00 | 18.56 | 13.53 | 15.00 | 15.67 |
| **RETURN ON EQUITY** | | | | | |
| Return on equity | 23.0% | 25.0% | 21.0% | 20.7% | 23.0% |

ating profitability, financing, and profits for the owners. As before, we use some ratios for more than one purpose—namely, the turnover ratios for accounts receivable and inventories. These ratios have implications both for the firm's liquidity and its profitability; thus they are listed in both areas. Also, we have included both average collection period and accounts receivable turnover; typically, we would only use one in our analysis, because they are just different ways of expressing the same thing.

## Conducting Financial Analysis Over Time

To this point, we have been comparing Harley-Davidson with a peer group as of 1999. As mentioned earlier, we should also be interested in a firm's performance over time. To illustrate this process, Table 3-4 shows the financial ratios for Harley-Davidson for the years 1995 through 1999. Based on the trends, we can draw the following conclusions:

1. The firm's liquidity, as measured by the current and quick ratios, has been relatively stable over time, with some slight improvement. However, accounts receivable turnover declined sharply from 10.09 to 4.77. In other words, the average collection period has increased from 36 days to 77 days. Inventory turnover has declined as well, but not nearly as much as for accounts receivables.
2. We see a nice increase in operating income return on investment (OIROI) in 1999 compared to the previous 4 years. This improvement was largely the result of a better operating profit margin.
3. Harley-Davidson reduced its use of debt somewhat over the past 5 years. During this same time, the firm's operating income increased. Given these two trends, we would expect the firm's times interest earned (operating income ÷ interest expense) to increase, which did not happen. While we cannot say for certain, such a finding suggests that the firm is paying a higher interest rate on its debt.

4. The firm's return on equity has fluctuated between 20 percent and 25 percent, with the last year being pretty typical. Thus, for these 5 years, management has been able to consistently provide very attractive returns to the owners.

From the forgoing trend analysis we are able to see clearly how the firm is performing financially over time, which gives us additional insights not possible from only looking at industry norms.

**CONCEPT CHECK**

1. How can financial ratios be used to make valuable comparisons?
2. The financial ratios outlined in this chapter have been developed to answer what four important questions?
3. Which number in the income statement should be used to measure profitability relative to total assets, and why? What are the two driving forces behind the operating income return on investment?
4. What is the relationship between the use of debt and the return on common equity for shareholders?

## THE DUPONT ANALYSIS: AN INTEGRATIVE APPROACH TO RATIO ANALYSIS

In the previous section, we used ratio analysis to answer four questions thought to be important in understanding a company's financial position. The last three of the four questions dealt with a company's earnings capabilities and the common stockholders' return on the equity capital. In our analysis, we measured the return on equity as follows:

$$\text{return on equity} = \frac{\text{net income}}{\text{common equity}} \tag{3-13}$$

**DuPont analysis** The DuPont analysis is an approach to evaluate a firm's profitability and return on equity.

Another approach can be used to evaluate a firm's return on equity. The **DuPont analysis** is a method used to analyze a firm's profitability and return on equity. Figure 3-1 shows graphically the DuPont technique, along with the numbers for Harley-Davidson. Beginning at the top of the figure, we see that the return on equity is calculated as follows:

$$\text{return on equity} = \left(\begin{matrix}\text{return}\\ \text{on assets}\end{matrix}\right) \div \left(1 - \frac{\text{total debt}}{\text{total assets}}\right) \tag{3-14}$$

where the return on assets, or ROA, equals:

$$\text{return on assets} = \frac{\text{net income}}{\text{total assets}} \tag{3-15}$$

Thus we see that the return on equity is a function of (1) the firm's overall profitability (net income relative to the amount invested in assets), and (2) the amount of debt used to finance the assets. We also know that the return on assets may be represented as follows:

$$\begin{aligned}\text{return on assets} &= \left(\begin{matrix}\text{net profit}\\ \text{margin}\end{matrix}\right) \times \left(\begin{matrix}\text{total asset}\\ \text{turnover}\end{matrix}\right) \\ &= \left(\frac{\text{net income}}{\text{sales}}\right) \times \left(\frac{\text{sales}}{\text{total assets}}\right)\end{aligned} \tag{3-16}$$

**FIGURE 3-1**
DuPont Analysis: Harley-Davidson

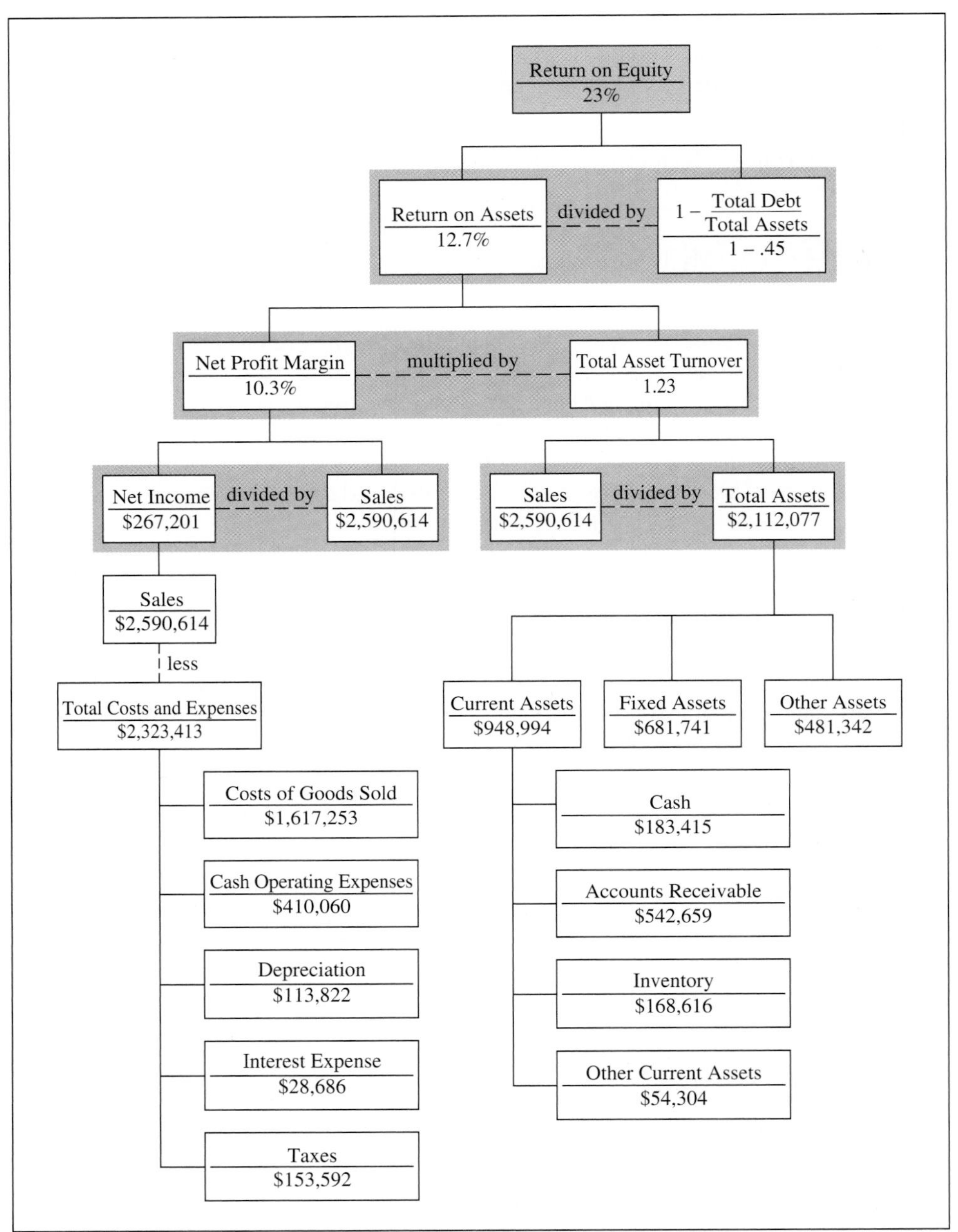


Combining equations (3-14) and (3-16) gives us the basic DuPont equation that shows the firm's return on equity as follows:

$$\text{return on equity} = \left(\begin{array}{c}\text{net profit}\\ \text{margin}\end{array}\right) \times \left(\begin{array}{c}\text{total asset}\\ \text{turnover}\end{array}\right) \div \left(1 - \frac{\text{total debt}}{\text{total assets}}\right) \tag{3-17}$$

$$= \left(\frac{\text{net income}}{\text{sales}}\right) \times \left(\frac{\text{sales}}{\text{total assets}}\right) \div \left(1 - \frac{\text{total debt}}{\text{total assets}}\right)$$

Using the DuPont equation and the diagram in Figure 3-1 allows management to see more clearly what drives the return on equity and the interrelationships among the net profit margin, the asset turnover, and the debt ratio. Management is provided with a road map to follow in determining its effectiveness in managing the firm's resources to maximize the return earned on the owners' investment. In addition, the manager or owner can determine why that particular return was earned.

Let's return to Harley-Davidson to demonstrate the use of the DuPont analysis. Taking the information from Harley-Davidson's income statement (Table 3-1) and balance sheet as of December 31, 1999 (Table 3-2), we can calculate the company's return on equity as follows:

$$\text{return on equity} = \left(\frac{\text{net income}}{\text{sales}}\right) \times \left(\frac{\text{sales}}{\text{total assets}}\right) \div \left(1 - \frac{\text{total debt}}{\text{total assets}}\right)$$

$$= \frac{267{,}201}{2{,}590{,}614} \times \frac{2{,}590{,}614}{2{,}112{,}077} \div \left[1 - \frac{950{,}997}{2{,}112{,}077}\right]$$

$$= .103 \times 1.23 \div .55$$

$$= 23\%$$

We can also visualize the relationships graphically for Harley-Davidson, as shown in Figure 3-1.

If Harley-Davidson's management wants to improve the company's return on equity, it should carefully examine Figure 3-1 for possible avenues. As we study the figure, we quickly see that improvement in the return on equity can come in one or more of four ways:

1. Increase sales without a disproportionate increase in costs and expenses.
2. Reduce the firm's cost of goods sold or operating expenses shown in the left side of Figure 3-1.
3. Increase the sales relative to the asset base, either by increasing sales or by reducing the amounts invested in company assets. From our earlier examination of Harley-Davidson, we learned that the firm had excessive accounts receivables and fixed assets. Thus management needs to reduce these assets to the lowest point possible, which would in turn result in an increase in the return on assets and then the return on equity.
4. Increase the use of debt relative to equity, but only to the extent that it does not unduly jeopardize the firm's financial position.

The choice between using the four-question approach as described earlier or the DuPont analysis is largely a matter of personal preference. Both approaches are intended to let us see the variables that determine a firm's profitability. There are, however, limitations to either technique because of the inherent limitations in using financial ratios—a topic addressed in the next section.

## CONCEPT CHECK

1. In the DuPont analysis, the return on equity is the function of what two factors?
2. What four methods can a firm utilize to improve return on equity?

## Limitations of Ratio Analysis

OBJECTIVE 3

We have shown how financial ratios may be used to understand a company's financial position, but anyone who works with these ratios ought to be aware of the limitations involved in their use. The following list includes some of the more important pitfalls that may be encountered in computing and interpreting financial ratios:

1. It is sometimes difficult to identify the industry category to which a firm belongs when the firm engages in multiple lines of business. Thus, we frequently must select our own set of peer firms and construct tailor-made norms. Such was the case with our analysis of Harley-Davidson.
2. Published industry averages are only approximations and provide the user with general guidelines rather than scientifically determined averages of the ratios of all or even a representative sample of the firms within an industry.
3. Accounting practices differ widely among firms and can lead to differences in computed ratios. In addition, firms may choose different methods of depreciating their fixed assets.
4. An industry average may not provide a desirable target ratio or norm. At best, an industry average provides a guide to the financial position of the average firm in the industry, which includes all the dogs and the stars. It does not mean it is the ideal or best value for the ratio. Thus, we may choose to compare our firm's ratios with a self-determined peer group or even a single competitor.[9]
5. Many firms experience seasonality in their operations. Thus, balance sheet entries and their corresponding ratios will vary with the time of year when the statements are prepared. For example, a firm may have a fiscal year that ends on June 30, whereas another company in the same industry may have a December 31 fiscal-year end. To avoid this problem, an average account balance should be used (for several months or quarters during the year) rather than the year-end total. For example, an average of month-end inventory balances might be used to compute a firm's inventory turnover ratio when the firm is subject to a significant seasonality in its sales (and correspondingly in its investment in inventories).

In spite of their limitations, financial ratios provide us with a very useful tool for assessing a firm's financial conditions. We should, however, be aware of these potential weaknesses when performing a ratio analysis. In many cases, the real value derived from analyzing financial ratios is that they tell us what questions to ask and what avenues to pursue.

### CONCEPT CHECK

1. Why is it difficult to create industry categories, especially among larger companies?
2. What differences in accounting practices create problems in using financial ratios?
3. Why should a firm be careful when making comparisons with industry norms?

[9]See Donald F. Cunningham and John T. Rose, "Industry Norms in Financial Statement Analysis: A Comparison of RMA and D&B Benchmark Data," *The Credit and Financial Management Review,* 1995, pp. 42–48, for a comparison of the industry financial ratios provided by Robert Morris Associates with those of Dun and Bradstreet. They find significant differences within the same industry classifications. This finding points out the need to carefully consider the choice of an industry norm. In fact, your analysis may require that you construct your own norm from, say, a list of the four or five firms in a particular industry that might provide the most appropriate standard of comparison for the firm being analyzed.

## How Financial Managers Use this Material

In this chapter, we provided a framework for using the information in evaluating a firm's performance. As stated in Chapter 2, accounting data is the basis for so much that is done in finance. The consequences of certain important management decisions can only be verified by the relationships shown in the financial statements. Such measurements as gross profit margin, operating profit margin, the different asset turnover ratios, debt ratios, and return on investment provide important information about the effectiveness of a management's strategies. For instance, Michael Eisner, the CEO for Disney, received large bonuses based on the company earning a superior return on the common stockholders' investment, as did Al Dunlap when he went to Scott Paper to turn the company around and make it more profitable. Eisner was successful, but Dunlap was not. So, if a manager or a common stockholder wants to know the effectiveness of a firm's strategies, the ultimate test is the rate of return being earned on the company's assets, which is measured, to a large extent, by the accounting data. Without such information, managers cannot make any definite conclusions as to the success of their strategies.

## SUMMARY

Financial ratios are the principal tools of financial analysis. Sometimes referred to simply as benchmarks, ratios standardize financial information so that comparisons can be made between firms of varying sizes.

Two groups find financial ratios useful. The first is comprised of managers who use them to measure and track company performance over time. The focus of their analysis is frequently related to various measures of profitability used to evaluate the performance of the firm from the perspective of the owners. The second group of users of financial ratios includes analysts external to the firm who, for one reason or another, have an interest in the firm's economic well-being. An example of this group would be a loan officer of a commercial bank who wishes to determine the creditworthiness of a loan applicant. Here the focus of the analysis is on the firm's previous use of financial leverage and its ability to pay the interest and principal associated with the loan request.

Financial ratios may be used to answer at least four questions: (1) How liquid is the company? (2) Is management effective at generating operating profits on the firm's assets? (3) How is the firm financed? (4) Are the returns earned by the common stockholders adequate?

Two methods may be used in analyzing financial ratios. The first involves trend analysis for the firm over time; the second involves making ratio comparisons with a selected peer group of similar firms. In our example, a peer group was chosen for analyzing the financial position of Harley-Davidson.

Another approach frequently used to evaluate a firm's profitability and the return on equity is the DuPont analysis. The basic format of the DuPont analysis dissects the return on equity into three drivers, represented as follows:

$$\text{return on equity} = \left(\frac{\text{net income}}{\text{sales}}\right) \times \left(\frac{\text{sales}}{\text{total assets}}\right) \div \left(1 - \frac{\text{total debt}}{\text{total assets}}\right)$$

The following limitations may be encountered in computing and interpreting financial ratios:

1. It is sometimes difficult to identify an appropriate industry category.
2. Published industry averages are only approximations rather than scientifically determined averages.
3. Accounting practices differ widely among firms and can lead to differences in computed ratios.

4. An industry average may not provide a desirable target ratio or norm.
5. Many firms experience seasonality in their operations. Thus, ratios will vary with the time of year when the statements are prepared.

In spite of their limitations, financial ratios provide us with very useful tools for assessing a firm's financial condition.

## KEY TERMS

**Accounts receivable turnover ratio, 67**
**Acid-test (quick) ratio, 65**
**Average collection period, 66**
**Current ratio, 65**
**Debt ratio, 72**
**DuPont analysis, 77**
**Financial ratios, 63**
**Inventory turnover ratio, 67**
**Net profit margin, 70**
**Operating income return on investment, 68**
**Operating profit margin, 69**
**Return on assets, 69**
**Return on common equity, 73**
**Times interest earned, 72**
**Total asset turnover, 70**

myPHLIP

Go To:
http://www.prenhall.com/keown
for downloads and current events associated with this chapter

## STUDY QUESTIONS

**3-1.** Describe the "four-question approach" to using financial ratios.

**3-2.** Discuss briefly the two perspectives that can be taken in performing ratio analyses.

**3-3.** Where can we obtain industry norms? What are the limitations of industry average ratios? Discuss briefly.

**3-4.** What is liquidity, and what is the rationale for its measurement?

**3-5.** Distinguish between the operating income return on investment and the operating profit margin.

**3-6.** Why is operating income return on investment a function of operating profit margin and total asset turnover?

**3-7.** What are the differences among gross profit margin, operating profit margin, and net profit margin?

**3-8.** Explain what drives a company's return on common equity.

## SELF-TEST PROBLEMS

**ST-1.** (*Ratio analysis and short-term liquidity*) Ray's Tool and Supply Company of Austin, Texas, has been expanding its level of operation for the past 2 years. The firm's sales have grown rapidly as a result of the expansion in the Austin economy. However, Ray's is a privately held company, and its only source of available funds is a line of credit with the firm's bank. The company needs to expand its inventories to meet the needs of its growing customer base but also wishes to maintain a current ratio of at least 3. If Ray's current assets are $6 million, and its current ratio is now 4, how much can it expand its inventories (financing the expansion with its line of credit) before the target current ratio is violated?

**ST-2.** Given the following information for Neff Industries, evaluate the firm's performance for the years 2000 and 2001 by using the "four-question approach."

Neff Industries Balance Sheet
For December 31, 2000, and December 31, 2001

| | 2000 | 2001 |
|---|---|---|
| Cash | $ 9,000 | $ 500 |
| Accounts receivable | 12,500 | 16,000 |
| Inventories | 29,000 | 45,500 |
| Total current assets | $ 50,500 | $ 62,000 |
| Land | 20,000 | 26,000 |
| Buildings and equipment | 70,000 | 100,000 |
| Less: allowance for depreciation | 28,000 | 38,000 |
| Total fixed assets | $ 62,000 | $ 88,000 |
| Total assets | $112,500 | $150,000 |
| Accounts payable | $ 10,500 | $ 22,000 |
| Bank notes | 17,000 | 47,000 |
| Total current liabilities | $ 27,500 | $ 69,000 |
| Long-term debt | 28,750 | 22,950 |
| Common stock | 31,500 | 31,500 |
| Retained earnings | 24,750 | 26,550 |
| Total liabilities and equity | $112,500 | $150,000 |

Neff Industries Income Statement
For the Years Ended December 31, 2000, and December 31, 2001

| | 2000 | 2001 |
|---|---|---|
| Sales | $125,000 | $160,000 |
| Cost of goods sold | 75,000 | 96,000 |
| Gross profit | $ 50,000 | $ 64,000 |
| Operating expenses | | |
| Fixed cash operating expense | 21,000 | 21,000 |
| Variable operating expense | 12,500 | 16,000 |
| Depreciation | 4,500 | 10,000 |
| Total operating expense | $ 38,000 | $ 47,000 |
| Earnings before interest and taxes | $ 12,000 | $ 17,000 |
| Interest | 3,000 | 6,100 |
| Earnings before taxes | $ 9,000 | $ 10,900 |
| Taxes | 4,500 | 5,450 |
| Net income | $ 4,500 | $ 5,450 |

**INDUSTRY NORMS:**

| | |
|---|---|
| Current ratio | 1.80 |
| Acid-test ratio | 0.70 |
| Average collection period | 37.00 |
| Inventory turnover | 2.50 |
| Debt ratio | 0.58 |
| Times interest earned | 3.80 |
| Gross profit margin | 38% |
| Operating profit margin | 10% |
| Total asset turnover | 1.14 |
| Fixed asset turnover | 1.40 |
| Operating income return on investment | 11.4% |
| Return on total assets | 4.0% |
| Return on common equity | 9.5% |

## STUDY PROBLEMS (SET A)

**3-1A.** (*Balance sheet analysis*) Complete the following balance sheet using the following information provided:

| | | | |
|---|---|---|---|
| Cash | | Accounts payable | 100,000 |
| Accounts receivable | | Long-term debt | |
| Inventory | | Total liabilities | |
| Current assets | | Common equity | |
| Net fixed assets | 1,500,000 | Total | $2,100,000 |
| Total | $2,100,000 | | |

| | |
|---|---|
| Current ratio = 6.0 | Total asset turnover = 1.0 |
| Inventory turnover = 8.0 | Average collection period = 30 days |
| Debt ratio = 20% | Gross profit margin = 15% |

**3-2A.** (*Ratio analysis*) The Mitchem Marble Company has a target current ratio of 2.0 but has experienced some difficulties financing its expanding sales in the past few months. The firm has a current ratio of 2.5 with current assets of $2.5 million. If Mitchem expands its receivables and inventories using its short-term line of credit, how much additional short-term funding can it borrow before its current ratio standard is reached?

**3-3A.** (*Ratio analysis*) The balance sheet and income statement for the J. P. Robard Mfg. Company are as follows:

Balance Sheet ($000)

| | |
|---|---|
| Cash | $ 500 |
| Accounts receivable | 2,000 |
| Inventories | 1,000 |
| Current assets | 3,500 |
| Net fixed assets | 4,500 |
| Total assets | $8,000 |
| Accounts payable | $1,100 |
| Accrued expenses | 600 |
| Short-term notes payable | 300 |
| Current liabilities | $2,000 |
| Long-term debt | 2,000 |
| Owners' equity | 4,000 |
| Total liabilities and owners' equity | $8,000 |

Income Statement ($000)

| | |
|---|---|
| Net sales (all credit) | $8,000 |
| Cost of goods sold | (3,300) |
| Gross profit | $4,700 |
| Operating expenses[a] | (3,000) |
| Operating income | $1,700 |
| Interest expense | (367) |
| Earnings before taxes | $1,333 |
| Income taxes (40%) | (533) |
| Net income | $ 800 |

[a]Includes depreciation expense of $500 for the year.

Calculate the following ratios:

| | |
|---|---|
| Current ratio | Debt ratio |
| Times interest earned | Average collection period |
| Inventory turnover | Fixed asset turnover |
| Total asset turnover | Gross profit margin |
| Operating profit margin | Return on equity |
| Operating income return on investment | |

**3-4A.** (*Analyzing operating income return on investment*) The R. M. Smithers Corporation earned an operating profit margin of 10 percent based on sales of $10 million and total assets of $5 million last year.

**a.** What was Smithers's total asset turnover ratio?

**b.** During the coming year, the company president has set a goal of attaining a total asset turnover of 3.5. How much must firm sales rise, other things being the same, for the goal to be achieved? (State your answer in both dollars and percentage increase in sales.)

**c.** What was Smithers's operating income return on investment last year? Assuming the firm's operating profit margin remains the same, what will the operating income return on investment be next year if the total asset turnover goal is achieved?

**3-5A.** (*Using financial ratios*) The Brenmar Sales Company had a gross profit margin (gross profits/sales) of 30 percent and sales of $9 million last year. Seventy-five percent of the firm's sales are on credit and the remainder are cash sales. Brenmar's current assets equal $1.5 million, its current liabilities equal $300,000, and it has $100,000 in cash plus marketable securities.

**a.** If Brenmar's accounts receivable are $562,500, what is its average collection period?

**b.** If Brenmar reduces its average collection period to 20 days, what will be its new level of accounts receivable?

**c.** Brenmar's inventory turnover ratio is nine times. What is the level of Brenmar's inventories?

**3-6A.** (*Ratio analysis*) Using the following financial statements for Pamplin Inc.:

**a.** Compute the following ratios for both 2000 and 2001.

| | Industry Norm |
|---|---|
| Current ratio | 5.00 |
| Acid-test (quick) ratio | 3.00 |
| Inventory turnover | 2.20 |
| Average collection period | 90.00 |
| Debt ratio | 0.33 |
| Times interest earned | 7.00 |
| Total asset turnover | 0.75 |
| Fixed asset turnover | 1.00 |
| Operating profit margin | 20% |
| Return on common equity | 9% |

**b.** How liquid is the firm?

**c.** Is management generating adequate operating profit on the firm's assets?

**d.** How is the firm financing its assets?

**e.** Are the common stockholders receiving a good return on their investment?

Pamplin, Inc., Balance Sheet at 12/31/00 and 12/31/01

| Assets | 2000 | 2001 |
|---|---|---|
| Cash | $ 200 | $ 150 |
| Accounts receivable | 450 | 425 |
| Inventory | 550 | 625 |
| Current assets | $1,200 | $1,200 |
| Plant and equipment | $2,200 | $2,600 |
| Less: accumulated depreciation | (1,000) | (1,200) |
| Net plant and equipment | $1,200 | $1,400 |
| Total assets | $2,400 | $2,600 |

(*continued*)

| Liabilities and Owners' Equity | 2000 | 2001 |
|---|---|---|
| Accounts payable | $ 200 | $ 150 |
| Notes payable—current (9%) | 0 | 150 |
| Current liabilities | $ 200 | $ 300 |
| Bonds (8 1/3% interest) | $ 600 | $ 600 |
| Owners' equity | | |
| Common stock | $ 300 | $ 300 |
| Paid-in capital | 600 | 600 |
| Retained earnings | 700 | 800 |
| Total owners' equity | $1,600 | $1,700 |
| Total liabilities and owners' equity | $2,400 | $2,600 |

Pamplin, Inc., Income Statement for Years Ending 12/31/00 and 12/31/01

| | | 2000 | | 2001 |
|---|---|---|---|---|
| Sales (all credit) | | $1,200 | | $1,450 |
| Cost of goods sold | | 700 | | 850 |
| Gross profit | | $ 500 | | $ 600 |
| Operating expenses | 30 | | 40 | |
| Depreciation | 220 | 250 | 200 | 240 |
| Operating income | | $ 250 | | $ 360 |
| Interest expense | | 50 | | 64 |
| Net income before taxes | | $ 200 | | $ 296 |
| Taxes (40%) | | 80 | | 118 |
| Net income | | $ 120 | | $ 178 |

**3-7A.** (*Financial ratios—investment analysis*) The annual sales for Salco, Inc., were $4.5 million last year. The firm's end-of-year balance sheet appeared as follows:

| | | | |
|---|---|---|---|
| Current assets | $ 500,000 | Liabilities | $1,000,000 |
| Net fixed assets | 1,500,000 | Owners' equity | 1,000,000 |
| | $2,000,000 | | $2,000,000 |

The firm's income statement for the year was as follows:

| | |
|---|---|
| Sales | $4,500,000 |
| Less: cost of goods sold | (3,500,000) |
| Gross profit | $1,000,000 |
| Less: operating expenses | (500,000) |
| Operating income | $ 500,000 |
| Less: interest expense | (100,000) |
| Earnings before taxes | $ 400,000 |
| Less: taxes (50%) | (200,000) |
| Net income | $ 200,000 |

**a.** Calculate Salco's total asset turnover, operating profit margin, and operating income return on investment.

**b.** Salco plans to renovate one of its plants, which will require an added investment in plant and equipment of $1 million. The firm will maintain its present debt ratio of .5 when financing the new investment and expects sales to remain constant, while the operating profit margin will rise to 13 percent. What will be the new operating income return on investment for Salco after the plant renovation?

**c.** Given that the plant renovation in part (b) occurs and Salco's interest expense rises by $50,000 per year, what will be the return earned on the common stockholders' investment? Compare this rate of return with that earned before the renovation.

**3-8A.** (*Ratio analysis of loan request*) The T. P. Jarmon Company manufactures and sells a line of exclusive sportswear. The firm's sales were $600,000 for the year just ended, and its total assets exceeded $400,000. The company was started by Mr. Jarmon just 10 years ago and has been profitable every year since its inception. The Chief Financial Officer for the firm, Brent Vehlim, has decided to seek a line of credit from the firm's bank totaling $80,000. In the past, the company has relied on its suppliers to finance a large part of its needs for inventory. However, in recent months, tight money conditions have led the firm's suppliers to offer sizable cash discounts to speed up payments for purchases. Mr. Vehlim wants to use the line of credit to supplant a large portion of the firm's payables during the summer months, which are the firm's peak seasonal sales period.

The firm's two most recent balance sheets were presented to the bank in support of its loan request. In addition, the firm's income statement for the year just ended was provided to support the loan request. These statements are as follows:

T. P. Jarmon Company, Balance Sheet for 12/31/00 and 12/31/01

| **Assets** | **2000** | **2001** |
|---|---|---|
| Cash | $ 15,000 | $ 14,000 |
| Marketable securities | 6,000 | 6,200 |
| Accounts receivable | 42,000 | 33,000 |
| Inventory | 51,000 | 84,000 |
| Prepaid rent | 1,200 | 1,100 |
| Total current assets | $115,200 | $138,300 |
| Net plant and equipment | 286,000 | 270,000 |
| Total assets | $401,200 | $408,300 |

| **Liabilities and Equity** | **2000** | **2001** |
|---|---|---|
| Accounts payable | $ 48,000 | $ 57,000 |
| Notes payable | 15,000 | 13,000 |
| Accruals | 6,000 | 5,000 |
| Total current liabilities | $ 69,000 | $ 75,000 |
| Long-term debt | $160,000 | $150,000 |
| Common stockholders' equity | $172,200 | $183,300 |
| Total liabilities and equity | $401,200 | $408,300 |

T. P. Jarmon Company, Income Statement for the Year Ended 12/31/01

| | | |
|---|---|---|
| Sales (all credit) | | $600,000 |
| Less: cost of goods sold | | 460,000 |
| Gross profits | | $140,000 |
| Less: operating and interest expenses | | |
| General and administrative | $30,000 | |
| Interest | 10,000 | |
| Depreciation | 30,000 | |
| Total | | 70,000 |
| Earnings before taxes | | $ 70,000 |
| Less: taxes | | 27,100 |
| Net income available to common stockholders | | $ 42,900 |
| Less: cash dividends | | 31,800 |
| Change in retained earnings | | $ 11,100 |

Jan Fama, associate credit analyst for the Merchants National Bank of Midland, Michigan, was assigned the task of analyzing Jarmon's loan request.

**a.** Calculate the financial ratios for 2001 corresponding to the industry norms provided as follows:

| | Ratio Norm |
|---|---|
| Current ratio | 1.8 |
| Acid-test ratio | 0.9 |
| Debt ratio | 0.5 |
| Times interest earned | 10.0 |
| Average collection period | 20.0 |
| Inventory turnover (based on cost of goods sold) | 7.0 |
| Return on common equity | 12.0% |
| Gross profit margin | 25.0% |
| Operating income return on investment | 16.8% |
| Operating profit margin | 14.0% |
| Total asset turnover | 1.20 |
| Fixed asset turnover | 1.80 |
| Return on assets | 6.0% |
| Return on equity | 12.0% |

**b.** Which of the ratios reported in the industry norms do you feel should be most crucial in determining whether the bank should extend the line of credit?

**c.** Use the DuPont analysis to evaluate the firm's financial position.

**3-9A.** (*Ratio analysis*) Intel's income statement for 1999 and the balance sheet for December 31, 1999 follow.

Compute the financial ratios for Intel for 1999, and using the industry norms, evaluate the firm in the following areas:

(1) liquidity
(2) operating profitability
(3) financing policies
(4) return on the shareholders' investment

Intel Income Statement for Year Ending 1999 ($ millions)

| | 1999 |
|---|---|
| Sales | $29,389,000 |
| Cost of goods sold | 9,061,000 |
| Gross profit | $20,328,000 |
| Selling, general, and administrative expense | 6,983,000 |
| Depreciation | 3,186,000 |
| Operating profit | $10,159,000 |
| Interest expense | 41,000 |
| Nonoperating income (expense) | 1,502,000 |
| Special items | (392,000) |
| Pretax income | $11,228,000 |
| Total income taxes | 3,914,000 |
| Net income | $ 7,314,000 |

Intel Balance Sheet, for December 31, 1999 ($ millions)

| | 1999 |
|---|---|
| **ASSETS** | |
| Cash and equivalents | $11,788,000 |
| Accounts receivable | 3,700,000 |
| Inventories | 1,478,000 |
| Other current assets | 853,000 |
| Total current assets | $17,819,000 |
| Gross plant, property, and equipment | 24,360,000 |
| Accumulated depreciation | 12,645,000 |
| Net plant, property, and equipment | $11,715,000 |
| Other investments | 7,911,000 |
| Intangibles | 4,322,000 |
| Other assets | 2,082,000 |
| Total assets | $43,849,000 |
| **LIABILITIES** | |
| Notes payable | $ 230,000 |
| Accounts payable | 1,370,000 |
| Taxes payable | 1,695,000 |
| Accrued expenses | 3,195,000 |
| Other current liabilities | 609,000 |
| Total current liabilities | $ 7,099,000 |
| Long-term debt | 955,000 |
| Deferred taxes | 3,130,000 |
| Total liabilities | $11,184,000 |
| **EQUITY** | |
| Preferred stock | 130,000 |
| Common stock | 3,334 |
| Capital surplus | 7,312,666 |
| Retained earnings | 25,219,000 |
| Common equity | $32,535,000 |
| Total equity | 32,665,000 |
| Total liabilities and equity | $43,849,000 |

| Industry Norms | |
|---|---|
| **Firm liquidity** | |
| Current ratio | 2.01 |
| Acid-test ratio | 1.66 |
| Average collection period | 72.64 |
| Accounts receivable turnover | 5.02 |
| Inventory turnover | 4.42 |
| **Operating profitability** | |
| Operating income return on investment | 9% |
| Operating profit margin | 13% |
| Total asset turnover | 0.69 |
| Accounts receivable turnover | 5.02 |
| Inventory turnover | 4.42 |
| Fixed asset turnover | 2.27 |
| **Financing decisions** | |
| Debt ratio | 0.44 |
| Times interest earned | 8.87 |
| **Return on equity** | |
| Return on equity | 12% |

## INTEGRATIVE PROBLEM

Following are the 1995 to 1999 financial statements for both Reebok International LTD and Nike, two head-to-head competitors in the athletic footwear industry.

1. Evaluate the two respective firms in terms of their financial performance over time (1995–1999) as it relates to (1) liquidity, (2) operating profitability, (3) financing assets, and (4) the shareholders' (common equity) return on investment. (A computer spreadsheet is extremely helpful here and will save you some time in doing the assignment.) In fact, the financial statements for these two companies are available at *http://nikebiz.com/invest/main_ar.shtml* and *http://www.reebok.com/about_reebok/investor_relations/default.asp.*
2. Compare the two firms' financial performance. How are they different and how are they similar?

Reebok International LTD, Financial Statements, 1995–1999

**Income Statements ($ millions)**

| | 1995 | 1996 | 1997 | 1998 | 1999 |
|---|---|---|---|---|---|
| Sales | $3,481 | $3,479 | $3,644 | $3,225 | $2,900 |
| Cost of goods sold | 2,084 | 2,108 | 2,255 | 1,996 | 1,746 |
| Gross profit | $1,398 | $1,370 | $1,389 | $1,228 | $1,154 |
| Selling, general, and administrative expense | 1,000 | 1,066 | 1,069 | 1,043 | 972 |
| Depreciation | 35 | 40 | 43 | 45 | 43 |
| Operating profit | $ 364 | $ 265 | $ 276 | $ 140 | $ 139 |
| Interest expense | 26 | 42 | 64 | 61 | 50 |
| Nonoperating income/expense | 10 | 15 | 5 | (8) | 1 |
| Special items | (72) | 0 | (58) | (35) | (62) |
| Pretax income | $ 276 | $ 238 | $ 158 | $ 37 | $ 28 |
| Total income taxes | 100 | 84 | 12 | 12 | 10 |
| Minority interest | 11 | 15 | 10 | 1 | 7 |
| Net income | $ 165 | $ 139 | $ 135 | $ 24 | $ 11 |

**Balance Sheets ($ millions)**

| | 1995 | 1996 | 1997 | 1998 | 1999 |
|---|---|---|---|---|---|
| Assets | | | | | |
| Cash and equivalents | $ 80 | $ 232 | $ 210 | $ 180 | $ 282 |
| Net receivables | 507 | 591 | 562 | 518 | 417 |
| Inventories | 635 | 545 | 564 | 535 | 415 |
| Other current assets | 121 | 96 | 130 | 129 | 129 |
| Total current assets | $1,343 | $1,463 | $1,465 | $1,362 | $1,243 |
| Gross plant, property, and equipment | 336 | 357 | 354 | 399 | 422 |
| Accumulated depreciation | 144 | 172 | 197 | 226 | 244 |
| Net plant, property, and equipment | $ 192 | $ 185 | $ 157 | $ 173 | $ 178 |
| Other assets | 121 | 138 | 134 | 205 | 143 |
| Total assets | $1,656 | $1,786 | $1,756 | $1,740 | $1,564 |
| Liabilities | | | | | |
| Long-term debt due in 1 year | $ 1 | $ 53 | $ 121 | $ 87 | $ 185 |
| Notes payable | 67 | 33 | 41 | 48 | 28 |
| Accounts payable | 166 | 196 | 192 | 203 | 154 |
| Taxes payable | 48 | 66 | 4 | 83 | 8 |
| Accrued expenses | 145 | 169 | 219 | 192 | 249 |
| Total current liabilities | $ 432 | $ 517 | $ 577 | $ 612 | $ 624 |
| Long-term debt | 254 | 854 | 639 | 554 | 370 |
| Minority interest | 31 | 34 | 32 | 32 | — |
| Other liabilities | — | — | — | — | 41 |
| Total liabilities | $ 717 | $1,405 | $1,249 | $1,199 | $1,035 |

*(continued)*

| Balance Sheets ($ millions) | 1995 | 1996 | 1997 | 1998 | 1999 |
|---|---|---|---|---|---|
| Equity | | | | | |
| Preferred stock | $ 39 | $ — | $ — | $ 17 | $ — |
| Common stock | 1 | 1 | 1 | 1 | 1 |
| Retained earnings | 1,497 | 998 | 1,124 | 1,141 | 1,146 |
| Less: treasury stock | 603 | 618 | 618 | 618 | 618 |
| Total equity | $ 934 | $ 381 | $ 507 | $ 541 | $ 529 |
| Total liabilities and equity | $1,656 | $1,786 | $1,756 | $1,740 | $1,564 |

Nike Financial Statements, 1995–1999

| Income Statements ($ millions) | 1995 | 1996 | 1997 | 1998 | 1999 |
|---|---|---|---|---|---|
| Sales | $4,761 | $6,471 | $9,187 | $9,553 | $8,777 |
| Cost of goods sold | 2,805 | 3,825 | 5,365 | 5,881 | 5,295 |
| Gross profit | $1,955 | $2,646 | $3,822 | $3,672 | $3,482 |
| Selling, general, and administrative expense | 1,210 | 1,589 | 2,304 | 2,624 | 2,427 |
| Depreciation | 84 | 119 | 158 | 204 | 218 |
| Operating profit | $ 661 | $ 938 | $1,360 | $ 844 | $ 837 |
| Interest expense | 24 | 40 | 55 | 67 | 51 |
| Nonoperating income/expense | 24 | 1 | 8 | 5 | (10) |
| Special items | (11) | — | (18) | (130) | (30) |
| Pretax income | $650 | $ 899 | $1,295 | $ 653 | $ 746 |
| Total income taxes | 250 | 346 | 499 | 253 | 295 |
| Preferred dividends | 0 | 0 | 0 | 0 | 0 |
| Net income | $400 | $ 553 | $ 796 | $ 400 | $ 451 |

| Balance Sheets ($ millions) | 1995 | 1996 | 1997 | 1998 | 1999 |
|---|---|---|---|---|---|
| Assets | | | | | |
| Cash and equivalents | $ 216 | $ 262 | $ 445 | $ 109 | $ 198 |
| Net receivables | 1,053 | 1,346 | 1,754 | 1,674 | 1,556 |
| Inventories | 630 | 931 | 1,339 | 1,397 | 1,199 |
| Prepaid expenses | 74 | 94 | 157 | 196 | 191 |
| Other current assets | 73 | 93 | 136 | 157 | 121 |
| Total current assets | $2,046 | $2,727 | $3,831 | $3,533 | $3,265 |
| Gross plant, property, and equipment | 891 | 1,048 | 1,426 | 1,820 | 2,001 |
| Accumulated depreciation | 336 | 404 | 503 | 667 | 736 |
| Net plant, property, and equipment | $ 555 | $ 643 | $ 922 | $1,153 | $1,266 |
| Intangibles | 496 | 475 | 464 | 436 | 427 |
| Other assets | 46 | 106 | 144 | 276 | 290 |
| Total assets | $3,143 | $3,952 | $5,361 | $5,397 | $5,248 |
| Liabilities | | | | | |
| Long-term debt due in one year | $ 32 | $ 7 | $ 2 | $ 2 | $ 1 |
| Notes payable | 397 | 445 | 553 | 480 | 419 |
| Accounts payable | 298 | 455 | 687 | 585 | 373 |
| Taxes payable | 36 | 79 | 54 | 29 | — |
| Accrued expenses | 345 | 480 | 571 | 609 | 654 |
| Total current liabilities | $1,108 | $1,467 | $1,867 | $1,704 | $1,447 |
| Long-term debt | 11 | 10 | 296 | 379 | 386 |
| Deferred taxes | 18 | 2 | 5 | — | — |
| Other liabilities | 42 | 41 | 37 | 52 | 80 |
| Total liabilities | $1,178 | $1,520 | $2,205 | $2,136 | $1,913 |

*(continued)*

**Balance Sheets ($ millions)**

| | 1995 | 1996 | 1997 | 1998 | 1999 |
|---|---|---|---|---|---|
| Equity | | | | | |
| Common stock | 3 | 3 | 3 | 3 | 3 |
| Capital surplus | 122 | 155 | 211 | 263 | 334 |
| Retained earnings | 1,839 | 2,274 | 2,942 | 2,996 | 2,998 |
| Total equity | $1,965 | $2,432 | $3,156 | $3,262 | $3,335 |
| Total liabilities and equity | $3,143 | $3,952 | $5,361 | $5,397 | $5,248 |

## STUDY PROBLEMS (SET B)

**3-1B.** (*Balance sheet analysis*) Complete the following balance sheet using this information:

| | | | |
|---|---|---|---|
| Cash | | Accounts payable | 100,000 |
| Accounts receivable | | Long-term debt | |
| Inventory | | Total liabilities | |
| Current assets | | Common equity | |
| Net fixed assets | 1,000,000 | Total | 1,300,000 |
| Total | $1,300,000 | | |

| | |
|---|---|
| Current ratio = 3.0 | Total asset turnover = .5 |
| Inventory turnover = 10.0 | Average collection period = 45 days |
| Debt ratio = 30% | Gross profit margin = 30% |

**3-2B.** (*Ratio analysis*) The Allandale Office Supply Company has a target current ratio of 2.0 but has experienced some difficulties financing its expanding sales in the past few months. At present, the firm has a current ratio of 2.75 with current assets of $3 million. If Allandale expands its receivables and inventories using its short-term bank loan (a current liability), how much additional short-term funding can it borrow before its current ratio standard is reached?

**3-3B.** (*Ratio analysis*) The balance sheet and income statement for the Simsboro Paper Company are as follows:

| **Balance Sheet ($000)** | | **Income Statement ($000)** | |
|---|---|---|---|
| Cash | $1,000 | Net sales (all credit) | $7,500 |
| Accounts receivable | 1,500 | Cost of goods sold | (3,000) |
| Inventories | 1,000 | Gross profit | $4,500 |
| Current assets | $3,500 | Operating expenses[a] | (3,000) |
| Net fixed assets | 4,500 | Operating income (EBIT) | $1,500 |
| Total assets | $8,000 | Interest expense | (367) |
| Accounts payable | $1,000 | Earnings before taxes | $1,133 |
| Accrued expenses | 600 | Income taxes (40%) | (453) |
| Short-term notes payable | 200 | Net income | $ 680 |
| Current liabilities | $1,800 | | |
| Long-term debt | 2,100 | | |
| Owners' equity | 4,100 | | |
| Total liabilities and owners' equity | $8,000 | | |

[a]Includes depreciation expense of $500 for the year.

Calculate the following ratios:

| | |
|---|---|
| Current ratio | Debt ratio |
| Times interest earned | Average collection period |
| Inventory turnover | Fixed asset turnover |
| Total asset turnover | Gross profit margin |
| Operating profit margin | Return on equity |
| Operating income return on investment | |

**3-4B.** (*Analyzing operating income return on investment*) The R. M. Senchack Corporation earned an operating profit margin of 6 percent based on sales of $11 million and total assets of $6 million last year.

**a.** What was Senchack's total asset turnover ratio?

**b.** During the coming year, the company president has set a goal of attaining a total asset turnover of 2.5. How much must firm sales rise, other things being the same, for the total asset goal to be achieved? (State your answer in both dollars and as a percent increase in sales.)

**c.** What was Senchack's operating income return on investment last year? Assuming the firm's operating profit margin remains the same, what will the operating income return on investment be next year if the total asset turnover goal is achieved?

**3-5B.** (*Using financial ratios*) Brenda Smith, Inc. had a gross profit margin (gross profits ÷ sales) of 25 percent and sales of $9.75 million last year. Seventy-five percent of the firm's sales are on credit and the remainder are cash sales. Smith's current assets equal $1,550,000, its current liabilities equal $300,000, and it has $150,000 in cash plus marketable securities.

**a.** If Smith's accounts receivable are $562,500, what is its average collection period?

**b.** If Smith reduces its average collection period to 20 days, what will be its new level of accounts receivable?

**c.** Smith's inventory turnover ratio is eight times. What is the level of Smith's inventories?

**3-6B.** (*Ratio analysis*) Using J. B. Chavez Corporation's financial statements:

**a.** Compute the following ratios for both 2000 and 2001.

| | Industry Norm |
|---|---|
| Current ratio | 5.00 |
| Acid-test (quick) ratio | 3.00 |
| Inventory turnover | 2.20 |
| Average collection period | 90.00 |
| Debt ratio | 0.33 |
| Times interest earned | 7.00 |
| Total asset turnover | 0.75 |
| Fixed asset turnover | 1.00 |
| Operating profit margin | 20% |
| Operating income return on investment | 15% |
| Return on common equity | 13.43% |

**b.** How liquid is the firm?

**c.** Is management generating adequate operating profit on the firm's assets?

**d.** How is the firm financing its assets?

**e.** Are the common stockholders receiving a good return on their investment?

J. B. Chavez Corporation, Balance Sheet at 12/31/00 and 12/31/01

| Assets | 12/31/00 | 12/31/01 | Liabilities and Owners' Equity | 12/31/00 | 12/31/01 |
|---|---|---|---|---|---|
| Cash | $ 225 | $ 175 | Accounts payable | $ 250 | $ 115 |
| Accounts receivable | 450 | 430 | Notes payable—current (9%) | 0 | 115 |
| Inventory | 575 | 625 | Current liabilities | $ 250 | $ 230 |
| Current assets | $1,250 | $1,230 | Bonds | $ 600 | $ 600 |
| Plant and equipment | $2,200 | $2,500 | Owners' equity | | |
| Less: accumulated depreciation | (1,000) | (1,200) | Common stock | $ 300 | $ 300 |
| Net plant and equipment | $1,200 | $1,300 | Paid-in capital | 600 | 600 |
| Total assets | $2,450 | $2,530 | Retained earnings | 700 | 800 |
| | | | Total owners' equity | $1,600 | $1,700 |
| | | | Total liabilities and owners' equity | $2,450 | $2,530 |

J. B. Chavez Corporation, Income Statement for the Years Ending 12/31/00 and 12/31/01

| | | 2000 | | 2001 |
|---|---|---|---|---|
| Sales | | $1,250 | | $1,450 |
| Cost of goods sold | | 700 | | 875 |
| Gross profit | | $ 550 | | $ 575 |
| Operating expenses | 30 | | 45 | |
| Depreciation | 220 | 250 | 200 | 245 |
| Net operating income | | $ 300 | | $ 330 |
| Interest expense | | 50 | | 60 |
| Net income before taxes | | $ 250 | | $ 270 |
| Taxes (40%) | | 100 | | 108 |
| Net income | | $ 150 | | $ 162 |

**3-7B.** (*Financial ratios—investment analysis*) The annual sales for Mel's, Inc. were $5 million last year. The firm's end-of-year balance sheet appeared as follows:

| | | | |
|---|---|---|---|
| Current assets | $ 500,000 | Liabilities | $1,000,000 |
| Net fixed assets | $1,500,000 | Owners' equity | $1,000,000 |
| | $2,000,000 | | $2,000,000 |

The firm's income statement for the year was as follows:

| | |
|---|---|
| Sales | $5,000,000 |
| Less: cost of goods sold | 3,000,000 |
| Gross profit | $2,000,000 |
| Less: operating expenses | 1,500,000 |
| Operating income | $ 500,000 |
| Less: interest expense | 100,000 |
| Earnings before taxes | $ 400,000 |
| Less: taxes (40%) | 160,000 |
| Net income | $ 240,000 |

**a.** Calculate Mel's total asset turnover, operating profit margin, and operating income return on investment.

**b.** Mel's plans to renovate one of its plants, which will require an added investment in plant and equipment of $1 million. The firm will maintain its present debt ratio of .5 when financing the new investment and expects sales to remain constant, whereas the operating profit margin will rise to 13 percent. What will be the new operating income return on investment for Mel's after the plant renovation?

**c.** Given that the plant renovation in part (b) occurs and Mel's interest expense rises by $40,000 per year, what will be the return earned on the common stockholders' investment? Compare this rate of return with that earned before the renovation.

**3-8B.** (*Ratio analysis of loan request*) RPI Inc. is a manufacturer and retailer of high-quality sports clothing and gear. The firm was started several years ago by a group of serious outdoors enthusiasts who felt there was a need for a firm that could provide quality products at reasonable prices. The result was RPI Inc. Since its inception, the firm has been profitable, with sales that last year totaled $700,000 and assets in excess of $400,000. The firm now finds its growing sales outstrip its ability to finance its inventory needs and estimates that it will need to borrow $100,000 in a short-term loan from its bank during the coming year.

The firm's most recent financial statements were provided to its bank as support for the firm's loan request. Joanne Peebie, a loan analyst trainee for the Morristown Bank and Trust, has been assigned the task of analyzing the firm's loan request.

RPI Inc., Balance Sheets for 12/31/00 and 12/31/01

| Assets | 2000 | 2001 | Liabilities and Stockholders' Equity | 2000 | 2001 |
|---|---|---|---|---|---|
| Cash | $ 16,000 | $ 17,000 | Accounts payable | $ 48,000 | $ 55,000 |
| Marketable securities | 7,000 | 7,200 | Notes payable | 16,000 | 13,000 |
| Accounts receivable | 42,000 | 38,000 | Accruals | 6,000 | 5,000 |
| Inventory | 50,000 | 93,000 | Total current liabilities | $ 70,000 | $ 73,000 |
| Prepaid rent | 1,200 | 1,100 | Long-term debt | $160,000 | $150,000 |
| Total current assets | $116,200 | $156,300 | Common stockholders' equity | $172,200 | $223,300 |
| Net plant and equipment | 286,000 | 290,000 | Total liabilities and equity | $402,200 | $446,300 |
| Total assets | $402,200 | $446,300 | | | |

RPI Inc., Income Statement for the Year Ended 12/31/01

| | | |
|---|---|---|
| Sales (all credit) | | $700,000 |
| Less: cost of goods sold | | 500,000 |
| Gross profits | | $200,000 |
| Less: operating and interest expenses | | |
| General and administrative | $50,000 | |
| Interest | 10,000 | |
| Depreciation | 30,000 | |
| Total | | 90,000 |
| Profit before taxes | | $110,000 |
| Less: taxes | | 27,100 |
| Net income available to common stockholders | | $ 82,900 |
| Less: cash dividends | | 31,800 |
| Change in retained earnings | | $ 51,100 |

**a.** Calculate RPI's financial ratios corresponding to these industry norms provided for 2001:

| | Ratio Norm | | Ratio Norm |
|---|---|---|---|
| Current ratio | 1.80 | Return on total assets | 6.0% |
| Acid-test ratio | 0.90 | Gross profit margin | 25.0% |
| Debt ratio | 0.50 | Operating income return on investment | 16.8% |
| Times interest earned | 10.00 | Operating profit margin | 14.0% |
| Average collection period | 20.00 | Total asset turnover | 1.20 |
| Inventory turnover (based on cost of goods sold) | 7.00 | Fixed asset turnover | 1.80 |
| | | Return on equity | 12.0% |

b. Which of the ratios reported in these industry norms do you feel should be most crucial in determining whether the bank should extend the loan?

**c.** Use the DuPont analysis to evaluate the firm's financial position as of December 31, 2001.

**3-9B.** (*Ratio analysis*) Dell Computer's income statement for 1999 and the balance sheet for December 31, 1999 follow.

Compute the financial ratios for Dell Computer for 1999, and using your industry norms, evaluate the firm in the following areas:

**(1)** liquidity
**(2)** operating profitability
**(3)** financing policies
**(4)** return on the shareholders' investment

Dell Computer Income Statement for Year Ending 1999

| | 1999 |
|---|---|
| Sales | $25,265,000 |
| Cost of goods sold | 19,891,000 |
| Gross profit | $ 5,374,000 |
| Selling, general, and administrative expense | 2,761,000 |
| Depreciation | 156,000 |
| Operating profit | $ 2,457,000 |
| Interest expense | 34,000 |
| Nonoperating income (expense) | 222,000 |
| Special items | (194,000) |
| Pretax income | $ 2,451,000 |
| Total income taxes | 785,000 |
| Net income | $ 1,666,000 |

Dell Computer Balance Sheet for December 31, 1999 ($ in thousands)

| | 1999 |
|---|---|
| **ASSETS** | |
| Cash and equivalents | $ 4,132,000 |
| Accounts receivable | 2,678,000 |
| Inventories | 391,000 |
| Other current assets | 480,000 |
| Total current assets | $ 7,681,000 |
| Gross plant, property, and equipment | 1,059,000 |
| Accumulated depreciation | 294,000 |
| Net plant, property, and equipment | $ 765,000 |
| Other investments | 2,721,000 |
| Intangibles | 304,000 |
| Other assets | — |
| Total assets | $11,471,000 |
| **LIABILITIES** | |
| Accounts payable | $ 3,538,000 |
| Accrued expenses | 337,000 |
| Other current liabilities | 1,317,000 |
| Total current liabilities | $ 5,192,000 |
| Long-term debt | 508,000 |
| Other liabilities | 463,000 |
| Total liabilities | $ 6,163,000 |
| **EQUITY** | |
| Common stock | $ 25,750 |
| Capital surplus | 3,557,250 |
| Retained earnings | 1,725,000 |
| Total equity | $ 5,308,000 |
| Total liabilities and equity | $11,471,000 |

| Industry Norms | |
|---|---|
| **Firm liquidity** | |
| Current ratio | 1.49 |
| Acid-test ratio | 1.36 |
| Average collection period | 53.38 |
| Accounts receivable turnover | 6.84 |
| Inventory turnover | 20.87 |
| **Operating profitability** | |
| Operating income return on investment | 9% |
| Operating profit margin | 6% |
| Total asset turnover | 1.58 |
| Accounts receivable turnover | 6.84 |
| Inventory turnover | 20.87 |
| Fixed asset turnover | 13.02 |
| **Financing decisions** | |
| Debt ratio | 0.47 |
| Times interest earned | 14.79 |
| **Return on equity** | |
| Return on equity | 13% |

## SELF-TEST SOLUTIONS

**ST-1.** Note that Ray's current inventory expansion is as follows:

$$\text{current ratio} = \$6{,}000{,}000/\text{current liabilities} = 4$$

Thus, the firm's level of current liabilities is $1,500,000. If the expansion in inventories is financed entirely with borrowed funds, then the change in inventories is equal to the change in current liabilities, and the firm's current ratio after the expansion can be defined as follows:

$$\text{current ratio} = \frac{\$6{,}000{,}000 + \text{change in inventory}}{\$1{,}500{,}000 + \text{change in inventory}} = 3$$

Note that we set the new current ratio equal to the firm's target of 3. Solving for the change in inventory in the previous equation, we determine that the firm can expand its inventories by $750,000, finance the expansion with current liabilities, and still maintain its target current ratio.

**ST-2.a.**

Neff Industries, Ratio Analysis

| | Industry Averages | Actual 2000 | Actual 2001 |
|---|---|---|---|
| Current ratio | 1.80 | 1.84 | 0.90 |
| Acid-test ratio | 0.70 | 0.78 | 0.24 |
| Average collection periods (based on a 365-day year and end-of-year figures) | 37.00 | 36.50 | 36.50 |
| Inventory turnover | 2.50 | 2.59 | 2.11 |
| Debt ratio | 58% | 50% | 61.3% |
| Times interest earned | 3.80 | 4.00 | 2.79 |
| Gross profit margin | 38% | 40% | 40% |
| Operating profit margin | 10% | 9.6% | 10.6% |
| Total asset turnover | 1.14 | 1.11 | 1.07 |
| Fixed asset turnover | 1.40 | 2.02 | 1.82 |
| Operating income return on investment | 11.4% | 10.7% | 11.3% |
| Return on common equity | 9.5% | 8.0% | 9.4% |
| Return on total assets | 4.0% | 4.0% | 3.6% |

**b.** Neff's liquidity in 2001 is poor, as suggested by the low current ratio and acid-test ratio: also, inventories are turning slowly. In 2001, management is doing a satisfactory job at generating profits on the firm's operating assets, as indicated by the operating income return on investment. Note that the operating income return on investment in 2001 is average, owing to a slightly above-average operating profit margin combined with a slightly below-average asset turnover. The problem with the asset turnover ratio comes from a slow inventory turnover.

Neff has increased its use of debt to the point of using slightly more debt than the average company in the industry. As a result, the firm's coverage of interest has decreased to a point well below the industry norm.

As of 2001, Neff's return on equity is average because the operating income return on investment and the debt ratio are average.

# FINANCIAL FORECASTING, PLANNING, AND BUDGETING

Forecasting is an integral part of the planning process, yet there are countless examples where our ability to predict the future has been simply awful. During the mid-1980s oil prices were roughly $30 a barrel, and many firms were developing new reserves that would cost well over this amount to produce. Why? Oil prices were projected to continue to rise and many thought the price might eventually reach $50 a barrel by the end of the decade. Then in January 1986, the collapse of the oil producer's cartel, in combination with the benefits of energy conservation efforts, produced a dramatic drop in oil prices to below $10 a barrel. ● If forecasting the future is so difficult, and plans are built on forecasts, why do firms engage in planning efforts? The answer, oddly enough, does not lie in the accuracy of the firm's projections, for planning offers its greatest value when the future is the most uncertain. The reason is that planning is the process of thinking about what the future might bring and devising strategies for dealing with the likely outcomes. Planning is thinking in advance, and thinking in advance provides an opportunity to devise contingency plans that can be quickly and easily initiated should the need arise. This increased speed of response to uncertain events means that the firm can reduce the costs of responding to adverse circumstances and quickly respond to take advantage of unexpected opportunities. ● Financial managers spend a significant portion of their time planning for their firm's uncertain future. Financial planning entails collecting sales forecasts from marketing

**LEARNING OBJECTIVES**

After reading this chapter, you should be able to

1. Use the percent of sales method to forecast the financing requirements of a firm.
2. Describe the limitations of the percent of sales forecast method.
3. Calculate a firm's sustainable rate of growth.
4. Prepare a cash budget and use it to evaluate the amount and timing of a firm's financing needs.

personnel and production plans from operations, and then combining them to make projections of the firm's future financing requirements. In this chapter, we will see that the financial plan takes the form of a set of pro forma or planned financial statements and a cash budget. These statements provide a benchmark to which day-to-day actual results can be compared. If actual performance results begin to deviate from the plan, then this provides the financial manager with an early warning signal that her financing plans may be inadequate and appropriate actions can be taken: for example, contacting the firm's banker to request an increase in the firm's prearranged credit line.

**CHAPTER PREVIEW**

Chapter 4 has two primary objectives: First, we develop an appreciation for the financial manager's role in financial forecasting. Firms go through an annual planning and budgeting exercise in which the financial manager is asked to bring together revenue forecasts from marketing and production plans from operations to develop a forecast of the firm's cash flow. This cash flow forecast then becomes the basis for estimating the firm's financing requirements. Second, we review the pro forma (planned) income statement, the pro forma balance sheet, and the cash budget. These statements constitute the principal elements of the firm's financial forecast and serve as a benchmark against which future performance can be compared.

This chapter emphasizes **Principle 3: Cash—Not Profits—Is King,** and **Principle 7: The Agency Problem—Managers won't work for owners unless it's in their best interest.** Firms pay bills and dividends with cash and investors make mortgage payments using cash not profits. In addition, financial planning entails the construction of detailed budgets that can be used as an oversight tool for monitoring the activities of the firm's employees.

**RELATE TO THE BIG PICTURE**

Financial decisions are made today in light of our expectations of an uncertain future. Financial forecasting involves making estimates of the future financing requirements of the firm. **Principle 3: Cash—Not Profits—Is King** speaks directly to this problem. Remember that effective financial management requires that consideration be given to cash flow and when it is received or dispersed.

## FINANCIAL FORECASTING

OBJECTIVE 1 

Forecasting in financial management is used to estimate a firm's future financial needs. If the financial manager has not attempted to anticipate his firm's future financing requirements, then a crisis occurs every time the firm's cash inflows fall below its cash outflows. Proper planning means anticipating and preparing for those times in every firm's future when it will need to obtain additional financing and also when the firm will have excess cash. For example, the financing requirements of growth firms frequently outstrip the firm's ability to generate cash. Planning for growth means that the financial manager can anticipate the firm's financing requirements and plan for them well in advance of the need. Advance planning means the financial manager can explore more alternatives and obtain the most favorable set of financing terms available.

The basic steps involved in predicting those financing needs are the following: **Step 1:** Project the firm's sales revenues and expenses over the planning period. **Step 2:** Estimate the levels of investment in current and fixed assets that are necessary to support the projected sales. **Step 3:** Determine the firm's financing needs throughout the planning period.

## Sales Forecast

The key ingredient in the firm's planning process is the *sales forecast.* This projection is generally derived using information from a number of sources. At a minimum, the sales forecast for the coming year would reflect (1) any past trends in sales that are expected to carry through into the new year, and (2) the influence of any events that might materially affect those trends.[1] An example of the latter would be the initiation of a major advertising campaign or a change in the firm's pricing policy.

## Forecasting Financial Variables

Traditional financial forecasting takes the sales forecast as a given and makes projections of its impact on the firm's various expenses, assets, and liabilities. The amount of financing—as we will see—can vary greatly if sales grow by 1 percent versus 5 percent or 10 percent. The amount of the variation depends on the interplay of the key variables that determine the firm's financing requirements.

## Percent of Sales Method of Financial Forecasting

The most commonly used method for making these projections is the percent of sales method. The **percent of sales method** involves estimating the level of an expense, asset, or liability for a future period as a percent of the sales forecast. The percentage used can come from the most recent financial statement as a percent of current sales, from an average computed over several years, from the judgment of the analyst, or from some combination of these sources.

**Percent of sales method** Estimating the level of an expense, asset, or liability for a future period as a percent of the sales forecast.

Table 4-1 presents a complete example of the use of the percent of sales method of financial forecasting. In this example, each item in the firm's balance sheet that varies with sales is converted to a percentage of 2000 sales of $10 million. The forecast of the new balance for each item is then calculated by multiplying this percentage times the $12 million in projected sales for the 2001 planning period. This method of forecasting future financing is not as precise or detailed as the method using a cash budget, which is presented later; however, it offers a relatively low-cost and easy-to-use first approximation of the firm's financing needs for a future period.

Note that in the example in Table 4-1, both current and fixed assets are assumed to vary with the level of firm sales. This means that the firm does not have sufficient productive capacity to absorb a projected increase in sales. Thus, if sales were to rise by $1, fixed assets would rise by 40¢, or 40 percent of the projected increase in sales. Note that if the fixed assets the firm currently owns were sufficient to support the projected level of new sales (such as when the firm has excess capacity), these assets should not be allowed to vary with sales. If this were the case, then fixed assets would not be converted to a percent of sales and would be projected to remain unchanged for the period being forecast.

Also, we note that accounts payable and accrued expenses are the only liabilities allowed to vary with sales. Both of these accounts might reasonably be expected to rise and fall with

[1]A complete discussion of forecast methodologies is outside the scope of this book. The interested reader will find the following references helpful: F. Gerard Adams, *The Business Forecasting Revolution* (Oxford: Oxford University Press, 1986); C. W. J. Granger, *Forecasting in Business and Economics,* 2d ed. (Boston: Academic Press, 1989); and Paul Newbold and Theodore Bos, *Introductory Business Forecasting* (Cincinnati: Southwestern, 1990).

**TABLE 4-1**
Using the Percent of Sales Method to Forecast Future Financing Requirements

| Assets | Present (2000) | Percent of Sales (2000 Sales = $10M) | Projected (Based on 2001 Sales = $12M) | |
|---|---|---|---|---|
| Current assets | $2.0M | $\frac{\$2M}{\$10M} = 20\%$ | | $.2 \times \$12M = \$2.4M$ |
| Net fixed assets | $4.0M | $\frac{\$4M}{\$10M} = 40\%$ | | $.4 \times \$12M = \$4.8M$ |
| Total | $6.0M | | | $7.2M |
| **Liabilities and Owners' Equity** | | | | |
| Accounts payable | $1.0M | $\frac{\$1M}{\$10M} = 10\%$ | | $.10 \times \$12M = \$1.2M$ |
| Accured expenses | 1.0M | $\frac{\$1M}{\$10M} = 10\%$ | | $.10 \times \$12M = \$1.2M$ |
| Notes payable | .5M | NA[a] | no change | .5M |
| Long-term debt | $2.0M | NA[a] | no change | 2.0M |
| Total liabilities | $4.5M | | | $4.9M |
| Common stock | $ .1M | NA[a] | no change | $ .1M |
| Paid-in capital | .2M | NA[a] | no change | .2M |
| Retained earnings | 1.2M | | $\$1.2M + [.05 \times \$12M \times (1 - .5)] =$ | 1.5M[b] |
| Common equity | $1.5M | | | $1.8M |
| Total | $6.0M | | Total financing provided | $6.7M |
| | | | Discretionary financing needed | .5M[c] |
| | | | Total | $7.2M |

[a]Not applicable. These account balances are assumed not to vary with sales.
[b]Projected retained earnings equals the beginning level ($1.2M) plus projected net income less any dividends paid. In this case, net income is projected to equal 5 percent of sales, and dividends are projected to equal half of net income: $.05 \times \$12M \times (1 - .5) = \$300{,}000$.
[c]Discretionary financing needed equals projected total assets ($7.2M) less projected total liabilities ($4.9M) less projected common equity ($1.8), or $\$7.2M - 4.9M - 1.8M = \$500{,}000$.

**Spontaneous sources of financing**
Sources of financing that arise naturally during the course of business. Accounts payable is a primary example.

**Discretionary financing**
Sources of financing that require an explicit decision on the part of the firm's management every time funds are raised.

the level of firm sales; hence the use of the percent of sales forecast. Because these two categories of current liabilities normally vary directly with the level of sales, they are often referred to as **spontaneous sources of financing.** Chapter 18, which discusses working-capital management, has more to say about these forms of financing. Notes payable, long-term debt, common stock, and paid-in capital are not assumed to vary directly with the level of firm sales. These sources of financing are termed **discretionary,** in that the firm's management must make a conscious decision to seek additional financing using any one of them. An example of discretionary financing is a bank note that requires that negotiations be undertaken and an agreement signed setting forth the terms and conditions for the financing. Finally, we note that the level of retained earnings does vary with estimated sales. The predicted change in the level of retained earnings equals the estimated after-tax profits (projected net income) equal to 5 percent of sales, or $600,000 less the common stock dividends of $300,000.

Thus using the example from Table 4-1, we estimate that firm sales will increase from $10 million to $12 million, which will cause the firm's needs for total assets to rise to $7.2 million. These assets will then be financed by $4.9 million in existing liabilities plus spontaneous liabilities; $1.8 million in owner funds, including $300,000 in retained earnings from next year's sales; and finally, $500,000 in discretionary financing, which can be raised by issuing notes payable, selling bonds, offering an issue of stock, or some combination of these sources. By far the most frequently used source of discretionary financing

**FINANCE MATTERS**

## Alcoa Implements Real Time Manufacturing System to Replace Forecasts

In 1998, Alcoa announced it would reduce manufacturing costs by \$1.1 billion by the end of 2000. By mid-2000, the firm had realized savings of \$832 million. The key to its success has been implementation of the Alcoa Business System, an adaptation of Toyota's production methods that focus on managing the business in real time.

Managing in real time requires accurate, live information in order to produce in response to actual demand rather than to forecasts. It also means the use of lots of other modern manufacturing techniques like just-in-time inventory control, small-batch production, flexible production lines, quick machine tool changes, and minimal waste of materials. This all sounds great, but how do you make it work? The key to Alcoa's success has been moving production decisions to the workers. A worker who has a problem with equipment or product defect summons a leader who is charged with fixing the problem on the spot. The manufacturing process is a 'pull' system in which workers in upstream processes respond to demand requests from workers downstream. Workers often negotiate with coworkers to buy and sell their inputs and outputs with others in the process.

Results of the change in the manufacturing process have increased inventory turns in Brazil to 60 times per year, and in Mississippi, the customer delivery time has been reduced from 3 weeks to just 2 days. At its Massena, New York, plant, the speed of production increased fourfold while work-in-process inventories were reduced by 85 percent. Company-wide, Alcoa was able to reduce inventories by more than \$250 million while increasing sales to just under \$1 billion.

Furthermore, Alcoa believes it can multiply these savings when suppliers and customers are integrated into the system. Integrating supplier and customer systems requires trust and impeccable reliability from all parties. By focusing on reducing costs and improving responsiveness, Alcoa will continue to revolutionize its manufacturing process and be a leader in the aluminum industry.

Source: Adapted from Thomas A. Stewart, "How Cisco and Alcoa Make Real Time Work." *Fortune,* May 29, 2000.

is a bank loan. As we learn later when we study financial policy, if the need for financing persists, then the firm may later issue bonds or stock to retire the bank loan.

In summary, we can estimate the firm's needs for discretionary financing, using the percent of sales method of financial forecasting, by following a four-step procedure:

Step 1: Convert each asset and liability account that varies directly with firm sales to a percent of the current year's sales, for example:

$$\frac{\text{current assets}}{\text{sales}} = \frac{\$2\text{M}}{\$10\text{M}} = .2 \text{ or } 20\%$$

Step 2: Project the level of each asset and liability account in the balance sheet using its percent of sales multiplied by projected sales or by leaving the account balance unchanged where the account does not vary with the level of sales, for example:

projected current assets =

$$\text{projected sales} + \frac{\text{current assets}}{\text{sales}} = \$12\text{M} \times .2 = \$2.4\text{M}$$

Step 3: Project the addition to retained earnings available to help finance the firm's operations. This equals projected net income for the period less planned common stock dividends, for example:

projected addition to retained earnings =

$$\text{projected sales} \times \frac{\text{net income}}{\text{sales}} \times \left(1 - \frac{\text{cash dividends}}{\text{net income}}\right)$$

$$= \$12\text{M} \times .05 \times [1 - .5] = \$300{,}000$$

Step 4: Project the firm's need for discretionary financing as the projected level of total assets less projected liabilities and owners' equity, for example:

discretionary financing needed =

projected total assets − projected total liabilities − projected owners' equity

= \$7.2M − \$4.9M − \$1.8M = \$500,000

## The Discretionary Financing Needed (DFN) Model

In the preceding discussion, we estimated *DFN* (discretionary financing needed) as the difference in projected total assets and the sum of projected liabilities and owners' equity. We can estimate the projected discretionary financing needs, $DFN_{t+1}$, directly using the predicted change in sales and corresponding changes in assets, liabilities, and owners' equity as follows:

$$DFN_{t+1} = \begin{matrix}\text{projected}\\ \text{change in}\\ \text{assets}_{t+1}\end{matrix} - \begin{matrix}\text{projected}\\ \text{change in}\\ \text{liabilities}_{t+1}\end{matrix} - \begin{matrix}\text{projected}\\ \text{change in}\\ \text{owners' equity}_{t+1}\end{matrix} \quad \textbf{(4-1)}$$

To calculate $DFN_{t+1}$ we must estimate each of the components found in equation 4-1. For example, we can project the firm's need for assets using the relationship between assets and sales for the current year multiplied by the projected change in sales for the coming year:

$$\begin{matrix}\text{projected}\\ \text{change in}\\ \text{assets}_{t+1}\end{matrix} = \left[\frac{\text{assets}_t}{\text{sales}_t}\right] \times [\text{sales}_{t+1} - \text{sales}_t]$$

Similarly, the projected change in liabilities can be calculated as the product of the ratio of total firm liabilities to sales for the current year and the projected change in firm sales:

$$\begin{matrix}\text{projected}\\ \text{change in}\\ \text{liabilities}_{t+1}\end{matrix} = \left[\frac{\text{liabilities}_t}{\text{sales}_t}\right] \times [\text{sales}_{t+1} - \text{sales}_t]$$

We can project the anticipated change in the firm's common equity for the coming year by first estimating net income for the coming year as the product of the net profit margin for the coming year, $NPM_{t+1}$, and the projected level of firm sales, and then multiplying projected net income by the percent of net income that is retained and not paid out in dividends. Note that $b$ is the percent of firm net income paid in dividends such that $(1 - b)$ is the fraction of net income that is retained. How are we to estimate $NPM_{t+1}$? One approach that can be used is to simply use the net profit margin for the current period, $NPM_t$. However, if sales are expected to change, then the firm's net profit margin will probably change as well, so using $NPM_t$ is only a rough approximation.

$$\begin{matrix}\text{projected}\\ \text{change in}\\ \text{owners' equity}_{t+1}\end{matrix} = [NPM_{t+1} \times \text{sales}_{t+1}] \times (1 - b)$$

Now let's define the terms we have been using with some care:

- $assets_t$ = those assets in period $t$ that are expected to change in proportion to the level of sales
- $sales_t$ = the level of sales for the period $t$
- $liabilities_t$ = the liabilities in period $t$ that are expected to change in proportion to the level of sales

- $NPM_{t+1}$ = net profit margin projected for period $t+1$
- $b$ = dividend payout ratio or dividends as a percent of net income; the fraction of the firm's net income that it plans to retain, therefore, is $(1-b)$

In the preceding example, we assumed that all of the firm's assets, accounts payable, and accrued expenses vary in proportion to sales. Notes payable and long-term debt did not change from the current to projected year. Using the numbers from our example, we estimate $DFN_{2001}$ as follows:

$$\text{projected change in assets}_{2001} = \left[\frac{\$2M + 4M}{10M}\right] \times [\$12M - 10M] = \$1.2M$$

$$\text{projected change in liabilities}_{2001} = \left[\frac{\$1M + 1M}{\$10M}\right] \times [\$12M - 10M] = \$.4M$$

$$\text{projected change in owners' equity}_{2001} = [0.5 \times \$12M] \times (1 - .5) = \$.3M$$

$$DFN_{2001} = \$1.2M - .4M - .3M = \$.5M \text{ or } \$500{,}000$$

## Analyzing the Effects of Profitability and Dividend Policy on DFN

Using the *DFN* model, we can quickly and easily evaluate the sensitivity of our projected financing requirements to changes in key variables. For example, using the information from the preceding example, we evaluate the effect of net profit margins (*NPM*) equal to 1 percent, 5 percent, and 10 percent in combination with dividend payout ratios of 30 percent, 50 percent, and 70 percent as follows:

Discretionary Financing Needed for Various Net Profit Margins and Dividend Payout Ratios

| Net Profit Margin | Dividend Payout Ratios (Dividends ÷ Net Income) | | |
|---|---|---|---|
| | **30%** | **50%** | **70%** |
| 1% | $716,000 | $740,000 | $764,000 |
| 5% | 380,000 | 500,000 | 620,000 |
| 10% | (40,000) | 200,000 | 440,000 |

Let's first consider the dividend payout ratio. The higher the dividend payout percentage ($b$), the lower the retention percentage $(1-b)$. Thus, as we just saw earlier when discussing the *DFN* model, this means that the firm will have less to reinvest and will need more discretionary financing. Consider the row corresponding to a 5 percent net profit margin. If the firm pays out 30 percent of its earnings in dividends (retains 70 percent), then its need for discretionary financing is estimated to be $380,000, whereas a 70 percent dividend payout ratio requires $620,000 in discretionary financing. Later, in Chapter 17, we will learn that firms tend to have dividend policies that are similar to other firms in their industry. For example, firms in high-growth industries such as Intel pay out a very small fraction of their earnings in dividends. In fact, until 1992 Intel paid no dividends to its common stockholders, and the firm currently pays less than 6 percent of its earnings in dividends. Thus, a firm's discretionary financing needs are in part a function of its growth prospects and industry practice with respect to the payment of dividends.

Discretionary financing needs are also a function of the firm's profitability. The higher the net profit margin is, all things being the same, the lower the firm's need for discretionary financing will be. For example, with a 1 percent net profit margin and 30 percent dividend payout ratio, the firm will require $716,000 in discretionary financing. If the net profit margin were 10 percent with the same payout ratio, the firm would have surplus funds of $40,000. Thus a firm's discretionary financing needs swing from year to year with the firm's profitability, which is, to a large degree, due to economy-wide and industry influences, and are outside the control of the firm's management. Financial planning is particularly crucial for firms subject to wide variability in their year to year profitability.

**CONCEPT CHECK**

1. If we cannot predict the future perfectly, then why do firms engage in financial forecasting?
2. Why are sales forecasts so important to developing a firm's financial forecast?
3. What is the percent of sales method of financial forecasting?
4. What are some examples of spontaneous and discretionary sources of financing?

## LIMITATIONS OF THE PERCENT OF SALES FORECAST METHOD

OBJECTIVE 2 

The percent of sales method of financial forecasting provides reasonable estimates of a firm's financing requirements only where asset requirements and financing sources can be accurately forecast as a constant percent of sales. For example, predicting inventories using the percent of sales method involves the following predictive equation:

$$\text{inventories}_{t+1} = \frac{\text{inventories}_t}{\text{sales}_t} \times \text{sales}_{t+1}$$

Figure 4-1a depicts this predictive relationship. Note that the percent of sales predictive model is simply a straight line that passes through the origin (that is, has a zero intercept). Thus the percent of sales model is appropriate where there is no level of inventories that remains constant regardless of the level of firm sales, and inventories rise and fall in direct proportion to changes in the level of sales.

There are some fairly common instances in which this type of relationship fails to describe the relationship between an asset category and sales. Two such examples involve assets for which there are scale economics and assets that must be purchased in discrete quantities ("lumpy assets").

Economies of scale are sometimes realized from investing in certain types of assets such as finished goods inventories. For example, a retail drugstore requires a full range of drug products in order to operate. This inventory can be replenished on a daily basis in response to firm sales. However, a constant level of investment is necessary to open the doors of the enterprise. This means that these assets do not increase in direct proportion to sales. Figure 4-1b reflects one instance in which the firm realizes economies of scale from its investment in inventory. Note that inventories as a percent of sales decline from 120 percent where sales are $100, to 30 percent where sales equal $1,000. This reflects the fact that there is a fixed component of inventories (in this case $100) that the firm must have on hand regardless of the level of sales, plus a variable component (20 percent of sales). In this instance, the predictive equation for inventories is as follows:

$$\text{inventories}_t = \text{a} + \text{b sales}_t$$

In this example, a is equal to 100 and b equals .20.

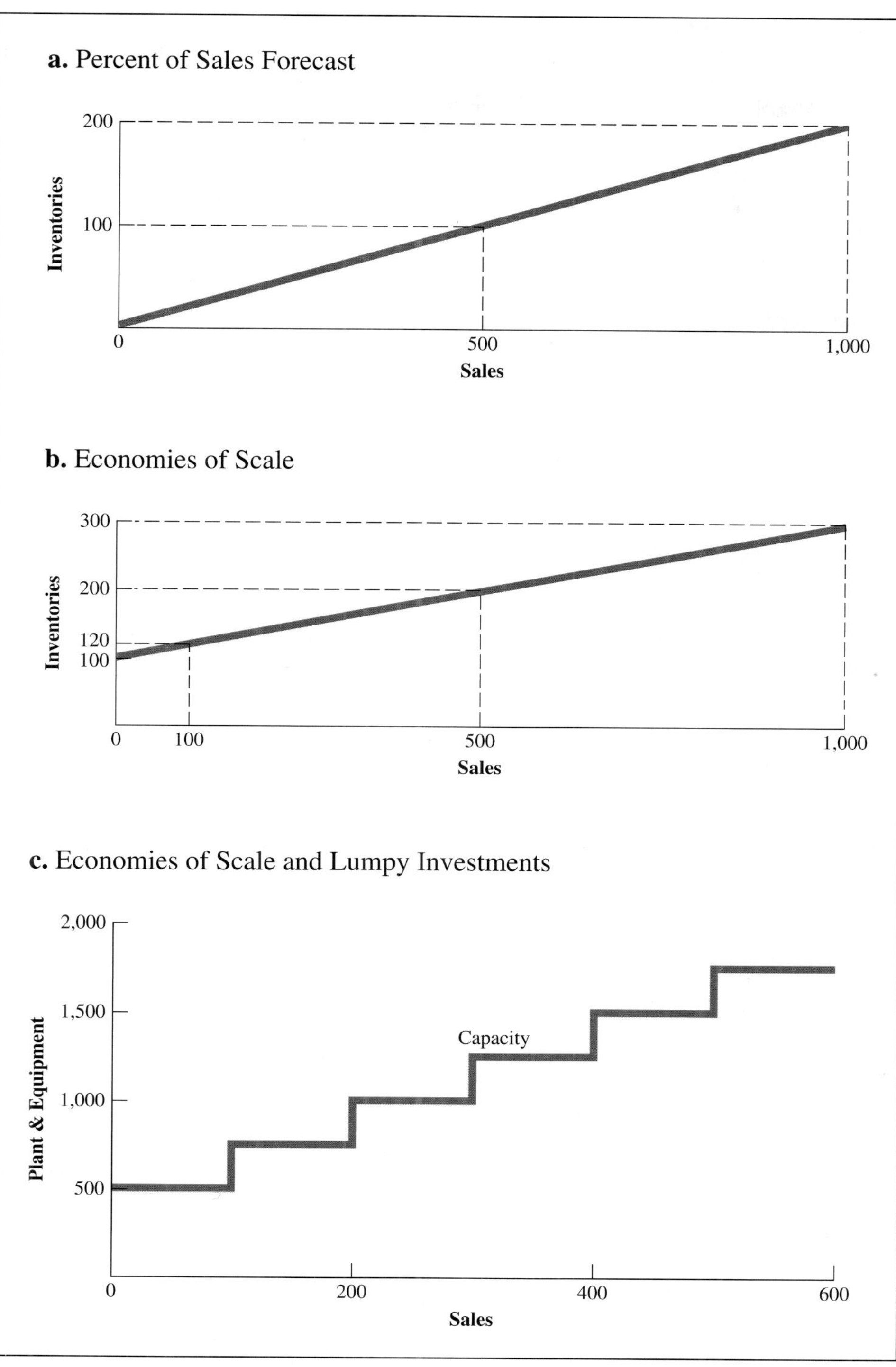


**FIGURE 4-1**
The Relationship Between Inventories and Sales

Figure 4-1c is an example of *lumpy assets*—that is, assets that must be purchased in large, nondivisible components such as plant and equipment. For example, firms in the semiconductor industry now invest approximately $2 billion in each new wafer fab (factory) they build. They then spend the next 2 to 3 years filling the fab's productive capacity with production. Consequently, when a block of assets is purchased, it creates excess capacity until sales grow to the point where the capacity is fully used. The result is a step function such as the one depicted in Figure 4-1c. Thus, if the firm does not expect sales to exceed the current capacity of its plant and equipment, there would be no projected need for added plant and equipment capacity.

**CONCEPT CHECK**

1. What, in words, is the fundamental relationship (equation) used in making percent of sales forecasts?
2. Under what circumstances does a firm violate the basic relationship underlying the percent of sales forecast method?

## THE SUSTAINABLE RATE OF GROWTH

OBJECTIVE 3 

Growing firms require expenditures for new assets that outstrip the firm's ability to finance those purchases using internally generated profits. This means that the firm must go out and borrow the additional funds or issue new equity. Because selling new shares of stock is a very involved and expensive endeavor, the question arises as to how fast a firm can grow without having to borrow more than the firm's desired debt ratio and without having to sell more stock. This growth rate is referred to as the sustainable rate of growth. Specifically, the **sustainable rate of growth** ($g^*$) represents the rate at which a firm's sales can grow if it wants to maintain its present financial ratios and does not want to resort to the sale of new equity shares.[2] A simple formula can be derived for $g^*$ where we assume that a firm's assets and liabilities all grow at the same rate as its sales; that is,

**Sustainable rate of growth** The maximum rate of growth in sales that the firm can sustain while maintaining its present capital structure (debt and equity mix) and without having to sell new common stock.

$$\text{sustainable rate of growth } (g^*) = ROE(1 - b) \tag{4-2}$$

*ROE* is the firm's return on equity, which was defined in Chapter 3 as follows:

$$ROE = \frac{\text{net income}}{\text{common equity}}$$

and $b$ is the firm's dividend payout ratio, that is, $\frac{\text{dividends}}{\text{net income}}$. The term $(1 - b)$ is sometimes referred to as the **plowback ratio** because it indicates the fraction of earnings that are reinvested or plowed back into the firm. Thus, $g^* = ROE \times \text{plowback ratio}$.

**Plowback ratio** The percent of a firm's earnings that are reinvested in the firm.

Equation (4-2) is deceptively simple. Recall that *ROE* can also be written as follows:

$$ROE = \left(\frac{\text{net income}}{\text{sales}}\right) \times \left(\frac{\text{sales}}{\text{assets}}\right) \times \left(\frac{\text{assets}}{\text{common equity}}\right)$$

Consequently, a firm's sustainable rate of growth is determined by its *ROE* (i.e., its anticipated net profit margin, asset turnover, and capital structure), as well as its dividend policy.

[2]For an extensive discussion of this concept, see Robert C. Higgins, "Sustainable Growth with Inflation," *Financial Management* (Autumn 1981): 36–40.

### EXAMPLE: CALCULATING THE SUSTAINABLE RATE OF GROWTH

Consider the following three firms:

| Firm | Net Profit Margin | Asset Turnover | Leverage (assets/equity) | Plowback Ratio | $g^*$ |
|---|---|---|---|---|---|
| A | 15% | 1 | 1.2 | 50% | 9.0% |
| B | 15% | 1 | 1.2 | 100% | 18.0% |
| C | 15% | 1 | 1.5 | 100% | 22.5% |

Comparing Firms A and B, we see that the only difference is that Firm A pays out half its earnings in common dividends (i.e., plows back half its earnings) whereas Firm B retains or plows back all of its earnings. The net result is that Firm B, with its added source of internal equity financing, can grow at twice the rate of Firm A (18 percent compared to only 9 percent). Similarly, comparing Firms B and C, we note that they differ in that Firm B finances 83 percent of its assets with equity (i.e., 1 ÷ 1.2 = .83) whereas Firm C finances 67 percent (1 ÷ 1.5 = .67) of its assets with equity. The result is that Firm C's sustainable rate of growth is 22.5 percent since it needs $0.67 per $1.00 of assets financed from equity versus $0.83 in equity financing for firm B. This compares to only 18 percent for Firm B.

Before leaving our discussion of the sustainable rate of growth concept, it is important that we stress the underlying assumptions behind equation 4-2. For this equation to accurately depict a firm's sustainable rate of growth, the following assumptions must hold: First, the firm's assets must vary as a constant percent of sales (i.e., even fixed assets expand and contract directly with the level of firm sales). Second, the firm's liabilities must all vary directly with firm sales. This means that the firm's management will expand its borrowing (both spontaneous and discretionary) in direct proportion with sales to maintain its present ratio of debt to assets. Finally, the firm pays out a constant proportion of its earnings in common stock dividends regardless of the level of firm sales. Since all three of these assumptions are only rough approximations to the way that firms actually behave, equation 4-2 provides a crude approximation of the firm's actual sustainable rate of growth. However, an estimate of $g^*$ using equation 4-2 can be a very useful first step in the firm's financial planning process.

### CONCEPT CHECK

1. What is a firm's sustainable rate of growth?
2. How is a firm's sustainable rate of growth related to the firm's profitability and dividend policy?

## FINANCIAL PLANNING AND BUDGETING

As we noted earlier, the primary virtue of the percent of sales method of financial forecasting is its simplicity. To obtain a more precise estimate of the amount and timing of a firm's future financing requirements requires that a cash budget be prepared. The percent of sales method of financial forecasting provides a very useful, low-cost forerunner to the development of the more detailed cash budget, which the firm will ultimately use to estimate its financing needs.

### RELATE TO THE BIG PICTURE

Elaborate cash budgets are needed so that firms can avoid a cash crisis when anticipated cash inflows fall below cash outflows. This is a direct reflection of **Principle 3: Cash—Not Profits—Is King.** It is cash flow and not accounting profits that pay the firm's bills. In addition, budgets are the critical tool of managerial control. **Principle 7: The Agency Problem—Managers won't work for owners unless it's in their best interest** speaks to the root source of the problem, and budgets provide one tool for attempting to deal with it. Specifically, budgets provide management with a tool for evaluating performance and consequently maintaining a degree of control over employee actions.

## Budget Functions

A *budget* is simply a forecast of future events. For example, students preparing for final exams make use of time budgets, which help them allocate their limited preparation time among their courses. Students also must budget their financial resources among competing uses, such as books, tuition, food, rent, clothes, and extracurricular activities.

Budgets perform three basic functions for a firm. First, they indicate the amount and timing of the firm's needs for future financing. Second, they provide the basis for taking corrective action in the event budgeted figures do not match actual or realized figures. Third, budgets provide the basis for performance evaluation. Plans are carried out by people, and budgets provide benchmarks that management can use to evaluate the performance of those responsible for carrying out those plans and, in turn, to control their actions. Thus budgets are valuable aids in both the planning and controlling aspects of the firm's financial management.

## The Cash Budget

**Cash budget**
A detailed plan of future cash receipts and disbursements.

The **cash budget** represents a detailed plan of future cash flows and is composed of four elements: cash receipts, cash disbursements, net change in cash for the period, and new financing needed.

To demonstrate the construction and use of the cash budget, consider Salco Furniture Company, Inc., a regional distributor of household furniture. Management is in the process of preparing a monthly cash budget for the upcoming period (January through April 2001). Salco's sales are highly seasonal, peaking in the months of February and March. The following information is used to prepare a cash budget:

- Roughly 30 percent of Salco's sales are collected 1 month after the sale and the balance (70 percent) is collected 2 months after the sale.
- Salco attempts to pace its purchases with its forecast of future sales. Purchases generally equal 60 percent of sales and are made 1 month in advance of anticipated sales. Payments are made in the month following the purchase. For example, January sales are estimated at \$60,000, thus December purchases are \$36,000 (.60 × \$60,000) and are paid in January.
- Wages, salaries, rent, and other cash expenses are recorded in Table 4-2, which gives Salco's cash budget for the 4-month period ended in April 2001.
- Additional expenditures are recorded in the cash budget related to the purchase of equipment in the amount of \$10,000 in January and the repayment of an \$8,000 loan in March.
- In January, Salco will pay \$4,000 in interest on its long-term debt. This interest expense corresponds to the period of January through March.

**TABLE 4-2**
Salco Furniture Co., Inc., Cash Budget for the 4 Months Ended April 30, 2001

| Worksheet | November | December | January | February | March | APRIL |
|---|---|---|---|---|---|---|
| Sales | $62,000 | $50,000 | $60,000 | $80,000 | $85,000 | $70,000 |
| Collections: | | | | | | |
| First month (30%) | | $18,600 | $15,000 | $18,000 | $24,000 | $25,500 |
| Second month (70%) | | $38,500 | $43,400 | $35,000 | $42,000 | $56,000 |
| Total collections | | $57,100 | $58,400 | $53,000 | $66,000 | $81,500 |
| Purchases (60% of next month's sales) | $30,000 | $36,000 | $48,000 | $51,000 | $42,000 | $39,000 |
| Payments (1-month lag) | | $30,000 | $36,000 | $48,000 | $51,000 | $42,000 |
| **CASH BUDGET** | | | | | | |
| **Cash receipts** | | | | | | |
| Collections (see above) | | $57,100 | $58,400 | $53,000 | $66,000 | $81,500 |
| **CASH DISBURSEMENTS** | | | | | | |
| Purchases | | $30,000 | $36,000 | $48,000 | $51,000 | $42,000 |
| Wages and salaries | | | 4,000 | 5,000 | 6,000 | 4,000 |
| Rent | | | 3,000 | 3,000 | 3,000 | 3,000 |
| Other expenses | | | 1,000 | 500 | 1,200 | 1,500 |
| Interest expense on existing debt | | | 4,000 | | 200 | |
| Taxes | | | | | 5,200 | |
| Purchases of equipment | | | 10,000 | | | |
| Loan repayment | | | | | 8,000 | |
| Total disbursements | | | $58,000 | $56,500 | $74,600 | $50,500 |
| Net monthly change | | | $400 | $(3,500) | $(8,600) | $31,000 |
| Plus: beginning cash balance | | | 10,000 | 10,400 | 10,000 | 10,000 |
| Less: interest on short-term borrowing | | | 0 | 0 | 31 | 117 |
| Equals: ending cash balance before short-term borrowing | | | 10,400 | 6,900 | 1,369 | 40,883 |
| Financing needed[a] | | | 0 | 3,100 | 8,631 | (11,731)[b] |
| Ending cash balance | | | 10,400 | 10,000 | 10,000 | 29,152 |
| Cumulative borrowing | | | 0 | 3,100 | 11,731 | 0 |

[a]The amount of financing that is required to raise the firm's ending cash balance up to its $10,000 desired cash balance.
[b]Negative financing needed simply means the firm has excess cash that can be used to retire a part of its short-term borrowing from prior months.

- Interest on the $8,000 short-term note for the period January through March equals $200 and is paid in March.
- A tax payment of $5,200 is made in March.
- Salco currently has a cash balance of $10,000 and maintains a minimum balance of $10,000 to meet any unanticipated shortfall in net cash flow.
- Additional borrowing necessary to maintain that minimum balance is estimated in the final section of Table 4-2. Borrowing takes place at the beginning of the month in which the funds are needed. Interest on borrowed funds equals 12 percent per annum, or 1 percent per month, and is paid in the month following the month in which funds are borrowed. Thus, interest on funds borrowed in February will be paid in March equal to 1 percent of the loan amount outstanding in February.
- The financing needed in Salco's cash budget indicates that the firm's cumulative short-term borrowing will be $3,100 at the end of February and $11,731 in March. In April, the firm will be able to repay all short-term debt incurred in February and March. Note

**FINANCE $ MATTERS**

### To Bribe or Not to Bribe

In many parts of the world, bribes and payoffs to public officials are considered the norm in business transactions. This raises a perplexing ethical question. If paying bribes is not considered unethical in a foreign country, should you consider it unethical to make these payments?

This situation provides an example of an ethical issue that gave rise to legislation. The Foreign Corrupt Practices Act of 1977 (as amended in the Omnibus Trade and Competitiveness Act of 1988) established criminal penalties for making payments to foreign officials, political parties, or candidates in order to obtain or retain business. Ethical problems are frequently found in the gray areas just outside the boundaries of current legislation and often lead to the passage of new legislation.

Consider the following question: If you were involved in negotiating an important business deal in a foreign country, and the success or failure of the deal hinged on whether you paid a local government official to help you consummate the deal, would you authorize the payment? Assume that the form of the payment is such that you do not expect to be caught and punished; for example, your company agrees to purchase supplies from a family member of the government official at a price slightly above the competitive price.

that the cash budget indicates not only the amount of financing needed during the period but also when the funds will be needed.

### Budget Period

There are no strict rules for determining the length of the budget period. However, as a general rule, it should be long enough to show the effect of management policies, yet short enough so that estimates can be made with reasonable accuracy. Applying this rule of thumb to the Salco example in Table 4-2, it appears that the 4-month budget period is too short. The reason is that we cannot tell whether the planned operations of the firm will be successful over the coming fiscal year. That is, for most of the first 4-month period, the firm is operating with a cash flow deficit. If this does not reverse in the latter 8 months of the year, then a reevaluation of the firm's plans and policies is clearly in order.

Longer-range budgets are also prepared in the form of the capital-expenditure budget. These budgets detail the firm's plans for acquiring plant and equipment over a 5-year, 10-year, or even longer period. Furthermore, firms often develop comprehensive long-range plans extending up to 10 years into the future. These plans are generally not as detailed as the annual cash budget, but they do consider such major components as sales, capital expenditures, new-product development, capital funds acquisition, and employment needs.

**CONCEPT CHECK**

1. What is a cash budget and how is it used in financial planning?
2. How long should a firm's budget period be?

## HOW FINANCIAL MANAGERS USE THIS MATERIAL

In the introduction, we pointed out examples that illustrate the difficulties involved in making financial forecasts. The difficulty of making a forecast, we learned, often varied directly with the value of the effort. That is, it is precisely where forecasts are most difficult that our attempts and the plans we formulate based upon the forecast are the most valuable.

Every business of any size makes and uses financial forecasts as an integral part of its planning process. The typical firm makes revenue and expense projections for at least 1 and usually 5 years. These forecasts are then used to develop pro forma financial statements that can be used to evaluate the financial condition of the firm if the forecast proves to be accurate. In addition, it is common practice to develop one or more contingency plans based on alternative sales and cost outcomes. The alternative scenarios frequently reflect optimistic and pessimistic scenarios.

The forecast methods used in practice can be varied. The firm may actually contract with a consulting firm for long-run forecasts that they feel demand skills not possessed by the finance staff. In the majority of the cases, however, the firm's finance personnel gather information concerning historical revenue and cost relationships and use this as the basis for developing the firm's financial forecast in conjunction with the firm's sales forecast. The sales forecast is frequently constructed by polling the heads of the firm's various operating divisions and then combining the results. In this way, the finance staff relies on the individuals who are directly responsible for the revenues being forecast.

## SUMMARY

This chapter develops the role of forecasting within the context of the firm's financial planning activities. Forecasts of the firm's sales revenues and related expenses provide the basis for projecting future financing needs. The most popular method for forecasting financial variables is the percent of sales method.

The percent of sales method presumes that the asset or liability being forecast is a constant percent of sales for all future levels of sales. There are instances where this assumption is not reasonable, and consequently, the percent of sales method does not provide reasonable predictions. One such instance arises where there are economies of scale in the use of the asset being forecast. For example, the firm may need at least $10 million in inventories to open its doors and operate even for sales as low as $100 million per year. If sales double to $200 million, inventories may only increase to $15 million. Thus, inventories do not increase with sales in a constant proportion. A second situation where the percent of sales method fails to work properly is where asset purchases are lumpy. That is, if plant capacity must be purchased in $50 million increments, then plant and equipment will not remain a constant percent of sales.

How serious are these possible problems and should we use the percent of sales method at all? Even in the face of these problems, the percent of sales method predicts reasonably well where predicted sales levels do not differ drastically from the level used to calculate the percent of sales. For example, if the current sales level used in calculating percent of sales for inventories is $40 million, then we can feel more comfortable forecasting the level of inventories corresponding to a new sales level of $42 million than if sales were predicted to rise to $60 million.

A firm's sustainable rate of growth is the maximum rate at which its sales can grow if it is to maintain its present financial ratios and not have to resort to issuing new equity. We calculate the sustainable rate of growth as follows:

$$\text{sustainable rate of growth } (g^*) = ROE\,(1 - b)$$

where $ROE$ is the return earned on common equity and $b$ is the dividend payout ratio (that is, the ratio of dividends to earnings). Consequently, a firm's sustainable rate of growth increases with ROE and decreases with a higher fraction of its earnings paid out in dividends.

The cash budget is the primary tool of financial forecasting and planning. It contains a detailed plan of future cash flow estimates and is comprised of four elements or segments: cash receipts, cash disbursements, net change in cash for the period, and new financing needed. Once prepared, the cash budget also serves as a tool for monitoring and controlling the firm's operations. By comparing actual cash receipts and disbursements to those in the cash budget, the financial manager can gain an appreciation for how well the firm is performing. In addition, deviations from the plan serve as an early warning system to signal the need for external financing in response to either the presence of future investment opportunities or poor business performance.

## KEY TERMS



**Cash budget, 110**
**Discretionary financing, 102**
**Percent of sales method, 101**
**Plowback ratio, 108**
**Spontaneous sources of financing, 102**
**Sustainable rate of growth, 108**

## STUDY QUESTIONS

**4-1.** Discuss the shortcomings of the percent of sales method of financial forecasting.

**4-2.** Explain how a fixed cash budget differs from a variable or flexible cash budget.

**4-3.** What two basic needs does a flexible (variable) cash budget serve?

**4-4.** What would be the probable effect on a firm's cash position of the following events?

- **a.** Rapidly rising sales
- **b.** A delay in the payment of accounts payable
- **c.** A more liberal credit policy on sales (to the firm's customers)
- **d.** Holding larger inventories

**4-5.** How long should the budget period be? Why would a firm not set a rule that all budgets be for a 12-month period?

**4-6.** A cash budget is usually thought of as a means of planning for future financing needs. Why would a cash budget also be important for a firm that had excess cash on hand?

**4-7.** Explain why a cash budget would be of particular importance to a firm that experiences seasonal fluctuations in its sales.

## SELF-TEST PROBLEMS

**ST-1.** (*Financial forecasting*) Use the percent of sales method to prepare a pro forma income statement for Calico Sales Co., Inc. Projected sales for next year equal $4 million. Cost of goods sold is expected to be 70 percent of sales, administrative expense equals $500,000, and depreciation expense is $300,000. Interest expense equals $50,000 and income is taxed at a rate of 40 percent. The firm plans to spend $200,000 during the period to renovate its office facility and will retire $150,000 in notes payable. Finally, selling expense equals 5 percent of sales.

**ST-2.** (*Cash budget*) Stauffer, Inc., has estimated sales and purchase requirements for the last half of the coming year. Past experience indicates that it will collect 20 percent of its sales in the month of the sale, 50 percent of the remainder 1 month after the sale, and the balance in the second month following the sale. Stauffer prefers to pay for half its purchases in the month of the purchase and the other half the following month. Labor expense for each month is expected to equal 5 percent of that month's sales, with cash payment being made in the month in which the expense is incurred. Depreciation expense is $5,000 per month; miscellaneous cash expenses are $4,000 per month and are paid in the month incurred. General and administrative expenses of $50,000 are recognized and paid monthly. A $60,000 truck is to be purchased in August and is to be depreciated on a straight-line basis over 10 years with no expected salvage value. The company also plans to pay a $9,000 cash dividend to stockholders in July. The company feels that a minimum cash balance of $30,000 should be maintained. Any borrowing will cost 12 percent annually, with interest paid in the month following the month in which the funds are borrowed. Borrowing takes place at the beginning of the month in which the need for funds arises. For example, if during the month of July, the firm should need to borrow $24,000 to maintain its $30,000 desired minimum balance, then $24,000 will be taken out on July 1 with interest owed for the entire month of July. Interest for the month of July would then be paid on August 1. Sales and purchase estimates are shown in the following chart. Prepare a cash budget for the months of July and August (cash on hand June 30 was $30,000, whereas sales for May and June were $100,000 and purchases were $60,000 for each of these months).

| Month | Sales | Purchases |
|---|---|---|
| July | $120,000 | $50,000 |
| August | 150,000 | 40,000 |
| September | 110,000 | 30,000 |

## STUDY PROBLEMS (SET A)

**4-1A.** (*Financial forecasting*) Zapatera Enterprises is evaluating its financing requirements for the coming year. The firm has only been in business for 1 year, but its Chief Financial Officer predicts that the firm's operating expenses, current assets, net fixed assets, and current liabilities will remain at their current proportion of sales.

Last year Zapatera had $12 million in sales with net income of $1.2 million. The firm anticipates that next year's sales will reach $15 million with net income rising to $2 million. Given its present high rate of growth, the firm retains all of its earnings to help defray the cost of new investments.

The firm's balance sheet for the year just ended is as follows:

Zapatera Enterprises, Inc.

| Balance Sheet | | |
|---|---|---|
| | **12/31/00** | **% of Sales** |
| Current assets | $3,000,000 | 25% |
| Net fixed assets | 6,000,000 | 50% |
| Total | $9,000,000 | |

| Liabilities and Owners' Equity | | |
|---|---|---|
| Accounts payable | $3,000,000 | 25% |
| Long-term debt | 2,000,000 | NA[a] |
| Total liabilities | $5,000,000 | |
| Common stock | 1,000,000 | NA* |
| Paid-in capital | 1,800,000 | NA* |
| Retained earnings | 1,200,000 | |
| Common equity | 4,000,000 | |
| Total | $9,000,000 | |

[a]Not applicable. This figure does not vary directly with sales and is assumed to remain constant for purposes of making next year's forecast of financing requirements.

Estimate Zapatera's total financing requirements (i.e., total assets) for 2001 and its net funding requirements (discretionary financing needed).

**4-2A.** (*Pro forma accounts receivable balance calculation*) On March 31, 2000, the Sylvia Gift Shop had outstanding accounts receivable of $20,000. Sylvia's sales are roughly evenly split between credit and cash sales, with half the credit sales collected in the month after the sale and the remainder 2 months after the sale. Historical and projected sales for the gift shop are:

| Month | Sales | Month | Sales |
|---|---|---|---|
| January | $15,000 | March | 30,000 |
| February | 20,000 | April (projected) | 40,000 |

**a.** Under these circumstances, what should the balance in accounts receivable be at the end of April?

**b.** How much cash did Sylvia realize during April from sales and collections?

**4-3A.** (*Financial forecasting*) Sambonoza Enterprises projects its sales next year to be $4 million and expects to earn 5 percent of that amount after taxes. The firm is currently in the process of projecting its financing needs and has made the following assumptions (projections):

1. Current assets will equal 20 percent of sales, and fixed assets will remain at their current level of $1 million.
2. Common equity is currently $0.8 million, and the firm pays out half of its after-tax earnings in dividends.
3. The firm has short-term payables and trade credit that normally equal 10 percent of sales, and it has no long-term debt outstanding.

What are Sambonoza's financing needs for the coming year?

**4-4A.** (*Financial forecasting—percent of sales*) Tulley Appliances, Inc., projects next year's sales to be $20 million. Current sales are at $15 million based on current assets of $5 million and fixed assets of $5 million. The firm's net profit margin is 5 percent after taxes. Tulley forecasts that current assets will rise in direct proportion to the increase in sales, but fixed assets will increase by only $100,000. Currently, Tulley has $1.5 million in accounts payable (which vary directly with sales), $2 million in long-term debt (due in 10 years), and common equity (including $4 million in retained earnings) totaling $6.5 million. Tulley plans to pay $500,000 in common stock dividends next year.

**a.** What are Tulley's total financing needs (that is, total assets) for the coming year?

**b.** Given the firm's projections and dividend payment plans, what are its discretionary financing needs?

**c.** Based on your projections, and assuming that the $100,000 expansion in fixed assets will occur, what is the largest increase in sales the firm can support without having to resort to the use of discretionary sources of financing?

**4-5A.** (*Pro forma balance sheet construction*) Use the following industry average ratios to construct a pro forma balance sheet for Carlos Menza, Inc.

| | |
|---|---|
| Total asset turnover | 2 times |
| Average collection period (assume a 365-day year) | 9 days |
| Fixed asset turnover | 5 times |
| Inventory turnover (based on cost of goods sold) | 3 times |
| Current ratio | 2 times |
| Sales (all on credit) | $4.0 million |
| Cost of goods sold | 75% of sales |
| Debt ratio | 50% |

| | | | |
|---|---|---|---|
| Cash | _____ | Current liabilities | _____ |
| Inventory | _____ | Long-term debt | _____ |
| Accounts receivable | _____ | Common stock plus | _____ |
| Net fixed assets | _____ | Retained earnings | _____ |
| Total | $_____ | Total | $_____ |

**4-6A.** (*Cash budget*) The Sharpe Corporation's projected sales for the first 8 months of 2001 are as follows:

| | | | |
|---|---|---|---|
| January | $ 90,000 | May | $300,000 |
| February | 120,000 | June | 270,000 |
| March | 135,000 | July | 225,000 |
| April | 240,000 | August | 150,000 |

Of Sharpe's sales, 10 percent is for cash, another 60 percent is collected in the month following sale, and 30 percent is collected in the second month following sale. November and December sales for 2000 were $220,000 and $175,000, respectively.

Sharpe purchases its raw materials 2 months in advance of its sales equal to 60 percent of their final sales price. The supplier is paid 1 month after it makes delivery. For example, purchases for April sales are made in February and payment is made in March.

In addition, Sharpe pays $10,000 per month for rent and $20,000 each month for other expenditures. Tax prepayments of $22,500 are made each quarter, beginning in March.

The company's cash balance at December 31, 2000, was $22,000; a minimum balance of $15,000 must be maintained at all times. Assume that any short-term financing needed to maintain the cash balance is paid off in the month following the month of financing if sufficient funds are available. Interest on short-term loans (12 percent) is paid monthly. Borrowing to meet estimated monthly cash needs takes place at the beginning of the month. Thus, if in the month of April the firm expects to have a need for an additional $60,500, these funds would be borrowed at the beginning of April with interest of $605 (.12 × 1/12 × $60,500) owed for April and paid at the beginning of May.

**a.** Prepare a cash budget for Sharpe covering the first 7 months of 2001.

**b.** Sharpe has $200,000 in notes payable due in July that must be repaid or renegotiated for an extension. Will the firm have ample cash to repay the notes?

**4-7A.** (*Percent of sales forecasting*) Which of the following accounts would most likely vary directly with the level of firm sales? Discuss each briefly.

| | Yes | No | | Yes | No |
|---|---|---|---|---|---|
| Cash | ______ | ______ | Notes payable | ______ | ______ |
| Marketable securities | ______ | ______ | Plant and equipment | ______ | ______ |
| Accounts payable | ______ | ______ | Inventories | ______ | ______ |

**4-8A.** (*Financial forecasting—percent of sales*) The balance sheet of the Thompson Trucking Company (TTC) follows:

Thompson Trucking Company Balance Sheet, December 31, 2000 ($ millions)

| | | | |
|---|---|---|---|
| Current assets | $10 | Accounts payable | $ 5 |
| Net fixed assets | 15 | Notes payable | 0 |
| Total | $25 | Bonds payable | 10 |
| | | Common equity | 10 |
| | | Total | $25 |

TTC had sales for the year ended 12/31/00 of $50 million. The firm follows a policy of paying all net earnings out to its common stockholders in cash dividends. Thus, TTC generates no funds from its earnings that can be used to expand its operations. (Assume that depreciation expense is just equal to the cost of replacing worn-out assets.)

**a.** If TTC anticipates sales of $80 million during the coming year, develop a pro forma balance sheet for the firm for 12/31/01. Assume that current assets vary as a percent of sales, net fixed assets remain unchanged, and accounts payable vary as a percent of sales. Use notes payable as a balancing entry.

**b.** How much "new" financing will TTC need next year?

**c.** What limitations does the percent of sales forecast method suffer from? Discuss briefly.

**4-9A.** (*Financial forecasting—discretionary financing needed*) The most recent balance sheet for the Armadillo Dog Biscuit Co. is shown in the following table. The company is about to embark on an advertising campaign, which is expected to raise sales from the current level of $5 million to $7 million by the end of next year. The firm is currently operating at full capacity and will have to increase its investment in both current and fixed assets to support the projected level of new sales. In fact, the firm estimates that both categories of assets will rise in direct proportion to the projected increase in sales.

Armadillo Dog Biscuit Co., Inc. ($ millions)

| | Present Level | Percent of Sales | Projected Level |
|---|---|---|---|
| Current assets | $2.0 | | |
| Net fixed assets | 3.0 | | |
| Total | $5.0 | | |
| Accounts payable | $0.5 | | |
| Accrued expenses | 0.5 | | |
| Notes payagle | — | | |
| Current liabilities | $1.0 | | |
| Long-term debt | $2.0 | | |
| Common stock | 0.5 | | |
| Retained earnings | 1.5 | | |
| Common equity | $2.0 | | |
| Total | $5.0 | | |

The firm's net profits were 6 percent of current year's sales but are expected to rise to 7 percent of next year's sales. To help support its anticipated growth in asset needs next year, the firm has suspended plans to pay cash dividends to its stockholders. In past years, a $1.50 per share dividend has been paid annually.

Armadillo's payables and accrued expenses are expected to vary directly with sales. In addition, notes payable will be used to supply the funds that are needed to finance next year's operations and that are not forthcoming from other sources.

**a.** Fill in the table and project the firm's needs for discretionary financing. Use notes payable as the balancing entry for future discretionary financing needed.

**b.** Compare Armadillo's current ratio and debt ratio (total liabilities/total assets) before the growth in sales and after. What was the effect of the expanded sales on these two dimensions of Armadillo's financial condition?

**c.** What difference, if any, would have resulted if Armadillo's sales had risen to $6 million in 1 year and $7 million only after 2 years? Discuss only; no calculations are required.

**4-10A.** (*Forecasting discretionary financing needs*) Fishing Charter, Inc., estimates that it invests 30¢ in assets for each dollar of new sales. However, 5¢ in profits are produced by each dollar of additional sales, of which 1¢ can be reinvested in the firm. If sales rise from their current level of $5 million by $500,000 next year, and the ratio of spontaneous liabilities to sales is .15, what will be the firm's need for discretionary financing? (*Hint:* In this situation you do not know what the firm's existing level of assets is, nor do you know how those assets have been financed. Thus, you must estimate the change in financing needs and match this change with the expected changes in spontaneous liabilities, retained earnings, and other sources of discretionary financing.)

**4-11A.** (*Preparation of a cash budget*) Harrison Printing has projected its sales for the first eight months of 2001 as follows:

| | | | | | |
|---|---|---|---|---|---|
| January | $100,000 | April | $300,000 | July | $200,000 |
| February | 120,000 | May | 275,000 | August | 180,000 |
| March | 150,000 | June | 200,000 | | |

Harrison collects 20 percent of its sales in the month of the sale, 50 percent in the month following the sale, and the remaining 30 percent 2 months following the sale. During November and December of 2000 Harrison's sales were \$220,000 and \$175,000, respectively.

Harrison purchases raw materials 2 months in advance of its sales equal to 65 percent of its final sales. The supplier is paid 1 month after delivery. Thus, purchases for April sales are made in February and payment is made in March.

In addition, Harrison pays \$10,000 per month for rent and \$20,000 each month for other expenditures. Tax prepayments of \$22,500 are made each quarter beginning in March. The company's cash balance as of December 31, 2000, was \$22,000; a minimum balance of \$20,000 must be maintained at all times to satisfy the firm's bank line of credit agreement. Harrison has arranged with its bank for short-term credit at an interest rate of 12 percent per annum (1 percent per month) to be paid monthly. Borrowing to meet estimated monthly cash needs takes place at the end of the month, and interest is not paid until the end of the following month. Consequently, if the firm were to need to borrow \$50,000 during the month of April, then it would pay \$500 (= .01 × \$50,000) in interest during May. Finally, Harrison follows a policy of repaying its outstanding short-term debt in any month in which its cash balance exceeds the minimum desired balance of \$20,000.

**a.** Harrison needs to know what its cash requirements will be for the next 6 months so that it can renegotiate the terms of its short-term credit agreement with its bank, if necessary. To evaluate this problem, the firm plans to evaluate the impact of a ± 20 percent variation in its monthly sales efforts. Prepare a 6-month cash budget for Harrison and use it to evaluate the firm's cash needs.

**b.** Harrison has a \$200,000 note due in June. Will the firm have sufficient cash to repay the loan?

**4-12A.** (*Sustainable rate of growth*) ADP, Inc., is a manufacturer of specialty circuit boards in the personal computer industry. The firm has experienced phenomenal sales growth over its short 5-year life. Selected financial statement data are found in the following table:

| | 2000 | 1999 | 1998 | 1997 | 1996 |
|---|---|---|---|---|---|
| Sales | \$3,000 | \$2,200 | \$1,800 | \$1,400 | \$1,200 |
| Net income | 150 | 110 | 90 | 70 | 60 |
| Assets | 2,700 | 1,980 | 1,620 | 1,260 | 1,080 |
| Dividends | 60 | 44 | 36 | 28 | 24 |
| Common equity | 812 | 722 | 656 | 602 | 560 |
| Liabilities | 1,888 | 1,258 | 964 | 658 | 520 |
| Liabilities and equity | 2,700 | 1,980 | 1,620 | 1,260 | 1,080 |

**a.** Calculate ADP's sustainable rate of growth for each of the 5 years of its existence.

**b.** Compare the actual rates of growth in sales to the firm's sustainable rates calculated in part a. How has ADP been financing its growing asset needs?

**4-13A.** (*Sustainable rate of growth*) The Carrera Game Company has experienced a 100 percent increase in sales over the last 5 years. The company president, Jack Carrera, has become increasingly alarmed by the firm's rising debt level even in the face of continued profitability.

| | 2000 | 1999 | 1998 | 1997 | 1996 |
|---|---|---|---|---|---|
| Sales | \$60,000 | \$56,000 | \$48,000 | \$36,000 | \$30,000 |
| Net income | 3,000 | 2,800 | 2,400 | 1,800 | 1,500 |
| Assets | 54,000 | 50,400 | 43,200 | 32,400 | 27,000 |
| Dividends | 1,200 | 1,120 | 960 | 720 | 600 |
| Common equity | 21,000 | 19,200 | 17,520 | 16,080 | 15,000 |
| Liabilities | 33,000 | 31,200 | 25,680 | 16,320 | 12,000 |
| Liabilities and equity | 54,000 | 50,400 | 43,200 | 32,400 | 27,000 |

**a.** Calculate the debt to asset ratio, return on common equity, actual rate of growth in firm sales, and retention ratio for each of the 5 years of data provided.

**b.** Calculate the sustainable rates of growth for Carrera for each of the last 5 years. Why has the firm's borrowing increased so dramatically?

**4-14A.** (*Forecasting inventories*) Findlay Instruments produces a complete line of medical instruments used by plastic surgeons and has experienced rapid growth over the last 5 years. In an effort to make more accurate predictions of its financing requirements, Findlay is currently attempting to construct a financial planning model based on the percent of sales forecasting method. However, the firm's Chief Financial Analyst (Sarah Macias) is concerned that the projections for inventories will be seriously in error. She recognizes that the firm has begun to accrue substantial economies of scale in its inventory investment and has documented this fact in the following data and calculations:

| Year | Sales (000) | Inventory (000) | % of Sales |
|---|---|---|---|
| 1996 | $15,000 | 1,150 | 7.67% |
| 1997 | 18,000 | 1,180 | 6.56% |
| 1998 | 17,500 | 1,175 | 6.71% |
| 1999 | 20,000 | 1,200 | 6.00% |
| 2000 | 25,000 | 1,250 | 5.00% |
| | | Average | 6.39% |

**a.** Plot Findlay's sales and inventories for the last 5 years. What is the relationship between these two variables?

**b.** Estimate firm inventories for 2001, when firm sales are projected to reach $30,000,000. Use the average percent of sales for the last 5 years, the most recent percent of sales, and your evaluation of the true relationship between the sales and inventories from part a to make three predications.

## INTEGRATIVE PROBLEM

Phillips Petroleum is an integrated oil and gas company with headquarters in Bartlesville, Oklahoma, where it was founded in 1917. The company engages in petroleum exploration and production worldwide. In addition, it engages in natural gas gathering and processing, as well as petroleum refining and marketing primarily in the United States. The company has three operating groups—Exploration and Production, Gas and Gas Liquids, and Downstream Operations, which encompasses Petroleum Products and Chemicals.

In the mid-1980s, Phillips engaged in a major restructuring following two failed takeover attempts, one led by T. Boone Pickens and the other by Carl Icahn.[a] The restructuring resulted in a $4.5 billion plan to exchange a package of cash and debt securities for roughly half the company's shares and to sell $2 billion worth of assets. Phillips's long-term debt increased from $3.4 billion in late 1984 to a peak of $8.6 billion in April 1985.

During 1992, Phillips was able to strengthen its financial structure dramatically. Its subsidiary Phillips Gas Company completed an offering of $345 million of Series A 9.32% Cumulative Preferred Stock. As a result of these actions and prior years' debt reductions, the company lowered its long-term debt to capital ratio over the last 5 years from 75 to 55 percent. In addition, the firm refinanced over a billion dollars of its debt at reduced rates. A company spokesman said that "Our debt-to-capital ratio is still on the high side, and we'll keep working to bring it down. But

[a]This discussion is based on a story in *The New York Times*, January 7, 1986.

Summary Financial Information for Phillips Petroleum Corporation: 1986–1992 (in millions of dollars except for per share figures)

| | 1986 | 1987 | 1988 | 1989 | 1990 | 1991 | 1992 |
|---|---|---|---|---|---|---|---|
| Sales | 10,018.00 | 10,917.00 | 11,490.00 | 12,492.00 | 13,975.00 | 13,259.00 | 12,140.00 |
| Net income | 228.00 | 35.00 | 650.00 | 219.00 | 541.00 | 98.00 | 270.00 |
| EPS | 0.89 | 0.06 | 2.72 | 0.90 | 2.18 | 0.38 | 1.04 |
| Current assets | 2,802.00 | 2,855.00 | 3,062.00 | 2,876.00 | 3,322.00 | 2,459.00 | 2,349.00 |
| Total assets | 12,403.00 | 12,111.00 | 11,968.00 | 11,256.00 | 12,130.00 | 11,473.00 | 11,468.00 |
| Current liabilities | 2,234.00 | 2,402.00 | 2,468.00 | 2,706.00 | 2,910.00 | 2,603.00 | 2,517.00 |
| Long-term liabilities | 8,175.00 | 7,887.00 | 7,387.00 | 6,418.00 | 6,501.00 | 6,113.00 | 5,894.00 |
| Total liabilities | 10,409.00 | 10,289.00 | 9,855.00 | 9,124.00 | 9,411.00 | 8,716.00 | 8,411.00 |
| Preferred stock | 270.00 | 205.00 | 0.00 | 0.00 | 0.00 | 0.00 | 359.00 |
| Common equity | 1,724.00 | 1,617.00 | 2,113.00 | 2,132.00 | 2,719.00 | 2,757.00 | 2,698.00 |
| Dividends per share | 2.02 | 1.73 | 1.34 | 0.00 | 1.03 | 1.12 | 1.12 |

Source: Phillips Annual Reports for the years 1987–1992.

the cost of debt is manageable, and we're beyond the point where debt overshadows everything else we do."[b]

Highlights of Phillips's financial condition spanning the years 1986–1992 are found in the preceding table.[c] These data reflect the modern history of the company as a result of its financial restructuring following the downsizing and reorganization of Phillips's operations begun in the mid-1980s.

Phillips's management is currently developing its financial plans for the next 5 years and wants to develop a forecast of its financing requirements. As a first approximation, they have asked you to develop a model that can be used to make "ballpark" estimates of the firm's financing needs under the proviso that existing relationships found in the firm's financial statements remain the same over the period. Of particular interest is whether or not Phillips will be able to further reduce its reliance on debt financing. You may assume that Phillips's projected sales (in millions) for 1993 through 1997 are as follows: \$13,000, \$13,500, \$14,000, \$14,500, and \$15,500.

1. Project net income for 1993 to 1997 using the percent of sales method based on an average of this ratio for 1986 to 1992.
2. Project total assets and current liabilities for the period 1993 to 1997 using the percent of sales method and your sales projections from part 1.
3. Assuming that common equity increases only as a result of the retention of earnings and holding long-term liabilities and preferred stock equal to their 1992 balances, project Phillips's discretionary financing needs for 1993 to 1997. (*Hint:* Assume that total assets and current liabilities vary as a percent of sales as per your answer. In addition, assume that Phillips plans to continue to pay its dividend of \$1.12 per share in each of the next 5 years.)

## STUDY PROBLEMS (SET B)

**4-1B.** (*Financial forecasting*) Hernandez Trucking Company is evaluating its financing requirements for the coming year. The firm has only been in business for 3 years and the firm's Chief Financial Officer (Eric Stevens) predicts that the firm's operating expenses, current assets, and current liabilities will remain at their current proportion of sales.

Last year, Hernandez had \$20 million in sales with net income of \$1 million. The firm anticipates that next year's sales will reach \$25 million with net income rising to \$2 million. Given its present high rate of growth, the firm retains all its earnings to help defray the cost of new investments.

[b]From *SEC Online*, 1992.

[c]Extracted from Phillips's Annual Reports for the years represented.

The firm's balance sheet for the year just ended follows:

Hernandez Trucking Company, Inc., Balance Sheet

| | 12/31/00 | % of Sales |
|---|---|---|
| Current assets | $ 4,000,000 | 20% |
| Net fixed assets | 8,000,000 | 40% |
| Total | $12,000,000 | |
| **Liabilities and Owners' Equity** | | |
| Accounts payable | $ 3,000,000 | 15% |
| Long-term debt | 2,000,000 | NA[a] |
| Total liabilities | $ 5,000,000 | |
| Common stock | 1,000,000 | NA |
| Paid-in capital | 1,800,000 | NA |
| Retained earnings | 4,200,000 | |
| Common equity | 7,000,000 | |
| Total | $12,000,000 | |

[a]Not applicable. This figure does not vary directly with sales and is assumed to remain constant for purposes of making next year's forecast of financing requirements.

Estimate Hernandez's total financing requirements for 2001 and its net funding requirements (discretionary financing needed).

**4-2B.** (*Pro forma accounts receivable balance calculation*) On March 31, 2001, the Floydata Food Distribution Company had outstanding accounts receivable of $52,000. Sales are roughly 40 percent credit and 60 percent cash, with half of the credit sales collected in the month after the sale and the remainder 2 months after the sale. Historical and projected sales for Floydata Food follow:

| Month | Sales |
|---|---|
| January | $100,000 |
| February | 100,000 |
| March | 80,000 |
| April (projected) | 60,000 |

**a.** Under these circumstances, what should the balance in accounts receivable be at the end of April?
**b.** How much cash did Floydata realize during April from sales and collections?

**4-3B.** (*Financial forecasting*) Simpson, Inc., projects its sales next year to be $5 million and expects to earn 6 percent of that amount after taxes. The firm is currently in the process of projecting its financing needs and has made the following assumptions (projections):

**a.** Current assets will equal 15 percent of sales and fixed assets will remain at their current level of $1 million.
**b.** Common equity is presently $0.7 million, and the firm pays out half its after-tax earnings in dividends.
**c.** The firm has short-term payables and trade credit that normally equal 11 percent of sales and has no long-term debt outstanding.

What are Simpson's financing needs for the coming year?

**4-4B.** (*Financial forecasting—percent of sales*) Carson Enterprises is in the midst of its annual planning exercise. Bud Carson, the owner, is a mechanical engineer by education and has only modest skills in financial planning. In fact, the firm has operated in the past on a "crisis" basis with little attention paid to the firm's financial affairs until a problem arose. This worked reasonably well for several years, until the firm's growth in sales created a serious cash flow shortage last year. Bud was able to convince the firm's bank to come up with the needed funds, but an outgrowth of the agreement was that the firm would begin to make forecasts of its financing requirements annually. To support its first such effort, Bud has made the following estimates for next year: Sales are currently $18 million with projected sales of $25 million for next year. The firm's current assets equal $7 million, and its fixed assets are $6 million. The best estimate Bud can make is that current assets will equal the current proportion of sales and fixed assets will rise by $100,000. At the present time, the firm has accounts payable of $1.5 million, $2 million in long-term debt, and common equity totaling $9.5 million (including $4 million in retained earnings). Finally, Carson Enterprises plans to continue paying its dividend of $600,000 next year and has a 5 percent profit margin.

**a.** What are Carson's total financing needs (that is, total assets) for the coming year?

**b.** Given the firm's projections and dividend payment plans, what are its discretionary financing needs?

**c.** Based on the projections given and assuming that the $100,000 expansion in fixed assets will occur, what is the largest increase in sales the firm can support without having to resort to the use of discretionary sources of financing?

**4-5B.** (*Pro forma balance sheet construction*) Use the following industry average ratios to construct a pro forma balance sheet for the V. M. Willet Co.

| | |
|---|---|
| Total asset turnover | 2.5 times |
| Average collection period (assume a 365-day year) | 10 days |
| Fixed asset turnover | 6 times |
| Inventory turnover (based on cost of goods sold) | 4 times |
| Current ratio | 3 times |
| Sales (all on credit) | $5 million |
| Cost of goods sold | 80% of sales |
| Debt ratio | 60% |

| | | | |
|---|---|---|---|
| Cash | _____ | Current liabilities | _____ |
| Accounts receivables | _____ | Long-term debt | _____ |
| Inventories | _____ | Common stock plus | _____ |
| Net fixed assets | $_____ | retained earnings | $_____ |
| | $_____ | | $_____ |

**4-6B.** (*Cash budget*) The Carmel Corporation's projected sales for the first 8 months of 2001 are as follows:

| | | | |
|---|---|---|---|
| January | $100,000 | May | $275,000 |
| February | 110,000 | June | 250,000 |
| March | 130,000 | July | 235,000 |
| April | 250,000 | August | 160,000 |

Of Carmel's sales, 20 percent is for cash, another 60 percent is collected in the month following sale, and 20 percent is collected in the second month following sale. November and December sales for 2000 were $220,000 and $175,000, respectively.

Carmel purchases its raw materials 2 months in advance of its sales equal to 70 percent of their final sales price. The supplier is paid 1 month after it makes delivery. For example, purchases for April sales are made in February and payment is made in March.

In addition, Carmel pays $10,000 per month for rent and $20,000 each month for other expenditures. Tax prepayments for $23,000 are made each quarter beginning in March.

The company's cash balance at December 31, 2000, was $22,000; a minimum balance of $20,000 must be maintained at all times. Assume that any short-term financing needed to maintain cash balance would be paid off in the month following the month of financing if sufficient funds are available. Interest on short-term loans (12 percent) is paid monthly. Borrowing to meet estimated monthly cash needs takes place at the beginning of the month. Thus, if in the month of April the firm expects to have a need for an additional $60,500, these funds would be borrowed at the beginning of April with interest of $605 (.12 × 1/12 × $60,500) owed for April and paid at the beginning of May.

**a.** Prepare a cash budget for Carmel covering the first 7 months of 2001.

**b.** Carmel has $250,000 in notes payable due in July that must be repaid or renegotiated for an extension. Will the firm have ample cash to repay the notes?

**4-7B.** (*Percent of sales forecasting*) Which of the following accounts would most likely vary directly with the level of firm sales? Discuss each briefly.

| | Yes | No | | Yes | No |
|---|---|---|---|---|---|
| Cash | _____ | _____ | Notes payable | _____ | _____ |
| Marketable securities | _____ | _____ | Plant and equipment | _____ | _____ |
| Accounts payable | _____ | _____ | Inventories | _____ | _____ |

**4-8B.** (*Financial forecasting—percent of sales*) The balance sheet of the Chavez Drilling Company (CDC) follows:

Chavez Drilling Company Balance Sheet for January 31, 2000 ($ millions)

| | | | |
|---|---|---|---|
| Current assets | $15 | Accounts payable | $10 |
| Net fixed assets | 15 | Notes payable | 0 |
| Total | $30 | Bonds payable | 10 |
| | | Common equity | 10 |
| | | Total | $30 |

CDC had sales for the year ended 1/31/00 of $60 million. The firm follows a policy of paying all net earnings out to its common stockholders in cash dividends. Thus, CDC generates no funds from its earnings that can be used to expand its operations (assume that depreciation expense is just equal to the cost of replacing worn-out assets).

**a.** If CDC anticipates sales of $80 million during the coming year, develop a pro forma balance sheet for the firm for 1/31/01. Assume that current assets vary as a percent of sales, net fixed assets remain unchanged, and accounts payable vary as a percent of sales. Use notes payable as a balancing entry.

**b.** How much "new" financing will CDC need next year?

**c.** What limitations does the percent of sales forecast method suffer from? Discuss briefly.

**4-9B.** (*Financial forecasting—discretionary financing needed*) Symbolic Logic Corporation (SLC) is a technological leader in the application of surface mount technology in the manufacture of printed circuit boards used in the personal computer industry. The firm has recently patented an advanced version of its original path-finding technology and expects sales to grow from their present level of $5 million to $8 million in the coming year. Since the firm is at present operating at full capacity, it expects to have to increase its investment in both current and fixed assets in proportion to the predicted increase in sales.

The firm's net profits were 7 percent of current year's sales and are expected to be the same next year. To help support its anticipated growth in asset needs next year, the firm has suspended plans to pay cash dividends to its stockholders. In years past, a $1.25 per share dividend has been paid annually.

Symbolic Logic Corporation ($ millions)

| | Present Level | Percent of Sales | Projected Level |
|---|---|---|---|
| Current assets | $2.5 | | |
| Net fixed assets | 3.0 | | |
| Total | 5.5 | | |
| Accounts payable | $1.0 | | |
| Accrued expenses | 0.5 | | |
| Notes payable | — | | |
| Current liabilities | $1.5 | | |
| Long-term debt | $2.0 | | |
| Common stock | 0.5 | | |
| Retained earnings | 1.5 | | |
| Common equity | $2.0 | | |
| Total | $5.5 | | |

SLC's payables and accrued expenses are expected to vary directly with sales. In addition, notes payable will be used to supply the funds needed to finance next year's operations and that are not forthcoming from other sources.

**a.** Fill in the table and project the firm's needs for discretionary financing. Use notes payable as the balancing entry for future discretionary financing needed.

**b.** Compare SLC's current ratio and debt ratio (total liabilities/total assets) before the growth in sales and after. What was the effect of the expanded sales on these two dimensions of SLC's financial condition?

**c.** What difference, if any, would have resulted if SLC's sales had risen to $6 million in 1 year and $8 million only after 2 years? Discuss only; no calculations are required.

**4-10B.** (*Forecasting discretionary financing needs*) Royal Charter, Inc., estimates that it invests 40¢ in assets for each dollar of new sales. However, 5¢ in profits are produced by each dollar of additional sales, of which 1¢ can be reinvested in the firm. If sales rise from their present level of $5 million by $500,000 next year, and the ratio of spontaneous liabilities to sales is .15, what will be the firm's need for discretionary financing? (*Hint:* In this situation you do not know what the firm's existing level of assets is, nor do you know how those assets have been financed. Thus, you must estimate the change in financing needs and match this change with the expected changes in spontaneous liabilities, retained earnings, and other sources of discretionary financing. Note that spontaneous liabilities are those liabilities that vary with sales.)

**4-11B.** (*Preparation of a cash budget*) Halsey Enterprises has projected its sales for the first eight months of 2001 as follows:

| | | | |
|---|---|---|---|
| January | $120,000 | May | $225,000 |
| February | 160,000 | June | 250,000 |
| March | 140,000 | July | 210,000 |
| April | 190,000 | August | 220,000 |

Halsey collects 30 percent of its sales in the month of the sale, 30 percent in the month following the sale, and the remaining 40 percent 2 months following the sale. During November and December of 2000, Halsey's sales were $230,000 and $225,000, respectively.

Halsey purchases raw materials 2 months in advance of its sales equal to 75 percent of its final sales. The supplier is paid in the month after delivery. Thus, purchases for April sales are made in February and payment is made in March.

In addition, Halsey pays $12,000 per month for rent and $20,000 each month for other expenditures. Tax prepayments of $26,500 are made each quarter beginning in March. The company's cash balance as of December 31, 2000, was $28,000; a minimum balance of $25,000 must be maintained at all times to satisfy the firm's bank line of credit agreement. Halsey has arranged with its bank for short-term credit at an interest rate of 12 percent per annum (1 percent per month) to be paid monthly. Borrowing to meet estimated monthly cash needs takes place at the beginning of the month, but interest is not paid until the end of the following month. Consequently, if the firm were to need to borrow $50,000 during the month of April, then it would pay $500 (= .01 × $50,000) in interest during May. Finally, Halsey follows a policy of repaying any outstanding short-term debt in any month in which its cash balance exceeds the minimum desired balance of $25,000.

**a.** Halsey needs to know what its cash requirements will be for the next 6 months so that it can renegotiate the terms of its short-term credit agreement with its bank, if necessary. To evaluate this problem the firm plans to assess the impact of a ± 20 percent variation in its monthly sales efforts. Prepare a 6-month cash budget for Halsey and use it to evaluate the firm's cash needs.

**b.** Halsey has a $200,000 note due in July. Will the firm have sufficient cash to repay the loan?

## SELF-TEST SOLUTIONS

**ST-1.**

Calico Sales Co., Inc., Pro Forma Income Statement

| | | |
|---|---|---|
| Sales | | $4,000,000 |
| Cost of goods sold (70%) | | (2,800,000) |
| Gross profit | | 1,200,000 |
| Operating expense | | |
| Selling expense (5%) | $ 200,000 | |
| Administrative expense | 500,000 | |
| Depreciation expense | 300,000 | (1,000,000) |
| Net operating income | | 200,000 |
| Interest | | (50,000) |
| Earnings before taxes | | 150,000 |
| Taxes (40%) | | (60,000) |
| Net income | | $ 90,000 |

Although the office renovation expenditure and debt retirement are surely cash outflows, they do not enter the income statement directly. These expenditures affect expenses for the period's income statement only through their effect on depreciation and interest expense. A cash budget would indicate the full cash impact of the renovation and debt retirement expenditures.

**ST-2.**

| | May | June | July | August |
|---|---|---|---|---|
| Sales | $100,000 | $100,000 | $ 120,000 | $ 150,000 |
| Purchases | 60,000 | 60,000 | 50,000 | 40,000 |
| Cash receipts: | | | | |
| Collections from month of sale (20%) | 20,000 | 20,000 | 24,000 | 30,000 |
| 1 month later (50% of uncollected amount) | | 40,000 | 40,000 | 48,000 |
| 2 months later (balance) | | | 40,000 | 40,000 |
| Total receipts | | | $ 104,000 | $ 118,000 |
| Cash disbursements: | | | | |
| Payments for purchases— | | | | |
| From 1 month earlier | | | $ 30,000 | $ 25,000 |
| From current month | | | 25,000 | $ 20,000 |
| Total | | | $ 55,000 | $ 45,000 |
| Miscellaneous cash expenses | | | 4,000 | 4,000 |
| Labor expense (5% of sales) | | | 6,000 | 7,500 |
| General and administrative expense ($50,000 per month) | | | 50,000 | 50,000 |
| Truck purchase | | | 0 | 60,000 |
| Cash dividends | | | 9,000 | — |
| Total disbursements | | | $ (124,000) | $ (166,500) |
| Net change in cash | | | (20,000) | (48,550) |
| Plus: Beginning cash balance | | | 30,000 | 30,000 |
| Less: Interest on short-term borrowing (1% of prior month's borrowing) | | | | (200) |
| Equals: ending cash balance—without borrowing | | | 10,000 | (18,700) |
| Financing needed to reach target cash balance | | | 20,000 | 48,700 |
| Cumulative borrowing | | | $ 20,000 | $ 68,700 |

PART 2: VALUATION OF FINANCIAL ASSETS

# THE TIME VALUE OF MONEY

For Harley-Davidson, and in fact for every company, the concept of the time value of money appears everywhere. That's because the time value of money allows you to compare cash flows that occur in different time periods. In business this practice occurs all the time. Businesses are always investing money today in hopes of reaping a big return in later years. For example, in 1997, Harley began the costly development of a new sport bike, the Buell Blast, that would take several years to bring to market. In effect, Harley spent a good deal of money in 1997, hoping it would pay off in 2000 and beyond. How did Harley go about comparing dollars it spent in 1997 with dollars it would receive in the year 2000 and beyond? The answer is with the help of the time value of money. With the tools and techniques that we will develop in this chapter, we will be able to move money through time and compare cash flows that occur in different time periods. In Harley's case, it hopes the Buell Blast not only pays for its development, but also provides Harley with a good return. How does Harley calculate the return on an investment? Again, the answer is with the help of the time value of money. ● We will also use the time value of money tools to understand how Harley determines what a customer's monthly payments will be when he or she buys a motorcycle that is financed by Harley-Davidson Credit, when Harley should build a new plant, how much payments will be on a Harley-Davidson Chrome Visa card, and how much Harley might want to pay for a company it is considering purchasing. In addition, as we will see in upcoming chapters, the time value of

**LEARNING OBJECTIVES**

After reading this chapter, you should be able to

1. Explain the mechanics of compounding: how money grows over time when it is invested.
2. Determine the future or present value of a sum when there are nonannual compounding periods.
3. Discuss the relationship between compounding (future value) and bringing money back to the present (present value).
4. Define an ordinary annuity and calculate its compound or future value.
5. Differentiate between an ordinary annuity and an annuity due, and determine the future and present value of an annuity due.
6. Deal with complex cash flows.
7. Work with annuities and perpetuities.
8. Calculate the annual percentage yield or effective annual rate of interest and then explain how it differs from the nominal or stated interest rate.

money plays a major role in valuing Harley's debt and common stock. The bottom line is that the time value of money is everywhere in business. In fact, the time value of money is important not only to you in business, but also in your personal financial life, regardless of whether you are a marketing, management, management science, or accounting major. You will see that only through an understanding of the time value of money will you be able to understand how stocks and bonds are valued, determine how much you should save for your children's education, how much your mortgage payments will be, and how much you should save for retirement. In addition, gaining an understanding of the power of compounding will demonstrate the importance of starting to save for your personal goals as soon as possible.

**CHAPTER PREVIEW**

In the next six chapters, we will focus on determining the value of the firm and the value of investment proposals. A key concept that underlies this material is the *time value of money*; that is, a dollar today is worth more than a dollar received a year from now because a dollar today can be invested and earn interest. Intuitively this idea is easy to understand. We are all familiar with the concept of interest. This concept illustrates what economists call an *opportunity cost* of passing up the earning potential of a dollar today. This opportunity cost is the time value of money.

Different investment proposals produce different sets of cash flows over different time periods. How does the manager compare these? We will see that the concept of the time value of money will let us do this. Thus, an understanding of the time value of money is essential to an understanding of financial management, whether basic or advanced. In this chapter, we develop the tools to incorporate **Principle 2: The Time Value of Money—A dollar received today is worth more than a dollar received in the future** into our calculations. In coming chapters, we will use this concept to measure value by bringing the benefits and costs from a project back to the present.

## COMPOUND INTEREST AND FUTURE VALUE

OBJECTIVE 1 

**Compound interest**
Interest that occurs when interest paid on the investment during the first period is added to the principal; then, during the second period, interest is earned on this new sum.

Most of us encounter the concept of compound interest at an early age. Anyone who has ever had a savings account or purchased a government savings bond has received compound interest. **Compound interest** occurs when interest paid on the investment during the first period is added to the principal; then, during the second period, interest is earned on this new sum.

For example, suppose we place \$100 in a savings account that pays 6 percent interest, compounded annually. How will our savings grow? At the end of the first year we have earned 6 percent, or \$6 on our initial deposit of \$100, giving us a total of \$106 in our savings account. The mathematical formula illustrating this relationship is

$$FV_1 = PV(1 + i) \tag{5-1}$$

where $FV_1$ = the future value of the investment at the end of 1 year
$i$ = the annual interest (or discount) rate
$PV$ = the present value, or original amount invested at the beginning of the first year

In our example

$$\begin{aligned} FV_1 &= PV(1 + i) \\ &= \$100(1 + .06) \\ &= \$100(1.06) \\ &= \$106 \end{aligned}$$

Carrying these calculations one period further, we find that we now earn the 6 percent interest on a principal of \$106, which means we earn \$6.36 in interest during the second year. Why do we earn more interest during the second year than we did during the first? Simply because we now earn interest on the sum of the original principal, or present value, and the interest we earned in the first year. In effect, we are now earning interest on interest—this is the concept of compound interest. Examining the mathematical formula illustrating the earning of interest in the second year, we find

$$FV_2 = FV_1(1 + i) \qquad \textbf{(5-2)}$$

which for our example, gives

$$\begin{aligned} FV_2 &= \$106(1.06) \\ &= \$112.36 \end{aligned}$$

Looking back at equation 5-1 we can see that $FV_1$, or \$106, is actually equal to $PV(1 + i)$, or \$100 (1 + .06). If we substitute these values into equation 5-2, we get

$$\begin{aligned} FV_2 &= PV(1 + i)(1 + i) \\ &= PV(1 + i)^2 \end{aligned} \qquad \textbf{(5-3)}$$

Carrying this forward into the third year, we find that we enter the year with \$112.36 and we earn 6 percent, or \$6.74, in interest, giving us a total of \$119.10 in our savings account. Expressing this mathematically

$$\begin{aligned} FV_3 &= FV_2(1 + i) \\ &= \$112.36(1.06) \\ &= \$119.10 \end{aligned} \qquad \textbf{(5-4)}$$

If we substitute the value in equation 5-3 for $FV_2$ into equation 5-4, we find

$$\begin{aligned} FV_3 &= PV(1 + i)(1 + i)(1 + i) \\ &= PV(1 + i)^3 \end{aligned} \qquad \textbf{(5-5)}$$

By now a pattern is beginning to be evident. We can generalize this formula to illustrate the value of our investment if it is compounded annually at a rate of $i$ for $n$ years to be

$$FV_n = PV(1 + i)^n \qquad \textbf{(5-6)}$$

where $FV_n$ = the future value of the investment at the end of $n$ years
$n$ = the number of years during which the compounding occurs
$i$ = the annual interest (or discount) rate
$PV$ = the present value or original amount invested at the beginning of the first year

Table 5-1 illustrates how this investment of \$100 would continue to grow for the first 10 years at a compound interest rate of 6 percent. Notice how the amount of interest earned annually increases each year. Again, the reason is that each year interest is received on the sum of the original investment plus any interest earned in the past.

When we examine the relationship between the number of years an initial investment is compounded for and its future value, as shown graphically in Figure 5-1, we see that we can increase the future value of an investment by increasing the number of years we let it compound or by compounding it at a higher interest rate. We can also see this from equation 5-6, because an increase in either $i$ or $n$ while $PV$ is held constant will result in an increase in $FV_n$.

Keep in mind that future cash flows are assumed to occur at the end of the time period during which they accrue. For example, if a cash flow of \$100 occurs in time period 5, it is assumed to occur at the end of time period 5, which is also the beginning of time period 6. In addition, cash flows that occur in time $t = 0$ occur right now; that is, they are already in present dollars.

**TABLE 5-1**
Illustration of Compound Interest Calculations

| Year | Beginning Value | Interest Earned | Ending Value |
|---|---|---|---|
| 1 | $100.00 | $ 6.00 | $106.00 |
| 2 | 106.00 | 6.36 | 112.36 |
| 3 | 112.36 | 6.74 | 119.10 |
| 4 | 119.10 | 7.15 | 126.25 |
| 5 | 126.25 | 7.57 | 133.82 |
| 6 | 133.82 | 8.03 | 141.85 |
| 7 | 141.85 | 8.51 | 150.36 |
| 8 | 150.36 | 9.02 | 159.38 |
| 9 | 159.38 | 9.57 | 168.95 |
| 10 | 168.95 | 10.13 | 179.08 |

**EXAMPLE**

If we place $1,000 in a savings account paying 5 percent interest compounded annually, how much will our account accrue in 10 years? Substituting $PV = \$1{,}000$, $i = 5$ percent, and $n = 10$ years into equation 5-6, we get

$$\begin{aligned} FV_n &= PV(1 + i)^n \\ &= \$1{,}000(1 + .05)^{10} \\ &= \$1{,}000(1.62889) \\ &= \$1{,}628.89 \end{aligned}$$

Thus, at the end of 10 years, we will have $1,628.89 in our savings account.

**FIGURE 5-1**
Future Value of $100 Initially Deposited and Compounded at 0, 5, and 10 Percent

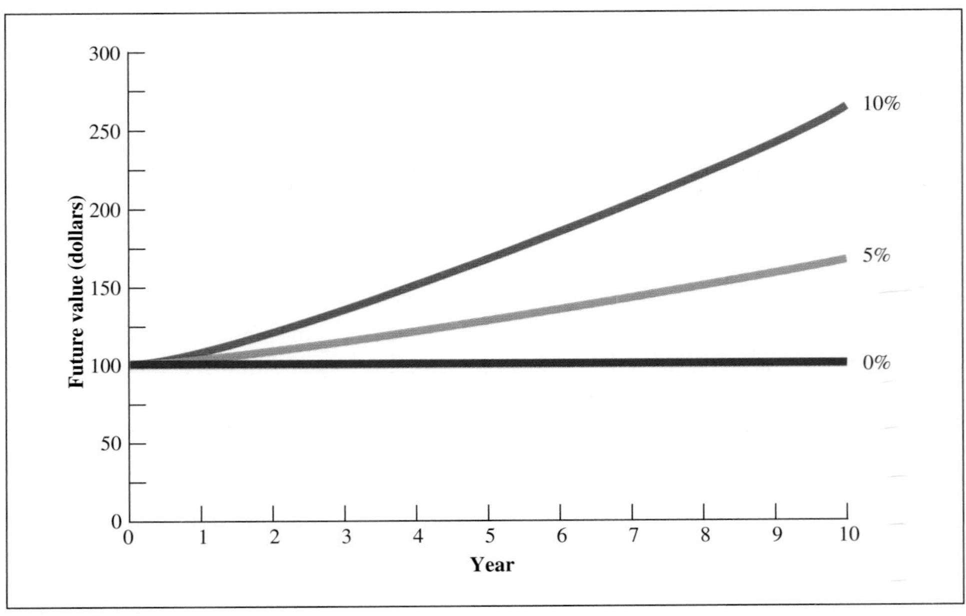

**TABLE 5-2**
$FVIF_{i,n}$ or the Compound Sum of $1

| n | 1% | 2% | 3% | 4% | 5% | 6% | 7% | 8% | 9% | 10% |
|---|---|---|---|---|---|---|---|---|---|---|
| 1 | 1.010 | 1.020 | 1.030 | 1.040 | 1.050 | 1.060 | 1.070 | 1.080 | 1.090 | 1.100 |
| 2 | 1.020 | 1.040 | 1.061 | 1.082 | 1.102 | 1.124 | 1.145 | 1.166 | 1.188 | 1.210 |
| 3 | 1.030 | 1.061 | 1.093 | 1.125 | 1.158 | 1.191 | 1.225 | 1.260 | 1.295 | 1.331 |
| 4 | 1.041 | 1.082 | 1.126 | 1.170 | 1.216 | 1.262 | 1.311 | 1.360 | 1.412 | 1.464 |
| 5 | 1.051 | 1.104 | 1.159 | 1.217 | 1.276 | 1.338 | 1.403 | 1.469 | 1.539 | 1.611 |
| 6 | 1.062 | 1.126 | 1.194 | 1.265 | 1.340 | 1.419 | 1.501 | 1.587 | 1.677 | 1.772 |
| 7 | 1.072 | 1.149 | 1.230 | 1.316 | 1.407 | 1.504 | 1.606 | 1.714 | 1.828 | 1.949 |
| 8 | 1.083 | 1.172 | 1.267 | 1.369 | 1.477 | 1.594 | 1.718 | 1.851 | 1.993 | 2.144 |
| 9 | 1.094 | 1.195 | 1.305 | 1.423 | 1.551 | 1.689 | 1.838 | 1.999 | 2.172 | 2.358 |
| 10 | 1.105 | 1.219 | 1.344 | 1.480 | 1.629 | 1.791 | 1.967 | 2.159 | 2.367 | 2.594 |
| 11 | 1.116 | 1.243 | 1.384 | 1.539 | 1.710 | 1.898 | 2.105 | 2.332 | 2.580 | 2.853 |
| 12 | 1.127 | 1.268 | 1.426 | 1.601 | 1.796 | 2.012 | 2.252 | 2.518 | 2.813 | 3.138 |
| 13 | 1.138 | 1.294 | 1.469 | 1.665 | 1.886 | 2.133 | 2.410 | 2.720 | 3.066 | 3.452 |
| 14 | 1.149 | 1.319 | 1.513 | 1.732 | 1.980 | 2.261 | 2.579 | 2.937 | 3.342 | 3.797 |
| 15 | 1.161 | 1.346 | 1.558 | 1.801 | 2.079 | 2.397 | 2.759 | 3.172 | 3.642 | 4.177 |

As the determination of future value can be quite time consuming when an investment is held for a number of years, the **future-value interest factor** for $i$ and $n$ ($FVIF_{i,n}$), defined as $(1 + i)^n$, has been compiled in the back of the book for various values of $i$ and $n$. An abbreviated compound interest or future-value interest factor table appears in Table 5-2, with a more comprehensive version of this table appearing in Appendix B at the back of this book. Alternatively, the $FVIF_{i,n}$ values could easily be determined using a calculator. Note that the compounding factors given in these tables represent the value of $1 compounded at rate $i$ at the *end* of the $n$th period. Thus, to calculate the future value of an initial investment, we need only determine the $FVIF_{i,n}$, using a calculator or the tables in Appendix B, and multiply this times the initial investment. In effect, we can rewrite equation 5-6 as follows:

**Future-value interest factor ($FVIF_{i,n}$)**
The value $(1 + i)^n$ used as a multiplier to calculate an amount's future value.

$$FV_n = PV(FVIF_{i,n}) \quad \textbf{(5-6a)}$$

**EXAMPLE**

If we invest $500 in a bank where it will earn 8 percent compounded annually, how much will it be worth at the end of 7 years? Looking at Table 5-2 in row $n = 7$ and column $i = 8\%$, we find that $FVIF_{8\%,7yrs}$ has a value of 1.714. Substituting this in equation 5-6a, we find

$$\begin{aligned} FV_n &= PV(FVIF_{8\%,7yrs}) \\ &= \$500(1.714) \\ &= \$857 \end{aligned}$$

Thus, we will have $857 at the end of 7 years.

We will find several uses for equation 5-6: Not only will we find the future value of an investment, but we can also solve for $PV$, $i$, or $n$. When we are given three of the four variables, we can solve for the fourth.

**EXAMPLE**

Let's assume that the Chrysler Corporation has guaranteed that the price of a new Jeep will always be \$20,000, and you'd like to buy one but currently have only \$7,752. How many years will it take for your initial investment of \$7,752 to grow to \$20,000 if it is invested at 9 percent compounded annually? We can use equation 5-6a to solve for this problem as well. Substituting the known values in equation 5-6a, you find

$$FV_n = PV(FVIF_{i,n})$$
$$\$20{,}000 = \$7{,}752(FVIF_{9\%,\,n\text{yrs}})$$
$$\frac{\$20{,}000}{\$7{,}752} = \frac{\$7{,}752(FVIF_{9\%,\,n\text{yrs}})}{\$7{,}752}$$
$$2.58 = FVIF_{9\%,\,n\text{yrs}}$$

Thus, you are looking for a value of 2.58 in the $FVIF_{i,n}$ tables, and you know it must be in the 9% column. To finish solving the problem, look down the 9% column for the value closest to 2.58. You find that it occurs in the $n = 11$ row. Thus, it will take 11 years for an initial investment of \$7,752 to grow to \$20,000 if it is invested at 9 percent compounded annually.

**EXAMPLE**

Now let's solve for the compound annual growth rate, and let's go back to that Jeep that always costs \$20,000. In 10 years, you'd really like to have \$20,000 to buy a new Jeep, but you only have \$11,167. At what rate must your \$11,167 be compounded annually for it to grow to \$20,000 in 10 years? Substituting the known variables into equation 5-6a, you get

$$FV_n = PV(FVIF_{i,n})$$
$$\$20{,}000 = \$11{,}167(FVIF_{i,\,10\text{yrs}})$$
$$\frac{\$20{,}000}{\$11{,}167} = \frac{\$11{,}167(FVIF_{i,\,10\text{yrs}})}{\$11{,}167}$$
$$1.791 = FVIF_{i,\,10\text{yrs}}$$

You know you are looking in the $n = 10$ row of the $FVIF_{i,n}$ tables for a value of 1.791, and you find this in the $i = 6\%$ column. Thus, if you want your initial investment of \$11,167 to grow to \$20,000 in 10 years, you must invest it at 6 percent.

Just how powerful is the time value of money? Manhattan Island was purchased by Peter Minuit from the Indians in 1624 for \$24 in "knickknacks" and jewelry. If at the end of 1624 the Indians had invested their \$24 at 8 percent compounded annually, it would be worth over \$88.6 trillion today (by the end of 2000, 376 years later). That's certainly enough to buy back all of Manhattan. In fact, with \$70 trillion in the bank, the \$80 to

$90 billion you'd have to pay to buy back all of Manhattan would only seem like pocket change. This story illustrates the incredible power of time in compounding. There simply is no substitute for it.

**CONCEPT CHECK**

1. Principle 2 states that "A Dollar Received Today Is Worth More Than a Dollar Received in the Future." Explain this statement.
2. How does compound interest differ from simple interest?
3. Explain the formula $FV_n = PV(1 + i)^n$

## Moving Money Through Time with the Aid of a Financial Calculator

Time value of money calculations can be made simple with the aid of a *financial calculator.* In solving time value of money problems with a financial calculator, you will be given three of four variables and will have to solve for the fourth. Before presenting any solutions using a financial calculator, we will introduce the calculator's five most common keys. (In most time value of money problems, only four of these keys are relevant.) These keys are:

| Menu Key | Description |
|---|---|
| N | Stores (or calculates) the total number of payments or compounding periods. |
| I/Y | Stores (or calculates) the interest or discount rate. |
| PV | Stores (or calculates) the present value of a cash flow or series of cash flows. |
| FV | Stores (or calculates) the future value, that is, the dollar amount of a final cash flow or the compound value of a single flow or series of cash flows. |
| PMT | Stores (or calculates) the dollar amount of each annuity payment deposited or received at the end of each year. |

When you use a financial calculator, remember that outflows generally have to be entered as negative numbers. In general, each problem will have two cash flows: one an outflow with a negative value, and one an inflow with a positive value. The idea is that you deposit money in the bank at some point in time (an outflow), and at some other point in time you take money out of the bank (an inflow). Also, every calculator operates a bit differently with respect to entering variables. Needless to say, it is a good idea to familiarize yourself with exactly how your calculator functions.

In any problem, you will be given three of four variables. These four variables will always include *N* and *I/Y;* in addition, two out of the final three variables *PV, FV,* and *PMT* will also be included. To solve a time value of money problem using a financial calculator, all you need to do is enter the appropriate numbers for three of the four variables, and press the key of the final variable to calculate its value. It is also a good idea to enter zero for any of the five variables not included in the problem in order to clear that variable.

Now let's solve the previous example using a financial calculator. We were trying to find at what rate $100 must be compounded annually for it to grow to $179.10 in 10 years. The solution using a financial calculator would be as follows:

**Step 1:** Input values of known variables

| Data Input | Function Key | Description |
|---|---|---|
| 10 | N | Stores $N = 10$ years |
| −100 | PV | Stores $PV = -\$100$ |
| 179.10 | FV | Stores $FV = \$179.10$ |
| 0 | PMT | Clears $PMT$ to $= 0$ |

**Step 2:** Calculate the value of the unknown variable

| Function Key | Answer | Description |
|---|---|---|
| CPT | | |
| I/Y | 6.00% | Calculates $I/Y = 6.00\%$ |

Any of the problems in this chapter can easily be solved using a financial calculator, and the solutions to many examples using a Texas Instrument (TI) BAII Plus financial calculator are provided in the margins. If you are using the TI BAII Plus, make sure that you have selected both the "END MODE" and "one payment per year" ($P/Y = 1$). This sets the payment conditions to a maximum of one payment per period occurring at the end of the period. One final point: You will notice that solutions using the present-value tables versus solutions using a calculator may vary slightly—a result of rounding errors in the tables.

For further explanation of the TI BAII Plus, see Appendix A at the end of the book.

## Spreadsheets and the Time Value of Money

Without question, in the real world most calculations involving moving money through time will be carried out with the help of a spreadsheet. While there are several competing spreadsheets, the most popular one is Microsoft Excel. Just as with the keystroke calculations on a financial calculator, a spreadsheet can make easy work of most common financial calculations. Following are some of the most common functions used with Excel when moving money through time:

| **Calculation** | **Formula** |
|---|---|
| Present value | =*PV*(rate,number of periods,payment,future value,type) |
| Future value | =*FV*(rate,number of periods,payment,present value,type) |
| Payment | =*PMT*(rate,number of periods,present value,future value,type) |
| Number of periods | =*NPER*(rate,payment,present value,future value,type) |
| Interest rate | =*RATE*(number of periods,payment,present value,future value,type,guess) |

where:

| | |
|---|---|
| Rate | = *i*, the interest rate or discount rate |
| Number of periods | = *n*, the number of years or periods |
| Payment | = *PMT*, the annuity payment deposited or received at the end of each period |
| Future value | = *FV*, the future value of the investment at the end of *n* periods or years |
| Present value | = *PV*, the present value of the future sum of money |
| Type | = when the payment is made (0 if omitted)<br>0 = at end of period<br>1 = at beginning of period |
| Guess | = a starting point when calculating the interest rate; if omitted, the calculations begin with a value of 0.1, or 10% |

Just like with a financial calculator, the outflows have to be entered as negative numbers. In general, each problem will have two cash flows—one positive and one negative. The idea is that you deposit money at some point in time (an outflow or negative value) and at some point later in time, you withdraw your money (an inflow or positive value). For example, let's look back on the example on page 131.

| | A–C | D |
|---|---|---|
| 1 | | |
| 2 | Spreadsheets and the Time Value of Money | |
| 3 | | |
| 4 | If we invest $500 in a bank where it will earn 8 percent compounded | |
| 5 | annually, how much will it be worth at the end of 7 years? | |
| 6 | | |
| 7 | rate (i) = | 8% |
| 8 | number of periods (n) = | 7 |
| 9 | payment (PMT) = | $0 |
| 10 | present value (PV) = | $500 |
| 11 | type (0 = at end of period) = | 0 |
| 12 | | |
| 13 | Future value = | $856.91 |
| 14 | | |
| 15 | Excel formula: =FV(rate,number of periods,payment,present value,type) | |
| 16 | | |
| 17 | Entered value in cell d13: =FV(d7,d8,d9,-d10,d11) | |
| 18 | Notice that present value ($500) took on a negative value. | |
| 19 | | |

Sheet1 / Sheet2 / Sheet3

| | A–C | D |
|---|---|---|
| 1 | Now let's solve for the value of i, just as we did on page 132. | |
| 2 | | |
| 3 | Spreadsheets: Solving for i | |
| 4 | | |
| 5 | In 10 years you'd like to have $20,000 to buy a new Jeep, but you only | |
| 6 | have $11,167. At what rate must your $11,167 be compounded | |
| 7 | annually for it to grow to $20,000 in 10 years? | |
| 8 | | |
| 9 | number of periods (n) = | 10 |
| 10 | payment (PMT) = | $0 |
| 11 | present value (PV) = | $11,167 |
| 12 | future value (FV) = | $20,000 |
| 13 | type (0 = at end of period) = | 0 |
| 14 | guess = | |
| 15 | | |
| 16 | i = | 6.00% |
| 17 | | |
| 18 | Excel formula: =RATE(number of periods,payment,present value,future value,type,guess) | |
| 19 | | |
| 20 | Entered value in cell d35: =RATE(d28,d29,-d30,d31,d32,d33) | |
| 21 | | |
| 22 | Notice that present value ($11,167) took on a negative value. | |
| 23 | Also note that if you didn't assign a value to guess, it would begin calculations | |
| 24 | with a value of 0.1 or 10%. If it could not come up with a value for i after | |
| 25 | 20 itterations, you would receive the #NUM! error message. Generally a | |
| 26 | guess between 10 and 100 percent will work. | |
| 27 | | |

Sheet1 / Sheet2 / Sheet3

## COMPOUND INTEREST WITH NONANNUAL PERIODS

OBJECTIVE 2 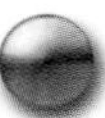

Until now, we have assumed that the compounding period is always annual; however, it need not be, as evidenced by savings and loan associations and commercial banks that compound on a quarterly, and in some cases a daily, basis. Fortunately, this adjustment of the compounding period follows the same format as that used for annual compounding. If we invest our money for 5 years at 8 percent interest compounded semiannually, we are really investing our money for 10 six-month periods during which we receive 4 percent interest each period. If it is compounded quarterly, we receive 2 percent interest per period for 20 three-month periods. Table 5-3 illustrates the importance of nonannual compounding. For example, if you invested $100 at 15 percent you would end up with about 5 percent more if it was compounded semiannually instead of annually, and about 10 percent more if the compounding occurred daily. This process can easily be generalized, giving us the following formula for finding the future value of an investment for which interest is compounded in nonannual periods:

$$FV_n = PV\left(1 + \frac{i}{m}\right)^{mn} \quad \textbf{(5-7)}$$

where $FV_n$ = the future value of the investment at the end of $n$ years
$n$ = the number of years during which the compounding occurs
$i$ = annual interest (or discount) rate
$PV$ = the present value or original amount invested at the beginning of the first year
$m$ = the number of times compounding occurs during the year

**CALCULATOR SOLUTION**

| Data Input | Function Key |
|---|---|
| 20 | N |
| 3 | I/Y |
| 100 | PV |
| 0 | PMT |

| Function Key | Answer |
|---|---|
| CPT | |
| FV | −180.61 |

### EXAMPLE

If we place $100 in a savings account that yields 12 percent compounded quarterly, what will our investment grow to at the end of 5 years? Substituting $n = 5$, $m = 4$, $i = 12$ percent, and $PV = \$100$ into equation 5-7, we find

$$FV_5 = \$100\left(1 + \frac{.12}{4}\right)^{4\cdot 5}$$

$$= \$100(1 + .03)^{20}$$
$$= \$100(1.806)$$
$$= \$180.60$$

Thus, we will have $180.60 at the end of 5 years. Notice that the calculator solution is slightly different because of rounding errors in the tables, as explained in the previous section, and that it also takes on a negative value.

Obviously, the choice of the interest rate plays a critical role in how much an investment grows, but do small changes in the interest rate have much of an impact on future values? To answer this question, let's look back to Peter Minuit's purchase of Manhattan. If the Indians had invested their $24 at 10 percent rather than 8 percent compounded annually at the end of 1624, they would have over $88 quadrillion by the end of 2000 (376 years). That is 88 followed by 15 zeros, or $88,000,000,000,000,000. Actually, that is enough to buy back not only Manhattan Island, but the entire world and still have plenty

**TABLE 5-3**
The Value of $100 Compounded at Various Nonannual Periods

| For 1 Year at *i* Percent | *i* = | 2% | 5% | 10% | 15% |
|---|---|---|---|---|---|
| Compounded annually | | $102.00 | $105.00 | $110.00 | $115.00 |
| Compounded semiannually | | 102.01 | 105.06 | 110.25 | 115.56 |
| Compounded quarterly | | 102.02 | 105.09 | 110.38 | 115.87 |
| Compounded monthly | | 102.02 | 105.12 | 110.47 | 116.08 |
| Compounded weekly (52) | | 102.02 | 105.12 | 110.51 | 116.16 |
| Compounded daily (365) | | 102.02 | 105.13 | 110.52 | 116.18 |

| For 10 Years at *i* Percent | *i* = | 2% | 5% | 10% | 15% |
|---|---|---|---|---|---|
| Compounded annually | | $121.90 | $162.89 | $259.37 | $404.56 |
| Compounded semiannually | | 122.02 | 163.86 | 265.33 | 424.79 |
| Compounded quarterly | | 122.08 | 164.36 | 268.51 | 436.04 |
| Compounded monthly | | 122.12 | 164.70 | 270.70 | 444.02 |
| Compounded weekly (52) | | 122.14 | 164.83 | 271.57 | 447.20 |
| Compounded daily (365) | | 122.14 | 164.87 | 271.79 | 448.03 |

left over! Now let's assume a lower interest rate—say, 6 percent. In that case, the $24 would have only grown to a mere $78.6 billion—less than 1/100th of what it grew to at 8 percent, and only one-millionth of what it would have grown to at 10 percent. With today's real estate prices, you'd have a tough time buying Manhattan, but if you did, you probably couldn't pay your taxes! To say the least, the interest rate is extremely important in investing.

**CONCEPT CHECK**

1. Why does the future value of a given amount increase when interest is compounded nonannually as opposed to annually?
2. How do you adjust the present and future value formulas when interest is compounded monthly?

## PRESENT VALUE

Up until this point, we have been moving money forward in time; that is, we know how much we have to begin with and are trying to determine how much that sum will grow in a certain number of years when compounded at a specific rate. We are now going to look at the reverse question: What is the value in today's dollars of a sum of money to be received in the future? The answer to this question will help us determine the desirability of investment projects in Chapters 9 through 11. In this case, we are moving future money back to the present. We will be determining the **present value** of a lump sum, which in simple terms is the current value of a future payment. What we will be doing is, in fact, nothing other than inverse compounding. The differences in these techniques come about merely from the investor's point of view. In compounding, we talked about the compound interest rate and the initial investment; in determining the present value, we will talk about the discount rate, and the present value of future cash flows. Determination of the discount rate is the subject of Chapter 6, and can be defined as the rate of return available on an investment of equal risk to what is being discounted. Other

**Present value**
The current value of a future sum.

than that, the technique and the terminology remain the same, and the mathematics are simply reversed. In equation 5-6, we attempt to determine the future value of an initial investment. We now want to determine the initial investment or present value. By dividing both sides of equation 5-6 by $(1 + i)^n$, we get

$$PV = FV_n\left[\frac{1}{(1 + i)^n}\right] \tag{5-8}$$

where $PV$ = the present value of the future sum of money
$FV_n$ = the future value of the investment at the end of $n$ years
$n$ = the number of years until the payment will be received
$i$ = the annual discount (or interest) rate

Because the mathematical procedure for determining the present value is exactly the inverse of determining the future value, we also find that the relationships among $n$, $i$, and $PV$ are just the opposite of those we observed in future value. The present value of a future sum of money is inversely related to both the number of years until the payment will be received and the discount rate. Graphically, this relationship can be seen in Figure 5-2. Although the present value equation (equation 5-8) will be used extensively in evaluating new investment proposals, it should be stressed that the present value equation is actually the same as the future value or compounding equation (equation 5-6) where it is solved for $PV$.

**CALCULATOR SOLUTION**

| Data Input | Function Key |
|---|---|
| 10 | N |
| 6 | I/Y |
| 500 | FV |
| 0 | PMT |

| Function Key | Answer |
|---|---|
| CPT | |
| PV | −279.20 |

**EXAMPLE**

What is the present value of \$500 to be received 10 years from today if our discount rate is 6 percent? Substituting $FV_{10}$ = \$500, $n$ = 10, and $i$ = 6 percent into equation 5-8, we find

$$\begin{aligned} PV &= \$500\left[\frac{1}{(1 + .06)^{10}}\right] \\ &= \$500\left(\frac{1}{1.791}\right) \\ &= \$500(.558) \\ &= \$279 \end{aligned}$$

Thus, the present value of the \$500 to be received in 10 years is \$279.

**Present-value interest factor ($PVIF_{i,n}$)** The value $[1/(1 + i)^n]$ used as a multiplier to calculate an amount's present value.

To aid in the computation of present values, the **present-value interest factor** for $i$ and $n$, or $PVIF_{i,n}$, which is equal to $[1/(1 + i)^n]$, has been compiled for various combinations of $i$ and $n$ and appears in Appendix C at the back of this book. An abbreviated version of Appendix C appears in Table 5-4. A close examination shows that the values in Table 5-4 are merely the inverse of those found in Appendix B. This, of course, is as it should be, as the values in Appendix B are $(1 + i)^n$ and those in Appendix C are $[1/(1 + i)^n]$. Now to determine the present value of a sum of money to be received at some future date, we need only determine the value of the appropriate $PVIF_{i,n}$, either by using a calculator or consulting the tables, and multiply it by the future value. In effect, we can use our new notation and rewrite equation 5-8 as follows:

$$PV = FV_n(PVIF_{i,n}) \tag{5-8a}$$

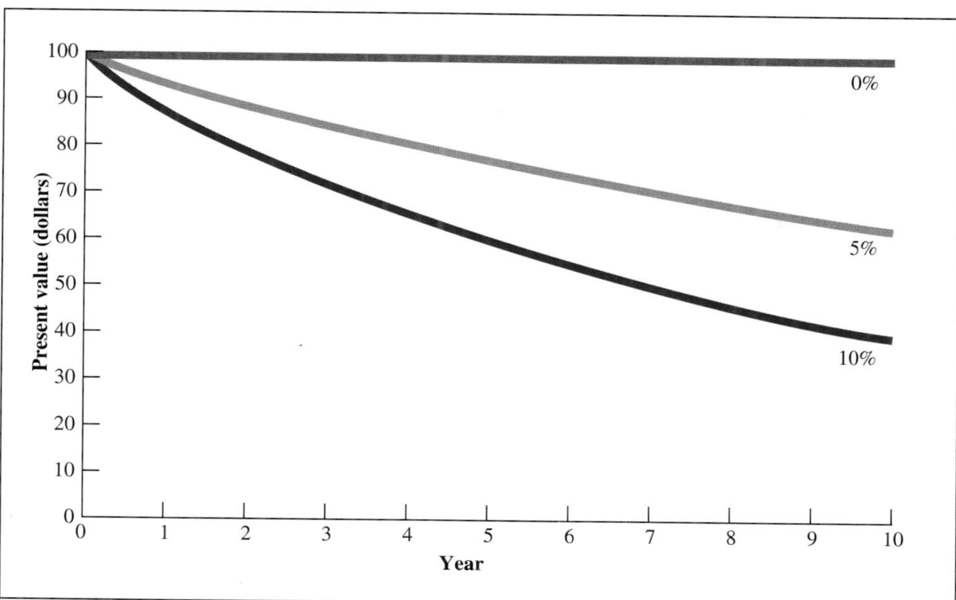


**FIGURE 5-2**
Present Value of $100 to Be Received at a Future Date and Discounted Back to the Present at 0, 5, and 10 Percent

## EXAMPLE

You're on vacation in a rather remote part of Florida and see an advertisement stating that if you take a sales tour of some condominiums, "you will be given $100 just for taking the tour." However, the $100 that you get is in the form of a savings bond that will not pay you the $100 for 10 years. What is the present value of $100 to be received 10 years from today if your discount rate is 6 percent? By looking at the $n$ = 10 row and $i$ = 6% column of Table 5-4, you find the $PVIF_{6\%,10\text{yrs}}$ is .558. Substituting $FV_{10}$ = $100 and $PVIF_{6\%,10\text{yrs}}$ = .558 into equation 5-8a, you find

$$
\begin{aligned}
PV &= \$100\,(PVIF_{6\%,10\text{yrs}}) \\
&= \$100(.558) \\
&= \$55.80
\end{aligned}
$$

Thus, the value in today's dollars of that $100 savings bond is only $55.80.

**CALCULATOR SOLUTION**

| Data Input | Function Key |
|---|---|
| 10 | N |
| 6 | I/Y |
| 100 | FV |
| 0 | PMT |

| Function Key | Answer |
|---|---|
| CPT | |
| PV | −55.84 |

**TABLE 5-4**
$PVIF_{i,n}$ or the Present Value of $1

| n | 1% | 2% | 3% | 4% | 5% | 6% | 7% | 8% | 9% | 10% |
|---|---|---|---|---|---|---|---|---|---|---|
| 1 | .990 | .980 | .971 | .962 | .952 | .943 | .935 | .926 | .917 | .909 |
| 2 | .980 | .961 | .943 | .925 | .907 | .890 | .873 | .857 | .842 | .826 |
| 3 | .971 | .942 | .915 | .889 | .864 | .840 | .816 | .794 | .772 | .751 |
| 4 | .961 | .924 | .888 | .855 | .823 | .792 | .763 | .735 | .708 | .683 |
| 5 | .951 | .906 | .863 | .822 | .784 | .747 | .713 | .681 | .650 | .621 |
| 6 | .942 | .888 | .837 | .790 | .746 | .705 | .666 | .630 | .596 | .564 |
| 7 | .933 | .871 | .813 | .760 | .711 | .655 | .623 | .583 | .547 | .513 |
| 8 | .923 | .853 | .789 | .731 | .677 | .627 | .582 | .540 | .502 | .467 |
| 9 | .914 | .837 | .766 | .703 | .645 | .592 | .544 | .500 | .460 | .424 |
| 10 | .905 | .820 | .744 | .676 | .614 | .558 | .508 | .463 | .422 | .386 |
| 11 | .896 | .804 | .722 | .650 | .585 | .527 | .475 | .429 | .388 | .350 |
| 12 | .887 | .789 | .701 | .625 | .557 | .497 | .444 | .397 | .356 | .319 |
| 13 | .879 | .773 | .681 | .601 | .530 | .469 | .415 | .368 | .326 | .290 |
| 14 | .870 | .758 | .661 | .577 | .505 | .442 | .388 | .340 | .299 | .263 |
| 15 | .861 | .743 | .642 | .555 | .481 | .417 | .362 | .315 | .275 | .239 |

## Dealing with Multiple, Uneven Cash Flows

Again, we only have one present value–future value equation; that is, equations 5-6 and 5-8 are identical. We have introduced them as separate equations to simplify our calculations; in one case, we are determining the value in future dollars and in the other case, the value in today's dollars. In either case, the reason is the same: To compare values on alternative investments and to recognize that the value of a dollar received today is not the same as that of a dollar received at some future date, we must measure the dollar values in dollars of the same time period.

In the chapter opening we discussed Harley-Davidson investing in the costly development of the Buell Blast in 1997 and receiving income on that investment in the year 2000 and beyond. The concept of present value allows us to bring those future cash flows back to the present and view them in terms of today's dollars. Moreover, because all present values are comparable (they are all measured in dollars of the same time period), we can add and subtract the present value of inflows and outflows to determine the present value of an investment. Let's now look at an example of an investment that has two cash flows in different time periods and determine the present value of this investment.

**EXAMPLE**

What is the present value of an investment that yields \$500 to be received in 5 years and \$1,000 to be received in 10 years if the discount rate is 4 percent? Substituting the values of $n = 5$, $i = 4$ percent, and $FV_5 = \$500$; and $n = 10$, $i = 4$ percent, and $FV_{10} = \$1,000$ into equation 5-8 and adding these values together, we find

$$\begin{aligned} PV &= \$500\left[\frac{1}{(1 + .04)^5}\right] + \$1,000\left[\frac{1}{(1 + .04)^{10}}\right] \\ &= \$500(PVIF_{4\%,5\text{yrs}}) + \$1,000(PVIF_{4\%,10\text{yrs}}) \\ &= \$500(.822) + \$1,000(.676) \\ &= \$411 + \$676 \\ &= \$1,087 \end{aligned}$$

Again, present values are comparable because they are measured in the same time period's dollars.

**CONCEPT CHECK**

1. What is the relationship between the present value equation (5-7) and the future value or compounding equation (5-6)?
2. Why is the present value of a future sum always less than that sum's future value?

## ANNUITIES—A LEVEL STREAM

OBJECTIVE 4 

**Annuity**
A series of equal dollar payments for a specified number of years.

An **annuity** is a series of equal dollar payments for a specified number of years. Because annuities occur frequently in finance—for example, interest payments on bonds are in effect annuities—we will treat them specially. Although compounding and determining the present value of an annuity can be dealt with using the methods we have just described, these processes can be time consuming, especially for larger annuities. Thus we have modified the formulas to deal directly with annuities.

Although all annuities involve a series of equal dollar payments for a specified number of years, there are two basic types of annuities: an **ordinary annuity** and an **annuity due.** With an ordinary annuity, we assume that the payments occur at the end of each period; with an annuity due, the payments occur at the beginning of each period. Because an annuity due provides the payments earlier (at the beginning of each period instead of the end as with an ordinary annuity), it has a greater present value. After we master ordinary annuities, we will examine annuities due. However, in finance, ordinary annuities are used much more frequently than are annuities due. Thus, in this text, whenever the term "annuity" is used, you should assume that we are referring to an ordinary annuity unless otherwise specified.

**Ordinary annuity**
An annuity in which the payments occur at the end of each period.

**Annuity due**
An annuity in which the payments occur at the beginning of each period.

## Compound Annuities

A **compound annuity** involves depositing or investing an equal sum of money at the end of each year for a certain number of years and allowing it to grow. Perhaps we are saving money for education, a new car, or a vacation home. In any case, we want to know how much our savings will have grown by some point in the future.

**Compound annuity**
Depositing an equal sum of money at the end of each year for a certain number of years and allowing it to grow.

Actually, we can find the answer by using equation 5-6, our compounding equation, and compounding each of the individual deposits to its future value. For example, if to provide for a college education we are going to deposit \$500 at the end of each year for the next 5 years in a bank where it will earn 6 percent interest, how much will we have at the end of 5 years? Compounding each of these values using equation 5-6, we find that we will have \$2,818.50 at the end of 5 years.

$$\begin{aligned} FV_5 &= \$500(1+.06)^4 + \$500(1+.06)^3 + \$500(1+.06)^2 + \$500(1+.06) + \$500 \\ &= \$500(1.262) + \$500(1.191) + \$500(1.124) + \$500(1.060) + \$500 \\ &= \$631.00 + \$595.50 + \$562.00 + \$530.00 + \$500.00 \\ &= \$2{,}818.50 \end{aligned}$$

**CALCULATOR SOLUTION**

| Data Input | Function Key |
|---|---|
| 5 | N |
| 6 | I/Y |
| 0 | PV |
| 500 | PMT |
| **Function Key** | **Answer** |
| CPT | |
| FV | −2,818.55 |

To better understand what's happening, let's look at this problem using a time line. A time line is simply a horizontal line on which the present—time period zero—is at the leftmost end. Future time periods are then shown along the line moving from left to right. The dollar amount of the cash flow is shown below the line, with positive values representing cash inflows, and negative values representing cash outflows. We will frequently use time lines to illustrate the timing of an investment's cash flows. In the present example, cash flows of \$500 are received at the end of years 1 through 5 and are presented graphically in Table 5-5. From examining the mathematics involved and the graph of the movement of money through time in Table 5-5, we can see that this procedure can be generalized to

$$FV_n = PMT\left[\sum_{t=0}^{n-1}(1+i)^t\right] \tag{5-9}$$

where $FV_n$ = the future value of the annuity at the end of the $n$th year
$PMT$ = the annuity payment deposited or received at the end of each year
$i$ = the annual interest (or discount) rate
$n$ = the number of years for which the annuity will last

To aid in compounding annuities, the **future-value interest factor for an annuity** for $i$ and $n$ ($FVIFA_{i,n}$), defined as $\left[\sum_{t=0}^{n-1}(1+i)^t\right]$, is provided in Appendix D for various combinations of $n$ and $i$. An abbreviated version is shown in Table 5-6.

**Future-value interest factor for an annuity ($FVIFA_{i,n}$)**
The value $\left[\sum_{t=0}^{n-1}(1+i)^t\right]$ used as a multiplier to calculate the future value of an annuity.

**TABLE 5-5**
Illustration of a 5-Year $500 Annuity Compounded at 6 Percent

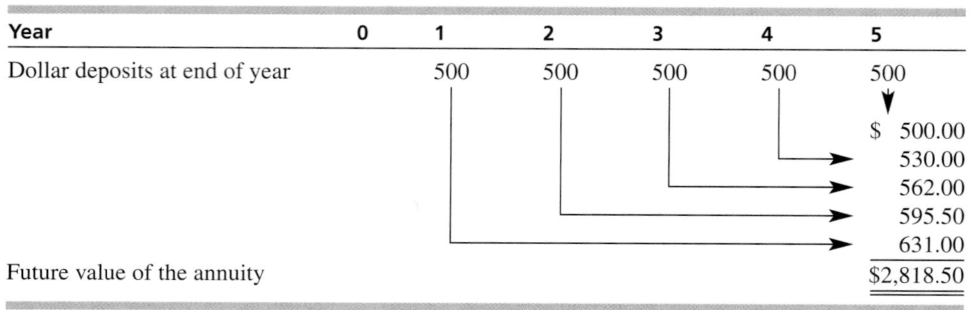


Using this new notation, we can rewrite equation 5-9 as follows:

$$FV_n = PMT(FVIFA_{i,n}) \tag{5-9a}$$

The $FVIFA_{i,n}$ can also be calculated as follows:

$$FVIFA_{i,n} = \frac{(1+i)^n - 1}{i} \tag{5-9b}$$

This formula is useful if you don't have a financial calculator or tables.

Reexamining the previous example, in which we determined the value after 5 years of $500 deposited at the end of each of the next 5 years in the bank at 6 percent, we would look in the $i = 6\%$ column and $n = 5$ year row and find the value of the $FVIFA_{6\%,5\text{yrs}}$ to be 5.637. Substituting this value into equation 5-9a, we get

$$\begin{aligned} FV_5 &= \$500(5.637) \\ &= \$2{,}818.50 \end{aligned}$$

This is the same answer we obtained earlier.

Rather than asking how much we will accumulate if we deposit an equal sum in a savings account each year, a more common question is how much we must deposit each year to accumulate a certain amount of savings. This problem frequently occurs with respect to saving for large expenditures and pension funding obligations.

**TABLE 5-6**
*$FVIFA_{i,n}$* or the Sum of an Annuity of $1 for *n* Years

| *n* | 1% | 2% | 3% | 4% | 5% | 6% | 7% | 8% | 9% | 10% |
|---|---|---|---|---|---|---|---|---|---|---|
| 1 | 1.000 | 1.000 | 1.000 | 1.000 | 1.000 | 1.000 | 0.000 | 1.000 | 1.000 | 1.000 |
| 2 | 2.010 | 2.020 | 2.030 | 2.040 | 2.050 | 2.060 | 2.070 | 2.080 | 2.090 | 2.100 |
| 3 | 3.030 | 3.060 | 3.091 | 3.122 | 3.152 | 3.184 | 3.215 | 3.246 | 3.278 | 3.310 |
| 4 | 4.060 | 4.122 | 4.184 | 4.246 | 4.310 | 4.375 | 4.440 | 4.506 | 4.573 | 4.641 |
| 5 | 5.101 | 5.204 | 5.309 | 5.416 | 5.526 | 5.637 | 5.751 | 5.867 | 5.985 | 6.105 |
| 6 | 6.152 | 6.308 | 6.468 | 6.633 | 6.802 | 6.975 | 7.153 | 7.336 | 7.523 | 7.716 |
| 7 | 7.214 | 7.434 | 7.662 | 7.898 | 8.142 | 8.394 | 8.654 | 8.923 | 9.200 | 9.487 |
| 8 | 8.286 | 8.583 | 8.892 | 9.214 | 9.549 | 9.897 | 10.260 | 10.637 | 11.028 | 11.436 |
| 9 | 9.368 | 9.755 | 10.159 | 10.583 | 11.027 | 11.491 | 11.978 | 12.488 | 13.021 | 13.579 |
| 10 | 10.462 | 10.950 | 11.464 | 12.006 | 12.578 | 13.181 | 13.816 | 14.487 | 15.193 | 15.937 |
| 11 | 11.567 | 12.169 | 12.808 | 13.486 | 14.207 | 14.972 | 15.784 | 16.645 | 17.560 | 18.531 |
| 12 | 12.682 | 13.412 | 14.192 | 15.026 | 15.917 | 16.870 | 17.888 | 18.977 | 20.141 | 21.384 |
| 13 | 13.809 | 14.680 | 15.618 | 16.627 | 17.713 | 18.882 | 20.141 | 21.495 | 22.953 | 24.523 |
| 14 | 14.947 | 15.974 | 17.086 | 18.292 | 19.598 | 21.015 | 22.550 | 24.215 | 26.019 | 27.975 |
| 15 | 16.097 | 17.293 | 18.599 | 20.023 | 21.578 | 23.276 | 25.129 | 27.152 | 29.361 | 31.772 |

For example, we may know that we need $10,000 for education in 8 years; how much must we deposit at the end of each year in the bank at 6 percent interest to have the college money ready? In this case, we know the values of $n$, $i$, and $FV_n$ in equation 5-9; what we do not know is the value of *PMT*. Substituting these example values in equation 5-9, we find

$$\$10{,}000 = PMT\left[\sum_{t=0}^{8-1}(1+.06)^t\right]$$

$$\$10{,}000 = PMT(FVIFA_{6\%,8yrs})$$

$$\$10{,}000 = PMT(9.897)$$

$$\frac{\$10{,}000}{9.897} = PMT$$

$$PMT = \$1{,}010.41$$

Thus, we must deposit $1,010.41 in the bank at the end of each year for 8 years at 6 percent interest to accumulate $10,000 at the end of 8 years.

**CALCULATOR SOLUTION**

| Data Input | Function Key |
| --- | --- |
| 8 | N |
| 6 | I/Y |
| 10,000 | FV |
| 0 | PV |

| Function Key | Answer |
| --- | --- |
| CPT | |
| PMT | −1,010.36 |

**EXAMPLE**

How much must we deposit in an 8 percent savings account at the end of each year to accumulate $5,000 at the end of 10 years? Substituting the values $FV_{10} = \$5{,}000$, $n = 10$, and $i = 8$ percent into equation 5-9, we find

$$\$5{,}000 = PMT\left[\sum_{t=0}^{10-1}(1+.08)^t\right] = PMT(FVIFA_{8\%,10yrs})$$

$$\$5{,}000 = PMT(14.487)$$

$$\frac{\$5{,}000}{14.487} = PMT$$

$$PMT = \$345.14$$

Thus, we must deposit $345.14 per year for 10 years at 8 percent to accumulate $5,000.

**CALCULATOR SOLUTION**

| Data Input | Function Key |
| --- | --- |
| 10 | N |
| 8 | I/Y |
| 5,000 | FV |
| 0 | PV |

| Function Key | Answer |
| --- | --- |
| CPT | |
| PMT | −345.15 |

## Present Value of an Annuity

Pension funds, insurance obligations, and interest received from bonds all involve annuities. To value them, we need to know the present value of each. Although we can find this by using the present-value table in Appendix C, this can be time consuming, particularly when the annuity lasts for several years. For example, if we wish to know what $500 received at the end of the next 5 years is worth to us today given the appropriate discount rate of 6 percent, we can simply substitute the appropriate values into equation 5-8, such that

$$PV = \$500\left[\frac{1}{(1+.06)^1}\right] + \$500\left[\frac{1}{(1+.06)^2}\right] + \$500\left[\frac{1}{(1+.06)^3}\right]$$

$$+ \$500\left[\frac{1}{(1+.06)^4}\right] + \$500\left[\frac{1}{(1+.06)^5}\right]$$

$$= \$500(.943) + \$500(.890) + \$500(.840) + \$500(.792) + \$500(.747)$$

$$= \$2{,}106$$

**FINANCE MATTERS**

## Make a Child (or Yourself) a Millionaire

Thanks a million.

Even if you haven't got a lot of money, you can easily give \$1 million or more to your children, grandchildren, or favorite charity. All it takes is a small initial investment and a lot of time.

Suppose your 16-year-old daughter plans to take a summer job, which will pay her at least \$2,000. Because she has earned income, she can open an individual retirement account. If you would like to help fund her retirement, Kenneth Klegon, a financial planner in Lansing, Michigan, suggests giving her \$2,000 to set up the IRA. He then advises doing the same in each of the next 5 years, so that your daughter stashes away a total of \$12,000.

Result? If the money is invested in stocks, and stocks deliver their historical average annual return of 10%, your daughter will have more than \$1 million by the time she turns 65.

Using the principles and techniques set out in this chapter, we can easily see how much this IRA investment will accumulate to. We can first take the \$2,000 6-year annuity and determine its future value—that is, its value when your daughter is 21 and receives the last payment. This would be done as follows:

$$\begin{aligned} FV &= PMT(FVIFA_{10\%,\, 6yrs}) \\ &= \$2{,}000(FVIFA_{10\%,\, 6yrs}) \\ &= \$15{,}431.22 \end{aligned}$$

We could then take this amount that your daughter has when she is 21 and compound it out 44 years to when she is 65, as follows:

$$\begin{aligned} FV &= PV(FVIF_{10\%,\, 44yrs}) \\ &= \$15{,}431.22(FVIF_{10\%,44yrs}) \\ &= \$1{,}022{,}535.54 \end{aligned}$$

Thus, your daughter's IRA would have accumulated to \$1,022,535.54 by age 65 if it grew at 10 percent compounded annually.

Because of the corrosive effect of inflation, that \$1 million will only buy a quarter of what \$1 million buys today, presuming the cost of living rises at 3 percent a year.

To determine how much this is worth in today's dollars, if inflation increases at an annual rate of 3 percent over this period, we need only calculate the present value of \$1,022,535.54 to be received 49 years from now given a discount rate of 3 percent. This would determine the future value of this IRA measured in dollars with the same spending power as those around when your daughter was 16. This is done as follows:

$$\begin{aligned} PV &= FV(PVIF_{3\%,\, 49yrs}) \\ &= \$1{,}022{,}535.54(PVIF_{3\%,\, 49yrs}) \\ &= \$240{,}245.02 \end{aligned}$$

You can change the growth and inflation rates and come up with all kinds of numbers, but one thing holds: There is incredible power in compounding! Nonetheless, your \$12,000 gift will go a long way toward paying for your daughter's retirement. The huge gain is possible because of the way stock market compounding works, with money earned each year not only on your initial investment, but also on the gains accumulated from earlier years.

"The beauty of this strategy is that it will grow tax-deferred," Klegon says. "There's no cost. You can set up an IRA with a no-load mutual fund for nothing." Similarly, Mr. Klegon says, once your children enter the workforce full time, you can encourage them to participate in their company's 401(k) plan by reimbursing them for their contributions.

Source: Jonathan Clements, "Make a Child a Millionaire," *The Wall Street Journal* (April 22, 1994): C1. Reprinted by permission of *The Wall Street Journal,* 

Thus, the present value of this annuity is \$2,106.00. From examining the mathematics involved and the graph of the movement of these funds through time in Table 5-7, we see that we are simply summing up the present values of each cash flow. Thus, this procedure can be generalized to

$$PV = PMT\left[\sum_{t=1}^{n} \frac{1}{(1+i)^t}\right] \tag{5-10}$$

where $PMT$ = the annuity payment deposited or received at the end of each year
$i$ = the annual discount (or interest) rate
$PV$ = the present value of the future annuity
$n$ = the number of years for which the annuity will last

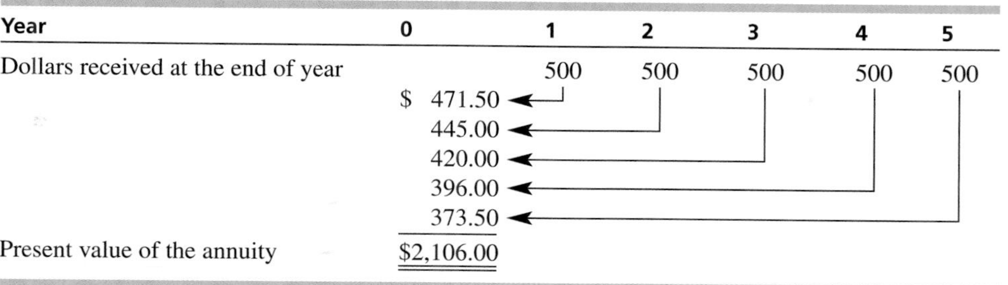

| Year | 0 | 1 | 2 | 3 | 4 | 5 |
|---|---|---|---|---|---|---|
| Dollars received at the end of year | | 500 | 500 | 500 | 500 | 500 |
| | $ 471.50 ← (year 1) | | | | | |
| | 445.00 ← (year 2) | | | | | |
| | 420.00 ← (year 3) | | | | | |
| | 396.00 ← (year 4) | | | | | |
| | 373.50 ← (year 5) | | | | | |
| Present value of the annuity | $2,106.00 | | | | | |

**TABLE 5-7**
Illustration of a 5-Year $500 Annuity Discounted Back to the Present at 6 Percent

To simplify the process of determining the present value for an annuity, the **present-value interest factor for an annuity** for $i$ and $n$ ($PVIFA_{i,n}$), defined as $\left[\sum_{t=1}^{n} \frac{1}{(1+i)^t}\right]$, has been compiled for various combinations of $i$ and $n$ in Appendix E, with an abbreviated version provided in Table 5-8.

**Present-value interest factor for an annuity ($PVIFA_{i,n}$)**
The value $\left[\sum_{t=1}^{n} \frac{1}{(1+i)^t}\right]$ used as a multiplier to calculate the present value of an annuity.

Using this new notation, we can rewrite equation 5-10 as follows:

$$PV = PMT(PVIFA_{i,n}) \tag{5-10a}$$

The $PVIFA_{i,n}$ can also be calculated as follows:

$$PVIFA_{i,n} = \frac{1 - \frac{1}{(1+i)^n}}{i} \tag{5-10b}$$

This formula is useful if you don't have a financial calculator or tables.

Solving the previous example to find the present value of $500 received at the end of each of the next 5 years discounted back to the present at 6 percent, we look in the $i = 6\%$ column and $n = 5$ year row and find the $PVIFA_{6\%,5yr}$ to be 4.212. Substituting the appropriate values into equation 5-10a, we find

$$PV = \$500(4.212)$$
$$= \$2,106$$

**TABLE 5-8**
$PVIFA_{i,n}$ or the Present Value of an Annuity of $1

| n | 1% | 2% | 3% | 4% | 5% | 6% | 7% | 8% | 9% | 10% |
|---|---|---|---|---|---|---|---|---|---|---|
| 1 | 0.990 | 0.980 | 0.971 | 0.962 | 0.952 | 0.943 | 0.935 | 0.926 | 0.917 | 0.909 |
| 2 | 1.970 | 1.942 | 1.913 | 1.886 | 1.859 | 1.833 | 1.808 | 1.783 | 1.759 | 1.736 |
| 3 | 2.941 | 2.884 | 2.829 | 2.775 | 2.723 | 2.673 | 2.624 | 2.577 | 2.531 | 2.487 |
| 4 | 3.902 | 3.808 | 3.717 | 3.630 | 3.546 | 3.465 | 3.387 | 3.312 | 3.240 | 3.170 |
| 5 | 4.853 | 4.713 | 4.580 | 4.452 | 4.329 | 4.212 | 4.100 | 3.993 | 3.890 | 3.791 |
| 6 | 5.795 | 5.601 | 5.417 | 5.242 | 5.076 | 4.917 | 4.767 | 4.623 | 4.486 | 4.355 |
| 7 | 6.728 | 6.472 | 6.230 | 6.002 | 5.786 | 5.582 | 5.389 | 5.206 | 5.033 | 4.868 |
| 8 | 7.652 | 7.326 | 7.020 | 6.733 | 6.463 | 6.210 | 5.971 | 5.747 | 5.535 | 5.335 |
| 9 | 8.566 | 8.162 | 7.786 | 7.435 | 7.108 | 6.802 | 6.515 | 6.247 | 5.995 | 5.759 |
| 10 | 9.471 | 8.983 | 8.530 | 8.111 | 7.722 | 7.360 | 7.024 | 6.710 | 6.418 | 6.145 |
| 11 | 10.368 | 9.787 | 9.253 | 8.760 | 8.306 | 7.887 | 7.499 | 7.139 | 6.805 | 6.495 |
| 12 | 11.255 | 10.575 | 9.954 | 9.385 | 8.863 | 8.384 | 7.943 | 7.536 | 7.161 | 6.814 |
| 13 | 12.134 | 11.348 | 10.635 | 9.986 | 9.394 | 8.853 | 8.358 | 7.904 | 7.487 | 7.103 |
| 14 | 13.004 | 12.106 | 11.296 | 10.563 | 9.899 | 9.295 | 8.746 | 8.244 | 7.786 | 7.367 |
| 15 | 13.865 | 12.849 | 11.938 | 11.118 | 10.380 | 9.712 | 9.108 | 8.560 | 8.061 | 7.606 |

**TABLE 5-9**
Present Value of a 6-Year Annuity Discounted at 8 Percent

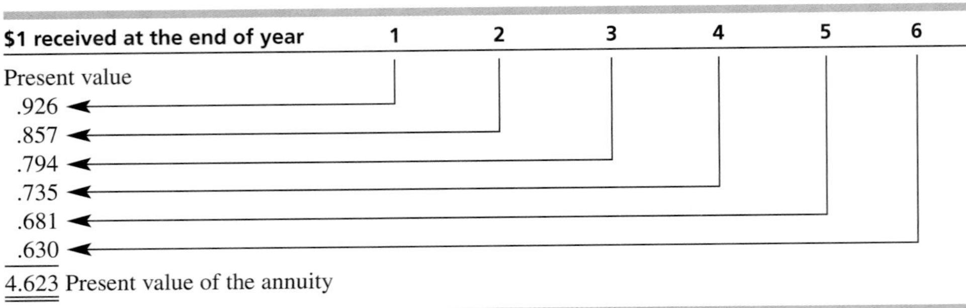

| $1 received at the end of year | 1 | 2 | 3 | 4 | 5 | 6 |
|---|---|---|---|---|---|---|
| Present value | | | | | | |
| .926 | ← | | | | | |
| .857 | | ← | | | | |
| .794 | | | ← | | | |
| .735 | | | | ← | | |
| .681 | | | | | ← | |
| .630 | | | | | | ← |
| 4.623 Present value of the annuity | | | | | | |

This, of course, is the same answer we calculated when we individually discounted each cash flow to the present. The reason is that we really only have one table: All of the tables are derived from Table 5-2; the Table 5-8 value for an $n$-year annuity for any discount rate $i$ is merely the sum of the first $n$ values in Table 5-4. We can see this by comparing the value in the present-value-of-an-annuity table (Table 5-8) for $i = 8$ percent and $n = 6$ years, which is 4.623, with the sum of the values in the $i = 8\%$ column and $n = 1, \ldots,$ six rows of the present-value table (Table 5-4), which is equal to 4.623, as shown in Table 5-9.

**CALCULATOR SOLUTION**

| Data Input | Function Key |
|---|---|
| 10 | N |
| 5 | I/Y |
| 1,000 | PMT |
| 0 | FV |
| **Function Key** | **Answer** |
| CPT | |
| PV | −7,721.73 |

**EXAMPLE**

What is the present value of a 10-year $1,000 annuity discounted back to the present at 5 percent? Substituting $n = 10$ years, $i = 5$ percent, and $PMT = \$1{,}000$ into equation 5-10, we find

$$PV = \$1{,}000\left[\sum_{t=1}^{10} \frac{1}{(1 + .05)^t}\right] = \$1{,}000(PVIFA_{5\%,10\text{yrs}})$$

Determining the value for the $PVIFA_{5\%,10\text{yrs}}$ from Table 5-8, row $n = 10$, column $i = 5\%$, and substituting it in, we get

$$\begin{aligned} PV &= \$1{,}000(7.722) \\ &= \$7{,}722 \end{aligned}$$

Thus, the present value of this annuity is $7,722.

**CALCULATOR SOLUTION**

| Data Input | Function Key |
|---|---|
| 5 | N |
| 8 | I/Y |
| 5,000 | PV |
| 0 | FV |
| **Function Key** | **Answer** |
| CPT | |
| PMT | −1,252.28 |

As with our other compounding and present-value tables, given any three of the four unknowns in equation 5-10, we can solve for the fourth. In the case of the present-value-of-an-annuity table, we may be interested in solving for $PMT$ if we know $i$, $n$, and $PV$. The financial interpretation of this action would be: How much can be withdrawn, perhaps as a pension or to make loan payments, from an account that earns $i$ percent compounded annually for each of the next $n$ years if we wish to have nothing left at the end of $n$ years? For an example, if we have $5,000 in an account earning 8 percent interest, how large an annuity can we draw out each year if we want nothing left at the end of 5 years? In this case, the present value, $PV$, of the annuity is $5,000, $n = 5$ years, $i = 8$ percent, and $PMT$ is unknown. Substituting this into equation 5-10, we find

$$\begin{aligned} \$5{,}000 &= PMT(3.993) \\ \$1{,}252.19 &= PMT \end{aligned}$$

Thus, this account will fall to zero at the end of 5 years if we withdraw $1,252.19 at the end of each year.

**CONCEPT CHECK**

1. How could you determine the future value of a 3-year annuity using the formula for the future value of a single cash flow?
2. What is the $PVIFA_{10\%,\,3yr.}$? Now add up the values for the $PVIF_{10\%,\,nyr}$ for $n = 1, 2,$ and 3. What is this value? Why do these values have the relationship they do?

## ANNUITIES DUE

Because annuities due are really just ordinary annuities in which all the annuity payments have been shifted forward by 1 year, compounding them and determining their present value is actually quite simple. Remember, with an annuity due, each annuity payment occurs at the beginning of each period rather than at the end of the period. Let's first look at how this affects our compounding calculations.

Because an annuity due merely shifts the payments from the end of the year to the beginning of the year, we now compound the cash flows for 1 additional year. Therefore, the compound sum of an annuity due is simply

$$FV_n(\text{annuity due}) = PMT(FVIFA_{i,n})(1 + i)$$

For example, earlier we calculated the value of a 5-year ordinary annuity of $500 invested in the bank at 6 percent to be $2,818.50. If we now assume this to be a 5-year annuity due, its future value increases from $2,818.50 to $2,987.61.

$$\begin{aligned} FV_5 &= \$500(FVIFA_{6\%,5yrs})(1 + .06) \\ &= \$500(5.637)(1.06) \\ &= \$2{,}987.61 \end{aligned}$$

Likewise, with the present value of an annuity due, we simply receive each cash flow 1 year earlier—that is, we receive it at the beginning of each year rather than at the end of each year. Thus, since each cash flow is received 1 year earlier, it is discounted back for one less period. To determine the present value of an annuity due, we merely need to find the present value of an ordinary annuity and multiply that by $(1 + i)$, which in effect cancels out 1 year's discounting.

$$PV(\text{annuity due}) = PMT(PVIFA_{i,n})(1 + i)$$

Reexamining the earlier example where we calculated the present value of a 5-year ordinary annuity of $500 given an appropriate discount rate of 6 percent, we now find that if it is an annuity due rather than an ordinary annuity, the present value increases from $2,106 to $2,232.36.

$$\begin{aligned} PV &= \$500(PVIFA_{6\%,\,5yrs})(1 + .06) \\ &= \$500(4.212)(1.06) \\ &= \$2{,}232.36 \end{aligned}$$

The result of all this is that both the future and present values of an annuity due are larger than that of an ordinary annuity because in each case all payments are received earlier. Thus, when *compounding* an annuity due, it compounds for 1 additional year; whereas when *discounting* an annuity due, the cash flows are discounted for 1 less year. Although annuities due are used with some frequency in accounting, their usage is quite limited in finance. Therefore, in the remainder of this text, whenever the term *annuity* is used, you should assume that we are referring to an ordinary annuity.

## EXAMPLE

The Virginia State Lottery runs like most other state lotteries: You must select six out of 44 numbers correctly in order to win the jackpot. If you come close, there are some significantly lesser prizes—we will ignore them for now. For each million dollars in the lottery jackpot, you receive \$50,000 per year for 20 years, and your chance of winning is 1 in 7.1 million. One of the recent advertisements for the Virginia State Lottery went as follows: "Okay, you got two kinds of people. You've got the kind who play Lotto all the time and the kind who play Lotto some of the time. You know, like only on a Saturday when they stop in at the store on the corner for some peanut butter cups and diet soda and the jackpot happens to be really big. I mean, my friend Ned? He's like, 'Hey, it's only 2 million dollars this week.' Well, hellloooo, anybody home? I mean, I don't know about you, but I wouldn't mind having a measly 2 mill coming *my* way. . . . "

What is the present value of these payments? The answer to this question depends upon what assumption you make as to the time value of money—in this case, let's assume that your required rate of return on an investment with this level of risk is 10 percent. Keep in mind that the Lotto is an annuity due—that is, on a \$2 million lottery you would get \$100,000 immediately and \$100,000 at the end of each of the next 19 years. Thus, the present value of this 20-year annuity due discounted back to present at 10 percent becomes:

$$
\begin{aligned}
PV_{\text{annuity due}} &= PMT(PVIFA_{i\%,\, n\text{yrs}})(1 + i) \\
&= \$100{,}000(PVIFA_{10\%,\, 20\text{yrs}})(1 + .10) \\
&= \$100{,}000(8.514)(1.10) \\
&= \$851{,}400(1.10) \\
&= \$936{,}540
\end{aligned}
$$

Thus, the present value of the \$2 million Lotto jackpot is less than \$1 million if 10 percent is the appropriate discount rate. Moreover, because the chance of winning is only 1 in 7.1 million, the expected value of each dollar "invested" in the lottery is only (1/7.1 million) × (\$936,540) = 13.19¢. That is, for every dollar you spend on the lottery, you should expect to get (*on average*) about 13¢ back—not a particularly good deal. Although this ignores the minor payments for coming close, it also ignores taxes. In this case, it looks like "my friend Ned" is doing the right thing by staying clear of the lottery. Obviously, the main value of the lottery is entertainment. Unfortunately, without an understanding of the time value of money, it can sound like a good investment.

## CONCEPT CHECK

1. How does an annuity due differ from an ordinary annuity?
2. Why are both the future and present values greater for an annuity due than for an ordinary annuity?

## Amortized Loans

The procedure of solving for *PMT* is also used to determine what payments are associated with paying off a loan in equal installments over time. Loans that are paid off this way, in equal periodic payments, are called **amortized loans.** For example, suppose you want to buy a used car. To do this, you borrow $6,000 to be repaid in four equal payments at the end of each of the next 4 years, and the interest rate that is paid to the lender is 15 percent on the outstanding portion of the loan. To determine what the annual payment associated with the repayment of this debt will be, we simply use equation 5-10 and solve for the value of *PMT,* the annual annuity. Again, we know three of the four values in that equation, *PV, i,* and *n. PV,* the present value of the future annuity, is $6,000; *i,* the annual interest rate, is 15 percent; and *n,* the number of years for which the annuity will last, is 4 years. *PMT,* the annuity payment received (by the lender and paid by you) at the end of each year, is unknown. Substituting these values into equation 5-10, we find

**Amortized loan**
A loan paid off in equal installments.

CALCULATOR SOLUTION

| Data Input | Function Key |
|---|---|
| 4 | N |
| 15 | I/Y |
| 6,000 | PV |
| 0 | FV |
| **Function Key** | **Answer** |
| CPT | |
| PMT | −2,101.59 |

$$\$6{,}000 = PMT\left[\sum_{t=1}^{4} \frac{1}{(1 + .15)^t}\right]$$

$$\$6{,}000 = PMT(PVIFA_{15\%,4yrs})$$

$$\$6{,}000 = PMT(2.855)$$

$$\$2{,}101.58 = PMT$$

To repay the principal and interest on the outstanding loan in 4 years, the annual payments would be $2,101.58. The breakdown of interest and principal payments is given in the **loan amortization schedule** in Table 5-10, with very minor rounding errors. As you can see, the interest payment declines each year as the loan outstanding declines, and more of the principal is repaid each year.

**Loan amortization schedule**
A breakdown of loan payments into interest and principal payments.

### CONCEPT CHECK

1. What is an amortized loan?

| | A–G | D |
|---|---|---|
| 1 | Now let's look at a loan amortization problem where the payments occur | |
| 2 | monthly using a spreadsheet. | |
| 3 | | |
| 4 | Spreadsheets: the Loan Amortization Problem | |
| 5 | | |
| 6 | To buy a new house you take out a 25 year mortgage for $100,000. | |
| 7 | What will your monthly interest rate payments be if the interest rate | |
| 8 | on your mortgage is 8 percent? | |
| 9 | | |
| 10 | Two things to keep in mind when you're working this problem: first, you'll | |
| 11 | have to convert the annual rate of 8 percent into a monthly rate by dividing it | |
| 12 | by 12, and second, you'll have to convert the number of periods into months | |
| 13 | by multiplying 25 times 12 for a total of 300 months. | |
| 14 | | |
| 15 | Excel formula: =PMT(rate,number of periods,present value,future value,type) | |
| 16 | | |
| 17 | rate (I) = | 8%/12 |
| 18 | number of periods (n) = | 300 |
| 19 | present value (PV) = | $100,000 |
| 20 | future value (FV) = | $0 |
| 21 | type (0 = at end of period) = | 0 |
| 22 | | |
| 23 | Entered values in cell d25: =PMT((8/12)%,d18,d19,d20,d21) | |
| 24 | | |
| 25 | monthly mortgage payment = | ($771.82) |
| 26 | | |
| 27 | Notice that monthly payments take on a negative value because you | |
| 28 | pay them. | |
| 29 | | |

Sheet1 / Sheet2 / Sheet3

**TABLE 5-10**
Loan Amortization Schedule Involving a $6,000 Loan at 15 Percent to Be Repaid in 4 Years

| Year | Annuity | Interest Portion of the Annuity[a] | Repayment of the Principal Portion of the Annuity[b] | Outstanding Loan Balance after the Annuity Payment |
|---|---|---|---|---|
| 1 | $2,101.58 | $900.00 | $1,201.58 | $4,798.42 |
| 2 | 2,101.58 | 719.76 | 1,381.82 | 3,416.60 |
| 3 | 2,101.58 | 512.49 | 1,589.09 | 1,827.51 |
| 4 | 2,101.58 | 274.07 | 1,827.51 | |

[a]The interest portion of the annuity is calculated by multiplying the outstanding loan balance at the beginning of the year by the interest rate of 15 percent. Thus, for year 1 it was $6,000.00 × .15 = $900.00, for year 2 it was $4,798.42 × .15 = $719.76, and so on.

[b]Repayment of the principal portion of the annuity was calculated by subtracting the interest portion of the annuity (column 2) from the annuity (column 1).

| | A | B | C | D | E | F | G | H | I | J |
|---|---|---|---|---|---|---|---|---|---|---|
| 29 | | | | | | | | | | |
| 30 | You can also use Excel to calculate the interest and principal portion of any | | | | | | | | | |
| 31 | loan amortization payment. You can do this using the | | | | | | | | | |
| 32 | following Excel functions: | | | | | | | | | |
| 33 | | | | | | | | | | |
| 34 | Calculation: | | | Formula: | | | | | | |
| 35 | | | | | | | | | | |
| 36 | Interest portion of payment | | | =IPMT(rate,period,number of periods,present value,future value,type) | | | | | | |
| 37 | Principal portion of payment | | | =PPMT(rate,period,number of periods,present value,future value,type) | | | | | | |
| 38 | | | | | | | | | | |
| 39 | where period refers to the number of an individual periodic payment. | | | | | | | | | |
| 40 | | | | | | | | | | |
| 41 | Thus, if you would like to determine how much of the 48th monthly | | | | | | | | | |
| 42 | payment went toward interest and principal you would solve as follows: | | | | | | | | | |
| 43 | | | | | | | | | | |
| 44 | Interest portion of payment 48: | | | | | | | | | |
| 45 | | | | | | | | | | |
| 46 | | | ($628.12) | | | | | | | |
| 47 | | | | | | | | | | |
| 48 | Entered values in cell c46: =IPMT((8/12)%,48,d18,d19,d20,d21) | | | | | | | | | |
| 49 | | | | | | | | | | |
| 50 | The principal portion of payment 48: | | | | | | | | | |
| 51 | | | | | | | | | | |
| 52 | | | ($143.69) | | | | | | | |
| 53 | | | | | | | | | | |
| 54 | Entered values in cell c52: =PPMT((8/12)%,48,d18,d19,d20,d21) | | | | | | | | | |
| 55 | | | | | | | | | | |
| 56 | | | | | | | | | | |
| 57 | | | | | | | | | | |

Sheet1 / Sheet2 / Sheet3

## PRESENT VALUE OF COMPLEX STREAM

OBJECTIVE 6 

Although some projects will involve a single cash flow and some annuities, many projects will involve uneven cash flows over several years. Chapter 9, which examines investments in fixed assets, presents this situation repeatedly. There we will be comparing not only the present value of cash flows between projects, but also the cash inflows and outflows within a particular project, trying to determine that project's present value. However, this will not be difficult because the present value of any cash flow is measured in today's dollars and

**TABLE 5-11**
Illustration of an Example of Present Value of an Uneven Stream Involving One Annuity Discounted to Present at 6 Percent

| Year | 0 | 1 | 2 | 3 | 4 | 5 | 6 | 7 | 8 | 9 | 10 |
|---|---|---|---|---|---|---|---|---|---|---|---|
| Dollars received at end of year | | 500 | 200 | −400 | 500 | 500 | 500 | 500 | 500 | 500 | 500 |
| | $ 471.50 | | | | | | | | | | |
| | 178.50 | | | | | | | | | | |
| | −336.00 | | | | | | | | | | |
| | | | | $2,791 | | | | | | | |
| | $2,344.44 | | | | | | | | | | |
| Total present value | $2,657.94 | | | | | | | | | | |

thus can be compared, through addition for inflows and subtraction for outflows, to the present value of any other cash flow also measured in today's dollars.

| Year | Cash Flow | Year | Cash Flow |
|---|---|---|---|
| 1 | $500 | 6 | $500 |
| 2 | 200 | 7 | 500 |
| 3 | −400 | 8 | 500 |
| 4 | 500 | 9 | 500 |
| 5 | 500 | 10 | 500 |

For example, if we wished to find the present value of the cash flows provided above given a 6 percent discount rate, we would merely discount the flows back to the present and total them by adding in the positive flows and subtracting the negative ones. However, this problem also contains the annuity of $500 that runs from years 4 through 10. To accommodate this, we can first discount the annuity back to the beginning of period 4 (or end of period 3) by multiplying it by the value of $PVIFA_{6\%,\ 7\text{yrs}}$ and get its present value at that point in time. We then multiply this value times the $PVIF_{6\%,\ 3\text{yrs}}$ in order to bring this single cash flow (which is the present value of the 7-year annuity) back to the present. In effect, we discount twice—first back to the end of period 3, then back to the present. This is shown graphically in Table 5-11 and numerically in Table 5-12. Thus, the present value of this uneven stream of cash flows is $2,657.94.

**TABLE 5-12**
Determination of the Present Value of an Uneven Stream Involving One Annuity Discounted to Present at 6 Percent

| | |
|---|---|
| **1.** Present value of $500 received at the end of 1 year = $500(.943) = | $ 471.50 |
| **2.** Present value of $200 received at the end of 2 years = $200(.890) = | 178.00 |
| **3.** Present value of a $400 outflow at the end of 3 years = −$400(.840) = | −336.00 |
| **4.** (a) Value at the end of year 3 of a $500 annuity, years 4 through 10 = $500(5.582) = $2,791 | |
| (b) Present value of $2,791 received at the end of year 3 = $2,791(.840) = | $2,344.44 |
| **5.** Total present value = | $2,657.94 |

**EXAMPLE**

What is the present value of an investment involving $200 received at the end of years 1 through 5, a $300 cash outflow at the end of year 6, and $500 received at the end of years 7 through 10, given a 5 percent discount rate? Here we have two annuities, one that can be discounted directly back to the present by multiplying it by the value of the $PVIFA_{5\%,5yrs}$ and one that must be discounted twice to bring it back to the present. This second annuity, which is a 4-year annuity, must first be discounted back to the beginning of period 7 (or end of period 6) by multiplying it by the value of the $PVIFA_{5\%,4yrs}$. Then the present value of this annuity at the end of period 6 (which can be viewed as a single cash flow) must be discounted back to the present by multiplying it by the value of the $PVIF_{5\%,6yrs}$. To arrive at the total present value of this investment, we subtract the present value of the $300 cash outflow at the end of year 6 from the sum of the present value of the two annuities. Table 5-13 shows this graphically; Table 5-14 gives the calculations. Thus, the present value of this series of cash flows is $1,964.66.

Remember, once the cash flows from an investment have been brought back to present they can be combined by adding and subtracting to determine the project's total present value.

**CONCEPT CHECK**

1. If you wanted to calculate the present value of an investment that produced cash flows of $100 received at the end of year 1 and $700 at the end of year 2, how would you do it?

**TABLE 5-13**
Illustration of an Example of Present Value of an Uneven Stream Involving Two Annuities Discounted to Present at 5 Percent

| Year | 0 | 1 | 2 | 3 | 4 | 5 | 6 | 7 | 8 | 9 | 10 |
|---|---|---|---|---|---|---|---|---|---|---|---|
| Dollars received at end of year | | 200 | 200 | 200 | 200 | 200 | −300 | 500 | 500 | 500 | 500 |
| | $ 865.80 ← | | | | | | | | | | |
| | −223.80 ← | | | | | | | | | | |
| | | | | | | | $1,773 ← | | | | |
| | 1,322.66 ← | | | | | | | | | | |
| Total present value | $1,964.66 | | | | | | | | | | |

**TABLE 5-14**
Determination of Present Value of an Example with Uneven Stream Involving Two Annuities Discounted to Present at 5 Percent

| | |
|---|---|
| **1.** Present value of first annuity, years 1 through 5 = $200(4.329) = | $ 865.80 |
| **2.** Present value of $300 cash outflow = −$300(.746) = | −223.80 |
| **3.** (a) Value at end of year 6 of second annuity, years 7 through 10 = $500(3.546) = $1,773 | |
| (b) Present value of $1,773 received at the end of year 6 = $1,773(.746) = | 1,322.66 |
| **4.** Total present value = | $1,964.66 |

## PERPETUITIES AND INFINITE ANNUITIES

**Perpetuity**
An annuity that continues forever.

A **perpetuity** is an annuity that continues forever; that is, every year from its establishment, this investment pays the same dollar amount. An example of a perpetuity is preferred stock that yields a constant dollar dividend infinitely. Determining the present value of a perpetuity is delightfully simple; we merely need to divide the constant flow by the discount rate.[1] For example, the present value of a $100 perpetuity discounted back to the present at 5 percent is $100/.05 = $2,000. Thus, the equation representing the present value of a perpetuity is

$$PV = \frac{PP}{i} \tag{5-11}$$

where $PV$ = the present value of the perpetuity
$PP$ = the constant dollar amount provided by the perpetuity
$i$ = the annual interest (or discount) rate

### EXAMPLE

What is the present value of a $500 perpetuity discounted back to the present at 8 percent? Substituting $PP$ = $500 and $i$ = .08 into equation (5-11), we find

$$PV = \frac{\$500}{.08} = \$6{,}250$$

Thus, the present value of this perpetuity is $6,250.

### CONCEPT CHECK

1. What is a perpetuity?
2. When $i$, the annual interest (or discount) rate, increases, what happens to the present value of a perpetuity? Why?

## MAKING INTEREST RATES COMPARABLE

In order to make intelligent decisions about where to invest or borrow money, it is important that we make the stated interest rates comparable. Unfortunately, some rates are quoted as compounded annually, whereas others are quoted as compounded quarterly or compounded daily. But we already know that it is not fair to compare interest rates with different compounding periods to each other. Thus, the only way interest rates can logically be compared is to convert them to some common compounding period and then compare them. That is what is done with the *annual percentage yield.* In order to understand the process of making different interest rates comparable, it is first necessary to define the **nominal** or **quoted interest rate.**

**Nominal or quoted interest rate**
The stated rate of interest on the contract.

The nominal or quoted rate is the rate of interest stated on the contract. For example, if you shop around for loans and are quoted 8 percent compounded annually and 7.85 percent

[1]See Chapter 8 for a mathematical derivation.

compounded quarterly, then 8 percent and 7.85 percent would both be nominal rates. Unfortunately, because on one the interest is compounded annually, but on the other interest is compounded quarterly, they are not comparable. In fact, it is never appropriate to compare nominal rates *unless* they include the same number of compounding periods per year. To make them comparable, we must calculate their equivalent rate at some common compounding period. We do this by calculating the **annual percentage yield** (**APY**) or **effective annual rate.** This is the annual compound rate that produces the same return as the nominal or quoted rate.

**Annual percentage yield (APY) or effective annual rate**
The annual compound rate that produces the same return as the nominal or quoted rate.

Let's assume that you are considering borrowing money from a bank at 12 percent compounded monthly. To convert this to an *APY,* we must determine the annual rate that would produce the same return as the nominal rate. In the case of a 12 percent loan compounded monthly, by looking in the *FVIF* table in the back of the book, we see that the future value of $1 in 1 year at 12 percent compounded monthly (that is, compounded at 1 percent per month for 12 1-month periods) is $1.1268 ($FVIF_{1\%,12\text{periods}} = 1.1268$). This tells us that 12.68 percent is the APY, because if we compound $1 at the nominal rate of 12 percent compounded monthly, we would have $1.1268 after 1 year.

Generalizing on this process, we can calculate the *APY* using the following equation:

$$APY = (1 + \text{quoted rate}/m)^m - 1 \tag{5-12}$$

where *APY* is the annual percentage yield and *m* is the number of compounding periods within a year. Given the wide variety of compounding periods used by businesses and banks, it is important to know how to make these rates comparable so that logical decisions can be made.

## THE MULTINATIONAL FIRM: THE TIME VALUE OF MONEY

OBJECTIVE 9 

From **Principle 1: The Risk-Return Tradeoff—We won't take on additional risk unless we expect to be compensated with additional return,** we found that investors demand a return for delaying consumption, as well as an additional return for taking on added risk. The discount rate that we use to move money through time should reflect this return for delaying consumption; and it should reflect anticipated inflation. In the United States, anticipated inflation is quite low, although it does tend to fluctuate over time. Elsewhere in the world, however, the inflation rate is difficult to predict because it can be dramatically high and undergo huge fluctuations.

Let's look at Argentina, keeping in mind that similar examples abound in Central and South America and Eastern Europe. At the beginning of 1992, Argentina introduced the fifth currency in 22 years, the new peso. The austral, the currency that was replaced, was introduced in June 1985 and was initially equal in value to $1.25 U.S. currency. Five and a half years later, it took 100,000 australs to equal $1. Inflation had reached the point where the stack of money needed to buy a candy bar was bigger and weighed more than the candy bar itself, and many workers received their weeks' wages in grocery bags. Needless to say, if we were to move australs through time, we would have to use an extremely high interest or discount rate. Unfortunately, in countries suffering from hyperinflation, inflation rates tend to fluctuate dramatically, and this makes estimating the expected inflation rate even more difficult. For example, in 1989 the inflation rate in Argentina was 4,924 percent; in 1990 it dropped to 1,344 percent; in 1991 it was only 84 percent; in 1992, only 18 percent; and in 1997 it had fallen to 0.3 percent. However, as inflation in Argentina dropped, inflation in Brazil heated up, going from 426 percent in 1991 to 1,094 percent in 1995, and finally coming under control in 1999 and 2000. But while inflation in one area of the world is finally controlled, it pops up in another area—for example, in mid-2000 inflation in Turkey was over 60 percent. Finally, at the extreme, in 1993 in Serbia the inflation rate reached 360,000,000,000,000,000 percent.

The bottom line on all this is that because of the dramatic fluctuations in inflation that can take place in the international setting, choosing the appropriate discount rate of moving money through time is an extremely difficult process.

**CONCEPT CHECK**

1. How does the international setting complicate the choice of the appropriate interest rate to use when discounting cash flows back to the present?

## HOW FINANCIAL MANAGERS USE THIS MATERIAL

Almost all business decisions involve cash flow occurring in different time periods. It is the techniques and tools introduced in this chapter that allow you to compare these cash flows and, therefore, make the appropriate decision. Perhaps you'll work for Marriott and you'll be deciding whether to build a hotel resort or some new time-share units on the beachfront land Marriott owns on Hilton Head Island. That's a decision that involves spending the money right now to build the complex and then, sometime in the future, either selling the time-share units or receiving rent from tourists at the new hotel resort. It's an understanding of the time value of money that allows you to compare these cash flows that occur in different time periods. In fact, any time you're evaluating a new product, the time value of money comes into play. In short, there isn't another tool in business that is more essential to making good decisions.

As you will see later, the time value of money also plays a central role in determining the price that a share of common stock sells for. That is to say, it was an understanding of the time value of money that allowed the folks at Friendly Ice Cream to determine that Friendly's common stock should be offered to the public at $18 per share when it was first sold. Those same people use the time value of money to determine how much they should save for their children's college education and for retirement, and whether they should refinance their home mortgage. Truly, the concept of the time value of money is one that not only affects all corporate finance decisions, but also affects all personal finance decisions.

## SUMMARY

To make decisions, financial managers must compare the costs and benefits of alternatives that do not occur during the same time period. Whether to make profitable investments or to take advantage of favorable interest rates, financial decision making requires an understanding of the time value of money. Managers who use the time value of money in all of their financial calculations assure themselves of more logical decisions. The time value process first makes all dollar values comparable; because money has a time value, it moves all dollar flows either back to the present or out to a common future date. All time value formulas presented in this chapter actually stem from the single compounding formula $FV_n = PV(1 + i)^n$. The formulas are used to deal simply with common financial situations, for example, discounting single flows, compounding annuities, and discounting annuities. Table 5-15 provides a summary of these calculations.

**TABLE 5-15**
Summary of Time Value of Money Equations[a]

| | Calculation | Equation |
|---|---|---|
| OBJECTIVE 1 | Future value of a single payment | $FV_n = PV(1+i)^n$ or $PV(FVIF_{i,n})$ |
| OBJECTIVE 2 | Future value of a single payment with nonannual compounding | $FV_n = PV\left(1+\frac{i}{m}\right)^{mn}$ |
| OBJECTIVE 3 | Present value of a single payment | $PV = FV_n\left[\frac{1}{(1+i)^n}\right]$ or $FV_n(PVIF_{i,n})$ |
| OBJECTIVE 4 | Future value of an annuity | $FV_n = PMT\left[\sum_{t=0}^{n-1}(1+i)^t\right]$ or $PMT(FVIFA_{i,n})$ |
| OBJECTIVE 5 | Present value of an annuity | $PV = PMT\left[\sum_{t=1}^{n}\frac{1}{(1+i)^t}\right]$ or $PMT(PVIFA_{i,n})$ |
| | Present value of a perpetuity | $PV = \frac{PP}{i}$ |
| OBJECTIVE 6 | Annual percentage yield ($APY$) | $APY = \left(1+\frac{\text{quoted rate}}{m}\right)^m - 1$ |

**Notation:** $FV_n$ = the future value of the investment at the end of $n$ years
$n$ = the number of years until payment will be received or during which compounding occurs
$i$ = the annual interest or discount rate
$PV$ = the present value of the future sum of money
$m$ = the number of times compounding occurs during the year
$PMT$ = the annuity payment deposited or received at the end of each year
$PP$ = the constant dollar amount provided by the perpetuity

[a]Related tables appear in Appendices B through E at the end of the book.

## KEY TERMS

myPHLIP

Go To: http://www.prenhall.com/keown for downloads and current events associated with this chapter

**Amortized loan, 149**
**Annual percentage yield (APY) or effective annual rate, 154**
**Annuity, 140**
**Annuity due, 141**
**Compound annuity, 141**
**Compound interest, 128**
**Future-value interest factor ($FVIF_{i,n}$), 131**
**Future-value interest factor for an annuity ($FVIFA_{i,n}$), 141**
**Nominal or quoted interest rate, 153**
**Ordinary annuity, 141**
**Perpetuity, 153**
**Present value, 137**
**Present-value interest factor ($PVIF_{i,n}$), 138**
**Present-value interest factor for an annuity ($PVIFA_{i,n}$), 145**

## STUDY QUESTIONS

**5-1.** What is the time value of money? Why is it so important?

**5-2.** The processes of discounting and compounding are related. Explain this relationship.

**5-3.** How would an increase in the interest rate ($i$) or a decrease in the holding period ($n$) affect the future value ($FV_n$) of a sum of money? Explain why.

**5-4.** Suppose you were considering depositing your savings in one of three banks, all of which pay 5 percent interest; bank A compounds annually, bank B compounds semiannually, and bank C compounds daily. Which bank would you choose? Why?

**5-5.** What is the relationship between the $PVIF_{i,n}$ (Table 5-4) and the $PVIFA_{i,n}$ (Table 5-8)? What is the $PVIFA_{10\%, 10yr}$? Add up the values of the $PVIF_{10\%, n}$ for $n = 1, \ldots, 10$. What is this value? Why do these values have the relationship they do?

**5-6.** What is an annuity? Give some examples of annuities. Distinguish between an annuity and a perpetuity.

## SELF-TEST PROBLEMS

**ST-1.** You place $25,000 in a savings account paying annual compound interest of 8 percent for 3 years and then move it into a savings account that pays 10 percent interest compounded annually. How much will your money have grown at the end of 6 years?

**ST-2.** You purchase a boat for $35,000 and pay $5,000 down and agree to pay the rest over the next 10 years in 10 equal annual payments that include principal payments plus 13 percent of compound interest on the unpaid balance. What will be the amount of each payment?

**ST-3.** For an investment to grow eightfold in 9 years, at what rate would it have to grow?

## STUDY PROBLEMS (SET A)

**5-1A.** (*Compound interest*) To what amount will the following investments accumulate?
- **a.** $5,000 invested for 10 years at 10 percent compounded annually
- **b.** $8,000 invested for 7 years at 8 percent compounded annually
- **c.** $775 invested for 12 years at 12 percent compounded annually
- **d.** $21,000 invested for 5 years at 5 percent compounded annually

**5-2A.** (*Compound value solving for* n) How many years will the following take?
- **a.** $500 to grow to $1,039.50 if invested at 5 percent compounded annually
- **b.** $35 to grow to $53.87 if invested at 9 percent compounded annually
- **c.** $100 to grow to $298.60 if invested at 20 percent compounded annually
- **d.** $53 to grow to $78.76 if invested at 2 percent compounded annually

**5-3A.** (*Compound value solving for* i) At what annual rate would the following have to be invested?
- **a.** $500 to grow to $1,948.00 in 12 years
- **b.** $300 to grow to $422.10 in 7 years
- **c.** $50 to grow to $280.20 in 20 years
- **d.** $200 to grow to $497.60 in 5 years

**5-4A.** (*Present value*) What is the present value of the following future amounts?
- **a.** $800 to be received 10 years from now discounted back to the present at 10 percent
- **b.** $300 to be received 5 years from now discounted back to the present at 5 percent
- **c.** $1,000 to be received 8 years from now discounted back to the present at 3 percent
- **d.** $1,000 to be received 8 years from now discounted back to the present at 20 percent

**5-5A.** (*Compound annuity*) What is the accumulated sum of each of the following streams of payments?
- **a.** $500 a year for 10 years compounded annually at 5 percent
- **b.** $100 a year for 5 years compounded annually at 10 percent
- **c.** $35 a year for 7 years compounded annually at 7 percent
- **d.** $25 a year for 3 years compounded annually at 2 percent

**5-6A.** (*Present value of an annuity*) What is the present value of the following annuities?
- **a.** $2,500 a year for 10 years discounted back to the present at 7 percent
- **b.** $70 a year for 3 years discounted back to the present at 3 percent
- **c.** $280 a year for 7 years discounted back to the present at 6 percent
- **d.** $500 a year for 10 years discounted back to the present at 10 percent

**5-7A.** (*Compound value*) Brian Mosallam, who recently sold his Porsche, placed $10,000 in a savings account paying annual compound interest of 6 percent.

**a.** Calculate the amount of money that will have accrued if he leaves the money in the bank for 1, 5, and 15 years.

**b.** If he moves his money into an account that pays 8 percent or one that pays 10 percent, rework part (a) using these new interest rates.

**c.** What conclusions can you draw about the relationship between interest rates, time, and future sums from the calculations you have done above?

**5-8A.** (*Compound interest with nonannual periods*) Calculate the amount of money that will be in each of the following accounts at the end of the given deposit period:

| Account | Amount Deposited | Annual Interest Rate | Compounding Period (Compounded Every __Months) | Deposit Period (Years) |
|---|---|---|---|---|
| Theodore Logan III | $ 1,000 | 10% | 12 | 10 |
| Vernell Coles | 95,000 | 12 | 1 | 1 |
| Thomas Elliott | 8,000 | 12 | 2 | 2 |
| Wayne Robinson | 120,000 | 8 | 3 | 2 |
| Eugene Chung | 30,000 | 10 | 6 | 4 |
| Kelly Cravens | 15,000 | 12 | 4 | 3 |

**5-9A.** (*Compound interest with nonannual periods*)

**a.** Calculate the future sum of $5,000, given that it will be held in the bank 5 years at an annual interest rate of 6 percent.

**b.** Recalculate part (a) using a compounding period that is (1) semiannual and (2) bimonthly.

**c.** Recalculate parts (a) and (b) for a 12 percent annual interest rate.

**d.** Recalculate part (a) using a time horizon of 12 years (annual interest rate is still 6 percent).

**e.** With respect to the effect of changes in the stated interest rate and holding periods on future sums in parts (c) and (d), what conclusions do you draw when you compare these figures with the answers found in parts (a) and (b)?

**5-10A.** (*Solving for* i *in annuities*) Nicki Johnson, a sophomore mechanical engineering student, receives a call from an insurance agent who believes that Nicki is an older woman ready to retire from teaching. He talks to her about several annuities that she could buy that would guarantee her an annual fixed income. The annuities are as follows:

| Annuity | Initial Payment into Annuity (at $t = 0$) | Amount of Money Received per Year | Duration of Annuity (Years) |
|---|---|---|---|
| A | $50,000 | $8,500 | 12 |
| B | $60,000 | $7,000 | 25 |
| C | $70,000 | $8,000 | 20 |

If Nicki could earn 11 percent on her money by placing it in a savings account, should she place it instead in any of the annuities? Which ones, if any? Why?

**5-11A.** (*Future value*) Sales of a new finance book were 15,000 copies this year and were expected to increase by 20 percent per year. What are expected sales during each of the next 3 years? Graph this sales trend and explain.

**5-12A.** (*Future value*) Reggie Jackson, formerly of the New York Yankees, hit 41 home runs in 1980. If his home-run output grew at a rate of 10 percent per year, what would it have been over the following 5 years?

**5-13A.** (*Loan amortization*) Mr. Bill S. Preston, Esq., purchased a new house for $80,000. He paid $20,000 down and agreed to pay the rest over the next 25 years in 25 equal annual payments that include principal payments plus 9 percent compound interest on the unpaid balance. What will these equal payments be?

**5-14A.** (*Solving for* PMT *in an annuity*) To pay for your child's education, you wish to have accumulated $15,000 at the end of 15 years. To do this, you plan to deposit an equal amount into the bank at the end of each year. If the bank is willing to pay 6 percent compounded annually, how much must you deposit each year to obtain your goal?

**5-15A.** (*Solving for* i *in compound interest*) If you were offered $1,079.50 10 years from now in return for an investment of $500 currently, what annual rate of interest would you earn if you took the offer?

**5-16A.** (*Future value of an annuity*) In 10 years, you plan to retire and buy a house in Oviedo, Florida. The house you are looking at currently costs $100,000 and is expected to increase in value each year at a rate of 5 percent. Assuming you can earn 10 percent annually on your investments, how much must you invest at the end of each of the next 10 years to be able to buy your dream home when you retire?

**5-17A.** (*Compound value*) The Aggarwal Corporation needs to save $10 million to retire a $10 million mortgage that matures in 10 years. To retire this mortgage, the company plans to put a fixed amount into an account at the end of each year for 10 years. The Aggarwal Corporation expects to earn 9 percent annually on the money in this account. What equal annual contribution must it make to this account to accumulate the $10 million by the end of 10 years?

**5-18A.** (*Compound interest with nonannual periods*) After examining the various personal loan rates available to you, you find that you can borrow funds from a finance company at 12 percent compounded monthly or from a bank at 13 percent compounded annually. Which alternative is the most attractive?

**5-19A.** (*Present value of an uneven stream of payments*) You are given three investment alternatives to analyze. The cash flows from these three investments are as follows:

| Investment | | | |
|---|---|---|---|
| **End of Year** | **A** | **B** | **C** |
| 1 | $10,000 | | $10,000 |
| 2 | 10,000 | | |
| 3 | 10,000 | | |
| 4 | 10,000 | | |
| 5 | 10,000 | $10,000 | |
| 6 | | 10,000 | 50,000 |
| 7 | | 10,000 | |
| 8 | | 10,000 | |
| 9 | | 10,000 | |
| 10 | | 10,000 | 10,000 |

Assuming a 20 percent discount rate, find the present value of each investment.

**5-20A.** (*Present value*) The Kumar Corporation plans to issue bonds that pay no interest but can be converted into $1,000 at maturity, 7 years from their purchase. To price these bonds competitively with other bonds of equal risk, it is determined that they should yield 10 percent, compounded annually. At what price should the Kumar Corporation sell these bonds?

**5-21A.** (*Perpetuities*) What is the present value of the following?

**a.** A $300 perpetuity discounted back to the present at 8 percent
**b.** A $1,000 perpetuity discounted back to the present at 12 percent
**c.** A $100 perpetuity discounted back to the present at 9 percent
**d.** A $95 perpetuity discounted back to the present at 5 percent

**5-22A.** (*Present value of an annuity due*) What is the present value of a 10-year annuity due of $1,000 annually given a 10 percent discount rate?

**5-23A.** (*Solving for* n *with nonannual periods*) About how many years would it take for your investment to grow fourfold if it were invested at 16 percent compounded semiannually?

**5-24A.** (*Present value of an uneven stream of payments*) You are given three investment alternatives to analyze. The cash flows from these three investments are as follows:

| | Investment | | |
|---|---|---|---|
| **End of Year** | **A** | **B** | **C** |
| 1 | $2,000 | $2,000 | $5,000 |
| 2 | $3,000 | $2,000 | $5,000 |
| 3 | $4,000 | $2,000 | −$5,000 |
| 4 | −$5,000 | $2,000 | −$5,000 |
| 5 | $5,000 | $5,000 | $15,000 |

What is the present value of each of these three investments if 10 percent is the appropriate discount rate?

**5-25A.** (*Complex present value*) How much do you have to deposit today so that beginning 11 years from now you can withdraw $10,000 a year for the next 5 years (periods 11 through 15) plus an *additional* amount of $20,000 in the last year (period 15)? Assume an interest rate of 6 percent.

**5-26A.** (*Loan amortization*) On December 31, Beth Klemkosky bought a yacht for $50,000, paying $10,000 down and agreeing to pay the balance in 10 equal annual installments that include both the principal and 10 percent interest on the declining balance. How big would the annual payments be?

**5-27A.** (*Solving for* i *in an annuity*) You lend a friend $30,000, which your friend will repay in 5 equal annual payments of $10,000, with the first payment to be received 1 year from now. What rate of return does your loan receive?

**5-28A.** (*Solving for* i *in compound interest*) You lend a friend $10,000, for which your friend will repay you $27,027 at the end of 5 years. What interest rate are you charging your "friend"?

**5-29A.** (*Loan amortization*) A firm borrows $25,000 from the bank at 12 percent compounded annually to purchase some new machinery. This loan is to be repaid in equal annual installments at the end of each year over the next 5 years. How much will each annual payment be?

**5-30A.** (*Present-value comparison*) You are offered $1,000 today, $10,000 in 12 years, or $25,000 in 25 years. Assuming that you can earn 11 percent on your money, which should you choose?

**5-31A.** (*Compound annuity*) You plan to buy some property in Florida 5 years from today. To do this, you estimate that you will need $20,000 at that time for the purchase. You would like to accumulate these funds by making equal annual deposits in your savings account, which pays 12 percent annually. If you make your first deposit at the end of this year, and you would like your account to reach $20,000 when the final deposit is made, what will be the amount of your deposits?

**5-32A.** (*Complex present value*) You would like to have $50,000 in 15 years. To accumulate this amount, you plan to deposit each year an equal sum in the bank, which will earn 7 percent interest compounded annually. Your first payment will be made at the end of the year.

**a.** How much must you deposit annually to accumulate this amount?

**b.** If you decide to make a large lump-sum deposit today instead of the annual deposits, how large should this lump-sum deposit be? (Assume you can earn 7 percent on this deposit.)

**c.** At the end of 5 years, you will receive $10,000 and deposit this in the bank toward your goal of $50,000 at the end of 15 years. In addition to this deposit, how much must you deposit in equal annual deposits to reach your goal? (Again, assume you can earn 7 percent on this deposit.)

**5-33A.** (*Comprehensive present value*) You are trying to plan for retirement in 10 years and currently you have $100,000 in a savings account and $300,000 in stocks. In addition, you plan to add to your savings by depositing $10,000 per year in your *savings account* at the end of each of the next 5 years and then $20,000 per year at the end of each year for the final 5 years until retirement.

**a.** Assuming your savings account returns 7 percent compounded annually and your investment in stocks will return 12 percent compounded annually, how much will you have at the end of 10 years? (Ignore taxes.)

**b.** If you expect to live for 20 years after you retire, and at retirement you deposit all of your savings in a bank account paying 10 percent, how much can you withdraw each year after retirement (20 equal withdrawals beginning 1 year after you retire) to end up with a zero balance at death?

**5-34A.** (*Loan amortization*) On December 31, Son-Nan Chen borrowed $100,000, agreeing to repay this sum in 20 equal annual installments that include both the principal and 15 percent interest on the declining balance. How large will the annual payments be?

**5-35A.** (*Loan amortization*) To buy a new house you must borrow $150,000. To do this, you take out a $150,000, 30-year, 10 percent mortgage. Your mortgage payments, which are made at the end of each year (one payment each year), include both principal and 10 percent interest on the declining balance. How large will your annual payments be?

**5-36A.** (*Present value*) The state lottery's million-dollar payout provides for $1 million to be paid over 19 years in $50,000 amounts. The first $50,000 payment is made immediately and the 19 remaining $50,000 payments occur at the end of each of the next 19 years. If 10 percent is the appropriate discount rate, what is the present value of this stream of cash flows? If 20 percent is the appropriate discount rate, what is the present value of the cash flows?

**5-37A.** (*Compounding an annuity due*) Find the future value at the end of year 10 of an annuity due of $1,000 per year for 10 years compounded annually at 10 percent. What would be the future value of this annuity if it were compounded annually at 15 percent?

**5-38A.** (*Present value of an annuity due*) Determine the present value of an annuity due of $1,000 per year for 10 years discounted back to the present at an annual rate of 10 percent. What would be the present value of this annuity due if it were discounted at an annual rate of 15 percent?

**5-39A.** (*Present value of a future annuity*) Determine the present value of an ordinary annuity of $1,000 per year for 10 years with the first cash flow from the annuity coming at the end of year 8 (that is, no payments at the end of years 1 through 7 and annual payments at the end of years 8 through 17) given a 10 percent discount rate.

**5-40A.** (*Solving for* i *in compound interest—financial calculator needed*) In September 1963, the first issue of the comic book *X-MEN* was issued. The original price for the issue was 12¢. By September 2000, 38 years later, the value of this comic book had risen to $6,500. What annual rate of interest would you have earned if you had bought the comic in 1963 and sold it in 2000?

**5-41A.** (*Comprehensive present value*) You have just inherited a large sum of money, and you are trying to determine how much you should save for retirement and how much you can spend now. For retirement, you will deposit today (January 1, 2002) a lump sum in a bank account paying 10 percent compounded annually. You don't plan on touching this deposit until you retire in 5 years (January 1, 2007), and you plan on living for 20 additional years and then to drop dead on December 31, 2026. During your retirement, you would like to receive income of $50,000 per year to be received the first day of each year, with the first payment on January 1, 2007, and the last payment on January 1, 2026. Complicating this objective is your desire to have one final 3-year fling during which time you'd like to track down all the original members of *Leave It to Beaver* and *The Brady Bunch* and get their autographs. To finance this, you want to receive $250,000 on January 1, 2022, and *nothing* on January 1, 2023 and January 1, 2024, because you will be on the road. In addition, after you pass on (January 1, 2027), you would like to have a total of $100,000 to leave to your children.

- **a.** How much must you deposit in the bank at 10 percent on January 1, 2002, to achieve your goal? (Use a time line to answer this question.)
- **b.** What kinds of problems are associated with this analysis and its assumptions?

**5-42A.** (*Spreadsheet problem*) If you invest $900 in a bank where it will earn 8 percent compounded annually, how much will it be worth at the end of 7 years? Use a spreadsheet to do your calculations.

**5-43A.** (*Spreadsheet problem*) In 20 years you would like to have $250,000 to buy a vacation home, but you have only $30,000. At what rate must your $30,000 be compounded annually for it to grow to $250,000 in 20 years? Use a spreadsheet to calculate your answer.

**5-44A.** (*Spreadsheet problem*) You take out a 25-year mortgage for $300,000 to buy a new house. What will your monthly interest rate payments be if the interest rate on your mortgage is 8 percent? Use a spreadsheet to calculate your answer. Now, calculate the portion of the 48th monthly payment that goes toward interest and principal.

## INTEGRATIVE PROBLEM

For your job as the business reporter for a local newspaper, you are given the task of putting together a series of articles that explains the power of the time value of money to your readers. Your editor would like you to address several specific questions in addition to demonstrating for the readership the use of the time value of money techniques by applying them to several problems. What would be your response to the following memorandum from your editor?

TO: Business Reporter

FROM: Perry White, Editor, *Daily Planet*

RE: Upcoming Series on the Importance and Power of the Time Value of Money

In your upcoming series on the time value of money, I would like to make sure you cover several specific points. In addition, before you begin this assignment, I want to make sure we are all reading from the same script, because accuracy has always been the cornerstone of the *Daily Planet.* In this regard, I'd like responses to the following questions before we proceed:

1. What is the relationship between discounting and compounding?
2. What is the relationship between the $PVIF_{i,n}$ and $PVIFA_{i,n}$?
3. **a.** What will $5,000 invested for 10 years at 8 percent compounded annually grow to?
   **b.** How many years will it take $400 to grow to $1,671, if it is invested at 10 percent compounded annually?
   **c.** At what rate would $1,000 have to be invested to grow to $4,046 in 10 years?
4. Calculate the future sum of $1,000, given that it will be held in the bank for 5 years and earn 10 percent compounded semiannually.
5. What is an annuity due? How does this differ from an ordinary annuity?
6. What is the present value of an ordinary annuity of $1,000 per year for 7 years discounted back to the present at 10 percent? What would be the present value if it were an annuity due?
7. What is the future value of an ordinary annuity of $1,000 per year for 7 years compounded at 10 percent? What would be the future value if it were an annuity due?
8. You have just borrowed $100,000, and you agree to pay it back over the next 25 years in 25 equal end-of-year annual payments that include the principal payments plus 10 percent compound interest on the unpaid balance. What will be the size of these payments?
9. What is the present value of a $1,000 perpetuity discounted back to the present at 8 percent?
10. What is the present value of a $1,000 annuity for 10 years with the first payment occurring at the end of year 10 (that is, ten $1,000 payments occurring at the end of year 10 through year 19) given an appropriate discount rate of 10 percent?
11. Given a 10 percent discount rate, what is the present value of a perpetuity of $1,000 per year if the first payment does not begin until the end of year 10?
12. What is the annual percentage yield (*APY*) on an 8 percent bank loan compounded quarterly?

## STUDY PROBLEMS (SET B)

**5-1B.** (*Compound interest*) To what amount will the following investments accumulate?

- **a.** $4,000 invested for 11 years at 9 percent compounded annually
- **b.** $8,000 invested for 10 years at 8 percent compounded annually
- **c.** $800 invested for 12 years at 12 percent compounded annually
- **d.** $21,000 invested for 6 years at 5 percent compounded annually

**5-2B.** (*Compound value solving for* n) How many years will the following take?

- **a.** $550 to grow to $1,043.90 if invested at 6 percent compounded annually
- **b.** $40 to grow to $88.44 if invested at 12 percent compounded annually

**c.** \$110 to grow to \$614.79 if invested at 24 percent compounded annually
**d.** \$60 to grow to \$78.30 if invested at 3 percent compounded annually

**5-3B.** (*Compound value solving for* i) At what annual rate would the following have to be invested?

**a.** \$550 to grow to \$1,898.60 in 13 years
**b.** \$275 to grow to \$406.18 in 8 years
**c.** \$60 to grow to \$279.66 in 20 years
**d.** \$180 to grow to \$486.00 in 6 years

**5-4B.** (*Present value*) What is the present value of the following future amounts?

**a.** \$800 to be received 10 years from now discounted back to the present at 10 percent
**b.** \$400 to be received 6 years from now discounted back to the present at 6 percent
**c.** \$1,000 to be received 8 years from now discounted back to the present at 5 percent
**d.** \$900 to be received 9 years from now discounted back to the present at 20 percent

**5-5B.** (*Compound annuity*) What is the accumulated sum of each of the following streams of payments?

**a.** \$500 a year for 10 years compounded annually at 6 percent
**b.** \$150 a year for 5 years compounded annually at 11 percent
**c.** \$35 a year for 8 years compounded annually at 7 percent
**d.** \$25 a year for 3 years compounded annually at 2 percent

**5-6B.** (*Present value of an annuity*) What is the present value of the following annuities?

**a.** \$3,000 a year for 10 years discounted back to the present at 8 percent
**b.** \$50 a year for 3 years discounted back to the present at 3 percent
**c.** \$280 a year for 8 years discounted back to the present at 7 percent
**d.** \$600 a year for 10 years discounted back to the present at 10 percent

**5-7B.** (*Compound value*) Trish Nealon, who recently sold her Porsche, placed \$20,000 in a savings account paying annual compound interest of 7 percent.

**a.** Calculate the amount of money that will have accrued if she leaves the money in the bank for 1, 5, and 15 years.
**b.** If she moves her money into an account that pays 9 percent or one that pays 11 percent, rework part (a) using these new interest rates.
**c.** What conclusions can you draw about the relationship among interest rates, time, and future sums from the calculations you have done?

**5-8B.** (*Compound interest with nonannual periods*) Calculate the amount of money that will be in each of the following accounts at the end of the given deposit period:

| Account | Amount Deposited | Annual Interest Rate | Compounding Period (Compounded Every __Months) | Deposit Period (Years) |
|---|---|---|---|---|
| Korey Stringer | \$ 2,000 | 12% | 2 | 2 |
| Erica Moss | 50,000 | 12 | 1 | 1 |
| Ty Howard | 7,000 | 18 | 2 | 2 |
| Rob Kelly | 130,000 | 12 | 3 | 2 |
| Mary Christopher | 20,000 | 14 | 6 | 4 |
| Juan Diaz | 15,000 | 15 | 4 | 3 |

**5-9B.** (*Compound interest with nonannual periods*)

**a.** Calculate the future sum of \$6,000, given that it will be held in the bank 5 years at an annual interest rate of 6 percent.
**b.** Recalculate part (a) using a compounding period that is (1) semiannual and (2) bimonthly.
**c.** Recalculate parts (a) and (b) for a 12 percent annual interest rate.
**d.** Recalculate part (a) using a time horizon of 12 years (annual interest rate is still 6 percent).
**e.** With respect to the effect of changes in the stated interest rate and holding periods on future sums in parts (c) and (d), what conclusions do you draw when you compare these figures with the answers found in parts (a) and (b)?

**5-10B.** (*Solving for* i *in annuities*) Ellen Denis, a sophomore mechanical engineering student, receives a call from an insurance agent, who believes that Ellen is an older woman ready to retire from teaching. He talks to her about several annuities that she could buy that would guarantee her an annual fixed income. The annuities are as follows:

| Annuity | Initial Payment into Annuity (at $t = 0$) | Amount of Money Received per year | Duration of Annuity (Years) |
|---|---|---|---|
| A | \$50,000 | \$8,500 | 12 |
| B | \$60,000 | \$7,000 | 25 |
| C | \$70,000 | \$8,000 | 20 |

If Ellen could earn 12 percent on her money by placing it in a savings account, should she place it instead in any of the annuities? Which ones, if any? Why?

**5-11B.** (*Future value*) Sales of a new marketing book were 10,000 copies this year and were expected to increase by 15 percent per year. What are expected sales during each of the next 3 years? Graph this sales trend and explain.

**5-12B.** (*Future value*) Reggie Jackson, formerly of the New York Yankees, hit 41 home runs in 1980. If his home-run output grew at a rate of 12 percent per year, what would it have been over the following 5 years?

**5-13B.** (*Loan amortization*) Stefani Moore purchased a new house for \$150,000. She paid \$30,000 down and agreed to pay the rest over the next 25 years in 25 equal annual payments that include principal payments plus 10 percent compound interest on the unpaid balance. What will these equal payments be?

**5-14B.** (*Solving for* PMT *in an annuity*) To pay for your child's education, you wish to have accumulated \$25,000 at the end of 15 years. To do this, you plan to deposit an equal amount into the bank at the end of each year. If the bank is willing to pay 7 percent compounded annually, how much must you deposit each year to obtain your goal?

**5-15B.** (*Solving for* i *in compound interest*) If you were offered \$2,376.50 10 years from now in return for an investment of \$700 currently, what annual rate of interest would you earn if you took the offer?

**5-16B.** (*Future value of an annuity*) In 10 years, you plan to retire and buy a house in Marco Island, Florida. The house you are looking at currently costs \$125,000 and is expected to increase in value each year at a rate of 5 percent. Assuming you can earn 10 percent annually on your investments, how much must you invest at the end of each of the next 10 years to be able to buy your dream home when you retire?

**5-17B.** (*Compound value*) The Knutson Corporation needs to save \$15 million to retire a \$15 million mortgage that matures in 10 years. To retire this mortgage, the company plans to put a fixed amount into an account at the end of each year for 10 years. The Knutson Corporation expects to earn 10 percent annually on the money in this account. What equal annual contribution must it make to this account to accumulate the \$15 million by the end of 10 years?

**5-18B.** (*Compound interest with nonannual periods*) After examining the various personal loan rates available to you, you find that you can borrow funds from a finance company at 24 percent compounded monthly or from a bank at 26 percent compounded annually. Which alternative is the most attractive?

**5-19B.** (*Present value of an uneven stream of payments*) You are given three investment alternatives to analyze. The cash flows from these three investments are as follows:

Investment

| End of Year | A | B | C |
|---|---|---|---|
| 1 | $15,000 | | $20,000 |
| 2 | 15,000 | | |
| 3 | 15,000 | | |
| 4 | 15,000 | | |
| 5 | 15,000 | $15,000 | |
| 6 | | 15,000 | 60,000 |
| 7 | | 15,000 | |
| 8 | | 15,000 | |
| 9 | | 15,000 | |
| 10 | | 15,000 | 20,000 |

Assuming a 20 percent discount rate, find the present value of each investment.

**5-20B.** (*Present value*) The Shin Corporation is planning on issuing bonds that pay no interest but can be converted into $1,000 at maturity, 8 years from their purchase. To price these bonds competitively with other bonds of equal risk, it is determined that they should yield 9 percent, compounded annually. At what price should the Shin Corporation sell these bonds?

**5-21B.** (*Perpetuities*) What is the present value of the following?

**a.** A $400 perpetuity discounted back to the present at 9 percent
**b.** A $1,500 perpetuity discounted back to the present at 13 percent
**c.** A $150 perpetuity discounted back to the present at 10 percent
**d.** A $100 perpetuity discounted back to the present at 6 percent

**5-22B.** (*Present value of an annuity due*) What is the present value of a 5-year annuity due of $1,000 annually given a 10 percent discount rate?

**5-23B.** (*Solving for* n *with nonannual periods*) About how many years would it take for your investment to grow sevenfold if it were invested at 10 percent compounded semiannually?

**5-24B.** (*Present value of an uneven stream of payments*) You are given three investment alternatives to analyze. The cash flows from these three investments are as follows:

Investment

| End of Year | A | B | C |
|---|---|---|---|
| 1 | $5,000 | $1,000 | $10,000 |
| 2 | $5,000 | $3,000 | $10,000 |
| 3 | $5,000 | $5,000 | $10,000 |
| 4 | −$15,000 | $10,000 | $10,000 |
| 5 | $15,000 | −$10,000 | −$40,000 |

What is the present value of each of these three investments if 10 percent is the appropriate discount rate?

**5-25B.** (*Complex present value*) How much do you have to deposit today so that beginning 11 years from now you can withdraw $10,000 a year for the next 5 years (periods 11 through 15), plus an *additional* amount of $15,000 in the last year (period 15)? Assume an interest rate of 7 percent.

**5-26B.** (*Loan amortization*) On December 31, Loren Billingsley bought a yacht for $60,000, paying $15,000 down and agreeing to pay the balance in 10 equal annual installments that include both the principal and 9 percent interest on the declining balance. How big will the annual payments be?

**5-27B.** (*Solving for* i *in an annuity*) You lend a friend $45,000, which your friend will repay in five equal annual payments of $9,000 with the first payment to be received 1 year from now. What rate of return does your loan receive?

**5-28B.** (*Solving for* i *in compound interest*) You lend a friend $15,000, for which your friend will repay you $37,313 at the end of 5 years. What interest rate are you charging your "friend"?

**5-29B.** (*Loan amortization*) A firm borrows $30,000 from the bank at 13 percent compounded annually to purchase some new machinery. This loan is to be repaid in equal annual installments at the end of each year over the next 4 years. How much will each annual payment be?

**5-30B.** (*Present value comparison*) You are offered $1,000 today, $10,000 in 12 years, or $25,000 in 25 years. Assuming that you can earn 11 percent on your money, which should you choose?

**5-31B.** (*Compound annuity*) You plan to buy some property in Florida 5 years from today. To do this, you estimate that you will need $30,000 at that time for the purchase. You would like to accumulate these funds by making equal annual deposits in your savings account, which pays 10 percent annually. If you make your first deposit at the end of this year and you would like your account to reach $30,000 when the final deposit is made, what will be the amount of your deposits?

**5-32B.** (*Complex present value*) You would like to have $75,000 in 15 years. To accumulate this amount, you plan to deposit each year an equal sum in the bank, which will earn 8 percent interest compounded annually. Your first payment will be made at the end of the year.

**a.** How much must you deposit annually to accumulate this amount?

**b.** If you decide to make a large lump-sum deposit today instead of the annual deposits, how large should this lump-sum deposit be? (Assume you can earn 8 percent on this deposit.)

**c.** At the end of 5 years, you will receive $20,000 and deposit this in the bank toward your goal of $75,000 at the end of 15 years. In addition to this deposit, how much must you deposit in equal annual deposits to reach your goal? (Again, assume you can earn 8 percent on this deposit.)

**5-33B.** (*Comprehensive present value*) You are trying to plan for retirement in 10 years and currently you have $150,000 in a savings account and $250,000 in stocks. In addition, you plan to add to your savings by depositing $8,000 per year in your *savings account* at the end of each of the next 5 years and then $10,000 per year at the end of each year for the final 5 years until retirement.

**a.** Assuming your savings account returns 8 percent compounded annually and your investment in stocks will return 12 percent compounded annually, how much will you have at the end of 10 years? (Ignore taxes.)

**b.** If you expect to live 20 years after you retire, and at retirement you deposit all of your savings in a bank account paying 11 percent, how much can you withdraw each year after retirement (20 equal withdrawals beginning 1 year after you retire) to end up with a zero-balance at death?

**5-34B.** (*Loan amortization*) On December 31, Eugene Chung borrowed $200,000, agreeing to repay this sum in 20 equal annual installments that include both the principal and 10 percent interest on the declining balance. How large will the annual payments be?

**5-35B.** (*Loan amortization*) To buy a new house, you must borrow $250,000. To do this, you take out a $250,000, 30-year, 9 percent mortgage. Your mortgage payments, which are made at the end of each year (one payment each year), include both principal and 9 percent interest on the declining balance. How large will your annual payments be?

**5-36B.** (*Present value*) The state lottery's million-dollar payout provides for $1 million to be paid over 24 years in $40,000 amounts. The first $40,000 payment is made immediately with the 24 remaining $40,000 payments occurring at the end of each of the next 24 years. If 10 percent is the appropriate discount rate, what is the present value of this stream of cash flows? If 20 percent is the appropriate discount rate, what is the present value of the cash flows?

**5-37B.** (*Compounding an annuity due*) Find the future value at the end of year 5 of an annuity due of $1,000 per year for 5 years compounded annually at 5 percent. What would be the future value of this annuity if it were compounded annually at 8 percent?

**5-38B.** (*Present value of an annuity*) Determine the present value of an annuity due of $1,000 per year for 15 years discounted back to the present at an annual rate of 12 percent. What would be the present value of this annuity due if it were discounted at an annual rate of 15 percent?

**5-39B.** (*Present value of a future annuity*) Determine the present value of an ordinary annuity of $1,000 per year for 10 years with the first cash flow from the annuity coming at the end of year 8 (that is, no payments at the end of years 1 through 7 and annual payments at the end of years 8 through 17) given a 15 percent discount rate.

**5-40B.** (*Solving for* i *in compound interest—financial calculator needed*) In March 1963, issue number 39 of *Tales of Suspense* was issued. The original price for that issue was 12¢. By March of 2001,

38 years later, the value of this comic book had risen to \$3,500. What annual rate of interest would you have earned if you had bought the comic in 1963 and sold it in 2001?

**5-41B.** (*Comprehensive present value*) You have just inherited a large sum of money and you are trying to determine how much you should save for retirement and how much you can spend now. For retirement you will deposit today (January 1, 2002) a lump sum in a bank account paying 10 percent compounded annually. You don't plan on touching this deposit until you retire in 5 years (January 1, 2007), and you plan on living for 20 additional years and then drop dead on December 31, 2026. During your retirement, you would like to receive income of \$60,000 per year to be received the first day of each year, with the first payment on January 1, 2007, and the last payment on January 1, 2026. Complicating this objective is your desire to have one final 3-year fling, during which time you'd like to track down all the original members of *The Mr. Ed Show* and *The Monkees* and get their autographs. To finance this, you want to receive \$300,000 on January 1, 2022, and *nothing* on January 1, 2023, and January 1, 2024, as you will be on the road. In addition, after you pass on (January 1, 2027), you would like to have a total of \$100,000 to leave to your children.

- **a.** How much must you deposit in the bank at 10 percent on January 1, 2002, in order to achieve your goal? (Use a time line in order to answer this question.)
- **b.** What kinds of problems are associated with this analysis and its assumptions?

## SELF-TEST SOLUTIONS

**ST-1.** This is a compound interest problem in which you must first find the future value of \$25,000 growing at 8 percent compounded annually for 3 years and then allow that future value to grow for an additional 3 years at 10 percent. First, the value of the \$25,000 after 3 years growing at 8 percent is

$$FV_3 = PV(1 + i)^n$$
$$FV_3 = \$25{,}000(1 + .08)^3$$
$$FV_3 = \$25{,}000(1.260)$$
$$FV_3 = \$31{,}500$$

Thus, after 3 years, you have \$31,500. Now this amount is allowed to grow for 3 years at 10 percent. Plugging this into equation 5-6, with $PV = \$31{,}500$, $i = 10$ percent, $n = 3$ years, we solve for $FV_3$:

$$FV_3 = \$31{,}500(1 + .10)^3$$
$$FV_3 = \$31{,}500(1.331)$$
$$FV_3 = \$41{,}926.50$$

Thus, after 6 years, the \$25,000 will have grown to \$41,926.50.

**ST-2.** This loan amortization problem is actually just a present-value-of-an-annuity problem in which we know the values of *i, n,* and *PV,* and are solving for *PMT.* In this case, the value of *i* is 13 percent, *n* is 10 years, and *PV* is \$30,000. Substituting these values into equation 5-10, we find

$$\$30{,}000 = PMT\left[\sum_{t=1}^{10} \frac{1}{(1 + .13)^t}\right]$$
$$\$30{,}000 = PMT(5.426)$$
$$\$5{,}528.93 = PMT$$

**ST-3.** This is a simple compound interest problem in which $FV_9$ is eight times larger than *PV.* Here again, three of the four variables are known: $n = 9$ years, $FV_9 = 8$, and $PV = 1$, and we are solving for *i.* Substituting these values into equation 5-6, we find

$$FV_9 = PV(1 + i)^n$$
$$FV_9 = PV(FVIF_{i,n})$$
$$8 = 1(FVIF_{i,9yr})$$
$$8.00 = FVIF_{i,9y}$$

Thus, we are looking for an $FVIF_{i,9yr}$ with a value of 8 in Appendix B, which occurs in the 9-year row. If we look in the 9-year row for a value of 8.00, we find it in the 26% column (8.004). Thus, the answer is 26 percent.

# RISK AND RATES OF RETURN

**LEARNING OBJECTIVES**

After reading this chapter, you should be able to

1. Describe the relationship between the average returns that investors have earned and riskiness of these returns.
2. Explain the effects of inflation on rates of return.
3. Describe *term structure of interest rates.*
4. Define and measure the expected rate of return of an individual investment.
5. Define and measure the riskiness of an individual investment.
6. Explain how diversifying investments affects the riskiness and expected rate of return of a portfolio or combination of assets.
7. Measure the market risk of an individual asset.
8. Calculate the market risk of a portfolio of investments.
9. Explain the relationship between an investor's required rate of return on an investment and the riskiness of the investment.

One of the most important concepts in all of finance deals with risk and return, and our first principle addresses this topic. As an illustration of risk and return, consider what was happening to the stock price of many of the high-tech stocks during

2000. From January 1, 2000, through March 10, 2000, the Nasdaq Composite Index, dominated by such firms as Microsoft, Oracle, and Intel, increased 25 percent in value—not bad for a mere 2 months. Many of us probably wished that we had been so "smart" as to buy a group of these high-tech stocks. But by October 2000, the Nasdaq was down 33 percent from its March high. Imagine how you would feel if you had jumped on the bandwagon in March. However, these highly volatile price changes were part of the 1999–2000 landscape if you bought and sold high-tech stocks. In other words, these stocks may produce high rates of return to their owners, but they are risky investments, as signified by their high volatility. As the owner of high-tech stocks during this time, you may have eaten well on the good days, but you certainly didn't sleep very well some nights. Welcome to the world where high rates of return go hand in hand with high risk.

## CHAPTER PREVIEW

The need to recognize risk in financial decisions has already been apparent in earlier chapters. In Chapter 1, we introduced **Principle 1: The Risk-Return Trade-Off—We won't take an additional risk unless we expect to be compensated with additional returns.** In the previous chapter, we observed the importance of the discount rate in comparing financial assets and investment proposals. But we assumed the interest rate to be a given. Now we want to examine where the appropriate rate comes from. We will see that risk is a prime factor in setting the appropriate rate.

There is an intuitive aspect to thinking about risk. Let's approach this by looking at an industry, a firm, and an individual investment proposal. For instance, think intuitively about different industries, such as soft drinks, computers, and biotechs. Which one would we expect to be the most stable? The obvious answer is soft drinks. We can reasonably anticipate this industry to keep chugging along. The computer industry, on the other hand, is more volatile. What happens if Intel introduces a faster chip? Will people buy it in large numbers? And the biotech industry is more volatile still—will a cure for AIDS be found? If so, we can imagine that there would be a big payoff, but a lot of money could be spent along the way.

Now consider individual companies involved in seeking an AIDS cure. There are large companies, such as GlaxoSmithKline Beecham and Pfizer, and small startups. Do we have any basis for thinking the larger companies have a better chance than the smaller ones? Does size imply financial commitment or superior resources?

Now think about a particular company, such as Pfizer. Finding an AIDS cure could give it a huge boost in profits. But Pfizer has many different products. An AIDS cure may not be as important to Pfizer's future as it would be for a one-product startup company.

In all of these cases, we have an intuitive sense of differences in prospects. We will now turn to how this intuitive sense flows into the returns one can expect to receive from a particular investment proposal. We will see the relationship between risk and average returns of different investments. We will show how we can quantify this concept of risk, and how this determines the interest rate we used in discounting to compare projects. The concept of risk is a crucial one for the financial manager. This chapter will show where it comes from and how it can be used to compare financial assets.

Three principles will serve as the foundation for this chapter. Keeping them in mind throughout will be helpful in your study. These axioms are **Principle 1: The Risk-Return Trade-Off—We won't take on additional risk unless we expect to be compensated with additional returns; Principle 3: Cash—Not Profits—Is King; Principle 9: All Risk Is Not Equal—Some risk can be diversified away, and some cannot.**

Watch for these principles and let them be the threads that connect the ideas presented in this chapter. Let's now begin our study by looking at what we mean by the expected rate of return and how it can be measured.

# RATES OF RETURN IN THE FINANCIAL MARKETS

In the financial markets where stocks and bonds are sold, net users of money, such as companies that make investments, have to compete with one another for capital. To obtain financing for projects that will benefit a firm's stockholders, a company must offer investors a rate of return that is *competitive* with the next best investment alternative available to the investor. This rate of return on the next best investment alternative to the saver is known as the investor's **opportunity cost of funds.**

**Opportunity cost of funds** The next best rate of return available to the investor for a given level of risk.

As managers, we need to understand the investor's opportunity cost of investing; that is, what could an investor earn by investing in another company of similar risk? Only by answering this question can a financial manager begin to understand whether the shareholders are receiving a fair return on their investments. Also, from an investor's perspective, there is a need to know the historical experience of other investors in the capital markets; otherwise, there is no basis for knowing what can be reasonably expected in terms of rates of returns.

## The Relationship Between Risk and Rates of Return

History can tell us a great deal about the returns that investors earn in the financial markets. A primary source for an historical perspective comes from Ibbotson and Sinquefield's *Stocks, Bonds, Bills, and Inflation,* which examines the realized rates of return for a wide variety of securities spanning the period from 1926 through 1999. Their data are comprehensive and extremely useful both to investors and financial managers in their respective needs for understanding rates of returns in the capital markets. In their results, they summarize, among other things, the annual returns for different portfolios of securities, five of them being:[1]

1. Common stocks of small firms
2. Common stocks of large companies
3. Long-term corporate bonds
4. Long-term U.S. government bonds
5. U.S. Treasury bills

Before comparing the actual rates of returns and their variability (risk), we should first think about what to expect. First, we would intuitively expect a Treasury bill to be the least risky of the five portfolios. Because a Treasury bill has a short-term maturity date, the price is less volatile (less risky) than the price of a long-term government security.[2] In turn, because there is a chance of default on a corporate bond, which is essentially nonexistent for government securities, a long-term government bond is less risky than a long-term corporate bond. Finally, common stock of large companies is more risky than a corporate bond, with small-company stocks being more risky than the portfolio of large-firm stocks.

By smaller firm, we do not mean the "mom-and-pop" store down on the corner, but rather the smallest companies listed on the New York Stock Exchange (the bottom 20 percent, to be exact). It is believed that these smaller companies are more risky than the really large firms. Why might that be? First, smaller businesses experience greater risk in their operations—they are more sensitive to business downturns and some operate in niche markets that can quickly appear and then quickly disappear. Second, they rely more heavily on debt financing than do larger firms. These differences create more variability in their profits and cash flows, which translates into greater risk.

With the forgoing in mind, we should expect different rates of return to the holders of these varied securities. If the market rewards an investor for assuming risk, the average annual rates of return should increase as risk increases.

A comparison of the annual rates of return for the five portfolios listed previously for the years 1926 to 1999 is provided in Table 6-1. Four attributes of these returns are included: (1) the *nominal* average annual rate of return; (2) the standard deviation of the returns, which measures the volatility or riskiness of the portfolios; (3) the *real* average annual rate of return, which is the nominal return less the inflation rate; and (4) the risk premium, which represents the additional return received beyond the risk-free rate (Treasury bill rate) for assuming risk.

Looking first at the two columns of average annual returns and standard deviations, we gain an overview of the risk-return relationships that have existed over the 74 years ending in 1999. For the most part, there has been a positive relationship between risk and return, with Treasury bills being the least risky and common stocks of small companies being the most risky.

The return information in Table 6-1 demonstrates that common stock has been the investor's primary inflation hedge in the long run—the average inflation rate has been 3.2 percent—and offered the highest risk premium. However, it is equally apparent that the common stockholder is exposed to sizable risk, as demonstrated by a 20.1 percent standard deviation for large-company stocks and a 33.6 percent standard deviation for small-company stocks. In fact, in the 1926 to 1999 time frame, large-company common shareholders received negative returns in 20 of the 74 years, compared with only 1 in 74 for Treasury bills.

[1]Roger G. Ibbotson and Rex A. Sinquefield, *Stocks, Bonds, Bills, and Inflation: Historical Return* (1926–1999) (Chicago, IL: Ibbotson Associates, 2000).

[2]For an explanation of the greater volatility for long-term bonds relative to short-term bonds, see Chapter 7.

**TABLE 6-1**
Annual Rates of Return 1926–1999

| Securities | Nominal Average Annual Returns | Standard Deviation of Returns | Real Average Annual Returns[a] | Risk Premium[b] |
|---|---|---|---|---|
| Small-company Stocks | 17.6% | 33.6% | 14.4% | 13.8% |
| Large-company Stocks | 13.3 | 20.1 | 10.1 | 9.5 |
| Long-term Corporate Bonds | 5.9 | 8.7 | 2.7 | 2.1 |
| Long-term Government Bonds | 5.5 | 9.3 | 2.3 | 1.7 |
| U.S. Treasury Bills | 3.8 | 3.2 | 0.6 | 0 |

[a]Real return equals the nominal return less the average inflation rate from 1926 through 1999 of 3.2 percent.
[b]Risk premium equals the nominal return less the average risk-free rate (Treasury bills) of 3.8 percent.

Source: R. G. Ibbotson and R. A. Sinquefield, *Stocks, Bonds, Bills, and Inflation: Historical Returns* (Chicago, IL: Ibbotson Associates, 2000): 14. © Ibbotson Associates.

## THE EFFECTS OF INFLATION ON RATES OF RETURN AND THE FISHER EFFECT

When a rate of interest is quoted, it is generally the nominal, or observed rate. The **real rate of interest,** on the other hand, represents the rate of increase in actual purchasing power, after adjusting for inflation. For example, if you have \$100 today and lend it to someone for a year at a nominal rate of interest of 11.3 percent, you will get back \$111.30 in 1 year. But if during the year prices of goods and services rise by 5 percent, it will take \$105 at year end to purchase the same goods and services that \$100 purchased at the beginning of the year. What was your increase in purchasing power over the year? The quick and dirty answer is found by subtracting the inflation rate from the nominal rate, 11.3% − 5% = 6.3%, but this is not exactly correct. To be more precise, let the nominal rate of interest be represented by $k_{rf}$, the anticipated rate of inflation by *IRP,* and the real rate of interest by $k^*$. Using these notations, we can express the relationship among the nominal interest rate, the rate of inflation, and the real rate of interest as follows:

**Real rate of interest** The nominal rate of interest less the expected rate of inflation over the maturity of the fixed-income security. This represents the expected increase in actual purchasing power to the investor.

$$1 + k_{rf} = (1 + k^*)(1 + IRP) \qquad \textbf{(6-1)}$$

or

$$k_{rf} = k^* + IRP + (k^* \times IRP)$$

Consequently, the nominal rate of interest ($k_{rf}$) is equal to the sum of the real rate of interest ($k^*$), the inflation rate (*IRP*), and the product of the real rate and the inflation rate. This relationship among nominal rates, real rates, and the rate of inflation has come to be called the *Fisher effect.*[3] It means that the observed nominal rate of interest includes both the real rate and an *inflation premium,* as noted in the previous section.

[3]This relationship was analyzed many years ago by Irving Fisher. For those who want to explore "Fisher's theory of interest" in more detail, a fine overview is contained in Peter N. Ireland, "Long-Term Interest Rates and Inflation: A Fisherian Approach," *Federal Reserve Bank of Richmond, Economic Quarterly* 82 (Winter 1996), pp. 22–26.

Substituting into equation 6-1 using a nominal rate of 11.3 percent and an inflation rate of 5 percent, we can calculate the real rate of interest, $k^*$, as follows:

$$k_{rf} = k^* + IRP + (k^* \times IRP)$$
$$.113 = k^* + .05 + .05k^*$$
$$k^* = .06 = 6\%$$

Thus, at the new higher prices, your purchasing power will have increased by only 6 percent, although you have \$11.30 more than you had at the start of the year. To see why, let's assume that at the outset of the year one unit of the market basket of goods and services costs \$1, so you could purchase 100 units with your \$100. At the end of the year you have \$11.30 more, but each unit now costs 1.05 (remember the 5 percent rate of inflation). How many units can you buy at the end of the year? The answer is \$111.30 ÷ \$1.05 = 106, which represents a 6 percent increase in real purchasing power.[4]

## THE TERM STRUCTURE OF INTEREST RATES

OBJECTIVE 3 

**Term structure of interest rates (yield to maturity)** Relationship between a debt security's rate of return and the length of time until the debt matures.

The relationship between a debt security's rate of return and the length of time until the debt matures is known as the **term structure of interest rates** or the **yield to maturity.** For the relationship to be meaningful to us, all the factors other than maturity, meaning factors such as the chance of the bond defaulting, must be held constant.

Thus, the term structure reflects observed rates or yields on similar securities, except for the length of time until maturity, at a particular moment in time.

Figure 6-1 shows an example of the term structure of interest rates. The curve is upward sloping, indicating that longer terms to maturity command higher returns, or yields. In this hypothetical term structure, the rate of interest on a 5-year note or bond is 11.5 percent, whereas the comparable rate on a 20-year bond is 13 percent.

As we might expect, the term structure of interest rates changes over time, depending on the environment. The particular term structure observed today may be quite different from the term structure a month ago and different still from the term structure 1 month from now. A perfect example of the changing term structure, or yield curve, was witnessed

**FIGURE 6-1**
The Term Structure of Interest Rates

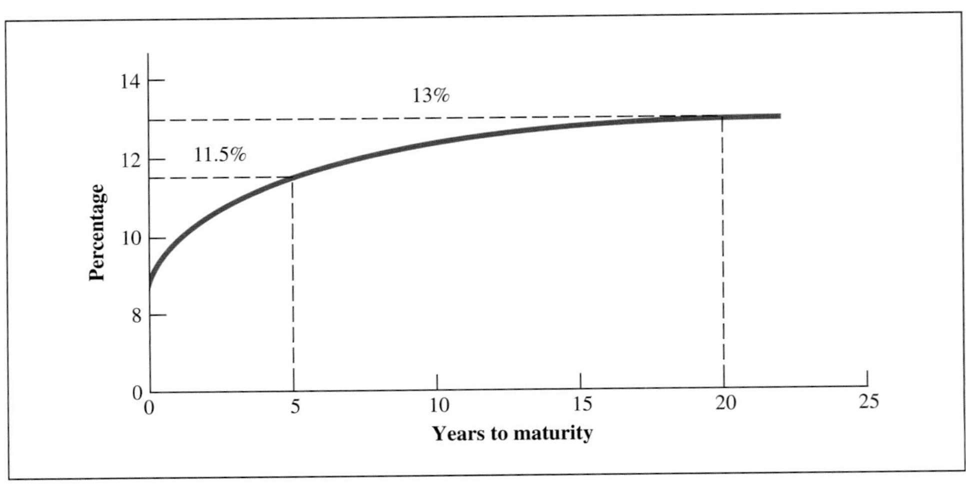


[4]Recall our discussion of the time value of money in Chapter 5.

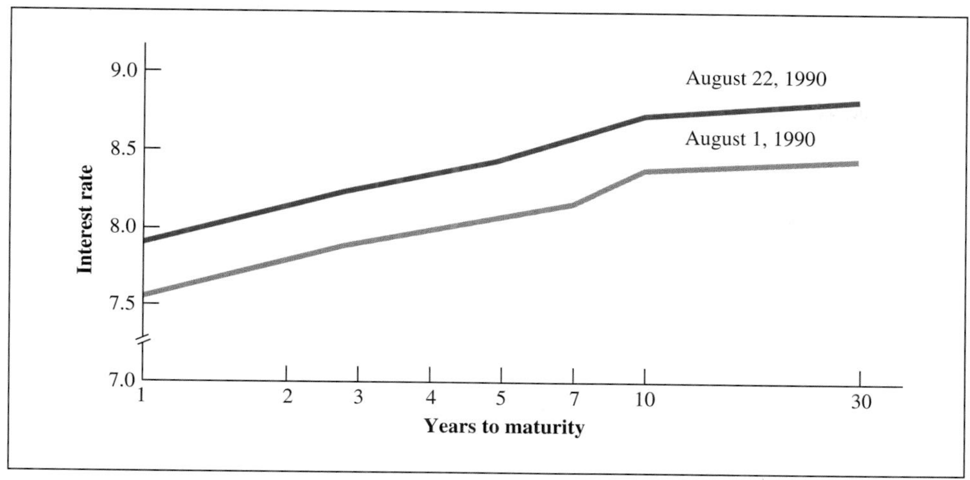


**FIGURE 6-2**
Changes in the Term Structure of Interest Rates for Government Securities at the Outbreak of the Persian Gulf Crisis

during the early days of the Persian Gulf crisis in August 1990. Figure 6-2 shows the yield curves 1 day before the Iraqi invasion of Kuwait and then again just 3 weeks later. The change is noticeable, particularly for long-term interest rates. Investors quickly developed new fears about the prospect of increased inflation to be caused by the crisis and consequently increased their required rates of return. Although the upward-sloping term-structure curves in Figures 6-1 and 6-2 are the ones most commonly observed, yield curves can assume several shapes. Sometimes the term structure is downward sloping; at other times it rises and then falls (hump-backed); and at still other times it may be relatively flat. Figure 6-3 shows some yield curves at different points in time.

Now that we have looked at actual rates of returns earned by investors, let's next examine specifically how risk and return are measured, both for individual assets and a portfolio of assets. In so doing, we will gain a better understanding of the underlying concepts relating to risk and returns.

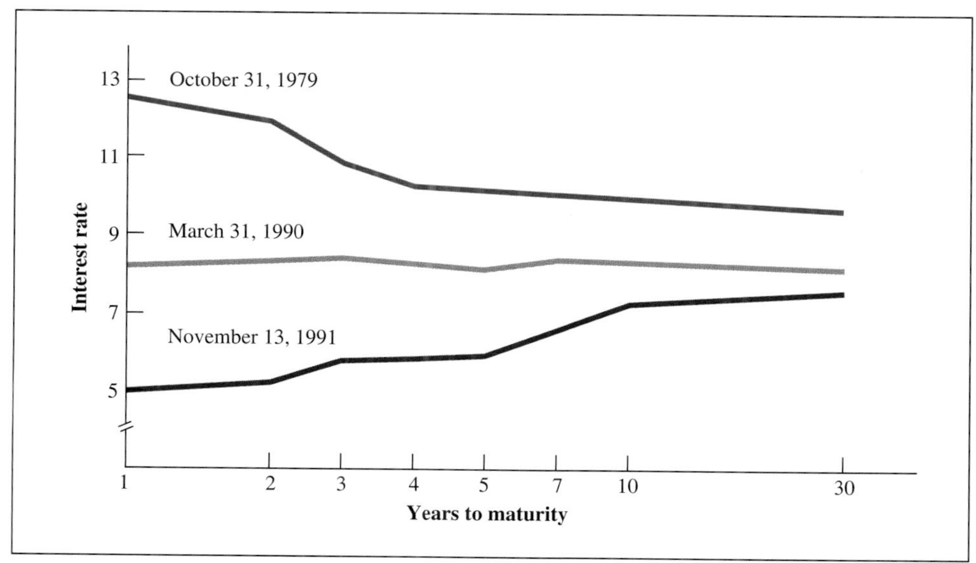


**FIGURE 6-3**
Historical Term Structures of Interest Rates for Government Securities

**TABLE 6-2**
Measuring the Expected Return

| State of the Economy | Probability of the State[a] | Cash Flows from the Investment | Percentage Return (Cash Flow ÷ Investment Cost) |
|---|---|---|---|
| Economic recession | 20% | $1,000 | 10% (= $1,000 ÷ $10,000) |
| Moderate economic growth | 30% | 1,200 | 12% (= $1,200 ÷ $10,000) |
| Strong economic growth | 50% | 1,400 | 14% (= $1,400 ÷ $10,000) |

[a]The probabilities assigned to the three possible economic conditions have to be determined subjectively, which requires management to have a thorough understanding of both the investment cash flows and the general economy.

## EXPECTED RETURN

OBJECTIVE 4 

The *expected return* from an investment, either by an individual investor or a company, is determined by the different possible outcomes that could occur from making the investment. The expected benefits or returns that an investment generates come in the form of cash flows. *Cash flows,* not accounting profits, should be used to measure returns. This principle holds true regardless of the type of security, whether it is a debt instrument, preferred stock, common stock, or any mixture of these (such as convertible bonds).

In an uncertain world, an accurate measurement of expected future cash flows is not easy for an investor to ascertain. The uncertainty of making an investment is apparent when we use our savings to purchase a share of General Electric stock, or even more so when we buy a share of stock of a privately held company where the shares are not actively traded in any market. At the firm level, uncertainty comes to play in almost any decision made, but particularly when investing in new product lines or entering a new geographical market. At the extreme, how would Motorola predict its cash flows in China, where the government is prone to imposing regulations restricting foreign expansion? With a lot of *uncertainty,* we can say without hesitation (that is, with certainty).

While we can talk about uncertainty in general terms, it helps to crystallize our thoughts by an illustration: Assume you are considering an investment costing $10,000, where the future cash flows from owning the security depend on the state of the economy, as estimated in Table 6-2.

In any given year, the investment could produce any one of three possible cash flows depending on the particular state of the economy. With this information, how should we select the cash flow estimate that means the most for measuring the investment's expected rate of return? One approach is to calculate an *expected* cash flow. The expected cash flow is simply the weighted average of the *possible* cash flow outcomes such that the weights are the probabilities of the occurrence of the various states of the economy. Let $X_i$ designate the $i$th possible cash flow, $n$ reflects the number of possible states of the economy, and $P(X_i)$ indicates the probability that the $i$th cash flow or state of economy will occur. The expected cash flow, $\overline{X}$, can then be calculated as follows:

$$\overline{X} = X_1P(X_1) + X_2P(X_2) + \ldots + X_nP(X_n) \tag{6-2}$$

or

$$\overline{X} = \sum_{i=1}^{n} X_iP(X_i)$$

For the present illustration,

$$\overline{X} = (.2)(\$1{,}000) + (.3)(\$1{,}200) + (.5)(\$1{,}400) = \$1{,}260$$

In addition to computing an expected dollar return from an investment, we can also calculate an **expected rate of return** earned on the \$10,000 investment. As the last column in Table 6-2 shows, the \$1,400 cash inflow, assuming strong economic growth, represents a 14 percent return (\$1,400 ÷ \$10,000). Similarly, the \$1,200 and \$1,000 cash flows result in 12 percent and 10 percent returns, respectively. Using these percentage returns in place of the dollar amounts, the expected rate of return, $\bar{k}$, may be expressed as follows:

**Expected rate of return** The weighted average of all possible returns where the returns are weighted by the probability that each will occur.

$$\bar{k} = k_1P(k_1) + k_2P(k_2) + \ldots + k_nP(k_n) \quad \textbf{(6-3)}$$

$$\bar{k} = \sum_{i=1}^{n} k_iP(k_i)$$

where $k_i$ = the $i$th possible rate of return
$P(k_i)$ = the probability of the $i$th possible rate of return

In our example:

$$\bar{k} = (.2)(10\%) + (.3)(12\%) + (.5)(14\%) = 12.6\%$$

Now let's consider the other side of the investment coin: risk.

**RELATE TO THE BIG PICTURE**

In the forgoing example, we were interested in cash flows—not earnings—in computing the investment's rate of return. This is not an unimportant distinction, as noted in **Principle 3: Cash—Not Profits—Is King.** Since we spend cash to make an investment, we want to receive cash in return. Thus, cash is what matters.

**CONCEPT CHECK**

1. When we speak of "benefits" from investing in an asset, what do we mean?
2. Why is it difficult to measure future cash flows?
3. Define "expected rate of return."

## RISK

Because we live in a world of uncertainty, how we perceive risk and integrate it into our decisions is vitally important in almost all dimensions of our life; certainly, risk must be considered in financial decision making. The Greek poet and statesman Solon, writing in the sixth century B.C., stated:

> There is risk in everything that one does, and no one knows where he will make his landfall when his enterprise is at its beginning. One man, trying to act effectively, fails to foresee something and falls into great and grim ruination, but to another man, one who is acting ineffectively, a god gives good fortune in everything and escape from his folly.[5]

Although Solon would have given more of the credit to Zeus than we might for the outcomes of our ventures, his insight reminds us that life has always been uncertain; thus we need to acknowledge and compensate as best we can for the risks we encounter.

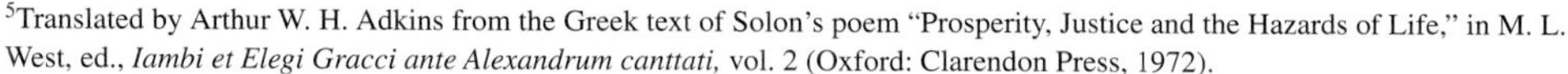
[5]Translated by Arthur W. H. Adkins from the Greek text of Solon's poem "Prosperity, Justice and the Hazards of Life," in M. L. West, ed., *Iambi et Elegi Gracci ante Alexandrum canttati,* vol. 2 (Oxford: Clarendon Press, 1972).

FINANCE $ MATTERS

### Whim of the Gods?

What is it that distinguishes the thousands of years of history from what we think of as modern times? The answer goes way beyond the progress of science, technology, capitalism, and democracy.

The distant past was studded with brilliant scientists, mathematicians, inventors, technologists, and political philosophers. Hundreds of years before the birth of Christ, the skies had been mapped, the great library of Alexandria built, and Euclid's geometry taught. Demand for technological innovation in warfare was as insatiable then as it is today. Coal, oil, iron, and copper have been at the service of human beings for millennia, and travel and communication mark the very beginnings of recorded civilization.

The revolutionary idea that defines the boundary between modern times and the past is the mastery of risk: the notion that the future is more than a whim of the gods and that men and women are not passive before nature. Until human beings discovered a way across that boundary, the future was a mirror of the past or the murky domain of oracles and soothsayers who held a monopoly over knowledge of anticipated events.

Peter Bernstein in *Against the Gods, the Remarkable Story of Risk.* John Wiley & Sons (October 1996).

Without intending to be trite, risk means different things to different people, depending on the context and on how they feel about taking chances. For the student, risk is the possibility of failing an exam, or the chance of not making his or her best grades. For the coal miner or the oil field worker, risk is the chance of an explosion in the mine or at the well site. For the retired person, risk means perhaps not being able to live comfortably on a fixed income. For the entrepreneur, risk is the chance that a new venture will fail. In a financial context, we want to understand risk so that we can assess the level of risk inherent in an investment.

To gain a basic understanding of investment risk, we might ask: "What is risk and how is it measured?" To begin, we will answer this question when we are only making a single investment, and then for a portfolio, or group of investments.

## Risk and a Single Investment

To help us grasp the fundamental meaning of risk, consider two possible investments:

1. The first investment is a U.S. Treasury bill, which is a government security that matures in 90 days and promises to pay an annual return of 6 percent. If we purchase and hold this security for 90 days, we are virtually assured of receiving no more and no less than 6 percent. For all practical purposes, the risk of loss is nonexistent.
2. The second investment involves the purchase of the stock of a local publishing company. Looking at the past returns of the firm's stock, we have made the following estimate of the annual returns from the investment:

| Chance (Probability) of Occurrence | Rate of Return on Investment |
|---|---|
| 1 chance in 10 (10%) | −10% |
| 2 chances in 10 (20%) | 5% |
| 4 chances in 10 (40%) | 15% |
| 2 chances in 10 (20%) | 25% |
| 1 chance in 10 (10%) | 40% |

Investing in the publishing company could conceivably provide a return as high as 40 percent if all goes well, or we could lose 10 percent if everything goes against the firm.

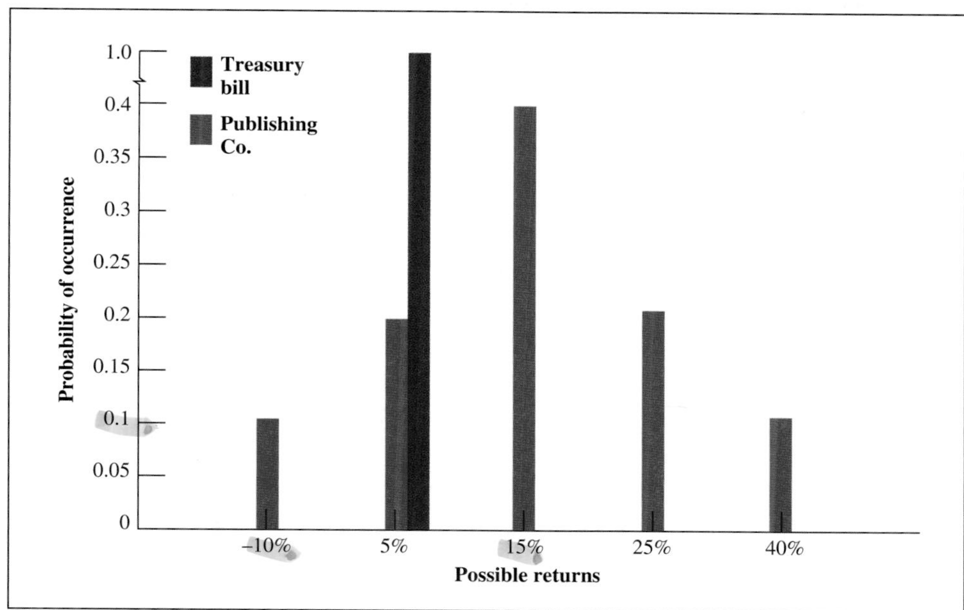


**FIGURE 6-4**
Probability Distribution of Returns for a Treasury bill and a Publishing Company

However, in future years, both good and bad, we could expect a 15 percent return on average computed as follows:[6]

$$\bar{k} = (.10)(-10\%) + (.20)(5\%) + (.40)(15\%) + (.20)(25\%) + (.10)(40\%)$$
$$= 15\%$$

Comparing the Treasury bill investment with the publishing company investment, we see that the Treasury bill offers an expected 6 percent rate of return, whereas the publishing company has an expected rate of return of 15 percent. However, our investment in the publishing firm is clearly more "risky"—that is, there is greater uncertainty about the final outcome. Stated somewhat differently, there is a greater variation or dispersion of possible returns, which in turn implies greater **risk.**[7] Figure 6-4 shows these differences graphically in the form of discrete probability distributions.

**Risk**
The prospect of an unfavorable outcome. This concept has been measured operationally as the standard deviation or beta, which will be explained later.

Although the return from investing in the publishing firm is clearly less certain than for Treasury bills, quantitative measures of risk are useful when the difference between two investments is not so evident. Just as we used the time value of money in Chapter 5 to compare cash flow streams of different investments, we need a way to compare the riskiness of different projects. Furthermore, the problem is similar for a financial manager who must consider different investments. At times the choice is obvious, but at others it is not—so the manager needs a way to be more precise in analyzing a project's level of risk. The standard deviation ($\sigma$) is such a measure. The **standard deviation** is

**Standard deviation**
A measure of the spread or dispersion about the mean of a probability distribution. We calculate it by squaring the difference between each outcome and its expected value, weighting each squared difference by its associated probability, summing over all possible outcomes, and taking the square root of this sum.

[6]We assume that the particular outcome or return earned in 1 year does *not* affect the return earned in the subsequent year. Technically speaking, the distribution of returns in any year is assumed to be independent of the outcome in any prior year.

[7]How can we possibly view variations above the expected return as risk? Should we not be concerned only with the negative deviations? Some would agree and view risk as only the negative variability in returns from a predetermined minimum acceptable rate of return. However, as long as the distribution of returns is symmetrical, the same conclusions will be reached.

simply the square root of the average squared deviation of each possible return from the expected return; that is

$$\sigma = \sqrt{\sum_{i=1}^{n} (k_i - \bar{k})^2 P(k_i)} \tag{6-4}$$

where $n$ = the number of possible outcomes or different rates of return on the investment
$k_i$ = the value of the $i$th possible rate of return
$\bar{k}$ = the expected rate of return
$P(k_i)$ = the chance or probability that the $i$th outcome or return will occur

For the publishing company, the standard deviation would be 12.85 percent, determined as follows:

$$\sigma = \begin{bmatrix} (-10\% - 15\%)^2(.10) + (5\% - 15\%)^2(.20) \\ + (15\% - 15\%)^2(.40) + (25\% - 15\%)^2(.20) \\ + (40\% - 15\%)^2(.10) \end{bmatrix}^{\frac{1}{2}}$$

$$= \sqrt{165\%} = 12.85\%$$

Although the standard deviation of returns provides us with a quantitative measure of an asset's riskiness, how should we interpret the result? What does it mean? Is the 12.85 percent standard deviation for the publishing company investment good or bad? First, we should remember that statisticians tell us that two-thirds of the time, an event will fall within plus or minus one standard deviation of the expected value (assuming the distribution is normally distributed; that is, it is shaped like a bell). Thus, given a 15 percent expected return and a standard deviation of 12.85 percent for the publishing company investment, we may reasonably anticipate that the actual returns will fall between 2.15 percent and 27.85 percent (15% ± 12.85%) two-thirds of the time—not much certainty with this investment.

A second way to interpret the standard deviation as a measure of risk is to compare the investment in the publishing firm against other investments. The attractiveness of a security with respect to its return and risk cannot be determined in isolation. Only by examining other available alternatives can we reach a conclusion about a particular investment's risk. For example, if another investment—say, an investment in a firm that owns a local radio station—has the same expected return as the publishing company, 15 percent, but with a standard deviation of 7 percent, we would consider the risk associated with the publishing firm, 12.85 percent, to be excessive. In the technical jargon of modern portfolio theory, the radio company investment is said to "dominate" the publishing firm investment. In commonsense terms, this means that the radio company investment has the same expected return as the publishing company investment but is less risky.

What if we compare the investment in the publishing company with one in a quick oil-change franchise, an investment in which the expected rate of return is an attractive 24 percent, but in which the standard deviation is estimated at 18 percent? Now what should we do? Clearly, the oil-change franchise has a higher expected rate of return, but it also has a larger standard deviation. In this example, we see that the real challenge in selecting the better investment comes when one investment has a higher expected rate of return but also exhibits greater risk. *Here the final choice is determined by our attitude toward risk, and there is no single right answer.* You might select the publishing company, whereas I might choose the oil-change investment, and neither of us would be wrong. We would simply be expressing our tastes and preferences about risk and return.

**CONCEPT CHECK**

1. Define "risk."
2. How does the standard deviation help us to measure the riskiness of an investment?
3. Does greater risk imply a bad investment?

## RISK AND DIVERSIFICATION

In the preceding discussion, we defined risk as the variability of anticipated returns as measured by the standard deviation. However, more can be said about risk, especially as to its nature, when either an individual or a firm holds more than one asset. Let's consider for the moment how risk is affected if we diversify our investment by holding a variety of securities.

To begin, assume that the date is September 8, 2000. When you awake this morning you follow your daily routine, which includes reading *The Wall Street Journal.* You always begin by scanning "What's News—Business and Finance," with an eye for anything related to the stocks you own—and there they are. Two of your stocks made the front page, the first being DuPont. The firm lowered profit projections for the third and fourth periods because of higher costs of oil-based raw materials. The result: DuPont's stock fell 12 percent on the announcement. That hurts! The only consolation is the article on General Electric, another one of your investments. General Electric's NBC reported a record $900 million in gross sales for its coverage of the 2000 Olympic Games in Sydney, Australia. In response, the company's stock increased 2 percent—not as much as your loss in DuPont, but it helps. You also notice that these events occurred on a day that the overall market on the New York Stock Exchange decreased less than 1 percent.

Clearly, what we have described about DuPont and General Electric were events unique to these two companies, and as we would expect, the investors reacted accordingly; that is, the value of the stock changed in light of the new information. Although we might have wished we had owned only GE stock at the time, most of us would prefer to avoid such uncertainties; that is, we are risk averse. Instead, we would like to reduce the risk associated with our investment portfolio without having to accept a lower expected return. Good news: It is possible by diversifying our portfolio!

If we diversify our investments across different securities rather than invest in only one stock, the variability in the returns of our portfolio should decline. The reduction in risk will occur if the stock returns within our portfolio do not move precisely together over time—that is, if they are not perfectly correlated. Figure 6-5 shows graphically what we can expect to happen to the variability of returns as we add additional stocks to the portfolio. The reduction occurs because some of the volatility in returns of a stock are unique to that security. The unique return variability of a single stock tends to be countered by the unique variability of another security. However, we should not expect to eliminate all risk from our portfolio. In practice, it would be rather difficult to cancel all the variations in returns of a portfolio, because stock prices have some tendency to move together; that is, a rising stock market tends to boost *most* (not all) stocks. Furthermore, investing in Intel, Microsoft, and Dell Computer would provide little reduction in the variability of returns. These firms are concentrated in the same industry, and as a result, their stocks tend to move together. On the other hand, investing in Coca-Cola, ExxonMobil, and Citibank would have a greater effect on the variability of returns. To be even more effective at reducing the variability of returns, we could invest in various large and small firms in different industries, as well as foreign

**FIGURE 6-5**
Variability of Returns Compared with Size of Portfolio

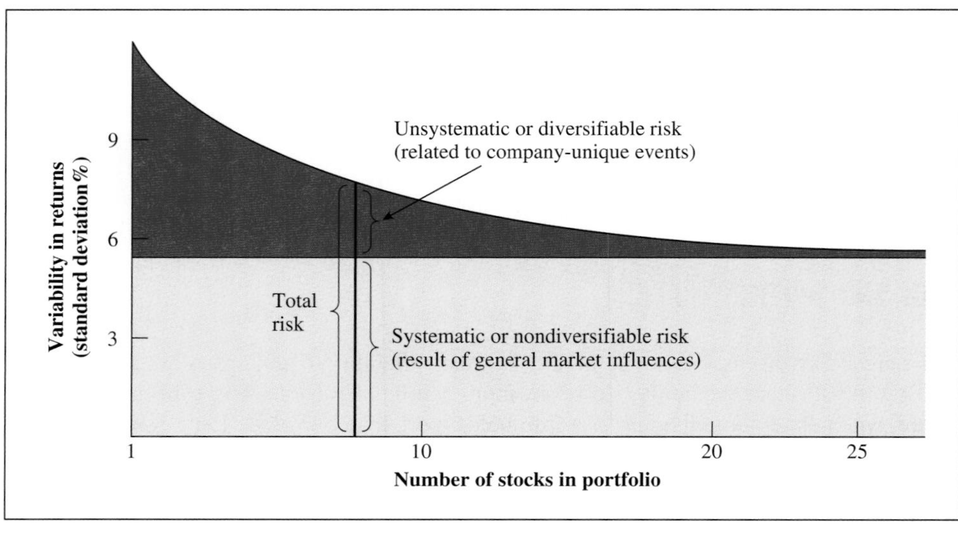


**Firm-specific risk or company-unique risk (diversifiable risk or unsystematic risk)**
The portion of the variation in investment returns that can be eliminated through investor diversification. This diversifiable risk is the result of factors that are unique to the particular firm.

**Market-related risk (nondiversifiable risk or systematic risk)**
The portion of variations in investment returns that cannot be eliminated through investor diversification. This variation results from factors that affect all stocks.

companies. But even then, you will not be able to remove all the risk (variation in returns). Thus we can divide the total risk (total variability) of our portfolio into two types of risk: (1) **firm-specific** or **company-unique risk** and (2) **market-related risk.** Company-unique risk might also be called **diversifiable risk,** because it can be diversified away. Market risk is **nondiversifiable risk;** it cannot be eliminated, no matter how much we diversify. These two types of risk are shown graphically in Figure 6-5.

Total risk declines until we have approximately 20 securities, and then the decline becomes very slight. The remaining risk, which would typically be about 40 percent of the total risk, is the portfolio's market risk. At this point, our portfolio is highly correlated with all securities in the marketplace. Events that affect our portfolio now are not so much unique events but changes in the general economy or major political events. Examples include changes in general interest rates, changes in tax legislation that affects companies, or increasing public concern about the effect of business practices on the environment.

Because we can remove the company-unique, or unsystematic risk, there is no reason to believe that the market will reward us with additional returns for assuming risk that could be avoided by simply diversifying. Our new measure of risk should therefore measure how responsive a stock or portfolio is to changes in a *market portfolio,* such as the New York Stock Exchange or the S&P 500 Index.[8] This relationship could be determined by plotting past returns—say, on a monthly basis—of a particular stock or a portfolio of stocks against the returns of the *market portfolio* for the same period. The market portfolio is one that only has systematic (nondiversifiable) risk. We frequently use the stocks making up the S&P 500 Index (500 largest U.S. companies) as a surrogate for the overall market portfolio.

**RELATE TO THE BIG PICTURE**

We have just explained **Principle 9: All Risk Is Not Equal—Some risk can be diversified away, and some cannot.** As we diversify our portfolio, we reduce the effects of company-unique risk, but some risk—nondiversifiable or market risk—still remains, no matter how much we diversify.

[8]The New York Stock Exchange Index is an index that reflects the performance of all stocks listed on the New York Stock Exchange. The Standard & Poor's (S&P) 500 Index is similarly an index that measures the combined performance of the companies that constitute the largest 500 companies in the United States, as designated by Standard & Poor's.

## Risk and Diversification Illustrated[9]

To see an actual case of the effects of diversification on rates of return, we can draw on a study by Ibbotson Associates. To demonstrate the effect of diversification on risk and rates of return, compare three portfolios (A, B, and C) consisting of the following investments:

| | Investment Mix in Portfolio: | | |
|---|---|---|---|
| **Types of securities** | **A** | **B** | **C** |
| Short-term government securities (Treasury bills) | 0% | 63% | 34% |
| Long-term government bonds | 100% | 12% | 14% |
| Large-company stocks | 0% | 25% | 52% |
| | 100% | 100% | 100% |

Figure 6-6 shows the average returns and standard deviations of the three portfolios. The results show that an investor can use diversification to improve the risk-return characteristics of a portfolio. Specifically, we see that:

1. Portfolio A, which consists entirely of long-term government bonds, had an average annual return of 5.5 percent with a standard deviation of 11.3 percent.[10]
2. In Portfolio B, we have diversified across all three security types, with the majority of the funds (63 percent) now invested in Treasury bills and a lesser amount (25 percent) in stocks. The effects are readily apparent. The average returns of the two portfolios, A

**FIGURE 6-6**
The Effect of Diversification on Average Returns and Risk

| Portfolio | | Average Annual Return | Risk (Standard Deviation) |
|---|---|---|---|
| A | 100% Long-term government bonds | 5.5% | 11.3% |
| B |  25% Large company stocks<br>12% Long-term government bonds<br>63% Treasury bills | 5.5% | 6.1% |
| C | 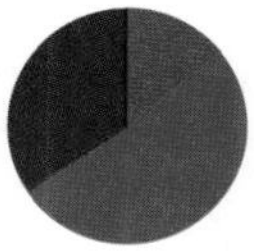 52% Large company stocks<br>14% Long-term government bonds<br>34% Treasury bills | 8.0% | 11.3% |

Large company stocks　Long-term government bonds　Treasury bills

NOTE: Adapted from Ibbotson Associates, Copyright 1994, Chicago, Illinois.

[9]This presentation is based on material developed by Ibbotson Associates. Copyright 1994.

[10]In this example, Ibbotson Associates use 1970–1993 data to compute the standard deviation for the long-term government bonds; all other computations use the total 1926–1993 time frame.

and B, are identical, but the risk associated with Portfolio B is almost half that of Portfolio A—standard deviation of 6.1 percent for Portfolio B compared to 11.3 percent for Portfolio A. Notice that risk has been reduced in Portfolio B even though stocks, a far more risky security, have been included in the portfolio. How could this be? Simple: Stocks behave differently than both government bonds and Treasury bills, with the effect being a less risky (lower standard deviation) portfolio.

3. Portfolio B demonstrates how an investor can reduce risk while keeping returns constant, and Portfolio C, with its increased investment in stocks (52 percent), shows how an investor can increase average returns while keeping risk constant. This portfolio has a risk level identical to that of long-term government bonds alone (Portfolio A), but achieves a higher average return of 8 percent, compared to 5.5 percent for the government bond portfolio.

The conclusion to be drawn from this example is clear: The market rewards diversification. By diversifying our investments, we can indeed lower risk without sacrificing expected return, or we can increase expected return without having to assume more risk.

The preceding example gives us real-world evidence as to the merits of diversification; however, a clarification is in order. Note that the diversification in the preceding example is across different asset types—Treasury bills versus long-term government bonds versus common stocks. Diversifying among different kinds of assets—such as stocks, bonds, and real estate—is called **asset allocation,** as compared to diversification within the different asset classes—such as investing only in PepsiCo, National Semiconductor, and American Airlines. The benefit we receive from diversifying is far greater through effective asset allocation than through merely selecting individual securities (e.g., stocks) to include within an asset category. For instance, Brinson, Singer, and Beebower studied quarterly data from 82 large U.S. pension funds over the period 1977 to 1987.[11] They found that the asset allocation decision accounted for over 91 percent of the differences among the returns of pension funds. Deciding what specific securities to hold accounted for only 4.6 percent of the variation in the different pension returns.[12]

**Asset allocation**
Identifying and selecting the asset classes appropriate for a specific investment portfolio and determining the proportions of these assets within the given portfolio.

**CONCEPT CHECK**

1. Give specific examples of systematic and unsystematic risk. How many different securities must be owned to essentially diversify away unsystematic risk?
2. What method is used to measure a firm's market risk?
3. What is a measure of a market portfolio? Is the risk of this portfolio systematic, unsystematic, or a combination of both?

## MEASURING MARKET RISK

OBJECTIVE 7 

To help clarify the idea of systematic risk, let's examine the relationship between the common stock returns of Harley-Davidson, Inc., and the returns of the S&P 500 Index. The

[11]Gary P. Brinson, Brian D. Singer, and Gilbert L. Beebower, "Determinants of Portfolio Performance," *Financial Analysts Journal* (May–June 1991).

[12]It is also interesting to know that Brinson, Singer, and Beebower found that timing investments explained a meager 1.8 percent of the variation in pension fund returns. That is, none of the investors of these pension funds were any better than their peers at timing market movements when making investments.

**TABLE 6-3**
Monthly Holding-Period Returns, Harley-Davidson and the S&P 500 Index, July 1998–July 2000

| | Harley-Davidson | | S&P 500 Index | |
|---|---|---|---|---|
| **Month and Year** | **Price** | **Return** | **Price** | **Return** |
| ***1998*** | | | | |
| July | \$19.81 | — | \$1,120.67 | — |
| August | 15.38 | −22.36% | 957.28 | −14.58% |
| September | 14.81 | −3.71% | 1,017.01 | 6.24% |
| October | 19.38 | 30.86% | 1,098.67 | 8.03% |
| November | 20.97 | 8.20% | 1,163.63 | 5.91% |
| December | 23.69 | 12.97% | 1,229.23 | 5.64% |
| ***1999*** | | | | |
| January | \$26.00 | 9.75% | \$1,279.64 | 4.10% |
| February | 28.94 | 11.31% | 1,238.33 | −3.23% |
| March | 28.69 | −0.86% | 1,286.37 | 3.88% |
| April | 29.94 | 4.36% | 1,335.18 | 3.79% |
| May | 25.53 | −14.73% | 1,301.84 | −2.50% |
| June | 27.19 | 6.50% | 1,372.71 | 5.44% |
| July | 27.69 | 1.84% | 1,328.72 | −3.20% |
| August | 27.25 | −1.59% | 1,320.41 | −0.63% |
| September | 25.03 | −8.15% | 1,282.71 | −2.86% |
| October | 29.66 | 18.50% | 1,362.93 | 6.25% |
| November | 30.50 | 2.83% | 1,388.91 | 1.91% |
| December | 32.03 | 5.02% | 1,469.25 | 5.78% |
| ***2000*** | | | | |
| January | \$35.09 | 9.55% | \$1,394.46 | −5.09% |
| February | 34.06 | −2.94% | 1,366.42 | −2.01% |
| March | 39.69 | 16.53% | 1,498.58 | 9.67% |
| April | 39.81 | 0.30% | 1,452.43 | −3.08% |
| May | 37.25 | −6.43% | 1,420.60 | −2.19% |
| June | 38.50 | 3.36% | 1,454.60 | 2.39% |
| July | 44.88 | 16.57% | 1,430.83 | −1.63% |
| Average monthly return | | 3.53% | | 1.29% |
| Standard deviation | | 11.26% | | 5.54% |

monthly returns for Harley-Davidson and for the S&P 500 Index for the 24 months ending July 2000 are presented in Table 6-3 and in Figure 6-7. These monthly returns, or holding-period returns, as they are often called, are calculated as follows:[13]

$$k_t = \frac{P_t}{P_{t-1}} - 1 \qquad \textbf{(6-5)}$$

where $k_t$ = the holding-period return in month $t$ for a particular firm such as Harley-Davidson or for a market portfolio such as the S&P 500 Index

$P_t$ = a firm's stock price such as Harley-Davidson (or the S&P 500 Index) at the end of month $t$

[13]For simplicity's sake, we are ignoring the dividend that the investor receives from the stock as part of the total return. In other words, letting $D_t$ equal the dividend received by the investor in month $t$, the holding period return would more accurately be measured as:

$$k_t = \frac{P_t + D_t}{P_{t-1}} - 1$$

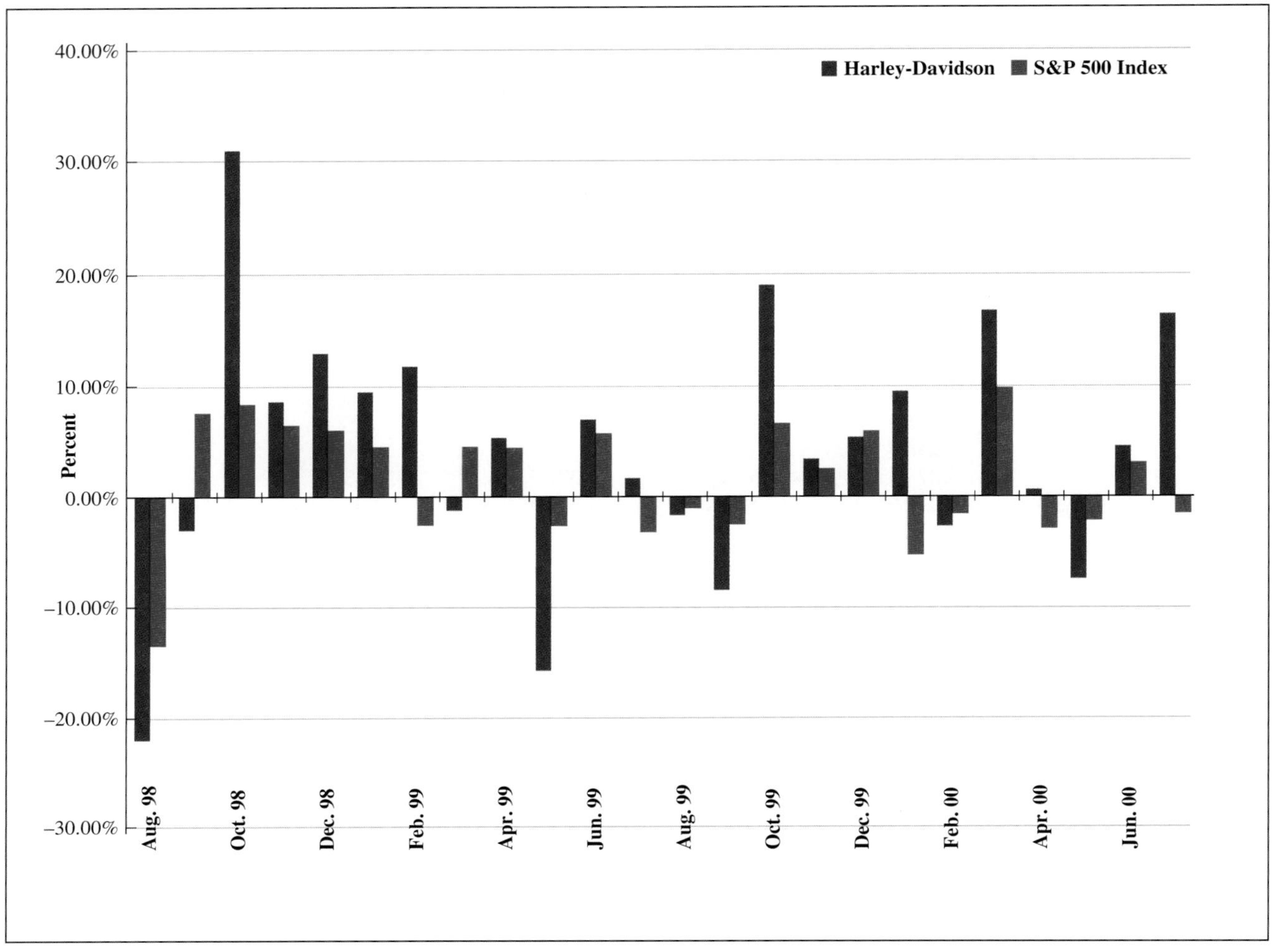


**FIGURE 6-7**
Monthly Holding-Period Returns: Harley-Davidson and the S&P 500 Index, August 1998 through July 2000

For instance, the holding-period return for Harley-Davidson and the S&P 500 Index for December 1999 is computed as follows:

$$\text{Harley-Davidson return} = \frac{\text{stock price at the end of December 1999}}{\text{stock price at the end of November 1999}} - 1$$

$$= \frac{\$32.03}{\$30.50} - 1 = .0502 = 5.02\%$$

$$\text{S\&P 500 index return} = \frac{\text{index value at the end of December 1999}}{\text{index value at the end of November 1999}} - 1$$

$$= \frac{\$1{,}469.25}{\$1{,}388.91} - 1 = .0578 = 5.78\%$$

At the bottom of Table 6-3, we have also computed the average of the returns for the 24 months, both for Harley-Davidson and for the S&P 500, and the standard deviation for these returns. Because we are using historical return data, we assume each observation has an equal probability of occurrence. Thus, the average return, $\bar{k}$, is found by summing the returns and dividing by the number of months; that is,

$$\text{average return} = \frac{\sum_{t=1}^{n} \text{return in month } t}{\text{number of months}} = \frac{\sum_{t=1}^{n} (k_t)}{n} \tag{6-6}$$

and the standard deviation is computed as:

$$\text{standard deviation} = \sqrt{\frac{\sum_{t=1}^{n} (\text{return in month } t - \text{averge return})^2}{\text{number of months} - 1}} \tag{6-7}$$

$$= \sqrt{\frac{\sum_{t=1}^{n} (k_t - \bar{k})^2}{n - 1}}$$

In looking at Table 6-3 and Figure 6-7, we notice the following things about Harley-Davidson's holding-period returns over the 2 years ending in July 2000:

1. Harley-Davidson's stockholders have had higher average monthly returns than the average stock in the S&P 500 Index, 3.53 percent compared to 1.29 percent. That's the good news.
2. The bad news is Harley-Davidson's greater volatility of returns—in other words, greater risk—as evidenced by Harley-Davidson's higher standard deviation. As shown at the bottom of Table 6-3, the standard deviation of the returns is 11.26 percent for Harley-Davidson versus 5.54 percent for the S&P 500 Index. Harley-Davidson's more volatile returns are also evident in Figure 6-3, where we see Harley-Davidson's returns frequently being higher and lower than the corresponding S&P 500 returns.
3. We should also notice the tendency of Harley-Davidson's stock price to increase (decrease) when the value of the S&P 500 Index increases (decreases). In 17 of the 24 months, Harley-Davidson's returns were positive (negative) when the S&P 500 Index returns were positive (negative). That is, there is a positive, although not perfect, relationship between Harley-Davidson's stock returns and the S&P 500 Index returns.

With respect to our third observation, that there is a relationship between the stock returns for Harley-Davidson and the S&P 500 Index, it is helpful to see this relationship by graphing Harley-Davidson's returns against the S&P 500 Index returns. We provide such a graph in Figure 6-8. In the figure, we have plotted Harley-Davidson's returns on the vertical axis and the returns for the S&P 500 Index on the horizontal axis. Each of the 24 dots in the figure represents the returns for Harley-Davidson and the S&P 500 Index for a particular month. For instance, the returns for November 1998 for Harley-Davidson and the S&P 500 Index were 8.20 percent and 5.91 percent, respectively, which are noted in the figure.

In addition to the dots in the graph, we have drawn a line of "best fit," which we call the **characteristic line.** The slope of the characteristic line measures the average relationship between a stock's returns and those of the S&P 500 Index; or stated differently, the slope of the line indicates the average movement in a stock's price to a movement in the S&P 500 Index price. For Harley-Davidson, the slope of the line is 1.4, which simply

**Characteristic line**
The line of "best fit" through a series of returns for a firm's stock relative to the market returns. The slope of the line, frequently called beta, represents the average movement of the firm's stock returns in response to a movement in the market's returns.

**FIGURE 6-8**
Monthly Holding-Period Returns: Harley-Davidson and the S&P 500 Index

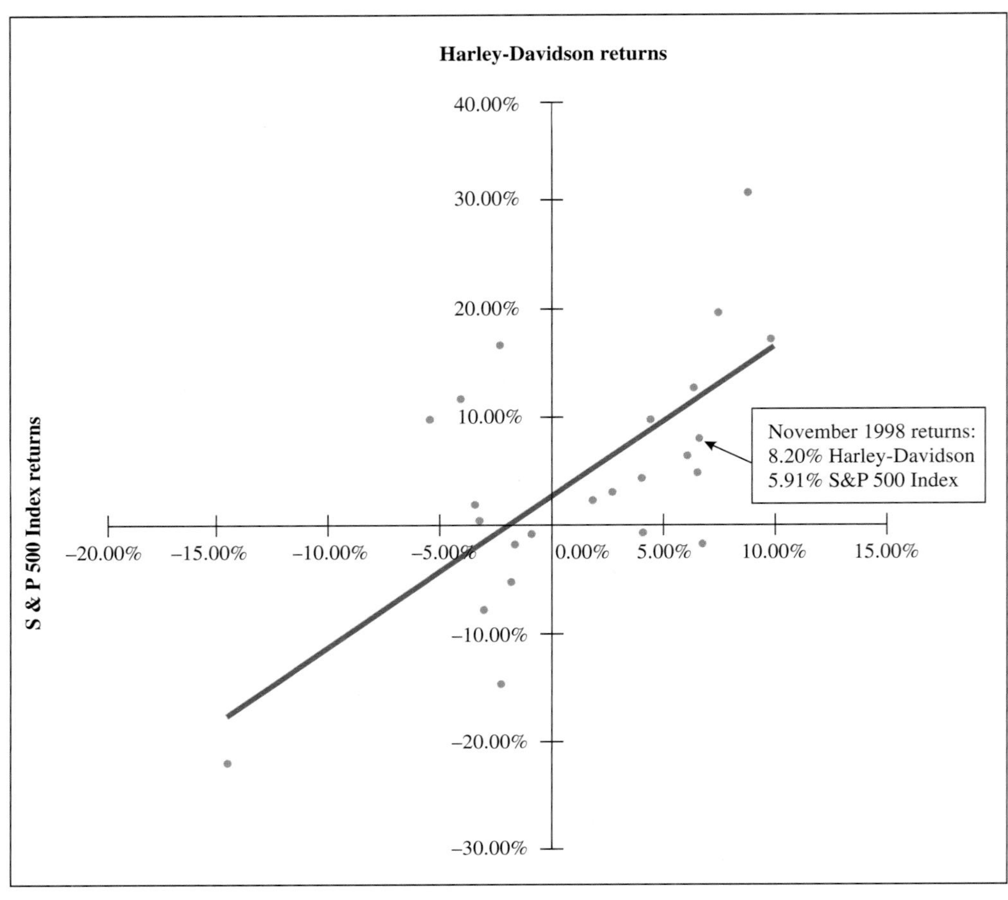


equals the rise of the line relative to the run of the line.[14] A slope of 1.4, as for Harley-Davidson, means that as the market return (S&P 500 Index returns) increases or decreases 1 percentage point, the return for Harley-Davidson on average increases or decreases 1.4 percentage points.

We can also think of the 1.4 slope of the characteristic line as indicating that Harley-Davidson's returns are 1.4 times as volatile on average as those of the overall market (S&P 500 Index). This slope has come to be called **beta** in investor jargon, and measures the average relationship between a stock's returns and the market's returns. It is a term you will see almost anytime you read an article written by a financial analyst about the riskiness of a stock.

**Beta**
A measure of the relationship between an investment's returns and the market's returns. This is a measure of the investment's nondiversifiable risk.

Looking once again at Figure 6-8, we see that the dots (returns) are scattered all about the characteristic line—most of the returns do not fit neatly on the characteristic line. That is, the average relationship may be 1.4, but the variation in Harley-Davidson's returns is only partly explained by the stock's average relationship with the S&P 500 Index. There are other driving forces unique to Harley-Davidson that also affect the firm's stock returns. (Earlier, we called this company-unique risk.) If we were, however, to diversify our holdings and own, say, 20 stocks with betas of 1.4, we could essentially eliminate the variation about the characteristic line. That is, we would remove almost all the volatility in returns,

[14]Linear regression analysis is the statistical technique used to determine the slope of the line of best fit.

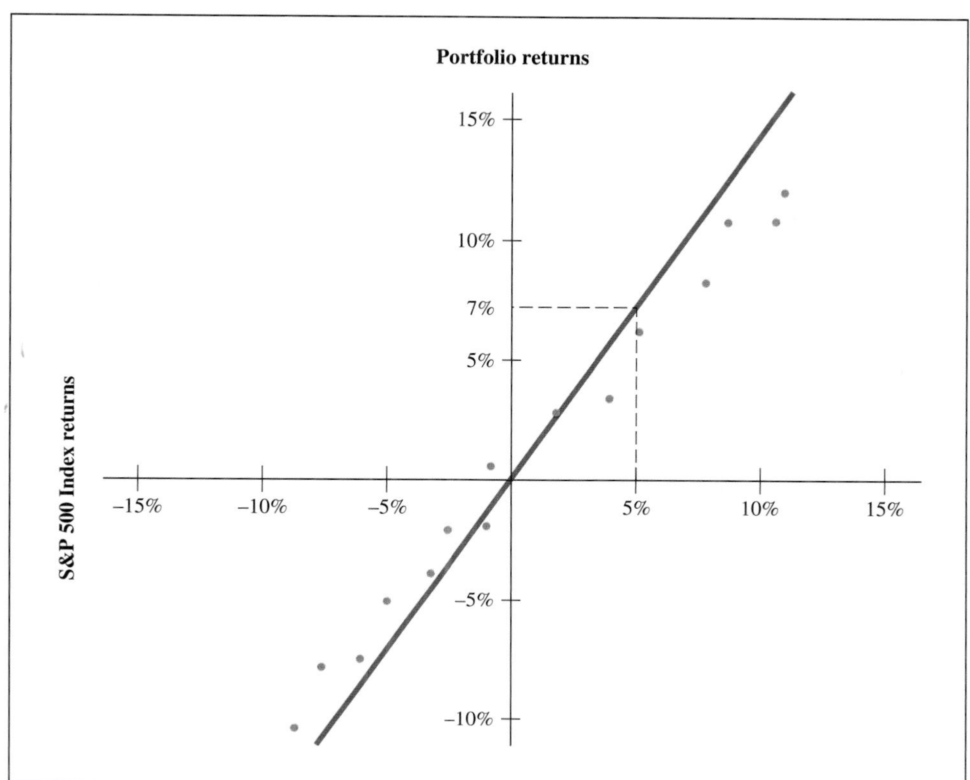


**FIGURE 6-9**
Holding-Period Returns: Hypothetical 20-Stock Portfolio and the S&P 500 Index

except for what is caused by the general market, which is represented by the slope of the line in Figure 6-8. If we plotted the returns of our 20-stock portfolio against the S&P 500 Index, the points in our new graph would fit nicely along a straight line with a slope of 1.4, which means that the beta of the portfolio is also 1.4. The new graph would look something like the one shown in Figure 6-9. In other words, by diversifying our portfolio, we can essentially eliminate the variations about the characteristic line, leaving only the variation in returns for a company that comes from variations in the general market returns.

So beta—the slope of the characteristic line—is a measure of a firm's market risk or systematic risk, which is the risk that remains for a company even after we have diversified our portfolio. It is this risk—and only this risk—that matters for any investors who have broadly diversified portfolios.

We have said that beta is a measure of a stock's systematic risk, but how should we interpret a specific beta? For instance, when is a beta considered low and when is it considered high? In general, a stock with a beta of 0 has no systematic risk; a stock with a beta of 1 has systematic or market risk equal to the "typical" stock in the marketplace; and a stock with a beta exceeding 1 has more market risk than the typical stock. Most stocks, however, have betas between 0.60 and 1.60.

We should also realize that calculating beta is no exact science. The final estimate of a firm's beta is heavily dependent on one's methodology. For instance, it matters whether you use 24 months in your measurement or 60 months, as most professional investment companies do. Take our computation of Harley-Davidson's beta. We said Harley-Davidson's beta was 1.4 but Standard & Poor's and Value Line, two well-known investment services, have estimated Harley-Davidson's beta to be 1.22 and 1.15, respectively.

The difference in results can be observed by comparing Standard & Poor's and Value Line's beta estimates for a number of firms as follows:

| | S&P | Value Line |
|---|---|---|
| Starbucks | 1.49 | 1.10 |
| McDonald's | 0.91 | 0.90 |
| Briggs & Stratton | 0.64 | 0.85 |
| ExxonMobil | 0.48 | 0.80 |
| Fossil | 1.90 | 1.05 |
| Dell | 1.96 | 1.30 |

Thus, although close in many instances, even the professionals may not agree in their measurement of a given firm's beta.

In conclusion, remember that the slope of the characteristic line is called beta and it is a measure of a stock's systematic or market risk. The slope of the characteristic line indicates the average response of a stock's returns to the change in the market as a whole. How an investor and a financial manager use beta will be explained in the section that follows. We will see it again in Chapter 12 when we explain how a firm computes its cost of capital.

To this point, we have talked about measuring an individual stock's beta. We will now consider how to measure the beta for a portfolio of stocks.

**CONCEPT CHECK**

1. Explain the meaning of a stock's holding-period return.
2. After reviewing Figure 6-8, explain the difference between the plotted dots and the firm's characteristic line. What must be done to eliminate the variations?

## MEASURING A PORTFOLIO'S BETA

OBJECTIVE 8 

From Figure 6-8, we see that the stock price of Harley-Davidson moves 1.4 percent on average for a 1 percent change in the market. However, we also see a lot of fluctuation around this characteristic line. If we were to diversify our holdings and own 20 stocks with betas of about 1.4, like that of Harley-Davidson, we could essentially eliminate the variation around the line; that is, we would remove almost all the volatility in returns, except for what is caused by the general market, represented by the slope of the line. If we plotted the returns of our 20-stock portfolio against the S&P 500 Index, the points in our new graph would fit nicely along a straight line with a slope of 1.4. The new graph would look something like the one that was shown in Figure 6-9.

**Portfolio beta**
The relationship between a portfolio's returns and the market's different returns. It is a measure of the portfolio's nondiversifiable risk.

What if we were to diversify our portfolio, as we have just suggested, but instead of acquiring stocks with the same beta as Harley-Davidson (1.4), we buy eight stocks with betas of 1 and 12 stocks with betas of 1.5. What is the beta of our portfolio? As it works out, the **portfolio beta** is merely the average of the individual stock betas. Actually, the portfolio beta is a weighted average of the individual securities' betas, the weights being equal to the proportion of the portfolio invested in each security. Thus the beta ($\beta$) of a portfolio consisting of $n$ stocks is equal to:

$$\beta_{portfolio} = \sum_{j=1}^{n} (\text{percentage invested in stock } j) \times (\beta \text{ of stock } j) \tag{6-8}$$

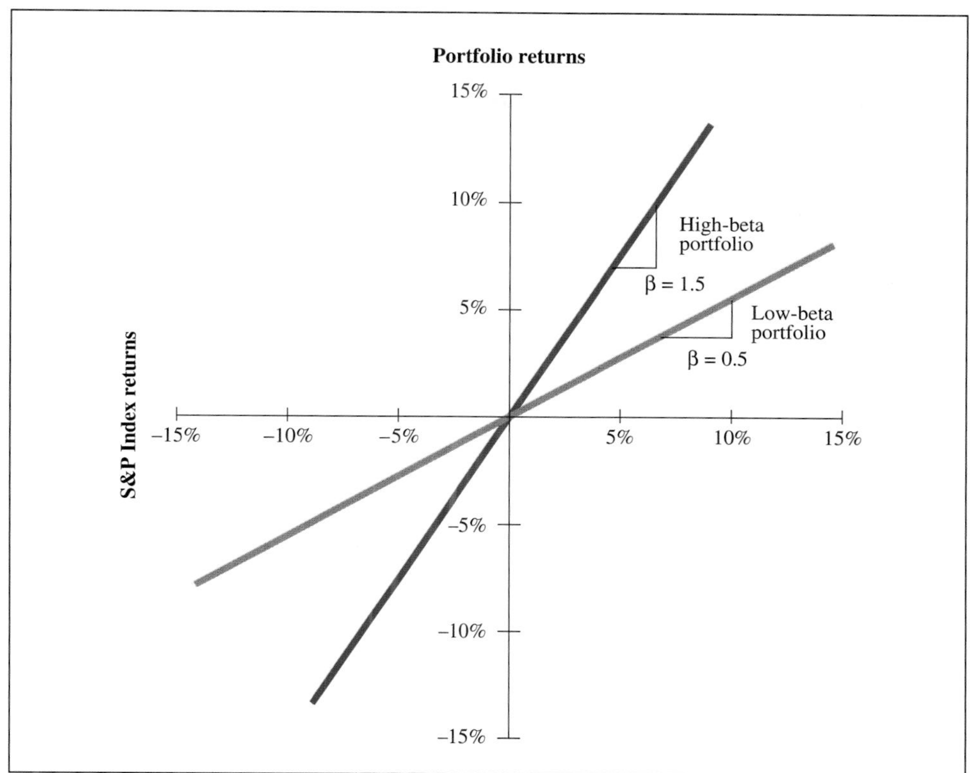


**FIGURE 6-10**
Holding-Period Returns: High- and Low-Beta Portfolios and the S&P 500 Index

So, assuming we bought equal amounts of each stock in our new 20-stock portfolio, the beta would simply be 1.3, calculated as follows:

$$\beta_{\text{portfolio}} = \left(\frac{8}{20} \times 1.0\right) + \left(\frac{12}{20} \times 1.50\right)$$
$$= 1.3$$

Thus, whenever the general market increases or decreases 1 percent, our new portfolio's returns would on average change 1.3 percent, which says that our new portfolio has more systematic or market risk than has the market as a whole.

We can conclude that the beta of a portfolio is determined by the betas of the individual stocks. If we have a portfolio consisting of stocks with low betas, then our portfolio will have a low beta. The reverse is true as well. Figure 6-10 presents these situations graphically.

Although portfolio betas tend to be stable, individual betas are not necessarily stable and not always particularly meaningful. A classic example of how individual stock betas can be misleading comes from Burton G. Malkiel's book *A Random Walk Down Wall Street.*[15] Malkiel describes how Meade Johnson (following its takeover by Bristol-Myers) had a negative beta in the 1960s. Apparently, Meade Johnson introduced a product called "Metrecal," a dietary supplement that Meade Johnson sold to consumers, who drank this instead of eating their normal lunches. In any case, the public loved it, and Meade Johnson's stock shot up in price just as the market sank into a deep slump. As the market rebounded in 1963 and 1964, the Metrecal fad died and Meade Johnson dropped in price, again moving in an opposite

[15]Burton Malkiel, *A Random Walk Down Wall Street,* 4th ed. (New York: W.W. Norton, 1996).

direction from the market. Later in the 1960s, just as the market began to drop, Meade Johnson reintroduced the exact same product, this time called "Nutrament," telling consumers to buy it and drink it in addition to their normal lunch to put on weight. Once again, Meade Johnson's stock price went up as the market went down. The result of all this was that Meade Johnson had a negative beta. Needless to say, it would be unfortunate if capital-budgeting decisions were made using Meade Johnson's beta as the yardstick by which they were measured. The point here is that betas for individual stocks are not always reliable. In fact, typically only about 30 percent of the variation in returns of a stock can be statistically related (correlated) to the market portfolio, and sometimes as low as 5 percent.

In summary, beta is the underlying basis often used for measuring a security's or a portfolio's risk. It also proves useful to a financial manager when attempting to specify what the relationship should be between an investor's required rate of return and the stock's or portfolio's risk—market risk, that is. In other words, a financial manager can use beta to estimate an *appropriate* required rate of return for the firm's stockholders. The use of beta in this regard is the topic of the following section and will be seen again in later chapters.

**CONCEPT CHECK**

1. How is the beta of a portfolio determined?
2. Explain what a portfolio beta of 1.5 means.

## THE INVESTOR'S REQUIRED RATE OF RETURN

OBJECTIVE 9 

In this section, we examine the concept of the investor's required rate of return, especially as it relates to the riskiness of the asset, and then we see how the required rate of return is measured.

**RELATE TO THE BIG PICTURE**

The point should be increasingly clear: In the words of **Principle 9: All Risk Is Not Equal—Some risk can be diversified away, and some cannot.** As we diversify our portfolio, we reduce the effects of company-unique risk, but some risk—called by different names such as nondiversifiable, systematic, or market risk—still remains no matter how much we diversify. It is therefore the market risk that we must be concerned about. Beta is a measure of this risk and is represented by the slope of the characteristic line. The slope of the characteristic line indicates the average response of a stock's returns to the change in the market as a whole.

### The Required Rate of Return Concept

**Investor's required rate of return**
The minimum rate of return necessary to attract an investor to purchase or hold a security. It is also the discount rate that equates the present value of the cash flows with the value of the security.

The **investor's required rate of return** can be defined as the minimum rate of return necessary to attract an investor to purchase or hold a security. This definition considers the investor's opportunity cost of making an investment; that is, if an investment is made, the investor must forgo the return available from the next best investment. This forgone return is the opportunity cost of funds and consequently is the investor's required rate of return. In other words, we invest with the intention of achieving a rate sufficient to warrant making the investment. The investment will be made only if the purchase price is low enough relative to expected future cash flows to provide a rate of return greater than or equal to our required rate of return. To help us better understand the nature of an investor's required rate of return, we can separate the return into its basic components: the *risk-free rate of return* plus a *risk premium.* Expressed as an equation:

$$k = k_{rf} + k_{rp} \quad \textbf{(6-9)}$$

where $k$ = the investor's required rate of return
$k_{rf}$ = the risk-free return
$k_{rp}$ = the risk premium

**Risk-free or riskless rate of return**
The rate of return on risk-free investments. The interest rate on short-term U.S. government securities is commonly used to measure this rate.

**Risk premium**
The additional rate of return we expect to earn above the risk-free rate for assuming risk.

As noted earlier in the chapter, the **risk-free rate of return,** $k_{rf}$, rewards us for deferring consumption, and not for assuming risk; that is, the risk-free return reflects the basic fact that we invest today so that we can consume more later. By itself, the risk-free rate should be used only as the required rate of return, or discount rate, for *riskless* investments. Typically, our measure for the risk-free rate is the rate of return on a U.S. government security.

The **risk premium,** $k_{rp}$, is the additional return we expect to receive for assuming risk.[16] As the level of risk increases, we will demand additional expected returns. Even though we may or may not actually receive this incremental return, we must have reason to expect it; otherwise, why expose ourselves to the chance of losing all or part of our money?

**EXAMPLE**

To demonstrate the required rate of return concept, let us take Polaroid, which has bonds that mature in 2006. Based on the market price of these bonds on September 19, 2000, we can determine that investors were expecting an 11-percent return. The 90-day Treasury bill rate at that time was about 6 percent, which means that Polaroid bondholders were requiring a risk premium of 5 percent. Stated as an equation, we have

$$\begin{aligned} \text{required rate } (k) &= \text{risk-free rate } (k_{rf}) + \text{risk premium } (k_{rp}) \\ &= 6\% \qquad\qquad\qquad + 5\% \\ &= 11\% \end{aligned}$$

## Measuring the Required Rate of Return

**Capital asset pricing model (CAPM)**
An equation stating that the expected rate of return on an investment is a function of (1) the risk-free rate, (2) the investment's systematic risk, and (3) the expected risk premium for the market portfolio of all risky securities.

We have seen that (1) systematic risk is the only relevant risk—the rest can be diversified away, and (2) the required rate of return, $k$, equals the risk-free rate, $k_{rf}$, plus a risk premium, $k_{rp}$. We can now put these elements together to estimate required rates of return. Looking at equation 6-9, the really tough task is how to estimate the risk premium.

The finance profession has had difficulty in developing a practical approach to measure the investor's required rates of return; however, financial managers often use a method called the **capital asset pricing model (CAPM).** The capital asset pricing model is an equation that equates the expected rate of return on a stock to the risk-free rate plus a risk premium for the stock's systematic risk. Although not without its critics, the CAPM provides an intuitive approach for thinking about the return that an investor should require on an investment, given the asset's systematic or market risk.

Equation 6-9, as previously shown, provides the natural starting point for measuring the investor's required rate of return and sets us up to use the CAPM. Rearranging this equation to solve for the risk premium ($k_{rp}$), we have

$$k_{rp} = k - k_{rf} \quad \textbf{(6-10)}$$

[16]The risk premium here can be thought of as a composite of a "default risk premium" (reflected in the difference in the bond's rate of return and the rate on a similar maturity government bond) and "term structure" premium (reflected in the difference in the 90-day Treasury bill rate and the long-term government bond rate).

**FIGURE 6-11**
Security Market Line

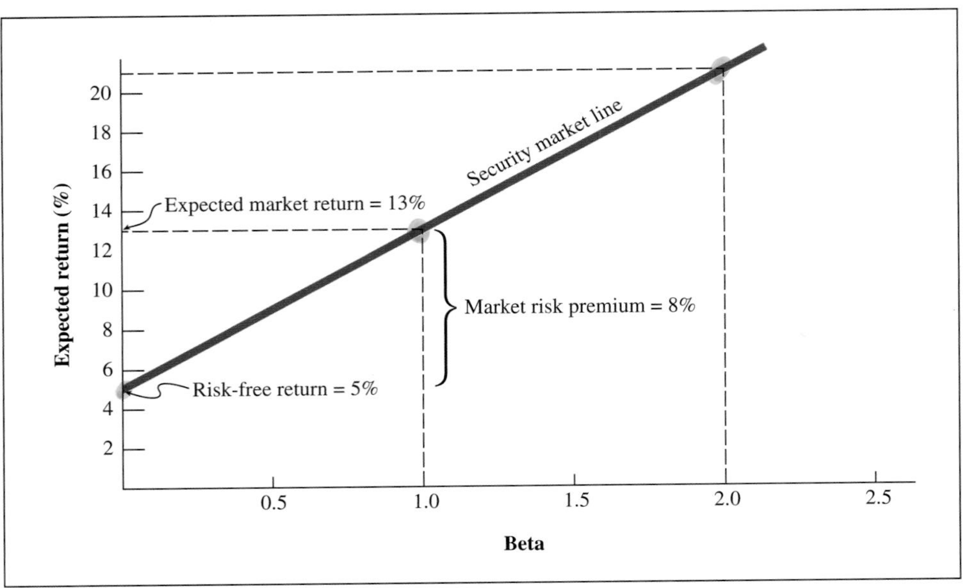


which simply says that the risk premium for a security, $k_{rp}$, equals the security's expected return, $k$, less the risk-free rate existing in the market, $k_{rf}$. For example, if the expected return for a security is 15 percent and the risk-free rate is 5 percent, the risk premium is 10 percent. Also, if the expected return for the market, $k_m$, is 13 percent, and the risk-free rate, $k_{rf}$, is 5 percent, the risk premium, $k_{rp}$, for the general market would be 8 percent. This 8 percent risk premium would apply to any security having systematic (nondiversifiable) risk equivalent to the general market, or a beta of 1.

In the same market, a security with a beta of 2 should provide a risk premium of 16 percent, or twice the 8 percent risk premium existing for the market as a whole. Hence, in general, the appropriate required rate of return for the $j$th security, $k_j$, should be determined by

$$k_j = k_{rf} + \beta_j(k_m - k_{rf}) \tag{6-11}$$

Equation 6-11 is the CAPM. This equation designates the risk-return trade-off existing in the market, where risk is defined in terms of beta. Figure 6-11 graphs the CAPM as the **security market line.**[17] As presented in this figure, securities with betas equal to 0, 1, and 2 should have required rates of return as follows:

**Security market line**
The return line that reflects the attitudes of investors regarding the minimal acceptable return for a given level of systematic risk.

$$\textit{If } \beta_j = 0: k_j = 5\% + 0(13\% - 5\%) = 5\%$$
$$\textit{If } \beta_j = 1: k_j = 5\% + 1(13\% - 5\%) = 13\%$$
$$\textit{If } \beta_j = 2: k_j = 5\% + 2(13\% - 5\%) = 21\%$$

where the risk-free rate, $k_{rf}$, is 5 percent and the expected market return, $k_m$, is 13 percent.[18]

[17]Two key assumptions are made in using the security market line. First, we assume that the marketplace where securities are bought and sold is highly efficient. Market efficiency indicates that the price of an asset responds quickly to new information, thereby suggesting that the price of a security reflects all available information. As a result, the current price of a security is considered to represent the best estimate of its future price. Second, the model assumes that a perfect market exists. A perfect market is one in which information is readily available to all investors at a nominal cost. Also, securities are assumed to be infinitely divisible, with any transaction costs incurred in purchasing or selling a security being negligible. Furthermore, investors are assumed to be single-period wealth maximizers who agree on the meaning and the significance of the available information. Finally, within the perfect market, all investors are *price takers,* which simply means that a single investor's actions cannot affect the price of a security. These assumptions are obviously not descriptive of reality. However, from the perspective of positive economics, the mark of a good theory is the accuracy of its predictions, not the validity of the simplifying assumptions that underlie its development.

[18]For a more in-depth explanation of the CAPM, see B. Rosenberg, "The Capital Asset Pricing Model and the Market Model," *Journal of Portfolio Management* (Winter 1981):5–16.

**EXAMPLE**

To illustrate the use of beta in estimating a fair rate of return for a given stock, consider General Electric. Standard and Poor's estimates GE's beta to be 1.25. As we saw earlier in the chapter the risk premium for large company stocks (return on large company stocks less a risk-free rate) has been about 9.5 percent over the last seven decades. The risk-free rate of return (U.S. Treasury bill) in late 2000 was about 6 percent. Thus, an investor should expect a 17.88 percent rate of return from investing in GE, computed as follows:

$$\begin{aligned} k_{GE} &= k_{rf} + \beta_{GE}(k_m - k_{rf}) \\ &= 6\% + 1.25\,(9.5\%) \\ &= 6\% + 11.88\% = 17.88\% \end{aligned}$$

The previous explanations rely on the capital asset pricing model (CAPM)—and beta—as our standard bearer for estimating a stock's market risk and the rate of return that we should expect for a given beta.

**RELATE TO THE BIG PICTURE**

The conclusion of the matter is that **Principle 1** is alive and well. It tells us, **We won't take on additional risk unless we expect to be compensated with additional return.** That is, there is a risk-return trade-off in the market.

**CONCEPT CHECK**

1. How does opportunity cost affect an investor's required rate of return?
2. What are the two components of the investor's required rate of return?
3. How does beta fit into factoring the risk premium in the CAPM equation?
4. Assuming the market is efficient, what is the relationship between a stock's price and the security market line?

## HOW FINANCIAL MANAGERS USE THIS MATERIAL

We have now completed our study of risk, and most importantly, how rates of return for investments are explicitly tied to risk. The greater the risk, the greater the required rate of return needed to attract investors. This concept, although presented at this point mostly from an investor's perspective, holds equally well for a financial manager considering an investment to develop a new product line. Thus, this chapter will serve as the basis for much that we do in later chapters when it comes to evaluating investment decisions. However, because any investment decision made by a firm should be linked to the goal of enhancing shareholder value, we will next study the concepts and procedures for valuing bonds and stocks.

## FINANCE MATTERS

### Does Beta Always Work?

At the start of 1998, Apple Computer was in deep trouble. As a result, its stock price fluctuated wildly—far more than that of other computer firms, such as IBM. However, based on the capital asset pricing model (CAPM) and its measure of beta, the required return of Apple's investors would have been only 8 percent at the time, compared to 12 percent for IBM's stockholders. Equally interesting, when Apple's situation improved in the spring of that year, and its share price became less volatile, Apple's investors—at least according to the CAPM—would have required a rate of return of 11 percent—a 3-percentage-point increase from the earlier required rate of return. That is not what intuition would suggest should have happened.

So what should we think? Just when Apple's future was most in doubt and its shares most volatile, its beta was only 0.47, suggesting that Apple's stock was only half as volatile as the overall stock market. In reality, beta is meaningless here. The truth is that Apple was in such a dire condition that its stock price simply decoupled itself from the stock market. So as IBM and its peer-stock prices moved up and down with the rest of the market, Apple shares reacted solely to news about the company, without regard for the market's movements. Beta thus created the false impression that Apple shares were more stable than the stock market.

The lesson here is that beta may at times be misleading when used with individual companies. Instead, its use is far more reliable when applied to a portfolio of companies. A firm that was interested in acquiring Apple Computer in 1998, for instance, would, most likely, not have been planning to buy other computer companies in the same circumstances. If an interested acquirer used beta in computing the required rate of return for the acquisition, it would without a doubt have overvalued Apple.

So does that mean that CAPM is worthless? No, not as long as company-unique risk is not the main driving force in a company's stock price movements, or if investors are able to diversify away specific company risk. Then they would bid up the price of such shares until they reflect only market risk. For example, a mutual fund that specializes in "distress stocks" might purchase a number of Apple Computer-type companies, each with its own problems, but for different reasons. For such investors, beta works pretty well. Thus, the moral of the story is: Don't use beta without some common sense and good judgment.

## SUMMARY

We have referred to the discount rate as the interest rate or the opportunity cost of funds. At that point, we considered a number of important factors that influence interest rates, including the price of time, expected or anticipated inflation, the risk premium related to maturity (liquidity) and variability of future returns.

In this chapter, we looked at the relationship between risk and rates of returns.

OBJECTIVE 1 

Ibbotson Associates has provided us with annual rates of return earned on different types of security investments as far back as 1926. They summarize, among other things, the annual returns for five portfolios of securities made up of (1) common stocks of small firms, (2) common stocks of large companies, (3) long-term corporate bonds, (4) long-term U.S. government bonds, and (5) U.S. Treasury bills. A comparison of the annual rates of return for these respective portfolios for the years 1926 to 1999 shows there to be a positive relationship between risk and return, with Treasury bills being least risky and common stocks of small firms being most risky.

OBJECTIVE 2 

The rate of inflation has an effect of the nominal rate of return that an investor receives on an investment. That is, part of the return on an investment is to keep an investor from losing purchasing power from holding an investment.

OBJECTIVE 3 

The term structure of interest rates (also called the yield to maturity) compares the rates of return of similar securities to their respective times to maturity. For instance, if long-term government bonds offer a higher rate of return than do U.S. Treasury bills, then the yield curve is upward sloping. But if the Treasury bill is paying a higher rate of interest than its long-term counterparts are, then the yield curve is downward sloping.

In a world of uncertainty, we cannot make forecasts with certainty. Thus, we must speak in terms of *expected* events. The expected return on an investment may therefore be stated as the arithmetic mean or average of all possible outcomes where those outcomes are weighted by the probability that each will occur. OBJECTIVE 4

Risk, for our purposes, is the prospect of an unfavorable outcome and may be measured by the standard deviation. OBJECTIVE 5

We have made an important distinction between nondiversifiable risk and diversifiable risk. We concluded that the only relevant risk given the opportunity to diversify our portfolio is a security's nondiversifiable risk, which we called by two other names: systematic risk and market risk. OBJECTIVE 6

A security's market risk is represented by beta, the slope of the characteristic line. Beta measures the average responsiveness of a security's returns to the movement of the general market, such as the S&P 500. If beta is 1, the security's returns move 1-to-1 with the market returns; if beta is 1.5, the security's returns move up and down 1.5 percent for every 1 percent change in the market's returns. OBJECTIVE 7

A portfolio's beta is simply a weighted average of the individual stock's betas, where the weights are the percentage of funds invested in each stock. The portfolio beta measures the average responsiveness of the portfolio's returns to the movement of the general market, such as the S&P 500. OBJECTIVE 8

The capital asset pricing model (CAPM), even with its weaknesses, provides an intuitive framework for understanding the risk-return relationship. The CAPM suggests that investors determine an appropriate required rate of return, depending upon the amount of systematic risk inherent in a security. This minimum acceptable rate of return is equal to the risk-free rate plus a return premium for assuming risk. OBJECTIVE 9

## KEY TERMS

**Asset allocation, 182**

**Beta, 186**

**Capital asset pricing model (CAPM), 191**

**Characteristic line, 185**

**Expected rate of return, 175**

**Firm-specific risk or company-unique risk (diversifiable risk or unsystematic risk), 180**

**Investor's required rate of return, 190**

**Market-related risk (nondiversifiable risk or systematic risk), 180**

**Opportunity cost of funds, 169**

**Portfolio beta, 188**

**Real rate of interest, 171**

**Risk, 177**

**Risk-free or riskless rate of return, 191**

**Risk premium, 191**

**Security market line, 192**

**Standard deviation, 177**

**Term structure of interest rates (yield to maturity), 172**

myPHLIP

Go To:
http://www.prenhall.com/keown
for downloads and current events associated with this chapter

## STUDY QUESTIONS

**6-1.** Over the past 7 decades, we have had the opportunity to observe the rates of return and variability of these returns for different types of securities. Summarize these observations.

**6-2.** Explain the effect of inflation on rates of return.

**6-3.** Explain the concept "term structure of interest rates."

**6-4.** **a.** What is meant by the investor's required rate of return?
**b.** How do we measure the riskiness of an asset?
**c.** How should the proposed measurement of risk be interpreted?

**6-5.** What is (a) unsystematic risk (company-unique or diversifiable risk) and (b) systematic risk (market or nondiversifiable risk)?

**6-6.** What is the meaning of beta? How is it used to calculate *k*, the investor's required rate of return?

**6-7.** Define the security market line. What does it represent?

**6-8.** How do we measure the beta for a portfolio?

**6-9.** If we were to graph the returns of a stock against the returns of the S&P 500 Index, and the points did not follow a very ordered pattern, what could we say about that stock? If the stock's returns tracked the S&P 500 returns very closely, then what could we say?

## SELF-TEST PROBLEMS

**ST-1.** (*Expected return and risk*) Universal Corporation is planning to invest in a security that has several possible rates of return. Given the following probability distribution of the returns, what is the expected rate of return on the investment? Also, compute the standard deviation of the returns. What do the resulting numbers represent?

| Probability | Return |
|---|---|
| .10 | −10% |
| .20 | 5% |
| .30 | 10% |
| .40 | 25% |

**ST-2.** (*Capital asset pricing model*) Using the CAPM, estimate the appropriate required rate of return for the following three stocks, given that the risk-free rate is 5 percent, and the expected return for the market is 17 percent.

| Stock | Beta |
|---|---|
| A | .75 |
| B | .90 |
| C | 1.40 |

**ST-3.** (*Expected return and risk*) Given the following holding-period returns, calculate the average returns and the standard deviations for the Kaifu Corporation and for the market.

| Month | Kaifu Corp. | Market |
|---|---|---|
| 1 | 4% | 2% |
| 2 | 6 | 3 |
| 3 | 0 | 1 |
| 4 | 2 | −1 |

**ST-4.** (*Holding-period returns*) From the following price data, compute the holding-period returns.

| Time | Stock Price |
|---|---|
| 1 | $10 |
| 2 | 13 |
| 3 | 11 |
| 4 | 15 |

**ST-5. a.** (*Security market line*) Determine the expected return and beta for the following portfolio:

| Stock | Percentage of Portfolio | Beta | Expected Return |
|---|---|---|---|
| 1 | 40% | 1.00 | 12% |
| 2 | 25 | 0.75 | 11 |
| 3 | 35 | 1.30 | 15 |

**b.** Given the preceding information, draw the security market line and show where the securities fit on the graph. Assume that the risk-free rate is 8 percent and that the expected return on the market portfolio is 12 percent. How would you interpret these findings?

## STUDY PROBLEMS (SET A)

**6-1A.** (*Inflation and interest rates*) What would you expect the nominal rate of interest to be if the real rate is 4.5 percent and the expected inflation rate is 7.3 percent?

**6-2A.** (*Inflation and interest rates*) Assume the expected inflation rate is 3.8 percent. If the current real rate of interest is 6.4 percent, what should the nominal rate of interest be?

**6-3A.** (*Expected rate of return and risk*) Pritchard Press, Inc., is evaluating a security. One-year Treasury bills are currently paying 9.1 percent. Calculate the following investment's expected return and its standard deviation. Should Pritchard invest in this security?

| Probability | Return |
|---|---|
| .15 | 5% |
| .30 | 7% |
| .40 | 10% |
| .15 | 15% |

**6-4A.** (*Expected rate of return and risk*) Syntex, Inc., is considering an investment in one of two common stocks. Given the information that follows, which investment is better, based on risk (as measured by the standard deviation) and return?

| Common Stock A | | Common Stock B | |
|---|---|---|---|
| Probability | Return | Probability | Return |
| .30 | 11% | .20 | −5% |
| .40 | 15% | .30 | 6% |
| .30 | 19% | .30 | 14% |
| | | .20 | 22% |

**6-5A.** (*Expected rate of return and risk*) Friedman Manufacturing, Inc., has prepared the following information regarding two investments under consideration. Which investment should be accepted?

| Common Stock A | | Common Stock B | |
|---|---|---|---|
| Probability | Return | Probability | Return |
| .20 | −2% | .10 | 4% |
| .50 | 18% | .30 | 6% |
| .30 | 27% | .40 | 10% |
| | | .20 | 15% |

**6-6A.** (*Required rate of return using CAPM*)

**a.** Compute a fair rate of return for Intel common stock, which has a 1.2 beta. The risk-free rate is 6 percent and the market portfolio (New York Stock Exchange stocks) has an expected return of 16 percent.

**b.** Why is the rate you computed a fair rate?

**6-7A.** (*Estimating beta*) From the following graph relating the holding-period returns for Aram, Inc., to the S&P 500 Index, estimate the firm's beta.

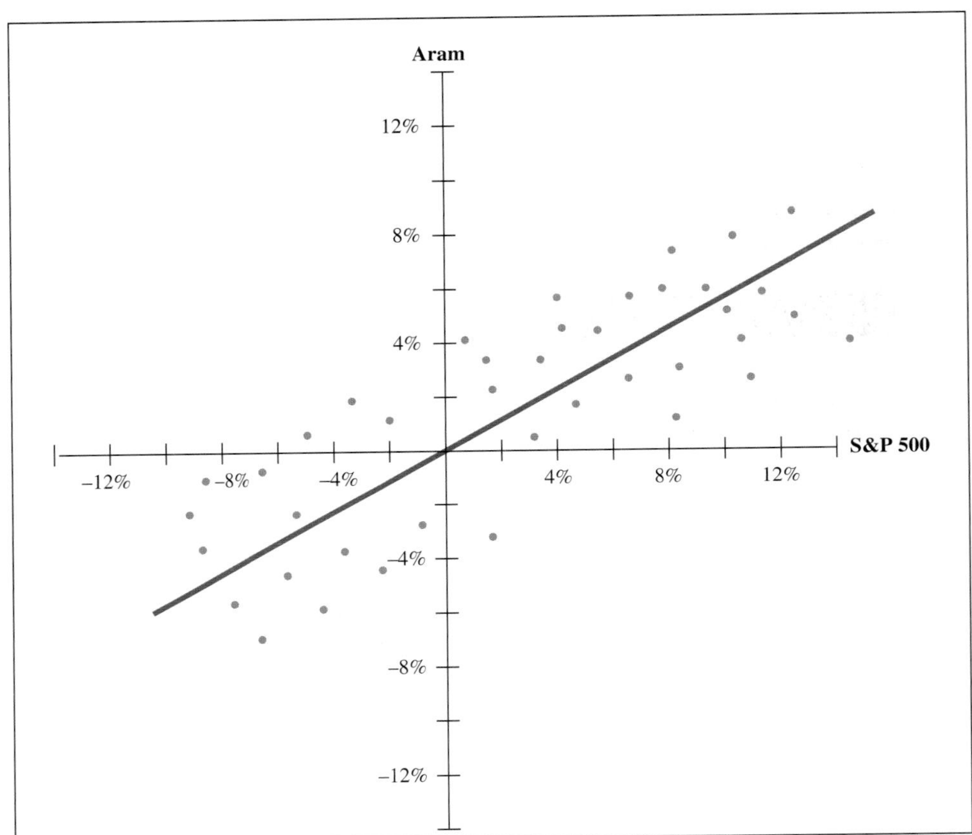


**6-8A.** (*Capital asset pricing model*) Johnson Manufacturing, Inc., is considering several investments. The rate on Treasury bills is currently 6.75 percent, and the expected return for the market is 12 percent. What should be the required rates of return for each investment (using the CAPM)?

| Security | Beta |
|---|---|
| A | 1.50 |
| B | .82 |
| C | .60 |
| D | 1.15 |

**6-9A.** (*Capital asset pricing model*) CSB, Inc. has a beta of .765. If the expected market return is 11.5 percent and the risk-free rate is 7.5 percent, what is the appropriate required rate of return of CSB (using the CAPM)?

**6-10A.** (*Capital asset pricing model*) The expected return for the general market is 12.8 percent, and the risk premium in the market is 4.3 percent. Tasaco, LBM, and Exxos have betas of

.864, .693, and .575, respectively. What are the appropriate required rates of return for the three securities?

**6-11A.** (*Computing holding-period returns*) From the following price data, compute the holding-period returns for Asman and Salinas.

| Time | Asman | Salinas |
|---|---|---|
| 1 | $10 | $30 |
| 2 | 12 | 28 |
| 3 | 11 | 32 |
| 4 | 13 | 35 |

How would you interpret the meaning of a holding-period return?

**6-12A.** (*Measuring risk and rates of return*)

**a.** Given the following holding-period returns, compute the average returns and the standard deviations for the Zemin Corporation and for the market.

| Month | Zemin Corp. | Market |
|---|---|---|
| 1 | 6% | 4% |
| 2 | 3 | 2 |
| 3 | 1 | −1 |
| 4 | −3 | −2 |
| 5 | 5 | 2 |
| 6 | 0 | 2 |

**b.** If Zemin's beta is 1.54 and the risk-free rate is 8 percent, what would be an appropriate required return for an investor owning Zemin? (*Note:* Because the preceding returns are based on monthly data, you will need to annualize the returns to make them comparable with the risk-free rate. For simplicity, you can convert from monthly to yearly returns by multiplying the average monthly returns by 12.)

**c.** How does Zemin's historical average return compare with the return you believe to be a fair return, given the firm's systematic risk?

**6-13A.** (*Portfolio beta and security market line*) You own a portfolio consisting of the following stocks:

| Stock | Percentage of Portfolio | Beta | Expected Return |
|---|---|---|---|
| 1 | 20% | 1.00 | 16% |
| 2 | 30% | 0.85 | 14% |
| 3 | 15% | 1.20 | 20% |
| 4 | 25% | 0.60 | 12% |
| 5 | 10% | 1.60 | 24% |

The risk-free rate is 7 percent. Also, the expected return on the market portfolio is 15.5 percent.

**a.** Calculate the expected return of your portfolio. (*Hint:* The expected return of a portfolio equals the weighted average of the individual stock's expected return, where the weights are the percentage invested in each stock.)

**b.** Calculate the portfolio beta.

**c.** Given the information preceding, plot the security market line on paper. Plot the stocks from your portfolio on your graph.

**d.** From your plot in part (c), which stocks *appear* to be your winners and which ones appear to be losers?

**e.** Why should you consider your conclusion in part (d) to be less than certain?

**6-14A.** (*Expected return, standard deviation, and capital asset pricing model*) Following you will find the end-of-month prices, both for the S&P 500 Index and for Intel common stock.

**a.** Using the following data, calculate the holding-period returns for each month from August 1999 to July 2000.

| | Month and year | Prices | |
|---|---|---|---|
| | | S&P 500 | Intel Corp. |
| 1999 | July | $1,328.72 | $34.50 |
| | August | $1,320.41 | $41.09 |
| | September | $1,282.71 | $37.16 |
| | October | $1,362.93 | $38.72 |
| | November | $1,388.91 | $38.34 |
| | December | $1,469.25 | $41.16 |
| 2000 | January | $1,394.46 | $49.47 |
| | February | $1,366.42 | $56.50 |
| | March | $1,498.58 | $65.97 |
| | April | $1,452.43 | $63.41 |
| | May | $1,420.60 | $62.34 |
| | June | $1,454.60 | $66.84 |
| | July | $1,430.83 | $66.75 |

**b.** Calculate the average monthly return and the standard deviation of these returns both for the S&P 500 and Intel.

**c.** Develop a graph that shows the relationship between the Intel stock returns and the S&P 500 Index. (Show the Intel returns on the vertical axis and the S&P 500 Index returns on the horizontal, as done in Figure 6-8.)

**d.** From your graph, describe the nature of the relationship between Intel stock returns and the returns for the S&P 500 Index.

## INTEGRATIVE PROBLEM

*Note:* Although not absolutely necessary, you are advised to use a computer spreadsheet to work the following problems.

1. Use the following price data for the S&P 500 Index, Dell Computer, and Starbucks to calculate the holding-period returns for the 24 months ending May 2000.
2. Calculate the average monthly holding-period return and the standard deviation of these returns for the S&P 500 Index, Dell Computer, and Starbucks.
3. Plot (a) the holding-period returns for Dell Computer against the S&P 500 Index, and (b) plot the Starbucks holding-period returns against the S&P 500 Index. (Use Figure 6-8 as the format for the graph.)
4. From your graphs in question 3, describe the nature of the relationship between the Dell Computer stock returns and the returns for the S&P 500 Index. Make the same comparison for Starbucks.
5. Assume that you have decided to invest one-half of your money in Dell Computer and the remaining amount in Starbucks. Calculate the monthly holding-period returns for your two-stock portfolio. (*Hint:* The monthly return for the portfolio is the average of the two stocks' monthly returns.)
6. Plot the returns of your two-stock portfolio against the S&P 500 Index as you did for the individual stocks in question 3. How does this graph compare to the graphs for the individual stocks? Explain the difference.
7. Following are the returns on an *annualized* basis that were realized from holding long-term government bonds for the 24 months ending May 2000. Calculate the average *monthly* holding-

period return and the standard deviation of these returns. (*Hint:* You will need to convert the annual returns to monthly returns by dividing each return by 12 months.)

8. Now assume that you have decided to invest equal amounts of money in Dell Computer, Starbucks, and the long-term government securities. Calculate the monthly returns for your three-asset portfolio. What are the average return and standard deviation?
9. Make a comparison of the average returns and the standard deviations for the individual assets and the two portfolios that we designed. What conclusions can be reached by your comparisons?
10. The betas for Dell Computer and Starbucks are 1.96 and 1.49, respectively. Compare the meaning of these betas relative to the preceding standard deviations calculated.
11. The Treasury bill rate at the end of May 2000 was approximately 6 percent. Given the betas for Dell Computer and Starbucks and using the preceding data for the S&P 500 Index as a measure for the market portfolio expected return, estimate an appropriate required rate of return given the level of systematic risk for each stock.

| | Month | S&P 500 | Dell | Starbucks |
|---|---|---|---|---|
| 1998 | May | $1,090.82 | $20.60 | $24.00 |
| | June | 1,133.84 | 23.20 | 26.72 |
| | July | 1,120.67 | 27.15 | 20.94 |
| | August | 957.28 | 25.00 | 15.78 |
| | September | 1,017.01 | 32.88 | 18.09 |
| | October | 1,098.67 | 32.75 | 21.69 |
| | November | 1,163.63 | 30.41 | 23.06 |
| | December | 1,229.23 | 36.59 | 28.06 |
| 1999 | January | 1,279.64 | 50.00 | 26.03 |
| | February | 1,238.33 | 40.06 | 26.44 |
| | March | 1,286.37 | 40.88 | 28.06 |
| | April | 1,335.18 | 41.19 | 36.94 |
| | May | 1,301.84 | 34.44 | 36.88 |
| | June | 1,372.71 | 37.00 | 37.56 |
| | July | 1,328.72 | 40.88 | 23.25 |
| | August | 1,320.41 | 48.81 | 22.88 |
| | September | 1,282.71 | 41.81 | 24.78 |
| | October | 1,362.93 | 40.13 | 27.19 |
| | November | 1,388.91 | 43.00 | 26.56 |
| | December | 1,469.25 | 51.00 | 24.25 |
| 2000 | January | 1,394.46 | 38.44 | 32.00 |
| | February | 1,366.42 | 40.81 | 35.13 |
| | March | 1,498.58 | 53.94 | 44.81 |
| | April | 1,452.43 | 50.13 | 30.23 |
| | May | 1,420.60 | 43.13 | 34.00 |

| | Month | Annualized Rate of Return | | Month | Annualized Rate of Return |
|---|---|---|---|---|---|
| 1998 | June | 5.70% | 1999 | June | 6.04% |
| | July | 5.68 | | July | 5.98 |
| | August | 5.54 | | August | 6.07 |
| | September | 5.20 | | September | 6.07 |
| | October | 5.01 | | October | 6.26 |
| | November | 5.25 | | November | 6.15 |
| | December | 5.06 | | December | 6.35 |
| 1999 | January | 5.16 | 2000 | January | 6.63 |
| | February | 5.37 | | February | 6.23 |
| | March | 5.58 | | March | 6.05 |
| | April | 5.55 | | April | 5.85 |
| | May | 5.81 | | May | 6.15 |

## STUDY PROBLEMS (SET B)

**6-1B.** (*Inflation and interest rates*) Assume the expected inflation rate is 5 percent. If the current real rate of interest is 7 percent, what should the nominal rate of interest be?

**6-2B.** (*Inflation and interest rates*) What would you expect the nominal rate of interest to be if the real rate is 5 percent and the expected inflation rate is 3 percent?

**6-3B.** (*Expected rate of return and risk*) B. J. Gautney Enterprises is evaluating a security. One-year Treasury bills are currently paying 8.9 percent. Calculate the following investment's expected return and its standard deviation. Should Gautney invest in this security?

| Probability | Return |
|---|---|
| .15 | 6% |
| .30 | 5% |
| .40 | 11% |
| .15 | 14% |

**6-4B.** (*Expected rate of return and risk*) Kelly B. Stites, Inc., is considering an investment in one of two common stocks. Given the information that follows, which investment is better, based on risk (as measured by the standard deviation) and return?

| Security A | | Security B | |
|---|---|---|---|
| Probability | Return | Probability | Return |
| .20 | −2% | .10 | 5% |
| .50 | 19% | .30 | 7% |
| .30 | 25% | .40 | 12% |
| | | .20 | 14% |

**6-5B.** (*Expected rate of return and risk*) Clevenger Manufacturing, Inc., has prepared the following information regarding two investments under consideration. Which investment should be accepted?

| Common Stock A | | Common Stock B | |
|---|---|---|---|
| Probability | Return | Probability | Return |
| .20 | 10% | .15 | 6% |
| .60 | 13% | .30 | 8% |
| .20 | 20% | .40 | 15% |
| | | .15 | 19% |

**6-6B.** (*Required rate of return using CAPM*)

**a.** Compute a *fair* rate of return for Compaq common stock, which has a 1.5 beta. The risk-free rate is 8 percent and the market portfolio (New York Stock Exchange stocks) has an expected return of 16 percent.

**b.** Why is the rate you computed a fair rate?

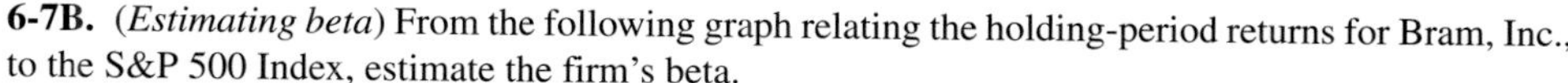

**6-7B.** (*Estimating beta*) From the following graph relating the holding-period returns for Bram, Inc., to the S&P 500 Index, estimate the firm's beta.

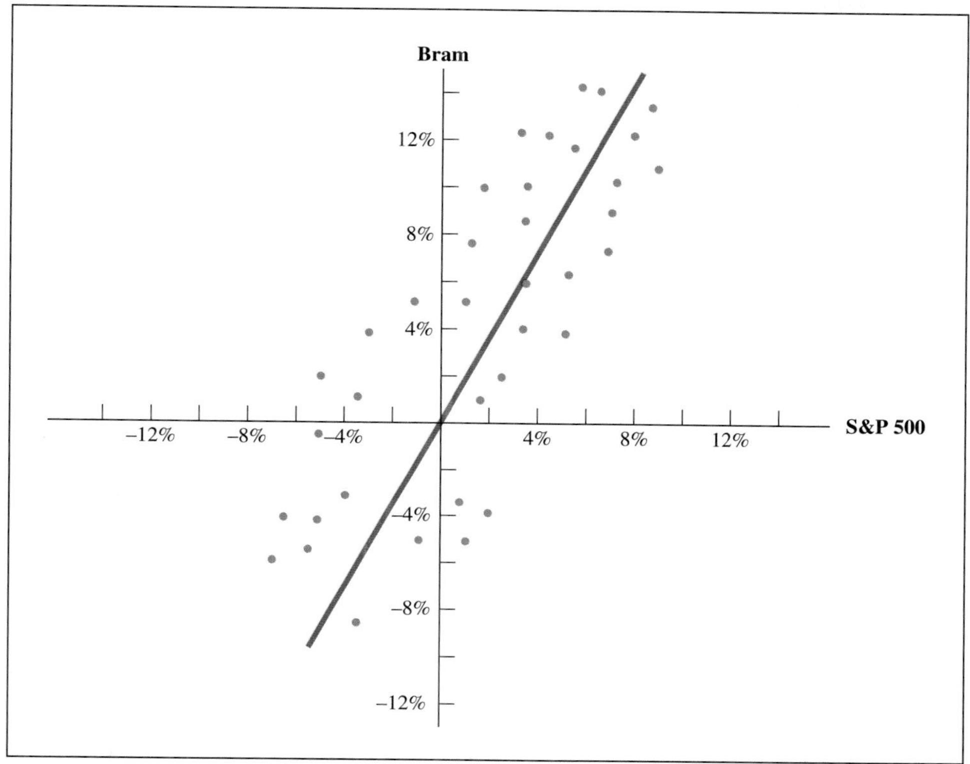


**6-8B.** (*Capital asset pricing model*) Bobbi Manufacturing, Inc., is considering several investments. The rate on Treasury bills is currently 6.75 percent, and the expected return for the market is 12 percent. What should be the required rates of return for each investment (using the CAPM)?

| Security | Beta |
|---|---|
| A | 1.40 |
| B | .75 |
| C | .80 |
| D | 1.20 |

**6-9B.** (*Capital asset pricing model*) Breckenridge, Inc., has a beta of .85. If the expected market return is 10.5 percent and the risk-free rate is 7.5 percent, what is the appropriate required return of Breckenridge (using the CAPM)?

**6-10B.** (*Capital asset pricing model*) The expected return for the general market is 12.8 percent, and the risk premium in the market is 4.3 percent. Dupree, Yofota, and MacGrill have betas of .82, .57, and .68, respectively. What are the appropriate required rates of return for the three securities?

**6-11B.** (*Computing holding-period returns*) From the following price data, compute the holding-period returns for O'Toole and Baltimore.

| Time | O'Toole | Baltimore |
|---|---|---|
| 1 | $22 | $45 |
| 2 | 24 | 50 |
| 3 | 20 | 48 |
| 4 | 25 | 52 |

How would you interpret the meaning of a holding-period return?

**6-12B.** (*Measuring risk and rates of return*)

**a.** Given the following holding-period returns, compute the average returns and the standard deviations for the Sugita Corporation and for the market.

| Month | Sugita Corp. | Market |
|---|---|---|
| 1 | 1.8% | 1.5% |
| 2 | −0.5 | 1.0 |
| 3 | 2.0 | 0.0 |
| 4 | −2.0 | −2.0 |
| 5 | 5.0 | 4.0 |
| 6 | 5.0 | 3.0 |

**b.** If Sugita's beta is 1.18 and the risk-free rate is 8 percent, what would be an appropriate required return for an investor owning Sugita? (*Note:* Because the preceding returns are based on monthly data, you will need to annualize the returns to make them comparable with the risk-free rate. For simplicity, you can convert from monthly to yearly returns by multiplying the average monthly returns by 12.)

**c.** How does Sugita's historical average return compare with the return you believe to be a fair return, given the firm's systematic risk?

**6-13B.** (*Portfolio beta and security market line*) You own a portfolio consisting of the following stocks:

| Stock | Percentage of Portfolio | Beta | Expected Return |
|---|---|---|---|
| 1 | 10% | 1.00 | 12% |
| 2 | 25 | 0.75 | 11 |
| 3 | 15 | 1.30 | 15 |
| 4 | 30 | 0.60 | 9 |
| 5 | 20 | 1.20 | 14 |

The risk-free rate is 8 percent. Also, the expected return on the market portfolio is 11.6 percent.

**a.** Calculate the expected return of your portfolio. (*Hint:* The expected return of a portfolio equals the weighted average of the individual stock's expected return, where the weights are the percentage invested in each stock.)

**b.** Calculate the portfolio beta.

**c.** Given the preceding information, plot the security market line on paper. Plot the stocks from your portfolio on your graph.

**d.** From your plot in part (c), which stocks *appear* to be your winners and which ones *appear* to be losers?

**e.** Why should you consider your conclusion in part (d) to be less than certain?

**6-14B.** (*Expected return, standard deviation, and capital asset pricing model*) Following you will find the end-of-month prices, both for the S&P 500 Index and for Ben & Jerry's common stock.

**a.** Using the following data, calculate the holding-period returns for each month from August 1999 to July 2000.

| | Month | Prices S&P 500 | Prices Ben & Jerry's |
|---|---|---|---|
| 1999 | July | \$1,328.72 | \$21.00 |
| | August | \$1,320.41 | \$19.50 |
| | September | \$1,282.71 | \$17.19 |
| | October | \$1,362.93 | \$16.88 |
| | November | \$1,388.91 | \$18.06 |
| | December | \$1,469.25 | \$24.88 |
| 2000 | January | \$1,394.46 | \$22.75 |
| | February | \$1,366.42 | \$26.25 |
| | March | \$1,498.58 | \$33.56 |
| | April | \$1,452.43 | \$43.31 |
| | May | \$1,420.60 | \$43.50 |
| | June | \$1,454.60 | \$43.50 |
| | July | \$1,430.83 | \$43.63 |

**b.** Calculate the average monthly return and the standard deviation of these returns both for the S&P 500 and Ben & Jerry's.

**c.** Develop a graph that shows the relationship between the Ben & Jerry's stock returns and the S&P 500 Index. (Show the Ben & Jerry's returns on the vertical axis and the S&P 500 Index returns on the horizontal as done in Figure 6-8.)

**d.** From your graph, describe the nature of the relationship between Ben & Jerry's stock returns and the returns for the S&P 500 Index.

## SELF-TEST SOLUTIONS

**ST-1.**

| (A) Probability $P(k_i)$ | (B) Return $(k_i)$ | Expected Return $(\bar{k})$ (A) × (B) | Weighted Deviation $(k_i - \bar{k})^2 P(k_i)$ |
|---|---|---|---|
| .10 | −10% | −1% | 52.9% |
| .20 | 5% | 1% | 12.8% |
| .30 | 10% | 3% | 2.7% |
| .40 | 25% | 10% | 57.6% |
| | | $\bar{k}$ = 13% | $\sigma^2$ = 126.0% |
| | | | $\sigma$ = 11.22% |

From our studies in statistics, we know that if the distribution of returns were normal, then Universal could expect a return of 13 percent with a 67 percent possibility that this return would vary up or down by 11.22 percent between 1.78 percent (13% − 11.22%) and 24.22 percent (13% + 11.22%). However, it is apparent from the probabilities that the distribution is not normal.

**ST-2.**

| | |
|---|---|
| Stock A | 5% + .75(17% − 5%) = 14% |
| Stock B | 5% + .90(17% − 5%) = 15.8% |
| Stock C | 5% + 1.40(17% − 5%) = 21.8% |

**ST-3.**

*Kaifu*

Average return:

$$\frac{4\% + 6\% + 0\% + 2\%}{4} = 3\%$$

Standard deviation:

$$\sqrt{\frac{\begin{array}{r}(4\% - 3\%)^2 \\ + (6\% - 3\%)^2 \\ + (0\% - 3\%)^2 \\ + (2\% - 3\%)^2\end{array}}{4 - 1}} = 2.58$$

*Market*

Average return:

$$\frac{2\% + 3\% + 1\% - 1\%}{4} = 1.25$$

Standard deviation:

$$\sqrt{\frac{\begin{array}{r}(2\% - 1.25\%)^2 \\ + (3\% - 1.25\%)^2 \\ + (1\% - 1.25\%)^2 \\ + (-1\% - 1.25\%)^2\end{array}}{4 - 1}} = 1.71\%$$

**ST-4.**

| Time | Stock Price | Holding-Period Return |
|---|---|---|
| 1 | \$10 | |
| 2 | 13 | (\$13 ÷ \$10) − 1 = 30.0% |
| 3 | 11 | (\$11 ÷ \$13) − 1 = −15.4% |
| 4 | 15 | (\$15 ÷ \$11) − 1 = 36.4% |

**ST-5. a.** Portfolio expected return:

$$(.4 \times 12\%) + (.25 \times 11\%) + (.35 \times 15\%) = 12.8\%$$

Portfolio beta:

$$(.4 \times 1) + (.25 \times .75) + (.35 \times 1.3) = 1.04$$

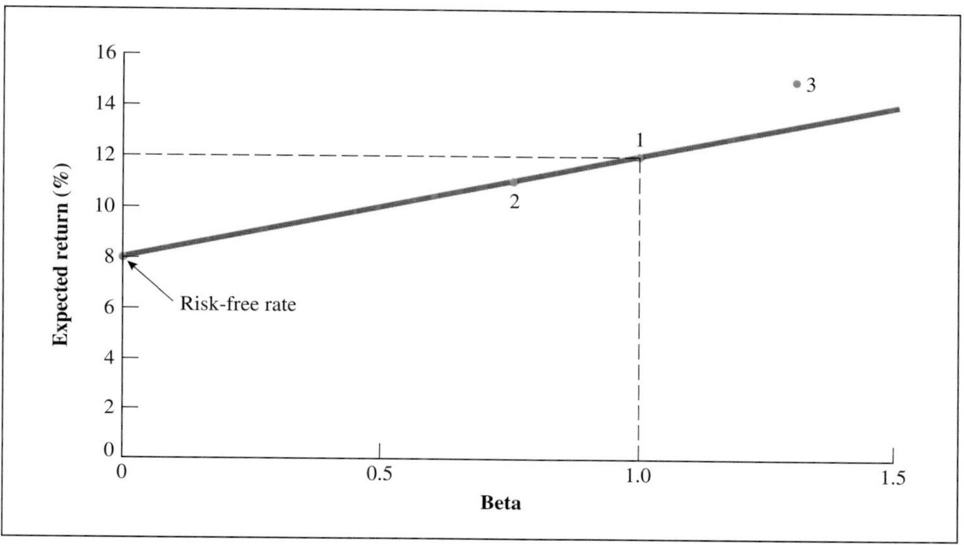


**b.** Stocks 1 and 2 seem to be right in line with the security market line, which suggests that they are earning a fair return, given their systematic risk. Stock 3, on the other hand, is earning more than a fair return (above the security market line). We might be tempted to conclude that security 3 is undervalued. However, we may be seeing an illusion; it is possible to misspecify the security market line by using bad estimates in our data.

## APPENDIX 6A

# MEASURING THE REQUIRED RATE OF RETURN: THE ARBITRAGE PRICING MODEL

The basic theme of the arbitrage pricing model (APM) may be summarized as follows:[18]

1. Actual security returns vary from their expected amounts because *of unanticipated* changes—anticipated changes are already reflected in the stock price—in a number of basic economic forces, such as industrial production, inflation rates, the term structure of interest rates, and the difference in interest rates between high- and low-risk bonds.[19]
2. Just as the CAPM defined a portfolio's systematic risk to be its sensitivity to the general-market returns (that is, its beta coefficient), APM suggests that the risk of a security is reflected in its sensitivity to the unexpected changes in important economic forces.
3. Any two stocks or portfolios that have the same sensitivity to meaningful economic forces (that is, the same relevant or systematic risk) must have the same expected return. Otherwise, we could replace some of the stocks in our portfolio with other stocks having the same sensitivities but higher expected returns and earn riskless profits.
4. We would expect portfolios that are highly sensitive to unexpected changes in macroeconomic forces to offer investors high expected returns. This relationship may be represented quantitatively as follows:

$$E(k_i) = k_{rf} + (S_{i1})(RP_1) + (S_{i2})(RP_2) + \dots + (S_{ij})(RP_j) + \dots + (S_{in})(RP_n) \tag{6A-1}$$

where $E(k_i)$ = the expected return for stock or portfolio $i$
$k_{rf}$ = the risk-free rate
$S_{ij}$ = the sensitivity of stock $i$ returns to unexpected changes in economic force $j$
$RP_j$ = the market risk premium associated with an unexpected change in the $j$th economic force
$n$ = the number of relevant economic forces

To help understand the APM model, we will draw from the actual research of Bower, Bower, and Logue (BBL).[20] After computing returns for 815 stocks from 1970 through 1979, BBL used a technique called factor analysis to study the general movement of monthly returns for the 815 stocks. The technique identified four factors that help explain the movement of the returns and also used equation 6A-1 to represent the risk-return relationship in an APM format. The actual model appears as follows:

$$\text{expected return for stock } i = 6.2\% - 185.5\%\,(S_{i1}) + 144.5\%\,(S_{i2}) + 12.4\%\,(S_{i3}) - 274.4\%\,(S_{i4})$$

The value 6.2% in the equation is an estimate of the risk-free rate, as determined by the model; the remaining values, −185.5%, . . . , −274.4%, signify the market risk premiums for each of the four factors; and the $S_{i1}, \dots, S_{i4}$ represent the sensitivities of stock $i$ to the four factors.

The BBL factors are determined statistically from past return data and were not intuitively or economically identified; that is, the technique provides *factors* that tell us more about the movement in the returns than would any other factors. Each factor could conceivably relate to a single

[18]The following description of the APM is taken in part from Dorothy H. Bower, Richard S. Bower, and Dennis E. Logue, "A Primer on Arbitrage Pricing Theory," in Joel M. Stern and Donald H. Chew, Jr., eds., *The Revolution in Corporate Finance* (New York: Basil Blackwell, 1986), 69–77.

[19]See R. Roll and S. Ross, "The Arbitrage Pricing Theory Approach to Strategic Portfolio Planning," *Financial Analysts Journal* (May–June 1984):14–26.

[20]Dorothy A. Bower, Richard S. Bower, and Dennis E. Logue, "Equity Screening Rates Using Arbitrage Pricing Theory," in C. F. Lee, ed., *Advances in Financial Planning* (Greenwich, CT: JAI Press, 1984).

economic variable; however, it is more likely that each factor represents the influence of several economic variables.

Having specified the APM risk-return relationship, BBL then used the model to estimate the expected (required) rates of return for 17 stocks. This estimation required BBL to use regression analysis to study the relationships of the returns of the 17 stocks to the four factors. From this regression analysis, they were able to measure the sensitivity of each security's return to a particular factor. These *sensitivity coefficients* for a particular stock may then be combined with the APM model in equation 6A-1 to estimate the investor's required rate of return.

Using 3 of the 17 stocks to demonstrate the calculation, the regression coefficients (sensitivity coefficients) for American Hospital Supply, CBS, and Western Union are shown here:

Stock Sensitivity Coefficients (S)

| | Factor 1 | Factor 2 | Factor 3 | Factor 4 |
|---|---|---|---|---|
| American Hospital Supply | −0.050 | 0.010 | 0.040 | 0.020 |
| CBS | −0.050 | 0.002 | 0.005 | 0.010 |
| Western Union | −0.050 | −0.020 | −0.010 | 0.009 |

Using these stock sensitivity coefficients and the APM model, as developed by BBL, we can estimate the investors' expected (required) rate of return for each stock as follows:

$$\text{American Hospital Supply} = 6.2\% - 185.5\%(-0.050) + 144.5\%(0.010) + 12.4\%(0.040) - 274.4\%(.020) = 11.93\%$$

$$\text{CBS} = 6.2\% - 185.5\%(-0.050) + 144.5\%(0.002) + 12.4\%(0.005) - 274.4\%(0.010) = 13.08\%$$

$$\text{Western Union} = 6.2\% - 185.5\%(-0.050) + 144.5\%(-0.020) + 12.4\%(-0.010) - 274.4\%(0.009) = 9.99\%$$

## STUDY PROBLEMS

**6A-1.** (*Arbitrage pricing model*) Using the APM along with the results of the Bower, Bower, and Logue research just discussed, estimate the appropriate required rates of return for the following three stocks:

Sensitivity Factor

| Stock | Factor 1 | Factor 2 | Factor 3 | Factor 4 |
|---|---|---|---|---|
| A | −0.070 | −0.020 | 0.010 | 0.003 |
| B | −0.070 | 0.030 | 0.005 | 0.010 |
| C | −0.070 | −0.010 | 0.006 | 0.009 |

**6A-2.** (*Required rate of return using APM*)

**a.** If we use the arbitrage pricing model to measure investor's required rate of return, what is our concept of risk?

**b.** Using the results of the Bower, Bower, and Logue study of return variability, as captured in equation 6A-1, calculate the investor's required rate of return for the following stocks:

Sensitivity Factor

| Stock | Factor 1 | Factor 2 | Factor 3 | Factor 4 |
|---|---|---|---|---|
| A | −0.070 | 0.030 | 0.005 | 0.010 |
| B | −0.070 | −0.010 | 0.006 | 0.009 |
| C | −0.050 | −0.004 | −0.010 | −0.007 |
| D | −0.060 | −0.007 | −0.006 | 0.006 |

**c.** Assuming (1) a risk-free rate of 6.1 percent and (2) an expected market return of 17.25 percent, estimate the investor's required rate of return for the four stocks in part (b), using the CAPM.

| Stock | Beta |
|---|---|
| A | 1.40 |
| B | 1.70 |
| C | 1.20 |
| D | 1.10 |

**d.** What might explain the differences in your answers to parts (b) and (c)?

# VALUATION AND CHARACTERISTICS OF BONDS

Practically all companies use debt to finance their firms, and many of those companies issue bonds, just one form of debt. Bonds provide investors a fixed income each year in the form of interest. Just as you can open a savings account at a bank and earn

interest on your savings, so can you buy a bond that pays interest and then repays your principal on a designated date when the bond matures. Many of these bonds are traded in the public capital markets. Three examples of companies that have issued bonds to investors include the computer firm, IBM; the telephone company, Pacific Bell; and the athletic wear business, Converse. Each of these bonds pays $70 in interest each year on a bond that will repay the investor $1,000 when it matures. However, while these bonds are similar in terms of their interest payment, investors do not value them the same. In mid-2000, they were selling for the following amounts:

| | |
|---|---|
| Pacific Bell | $1,014 |
| IBM | $ 949 |
| Converse | $ 150 |

Why would there be differences in the values of these bonds? Why would Pacific Bell's bonds be worth more than IBM's bonds? And why would the Converse

**LEARNING OBJECTIVES**

After reading this chapter, you should be able to

1. Distinguish between different kinds of bonds.
2. Explain the more popular features of bonds.
3. Define the term *value* as used for several different purposes.
4. Explain the factors that determine value.
5. Describe the basic process for valuing assets.
6. Estimate the value of a bond.
7. Compute a bondholder's expected rate of return.
8. Explain five important relationships that exist in bond valuation.

bonds be so "cheap"? They all pay the same amount of interest. Why would investors pay $1,014 for a bond that promises $70 in interest, when they could buy Converse bonds for only $150? Or a more general question, "What determines a bond's value?" Read on and you will find the answer to this puzzle.

**CHAPTER PREVIEW**

Knowing the fair value or price of an asset is no easy matter. The *Maxims* of the French writer La Rochefoucauld, written over three centuries ago, still speak to us: "The greatest of all gifts is the power to estimate things at their true worth." Understanding how to value financial securities is essential if managers are to meet the objective of maximizing the value of the firm. If they are to maximize the investors' value, they must know what drives the value of an asset. Specifically, they need to understand how bonds and stocks are valued in the marketplace; otherwise, they cannot act in the best interest of the firm's investors.

A bond is one form of a company's long-term debt. In this chapter, we begin by identifying the different kinds of bonds. We next look at the features or characteristics of most bonds. We then examine the concepts of and procedures for valuing an asset and apply these ideas to valuing bonds, one form of a company's long-term debt. We now begin our study by considering the different kinds of bonds.

## TYPES OF BONDS

OBJECTIVE 1 

**Bond**
A type of debt or a long-term promissory note, issued by the borrower, promising to pay its holder a predetermined and fixed amount of interest each year.

A **bond** is a type of debt or long-term promissory note, issued by the borrower, promising to pay its holder a predetermined and fixed amount of interest per year. However, there are a wide variety of such creatures. Just to mention a few, we have:

- Debentures
- Subordinated debentures
- Mortgage bonds
- Eurobonds
- Zero and very low coupon bonds
- Junk bonds

The following sections briefly explain each of these types of bonds.

### Debentures

**Debenture**
Any unsecured long-term debt.

The term **debenture** applies to any unsecured long-term debt. Because these bonds are unsecured, the earning ability of the issuing corporation is of great concern to the bondholder. They are also viewed as being more risky than secured bonds and as a result must provide investors with a higher yield than secured bonds provide. Often, the issuing firm attempts to provide some protection to the holder of the bond by prohibiting the firm from issuing more secured long-term debt that would further tie up the firm's assets and leave the bondholders less protected. To the issuing firm, the major advantage of debentures is that no property has to be secured by them. This allows the firm to issue debt and still preserve some future borrowing power.

### Subordinated Debentures

Many firms have more than one issue of debentures outstanding. In this case a hierarchy may be specified, in which some debentures are given subordinated standing in case of insolvency. The claims of the **subordinated debentures** are honored only after the claims of secured debt and unsubordinated debentures have been satisfied.

**Subordinated debenture**
A debenture that is subordinated to other debentures in being paid in the case of insolvency.

## Mortgage Bonds

A **mortgage bond** is a bond secured by a lien on real property. Typically, the value of the real property is greater than that of the mortgage bonds issued. This provides the mortgage bondholders with a margin of safety in the event the market value of the secured property declines. In the case of foreclosure, the trustees have the power to sell the secured property and use the proceeds to pay the bondholders. In the event that the proceeds from this sale do not cover the bonds, the bondholders become general creditors, similar to debenture bondholders, for the unpaid portion of the debt.

**Mortgage bond**
A bond secured by a lien on real property

## Eurobonds

**Eurobonds** are not so much a different type of security. They are simply securities, in this case bonds, issued in a country different from the one in whose currency the bond is denominated. For example, a bond that is issued in Europe or in Asia by an American company and that pays interest and principal to the lender in U.S. dollars would be considered a Eurobond. Thus, even if the bond is not issued in Europe, it merely needs to be sold in a country different from the one in whose currency it is denominated to be considered a Eurobond. The Eurobond market actually had its roots in the 1950s and 1960s as the U.S. dollar became increasingly popular because of its role as the primary international reserve. In recent years, as the U.S. dollar has gained a reputation for being one of the most stable currencies, demand for Eurobonds has increased. The primary attractions of Eurobonds to borrowers, aside from favorable rates, are the relative lack of regulation (Eurobonds are not registered with the Securities and Exchange Commission [SEC]), less rigorous disclosure requirements than those of the SEC, and the speed with which they can be issued. Interestingly, not only are Eurobonds not registered with the SEC, but U.S. citizens and residents may not be offered them during their initial distribution.

**Eurobonds**
Bonds issued in a country different from the one in whose currency the bond is denominated—for instance, a bond issued in Europe or in Asia by an American company that pays interest and principal to the lender in U.S. dollars.

## Zero and Very Low Coupon Bonds

**Zero and very low coupon bonds** allow the issuing firm to issue bonds at a substantial discount from their $1,000 face value with a zero or very low coupon rate. The investor receives a large part (or all with zero coupon bonds) of the return from the appreciation of the bond. For example, in 1998, 21st Century Telecom Group, Inc., a telecommunications firm, issued $43 million of debt maturing in 2008 with a zero coupon rate. These bonds were sold at a 57 percent discount from their par value; that is, investors only paid $433 for a bond with a $1,000 par value. Investors who purchased these bonds for $433 and hold them until they mature in 2008 will receive an 8.8 percent yield to maturity, with all of this yield coming from appreciation of the bond. On the other hand, 21st Century Telecom Group, Inc., will have no cash outflows until these bonds mature; however, at that time it will have to pay back $100 million even though it only received $43 million when the bonds were first issued.

**Zero and very low coupon bonds**
Bonds issued at a substantial discount from their $1,000 face value that pay no or little interest.

As with any form of financing, there are both advantages and disadvantages of issuing zero or very low coupon bonds. As already mentioned, the disadvantage is when the bonds mature, 21st Century Telecom Group will face an extremely large cash outflow, much greater than the cash inflow it experienced when the bonds were first issued. The advantages of zero and low coupon bonds are, first, that annual cash outflows associated with interest payments do not occur with zero coupon bonds and are at a relatively low level with low coupon bonds. Second, because there is relatively strong investor demand for this type of debt, prices tend to be bid up and yields tend to be bid down. That is to say, 21st Century Telecom Group was able to issue zero coupon bonds at about half a percent less than it would have been if they had been traditional coupon bonds. Finally, 21st Century Telecom Group is able to deduct the annual amortization of the discount from taxable income, which will provide a positive annual cash flow to 21st Century Telecom Group.

## Junk Bonds (High-Yield Bonds)

**Junk or high-yield bonds** Bonds rated BB or below.

**Junk bonds** are high-risk debt with ratings of BB or below by Moody's and Standard & Poor's. The lower the rating, the higher the chance of default; the lowest class is CC for Standard & Poor's and Ca for Moody's. Originally, the term was used to describe bonds issued by "fallen angels"; that is, firms with sound financial histories that were facing severe financial problems and suffering from poor credit ratings.

Junk bonds are also called **high-yield bonds** for the high interest rates they pay the investor, typically having an interest rate of between 3 and 5 percent more than AAA grade long-term debt.

Before the mid-1970s, smaller firms simply did not have access to the capital markets because of the reluctance of investors to accept speculative grade bonds. However, by the late 1980s, junk bonds became the way to finance hostile takeovers—buying a firm without the management's approval. For example, the purchase of RJR Nabisco for some $20 billion by the investment group KKR was largely accomplished by junk bond financing. However, the eventual bankruptcy of Drexel Burnham Lambert, the investment bank most responsible for developing a large junk bond market, the jailing of the "king of junk bonds" Michael Milken, and increasing interest rates brought an end to the extensive use of junk bonds for financing corporate takeovers. (Michael Milken, a partner at Drexel Burnham Lambert, used to have an annual conference in Beverly Hills, California, nicknamed "The Predator's Ball" for attracting takeover investors and corporate raiders who needed junk bond financing to accomplish their takeovers.)

When corporate takeovers subsided from their highs, most people thought the junk bond was forever dead. By 1990, the junk bond market was virtually nonexistent. Then, in 1992, with investors looking for higher interest rates and a rebounding economy, the junk bond market was revitalized. The following year, new junk bond issues reached a record $62 billion. Also, by 1995, less than 20 percent of the proceeds from junk bonds were being used to finance mergers and acquisitions, compared to 60 percent in the 1980s. In addition, in 1995, more than 800 companies had issued junk bonds, up from several hundred in the 1980s. Then in early 1998, the junk bond market suffered a sudden, jarring setback that led to the market for these bonds essentially dying. By year-end 1998, the capital market had returned to relatively moderate levels, in part because the Federal Reserve lowered interest rates. The borrowers in the 1990s came from a variety of industries, including manufacturing, media, retailing, consumer products, financial services, and housing. Also, credit quality improved. Only 17 percent of new issues in 1995 fell into the lower ratings of creditworthiness, compared with 66 percent in 1988.

### RELATE TO THE BIG PICTURE

Some have thought junk bonds were fundamentally different from other securities, but they are not. They are bonds with a great amount of risk, and therefore promise high expected returns. Thus, **Principle 1: The Risk-Return Trade-off—We won't take on additional risk unless we expect to be compensated with additional return.**

FINANCE $ MATTERS

## Issuing Junk Bonds: A Case Example

On the matter of junk bonds, Lea Carty, an economist at the bond-rating agency Moody's Investors Service in New York, says, "The junk bond market is here to stay. It's become a very important form of financing for younger, riskier firms." One such young, risky company is CommNet.

CommNet, which went public in 1986 and had yet to make a profit by 1995, is an example of a hot, young company that issued junk bonds. A 10-year-old firm with $90 million in sales was one of the first companies in the cellular telephone industry to use junk bond financing in 1993. The company's first issue raised $100 million to expand CommNet's eight-state rural telephone systems. The company sold more junk bonds in 1995, raising $80 million by selling 10-year notes with an 11.25 percent coupon.

Proceeds from CommNet's second junk bond sale were used to pay investors of convertible stock. A conventional bank loan wasn't a viable alternative because banks don't allow companies to buy back stock with bank proceeds, he said.

The firm's chief financial officer, Dan Dwyer, remembers the experience this way: "I think it was a combination of the quality of our company and market timing. The company's philosophy chose to sell bonds instead of stock in hopes of increasing value to shareholders."

Dwyer doesn't rule out a third junk bond issue in the future. "If we see an acquisition opportunity out there, we may well be back in the high-yield market," he said.

Source: John Accola, "Junk is Looking Good: Denver Companies Find Raising Cash with Risky Securities Easy as ATM," *Rocky Mountain News*, January 14, 1996, p. 80A. Denver: Denver Publishing Company. Reprinted with permission of the Denver *Rocky Mountain News*.

In the new millennium, junk bonds continue to play an important role in the financing of many middle-sized firms. Mutual funds and pension funds, which owned 40 percent of all junk bonds in 1995, should continue to provide an active market for such securities. So, contrary to the conventional wisdom of the early 1990s, the junk bond market is alive and well.

**CONCEPT CHECK**

1. What is the difference in the nature and associated risk among debentures, subordinated debentures, and mortgage bonds? How would investors respond to the varying types of risk?
2. How does an investor receive a return from a zero or very low coupon bond? Why would a company be able to deduct amortized interest over the life of the bond even though there are no cash outflows associated with interest?
3. Why do junk bonds typically have a higher interest rate than other types of bonds? Why has this market been revitalized?

Now that you have an understanding of the kinds of bonds firms might issue, let's look at some of the characteristics and terminology of bonds.

## TERMINOLOGY AND CHARACTERISTICS OF BONDS

Now that we have learned about the types of bonds, we need to look at the specific characteristics and terminology used in describing bonds. Only then will we be prepared to learn how to value a bond.

When a firm or nonprofit institution needs financing, one source is bonds. As already noted, this type of financing instrument is simply a long-term promissory note, issued by the borrower, promising to pay its holder a predetermined and fixed amount of interest each year. Some of the more important terms and characteristics that you might hear about bonds are as follows:

- Claims on assets and income
- Par value
- Coupon interest rate
- Maturity
- Indenture
- Current yield
- Bond ratings

Let's consider each in turn.

## Claims on Assets and Income

In the case of insolvency, claims of debt in general, including bonds, are honored before those of both common stock and preferred stock. However, different types of debt may also have a hierarchy among themselves as to the order of their claim on assets.

Bonds also have a claim on income that comes ahead of common and preferred stock. In general, if interest on bonds is not paid, the bond trustees can classify the firm as insolvent and force it into bankruptcy. Thus, the bondholder's claim on income is more likely to be honored than that of common and preferred stockholders, whose dividends are paid at the discretion of the firm's management.

## Par Value

**Par value of a bond** The bond's face value that is returned to the bondholder at maturity, usually $1,000.

The **par value of a bond** is its face value that is returned to the bondholder at maturity. In general, corporate bonds are issued in denominations of $1,000, although there are some exceptions to this rule. Also, when bond prices are quoted, either by financial managers or in the financial press, prices are generally expressed as a percentage of the bond's par value. For example, a Lucent bond was recently quoted in the *Wall Street Journal* as selling for $102\frac{5}{8}$. That does not mean you can buy the bond for $102.63. It means that this bond is selling for $102\frac{5}{8}$ percent of its par value of $1,000. Hence, the market price of this bond is actually $1,026.25. At maturity in 2006, the bondholder will receive the $1,000.

## Coupon Interest Rate

**Coupon interest rate** A bond's coupon interest rate indicates what percentage of the par value of the bond will be paid out annually in the form of interest.

The **coupon interest rate** on a bond indicates the percentage of the par value of the bond that will be paid out annually in the form of interest. Thus, regardless of what happens to the price of a bond with an 8 percent coupon interest rate and a $1,000 par value, it will pay out $80 annually in interest until maturity ($.08 \times \$1,000 = \$80$).

## Maturity

**Maturity** The length of time until the bond issuer returns the par value to the bondholder and terminates the bond.

The **maturity** of a bond indicates the length of time until the bond issuer returns the par value to the bondholder and terminates or redeems the bond.

## Indenture

**Indenture** The legal agreement or contract between the firm issuing the bonds and the bond trustee who represents the bondholders.

An **indenture** is the legal agreement between the firm issuing the bonds and the bond trustee who represents the bondholders. The indenture provides the specific terms of the loan agreement, including a description of the bonds, the rights of the bondholders, the

**FINANCE MATTERS**

### Bond Rating: Moody's Changes Outlook on Sprint Corporation's Ratings to Negative

The following news announcement was released regarding Moody's Investors Service changing its rating outlook on Sprint Corporation's long-term securities. The following is an excerpt from the announcement.

> Moody's Investors Service has confirmed the ratings of Sprint Corporation (Baal, senior unsecured) and its subsidiaries, but has changed the rating outlook on the long-term securities to negative from stable. The outlook change reflects the pressure Sprint's capital needs place on its long-term debt ratings. These capital needs are the direct result of intensifying industry-wide competition. As a result, deleveraging through cash flow growth has occurred at a slower pace than Moody's expected. The combined effect of increased capital spending and slower than expected cash flow growth will require Sprint to seek $5 billion of additional financing in 2001, in a capital market environment that is currently difficult.

Source: "Moody's Changes Outlook on Sprint Corporation's Ratings to Negative, Confirms Sr. Unsec. Ratings at Baal," Moody's Investors Service, November 22, 2000.

rights of the issuing firm, and the responsibilities of the trustee. This legal document may run 100 pages or more in length, with the majority of it devoted to defining protective provisions for the bondholder. The bond trustee, usually a banking institution or trust company, is then assigned the task of overseeing the relationship between the bondholder and the issuing firm, protecting the bondholder, and seeing that the terms of the indenture are carried out.

Typically, the restrictive provisions included in the indenture attempt to protect the bondholders' financial position relative to that of other outstanding securities. Common provisions involve (1) prohibiting the sale of accounts receivable, (2) limiting common stock dividends, (3) restricting the purchase or sale of fixed assets, and (4) setting limits on additional borrowing. Not allowing the sale of accounts receivable is specified because such sales would benefit the firm's short-run liquidity position at the expense of its future liquidity position. Common stock dividends may not be allowed if the firm's liquidity falls below a specified level, or the maximum dividend payout may be limited to some fraction, say 50 percent or 60 percent of earnings under any circumstance. Fixed-asset restrictions generally require lender permission before the liquidation of any fixed asset or prohibit the use of any existing fixed asset as collateral on new loans. Constraints on additional borrowing usually involve limiting the amount and type of additional long-term debt that can be issued. All of these restrictions have one thing in common: They attempt to prohibit actions that would improve the status of other securities at the expense of bonds and to protect the status of bonds from being weakened by any managerial action.

## Current Yield

**Current yield**
The ratio of the annual interest payment to the bond's market price.

The **current yield** on a bond refers to the ratio of the annual interest payment to the bond's current market price. If, for example, we have a bond with an 8 percent coupon interest rate, a par value of $1,000, and a market price of $700, it would have a current yield of

$$\text{Current yield} = \frac{\text{annual interest payment}}{\text{market price of the bond}} \quad \textbf{(7-1)}$$

$$= \frac{0.08 \times \$1000}{\$700} = \frac{\$80}{\$700} = 0.114 = 11.4\%$$

## Bond Ratings

John Moody first began to rate bonds in 1909. Since that time three rating agencies—Moody's, Standard & Poor's, and Fitch Investor Services—have provided ratings on corporate bonds. These ratings involve a judgment about the future risk potential of the bond. Although they deal with expectations, several historical factors seem to play a significant role in their determination. Bond ratings are favorably affected by (1) a greater reliance on equity as opposed to debt in financing the firm, (2) profitable operations, (3) a low variability in past earnings, (4) large firm size, and (5) little use of subordinated debt. In turn, the rating a bond receives affects the rate of return demanded on the bond by the investors. The poorer the bond rating, the higher the rate of return demanded in the capital markets. Table 7-1 provides an example and description of these ratings. Thus, bond ratings are extremely important for the financial manager. They provide an indicator of default risk that in turn affects the rate of return that must be paid on borrowed funds.

**RELATE TO THE BIG PICTURE**

When we say that a lower bond rating means a higher interest rate charged by the investors (bondholders), we are observing an application of **Principle 1: The Risk-Return Trade-off—We won't take on additional risk unless we expect to be compensated with additional return.**

We are now ready to think about bond valuation. But, to begin, we must first clarify precisely what we mean by value. Next, we need to understand the basic concepts of valuation and the process for valuing an asset. Then we may apply these concepts to valuing a bond—and in Chapter 8 to valuing stocks.

**CONCEPT CHECK**

1. What are some of the important features of a bond? Which features determine the cash flows associated with a bond?
2. What restrictions are typically included in an indenture in order to protect the bondholder?
3. How does the bond rating affect an investor's required rate of return? What actions could a firm take to receive a more favorable rating?

OBJECTIVE 3 

## DEFINITIONS OF VALUE

**Book value**
The value of an asset as shown on a firm's balance sheet. It represents the historical cost of the asset rather than its current market value or replacement cost.

**Liquidation value**
The amount that could be realized if an asset were sold individually and not as a part of a going concern.

The term *value* is often used in different contexts, depending on its application. Examples of different uses of this term include the following:

**Book value** is the value of an asset as shown on a firm's balance sheet. It represents the historical cost of the asset rather than its current worth. For instance, the book value of a company's preferred stock is the amount the investors originally paid for the stock and therefore the amount the firm received when the stock was issued.

**Liquidation value** is the dollar sum that could be realized if an asset were sold individually and not as part of a going concern. For example, if a firm's operations were discontinued and its assets were divided up and sold, the sales price would represent the asset's liquidation value.

**TABLE 7-1**
Standard & Poor's Corporate Bond Ratings

| Rating | Description |
|---|---|
| AAA | This is the highest rating assigned by Standard & Poor's for debt obligation and indicates an extremely strong capacity to pay principal and interest. |
| AA | Bonds rated AA also qualify as high-quality debt obligations. Their capacity to pay principal and interest is very strong, and in the majority of instances, they differ from AAA issues only in small degree. |
| A | Bonds rated A have a strong capacity to pay principal and interest, although they are somewhat more susceptible to the adverse effects of changes in circumstances and economic conditions. |
| BBB | Bonds rated BBB are regarded as having an adequate capacity to pay principal and interest. Whereas they normally exhibit adequate protection parameters, adverse economic conditions or changing circumstances are more likely to lead to a weakened capacity to pay principal and interest for bonds in this category than for bonds in the A category. |
| BB<br>B<br>CCC<br>CC | Bonds rated BB, B, CCC, and CC are regarded, on balance, as predominantly speculative with respect to the issuer's capacity to pay interest and repay principal in accordance with the terms of the obligation. BB indicates the lowest degree of speculation and CC the highest. While such bonds will likely have some quality and protective characteristics, these are outweighed by large uncertainties or major risk exposures to adverse conditions. |
| C | The rating C is reserved for income bonds on which no interest is being paid. |
| D | Bonds rated D are in default, and payment of principal and/or interest is in arrears. |

Plus (+) or Minus (−): To provide more detailed indications of credit quality, the ratings from AA to BB may be modified by the addition of a plus or minus sign to show relative standing within the major rating categories.

Source: *Standard & Poor's Fixed Income Investor,* Vol. 8 (1980). Reprinted by permission.

The **market value** of an asset is the observed value for the asset in the marketplace. This value is determined by supply and demand forces working together in the marketplace, where buyers and sellers negotiate a mutually acceptable price for the asset. For instance, the market price for Ford Motor Company common stock on September 27, 2000, was $24.38. This price was reached by a large number of buyers and sellers working through the New York Stock Exchange. In theory, a market price exists for all assets. However, many assets have no readily observable market price because trading seldom occurs. For instance, the market price for the common stock of Blanks Engraving, a Dallas-based, family-owned firm, would be more difficult to establish than the market value of J. C. Penney's common stock.

**Market value**
The observed value for the asset in the marketplace.

The **intrinsic** or **economic value** of an asset—also called the fair value—is the present value of the asset's expected future cash flows. This value is the amount an investor should be willing to pay, given the amount, timing, and riskiness of future cash flows. Once the investor has estimated the intrinsic value of a security, this value could be compared with its market value when available. If the intrinsic value is greater than the market value, then the security is undervalued in the eyes of the investor. Should the market value exceed the investor's intrinsic value, then the security is overvalued.

**Intrinsic or economic value**
The present value of the asset's expected future cash flows. This value is the amount the investor considers to be a fair value, given the amount, timing, and riskiness of future cash flows.

We hasten to add that if the securities market is working efficiently, the market value and the intrinsic value of a security will be equal. Whenever a security's intrinsic value differs from its current market price, the competition among investors seeking opportunities to make a profit will quickly drive the market price back to its intrinsic value. Thus, we may define an **efficient market** as one in which the values of all securities at any instant fully reflect all available public information, which results in the market value and the intrinsic value being the same. If the markets are efficient, it is extremely difficult for an investor to make extra profits from an ability to predict prices.

**Efficient market**
A market in which the values of securities at any instant in time fully reflect all available information, which results in the market value and the intrinsic value being the same.

**RELATE TO THE BIG PICTURE**

The fact that investors have difficulty identifying securities that are undervalued relates to **Principle 6: Efficient Capital Markets—The Markets are quick and the prices are right.** In an efficient market, the price reflects all available public information about the security, and therefore, it is priced fairly.

The idea of market efficiency has been the backdrop for an intense battle between professional investors and university professors. The academic community has contended that someone throwing darts at the list of securities in the *Wall Street Journal* could do as well as a professional money manager. Market professionals retort that academicians are grossly mistaken in this view. The war has been intense but also one that the student of finance should find intriguing, and it can be followed each month in the *Wall Street Journal,* where the investment performances of dart throwers and different professional investors are compared. Through September 2000, there had been 123 contests between these rivals. The score: 76 for the professional managers and 47 for the dart throwers. Also, as aptly expressed by one teacher, the real point about efficient markets is that an investor should throw a large wet towel at the *Wall Street Journal,* not a dart. That is, we want to be broadly diversified with a large group of stocks, not just one. For example, when the professional investors are compared with the performance of the 30 companies represented on the Dow Jones Industrial Index, they have won only 64 of the contests. The importance of diversification was explained in Chapter 6.

**CONCEPT CHECK**

1. Explain the difference between the four different values of a bond. Why should the market value equal the intrinsic value?
2. How does risk play a role in the three basic factors of asset valuation?

## DETERMINANTS OF VALUE

OBJECTIVE 4 

For our purposes, the value of an asset is its intrinsic value or the present value of its expected future cash flows, where these cash flows are discounted back to the present using the investor's required rate of return. This statement is true for valuing all assets and serves as the basis of almost all that we do in finance. Thus, value is affected by three elements:

1. The amount and timing of the asset's expected cash flows
2. The riskiness of these cash flows
3. The investor's required rate of return for undertaking the investment

The first two factors are characteristics of the asset; the third one, the required rate of return, is the minimum rate of return necessary to attract an investor to purchase or hold a security, which is determined by the rates of return available on similar investments, or what is called the **opportunity cost of funds.** This rate must be high enough to compensate the investor for the risk perceived in the asset's future cash flows. (The required rate of return was explained in Chapter 6.)

**Opportunity cost of funds** The next best rate of return available to the investor for a given level of risk.

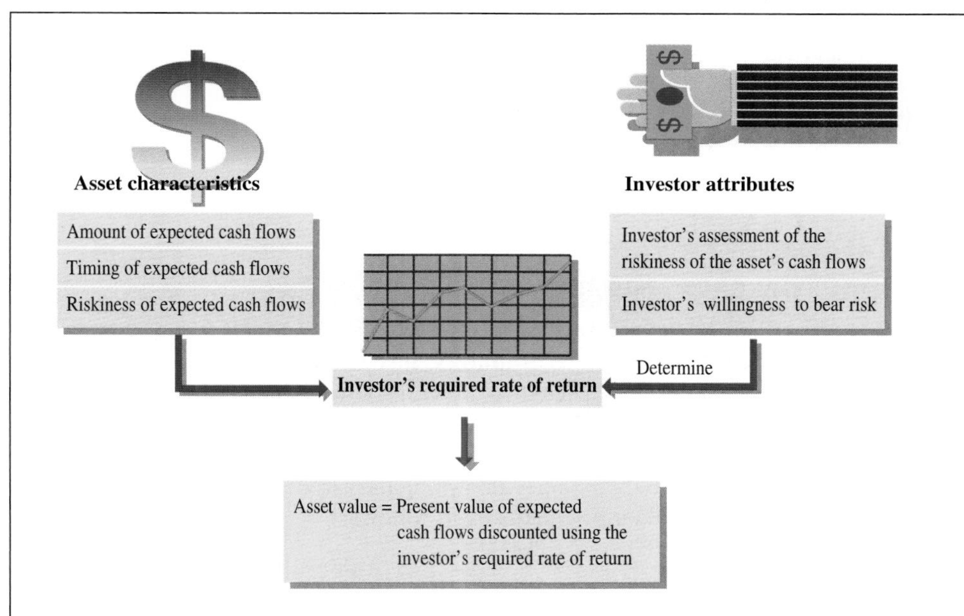


**FIGURE 7-1**
Basic Factors Determining an Asset's Value

## RELATE TO THE BIG PICTURE

Our discussions should remind us of three of our principles that help us understand finance:

**Principle 1: The Risk-Return Trade-off—We won't take on additional risk unless we expect to be compensated with additional return.**

**Principle 2: The Time Value of Money—A dollar received today is worth more than a dollar received in the future.**

**Principle 3: Cash—Not Profits—Is King.**

Determining the economic worth or value of an asset always relies on these three principles. Without them, we would have no basis for explaining value. With them, we can know that the amount and timing of cash, not earnings, drive value. Also, we must be rewarded for taking risk; otherwise, we will not invest.

Figure 7-1 depicts the basic factors involved in valuation. As the figure shows, finding the value of an asset involves the following steps:

1. Assessing the asset's characteristics, which include the amount and timing of the expected cash flows and the riskiness of these cash flows
2. Determining the investor's required rate of return, which embodies the investor's attitude about assuming risk and perception of the riskiness of the asset
3. Discounting the expected cash flows back to the present, using the investor's required rate of return as the discount rate

Thus, intrinsic value is a function of the cash flows yet to be received, the riskiness of these cash flows, and the investor's required rate of return.

**CONCEPT CHECK**

1. What are the three important elements of asset valuation?

## VALUATION: THE BASIC PROCESS

OBJECTIVE 5 

The valuation process can be described as follows: It is assigning value to an asset by calculating the present value of its expected future cash flows using the investor's required rate of return as the discount rate. The investor's required rate of return, $k$, is determined by the level of the risk-free rate of interest and the risk premium that the investor feels is necessary to compensate for the risks assumed in owning the asset. Therefore, a basic security valuation model can be defined mathematically as follows:

$$V = \frac{C_1}{(1+k)^1} + \frac{C_2}{(1+k)^2} + \dots + \frac{C_n}{(1+k)^n} \quad \textbf{(7-2)}$$

or

$$V = \sum_{t=1}^{n} \frac{C_t}{(1+k)^t}$$

where $C_t$ = cash flow to be received at time $t$
$V$ = the intrinsic value or present value of an asset producing expected future cash flows, $C_t$, in years 1 through $n$
$k$ = the investor's required rate of return

Using equation 7-2, there are three basic steps in the valuation process:

Step 1: Estimate $C_t$ in equation 7-2, which is the amount and timing of the future cash flows the security is expected to provide.
Step 2: Determine $k$, the investor's required rate of return.
Step 3: Calculate the intrinsic value, $V$, as the present value of expected future cash flows discounted at the investor's required rate of return.

Equation 7-2, which measures the present value of future cash flows, is the basis of the valuation process. It is the most important equation in this chapter, because all the remaining equations in this chapter and in Chapter 8 are merely reformulations of this one equation. If we understand equation 7-2, all the valuation work we do, and a host of other topics as well, will be much clearer in our minds.

**CONCEPT CHECK**

1. What two factors determine an investor's required rate of return?
2. How does the required rate of return affect an asset's value?

With the foregoing principles of valuation as our foundation, let's now look at how bonds are valued.

| | |
|---|---|
| (A) Cash Flow Information | Periodic interest payments<br>For example, $65 per year<br>Principal amount or par value<br>For example, $1,000 |
| (B) Time to Maturity | For example, 12 years |
| (C) Investor's Required Rate of Return | For example, 8 percent |

**FIGURE 7-2**
Data Requirements for Bond Valuation

## BOND VALUATION

The value of a bond is the present value both of future interest to be received and the par or maturity value of the bond. It's that simple.

The process for valuing a bond, as depicted in Figure 7-2, requires knowing three essential elements: (1) the amount and timing of the cash flows to be received by the investor, (2) the time to maturity of the loan, and (3) the investor's required rate of return. The amount of cash flows is dictated by the periodic interest to be received and by the par value to be paid at maturity. Given these elements, we can compute the value of the bond, or the present value.

### EXAMPLE

Consider a bond issued by SBC (Southwestern Bell) with a maturity date of 2020 and a stated coupon rate of 7 percent.[1] In 2000, with 20 years left to maturity, investors owning the bonds are requiring a 7.5 percent rate of return. We can calculate the value of the bonds to these investors using the following three-step valuation procedure:

**Step 1:** Estimate the amount and timing of the expected future cash flows. Two types of cash flows are received by the bondholder:

**a.** Annual interest payments equal to the coupon rate of interest times the face value of the bond. In this example, the bond's coupon interest rate is 7 percent; thus the annual interest payment is $70 = .07 \times \$1,000$. Assuming that 2000 interest payments have already been made, these cash flows will be received by the bondholder in each of the 20 years before the bond matures (2001 through 2020 = 20 years).

**b.** The face value of the bond of $1,000 to be received in 2020. To summarize, the cash flows received by the bondholder are as follows:

| YEAR | 1 | 2 | 3 | 4 | . . . | 19 | 20 |
|---|---|---|---|---|---|---|---|
| | $70 | $70 | $70 | $70 | . . . | $70 | $ 70 |
| | | | | | | | $1,000 |
| | | | | | | | $1,070 |

[1] SBC pays interest to its bondholders on a semiannual basis on January 15 and July 15. However, for the moment, assume the interest is to be received annually. The effect of semiannual payments is examined later.

**Step 2:** Determine the investor's required rate of return by evaluating the riskiness of the bond's future cash flows. A 7.5 percent required rate of return for the bondholders is given. In Chapter 6, we learned how this rate is determined. For now, simply realize that the investor's required rate of return is equal to a rate earned on a risk-free security plus a risk premium for assuming risk.

**Step 3:** Calculate the intrinsic value of the bond as the present value of the expected future interest and principal payments discounted at the investor's required rate of return.

The present value of SBC bonds is as follows:

$$\text{bond value} = V_b = \frac{\$\text{ interest in year 1}}{(1 + \text{required rate of return})^1} + \frac{\$\text{ interest in year 2}}{(1 + \text{required rate of return})^2} + \cdots + \frac{\$\text{ interest in year 20}}{(1 + \text{required rate of return})^{20}} + \frac{\$\text{ par value of bond}}{(1 + \text{required rate of return})^{20}} \qquad \textbf{(7-3a)}$$

or, summing over the interest payments,

$$V_b = \underbrace{\sum_{t=1}^{20} \frac{\$\text{ interest in year } t}{(1 + \text{required rate of return})^t}}_{\text{present value of interest}} + \underbrace{\frac{\$\text{ par value of bond}}{(1 + \text{required rate of return})^{20}}}_{\text{present value of par value}}$$

The foregoing equation is a restatement in a slightly different form of equation 7-2. Recall that equation 7-2 states that the value of an asset is the present value of future cash flows to be received by the investor.

Using $I_t$ to represent the interest payment in year $t$, $M$ to represent the bond's maturity (or par) value, and $k_b$ to equal the bondholder's required rate of return, we may express the value of a bond maturing in year $n$ as follows:

$$V_b = \sum_{t=1}^{n} \frac{\$I_t}{(1 + k_b)^t} + \frac{\$M}{(1 + k_b)^n} \qquad \textbf{(7-3b)}$$

Finding the value of SBC's bonds may be represented graphically as follows:

| YEAR | 0 | 1 | 2 | 3 | 4 | 5 | 6 | . . . | 20 |
|---|---|---|---|---|---|---|---|---|---|
| Dollars received at end of year | | $70 | $70 | $70 | $70 | $70 | $70 | . . . | $70<br>$1,000<br>$1,070 |
| Present value | $949 | | | | | | | | |

**CALCULATOR SOLUTION**

| Data Input | Function Key |
|---|---|
| 20 | N |
| 7.5 | I/Y |
| 70 | PMT |
| 1000 | FV |

| Function Key | Answer |
|---|---|
| CPT PV | −949 |

Using the TI BAII Plus, we find the value of the bond to be $949, as calculated in the margin.[2] Thus, if investors consider 7.5 percent to be an appropriate required rate of return in view of the risk level associated with SBC bonds, paying a price of $949 would satisfy their return requirement.

[2] As noted in Chapter 5, we are using the TI BAII Plus. You may want to return to the Chapter 5 section "Moving Money through Time with the Aid of a Financial Calculator" or Appendix A to see a more complete explanation of using the TI BAII Plus.

## FINANCE MATTERS

### Reading a Bond Quote in *The Wall Street Journal*

Following is a section of *The Wall Street Journal* that gives the quotes for October 19, 2000, for some of the corporate bonds traded on the New York Stock Exchange on that date.

U.S. Exchange Bonds

| BONDS | CUR YLD. | VOL. | CLOSE | | NET CHG. |
|---|---|---|---|---|---|
| NYTel 7⅜11 | 7.5 | 75 | 99 | + | ⅛ |
| OcciP 10⅛01 | 9.9 | 10 | 102 | – | ½ |
| OreStl 11s03 | 16.9 | 203 | 65 | – | 2 |
| ParkElc 5½06 | cv | 90 | 127 | + | 4 |
| ParkerD 5½04 | cv | 10 | 85⅛ | + | ⅛ |
| PhilPt 7.92s23 | 8.2 | 39 | 97 | + | 1¼ |
| PhilPt 7.2s23 | 8.0 | 15 | 89⅞ | + | 1⅞ |
| Polaroid 11½06 | 14.3 | 479 | 80¼ | + | 1¼ |
| PotEl 5s02 | cv | 250 | 96 | – | ¼ |
| PSvEG 6⅛02 | 6.3 | 35 | 97⅞ | – | ⅛ |
| Quanx 6.88s07 | cv | 45 | 87⅞ | + | 1⅞ |
| RalsP 7⅞25 | 8.2 | 13 | 96⅛ | + | ⅛ |

The bonds shown in the list as "Polaroid 11½ 06" were issued by Polaroid Corporation. They pay an 11½ percent coupon interest rate (indicated by the "11½"), or $115 interest paid annually (actually $57.50 paid semiannually) on a par value of $1,000, and they mature in 2006 (06 is the last two digits of the year the bonds mature). The closing price of the bonds on October 19, 2000 was 80¼, which is stated as a percentage of the bond's $1,000 par value; thus, the bond's closing price on October 19 was $802.50 = .8025 × 1000. The current yield on the bond is 14.3 percent, calculated as the annual interest divided by the closing price, or $115/$802.50 = 14.3 percent. During the day, 479 bonds were traded on the exchange, as reflected by the "VOL." heading.* Finally, the net change ("NET CHG.") in the price of the bond from the previous day's close was an increase of 1¼ percent.

*There may have been more than 479 bonds changing hands on October 19, 2000. Many bond trades are negotiated directly between institutional investors or through bankers and are not listed in *The Wall Street Journal.*

We can also solve for the value of SBC's bonds using a spreadsheet. The solution using Excel appears as follows:

| | A | B | C | D |
|---|---|---|---|---|
| 1 | Required rate of return | Rate | 0.075 | |
| 2 | Years left to maturity | Nper | 20 | |
| 3 | Annual interest payment | Pmt | 70 | |
| 4 | Future value | FV | 1,000 | |
| 5 | Present value | PV | ($949) | |
| 6 | | | | |
| 7 | | | | |
| 8 | | | | |
| 9 | Equation: = PV (Rate, Nper, Pmt, FV) = PV (C1, C2, C3, C4) | | | |

## Semiannual Interest Payments

In the preceding SBC illustration, the interest payments were assumed to be paid annually. However, companies typically pay interest to bondholders semiannually. For example, consider Alaskan Airlines' bonds maturing in 14 years that pay \$68.75 per year, but the interest is dispersed semiannually (\$34.375 each January 15 and July 15).

Several steps are involved in adapting equation 7-3b for semiannual interest payments.[3] First, thinking in terms of *periods* instead of years, a bond with a life of $n$ years paying interest semiannually has a life of $2n$ periods. In other words, a 5-year bond ($n = 5$) that remits its interest on a semiannual basis actually makes 10 payments. Yet although the number of periods has doubled, the *dollar* amount of interest being sent to the investors for each period and the bondholders' required rate of return are half of the equivalent annual figures. $I_t$ becomes $I_t/2$ and $k_b$ is changed to $k_b/2$; thus, for semiannual compounding, equation 7-3b becomes

$$V_b = \sum_{t=1}^{2n} \frac{\$I_t/2}{\left(1 + \frac{k_b}{2}\right)^t} + \frac{\$M}{\left(1 + \frac{k_b}{2}\right)^{2n}} \quad \textbf{(7-4)}$$

**CALCULATOR SOLUTION**

| Data Input | Function Key |
|---|---|
| 2n → 2 × 14 = 28 | N |
| 7.2% ÷ 2 = 3.6 | I/Y |
| \$68.75 ÷ 2 = 34.375 | PMT |
| 1000 | FV |
| **Function Key** | **Answer** |
| CPT PV | −972 |

Alternatively, using the notations introduced in Chapter 5 for discounting cash flows, equation 7-4 may be restated as follows:

$$V_b = (\$I_t \div 2)\,(PVIFA_{k_b/2,\,2n}) + \$M(PVIF_{k_b/2,\,2n}) \quad \textbf{(7-5)}$$

Assuming the Alaskan Airlines bondholders' annual required rate of return is 7.2 percent, we can use the TI BAII Plus calculator, as shown in the margin, to find the bond value, but now assuming semiannual interest payments. Thus, the value of a bond paying \$34.375 in semiannual interest for 14 years, where the investor has a 7.2 percent required rate of return, would be \$972.

This solution can be found using a spreadsheet that would look as follows:

| | A | B | C | D |
|---|---|---|---|---|
| 1 | Required rate of return | Rate | 0.036 | |
| 2 | Periods left to maturity | Nper | 28 | |
| 3 | Semiannual interest payment | Pmt | 34.375 | |
| 4 | Future value | FV | 1,000 | |
| 5 | Present value | PV | (\$972) | |
| 6 | | | ↑ | |
| 7 | | | | |
| 8 | | | | |
| 9 | Equation: = PV (Rate, Nper, Pmt, FV) = PV (C1, C2, C3, C4) | | | |

**CONCEPT CHECK**

1. What does it mean if your required rate of return for investing in a bond is different from the expected rate of return implied by its current market price? As an investor, what would you do if this were true?
2. How do semiannual payments affect the asset valuation equation?

## THE BONDHOLDER'S EXPECTED RATE OF RETURN (YIELD TO MATURITY)

OBJECTIVE 7 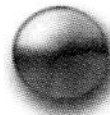

Theoretically, each investor could have a different required rate of return for a particular security. However, the financial manager is only interested in the required rate of return that is implied by the market prices of the firm's securities. In other words, the consensus

[3]The logic for calculating the value of a bond that pays interest semiannually is similar to the material presented in Chapter 5 where compound interest with nonannual periods was discussed.

of a firm's investors about the expected rate of return is reflected in the current market price of the stock.

To measure the bondholder's **expected rate of return,** $\bar{k}_b$, we would find the discount rate that equates the present value of the future cash flows (interest and maturity value) with the current market price of the bond.[4] The expected rate of return for a bond is also the rate of return the investor will earn if the bond is held to maturity, or the **yield to maturity.** Thus, when referring to bonds, the terms *expected rate of return* and *yield to maturity* are often used interchangeably.

**Expected rate of return**
The discount rate that equates the present value of the future cash flows (interest and maturity value) with the current market price of the bond. It is the rate of return an investor will earn if a bond is held to maturity.

**Yield to maturity**
The same as the expected rate of return.

To illustrate this concept, consider the Brister Corporation's bonds, which are selling for $1,100. The bonds carry a coupon interest rate of 9 percent and mature in 10 years. (Remember, the coupon rate determines the interest payment—coupon rate × par value.)

In determining the expected rate of return ($\bar{k}_b$) implicit in the current market price, we need to find the rate that discounts the anticipated cash flows back to a present value of $1,100, the current market price ($P_0$) for the bond.

Finding the expected rate of return for a bond using the present value tables is done by trial and error. We have to keep trying new rates until we find the discount rate that results in the present value of the future interest and maturity value of the bond just equaling the current market value of the bond. If the expected rate is somewhere between rates in the present value tables, we then must interpolate between the rates.

For our example, if we try 7 percent, the bond's present value is $1,140.16. Because the present value of $1,140.16 is greater than the market price of $1,100, we should next try a higher rate. Increasing the discount rate, say, to 8 percent gives a present value of $1,066.90. (These computations are shown in the following chart.) Now the present value is less than the market price; thus, we know that the investor's expected rate of return is between 7 percent and 8 percent.

| Years | Cash Flow | 7% Present Value Factors | Present Value | 8% Present Value Factors | Present Value |
|---|---|---|---|---|---|
| 1–10 | $90 per year | 7.024 | $ 632.16 | 6.710 | $ 603.90 |
| 10 | $1,000 in year 10 | 0.508 | 508.00 | 0.463 | $ 463.00 |
| | | Present value at 7% | $1,140.16 | Present value at 8% | $1,066.90 |

**CALCULATOR SOLUTION**

| Data Input | Function Key |
|---|---|
| 10 | N |
| 1100 | PV |
| 90 | +/– PMT |
| 1000 | +/– FV |
| **Function Key** | **Answer** |
| CPT I/Y | 7.54 |

The actual expected return for the Brister Corporation bondholders is 7.54 percent, which may be found by using the TI BAII Plus calculator as presented in the margin, or by using a computer spreadsheet as follows:

| | A | B | C | D |
|---|---|---|---|---|
| 1 | Years left to maturity | Nper | 10 | |
| 2 | Annual interest payment | Pmt | 90 | |
| 3 | Present value | PV | −1100 | |
| 4 | Future value | FV | 1,000 | |
| 5 | Required rate of return | Rate | 7.54% | |
| 6 | | | ↑ | |
| 7 | | | | |
| 8 | | | | |
| 9 | | | | |
| 10 | Equation: = RATE (Nper, Pmt, −PV, FV) = RATE (C1, C2, C3, C4) | | | |

[4]When we speak of computing an expected rate of return, we are not describing the situation very accurately. Expected rates of return are ex ante (before the fact) and are based on "expected and unobservable future cash flows" and, therefore, can only be "estimated."

Given our understanding of bond valuation and a bondholder's expected rate of return, let's discover what else a financial manager needs to know to understand why bond prices and interest rates perform as they do.

## BOND VALUATION: FIVE IMPORTANT RELATIONSHIPS

OBJECTIVE 8 

We have now learned to find the value of a bond ($V_b$), given (1) the amount of interest payments, (2) the maturity or par value, (3) the length of time to maturity, and (4) the investor's required rate of return. We also know how to compute the expected rate of return, $\bar{k}_b$, which also happens to be the *current interest rate* on the bond, given (1) the current market value, (2) the amount of interest payments, (3) the maturity value, and (4) the length of time to maturity. We now have the basics. However, a financial manager needs to know more in order to understand how the firm's bonds will react to changing conditions. So let's go further in our understanding of bond valuation by studying several important relationships.

### First Relationship

The value of a bond is inversely related to changes in the investor's present required rate of return (the current interest rate). In other words, as interest rates increase (decrease), the value of the bond decreases (increases).

To illustrate, assume that an investor's required rate of return for a given bond is 12 percent. The bond has a par value of \$1,000 and annual interest payments of \$120, indicating a 12 percent coupon interest rate (\$120 ÷ \$1,000 = 12%). Assuming a 5-year maturity date, the bond would be worth \$1,000, computed as follows by using equation 7-3a:

$$V_b = \frac{I_1}{(1+k_b)^1} + \ldots + \frac{I_n}{(1+k_b)^n} + \frac{M}{(1+k_b)^n}$$

$$= \sum_{t=1}^{n} \frac{I_t}{(1+k_b)^t} + \frac{M}{(1+k_b)^n}$$

$$= \sum_{t=1}^{5} \frac{\$120}{(1+.12)^t} + \frac{\$1{,}000}{(1+.12)^5} = \$1{,}000$$

Using present value tables, we have:

$$V_b = \$120\,(PVIFA_{12\%,5yr}) + \$1{,}000\,(PVIF_{12\%,5yr})$$
$$V_b = \$120(3.605) + \$1{,}000(.567)$$
$$= \$432.60 + \$567.00$$
$$= \$999.60 \cong \$1{,}000.00$$

If, however, the investor's required rate of return increases from 12 percent to 15 percent, the value of the bond would decrease to \$899.24, computed as follows:

$$V_b = \$120\,(PVIFA_{15\%,5yr}) + \$1{,}000(PVIF_{15\%,5yr})$$
$$V_b = \$120(3.352) + \$1{,}000(.497)$$
$$= \$402.24 + \$497.00$$
$$= \$899.24$$

On the other hand, if the investor's required rate of return decreases to 9 percent, the bond would increase in value to \$1,116.80:

$$V_b = \$120\,(PVIFA_{9\%,5yr}) + \$1{,}000(PVIF_{9\%,5yr})$$
$$V_b = \$120(3.890) + \$1{,}000(.650)$$
$$= \$466.80 + \$650.00$$
$$= \$1{,}116.80$$

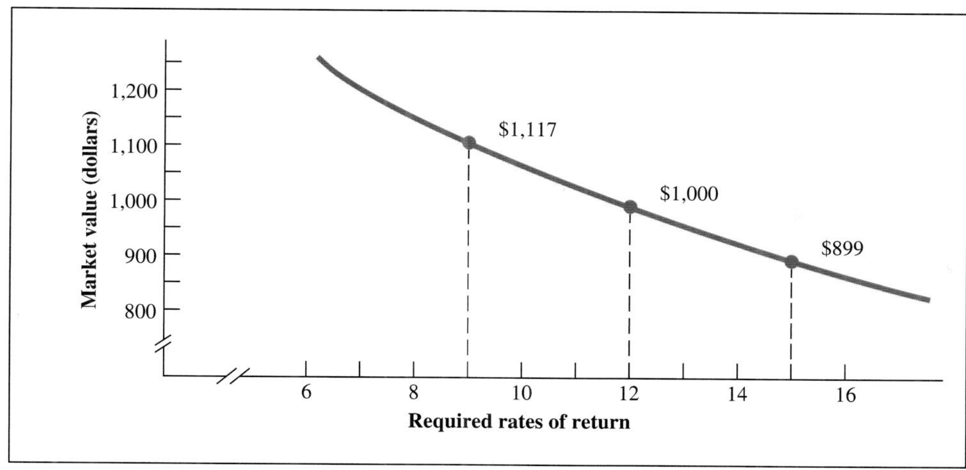


**FIGURE 7-3**
Value and Required Rates for a 5-Year Bond at 12 Percent Coupon Rate

This inverse relationship between the investor's required rate of return and the value of a bond is presented in Figure 7-3. Clearly, as an investor demands a higher rate of return, the value of the bond decreases. Because the interest payments and par value are fixed, the higher rate of return the investor desires can be achieved only by paying less for the bond. Conversely, a lower required rate of return yields a higher market value for the bond.

Changes in bond prices represent an element of uncertainty for the bond investor as well as the financial manager. If the current interest rate (required rate of return) changes, the price of the bond also fluctuates. An increase in interest rates causes the bondholder to incur a loss in market value. Because future interest rates and the resulting bond value cannot be predicted with certainty, a bond investor is exposed to the risk of changing values as interest rates vary. This risk has come to be known as **interest-rate risk.**

**Interest-rate risk**
The variability in a bond's value (risk) caused by changing interest rates.

## Second Relationship

The market value of a bond will be less than the par value if the investor's required rate is above the coupon interest rate; but it will be valued above par value if the investor's required rate of return is below the coupon interest rate.

Using the previous example, we observed that:

1. The bond has a *market* value of $1,000, equal to the par or maturity value, when the investor's required rate of return equals the 12 percent coupon interest rate. In other words, if

   *required rate* = *coupon rate,* then *market value* = *par value*
   12% = 12%, then $1,000 = $1,000

2. When the required rate is 15 percent, which exceeds the 12 percent coupon rate, the market value falls below par value to $899.24; that is, if

   *required rate* > *coupon rate,* then *market value* < *par value*
   15% > 12%, then $899.24 < $1,000

In this case, the bond sells at a discount below par value; thus it is called a **discount bond.**

**Discount bond**
A bond that is selling below its par value.

**TABLE 7-2**
Values Relative to Maturity Dates

| | Market Value If Maturity Is: | | |
|---|---|---|---|
| **Required Rate** | **5 Years** | **2 Years** | **Change in Value** |
| 9% | $1,116.80 | $1,053.08 | −$63.72 |
| 12 | 1,000.00 | 1,000.00 | .00 |
| 15 | 899.24 | 951.12 | 51.88 |

3. When the required rate is 9 percent, or less than the 12 percent coupon rate, the market value, $1,116.80, exceeds the bond's par value. In this instance, if

*required rate* < *coupon rate,* then *market value* > *par value*

9% < 12%, then $1,116.80 > $1,000

**Premium bond**
A bond that is selling above its par value.

The bond is now selling at a premium above par value; thus it is a **premium bond.**

## Third Relationship

As the maturity date approaches, the market value of a bond approaches its par value.

Continuing to draw from our example, the bond has 5 years remaining until the maturity date. The bond sells at a discount below par value ($899.24) when the required rate is 15 percent; it sells at a premium above par value ($1,116.80) when the required rate is only 9 percent.

In addition to knowing value today, an investor would also be interested in knowing how these values would change over time, assuming no change in the current interest rates. For example, how will these values change when only 2 years remain until maturity rather than 5 years? Table 7-2 shows (1) the values with 5 years remaining to maturity, (2) the values as recomputed with only 2 years left until the bonds mature, and (3) the changes in values between the 5-year bonds and the 2-year bonds. The following conclusions can be drawn from these results:

1. The premium bond sells for less as maturity approaches. The price decreases from $1,116.80 to $1,053.08 over the 3 years.
2. The discount bond sells for more as maturity approaches. The price increases from $899.24 to $951.12 over the 3 years.

The change in prices over the entire life of the bond is shown in Figure 7-4. The graph clearly demonstrates that the value of a bond, either a premium or a discount bond, approaches par value as the maturity date becomes closer in time.

## Fourth Relationship

Long-term bonds have greater interest rate risk than do short-term bonds.

As already noted, a change in current interest rates (required rate of return) causes a change in the market value of a bond. However, the impact on value is greater for long-term bonds than it is for short-term bonds.

In Figure 7-3, we observed the effect of interest rate changes on a 5-year bond paying a 12 percent coupon interest rate. What if the bond did not mature until 10 years from today instead of 5 years? Would the changes in market value be the same? Absolutely not. The changes in value would be more significant for the 10-year bond. For example, if we vary the current interest rates (the bondholder's required rate of return) from 9 percent to

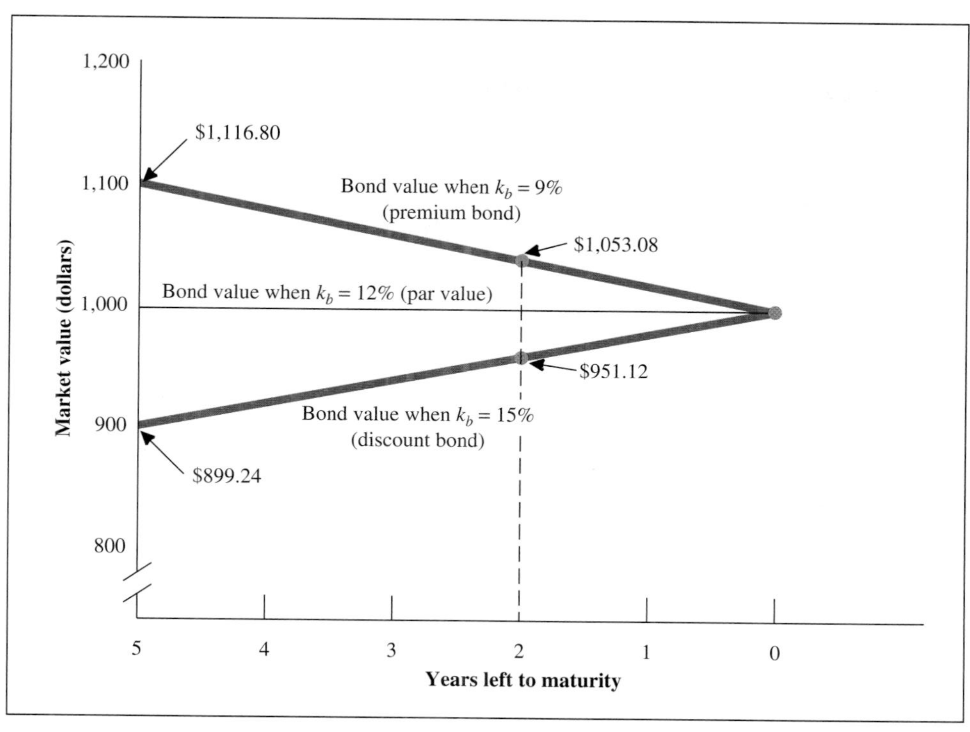


**FIGURE 7-4**
Value of a 12-percent Coupon Bond During the Life of the Bond

12 percent and then to 15 percent, as we did earlier with the 5-year bond, the values for both the 5-year and the 10-year bonds would be as follows:

| | Market Value for a 12% Coupon Rate Bond Maturing in | |
|---|---|---|
| **Required Rate** | **5 Years** | **10 Years** |
| 9% | $1,116.80 | $1,192.16 |
| 12 | 1,000.00 | 1,000.00 |
| 15 | 899.24 | 849.28 |

Using these values and the required rates, we can graph the changes in values for the two bonds relative to different interest rates. These comparisons are provided in Figure 7-5. The figure clearly illustrates that the price of the long-term bond (say, 10 years) is more responsive or sensitive to interest rate changes than the price of a short-term bond (say, 5 years).

The reason long-term bond prices fluctuate more than short-term bond prices in response to interest rate changes is simple. Assume an investor bought a 10-year bond yielding a 12 percent interest rate. If the current interest rate for bonds of similar risk increased to 15 percent, the investor would be locked into the lower rate for 10 years. If, on the other hand, a shorter-term bond had been purchased—say, one maturing in 2 years—the investor would have to accept the lower return for only 2 years and not the full 10 years. At the end of year 2, the investor would receive the maturity value of $1,000 and could buy a bond offering the higher 15 percent rate for the remaining 8 years. Thus, interest rate risk is determined, at least in part, by the length of time an investor is required to commit to an investment. However, the holder of a long-term bond may take some comfort from the fact that long-term interest rates are usually not as volatile as short-term rates. If the short-term

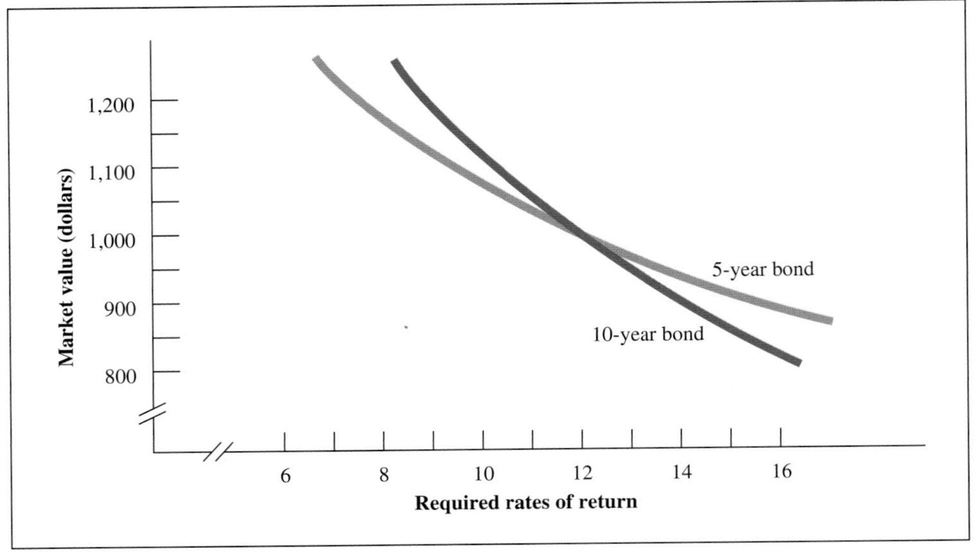


**FIGURE 7-5**
Market Values of a 5-Year and a 10-Year Bond at Different Required Rates

rate changed 1 percentage point, for example, it would not be unusual for the long-term rate to change only 0.3 percentage points.

## Fifth Relationship

The sensitivity of a bond's value to changing interest rates depends not only on the length of time to maturity, but also on the pattern of cash flows provided by the bond.

It is not at all unusual for two bonds with the same maturity to react differently to a change in interest rates. Consider two bonds, A and B, both with 10-year maturities. Although the bonds are similar in terms of maturity date and the contractual interest rate, the structure of the interest payments is different for each bond. Bond A pays $100 interest annually, with the $1,000 principal being repaid at the end of the tenth year. Bond B is a zero-coupon bond; it pays no interest until the bond matures. At that time, the bondholder receives $1,593.70 in interest plus $1,000 in principal. The value of both bonds, assuming a market interest rate (required rate of return) of 10 percent, is $1,000. However, if interest rates fell to 6 percent, bond A's market value would be $1,294, compared with $1,447 for bond B. Why the difference? Both bonds have the same maturity, and each promises the same 10 percent rate of return. The answer lies in the differences in their cash flow patterns. Bond B's cash flows are received in the more distant future on average than are the cash flows for bond A. Because a change in interest rates always has a greater impact on the present value of later cash flows than on earlier cash flows (due to the effects of compounding), bonds with cash flows coming later, on average, will be more sensitive to interest rate changes than will bonds with earlier cash flows. This phenomenon was recognized in 1938 by Macaulay, who devised the concept of duration.

**Duration**
A measure of how responsive a bond's price is to changing interest rates. Also, it is a weighted average time to maturity in which the weight attached to each year is the present value of the cash flow for that year.

The **duration** of a bond is simply a measure of the responsiveness of its price to a change in interest rates. The greater the relative percentage change in a bond price in response to a given percentage change in the interest rate, the longer the duration. In computing duration, we consider not only the maturity or term over which cash flows are received but also the time pattern of interim cash flows. Specifically, duration is a weighted average time to maturity in which the weight attached to each year is the present value of the cash flow for that year. A measurement of duration may be represented as follows:

$$\text{duration} = \frac{\displaystyle\sum_{t=1}^{n} \frac{tC_t}{(1 + k_b)^t}}{P_0} \qquad \textbf{(7-6)}$$

where $t$ = the year the cash flow is to be received

$n$ = the number of years to maturity
$C_t$ = the cash flow to be received in year $t$
$k_b$ = the bondholder's required rate of return
$P_0$ = the bond's present value

For our two bonds, A and B, duration would be calculated as follows:

$$\text{duration bond A} = \left( \frac{(1)\dfrac{\$100}{(1.1)^1} + (2)\dfrac{\$100}{(1.1)^2} + (3)\dfrac{\$100}{(1.1)^3} + \ldots + (9)\dfrac{\$100}{(1.1)^9} + (10)\dfrac{\$1{,}100}{(1.1)^{10}}}{\$1{,}000} \right)$$

$$= 6.759$$

$$\text{duration bond B} = \left( \frac{(1)\dfrac{0}{(1.1)^1} + (2)\dfrac{0}{(1.1)^2} + (3)\dfrac{0}{(1.1)^3} + \ldots + (9)\dfrac{0}{(1.1)^9} + (10)\dfrac{\$2{,}593.70}{(1.1)^{10}}}{\$1{,}000} \right)$$

$$= 10$$

Thus, although both bonds have the same maturity, 10 years, the zero coupon bond (bond B) is more sensitive to interest rate changes, as suggested by its higher duration, which in this instance equals its maturity. The lesson learned: in assessing a bond's sensitivity to changing interest rates, the bond's duration is the more appropriate measure, not the term to maturity.

## CONCEPT CHECK

1. Explain the relationship between bond value and investor's required rate of return.
2. As interest rates increase, why does the price of a long-term bond decrease more than the price of a short-term bond?
3. Why does a bond sell at a premium when the coupon rate is higher than the required rate of return, and vice versa?
4. As the maturity date of a bond approaches, what happens to the price of a discount bond? Is the result the same if the bond is a premium bond?
5. What bond characteristics influence the duration measurement? Why is duration the more appropriate measure of a bond's sensitivity to interest rates than term to maturity?

## HOW FINANCIAL MANAGERS USE THIS MATERIAL

To be effective as a financial manager, we must have a good understanding of the capital markets, where a company's bonds and stocks are issued and are bought and sold. The foregoing presentation has provided us the foundation to that understanding. Much of what has been said has been from an investor's perspective, but it is crucial that the financial manager see the "territory" from that perspective as well. Otherwise, the manager is likely to be blindsided by the markets. Also, many firms not only issue bonds, but also buy and sell bonds of other companies as well as the federal and state governments. The financial manager then becomes an investor in his or her own right.

## SUMMARY

Valuation is an important issue if we are to manage the company effectively. An understanding of the concepts and how to compute the value of a security underlie much of what we do in finance and in making correct decisions for the firm as a whole. Only if we know what matters to our investors can we maximize the firm's value.

OBJECTIVE 1 

There are a variety of types of bonds, including:

- Debentures
- Subordinated debentures
- Mortgage bonds
- Eurobonds
- Zero and very low coupon bonds
- Junk bonds

OBJECTIVE 2 

Some of the more popular terms and characteristics that you might hear about bonds include the following:

- Claims on assets and income
- Par value
- Coupon interest rate
- Maturity
- Indenture
- Current yield
- Bond ratings

OBJECTIVE 3 

Value is defined differently depending on the context. But for us, value is the present value of future cash flows expected to be received from an investment discounted at the investor's required rate of return.

OBJECTIVE 4 

Three basic factors determine an asset's value: (1) the amount and timing of future cash flows, (2) the riskiness of the cash flows, and (3) the investor's attitude about the risk.

OBJECTIVE 5 

The valuation process can be described as follows: It is assigning value to an asset by calculating the present value of its expected future cash flows using the investor's required rate of return as the discount rate. The investor's required rate of return, $k$, equals the risk-free rate of interest plus a risk premium to compensate the investor for assuming risk.

OBJECTIVE 6 

The value of a bond is the present value both of future interest to be received and the par or maturity value of the bond.

OBJECTIVE 7 

To measure the bondholder's expected rate of return, we find the discount rate that equates the present value of the future cash flows (interest and maturity value) with the current market price of the bond. The expected rate of return for a bond is also the rate of return the investor will earn if the bond is held to maturity, or the yield to maturity.

Five key relationships exist in bond valuation:

OBJECTIVE 8

1. A decrease in interest rates (required rates of return) will cause the value of a bond to increase; an interest rate increase will cause a decrease in value. The change in value caused by changing interest rates is called interest rate risk.
2. If the bondholder's required rate of return (current interest rate):
   a. Equals the coupon interest rate, the bond will sell at par, or maturity value.
   b. Exceeds the bond's coupon rate, the bond will sell below par value, or at a *discount*.
   c. Is less than the bond's coupon rate, the bond will sell above par value, or at a *premium*.
3. As a bond approaches maturity, the market price of the bond approaches the par value.
4. A bondholder owning a long-term bond is exposed to greater interest rate risk than one owning a short-term bond.
5. The sensitivity of a bond's value to interest rate changes is not only affected by the time to maturity, but also by the time pattern of interim cash flows, or its *duration*.

## KEY TERMS

**Bond, 212**
**Book value, 218**
**Coupon interest rate, 216**
**Current yield, 217**
**Debenture, 212**
**Discount bond, 229**
**Duration, 232**
**Efficient market, 219**
**Eurobonds, 213**
**Expected rate of return, 227**
**Indenture, 216**
**Interest-rate risk, 229**
**Intrinsic or economic value, 219**
**Junk or high yield bonds, 214**
**Liquidation value, 218**
**Market value, 219**
**Maturity, 216**
**Mortgage bond, 213**
**Opportunity cost of funds, 219**
**Par value of a bond, 216**
**Premium bond, 230**
**Subordinated debenture, 213**
**Yield to maturity, 227**
**Zero and very low coupon bonds, 213**

myPHLIP

Go To:
http://www.prenhall.com/keown
for downloads and current events associated with this chapter

## STUDY QUESTIONS

**7-1.** What are the basic differences among book value, liquidation value, market value, and intrinsic value?

**7-2.** What is a general definition of the intrinsic value of a security?

**7-3.** Explain the three factors that determine the intrinsic or economic value of an asset.

**7-4.** Explain the relationship between an investor's required rate of return and the value of a security.

**7-5.** **a.** How does a bond's par value differ from its market value?
**b.** Explain the difference between a bond's coupon interest rate, the current yield, and a bondholder's required rate of return.

**7-6.** Describe the bondholder's claim on the firm's assets and income.

**7-7.** What factors determine a bond's rating? Why is the rating important to the firm's manager?

**7-8.** Distinguish between debentures and mortgage bonds.

**7-9.** Define (a) Eurobonds, (b) zero coupon bonds, and (c) junk bonds.

**7-10.** Define the bondholder's expected rate of return.

**7-11.** How does the market value of a bond differ from its par value when the coupon interest rate does not equal the bondholder's required rate of return?

**7-12.** Differentiate between a premium bond and discount bond. What happens to the premium or discount for a given bond over time?

**7-13.** Why is the value of a long-term bond more sensitive to a change in interest rates than that of a short-term bond?

**7-14.** Explain duration.

## SELF-TEST PROBLEMS

**ST-1.** (*Bond valuation*) Trico bonds have a coupon rate of 8 percent, a par value of $1,000, and will mature in 20 years. If you require a return of 7 percent, what price would you be willing to pay for the bond? What happens if you pay *more* for the bond? What happens if you pay *less* for the bond?

**ST-2.** (*Bond valuation*) Sunn Co.'s bonds, maturing in 7 years, pay 8 percent on a $1,000 face value. However, interest is paid semiannually. If your required rate of return is 10 percent, what is the value of the bond? How would your answer change if the interest were paid annually?

**ST-3.** (*Bondholder's expected rate of return*) Sharp Co. bonds are selling in the market for $1,045. These 15-year bonds pay 7 percent interest annually on a $1,000 par value. If they are purchased at the market price, what is the expected rate of return?

**ST-4.** (*Duration*) Calculate the value and the duration for the following bonds:

| Bond | Years to Maturity | Annual Interest | Maturity Value |
|---|---|---|---|
| Argile | 10 | $80 | $1,000 |
| Terathon | 15 | 65 | 1,000 |

The required rate of return is 8 percent.

## STUDY PROBLEMS (SET A)

**7-1A.** (*Bond valuation*) Calculate the value of a bond that expects to mature in 12 years and has a $1,000 face value. The coupon interest rate is 8 percent and the investor's required rate of return is 12 percent.

**7-2A.** (*Bond valuation*) Enterprise, Inc., bonds have a 9 percent coupon rate. The interest is paid semiannually and the bonds mature in 8 years. Their par value is $1,000. If your required rate of return is 8 percent, what is the value of the bond? What is its value if the interest is paid annually?

**7-3A.** (*Bondholder's expected rate of return*) The market price is $900 for a 10-year bond ($1,000 par value) that pays 8 percent interest (4 percent semiannually). What is the bond's expected rate of return?

**7-4A.** (*Bondholder's expected rate of return*) Exxon 20-year bonds pay 9 percent interest annually on a $1,000 par value. If bonds sell at $945, what is the bond's expected rate of return?

**7-5A.** (*Bondholder's expected rate of return*) Zenith Co.'s bonds mature in 12 years and pay 7 percent interest annually. If you purchase the bonds for $1,150, what is your expected rate of return?

**7-6A.** (*Bond valuation*) National Steel 15-year, $1,000 par value bonds pay 8 percent interest annually. The market price of the bonds is $1,085, and your required rate of return is 10 percent.

- **a.** Compute the bond's expected rate of return.
- **b.** Determine the value of the bond to you, given your required rate of return.
- **c.** Should you purchase the bond?

**7-7A.** (*Bond valuation*) You own a bond that pays $100 in annual interest, with a $1,000 par value. It matures in 15 years. Your required rate of return is 12 percent.

- **a.** Calculate the value of the bond.
- **b.** How does the value change if your required rate of return (*i*) increases to 15 percent or (*ii*) decreases to 8 percent?

**c.** Explain the implications of your answers in part (b) as they relate to interest rate risk, premium bonds, and discount bonds.

**d.** Assume that the bond matures in 5 years instead of 15 years. Recompute your answers in part (b).

**e.** Explain the implications of your answers in part (d) as they relate to interest rate risk, premium bonds, and discount bonds.

**7-8A.** (*Bondholder's expected return*) Abner Corporation's bonds mature in 15 years and pay 9 percent interest annually. If you purchase the bonds for $1,250, what is your expected rate of return?

**7-9A.** (*Bond valuation*) Telink Corporation bonds pay $110 in annual interest, with a $1,000 par value. The bonds mature in 20 years. Your required rate of return is 9 percent.

**a.** Calculate the value of the bond.

**b.** How does the value change if (*i*) your required rate of return (*k*) increases to 12 percent or (*ii*) decreases to 6 percent?

**c.** Interpret your findings in parts (a) and (b).

**7-10A.** (*Duration*) Calculate the value and the duration for the following bonds:

| Bond | Years to Maturity | Annual Interest | Maturity Value |
|---|---|---|---|
| P | 5 | $100 | $1,000 |
| Q | 5 | 70 | 1,000 |
| R | 10 | 120 | 1,000 |
| S | 10 | 80 | 1,000 |
| T | 15 | 65 | 1,000 |

Your required rate of return is 8 percent.

## INTEGRATIVE PROBLEM

Following you will find data on $1,000 par value bonds issued by Bank of America, Hilton Hotels, and Time Warner at the end of 2000. Assume you are thinking about buying these bonds as of January 2001. Answer the following questions for each of these bonds:

1. Calculate the values of the bonds if your required rates of return are as follows: Bank of America, 6 percent; Hilton Hotels, 9 percent; and Time Warner, 8 percent:

| | Bank of America | Hilton Hotels | Time Warner |
|---|---|---|---|
| Coupon interest rates | 7.8% | 7.5% | 7.975% |
| Years to maturity | 10 | 17 | 4 |

2. In December 2000, the bonds were selling for the following amounts:

| | |
|---|---|
| Bank of America | $1,030 |
| Hilton Hotels | $ 973 |
| Time Warner | $1,035 |

   What were the expected rates of return for each bond?

3. How would the values of the bonds change if (*i*) your required rate of return (*k*) increases 3 percentage points or (*ii*) your required rate of return (*k*) decreases 3 percentage points?
4. Explain the implications of your answers in questions 2 and 3 as they relate to interest rate risk, premium bonds, and discount bonds.
5. Compute the duration for each of the bonds. Interpret your results.
6. What are some of the things you can conclude from these computations?
7. Should you buy the bonds? Explain.

## STUDY PROBLEMS (SET B)

**7-1B.** (*Bond valuation*) Calculate the value of a bond that expects to mature in 10 years and has a $1,000 face value. The coupon interest rate is 9 percent and the investor's required rate of return is 15 percent.

**7-2B.** (*Bond valuation*) Pybus, Inc., bonds have a 10 percent coupon rate. The interest is paid semiannually and the bonds mature in 11 years. Their par value is $1,000. If your required rate of return is 9 percent, what is the value of the bond? What is it if the interest is paid annually?

**7-3B.** (*Bondholder's expected return*) A bond's market price is $950. It has a $1,000 par value, will mature in 8 years, and pays 9 percent interest (4.5 percent semiannually). What is your expected rate of return?

**7-4B.** (*Bondholder's expected rate of return*) Doisneau 20-year bonds pay 10 percent interest annually on a $1,000 par value. If you buy the bonds at $975, what is your expected rate of return?

**7-5B.** (*Bondholder's expected return*) Hoyden Co.'s bonds mature in 15 years and pay 8 percent interest annually. If you purchase the bonds for $1,175, what is your expected rate of return?

**7-6B.** (*Bond valuation*) Fingen 14-year, $1,000 par value bonds pay 9 percent interest annually. The market price of the bonds is $1,100 and your required rate of return is 10 percent.

**a.** Compute the bond's expected rate of return.
**b.** Determine the value of the bond to you, given your required rate of return.
**c.** Should you purchase the bond?

**7-7B.** (*Bond valuation*) Arizona Public Utilities issued a bond that pays $80 in interest, with a $1,000 par value. It matures in 20 years. Your required rate of return is 7 percent.

**a.** Calculate the value of the bond.
**b.** How does the value change if your required rate of return (*i*) increases to 10 percent or (*ii*) decreases to 6 percent?
**c.** Explain the implications of your answers in part (b) as they relate to interest rate risk, premium bonds, and discount bonds.
**d.** Assume that the bond matures in 10 years instead of 20 years. Recompute your answers in part (b).
**e.** Explain the implications of your answers in part (d) as they relate to interest rate risk, premium bonds, and discount bonds.

**7-8B.** (*Bondholder's expected return*) Zebner Corporation's bonds mature in 14 years and pay 7 percent interest annually. If you purchase the bonds for $1,110, what is your expected rate of return?

**7-9B.** (*Bond valuation*) Visador Corporation bonds pay $70 in annual interest, with a $1,000 par value. The bonds mature in 17 years. Your required rate of return is 8.5 percent.

**a.** Calculate the value of the bond.
**b.** How does the value change your required rate of return (*k*) if (*i*) increases to 11 percent or (*ii*) decreases to 6 percent?
**c.** Interpret your finding in parts (a) and (b).

**7-10B.** (*Duration*) Calculate the value and the duration for the following bonds:

| Bond | Years to Maturity | Annual Interest | Maturity Value |
|---|---|---|---|
| A | 5 | $90 | $1,000 |
| B | 5 | 60 | 1,000 |
| C | 10 | 120 | 1,000 |
| D | 15 | 90 | 1,000 |
| E | 15 | 75 | 1,000 |

Your required rate of return is 7 percent.

## SELF-TEST SOLUTIONS

**ST-1.**

$$\text{Value } (V_b) = \sum_{t=1}^{20} \frac{\$80}{(1.07)^t} + \frac{\$1{,}000}{(1.07)^{20}}$$

Thus,

$$\begin{aligned} \text{present value of interest:} \quad \$80(10.594) &= \$\ \ 847.52 \\ \text{present value of par value:} \quad \$1{,}000(0.258) &= \underline{\ \ 258.00} \\ \text{Value } (V_b) &= \underline{\underline{\$1{,}105.52}} \end{aligned}$$

If you pay more for the bond, your required rate of return will not be satisfied. In other words, by paying an amount for the bond that exceeds $1,105.52, the expected rate of return for the bond is less than the required rate of return. If you have the opportunity to pay less for the bond, the expected rate of return exceeds the 7 percent required rate of return.

**ST-2.** If interest is paid semiannually:

$$\text{Value } (V_b) = \sum_{t=1}^{14} \frac{\$40}{(1 + 0.05)^t} + \frac{\$1{,}000}{(1 + 0.05)^{14}}$$

Thus,

$$\begin{aligned} \$40(9.899) &= \$395.96 \\ \$1{,}000(0.505) &= \underline{\ \ 505.00} \\ \text{value } (V_b) &= \underline{\underline{\$900.96}} \end{aligned}$$

If interest is paid annually:

$$\text{Value } (V_b) = \sum_{t=1}^{7} \frac{\$80}{(1.10)^t} + \frac{\$1{,}000}{(1.10)^7}$$

$$V_b = \$80\ (4.868) + \$1{,}000\ (0.513)$$

$$V_b = \$902.44$$

**ST-3.**

$$\$1{,}045 = \sum_{t=1}^{15} \frac{\$70}{(1 + \bar{k}_b)^t} + \frac{\$1{,}000}{(1 + \bar{k}_b)^{15}}$$

At 6%: $70(9.712) + $1,000(0.417) = $1,096.84

At 7%: Value must equal $1,000.

Interpolation:

$$\text{Expected rate of return: } \bar{k} = 6\% + \frac{\$51.84}{\$96.84}(1\%) = 6.54\%$$

**CALCULATOR SOLUTION**

| Data Input | Function Key |
|---|---|
| 15 | N |
| 70 | +/− PMT |
| 1,000 | +/− FV |
| 1,045 | PV |
| **Function Key** | **Answer** |
| CPT I/Y | 6.52 |

**ST-4.**

| | Bond | | | |
|---|---|---|---|---|
| | Argile $1,000 (value) | | Terathon $872 (value) | |
| Year | $C_t$ | $(t)(PV(C_t))$ | $C_t$ | $(t)(PV(C_t))$ |
| 1 | $ 80 | $ 74 | $ 65 | $ 60 |
| 2 | 80 | 137 | 65 | 111 |
| 3 | 80 | 191 | 65 | 155 |
| 4 | 80 | 235 | 65 | 191 |
| 5 | 80 | 272 | 65 | 221 |
| 6 | 80 | 302 | 65 | 246 |
| 7 | 80 | 327 | 65 | 265 |
| 8 | 80 | 346 | 65 | 281 |
| 9 | 80 | 360 | 65 | 293 |
| 10 | 1,080 | 5,002 | 65 | 301 |
| 11 | | | 65 | 307 |
| 12 | | | 65 | 310 |
| 13 | | | 65 | 311 |
| 14 | | | 65 | 310 |
| 15 | | | 1,065 | 5,036 |
| Sum of $(t)(PV(C_t))$ | | $7,246 | | $8,398 |
| Duration | | 7.25 | | 9.63 |

# STOCK VALUATION

If you had invested $100 in Harley-Davidson, Inc., common stock at the time its stock began trading publicly on July 8, 1986, and reinvested all dividends, the value of your investment on December 31, 2000, would have been approximately $11,980. Compared to the average share price for the firms included in the Standard & Poor's 500, that is excellent performance, as shown in the following graph. ● In this chapter, we look closely at common stock and what determines the value investors think a stock is worth.

Year-end market value of $100 invested on July 8, 1986

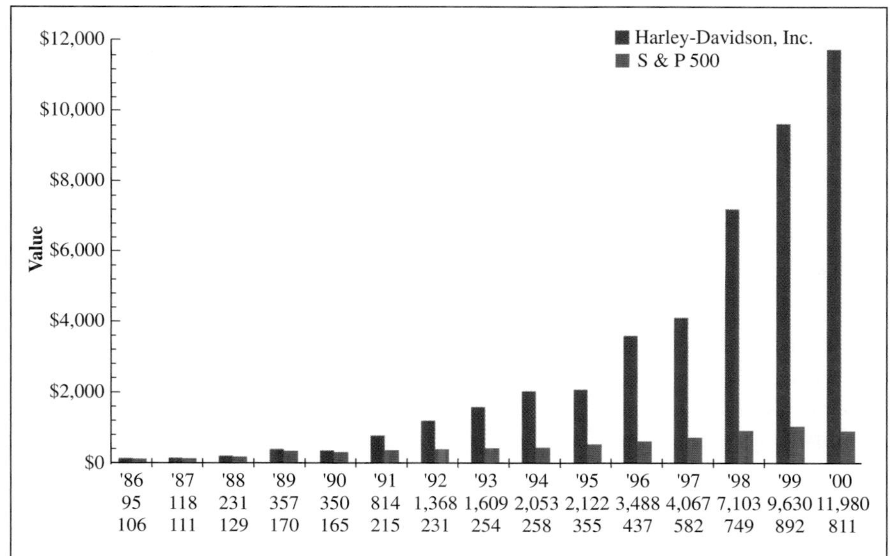


**LEARNING OBJECTIVES**

After reading this chapter, you should be able to

1. Identify the basic characteristics and features of preferred stock.
2. Value preferred stock.
3. Identify the basic characteristics and features of common stock.
4. Value common stock.
5. Calculate a stock's expected rate of return.

In Chapter 7, we developed a general concept about valuation, where economic value was defined as the present value of the expected future cash flows generated by the asset. We then applied that concept to valuing bonds.

CHAPTER PREVIEW

We now give our attention to valuing stocks, both preferred stock and common stock. As already noted at the outset of our study of finance and on several occasions since, the financial manager's objective should be to maximize the value of the firm's common stock. Thus, we need to understand what determines stock value.

As we have done in all other chapters, it is important to begin by identifying the principles that are important in understanding the topic to be studied—in this case, the basic considerations in issuing and valuing stock. These principles are as follows: **Principle 1: The Risk-Return Trade-Off—We won't take on additional risk unless we expect to be compensated with additional return; Principle 2: The Time Value of Money—A dollar received today is worth more than a dollar received in the future; Principle 3: Cash—Not Profits—Is King; Principle 7: The Agency Problem—Managers won't work for the owners unless it's in their best interest.**

The first three principles relate to our definition of value—present value of cash flows. The last principle, Principle 7, indicates that the value of a firm's stock is in part dictated by the willingness of management to work in the best interest of the owners, which for most large companies are not the same group.

## FEATURES AND TYPES OF PREFERRED STOCK

OBJECTIVE 1 

**Preferred stock**
A hybrid security with characteristics of both common stock and bonds. It is similar to common stock because it has no fixed maturity date, the nonpayment of dividends does not bring on bankruptcy, and dividends are not deductible for tax purposes. Preferred stock is similar to bonds in that dividends are limited in amount.

**Preferred stock** is often referred to as a hybrid security because it has many characteristics of both common stock and bonds. Preferred stock is similar to common stock in that it has no fixed maturity date, the nonpayment of dividends does not bring on bankruptcy, and dividends are not deductible for tax purposes. On the other hand, preferred stock is similar to bonds in that dividends are fixed in amount.

The size of the preferred stock dividend is generally fixed either as a dollar amount or as a percentage of the par value. For example, Texas Power and Light has issued $4 preferred stock, whereas Toledo Edison has some 4.25 percent preferred stock outstanding. The par value on the Toledo Edison preferred stock is $100; hence each share pays 4.25% × 100, or $4.25 in dividends annually. Because these dividends are fixed, preferred stockholders do not share in the residual earnings of the firm but are limited to their stated annual dividend.

In examining preferred stock, we will first discuss several features common to almost all preferred stock. Next we will investigate features less frequently included and take a brief look at methods of retiring preferred stock. We will then learn how to value preferred stock.

Although each issue of preferred stock is unique, a number of characteristics are common to almost all issues. Some of these more frequent traits include:

- multiple classes of preferred stock
- preferred stock's claim on assets and income
- cumulative dividends
- protective provisions
- convertibility

Other features that are less common include:

- adjustable rates
- participation
- payment-in-kind (PIK)

In addition, there are provisions frequently used to retire an issue of preferred stock, including the ability of the firm to call its preferred stock or to use a sinking-fund provision to repurchase preferred shares. All of these features are presented in the discussion that follows.

## Multiple Classes

If a company desires, it can issue more than one series or class of preferred stock, and each class can have different characteristics. In fact, it is quite common for firms that issue preferred stock to issue more than one series. For example, Philadelphia Electric has 13 different issues of preferred stock outstanding. These issues can be further differentiated in that some are convertible into common stock and others are not, and they have varying priority status regarding assets in the event of bankruptcy.

## Claim on Assets and Income

Preferred stock has priority over common stock with regard to claims on assets in the case of bankruptcy. If a firm is liquidated, the preferred stock claim is honored after that of bonds and before that of common stock. Multiple issues of preferred stock may be given an order of priority. Preferred stock also has a claim on income prior to common stock. That is, the firm must pay its preferred stock dividends before it pays common stock dividends. Thus, in terms of risk, preferred stock is safer than common stock because it has a prior claim on assets and income. However, it is riskier than long-term debt because its claims on assets and income come after those of bonds.

## Cumulative Feature

Most preferred stocks carry a cumulative feature. **Cumulative preferred stock** requires all past unpaid preferred stock dividends be paid before any common stock dividends are declared. This feature provides some degree of protection for the preferred shareholder. Without a cumulative feature, management might be tempted not to pay preferred dividends when common stock dividends were passed. Because preferred stock does not have the dividend enforcement power of interest from bonds, the cumulative feature is necessary to protect the rights of preferred stockholders.

**Cumulative preferred stock**
Requires all past unpaid preferred stock dividends be paid before any common stock dividends are declared.

## Protective Provisions

In addition to the cumulative feature, protective provisions are common to preferred stock. These **protective provisions** generally allow for voting rights in the event of nonpayment of dividends, or they restrict the payment of common stock dividends if sinking-fund payments are not met or if the firm is in financial difficulty. In effect, the protective features included with preferred stock are similar to the restrictive provisions included with long-term debt.

**Protective provisions**
Provisions for preferred stock that are included in the terms of the issue to protect the investor's interest.

To examine typical protective provisions, consider Tenneco Corporation and Reynolds Metals preferred stocks. The Tenneco preferred stock has a protective provision that provides preferred stockholders with voting rights whenever six quarterly dividends are in arrears. At that point, the preferred shareholders are given the power to elect a majority of the board of directors. The Reynolds Metals preferred stock includes a protective provision that precludes the payment of common stock dividends during any period in which the preferred stock sinking fund is in default. Both provisions, which yield protection beyond that provided by the cumulative provision and thereby reduce shareholder risk, are desirable. Given these protective provisions for the investor, they reduce the cost of preferred stock to the issuing firm.

## Convertibility

Much of the preferred stock that is issued today is **convertible** at the discretion of the holder into a predetermined number of shares of common stock. In fact, today about one-third of all

**Convertible preferred stock**
Convertible preferred stock allows the preferred stockholder to convert the preferred stock into a predetermined number of shares of common stock, if he or she so chooses.

preferred stock issued has a convertibility feature. The convertibility feature is, of course, desirable to the investor and thus reduces the cost of the preferred stock to the issuer.

## Adjustable Rate Preferred Stock

**Adjustable rate preferred stock**
Preferred stock intended to provide investors with some protection against wide swings in the stock value that occur when interest rates move up and down. The dividend rate changes along with prevailing interest rates.

**Adjustable rate preferred stock** was developed to provide investors with some protection against wide swings in principal that occur when interest rates move up and down. With this kind of preferred stock, quarterly dividends fluctuate with interest rates under a formula that ties the dividend payment at either a premium or discount to the highest of (1) the 3-month Treasury bill rate, (2) the 10-year Treasury bond rate, or (3) the 20-year Treasury bond rate. For instance, BankAmerica has adjustable rate preferred stock, where the dividend rate is adjusted every 3 months to 2 percentage points below the highest of the interest rates on three U.S. Treasury securities, but no lower than 6.5 percent and no greater than 14.5 percent.

Although adjustable rate preferred stock allows dividend rates to be tied to the rates on Treasury securities, it also provides a maximum and a minimum level to which they can climb or fall, called the *dividend rate band.* The purpose of allowing the dividend rate on this preferred stock to fluctuate is, of course, to minimize the fluctuation in the value of the preferred stock. In times of high and fluctuating interest rates, this is a very appealing feature indeed.

**Auction rate preferred stock**
Variable rate preferred stock in which the dividend rate is set by an auction process.

Another type of adjustable rate preferred stock is **auction rate preferred stock.** With this stock, the dividend rate is set every 49 days by an auction process. At each auction, buyers and sellers place bids for shares, specifying the yield they are willing to accept for the next 7-week period. The yield is then set at the lowest level necessary to match buyers and sellers. As a result, the yield offered on auction rate preferred stock accurately reflects current interest rates, while keeping the market price of these securities at par.

## Participation

**Participating preferred stock**
Allows the preferred stockholder to participate in earnings beyond the payment of the stated dividend.

Although *participating* features are infrequent in preferred stock, their inclusion can greatly affect its desirability to investors and cost to the issuing firm. The **participation feature** allows the preferred stockholder to participate in earnings beyond the payment of the stated dividend. This is usually done in accordance with some set formula. For example, Borden Series A preferred stock currently provides for a dividend of *no less than* 60¢ per share, to be determined by the board of directors.[1] Preferred stock of this sort actually resembles common stock as much as it does normal preferred stock. Although a participating feature is certainly desirable from the point of view of the investor, it is infrequently included in preferred stock.

## PIK Preferred

**PIK preferred stock**
Investors receive no dividends initially; they merely get more preferred stock, which in turn pays dividends in even more preferred stock.

One byproduct of the acquisition boom of the late 1980s was the creation of payment-in-kind (PIK) preferred stock. With **PIK preferred,** investors receive no dividends initially; they merely get more preferred stock, which in turn pays dividends in even more preferred stock. Eventually (usually after 5 or 6 years if all goes well for the issuing company), cash dividends should replace the preferred stock dividends. Needless to say, the issuing firm has to offer hefty dividends, generally ranging from 12 percent to 18 percent, to entice investors to purchase PIK preferred.

[1]During the early 1990s, Borden ran into financial problems. By fall of 1994, the firm was being restructured financially and later acquired, which altered some of the agreements with investors. As a result, the Borden Series A preferred shareholders did not participate in earnings in the ensuing years.

## Retirement Features

Although preferred stock does not have a set maturity associated with it, issuing firms generally provide for some method of retirement. If preferred stock could not be retired, issuing firms could not take advantage of falling interest rates. In other words, if interest rates decline, a financial manager would want to retire (pay off) the preferred stock that is currently outstanding and issue new debt or preferred stock at the lower rate. Without the retirement feature, the manager would be unable to do so.

Most preferred stock has some type of **call provision** associated with it. A call provision allows a company to repurchase its preferred stock (or bonds) from holders at stated prices over a given time period. In fact, the Securities and Exchange Commission discourages the issuance of preferred stock without some call provision. The SEC has taken this stance on the grounds that if a method of retirement is not provided, the issuing firm will not be able to retire its preferred stock if interest rates fall.

**Call provision**
Lets the company buy its preferred stock back from the investor, usually at a premium price above the stock's par value.

The call feature on preferred stock usually involves an initial premium above the par value or issuing price of the preferred of approximately 10 percent. Then over time, the call premium generally falls. By setting the initial call price above the initial issue price and allowing it to decline slowly over time, the firm protects the investor from an early call that carries no premium. A call provision also allows the financial manager to plan the retirement of its preferred stock at predetermined prices.

A **sinking fund** provision requires the firm periodically to set aside an amount of money for the retirement of its preferred stock. This money is then used to purchase the preferred stock in the open market or through the use of the call provision, whichever method is cheaper. Although preferred stock does not have a maturity date associated with it, the use of a call provision in addition to a sinking fund can effectively create a maturity date. For example, a Quaker Oats issue of preferred stock has an annual sinking fund, operating between the years 1981 and 2005, which requires the annual elimination of a minimum of 20,000 shares and a maximum of 40,000 shares. The minimum payments are designed so that the entire issue will be retired by the year 2005. If any sinking fund payments are made above the minimum amount, the issue will be retired prior to 2005. Thus, the size of the outstanding issue decreases each year after 1981.

**Sinking fund**
A fund that requires the firm periodically to set aside an amount of money for the retirement of its preferred stock. This money is then used to purchase the preferred stock in the open market or through the use of the call provision, whichever method is cheaper.

## VALUING PREFERRED STOCK

OBJECTIVE 2

As already explained, the owner of preferred stock generally receives a *constant income* from the investment in each period. However, the return from preferred stock comes in the form of *dividends* rather than *interest*. In addition, whereas bonds generally have a specific maturity date, most preferred stocks are perpetuities (nonmaturing). In this instance, finding the value (present value) of preferred stock, $V_{ps}$, with a level cash flow stream continuing indefinitely, may best be explained by an example.

### EXAMPLE

Consider AT&T's preferred stock issue. In the same way that we valued bonds in Chapter 7, we will use a three-step valuation procedure.

**Step 1:** Estimate the amount and timing of the receipt of the future cash flows the preferred stock is expected to provide. AT&T's preferred stock pays an annual dividend of $3.64. The shares do not have a maturity date; that is, they go to perpetuity.

**Step 2:** Evaluate the riskiness of the preferred stock's future dividends and determine the investor's required rate of return. For AT&T, assume that the investor's required rate of return is 7 percent.[2]

**Step 3:** Calculate the economic or intrinsic value of the share of preferred stock, which is the present value of the expected dividends discounted at the investor's required rate of return. The valuation model for a share of preferred stock ($V_{ps}$) is therefore defined as follows:

$$V_{ps} = \frac{\text{dividend in year 1}}{(1 + \text{required rate of return})^1} + \frac{\text{dividend in year 2}}{(1 + \text{required rate of return})^2} + \ldots + \frac{\text{dividend in infinity}}{(1 + \text{required rate of return})^\infty}$$

$$= \frac{D_1}{(1 + k_{ps})^1} + \frac{D_2}{(1 + k_{ps})^2} + \ldots + \frac{D_\infty}{(1 + k_{ps})^\infty}$$

$$V_{ps} = \sum_{t=1}^{\infty} \frac{D_t}{(1 + k_{ps})^t} \quad \textbf{(8-1)}$$

Because the dividends for preferred stock represent a perpetuity—they continue indefinitely—equation 8-1 can be reduced to the following relationship:[3]

$$V_{ps} = \frac{\text{annual dividend}}{\text{required rate of return}} = \frac{D}{k_{ps}} \quad \textbf{(8-2)}$$

Equation 8-2 represents the present value of an infinite stream of constant cash flows. We can determine the value of the AT&T preferred stock, using equation 8-2, as follows:

$$V_{ps} = \frac{D}{k_{ps}} = \frac{\$3.64}{.07} = \$52$$

[2]How do we know the investor's required rate of return is 7 percent? Return to Chapter 6 for an explanation of how we ascertain an investor's required rate of return.

[3]To verify this result, consider the following equation:

(i) $$V_{ps} = \frac{D_1}{(1 + k_{ps})^1} + \frac{D_2}{(1 + k_{ps})^2} + \ldots + \frac{D_n}{(1 + k_{ps})^n}$$

If we multiply both sides of this equation by $(1 + k_{ps})$, we have

(ii) $$V_{ps}(1 + k_{ps}) = D_1 + \frac{D_2}{(1 + k_{ps})} + \ldots + \frac{D_n}{(1 + k_{ps})^{n-1}}$$

Subtracting (i) from (ii) yields

$$V_{ps}(1 + k_{ps} - 1) = D_1 + \frac{D_n}{(1 + k_{ps})^n}$$

As $n$ approaches infinity, $D_n/(1 + k_{ps})^n$ approaches zero. Consequently,

$$V_{ps}k_{ps} = D_1 \text{ and } V_{ps} = \frac{D_1}{k_{ps}}$$

Because $D_1 = D_2 = \ldots = D_n$, we need not designate the year. Therefore,

(iii) $$V_{ps} = \frac{D}{k_{ps}}$$

In summary, the value of a preferred stock is the present value of all future dividends. But because most preferred stocks are nonmaturing—the dividends continue to infinity—we therefore have to come up with another way for finding value as represented by equation 8-2.

**RELATE TO THE BIG PICTURE**

Valuing preferred stock relies on three of our principles presented in Chapter 1, namely:

- **Principle 1: The Risk-Return Trade-Off—We won't take on additional risk unless we expect to be compensated with additional return.**
- **Principle 2: The Time Value of Money—A dollar received today is worth more than a dollar received in the future.**
- **Principle 3: Cash—Not Profits—Is King.**

As we have already observed with bonds, determining the economic worth or value of an asset always relies on these three principles. Without them, we would have no basis for explaining value. With them, we can know that the amount and timing of cash, not earnings, drives value. Also, we must be rewarded for taking risk; otherwise, we will not invest.

**CONCEPT CHECK**

1. What features of preferred stock are different from bonds?
2. What provisions are available to protect a preferred stockholder?
3. What cash flows associated with preferred stock are included in the valuation model (equation 8-1)? Why is the valuation model simplified in equation 8-2?

## CHARACTERISTICS OF COMMON STOCK

**Common stock** represents ownership in the corporation. Bondholders can be viewed as creditors, whereas the common stockholders are the true owners of the firm. Common stock does not have a maturity date, but exists as long as the firm does. Nor does common stock have an upper limit on its dividend payments. Dividend payments must be declared by the firm's board of directors before they are issued. In the event of bankruptcy, the common stockholders—as owners of the corporation—cannot exercise claims on assets until the firm's creditors, including the bondholders and preferred shareholders, have been satisfied.

**Common stock**
Common stock shares represent the ownership in a corporation.

In examining common stock, we will look first at several of its features or characteristics. Then we will focus on valuing common stock.

### Claim on Income

As the owners of the corporation, the common shareholders have the right to the residual income after bondholders and preferred stockholders have been paid. This income may be paid directly to the shareholders in the form of dividends or retained and reinvested by the firm. Although it is obvious the shareholder benefits immediately from the distribution of income in the form of dividends, the reinvestment of earnings also benefits the shareholder.

ROAD RULES

A FOCUS ON HARLEY-DAVIDSON

ROAD RULES

## A Conversation with Pat Davidson, Director of Investor Relations at Harley-Davidson

1. **Could you tell us about your background and how you came to be Director of Investor Relations at Harley-Davidson?**
Let me begin by stating that I am not a member of the founding Davidson family and yes, I do own and ride a Harley. I came to Harley-Davidson in 1992 after graduating from the MBA program at the Kellogg School at Northwestern University. Before that I had worked for Motorola in Austin, Texas for 3 years as a product engineer. After I arrived at Harley-Davidson I worked in a number of jobs, gaining a broad exposure to the firm, its business, and its culture. In 1999, I was appointed to the job of Director of Investor Relations.

2. **Just what is investor relations?**
When compared to most other business functions like marketing, accounting, finance, or human resources, the Investor Relations function is a relatively new one in many businesses. However, the importance of investor relations has increased dramatically in recent years with the rise of the common stock ownership and the growing importance of institutional investors, including mutual fund managers.

The primary function of Investor Relations is to serve as the interface between the company and the Wall Street investor community. However, the company's IRO (Investor Relations Officer) has many other responsibilities. For example, the IRO is responsible for helping to develop and communicate the company's key messages to the investing public concerning the firm's strategic direction and its prospects for future performance. This includes company statements regarding its strategy, budgets, and forecasts as well as developments that are under consideration. At Harley-Davidson, this is done primarily with the CFO and our Communications group, but also includes interaction with other members of our Functional Leadership Group and our CEO.

The Investor Relations officer is responsible for a company's disclosure record, so the IRO is always involved when information regarding the company is disclosed to the investment community. It is important that companies do not improperly or inadvertently disclose information that is material. This requires a policing effort to make certain that the company is acting responsibly and within the law.

The Investor Relations office is also a key conduit for information about company performance and strategy back to management from the street. Thus, Investor Relations can often present an external view of the company, which can be helpful in gauging investor sentiment.

3. **How does the Investor Relations officer communicate with "the street"?**
We use three principal methods to communicate with investors and security analysts:

- Broker-sponsored investor conferences where the CEO or CFO presents the Harley-Davidson story
- One-on-one meetings between the company and an institutional investor
- Company-sponsored meetings

Whenever we disclose material information, we take steps to do it publicly and obey all relevant securities regulations. Before moving on to your next question, let me also point out that Harley-Davidson has an active individual investor program run by Michelle Updike. Through this program we receive a large number of information requests from a variety of sources. For example, students often contact us and we are happy to help, provided they have performed some initial background work trying to understand Harley-Davidson.

4. **Would you recommend that students target a career in investor relations?**
Like most things in life, the answer is "it depends." Investor relations can be a great career for people with a hunger for knowledge and the curiosity for understanding how things work. An effective IRO must possess superior knowledge about the company and its industry. This requires that the IRO work with the company's marketing research team to develop a better understanding of the company's competitors and the strategic threat they pose.

In total, the Investor Relations position requires a person who is very familiar with the company and its industry. This requires an understanding of the big picture, as well as enough detailed knowledge to be able to provide information valued by investors. Investor Relations officer gets too much credit when the stock price goes up and too much blame when the stock price goes down, but it sure makes for an interesting job.

5. **To give us a better understanding of your job, please trace through the events in a typical day.**

- Stop by Jim Ziemer's (CFO) office to chat with him and Jim Brostowitz (Treasurer) on the upcoming week.
- Talk with analyst in Boston regarding next week's one-on-one meeting with our CEO and CFO.

- Discuss upcoming conference particulars with analyst in Milwaukee.
- Meet with Vice President of Dealer Service and Director of Business Planning to review recent activity in the heavyweight motorcycle market.
- Review internal income statements and cash-flow models with Michelle Updike (Assistant IR officer).
- Review the investor relations portion of Harley-Davidson.com to determine if any changes or updating are required.
- Set up a plant tour for portfolio managers from Denver who are visiting next week and need to be on a plane by 4:30 pm. And, of course, there is a significant portion of my time spent on the phone and on the computer responding to email.

Plowing back earnings into the firm should result in an increase in the value of the firm, in its earning power, and in its future dividends. This action in turn results in an increase in the value of the stock. In effect, residual income is distributed directly to shareholders in the form of dividends or indirectly in the form of capital gains (a rising stock price) on their common stock.

The right to residual income has both advantages and disadvantages for the common stockholder. The advantage is that the potential return is limitless. Once the claims of the more senior securities (bonds and preferred stock) have been satisfied, the remaining income flows to the common stockholders in the form of dividends or capital gains. The disadvantage: If the bond and preferred stock claims on income totally absorb earnings, common shareholders receive nothing. In years when earnings fall, it is the common shareholder who suffers first.

## Claim on Assets

Just as common stock has a residual claim on income, it also has a residual claim on assets in the case of liquidation. Only after the claims of debt holders and preferred stockholders have been satisfied do the claims of common shareholders receive attention. Unfortunately, when bankruptcy does occur, the claims of the common shareholders generally go unsatisfied. This residual claim on assets adds to the risk of common stock. Thus, although common stock has historically provided a higher return than other securities, averaging 12 percent annually since the late 1920s, it also has more risks associated with it.

## Voting Rights

The common shareholders elect the board of directors and are in general the only security holders given a vote. Early in this century, it was not uncommon for a firm to issue two classes of common stock that were identical, except that only one carried voting rights. For example, both the Parker Pen Co. and the Great Atlantic and Pacific Tea Co. (A&P) had two such classes of common stock. This practice was virtually eliminated by (1) the Public Utility Holding Company Act of 1935, which gave the Securities and Exchange Commission the power to require that newly issued common stock carry voting rights; (2) the New York Stock Exchange's refusal to list common stock without voting privileges; and (3) investor demand for the inclusion of voting rights. However, with the merger boom of the 1980s, dual classes of common stock with different voting rights again emerged, this time as a defensive tactic used to prevent takeovers.

FINANCE $ MATTERS

## Buffett on the Stock Market

During the 17-year period from 1981 to 1998, bond investors realized an annual return of more than 13% while stock investors earned a return of 19%. But should investors expect these investments to continue to provide such phenomenal returns? No, according to Warren Buffett, chairman of Berkshire Hathaway. While Buffett usually avoids speaking of market projections, in 1999 he addressed the reasons he believed stock and bond returns were likely to be well below the returns of the prior 17-year period.

One reason that returns are likely to fall is that stocks are overvalued. In 1998 profits for the Fortune 500 companies were $334,335,000,000 and market value on March 15, 1999 was $9,907,233,000,000. This implies that investors are paying $30 for each $1 in profits. This overvaluation has been a factor in the extraordinary returns of the past and is not likely to continue into the future. While markets sometimes behave in ways not linked to value, eventually value does become important. Investors cannot get out of a firm more than what the business earns.

In July 1999 Paine Webber and Gallup Organization surveyed investors and found that those with less than five years experience expected stock returns to be 22.6% over the next ten years. More experienced investors believed a return of 12.9% was more reasonable. Mr. Buffett believes that both estimates are too high. He says that in order for an investor to realize such high returns three doubtful conditions must occur.

First, interest rates must fall. The return an investor realizes from their investment is tied to the risk-free rate earned from government securities. When interest rates fall, security prices increase. Therefore, for investors to earn a significantly higher return on their investments, the government must lower the rate on government securities well below the 6% level in 1999.

Second, corporate profits in relation to GDP would have to rise. Since 1990, after-tax corporate profits as a percent of GDP have been around 6%. Buffett expects this rate to remain within the range of 4% to 6.5% as a result of competition among firms. If GDP is expected to grow at 5% per year and corporate profits remain at 6% of GDP, firm values will not grow at the 12.9%—or 22.6%—rate investors expect. After all, a firm's value cannot grow faster than its earnings do.

Finally, Buffett says that the key to earning significant profits from investments is not in selecting the industry but rather in selecting the company that has the competitive advantage and can provide persistent growth for the investors. Historically, industries that have impacted the economy, such as automobiles and aviation, have seen more companies fail than succeed. Identifying the companies that are sustainable over the long term is difficult at best.

While investors may not see double digit-returns long term, the securities market still provides an opportunity to increase wealth and to enjoy a progressively higher standard of living.

Source: "Mr. Buffett on the Stock Market," *Fortune,* November 22, 1999.

**Proxy**
A proxy gives a designated party the temporary power of attorney to vote for the signee at the corporation's annual meeting.

**Proxy fights**
When rival groups compete for proxy votes in order to control the decisions made in a stockholder meeting.

**Majority voting**
Each share of stock allows the shareholder one vote, and each position on the board of directors is voted on separately. As a result, a majority of shares has the power to elect the entire board of directors.

**Cumulative voting**
Each share of stock allows the shareholder a number of votes equal to the number of directors being elected. The shareholder can then cast all of his or her votes for a single candidate or split them among the various candidates.

Common shareholders not only have the right to elect the board of directors, they also must approve any change in the corporate charter. A typical charter change might involve the authorization to issue new stock or perhaps a merger proposal.

Voting for directors and charter changes occur at the corporation's annual meeting. Whereas shareholders may vote in person, the majority generally vote by proxy. A **proxy** gives a designated party the temporary power of attorney to vote for the signee at the corporation's annual meeting. The firm's management generally solicits proxy votes and, if the shareholders are satisfied with its performance, has little problem securing them. However, in times of financial distress or when management takeovers are being attempted, **proxy fights**—battles between rival groups for proxy votes—occur.

Although each share of stock carries the same number of votes, the voting procedure is not always the same from company to company. The two procedures commonly used are majority and cumulative voting. Under **majority voting,** each share of stock allows the shareholder one vote, and each position on the board of directors is voted on separately. Because each member of the board of directors is elected by a simple majority, a majority of shares has the power to elect the entire board of directors.

With **cumulative voting,** each share of stock allows the shareholder a number of votes equal to the number of directors being elected. The shareholder can then cast all of his or her votes for a single candidate or split them among the various candidates. The advantage of a cumulative voting procedure is that it gives minority shareholders the power to elect a director.

## FINANCE MATTERS

### Reading a Stock Quote in *The Wall Street Journal*

Following is a section of *The Wall Street Journal* that gives the quotes for some of the stocks traded on the New York Stock Exchange on October 19, 2000.

| | 52 WEEKS HI | LO | STOCK | SYM | DIV | YLD % | PE | VOL 100s | HI | LO | CLOSE | | NET CHG |
|---|---|---|---|---|---|---|---|---|---|---|---|---|---|
| s | $50^{63}$ | $27^{88}$ | HarleyDav | HDI | .10 | .2 | 44 | 8582 | $47^{31}$ | $45^{13}$ | $46^{88}$ | + | $1^{13}$ |
| s | $42^{38}$ | $18^{38}$ | Harmanlnt | HAR | .10 | .3 | 17 | 1292 | $35^{75}$ | $34^{55}$ | $35^{15}$ | – | $0^{10}$ |
| | $30^{75}$ | 17 | HarrahEntn | HET | | ... | 15 | 6622 | $26^{63}$ | $25^{56}$ | $26^{25}$ | + | $0^{75}$ |
| s | **$39^{38}$** | **$17^{62}$** | **Harris** | **HRS** | **.20** | **.9** | **96** | **3490** | **$22^{94}$** | **22** | **$22^{94}$** | + | **$1^{44}$** |
| | $22^{88}$ | $18^{94}$ | HarrisPfCap | pfA | 1.84 | 8.5 | ... | 106 | $21^{69}$ | $21^{38}$ | $21^{63}$ | – | $0^{13}$ |
| | $31^{88}$ | $17^{88}$ | Harsco | HSC | .94 | 5.1 | 7 | 1668 | $19^{25}$ | $18^{31}$ | $18^{44}$ | – | $0^{44}$ |
| | **$28^{44}$** | **$19^{06}$** | **HarteHanks** | **HHS** | **.10** | **.4** | **25** | **490** | **$27^{94}$** | **$26^{19}$** | **$27^{88}$** | + | **$1^{56}$** |

These stocks include Harley-Davidson and others that are listed in *The Wall Street Journal* on a daily basis. To help us understand how to read the quotes, consider Harley-Davidson:

- The *s* in the left margin indicates there has been a stock split or stock dividend, or cash or cash equivalent distribution, amounting to 10 percent or more in the past 52 weeks.
- The 52-week *Hi* column shows that Harley-Davidson stock reached a high of 50.63 during the past year.
- The 52-week *Lo* column shows that Harley-Davidson stock sold for a low of 27.88 during the past year. Both the high and low prices have been adjusted for the stock split.
- The *Stock* (HarleyDav) and *Sym* (HDI) columns give an abbreviated version of the corporation's name and the ticker symbol, respectively.
- *Div,* the dividend column, gives the amount of dividend that Harley-Davidson paid its common stockholders in the last year, 10¢ per share.
- *Yld%* (.2) is the stock's dividend yield – the amount of the dividend divided by the day's closing price (10¢ ÷ 46.88).
- *PE* (44) gives the current market price (46.88) divided by the firm's earnings per share.
- The amount of Harley-Davidson stock traded on October 19, 2000, is represented in the *Vol 100s* column. On this day 858,200 shares were traded.
- Harley-Davidson stock traded at a high price of 47.31 *(Hi)* and a low price of 45.13 *(Lo)* during the day.
- The previous day's closing price is subtracted from the closing price *(Close)* of 46.88 on October 19, 2000, for a net change *(Net Chg)* of 1.13.

## RELATE TO THE BIG PICTURE

In theory, the shareholders pick the corporate board of directors, generally through proxy voting, and the board of directors in turn picks the management. Unfortunately, in reality the system frequently works the other way around. Shareholders are offered a slate of nominees selected by management from which to choose. The end result is that management effectively selects the directors, who then may have more allegiance to the managers than to the shareholders. This in turn sets up the potential for agency problems in which a divergence of interests between managers and shareholders is allowed to exist, with the board of directors not monitoring the managers on behalf of the shareholders as they should. The result: **Principle 7: The Agency Problem—Managers won't work for the owners unless it's in their best interest.** A former president for Archer-Daniels-Midland is one example among many of the agency problem. At one time, he would place his own family members and personal friends on the firm's board, paying them at rates twice the norm.

**FINANCE MATTERS**

### Ethics: Keeping Perspective

Ethical and moral lapses in the business and financial community, academia, politics, and religion fill the daily press. But the rash of insider-trading cases on Wall Street against recent graduates of top business and law schools seems particularly disturbing because the cream of the crop, with six-figure incomes and brilliant careers ahead, is being convicted.

Most appear to have been very bright, highly motivated overachievers, driven by peer rivalries to win a game in which the score had a dollar sign in front of it. Although there have been a few big fish, most sold their futures for $20,000 to $50,000 of illicit profits. They missed the point—that life is a marathon, not a sprint.

In fact, most business school graduates become competent executives, managing people and resources for the benefit of society. The rewards—the titles and money—are merely byproducts of doing a good job.

To illustrate the point, consider the owner of a small company who had the opportunity to acquire a contract with a large Fortune 500 company to produce a product for the large firm. Verbal agreement was reached on the deal, but when the owner met with the president of the large company to sign the contract, the price of the product to be produced by the small firm was $0.25 per unit higher than originally agreed upon—in the small company owner's favor. When questioned, the president of the large firm informed the small firm owner she was to deposit the difference in a personal account and then periodically send the money to the president's personal bank account. Because the small firm owner was not directly profiting from the president's clearly unethical behavior, should she have accepted the terms? It would have increased her firm's profits—but only by a legitimate amount. How about the president of the large company? Why would he be willing to act unethically for what would have meant $40,000 or $50,000 to him?

## Preemptive Rights

**Preemptive rights**
The right of a common shareholder to maintain a proportionate share of ownership in the firm. When new shares are issued, common shareholders have the first right of refusal.

**Rights**
Certificates issued to shareholders giving them an option to purchase a stated number of new shares of stock at a specified price during a 2- to 10-week period.

The **preemptive right** entitles the common shareholder to maintain a proportionate share of ownership in the firm. When new shares are issued, common shareholders have the first right of refusal. If a shareholder owns 25 percent of the corporation's stock, then he or she is entitled to purchase 25 percent of the new shares. Certificates issued to the shareholders giving them an option to purchase a stated number of new shares of stock at a specified price typically during a 2- to 10-week period are called **rights.** These rights can be exercised (generally at a price set by management below the common stock's current market price), can be allowed to expire, or can be sold in the open market.

## Limited Liability

Although the common shareholders are the actual owners of the corporation, their liability in the case of bankruptcy is limited to the amount of their investment. The advantage is that investors who might not otherwise invest their funds in the firm become willing to do so.

# VALUING COMMON STOCK

OBJECTIVE 4 

Like both bonds and preferred stock, a common stock's value is equal to the present value of all future cash flows expected to be received by the stockholder. However, in contrast to bonds, common stock does not promise its owners interest income or a maturity payment at some specified time in the future. Nor does common stock entitle the holder to a predetermined constant dividend, as does preferred stock. For common stock, the dividend is based on (1) the profitability of the firm, and (2) on management's decision to pay dividends or to retain the profits to grow the firm.

Thus, dividends will vary with a firm's profitability and its stage of growth. In a company's early years, little if any dividends are typically paid. The funds are needed to finance the firm's growth—to capture the opportunity that was identified by the founders. As a company's growth slows—additional investment opportunities become less attractive—and the business becomes more profitable, the financial manager will then begin paying dividends to the common stockholders. As the firm eventually reaches maturity and growth is no longer a priority, the financial manager should increase the dividends even more. In short, a firm's stage of growth has direct implications on the dividends to be paid and on the value of the stock.

## The Growth Factor in Valuing Common Stock

What is meant by the term *growth* when used in the context of valuing common stock? A company can grow in a variety of ways. It can become larger by borrowing money to invest in new projects. Likewise, it can issue new stock for expansion. Management could also acquire another company to merge with the existing firm, which would increase the firm's assets. In all of these cases, the firm is growing through the use of new financing, by issuing debt or common stock. Although management could accurately say that the firm has grown, the original stockholders may or may not participate in this growth. Growth is realized through the infusion of new capital. The firm's assets have clearly increased, but unless the original investors increase their investment in the firm, they will own a smaller portion of the expanded business.

Another means of growing is internal growth, which comes from management retaining some or all of the firm's profits for reinvestment in the firm, in turn resulting in the growth of future earnings and hopefully the value of the existing common stock. Although not a direct investment in the company—the shareholders did not send the firm any additional money—the retention of profits is a form of investment by the current common stockholders. The money made from existing product lines could be distributed to the shareholders, but instead is retained as a source of financing future growth. In this way, the current stockholders participate in the growth of the company. It is this internal growth (no financing was acquired from new external sources) that matters in valuing the shares of the present common stockholders.[4]

### EXAMPLE

To illustrate the nature of internal growth, assume that the return on equity for PepsiCo is 16 percent.[5] If PepsiCo's management decides to pay all the profits out in dividends to its stockholders, the firm will experience no growth internally. It might become larger by borrowing more money or issuing new stock, but internal growth will come only through the retention of profits. If, on the other hand, PepsiCo retains all the profits, the stockholders' investment in the firm would grow by the amount of profits retained, or by 16 percent. If, however, management kept only 50 percent of the profits for reinvestment, the common shareholders' investment would increase

[4]We are not arguing that the existing common stockholders never benefit from the use of external financing; however, such benefit is more evasive when dealing with competitive capital markets.

[5]The return on equity is the percentage return on the common shareholders' investment in the company and is computed as follows:

$$\text{return on equity} = \frac{\text{net income}}{(\text{par value} + \text{paid-in capital} + \text{retained earnings})}$$

only by half of the 16 percent return on equity, or by 8 percent. Generalizing this relationship, we have

$$g = ROE \times r, \tag{8-3}$$

where $g$ = the growth rate of future earnings and the growth in the common stockholders' investment in the firm

$ROE$ = the return on equity (net income/common book value)

$r$ = the company's percentage of profits retained, called the profit-retention rate.[6]

Therefore, if only 25 percent of the profits were retained by PepsiCo, we would expect the common stockholders' investment in the firm and the value of the stock price to increase or grow by only 4 percent; that is,

$$g = 16\% \times 0.25 = 4\%$$

In summary, common stockholders frequently rely on an increase in the stock price as a source of return. If the company is retaining a portion of its earnings for reinvestment, future profits and dividends should grow. This growth should be reflected in an increased market price of the common stock in future periods, provided that the return on the funds reinvested exceeds the investor's required rate of return. Therefore, both types of return (dividends and price appreciation) are necessary in the development of a valuation model for common stock.

To explain this process, let us begin by examining how an investor—and financial manager—might value a common stock that is to be held for only 1 year.

## Common Stock Valuation—Single Holding Period

For an investor holding a common stock for only 1 year, the value of the stock should equal the present value of both the expected dividend to be received in 1 year, $D_1$, and the anticipated market price of the share at year end, $P_1$. If $k_{cs}$ represents a common stockholder's required rate of return, the value of the security, $V_{cs}$, would be

$$V_{cs} = \begin{bmatrix} \text{present value of dividend} \\ \text{received in 1 year } (D_1) \end{bmatrix} + \begin{bmatrix} \text{present value of market price} \\ \text{received in 1 year } (P_1) \end{bmatrix}$$

$$= \frac{D_1}{(1 + k_{cs})} + \frac{P_1}{(1 + k_{cs})}$$

### EXAMPLE

Suppose an investor is contemplating the purchase of RMI common stock at the beginning of this year. The dividend at year end is expected to be \$1.64, and the market price by the end of the year is projected to be \$22. If the investor's required rate of return is 18 percent, the value of the security would be

$$V_{cs} = \frac{\$1.64}{(1 + .18)} + \frac{\$22}{(1 + .18)}$$

$$= \$1.39 + \$18.64$$

$$= \$20.03$$

[6] The retention rate is also equal to (1 − the percentage of profits paid out in dividends). The percentage of profits paid out in dividends is often called the dividend-payout ratio.

Once again we see that valuation is a three-step process. First, we estimate the expected future cash flows from common stock ownership (a \$1.64 dividend and a \$22 end-of-year expected share price). Second, we estimate the investor's required rate of return by assessing the riskiness of the expected cash flows (assumed to be 18 percent). Finally, we discount the expected dividend and end-of-year share price back to the present at the investor's required rate of return.

## Common Stock Valuation—Multiple Holding Periods

Because common stock has no maturity date and is frequently held for many years, a multiple-holding-period valuation model is needed. This model is an equation used to value stock that has no maturity date, but continues in perpetuity (or as long as the firm exists). The general common stock valuation model can be defined as follows:

$$V_{cs} = \frac{D_1}{(1 + k_{cs})^1} + \frac{D_2}{(1 + k_{cs})^2} + \ldots + \frac{D_n}{(1 + k_{cs})^n} + \ldots + \frac{D_\infty}{(1 + k_{cs})^\infty} \qquad \textbf{(8-4)}$$

Equation 8-4 indicates that we are discounting the dividend at the end of the first year, $D_1$, back 1 year; the dividend in the second year, $D_2$, back 2 years; the dividend in the $n$th year back $n$ years; and the dividend in infinity back an infinite number of years. The required rate of return is $k_{cs}$. In using equation 8-4, note that the value of the stock is established at the beginning of the year, say January 1, 2002. The most recent past dividend $D_0$ would have been paid the previous day, December 31, 2001. Thus, if we purchased the stock on January 1, the first dividend would be received in 12 months, on December 31, 2002, which is represented by $D_1$.

Fortunately, equation 8-4 can be reduced to a much more manageable form if dividends grow each year at a constant rate, $g$. The constant-growth common stock valuation equation may be represented as follows:[7]

$$\text{common stock value} = \frac{\text{dividend in year 1}}{\text{required rate of return} - \text{growth rate}} \qquad \textbf{(8-5)}$$

$$V_{cs} = \frac{D_1}{k_{cs} - g}$$

Consequently, the intrinsic value (present value) of a share of common stock whose dividends grow at a constant annual rate in perpetuity can be calculated using equation 8-5.

[7]Where common stock dividends grow at a constant rate of $g$ every year, we can express the dividend in any year in terms of the dividend paid at the end of the previous year, $D_0$. For example, the expected dividend 1 year hence is simply $D_0(1 + g)$. Likewise, the dividend at the end of $t$ years is $D_0(1 + g)^t$. Using this notation, the common stock valuation equation in equation 8-4 can be written as follows:

$$V_{cs} = \frac{D_0(1 + g)^1}{(1 + k_{cs})^1} + \frac{D_0(1 + g)^2}{(1 + k_{cs})^2} + \ldots + \frac{D_0(1 + g)^n}{(1 + k_{cs})^n} + \ldots + \frac{D_0(1 + g)^\infty}{(1 + k_{cs})^\infty}$$

If both sides of equation 8-5 are multiplied by $(1 + k_{cs})/(1 + g)$ and then equation 8-4 is subtracted from the product, the result is

$$\frac{V_{cs}(1 + k_{cs})}{(1 + g)} - V_{cs} = D_0 - \frac{D_0(1 + g)^\infty}{(1 + k_{cs})^\infty}$$

If $k_{cs} > g$, which normally should hold, $[D_0(1 + g)^\infty/(1 + k_{cs})^\infty]$ approaches zero. As a result,

$$\frac{V_{cs}(1 + k_{cs})}{(1 + g)} - V_{cs} = D_0$$

$$V_{cs}\left(\frac{1 + k_{cs}}{1 + g}\right) - V_{cs}\left(\frac{1 + g}{1 + g}\right) = D_0$$

$$V_{cs}\left[\frac{(1 + k_{cs}) - (1 + g)}{1 + g}\right] = D_0$$

$$V_{cs}(k_{cs} - g) = D_0(1 + g)$$

$$V_{cs} = \frac{D_1}{k_{cs} - g}$$

Although the interpretation of this equation may not be intuitively obvious, simply remember that it solves for the present value of the future dividend stream growing at a rate, $g$, to infinity, assuming that $k_{cs}$ is greater than $g$.

**EXAMPLE**

Consider the valuation of a share of common stock that paid a \$2 dividend at the end of last year and is expected to pay a cash dividend every year from now to infinity. Each year the dividends are expected to grow at a rate of 10 percent. Based on an assessment of the riskiness of the common stock, the investor's required rate of return is 15 percent. Using this information, we would compute the value of the common stock as follows:

1. Because the \$2 dividend was paid last year (actually yesterday), we must compute the next dividend to be received, that is, $D_1$, where

$$\begin{aligned} D_1 &= D_0(1 + g) \\ &= \$2(1 + .10) \\ &= \$2.20 \end{aligned}$$

2. Now, using equation 8-5

$$\begin{aligned} V_{cs} &= \frac{D_1}{k_{cs} - g} \\ &= \frac{\$2.20}{.15 - .10} \\ &= \$44 \end{aligned}$$

We have argued that the value of a common stock is equal to the present value of all future dividends, which is without question a fundamental premise of finance. In practice, however, managers, along with many security analysts, often talk about the relationship between stock value and earnings, rather than dividends. We would encourage you to be very cautious in using earnings to value a stock. Even though it may be a popular practice, the evidence available suggests that investors look to the cash flows generated by the firm, not the earnings, for value. A firm's value truly is the present value of the cash flows it produces. (We look at this issue in Appendix 8A.)

We now turn to our last issue in stock valuation, that of the stockholder's expected returns, a matter of key importance to the financial manager.

**RELATE TO THE BIG PICTURE**

Valuing common stock is no different from valuing preferred stock; the pattern of the cash flows changes, but nothing else. Thus, the valuation of common stock relies on the same three principles that were used in valuing preferred stock:

- **Principle 1: The Risk-Return Trade-Off—We won't take on additional risk unless we expect to be compensated with additional return.**
- **Principle 2: The Time Value of Money—A dollar received today is worth more than a dollar received in the future.**
- **Principle 3: Cash—Not Profits—Is King.**

ROAD RULES

A FOCUS ON HARLEY-DAVIDSON

ROAD RULES

## The Value of the Harley-Davidson Brand

Take the following test: If you want to buy a book, what company or store name comes to mind? Chances are it's one of the big book retailers like Barnes & Noble or perhaps Amazon.com. The fact that you are aware of these companies when book purchases come to mind is very valuable to the respective firms. Thus, owning a brand name can be a tremendous source of value. Furthermore, the brand is a source of valuable assets to the firm that doesn't appear on a traditional balance sheet. These assets are sometimes referred to as market-based assets and include customer loyalty, name awareness, and perceived quality. In addition, owning a brand can be a source of new and valuable opportunities for the firm. For example, Harley-Davidson is the leading producer of heavyweight motorcycles in the world. Virtually since its inception, the company sold functional riding gear, including riding jackets dating back to 1906. However, in 1989 the company introduced an expanded line of clothing called "Harley-Davidson MotorClothes" that carry the Harley-Davidson brand and are sold in motorcycle dealerships and specialty Harley-Davidson clothing shops around the world. A large part of this decision was predicated on the brand image that the company enjoyed based on its motorcycle product line. To date, the venture has proven very successful, producing over $151 million in revenues during 2000.

### PROTECTING THE BRAND

Something so valuable as the company brand must be cherished and carefully managed and protected. At Harley-Davidson, for example, the "Bar & Shield" company emblem doesn't go on just anything. In fact, one of the company's corporate strategic objectives is to "Strengthen the Harley-Davidson brand." In producing a Harley-Davidson product, whether branded or licensed, the company looks for authentic products that are consistent with, and relevant to, the Harley-Davidson brand image.

### BRAND MANAGEMENT AND THE CREATION OF SHAREHOLDER VALUE

Expenditures made on advertising that are directed at enhancing customer awareness of the firm and its products are really investments in the firm's brand. However, the accounting profession doesn't see it this way. That is, generally accepted accounting principles (GAAP) call for the expensing of all advertising expenditures in the period in which they are made such that no asset is ever recorded on the firm's balance sheet to reflect the value that these expenditures might have created by enhancing the value of the firm's brand.

But what exactly is the value of a firm's brand and how should we think about its determinants? Conceptually, it is quite easy to imagine that a firm's brand has value when it leads customers to think of the firm's products and services when a need arises. However, coming to understand how much value the brand has is a really tough problem. Perhaps the best way to begin is to review briefly the sources of value from any productive asset. These include the amount, timing, and riskiness of future cash-flow expectations. Thus, the firm's brand has value insofar as it can increase future cash-flow expectations, shorten the time until customers make their purchases (thus shortening the time to receipt of future cash flows), and reduce the risk of future cash flows by increasing the loyalty of customers and the likelihood that they will purchase the firm's product.

### WANT TO KNOW MORE ABOUT THE INTERFACE BETWEEN MARKETING AND FINANCE?

The following references address the marketing-finance interface and provide valuable grounding for financial specialists and marketers. In fact, these papers received the prize for best practical and theoretical article from the *Journal of Marketing,* the premier journal of marketers.

Rajendra K. Srivastava, Tasadduz A. Shervani, and Liam Fahey, 1998. Market-based assets and shareholder value: A framework for analysis. *Journal of Marketing* 62 (January), 2–18.

Rajendra K. Srivastava, Tasadduz A. Shervani, and Liam Fahey, 1999. Marketing, business processes, and shareholder value: An organizationally embedded view of marketing activities and the discipline of marketing. *Journal of Marketing* 63 (Special Issue), 168–179.

## CONCEPT CHECK

1. What features of common stock indicate ownership in the corporation versus preferred stock or bonds?
2. What are the two ways that a shareholder benefits from ownership?
3. How does internal growth versus the infusion of new capital affect the original shareholders?
4. If a corporation decides to retain its earnings, when would the value of the market price actually decrease?
5. What is the three-step process for common stock valuation? Explain the difference in the equations for a single holding period and multiple holding periods.

## STOCKHOLDER'S EXPECTED RATE OF RETURN

OBJECTIVE 5 

As stated in Chapter 7, the expected rate of return on a bond is the return the bondholder expects to receive on the investment by paying the existing market price for the security. This rate of return is of interest to the financial manager because it tells the manager about the investor's expectations, which in turn affects the firm's cost of financing new projects. The same can be said for the financial manager needing to know the expected rate of return of the firm's stockholders, which is the topic of this next section.

### The Preferred Stockholder's Expected Rate of Return

In computing the preferred stockholder's expected rate of return, we use the valuation equation for preferred stock. Earlier, equation 8-2 specified the value of a preferred stock $(V_{ps})$ as

$$V_{ps} = \frac{\text{annual dividend}}{\text{required rate of return}} = \frac{D}{k_{ps}}$$

Solving equation 8-2 for the preferred stockholder's required rate of return $(k_{ps})$, we have:

$$k_{ps} = \frac{\text{annual dividend}}{\text{intrinsic value}} = \frac{D}{V_{ps}} \tag{8-7}$$

That is, the preferred stockholder's *required* rate of return simply equals the stock's annual dividend divided by the intrinsic value. We may also restate equation 8-7 to solve for a preferred stock's *expected* rate of return, $\bar{k}_{ps}$, as follows:[8]

$$\bar{k}_{ps} = \frac{\text{annual dividend}}{\text{market price}} = \frac{D}{P_0} \tag{8-8}$$

Note that we have merely substituted the current market price, $P_0$, for the intrinsic value, $V_{ps}$. The expected rate of return $\bar{k}_{ps}$, therefore, equals the annual dividend relative to the price the stock is presently selling for, $P_0$. Thus, the expected rate of return $\bar{k}_{ps}$, is the rate of return the investor can expect to earn from the investment if bought at the current market price. For example, if the present market price of preferred stock is \$50 and it pays a \$3.64 annual dividend, the expected rate of return implicit in the present market price is

$$\bar{k}_{ps} = \frac{D}{P_0} = \frac{\$3.64}{\$50} = 7.28\%$$

Therefore, investors at the margin (who pay \$50 per share for a preferred security that is paying \$3.64 in annual dividends) are expecting a 7.28 percent rate of return.

### The Common Stockholder's Expected Rate of Return

The valuation equation for common stock was defined earlier in equation 8-4 as

$$\text{value} = \frac{\text{dividend in year 1}}{(1 + \text{required rate of return})^1} + \frac{\text{dividend in year 2}}{(1 + \text{required rate of return})^2}$$

$$+ \ldots + \frac{\text{dividend in year infinity}}{(1 + \text{required rate of return})^\infty}$$

$$V_{cs} = \frac{D_1}{(1 + k_{cs})^1} + \frac{D_2}{(1 + k_{cs})^2} + \ldots + \frac{D_\infty}{(1 + k_{cs})^\infty}$$

[8]We will use $\bar{k}$ to represent a security's expected rate of return versus $k$ for the investor's required rate of return.

$$V_{cs} = \sum_{t=1}^{\infty} \frac{D_t}{(1 + k_{cs})^t}$$

Owing to the difficulty of discounting to infinity, we made the key assumption that the dividends, $D_t$, increase at a constant annual compound growth rate of $g$. If this assumption is valid, equation 8-4 was shown to be equivalent to

$$\text{value} = \frac{\text{dividend in year 1}}{\text{required rate of return} - \text{growth rate}}$$

$$V_{cs} = \frac{D_1}{k_{cs} - g}$$

Thus, $V_{cs}$ represents the maximum value that an investor having a required rate of return of $k_{cs}$ would pay for a security having an anticipated dividend in year 1 of $D_1$ that is expected to grow in future years at rate $g$. Solving for $k_{cs}$, we can compute the common stockholder's required rate of return as follows:[9]

$$k_{cs} = \underset{\substack{\uparrow \\ \text{dividend} \\ \text{yield}}}{\left(\frac{D_1}{V_{cs}}\right)} + \underset{\substack{\uparrow \\ \text{annual} \\ \text{growth rate}}}{g} \tag{8-9}$$

From this equation, the common stockholder's required rate of return is equal to the dividend yield plus a growth factor. Although the growth rate, $g$, applies to the growth in the company's dividends, given our assumptions the stock's value may also be expected to increase at the same rate. For this reason, $g$ represents the annual percentage growth in the stock value. In other words, the investor's required rate of return is satisfied by receiving dividends and capital gains, as reflected by the expected percentage growth rate in the stock price.

As was done for preferred stock earlier, we may revise equation 8-9 to measure a common stock's *expected* rate of return, $\bar{k}_{cs}$. Replacing the intrinsic value, $V_{cs}$, in equation 8-9 with the stock's current market price, $P_0$, we may express the stock's expected rate of return as follows:

$$\bar{k}_{cs} = \frac{\text{dividend in year 1}}{\text{market price}} + \text{growth rate} = \frac{D_1}{P_0} + g$$

**EXAMPLE**

As an example of computing the expected rate of return for a common stock where dividends are anticipated to grow at a constant rate to infinity, assume that a firm's common stock has a current market price of \$44. If the expected dividend at the conclusion of this year is \$2.20 and dividends and earnings are growing at a 10 percent annual rate (last year's dividend was \$2), the expected rate of return implicit in the \$44 stock price is as follows:

$$\bar{k}_{cs} = \frac{\$2.20}{\$44} + 10\% = 15\%$$

[9]At times, the expected dividend at year end ($D_1$) is not given. Instead, we might only know the most recent dividend (paid yesterday), that is, $D_0$. If so, we must restate the equation as follows:

$$V_{cs} = \frac{D_1}{(k_{cs} - g)} = \frac{D_0(1 + g)}{(k_{cs} - g)}$$

As a final note, we should understand that the *expected* rate of return implied by a given market price equals the *required* rate of return for investors at the margin. For these investors, the expected rate of return is just equal to their required rate of return, and therefore they are willing to pay the current market price for the security. These investors' required rate of return is of particular significance to the financial manager, because it represents the cost of new financing to the firm.

**CONCEPT CHECK**

1. In computing the required rate of return, why should the growth factor be added to the dividend yield?
2. How does an efficient market affect the required and expected rates of return?

## HOW FINANCIAL MANAGERS USE THIS MATERIAL

In this chapter, we have looked at the nature and process for valuing both preferred stock and common stock—sources of equity capital for a business. Although we have taken an investor perspective in much of what we have said, we are ultimately interested in the implications of valuation for a financial manager. But a financial manager must first and foremost view valuation from the investor's vantage point. What matters to the investor should matter to the financial manager. Otherwise, a financial manager cannot be effective in enhancing firm value—the criterion for evaluating much that the financial manager does. This relationship will become increasingly clear as we move into future chapters dealing with making capital investments and financing these expenditures.

## SUMMARY

OBJECTIVE 1 

Valuation is an important process in financial management. An understanding of valuation, both the concepts and procedures, supports the financial officer's objective of maximizing the value of the firm.

Preferred stock has no fixed maturity date and the dividends are fixed in amount. Following are some of the more frequent characteristics of preferred stock:

- There are multiple classes of preferred stock.
- Preferred stock has a priority of claim on assets and income over common stock.
- Any dividends, if not paid as promised, must be paid before any common stock dividends may be paid. That is, they are cumulative.
- Protective provisions are included in the contract for the preferred shareholder in order to reduce the investor's risk.
- Many preferred stocks are convertible into common stock shares.

For a few preferred stocks:

- The dividend rate may be adjustable as interest rates change.
- The preferred stockholder may be allowed to participate in the firm's earnings in certain situations.
- The preferred stockholder may receive dividends in the form of more shares—payment-in-kind (PIK).

In addition, there are provisions frequently used to retire an issue of preferred stock, such as the ability for the firm to call its preferred stock or to use a sinking fund provision.

OBJECTIVE 2

*Value* is the present value of future cash flows discounted at the investor's required rate of return. Although the valuation of any security entails the same basic principles, the procedures used in each situation vary. For example, we learned in Chapter 7 that valuing a bond involves calculating the present value of future interest to be received plus the present value of the principal returned to the investor at the maturity of the bond.

For securities with cash flows that are constant in each year but with no specified maturity, such as preferred stock, the present value equals the dollar amount of the annual dividend divided by the investor's required rate of return; that is,

$$\text{preferred stock value} = \frac{\text{dividend}}{\text{required rate of return}}$$

Bondholders and preferred stockholders can be viewed as creditors, whereas the common stockholders are the owners of the firm. Common stock does not have a maturity date, but exists as long as the firm does. Nor does common stock have an upper limit on its dividend payments. Dividend payments must be declared by the firm's board of directors before they are issued. In the event of bankruptcy, the common stockholders, as owners of the corporation, cannot exercise claims on assets until the firm's creditors, including the bondholders and preferred shareholders, have been satisfied. However, common stockholders' liability is limited to the amount of their investment.

The common shareholders are in general the only security holders given a vote. Common shareholders have the right to elect the board of directors and to approve any change in the corporate charter. Although each share of stock carries the same number of votes, the voting procedure is not always the same from company to company.

The preemptive right entitles the common shareholder to maintain a proportionate share of ownership in the firm.

For common stock where the future dividends are expected to increase at a constant growth rate, value may be given by the following equation:

$$\text{common stock value} = \frac{\text{dividend in year 1}}{\text{required rate of return} - \text{growth rate}}$$

Growth here relates to *internal* growth only, where management retains part of the firm's profits to be reinvested and thereby grow the firm—as opposed to growth through issuing new stock or acquiring another firm.

Growth in and of itself does not mean that we are creating value for the stockholders. Only if we are reinvesting at a rate of return that is greater than the investors' required rate of return will growth result in increased value to the firm. In fact, if we are investing at rates less than the required rate of return for our investors, the value of the firm will actually decline.

The expected rate of return on a security is the required rate of return of investors who are willing to pay the present market price for the security, but no more. This rate of return is important to the financial manager because it equals the required rate of return of the firm's investors.

The expected rate of return for preferred stock is computed as follows:

$$\text{expected return preferred stock} = \frac{\text{annual dividend}}{\text{stock market price}}$$

The expected rate of return for common stock is calculated as follows:

$$\text{expected return common stock} = \frac{\text{dividend in year 1}}{\text{stock market price}} + \text{dividend growth rate}$$

## KEY TERMS

**Adjustable rate preferred stock, 244**

**Auction rate preferred stock, 244**

**Call provision, 245**

**Common stock, 247**

**Convertible preferred stock, 243**

**Cumulative preferred stock, 243**

**Cumulative voting, 250**

**Majority voting, 250**

my**PHLIP**

Go To:
http://www.prenhall.com/keown
for downloads and current events associated with this chapter

**Participating preferred stock, 244**
**PIK preferred stock, 244**
**Preemptive rights, 252**
**Preferred stock, 242**
**Protective provisions, 243**
**Proxy, 250**
**Proxy fights, 250**
**Rights, 252**
**Sinking fund, 245**

## STUDY QUESTIONS

**8-1.** Why is preferred stock referred to as a hybrid security? It is often said to combine the worst features of common stock and bonds. What is meant by this statement?

**8-2.** Because preferred stock dividends in arrears must be paid before common stock dividends, should they be considered a liability and appear on the right side of the balance sheet?

**8-3.** Why would a preferred stockholder want the stock to have a cumulative dividend feature and other protective provisions?

**8-4.** Distinguish between fixed rate preferred stock and adjustable rate preferred stock. What is the rationale for a firm issuing adjustable rate preferred stock?

**8-5.** What is PIK preferred stock?

**8-6.** Why is preferred stock frequently convertible? Why would it be callable?

**8-7.** Compare valuing preferred stock and common stock.

**8-8.** Define the investor's *expected* rate of return.

**8-9.** State how the investor's required rate of return is computed.

**8-10.** The common stockholders receive two types of return from their investment. What are they?

## SELF-TEST PROBLEMS

**ST-1.** *(Preferred stock valuation)* What is the value of a preferred stock where the dividend rate is 16 percent on a $100 par value? The appropriate discount rate for a stock of this risk level is 12 percent.

**ST-2.** *(Preferred stockholder expected return)* You own 250 shares of Dalton Resources' preferred stock, which currently sells for $38.50 per share and pays annual dividends of $3.25 per share.

**a.** What is your expected return?

**b.** If you require an 8 percent return, given the current price, should you sell or buy more stock?

**ST-3.** *(Preferred stock valuation)* The preferred stock of Armlo pays a $2.75 dividend. What is the value of the stock if your required return is 9 percent?

**ST-4.** *(Common stock valuation)* Crosby Corporation's common stock paid $1.32 in dividends last year and is expected to grow indefinitely at an annual 7 percent rate. What is the value of the stock if you require an 11 percent return?

**ST-5.** *(Common stockholder expected return)* Blackburn & Smith's common stock currently sells for $23 per share. The company's executives anticipate a constant growth rate of 10.5 percent and an end-of-year dividend of $2.50.

**a.** What is your expected rate of return?

**b.** If you require a 17 percent return, should you purchase the stock?

## STUDY PROBLEMS (SET A)

**8-1A.** *(Preferred stock valuation)* Calculate the value of a preferred stock that pays a dividend of $6 per share and your required rate of return is 12 percent.

**8-2A.** *(Measuring growth)* If Pepperdine, Inc.'s return on equity is 16 percent and the management plans to retain 60 percent of earnings for investment purposes, what will be the firm's growth rate?

**8-3A.** *(Preferred stock valuation)* What is the value of a preferred stock where the dividend rate is 14 percent on a $100 par value? The appropriate discount rate for a stock of this risk level is 12 percent.

**8-4A.** *(Preferred stockholder expected return)* Solitron's preferred stock is selling for $42.16 and pays $1.95 in dividends. What is your expected rate of return if you purchase the security at the market price?

**8-5A.** *(Preferred stockholder expected return)* You own 200 shares of Somner Resources' preferred stock, which currently sells for $40 per share and pays annual dividends of $3.40 per share.

**a.** What is your expected return?

**b.** If you require an 8 percent return, given the current price should you sell or buy more stock?

**8-6A.** *(Common stock valuation)* You intend to purchase Marigo common stock at $50 per share, hold it 1 year, and sell after a dividend of $6 is paid. How much will the stock price have to appreciate for you to satisfy your required rate of return of 15 percent?

**8-7A.** *(Common stockholder expected return)* Made-It's common stock currently sells for $22.50 per share. The company's executives anticipate a constant growth rate of 10 percent and an end-of-year dividend of $2.

**a.** What is your expected rate of return if you buy the stock for $22.50?

**b.** If you require a 17 percent return, should you purchase the stock?

**8-8A.** *(Common stock valuation)* Header Motor, Inc., paid a $3.50 dividend last year. At a constant growth rate of 5 percent, what is the value of the common stock if the investors require a 20 percent rate of return?

**8-9A.** *(Measuring growth)* Given that a firm's return on equity is 18 percent and management plans to retain 40 percent of earnings for investment purposes, what will be the firm's growth rate?

**8-10A.** *(Common stockholder expected return)* The common stock of Zaldi Co. is selling for $32.84. The stock recently paid dividends of $2.94 per share and has a projected constant growth rate of 9.5 percent. If you purchase the stock at the market price, what is your expected rate of return?

**8-11A.** *(Common stock valuation)* Honeywag common stock is expected to pay $1.85 in dividends next year, and the market price is projected to be $42.50 by year end. If the investor's required rate of return is 11 percent, what is the current value of the stock?

**8-12A.** *(Common stockholder expected return)* The market price for Hobart common stock is $43. The price at the end of 1 year is expected to be $48, and dividends for next year should be $2.84. What is the expected rate of return?

**8-13A.** *(Preferred stock valuation)* Pioneer's preferred stock is selling for $33 in the market and pays a $3.60 annual dividend.

**a.** What is the expected rate of return on the stock?

**b.** If an investor's required rate of return is 10 percent, what is the value of the stock for that investor?

**c.** Should the investor acquire the stock?

**8-14A.** *(Common stock valuation)* The common stock of NCP paid $1.32 in dividends last year. Dividends are expected to grow at an 8 percent annual rate for an indefinite number of years.

**a.** If NCP's current market price is $23.50, what is the stock's expected rate of return?

**b.** If your required rate of return is 10.5 percent, what is the value of the stock for you?

**c.** Should you make the investment?

**8-15A.** *(Common stockholder expected return)* In October 1997, Briggs & Stratton, a small engine manufacturer, was expecting to pay an annual dividend of $1.12 in 1998. The firm's stock was selling for $49. The stock's beta is 1.10.

**a.** What is Briggs & Stratton's dividend yield?

**b.** Based on the Ibbotson Associates data presented in Chapter 6 (Table 6-1, p. 171), compute the expected rate of return for this stock. (Use the CAPM approach described in Chapter 6.)

**c.** What growth rate would you have to use in the multiple-period valuation model to get the same expected return as in part (b)?

**8-16A.** *(Common stockholder expected return)* Access the Internet to gather the following information for Johnson & Johnson.

- **a.** The earnings per share and dividends per share for the past 5 years.
- **b.** The common stock price.

Assuming that the annual growth rate in earnings per share for the past 4 years is a reasonable estimate of the growth in share price for the indefinite future, which it may not be, estimate the expected rate of return for the stock.

## INTEGRATIVE PROBLEM

You are considering three investments. The first is a bond that is selling in the market at $1,200. The bond has a $1,000 par value, pays interest at 14 percent, and is scheduled to mature in 12 years. For bonds of this risk class, you believe that a 12 percent rate of return should be required. The second investment that you are analyzing is a preferred stock ($100 par value) that sells for $80 and pays an annual dividend of $12. Your required rate of return for this stock is 14 percent. The last investment is a common stock ($25 par value) that recently paid a $3 dividend. The firm's earnings per share have increased from $4 to $8 in 10 years, which also reflects the expected growth in dividends per share for the indefinite future. The stock is selling for $25, and you think a reasonable required rate of return for the stock is 20 percent.

1. Calculate the value of each security based on your required rate of return.
2. Which investment(s) should you accept? Why?
3. If your required rates of return changed to 14 percent for the bond, 16 percent for the preferred stock, and 18 percent for the common stock, how would your answers change to parts 1 and 2?
4. Assuming again that your required rate of return for the common stock is 20 percent, but the anticipated constant growth rate changes to 12 percent, how would your answers to questions 1 and 2 change?

## STUDY PROBLEMS (SET B)

**8-1B.** *(Preferred stock valuation)* Calculate the value of a preferred stock that pays a dividend of $7 per share when your required rate of return is 10 percent.

**8-2B.** *(Measuring growth)* If the Stanford Corporation's return on equity is 24 percent and management plans to retain 70 percent of earnings for investment purposes, what will be the firm's growth rate?

**8-3B.** *(Preferred stock valuation)* What is the value of a preferred stock where the dividend rate is 16 percent on a $100 par value? The appropriate discount rate for a stock of this risk level is 12 percent.

**8-4B.** *(Preferred stockholder expected return)* Shewmaker's preferred stock is selling for $55.16 and pays $2.35 in dividends. What is your expected rate of return if you purchase the security at the market price?

**8-5B.** *(Preferred stockholder expected return)* You own 250 shares of McCormick Resources' preferred stock, which currently sells for $38.50 per share and pays annual dividends of $3.25 per share.

- **a.** What is your expected return?
- **b.** If you require an 8 percent return, given the current price, should you sell or buy more stock?

**8-6B.** *(Common stock valuation)* You intend to purchase Bama, Inc., common stock at $52.75 per share, hold it 1 year, and sell after a dividend of $6.50 is paid. How much will the stock price have to appreciate if your required rate of return is 16 percent?

**8-7B.** *(Common stockholder expected return)* Blackburn & Smith's common stock currently sells for $23 per share. The company's executives anticipate a constant growth rate of 10.5 percent and an end-of-year dividend of $2.50.

- **a.** What is your expected rate of return?
- **b.** If you require a 17 percent return, should you purchase the stock?

**8-8B.** *(Common stock valuation)* Gilliland Motor, Inc., paid a $3.75 dividend last year. At a growth rate of 6 percent, what is the value of the common stock if the investors require a 20 percent rate of return?

**8-9B.** *(Measuring growth)* Given that a firm's return on equity is 24 percent and management plans to retain 60 percent of earnings for investment purposes, what will be the firm's growth rate?

**8-10B.** *(Common stockholder expected return)* The common stock of Bouncy-Bob Moore Co. is selling for $33.84. The stock recently paid dividends of $3 per share and has a projected growth rate of 8.5 percent. If you purchase the stock at the market price, what is your expected rate of return?

**8-11B.** *(Common stock valuation)* Honeybee common stock is expected to pay $1.85 in dividends next year, and the market price is projected to be $40 by year end. If the investor's required rate of return is 12 percent, what is the current value of the stock?

**8-12B.** *(Common stock valuation)* The market price for M. Simpson & Co.'s common stock is $44. The price at the end of 1 year is expected to be $47, and dividends for next year should be $2. What is the expected rate of return?

**8-13B.** *(Preferred stock valuation)* Green's preferred stock is selling for $35 in the market and pays a $4 annual dividend.

**a.** What is the expected rate of return on the stock?

**b.** If an investor's required rate of return is 10 percent, what is the value of the stock for that investor?

**c.** Should the investor acquire the stock?

**8-14B.** *(Common stock valuation)* The common stock of KPD paid $1 in dividends last year. Dividends are expected to grow at an 8 percent annual rate for an indefinite number of years.

**a.** If KPD's current market price is $25, what is the stock's expected rate of return?

**b.** If your required rate of return is 11 percent, what is the value of the stock for you?

**c.** Should you make the investment?

**8-15B.** *(Common stockholder expected return)* In October 1997, CSX, a transportation firm (mostly railroads), was expecting to pay an annual dividend of $1.20 in 1998. The firm's stock was selling for $54. The stock's beta is 0.90.

**a.** What is CSX's dividend yield?

**b.** Based on the Ibbotson Associates data presented in Chapter 6 (Table 6-1, p. 171), compute the expected rate of return for this stock. (Use the CAPM approach described in Chapter 6.)

**c.** What growth rate would you have to use in the multiple-period valuation model to get the same expected return as in part (b)?

**8-16B.** *(Expected rate of return)* Access the Internet to gather the following information for First Union Corporation.

**a.** The earnings per share and dividends per share for the past 5 years.

**b.** The common stock price.

Assuming that the annual growth rate in earnings per share for the past 4 years is a reasonable estimate of the growth in share price for the indefinite future, which it may not be, estimate the expected rate of return for the stock.

## SELF-TEST SOLUTIONS

**ST-1.**

$$\text{value } (V_{ps}) = \frac{.16 \times \$100}{.12}$$

$$= \frac{\$16}{.12}$$

$$= \$133.33$$

**ST-2.**

**a.** $\text{expected return} = \dfrac{\text{dividend}}{\text{market price}} = \dfrac{\$3.25}{\$38.50} = 0.0844 = 8.44\%$

**b.** Given your 8 percent required rate of return, the stock is worth \$40.62 to you:

$$\text{value} = \frac{\text{dividend}}{\text{required rate of return}} = \frac{\$3.25}{0.08} = \$40.62$$

Because the expected rate of return (8.44%) is greater than your required rate of return (8%) or because the current market price (\$38.50) is less than \$40.62, the stock is undervalued and you should buy.

**ST-3.**

$$\text{value } (V_{ps}) = \frac{\text{dividend}}{\text{required rate of return}} = \frac{\$2.75}{0.09} = \$30.56$$

**ST-4.**

$$\text{value } (V_{cs}) = \left(\frac{\text{last year dividend } (1 + \text{growth rate})}{\text{required rate of return} - \text{growth rate}}\right)$$

$$= \frac{\$1.32(1.07)}{0.11 - 0.07}$$

$$= \$35.31$$

**ST-5.**

**a.** $\text{expected rate of return } (\bar{k}_{cs}) = \dfrac{\text{dividend in year 1}}{\text{market price}} + \text{growth rate}$

$$\bar{k}_{cs} = \frac{\$2.50}{\$23.00} + 0.105 = .2137$$

$$\bar{k}_{cs} = 21.37\%$$

**b.** The value of the stock for you would be \$38.46. Thus, the expected rate of return exceeds your required rate of return, which means that the value of the security to you is greater than the current market price. Thus, you should buy the stock.

$$V_{cs} = \frac{\$2.50}{.17 - .105} = \$38.46$$

## APPENDIX 8A

# THE RELATIONSHIP BETWEEN VALUE AND EARNINGS

In understanding the relationship between a firm's earnings and the market price of its stock, it is helpful to look first at the relationship for a nongrowth firm and then expand our view to include the growth firm.

## THE RELATIONSHIP BETWEEN EARNINGS AND VALUE FOR THE NONGROWTH COMPANY

When we speak of a nongrowth firm, we mean one that retains no profits for the purpose of reinvestment. The only investments made are for the purpose of maintaining status quo—that is, investing the amount of the depreciation taken on fixed assets so that the firm does not lose its current earnings capacity. The result is both constant earnings and a constant dividend stream to the common stockholder, because the firm is paying all earnings out in the form of dividends (dividend in year *t* equals earnings in year *t*). This type of common stock is essentially no different from a preferred stock. Recalling our earlier discussion about valuing a preferred stock, we may value the nongrowth common stock similarly, expressing our valuation in one of two ways:

$$\text{value of a nongrowth common stock } (V_{ng}) = \frac{\text{earnings per share}_1}{\text{required rate of return}} \quad \textbf{(8A-1)}$$

$$= \frac{\text{dividend per share}_1}{\text{required rate of return}} \quad \textbf{(8A-2)}$$

or

$$V_{ng} = \frac{EPS_1}{k_{cs}} = \frac{D_1}{k_{cs}}$$

### EXAMPLE

The Reeves Corporation expects its earnings per share this year to be $12, which is to be paid out in total to the investors in the form of dividends. If the investors have a required rate of return of 14 percent, the value of the stock would be $85.71:

$$V_{ng} = \frac{\$12}{.14} = \$85.71$$

In this instance, the relationship between value and earnings per share is direct and unmistakable. If earnings per share increases (decreases) 10 percent, then the value of the share should increase (decrease) 10 percent; that is, the ratio of price to earnings will be a constant, as will the ratio of earnings to price. A departure from the constant relationship would occur only if the investors change their required rate of return, owing to a change in their perception about such things as risk or anticipated inflation. Thus, there is good reason to perceive a relationship between next year's earnings and share price for the nongrowth company.

## THE RELATIONSHIP BETWEEN EARNINGS AND VALUE FOR THE GROWTH FIRM

Turning our attention now to the growth firm, one that does reinvest its profits back into the business, we will recall that our valuation model depended on dividends and earnings increasing at a constant growth rate. Returning to equation 8-5, we valued a common stock where dividends were expected to increase at a constant growth rate as follows:

$$\text{value} = \frac{\text{dividend}_1}{\text{required rate of return} - \text{growth rate}}$$

or

$$V_{cs} = \frac{D_1}{k_{cs} - g}$$

Although equation 8-5 is certainly the conventional way of expressing value of the growth stock, it is not the only means. We could also describe the value of a stock as the present value of the dividend stream provided from the firm's existing assets plus the present value of any future growth resulting from the reinvestment of future earnings. We could represent this concept notationally as follows:

$$V_{cs} = \frac{EPS_1}{k_{cs}} + NVDG \tag{8A-3}$$

where $EPS_1/k_{cs}$ = the present value of the cash flow stream provided by the existing assets
$NVDG$ = the net value of any dividend growth resulting from the reinvestment of future earnings

The first term, $EPS_1/k_{cs}$, is immediately understandable given our earlier rationale about non-growth stocks. The second term, the net value of future dividend growth *(NVDG),* needs some clarification.

To begin our explanation of *NVDG,* let $r$ equal the fraction of a firm's earnings that are retained in the business, which implies that the dividend in year 1 ($D_1$) would equal $(1 - r) \times EPS_1$. Next assume that any earnings that are reinvested yield a rate of *ROE* (return on equity). Thus, from the earnings generated in year 1, we would be investing the percentage of earnings retained, $r$, times the firm's earnings per share, $EPS_1$, or $r \times EPS_1$. In return, we should expect to receive a cash flow in all future years equal to the expected return on our investment, *ROE,* times the amount of our investment, or $r \times EPS_1 \times ROE$. Because cash inflows represent an annuity continuing in perpetuity, the present value from reinvesting a part of the firm's earnings in year 1 ($PV_1$) would be equal to the present value of the new cash flows less the cost of the investment:

$$PV_1 = \underbrace{\left(\frac{r \times EPS_1 \times ROE}{k_{cs}}\right)}_{\substack{\text{present value}\\\text{of increased}\\\text{cash flows}}} \underbrace{-r \times EPS}_{\substack{\text{amount of cash}\\\text{retained and}\\\text{reinvested}}} \tag{8A-4}$$

If we continued to reinvest a fixed percentage of earnings each year and earned *ROE* on these investments, there would also be a net present value in all the following years; that is, we would have a $PV_2, PV_3, PV_4 \ldots PV_\infty$. Also, because $r$ and *ROE* are both constant, the series of *PV*s will increase at a constant growth rate of $r \times ROE$. We may therefore use the *constant-growth valuation model* to value *NVDG* as follows:

$$NVDG = \frac{PV_1}{k_{cs} - g} \tag{8A-5}$$

Thus, we may now establish the value of a common stock as the sum of (1) a present value of a constant stream of earnings generated from the firm's assets already in place and (2) the present value of an increasing dividend stream coming from the retention of profits; that is,

$$V_{cs} = \frac{EPS_1}{k_{cs}} + \frac{PV_1}{k_{cs} - g} \quad \text{(8A-6)}$$

**EXAMPLE**

The Upp Corporation should earn \$8 per share this year, of which 40 percent will be retained within the firm for reinvestment and 60 percent paid in the form of dividends to the stockholders. Management expects to earn an 18 percent return on any funds retained. Let us use both the constant-growth dividend model and the *NVDG* model to compute Upp's stock value, assuming the investors have a 12 percent required rate of return.

## Constant-Growth Dividend Model

Because we are assuming that the Upp's *ROE* will be constant and that management faithfully intends to retain 40 percent of earnings each year to be used for new investments, the dividend stream flowing to the investor should increase by 7.2 percent each year, which we know by solving for $r \times ROE$, or (.4)(18%). The dividend for this year will be \$4.80, which is the dividend-payout ratio of $(1 - r)$ times the expected earnings per share of \$8 (.60 × \$8 = \$4.80). Given a 12 percent required rate of return for the investors, the value of the security may be shown to be \$100.

$$V_{cs} = \frac{D_1}{k_{cs} - g}$$

$$= \frac{\$4.80}{.12 - .072}$$

$$= \$100$$

## *NVDG* Model

Restructuring the problem to compute separately the present value of the no-growth stream and the present value of future growth opportunities, we may again determine the value of the stock to be \$100. Solving first for value assuming a no-growth scenario,

$$V_{ng} = \frac{EPS_1}{k_{cs}} \quad \text{(8A-7)}$$

$$= \frac{\$8}{.12}$$

$$= \$66.67$$

We next estimate the value of the future growth opportunities coming from reinvesting corporate profits each year, which is

$$NVDG = \frac{PV_1}{k_{cs} - g} \quad \text{(8A-8)}$$

Knowing $k_{cs}$ to be 12 percent and the growth rate to be 7.2 percent, we lack knowing only $PV_1$, which can easily be determined using equation 8A-4:

$$PV_1 = \left(\frac{r \times EPS_1 \times ROE}{k_{cs}}\right) - r \times EPS_1$$

$$= \left(\frac{(.4)(\$8)(.18)}{.12}\right) - (.4)(\$8)$$

$$= \$4.80 - \$3.20$$

$$= \$1.60$$

The *NVDG* may now be computed:

$$NVDG = \frac{\$1.60}{.12 - .072}$$

$$= \$33.33$$

Thus, the value of the combined streams is \$100:

$$V_{cs} = \$66.67 + \$33.33 = \$100$$

From the preceding example, we see that the value of the growth opportunities represents a significant portion of the total value, 33 percent to be exact. Furthermore, in looking at the *NVDG* model, we observe that value is influenced by the following: (1) the size of the firm's beginning earnings per share, (2) the percentage of profits retained, and (3) the spread between the return generated on new investments and the investor's required rate of return. The first factor relates to firm size; the second to management's decision about the firm's earnings retention rate. Although the first two factors are not unimportant, the last one is the key to wealth creation by management. *Simply because management retains profits does not mean that wealth is created for the stockholders.* Wealth comes only if the return on equity from the investments, *ROE,* is greater than the investor's required rate of return, $k_{cs}$. Thus we should expect the market to assign value not only to the reported earnings per share for the current year but also to the anticipated growth opportunities that have a marginal rate of return that exceed the required rate of return of the firm's investors.

## STUDY PROBLEMS

**8A-1.** *(Valuation of common stock—*NVDG *model)* The Burgon Co. management expects the firm's earnings per share to be \$5 this forthcoming year. The firm's policy is to pay out 35 percent of its earnings in the form of dividends. In looking at the investment opportunities available to the firm, the return on equity should be 20 percent for the foreseeable future. Use the *NVDG* model to find the value of the company's stock. The stockholder's required rate of return is 16 percent. Verify your results with the constant-growth dividend model.

**8A-2.** *(Valuation of common stock—*NVDG *model)* You want to know the impact of retaining earnings on the value of your firm's stock. Given the following information, calculate the value of the stock under the different scenarios described in part d.

- **a.** Earnings per share on existing assets should be about \$7 this forthcoming year.
- **b.** The stockholder's required rate of return is 18 percent.
- **c.** The expected return on equity may be as low as 16 percent or as high as 24 percent, with an expected return of 18 percent.
- **d.** You are considering three earnings-retention policies on a long-term basis: (1) retain no earnings, instead distributing all earnings to stockholders in the form of dividends; (2) retain 30 percent of earnings; or (3) retain 60 percent of earnings.

PART 3: INVESTMENT IN LONG-TERM ASSETS

# CAPITAL-BUDGETING DECISION CRITERIA

Expanding your market is always a difficult thing to do, and it's more difficult when your product is a motorcycle. For the first-time rider, a Harley can be a bit intimidating. Moreover, for young riders, it can also be out of their price range.

The answer to both of these problems was to introduce a low-cost, lightweight motorcycle. The idea is to hook the new riders on cycling, and then let nature take its course, eventually moving them into a full-fledged Harley. ● In 2000, Harley-Davidson did just that by introducing the Buell Blast, a smaller, lighter motorcycle selling for under $4,400 and designed specifically for the male or female new rider or novice rider who is not yet ready for the traditionally heavier Harley-Davidson cruising or touring bikes. The Buell Blast marked a change in this philosophy, going directly at younger men and women who like the outdoors and are physically active with a bike that is fun to ride. Not only did Harley introduce a new product to a market it had not been aiming at in the past, but it also packaged it with a training program aimed at uninitiated nonriders or novices to help minimize any fear of the unknown. From early reviews it appears that Harley has come up with a winner. How did Harley-Davidson go about deciding to spend millions of dollars to introduce a lightweight bike? It did it using the decision criteria we will examine in this chapter. ● This chapter is actually the first of three chapters that deal with the process of decision making with respect to investment in fixed assets—that is, should a proposal be accepted or should it be rejected? We will refer to this

**LEARNING OBJECTIVES**

After reading this chapter, you should be able to

1. Discuss the difficulty of finding profitable projects in competitive markets.
2. Determine whether a new project should be accepted using the payback period.
3. Determine whether a new project should be accepted using the net present value.
4. Determine whether a new project should be accepted using the profitability index.
5. Determine whether a new project should be accepted using the internal rate of return.
6. Explain the importance of ethical considerations in capital-budgeting decisions.
7. Discuss the trends in the use of different capital-budgeting criteria.

process as capital budgeting. In this chapter, we will look at evaluating a project. In deciding whether to accept a new project, we will focus on free cash flows. Free cash flows represent the benefits generated from accepting a capital-budgeting proposal. In this chapter, we will assume we know what level of cash flows are generated by a project and work on determining whether that project should be accepted. In the next chapter we will examine what is a relevant cash flow and how we measure it. Then, in Chapter 11, we will look at how risk enters into this process. ● Typically, these investments involve rather large cash outlays at the outset and commit the firm to a particular course of action over a relatively long period. Thus, if a capital-budgeting decision is incorrect, reversing it tends to be costly. In evaluating capital investment proposals, we compare the cost and benefits of each in a number of ways. Some of these methods take into account the time value of money, one does not; however, each of these methods is used frequently in the real world. As you will see, our preferred method of analysis will be the net present value (*NPV*) method, which compares the present value of inflows and outflows.

**CHAPTER PREVIEW**

**Capital budgeting** is the process by which the firm renews and reinvents itself—adapting old projects to the times and finding new ones. It involves comparing cash inflows that may spread out over many years with cash outflows that generally occur close to the present. As a result, much of this chapter relies heavily on **Principle 2: The Time Value of Money—A dollar received today is worth more than a dollar received in the future.** We will begin this chapter with a look at finding profitable projects. As you will see, **Principle 5: The Curse of Competitive Markets—Why it's hard to find exceptionally profitable projects** helps explain this. Next we will look at the purpose and importance of capital budgeting. We will then consider four commonly used criteria for determining acceptability of investment proposals. Keep in mind during all this that what we are actually doing is developing a framework for decision making.

## FINDING PROFITABLE PROJECTS

OBJECTIVE 1 

**Capital budgeting**
The decision-making process with respect to investment in fixed assets.

Without question, it is easier to *evaluate* profitable projects than it is to *find* them. In competitive markets, generating ideas for profitable projects is extremely difficult. The competition is brisk for new profitable projects, and once they have been uncovered competitors generally rush in, pushing down prices and profits. For this reason, a firm must have a systematic strategy for generating **capital-budgeting** projects. Without this flow of new projects and ideas, the firm cannot grow or even survive for long, being forced to live off the profits from existing projects with limited lives. So where do these ideas come from for new products, for ways to improve existing products, or for ways to make existing products more profitable? The answer is from inside the firm—from everywhere inside the firm.

FINANCE MATTERS

### The Green-and-Bear-It Approach to Finding New Projects

How do you expand the market for a product like ketchup? It seems like there is only so much ketchup a person will use and the goal might just be to take market share away from your competitors. That's not an answer that Heinz was satisfied with, and so in the fall of 2000, Heinz introduced green ketchup. How and why did Heinz come up with the idea of green ketchup?

The answer is through simple capital budgeting. In the food industry, one of the recent trends has been toward "eatertainment"—that is, making kids' food more fun to eat. Market research has shown that kids just like to be entertained when they eat. That's the reason behind the success of Dannon Sprinkl'ins Color Creations, a vanilla yogurt packaged with a different colored sprinkle under each cup lid—stir in the sprinkle and the yogurt changes colors, the green crystals turn the yogurt blue and the red turns it yellow. It is also the reason behind the success of Quaker Oats Sea Adventures, which advertises, "a blue sea with sharks, treasures, and divers magically appears as you stir!" It even hit the computer industry with the introduction of the iMac.

To say the least, the people at Heinz were a bit taken back when they found out that grade school children in test groups from coast to coast said they wanted their ketchup in colors. According to Kelly Stitt, the brand manager for Heinz, "Kids live a world of color. Everything is bright, bold color." The bottom line is that kids wanted ketchup in green, and also in blue. For Heinz, it's one step at a time—it initially just went with the green, and in a plastic bottle that squirts a stream so thin that kids that can draw with it.

What techniques did Heinz use to make its decision to go forward with this project? It used the same capital-budgeting techniques we introduce in this chapter. Many times good capital-budgeting projects are not just a great idea for a new project, but are instead the result of good marketing research. In effect, although our capital-budgeting techniques can do a good job of evaluating projects, a good project has its roots in good product development—knowing what the consumer wants and delivering it. That means coming up with sales forecasts that are accurate—that anticipate moves by competitors—because although our capital-budgeting criteria are good at evaluating proposals, the results are only as good as what is input into the models.

Source: Based on Paul Lukas, "The Color Of Money And Ketchup," *Fortune Magazine* (August 14, 2000): 38; Constance L. Hays, "Go Play With Your Food, Dear," *The New York Times* (July 16, 2000): 2; Lisa Gutierrez, "In living color it's fast becoming a mix-and-match world, from food to appliances," *The Kansas City Star* (July 18, 2000): E1; Damian Whitworth, "Green ketchup is latest Heinz variety, *The Times of London* (July 11, 2000): 4m; and Kristen Hays, "Heinz looks to new green ketchup for a pot of gold," Chicago Sun-Times (July 10, 2000): 4.

### RELATE TO THE BIG PICTURE

The fact that profitable projects are difficult to find relates directly to **Principle 5: The Curse of Competitive Markets—Why it's hard to find exceptionally profitable projects.** When we introduced that principle we stated that successful investments involve the reduction of competition by creating barriers to entry either through product differentiation or cost advantages. The key to locating profitable projects is to understand how and where they exist.

Typically, a firm has a research and development department that searches for ways to improve existing products or find new products. These ideas may come from within the R&D department or be based on referral ideas from executives, sales personnel, anyone in the firm, or even from customers. For example, at Ford Motor Company prior to the 1980s, ideas for product improvement had typically been generated in Ford's research and development department. Unfortunately, this strategy was not enough to keep Ford from losing much of its market share to the Japanese. In an attempt to cut costs and improve product quality, Ford moved from strict reliance on an R&D department to seeking the input of employees at all levels for new ideas. Bonuses are now provided to workers for their cost-cutting suggestions, and assembly line personnel who can see the production process from a hands-on point of view are now brought into the hunt for new projects. The effect on Ford has been positive and significant. Although not all suggested projects prove to be profitable, many new ideas generated from within the firm turn out to be good ones.

Keep in mind that new capital-budgeting projects don't necessarily mean coming up with a new product, it may be taking an existing product and applying it to a new market. That's certainly been the direction that McDonald's has taken in recent years. Today, McDonald's operates in over 51 countries with more than 11,000 restaurants. One of the biggest is a 700-seat McDonald's in Moscow. Was this an expensive venture? It certainly was, in fact, the food plant that McDonald's built to supply burgers, buns, fries, and everything else sold there cost over $60 million. In addition to the costs, it differs from opening an outlet in the United States in a number of ways. First, in order to keep the quality of what McDonald's sells identical to what is served at any McDonald's anywhere in the world, McDonald's spent 6 years in putting together a supply chain that would provide the necessary raw materials at the quality level McDonald's demanded. On top of that, there are risks associated with the Russian economy and its currency that are well beyond the scope of what is experienced in the United States. However, since it opened, it has proven to be enormously successful. It all goes to show that not all capital-budgeting projects have to be new products, they can also be existing products in new markets.

We will consider four commonly used criteria for determining acceptability of investment proposals. The first is the payback period and it is the least sophisticated, in that it does not incorporate the time value of money into its calculations; the remaining three do take it into account. For the time being, the problem of incorporating risk into the capital-budgeting decision is ignored. This issue will be examined in Chapter 11. In addition, we will assume that the appropriate discount rate, required rate of return, or cost of capital is given. The determination of this rate is the topic of Chapter 12.

**CONCEPT CHECK**

1. Why is it so difficult to find an exceptionally profitable project?
2. Why is the search for new, profitable projects so important?

## PAYBACK PERIOD

OBJECTIVE 2 

**Payback period**
A capital-budgeting criterion defined as the number of years required to recover the initial cash investment.

The **payback period** is the number of years needed to recover the initial cash outlay. As this criterion measures how quickly the project will return its original investment, it deals with free cash flows, which measure the true timing of the benefits, rather than accounting profits. Unfortunately, it also ignores the time value of money and does not discount these free cash flows back to the present. The accept-reject criterion centers on whether the project's payback period is less than or equal to the firm's maximum desired payback period. For example, if a firm's maximum desired payback period is 3 years and an investment proposal requires an initial cash outlay of $10,000 and yields the following set of annual free cash flows, what is its payback period? Should the project be accepted?

| | After-Tax Free Cash Flow |
|---|---|
| Year 1 | $ 2,000 |
| Year 2 | 4,000 |
| Year 3 | 3,000 |
| Year 4 | 3,000 |
| Year 5 | 10,000 |

In this case, after 3 years the firm will have recaptured $9,000 on an initial investment of $10,000, leaving $1,000 of the initial investment still to be recouped. During the fourth year, a total of $3,000 will be returned from this investment. Assuming cash will flow into the firm at a constant rate over the year, it will take one-third of the year ($1,000/$3,000) to recapture the remaining $1,000. Thus, the payback period on this project is 3⅓ years, which is more than the desired payback period. Using the payback period criterion, the firm would reject this project without even considering the $10,000 cash flow in year 5.

Although the payback period is used frequently, it does have some rather obvious drawbacks, which can best be demonstrated through the use of an example. Consider two investment projects, A and B, which involve an initial cash outlay of $10,000 each and produce the annual free cash flows shown in Table 9-1. Both projects have a payback period of 2 years; therefore, in terms of the payback period criterion, both are equally acceptable. However, if we had our choice, it is clear we would select A over B, for at least two reasons. First, regardless of what happens after the payback period, project A returns our initial investment to us earlier within the payback period. Thus, because there is a time value of money, the cash flows occurring within the payback period should not be weighted equally, as they are. In addition, all cash flows that occur after the payback period are ignored. This violates the principle that investors desire more in the way of benefits rather than less—a principle that is difficult to deny, especially when we are talking about money.

To deal with the criticism that the payback period ignores the time value of money, some firms use the **discounted payback period** approach. The discounted payback period method is similar to the traditional payback period except that it uses discounted free cash flows rather than actual undiscounted free cash flows in calculating the payback period. The discounted payback period is defined as the number of years needed to recover the initial cash outlay from the *discounted free cash flows*. The accept-reject criterion then becomes whether the project's discounted payback period is less than or equal to the firm's maximum desired discounted payback period. Using the assumption that the required rate of return on projects A and B illustrated in Table 9-1 is 17 percent, the discounted cash flows from these projects are given in Table 9-2. On project A, after 3 years, only $74 of the initial outlay remain to be recaptured, whereas year 4 brings in a discounted free cash flow of $1,068. Thus, if the $1,068 comes in a constant rate over the year, it will take 7/100s of the year ($74/$1,068) to recapture the remaining $74. The discounted payback period for project A is 3.07 years, calculated as follows:

**Discounted payback period**
A variation of the payback period decision criterion defined as the number of years required to recover the initial cash outlay from the discounted net cash flows.

$$\text{discounted payback period}_A = 3.0 + \$74/\$1{,}068 = 3.07 \text{ years}$$

If project A's discounted payback period was less than the firm's maximum desired discounted payback period, then project A would be accepted. Project B, on the other hand, does not have a discounted payback period because it never fully recovers the project's initial cash outlay, and thus should be rejected. The major problem with the discounted payback period comes in setting the firm's maximum desired discounted payback

**TABLE 9-1**
Payback Period Example

| Projects | A | B |
|---|---|---|
| Initial cash outlay | −$10,000 | −$10,000 |
| Annual free cash flows: | | |
| Year 1 | $ 6,000 | $ 5,000 |
| 2 | 4,000 | 5,000 |
| 3 | 3,000 | 0 |
| 4 | 2,000 | 0 |
| 5 | 1,000 | 0 |

**TABLE 9-2**
Discounted Payback Period Example Using a 17 Percent Required Rate of Return

**PROJECT A**

| Year | Undiscounted Free Cash Flows | $PVIF_{17\%,n}$ | Discounted Free Cash Flows | Cumulative Discounted Free Cash Flows |
|---|---|---|---|---|
| 0 | −$10,000 | 1.0 | −$10,000 | −$10,000 |
| 1 | 6,000 | .855 | 5,130 | − 4,870 |
| 2 | 4,000 | .731 | 2,924 | − 1,946 |
| 3 | 3,000 | .624 | 1,872 | −74 |
| 4 | 2,000 | .534 | 1,068 | 994 |
| 5 | 1,000 | .456 | 456 | 1,450 |

**PROJECT B**

| Year | Undiscounted Free Cash Flows | $PVIF_{17\%,n}$ | Discounted Free Cash Flows | Cumulative Discounted Free Cash Flows |
|---|---|---|---|---|
| 0 | −$10,000 | 1.0 | −$10,000 | −$10,000 |
| 1 | 5,000 | .855 | 4,275 | − 5,725 |
| 2 | 5,000 | .731 | 3,655 | − 2,070 |
| 3 | 0 | .624 | 0 | − 2,070 |
| 4 | 0 | .534 | 0 | − 2,070 |
| 5 | 0 | .456 | 0 | − 2,070 |

period. This is an arbitrary decision that affects which projects are accepted and which ones are rejected. Thus, although the discounted payback period is superior to the traditional payback period, in that it accounts for the time value of money in its calculations, its use is limited by the arbitrariness of the process used to select the maximum desired payback period. Moreover, as we will soon see, the net present value criterion is theoretically superior and no more difficult to calculate.

Although these deficiencies limit the value of the payback period and discounted payback period as tools for investment evaluation, these methods do have several positive features. First, they deal with free cash flows, as opposed to accounting profits, and therefore focus on the true timing of the project's benefits and costs, even though the traditional payback period does not adjust the cash flows for the time value of money. Second, they are easy to visualize, quickly understood, and easy to calculate. Finally, although the payback period and discounted payback period methods have serious deficiencies, they are often used as rough screening devices to eliminate projects whose returns do not materialize until later years. These methods emphasize the earliest returns, which in all likelihood are less uncertain, and provide for the liquidity needs of the firm. Although their advantages are certainly significant, their disadvantages severely limit their value as discriminating capital-budgeting criteria.

## RELATE TO THE BIG PICTURE

The final three capital-budgeting criteria all incorporate **Principle 2: The Time Value of Money—A dollar received today is worth more than a dollar received in the future** in their calculations. If we are at all to make rational business decisions we must recognize that money has a time value. In examining the following three capital-budgeting techniques, you will notice that this principle is the driving force behind each of them.

**CONCEPT CHECK**

1. What are some of the shortcomings of the payback period?
2. Why do you think the payback period is used as frequently as it is?
3. What is the major problem with the discounted payback period?

## NET PRESENT VALUE

OBJECTIVE 3

**Net present value (*NPV*)** A capital-budgeting decision criterion defined as the present value of the future net cash flows after tax less the project's initial outlay.

The **net present value (*NPV*)** of an investment proposal is equal to the present value of its annual after-tax net cash flows less the investment's initial outlay. The net present value can be expressed as follows:

$$NPV = \sum_{t=1}^{n} \frac{FCF_t}{(1+k)^t} - IO \quad \textbf{(9-1)}$$

where $FCF_t$ = the annual free cash flow in time period $t$ (this can take on either positive or negative values)
$k$ = the appropriate discount rate; that is, the required rate of return or cost of capital[1]
$IO$ = the initial cash outlay
$n$ = the project's expected life

The project's net present value gives a measurement of the *net value* of an investment proposal in terms of today's dollars. Because all cash flows are discounted back to the present, comparing the difference between the present value of the annual free cash flows and the investment outlay is appropriate. The difference between the present value of the annual free cash flows and the initial outlay determines the net value of accepting the investment proposal in terms of today's dollars. Whenever the project's *NPV* is greater than or equal to zero, we will accept the project; whenever the *NPV* is negative, we will reject the project. Note that if the project's net present value is zero, then it returns the required rate of return and should be accepted. This accept-reject criterion can be stated as:

$NPV \geq 0.0$: Accept
$NPV < 0.0$: Reject

The following example illustrates the use of the net present value capital-budgeting criterion.

**EXAMPLE**

Ski-Doo is considering new machinery that would reduce manufacturing costs associated with its Mach Z snowmobile, for which the after-tax cash flows are shown in Table 9-3. If the firm has a 12 percent required rate of return, the present value of the free cash flows is $47,678, as calculated in Table 9-4. Subtracting the $40,000 initial outlay leaves a net present value of $7,678. Because this value is greater than zero, the net present value criterion indicates that the project should be accepted.

[1]The required rate of return or cost of capital is the rate of return necessary to justify raising funds to finance the project or, alternatively, the rate of return necessary to maintain the firm's current market price per share. These terms will be defined in greater detail in Chapter 12.

**TABLE 9-3**
*NPV* Illustration of Investment in New Machinery

| | Free Cash Flow | | Free Cash Flow |
|---|---|---|---|
| Initial outlay | −$40,000 | Year 3 | 13,000 |
| Year 1 | 15,000 | Year 4 | 12,000 |
| Year 2 | 14,000 | Year 5 | 11,000 |

**TABLE 9-4**
Calculation for *NPV* Illustration of Investment in New Machinery

| | Free Cash Flow | Present Value Factor at 12 Percent | Present Value |
|---|---|---|---|
| Year 1 | $15,000 | .893 | $13,395 |
| Year 2 | 14,000 | .797 | 11,158 |
| Year 3 | 13,000 | .712 | 9,256 |
| Year 4 | 12,000 | .636 | 7,632 |
| Year 5 | 11,000 | .567 | 6,237 |
| Present value of free cash flows | | | $47,678 |
| Initial outlay | | | −40,000 |
| Net present value | | | $7,678 |

Note in the Ski-Doo example that the worth of the net present value calculation is a function of the accuracy of cash-flow predictions.

The *NPV* criterion is the capital-budgeting decision tool we will find most favorable. First of all, it deals with free cash flows rather than accounting profits. Also, it is sensitive to the true timing of the benefits resulting from the project. Moreover, recognizing that, the time value of money allows comparison of the benefits and costs in a logical manner. Finally, because projects are accepted only if a positive net present value is associated with them, the acceptance of a project using this criterion will increase the value of the firm, which is consistent with the goal of maximizing the shareholders' wealth.

**EXAMPLE**

A firm is considering the purchase of a new computer system, which will cost $30,000 initially, to aid in credit billing and inventory management. The free cash flows resulting from this project are provided in Table 9-5. The required rate of return demanded by the firm is 10 percent. To determine the system's net present value, the 3-year $15,000 cash flow annuity is first discounted back to the present at 10 percent. From Appendix E in the back of this book, we find that $PVIFA_{10\%,3yr}$ is 2.487. Thus, the present value of this $15,000 annuity is $37,305 ($15,000 × 2.487).

**TABLE 9-5**
*NPV* Example Problem of Computer System

| | Free Cash Flow | | Free Cash Flow |
|---|---|---|---|
| Initial outlay | −$30,000 | Year 2 | 15,000 |
| Year 1 | 15,000 | Year 3 | 15,000 |

Seeing that the cash inflows have been discounted back to the present, they can now be compared with the initial outlay, because both of the flows are now stated in terms of today's dollars. Subtracting the initial outlay ($30,000) from the present value of the free cash flows ($37,305), we find that the system's net present value is $7,305. Because the *NPV* on this project is positive, the project should be accepted.

The disadvantage of the *NPV* method stems from the need for detailed, long-term forecasts of free cash flows accruing from the project's acceptance. Despite this drawback, the net present value is the theoretically correct criterion in that it measures the impact of a project's acceptance on the value of the firm's equity. The following example provides an additional illustration of its application.

## Spreadsheets and the Net Present Value

While we can calculate the *NPV* by hand, it is more common that it will be done with the help of a spreadsheet. Just as with the keystroke calculations on a financial calculator, a spreadsheet can make easy work of the *NPV* calculations. The only real glitch here is that Excel, along with most other spreadsheets, only calculates the present value of the future cash flows and ignores the initial outlay in its *NPV* calculations. Sound strange? Well, it is. It is essentially just a carry-forward of an error in one of the first spreadsheets. That means that the actual *NPV* is the Excel calculated *NPV*, minus the initial outlay:

actual *NPV* = Excel calculated *NPV* − initial outlay

This can be input into a spreadsheet cell as: =*NPV*(rate, inflow 1, inflow 2, . . . inflow 29) − initial outlay.

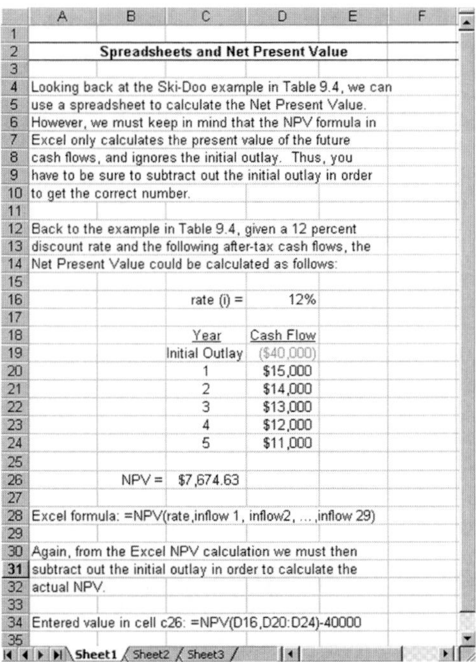

**Spreadsheets and Net Present Value**

Looking back at the Ski-Doo example in Table 9.4, we can use a spreadsheet to calculate the Net Present Value. However, we must keep in mind that the NPV formula in Excel only calculates the present value of the future cash flows, and ignores the initial outlay. Thus, you have to be sure to subtract out the initial outlay in order to get the correct number.

Back to the example in Table 9.4, given a 12 percent discount rate and the following after-tax cash flows, the Net Present Value could be calculated as follows:

rate (i) = 12%

| Year | Cash Flow |
|---|---|
| Initial Outlay | ($40,000) |
| 1 | $15,000 |
| 2 | $14,000 |
| 3 | $13,000 |
| 4 | $12,000 |
| 5 | $11,000 |

NPV = $7,674.63

Excel formula: =NPV(rate,inflow 1, inflow2, ... ,inflow 29)

Again, from the Excel NPV calculation we must then subtract out the initial outlay in order to calculate the actual NPV.

Entered value in cell c26: =NPV(D16,D20:D24)-40000

### CONCEPT CHECK

1. Provide an intuitive definition of the net present value of a project.
2. Suppose a project has a net present value of $10 million. What does that mean?

## PROFITABILITY INDEX (BENEFIT/COST RATIO)

OBJECTIVE 4 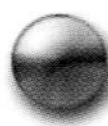

**Profitability index (*PI*) (or Benefit/Cost Ratio)**
A capital-budgeting decision criterion defined as the ratio of the present value of the future free cash flows to the initial outlay.

The **profitability index (PI),** or **benefit/cost ratio,** is the ratio of the present value of the future free cash flows to the initial outlay. Although the net present value investment criterion gives a measure of the absolute dollar desirability of a project, the profitability index provides a relative measure of an investment proposal's desirability—that is, the ratio of the present value of its future benefits to its initial cost. The profitability index can be expressed as follows:

$$PI = \frac{\sum_{t=1}^{n} \frac{FCF_t}{(1+k)^t}}{IO} \tag{9-2}$$

where $FCF_t$ = the annual free cash flow in time period $t$ (this can take on either positive or negative values)
$k$ = the appropriate discount rate; that is, the required rate of return or cost of capital
$IO$ = the initial cash outlay
$n$ = the project's expected life

The decision criterion is this: Accept the project if the *PI* is greater than or equal to 1.00, and reject the project if the *PI* is less than 1.00.

$PI \geq 1.0$: Accept
$PI < 1.0$: Reject

Looking closely at this criterion, we see that it yields the same accept-reject decision as the net present value criterion. Whenever the present value of the project's net cash flows is greater than its initial cash outlay, the project's net present value will be positive, signaling a decision to accept. When this is true, the project's profitability index will also be greater than 1, as the present value of the free cash flows (the *PI*'s numerator) is greater than its initial outlay (the *PI*'s denominator). Thus, these two decision criteria will always yield the same accept-reject decision, although they will not necessarily rank acceptable projects in the same order. This problem of conflicting ranking will be dealt with at a later point.

Because the net present value and profitability index criteria are essentially the same, they have the same advantages over the other criteria examined. Both employ cash flows, recognize the timing of the cash flows, and are consistent with the goal of maximization of shareholders' wealth. The major disadvantage of this criterion, similar to the net present value criterion, is that it requires detailed free cash flow forecasts over the entire life of the project.

### EXAMPLE

A firm with a 10 percent required rate of return is considering investing in a new machine with an expected life of 6 years. The after-tax cash flows resulting from this investment are given in Table 9-6. Discounting the project's future free cash flows back to the present yields a present value of $53,667; dividing this value by the initial outlay of $50,000 gives a profitability index of 1.0733, as shown in Table 9-7. This tells us that the present value of the future benefits accruing from this project is 1.0733 times the level of the initial outlay. Because the profitability index is greater than 1.0, the project should be accepted.

**TABLE 9-6**
*PI* Illustration of Investment in New Machinery

| | Free Cash Flow | | Free Cash Flow |
|---|---|---|---|
| Initial outlay | −$50,000 | Year 4 | 12,000 |
| Year 1 | 15,000 | Year 5 | 14,000 |
| Year 2 | 8,000 | Year 6 | 16,000 |
| Year 3 | 10,000 | | |

**TABLE 9-7**
Calculation for *PI* Illustration of Investment in New Machinery

| | Free Cash Flow | Present Value Factor at 10 Percent | Present Value |
|---|---|---|---|
| Initial outlay | −$50,000 | 1.000 | −$50,000 |
| Year 1 | 15,000 | 0.909 | 13,635 |
| Year 2 | 8,000 | 0.826 | 6,608 |
| Year 3 | 10,000 | 0.751 | 7,510 |
| Year 4 | 12,000 | 0.683 | 8,196 |
| Year 5 | 14,000 | 0.621 | 8,694 |
| Year 6 | 16,000 | 0.564 | 9,024 |

$$PI = \frac{\sum_{t=1}^{n} \frac{FCF_t}{(1+k)^t}}{IO}$$

$$= \frac{\$13{,}635 + \$6{,}608 + \$7{,}510 + \$8{,}196 + \$8{,}694 + \$9{,}024}{\$50{,}000}$$

$$= \frac{\$53{,}667}{\$50{,}000}$$

$$= 1.0733$$

**CONCEPT CHECK**

1. Provide an intuitive definition of the profitability index of a project.
2. Suppose a project has a profitability index of 0.94. What does that mean?
3. Why do the net present value and profitability index always give the same accept or reject decision for any project?

## INTERNAL RATE OF RETURN

The **internal rate of return (*IRR*)** attempts to answer this question: What rate of return does this project earn? For computational purposes, the internal rate of return is defined as the discount rate that equates the present value of the project's future net cash flows with the project's initial cash outlay. Mathematically, the internal rate of return is defined as the value of *IRR* in the following equation:

**Internal rate of return (*IRR*)**
A capital-budgeting decision criterion that reflects the rate of return a project earns. Mathematically, it is the discount rate that equates the present value of the inflows with the present value of the outflows.

$$IO = \sum_{t=1}^{n} \frac{FCF_t}{(1+IRR)^t} \quad \textbf{(9-3)}$$

where $FCF_t$ = the annual free cash flow in time period $t$ (this can take on either positive or negative values)
$IO$ = the initial cash outlay
$n$ = the project's expected life
$IRR$ = the project's internal rate of return

In effect, the *IRR* is analogous to the concept of the yield to maturity for bonds, which was examined in Chapter 7. In other words, a project's internal rate of return is simply the rate of return that the project earns.

The decision criterion is this: Accept the project if the internal rate of return is greater than or equal to the required rate of return. We reject the project if its internal rate of return is less than this required rate of return. This accept-reject criterion can be stated as:

$IRR \geq$ required rate of return: Accept
$IRR <$ required rate of return: Reject

If the internal rate of return on a project is equal to the shareholders' required rate of return, then the project should be accepted, because the firm is earning the rate that its shareholders require. However, the acceptance of a project with an internal rate of return below the investors' required rate of return will decrease the firm's stock price.

If the *NPV* is positive, then the *IRR* must be greater than the required rate of return, $k$. Thus, all the discounted cash flow criteria are consistent and will give similar accept-reject decisions. In addition, because the internal rate of return is another discounted cash flow criterion, it exhibits the same general advantages and disadvantages as both the net present value and profitability index, but has an additional disadvantage of being tedious to calculate if a financial calculator is not available.

An additional disadvantage of the *IRR* relative to the *NPV* deals with the implied reinvestment rate assumptions made by these two methods. The *NPV* method implicitly assumes that cash flows received over the life of the project are reinvested back in projects that earn the required rate of return. That is, if we have a mining project with a 10-year expected life that produces a $100,000 cash flow at the end of the second year, the *NPV* technique assumes that this $100,000 is reinvested over the period years 3 through 10 at the required rate of return. The use of the *IRR,* on the other hand, implies that cash flows over the life of the project can be reinvested at the *IRR*. Thus, if the mining project we just looked at has a 40 percent *IRR,* the use of the *IRR* implies that the $100,000 cash flow that is received at the end of year 2 could be reinvested at 40 percent over the remaining life of the project. In effect, *the* NPV *method implicitly assumes that cash flows over the life of the project can be reinvested at the firm's required rate of return, whereas the use of the* IRR *method implies that these cash flows could be reinvested at the* IRR. The better assumption is the one made by the *NPV,* that cash flows could be reinvested at the required rate of return, because these cash flows will either be (1) returned in the form of dividends to shareholders who demand the required rate of return on their investment, or (2) reinvested in a new investment project. If these cash flows are invested in a new project, then they are simply substituting for external funding on which the required rate of return is demanded. Thus, the opportunity cost of these funds is the required rate of return. The bottom line to all this is that the *NPV* method makes the best reinvestment rate assumption and, as such, is superior to the *IRR* method. Why should we care which method is used if both methods give similar accept-reject decisions? The answer, as we will see in the next chapter, is that although they may give the same accept-reject decision, they may rank projects differently in terms of desirability.

## Computing the IRR with a Financial Calculator

With today's calculators, the determination of an internal rate of return is merely a matter of a few keystrokes. In Chapter 5, whenever we were solving time value of money problems for *i,* we were really solving for the internal rate of return. For instance, in Chapter 5, when we solved for the rate that $100 must be compounded annually for it to grow to $179.10 in 10 years, we were actually solving for that problem's internal rate of return. Thus, with financial calculators we need only input the initial outlay, the cash flows, and their timing, and then press the function key ***I/Y*** or the ***IRR*** button to calculate the internal rate of return. On some calculators, it is necessary to press the compute key, ***CPT,*** before pressing the function key to be calculated.

## Computing the IRR for Even Cash Flows

In this section, we are going to put our spreadsheets and calculators aside and obtain a better understanding of the *IRR* by examining the mathematical process of calculating internal rates of return.

The calculation of a project's internal rate of return can either be very simple or relatively complicated. As an example of a straightforward solution, assume that a firm with a required rate of return of 10 percent is considering a project that involves an initial outlay of $45,555. If the investment is taken, the free cash flows are expected to be $15,000 per annum over the project's 4-year life. In this case, the internal rate of return is equal to *IRR* in the following equation:

$$\$45{,}555 = \frac{\$15{,}000}{(1 + IRR)^1} + \frac{\$15{,}000}{(1 + IRR)^2} + \frac{\$15{,}000}{(1 + IRR)^3} + \frac{\$15{,}000}{(1 + IRR)^4}$$

From our discussion of the present value of an annuity in Chapter 5, we know that this equation can be reduced to

$$\$45{,}555 = \$15{,}000\left[\sum_{t=1}^{4}\frac{1}{(1 + IRR)^t}\right]$$

Appendix E gives values for the $PVIFA_{i,n}$ for various combinations of *i* and *n,* which further reduces this equation to

$$\$45{,}555 = \$15{,}000\,(PVIFA_{i,4\text{yr}})$$

Dividing both sides by $15,000, this becomes

$$3.037 = PVIFA_{i,4\text{yr}}$$

Hence we are looking for a $PVIFA_{i,4\text{yr}}$ of 3.037 in the 4-year row of Appendix E. This value occurs when *i* equals 12 percent, which means that 12 percent is the internal rate of return for the investment. Therefore, because 12 percent is greater than the 10 percent required return, the project should be accepted.

## Computing the IRR for Uneven Cash Flows

Unfortunately, although solving for the *IRR* is quite easy when using a financial calculator or spreadsheet, it can be solved directly in the tables only when the future after-tax net cash flows are in the form of an annuity or a single payment. With a calculator, the process is simple: One need only key in the initial cash outlay, the cash flows, and their timing, and press the ***IRR*** button. When a financial calculator is not available and these flows are in the form of an uneven series of flows, a trial-and-error approach is necessary. To do this, we first determine the present value of the future free cash flows using an arbitrary discount rate. If the present value of the future free cash flows at this discount rate is larger than the initial outlay, the rate is increased; if it is smaller than the initial outlay, the discount rate is lowered and the process begins again. This search routine is continued until the present value of the future free cash flows is equal to the initial outlay. The interest rate that creates this situation is the internal rate of return. This is the same basic process that a financial calculator uses to calculate an *IRR*.

To illustrate the procedure, consider an investment proposal that requires an initial outlay of $3,817 and returns $1,000 at the end of year 1, $2,000 at the end of year 2, and $3,000 at the end of year 3. In this case, the internal rate of return must be determined using trial and error. This process is presented in Table 9-8, in which an arbitrarily selected discount rate of 15 percent was chosen to begin the process.

**TABLE 9-8**
Computing *IRR* for Uneven Free Cash Flows Without a Financial Calculator

| | | | |
|---|---|---|---|
| Initial outlay | −$3,817 | *FCF* year 2 | 2,000 |
| *FCF* year 1 | 1,000 | *FCF* year 3 | 3,000 |

Solution:
Step 1: Pick an arbitrary discount rate and use it to determine the present value of the free cash flows.
Step 2: Compare the present value of the free cash flows with the initial outlay; if they are equal you have determined the *IRR*.
Step 3: If the present value of the free cash flows is larger than (less than) the initial outlay, raise (lower) the discount rate.
Step 4: Determine the present value of the free cash flows and repeat step 2.

**1. TRY *i* = 15 PERCENT:**

| | Free Cash Flows | Present Value Factor at 15 Percent | Present Value |
|---|---|---|---|
| Year 1 | $1,000 | .870 | $ 870 |
| Year 2 | 2,000 | .756 | 1,512 |
| Year 3 | 3,000 | .658 | 1,974 |
| Present value of inflows | | | $4,356 |
| Initial outlay | | | −$3,817 |

**2. TRY *i* = 20 PERCENT:**

| | Free Cash Flows | Present Value Factor at 20 Percent | Present Value |
|---|---|---|---|
| Year 1 | $1,000 | .833 | $ 833 |
| Year 2 | 2,000 | .694 | 1,388 |
| Year 3 | 3,000 | .579 | 1,737 |
| Present value of inflows | | | $3,958 |
| Initial outlay | | | −$3,817 |

**3. TRY *i* = 22 PERCENT:**

| | Free Cash Flows | Present Value Factor at 22 Percent | Present Value |
|---|---|---|---|
| Year 1 | $1,000 | .820 | $ 820 |
| Year 2 | 2,000 | .672 | 1,344 |
| Year 3 | 3,000 | .551 | 1,653 |
| Present value of inflows | | | $3,817 |
| Initial outlay | | | −$3,817 |

Obviously, 15 percent isn't the *IRR* for this project, because the present value of the free cash flows discounted back to present at 15 percent ($4,356) doesn't equal the initial outlay ($3,815). How do we make the present value of the future free cash flows smaller? We raise the discount rate. Thus we tried 20 percent next. Again, 20 percent isn't the *IRR* for this project because the present value of the free cash flows discounted back to present at 20 percent ($3,958) doesn't equal the initial outlay ($3,815)—although it's closer than it was at 15 percent. Once more, we need to make the present value of the future free cash flows smaller so we try a higher discount rate—22 percent. At 22 percent, we have found the project's internal rate of return, because the present value of the future free cash flows equals the initial outlay. The project's internal rate of return is then compared with the firm's required rate of return, and if the *IRR* is the larger, the project is accepted.

## EXAMPLE

A firm with a required rate of return of 10 percent is considering three investment proposals. Given the information in Table 9-9, management plans to calculate the internal rate of return for each project and determine which projects should be accepted.

**TABLE 9-9**
Three *IRR* Investment Proposal Examples

| | A | B | C |
|---|---|---|---|
| Initial outlay | −$10,000 | −$10,000 | −$10,000 |
| *FCF* year 1 | 3,362 | 0 | 1,000 |
| *FCF* year 2 | 3,362 | 0 | 3,000 |
| *FCF* year 3 | 3,362 | 0 | 6,000 |
| *FCF* year 4 | 3,362 | 13,605 | 7,000 |

Because project A is an annuity, we can easily calculate its internal rate of return by determining the $PVIFA_{i,4\text{yr}}$ necessary to equate the present value of the future free cash flows with the initial outlay. This computation is done as follows:

$$IO = \sum_{t=1}^{n} \frac{FCF_t}{(1 + IRR)^t}$$

$$\$10{,}000 = \sum_{t=1}^{4} \frac{\$3{,}362}{(1 + IRR)^t}$$

$$\$10{,}000 = \$3{,}362(PVIFA_{i,4\text{yr}})$$

$$2.974 = (PVIFA_{i,4\text{yr}})$$

We are looking for a $PVIFA_{i,4\text{yr}}$ of 2.974, in the 4-year row of Appendix E, which occurs in the $i = 13$ percent column. Thus, 13 percent is the internal rate of return. Because this rate is greater than the firm's required rate of return of 10 percent, the project should be accepted.

Project B involves a single future free cash flow of $13,605, resulting from an initial outlay of $10,000; thus, its internal rate of return can be determined directly from the present-value table in Appendix C, as follows:

$$IO = \frac{FCF_t}{(1 + IRR)^t}$$

$$\$10{,}000 = \frac{\$13{,}605}{(1 + IRR)^4}$$

$$\$10{,}000 = \$13{,}605(PVIF_{i,4yr})$$

$$.735 = (PVIF_{i,4yr})$$

This tells us that we should look for a $PVIF_{i,4yr}$ of .735 in the 4-year row of Appendix C, which occurs in the $i = 8$ percent column. We may therefore conclude that 8 percent is the internal rate of return. Because this rate is less than the firm's required rate of return of 10 percent, project B should be rejected.

The uneven nature of the future free cash flows associated with project C necessitates the use of the trial-and-error method. The internal rate of return for project C is equal to the value of *IRR* in the following equation:

$$\$10{,}000 = \frac{\$1{,}000}{(1 + IRR)^1} + \frac{\$3{,}000}{(1 + IRR)^2} + \frac{\$6{,}000}{(1 + IRR)^3} + \frac{\$7{,}000}{(1 + IRR)^4}$$

Arbitrarily selecting a discount rate of 15 percent and substituting it for *IRR* reduces the right side of the equation to \$11,090, as shown in Table 9-10 (page 000). Therefore, because the present value of the future free cash flows is larger than the initial outlay, we must raise the discount rate to find the project's internal rate of return. Substituting 20 percent for the discount rate, the right side of the equation now becomes \$9,763. As this is less than the initial outlay of \$10,000, we must now decrease the discount rate. In other words, we know that the internal rate of return for this project is between 15 and 20 percent. Because the present value of the future flows discounted back to present at 20 percent was only \$237 too low, a discount rate of 19 percent is selected. As shown in Table 9-10, a discount rate of 19 percent reduces the present value of the future inflows down to \$10,009, which is approximately the same as the initial outlay. Consequently, project C's internal rate of return is approximately 19 percent.[2] Because the internal rate of return is greater than the firm's required rate of return of 10 percent, this investment should be accepted.

[2]If desired, the actual rate can be more precisely approximated through interpolation as follows:

| Discount Rate | Present Value | | |
|---|---|---|---|
| 19% | \$10,009 | difference \$9 (19% to IRR) | difference \$246 (19% to 20%) |
| IRR | 10,000 | | |
| 20% | 9,763 | | |

Thus IRR = 19% + (\$9/\$246) · 1% = 19.04%

**TABLE 9-10**
Computing IRR for Project C

**TRY *i* = 15 PERCENT:**

| | Free Cash Flows | Present Value Factor at 15 Percent | Present Value |
|---|---|---|---|
| Year 1 | $1,000 | .870 | $ 870 |
| Year 2 | 3,000 | .756 | 2,268 |
| Year 3 | 6,000 | .658 | 3,948 |
| Year 4 | 7,000 | .572 | 4,004 |
| Present value of free cash flows | | | $11,090 |
| Initial outlay | | | −$10,000 |

**TRY *i* = 20 PERCENT:**

| | Free Cash Flows | Present Value Factor at 20 Percent | Present Value |
|---|---|---|---|
| Year 1 | $1,000 | .833 | $ 833 |
| Year 2 | 3,000 | .694 | 2,082 |
| Year 3 | 6,000 | .579 | 3,474 |
| Year 4 | 7,000 | .482 | 3,374 |
| Present value of free cash flows | | | $ 9,763 |
| Initial outlay | | | −$10,000 |

**TRY *i* = 19 PERCENT:**

| | Free Cash Flows | Present Value Factor at 19 Percent | Present Value |
|---|---|---|---|
| Year 1 | $1,000 | .840 | $ 840 |
| Year 2 | 3,000 | .706 | 2,118 |
| Year 3 | 6,000 | .593 | 3,558 |
| Year 4 | 7,000 | .499 | 3,493 |
| Present value of free cash flows | | | $10,009 |
| Initial outlay | | | −$10,000 |

## Spreadsheets and the Internal Rate of Return

Calculating the *IRR* using a spreadsheet is extremely simple. Once the cash flows have been entered on the spreadsheet, all you need to do is input the Excel *IRR* formula into a spreadsheet cell and let the spreadsheet do the calculations for you. Of course, at least one of the cash flows must be positive and at least one must be negative. The *IRR* formula to be input into a spreadsheet cell is: ***=IRR*(values),** where values is simply the range of cells where the cash flows are stored.

| | A | B | C | D | E | F | G |
|---|---|---|---|---|---|---|---|
| 1 | | | | | | | |
| 2 | | Spreadsheets and the IRR | | | | | |
| 3 | | | | | | | |
| 4 | The three investment proposals just examined have the following | | | | | | |
| 5 | cash flows: | | | | | | |
| 6 | | | | | | | |
| 7 | Year | Project A | Project B | Project C | | | |
| 8 | Initial Outlay | ($10,000) | ($10,000) | ($10,000) | | | |
| 9 | 1 | 3,362 | 0 | 1,000 | | | |
| 10 | 2 | 3,362 | 0 | 3,000 | | | |
| 11 | 3 | 3,362 | 0 | 6,000 | | | |
| 12 | 4 | 3,362 | 13,605 | 7,000 | | | |
| 13 | | | | | | | |
| 14 | IRR= | 13.001% | 8.000% | 19.040% | | | |
| 15 | | | | | | | |
| 16 | Excel Formula: =IRR(values) | | | | | | |
| 17 | | | | | | | |
| 18 | where: | | | | | | |
| 19 | values = | the range of cells where the cash flows are stored. | | | | | |
| 20 | | Note: There must be at least one positive and one | | | | | |
| 21 | | negative cash flow. | | | | | |
| 22 | | | | | | | |
| 23 | Entered value in cell B14:=IRR(B8:B12) | | | | | | |
| 24 | Entered value in cell C14:=IRR(C8:C12) | | | | | | |
| 25 | Entered value in cell D14:=IRR(D8:D12) | | | | | | |
| 26 | | | | | | | |
| 27 | | | | | | | |

Sheet1 / Sheet2 / Sheet3

## Viewing the NPV–IRR Relationship: The Net Present Value Profile

**Net present value profile** A graph showing how a project's net present value changes as the discount rate changes.

Perhaps the easiest way to understand the relationship between the internal rate of return the net present value is to view it graphically through the use of a **net present value profile.** A net present value profile is simply a graph showing how a project's net present value changes as the discount rate changes. To graph a project's net present value profile, you simply need to determine the project's net present value first using a zero percent discount rate, then slowly increase the discount rate until a representative curve has been plotted. How does the *IRR* enter into the net present value profile? The *IRR* is the discount rate at which the net present value is zero.

Let's look at an example of a project that involves an after-tax initial outlay of $105,517 with free cash flows expected to be $30,000 per year over the project's 5-year life. Calculating the *NPV* of this project at several different discounts rates results in the following:

| Discount Rate | Project's *NPV* |
|---|---|
| 0% | $44,483 |
| 5% | $24,367 |
| 10% | $ 8,207 |
| 13% | $ 0 |
| 15% | −$ 4,952 |
| 20% | −$15,798 |
| 25% | −$24,839 |

Plotting these values, we get the net present value profile in Figure 9-1.

Where is the *IRR* in this figure? Recall that the *IRR* is the discount rate that equates the present value of the inflows with the present value of the outflows; thus, the *IRR* is the point where the *NPV* is equal to zero. In this case, 13 percent.

From the net present value profile, you can easily see how a project's net present value varies inversely with the discount rate—as the discount rate is raised, the net present value drops. From looking at a project's net present value profile, you can also

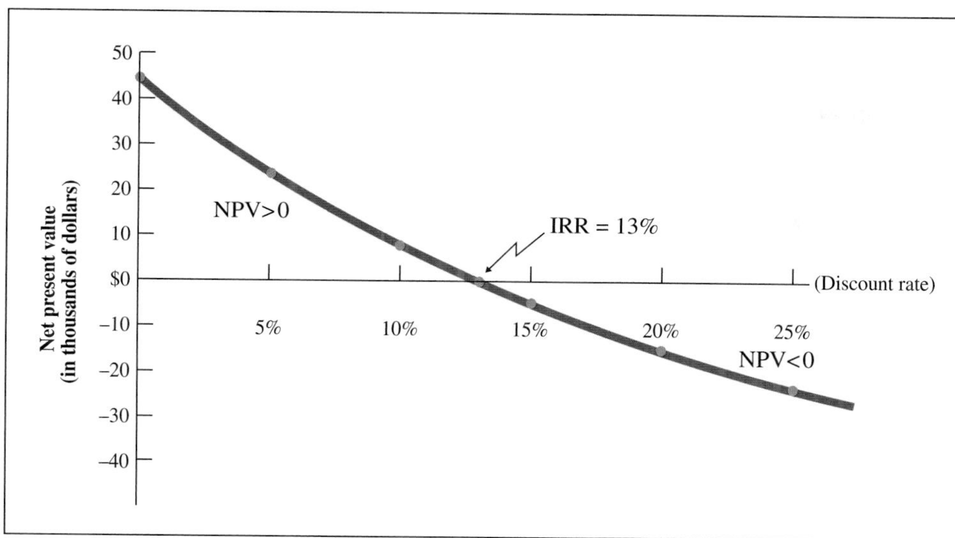


**FIGURE 9-1**
Net Present Value Profile

see how sensitive the project is to your selection of the discount rate. The more sensitive the *NPV* is to the discount rate, the more important it is that you use the correct one in your calculations.

## Complications with IRR: Multiple Rates of Return

Although any project can have only one *NPV* and one *PI,* a single project under certain circumstances can have more than one *IRR.* The reason for this can be traced to the calculations involved in determining the *IRR.* Equation 9-3 states that the *IRR* is the discount rate that equates the present value of the project's future free cash flows with the project's initial outlay:

$$IO = \sum_{t=1}^{n} \frac{FCF_t}{(1 + IRR)^t}$$

However, because equation 9-3 is a polynomial of a degree $n$, it has $n$ solutions. Now if the initial outlay (*IO*) is the only negative cash flow and all the annual free cash flows ($FCF_t$) are positive, then all but one of these $n$ solutions is either a negative or an imaginary number, and there is no problem. But problems occur when there are sign reversals in the cash flow stream; in fact, there can be as many solutions as there are sign reversals. A normal pattern with a negative initial outlay and positive annual free cash flows after that (−, +, +, . . . , +) has only one sign reversal, hence only one positive *IRR.* However, a pattern with more than one sign reversal can have more than one *IRR.*[3]

| | Free Cash Flow |
|---|---|
| Initial outlay | −$ 1,600 |
| Year 1 | +$10,000 |
| Year 2 | −$10,000 |

[3]This example is taken from James H. Lorie and Leonard J. Savage, "Three Problems in Rationing Capital," *Journal of Business* 28 (October 1955): 229–39.

ROAD RULES

A FOCUS ON HARLEY-DAVIDSON

ROAD RULES

### Decision Making at Harley-Davidson—An Interview with Dave Cotteleer

Dave Cotteleer took his first finance class at Northern Illinois University, and in that class was introduced to discounted cash-flow decision techniques like net present value and the internal rate of return. Little did he know then that he would actually be using what he learned in that undergraduate finance course years later in his job as Manager for Planning and Control for Materials Management at Harley-Davidson, where he oversees major initiatives in materials management. As Dave says "It is vitally important to understand these techniques when making a multi-million dollar expenditure. To boil a decision down to its value today is critical."

As Manager for Planning and Control, the job of deciding whether or not to buy purchasing software for Harley fell into his lap. In the past, Harley had used different packages to handle purchasing in different parts of the firm. The software package that Harley was considering was extremely comprehensive in nature, overseeing purchasing for all areas of Harley business. It would result in common systems across the company that would reduce support and maintenance costs in addition to reducing the amount of integration needed.

How did Dave go about making this decision? His first task was to identify all the benefits to Harley from the system being considered. That meant asking the purchasing people to identify any and all benefits and the timing of those benefits. For example, if this purchasing software allowed for inventory to be reduced by 30 percent, what was the timing of that 30 percent reduction? Once the benefits and their timing were identified, they were quantified. Finally, the costs of the purchase and installation of the software and the timing of those costs had to be identified, since all costs weren't expected to occur at the same time. Once this was done, these cash flows were discounted back to the present and the final decision was made. What is the key to making good decisions? A strong understanding of basic finance and capital budgeting. As Dave Cotteleer says, "Finance is in everything—in marketing, purchasing, management, production and accounting. You've got to understand it if you're to be successful."

In the preceding pattern of free cash flows, there are two sign reversals, from −\$1,600 to +\$10,000 and then from +\$10,000 to −\$10,000, so there can be as many as two positive *IRR*s that will make the present value of the future cash flows equal to the initial outlay. In fact, two internal rates of return solve this problem, 25 and 400 percent. Graphically, what we are solving for is the discount rate that makes the project's *NPV* equal to zero; as Figure 9-2 illustrates, this occurs twice.

Which solution is correct? The answer is that neither solution is valid. Although each fits the definition of *IRR*, neither provides any insight into the true project returns. In summary, when there is more than one sign reversal in the cash flow stream, the possibility of multiple *IRR*s exists, and the normal interpretation of the *IRR* loses its meaning. In this case, try the *NPV* criterion instead.

## Modified Internal Rate of Return

**Modified internal rate of return (*MIRR*)**
A variation of the *IRR* capital-budgeting decision criterion defined as the discount rate that equates the present value of the project's annual cash outlays with the present value of the project's terminal value, where the terminal value is defined as the sum of the future value of the project's free cash flows compounded to the project's termination at the project's required rate of return.

The primary drawback of the internal rate of return relative to the net present value method is the reinvestment rate assumption made by the internal rate of return. Recently, a new technique, the **modified internal rate of return *(MIRR)***, has gained popularity as an alternative to the *IRR* method because it allows the decision-maker to directly specify the appropriate reinvestment rate. As a result, the *MIRR* provides the decision-maker with the intuitive appeal of the *IRR* coupled with an improved reinvestment rate assumption.

The driving force behind the *MIRR* is the assumption that all free cash flows over the life of the project are reinvested at the required rate of return until the termination of the project. Thus, to calculate the *MIRR*, we take all the annual free cash *inflows*, $ACIF_t$s, and find their future value at the end of the project's life, compounded at the required rate of return. We will call this the project's *terminal value*, or *TV*. We then cal-

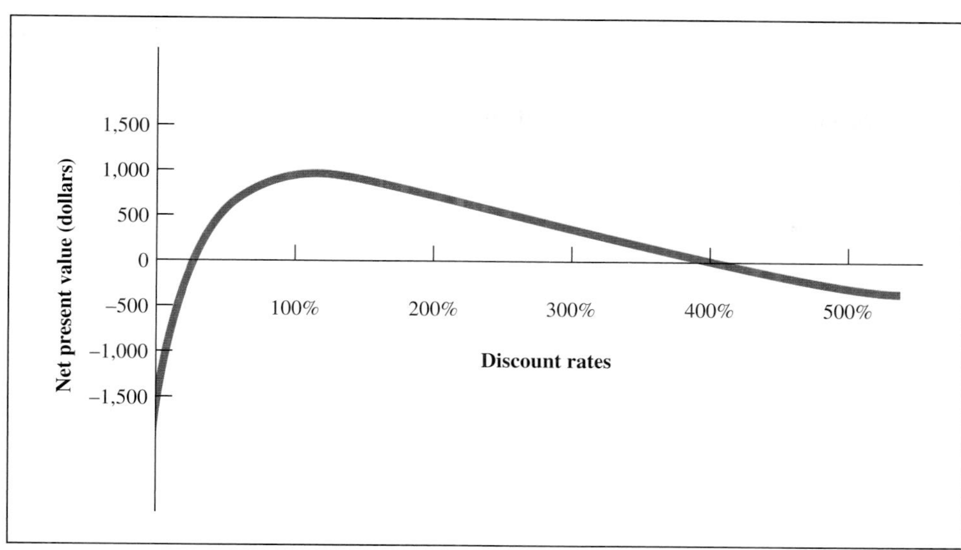


**FIGURE 9-2**
Multiple *IRRs*

culate the present value of the project's free cash *out*flows. We do this by discounting all free cash *out*flows, $ACOF_t$, back to present at the required rate of return. If the initial outlay is the only free cash *out*flow, then the initial outlay is the present value of the free cash *out*flows. The *MIRR* is the discount rate that equates the present value of the free cash *out*flows with the present value of the project's *terminal value*.[4] Mathematically, the modified internal rate of return is defined as the value of *MIRR* in the following equation:

$$PV_{outflows} = PV_{inflows}$$

$$\sum_{t=0}^{n} \frac{ACOF_t}{(1+k)^t} = \frac{\sum_{t=0}^{n} ACIF_t(1+k)^{n-t}}{(1+MIRR)^n} \quad \textbf{(9-4)}$$

$$PV_{outflows} = \frac{TV}{(1+MIRR)^n}$$

where $ACOF_t$ = the annual free cash *out*flow in time period $t$
$ACIF_t$ = the annual free *in*flow in time period $t$
$TV$ = the terminal value of the *ACIF*s compounded at the required rate of return to the end of the project
$n$ = the project's expected life
$MIRR$ = the project's modified internal rate of return
$k$ = the appropriate discount rate; that is, the required rate of return or cost of capital

[4]You will notice that we differentiate between annual cash *in*flows and annual cash *out*flows, compounding all the *in*flows to the end of the project and bringing all the *out*flows back to present as part of the present value of the costs. Although there are alternative definitions of the *MIRR*, this is the most widely accepted definition. For an excellent discussion of the *MIRR*, see William R. McDaniel, Daniel E. McCarty, and Kenneth A. Jessell, "Discounted Cash Flow with Explicit Reinvestment Rates: Tutorial and Extension," *The Financial Review* (August 1988): 369–85.

## EXAMPLE

Let's look at an example of a project with a 3-year life and a required rate of return of 10 percent assuming the following cash flows are associated with it:

| | Free Cash Flows | | Free Cash Flows |
|---|---|---|---|
| Initial outlay | −$6,000 | Year 2 | 3,000 |
| Year 1 | 2,000 | Year 3 | 4,000 |

The calculation of the *MIRR* can be viewed as a three-step process, which is also shown graphically in Figure 9-3.

**Step 1:** Determine the present value of the project's free cash *out*flows. In this case, the only *out*flow is the initial outlay of $6,000, which is already at the present, thus it becomes the present value of the cash *out*flows.

**Step 2:** Determine the terminal value of the project's free cash *in*flows. To do this, we merely use the project's required rate of return to calculate the future value of the project's three cash *in*flows at the termination of the project. In this case, the *terminal value* becomes $9,720.

**Step 3:** Determine the discount rate that equates the present value of the *terminal value* and the present value of the project's cash *out*flows. Thus the *MIRR* is calculated to be 17.446 percent.

For our example, the calculations are as follows:

$$\$6{,}000 = \frac{\sum_{t=1}^{3} ACIF_t(1 + k)^{n-t}}{(1 + MIRR)^n}$$

$$\$6{,}000 = \frac{\$2{,}000(1 + .10)^2 + \$3{,}000(1 + .10)^1 + \$4{,}000(1 + .10)^0}{(1 + MIRR)^3}$$

$$\$6{,}000 = \frac{\$2{,}420 + \$3{,}300 + \$4{,}000}{(1 + MIRR)^3}$$

$$\$6{,}000 = \frac{\$9{,}720}{(1 + MIRR)^3}$$

$$MIRR = 17.446\%$$

Thus, the *MIRR* for this project (17.446 percent) is less than its *IRR,* which comes out to 20.614 percent. In this case, it only makes sense that the *IRR* should be greater than the *MIRR,* because the *IRR* allows intermediate cash *in*flows to grow at the *IRR* rather than the required rate of return.

In terms of decision rules, if the project's *MIRR* is greater than or equal to the project's required rate of return, then the project should be accepted; if not, it should be rejected:

*MIRR* ≥ required rate of return: Accept
*MIRR* < required rate of return: Reject

Because of the frequent use of the *IRR* in the real world as a decision-making tool and its limiting reinvestment rate assumption, the *MIRR* has become increasingly popular as an alternative decision-making tool.

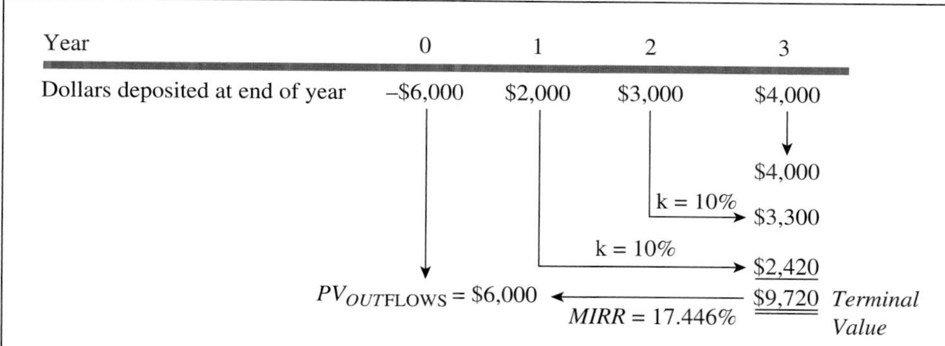


**FIGURE 9-3**
Calculation of the *MIRR*

## Spreadsheets and the Modified Internal Rate of Return

As with other financial calculations using a spreadsheet, calculating the *MIRR* is extremely simple. The only difference between this calculation and that of the traditional *MIRR* is that with a spreadsheet you also have the option of specifying both a *financing rate* and a *reinvestment rate.* The financing rate refers to the rate at which you borrow the money needed for the investment, while the reinvestment rate is the rate at which you reinvest the cash flows. Generally, it is assumed that these two values are one and the same. Thus, we enter in the value of *k,* the appropriate discount rate, for both of these values. Once the cash flows have been entered on the spreadsheet, all you need to do is input the Excel *MIRR* formula into a spreadsheet cell and let the spreadsheet do the calculations for you. Of course, as with the *IRR* calculation, at least one of the cash flows must be positive and at least one must be negative. The *MIRR* formula to be input into a spreadsheet cell is: **=*MIRR* (values, finance rate, reinvestment rate)**, where values is simply the range of cells where the cash flows are stored, and *k* is entered for both the finance rate and the reinvestment rate.

**Using a Spreadsheet to Calculate the MIRR**

Looking back on the previous example, we can also calculate the MIRR using a spreadsheet. However, with a spreadsheet you also have the option of specifying both a financing rate and a reinvestment rate. The *financing rate* would be the rate you borrow the money you need for the investment, while the *reinvestment rate* is the rate at which you reinvest the cash flows. In our calculations we assume these values to be identical. Thus we will put *k*, the appropriate discount rate in for both of these values. Going back to the previous example:

| Year | Cash Flow |
|---|---|
| Initial Outlay | ($6,000) |
| 1 | 2000 |
| 2 | 3000 |
| 3 | 4000 |
| | |
| MIRR = | 17.446% |

Excel formula: =MIRR(values, finance rate, reinvestment rate)

Entered value in cell C20: =MIRR(C15:C18,10%,10%)

where:

| | |
|---|---|
| values = | the range of cells where the cash flows are stored. Note: There must be at least one positive and one cash flow. |
| finance rate = | the rate at which you borrow the money needed for the investment. Generally assumed to be *k*. |
| reinvestment rate = | the reinvestment rate. Generally assumed to be *k*. |

Sheet1 / Sheet2 / Sheet3

### CONCEPT CHECK

1. Provide an intuitive definition of an internal rate of return for a project.
2. What does a net present value profile tell you and how is it constructed?
3. What is the difference between the *IRR* and the *MIRR?*
4. Why do the net present value and profitability index always give the same accept or reject decision for any project?

## ETHICS IN CAPITAL BUDGETING

OBJECTIVE 6 

Although it may not seem obvious, ethics has a role in capital budgeting. Any actions that violate ethical standards can cause a loss of trust, which can, in turn, have a negative and long-lasting effect on the firm. The Finance Matters "Bad Apple for Baby" story outlines one such violation. In this case, it deals with ethical lapses at Beech-Nut and demonstrates the consequences of those actions. No doubt the decisions of the Beech-Nut executives were meant to create wealth, but in fact, they cost Beech-Nut tremendously.

### RELATE TO THE BIG PICTURE

Ethics and ethical considerations continually crop up when capital-budgeting decisions are being made. This brings us back to the fundamental **Principle 10: Ethical Behavior Is Doing the Right Thing, and Ethical Dilemmas Are Everywhere in Finance.** As "Bad Apple for Baby" points out, the most damaging event a business can experience is a loss of the public's confidence in its ethical standards. In making capital-budgeting decisions we must be aware of this, and that ethical behavior is doing the right thing and it is the right thing to do.

FINANCE MATTERS

## Bad Apple for Baby

When we introduced **Principle 10: Ethical Behavior Is Doing the Right Thing, and Ethical Dilemmas Are Everywhere in Finance** in Chapter 1, we noted that acting in an ethical manner is not only morally correct, but that it is congruent with our goal of maximization of shareholder wealth. In this case, we can directly relate unethical behavior to a loss of shareholder wealth.

It's a widely held, but hard-to-prove belief that a company gains because it is perceived as more socially responsive than its competitors. Over the years, the three major manufacturers of baby food—Gerber Products, Beech-Nut Nutrition, and H. J. Heinz—had, with almost equal success, gone out of their way to build an image of respectability.

Theirs is an almost perfect zero-sum business. They know, at any given time, how many babies are being born. They all pay roughly the same price for their commodities, and their manufacturing and distribution costs are almost identical. So how does one company gain a market share edge over another, especially in a stagnant or declining market?

The answer for Beech-Nut was to sell a cheaper, adulterated product. Beginning in 1977, the company began buying a chemical concoction, made up mostly of sugar and water, and labeling it as apple juice. Sales of that product brought Beech-Nut an estimated $60 million between 1977 and 1982, while reducing material costs about $250,000 annually.

When various investigators tried to do something about it, the company stonewalled. Among other things, they shipped the bogus juice out of a plant in New York to Puerto Rico, to put it beyond the jurisdiction of federal investigators, and they even offered the juice as a give-away to reduce their stocks after they were finally forced to discontinue selling it.

In the end, the company pleaded guilty to 215 counts of introducing adulterated food into commerce and violating the Federal Food Drug and Cosmetic Act. The FDA fined Beech-Nut $2 million.

In addition, Beech-Nut's president, Neils Hoyvald, and its vice president of operations, John Lavery, were found guilty of similar charges. Each faces a year and one day in jail and a $100,000 fine. Both are now out on appeal on a jurisdiction technicality.

Why did they do it? The Fort Washington, Pa.-based company will not comment. But perhaps some portion of motive can be inferred from a report Hoyvald wrote to Nestle, the company which had acquired Beech-Nut in the midst of his cover-up. "It is our feeling that we can report safely now that the apple juice recall has been completed. If the recall had been effectuated in early June [when the FDA had first ordered it], over 700,000 cases in inventory would have been affected; due to our many delays, we were only faced with having to destroy 20,000 cases."

One thing is clear: Two executives of a company with an excellent reputation breached a trust and did their company harm.

The most damaging event a business can suffer is a loss of the public's confidence in its ethical standards. In the financial world, we have seen this happen with the insider trading scandal at Drexel Burnham Lambert that brought down the firm and at Bridgestone/Firestone when it kept silent about problems with ATX and Wilderness tires, used mainly on Ford Explorers. At Beech-Nut, the loss in consumer confidence that accompanied this scandal resulted in a drop of Beech-Nut's share of the overall baby food market from 19.1 percent to 15.8 percent. Thus, although this violation of ethics resulted in a short-run gain for Beech-Nut, much more was lost in the long run for many years to come.

Source: Stephen Kindel, "Bad Apple for Baby," *Financial World* (June 27, 1989): 48. Reprinted by permission. © 1989 *Financial World*.

# A GLANCE AT ACTUAL CAPITAL-BUDGETING PRACTICES

During the past 50 years, the popularity of each of the capital-budgeting methods has shifted rather dramatically. In the 1950s and 1960s, the payback period method dominated capital budgeting; but through the 1970s and 1980s, the internal rate of return and the net present value techniques slowly gained in popularity until they are today used by virtually all major corporations in decision making. Table 9-11 provides the results of a 1992 survey of the 100 largest Fortune 500 firms, showing the popularity of the internal rate of return and net present value methods.

Interestingly, although most firms use the *NPV* and *IRR* as their primary techniques, most firms also use the payback period as a secondary decision method for capital budgeting. In a sense, they are using the payback period to control for risk. The logic behind this is that because the payback period dramatically emphasizes early cash

**TABLE 9-11**
1992 Survey of Capital-Budgeting Practices of the 100 Largest Fortune 500 Industrial Firms

| | Percent of Firms | | |
|---|---|---|---|
| **Investment Evaluation Methods Used:** | **A Primary Method** | **A Secondary Method** | **Total Using This Method** |
| Internal rate of return | 88% | 11% | 99% |
| Net present value | 63% | 22% | 85% |
| Payback period | 24% | 59% | 83% |
| Profitability index | 15% | 18% | 33% |

*Source:* Harold Bierman, Jr., "Capital Budgeting in 1992: A Survey," *Financial Management* (Autumn 1993): 24.

flows, which are presumably more certain—that is, have less risk—than cash flows occurring later in a project's life. Managers believe its use will lead to projects with more certain cash flows.

A reliance on the payback period came out even more dramatically in a study of the capital-budgeting practices of 12 large manufacturing firms.[5] This study also showed that, although the discounted cash flow methods are used at most firms, the simple payback criterion was the measure relied on primarily in one third of the firms examined. The use of the payback period seemed to be even more common for smaller projects, with firms severely simplifying the discounted cash flow analysis or relying primarily on the payback period. Thus, although discounted cash flow decision techniques have become more widely accepted, their use depends to an extent on the size of the project.

**CONCEPT CHECK**

1. What capital-budgeting criteria seem to be used most frequently in the real world? Why do you think this is so?

## The Multinational Firm: Capital Budgeting

Without question, the key to success in capital budgeting is to identify good projects, and for many companies, these good projects are found overseas. Just look at the success that Coca-Cola has had in the international markets, with over 80 percent of its beverage profit coming from foreign markets and earning more in Japan than in the United States. This success abroad also holds true for Exxon, which earns over half its profits from abroad and is involved in gas and oil exploration projects in West Africa, the Caspian Sea, Russia, the Gulf of Mexico, and South America.

But how do you enter those markets initially? One approach that has been used successfully is through international joint ventures or strategic alliances. Under these arrangements, two or more corporations merge their skills and resources on a specific project, trading things like technology and access to marketing channels. For example, GM and Suzuki Motors recently announced a strategic alliance that will provide Suzuki with access to Europe, North America, South America, and Africa, where GM has a strong presence, and provide GM with access to the Asia Pacific region, where Suzuki is well established. As John F. Smith, Jr., the GM Chairman and CEO, said at the

[5]Marc Ross, "Capital Budgeting Practices of Twelve Large Manufacturers," *Financial Management* 15 (Winter 1986): 15–22.

announcement of this joint venture, "Each company has specific competencies and market strengths, which can be better leveraged to the mutual benefit of both parties through this agreement."

An example of a successful market penetration using joint ventures is that of the U.S. oil giant Armco, which formed a joint venture with Mitsubishi to sell Armco's lightweight plastics in Japan. Similarly, Georgia Pacific and Canfor Japan Corporation recently announced a joint venture in which Georgia Pacific will gain access to Canfor's marketing expertise in Japan to sell pulp and paper products there. H. J. Heinz Co. announced a joint venture with an Indonesian firm to gain access to its Indonesian marketing channels. Joint ventures also provide a way to get around trade barriers. For example, India and Mexico require joint ventures for entry into their markets. As a result, U.S. firms like Apple Computer and Hewlett-Packard have been forced to enter into Mexican joint ventures in order to be allowed to ship their products into Mexico.

What is the alternative to not looking abroad for projects? It is losing out on potential revenues. Keep in mind that firms like Xerox, Hewlett-Packard, Dow Chemical, IBM, and Gillette all earn more than 50 percent of their profits from sales abroad. International boundaries no longer apply in finance.

**CONCEPT CHECK**

1. What methods do corporations use to enter the international markets?

## HOW FINANCIAL MANAGERS USE THIS MATERIAL

Without taking on new projects, a company simply wouldn't continue to exist. For example, Smith-Corona's inability to come up with a product to replace the typewriters that it produced resulted in that company going under in 1996. Finding new profitable projects and correctly evaluating them are central to the firm's continued existence—and that's what capital budgeting is all about. It may be your decision to buy a Burger King franchise and open a Burger King restaurant. Or you may decide to help in Burger King's introduction of the Big King, a new burger that looks an awful lot like the Big Mac. Whatever your decision, when you're making an investment in fixed assets, it's a capital-budgeting decision. It may also involve taking a product that didn't work and trying to redesign it in such a way that it does. That's what 3Com Corporation did with the Palm Pilot electronic datebook and scheduler, which succeeded with small size and simplicity where Apple's Newton and Motorola's Envoy failed.

Much of what is done within a business involves the capital-budgeting process. Many times it's referred to as strategic planning, but it generally involves capital-budgeting decisions. You may be involved in market research dealing with a proposed new product, on its marketing plan, or in analyzing its costs—these are all part of the capital-budgeting process. Once all this information has been gathered, it is analyzed using the techniques and tools that we have presented in this chapter. Actually, almost any decision can be analyzed using the framework we presented here. That's because the net present value method "values" the project under consideration. That is, it looks at the present value of its benefits relative to the present value of its costs, and if the present value of the benefits outweighs the costs, the project is accepted. That's a pretty good decision rule, and it can be applied to any decision a business faces.

## SUMMARY

Before a profitable project can be adopted, it must be identified or found. Unfortunately, coming up with ideas for new products, for ways to improve existing products, or for ways to make existing products more profitable is extremely difficult. In general, the best source of ideas for these new, potentially profitable products is found within the firm.

OBJECTIVE 1 

The process of capital budgeting involves decision making with respect to investment in fixed assets. We examine four commonly used criteria for determining the acceptance or rejection of capital-budgeting proposals. The first method, the payback period, does not incorporate the time value of money into its calculations, although a variation of it, the discounted payback period, does. The discounted methods, net present value, profitability index, and internal rate of return, do account for the time value of money. These methods are summarized in Table 9-12.

**TABLE 9-12**
Capital-Budgeting Criteria

OBJECTIVE 2 

1. A. Payback period = number of years required to recapture the initial investment

Accept if payback ≤ maximum acceptable payback period
Reject if payback > maximum acceptable payback period

Advantages:
- Uses free cash flows
- Is easy to calculate and understand
- May be used as rough screening device

Disadvantages:
- Ignores the time value of money
- Ignores free cash flows occurring after the payback period
- Selection of the maximum acceptable payback period is arbitrary

B. Discounted payback period = the number of years needed to recover the initial cash outlay from the *discounted free cash flows*

Accept if discounted payback ≤ maximum acceptable discounted payback period
Reject if discounted payback > maximum acceptable discounted payback period

Advantages:
- Uses free cash flows
- Is easy to calculate and understand
- Considers time value of money

Disadvantages:
- Ignores free cash flows occurring after the payback period
- Selection of the maximum acceptable discounted payback period is arbitrary

OBJECTIVE 3 

2. Net present value = present value of the annual free cash flows less the investment's initial outlay

$$NPV = \sum_{t=1}^{n} \frac{FCF_t}{(1 + k)^t} - IO$$

where $FACF_t$ = the annual free cash flow in time period $t$ (this can take on either positive or negative values)
$k$ = the appropriate discount rate; that is, the required rate of return or the cost of capital
$IO$ = the initial cash outlay
$n$ = the project's expected life

**TABLE 9-12** (Continued)

Accept if $NPV \geq 0.0$
Reject if $NPV < 0.0$

Advantages:
- Uses free cash flows
- Recognizes the time value of money
- Is consistent with the firm's goal of shareholder wealth maximization

Disadvantages:
- Requires detailed long-term forecasts of a project's free cash flows

3. Profitability index = the ratio of the present value of the future free cash flows to the initial outlay

$$PI = \frac{\sum_{t=1}^{n} \frac{FCF_t}{(1+k)^t}}{IO}$$

Accept if $PI \geq 1.0$
Reject if $PI < 1.0$

Advantages:
- Uses free cash flows
- Recognizes the time value of money
- Is consistent with the firm's goal of shareholder wealth maximization

Disadvantages:
- Requires detailed long-term forecasts of a project's free cash flows

4. A. Internal rate of return = the discount rate that equates the present value of the project's future free cash flows with the project's initial outlay

$$IO = \sum_{t=1}^{n} \frac{FCF_t}{(1+IRR)^t}$$

where $IRR$ = the project's internal rate of return

Accept if $IRR \geq$ required rate of return
Reject if $IRR <$ required rate of return

Advantages:
- Uses free cash flows
- Recognizes the time value of money
- Is in general consistent with the firm's goal of shareholder wealth maximization

Disadvantages:
- Requires detailed long-term forecasts of a project's free cash flows
- Possibility of multiple *IRR*s
- Assumes cash flows over the life of the project are reinvested at the *IRR*

B. Modified internal rate of return = the discount rate that equates the present value of the project's cash *out*flows with the present value of the project's *terminal value*

$$\sum_{t=0}^{n} \frac{ACOF_t}{(1+k)^t} = \frac{\sum_{t=0}^{n} ACIF_t(1+k)^{n-t}}{(1+MIRR)^n}$$

$$PV_{OUTFLOWS} = \frac{TV}{(1+MIRR)^n}$$

**TABLE 9-12** (Continued)

where $ACOF_t$ = the annual free cash *outflow* in time period $t$
$ACIF_t$ = the annual free cash *inflow* in time period $t$
$TV$ = the terminal value of *ACIF*s compounded at the required rate of return to the end of the project

Accept if $MIRR \geq$ the required rate of return
Reject if $MIRR <$ required rate of return

Advantages:
- Uses free cash flows
- Recognizes the time value of money
- In general, is consistent with the goal of maximization of shareholder wealth

Disadvantages:
- Requires detailed long-term forecasts of a project's free cash flows

OBJECTIVE 6 

Ethics and ethical decisions crop up in capital budgeting. Just as with all other areas of finance, violating ethical considerations results in a loss of public confidence, which can have a significant negative effect on shareholder wealth.

OBJECTIVE 7 

Over the past 40 years, the discounted capital-budgeting decision criteria have continued to gain in popularity and today dominate in the decision-making process.

## KEY TERMS

myPHLIP

Go To: http://www.prenhall.com/keown for downloads and current events associated with this chapter

**Capital budgeting, 272**

**Discounted payback period, 275**

**Internal rate of return (*IRR*), 281**

**Modified internal rate of return (*MIRR*), 290**

**Net present value (*NPV*), 277**

**Net present value profile, 288**

**Payback period, 274**

**Profitability index (*PI*) (or benefit/cost ratio), 280**

## STUDY QUESTIONS

**9-1.** Why is the capital-budgeting decision so important? Why are capital-budgeting errors so costly?

**9-2.** What are the criticisms of the use of the payback period as a capital-budgeting technique? What are its advantages? Why is it so frequently used?

**9-3.** In some countries, expropriation of foreign investments is a common practice. If you were considering an investment in one of those countries, would the use of the payback period criterion seem more reasonable than it otherwise might? Why?

**9-4.** Briefly compare and contrast the *NPV, PI,* and *IRR* criteria. What are the advantages and disadvantages of using each of these methods?

**9-5.** What is the advantage of using the *MIRR* as opposed to the *IRR* decision criteria?

## SELF-TEST PROBLEMS

**ST-1.** You are considering a project that will require an initial outlay of $54,200. This project has an expected life of 5 years and will generate after-tax cash flows to the company as a whole of $20,608 at the end of each year over its 5-year life. In addition to the $20,608 free cash flow from operations during the fifth and final year, there will be an additional cash inflow of $13,200 at the end of the fifth year associated with the salvage value of a machine, making the cash flow in year 5 equal to $33,808. Thus the free cash flows associated with this project look like this:

| Year | Free Cash Flow | Year | Free Cash Flow |
|---|---|---|---|
| 0 | −$54,200 | 3 | 20,608 |
| 1 | 20,608 | 4 | 20,608 |
| 2 | 20,608 | 5 | 33,808 |

Given a required rate of return of 15 percent, calculate the following:

**a.** Payback period
**b.** Net present value
**c.** Profitability index
**d.** Internal rate of return

Should this project be accepted?

## STUDY PROBLEMS (SET A)

**9-1A.** (IRR *calculation*) Determine the internal rate of return on the following projects:

**a.** An initial outlay of $10,000 resulting in a single cash flow of $17,182 after 8 years
**b.** An initial outlay of $10,000 resulting in a single cash flow of $48,077 after 10 years
**c.** An initial outlay of $10,000 resulting in a single cash flow of $114,943 after 20 years
**d.** An initial outlay of $10,000 resulting in a single cash flow of $13,680 after 3 years

**9-2A.** (IRR *calculation*) Determine the internal rate of return on the following projects:

**a.** An initial outlay of $10,000 resulting in a cash flow of $1,993 at the end of each year for the next 10 years
**b.** An initial outlay of $10,000 resulting in a cash flow of $2,054 at the end of each year for the next 20 years
**c.** An initial outlay of $10,000 resulting in a cash flow of $1,193 at the end of each year for the next 12 years
**d.** An initial outlay of $10,000 resulting in a cash flow of $2,843 at the end of each year for the next 5 years

**9-3A.** (IRR *calculation*) Determine the internal rate of return to the nearest percent on the following projects:

**a.** An initial outlay of $10,000 resulting in a cash flow of $2,000 at the end of year 1, $5,000 at the end of year 2, and $8,000 at the end of year 3
**b.** An initial outlay of $10,000 resulting in a cash flow of $8,000 at the end of year 1, $5,000 at the end of year 2, and $2,000 at the end of year 3
**c.** An initial outlay of $10,000 resulting in a cash flow of $2,000 at the end of years 1 through 5 and $5,000 at the end of year 6

**9-4A.** (NPV, PI, *and* IRR *calculations*) Fijisawa, Inc., is considering a major expansion of its product line and has estimated the following cash flows associated with such an expansion. The initial outlay associated with the expansion would be $1,950,000, and the project would generate free cash flows of $450,000 per year for 6 years. The appropriate required rate of return is 9 percent.

**a.** Calculate the net present value.
**b.** Calculate the profitability index.
**c.** Calculate the internal rate of return.
**d.** Should this project be accepted?

**9-5A.** (*Payback period, net present value, profitability index, and internal rate of return calculations*) You are considering a project with an initial cash outlay of $80,000 and expected free cash flows of $20,000 at the end of each year for 6 years. The required rate of return for this project is 10 percent.

**a.** What are the project's payback and discounted payback periods?
**b.** What is the project's *NPV?*
**c.** What is the project's *PI?*
**d.** What is the project's *IRR?*

**9-6A.** (*Net present value, profitability index, and internal rate of return calculations*) You are considering two independent projects, project A and project B. The initial cash outlay associated with project A is $50,000 and the initial cash outlay associated with project B is $70,000. The required rate of return on both projects is 12 percent. The expected annual free cash flows from each project are as follows:

| Year | Project A | Project B |
|---|---|---|
| 0 | −$50,000 | −$70,000 |
| 1 | 12,000 | 13,000 |
| 2 | 12,000 | 13,000 |
| 3 | 12,000 | 13,000 |
| 4 | 12,000 | 13,000 |
| 5 | 12,000 | 13,000 |
| 6 | 12,000 | 13,000 |

Calculate the *NPV, PI,* and *IRR* for each project and indicate if the project should be accepted.

**9-7A.** (*Payback period calculations*) You are considering three independent projects, project A, project B, and project C. The required rate of return is 10 percent on each. Given the following free cash flow information, calculate the payback period and discounted payback period for each.

| Year | Project A | Project B | Project C |
|---|---|---|---|
| 0 | −$1,000 | −$10,000 | −$5,000 |
| 1 | 600 | 5,000 | 1,000 |
| 2 | 300 | 3,000 | 1,000 |
| 3 | 200 | 3,000 | 2,000 |
| 4 | 100 | 3,000 | 2,000 |
| 5 | 500 | 3,000 | 2,000 |

If you require a 3-year payback for both the traditional and discounted payback period methods before an investment can be accepted, which projects would be accepted under each criterion?

**9-8A.** (NPV *with varying rates of return*) Dowling Sportswear is considering building a new factory to produce aluminum baseball bats. This project would require an initial cash outlay of $5,000,000 and will generate annual free cash inflows of $1 million per year for 8 years. Calculate the project's *NPV* given:

**a.** A required rate of return of 9 percent
**b.** A required rate of return of 11 percent
**c.** A required rate of return of 13 percent
**d.** A required rate of return of 15 percent

**9-9A.** (*Internal rate of return calculations*) Given the following free cash flows, determine the internal rate of return for the three independent projects A, B, and C.

| | Project A | Project B | Project C |
|---|---|---|---|
| Initial Investment: | −$50,000 | −$100,000 | −$450,000 |
| Cash Inflows: | | | |
| Year 1 | $10,000 | $ 25,000 | $200,000 |
| Year 2 | 15,000 | 25,000 | 200,000 |
| Year 3 | 20,000 | 25,000 | 200,000 |
| Year 4 | 25,000 | 25,000 | — |
| Year 5 | 30,000 | 25,000 | — |

**9-10A.** (NPV *with varying required rates of return*) Big Steve's, makers of swizzle sticks, is considering the purchase of a new plastic stamping machine. This investment requires an initial outlay of $100,000 and will generate free cash inflows of $18,000 per year for 10 years. For each of the listed required rates of return, determine the project's net present value.

**a.** The required rate of return is 10 percent.
**b.** The required rate of return is 15 percent.
**c.** Would the project be accepted under part (a) or (b)?
**d.** What is this project's internal rate of return?

**9-11A.** (MIRR *calculation*) Emily's Soccer Mania is considering building a new plant. This project would require an initial cash outlay of $10 million and will generate annual free cash inflows of $3 million per year for 10 years.

Calculate the project's *MIRR*, given:

**a.** A required rate of return of 10 percent
**b.** A required rate of return of 12 percent
**c.** A required rate of return of 14 percent

## INTEGRATIVE PROBLEM

Your first assignment in your new position as assistant financial analyst at Caledonia Products is to evaluate two new capital-budgeting proposals. Because this is your first assignment, you have been asked not only to provide a recommendation, but also to respond to a number of questions aimed at judging your understanding of the capital-budgeting process. This is a standard procedure for all new financial analysts at Caledonia and will serve to determine whether you are moved directly into the capital-budgeting analysis department or are provided with remedial training. The memorandum you received outlining your assignment follows:

TO: The New Financial Analysts
FROM: Mr. V. Morrison, CEO, Caledonia Products
RE: Capital-Budgeting Analysis

Provide an evaluation of two proposed projects, both with 5-year expected lives and identical initial outlays of $110,000. Both of these projects involve additions to Caledonia's highly successful Avalon product line, and as a result, the required rate of return on both projects has been established at 12 percent. The expected free cash flows from each project are as follows:

| 3 | Project A | Project B |
|---|---|---|
| Initial Outlay | −$110,000 | −$110,000 |
| Year 1 | 20,000 | 40,000 |
| Year 2 | 30,000 | 40,000 |
| Year 3 | 40,000 | 40,000 |
| Year 4 | 50,000 | 40,000 |
| Year 5 | 70,000 | 40,000 |

In evaluating these projects, please respond to the following questions:

1. Why is the capital-budgeting process so important?
2. Why is it difficult to find exceptionally profitable projects?
3. What is the payback period on each project? If Caledonia imposes a 3-year maximum acceptable payback period, which of these projects should be accepted?
4. What are the criticisms of the payback period?
5. What are the discounted payback periods for each of these projects? If Caledonia requires a 3-year maximum acceptable discounted payback period on new projects, which of these projects should be accepted?
6. What are the drawbacks or deficiencies of the discounted payback period? Do you feel either the payback or discounted payback period should be used to determine whether or not these projects should be accepted? Why or why not?
7. Determine the net present value for each of these projects. Should they be accepted?
8. Describe the logic behind the net present value.
9. Determine the profitability index for each of these projects. Should they be accepted?
10. Would you expect the net present value and profitability index methods to give consistent accept-reject decisions? Why or why not?
11. What would happen to the net present value and profitability index for each project if the required rate of return increased? If the required rate of return decreased?
12. Determine the internal rate of return for each project. Should they be accepted?
13. How does a change in the required rate of return affect the project's internal rate of return?
14. What reinvestment rate assumptions are implicitly made by the net present value and internal rate of return methods? Which one is better?
15. Determine the modified internal rate of return for each project. Should they be accepted? Do you feel it is a better evaluation technique than is the internal rate of return? Why or why not?

## STUDY PROBLEMS (SET B)

**9-1B.** (IRR *calculation*) Determine the internal rate of return on the following projects:

**a.** An initial outlay of $10,000 resulting in a single cash flow of $19,926 after 8 years
**b.** An initial outlay of $10,000 resulting in a single cash flow of $20,122 after 12 years
**c.** An initial outlay of $10,000 resulting in a single cash flow of $121,000 after 22 years
**d.** An initial outlay of $10,000 resulting in a single cash flow of $19,254 after 5 years

**9-2B.** (IRR *calculation*) Determine the internal rate of return on the following projects:

**a.** An initial outlay of $10,000 resulting in a cash flow of $2,146 at the end of each year for the next 10 years
**b.** An initial outlay of $10,000 resulting in a cash flow of $1,960 at the end of each year for the next 20 years
**c.** An initial outlay of $10,000 resulting in a cash flow of $1,396 at the end of each year for the next 12 years
**d.** An initial outlay of $10,000 resulting in a cash flow of $3,197 at the end of each year for the next 5 years

**9-3B.** (IRR *calculation*) Determine the internal rate of return to the nearest percent on the following projects:

**a.** An initial outlay of $10,000 resulting in a cash flow of $3,000 at the end of year 1, $5,000 at the end of year 2, and $7,500 at the end of year 3
**b.** An initial outlay of $12,000 resulting in a cash flow of $9,000 at the end of year 1, $6,000 at the end of year 2, and $2,000 at the end of year 3
**c.** An initial outlay of $8,000 resulting in a cash flow of $2,000 at the end of years 1 through 5 and $5,000 at the end of year 6

**9-4B.** (NPV, PI, *and* IRR *calculations*) Gecewich, Inc., is considering a major expansion of its product line and has estimated the following cash flows associated with such an expansion. The initial outlay associated with the expansion would be $2,500,000 and the project would generate incremental free cash flows of $750,000 per year for 6 years. The appropriate required rate of return is 11 percent.

**a.** Calculate the net present value.
**b.** Calculate the profitability index.
**c.** Calculate the internal rate of return.
**d.** Should this project be accepted?

**9-5B.** (*Payback period, net present value, profitability index, and internal rate of return calculations*) You are considering a project with an initial cash outlay of $160,000 and expected free cash flows of $40,000 at the end of each year for 6 years. The required rate of return for this project is 10 percent.

**a.** What is the project's payback period?
**b.** What is the project's *NPV?*
**c.** What is the project's *PI?*
**d.** What is the project's *IRR?*

**9-6B.** (*Net present value, profitability index, and internal rate of return calculations*) You are considering two independent projects, project A and project B. The initial cash outlay associated with project A is $45,000, whereas the initial cash outlay associated with project B is $70,000. The required rate of return on both projects is 12 percent. The expected annual free cash inflows from each project are as follows:

| Year | Project A | Project B | Year | Project A | Project B |
|---|---|---|---|---|---|
| 0 | −$45,000 | −$70,000 | 4 | $12,000 | $14,000 |
| 1 | 12,000 | 14,000 | 5 | 12,000 | 14,000 |
| 2 | 12,000 | 14,000 | 6 | 12,000 | 14,000 |
| 3 | 12,000 | 14,000 | | | |

Calculate the *NPV, PI,* and *IRR* for each project and indicate if the project should be accepted.

**9-7B.** (*Payback period calculations*) You are considering three independent projects, project A, project B, and project C. Given the following free cash flow information calculate the payback period for each.

| Year | Project A | Project B | Project C |
|---|---|---|---|
| 0 | −900 | −$9,000 | −$7,000 |
| 1 | 600 | 5,000 | 2,000 |
| 2 | 300 | 3,000 | 2,000 |
| 3 | 200 | 3,000 | 2,000 |
| 4 | 100 | 3,000 | 2,000 |
| 5 | 500 | 3,000 | 2,000 |

If you require a 3-year payback period before an investment can be accepted, which projects would be accepted?

**9-8B.** (NPV *with varying required rates of return*) Mo-Lee's Sportswear is considering building a new factory to produce soccer equipment. This project would require an initial cash outlay of $10,000,000 and will generate annual free cash inflows of $2,500,000 per year for 8 years. Calculate the project's *NPV* given:

**a.** A required rate of return of 9 percent
**b.** A required rate of return of 11 percent
**c.** A required rate of return of 13 percent
**d.** A required rate of return of 15 percent

**9-9B.** (*Internal rate of return calculations*) Given the following cash flows, determine the internal rate of return for projects A, B, and C.

| Year | Project A | Project B | Project C |
|---|---|---|---|
| Initial Investment: | −$75,000 | −$95,000 | −$395,000 |
| Cash inflows: | | | |
| Year 1 | $10,000 | $25,000 | $150,000 |
| Year 2 | 10,000 | 25,000 | 150,000 |
| Year 3 | 30,000 | 25,000 | 150,000 |
| Year 4 | 25,000 | 25,000 | — |
| Year 5 | 30,000 | 25,000 | — |

**9-10B.** (NPV *with varying required rates of return*) Bert's, makers of gourmet corn dogs, is considering the purchase of a new corn dog "molding" machine. This investment requires an initial outlay of $150,000 and will generate free cash inflows of $25,000 per year for 10 years. For each of the listed required rates of return, determine the project's net present value.

**a.** The required rate of return is 9 percent.
**b.** The required rate of return is 15 percent.
**c.** Would the project be accepted under part (a) or (b)?
**d.** What is this project's internal rate of return?

**9-11B.** (MIRR *calculation*) Artie's Soccer Stuff is considering building a new plant. This plant would require an initial cash outlay of $8 million and will generate annual free cash inflows of $2 million per year for 8 years. Calculate the project's *MIRR* given:

**a.** A required rate of return of 10 percent
**b.** A required rate of return of 12 percent
**c.** A required rate of return of 14 percent

## CASE PROBLEM

### Ford's Pinto

Ethics Case: The Value of Life

There was a time when the "made in Japan" label brought a predictable smirk of superiority to the face of most Americans. The quality of most Japanese products usually was as low as their price. In fact, few imports could match their domestic counterparts, the proud products of "Yankee know-how." But by the late 1960s, an invasion of foreign-made goods chiseled a few worry lines into the countenance of American industry. And in Detroit, worry was fast fading to panic as the Japanese, not to mention the Germans, began to gobble up more and more of the subcompact auto market.

Never one to take a back seat to the competition, Ford Motor Company decided to meet the threat from abroad head-on. In 1968, Ford executives decided to produce the Pinto. Known inside the company as "Lee's car," after Ford president Lee Iacocca, the Pinto was to weigh no more than 2,000 pounds and cost no more than $2,000.

Eager to have its subcompact ready for the 1971 model year, Ford decided to compress the normal drafting-board-to-showroom time of about three-and-a-half years into two. The compressed schedule meant that any design changes typically made before production-line tooling would have to be made during it.

Before producing the Pinto, Ford crash-tested eleven of them, in part to learn if they met the National Highway Traffic Safety Administration (NHTSA) proposed safety standard that all autos be able to withstand a fixed-barrier impact of 20 miles per hour without fuel loss. Eight standard-design Pintos failed the tests. The three cars that passed the test all had some kind of gas-tank modification. One had a plastic baffle between the front of the tank and the differential housing; the second had a piece of steel between the tank and the rear bumper; and the third had a rubber-lined gas tank.

Ford officials faced a tough decision. Should they go ahead with the standard design, thereby meeting the production time table but possibly jeopardizing consumer safety? Or should they delay production of the Pinto by redesigning the gas tank to make it safer and thus concede another year of subcompact dominance to foreign companies?

To determine whether to proceed with the original design of the Pinto fuel tank, Ford decided to use a capital-budgeting approach, examining the expected costs and the social benefits of making the change. Would the social benefits of a new tank design outweigh design costs, or would they not?

To find the answer, Ford had to assign specific values to the variables involved. For some factors in the equation, this posed no problem. The costs of design improvement, for example, could be estimated at eleven dollars per vehicle. But what about human life? Could a dollar-and-cents figure be assigned to a human being?

NHTSA thought it could. It had estimated that society loses $200,725 every time a person is killed in an auto accident. It broke down the costs as follows:

| Future productivity losses | |
|---|---|
| Direct | $ 132,000 |
| Indirect | 41,300 |
| **Medical Costs** | |
| Hospital | 700 |
| Other | 425 |
| Property damage | 1,500 |
| Insurance administration | 4,700 |
| Legal and court expenses | 3,000 |
| Employer losses | 1,000 |
| Victim's pain and suffering | 10,000 |
| Funeral | 900 |
| Assets (lost consumption) | 5,000 |
| Miscellaneous accident costs | 200 |
| Total per fatality | $200,725[a] |

[a]Ralph Drayton, "One Manufacturer's Approach to Automobile Safety Standards," *CTLA News 8* (February 1968): 11.

Ford used NHTSA and other statistical studies in its cost-benefit analysis, which yielded the following estimates:

| Benefits | |
|---|---|
| Savings: | 180 burn deaths, 180 serious burn injuries, 2,100 burned vehicles |
| Unit cost: | $200,000 per death, $67,000 per injury, $700 per vehicle |
| Total benefit: | (180 × $200,000) + (180 × $67,000) + (2,100 × $700) = $49.5 million |

| Costs | |
|---|---|
| Sales: | 11 million cars, 1.5 million light trucks |
| Unit cost: | $11 per car, $11 per truck |
| Total cost: | 12.5 million × $11 = $137.5 million[a] |

[a]Mark Dowie, "Pinto Madness," *Mother Jones* (September–October 1977): 20. See also Russell Mokhiber, *Corporate Crime and Violence* (San Francisco: Sierra Club Books, 1988): 373–82, and Francis T. Cullen, William J. Maakestad, and Gary Cavender, *Corporate Crime Under Attack: The Ford Pinto Case and Beyond* (Cincinnati: Anderson Publishing, 1987).

Because the costs of the safety improvement outweighed its benefits, Ford decided to push ahead with the original design.

Here is what happened after Ford made this decision:

> Between 700 and 2,500 persons died in accidents involving Pinto fires between 1971 and 1978. According to sworn testimony of Ford engineer Harley Copp, 95 percent of them would have survived if Ford had located the fuel tank over the axle (as it had done on its Capri automobiles).
>
> NHTSA's standard was adopted in 1977. The Pinto then acquired a rupture-proof fuel tank. The following year Ford was obliged to recall all 1971–1976 Pintos for fuel-tank modifications.
>
> Between 1971 and 1978, approximately fifty lawsuits were brought against Ford in connection with rear-end accidents in the Pinto. In the Richard Grimshaw case, in addition to awarding over $3 million in compensatory damages to the victims of a Pinto crash, the jury awarded a landmark $125 million in punitive damages against Ford. The judge reduced punitive damages to $3.5 million.
>
> On August 10, 1978, eighteen-year-old Judy Ulrich, her sixteen-year-old sister Lynn, and their eighteen-year-old cousin Donna, in their 1973 Ford Pinto, were struck from the rear by a van near Elkhart, Indiana. The gas tank of the Pinto exploded on impact. In the fire that resulted, the three teenagers were burned to death. Ford was charged with criminal homicide. The judge presiding over the twenty-week trial advised jurors that Ford should be convicted if it had clearly disregarded the harm that might result from its actions and that disregard represented a substantial deviation from acceptable standards of conduct. On March 13, 1980, the jury found Ford not guilty of criminal homicide.

For its part, Ford has always denied that the Pinto is unsafe compared with other cars of its type and era. The company also points out that in every model year the Pinto met or surpassed the government's own standards. But what the company doesn't say is that successful lobbying by it and its industry associates was responsible for delaying for nine years the adoption of NHTSA's 20 miles-per-hour crash standard. And Ford critics claim that there were more than forty European and Japanese models in the Pinto price and weight range with a safer gas-tank position. "Ford made an extremely irresponsible decision," concludes auto safety expert Byron Bloch, "when they placed such a weak tank in such a ridiculous location in such a soft rear end."

## QUESTIONS

1. Do you think Ford approached this question properly?
2. What responsibilities to its customers do you think Ford had? Were their actions ethically appropriate?
3. Would it have made a moral or ethical difference if the $11 savings had been passed on to Ford's customers? Could a rational customer have chosen to save $11 and risk the more dangerous gas tank? Would that have been similar to making air bags optional? What if Ford had told potential customers about its decision?
4. Should Ford have been found guilty of criminal homicide in the Ulrich case?
5. If you, as a financial manager at Ford, found out about what had been done, what would you do?

SOURCE: Reprinted by permission from William Shaw and Vincent Barry, "Ford's Pinto," *Moral Issues in Business*, 6th ed. (New York: Wadsworth, 1995), 84–86. 

## SELF-TEST SOLUTIONS

**ST-1.**

**a.** Payback period $= \dfrac{\$54{,}000}{\$20{,}608} = 2.630$ years

**b.** $NPV = \sum_{t=1}^{n} \dfrac{FCF_t}{(1+k)^t} - IO$

$= \sum_{t=1}^{4} \dfrac{\$20{,}608}{(1+.15)^t} + \dfrac{\$33{,}808}{(1+.15)^5} - \$54{,}200$

$= \$20{,}608(2.855) + \$33{,}808\,(.497) - \$54{,}200$

$= \$58{,}836 + \$16{,}803 - \$54{,}200$

$= 21{,}439$

**c.** $PI = \dfrac{\sum_{t=1}^{n} \dfrac{FCF_t}{(1+k)^t}}{IO}$

$= \dfrac{\$75{,}639}{\$54{,}200}$

$= 1.396$

**d.** $IO = \sum_{t=1}^{n} \dfrac{FCF_t}{(1+IRR)^t}$

$\$54{,}200 = \$20{,}608\,(PVIFA_{IRR\%,\,4\text{yr}}) + \$33{,}808\,(PVIF_{IRR\%,\,5\text{yr}})$

Try 29 percent:

$\$54{,}200 = \$20{,}608\,(2.203) + \$33{,}808\,(.280)$

$= \$45{,}399 + 9{,}466$

$= \$54{,}865$

Try 30 percent:

$\$45{,}200 = \$20{,}608\,(2.166) + \$33{,}808\,(.269)$

$= \$44{,}637 + 9{,}094$

$= 53{,}731$

Thus, the *IRR* is just below 30 percent. The project should be accepted because the *NPV* is positive, the *PI* is greater than 1.0, and the *IRR* is greater than the required rate of return of 15 percent.

# CASH FLOWS AND OTHER TOPICS IN CAPITAL BUDGETING

A major capital-budgeting decision led Harley-Davidson to introduce the Buell Blast in 2000. In the introduction to the previous chapter, we talked about the importance of this multi-million dollar investment by Harley that was targeted directly at new and younger riders. Although this capital-budgeting decision may, on the surface, seem like a relatively simple decision, the forecasting of the expected cash flows associated with the Buell Blast were, in fact, quite complicated. ● To begin with, Harley-Davidson had two goals in mind when it introduced the Buell Blast. First, it was trying to expand into a new market made up of Generation X-ers. Second, it wanted to expand the market for existing products by introducing more people to motorcycling. That is, the Buell Blast should not only produce its own sales, but its introduction should eventually result in increased sales in Harley's heavier cruiser and touring bikes as the Blast customers move up to these larger bikes. ● While the motorcycle industry has enjoyed tremendous growth over the past 10 years with over 7 million riders out there now, representing an increase of 30 percent in just 10 years, the demographics of the motorcycle rider has changed considerably. In particular, the median age of a rider has risen 8 years over the past 10 years. This aging of the motorcycle-riding population played a major role in the decision to go forward with the Blast, and from early returns, it looks like it was, in fact, an excellent decision. ● How exactly do you measure the cash flows that come from the introduction of a new product line? What do you do about cash flows that the new

**LEARNING OBJECTIVES**

After reading this chapter, you should be able to

1. Identify the guidelines by which we measure cash flows.
2. Explain how a project's benefits and costs—that is, its incremental after-tax cash flows—are calculated.
3. Explain how the capital-budgeting decision process changes when a limit is placed on the dollar size of the capital budget, or there are mutually exclusive projects.

product brings to other product lines? In the previous chapter, we looked at decision criteria, assuming the cash flows were known. In this chapter, we will see how difficult and complex it is estimating those cash flows. We will also gain an understanding of what a relevant cash flow is. We will evaluate projects relative to their base case—that is, what will happen to the company as a whole if the project is not carried out. In the case of Harley's Buell Blast, we will also look at the sales that this new product brings down the line to Harley's cruising and touring bikes. Does the introduction of the Buell Blast result in eventual sales to Harley's other lines? What is the future level of cash flows to Harley-Davidson as a whole versus the level without the introduction of the Buell Blast? Questions such as these lead us to an understanding of what are and what are not relevant cash flows. As you will see in the future, these questions are generally answered by those in marketing and management, but regardless of your area of concentration, they are important questions to understand.

This chapter continues our discussion of decision rules for deciding when to invest in new projects. First we will examine what is a relevant cash flow and how to calculate the relevant cash flow. This will be followed by a discussion of the problems created when the number of projects that can be accepted or the total budget is limited. This chapter will rely on **Principle 3: Cash—Not Profits—Is King, Principle 4: Incremental Cash Flows—It's only what changes that counts,** and **Principle 5: The Curse of Competitive Markets.** Be on the lookout for these important concepts.

## GUIDELINES FOR CAPITAL BUDGETING

OBJECTIVE 1 

To evaluate investment proposals, we must first set guidelines by which we measure the value of each proposal. In effect, we will be deciding what is and what isn't a relevant cash flow.

### Use Free Cash Flows Rather than Accounting Profits

We will use free cash flows, not accounting profits, as our measurement tool. The firm receives and is able to reinvest free cash flows, whereas accounting profits are shown when they are earned rather than when the money is actually in hand. Unfortunately, a firm's accounting profits and cash flows may not be timed to occur together. For example, capital expenses, such as vehicles and plant and equipment, are depreciated over several years, with their annual depreciation subtracted from profit. Free cash flows correctly reflect the timing of benefits and costs—that is, when the money is received, when it can be reinvested, and when it must be paid out.

**RELATE TO THE BIG PICTURE**

If we are to make intelligent capital-budgeting decisions, we must accurately measure the timing of the benefits and costs, that is, when we receive money and when it leaves our hands. **Principle 3: Cash—Not Profits—Is King** speaks directly to this. Remember, it is cash inflows that can be reinvested and cash outflows that involve paying out money.

## Think Incrementally

Unfortunately, calculating cash flows from a project may not be enough. Decision makers must ask: What new cash flows will the company as a whole receive if the company takes on a given project? What if the company does not take on the project? Interestingly, we may find that not all cash flows a firm expects from an investment proposal are incremental in nature. In measuring cash flows, however, the trick is to *think* incrementally. In doing so, we will see that only *incremental after-tax cash flows* matter. As such, our guiding rule in deciding if a cash flow is incremental will be to look at the company with, versus without, the new product. These incremental after-tax cash flows to the company as a whole are many times referred to as *free cash flows*. As you will see in the upcoming sections, this may be easier said than done.

**RELATE TO THE BIG PICTURE**

In order to measure the true effects of our decisions, we will analyze the benefits and costs of projects on an incremental basis, which relates directly to **Principle 4: Incremental Cash Flows—It's only what changes that counts.** In effect, we will ask ourselves what the cash flows will be if the project is taken on versus what they will be if the project is not taken on.

## Beware of Cash Flows Diverted from Existing Products

Assume for a moment that we are managers of a firm considering a new product line that might compete with one of our existing products and possibly reduce its sales. In determining the cash flows associated with the proposed project, we should consider only the incremental sales brought to the company as a whole. New-product sales achieved at the cost of losing sales of other products in our line are not considered a benefit of adopting the new product. For example, when General Foods's Post Cereal Division introduced its Dino Pebbles, the product competed directly with the company's Fruity Pebbles. (In fact, the two were actually the same product, with an addition to the former of dinosaur-shaped marshmallows.) Post meant to target the market niche held by Kellogg's Marshmallow Krispies, but there was no question that sales recorded by Dino Pebbles bit into—literally cannibalized—Post's existing product line.

Remember that we are only interested in the sales dollars to the firm if this project is accepted, as opposed to what the sales dollars would be if the project is rejected. Just moving sales from one product line to a new product line does not bring anything new into the company, but if sales are captured from our competitors or if sales that would have been lost to new competing products are retained, then these are relevant incremental cash flows. In each case, these are the incremental cash flows to the firm—looking at the firm as a whole with the new product versus without the new product.

## Look for Incidental or Synergistic Effects

Although in some cases a new project may take sales away from a firm's current projects, in other cases a new effort may actually bring new sales to the existing line. For example, in 2000 GM's Pontiac division introduced the Aztek, an in-your-face looking sport-ute. The idea was not only to sell lots of Azteks, but also to help lure back young customers to Pontiac's other car lines. From 1994 until the introduction of the Aztek, the average age of Pontiac buyers had risen from 40 to 42. Thus, the hope was that Aztek would bring younger customers into showrooms, who would in turn either buy an Aztek, or lock onto another one of Pontiac's products. Thus, in evaluating the Aztek, if managers were to look only at the revenue from new Aztek sales, they would miss the incremental cash flow to Pontiac as a whole that results from new customers who would not have otherwise purchased a Pontiac automobile, but did so only after being lured into a Pontiac showroom to see an Aztek. This is called a *synergistic effect.* The cash flow comes from any Pontiac sale that would not have occurred if a customer had not visited a Pontiac showroom to see an Aztek.

This is very similar to what Harley-Davidson did with the Buell Blast. This youth-oriented sports bike is not only intended to generate sales on its own, but also to serve as a feeder for Harley-Davidson's cruising and touring bikes, as Blast riders grow older and trade up. Thus, the incremental sales from the Buell Blast can only be measured by looking at all cash flows that accrue to Harley-Davidson as a whole from its introduction. The bottom line: Any cash flow to any part of the company that may result from the decision at hand must be considered when making that decision.

## Work in Working-Capital Requirements

Many times, a new project will involve additional investment in working capital. This may take the form of new inventory to stock a sales outlet, additional investment in accounts receivable resulting from additional credit sales, or increased investment in cash to operate additional cash registers, and more. For most projects, some of the funds to support the new level of working capital will come from money owed to suppliers (accounts receivable). Still, the firm will generally have to provide some funds to working capital. Working-capital requirements are considered a cash flow even though they do not leave the company. How can investment in inventory be considered a cash outflow when the goods are still in the store? Because the firm does not have access to the inventory's cash value, the firm cannot use the money for other investments. Generally, working-capital requirements are tied up over the life of the project. When the project terminates, there is usually an offsetting cash inflow as the working capital is recovered. (Although this offset is not perfect because of the time value of money.)

## Consider Incremental Expenses

Just as cash inflows from a new project are measured on an incremental basis, expenses should also be measured on an incremental basis. For example, if introducing a new product line necessitates training the sales staff, the after-tax cash flow associated with the training program must be considered a cash outflow and charged against the project. If accepting a new project dictates that a production facility be reengineered, the after-tax cash flows associated with that capital investment should be charged against the project. Again, any incremental after-tax cash flow affecting the company as a whole is a relevant cash flow whether it is flowing in or flowing out.

For example, Harley-Davidson offers buyers of the Buell Blast a "Riders Edge" schooling program to help them learn how to drive a motorcycle safely and minimize any fear of the unknown. The idea here is, of course, to make it easier for nonriders or novices to enter biking. This is also an incremental expense, one that would not have happened if the Buell Blast had not been introduced. As such it is a relevant cash flow. The bottom line is to look at the company's cash flows as a whole with this project versus without this project. The decision is then based on the difference in those cash flows.

## Remember That Sunk Costs Are Not Incremental Cash Flows

Only cash flows that are affected by the decision made at the moment are relevant in capital budgeting. The manager asks two questions: (1) Will this cash flow occur if the project is accepted? (2) Will this cash flow occur if the project is rejected? *Yes* to the first question and *no* to the second equals an incremental cash flow. For example, let's assume you are considering introducing a new taste treat called "Puddin' in a Shoe." You would like to do some test marketing before production. If you are considering the decision to test market and have not yet done so, the costs associated with the test marketing are relevant cash flows. Conversely, if you have already test marketed, the cash flows involved in test marketing are no longer relevant in project evaluation. It's a matter of timing. Regardless of what you might decide about future production, the cash flows allocated to marketing have already occurred. Cash flows that have already taken place are often referred to as "sunk costs" because they have been sunk into the project and cannot be undone. As a rule, any cash flows that are not affected by the accept-reject decision should not be included in capital-budgeting analysis.

## Account for Opportunity Costs

Now we will focus on the cash flows that are lost because a given project consumes scarce resources that would have produced cash flows if that project had been rejected. This is the opportunity cost of doing business. For example, a product may use valuable floor space in a production facility. Although the cash flow is not obvious, the real question remains: What else could be done with this space? The space could have been rented out, or another product could have been stored there. The key point is that opportunity-cost cash flows should reflect net cash flows that would have been received if the project under consideration were rejected. Again, we are analyzing the cash flows to the company as a whole, with or without the project.

## Decide If Overhead Costs Are Truly Incremental Cash Flows

Although we certainly want to include any incremental cash flows resulting in changes from overhead expenses such as utilities and salaries, we also want to make sure that these are truly incremental cash flows. Many times, overhead expenses—heat, light, rent—would occur whether a given project were accepted or rejected. There is often not a single specific project to which these expenses can be allocated. Thus, the question is not whether the project benefits from overhead items, but whether the overhead costs are incremental cash flows associated with the project—and relevant to capital budgeting.

## Ignore Interest Payments and Financing Flows

In evaluating new projects and determining cash flows, we must separate the investment decision from the financing decision. Interest payments and other financing cash flows that might result from raising funds to finance a project should not be considered

## FINANCE MATTERS

### Universal Studios

A major capital-budgeting decision led Universal Studios to build its Islands of Adventures theme park. The purpose of this $2.6 billion investment by Universal was to take direct aim at the first crack of the tourist's dollar in Orlando. Although this capital-budgeting decision may, on the surface, seem like a relatively simple decision, forecasting the expected cash flows associated with this theme park was, in fact, quite complicated.

To begin with, Universal was introducing a product that competes directly with itself. The original Universal Studios features rides like "Back to the Future" and "Jaws." Are there enough tourist dollars to support both theme parks, or will the new Islands of Adventure park simply cannibalize ticket sales to the older Universal Studios? In addition, what happens when Disney counters with a new park of its own? We will evaluate projects relative to their base case—that is, what will happen if the project is not carried out? In the case of Universal's Islands of Adventure, we could ask what would happen to attendance at the original Universal Studios if the new park was not opened, versus what the attendance would be with the new park. Will tourist traffic through the Islands of Adventure lead to additional sales of the brands and businesses visibly promoted and available in the new park that fall under Universal's and Seagrams's corporate umbrella?

From Universal's point of view, the objective may be threefold: to increase its share of the tourist market; to keep from losing market share as the tourists look for the latest in technological rides and entertainment; and to promote Universal's, and its parent company Seagrams, other brands and products. However, for companies in very competitive markets, the evolution and introduction of new products may serve more to preserve market share than to expand it. Certainly, that's the case in the computer market, where Dell, Compaq, and IBM introduce upgraded models that continually render current models obsolete. The bottom line here is that, with respect to estimating cash flows, things are many times more complicated than they first appear. As such, we have to dig deep to understand how a firm's free cash flows are affected by the decision at hand.

incremental cash flows. If accepting a project means we have to raise new funds by issuing bonds, the interest charges associated with raising funds are not a relevant cash outflow. When we discount the incremental cash flows back to the present at the required rate of return, we are implicitly accounting for the cost of raising funds to finance the new project. In essence, the required rate of return reflects the cost of the funds needed to support the project. Managers first determine the desirability of the project and then determine how best to finance it.

### CONCEPT CHECK

1. What is an incremental cash flow? What is a sunk cost? What are opportunity costs?
2. If Ford introduces a new auto line, might some of the cash flows from that new car line be diverted from existing product lines? How should you deal with this?

## AN OVERVIEW OF THE CALCULATIONS OF A PROJECT'S FREE CASH FLOWS

OBJECTIVE 2 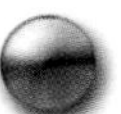

In measuring cash flows, we will be interested only in the *incremental,* or differential, *after-tax cash flows* that can be attributed to the proposal being evaluated. That is, we will focus our attention on the difference in the firm's after-tax cash flows *with* versus *without* the project—the project's free cash flows. The worth of our decision depends on the accuracy of our cash flow estimates. For this reason, we first examined the question of what cash flows are relevant. Now we will see that, in general, a project's free cash flows will fall into one of three categories: (1) the initial outlay, (2) the differential flows over the project's life, and

**TABLE 10-1**
Summary of Typical Initial Outlay Incremental After-Tax Cash Flows

1. Installed cost of asset
2. Additional nonexpense outlays incurred (for example, working-capital investments)
3. Additional expenses on an after-tax basis (for example, training expenses)
4. In a replacement decision, the *after-tax* cash flow associated with the sale of the old machine

(3) the terminal cash flow. Once we have taken a look at these categories, we will take on the task of measuring these free cash flows.

## Initial Outlay

**Initial outlay**
The immediate cash outflow necessary to purchase the asset and put it in operating order.

The **initial outlay** involves the immediate cash outflow necessary to purchase the asset and put it in operating order. This amount includes the cost of installing the asset (the asset's purchase price plus any expenses associated with shipping or installation) and any nonexpense cash outlays, such as increased working-capital requirements. If we are considering a new sales outlet, there might be additional cash flows associated with net investment in working capital in the form of increased inventory and cash necessary to operate the sales outlet. Although these cash flows are not included in the cost of the asset or even expensed on the books, they must be included in our analysis. The after-tax cost of expense items incurred as a result of new investment must also be included as cash outflows—for example, any training expenses or special engineering expenses that would not have been incurred otherwise.

Finally, if the investment decision is a replacement decision, the cash inflow associated with the selling price of the old asset, in addition to any tax effects resulting from its sale, must be included.

Determining the initial outlay is a complex matter. Table 10-1 summarizes some of the more common calculations involved in determining the initial outlay. This list is by no means exhaustive, but it should give you a framework for thinking about the initial outlay. At this point, we should realize that the incremental nature of the cash flow is of great importance. In many cases, if the project is not accepted, then status quo for the firm will simply not continue. In calculating incremental cash flows, we must be realistic in estimating what the cash flows to the company would be if the new project is not accepted.

TAX EFFECTS—SALE OF OLD MACHINE Potentially, one of the most confusing initial outlay calculations is for a replacement project involving the incremental tax payment associated with the sale of an old machine. There are three possible tax situations dealing with the sale of an old asset:

1. The old asset is sold for a price above the depreciated value. Here the difference between the old machine's selling price and its depreciated value is considered a taxable gain and taxed at the marginal corporate tax rate. If, for example, the old machine was originally purchased for \$15,000, had a book value of \$10,000, and was sold for \$17,000, assuming the firm's marginal corporate tax rate is 34 percent, the taxes due from the gain would be (\$17,000 − \$10,000) × (.34), or \$2,380.
2. The old asset is sold for its depreciated value. In this case, no taxes result, as there is neither a gain nor a loss in the asset's sale.
3. The old asset is sold for less than its depreciated value. In this case, the difference between the depreciated book value and the salvage value of the asset is a taxable loss and may be used to offset capital gains and thus results in tax savings. For example, if the depreciated book value of the asset is \$10,000 and it is sold for \$7,000 we have a \$3,000 loss. Assuming the firm's marginal corporate tax rate is 34 percent, the cash inflow from tax savings is (\$10,000 − \$7,000) × (.34), or \$1,020.

**TABLE 10-2**
Summary of Typical Differential After-Tax Cash Flows

1. Added revenue offset by increased expenses
2. Labor and material savings
3. Increases in overhead incurred
4. Change in taxes
5. Change in net working capital
6. Change in capital spending
7. Make sure calculations reflect the fact that while depreciation is an expense, it does not involve any cash flows.
8. Do *not* include interest expenses if the project is financed by issuing debt, as this is accounted for in the required rate of return.

## Differential Flows over a Project's Life

The differential cash flows over the project's life involve the incremental after-tax cash flows resulting from increased revenues, plus savings in labor or material and reductions in selling expenses. Overhead items, such as utilities, heat, light, and executive salaries, are generally not affected. However, any resultant change in any of these categories should be reflected in the calculation of the cash flows. Any increase in interest payments incurred as a result of issuing bonds to finance the project will *not* be included, as the costs of funds needed to support the project are implicitly accounted for by discounting the project back to the present using the required rate of return. Finally, an adjustment for the incremental change in taxes should be included. In addition, we must make sure our calculations reflect the fact that while depreciation is considered an expense from an accounting perspective, it does not involve any cash flows. We must also take note of any changes in working capital or capital spending that take place. Table 10-2 lists some of the factors that might be involved in determining a project's differential cash flows. However, before we look at the actual calculation, we will briefly examine the calculation of depreciation and the net change in working capital.

Depreciation plays an important role in the calculation of cash flows. Although it is not a cash flow item, it lowers profits, which in turn lowers taxes. For students developing a foundation in corporate finance, it is the concept of depreciation, not the calculation of it, that is important. The reason the calculation of depreciation is deemphasized is that it is extremely complicated, and its calculation changes every few years as Congress enacts new tax laws. Through all this, bear in mind that although depreciation is not a cash flow item, it does affect cash flows by lowering the level of profits on which taxes are calculated.

DEPRECIATION The Revenue Reconciliation Act of 1993 largely left intact the modified version of the Accelerated Cost Recovery System introduced in the Tax Reform Act of 1986. Although this was examined earlier, a review is appropriate here. This modified version of the old accelerated cost recovery system (ACRS) is used for most tangible depreciable property placed in service beginning in 1987. Under this method, the life of the asset is determined according to the asset's class life, which is assigned by the IRS; for example, most computer equipment has a 5-year asset life. It also allows for only a half-year's deduction in the first year and a half-year's deduction in the year after the recovery period. The asset is then depreciated using the 200 percent declining balance method or an optional straight-line method.

For our purposes, depreciation is calculated using a simplified straight-line method. This simplified process ignores the half-year convention that allows only a half-year's deduction in the year the project is placed in service and a half-year's deduction in the first year after the recovery period. By ignoring the half-year convention and assuming a zero salvage value, we are able to calculate annual depreciation by taking the project's initial depreciable value and dividing by its depreciable life as follows:

$$\text{annual depreciation using the simplified straight-line method} = \frac{\text{initial depreciable value}}{\text{depreciable life}}$$

The initial depreciable value is equal to the cost of the asset plus any expenses necessary to get the new asset into operating order.

This is not how depreciation would actually be calculated. The reason we have simplified the calculation is to allow you to focus directly on what should and should not be included in the cash flow calculations. Moreover, because the tax laws change rather frequently, we are more interested in recognizing the tax implications of depreciation than in understanding the specific depreciation provisions of the current tax laws.

Our concern with depreciation is to highlight its importance in generating cash flow estimates and to indicate that the financial manager must be aware of the current tax provisions when evaluating capital-budgeting proposals.

While depreciation is an expense, but not a cash-flow item, working capital is a cash-flow item, but not an expense. In fact, very few projects do not require some increased investment in working capital. It is only natural for inventory levels to increase as a firm begins production of a new product. Likewise, much of the sales of the new product may be on credit, resulting in an increase in accounts receivable. Offsetting some of this may be a corresponding increase in accounts payable, as the firm buys raw materials on credit.

The increased working capital minus any additional short-term liabilities that were generated is the change in net working capital. Thus, we need only look at the difference between the beginning and ending levels of investment in working capital less any additional short-term liabilities to calculate the change in net working capital. Complicating all of this are two things: the current portion of long-term debt and cash. Because the current portion of long-term debt is already counted as part of the financing for the project, including it as part of working capital would double-count it.

Cash is more complicated. The only change in the level of cash held that should be considered to be a cash flow is cash that is required for the operation of the business and does not earn interest. For example, an increase in teller cash associated with opening a new sales outlet would be a relevant cash-flow item. However, if as a result of the operation of the new project the firm increases its level of idle cash, this would not be considered a cash-flow item. The firm can earn interest on this idle cash, so it would be inappropriate to consider it a cash-outflow item.

## Terminal Cash Flow

The calculation of the terminal cash flow is in general quite a bit simpler than the preceding two calculations. Flows associated with the project's termination generally include the salvage value of the project plus or minus any taxable gains or losses associated with its sale.

Under the current tax laws, in most cases there will be tax payments associated with the salvage value at termination. This is because the current laws allow all projects to be depreciated to zero, and if a project has a book value of zero at termination and a positive salvage value, then that salvage value will be taxed. The tax effects associated with the salvage value of the project at termination are determined exactly like the tax effects on the sale of the old machine associated with the initial outlay. The salvage value proceeds are compared with the depreciated value, in this case zero, to determine the tax.

In addition to the salvage value, there may be a cash outlay associated with the project termination. For example, at the close of a strip-mining operation, the mine must be refilled in an ecologically acceptable manner. Finally, any working capital outlay

**TABLE 10-3**
Summary of Typical Terminal Cash Flows on After-Tax Basis

1. The after-tax salvage value of the project
2. Cash outlays associated with the project's termination
3. Recapture of nonexpense outlays that occurred at the project's initiation (for example, working capital investments)

required at the initiation of the project—for example, increased inventory needed for the operation of a new plant—will be recaptured at the termination of the project. In effect, the increased inventory required by the project can be liquidated when the project expires. Table 10-3 provides a general list of some of the factors that might affect a project's terminal cash flow.

## Measuring the Cash Flows

Fortunately, the calculations for each cash flow category are very similar. In fact, the only reason we have divided our discussion into these three categories based upon timing is because there tend to be some unusual cash flows associated with the initial outlay and the terminal cash flow. For example, in addition to the cost of the fixed assets associated with the new project, there may be some other cash flows, perhaps training costs or marketing research expenses, that are associated with the start-up of the new project. Similarly, the terminal cash flow may involve some unusual cash flow, perhaps making the project site environmentally safe after the plant closes.

We are trying to measure the after-tax incremental cash flows to the company as a whole that accrue from the new project. That is, we look at the cash flows to the company with and without this project and measure the difference.

In general, these cash flows can be divided into three types:

1. *The project's change in operating cash flows.* These include any after-tax savings or earnings that result from the new project. It should take into account any new sales or cost savings offset by any increased expenses, all on an after-tax basis. It should also include any increases in overhead that are required. For example, if taking on the new project requires that the accounting staff must be increased by two, then that cash flow associated with the increased salaries from the additional staff should be included in the analysis. Likewise, if this project produces sales increases in other product lines, those cash flows will also be relevant.

   What we are trying to measure with the change in operating cash flows is simply the change in sales minus costs minus taxes:

$$\begin{aligned}\text{operating cash flows} &= \text{change in sales}\\ &\quad - \text{change in costs}\\ &\quad - \text{change in taxes}\end{aligned}$$

The easiest way to calculate this is to use a pro forma statement and simply convert the accounting information into cash-flow information.[1]

The calculation of a project's operating cash flow actually involves three steps. First, we determine the company's *earnings before interest and taxes* (EBIT) with and without this project. Second, we subtract out the change in taxes. Keep in mind that in calculating the change in taxes, we will ignore any interest expenses. Third, we adjust this value for the fact that depreciation, a noncash-flow item, has been subtracted out in the calcu-

[1]To do this we take advantage of the fact that the difference between the change in sales and the change in costs should be equal to the change in EBIT plus depreciation.

lation of EBIT. We do this by adding back depreciation. Thus, operating cash flows are calculated as follows:

operating cash flows = change in earnings before interest and taxes
− change in taxes
+ change in depreciation

2. *Change in net working capital.* As we mentioned earlier in this chapter, many times a new project will involve additional investment in working capital—perhaps new inventory to stock a new sales outlet or simply additional investment in accounts receivable. There also may be some spontaneous short-term financing—for example, increases in accounts receivable—that results from the new project. Thus, the change in net working capital is the additional investment in working capital minus any additional short-term liabilities that were generated.
3. *Change in capital spending.* While there is generally a large cash outflow associated with a project's initial outlay, there may also be additional capital spending requirements over the life of the project. For example, you may know ahead of time that the plant will need some minor retooling in the second year of the project in order to keep the project abreast of new technological changes that are expected to take place. In effect, we will look at the company with and without the new project. Any changes in capital spending that occur are relevant.

Thus, a project's free cash flows are:

project's free cash flows = project's change in operating cash flows
− change in net working capital
− change in capital spending

If we rewrite this, inserting our calculation for the project's change in operating cash flows, we get:

project's free cash flows = change in earnings before interest and taxes
− change in taxes
+ change in depreciation
− change in net working capital
− change in capital spending

How do we go about estimating the changes in EBIT, taxes, depreciation, net working capital, and capital spending? We start with estimates of how many units we expect to sell, what the costs—both fixed and variable—will be, what the selling price will be, and what the required capital investment will be. From there we can put together a pro forma statement that should provide us with the data we need to estimate the project's free cash flows. However, you must keep in mind that our capital-budgeting decision will only be as good as our estimates of the costs and future demand. In fact, most capital-budgeting decisions that turn out to be bad decisions are not bad decisions because the decision maker used a bad decision rule, but because the estimates of future demand and costs were inaccurate.

Let's look at a simple example. You are considering expanding your product line, which currently consists of Lee's Press-on Nails, to take advantage of the fitness craze. The new product you are considering introducing is "Press-on Abs." You feel you can sell 100,000 of these per year for 4 years (after which time this project is expected to shut down because forecasters predict healthy looks will no longer be in vogue, being replaced with a couch-potato look). The press-on abs will sell for $6 each, with variable costs of $3 for each one produced, while annual fixed costs associated with production will be $90,000. In addition, there will be a $200,000 initial expenditure associated with the purchase of new

**TABLE 10-4** Calculation of the Annual Change in Earnings Before Interest and Taxes for the Press-on Abs Project

| | |
|---|---|
| Δ Sales (100,000 units at $6/unit) | $600,000 |
| Less: Δ Variable costs (variable cost $3.00/unit) | − 300,000 |
| Less: Δ Fixed costs | − 90,000 |
| Equals: | 210,000 |
| Less: Δ Depreciation ($200,000/4 years) | − 50,000 |
| Equals: Δ EBIT | 160,000 |
| Δ Taxes: (taxed at 34%) | 54,400 |

**TABLE 10-5** Annual Change in Operating Cash Flow for the Press-on Abs Project

| | |
|---|---|
| Δ Earnings before interest and taxes (EBIT) | $160,000 |
| Minus: Δ Taxes | − 54,400 |
| Plus: Δ Depreciation | + 50,000 |
| Equals: Δ Operating cash flow | 155,600 |

production equipment. It is assumed that this initial expenditure will be depreciated using the simplified straight-line method down to zero over 4 years. This project will also require a one-time initial investment of $30,000 in net working capital associated with inventory. Finally, assume that the firm's marginal tax rate is 34 percent.

Let's begin by estimating the initial outlay. In this example, the initial outlay will be the $200,000 initial expenditure plus the investment of $30,000 in net working capital, for a total of $230,000. Table 10-4 calculates the annual change in earnings before interest and taxes. This calculation begins with the change in sales (Δ Sales) and subtracts the change in fixed and variable costs, in addition to the change in depreciation, to calculate the change in earnings before interest and taxes, or EBIT. Depreciation is calculated using the simplified straight-line method, which is simply the depreciable value of the asset ($200,000) divided by the asset's expected life, which is 4 years. Taxes are then calculated assuming a 34 percent marginal tax rate. Once we have calculated EBIT and taxes we don't need to go any further, since these are the only two values from the pro forma income statement that we need. In addition, there is not any annual increase in working capital associated with the project under consideration in this example. Also notice that we have ignored any interest payments and financing flows that might have occurred. As mentioned earlier, when we discount the free cash flows back to present at the required rate of return, we are implicitly accounting for the cost of the funds needed to support the project.

The project's annual change in operating cash flow, which is simply the change in earnings before interest and taxes *minus* the change in taxes *plus* the change in depreciation, is calculated in Table 10-5.

The project's annual free cash flow is simply the change in operating cash flow less any change in net working capital and less any change in capital spending. In this example, there are no changes in net working capital and capital spending over the life of the project. This is not the case for all projects that you will consider. For example, on a project in which sales increase annually, it is likely that working capital will also increase each year to support a larger inventory and a higher level of accounts receivable. Similarly, on some projects the capital expenditures may be spread out over several years. The point here is that what we are trying to do is look at the firm with this project and without this project and measure the change in cash flows other than any interest payments and financing flows that might have occurred.

The terminal cash flow for this project is quite simple. The only unusual cash flow at the project's termination is the recapture of the net working capital associated with the

| | |
|---|---|
| Δ Earning before interest and taxes (EBIT) | $160,000 |
| Minus: Δ Taxes | − 54,400 |
| Plus: Δ Depreciation | + 50,000 |
| Minus: Change in net working capital | − (30,000) |
| Equals: Δ Free cash flow | 185,600 |

**TABLE 10-6**
Terminal Free Cash Flow for the Press-on Abs Project

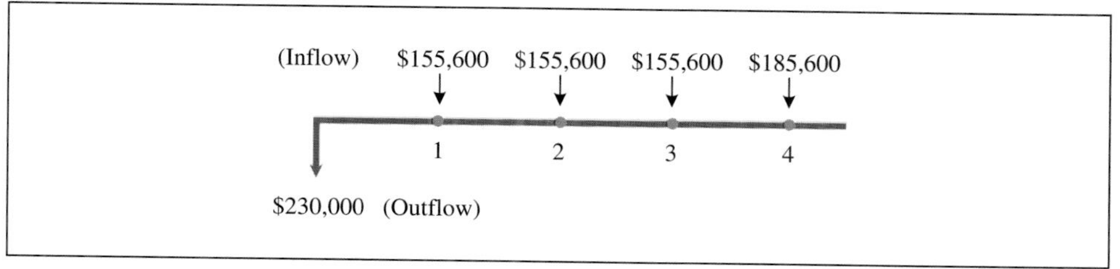


**FIGURE 10-1**
Free Cash Flow Diagram for Press-on Abs

project. In effect, the investment in inventory of $30,000 is liquidated when the project is shut down in 4 years. Keep in mind that in calculating free cash flow, we subtract out the change in net working capital, but because the change in net working capital is negative (we are reducing our investment in inventory), we are subtracting a negative number, which has the effect of adding it back in. Thus, working capital was a negative cash flow when the project began and we invested in inventory. At termination it becomes a positive offsetting cash flow when the inventory is liquidated. The calculation of the terminal free cash flow is shown in Table 10-6.

If we were to construct a free cash-flow diagram from this example (Figure 10-1), it would have an initial outlay of $230,000, the free cash flows during years 1 through 3 would be $155,600, and the free cash flow in the terminal year would be $185,600. Free cash-flow diagrams similar to that shown in Figure 10-1 will be used through the remainder of this chapter. Arrows above the time line indicate cash inflows and arrows below the time line denote outflows.

## A Comprehensive Example: Calculating Free Cash Flows

Now let's put what we know about capital budgeting together and look at a capital-budgeting decision for a firm in the 34 percent marginal tax bracket with a 15 percent required rate of return or cost of capital. The project we are considering involves the introduction of a new electric scooter line by Raymobile. Our first task is that of estimating cash flows. This project is expected to last 5 years and then, because of this is somewhat of a fad project, to be terminated. Thus, our first task becomes that of estimating the initial outlay, the annual free cash flows, and the terminal free cash flow. Given the information in Table 10-7, we want to determine the free cash flows associated with the project. Once we had that, we could easily calculate the project's net present value, the profitability index, and the internal rate of return, and apply the appropriate decision criteria.

To determine the differential annual free cash flows, we first need to determine the annual change in operating cash flow. To do this we will take the change in EBIT, subtract out the change in taxes, and then add in the change in depreciation. This is shown in Section I of Table 10-8 on page 323. We first determine what the change in sales revenue will be by multiplying the units sold times the sale price. From the change in sales revenue we subtract

**TABLE 10-7**
Raymobile Scooter Line Capital-Budgeting Example

**Cost of new plant and equipment:** $9,700,000

**Shipping and installation costs:** $ 300,000

**Unit Sales:**

| *Year* | *Units Sold* |
|---|---|
| 1 | 50,000 |
| 2 | 100,000 |
| 3 | 100,000 |
| 4 | 70,000 |
| 5 | 50,000 |

**Sales price per Unit:** $150/unit in years 1–4, $130/unit in year 5

**Variable cost per unit:** $80/unit

**Annual fixed costs:** $500,000

**Working capital requirements:** There will be an initial working capital requirement of $100,000 just to get production started. Then, for each year, the *total* investment in net working capital will be equal to 10 percent of the dollar value of sales for that year. Thus, the investment in working capital will increase during years 1 through 3, then decrease in year 4. Finally, all working capital is liquidated at the termination of the project at the end of year 5.

**The depreciation method:** We use the simplified straight-line method over 5 years. It is assumed that the plant and equipment will have no salvage value after 5 years. Thus, annual depreciation is $2,000,000/year for 5 years.

out variable costs, which were given as a percent of sales. Then, the change in fixed costs is subtracted out, and the result is earnings before depreciation, interest, and taxes (EBDIT). Subtracting the change in depreciation from EBDIT then leaves us with the change in earnings before interest and taxes (EBIT). From the change in EBIT we can then calculate the change in taxes, which are assumed to be 34 percent of EBIT.

Using the calculations provided in Section I of Table 10-8, we then calculate the operating cash flow in Section II of Table 10-8. As you recall, the operating cash flow is simply EBIT minus taxes, plus depreciation.

To calculate the free cash flow from this project, we subtract the change in net working capital and the change in capital spending from operating cash flow. Thus, the first step becomes determining the change in net working capital, which is shown in Section III of Table 10-8. The change in net working capital generally includes both increases in inventory and increases in accounts receivable that naturally occur as sales increase from the introduction of the new product line. Some of the increase in accounts receivable may be offset by increases in accounts payable, but, in general, most new projects involve some type of increase in net working capital. In this example, there is an initial working capital requirement of $100,000. In addition, for each year the total investment in net working capital will be equal to 10 percent of sales for each year. Thus, the investment in working capital for year 1 is $750,000 (because sales are estimated to be $7,500,000). Working capital will already be at $100,000, so the change in net working capital will be $650,000. Net working capital will continue to increase during years 1 through 3, then decrease in year 4. Finally, all working capital is liquidated at the termination of the project at the end of year 5.

With the operating cash flow and the change in net working capital already calculated, the calculation of the project's free cash flow becomes easy. All that is missing is the change in capital spending, which in this example will simply be the $9,700,000 for plant and equipment plus the $300,000 for shipping and installation. Thus, change in capital spending becomes $10,000,000. We then need to merely take operating cash flow

**TABLE 10-8**
Calculation of Free Cash Flow for Raymobile Scooters

**Section I.** Calculate the change in EBIT, taxes, and depreciation (this becomes an input in the calculation of operating cash flow in Section II)

| YEAR | 0 | 1 | 2 | 3 | 4 | 5 |
|---|---|---|---|---|---|---|
| Units sold | | 50,000 | 100,000 | 100,000 | 70,000 | 50,000 |
| Sale price | | $150 | $150 | $150 | $150 | $130 |
| Sales revenue | | 7,500,000 | 15,000,000 | 15,000,000 | 10,500,000 | 6,500,000 |
| Less: variable costs | | 4,000,000 | 8,000,000 | 8,000,000 | 5,600,000 | 4,000,000 |
| Less: fixed costs | | 500,000 | 500,000 | 500,000 | 500,000 | 500,000 |
| Equals: EBDIT | | 3,000,000 | 6,500,000 | 6,500,000 | 4,400,000 | 2,000,000 |
| Less: depreciation | | 2,000,000 | 2,000,000 | 2,000,000 | 2,000,000 | 2,000,000 |
| Equals: EBIT | | 1,000,000 | 4,500,000 | 4,500,000 | 2,400,000 | 0 |
| Taxes (@34%) | | 340,000 | 1,530,00 | 1,530,000 | 816,000 | 0 |

**Section II.** Calculate operating cash flow (this becomes an input in the calculation of free cash flow in Section IV)

| Operating Cash Flow: | 0 | 1 | 2 | 3 | 4 | 5 |
|---|---|---|---|---|---|---|
| EBIT | | $1,000,000 | $4,500,000 | $4,500,000 | $2,400,000 | $0 |
| Minus: taxes | | 340,000 | 1,530,00 | 1,530,00 | 816,000 | 0 |
| Plus: depreciation | | 2,000,000 | 2,000,000 | 2,000,000 | 2,000,000 | 2,000,000 |
| Equals: operating cash flows | | 2,660,000 | 4,970,000 | 4,970,000 | 3,584,000 | 2,000,000 |

**Section III.** Calculate the net working capital (this becomes an input in the calculation of free cash flows in Section IV)

| Change in Net Working Capital: | 0 | 1 | 2 | 3 | 4 | 5 |
|---|---|---|---|---|---|---|
| Revenue | | $7,500,000 | $15,000,000 | $15,000,000 | $10,500,000 | $6,500,000 |
| Initial working capital requirement | 100,000 | | | | | |
| Net working capital needs | | 750,000 | 1,500,000 | 1,500,000 | 1,050,000 | 650,000 |
| Liquidation of working capital | | | | | | 650,000 |
| Change in working capital | 100,000 | 650,000 | 750,000 | 0 | (450,000) | (1,050,000) |

**Section IV.** Calculate free cash flow (using information calculated in Sections II and III, in addition to the change in capital spending)

| Free Cash Flow: | 0 | 1 | 2 | 3 | 4 | 5 |
|---|---|---|---|---|---|---|
| Operating cash flow | | $2,660,000 | $4,970,000 | $4,970,000 | $3,584,000 | $2,000,000 |
| Minus: change in net working capital | 100,000 | 650,000 | 750,000 | 0 | (450,000) | (1,050,000) |
| Minus: change in capital spending | 10,000,000 | 0 | $0 | 0 | 0 | 0 |
| **Free cash flow** | **(10,100,000)** | **2,010,000** | **4,220,000** | **4,970,000** | **4,034,000** | **3,050,000** |

and subtract from it both the change in net working capital and the change in capital spending. This is done in Section IV of Table 10-8. A free cash-flow diagram for this project is provided in Figure 10-2.

Using the information provided in Section IV of Table 10-8 and Figure 10-2, we easily calculate the *NPV, PI,* and *IRR* for this project.

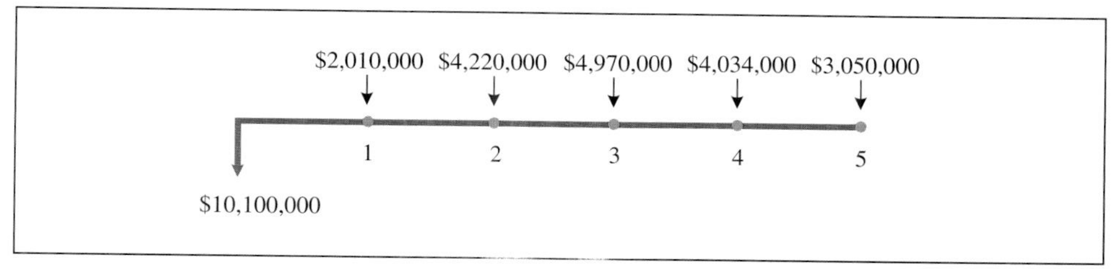


**FIGURE 10-2**
Free Cash-Flow Diagram for the Raymobile Scooter Line

**CONCEPT CHECK**

1. In general, a project's cash flows will fall into one of three categories. What are these categories?
2. What is a free cash flow? How do we calculate it?
3. What is depreciation? Where does it come from?
4. Although depreciation is not a cash flow item, it plays an important role in the calculation of cash flows. How does depreciation affect a project's cash flows?

**RELATE TO THE BIG PICTURE**

In this chapter, it is easy to get caught up in the calculations and forget that before the calculations can be made, someone has to come up with the idea for the project. In some of the example problems, you may see projects that appear to be extremely profitable. Unfortunately, as we learned in **Principle 5: The Curse of Competitive Markets—Why it's hard to find exceptionally profitable projects,** it is unusual to find projects with dramatically high returns because of the very competitive nature of business. Thus, keep in mind that capital budgeting not only involves the estimation and evaluation of the project's cash flows, but it also includes the process of coming up with the idea for the project in the first place.

## COMPLICATIONS IN CAPITAL BUDGETING: CAPITAL RATIONING AND MUTUALLY EXCLUSIVE PROJECTS

OBJECTIVE 3 

**Capital rationing**
The placing of a limit by the firm on the dollar size of the capital budget.

The use of our capital-budgeting decision rules implies that the size of the capital budget is determined by the availability of acceptable investment proposals. However, a firm may place a limit on the dollar size of the capital budget. This situation is called **capital rationing.** As we will see, an examination of capital rationing will not only enable us to deal with complexities of the real world but will also serve to demonstrate the superiority of the NPV method over the IRR method for capital budgeting.

Using the internal rate of return as the firm's decision rule, a firm accepts all projects with an internal rate of return greater than the firm's required rate of return. This rule is illustrated in Figure 10-3, where projects A through E would be chosen. However, when capital rationing is imposed, the dollar size of the total investment is limited by the budget

**FIGURE 10-3**
Projects Ranked by *IRR*

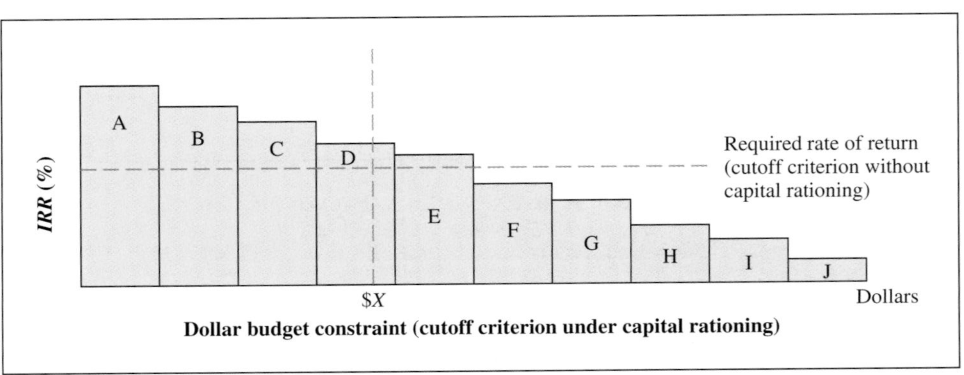

constraint. In Figure 10-3, the budget constraint of $\$X$ precludes the acceptance of an attractive investment, project E. This situation obviously contradicts prior decision rules. Moreover, the solution of choosing the projects with the highest internal rate of return is complicated by the fact that some projects may be indivisible; for example, it is meaningless to recommend that half of project D be acquired.

## Rationale for Capital Rationing

We will first ask why capital rationing exists and whether or not it is rational. In general, three principal reasons are given for imposing a capital-rationing constraint. First, management may think market conditions are temporarily adverse. In the period surrounding the stock market crash of 1987, this reason was frequently given. At that time, interest rates were high, and stock prices were depressed, which made the cost of funding projects high. Second, there may be a shortage of qualified managers to direct new projects; this can happen when projects are of a highly technical nature. Third, there may be intangible considerations. For example, management may simply fear debt, wishing to avoid interest payments at any cost. Or perhaps issuance of common stock may be limited to maintain a stable dividend policy.

Despite strong evidence that capital rationing exists in practice, the question remains as to its effect on the firm. In brief, the effect is negative, and to what degree depends on the severity of the rationing. If the rationing is minor and short-lived, the firm's share price will not suffer to any great extent. In this case, capital rationing can probably be excused, although it should be noted that any capital rationing that rejects projects with positive net present values is contrary to the firm's goal of maximization of shareholders' wealth. If the capital rationing is a result of the firm's decision to limit dramatically the number of new projects or to limit total investment to internally generated funds, then this policy will eventually have a significantly negative effect on the firm's share price. For example, a lower share price will eventually result from lost competitive advantage if, owing to a decision to limit arbitrarily its capital budget, a firm fails to upgrade its products and manufacturing process.

## Capital Rationing and Project Selection

If the firm decides to impose a capital constraint on investment projects, the appropriate decision criterion is to select the set of projects with the highest net present value subject to the capital constraint. In effect, you are selecting the projects that increase shareholder wealth the most, because the net present value is the amount of wealth that is created when a project is accepted. This guideline may preclude merely taking the highest-ranked projects in terms of the profitability index or the internal rate of return. If the projects shown in Figure 10-3 are divisible, the last project accepted may be only partially accepted. Although partial acceptances may be possible in some cases, the indivisibility of most capital investments prevents it. If a project is a sales outlet or a truck, it may be meaningless to purchase half a sales outlet or half a truck.

To illustrate this procedure, consider a firm with a budget constraint of \$1 million and five indivisible projects available to it, as given in Table 10-9. If the highest-ranked projects were taken, projects A and B would be taken first. At that point, there would not be enough funds available to take project C; hence projects D and E would be taken. However, a higher total net present value is provided by the combination of projects A and C. Thus, projects A and C should be selected from the set of projects available. This illustrates our guideline: to select the set of projects that maximize the firm's net present value.

**TABLE 10-9**
Capital-Rationing Example of Five Indivisible Projects

| Project | Initial Outlay | Profitability Index | Net Present Value |
|---|---|---|---|
| A | $200,000 | 2.4 | $280,000 |
| B | 200,000 | 2.3 | 260,000 |
| C | 800,000 | 1.7 | 560,000 |
| D | 300,000 | 1.3 | 90,000 |
| E | 300,000 | 1.2 | 60,000 |

## Project Ranking

In the past, we have proposed that all projects with a positive net present value, a profitability index greater than 1.0, or an internal rate of return greater than the required rate of return be accepted, assuming there is no capital rationing. However, this acceptance is not always possible. In some cases, when two projects are judged acceptable by the discounted cash flow criteria, it may be necessary to select only one of them, as they are mutually exclusive.

**Mutually exclusive projects**
A set of projects that perform essentially the same task, so that acceptance of one will necessarily mean rejection of the others.

**Mutually exclusive projects** occur when a set of investment proposals perform essentially the same task; acceptance of one will necessarily mean rejection of the others. For example, a company considering the installation of a computer system may evaluate three or four systems, all of which may have positive net present values; however, the acceptance of one system will automatically mean rejection of the others. In general, to deal with mutually exclusive projects, we will simply rank them by means of the discounted cash flow criteria and select the project with the highest ranking. On occasion, however, problems of conflicting ranking may arise. As we will see, in general the net present value method is the preferred decision-making tool because it leads to the selection of the project that increases shareholder wealth the most.

## Problems in Project Ranking

There are three general types of ranking problems: the size disparity problem, the time disparity problem, and the unequal lives problem. Each involves the possibility of conflict in the ranks yielded by the various discounted cash flow capital-budgeting decision criteria. As noted previously, when one discounted cash flow criterion gives an accept signal, they will all give an accept signal, but they will not necessarily rank all projects in the same order. In most cases, this disparity is not critical; however, for mutually exclusive projects, the ranking order is important.

SIZE DISPARITY The *size disparity problem* occurs when mutually exclusive projects of unequal size are examined. This problem is most easily clarified with an example.

### EXAMPLE

Suppose a firm is considering two mutually exclusive projects, A and B, both with required rates of return of 10 percent. Project A involves a $200 initial outlay and cash inflow of $300 at the end of 1 year, whereas project B involves an initial outlay of $1,500 and a cash inflow of $1,900 at the end of 1 year. The net present value, profitability index, and internal rate of return for these projects are given in Figure 10-4.

**FIGURE 10-4**
Size Disparity Ranking Problem

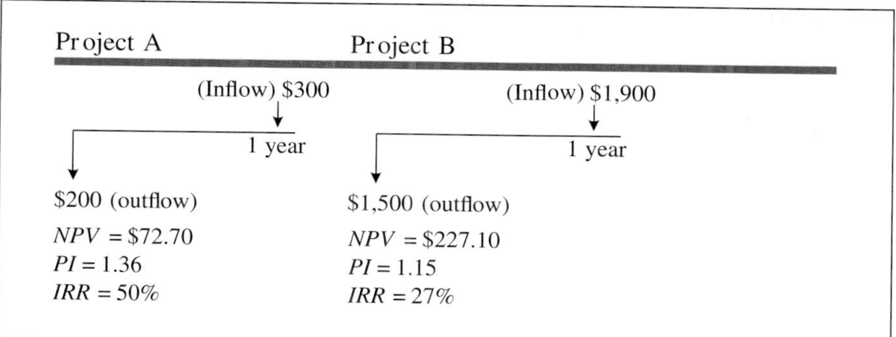


*NPV* = $72.70
*PI* = 1.36
*IRR* = 50%

*NPV* = $227.10
*PI* = 1.15
*IRR* = 27%

In this case, if the net present value criterion is used, project B should be accepted, whereas if the profitability index or the internal rate of return criterion is used, project A should be chosen. The question now becomes: Which project is better? The answer depends on whether capital rationing exists. Without capital rationing, project B is better because it provides the largest increase in shareholders' wealth; that is, it has a larger net present value. If there is a capital constraint, the problem then focuses on what can be done with the additional $1,300 that is freed if project A is chosen (costing $200, as opposed to $1,500). If the firm can earn more on project A plus the project financed with the additional $1,300 ($1,500 − $200) freed up if project A as opposed to project B is chosen, then project A and the marginal project should be accepted. In effect, we are attempting to select the set of projects that maximize the firm's *NPV*. Thus, if the marginal project has a net present value greater than $154.40 ($227.10 − $72.70), selecting it plus project A with a net present value of $72.70 will provide a net present value greater than $227.10, the net present value for project B.

In summary, whenever the size disparity problem results in conflicting rankings between mutually exclusive projects, the project with the largest net present value will be selected, provided there is no capital rationing. When capital rationing exists, the firm should select the set of projects with the largest net present value.

**TIME DISPARITY** The *time disparity problem* and the conflicting rankings that accompany it result from the differing reinvestment assumptions made by the net present value and internal rate of return decision criteria. The *NPV* criterion assumes that cash flows over the life of the project can be reinvested at the required rate of return or cost of capital, whereas the *IRR* criterion implicitly assumes that the cash flows over the life of the project can be reinvested at the internal rate of return. Again, this problem may be illustrated through the use of an example.

Suppose a firm with a required rate of return or cost of capital of 10 percent and with no capital constraint is considering the two mutually exclusive projects illustrated in Figure 10-5. The net present value and profitability index indicate that project A is the better of the two, whereas the internal rate of return indicates that project B is the better. Project B receives its cash flows earlier than project A, and the different assumptions made as to how these flows can be reinvested result in the difference in rankings. Which criterion should be followed depends on which reinvestment assumption is used. The net present value criterion is preferred in this case because it makes the most acceptable assumption for the wealth-

**FIGURE 10-5**
Time Disparity Ranking Problem

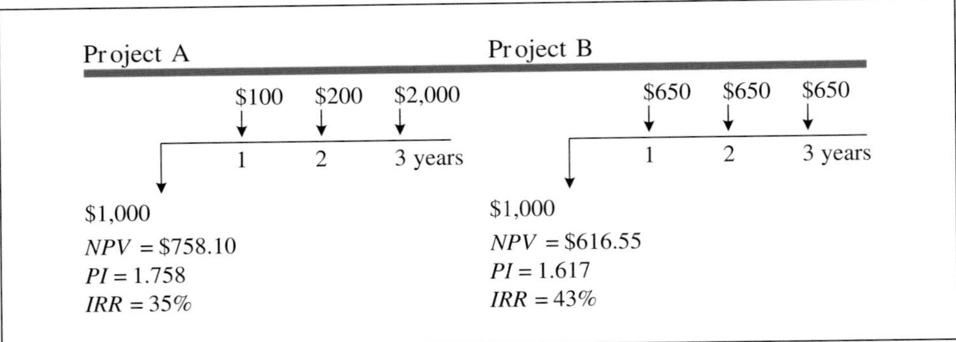


maximizing firm. It is certainly the most conservative assumption that can be made, because the required rate of return is the lowest possible reinvestment rate. Moreover, as we have already noted, the net present value method maximizes the value of the firm and the shareholders' wealth. An alternate solution, as discussed in Chapter 9, is to use the *MIRR* method.

**UNEQUAL LIVES** The final ranking problem to be examined centers on the question of whether it is appropriate to compare mutually exclusive projects with different life spans.

Suppose a firm with a 10 percent required rate of return is faced with the problem of replacing an aging machine and is considering two replacement machines, one with a 3-year life and one with a 6-year life. The relevant cash flow information for these projects is given in Figure 10-6.

Examining the discounted cash flow criteria, we find that the net present value and profitability index criteria indicate that project B is the better project, whereas the internal rate of return favors project A. This ranking inconsistency is caused by the different life spans of the projects being compared. In this case, the decision is a difficult one because the projects are not comparable.

The problem of incomparability of projects with different lives arises because future profitable investment proposals may be rejected without being included in the analysis. This can easily be seen in a replacement problem such as the present example, in which two mutually exclusive machines with different lives are being considered. In this case, a comparison of the net present values alone on each of these projects would be misleading. If the project with the shorter life were taken, at its termination the firm could replace the machine and receive additional benefits, whereas acceptance of the project with the longer life would exclude this possibility, a possibility that is not included in the analysis. The key

**FIGURE 10-6**
Unequal Lives Ranking Problem

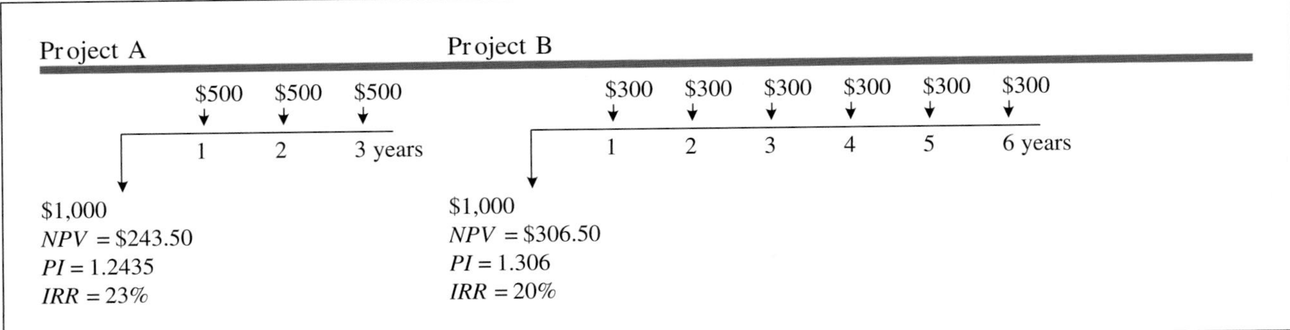

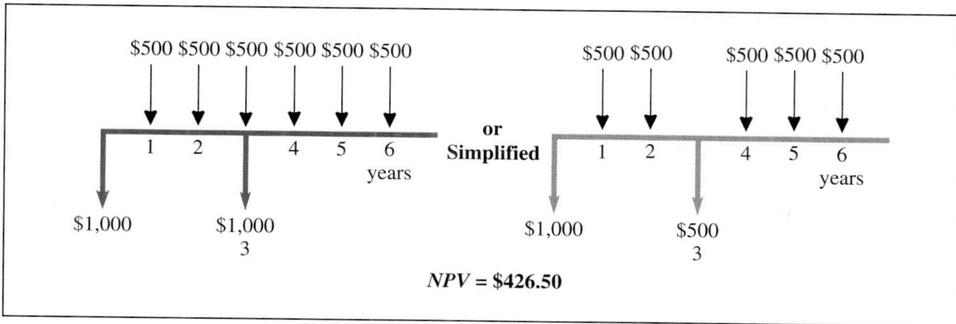


**FIGURE 10-7**
Replacement Chain Illustration: Two Project A's Back to Back

question thus becomes: Does today's investment decision include all future profitable investment proposals in its analysis? If not, the projects are not comparable. In this case, if project B is taken, then the project that could have been taken after 3 years when project A terminates is automatically rejected without being included in the analysis. Thus acceptance of project B not only forces rejection of project A, but also forces rejection of any replacement machine that might have been considered for years 4 through 6 without including this replacement machine in the analysis.

There are several methods to deal with this situation. The first option is to assume that the cash inflows from the shorter-lived investment will be reinvested at the required rate of return until the termination of the longer-lived asset. Although this approach is the simplest, merely calculating the net present value, it actually ignores the problem at hand—that of allowing for participation in another replacement opportunity with a positive net present value. The proper solution thus becomes the projection of reinvestment opportunities into the future—that is, making assumptions about possible future investment opportunities. Unfortunately, whereas the first method is too simplistic to be of any value, the second is extremely difficult, requiring extensive cash flow forecasts. The final technique for confronting the problem is to assume that reinvestment opportunities in the future will be similar to the current ones. The two most common ways of doing this are by creating a replacement chain to equalize life spans or calculating the project's equivalent annual annuity (EAA). Using a replacement chain, the present example would call for the creation of a two-chain cycle for project A; that is, we assume that project A can be replaced with a similar investment at the end of 3 years. Thus, project A would be viewed as two A projects occurring back to back, as illustrated in Figure 10-7. The net present value on this replacement chain is $426.50, which can be compared with project B's net present value. Therefore, project A should be accepted because the net present value of its replacement chain is greater than the net present value of project B.

One problem with replacement chains is that, depending on the life of each project, it can be quite difficult to come up with equivalent lives. For example, if the two projects had 7- and 13-year lives, because the lowest common denominator is $7 \times 13 = 91$, a 91-year replacement chain would be needed to establish equivalent lives. In this case, it is easier to determine the project's **equivalent annual annuity (*EAA*)**. A project's *EAA* is simply an annuity cash flow that yields the same present value as the project's *NPV*. To calculate a project's *EAA*, we need only calculate a project's *NPV* and then divide that number by the $PVIFA_{i,n}$ to determine the dollar value of an $n$-year annuity that would produce the same *NPV* as the project. This can be done in two steps as follows:

**Equivalent annual annuity (*EAA*)**
An annual cash flow that yields the same present value as the project's *NPV*. It is calculated by dividing the project's *NPV* by the appropriate $PVIFA_{i,n}$.

Step 1: *Calculate the project's NPV.* In Figure 10-6 we determined that project A had an *NPV* of $243.50, whereas project B had an *NPV* of $306.50.

Step 2: *Calculate the EAA.* The *EAA* is determined by dividing each project's *NPV* by the $PVIFA_{i,n}$ where *i* is the required rate of return and *n* is the project's life. This determines the level of an annuity cash flow that would produce the same *NPV* as the project. For project A the $PVIFA_{10\%,3yr}$ is equal to 2.487, whereas the $PVIFA_{10\%,6yr}$ for project B is equal to 4.355. By dividing each project's *NPV* by the appropriate $PVIFA_{i,n}$ we determine the EAA for each project:

$$
\begin{aligned}
EAA_A &= NPV/PVIFA_{i,n} \\
&= \$243.50/2.487 \\
&= \$97.91 \\
EAA_B &= \$306.50/4.355 \\
&= \$70.38
\end{aligned}
$$

How do we interpret the *EAA*? For a project with an *n*-year life, it tells us what the dollar value is of an *n*-year annual annuity that would provide the same *NPV* as the project. Thus, for project A, it means that a 3-year annuity of $97.91 given a discount rate of 10 percent would produce a net present value the same as project A's net present value, which is $243.50. We can now compare the equivalent annual annuities directly to determine which project is better. We can do this because we now have found the level of annual annuity that produces an *NPV* equivalent to the project's *NPV.* Thus, because they are both annual annuities, they are comparable. An easy way to see this is to use the *EAAs* to create infinite-life replacement chains. To do this, we need only calculate the present value of an infinite stream or perpetuity of equivalent annual annuities. This is done by using the present value of an infinite annuity formula—that is, simply dividing the equivalent annual annuity by the appropriate discount rate. In this case we find:

$$
\begin{aligned}
NPV_{\infty,A} &= \$97.91/.10 \\
&= \$979.10 \\
NPV_{\infty,B} &= \$70.38/.10 \\
&= \$703.80
\end{aligned}
$$

Here we have calculated the present value of an infinite-life replacement chain. Because the *EAA* method provides the same results as the infinite-life replacement chain, it really doesn't matter which method you prefer to use.

**CONCEPT CHECK**

1. What is capital rationing and why does it occur?
2. What are mutually exclusive projects? Give an example.

## Options in Capital Budgeting

The use of our discounted cash-flow decision criteria like the *NPV* method provides an excellent framework within which to evaluate projects. However, what happens if the project being analyzed has the potential to be modified after some future uncertainty has been resolved? For example, if a project that had an expected life of 10 years turns out to be better than anticipated, it may be expanded or continued past 10 years, perhaps going for 20 years. On the other hand, if its cash flows do not meet expectations, it may not last a full 10 years—it might be scaled back, abandoned, or sold. In addition, it might be delayed for a year or two. This flexibility is something that the *NPV* and our other decision criteria had a difficult time dealing with. In fact, the *NPV* may actually understate the value of the project because the future opportunities associated with the possibility of modifying the project may have a positive value. It is this value of flexibility that we will be examining using options.

Three of the most common option types that can add value to a capital-budgeting project are (1) the option to delay a project until the future cash flows are more favorable—this option is common when the firm has exclusive rights, perhaps a patent, to a product or technology; (2) the option to expand a project, perhaps in size or even to new products that would not have otherwise been feasible; and (3) the option to abandon a project if the future cash flows fall short of expectations.

**THE OPTION TO DELAY A PROJECT** There is no question that the estimated cash flows associated with a project can change over time. In fact, as a result of changing expected cash flows, a project that currently has a negative net present value may have a positive net present value in the future. Let's look at the example of an eco-car—a car with a hybrid gasoline engine and an electric motor. Perhaps you've developed a high-voltage nickel-metal hydride battery that you plan on using, coupled with a gasoline engine, to power an automobile. However, as you examine the costs of introducing an eco-car capable of producing 70 miles per gallon, you realize that it is still relatively expensive to manufacture the nickel-metal hydride battery and the market for such a car would be quite small. Thus, this project seems to have a negative net present value. Does that mean that the rights to the high-voltage nickel-metal hydride battery have no value? No, they have value because you may be able to improve on this technology in the future and make the battery more efficient and less expensive, and they also have value because oil prices may rise, which would lead to a bigger market for fuel-efficient cars. In effect, the ability to delay this project with the hope that technological and market conditions will change, making this project profitable, lends value to this project.

Another example of the option to delay a project until the future cash flows are more favorable involves a firm that owns the oil rights to some oil-rich land and is considering an oil-drilling project. After all of the costs and the expected oil output are considered, this project may have a negative net present. Does that mean the firm should give away its oil rights or that those oil rights have no value? Certainly not; there is a chance that in the future oil prices could rise to the point that this negative net present value project could become a positive net present value project. It is this ability to delay development that provides value. Thus, the value in this seemingly negative *NPV* project is provided by the option to delay the project until the future cash flows are more favorable.

**THE OPTION TO EXPAND A PROJECT** Just as we saw with the option to delay a project, the estimated cash flows associated with a project can change over time, making it valuable to expand a project. Again, this flexibility to adjust production to demand has value. For example, a firm may build a production plant with excess capacity so that if the product has more than anticipated demand, it can simply increase production. Alternatively, taking on this project may provide the firm with a foothold in a new industry and lead to other products that would not have otherwise been feasible. This reasoning has led many firms to expand into e-businesses, hoping to gain know-how and expertise that will lead to other profitable projects down the line. It also provides some of the rationale for research and development expenditures in which the future project is not well defined.

Let's go back to our example of the eco-car and examine the option to expand that project. One of the reasons that most of the major automobile firms are introducing eco-cars is that they feel that if gas prices surge beyond the $2 per gallon price, these hybrids may be the future of the industry, and the only way to gain the know-how and expertise to produce an eco-car is to do it. If the cost of technology declines and the demands increase—perhaps pushed on by increases in gas prices—then they will be ready to expand into full-fledged production. This point becomes clear when you look at the new Honda Insight, which was introduced in January 2000. This is a two-passenger, 3-cylinder car with a gas engine and electric motor. It provides 65 miles per gallon, and Honda expects to sell between 7,000 and 8,000 during 2000.

On every Insight that Honda sells, analysts estimate that Honda loses about $8,000. A Honda spokesman says that Honda expects to break even "in a couple of years." Still, this project makes sense because only through it can Honda gain the technological and production expertise to produce an eco-car profitably. Moreover, the technology Honda develops with the Insight may have profitable applications for other cars or in other areas. In effect, it is the option of expanding production in the future that brings value to this project.

**THE OPTION TO ABANDON A PROJECT** The option to abandon a project as the estimated cash flows associated with a project can change over time also has value. Again, it is this flexibility to adjust to new information that provides the value. For example, a project's sales in the first year or two may not live up to expectations, with the project being barely profitable. The firm may then decide to liquidate the project and sell the plant and all of the equipment, and that liquidated value may be more than the value of keeping the project going.

Again, let's go back to our example of the eco-car and, this time, examine the option to abandon that project. If after a few years the cost of gas falls dramatically while the cost of technology remains high, the eco-car may not become profitable. At that point Honda may decide to abandon the project and sell the technology, including all the patent rights it has developed. In effect, the original project, the eco-car, may not be of value, but the technology that has been developed may be. In effect, the value of abandoning the project and selling the technology may be more than the value of keeping the project running. Again, it is the value of flexibility associated with the possibility of modifying the project in the future—in this case abandoning the project—that can produce positive value.

**OPTIONS IN CAPITAL BUDGETING: THE BOTTOM LINE** Because of the potential to be modified in the future after some future uncertainty has been resolved, we may find that a project with a negative net present value based upon its expected free cash flows is a "good" project and should be accepted—this demonstrates the value of options. In addition, we may find that a project with a positive net present value may be of more value if its acceptance is delayed. Options also explain the logic that drives firms to take on negative net present value projects that allow them to enter new markets. The option to abandon a project explains why firms hire employees on a temporary basis rather than permanently, why they may lease rather than buy equipment, and why they may enter into contracts with suppliers on an annual basis rather than long term.

**CONCEPT CHECK**

1. Give an example of an option to delay a project. Why might this be of value?
2. Give an example of an option to expand a project. Why might this be of value?
3. Give an example of an option to abandon a project. Why might this be of value?

## THE MULTINATIONAL FIRM: INTERNATIONAL COMPLICATIONS IN CALCULATING EXPECTED FREE CASH FLOWS

The process of measuring the incremental after-tax cash flows to the company as a whole gets a bit more complicated when we are dealing with competition from abroad. One area in which this is certainly true is in calculating the right base case; that is, what the firm's free cash flows would be if the project is not taken on. In determining what free cash flows will be in the future, we must always be aware of potential competition from abroad. We need only look to the auto industry to see that competition from abroad can be serious. During the

1970s, who would have thought that firms like Toyota, Honda, and Nissan could enter the U.S. markets and actually challenge the likes of Ford and GM? The end result of this is that the opening of the markets to international competition has not only led to increased opportunities, but it has also led to increased difficulties in estimating expected free cash flows.

There are also other intangible benefits from investing in countries like Germany and Japan, where cutting-edge technology is making its way into the marketplace. Here, investment abroad provides a chance to observe the introduction of new innovations on a first-hand basis. This allows firms like IBM, GE, and 3Com to react more quickly to any technological advances and product innovations that might come out of Germany or Japan.

Finally, international markets can be viewed as an option to expand if a product is well received at home. For example, McDonalds was much more of a hit at home than anyone ever expected 30 years ago. Once it conquered the United States, it moved abroad. There is much uncertainty every time McDonalds opens a new store in another country; it is unlikely that any new store will be without problems stemming from cultural differences. What McDonald's learns in the first store opened in a new country is then used in modifying any new stores that it opens in that country. In effect, opening that first store in a new country provides the option to expand, and that option to expand and the value of the flexibility to adjust to the future make opening that first store in a new country a good project.

## HOW FINANCIAL MANAGERS USE THIS MATERIAL

Not only is the financial manager responsible for finding and then properly evaluating new projects, but the financial manager must be certain that the numbers going into the analysis are correct. Let's look at what the financial managers at Burger King faced when they decided to introduce the Big King, a new burger that looks an awful lot like the Big Mac. The first task they face is to estimate what the sales from this new product will be—a task that is easier said than done. Not only will sales be dependent upon how good the product is, or in this case, how good the product tastes, but they will also be dependent upon how good a job the marketing department does in selling the public on this new product. But just looking at sales is not enough. To properly perform the analysis on this product, Burger King needs to know what portion of sales will simply be sales diverted from Whoppers, and what portion of sales will be new to Burger King as a whole. In other words, when it introduces the Big King, how much of the sales are from new customers—those "Big Mac attack" eaters?

This is truly an area where finance and marketing meet. Much of the job of the financial manager is to make sure that the numbers are correct. That is, have the marketing people considered any synergistic effects? If new customers are drawn into Burger King, are they likely to buy a drink and some fries—two very high markup sales? Will they bring in their families or friends when they make their Big King purchase? How about the increased inventory associated with carrying the Big King line? If it all sounds pretty complex, that's because it *is* complex. But more important, it is a decision that has a dramatic effect on the future direction of the firm, and it is an ongoing decision. That is, once the product is introduced and you see how the public reacts, you will continuously reevaluate the product to determine if it should be abandoned or expanded.

Look at the "New Coke." Cola-Cola spent an enormous amount of money test marketing and promoting that product, only to find the public didn't really like it after all. Once it realized that, the next capital-budgeting decision it made was, given the new sales estimates, to abandon the product. In effect, capital budgeting involves reinventing the company, and in order to make a good decision, you've got to have good information going into your capital-budgeting decision model. An awful lot of time and many jobs—maybe your job—revolve around making these decisions.

## SUMMARY

OBJECTIVE 1 

In this chapter, we examined the measurement of free cash flows associated with a firm's investment proposals that are used to evaluate those proposals. Relying on **Principle 3: Cash—Not Profits—Is King,** and **Principle 4: Incremental Cash Flows—It's only what changes that counts,** we focused only on free cash flows—that is, the incremental or different after-tax cash flows attributed to the investment proposal. Care was taken to be wary of cash flows diverted from existing products, look for incidental or synergistic effects, consider working-capital requirements, consider incremental expenses, ignore sunk costs, account for opportunity costs, examine overhead costs carefully, and ignore interest payments and financing flows.

OBJECTIVE 2 

In general, a project's free cash flows fall into one of three categories: (1) the initial outlay, (2) the differential flows over the project's life, and (3) the terminal cash flow.

To measure a project's benefits, we use the project's free cash flows. These free cash flows include:

$$
\begin{aligned}
\text{project's free cash flows} = {} & \text{project's change in operating cash flows} \\
& - \text{change in net working capital} \\
& - \text{change in capital spending}
\end{aligned}
$$

We can rewrite this, inserting our calculation for project's change in operating cash flows:

$$
\begin{aligned}
\text{Project's free cash flows} = {} & \text{change in earnings before interest and taxes} \\
& - \text{change in taxes} \\
& + \text{change in depreciation} \\
& - \text{change in net working capital} \\
& - \text{change in capital spending}
\end{aligned}
$$

OBJECTIVE 3 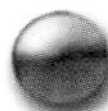

We also examined capital rationing and the problems it can create by imposing a limit on the dollar size of the capital budget. Although capital rationing does not, in general, lead to the goal of maximization of shareholders' wealth, it does exist in practice. We discussed problems associated with the evaluation of mutually exclusive projects. Mutually exclusive projects occur when we have a set of investment proposals that perform essentially the same task. In general, to deal with mutually exclusive projects, we rank them by means of the discounted cash flow criteria and select the project with the highest ranking. Conflicting rankings may arise because of the size disparity problem, the time disparity problem, and unequal lives. The problem of incomparability of projects with different lives is not simply a result of the different lives; rather, it arises because future profitable investment proposals may be rejected without being included in the analysis. Replacement chains and equivalent annual annuities are possible solutions to this problem.

How do we deal with a project that has the potential to be modified after some future uncertainty has been resolved? This flexibility to be modified is something that the *NPV* and our other decision criteria had a difficult time dealing with. It is this value of flexibility that we examined using options. Three of the most common types of options that can add value to a capital budgeting project are (1) the option to delay a project until the future cash flows are more favorable—this option is common when the firm has exclusive rights, perhaps a patent, to a product or technology; (2) the option to expand a project, perhaps in size or even to new products that would not have otherwise been feasible; and (3) the option to abandon a project if the future cash flows fall short of expectations.

myPHLIP

Go To:
http://www.prenhall.com/keown
for downloads and current events associated with this chapter

## KEY TERMS

**Capital rationing, 324**

**Equivalent annual annuity (*EAA*), 329**

**Initial outlay, 315**

**Mutually exclusive projects, 326**

## STUDY QUESTIONS

**10-1.** Why do we focus on cash flows rather than accounting profits in making our capital-budgeting decisions? Why are we interested only in incremental cash flows rather than total cash flows?

**10-2.** If depreciation is not a cash flow item, why does it affect the level of cash flows from a project in any way? Why?

**10-3.** If a project requires additional investment in working capital, how should this be treated in calculating cash flows?

**10-4.** How do sunk costs affect the determination of cash flows associated with an investment proposal?

**10-5.** What are mutually exclusive projects? Why might the existence of mutually exclusive projects cause problems in the implementation of the discounted cash flow capital-budgeting decision criteria?

**10-6.** What are common reasons for capital rationing? Is capital rationing rational?

**10-7.** How should managers compare two mutually exclusive projects of unequal size? Would your approach change if capital rationing existed?

**10-8.** What causes the time disparity ranking problem? What reinvestment rate assumptions are associated with the net present value and internal rate of return capital-budgeting criteria?

**10-9.** When might two mutually exclusive projects having unequal lives be incomparable? How should managers deal with this problem?

## SELF-TEST PROBLEMS

**ST-1.** The Easterwood Corporation, a firm in the 34 percent marginal tax bracket with a 15 percent required rate of return or cost of capital, is considering a new project. This project involves the introduction of a new product. This project is expected to last 5 years and then, because this is somewhat of a fad project, to be terminated. Given the following information, determine the free cash flows associated with the project, the project's net present value, the profitability index, and the internal rate of return. Apply the appropriate decision criteria.

**Cost of new plant and equipment:** $20,900,000

**Shipping and installation costs:** $ 300,000

**Unit sales:**

| Year | Units Sold |
|---|---|
| 1 | 100,000 |
| 2 | 130,000 |
| 3 | 160,000 |
| 4 | 100,000 |
| 5 | 60,000 |

**Sales price per unit:** $500/unit in years 1–4, $380/unit in year 5

**Variable cost per unit:** $260/unit

**Annual fixed costs:** $300,000

**Working-capital requirements:** There will be an initial working-capital requirement of $500,000 just to get production started. For each year, the total investment in net working capital will be equal to 10 percent of the dollar value of sales for that year. Thus, the investment in working capital will increase during years 1 through 3, then decrease in year 4. Finally, all working capital is liquidated at the termination of the project at the end of year 5.

**The depreciation method:** Use the simplified straight-line method over 5 years. It is assumed that the plant and equipment will have no salvage value after 5 years.

**ST-2.** The J. Serrano Corporation is considering signing a 1-year contract with one of two computer-based marketing firms. Although one is more expensive, it offers a more extensive program and thus will provide higher after-tax net cash flows. Assume these two options are mutually exclusive and that the required rate of return is 12 percent. Given the following after-tax net cash flows:

| Year | Option A | Option B |
|---|---|---|
| 0 | −$50,000 | −$100,000 |
| 1 | 70,000 | 130,000 |

**a.** Calculate the net present value.
**b.** Calculate the profitability index.
**c.** Calculate the internal rate of return.
**d.** If there is no capital-rationing constraint, which project should be selected? If there is a capital-rationing constraint, how should the decision be made?

## STUDY PROBLEMS (SET A)

**10-1A.** (*Capital gains tax*) The J. Harris Corporation is considering selling one of its old assembly machines. The machine, purchased for $30,000 5 years ago, had an expected life of 10 years and an expected salvage value of zero. Assume Harris uses simplified straight-line depreciation, creating depreciation of $3,000 per year, and could sell this old machine for $35,000. Also assume a 34 percent marginal tax rate.

**a.** What would be the taxes associated with this sale?
**b.** If the old machine were sold for $25,000, what would be the taxes associated with this sale?
**c.** If the old machine were sold for $15,000, what would be the taxes associated with this sale?
**d.** If the old machine were sold for $12,000, what would be the taxes associated with this sale?

**10-2A.** (*Relevant cash flows*) Captins' Cereal is considering introducing a variation of its current breakfast cereal, Crunch Stuff. This new cereal will be similar to the old with the exception that it will contain sugarcoated marshmallows shaped in the form of stars. The new cereal will be called Crunch Stuff n' Stars. It is estimated that the sales for the new cereal will be $25 million; however, 20 percent of those sales will be former Crunch Stuff customers who have switched to Crunch Stuff n' Stars who would not have switched if the new product had not been introduced. What is the relevant sales level to consider when deciding whether or not to introduce Crunch n' Stars?

**10-3A.** (*Calculating free cash flows*) Racin' Scooters is introducing a new product and has an expected change in EBIT of $475,000. Racin' Scooters has a 34 percent marginal tax rate. This project will also produce $100,000 of depreciation per year. In addition, this project will also cause the following changes:

| | Without the Project | With the Project |
|---|---|---|
| Accounts receivable | $45,000 | $63,000 |
| Inventory | 65,000 | 80,000 |
| Accounts payable | 70,000 | 94,000 |

What is the project's free cash flow?

**10-4A.** (*Calculating free cash flows*) Visible Fences is introducing a new product and has an expected change in EBIT of $900,000. Visible Fences has a 34 percent marginal tax rate. This project will also produce $300,000 of depreciation per year. In addition, this project will also cause the following changes:

| | Without the Project | With the Project |
|---|---|---|
| Accounts receivable | $55,000 | $63,000 |
| Inventory | 55,000 | 70,000 |
| Accounts payable | 90,000 | 106,000 |

What is the project's free cash flow?

**10-5A.** (*New project analysis*) The Chung Chemical Corporation is considering the purchase of a chemical analysis machine. Although the machine being considered will result in an increase in earnings before interest and taxes of $35,000 per year, it has a purchase price of $100,000, and it would cost an additional $5,000 after tax to properly install this machine. In addition, to properly operate this machine, inventory must be increased by $5,000. This machine has an expected life of 10 years, after which it will have no salvage value. Also, assume simplified straight-line depreciation and that this machine is being depreciated down to zero, a 34 percent marginal tax rate, and a required rate of return of 15 percent.

- **a.** What is the initial outlay associated with this project?
- **b.** What are the annual after-tax cash flows associated with this project, for years 1 through 9?
- **c.** What is the terminal cash flow in year 10 (what is the annual after-tax cash flow in year 10 plus any additional cash flows associated with termination of the project)?
- **d.** Should this machine be purchased?

**10-6A.** (*New project analysis*) Raymobile Motors is considering the purchase of a new production machine for $500,000. The purchase of this machine will result in an increase in earnings before interest and taxes of $150,000 per year. To operate this machine properly, workers would have to go through a brief training session that would cost $25,000 after tax. In addition, it would cost $5,000 after tax to install this machine properly. Also, because this machine is extremely efficient, its purchase would necessitate an increase in inventory of $30,000. This machine has an expected life of 10 years, after which it will have no salvage value. Assume simplified straight-line depreciation and that this machine is being depreciated down to zero, a 34 percent marginal tax rate, and a required rate of return of 15 percent.

- **a.** What is the initial outlay associated with this project?
- **b.** What are the annual after-tax cash flows associated with this project, for years 1 through 9?
- **c.** What is the terminal cash flow in year 10 (what is the annual after-tax cash flow in year 10 plus any additional cash flows associated with termination of the project)?
- **d.** Should this machine be purchased?

**10-7A.** (*New project analysis*) Garcia's Truckin' Inc. is considering the purchase of a new production machine for $200,000. The purchase of this machine will result in an increase in earnings before interest and taxes of $50,000 per year. To operate this machine properly, workers would have to go through a brief training session that would cost $5,000 after tax. In addition, it would cost $5,000 after tax to install this machine properly. Also, because this machine is extremely efficient, its purchase would necessitate an increase in inventory of $20,000. This machine has an expected life of 10 years, after which it will have no salvage value. Finally, to purchase the new machine, it appears that the firm would have to borrow $100,000 at 8 percent interest from its local bank, resulting in additional interest payments of $8,000 per year. Assume simplified straight-line depreciation and that this machine is being depreciated down to zero, a 34 percent marginal tax rate, and a required rate of return of 10 percent.

- **a.** What is the initial outlay associated with this project?
- **b.** What are the annual after-tax cash flows associated with this project, for years 1 through 9?
- **c.** What is the terminal cash flow in year 10 (what is the annual after-tax cash flow in year 10 plus any additional cash flows associated with termination of the project)?
- **d.** Should this machine be purchased?

**10-8A.** (*Comprehensive problem*) Traid Winds Corporation, a firm in the 34 percent marginal tax bracket with a 15 percent required rate of return or cost of capital, is considering a new project. This project involves the introduction of a new product. This project is expected to last 5 years and then, because this is somewhat of a fad project, to be terminated. Given the following information, determine the free cash flows associated with the project, the project's net present value, the profitability index, and the internal rate of return. Apply the appropriate decision criteria.

**Cost of new plant and equipment:** $14,800,000

**Shipping and installation costs:** $ 200,000

**Unit sales:**

| Year | Units Sold |
|---|---|
| 1 | 70,000 |
| 2 | 120,000 |
| 3 | 120,000 |
| 4 | 80,000 |
| 5 | 70,000 |

**Sales price per unit:** $300/unit in years 1–4, $250/unit in year 5

**Variable cost per unit:** $140/unit

**Annual fixed costs:** $700,000

**Working-capital requirements:** There will be an initial working-capital requirement of $200,000 just to get production started. For each year, the total investment in net working capital will be equal to 10 percent of the dollar value of sales for that year. Thus, the investment in working capital will increase during years 1 through 3, then decrease in year 4. Finally, all working capital is liquidated at the termination of the project at the end of year 5.

**The depreciation method:** Use the simplified straight-line method over 5 years. It is assumed that the plant and equipment will have no salvage value after 5 years.

**10-9A.** (*Comprehensive problem*) The Shome Corporation, a firm in the 34 percent marginal tax bracket with a 15 percent required rate of return or cost of capital, is considering a new project. This project involves the introduction of a new product. This project is expected to last 5 years and then, because this is somewhat of a fad project, to be terminated. Given the following information, determine the free cash flows associated with the project, the project's net present value, the profitability index, and the internal rate of return. Apply the appropriate decision criteria.

**Cost of new plant and equipment:** $6,900,000

**Shipping and installation costs:** $ 100,000

**Unit sales:**

| Year | Units Sold |
|---|---|
| 1 | 80,000 |
| 2 | 100,000 |
| 3 | 120,000 |
| 4 | 70,000 |
| 5 | 70,000 |

**Sales price per unit:** $250/unit in years 1–4, $200/unit in year 5

**Variable cost per unit:** $130/unit

**Annual fixed costs:** $300,000

**Working-capital requirements:** There will be an initial working-capital requirement of $100,000 just to get production started. For each year, the total investment in net working capital will be equal to 10 percent of the dollar value of sales for that year. Thus, the investment in working capital will increase during years 1 through 3, then decrease in year 4. Finally, all working capital is liquidated at the termination of the project at the end of year 5.

**The depreciation method:** Use the simplified straight-line method over 5 years. It is assumed that the plant and equipment will have no salvage value after 5 years.

**10-10A.** (*Size disparity ranking problem*) The D. Dorner Farms Corporation is considering purchasing one of two fertilizer-herbicides for the upcoming year. The more expensive of the two is better and will produce a higher yield. Assume these projects are mutually exclusive and that the required rate of return is 10 percent. Given the following after-tax net cash flows:

| Year | Project A | Project B |
|---|---|---|
| 0 | −$500 | −$5,000 |
| 1 | 700 | 6,000 |

**a.** Calculate the net present value.
**b.** Calculate the profitability index.
**c.** Calculate the internal rate of return.
**d.** If there is no capital-rationing constraint, which project should be selected? If there is a capital-rationing constraint, how should the decision be made?

**10-11A.** (*Time disparity ranking problem*) The State Spartan Corporation is considering two mutually exclusive projects. The cash flows associated with those projects are as follows:

| Year | Project A | Project B |
|---|---|---|
| 0 | −$50,000 | −$50,000 |
| 1 | 15,625 | 0 |
| 2 | 15,625 | 0 |
| 3 | 15,625 | 0 |
| 4 | 15,625 | 0 |
| 5 | 15,625 | $100,000 |

The required rate of return on these projects is 10 percent.
**a.** What is each project's payback period?
**b.** What is each project's net present value?
**c.** What is each project's internal rate of return?
**d.** What has caused the ranking conflict?
**e.** Which project should be accepted? Why?

**10-12A.** (*Unequal lives ranking problem*) The B. T. Knight Corporation is considering two mutually exclusive pieces of machinery that perform the same task. The two alternatives available provide the following set of after-tax net cash flows:

| Year | Equipment A | Equipment B |
|---|---|---|
| 0 | −$20,000 | −$20,000 |
| 1 | 12,590 | 6,625 |
| 2 | 12,590 | 6,625 |
| 3 | 12,590 | 6,625 |
| 4 | | 6,625 |
| 5 | | 6,625 |
| 6 | | 6,625 |
| 7 | | 6,625 |
| 8 | | 6,625 |
| 9 | | 6,625 |

Equipment A has an expected life of 3 years, whereas equipment B has an expected life of 9 years. Assume a required rate of return of 15 percent.
**a.** Calculate each project's payback period.
**b.** Calculate each project's net present value.
**c.** Calculate each project's internal rate of return.
**d.** Are these projects comparable?
**e.** Compare these projects using replacement chains and *EAA*. Which project should be selected? Support your recommendation.

**10-13A.** (*EAAs*) The Andrzejewski Corporation is considering two mutually exclusive projects, one with a 3-year life and one with a 7-year life. The after-tax cash flows from the two projects are as follows:

| Year | Project A | Project B |
|---|---|---|
| 0 | −$50,000 | −$50,000 |
| 1 | 20,000 | 36,000 |
| 2 | 20,000 | 36,000 |
| 3 | 20,000 | 36,000 |
| 4 | 20,000 | |
| 5 | 20,000 | |
| 6 | 20,000 | |
| 7 | 20,000 | |

**a.** Assuming a 10 percent required rate of return on both projects, calculate each project's *EAA*. Which project should be selected?
**b.** Calculate the present value of an infinite-life replacement chain for each project.

**10-14A.** (*Capital rationing*) Cowboy Hat Company of Stillwater, Oklahoma, is considering seven capital investment proposals, for which the funds available are limited to a maximum of $12 million. The projects are independent and have the following costs and profitability indexes associated with them:

| Project | Cost | Profitability Index |
|---|---|---|
| A | $4,000,000 | 1.18 |
| B | 3,000,000 | 1.08 |
| C | 5,000,000 | 1.33 |
| D | 6,000,000 | 1.31 |
| E | 4,000,000 | 1.19 |
| F | 6,000,000 | 1.20 |
| G | 4,000,000 | 1.18 |

**a.** Under strict capital rationing, which projects should be selected?
**b.** What problems are there with capital rationing?

## INTEGRATIVE PROBLEM

It's been 2 months since you took a position as an assistant financial analyst at Caledonia Products. Although your boss has been pleased with your work, he is still a bit hesitant about unleashing you without supervision. Your next assignment involves both the calculation of the cash flows associated with a new investment under consideration and the evaluation of several mutually exclusive projects. Given your lack of tenure at Caledonia, you have been asked not only to provide a recommendation, but also to respond to a number of questions aimed at judging your understanding of the capital-budgeting process. The memorandum you received outlining your assignment follows:

TO: The Assistant Financial Analyst

FROM: Mr. V. Morrison, CEO, Caledonia Products

RE: Cash Flow Analysis and Capital Rationing

We are considering the introduction of a new product. Currently we are in the 34 percent marginal tax bracket with a 15 percent required rate of return or cost of capital. This project is expected to last 5 years and then, because this is somewhat of a fad project, to be terminated. The following information describes the new project:

**Cost of new plant and equipment:** $7,900,000

**Shipping and installation costs:** $100,000

**Unit sales:**

| Year | Units Sold |
|---|---|
| 1 | 70,000 |
| 2 | 120,000 |
| 3 | 140,000 |
| 4 | 80,000 |
| 5 | 60,000 |

**Sales price per unit:** $300/unit in years 1–4, $260/unit in year 5

**Variable cost per unit:** $180/unit

**Annual fixed costs:** $200,000

**Working-capital requirements:** There will be an initial working-capital requirement of $100,000 just to get production started. For each year, the total investment in net working capital will be equal to 10 percent of the dollar value of sales for that year. Thus, the investment in working capital will increase during years 1 through 3, then decrease in year 4. Finally, all working capital is liquidated at the termination of the project at the end of year 5.

**The depreciation method:** Use the simplified straight-line method over 5 years. It is assumed that the plant and equipment will have no salvage value after 5 years.

1. Should Caledonia focus on cash flows or accounting profits in making our capital-budgeting decisions? Should we be interested in incremental cash flows, incremental profits, total free cash flows, or total profits?
2. How does depreciation affect free cash flows?
3. How do sunk costs affect the determination of cash flows?
4. What is the project's initial outlay?
5. What are the differential cash flows over the project's life?
6. What is the terminal cash flow?
7. Draw a cash flow diagram for this project.
8. What is its net present value?
9. What is its internal rate of return?
10. Should the project be accepted? Why or why not?

You have also been asked for your views on three unrelated sets of projects. Each set of projects involves two mutually exclusive projects. These projects follow:

11. Caledonia is considering two investments with 1-year lives. The more expensive of the two is the better and will produce more savings. Assume these projects are mutually exclusive and that the required rate of return is 10 percent. Given the following after-tax net cash flows:

| Year | Project A | Project B |
|---|---|---|
| 0 | −$195,000 | −$1,200,000 |
| 1 | 240,000 | 1,650,000 |

a. Calculate the net present value.
b. Calculate the profitability index.
c. Calculate the internal rate of return.
d. If there is no capital-rationing constraint, which project should be selected? If there is a capital-rationing constraint, how should the decision be made?

**12.** Caledonia is considering two additional mutually exclusive projects. The cash flows associated with these projects are as follows:

| Year | Project A | Project B |
|---|---|---|
| 0 | −$100,000 | −$100,000 |
| 1 | 32,000 | 0 |
| 2 | 32,000 | 0 |
| 3 | 32,000 | 0 |
| 4 | 32,000 | 0 |
| 5 | 32,000 | $200,000 |

The required rate of return on these projects is 11 percent.

**a.** What is each project's payback period?
**b.** What is each project's net present value?
**c.** What is each project's internal rate of return?
**d.** What has caused the ranking conflict?
**e.** Which project should be accepted? Why?

**13.** The final two mutually exclusive projects that Caledonia is considering involve mutually exclusive pieces of machinery that perform the same task. The two alternatives available provide the following set of after-tax net cash flows:

| Year | Equipment A | Equipment B |
|---|---|---|
| 0 | −$100,000 | −$100,000 |
| 1 | 65,000 | 32,500 |
| 2 | 65,000 | 32,500 |
| 3 | 65,000 | 32,500 |
| 4 | | 32,500 |
| 5 | | 32,500 |
| 6 | | 32,500 |
| 7 | | 32,500 |
| 8 | | 32,500 |
| 9 | | 32,500 |

Equipment A has an expected life of 3 years, whereas equipment B has an expected life of 9 years. Assume a required rate of return of 14 percent.

**a.** Calculate each project's payback period.
**b.** Calculate each project's net present value.
**c.** Calculate each project's internal rate of return.
**d.** Are these projects comparable?
**e.** Compare these projects using replacement chains and *EAAs*. Which project should be selected? Support your recommendation.

## STUDY PROBLEMS (SET B)

**10-1B.** (*Capital gains tax*) The R. T. Kleinman Corporation is considering selling one of its old assembly machines. The machine, purchased for $40,000 5 years ago, had an expected life of 10 years and an expected salvage value of zero. Assume Kleinman uses simplified straight-line depreciation, creating depreciation of $4,000 per year, and could sell this old machine for $45,000. Also assume a 34 percent marginal tax rate.

**a.** What would be the taxes associated with this sale?
**b.** If the old machine were sold for $40,000, what would be the taxes associated with this sale?

**c.** If the old machine were sold for $20,000, what would be the taxes associated with this sale?
**d.** If the old machine were sold for $17,000, what would be the taxes associated with this sale?

**10-2B.** (*Relevant cash flows*) Fruity Stones is considering introducing a variation of its current breakfast cereal, Jolt 'n Stones. This new cereal will be similar to the old with the exception that it will contain more sugar in the form of small pebbles. The new cereal will be called Jolt 'n Stones. It is estimated that the sales for the new cereal will be $100 million; however, 40 percent of those sales will be from former Fruity Stones customers who have switched to Stones 'n Stuff who would not have switched if the new product had not been introduced. What is the relevant sales level to consider when deciding whether or not to introduce Stone 'n Stuff?

**10-3B.** (*Calculating free cash flows*) Tetious Dimensions is introducing a new product and has an expected change in EBIT of $775,000. Tetious Dimensions has a 34 percent marginal tax rate. This project will also produce $200,000 of depreciation per year. In addition, this project will also cause the following changes:

| | Without the Project | With the Project |
|---|---|---|
| Accounts receivable | $55,000 | $89,000 |
| Inventory | 100,000 | 180,000 |
| Accounts payable | 70,000 | 120,000 |

What is the project's free cash flow?

**10-4B.** (*Calculating free cash flows*) Duncan Motors is introducing a new product and has an expected change in EBIT of $300,000. Duncan Motors has a 34 percent marginal tax rate. This project will also produce $50,000 of depreciation per year. In addition, this project will also cause the following changes:

| | Without the Project | With the Project |
|---|---|---|
| Accounts receivable | $33,000 | $23,000 |
| Inventory | 25,000 | 40,000 |
| Accounts payable | 50,000 | 86,000 |

What is the project's free cash flow?

**10-5B.** (*New project analysis*) The Guo Chemical Corporation is considering the purchase of a chemical analysis machine. The purchase of this machine will result in an increase in earnings before interest and taxes of $70,000 per year. The machine has a purchase price of $250,000, and it would cost an additional $10,000 after tax to install this machine properly. In addition, to operate this machine properly, inventory must be increased by $15,000. This machine has an expected life of 10 years, after which it will have no salvage value. Also, assume simplified straight-line depreciation and that this machine is being depreciated down to zero, a 34 percent marginal tax rate, and a required rate of return of 15 percent.

**a.** What is the initial outlay associated with this project?
**b.** What are the annual after-tax cash flows associated with this project, for years 1 through 9?
**c.** What is the terminal cash flow in year 10 (what is the annual after-tax cash flow in year 10 plus any additional cash flow associated with termination of the project)?
**d.** Should this machine be purchased?

**10-6B.** (*New project analysis*) El Gato's Motors is considering the purchase of a new production machine for $1 million. The purchase of this machine will result in an increase in earnings before interest and taxes of $400,000 per year. To operate this machine properly, workers would have to go through a brief training session that would cost $100,000 after tax. In addition, it would cost $50,000 after tax to install this machine properly. Also, because this machine is extremely efficient, its purchase would necessitate an increase in inventory of $150,000. This machine has an expected life of 10 years, after which it will have no salvage value. Assume simplified straight-line depreciation and that this machine is being depreciated down to zero, a 34 percent marginal tax rate, and a required rate of return of 12 percent.

**a.** What is the initial outlay associated with this project?
**b.** What are the annual after-tax cash flows associated with this project, for years 1 through 9?
**c.** What is the terminal cash flow in year 10 (what is the annual after-tax cash flow in year 10 plus any additional cash flows associated with termination of the project)?
**d.** Should this machine be purchased?

**10-7B.** (*New project analysis*) Weir's Truckin' Inc. is considering the purchase of a new production machine for $100,000. The purchase of this new machine will result in an increase in earnings before interest and taxes of $25,000 per year. To operate this machine properly, workers would have to go through a brief training session that would cost $5,000 after tax. In addition, it would cost $5,000 after-tax to install this machine properly. Also, because this machine is extremely efficient, its purchase would necessitate an increase in inventory of $25,000. This machine has an expected life of 10 years, after which it will have no salvage value. Finally, to purchase the new machine, it appears that the firm would have to borrow $80,000 at 10 percent interest from its local bank, resulting in additional interest payments of $8,000 per year. Assume simplified straight-line depreciation and that this machine is being depreciated down to zero, a 34 percent marginal tax rate, and a required rate of return of 12 percent.

**a.** What is the initial outlay associated with this project?
**b.** What are the annual after-tax cash flows associated with this project, for years 1 through 9?
**c.** What is the terminal cash flow in year 10 (what is the annual after-tax cash flow in year 10 plus any additional cash flows associated with termination of the project)?
**d.** Should this machine be purchased?

**10-8B.** (*Comprehensive problem*) The Dophical Corporation, a firm in the 34 percent marginal tax bracket with a 15 percent required rate of return or cost of capital, is considering a new project. This project involves the introduction of a new product. This project is expected to last 5 years and then, because this is somewhat of a fad product, to be terminated. Given the following information, determine the free cash flows associated with the project, the project's net present value, the profitability index, and the internal rate of return. Apply the appropriate decision criteria.

**Cost of new plant and equipment:** $198,000,000

**Shipping and installation costs:** $2,000,000

| **Unit sales:** | Year | Units Sold |
|---|---|---|
| | 1 | 1,000,000 |
| | 2 | 1,800,000 |
| | 3 | 1,800,000 |
| | 4 | 1,200,000 |
| | 5 | 700,000 |

**Sales price per unit:** $800/unit in years 1–4, $600/unit in year 5

**Variable cost per unit:** $400/unit

**Annual fixed costs:** $10,000,000

**Working-capital requirements:** There will be an initial working-capital requirement of $2,000,000 just to get production started. For each year, the total investment in net working capital will equal 10 percent of the dollar value of sales for that year. Thus, the investment in working capital will increase during years 1 through 3, then decrease in year 4. Finally, all working capital is liquidated at the termination of the project at the end of year 5.

**The depreciation method:** Use the simplified straight-line method over 5 years. It is assumed that the plant and equipment will have no salvage value after 5 years.

**10-9B.** (*Comprehensive problem*) The Kumar Corporation, a firm in the 34 percent marginal tax bracket with a 15 percent required rate of return or cost of capital, is considering a new project. This project involves the introduction of a new product. This project is expected to last 5 years and then, because this is somewhat of a fad product, to be terminated. Given the following information, determine the free cash flows associated with the project, the project's net present value, the profitability index, and the internal rate of return. Apply the appropriate decision criteria.

**Cost of new plant and equipment:** $9,900,000

**Shipping and installation costs:** $100,000

**Unit sales:**

| Year | Units Sold |
|---|---|
| 1 | 70,000 |
| 2 | 100,000 |
| 3 | 140,000 |
| 4 | 70,000 |
| 5 | 60,000 |

**Sales price per unit:** $280/unit in years 1–4, $180/unit in year 5

**Variable cost per unit:** $140/unit

**Annual fixed costs:** $300,000

**Working-capital requirements:** There will be an initial working-capital requirement of $100,000 just to get production started. For each year, the total investment in net working capital will equal 10 percent of the dollar value of sales for that year. Thus, the investment in working capital will increase during years 1 through 3, then decrease in year 4. Finally, all working capital is liquidated at the termination of the project at the end of year 5.

**The depreciation method:** Use the simplified straight-line method over 5 years. It is assumed that the plant and equipment will have no salvage value after 5 years.

**10-10B.** (*Size disparity ranking problem*) The Unk's Farms Corporation is considering purchasing one of two fertilizer-herbicides for the upcoming year. The more expensive of the two is the better and will produce a higher yield. Assume these projects are mutually exclusive and that the required rate of return is 10 percent. Given the following after-tax net cash flows:

| Year | Project A | Project B |
|---|---|---|
| 0 | −$650 | −$4,000 |
| 1 | 800 | 5,500 |

**a.** Calculate the net present value.
**b.** Calculate the profitability index.
**c.** Calculate the internal rate of return.
**d.** If there is no capital-rationing constraint, which project should be selected? If there is a capital-rationing constraint, how should the decision be made?

**10-11B.** (*Time disparity ranking problem*) The Z. Bello Corporation is considering two mutually exclusive projects. The cash flows associated with those projects are as follows:

| Year | Project A | Project B |
|---|---|---|
| 0 | −$50,000 | −$50,000 |
| 1 | 16,000 | 0 |
| 2 | 16,000 | 0 |
| 3 | 16,000 | 0 |
| 4 | 16,000 | 0 |
| 5 | 16,000 | $100,000 |

The required rate of return on these projects is 11 percent.

**a.** What is each project's payback period?
**b.** What is each project's net present value?
**c.** What is each project's internal rate of return?
**d.** What has caused the ranking conflict?
**e.** Which project should be accepted? Why?

**10-12B.** (*Unequal lives ranking problem*) The Battling Bishops Corporation is considering two mutually exclusive pieces of machinery that perform the same task. The two alternatives available provide the following set of after-tax net cash flows:

| Year | Equipment A | Equipment B |
|---|---|---|
| 0 | −$20,000 | −$20,000 |
| 1 | 13,000 | 6,500 |
| 2 | 13,000 | 6,500 |
| 3 | 13,000 | 6,500 |
| 4 | | 6,500 |
| 5 | | 6,500 |
| 6 | | 6,500 |
| 7 | | 6,500 |
| 8 | | 6,500 |
| 9 | | 6,500 |

Equipment A has an expected life of 3 years, whereas equipment B has an expected life of 9 years. Assume a required rate of return of 14 percent.

**a.** Calculate each project's payback period.
**b.** Calculate each project's net present value.
**c.** Calculate each project's internal rate of return.
**d.** Are these projects comparable?
**e.** Compare these projects using replacement chains and *EAAs*. Which project should be selected? Support your recommendation.

**10-13B.** (*EAAs*) The Anduski Corporation is considering two mutually exclusive projects, one with a 5-year life and one with a 7-year life. The after-tax cash flows from the two projects are as follows:

| Year | Project A | Project B |
|---|---|---|
| 0 | −$40,000 | −$40,000 |
| 1 | 20,000 | 25,000 |
| 2 | 20,000 | 25,000 |
| 3 | 20,000 | 25,000 |
| 4 | 20,000 | 25,000 |
| 5 | 20,000 | 25,000 |
| 6 | 20,000 | |
| 7 | 20,000 | |

**a.** Assuming a 10 percent required rate of return on both projects, calculate each project's *EAA*. Which project should be selected?
**b.** Calculate the present value of an infinite-life replacement chain for each project.

**10-14B.** (*Capital rationing*) The Taco Toast Company is considering seven capital investment projects, for which the funds available are limited to a maximum of $12 million. The projects are independent and have the following costs and profitability indexes associated with them:

**a.** Under strict capital rationing, which projects should be selected?
**b.** What problems are associated with imposing capital rationing?

| Project | Cost | Profitability Index |
|---|---|---|
| A | $4,000,000 | 1.18 |
| B | 3,000,000 | 1.08 |
| C | 5,000,000 | 1.33 |
| D | 6,000,000 | 1.31 |
| E | 4,000,000 | 1.19 |
| F | 6,000,000 | 1.20 |
| G | 4,000,000 | 1.18 |

## SELF-TEST SOLUTIONS

**ST-1:** STEP 1: First calculate the initial outlay.

**Section I. Calculate the change in EBIT, Taxes, and Depreciation (this becomes an input in the calculation of operating cash flow in Section II).**

| Year | 0 | 1 | 2 | 3 | 4 | 5 |
|---|---|---|---|---|---|---|
| Units sold | | 100,000 | 130,000 | 160,000 | 100,000 | 60,000 |
| Sale price | | $500 | $500 | $500 | $500 | $380 |
| Sales revenue | | $50,000,000 | $65,000,000 | $80,000,000 | $50,000,000 | $22,800,000 |
| Less: variable costs | | 26,000,000 | 33,800,000 | 41,600,000 | 26,000,000 | 15,600,000 |
| Less: fixed costs | | $ 300,000 | $ 300,000 | $ 300,000 | $ 300,000 | $ 300,000 |
| Equals: EBDIT | | $23,700,000 | $30,900,000 | $38,100,000 | $23,700,000 | $ 6,900,000 |
| Less: depreciation | | $ 4,240,000 | $ 4,240,000 | $ 4,240,000 | $4,240,000 | $ 4,240,000 |
| Equals: EBIT | | $19,450,000 | $26,660,000 | $33,860,000 | $19,460,000 | $ 2,660,000 |
| Taxes (@34%) | | $ 6,616,400 | $ 9,064,400 | $11,512,400 | $ 6,616,400 | $ 904,400 |
| **Section II. Calculate Operating Cash Flow (this becomes an input in the calculation of free cash flow in Section IV).** | | | | | | |
| **Operating cash flow:** | | | | | | |
| EBIT | | $19,460,000 | $26,660,000 | $33,860,000 | $19,460,000 | $ 2,660,000 |
| Minus: taxes | | $ 6,616,400 | $ 9,064,400 | $11,512,400 | $ 6,616,400 | $ 904,400 |
| Plus: depreciation | | $ 4,240,000 | $ 4,240,000 | $ 4,240,000 | $ 4,240,000 | $ 4,240,000 |
| Equals: operating cash flow | | $17,083,600 | $21,835,600 | $26,587,600 | $17,083,600 | $ 5,995,600 |
| **Section III. Calculate the Net Working Capital (this becomes an input in the calculation of free cash flows in Section IV).** | | | | | | |
| **Change in net working capital:** | | | | | | |
| Revenue: | | $50,000,000 | $65,000,000 | $80,000,000 | $50,000,000 | $22,800,000 |
| Initial working-capital requirement | $ 500,000 | | | | | |
| Net working-capital needs: | | $ 5,000,000 | $ 6,500,000 | $ 8,000,000 | $ 5,000,000 | $ 2,280,000 |
| Liquidation of working capital | | | | | | $ 2,280,000 |
| Change in working capital: | $ 500,000 | $ 4,500,000 | $ 1,500,000 | $ 1,500,000 | ($3,000,000) | ($5,000,000) |
| **Section IV. Calculate Free Cash Flow (using information calculated in Sections II and III, in addition to change in capital spending).** | | | | | | |
| **Free cash flow:** | | | | | | |
| Operating cash flow | | $17,083,600 | $21,835,600 | $26,587,600 | $17,083, 600 | $ 5,995,600 |
| Minus: change in net working capital | $ 500,000 | $ 4,500,000 | $ 1,500,000 | $ 1,500,000 | ($3,000,000) | ($5,000,000) |
| Minus: change in capital spending | $ 21,200,000 | 0 | $0 | 0 | 0 | 0 |
| **Free cash flow:** | ($ 21,700,000) | **$12,583,600** | **$20,335,600** | **$25,087,600** | **$20,083,600** | **$10,995,600** |
| *NPV* | **$38,064,020** | | | | | |

STEP 2: Calculate the differential cash flows over the project's life.

Thus the cash flow in the final year will be equal to the annual net cash flow in that year of $20,608 plus the terminal cash flow of $13,200 for a total of $33,808.

**ST-2. a.** 
$$
\begin{aligned}
NPV_A &= \$70{,}000\left[\frac{1}{(1+.12)^1}\right] - \$50{,}000\\
&= \$70{,}000\,(.893) - \$50{,}000\\
&= \$62{,}510 - \$50{,}000\\
&= \$12{,}510
\end{aligned}
$$

$$
\begin{aligned}
NPV_B &= \$130{,}000\left[\frac{1}{(1+.12)^1}\right] - \$100{,}000\\
&= \$130{,}000\,(.893) - \$100{,}000\\
&= \$116{,}090 - \$100{,}000\\
&= \$16{,}090
\end{aligned}
$$

**b.** 
$$
\begin{aligned}
PI_A &= \frac{\$62{,}510}{\$50{,}000}\\
&= 1.2502
\end{aligned}
$$

$$
\begin{aligned}
PI_B &= \frac{\$116{,}090}{\$100{,}000}\\
&= 1.1609
\end{aligned}
$$

**c.** 
$$
\begin{aligned}
\$50{,}000 &= \$70{,}000\,(PVIF_{i,1\text{yr}})\\
.7143 &= PVIF_{i,1\text{yr}}
\end{aligned}
$$

Looking for a value of $PVIF_{i,1\text{yr}}$ in appendix C, a value of .714 is found in the 40 percent column. Thus, the *IRR* is 40 percent.

$$
\begin{aligned}
\$100{,}000 &= \$130{,}000(PVIF_{i,1\text{yr}})\\
.7692 &= PVIF_{i,1\text{yr}}
\end{aligned}
$$

Looking for a value of $PVIF_{i,1\text{yr}}$ in appendix C, a value of .769 is found in the 30 percent column. Thus, the *IRR* is 30 percent.

**d.** If there is no capital rationing, project B should be accepted because it has a larger net present value. If there is a capital constraint, the problem focuses on what can be done with the additional $50,000 (the additional money that could be invested if project A, with an initial outlay of $50,000, were selected over project B, with an initial outlay of $100,000). In the capital constraint case, if Serrano can earn more on project A plus the marginal project financed with the additional $50,000 than it can on project B, then project A and the marginal project should be accepted.

# CAPITAL BUDGETING AND RISK ANALYSIS

In the previous two chapters, we assumed that all projects had the same level of risk. In this chapter, we will discard that assumption and incorporate risk into the capital-budgeting decision. As international competition increases and technology changes at an ever-quickening pace, risk and uncertainty play an increasingly important role in business decisions. In this chapter, we will examine problems in measuring risk and approaches for dealing with it as it affects business decisions. ● We will look at risks faced in decisions like the one made by Harley-Davidson to develop and introduce

the Harley-Davidson Buell Blast model, a lightweight, one-cylinder motorcycle, priced at under $4,400, and designed specifically for first-time riders—a group not targeted by Harley-Davidson in over 30 years. How would the public react to a lightweight bike from Harley? Harley-Davidson hopes that the Blast will get more young people and women on an easy-to-handle, fun bike and give them the new excitement of motorcycling. Will it accomplish this task? Because the Blast is easier to ride and light as a feather compared with the heavier cruising and touring "Harley Hogs," will it take away from Harley's big-bike image? The bottom line is that before Harley-Davidson introduced the Buell Blast, it didn't know how the public would react to it. That is, the expected future free cash flows from this project were far from certain. How should Harley evaluate projects with uncertain returns that stretch well into the future? Certainly, it shouldn't treat all projects in the same way, but how should Harley ensure that the decisions it makes correctly reflect a project's uncertainty? Complicating Harley's task is the question of what is the appropriate measure of risk for a new project. How well a firm does in answering these ques-

**LEARNING OBJECTIVES**

After reading this chapter, you should be able to

1. Explain what the appropriate measure of risk is for capital-budgeting purposes.
2. Determine the acceptability of a new project using both the certainty equivalent and risk-adjusted discount rate methods of adjusting for risk.
3. Explain the use of simulation and probability trees for imitating the performance of a project under evaluation.

tions and evaluating capital-budgeting projects will determine its future. These are "strategic" decisions that are made by all of the firm's employees—those in management, accounting, information technology, and marketing—working together. **Principle 1: The Risk-Return Trade-Off** states that investors demand a higher return for taking on additional risk; in this chapter, we modify our capital-budgeting decision criterion to allow for different levels of risk for different projects. In so doing we will try to understand how a company like Harley-Davidson, or any other firm, deals with the risk and uncertainty that surrounds its capital-budgeting decisions.

**CHAPTER PREVIEW**

This chapter completes our discussion of decision rules for when to invest in new projects. In Chapter 9, we introduced the different capital-budgeting decision criteria, and in Chapter 10, we looked at measuring a project's relevant cash flows. Through all of this discussion of capital-budgeting techniques, we implicitly assumed that the level of risk associated with each investment was the same. In this chapter, we lift that assumption. We begin with a discussion of what measure of risk is relevant in capital-budgeting decisions. We then look at various ways of incorporating risk into the capital-budgeting decision and how to measure that risk.

To do this, we will be relying heavily on **Principle 1: The Risk-Return Trade-Off—We won't take on additional risk unless we expect to be compensated with additional return and Principle 9: All Risk Is Not Equal—Some risk can be diversified away, and some cannot.**

## RISK AND THE INVESTMENT DECISION

OBJECTIVE 1 

Up to this point, we have ignored risk in capital budgeting; that is, we have discounted expected cash flows back to the present and ignored any uncertainty that there might be surrounding that estimate. In reality, the future cash flows associated with the introduction of a new sales outlet or a new product are estimates of what is *expected* to happen in the future, not necessarily what *will* happen in the future. For example, when Coca-Cola decided to replace Classic Coke with its "New Coke," you can bet that the expected cash flows it based its decision on were nothing like the cash flows it realized. As a result, it didn't take Coca-Cola long to reintroduce Classic Coke. In effect, the cash flows we have discounted back to the present have been our best estimate of the expected future cash flows. A cash-flow diagram based on the possible outcomes of an investment proposal rather than the expected values of these outcomes appears in Figure 11-1.

In this section, we will assume that under conditions of risk we do not know beforehand what cash flows will actually result from a new project. However, we do have expectations concerning the possible outcomes and are able to assign probabilities to these outcomes. Stated another way, although we do not know the cash flows resulting from the acceptance of a new project, we can formulate the probability distributions from which the flows will be drawn.

As we learned in Chapter 6, risk occurs when there is some question as to the future outcome of an event. We will now proceed with an examination of the logic behind this definition. Again, risk is defined as the potential variability in future cash flows.

The fact that variability reflects risk can easily be shown with a coin toss. Consider the possibility of flipping a coin—heads you win, tails you lose—for 25¢ with your finance

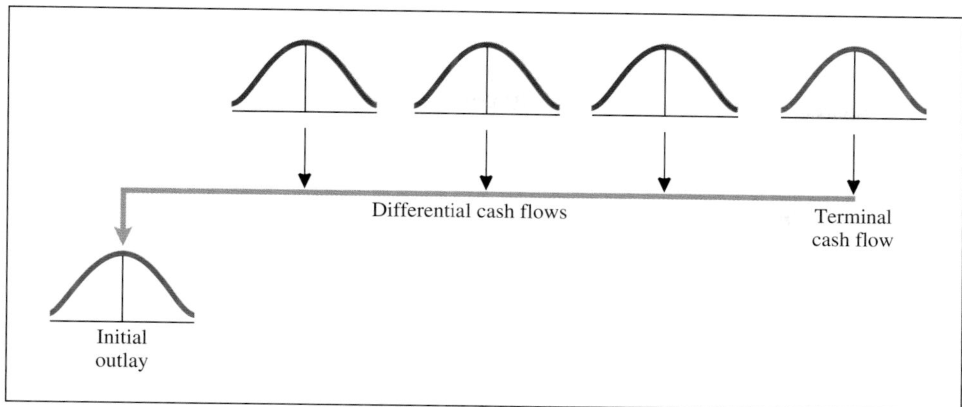


**FIGURE 11-1**
Cash-Flow Diagram Based on Possible Outcomes

professor. Most likely, you would be willing to take on this game because the utility gained from winning 25¢ is about equal to the utility lost if you lose 25¢. Conversely, if the flip is for $1,000, you may be willing to play only if you are offered more than $1,000 if you win—say, you win $1,500 if it turns out heads and lose $1,000 if it turns out tails. In each case, the probability of winning and losing is the same; that is, there is an equal chance that the coin will land heads or tails. In each case, however, the width of the dispersion changes, which is why the second coin toss is more risky and why you may not take the chance unless the payoffs are altered. The key here is the fact that only the dispersion changes; the probability of winning or losing is the same in each case. Thus, the potential variability in future returns reflects the risk.

The final question to be addressed is whether or not individuals are in fact risk averse. Although we do see people gambling when the odds of winning are against them, it should be stressed that monetary return is not the only possible return they may receive. A non-monetary, psychic reward accrues to some gamblers, allowing them to fantasize that they will break the bank, never have to work again, and retire to some island. Actually, the heart of the question is how wealth is measured. Although gamblers appear to be acting as risk seekers, they actually attach an additional nonmonetary return to gambling; the risk is in effect its own reward. When this is considered, their actions seem totally rational. It should also be noted that although gamblers appear to be pursuing risk on one hand, on the other hand in other endeavors they are also eliminating some risk by purchasing insurance and diversifying their investments.

In the remainder of this chapter, we assume that although future cash flows are not known with certainty, the probability distribution from which they come can be estimated. Also, as illustrated in Chapter 6, because the dispersion of possible outcomes reflects risk, we are prepared to use a measure of dispersion or variability later in the chapter when we quantify risk.

In the pages that follow, there are only two basic issues that we address: (1) What is risk in terms of capital-budgeting decisions, and how should it be measured? (2) How should risk be incorporated into capital-budgeting analysis?

## What Measure of Risk Is Relevant in Capital Budgeting?

Before we begin our discussion of how to adjust for risk, it is important to determine just what type of risk we are to adjust for. In capital budgeting, a project's risk can be looked at on three levels. First, there is the **project standing alone risk,** which is a project's risk ignoring the fact that much of this risk will be diversified away as the project is combined with the firm's other projects and assets.

**Project standing alone risk**
The risk of a project standing alone is measured by the variability of the asset's expected returns. That is, it is the risk of a project ignoring the fact that it is only one of many projects within the firm, and the firm's stock is but one of many stocks within a stockholder's portfolio.

**FIGURE 11-2**
Looking at Three Measures of a Project's Risk

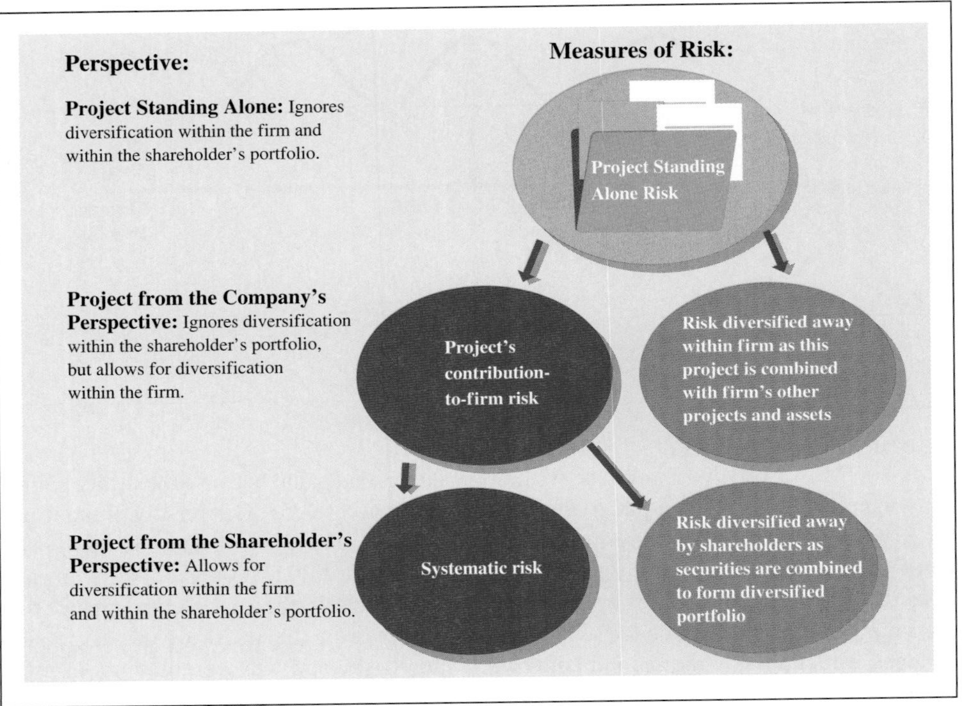


**Project's contribution-to-firm risk**
The amount of risk that a project contributes to the firm as a whole. That is, it is a project's risk considering the effects of diversification among different projects within the firm, but ignoring the effects of shareholder diversification within the portfolio.

**Systematic risk**
The risk of a project measured from the point of view of a well-diversified shareholder. That is, it is a project's risk taking into account the fact that this project is only one of many projects within the firm, and the firm's stock is but one of many stocks within a stockholder's portfolio.

Second, we have the **project's contribution-to-firm risk,** which is the amount of risk that the project contributes to the firm as a whole; this measure considers the fact that some of the project's risk will be diversified away as the project is combined with the firm's other projects and assets, but *ignores* the effects of diversification of the firm's shareholders. Finally, there is **systematic risk,** which is the risk of the project from the viewpoint of a well-diversified shareholder; this measure considers the fact that some of a project's risk will be diversified away as the project is combined with the firm's other projects, and, in addition, some of the remaining risk will be diversified away by shareholders as they combine this stock with other stocks in their portfolios. This is shown graphically in Figure 11-2.

Should we be interested in the project standing alone risk? The answer is *no.* Perhaps the easiest way to understand why not is to look at an example. Let's take the case of research and development projects at Johnson & Johnson. Each year, Johnson & Johnson takes on hundreds of new R&D projects, knowing that they only have about a 10 percent probability of being successful. If they are successful, the profits can be enormous; if they fail, the investment is lost. If the company has only one project, and it is an R&D project, the company would have a 90 percent chance of failure. Thus, if we look at these R&D projects individually and measure their project standing alone risk, we would have to judge them to be enormously risky. However, if we consider the effect of the diversification that comes about from taking on several hundred independent R&D projects a year, all with a 10 percent chance of success, we can see that each R&D project does not add much in the way of risk to Johnson & Johnson. In short, because much of a project's risk is diversified away within the firm, project standing alone risk is an inappropriate measure of the level of risk of a capital-budgeting project.

Should we be interested in the project's contribution-to-firm risk? Once again, the answer is *no,* provided investors are well diversified, and there is no chance of bankruptcy. From our earlier discussion of risk in Chapter 6, we saw that, as shareholders, if we combined our stocks with other stocks to form a diversified portfolio, much of the risk of our security would be diversified away. Thus, all that affects the shareholders is the systematic risk of the project and, as such, it is all that is theoretically relevant for capital budgeting.

**CONCEPT CHECK**

1. In capital budgeting, a project's risk can be looked at on three levels. What are they and what are the measures of risk?
2. Is a project's stand alone risk the appropriate level of risk for capital budgeting? Why or why not?
3. What is systematic risk?
4. What type of risk affects all shareholders and is theoretically the correct measure for capital budgeting?

**RELATE TO THE BIG PICTURE**

Our discussion of capital budgeting and risk is based on **Principle 9: All Risk Is Not Equal—Some risk can be diversified away, and some cannot.** That principle describes how difficult it is to measure a project's risk as a result of diversification. This is because diversification takes place both within the firm, where the new project is just one of many projects, and in the shareholder's portfolio, where the company's stock is just one of many stocks he or she holds.

## Measuring Risk for Capital-Budgeting Purposes and a Dose of Reality—Is Systematic Risk All There Is?

According to the capital asset pricing model (CAPM), systematic risk is the only relevant risk for capital-budgeting purposes; however, reality complicates this somewhat. In many instances, a firm will have undiversified shareholders, including owners of small corporations. Because they are not diversified, for those shareholders the relevant measure of risk is the project's contribution-to-firm risk.

The possibility of bankruptcy also affects our view of what measure of risk is relevant. Because the project's contribution-to-firm risk can affect the possibility of bankruptcy, this may be an appropriate measure of risk in the real world, where there is a cost associated with bankruptcy. First, if a firm fails, its assets, in general, cannot be sold for their true economic value. Moreover, the amount of money actually available for distribution to stockholders is further reduced by liquidation and legal fees that must be paid. Finally, the opportunity cost associated with the delays related to the legal process further reduces the funds available to the shareholder. Therefore, because there are costs associated with bankruptcy, reduction of the chance of bankruptcy has a very real value associated with it.

Indirect costs of bankruptcy also affect other areas of the firm, including production, sales, and the quality and efficiency of management. For example, firms with a higher probability of bankruptcy may have a more difficult time recruiting and retaining quality managers because jobs with that firm are viewed as being less secure. Suppliers also may be less willing to sell on credit. Finally, customers may lose confidence and fear that the firm may not be around to honor the warranty or to supply spare parts for the product in the future. As a result, as the probability of bankruptcy increases, the eventual bankruptcy may become self-fulfilling as potential customers and suppliers flee. The end result is that the project's contribution-to-firm risk is also a relevant risk measure for capital budgeting.

Finally, problems in measuring a project's systematic risk make its implementation extremely difficult. As we will see later on in this chapter, it is much easier talking about a project's systematic risk than it is measuring it.

Given all this, what do we use? The answer is that we will give consideration to both measures. We know in theory systematic risk is correct. We also know that bankruptcy costs and undiversified shareholders violate the assumptions of the theory, which brings us back to the concept of a project's contribution-to-firm risk. Still, the concept of systematic risk holds value for capital-budgeting decisions, because that is the risk for which shareholders are compensated. As such, we will concern ourselves with both the project's contribution-to-firm risk and the project's systematic risk, and not try to make any specific allocation of importance between the two for capital-budgeting purposes.

### RELATE TO THE BIG PICTURE

All the methods used to compensate for risk in capital budgeting find their roots in fundamental **Principle 1: The Risk-Return Trade-Off.** In fact, the risk-adjusted discount method, to be described later, puts this concept directly into play.

## METHODS FOR INCORPORATING RISK INTO CAPITAL BUDGETING

OBJECTIVE 2 

In the past two chapters, we ignored any risk differences between projects. This assumption is simple but not valid; different investment projects do in fact contain different levels of risk. We will now look at two methods for incorporating risk into the analysis. The first method, the *certainty equivalent approach,* attempts to incorporate the manager's utility function into the analysis. The second method, the *risk-adjusted discount rate,* is based on the notion that investors require higher rates of return on more risky projects.

**Certainty equivalent approach**
A method for incorporating risk into the capital-budgeting decision in which the decision maker substitutes a set of equivalent riskless cash flows for the expected cash flows and then discounts these cash flows back to the present.

**Certainty equivalent**
The amount of cash a person would require with certainty to make him or her indifferent between this certain sum and a particular risky or uncertain sum.

### Certainty Equivalent Approach

The **certainty equivalent approach** involves a direct attempt to allow the decision maker to incorporate his or her utility function into the analysis. The financial manager is allowed to substitute the certain dollar amount that he or she feels is equivalent to the expected but risky cash flow offered by the investment for that risky cash flow in the capital-budgeting analysis. In effect, a set of riskless cash flows is substituted for the original risky cash flows, between both of which the financial manager is indifferent. The key here is that the financial manager is indifferent between picking from the risky distribution and the certain cash flow.

To illustrate the concept of a **certainty equivalent,** let us look at a simple coin toss. Assume you can play the game only once and if it comes out heads, you win $10,000, and if it comes out tails, you win nothing. Obviously, you have a 50 percent chance of winning $10,000 and a 50 percent chance of winning nothing, with an expected value of $5,000. Thus $5,000 is your uncertain expected value outcome. The certainty equivalent then becomes the amount you would demand to make you indifferent with regard to playing and not playing the game. If you are indifferent with respect to receiving $3,000 for certain and not playing the game, then $3,000 is the certainty equivalent. However, someone else may not have as much fear of risk as you do and as a result, will have a different certainty equivalent.

To simplify future calculations and problems, let us define certainty equivalent coefficient ($\alpha_t$) that represents the ratio of the certain outcome to the risky or expected outcome, between which the financial manager is indifferent. In equation form, $\alpha_t$ can be represented as follows:

$$\alpha_t = \frac{\text{certain cash flow}_t}{\text{risky or expected cash flow}_t} \tag{11-1}$$

Thus, the alphas ($\alpha_t$) can vary between 0, in the case of extreme risk, and 1, in the case of certainty. To obtain the value of the equivalent certain cash flow, we need only multiply the risky cash flow in years $t$ times the $\alpha_t$. When this is done, we are indifferent with respect to this certain cash flow and the risky cash flow. In the preceding example of the simple coin toss, the certain cash flow was $3,000, whereas the risky cash flow was $5,000, the expected value of the coin toss; thus the certainty equivalent coefficient is $3,000/$5,000 = 0.6. In summary, by multiplying the certainty equivalent coefficient ($\alpha_t$) times the expected but risky cash flow, we can determine an equivalent certain cash flow.

Once this risk is taken out of the project's cash flows, those cash flows are discounted back to present at the risk-free rate of interest, and the project's net present value or profitability index is determined. If the internal rate of return is calculated, it is then compared with the risk-free rate of interest rather than the firm's required rate of return in determining whether or not it should be accepted or rejected. The certainty equivalent method can be summarized as follows:

$$NPV = \sum_{t=1}^{n} \frac{\alpha_t FCF_t}{(1 + k_{rf})^t} - IO \tag{11-2}$$

where $\alpha_t$ = the certainty equivalent coefficient in period $t$
$FCF_t$ = the annual expected free cash flow in period $t$
$IO$ = the initial cash outlay
$n$ = the project's expected life
$k_{rf}$ = the risk-free interest rate

The certainty equivalent approach can be summarized as follows:

Step 1: Risk is removed from the cash flows by substituting equivalent certain cash flows for the risky cash flows. If the certainty equivalent coefficient ($\alpha_t$) is given, this is done by multiplying each risky cash flow by the appropriate $\alpha_t$ value.

Step 2: These riskless cash flows are then discounted back to the present at the riskless rate of interest.

Step 3: The normal capital-budgeting criteria are then applied, except in the case of the internal rate of return criterion, where the project's internal rate of return is compared with the risk-free rate of interest rather than the firm's required rate of return.

**EXAMPLE**

A firm with a 10 percent required rate of return is considering building new research facilities with an expected life of 5 years. The initial outlay associated with this project involves a certain cash outflow of $120,000. The expected cash inflows and certainty equivalent coefficients, $\alpha_t$ are as follows:

| Year | Expected Cash Flow | Certainty Equivalent Coefficient $\alpha_t$ |
|---|---|---|
| 1 | $10,000 | 0.95 |
| 2 | 20,000 | 0.90 |
| 3 | 40,000 | 0.85 |
| 4 | 80,000 | 0.75 |
| 5 | 80,000 | 0.65 |

The risk-free rate of interest is 6 percent. What is the project's net present value?

To determine the net present value of this project using the certainty equivalent approach, we must first remove the risk from the future cash flows. We do so by multiplying each expected cash flow by the corresponding certainty equivalent coefficient, $\alpha_t$, as shown below:

| Expected Cash Flow | Certainty Equivalent Coefficient $\alpha_t$ | $\alpha_t$ (Expected Cash Flow) = Equivalent Riskless Cash Flow |
|---|---|---|
| $10,000 | 0.95 | $ 9,500 |
| 20,000 | 0.90 | 18,000 |
| 40,000 | 0.85 | 34,000 |
| 80,000 | 0.75 | 60,000 |
| 80,000 | 0.65 | 52,000 |

The equivalent riskless cash flows are then discounted back to the present at the riskless interest rate, not the firm's required rate of return. The required rate of return would be used if this project had the same level of risk as a typical project for this firm. However, these equivalent cash flows have no risk at all; hence the appropriate discount rate is the riskless rate of interest. The equivalent riskless cash flows can be discounted back to the present at the riskless rate of interest, 6 percent, as follows:

| Year | Equivalent Riskless Cash Flow | Present Value Factor at 6 Percent | Present Value |
|---|---|---|---|
| 1 | $ 9,500 | 0.943 | $ 8,958.50 |
| 2 | 18,000 | 0.890 | 16,020.00 |
| 3 | 34,000 | 0.840 | 28,560.00 |
| 4 | 60,000 | 0.792 | 47,520.00 |
| 5 | 52,000 | 0.747 | 38,844.00 |

$NPV = -\$120{,}000 + \$8958.50 + \$16{,}020 + \$28{,}560 + \$47{,}520 + \$38{,}844 = \$19{,}902.50$

Applying the normal capital-budgeting decision criteria, we find that the project should be accepted, as its net present value is greater than zero.

The real problem with the certainty equivalent risk adjustment technique is that it is so arbitrary. That is, two excellent managers might look at the same project and come up with different certainty equivalent values. Which one is right? The answer is that they are both right, they just have different levels of risk aversion. Because it is so slippery, the certainty equivalent method is not used very often.

## Risk-Adjusted Discount Rates

The use of risk-adjusted discount rates is based on the concept that investors demand higher returns for more risky projects. This is the basic axiom behind **Principle 1: The Risk-Return Trade-Off** and the CAPM.

The required rate of return on any investment should include compensation for delaying consumption equal to the risk-free rate of return, plus compensation for any risk taken on. If the risk associated with the investment is greater than the risk involved in a typical endeavor, the discount rate is adjusted upward to compensate for this added risk. Once the firm determines the appropriate required rate of return for a project with a given level of risk, cash flows are discounted back to the present at the **risk-adjusted discount rate.** Then the normal capital-budgeting criteria are applied, except in the case of the internal rate of return. For the *IRR,* the hurdle rate with which the project's internal rate of return is compared now becomes the risk-adjusted discount rate. Expressed mathematically, the net present value using the risk-adjusted discount rate becomes

**Risk-adjusted discount rate**
A method for incorporating the project's level of risk into the capital-budgeting process, in which the discount rate is adjusted upward to compensate for higher than normal risk or downward to adjust for lower than normal risk.

$$NPV = \sum_{t=1}^{n} \frac{FCF_t}{(1 + k^*)^t} - IO \qquad \textbf{(11-3)}$$

where $FCF_t$ = the annual expected free cash flow in time period $t$
$IO$ = the initial cash outlay
$k^*$ = the risk-adjusted discount rate
$n$ = the project's expected life

The logic behind the risk-adjusted discount rate stems from the idea that if the level of risk in a project is different from that in the firm's typical project, then management must incorporate the shareholders' probable reaction to this new endeavor into the decision-making process. If the project has more risk than a typical project, then a higher required rate of return should apply. Otherwise, a project may appear to have a positive net present value, but if you had used the appropriate, higher required rate of return, the project may actually have a negative net present value. Thus, marginal projects may lower the firm's share price—that is, reduce shareholders' wealth. This will occur as the market raises its required rate of return on the firm to reflect the addition of a more risky project, whereas the incremental cash flows resulting from the acceptance of the new project are not large enough to offset this change fully. By the same logic, if the project has less than normal risk, a reduction in the required rate of return is appropriate. Thus, the risk-adjusted discount method attempts to apply more stringent standards—that is, require a higher rate of return—to projects that will increase the firm's risk level.

### EXAMPLE

A toy manufacturer is considering the introduction of a line of fishing equipment with an expected life of 5 years. In the past, this firm has been quite conservative in its investment in new products, sticking primarily to standard toys. In this context, the introduction of a line of fishing equipment is considered an abnormally risky project. Management thinks that the normal required rate of return for the firm of 10 percent is not sufficient. Instead, the minimally acceptable rate of return on this project should be 15 percent. The initial outlay would be \$110,000, and the expected free cash flows from this project are as given below:

| Year | Expected Cash Flow |
|---|---|
| 1 | \$30,000 |
| 2 | \$30,000 |
| 3 | \$30,000 |
| 4 | \$30,000 |
| 5 | \$30,000 |

Discounting this annuity back to the present at 15 percent yields a present value of the future cash flows of \$100,560. Because the initial outlay on this project is \$110,000, the net present value becomes −\$9,440, and the project should be rejected. If the normal required rate of return of 10 percent had been used as the discount rate, the project would have been accepted with a net present value of \$3,730.

In practice, when the risk-adjusted discount rate is used, projects are generally grouped according to purpose, or risk class; then the discount rate preassigned to that purpose or risk class is used. For example, a firm with an overall required rate of return of 12 percent might use the following rate-of-return categorization:

| Project | Required Rate of Return |
|---|---|
| Replacement decision | 12% |
| Modification or expansion of existing product line | 15 |
| Project unrelated to current operations | 18 |
| Research and development operations | 25 |

The purpose of this categorization of projects is to make their evaluation easier, but it also introduces a sense of the arbitrary into the calculations that makes the evaluation less meaningful. The trade-offs involved in the preceding classification are obvious; time and effort are minimized, but only at the cost of precision.

## Certainty Equivalent versus Risk-Adjusted Discount Rate Methods

The primary difference between the certainty equivalent approach and the risk-adjusted discount rate approach involves the point at which the adjustment for risk is incorporated into the calculations. The certainty equivalent penalizes or adjusts downward the value of the expected annual free cash flows, $FCF_t$, which results in a lower net present value for a risky project. The risk-adjusted discount rate, conversely, leaves the cash flows at their expected value and adjusts the required rate of return, $k$, upward to compensate for added risk. In either case, the project's net present value is being adjusted downward to compensate for additional risk. The computational differences are illustrated in Table 11-1.

In addition to the difference in point of adjustment for risk, the risk-adjusted discount rate makes the implicit assumption that risk becomes greater as we move further out in time. Although this is not necessarily a good or bad assumption, we should be aware of it

**TABLE 11-1**
Computational Steps in Certainty Equivalent and Risk-Adjusted Discount Rate Methods

| Certainty Equivalent | Risk-Adjusted Discount Rate |
|---|---|
| STEP 1: Adjust the free cash flows, $FCF_t$, downward for risk by multiplying them by the corresponding certainty equivalent coefficient, $\alpha_t$. | STEP 1: Adjust the discount rate upward for risk, or down in the case of less than normal risk. |
| STEP 2: Discount the certainty equivalent riskless cash flows back to the present using the risk-free rate of interest. | STEP 2: Discount the expected free cash flows back to the present using the risk-adjusted discount rate. |
| STEP 3: Apply the normal decision criteria, except in the case of the internal rate of return, where the risk-free rate of interest replaces the required rate of return as the hurdle rate. | STEP 3: Apply the normal decision criteria except in the case of the internal rate of return, where the risk-adjusted discount rate replaces the required rate of return as the hurdle rate. |

and understand it. Let's look at an example in which the risk-adjusted discount rate is used and then determine what certainty equivalent coefficients, $\alpha_t$, would be necessary to arrive at the same solution.

## EXAMPLE

Assume that a firm with a required rate of return of 10 percent is considering introducing a new product. This product has an initial outlay of $800,000, an expected life of 10 years, and free cash flows of $100,000 each year during its life. Because of the increased risk associated with this project, management is requiring a 15 percent rate of return. Let us also assume that the risk-free rate of return is 6 percent.

If the firm chose to use the certainty equivalent method, the certainty equivalent cash flows would be discounted back to the present at 6 percent, the risk-free rate of interest. The present value of the $100,000 cash flow occurring at the end of the first year discounted back to the present at 15 percent is $87,000. The present value of this $100,000 flow discounted back to the present at the risk-free rate of 6 percent is $94,300. Thus, if the certainty equivalent approach were used, a certainty equivalent coefficient, $\alpha_1$, of .9226 ($87,000 ÷ $94,300 = 0.9226) would be necessary to produce a present value of $87,000. In other words, the same results can be obtained in the first year by using the risk-adjusted discount rate and adjusting the discount rate up to 15 percent or by using the certainty equivalent approach and adjusting the expected cash flows by a certainty equivalent coefficient of 0.9226.

Under the risk-adjusted discount rate, the present value of the $100,000 cash flow occurring at the end of the second year becomes $75,600. To produce an identical present value under the certainty equivalent approach, a certainty equivalent coefficient of 0.8494 would be needed. Following this through for the life of the project yields the certainty equivalent coefficients given in Table 11-2.

**TABLE 11-2**
Certainty Equivalent Coefficients Yielding Same Results as Risk-Adjusted Discount Rate of 15 Percent in Illustrative Example

| Year | 1 | 2 | 3 | 4 | 5 | 6 | 7 | 8 | 9 | 10 |
|---|---|---|---|---|---|---|---|---|---|---|
| $\alpha_t$: | 0.9226 | 0.8494 | 0.7833 | 0.7222 | 0.6653 | 0.6128 | 0.5654 | 0.5215 | 0.4797 | 0.4427 |

What does this analysis suggest? It indicates that if the risk-adjusted discount rate method is used, we are adjusting downward the value of future cash flows that occur further in the future more severely than earlier cash flows.

In summary, the use of the risk-adjusted discount rate assumes that risk increases over time and that cash flows occurring further in the future should be more severely penalized. If performed properly, either of these methods can do a good job of adjusting for risk. However, by far the most popular method of risk adjustment is the risk-adjusted discount rate. The reason for the popularity of the risk-adjusted discount rate over the certainty equivalent approach is purely and simply its ease of implementation.

## Risk-Adjusted Discount Rate and Measurement of a Project's Systematic Risk

When we initially talked about systematic risk or a beta, we were talking about measuring it for the entire firm. As you recall, although we could estimate a firm's beta using historical data, we did not have complete confidence in our results. As we will see, estimating the appropriate level of systematic risk for a single project is even more fraught with difficulties. To truly understand what it is that we are trying to do and the difficulties that we will encounter, let us step back a bit and examine systematic risk and the risk adjustment for a project.

What we are trying to do is to use the CAPM to determine the level of risk and the appropriate risk-return trade-offs for a particular project. We will then take the expected return on this project and compare it to the risk-return trade-offs suggested by the CAPM to determine whether or not the project should be accepted. If the project appears to be a typical one for the firm, using the CAPM to determine the appropriate risk-return trade-offs and then judging the project against them may be a warranted approach. But if the project is not a typical project, what do we do? Historical data generally do not exist for a new project. In fact, for some capital investments, for example, a truck or a new building, historical data would not have much meaning. What we need to do is make the best out of a bad situation. We either (1) fake it—that is, use historical accounting data, if available, to substitute for historical price data in estimating systematic risk; or (2) we attempt to find a substitute firm in the same industry as the capital-budgeting project and use the substitute firm's estimated systematic risk as a proxy for the project's systematic risk.

**BETA ESTIMATION USING ACCOUNTING DATA** When we are dealing with a project that is identical to the firm's other projects, we need only estimate the level of systematic risk for the firm and use that estimate as a proxy for the project's risk. Unfortunately, when projects are not typical of the firm, this approach does not work. For example, when R. J. Reynolds introduces a new food through one of its food products divisions, this new product most likely carries with it a different level of systematic risk than is typical for Reynolds as a whole.

To get a better approximation of the systematic risk level on this project, we could estimate the level of systematic risk for the food division and use that as a proxy for the project's systematic risk. Unfortunately, historical stock price data are available only for the company as a whole and, as you recall, historical stock return data are generally used to estimate a firm's beta. Thus, we are forced to use *accounting return data* rather than historical stock return data for the division to estimate the division's systematic risk. To estimate a project's beta using accounting data we need only run a time series regression of the division's return on assets (net income/total assets) on the market index (the S&P 500). The regression coefficient from this equation would be the project's accounting beta and would serve as an approximation for the project's true beta or measure of systematic risk. Alternatively, a multiple regression model based on accounting data could be developed to explain betas. The results of this model could then be applied to firms that are not publicly traded to estimate their betas.

How good is the accounting beta technique? It certainly is not as good as a direct calculation of the beta. In fact, the correlation between the accounting beta and the beta calculated on historical stock return data is only about 0.6; however, better luck has been experienced with multiple regression models used to predict betas. Unfortunately, in many cases, there may not be any realistic alternative to the calculation of the accounting beta. Owing to the importance of adjusting for a project's risk, the accounting beta method is much preferred to doing nothing.

THE PURE PLAY METHOD FOR ESTIMATING A PROJECT'S BETA Whereas the accounting beta method attempts to directly estimate a project's or division's beta, the **pure play method** attempts to identify publicly traded firms that are engaged solely in the same business as the project or division. Once the proxy or pure play firm is identified, its systematic risk is determined and then used as a proxy for the project's or division's level of systematic risk. What we are doing is looking for a publicly traded firm on the outside that looks like our project, and using that firm's required rate of return to judge our project. In doing so, we are presuming that the systematic risk of the proxy firm is identical to that of the project.

**Pure play method**
A method of estimating a project's beta that attempts to identify a publicly traded firm that is engaged solely in the same business as the project, and uses that beta as a proxy for the project's beta.

In using the pure play method, it should be noted that a firm's capital structure (that is, the way it raises money in the capital markets) is reflected in its beta. When the capital structure of the proxy firm is different from that of the project's firm, some adjustment must be made for this difference. Although not a perfect approach, it does provide some insights as to the level of systematic risk a project might have. It also provides a good framework from which to view risk.

**CONCEPT CHECK**

1. What is the most commonly used method for incorporating risk into the capital-budgeting decision? How is this technique related to Principle 1?
2. Describe two methods for estimating a project's systematic risk.

## OTHER APPROACHES TO EVALUATING RISK IN CAPITAL BUDGETING

### Simulation

**Simulation**
The process of imitating the performance of an investment project under evaluation using a computer. This is done by randomly selecting observations from each of the distributions that affect the outcome of the project, combining those observations to determine the final output of the project, and continuing with this process until a representative record of the project's probable outcome is assembled.

Another method for evaluating risk in the investment decision is through the use of **simulation.** The certainty equivalent and risk-adjusted discount rate approaches provided us with a single value for the risk-adjusted net present value, whereas a simulation approach gives us a probability distribution for the investment's net present value or internal rate of return. Simulation imitates the performance of the project under evaluation. This is done by randomly selecting observations from each of the distributions that affect the outcome of the project, combining those observations to determine the final output of the project, and continuing with this process until a representative record of the project's probable outcome is assembled. Today this process is much simpler due to the fact that spreadsheets like Excel have add-in programs that allow for simulations. In effect, what was once a major effort is now a simple task with spreadsheets.

The easiest way to develop an understanding of the computer simulation process is to follow through an example simulation for an investment project evaluation. Suppose Merck is considering a new drug for the treatment of Alzheimer's disease. The simulation process is portrayed in Figure 11-3. First, the probability distributions are determined for all the factors that affect the project's returns; in this case, let us assume these include the market size, selling price, fixed costs, market growth rate, investment required, residual value of investment, share of market (which results in physical sales volume), operating costs, and useful life of facilities.

Then the computer randomly selects one observation from each of the probability distributions, according to its chance of actually occurring in the future. These nine observations are combined, and a net present value or internal rate of return figure is calculated. This process is repeated as many times as desired, until a representative distribution of possible future outcomes is assembled. Thus, the inputs to a simulation include all the principal factors affecting the project's profitability, and the simulation output is a probability distribution of net present values or internal rates of return for the project. The decision maker bases the decision on the full range of possible outcomes. The project is accepted if the decision maker feels that enough of the distribution lies above the normal cutoff criteria ($NPV \geq 0$, $IRR \geq$ required rate of return).

Suppose that the output from the simulation of Merck's Alzheimer's disease drug project is as given in Figure 11-4. This output provides the decision maker with the probability of different outcomes occurring in addition to the range of possible outcomes. Sometimes called **scenario analysis,** this examination identifies the range of possible outcomes under the worst, best, and most likely case. Merck's management will examine the distribution to determine the project's level of risk and then make the appropriate adjustment.

**Scenario analysis**
Simulation analysis that focuses on an examination of the range of possible outcomes.

You'll notice that although the simulation approach helps us to determine the amount of total risk that a project has, it does not differentiate between systematic and unsystematic risk. Because systematic risk cannot be diversified away for free, the simulation approach does not provide a complete method of risk assessment. However, it does provide important insights as to the total risk level of a given investment project. Now we will look briefly at how the simulation approach can be used to perform sensitivity analysis.

**Sensitivity analysis**
The process of determining how the distribution of possible returns for a particular project is affected by a change in one particular input variable.

SENSITIVITY ANALYSIS THROUGH THE SIMULATION APPROACH **Sensitivity analysis** involves determining how the distribution of possible net present values or internal rates of returns for a particular project is affected by a change in one particular input variable. This is done by changing the value of one input variable while holding all other input variables constant. The distribution of possible net present values or internal rates of return that is generated is then compared with the distribution of possible returns generated before the change was made to determine the effect of the change. For this reason, sensitivity analysis is commonly called "*What if?*" analysis.

For example, in analyzing the proposal for a new drug for the treatment of Alzheimer's disease, Merck's management may wish to determine the effect of a more pessimistic forecast of the anticipated market growth rate. After the more pessimistic forecast replaces the original forecast in the model, the simulation is rerun. The two outputs are then compared to determine how sensitive the results are to the revised estimate of the market growth rate.

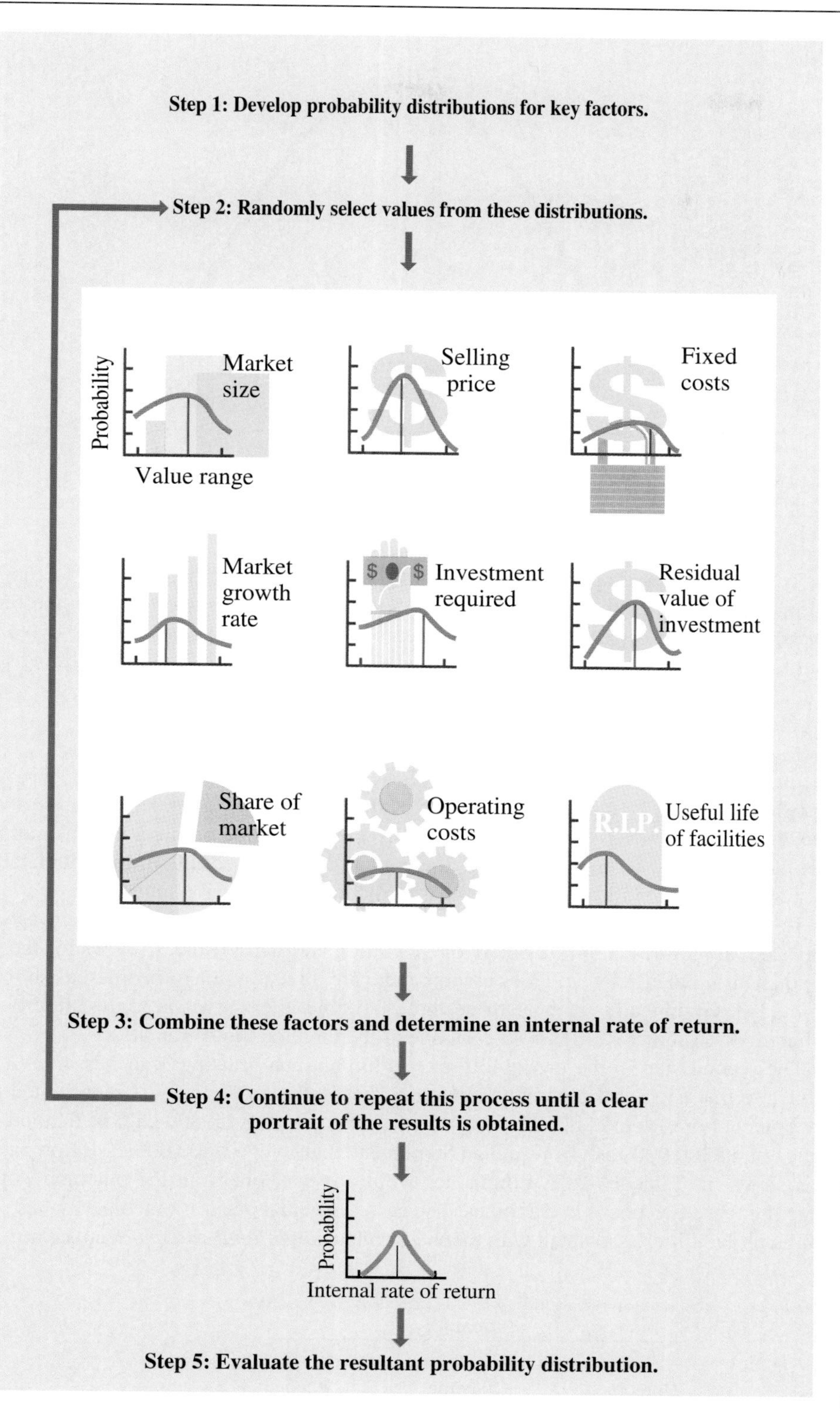


**FIGURE 11-3**
Capital-Budgeting Simulation for Proposed New Alzheimer's Drug

**FIGURE 11-4**
Output from Simulation of a Proposed New Drug for the Treatment of Alzheimer's Disease

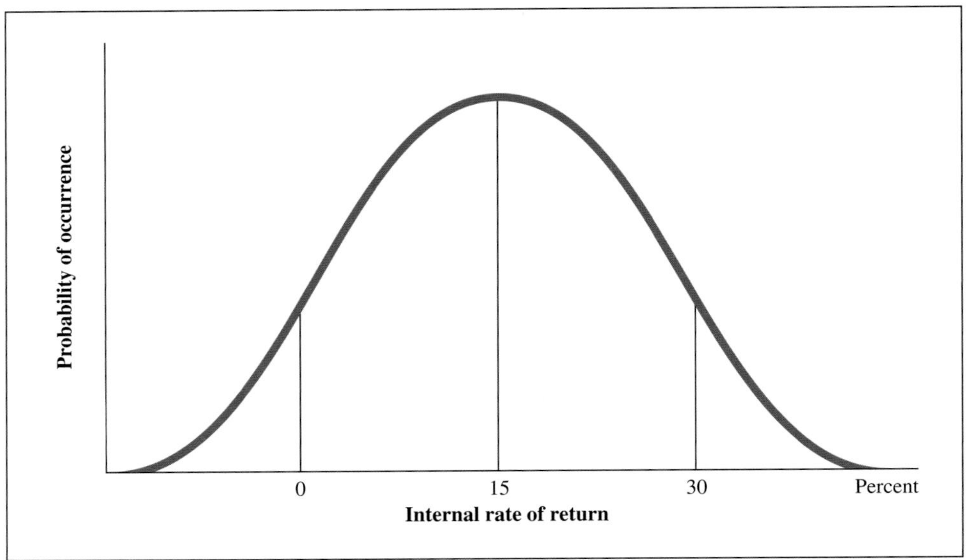


By modifying assumptions made about the values and ranges of the input factors and rerunning the simulation, management can determine how sensitive the outcome of the project is to these changes. If the output appears to be highly sensitive to one or two of the input factors, the financial managers may then wish to spend additional time refining those input estimates to make sure they are accurate.

## Probability Trees

**Probability tree**
A schematic representation of a problem in which all possible outcomes are graphically displayed.

A **probability tree** is a graphic exposition of the sequence of possible outcomes; it presents the decision maker with a schematic representation of the problem in which all possible outcomes are pictured. Moreover, the computations and results of the computations are shown directly on the tree, so that the information can be easily understood.

To illustrate the use of a probability tree, suppose a firm is considering an investment proposal that requires an initial outlay of $1 million and will yield cash flows for the next 2 years. During the first year, let us assume there are three possible outcomes, as shown in Table 11-3. Graphically, each of these three possible alternatives is represented on the probability tree shown in Figure 11-5 as one of the three possible branches.

The second step in the probability tree is to continue drawing branches in a similar manner so that each of the possible outcomes during the second year is represented by a new branch. For example, if outcome 1 occurs in year 1, then there would be a 20 percent chance of a $300,000 cash flow and an 80 percent chance of a $600,000 cash flow in year 2, as shown in Table 11-4. Two branches would be sent out from the outcome 1 node, reflecting these two possible outcomes. The cash flows that occur if outcome 1 takes place and the probabilities associated with them are called *conditional outcomes* and *conditional*

**TABLE 11-3**
Possible Outcomes in Year 1

| | Probability | | |
|---|---|---|---|
| | .5 | .3 | .2 |
| | Outcome 1 | Outcome 2 | Outcome 3 |
| Cash flow | $600,000 | $700,000 | $800,000 |

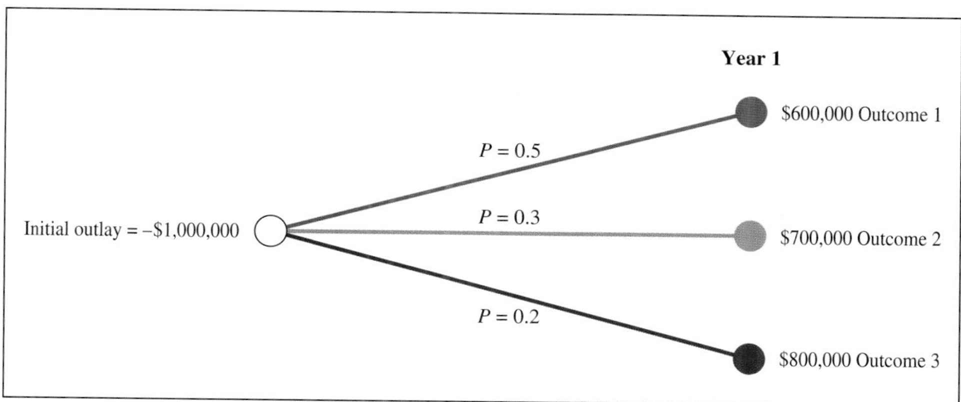


**FIGURE 11-5**
First Stage of a Probability-Tree Diagram

**TABLE 11-4**
Conditional Outcomes and Probabilities for Year 2

| | If Outcome 1 | | If Outcome 2 | | If Outcome 3 | |
|---|---|---|---|---|---|---|
| Year 1 | $ACF_1$ = $600,000 | | $ACF_1$ = $700,000 | | $ACF_1$ = $800,000 | |
| | Then | | Then | | Then | |
| Year 2 | $ACF_2$ | Probability | $ACF_2$ | Probability | $ACF_2$ | Probability |
| | $300,000 | .2 | $300,000 | .2 | $400,000 | .2 |
| | 600,000 | .8 | 500,000 | .3 | 600,000 | .7 |
| | | | 700,000 | .5 | 800,000 | .1 |

*probabilities* because they can occur only if outcome 1 occurs during the first year. Finally, to determine the probability of the sequence of a $600,000 flow in year 1 and a $300,000 outcome in year 2, the probability of the $600,000 flow (.5) is multiplied by the conditional probability of the second flow (.2), telling us that this sequence has a 10 percent chance of occurring; this is called its **joint probability.** Letting the values in Table 11-4 represent the conditional outcomes and their respective conditional probabilities, we can complete the probability tree, as shown in Figure 11-6.

**Joint probability**
The probability of two different sequential outcomes occurring.

The financial manager, by examining the probability tree, is provided with the expected internal rate of return for the investment, the range of possible outcomes, and a listing of each possible outcome with the probability associated with it. In this case, the expected internal rate of return is 14.74 percent, and there is a 10 percent chance of incurring the worst possible outcome with an internal rate of return of −7.55 percent. There is a 2 percent probability of achieving the most favorable outcome, an internal rate of return of 37.98 percent.

Decision making with probability trees does not mean simply the acceptance of any project with an internal rate of return greater than the firm's required rate of return, because the project's required rate of return has not yet been adjusted for risk. As a result, the financial decision maker must examine the entire distribution of possible internal rates of return. Then, based on that examination, he or she must decide, given her or his aversion to risk, if enough of this distribution is above the appropriate (risk-adjusted) required rate of return to warrant acceptance of the project. Thus, the probability tree allows the manager to quickly visualize the possible future events, their probabilities, and their outcomes. In addition, the calculation of the expected internal rate of return and enumeration of the distribution should aid the financial manager in determining the risk level of the project. However, just as with the simulation approach, probability trees do not differentiate between systematic and unsystematic risk.

**FIGURE 11-6**
Probability Tree

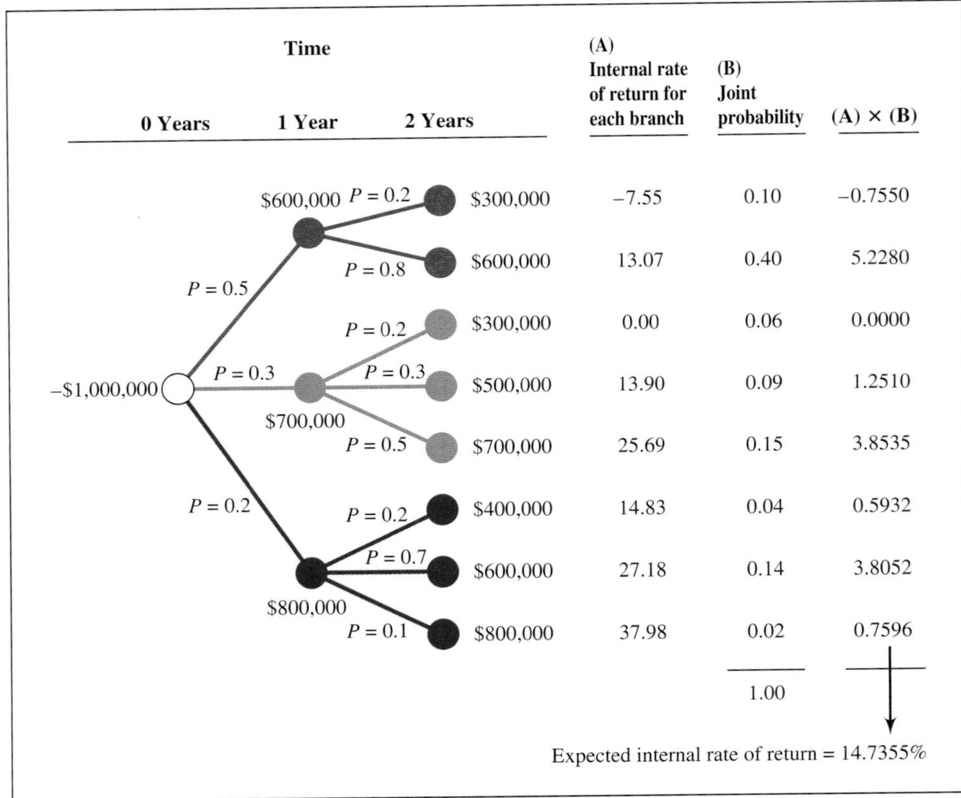


## Other Sources of Risk: Time Dependence of Cash Flows

Up to this point, in all approaches other than the probability tree, we have assumed that the cash flow in one period is independent of the cash flow in the previous period. Although this assumption is appealing because it is simple, in many cases it is also invalid. For example, if a new product is introduced and the initial public reaction is poor, resulting in low initial cash flows, then cash flows in future periods are likely to be low. An extreme example of this is Coca-Cola's experience with the "New Coke." Poor consumer acceptance and sales in the first year were followed by even poorer results in the second year. If the New Coke had been received favorably during its first year, it quite likely would have done well in the second year. The end effect of time dependence of cash flows is to increase the risk of the project over time. That is, because large cash flows in the first period lead to large cash flows in the second period, and low cash flows in the first period lead to low cash flows in the second period, the probability distribution of possible net present values tends to be wider than if the cash flows were not dependent over time. The greater the degree of correlation between flows over time, the greater will be the dispersion of the probability distribution.

### CONCEPT CHECK

1. Explain how simulations work.
2. What is scenario analysis? What is sensitivity analysis? When would you perform sensitivity analysis?

FINANCE MATTERS

## Financial Engineering at Merck

The risks that pharmaceutical firms face in product development are great. It costs $359 million and takes 10 years to bring a new drug to market. Then, once the drug has reached the market, 70 percent of the new drugs introduced do not cover their costs. Rather than simply using an estimate of the project's expected net present value, Merck relies on a simulation approach. It examines the returns on proposed new drugs over a 20-year period, allowing for any and all complexities that it can foresee. The excerpt that follows illustrates this.

Last year Merck & Co., Inc., invested well over $2 billion in R&D and capital expenditures combined. The company spent much of the money on risky, long-term projects that are notoriously difficult to evaluate. Indeed, the critics of modern finance would argue that such projects should not be subjected to rigorous financial analysis, because such analysis fails to reflect the strategic value of long-term investments. Yet at Merck, it is those projects with the longest time horizon that receive the most intense and financially sophisticated analyses. In fact, Merck's financial function is active and influential with a highly quantitative, analytical orientation. The company is seldom, if ever, criticized for being shortsighted.

Why doesn't all this analysis choke off long-term investing, as critics of modern finance theory say it should? In part because Merck is a leader in building financial models of scientific and commercial processes and in using those models to improve business decisions. Rather than relying on static, single-point forecasts, Merck's models use probability distributions for numerous variables and come up with a range of possible outcomes that both stimulate discussion and facilitate decision making.

For example, Merck's Research Planning Model, now ten years old, and its Revenue Hedging Model, now four years old, integrate economics, finance, statistics, and computer science to produce disciplined, quantitative analyses of specific elements of Merck's business. These models do not make decisions. Instead, they provide Merck executives with cogent information both about risks and returns and about financial performance for specific projects and activities.

One of the key aspects of the simulation approach used by Merck is the ability to perform sensitivity analysis by changing the value of specific variables and seeing how the results are affected. In this way, Merck can determine where to spend more time in forecasting and where they should spend time and money trying to improve efficiency.

Source: Timothy A. Luehrman, "Financial Engineering at Merck," *Harvard Business Review* (January–February 1993): 93. Reprinted by permission of *Harvard Business Review*. An excerpt from "Scientific Management at Merck: An Interview with CFO Judy Lewent" by Nancy A. Nichols (1993). 

## THE MULTINATIONAL FIRM: CAPITAL BUDGETING AND RISK

Along with all the benefits from going multinational come the risks. One of the major risks involves currency fluctuations. For example, in 1998, Boeing introduced the Boeing Business Jet, a new versatile business jet that combines fuel efficiency for short flights with globe-spanning range. Boeing produces these planes in the United States, paying workers and suppliers in U.S. dollars. Boeing then exports them all over the world in many different currencies. What happens if the value of the foreign currency falls in the time between placement of the order and receipt of the payment? Can this happen? The answer is that it can happen. In fact, on April 1, 1998, the value of the Yugoslav dinar fell by 43 percent against the U.S. dollar. That means if Boeing had sold a Business Jet to a customer in Yugoslavia for Yugoslav dinars, Boeing would have received the same number of dinars stated in the contract, but they would have been worth 43 percent less. Risks from economic and currency problems abroad can be devastating. For example, the Asian and Latin American economic crisis of 1998 resulted in GM's Latin America/Africa/Mid-East division showing a loss of $161 million in the fourth quarter of 1998 compared with income of $192 million in the fourth quarter of 1997. Also, GM's Asia/Pacific's losses totaled $116 million in the fourth quarter of 1998, compared with a loss of $27 million in the prior-year period. Currency risks also came into play in 2000, but this time from a place that might at first appear safe—Europe. In fact, between January 1, 1999, and the end of 2000, the value of the currency of the European Union, the Euro, fell by about 28 percent. This dramatic drop in the Euro had a major impact on the bottom-line profits of almost every company that did business in Europe. For example, Harley-Davidson, which posted record profits in the third quarter of 2000, pointed out the "negative effects of European currencies" on its profits. McDonald's, on the other hand, reported that the Euro's fall would slash its full-year earnings by about 5 percent, while Goodyear's third quarter profits dropped by 30 percent as a result of the Euro. The bottom line here is that when a firm's capital budgeting goes across its border, it adds some new risks to the decision.

## HOW FINANCIAL MANAGERS USE THIS MATERIAL

If financial managers could see into the future, the material in this chapter would be unnecessary. Unfortunately, they can't—in fact, no one can. What that means for capital-budgeting decision is that you're never really sure how the market will react to your new project. Moreover, not all projects have the same level of risk and, as a result, you have to look at each project individually and make some adjustment for risk. On top of all that, we have the problem of measuring risk.

What does all this mean for you as a financial manager? It means that you not only must understand how risk is measured and the fact that all risk is not the same (in effect, **Principle 9**), but you must also make an adjustment for risk within the capital-budgeting process.

Looking back at Burger King and its introduction of the Big King burger aimed at competing with the McDonald's Big Mac, after all the test marketing, there is still a good deal of uncertainty as to how the public will react to this product. Remember, when McDonald's introduced the Arch Deluxe a couple years ago? That was McDonald's attempt to bring older customers back into McDonald's by providing a more sophisticated burger. They went through extensive test marketing and thought they had a winner, but it didn't sell that way. To determine how much risk and uncertainty there is with a new product, the financial manager much rely heavily on those making the sales forecast. Once they provide the estimate of risk, it is the financial manager's job to react to this and incorporate it into the capital-budgeting process, looking at the best and worst case scenarios and trying to determine just how risky the project is. That may be your job.

## SUMMARY

OBJECTIVE 1 

In this chapter, we examine the problem of incorporating risk into the capital-budgeting decision. First we explore just what type of risk to adjust for: project standing alone risk, the project's contribution-to-firm risk, or the project's systematic risk. In theory, systematic risk is the appropriate risk measure, but bankruptcy costs and the issue of undiversified shareholders also give weight to considering a project's contribution-to-firm risk as the appropriate risk measure. Both measures of risk have merit, and we avoid making any specific allocation of importance between the two in capital budgeting.

OBJECTIVE 2 

Two commonly used methods for incorporating risk into capital budgeting are (1) the certainty equivalent method and (2) risk-adjusted discount rates. The certainty equivalent approach involves a direct attempt to incorporate the decision maker's utility function into the analysis. Under this method, cash flows are adjusted downward by multiplying them by certainty equivalent coefficients, $\alpha_t$'s, which transform the risky cash flows into equivalent certain cash flows in terms of desirability. A project's net present value using the certainty equivalent method for adjusting for risk becomes

$$NPV = \sum_{t=1}^{n} \frac{\alpha_t FCF_t}{(1 + k_{rf})^t} - IO \quad \textbf{(11-2)}$$

The risk-adjusted discount rate involves an upward adjustment of the discount rate to compensate for risk. This method is based on the concept that investors demand higher returns for riskier projects.

OBJECTIVE 3

The simulation and probability tree methods are used to provide information as to the location and shape of the distribution of possible outcomes. Decisions could be based directly on these methods, or they could be used to determine input into either certainty equivalent or risk-adjusted discount method approaches.

## KEY TERMS

**Certainty equivalent approach, 354**

**Certainty equivalents, 354**

**Joint probability, 365**

**Probability tree, 364**

**Project's contribution-to-firm risk, 352**

**Project standing alone risk, 351**

**Pure play method, 361**

**Risk-adjusted discount rate, 357**

**Scenario analysis, 362**

**Sensitivity analysis, 362**

**Simulation, 361**

**Systematic risk, 352**

Go To: http://www.prenhall.com/keown for downloads and current events associated with this chapter

## STUDY QUESTIONS

**11-1.** In Chapter 9, we examined the payback period capital-budgeting decision criterion. Often this capital-budgeting criterion is used as a risk-screening device. Explain the rationale behind its use.

**11-2.** The use of the risk-adjusted discount rate assumes that risk increases over time. Justify this assumption.

**11-3.** What are the similarities and differences between the risk-adjusted discount rate and the certainty equivalent methods for incorporating risk into the capital-budgeting decision?

**11-4.** What is the value of using the probability tree method for evaluating capital-budgeting projects?

**11-5.** Explain how simulation works. What is the value in using a simulation approach?

**11-6.** What does time dependence of cash flows mean? Why might cash flows be time dependent? Give some examples.

## SELF-TEST PROBLEMS

**ST-1.** G. Norohna and Co. is considering two mutually exclusive projects. The expected values for each project's cash flows are as follows:

| Year | Project A | Project B |
|---|---|---|
| 0 | −\$300,000 | −\$300,000 |
| 1 | 100,000 | 200,000 |
| 2 | 200,000 | 200,000 |
| 3 | 200,000 | 200,000 |
| 4 | 300,000 | 300,000 |
| 5 | 300,000 | 400,000 |

The company has decided to evaluate these projects using the certainty equivalent method. The certainty equivalent coefficients for each project's cash flows are as follows:

| Year | Project A | Project B |
|---|---|---|
| 0 | 1.00 | 1.00 |
| 1 | .95 | .90 |
| 2 | .90 | .80 |
| 3 | .85 | .70 |
| 4 | .80 | .60 |
| 5 | .75 | .50 |

Given that this company's normal required rate of return is 15 percent and the after-tax risk-free rate is 8 percent, which project should be selected?

## STUDY PROBLEMS (SET A)

**11-1A.** (*Risk-adjusted* NPV) The Hokie Corporation is considering two mutually exclusive projects. Both require an initial outlay of $10,000 and will operate for 5 years. The probability distributions associated with each project for years 1 through 5 are given as follows:

Probability Distribution for Cash Flow Years 1–5 (the same cash flow each year)

| Project A | | Project B | |
|---|---|---|---|
| Probability | Cash Flow | Probability | Cash Flow |
| .15 | $4,000 | .15 | $ 2,000 |
| .70 | 5,000 | .70 | 6,000 |
| .15 | 6,000 | .15 | 10,000 |

Because project B is the riskier of the two projects, the management of Hokie Corporation has decided to apply a required rate of return of 15 percent to its evaluation but only a 12 percent required rate of return to project A.

**a.** Determine the expected value of each project's annual cash flows.

**b.** Determine each project's risk-adjusted net present value.

**c.** What other factors might be considered in deciding between these two projects?

**11-2A.** (*Risk-adjusted* NPV) The Goblu Corporation is evaluating two mutually exclusive projects, both of which require an initial outlay of $100,000. Each project has an expected life of 5 years. The probability distributions associated with the annual cash flows from each project are as follows:

Probability Distribution for Cash Flow Years 1–5 (the same cash flow each year)

| Project A | | Project B | |
|---|---|---|---|
| Probability | Cash Flow | Probability | Cash Flow |
| .10 | $35,000 | .10 | $10,000 |
| .40 | 40,000 | .20 | 30,000 |
| .40 | 45,000 | .40 | 45,000 |
| .10 | 50,000 | .20 | 60,000 |
| | | .10 | 80,000 |

The normal required rate of return for Goblu is 10 percent, but because these projects are riskier than most, it is requiring a higher-than-normal rate of return on them. Project A requires a 12 percent rate of return and project B requires a 13 percent rate of return.

**a.** Determine the expected value for each project's cash flows.

**b.** Determine each project's risk-adjusted net present value.
**c.** What other factors might be considered in deciding between these projects?

**11-3A.** (*Certainty equivalents*) The V. Coles Corp. is considering two mutually exclusive projects. The expected values for each project's cash flows are as follows:

| Year | Project A | Project B |
|---|---|---|
| 0 | −$1,000,000 | −$1,000,000 |
| 1 | 500,000 | 500,000 |
| 2 | 700,000 | 600,000 |
| 3 | 600,000 | 700,000 |
| 4 | 500,000 | 800,000 |

Management has decided to evaluate these projects using the certainty equivalent method. The certainty equivalent coefficients for each project's cash flows are as follows:

| Year | Project A | Project B |
|---|---|---|
| 0 | 1.00 | 1.00 |
| 1 | .95 | .90 |
| 2 | .90 | .70 |
| 3 | .80 | .60 |
| 4 | .70 | .50 |

Given that this company's normal required rate of return is 15 percent and the after-tax risk-free rate is 5 percent, which project should be selected?

**11-4A.** (*Certainty equivalents*) Neustal, Inc., has decided to use the certainty equivalent method in determining whether or not a new investment should be made. The expected cash flows associated with this investment and the estimated certainty equivalent coefficients are as follows:

| Year | Expected Values for Cash Flows | Certainty Equivalent Coefficients |
|---|---|---|
| 0 | −$90,000 | 1.00 |
| 1 | 25,000 | 0.95 |
| 2 | 30,000 | 0.90 |
| 3 | 30,000 | 0.83 |
| 4 | 25,000 | 0.75 |
| 5 | 20,000 | 0.65 |

Given that Neustal's normal required rate of return is 18 percent and that the after-tax risk free rate is 7 percent, should this project be accepted?

**11-5A.** (*Risk-adjusted discount rates and risk classes*) The G. Wolfe Corporation is examining two capital-budgeting projects with 5-year lives. The first, project A, is a replacement project; the second, project B, is a project unrelated to current operations. The G. Wolfe Corporation uses the risk-adjusted discount rate method and groups projects according to purpose and then uses a required rate of return or discount rate that has been preassigned to that purpose or risk class. The expected cash flows for these projects are as follows:

| | Project A | Project B |
|---|---|---|
| Initial Investment: | $250,000 | $400,000 |
| Cash inflows: | | |
| Year 1 | $ 30,000 | $135,000 |
| Year 2 | 40,000 | 135,000 |
| Year 3 | 50,000 | 135,000 |
| Year 4 | 90,000 | 135,000 |
| Year 5 | 130,000 | 135,000 |

The purpose or risk classes and preassigned required rates of return are as follows:

| Purpose | Required Rate of Return |
|---|---|
| Replacement decision | 12% |
| Modification or expansion of existing product line | 15 |
| Project unrelated to current operations | 18 |
| Research and development operations | 20 |

Determine the project's risk-adjusted net present value.

**11-6A.** (*Certainty equivalents*) Nacho Nachtmann Company uses the certainty equivalent approach when it evaluates risky investments. The company presently has two mutually exclusive investment proposals with an expected life of 4 years each to choose from with money it received from the sale of part of its toy division to another company. The expected net cash flows are as follows:

| Year | Project A | Project B |
|---|---|---|
| 0 | −$50,000 | −$50,000 |
| 1 | 15,000 | 20,000 |
| 2 | 15,000 | 25,000 |
| 3 | 15,000 | 25,000 |
| 4 | 45,000 | 30,000 |

The certainty equivalent coefficients for the net cash flows are as follows:

| Year | Project A | Project B |
|---|---|---|
| 0 | 1.00 | 1.00 |
| 1 | .95 | .90 |
| 2 | .85 | .85 |
| 3 | .80 | .80 |
| 4 | .70 | .75 |

Which of the two investment proposals should be chosen, given that the after-tax risk-free rate of return is 6 percent?

**11-7A.** (*Probability trees*) The M. Solt Corporation is evaluating an investment proposal with an expected life of 2 years. This project will require an initial outlay of $1,200,000. The resultant possible cash flows are as follows:

Possible Outcomes in Year 1

| | Probability | | |
|---|---|---|---|
| | .6 | .3 | .1 |
| | Outcome 1 | Outcome 2 | Outcome 3 |
| Cash flow = | $700,000 | $850,000 | $1,000,000 |

Conditional Outcomes and Probabilities for Year 2

| If $ACF_1$ = $700,000 | | If $ACF_1$ = $850,000 | | If $ACF_1$ = $1,000,000 | |
|---|---|---|---|---|---|
| $ACF_2$ | Probability | $ACF_2$ | Probability | $ACF_2$ | Probability |
| $ 300,000 | .3 | $ 400,000 | .2 | $ 600,000 | .1 |
| 700,000 | .6 | 700,000 | .5 | 900,000 | .5 |
| 1,100,000 | .1 | 1,000,000 | .2 | 1,100,000 | .4 |
| | | 1,300,000 | .1 | | |

**a.** Construct a probability tree representing the possible outcomes.

**b.** Determine the joint probability of each possible sequence of events taking place.

**c.** What is the expected *IRR* of this project?
**d.** What is the range of possible *IRR*s for this project?

**11-8A.** (*Probability trees*) Sega, Inc. is considering expanding its operations into computer-based lacrosse games. Sega feels that there is a 3-year life associated with this project, and it will initially involve an investment of $100,000. It also believes there is a 60 percent chance of success and a cash flow of $100,000 in year 1 and a 40 percent chance of failure and a $10,000 cash flow in year 1. If the project fails in year 1, there is a 60 percent chance that it will produce cash flows of only $10,000 in years 2 and 3. There is also a 40 percent chance that it will *really* fail and Sega will earn nothing in year 2 and get out of this line of business, with the project terminating and no cash flow occurring in year 3. If, conversely, this project succeeds in the first year, then cash flows in the second year are expected to be $200,000, $175,000, or $150,000 with probabilities of .30, .50, and .20, respectively. Finally, if the project succeeds in the third and final year of operation, the cash flows are expected to be either $30,000 more or $20,000 less than they were in year 2, with an equal chance of occurrence.

**a.** Construct a probability tree representing the possible outcomes.
**b.** Determine the joint probability of each possible sequence of events.
**c.** What is the expected *IRR*?
**d.** What is the range of possible *IRR*s for this project?

## INTEGRATIVE PROBLEM

It's been 4 months since you took a position as an assistant financial analyst at Caledonia Products. During that time, you've had a promotion and now are working as a special assistant for capital budgeting to the CEO. Your latest assignment involves the analysis of several risky projects. Because this is your first assignment dealing with risk analysis, you have been asked not only to provide a recommendation on the projects in question, but also to respond to a number of questions aimed at judging your understanding of risk analysis and capital budgeting. The memorandum you received outlining your assignment follows:

TO: The Special Assistant for Capital Budgeting
FROM: Mr. V. Morrison, CEO, Caledonia Products
RE: Capital Budgeting and Risk Analysis

Provide a written response to the following questions:

1. In capital budgeting, risk can be measured from three perspectives. What are those three measures of a project's risk?
2. According to the CAPM, which measurement of a project's risk is relevant? What complications does reality introduce into the CAPM view of risk and what does that mean for our view of the relevant measure of a project's risk?
3. What are the similarities and differences between the risk-adjusted discount rate and certainty equivalent methods for incorporating risk into the capital-budgeting decision?
4. Why might we use the probability tree technique for evaluating capital-budgeting projects?
5. Explain how simulation works. What is the value of using a simulation approach?
6. What is sensitivity analysis and what is its purpose?
7. What does time dependence of cash flows mean? Why might cash flows be time dependent? Give some examples.
8. Caledonia Products is using the certainty equivalent approach to evaluate two mutually exclusive investment proposals with an expected life of 4 years. The expected net cash flows are as follows:

| Year | Project A | Project B |
|---|---|---|
| 0 | −$150,000 | −$200,000 |
| 1 | 40,000 | 50,000 |
| 2 | 40,000 | 60,000 |
| 3 | 40,000 | 60,000 |
| 4 | 100,000 | 50,000 |

The certainty equivalent coefficients for the net cash flows are as follows:

| Year | Project A | Project B |
|---|---|---|
| 0 | 1.00 | 1.00 |
| 1 | .90 | .95 |
| 2 | .85 | .85 |
| 3 | .80 | .80 |
| 4 | .70 | .75 |

Which of the two investment proposals should be chosen, given that the after-tax risk-free rate of return is 7 percent?

**9.** Caledonia is considering an additional investment project with an expected life of 2 years and would like some insights on the level of risk this project has using the probability tree method. The initial outlay on this project would be $600,000, and the resultant possible cash flows are as follows:

Possible Outcomes in Year 1

| | Probability | | |
|---|---|---|---|
| | .4 | .4 | .2 |
| | Outcome 1 | Outcome 2 | Outcome 3 |
| Cash flow = | $300,000 | $350,000 | $450,000 |

Conditional Outcomes and Probabilities for Year 2

| If $ACF_1$ = $300,000 | | If $ACF_1$ = $350,000 | | If $ACF_1$ = $450,000 | |
|---|---|---|---|---|---|
| $ACF_2$ | Probability | $ACF_2$ | Probability | $ACF_2$ | Probability |
| $200,000 | .3 | $250,000 | .2 | $ 300,000 | .2 |
| 300,000 | .7 | 450,000 | .5 | 500,000 | .5 |
| | | 650,000 | .3 | 700,000 | .2 |
| | | | | 1,000,000 | .1 |

**a.** Construct a probability tree representing the possible outcomes.
**b.** Determine the joint probability of each possible sequence of events taking place.
**c.** What is the expected *IRR* of this project?
**d.** What is the range of possible *IRR*s for this project?

## STUDY PROBLEMS (SET B)

**11-1B.** (*Risk-adjusted* NPV) The Cake-O-Las Corporation is considering two mutually exclusive projects. Each of these projects requires an initial outlay of $10,000 and will operate for 5 years. The probability distributions associated with each project for years 1 through 5 are given as follows:

Probability Distribution for Cash Flow Years 1–5 (the same cash flow each year)

| Project A | | Project B | |
|---|---|---|---|
| Probability | Cash Flow | Probability | Cash Flow |
| .20 | $5,000 | .20 | $ 3,000 |
| .60 | 6,000 | .60 | 7,000 |
| .20 | 7,000 | .20 | 11,000 |

Because project B is the riskier of the two projects, the management of Cake-O-Las Corporation has decided to apply a required rate of return of 18 percent to its evaluation but only a 13 percent required rate of return to project A.

**a.** Determine the expected value of each project's annual cash flows.

**b.** Determine each project's risk-adjusted net present value.

**c.** What other factors might be considered in deciding between these two projects?

**11-2B.** (*Risk-adjusted* NPV) The Dorf Corporation is evaluating two mutually exclusive projects, both of which require an initial outlay of $125,000. Each project has an expected life of 5 years. The probability distributions associated with the annual cash flows from each project are as follows:

Probability Distribution for Cash Flow Years 1–5 (the same cash flow each year)

| Project A | | Project B | |
|---|---|---|---|
| **Probability** | **Cash Flow** | **Probability** | **Cash Flow** |
| .10 | $40,000 | .10 | $20,000 |
| .40 | 45,000 | .20 | 40,000 |
| .40 | 50,000 | .40 | 55,000 |
| .10 | 55,000 | .20 | 70,000 |
| | | .10 | 90,000 |

The normal required rate of return for Dorf is 10 percent, but because these projects are riskier than most, Dorf is requiring a higher-than-normal rate of return on them. On project A, it is requiring an 11 percent rate of return, and on project B, a 13 percent rate of return.

**a.** Determine the expected value for each project's cash flows.

**b.** Determine each project's risk-adjusted net present value.

**c.** What other factors might be considered in deciding between these projects?

**11-3B.** (*Certainty equivalents*) The Temco Corp. is considering two mutually exclusive projects. The expected values for each project's cash flows are as follows:

| Year | Project A | Project B |
|---|---|---|
| 0 | −$1,000,000 | −$1,000,000 |
| 1 | 600,000 | 600,000 |
| 2 | 750,000 | 650,000 |
| 3 | 600,000 | 700,000 |
| 4 | 550,000 | 750,000 |

Temco has decided to evaluate these projects using the certainty equivalent method. The certainty equivalent coefficients for each project's cash flows are as follows:

| Year | Project A | Project B |
|---|---|---|
| 0 | 1.00 | 1.00 |
| 1 | .90 | .95 |
| 2 | .90 | .75 |
| 3 | .75 | .60 |
| 4 | .65 | .60 |

Given that this company's normal required rate of return is 15 percent and the after-tax risk-free rate is 5 percent, which project should be selected?

**11-4B.** (*Certainty equivalents*) Perumperal, Inc., has decided to use the certainty equivalent method in determining whether or not a new investment should be made. The expected cash flows associated with this investment and the estimated certainty equivalent coefficients are as follows:

| Year | Expected Values for Cash Flows | Certainty Equivalent Coefficients |
|---|---|---|
| 0 | −$100,000 | 1.00 |
| 1 | 30,000 | .95 |
| 2 | 25,000 | .90 |
| 3 | 30,000 | .83 |
| 4 | 20,000 | .75 |
| 5 | 25,000 | .65 |

Given that Perumperal's normal required rate of return is 18 percent and that the after-tax risk free rate is 8 percent, should this project be accepted?

**11-5B.** (*Risk-adjusted discount rates and risk classes*) The Kick 'n' MacDonald Corporation is examining two capital-budgeting projects with 5-year lives. The first, project A, is a replacement project; the second, project B, is a project unrelated to current operations. The Kick 'n' MacDonald Corporation uses the risk-adjusted discount rate method and groups projects according to purpose and then uses a required rate of return or discount rate that has been preassigned to that purpose or risk class. The expected cash flows for these projects are as follows:

| | Project A | Project B |
|---|---|---|
| Initial Investment: | $300,000 | $450,000 |
| Cash Inflows: | | |
| Year 1 | $ 30,000 | $130,000 |
| Year 2 | 40,000 | 130,000 |
| Year 3 | 50,000 | 130,000 |
| Year 4 | 80,000 | 130,000 |
| Year 5 | 120,000 | 130,000 |

The purpose-risk classes and preassigned required rates of return are as follows:

| Purpose | Required Rate of Return |
|---|---|
| Replacement decision | 13% |
| Modification or expansion of existing product line | 16 |
| Project unrelated to current operations | 18 |
| Research and development operations | 20 |

Determine the project's risk-adjusted net present value.

**11-6B.** (*Certainty equivalents*) The M. Jose Company uses the certainty equivalent approach when it evaluates risky investments. The company presently has two mutually exclusive investment proposals, with an expected life of 4 years each, to choose from with money it received from the sale of part of its toy division to another company. The expected net cash flows are as follows:

| Year | Project A | Project B |
|---|---|---|
| 0 | −$75,000 | −$75,000 |
| 1 | 20,000 | 25,000 |
| 2 | 20,000 | 30,000 |
| 3 | 15,000 | 30,000 |
| 4 | 50,000 | 25,000 |

The certainty equivalent coefficients for the net cash flows are as follows:

| Year | Project A | Project B |
|---|---|---|
| 0 | 1.00 | 1.00 |
| 1 | .95 | .95 |
| 2 | .85 | .85 |
| 3 | .80 | .80 |
| 4 | .70 | .75 |

Which of the two investment proposals should be chosen, given that the after-tax risk-free rate of return is 7 percent?

**11-7B.** (*Probability trees*) The Buckeye Corporation is evaluating an investment proposal with an expected life of 2 years. This project will require an initial outlay of $1,300,000. The resultant possible cash flows are as follows:

Possible Outcomes in Year 1

| | Probability | | |
|---|---|---|---|
| | .6 | .3 | .1 |
| | Outcome 1 | Outcome 2 | Outcome 3 |
| Cash flow = | $750,000 | $900,000 | $1,500,000 |

Conditional Outcomes and Probabilities for Year 2

| If $ACF_1$ = $750,000 | | If $ACF_1$ = $900,000 | | If $ACF_1$ = $1,500,000 | |
|---|---|---|---|---|---|
| $ACF_2$ | Probability | $ACF_2$ | Probability | $ACF_2$ | Probability |
| $ 300,000 | .10 | $ 400,000 | .2 | $ 600,000 | .3 |
| 700,000 | .50 | 700,000 | .5 | 900,000 | .6 |
| 1,100,000 | .40 | 900,000 | .2 | 1,100,000 | .1 |
| | | 1,300,000 | .1 | | |

**a.** Construct a probability tree representing the possible outcomes.
**b.** Determine the joint probability of each possible sequence of events taking place.
**c.** What is the expected *IRR* of this project?
**d.** What is the range of possible *IRR*s for this project?

**11-8B.** (*Probability trees*) Mac's Buffaloes, Inc., is considering expanding its operations into computer-based basketball games. Mac's Buffaloes feels that there is a 3-year life associated with this project, and it will initially involve an investment of $120,000. It also feels there is a 70 percent chance of success and a cash flow of $100,000 in year 1 and a 30 percent chance of "failure" and a $10,000 cash flow in year 1. If the project "fails" in year 1, there is a 60 percent chance that it will produce cash flows of only $10,000 in years 2 and 3. There is also a 40 percent chance that it will really fail and Mac's Buffaloes will earn nothing in year 2 and get out of this line of business, with the project terminating and no cash flow occurring in year 3. If, on the other hand, this project succeeds in the first year, then cash flows in the second year are expected to be $225,000, $180,000, or $140,000 with probabilities of .30, .50, and .20, respectively. Finally, if the project succeeds in the third and final year of operation, the cash flows are expected to be either $30,000 more or $20,000 less than they were in year 2, with an equal chance of occurrence.

**a.** Construct a probability tree representing the possible outcomes.
**b.** Determine the joint probability of each possible sequence of events.
**c.** What is the expected *IRR?*
**d.** What is the range of possible *IRR*s for this project?

## CASE PROBLEM

### Made in the U.S.A.: Dumped in Brazil, Africa . . .
Ethics in Dealing with Uncertainty in Capital Budgeting, or What Happens When a Project Is No Longer Sellable

In an uncertain world, capital budgeting attempts to determine what the future of a new product will bring and how then to act on that forecast. We never know for certain what the future will bring, but we do arrive at some idea of what the distribution of possible outcomes looks like. Unfortunately, when there is uncertainty, the outcome is not always a good one. For example, what happens if the government rules that our product is not safe? The answer is that we must abandon the product. The question then becomes what to do with the inventory we currently have on hand. We certainly want to deal with it in a way that is in the best interests of our shareholders. We also want to obey the law and act ethically. As with most ethical questions, there isn't necessarily a right or wrong answer.

When it comes to the safety of young children, fire is a parent's nightmare. Just the thought of their young ones trapped in their cribs and beds by a raging nocturnal blaze is enough to make most mothers and fathers take every precaution to ensure their children's safety. Little wonder that when fire-retardant children's pajamas hit the market in the mid-1970s, they proved an overnight success. Within a few short years, more than 200 million pairs were sold, and the sales of millions more were all but guaranteed. For their manufacturers, the future could not have been brighter. Then, like a bolt from the blue, came word that the pajamas were killers.

In June 1977, the U.S. Consumer Product Safety Commission (CPSC) banned the sale of these pajamas and ordered the recall of millions of pairs. Reason: The pajamas contained the flame-retardant chemical Tris (2,3-dibromoprophyl), which had been found to cause kidney cancer in children.

Whereas just months earlier the 100 medium- and small-garment manufacturers of the Tris-impregnated pajamas couldn't fill orders fast enough, suddenly they were worrying about how to get rid of the millions of pairs now sitting in warehouses. Because of its toxicity, the sleepwear couldn't even be thrown away, let alone be sold. Indeed, the CPSC left no doubt about how the pajamas were to be disposed of—buried or burned or used as industrial wiping cloths. All meant millions of dollars in losses for manufacturers.

The companies affected—mostly small, family-run operations employing fewer than 100 workers—immediately attempted to shift blame to the mills that made the cloth. When that attempt failed, they tried to get the big department stores that sold the pajamas and the chemical companies that produced Tris to share the financial losses. Again, no sale. Finally, in desperation, the companies lobbied in Washington for a bill making the federal government partially responsible for the losses. It was the government, they argued, that originally had required the companies to add Tris to pajamas and then had prohibited their sale. Congress was sympathetic; it passed a bill granting companies relief. But President Carter vetoed it.

While the small firms were waging their political battle in the halls of Congress, ads began appearing in the classified pages of *Women's Wear Daily.* "Tris-Tris-Tris . . . We will buy any fabric containing Tris," read one. Another said, "Tris—we will purchase any large quantities of garments containing Tris."[1] The ads had been placed by exporters, who began buying up the pajamas, usually at 10 to 30 percent of the normal wholesale price. Their intent was clear: to dump[2] the carcinogenic pajamas on overseas markets.[3]

Tris is not the only example of dumping. In 1972, 400 Iraqis died and 5,000 were hospitalized after eating wheat and barley treated with a U.S.-banned organic mercury fungicide. Winstrol, a synthetic male hormone that had been found to stunt the growth of American children, was made available in Brazil as an appetite stimulant for children. Depo-Provera, an injectable contraceptive known to cause malignant tumors in animals, was shipped overseas to 70 countries where it was used in U.S.-sponsored population control programs. And 450,000 baby pacifiers, of the type known to have caused choking deaths, were exported for sale overseas.

Manufacturers that dump products abroad clearly are motivated by profit or at least by the hope of avoiding financial losses resulting from having to withdraw a product from the market. For government and health agencies that cooperate in the exporting of dangerous products, the motives are more complex.

For example, as early as 1971, the dangers of the Dalkon Shield intrauterine device were well documented.[4] Among the adverse reactions were pelvic inflammation, blood poisoning, pregnancies resulting in spontaneous abortions, tubal pregnancies, and uterine perforations. A number of deaths were even attributed to the device. Faced with losing its domestic market, A. H. Robins Co., manufacturer of the Dalkon Shield, worked out a deal with the Office of Population within the U. S. Agency for International Development (AID), whereby AID bought thousands of the devices at a reduced price for use in population-control programs in 42 countries.

Why do governmental and population-control agencies approve for sale and use overseas birth control devices proved dangerous in the United States? They say their motives are humanitarian. Because the rate of dying in childbirth is high in Third World countries, almost any birth control device is prefer-

[1]Mark Hosenball, "Karl Marx and the Pajama Game," *Mother Jones* (November 1979): 47.

[2]"Dumping" is a term apparently coined by *Mother Jones* magazine to refer to the practice of exporting to overseas countries products that have been banned or declared hazardous in the United States.

[3]Unless otherwise noted, the facts and quotations reported in this case are based on Mark Dowie, "The Corporate Crime of the Century," *Mother Jones* (November 1971) and Russell Mokhiber, *Corporate Crime and Violence* (San Francisco: Sierra Club Books, 1988): 181–95. See also Jane Kay, "Global Dumping of U.S. Toxics Is Big Business," *San Francisco Examiner* (September 23, 1990): A2.

[4]See Mark Dowie and Tracy Johnston, "A Case of Corporate Malpractice," *Mother Jones* (November 1976).

able to none. Third World scientists and government officials frequently support this argument. They insist that denying their countries access to the contraceptives of their choice is tantamount to violating their countries' national sovereignty.

Apparently this argument has found a sympathetic ear in Washington, for it turns up in the "notification" system that regulates the export of banned or dangerous products overseas. Based on the principles of national sovereignty, self-determination, and free trade, the notification system requires that foreign governments be notified whenever a product is banned, deregulated, suspended, or canceled by an American regulatory agency. The State Department, which implements the system, has a policy statement on the subject that reads in part: "No country should establish itself as the arbiter of others' health and safety standards. Individual governments are generally in the best position to establish standards of public health and safety."

Critics of the system claim that notifying foreign health officials is virtually useless. For one thing, other governments rarely can establish health standards or even control imports into their countries. Indeed, most of the Third World countries where banned or dangerous products are dumped lack regulatory agencies, adequate testing facilities, and well-staffed customs departments.

Then there's the problem of getting the word out about hazardous products. In theory, when a government agency such as the Environmental Protection Agency or the Food and Drug Administration (FDA) finds a product hazardous, it is supposed to inform the State Department, which is to notify local health officials. But agencies often fail to inform the State Department of the product they have banned or found harmful. And when it is notified, its communiqués typically go no further than the U.S. embassies abroad. One embassy official even told the General Accounting Office that he "did not routinely forward notification of chemicals not registered in the host country because it may adversely affect U.S. exporting." When foreign officials are notified by U.S. embassies, they sometimes find the communiqués vague or ambiguous or too technical to understand.

In an effort to remedy these problems, at the end of his term in office, President Jimmy Carter issued an executive order that (1) improved export notice procedures; (2) called for publishing an annual summary of substances banned or severely restricted for domestic use in the United States; (3) directed the State Department and other federal agencies to participate in the development of international hazards alert systems; and (4) established procedures for placing formal export licensing controls on a limited number of extremely hazardous substances. In one of his first acts as president, however, Ronald Reagan rescinded the order. Later in his administration, the law that formerly prohibited U.S. pharmaceutical companies from exporting drugs that are banned or not registered in this country was weakened to allow the export to 21 countries of drugs not yet approved for use in the United States.

But even if communication procedures were improved or the export of dangerous products forbidden, there are ways that companies can circumvent these threats to their profits—for example, by simply changing the name of the product or by exporting the individual ingredients of a product to a plant in a foreign country. Once there, the ingredients can be reassembled and the product dumped.[5] Upjohn, for example, through its Belgian subsidiary, continues to produce Depo-Provera, which the FDA has consistently refused to approve for use in this country. And the prohibition on the export of dangerous drugs is not that hard to sidestep. "Unless the package bursts open on the dock," one drug company executive observes, "you have no chance of being caught."

Unfortunately for us, in the case of pesticides, the effects of overseas dumping are now coming home. The Environmental Protection Agency bans from the United States all crop uses of DDT and Dieldrin, which kill fish, cause tumors in animals, and build up in the fatty tissue of humans. It also bans heptachlor, chlordane, leptophos, endrin, and many other pesticides, including 2,4,5-T (which contains the deadly poison dioxin, the active ingredient in Agent Orange, the notorious defoliant used in Vietnam) because they are dangerous to human beings. No law, however, prohibits the sale of DDT and these other U.S.-banned pesticides overseas, where—thanks to corporate dumping—they are routinely used in agriculture. The FDA now estimates, through spot checks, that 10 percent of our imported food is contaminated with illegal residues of banned pesticides. And the FDA's most commonly used testing procedure does not even check for 70 percent of the pesticides known to cause cancer.

## QUESTIONS

1. Was the dumping in this case ethical? Those involved in the dumping might have argued that the people receiving the pajamas would not have otherwise had access to such clothing and were notified of the health and safety hazards. Does this affect your feelings about the case? What do you think about the exportation of the Dalkon Shield? Can it be justified because the rate of dying during childbirth in Third World countries is extremely high, and, as such, any effective birth control device is better than none?
2. What obligations did the financial managers have to their shareholders to do whatever is possible to avoid major financial losses associated with these products?
3. Is it still immoral or unethical to dump goods when doing so does not violate any U.S. laws? How about when those receiving the goods know the dangers? Why do you think dumpers dump? Do you think they believe what they are doing is ethically acceptable?

[5]Mark Dowie, "A Dumper's Guide to Tricks of the Trade," *Mother Jones* (November 1979): 25.

Source: Adapted by permission from William Shaw and Vincent Barry, "Made in the U.S.A.: Dumped in Brazil, Africa . . .", *Moral Issues in Business,* 6th ed. (New York: Wadsworth, 1995): 28–31. 

## SELF-TEST SOLUTIONS

**ST-1:** Project A:

| Year | (A) Expected Cash Flow | (B) $\alpha_t$ | (A · B) (Expected Cash Flow) × ($\alpha_t$) | Present Value Factor at 8% | Present Value |
|---|---|---|---|---|---|
| 0 | −$300,000 | 1.00 | −$300,000 | 1.000 | −$300,000 |
| 1 | 100,000 | .95 | 95,000 | 0.926 | 87,970 |
| 2 | 200,000 | .90 | 180,000 | 0.857 | 154,260 |
| 3 | 200,000 | .85 | 170,000 | 0.794 | 134,980 |
| 4 | 300,000 | .80 | 240,000 | 0.735 | 176,400 |
| 5 | 300,000 | .75 | 225,000 | 0.681 | 153,225 |
| | | | | | $NPV_A$ = $406,835 |

Project B:

| Year | (A) Expected Cash Flow | (B) $\alpha_t$ | (A · B) (Expected Cash Flow) × ($\alpha_t$) | Present Value Factor at 8% | Present Value |
|---|---|---|---|---|---|
| 0 | −$300,000 | 1.00 | −$300,000 | 1.000 | −$300,000 |
| 1 | 200,000 | .90 | 180,000 | 0.926 | 166,680 |
| 2 | 200,000 | .80 | 160,000 | 0.857 | 137,120 |
| 3 | 200,000 | .70 | 140,000 | 0.794 | 111,160 |
| 4 | 300,000 | .60 | 180,000 | 0.735 | 132,300 |
| 5 | 400,000 | .50 | 200,000 | 0.681 | 136,460 |
| | | | | | $NPV_A$ = $383,460 |

Thus, project A should be selected, because it has the higher *NPV.*

# COST OF CAPITAL

Harley-Davidson and Briggs & Stratton are both headquartered in Milwaukee, Wisconsin. However, this is not the only thing these two firms have in common. Both firms are faced with the need to assess two types of financial performance. In one instance, it is the anticipated performance of what seems like a never-ending stream of new capital investment opportunities, and in the other, it is the operating performance of the firm as a whole. Consider the following scenarios:

- In the face of demand that continues to outstrip its ability to produce motorcycles, Harley-Davidson is ever faced with the opportunity to commit additional funds to plant and equipment. Funds are required to update and replace worn-out equipment as well as to expand production capacity. How should the firm choose among its many investment opportunities?
- Briggs & Stratton, on the other hand, tries to reward its employees with bonuses that reflect value created during the year. To properly assess the bonuses, the firm must first know what is expected of it by the firm's investors. That is, what minimum rate of return must the firm earn if it is to be assured of creating value for the firm's shareholders?

Harley-Davidson needs a benchmark return that can be used to evaluate new project proposals. Similarly, Briggs & Stratton needs a benchmark return to use in evaluating whether the firm's ongoing operations are creating additional shareholder value. In both of these instances, the firm needs an estimate of its cost of

**LEARNING OBJECTIVES**

After reading this chapter, you should be able to

1. Describe the concepts underlying the firm's cost of capital (technically, its weighted average cost of capital) and the purpose for its calculation.
2. Calculate the after-tax cost of debt, preferred stock, and common equity.
3. Calculate a firm's weighted average cost of capital.
4. Describe the procedure used by PepsiCo to estimate the cost of capital for a multiple division firm.
5. Use the cost of capital to evaluate new investment opportunities.

capital. We discussed the use of the cost of capital in the context of a firm's investment decisions in Chapters 9–11 and we return to a discussion of the use of the cost of capital in evaluating a firm's operating performance in Chapter 13.

## CHAPTER PREVIEW

Having studied the linkage between risk and rates of return for securities (Chapter 6) and the valuation of bonds and stocks (Chapters 7 and 8), we are prepared to consider the firm's cost of capital. A firm's cost of capital serves as the linkage between its financing and investment decisions. The cost of capital becomes the hurdle rate that must be achieved by an investment before it will increase shareholder wealth. The term *cost of capital* is frequently used interchangeably with the firm's *required rate of return*, the *hurdle rate for new investments*, the *discount rate for evaluating a new investment*, and the firm's *opportunity cost of funds*. Regardless of the term used, the basic concept is the same. The cost of capital is the rate that must be earned on an investment project if the project is to increase the value of the common stockholder's investment.

The cost of capital is also the appropriate basis for evaluating the periodic performance of a division or even an entire firm. In this case, the cost of capital becomes the key determinant of the capital cost associated with a firm's investments.

In this chapter, we will discuss the fundamental determinants of a firm's cost of capital as well as the rationale for its calculation and use. This will entail estimating the cost of debt capital, preferred stock, and common stock. Chapter 16 takes up consideration of the impact of the firm's financing mix on the cost of capital.

This chapter emphasizes principles 1, 2, 3, 6, 8, and 9: **Principle 1: The Risk-Return Trade-Off—We won't take on additional risk unless we expect to be compensated with additional return; Principle 2: The Time Value of Money—A dollar received today is worth more than a dollar received in the future; Principle 3: Cash—Not Profits—Is King; Principle 6: Efficient Capital Markets—The markets are quick and the prices are right; Principle 8: Taxes Bias Business Decisions; Principle 9: All Risk Is Not Equal—Some risk can be diversified away, and some cannot.**

# THE COST OF CAPITAL: KEY DEFINITIONS AND CONCEPTS

## Investor Opportunity Costs, Required Rates of Return, and the Cost of Capital

OBJECTIVE 1 

**Investor's required rate of return**
The minimum rate of return necessary to attract an investor to purchase or hold a security.

In Chapter 9, we referred to the discount rate used in calculating *NPV* simply as the appropriate discount rate. In this chapter, we define what we mean by this term. Specifically, the appropriate discount rate primarily reflects the **investor's required rate of return**. In Chapter 6, we defined the investor's required rate of return for a security as the *minimum rate of return necessary to attract an investor to purchase or hold a security*. This rate of return considers the investor's opportunity cost of making an investment; that is, if an investment is made, the investor must forgo the return available on the next-best investment. This forgone return then is the opportunity cost of undertaking the investment and, consequently, is the investor's required rate of return.

Is the investor's required rate of return the same thing as the cost of capital? Not exactly. Two basic considerations drive a wedge between the investor's required rate of return and the cost of capital to the firm. First, there are taxes. When a firm borrows money to finance the purchase of an asset, the interest expense is deductible for federal income tax calculations. Consider a firm that borrows at 9 percent and then deducts its interest expense from its revenues before paying taxes at a rate of 34 percent. For each dollar of interest it pays, the firm reduces its taxes by 34¢. Consequently, the actual cost of borrowing to the firm is only 5.94%. We calculate the after-tax cost of debt in this case as follows: $.09 - (.34 \times .09) = .09(1 - .34) = 0.0594 = 5.94\%$. The second thing that causes the firm's cost of capital to differ from the investor's required rate of return is any transaction costs incurred when a firm raises funds by issuing a particular type of security, sometimes called **flotation costs**. For example, if a firm sells new shares of common stock for \$25 per share but incurs transaction costs of \$5 per share, then the cost of capital for the new common equity is increased. Assume that the investor's required rate of return is 15 percent for each \$25 share, then .15 × \$25 = \$3.75 must be earned each year to satisfy the investor's required return. However, the firm has only \$20 to invest, so the cost of capital ($k$) is calculated as the rate of return that must be earned on the \$20 net proceeds, which will produce a dollar return of \$3.75; that is,

**Flotation costs**
The underwriter's spread and issuing costs associated with the issuance and marketing of new securities.

$$\$20k = \$25 \times .15 = \$3.75$$

$$k = \frac{\$3.75}{\$20.00} = .1875 = 18.75\%$$

We will have more to say about both of these considerations as we discuss the costs of the individual sources of capital to the firm.

## Financial Policy and the Cost of Capital

A firm's **financial policy**—that is, the policies regarding the sources of finances it plans to use and the particular mix (proportions) in which they will be used—governs its use of debt and equity financing. The particular mixture of debt and equity that the firm utilizes can impact the firm's cost of capital. However, in this chapter, we will assume that the firm maintains a fixed financial policy that is defined by the firm's debt-to-equity ratio. Determination of the target mix of debt and equity financing is the subject of Chapter 16.

**Financial policy**
The firm's policies regarding the sources of financing and the particular mix in which they will be used.

The firm's overall cost of capital will reflect the combined costs of all the sources of financing used by the firm. We refer to this overall cost of capital as the firm's **weighted average cost of capital**. The weighted average cost of capital is the weighted average of the after-tax costs of each of the sources of capital used by a firm to finance a project where the weights reflect the proportion of total financing raised from each source. Consequently, the weighted average cost of capital is the rate of return that the firm must earn on its investments so that it can compensate both its creditors and stockholders with their individual required rates of return. Let's now turn to a discussion of how the costs of debt and equity can be estimated.

**Weighted average cost of capital**
The average of the after-tax costs of each of the sources of capital used by a firm to finance a project. The weights reflect the proportion of the total financing raised from each source.

### CONCEPT CHECK

1. Define the concept of an investor's required rate of return.
2. How is the investor's required rate of return related to the firm's cost of capital?
3. Define a firm's financial policy.
4. What is meant by the phrase "a firm's weighted average cost of capital"?

## DETERMINING INDIVIDUAL COSTS OF CAPITAL

In order to attract new investors, companies have created a wide variety of financing instruments or securities. In this chapter, we will stick to three basic types: debt, preferred stock, and common stock. In calculating the respective cost of financing from each of these financing instruments, we estimate the investor's required rate of return properly adjusted for any transaction or flotation costs associated with each funding source. In addition, because we will be discounting after-tax cash flows, we should adjust our cost of capital for any influence of corporate taxes. In summary, the cost of a particular source of capital is equal to the investor's required rate of return after adjusting for the effects of both flotation costs and corporate taxes.

## The Cost of Debt

The investor's required rate of return on debt is simply the return that creditors demand when they lend to the firm. In Chapter 7 we estimated this required rate of return by solving the following bond valuation equation:

$$P_d = \sum_{t=1}^{n} \frac{\text{interest paid in period } t(I_t)}{(1 + \text{bondholder's required rate of return } (k_d))^t} + \frac{\text{maturity value of the debt } (\$M)}{(1 + \text{bondholder's required rate of return } (k_d))^n} \tag{12-1}$$

where $P_d$ is the market price of the debt security and $n$ is the number of periods to maturity. Should the firm incur flotation costs such as brokerage commissions and legal and accounting fees in issuing the debt, then the cost of debt capital, $k_d$, is found as follows:

$$\begin{array}{c}\text{net proceeds}\\ \text{per bond } (NP_d)\end{array} = \sum_{t=1}^{n} \frac{\$I_t}{(1 + \$k_d)^t} + \frac{\$M}{(1 + k_d)^n} \tag{12-2}$$

The adjustment for flotation costs simply involves replacing the market price of the bond with the net proceeds per bond ($NP_d$) received by the firm after paying these costs. The result of this adjustment is that the discount rate that solves equation 12-2 is now the firm's cost of debt financing before adjusting for the effect of corporate taxes—that is, the before-tax cost of debt ($k_d$). The final adjustment we make is to account for the fact that interest is tax deductible. Thus the after-tax cost of debt capital is simply $k_d(1 - T_c)$, where $T_c$ is the corporate tax rate.

As we learned in Chapter 6, the interest payments on bonds are generally the same for each period. Under these conditions, equation 12-2 can be restated using the interest factors in the present value tables in Appendices B and C as follows:

$$NP_d = \$I_t(PVIFAk_{d,n}) + \$M(PVIFk_{d,n}) \tag{12-2a}$$

**RELATE TO THE BIG PICTURE**

When we calculate the bondholder's required rate of return, we are discounting the interest and principal payments to the bondholder back to the present using a discount rate that makes this present value equal the current price of the firm's bonds. In essence, we are valuing the bond, which relies on two basic principles of finance: **Principle 1: The Risk-Return Trade-Off—We won't take on additional risk unless we expect to be compensated with additional return**, and **Principle 2: The Time Value of Money—A dollar received today is worth more than a dollar received in the future**.

In addition, the calculation of the bondholder's required rate of return relies on the observed market price of the firm's bonds to be an accurate reflection of their worth. Buyers and sellers only stop trading when they are convinced that the price properly reflects all available information. **Principle 6: Efficient Capital Markets—The markets are quick and the prices are right**. What we mean here, very simply, is that investors are ever vigilant and quickly act on information that affects the riskiness and, consequently, the price of a firm's bonds and other securities.

## EXAMPLE: THE COST OF DEBT CAPITAL

TRW, Inc., plans to offer a new bond issue but first wants to estimate the cost of new debt capital. The firm's investment banker estimates that a 30-year bond with a \$1,000 face value and 7.75 percent coupon paid annually (7.75% × \$1,000 = 77.50) could be sold to investors for \$990.81. Equation 12-1 can be used to solve for the investor's required rate of return, as illustrated in Chapter 6. In this case, TRW's creditors require a 7.83 percent rate of return. The cost of capital to the firm is higher than 7.83 percent, however, because the firm will have to pay flotation costs of \$12.50 per bond when it issues the security. The flotation costs reduce the net proceeds to TRW to \$978.31 = \$990.81 − \$12.50. Substituting into equation 12-2, we estimate the before-tax cost of capital for the bond issue is 7.94 percent. One again, we can solve equation 12-2 using a financial calculator, as illustrated in the margin.

One final adjustment is necessary to obtain an estimate of the firm's after-tax cost of debt capital. Assuming that TRW is in the 34 percent corporate income tax bracket, we estimate the after-tax cost of debt capital as follows:

$$\text{after-tax cost of debt} = k_d(1 - T_c)$$

$$\text{after-tax cost of debt} = 7.94\%(1 - .34) = 5.24\%$$

**CALCULATOR SOLUTION**

| Data Input | Function Key |
|---|---|
| 30 | N |
| 978.31 | +/– PV |
| 77.50 | PMT |
| 1,000 | FV |

| Function Key | Answer |
|---|---|
| CPT I/Y | 7.94% |

### RELATE TO THE BIG PICTURE

The tax deductibility of interest expense makes debt financing less costly to the firm. This is an example of **Principle 8: Taxes Bias Business Decisions**. The tax deductibility of interest, other things remaining constant, serves to encourage firms to use more debt in their capital structure than they might otherwise use.

## The Cost of Preferred Stock

Determining the cost of preferred stock is very straightforward because of the simple nature of the cash flows paid to the holders of preferred shares. You will recall from Chapter 7 that the value of a preferred stock is simply

$$\begin{array}{c}\text{price of}\\ \text{preferred stock } (P_{ps})\end{array} = \frac{\text{preferred stock dividend}}{\text{required rate of return for preferred stockholder}} \quad \textbf{(12-3)}$$

where $P_{ps}$ is the current market price of the preferred shares. Solving for the preferred stockholder's required rate of return, we get the following:

$$\begin{array}{c}\text{required rate of return}\\ \text{for preferred stockholder}\end{array} = \frac{\text{preferred stock dividend}}{\text{price of preferred stock}} \quad \textbf{(12-4)}$$

Once again, where flotation costs are incurred when new preferred shares are sold, the investor's required rate of return is less than the cost of preferred capital to the firm. To calculate the cost of preferred stock, we must adjust the required rate of return to reflect these flotation costs. We replace the price of a preferred share in equation 12-4 with the net proceeds per share from the sale of new preferred shares ($NP_{ps}$). The resulting formula can be used to calculate the cost of preferred stock to the firm.

$$\text{cost of preferred stock } (k_{ps}) = \frac{\text{preferred stock dividend}}{\text{net proceeds per preferred share}} \quad \textbf{(12-5)}$$

What about corporate taxes? In the case of preferred stock, no tax adjustment must be made because preferred dividends are not tax deductible.

**EXAMPLE: THE COST OF PREFERRED STOCK**

On August 29, 2000, Ford Motor Company had an issue of preferred stock trading on the NYSE that had a closing price of \$26.25 and paid an annual dividend of \$2.06 per share. Assume that if the firm were to sell an issue of preferred stock with the same characteristics as its outstanding issue, it would incur flotation costs of \$2.00 per share and the shares would sell for their August 29, 2000, closing price. What is Ford's cost of preferred stock?

Substituting into equation 12-5, we get the following cost of preferred stock for Ford:

$$k_{ps} = \frac{\$2.06}{(\$26.25 - \$2.00)} = .085 \text{ or } 8.5\%$$

Note that there is no adjustment for taxes, as preferred dividends are not tax deductible—that is, preferred dividends are paid after corporate taxes, unlike bond interest, which is paid with before-tax dollars.

## The Cost of Common Equity

Common equity is unique in two respects. First, the cost of common equity is more difficult to estimate than the cost of debt or preferred stock because the common stockholder's required rate of return is not observable. This results from the fact that common stockholders are the residual owners of the firm, which means that their return is equal to what is left of the firm's earnings after paying the firm's bondholders their contractually set interest and principal payments and the preferred stockholders their promised dividends. Second, common equity can be obtained from either the retention of firm earnings or through the sale of new shares. The cost associated with each of these sources is different because the firm does not incur any flotation costs when it retains earnings but does when it sells new common shares.

We discuss two methods for estimating the common stockholder's required rate of return, which is the foundation for our estimate of the firm's cost of equity capital. These methods are based on the dividend growth model and the capital asset pricing model, which were both discussed earlier in Chapter 8 when we discussed stock valuation.

## The Dividend Growth Model

Recall from Chapter 8 that the value of a firm's common stock is equal to the present value of all future dividends. Where dividends are expected to grow at a rate $g$ forever and this rate $g$ is less than the investor's required rate of return, $k_{cs}$, then the value of a share of common stock, $P_{cs}$, can be written as:

$$P_{cs} = \frac{D_1}{k_{cs} - g} \qquad \textbf{(12-6)}$$

where $D_1$ is the dividend expected to be received by the firm's common shareholders 1 year hence. The expected dividend is simply equal to the current dividend multiplied by 1 plus the annual rate of growth in dividends (i.e., $D_1 = D_0(1 + g)$). The investor's required rate of return then is found by solving equation 12-6 for $k_{cs}$.

$$k_{cs} = \frac{D_1}{P_{cs}} + g \qquad \textbf{(12-7)}$$

Note that $k_{cs}$ is the investor's required rate of return for investing in the firm's stock. It also serves as our estimate of the cost of equity capital, where new equity capital is obtained by retaining a part of the firm's current period earnings. Recall that common equity financing can come from one of two sources: the retention of earnings (i.e., earnings not paid out in dividends to the common stockholders) or from the sale of new common shares. When the firm retains earnings, it doesn't incur any flotation costs, thus the investor's required rate of return is the same as the firm's cost of new equity capital in this instance.

If the firm issues new shares to raise equity capital, then it incurs flotation costs. Once again we adjust the investor's required rate of return for flotation costs by substituting the net proceeds per share, $NP_{cs}$, for the stock price, $P_{cs}$, in equation 12-7 to estimate the cost of new common stock, $k_{ncs}$.

$$k_{ncs} = \frac{D_1}{NP_{cs}} + g \qquad \textbf{(12-8)}$$

## EXAMPLE: ESTIMATING THE COST OF COMMON STOCK USING THE DIVIDEND GROWTH MODEL

On September 1, 2000, the common stock of Wal-Mart closed at \$49.00 per share. In 1999 Wal-Mart paid a dividend of \$0.22. If dividends are expected to grow at a rate of 14.6 percent per year into the foreseeable future, then the expected dividend for 2000 is 25¢. What is the investor's required rate of return (i.e., the cost of retained earnings) for Wal-Mart?

$$k_{cs} = \frac{D_1}{P_{cs}} + g = \frac{\$0.25}{\$49.00} + .146 = .1511 \text{ or } 15.11\%$$

Should Wal-Mart decide to issue new common stock, it will incur a flotation cost. If these costs are approximately 6 percent of the share price or \$3.00 per share, what is the resulting cost of new common equity capital?

$$k_{ncs} = \frac{D_1}{NP_{cs}} + g = \frac{\$.25}{\$49.00 - \$3.00} + .146 = .1515 \text{ or } 15.15\%$$

Thus, when Wal-Mart retains earnings, we estimate its cost of equity to be 15.11 percent compared to 15.15 percent should the firm issue new equity.

## RELATE TO THE BIG PICTURE

The dividend growth model for common stock valuation relies on three of the fundamental principles of finance. First, stock value is equal to the present value of expected future dividends. This reflects **Principle 2: The Time Value of Money—A dollar received today is worth more than a dollar received in the future**. Furthermore, dividends represent actual cash receipts to stockholders and are incorporated into the valuation model in a manner that reflects the timing of their receipt. This attribute of the dividend growth model reflects **Principle 3: Cash—Not Profits—Is King**. Finally, the rate used to discount the expected future dividends back to the present reflects the riskiness of the dividends. The higher the riskiness of the dividend payments, the higher the investor's required rate of return. This reflects **Principle 1: The Risk-Return Trade-Off—We won't take on additional risk unless we expect to be compensated with additional return.**

## Issues in Implementing the Dividend Growth Model

The principal advantage of the dividend growth model is its simplicity. To estimate an investor's required rate of return, the analyst needs only to observe the current dividend and stock price and to estimate the rate of growth in future dividends. The primary drawback relates to the applicability or appropriateness of the valuation model. That is, the dividend growth model is based on the fundamental assumption that dividends are expected to grow at a constant rate $g$ forever. To avoid this assumption, analysts frequently utilize more complex valuation models in which dividends are expected to grow for, say, 5 years at one rate and then grow at a lower rate from year 6 forward. We will not consider these more complex models here.

Even if the constant growth rate assumption is acceptable, we must arrive at an estimate of that growth rate. We could estimate the rate of growth in historical dividends ourselves or go to published sources of growth rate expectations. Investment advisory services such as Value Line provide their own analysts' estimates of earnings growth rates (generally spanning up to 5 years), and the Institutional Brokers' Estimate System (I/B/E/S) collects and publishes earnings per share forecasts made by over 1,000 analysts for a broad list of stocks. These estimates are helpful but still require the careful judgment of the analyst in their use, because they relate to earnings (not dividends) and only extend 5 years into the future (not forever, as required by the dividend growth model). Nonetheless, these estimates provide a useful guide to making your initial dividend growth rate estimate.

## The Capital Asset Pricing Model

**Capital asset pricing model (CAPM)**
A statement of the relationship between expected returns and risk in which risk is captured by the systematic risk (beta) for the risky asset. The expected return is equal to the sum of the risk-free rate of interest and a risk premium equal to the product of beta and the market risk premium.

Recall from Chapter 6 that the **capital asset pricing model (CAPM)** provides a basis for determining the investor's expected or required rate of return from investing in common stock. The model depends on three things:

1. the risk-free rate, $k_{rf}$,
2. the systematic risk of the common stock's returns relative to the market as a whole or the stock's beta coefficient, $\beta$; and
3. the market risk premium, which is equal to the difference in the expected rate of return for the market as a whole—that is, the expected rate of return for the "average security" minus the risk-free rate, or in symbols, $k_m - k_{rf}$.

Using the CAPM, the investor's required rate of return can be written as follows:

$$k_c = k_{rf} + \beta(k_m - k_{rf}) \tag{12-9}$$

**EXAMPLE: ESTIMATING THE COST OF COMMON STOCK USING THE CAPM**

Wal-Mart's common stock has a beta coefficient of 1.198. Furthermore, on September 1, 2000, the risk-free rate was 6.23 percent, and the expected rate of return on the market portfolio of all risky assets was approximately 14 percent. Using the CAPM from equation 12-9, we can estimate Wal-Mart's cost of capital as follows:

$$\begin{aligned} k_c &= k_{rf} + \beta(k_m - k_{rf}) \\ &= 0.0623 + 1.198(0.14 - 0.0623) = .1553 \text{ or } 15.53\% \end{aligned}$$

Note that the required rate of return we have estimated is the cost of internal common equity because no transaction costs are considered.

FINANCE $ MATTERS

## IPOs: Should a Firm Go Public?

When a privately owned company decides to distribute its shares to the general public, it goes through a process known as an initial public offering or IPO. There are a number of advantages to having a firm's shares traded in the public equity market. These include the following:

- New capital is raised. When the firm sells its shares to the public, it acquires new capital that can be invested in the firm.
- The firm's owners gain liquidity of their share holdings. Publicly traded shares are more easily bought and sold so that the owners can more easily liquidate all or a part of their interest in the firm.
- The firm gains future access to the public capital market. Once a firm has raised capital in the public markets, it is easier to go back a second and third time.
- Being a publicly traded firm may benefit the firm's business. Public firms tend to enjoy a higher profile than their privately held counterparts. This may make it easier to make sales and attract vendors to supply goods and services to the firm.

However, all is not rosy as a publicly held firm. There are a number of potential disadvantages including the following:

- Reporting requirements can be onerous. Publicly held firms are required to file periodic reports with the Securities and Exchange Commission (SEC). This is not only onerous in terms of the time and effort required, but some business owners feel they must reveal information to their competitors that could be potentially damaging.
- Private equity investors now must share any new wealth with the new public investors. Now that the firm is a publicly held company, the new shareholders share on an equal footing with the company founders in the good (and bad) fortune of the firm.
- The private investors lose a degree of control of the organization. Outsiders gain voting control over the firm to the extent that they own its shares.
- An IPO is expensive. A typical firm may spend 15 to 25 percent of the money raised on expenses directly connected to the IPO. This cost is increased further if we consider the cost of lost management time and disruption of business associated with the IPO process.
- Exit of company owners is usually limited. The company founders may want to sell their shares through the IPO, but this is not allowed for an extended period of time. Therefore, the IPO is not usually a good mechanism for cashing out the company founders.
- Everyone involved faces legal liability. The IPO participants are jointly and severally liable for each others' actions. This means that they can be sued for any omissions from the IPO prospectus should the public market valuation fall below the IPO offering price.

A careful weighing of the financial consequences of each of these advantages and disadvantages can provide a company's owners (and management) with some basis for answering the question of whether they want to become a public corporation.

Other sources: Professor Ivo Welch's Web site at http://welch.som.yale.edu provides a wealth of information concerning IPOs.

## Issues in Implementing the CAPM

The CAPM approach has two primary advantages. First, the model is simple and easy to understand and implement. The model variables are readily available from public sources with the possible exception of beta coefficients for small and/or nonpublicly traded firms. Second, because the model does not rely on dividends or any assumption about the growth rate in dividends, it can be applied to companies that do not currently pay dividends or are not expected to experience a constant rate of growth in dividends.

Using the CAPM requires that we obtain estimates of each of the three model variables—$k_{rf}$, $\beta$, and $k_m - k_{rf}$. Let's consider each in turn. First, the analyst has a wide range of U.S. government securities upon which to base an estimate of the risk-free rate. Treasury securities with maturities from 30 days to 20 years are readily available, but the CAPM offers no guidance as to the appropriate choice. In fact, the model itself assumes that there is but one risk-free rate, and it corresponds to a one-period return (the length of the period is not specified, however). Consequently, we are left to our own judgment as to which maturity we should use to represent the risk-free rate. For applications of the cost of capital involving long-term capital expenditure decisions, it seems reasonable to select a risk-free rate of comparable maturity. So, if we are calculating the cost of capital to be used as the basis for evaluating investments that will provide returns over the next 20 years, it seems appropriate to use a risk-free rate corresponding to a U.S. Treasury bond of comparable maturity.

Second, estimates of security beta coefficients are available from a wide variety of investment advisory services, including Merrill Lynch and Value Line, among others. Alternatively, we could collect historical stock market returns for the company of interest as well as a general market index (such as the Standard and Poor's 500 Index) and estimate the stock's beta as the slope of the relationship between the two return series—as we did in Chapter 6. However, because beta estimates are widely available for a large majority of publicly traded firms, analysts frequently rely on published sources for betas.

Finally, estimation of the market risk premium can be accomplished by looking at the history of stock returns and the premium earned over (under) the risk-free rate of interest. In Chapter 6, we reported a summary of the historical returns earned on risk-free securities and common stocks in Figure 6-2. We saw that on average over the last 74 years, common stocks have earned a premium of roughly 7.5 percent over long-term government bonds. Thus, for our purposes, we will utilize this estimate of the market risk premium $(k_m - k_{rf})$ when estimating the investor's required rate of return on equity using the CAPM.

**RELATE TO THE BIG PICTURE**

The capital asset pricing model, or CAPM, is a formal representation of **Principle 1: The Risk-Return Trade-Off—We won't take on additional risk unless we expect to be compensated with additional return**. By "formal" we mean that the specific method of calculating the additional returns needed to compensate for additional risk is specified in the form of an equation—the CAPM. The CAPM's recognition of systematic or nondiversifiable risk as the source of risk that is rewarded in the capital market is a reflection of **Principle 9: All Risk Is Not Equal—Some risk can be diversified away, and some cannot**.

**CONCEPT CHECK**

1. How do you estimate a firm's cost of new debt financing?
2. What are two alternative approaches to estimating a firm's cost of equity financing?
3. What are flotation costs and how do they impact a firm's cost of capital when it issues new bonds or equity?

## THE WEIGHTED AVERAGE COST OF CAPITAL

OBJECTIVE 3 

**Capital structure**
The mix of long-term sources of funds used by the firm.

Now that we have calculated the individual costs of capital for each of the sources of financing the firm might use, we now turn to the combination of these capital costs into a single weighted average cost of capital. To estimate the weighted average cost of capital, we need to know the cost of each of the sources of capital used and the capital structure mix. We use the term **capital structure** to refer to the proportions of each source of financing used by the firm. Although a firm's capital structure can be quite complex, we will focus our examples on the three basic sources of capital: bonds, preferred stock, and common equity.

In words, we calculate the weighted average cost of capital for a firm that uses only debt and common equity using the following equation:

$$\begin{matrix}\textit{weighted}\\ \textit{average cost}\\ \textit{of capital}\end{matrix} = \left[\begin{matrix}\textit{after-tax}\\ \textit{cost of}\\ \textit{debt}\end{matrix} \times \begin{matrix}\textit{proportion}\\ \textit{of debt}\\ \textit{financing}\end{matrix}\right] + \left[\begin{matrix}\textit{cost of}\\ \textit{equity}\end{matrix} \times \begin{matrix}\textit{proportion}\\ \textit{of equity}\\ \textit{financing}\end{matrix}\right]$$

For example, if a firm borrows money at 6 percent after taxes, pays 10 percent for equity, and raises its capital in equal proportions from debt and equity, its weighted average cost of capital is 8 percent, that is,

$$\begin{matrix}\textit{weighted}\\ \textit{average cost}\\ \textit{of capital}\end{matrix} = [.06 \times .5] + [.10 \times .5] = .08 \textit{ or } 8\%$$

In practice, the calculation of the cost of capital is generally more complex than this example. For one thing, firms often have multiple debt issues with different required rates of return, and they also use preferred equity as well as common equity financing. Furthermore, when new common equity capital is raised, it is sometimes the result of retaining and reinvesting the firm's current period earnings and, at other times, it involves a new stock offering. In the case of retained earnings, the firm does not incur the costs associated with selling new common stock. This means that equity from retained earnings is less costly than a new stock offering. In the examples that follow, we will address each of these complications.

## Capital Structure Weights

A critical element in the analysis of new investments is an estimate of the cost of capital—the discount rate—to be used to calculate the *NPV* for the project. We calculate a cost of capital so we can evaluate the firm's investment opportunities. Remember that the cost of capital should reflect the riskiness of the project being evaluated, so that a firm may calculate multiple costs of capital where it makes investments in multiple divisions or business units having different risk characteristics. Thus, for the calculated cost of capital to be meaningful, it must correspond directly to the riskiness of the particular project being analyzed. That is, in theory the cost of capital should reflect the particular way in which the funds are raised (the capital structure used) and the systematic risk characteristics of the project. Consequently, the correct way to calculate capital structure weights is to use the actual dollar amounts of the various sources of capital actually used by the firm.[1]

In practice, the mixture of financing sources used by a firm will vary from year to year. For this reason, many firms find it expedient to use **target capital structure proportions** in calculating the firm's weighted average cost of capital. For example, a firm might use its target mix of 40 percent debt and 60 percent equity to calculate its weighted average cost of capital even though, in that particular year, it raised the majority of its financing requirements by borrowing. Similarly, it would continue to use the target proportions in the subsequent year when it might raise the majority of its financing needs by reinvesting earnings or through a new stock offering.

**Target capital structure proportions**
The mix of financing sources that the firm plans to maintain through time.

[1]There are instances when we will want to calculate the cost of capital for the firm as a whole. In this case, the appropriate weights to use are based upon the market value of the various capital sources used by the firm. Market values rather than book values properly reflect the sources of financing used by a firm at any particular point in time. However, where a firm is privately owned, it is not possible to get market values of its securities, and book values are often used.

**TABLE 12-1**
Calculating the Weighted Average Cost of Capital

**Panel A: Common equity raised by retaining earnings**

| Source of Capital | Capital Structure Weights | × | Cost of Captial | = | Product |
|---|---|---|---|---|---|
| Bonds | $w_d$ | | $k_d(1 - T_c)$ | | $w_d \cdot k_d(1 - T_c)$ |
| Preferred stock | $w_{ps}$ | | $k_{ps}$ | | $w_{ps} \cdot k_{ps}$ |
| Common equity | | | | | |
| Retained earnings | $w_{cs}$ | | $k_{cs}$ | | $w_{cs} \cdot k_{cs}$ |
| Sum = | 100% | | | | $k_{wacc}$ |

**Panel B: Common equity raised by selling new common stock**

| Source of Capital | Capital Structure Weights | × | Cost of Captial | = | Product |
|---|---|---|---|---|---|
| Bonds | $w_d$ | | $k_d(1 - T_c)$ | | $w_d \cdot k_d(1 - T_c)$ |
| Preferred stock | $w_{ps}$ | | $k_{ps}$ | | $w_{ps} \cdot k_{ps}$ |
| Common equity | | | | | |
| New stock offering | $w_{ncs}$ | | $k_{ncs}$ | | $w_{ncs} \cdot k_{ncs}$ |
| Sum = | 100% | | | | $k_{wacc}$ |

## Calculating the Weighted Average Cost of Capital

The weighted average cost of capital, $k_{wacc,}$ is simply a weighted average of all the capital costs incurred by the firm. Table 12-1 illustrates the procedure used to esimate $k_{wacc}$, for a firm that has debt, preferred stock, and common equity in its target capital structure mix. Note that in Panel A, the firm is able to finance all its target capital structure requirements for common equity through the retention of firm earnings, and in Panel B, it utilizes a new equity offering. For example, if the firm targets 75 percent equity financing and has current earnings of \$750,000, then it can raise up to \$750,000/.75 = \$1,000,000 in new financing before it has to sell new equity. For \$1,000,000 or less in capital spending, the firm's weighted average cost of capital would be calculated using the cost of equity from retained earnings (following Panel A of Table 12-1). For more than \$1,000,000 in new capital, the cost of capital would rise to reflect the impact of the higher cost of using new common stock (following Panel B of Table 12-1).

### EXAMPLE: ESTIMATING THE WEIGHTED AVERAGE COST OF CAPITAL

Ash, Inc.'s capital structure and estimated capital costs are found in Table 12-2. Note that the sum of the capital structure weights must sum to 100 percent if we have properly accounted for all sources of financing and in the correct amounts. For example, Ash plans to invest a total of \$3 million in common equity into the \$5 million investment. Because Ash has earnings equal to the \$3,000,000 it needs in new equity financing, the entire amount of new equity will be raised by retaining earnings.

We calculate the weighted average cost of capital following the procedure described in Panel A of Table 12-1 and using the information found in Table 12-2. The resulting calculations are found in Panel A of Table 12-3, in which Ash, Inc.'s weighted average cost of capital for up to \$5,000,000 in new financing is found to be 12.7 percent.

If Ash needs more than $5,000,000, then it will not have any retained earnings to provide the additional equity capital. Thus, to maintain its desired 60 percent equity financing proportion, Ash will now have to issue new equity that costs 18 percent. Panel B of Table 12-3 contains the calculation of Ash's weighted average cost of capital for more than $5,000,000. The resulting cost is 13.9 percent.

In practice, many firms calculate only one cost of capital using a cost of equity capital that ignores the transaction costs associated with raising new equity capital. In essence, they would use the capital cost calculated for Ash in Panel A of Table 12-3 regardless of the level of new financing for the year. Although this is technically incorrect, it is understandable given the difficulties involved in estimating equity capital costs.[2]

**TABLE 12-2**
Calculating Structure and Capital Costs for Ash, Inc.

| Source of Capital | Amount of Funds Raised ($) | Percentage of Total | After-tax Cost of Capital |
|---|---|---|---|
| Bonds | $1,750,000 | 35% | 7% |
| Preferred stock | 250,000 | 5% | 13% |
| Common equity | | | |
| Retained earnings | 3,000,000 | 60% | 16% |
| | $5,000,000 | 100% | |

**TABLE 12-3**
Weighted Average Cost of Capital for Ash, Inc.

**Panel A: Cost of capital for $0 to $5,000,000 in new capital**

| Source of Capital | Capital Structure Weights | After-tax Cost of Capital | Product |
|---|---|---|---|
| Bonds | 35% | 7% | 2.45% |
| Preferred stock | 5% | 13% | 0.65% |
| Common equity | | | |
| Retained earnings | 60% | 16% | 9.60% |
| | 100% | $k_{wacc}$ | = 12.70% |

**Panel B: Cost of capital for more than $5,000,000**

| Source of Capital | Capital Structure Weights | After-tax Cost of Capital | Product |
|---|---|---|---|
| Bonds | 35% | 7% | 2.45% |
| Preferred stock | 5% | 13% | 0.65% |
| Common equity | | | |
| Common stock | 60% | 18% | 10.80% |
| | 100% | $k_{wacc}$ | = 13.90% |

[2]For a discussion of the imprecise nature of equity capital cost estimates, see Eugene F. Fama and Kenneth R. French, 1997 "Industry costs of equity," *Journal of Financial Economics* 43, 153–193.

## COST OF CAPITAL IN PRACTICE: BRIGGS & STRATTON

Briggs & Stratton is the world's largest producer of air-cooled gasoline engines. For many years, the firm also was the world's largest producer of locks for automobiles and trucks. However, on February 27, 1995, the automobile lock business was spun off to the stockholders, leaving Briggs & Stratton in a single business (producing air-cooled gasoline engines for outdoor power equipment).

Each year Briggs & Stratton engages in the exercise of estimating its cost of capital. The process entails a calculation very similar to that used by the hypothetical Ash, Inc. The differences, as we shall see, relate to simplifications, not additional complexities. The example calculations we present here are for 2001 and reflect the procedure used by the firm.

### Cost of Equity

Briggs & Stratton uses the CAPM to estimate its cost of equity capital as follows:

$$k_c = k_{rf} + \beta(k_m - k_{rf}) \quad \textbf{(12-9)}$$

$$k_c = .0605 + .83(.06) = .1103 \text{ or } 11.03\%$$

The risk-free rate ($k_{rf}$) is estimated as a weighted average of 30-year government bond interest rates from March 2000. The firm's beta coefficient ($\beta$) is taken from *Value Line*. Finally, the market risk premium ($k_m - k_{rf}$) is estimated as the historical average difference in the return to equities and long-term government bonds.

Note that Briggs & Stratton does not make any adjustment for the influence of transaction costs nor does it bother with the nuance of estimating the fraction of its target equity component that could come from retained earnings.

### Cost of Debt

Briggs & Stratton estimates the before-tax cost of debt financing to be 7.5 percent. The firm uses its tax rate of 38 percent to calculate the after-tax cost of debt financing as follows:

$$k_d (1 - \text{tax rate}) = .075\ (1 - .38) = .0465 \text{ or } 4.65\%$$

### Weighted Average Cost of Capital for 2001

The weighted average cost of capital is calculated using a formula very similar to the one laid out in equation 12-2. The only difference—as we see following—is the lumping of all equity financing into one component with no special consideration being given to the cost of retained earnings versus the sale of new equity, that is,

$$k_{wacc} = K_d (1 - T_c)\, w_d + k_c w_{cs} \quad \textbf{(12-10)}$$

where $k_d$ and $k_c$ are the costs of debt and equity, $T_c$ is the corporate tax rate, and $w_d$ and $w_{cs}$ are the weights attached to debt and equity, respectively.

Briggs & Stratton bases its capital structure weights upon its target capital structure. The weighted average cost of capital for 2001 is calculated in Table 12-4.

FINANCE MATTERS

## How Do Managers Resolve Ethical Decisions?

What makes a managerial choice an ethical one? Brief et al.[a] (1991) suggest that if the decision entails reflection on the moral significance of the choice, then the choice is an ethical one. How do managers resolve ethical dilemmas? There is some evidence suggesting that two factors come to bear on ethical choices: values and accountability.

We will consider two social value systems that are present in Western society, which are particularly relevant to the study of finance. These are the Smithian and Humanitarian value systems. The Smithian system is derived from the writings of the 19th-century moral philosopher and political economist Adam Smith. This value system is reflected in the current-day teachings of economists such as Milton Friedman[b] (1962). Briefly, this system holds that when individuals pursue their own self-interest in the marketplace, they contribute to the good of society. At the firm level, this system provides the basis for the market system and is used as the basis for corporate self-interest. In contrast, the Humanitarian system is based on the fundamental premise of the equality of individuals in society. This system seeks to protect individuals from the harshness of the market system and to promote equality of opportunity.

Personal value systems are not the only influence on managerial decisions that have ethical implications. Managers are influenced by their perception of the value systems of the individuals to whom they are held accountable. That is, ethical choices made by managers are influenced by the values they believe are held by the person to whom they are accountable.[c] Arendt (1951, 1977) provides evidence that suggests that the effects of accountability may be more profound than those of the individual manager's values. Consequently, the potentially overpowering effects of hierarchical accountability may lead individual managers not to construe the moral significance attached to the choices they make. They may see no choice but to comply with the higher authority. Brief et al. (1991) provide empirical evidence bearing on the question of the relative importance of personal values versus accountability in the choices made by individuals. Using a set of experiments involving 135 M.B.A. students, they concluded that personal values may not be related to how an individual chooses to resolve ethical dilemmas when the choices (values) of the higher authority are known explicitly.

Note that we have not addressed the normative issue: How should ethical dilemmas be resolved? Instead, we have addressed the question, How do managers actually deal with ethical choices? The principal finding of the studies we have reviewed is that the *perceived values of one's superiors* have a profound impact on the way in which a subordinate resolves ethical dilemmas. So choose your superior carefully.

Sources: [a]A. Brief, J. M. Dukerich, and L. I. Doran, "Resolving Ethical Dilemmas in Management: Experimental Investigations of Values, Accountability and Choice," *Journal of Applied Social Psychology* 21 (1991): 380–96; [b]M. Friedman, *Capitalism and Freedom* (Chicago: University of Chicago Press, 1962); [c]H. Arendt, *The Origins of Totalitarianism* (New York: Harcourt Brace, 1951); H. Arendt, *Eichmann in Jerusalem* (New York: Penguin Books, 1977).

**TABLE 12-4**
Weighted Average Cost of Capital for Briggs & Stratton, 2001

| Source of Capital | Capital Sources | Percent of Capital | | Cost of Capital | | Weighted Cost of Capital |
|---|---|---|---|---|---|---|
| Debt | $251.6 million | 23% | × | 4.65% | = | 1.1% |
| Equity | 843.4 million | 77% | × | 11.03% | = | 8.5% |
| | $1,095.0 million | 100.0% | | | | 9.6% |

**CONCEPT CHECK**

1. What does the term "capital structure" mean and how is it used in evaluating a firm's weighted average cost of capital?
2. What is the source of capital structure weights that a firm should use when calculating its weighted average cost of capital?

**TABLE 12-5**
Estimating PepsiCo's Cost of Debt

| | Pretax Cost of Debt | × | (1−Tax Rate) | After-Tax Cost of Debt |
|---|---|---|---|---|
| Restaurants | 8.93% | × | .62 | 5.54% |
| Snack foods | 8.43% | × | .62 | 5.23% |
| Beverages | 8.51% | × | .62 | 5.28% |

**TABLE 12-6**
Cost of Equity Capital for PepsiCo's Operating Divisions

| | Risk-Free Rate | + | Beta | Expected Market Return | − | Risk-Free Rate | = | Cost of Equity |
|---|---|---|---|---|---|---|---|---|
| Restaurants | 7.28% | + | 1.17 | (11.48% | − | 7.28%) | = | 12.20% |
| Snack foods | 7.28% | + | 1.02 | (11.48% | − | 7.28%) | = | 11.56% |
| Beverages | 7.28% | + | 1.07 | (11.48% | − | 7.28%) | = | 11.77% |

## CALCULATING DIVISIONAL COSTS OF CAPITAL: PEPSICO, INC.

If a firm operates in multiple industries where each has its own particular risk characteristics, should it use different capital costs for each division? **Principle 1** suggests that the financial manager should recognize these risk differences in estimating the cost of capital to use in each division. This is exactly what PepsiCo did prior to February 1997, when it operated in three basic industries.

PepsiCo went to great lengths to estimate the cost of capital for each of its three major operating divisions (restaurants, snack foods, and beverages).[3] We will briefly summarize the basic elements of the calculations involved in these estimates, including the cost of debt financing, the cost of common equity, the target capital structure weights, and the weighted average cost of capital.

Table 12-5 contains the estimates of the after-tax cost of debt for each of PepsiCo's three divisions. Table 12-6 contains the estimates of the cost of equity capital using the CAPM. We will not explain the intricacies of their method for estimating divisional betas, except to say that they make use of beta estimates for a number of competitor firms from each of the operating divisions, which involves making appropriate adjustments for differences in the use of financial leverage across the competitor firms used in the analysis.[4]

The weighted average cost of capital for each of the divisions is estimated in Table 12-7 using the capital costs estimated in Tables 12-5 and 12-6 and using PepsiCo's target capital structure weights for each operating division. Note that the weighted average costs of capital for all three divisions fall within a very narrow range, between 10.08 percent and 10.29 percent.

[3]PepsiCo spun off its restaurants division in February 1997. However, the example used here was based on the pre-spinoff company.

[4]This method of using betas from comparable firms is sometimes referred to as the pure play method, because the analyst seeks independent beta estimates for firms engaged in only one business (i.e., restaurants or beverages). The betas for these pure play companies are then used to estimate the beta for a business or division.

**TABLE 12-7**
PepsiCo's Weighted Average Cost of Captial for Each of Its Operating Divisions

| | Cost of Equity Times the Target Equity Ratio | + | Cost of Debt Times the Target Debt Ratio | = | Weighted Average Cost of Capital |
|---|---|---|---|---|---|
| Restaurants | (12.20%)(0.70) | + | (5.54%)(0.30) | = | 10.20% |
| Snack foods | (11.56%)(0.80) | + | (5.23%)(0.20) | = | 10.29% |
| Beverages | (11.77%)(0.74) | + | (5.28%)(0.26) | = | 10.08% |

**CONCEPT CHECK**

1. Why do firms calculate individual costs of capital for their operating divisions?
2. How should divisional costs of capital be used in evaluating a firm's new investment opportunities?

## USING A FIRM'S COST OF CAPITAL TO EVALUATE NEW CAPITAL INVESTMENTS

Now that we have learned the principles used to estimate a firm's cost of capital, it is tempting to use this capital cost to evaluate all the firm's investment opportunities. This can produce some very expensive mistakes. *Recall that the cost of capital depends pri-marily on the use of the funds, not their source*. Consequently, the appropriate cost of capital for individual investment opportunities should, in theory and practice, reflect the individual risk characteristics of the investment. With this principle in mind, we reason that the firm's weighted average cost of capital is the appropriate discount rate for estimating a project's *NPV* only when the project has similar risk characteristics to the firm. This would be true, for example, when the investment involves expanding an existing facility but would not be true when the investment involves entering into a completely new business with different risk characteristics.

What does it mean to say that a firm and an investment opportunity have similar risk characteristics? We can think of an investment's risk characteristics as coming from two sources: business risk and financial risk. By **business risk** we mean the potential variability in the firm's expected earnings before interest and taxes (EBIT). In Chapter 6, we learned that investors should not be worried about total variability but should only be concerned about systematic variability. **Financial risk** refers to the added variability in earnings available to a firm's shareholders and the added chance of insolvency caused by the use of securities bearing a fixed rate of return in the firm's financial structure. For example, in Chapter 3, we learned that firms that use higher levels of financial leverage also experience higher volatility in earnings available to the common stockholders. This higher volatility leads investors to require higher rates of return, which means a higher cost of capital for the project.

**Business risk**
The potential variability in a firm's earnings before interest and taxes resulting from the nature of the firm's business endeavors.

**Financial risk**
The added variability in earnings available to a firm's shareholders and the additional risk of insolvency caused by the use of financing sources that require a fixed return.

In summary, the firm's weighted average cost of capital is the appropriate discount rate for evaluating the *NPV* of investments whose business and financial risks are similar to those of the firm as a whole. See Table 12-8 on page 398 for a summary of the formulas involved in estimating the weighted average cost of capital. If either of these sources of project risk is different from the risks of the firm, then the analyst must alter the estimate of the cost of capital to reflect these differences. If financial risk is different, then this calls for the use of different financial mix ratios when calculating the weighted average cost of capital, as well as estimates of individual capital costs that properly reflect these financial

**TABLE 12-8**
Summary of Cost of Capital Formulas

1. The After-Tax Cost of Debt, $k_d(1 - T_c)$
   a. Calculate the before-tax cost of debt, $k_d$, as follows:

$$NP_d = \sum_{t=1}^{n} \frac{\$I_t}{(1 + k_d)^t} + \frac{\$M}{(1 + k_d)^n} \tag{12-2}$$

where $NP_d$ is the net proceeds received by the firm from the sale of each bond; $\$I_t$ is the dollar amount of interest paid to the investor in period $t$ for each bond; $\$M$ is the maturity value of each bond paid in period $n$; $k_d$ is the before-tax cost of debt to the firm; and $n$ is the number of periods to maturity.

   b. Calculate the after-tax cost of debt as follows:

after-tax cost of debt $= k_d(1 - T_c)$
where $T_c$ is the corporate tax rate.

2. The Cost of Preferred Stock, $k_{ps}$

$$k_{ps} = \frac{\text{preferred stock dividend}}{NP_{ps}} \tag{12-5}$$

where $NP_{ps}$ is the net proceeds per share of new preferred stock sold after flotation costs.

3. The Cost of Common Equity
   a. Method 1: dividend growth mode
   Calculate the cost of internal common equity (retained earnings), $k_c$, as follows:

$$k_{cs} = \frac{D_1}{P_{cs}} + g \tag{12-7}$$

where $D_1$ is the expected dividend for the next year, $P_{cs}$ is the current price of the firm's common stock, and $g$ is the rate of growth in dividends per year.
Calculate the cost of external common equity (new stock offering), $k_{ncs}$, as follows:

$$k_{ncs} = \frac{D_1}{NP_{cs}} + g \tag{12-8}$$

where $NP_{cs}$ is the net proceeds to the firm after flotation costs per share of stock sold.

   b. Method 2: capital asset pricing model, $k_c$

$$k_c = k_{rf} + \beta(k_m - k_{rf}) \tag{12-9}$$

where the risk-free rate is $k_{rf}$; the systematic risk of the common stock's returns relative to the market as a whole or the stock's beta coefficient is $\beta$; and the market risk premium, which is equal to the difference in the expected rate of return for the market as a whole (i.e., the expected rate of return for the "average security" minus the risk-free rate), is $k_m - k_{rf}$.

4. The Weighted Average Cost of Capital

$$k_{wacc} = w_d \times k_d(1 - T_c) + w_{ps} \times k_{ps} + w_{cs} \times k_{cs} + w_{ncs} \times k_{ncs}$$

where the $w_i$ terms represent the market value weights associated with the firm's use of each of its sources of financing. Note that we are simply calculating a weighted average of the costs of each of the firm's sources of capital where the weights reflect the firm's relative use of each source.

risks. If operating-risk characteristics differ, then once again capital costs must be adjusted to reflect this difference. In our discussion of PepsiCo, we saw that it estimates three different weighted average costs of capital to reflect what it feels are meaningful differences in the operating and financial risk characteristics of its three operating divisions. This practice reflects PepsiCo's adherence to the principle that the cost of capital is primarily a function of the use of the capital (i.e., the riskiness of the different operating divisions).

## RELATE TO THE BIG PICTURE

The firm's weighted average cost of capital provides the appropriate discount rate for evaluating new projects only where the projects offer the same riskiness as the firm as a whole. This limitation of the usefulness of the firm's weighted average cost of capital is a direct extension of **Principle 1: The Risk-Return Trade-Off—We won't take on additional risk unless we expect to be compensated with additional return**. If project risk differs from that of the firm, then the firm's cost of capital (which reflects the risk of the firm's investment portfolio) is no longer the appropriate cost of capital for the project. For this reason, firms that invest in multiple divisions or business units that have different risk characteristics should calculate a different cost of capital for each division. In theory, each individual investment opportunity has its own unique risk attributes and correspondingly should have a unique cost of capital. However, given the impreciseness with which we estimate the cost of capital, we generally calculate the cost of capital for each operating division of the firm, not each project.

## CONCEPT CHECK

1. What determines a firm's business risk?
2. What is meant by a firm's financial risk?

## FINANCE MATTERS

### Why Do Interest Rates Differ Between Countries?

If borrowers and lenders can freely obtain money in one country and invest it in another, why are interest rates not the same the world over? Stated somewhat differently, if capital markets are fully integrated and money flows to the highest rate of interest, it would seem that the forces of competition would make interest rates the same for a given risk borrower.

Let's consider a hypothetical example to see how this might work. Assume that a U.S. borrower can borrow 1,000 yen in Japan for a 5 percent interest paying back 1,050 yen in 1 year. Alternatively, the U.S. firm can borrow an equivalent amount in the United States and pay 15.5 percent interest. Why the big difference? Is capital 10.5 percent cheaper in Japan, and if so, why don't U.S. firms simply switch to the Japanese capital market for their funds? The answer, as we will now illustrate, lies in the differences in the anticipated rates of inflation for Japan versus the United States.

Although it was not obvious in the preceding example, we assumed a zero rate of inflation for the Japanese economy and

(continued)

FINANCE MATTERS

## Why Do Interest Rates Differ Between Countries? *(continued)*

a 10 percent rate of inflation for the U.S. economy. With a zero anticipated rate of inflation, the nominal rate of interest in Japan is equal to the real rate of 5 percent. Under these assumptions, the nominal rate in the United States can be calculated using the Fisher model as follows:*

$$\text{U.S. nominal rate of interest} = \frac{(1 + \text{real rate, U.S.})}{(1 + \text{inflation rate, U.S.})} - 1$$
$$= (1 + .05)(1 + .10) - 1 = .155 \text{ or } 15.5\%$$

To understand the reason for the different interest rates in Japan and the United States, we must extend the Fisher model to its international counterpart.

**The International Fisher Effect**

In an international context, we must recognize that there can be different rates of inflation among the different countries of the world. For example, the Fisher model for the nominal rate in the home or domestic country ($r_{n,h}$) is a function of the real interest rate in the home country ($r_{r,h}$) and the anticipated rate of inflation in the home country ($i_h$). For the domestic economy, the Fisher relationship can be described as follows:

$$r_{n,h} = (1 + r_{r,h})(1 + i_h) - 1 = r_{r,h} + (i_h)(r_{r,h}) + i_h \quad (1a)$$

Using "*f*" as a subscript to denote a foreign country, we can define a similar relationship for any foreign country (Japan in our previous example):

$$r_{n,f} = (1 + r_{r,f})(1 + i_f) - 1 = r_{r,f} + (i_f)(r_{r,f}) + i_f \quad (1b)$$

The international version of the Fisher model prescribes that real returns will be equalized across countries through arbitrage, that is,

$$r_{r,h} = r_{r,f}$$

Solving for the real rates of interest in equations 1a and 1b and equating the results produces the international version of the Fisher model, that is,

$$r_{n,h} - (i_h)(r_{r,h}) - i_h = r_{n,f} - (i_f)(r_{r,f}) - i_f \quad (2)$$

For simplicity analysts frequently ignore the intermediate product terms on both sides of equation 3 such that equation 2 reduces to the following:

$$r_{n,h} - i_h = r_{n,f} - i_f$$

*The Fisher model or Fisher effect was introduced earlier in Chapter 2.

Rearranging terms, we get the following relationship between nominal interest rates in the domestic and foreign country and the differences in anticipated inflation in the two countries:

$$r_{n,h} - r_{n,f} = i_h - i_f \quad (3)$$

Thus differences in observed nominal rates of interest should equal differences in the expected rates of inflation between the two countries. This means that when we compare the interest rates for similar loans in two countries and they are not the same, we should immediately suspect that the expected rates of inflation for the two economies differ by an amount roughly equal to the interest rate differential!

**Interest Rates and Currency Exchange Rates: Interest Rate Parity**

Economists have formalized the relationship between interest rates of different countries in the interest rate parity theorem. This theorem is as follows:

$$\frac{(1 + r_{n,h})}{(1 + r_{n,f})} = \frac{E_1}{E_0} \quad (4)$$

where $r_{n,h}$ is the domestic one-period rate of interest, $r_{n,f}$ is the corresponding rate of interest in a foreign country, and the $E_j$ are exchange rates corresponding to the current period (i.e., the spot rate, $E_0$) and one-period hence (i.e., the one-period forward rate, $E_1$).

To illustrate, let's consider the previous example where the domestic one-period interest rate ($r_{n,h}$) is 15.5 percent, the Japanese rate of interest ($r_{n,f}$) is 5 percent, the spot exchange ratio ($E_0$) is \$1 to 1 yen, and the forward exchange rate ($E_1$) is \$1.10 to 1 yen. Substituting into equation 1 produces the following result:

$$\frac{(1 + .155)}{(1 + .05)} = \frac{1.1}{1} = 1.10$$

The key thing to note here is that nominal interest rates are tied to exchange rates, and as we learned earlier, differences in nominal rates of interest are tied to expected rates of inflation.

Why would we expect the interest rate parity relationship to hold? The answer lies in the greed of investors who stand ready to engage in arbitrage (trading) to enforce this relationship (within the bounds of transaction costs). Formally, we rely on the fundamental dictum of an efficient market (the law of one price). Very simply, the exchange-adjusted prices of identical loans must be within transaction costs of equality or the opportunity exists for traders to buy the low cost loan and sell the higher priced loan for a profit.

Source: W. Carl Kester and Timothy A. Luehrman, "What Makes You Think U.S. Capital Is So Expensive?" *Journal of Applied Corporate Finance* (Summer 1992): 29–41.

## HOW FINANCIAL MANAGERS USE THIS MATERIAL

The opportunity cost of capital is critically important for every firm, and most publicly traded firms estimate it at least annually and some revise their estimate quarterly. The cost of capital is not an abstract concept but a very important factor of corporate business decision making. Most firms rely on the weighted average cost of capital (calculated using current investor required rates of return and target financing proportions or weights).

Our discussion was kept purposely basic because this reflects the way in which the cost of capital is actually calculated. Specifically, firms that have two or more operating divisions will usually estimate a cost of capital for each division. However, when using the cost of capital for evaluating operating results and determining incentive compensation, even multi-division firms sometimes use a single weighted average cost of capital. This is sometimes done to simplify the basis for determining bonuses, and in other instances, it is done in an effort to remove the cost of capital as an element of discussion in determining compensation. The key fact here is that firms do calculate their cost of capital, they use it to make investment decisions and to determine incentive compensation, and they "try to keep it simple."

## SUMMARY

Consider the following investment opportunity. The investment requires that the firm invest $75 million to renovate a production facility that will provide after-tax savings to the firm of $25 million per year over the next 5 years. In Chapter 9, we learned that the proper way to evaluate whether or not to undertake the investment involves calculating its net present value (*NPV*). To calculate *NPV*, we must estimate both project cash flows and an appropriate discount rate. In this chapter, we have learned that the proper discount rate is a weighted average of the after-tax costs of all the firm's sources of financing. In addition, we have learned that the cost of capital for any source of financing is estimated by first calculating the investor's required rate of return, then making appropriate adjustments for flotation costs and corporate taxes (where appropriate). If the weighted average cost of capital is 12 percent, then the *NPV* of the plant renovation is $15,120 and the investment should be made. The reason is that the project is expected to increase the wealth of the firm's shareholders by $15,120. Very simply, the project is expected to return a present value amount of $15,120 more than the firm's sources of capital require, and since the common stockholders get any residual value left after returning the promised return to each of the other sources of capital, they receive the *NPV*.

To calculate the after-tax cost of debt capital, we must first calculate the before-tax cost of capital using the following formula:

$$NP_d = \sum_{t=1}^{n} \frac{\$I_t}{(1 + k_d)^t} + \frac{\$M}{(1 + k_d)^n} \quad \textbf{(12-2)}$$

where $NP_d$ = the net proceeds received by the firm from the sale of each bond

$\$I_t$ = the dollar amount of interest paid to the investor in period $t$ for each bond

$\$M$ = the maturity value of each bond paid in period $n$

$k_d$ = the before-tax cost of debt to the firm

$n$ = the number of periods to maturity

Next, we adjust for the effects of corporate taxes because the bond interest is deducted from the firm's taxable income.

after-tax cost of debt = $k_d(1 - \text{corporate tax rate})$

The cost of preferred stock is relatively easy to calculate. We calculate the dividend yield on the preferred issue using net proceeds from the sale of each new share as follows:

$$\text{cost of preferred stock} = \frac{\text{preferred stock dividend}}{\text{net proceeds per preferred share}} \quad \textbf{(12-5)}$$

Note that no adjustment is made for corporate taxes because preferred stock dividends, unlike bond interest, are paid with after-tax earnings.

Common equity can be obtained by the firm in one of two ways. First, the firm can retain a portion of its net income after paying common dividends. The retention of earnings constitutes a means of raising common-equity financing internally—that is, no capital market issuance of securities is involved. Second, the firm can also raise equity capital through the sale of a new issue of common stock.

We discussed two methods for estimating the cost of common equity. The first involved using the dividend growth model:

$$k_{cs} = \frac{D_1}{P_{cs}} + g \quad \textbf{(12-7)}$$

where $g$ is the rate at which dividends are expected to grow forever, $k_{cs}$ is the investor's required rate of return, and $P_{cs}$ is the current price of a share of common stock. When a new issue of common shares is issued, the firm incurs flotation costs. These costs reduce the amount of funds the firm receives per share. Consequently, the cost of external common equity using the dividend growth model requires that we substitute the new proceeds per share, $NP_{cs}$, for share price:

$$k_{ncs} = \frac{D_1}{NP_{cs}} + g \quad \textbf{(12-8)}$$

The second method for estimating the cost of common equity involves the use of capital asset pricing model (CAPM), which we first discussed in Chapter 6. There we learned that the CAPM provides a basis for evaluating investor's required rates of return on common equity, $k_c$, using three variables:

1. the risk-free rate, $k_{rf}$;
2. the systematic risk of the common stock's returns relative to the market as a whole or the stock's beta coefficient, $\beta$; and
3. the market risk premium which is equal to the difference in the expected rate of return for the market as a whole—that is, the expected rate of return for the "average security" minus the risk-free rate, $k_m - k_{rf}$

The CAPM is written as follows:

$$k_c = k_{rf} + \beta(k_m - k_{rf}) \quad \textbf{(12-9)}$$

We found that all of the variables on the right side of equation (12-9) could be obtained from public sources for larger, publicly traded firms. However, for non–publicly traded firms, the CAPM is more difficult to apply in the estimation of investor-required rates of return.

**OBJECTIVE 3** 

The firm's weighted average cost of capital, $k_{wacc}$, can be defined as follows:

$$k_{wacc} = w_d \times k_d(1 - T_c) + w_{ps} \times k_{ps} + w_{cs} \times k_{cs} + w_{ncs} \times k_{ncs}$$

where the $w$ terms represent the market value weights associated with the firm's use of each of its sources of financing. Note that we are simply calculating a weighted average of the costs of each of the firm's sources of capital where the weights reflect the firm's relative use of each source.

The weights used to calculate $k_{wacc}$ should theoretically reflect the market values of each capital source as a fraction of the total market value of all capital sources (i.e., the market value of the firm). However, the analyst frequently finds the use of market value weights is impractical, either because the firm's securities are not publicly traded or because all capital sources are not used in proportion to their makeup of the firm's target capital structure in every financing episode. In these instances, we found that the weights should be the firm's long-term target financial mix.

The firm's weighted average cost of capital will reflect the operating or business risk of the firm's present set of investments and the financial risks attendant upon the way in which those assets are financed. Therefore, this cost of capital estimate is useful only for evaluating new investment opportunities that have similar business and financial risks. Remember that the primary determinant of the cost of capital for a particular investment is the risk of the investment itself, not the source of the capital. Multidivision firms such as PepsiCo resolve this problem by calculating a different cost of capital for each of their major operating divisions.

## KEY TERMS

**Business risk, 397**

**Capital asset pricing model, 388**

**Capital structure, 390**

**Financial policy, 383**

**Financial risk, 397**

**Flotation costs, 383**

**Investor's required rate of return, 382**

**Target capital structure proportions, 391**

**Weighted average cost of capital, 383**

my**PHLIP**

Go To:
http://www.prenhall.com/keown
for downloads and current events associated with this chapter

## STUDY QUESTIONS

**12-1.** Define the term *cost of capital.*

**12-2.** Why do we calculate a firm's weighted average cost of capital?

**12-3.** In computing the cost of capital, which sources of capital do we consider?

**12-4.** How does a firm's tax rate affect its cost of capital? What is the effect of the flotation costs associated with a new security issue?

**12-5.** **a.** Distinguish between internal common equity and new common stock.

**b.** Why is a cost associated with internal common equity?

**c.** Describe the two approaches that could be used in computing the cost of common equity.

**12-6.** What might we expect to see in practice in the relative costs of different sources of capital?

## SELF-TEST PROBLEMS

**ST-1.** (*Individual costs of capital*) Compute the cost for the following sources of financing:

**a.** A \$1,000 par value bond with a market price of \$970 and a coupon interest rate of 10 percent. Flotation costs for a new issue would be approximately 5 percent. The bonds mature in 10 years and the corporate tax rate is 34 percent.

**b.** A preferred stock selling for \$100 with an annual dividend payment of \$8. If the company sells a new issue, the flotation cost will be \$9 per share. The company's marginal tax rate is 30 percent.

**c.** Internally generated common stock totaling \$4.8 million. The price of the common stock is \$75 per share, and the dividend per share was \$9.80 last year. The dividend is not expected to change in the future.

**d.** New common stock where the most recent dividend was \$2.80. The company's dividends per share should continue to increase at an 8 percent growth rate into the indefinite future. The market price of the stock is currently \$53; however, flotation costs of \$6 per share are expected if the new stock is issued.

**ST-2.** (*Weighted average cost of capital*) The capital structure for the Carion Corporation is provided below. The company plans to maintain its debt structure in the future. If the firm has a 5.5 percent after-tax cost of debt, a 13.5 percent cost of preferred stock, and an 18 percent cost of common stock, what is the firm's weighted average cost of capital?

| Capital Structure ($000) | |
|---|---|
| Bonds | $1,083 |
| Preferred stock | 268 |
| Common stock | 3,681 |
| | $5,032 |

## STUDY PROBLEMS (SET A)

**12-1A.** (*Individual or component costs of capital*) Compute the cost for the following:

**a.** A bond that has a $1,000 par value (face value) and a contract or coupon interest rate of 11 percent. A new issue would have a flotation cost of 5 percent of the $1,125 market value. The bonds mature in 10 years. The firm's average tax rate is 30 percent and its marginal tax rate is 34 percent.

**b.** A new common stock issue that paid a $1.80 dividend last year. The par value of the stock is $15, and earnings per share have grown at a rate of 7 percent per year. This growth rate is expected to continue into the foreseeable future. The company maintains a constant dividend-earnings ratio of 30 percent. The price of this stock is now $27.50, but 5 percent flotation costs are anticipated.

**c.** Internal common equity where the current market price of the common stock is $43. The expected dividend this coming year should be $3.50, increasing thereafter at a 7 percent annual growth rate. The corporation's tax rate is 34 percent.

**d.** A preferred stock paying a 9 percent dividend on a $150 par value. If a new issue is offered, flotation costs will be 12 percent of the current price of $175.

**e.** A bond selling to yield 12 percent after flotation costs, but prior to adjusting for the marginal corporate tax rate of 34 percent. In other words, 12 percent is the rate that equates the net proceeds from the bond with the present value of the future cash flows (principal and interest).

**12-2A.** (*Individual or component costs of capital*) Compute the cost for the following:

**a.** A bond selling to yield 8 percent after flotation costs, but prior to adjusting for the marginal corporate tax rate of 34 percent. In other words, 8 percent is the rate that equates the net proceeds from the bond with the present value of the future cash flows (principal and interest).

**b.** A new common stock issue that paid a $1.05 dividend last year. The par value of the stock is $2, and the earnings per share have grown at a rate of 5 percent per year. This growth rate is expected to continue into the foreseeable future. The company maintains a constant dividend-earnings ratio of 40 percent. The price of this stock is now $25, but 9 percent flotation costs are anticipated.

**c.** A bond that has a $1,000 par value and a contract or coupon interest rate of 12 percent. A new issue would net the company 90 percent of the $1,150 market value. The bonds mature in 20 years, the firm's average tax rate is 30 percent, and its marginal tax rate is 34 percent.

**d.** A preferred stock paying a 7 percent dividend on a $100 par value. If a new issue is offered, the company can expect to net $85 per share.

**e.** Internal common equity where the current market price of the common stock is $38. The expected dividend this forthcoming year should be $3, increasing thereafter at a 4 percent annual growth rate. The corporation's tax rate is 34 percent.

**12-3A.** (*Cost of equity*) Salte Corporation is issuing new common stock at a market price of $27. Dividends last year were $1.45 and are expected to grow at an annual rate of 6 percent forever. Flotation costs will be 6 percent of market price. What is Salte's cost of equity?

**12-4A.** (*Cost of debt*) Belton is issuing a $1,000 par value bond that pays 7 percent annual interest and matures in 15 years. Investors are willing to pay $958 for the bond. Flotation costs will be 11 percent of market value. The company is in an 18 percent tax bracket. What will be the firm's after-tax cost of debt on the bond?

**12-5A.** (*Cost of preferred stock*) The preferred stock of Walter Industries sells for $36 and pays $2.50 in dividends. The net price of the security after issuance costs is $32.50. What is the cost of capital for the preferred stock?

**12-6A.** (*Cost of debt*) The Zephyr Corporation is contemplating a new investment to be financed 33 percent from debt. The firm could sell new $1,000 par value bonds at a net price of $945. The coupon interest rate is 12 percent, and the bonds would mature in 15 years. If the company is in a 34 percent tax bracket, what is the after-tax cost of capital to Zephyr for bonds?

**12-7A.** (*Cost of preferred stock*) Your firm is planning to issue preferred stock. The stock sells for $115; however, if new stock is issued, the company would receive only $98. The par value of the stock is $100 and the dividend rate is 14 percent. What is the cost of capital for the stock to your firm?

**12-8A.** (*Cost of internal equity*) Pathos Co.'s common stock is currently selling for $21.50. Dividends paid last year were $.70. Flotation costs on issuing stock will be 10 percent of market price. The dividends and earnings per share are projected to have an annual growth rate of 15 percent. What is the cost of internal common equity for Pathos?

**12-9A.** (*Cost of equity*) The common stock for the Bestsold Corporation sells for $58. If a new issue is sold, the flotation costs are estimated to be 8 percent. The company pays 50 percent of its earnings in dividends, and a $4 dividend was recently paid. Earnings per share 5 years ago were $5. Earnings are expected to continue to grow at the same annual rate in the future as during the past 5 years. The firm's marginal tax rate is 34 percent. Calculate the cost of (a) internal common and (b) external common.

**12-10A.** (*Cost of debt*) Sincere Stationery Corporation needs to raise $500,000 to improve its manufacturing plant. It has decided to issue a $1,000 par value bond with a 14 percent annual coupon rate and a 10-year maturity. The investors require a 9 percent rate of return.

- **a.** Compute the market value of the bonds.
- **b.** What will the net price be if flotation costs are 10.5 percent of the market price?
- **c.** How many bonds will the firm have to issue to receive the needed funds?
- **d.** What is the firm's after-tax cost of debt if its average tax rate is 25 percent and its marginal tax rate is 34 percent?

**12-11A.** (*Cost of debt*)

- **a.** Rework problem 12-10A assuming a 10 percent coupon rate. What effect does changing the coupon rate have on the firm's after-tax cost of capital?
- **b.** Why is there a change?

**12-12A.** (*Weighted average cost of capital*) The target capital structure for QM Industries is 40 percent common stock, 10 percent preferred stock, and 50 percent debt. If the cost of equity for the firm is 18 percent, the cost of preferred stock is 10 percent, the before-tax cost of debt is 8 percent, and the firm's tax rate is 35 percent, what is QM's weighted average cost of capital?

**12-13A.** (*Weighted average cost of capital*) Crypton Electronics has a capital structure consisting of 40 percent common stock and 60 percent debt. A debt issue of $1,000 par value 6 percent bonds, maturing in 15 years and paying annual interest, will sell for $975. Flotation costs for the bonds will be $15 per bond. Common stock of the firm is currently selling for $30 per share. The firm expects to pay a $2.25 dividend next year. Dividends have grown at the rate of 5 percent per year and are expected to continue to do so for the foreseeable future. Flotation costs for the stock issue are 5 percent of the market price. What is Crypton's cost of capital where the firm's tax rate is 30 percent?

**12-14A.** (*Weighted average cost of capital*) As a member of the Finance Department of Ranch Manufacturing, your supervisor has asked you to compute the appropriate discount rate of use when evaluating the purchase of new packaging equipment for the plant. You have determined the market value of the firm's capital structure as follows:

| Source of Capital | Market Values |
|---|---|
| Bonds | $4,000,000 |
| Preferred stock | $2,000,000 |
| Common stock | $6,000,000 |

To finance the purchase, Ranch Manufacturing will sell 10-year bonds paying 7 percent per year at the market price of $1,050. Flotation costs for issuing the bonds are 4 percent of the market price. Preferred stock paying a $2.00 dividend can be sold for $25; the cost of issuing these shares is $3 per share. Common stock for Ranch Manufacturing is currently selling for $55 per share. The firm paid a $3 dividend last year and expects dividends to continue growing at a rate of 10 percent per year. Flotation costs for issuing new common stock will be $5 per share and the firm's tax rate is 30 percent. What discount rate should you use to evaluate the equipment purchase?

## INTEGRATIVE PROBLEM

The capital structure for Nealon, Inc., follows:

Nealon, Inc., Balance Sheet

| Type of Financing | Percentage of Future Financing |
|---|---|
| Bonds (8%, $1,000 par, 16-year maturity) | 38% |
| Preferred stock (5,000 shares outstanding, $50 par, $1.50 dividend) | 15% |
| Common stock | 47% |
| Total | 100% |

Flotation costs are (a) 15 percent of market value for a new bond issue, (b) $1.21 per share for common stock, and (c) $2.01 per share for preferred stock. The dividends for common stock were $2.50 last year and are projected to have an annual growth rate of 6 percent. The firm is in a 34 percent tax bracket. What is the weighted average cost of capital if the firm finances are in the following proportions?

Market prices are $1,035 for bonds, $19 for preferred stock, and $35 for common stock. There will be sufficient internal common equity funding (i.e., retained earnings) available such that the firm does not plan to issue new common stocks.

## STUDY PROBLEMS (SET B)

**12-1B.** (*Individual or component costs of capital*) Compute the cost for the following:

**a.** A bond that has a $1,000 par value (face value) and a contract or coupon interest rate of 12 percent. A new issue would have a flotation cost of 6 percent of the $1,125 market value. The bonds mature in 10 years. The firm's average tax rate is 30 percent and its marginal tax rate is 34 percent.

**b.** A new common stock issue that paid a $1.75 dividend last year. The par value of the stock is $15, and earnings per share have grown at a rate of 8 percent per year. This growth rate is expected to continue into the foreseeable future. The company maintains a constant dividend/earnings ratio of 30 percent. The price of this stock is now \$28, but 5 percent flotation costs are anticipated.

**c.** Internal common equity in which the current market price of the common stock is \$43.50. The expected dividend this coming year should be \$3.25, increasing thereafter at a 7 percent annual growth rate. The corporation's tax rate is 34 percent.

**d.** A preferred stock paying a 10 percent dividend on a \$125 par value. If a new issue is offered, flotation costs will be 12 percent of the current price of \$150.

**e.** A bond selling to yield 13 percent after flotation costs, but prior to adjusting for the marginal corporate tax rate of 34 percent. In other words, 13 percent is the rate that equates the net proceeds from the bond with the present value of the future cash flows (principal and interest).

**12-2B.** (*Individual or component costs of capital*) Compute the cost of the following:

**a.** A bond selling to yield 9 percent after flotation costs, but prior to adjusting for the marginal corporate tax rate of 34 percent. In other words, 9 percent is the rate that equates the net proceeds from the bond with the present value of the future flows (principal and interest).

**b.** A new common stock issue that paid a \$1.25 dividend last year. The par value of the stock is \$2, and the earnings per share have grown at a rate of 6 percent per year. This growth rate is expected to continue into the foreseeable future. The company maintains a constant dividend/earnings ratio of 40 percent. The price of this stock is now \$30, but 9 percent flotation costs are anticipated.

**c.** A bond that has a \$1,000 par value (face value) and a contract or coupon interest rate of 13 percent. A new issue would net the company 90 percent of the \$1,125 market value. The bonds mature in 20 years, the firm's average tax rate is 30 percent, and its marginal tax rate is 34 percent.

**d.** A preferred stock paying a 7 percent dividend on a \$125 par value. If a new issue is offered, the company can expect to net \$90 per share.

**e.** Internal common equity where the current market price of the common stock is \$38. The expected dividend this coming year should be \$4, increasing thereafter at a 5 percent annual growth rate. This corporation's tax rate is 34 percent.

**12-3B.** (*Cost of equity*) Falon Corporation is issuing new common stock at a market price of \$28. Dividends last year were \$1.30 and are expected to grow at an annual rate of 7 percent forever. Flotation costs will be 6 percent of market price. What is Falon's cost of equity?

**12-4B.** (*Cost of debt*) Temple is issuing a \$1,000 par value bond that pays 8 percent annual interest and matures in 15 years. Investors are willing to pay \$950 for the bond. Flotation costs will be 11 percent of market value. The company is in a 19 percent tax bracket. What will be the firm's after-tax cost of debt on the bond?

**12-5B.** (*Cost of preferred stock*) The preferred stock of Gator Industries sells for \$35 and pays \$2.75 in dividends. The net price of the security after issuance costs is \$32.50. What is the cost of capital for the preferred stock?

**12-6B.** (*Cost of debt*) The Walgren Corporation is contemplating a new investment to be financed 33 percent from debt. The firm could sell new \$1,000 par value bonds at a net price of \$950. The coupon interest rate is 13 percent, and the bonds would mature in 15 years. If the company is in a 34 percent tax bracket, what is the after-tax cost of capital to Walgren for bonds?

**12-7B.** (*Cost of preferred stock*) Your firm is planning to issue preferred stock. The stock sells for \$120; however, if new stock is issued, the company would receive only \$97. The par value of the stock is \$100, and the dividend rate is 13 percent. What is the cost of capital for the stock to your firm?

**12-8B.** (*Cost of internal equity*) The common stock or Oxford, Inc., is currently selling for \$22.50. Dividends last year were \$.80. Flotation costs on issuing stock will be 10 percent of market price. The dividends and earnings per share are projected to have an annual growth rate of 16 percent. What is the cost of internal common equity for Oxford?

**12-9B.** (*Cost of equity*) The common stock for the Hetterbrand Corporation sells for \$60. If a new issue is sold, the flotation cost is estimated to be 9 percent. The company pays 50 percent of its earnings in dividends, and a \$4.50 dividend was recently paid. Earnings per share 5 years ago were \$5. Earnings are expected to continue to grow at the same annual rate in the future as during the past 5 years. The firms' marginal tax rate is 35 percent. Calculate the cost of (a) internal common and (b) external common stock.

**12-10B.** (*Cost of debt*) Gillian Stationery Corporation needs to raise $600,000 to improve its manufacturing plant. It has decided to issue a $1,000 par value bond with a 15 percent annual coupon rate and a 10-year maturity. If the investors require a 10 percent rate of return:

**a.** Compute the market value of the bonds.

**b.** What will the net price be if flotation costs are 11.5 percent of the market price?

**c.** How many bonds will the firm have to issue to receive the needed funds?

**d.** What is the firm's after-tax cost of debt if its average tax rate is 25 percent and its marginal tax rate is 34 percent?

**12-11B.** (*Cost of debt*)

**a.** Rework problem 12-10B assuming a 10 percent coupon rate. What effect does changing the coupon rate have on the firm's after-tax cost of capital?

**b.** Why is there a change?

**12-12B.** (*Weighted cost of capital*) The capital structure for the Bias Corporation follows. The company plans to maintain its debt structure in the future. If the firm has a 6 percent after-tax cost of debt, a 13.5 percent cost of preferred stock, and a 19 percent cost of common stock, what is the firm's weighted cost of capital?

| Capital Structure ($000) | |
|---|---|
| Bonds | $1,100 |
| Preferred stock | 250 |
| Common stock | 3,700 |
| | $5,050 |

**12-13B.** The target capital structure for Jowers Manufacturing is 50 percent common stock, 15 percent preferred stock, and 35 percent debt. If the cost of equity for the firm is 20 percent, the cost of preferred stock is 12 percent, and the before-tax cost of debt is 10 percent, what is Jower's cost of capital? The firm's marginal tax rate is 34 percent.

**12-14B.** Bane Industries has a capital structure consisting of 60 percent common stock and 40 percent debt. A debt issue of $1,000 par value, 8 percent bonds, maturing in 20 years and paying semi-annually, will sell for $1,100. Flotation costs for the bonds will be $20 per bond. Common stock of the firm is currently selling for $80 per share. The firm expects to pay a $2 dividend next year. Dividents have grown at the rate of 8 percent per year and are expected to continue to do so for the foreseeable future. Flotation costs for the stock issue are 10 percent of the market price. What is Bane's cost of capital? The firm's marginal tax rate is 34 percent.

**12-15B.** As a consultant to GBH Skiwear, you have been asked to compute the appropriate discount rate to use to evaluate the purchase of a new warehouse facility. You have determined the market value of the firm's capital structure as follows:

| Source of Capital | Market Value |
|---|---|
| Bonds | $500,000 |
| Preferred stock | $100,000 |
| Common stock | $400,000 |

To finance the purchase, GBH will sell 20-year bonds, paying 8 percent per year, at the market price of $950. Flotation costs for issuing the bonds are 6 percent of the market price. Preferred stock paying a $2.50 dividend can be sold for $35; the cost of issuing these shares is $5 per share. Common stock for GBH is currently selling for $50 per share. The firm paid a $2 dividend last year and expects dividends to continue growing at a rate of 8 percent per year. Flotation costs for issuing new common stock will be 10 percent of the market price. The firm's marginal tax rate is 34 percent. What discount rate should you use to evaluate the warehouse project? What discount rate should you use to evaluate the equipment purchase?

## SELF-TEST SOLUTIONS

The following notations are used in this group of problems:

$k_d$ = the before-tax cost of debt
$k_{ps}$ = the cost of preferred stock
$k_{cs}$ = the cost of internal common stock
$k_{ncs}$ = the cost of new common stock
$t$ = the marginal tax rate
$D_t$ = the dollar dividend per share, where $D_0$ is the most recently paid dividend and $D_1$ is the forthcoming dividend
$P_0$ = the value (present value) of a security
$NP_0$ = the value of a security less any flotation costs incurred in issuing the security

**ST-1.**

**a.** $$\$921.50 = \sum_{t=1}^{n} \frac{\$100}{(1 + k_d)^t} + \frac{\$1,000}{(1 + k_d)^{10}}$$

| Rate | Value | | |
|---|---|---|---|
| 11% | \$940.90 | \$19.40 (11% to $k_d$%) | \$53.90 (11% to 12%) |
| $k_d$% | \$921.50 | | |
| 12% | \$887.00 | | |

$$k_d = 0.11 + \left(\frac{\$19.40}{\$53.90}\right)0.01 = .1136 = 11.36\%$$

$$k_d(1 - t) = 11.36\% \ (1 - 0.34) = 7.50\%$$

**b.** $$k_{ps} = \frac{D}{NP_0}$$

$$k_{ps} = \frac{\$8}{\$100 - \$9} = .0879 = 8.79\%$$

**c.** $$k_{cs} = \frac{D_1}{P_0} + g$$

$$k_{cs} = \frac{\$9.80}{\$75} + 0\% = .1307 = 13.07\%$$

**d.** $$k_{ncs} = \frac{D_1}{NP_0} + g$$

$$k_{ncs} = \frac{\$2.80(1 + 0.08)}{\$53 - \$6} + 0.08 = .1443 = 14.43\%$$

**ST-2.**

Carion Corporation—Weighted Cost of Capital

| | Capital Structure | Weights | Individual Costs | Weighted Costs |
|---|---|---|---|---|
| Bonds | \$1,083 | 0.2152 | 5.5% | 1.18% |
| Preferred stock | 268 | 0.0533 | 13.5% | 0.72% |
| Common stock | 3,681 | 0.7315 | 18.0% | 13.17% |
| | \$5,032 | 1.0000 | | 15.07% |

# MANAGING FOR SHAREHOLDER VALUE

We are a nation of stockholders. More than 41 percent of American families own shares of common stock in either their personal portfolio, their retirement portfolio, or both.[2] Furthermore, these equity holdings constitute about 40 percent of their total

financial assets, and this fraction has been growing. The reason for investing in the common shares of a firm are obvious, as Danny DeVito, playing the role of "Larry the Liquidator" in the movie *Other Peoples Money,* stated when addressing the annual shareholders meeting of the New England Wire and Cable Company: "Lest we forget, the reason you became a stockholder in the first place was to make money." In the movie, Larry the Liquidator was unhappy with the past performance of the New England Wire and Cable Company and he saw the opportunity to "make a buck or two" by buying the firm and restructuring it. ● In real life, the Harley-Davidson Company offers a shareholder experience that has been totally different from the fictional New England Wire and Cable Company. Harley's CEO and President, Jeffrey Bleustein, describes the firm's stockholder performance in the following quote from his letter to the shareholders contained in the company's 1999 annual report:

> Dear Fellow Shareholder: It is my privilege to share with you in this Annual Report the results of Harley-Davidson's fourteenth consecutive record year of financial performance. Our consistent growth has had a clear benefit to investors—a shareholder who purchased $10,000 of Harley-Davidson stock when we first went public in 1986 would be a millionaire today—for many, a dream came true. (Harley-Davidson Annual Report, 1999)

**LEARNING OBJECTIVES**

After reading this chapter, you should be able to

1. Use Market Value Added to identify the value created for shareholders by a publicly held firm.
2. Estimate the value of the firm, which we will refer to as its enterprise value, using the discounted free cash-flow model.
3. Identify the value drivers that can be managed to create shareholder value.
4. Define, compute, and interpret a firm's return on invested capital, and Economic Value Added (EVA)®.[1]
5. Discuss the structure of typical managerial compensation packages and the issues that arise in designing them.

[1]EVA® is a registered trademark of the Stern Stewart and Company.

[2]Based on the Survey of Consumer Finances and reported by Kennickell, Martha Starr-McCluer, and Annika E. Sunden, Family Finances in the U.S.: Recent Evidence from the Survey of Consumer Finances, *Federal Reserve Bulletin,* January 1997, 1–28.

You would not expect to find Larry the Liquidator making an appearance at the Harley-Davidson shareholders meeting unless it was to lead a cheer! Harley's shares had increased in value from 65¢ to $64.06 over the 1986–1999 period, providing an average compound rate of return of 39 percent per year! Thus, Harley's management has been very successful in managing the firm to create shareholder value. How did this happen? In our discussions of capital budgeting and the cost of capital (Chapters 9–12), we learned that managers create shareholder value by identifying and undertaking investments that earn returns greater than the firm's cost of raising money (i.e., the firm's weighted average cost of capital). Let's put this notion to the test by reviewing Harley's performance during 1998. In that year, the firm earned an annual rate of return of 18.92 percent on its investments while its cost of capital was only 12.23 percent.[3] Clearly, shareholder value was created during 1998. The issue we address in this chapter then boils down to addressing the problems associated with making sure that the firm maintains a return on its investments that meets or exceeds its cost of capital. We present economic value added, or *EVA®*, as a performance measure that is designed to accomplish this goal. Throughout the text we have promoted the notion that a firm's management should make decisions that lead to increased shareholder value. To investors, this is not a controversial statement. After all, the common shareholders do "own" the firm. In fact, it is not uncommon to see corporate mission statements that endorse shareholder value maximization as the firm's primary goal. For example, the Disney 1999 annual report states "Disney's overriding objective is to create shareholder value by continuing to be the world's premier entertainment company from a creative, strategic, and financial standpoint." Unfortunately, the incentives of a firm's management are not always aligned with those of the firm's stockholders. As a consequence, many (perhaps even most) large corporations are not run on a day-to-day basis so as to maximize shareholder wealth.[4] In fact, many proceed to destroy shareholder value year after year. In this chapter we use the free cash-flow valuation model that serves as the basis for estimating project value in an analysis of new capital expenditure proposals to estimate the value of the business enterprise. We then link this valuation to value drivers that can be used by managers for setting performance goals that can be tied directly to firm value. Next we look at *EVA®* as a measure of firm or business unit performance. This performance measure has become very popular

[3]Reported in Shawn Tully, MVA Performance Ranking: United States, *Fortune Magazine,* 1999.

[4]In their book on value-based management, McTaggart, Kontes, and Mankins go so far as to assert that "the great majority of large corporations throughout the world are not managed with the objective of maximizing wealth or shareholder value," *Managing for Shareholder Returns: The Value Imperative* (New York: Free Press, 1994), p. 41.

among firms that have focused their efforts on the creation of shareholder value. Finally, we discuss the fundamental issues arising in establishing an incentive compensation program that encourages employees to engage in activities that create shareholder value. Here we learn that compensation based on performance measures that are linked directly to the creation of shareholder value is critical. In fact, if compensation is not tied to performance measures, the value creation process is ultimately doomed to failure. The old adage that what gets measured and rewarded gets done is the guiding principle behind managing the firm to create value for its shareholders.

**CHAPTER PREVIEW**

We have spent a lot of time addressing the problems that firms encounter when making investment decisions designed to maximize shareholder wealth. In Chapters 9 through 11, we discussed the use of net present value and other tools of discounted cash-flow analysis to analyze project cash flows and compare them to the investments required. Furthermore, in Chapter 12, we addressed the problem of assessing the proper required rate of return for a firm's investments. What happens once the investment is made and the firm has bought and put into operation the new assets that were the object of the capital expenditure analysis? How can we be sure that these assets will be managed and operated so as to maximize shareholder value? This chapter answers these questions. Specifically, we address the fundamental problem of managing a firm's operations to create as much shareholder value as possible.

We introduce the subject of managing for shareholder value by introducing the free cash-flow model of firm value. This model is widely used to develop an understanding of the value of the business. We then identify the basic determinants of firm value in this model and then provide the value drivers that managers can focus upon.

Firm performance is evaluated periodically in an effort to determine whether the firm's management is on track to create shareholder value. As a consequence, we need measures of quarterly and annual performance that can be used to assess that performance and pay for success or penalize failure. Firms have used a wide variety of performance measures including firm earnings, earnings growth, and return on investment, to name a few. Recently, however, economic value added has been widely recommended as an improvement on traditional accounting-based performance measures.

This chapter emphasizes **Principle 1: The Risk-Return Tradeoff—We won't take on additional risk unless we expect to be compensated with additional return; Principle 2: The Time Value of Money—A dollar received today is worth more than a dollar received in the future; Principle 3: Cash—Not Profits—Is King; and Principle 7: The Agency Problem—Managers won't work for owners unless it's in their best interest.** We are particularly attentive to Principle 7 as it describes the agency problem that arises between managers and stockholders. In fact, there would be no need for the use of periodic performance measures and reward (compensation) systems based upon them if it were not for this basic problem.

## WHO ARE THE TOP CREATORS OF SHAREHOLDER VALUE?

OBJECTIVE 1 

**Market value added (*MVA*)**
The difference in the market value of the firm and the capital that has been invested in it.

Table 13-1 contains a list of the five top and bottom wealth creators for 1998 among the 1,000 largest U.S. corporations. The ranking is based on **market value added (*MVA*),** which was devised by Stern Stewart and Company to measure how much wealth a firm has created at a particular moment in time.[5] *MVA* is computed as follows:

$$\begin{matrix}\text{market}\\ \text{value}\\ \text{added}\end{matrix} = \begin{matrix}\text{firm}\\ \text{value}\end{matrix} - \begin{matrix}\text{invested}\\ \text{capital}\end{matrix} \qquad \textbf{(13-1)}$$

[5]Although we do not report it here, a similar ranking called the Shareholder Scoreboard is prepared by L.E.K. Consulting LLC and published in the *Wall Street Journal.* This ranking, however, uses the total return to shareholders over 1-, 3-, 5-, and 10-year holding periods to assess wealth creation/destruction. Total return includes price appreciation or depreciation, and any reinvestment from cash dividends, rights and warrant offerings, and cash equivalents, such as stock received in spinoffs. Returns are also adjusted for stock splits, stock dividends, and recapitalizations. (See *Wall Street Journal* Interactive edition, February 24, 2000.)

**TABLE 13-1**
America's Top and Bottom Creators of Shareholder Value for 1998 ($ Millions)

| Company Name | Market Value Added (*MVA*) | Invested Capital | Return on Invested Capital | Cost of Capital (*WACC*) |
|---|---|---|---|---|
| **Top Five Wealth Creators for 1998** | | | | |
| Microsoft | 328,257 | 10,954 | 56.16% | 12.64% |
| General Electric | 285,320 | 65,298 | 19.29% | 11.92% |
| Intel | 166,902 | 23,626 | 35.44% | 12.92% |
| Wal-Mart Stores | 159,444 | 36,188 | 13.24% | 9.82% |
| Coca-Cola | 157,536 | 13,311 | 31.22% | 11.24% |
| **Bottom Five Wealth Creators for 1998** | | | | |
| Union Pacific | (5,286) | 30,191 | 2.42% | 7.26% |
| Loews Corporation | (11,425) | 22,486 | 2.13% | 9.94% |
| Nabisco | (12,171) | 35,041 | 3.42% | 7.52% |
| CNA Financial Corp | (12,948) | 20,349 | −0.28% | 10.24% |
| General Motors | (17,943) | 85,173 | 1.99% | 9.36% |

Source: Stern Stewart and Company, 1999.

By *firm value,* we mean the market values of the firm's outstanding debt and equity securities. Invested capital is a bit more problematic. Conceptually, a firm's **invested capital** is the sum of all the funds that have been invested in it. Although this sum is related to the firm's total assets, it is not quite the same thing.[6] But for right now, let's just think of invested capital as total assets.

**Invested capital**
Total amount of funds invested in a firm.

Let's take a look at the firms listed in Table 13-1 whose performance places them at the top and bottom of the list of wealth creators. The names of the firms at the top of the list are probably very familiar to you. For example, investors have invested roughly $11 billion in the assets of top-ranked Microsoft. The market value of this investment at the end of 1998 was over $328 billion. On the other end of the spectrum we see General Motors, whose investors have entrusted over $85 billion to the firm's management, which is worth almost $18 billion less than their investment at the end of 1998. Table 13-1 also provides information concerning the rates of return earned on each firm's invested capital as well as the market's assessment of the firm's cost of capital. These last two pieces of information highlight the fundamental paradigm of creating shareholder value—that is, firms that earn higher rates of return than their capital costs create shareholder wealth, while those that fail this simple test destroy it.

How is it that some firms can create so much value for their shareholders while others destroy it?[7] Value creation, very simply, results from the marriage of opportunity and

[6]Accounting conventions used in constructing the firm's balance sheet distort the reporting of the firm's invested capital, so that we have to make some adjustments to the firm's total assets from its balance sheet. Stern Stewart has identified over 160 such adjustments; however, we will mention only one important one here to provide a flavor for the types of adjustments that are required. The example we use is the adjustment made for research and development (R&D) expenditures. Generally accepted accounting principles (GAAP) call for the expensing of 100 percent of the firm's R&D expenditures in the year in which the expenditure is made. This practice fails to recognize the future value that the firm's management anticipates receiving from these expenditures. As a consequence, expenditures for R&D, unlike expenditures made for new plant and equipment, are not reflected in the total assets of the company. This treatment of R&D has the effect of understating the total investment that has been made in the firm. Stern Stewart adds R&D back to the firm's total assets and amortizes it over several future years. The net effect of this adjustment is to inflate book value to be more clearly reflective of the total investment that has been made in the firm.

[7]Although the 1990s produced the longest bull market for common stock in recorded history, many firms have struggled and even lost value for their shareholders. The manufacturing sector was particularly hard hit with only one in eight manufacturers outperforming the S&P 500 since 1988 and one-third experiencing a decline in the value of their shares (Wise and Baumgartner, 1999).

execution. Opportunities must be recognized and, in some cases, created, and this is the stuff of which business strategy is made. However, opportunity is not enough. Firms have to have employees who are ready, willing, and able to take advantage of business opportunities. It is on this side of the value creation equation that we focus our attention. Specifically, managing for shareholder value requires that we resolve two separate issues: First, we must identify a set of performance measures that are both linked to value creation and are under the control of the firm's management. Second, we must design a system of incentives that encourages employees to base their decisions on these performance metrics in their day-to-day decisions. In essence, we must develop a performance measurement and reward system that encourages managers to think and act like business owners. Let's consider how this might be accomplished.

**CONCEPT CHECK**

1. What is Market Value Added and how is it calculated?
2. What is the fundamental paradigm for creating shareholder value?

## BUSINESS VALUATION—THE KEY TO CREATING SHAREHOLDER VALUE

OBJECTIVE 2 

To understand how shareholder value is created we must first understand how firms are valued in the capital markets. There are two competing valuation paradigms that have been used to explain the value of a firm's common stock in the capital market: the accounting model and the discounted cash flow model. Figure 13-1 captures the essential elements of both.

### The Accounting Model

Although both the accounting and discounted cash flow models *can be* consistent in theory, they are not generally used in a consistent manner and they can lead management to act in very different ways as it tries to manage for shareholder value. If management uses the accounting model to think about the value of its equity, then it will focus on reported earnings in conjunction with the market's valuation of those earnings as reflected in the price-earnings ratio. For example, if the price-earnings ratio is 20, then a $1 increase in earnings per share will create $20 in additional equity value per share. Similarly, a $1 loss in earnings per share will lead to a drop of $20 in share value. To see what's wrong with this theory of equity valuation, consider the following scenario. In 1999, Intel Corporation spent $3.503 billion on research and development (R&D) designed to identify the products that would become the source of future revenues for the company. This total represents 69¢ per share after taxes. On March 20, 1999, the firm's price-earnings multiple was 61.36, reflecting 1999 earnings per share of $2.20 and a share price of $135. Ask yourself the following question: "Do you believe that Intel's stock price would have been $42.34 higher (i.e., 69¢ in R&D per share times 61.36), or $177.34, if Intel had not spent anything on R&D? Of course not! Intel's expenditures for R&D are its life's blood in creating new products that drive its future profitability. Without its R&D, the firm's stream of new products would evaporate, as would its future cash flows. This simple example serves to caution against managing for shareholder value by managing the firm's reported accounting earnings.

We learned in our discussion of capital budgeting that the discounted cash-flow valuation model incorporates investor expectations of future cash flows into the indefinite future as well as the opportunity cost of funds when estimating value. In this model, the R&D investment used in the previous example would lead to a reduction in cash flow during the

| | Accounting (earnings) Model | Discounted Cash Flow Model |
|---|---|---|
| Equity value | [price-earnings ratio] × [earnings per share] | Present value of future cash flows |
| Value drivers | Determinants of accounting earnings and the price-earnings ratio | Determinants of firm future cash flows and the opportunity cost of capital |

**FIGURE 13-1**
Competing Models of Equity Valuation

period in which the expenditure is being made, but would correspondingly increase future cash flows when the anticipated rewards of the investment are being reaped. Hence, the appropriate model for our use in managing the firm for shareholder value is one that focuses on the cash-flow consequences of the firm's decisions for the future, not just the current period, because this is how investors view their investments.

## Free Cash-Flow Valuation Model

The **free cash-flow model** for valuing a firm provides a method for analyzing value as the present value of the firm's projected free cash flows for all future years (1 through infinity). Pragmatically, of course, we cannot forecast free cash flows for an infinite future, so we generally project them for a finite number of years called the *planning period,* and then capture the value of all subsequent free cash flows using the concept of a **terminal value.**[8]

**Free cash-flow model** Method of valuing a firm by calculating the present value of all future free cash flows.

**Terminal value** The estimated value of the firm at the end of the planning period or the present value of the firm's free cash flows to be received after the end of the planning period.

To illustrate the use of the free cash-flow valuation model, let's consider a model based on a 4-year planning period; that is, we project free cash flows for a firm over a period of 4 years into the future. For years 5 and beyond we capture the value of the estimated free cash flows in the terminal value of the firm at the end of year 4. The value of the firm under this circumstance is reflected in the following model:

$$\text{firm value} = \frac{\text{free cash flow}_1}{(1 + k_{wacc})^1} + \frac{\text{free cash flow}_2}{(1 + k_{wacc})^2} + \frac{\text{free cash flow}_3}{(1 + k_{wacc})^3} + \frac{\text{free cash flow}_4}{(1 + k_{wacc})^4} + \frac{\text{terminal value}_4}{(1 + k_{wacc})^4} \quad \textbf{(13-2)}$$

To estimate the value of the firm, we discount future free cash flows for years 1 through 4, as well as the terminal value, back to the present using the firm's weighted average cost of

[8]Free cash flow provides the basis for valuing the firm as an entity and is calculated as follows:

| Calculation of Free Cash Flow | | Explanation |
|---|---|---|
| Net operating income (NOI) | | Estimated as revenues less cost of goods sold and operating expenses |
| Less: | taxes | Taxes estimated on the level of NOI |
| Equals: | net operating income after tax | NOPAT |
| Plus: | depreciation expense | Add back noncash depreciation |
| Less: | new investments made during the period | |
| | Additional net working capital | Increases in current assets less accounts payable and other noninterest-bearing liabilities |
| | Capital expenditures (CAPEX) | New investments made in plant and equipment during the period |
| Equals: | free cash flow | Cash available to pay dividends, interest and principal. |

capital ($k_{wacc}$). Let's now consider how the terminal value component of the model captures the firm's free cash flows for years 5 and beyond.

There are many ways to estimate the terminal value at the end of year 4 depending upon the pattern of future free cash flows the firm is expected to generate. For simplicity, we will assume that the firm's free cash flows for years 5 through infinity are all equal to the free cash flow for year 4. In other words, free cash flows for years 5, 6, and so forth do not grow after year 4. Technically, this means that terminal value at the end of year 3 is equal to the present value of a level perpetuity. We learned in Chapter 5 that the present value of a level perpetuity is calculated as follows:

$$\text{terminal value}_4 = \frac{\text{free cash flow}_5}{k_{wacc}} \tag{13-3}$$

Recall that free cash $\text{flow}_5$ is equal to free cash $\text{flow}_4$.

**RELATE TO THE BIG PICTURE**

When we calculate the value of the firm using the free cash-flow model, we are using the same basic model we used earlier to estimate the value of a capital investment proposal. The three basic determinants of value are the same. We rely on two fundamental principles of finance when we utilize the free cash flow model to value a firm: **Principle 1: The Risk-Return Trade-Off,** because we discount the expected firm free cash flows using the firm's risk adjusted weighted average cost of capital, and **Principle 3: Cash—Not Profits—Is King,** as we estimate firm free cash flow and not firm profits as the basis for valuation.

## Example of Free Cash-Flow Valuation

Table 13-2 contains projections for Kramerica, Inc., spanning the next 4 years of the firm's operations. Specifically, the table includes pro forma income statements (Panel A), current and pro forma balance sheets (Panel B), and free cash-flow estimates (Panel C). Note that the calculation of free cash flow follows the procedure laid out earlier in Chapter 2 and used in our earlier discussions of capital budgeting. Let's consider the underlying basis for the projections:

- *Estimated revenues.* Kramerica's sales are predicted to grow at a rate of 12 percent per year over the first 3 years before leveling off in year 4. For example, revenue for year 1 is predicted to be $56,000 = $50,000 (1 + .12).
- *Estimated gross profits.* Gross profits are projected to equal 60 percent of firm sales such that in year 1, gross profit = .60 × $56,000 = $33,600.
- *Estimated operating expenses.* We estimate operating expenses before depreciation to be 30 percent of revenues. Depreciation expense for the year is based on the level of property, plant, and equipment for the previous year. This total grows over the years as the firm acquires more depreciable assets.
- *Investment in net working capital.* Each year the firm must invest in additional current assets to support its growth in sales. However, at least a part of this investment is financed by noninterest-bearing liabilities such as accounts payable and accrued expenses. Thus, each year Kramerica will have to invest an amount in net working capital equal to the difference in the new current assets it needs to support the firm's

**TABLE 13-2**
Income Statements, Balance Sheets, and Free Cash-Flow Estimates for Kramerica, Inc.

**PANEL A. PRO FORMA INCOME STATEMENTS**

| | Years | | | |
|---|---|---|---|---|
| | 1 | 2 | 3 | 4 |
| Sales | $56,000 | $62,720 | $70,246 | $70,246 |
| Cost of goods sold | (22,400) | (25,088) | (28,099) | (28,099) |
| Gross profit | $33,600 | $37,632 | $42,148 | $42,148 |
| Operating expenses (excluding depreciation) | (16,800) | (18,816) | (21,074) | (21,074) |
| Depreciation expense | (4,000) | (4,240) | (4,509) | (4,810) |
| Operating income (earnings before interest and taxes) | $12,800 | $14,576 | $16,565 | $16,264 |
| Less: interest expense | (1,000) | (1,400) | (1,568) | (1,756) |
| Earnings before taxes | $11,800 | $13,176 | $14,997 | $14,508 |
| Less: taxes | (3,540) | (3,953) | (4,499) | (4,352) |
| Net income | $ 8,260 | $ 9,223 | $10,498 | $10,156 |

**PANEL B. CURRENT AND PRO FORMA BALANCE SHEETS**

| | Current Period | Pro Forma Balance Sheets | | | | |
|---|---|---|---|---|---|---|
| | 0 | 1 | 2 | 3 | 4 | 5 |
| Current assets | $ 7,500.00 | $ 8,400.00 | $ 9,408.00 | $10,536.96 | $10,536.96 | $10,536.96 |
| Property, plant, and Equipment | 20,000.00 | 22,400.00 | 25,088.00 | 28,098.56 | 28,098.56 | 28.098.56 |
| Total | $22,500.00 | $30,800.00 | $34,496.00 | $38,635.52 | $38,635.52 | $38,635.52 |
| Accruals and payables | $ 2,500.00 | $ 2,800.00 | $ 3,136.00 | $ 3,512.32 | $ 3,512.32 | $ 3,512.32 |
| Long-term debt | 10,000.00 | 14,000.00 | 15,680.00 | 17,561.60 | 17,561.60 | 17,561.60 |
| Equity | 10,000.00 | 14,000.00 | 15,680.00 | 17,561.60 | 17,561.60 | 17,561.60 |
| Total | $22,500.00 | $30,800.00 | $34,496.00 | $38,635.52 | $38,635.52 | $38,635.52 |
| Invested capital[a] | $20,000.00 | $28,000.00 | $31,360.00 | $35,123.20 | $35,123.20 | $35,123.20 |

**PANEL C. ESTIMATION OF FREE CASH FLOW**

| | 1 | 2 | 3 | 4 and beyond |
|---|---|---|---|---|
| Sales | $56,000 | $62,720 | $70,246 | $70,246 |
| Operating income (earnings before interest and taxes) | 12,800 | 14,576 | 16,565 | 16,264 |
| Less: cash tax payments | (3,840) | (4,373) | (4,970) | (4,879) |
| Net operating profits after taxes (NOPAT) | $ 8,960 | $10,203 | $11,596 | $11,385 |
| Plus: depreciation expense | 4,000 | 4,240 | 4,509 | 4,810 |
| Less investments: | | | | |
| In net working capital | $ (600) | $ (672) | $ (753) | $ — |
| In new capital (CAPEX) | (6,400) | (6,928) | (7,519) | (4,810) |
| Total net investment for the period | $(7,000) | $(7,600) | $(8,272) | $(4,810) |
| Free cash flow[b] | $ 5,960 | $ 6,843 | $ 7,832 | $11,385 |

[a]Invested capital is the total amount of funds invested in the assets of the firm that is financed by interest-bearing liabilities such as notes payable and bonds plus equity invested by the firm's preferred and common shareholders. In this example, invested capital = total assets − accruals & payables.
[b]Free cash flow = NOPAT + depreciation expense − total net investment for the period.

growing sales and the corresponding change in noninterest-bearing current liabilities. We refer to this total as the firm's investment in net working capital for the period.[9] Kramerica is assumed to invest 15 percent of each additional dollar in firm sales in current assets. However, 5 percent of this amount is spontaneously financed by accruals and payables. Thus, for each dollar in sales, Kramerica needs to raise 10¢ in new capital. For example, firm sales are expected to increase by $6,000 over the first year from $50,000 to $56,000. Thus, the anticipated need for new investment in net working capital for the first year of the planning period will be 10 percent of $6,000, or $600.

- *Capital expenditures (CAPEX).* New expenditures for property, plant, and equipment are included in Panel C of Table 13-2. To simplify our analysis, we follow common practice and assume that accounting depreciation expense on the firm's investment in plant and equipment at the beginning of each year is just equal to the cost of replacing plant and equipment that wears out during the year. This assumption is obvious when we look at the *CAPEX* for year 4, which is equal to depreciation expense for the year. The reason for this, you will recall, is that sales stop growing after year 3, and the only *CAPEX* the firm incurs is to replace worn-out assets. In addition, during the first 3 years when sales are growing at 12 percent per year, we estimate that Kramerica will have to invest an amount equal to 40 percent of the year-to-year increase in sales. Thus, in year 1 when sales rise by $6,000 over year 0, we estimate that the firm will have to spend $2,400 = .40 × $6,000 on new property, plant, and equipment in addition to the cost of replacing worn-out fixed assets in an amount equal to year 1's depreciation expense of $4,000. The net result is *CAPEX* equal to $6,400 in year 1.

Substituting Kramerica's weighted average cost of capital of 15 percent and the year 5 (same as year 4) free cash flow of $11,385 into equation 13-3, we estimate Kramerica's terminal value at the end of year 4 (i.e., the present value of the firm's free cash flows for years 5 through infinity) to be $75,899:

$$\text{terminal value}_4 = \frac{\textit{free cash flow}_5}{K_{wacc}} = \frac{\$11{,}385}{.15} = \$75{,}899$$

Finally, substituting our estimate of the terminal value into equation 13-2 along with the free cash flows for years 1 through 4 from Table 13-2, we estimate the firm's enterprise value to be $65,412:

$$\begin{array}{c}\text{firm}\\\text{value}\end{array} = \left[\frac{\$5{,}960}{(1+.15)^1} + \frac{\$6{,}843}{(1+.15)^2} + \frac{\$7{,}832}{(1+.15)^3} + \frac{\$11{,}385}{(1+.15)^4} + \frac{\$75{,}899}{(1+.15)^4}\right.$$

$$\begin{array}{c}\text{firm}\\\text{value}\end{array} = \$22{,}016 + 43{,}396 = \$65{,}412$$

We estimate the value of the firm's equity by subtracting the value of Kramerica's interest-bearing liabilities from firm value.[10] In our example, we assume that Kramerica has interest-

[9]Traditionally, net working capital is defined to be the difference in current assets and current liabilities. However, for purposes of valuing the firm, we are interested only in the financing provided by noninterest-bearing current liabilities (e.g., accounts payable and deferred expenses). Thus, when a firm's sales increase and it needs additional current assets (such as accounts receivable and inventories) to support the added sales, this need is partially offset by noninterest-bearing current liabilities. Thus, the net new investment a firm must make to finance current assets as its sales grow is represented by the difference between the added current assets and additional noninterest-bearing current liabilities.

[10]Technically, we have estimated the value of the firm's invested capital to be $65,412. To get the value of the entire firm we have to add back to this total the firm's accruals and payables of $2,500, or $65,412 + 2,500 = $67,912.

bearing liabilities of \$10,000, such that the equity value is \$55,412. To value Kramerica's equity we make use of the following relationship:[11]

$$\text{firm value} = \text{debt value} + \text{equity value} \tag{13-4}$$

Recall that this is simply the balance sheet equation for the firm, with one significant difference. In this case we are using market, as opposed to book, values. Solving for equity value:

$$\text{equity value} = \$65{,}412 - \$10{,}000 = \$55{,}412$$

Kramerica, Inc., has a total of 2,000 shares of outstanding stock. Thus, we calculate the value per share of the firm's equity to be \$27.71:

$$\text{share value} = \frac{\text{equity value}}{\text{number of shares}} = \frac{\$55{,}412}{2{,}000} = \$27.71$$

**CONCEPT CHECK**

1. What is the free cash-flow valuation model?
2. What does the terminal value in the free cash-flow valuation model represent?

## VALUE DRIVERS

Let's now consider how we can use our free cash-flow valuation model to manage the firm for shareholder value. Stated differently, what are the "knobs and controls" that managers can tweak to increase firm value? We will refer to these knobs and controls as *value drivers* and can identify them by reviewing the assumptions that underlie the free cash-flow estimates for Kramerica, Inc., that were presented in Table 13-2. Consider the following list of model assumptions—parameter values used in Table 13-2—and classification as either value driver or historical value:

Model Assumptions and Forecast Variables

| | Value | Value Driver or Historical Value |
|---|---|---|
| **Sales growth for years 1–3** | **12%** | **Value driver** |
| Gross profit margin | 60% | Value driver |
| Operating expenses (before depreciation) | 30% | Value driver |
| Net working capital to sales ratio | 10% | Value driver |
| Property, plant, and equipment to sales ratio | 40% | Value driver |
| Beginning sales | \$50,000 | Historical value |
| Cash tax rate | 30% | Historical value |
| Total liabilities | \$10,000 | Historical value |
| Cost of capital | 15.0% | Value driver |
| Number of shares | 2,000 | Historical value |

Note that four of the items represent historical values (sales, total liabilities, the corporate tax rate, and the number of common shares outstanding) for the previous year. These four items

[11] See footnote 9 for an explanation as to why we only deduct only long-term interest-bearing debt rather than total liabilities.

**TABLE 13-3**
Value Drivers and Managing for Shareholder Value

| Value Drivers | Value-enhancing Strategies |
|---|---|
| Sales growth for years 1–3 | • Implement a new promotional campaign to promote exciting or new products<br>• Form a distributional alliance to enter a new market<br>• Invest in R&D to create new products<br>• Acquire a competitor firm |
| Operating profit margin | • Initiate cost-control programs to reduce operating and administrative expenses<br>• Invest in a promotional campaign aimed at improving the brand image of your products or services in an effort to support premium pricing policies |
| Net working capital-to-sales ratio | • Initiate inventory control policies designed to reduce the time that inventory is held before sale<br>• Implement a program of credit analysis and control designed to either decrease the time customers take to pay for their purchases or to incorporate penalties for late payment<br>• Negotiate more lenient credit terms from the firm's suppliers |
| Property, plant, and equipment-to-sales ratio | • Consider outsourcing of production to strategic partners who might be more efficient in their operations in an effort to reduce the firm's need for plant and equipment<br>• Implement stringent controls over the acquisition of new plant and equipment to assure that all purchases are economically viable<br>• Improve maintenance of existing plant and equipment to improve up time, which reduces the need for additional plant and equipment |
| Cost of capital | • Review the firm's financial policies to assure that financing is being obtained from the lowest-cost sources<br>• Approach large institutional investors in an effort to develop direct sources of financing for the firm's new capital needs, thus bypassing the significant costs associated with using the public capital markets |

**Value drivers**
Variables that affect firm value and can be controlled or influenced by the firm's management.

provide the base values for our analysis and are not decision variables over which management has any control.[12] The remaining five items represent **value drivers.**

The value drivers represent the variables that are in some degree under the control or influence of the firm's management and that are connected in some meaningful way to the determinants of firm value. For example, management may be able to initiate a new compensation program for the firm's sales force that would increase the projected rate of growth in firm sales. It might institute cost-control procedures that would lead to an increase in the gross profit margin or a decrease in the ratio of operating expenses to sales. Or it might engage in a repurchase of the firm's shares financed by borrowing (a leveraged recapitalization) that could lead to a reduction in the firm's cost of capital. Thus, the value drivers meet all the requirements we set forth previously. The firm's management can influence them and each is linked to the determination of the value of the firm and, consequently, equity value.

Table 13-3 contains a list of potential strategies that the firm's management might consider in an effort to manage each of the value drivers that we have identified here. While these strategies have the potential for impacting firm value in a beneficial way, it is not certain that they will. For example, the firm might spend $40 million on a new advertising campaign that

[12]The tax rate paid by the firm is, to some degree, a manageable variable because the tax code is a very complex structure that provides some decision flexibility on the part of the firm's tax specialists. However, we will eschew further consideration of tax management issues here—they should be left to the tax specialists, although the issues raised are real and consequential in their value impact on the firm.

only leads to improvements in firm cash flow valued at $35 million, in which case $5 million in value would be destroyed. Thus, each of these strategies must be analyzed by management and decisions made based upon the anticipated merits of the specific proposal.

**CONCEPT CHECK**

1. What are value drivers? Give some examples.
2. How can management use value drivers to improve firm performance?

## ECONOMIC VALUE ADDED (EVA)®

Earlier we used Market Value Added (*MVA*) to measure the total wealth created by a firm at a particular point in time. As such, *MVA* is a reflection of investor expectations regarding the total value they expect the firm to create in the future less the total capital invested in the firm. Stated like this, we can see a direct analogy between *MVA* and net present value (*NPV*) for the firm as a whole. However, the manager must evaluate the performance of the firm over specific intervals of time—say, 1 year. For this purpose, we calculate the firm's **economic value added,** or *EVA*®. *EVA* for year *t* is defined as follows:

**Economic value added**
The difference in a firm's net operating profit after taxes (NOPAT) and the capital charge for the period (i.e., the product of the firm's cost of capital and its invested capital at the beginning of the period).

$$EVA_t = \begin{bmatrix} \text{net operating} \\ \text{profit after} \\ \text{tax } (NOPAT)_t \end{bmatrix} - \begin{bmatrix} \text{weighted average} \\ \text{cost of} \\ \text{capital } (k_{wacc}) \end{bmatrix} \times \begin{matrix} \text{invested} \\ \text{capital}_{t-1} \end{matrix} \tag{13-5}$$

Note that *EVA* is related to accounting profits (i.e., *NOPAT* = net operating income ([1 − tax rate]) but differs in that it incorporates a charge for the capital invested in the firm. This **capital charge** is equal to the product of the firm's invested capital at the beginning of the period and the firm's weighted average cost of capital and is deducted from the period's net operating profit after tax (*NOPAT*) to estimate *EVA*. The result is a measure of the contribution of the firm's operations for the period to the value of the firm.

**Capital charge**
The firm's invested capital at the beginning of the period multiplied by the firm's weighted average cost of capital. This value is deducted from the firm's net operating profit after taxes (*NOPAT*) to estimate *EVA*.

The relationship between the future *EVA*s and *MVA* is an important one, the reason being that managing for shareholder value entails increasing *MVA*. However, we manage a firm's *EVA*, which is related to *MVA* in the following way: *MVA* is the present value of all future *EVA*s over the life of the firm. Thus, managing the firm in ways that increase *EVA* will generally lead to a higher *MVA*.[13]

### Example Calculation of EVA

Let's take a look at the *EVA*s anticipated by Kramerica, Inc., based on the projections of future performance discussed earlier regarding free cash-flow valuation. Table 13-4 contains estimates of Kramerica's *EVA* for years 1–4. In Panel A we see that *EVA* is positive for every year, indicating that value is being created in each period. For example, in year 1 Kramerica's *EVA* is $5,960, reflecting the fact that during this year Kramerica expects to earn $8,960 in after-tax operating income (*NOPAT*), which exceeds capital costs of $3,750 (i.e., .15 × $25,000) by $5,210. Kramerica's capital cost for year 1 is computed as the product of the firm's weighted average cost of capital of 15 percent and its invested capital of $25,000.

[13]This is a simplistic interpretation of the use of *EVA* that sometimes does not hold. For example, there are situations in which very large capital investments lead to a decrease in *EVA* in the near term that is more than offset by future increases in *EVA*. Thus, simply maximizing *EVA* is not always the same thing as maximizing *MVA*. Discussion of the limitations of *EVA* as an indicator of value creation is beyond the scope of this text. The interested reader is referred to Martin and Petty (2001) for a detailed treatment of these and other related issues.

**TABLE 13-4**
Calculation of Economic Value Added (*EVA*) for *Kramerica, Inc.*

**PANEL A. METHOD I FOR CALCULATING *EVA*®**

| | Years | | | | |
|---|---|---|---|---|---|
| | 0 | 1 | 2 | 3 | 4 and beyond |
| Sales | | $56,000 | $62,720 | $70,246 | $70,246 |
| Operating income | | $12,800 | $14,576 | $16,565 | 16,264 |
| Less cash tax payments | | (3,840) | (4,373) | (4,970) | (4,879) |
| Net operating profits after taxes (*NOPAT*) | | $ 8,960 | $10,203 | $11,596 | $11,385 |
| Less capital charge = invested capital × $K_{wacc}$ | | (3,750) | (4,200) | (4,704) | (5,268) |
| Economic value added | | $ 5,210 | $ 6,003 | $ 6,892 | $ 6,116 |

**PANEL B. METHOD II FOR CALCULATING *EVA*®**

| | 0 | 1 | 2 | 3 | 4 and beyond |
|---|---|---|---|---|---|
| Return on invested capital $(ROIC) = NOPAT_{(t)} \div IC_{(t-1)}$ | | 44.80% | 36.44% | 36.98% | 32.41% |
| Cost of capital ($K_{wacc}$) | | 15% | 15% | 15% | 15% |
| Invested capital (Table 13-2) | $20,000 | $28,000 | $31,360 | $35,123 | $35,123 |
| Economic value added | | $ 5,210 | $ 6,003 | $ 6,892 | $ 6,116 |

$EVA(1) = (.3584 - .15) \times \$25{,}000 = \$5{,}210$

Earlier, when we introduced the notion of a firm's invested capital, we indicated that it was related to the firm's total assets, but because of the way that accountants prepare the firm's balance sheet, this was not exactly the case. For example, Stern Stewart recommends a number of adjustments to the firm's reported accounting numbers for the express purpose of converting both *NOPAT* and capital from an accounting book value to economic book value.[14] In the Kramerica example used here, none of these adjustments is required.

Panel B of Table 13-4 contains an alternative definition of *EVA* that is completely equivalent to the definition found in equation 13-5. The alternative definition is:

$$EVA_t = \left(\begin{array}{c}\text{return on invested}\\ \text{capital } (ROIC)_t\end{array} - \begin{array}{c}\text{weighted average}\\ \text{cost of capital } (k_{wacc})\end{array}\right) \times \begin{array}{c}\text{invested}\\ \text{capital } (IC)_{t-1}\end{array} \qquad \textbf{(13-6)}$$

**Return on invested capital** The ratio of net operating income after tax for the period divided by the firm's invested capital at the end of the previous period.

In this alternative format, we can see that a firm creates value only when it earns a rate of **return on invested capital** (i.e., $NOPAT_t$/invested capital$_{t-1}$) that exceeds the firm's cost of capital. If this difference is positive, then *EVA* is positive. Going back to Table 13-1, we can see that all five of the top wealth creators earned rates of return on their invested capital that far exceeded their cost of capital during 1998. Similarly, the bottom five wealth creators all failed to earn a rate of return on their invested capital that was as high as their cost of capital. In fact, in the case of CNA Financial Corporation, the return earned was actually negative.

**CONCEPT CHECK**

1. Define economic value added and explain how to interpret it.
2. How is market value added related to economic value added?

[14]While Stern Stewart mentions some 162 adjustments, only 10 to 15 adjustments are more typically made. These adjustments are made for three reasons: (1) To convert from accrual to cash accounting (eliminating many of the reserves that the accountants have created in the financial statements; e.g., reserves for bad debt or LIFO reserves). (2) To capitalize market-building expenditures that have been expensed in the past (converting from a liquidating perspective to a going-concern perspective; e.g., capitalizing expensed R&D). (3) To remove cumulative unusual losses or gains after taxes (converting from successful-efforts to full-cost accounting)

**TABLE 13-5**
Value Drivers for the Top and Bottom Five Wealth Creators for 1998

| | 3-year Growth Rate in Sales | Fixed Asset Turnover | | Net Profit Margin | | Return on Invested Capital | Cost of Capital |
|---|---|---|---|---|---|---|---|
| | | Firm | Industry | Firm | Industry | | |
| Microsoft | 34.62% | 9.80 | 8.90 | 31.00% | 17.54% | 56.16% | 12.64% |
| General Electric | 12.95% | 2.90 | 3.10 | 9.31% | 9.29% | 19.29% | 11.92% |
| Intel | 17.48% | 2.40 | 2.00 | 23.10% | 11.82% | 35.44% | 12.92% |
| Wal-Mart Stores | 12.66% | 5.40 | 5.40 | 2.99% | 2.55% | 13.24% | 9.82% |
| Coca-Cola | 1.45% | 5.10 | NA | 18.75% | NA | 31.22% | 11.24% |
| Average | 15.83% | 5.12 | 4.85 | 17.03% | 10.30% | 31.07% | 11.71% |
| Union Pacific | 12.13% | 0.40 | 0.50 | −6.00% | 5.20% | 2.42% | 7.26% |
| Lowes | 6.31% | 7.60 | 6.10 | 2.24% | 8.60% | 2.13% | 9.94% |
| Nabisco | 2.10% | 3.00 | 3.30 | −3.39% | −2.28% | 3.42% | 7.52% |
| CNA Financial | 5.12% | 21.70 | 6.10 | 1.65% | 8.60% | −0.28% | 10.24% |
| General Motors | −1.40% | 2.30 | 3.00 | 1.86% | 8.04% | 1.99% | 9.36% |
| Average | 4.85% | 7.00 | 3.80 | −0.73% | 5.63% | 1.94% | 8.86% |

## How Do They Do It?

Back in Table 13-1 we identified the top and bottom five wealth creators among America's 1,000 largest corporations. Let's see how they faired in managing the value drivers we identified using our free cash-flow valuation model and EVA analysis. Table 13-5 contains selected value drivers for each of these firms. Note that the 3-year growth rate in sales for the top performers is much higher than that of the bottom performer group with one exception (Coca-Cola). Although the bottom performers appear to compare favorably with their industry in terms of their fixed asset turnover, a closer look indicates that one firm (CNA Financial) is driving this conclusion. In addition, the net profit margins for the top group average 17.03 percent compared to an average for their respective industries of only 10.30 percent. Compare this with the bottom performers whose average net profit margin is −0.73 percent versus 5.63 percent for their respective industries. Finally, when we analyze the return on invested capital for the top performers, we find that all five firms earned rates of return that far exceeded their cost of capital, whereas none of the bottom tier performers earned a return as high as their cost of capital. The message is clear. Manage your value drivers to beat the competition and you will create shareholder value.

**RELATE TO THE BIG PICTURE**

The basic problem we attempt to address in paying for performance relates to **Principle 7: The Agency Problem.** Specifically, individual managers will seek to follow their own self-interests whenever self-interest and shareholder interests come into conflict unless they are paid to do otherwise. Consequently, the theory behind paying for performance relies on developing methods for paying employees to make decisions that favor shareholder interests as well as their own.

**FINANCE MATTERS**

## EVA Success Story—Manitowoc Co.

Manitowoc is a manufacturer of construction cranes, ice machines and Great Lakes shipping vessels that a decade ago was suffering from the effects of the construction recession of the mid-1980s. However, since 1995 Manitowoc's share price has increased fivefold. The booming economy of the 1990s certainly helped produce this result but that's not all. Manitowoc got religion—EVA religion, that is. Here's their inspiring store of shareholder value creation.

In 1986 and 1987 Manitowoc did not receive a single order for a new crane. Not to worry, the firm had a $100 million cash reserve that allowed the firm to ride out the recession until 1990, when the board promoted a newly hired Chief Operating Officer to replace the retiring CEO. The new CEO inherited a firm with a debt-free balance sheet so when tough times came, no creditors showed up at the door demanding control over the firm to repay their claims. In addition, the firm had storerooms crammed full of dusty parts dating to the 1940s. To make matters even worse Manitowoc's customers used the firm like a bank by taking two months to pay their bills.

In 1991 the firm's CFO heard a talk about EVA® and the CEO adopted the concept. The results were striking. Headquarters staff was cut from 127 to 30, Manitowoc's two crane factories were consolidated into one plant, and inventories were reduced from $84 million to $34 million over a period of two years. In addition, the firm started charging interest on late payments. These changes have shown up in dramatically improved firm performance. For example, the crane division's operating margin (net operating income before depreciation, interest and taxes, as a percent of sales) is 16% compared to rival Terex's 11.5%.

Source: Abstracted from Michelle Conlin, "Manitowoc Co. used to be a Rust Belt bum—until management got evangelical about not wasting capital." *Forbes Magazine,* (April 19, 1999).

# PAYING FOR PERFORMANCE

OBJECTIVE 5 

Financial economists beginning with Berle and Means (1932) have recognized the fundamental problems that arise where ownership and control of the modern corporation are separated. Where a firm's owners (stockholders) are different than its management, an agency problem arises. In essence, managers control the firm and can at times make decisions that benefit themselves at the expense of the firm's stockholders. The proponents of *EVA* propose that where the contributions of individuals and groups toward the creation of shareholder value are measured using *EVA* and rewards are structured accordingly, shareholder and manager interests will be aligned. In essence, they argue that such a reward system pays employees to behave like owners. The benefits of getting employees to act like owners is summed up in the following quote from Robert Kidder, CEO of Duracell:[15]

> When managers become owners, they begin to think a lot harder about taking money out of mature businesses and investing in growth areas. And I think that happens as a fairly natural consequence of greater ownership. It's certainly not happening because all of a sudden we put in new controls at headquarters. In fact, today we have fewer controls than we had as part of Kraft. What's different is that the proposals for change are coming from the bottom up rather than from the top down.

## Basic Components of a Firm's Compensation Policy

Before we delve into the intricacies of linking pay to performance, let's first step back and review the basic elements of a firm's compensation program. Managerial compensation plans generally provide for three types of compensation, as depicted in Figure 13-2.

[15]This quote was taken from The Stern Steward Roundtables, *Discussing the Revolution in Corporate Finance,* edited by Donald H. Chew, Jr., (Malden, MA: Blackwell Business, 1998).

- **Base pay** is the fixed salary component of compensation.
- The **bonus payment** is generally a quarterly, semi-annual, or annual cash payment that is dependent upon firm performance compared to targets set at the beginning of the period. *EVA* provides one such performance measure that can be used in this regard.
- **Long-term compensation** consists of stock options and grants that are also made periodically to employees.[16] This type of compensation is the most direct method available to the firm to align the interests of the firm's employees with those of its shareholders.

**Base pay**
Fixed amount of compensation paid to an employee.

**Bonus payment**
Compensation paid to an employee that is dependent upon the firm's performance compared to predetermined targets.

**Long-term compensation**
Compensation paid to the employee as an incentive to align the employee's actions to the firm's goal of maximizing shareholder wealth. The most common form of long-term compensation is stock options.

Note that both bonus and long-term compensation are "at-risk" in that both depend upon performance of the individual and the firm. We often use the term **incentive,** or **performance-based compensation,** to describe this at-risk component of managerial compensation.

**Incentive (performance-based) compensation**
Compensation such as bonus and long-term compensation that is designed to motivate the employee to align employee actions with shareholder wealth creation.

## Designing a Compensation Program

A firm's compensation program can be very complex. In this section we lay out the fundamental issues that every firm's program must address in terms of four issues:

1. How much should be paid for a particular job?
2. What portion of the total compensation package should be in base salary and what part should be incentive based?
3. How should incentive pay be linked to performance?
4. Finally, what portion of the incentive pay should be paid as a cash bonus and what portion should be in long-term (equity) compensation?

The design of a compensation program that supports the creation of shareholder value must arrive at satisfactory answers to all four of these questions. We will touch on each issue briefly; however, from the perspective of creating shareholder value, our primary focus is on issue number 3.

ISSUE 1: HOW MUCH TO PAY? How much to pay for a particular job is dictated by market forces outside the firm's control. That is, the total value of the entire compensation package for a given employee must meet a market test. The firm will only be able to hire good employees if it offers a competitive level of total compensation.[17] This means that companies must be ever vigilant in comparing their pay scales with their competitors in the labor market. The size of the total compensation package may determine where you go to work, but the mix of base pay and performance-based pay will determine how hard you

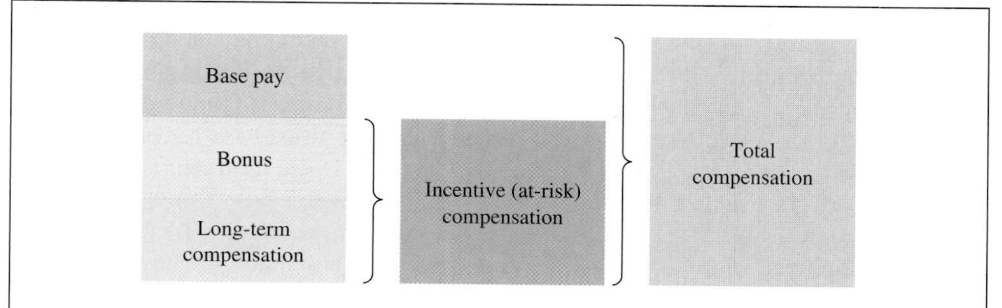


**FIGURE 13-2**
Components of the Typical Managerial Compensation Package

[16]We discuss options in Chapter 21, where we review the tools of risk management. At this point it is sufficient to understand that a stock option provides the holder with the right to buy (a call option) shares of the firm's stock at a specified price (the exercise or strike price).

[17]For example, the Dana Corporation's 1999 proxy statement indicates that the firm ". . . compares Dana's compensation practices to those of a group of comparable companies. The comparison group . . . currently consists of 22 companies . . ." (p. 11).

will work. Thus, the key to creating shareholder value lies in linking the incentive portion of the compensation package to the value drivers identified earlier in the chapter.

**ISSUE 2: BASE PAY VERSUS AT-RISK OR INCENTIVE COMPENSATION** What fraction of the total compensation package should be tied to performance or placed at-risk? There are no hard-and-fast rules for determining the mix of variable (at-risk) versus fixed compensation. However, in practice, the firm's highest-ranking employees generally have a larger fraction of their total compensation "at-risk" and the fraction declines with the employee's rank in the firm. For example, in 1999, Johnson & Johnson Medical (annual report) used the following scheme to define its target percent of base pay for its incentive pool:

| Base Salary | Target % of Base Pay |
|---|---|
| $64,000–88,999 | 10% |
| 89,000–112,999 | 15% |
| 113,000–156,999 | 20% |

On the other hand, in 1999, Motel 6 set its incentive pay based on employee responsibilities and title. A manager had 10 percent of base salary subject to incentive compensation while a vice president had 25 percent subject to incentive compensation (annual report for 1999). For most firms, basing the fraction of an employee's compensation that is at-risk on either salary level or responsibilities simply mirrors the responsibilities of the firm's top managers and their ability to control firm performance.

**ISSUE 3: LINKING PAY TO PERFORMANCE** The procedure used to link the level of incentive compensation to performance is the same regardless of the particular performance measure that is chosen, so let's begin by looking at an unbounded incentive compensation payout formula.[18]

$$\text{incentive pay} = \begin{pmatrix}\text{base}\\ \text{pay}\end{pmatrix}\begin{pmatrix}\text{fraction}\\ \text{of pay}\\ \text{at-risk}\end{pmatrix}\left(\frac{\text{actual performance}}{\text{target performance}}\right) \quad \textbf{(13-7)}$$

Note that in equation 13-7 incentive pay is unbounded. That is, there are no limits specified as to the maximum or minimum levels of incentive pay that can be earned. Incentive pay is a function of the portion of the employee's compensation that is at-risk or subject to firm performance (the product of base pay and fraction of pay at-risk) and the firm's actual performance for the period relative to a target level of performance. Note that we have not yet specified the measure of firm performance. Historically, it should be noted that performance has been measured in terms of profits or revenue growth. For example, see the description of the Harley-Davidson Short-Term Incentive Program found in the Finance Matters discussion later in this chapter. Alternatively, some firms base performance on a return on investment measure. For example, in 1996, John Deere used return on assets as its primary performance metric.

To illustrate this basic model of incentive pay found in equation 13-7, consider the case of an employee whose base pay is $40,000 and who has a target bonus equal to 25 percent of his base pay or expected incentive compensation (i.e., dependent on firm performance) equal to $10,000. The employee's expected total compensation *if* the firm meets its performance target will equal $50,000, which is the sum of the $40,000 base

[18]The discussion that follows is very basic. In most firms incentive pay is based on multiple performance metrics. For example, executives may receive 75 percent of their incentive pay based on financial results and 25 percent based on personal objectives. In other cases incentive pay might be based on individual performance, financial performance, and strategic performance.

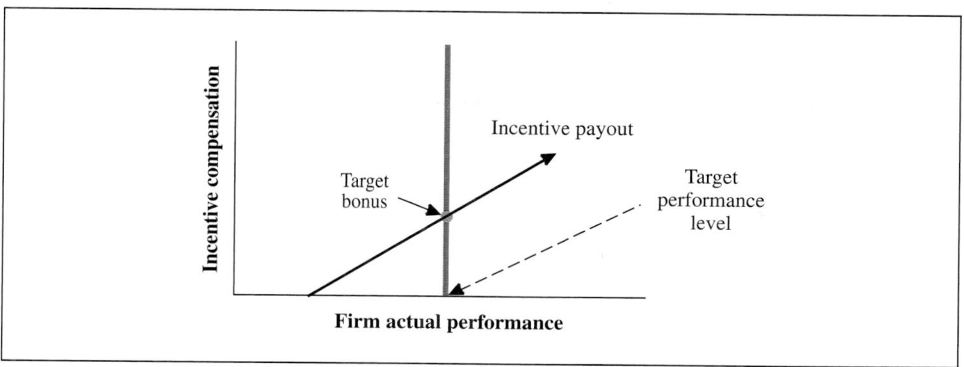


**FIGURE 13-3**
Pure (Unbounded) Incentive Pay for Performance System

pay plus the $10,000 incentive compensation. Substituting into equation 13-7 to calculate the incentive compensation, we get:

$$\text{incentive pay} = \$40{,}000 \times .25 \times 1.0 = \$10{,}000$$

If we assume that the ratio of actual to target performance is 1.1, then his incentive or at-risk pay for the year is $11,000 (i.e., $40,000 × .25 × 1.1 = $11,000) and total compensation for the period will equal $51,000. The basic system would differ across employees only in terms of the level of employee base pay and the percent of that base pay that is at-risk or subject to incentive compensation.

Figure 13-3 illustrates how incentive compensation varies with firm performance. This example represents an **unbounded incentive compensation plan** because it varies directly with actual performance in relation to target performance with no floor (minimum) or cap (maximum).[19] Employees are "incentivized" to improve firm performance regardless of the level of firm performance in such a system.

**Unbounded incentive compensation plan**
An incentive program that has no minimum or maximum performance targets that limit the payment of incentive pay.

Most firms, however, do not use an unbounded incentive pay program. Instead they use a system that provides for a minimum, or threshold, level of performance (in relation to the target level) before the incentive plan kicks in, and a maximum level of performance (again in relation to the target) above which no incentive pay is rewarded. We refer to these plans as **bounded incentive pay programs.** The minimum and maximum performance levels are sometimes referred to as "golfing points" because of the adverse incentives that they have on employee work effort (i.e., they go play golf rather than work harder).

**Bounded incentive pay programs**
Incentive pay programs that place upper and lower limits on the levels of firm performance for which incentive compensation will be awarded to employees.

Figure 13-4 contains an example of an 80/120 plan for which the minimum or threshold level of performance at which incentive compensation will be paid is 80 percent of the target level of performance. The maximum performance for which incentive pay will be awarded is 120 percent of the target performance. Incentive compensation is only paid for performance levels that fall within the 80/120 range. Consequently, there is a wide range of performance for which no incentive pay is awarded (i.e., performance above 120 percent or below 80 percent of the target level). As a result of the boundaries, this type of program encourages employees to work to meet their performance targets only within the range of performance for which the payout varies with performance.

This type of bounded incentive payment plan also has some unfortunate effects on employee incentives to improve firm performance. Specifically, consider the effects on employee incentives under an 80/120 bonus plan that uses firm earnings to measure performance. Under this plan, managers have an incentive to select accounting procedures and accruals to increase the present value of their bonus. For example, as it becomes obvious that the firm's performance for the evaluation period (usually 1 quarter or 1 year) will fall below the

[19]Implicit in our discussion is the assumption that the performance metric is bounded from below at zero.

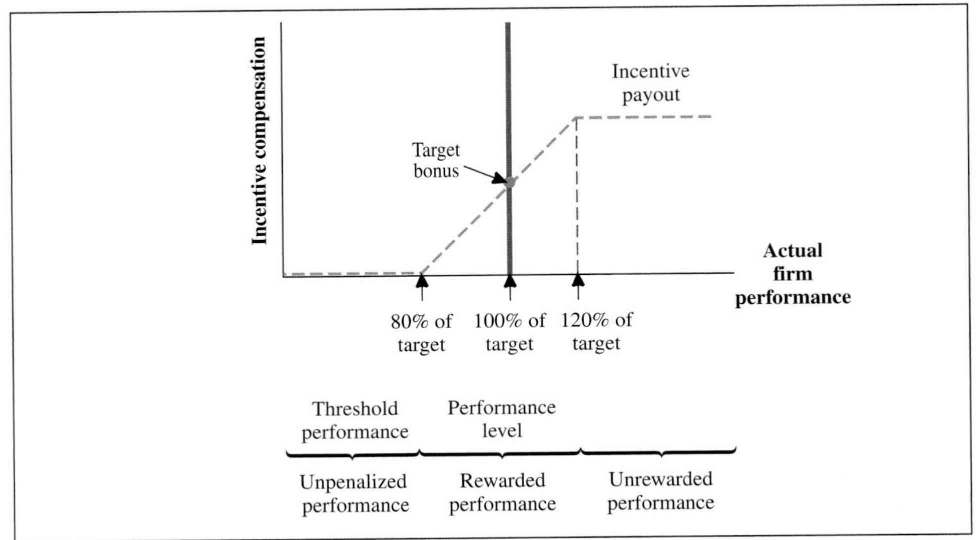


**FIGURE 13-4**
An 80/120 (Bounded) Incentive Pay for Performance System

80 percent threshold, employees have no direct pay-for-performance incentive to work harder in order to raise firm performance during the remainder of the performance evaluation period. In fact, they have an incentive to reduce current period performance even further in the hopes that it will lower the performance target for the coming period. In addition, reducing current period performance may allow management to shift some or all of the unrewarded performance from the current to the subsequent evaluation period when it hopes to be rewarded for it.

A similar perversity arises at the upper end of the performance spectrum when management sees that the firm may exceed the upper bound on the incentive compensation program. For example, if it looks like the firm's performance is going to surpass the maximum payout level, then the employees once again lose the incentive to improve performance. This occurs for two reasons. First of all, they are not paid for performance above the maximum, and second, they may be able to postpone some of the current period's business until the coming period when they can count it toward incentive pay for that period.

**ISSUE 4: PAYING WITH A CASH BONUS VERSUS EQUITY** The amount of incentive pay is determined by firm performance and the particulars of the payout function (i.e., whether it is bounded or not). However, the form of the compensation is also an important component of a firm's compensation program. Specifically, the firm can pay in cash, stock, or some mixture of the two. If the firm chooses stock, then the employees are rewarded for current performance and are also provided with a long-term incentive to improve performance.

The importance of stock options is reflected in the fact that they currently account for more than half of total CEO compensation in the largest U.S. companies and about 30 percent of senior operating managers' pay. Furthermore, options and stock grants now constitute almost half of board of directors' pay. Obviously, equity-based compensation is an important and valuable tool in a firm's compensation package. Baker, Jensen, and Murphy (1988) summarize the case for equity-based compensation as follows:

> Compensation practitioners argue that fundamental changes in the "corporate culture" occur when employees are made partial owners of the firm. The effects of these plans include "rooting for the home team" and a growing awareness of and interest in the corporate bottom line. We do not understand how these effects translate into increased productivity, nor do we have a well-developed economic theory of the creation and effects of corporate culture.

This is a very brief overview of the use of equity-based pay as an important component of a firm's overall compensation program. There are a number of important issues that

ROAD RULES

A FOCUS ON HARLEY-DAVIDSON

ROAD RULES

### The Annual Bonus Program for Harley-Davidson Employees

The employees at Harley-Davidson participate in an annual bonus program called STIP, for Short Term Incentive Plan.[1] The STIP program is a variable compensation program that rewards financial performance and continuous improvement of defined measures. The program was designed to provide eligible employees with cash rewards when company performance improves. Furthermore, the program is continually reviewed and may be amended annually. For our purposes, we review the basic elements of the system in place for 2000 to illustrate the fundamental characteristics of the program.

#### HOW IS THE STIP PAYOUT DETERMINED?

The cash payout for 2000 is determined by company-wide performance based on both financial and quality measures. The specific payout reflects how the company performs against the 2000 STIP measures.

For 2000, the financial performance measure for the STIP plan is based on earnings growth rate (EGR), which is calculated by comparing 2000 earnings before interest and taxes (EBIT) to 1999 EBIT. The amount of the payout is then based on the company's actual EGR for the year. The higher is the EGR, the higher the bonus payout.

The second performance measure in the STIP program for 2000 is based on quality and, for 2000, is comprised of two quality measures. The first quality performance standard relates to the number of warranty claims received within 30 days following registration, per hundred motorcycles produced from January through September 2000. The second quality measure relates to the establishment of a companywide, five-year Quality Plan. With this standard a bonus is awarded for completing the plan.

#### SUMMING UP

The STIP program at Harley-Davidson constitutes the firm's annual bonus program and is but one form of compensation paid to employees. They also receive pay that is subject to merit raises and some employees participate in a stock option program. Note also that the STIP payout is based on overall company performance and not the perfor-mance of the individual or group in which the individual participates. Another interesting feature of the program is that it is "uncapped." That is, the maximum bonus depends on firm performance and is not limited or capped at any particular percentage of target bonus pay. Finally, the program is very flexible in that the performance measures can be changed from year to year depending upon the perceived needs of the firm. For 2000 the performance measures reflect both financial performance (operating earnings) and quality.

[1]The description given here is a simplification of the actual program but captures the essence of the program for 2000.

arise in determining just who should receive equity-based pay within the organization and how that pay should be structured. However, discussion of these issues is beyond the scope of this book. The interested reader will find the discussion by Rappaport (1999) very helpful in coming to understand these issues.

### CONCEPT CHECK

1. Define each of the following components of a firm's compensation plan: base pay, bonus, long-term compensation, incentive-based compensation, and at-risk compensation.
2. Describe a bounded and an unbounded incentive pay program. What are the behavioral implications of the bounded program?

## HOW FINANCIAL MANAGERS USE THIS MATERIAL

Capital-budgeting procedures are designed to help managers make new investments that promise returns that are higher than the firm's cost of capital. However, promising and delivering these returns are not always the same thing. Forecast project benefits and costs are not always realized, and it is up to the firm's management to oversee operations so as to achieve the greatest value possible from its investments. However, when firms are managed by non-owner employees, the problem of properly motivating employees to make shareholder wealth-maximizing decisions arises. This is where managing for shareholder value comes into prominence. Firms must measure and reward periodic performance of the firm in a way that encourages good decisions. This is a difficult task, but recent developments in the use of economic value added have helped a number of firms in this regard. In addition, most publicly held firms choose to make owners out of their employees by granting them shares of stock or giving them the option to buy shares.

Shareholder value maximization represents a melding of multiple business disciplines by focusing on the measurement and rewarding of performance that creates shareholder value. Traditionally, the periodic measurement of firm performance has been discussed in managerial accounting classes while compensation programs were discussed in human relations management courses. Stock options are discussed in finance courses and the overall design of business strategy falls within the realm of strategic management. Shareholder value management represents an attempt to bring all of these topics together in the context of managing the firm for value creation.

## SUMMARY

Using performance measures that are directly linked to firm value as the basis for compensating managers has been found to be a very powerful tool for focusing behavior on the goal of shareholder wealth maximization. However, as simple as the idea might sound, its implementation can be fraught with difficulties. In this chapter, we laid out a framework for analyzing both the choice of a performance measure and a discussion of the issues that must be addressed when linking performance to pay.

**OBJECTIVE 1** 

Which firms create shareholder value and which ones destroy it? This sounds like a very difficult question but, in fact, it is pretty easy to address. Recalling our discussion of project net present value, we determined that a new investment was expected to create value for the firm's shareholders if the anticipated value of its cash flows (i.e., the present value of expected future cash flows) was greater than the amount of money required to undertake the investment. Well, it may surprise you to learn that there is an analogous measure for the firm as a whole and it is called market value added, or *MVA*. However, when we measure *MVA* for a publicly held firm (i.e., a firm whose shares of stock are traded in the public capital market) we don't have to do the discounting of future cash flows to estimate the market value of the firm. So, we can assess the market's assessment of whether a firm is creating value for its shareholders directly using *MVA,* which is calculated as the difference in the market value of the firm (i.e., the sum of the market values of all the firm's securities—debt and equity) less the total capital invested in the firm.

**OBJECTIVE 2** 

Throughout this text we have argued that the underlying basis for understanding the determinants of firm value lie in the discounted cash-flow model. The model was described as follows:

$$\text{firm value} = \frac{\text{free cash flow}_1}{(1 + k_{wacc})^1} + \frac{\text{free cash flow}_2}{(1 + k_{wacc})^2} + \frac{\text{free cash flow}_3}{(1 + k_{wacc})^3} + \frac{\text{terminal value}_3}{(1 + k_{wacc})^3} \tag{13-2}$$

With this model of firm value in mind, we then considered the underlying drivers of free cash flow. We referred to these as value drivers.

**OBJECTIVE 3** 

We identified a key set of value drivers in the free cash-flow valuation model including operating profit margins and asset intensity (i.e., the efficiency with which the firm uses its assets to generate sales). These drivers, in turn, have their determinants in the actions taken by the firm's management. For example, instituting a just-in-time inventory control program can lead to reductions in inventories and, consequently, an increase in the efficiency with which assets are utilized. Other things remaining the same, this could lead to a reduction in expenses and an increase in firm value.

**OBJECTIVE 4** 

Economic value added represents a measure of performance that can be used to capture the success or failure of the firm (or a business unit) to create shareholder value over a specific interval of time such as 1 year. *EVA* is defined in either of two equivalent ways:

$$EVA_t = \left[\begin{array}{c}\text{net operating}\\ \text{profit after}\\ \text{tax } (NOPAT)_t\end{array}\right] - \left[\begin{array}{c}\text{weighted average}\\ \text{cost of}\\ \text{capital } (k_{wacc})\end{array} \times \begin{array}{c}\text{invested}\\ \text{capital}_{t-1}\end{array}\right] \tag{13-5}$$

We observed that although *EVA* is related to accounting profits, it differs in that it incorporates a charge for the capital invested in the firm equal to the product of the firm's invested capital at the beginning of the period and the firm's weighted average cost of capital. The result is a measure of the contribution of the firm's operations for the period to the value of the firm. If *EVA* is positive, then value was created in the period, and if it is negative, value was destroyed.[20] An alternative definition of *EVA* focuses on the rates of return earned on capital compared to the cost of capital:

$$EVA_t = \left(\begin{array}{c}\text{return on invested}\\ \text{capital } (ROIC)_t\end{array} - \begin{array}{c}\text{weighted average}\\ \text{cost of capital } (k_{wacc})\end{array}\right) \times \begin{array}{c}\text{invested}\\ \text{capital } (IC)_{t-1}\end{array} \quad \textbf{(13-6)}$$

Either formulation provides the same estimate of *EVA,* which can then be used as a measure of the performance of the firm for a specific period of time. A growing number of firms are now using *EVA* and similar performance measures as the basis for determining incentive or at-risk compensation for their employees.

Managerial compensation programs typically are comprised of three basic components: base pay, bonus, and long-term compensation. Base pay is the salary component that does not vary with the performance of the firm. The bonus and long-term compensation components are based on the performance of the firm compared to a target set prior to the start of the period. Because these latter components of compensation vary with firm performance, they are considered to be *at-risk.*

There are four fundamental issues that every managerial compensation program must address:

- *How much should be paid for a particular job?* We found that this issue is generally addressed by deferring to the labor market and the going rate of pay for the job.
- *What portion of the total compensation package should be in base salary and what part should be incentive based?* Although no strict guidelines were given, we do know that, in general, the higher the position in the firm's managerial hierarchy, the greater the proportion of pay that is based on firm performance.
- *How should incentive pay be linked to performance?* Typically, firms pay out incentive compensation to their employees over a limited range of performance. For example, if performance exceeds 80 percent of the target performance level set by upper management but is less than 120 percent of the target, incentive compensation will be paid. However, should firm performance drop below 80 percent of the target level, no incentive pay will be awarded for the period. Should performance exceed 120 percent of the target, no incentive pay is awarded for performance in excess of the 120 percent cap. These upper and lower bounds on incentive pay are often referred to by those affected as *golfing points* because the employees have no financial incentive to work hard once it becomes obvious that one of these boundaries will be violated.
- *What portion of the incentive pay should be paid as a cash bonus and what portion should be in long-term (equity) compensation?* Equity in the company is growing in popularity as a medium of payment for incentive-based compensation. Giving employees shares of stock has the double effect of both compensating them for superior performance in the current period and also giving them an added incentive to perform well in the future.

## KEY TERMS

**Base pay, 425**
**Bonus payment, 425**
**Bounded incentive pay programs, 427**
**Capital charge, 421**
**Economic value added, 421**
**Free cash-flow model, 415**
**Incentive (performance-based compensation), 425**
**Invested capital, 413**
**Long-term compensation, 425**
**Market value added (MVA), 412**

myPHLIP

Go To:
http://www.prenhall.com/keown
for downloads and current events associated with this chapter

[20]This is a simplistic interpretation of *EVA* that sometimes does not hold. Discussion of the limitations of *EVA* as an indicator of value creation is beyond the scope of this text. The interested reader is referred to Martin and Petty (2001) for a detailed treatment of these and other related issues.

**Return on invested capital, 422**

**Terminal value, 415**

**Unbounded incentive compensation plan, 427**

**Value drivers, 420**

## STUDY QUESTIONS

**13-1.** What is the accounting model of equity valuation and what are its limitations?

**13-2.** What is the free cash-flow valuation model?

**13-3.** List and describe four value drivers. How can a firm's management take explicit steps to manage these value drivers?

**13-4.** What is Economic Value Added, how is it calculated, and how is it related to market value added?

**13-5.** List and discuss the fundamental components of a firm's compensation program.

**13-6.** List and discuss the four basic issues that must be addressed in designing a firm's compensation program.

## SELF-TEST PROBLEMS

**ST-1.** The earnings per share of Creamco, Inc., for the current year are $2 per share and the firm has 4 million shares outstanding. The dairy products industry in which Creamco competes consists of a relatively small number of producers and the common stock of those that are publicly traded generally trade at price multiples of about 18 times earnings.

**a.** Based on the information provided, what price would you expect Creamco's shares to sell for?

**b.** Creamco has an opportunity to construct a new dairy processing plant in nearby Weatherford, Texas. The new plant will offer state-of-the-art facilities and allow the firm to reduce its waste by 15 percent. However, if plant construction begins next year, it will interrupt the firm's operations such that earnings per share may drop by as much as 10¢ for the year. What effect, if any, would you anticipate that the decision to undertake the new investment will have on Creamco's stock price?

**ST-2.** Zaap.com, Inc. is a privately held B2B startup that offers inventory management services to clients. Client firms are generally small- to medium-sized manufacturing firms that cannot afford sophisticated inventory control practices. Zaap.com provides its services via the Internet by connecting the manufacturers directly to their suppliers and managing the ordering and payment interface. Zaap.com plans to sell its shares to the general public within the next 18 months and wants to get some idea what the firm's stock will be worth. An investment banker located in Dallas who specializes in assisting high-tech startups to go public has evaluated the company's future prospects and made the following estimates of future free cash flows:

| | Years | | | |
|---|---|---|---|---|
| | 1 | 2 | 3 | 4 |
| Sales | $100,000.00 | $115,000.00 | $132,250.00 | $132,250.00 |
| Operating income (earnings before interest and taxes) | 16,000.00 | 18,400.00 | 21,160.00 | 21,160.00 |
| Less cash tax payments | (4,800.00) | (5,520.00) | (6,348.00) | (6,348.00) |
| Net operating profits after taxes (*NOPAT*) | $ 11,200.00 | $ 12,880.00 | $ 14,812.00 | $ 14,812.00 |
| Less investments: | | | | |
| Investment in net working capital | (1,695.65) | (1,950.00) | (2,242.50) | — |
| Capital expenditures (*CAPEX*) | (2,347.83) | (2,700.00) | (3,105.00) | — |
| Total investments | $ (4,043.48) | $ (4,650.00) | $ (5,347.50) | $ — |
| Free cash flow | $ 7,156.52 | $ 8,230.00 | $ 9,464.50 | $ 14,812.00 |

Furthermore, the firm's investment banker had done a study of the firm's cost of capital and estimated the weighted average cost of capital to be approximately 12 percent.

**a.** What is the value of Zaap.com based on these estimates?

**b.** Given that Zaap.com's invested capital in year 0 is \$31,304.35, what is the firm's market value added?

**c.** If Zaap.com has 2,000 shares of common stock outstanding and liabilities valued at \$4,000, what is the value per share of its stock?

**ST-3.** The management of the Zaap.com (from ST-2) wishes to estimate *EVA* for each of the next 4 years of the firm's operations. An evaluation of the firm's invested capital reveals the following values beginning with the current period (year 0):

| | Years | | | | |
|---|---|---|---|---|---|
| | 0 | 1 | 2 | 3 | 4 |
| Current assets | \$15,652.17 | \$17,347.83 | \$19,297.83 | \$21,540.33 | \$21,540.33 |
| Property, plant, and equipment | 15,652.17 | \$18,000.00 | \$20,700.00 | \$23,805.00 | \$23,805.00 |
| Invested capital | \$31,304.35 | \$35,347.83 | \$39,997.83 | \$45,345.33 | \$45,345.33 |

**a.** Calculate Zaap.com's *EVA*s for years 1 through 4. What do these values tell you about the value being created by Zaap.com?

**b.** What is Zaap.com's return on invested capital (*ROIC*) for each of the years 1 through 4? Relate the firm's *ROIC* to your *EVA* estimates.

## STUDY PROBLEMS (SET A)

**13-1A.** (*Accounting model valuation*) The Enron Corporation's earnings for 1999 were \$1.18 per share and its closing stock price for the year was \$44.375. Analysts' estimates of 2000 earnings per share are about \$1.41. Use the accounting valuation model to estimate Enron's stock price.

**13-2A.** (*Free cash flow model valuation*) The Bergman Corporation sold its shares to the general public in 1995. The firm's estimated free cash flows for the next 4 years are as follows:

| | Years | | | |
|---|---|---|---|---|
| | 1 | 2 | 3 | 4 |
| Sales | \$30,000.00 | \$33,000.00 | \$36,300.00 | \$36,300.00 |
| Operating income | 4,800.00 | 5,280.00 | 5,808.00 | 5,808.00 |
| Less cash tax payments | (1,440.00) | (1,584.00) | (1,742.40) | (1,742.40) |
| Net operating profits after taxes (*NOPAT*) | \$ 3,360.00 | \$ 3,696.00 | \$ 4,065.60 | \$ 4,065.60 |
| Less investments: | | | | |
| Investment in net working capital | (354.55) | (390.00) | (429.00) | — |
| Capital expenditures (*CAPEX*) | (490.91) | (540.00) | (594.00) | — |
| Total investments | \$ (845.46) | \$ (930.00) | \$(1,023.00) | \$ — |
| Free cash flow | \$ 2,514.55 | \$ 2,766.00 | \$ 3,042.60 | \$ 4,065.60 |

Bergman estimated that its revenues and free cash flows would stop growing in year 4 and form a level perpetuity. Furthermore, the firm's investment banker conducted a study of the firm's cost of capital and estimated the weighted average cost of capital to be approximately 12 percent.

**a.** What is the value of Bergman using the free cash flow valuation model?

**b.** Given that Bergman's invested capital in year 0 is \$9,818.18, what is the market value added for Bergman?

**c.** If Bergman has 2,000 shares of common stock outstanding and liabilities valued at \$4,000, what is the value per share of its stock?

**13-3A.** (*Calculating economic value added*) The management of the Bergman Corporation (from problem 13-2A) wishes to estimate *EVA* for each of the next 3 years of the firm's operations. An evaluation of the firm's invested capital reveals the following values beginning with the current period (year 0):

| | Years | | | | |
|---|---|---|---|---|---|
| | 0 | 1 | 2 | 3 | 4 |
| Current assets | $4,909.09 | $ 5,263.64 | $ 5,653.64 | $ 6,082.64 | $ 6,082.64 |
| Property, plant, and equipment | 4,909.09 | 5,400.00 | 5,940.00 | 6,534.00 | 6,534.00 |
| Invested capital | $9,818.18 | $10,663.64 | $11,593.64 | $12,616.64 | $12,616.64 |

**a.** Calculate Bergman's *EVA*s for years 1 through 4. What do these values tell you about the value being created by Bergman?

**b.** What is Bergman's return on invested capital (*ROIC*) for each of the years 1 through 4? Relate the firm's *ROIC* to your *EVA* estimates.

**c.** Bergman's *EVA*s for years 4 and beyond form a level perpetuity equal to the *EVA* for year 3. Calculate the present value of the firm's *EVA*s for years 1 through infinity. How does this present value compare to the market value added for the firm (see part *b* of problem 13-2A)? You can assume that the free cash flow value of Bergman from problem 13-2a is $30,730.95.

**13-4A.** (*Incentive compensation*) The management of Seligman Manufacturing has decided to tie employee compensation to *EVA* performance of the firm. The firm's CFO, Virginia Whitten, is to make a presentation to the CEO and board of directors illustrating how the program will work under both an unbounded and a bounded plan for awarding incentive compensation. To illustrate the two plans, Virginia has chosen to use the compensation for a typical plant manager. Under the proposed compensation plan, a plant manager would receive a base pay level of $100,000 plus incentive pay equal to 20 percent of this base pay if the firm hits its *EVA* performance targets exactly.

**a.** Calculate the plant manager's incentive pay and total compensation for actual *EVA* performance of $15,000,000; $20,000,000; and $30,000,000 if the target level of *EVA* performance is set at $20,000,000.

**b.** Now estimate the plant manager's incentive pay and total compensation for the same three levels of *EVA* performance and target *EVA* but with a bounded incentive pay system that has a floor equal to 80 percent of the target performance level and a cap at 120 percent. What are the incentive effects for the plant manager of placing the floor and cap on target performance when determining the incentive pay?

## INTEGRATIVE PROBLEM

Jason Jeffries was still a bit stunned as he pressed the lever on the water cooler just outside his boss's office. Just minutes before, Jason had left the office of Sarah Burchette, a partner at PerformancePlus and Jason's immediate supervisor. During their brief visit, Sarah had informed him that the firm wanted to broaden its practice to include new-economy Internet firms. To get the ball rolling for the firm's new target market, she asked Jason to work up a performance analysis for RealNetworks Inc. and present it to the company's partners in 2 weeks. This meant that Jason would have to come to grips with just how much value RealNetworks was creating and how it was doing it. Jason was thrilled with the opportunity to lead the effort but very concerned that he would have enough time to come up with anything meaningful. After all, rationalizing the market valuations of Internet firms was not easy even to the most savvy investors.

After graduating with an MBA from a well-known university in the southwestern United States, Jason had joined the staff of a regional consulting firm, PerformancePlus, where he entered the firm's practice as an associate with a specialty in finance. PerformancePlus specializes in the design of compensation programs that provide greater employee incentives to create shareholder value. The principal tool used in its performance appraisal practice is economic value added, or *EVA*®, which was developed by Stern Stewart and Company.

RealNetworks Inc. is a Washington corporation that provides software products for "streaming" audio, video, text, animation, and other media content over the Internet. Its products include RealAudio and RealVideo. The leadership of the firm, and many industry watchers, believe that streaming media technology is essential to the evolution of the World Wide Web as a mass communications medium because it allows the Internet to compete more effectively with traditional media.[21]

The historical performance of RealNetworks is similar to that of many other new economy Internet firms. The company has experienced very rapid sales growth but has yet to produce a profit (see Panel A of Exhibit 1). In fact, the firm has experienced increasing losses in every year; in 1998, the firm lost over $20 million. In spite of these continued and growing losses, RealNetworks's stock price closed just under $9 per share in 1998, giving the firm a market capitalization of $1,204,467.

Exhibit 1. Selected Financial Statements—RealNetworks, Inc.

**PANEL A. GAAP ACCOUNTING EARNINGS**

| | (US $ thousands) | | |
|---|---|---|---|
| | **1996** | **1997** | **1998** |
| Revenue | $14,012 | $ 32,720 | $ 64,839 |
| Cost of sales | (2,185) | (6,465) | (12,390) |
| Gross profit | $11,827 | $26,255 | $52,449 |
| General and administration | (3,491) | (6,024) | (9,841) |
| Selling, marketing, and advertising | (7,540) | (20,124) | (32,451) |
| Research and development | (4,812) | (13,268) | (29,401) |
| Goodwill amortization | — | — | (1,596) |
| Net operating profit | $(4,016) | $(13,161) | $(20,840) |

**PANEL B. GAAP BALANCE SHEETS**

| | (U.S. $ thousands) | | | |
|---|---|---|---|---|
| | **Dec-95** | **Dec-96** | **Dec-97** | **Dec-98** |
| **ASSETS** | | | | |
| Cash and equivalents | $6,116 | $19,595 | $ 92,028 | $ 89,777 |
| Net receivables | 717 | 3,381 | 15,779 | 4,941 |
| Inventories | 3 | 61 | 167 | — |
| Other current assets | 143 | 491 | 1,885 | 3,212 |
| Total current assets | $6,979 | $23,528 | $109,859 | $ 97,930 |
| Gross plant, property, and equipment | 692 | 3,462 | 7,896 | 12,355 |
| Accumulated depreciation | 98 | 783 | 2,753 | 6,082 |
| Net plant, property, and equipment | $ 594 | $ 2,679 | $ 5,143 | $ 6,273 |
| Investments at equity | — | — | 816 | — |
| Intangibles | — | — | — | 9,048 |
| Other assets | 1 | 261 | 886 | 14,808 |
| **TOTAL ASSETS** | $7,574 | $26,468 | $116,704 | $128,059 |
| **LIABILITIES** | | | | |
| Accounts payable | $ 185 | $ 2,405 | $ 2,136 | $ 3,563 |
| Accrued expenses | 200 | 1,318 | 3,653 | 10,418 |
| Other current liabilities | 646 | 2,912 | 16,550 | 23,742 |
| Total current liabilities | 1,031 | 6,635 | 22,339 | 37,723 |
| Long-term debt | — | — | 963 | 987 |
| Other liabilities | — | — | 15,500 | 5,833 |

*(continued)*

[21]Based on RealNetworks's 10K filing for the period ended December 31, 1998.

| | (U.S. $ thousands) | | | |
|---|---|---|---|---|
| | Dec-95 | Dec-96 | Dec-97 | Dec-98 |
| **EQUITY** | | | | |
| Preferred stock—redeemable | $ 7,654 | $23,153 | — | — |
| Preferred stock—nonredeemable | 14 | 14 | — | — |
| Total preferred stock | $ 7,668 | $23,167 | — | — |
| Common stock | — | 1 | 31 | 34 |
| Capital surplus | 921 | 2,543 | 95,557 | 117,546 |
| Retained earnings | (2,046) | (5,878) | (17,686) | (34,064) |
| Common equity | $(1,125) | $ (3,334) | $77,902 | $ 83,516 |
| **TOTAL EQUITY** | $ 6,543 | $19,833 | $77,902 | $ 83,516 |
| **TOTAL LIABILITIES AND EQUITY** | 7,574 | 26,468 | 116,704 | 128,059 |
| **COMMON SHARES OUTSTANDING** | 148 | 2,140 | 123,464 | 134,296 |

**a.** Evaluate RealNetworks' profitability over the 1996–98 period.

**b.** What do you think is the appropriate number for RealNetworks' invested capital at the end of 1998? Note that both marketing and R&D expenditures are expensed fully against revenues in the year in which the expenditures are made. Do you think that this distorts total assets as an indication of the firm's invested capital? Explain.

**c.** Explain how you would go about evaluating the *EVA* for 1996–98. What problems do you see in carrying out the analysis?

## STUDY PROBLEMS (SET B)

**13-1B.** (*Accounting model valuation*) The Harley-Davidson Corporation's earnings for 1999 were 87¢ per share and its closing stock price for the year was $16-1/16. Analyst estimates of 2000 earnings per share are about $1.09. Use the accounting valuation model to estimate Harley-Davidson's stock price.

**13-2B.** (*Free cash flow model valuation*) The Hackberg Corporation sold its shares to the general public in 1996. The firm's estimated free cash flows for the next 4 years are as follows:

| | Years | | | |
|---|---|---|---|---|
| | 1 | 2 | 3 | 4 |
| Sales | $34,500.00 | $37,950.00 | $41,745.00 | $41,745.00 |
| Operating income | 5,865.00 | 6,451.50 | 7,096.65 | 7,096.65 |
| Less cash tax payments | (1,6542.20) | (1,806.42) | (1,987.06) | (1,987.06) |
| Net operating profits after taxes (*NOPAT*) | $ 4,222.80 | $ 4,645.08 | $ 5,109.59 | $ 5,109.59 |
| Less investments: | | | | |
| Investment in net working capital | (407.73) | (448.50) | (493.35) | — |
| Capital expenditures (*CAPEX*) | (564.55) | (621.00) | (683.10) | — |
| Total investments | $ (972.27) | $ (1,069.50) | $ (1,176.45) | $ — |
| Free cash flow | $ 3,250.53 | $ 3,575.58 | $ 3,933.14 | $ 5,109.59 |

Hackberg estimated that its revenues and free cash flows would stop growing in year 3 and form a level perpetuity. Furthermore, the firm's investment banker did a study of the firm's cost of capital and estimated the weighted average cost of capital to be approximately 15 percent.

**a.** What is the value of Hackberg?

**b.** Given that Hackberg's invested capital in year 0 is $11,290.91, what is the market value added for Hackberg?

**c.** If Hackberg has 4,000 shares of common stock outstanding and liabilities valued at $6,000, what is the value per share of its stock?

**13-3B.** (*Calculating economic value added*) The management of the Hackberg Corporation (from problem 13-2B) wishes to estimate *EVA* for each of the next 4 years of the firm's operations. An evaluation of the firm's invested capital reveals the following values beginning with the current period (year 0):

| | Years | | | | |
|---|---|---|---|---|---|
| | 0 | 1 | 2 | 3 | 4 |
| Current assets | \$ 5,645.45 | \$ 6,053.18 | \$ 6,501.68 | \$ 6,995.03 | \$ 6,995.03 |
| Property, plant and equipment | 5,645.45 | 6,210.00 | \$ 6,831.00 | 7,514.10 | 7,514.10 |
| Invested capital | \$11,290.91 | \$12,263.18 | \$13,332.68 | \$14,509.13 | \$14,509.13 |

**a.** Calculate Hackberg's *EVA*s for years 1 through 4. What do these values tell you about the value being created by Hackberg?

**b.** What is Hackberg's return on invested capital (*ROIC*) for each of the years 1 through 4? Relate the firm's *ROIC* to your *EVA* estimates.

**c.** Hackberg's *EVA*s for years 4 and beyond form a level perpetuity equal to the *EVA* for year 3. Calculate the present value of the firm's *EVA*s for years 1 through infinity. How does this present value compare to the market value added for the firm (see part *b* of problem 13-2B)? You can assume that the free cash flow value of Hackberg from problem 13-2B is \$41,745.25.

**13-4B.** (*Incentive compensation*) The management of Shook Manufacturing has decided to tie employee compensation to *EVA* performance of the firm. The firm's CFO, Mark Shephard, is to make a presentation to the CEO and board of directors illustrating how the program will work under both an unbounded and a bounded plan for awarding incentive compensation. To illustrate the two plans, Mark has chosen to use the compensation for a typical division manager. Under the proposed compensation plan, a division manager would receive a base pay level of \$150,000 plus incentive pay equal to 30 percent of this base pay if the firm hits its *EVA* perfor-mance targets exactly.

**a.** Calculate the division manager's incentive pay and total compensation for actual *EVA* performance of \$20,000,000; \$30,000,000; and \$40,000,000 if the target level of *EVA* performance is set at \$30,000,000.

**b.** Now estimate the division manager's incentive pay and total compensation for the same three levels of *EVA* performance and target *EVA* but with a bounded incentive pay system that has a floor equal to 80 percent of the target performance level and a cap at 120 percent. What are the incentive effects for the division manager of placing the floor and cap on target performance when determining the incentive pay?

## SELF-TEST SOLUTIONS

**ST-1. a.** $$\text{price-earnings multiple} = \frac{\text{stock price}}{\text{earnings per share}}$$

$$18 = \frac{\text{stock price}}{\$2.00}$$

$$\text{stock price} = 18 \times \$2.00 = \$36.00$$

**b.** Although the new processing plant will reduce earnings per share by 10¢, this project should not have a negative impact on the stock price. It is reasonable to think the stock price may increase as a result of the new facility and the reduction in waste.

**ST-2. a.** $$\text{terminal value} = \frac{\$14{,}812}{.12} = 123{,}433.33$$

$$\text{value of the firm} = PV \text{ of free cash flows} = \frac{\$7{,}156.52}{(1.12)^1} + \frac{\$8{,}230.00}{(1.12)^2} + \frac{\$9{,}464.50}{(1.12)^3} + \frac{\$123{,}433.33}{(1.12)^3}$$

$$= \$107{,}544.71$$

**b.** $MVA$ = firm value − invested capital
= $107,544.71 − $31,304.05
= $76,240.66

**c.** firm value = debt value + equity value
$107,544.71 = $4,000 + equity value
equity value = $103,544.71

$$\text{value per share of stock} = \frac{\text{equity value}}{\text{shares outstanding}} = \frac{\$103{,}544.71}{2{,}000} = \$51.77$$

**ST-3. a.** $EVA_t = NOPAT_t - (k_{wacc} \times IC_{t-1})$

$k_{wacc} = 12\%$

| | Year 1 | Year 2 | Year 3 | Year 4 |
|---|---|---|---|---|
| $NOPAT_t$ | $11,200 | $12,880 | $14,812 | $14,812 |
| $IC_{t-1}$ | $31,304.35 | $35,347.83 | $39,997.83 | $45,345.33 |
| $EVA_t$ | $ 7,443.48 | $ 8,638.61 | $10,012.26 | $ 9,370.56 |

*EVA* is positive for each of the 4 years under review, indicating that Zaap.com is creating value for its shareholders.

**b.** $ROIC_t = \dfrac{NOPAT_t}{IC_{t-1}}$

| | Year 1 | Year 2 | Year 3 | Year 4 |
|---|---|---|---|---|
| $NOPAT_t$ | $11,200 | $12,880 | $14,812 | $14,812 |
| $IC_{t-1}$ | $31,304.35 | $35,347.83 | $39,997.83 | $45,345.33 |
| $ROIC_t$ | 35.8% | 36.4% | $37.0% | 32.7% |

As we would expect, the firm's *ROIC* is greater than its cost of capital and, thus, the firm is creating value for its shareholders. When *ROIC* is greater than the firm's cost of capital, we would see positive *EVA*s, which we did in part *a* of this problem.

## Suggested Readings

Berle, Adolph., and Gardner Means. 1932. *The modern corporation and private property* (New York: Macmillan).

Copeland, Tom, Tim Koller, and Jack Murrin. 1994. *Valuation: Measuring and managing the value of companies,* 2nd edition. (New York: John Wiley & Sons, Inc.).

Martin, John D., and J. William Petty. 2001. *Value-based management: The corporate response to the shareholder revolution.* (Boston: Harvard Business School Press).

McTaggart, James M., Peter W. Kontes, and Michael C. Mankins. 1994. *The value imperative: Managing for superior shareholder returns.* (New York: The Free Press).

Rappaport, Alfred. 1986. *Creating shareholder value: The new standard for business performance.* (New York: The Free Press).

Rappaport, Alfred. 1999. New thinking on how to link executive pay with performance. *Harvard Business Review,* March/April: 91–101.

Stewart, G. Bennett III. 1991. *The quest for value.* (New York: Harper Business).

# RAISING CAPITAL IN THE FINANCIAL MARKETS

From February 4, 1994, through May 16, 2000, the Federal Reserve System (Fed), the nation's central bank, voted to change the "target" federal funds rate on 20 different occasions. Fourteen of these interest rate changes were in the upward direction. The federal funds rate is a short-term market rate of interest, influenced by the Fed, that serves as a sensitive indicator of the direction of future changes in interest rates. We will review here four different interest rate cycles that have confronted major corporate officers, like those at Harley-Davidson or The Walt Disney Company. This will emphasize how alert and flexible top-level executives must be in planning their firms' cash availability and cash distributions within an always-uncertain global economic environment. The discussion also stresses that interest rate changes induce changes in the cost of capital to firms and thereby affect their capital-budgeting decisions. The funds-management process, as you will shortly see, is continual. Following is an overview of the four distinct cycles: In early 1994, the central bank feared that inflationary pressures were building up in the U.S. economy and decided to take action, via raising nominal short-term interest rates, to stem those pressures by slowing down aggregate economic growth. The Fed remained committed to a course of higher interest rates throughout 1994 and the first half of 1995; then on July 6, 1995, these monetary policymakers reversed course and began a series of three interest rate decreases. For over a year, from

**LEARNING OBJECTIVES**

After reading this chapter, you should be able to

1. Understand the historical relationship between internally generated corporate sources of funds and externally generated sources of funds.
2. Understand the financing mix that tends to be used by firms raising long-term financial capital.
3. Explain why financial markets exist in a developed economy.
4. Explain the financing process by which savings are supplied and raised by major sectors in the economy.
5. Describe the key components of the U.S. financial market system.
6. Understand the role of the investment banking business in the context of raising corporate capital.
7. Distinguish between privately placed securities and publicly offered securities.
8. Be acquainted with the concepts of securities flotation costs and securities markets regulations.

January 31, 1996, to March 25, 1997, the Fed stayed on the sidelines and let the nation's financial markets direct the course of interest rates. ● However, during the first quarter of 1997, the Fed again became concerned that increased inflationary pressures were building up within the U.S. economic system. For example, the national economy was growing at a faster inflation-adjusted rate in the first quarter of 1997 than was experienced in the first quarter of 1987—the year of the major equity market crash, which later occurred during October of that year. As a result, the Fed chose to raise the target federal funds rate on March 25, 1997. The March 1997 interest rate increase directed by the Fed was followed by almost a year and a half of the central bank returning to the sidelines and observing the important relationship between the rate of inflation and real economic growth. ● Then, during the fall months of 1998, unfavorable international pressures from Brazil and Russia, among others, caused the commercial lending system to pull in the reigns. This put financing strains on corporate America. Fearing a widening international economic slowdown, the Fed engineered a quick sequence of three more interest rate decreases that ended on November 17, 1998, aimed at stabilizing both the credit and equity markets. By the way, this maneuvering by the central bank in 1998 did, in fact, work. ● Once again, commencing on June 30, 1999, the Fed became concerned about the relationship among (a) tight labor markets, (b) strong aggregate real economic growth, usually monitored by rates of change in real gross domestic product (GDP), and (c) the rate of observed inflation as well as inflationary expectations. During this phase of the business cycle, the Fed chose to increase short-term interest rates on six different occasions over the period ended May 16, 2000. ●

Recent Interest Rate Cycles

| Phase and Time Period | Main Concern or Risk | Policy Action |
|---|---|---|
| 1. Early 1994 | Inflation | Raise interest rates |
| 2. Early 1997 | Inflation | Raise interest rates |
| 3. Fall 1998 | International pressures | Lower interest rates |
| 4. Summer 1999 | Tight labor markets, strong aggregate, real growth, and inflation | Raise interest rates |

Realize that at this state of the business cycle, the U.S. economy was in uncharted territory, as the remarkable economic expansion that began in March 1991 entered its tenth year at the close of the 2000 first quarter. Such good performance within the aggregate domestic economy stood out, as it marked the longest uninterrupted period of expansion in the United States dating back to 1854 when reliable records began to be maintained. Thus, the Fed continued its vigilant monitoring stance by putting upward pressure on short-term interest rates in hopes of meeting its twin objectives of supporting (a) maximum sustainable employment and (b) price stability. The 20 policy actions and resultant interest rate changes discussed here are shown in

Changes in the Target Federal Funds Rate and Commercial Bank Prime Lending Rate
February 1994–June 2000

| Date | Old Target Rate % | New Target Rate % | Prime Lending Rate % |
|---|---|---|---|
| | | **1994** | |
| February 4 | 3.00 | 3.25 | No change 6.00 |
| March 22 | 3.25 | 3.50 | 6.25 |
| April 18 | 3.50 | 3.75 | 6.75 |
| May 17 | 3.75 | 4.25 | 7.25 |
| August 16 | 4.25 | 4.75 | 7.75 |
| November 19 | 4.75 | 5.50 | 8.50 |
| | | **1995** | |
| February 1 | 5.50 | 6.00 | 9.00 |
| July 6 | 6.00 | 5.75 | 8.75 |
| December 19 | 5.75 | 5.50 | 8.50 |
| | | **1996** | |
| January 31 | 5.50 | 5.25 | 8.25 |
| | | **1997** | |
| March 25 | 5.25 | 5.50 | 8.50 |
| | | **1998** | |
| September 29 | 5.50 | 5.25 | 8.25 |
| October 15 | 5.25 | 5.00 | 8.00 |
| November 17 | 5.00 | 4.75 | 7.75 |
| | | **1999** | |
| June 30 | 4.75 | 5.00 | 8.00 |
| August 24 | 5.00 | 5.25 | 8.25 |
| November 16 | 5.25 | 5.50 | 8.50 |
| | | **2000** | |
| February 2 | 5.50 | 5.75 | 8.75 |
| March 21 | 5.75 | 6.00 | 9.00 |
| May 16 | 6.00 | 6.50 | 9.50 |

the accompanying table. • From a financial management viewpoint, the 14 overt actions by the Fed to raise rates caused the *opportunity cost of funds* to rise. This means that firms like Harley-Davidson and The Walt Disney Company endured increases in their respective cost of capital funds. This, in turn, made it more difficult for real capital projects to be financed and be included in those firms' capital budgets. • The six decisions to lower the target federal funds rate had the exact opposite effect; that is, the given firm's cost of capital funds decreased. In this latter case, the company can take on more capital projects. • Also note in the far right column of the table that the commercial bank prime lending rate typically changes in the same direction and at about the same time that a shift in the federal funds rate occurs. The prime lending rate is the interest rate that banks charge their *most* creditworthy customers. Thus, the transmission of the central bank's policy move to the explicit cost of funds that the firm faces in the financial markets happens quickly. The commercial banking industry helps it along. • As you read this chapter you will learn about (a) the importance of financial markets to a developed economy and (b) how funds are raised in the financial markets. This will help you, as an emerging business executive specializing in accounting, finance, marketing, or strategy, understand the basics of acquiring financial capital in the funds marketplace.

**CHAPTER PREVIEW**

This chapter focuses on the market environment in which long-term financial capital is raised. Long-term funds are raised in the capital market. By the term *capital-market,* we mean all institutions and procedures that facilitate transactions in long-term financial instruments (such as common stocks and bonds).

The sums involved in tapping the capital markets can be vast. For example, new corporate securities offered to the investing marketplace for cash during 1999 totaled $1.07 trillion. To be able to distribute and absorb security offerings of such enormous size, an economy must have a well-developed financial market system. To use that system effectively, the financial manager must possess a basic understanding of its structure. This chapter will help you gain that understanding.

As you work through this chapter, be on the lookout for direct applications of several of our principles that form the basics of business financial management. Specifically, your attention will be directed to: **Principle 1: The Risk-Return Trade-Off—We won't take on additional risk unless we expect to be compensated with additional return; Principle 6: Efficient Capital Markets—The markets are quick and the prices are right;** and **Principle 10: Ethical Behavior Is Doing the Right Thing, and Ethical Dilemmas Are Everywhere in Finance.**

## THE FINANCIAL MANAGER, INTERNAL AND EXTERNAL FUNDS, AND FLEXIBILITY

OBJECTIVE 1 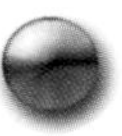

At times, internally generated funds will not be sufficient to finance all of the firm's proposed expenditures. In these situations, the corporation may find it necessary to attract large amounts of financial capital externally or otherwise forgo projects that are forecast to

**TABLE 14-1**
Nonfinancial Corporate Business Sources of Funds: 1981–1999

| Year | Total Sources ($ Billions) | Percent Internal Funds | Percent External Funds |
|---|---|---|---|
| 1999 | 1,210.3 | 66.0 | 34.0 |
| 1998 | 886.4 | 86.0 | 14.0 |
| 1997 | 967.6 | 75.6 | 24.4 |
| 1996 | 812.0 | 83.4 | 16.6 |
| 1995 | 878.4 | 70.7 | 29.3 |
| 1994 | 733.7 | 77.3 | 22.7 |
| 1993 | 593.1 | 81.6 | 18.4 |
| 1992 | 560.5 | 78.2 | 21.8 |
| 1991 | 471.7 | 90.3 | 9.7 |
| 1990 | 535.5 | 76.9 | 23.1 |
| 1989 | 567.9 | 70.4 | 29.6 |
| 1988 | 634.2 | 63.7 | 36.3 |
| 1987 | 564.7 | 66.6 | 33.4 |
| 1986 | 538.8 | 62.5 | 37.5 |
| 1985 | 493.8 | 71.3 | 28.7 |
| 1984 | 511.4 | 65.8 | 34.2 |
| 1983 | 444.6 | 65.7 | 34.3 |
| 1982 | 331.7 | 74.6 | 25.4 |
| 1981 | 394.4 | 60.6 | 39.4 |
| Mean | — | 73.0 | 27.0 |

Sources: *Economic Report of the President,* February 1995, p. 384; *Federal Reserve Bulletin,* June 2000, Table 1.57; and *Flow of Funds Accounts of the U.S.,* First Quarter 2000, Table F. 102.

be profitable.[1] Year in and year out, business firms in the nonfinancial corporate sector of the U.S. economy rely heavily on the nation's financial market system to raise cash.

Table 14-1 displays the relative internal and external sources of funds for such corporations over the 1981 to 1999 period. Notice that the percentage of external funds raised in any given year can vary substantially from that of other years. In 1982, for example, the nonfinancial business sector raised 25.4 percent of its funds in the financial markets. This was substantially less than the 39.4 percent raised externally only 1 year earlier, during 1981. After that, the same type of significant adjustment made by financial managers is evident. During 1988, we see that nonfinancial firms raised 36.3 percent of new funds in the external markets. By the end of 1991, this proportion dropped drastically to 9.7 percent.

Such adjustments illustrate an important point: Financial executives are perpetually on their toes regarding market conditions and the state of the overall economy. Both are reflected in interest rate levels and changes, which were discussed in Chapter 6. Changes in market conditions influence the precise way corporate funds will be raised. High relative interest rates, for instance, will deter use of debt instruments by the financial manager.

The financial market system must be both organized and resilient. Periods of economic recession test the financial markets and those firms that continually use the markets. Economic contractions are especially challenging to financial decision makers because all recessions are unique. This forces financing policies to become unique.

During the 1981 to 1982 recession, which lasted 16 months, interest rates remained high by historic standards during the worst phases of the downturn. This occurred because policy makers at the Fed decided to wring a high rate of inflation out of the economy by means of a tight monetary policy. Simultaneously, stock prices were depressed. These

[1]By *externally generated,* we mean that the funds are obtained by means other than through retentions or depreciation. Funds from these latter two sources are commonly called *internally generated funds.*

**FIGURE 14-1**
Nonfinancial Corporate Business Sources of Funds 1981–1999 vs. 1994–1999

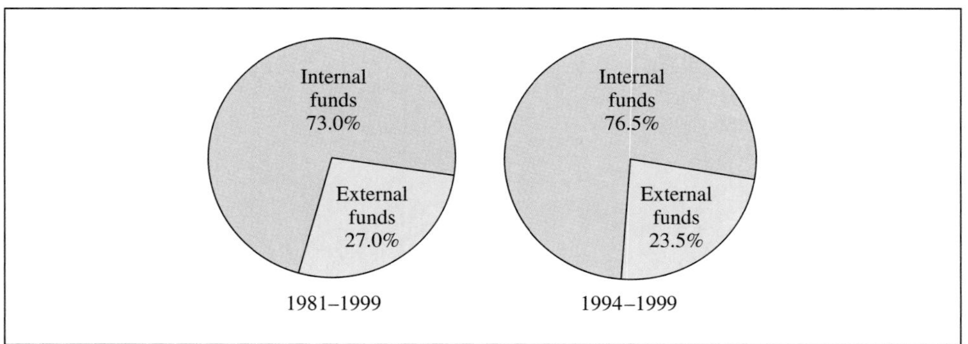


business conditions induced firms to forgo raising funds via external means. During 1982, 74.6 percent of corporate funds were generated internally (see Table 14-1). The same general pattern followed after the 1990 to 1991 recession ended in the first quarter of 1991. During 1991, businesses paid down their short-term borrowing and relied on internally generated sources for 90.3 percent of their net financing needs.

Corporate profitability also plays a role in the determination of the internal-external financing choice. In March 2000, the U.S. economy began the tenth year of economic expansion, making it the longest expansion on record. The good economy translated into good corporate profits. Other things held equal, greater profits reduce the need for external financing. Thus, over the 1993 to 1996 period, the reliance on external finance averaged 22 percent. Whereas, when profits were more strained over the 1981 to 1984 period, financial managers relied more heavily on the market system for an average of 33 percent of their total funds needed.

The collective behavior of companies that results in firms retaining internally generated cash rather than paying it to stockholders as dividends or to creditors (bondholders) as interest is referred to by financial economists and analysts as the *internal capital market.*[2] This is because the firm allocates the cash flows to new projects. On the other hand, if the cash payments were made directly to stockholders and creditors, the funds would ultimately be allocated to new projects through the external capital markets.

As Figure 14-1 shows, the internal capital market accounted for 76.5 percent of nonfinancial corporations' sources of funds over the more recent 1994–1999 period compared to 73.0 percent over the longer 1981–1999 period. Changing economic conditions will cause this relationship to shift persistently because financial executives will continually adjust to the new information that encompasses the business cycle, interest rates, and stock prices.

The point here is an important one for the executive: As economic activity and policy shape the environment of the financial markets, financial managers must understand the meaning of the economic ups and downs and remain flexible in their decision-making processes. Remaining excessively rigid leads to financing mistakes. Those mistakes will generate costs that are ultimately borne by the firm's stockholders.

**CONCEPT CHECK**

1. What distinguishes the internal capital market from the external capital market?
2. What important factor(s) might affect a firm's internal-external financing choice?

[2]A lengthier discussion on the relationship of the internal capital market to the external capital market is found in M. Berlin, "Jack of All Trades? Product Diversification in Nonfinancial Firms," *Business Review,* Federal Reserve Bank of Philadelphia (May–June 1999), pp. 19, 23.

**TABLE 14-2**
Corporate Securities Offered for Cash—Nonfinancial Corporations, 4-Year Cash Weighted Average, 1996–1999

| Total Volume ($ Millions) | Percent Equities | Percent Bonds and Notes |
|---|---|---|
| $1,317,648 | 24.7 | 75.3 |

Source: *Federal Reserve Bulletin,* Table 1.46, June 2000, A31.

## THE MIX OF CORPORATE SECURITIES SOLD IN THE CAPITAL MARKET

OBJECTIVE 2

When corporations decide to raise cash in the capital market, what type of financing vehicle is most favored? Many individual investors think that common stock is the answer to this question. This is understandable, given the coverage of the level of common stock prices by the popular news media. All of the major television networks, for instance, quote the closing price of the Dow Jones Industrial Average on their nightly news broadcasts. Common stock, though, is not the financing method relied on most heavily by corporations. The answer to this question is *corporate bonds. The corporate debt markets clearly dominate the corporate equity markets when new funds are being raised.* This is a long-term relationship—it occurs year after year. Table 14-2 highlights this fact for the recent time period of 1996–1999.

In Table 14-2, we see the annual average volume (in millions of dollars) of corporate securities sold for cash over the 1996 to 1999 period. The percentage breakdown between equities (both common and preferred stocks) and bonds and notes (corporate debt) is also displayed. Notice that debt-type instruments represented a full 75.3 percent of the annual average dollar amount offered to investors by nonfinancial corporations over this 4-year time frame. Equities, therefore, represented the other 24.7 percent. We learned from our discussions of the cost of capital and planning the firm's financing mix that the U.S. tax system inherently favors debt as a means of raising capital. Quite simply, interest expense is deductible from other income when computing the firm's federal tax liability, whereas the dividends paid on both preferred and common stock are not.

Financial executives responsible for raising corporate cash know this. When they have a choice between marketing new bonds and marketing new preferred stock, the outcome is usually in favor of bonds. The after-tax cost of capital on the debt is less than that incurred on preferred stock. Likewise, if the firm has unused debt capacity and the general level of equity prices is depressed, financial executives favor the issuance of debt securities over the issuance of new common stock.

**CONCEPT CHECK**

1. Why might firms prefer to issue new debt securities rather than new common stock?
2. How does the U.S. tax system affect a firm's financing choices?

## WHY FINANCIAL MARKETS EXIST

**Financial markets** are institutions and procedures that facilitate transactions in all types of financial claims. The purchase of your home, the common stock you may own, and your life insurance policy all took place in some type of financial market. Why do financial markets exist? What would the economy lose if our complex system of financial markets were not developed? We will address these questions here.

**Financial markets**
Those institutions and procedures that facilitate transactions in all types of financial claims (securities).

Some *economic units,* such as households, firms, or governments, spend more during a given period than they earn. Other economic units spend less on current consumption than they earn. For example, business firms in the aggregate usually spend more during a specific period than they earn. Households in the aggregate spend less on current consumption than they earn. As a result, some mechanism is needed to facilitate the transfer of savings from those economic units with a surplus to those with a deficit. That is precisely the function of financial markets. Financial markets exist in order to allocate the supply of savings in the economy to the demanders of those savings. The central characteristic of a financial market is that it acts as the vehicle through which the forces of demand and supply for a specific type of financial claim (such as a corporate bond) are brought together.

## RELATE TO THE BIG PICTURE

In this chapter, we cover material that introduces the financial manager to the process involved in raising funds in the nation's capital markets and also rely on the logic that lies behind the determination of interest rates and required rates of return in those capital markets.

We will see that the United States has a highly developed, complex, and competitive system of financial markets that allows for the quick transfer of savings from those economic units with a surplus of savings to those economic units with a savings deficit. Such a system of highly developed financial markets allows great ideas (such as the personal computer) to be financed and increases the overall wealth of the economy. Consider your wealth, for example, compared to that of the average family in Russia. Russia lacks a complex system of financial markets to facilitate transactions in financial claims (securities). As a result, real capital formation there has suffered.

Thus we return now to **Principle 6: Efficient Capital Markets—The markets are quick and the prices are right.** Financial managers like our system of capital markets because they trust it. This trust stems from the fact that the markets are "efficient." Managers trust prices in the securities markets because those prices quickly and accurately reflect all available information about the value of the underlying securities. This means that expected risks and expected cash flows matter more to market participants than do simpler things such as accounting changes and the sequence of past price changes in a specific security. With security prices and returns (such as interest rates) competitively determined, more financial managers (rather than fewer) participate in the markets and help ensure the basic concept of efficiency.

Now, why would the economy suffer without a developed financial market system? The answer is that the wealth of the economy would be less without the financial markets. The rate of capital formation would not be as high if financial markets did not exist. This means that the net additions during a specific period to the stocks of (1) dwellings, (2) productive plant and equipment, (3) inventory, and (4) consumer durables would occur at lower rates. Figure 14-2 helps clarify the rationale behind this assertion. The abbreviated balance sheets in the figure refer to firms or any other type of economic units that operate in the private as opposed to governmental sectors of the economy. This means that such units cannot issue money to finance their own activities.

**Real assets**
Tangible assets such as houses, equipment, and inventories.

**Financial assets**
Claims for future payment by one economic unit on another.

At stage 1 in Figure 14-2, only real assets exist in the hypothetical economy. **Real assets** are tangible assets, such as houses, equipment, and inventories. They are distinguished from **financial assets,** which represent claims for future payment on other economic units. Common and preferred stocks, bonds, bills, and notes all are types of financial assets. If only real assets exist, then savings for a given economic unit, such as a firm,

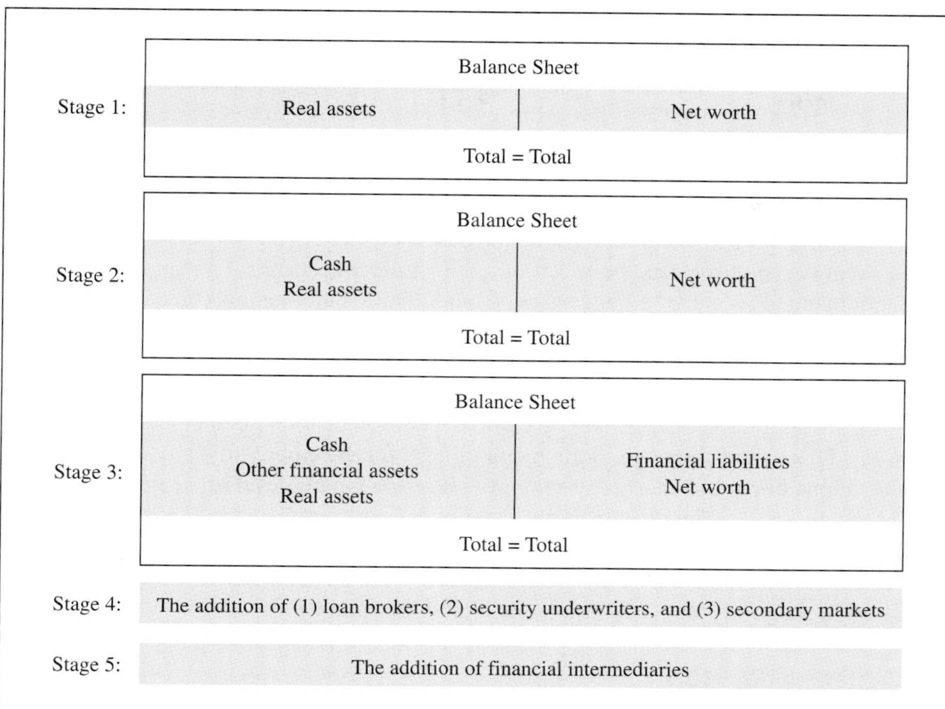


**FIGURE 14-2**
Development of a Financial Market System

must be accumulated in the form of real assets. If the firm has a great idea for a new product, that new product can be developed, produced, and distributed only out of company savings (retained earnings). Furthermore, all investment in the new product must occur simultaneously as the savings are generated. If you have the idea, and we have the savings, there is no mechanism to transfer our savings to you. This is not a good situation.

At stage 2, paper money (cash) comes into existence in the economy. Here, at least, you can *store* your own savings in the form of money.

Thus, you can finance your great idea by drawing down your cash balances. This is an improvement over stage 1, but there is still no effective mechanism to transfer our savings to you. You see, we will not just hand you our dollar bills. We will want a receipt.

The concept of a receipt that represents the transfer of savings from one economic unit to another is a monumental advancement. The economic unit with excess savings can lend the savings to an economic unit that needs them. To the lending unit, these receipts are identified as "other financial assets" in stage 3 of Figure 14-2. To the borrowing unit, the issuance of financial claims (receipts) shows up as "financial liabilities" on the stage 3 balance sheet. The economic unit with surplus savings will earn a rate of return on those funds. The borrowing unit will pay that rate of return, but it has been able to finance its great idea.

In stage 4, the financial market system moves further toward full development. Loan brokers come into existence. These brokers help locate pockets of excess savings and channel such savings to economic units needing the funds. Some economic units will actually purchase the financial claims of borrowing units and sell them at a higher price to other investors; this process is called **underwriting.** Underwriting is discussed in more detail later in this chapter. In addition, **secondary markets** develop. Secondary markets simply represent trading existing financial claims. If you buy your brother's General Motors common stock, you have made a secondary market transaction. Secondary markets

**Underwriting**
The purchase and subsequent resale of a new security issue. The risk of selling the new issue at a profitable price is assumed (underwritten) by an investment banker.

**Secondary markets**
Transactions in currently outstanding securities.

reduce the risk of investing in financial claims. Should you need cash, you can liquidate your claims in the secondary market. This induces savers to invest in securities.

The progression toward a developed and complex system of financial markets ends with stage 5. Here, financial intermediaries come into existence. You can think of financial intermediaries as the major financial institutions with which you are used to dealing. These include commercial banks, savings and loan associations, credit unions, life insurance companies, and mutual funds. Financial intermediaries share a common characteristic: They offer their own financial claims, called **indirect securities,** to economic units with excess savings. The proceeds from selling their indirect securities are then used to purchase the financial claims of other economic units. These latter claims can be called **direct securities.** Thus, a mutual fund might sell mutual fund shares (its indirect security) and purchase the common stocks (direct securities) of some major corporations. A life insurance company sells life insurance policies and purchases huge quantities of corporate bonds. Financial intermediaries thereby involve many small savers in the process of capital formation. This means there are more "good things" for everybody to buy.

**Indirect securities**
The unique financial claims issued by financial intermediaries. Mutual fund shares are an example.

**Direct securities**
The pure financial claims issued by economic units to savers. These can later be transformed into indirect securities.

A developed financial market system provides for a greater level of wealth in the economy. In the absence of financial markets, savings are not transferred to the economic units most in need of those funds. It is difficult, after all, for a household to build its own automobile. The financial market system makes it *easier* for the economy to build automobiles and all the other goods that economic units like to accumulate.

**CONCEPT CHECK**

1. What are financial markets?
2. Why will an economy suffer without a developed financial market system?
3. What distinguishes a real asset from a financial asset?
4. Can you distinguish between direct securities and indirect securities?

## FINANCING OF BUSINESS: THE MOVEMENT OF FUNDS THROUGH THE ECONOMY

OBJECTIVE 4 

We now understand the crucial role that financial markets play in a capitalist economy. At this point, we will take a brief look at how funds flow across some selected sectors of the U.S. economy. In addition, we will focus a little more closely on the process of financial intermediation that was introduced in the preceding section. Some actual data are used to sharpen our knowledge of the financing process. We will see that financial institutions play a major role in bridging the gap between savers and borrowers in the economy. Nonfinancial corporations, we already know, are significant borrowers of financial capital.

### The Financing Process

Table 14-3 shows how funds were supplied and raised by the major sectors of the U.S. economy over the 5-year period from 1995 through 1999. The dollar amounts (in billions) are annual averages over those 5 years. We will specifically make comments on three of the five sectors identified in the table.

Households' net increase in financial liabilities exceeded their net increase in financial assets to the extent of $50.3 billion, as shown in the right-hand column of the table. In the jargon of economics, the household sector was a *savings-deficit* sector over this period.

**TABLE 14-3**
Sector View of Flow of Funds in U.S. Financial Markets for 1995–1999

(Billions of Dollars, 5-Year Averages)

| Sector | [1] Funds Raised $ Billions | [2] Funds Supplied $ Billions | [2] − [1] Net Funds Supplied $ Billions |
|---|---|---|---|
| Households[a] | 447.4 | 397.1 | −50.3 |
| Nonfinancial corporate business | 447.5 | 383.8 | −63.7 |
| U.S. government | 73.9 | 62.9 | −11.0 |
| State and local governments | 56.4 | 48.4 | −8.0 |
| Foreign | 320.2 | 561.7 | 241.5 |

[a]Includes personal trusts and nonprofit organizations.

Source: *Flow of Funds Accounts, First Quarter 2000,* Flow of Funds Section, Statistical Release Z.1 (Washington, DC; Board of Governors of the Federal Reserve System, June 9, 2000).

This financing behavior was unusual because the household sector over long periods of time is typically a major *savings-surplus* sector. This means the household sector normally is a key net supplier of funds to the financial markets. Actually, and for example, over the 6-year period of 1991 through 1996, the household sector supplied an annual average of $170.0 billion to the markets. Since 1991, the household sector has been a savings-surplus sector for all years except the recent 3 covering the period 1997 through 1999. So why were those most-recent 3 years any different? We can see and understand the difference merely by looking at data from 1999. Because of prevailing low interest rates in the U.S. credit markets, households took on a huge $411.0 billion in mortgages to finance home purchases. The result made the household sector a net user of financial capital in that year, and similar financing behavior was followed in the previous 2 years.

Notice that over the subject 5 years, as detailed in Table 14-3, the nonfinancial business sector was likewise a savings-deficit sector to the net extent of $63.7 billion on average for each year. This means nonfinancial firms, such as General Motors, raised $63.7 billion more in the financial markets than they supplied to the markets. While the nonfinancial business sector often is a savings-deficit sector, it can at times be a savings-surplus sector depending on aggregate economic conditions. The most important of those conditions is the level of corporate profitability.

Table 14-3 further highlights how important foreign financial investment is to the activity of the U.S. economy. On average, the foreign sector supplied a net $241.5 billion to the domestic capital markets for each year of the 1995 through 1999 period. Thus, it was a crucial *savings-surplus* sector. Back in 1982, the foreign sector raised—rather than supplied—$29.9 billion in the U.S. financial markets! This illustrates the dynamic nature of financial management and why financial-management practitioners have to be in tune with current business conditions. Actual capital-budgeting decisions, like those explored in earlier chapters, are made in the corporate board room—not within the rather sterile confines of an end-of-chapter problem.

We have seen here that the financial market system must exist to facilitate the orderly and efficient flow of savings from the surplus sectors to the deficit sectors of the economy. Over long periods, the nonfinancial business sector is typically dependent on the household sector to finance its investment needs. And, foreign financing plays an important role in the U.S. economy.

## Movement of Savings

Figure 14-3 provides a useful way to summarize our discussion of (1) why financial markets exist and (2) the movement of funds through the economy. It also serves as an introduction to the role of the investment banker—a subject discussed in detail later in this chapter.

**FIGURE 14-3**
Three Ways to Transfer Financial Capital in the Economy

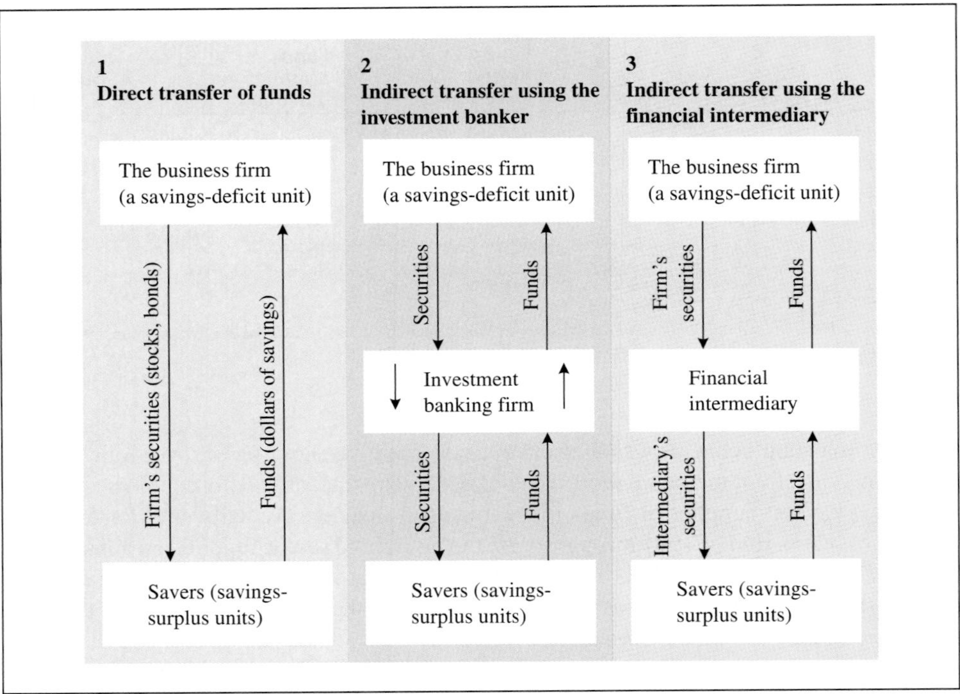


We see that savings are ultimately transferred to the business firm in need of cash in three ways:

1. **The direct transfer of funds.** Here the firm seeking cash sells its securities directly to savers (investors) who are willing to purchase them in hopes of earning a reasonable rate of return. New business formation is a good example of this process at work. The new business may go directly to a saver or group of savers called *venture capitalists.* The venture capitalists will lend funds to the firm or take an equity position in the firm if they feel the product or service the new firm hopes to market will be successful.
2. **Indirect transfer using the investment banker.** In a common arrangement under this system, the managing investment banking house will form a syndicate of several investment bankers. The syndicate will buy the entire issue of securities from the firm that is in need of financial capital. The syndicate will then sell the securities at a higher price than it paid for them to the investing public (the savers). Merrill Lynch Capital Markets and Goldman Sachs are examples of investment banking firms. They tend to be called "houses" by those who work in the financial community. Notice that under this second method of transferring savings, the securities being issued just pass through the investment banking firm. They are not transformed into a different type of security.
3. **Indirect transfer using the financial intermediary.** This is the type of system life insurance companies and pension funds operate within. The financial intermediary collects the savings of individuals and issues its own (indirect) securities in exchange for these savings. The intermediary then uses the funds collected from the individual savers to acquire the business firm's (direct) securities, such as stocks and bonds.

We all benefit from the three transfer mechanisms displayed in Figure 14-3. Capital formation and economic wealth are greater than they would be in the absence of this financial market system.

**CONCEPT CHECK**

1. What is the difference between a savings-surplus sector and a savings-deficit sector? Give an example of each.
2. Why cannot all sectors be savings-deficit sectors?

## COMPONENTS OF THE U.S. FINANCIAL MARKET SYSTEM

Numerous approaches exist for classifying the securities markets. At times, the array can be confusing. An examination of four sets of dichotomous terms can help provide a basic understanding of the structure of the U.S. financial markets.

### Public Offerings and Private Placements

When a corporation decides to raise external capital, those funds can be obtained by making a public offering or a private placement. In a **public offering,** both individual and institutional investors have the opportunity to purchase the securities. The securities are usually made available to the public at large by a managing investment banking firm and its underwriting (risk-taking) syndicate. The firm does not meet the ultimate purchasers of the securities in the public offering. The public market is an impersonal market.

**Public offering**
A security offering where all investors have the opportunity to acquire a portion of the financial claims being sold.

In a **private placement,** also called a **direct placement,** the securities are offered and sold to a limited number of investors. The firm will usually hammer out, on a face-to-face basis with the prospective buyers, the details of the offering. In this setting, the investment banking firm may act as a finder by bringing together potential lenders and borrowers. The private placement market is a more personal market than its public counterpart. We will now relate the private placement market to the need by firms for venture capital.

**Private placement (direct placement)**
A security offering limited to a small number of potential investors.

THE PRIVATE PLACEMENT MARKET AND VENTURE CAPITAL Private placements can be separated logically into two forms: (1) the organized private equity market and (2) the organized private debt market. Both of these markets are actively participated in by venture capitalists. Because issuing public equity or debt is not workable for new, small, or even most medium-sized firms, these younger business units seek out the financial capital of firms that specialize in rather risky company investments—the so-called venture capitalists.

The unseasoned firm finds that its need for financial capital is not appealing to the broader public markets owing to: (1) small absolute size, (2) a very limited or no historical track record of operating results, and (3) obscure growth prospects.[3] Thus, the venture capitalist who is willing to accept such risks jumps into these more cloudy markets in hopes of a greater return (reward). This economic logic should remind you of **Principle 1: The Risk-Return Trade-Off—We won't take on additional risk unless we expect to be compensated with additional return.**

On the equity investment side, the venture capitalist firm will frequently acquire a meaningful dollar stake in the start-up firm. In exchange for this risk-taking, the venture capital firm will occupy a seat or seats on the young firm's board of directors and will take an active part in monitoring management activities, strategies, and capital-budgeting decisions. Other private equity investors with less financial capital committed to the venture will be given "observational rights" (as distinct from voting rights) at regular meetings of

[3]A useful discussion on financing challenges to younger firms is provided by Stephen Prowse, "Equity Capital and Entrepreneurs," in *Equity for Rural America: From Wall Street to Main Street,* Federal Reserve Bank of Kansas City, August 1999, pp. 10–26.

**TABLE 14-4**
Why Major Companies Participate in the Organized Private Equity Market

**Question**

If you have made equity investments in other companies during the previous year, what were your objectives?

| Responses | Percent |
|---|---|
| 1. Capital appreciation | 34.2 |
| 2. Strategic alliance | 76.3 |
| 3. An alternative/precursor to outright acquisition | 15.8 |
| 4. To outsource research and development | 21.1 |
| 5. To boost exposure to the Internet/technology | 23.7 |
| 6. To acquire a minority stake as part of a separate acquisition or as consideration in another deal | 10.5 |

the board. This tendency reminds you of **Principle 7: The Agency Problem—Managers won't work for owners unless it's in their best interest.**

The private equity market is not the sole province of pure venture capital firms. Numerous established and well-known companies such as Microsoft, Intel, and Xerox have for years taken "minority investment positions" in emerging corporations or have created their own separate venture capital subsidiaries. The subsidiary approach has two major benefits to the seasoned company: (1) An incentive is created for human capital to remain with the firm, and (2) great ideas are retained as intellectual capital rather than departing as the basis for a start-up operation.

The other side of the subsidiary approach is for the seasoned company to acquire a minority equity interest in an emerging firm. This choice allows the established corporation to use the private equity market and gain access to new technology by investing directly in start-up organizations rather than taking the risks associated with internal research and development.

Along these lines, a survey of 1,600 Chief Financial Officers published in August 2000 reported that a whopping 76.3 percent of the responding CFOs said that the main objective of taking an equity position in another firm was to create some form of a strategic alliance.[4] Other reasons for participating in the private equity market through minority investments are displayed in Table 14-4.

So we see that investment in young firms does not just come from venture capital companies; numerous established corporations use the private equity market to help fund start-up firms.

In recent years, the dollar volume of financing activity in the private equity market has benefited enormously from the rapid growth of the venture capital industry. We know that the U.S. economy emerged from its last recession during the winter of 1991. That roughly dates the beginning of the hot growth pattern of pure (dedicated) U.S. venture capital firms.[5]

Notice in Figure 14-4 that U.S.-based venture capital companies had $134.5 billion of financial capital under management at the end of 1999. Also observe that, back in 1992, the amount under management was a significantly lesser $28.1 billion. Uninterrupted domestic economic growth provides a stable environment for venture capital activities, whether it be on the investment side by the venture capital fund, or on the operations side by the start-up firm with the great idea that needs financing.

[4]CFO Forum, "The New R&D: Corporations Are Making More Minority Investments in Strategic Partners," *Institutional Investor,* August 2000, p. 34.

[5]Additional information and data on venture capital are available from the National Venture Capital Association and Venture Economics. Their Internet sites are *www.nvca.org* and *www.ventureeconomics.com,* respectively.

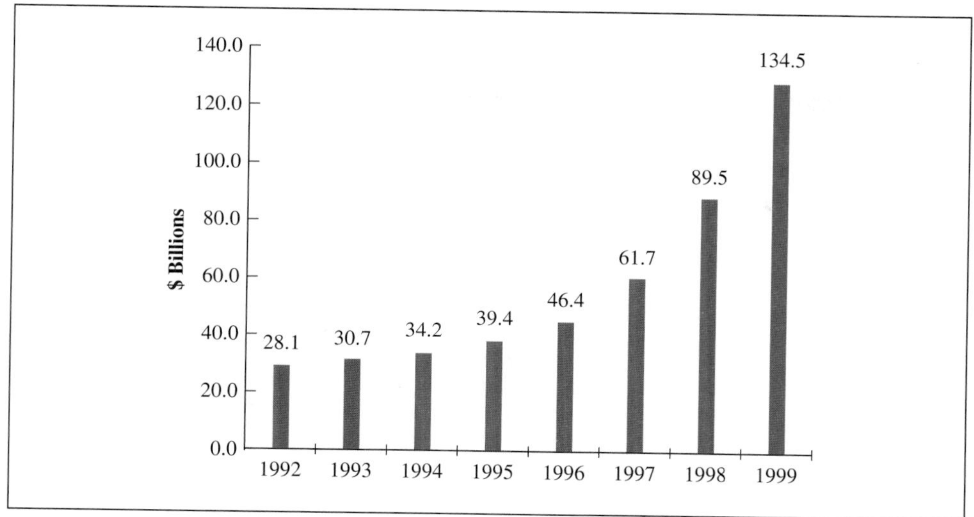


**FIGURE 14-4**
Financial Capital Under Management ($ Billions) U.S. Venture Funds, 1992–1999

Source: *National Venture Capital Association 2000 Yearbook*, p. 9.

## Primary Markets and Secondary Markets

**Primary markets** are those in which securities are offered for the *first* time to potential investors. A new issue of common stock by AT&T is a primary market transaction. This type of transaction increases the total stock of financial assets outstanding in the economy.

**Primary markets**
Transactions in securities offered for the first time to potential investors.

As mentioned in our discussion of the development of the financial market system, *secondary markets* represent transactions in currently outstanding securities. If the first buyer of the AT&T stock subsequently sells it, he or she does so in the secondary market. All transactions after the initial purchase take place in the secondary market. The sales do *not* affect the total stock of financial assets that exist in the economy. Both the money market and the capital market, described next, have primary and secondary sides.

## Money Market and Capital Market

The key distinguishing feature between the money and capital markets is the maturity period of the securities traded in them. The **money market** refers to all institutions and procedures that provide for transactions in short-term debt instruments generally issued by borrowers with very high credit ratings. By financial convention, *short-term* means maturity periods of 1 year or less. Notice that equity instruments, either common or preferred, are not traded in the money market. The major instruments issued and traded are U.S. Treasury bills, various federal agency securities, bankers' acceptances, negotiable certificates of deposit, and commercial paper. Keep in mind that the money market is an intangible market. You do not walk into a building on Wall Street that has the words "Money Market" etched in stone over its arches. Rather, the money market is primarily a telephone and computer market.

**Money market**
All institutions and procedures that facilitate transactions in short-term credit instruments.

The **capital market** refers to all institutions and procedures that provide for transactions in long-term financial instruments. *Long-term* here means having maturity periods that extend beyond 1 year. In the broad sense, this encompasses term loans and financial leases, corporate equities, and bonds. The funds that comprise the firm's capital structure are raised in the capital market. Important elements of the capital market are the organized security exchanges and the over-the-counter markets.

**Capital market**
All institutions and procedures that facilitate transactions in long-term financial instruments.

## Organized Security Exchanges and Over-the-Counter Markets

**Organized security exchanges**
Formal organizations involved in the trading of securities. They are tangible entities that conduct auction markets in listing securities.

**Over-the-counter markets**
All security markets except the organized exchanges.

**Organized security exchanges** are tangible entities; they physically occupy space (such as a building or part of a building), and financial instruments are traded on their premises. The **over-the-counter markets** include all security markets *except* the organized exchanges. The money market, then, is an over-the-counter market. Because both markets are important to financial officers concerned with raising *long-term capital,* some additional discussion is warranted.

## Organized Security Exchanges

For practical purposes there are seven major security exchanges in the United States. These are the (1) New York Stock Exchange, (2) American Stock Exchange, (3) Chicago Stock Exchange, (4) Pacific Stock Exchange, (5) Philadelphia Stock Exchange, (6) Boston Stock Exchange, and (7) Cincinnati Stock Exchange. The New York Stock Exchange (NYSE) and the American Stock Exchange (AMEX) are called *national* exchanges, whereas the others are loosely described as *regionals.* All of these seven active exchanges are registered with the Securities and Exchange Commission (SEC). Firms whose securities are traded on the registered exchanges must comply with reporting requirements of both the specific exchange and the SEC.

The business of an exchange, including securities transactions, is conducted by its *members.* Members are said to occupy "seats." There are 1,366 seats on the NYSE, a number that has remained constant since 1953. Major brokerage firms own seats on the exchanges. An officer of the firm is designated to be the member of the exchange, and this membership permits the brokerage house to use the facilities of the exchange to effect trades. During 1999, the prices of seats that were exchanged for cash ranged from a low of $2.0 million to a high of $2.65 million.[6] The high price in 1999 was an all-time high.

STOCK EXCHANGE BENEFITS. Both corporations and investors enjoy several benefits provided by the existence of organized security exchanges. These include

1. **Providing a continuous market.** This may be the most important function of an organized security exchange. A continuous market provides a series of continuous security prices. Price changes from trade to trade tend to be smaller than they would be in the absence of organized markets. The reasons are that there is a relatively large sales volume in each security, trading orders are executed quickly, and the range between the price asked for a security and the offered price tends to be narrow. The result is that price volatility is reduced.
2. **Establishing and publicizing fair security prices.** An organized exchange permits security prices to be set by competitive forces. They are not set by negotiations off the floor of the exchange, where one party might have a bargaining advantage. The bidding process flows from the supply and demand underlying each security. This means the specific price of a security is determined in the manner of an auction. In addition, the security prices determined at each exchange are widely publicized.
3. **Helping business raise new capital.** Because a continuous secondary market exists where prices are competitively determined, it is easier for firms to float new security offerings successfully. This continuous pricing mechanism also facilitates the determination of the offering price of a new issue. This means that comparative values are easily observed.

[6]New York Stock Exchange, *1999 Fact Book* (New York, 2000), 102.

**TABLE 14-5**
A Sample of NYSE Listing Requirements for Domestic (U.S.) Companies

**PROFITABILITY (EARNINGS)**

Earnings before taxes (EBT) for the most recent year must be at least $2.5 million. For the 2 years preceding that, EBT must be at least $2.0 million.

**MARKET VALUE**

The market value of publicly held stock must be at least $100.0 million. For initial public offerings (IPOs), the value must be at least $60.0 million.

**PUBLIC OWNERSHIP (DISTRIBUTION CRITERIA)**

There must be at least 1.1 million publicly held common shares.
There must be at least 2,000 holders of 100 shares or more.

Source: New York Stock Exchange, *2000 Fact Book for 1999 Data* (New York, 2000), 37.

**LISTING REQUIREMENTS.** To receive the benefits provided by an organized exchange, the firm must seek to have its securities listed on the exchange. An application for listing must be filed and a fee paid. The requirements for listing vary from exchange to exchange; those of the NYSE are the most stringent. The general criteria for listing fall into these categories: (1) profitability, (2) size, (3) market value, and (4) public ownership. To give you the flavor of an actual set of listing requirements, those set forth by the NYSE are displayed in Table 14-5.

## Over-the-Counter Markets

Many publicly held firms do not meet the listing requirements of major stock exchanges. Others may want to avoid the reporting requirements and fees required to maintain listing. As an alternative, their securities may trade in the over-the-counter markets. On the basis of sheer numbers (not dollar volume), more stocks are traded over-the-counter than on organized exchanges. As far as secondary trading in corporate bonds is concerned, the over-the-counter markets are where the action is. In a typical year, more than 90 percent of corporate bond business takes place over-the-counter.

Most over-the-counter transactions are done through a loose network of security traders who are known as broker-dealers and brokers. Brokers do not purchase securities for their own account, whereas dealers do. Broker-dealers stand ready to buy and sell specific securities at selected prices. They are said to "make a market" in those securities. Their profit is the spread or difference between the price they will pay for a security (bid price) and the price at which they will sell the security (asked price).

**PRICE QUOTES AND THE NASDAQ.** The availability of prices is not as continuous in the over-the-counter market as it is on an organized exchange. Since February 8, 1971, however, when a computerized network called NASDAQ came into existence, the availability of prices in this market has improved substantially. NASDAQ stands for National Association of Security Dealers Automated Quotation System. It is a telecommunications system that provides a national information link among the brokers and dealers operating in the over-the-counter markets. Subscribing traders have a terminal that allows them to obtain representative bids and ask prices for thousands of securities traded over-the-counter. NASDAQ is a quotation system, not a transactions system. The final trade is still consummated by direct negotiation between traders.

The NASDAQ system has become an increasingly important element of the U.S. financial market system in recent years. It provides a nationwide communications element that was lacking in the over-the-counter side of the securities markets. When the NASDAQ, AMEX, and NYSE are considered collectively, the NASDAQ accounted for 43 percent of equity market trading in the United States as measured in dollar volume for the year of 1998. The following display shows the respective percentage totals. These totals do not include the regional exchanges.

| Exchange or System | Percent of Equity Dollar Volume |
|---|---|
| NASDAQ | 43.1 |
| AMEX | 2.2 |
| NYSE | 54.7 |

The Nasdaq Stock Market, Inc., describes itself as a "screen-based, floorless market." It now is actually home to the securities of more companies than the NYSE; in 1998 some 5,100 public companies had securities traded by means of the NASDAQ system. It has become highly popular as the trading mechanism of choice of several fast-growth sectors in the United States, including the high-technology sector. The common stock of computer chip maker Intel Corporation, for example, is traded via the NASDAQ.[7]

In June 1998, the Nasdaq Stock Market, Inc. and the AMEX announced the creation of a strategic alliance to provide market participants with timely information and enhanced order-execution capabilities. The latter extended to international trading. The merger was completed later in 1998. The Nasdaq-Amex Market Group allowed the traditional NASDAQ system and AMEX to continue to operate as separate markets, but under one corporate shell.[8]

NASDAQ price quotes for many stocks are published daily in *The Wall Street Journal.* This same financial newspaper also publishes prices on hundreds of other stocks traded over-the-counter. Local papers supply prices on stocks of regional interest.

**CONCEPT CHECK**

1. What are the differences between (a) public offerings and private placements, (b) primary markets and secondary markets, (c) the money market and the capital market, and (d) tangible-organized security exchanges and over-the-counter markets?
2. What benefits are derived from the existence of stock exchanges?
3. Briefly describe what is meant by the "NASDAQ system."

## THE INVESTMENT BANKER

OBJECTIVE 6 

We touched briefly on the investment banking industry and the investment banker earlier in this chapter when we described various methods for transferring financial capital (see Figure 14-3). The investment banker is to be distinguished from the commercial banker in that the former's organization is not a permanent depository for funds. For the moment, it is important for you to learn about the role of the investment banker in the funding of commercial activity because of the importance of this institution within the financial market system.

[7]The NASDAQ Stock Market, *1999 NASDAQ-AMEX Fact Book & Company Directory* (Washington, D.C.), pp. 1, 9.

[8]More information on this combined market structure is given in the *1999 NASDAQ-AMEX Fact Book & Company Directory,* pp. 1–4. Further, the NASDAQ-AMEX Web site is particularly useful. It is located at www.nasdaq-amex.com.

Most corporations do not raise long-term capital frequently. The activities of working-capital management go on daily, but attracting long-term capital is, by comparison, episodic. The sums involved can be huge, so these situations are considered of great importance to financial managers. Because most managers are unfamiliar with the subtleties of raising long-term funds, they enlist the help of an expert. That expert is an investment banker.

## Definition

The **investment banker** is a financial specialist involved as an intermediary in the merchandising of securities. He or she acts as a "middle person" by facilitating the flow of savings from those economic units that want to invest to those units that want to raise funds. We use the term *investment banker* to refer both to a given individual and to the organization for which such a person works, variously known as an *investment banking firm* or an *investment banking house.* Although these firms are called investment bankers, they perform no depository or lending functions. The activities of commercial banking and investment banking as we know them today were separated by the Banking Act of 1933 (also known as the Glass-Steagall Act of 1933). Then, after considerable political debate, the Financial Modernization Act was passed by the U.S. Congress on November 12, 1999. This recent legislation is also referred to as the Gramm-Leach-Bliley Act of 1999, in honor of its congressional sponsors. The act actually repealed significant portions of the Depression-era Glass-Steagall Act and is aimed at increasing competitiveness among modern financial services companies. Through the creation of operating subsidiaries, the act provides for business combinations among banks, underwriters of financial securities (investment bankers), insurance firms, and securities brokers. Here we focus on investment banking and its important middleman role. That is most easily understood in terms of the basic functions of investment banking.

**Investment banker**
A financial specialist who underwrites and distributes new securities and advises corporate clients about raising external financial capital.

## Functions

The investment banker performs three basic functions: (1) underwriting, (2) distributing, and (3) advising.

UNDERWRITING. The term *underwriting* is borrowed from the field of insurance. It means "assuming a risk." The investment banker assumes the risk of selling a security issue at a satisfactory price. A satisfactory price is one that will generate a profit for the investment banking house.

The procedure goes like this. The managing investment banker and its syndicate will buy the security issue from the corporation in need of funds. The **syndicate** is a group of other investment bankers who are invited to help buy and resell the issue. The managing house is the investment banking firm that originated the business because its corporate client decided to raise external funds. On a specific day, the firm that is raising capital is presented with a check (cash) in exchange for the securities being issued. At this point, the investment banking syndicate owns the securities. The corporation has its cash and can proceed to use it. The firm is now immune from the possibility that the security markets might turn sour. If the price of the newly issued security falls below that paid to the firm by the syndicate, the syndicate will suffer a loss. The syndicate, of course, hopes that the opposite situation will result. Its objective is to sell the new issue to the investing public at a price per security greater than its cost.

**Syndicate**
A group of investment bankers who contractually assist in the buying of a new security issue.

DISTRIBUTING. Once the syndicate owns the new securities, it must get them into the hands of the ultimate investors. This is the distribution or selling function of investment banking. The investment banker may have branch offices across the United States, or it may have an informal arrangement with several security dealers who regularly buy a portion of each new offering for final sale. It is not unusual to have 300 to 400 dealers involved in the selling effort. The syndicate can properly be viewed as the security wholesaler, and the dealer organization can be viewed as the security retailer.

**ADVISING.** The investment banker is an expert in the issuance and marketing of securities. A sound investment banking house will be aware of prevailing market conditions and can relate those conditions to the particular type of security that should be sold at a given time. Business conditions may be pointing to a future increase in interest rates. The investment banker might advise the firm to issue its bonds in a timely fashion to avoid the higher yields that are forthcoming. The banker can analyze the firm's capital structure and make recommendations as to what general source of capital should be issued. In many instances, the firm will invite its investment banker to sit on the board of directors. This permits the banker to observe corporate activity and make recommendations on a regular basis.

## Distribution Methods

Several methods are available to the corporation for placing new security offerings in the hands of final investors. The investment banker's role is different in each of these. Sometimes, in fact, it is possible to bypass the investment banker. These methods are described in this section. Private placements, because of their importance, are treated separately later in the chapter.

**NEGOTIATED PURCHASE.** In a negotiated underwriting, the firm that needs funds makes contact with an investment banker, and deliberations concerning the new issue begin. If all goes well, a *method* is negotiated for determining the price the investment banker and the syndicate will pay for the securities. For example, the agreement might state that the syndicate will pay $2 less than the closing price of the firm's common stock on the day before the offering date of a new stock issue. The negotiated purchase is the most prevalent method of securities distribution in the private sector. It is generally thought to be the most profitable technique as far as investment bankers are concerned.

**COMPETITIVE BID PURCHASE.** The method by which the underwriting group is determined distinguishes the competitive bid purchase from the negotiated purchase. In a competitive underwriting, several underwriting groups bid for the right to purchase the new issue from the corporation that is raising funds. The firm does not directly select the investment banker. The investment banker that underwrites and distributes the issue is chosen by an auction process. The syndicate willing to pay the greatest dollar amount per new security will win the competitive bid.

Most competitive bid purchases are confined to three situations, compelled by legal regulations: (1) railroad issues, (2) public utility issues, and (3) state and municipal bond issues. The argument in favor of competitive bids is that any undue influence of the investment banker over the firm is mitigated and the price received by the firm for each security should be higher. Thus, we would intuitively suspect that the cost of capital in a competitive bid situation would be less than in a negotiated purchase situation. Evidence on this question, however, is mixed. One problem with the competitive bid purchase as far as the fundraising firm is concerned is that the benefits gained from the advisory function of the investment banker are lost. It may be necessary to use an investment banker for advisory purposes and then by law exclude that same banker from the competitive bid process.

**COMMISSION OR BEST-EFFORTS BASIS.** Here, the investment banker acts as an agent rather than as a principal in the distribution process. The securities are *not* underwritten. The investment banker attempts to sell the issue in return for a fixed commission on each security actually sold. Unsold securities are returned to the corporation. This arrangement is typically used for more speculative issues. The issuing firm may be smaller or less established than the investment banker would like. Because the underwriting risk is not passed on to the investment banker, this distribution method is less costly to the issuer than a negotiated or competitive bid purchase. On the other hand, the investment banker only has to give it his or her "best effort." A successful sale is not guaranteed.

**PRIVILEGED SUBSCRIPTION.** Occasionally, the firm may feel that a distinct market already exists for its new securities. When a new issue is marketed to a definite and select group of investors, it is called a **privileged subscription.** Three target markets are typically involved: (1) current stockholders, (2) employees, or (3) customers. Of these, distributions directed at current stockholders are the most prevalent. Such offerings are called *rights offerings.* In a privileged subscription, the investment banker may act only as a selling agent. It is also possible that the issuing firm and the investment banker might sign a *standby agreement,* which would obligate the investment banker to underwrite the securities that are not accepted by the privileged investors.

**Privileged subscription**
The process of marketing a new security issue to a select group of investors.

**DIRECT SALE.** In a **direct sale,** the issuing firm sells the securities directly to the investing public without involving an investment banker. Even among established corporate giants, this procedure is relatively rare. A variation of the direct sale, though, was used more frequently in the 1970s than in previous decades. This involves the private placement of a new issue by the fundraising corporation *without* use of an investment banker as an intermediary. Texaco, Mobil Oil (prior to its merger with Exxon), and International Harvester (now Navistar) are examples of large firms that have followed this procedure.

**Direct sale**
The sale of securities by the corporation to the investing public without the services of an investment banking firm.

**INDUSTRY LEADERS.** All industries have their leaders, and investment banking is no exception. We have discussed investment bankers at some length in this chapter. Table 14-6 gives us some idea who the major players are within the investment banking industry. It lists the top 10 houses in 1999 based on the dollar volume of security issues that were managed. Notice in the table that the U.S. investment banking industry is a highly concentrated one. The top four bankers with regard to underwriting volume during 1999 accounted for a full 46.7 percent of the total market. This degree of concentration is pervasive over time.

**TABLE 14-6**
Leading U.S. Investment Bankers, 1999

| Firm | Underwriting Volume (Billions of Dollars) | Percent of Market |
|---|---|---|
| 1. Merrill Lynch | $331.78 | 15.4% |
| 2. Salomon Smith Barney | 268.07 | 12.5 |
| 3. Morgan Stanley Dean Witter | 210.99 | 9.8 |
| 4. Goldman Sachs | 192.44 | 9.0 |
| 5. Credit Suisse First Boston | 181.40 | 8.4 |
| 6. Lehman Brothers | 169.71 | 7.9 |
| 7. Chase Manhattan | 109.40 | 5.1 |
| 8. J.P. Morgan | 90.73 | 4.2 |
| 9. Bear Stearns | 86.34 | 4.0 |
| 10. Banc of America Securities | 75.90 | 3.5 |

Source: Thomson Financial Securities Data as reported in *The Wall Street Journal* (January 3, 2000), p. R24.

**CONCEPT CHECK**

1. What is the main difference between an investment banker and a commercial banker?
2. What are the three major functions that an investment banker performs?
3. What are the five key methods by which securities are distributed to final investors?

## MORE ON PRIVATE PLACEMENTS: THE DEBT SIDE

OBJECTIVE 7 

Earlier in this chapter we discussed the private placement market and its important relationship to the market for venture capital. There we emphasized the private equity side of private placements. Here we take a closer look at the debt side of the private placement market and how it is used by more seasoned corporations as distinct from "start-ups." Thus, when we talk of private placements, we are focusing on debt contracts.

This debt side of the private placement market is always a significant portion of the total private market. According to the Federal Reserve, (1) bonds and notes made up 35.5 percent of private securities offered for cash over the 1997 to 1999 period, and (2) the private placement side of the corporate debt market represented 26.6 percent of total domestically placed debt issues for the 10-year period ended 1994. So, as financial managers, we have to be acquainted with this market for financial capital.

Private placements are an alternative to the sale of securities to the public or to a restricted group of investors through a privileged subscription. Any type of security can be privately placed (directly placed). The major investors in private placements are large financial institutions. Based on the volume of securities purchased, the three most important investor groups are (1) life insurance companies, (2) state and local retirement funds, and (3) private pension funds.

In arranging a private placement, the firm may (1) avoid the use of an investment banker and work directly with the investing institutions or (2) engage the services of an investment banker. If the firm does not use an investment banker, of course, it does not have to pay a fee. Conversely, investment bankers can provide valuable advice in the private placement process. They are usually in contact with several major institutional investors; thus, they will know if a firm is in a position to invest in its proposed offering, and they can help the firm evaluate the terms of the new issue.

Private placements have advantages and disadvantages compared with public offerings. The financial manager must carefully evaluate both sides of the question. The advantages associated with private placements are these:

1. **Speed.** The firm usually obtains funds more quickly through a private placement than a public offering. The major reason is that registration of the issue with the SEC is not required.
2. **Reduced flotation costs.** These savings result because the lengthy registration statement for the SEC does not have to be prepared, and the investment banking underwriting and distribution costs do not have to be absorbed.
3. **Financing flexibility.** In a private placement, the firm deals on a face-to-face basis with a small number of investors. This means that the terms of the issue can be tailored to meet the specific needs of the company. For example, all of the funds need not be taken by the firm at once. In exchange for a commitment fee, the firm can "draw down" against the established amount of credit with the investors. This provides some insurance against capital market uncertainties, and the firm does not have to borrow the funds if the need does not arise. There is also the possibility of renegotiation. The

terms of the debt issue can be altered. The term to maturity, the interest rate, or any restrictive covenants can be discussed among the affected parties.

The following disadvantages of private placements must be evaluated:

1. **Interest costs.** It is generally conceded that interest costs on private placements exceed those of public issues. Whether this disadvantage is enough to offset the reduced flotation costs associated with a private placement is a determination the financial manager must make. There is some evidence that on smaller issues—say, $500,000 as opposed to $30 million—the private placement alternative would be preferable.
2. **Restrictive covenants.** Dividend policy, working-capital levels, and the raising of additional debt capital may all be affected by provisions in the private-placement debt contract. That is not to say that such restrictions are always absent in public debt contracts. Rather, the financial officer must be alert to the tendency for these covenants to be especially burdensome in private contracts.
3. **The possibility of future SEC registration.** If the lender (investor) should decide to sell the issue to a public buyer before maturity, the issue must be registered with the SEC. Some lenders, then, require that the issuing firm agree to a future registration at their option.

**CONCEPT CHECK**

1. Within the financial markets, what do we mean by "private placements"?
2. What are the possible advantages and disadvantages of private placements?

## FLOTATION COSTS

**Flotation costs**
The underwriter's spread and issuing costs associated with the issuance and marketing of new securities.

The firm raising long-term capital incurs two types of **flotation costs:** (1) the underwriter's spread and (2) issuing costs. Of these two costs, the underwriter's spread is the larger. The *underwriter's spread* is simply the difference between the gross and net proceeds from a given security issue expressed as a percent of the gross proceeds. The *issue costs* include (1) printing and engraving, (2) legal fees, (3) accounting fees, (4) trustee fees, and (5) several other miscellaneous components. The two most significant issue costs are printing and engraving and legal fees.

Data published by the SEC have consistently revealed two relationships about flotation costs. First, the costs associated with issuing common stock are notably greater than the costs associated with preferred stock offerings. In turn, preferred stock costs exceed those of bonds. Second, flotation costs (expressed as a percent of gross proceeds) decrease as the size of the security issue increases.

In the first instance, the stated relationship reflects the fact that issue costs are sensitive to the risks involved in successfully distributing a security issue. Common stock is riskier to own than corporate bonds. Underwriting risk is, therefore, greater with common stock than with bonds. Thus, flotation costs just mirror these risk relationships. In the second case, a portion of the issue costs is fixed. Legal fees and accounting costs are good examples. So, as the size of the security issue rises, the fixed component is spread over a larger gross proceeds base. As a consequence, average flotation costs vary inversely with the size of the issue.

**CONCEPT CHECK**

1. What are the two major categories of flotation costs?
2. Are flotation costs greater for a new bond issue or a new common stock issue?

# REGULATION

Since late 1986, there has been a renewal of public interest in the regulation of the country's financial markets. The key event was a massive insider trading scandal that made the name Ivan F. Boesky one of almost universal recognition—but unfortunately, in a negative sense. This was followed by the October 19, 1987, crash of the equity markets. In early 1990, the investing community (both institutional and individual) became increasingly concerned over a weakening in the so-called "junk bond market." The upshot of all of this enhanced awareness is a new appreciation of the crucial role that regulation plays in the financial system.

Following the severe economic downturn of 1929 to 1932, Congressional action was taken to provide for federal regulation of the securities markets. State statutes (blue sky laws) also govern the securities markets where applicable, but the federal regulations are clearly more pressing and important. The major federal regulations are reviewed here.

## Primary Market Regulations

The new issues market is governed by the Securities Act of 1933. The intent of the act is important. It aims to provide potential investors with accurate, truthful disclosure about the firm and the new securities being offered to the public. This does *not* prevent firms from issuing highly speculative securities. The SEC says nothing whatsoever about the possible investment worth of a given offering. It is up to the investor to separate the junk from the jewels. The SEC does have the legal power and responsibility to enforce the 1933 act.

Full public disclosure is achieved by the requirement that the issuing firm file a registration statement with the SEC containing requisite information. The statement details particulars about the firm and the new security being issued. During a minimum 20-day waiting period, the SEC examines the submitted document. In numerous instances, the 20-day wait has been extended by several weeks. The SEC can ask for additional information that was omitted in order to clarify the original document. The SEC can also order that the offering be stopped.

During the registration process, a preliminary prospectus (the "red herring") may be distributed to potential investors. When the registration is approved, the final prospectus must be made available to the prospective investors. The prospectus is actually a condensed version of the full registration statement. If, at a later date, the information in the registration statement and the prospectus is found to be lacking, purchasers of the new issue who incurred a loss can sue for damages. Officers of the issuing firm and others who took part in the registration and marketing of the issue may suffer both civil and criminal penalties.

Generally, the SEC defines public issues as those that are sold to more than 25 investors. Some public issues need not be registered. These include

1. Relatively small issues, where the firm sells less than $1.5 million of new securities per year. Such issues of less than $1.5 million are not entirely regulation-free. They are monitored through what is usually called the *small-issues exemption.* These small issues, then, fall under the auspicies of Regulation A, which is just a very short offering statement compared to the full-blown registration statement. The latter is very onerous; it often ends up in the 50–100 page range.
2. Issues that are sold entirely intrastate.
3. Issues that are basically short-term instruments. This translates into maturity periods of 270 days or less.
4. Issues that are already regulated or controlled by some other federal agency. Examples here are the Federal Power Commission (public utilities) and the Interstate Commerce Commission (railroads).

## Secondary Market Regulations

Secondary trading is regulated by the Securities Exchange Act of 1934. This act created the SEC to enforce securities laws. The Federal Trade Commission enforced the 1933 act for 1 year. The major aspects of the 1934 act can be best presented in outline form:

1. Major security exchanges must register with the SEC. This regulates the exchanges and places reporting requirements on the firms whose securities are listed on them.
2. Insider trading is regulated. Insiders can be officers, directors, employees, relatives, major investors, or anyone having information about the operation of the firm that is not public knowledge. If an investor purchases the security of the firm in which the investor is an insider, he or she must hold it for at least 6 months before disposing of it. Otherwise, profits made from trading the stock within a period of less than 6 months must be returned to the firm. Furthermore, insiders must file with the SEC a monthly statement of holdings and transactions in the stock of their corporation.[9]
3. Manipulative trading of securities by investors to affect stock prices is prohibited.
4. The SEC is given control over proxy procedures.
5. The Board of Governors of the Federal Reserve System is given responsibility for setting margin requirements. This affects the flow of credit into the securities markets. Buying securities on margin simply means using credit to acquire a portion of the subject financial instruments.

## Securities Acts Amendments of 1975

The Securities Acts Amendments of 1975 touched on three important issues. First, Congress mandated the creation of a national market system (NMS). Only broad goals for this national exchange were identified by Congress. Implementation details were left to the SEC and, to a much lesser extent, the securities industry in general. Congress was really expressing its desire for (1) widespread application of auction market trading principles, (2) a high degree of competition across markets, and (3) the use of modern electronic communication systems to link the fragmented markets in the country into a true NMS. The NMS is still a goal toward which the SEC and the securities industry are moving. Agreement as to its final form and an implementation date have not occurred.

A second major alteration in the habits of the securities industry also took place in 1975. This was the elimination of fixed commissions (fixed brokerage rates) on public transactions in securities. This was closely tied to the desire for an NMS in that fixed brokerage fees provided no incentive for competition among brokers. A third consideration of the 1975 amendments focused on such financial institutions as commercial banks and insurance firms. These financial institutions were prohibited from acquiring membership on stock exchanges in order to reduce or save commissions on their own trades.

## Shelf Registration

**Shelf registration (shelf offering)**
A procedure for issuing new securities where the firm obtains a master registration statement approved by the SEC.

On March 16, 1982, the SEC began a new procedure for registering new issues of securities. Formally it is called SEC Rule 415; informally the process is known as a **shelf registration,** or a **shelf offering.** The essence of the process is rather simple. Rather than go

[9]On November 14, 1986, the SEC announced that Ivan F. Boesky had admitted to illegal insider trading after an intensive investigation. Boesky at the time was a very well-known Wall Street investor, speculator, and arbitrageur. Boesky was an owner or part owner in several companies, including an arbitrage fund named Ivan F. Boesky & Co. L. P. Boesky agreed to pay the U.S. government $50 million, which represented a return of illegal profits, another $50 million in civil penalties; to withdraw permanently from the securities industry; and to plead guilty to criminal charges. The far-reaching investigation continued into 1987 and implicated several other prominent investment figures.

through the lengthy, full registration process each time the firm plans an offering of securities, it can get a blanket order approved by the SEC. A master registration statement that covers the financing plans of the firm over the coming 2 years is filed with the SEC. On approval, the firm can market some or all of the securities over this 2-year period. The securities are sold in a piecemeal fashion, or "off the shelf." Prior to each specific offering, a short statement about the issue is filed with the SEC.

Corporations raising funds approve of this new procedure. The tedious, full registration process is avoided with each offering pulled off the shelf. This should result in a saving of fees paid to investment bankers. Moreover, an issue can more quickly be brought to the market. Also, if market conditions change, an issue can easily be redesigned to fit the specific conditions of the moment.

As is always the case, there is another side to the story. Recall that the reason for the registration process in the first place is to give investors useful information about the firm and the securities being offered. Under the shelf registration procedure, some of the information about the issuing firm becomes old as the 2-year horizon unfolds. Some investment bankers feel they do not have the proper amount of time to study the firm when a shelf offering takes place. This is one of those areas of finance where more observations are needed before any final conclusions can be made.

**CONCEPT CHECK**

1. What are the main elements of the Securities Act of 1933 and the Securities Exchange Act of 1934?
2. What is meant by "insider trading"?
3. What is a "shelf registration"?

## THE MULTINATIONAL FIRM: EFFICIENT FINANCIAL MARKETS AND INTERCOUNTRY RISK

We have discussed and demonstrated in this chapter that the United States has a highly developed, complex, and competitive system of financial markets that allows for the quick transfer of savings from those economic units with a surplus of savings to those economic units with a savings deficit. Such a system of robust and credible financial markets allows great ideas (like the personal computer) to be financed and increases the overall wealth of the given economy. Real capital formation—for example, a Ford Motor Company manufacturing plant in Livonia, Michigan—is enhanced by the financial market mechanism.

One major reason why underdeveloped countries are indeed underdeveloped is that they lack a financial market system that has the confidence of those who must use it—like the multinational firm. The multinational firm with cash to invest in foreign markets will weigh heavily the integrity of both the financial system and the political system of the prospective foreign country.

A lack of integrity on either the financial side or the political stability side will retard direct investment in the lesser-developed nation. Consider The Walt Disney Company headquartered in Burbank, California. Disney common stock trades on the NYSE (ticker symbol DIS), while the firm has significant overseas real investments in projects known as the Disneyland Paris Resort and Tokyo Disneyland. Disney has confidence in the French financial markets, and those of western Europe and Japan. As an example, that confidence led Disney executives to launch three new projects in Japan during 1998—a new theme park and two new hotels.[10]

[10]The Walt Disney Company, *Annual Report,* 1998, pp. 24–25, 57.

However, Disney did not launch any new projects in Thailand because the basic currency in Thailand, called the "baht," lost a full 98 percent of its value against the U.S. dollar over the short period from June 1997 to February 1998. Profits generated in Thailand and measured by the baht would have bought significantly fewer U.S. dollars after the devaluation. This type of situation is typically referred to as *exchange rate risk.* Currencies, too, trade within financial markets and those risks are closely studied by wise multinational firms.

**CONCEPT CHECK**

1. Identify one major reason why underdeveloped countries remain underdeveloped.
2. Give an example of "foreign exchange risk."

## HOW FINANCIAL MANAGERS USE THIS MATERIAL

Corporate financial executives are constantly balancing the internal demand for funds against the costs of raising external financial capital. In order to finance favorable projects, the financial executive at times will have to choose between issuing new debt, preferred stock, or common stock. Further, the executive will decide whether to raise the external capital via a public offering or private placement of the new securities to a limited number of potential investors. Most of these activities will involve the counsel of an investment banking firm and an awareness of securities markets regulations.

We know that when financial executives decide to raise cash in the capital market, the issuance of corporate debt clearly dominates other forms of financing instruments. This preference rests on economic logic: Interest expense is deductible from other taxable income when computing the firm's tax liability; dividends paid on either preferred stock or common stock are not. This puts **Principle 8: Taxes Bias Business Decisions** into action. Stated alternatively, firms would rather suffer a lower tax bill as opposed to a higher tax bill. Wouldn't you? As a result of this knowledge, U.S. corporate executives raised 75.3 percent of their external cash from bonds and notes (debt capital) during the 1996–1999 period.

Financial executives are fully aware of **Principle 8,** but also the need to create wealth for their common stock investors. The use of fixed-income financing (leverage) has to be wisely done—not overdone, or it will ultimately raise overall capital costs and the risk of bankruptcy. The Walt Disney Company displays this perspective in the following statement: "Disney shareholders benefit from the prudent leverage in the company's capital structure represented by total borrowings of $11.1 billion at year end. Attractive borrowing rates help to reduce the company's overall cost of capital, thereby creating value for shareholders. Disney still has substantial financial flexibility to borrow, should sound business opportunities present themselves."[11]

## SUMMARY

This chapter centers on the market environment in which corporations raise long-term funds, including the structure of the U.S. financial markets, the institution of investment banking, and the various methods for distributing securities.

[11]The Walt Disney Company, *Annual Report* (1997), 17.

**OBJECTIVE 1**

**OBJECTIVE 2** 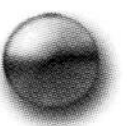

**OBJECTIVE 3** 

When corporations go to the capital market for cash, the most favored financing method is debt. The corporate debt markets clearly dominate the equity markets when new funds are raised. The U.S. tax system inherently favors debt capital as a fundraising method. In an average year over the 1981 to 1996 period, bonds and notes made up 75.6 percent of external cash that was raised, and 75.3 percent over the more recent 1996 to 1999 period.

The function of financial markets is to allocate savings efficiently in the economy to the ultimate demander (user) of the savings. In a financial market, the forces of supply and demand for a specific financial instrument are brought together. The wealth of an economy would not be as great as it is without a fully developed financial market system.

**OBJECTIVE 4** 

Most years, households are a net supplier of funds to the financial markets. The nonfinancial business sector is most always a net borrower of funds. Both life insurance companies and private pension funds are important buyers of corporate securities. Savings are ultimately transferred to the business firm seeking cash by means of (1) the direct transfer, (2) the indirect transfer using the investment banker, or (3) the indirect transfer using the financial intermediary.

**OBJECTIVE 5** 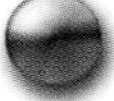

Corporations can raise funds through public offerings or private placements. The public market is impersonal in that the security issuer does not meet the ultimate investors in the financial instruments. In a private placement, the securities are sold directly to a limited number of institutional investors.

The primary market is the market for new issues. The secondary market represents transactions in currently outstanding securities. Both the money and capital markets have primary and secondary sides. The *money market* refers to transactions in short-term debt instruments. The *capital market,* on the other hand, refers to transactions in long-term financial instruments. Trading in the money and capital markets can occur in either the organized security exchanges or the over-the-counter market. The money market is exclusively an over-the-counter market.

**OBJECTIVE 6** 

The investment banker is a financial specialist involved as an intermediary in the merchandising of securities. He or she performs the functions of (1) underwriting, (2) distributing, and (3) advising. Major methods for the public distribution of securities include (1) the negotiated purchase, (2) the competitive bid purchase, (3) the commission or best-efforts basis, (4) privileged subscriptions, and (5) direct sales. The direct sale bypasses the use of an investment banker. The negotiated purchase is the most profitable distribution method to the investment banker. It also provides the greatest amount of investment banking services to the corporate client.

**OBJECTIVE 7** 

Privately placed debt provides an important market outlet for corporate bonds. Major investors in this market are (1) life insurance firms, (2) state and local retirement funds, and (3) private pension funds. Several advantages and disadvantages are associated with private placements. The financial officer must weigh these attributes and decide if a private placement is preferable to a public offering.

**OBJECTIVE 8** 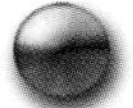

Flotation costs consist of the underwriter's spread and issuing costs. The flotation costs of common stock exceed those of preferred stock, which, in turn, exceed those of debt. Moreover, flotation costs as a percent of gross proceeds are inversely related to the size of the security issue.

The new issues market is regulated at the federal level by the Securities Act of 1933. It provides for the registration of new issues with the SEC. Secondary market trading is regulated by the Securities Exchange Act of 1934. The Securities Acts Amendments of 1975 placed on the SEC the responsibility for devising a national market system. This concept is still being studied. The shelf registration procedure (SEC Rule 415) was initiated in March 1982. Under this regulation and with the proper filing of documents, firms that are selling new issues do not have to go through the old, lengthy registration process each time the firm plans an offering of securities.

## KEY TERMS

Capital market, 453
Direct sale, 459
Direct securities, 448
Financial assets, 446
Financial markets, 445
Flotation costs, 461
Indirect securities, 448
Investment banker, 457
Money market, 453
Organized security exchanges, 454
Over-the-counter markets, 454
Primary markets, 453
Private placement, 451
Privileged subscription, 459
Public offering, 451
Real assets, 446
Secondary markets, 447
Shelf registration (shelf offering), 463
Syndicate, 457
Underwriting, 447

Go To:
http://www.prenhall.com/keown
for downloads and current events associated with this chapter

## STUDY QUESTIONS

**14-1.** What are financial markets? What function do they perform? How would an economy be worse off without them?

**14-2.** Define in a technical sense what we mean by *financial intermediary.* Give an example of your definition.

**14-3.** Distinguish between the money and capital markets.

**14-4.** What major benefits do corporations and investors enjoy because of the existence of organized security exchanges?

**14-5.** What are the general categories examined by an organized exchange in determining whether an applicant firm's securities can be listed on it?

(Specific numbers are not needed here, but rather areas of investigation.)

**14-6.** Why do you think most secondary market trading in bonds takes place over-the-counter?

**14-7.** What is an investment banker, and what major functions does he or she perform?

**14-8.** What is the major difference between a negotiated purchase and a competitive bid purchase?

**14-9.** Why is an investment banking syndicate formed?

**14-10.** Why might a large corporation want to raise long-term capital through a private placement rather than a public offering?

**14-11.** As a recent business school graduate, you work directly for the corporate treasurer. Your corporation is going to issue a new security plan and is concerned with the probable flotation costs. What tendencies about flotation costs can you relate to the treasurer?

**14-12.** When corporations raise funds, what type of financing vehicle (instrument or instruments) is most favored?

**14-13.** What is the major (most significant) savings-surplus sector in the U.S. economy?

**14-14.** Identify three distinct ways that savings are ultimately transferred to business firms in need of cash.

# ANALYSIS AND IMPACT OF LEVERAGE

**LEARNING OBJECTIVES**

After reading this chapter, you should be able to

1. Understand the difference between business risk and financial risk.
2. Use the technique of break-even analysis in a variety of analytical settings.
3. Distinguish among the financial concepts of operating leverage, financial leverage, and combined leverage.
4. Calculate the firm's degree of operating leverage, financial leverage, and combined leverage.
5. Explain why a firm with a high business risk exposure might logically choose to employ a low degree of financial leverage in its financial structure.
6. Understand how business risk and global sales impact the multinational firm.

On July 12, 2000, Harley-Davidson, Inc., issued a press release to the financial community and media that discussed its financial performance for the quarter ended June 25. Harley posted a second-quarter fiscal increase in net income of 32 percent

over the 1999 second quarter. Harley noted that its sales revenue jumped by a pleasant 24 percent over the like comparison. Note that Harley's increase in reported net income was 1.333 times the percentage increment in sales. Such disparate relationships between earnings increments and sales increments are commonly reported by numerous firms. Some other actual examples follow here. ● In 1996, the Coca-Cola Company posted only a moderate sales increase of 2.9 percent over the level of reported sales for 1995. This firm's change in net income, however, rose by a pleasant 16.9 percent over the same 1-year period. Thus, the relative change in net income was 5.83 times the relative fluctuation in sales (i.e., 16.9 percent/2.9 percent). Such disparity in the relationship between sales fluctuations and net income fluctuations is not peculiar to Coca-Cola. ● Consider that in 1993, Phillips Petroleum saw its sales rise by only 3.2 percent, yet its net income rose by a whopping 35 percent. Further, Archer Daniels Midland experienced a sales rise of 6.3 percent and a 12.7 percent increase in net income. ● We know that sales fluctuations are not always in the positive direction. Over the 1992 to 1993 time frame, Chevron

Corporation, the large integrated oil company, endured a 3.6 percent contraction in sales revenues; yet its net income contracted by a larger and more painful 19.4 percent. ● What is it about the nature of businesses that causes changes in sales revenues to translate into larger variations in net income and finally the earnings available to the common shareholders? It would actually be a good planning tool for managers to be able to decompose such fluctuations into those policies that are associated with the operating side of the business, as distinct from those policies associated with the financing side of the business. Such knowledge could be put to effective use when the firm builds its strategic plan. This chapter will show you how to do just that.

Our work in earlier chapters allowed us to develop an understanding of how financial assets are valued in the marketplace. Drawing on the tenets of valuation theory, we presented various approaches to measuring the cost of funds to the business organization. This chapter presents concepts that relate to the valuation process and the cost of capital; it also discusses the crucial problem of planning the firm's financing mix.

The cost of capital provides a direct link between the formulation of the firm's asset structure and its financial structure. This is illustrated in Figure 15-1. Recall that the cost of capital is a basic input to the time-adjusted capital-budgeting models. It therefore affects the capital-budgeting, or asset-selection, process. The cost of capital is affected, in turn, by the composition of the right side of the firm's balance sheet—that is, its financial structure.

This chapter examines tools that can be useful aids to the financial manager in determining the firm's proper financial structure. First, we review the technique of breakeven analysis. This provides the foundation for the relationships to be highlighted in the remainder of the chapter. We then examine the concept of operating leverage, some consequences of the firm's use of financial leverage, and the impact on the firm's earnings stream when operating and financial leverage are combined in various patterns.

As you work through this chapter, you will be reminded of several of the principles that form the basics of business financial management and decision making. These will be emphasized: **Principle 1: The Risk-Return Trade-Off—We won't take on additional risk unless we expect to be compensated with additional return; Principle 3: Cash—Not Profits—Is King; and Principle 6: Efficient Capital Markets—The markets are quick and the prices are right.** Our immediate tasks are to distinguish two types of risk that confront the firm and to clarify some key terminology that will be used throughout this and the subsequent chapter.

## BUSINESS AND FINANCIAL RISK

In this chapter, we become more precise in assessing the causes of variability in the firm's expected revenue streams. It is useful to think of business risk as induced by the firm's investment decisions. That is, the composition of the firm's assets determines its exposure to business risk. In this way, business risk is a direct function of what appears on the left side of the company's balance sheet. Financial risk is properly attributed to the manner in which the firm's managers have decided to arrange the right side of the company's balance sheet. The choice to use more financial leverage means that the firm will experience greater exposure to financial risk. The tools developed here will help you quantify the firm's business and financial risk. A solid understanding of these tools will make you a better financial manager.

In studying capital-budgeting techniques, we referred to **risk** as the likely variability associated with expected revenue or income streams. As our attention is now focused on

**Risk**
The likely variability associated with expected revenue or income streams.

**FIGURE 15-1**
Cost of Capital As a Link between Firm's Asset Structure and Financial Structure

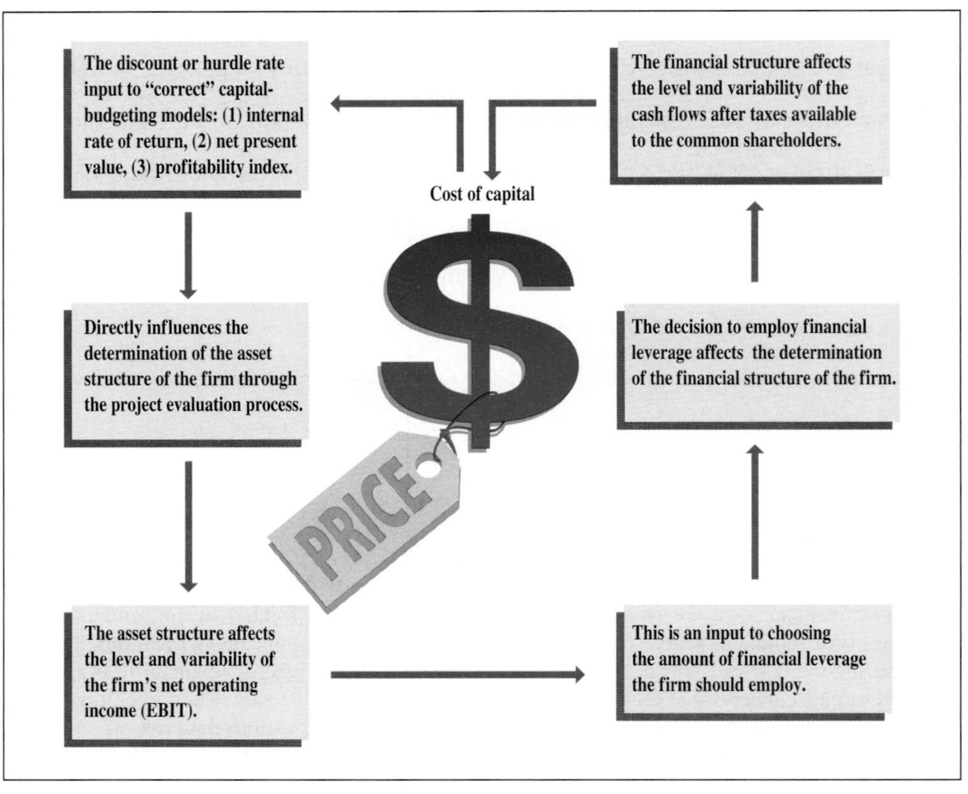


the firm's financing decision rather than its investment decision, it is useful to separate the income stream variations attributable to (1) the company's exposure to business risk and (2) its decision to incur financial risk.

**Business risk**
The relative dispersion in the firm's expected earnings before interest and taxes.

**Business risk** refers to the relative dispersion (variability) in the firm's expected earnings before interest and taxes (EBIT).[1] Figure 15-2 shows a subjectively estimated probability distribution of next year's EBIT for the Pierce Grain Company and the same type of projection for Pierce's larger competitor, the Blackburn Seed Company. The expected value of EBIT for Pierce is \$100,000, with an associated standard deviation of \$20,000. If next year's EBIT for Pierce fell one standard deviation short of the expected \$100,000, the actual EBIT would equal \$80,000. Blackburn's expected EBIT is \$200,000, and the size of the associated standard deviation is \$20,000. The standard deviation for the expected level of EBIT is the same for both firms. We would say that Pierce's degree of business risk exceeds Blackburn's because of its larger coefficient of variation of expected EBIT as follows:

$$\text{Pierce's coefficient of variation of expected EBIT} = \frac{\$12{,}000}{\$100{,}000} = .20$$

$$\text{Blackburn's coefficient of variation of expected EBIT} = \frac{\$20{,}000}{\$200{,}000} = .10$$

[1]If what the accountants call "other income" and "other expenses" are equal to zero, then EBIT is equal to net operating income. These terms will be used interchangeably.

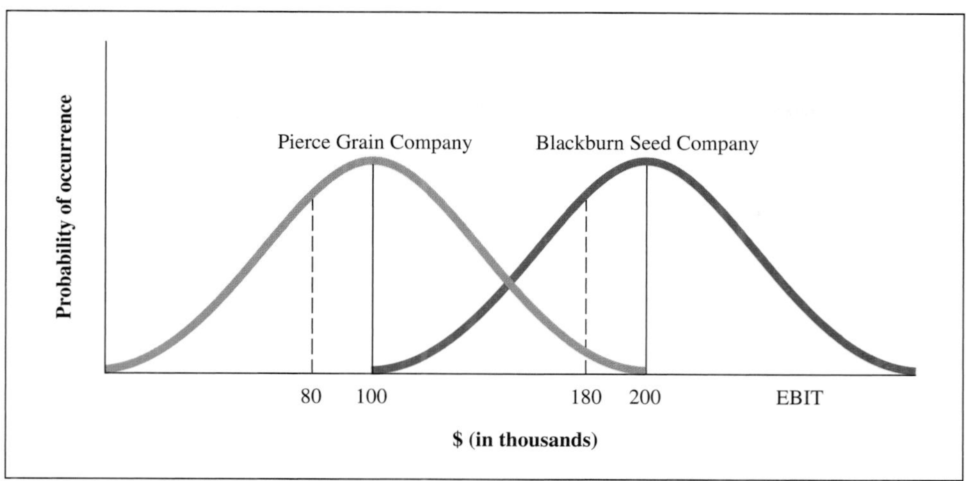


**FIGURE 15-2**
Subjective Probability Distribution of Next Year's EBIT

The relative dispersion in the firm's EBIT stream, measured here by its expected coefficient of variation, is the *residual* effect of several causal influences. Dispersion in operating income does not *cause* business risk; rather, this dispersion, which we call business risk, is the *result* of several influences. Some of these are listed in Table 15-1, along with an example of each particular attribute. Notice that the company's cost structure, product demand characteristics, and intra-industry competitive position all affect its business risk exposure. Such business risk is a direct result of the firm's investment decision. It is the firm's asset structure, after all, that gives rise to both the level and variability of its operating profits.

**Financial risk**
The additional variability in earnings available to the firm's common stockholders, and the additional chance of insolvency borne by the common stockholder caused by the use of financial leverage.

**Financial risk,** conversely, is a direct result of the firm's financing decision**.** In the context of selecting a proper financing mix, this risk applies to (1) the additional variability in earnings available to the firm's common shareholders; and (2) the additional chance of insolvency borne by the common shareholder caused by the use of financial leverage.[2]

**TABLE 15-1**
Concept of Business Risk

| Business Risk Attribute | Example[a] |
|---|---|
| 1. Sensitivity of the firm's product demand to general economic conditions | If GDP declines, does the firm's sales level decline by a greater percentage? |
| 2. Degree of competition | Is the firm's market share small in comparison with other firms that produce and distribute the same product(s)? |
| 3. Product diversification | Is a large proportion of the firm's sales revenue derived from a single major product or product line? |
| 4. Operating leverage | Does the firm utilize a high level of operating leverage resulting in a high level of fixed costs? |
| 5. Growth prospects | Are the firm's product markets expanding and (or) changing, making income estimates and prospects highly volatile? |
| 6. Size | Does the firm suffer a competitive disadvantage due to lack of size in assets, sales, or profits that translates into (among other things) difficulty in tapping the capital market for funds? |

[a]Affirmative responses indicate greater business risk exposure.

[2]Note that the concept of financial risk used here differs from that used in our examination of cash and marketable securities management in chapter 19.

**Financial leverage**
Financing a portion of the firm's assets with securities bearing a fixed or limited rate of return.

**Financial leverage** means financing a portion of the firm's assets with securities bearing a fixed (limited) rate of return in hopes of increasing the ultimate return to the common stockholders. The decision to use debt or preferred stock in the financial structure of the corporation means that those who own the common shares of the firm are exposed to financial risk. Any given level of variability in EBIT will be *magnified* by the firm's use of financial leverage, and such additional variability will be embodied in the variability of earnings available to the common stockholder and earnings per share. If these magnifications are negative, the common stockholder has a higher chance of insolvency than would have existed had the use of fixed-charge securities (debt and preferred stock) been avoided.

The closely related concepts of business and financial risk are crucial to the problem of financial structure design. This follows from the impact of these types of risk on the variability of the earnings stream flowing to the company's shareholders. In the rest of this chapter, we study techniques that permit a precise assessment of the earnings stream variability caused by (1) operating leverage and (2) financial leverage. We have already defined financial leverage. Table 15-1 shows that the business risk of the enterprise is influenced by the use of what is called *operating leverage.* **Operating leverage** refers to the incurrence of fixed operating costs in the firm's income stream. To understand the nature and importance of operating leverage, we need to draw upon the basics of cost-volume-profit analysis, or *break-even analysis.*

**Operating leverage**
The incurrence of fixed operating costs in the firm's income stream.

**CONCEPT CHECK**

1. Explain the concept of "business risk" within the context of financial structure management.
2. Explain the concept of "financial risk" within the context of financial structure management.
3. Distinguish between "financial leverage" and "operating leverage."

## BREAK-EVEN ANALYSIS

OBJECTIVE 2 

The break-even analysis concepts presented in this section are often covered in many of your other classes, such as basic accounting principles and managerial economics. This just shows you how important and accepted this tool is within the realm of business decision making. The "Objective and Uses" section identifies five typical uses of the break-even model. You can probably add an application or two of your own. Hotels and motels, for instance, know exactly what their break-even occupancy rate is. This break-even occupancy rate gives them an operating target. This operating target, in turn, often becomes a crucial input to the hotel's advertising strategy. You may not want to become a financial manager—but you do want to understand how to compute break-even points.

The technique of break-even analysis is familiar to legions of businesspeople. It is usefully applied in a wide array of business settings, including both small and large organizations. This tool is widely accepted by the business community for two reasons: It is based on straightforward assumptions, and companies have found that the information gained from the break-even model is beneficial in decision-making situations.

### Objective and Uses

The objective of *break-even analysis* is to determine the *break-even quantity of output* by studying the relationships among the firm's cost structure, volume of output, and profit.

Alternatively, the firm ascertains the break-even level of sales dollars that corresponds to the break-even quantity of output. We will develop the fundamental relationships by concentrating on units of output, and then extend the procedure to permit direct calculation of the break-even sales level.

What is meant by the break-even quantity of output? It is that quantity of output, denominated in units, that results in an EBIT level equal to zero. Use of the break-even model, therefore, enables the financial officer (1) to determine the quantity of output that must be sold to cover all operating costs, as distinct from financial costs, and (2) to calculate the EBIT that will be achieved at various output levels.

The many actual and potential applications of the break-even approach include the following:

1. **Capital expenditure analysis.** As a complementary technique to discounted cash flow evaluation models, the break-even model locates in a rough way the sales volume needed to make a project economically beneficial to the firm. It should not be used to replace the time-adjusted evaluation techniques.
2. **Pricing policy.** The sales price of a new product can be set to achieve a target EBIT level. Furthermore, should market penetration be a prime objective, a price could be set that would cover slightly more than the variable costs of production and provide only a partial contribution to the recovery of fixed costs. The negative EBIT at several possible sales prices can then be studied.
3. **Labor contract negotiations.** The effect of increased variable costs resulting from higher wages on the break-even quantity of output can be analyzed.
4. **Cost structure.** The choice of reducing variable costs at the expense of incurring higher fixed costs can be evaluated. Management might decide to become more capital-intensive by performing tasks in the production process through use of equipment rather than labor. Application of the break-even model can indicate what the effects of this trade-off will be on the break-even point for the given product.
5. **Financing decisions.** Analysis of the firm's cost structure will reveal the proportion that fixed operating costs bear to sales. If this proportion is high, the firm might reasonably decide not to add any fixed financing costs on top of the high fixed operating costs.

## Essential Elements of the Break-Even Model

To implement the break-even model, we must separate the production costs of the company into two mutually exclusive categories: fixed costs and variable costs. You will recall from your study of basic economics that in the long run, all costs are variable. Break-even analysis, therefore, is a short-run concept.

## Assumed Behavior of Costs

FIXED COSTS **Fixed costs,** also referred to as **indirect costs,** do not vary in total amount as sales volume or the quantity of output changes over some *relevant* range of output. Total fixed costs are independent of the quantity of product produced and equal some constant dollar amount. As production volume increases, fixed cost per unit of product falls, as fixed costs are spread over larger and larger quantities of output. Figure 15-3 graphs the behavior of total fixed costs with respect to the company's relevant range of output. This total is shown to be unaffected by the quantity of product that is manufactured and sold. Over some other relevant output range, the amount of total fixed costs might be higher or lower for the same company.

**Fixed costs (indirect costs)** Costs that do not vary in total dollar amount as sales volume or quantity of output changes.

**FIGURE 15-3**
Fixed-Cost Behavior over Relevant Range of Output

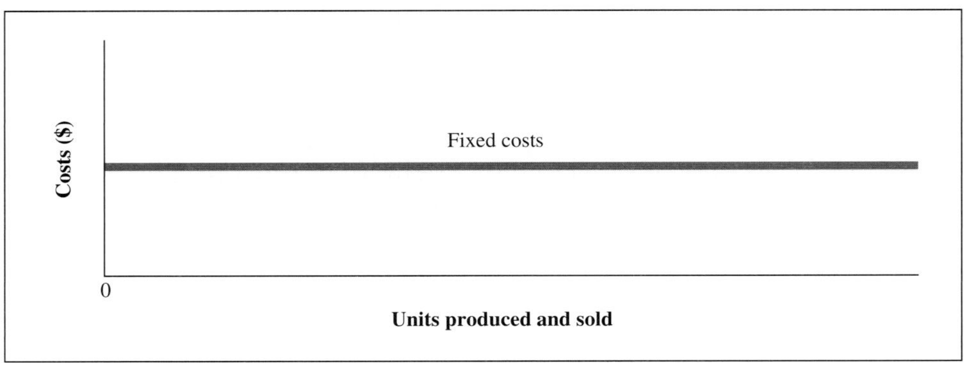


In a manufacturing setting, some specific examples of fixed costs are:

1. Administrative salaries
2. Depreciation
3. Insurance
4. Lump sums spent on intermittent advertising programs
5. Property taxes
6. Rent

**Variable costs (direct costs)** Costs that are fixed per unit of output but vary in total as output changes.

VARIABLE COSTS **Variable costs** are sometimes referred to as **direct costs.** Variable costs are fixed per unit of output but vary in total as output changes. Total variable costs are computed by taking the variable cost per unit and multiplying it by the quantity produced and sold. The break-even model assumes proportionality between total variable costs and sales. Thus, if sales rise by 10 percent, it is assumed that variable costs will rise by 10 percent. Figure 15-4 graphs the behavior of total variable costs with respect to the company's relevant range of output. Total variable costs are seen to depend on the quantity of product that is manufactured and sold. Notice that if zero units of the product are manufactured, then variable costs are zero, but fixed costs are greater than zero. This implies that some contribution to the coverage of fixed costs occurs as long as the selling price per unit exceeds the variable cost per unit. This helps explain why some firms will operate a plant even when sales are temporarily depressed—that is, to provide some increment of revenue toward the coverage of fixed costs.

For a manufacturing operation, some examples of variable costs include:

1. Direct labor
2. Direct materials

**FIGURE 15-4**
Variable-Cost Behavior over Relevant Range of Output

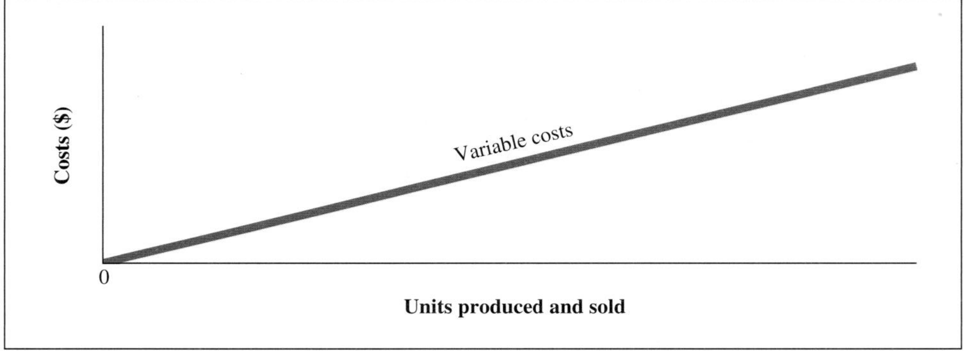

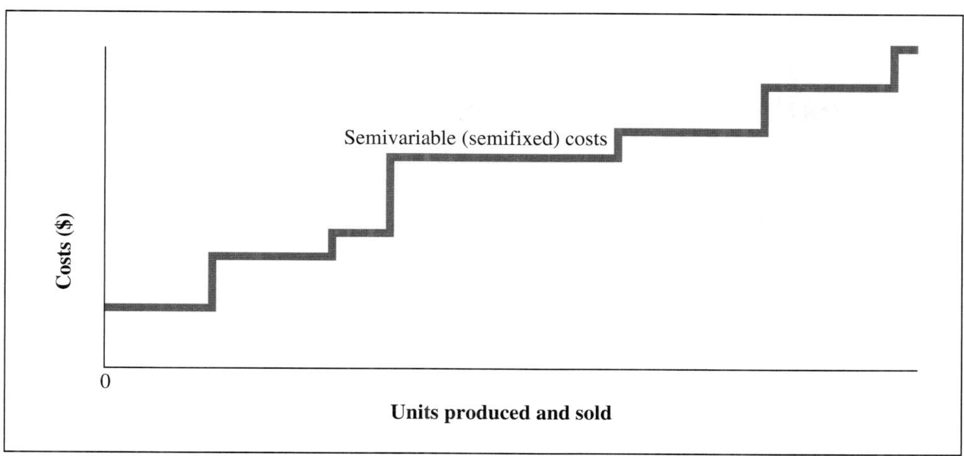


**FIGURE 15-5**
Semivariable Cost Behavior over Relevant Range of Output

3. Energy costs (fuel, electricity, natural gas) associated with the production area
4. Freight costs for products leaving the plant
5. Packaging
6. Sales commissions

MORE ON BEHAVIOR OF COSTS No one believes that all costs behave as neatly as we have illustrated the fixed and variable costs in Figures 15-3 and 15-4. Nor does any law or accounting principle dictate that a certain element of the firm's total costs always be classified as fixed or variable. This will depend on each firm's specific circumstances. In one firm, energy costs may be predominantly fixed, whereas in another they may vary with output.[3]

Furthermore, some costs may be fixed for a while, then rise sharply to a higher level as a higher output is reached, remain fixed, and then rise again with further increases in production. Such costs may be termed either **semivariable** or **semifixed.**

**Semivariable costs (semifixed costs)** Costs that exhibit the joint characteristics of both fixed and variable costs over different ranges of output.

The label is your choice, because both are used in industrial practice. An example might be the salaries paid production supervisors. Should output be cut back by 15 percent for a short period, the management of the organization is not likely to lay off 15 percent of the supervisors. Similarly, commissions paid to salespeople often follow a stepwise pattern over wide ranges of success. This sort of cost behavior is shown in Figure 15-5.

To implement the break-even model and deal with such a complex cost structure, the financial manager must (1) identify the most relevant output range for planning purposes, and then (2) approximate the cost effect of semivariable items over this range by segregating a portion of them to fixed costs and a portion to variable costs. In the actual business setting this procedure is not fun. It is not unusual for the analyst who deals with the figures to spend considerably more time allocating costs to fixed and variable categories than in carrying out the actual breakeven calculations.

## Total Revenue and Volume of Output

Besides fixed and variable costs, the essential elements of the break-even model include total revenue from sales and volume of output. **Total revenue** means sales dollars and is equal to

**Total revenue** Total sales dollars.

[3]In a greenhouse operation, where plants are grown (manufactured) under strictly controlled temperatures, heat costs will tend to be fixed whether the building is full or only half full of seedlings. In a metal stamping operation, where levers are being produced, there is no need to heat the plant to as high a temperature when the machines are stopped and the workers are not there. In this latter case, the heat costs will tend to be variable.

**Volume of output**
The firm's level of operations expressed either in sales dollars or as units of output.

the selling price per unit multiplied by the quantity sold. The **volume of output** refers to the firm's level of operations and may be indicated either as a unit quantity or as sales dollars.

## Finding the Break-Even Point

Finding the break-even point in terms of units of production can be accomplished in several ways. All approaches require the essential elements of the break-even model just described. The break-even model is a simple adaptation of the firm's income statement expressed in the following analytical format:

$$\text{sales} - (\text{total variable cost} + \text{total fixed cost}) = \text{profit} \quad \textbf{(15-1)}$$

On a units of production basis, it is necessary to introduce (1) the price at which each unit is sold and (2) the variable cost per unit of output. Because the profit item studied in break-even analysis is EBIT, we will use that acronym instead of the word "profit." In terms of units, the income statement shown in equation (15-1) becomes the break-even model by setting EBIT equal to zero:

$$(\text{sales price per unit})\,(\text{units sold}) - [(\text{variable cost per unit})\,(\text{units sold}) + (\text{total fixed cost})] = \text{EBIT} = \$0 \quad \textbf{(15-2)}$$

Our task now becomes finding the number of units that must be produced and sold in order to satisfy equation (15-2)—that is, to arrive at an EBIT = \$0. This can be done by (1) trial-and-error analysis, (2) contribution-margin analysis, or (3) algebraic analysis. Each approach will be illustrated using the same set of circumstances.

## Problem Situation

Even though the Pierce Grain Company manufactures several different products, it has observed over a lengthy period that its product mix is rather constant. This allows management to conduct its financial planning by use of a "normal" sales price per unit and "normal" variable cost per unit. The "normal" sales price and variable cost per unit are calculated from the constant product mix. It is like assuming that the product mix is one big product. The selling price is \$10 and the variable cost is \$6. Total fixed costs for the firm are \$100,000 per year. What is the break-even point in units produced and sold for the company during the coming year?

**TRIAL-AND-ERROR ANALYSIS** The most cumbersome approach to determining the firm's break-even point is to employ the trial-and-error technique illustrated in Table 15-2. The process simply involves the arbitrary selection of an output level and the calculation of a corresponding EBIT amount. When the level of output is found that results in an EBIT = \$0, the break-even point has been located. Notice that Table 15-2 is just equation 15-2 in worksheet form. For the Pierce Grain Company, total operating costs will be covered when 25,000 units are manufactured and sold. This tells us that if sales equal \$250,000, the firm's EBIT will equal \$0.

**Contribution margin**
Unit sales price minus unit variable cost.

**CONTRIBUTION-MARGIN ANALYSIS** Unlike trial and error, use of the contribution-margin technique permits direct computation of the break-even quantity of output. The **contribution margin** is the difference between the unit selling price and unit variable costs, as follows:

| | |
|---|---|
| | Unit sales price |
| − | Unit variable cost |
| = | Unit contribution margin |

**TABLE 15-2**
Pierce Grain Company Sales, Cost, and Profit Schedule

| (1) Units Sold | (2) Unit Sales Price | (3) = (1) × (2) Sales | (4) Unit Variable Cost | (5) = (1) × (4) Total Variable Cost | (6) Total Fixed Cost | (7) = (5) + (6) Total Cost | (8) = (3) − (7) EBIT | |
|---|---|---|---|---|---|---|---|---|
| 1. 10,000 | $10 | $100,000 | $6 | $ 60,000 | $100,000 | $160,000 | $−60,000 | 1. |
| 2. 15,000 | 10 | 150,000 | 6 | 90,000 | 100,000 | 190,000 | −40,000 | 2. |
| 3. 20,000 | 10 | 200,000 | 6 | 120,000 | 100,000 | 220,000 | −20,000 | 3. |
| 4. 25,000 | 10 | 250,000 | 6 | 150,000 | 100,000 | 250,000 | 0 | 4. |
| 5. 30,000 | 10 | 300,000 | 6 | 180,000 | 100,000 | 280,000 | 20,000 | 5. |
| 6. 35,000 | 10 | 350,000 | 6 | 210,000 | 100,000 | 310,000 | 40,000 | 6. |

| Input Data | Output Data |
|---|---|
| Unit sales price = $10 | Break-even point in units = 25,000 units produced and sold |
| Unit variable cost = $ 6 | Break-even point in sales = $250,000 |
| Total fixed cost = $100,000 | |

The use of the word "contribution" in the present context means contribution to the coverage of fixed operating costs. For the Pierce Grain Company, the unit contribution margin is:

| | |
|---|---|
| Unit sales price | $10 |
| Unit variable cost | − 6 |
| Unit contribution margin | $ 4 |

If the annual fixed costs of $100,000 are divided by the unit contribution margin of $4, we find the break-even quantity of output for Pierce Grain is 25,000 units. With much less effort, we have arrived at the identical result found by trial and error. Figure 15-6 portrays the contribution-margin technique for finding the break-even point.

**ALGEBRAIC ANALYSIS** To explain the algebraic method for finding the break-even output level, we need to adopt some notation. Let:

$Q$ = the number of units sold
$Q_B$ = the break-even level of $Q$
$P$ = the unit sales price
$F$ = total fixed costs anticipated over the planning period
$V$ = the unit variable cost

Equation 15-2, the break-even model, is repeated as equation 15-2a with the model symbols used in place of words. The break-even model is then solved for $Q$, the number of units that must be sold in order that EBIT will equal $0. We label the break-even point quantity $Q_B$.

$$(P \cdot Q) - [(V \cdot Q) + (F)] = \text{EBIT} = \$0 \tag{15-2a}$$

$$(P \cdot Q) - (V \cdot Q) - F = \$0$$

$$Q(P - V) = F$$

$$Q_B = \frac{F}{P - V} \tag{15-3}$$

**FIGURE 15-6**
Contribution-Margin Approach to Break-Even Analysis

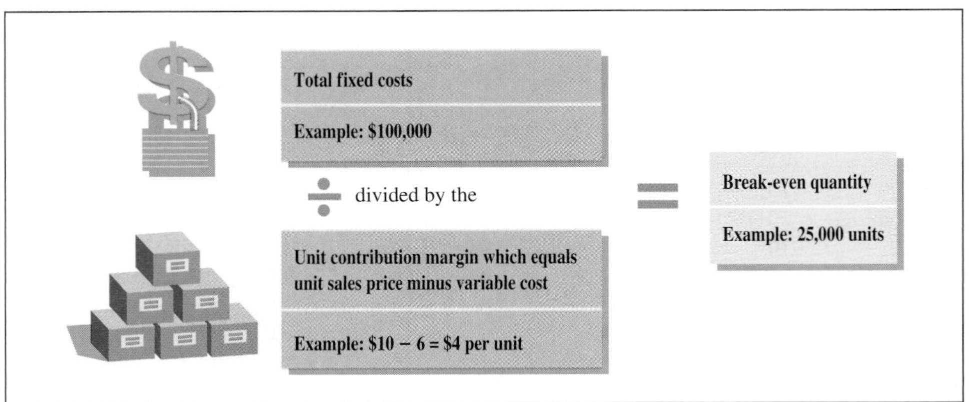


Observe that equation 15-3 says: divide total fixed operating costs, $F$, by the unit contribution margin, $P - V$, and the break-even level of output, $Q_B$, will be obtained. The contribution-margin analysis is nothing more than equation 15-3 in different garb.

Application of equation 15-3 permits direct calculation of Pierce Grain's break-even point, as follows:

$$Q_B = \frac{F}{P - V} = \frac{\$100{,}000}{\$10 - \$6} = 25{,}000 \text{ units}$$

## Break-Even Point in Sales Dollars

In dealing with the multiproduct firm, it is convenient to compute the break-even point in terms of sales dollars rather than units of output. Sales, in effect, become a common denominator associated with a particular product mix. Furthermore, an outside analyst may not have access to internal unit cost data. He or she may, however, be able to obtain annual reports for the firm. If the analyst can separate the firm's total costs as identified from its annual reports into their fixed and variable components, he or she can calculate a general break-even point in sales dollars.

**Analytical income statement**
A financial statement used by internal analysts that differs in composition from audited or published financial statements.

We will illustrate the procedure using the Pierce Grain Company's cost structure, contained in Table 15-2. Suppose that the information on line 5 of Table 15-2 is arranged in the format shown in Table 15-3. We will refer to this type of financial statement as an **analytical income statement.** This distinguishes it from audited income statements published, for example, in the annual reports of public corporations. If we are aware of the simple mathematical relationships on which cost-volume-profit analysis is based, we can use Table 15-3 to find the break-even point in sales dollars for the Pierce Grain Company.

First, let us explore the logic of the process. Recall from equation 15-1 that

sales − (total variable cost + total fixed cost) = EBIT

If we let total sales = $S$, total variable cost = $VC$, and total fixed cost = $F$, the preceding relationship becomes

$$S - (VC + F) = \text{EBIT}$$

Because variable cost per unit of output and selling price per unit are *assumed* constant over the relevant output range in break-even analysis, the ratio of total sales to total vari-

**TABLE 15-3**
Pierce Grain Company Analytical Income Statement

| | |
|---|---|
| Sales | $300,000 |
| Less: total variable costs | 180,000 |
| Revenue before fixed costs | $120,000 |
| Less: total fixed costs | 100,000 |
| EBIT | $20,000 |

able cost, $VC/S$, is a constant for any level of sales. This permits us to rewrite the previous expression as:

$$S - \left[\left(\frac{VC}{S}\right)S\right] - F = \text{EBIT}$$

and

$$S\left(1 - \frac{VC}{S}\right) - F = \text{EBIT}$$

At the break-even point, however, EBIT $= 0$, and the corresponding break-even level of sales can be represented as $S^*$. At the break-even level of sales, we have

$$S^*\left(1 - \frac{VC}{S}\right) - F = 0$$

or

$$S^*\left(1 - \frac{VC}{S}\right) = F$$

Therefore,

$$S^* = \frac{F}{1 - \dfrac{VC}{S}} \tag{15-4}$$

The application of equation 15-4 to Pierce Grain's analytical income statement in Table 15-3 permits the break-even sales level for the firm to be directly computed, as follows:

$$S^* = \frac{\$100{,}000}{1 - \dfrac{\$180{,}000}{\$300{,}000}}$$

$$= \frac{\$100{,}000}{1 - .60} = \$250{,}000$$

Notice that this is indeed the same break-even sales level for Pierce Grain that is indicated on line 4 of Table 15-2.

## Graphic Representation, Analysis of Input Changes, and Cash Break-Even Point

In making a presentation to management, it is often effective to display the firm's cost-volume-profit relationships in the form of a chart. Even those individuals who truly enjoy analyzing financial problems find figures and equations dry material at times. Furthermore, by

**FIGURE 15-7**
Pierce Grain Company's Break-Even Chart

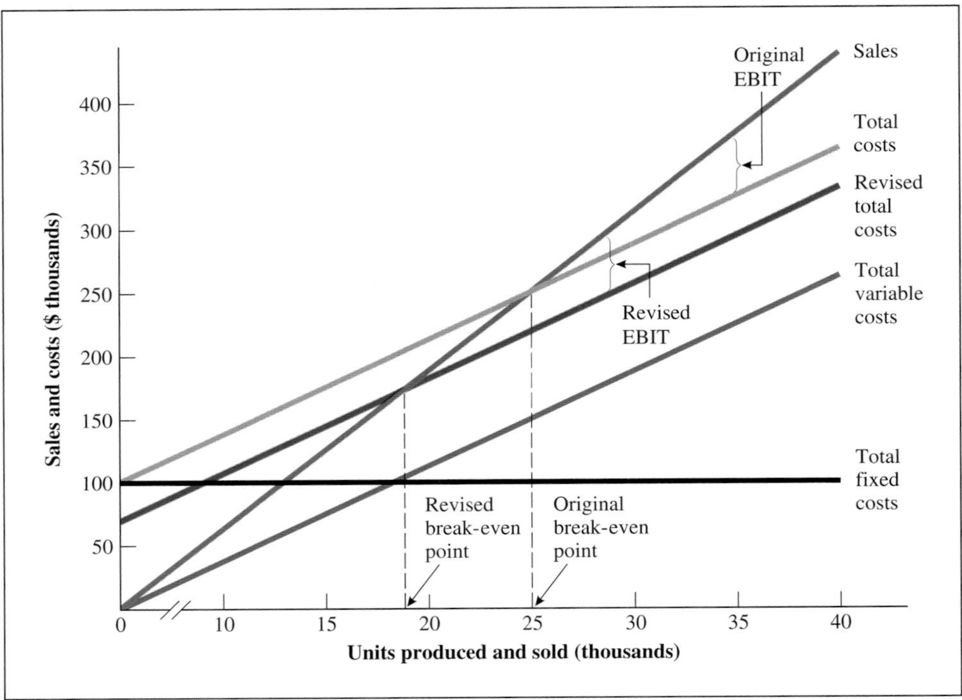


quickly scanning the basic break-even chart, the manager can approximate the EBIT amount that will prevail at different sales levels.

Such a chart has been prepared for the Pierce Grain Company. Figure 15-7 has been constructed for this firm using the input data contained in Table 15-2. Total fixed costs of \$100,000 are added to the total variable costs associated with each production level to form the total costs line. When 25,000 units of product are manufactured and sold, the sales line and total costs line intersect. This means, of course, the EBIT that would exist at that volume of output is zero. Beyond 25,000 units of output, notice that sales revenues exceed the total costs line. This causes a positive EBIT. This positive EBIT, or profits, is labeled "original EBIT" in Figure 15-7.

The unencumbered nature of the break-even model makes it possible to quickly incorporate changes in the requisite input data and generate the revised output. Suppose a favorable combination of events causes Pierce Grain's fixed costs to decrease by \$25,000. This would put total fixed costs for the planning period at a level of \$75,000 rather than the \$100,000 originally forecast. Total costs, being the sum of fixed and variable costs, would be lower by \$25,000 at all output levels. The revised total costs line in Figure 15-7 reflects Pierce Grain's reduction in fixed costs. Under these revised conditions, the new break-even point in units would be as follows:

$$Q_B = \frac{\$75{,}000}{\$10 - \$6} = 18{,}750 \text{ units}$$

The revised break-even point of 18,750 units is identified in Figure 15-7, along with the revised EBIT amounts that would prevail at differing output and sales levels. The chart clearly indicates that at any specific production and sales level, the revised EBIT would exceed the original EBIT. This must be the case, as the revised total costs line lies below the original total costs line over the entire relevant output range. The effect on the break-even point caused by other changes in (1) the cost structure or (2) the pricing policy can be analyzed in a similar fashion.

The data in Figure 15-7 can be used to demonstrate another version of basic cost-volume-profit analysis. This can be called **cash break-even analysis.** If the company's fixed- or variable-cost estimates allow for any noncash expenses, then the resultant break-even point is higher on an accounting profit basis than on a cash basis. This means the firm's production and sales levels do not have to be as great to cover the cash costs of manufacturing the product.

**Cash break-even analysis** A variation from traditional break-even analysis that removes (deducts) noncash expenses from the cost items.

What are these noncash expenses? The largest and most significant is depreciation expense. Another category is prepaid expenses. Insurance policies are at times paid to cover a 3-year cycle. Thus, the time period for which the break-even analysis is being performed might *not* involve an actual cash outlay for insurance coverage.

For purposes of illustration, assume that noncash expenses for Pierce Grain amount to $25,000 over the planning period and that all of these costs are fixed. We can compare the revised total costs line in Figure 15-7, which implicitly assumes a lower fixed *cash* cost line, with the sales revenue line to find the cash break-even point. Provided Pierce Grain can produce and sell 18,750 units over the planning horizon, revenues from sales will be equal to cash operating costs.

**RELATE TO THE BIG PICTURE**

The preceding discussion on cash break-even analysis reinforces the importance of **Principle 3: Cash—Not Profits—Is King.** By use of this modified version of regular break-even analysis, we are reminded that only cash can be reinvested into the firm's operations, as distinct from retained earnings. Cash is used to pay operating expenses, acquire real capital, and distribute earnings in the form of cash dividends. Another way of understanding **Principle 3** is as follows: Accounting profits are an opinion—cash is reality. Financial asset values are based on the firm's ability to generate cash flows. You cannot be misled over long time periods by cash-flow generation. Note that this emphasis on reality also relates to our discussion of value-based management techniques (economic value added and market value added).

## Limitations of Break-Even Analysis

Earlier we identified some of the applications of break-even analysis. This technique is a useful tool in many settings. It must be emphasized, however, that break-even analysis provides a *beneficial guide* to managerial action, not the final answer. The use of cost-volume-profit analysis has limitations, which should be kept in mind. These include the following:

1. The cost-volume-profit relationship is assumed to be linear. This is realistic only over narrow ranges of output.
2. The total revenue curve (sales curve) is presumed to increase linearly with the volume of output. This implies any quantity can be sold over the relevant output range at that *single* price. To be more realistic, it is necessary in many situations to compute *several* sales curves and corresponding break-even points at differing prices.
3. A constant production and sales mix is assumed. Should the company decide to produce more of one product and less of another, a new break-even point would have to be found. Only if the variable cost-to-sales ratios were identical for products involved would the new calculation be unnecessary.

4. The break-even chart and the break-even computation are static forms of analysis. Any alteration in the firm's cost or price structure dictates that a new break-even point be calculated. Break-even analysis is more helpful, therefore, in stable industries than in dynamic ones.

**CONCEPT CHECK**

1. Distinguish among "fixed costs," "variable costs," and "semivariable costs."
2. Define the term "contribution margin."
3. When is it useful or necessary to compute the break-even point in terms of sales dollars rather than units of output?

## OPERATING LEVERAGE

OBJECTIVE 3 

If *fixed* operating costs are present in the firm's cost structure, so is *operating leverage.* Fixed operating costs do not include interest charges incurred from the firm's use of debt financing. Those costs will be incorporated into the analysis when financial leverage is discussed.

So operating leverage arises from the firm's use of fixed operating costs. But what is operating leverage? Operating leverage is the responsiveness of the firm's EBIT to fluctuations in sales. By continuing to draw on our data for the Pierce Grain Company, we can illustrate the concept of operating leverage. Table 15-4 contains data for a study of a possible fluctuation in the firm's sales level. It is assumed that Pierce Grain is currently operating at an annual sales level of $300,000. This is referred to in the tabulation as the base sales level at $t$ (time period zero). The question is: How will Pierce Grain's EBIT level respond to a positive 20 percent change in sales? A sales volume of $360,000, referred to as the forecast sales level at $t+1$, reflects the 20 percent sales rise anticipated over the planning period. Assume that the planning period is 1 year.

Operating leverage relationships are derived within the mathematical assumptions of cost-volume-profit analysis. In the present example, this means that Pierce Grain's variable cost-to-sales ratio of .6 will continue to hold during time period $t+1$, and the fixed costs will hold steady at $100,000.

Given the forecasted sales level for Pierce Grain and its cost structure, we can measure the responsiveness of EBIT to the upswing in volume. Notice in Table 15-4 that EBIT is expected to be $44,000 at the end of the planning period. The percentage change in EBIT from $t$ to $t+1$ can be measured as follows:

$$\text{percentage change in EBIT} = \frac{\$44{,}000_{t+1} - \$20{,}000_t}{\$20{,}000_t} = \frac{\$24{,}000}{\$20{,}000} = 120\%$$

We know that the projected fluctuation in sales amounts to 20 percent of the base period, $t$, sales level. This is verified:

$$\text{percentage change in sales} = \frac{\$360{,}000_{t+1} - \$300{,}000_t}{\$300{,}000_t} = \frac{\$60{,}000}{\$300{,}000} = 20\%$$

**TABLE 15-4**
Concept of Operating Leverage: Increase in Pierce Grain Company Sales

| Item | Base Sales Level, *t* | Forecast Sales Level, *t* + 1 |
|---|---|---|
| Sales | $300,000 | $360,000 |
| Less: total variable costs | 180,000 | 216,000 |
| Revenue before fixed costs | $120,000 | $144,000 |
| Less: total fixed costs | 100,000 | 100,000 |
| EBIT | $ 20,000 | $44,000 |

By relating the percentage fluctuation in EBIT to the percentage fluctuation in sales, we can calculate a specific measure of operating leverage. Thus, we have:

$$\text{degree of operating leverage from the base sales level}_{(s)} = DOL_s = \frac{\text{percentage change in EBIT}}{\text{percentage change in sales}} \qquad \textbf{(15-5)}$$

Applying equation 15-5 to our Pierce Grain data gives:

$$DOL_{\$300{,}000} = \frac{120\%}{20\%} = 6 \text{ times}$$

Unless we understand what the specific measure of operating leverage tells us, the fact that we may know it is equal to six times is nothing more than sterile information. For Pierce Grain, the inference is that for *any* percentage fluctuation in sales from the base level, the percentage fluctuation in EBIT will be six times as great. If Pierce Grain expected only a 5 percent rise in sales over the coming period, a 30 percent rise in EBIT would be anticipated as follows:

$$(\text{percentage change in sales}) \times (DOL_s) = \text{percentage change in EBIT}$$
$$(5\%) \times (6) = 30\%$$

We will now return to the postulated 20 percent change in sales. What if the direction of the fluctuation is expected to be negative rather than positive? What is in store for Pierce Grain? Unfortunately for Pierce Grain (but fortunately for the analytical process), we will see that the operating leverage measure holds in the negative direction as well. This situation is displayed in Table 15-5.

At the $240,000 sales level, which represents the 20 percent decrease from the base period, Pierce Grain's EBIT is expected to be −$4,000. How sensitive is EBIT to this sales change? The magnitude of the EBIT fluctuation is calculated as:[4]

$$\text{percentage change in EBIT} = \frac{-\$4{,}000_{t+1} - \$20{,}000_t}{\$20{,}000_t} = \frac{-\$24{,}000}{\$20{,}000} = -120\%$$

**TABLE 15-5**
Concept of Operating Leverage: Decrease in Pierce Grain Company Sales

| Item | Base Sales Level, *t* | Forecast Sales Level, *t* + 1 |
|---|---|---|
| Sales | $300,000 | $240,000 |
| Less: total variable costs | 180,000 | 144,000 |
| Revenue before fixed costs | $120,000 | $ 96,000 |
| Less: total fixed costs | 100,000 | 100,000 |
| EBIT | $ 20,000 | $ −4,000 |

[4]Some students have conceptual difficulty in computing these percentage changes when negative amounts are involved. Notice by inspection in Table 15-5 that the *difference* between an EBIT amount of +$20,000 at *t* and −$4,000 at *t* + 1 is −$24,000.

Making use of our knowledge that the sales change was equal to −20 percent permits us to compute the specific measure of operating leverage as:

$$DOL_{\$300{,}000} = \frac{-120\%}{-20\%} = 6 \text{ times}$$

What we have seen, then, is that the degree of operating leverage measure works in the positive or the negative direction. A negative change in production volume and sales can be magnified severalfold when the effect on EBIT is calculated.

To this point, our calculations of the degree of operating leverage have required two analytical income statements: one for the base period and a second for the subsequent period that incorporates the possible sales alteration. This cumbersome process can be simplified. If unit cost data are available to the financial manager, the relationship can be expressed directly in the following manner:

$$DOL_s = \frac{Q(P - V)}{Q(P - V) - F} \tag{15-6}$$

Observe in equation 15-6 that the variables were all previously defined in our algebraic analysis of the break-even model. Recall that Pierce sells its product at \$10 per unit, the unit variable cost is \$6, and total fixed costs over the planning horizon are \$100,000. Still assuming that Pierce is operating at a \$300,000 sales volume, which means output ($Q$) is 30,000 units, we can find the degree of operating leverage by application of equation 15-6:

$$DOL_{\$300{,}000} = \frac{30{,}000(\$10 - \$6)}{30{,}000(\$10 - \$6) - \$100{,}000} = \frac{\$120{,}000}{\$20{,}000} = 6 \text{ times}$$

Whereas equation 15-6 requires us to know unit cost data to carry out the computations, the next formulation we examine does not. If we have an analytical income statement for the base period, then equation 15-6 can be employed to find the firm's degree of operating leverage:

$$DOL_s = \frac{\text{revenue before fixed costs}}{\text{EBIT}} = \frac{S - VC}{S - VC - F} \tag{15-7}$$

Use of equation 15-7 in conjunction with the base period data for Pierce Grain shown in either Table 15-4 or 15-5 gives:

$$DOL_{\$300{,}000} = \frac{\$120{,}000}{\$20{,}000} = 6 \text{ times}$$

The three versions of the operating leverage measure all produce the same result. Data availability will sometimes dictate which formulation can be applied. The crucial consideration, though, is that you grasp what the measurement tells you. For Pierce Grain, a 1 percent change in sales will produce a 6 percent change in EBIT.

Before we complete our discussion of operating leverage and move on to the subject of financial leverage, ask yourself, "Which type of leverage is more under the control of management?" You will probably (and correctly) come to the conclusion that the firm's managers have less control over its operating cost structure and almost complete control over its financial structure. What the firm actually produces, for example, will determine to a significant degree the division between fixed and variable costs. There is more room for substitution among the various sources of financial capital than there is among the labor and real capital inputs that enable the firm to meet its production requirements. Thus, you can anticipate more arguments over the choice to use a given degree of financial leverage than the corresponding choice over operating leverage use.

**TABLE 15-6**
Pierce Grain Company Degree of Operating Leverage Relative to Different Sales Bases

| Units Produced and Sold | Sales Dollars | $DOL_s$ |
|---|---|---|
| 25,000 | $ 250,000 | Undefined |
| 30,000 | 300,000 | 6.00 |
| 35,000 | 350,000 | 3.50 |
| 40,000 | 400,000 | 2.67 |
| 45,000 | 450,000 | 2.25 |
| 50,000 | 500,000 | 2.00 |
| 75,000 | 750,000 | 1.50 |
| 100,000 | 1,000,000 | 1.33 |

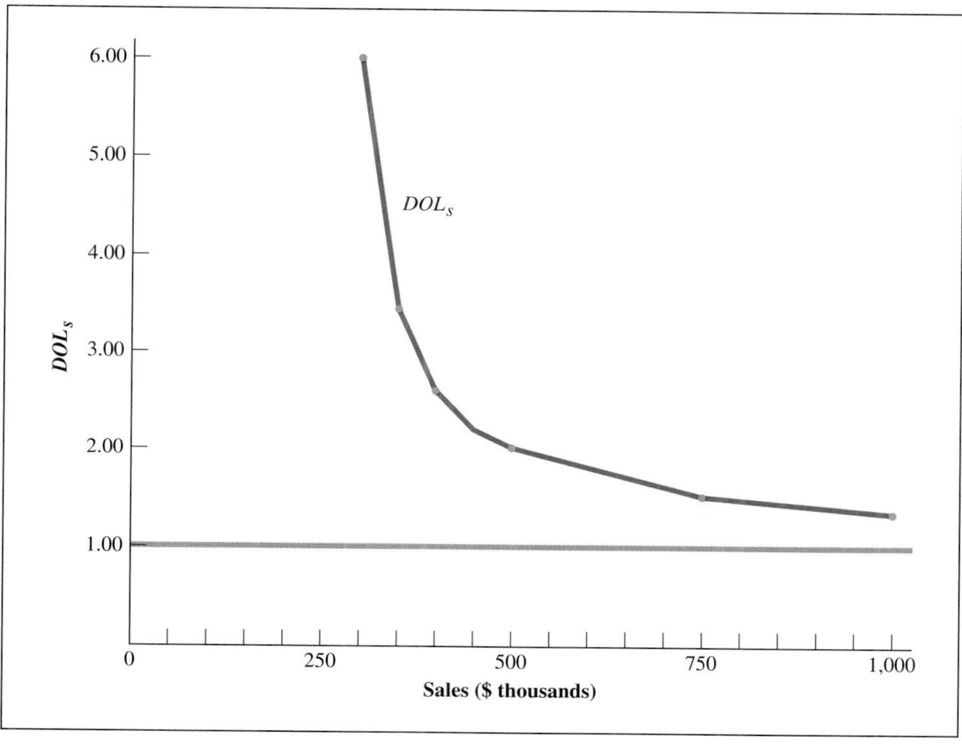


**FIGURE 15-8**
Pierce Grain Company Degree of Operating Leverage Relative to Different Sales Bases

## Implications

As the firm's scale of operations moves in a favorable manner above the break-even point, the degree of operating leverage at each subsequent (higher) sales base will decline. In short, the greater the sales level, the lower the degree of operating leverage. This is demonstrated in Table 15-6 for the Pierce Grain Company. At the break-even sales level for Pierce Grain, the degree of operating leverage is *undefined,* because the denominator in any of the computational formulas is zero. Notice that beyond the break-even point of 25,000 units, the degree of operating leverage declines. It will decline at a decreasing rate and asymptotically approach a value of 1.00. As long as some fixed operating costs are present in the firm's cost structure, however, operating leverage exists, and the degree of operating leverage ($DOL_s$) will exceed 1.00. Operating leverage is present, then, whenever the firm faces the following situation:

$$\frac{\text{percentage change in EBIT}}{\text{percentage change in sales}} > 1.00$$

The data in Table 15-6 are presented in graphic form in Figure 15-8.

**CONCEPT CHECK**

1. If a firm's degree of operating leverage happens to be six times, what precisely does that mean?
2. What does the degree of operating leverage concept suggest when a negative shock in production volume and sales occurs?
3. When is operating leverage present in the firm's cost structure? What condition is necessary for operating leverage not to be present in the firm's cost structure?

The greater the firm's degree of operating leverage, the more its profits will vary with a given percentage change in sales. Thus, operating leverage is definitely an attribute of the business risk that confronts the company. From Table 15-6 and Figure 15-8, we have seen that the degree of operating leverage falls as sales increase past the firm's break-even point. The sheer size and operating profitability of the firm, therefore, affect and can lessen its business-risk exposure.

The manager considering an alteration in the firm's cost structure will benefit from an understanding of the operating leverage concept. It might be possible to replace part of the labor force with capital equipment (machinery). A possible result is an increase in fixed costs associated with the new machinery and a reduction in variable costs attributable to a lower labor bill. This conceivably could raise the firm's degree of operating leverage at a specific sales base. If the prospects for future sales increases are high, then increasing the degree of operating leverage might be a prudent decision. The opposite conclusion will be reached if sales prospects are unattractive.

## FINANCIAL LEVERAGE

OBJECTIVE 4 

We have defined *financial leverage* as the practice of financing a portion of the firm's assets with securities bearing a fixed rate of return in hope of increasing the ultimate return to the common shareholders. In the present discussion, we focus on the responsiveness of the company's earnings per share to changes in its EBIT. For the time being, then, the return to the common stockholder being concentrated upon is earnings per share. We are *not* saying that earnings per share is the appropriate criterion for all financing decisions. In fact, the weakness of such a contention will be examined in the next chapter. Rather, the use of financial leverage produces a certain type of *effect.* This effect can be illustrated clearly by concentrating on an earnings-per-share criterion.

Let us assume that the Pierce Grain Company is in the process of getting started as a going concern. The firm's potential owners have calculated that $200,000 is needed to purchase the necessary assets to conduct the business. Three possible financing plans have been identified for raising the $200,000; they are presented in Table 15-7. In plan A, no financial risk is assumed: The entire $200,000 is raised by selling 2,000 common shares, each with a $100 par value. In plan B, a moderate amount of financial risk is assumed: 25 percent of the assets are financed with a debt issue that carries an 8 percent annual interest rate. Plan C would use the most financial leverage: 40 percent of the assets would be financed with a debt issue costing 8 percent.[5]

[5]In actual practice, moving from a 25 to a 40 percent debt ratio would probably result in a higher interest rate on the additional bonds. That effect is ignored here to let us concentrate on the ramifications of using different proportions of debt in the financial structure.

**TABLE 15-7**
Pierce Grain Company Possible Financial Structures

| | | | |
|---|---|---|---|
| **Plan A: 0% debt** | | | |
| | | Total debt | $ 0 |
| | | Common equity | 200,000[a] |
| Total assets | $200,000 | Total liabilities and equity | $200,000 |
| **Plan B: 25% debt at 8% interest rate** | | | |
| | | Total debt | $ 50,000 |
| | | Common equity | 150,000[b] |
| Total assets | $200,000 | Total liabilities and equity | $200,000 |
| **Plan C: 40% debt at 8% interest rate** | | | |
| | | Total debt | $ 80,000 |
| | | Common equity | 120,000[c] |
| Total assets | $200,000 | Total liabilities and equity | $200,000 |

[a]2,000 common shares outstanding [b]1,500 common shares outstanding [c]1,200 common shares outstanding

Table 15-8 presents the impact of financial leverage on earnings per share associated with each fund-raising alternative. If EBIT should increase from $20,000 to $40,000, then earnings per share would rise by 100 percent under plan A. The same positive fluctuation in EBIT would occasion an earnings per share rise of 125 percent under plan B, and 147 percent under plan C. In plans B and C, the 100 percent increase in EBIT (from $20,000 to $40,000) is magnified to a greater than 100 percent increase in earnings per share. The firm is employing financial leverage, and exposing its owners to financial risk, when the following situation exists:

$$\frac{\text{percentage change in earnings per share}}{\text{percentage change in EBIT}} > 1.00$$

By following the same general procedures that allowed us to analyze the firm's use of operating leverage, we can lay out a precise measure of financial leverage. Such a measure deals with the sensitivity of earnings per share to EBIT fluctuations. The relationship can be expressed as:

$$\text{degree of financial leverage } (DFL) \text{ from base EBIT level} = DFL_{EBIT} = \frac{\text{percentage change in earnings per share}}{\text{percentage change in EBIT}} \quad \textbf{(15-8)}$$

Use of equation 15-8 with each of the financing choices outlined for Pierce Grain is shown subsequently. The base EBIT level is $20,000 in each case.

$$\text{Plan A: } DFL_{\$20{,}000} = \frac{100\%}{100\%} = 1.00 \text{ time}$$

$$\text{Plan B: } DFL_{\$20{,}000} = \frac{125\%}{100\%} = 1.25 \text{ times}$$

$$\text{Plan C: } DFL_{\$20{,}000} = \frac{147\%}{100\%} = 1.47 \text{ times}$$

Like operating leverage, the *degree of financial leverage* concept performs in the negative direction as well as the positive. Should EBIT fall by 10 percent, the Pierce Grain Company would suffer a 12.5 percent decline in earnings per share under plan B. If plan C were chosen to raise the necessary financial capital, the decline in earnings would be 14.7 percent. Observe that the greater the *DFL*, the greater the fluctuations (positive or negative) in earnings per share. The common stockholder is required to endure greater variations in returns when the

FINANCE MATTERS

## IBM: International Influences on Revenue Growth

In 1996, IBM posted an increase in sales of some 5.6 percent. But the company's change in net income was a much greater 30.0 percent. This is exactly the type of magnification effect that we are studying within this chapter. The management discussion from IBM's 1996 *Annual Report* highlights several concepts explored in this and other chapters of the text.

IBM's management identifies the building blocks of its strategic plan. The emphasis on sales growth remains intact. Notice the closing reference to cash-flow generation—this should remind you of **Principle 3: Cash—Not Profits—Is King.** Companies do, in fact, think about the important concepts that we discuss in this text.

---

IBM's financial performance in 1996 reflects continued progress towards its strategic goals of revenue growth, an expanded portfolio of industry-specific customer solutions, (especially through network computing), and an increasingly competitive cost and expense structure.

The company reported record revenue of nearly $76 billion, 30 percent net earnings growth over 1995, and ended the year with over $8 billion in cash. The company also continued to align itself for strategic growth by investing almost $20 billion in critical high-growth and advanced technology businesses, research and development, acquisitions, and repurchases of its common shares.

The company's results were also affected adversely by the continued weakness of the European economy and the continued strengthening of the U.S. dollar. Without the currency effect, year-to-year revenue growth would have been 9 percent compared with the reported growth of 6 percent.

Although excellent progress was made in 1996, the company must continue to implement strategic actions to further improve its competitiveness. These actions include an ongoing focus on revenue growth and stable net income margins, while at the same time maintaining a strong balance sheet and cash flows for long-term growth.

Source: IBM *Annual Report* (1996): 44.

**TABLE 15-8**
Pierce Grain Company Analysis of Financial Leverage at Different EBIT Levels

| (1) EBIT | (2) Interest | (3) = (1) − (2) EBT | (4) = (3) × .5 Taxes | (5) = (3) − (4) Net Income to Common | (6) Earnings per Share | |
|---|---|---|---|---|---|---|
| **Plan A: 0% debt; $200,000 common equity; 2,000 shares** | | | | | | |
| $ 0 | $ 0 | $ 0 | $ 0 | $ 0 | $ 0 | |
| 20,000 | 0 | 20,000 | 10,000 | 10,000 | 5.00 | 100% |
| 40,000 | 0 | 40,000 | 20,000 | 20,000 | 10.00 | |
| 60,000 | 0 | 60,000 | 30,000 | 30,000 | 15.00 | |
| 80,000 | 0 | 80,000 | 40,000 | 40,000 | 20.00 | |
| **Plan B: 25% debt; 8% interest rate; $150,000 common equity, 1,500 shares** | | | | | | |
| $ 0 | $4,000 | $(4,000) | $(2,000)[a] | $(2,000) | $(1.33) | |
| 20,000 | 4,000 | 16,000 | 8,000 | 8,000 | 5.33 | 125% |
| 40,000 | 4,000 | 36,000 | 18,000 | 18,000 | 12.00 | |
| 60,000 | 4,000 | 56,000 | 28,000 | 28,000 | 18.67 | |
| 80,000 | 4,000 | 76,000 | 38,000 | 38,000 | 25.33 | |
| **Plan C: 40% debt; 8% interest rate; $120,000 common equity; 1,200 shares** | | | | | | |
| $ 0 | $6,400 | $(6,400) | $ (3,200)[a] | $(3,200) | $(2.67) | |
| 20,000 | 6,400 | 13,600 | 6,800 | 6,800 | 5.67 | 147% |
| 40,000 | 6,400 | 33,600 | 16,800 | 16,800 | 14.00 | |
| 60,000 | 6,400 | 53,600 | 26,800 | 26,800 | 22.33 | |
| 80,000 | 6,400 | 73,600 | 36,800 | 36,800 | 30.67 | |

[a]The negative tax bill recognizes the credit arising from the carryback and carryforward provision of the tax code.

firm's management chooses to use more financial leverage rather than less. The *DFL* measure allows the variation to be quantified.

Rather than taking the time to compute percentage changes in EBIT and earnings per share, the *DFL* can be found directly, as follows:

$$DFL_{EBIT} = \frac{EBIT}{EBIT - I} \quad \textbf{(15-9)}$$

In equation 15-9, the variable, *I*, represents the total interest expense incurred on *all* the firm's contractual debt obligations. If six bonds are outstanding, *I* is the sum of the interest expense on all six bonds. If the firm has preferred stock in its financial structure, the dividend on such issues must be inflated to a before-tax basis and included in the computation of *I*.[6] In this latter instance, *I* is in reality the sum of all fixed financing costs.

Equation 15-9 has been applied to each of Pierce Grain's financing plans (Table 15-8) at a base EBIT level of $20,000. The results are as follows:

$$\text{Plan A: } DFL_{\$20{,}000} = \frac{\$20{,}000}{\$20{,}000 - 0} = 1.00 \text{ time}$$

$$\text{Plan B: } DFL_{\$20{,}000} = \frac{\$20{,}000}{\$20{,}000 - \$4{,}000} = 1.25 \text{ times}$$

$$\text{Plan C: } DFL_{\$20{,}000} = \frac{\$20{,}000}{\$20{,}000 - \$6{,}400} = 1.47 \text{ times}$$

As you probably suspected, the measures of financial leverage shown previously are identical to those obtained by use of equation 15-8. This will always be the case.

## RELATE TO THE BIG PICTURE

The effect on the earnings stream available to the firm's common stockholders from combining operating and financial leverage in large degrees is dramatic. When the use of both leverage types is indeed heavy, a large sales increase will result in a very large rise in earnings per share. Be aware, though, that the very same thing happens in the opposite direction should the sales change be negative! Piling heavy financial leverage use on a high degree of operating leverage, then, is a very risky way to do business.

Thus, the firm will not "fool the markets" by combining high degrees of operating and financial leverage. Recall **Principle 6: Efficient Capital Markets—The markets are quick and the prices are right.** We stated in Chapter 1 that efficient markets deal with the speed with which information is impounded into security prices. Should the firm become overlevered in the eyes of the markets—say, stemming from an overly large issue of new debt securities—then the company's stock price will quickly be adjusted downward. The capital markets fully understand the double-edged sword of leverage use. Things go well when revenues rise; things do not go well when revenues fall. And, leverage use, either operating or financial, magnifies the original fluctuations in the revenues. Be aware.

[6]Suppose (1) preferred dividends of $4,000 are paid annually by the firm and (2) it faces a 40 percent marginal tax rate. How much must the firm earn *before* taxes to make the $4,000 payment out of after-tax earnings? Because preferred dividends are not tax deductible to the paying company, we have $4,000/(1 − .40) = $6,666.67. The Tax Reform Act of 1986 provided for the taxation of corporate incomes at a maximum rate of 34 percent for tax years beginning after June 30, 1987. This maximum rate applies to taxable incomes over $75,000. Under this new tax provision, the firm would need to earn only $6,060.61 before taxes to make the $4,000 preferred dividend payment. That is, $4,000/(1 − .34) = $6,060.61. Note that from a financial policy viewpoint, the 1986 tax act reduced *somewhat* the tax shield advantages of corporate debt financing and simultaneously reduced the tax bias against preferred stock and common stock financing.

**CONCEPT CHECK**

1. If a firm's degree of financial leverage happens to be 1.25 times, what precisely does that mean?
2. What does the degree of financial leverage concept suggest when a negative shock in earnings before interest and taxes (EBIT) occurs?
3. From the viewpoint of the company's shareholders, explain the difference between enduring a degree of financial leverage of 5 times versus 2 times.

## COMBINATION OF OPERATING AND FINANCIAL LEVERAGE

OBJECTIVE 4 

Changes in sales revenues cause greater changes in EBIT. Additionally, changes in EBIT translate into larger variations in both earnings per share (EPS) and total earnings available to the common shareholders (EAC), if the firm chooses to use financial leverage. It should be no surprise, then, to find out that combining operating and financial leverage causes further large variations in earnings per share. This entire process is visually displayed in Figure 15-9.

Because the risk associated with possible earnings per share is affected by the use of combined or total leverage, it is useful to quantify the effect. For an illustration, we refer once more to the Pierce Grain Company. The cost structure identified for Pierce Grain in our discussion of break-even analysis still holds. Furthermore, assume that plan B, which carried a 25 percent debt ratio, was chosen to finance the company's assets. Turn your attention to Table 15-9.

In Table 15-9, an increase in output for Pierce Grain from 30,000 to 36,000 units is analyzed. This increase represents a 20 percent rise in sales revenues. From our earlier discussion of operating leverage and the data in Table 15-9, we can see that this 20 percent increase in sales is magnified into a 120 percent rise in EBIT. From this base sales level of \$300,000 the degree of operating leverage is 6 times.

The 120 percent rise in EBIT induces a change in earnings per share and earnings available to the common shareholders of 150 percent. The degree of financial leverage is therefore 1.25 times.

The upshot of the analysis is that the 20 percent rise in sales has been magnified to 150 percent, as reflected by the percentage change in earnings per share. The formal measure of combined leverage can be expressed as follows:

$$\begin{pmatrix}\text{degree of combined}\\ \text{leverage from the}\\ \text{base sales level}\end{pmatrix} = DCL_s = \left(\frac{\text{percentage change in earnings per share}}{\text{percentage change in sales}}\right) \tag{15-10}$$

**FIGURE 15-9**
Leverage and Earnings Fluctuations

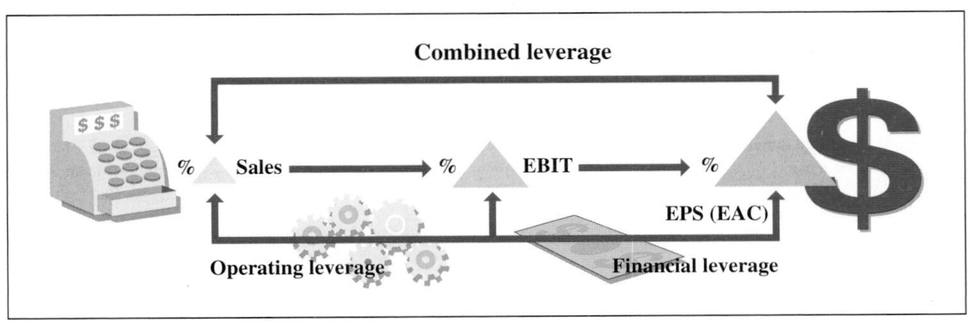

**TABLE 15-9**
Pierce Grain Company Combined Leverage Analysis

| Item | Base Sales Level, $t$ | Forecast Sales Level, $t + 1$ | Selected Percentage Changes |
|---|---|---|---|
| Sales | $300,000 | $360,000 | +20 |
| Less: total variable costs | 180,000 | 216,000 | |
| Revenue before fixed costs | $120,000 | $144,000 | |
| Less: total fixed costs | 100,000 | 100,000 | |
| EBIT | $ 20,000 | $ 44,000 | +120 |
| Less: interest expense | 4,000 | 4,000 | |
| Earnings before taxes (EBT) | $ 16,000 | $ 40,000 | |
| Less: taxes at 50% | 8,000 | 20,000 | |
| Net income | $ 8,000 | $ 20,000 | +150 |
| Less: preferred dividends | 0 | 0 | |
| Earnings available to common (EAC) | $ 8,000 | $ 20,000 | +150 |
| Number of common shares | 1,500 | 1,500 | |
| Earnings per share (EPS) | $ 5.33 | $ 13.33 | +150 |

$$\text{Degree of operating leverage} = DOL_{\$300,000} = \frac{120\%}{20\%} = 6 \text{ times}$$

$$\text{Degree of financial leverage} = DFL_{\$20,000} = \frac{150\%}{120\%} = 1.25 \text{ times}$$

$$\text{Degree of combined leverage} = DCL_{\$300,000} = \frac{150\%}{20\%} = 7.50 \text{ times}$$

This equation was used in the bottom portion of Table 15-9 to determine that the degree of combined leverage from the base sales level of $300,000 is 7.50 times. Pierce Grain's use of both operating and financial leverage will cause any percentage change in sales (from the specific base level) to be magnified by a factor of 7.50 when the effect on earnings per share is computed. A 1 percent change in sales, for example, will result in a 7.50 percent change in earnings per share.

Notice that the degree of combined leverage is actually the *product* (not the simple sum) of the two independent leverage measures. Thus, we have:

$$(DOL_s) \times (DFL_{EBIT}) = DCL_s \qquad \textbf{(15-11)}$$

or

$$(6) \times (1.25) = 7.50 \text{ times}$$

It is possible to ascertain the degree of combined leverage in a direct fashion, without determining any percentage fluctuations or the separate leverage values. We need only substitute the appropriate values into equation 15-12:[7]

$$DCL_s = \frac{Q(P - V)}{Q(P - V) - F - I} \qquad \textbf{(15-12)}$$

[7]As was the case with the degree of financial leverage metric, the variable, $I$, in the combined leverage measure, must include the before-tax equivalent of any preferred dividend payments when preferred stock is in the financial structure.

FINANCE MATTERS

## The Coca-Cola Company Financial Policies

The fact that financial leverage effects can be measured provides management the opportunity to shape corporate policy formally around the decision to use or avoid the use of leverage-inducing financial instruments. The Coca-Cola Company has very specific policies on the use of financial leverage. The learning objectives of this chapter, then, comprise more than mere academic, intellectual exercises. The material is, in fact, the stuff of boardroom-level discussion.

We stated in Chapter 1 that the goal of the firm is to maximize shareholder wealth, and this means maximizing the price of the firm's existing common stock. The Coca-Cola Company has accepted this approach to management as its "primary objective." To accomplish the objective, the company has developed a strategy that centers on investment in its core business—the high-return soft drink business. Notice that Coca-Cola also speaks clearly about "optimizing" its cost of capital through properly designed financial policies. This is a good time to review the cost of capital linkage identified in Figure 15-1 and ponder its meaning.

Determining an appropriate (optimal) financing mix is a crucial activity of financial management. Companies use different approaches to seek an optimal range of financial leverage use. The Coca-Cola Company searches for a "prudent" level of debt use that is affected by (1) its projected cash flows, (2) interest coverage ratios, and (3) ratio of long-term debt to total capitalization. Further, the company is highly concerned about the bond ratings that it receives from major rating agencies.

---

Management's primary objective is to maximize share-owner value over time. To accomplish this objective, the Coca-Cola Company and subsidiaries (the Company) have developed a comprehensive business strategy that emphasizes maximizing long-term cash flows. This strategy focuses on continuing aggressive investment in the high-return soft drink business, increasing returns on existing investments and optimizing the cost of capital through appropriate financial policies. The success of this strategy is evidenced by the growth in the Company's cash flows and earnings, its increased returns on total capital and equity, and the total return to its share owners over time.

Management seeks investments that strategically enhance existing operations and offer cash returns that exceed the Company's long-term after-tax weighted average cost of capital, estimated by management to be approximately 11 percent as of January 1, 1994. The Company's soft drink business generates inherent high returns on capital, providing an attractive area for continued investment.

Maximizing share-owner value necessitates optimizing the Company's cost of capital through appropriate financial policies.

The Company maintains debt levels considered prudent based on the Company's cash flows, interest coverage, and the percentage of debt to the Company's total capital. The Company's overall cost of capital is lowered by the use of debt financing, resulting in increased return to share owners.

The Company's capital structure and financial policies have resulted in long-term credit ratings of "AA" from Standard & Poor's and "Aa3" from Moody's, as well as the highest credit ratings available for its commercial paper programs. The Company's strong financial position and cash flows allow for opportunistic access to financing in financial markets around the world.

Source: The Coca-Cola Company, *Annual Report* (1993): 44–46.

The variable definitions in equation 15-12 are the same ones that have been employed throughout this chapter. Use of equation 15-12 with the information in Table 15-9 gives:

$$DCL_{\$300,000} = \frac{\$30,000(\$10 - \$6)}{\$30,000(\$10 - \$6) - \$100,000 - \$4,000}$$

$$= \frac{\$120,000}{\$16,000}$$

$$= 7.5 \text{ times}$$

### Implications

The total risk exposure the firm assumes can be managed by combining operating and financial leverage in different degrees. Knowledge of the various leverage measures aids the financial officer in determining the proper level of overall risk that should be accepted. If a high degree of business risk is inherent to the specific line of commercial activity, then a low posture regarding financial risk would minimize *additional* earnings fluctuations stemming from sales changes. Conversely, the firm that by its very nature incurs a low level of fixed operating costs might choose to use a high degree of financial leverage in the hope of increasing earnings per share and the rate of return on the common equity investment.

## CONCEPT CHECK

1. Explain the degree of combined leverage concept.
2. When would the degree of operating leverage and the degree of combined leverage be equal?

## RELATE TO THE BIG PICTURE

Our analysis of business risk, financial risk, and the three measurements of leverage use all relate directly to **Principle 1: The Risk-Return Trade-Off—We won't take on additional risk unless we expect to be compensated with additional return.** Should the firm decide to "pile on" heavy financial leverage use on top of a high degree of business risk exposure, then we would expect the firm's overall cost of capital to rise and its stock price to fall. This underscores the critical nature of designing the firm's financing mix to both the financial manager and the stockholders. This central area of financial decision making is explored further in the next chapter on "Planning the Firm's Financing Mix."

# THE MULTINATIONAL FIRM: BUSINESS RISK AND GLOBAL SALES

Early in this chapter we defined business risk as the relative dispersion (variability) in the firm's expected earnings before interest and taxes (EBIT). When we discussed operating leverage and the degree of operating leverage concept, we learned that changes or shocks to the firm's overall sales level will cause a greater percentage change in EBIT if fixed operating costs are present in the firm's cost structure. Thus, any event that induces a fluctuation in measured sales will impact a firm's business risk and its resulting EBIT.

Business risk is multidimensional and international. It is directly affected by several factors, including (1) the sensitivity of the firm's product demand to general economic conditions, (2) the degree of competition to which the firm is exposed, (3) product diversification, (4) growth prospects, and (5) global sales volume and production output. The latter factor is especially important to the multinational firm, and such firms are aware of it. Some seek to take advantage of it in an aggressive manner.

Consider the Coca-Cola Company. In his statement to shareholders published in 1998, Mr. M. Douglas Ivester, the Chairman of Coke's Board of Directors and its Chief Executive Officer, commented on the firm's commercial strategy in both China and Russia.[8] He said: "In China, the world's largest market, our volume soared another 30 percent in 1997. But the average resident of China still drinks just six of our products a year—certainly a business in its infancy." Notice that while Coke's presence in China increases its total business risk exposure, this exposure is viewed by Mr. Ivester as a commercial opportunity for the firm.

[8]The Coca-Cola Company, *Annual Report,* 1997: 5–6.

FINANCE MATTERS

## The Relationship Among Sales, Cash Flow, and Leverage

We spent considerable time in earlier chapters studying capital-budgeting techniques and discussed the search by firms for projects with positive net present values. The spending by firms on real capital projects is an important topic not only for the specific firms involved, but also for the aggregate economy. This is because high levels of real capital spending over time are associated with high levels of societal wealth. Societies that do not invest tend to be poor. So, it follows that national economic policymaking is concerned with what variables do affect the spending by companies on projects.

Mr. Kopcke and Mr. Howrey of the Federal Reserve Bank of Boston studied the investment spending of 396 domestic manufacturing corporations and found some interesting relationships among the variables that seem to influence the size of firms' capital budgets.

The authors of this study have put forth a reasonable conclusion concerning the relationship between capital spending and the firm's choice to use or avoid financial leverage. They suggest that *both* capital budgets and financial leverage use depend on expected profits. This is close to asserting that the specific firm's capacity to generate future cash flows is a major determinant of its financing mix. This should remind you of **Principle 3: Cash—Not Profits—Is King.** In the present context, the firm's ability to service its debt contracts depends on its ability to generate future cash flows.

Also, we see that these researchers suggest that general business conditions (that is, strong or weak) affect not only the size of the firm's capital budget, but also management's decision to use financial leverage in the financing of that capital budget. Such a logical combination of (1) the state of business conditions and (2) the expectation of future profits (cash flows) means that the underlying nature of the business in which the firm operates should be the most important factor affecting its ultimate financing mix. That is, *business risk* and commercial strategy directly affect the specific firm's decision to use financial leverage.

---

Perhaps it is not surprising that leverage, liquidity, and other variables should influence capital spending so little once the general business climate (represented by sales or cash flow) has been taken into account. The choice of leverage, like capital spending, depends on the prospect for profit. A good business climate can foster both investment and debt financing. In these cases, higher leverage does not deter investment; instead, it may appear to facilitate investment.

At other times, companies may increase their leverage while they reduce their capital spending, if the return on existing capital is great compared to that foreseen on new investments. In these cases, higher leverage may appear to deter investment. In any of these cases, appearances can be deceiving, because investment and leverage jointly depend on business conditions, and this dependency entails no consistent relationship between indebtedness and investment.

For the making of economic policy, the evidence suggests that the familiar macroeconomic incentives for investment would be no less effective today than they have been in the past. In particular, the volume of investment spending would appear to respond to monetary and fiscal policies in the customary way. Profits and cash flow might increase as a result of either rising sales or a tax cut.

Source: R. W. Kopcke with M. M. Howrey, "A Panel Study of Investment: Sales, Cash Flow, the Cost of Capital, and Leverage," *New England Economic Review* (January/February 1994): 23.

Next, in his discussion of the Russian market, Mr. Ivester offered: "In Russia, where we took the lead over our largest competitor in 1996, we widened that lead to 3-to-1 in 1997; we opened four more plants there on October 1, bringing our system's Russian investment to $650 million and pointing to strong future growth." Here we see that Coke is both cultivating the Russian consumer and simultaneously investing in plant and equipment there. Thus, Coke's broad commercial strategy, which impacts business risk, also encompasses the capital-budgeting decision discussed earlier in this text.

**CONCEPT CHECK**

1. Identify several factors that directly affect a firm's business risk.
2. How might a firm's commercial strategy be influenced by its presence in foreign markets?

## HOW FINANCIAL MANAGERS USE THIS MATERIAL

The introduction to this chapter pointed out how fluctuations of specific magnitudes in sales at Harley-Davidson, Coca-Cola, Phillips Petroleum, Archer Daniels Midland, and Chevron actually became even *larger* relative changes in net income and earnings available to the respective firm's common stockholders. The material presented in the chapter allows financial managers to explain this phenomenon to various constituencies such as other managers, shareholders, and financial analysts who follow their firm's stock performance.

Based on the logic, models, and inherent assumptions within the models, managers can more precisely *estimate* the interaction that stems from combining operating leverage with financial leverage. The risks that shareholders are asked to assume because of management choices involving cost structure and financial structure are clarified.

Using some of the same theory and logic, managers develop a distinct linkage among the firm's forecasted sales revenues, cost structure, pricing decisions, and advertising programs. The break-even model, although conceptually simple, is operationally powerful. Its understandability is its strength.

In the hotel industry, managers use the break-even model to determine the property's break-even occupancy rate. This becomes an input to the hotel's pricing policy. To achieve a desired total break-even sales revenue might require a change in the rate charged per room night. In this instance, the hotel's competition has to be assessed and an advertising program put in place that on a forecast basis will permit the break-even occupancy rate to be achieved.

Because firms are in business to generate a profit (and not just "break-even"), the break-even analysis will then extend into a format for achieving minimum target profit levels. So, the break-even model is an essential part of the manager's strategy formulation toolkit.

## SUMMARY

In this chapter, we begin to study the process of arriving at an appropriate financial structure for the firm. We examine tools that can assist the financial manager in this task. We are mainly concerned with assessing the variability in the firm's residual earnings stream (either earnings per share or earnings available to the common shareholders) induced by the use of operating and financial leverage. This assessment builds on the tenets of break-even analysis.

Break-even analysis permits the financial manager to determine the quantity of output or the level of sales that will result in an EBIT level of zero. This means the firm has neither a profit nor a loss before any tax considerations. The effect of price changes, cost structure changes, or volume changes on profits (EBIT) can be studied. To make the technique operational, it is necessary that the firm's costs be classified as fixed or variable. Not all costs fit neatly into one of these two categories. Over short planning horizons, though, the preponderance of costs can be assigned to either the fixed or variable classification. Once the cost structure has been identified, the break-even point can be found by use of (1) trial-and-error analysis, (2) contribution-margin analysis, or (3) algebraic analysis.

Operating leverage is the responsiveness of the firm's EBIT to changes in sales revenues. It arises from the firm's use of fixed operating costs. When fixed operating costs are present in the company's cost structure, changes in sales are magnified into even greater changes in EBIT. The firm's degree of operating leverage from a base sales level is the percentage change in EBIT divided by the percentage change in sales. All types of leverage are two-edged swords. When sales decrease by some percentage, the negative impact upon EBIT will be even larger.

OBJECTIVE 4 

A firm employs financial leverage when it finances a portion of its assets with securities bearing a fixed rate of return. The presence of debt and/or preferred stock in the company's financial structure means that it is using financial leverage. When financial leverage is used, changes in EBIT translate into larger changes in earnings per share. The concept of the degree of financial leverage dwells on the sensitivity of earnings per share to changes in EBIT. The DFL from a base EBIT level is defined as the percentage change in earnings per share divided by the percentage change in EBIT. All other things equal, the more fixed-charge securities the firm employs in its financial structure, the greater its degree of financial leverage. Clearly, EBIT can rise or fall. If it falls, and financial leverage is used, the firm's shareholders endure negative changes in earnings per share that are larger than the relative decline in EBIT. Again, leverage is a two-edged sword.

OBJECTIVE 5 

Firms use operating and financial leverage in various degrees. The joint use of operating and financial leverage can be measured by computing the degree of combined leverage, defined as the percentage change in earnings per share divided by the percentage change in sales. This measure allows the financial manager to ascertain the effect on total leverage caused by adding financial leverage on top of operating leverage. Effects can be dramatic, because the degree of combined leverage is the product of the degrees of operating and financial leverage. Table 15-10 summarizes the salient concepts and calculation formats discussed in this chapter.

OBJECTIVE 6 

Business risk is both multidimensional and international. It is directly affected by several factors, including (1) the sensitivity of the firm's product demand to general economic conditions, (2) the degree of competition to which the firm is exposed, (3) product diversification, (4) growth prospects, and (5) global sales. On the latter factor, we explored how the Coca-Cola Company related the firm's commercial strategy to include sales prospects in the huge markets of both China and Russia.

**TABLE 15-10**
Summary of Leverage Concepts and Calculations

| Technique | Description or Concept | Calculation | Text Reference |
|---|---|---|---|
| **BREAK-EVEN ANALYSIS** | | | |
| 1. Break-even point quantity | Total fixed costs divided by the unit contribution margin | $Q_B = \frac{F}{P - V}$ | (15-3) |
| 2. Break-even sales level | Total fixed costs divided by 1 minus the ratio of total variable costs to the associated level of sales | $S^* = \frac{F}{1 - \frac{VC}{S}}$ | (15-4) |
| **OPERATING LEVERAGE** | | | |
| 3. Degree of operating leverage | Percentage change in EBIT divided by the percentage change in sales; or revenue before fixed costs divided by revenue after fixed costs, EBIT | $DOL_s = \frac{Q(P - V)}{Q(P - V) - F}$ | (15-6) |
| **FINANCIAL LEVERAGE** | | | |
| 4. Degree of financial leverage | Percentage change in earnings per share divided by the percentage change in EBIT; or EBIT divided by EBT.[a] | $DFL_{EBIT} = \frac{EBIT}{EBIT - I}$ | (15-9) |
| **COMBINED LEVERAGE** | | | |
| 5. Degree of combined leverage | Percentage change in earnings per share divided by the percentage change in sales; or revenue before fixed costs divided by EBT.[a] | $DCL_s = \frac{Q(P - V)}{Q(P - V) - F - I}$ | (15-12) |

[a]The use of EBT here presumes no preferred dividend payments. In the presence of preferred dividend payments, replace EBT with earnings available to common stock (EAC).

## KEY TERMS

**Analytical income statement, 478**
**Business risk, 470**
**Cash break-even analysis, 481**
**Contribution margin, 476**
**Financial leverage, 472**
**Financial risk, 471**
**Fixed costs (indirect costs), 473**
**Operating leverage, 472**
**Risk, 469**
**Semivariable costs (semifixed costs), 475**
**Total revenue, 475**
**Variable costs (direct costs), 474**
**Volume of output, 476**

my**PHLIP**

Go To:
http://www.prenhall.com/keown
for downloads and current events associated with this chapter

## STUDY QUESTIONS

**15-1.** Distinguish between business risk and financial risk. What gives rise to, or causes, each type of risk?

**15-2.** Define the term *financial leverage.* Does the firm use financial leverage if preferred stock is present in the capital structure?

**15-3.** Define the term *operating leverage.* What type of effect occurs when the firm uses operating leverage?

**15-4.** What is the difference between the (ordinary) break-even point and the cash break-even point? Which will be the greater?

**15-5.** A manager in your firm decides to employ break-even analysis. Of what shortcomings should this manager be aware?

**15-6.** What is meant by total risk exposure? How may a firm move to reduce its total risk exposure?

**15-7.** If a firm has a degree of combined leverage of 3 times, what does a negative sales fluctuation of 15 percent portend for the earnings available to the firm's common stock investors?

**15-8.** Break-even analysis assumes linear revenue and cost functions. In reality, these linear functions over large output and sales levels are highly improbable. Why?

## SELF-TEST PROBLEMS

**ST-1.** (*Break-even point*) You are a hard-working analyst in the office of financial operations for a manufacturing firm that produces a single product. You have developed the following cost structure information for this company. All of it pertains to an output level of 10 million units. Using this information, find the break-even point in units of output for the firm.

| | |
|---|---|
| Return on operating assets | = 30% |
| Operating asset turnover | = 6 times |
| Operating assets | = \$20 million |
| Degree of operating leverage | = 4.5 times |

**ST-2.** (*Leverage analysis*) You have developed the following analytical income statement for your corporation. It represents the most recent year's operations, which ended yesterday. Your supervisor in the financial studies office has just handed you a memorandum that asked for written responses to the following questions:

**a.** At this level of output, what is the degree of operating leverage?
**b.** What is the degree of financial leverage?
**c.** What is the degree of combined leverage?

**d.** What is the firm's break-even point in sales dollars?

**e.** If sales should increase by 30 percent, by what percent would earnings before taxes (and net income) increase?

| | |
|---|---|
| Sales | $20,000,000 |
| Variable costs | 12,000,000 |
| Revenue before fixed costs | $ 8,000,000 |
| Fixed costs | 5,000,000 |
| EBIT | $ 3,000,000 |
| Interest expense | 1,000,000 |
| Earnings before taxes | $ 2,000,000 |
| Taxes (0.50) | 1,000,000 |
| Net income | $ 1,000,000 |

**f.** Prepare an analytical income statement that verifies the calculations from part (e).

**ST-3.** (*Fixed costs and the break-even point*) Bonaventure Manufacturing expects to earn $210,000 next year after taxes. Sales will be $4 million. The firm's single plant is located on the outskirts of Olean, New York. The firm manufactures a combined bookshelf and desk unit used extensively in college dormitories. These units sell for $200 each and have a variable cost per unit of $150. Bonaventure experiences a 30 percent tax rate.

**a.** What are the firm's fixed costs expected to be next year?

**b.** Calculate the firm's break-even point in both units and dollars.

## STUDY PROBLEMS (SET A)

**15-1A.** (*Sales mix and break-even point*) CheeMortal music store sells four kinds of musical instruments—pianos, violins, cellos, and flutes. The current sales mix for the store and the contribution margin ratio (unit contribution margin divided by unit sales price) for these product lines are as follows:

| Product Line | Percent of Total Sales | Contribution Margin Ratio |
|---|---|---|
| Piano | 24.5% | 32% |
| Violin | 15.0% | 40% |
| Cello | 39.5% | 38% |
| Flute | 21.0% | 51% |

Total sales for the next year are forecast to be $250,000. Total fixed costs will be $50,000.

**a.** Prepare a table showing (1) sales, (2) total variable costs, and (3) the total contribution margin associated with each product line.

**b.** What is the aggregate contribution margin ratio indicative of the sales mix? (Round off to two decimals.)

**c.** At this sales mix, what is the break-even point in dollars?

**15-2A.** (*Break-even point*) Napa Valley Winery (NVW) is a boutique winery that produces a high-quality, nonalcoholic red wine from organically grown cabernet sauvignon grapes. It sells each bottle for $30. NVW's chief financial officer, Jackie Cheng, has estimated variable costs to be 70 percent of sales. If NVW's fixed costs are $360,000, how many bottles of its wine must NVW sell to break even?

**15-3A.** (*Operating leverage*) In light of a sales agreement that Napa Valley Winery (see description in Problem 15-2A) just signed with a national chain of health food restaurants, NVW's CFO Jackie Cheng is estimating that NVW's sales in the next year will be 50,000 bottles at $30 per bottle. If variable costs are expected to be 70 percent of sales, what is NVW's expected degree of operating leverage?

**15-4A.** (*Break-even point and operating leverage*) Some financial data for each of three firms are as follows:

| | Jake's Lawn Chairs | Sarasota Sky Lights | Jefferson Wholesale |
|---|---|---|---|
| Average selling price per unit | $ 32.00 | $ 875.00 | $ 97.77 |
| Average variable cost per unit | $ 17.38 | $ 400.00 | $ 87.00 |
| Units sold | 18,770 | 2,800 | 11,000 |
| Fixed costs | $120,350 | $ 850,000 | $89,500 |

**a.** What is the profit for each company at the indicated sales volume?
**b.** What is the break-even point in units for each company?
**c.** What is the degree of operating leverage for each company at the indicated sales volume?
**d.** If sales were to decline, which firm would suffer the largest relative decline in profitability?

**15-5A.** (*Leverage analysis*) You have developed the following analytical income statement for your corporation. It represents the most recent year's operations, which ended yesterday.

| | |
|---|---|
| Sales | $45,750,000 |
| Variable costs | 22,800,000 |
| Revenue before fixed costs | $22,950,000 |
| Fixed costs | 9,200,000 |
| EBIT | $13,750,000 |
| Interest expense | 1,350,000 |
| Earnings before taxes | $12,400,000 |
| Taxes (.50) | 6,200,000 |
| Net income | $ 6,200,000 |

Your supervisor in the controller's office has just handed you a memorandum asking for written responses to the following questions:

**a.** At this level of output, what is the degree of operating leverage?
**b.** What is the degree of financial leverage?
**c.** What is the degree of combined leverage?
**d.** What is the firm's break-even point in sales dollars?
**e.** If sales should increase by 25 percent, by what percent would earnings before taxes (and net income) increase?

**15-6A.** (*Break-even point and operating leverage*) Footwear, Inc., manufactures a complete line of men's and women's dress shoes for independent merchants. The average selling price of its finished product is $85 per pair. The variable cost for this same pair of shoes is $58. Footwear, Inc., incurs fixed costs of $170,000 per year.

**a.** What is the break-even point in pairs of shoes for the company?
**b.** What is the dollar sales volume the firm must achieve to reach the break-even point?
**c.** What would be the firm's profit or loss at the following units of production sold: 7,000 pairs of shoes? 9,000 pairs of shoes? 15,000 pairs of shoes?
**d.** Find the degree of operating leverage for the production and sales levels given in part (c).

**15-7A.** (*Break-even point and operating leverage*) Zeylog Corporation manufactures a line of computer memory expansion boards used in microcomputers. The average selling price of its finished product is $180 per unit. The variable cost for these same units is $110. Zeylog incurs fixed costs of $630,000 per year.

**a.** What is the break-even point in units for the company?
**b.** What is the dollar sales volume the firm must achieve to reach the break-even point?
**c.** What would be the firm's profit or loss at the following units of production sold: 12,000 units? 15,000 units? 20,000 units?
**d.** Find the degree of operating leverage for the production and sales levels given in part (c) above.

**15-8A.** (*Break-even point and operating leverage*) Some financial data for each of three firms are as follows:

| | Blacksburg Furniture | Lexington Cabinets | Williamsburg Colonials |
|---|---|---|---|
| Average selling price per unit | $ 15.00 | $ 400.00 | $ 40.00 |
| Average variable cost per unit | $ 12.35 | $ 220.00 | $ 14.50 |
| Units sold | 75,000 | 4,000 | 13,000 |
| Fixed costs | $35,000 | $100,000 | $70,000 |

**a.** What is the profit for each company at the indicated sales volume?
**b.** What is the break-even point in units for each company?
**c.** What is the degree of operating leverage for each company at the indicated sales volume?
**d.** If sales were to decline, which firm would suffer the largest relative decline in profitability?

**15-9A.** (*Fixed costs and the break-even point*) A & B Beverages expects to earn $50,000 next year after taxes. Sales will be $375,000. The store is located near the shopping district surrounding Blowing Rock University. Its average product sells for $27 a unit. The variable cost per unit is $14.85. The store experiences a 40 percent tax rate.
**a.** What are the store's fixed costs expected to be next year?
**b.** Calculate the store's break-even point in both units and dollars.

**15-10A.** (*Break-even point and profit margin*) Mary Clark, a recent graduate of Clarion South University, is planning to open a new wholesaling operation. Her target operating profit margin is 26 percent. Her unit contribution margin will be 50 percent of sales. Average annual sales are forecast to be $3,250,000.
**a.** How large can fixed costs be for the wholesaling operation and still allow the 26 percent operating profit margin to be achieved?
**b.** What is the break-even point in dollars for the firm?

**15-11A.** (*Leverage analysis*) You have developed the following analytical income statement for your corporation. It represents the most recent year's operations, which ended yesterday. Your supervisor in the controller's office has just handed you a memorandum asking for written responses to the following questions:
**a.** At this level of output, what is the degree of operating leverage?
**b.** What is the degree of financial leverage?

| | |
|---|---|
| Sales | $30,000,000 |
| Variable costs | 13,500,000 |
| Revenue before fixed costs | $16,500,000 |
| Fixed costs | 8,000,000 |
| EBIT | $ 8,500,000 |
| Interest expense | 1,000,000 |
| Earnings before taxes | $ 7,500,000 |
| Taxes (.50) | 3,750,000 |
| Net income | $ 3,750,000 |

**c.** What is the degree of combined leverage?
**d.** What is the firm's break-even point in sales dollars?
**e.** If sales should increase by 25 percent, by what percent would earnings before taxes (and net income) increase?

**15-12A.** (*Break-even point*) You are a hard-working analyst in the office of financial operations for a manufacturing firm that produces a single product. You have developed the following cost structure information for this company. All of it pertains to an output level of 10 million units. Using this information, find the break-even point in units of output for the firm.

| | |
|---|---|
| Return on operating assets | = 25% |
| Operating asset turnover | = 5 times |
| Operating assets | = $20 million |
| Degree of operating leverage | = 4 times |

**15-13A.** (*Break-even point and operating leverage*) Allison Radios manufactures a complete line of radio and communication equipment for law enforcement agencies. The average selling price of its finished product is $180 per unit. The variable cost for these same units is $126. Allison Radios incurs fixed costs of $540,000 per year.

**a.** What is the break-even point in units for the company?

**b.** What is the dollar sales volume the firm must achieve in order to reach the break-even point?

**c.** What would be the firm's profit or loss at the following units of production sold: 12,000 units? 15,000 units? 20,000 units?

**d.** Find the degree of operating leverage for the production and sales levels given in part (c).

**15-14A.** (*Break-even point and operating leverage*) Some financial data for each of three firms are as follows:

| | Oviedo Seeds | Gainesville Sod | Athens Peaches |
|---|---|---|---|
| Average selling price per unit | $ 14.00 | $ 200.00 | $ 25.00 |
| Average variable cost per unit | $ 11.20 | $ 130.00 | $ 17.50 |
| Units sold | 100,000 | 10,000 | 48,000 |
| Fixed costs | $25,000 | $100,000 | $35,000 |

**a.** What is the profit for each company at the indicated sales volume?

**b.** What is the break-even point in units for each company?

**c.** What is the degree of operating leverage for each company at the indicated sales volume?

**d.** If sales were to *decline,* which firm would suffer the largest relative decline in profitability?

**15-15A.** (*Fixed costs and the break-even point*) Dot's Quik-Stop Party Store expects to earn $40,000 next year after taxes. Sales will be $400,000. The store is located near the fraternity-row district of Cambridge Springs State University and sells only kegs of beer for $20 a keg. The variable cost per keg is $8. The store experiences a 40 percent tax rate.

**a.** What are the Party Store's fixed costs expected to be next year?

**b.** Calculate the firm's break-even point in both units and dollars.

**15-16A.** (*Fixed costs and the break-even point*) Albert's Cooling Equipment hopes to earn $80,000 next year after taxes. Sales will be $2 million. The firm's single plant is located on the edge of Slippery Rock, Pennsylvania, and manufactures only small refrigerators. These are used in many of the dormitories found on college campuses. Refrigerators sell for $80 per unit and have a variable cost of $56. Albert's experiences a 40 percent tax rate.

**a.** What are the firm's fixed costs expected to be next year?

**b.** Calculate the firm's break-even point both in units and dollars.

**15-17A.** (*Break-even point and selling price*) Gerry's Tool and Die Company will produce 200,000 units next year. All of this production will be sold as finished goods. Fixed costs will total $300,000. Variable costs for this firm are relatively predictable at 75 percent of sales.

**a.** If Gerry's Tool and Die wants to achieve an earnings before interest and taxes level of $240,000 next year, at what price per unit must it sell its product?

**b.** Based on your answer to part (a), set up an analytical income statement that will verify your solution.

**15-18A.** (*Break-even point and selling price*) Parks Castings, Inc., will manufacture and sell 200,000 units next year. Fixed costs will total $300,000, and variable costs will be 60 percent of sales.

**a.** The firm wants to achieve an earnings before interest and taxes level of $250,000. What selling price per unit is necessary to achieve this result?

**b.** Set up an analytical income statement to verify your solution to part (a).

**15-19A.** (*Break-even point and profit margin*) A recent business graduate of Midwestern State University is planning to open a new wholesaling operation. His target operating profit margin is 28 percent. His unit contribution margin will be 50 percent of sales. Average annual sales are forecast to be $3,750,000.

- **a.** How large can fixed costs be for the wholesaling operation and still allow the 28 percent operating profit margin to be achieved?
- **b.** What is the break-even point in dollars for the firm?

**15-20A.** (*Operating leverage*) Rocky Mount Metals Company manufactures an assortment of wood-burning stoves. The average selling price for the various units is $500. The associated variable cost is $350 per unit. Fixed costs for the firm average $180,000 annually.

- **a.** What is the break-even point in units for the company?
- **b.** What is the dollar sales volume the firm must achieve to reach the break-even point?
- **c.** What is the degree of operating leverage for a production and sales level of 5,000 units for the firm? (Calculate to three decimal places.)
- **d.** What will be the projected effect upon earnings before interest and taxes if the firm's sales level should increase by 20 percent from the volume noted in part (c)?

**15-21A.** (*Break-even point and operating leverage*) The Portland Recreation Company manufactures a full line of lawn furniture. The average selling price of a finished unit is $25. The associated variable cost is $15 per unit. Fixed costs for Portland average $50,000 per year.

- **a.** What is the break-even point in units for the company?
- **b.** What is the dollar sales volume the firm must achieve to reach the break-even point?
- **c.** What would be the company's profit or loss at the following units of production sold: 4,000 units? 6,000 units? 8,000 units?
- **d.** Find the degree of operating leverage for the production and sales levels given in part (c).
- **e.** What is the effect on the degree of operating leverage as sales rise above the break-even point?

**15-22A.** (*Fixed costs*) Detroit Heat Treating projects that next year its fixed costs will total $120,000. Its only product sells for $12 per unit, of which $7 is a variable cost. The management of Detroit is considering the purchase of a new machine that will lower the variable cost per unit to $5. The new machine, however, will add to fixed costs through an increase in depreciation expense. How large can the *addition to* fixed costs be to keep the firm's break-even point in units produced and sold unchanged?

**15-23A.** (*Operating leverage*) The management of Detroit Heat Treating did not purchase the new piece of equipment (see problem 15-22A). Using the existing cost structure, calculate the degree of operating leverage at 30,000 units of output. Comment on the meaning of your answer.

**15-24A.** (*Leverage analysis*) An analytical income statement for Detroit Heat Treating is shown below. It is based on an output (sales) level of 40,000 units. You may refer to the original cost structure data in problem (15-22A).

| | |
|---|---|
| Sales | $480,000 |
| Variable costs | 280,000 |
| Revenue before fixed costs | $200,000 |
| Fixed costs | 120,000 |
| EBIT | $ 80,000 |
| Interest expense | 30,000 |
| Earnings before taxes | $ 50,000 |
| Taxes | 25,000 |
| Net income | $ 25,000 |

- **a.** Calculate the degree of operating leverage at this output level.
- **b.** Calculate the degree of financial leverage at this level of EBIT.
- **c.** Determine the combined leverage effect at this output level.

**15-25A.** (*Break-even point*) You are employed as a financial analyst for a single-product manufacturing firm. Your supervisor has made the following cost structure information available to you, all of which pertains to an output level of 1,600,000 units.

| | |
|---|---|
| Return on operating assets | = 15% |
| Operating asset turnover | = 5 times |
| Operating assets | = $3 million |
| Degree of operating leverage | = 8 times |

Your task is to find the break-even point in units of output for the firm.

**15-26A.** (*Fixed costs*) Des Moines Printing Services is forecasting fixed costs next year of $300,000. The firm's single product sells for $20 per unit and incurs a variable cost per unit of $14. The firm may acquire some new binding equipment that would lower variable cost per unit to $12. The new equipment, however, would add to fixed costs through the price of an annual maintenance agreement on the new equipment. How large can this increase in fixed costs be and still keep the firm's present break-even point in units produced and sold unchanged?

**15-27A.** (*Leverage analysis*) Your firm's cost analysis supervisor supplies you with the following analytical income statement and requests answers to the four questions listed following the statement.

| | |
|---|---|
| Sales | $12,000,000 |
| Variable costs | 9,000,000 |
| Revenue before fixed costs | $ 3,000,000 |
| Fixed costs | 2,000,000 |
| EBIT | $ 1,000,000 |
| Interest expense | 200,000 |
| Earnings before taxes | $ 800,000 |
| Taxes | 400,000 |
| Net income | $ 400,000 |

**a.** At this level of output, what is the degree of operating leverage?
**b.** What is the degree of financial leverage?
**c.** What is the degree of combined leverage?
**d.** What is the firm's break-even point in sales dollars?

**15-28A.** (*Leverage analysis*) You are supplied with the following analytical income statement for your firm. It reflects last year's operations.

| | |
|---|---|
| Sales | $16,000,000 |
| Variable costs | 8,000,000 |
| Revenue before fixed costs | $ 8,000,000 |
| Fixed costs | 4,000,000 |
| EBIT | $ 4,000,000 |
| Interest expense | 1,500,000 |
| Earnings before taxes | $ 2,500,000 |
| Taxes | 1,250,000 |
| Net income | $ 1,250,000 |

**a.** At this level of output, what is the degree of operating leverage?
**b.** What is the degree of financial leverage?
**c.** What is the degree of combined leverage?
**d.** If sales should increase by 20 percent, by what percent would earnings before taxes (and net income) increase?
**e.** What is your firm's break-even point in sales dollars?

**15-29A.** (*Sales mix and break-even point*) Toledo Components produces four lines of auto accessories for the major Detroit automobile manufacturers. The lines are known by the code letters A, B,

C, and D. The current sales mix for Toledo and the contribution margin ratio (unit contribution margin divided by unit sales price) for these product lines are as follows:

| Product Line | Percent of Total Sales | Contribution Margin Ratio |
|---|---|---|
| A | 33⅓% | 40% |
| B | 41⅔ | 32 |
| C | 16⅔ | 20 |
| D | 8⅓ | 60 |

Total sales for next year are forecast to be $120,000. Total fixed costs will be $29,400.

**a.** Prepare a table showing (1) sales, (2) total variable costs, and (3) the total contribution margin associated with each product line.

**b.** What is the aggregate contribution margin ratio indicative of this sales mix?

**c.** At this sales mix, what is the break-even point in dollars?

**15-30A.** (*Sales mix and break-even point*) Because of production constraints, Toledo Components (see problem 15-29A) may have to adhere to a different sales mix for next year. The alternative plan is outlined as follows:

| Product Line | Percent of Total Sales |
|---|---|
| A | 25% |
| B | 36⅔ |
| C | 33⅓ |
| D | 5 |

**a.** Assuming all other facts in problem 15-29A remain the same, what effect will this different sales mix have on Toledo's break-even point in dollars?

**b.** Which sales mix will Toledo's management prefer?

## INTEGRATIVE PROBLEM

Imagine that you were hired recently as a financial analyst for a relatively new, highly leveraged ski manufacturer located in the foothills of Colorado's Rocky Mountains. Your firm manufactures only one product, a state-of-the-art snow ski. The company has been operating up to this point without much quantitative knowledge of the business and financial risks it faces.

Ski season just ended, however, so the president of the company has started to focus more on the financial aspects of managing the business. He has set up a meeting for next week with the CFO, Maria Sanchez, to discuss matters such as the business and financial risks faced by the company. Accordingly, Maria has asked you to prepare an analysis to assist her in her discussions with the president.

As a first step in your work, you compiled the following information regarding the cost structure of the company.

| | |
|---|---|
| Output level | 50,000 units |
| Operating assets | $2,000,000 |
| Operating asset turnover | 7 times |
| Return on operating assets | 35% |
| Degree of operating leverage | 5 times |
| Interest expense | $ 400,000 |
| Tax rate | 35% |

As the next step, you need to *determine the break-even point in units of output* for the company. One of your strong points has been that you always prepare supporting workpapers, which show how you arrive at your conclusions. You know Maria would like to see such workpapers for this analysis to facilitate her review of your work.

Thereafter you will have the information you require to *prepare an analytical income statement* for the company. You are sure that Maria would like to see this statement; in addition, you know that you need it to be able to answer the following questions. You also know Maria expects you to prepare, in a format that is presentable to the president, answers to the questions to serve as a basis for her discussions with the president.

1. What is the degree of financial leverage?
2. What is the degree of combined leverage?
3. What is the firm's break-even point in sales dollars?
4. If sales should increase by 30 percent (as the president expects), by what percent would EBT (earnings before taxes) and net income increase?
5. Prepare another analytical income statement, this time to verify the calculations from question (4).

## STUDY PROBLEMS (SET B)

**15-1B.** (*Break-even point*) Roberto Martinez is the chief financial analyst at New Wave Pharmaceuticals (NWP), a company that produces a vitamin claimed to prevent the common cold. Roberto has been asked to determine the company's break-even point in units. He obtained the following information from the company's financial statements for the year just ended. In addition, he found out from NWP's production manager that the company produced 40 million units in that year. What will Roberto determine the break-even point to be?

| | |
|---|---|
| Sales | \$20,000,000 |
| Variable costs | 16,000,000 |
| Revenue before fixed costs | \$ 4,000,000 |
| Fixed costs | 2,400,000 |
| EBIT | \$ 1,600,000 |

**15-2B.** (*Leverage analysis*) New Wave Pharmaceuticals (see description and data in Problem 15-1B) is concerned that recent unfavorable publicity about the questionable medicinal benefits of other vitamins will temporarily hurt NWP's sales even though such assertions do not apply to NWP's vitamin. Accordingly, Roberto has been asked to determine the company's level of risk based on the financial information for the year just ended. In addition to the data described in Problem 15-1B, Roberto learned from the company's financial statements that the company incurred \$800,000 of interest expense in the year just ended. What will Roberto determine the (a) degree of operating leverage, (b) degree of financial leverage, and (c) degree of combined leverage to be?

**15-3B.** (*Break-even point and operating leverage*) Avitar Corporation manufactures a line of computer memory expansion boards used in microcomputers. The average selling price of its finished product is \$175 per unit. The variable cost for these same units is \$115. Avitar incurs fixed costs of \$650,000 per year.

**a.** What is the break-even point in units for the company?

**b.** What is the dollar sales volume the firm must achieve to reach the break-even point?

**c.** What would be the firm's profit or loss at the following units of production sold: 10,000 units? 16,000 units? 20,000 units?

**d.** Find the degree of operating leverage for the production and sales levels given in part (c).

**15-4B.** (*Break-even point and operating leverage*) Some financial data for each of three firms are as follows:

| | Durham Furniture | Raleigh Cabinets | Charlotte Colonials |
|---|---|---|---|
| Average selling price per unit | $ 20.00 | $ 435.00 | $ 35.00 |
| Average variable cost per unit | $ 13.75 | $ 240.00 | $ 15.75 |
| Units sold | 80,000 | 4,500 | 15,000 |
| Fixed costs | $40,000 | $150,000 | $60,000 |

**a.** What is the profit for each company at the indicated sales volume?
**b.** What is the break-even point in units for each company?
**c.** What is the degree of operating leverage for each company at the indicated sales volume?
**d.** If sales were to decline, which firm would suffer the largest relative decline in profitability?

**15-5B.** (*Fixed costs and the break-even point*) Cypress Books expects to earn $55,000 next year after taxes. Sales will be $400,008. The store is located near the shopping district surrounding Sheffield University. Its average product sells for $28 a unit. The variable cost per unit is $18. The store experiences a 45 percent tax rate.
**a.** What are the store's fixed costs expected to be next year?
**b.** Calculate the store's break-even point in both units and dollars.

**15-6B.** (*Break-even point and profit margin*) A recent graduate of Neeley University is planning to open a new wholesaling operation. Her target operating profit margin is 28 percent. Her unit contribution margin will be 45 percent of sales. Average annual sales are forecast to be $3,750,000.
**a.** How large can fixed costs be for the wholesaling operation and still allow the 28 percent operating profit margin to be achieved?
**b.** What is the break-even point in dollars for the firm?

**15-7B.** (*Leverage analysis*) You have developed the following analytical income statement for your corporation. It represents the most recent year's operations, which ended yesterday.

| | |
|---|---|
| Sales | $40,000,000 |
| Variable costs | 16,000,000 |
| Revenue before fixed costs | $24,000,000 |
| Fixed costs | 10,000,000 |
| EBIT | $14,000,000 |
| Interest expense | 1,150,000 |
| Earnings before taxes | $12,850,000 |
| Taxes | 3,750,000 |
| Net income | $ 9,100,000 |

Your supervisor in the controller's office has just handed you a memorandum asking for written responses to the following questions:
**a.** At this level of output, what is the degree of operating leverage?
**b.** What is the degree of financial leverage?
**c.** What is the degree of combined leverage?
**d.** What is the firm's break-even point in sales dollars?
**e.** If sales should increase by 20 percent, by what percent would earnings before taxes (and net income) increase?

**15-8B.** (*Break-even point*) You are a hard-working analyst in the office of financial operations for a manufacturing firm that produces a single product. You have developed the following cost structure information for this company. All of it pertains to an output level of 7 million units. Using this information, find the break-even point in units of output for the firm.

| | |
|---|---|
| Return on operating assets | = 25% |
| Operating asset turnover | = 5 times |
| Operating assets | = $18 million |
| Degree of operating leverage | = 6 times |

**15-9B.** (*Break-even point and operating leverage*) Matthew Electronics manufactures a complete line of radio and communication equipment for law enforcement agencies. The average selling price of its finished product is $175 per unit. The variable costs for these same units is $140. Matthew's incurs fixed costs of $550,000 per year.

**a.** What is the break-even point in units for the company?

**b.** What is the dollar sales volume the firm must achieve to reach the break-even point?

**c.** What would be the firm's profit or loss at the following units of production sold: 12,000 units? 15,000 units? 20,000 units?

**d.** Find the degree of operating leverage for the production and sales levels given in part (c).

**15-10B.** (*Break-even point and operating leverage*) Some financial data for each of three firms are as follows:

| | Farm City Seeds | Empire Sod | Golden Peaches |
|---|---|---|---|
| Average selling price per unit | $ 15.00 | $ 190.00 | $ 28.00 |
| Average variable cost per unit | $ 11.75 | $ 145.00 | $ 19.00 |
| Units sold | 120,000 | 9,000 | 50,000 |
| Fixed costs | $30,000 | $110,000 | $33,000 |

**a.** What is the profit for each company at the indicated sales volume?

**b.** What is the break-even point in units for each company?

**c.** What is the degree of operating leverage for each company at the indicated sales volume?

**d.** If sales were to *decline,* which firm would suffer the largest relative decline in profitability?

**15-11B.** (*Fixed costs and the break-even point*) Keller's Keg expects to earn $38,000 next year after taxes. Sales will be $420,002. The store is located near the fraternity-row district of Blue Springs State University and sells only kegs of beer for $17 a keg. The variable cost per keg is $9. The store experiences a 35 percent tax rate.

**a.** What are Keller's Keg's fixed costs expected to be next year?

**b.** Calculate the firm's break-even point both in units and in dollars.

**15-12B.** (*Fixed costs and the break-even point*) Mini-Kool hopes to earn $70,000 next year after taxes. Sales will be $2,500,050. The firm's single plant manufactures only small refrigerators. These are used in many recreational campers. The refrigerators sell for $75 per unit and have a variable cost of $58. Mini-Kool experiences a 45 percent tax rate.

**a.** What are the firm's fixed costs expected to be next year?

**b.** Calculate the firm's break-even point both in units and dollars.

**15-13B.** (*Break-even point and selling price*) Heritage Chain Company will produce 175,000 units next year. All of this production will be sold as finished goods. Fixed costs will total $335,000. Variable costs for this firm are relatively predictable at 80 percent of sales.

**a.** If Heritage Chain wants to achieve an earnings before interest and taxes level of $270,000 next year, at what price per unit must it sell its product?

**b.** Based on your answer to part (a), set up an analytical income statement that will verify your solution.

**15-14B.** (*Break-even point and selling price*) Thomas Appliances will manufacture and sell 190,000 units next year. Fixed costs will total $300,000, and variable costs will be 75 percent of sales.

**a.** The firm wants to achieve an earnings before interest and taxes level of $250,000. What selling price per unit is necessary to achieve this result?

**b.** Set up an analytical income statement to verify your solution to part (a).

**15-15B.** (*Break-even point and profit margin*) A recent business graduate of Dewey University is planning to open a new wholesaling operation. His target operating profit margin is 25 percent. His unit contribution margin will be 60 percent of sales. Average annual sales are forecast to be $4,250,000.

- **a.** How large can fixed costs be for the wholesaling operation and still allow the 25 percent operating profit margin to be achieved?
- **b.** What is the break-even point in dollars for the firm?

**15-16B.** (*Operating leverage*) The B. H. Williams Company manufactures an assortment of wood-burning stoves. The average selling price for the various units is $475. The associated variable cost is $350 per unit. Fixed costs for the firm average $200,000 annually.

- **a.** What is the break-even point in units for the company?
- **b.** What is the dollar sales volume the firm must achieve to reach the break-even point?
- **c.** What is the degree of operating leverage for a production and sales level of 6,000 units for the firm? (Calculate to three decimal places.)
- **d.** What will be the projected effect on earnings before interest and taxes if the firm's sales level should increase by 13 percent from the volume noted in part (c) above?

**15-17B.** (*Break-even point and operating leverage*) The Palm Patio Company manufactures a full line of lawn furniture. The average selling price of a finished unit is $28. The associated variable cost is $17 per unit. Fixed costs for Palm Patio average $55,000 per year.

- **a.** What is the break-even point in units for the company?
- **b.** What is the dollar sales volume the firm must achieve to reach the break-even point?
- **c.** What would be the company's profit or loss at the following units of production sold: 4,000 units? 6,000 units? 8,000 units?
- **d.** Find the degree of operating leverage for the production and sales levels given in part (c).
- **e.** What is the effect on the degree of operating leverage as sales rise above the break-even point?

**15-18B.** (*Fixed costs*) Tropical Sun projects that next year its fixed costs will total $135,000. Its only product sells for $13 per unit, of which $6 is a variable cost. The management of Tropical is considering the purchase of a new machine that will lower the variable cost per unit to $5. The new machine, however, will add to fixed costs through an increase in depreciation expense. How large can the *addition* to fixed costs be to keep the firm's break-even point in units produced and sold unchanged?

**15-19B.** (*Operating leverage*) The management of Tropical Sun did not purchase the new piece of equipment (see problem 15-18B). Using the existing cost structure, calculate the degree of operating leverage at 40,000 units of output. Comment on the meaning of your answer.

**15-20B.** (*Leverage analysis*) An analytical income statement for Tropical Sun follows. It is based on an output (sales) level of 50,000 units. You may refer to the original cost structure data in problem (15-18B).

| | |
|---|---|
| Sales | $650,000 |
| Variable costs | 300,000 |
| Revenue before fixed costs | $350,000 |
| Fixed costs | 135,000 |
| EBIT | $215,000 |
| Interest expense | 60,000 |
| Earnings before taxes | $155,000 |
| Taxes | 70,000 |
| Net income | $ 85,000 |

- **a.** Calculate the degree of operating leverage at this output level.
- **b.** Calculate the degree of financial leverage at this level of EBIT.
- **c.** Determine the combined leverage effect at this output level.

**15-21B.** (*Break-even point*) You are employed as a financial analyst for a single-product manufacturing firm. Your supervisor has made the following cost structure information available to you, all of which pertains to an output level of 1,700,000 units.

| | |
|---|---|
| Return on operating assets | = 16 percent |
| Operating asset turnover | = 6 times |
| Operating assets | = $3.25 million |
| Degree of operating leverage | = 9 times |

Your task is to find the break-even point in units of output for the firm.

**15-22B.** (*Fixed costs*) Sausalito Silkscreen is forecasting fixed costs next year of $375,000. The firm's single product sells for $25 per unit and incurs a variable cost per unit of $13. The firm may acquire some new binding equipment that would lower variable cost per unit to $11. The new equipment, however, would add to fixed costs through the price of an annual maintenance agreement on the new equipment. How large can this increase in fixed costs be and still keep the firm's present break-even point in units produced and sold unchanged?

**15-23B.** (*Leverage analysis*) Your firm's cost analysis supervisor supplies you with the following analytical income statement and requests answers to the four questions listed following the statement.

| | |
|---|---:|
| Sales | $13,750,000 |
| Variable costs | 9,500,000 |
| Revenue before fixed costs | $ 4,250,000 |
| Fixed costs | 3,000,000 |
| EBIT | $ 1,250,000 |
| Interest expense | 250,000 |
| Earnings before taxes | $ 1,000,000 |
| Taxes | 430,000 |
| Net income | $ 570,000 |

**a.** At this level of output, what is the degree of operating leverage?
**b.** What is the degree of financial leverage?
**c.** What is the degree of combined leverage?
**d.** What is the firm's break-even point in sales dollars?

**15-24B.** (*Leverage analysis*) You are supplied with the following analytical income statement for your firm. It reflects last year's operations.

| | |
|---|---:|
| Sales | $18,000,000 |
| Variable costs | 7,000,000 |
| Revenue before fixed costs | $11,000,000 |
| Fixed costs | 6,000,000 |
| EBIT | $ 5,000,000 |
| Interest expense | 1,750,000 |
| Earnings before taxes | $ 3,250,000 |
| Taxes | 1,250,000 |
| Net income | $ 2,000,000 |

**a.** At this level of output, what is the degree of operating leverage?
**b.** What is the degree of financial leverage?
**c.** What is the degree of combined leverage?
**d.** If sales should increase by 15 percent, by what percent would earnings before taxes (and net income) increase?
**e.** What is your firm's break-even point in sales dollars?

**15-25B.** *(Sales mix and the break-even point)* Wayne Automotive produces four lines of auto accessories for the major Detroit automobile manufacturers. The lines are known by the code letters A, B, C, and D. The current sales mix for Wayne and the contribution margin ratio (unit contribution margin divided by unit sales price) for these product lines are as follows:

| Product Line | Percent of Total Sales | Contribution Margin Ratio |
|---|---|---|
| A | 25⅔% | 40% |
| B | 41⅓ | 32 |
| C | 19⅔ | 20 |
| D | 13⅓ | 60 |

Total sales for next year are forecast to be $150,000. Total fixed costs will be $35,000.

**a.** Prepare a table showing (1) sales, (2) total variable costs, and (3) the total contribution margin associated with each product line.

**b.** What is the aggregate contribution margin ratio indicative of this sales mix?

**c.** At this sales mix, what is the break-even point in dollars?

**15-26B.** (*Sales mix and the break-even point*) Because of production constraints, Wayne Automotive (see problem 15-25B) may have to adhere to a different sales mix for next year. The alternative plan is outlined as follows:

| Product Line | Percent of Total Sales |
|---|---|
| A | 33⅓% |
| B | 41⅔ |
| C | 16⅔ |
| D | 8⅓ |

**a.** Assuming all other facts in problem 15-25B remain the same, what effect will this different sales mix have on Wayne's break-even point in dollars?

**b.** Which sales mix will Wayne's management prefer?

## SELF-TEST SOLUTIONS

**ST-1.** *Step 1: Compute the operating profit margin:*

$$(\text{margin}) \times (\text{turnover}) = \text{return on operating assets}$$
$$(\text{M}) \times (6) = 0.30$$
$$\text{M} = 0.30/6 = 0.05$$

*Step 2: Compute the sales level associated with the given output level:*

$$\frac{\text{sales}}{\$20{,}000{,}000} = 6$$
$$\text{sales} = \$120{,}000{,}000$$

*Step 3: Compute EBIT:*

$$(.05)\ (\$120{,}000{,}000) = \$6{,}000{,}000 = \text{EBIT}$$

*Step 4: Compute revenue before fixed costs. Because the degree of operating leverage is 4.5 times, revenue before fixed costs (RBF) is 4.5 times EBIT, as follows:*

$$\text{RBF} = (4.5)\ (\$6{,}000{,}000) = \$27{,}000{,}000$$

*Step 5: Compute total variable costs:*

$$(\text{sales}) - (\text{total variable costs}) = \$27{,}000{,}000$$
$$\$120{,}000{,}000 - (\text{total variable costs}) = \$27{,}000{,}000$$
$$\text{total variable costs} = \$93{,}000{,}000$$

*Step 6: Compute total fixed costs:*

$$\text{RBF} - \text{fixed costs} = \text{EBIT}$$
$$\$27{,}000{,}000 - \text{fixed costs} = \$6{,}000{,}000$$
$$\text{Fixed costs} = \$21{,}000{,}000$$

*Step 7: Find the selling price per unit (P), and the variable cost per unit (V):*

$$P = \frac{\text{sales}}{\text{output in units}} = \frac{\$120{,}000{,}000}{10{,}000{,}000} = \$12.00$$

$$V = \frac{\text{total variable costs}}{\text{output in units}} = \frac{\$93{,}000{,}000}{10{,}000{,}000} = \$9.30$$

*Step 8: Compute the break-even point:*

$$Q_B = \frac{F}{P - V} = \frac{\$21{,}000{,}000}{\$12.00 - \$9.30}$$

$$= \frac{\$21{,}000{,}000}{\$2.70} = 7{,}777{,}778 \text{ units}$$

The firm will break even when it produces and sells 7,777,778 units.

**ST-2. a.** $\frac{\text{Revenue before fixed costs}}{\text{EBIT}} = \frac{\$8{,}000{,}000}{\$3{,}000{,}000} = \underline{\underline{2.67 \text{ times}}}$

**b.** $\frac{\text{EBIT}}{\text{EBIT} - I} = \frac{\$3{,}000{,}000}{\$2{,}000{,}000} = \underline{\underline{1.50 \text{ times}}}$

**c.** $DCI_{\$20{,}000{,}000} = (2.67)(1.50) = \underline{\underline{4.00 \text{ times}}}$

**d.** $S^* = \frac{F}{1 - \frac{VC}{S}} = \frac{\$5{,}000{,}000}{1 - \frac{\$12M}{\$20M}} = \frac{\$5{,}000{,}000}{1 - 0.60} = \frac{\$5{,}000{,}000}{0.40} = \underline{\underline{\$12{,}500{,}000}}$

**e.** (30%)(4.00) = 120%

**f.**

| | |
|---|---|
| Sales | $26,000,000 |
| Variable costs | 15,600,000 |
| Revenue before fixed costs | $10,400,000 |
| Fixed costs | 5,000,000 |
| EBIT | $ 5,400,000 |
| Interest expense | 1,000,000 |
| Earnings before taxes | $ 4,400,000 |
| Taxes (0.50) | 2,200,000 |
| Net income | $ 2,200,000 |

We know that sales have increased by 30 percent to $26 million from the base sales level of $20 million. Let us focus now on the change in earnings before taxes. We can compute that change as follows:

$$\frac{\$4{,}400{,}000 - \$2{,}000{,}000}{\$2{,}000{,}000} = \frac{\$2{,}400{,}000}{\$2{,}000{,}000} = 120\%$$

Because the tax rate was held constant, the percentage change in net income will also equal 120 percent. The fluctuations implied by the degree of combined leverage measure are therefore accurately reflected in this analytical income statement.

**ST-3. a.**

$$\begin{aligned}\{(P \cdot Q) - [V \cdot Q + (F)]\}(1 - T) &= \$210{,}000\\ [(\$4{,}000{,}000) - (\$3{,}000{,}000) - F](.7) &= \$210{,}000\\ (\$1{,}000{,}000 - F)(.7) &= \$210{,}000\\ \$700{,}000 - .7F &= \$210{,}000\\ .7F &= \$490{,}000\\ F &= \underline{\underline{\$700{,}000}}\end{aligned}$$

Fixed costs next year, then, are expected to be $700,000.

**b.** $$Q_B = \frac{F}{P - V} = \frac{\$700{,}000}{\$50} = \underline{\underline{14{,}000 \text{ units}}}$$

$$S^* = \frac{F}{1 - \dfrac{VC}{S}} = \frac{\$700{,}000}{1 - .75} = \frac{\$700{,}000}{.25} = \underline{\underline{\$2{,}800{,}000}}$$

The firm will break even (EBIT = 0) when it sells 14,000 units. With a selling price of $200 per unit, the break-even sales level is $2,800,000.

# PLANNING THE FIRM'S FINANCING MIX

The United States was recession-free from November 1982 until July 1990, when a general business contraction did occur. It officially lasted until the end of February 1991, and the nation's labor markets didn't regain full speed until the first half of 1994. Essentially, business enterprises were going through a once in a lifetime global realignment. This period was an essentially challenging one for many American business firms that had loaded their balance sheets with debt over the "good times." ● Financial executives had to delicately manage cash flows to service existing debt contracts or face bankruptcy. These same executives had to give considerable thought as to how to finance the next (incremental) capital project. ● Along these lines, Harley-Davidson, Inc., has taken a rather moderate exposure to financial risk in the management of its funds sources. Harley has about 7,200 employees and for reporting year 1999 ranked 579th among the *Fortune* 1,000 largest domestic corporations with sales revenues of $2.45 billion. For 1999, Harley generated $450 million in earnings before interest and taxes (i.e., EBIT) and incurred interest expense of $29.0 million. This put its times interest earned ratio at 15.5 times (i.e., $450/$29) for 1999. So in an adverse economic year, Harley's EBIT could slip to about one-fifteenth of its 1999 amount and the firm would still be able to pay its contractual debt obligations. By the way, the times interest earned ratio is defined in Table 16-7 in this chapter, should you not already be familiar with it. ● Similarly, another company that pays explicit attention to managing its financing mix is the Georgia-Pacific Corporation. This firm is one of the world's leaders in the manufacturing and distribution of building products, pulp, and paper. The firm employs about

**LEARNING OBJECTIVES**

After reading this chapter, you should be able to

1. Understand the concept of an optimal capital structure.
2. Explain the main underpinnings of capital structure theory.
3. Distinguish between the independence hypothesis and dependence hypothesis as these concepts relate to capital structure theory; identify the Nobel Prize winners in economics who are the leading proponents of the independence hypothesis.
4. Understand and be able to graph the moderate position on capital structure importance.
5. Incorporate the concepts of agency costs and free cash flow into a discussion on capital structure management.
6. Use the basic tools of capital structure management.
7. Understand the relationship between exposure to foreign currency risk and financial risk.
8. Understand corporate financing policies in practice.

47,500 individuals and ranked exactly 100 among the *Fortune* 500 largest domestic corporations at the end of 1996. Georgia-Pacific posted sales revenues of $13 billion for 1996 and possessed $12.8 billion in assets. ● Georgia-Pacific's 1996 Annual Report contained a separate section on "Financial Strategy." On that subject, the management of the firm said: "Georgia-Pacific's objective is to provide superior returns to our shareholders. To achieve this goal, our financial strategy must complement our operating strategy. We must maintain a capital structure that minimizes our cost of capital while providing flexibility in financing our capital (expenditure) requirements." ● As you learn the material in this chapter, you will be able to make positive contributions to company financing strategies such as those put forth above by Harley and the Georgia-Pacific Corporation. In dealing with the firm's financing mix, you can help the firm avoid making serious financial errors, the consequences of which usually last for several years.

## CHAPTER PREVIEW

In this chapter, we direct our attention to the determination of an appropriate financing mix for the firm. Think of the right side of the firm's balance sheet as a big pie. That pie can be sliced into different-sized pieces. One piece might be labeled *long-term debt,* another labeled *preferred equity,* and yet another, *common equity.* We want to mix the pieces together in an optimal fashion that will make the pie as large as possible.

That task is the focal point of this chapter, and it is one that all chief financial officers confront. In some instances, just changing the labels on the slices of the pie might not change its size—but in other cases, it might. That is the challenge of financial structure management. The total value of the firm is represented by the ultimate size of the pie. More value (pie) is better than less value (pie). Keep this in mind while you work through the chapter.

As you study this chapter on financial structure theory, decision making, and policy, you will be made aware of a full five of the ten principles, first noted and explained in Chapter 1, that underlie the basics of business financial management. Specifically, your attention will be directed to: **Principle 1: The Risk-Return Trade-Off—We won't take on additional risk unless we expect to be compensated with additional return; Principle 3: Cash—Not Profits—Is King; Principle 6: Efficient Capital Markets—The markets are quick and prices are right; Principle 7: The Agency Problem—Managers won't work for the owners unless it's in their best interest; and Principle 8: Taxes Bias Business Decisions.**

## KEY TERMS AND GETTING STARTED

**Financial Structure**
The mix of all funds sources that appear on the right side of the balance sheet.

**Capital structure**
The mix of long-term sources of funds used by the firm. Basically, this concept omits short-term liabilities.

**Financial structure design**
The management activity of seeking the proper mix of all financing components in order to minimize the cost of raising a given amount of funds.

We now direct our attention to the determination of an appropriate financing mix for the firm. First, we must distinguish between financial structure and capital structure. **Financial structure** is the mix of all items that appear on the right side of the company's balance sheet. **Capital structure** is the mix of the *long-term* sources of funds used by the firm. The relationship between financial and capital structure can be expressed in equation form:

$$(\text{financial structure}) - (\text{current liabilities}) = \text{capital structure} \quad \textbf{(16-1)}$$

Prudent **financial structure design** requires answers to the following two questions:

1. What should be the maturity composition of the firm's sources of funds; in other words, how should a firm best divide its total fund sources between short- and long-term components?

**TABLE 16-1**
Balance Sheet

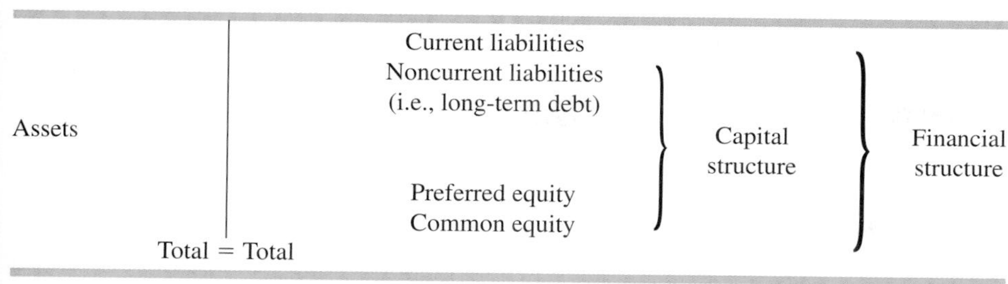

| Assets | Liabilities and equity | | |
|---|---|---|---|
| Assets | Current liabilities | | Financial structure |
| | Noncurrent liabilities (i.e., long-term debt) | Capital structure | Financial structure |
| | Preferred equity | Capital structure | Financial structure |
| | Common equity | Capital structure | Financial structure |
| Total | = Total | | |

2. In what proportions relative to the total should the various forms of permanent financing be utilized?

The major influence on the maturity structure of the financing plan is the nature of the assets owned by the firm. A company heavily committed to real capital investment, represented primarily by fixed assets on its balance sheet, *should* finance those assets with permanent (long-term) types of financial capital. Furthermore, the permanent portion of the firm's investment in current assets should likewise be financed with permanent capital. Alternatively, assets held on a temporary basis are to be financed with temporary sources. The present discussion assumes that the bulk of the company's current liabilities are comprised of temporary capital.

This hedging concept is discussed in Chapter 18. Accordingly, our focus in this chapter is an answer to the second of the two questions noted previously—this process is usually called *capital structure management.*

The *objective* of capital structure management is to mix the permanent sources of funds used by the firm in a manner that will maximize the company's common stock price. Alternatively, this objective may be viewed as a search for the funds mix that will minimize the firm's composite cost of capital. We can call this proper mix of funds sources the **optimal capital structure.**

**Optimal capital structure** The unique capital structure that minimizes the firm's composite cost of long-term capital.

Table 16-1 looks at equation 16-1 in terms of a simplified balance sheet format. It helps us visualize the overriding problem of capital structure management. The sources of funds that give rise to financing fixed costs (long-term debt and preferred equity) must be combined with common equity in the proportions most suitable to the investing marketplace. If that mix can be found, then, holding all other factors constant, the firm's common stock price will be maximized.

Whereas equation 16-1 quite accurately indicates that the corporate capital structure may be viewed as an absolute dollar *amount,* the *real* capital structure problem is one of balancing the array of funds sources in a proper manner. Our use of the term *capital structure* emphasizes this latter problem of relative magnitude, or proportions.

The rest of this chapter will cover three main areas. First, we discuss the theory of capital structure to provide a perspective. Second, we examine the basic tools of capital structure management. We conclude with a real-world look at actual capital structure management.

## CONCEPT CHECK

1. What is the objective of capital structure management?
2. What is the main attribute of a firm's optimal capital structure?

## A GLANCE AT CAPITAL STRUCTURE THEORY

It pays to understand the essential components of capital structure theory. The assumption of excessive financial risk can put the firm into bankruptcy proceedings. Some argue that the decision to use little financial leverage results in an undervaluation of the firm's shares in the marketplace. The effective financial manager must know how to find the area of optimum financial leverage use—this will enhance share value, all other considerations held constant. Thus, grasping the theory will make you better able to formulate a sound financial structure policy.

An enduring controversy within financial theory concerns the effect of financial leverage on the overall cost of capital to the enterprise. The heart of the argument may be stated in the form of a question: Can the firm affect its overall cost of funds, either favorably or unfavorably, by varying the mixture of financing sources used?

This controversy has taken many elegant forms in the finance literature. Most of these presentations appeal more to academics than to financial management practitioners. To emphasize the ingredients of capital structure theory that have practical applications for business financial management, we will pursue an intuitive, or nonmathematical, approach to reach a better understanding of the underpinnings of this *cost of capital–capital structure argument.*

### The Importance of Capital Structure

It makes economic sense for the firm to strive to minimize the cost of using financial capital. Both capital costs and other costs, such as manufacturing costs, share a common characteristic in that they potentially reduce the size of the cash dividend that could be paid to common stockholders.

We saw in Chapter 8 that the ultimate value of a share of common stock depends in part on the returns investors expect to receive from holding the stock. Cash dividends comprise all (in the case of an infinite holding period) or part (in the case of a holding period less than infinity) of these expected returns. Now hold constant all factors that could affect share price except capital costs. If these capital costs could be kept at a minimum, the dividend stream flowing to the common stockholders would be maximized. This, in turn, would maximize the firm's common stock price.

If the firm's cost of capital can be affected by its capital structure, then capital structure management is clearly an important subset of business financial management.

### Analytical Setting

The essentials of the capital structure controversy are best highlighted within a framework that economists would call a "partial equilibrium analysis." In a partial equilibrium analysis, changes that *do* occur in several factors and have an impact on a certain key item are ignored to study the effect of changes in a main factor on that same item of interest. Here, two items are simultaneously of interest: (1) $K_0$, the firm's composite cost of capital, and (2) $P_0$, the market price of the firm's common stock. The firm's use of financial leverage is the main factor that is allowed to vary in the analysis. This means that important financial decisions, such as investing policy and dividend policy, are held constant throughout the discussion. We are concerned with the effect of changes in the financing mix on share price and capital costs.

Our analysis will be facilitated if we adopt a *simplified* version of the basic dividend valuation model presented in Chapter 8 in our study of valuation principles, and in Chapter 12 in our assessment of the cost of capital. That model is shown as equation 16-2:

$$P_0 = \sum_{t=1}^{\infty} \frac{D_t}{(1 + K_c)^t} \tag{16-2}$$

where $P_0$ = the current price of the firm's common stock
$D_t$ = the cash dividend per share expected by investors during period $t$
$K_c$ = the cost of common equity capital

We can strip away some complications by making the following assumptions concerning the valuation process implicit in equation 16-2:

1. Cash dividends paid will not change over the infinite holding period. Thus $D_1 = D_2 = D_3 = \ldots = D_\infty$. There is no expected growth by investors in the dividend stream.
2. The firm retains none of its current earnings. This means that *all* of each period's per-share earnings are paid to stockholders in the form of cash dividends. The firm's dividend payout ratio is 100 percent. Cash dividends per share in equation 16-2, then, also equal earnings per share for the same period.

Under these assumptions, the cash dividend flowing to investors can be viewed as a level payment over an infinite holding period. The payment stream is perpetual, and according to the mathematics of perpetuities, equation 16-2 reduces to equation 16-3, where $E_t$ represents earnings per share during period $t$.

$$P_0 = \frac{D_t}{K_c} = \frac{E_t}{K_c} \tag{16-3}$$

In addition to the suppositions just noted, the analytical setting for the discussion of capital structure theory includes the following assumptions:

1. Corporate income is not subject to any taxation. The major implication of removing this assumption is discussed later.
2. Capital structures consist of only stocks and bonds. Furthermore, the degree of financial leverage used by the firm is altered by the issuance of common stock with the proceeds used to retire existing debt, or the issuance of debt with the proceeds used to repurchase stock. This permits leverage use to vary but maintains constancy of the total book value of the firm's capital structure.
3. The expected values of all investors' forecasts of the future levels of net operating income (EBIT) for each firm are identical. Say that you forecast the average level of EBIT to be achieved by General Motors over a very long period ($n \rightarrow \infty$). Your forecast will be the same as our forecast, and both will be equal to the forecasts of all other investors interested in General Motors common stock. In addition, we do not expect General Motors' EBIT to grow over time. Each year's forecast is the same as any other year's. This is consistent with our assumption underlying equation 16-3, where the firm's dividend stream is not expected to grow.
4. Securities are traded in perfect or efficient financial markets. This means that transaction costs and legal restrictions do not impede any investors' incentives to execute portfolio changes that they expect will increase their wealth. Information is freely available. Moreover, corporations and individuals that are equal credit risks can borrow funds at the same rates of interest.

This completes our description of the analytical setting. We now discuss three differing views on the relationship between use of financial leverage and common stock value.

The discussion and illustrations of the two extreme positions on the importance of capital structure that follow are meant to highlight the critical differences between differing viewpoints. This is not to say that the markets really behave in strict accordance with either position—they don't. The point is to identify polar positions on how things might work. Then by relaxing various restrictive assumptions, a more useful theory of how financing decisions are actually made becomes possible. That results in the third, or moderate, view.

## Extreme Position 1: Independence Hypothesis (NOI Theory)[1]

OBJECTIVE 3 

The crux of this position is that the firm's composite cost of capital, $K_0$, and common stock price, $P_0$, are both *independent* of the degree to which the company chooses to use financial leverage. In other words, no matter how modest or excessive the firm's use of debt financing, its common stock price will not be affected. Let us illustrate the mechanics of this point of view.

Suppose that Rix Camper Manufacturing Company has the following financial characteristics:

Shares of common stock outstanding = 2,000,000 shares
Common stock price, $P_0$ = \$10 per share
Expected level of net operating income (EBIT) = \$2,000,000
Dividend payout ratio = 100 percent

Currently, the firm uses no financial leverage; its capital structure consists entirely of common equity. Earnings per share and dividends per share equal \$1 each. When the capital structure is all common equity, the cost of common equity, $K_c$, and the weighted cost of capital, $K_0$ are equal. If equation 16-3 is restated in terms of the cost of common equity, we have for Rix Camper:

$$K_c = \frac{D_t}{P_0} = \frac{\$1}{\$10} = 10\%$$

Now, the management of Rix Camper decides to use some debt capital in its financing mix. The firm sells \$8 million worth of long-term debt at an interest rate of 6 percent. With no taxation of corporate income, this 6 percent interest rate is the cost of debt capital, $K_d$. The firm uses the proceeds from the sale of the bonds to repurchase 40 percent of its outstanding common shares. After the capital-structure change has been accomplished, Rix Camper Manufacturing Company has the financial characteristics displayed in Table 16-2.

Based on the preceding data, we notice that the recapitalization (capital structure change) of Rix Camper will result in a dividend paid to owners that is 26.7 percent higher than it was when the firm used no debt in its capital structure. Will this higher dividend result in a lower composite cost of capital to Rix and a higher common stock price? According to the principles of the independence hypothesis, the answer is "No."

The independence hypothesis suggests that the total market value of the firm's outstanding securities is *unaffected* by the manner in which the right side of the balance sheet is arranged. That is, the sum of the market value of outstanding debt plus the sum of the

[1]The net operating income and net income capitalization methods, which are referred to here as "extreme positions 1 and 2," were first presented in comprehensible form by Durand. See David Durand, "Costs of Debt and Equity Funds for Business: Trends and Problems of Measurement," *Conference on Research in Business Finance* (New York: National Bureau of Economic Research, 1952), reprinted in Ezra Solomon, ed., *The Management of Corporate Capital* (New York: Free Press), 91–116. The leading proponents of the independence hypothesis in its various forms are Professors Modigliani and Miller. See Franco Modigliani and Merton H. Miller, "The Cost of Capital, Corporation Finance and Theory of Investment," *American Economic Review* 48 (June 1958): 261–97; Franco Modigliani and Merton H. Miller, "Corporate Income Taxes and the Cost of Captial: A Correction," *American Economic Review* 53 (June 1963): 433–43; and Merton H. Miller, "Debt and Taxes," *Journal of Finance 32* (May 1977): 261–75.

**TABLE 16-2**
Rix Camper Manufacturing Company Financial Data Reflecting the Capital Structure Adjustment

| **Capital Structure Information** | |
|---|---|
| Shares of common stock outstanding = 1,200,000 | |
| Bonds at 6 percent = \$8,000,000 | |
| **Earnings Information** | |
| Expected level of net operating income (EBIT) | \$ 2,000,000 |
| Less: Interest expense | 480,000 |
| Earnings available to common stockholders | \$ 1,520,000 |
| Earnings per share $(E_t)$ | 1.267 |
| Dividends per share $(D_t)$ | 1.267 |
| Percentage change in both earnings per share and dividends per share relative to the unlevered capital structure | 26.7 percent |

market value of outstanding common equity will always be the *same* regardless of how much or little debt is actually used by the company. If capital structure has no impact on the total market value of the company, then that value is arrived at by the marketplace's capitalizing (discounting) the firm's expected net operating income stream. Therefore the independence hypothesis rests on what is called the **net operating income (NOI) approach to valuation.**

**Net operating income (NOI) approach to valuation**
The concept from financial theory that suggests the firm's capital structure has no impact on its market valuation.

The format is a very simple one, and the market value of the firm's common stock turns out to be a residual of the valuation process. Recall that before Rix Camper's recapitalization, the total market value of the firm was \$20 million (2 million common shares times \$10 per share). The firm's cost of common equity, $K_c$, and its weighted cost of capital, $K_0$, were each equal to 10 percent. The composite discount rate, $K_0$, is used to arrive at the market value of the firm's securities. After the recapitalization, we have for Rix Camper:

| | |
|---|---|
| Expected level of net operating income | \$ 2,000,000 |
| capitalized at $K_0$ = 10 percent | |
| = Market value of debt and equity | \$20,000,000 |
| − Market value of the new debt | 8,000,000 |
| = Market value of the common stock | \$12,000,000 |

With this valuation format, what is the market price of each share of common stock? Because we know that 1.2 million shares of stock are outstanding after the capital-structure change, the market price per share is \$10 (\$12 million/1.2 million). This is exactly the market value per share, $P_0$, that existed *before* the change.

Now, if the firm is using some debt that has an *explicit cost* of 6 percent, $K_d$, and the weighted (composite) cost of capital, $K_0$, is 10 percent, it stands to reason that the cost of common equity, $K_c$, has risen above its previous level of 10 percent. What will the cost of common equity be in this situation? As we did previously, we can take equation 16-3 and restate it in terms of $K_c$, the cost of common equity. After the recapitalization, the cost of common equity for Rix Camper is shown to *rise* to 12.67 percent:

$$K_c = \frac{D_t}{P_0} = \frac{\$1.267}{\$10} = 12.67\%$$

The cost of common equity for Rix Camper is 26.7 percent higher than it was before the capital structure shift. Notice in Table 16-2 that this is *exactly* equal to the percentage

**FIGURE 16-1**
Capital Cost and Financial Leverage No Taxes—Independence Hypothesis (NOI Theory)

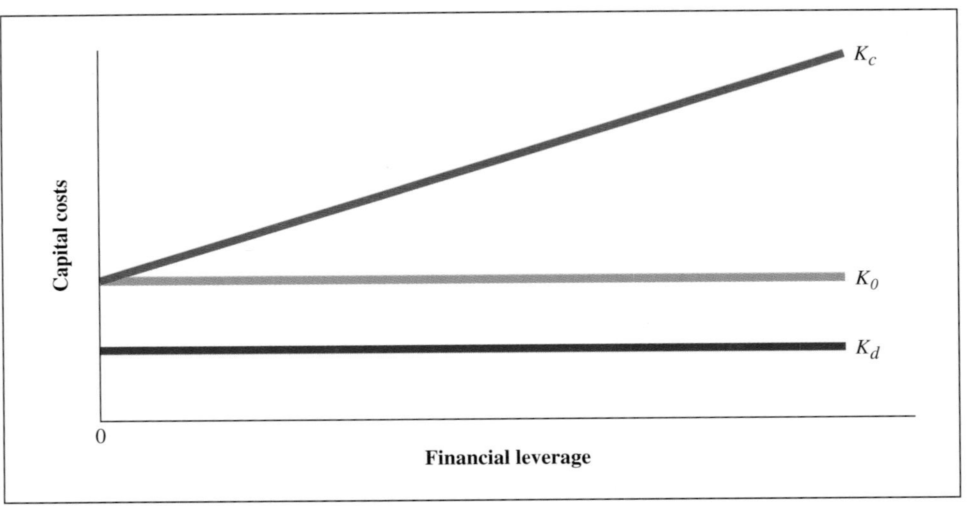


increase in earnings and dividends per share that accompanies the same capital structure adjustment. This highlights a fundamental relationship that is an integral part of the independence hypothesis. It concerns the perceived behavior in the firm's cost of common equity as expected dividends (earnings) increase relative to a financing mix change:

percentage change in $K_c$ = percentage change in $D_t$

In this framework, the use of a greater degree of financial leverage may result in greater earnings and dividends, but the firm's cost of common equity will rise at precisely the same rate as the earnings and dividends do. Thus, the inevitable trade-off between the higher expected return in dividends and earnings ($D_t$ and $E_t$) and increased risk that accompanies the use of debt financing manifests itself in a linear relationship between the cost of common equity ($K_c$) and financial leverage use. This view of the relationship between the firm's cost of funds and its financing mix is shown graphically in Figure 16-1. Figure 16-2 relates the firm's stock price to its financing mix under the same set of assumptions.

In Figure 16-1, the firm's overall cost of capital, $K_0$, is shown to be unaffected by an increased use of financial leverage. If more debt is used in the capital structure, the cost of common equity will rise at the same rate additional earnings are generated. This will keep the composite cost of capital to the corporation unchanged. Figure 16-2 shows that because the cost of capital will not change with the leverage use, neither will the firm's stock price.

**Explicit cost of capital**
The cost of capital for any funds source considered in isolation from other funds sources.

**Implicit cost of debt**
The change in the cost of common equity caused by the choice to use additional debt.

Debt financing, then, has two costs—its **explicit cost of capital,** $K_d$, calculated according to the formats outlined in Chapter 12 and an implicit cost. The **implicit cost of debt** is the change in the cost of common equity brought on by using financial leverage (additional debt). The real cost of debt is the sum of these explicit and implicit costs. In general, the real cost of *any* source of capital is its explicit cost, plus the change that it induces in the cost of any other source of funds.

Followers of the independence hypothesis argue that the use of financial leverage brings a change in the cost of common equity large enough to offset the benefits of higher dividends to investors. Debt financing is not as cheap as it first appears to be. This will keep the composite cost of funds constant. The implication for management is that one capital structure is as good as any other; financial officers should not waste time searching for an optimal capital structure. One capital structure, after all, is as beneficial as any other, because all result in the same weighted cost of capital.

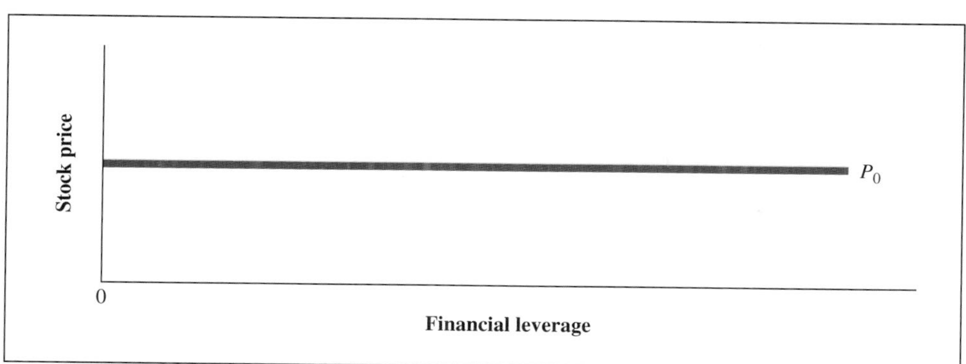


**FIGURE 16-2**
Stock Price and Financial Leverage: No Taxes—Independence Hypothesis (NOI Theory)

**RELATE TO THE BIG PICTURE**

The suggestion from capital-structure theory that one capital structure is just as good as any other within a perfect ("pure") market framework relies directly on **Principle 1: The Risk-Return Trade-Off—We won't take on additional risk unless we expect to be compensated with additional return.** This means that using more debt in the capital structure will not be ignored by investors in the financial markets. These rational investors will require a higher return on common stock investments in the firm that uses more leverage (rather than less), to compensate for the increased uncertainty stemming from the addition of the debt securities in the capital structure.

## Extreme Position 2: Dependence Hypothesis (NI Theory)

OBJECTIVE 3

The dependence hypothesis is at the opposite pole from the independence hypothesis. It suggests that both the weighted cost of capital, $K_0$, and common stock price, $P_0$, *are* affected by the firm's use of financial leverage. No matter how modest or excessive the firm's use of debt financing, both its cost of debt capital, $K_d$, and cost of equity capital, $K_c$, will not be affected by capital structure management. Because the cost of debt is less than the cost of equity, greater financial leverage will lower the firm's composite cost of capital indefinitely. Greater use of debt financing will thereby have a favorable effect on the company's common stock price. By returning to the Rix Camper situation, we can illustrate this point of view.

The same capital structure shift is being evaluated. That is, management will market $8 million of new debt at a 6 percent interest rate and use the proceeds to purchase its own common shares. Under this approach, the market is assumed to capitalize (discount) the expected earnings available to the common stockholders to arrive at the aggregate market value of the common stock. The market value of the firm's common equity is *not* a residual of the valuation process. After the recapitalization, the firm's cost of common equity, $K_c$, will still be equal to 10 percent. Thus, a 10 percent cost of common equity is applied in the following format:

| | |
|---|---|
| Expected level of net operating income | $ 2,000,000 |
| − Interest expense | 480,000 |
| = Earnings available to common stockholders capitalized at $K_c$ = 10 percent | $ 1,520,000 |
| = Market value of the common stock | $15,200,000 |
| + Market value of the new debt | 8,000,000 |
| = Market value of debt and equity | $23,200,000 |

**FIGURE 16-3**
Capital Costs and Financial Leverage: No Taxes—Dependence Hypothesis (NI Theory)

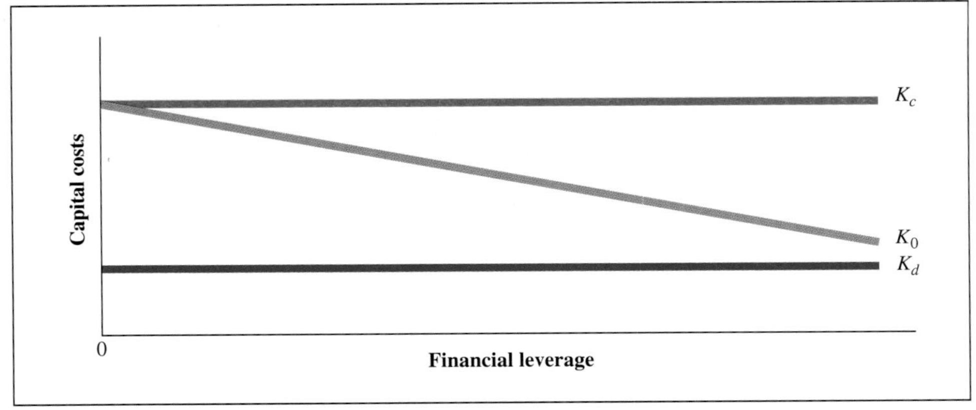


When we assume that the firm's capital structure consists only of debt and common equity, earnings available to the common stockholders is synonymous with net income. In the valuation process outlined previously, it is net income that is actually capitalized to arrive at the market value of the common equity. Because of this, the dependence hypothesis is also called the **net income (NI) approach to valuation.**

**Net income (NI) approach to valuation**
The concept from financial theory that suggests the firm's capital structure has a direct impact upon and can increase its market valuation.

Notice that the total market value of the firm's securities has risen to \$23.2 million from the \$20 million level that existed before the firm moved from the unlevered to the levered capital structure. The per-share value of the common stock is also shown to rise under this valuation format. With 1.2 million shares of stock outstanding, the market price per share is \$12.67 (\$15.2 million/1.2 million).

This increase in the stock price to \$12.67 represents a 26.7 percent rise over the previous level of \$10 per share. This is exactly equal to the percentage change in earnings per share and dividends per share calculated in Table 16-1. This permits us to characterize the dependence hypothesis in a very succinct fashion:

percentage change in $K_c$ = 0 percent < percentage change in $D_t$
(over all degrees of leverage)

percentage change in $P_0$ = percentage change in $D_t$

The dependence hypothesis suggests that the *explicit and implicit* costs of debt are one and the same. The use of more debt does *not* change the firm's cost of common equity. Using more debt, which is explicitly cheaper than common equity, will lower the firm's composite cost of capital, $K_0$. If you take the market value of Rix Camper's common stock according to the net income theory of \$15.2 million and express it as a percent of the total market value of the firm's securities, you get a market value weight of .655 (\$15.2 million/\$23.2 million). In a similar fashion, the market value weight of Rix Camper's debt is found to be .345 (\$8 million/\$23.2 million). After the capital structure adjustment, the firm's weighted cost of capital becomes:

$$K_0 = (.345)(6.00\%) + (.655)(10.00\%) = 8.62\%$$

So, changing the financing mix from all equity to a structure including both debt and equity lowered the composite cost of capital from 10 percent to 8.62 percent. The ingredients of the dependence hypothesis are illustrated in Figures 16-3 and 16-4.

The implication for management from Figures 16-3 and 16-4 is that the firm's cost of capital, $K_0$, will decline as the debt-to-equity ratio increases. This also implies that the company's common stock price will rise with increased leverage use. Because the cost of

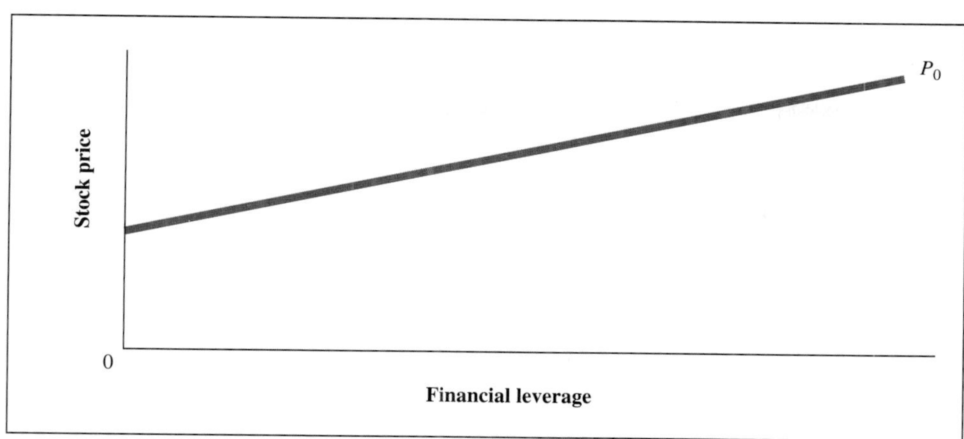


**FIGURE 16-4**
Stock Price and Financial Leverage: No Taxes—Dependence Hypothesis (NI Theory)

capital decreases continuously with leverage, the firm should use as much leverage as is possible. Next we will move toward reality in the analytical setting of our capital structure discussion. This is accomplished by relaxing some of the major assumptions that surrounded the independence and dependence hypotheses.

## Moderate Position: Corporate Income Is Taxed and Firms May Fail

In general, an analysis of extreme positions may be useful in that you are forced to sharpen your thinking not only about the poles, but also the situations that span the poles. In microeconomics, the study of perfect competition and monopoly provides a better understanding of the business activity that occurs in the wide area between these two model markets. In a similar fashion, the study of the independence and dependence hypotheses of the importance of capital structure helps us formulate a more informed view of the possible situations between those polar positions.

We turn now to a description of the cost of capital–capital structure relationship that has rather wide appeal to both business practitioners and academics. This moderate view (1) admits to the fact that interest expense is tax deductible, and (2) acknowledges that the probability of the firm's suffering bankruptcy costs is directly related to the company's use of financial leverage.

**TAX DEDUCTIBILITY OF INTEREST EXPENSE** This portion of the analysis recognizes that corporate income is subject to taxation. Furthermore, we assume that interest expense is tax deductible for purposes of computing the firm's tax bill. In this environment, the use of debt financing should result in a higher total market value for the firm's outstanding securities. We will see why subsequently.

We continue with our Rix Camper Manufacturing Company example. First, consider the total cash payments made to all security holders (holders of common stock plus holders of bonds). In the no-tax case, the sum of cash dividends paid to common shareholders plus interest expense amounted to \$2 million both (1) when financing was all by common equity, and (2) after the proposed capital structure adjustment to a levered situation was accomplished. The *sum* of the cash flows that Rix Camper could pay to its contributors of debt and equity capital was not affected by its financing mix.

When corporate income is taxed by the government, however, the sum of the cash flows made to *all* contributors of financial capital *is* affected by the firm's financing mix. Table 16-3 illustrates this point.

**TABLE 16-3**
Rix Camper Manufacturing Company Cash Flows to All Investors—The Case of Taxes

| | Unlevered Capital Structure | Levered Capital Structure |
|---|---|---|
| Expected level of net operating income | \$2,000,000 | \$2,000,000 |
| Less: Interest expense | 0 | 480,000 |
| Earning before taxes | \$2,000,000 | \$1,520,000 |
| Less: Taxes at 50% | 1,000,000 | 760,000 |
| Earning available to common stockholders | \$1,000,000 | \$ 760,000 |
| Expected payments to all security holders | \$1,000,000 | \$1,240,000 |

**Tax shield**
The element from the federal tax code that permits interest costs to be deductible when computing the firm's tax bill. The dollar difference (the shield) flows to the firm's security holders.

If Rix Camper makes the capital structure adjustment identified in the preceding sections of this chapter, the total payments to equity and debtholders will be \$240,000 *greater* than under the all-common-equity capitalization. Where does this \$240,000 come from? The government's take, through taxes collected, is lower by that amount. This difference, which flows to the Rix Camper security holders, is called the **tax shield** on interest. In general, it may be calculated by equation 16-4, where $r_d$ is the interest rate paid on the debt, $M$ is the principal amount of the debt, and $t$ is the firm's marginal tax rate:

$$\text{tax shield} = r_d(M)(t) \qquad \textbf{(16-4)}$$

The moderate position on the importance of capital structure presumes that the tax shield must have value in the marketplace. Accordingly, this tax benefit will increase the total market value of the firm's outstanding securities relative to the all-equity capitalization. Financial leverage does affect firm value. Because the cost of capital is just the other side of the valuation coin, financial leverage also affects the firm's composite cost of capital. Can the firm increase firm value indefinitely and lower its cost of capital continuously by using more and more financial leverage? Common sense would tell us "No!" So would most financial managers and academicians. The acknowledgment of bankruptcy costs provides one possible rationale.

**RELATE TO THE BIG PICTURE**

The preceding section on the "Tax Deductibility of Interest Expense" is a compelling example of **Principle 8: Taxes Bias Business Decisions.** We have just seen that corporations have an important incentive provided by the tax code to finance projects with debt securities rather than new issues of common stock. The interest expense on the debt issue will be tax deductible. The common stock dividends will not be tax deductible. So firms can indeed increase their total after-tax cash flows available to all investors in their securities by using financial leverage. This element of the U.S. tax code should also remind you of **Principle 3: Cash—Not Profits—Is King.**

**THE LIKELIHOOD OF FIRM FAILURE** The probability that the firm will be unable to meet the financial obligations identified in its debt contracts increases as more debt is employed. The highest costs would be incurred if the firm actually went into bankruptcy proceedings. Here, assets would be liquidated. If we admit that these assets might sell for something less than their perceived market values, equity investors and debtholders could both suffer losses. Other problems accompany bankruptcy proceedings. Lawyers and accountants have to be hired and paid. Managers must spend time preparing lengthy reports for those involved in the legal action.

Milder forms of financial distress also have their costs. As their firm's financial condition weakens, creditors may take action to restrict normal business activity. Suppliers may not deliver materials on credit. Profitable capital investments may have to be forgone, and dividend payments may even be interrupted. At some point, the expected cost of default will be large enough to outweigh the tax shield advantage of debt financing.[2] The firm will turn to other sources of financing, mainly common equity. At this point, the real cost of debt is thought to be higher than the real cost of common equity.

## Moderate View: Saucer-Shaped Cost of Capital Curve

This moderate view of the relationship between financing mix and the firm's cost of capital is depicted in Figure 16-5. The result is a saucer-shaped (or U-shaped) average cost of capital curve, $K_0$. The firm's average cost of equity, $K_{0,}$ is seen to rise over all positive degrees of financial leverage use. For a while, the firm can borrow funds at a relatively low cost of debt, $K_d$. Even though the cost of equity is rising, it does not rise at a fast enough rate to offset the use of the less expensive debt financing. Thus, between points 0 and A on the financial-leverage axis, the average cost of capital declines and stock price rises.

Eventually, the threat of financial distress causes the cost of debt to rise. In Figure 16-5, this increase in the cost of debt shows up in the average cost of debt curve, $K_d$, at point *A*. Between points *A* and *B*, mixing debt and equity funds produces an average cost of capital that is (relatively) flat. The firm's **optimal range of financial leverage** lies between points *A* and *B*. All capital structures between these two points are optimal because they produce the lowest composite cost of capital. As we said in the introduction to this chapter, finding this optimal range of financing mixes is the objective of capital structure management.

**Optimal range of financial leverage**
The range of various financial structure combinations that generate the lowest composite cost of capital for the firm.

Point *B* signifies the firm's debt capacity. **Debt capacity** is the maximum proportion of debt the firm can include in its capital structure and still maintain its lowest composite cost of capital. Beyond point *B*, additional fixed-charge capital can be attracted only at very costly interest rates. At the same time, this excessive use of financial leverage would cause

**Debt capacity**
The maximum proportion of debt that the firm can include in its capital structure and still maintain its lowest composite cost of capital.

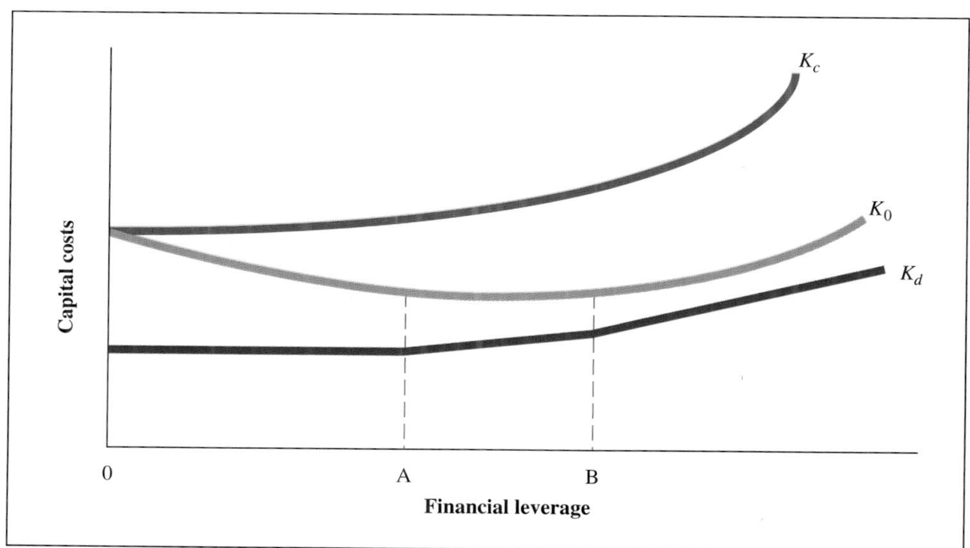


**FIGURE 16-5**
Capital Costs and Financial Leverage: The Moderate View, Considering Taxes and Financial Distress

[2]Even this argument that the trade-off between costs and the tax shield benefit of debt financing can lead to an optimal structure has its detractors. See Robert A. Haugen and Lemma W. Senbet, "The Insignificance of Bankruptcy Costs to the Theory of Optimal Capital Structure," *Journal of Finance* 33 (May 1978): 383–93.

the firm's cost of equity to rise at a faster rate than previously. The composite cost of capital would then rise quite rapidly, and the firm's stock price would decline.

This version of the moderate view as it relates to the firm's stock price is characterized subsequently. The notation is the same as that found in our discussion of the independence and dependence hypotheses.

1. Between points 0 and *A:* $0 <$ percentage change in $P_0 <$ percentage change in $D_t$
2. Between points *A* and *B:* percentage change in $P_0 = 0$
3. Beyond point *B:* percentage change in $P_0 < 0$

## Firm Value, Agency Costs, Static Trade-Off Theory, and the Pecking Order Theory

Given the same task or assignment, it is quite likely that you will do it better for yourself than for someone else. If you are paid well enough, you might do the job about as effectively for that other person. Once you receive compensation, your work will be evaluated by someone. This process of evaluation is called "monitoring" within most discussions on agency costs.

This describes the heart of what is called the "agency problem." As American businesses have grown in size, the owners and managers have become (for the most part) separate groups of individuals. An inherent conflict exists, therefore, between managers and shareholders for whom managers act as agents in carrying out their objectives (for example, corporate goals). The following discussion relates the agency problem to the financial decision-making process of the firm.

In Chapter 1 of this text, we mentioned the *agency problem.* Recall that the agency problem gives rise to *agency costs,* which tend to occur in business organizations because ownership and management control are often separate. Thus the firm's managers can be properly thought of as agents for the firm's stockholders.[3] To ensure that agent-managers act in the stockholders' best interests requires that they have (1) proper incentives to do so and (2) that their decisions are monitored. The incentives usually take the form of executive compensation plans and perquisites. The perquisites might be a bloated support staff, country club memberships, luxurious corporate planes, or other amenities of a similar nature. Monitoring requires that certain costs be borne by the stockholders, such as (1) bonding the managers, (2) auditing financial statements, (3) structuring the organization in unique ways that limit useful managerial decisions, and (4) reviewing the costs and benefits of management perquisites. This list is indicative, not exhaustive. The main point is that monitoring costs are ultimately covered by the owners of the company—its common stockholders.

Capital structure management also gives rise to agency costs. Agency problems stem from conflicts of interest, and capital-structure management encompasses a natural conflict between stockholders and bondholders. Acting in the stockholders' best interests might cause management to invest in extremely risky projects. Existing investors in the firm's bonds could logically take a dim view of such an investment policy. A change in the risk structure of the firm's assets would change the business risk exposure of the firm. This could lead to a downward revision of the bond rating the firm currently enjoys. A lowered

[3]Economists have studied the problems associated with control of the corporation for decades. An early, classic work on this topic was A. A. Berle, Jr., and G. C. Means, *The Modern Corporation and Private Property* (New York: Macmillan, 1932). The recent emphasis in corporate finance and financial economics stems from the important contribution of Michael C. Jensen and William H. Meckling, "Theory of the Firm: Managerial Behavior, Agency Costs and Ownership Structure," *Journal of Financial Economics* 3 (October 1976): 306–60. Professors Jensen and Smith have analyzed the bondholder-stockholder conflict in a very clear style. See Michael C. Jensen and Clifford W. Smith, Jr., "Stockholder, Manager, and Creditor Interests: Applications of Agency Theory," in Edward I. Altman and Marti G. Subrahmanyam, eds., *Recent Advances in Corporate Finance* (Homewood, IL: Richard D. Irwin, 1985): 93–131.

| No Protective Bond Covenants | Many Protective Bond Covenants |
|---|---|
| High interest rates | Low interest rates |
| Low monitoring costs | High monitoring costs |
| No lost operating efficiencies | Many lost operating efficiencies |

**FIGURE 16-6**
Agency Costs of Debt: Trade-Offs

bond rating in turn would lower the current market value of the firm's bonds. Clearly, bondholders would be unhappy with this result.

To reduce this conflict of interest, the creditors (bond investors) and stockholders may agree to include several protective covenants in the bond contract. These bond covenants were discussed in more detail in Chapter 7, but essentially they may be thought of as restrictions on managerial decision making. Typical covenants restrict payment of cash dividends on common stock, limit the acquisition or sale of assets, or limit further debt financing. To make sure that the protective covenants are complied with by management means that monitoring costs are incurred. Like all monitoring costs, they are borne by common stockholders. Further, like many costs, they involve the analysis of an important trade-off.

Figure 16-6 displays some of the trade-offs involved with the use of protective bond covenants. Note (in the left panel of Figure 16-6) that the firm might be able to sell bonds that carry no protective covenants only by incurring very high interest rates. With no protective covenants, there are no associated monitoring costs. Also, there are no lost operating efficiencies, such as being able to move quickly to acquire a particular company in the acquisitions market. Conversely, the willingness to submit to several covenants could reduce the explicit cost of the debt contract, but would involve incurring significant monitoring costs and losing some operating efficiencies (which also translates into higher costs). When the debt issue is first sold, then, a trade-off will be arrived at between incurring monitoring costs, losing operating efficiencies, and enjoying a lower explicit interest cost.

Next we have to consider the presence of monitoring costs at low levels of leverage and at higher levels of leverage. When the firm operates at a low debt-to-equity ratio, there is little need for creditors to insist on a long list of bond covenants. The financial risk is just not there to require that type of activity. The firm will likewise benefit from low explicit interest rates when leverage is low. When the debt-to-equity ratio is high, however, it is logical for creditors to demand a great deal of monitoring. This increase in agency costs will raise the implicit cost (the true total cost) of debt financing. It seems logical, then, to suggest that monitoring costs will rise as the firm's use of financial leverage increases. Just as the likelihood of firm failure (financial distress) raises a company's overall cost of capital ($K_0$), so do agency costs. On the other side of the coin, this means that total firm value (the total market value of the firm's securities) will be *lower* owing to the presence of agency costs of debt. Taken together, the presence of agency costs and the costs associated with financial distress argue in favor of the concept of an *optimal* capital structure for the individual firm.

This general approach to understanding or explaining capital-structure decision making has come to be known in the finance literature as the "static trade-off theory." The label follows the essential form of the implied model wherein the present value (benefits) of tax shields that stem from increased leverage use are "traded-off" against both the rising costs of the likelihood of financial distress and the rising agency costs associated with increased debt usage.[4]

[4]Portions of the static trade-off model were contained in the original Modigliani and Miller 1958 article noted in footnote 1 in this chapter. It drew much increased attention, however, after the publication of Stewart C. Myers presidential address to the American Finance Association. See Stewart C. Myers's, "The Capital Structure Puzzle," *Journal of Finance* 39 (July 1984): 575–92. As might be expected, not all of the attention is complimentary concerning the usefulness of the static trade-off model.

**FIGURE 16-7**
Firm Value Considering Taxes, Agency Costs, and Financial Distress Costs

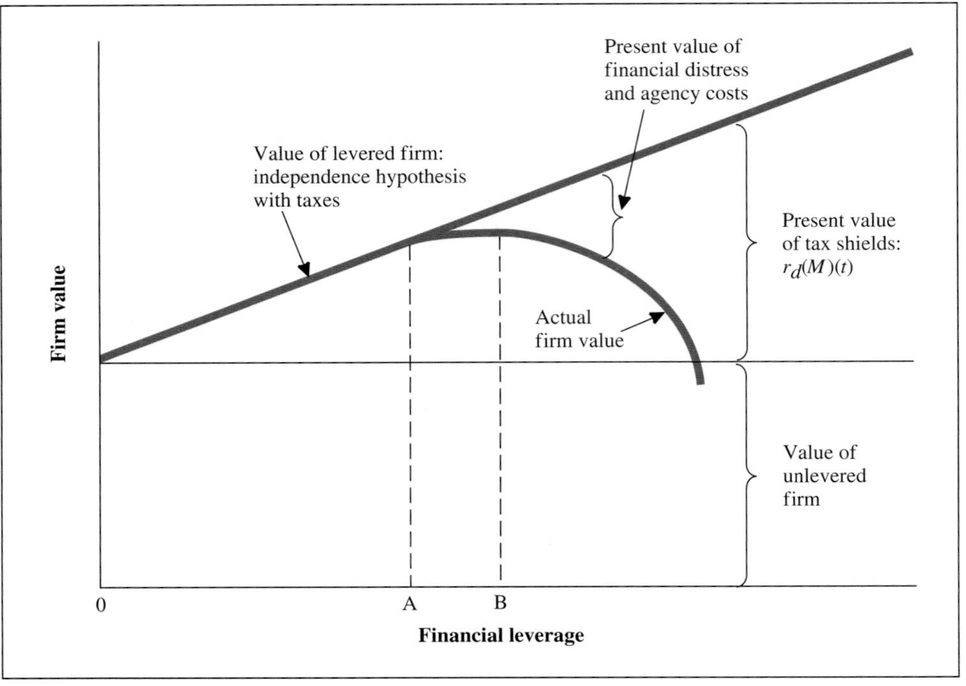


This discussion can be summarized by introducing equation 16-5 for the value of the levered firm. It represents the static trade-off model.

$$\begin{aligned}\begin{matrix}\text{market value}\\\text{of levered firm}\end{matrix} &= \begin{matrix}\text{market value of}\\\text{unlevered firm}\end{matrix} + \begin{matrix}\text{present value}\\\text{of tax shields}\end{matrix}\\ &\quad - \left(\begin{matrix}\text{present value}\\\text{of financial}\\\text{distress costs}\end{matrix} + \begin{matrix}\text{present value}\\\text{of agency}\\\text{costs}\end{matrix}\right)\end{aligned} \tag{16-5}$$

The relationship expressed in equation 16-5 is presented graphically in Figure 16-7. There we see that the tax shield effect is dominant until point *A* is reached. After point *A*, the rising costs of the likelihood of firm failure (financial distress) and agency costs cause the market value of the levered firm to decline. The objective for the financial manager here is to find point *B* by using all of his or her analytical skill; this must also include a good dose of seasoned judgment. At point *B*, the actual market value of the levered firm is maximized, and its composite cost of capital ($K_0$) is at a minimum. The implementation problem is that the precise costs of financial distress and monitoring can only be estimated by subjective means; a definite mathematical solution is not available. Thus, planning the firm's financing mix always requires good decision making and management judgment.

An alternative view aimed at predicting how managers will finance their firm's capital budgets is now known in the financial-economics literature as the "pecking order theory." The germ of this approach is found in the works of Gordon Donaldson. Specifically, see his two volumes: *Corporate Debt Capacity* (Cambridge, MA: Division of Research, Harvard University, 1961) and *Strategy for Financial Mobility* (Cambridge, MA: Division of Research, Harvard University, 1969).

Myers then expanded on Donaldson's insights in the "Capital Structure Puzzle," noted below, and in several other places, including "Still Searching for Optimal Capital Structure," which appeared in R. W. Kopcke and E. S. Rosengren, eds., *Are the Distinctions between Debt and Equity Disappearing?* (Boston: Federal Reserve Bank of Boston, 1989): 80–95.

In this latter article, Myers succinctly summarized the pecking order theory of capital structure with these four points (see pages 84–85):

1. Firms adapt dividend policy to investment opportunities. Note that this assumption is close to the concept of the *residual dividend theory* discussed in Chapter 17.
2. Firms prefer to finance investment opportunities with internally generated funds first; then external financial capital will be sought.
3. When external financing is needed, the firm will first choose to issue debt securities; issuing equity-type securities will be done last.
4. As more external financing is required to fund projects with positive net present values, the financing pecking order will be followed. This means a preference toward more risky debt, then to convertibles, preferred equity, and common equity as the last preference.

The upshot of this pecking order theory is that *no* precisely defined target leverage ratio really exists. This is because observed leverage ratios (that is, total debt to total assets) merely reflect the cumulative external financing needs of the firm over time.

## Agency Costs, Free Cash Flow, and Capital Structure

In 1986, Professor Michael C. Jensen further extended the concept of agency costs into the area of capital structure management. The contribution revolves around a concept that Jensen labels "free cash flow." Professor Jensen defines free cash flow as follows:[5]

> Free cash flow is cash flow in excess of that required to fund all projects that have positive net present values when discounted at the relevant cost of capital.

Jensen then puts forth that substantial free cash flow can lead to misbehavior by managers and poor decisions that are *not* in the best interests of the firm's common stockholders. In other words, managers have an incentive to hold on to the free cash flow and have "fun" with it, rather than "disgorging" it, say, in the form of higher cash dividend payments.

But all is not lost. This leads to what Jensen calls his "control hypothesis" for debt creation. By levering up, the firm's shareholders will enjoy increased control over their management team. For example, if the firm issues new debt and uses the proceeds to retire outstanding common stock, then management is obligated to pay out cash to service the debt—this simultaneously reduces the amount of free cash flow available to management with which to have fun.

We can also refer to this motive for financial leverage use as the "threat hypothesis." Management works under the threat of financial failure—therefore, according to the "free cash flow theory of capital structure," it works more efficiently. This is supposed to reduce the agency costs of free cash flow which will in turn be recognized by the marketplace in the form of greater returns on the common stock.

Note that the *free cash flow theory of capital structure* does not give a theoretical solution to the question of just how much financial leverage is enough. Nor does it suggest how much leverage is too much leverage. It is a way of thinking about why shareholders and their boards of directors might use more debt to control management behavior and decisions. The basic decision tools of capital structure management still have to be utilized. They will be presented later in this chapter.

[5]Michael Jensen, "Agency Costs of Free Cash Flow, Corporate Finance, and Takeovers," *American Economic Review* 76 (May 1986): 323–29.

**RELATE TO THE BIG PICTURE**

The discussions on agency costs, free cash flow, and the control hypothesis for debt creation return us to **Principle 7: The Agency Problem—Managers won't work for the owners unless it's in their best interest.** The control hypothesis put forth by Jensen suggests that managers will work harder for shareholder interests when they have to "sweat it out" to meet contractual interest payments on debt securities. But we also learned that managers and bond investors can have a conflict that leads to agency costs associated with using debt capital. Thus, the theoretical benefits that flow from minimizing the agency costs of free cash flow by using more debt will cease when the rising agency costs of debt exactly offset those benefits. You can see how very difficult it is, then, for financial managers to precisely identify their true optimal capital structure.

## Managerial Implications

Where does our examination of capital structure theory leave us? The upshot is that the determination of the firm's financing mix is centrally important to the financial manager. The firm's stockholders are affected by capital structure decisions.

At the very least, and before bankruptcy costs and agency costs become detrimental, the tax shield effect will cause the shares of a levered firm to sell at a higher price than they would if the company had avoided debt financing. Owing to both the risk of failure and agency costs that accompany the excessive use of leverage, the financial manager must exercise caution in the use of fixed-charge capital. This problem of searching for the optimal range of use of financial leverage is our next task.[6]

**CONCEPT CHECK**

1. What is the enduring controversy within the subject of capital structure theory?
2. Can you name the two financial economists, both of whom have won the Nobel Prize in economics, who back in 1958 challenged the importance of capital structure management?
3. Can you explain the independence hypothesis as it relates to capital structure management?
4. Can you explain the moderate view of the relationship between a firm's financing mix and its average cost of capital?
5. How do agency costs and free cash flow relate to capital structure management?

## BASIC TOOLS OF CAPITAL STRUCTURE MANAGEMENT

You have now developed a workable knowledge of capital structure theory. This makes you better equipped to search for your firm's optimal capital structure. Several tools are available to help you in this search process and simultaneously help you make prudent financing choices. These tools are decision oriented. They assist us in answering this

[6]The relationship between capital structure and enterprise valuation by the marketplace continues to stimulate considerable research output. The complexity of the topic is reviewed in Stewart C. Myers, "The Capital Structure Puzzle," *Journal of Finance* 39 (July 1984): 575–92. Ten useful papers are contained in Benjamin M. Friedman, ed., *Corporate Capital Structures in the United States* (Chicago: National Bureau of Economic Research and the University of Chicago Press, 1985).

**TABLE 16-4**
Pierce Grain Company Possible Capital Structures

| | | | |
|---|---|---|---|
| **Plan A: 0% debt** | | | |
| | | Total debt | $ 0 |
| | | Common equity | 200,000[a] |
| Total assets | $200,000 | Total liabilities and equity | $200,000 |
| **Plan B: 25% debt at 8% interest rate** | | | |
| | | Total debt | $ 50,000 |
| | | Common equity | 150,000[b] |
| Total assets | $200,000 | Total liabilities and equity | $200,000 |
| **Plan C: 40% debt at 8% interest rate** | | | |
| | | Total debt | $ 80,000 |
| | | Common equity | 120,000[c] |
| Total assets | $200,000 | Total liabilities and equity | $200,000 |

[a]2,000 common shares outstanding
[b]1,500 common shares outstanding
[c]1,200 common shares outstanding

**TABLE 16-5**
Pierce Grain Company Analysis of Financial Leverage at Different EBIT Levels

| (1) EBIT | (2) Interest | (3) = (1) − (2) EBT | (4) = (3) × .5 Taxes | (5) = (3)−(4) Net Income to Common | (6) Earnings per Share | |
|---|---|---|---|---|---|---|
| **Plan A: 0% debt; $200,000 common equity; 2,000 shares** | | | | | | |
| $ 0 | $ 0 | $ 0 | $ 0 | $ 0 | $ 0 | |
| 20,000 | 0 | 20,000 | 10,000 | 10,000 | 5.00 | } 100% |
| 40,000 | 0 | 40,000 | 20,000 | 20,000 | 10.00 | |
| 60,000 | 0 | 60,000 | 30,000 | 30,000 | 15.00 | |
| 80,000 | 0 | 80,000 | 40,000 | 40,000 | 20.00 | |
| **Plan B: 25% debt; 8% interest rate; $150,000 common equity, 1,500 shares** | | | | | | |
| $ 0 | $4,000 | $ (4,000) | $ (2,000)[a] | $ (2,000) | $ (1.33) | |
| 20,000 | 4,000 | 16,000 | 8,000 | 8,000 | 5.33 | } 125% |
| 40,000 | 4,000 | 36,000 | 18,000 | 18,000 | 12.00 | |
| 60,000 | 4,000 | 56,000 | 28,000 | 28,000 | 18.67 | |
| 80,000 | 4,000 | 76,000 | 38,000 | 38,000 | 25.33 | |
| **Plan C: 40% debt; 8% interest rate; $120,000 common equity; 1,200 shares** | | | | | | |
| $ 0 | $6,400 | $ (6,400) | $ (3,200)[a] | $ (3,200) | $ (2.67) | |
| 20,000 | 6,400 | 13,600 | 6,800 | 6,800 | 5.67 | } 147% |
| 40,000 | 6,400 | 33,600 | 16,800 | 16,800 | 14.00 | |
| 60,000 | 6,400 | 53,600 | 26,800 | 26,800 | 22.33 | |
| 80,000 | 6,400 | 73,600 | 36,800 | 36,800 | 30.67 | |

[a]The negative tax bill recognizes the credit arising from the carryback and carryforward provision of the tax code.

question: "The next time we need $20 million, should we issue common stock or sell long-term bonds?"

Recall from Chapter 15 that the use of financial leverage has two effects on the earnings stream flowing to the firm's common stockholders. For clarity of exposition, Tables 15-7 and 15-8 are repeated here as Tables 16-4 and 16-5. Three possible financing mixes for the Pierce Grain Company are contained in Table 16-4, and an analysis of the corresponding financial leverage effects is displayed in Table 16-5.

The *first financial leverage effect* is the added variability in the earnings-per-share stream that accompanies the use of fixed-charge securities in the company's capital structure. By means of the degree-of-financial-leverage measure ($DFL_{EBIT}$) we explained how

FINANCE MATTERS

## Ben Bernanke on the Free Cash Theory of Capital Structure and the Buildup in Corporate Debt

Business journalists and academic researchers alike generated several explanations for the seemingly heavy use of debt financing by corporations that persisted over most of the 1980s. Not all analysts accepted Jensen's control hypothesis for debt creation. Professor Bernanke had his doubts. He reviews Jensen's free cash flow theory and comments on the 1980s buildup in corporate leverage. The "incentive-based approach" is Bernanke's term for the free cash flow theory of capital structure.

---

The idea is that the financial structure of firms influences the incentives of "insiders" (managers, directors, and large shareholders with some operational interest in the business) and that, in particular, high levels of debt may increase the willingness of insiders to work hard and make profit-maximizing decisions. This incentive-based approach makes a valuable contribution to our understanding of a firm's capital structure. But while this theory might explain why firms like to use debt in general, does it explain why the use of debt has increased so much in recent years?

Michael Jensen, a founder and leading proponent of the incentive-based approach to capital structure, argues that it can. Jensen focuses on a recent worsening of what he calls the "free cash flow" problem. Free cash flow is defined as the portion of a corporation's cash flow that it is unable to invest profitably within the firm. Companies in industries that are profitable but no longer have much potential for expansion—the U.S. oil industry, for example—have a lot of free cash flow.

Why is free cash flow a problem? Jensen argues that managers are often tempted to use free cash flow to expand the size of the company, even if the expansion is not profitable. This is because managers feel that their power and job satisfaction are enhanced by a growing company; so given that most managers' compensation is at best weakly tied to the firm's profitability, Jensen argues that managers will find it personally worthwhile to expand even into money-losing operations. In principle, the board of directors and shareholders should be able to block these unprofitable investments; however, in practice, the fact that the management typically has far more information about potential investments than do outside directors and shareholders makes it difficult to second-guess the managers' recommendations.

**How More Leverage Can Help**

The company manager with lots of free cash flow may attempt to use that cash to increase his power and perquisites, at the expense of the shareholders. Jensen argues that the solution to the free cash-flow problem is more leverage. For example, suppose that management uses the free cash flow of the company, plus the proceeds of new debt issues, to repurchase stock from the outside shareholders—that is, to do a management buyout. This helps solve the free-cash-flow problem in several ways. The personal returns of the managers are now much more closely tied to the profits of the firm, which gives them incentives to be more efficient. Second, the releveraging process removes the existing free cash from the firm, so that any future investment projects will have to be financed externally; thus future projects will have to meet the market test of being acceptable to outside bankers or bond purchasers. Finally, the high interest payments implied by releveraging impose a permanent discipline on the managers; in order to meet these payments, they will have to ruthlessly cut money-losing operations, avoid questionable investments, and take other efficiency-promoting actions.

According to Jensen, a substantial increase in free-cash-flow problems—resulting from deregulation, the maturing of some large industries, and other factors—is a major source of the recent debt expansion. Jensen also points to a number of institutional factors that have promoted increased leverage. These include relaxed restrictions on mergers, which have lowered the barriers to corporate takeovers created by the antitrust laws and increased financial sophistication, such as the greatly expanded operations of takeover specialists like Drexel Burnham Lambert Inc. and the development of the market for "junk bonds." Jensen's diagnosis is not controversial: it's quite plausible that these factors, plus changing norms about what constitutes an "acceptable" level of debt, explain at least part of the trend toward increased corporate debt. One important piece of evidence in favor of this explanation is that net equity issues have been substantially negative since 1983. This suggests that much of the proceeds of the new debt issues is being used to repurchase outstanding shares. This is what we would expect if corporations are attempting to releverage their existing assets, rather than using debt to expand their asset holdings. However, the implied conclusion—that the debt buildup

this variability can be quantified. The firm that uses more financial leverage (rather than less) will experience larger relative changes in its earnings per share (rather than smaller) following EBIT fluctuations. Assume that Pierce Grain elected financing plan C rather than plan A. Plan C is highly levered and plan A is unlevered. A 100 percent increase in EBIT from \$20,000 to \$40,000 would cause earnings per share to rise by 147 percent under plan

FINANCE MATTERS

(continued)

is beneficial overall to the economy—is considerably more controversial.

**Criticisms of the Incentive-Based Rationale for Increased Debt**

Jensen and other advocates of the incentive-based approach to capital structure have made a cogent theoretical case for the beneficial effects of debt finance, and many architects of large-scale restructurings have given improved incentives and the promise of greater efficiency as a large part of the rationale for increased leverage. The idea that leverage is beneficial has certainly been embraced by the stock market: even unsubstantiated rumors of a potential leveraged buyout (LBO) have been sufficient to send the stock price of the targeted company soaring, often by 40 percent or more. At a minimum, this indicates that stock market participants *believe* that higher leverage increases profitability. Proponents of restructuring interpret this as evidence that debt is good for the economy.

There are, however, criticisms of this conclusion. First, the fact that the stock market's expectations of company profitability rise when there is a buyout is not proof that profits will rise in actuality. It is still too soon to judge whether the increased leverage of the 1980s will lead to a sustained increase in profitability. One might think of looking to historical data for an answer to this question. But buyouts in the 1960s and 1970s were somewhat different in character from more recent restructurings, and, in any case, the profitability evidence on the earlier episodes is mixed.

Even if the higher profits expected by the stock market do materialize, there is contention over where they are likely to come from. The incentive-based theory of capital structure says they will come from improved efficiency. But some opponents have argued that the higher profits will primarily reflect transfers to the shareholders from other claimants on the corporation—its employees, customers, suppliers, bondholders, and the government. Customers may be hurt if takeovers are associated with increased monopolization of markets. Bondholders have been big losers in some buyouts, as higher leverage has increased bankruptcy risk and thus reduced the value of outstanding bonds. The government may have lost tax revenue, as companies, by increasing leverage, have increased their interest deductions (although there are offsetting effects here, such as the taxes paid by bought-out shareholders on their capital gains). The perception that much of the profits associated with releveraging and buyouts comes from "squeezing" existing beneficiaries of the corporation explains much of the recent political agitation to limit these activities.

The debt buildup can also be criticized from the perspective of incentive-based theories themselves. Two points are worth noting: first, the principal problem that higher leverage is supposed to address is the relatively weak connection between firms' profits and managers' personal returns, which reduces managers' incentives to take profit-maximizing actions. But if this is truly the problem, it could be addressed more directly—without subjecting the company to serious bankruptcy risk—simply by changing managerial compensation schemes to include more profit-based incentives.

**The Downside of Debt Financing**

Increased debt is not the optimal solution to all incentive problems. For example, it has been shown, as a theoretical proposition, that managers of debt-financed firms have an incentive to choose riskier projects over safe ones; this is because firms with fixed-debt obligations enjoy all of the upside potential of high-risk projects but share the downside losses with the debt holders, who are not fully repaid if bad investment outcomes cause the firm to fail.

That high leverage does not always promote efficiency can be seen when highly leveraged firms suffer losses and find themselves in financial distress. When financial problems hit, the need to meet interest payments may force management to take a very short-run perspective, leading them to cut back production and employment, cancel even potentially profitable expansion projects, and sell assets at fire-sale prices. Because the risk of bankruptcy is so great, firms in financial distress cannot make long-term agreements; they lose customers and suppliers who are afraid they cannot count on an ongoing relationship, and they must pay wage premiums to hire workers.

These efficiency losses, plus the direct costs of bankruptcy (such as legal fees), are the potential downside of high leverage.

Source: Ben Bernanke, "Is There Too Much Corporate Debt?" *Business Review,* Federal Reserve Bank of Philadelphia (September–October 1989): 5–8.

C, but only 100 percent under plan A. Unfortunately, the effect would operate in the negative direction as well. A given change in EBIT is *magnified* by the use of financial leverage. This magnification is reflected in the variability of the firm's earnings per share.

The *second financial leverage effect* concerns the level of earnings per share at a given EBIT under a given capital structure. Refer to Table 16-5. At the EBIT level of

$20,000, earnings per share would be $5, $5.33, and $5.67 under financing arrangements A, B, and C, respectively. Above a critical level of EBIT, the firm's earnings per share will be higher if greater degrees of financial leverage are employed. Conversely, below some critical level of EBIT, earnings per share will suffer at greater degrees of financial leverage. Whereas the first financial-leverage effect is quantified by the degree-of-financial-leverage measure ($DFL_{EBIT}$), the second is quantified by what is generally referred to as EBIT–EPS analysis. EPS refers, of course, to earnings per share. The rationale underlying this sort of analysis is simple. Earnings is one of the key variables that influences the market value of the firm's common stock. The effect of a financing decision on EPS, then, should be understood because the decision will probably affect the value of the stockholders' investment.

## EBIT–EPS Analysis

**EXAMPLE**

Assume that plan B in Table 16-5 is the existing capital structure for Pierce Grain Company. Furthermore, the asset structure of the firm is such that EBIT is expected to be $20,000 per year for a very long time. A capital investment is available to Pierce Grain that will cost $50,000. Acquisition of this asset is expected to raise the projected EBIT level to $30,000, permanently. The firm can raise the needed cash by (1) selling 500 shares of common stock at $100 each or (2) selling new bonds that will net the firm $50,000 and carry an interest rate of 8.5 percent. These capital structures and corresponding EPS amounts are summarized in Table 16-6.

**TABLE 16-6**
Pierce Grain Company Analysis of Financing Choices

| Part A: Capital Structures | Existing Capital Structure | | With New Common Stock Financing | | With New Debt Financing |
|---|---|---|---|---|---|
| Long-term debt at 8% | $ 50,000 | Long-term debt at 8% | $ 50,000 | Long-term debt at 8% | $ 50,000 |
| Common stock | 150,000 | Common stock | 200,000 | Long-term debt at 8.5% | 50,000 |
| | | | | Common stock | 150,000 |
| Total liabilities and equity | $ 200,000 | Total liabilities and equity | $ 250,000 | Total liabilities and equity | $ 250,000 |
| Common shares outstanding | 1,500 | Common shares outstanding | 2,000 | Common shares outstanding | 1,500 |

| Part B: Projected EPS Levels | Existing Capital Structure | With New Common Stock Financing | With New Debt Financing |
|---|---|---|---|
| EBIT | $ 20,000 | $ 30,000 | $ 30,000 |
| Less: Interest expense | 4,000 | 4,000 | 8,250 |
| Earnings before taxes (EBT) | $ 16,000 | $ 26,000 | $ 21,750 |
| Less: Taxes at 50% | 8,000 | 13,000 | 10,875 |
| Net Income | $ 8,000 | $ 13,000 | $ 10,875 |
| Less: Preferred dividends | 0 | 0 | 0 |
| Earnings available to common | $ 8,000 | $ 13,000 | $ 10,875 |
| EPS | $ 5.33 | $ 6.50 | $ 7.25 |

At the projected EBIT level of $30,000, the EPS for the common stock and debt alternatives are $6.50 and $7.25, respectively. Both are considerably above the $5.33 that would occur if the new project were rejected and the additional financial capital were not raised. Based on a criterion of selecting the financing plan that will provide the highest EPS, the bond alternative is favored. But what if the basic business risk to which the firm is exposed causes the EBIT level to vary over a considerable range? Can we be sure that the bond alternative will *always* have the higher EPS associated with it? The answer, of course, is "No." When the EBIT level is subject to uncertainty, a graphic analysis of the proposed financing plans can provide useful information to the financial manager.

**GRAPHIC ANALYSIS** The EBIT–EPS analysis chart allows the decision maker to visualize the impact of different financing plans on EPS over a range of EBIT levels. The relationship between EPS and EBIT is linear. Therefore, to construct the chart we only need two points for each alternative. Part B of Table 16-6 already provides us with one of these points. The answer to the following question for each choice gives us the second point: At what EBIT level will the EPS for the plan be exactly zero? If the EBIT level just covers the plan's financing costs (on a before-tax basis), then EPS will be zero. For the stock plan, an EPS of zero is associated with an EBIT of $4,000. The $4,000 is the interest expense incurred under the existing capital structure. If the bond plan is elected, the interest costs will be the present $4,000 plus $4,250 per year arising from the new debt issue. An EBIT of $8,250, then, is necessary to provide a zero EPS with the bond plan.

The EBIT–EPS analysis chart representing the financing choices available to the Pierce Grain Company is shown as Figure 16-8. EBIT is charted on the horizontal axis and EPS on the vertical axis. The intercepts on the horizontal axis represent the before-tax equivalent financing charges related to each plan. The straight lines for each plan tell us the EPS amounts that will occur at different EBIT amounts.

Notice that the bond-plan line has a *steeper slope* than the stock-plan line. This ensures that the lines for each financing choice will *intersect.* Above the intersection point, EPS for the plan with greater leverage will exceed that for the plan with lesser leverage. The intersection point, encircled in Figure 16-8, occurs at an EBIT level of $21,000 and produces EPS of $4.25 for each plan. When EBIT is $30,000, notice that the bond plan produces EPS of $7.25 and the stock plan, $6.50. Below the intersection point, EPS with the stock plan will *exceed* that with the more highly levered bond plan. The steeper slope of the bond-plan line indicates that with greater leverage, EPS is more sensitive to EBIT changes. This same concept was discussed in Chapter 15 when we derived the degree of financial leverage measure.

**COMPUTING INDIFFERENCE POINTS** The point of intersection in Figure 16-8 is called the **EBIT–EPS indifference point.** It identifies the EBIT level at which the EPS will be the same regardless of the financing plan chosen by the financial manager. This indifference point, sometimes called the breakeven point, has major implications for financial planning. At EBIT amounts in excess of the EBIT indifference level, the more heavily levered financing plan will generate a higher EPS. At EBIT amounts below the EBIT indifference level, the financing plan involving less leverage will generate a higher EPS. It is important, then, to know the EBIT indifference level.

**EBIT–EPS indifference point**
The level of earnings before interest and taxes (EBIT) that will equate earnings per share (EPS) between two different financing plans.

We can find it graphically, as in Figure 16-8. At times it may be more efficient, though, to calculate the indifference point directly. This can be done by using the following equation:

$$\overset{\textit{EPS: Stock Plan}}{\frac{(EBIT - I)(1 - t) - P}{S_s}} = \overset{\textit{EPS: Bond Plan}}{\frac{(EBIT - I)(1 - t) - P}{S_b}} \tag{16-6}$$

**FIGURE 16-8**
EBIT–EPS Analysis Chart

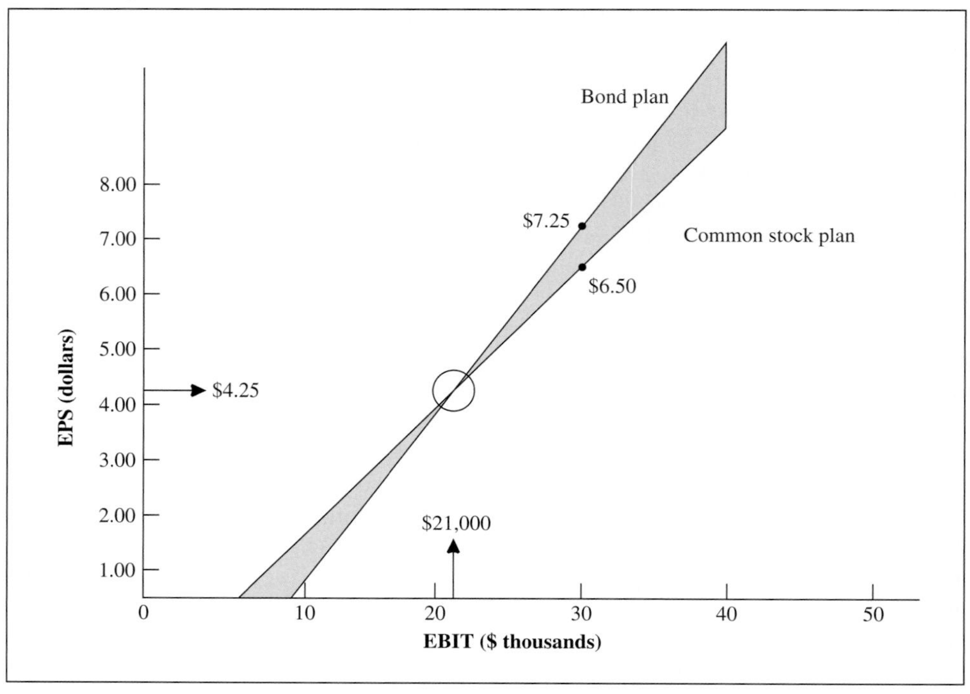


where $S_s$ and $S_b$ are the number of common shares outstanding under the stock and bond plans, respectively, $I$ is interest expense, $t$ is the firm's income tax rate, and $P$ is preferred dividends paid. In the present case, $P$ is zero because there is no preferred stock outstanding. If preferred stock is associated with one of the financing alternatives, keep in mind that the preferred dividends, $P$, are not tax deductible. Equation 16-6 *does* take this fact into consideration.

For the present example, we calculate the indifference level of EBIT as:

$$\frac{(EBIT - \$4{,}000)(1 - 0.5) - 0}{2{,}000} = \frac{(EBIT - \$8{,}250)(1 - 0.5) - 0}{1{,}500}$$

When the expression is solved for EBIT, we obtain $21,000. If EBIT turns out to be $21,000, then EPS will be $4.25 under both plans.

**UNCOMMITTED EARNINGS PER SHARE AND INDIFFERENCE POINTS** The calculations that permitted us to solve for Pierce Grain's EBIT–EPS indifference point made no explicit allowance for the repayment of the bond principal. This procedure is not that unrealistic. It only presumes the debt will be perpetually outstanding. This means that when the current bond issue matures, a new bond issue will be floated. The proceeds from the newer issue would be used to pay off the maturity value of the older issue.

**Sinking fund**
A cash reserve used for the orderly and early retirement of the principal amount of a bond issue. Payments into the fund are known as sinking fund payments.

Many bond contracts, however, require that **sinking fund payments** be made to a bond trustee. A **sinking fund** is a real cash reserve that is used to provide for the orderly and early retirement of the principal amount of the bond issue. Most often the sinking fund payment is a mandatory fixed amount and is required by a clause in the bond indenture. Sinking fund payments can represent a sizable cash drain on the firm's liquid resources. Moreover, sinking fund payments are a return of borrowed principal, so they are *not* tax deductible to the firm.

Because of the potentially serious nature of the cash drain caused by sinking fund requirements, the financial manager might be concerned with the uncommitted earnings per share (UEPS) related to each financing plan. The calculation of UEPS recognizes that sinking fund commitments have been honored. UEPS can be used, then, for discretionary spending—such as the payment of cash dividends to common stockholders or investment in capital facilities.

If we let *SF* be the sinking fund payment required in a given year, the EBIT–UEPS indifference point can be calculated as:

$$\overset{\textit{UEPS: Stock Plan}}{\frac{(EBIT - I)(1 - t) - P - SF}{S_s}} = \overset{\textit{UEPS: Bond Plan}}{\frac{(EBIT - I)(1 - t) - P - SF}{S_b}} \qquad \textbf{(16-7)}$$

If several bond issues are already outstanding, then *I* in equations 16-6 and 16-7 for the stock plan consists of the sum of their related interest payments. For the bond plan, *I* would be the sum of existing plus new interest charges. In equation 16-7 the same logic applies to the sinking fund variable, *SF.* The indifference level of EBIT based on UEPS will always exceed that based on EPS.

A WORD OF CAUTION Above the EBIT–EPS indifference point, a more heavily levered financial plan promises to deliver a larger EPS. Strict application of the criterion of selecting the financing plan that produces the highest EPS might have the firm issuing debt most of the time it raised external capital. Our discussion of capital structure theory taught us the dangers of that sort of action.

The primary weakness of EBIT–EPS analysis is that it disregards the implicit costs of debt financing. The effect of the specific financing decision on the firm's cost of common equity capital is totally ignored. Investors should be concerned with both the *level and variability* of the firm's expected earnings stream. EBIT–EPS analysis considers only the level of the earnings stream and ignores the variability (riskiness) inherent in it. Thus, this type of analysis must be used in conjunction with other basic tools in reaching the objective of capital structure management.

**RELATE TO THE BIG PICTURE**

The companion techniques of EBIT–EPS analysis and Uncommitted Earnings per Share analysis are well-known within the corporate financial planning groups of corporations. It is useful to emphasize that these tools of capital structure management are best utilized if we relate them to both **Principle 3: Cash—Not Profits—Is King,** and **Principle 6: Efficient Capital Markets—The markets are quick and the prices are right.**

Thus, the cash flows, as opposed to accounting profits, that are available to the firm after a financing choice is made will drive market prices. Recall from Chapter 1 that we said *efficient markets* will not be fooled by accounting changes that merely manipulate reported earnings. In the context of using these tools, then, the proper way to think of earnings per share and uncommitted earnings per share is on a cash basis rather than on an accounting accrual basis. The firm services its debt contracts not out of accounting earnings, but out of cash flows.

## Comparative Leverage Ratios

In Chapter 3, we explored the overall usefulness of financial ratio analysis. Leverage ratios are one of the categories of financial ratios identified in that chapter. We emphasize here that the computation of leverage ratios is one of the basic tools of capital structure management.

FINANCE MATTERS

## The Walt Disney Company on Capital Costs and Capital Structure

At the end of fiscal year 1998, The Walt Disney Company had a total market capitalization of $65 billion; this placed it among the 40 largest corporations in the United States, while its sales revenues of $23 billion placed it 53rd on the 1999 *Fortune* 500 list. This multinational giant with 117,000 employees provides several real examples of the capital structure concepts presented in this chapter.

In the discussion that follows from Disney management, notice how the firm (1) relates capital costs to shareholder value, (2) believes in the "prudent degree of leverage" concept, (3) is concerned with its interest coverage ratio—measured as earnings before net interest, taxes, depreciation, and amortization or EBITDA divided by net interest expense, and (4) strives to maintain a minimum desired or target bond rating. Within the accompanying graph you will see that Disney's coverage ratio for fiscal year 1998 of EBITDA to net interest expense is 8.1 times (i.e., $5,019 million/$622 million).

Disney's solid balance sheet allows the company to borrow at attractive rates, helping to reduce the overall cost of capital and thereby creating value for shareholders. As of year end, Disney maintained total borrowings of approximately $12 billion and a debt-to-total-capital ratio of 38 percent. The company believes that this level of debt represents a prudent degree of leverage, which provides for substantial financial flexibility to borrow should business opportunities present themselves. As measured by the ratio of earnings before net interest, taxes, depreciation, and amortization (EBITDA) to net interest expense, the company covered its interest costs by a factor of more than eight times for the year ended September 30.

The Walt Disney Company 1998
Net Interest Expense Coverage

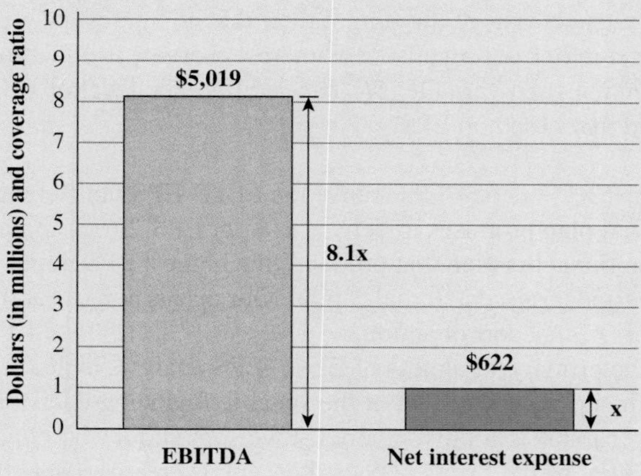


The company monitors its cash flow, interest coverage, and its debt-to-total-capital ratio with the long-term goal of maintaining a strong single-A or better credit rating.

Source: The Walt Disney Company, *1998 Annual Report*, 12.

Two types of leverage ratios must be computed when a financing decision faces the firm. We call these *balance sheet leverage ratios* and *coverage ratios.* The firm's balance sheet supplies inputs for computing the balance sheet leverage ratios. In various forms, these balance sheet metrics compare the firm's use of funds supplied by creditors with those supplied by owners.

Inputs to the coverage ratios *generally* come from the firm's income statement. At times, the external analyst may have to consult balance sheet information to construct some of these needed estimates. On a privately placed debt issue, for example, some fraction of the current portion of the firm's long-term debt might have to be used as an estimate of that issue's sinking fund. Coverage ratios provide estimates of the firm's ability to service its financing contracts. High coverage ratios, compared with a standard, imply unused debt capacity.

**A WORKSHEET** Table 16-7 is a sample worksheet used to analyze financing choices. The objective of the analysis is to determine the effect each financing plan will have on key financial ratios. The financial officer can compare the existing level of each ratio with its projected level, taking into consideration the contractual commitments of each alternative.

In reality, we know that EBIT might be expected to vary over a considerable range of outcomes. For this reason the coverage ratios should be calculated several times, each at a different level of EBIT. If this is accomplished over all possible values of EBIT, a proba-

**TABLE 16-7**
Comparative Leverage Ratios: Worksheet for Analyzing Financing Plans

| Ratios | Computation Method | Existing Ratio | Ratio with New Common Stock Financing | Ratio with New Debt Financing |
|---|---|---|---|---|
| **Balance sheet leverage ratios** | | | | |
| 1. Debt ratio | $\frac{\text{total liabilities}}{\text{total assets}}$ | ___% | ___% | ___% |
| 2. Long-term debt to total capitalization | $\frac{\text{long-term debt}}{\text{long-term debt} + \text{net worth}}$ | ___% | ___% | ___% |
| 3. Total liabilities to net worth | $\frac{\text{total liabilities}}{\text{net worth}}$ | ___% | ___% | ___% |
| 4. Common equity ratio | $\frac{\text{common equity}}{\text{total assets}}$ | ___% | ___% | ___% |
| **Coverage ratios** | | | | |
| 1. Times interest earned | $\frac{\text{EBIT}}{\text{annual interest expense}}$ | ___ times | ___ times | ___ times |
| 2. Times burden covered | $\frac{\text{EBIT}}{\text{interest} + \frac{\text{sinking fund}}{1 - t}}$ | ___ times | ___ times | ___ times |
| 3. Cash flow overall coverage ratio | $\frac{\text{EBIT} + \text{lease expense} + \text{depreciation}}{\text{interest} + \text{lease expense} + \frac{\text{preferred dividends}}{1 - t} + \frac{\text{principal payments}}{1 - t}}$ | ___ times | ___ times | ___ times |

bility distribution for each coverage ratio can be constructed. This provides the financial manager with much more information than simply calculating the coverage ratios based on the expected value of EBIT.

**INDUSTRY NORMS** The comparative leverage ratios calculated according to the format laid out in Table 16-7, or in a similar format, have additional utility to the decision maker if they can be compared with some standard. Generally, corporate financial analysts, investment bankers, commercial bank loan officers, and bond-rating agencies rely on industry classes from which to compute "normal" ratios. Although industry groupings may actually contain firms whose basic business risk exposure differs widely, the practice is entrenched in American business behavior.[7] At the very least, then, the financial officer must be interested in *industry standards* because almost everybody else is.

Several published studies indicate that capital structure ratios vary in a significant manner among industry classes.[8] For example, random samplings of the common equity ratios of

[7] An approach to grouping firms based on several component measures of business risk, as opposed to ordinary industry classes, is reported in John D. Martin, David F. Scott, Jr., and Robert F. Vandell, "Equivalent Risk Classes: A Multidimensional Examination," *Journal of Financial and Quantitative Analysis* 14 (March 1979): 101–18.

[8] See, for example, Eli Schwartz and J. Richard Aronson, "Some Surrogate Evidence in Support of the Concept of Optimal Financial Structure," *Journal of Finance* 22 (March 1967): 10–18; David F. Scott, Jr., "Evidence on the Importance of Financial Structure," *Financial Management* 1 (Summer 1972): 45–50; and David F. Scott, Jr., and John D. Martin, "Industry Influence on Financial Structure," *Financial Management* 4 (Spring 1975): 67–73.

**FINANCE MATTERS**

### Georgia-Pacific on Capital Structure

The introduction to this chapter referred to the Georgia-Pacific Corporation's financial strategies and management of its capital structure. The following discussion further illustrates the care that this firm's key officers place on managing its financing mix and also alerts you to the subject of the next section.

---

Georgia-Pacific tries to balance the mix of debt and equity in a way that will benefit our shareholders, by keeping our weighted average cost of capital low, while retaining the flexibility needed to finance attractive internal projects or acquisitions. Risk factors that contribute to the volatility of our cash flows include economic cycles, changes in industry capacity, environmental regulations, and litigation.

On a market-value basis, our debt-to-capital ratio was 47 percent (year-end 1996). By employing this capital structure, we believe that our weighted average cost of capital is nearly optimized—at approximately 10 percent. Although reducing debt significantly would somewhat reduce the marginal cost of debt, significant debt reduction would likely increase our weighted average cost of capital by raising the proportion of higher-cost equity.

Considering Georgia-Pacific's ability to generate strong cash flow—even at the bottom of the cycle—we believe the current debt structure is quite manageable. In fact, combining the lowest full-year cash flows from building products and pulp and paper operations over recent business cycles would still provide enough cash to pay taxes, cover interest on $5.5 billion of debt, pay dividends and fund several hundred million dollars of reinvestment needed to maintain our facilities in competitive condition.

Source: *Georgia-Pacific 1996 Annual Report,* 15.

large retail firms seem to differ statistically from those of major steel producers. The major steel producers use financial leverage to a lesser degree than do the large retail organizations. On the whole, firms operating in the *same* industry tend to exhibit capital structure ratios that cluster around a central value, which we call a norm. Business risk will vary from industry to industry. As a consequence, the capital structure norms will vary from industry to industry.

This is not to say that all companies in the industry will maintain leverage ratios "close" to the norm. For instance, firms that are very profitable may display *high* coverage ratios and *high* balance sheet leverage ratios. The moderately profitable firm, though, might find such a posture unduly risky. Here the usefulness of industry normal leverage ratios is clear. If the firm chooses to deviate in a material manner from the accepted values for the key ratios, it must have a sound reason.

## Companywide Cash Flows: What Is the Worst that Could Happen?

In Chapter 3, we noted that liquidity ratios are designed to measure the ability of the firm to pay its bills on time. Financing charges are just another type of bill that eventually comes due for payment. Interest charges, preferred dividends, lease charges, and principal payments all must be paid on time, or the company risks being caught in bankruptcy proceedings. To a lesser extent, dispensing with financing charges on an other than timely basis can result in severely restricted business operations. We have just seen that coverage ratios provide a measure of the safety of one general class of payment—financing charges. Coverage ratios, then, and liquidity ratios are very close in concept.

A more comprehensive method is available for studying the impact of capital structure decisions on corporate cash flows. The method is simple but nonetheless very valuable. It involves the preparation of a series of cash budgets under (1) different economic conditions and (2) different capital structures. The net cash flows under these different situations can be examined to determine if the financing requirements expose the firm to a degree of default risk too high to bear.

In work that has been highly acclaimed, Donaldson has suggested that the firm's debt-carrying capacity (defined in the broad sense here to include preferred dividend payments and lease payments) ought to depend on the net cash flows the firm could expect to receive during a recessionary period.[9] In other words, *target capital structure proportions* could be set by planning for the "worst that could happen." An example will be of help.

Suppose that a recession is expected to last for 1 year.[10] Moreover, the end of the year represents the bottoming-out, or worst portion of the recession. Equation 16-8 defines the cash balance, $CB_r$, the firm could expect to have at the end of the recession period.[11]

$$CB_r = C_0 + (C_s + OR) - (P_a + RM + \ldots + E_n) - FC \tag{16-8}$$

where $C_0$ = the cash balance at the beginning of the recession
$C_s$ = collection from sales
$OR$ = other cash receipts
$P_a$ = payroll expenditures
$RM$ = raw material payments
$E_n$ = the last of a long series of expenditures over which management has little control (nondiscretionary expenditures)
$FC$ = fixed financial charges associated with a specific capital structure

If we let the net of total cash receipts and nondiscretionary expenditures be represented by $NCF_r$, then equation 16-8 can be simplified to:

$$CB_r = C_0 + NCF_r - FC \tag{16-9}$$

The inputs to equation 16-9 come from a detailed cash budget. The variable representing financing costs, $FC$, can be changed in accordance with several alternative financing plans to ascertain if the net cash balance during the recession, $CB_r$, might fall below zero.

Suppose that some firm typically maintains \$500,000 in cash and marketable securities. This amount would be on hand at the start of the recession period. During the economic decline, the firm projects that its net cash flows from operations, $NCF_r$, will be \$2 million. If the firm currently finances its assets with an unlevered capital structure, its cash balance at the worst point of the recession would be:

$$CB_r = \$500{,}000 + \$2{,}000{,}000 - \$0 = \$2{,}500{,}000$$

This procedure allows us to study many different situations.[12] Assume that the same firm is considering a shift in its capitalization such that annual interest and sinking fund payments will be \$2,300,000. If a recession occurred, the firm's cash balance at the end of the adverse economic period would be:

$$CB_r = \$500{,}000 + \$2{,}000{,}000 - \$2{,}300{,}000 = \$200{,}000$$

The firm ordinarily maintains a liquid asset balance of \$500,000. Thus, the effect of the proposed capital structure on the firm's cash balance during adverse circumstances might seem too risky for management to accept. When the chance of being out of cash is too high for management to bear, the use of financial leverage has been pushed beyond a reasonable level. According to this tool, the appropriate level of financial leverage is reached when the chance of being out of cash is exactly equal to that which management will assume.

[9]Refer to Gordon Donaldson, "New Framework for Corporate Debt Policy," *Harvard Business Review* 40 (March–April 1962): 117–31; Gordon Donaldson, *Corporate Debt Capacity* (Boston: Division of Research, Graduate School of Business Administration, Harvard University, 1961), chap. 7; and Gordon Donaldson, "Strategy for Financial Emergencies," *Harvard Business Review 47* (November–December 1969): 67–79.

[10]The analysis can readily be extended to cover a recessionary period of several years. All that is necessary is to calculate the cash budgets over a similar period.

[11]For the most part, the present notation follows that of Donaldson.

[12]It is not difficult to improve the usefulness of this sort of analysis by applying the technique of simulation to the generation of the various cash budgets. This facilitates the construction of probability distributions of net cash flows under differing circumstances.

**CONCEPT CHECK**

1. Explain the meaning of the EBIT–EPS indifference point.
2. How are various leverage ratios and industry norms used in capital structure management?

## THE MULTINATIONAL FIRM: BEWARE OF CURRENCY RISK

OBJECTIVE 7 

When the euro was introduced as a new currency by the 11 countries comprising the European Union on January 1, 1999, it took .8455 euros to buy $1 in foreign exchange markets. By November 15, 2000, it took a greater 1.1663 euros to acquire that same U.S. dollar. That amounted to a relative increase of 37.94 percent as measured in euros to buy that dollar ([1.1663/.8455] − 1). The euro depreciated in value against the dollar; the dollar appreciated against the euro. Such variations in the value of foreign currencies can at times cause big headaches for U.S. financial executives.

The financial-economic reason underlying the headache is straightforward. The U.S. multinational firm, for financial reporting purposes, must convert earnings denominated in foreign currencies into dollars. So, firms with large volumes of sales in non-U.S. markets are exposed to a large degree of currency risk. You can understand, then, that firms with an already high exposure to currency value changes might reasonably choose to avoid incurring high levels of financial risk. The currency risk challenge occurs quite often.

Consider that on September 14, 2000, the common stock price of Colgate-Palmolive declined by 16 percent after security analysts warned of likely lower reported earnings due to a high level of European sales exposure and euro conversion risk. On that same day, McDonalds' common stock fell by 5 percent for the same reason—a decline in the relative value of the euro. And, a few weeks earlier, Harley-Davidson reported on July 12, 2000, that its gross profit margin declined due partially to "weakening European currencies." Managing currency risk, then, is a daily activity for the finance function of the multinational firm. Note that Chapter 22 on International Finance includes a more detailed discussion of currency risk and management.

**CONCEPT CHECK**

1. Why can a stronger value of the U.S. dollar relative to a foreign currency like the euro pose a problem for financial executives of multinational firms?
2. Why might firms that derive a large proportion of their total sales from overseas markets choose not to utilize large degrees of financial leverage?

## HOW FINANCIAL MANAGERS USE THIS MATERIAL

OBJECTIVE 8 

Our study of capital structure management has included examples of actual practice from several corporations including Georgia-Pacific, Texas Instruments, Medtronic, and General Mills. More emphasis and examples dealing with how financial managers use the main concepts from this chapter are presented in this section.

We have discussed (1) the concept of an optimal capital structure, (2) the search for an appropriate range of financial leverage, and (3) the fundamental tools of capital structure management. Now we will examine some opinions and practices of financial executives that support our emphasis on the importance of capital structure management.

FINANCE MATTERS

## Corporate Policies on Using Financial Leverage

Managements continually face the challenge of determining how much financial leverage is enough. The statements that follow from Texas Instruments, General Mills, and Medtronic, Inc., deal with this difficult financial policy question.

**Texas Instruments**

TI's financial condition continued to strengthen in 1993. The company made further progress toward management's goal of reducing TI's debt-to-total capital ratio and generated positive cash flow net of additions to property, plant, and equipment.

TI's debt-to-total-capital ratio was .28 at the end of the year, down .01 from the third quarter and down .05 from year-end 1992. TI's goal is to reduce this ratio to about .25.

**General Mills**

Our major financial targets for top-decile performance include: Meeting or exceeding a 20 percent after-tax return on invested capital and 38 percent return on equity. Our ROC and ROE, before unusual items, have averaged 21 percent and 43 percent, respectively, during the past 3 years.

Maintaining a balance sheet with a strong A bond rating. Financial ratios, including a cash flow to debt ratio of 53 percent and a fixed charge coverage of 7.8 times, continued strong in 1993. The purchase of 6.3 million shares for our treasury, which both increased debt and reduced stockholders' equity, increased our debt-to-capital ratio to 63 percent.

**Medtronic**

The company's capital structure consists of equity and interest-bearing debt. The company utilizes long-term debt minimally. Interest-bearing debt as a percent of total capital was 10.9 percent at April 30, 1993, compared with 10.1 percent and 12.6 percent at April 30, 1992 and 1991, respectively. These ratios are well within the company's financial objective of maintaining a debt-to-total-capital ratio not exceeding 30 percent.

Source: *Texas Instruments, 1993 Annual Report,* 36; *General Mills, 1993 Annual Report,* 19; and *Medtronic, 1993 Annual Report,* 36.

The Conference Board has surveyed 170 senior financial officers with respect to their capital structure practices.[13] Of these 170 executives, 102, or 60 percent, stated that they *do* believe there is an optimum capital structure for the corporation. Sixty-five percent of the responding practitioners worked for firms with annual sales in excess of $200 million. One executive who subscribed to the optimal capital structure concept stated:

> In my opinion, there is an optimum capital structure for companies. However, this optimum capital structure will vary by individual companies, industries, and then is subject to changing economies, by money markets, earnings trends, and prospects . . . the circumstances and the lenders will determine an optimum at different points in time.[14]

This survey and others consistently point out that (1) financial officers set target debt ratios for their companies, and (2) the values for those ratios are influenced by a conscious evaluation of the basic business risk to which the firm is exposed.

## Target Debt Ratios

Selected comments from financial executives point to the widespread use of target debt ratios. A vice-president and treasurer of the American Telephone and Telegraph Company (AT&T) described his firm's debt ratio policy in terms of a range:

> All of the foregoing considerations led us to conclude, and reaffirm for a period of many years, that the proper range of our debt was 30 percent to 40 percent of total capital. Reasonable success in meeting financial needs under the diverse market and economic conditions that we have faced attests to the appropriateness of this conclusion.[15]

[13]Francis J. Walsh, Jr., *Planning Corporate Capital Structures* (New York: The Conference Board, 1972).

[14]Walsh, *Planning Corporate Capital Structures,* 14.

[15]John J. Scanlon, "Bell System Financial Policies," *Financial Management* 1 (Summer 1972): 16–26.

**TABLE 16-8**
Setting Target Financial Structure Ratios

| Type of Influence | Rank 1 | Rank 2 |
|---|---|---|
| Internal management and staff analysts | 85% | 7% |
| Investment bankers | 3 | 39 |
| Commercial bankers | 0 | 9 |
| Trade creditors | 1 | 0 |
| Security analysts | 1 | 4 |
| Comparative industry ratios | 3 | 23 |
| Other | 7 | 18 |
| Total | 100% | 100% |

Source: David F. Scott, Jr., and Dana J. Johnson, "Financing Policies and Practices in Large Corporations," *Financial Management* 11 (Summer 1982), p.53.

In a similar fashion, the president of Fibreboard Corporation identified his firm's target debt ratio and noted how it is related to the uncertain nature of the company's business:

> Our objective is a 30 percent ratio of debt to capitalization. We need that kind of flexibility to operate in the cyclical business we are in.[16]

In the Conference Board survey mentioned earlier, 84 of the 102 financial officers who subscribed to the optimal capital structure concept stated that their firm *has* a target debt ratio.[17] The most frequently mentioned influence on the level of the target debt ratio was ability to meet financing charges. Other factors identified as affecting the target were (1) maintaining a desired bond rating, (2) providing an adequate borrowing reserve, and (3) exploiting the advantages of financial leverage.

## Who Sets Target Debt Ratios?

From the preceding discussion, we know that firms *do* use target debt ratios in arriving at financing decisions. But who sets or influences these target ratios? This and other questions concerning corporate financing policy were investigated in one study published in 1982.[18] This survey of the 1,000 largest industrial firms in the United States (as ranked by total sales dollars) involved responses from 212 financial executives.

In one portion of this study, the participants were asked to rank several possible influences on their target leverage (debt) ratios. Table 16-8 displays the percentage of responses ranked either number one or number two in importance. Ranks past the second are omitted in that they were not very significant. Notice that the most important influence is the firm's own management group and staff of analysts. This item accounted for 85 percent of the responses ranked number one. Of the responses ranked number two in importance, investment bankers dominated the outcomes and accounted for 39 percent of such replies. The role of investment bankers in the country's capital market system is explored in some detail in Chapter 14. Also notice that comparisons with ratios of industry competitors and commercial bankers have some impact on the determination of leverage targets.

[16] *Business Week* (December 6, 1976): 30.

[17] Walsh, *Planning Corporate Capital Structures,* 17.

[18] David F. Scott, Jr., and Dana J. Johnson, "Financing Policies and Practices in Large Corporations," *Financial Management* 11 (Summer 1982): 51–59.

**TABLE 16-9**
Definitions of Debt Capacity in Practice

| Standard or Method | 1,000 Largest Corporations (Percent Using) |
|---|---|
| Target percent of total capitalization (long-term debt to total capitalization) | 27% |
| Long-term debt to net worth ratio (or its inverse) | 14 |
| Long-term debt to total assets | 2 |
| Interest (or fixed charge) coverage ratio | 6 |
| Maintain bond ratings | 14 |
| Restrictive debt covenants | 4 |
| Most adverse cash flow | 4 |
| Industry standard | 3 |
| Other | 10 |
| No response | 16 |
| Total | 100% |

Source: Derived from David F. Scott, Jr., and Dana J. Johnson, "Financing Policies and Practices in Large Corporations," *Financial Management* 11 (Summer 1982), pp. 51–59.

## Debt Capacity

Previously in this chapter, we noted that the firm's debt capacity is the maximum proportion of debt that it can include in its capital structure and still maintain its lowest composite cost of capital. But how do financial executives make the concept of debt capacity operational? Table 16-9 is derived from the same 1982 survey, involving 212 executives, mentioned previously. These executives defined debt capacity in a wide variety of ways. The most popular approach was as a target percentage of total capitalization. Twenty-seven percent of the respondents thought of debt capacity in this manner. Forty-three percent of the participating executives remarked that debt capacity is defined in terms of some balance-sheet-based financial ratio (see the first three items in Table 16-9). Maintaining a specific bond rating was also indicated to be a popular approach to implementing the debt capacity concept.

## Business Cycles

Effective financial managers—those who assist in creating value for the firm's common shareholders—are perceptive about and in constant communication with the financial marketplace. When market conditions change abruptly, company financial policies and decisions must adapt to the new conditions. Some firms, however, do a better job of adjusting than others. Companies that are slow to adapt to changes in the aggregate, or overall, business environment face a lower level of cash flow generation and increased risk of financial distress.

Changes in the aggregate business environment are often referred to as *business cycles.* There are many useful definitions of such cycles. For example, the late Dr. Fischer Black, a former finance professor and later an executive with the well-known investment banking firm of Goldman, Sachs & Co., defined business cycles as follows:[19]

> Business cycles are fluctuations in economic activity. Business cycles show up in virtually all measures of economic activity—output, income, employment, unemployment, retail sales, new orders by manufacturers, even housing starts. When times are good, they tend to be good all over; and when times are bad, they tend to be bad all over.

[19]Fischer Black, "The ABCs of Business Cycles," *Financial Analysts Journal* 37 (November–December 1981): 75–80. Dr. Black touched on similar points and other far-reaching points in his compelling presidential address to the American Finance Association; see Fischer Black, "Noise," *Journal of Finance* 41 (July 1986): 529–43.

**TABLE 16-10**
Post–World War II U.S Business Cycles

| Start of Recession (Peaks) | End (Troughs) | Length (Months) |
|---|---|---|
| November 1948 | October 1949 | 11 |
| July 1953 | May 1954 | 10 |
| August 1957 | April 1958 | 8 |
| April 1960 | February 1961 | 10 |
| December 1969 | November 1970 | 11 |
| November 1973 | March 1975 | 16 |
| January 1980 | July 1980 | 6 |
| July 1981 | November 1982 | 16 |
| July 1990 | March 1991 | 8 |

Source: National Bureau of Economic Research (NBER).

**Business cycles**
A series of commercial adjustments to unanticipated new information accentuated by both public policy decisions and private-sector decisions.

A slightly different but compatible definition of business cycles that we will use is: **Business cycles** are a series of commercial adjustments to unanticipated new information accentuated by *both* public policy decisions and private-sector decisions. When the decisions, on balance, are correct, the economy expands. When the decisions, on balance, are incorrect, the economy contracts.

Since the end of World War II, the United States has endured nine recessions. Recessions are the contractionary or negative phase of the entire business cycle. Those nine recessions are documented in Table 16-10.

Typically, different stages of the business cycle induce a different set of relationships in the financial markets. These different relationships are reflected in the different capital structure decisions managers make. For example, relationships between interest rates and equity prices may differ sharply over different phases of the cycle. Some phases of the cycle favor the issuance of debt securities over equity instruments, and vice versa. Complicating the decision-making setting for the manager is the fact that financial relationships will be *dissimilar* over each cycle.[20]

The last "official" recession, which began in July 1990, produced its own set of unique financial characteristics. Accordingly, financial managers altered their firms' capital structures in response to new information that included capital cost relationships in the financial markets. Managers began to reverse some of the financial leverage buildup that occurred in the 1980s. Specifically, by early 1991, corporations began to take advantage of an improved market for common equities and brought to the marketplace substantial amounts of new common stock issues.

## Business Risk

The single most important factor that should affect the firm's financing mix is the underlying nature of the business in which it operates. In Chapter 15, we defined business risk as the relative dispersion in the firm's expected stream of EBIT. If the nature of the firm's business is such that the variability inherent in its EBIT stream is high, then it would be unwise to impose a high degree of financial risk on top of this already uncertain earnings stream.

Corporate executives are likely to point this out in discussions of capital structure management. A financial officer in a large steel firm related:

> The nature of the industry, the marketplace, and the firm tend to establish debt limits that any prudent management would prefer not to exceed. Our industry is capital intensive and our markets

[20]Available discussions and studies on the relationship between business cycles and corporate financing patterns are not plentiful. One such study is Robert A. Taggart, Jr., "Corporate Financing: Too Much Debt?" *Financial Analysts Journal* 42 (May–June 1986): 35–42.

> tend to be cyclical. . . . The capability to service debt while operating in the environment described dictates a conservative financial structure.[21]

Notice how that executive was concerned with both his firm's business risk exposure and its cash flow capability for meeting any financing costs. The AT&T financial officer referred to earlier also has commented on the relationship between business and financial risk:

> In determining how much debt a firm can safely carry, it is necessary to consider the basic risks inherent in that business. This varies considerably among industries and is related essentially to the nature and demand for an industry's product, the operating characteristics of the industry, and its ability to earn an adequate return in an unknown future.[22]

Also, refer back to the introduction to this chapter. Recall that the management of Georgia-Pacific said:

> Georgia-Pacific's objective is to provide superior returns to our shareholders. To achieve this goal, our financial strategy must complement our operating strategy.[23]

It appears clear that the firm's capital structure cannot be properly designed without a thorough understanding of its commercial strategy.

## Financial Managers and Theory

Earlier in this chapter, we discussed a moderate view of capital structure theory. The saucer-shaped cost of capital curve implied by this theory (Figure 16-9) predicts that managers will add debt to the firm's capital structure when current leverage use is *below* the firm's optimal range of leverage use at the base of the overall cost of capital curve. Conversely, managers will add equity when leverage use is above this optimal range. Under these conditions above, *both* financing activities lower the cost of capital to the firm and increase shareholder wealth.

A 1991 survey of chief financial officers of the top (largest) nonfinancial, nonregulated U.S. firms addressed these predicted activities. Of the 800 firms surveyed, 117 responded, for a response rate of 14.6 percent. These decision makers were asked how their firms would respond if confronted with certain, specific financing situations.

It should be noted that the moderate view does not distinguish between internal equity (retained earnings and depreciation) and external equity (the sale of common stock). The questions posed to the financial managers, however, *do* make this distinction. Based on our financial asset valuation models, common equity is generally considered the most *expensive* source of funds, exceeding the costs of both debt and preferred stock. The cost of external equity exceeds internal equity by the addition of flotation costs. (Recall our discussion in Chapter 12 on these relationships.)

Addressing the downward-sloping portion of the cost of capital curve, managers were asked what their financing choice would be if (1) the firm has internal funds *sufficient* for investment requirements (capital budgeting needs), but (2) the debt ratio is *below* the level preferred by the firm. The moderate theory predicts that managers will add debt to the firm's capital structure in this situation. However, 81 percent of the respondents said they would use internal equity to finance their investments. Only 17 percent suggested they would use long-term debt, and 11 percent selected short-term debt. In this situation, most managers indicated they would choose to use the more expensive internal equity rather than the (seemingly) less expensive debt for investments.

[21]Walsh, *Capital Structures,* 18.

[22]Scanlon, "Bell System Financial Policies," 19.

[23]*Georgia-Pacific 1996 Annual Report,* 15.

**FIGURE 16-9**
Capital Costs: The Moderate View

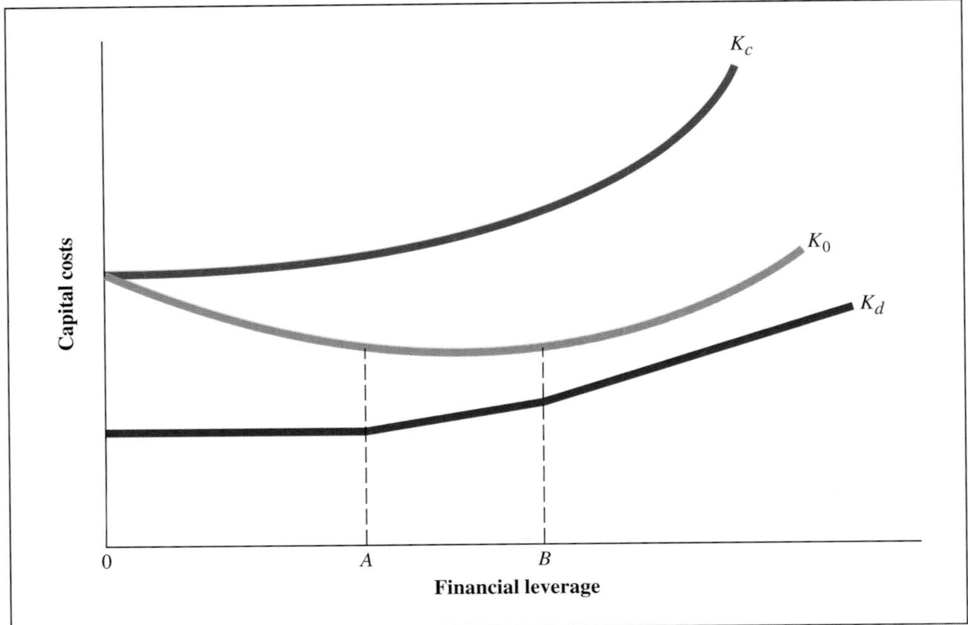


Similarly, when internal funds are sufficient for new investment and the debt level *exceeds* the firm's optimum range of leverage use, managers again chose to use internal equity in 81 percent of the responses. Seventeen percent would issue new equity if market conditions were favorable. Because the debt level is currently excessive, the moderate theory would predict that external equity would be added to minimize the cost of capital. Instead, most firms preferred to fund investment with the internal funds. This is a prevalent tendency in American industry.

Responses to the preceding questions imply that, if managers follow the financing activity prescribed by the moderate view, it is *only* after internal funds have been exhausted. Because these internal funds are relatively expensive (compared with new debt), their use as the *initial* financing option indicates that either: (1) managers do not view their financing goal to be the minimization of the firm's cost of capital or (2) the explicit and implicit costs of new security issues are understated. If this is actually the case, internal funds may be the *least* expensive source of funds from the perspective of financial managers. This may be a form of the agency problem that we previously discussed in this chapter.

The chief financial officers were also asked what their financing decision would be under these conditions: (1) the firm requires external funds, (2) financial leverage use *exceeds* the desired level, and (3) equity markets are underpricing the firm's stock. Table 16-11 contains the responses to this question.

In this difficult situation, 68 percent of the managers indicated that they would *reduce* their investment plans. That is, capital budgets would shrink. The primary explanations for such investment restriction were (1) that it was in the best interest of current shareholders, and (2) that it controlled risk.

The next-favored choice (28 percent) was the use of short-term debt, sometimes combined with investment reduction. This suggests that managers attempt to wait out difficult market conditions by adopting short-term solutions. The timing of security

**TABLE 16-11**
Managers and Theory: Some Responses

| **Question** | |
|---|---|
| Your firm requires external funds to finance the next period's capital investments. | |
| Financial leverage use exceeds that preferred by the firm. | |
| Equity markets are underpricing your securities. Would your firm: | |
| **Choices** | **Responses** |
| Reduce your investment plans? | 68% |
| Obtain short-term debt? | 28 |
| Attempt to provide the market with adequate information to correctly price your securities before issuing equity? | 13 |
| Issue long-term debt? | 13 |
| Issue equity anyway? | 4 |
| Reduce your dividend payout? | 4 |

Source: Adapted from David F. Scott, Jr., and Nancy Jay, "Financial Managers and Capital Structure Theories" *Working Paper* 9203, Orlando, FL: Dr. Phillips Institute for the Study of American Business Activity, University of Central Florida, March 1992.

issues with favorable market conditions is a major objective of financial managers and entirely consistent with the optimal capital structure range defined under the moderate theory (Figure 16-9).

Some 4 percent of the respondents indicated that they would issue equity, despite the underpricing of the firm's stock. Thirteen percent of the firms indicated that they would attempt to correct the adverse pricing by providing the market with adequate information before attempting to issue equity.

Another 13 percent of the respondents indicated that they would add long-term debt, moving leverage use further beyond the optimal range.

Only 4 percent of the executives responding to this situation stated they would obtain needed funds by *reducing* the cash dividend payout. To managers, the shareholders' cash dividends are quite important. Firms prefer to forgo profitable projects rather than to reallocate the shareholders' expected cash dividends to investment. Dividend policies are discussed extensively in Chapter 17.

You can see that our ability as analysts to *predict* financing choices, as opposed to *prescribing* them, is far from perfect. In many instances, managers appear to react as popular capital structure theories suggest. In other instances, though, managers either are rejecting some aspects of the theories, or the theories need more work. Understanding these aberrations is useful to the analyst.

A thorough grounding in both the theory of financing decisions and in the tools of capital structure management will assist you in making sound choices that maximize shareholder wealth. This combination of theory and practical tools also permits you to ask some very perceptive questions when faced with a decision-making situation.

**CONCEPT CHECK**

1. Identify several factors that influence target debt ratios in actual business practice.
2. Identify several methods used by executives to make the concept of debt capacity operational.

## SUMMARY

OBJECTIVE 1 

This chapter deals with the design of the firm's financing mix, particularly emphasizing management of the firm's permanent sources of funds—that is, its capital structure. The objective of capital structure management is to arrange the company's sources of funds so that its common stock price will be maximized, all other factors held constant.

OBJECTIVES 2, 3, 4 

Can the firm affect its composite cost of capital by altering its financing mix? Attempts to answer this question have comprised a significant portion of capital structure theory for over three decades. Extreme positions show that the firm's stock price is either unaffected or continually affected as the firm increases its reliance on leverage-inducing funds. In the real world, an operating environment where interest expense is tax deductible and market imperfections operate to restrict the amount of fixed-income obligations a firm can issue, most financial officers and financial academics subscribe to the concept of an optimal capital structure. The optimal capital structure minimizes the firm's composite cost of capital. Searching for a proper range of financial leverage, then, is an important financial management activity.

Complicating the manager's search for an optimal capital structure are conflicts that lead to agency costs. A natural conflict exists between stockholders and bondholders (the agency costs of debt). To reduce excessive risk taking by management on behalf of stockholders, it may be necessary to include several protective covenants in bond contracts that serve to restrict managerial decision making.

OBJECTIVE 5 

Another type of agency cost is related to "free cash flow." Managers, for example, have an incentive to hold on to free cash flow and enjoy it, rather than paying it out in the form of higher cash-dividend payments. This conflict between managers and stockholders leads to the concept of the *free cash flow theory of capital structure.* This same theory is also known as the *control hypothesis* and the *threat hypothesis.* The ultimate resolution of these agency costs affects the specific form of the firm's capital structure.

OBJECTIVE 6 

The decision to use senior securities in the firm's capitalization causes two types of financial leverage effects. The first is the added variability in the earnings-per-share stream that accompanies the use of fixed-charge securities. We explained in Chapter 15 how this could be quantified by use of the degree of financial leverage metric. The second financial leverage effect relates to the level of earnings per share (EPS) at a given EBIT under a specific capital structure. We rely on EBIT–EPS analysis to measure this second effect. Through EBIT–EPS analysis the decision maker can inspect the impact of alternative financing plans on EPS over a full range of EBIT levels.

A second tool of capital structure management is the calculation of comparative leverage ratios. Balance sheet leverage ratios and coverage ratios can be computed according to the contractual stipulations of the proposed financing plans. Comparison of these ratios with industry standards enables the financial officer to determine if the firm's key ratios are materially out of line with accepted practice.

A third tool is the analysis of corporate cash flows. This process involves the preparation of a series of cash budgets that consider different economic conditions and different capital structures. Useful insight into the identification of proper target capital structure ratios can be obtained by analyzing projected cash flow statements that assume adverse operating circumstances.

OBJECTIVE 7 

The euro was introduced as a new currency by the 11 countries comprising the European Union on January 1, 1999. Swiftly, and by November 2000, the euro had depreciated (weakened) some 38 percent as measured against the U.S. dollar. Such variations in the value of foreign currencies pose huge forecasting problems for the financial executives of multinational firms. Managing currency risk is a daily activity for the finance function of such firms with a significant international presence. Firms with a high exposure to currency value changes might choose to avoid using large relative amounts of corporate debt in their financial structures.

OBJECTIVE 8 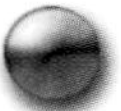

Surveys indicate that most financial officers in large firms believe in the concept of an optimal capital structure. The optimal capital structure is approximated by the identification of target debt ratios. The targets reflect the firm's ability to service fixed financing costs and also consider the business risk to which the firm is exposed.

Survey studies have provided information on who sets or influences the firm's target leverage ratios. The firm's own management group and staff of analysts are the major influence, followed in importance by investment bankers. Studies also show that executives operationalize the concept of debt capacity in many ways. The most popular approach is to define debt capacity in terms of a target long-term debt-to-total-capitalization ratio. Maintaining a specific bond rating (such as Aa or A) is also a popular approach to implementing the debt capacity concept.

Financing policies change in significant ways over time. During the 1980s, for example, most studies confirm that U.S. companies "levered up" when compared with past decades. Specifically, interest coverage ratios deteriorated during the 1980s when compared with the 1970s.

The early 1990s displayed a reversal of this trend. Effective financial managers have a sound understanding of business cycles. The recession that started in July 1990 produced a unique set of financial characteristics that led to relatively high common stock prices. Accordingly, financial managers reversed some of the leverage buildup incurred during the 1980s by bringing substantial amounts of new common stock to the marketplace.

Other studies of managers' financing tendencies suggest that (1) a tremendous preference for the use of internally generated equity to finance investments exists, (2) firms prefer to forgo seemingly profitable projects rather than reduce shareholders' expected cash dividends to finance a greater part of the capital budget, and (3) security issues are timed with favorable market conditions.

## KEY TERMS

**Business cycles, 546**
**Capital structure, 514**
**Debt capacity, 525**
**EBIT–EPS indifference point, 535**
**Explicit cost of capital, 520**
**Financial structure, 514**
**Financial structure design, 514**
**Implicit cost of debt, 520**
**Net income (NI) approach to valuation, 522**
**Net operating income (NOI) approach to valuation, 519**
**Optimal capital structure, 515**
**Optimal range of financial leverage, 525**
**Sinking fund, 536**
**Tax shield, 524**

Go To:
http://www.prenhall.com/keown
for downloads and current events associated with this chapter

## STUDY QUESTIONS

**16-1.** Define the following terms:
   **a.** Financial structure
   **b.** Capital structure
   **c.** Optimal capital structure
   **d.** Debt capacity

**16-2.** What is the primary weakness of EBIT–EPS analysis as a financing decision tool?

**16-3.** What is the objective of capital structure management?

**16-4.** Distinguish between (a) balance sheet leverage ratios and (b) coverage ratios. Give two examples of each and indicate how they would be computed.

**16-5.** Why might firms whose sales levels change drastically over time choose to use debt only sparingly in their capital structures?

**16-6.** What condition would cause capital structure management to be a meaningless activity?

**16-7.** What does the term *independence hypothesis* mean as it applies to capital structure theory?

**16-8.** Who have been the foremost advocates of the independence hypothesis?

**16-9.** A financial manager might say that the firm's composite cost of capital is saucer-shaped or U-shaped. What does this mean?

**16-10.** Define the EBIT–EPS indifference point.

**16-11.** What is UEPS?

**16-12.** Explain how industry norms might be used by the financial manager in the design of the company's financing mix.

**16-13.** Define the term *free cash flow.*

**16-14.** What is meant by the *free cash flow theory of capital structure?*

**16-15.** Briefly describe the trend in corporate use of financial leverage during the 1980s.

**16-16.** Why should the financial manager be familiar with the business cycle?

**16-17.** In almost every instance, what funds source do managers use first in the financing of their capital budgets?

## SELF-TEST PROBLEMS

**ST-1.** *(Analysis of recessionary cash flows)* The management of Story Enterprises is considering an increase in its use of financial leverage. The proposal on the table is to sell $6 million of bonds that would mature in 20 years. The interest rate on these bonds would be 12 percent. The bond issue would have a sinking fund attached to it requiring that one-twentieth of the principal be retired each year. Most business economists are forecasting a recession that will affect the entire economy in the coming year. Story's management has been saying, "If we can make it through this, we can make it through anything." The firm prefers to carry an operating cash balance of $750,000. Cash collections from sales next year will total $3 million. Miscellaneous cash receipts will be $400,000. Raw material payments will be $700,000. Wage and salary costs will be $1,200,000 on a cash basis. On top of this, Story will experience nondiscretionary cash outlays of $1.2 million, *including* all tax payments. The firm faces a 34 percent tax rate.

**a.** At present, Story is unlevered. What will be the total fixed financial charges the firm must pay next year?

**b.** If the bonds are issued, what is your forecast for the firm's expected cash balance at the end of the recessionary year (next year)?

**c.** As Story's financial consultant, do you recommend that it issue the bonds?

**ST-2.** *(Assessing leverage use)* Some financial data and the appropriate industry norm for three companies are shown in the following table:

| Measure | Firm X | Firm Y | Firm Z | Industry Norm |
|---|---|---|---|---|
| Total debt to total assets | 20% | 30% | 10% | 30% |
| Times interest and preferred dividend coverage | 8 times | 16 times | 19 times | 8 times |
| Price/earnings ratio | 9 times | 11 times | 9 times | 9 times |

**a.** Which firm appears to be employing financial leverage to the most appropriate degree?

**b.** In this situation, which "financial leverage effect" appears to dominate the market valuation process?

**ST-3.** *(EBIT–EPS analysis)* Four engineers from Martin-Bowing Company are leaving that firm in order to form their own corporation. The new firm will produce and distribute computer software on a national basis. The software will be aimed at scientific markets and at businesses desiring to install comprehensive information systems. Private investors have been lined up to finance the new company. Two financing proposals are being studied. Both of these plans involve the use of some financial leverage; however, one is much more highly levered than the other. Plan A requires the firm to sell bonds with an effective interest rate of 14 percent. One million dollars would be raised in this manner. In addition, under plan A, $5 million would be raised by selling stock at $50 per common share. Plan B also involves raising $6 million. This would be accomplished by selling $3 million of bonds at an interest rate of 16 percent. The other $3 million would come from selling common stock at $50 per share. In both cases, the use of financial leverage is considered to be a permanent part of the firm's capital structure, so no fixed maturity date is used in the analysis. The firm considers a 50 percent tax rate appropriate for planning purposes.

**a.** Find the EBIT indifference level associated with the two financing plans, and prepare an EBIT–EPS analysis chart.

**b.** Prepare an analytical income statement that demonstrates that EPS will be the same regardless of the plan selected. Use the EBIT level found in part (a) above.

**c.** A detailed financial analysis of the firm's prospects suggests that long-term EBIT will be above $1,188,000 annually. Taking this into consideration, which plan will generate the higher EPS?

**d.** Suppose that long-term EBIT is forecast to be $1,188,000 per year. Under plan A, a price/earnings ratio of 13 would apply. Under plan B, a price/earnings ratio of 11 would apply. If this set of financial relationships does hold, which financing plan would you recommend be implemented?

**e.** Again, assume an EBIT level of $1,188,000. What price/earnings ratio applied to the EPS of plan B would provide the same stock price as that projected for plan A? Refer to your data from part (d) above.

## STUDY PROBLEMS (SET A)

**16-1A.** (*Analysis of recessionary cash flows*) The management of Transpacific Inc. is considering an increase in its use of financial leverage to develop several investment projects. The proposal is to sell $15 million of bonds that would mature in 30 years. The interest rate on these bonds would be 18 percent. The bond issue would have a sinking fund attached to it requiring that one-thirtieth of the principal be retired each year. Most business economists are forecasting a recession that will affect the economy in the coming year. Transpacific's management has been maintaining an operating cash balance of $2 million. Cash collections from sales next year are estimated to be $4.5 million. Miscellaneous cash receipts will be $450,000. Raw material payments will be $900,000. Wage and salary cost will total $1.7 million on a cash basis. On top of this, Transpacific will experience nondiscretionary cash outflows of $1.4 million including all tax payments. The firm uses a 50 percent tax rate.

**a.** At present, Transpacific is unlevered. What will be the total fixed financial charges the firm must pay next year?

**b.** If the bonds are issued, what is your forecast for the firm's expected cash balance at the end of the recessionary year (next year)?

**c.** As Transpacific's financial consultant, do you recommend that it issue the bonds?

**16-2A.** (*Analysis of recessionary cash flows*) Ontherise, Inc. is considering expanding its bagel bakery business with the acquisition of new equipment to be financed entirely with debt. The company does not have any other debt or preferred stock outstanding. The company currently has a cash balance of $200,000, which is the minimum Baruch Chavez, the CFO of Ontherise, believes to be desirable. Baruch has determined that the following relationships exist among the company's various items of cash flow (except as noted, all are expressed as a percentage of cash collections on sales):

| | |
|---|---|
| Other cash receipts | 5% |
| **Cash Disbursements for:** | |
| Payroll | 30% |
| Raw materials | 25% |
| Nondiscretionary expenditures (essentially fixed, thus not percent of sales) | $500,000 |

The new debt would carry fixed financial charges of $140,000 the first year (interest, $90,000, plus principal–sinking fund, $50,000). To evaluate the sensitivity of the proposed debt plan to economic fluctuations, Baruch would like to determine how low cash collections from sales could be in the next year while ensuring that the cash balance at the end of the year is the minimum he considers necessary.

**16-3A.** (*EBIT–EPS analysis with sinking fund*) Due to his concern over the effect of the "worst that could happen" if he finances the equipment acquisition only with debt (he believes cash collections on sales could be as low as $1,100,000 in the coming year), Baruch Chavez, the CFO of Ontherise, Inc., (see Problem 16-2A) also has decided to consider a part debt/part equity alternative to the proposed all-debt plan described above. The combination would include 60 percent equity and 40 percent debt. The equity part of the plan would provide $20 per share to the company for 30,000 new shares. The debt portion of this plan would include $400,000 of new debt with fixed financial charges of $52,000 for the first year (interest, $32,000, plus principal–sinking fund, $20,000). The company is in the 35 percent tax bracket. The company currently has 100,000 shares of stock outstanding. Baruch has asked you to determine the EBIT indifference level associated with the two financing alternatives.

**16-4A.** (*EBIT–EPS analysis*) A group of retired college professors has decided to form a small manufacturing corporation. The company will produce a full line of traditional office furniture. Two financing plans have been proposed by the investors. Plan A is an all-common-equity alternative. Under this agreement, 1 million common shares will be sold to net the firm $20 per share. Plan B involves the use of financial leverage. A debt issue with a 20-year maturity period will be privately placed. The debt issue will carry an interest rate of 10 percent, and the principal borrowed will amount to $6 million. Under this alternative, another $14 million would be raised by selling 700,000 shares of common stock. The corporate tax rate is 50 percent.

- **a.** Find the EBIT indifference level associated with the two financing proposals.
- **b.** Prepare an analytical income statement that proves EPS will be the same regardless of the plan chosen at the EBIT level found in part (a).
- **c.** Prepare an EBIT–EPS analysis chart for this situation.
- **d.** If a detailed financial analysis projects that long-term EBIT will always be close to $2.4 million annually, which plan will provide for the higher EPS?

**16-5A.** (*Capital structure theory*) Deep End Pools & Supplies has an all-common-equity capital structure. Some financial data for the company are as follows:

Shares of common stock outstanding = 900,000
Common stock price, $P_0$ = $30 per share
Expected level of EBIT = $5,400,000
Dividend payout ratio = 100 percent

In answering the following questions, assume that corporate income is not taxed.

- **a.** Under the present capital structure, what is the total value of the firm?
- **b.** What is the cost of common equity capital, $K_c$? What is the composite cost of capital, $K_0$?
- **c.** Now suppose Deep End sells $1.5 million of long-term debt with an interest rate of 8 percent. The proceeds are used to retire the outstanding common stock. According to the net operating income theory (the independence hypothesis), what will be the firm's cost of common equity after the capital structure change?
    1. What will be the dividend per share flowing to the firm's common shareholders?
    2. By what percentage has the dividend per share changed owing to the capital structure change?
    3. By what percentage has the cost of common equity changed owing to the capital structure change?
    4. What will be the composite cost of capital after the capital structure change?

**16-6A.** (*EBIT–EPS analysis*) Four recent liberal arts graduates have interested a group of venture capitalists in backing a new business enterprise. The proposed operation would consist of a series of retail outlets to distribute and service a full line of vacuum cleaners and accessories. These stores would be located in Dallas, Houston, and San Antonio. Two financing plans have been proposed by the graduates. Plan A is an all-common-equity structure. Two million dollars would be raised by selling 80,000 shares of common stock. Plan B would involve the use of long-term debt financing. One million dollars would be raised by marketing bonds with an effective interest rate of 12 percent. Under this alternative, another million dollars would be raised by selling 40,000 shares of common stock. With both plans, then, $2 million is needed to launch the new firm's operations. The debt funds raised under plan B are considered to have no fixed maturity date, in that this portion of financial leverage is thought to be a permanent part of the company's capital structure. The fledgling executives have decided to use a 40 percent tax rate in their analysis, and they have hired you on a consulting basis to do the following:

**a.** Find the EBIT indifference level associated with the two financing proposals.

**b.** Prepare an analytical income statement that proves EPS will be the same regardless of the plan chosen at the EBIT level found in part (a) above.

**16-7A.** (*EBIT–EPS analysis*) Three recent graduates of the computer science program at Southern Tennessee Tech are forming a company to write and distribute software for various personal computers. Initially, the corporation will operate in the southern region of Tennessee, Georgia, North Carolina, and South Carolina. Twelve serious prospects for retail outlets have already been identified and committed to the firm. The firm's software products have been tested and displayed at several trade shows and computer fairs in the perceived operating region. All that is lacking is adequate financing to continue with the project. A small group of private investors in the Atlanta, Georgia, area is interested in financing the new company. Two financing proposals are being evaluated. The first (plan A) is an all-common-equity capital structure. Two million dollars would be raised by selling common stock at $20 per common share. Plan B would involve the use of financial leverage. One million dollars would be raised selling bonds with an effective interest rate of 11 percent (per annum). Under this second plan, the remaining $1 million would be raised by selling common stock at the $20 price per share. The use of financial leverage is considered to be a permanent part of the firm's capitalization, so no fixed maturity date is needed for the analysis. A 34 percent tax rate is appropriate for the analysis.

**a.** Find the EBIT indifference level associated with the two financing plans.

**b.** A detailed financial analysis of the firm's prospects suggests that the long-term EBIT will be above $300,000 annually. Taking this into consideration, which plan will generate the higher EPS?

**c.** Suppose long-term EBIT is forecast to be $300,000 per year. Under plan A, a price/earnings ratio of 19 would apply. Under plan B, a price/earnings ratio of 15 would apply. If this set of financial relationships does hold, which financing plan would you recommend?

**16-8A.** (*EBIT–EPS analysis*) Three recent liberal arts graduates have interested a group of venture capitalists in backing a new business enterprise. The proposed operation would consist of a series of retail outlets to distribute and service a full line of personal computer equipment. These stores would be located in southern New Jersey, New York, and Pennsylvania. Two financing plans have been proposed by the graduates. Plan A is an all-common-equity structure. Three million dollars would be raised by selling 75,000 shares of common stock. Plan B would involve the use of long-term debt financing. One million dollars would be raised by marketing bonds with an effective interest rate of 15 percent. Under this alternative, another $2 million would be raised by selling 50,000 shares of common stock. With both plans, then, $3 million is needed to launch the new firm's operations. The debt funds raised under plan B are considered to have no fixed maturity date, in that this proportion of financial leverage is thought to be a permanent part of the company's capital structure. The fledgling executives have decided to use a 34 percent tax rate in their analysis, and they have hired you on a consulting basis to do the following:

**a.** Find the EBIT indifference level associated with the two financing proposals.

**b.** Prepare an analytical income statement that proves EPS will be the same regardless of the plan chosen at the EBIT level found in part (a) above.

**16-9A.** (*EBIT–EPS analysis*) Two recent graduates of the computer science program at Ohio Tech are forming a company to write, market, and distribute software for various personal computers. Initially, the corporation will operate in Illinois, Indiana, Michigan, and Ohio. Twelve serious prospects for retail outlets in these different states have already been identified and committed to the firm. The firm's software products have been tested and displayed at several trade shows and computer fairs in the perceived operating region. All that is lacking is adequate financing to continue the project. A small group of private investors in the Columbus, Ohio, area is interested in financing the new company. Two financing proposals are being evaluated. The first (plan A) is an all-common-equity capital structure. Four million dollars would be raised by selling stock at $40 per common share. Plan B would involve the use of financial leverage. Two million dollars would be raised by selling bonds with an effective interest rate of 16 percent (per annum). Under this second plan, the remaining $2 million would be raised by selling common stock at the $40 price per share. This use of financial leverage is considered to be a permanent part of the firm's capitalization, so no fixed maturity date is needed for the analysis. A 50 percent tax rate is appropriate for the analysis.

**a.** Find the EBIT indifference level associated with the two financing plans.

**b.** Prepare an analytical income statement that proves EPS will be the same regardless of the plan chosen at the EBIT level found in part (a) above.

**c.** A detailed financial analysis of the firm's prospects suggests that long-term EBIT will be above $800,000 annually. Taking this into consideration, which plan will generate the higher EPS?

**d.** Suppose that long-term EBIT is forecast to be $800,000 per year. Under plan A, a price/earnings ratio of 12 would apply. Under plan B, a price/earnings ratio of 10 would apply. If this set of financial relationships does hold, which financing plan would you recommend be implemented?

**16-10A.** (*Analysis of recessionary cash flows*) The management of Idaho Produce is considering an increase in its use of financial leverage. The proposal on the table is to sell $10 million of bonds that would mature in 20 years. The interest rate on these bonds would be 15 percent. The bond issue would have a sinking fund attached to it requiring that one-twentieth of the principal be retired each year. Most business economists are forecasting a recession that will affect the entire economy in the coming year. Idaho's management has been saying, "If we can make it through this, we can make it through anything." The firm prefers to carry an operating cash balance of $1 million. Cash collections from sales next year will total $4 million. Miscellaneous cash receipts will be $300,000. Raw material payments will be $800,000. Wage and salary costs will total $1.4 million on a cash basis. On top of this, Idaho will experience nondiscretionary cash outflows of $1.2 million *including* all tax payments. The firm faces a 50 percent tax rate.

**a.** At present, Idaho is unlevered. What will be the total fixed financial charges the firm must pay next year?

**b.** If the bonds are issued, what is your forecast for the firm's expected cash balance at the end of the recessionary year (next year)?

**c.** As Idaho's financial consultant, do you recommend that it issue the bonds?

**16-11A.** (*EBIT–EPS analysis*) Four recent business school graduates have interested a group of venture capitalists in backing a small business enterprise. The proposed operation would consist of a series of retail outlets that would distribute and service a full line of energy-conservation equipment. These stores would be located in northern Virginia, western Pennsylvania, and throughout West Virginia. Two financing plans have been proposed by the graduates. Plan A is an all-common-equity capital structure. Three million dollars would be raised by selling 60,000 shares of common stock. Plan B would involve the use of long-term debt financing. One million dollars would be raised by marketing bonds with an interest rate of 10 percent. Under this alternative, another $2 million would be raised by selling 40,000 shares of common stock. With both plans, then, $3 million is needed to launch the new firm's operations. The debt funds raised under plan B are considered to have no fixed maturity date, in that this proportion of financial leverage is thought to be a permanent part of the company's capital structure. The fledgling executives have decided to use a 40 percent tax rate in their analysis.

**a.** Find the EBIT indifference level associated with the two financing proposals.

**b.** Prepare an analytical income statement that proves EPS will be the same regardless of the plan chosen at the EBIT level found in part (a).

**16-12A.** (*EBIT–EPS analysis*) A group of college professors has decided to form a small manufacturing corporation. The company will produce a full line of contemporary furniture. Two financing plans have been proposed by the investors. Plan A is an all-common-equity alternative. Under this arrangement, 1,400,000 common shares will be sold to net the firm $10 per share. Plan B involves the use of financial leverage. A debt issue with a 20-year maturity period will be privately placed. The debt issue will carry an interest rate of 8 percent and the principal borrowed will amount to $4 million. Under this plan, another $10 million would be raised by selling 1 million shares of common stock. The corporate tax rate is 50 percent.

**a.** Find the EBIT indifference level associated with the two financing proposals.
**b.** Prepare an analytical income statement that proves EPS will be the same regardless of the plan chosen at the EBIT level found in part (a).
**c.** Prepare an EBIT–EPS analysis chart for this situation.
**d.** If a detailed financial analysis projects that long-term EBIT will always be close to $1,800,000 annually, which plan will provide for the higher EPS?

**16-13A.** (*EBIT–EPS analysis*) The professors discussed in problem 16-12A contacted a financial consultant to provide them with some additional information. They felt that in a few years, the stock of the firm would be publicly traded over the counter, so they were interested in the consultant's opinion as to what the stock price would be under the financing plan outlined in problem 16-12A. The consultant agreed that the projected long-term EBIT level of $1,800,000 was reasonable. He also felt that if plan A were selected, the marketplace would apply a price/earnings ratio of 12 times to the company's stock; for plan B he estimated a price/earnings ratio of 10 times.
**a.** According to this information, which financing alternative would offer a higher stock price?
**b.** What price/earnings ratio applied to the EPS related to plan B would provide the same stock price as that projected for plan A?
**c.** Comment on the results of your analysis of problems 16-12A and 16-13A.

**16-14A.** (*Analysis of recessionary cash flows*) Cavalier Agriculture Supplies is undertaking a thorough cash flow analysis. It has been proposed by management that the firm expand by raising $5 million in the long-term debt markets. All of this would be immediately invested in new fixed assets. The proposed bond issue would carry an 8 percent interest rate and have a maturity period of 20 years. The bond issue would have a sinking fund provision that one-twentieth of the principal would be retired annually. Next year is expected to be a poor one for Cavalier. The firm's management feels, therefore, that the upcoming year would serve well as a model for the worst possible operating conditions that the firm can be expected to encounter. Cavalier ordinarily carries a $500,000 cash balance. Next year sales collections are forecast to be $3 million. Miscellaneous cash receipts will total $200,000. Wages and salaries will amount to $1 million. Payments for raw materials used in the production process will be $1,400,000. In addition, the firm will pay $500,000 in nondiscretionary expenditures including taxes. The firm faces a 50 percent tax rate.
**a.** Cavalier currently has no debt or preferred stock outstanding. What will be the total fixed financial charges that the firm must meet next year?
**b.** What is the expected cash balance at the end of the recessionary period (next year), assuming the debt is issued?
**c.** Based on this information, should Cavalier issue the proposed bonds?

**16-15A.** (*Assessing leverage use*) Some financial data for three corporations are as follows:

| Measure | Firm A | Firm B | Firm C | Industry Norm |
|---|---|---|---|---|
| Debt ratio | 20% | 25% | 40% | 20% |
| Times burden covered | 8 times | 10 times | 7 times | 9 times |
| Price/earnings ratio | 9 times | 11 times | 6 times | 10 times |

**a.** Which firm appears to be excessively levered?
**b.** Which firm appears to be employing financial leverage to the most appropriate degree?
**c.** What explanation can you provide for the higher price/earnings ratio enjoyed by firm B as compared with firm A?

**16-16A.** (*Assessing leverage use*) Some financial data and the appropriate industry norm are shown in the following table:

| Measure | Firm X | Firm Y | Firm Z | Industry Norm |
|---|---|---|---|---|
| Total debt to total assets | 35% | 30% | 10% | 35% |
| Times interest and preferred dividend coverage | 7 times | 14 times | 16 times | 7 times |
| Price/earnings ratio | 8 times | 10 times | 8 times | 8 times |

**a.** Which firm appears to be using financial leverage to the most appropriate degree?
**b.** In this situation which "financial leverage effect" appears to dominate the market's valuation process?

**16-17A.** (*Capital structure theory*) Boston Textiles has an all-common-equity capital structure. Pertinent financial characteristics for the company are shown below:

Shares of common stock outstanding = 1,000,000
Common stock price, $P_0$ = \$20 per share
Expected level of EBIT = \$5,000,000
Dividend payout ratio = 100 percent

In answering the following questions, assume that corporate income is not taxed.

**a.** Under the present capital structure, what is the total value of the firm?
**b.** What is the cost of common equity capital, $K_c$? What is the composite cost of capital, $K_0$?
**c.** Now suppose that Boston Textiles sells \$1 million of long-term debt with an interest rate of 8 percent. The proceeds are used to retire outstanding common stock. According to NOI theory (the independence hypothesis), what will be the firm's cost of common equity *after* the capital structure change?
1. What will be the dividend per share flowing to the firm's common shareholders?
2. By what percent has the dividend per share changed owing to the capital structure change?
3. By what percent has the cost of common equity changed owing to the capital structure change?
4. What will be the composite cost of capital after the capital structure change?

**16-18A.** (*Capital structure theory*) South Bend Auto Parts has an all-common-equity capital structure. Some financial data for the company are as follows:

Shares of common stock outstanding = 600,000
Common stock price, $P_0$ = \$40 per share
Expected level of EBIT = \$4,200,000
Dividend payout ratio = 100 percent

In answering the following questions, assume that corporate income is not taxed.

**a.** Under the present capital structure, what is the total value of the firm?
**b.** What is the cost of common equity capital, $K_c$? What is the composite cost of capital, $K_0$?
**c.** Now, suppose South Bend sells \$1 million of long-term debt with an interest rate of 10 percent. The proceeds are used to retire outstanding common stock. According to the net operating income theory (the independence hypothesis), what will be the firm's cost of common equity after the capital structure change?
1. What will be the dividend per share flowing to the firm's common shareholders?
2. By what percentage has the dividend per share changed owing to the capital structure change?
3. By what percentage has the cost of common equity changed owing to the capital structure change?
4. What will be the composite cost of capital after the capital structure change?

**16-19A.** (*EBIT–EPS analysis*) Albany Golf Equipment is analyzing three different financing plans for a newly formed subsidiary. The plans are described as follows:

| Plan A | Plan B | | Plan C | |
|---|---|---|---|---|
| Common stock: | Bonds at 9%: | \$20,000 | Preferred stock at 9%: | \$20,000 |
| \$100,000 | Common stock: | 80,000 | Common stock: | 80,000 |

In all cases, the common stock will be sold to net Albany $10 per share. The subsidiary is expected to generate an average EBIT per year of $22,000. The management of Albany places great emphasis on EPS performance. Income is taxed at a 50 percent rate.

**a.** Where feasible, find the EBIT indifference levels between the alternatives.

**b.** Which financing plan do you recommend that Albany pursue?

## INTEGRATIVE PROBLEM

Several biking enthusiasts recently left their defense industry jobs and grouped together to form a corporation, Freedom Cycle, Inc. (FCI), which will produce a new type of bicycle. These new bicycles are to be constructed using space-age technologies and materials so that they will never need repairs or maintenance. The FCI founders believe there is a need for such a bicycle due to their perception that many people today, especially middle-aged working couples such as themselves, really would like to ride bicycles for transportation as well as for pleasure, but are put off by the perceived high maintenance requirements of most bicycles today.

The founders believe such people would be quite willing to buy a maintenance-free bicycle for themselves as well as for their children, particularly after observing the repair and maintenance needs (for example, keeping spoked wheels trued and derailleurs and brakes adjusted) of the bikes they already have purchased for their children. Accordingly, the FCI group feels certain that their new-age bicycles will meet the needs of this market and will be a tremendous hit.

To assist them with the financial management of the company, the FCI founders have hired Mabra Jordan to be CFO. Mabra has considerable experience with start-up companies such as FCI, and she is well respected in the venture capital community. Indeed, based on the strength of her business plan, Mabra has convinced a local venture capital partnership to provide funding for FCI. Two alternatives have been proposed by the venture capitalists: a high leverage plan primarily using "junk" bonds (HLP), and a low leverage plan (LLP) primarily using equity.

HLP consists of $6 million of bonds carrying a 14 percent interest rate and $4 million of $20-per-share common stock. LLP, on the other hand, consists of $2 million of bonds with an interest rate of 11 percent and $8 million of common stock at $20 per share. Under either alternative, FCI is required to use a sinking fund to retire 10 percent of the bonds each year. FCI's tax rate is expected to be 35 percent.

1. Find the EBIT indifference level associated with the two financing alternatives, and prepare an EBIT–EPS analysis graph.
2. Prepare an analytical income statement that demonstrates that EPS will be the same regardless of the alternative selected. Use the EBIT level computed in part 1 above.
3. If an analysis of FCI's long-term prospects indicates that long-term EBIT will be $1,300,000 annually, which financing alternative will generate the higher EPS?
4. If the analysis of FCI's long-term prospects also shows that at a long-term EBIT of $1,300,000 a price/earnings ratio of 18 likely would apply under LLP, and a ratio of 14 would apply under HLP, which of the two financing plans would you recommend and why?
5. At an EBIT level of $1,300,000, what is the price/earnings ratio that would have to obtain under HLP for the EPS of HLP to provide the same stock price as that projected for LLP in part 4 above?

A concern of the venture capitalists, of course, is whether FCI would be able to survive its first year in business if for some reason—such as an economic recession or just an overly optimistic sales projection—the cash flow targets in FCI's business plan were not met. To allay such fears, Mabra included in the FCI business plan a worst-case scenario based on the following pessimistic projections.

Mabra believes FCI should maintain a $500,000 cash balance. Starting initially with zero cash, the company would obtain cash of $10,000,000 from either of the two financing alternatives described above. A total of $9,500,000 of such financing would be used for capital acquisitions; the balance is intended to be available to provide initial working capital. The pessimistic sales forecast indicates cash receipts would be $4 million. Miscellaneous cash receipts (for example, from the sale of scrap titanium and other materials) would be $200,000. Cash payments on raw materials purchases would be

$1 million; wage and salary cash outlays would be $1,500,000; nondiscretionary cash costs (not including tax payments) would be $700,000; and estimated tax payments would be $265,000 under LLP and $54,000 under HLP (note that the difference in estimated tax payments is attributable to the variation in taxable income, which reflects the difference in deductible interest expense).

6. What would be the total fixed financial charges under each of the two alternative financing plans being considered by FCI?
7. A significant issue is whether FCI will have a sufficient cash balance at the end of the possible recessionary year. What is your estimate of FCI's cash balance under each of the two financing plans at the end of such a year?
8. In light of the above and your knowledge of FCI's desired cash level, which financing plan, LLP or HLP, would you recommend?

## STUDY PROBLEMS (SET B)

**16-1B.** (*Analysis of recessionary cash flows*) Cappuccino Express, Inc., is considering expanding its cafe business by adding a number of new stores. Strong consideration is being given to financing the expansion entirely with debt. The company does not have any other debt or preferred stock outstanding. The company currently has a cash balance of $400,000, which is the minimum the CFO, Vanessa Jefferson, believes to be desirable. Vanessa has determined that the following relationships exist among the company's various items of cash flow (except as noted, all are expressed as a percentage of cash collections on sales):

| | |
|---|---|
| Other cash receipts | 5% |
| Cash Disbursements for: | |
| Payroll | 40% |
| Coffee, pastries, and other costs of items sold | 20% |
| Nondiscretionary expenditures (essentially fixed, thus not percent of sales) | $500,000 |

The new debt would carry fixed financial charges of $300,000 the first year (interest, $200,000, plus principal–sinking fund, $100,000). To evaluate the sensitivity of the proposed debt plan to economic fluctuations, Vanessa would like to determine how low cash collections from sales could be in the next year while ensuring that the cash balance at the end of the year is the minimum she considers necessary.

**16-2B.** (*EBIT–EPS analysis with sinking fund*) Due to her concern over the effect of the "worst that could happen" if she finances the expansion only with debt (she believes cash collections on sales could be as low as $1,300,000 in the coming year), Vanessa Jefferson, the CFO of Cappuccino Express, Inc. (see Problem 16-1B), also has decided to consider a part debt/part equity alternative to the proposed all-debt plan described above. The combination would include 70 percent equity and 30 percent debt. The equity part of the plan would provide $20 per share to the company for 70,000 new shares. The debt portion of this plan would include $600,000 of new debt with fixed financial charges of $78,000 for the first year (interest, $48,000, plus principal–sinking fund, $30,000). The company is in the 35 percent tax bracket. The company currently has 100,000 shares of stock outstanding. Vanessa has asked you to determine the EBIT indifference level associated with the two financing alternatives.

**16-3B.** (*EBIT–EPS analysis*) Three recent graduates of the computer science program at Midstate University are forming a company to write and distribute software for various personal computers. Initially, the corporation will operate in the region of Michigan, Illinois, Indiana, and Ohio. Twelve serious prospects for retail outlets have already been identified and committed to the firm. The firm's software products have been tested and displayed at several trade shows and computer fairs in the perceived operating region. All that is lacking is adequate financing to continue with the project. A small group of private investors in the Chicago, Illinois, area is interested in financing the new company. Two financing proposals are being evaluated. The first (plan A) is an all-common-equity capital structure. Three million dollars would be raised by selling common stock at $20 per common share. Plan B would involve the use of financial leverage. Two million dollars would be raised selling bonds with an effective interest rate of 11 percent (per annum). Under this second plan, the remaining $1 million would be raised by selling common stock at the $20 price per share. The use of financial leverage is considered to be a permanent part of the firm's capitalization, so no fixed maturity date is needed for the analysis. A 34 percent tax rate is appropriate for the analysis.

**a.** Find the EBIT indifference level associated with the two financing plans.

**b.** A detailed financial analysis of the firm's prospects suggests that the long-term EBIT will be above $450,000 annually. Taking this into consideration, which plan will generate the higher EPS?

**c.** Suppose long-term EBIT is forecast to be $450,000 per year. Under plan A, a price/earnings ratio of 19 would apply. Under plan B, a price/earnings ratio of 12.39 would apply. If this set of financial relationships does hold, which financing plan would you recommend?

**16-4B.** (*EBIT–EPS analysis*) Three recent liberal arts graduates have interested a group of venture capitalists in backing a new business enterprise. The proposed operation would consist of a series of retail outlets to distribute and service a full line of personal computer equipment. These stores would be located in Texas, Arizona, and New Mexico. Two financing plans have been proposed by the graduates. Plan A is an all-common-equity structure. Four million dollars would be raised by selling 80,000 shares of common stock. Plan B would involve the use of long-term debt financing. Two million dollars would be raised by marketing bonds with an effective interest rate of 16 percent. Under this alternative, another $2 million would be raised by selling 50,000 shares of common stock. With both plans, then, $4 million is needed to launch the new firm's operations. The debt funds raised under plan B are considered to have no fixed maturity date, in that this proportion of financial leverage is thought to be a permanent part of the company's capital structure. The fledgling executives have decided to use a 34 percent tax rate in their analysis, and they have hired you on a consulting basis to do the following:

**a.** Find the EBIT indifference level associated with the two financing proposals.

**b.** Prepare an analytical income statement that proves EPS will be the same regardless of the plan chosen at the EBIT level found in part (a) above.

**16-5B.** (*EBIT–EPS analysis*) Two recent graduates of the computer science program at Ohio Tech are forming a company to write, market, and distribute software for various personal computers. Initially, the corporation will operate in Missouri, Iowa, Nebraska, and Kansas. Eight prospects for retail outlets in these different states have already been identified and committed to the firm. The firm's software products have been tested. All that is lacking is adequate financing to continue the project. A small group of private investors are interested in financing the new company. Two financing proposals are being evaluated. The first (plan A) is an all-common-equity capital structure. Three million dollars would be raised by selling stock at $40 per common share. Plan B would involve the use of financial leverage. One million dollars would be raised by selling bonds with an effective interest rate of 14 percent (per annum). Under this second plan, the remaining $2 million would be raised by selling common stock at the $40 price per share. This use of financial leverage is considered to be a permanent part of the firm's capitalization, so no fixed maturity date is needed for the analysis. A 50 percent tax rate is appropriate for the analysis.

**a.** Find the EBIT indifference level associated with the two financing plans.

**b.** Prepare an analytical income statement that proves EPS will be the same regardless of the plan chosen at the EBIT level found in part (a) above.

**c.** A detailed financial analysis of the firm's prospects suggests that long-term EBIT will be above $750,000 annually. Taking this into consideration, which plan will generate the higher EPS?

**d.** Suppose that long-term EBIT is forecast to be $750,000 per year. Under plan A, a price/earnings ratio of 12 would apply. Under plan B, a price/earnings ratio of 9.836 would apply. If this set of financial relationships does hold, which financing plan would you recommend be implemented?

**16-6B.** (*Analysis of recessionary cash flows*) The management of Cincinnati Collectibles (CC) is considering an increase in its use of financial leverage. The proposal on the table is to sell $11 million of bonds that would mature in 20 years. The interest rate on these bonds would be 16 percent. The bond issue would have a sinking fund attached to it requiring that one-twentieth of the principal be retired each year. Most business economists are forecasting a recession that will affect the entire economy in the coming year. CC's management has been saying, "If we can make it through this, we can make it through anything." The firm prefers to carry an operating cash balance of $500,000. Cash collections from sales next year will total $3.5 million. Miscellaneous cash receipts will be $300,000. Raw material payments will be $800,000. Wage and salary costs will total $1.5 million on a cash basis. On top of this, CC will experience nondiscretionary cash outflows of $1.3 million *including* all tax payments. The firm faces a 50 percent tax rate.

**a.** At present, CC is unlevered. What will be the total fixed financial charges the firm must pay next year?

**b.** If the bonds are issued, what is your forecast for the firm's expected cash balance at the end of the recessionary year (next year)?

**c.** As CC's financial consultant, do you recommend that it issue the bonds?

**16-7B.** (*EBIT–EPS analysis*) Four recent business school graduates have interested a group of venture capitalists in backing a small business enterprise. The proposed operation would consist of a series of retail outlets that would distribute and service a full line of energy-conservation equipment. These stores would be located in northern California, western Nevada, and throughout Oregon. Two financing plans have been proposed by the graduates. Plan A is an all-common-equity capital structure. Five million dollars would be raised by selling 75,000 shares of common stock. Plan B would involve the use of long-term debt financing. Two million dollars would be raised by marketing bonds with an interest rate of 12 percent. Under this alternative, another $3 million would be raised by selling 55,000 shares of common stock. With both plans, then, $5 million is needed to launch the new firm's operations. The debt funds raised under plan B are considered to have no fixed maturity date, in that this proportion of financial leverage is thought to be a permanent part of the company's capital structure. The fledgling executives have decided to use a 40 percent tax rate in their analysis.

**a.** Find the EBIT indifference level associated with the two financing proposals.

**b.** Prepare an analytical income statement that proves EPS will be the same regardless of the plan chosen at the EBIT level found in part (a).

**16-8B.** (*EBIT–EPS analysis*) A group of college professors has decided to form a small manufacturing corporation. The company will produce a full line of contemporary furniture. Two financing plans have been proposed by the investors. Plan A is an all-common-equity alternative. Under this arrangement 1,200,000 common shares will be sold to net the firm $10 per share. Plan B involves the use of financial leverage. A debt issue with 20-year maturity period will be privately placed. The debt issue will carry an interest rate of 9 percent and the principal borrowed will amount to $3.5 million. Under this alternative, another $8.5 million would be raised by selling 850,000 shares of common stock. The corporate tax rate is 50 percent.

**a.** Find the EBIT indifference level associated with the two financing proposals.

**b.** Prepare an analytical income statement that proves EPS will be the same regardless of the plan chosen at the EBIT level found in part (a).

**c.** Prepare an EBIT–EPS analysis chart for this situation.

**d.** If a detailed financial analysis projects that long-term EBIT will always be close to $1,500,000 annually, which plan will provide for the higher EPS?

**16-9B.** (*EBIT–EPS analysis*) The professors in problem 16-8B contacted a financial consultant to provide them with some additional information. They felt that in a few years, the stock of the firm would be publicly traded over the counter, so they were interested in the consultant's opinion as to what the stock price would be under the financing plan outlined in problem 16-8B. The consultant agreed that the projected long-term EBIT level of $1,500,000 was reasonable. He also felt that if plan A were selected, the marketplace would apply a price/earnings ratio of 13 times to the company's stock; for plan B he estimated a price/earnings ratio of 11 times.

**a.** According to this information, which financing alternative would offer a higher stock price?

**b.** What price/earnings ratio applied to the EPS related to plan B would provide the same stock price as that projected for plan A?

**c.** Comment upon the results of your analysis of problems 16-8B and 16-9B.

**16-10B.** (*Analysis of recessionary cash flows*) Seville Cranes, Inc., is undertaking a thorough cash flow analysis. It has been proposed by management that the firm expand by raising $6 million in the long-term debt markets. All of this would be immediately invested in new fixed assets. The proposed bond issue would carry a 10 percent interest rate and have a maturity period of 20 years. The bond issue would have a sinking fund provision that one-twentieth of the principal would be retired annually. Next year is expected to be a poor one for Seville. The firm's management feels, therefore, that the upcoming year would serve well as a model for the worst possible operating conditions that the firm can be expected to encounter. Seville ordinarily carries a $750,000 cash balance. Next year sales collections are forecast to be $3.5 million. Miscellaneous cash receipts will total $200,000. Wages and salaries will amount to $1.2 million. Payments for raw materials used in the production process will be $1,500,000. In addition, the firm will pay $500,000 in nondiscretionary expenditures including taxes. The firm faces a 50 percent tax rate.

**a.** Seville currently has no debt or preferred stock outstanding. What will be the total fixed financial charges that the firm must meet next year?

**b.** What is the expected cash balance at the end of the recessionary period (next year), assuming the debt is issued?

**c.** Based on this information, should Seville issue the proposed bonds?

**16-11B.** (*Assessing leverage use*) Some financial data for three corporations are as follows:

| Measure | Firm A | Firm B | Firm C | Industry Norm |
|---|---|---|---|---|
| Debt ratio | 15% | 20% | 35% | 25% |
| Times burden covered | 9 times | 11 times | 6 times | 9 times |
| Price/earnings ratio | 10 times | 12 times | 5 times | 10 times |

**a.** Which firm appears to be excessively levered?

**b.** Which firm appears to be employing financial leverage to the most appropriate degree?

**c.** What explanation can you provide for the higher price/earnings ratio enjoyed by firm B as compared with firm A?

**16-12B.** (*Assessing leverage use*) Some financial data and the appropriate industry norm are shown in the following table:

| Measure | Firm X | Firm Y | Firm Z | Industry Norm |
|---|---|---|---|---|
| Total debt to total assets | 40% | 35% | 10% | 35% |
| Times interest and preferred dividend coverage | 8 times | 13 times | 16 times | 7 times |
| Price/earnings ratio | 8 times | 11 times | 8 times | 8 times |

**a.** Which firm appears to be using financial leverage to the most appropriate degree?

**b.** In this situation which "financial leverage effect" appears to dominate the market's valuation process?

**16-13B.** (*Capital structure theory*) Whittier Optical Labs has an all-common-equity capital structure. Pertinent financial characteristics for the company are as follows:

Shares of common stock outstanding = 1,000,000
Common stock price, $P_0$ = \$22 per share
Expected level of EBIT = \$4,750,000
Dividend payout ratio = 100 percent

In answering the following questions, assume that corporate income is not taxed.

**a.** Under the present capital structure, what is the total value of the firm?

**b.** What is the cost of common equity capital, $K_c$? What is the composite cost of capital, $K_0$?

**c.** Now suppose that Whittier sells $1 million of long-term debt with an interest rate of 9 percent. The proceeds are used to retire outstanding common stock. According to NOI theory (the independence hypothesis), what will be the firm's cost of common equity *after* the capital structure change?

1. What will be the dividend per share flowing to the firm's common shareholders?
2. By what percentage has the dividend per share changed owing to the capital structure change?
3. By what percentage has the cost of common equity changed owing to the capital structure change?
4. What will be the composite cost of capital after the capital structure change?

**16-14B.** (*Capital structure theory*) Fernando Hotels has an all-common-equity capital structure. Some financial data for the company are as follows:

Shares of common stock outstanding = 575,000
Common stock price, $P_0$ = \$38 per share
Expected level of EBIT = \$4,500,000
Dividend payout ratio = 100 percent

In answering the following questions, assume that corporate income is not taxed.

**a.** Under the present capital structure, what is the total value of the firm?

**b.** What is the cost of common equity capital, $K_c$? What is the composite cost of capital, $K_0$?

**c.** Now suppose Fernando sells \$1.5 million of long-term debt with an interest rate of 11 percent. The proceeds are used to retire outstanding common stock. According to the net operating income theory (the independence hypothesis), what will be the firm's cost of common equity after the capital structure change?

1. What will be the dividend per share flowing to the firm's common shareholders?
2. By what percent has the dividend per share changed owing to the capital structure change?
3. By what percent has the cost of common equity changed owing to the capital structure change?
4. What will be the composite cost of capital after the capital structure change?

**16-15B.** (*EBIT–EPS analysis*) Mount Rosemead Health Services, Inc., is analyzing three different financing plans for a newly formed subsidiary. The plans are described as follows:

| Plan A | Plan B | Plan C |
|---|---|---|
| Common stock: \$150,000 | Bonds at 10%: \$ 50,000<br>Common stock: \$100,000 | Preferred stock at 10%: \$ 50,000<br>Common stock: \$100,000 |

In all cases, the common stock will be sold to net Mount Rosemead \$10 per share. The subsidiary is expected to generate an average EBIT per year of \$36,000. The management of Mount Rosemead places great emphasis on EPS performance. Income is taxed at a 50 percent rate.

**a.** Where feasible, find the EBIT indifference levels between the alternatives.

**b.** Which financing plan do you recommend that Mount Rosemead pursue?

## SELF-TEST SOLUTIONS

**ST-1. a.** $FC$ = interest + sinking fund

$FC = (\$6{,}000{,}000)(.12) + (\$6{,}000{,}000/20)$

$FC = \$720{,}000 + \$300{,}000 = \underline{\underline{\$1{,}020{,}000}}$

**b.** $CB_r = C_0 + NCF_r - FC$

where $C_0 = \$750{,}000$

$FC = \$1{,}020{,}000$

and

$NCF_r = \$3{,}400{,}000 - \$3{,}100{,}000 = \$300{,}000$

so

$CB_r = \$750{,}000 + \$300{,}000 - \$1{,}020{,}000$

$CB_r = \underline{\underline{\$30{,}000}}$

**c.** We know that the firm has a preference for maintaining a cash balance of $750,000. The joint impact of the recessionary economic environment and the proposed issue of bonds would put the firm's recessionary cash balance ($CB_r$) at $30,000. Because the firm desires a minimum cash balance of $750,000 ($C_0$), the data suggest that the proposed bond issue should be postponed.

**ST-2. a.** Firm Y seems to be using financial leverage to the most appropriate degree. Notice that its price/earnings ratio of 16 times exceeds that of firm X (at 9 times) and firm Z (also at 9 times).

**b.** The first financial leverage effect refers to the added variability in the earnings per share stream caused by the use of leverage-inducing financial instruments. The second financial leverage effect concerns the level of earnings per share at a specific EBIT associated with a specific capital structure.

Beyond some critical EBIT level, earnings per share will be higher if more leverage is used. Based on the company data provided, the marketplace for financial instruments is weighing the second leverage effect more heavily. Firm Z, therefore, seems to be underlevered (is operating *below* its theoretical leverage capacity).

**ST-3. a.**

| Plan A | | Plan B |
|---|---|---|
| **EPS: Less-Levered Plan** | | **EPS: More-Levered Plan** |
| $\dfrac{(EBIT - I)(1 - t) - P}{S_A}$ | = | $\dfrac{(EBIT - I)(1 - t) - P}{S_B}$ |
| $\dfrac{(EBIT - \$140{,}000)(1 - 0.5)}{100{,}000\text{ (shares)}}$ | = | $\dfrac{(EBIT - \$480{,}000)(1 - 0.5)}{60{,}000\text{ (shares)}}$ |
| $\dfrac{0.5\,EBIT - \$70{,}000}{10}$ | = | $\dfrac{0.5\,EBIT - \$240{,}000}{6}$ |
| $EBIT = \underline{\underline{\$990{,}000}}$ | | |

**b.** The EBIT–EPS analysis chart for Martin-Bowing is presented in Figure 16-10.

| | Plan A | Plan B |
|---|---|---|
| EBIT | $990,000 | $990,000 |
| I | 140,000 | 480,000 |
| EBT | $850,000 | $510,000 |
| *T* (.5) | 425,000 | 255,000 |
| NI | $425,000 | $255,000 |
| *P* | 0 | 0 |
| EAC | $425,000 | $255,000 |
| ÷ No. of common shares | 100,000 | 60,000 |
| EPS | $ 4.25 | $ 4.25 |

**c.** Because $1,188,000 exceeds the calculated indifference level of $990,000, the more highly levered plan (plan B) will produce the higher EPS.

**d.** At this stage of the problem, it is necessary to compute EPS under each financing alternative. Then the relevant price/earnings ratio for each plan can be applied to project the common stock price for the plan at a specific EBIT level.

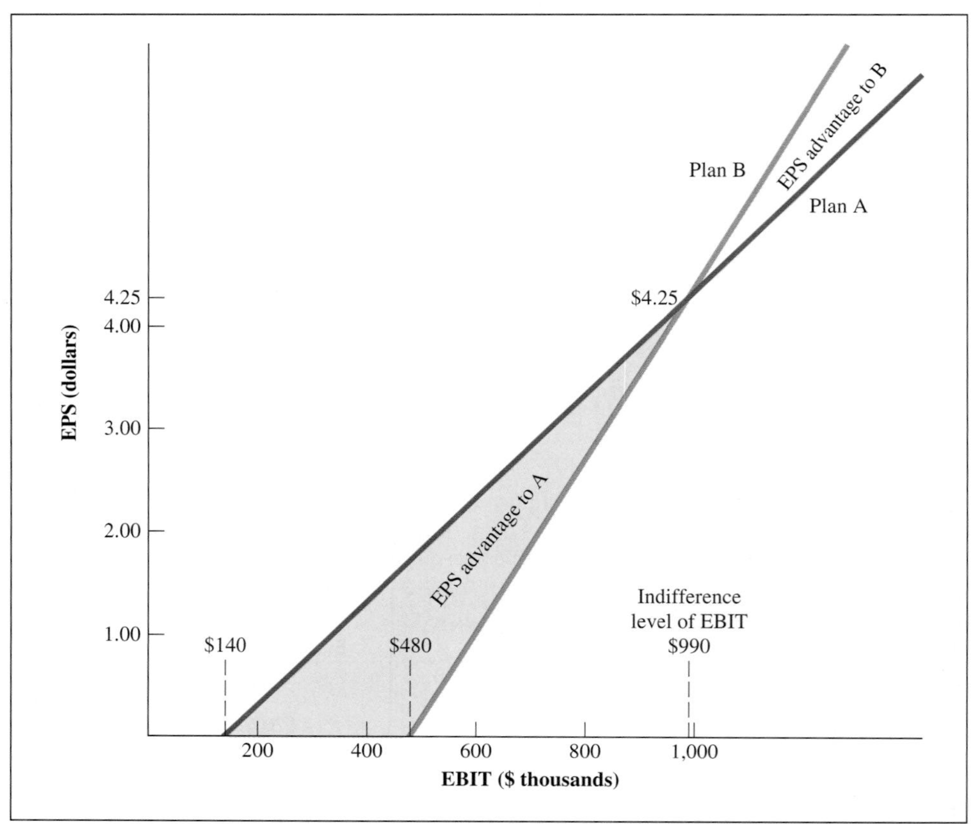


**FIGURE 16-10**
EBIT–EPS Analysis Chart for Martin-Bowing Company

| | Plan A | Plan B |
|---|---|---|
| EBIT | $1,188,000 | $1,188,000 |
| *I* | 140,000 | 480,000 |
| EBT | $1,048,000 | $ 708,000 |
| *T* (.5) | 524,000 | 354,000 |
| NI | $ 524,000 | $ 354,000 |
| *P* | 0 | 0 |
| EAC | $ 524,000 | $ 354,000 |
| ÷ No. of common shares | 100,000 | 60,000 |
| EPS | $ 5.24 | $ 5.90 |
| × P/E ratio | 13 | 11 |
| = Projected stock price | $ 68.12 | $ 64.90 |

Notice that the greater riskiness of plan B results in the market applying a lower price/earnings multiple to the expected EPS. Therefore, the investors would actually enjoy a higher stock price under plan A ($68.12) than they would under plan B ($64.90).

**e.** Here, we want to find the price/earnings ratio that would equate the common stock prices for both plans at an EBIT level of $1,188,000. All we have to do is take plan B's EPS and relate it to plan A's stock price. Thus:

$5.90 (P/E) = $68.12

(P/E) = $68.12/$5.90 = 11.546.

A price/earnings ratio of 11.546 when applied to plan B's EPS would give the same stock price as that of plan A ($68.12).

# DIVIDEND POLICY AND INTERNAL FINANCING

The corporate choice to pay or not to pay a cash dividend to stockholders and the further choice to increase the dividend, reduce the dividend, or keep it at the same dollar amount, represent one of the most challenging and perplexing areas of corporate

financial policy. Because stockholder returns only come in two forms: stock price change and cash dividends received, it follows that the dividend decision directly impacts shareholder wealth. ● We know that rational investors would rather be more wealthy rather than less wealthy. Accordingly, corporate boards of directors face a daunting decision every time the question of dividend policy and the possibility of changing the cash dividend is on the agenda. ● In the simplest form, increasing the cash dividend simultaneously reduces the stock of internal financial capital (cash) available for capital expenditures. Thus the firm's stockholders find themselves smack in the middle of **Principle 1: The Risk-Return Trade-Off—We won't take on additional risk unless we expect to be compensated with additional return.** The cash dividend, after all, is there in your hand to be spent today; the proposed capital expenditure is made based on the valuation of its expected incremental net cash flows. Recall **Principle 4.** ● The expected net present value of the proposed capital project will be impacted into the firm's stock price. But the arrival of new information over time about

**LEARNING OBJECTIVES**

After reading this chapter, you should be able to

1. Describe the trade-off between paying dividends and retaining the profits within the company.
2. Explain the relationship between a corporation's dividend policy and the market price of its common stock.
3. Describe practical considerations that may be important to the firm's dividend policy.
4. Distinguish among the types of dividend policies corporations frequently use.
5. Specify the procedures a company follows in administering the dividend payment.
6. Describe why and how a firm might choose to pay noncash dividends (stock dividends and stock splits) instead of cash dividends.
7. Explain the purpose and procedures related to stock repurchases.
8. Understand the relationship between a policy of low dividend payments and international capital-budgeting opportunities that confront the multinational firm.

the success (or lack of success) of the capital project will be digested by the capital market and subsequently reflected in its stock price. So to be better off in a wealth context, the investor needs the firm to earn a higher rate of return on a dollar that is retained in the firm than that same investor could earn by investing that dollar elsewhere, given all economic considerations, such as having to pay a personal tax on the dollar of cash dividends received. It is indeed a perplexing corporate choice. ● Over the years 1995 through 1999, the total return on the S&P 500 Stock index equaled 37.4, 23.1, 33.4, 28.6, and 21.0, percent, respectively.[1] Not since very precise records have been kept commencing in 1926 did this bellwether index exceed a 20 percent level for 5 consecutive years. Note that these 5 years of abnormally high nominal returns followed a run of 3 consecutive years, 1992 to 1994, in which the total return on this same stock index never exceeded 10 percent. The recent history of lofty total returns on equity investments (which ended in the presidential election year of 2000, by the way) induced corporate executives and their boards of directors to rein in their dividend payout policies. ● For example, in 1997, fewer firms increased their dividends from the previous year than had occurred since 1990. This tendency reflected widespread corporate sentiment that firms could increase shareholder wealth by retaining a larger proportion of earnings per share. Along these same lines, the management of the Coca-Cola Company said, "In 1996, our dividend payout ratio was approximately 36 percent of our net income. To free up additional cash for reinvestment in our high-return beverages business, our Board of Directors intends to gradually reduce our dividend payout ratio to 30 percent over time."[2] From Coca-Cola, above, you have an explicit statement that describes the firm's dividend policy. Another actual example follows. ● During periods of strong internal corporate growth, firms tend to maintain modest dividend payout ratios (i.e., cash dividends paid/earnings per share). Harley-Davidson, Inc., provides a sound example of such a financial policy. Over the 5-year period from 1995 through 1999, Harley-Davidson's dividend payout ratio averaged 11.25 percent. Notice that this was considerably less than Coca-Cola's target of 30 percent. But, while Harley-Davidson's payout ratio was quite stable over these 5 years, the firm did, in fact, increase the absolute amount paid out in cash dividends each year from $.09 per share in 1995 to $.175 per share in 1999. ● Harley-Davidson's dividend policy makes sense from the standpoint of its stated and planned capital-expenditure decisions. You will observe in this chapter that the capital-budgeting decision and the dividend decision are as closely linked as

[1] *The Wall Street Journal* (January 2, 1998): R12, and (January 3, 1999); R14.

[2] The Coca-Cola Company, *Annual Report* (1996), 42.

is possible within the framework of increasing shareholder wealth and increasing economic value.

In discussing the firm's financial condition and operating results for 1999, Harley-Davidson's management said: "The Company regularly invests in equipment to support and improve its various manufacturing processes. The Company estimates that capital expenditures required in 2000 will be in the range of \$150–\$170 million. The Company anticipates it will have the ability to fund all capital expenditures with internally generated funds and short-term financing."[3] Thus, the Harley-Davidson stated policy of financing the major proportion of its capital expenditures with internally generated financial capital means, simultaneously, that fewer dollars will be paid to shareholders in the form of cash dividends. Also notice how similar Harley-Davidson's retention and funding policy, here, is to that of Coca-Cola. These sorts of highly important corporate dividend policies, and the decisions that underlie them, are the focus of this chapter.

**CHAPTER PREVIEW**

The primary goal or objective of the firm should be to maximize the value, or price, of a firm's common stock. The success or failure of management's decisions can be evaluated only in light of their impact on the firm's common stock price. We observed that the company's investment (Chapters 9, 10, and 11) and financing decisions (Chapters 15 and 16) can increase the value of the firm. As we look at the firm's dividend and internal financing policies (*internal financing* means how much of the company's financing comes from cash flows generated internally), we return to the same basic question: "Can management influence the price of the firm's stock, in this case, through its dividend policies?" After addressing this important question, we then look at the practical side of the question, "What are the practices commonly followed by managers in making decisions about paying or not paying a dividend to the firm's stockholders?"

In the development of this chapter, you will be referred to several of the principles that form the basics of business financial management and decision making. These are emphasized: **Principle 1: The Risk-Return Trade-Off—We won't take on additional risk unless we expect to be compensated with additional return; Principle 2: The Time Value of Money—A dollar received today is worth more than a dollar received in the future; Principle 4: Incremental Cash Flows—It's only what changes that counts; Principle 7: The Agency Problem—Managers won't work for owners unless it's in their best interest; and Principle 8: Taxes Bias Business Decisions.**

## DIVIDEND PAYMENT VERSUS PROFIT RETENTION

Before taking up the particular issues relating to dividend policy, we must understand several key terms and interrelationships.

**Dividend payout ratio**
The amount of dividends relative to the company's net income or earnings per share.

A firm's dividend policy includes two basic components. First, the **dividend payout ratio** indicates the amount of dividends paid relative to the company's earnings. For instance, if the dividend per share is \$2 and the earnings per share is \$4, the payout ratio is 50 percent (\$2 ÷ \$4). The second component is the *stability* of the dividends over time. As will be observed later in the chapter, dividend stability may be almost as important to the investor as the amount of dividends received.

In formulating a dividend policy, the financial manager faces trade-offs. Assuming that management has already decided how much to invest and has chosen its debt-equity mix for financing these investments, the decision to pay a large dividend means simultaneously

[3] Harley-Davidson, Inc., *Annual Report* (1999), 62, 63.

**FIGURE 17-1**
Dividend-Retention-Financing Trade-Offs

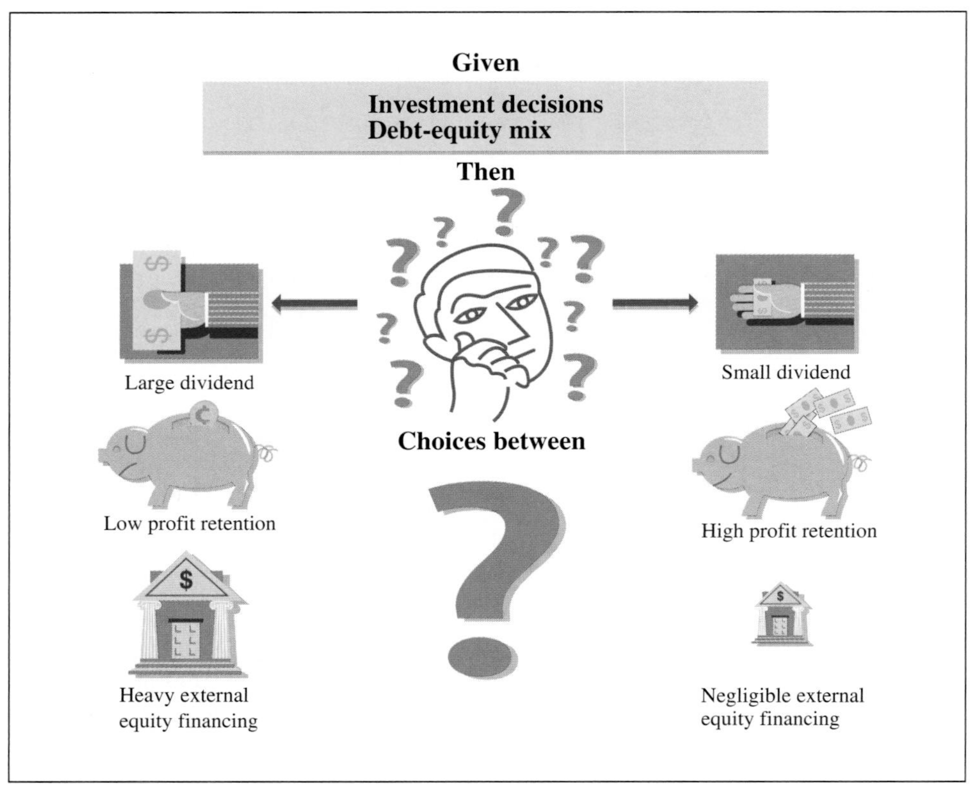


deciding to retain little, if any, profits; this in turn results in a greater reliance on external equity financing. Conversely, given the firm's investment and financing decisions, a small dividend payment corresponds to high profit retention with less need for externally generated equity funds. These trade-offs, which are fundamental to our discussion, are illustrated in Figure 17-1.

**CONCEPT CHECK**

1. Can you provide a financial executive a useful definition of the term *dividend payout ratio?*
2. How does the firm's actual dividend policy affect its need for externally generated financial capital?

## DOES DIVIDEND POLICY AFFECT STOCK PRICE?[4]

OBJECTIVE 2 

The fundamental question to be resolved in our study of the firm's dividend policy may be stated simply: What is a sound rationale or motivation for dividend payments? If we believe our objective should be to maximize the value of the common stock, we may

[4]The concepts of this section draw heavily from Donald H. Chew, Jr., ed., "Do Dividends Matter? A Discussion of Corporate Dividend Policy," in *Six Roundtable Discussions of Corporate Finance with Joel Stern* (New York: Quorum Books, 1986): 67–101; and a book of readings edited by Joel M. Stern and Donald H. Chew, Jr., *The Revolution in Corporate Finance* (New York: Basil Blackwell, 1986). Specific readings included Merton Miller, "Can Management Use Dividends to Influence the Value of the Firm?" 299–303; Richard Brealey, "Does Dividend Policy Matter?" 304–9; and Michael Rozeff, "How Companies Set Their Dividend Payout Ratios," 320–26.

restate the question as follows: Given the firm's capital-budgeting and borrowing decisions, what is the effect of the firm's dividend policies on the stock price? *Does a high dividend payment decrease stock value, increase it, or make no real difference?*

At first glance, we might reasonably conclude that a firm's dividend policy is important. We have already defined the value of a stock to be equal to the present value of future dividends (Chapter 8). How can we now suggest that dividends are not important? Why do so many companies pay dividends, and why is a page in *The Wall Street Journal* devoted to dividend announcements? Based on intuition, we could quickly conclude that dividend policy is important. However, we might be surprised to learn that the dividend question has been a controversial issue for well over three decades. It has even been called the "dividend puzzle."[5]

## Three Basic Views

Some would argue that the amount of the dividend is irrelevant, and any time spent on the decision is a waste of energy. Others contend that a high dividend will result in a high stock price. Still others take the view that dividends actually hurt the stock value. Let us look at these three views in turn.

**VIEW 1: DIVIDEND POLICY IS IRRELEVANT** Much of the controversy about the dividend issue is based in the time-honored disagreements between the academic and professional communities. Some experienced practitioners perceive stock price changes resulting from dividend announcements and therefore see dividends as important. Many within the academic community—namely, finance professors—who argue that dividends are irrelevant see the confusion about the matter resulting from not carefully defining what we mean by dividend policy. They would argue that the appearance of a relationship between dividends and stock price may be an illusion.[6]

The position that dividends are not important rests on two preconditions. First, we assume that investment and borrowing decisions have already been made, and that these decisions will not be altered by the amount of any dividend payments. Second, **"perfect" capital markets** are assumed to exist, which means that (1) investors can buy and sell stocks without incurring any transaction costs, such as brokerage commissions; (2) companies can issue stocks without any cost of doing so; (3) there are no corporate or personal taxes; (4) complete information about the firm is readily available; (5) there are no conflicts of interest between managements and stockholders; and (6) financial distress and bankruptcy costs are nonexistent.

**"Perfect" capital markets** Capital markets where (1) investors can buy and sell stock without incurring any transaction costs, such as brokerage commissions; (2) companies can issue stocks without any cost of doing so; (3) there are no corporate or personal taxes; (4) complete information about the firm is readily available; (5) there are no conflicts of interest between managements and stockholders; and (6) financial distress and bankruptcy costs are nonexistent.

The first assumption—that we have already made the investment and financing decisions—simply keeps us from confusing the issues. We want to know the effect of dividend decisions on a stand-alone basis, without mixing in other decisions. The second assumption, that of perfect markets, also allows us to study the effect of dividend decisions in isolation, much like a physicist studies motion in a vacuum to avoid the influence of friction.

Given these assumptions, the effect of a dividend decision on share price may be stated unequivocally: *There is no relationship between dividend policy and stock value.* One dividend policy is as good as another one. In the aggregate, investors are concerned only with *total* returns from investment decisions; they are indifferent whether these returns come from capital gains or dividend income. They also recognize that the dividend decision, given the investment policy, is really a choice of financing strategy. To finance growth, the firm (a) may choose to issue stock, allowing internally generated funds (profits) to be used to pay dividends; or (b) may

[5]See Fischer Black, "The Dividend Puzzle," *Journal of Portfolio Management 2* (Winter 1976): 5–8.

[6]For an excellent presentation of this issue, see Merton Miller, "Can Management Use Dividends to Influence the Value of the Firm?" in Joel M. Stern and Donald H. Chew, Jr., eds., *The Revolution in Corporate Finance* (New York: Basil Blackwell, 1986): 299–305.

**TABLE 17-1**
Dowell Venture, Inc., Financial Data

| | December 31, 1998 | |
|---|---|---|
| Total assets | $2,000,000 | |
| Common stock (100,000 shares) | $2,000,000 | |
| | **1999** | **2000** |
| Projected cash available from operations for paying dividends or for reinvesting | $400,000 | $460,000 |

use internally generated funds to finance its growth, while paying less in dividends, but not having to issue stock. In the first case, shareholders receive dividend income; in the second case, the value of their stock should increase, providing capital gains. The nature of the return is the only difference; total returns should be about the same. Thus, to argue that paying dividends can make shareholders better off is to argue that paying out cash with one hand and taking it back with the other hand is a worthwhile activity for management.

The firm's dividend payout could affect stock price if the shareholder has no other way to receive income from the investment. However, assuming the capital markets are relatively efficient, a stockholder who needs current income could always sell shares. If the firm pays a dividend, the investor could eliminate any dividend received, in whole or in part, by using the dividend to purchase stock. The investor can thus personally create any desired dividend stream, no matter what dividend policy is in effect.

*An example of dividend irrelevance.* To demonstrate the argument that dividends may not matter, come to the Land of Ez (pronounced "ease"), where the environment is quite simple. First, the king, being a kind soul, has imposed no income taxes on his subjects. Second, investors can buy and sell securities without paying any sales commissions. In addition, when a company issues new securities (stocks or bonds), there are no flotation costs. Furthermore, the Land of Ez is completely computerized, so that all information about firms is instantaneously available to the public at no cost. Next, all investors realize that the value of a company is a function of its investment opportunities and its financing decisions. Therefore, the dividend policy offers no new information about either the firm's ability to generate earnings or the riskiness of its earnings. Finally, all firms are owned and managed by the same parties; thus we have no potential conflict between owners and managers.

Within this financial utopia, would a change in a corporation's dividend stream have any effect on the price of the firm's stock? The answer is no. To illustrate, consider Dowell Venture, Inc., a corporation that received a charter at the end of 1998 to conduct business in the Land of Ez. The firm is to be financed by common stock only. Its life is to extend for only 2 years (1999 and 2000) at which time it will be liquidated.

Table 17-1 presents Dowell Venture's balance sheet at the time of its formation, as well as the projected cash flows from the short-term venture. The anticipated cash flows are based on an expected return on investment of 20 percent, which is exactly what the common shareholders require as a rate of return on their investment in the firm's stock.

At the end of 1999, an additional investment of $300,000 will be required, which may be financed by (1) retaining $300,000 of the 1999 profits, or (2) issuing new common stock, or (3) some combination of both of these. In fact, two dividend plans for 1999 are under consideration. The investors would receive either $100,000 or $250,000 in dividends. If $250,000 is paid out of 1999's $400,000 in earnings, the company would be required to issue $150,000 in new stock to make up the difference in the total $300,000 needed for reinvestment versus the $150,000 that is retained. Table 17-2 depicts these two dividend plans and the corresponding new stock issue. Our objective in analyzing the data is to answer this ques-

**TABLE 17-2**
Dowell Venture, Inc., 1999
Proposed Dividend Plans

| | Plan 1 | Plan 2 |
|---|---|---|
| Internally generated cash flow | $400,000 | $400,000 |
| Dividend for 1999 | 100,000 | 250,000 |
| Cash available for reinvestment | $300,000 | $150,000 |
| Amount of investment in 1999 | 300,000 | 300,000 |
| Additional external financing required | $ 0 | $150,000 |

**TABLE 17-3**
Dowell Venture, Inc., Step 1: Measurement of Proposed Dividend Streams

| | Plan 1 | | Plan 2 | |
|---|---|---|---|---|
| | Total Amount | Amount Per Share[a] | Total Amount | Amount Per Share[a] |
| **Year 1 (1999)** | | | | |
| (1) Dividend | $ 100,000 | $ 1.00 | $ 250,000 | $ 2.50 |
| **Year 2 (2000)** | | | | |
| **Total dividend consisting of:** | | | | |
| (2) Original investment: | | | | |
| (a) Old investors | $2,000,000 | | $2,000,000 | |
| (b) New investors | 0 | | 150,000 | |
| (3) Retained earnings from 1999 | 300,000 | | 150,000 | |
| (4) Profits for 2000 | 460,000 | | 460,000 | |
| (5) Total dividend to all investors in 2000 | $2,760,000 | | $2,760,000 | |
| **(6) Less dividends to new investors:** | | | | |
| (a) Original investment | 0 | | (150,000) | |
| (b) Profits for new investors (20% of $150,000 investment) | 0 | | (30,000) | |
| (7) Liquidating dividends available to original investors in 2000 | $2,760,000 | $27.60 | $2,580,000 | $25.80 |

[a]Number of original shares outstanding equals 100,000.

tion: Which dividend plan is preferable to the investors? In answering this question, we must take three steps: (1) Calculate the amount and timing of the dividend stream for the *original* investors. (2) Determine the present value of the dividend stream for each dividend plan. (3) Select the dividend alternative providing the higher value to the investors.

Step 1: *Computing the Dividend Streams.* The first step in this process is presented in Table 17-3. The dividends in 1999 (line 1, Table 17-3) are readily apparent from the data in Table 17-2. However, the amount of the dividend to be paid to the present shareholders in 2000 has to be calculated. To do so, we assume that investors receive (1) their original investments (line 2, Table 17-3), (2) any funds retained within the business in 1999 (line 3, Table 17-3), and (3) the profits for 2000 (line 4, Table 17-3). However, if additional stockholders invest in the company, as with plan 2, the dividends to be paid to these investors must be subtracted from the total available dividends (line 6, Table 17-3). The remaining dividends (line 7, Table 17-3) represent the amount current stockholders will receive in 2000. Therefore, the amounts of the dividend may be summarized as follows:

| Dividend Plan | 1999 | 2000 |
|---|---|---|
| 1 | $1.00 | $27.60 |
| 2 | $2.50 | $25.80 |

Step 2: *Determining the Present Value of the Cash Flow Streams.* For each of the dividend payment streams, the resulting common stock value is:

$$\text{stock price (plan 1)} = \frac{\$1.00}{(1 + .20)^1} + \frac{\$27.60}{(1 + .20)^2} = \$20$$

$$\text{stock price (plan 2)} = \frac{\$2.50}{(1 + .20)^1} + \frac{\$25.80}{(1 + .20)^2} = \$20$$

Therefore, the two approaches provide the same end product; that is, the market price of Dowell Venture's common stock is $20 regardless of the dividend policy chosen.

Step 3: *Select the Best Dividend Plan.* If the objective is to maximize the shareholders' wealth, either plan is acceptable. Alternatively, shifting the dividend payments between years by changing the dividend policy does not affect the value of the security. Thus, only if investments are made with expected returns exceeding 20 percent will the value of the stock increase. In other words, the only wealth-creating activity in the Land of Ez, where companies are financed entirely by equity, is management's investment decisions.

**VIEW 2: HIGH DIVIDENDS INCREASE STOCK VALUE** The belief that a firm's dividend policy is unimportant implicitly assumes that an investor should use the same required rate of return whether income comes through capital gains or through dividends. However, dividends are more predictable than capital gains; management can control dividends, but it cannot dictate the price of the stock. Investors are less certain of receiving income from capital gains than from dividends. The incremental risk associated with capital gains relative to dividend income implies a higher required rate for discounting a dollar of capital gains than for discounting a dollar of dividends. In other words, we would value a dollar of expected dividends more highly than a dollar of expected capital gains. We might, for example, require a 14 percent rate of return for a stock that pays its entire return from dividends, but a 20 percent return for a high-growth stock that pays no dividend. In so doing, we would give a higher value to the dividend income than we would to the capital gains. This view, which says dividends are more certain than capital gains, has been called the **"bird-in-the-hand" dividend theory.**

**"Bird-in-the-hand" dividend theory**
The belief that dividend income has a higher value to the investor than does capital gains income, because dividends are more certain than capital gains.

The position that dividends are less risky than capital gains, and should therefore be valued differently, is not without its critics. If we hold to our basic decision not to let the firm's dividend policy influence its investment and capital-mix decisions, the company's operating cash flows, both in expected amount and variability, are unaffected by its dividend policy. Because the dividend policy has no impact on the volatility of the company's overall cash flows, it has no impact on the riskiness of the firm.

Increasing a firm's dividend does not reduce the basic riskiness of the stock; rather, if a dividend payment requires management to issue new stock, it only transfers risk *and* ownership from the current owners to new owners. We would have to acknowledge that the current investors who receive the dividend trade an uncertain capital gain for a "safe" asset (the cash dividend). However, if risk reduction is the only goal, the investor could have kept the money in the bank and not bought the stock in the first place.

We might find fault with this "bird-in-the-hand" theory, but there is still a strong perception among many investors and professional investment advisors that dividends are important. They frequently argue their case based on their own personal experience. As expressed by one investment advisor:

> In advising companies on dividend policy, we're absolutely sure on one side that the investors in companies like the utilities and the suburban banks want dividends. We're absolutely sure on the other side that . . . the high-technology companies should have no dividends. For the high earners—the ones that have a high rate of return like 20 percent, or more—we think they should have a low

payout ratio. We think a typical industrial company which earns its cost of capital—just earns its cost of capital—probably should be in the average [dividend-payout] range of 40 to 50 percent.[7]

## RELATE TO THE BIG PICTURE

The preceding discussion that specifies the "bird-in-the-hand" theory between the relationship of stock price and the firm's dividend policy relates directly to **Principle 2: The Time Value of Money—A dollar received today is worth more than a dollar received in the future.** This theory suggests that because the dollar of dividends is received today it should be valued more highly than an uncertain capital gain that might be received in the future. The fundamental premise of this position is that the cash dividend in your hand (placed there today by the firm's payout policy) is more certain (less risky) than a possible capital gain. Many practitioners adhere to this theory; but many also adhere to the theory that is advanced in the next section. If nothing else, because it is controversial, dividend policy is important to the firm and its stockholders. And, in reality, many companies do pay cash dividends. Cash dividends are ubiquitous, so they are discussed in depth.

**VIEW 3: LOW DIVIDENDS INCREASE STOCK VALUE** The third view of how dividends affect stock price proposes that dividends actually hurt the investor. This argument has largely been based on the difference in tax treatment for dividend income and capital gains. Unlike the investors in the great Land of Ez, most other investors do pay income taxes. For these taxpayers, the objective is to maximize the *after-tax* return on investment relative to the risk assumed. This objective is realized by *minimizing* the effective tax rate on the income and, whenever possible, by *deferring* the payment of taxes.

Like most tax code complexities, Congress over the years has altered the outcome of whether capital gains are taxed at either (1) a lower or (2) a similar rate as "earned income." Think of a water faucet being randomly turned on and then off. From 1987 through 1992, no federal tax advantage was provided for capital gains income relative to dividend income. A revision in the tax code that took effect beginning in 1993 did provide a preference for capital gains income. Then, the Taxpayer Relief Act of 1997 made the difference (preference) even more favorable for capital gains as opposed to cash dividend income. For some taxpayers, if a minimum holding period has been reached, the tax rate applied to capital gains was reduced to 20 percent from the previous level of 28 percent.

Further, another distinct benefit exists for capital gains vis-a-vis dividend income. Taxes on dividend income are paid when the dividend is received, whereas taxes on price appreciation (capital gains) are deferred until the stock is actually sold. Thus when it comes to tax considerations, most investors prefer the retention of a firm's earnings as opposed to the payment of cash dividends. If earnings are retained within the firm, the stock price increases, but the increase is not taxed until the stock is sold.

Although the majority of investors are subject to taxes, certain investment companies, trusts, and pension plans are exempt on their dividend income. Also, for tax purposes, a corporation may exclude 70 percent of the dividend income received from another corporation. In these cases, investors may prefer dividends over capital gains.

[7]From a discussion by John Childs, an investment advisor at Kidder Peabody, in Donald H. Chew, Jr., ed., "Do Dividends Matter? A Discussion of Corporate Dividend Policy," in *Six Roundtable Discussions of Corporate Finance with Joel Stern* (New York: Quorum Books, 1986): 83–84.

To summarize, when it comes to taxes, we want to maximize our *after-tax* return, as opposed to the *before-tax* return. Investors try to defer taxes whenever possible. Stocks that allow tax deferral (low dividends—high capital gains) will possibly sell at a premium relative to stocks that require current taxation (high dividends—low capital gains). In this way, the two stocks may provide comparable after-tax returns. This suggests that a policy of paying low dividends will result in a higher stock price. That is, high dividends hurt investors, whereas low dividends and high retention help investors. This is the logic of advocates of the low-dividend policy.

**RELATE TO THE BIG PICTURE**

The presentation here of the argument that low cash dividends might increase common stock prices depends prominently on **Principle 8: Taxes Bias Business Decisions.** For most individual economic units, income received in the form of cash dividends is subject to taxation at the relevant personal income tax rate. But the amount received from the sale of common stock that represents a "capital gain" is subject to a lower and, thus, more favorable tax rate. So the argument suggests that taxpayers (investors) who find themselves in higher personal tax brackets will actually prefer to invest in companies that have dividend policies calling for low or no cash dividends being paid. Not only is the ultimate tax deferred until the gain is realized, but it enjoys a lower tax rate, leaving a larger residual gain for the investor who actually assumed the risk of the financial investment. **Principle 8** is also an important underpinning of something called "the clientele effect" that will be discussed later in this chapter.

## Improving Our Thinking

We have now looked at three views on dividend policy. Which is right? The argument that dividends are irrelevant is difficult to refute, given the perfect market assumptions. However, in the real world, it is not always easy to feel comfortable with such an argument. Conversely, the high-dividend philosophy, which measures risk by how we split the firm's cash flows between dividends and retention, is not particularly appealing when studied carefully. The third view, which is essentially a tax argument against high dividends, is persuasive. However, if low dividends are so advantageous and generous dividends are so hurtful, why do companies continue to pay dividends? It is difficult to believe that managers would forgo such an easy opportunity to benefit their stockholders. What are we missing?

The need to find the missing elements in our "dividend puzzle" has not been ignored. When we need to understand better an issue or a phenomenon, we have two options: improving our thinking or gathering more evidence about the topic. Scholars and practitioners have taken both approaches. Although no single definitive answer has yet been found that is acceptable to all, several plausible extensions have been developed. Some of the more popular additions include (1) the residual dividend theory, (2) the clientele effect, (3) information effects, (4) agency costs, and (5) expectations theory.

**THE RESIDUAL DIVIDEND THEORY** Within the Land of Ez, companies were blessed with professional consultants who were essentially charitable in nature; they did not seek any compensation when they helped a firm through the process of issuing stock. (Even in the Land of Ez, managers needed help from investment bankers, accountants, and attorneys to sell a new issue.) However, in reality, the process is quite expensive and may cost as much as 20 percent of the dollar issue size.[8]

If a company incurs flotation costs, that may have a direct bearing on the dividend decision. Because of these costs, a firm must issue a larger amount of securities in order to receive the amount required for investment. For example, if $300,000 is needed to finance proposed investments, an amount exceeding the $300,000 will have to be issued to offset flotation costs incurred in the sale of the new stock issue. This means, very simply, that new equity capital raised through the sale of common stock will be more expensive than capital raised through the retention of earnings. (Remember what we learned in Chapter 12?)

In effect, flotation costs eliminate our indifference between financing by internal capital and by new common stock. Earlier, the company could pay dividends and issue common stock or retain profits. However, when flotation costs exist, internal financing is preferred. Dividends are paid only if profits are not completely used for investment purposes—that is, only when there are "residual earnings" after the financing of new investments. This policy is called **residual dividend theory.**[9]

**Residual dividend theory** A theory asserting that the dividends to be paid should equal capital left over after the financing of profitable investments.

With the assumption of no flotation costs removed, the firm's dividend policy would be as follows:

1. Maintain the optimum debt ratio in financing future investments.
2. Accept an investment if the net present value is positive. That is, the expected rate of return exceeds the cost of capital.
3. Finance the equity portion of new investments first by internally generated funds. Only after this capital is fully utilized should the firm issue new common shares.
4. If any internally generated funds still remain after making all investments, pay dividends to the investors. However, if all internal capital is needed for financing the equity portion of proposed investments, pay no dividend.

In summary, dividend policy is influenced by (1) the company's investment opportunities, (2) the capital structure mix, and (3) the availability of internally generated capital. In the following Krista Corporation example, dividends were paid *only* after all acceptable investments had been financed. This logic, called the residual dividend theory, implies that the dividends to be paid should equal the equity capital *remaining* after financing investments. According to this theory, dividend policy is a passive influence, having by itself no direct influence on the market price of the common stock.

## EXAMPLE

Assume that the Krista Corporation finances 40 percent of its investments with debt and the remaining 60 percent with common equity. Two million dollars have been generated from operations and may be used to finance the common equity portion of new investments or to pay common dividends. The firm's management is considering five investment opportunities. Figure 17-2 graphs the expected rate of return for these investments, along with the firm's weighted marginal cost of capital curve. From the information contained in the figure, we would accept projects A, B, and C, requiring $2.5 million in total financing. Therefore, $1 million in new debt (40% × $2.5 million) would be needed, with common equity providing

[8]We discussed the costs of issuing securities in Chapter 12.

[9]The residual dividend theory is consistent with the "pecking order" theory of finance as described by Stewart Myers, "The Capital Structure Puzzle," *The Journal of Finance* (July 1984): 575–92.

$1.5 million (60% × $2.5 million). In this instance, the dividend payment decision would be to pay $500,000 in dividends, which is the residual, or remainder, of the $2 million internally generated capital.

To illustrate further, consider the dividend decision if project D had also been acceptable. If this investment were added to the firm's portfolio of proposed capital expenditures, then $4 million in new financing would be needed. Debt financing would constitute $1.6 million (40% × $4 million) and common equity would provide the additional $2.4 million (60% × $4 million). Because only $2 million is available internally, $400,000 in new common stock would be issued. The residual available for dividends would be zero, and no dividend would be paid.

**FIGURE 17-2**
Krista Corporation Investment Schedule

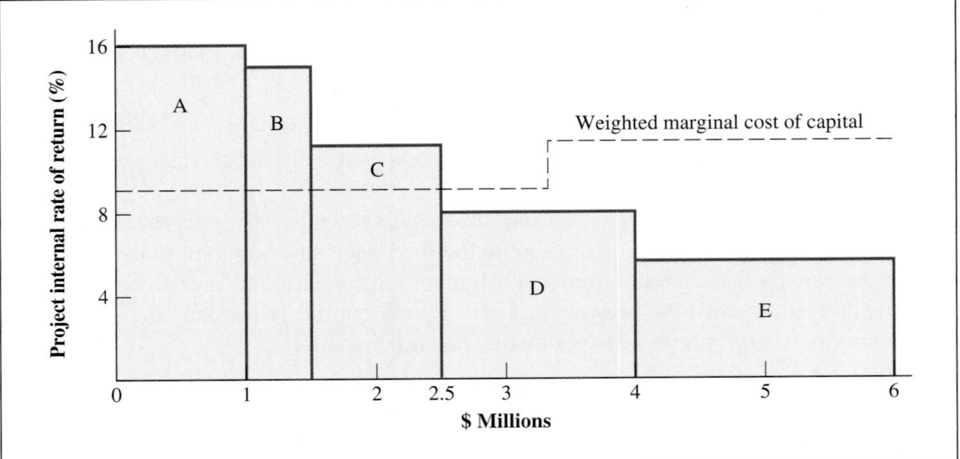


THE CLIENTELE EFFECT What if the investors living in the Land of Ez did not like the dividend policy chosen by Dowell's management? No problem. They could simply satisfy their personal income preferences by purchasing or selling securities when the dividends received did not satisfy their current needs for income. If an investor did not view the dividends received in any given year as sufficient, he or she could simply sell a portion of stock, thereby "creating a dividend." In addition, if the dividend were larger than the investor desired, he or she could purchase stock with the "excess cash" created by the dividend. However, once we leave the Land of Ez, we find that such adjustments in stock ownership are not cost-free. When an investor buys or sells stock, brokerage fees are incurred, ranging from approximately 1 to 10 percent. Even more costly, the investor who buys the stock with cash received from a dividend will have to pay taxes before reinvesting the cash. And when a stock is bought or sold, it must first be reevaluated. Acquisition of the information for decision making also may be time consuming and costly. Finally, aside from the cost of buying or selling part of the stock, some institutional investors, such as university endowment funds, are precluded from selling stock and "spending" the proceeds.

As a result of these considerations, investors may not be too inclined to buy stocks that require them to "create" a dividend stream more suitable to their purposes. Rather, if investors do in fact have a preference between dividends and capital gains, we could expect them to seek firms that have a dividend policy consistent with these preferences. They would, in essence, "sort themselves out" by buying stocks that satisfy their preferences for dividends and capital gains. Individuals and institutions that need current income would be drawn to companies that have high dividend payouts. Other investors, such as wealthy individuals, would much prefer to avoid taxes by holding securities that offer no or small dividend income but large capital gains. In other words, there would be a **clientele effect:** Firms draw a given clientele, given their stated dividend policy.

**Clientele effect**
The belief that individuals and institutions that need current income will invest in companies that have high dividend payouts. Other investors prefer to avoid taxes by holding securities that offer only small dividend income, but large capital gains. Thus we have a "clientele" of investors.

The possibility that clienteles of investors exist might lead us to believe that the firm's dividend policy matters. However, unless there is a greater aggregate demand for a particular policy than the market can satisfy, dividend policy is still unimportant; one policy is as good as the other. The clientele effect only warns firms to avoid making capricious changes in their dividend policy. Given that the firm's investment decisions are already made, the level of the dividend is still unimportant. The change in the policy matters only when it requires clientele to shift to another company.

**THE INFORMATION EFFECT** The investor in the Land of Ez would argue with considerable persuasion that a firm's value is determined strictly by its investment and financing decisions, and that the dividend policy has no impact on value. Yet we know from experience that a large, unexpected change in dividends can have a significant impact on the stock price. For instance, in August 1994, the Continental Corporation, a large insurance company, eliminated its annual dividend of $1. In response, the firm's stock price went from about $18 to $15. How can we suggest that dividend policy matters little, when we can cite numerous such examples of a change in dividend affecting the stock price, especially when the change is negative?

Despite such "evidence," we are not looking at the real cause and effect. It may be that investors use a change in dividend policy as a *signal* about the firm's financial condition, especially its earnings power. Thus, a dividend increase that is larger than expected might signal to investors that management expects significantly higher earnings in the future. Conversely, a dividend decrease, or even a less than expected increase, might signal that management is forecasting less favorable future earnings.

Some would argue that management frequently has inside information about the firm that it cannot make available to investors. This difference in accessibility to information between management and investors, called **information asymmetry,** may result in a lower stock price than would occur under conditions of certainty. This reasoning says that, by regularly increasing dividends, management is making a commitment to continue these cash flows to the stockholders for the foreseeable future. So in a risky marketplace, dividends become a means to minimize any "drag" on the stock price that might come from differences in the level of information available to managers and investors.

**Information asymmetry**
The difference in accessibility to information between management and investors may result in a lower stock price than would occur under conditions of certainty.

Dividends may therefore be important only as a communication tool; management may have no other credible way to inform investors about future earnings, or at least no convincing way that is less costly.

**AGENCY COSTS** Let us return again to the Land of Ez. We had avoided any potential conflict between the firm's investors and managers by assuming them to be one and the same. With only a cursory look at the real marketplace, we can see that managers and investors are typically not the same people, and as noted in the preceding section, these two groups do not have the same access to information about the firm. If the two groups are not the same, we must then assume that management is dedicated to maximizing shareholder wealth.[10] That is, we are making a presupposition that the market values of companies with separate owners and managers will not differ from those of owner-managed firms.

[10]This issue was addressed briefly in Chapter 1.

### RELATE TO THE BIG PICTURE

**Principle 7** warned us there may be a conflict between management and owners, especially in large firms where managers and owners have different incentives. That is: **Managers Won't Work for Owners Unless It's in Their Best Interest.** As we shall see in this section, the dividend policy may be one way to reduce this problem.

Two possibilities should help managers see things as the equity investors see them: (1) Low market values may attract takeover bids; and (2) a competitive labor market may allow investors to replace uncooperative managers. That is, if management is not sensitive to the need to maximize shareholder wealth, new investors may buy the stock, take control of the firm, and remove management.[11] If current management is being less than supportive of the owners, these owners can always seek other managers who will work in the investors' best interest. If these two market mechanisms worked perfectly without any cost, the potential conflict would be nonexistent. In reality, however, conflicts may still exist, and the stock price of a company owned by investors who are separate from management may be less than the stock value of a closely held firm. The difference in price is the cost of the conflict to the owners, which has come to be called **agency costs.**[12]

**Agency costs**
The costs, such as a reduced stock price, associated with potential conflict between managers and investors when these two groups are not the same.

Recognizing the possible problem, management, acting independently or at the insistence of the board of directors, frequently takes action to minimize the cost associated with the separation of ownership and management control. Such action, which in itself is costly, includes auditing by independent accountants, assigning supervisory functions to the company's board of directors, creating covenants in lending agreements that restrict management's powers, and providing incentive compensation plans for management that help "bond" the management with the owners.

A firm's dividend policy may be perceived by owners as a tool to minimize agency costs. Assuming that the payment of a dividend requires management to issue stock to finance new investments, new investors may be attracted to the company only if management provides convincing information that the capital will be used profitably. Thus the payment of dividends indirectly results in a closer monitoring of management's investment activities. In this case, dividends may make a meaningful contribution to the value of the firm.

**EXPECTATIONS THEORY**[13] A common thread throughout much of our discussion of dividend policy, particularly as it relates to information effects, is the word *expected.* We should not overlook the significance of this word when we are making any financial decision within the firm. No matter what the decision area, how the market price responds to management's actions is not determined entirely by the action itself; it is also affected by investors' expectations about the ultimate decision to be made by management. This idea is called the **expectations theory.**

**Expectations theory**
The effect of new information about a company on the firm's stock price depends more on how the new information compares to expectations than on the actual announcement itself.

As the time approaches for management to announce the amount of the next dividend, investors form expectations as to how much that dividend will be. These expectations are based on several factors internal to the firm, such as past dividend decisions, current and

[11]The "corporate control hypothesis," especially as it relates to companies merging or being acquired, has generated a great amount of interest. For example, see the April 1983 issue of *Journal of Financial Economics.*

[12]See M. C. Jenson, and W. H. Meckling, "Theory of the Firm: Managerial Behavior, Agency Costs, and Ownership Structure," *Journal of Financial Economics* (October 1976): 305–60.

[13]Much of the thoughts in this section came from Merton Miller, "Can Management Use Dividends to Influence the Value of the Firm?" in *The Revolution in Corporate Finance,* Joel M. Stern, and Donald H. Chew, Jr., eds. (New York: Basil Blackwell, 1986): 299–303.

expected earnings, investment strategies, and financing decisions. They also consider such things as the condition of the general economy, the strength or weakness of the industry at the time, and possible changes in government policies.

When the actual dividend decision is announced, the investor compares the actual decision with the expected decision. If the amount of the dividend is as expected, even if it represents an increase from prior years, the market price of the stock will remain unchanged. However, if the dividend is higher or lower than expected, investors will reassess their perceptions about the firm. They will question the meaning of the *unexpected* change in the dividend. They may use the unexpected dividend decision as a clue about unexpected changes in earnings; that is, the unexpected dividend change has information content about the firm's earnings and other important factors. In short, management's actual decision about the firm's dividend policy may not be terribly significant, unless it departs from investors' expectations. If there is a difference between actual and expected dividends, we will more than likely see a movement in the stock price.

## The Empirical Evidence

Our search for an answer to the question of dividend relevance has been less than successful. We have given it our best thinking, but still no single, definitive position has emerged. Maybe we could gather evidence to show the relationship between dividend practices and security prices. We might also inquire into the perceptions of financial managers who make decisions about dividend policies, with the idea that their beliefs affect their decision making. Then we could truly know that dividend policy is important or that it does not matter.

To test the relationship between dividend payments and security prices, we could compare a firm's dividend yield (dividend/stock price) and the stock's total return. The question is: Do stocks that pay high dividends provide higher or lower returns to investors? Such tests have been conducted with the use of highly sophisticated statistical techniques. Despite the use of these extremely powerful analytical tools, which involve intricate and complicated procedures, the results have been mixed.[14] However, over long periods, the results have given a slight advantage to the low-dividend stocks; that is, stocks that pay lower dividends appear to have higher prices. The findings are far from conclusive, however, owing to the relatively large standard errors of the estimates. (The apparent differences may be the result of random sampling error and not real differences.) We simply have been unable to disentangle the effect of dividend policy from other influences.

Several reasons may be given for our inability to arrive at conclusive results. First, to be accurate, we would need to know the amount of dividends investors *expected* to receive. Because these expectations cannot be observed, we can only use historical data, which may or may not relate to current expectations. Second, most empirical studies have assumed a linear relationship between dividend payments and stock prices. The actual relationship may be nonlinear, possibly even discontinuous. Whatever the reasons, the evidence to date is inconclusive and the jury is still out.

Because our statistical prowess does not provide any conclusive evidence, let's turn to our last hope. What do the financial managers of the world believe about the relevance of dividend policy? Although we may not conclude that a manager's opinion is necessarily the "final word on the matter," having these insights is helpful. If financial managers

[14]See F. Black and M. Scholes, "The Effects of Dividend Yield and Dividend Policy on Common Stock Prices and Returns," *Journal of Financial Economics* 1 (May 1974), 1–22; P. Hess, "The Ex-Dividend Behavior of Stock Returns: Further Evidence on Tax Effects," *Journal of Finance* 37 (May 1982), 445–56; R. H. Litzenberger and K. Ramaswamy, "The Effect of Personal Taxes and Dividends on Capital Asset Prices: Theory and Empirical Evidence," *Journal of Financial Economics* 7 (June 1979), 163–95; and M. H. Miller and M. Scholes, "Dividends and Taxes: Some Empirical Evidence," *Journal of Political Economy* 90 (1982): 1118–41.

**TABLE 17-4**
Management Opinion Survey on Dividends

| Statement of Managerial Beliefs | Level of Managers' Agreement | | |
|---|---|---|---|
| | Agreement | No Opinion | Disagreement |
| 1. A firm's dividend payout ratio affects the price of the common stock. | 61% | 33% | 6% |
| 2. Dividend payments provide a signaling device of future prospects. | 52 | 41 | 7 |
| 3. The market uses dividend announcements as information for assessing security value. | 43 | 51 | 6 |
| 4. Investors have different perceptions of the relative riskiness of dividends and retained earnings. | 56 | 42 | 2 |
| 5. Investors are basically indifferent with regard to returns from dividends versus those from capital gains. | 6 | 30 | 64 |
| 6. A stockholder is attracted to firms that have dividend policies appropriate to the stockholder's particular tax environment. | 44 | 49 | 7 |
| 7. Management should be responsive to its shareholders' preferences regarding dividends. | 41 | 49 | 10 |

Source: Adapted from H. Kent Baker, Gail E. Farrelly, and Richard B. Edelman, "A Survey of Management Views on Dividend Policy," *Financial Management* (Autumn 1985): 81.

believe that dividends matter and act consistently in accordance with that conviction, they could influence the relationship between stock value and dividend policy.

To help us gain some understanding of managements' perceptions, let's turn to a study by Baker, Farrelly, and Edelman, which surveyed financial executives at 318 firms listed on the New York Stock Exchange.[15] The study conducted in 1983 is summarized in Table 17-4. In looking at the Baker, Farrelly, and Edelman results, the evidence favors the relevance of dividend policy, but not overwhelmingly so. For the most part, managers are divided between believing that dividends are important and having no opinion in the matter.

Regarding the question about the price-dividend relationship, Baker et al. asked the financial managers straight up, "Does the firm's dividend policy affect the price of the common stock?" Slightly more than 60 percent of the responses were affirmative, which is significant, but there were still almost 40 percent who had no opinion or disagreed. Thus, we could conclude that most managers think that dividends matter, but they have no mandate. Similarly, when asked if dividends provide informational content about the firm's future (Statements 2 and 3), the managers are basically split between "no opinion" and "agreement." When asked about the trade-off between dividends and capital gains (Statements 4 and 5), almost two-thirds of the managers thought stockholders have a preference for dividend or capital gains, with a lesser number (56 percent) believing that investors perceive the relative riskiness of capital gains and dividends to be different. Interestingly enough, though, almost half of the managers felt no clear responsibility to be responsive to stockholders' preferences. Specifically, 56 percent of the financial executives either had no opinion or did not believe that stockholders are attracted to firms that have dividend policies appropriate to the stockholder's particular tax environment. Finally, Statement 7 suggests that the majority of managers are not true believers in the concept of a clientele effect.

[15]H. Kent Baker, Gail E. Farrelly, and Richard B. Edelman, "A Survey of Management Views on Dividend Policy," *Financial Management* (Autumn 1985): 78–84.

## What Are We to Conclude?

We have now looked carefully at the importance of a firm's dividend policy as management seeks to increase the shareholders' wealth. We have gone to great lengths to gain insight and understanding from our best thinking. We have even drawn from the empirical evidence on hand to see what the findings suggest.

A reasonable person cannot reach a definitive conclusion; nevertheless, management is left with no choice. A firm must develop a dividend policy, it is hoped, based on the best available knowledge. Although we can give advice only with some reservations, the following conclusions would appear reasonable:

1. As a firm's investment opportunities increase, the dividend payout ratio should decrease. In other words, an inverse relationship should exist between the amount of investments with an expected rate of return that exceeds the cost of capital and the dividends remitted to investors. Because of flotation costs associated with raising external capital, the retention of internally generated equity financing is preferable to selling stock (in terms of the wealth of the current common shareholders).
2. The firm's dividend policy appears to be important; however, appearances may be deceptive. The real issue may be the firm's *expected* earning power and the riskiness of these earnings. Investors may be using the dividend payment as a source of information about the company's *expected* earnings. Management's actions regarding dividends may carry greater weight than a statement by management that earnings will be increasing.
3. If dividends influence stock price, this is probably based on the investor's desire to minimize and defer taxes and from the role of dividends in minimizing agency costs.
4. If the expectations theory has merit, which we believe it does, management should avoid surprising investors when it comes to the firm's dividend decision. The firm's dividend policy might effectively be treated as a *long-term residual.* Rather than projecting investment requirements for a single year, management could anticipate financing needs for several years. Based upon the expected investment opportunities during the planning horizon, the firm's debt-equity mix, and the funds generated from operations, a *target* dividend payout ratio could be established. If internal funds remained after projection of the necessary equity financing, dividends would be paid. However, the planned dividend stream should distribute residual capital evenly to investors over the planning period. Conversely, if over the long term the entire amount of internally generated capital is needed for reinvestment in the company, then no dividend should be paid.

### CONCEPT CHECK

1. Can you summarize the position that dividend policy may be irrelevant with regard to the firm's stock price?
2. What is meant by the bird-in-the-hand dividend theory?
3. Why are cash dividend payments thought to be more certain than prospective capital gains?
4. How might personal taxes affect both the firm's dividend policy and its share price?
5. Distinguish between the residual dividend theory and the clientele effect.

# THE DIVIDEND DECISION IN PRACTICE

In setting a firm's dividend policy, financial managers must work in the world of reality with the concepts we have set forth so far in this chapter. Again, although these concepts do not provide an equation that explains the key relationships, they certainly give us a more complete view of the finance world, which can only help us make better decisions. Other considerations of a more practical nature also appear as part of the firm's decision making about its dividend policy.

## Other Practical Considerations

OBJECTIVE 3 

Many considerations may influence a firm's decision about its dividends, some of them unique to that company. Some of the more general considerations are given subsequently.

LEGAL RESTRICTIONS Certain legal restrictions may limit the amount of dividends a firm may pay. These legal constraints fall into two categories. First, *statutory restrictions* may prevent a company from paying dividends. Although specific limitations vary by state, generally a corporation may not pay a dividend (1) if the firm's liabilities exceed its assets, (2) if the amount of the dividend exceeds the accumulated profits (retained earnings), and (3) if the dividend is being paid from capital invested in the firm.

The second type of legal restriction is unique to each firm and results from restrictions in debt and preferred stock contracts. To minimize their risk, investors frequently impose restrictive provisions upon management as a condition to their investment in the company. These constraints may include the provision that dividends may not be declared prior to the debt being repaid. Also, the corporation may be required to maintain a given amount of working capital. Preferred stockholders may stipulate that common dividends may not be paid when any preferred dividends are delinquent.

LIQUIDITY POSITION Contrary to common opinion, the mere fact that a company shows a large amount of retained earnings in the balance sheet does not indicate that cash is available for the payment of dividends. The firm's current position in liquid assets, including cash, is basically independent of the retained earnings account. Historically, a company with sizable retained earnings has been successful in generating cash from operations. Yet these funds are typically either reinvested in the company within a short period or used to pay maturing debt. Thus, a firm may be extremely profitable and still be *cash poor.* Because dividends are paid with cash, and not with retained earnings, the firm must have cash available for dividends to be paid. Hence, the firm's liquidity position has a direct bearing on its ability to pay dividends.

ABSENCE OR LACK OF OTHER SOURCES OF FINANCING As already noted, a firm may (1) retain profits for investment purposes, or (2) pay dividends and issue new debt or equity securities to finance investments. For many small or new companies, this second option is not realistic. These firms do not have access to the capital markets, so they must rely more heavily upon internally generated funds. As a consequence, the dividend payout ratio is generally much lower for a small or newly established firm than for a large, publicly owned corporation.

EARNINGS PREDICTABILITY A company's dividend payout ratio depends to some extent on the predictability of a firm's profits over time. If earnings fluctuate significantly, management cannot rely on internally generated funds to meet future needs. When profits are realized, the firm may retain larger amounts to ensure that money is available when needed. Conversely, a firm with a stable earnings trend will typically pay a larger portion of its earnings out in dividends. This company has less concern about the availability of profits to meet future capital requirements.

OWNERSHIP CONTROL For many large corporations, control through the ownership of common stock is not an issue. However, for many small and medium-sized companies, maintaining voting control takes a high priority. If the present common shareholders are unable to participate in a new offering, issuing new stock is unattractive, in that the control of the current stockholders is diluted. The owners might prefer that management finance new investments with debt and through profits rather than by issuing new common stock. This firm's growth is then constrained by the amount of debt capital available and by the company's ability to generate profits.

INFLATION Before the late 1970s, inflationary pressures had not been a significant problem for either consumers or businesses. However, during much of the 1980s, the deterioration of the dollar's purchasing power had a direct impact on the replacement of fixed assets. In a period of inflation, ideally, as fixed assets become worn and obsolete, the funds generated from depreciation are used to finance the replacements. As the cost of equivalent equipment continues to increase, the depreciation funds are insufficient. This requires a greater retention of profits, which implies that dividends have to be adversely affected. In the late 1990s, inflation was not a primary concern.

## Alternative Dividend Policies

Regardless of a firm's long-term dividend policy, most firms choose one of several year-to-year dividend payment patterns:

1. **Constant dividend payout ratio.** In this policy, the percentage of earnings paid out in dividends is held constant. Although the dividend-to-earnings ratio is stable, the dollar amount of the dividend naturally fluctuates from year to year as profits vary.
2. **Stable dollar dividend per share payout.** This policy maintains a relatively stable dollar dividend over time. An increase in the dollar dividend usually does not occur until management is convinced that the higher dividend level can be maintained in the future. Management also will not reduce the dollar dividend until the evidence clearly indicates that a continuation of the present dividend cannot be supported.
3. **Small, regular dividend plus year-end extra dividend payout.** A corporation following this policy pays a small regular dollar dividend plus a year-end *extra dividend* in prosperous years. The extra dividend is declared toward the end of the fiscal year, when the company's profits for the period can be estimated. Management's objective is to avoid the connotation of a permanent dividend. However, this purpose may be defeated if *recurring* extra dividends come to be expected by investors.

Of the three dividend policies, the stable dollar dividend is by far the most common. In a study by Lintner, corporate managers were found to be reluctant to change the dollar amount of the dividend in response to temporary fluctuations in earnings from year to year. This aversion was particularly evident when it came to decreasing the amount of the dividend from the previous level.[16] In a separate study, Smith explained the tendency for stable dividend in terms of his **"increasing-stream hypothesis of dividend policy."**[17] He

**Constant dividend payout ratio**
A dividend payment policy in which the percentage of earnings paid out in dividends is held constant. The dollar amount fluctuates from year to year as profits vary.

**Stable dollar dividend per share payout**
A dividend policy that maintains a relatively stable dollar dividend per share over time.

**Small, regular dividend plus year-end extra dividend payout**
A dividend payment policy in which the firm pays a small regular dividend plus an extra dividend only if the firm has experienced a good year.

**"Increasing-stream hypothesis of dividend policy"**
A smoothing of the dividend stream in order to minimize the effect of company reversals. Corporate managers make every effort to avoid a dividend cut, attempting instead to develop a gradually increasing dividend series over the long-term future.

[16]John Lintner, "Distribution of Income of Corporations Among Dividends, Retained Earnings, and Taxes," *American Economic Review* 46 (May 1956): 97–113.

[17]Keith V. Smith, "Increasing-Stream Hypothesis of Corporate Dividend Policy," *California Management Review* 15 (Fall 1971): 56–64.

proposed that dividend stability is essentially a smoothing of the dividend stream to minimize the effect of other types of company reversals. Thus corporate managers make every effort to avoid a dividend cut, attempting instead to develop a gradually increasing dividend series over the long-term future. However, if a dividend reduction is absolutely necessary, the cut should be large enough to reduce the probability of future cuts.

### EXAMPLE DIVIDEND POLICY FROM HARLEY-DAVIDSON, INC.

We just discussed several alternative corporate dividend policies. Following are some actual data from Harley-Davidson that provide insight into that firm's payout policy. The table presents Harley's actual reported earnings and dividends per share, along with the calculated dividend payout ratio, which is shown in the last column.

Earnings per Share, Dividends per Share, and the Dividend Payout Ratio, Harley-Davidson, Inc., 1995–1999

| Year | Earnings per Share[a] | Dividends per Share | Payout Ratio |
|---|---|---|---|
| 1995 | $.73 | $.09 | 12.3% |
| 1996 | .94 | .11 | 11.7 |
| 1997 | 1.13 | .135 | 11.9 |
| 1998 | 1.38 | .155 | 11.2 |
| 1999 | 1.73 | .175 | 10.1 |

[a]This series represents "diluted" earnings.

Source: Basic data from Harley-Davidson, Inc., *Annual Report*, 1999, 55.

Now, which of the alternative dividend policies that we reviewed does the management of Harley seem to follow? Notice two important elements: (1) the payout ratio is quite stable over the given 5-year time frame, and (2) the actual cash dividend paid over time increased each year. Also be aware that the alternative policies we have discussed are not always mutually exclusive. Alternatively stated, the actual data may not *precisely* fit any of the three popular policies.

HINT: Think about the results of the study reported by Dr. K.V. Smith and incorporate that into your analysis.

## Dividend Policy and Corporate Strategy: Things Will Change—Even Dividend Policy

The recession of 1990 to 1991 induced a large number of American corporations to revisit their broadest corporate strategies that directly impact shareholder wealth. Today, the results of that "rethinking" are evident in many aspects of corporate behavior, including adjusted dividend policies.

One firm that altered its dividend policy in response to new strategies was W. R. Grace & Co., headquartered in Boca Raton, Florida. The firm's core businesses include packaging, catalysts and silica products, and construction products. Grace & Co. ranked number 271 within the 1997 *Fortune* 500 list of the largest U.S. corporations, with sales of $5.26 billion.

The new corporate plans involved (1) divesting or discontinuing several product lines and (2) initiating a significant repurchase program of its own common stock. Stock repurchase programs are discussed in depth later in this chapter.

**TABLE 17-5**
Earnings per Share, Dividends per Share, and the Dividend Payout Ratio W. R. Grace & Co., 1992–1996

| Year | Earnings per Share[a] | Dividends per Share | Payout Ratio |
|---|---|---|---|
| 1992 | $1.70 | $1.40 | 82.3% |
| 1993 | 1.39 | 1.40 | 101.0 |
| 1994 | 1.74 | 1.40 | 80.5 |
| 1995 | 2.14 | 1.175 | 54.9 |
| 1996 | 2.41 | 0.50 | 20.7 |

[a]This series represents earnings from continuing operations, but before special items.

Source: Basic data from W. R. Grace & Co., *Annual Report* (1996), 55.

As a result, both the firm's payout ratio and actual cash dividend paid per share declined in significant fashion. The change in observed dividend policy is evident in Table 17-5. Notice that over the 1992 to 1994 period, Grace & Co. provided a good example of what we have called a "stable dividend policy." During this period, the firm maintained a stable dollar dividend of $1.40 per share, whereas the payout ratio varied from 80.5 percent to 101.0 percent.

But when company policies changed dramatically, so did the associated dividend variables. The absolute dollar amount of the cash dividend per share was lowered to $0.50 in 1996 and the accompanying payout ratio fell to 20.7 percent. Importantly, the firm's total return to investors was a robust 30.9 percent during 1996, compared to its ten-year average of 16.4 percent. The market liked the change in dividend policy. So, although firms may be reluctant to change their dividend policies, with good planning and proper information dissemination it is possible to convince the financial markets that such a new direction might be good for investors.

**CONCEPT CHECK**

1. Can you identify some practical considerations that affect a firm's payout policy?
2. Identify and explain three different dividend policies. Hint: One of these is a constant dividend payout ratio.
3. What is the increasing-stream hypothesis of dividend policy?

## DIVIDEND PAYMENT PROCEDURES

After the firm's dividend policy has been structured, several procedural details must be arranged. For instance, how frequently are dividend payments to be made? If a stockholder sells the shares during the year, who is entitled to the dividend? To answer these questions, we need to understand dividend payment procedures.

Generally, companies pay dividends on a quarterly basis. To illustrate, IBM pays $1 per share in annual dividends. However, the firm actually issues a 25¢ dividend for a total yearly dividend of $1 (25¢ × 4 quarters).

**Declaration date**
The date upon which a dividend is formally declared by the board of directors.

**Date of record**
Date at which the stock transfer books are to be closed for determining which investor is to receive the next dividend payment.

The final approval of a dividend payment comes from the board of directors. As an example, Abbot Labs, on December 12, 1994, announced that holders of record as of January 13, 1995, would receive a 19¢ dividend. The dividend payment was to be made on February 15. December 12 is the **declaration date**—the date when the dividend is formally declared by the board of directors. The **date of record,** January 13, designates when the stock transfer books are to be closed. Investors shown to own stock on this date receive the dividend. If a notification of a transfer is recorded subsequent to January 13, the new

**Ex-dividend date**
The date upon which stock brokerage companies have uniformly decided to terminate the right of ownership to the dividend, which is 4 days prior to the record date.

**Payment date**
The date on which the company mails a dividend check to each investor.

owner is not entitled to the dividend. However, a problem could develop if the stock were sold on January 12, one day prior to the record date. Time would not permit the sale to be reflected on the stockholder list by the January 13 date of record. To avoid this problem, stock brokerage companies have uniformly decided to terminate the right of ownership to the dividend two working days prior to the record date. This prior date is the **ex-dividend date.** Therefore, any acquirer of Abbot Labs stock on January 11 or thereafter does not receive the dividend. Finally, the company mails the dividend check to each investor on February 15, the **payment date.** These events may be diagrammed as follows:

| Announcement Date | Ex-dividend Date | Record Date | Payment Date |
|---|---|---|---|
| December 12 | January 11 | January 13 | February 15 |

**CONCEPT CHECK**

1. What is the typical frequency with which cash dividends are paid to investors?
2. Distinguish among the (a) declaration date, (b) date of record, and (c) ex-dividend date.

## STOCK DIVIDENDS AND STOCK SPLITS

OBJECTIVE 6 

**Stock dividend**
A distribution of shares of up to 25 percent of the number of shares currently outstanding, issued on a pro rata basis to the current stockholders.

**Stock split**
A stock dividend exceeding 25 percent of the number of shares currently outstanding.

An integral part of dividend policy is the use of **stock dividends** and **stock splits.** Both involve issuing new shares of stock on a pro rata basis to the current shareholders, while the firm's assets, its earnings, and the risk assumed and the investor's percentage of ownership in the company remain unchanged. The only *definite* result from either a stock dividend or stock split is the increase in the number of shares of stock outstanding.

To illustrate the effect of a stock dividend, assume that the Katie Corporation has 100,000 shares outstanding. The firm's after-tax profits are $500,000, or $5 in earnings per share. At present, the company's stock is selling at a price/earnings multiple of 10, or $50 per share. Management is planning to issue a 20 percent stock dividend, so that a stockholder owning 10 shares would receive two additional shares. We might immediately conclude that this investor is being given an asset (two shares of stock) worth $100; consequently, his or her personal worth should increase by $100. This conclusion is erroneous. The firm will be issuing 20,000 new shares (100,000 shares × 20 percent). Because the $500,000 in after-tax profits does not change, the new earnings per share will be $4.167 ($500,000 ÷ 120,000 shares). If the price/earnings multiple remains at 10, the market price of the stock after the dividend should fall to $41.67 ($4.167 earnings per share × 10). The investor now owns 12 shares worth $41.67, which provides a $500 total value; thus he or she is neither better nor worse off than before the stock dividend.

This example may make us wonder why a corporation would even bother with a stock dividend or stock split if no one benefits. However, before we study the rationale for such distributions, we should understand the differences between a stock split and a stock dividend.

### Stock Dividend versus Stock Split

The only difference between a stock dividend and a stock split relates to their respective accounting treatment. Stated differently, *there is absolutely no difference on an economic*

**TABLE 17-6**
L. Bernard Corporation Balance Sheet Before Stock Dividend

| | |
|---|---|
| **Common stock** | |
| Par value (1,000,000 shares outstanding; $2 par value) | $ 2,000,000 |
| Paid-in capital | 8,000,000 |
| **Retained earnings** | 15,000,000 |
| Total equity | $25,000,000 |

**TABLE 17-7**
L. Bernard Corporation Balance Sheet After Stock Dividend

| | |
|---|---|
| **Common stock** | |
| Par value (1,150,000 shares outstanding; $2 par value) | $ 2,300,000 |
| Paid-in capital | 9,800,000 |
| **Retained earnings** | 12,900,000 |
| Total equity | $25,000,000 |

**TABLE 17-8**
L. Bernard Corporation Balance Sheet After Stock Split

| | |
|---|---|
| **Common stock** | |
| Par value (2,000,000 shares outstanding; $1 par value) | $ 2,000,000 |
| Paid-in capital | 8,000,000 |
| **Retained earnings** | 15,000,000 |
| Total equity | $25,000,000 |

*basis between a stock dividend and a stock split.* Both represent a proportionate distribution of additional shares to the present stockholders. However, *for accounting purposes,* the stock split has been defined as a stock dividend exceeding 25 percent.[18] Thus, a stock dividend is arbitrarily defined as a distribution of shares up to 25 percent of the number of shares currently outstanding.

The accounting treatment for a stock dividend requires the issuing firm to capitalize the "market value" of the dividend. In other words, the dollar amount of the dividend is transferred from retained earnings to the capital accounts (par and paid-in capital). This procedure may best be explained by an example. Assume that the L. Bernard Corporation is preparing to issue a 15 percent stock dividend. Table 17-6 presents the equity portion of the firm's balance sheet prior to the distribution. The market price for the stock has been $14. Thus, the 15 percent stock dividend increases the number of shares by 150,000 (1,000,000 shares × 15 percent). The "market value" of this increase is $2,100,000 (150,000 shares × $14 market price). To record this transaction, $2,100,000 would be transferred from retained earnings, resulting in a $300,000 increase in total par value (150,000 shares × $2 par value) and a $1,800,000 increment to paid-in capital. The $1,800,000 is the residual difference between $2,100,000 and $300,000. Table 17-7 shows the revised balance sheet.

What if the management of L. Bernard Corporation changed the plan and decided to split the stock two for one? In other words, a *100 percent increase* in the number of shares would result. In accounting for the split, the changes to be recorded are (1) the increase in the number of shares and (2) the decrease in the per-share par value from $2 to $1. The dollar amounts of each account do not change. Table 17-8 reveals the new balance sheet.

Thus, for a stock dividend, an amount equal to the market value of the stock dividend is transferred from retained earnings to the capital stock accounts. When stock is split, only

[18]The 25 percent standard applies only to corporations listed on the New York Stock Exchange. The American Institute of Certified Public Accountants states that a stock dividend greater than 20 or 25 percent is for all practical purposes a stock split.

the number of shares changes, and the par value of each share is decreased proportionately. Despite this dissimilarity in accounting treatment, remember that no real economic difference exists between a split and a dividend.

### Rationale for a Stock Dividend or Split

Although *stock* dividends and splits occur far less frequently than *cash* dividends, a significant number of companies choose to use these share distributions either with or in lieu of cash dividends. Because no economic benefit results, how do corporations justify these distributions?

Proponents of stock dividends and splits frequently maintain that stockholders receive a key benefit because the price of the stock will not fall precisely in proportion to the share increase. For a two-for-one split, the price of the stock might not decrease a full 50 percent, and the stockholder is left with a higher total value. There are two perceived reasons for this disequilibrium. First, many financial executives believe that an optimal price range exists. Within this range the total market value of the common stockholders is thought to be maximized. As the price exceeds this range, fewer investors can purchase the stock, thereby restraining the demand. Consequently, downward pressure is placed on its price. The second explanation relates to the *information content* of the dividend or split announcement. Stock dividends and splits have generally been associated with companies with growing earnings. The announcement of a stock dividend or split has therefore been perceived as favorable news. The empirical evidence, however, fails to verify these conclusions. Most studies indicate that investors are perceptive in identifying the true meaning of a share distribution. If the stock dividend or split is not accompanied by a positive trend in earnings and increases in cash dividends, price increases surrounding the stock dividend or split are insignificant.[19] Therefore, we should be suspicious of the assertion that a stock dividend or split can help increase the investors' worth.

A second reason for stock dividends or splits is the conservation of corporate cash. If a company is encountering cash problems, it may substitute a stock dividend for a cash dividend. However, as before, investors will probably look beyond the dividend to ascertain the underlying reason for conserving cash. If the stock dividend is an effort to conserve cash for attractive investment opportunities, the shareholder may bid up the stock price. If the move to conserve cash relates to financial difficulties within the firm, the market price will most likely react adversely.

**CONCEPT CHECK**

1. From an economic standpoint, is there any meaningful difference between a stock split and a stock dividend?
2. What managerial logic might lie behind a stock split or a stock dividend?

## STOCK REPURCHASES

OBJECTIVE 7 

For well over three decades, corporate managements have been active in repurchasing their own equity securities. For example, on September 14, 2000, the Ford Motor Company announced in a press release that it planned to buy back up to a full $5 billion of its stock. Immediately after the public announcement of this plan, shares of Ford com-

[19]See James A. Millar and Bruce D. Fielitz, "Stock Split and Stock-Dividend Decisions," *Financial Management* (Winter 1973): 35–45; and Eugene Fama, Lawrence Fisher, Michael Jensen, and Richard Roll, "The Adjustment of Stock Prices to New Information," *International Economic Review* (February 1969): 1–21.

mon stock rose by 2.2 percent in the financial markets. Now, a key word in such announcements is the word "plan." Companies give themselves room across time to execute these buybacks. And, Ford, at the time, you may recall, was mired in the midst of a major-league tire quality problem on some of its best-selling vehicles, so not all financial analysts and marketwatchers were sure of when the actual repurchases would commence. Several reasons have been given for a firm repurchasing its own stock. Examples of such benefits include:

1. Means for providing an internal investment opportunity
2. Approach for modifying the firm's capital structure
3. Favorable impact on earnings per share
4. Elimination of a minority ownership group of stockholders
5. Minimization of dilution in earnings per share associated with mergers and options
6. Reduction in the firm's costs associated with servicing small stockholders

Also, from the shareholders' perspective, a **stock repurchase,** as opposed to a cash dividend, has a potential tax advantage.

**Stock repurchase (stock buyback)**
The repurchase of common stock by the issuing firm for any of a variety of reasons resulting in a reduction of shares outstanding.

## Share Repurchase as a Dividend Decision

Clearly, the payment of a common stock dividend is the conventional method for distributing a firm's profits to its owners. However, it need not be the only way. Another approach is to repurchase the firm's stock. The concept may best be explained by an example.

### EXAMPLE

Telink, Inc., is planning to pay $4 million ($4 per share) in dividends to its common stockholders. The following earnings and market price information is provided for Telink:

| | |
|---|---|
| Net income | $7,500,000 |
| Number of shares | 1,000,000 |
| Earnings per share | $ 7.50 |
| Price/earnings ratio | 8 |
| Expected market price per share after proposed dividend payment | $ 60 |

In a recent meeting, several board members, who are also major stockholders, questioned the need for a dividend payment. They maintain that they do not need the income, so why not allow the firm to retain the funds for future investments? In response, management contends that the available investments are not sufficiently profitable to justify retention of the income. That is, the investors' required rates of return exceed the expected rates of return that could be earned with the additional $4 million in investments.

Because management opposes the idea of retaining the profits for investment purposes, one of the firm's directors has suggested that the $4 million be used to repurchase the company's stock. In this way, the value of the stock should increase. This result may be demonstrated as follows:

1. Assume that shares are repurchased by the firm at the $60 market price (ex-dividend price) plus the contemplated $4 dividend per share, or for $64 per share.

2. Given a \$64 price, 62,500 shares would be repurchased (\$4 million ÷ \$64 price).
3. If net income is not reduced, but the number of shares declines as a result of the share repurchase, earnings per share would increase from \$7.50 to \$8, computed as follows:

$$\begin{aligned}\text{earnings per share} &= \text{net income/outstanding shares}\\ \text{(before repurchase)} &= \$7{,}500{,}000/1{,}000{,}000\\ &= \$7.50\\ \text{(after repurchase)} &= \$7{,}500{,}000/(1{,}000{,}000 - 62{,}500)\\ &= \$8.00\end{aligned}$$

4. Assuming that the price/earnings ratio remains at 8, the new price after the repurchase would be \$64, up from \$60, where the increase exactly equals the amount of the dividend forgone.

In this example, Telink's stockholders are essentially provided the same value, whether a dividend is paid or stock is repurchased. If management pays a dividend, the investor will have a stock valued at \$60 plus \$4 received from the dividend. Conversely, if stock is repurchased in lieu of the dividend, the stock will be worth \$64. These results were based upon assuming (1) the stock is being repurchased at the exact \$64 price, (2) the \$7,500,000 net income is unaffected by the repurchase, and (3) the price/earnings ratio of 8 does not change after the repurchase. Given these assumptions, however, the stock repurchase serves as a perfect substitute for the dividend payment to the stockholders.

## The Investor's Choice

Given the choice between a stock repurchase and a dividend payment, which would an investor prefer? In perfect markets, where there are no taxes, no commissions when buying and selling stock, and no informational content assigned to a dividend, the investor would be indifferent with regard to the choices. The investor could create a dividend stream by selling stock when income is needed.

Because market imperfections do exist, the investor may have a preference for one of the two methods of distributing the corporate income. First, the firm may have to pay too high a price for the repurchased stock, which is to the detriment of the remaining stockholders. If a relatively large number of shares are being bought, the price may be bid up too high, only to fall after the repurchase operation. Second, as a result of the repurchase, the market may perceive the riskiness of the corporation as increasing, which would lower the price/earnings ratio and the value of the stock.

## Financing or Investment Decision

Repurchasing stock when the firm has excess cash may be regarded as a dividend decision. However, a stock repurchase may also be viewed as a financing decision. By issuing debt and then repurchasing stock, a firm can immediately alter its debt-equity mix toward a higher proportion of debt. Rather than choosing how to distribute cash to the stockholders, management is using a stock repurchase as a means to change the corporation's capital structure.

In addition to dividend and financing decisions, many managers consider a stock repurchase an investment decision. When equity prices are depressed in the marketplace,

FINANCE $ MATTERS

### Many Concerns Use Excess Cash to Repurchase Their Shares

Stock buybacks are back. Faced with the prospect of only modest economic growth, many companies are using excess cash to buy their own shares rather than build new plants.

Consider the case of Mattel Inc., the El Segundo, Calif, toy maker. It just announced plans to buy 10 million shares during the next four years, even though its stock, 24 3/8, is selling at a healthly 16.6 times its past twelve month earnings. The reason: Plant capacity is sufficient to handle current sales growth of 10 percent to 12 percent yearly and excess cash is building up at the rate of $200 million a year.

"We don't need the cash to grow so we've decided to give it back," says James Eskridge, Mattel's chief financial officer. Actually, Mattel plans to use about half of the $200 million each year for buybacks and dividends and the rest for growth.

The effect [of a stock repurchase] on individual stocks can be significant, says Robert Giordano, director of economic research at Goldman Sachs & Co. A case in point is General Dynamics Corp., which last summer began selling some divisions and using the proceeds to buy its stock when shares were trading at about $65 each. After nearly $1 billion in buybacks, the stock has gained about 37 percent, closing yesterday at 89 1/2.

"The market reacts positively to purchases, and it appreciates a firm that does not squander excess cash," says Columbia Business School professor Gailen Hite.

Some of the buybacks have come from companies whose stock prices have been hurt. Drug makers, for example, have seen their stocks pummeled by fears that health-care reform will sap profits. As a result, pharmaceutical companies have been big players in the buyback game.

But economists and analysts are much more intrigued by companies that are awash in cash, thanks to improving sales and several years of cost cutting and debt reduction. At this stage of an economic recovery, many such companies would be investing heavily in plant and equipment. Not this time.

"Companies are throwing off more cash than they can ever hope to invest in plant, equipment, or inventories," says Charles Clough, chief investment strategist for Merrill Lynch Capital Markets. Companies already have pared down debt, and now they're turning to equity, he says. His prediction: "He who shrinks his balance sheet the fastest will win in the '90s."

Source: Leslie Schism, "Many Concerns Use Excess Cash to Repurchase Their Shares," *The Wall Street Journal,* (September 2, 1993): C1, C10. Reprinted by permission of *The Wall Street Journal,* 

management may view the firm's own stock as being materially undervalued and representing a good investment opportunity. While the firm's management may be wise to repurchase stock at unusually low prices, this decision cannot and should not be viewed in the context of an investment decision. Buying its own stock cannot provide expected returns as other investments do. No company can survive, much less prosper, by investing only in its own stock.

## The Repurchase Procedure

If management intends to repurchase a block of the firm's outstanding shares, it should make this information public. All investors should be given the opportunity to work with complete information. They should be told the purpose of the repurchase, as well as the method to be used to acquire the stock.

Three methods for stock repurchase are available. First, the shares could be bought in the *market.* Here the firm acquires the stock through a stockbroker at the going market price. This approach may place an upward pressure on the stock price until the stock is acquired. Also, commissions must be paid to the stockbrokers as a fee for their services.

The second method is to make a tender offer to the firm's shareholders. A **tender offer** is a formal offer by the company to buy a specified number of shares at a predetermined and stated price. The tender price is set above the current market price in order to attract sellers. A tender offer is best when a relatively large number of shares are to be bought, because the company's intentions are clearly known and each shareholder has the opportunity to sell the stock at the tendered price.

**Tender offer**
The formal offer by the company to buy a specified number of shares at a predetermined and stated price.

The third and final method for repurchasing stock entails the purchase of the stock from one or more major stockholders. These purchases are made on a *negotiated basis.* Care should be taken to ensure a fair and equitable price. Otherwise, the remaining stockholders may be hurt as a result of the sale.

**CONCEPT CHECK**

1. Identify three reasons why a firm might buy back its own common stock shares.
2. What financial relationships must hold for a stock repurchase to be a perfect substitute for a cash dividend payment to stockholders?
3. Within the context of a stock repurchase, what is meant by a tender offer?

## THE MULTINATIONAL FIRM: THE CASE OF LOW DIVIDEND PAYMENTS—SO WHERE DO WE INVEST?

OBJECTIVE 8 

During the fourth quarter of 2000, the U.S. economy continued an outstanding period of aggregate expansion that made it the longest in domestic business cycle history. When such periods of relative prosperity occur, financially strong firms tend to focus their business strategies on growth; as a direct result, corporate dividend yields (i.e., cash dividends divided by common stock price) tend to decline. Firms retain more cash dollars for internal investment opportunities and disgorge less cash to investors. For growth-seeking companies, the capital-budgeting decision takes on greater importance, while the consequence of the dividend decision relative to both firm value and cash outflows shrinks. This might properly remind you of what we called the *residual dividend theory* earlier in this chapter.

During general economic prosperity, the multinational firm logically looks to international markets for prospectively high net present value projects. There are at least two solid reasons for such investing behavior: (1) to spread or dilute country-related economic risks by diversifying geographically and (2) to achieve a cost advantage over competitors. These two reasons for U.S. direct investment abroad should remind you of **Principle 9: All Risk is Not Equal—Some risk can be diversified away and some cannot;** and **Principle 5: The Curse of Competitive Markets—Why it's hard to find exceptionally profitable projects.**

Table 17-9 identifies those countries, apart from the United States, that make up the so-called "Group of Seven Industrialized Nations." Just think of them as the most advanced economies on the globe. They are referred to in the popular business press as the "G-7" countries. Government finance officials from the G-7 and sometimes their chief executive officers (like the President of the United States) usually meet twice a year to discuss multi-

**TABLE 17-9**
U.S. Direct Investment Abroad, 1998, Group of Seven Industrialized Nations

| Country | Amount ($ Billions) | Percent of Total | Percent in Manufacturing |
|---|---|---|---|
| Canada | $103.9 | 24.8% | 44.7% |
| France | 39.2 | 9.4 | 48.4 |
| Germany | 42.9 | 10.3 | 51.9 |
| Italy | 14.6 | 3.5 | 58.5 |
| Japan | 38.2 | 9.2 | 37.2 |
| United Kingdom | 178.6 | 42.8 | 26.0 |
| Total | $417.4 | 100.0% | |

Source: *U.S. Net International Position at Yearend, 1998,* U.S. Department of Commerce (June 30, 1999), 10.

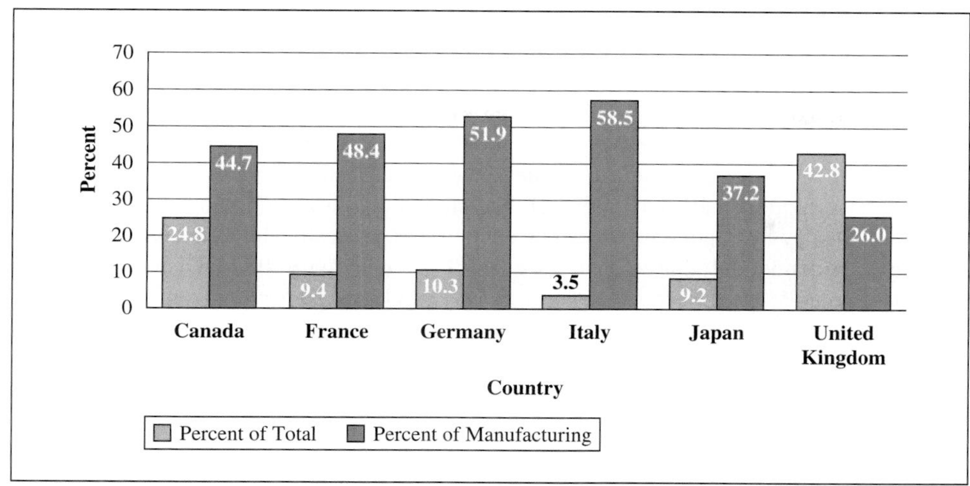


**FIGURE 17-3**
U.S. Direct Investment Abroad, 1998, Group of Seven Industrialized Nations

Source: *U.S. Net International Position at Yearend,* 1998. U.S. Department of Commerce (June 30, 1999), 10.

national economic policy. In Table 17-9 we can observe the historical dollar amounts in countries where U.S. multinational firms have invested internationally.

Notice that when corporate cash is available, U.S. multinational firms favor (1) the United Kingdom and (2) Canada as domiciles for direct investment. A full 67.6 percent of U.S. firms' investment in other G-7 countries is placed in those two countries. Also notice that the capital projects chosen by U.S. multinational firms tend to be concentrated in various manufacturing industries. For instance, in Italy, a full 58.5 percent of the U.S. investment lies within the manufacturing sector. These relationships and the dominance of international manufacturing projects are displayed in Figure 17-3. A perceived cost advantage associated with overseas manufacturing, usually related to lower labor costs, explains the bias toward manufacturing-oriented projects by U.S. multinational firms. The competitive nature of a capitalist-based economy induces U.S. firms to seek low-cost labor inputs from their direct international investments.

**CONCEPT CHECK**

1. Identify two reasons why multinational firms might turn to international markets in search of high net present value projects.
2. Among the Group of Seven countries, which two are most-favored with direct investment by U.S. companies?

## HOW FINANCIAL MANAGERS USE THIS MATERIAL

The introduction to this chapter presented a definite statement from the management of Coca-Cola concerning its outlook for the firm's dividend policy that was framed within the concept of its dividend payout ratio. We learned that Coca-Cola plans to gradually reduce its payout ratio.

Coca-Cola management further has said: "We reinvest our operating cash flow principally in three ways: by pumping it back into our own business, by paying dividends, and by buying back our own stock."[20] Note that this latter use of the firm's cash flow relates to our

[20]The Coca-Cola Company, *Annual Report* (1996), 27.

discussion of "stock repurchases" (objective 7) toward the end of the chapter. Again, the differential tax treatment of cash dividends as opposed to capital gains can give investors a potential tax advantage when shares are repurchased. We are reminded once more of **Principle 8: Taxes Bias Business Decisions.**

Another real example is provided by the Walt Disney Company. Recall our discussion of "Alternative Dividend Policies." Disney provides us with a concrete illustration of the stable dollar dividend per share approach in conjunction with an ongoing share repurchase program. Disney management said: "Disney paid out to its shareholders almost $1 billion through dividends and share repurchase in 1997. In January 1997, Disney's Board of Directors voted to increase the company *quarterly* dividend 20 percent from $.11 to $.1325 per share.[21]

In February 1996, Disney common stock was trading at around $106 per share. This put the firm's annual dividend yield at a tiny 0.5 percent (i.e., $0.53/$106.0). By comparison, the dividend yield on the S&P 500 Index at that same point in time was 1.64 percent or 3.28 times that of Disney. Clearly, Disney management perceives that investors are more interested in expected capital gains than cash dividends, even if they did raise the absolute dollar value of the dividend payout.

## SUMMARY

OBJECTIVE 1 

A company's dividend decision has an immediate impact upon the firm's financial mix. If the dividend payment is increased, less funds are available internally for financing investments. Consequently, if additional equity capital is needed, the company has to issue new common stock.

OBJECTIVE 2 

In trying to understand the effect of the dividend policy on a firm's stock price, we must realize the following:

- In perfect markets, the choice between paying or not paying a dividend does not matter. However, when we realize in the real world that there are costs of issuing stock, we have a preference to use internal equity to finance our investment opportunities. Here the dividend decision is simply a residual factor, where the dividend payment should equal the remaining internal capital after financing the equity portion of investments.
- Other market imperfections that may cause a company's dividend policy to affect the firm's stock price include: (1) the tax benefit of capital gains, (2) agency costs, (3) the clientele effect, and (4) the informational content of a given policy.

OBJECTIVE 3 

Other practical considerations that may affect a firm's dividend-payment decision include:

- The firm's liquidity position
- The company's accessibility to capital markets
- Inflation rates
- Legal restrictions
- The stability of earnings
- The desire of investors to maintain control of the company

OBJECTIVE 4 

In practice, managers have generally followed one of three dividend policies:

- Constant dividend payout ratio, where the percentage of dividends to earnings is held constant.
- Stable dollar dividend per share, where a relatively stable dollar dividend is maintained over time.
- Small, regular dividend plus a year-end extra, where the firm pays a small regular dollar dividend plus a year-end extra.

Of the three dividend policies, the stable dollar dividend is by far the most popular.

[21]The Walt Disney Company, *Annual Report* (1997), 18.

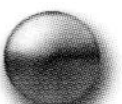 OBJECTIVE 5

Generally, companies pay dividends on a quarterly basis. The final approval of a dividend payment comes from the board of directors. The critical dates in this process are as follows:

- Declaration date—the date when the dividend is formally declared by the board of directors.
- Date of record—the date when the stock transfer books are to be closed to determine who owns the stock.
- Ex-dividend date—2 working days prior to the record date. After this date, the right to receive the dividend no longer goes with the stock.
- Payment date—the date the dividend check is mailed to the stockholders.

 OBJECTIVE 6

Stock dividends and stock splits have been used by corporations either in lieu of or to supplement cash dividends. At the present, no empirical evidence identifies a relationship between stock dividends and splits and the market price of the stock. Yet a stock dividend or split could conceivably be used to keep the stock price within an optimal trading range. Also, if investors perceive that the stock dividend contained favorable information about the firm's operations, the price of the stock could increase.

 OBJECTIVE 7

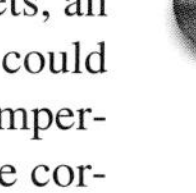

As an alternative to paying a dividend, management can repurchase stock. In perfect markets, an investor would be indifferent between receiving a dividend or a share repurchase. The investor could simply create a dividend stream by selling stock when income is needed. If, however, market imperfections exist, the investor may have a preference for one of the two methods of distributing the corporate income. A stock repurchase may also be viewed as a financing decision. By issuing debt and then repurchasing stock, a firm can immediately alter its debt-equity mix toward a higher proportion of debt. Also, many managers consider a stock repurchase an investment decision—buying the stock when they believe it to be undervalued.

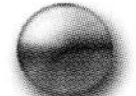 OBJECTIVE 8

During periods of general economic prosperity, financially strong firms tend to focus their business strategies on growth. As a result, dividend yields and cash dividend payments can decline. With internally generated cash to invest, the multinational firm will look to international markets for prospectively high *NPV* projects. This may allow the firm to (1) spread country-related economic risks by diversifying geographically and (2) achieve a cost advantage over competitors.

## KEY TERMS

**Agency costs, 580**
**"Bird-in-the-hand" dividend theory, 574**
**Clientele effect, 579**
**Constant dividend payout ratio, 585**
**Date of record, 587**
**Declaration date, 587**
**Dividend payout ratio, 569**
**Ex-dividend date, 588**
**Expectations theory, 580**
**"Increasing-stream hypothesis of dividend policy," 585**
**Information asymmetry, 579**
**Payment date, 588**
**"Perfect" capital markets, 571**
**Residual dividend theory, 577**
**Small, regular dividend plus a year-end extra dividend payout, 585**
**Stable dollar dividend per share payout, 585**
**Stock dividend, 588**
**Stock repurchase (stock buyback), 591**
**Stock split, 588**
**Tender offer, 593**

myPHLIP

Go To:
http://www.prenhall.com/keown
for downloads and current events associated with this chapter

## STUDY QUESTIONS

**17-1.** What is meant by the term *dividend payout ratio?*

**17-2.** Explain the trade-off between retaining internally generated funds and paying cash dividends.

**17-3.** **a.** What are the assumptions of a perfect market?

**b.** What effect does dividend policy have on the share price in a perfect market?

**17-4.** What is the impact of flotation costs on the financing decision?

**17-5.** **a.** What is the *residual dividend theory?*

**b.** Why is this theory operational only in the long term?

**17-6.** Why might investors prefer capital gains to the same amount of dividend income?

**17-7.** What legal restrictions may limit the amount of dividends to be paid?

**17-8.** How does a firm's liquidity position affect the payment of dividends?

**17-9.** How can ownership control constrain the growth of a firm?

**17-10.** **a.** Why is a stable dollar dividend policy popular from the viewpoint of the corporation?

**b.** Is it also popular with investors? Why?

**17-11.** Explain declaration date, date of record, and ex-dividend date.

**17-12.** What are the advantages of a stock split or dividend over a cash dividend?

**17-13.** Why would a firm repurchase its own stock?

## SELF-TEST PROBLEMS

**ST-1.** (*Dividend growth rate*) Schutz, Inc., maintains a constant dividend payout ratio of 35 percent. Earnings per share last year were $8.20 and are expected to grow indefinitely at a rate of 12 percent. What will be the dividend per share this year? In 5 years?

**ST-2.** (*Residual dividend theory*) Britton Corporation is considering four investment opportunities. The required investment outlays and expected rates of return for these investments are shown below. The firm's cost of capital is 14 percent. The investments are to be financed by 40 percent debt and 60 percent common equity. Internally generated funds totaling $750,000 are available for reinvestment.

**a.** Which investments should be accepted? According to the residual dividend theory, what amount should be paid out in dividends?

**b.** How would your answer change if the cost of capital were 10 percent?

| Investment | Investment Cost | Internal Rates of Return |
|---|---|---|
| A | $275,000 | 17.50% |
| B | 325,000 | 15.72 |
| C | 550,000 | 14.25 |
| D | 400,000 | 11.65 |

**ST-3.** (*Stock split*) The debt and equity section of the Robson Corporation balance sheet follows. The current market price of the common shares is $20. Reconstruct the financial statement assuming that (a) a 15 percent stock dividend is issued and (b) a two-for-one stock split is declared.

| Robson Corporation | |
|---|---|
| **Debt** | $1,800,000 |
| **Common** | |
| Par ($2 par; 100,000 shares) | 200,000 |
| Paid-in capital | 400,000 |
| Retained earnings | 900,000 |
| | $3,300,000 |

## STUDY PROBLEMS (SET A)

**17-1A.** (*Dividend policies*) The earnings for Harmony Pianos, Inc., have been predicted for the next 5 years and are listed in the following table. There are 1 million shares outstanding. Determine the yearly dividend per share to be paid if the following policies are enacted:

**a.** Constant dividend payout ratio of 40 percent.

**b.** Stable dollar dividend targeted at 40 percent of the earnings over the 5-year period.

**c.** Small, regular dividend of $0.50 per share plus a year-end extra when the profits in any year exceed $1,500,000. The year-end extra dividend will equal 50 percent of profits exceeding $1,500,000.

| Year | Profits after taxes |
|---|---|
| 1 | $1,000,000 |
| 2 | 2,000,000 |
| 3 | 1,600,000 |
| 4 | 900,000 |
| 5 | 3,000,000 |

**17-2A.** (*Flotation costs and issue size*) Your firm needs to raise $10 million. Assuming that flotation costs are expected to be $15 per share and that the market price of the stock is $120, how many shares would have to be issued? What is the dollar size of the issue?

**17-3A.** (*Flotation costs and issue size*) If flotation costs for a common stock issue are 18 percent, how large must the issue be so that the firm will net $5,800,000? If the stock sells for $85 per share, how many shares must be issued?

**17-4A.** (*Residual dividend theory*) Terra Cotta finances new investments by 40 percent debt and 60 percent equity. The firm needs $640,000 for financing new investments. If retained earnings available for reinvestment equal $400,000, how much money will be available for dividends in accordance with the residual dividend theory?

**17-5A.** (*Stock dividend*) RCB has 2 million shares of common stock outstanding. Net income is $550,000, and the P/E ratio for the stock is 10. Management is planning a 20 percent stock dividend. What will be the price of the stock after the stock dividend? If an investor owns 100 shares prior to the stock dividend, does the total value of his or her shares change? Explain.

**17-6A.** (*Dividends in perfect markets*) The management of Harris, Inc., is considering two dividend policies for the years 1996 and 1997, 1 and 2 years away. In 1998, the management is planning to liquidate the firm. One plan would pay a dividend of $2.50 in 1996 and 1997 and a liquidating dividend of $45.75 in 1998. The alternative would be to pay out $4.25 in dividends in 1996, $4.75 in dividends in 1997, and a final dividend of $40.66 in 1998. The required rate of return for the common stockholders is 18 percent. Management is concerned about the effect of the two dividend streams on the value of the common stock.

**a.** Assuming perfect markets, what would be the effect?

**b.** What factors in the real world might change your conclusion reached in part (a)?

**17-7A.** (*Long-term residual dividend policy*) Stetson Manufacturing, Inc., has projected its investment opportunities over a 5-year planning horizon. The cost of each year's investment and the amount of internal funds available for reinvestment for that year is as follows. The firm's debt-equity mix is 35 percent debt and 65 percent equity. There are currently 100,000 shares of common stock outstanding.

**a.** What would be the dividend each year if the residual dividend theory were used on a year-to-year basis?

**b.** What target stable dividend can Stetson establish by using the long-term residual dividend theory over the future planning horizon?

**c.** Why might a residual dividend policy applied to the 5 years as opposed to individual years be preferable?

| Year | Cost of Investments | Internal Funds Available for Reinvestment or for Dividends |
|---|---|---|
| 1 | $350,000 | $250,000 |
| 2 | 475,000 | 450,000 |
| 3 | 200,000 | 600,000 |
| 4 | 980,000 | 650,000 |
| 5 | 600,000 | 390,000 |

**17-8A.** (*Stock split*) You own 5 percent of the Trexco Corporation's common stock, which recently sold for $98 prior to a planned two-for-one stock split announcement. Before the split there are 25,000 shares of common stock outstanding.

**a.** Relative to now, what will be your financial position after the stock split? (Assume the stock price falls proportionately.)

**b.** The executive vice-president in charge of finance believes the price will only fall 40 percent after the split because she feels the price is above the optimal price range. If she is correct, what will be your net gain?

**17-9A.** (*Dividend policies*) The earnings for Crystal Cargo, Inc. have been predicted for the next 5 years and follow. There are 1 million shares outstanding. Determine the yearly dividend per share to be paid if the following policies are enacted:

**a.** Constant dividend payout ratio of 50 percent.

**b.** Stable dollar dividend targeted at 50 percent of the earnings over the 5-year period.

**c.** Small, regular dividend of $0.50 per share plus a year-end extra when the profits in any year exceed $1,500,000. The year-end extra dividend will equal 50 percent of profits exceeding $1,500,000.

| Year | Profits After Taxes |
|---|---|
| 1 | $1,400,000 |
| 2 | 2,000,000 |
| 3 | 1,860,000 |
| 4 | 900,000 |
| 5 | 2,800,000 |

**17-10A.** (*Repurchase of stock*) The Dunn Corporation is planning to pay dividends of $500,000. There are 250,000 shares outstanding, with an earnings per share of $5. The stock should sell for $50 after the ex-dividend date. If instead of paying a dividend, management decides to repurchase stock:

**a.** What should be the repurchase price?

**b.** How many shares should be repurchased?

**c.** What if the repurchase price is set below or above your suggested price in part (a)?

**d.** If you own 100 shares, would you prefer that the company pay the dividend or repurchase stock?

**17-11A.** (*Flotation costs and issue size*) D. Butler, Inc., needs to raise $14 million. Assuming that the market price of the firm's stock is $95 and flotation costs are 10 percent of the market price, how many shares would have to be issued? What is the dollar size of the issue?

**17-12A.** (*Residual dividend theory*) Martinez, Inc., finances new acquisitions with 70 percent debt and the rest in equity. The firm needs $1.2 million for a new acquisition. If retained earnings available for reinvestment are $450,000, how much money will be available for dividends according to the residual dividend theory?

**17-13A.** (*Stock split*) You own 20 percent of Rainy Corp., which recently sold for $86 before a planned two-for-one stock split announcement. Before the split there are 80,000 shares of common stock outstanding.

**a.** What is your financial position before the split, and what will it be after the stock split? (Assume the stock falls proportionately.)

**b.** Your stockbroker believes the market will react positively to the split and that the price will fall only 45 percent after the split. If she is correct, what will be your net gain?

## INTEGRATIVE PROBLEM

The following article appeared in the July 2, 1995, issue of the *Dallas Morning News.* Scott Burns, the author, argues the case for the importance of dividends.

> Let us now praise the lowly dividend.
>
> Insignificant to some. Small potatoes to others. An irksome sign of tax liability to many. However characterized, dividends are experiencing yet another round of defamation on Wall Street.
>
> Why pay out dividends, the current argument goes, when a dollar of dividend can be retained as a dollar of book value that the market will value at two, three or four dollars? With the average stock now selling at more than three times book value, investors should prefer companies that retain earnings rather than pay them out, even if they do nothing more with the money than repurchase shares.

### The New Wisdom

Instead, the New Wisdom says, the investor should go for companies that retain earnings, reinvest them and try to maximize shareholder value. Dividends should be avoided in the pursuit of long-term capital gains.

The only problem with this reasoning is that we've heard it before. And always at market tops.

- We heard it in the late 1960s as stock prices soared and dividend yields fell.
- We heard it again in the early '70s as investors fixated on the "Nifty Fifty" and analysts calmly projected that with growth companies yielding 1 percent or less, the most important part of the return was the certainty of 20 percent annual earnings growth.
- And we're hearing it now, with stock prices hitting new highs each day. The Standard & Poor's 500 Index, for instance, is up 19.7 percent since Dec. 31, the equivalent of more than seven years of dividends at the current yield of 2.6 percent.

### Tilting the Yield

Significantly, we didn't hear that dividends were irrelevant in the late '70s, as stock valuations moved to new lows. At that time, portfolio managers talked about "yield tilt"—running a portfolio with a bias toward dividend return to offset some of the risk of continuing stock market decline. Indeed, many of the best performing funds in the late '70s were Equity-Income funds, the funds that seek above-average dividend income.

You can understand how much dividends contribute to long-term returns by taking a look at the performance of a major index, with and without dividend reinvestment. If you had invested $10,000 in the S&P's 500 Index in January 1982 and taken all dividends in cash, your original investment would have grown to $37,475 by the end of 1994.

It doesn't get much better than that.

The gain clocks a compound annual return of 10.7 percent, and total gain of $27,475. During the same period you would have collected an additional $14,244 in dividends.

Not a trivial sum, either.

In other words, during one of the biggest bull markets in history, unreinvested dividend income accounted for more than one-third of your total return.

If you had reinvested those dividends in additional stock, the final score would be even better: $60,303. The appreciation of your original investment would have been $27,475 while the growth from reinvested dividends would have been $22,828. Nearly half—45 percent—of your total return came from reinvested dividends. And this happened during a stellar period of rising stock prices.

Now consider the same investment during a period of misery. If you had invested $10,000 in the S&P's Index stocks in January 1968, your investment would have grown to only $14,073 over the next 13 years, a gain of only $4,073. During much of that time, the value of your original investment would have been less than $10,000. Dividends during the period would have totaled $7,088—substantially more than stock appreciation. Reinvested, the same dividends would have grown to $9,705, helping your original investment grow to $23,778.

In a period of major ups and downs that many investors don't like to remember, dividends accounted for 70 percent of total return (see accompanying chart).

We could fiddle with these figures any number of ways. We could reduce the value of dividends by calculating income taxes. We could raise it by starting with the Dow Jones industrial average stocks, which tend to have higher dividends. But the point here is very simple: Whether you spend them or reinvest them, dividends are always an important part of the return on common stock.

A Close Look at Dividends in Two Markets

| **Anatomy of the bull market of 1982–1994** | | |
|---|---|---|
| Original investment | | $10,000 |
| Gain on original investment | | $27,475 |
| Total dividends | $14,244 | |
| Gain on reinvested dividends | $ 8,584 | |
| Total gain from dividends | | $22, 828 |
| **Total** | | **$60,303** |
| Compound annualized return equals 14.8%; 45% from dividends | | |

| **Anatomy of a bear market, 1968–1980** | | |
|---|---|---|
| Original investment | | $10,000 |
| Gain on original investment | | $ 4,073 |
| Total dividends | $ 7,088 | |
| Gain on reinvested dividends | $ 2,617 | |
| Total gain from dividends | | $ 9,705 |
| **Total** | | **$23,778** |
| Compound annualized return equals 6.9%; 70% from dividends. | | |

Source: Franklin/Templeton Group Hypothetical Illustration Program.

Based on your reading of this chapter, evaluate what Burns is saying. Do you agree or disagree with him? Why?

Source: Scott Burns, "Those Lowly Dividends," *Dallas Morning News* (July 2, 1995): 1H.

## STUDY PROBLEMS (SET B)

**17-1B.** (*Flotation costs and issue size*) Your firm needs to raise $12 million. Assuming that flotation costs are expected to be $17 per share and that the market price of the stock is $115, how many shares would have to be issued? What is the dollar size of the issue?

**17-2B.** (*Flotation costs and issue size*) If flotation costs for a common stock issue are 14 percent, how large must the issue be so that the firm will net $6,100,000? If the stock sells for $76 per share, how many shares must be issued?

**17-3B.** (*Residual dividend theory*) Steven Miller finances new investments by 35 percent debt and 65 percent equity. The firm needs $650,000 for financing new investments. If retained earnings available for reinvestment equal $375,000, how much money will be available for dividends in accordance with the residual dividend theory?

**17-4B.** (*Stock dividend*) DCA has 2.5 million shares of common stock outstanding. Net income is $600,000, and the P/E ratio for the stock is 10. Management is planning an 18 percent stock dividend. What will be the price of the stock after the stock dividend? If an investor owns 120 shares before the stock dividend, does the total value of his or her shares change? Explain.

**17-5B.** (*Dividends in perfect markets*) The management of Montford, Inc., is considering two dividend policies for the years 1997 and 1998, 1 and 2 years away. In 1999, the management is planning to liquidate the firm. One plan would pay a dividend of $2.55 in 1997 and 1998 and a liquidating dividend of $45.60 in 1999. The alternative would be to pay out $4.35 in dividends in 1997, $4.70 in dividends in 1998, and a final dividend of $40.62 in 1999. The required rate of return for the common stockholders is 17 percent. Management is concerned about the effect of the two dividend streams on the value of the common stock.

**a.** Assuming perfect markets, what would be the effect?
**b.** What factors in the real world might change your conclusion reached in part (a)?

**17-6B.** (*Long-term residual dividend policy*) Wells Manufacturing, Inc. has projected its investment opportunities over a 5-year planning horizon. The cost of each year's investment and the amount of internal funds available for reinvestment for that year follow. The firm's debt-equity mix is 40 percent debt and 60 percent equity. There are currently 125,000 shares of common stock outstanding.

**a.** What would be the dividend each year if the residual dividend theory were used on a year-to-year basis?
**b.** What target stable dividend can Wells establish by using the long-term residual dividend theory over the future planning horizon?
**c.** Why might a residual dividend policy applied to the 5 years as opposed to individual years be preferable?

| Year | Cost of Investments | Internal Funds Available for Reinvestment or for Dividends |
|---|---|---|
| 1 | $360,000 | $225,000 |
| 2 | 450,000 | 440,000 |
| 3 | 230,000 | 600,000 |
| 4 | 890,000 | 650,000 |
| 5 | 600,000 | 400,000 |

**17-7B.** (*Stock split*) You own 8 percent of the Standlee Corporation's common stock, which most recently sold for $98 before a planned two-for-one stock split announcement. Before the split there are 30,000 shares of common stock outstanding.

**a.** Relative to now, what will be your financial position after the stock split? (Assume the stock price falls proportionately.)
**b.** The executive vice-president in charge of finance believes the price will only fall 45 percent after the split because she thinks the price is above the optimal price range. If she is correct, what will be your net gain?

**17-8B.** (*Dividend policies*) The earnings for Carlson Cargo, Inc., have been predicted for the next 5 years and are listed in the following table. There are 1 million shares outstanding. Determine the yearly dividend per share to be paid if the following policies are enacted:

**a.** Constant dividend payout ratio of 40 percent.
**b.** Stable dollar dividend targeted at 40 percent of the earnings over the 5-year period.
**c.** Small, regular dividend of $0.50 per share plus a year-end extra when the profits in any year exceed $1,500,000. The year-end extra dividend will equal 50 percent of profits exceeding $1,500,000.

| Year | Profits After Taxes |
|---|---|
| 1 | $1,500,000 |
| 2 | 2,000,000 |
| 3 | 1,750,000 |
| 4 | 950,000 |
| 5 | 2,500,000 |

**17-9B.** (*Repurchase of stock*) The B. Phillips Corporation is planning to pay dividends of $550,000. There are 275,000 shares outstanding, with an earnings per share of $6. The stock should sell for \$45 after the ex-dividend date. If instead of paying a dividend, management decides to repurchase stock:

**a.** What should be the repurchase price?

**b.** How many shares should be repurchased?

**c.** What if the repurchase price is set below or above your suggested price in part (a)?

**d.** If you own 100 shares, would you prefer that the company pay the dividend or repurchase stock?

**17-10B.** (*Flotation costs and issue size*) D. B. Fool, Inc., needs to raise \$16 million. Assuming that the market price of the firm's stock is \$100 and flotation costs are 12 percent of the market price, how many shares would have to be issued? What is the dollar size of the issue?

**17-11B.** (*Residual dividend theory*) Maness, Inc., finances new acquisitions with 35 percent in equity and the rest in debt. The firm needs \$1.5 million for a new acquisition. If retained earnings available for reinvestment are \$525,000, how much money will be available for dividends according to the residual dividend theory?

**17-12B.** (*Stock split*) You own 25 percent of The Star Corporation, which recently sold for \$90 before a planned two-for-one stock split announcement. Before the split there are 90,000 shares of common stock outstanding.

**a.** What is your financial position before the split, and what will it be after the stock split? (Assume the stock falls proportionately.)

**b.** Your stockbroker believes the market will react positively to the split and that the price will fall only 45 percent after the split. If she is correct, what will be your net gain?

## SELF-TEST SOLUTIONS

**ST-1.** Dividend per share = 35% × \$8.20
= \$2.87

Dividends:

1 year = \$2.87 (1 + 0.12)
= \$3.21

5 years = \$2.87 $(1 + 0.12)^5$
= \$2.87 (1.762)
= \$5.06

**ST-2. a.** Investments A, B, and C will be accepted, requiring \$1,150,000 in total financing. Therefore, 40 percent of \$1,150,000 or \$460,000 in new debt will be needed, and common equity will have to provide \$690,000. The remainder of the \$750,000 internal funds will be \$60,000, which will be paid out in dividends.

**b.** Assuming a 10 percent cost of capital, all four investments would be accepted, requiring total financing of \$1,550,000. Equity would provide 60 percent, or \$930,000 of the total, which would not leave any funds to be paid out in dividends. New common would have to be issued.

**ST-3. a.** If a 15 percent stock dividend is issued, the financial statement would appear as follows:

Robson Corporation

| | |
|---|---|
| **Debt** | \$1,800,000 |
| **Common** | |
| Par (\$2 par, 115,000 shares) | 230,000 |
| Paid-in capital | 670,000 |
| Retained earnings | \$ 600,000 |
| | \$3,300,000 |

**b.** A two-for-one split would result in a 100 percent increase in the number of shares. Because the total par value remains at $200,000, the new par value per share is $1 ($200,000 ÷ 200,000 shares). The new financial statement would be as follows:

Robson Corporation

| | |
|---|---|
| **Debt** | $1,800,000 |
| **Common** | |
| Par ($1 par, 200,000 shares) | 200,000 |
| Paid-in capital | 400,000 |
| Retained earnings | 900,000 |
| | $3,300,000 |

# WORKING-CAPITAL MANAGEMENT AND SHORT-TERM FINANCING

**LEARNING OBJECTIVES**

After reading this chapter, you should be able to

1. List the determinants of a firm's net working capital and explain the risk-return trade-off involved in managing net working capital.
2. List the advantages and disadvantages of using current liabilities to finance a firm's working-capital requirements.
3. Describe the hedging principle or principle of self-liquidating debt, and the relevance of permanent and temporary sources of financing.
4. Calculate a firm's cash conversion cycle and interpret its component parts.
5. Calculate the effective cost of short-term credit.
6. List and describe the basic sources of short-term credit.
7. Describe the currency exchange risks faced by multinational firms when managing working capital.

U.S. companies, on average, invest more than 15 cents in current assets from each $1 of sales. In 1990, American Standard fit into this mold very well with over $735 million invested in working capital. By 1993, American Standard had revenues total-

ing $4.2 billion but had reduced its net working capital (current assets–current liabilities) roughly in half. ● In 1990, American Standard had three primary product lines: plumbing supplies, air conditioners, and brakes for trucks and buses. The firm faced static sales and huge interest payments (the result of a $3.1 billion junk bond issue used to stave off a hostile takeover attempt by Black & Decker in 1989). To improve the firm's operating performance, its chairman, Emmanuel Kampouris, introduced a strategy aimed at reducing the firm's $735 million in net working capital to zero by 1996. This is feasible if the company can reduce its inventories so low that they can be financed without borrowing. The idea is to deliver goods and bill customers more rapidly so that customer payments are sufficient to pay for minimal stocks of inventories. Kampouris sought to accomplish this ambitious goal through implementation of a lean manufacturing system known as demand flow technology. Under this system, plants manufacture products as customers order them. Suppliers deliver straight to the assembly line, thus reducing stocks of parts, and plants ship the products as soon as they are completed. The system dramatically reduces inventories of both parts and finished goods. To date, American Standard has reduced its inventories by more than one-half, down to $326 million since 1990. Thus American Standard invests only 5 cents out of each sales dollar in working capital compared to the norm of 15 cents. By saving interest payments on supplies, the company has increased its cash flow by $60 million a year.

Shawn Tully, "Raiding a Company's Hidden Cash," *Fortune* (August 22, 1994): 82–87.

**CHAPTER PREVIEW**

Chapter 18 is the first of three chapters that address short-term financing problems. Short-term financing decisions relate to the management of current assets, which, by definition, are converted into cash within a period of 1 year or less and current liabilities, which must be repaid in 1 year or less. This topic contrasts with capital budgeting, which is a long-term financing issue. We now want to look at short-term investing and financing issues. Short-term financing issues include such things as making sure that the firm has sufficient cash to pay its bills on time, managing the firm's collections of accounts receivable, extending credit to the firm's customers, and determining the proper amount and mix of short-term borrowing. Chapter 18 provides the framework for analyzing how much short-term financing the firm should use and what specific sources of short-term financing the firm should use. In Chapter 19, we discuss the management of cash and marketable securities followed in Chapter 20 by the discussion of managing the firm's investments in accounts receivable and inventories.

This chapter will emphasize these principles: **Principle 1: The Risk-Return Trade-Off—We won't take on additional risk unless we expect to be compensated with additional return; Principle 2: The Time Value of Money—A dollar received today is worth more than a dollar received in the future; Principle 3: Cash—Not Profits—Is King;** and **Principle 4: Incremental Cash Flows—It's only what changes that counts.**

## MANAGING CURRENT ASSETS AND LIABILITIES

Short-term financing problems arise in the management of a firm's investments in current assets (sometimes referred to as **working capital**) and its use of current liabilities. The firm's **net working capital** (which is the difference in a firm's current assets and its current liabilities) at any particular time provides a very useful summary measure of the firm's short-term financing decisions. As the firm's net working capital decreases, the firm's profitability tends to rise. However, this increase in profitability comes only at the expense of an increased risk of illiquidity. Consequently, short-term financing decisions impact a firm's net working capital and consequently entail a risk-return trade-off.

**Working capital**
The firm's total investment in current assets or assets that it expects to be converted into cash within a year or less.

**Net working capital**
The difference between the firm's current assets and its current liabilities. Frequently when the term *working capital* is used, it is actually intended to mean *net working capital*.

### Working-Capital Management and the Risk-Return Trade-Off

Figure 18-1 illustrates the risk-return trade-off that arises in the management of a firm's net working capital. A firm can increase its net working capital by adding to its current assets relative to its current liabilities (for example, holding larger levels of inventories or marketable securities) or by decreasing its current liabilities relative to its current assets (for

**FIGURE 18-1**
The Risk-Return Trade-Off in Managing a Firm's Net Working Capital

| | Firm Profitability | Firm Liquidity |
|---|---|---|
| Investing in additional marketable securities and inventories | Lower | Higher |
| Increasing the use of short- versus long-term sources of financing | Higher | Lower |

example, by using long-term sources of finance such as bonds rather than bank loans that must be repaid within the year).

Consider first the effects of increasing a firm's net working capital by holding larger investments in marketable securities and inventories without changing the firm's use of current liabilities. Other things remaining the same, this has the effect of increasing the firm's liquidity. That is, with the additional marketable securities, the firm has a ready source of funds should it experience an unexpected shortfall in its cash flow. In addition, the added inventories reduce the chance of production stoppages, and the loss of sales from inventory shortages. However, because these additional current asset investments earn very low returns, firm profitability is reduced.

Now consider the effects of reducing a firm's net working capital by substituting short-term financing such as notes payable that must be repaid in 1 year or less for long-term sources such as bonds. This has the net effects pointed out in Figure 18-1. The use of short-term financing increases firm profitability for two reasons. First, short-term financing usually carries a lower rate of interest than does long-term financing. In addition, when short-term sources of financing are used to finance a firm's seasonal needs for financing (such as the buildup of inventories for a retail firm prior to the Christmas season), the firm can repay the funds after the seasonal need has expired, thus requiring the firm to pay interest only during the periods when the funds are needed. If long-term financing is used, the firm will end up holding excess cash during those times of the year when seasonal financing needs are zero, thus incurring additional borrowing costs and reducing overall profitability.

Using short-term financing increases a firm's risk of not being able to pay its bills on time, or the risk of illiquidity. This corresponds to the commonsense notion that short-term financing must be repaid more frequently than long-term financing, thus exposing the firm to additional risk of having the financing come due at a time when its financial condition might make it difficult to repay the loan.

## RELATE TO THE BIG PICTURE

Working-capital decisions provide a classic example of the risk-return nature of financial decision making. Increasing the firm's net working capital (current assets less current liabilities) reduces the risk that the firm will not be able to pay its bills on time (i.e., the risk of illiquidity) but, at the same time, reduces the overall profitability of the firm. Thus, working-capital decisions involve **Principle 1: The Risk-Return Trade-Off—We won't take on additional risk unless we expect to be compensated with additional return.**

**CONCEPT CHECK**

1. What is net working capital and how does it impact firm profitability and liquidity?
2. What are the benefits and costs of increasing net working capital through the addition of current assets?

## FINANCING WORKING CAPITAL WITH CURRENT LIABILITIES

### Advantages of Current Liabilities: The Return

Current liabilities offer the firm a more flexible source of financing than do long-term liabilities or equity. They can be used to match the timing of a firm's needs for short-term financing. If, for example, a firm needs funds for a 3-month period during each year to finance a seasonal expansion in inventories, then a 3-month loan can provide substantial cost savings over a long-term loan (even if the interest rate on short-term financing should be higher). The use of long-term debt in this situation involves borrowing for the entire year rather than for the period when the funds are needed, which increases the amount of interest the firm must pay. This brings us to the second advantage generally associated with the use of short-term financing: interest cost.

In general, interest rates on short-term debt are lower than on long-term debt for a given borrower.

### Disadvantages of Current Liabilities: The Risk

The use of current liabilities, or short-term debt, as opposed to long-term debt, subjects the firm to a greater risk of illiquidity for two reasons. First, short-term debt, due to its very nature, must be repaid or rolled over more often, and so it increases the possibility that the firm's financial condition might deteriorate to a point where the needed funds might not be available.[1]

A second disadvantage of short-term debt is the uncertainty of interest costs from year to year. For example, a firm borrowing during a 6-month period each year to finance a seasonal expansion in current assets might incur a different rate of interest each year. This rate reflects the current rate of interest at the time of the loan, as well as the lender's perception of the firm's riskiness. If fixed rate long-term debt were used, the interest cost would be known for the entire period of the loan agreement.

**CONCEPT CHECK**

1. How does investing more heavily in current assets while not increasing the firm's current liabilities decrease both the firm's risk and the expected return on its investments?
2. How does the use of current liabilities enhance firm profitability and also increase the firm's risk of default on its financial obligations?

[1]The dangers of such a policy are readily apparent in the experiences of firms that have been forced into bankruptcy. Penn Central, for example, had $80 million in short-term debt that it was unable to refinance (roll over) at the time of its bankruptcy.

## APPROPRIATE LEVEL OF WORKING CAPITAL

OBJECTIVE 3 

**Hedging principle (principle of self-liquidating debt)**
Financing maturity should follow the cash-flow-producing characteristics of the asset being financed.

Managing the firm's net working capital (its liquidity) has been shown to involve simultaneous and interrelated decisions regarding investment in current assets and use of current liabilities. Fortunately, a guiding principle exists that can be used as a benchmark for the firm's working-capital policies: the **hedging principle,** or **principle of self-liquidating debt.** This principle provides managers with a guide to the maintenance of a level of liquidity sufficient for the firm to meet its maturing obligations on time.[2]

## HEDGING PRINCIPLES

Very simply, the hedging principle involves *matching* the cash-flow-generating characteristics of an asset with the maturity of the source of financing used to finance its acquisitions. For example, a seasonal expansion in inventories, according to the hedging principle, should be financed with a short-term loan or current liability. The rationale underlying the rule is straightforward. Funds are needed for a limited period and, when that time has passed, the cash needed to repay the loan will be generated by the sale of the extra inventory items. Obtaining the needed funds from a long-term source (longer than 1 year) would mean that the firm would still have the funds after the inventories they helped finance had been sold. In this case, the firm would have "excess" liquidity, which it either holds in cash or invests in low-yield marketable securities until the seasonal increase in inventories occurs again and the funds are needed. The result would be an overall lowering of firm profits.

Consider an example in which a firm purchases a new conveyor belt system, which is expected to produce cash savings to the firm by eliminating the need for two laborers and, consequently, their salaries. This amounts to an annual savings of $14,000, whereas the conveyor belt costs $150,000 to install and will last 20 years. If the firm chooses to finance this asset with a 1-year note, then it will not be able to repay the loan from the $14,000 cash flow generated by the asset. In accordance with the hedging principle, the firm should finance the asset with a source of financing that more nearly matches the expected life and cash-flow-generating characteristics of the asset. In this case, a 15- to 20-year loan would be more appropriate.

**Permanent asset investment**
An investment in an asset that the firm expects to hold for the foreseeable future, whether fixed assets or current assets. For example, the minimum level of inventory the firm plans to hold for the foreseeable future is a permanent investment.

**Temporary asset investment**
Investments in assets that the firm plans to sell (liquidate) within a period no longer than 1 year. Although temporary investments can be made in fixed assets, this is not the usual case. Temporary investments generally are made in inventories and receivables.

### Permanent and Temporary Assets

The notion of *maturity matching* in the hedging principle can be most easily understood when we think in terms of the distinction between **permanent** and **temporary asset investments** as opposed to the more traditional fixed and current asset categories. A permanent investment in an asset is an investment that the firm expects to hold for a period longer than 1 year. Note that we are referring to the period the firm plans to hold an investment, not the useful life of the asset. For example, permanent investments are made in the firm's minimum level of current assets, as well as in its fixed assets. Temporary asset investments, on the other hand, are composed of current assets that will be liquidated and not replaced within the current year. Thus, some part of the firm's current assets is perma-

[2]A value-maximizing approach to the management of the firm's liquidity involves assessing the value of the benefits derived from increasing the firm's investment in liquid assets and weighing them against the added costs to the firm's owners resulting from investing in low-yield current assets. Unfortunately, the benefits derived from increased liquidity relate to the expected costs of bankruptcy to the firm's owners, and these costs are "unmeasurable" by existing technology. Thus a "valuation" approach to liquidity management exists only in the theoretical realm.

nent and the remainder is temporary. For example, a seasonal increase in inventories is a temporary investment because the buildup in inventories will be eliminated when it is no longer needed.

## Temporary, Permanent, and Spontaneous Sources of Financing

Because total assets must always equal the sum of temporary, permanent, and spontaneous sources of financing, the hedging approach provides the financial manager with the basis for determining the sources of financing to use at any point.

Now, what constitutes a temporary, permanent, or spontaneous source of financing? **Temporary sources of financing** consist of current liabilities. Short-term notes payable is the most common example of a temporary source of financing. Notes payable include unsecured bank loans, commercial paper, and loans secured by accounts receivable and inventories. **Permanent sources of financing** include intermediate-term loans, long-term debt, preferred stock, and common equity.

**Temporary sources of financing**
Another term for current liabilities.

**Permanent sources of financing**
Sources of financing that do not mature or come due within the year, including intermediate term debt, long-term debt, preferred stock, and common stock.

**Spontaneous sources of financing**
Trade credit and other sources of accounts payable that arise in the firm's day-to-day operations.

**Spontaneous sources of financing** consist of trade credit and other accounts payable that arise in the firm's day-to-day operations. For example, as the firm acquires materials for its inventories, trade credit is often made available spontaneously or on demand from the firm's suppliers. Trade credit appears on the firm's balance sheet as accounts payable, and the size of the accounts payable balance varies directly with the firm's purchases of inventory items. In turn, inventory purchases are related to anticipated sales. Thus part of the financing needed by the firm is spontaneously provided in the form of trade credit.

In addition to trade credit, wages, and salaries payable, accrued interest and accrued taxes also provide valuable sources of spontaneous financing. These liabilities accrue throughout the period until they are paid. For example, if a firm has a wage expense of $10,000 a week and pays its employees monthly, then its employees effectively provide financing equal to $10,000 by the end of the first week following a payday, $20,000 by the end of the second week, and so forth. Because these expenses generally arise in direct conjunction with the firm's ongoing operations, they too are referred to as *spontaneous.*

## Hedging Principle: Graphic Illustration

The hedging principle can now be stated very succinctly: *Asset needs of the firm not financed by spontaneous sources should be financed in accordance with this rule: Permanent asset investments are financed with permanent sources, and temporary investments are financed with temporary sources.*

The hedging principle is depicted in Figure 18-2. Total assets are broken down into temporary and permanent asset investment categories. The firm's permanent investment in assets is financed by the use of permanent sources of financing (intermediate- and long-term debt, preferred stock, and common equity) or spontaneous sources (trade credit and other accounts payable). For illustration purposes, spontaneous sources of financing are treated as if their amount were fixed. In practice, of course, spontaneous sources of financing fluctuate with the firm's purchases and its expenditures for wages, salaries, taxes, and other items that are paid on a delayed basis. Its temporary investment in assets is financed with temporary (short-term) debt.

To summarize, note that the optimal financing mix involves the use of a combination of short- and long-term sources of financing. The particular mix according to the hedging principle relies on the nature of the firm's needs for financing—that is, whether the need is permanent or temporary.

**FIGURE 18-2**
Hedging Principle: Financing Strategy

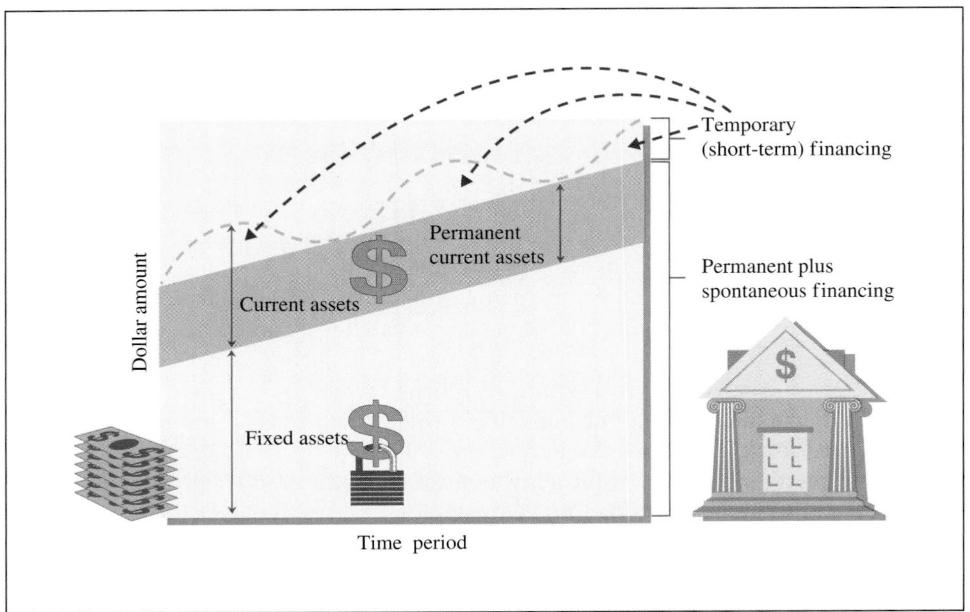


## RELATE TO THE BIG PICTURE

Although current liabilities provide financing for periods less than 1 year, the time value of money is still relevant and should be incorporated into our estimation of their cost. Thus, estimating the cost of short-term credit provides yet another case where we rely on **Principle 2: The Time Value of Money—A dollar received today is worth more than a dollar received in the future.** In addition, as we estimate the cost of credit, we will focus on cash received and paid. So we also rely on **Principle 3: Cash—Not Profits—Is King.** Finally, we must be careful to consider all the cash flow consequences of the use of a particular source of short-term credit. In particular, we are interested in all the incremental cash inflows and outflows associated with the financing source. This reflects our use of **Principle 4: Incremental Cash Flows—It's only what changes that counts.**

## CONCEPT CHECK

1. What is the hedging principle, or principle of self-liquidating debt?
2. What are some examples of permanent and temporary investments in current assets?
3. Is trade credit a permanent, temporary, or spontaneous source of financing? Explain.

## CASH CONVERSION CYCLE

Because firms vary widely with respect to their ability to manage their new working capital, there exists a need for an overall measure of effectiveness. An increasingly popular method for evaluating a firm's effective management of its working capital takes the approach that the firm's objective should be to minimize working capital subject to the constraint that it has sufficient working capital to support the firm's operations.

Minimizing working capital is accomplished by speeding up the collection of cash from sales, increasing inventory turns, and slowing down the disbursement of cash. We can incorporate all of these factors in a single measure called the *cash conversion cycle.*

## Measuring Working Capital Efficiency

The cash conversion cycle, or CCC, is simply the sum of days of sales outstanding and days of sales in inventory less days of payables outstanding:

$$\begin{matrix}\text{cash}\\ \text{conversion}\\ \text{cycle}\end{matrix}(\text{CCC}) = \begin{matrix}\text{days of}\\ \text{sales}\\ \text{outstanding}\end{matrix}(\text{DSO}) + \begin{matrix}\text{days of}\\ \text{sales in}\\ \text{inventory}\end{matrix}(\text{DSI}) - \begin{matrix}\text{days of}\\ \text{payables}\\ \text{outstanding}\end{matrix}(\text{DPO})$$

We calculate days of sales outstanding as follows:

$$\begin{matrix}\text{days of}\\ \text{sales}\\ \text{outstanding}\end{matrix}(\text{DSO}) = \frac{\text{accounts receivable}}{\text{sales}/365} \quad \textbf{(18-1)}$$

Recall from Chapter 4 that DSO can also be thought of as the average age of the firm's accounts receivable or the average collection period.

Days of sales in inventory is defined as follows:

$$\begin{matrix}\text{days of}\\ \text{sales in}\\ \text{inventory}\end{matrix}(\text{DSI}) = \frac{\text{inventories}}{\text{sales}/365} \quad \textbf{(18-2)}$$

Note that DSI can also be thought of as the average age of the firm's inventory; that is, the average number of days that a dollar of inventory is held by the firm.

Days of payables outstanding is defined as follows:

$$\begin{matrix}\text{days of}\\ \text{payables}\\ \text{outstanding}\end{matrix}(\text{DPO}) = \frac{\text{accounts payable}}{\text{sales}/365} \quad \textbf{(18-3)}$$

This ratio indicates the average age, in days, of the firm's accounts payable.

To illustrate the use of the CCC metric, consider Dell Computer Corporation. In 1989 Dell was a fledgling startup whose CCC was 121.88 days (Table 18-1). By 1998, Dell had reduced this number to −18.12 days. How, you might ask, does a firm reduce its CCC below zero? The answer is through very aggressive management of its working capital. As Table 18-1 indicates, Dell achieved this phenomenal reduction in CCC primarily through very effective management of inventories (days of sales in inventories dropped from 132.04 in 1989 to 9.13 in 1998) and more favorable trade credit payment practices (days of payables outstanding increased from 47.46 in 1989 to 62.13 in 1998). Specifically, Dell, a direct marketer of personal computers, does not build a computer until an order is received. It purchases its supplies using trade credit. This business model results in minimal investment in inventories. Dell has obviously improved its working-capital management practices over the 1989–1998 period, as evidenced in Figure 18-3 where we compare Dell with Compaq and Apple. The dramatic differences in CCC reflect both differences in business models (direct seller versus the use of more traditional channels of distribution involving the use of resellers such as CompUSA, Best Buy, and Computer City) as well as the relative efficiency of the firm in managing inventories, receivables, and payables.

**TABLE 18-1**
Determinants of Dell Computer Corporation's Cash Conversion Cycle for 1989–1998

cash conversion cycle (CCC) = days of sales outstanding (DSO) + days of sales in inventory (DSI) − days of payables outstanding (DPO).

| | Jan-89 | Jan-90 | Jan-91 | Jan-92 | Jan-93 | Jan-94 | Jan-95 | Jan-96 | Jan-97 | Jan-98 |
|---|---|---|---|---|---|---|---|---|---|---|
| Days of sales outstanding (DSO) | 37.30 | 44.66 | 49.34 | 51.51 | 48.17 | 49.17 | 49.14 | 42.96 | 37.79 | 34.88 |
| Days of sales in inventory (DSI) | 132.04 | 113.82 | 79.17 | 65.16 | 50.08 | 40.28 | 34.16 | 31.01 | 20.25 | 9.13 |
| Days of payables outstanding (DPO) | 47.46 | 78.31 | 74.49 | 55.47 | 61.72 | 45.10 | 57.96 | 38.77 | 63.80 | 62.13 |
| Cash conversion cycle (CCC) | 121.88 | 80.17 | 54.02 | 61.20 | 36.53 | 44.35 | 25.34 | 35.20 | −5.76 | −18.12 |

**FIGURE 18-3**
Cash Conversion Cycles for Apple, Compaq, and Dell: 1989–1998.

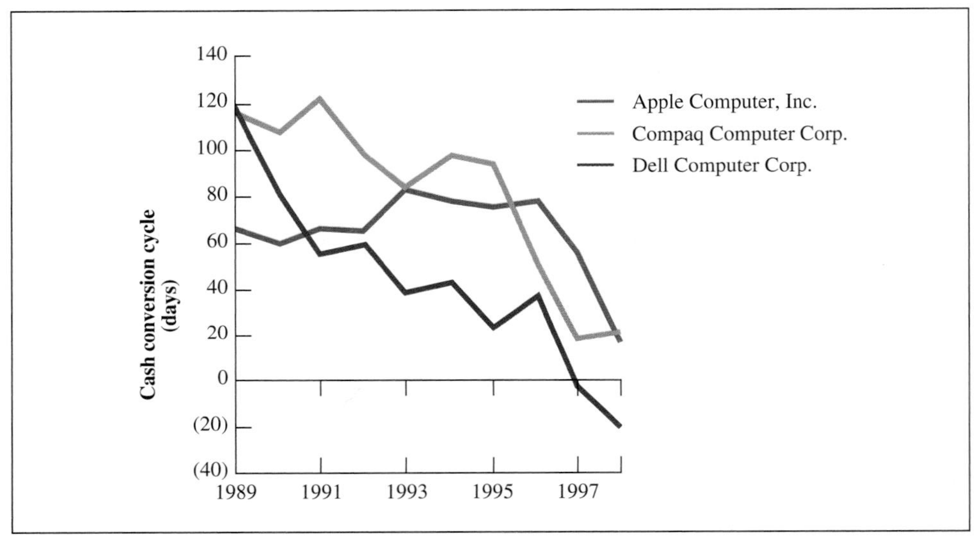


**CONCEPT CHECK**

1. What three actions can a firm take to minimize net working capital?
2. Define *days of sales outstanding, days of sales in inventory,* and *days of payables outstanding.*

## ESTIMATION OF THE COST OF SHORT-TERM CREDIT

OBJECTIVE 5 

There are a myriad of types of short-term financing sources. How is one to choose? A key factor is certainly the cost of credit.

### Approximate Cost-of-Credit Formula

The procedure for estimating the cost of short-term credit is a very simple one and relies on the basic interest equation:

$$\text{interest} = \text{principal} \times \text{rate} \times \text{time} \tag{18-4}$$

where *interest* is the dollar amount of interest on a *principal* that is borrowed at some annual *rate* for a fraction of a year (represented by *time*). For example, a 6-month loan for $1,000 at 8 percent interest would require an interest payment of $40:

$$\text{interest} = \$1{,}000 \times .08 \times 1/2 = \$40$$

We use this basic relationship to solve for the cost of a source of short-term financing, or the annual percentage rate (*APR*), where the interest amount, the principal sum, and the time period for financing are known. Thus, solving the basic interest equation for APR produces[3]

$$APR = \frac{\text{interest}}{\text{principal} \times \text{time}} \tag{18-5}$$

or

$$APR = \frac{\text{interest}}{\text{principal}} \times \frac{1}{\text{time}}$$

**EXAMPLE**

The SKC Corporation plans to borrow $1,000 for a 90-day period. At maturity, the firm will repay the $1,000 principal amount plus $30 interest. The effective annual rate of interest for the loan can be estimated using the *APR* equation, as follows:

$$APR = \frac{\$30}{\$1{,}000} \times \frac{1}{90/360}$$

$$= .03 \times \frac{360}{90} = .12, \text{ or } 12\%$$

The effective annual cost of funds provided by the loan is therefore 12 percent.

## Annual Percentage Yield Formula

The simple *APR* calculation does not consider compound interest. To account for the influence of compounding, we can use the following equation:

$$APY = \left(1 + \frac{i}{m}\right)^m - 1 \tag{18-6}$$

where *APY* is the annual percentage yield, *i* is the nominal rate of interest per year (12 percent in the previous example), and *m* is the number of compounding periods within a year [$m = 1/\text{time} = 1 \div (90/360) = 4$ in the preceding example]. Thus, the effective rate of interest on the example problem, considering compounding, is

$$APY = \left(1 + \frac{.12}{4}\right)^4 - 1 = .126, \text{ or } 12.6\%$$

Compounding effectively raises the cost of short-term credit. Because the differences between *APR* and *APY* are usually small, we use the simple interest version or *APR* to compute the cost of short-term credit.

[3]For ease of computation, we will assume a 30-day month and 360-day year in this chapter.

CONCEPT CHECK

1. What is the fundamental interest equation that underlies that calculation of the cost of credit formula?
2. What is the annual percentage yield (*APY*) and why is it preferred to the annual percentage rate (*APR*)?

## SOURCES OF SHORT-TERM CREDIT

OBJECTIVE 6 

**Secured and unsecured loans**
Secured loans are backed by the pledge of specific assets as collateral whereas unsecured loans are only backed by the promise of the borrower to honor the loan commitment.

Short-term credit is offered by a wide variety of financial intermediaries in many different forms. For purposes of our review, we will find it useful to categorize them into two basic groups: unsecured and secured. **Unsecured loans** include all those sources that have as their security only the lender's faith in the ability of the borrower to repay the funds when due. Major sources of unsecured short-term credit include accrued wages and taxes, trade credit, unsecured bank loans, and commercial paper. **Secured loans** involve the pledge of specific assets as collateral in the event the borrower defaults in payment of principal or interest. Commercial banks, finance companies, and factors are the primary suppliers of secured credit. The principal sources of collateral are accounts receivable and inventories.

### Unsecured Sources: Accrued Wages and Taxes

Because most businesses pay their employees only periodically (weekly, biweekly, or monthly), firms accrue a wages payable account that is, in essence, a loan from their employees. For example, if the wage expense for the Appleton Manufacturing Company is $450,000 per week and it pays its employees monthly, then by the end of a 4-week month, the firm will owe its employees $1.8 million in wages for services they have already performed during the month. Consequently, the employees finance their own efforts through waiting a full month for payment.

Similarly, firms generally make quarterly income tax payments for their estimated quarterly tax liability. This means that the firm has the use of the tax monies it owes based on quarterly profits up through the end of the quarter. In addition, the firm pays sales taxes and withholding (income) taxes for its employees on a deferred basis. The longer the period that the firm holds the tax payments, the greater the amount of financing they provide.

Note that these sources of financing *rise and fall spontaneously* with the level of firm sales. That is, as the firm's sales increase so do its labor expenses, sales taxes collected, and income taxes. Consequently, these accrued expense items provide the firm with automatic or spontaneous sources of financing.

### Unsecured Sources: Trade Credit

**Trade credit**
Accounts payable that arise out of the normal course of business when the firm purchases from its suppliers who allow the firm to make payment after the delivery of the merchandise or services.

**Trade credit** provides one of the most flexible sources of short-term financing available to the firm. We previously noted that trade credit is a primary source of spontaneous, or on-demand, financing. That is, trade credit arises spontaneously with the firm's purchases. To arrange for credit, the firm need only place an order with one of its suppliers. The supplier checks the firm's credit and, if it is good, sends the merchandise. The purchasing firm then pays for the goods in accordance with the supplier's credit terms.

CREDIT TERMS AND CASH DISCOUNTS Very often the credit terms offered with trade credit involve a cash discount for early payment. For example, a supplier might offer terms

**TABLE 18-2**
Effective Rates of Interest on Selected Trade Credit Terms

| Credit Terms | Effective Rate |
|---|---|
| 2/10, net 60 | 14.69% |
| 2/10, net 90 | 9.18 |
| 3/20, net 60 | 27.84 |
| 6/10, net 90 | 28.72 |

of 2/10, net 30, which means that a 2 percent discount is offered for payment within 10 days or the full amount is due in 30 days. Thus, a 2 percent penalty is involved for not paying within 10 days or for delaying payment from the tenth to the thirtieth day (that is, for 20 days). The effective annual cost of not taking the cash discount can be quite severe. Using a $1 invoice amount, the effective cost of passing up the discount period using the preceding credit terms and our *APR* equation can be estimated:

$$APR = \frac{\$.02}{\$.98} \times \frac{1}{20/360} = .3673, \text{ or } 36.73\%$$

Note that the 2 percent cash discount is the *interest* cost of extending the payment period an *additional* 20 days. Note also that the principal amount of the credit is 98¢. This amount constitutes the full principal amount as of the tenth day of the credit period, after which time the cash discount is lost. The effective cost of passing up the 2 percent discount for 20 days is quite expensive: 36.73 percent. Furthermore, once the discount period has passed, there is no reason to pay before the final due date (the thirtieth day). Table 18-2 lists the effective annual cost of alternative credit terms. Note that the cost of trade credit varies directly with the size of the cash discount and inversely with the length of time between the end of the discount period and the final due date.

STRETCHING OF TRADE CREDIT Some firms that use trade credit engage in a practice called *stretching* trade accounts. This practice involves delaying payments beyond the prescribed credit period. For example, a firm might purchase materials under credit terms of 3/10, net 60; however, when faced with a shortage of cash, the firm might extend payment to the eightieth day. Continued violation of trade terms can eventually lead to a loss of credit. However, for short periods, and at infrequent intervals, stretching may offer the firm an emergency source of short-term credit.

ADVANTAGES OF TRADE CREDIT As a source of short-term financing, trade credit has a number of advantages. First, trade credit is conveniently obtained as a normal part of the firm's operations. Second, no formal agreements are generally involved in extending credit. Furthermore, the amount of credit extended expands and contracts with the needs of the firm; this is why it is classified as a spontaneous, or on-demand, source of financing.

## Unsecured Sources: Bank Credit

Commercial banks provide unsecured short-term credit in two basic forms: lines of credit and transaction loans (notes payable). Maturities of both types of loans are usually 1 year or less, with rates of interest depending on the creditworthiness of the borrower and the level of interest rates in the economy as a whole.

**Line of credit agreement**
A line of credit agreement is an agreement between a firm and its banker to provide short-term financing to meet its temporary financing needs.

LINE OF CREDIT A **line of credit agreement** is a lending arrangement between a bank and a borrower in which the bank makes available a maximum amount of funds during a specified period of time. The actual borrowing is at the discretion of the borrowing firm and the bank usually requires that the line of credit have a zero balance for some specified period of time such as a month during each year. This requirement is designed to assure that the borrower is using the line of credit to finance working capital and not permanent asset acquisitions such as plant and equipment. **Revolving credit** or a **revolver** is a special type of line of credit agreement in which the line of agreements usually extend from 1 to 5 years in duration.

**Revolving credit or revolver**
A special type of line of credit agreement in which the line of credit is eventually converted into a term loan that requires periodic payments.

CREDIT TERMS Lines of credit generally do not involve fixed rates of interest; instead they state that credit will be extended *at 1/2 percent over prime* or some other spread over the bank's prime rate.[4] Furthermore, the agreement usually does not spell out the specific use that will be made of the funds beyond a general statement, such as *for working-capital purposes.*

Lines of credit usually require that the borrower maintain a minimum balance in the bank throughout the loan period, called a *compensating balance.* This required balance (which can be stated as a percent of the line of credit or the loan amount) increases the effective cost of the loan to the borrower, unless a deposit balance equal to or greater than this balance requirement is ordinarily maintained in the bank.

**EXAMPLE**

M&M Beverage Company has a $300,000 line of credit that requires a compensating balance equal to 10 percent of the loan amount. The rate paid on the loan is 12 percent per annum, $200,000 is borrowed for a 6-month period, and the firm does not currently have a deposit with the lending bank. The dollar cost of the loan includes the interest expense and, in addition, the opportunity cost of maintaining an idle cash balance equal to the 10 percent compensating balance. To accommodate the cost of the compensating balance requirement, assume that the added funds will have to be borrowed and simply left idle in the firm's checking account. Thus, the amount actually borrowed ($B$) will be larger than the $200,000 needed. In fact, the needed $200,000 will constitute 90 percent of the total borrowed funds because of the 10 percent compensating balance requirement, hence $.90B =$ $200,000, such that $B =$ $222,222. Thus, interest is paid on a $222,222 loan ($222,222 × .12 × 1/2 = $13,333.32) of which only $200,000 is available for use by the firm.[5] The effective annual cost of credit therefore is

$$APR = \frac{\$13,333.32}{\$200,000} \times \frac{1}{180/360} = 13.33\%$$

In the M&M Beverage Company example, the loan required the payment of principal ($222,222) plus interest ($13,333.32) at the end of the 6-month loan period. Frequently, bank loans will be made on a discount basis. That is, the loan interest will be deducted from the loan amount before the funds are transferred to the borrower. Extending the M & M Beverage Company example to consider discounted

[4]The *prime rate of interest* is the rate that a bank charges its most creditworthy borrowers.

[5]The same answer would have been obtained by assuming a total loan of $200,000, of which only 90 percent or $180,000 was available for use by the firm; that is,

$$APR = \frac{\$12,000}{\$180,000} \times \frac{1}{180/360} = 13.33\%$$

Interest is now calculated on the $200,000 loan amount ($12,000 = $200,000 × 12 × 1/2).

interest involves reducing the loan proceeds ($200,000) in the previous example by the amount of interest for the full 6 months ($13,333.32). The effective rate of interest on the loan is now:

$$APR = \frac{\$13{,}333.32}{\$200{,}000 - \$13{,}333.32} \times \frac{1}{180/360}$$

$$= .1429, \text{ or } 14.29\%$$

The effect of discounting interest raises the cost of the loan from 13.33 percent to 14.29 percent. This results from the fact that the firm pays interest on the same amount of funds as before ($222,222); however, this time it gets the use of $13,333.32 less, or $200,000 − $13,333.32 = $186,666.68.

If M&M needs the use of a full $200,000, then it will have to borrow more than $222,222 to cover both the compensating balance requirement *and* the discounted interest. In fact, the firm will have to borrow some amount *B* such that:

$$B - .10B - (.12 \times \tfrac{1}{2})\,B = \$200{,}000$$

$$.84B = \$200{,}000$$

$$B = \frac{\$200{,}000}{.84} = \$238{,}095$$

$$\text{and interest} = 0.12 \times \$238{,}095 \times 1/2 = \$14{,}285.70$$

The cost of credit remains the same at 14.29 percent, as follows:

$$APR = \frac{\$14{,}285.70}{\$238{,}095 - \$23{,}810 - \$14{,}285.70} \times \frac{1}{180/360}$$

$$= .1429, \text{ or } 14.29\%$$

## Transaction Loans

Still another form of unsecured short-term bank credit can be obtained in the form of *transaction loans.* Here the loan is made for a specific purpose. This is the type of loan that most individuals associate with bank credit and is obtained by signing a promissory note.

Unsecured transaction loans are very similar to a line of credit regarding cost, term to maturity, and compensating balance requirements. In both instances, commercial banks often require that the borrower *clean up* its short-term loans for a 30- to 45-day period during the year. This means, very simply, that the borrower must be free of any bank debt for the stated period. The purpose of such a requirement is to ensure that the borrower is not using short-term bank credit to finance a part of its permanent needs for funds.

## Unsecured Sources: Commercial Paper

Only the largest and most creditworthy companies are able to use **commercial paper,** which is simply a short-term *promise to pay* that is sold in the market for short-term debt securities.

**Commercial paper**
Short-term loans by the most creditworthy borrowers that are bought and sold in the market for short-term debt securities.

The maturity of this credit source is generally 6 months or less, although some issues carry 270-day maturities. The interest rate on commercial paper is generally slightly lower (.5 percent to 1 percent) than the prime rate on commercial bank loans. Also, interest is usually discounted, although sometimes interest-bearing commercial paper is available.

New issues of commercial paper are either placed directly (sold by the issuing firm directly to the investing public) or dealer placed. Dealer placement involves the use of a commercial paper dealer, who sells the issue for the issuing firm. Many major finance companies, such as General Motors Acceptance Corporation, place their commercial paper directly. The volume of direct versus dealer placements is roughly 4 to 1 in favor of direct placements. Dealers are used primarily by industrial firms that either make infrequent use of the commercial paper market or, owing to their small size, would have difficulty placing the issue without the help of a dealer.

Several advantages accrue to the user of commercial paper:

1. **Interest rate.** Commercial paper rates are generally lower than rates on bank loans and comparable sources of short-term financing.
2. **Compensating balance requirements.** No minimum balance requirements are associated with commercial paper. However, issuing firms usually find it desirable to maintain lines of credit agreements sufficient to back up their short-term financing needs in the event that a new issue of commercial paper cannot be sold or an outstanding issue cannot be repaid when due.
3. **Amount of credit.** Commercial paper offers the firm with very large credit needs a single source for all its short-term financing. Because of loan restrictions placed on the banks by the regulatory authorities, obtaining the necessary funds from a commercial bank might require dealing with a number of institutions.[6]
4. **Prestige.** Because it is widely recognized that only the most creditworthy borrowers have access to the commercial paper market, its use signifies a firm's credit status.

Using commercial paper for short-term financing, however, involves a very important *risk.* That is, the commercial paper market is highly impersonal and denies even the most creditworthy borrower any flexibility in terms of repayment. When bank credit is used, the borrowing firm has someone with whom it can work out any temporary difficulties that might be encountered in meeting a loan deadline. This flexibility simply does not exist for the user of commercial paper.

The cost of commercial paper can be estimated using the simple effective cost-of-credit equation (*APR*). The key points to remember are that commercial paper interest is usually discounted and that a fee is charged if a dealer is used to place the issue. Even if a dealer is not used, the issuing firm will incur costs associated with preparing and placing the issue, and these costs must be included in estimating the cost of credit.

**EXAMPLE**

The EPG Mfg. Company uses commercial paper regularly to support its needs for short-term financing. The firm plans to sell $100 million in 270-day-maturity paper on which it expects to have to pay discounted interest at a rate of 12 percent per annum ($9,000,000). In addition, EPG expects to incur a cost of approximately $100,000 in dealer placement fees and other expenses of issuing the paper. The effective cost of credit to EPG can be calculated as follows:

$$APR = \frac{\$9{,}000{,}000 + \$100{,}000}{\$100{,}000{,}000 - \$100{,}000 - \$9{,}000{,}000} \times \frac{1}{270/360}$$

$$= .1335, \text{ or } 13.35\%$$

[6]Member banks of the Federal Reserve System are limited to 10 percent of their total capital, surplus, and undivided profits when making loans to a single borrower. Thus, when a corporate borrower's needs for financing are very large, it may have to deal with a group of participating banks to raise the needed funds.

where the interest cost is calculated as $100,000,000 × .12 × [270/360] or $9,000,000 plus the $100,000 dealer placement fee. Thus, the effective cost of credit to EPG is 13.35 percent.

## Secured Sources: Accounts Receivable Loans

Secured sources of short-term credit have certain assets of the firm pledged as collateral to secure the loan. Upon default of the loan agreement, the lender has first claim to the pledged assets in addition to its claim as a general creditor of the firm. Hence, the secured credit agreement offers an added margin of safety to the lender.

Generally, a firm's receivables are among its most liquid assets. For this reason, they are considered by many lenders to be prime collateral for a secured loan. Two basic procedures can be used in arranging for financing based on receivables: pledging and factoring.

PLEDGING ACCOUNTS RECEIVABLE Under the pledging arrangement, the borrower simply pledges accounts receivable as collateral for a loan obtained from either a commercial bank or a finance company. The amount of the loan is stated as a percent of the face value of the receivables pledged. If the firm provides the lender with a *general line* on its receivables, then all of the borrower's accounts are pledged as security for the loan. This method of pledging is simple and inexpensive. However, because the lender has no control over the quality of the receivables being pledged, it will set the maximum loan at a relatively low percent of the total face value of the accounts, generally ranging downward from a maximum of around 75 percent.

Still another approach to pledging involves the borrower's presenting specific invoices to the lender as collateral for a loan. This method is somewhat more expensive in that the lender must assess the creditworthiness of each individual account pledged; however, given this added knowledge, the lender will be willing to increase the loan as a percent of the face value of the invoices. In this case, the loan might reach as high as 85 percent or 90 percent of the face value of the pledged receivables.

Accounts receivable loans generally carry an interest rate 2 percent to 5 percent higher than the bank's prime lending rate. Finance companies charge an even higher rate. In addition, the lender will usually charge a handling fee stated as a percent of the face value of the receivables processed, which may be as much as 1 percent to 2 percent of the face value.

**EXAMPLE**

The A. B. Good Company sells electrical supplies to building contractors on terms of net 60. The firm's average monthly sales are $100,000; thus, given the firm's 2-month credit terms, its average receivables balance is $200,000. The firm pledges all its receivables to a local bank, which in turn advances up to 70 percent of the face value of the receivables at 3 percent over prime and with a 1 percent processing charge on all receivables pledged. A. B. Good follows a practice of borrowing the maximum amount possible, and the current prime rate is 10 percent.

The *APR* of using this source of financing for a full year is computed as follows:

$$APR = \frac{\$18{,}200 + \$12{,}000}{\$140{,}000} \times \frac{1}{360/360} = .2157, \text{ or } 21.57\%$$

where the total dollar cost of the loan consists of both the annual interest expense (.13 × .70 × $200,000 = $18,200) and the annual processing fee (.01 × $100,000 × 12 months = $12,000). The amount extended is .70 × $200,000 = $140,000. Note that the processing charge applies to all receivables pledged. Thus, the A. B. Good Company pledges $100,000 each month, or $1,200,000 during the year, and a 1 percent fee must be paid, for a total annual charge of $12,000.

One more point: The lender, in addition to making advances or loans, may be providing certain credit services to the borrower. For example, the lender may provide billing and collection services. The value of these services should be considered in computing the cost of credit. In the preceding example, A. B. Good Company may save credit department expenses of $10,000 per year by pledging all its accounts and letting the lender provide those services. In this case, the cost of short-term credit is only

$$APR = \frac{\$18{,}200 + \$12{,}000 - \$10{,}000}{\$140{,}000} \times \frac{1}{360/360} = .1443, \text{ or } 14.43\%$$

The primary advantage of pledging as a source of short-term credit is the flexibility it provides the borrower. Financing is available on a continuous basis. The new accounts created through credit sales provide the collateral for the financing of new production. Furthermore, the lender may provide credit services that eliminate or at least reduce the need for similar services within the firm. The primary disadvantage associated with this method of financing is its cost, which can be relatively high compared with other sources of short-term credit, owing to the level of the interest rate charged on loans and the processing fee on pledged accounts.

**Factoring**
The sale of a firm's accounts receivable to a financial intermediary known as a *factor.*

FACTORING ACCOUNTS RECEIVABLE **Factoring** accounts receivable involves the outright sale of a firm's accounts to a financial institution, called a *factor.* A factor is a firm that acquires the receivables of other firms. The factoring institution may be a commercial finance company that engages solely in factoring receivables (known as an *old-line factor*) or it may be a commercial bank. The factor, in turn, bears the risk of collection and services the accounts for a fee. The fee is stated as a percent of the face value of all receivables factored (usually from 1 percent to 3 percent).

The factor firm typically does not make payment for factored accounts until the accounts have been collected or the credit terms have been met. Should the firm wish to receive immediate payment for factored accounts, it can borrow from the factor, using the factored accounts as collateral. The maximum loan the firm can obtain is equal to the face value of its factored accounts less the factor's fee (1 percent to 3 percent), less a reserve (6 percent to 10 percent), less the interest on the loan. For example, if $100,000 in receivables is factored, carrying 60-day credit terms, a 2 percent factor's fee, a 6 percent reserve, and interest at 1 percent per month on advances, then the maximum loan or advance the firm can receive is computed as follows:

| | |
|---|---|
| Face amount of receivables factored | $100,000 |
| Less: fee (.02 × $100,000) | (2,000) |
| reserve (.06 × $100,000) | (6,000) |
| interest (.01 × $92,000 × 2 months) | (1,840) |
| Maximum advance | $ 90,160 |

Note that interest is discounted and calculated based on a maximum amount of funds available for advance ($92,000 = $100,000 − $2,000 − $6,000). Thus, the effective cost of credit can be calculated as follows:

$$APR = \frac{\$1{,}840 + \$2{,}000}{\$90{,}160} \times \frac{1}{60/360}$$

$$= .2555 \text{ or } 25.55\%$$

## Secured Sources: Inventory Loans

**Inventory loans** provide a second source of security for short-term secured credit. The amount of the loan that can be obtained depends on both the marketability and perishability of the inventory. Some items, such as raw materials (grains, oil, lumber, and chemicals), are excellent sources of collateral, because they can easily be liquidated. Other items, such as work-in-process inventories, provide very poor collateral because of their lack of marketability.

**Inventory loans** Short-term loans that are secured by the pledge of inventories. The type of pledge or security agreement varies and can include floating liens, chattel mortgage agreements, field warehouse financing agreements, and terminal warehouse agreements.

There are several methods by which inventory can be used to secure short-term financing. These include a *floating* or *blanket lien, chattel mortgage, field warehouse receipt,* and *terminal warehouse receipt.*

Under a *floating lien* agreement, the borrower gives the lender a lien against all its inventories. This provides the simplest but least secure form of inventory collateral. The borrowing firm maintains full control of the inventories and continues to sell and replace them as it sees fit. Obviously, this lack of control over the collateral greatly dilutes the value of this type of security to the lender.

Under a *chattel mortgage agreement,* the inventory is identified (by serial number or otherwise) in the security agreement and the borrower retains title to the inventory but cannot sell the items without the lender's consent.

Under a *field warehouse financing agreement,* inventories used as collateral are separated from the firm's other inventories and placed under the control of a third-party field warehousing firm.

The *terminal warehouse agreement* differs from the field warehouse agreement in only one respect. Here the inventories pledged as collateral are transported to a public warehouse that is physically removed from the borrower's premises. The lender has an added degree of safety or security because the inventory is totally removed from the borrower's control. Once again, the cost of this type of arrangement is increased because the warehouse firm must be paid by the borrower; in addition, the inventory must be transported to and eventually from the public warehouse.

# MULTINATIONAL WORKING-CAPITAL MANAGEMENT

The basic principles of working-capital management are the same for multinational and domestic firms. However, since multinationals spend and receive money in different countries, the exchange rate between the firm's home country and each of the countries in which it does business poses an added source of concern when managing working capital.

Multinational firms, by definition, have assets that are denominated or valued in foreign currencies. This means that the multinational will lose value if that foreign currency declines in value vis-a-vis that of the home currency. Technically, the foreign assets of the firm are exposed to exchange rate risk—the risk that tomorrow's exchange rate will differ from today's rate. However, the possibility of a decline in asset value may be offset by the decline in value of any liability that is also denominated or valued in terms of that foreign currency. Thus, a firm would normally be interested in it net exposed position (exposed assets − exposed liabilities) for each period and in each currency to which the firm has exposure.

If a firm is to manage its foreign exchange risk exposure it needs good measures. There are three popular measures of foreign exchange risk that can be used: translation exposure, transaction exposure, and economic exposure. Translation exposure arises because the foreign operations of multinational corporations have accounting statements denominated in the local currency of the country in which the operation is located. For U.S. multinational corporations, the reporting currency for its consolidated financial statements is the dollar, so the assets, liabilities, revenues, and expenses of the foreign operations must be translated into dollars. Furthermore, international transactions often require a payment to be made or received in a foreign currency in the future, so these transactions are exposed to exchange rate risk. Economic exposure exists over the long term because the value of the future cash flows in the reporting currency (that is, the dollar) from foreign operations is exposed to exchange rate risk. Indeed, the whole stream of future cash flows is exposed.

**CONCEPT CHECK**

1. What are some examples of unsecured and secured sources of short-term credit?
2. What is the difference between a line of credit and a revolving credit agreement?
3. What are the types of credit agreements a firm can get that are secured by its accounts receivable as collateral?
4. What are some examples of loans secured by a firm's inventories?

## HOW FINANCIAL MANAGERS USE THIS MATERIAL

The very existence of the firm depends upon the ability of its leadership to manage the firm's working capital. Working-capital management involves managing the process of converting investments in inventories and accounts receivable into cash, which the firm can use to pay its bills as investments mature. As such, working-capital management is at the very heart of the firm's day-to-day operating environment.

The firm's management is involved daily in making decisions that will impact this cash flow cycle. New items of inventory are acquired to replace ones that have been sold or to increase the firm's available stock. The inventory may be automatically financed through the creation of accounts payable or it may require that the firm seek out another source. As the firm sells its product or service, it frequently offers credit to its customers, which allows them to pay later. All these decisions impact the firm's financial obligations (debts) and its ability to meet those obligations when due (its liquidity).

The management of the firm's working capital is closely tied to the firm's financial planning process (Chapter 4). Financial planning provides the firm with a means of foreseeing its future cash needs and sources of cash. Thus, the financial planning process provides a tool for preparing for the future working-capital requirements of the firm.

## SUMMARY

In this chapter, we studied the determinants of a firm's investment in working capital and the factors underlying the firm's choice among various sources of short-term financing. Working capital constitutes a significant determinant of most firms' total investment, and efforts to manage the level of the firm's investment can have a substantial impact on the firm's overall profitability.

OBJECTIVE 1

Traditionally, *working capital* is defined as the firm's total investment in current assets. Net *working capital,* on the other hand, is the difference between the firm's current assets and its current liabilities.

Net working capital arises out of a firm's investments in current assets and its decisions regarding the use of current liabilities. Investments in current assets are largely determined by the nature of the firm's business (that is, whether it is a manufacturing firm or a retail establishment) and how efficiently the firm is managed. A firm's use of current liabilities is a function of the availability of short-term sources of financing to the firm and management's willingness to expose itself to the risks of insolvency posed by the use of short-term as opposed to long-term or permanent sources of financing.

Managing working capital can be thought of as managing the firm's liquidity, which in turn entails managing the firm's investment in current assets and its use of current liabilities. Each of these decisions involves risk-return trade-offs. Investing in current assets reduces the risk of illiquidity because current assets (generally) can be quickly turned into cash with little loss of value should the need arise. Using short-term sources of financing increases a firm's risk of illiquidity in that these sources of financing must be renegotiated or repaid more frequently than longer-term sources of financing such as bonds and equity.

The principal advantage of using current liabilities for financing working capital is that their repayment term can be matched exactly to the period for which financing is needed. On the other hand, should the period for which funding is needed be uncertain, then the firm runs the risk of not having the necessary funds available to retire the short-term financing should it come due while the firm still needs the financing. A further disadvantage of using short-term financing arises when the need for funds extends beyond the term of the financing. This creates uncertainty with respect to the cost of financing. For example, should a firm borrow using a 6-month note and discover that it needs financing for a full year, then the firm not only must engage in the renegotiation of the terms of financing (or find a new source of financing), but it also faces the uncertainty as to the cost of credit 6 months hence. If the firm had borrowed with a 1-year maturity, it may have been able to lock in the rate of interest for the full year at the time the loan was taken out.

The hedging principle provides a benchmark for managing a firm's net working capital position. Very simply, the principle involves matching the cash-flow generating characteristics of an asset with the cash flow requirements of the financing source chosen.

The cash conversion cycle is a very useful measure of the overall effectiveness with which a firm is managing its working capital. It is calculated as the sum of the average number of days of sales outstanding in both accounts receivable and inventories less the average number of days of sales represented by the firm's accounts payable. Thus, a cash conversion cycle of 30 implies that the firm has tied up 30 times its average daily sales in accounts receivable and inventories after netting out the firm's use of trade credit or accounts payable.

The effective cost of short-term credit can be calculated using the annual percentage rate (*APR*) formula:

$$APR = \frac{\text{interest}}{\text{principal}} \times \frac{1}{\text{time}}$$

In this formulation, "interest" refers to the dollar amount of interest paid for the use of a sum equal to "principal" for the fraction of a year defined by "time." If interest is compounded, then the appropriate calculation involves computing the annual percentage yield (*APY*) using the following formula:

$$APY = \left(1 + \frac{i}{m}\right)^m - 1$$

where $i$ is the rate of interest per year and $m$ is the number of compounding periods within a year.

Short-term credit can be obtained from a variety of sources and in a wide array of forms. It is helpful to categorize these sources as either secured (repayment is assured by the pledge of specific assets) or unsecured (repayment is assured only by the pledge of the borrower to repay). Unsecured sources consist primarily of accrued expenses (such as wages and taxes) and accounts payable that arise in the normal course of business. Secured sources of short-term financing are generally secured by the pledge of a highly liquid asset. Frequently, the pledged asset is a current asset such as accounts receivable or inventories.

OBJECTIVE 7 

Multinational firms have the additional consideration of exchange rate factors that impact management of its working capital. An asset denominated in terms of foreign currency cash flows will lose value if that foreign currency declines. This decline may be offset by a decline in value of liabilities also denominated in terms of the foreign currency. Thus, a firm is interested in its net exposed position, exposed assets minus exposed liabilities.

## KEY TERMS

myPHLIP

Go To:
http://www.prenhall.com/keown
for downloads and current events associated with this chapter

**Commercial paper, 619**

**Factoring, 622**

**Hedging principle (principle of self-liquidating debt), 610**

**Inventory loans, 623**

**Line of credit agreement, 617**

**Net working capital, 607**

**Permanent asset investment, 610**

**Permanent sources of financing, 611**

**Revolving credit or revolver, 618**

**Secured and unsecured loans, 616**

**Spontaneous sources of financing, 611**

**Temporary asset investment, 610**

**Temporary sources of financing, 611**

**Trade credit, 616**

**Working capital, 607**

## STUDY QUESTIONS

**18-1.** Define and contrast the terms *working capital* and *net working capital.*

**18-2.** Discuss the risk-return relationship involved in managing the firm's working capital.

**18-3.** What is the primary advantage and disadvantage associated with the use of short-term debt? Discuss.

**18-4.** Explain what is meant by the statement, "The use of current liabilities as opposed to long-term debt subjects the firm to a greater risk of illiquidity."

**18-5.** Define the hedging principle. How can this principle be used in the management of working capital?

**18-6.** Define the following terms:
- **a.** Permanent asset investments
- **b.** Temporary asset investments
- **c.** Permanent sources of financing
- **d.** Temporary sources of financing
- **e.** Spontaneous sources of financing

**18-7.** What considerations should be used in selecting a source of short-term credit? Discuss each.

**18-8.** How can the formula "interest = principal × rate × time" be used to estimate the effective cost of short-term credit?

**18-9.** How can we accommodate the effects of compounding in our calculation of the effective cost of short-term credit?

**18-10.** What is meant by the following trade credit terms: 2/10, net 30? 4/20, net 60? 3/15, net 45?

**18-11.** Define the following:
- **a.** Line of credit
- **b.** Commercial paper

**c.** Compensating balance
**d.** Prime rate

**18-12.** List and discuss four advantages of the use of commercial paper.

**18-13.** What risk is involved in the firm's use of commercial paper as a source of short-term credit? Discuss.

**18-14.** List and discuss the distinguishing features of the principal sources of secured credit based on accounts receivable.

## SELF-TEST PROBLEMS

**ST-1.** (*Analyzing the cost of commercial paper*) The Marilyn Sales Company is a wholesale machine tool broker that has gone through a recent expansion of its activities resulting in a doubling of its sales. The company has determined that it needs an additional $200 million in short-term funds to finance peak season sales during roughly 6 months of the year. Marilyn's treasurer has recommended that the firm use a commercial paper offering to raise the needed funds. Specifically, he has determined that a $200 million offering would require 10 percent interest (paid in advance or discounted) plus a $125,000 placement fee. The paper would carry a 6-month (180-day) maturity. What is the effective cost of credit?

**ST-2.** (*Analyzing the cost of short-term credit*) The treasurer of the Lights-a-Lot Mfg. Company is faced with three alternative bank loans. The firm wishes to select the one that minimizes its cost of credit on a $200,000 note that it plans to issue in the next 10 days. Relevant information for the three loan configurations is as follows:

**a.** An 18 percent rate of interest with interest paid at the end of the loan period and no compensating balance requirement.
**b.** A 16 percent rate of interest and a 20 percent compensating balance requirement. This loan also calls for interest to be paid at the end of the loan period.
**c.** A 14 percent rate of interest that is discounted plus a 20 percent compensating balance requirement.

Analyze the cost of each of these alternatives. You may assume the firm would not normally maintain any bank balance that might be used to meet the 20 percent compensating balance requirements of alternatives (b) and (c). Finally, the loan period is 1 year.

## STUDY PROBLEMS (SET A)

**18-1A.** (*Liquidity and working-capital policy*) The balance sheets for two firms (A and B) are as follows:

**Firm A**

| | | | |
|---|---|---|---|
| Cash | $ 100,000 | Accounts payable | $ 200,000 |
| Accounts receivable | 100,000 | Notes payable | 200,000 |
| Inventories | 300,000 | Current liabilities | $ 400,000 |
| Net fixed assets | 1,500,000 | Bonds | 600,000 |
| Total | $2,000,000 | Common equity | 1,000,000 |
| | | Total | $2,000,000 |

**Firm B**

| | | | |
|---|---|---|---|
| Cash | $ 150,000 | Accounts payable | $ 400,000 |
| Accounts receivable | 50,000 | Notes payable | 200,000 |
| Inventories | 300,000 | Current liabilities | $ 600,000 |
| Net fixed assets | 1,500,000 | Bonds | 400,000 |
| Total | $2,000,000 | Common equity | 1,000,000 |
| | | Total | $2,000,000 |

Which of the two firms follows the most aggressive working-capital policy? Why?

**18-2A.** (*Cost of trade credit*) Sage Construction Company purchases $480,000 in doors and windows from Crenshaw Doors under credit terms of 1/15, net 45. Assuming that Sage takes advantage of the cash discount by paying on day 15, answer the following questions:

- **a.** What is Sage's average monthly payables balance? You may assume a 360-day year and that the accounts payable balance includes the gross amount owed (that is, no discount has been taken).
- **b.** If Sage were to decide to pass up the cash discount and extend payment until the end of the credit period, what would its payable balance become?
- **c.** What is the opportunity cost of not taking the cash discount?

**18-3A.** (*Estimating the cost of bank credit*) Paymaster Enterprises has arranged to finance its seasonal working-capital needs with a short-term bank loan. The loan will carry a rate of 12 percent per annum with interest paid in advance (discounted). In addition, Paymaster must maintain a minimum demand deposit with the bank of 10 percent of the loan balance throughout the term of the loan. If Paymaster plans to borrow $100,000 for a period of 3 months, what is the effective cost of the bank loan?

**18-4A.** (*Estimating the cost of commercial paper*) On February 3, Burlington Western Company plans a commercial paper issue of $20 million. The firm has never used commercial paper before but has been assured by the firm placing the issue that it will have no difficulty raising the funds. The commercial paper will carry a 270-day maturity and will require interest based on a rate of 11 percent per annum. In addition, the firm will have to pay fees totaling $200,000 in order to bring the issue to market. What is the effective cost of the commercial paper issue to Burlington Western?

**18-5A.** (*Cost of trade credit*) Calculate the effective cost of the following trade credit terms where payment is made on the net due date, using the annual percentage rate (*APR*) formula.

- **a.** 2/10, net 30
- **b.** 3/15, net 30
- **c.** 3/15, net 45
- **d.** 2/15, net 60

**18-6A.** (*Annual percentage yield*) Compute the cost of the trade credit terms in problem 18-5A using the compounding formula, or annual percentage yield.

**18-7A.** (*Cost of short-term financing*) The R. Morin Construction Company needs to borrow $100,000 to help finance a new $150,000 hydraulic crane used in the firm's commercial construction business. The crane will pay for itself in 1 year. The firm is considering the following alternatives for financing its purchase:

**Alternative A**—The firm's bank has agreed to lend the $100,000 at a rate of 14 percent. Interest would be discounted, and a 15 percent compensating balance would be required. However, the compensating balance requirement would not be binding on R. Morin because the firm normally maintains a minimum demand deposit (checking account) balance of $25,000 in the bank.

**Alternative B**—The equipment dealer has agreed to finance the equipment with a 1-year loan. The $100,000 loan would require payment of principal and interest totaling $116,300 at year end.

- **a.** Which alternative should R. Morin select?
- **b.** If the bank's compensating balance requirement were to necessitate idle demand deposits equal to 15 percent of the loan, what effect would this have on the cost of the bank loan alternative?

**18-8A.** (*Cost of short-term bank loan*) The Southwest Forging Corporation recently arranged for a line of credit with the First National Bank of Dallas. The terms of the agreement called for a $100,000 maximum loan with interest set at 1 percent over prime. In addition, the firm has to maintain a 20 percent compensating balance in its demand deposit account throughout the year. The prime rate is currently 12 percent.

- **a.** If Southwest normally maintains a $20,000 to $30,000 balance in its checking account with FNB of Dallas, what is the effective cost of credit through the line-of-credit agreement where the maximum loan amount is used for a full year?
- **b.** Re-compute the effective cost of credit to Southwest if the firm will have to borrow the compensating balance and it borrows the maximum possible under the loan agreement. Again, assume the full amount of the loan is outstanding for a whole year.

**18-9A.** (*Cost of commercial paper*) Tri-State Enterprises plans to issue commercial paper for the first time in the firm's 35-year history. The firm plans to issue $500,000 in 180-day maturity notes.

The paper will carry a 10-1/4 percent rate with discounted interest and will cost Tri-State $12,000 (paid in advance) to issue.

**a.** What is the cost of credit to Tri-State?

**b.** What other factors should the company consider in analyzing the use of commercial paper?

**18-10A.** (*Cost of accounts receivable*) Johnson Enterprises, Inc., is involved in the manufacture and sale of electronic components used in small AM-FM radios. The firm needs $300,000 to finance an anticipated expansion in receivables due to increased sales. Johnson's credit terms are net 60, and its average monthly credit sales are $200,000. In general, the firm's customers pay within the credit period; thus the firm's average accounts receivable balance is $400,000.

Chuck Idol, Johnson's comptroller, approached the firm's bank with a request for a loan for the $300,000 using the firm's accounts receivable as collateral. The bank offered to make the loan at a rate of 2 percent over prime plus a 1 percent processing charge on all receivables pledged ($200,000 per month). Furthermore, the bank agreed to lend up to 75 percent of the face value of the receivables pledged.

**a.** Estimate the cost of the receivables loan to Johnson where the firm borrows the $300,000. The prime rate is currently 11 percent.

**b.** Idol also requested a line of credit for $300,000 from the bank. The bank agreed to grant the necessary line of credit at a rate of 3 percent over prime and required a 15 percent compensating balance. Johnson currently maintains an average demand deposit of $80,000. Estimate the cost of the line of credit to Johnson.

**c.** Which source of credit should Johnson select? Why?

**18-11A.** (*Cost of factoring*) MDM, Inc., is considering factoring its receivables. The firm has credit sales of $400,000 per month and has an average receivables balance of $800,000 with 60-day credit terms. The factor has offered to extend credit equal to 90 percent of the receivables factored less interest on the loan at a rate of 1-1/2 percent per month. The 10 percent difference in the advance and the face value of all receivables factored consists of a 1 percent factoring fee plus a 9 percent reserve, which the factor maintains. In addition, if MDM decides to factor its receivables, it will sell them all, so that it can reduce its credit department costs by $1,500 a month.

**a.** What is the cost of borrowing the maximum amount of credit available to MDM, Inc., through the factoring agreement?

**b.** What considerations other than cost should be accounted for by MDM, Inc., in determining whether to enter the factoring agreement?

**18-12A.** (*Cost of secured short-term credit*) The Sean-Janeow Import Co. needs $500,000 for a 3-month period. The firm has explored two possible sources of credit:

**(1)** S-J has arranged with its bank for a $500,000 loan secured by accounts receivable. The bank has agreed to advance S-J 80 percent of the value of its pledged receivables at a rate of 11 percent plus a 1 percent fee based on all receivables pledged. S-J's receivables average a total of $1 million throughout the year.

**(2)** An insurance company has agreed to lend the $500,000 at a rate of 9 percent per annum, using a loan secured by S-J's inventory of salad oil. A field warehouse agreement would be used, which would cost S-J $2,000 a month.

Which source of credit should S-J select? Explain.

**18-13A.** (*Cost of short-term financing*) You plan to borrow $20,000 from the bank to pay for a gift shop you have just opened. The bank offers to lend you the money at 10 percent annual interest for the 6 months the funds will be needed.

**a.** Calculate the effective rate of interest on the loan.

**b.** In addition, the bank requires you to maintain a 15 percent compensating balance in the bank. Because you are just opening your business, you do not have a demand deposit account at the bank that can be used to meet the compensating balance requirement. This means that you will have to put 15 percent of the loan amount from your own personal money (which you had planned to use to help finance the business) in a checking account. What is the cost of the loan now?

**c.** In addition to the compensating balance requirement in (b), you are told that interest will be discounted. What is the effective rate of interest on the loan now?

**18-14A.** (*Cost of factoring*) A factor has agreed to lend the JVC Corporation funds by factoring \$300,000 in receivables. JVC's receivables average \$100,000 per month and have a ninety-day average collection period. (Note that JVC's credit terms call for payment in 90 days and accounts receivable average \$300,000 because of the 90-day average collection period.) The factor will charge 12 percent interest on any advance (1 percent per month paid in advance), will charge a 2 percent factoring fee on all receivables factored, and will maintain a 20 percent reserve. If JVC undertakes the loan, it will reduce its own credit department expenses by \$2,000 per month. What is the annual effective rate of interest to JVC on the factoring arrangement? Assume that the maximum advance is taken.

**18-15A.** *(Cash conversion cycle)* Mega PC, Inc., has been striving for the last 5 years to improve its management of working capital. Historical data for the firm's sales, accounts receivable, inventories, and accounts payable follow:

| | Jan-96 | Jan-97 | Jan-98 | Jan-99 | Jan-00 |
|---|---|---|---|---|---|
| Sales–Net | 2,873 | 3,475 | 5,296 | 7,759 | 12,327 |
| Receivables–Total | 411 | 538 | 726 | 903 | 1,486 |
| Accounts Payable | 283 | 447 | 466 | 1,040 | 1,643 |
| Inventories–Total | 220 | 293 | 429 | 251 | 233 |

**a.** Calculate Mega's days of sales outstanding and days of sales in inventory for each of the 5 years. What has Mega accomplished in its attempts to better manage its investments in accounts receivable and inventory?

**b.** Calculate Mega's cash conversion cycle for each of the 5 years. Evaluate Mega's overall management of its working capital.

## STUDY PROBLEMS (SET B)

**18-1B.** (*Liquidity and working-capital policy*) The balance sheets for two firms (A and B) are as follows:

**Firm A**

| | | | |
|---|---|---|---|
| Cash | \$ 200,000 | Accounts payable | \$ 400,000 |
| Accounts receivable | 200,000 | Notes payable | 400,000 |
| Inventories | 600,000 | Bonds | 1,200,000 |
| Net fixed assets | 3,000,000 | Common equity | 2,000,000 |
| Total | \$4,000,000 | Total | \$4,000,000 |

**Firm B**

| | | | |
|---|---|---|---|
| Cash | \$ 200,000 | Accounts payable | \$ 600,000 |
| Accounts receivable | 400,000 | Notes payable | 400,000 |
| Inventories | 400,000 | Bonds | 500,000 |
| Net fixed assets | 3,000,000 | Common equity | 2,500,000 |
| Total | \$4,000,000 | Total | \$4,000,000 |

Which of the two firms follows the most aggressive working-capital policy? Why?

**18-2B.** (*Cost of trade credit*) Clearwater Construction Company purchases \$600,000 in parts and supplies under credit terms of 2/30, net 60 every year. Assuming that Clearwater takes advantage of the cash discount by paying on day 30, answer the following questions:

**a.** What is Clearwater's average monthly payables balance? You may assume a 360-day year and that the accounts payable balance includes the gross amount owed (that is, no discount has been taken).

**b.** If Clearwater were to decide to pass up the cash discount and extend payment until the end of the credit period, what would its payable balance become?

**c.** What is the opportunity cost of not taking the cash discount?

**18-3B.** (*Estimating the cost of bank credit*) Dee's Christmas Trees, Inc., is evaluating options for financing its seasonal working-capital needs. A short-term loan from Liberty Bank would carry a 14 percent annual interest rate, with interest paid in advance (discounted). If this option is chosen, Dee's would also have to maintain a minimum demand deposit equal to 10 percent of the loan balance, throughout the term of the loan. If Dee's needs to borrow $125,000 for the upcoming 3 months before Christmas, what is the effective cost of the loan?

**18-4B.** (*Estimating the cost of commercial paper*) Duro Auto Parts would like to exploit a production opportunity overseas and is seeking additional capital to finance this expansion. The company plans a commercial paper issue of $15 million. The firm has never issued commercial paper before, but has been assured by the investment banker placing the issue that it will have no difficulty raising the funds, and that this method of financing is the least expensive option, even after the $150,000 placement fee. The issue will carry a 270-day maturity and will require interest based on an annual rate of 12 percent. What is the effective cost of the commercial paper issue to Duro?

**18-5B.** (*Cost of trade credit*) Calculate the effective cost of the following trade credit terms where payment is made on the net due date.

**a.** 1/10, net 30
**b.** 2/15, net 30
**c.** 2/15, net 45
**d.** 3/15, net 60

**18-6B.** (*Annual percentage yield*) Compute the cost of the trade credit terms in problem 18-5B using the compounding formula, or annual percentage yield.

**18-7B.** (*Cost of short-term financing*) Vitra Glass Company needs to borrow $150,000 to help finance the cost of a new $225,000 kiln to be used in the production of glass bottles. The kiln will pay for itself in 1 year, and the firm is considering the following alternatives for financing its purchase:

**Alternative A**—The firm's bank has agreed to lend the $150,000 at a rate of 15 percent. Interest would be discounted, and a 16 percent compensating balance would be required. However, the compensating balance requirement would not be binding on Vitra, because the firm normally maintains a minimum demand deposit (checking account) balance of $25,000 in the bank.

**Alternative B**—The kiln dealer has agreed to finance the equipment with a 1-year loan. The $150,000 loan would require payment of principal and interest totaling $180,000.

**a.** Which alternative should Vitra select?
**b.** If the bank's compensating balance requirement were to necessitate idle demand deposits equal to 16 percent of the loan, what effect would this have on the cost of the bank loan alternative?

**18-8B.** (*Cost of short-term bank loan*) Lola's Ice Cream recently arranged for a line of credit with the Longhorn State Bank of Dallas. The terms of the agreement called for a $100,000 maximum loan with interest set at 2.0 percent over prime. In addition, Lola's must maintain a 15 percent compensating balance in its demand deposit throughout the year. The prime rate is currently 12 percent.

**a.** If Lola's normally maintains a $15,000 to $25,000 balance in its checking account with LSB of Dallas, what is the effective cost of credit through the line-of-credit agreement where the maximum loan amount is used for a full year?
**b.** Recompute the effective cost of credit to Lola's Ice Cream if the firm has to borrow the compensating balance and it borrows the maximum possible under the loan agreement. Again, assume the full amount of the loan is outstanding for a whole year.

**18-9B.** (*Cost of commercial paper*) Luft, Inc., recently acquired production rights to an innovative sailboard design but needs funds to pay for the first production run, which is expected to sell briskly. The firm plans to issue $450,000 in 180-day maturity notes. The paper will carry an 11 percent rate with discounted interest and will cost Luft $13,000 (paid in advance) to issue.

**a.** What is the effective cost of credit to Luft?
**b.** What other factors should the company consider in analyzing whether to issue the commercial paper?

**18-10B.** (*Cost of accounts receivable*) TLC Enterprises, Inc., is a wholesaler of toys and curios. The firm needs $400,000 to finance an anticipated expansion in receivables. TLC's credit terms are net

60, and its average monthly credit sales are $250,000. In general, TLC's customers pay within the credit period; thus the firm's average accounts receivable balance is $500,000.

Kelly Leaky, TLC's comptroller, approached the firm's bank with a request for a loan for the $400,000, using the firm's accounts receivable as collateral. The bank offered to make the loan at a rate of 2 percent over prime plus a 1 percent processing charge on all receivables pledged ($250,000 per month). Furthermore, the bank agreed to lend up to 80 percent of the face value of the receivables pledged.

**a.** Estimate the cost of the receivables loan to TLC where the firm borrows the $400,000. The prime rate is currently 11 percent.

**b.** Leaky also requested a line of credit for $400,000 from the bank. The bank agreed to grant the necessary line of credit at a rate of 3 percent over prime and required a 15 percent compensating balance. TLC currently maintains an average demand deposit of $100,000. Estimate the cost of the line of credit.

**c.** Which source of credit should TLC select? Why?

**18-11B.** (*Cost of factoring*) To increase profitability, a management consultant has suggested to the Dal Molle Fruit Company that it consider factoring its receivables. The firm has credit sales of $300,000 per month and has an average receivables balance of $600,000 with 60-day credit terms. The factor has offered to extend credit equal to 90 percent of the receivables factored less interest on the loan at a rate of 1-1/2 percent per month. The 10 percent difference in the advance and the face value of all receivables factored consists of a 1 percent factoring fee plus a 9 percent reserve, which the factor maintains. In addition, if Dal Molle decides to factor its receivables, it will sell them all, so that it can reduce its credit department costs by $1,400 a month.

**a.** What is the cost of borrowing the maximum amount of credit available to Dal Molle, through the factoring agreement?

**b.** What considerations other than cost should be accounted for by Dal Molle, in determining whether or not to enter the factoring agreement?

**18-12B.** (*Cost of secured short-term credit*) DST, Inc., a producer of inflatable river rafts, needs $400,000 over the 3-month summer season. The firm has explored two possible sources of credit:

**a.** DST has arranged with its bank for a $400,000 loan secured by accounts receivable. The bank has agreed to advance DST 80 percent of the value of its pledged receivables at a rate of 11 percent plus a 1 percent fee based on all receivables pledged. DST's receivables average a total of $1 million year-round.

**b.** An insurance company has agreed to lend the $400,000 at a rate of 9 percent per annum, using a loan secured by DST's inventory. A field warehouse agreement would be used, which would cost DST $2,000 a month.

Which source of credit would DST select? Explain.

**18-13B.** (*Cost of secured short-term financing*) You are considering a loan of $25,000 to finance inventories for a janitorial supply store that you plan to open. The bank offers to lend you the money at 11 percent annual interest for the 6 months the funds will be needed.

**a.** Calculate the effective rate of interest on the loan.

**b.** In addition, the bank requires you to maintain a 15 percent compensating balance in the bank. Because you are just opening your business, you do not have a demand deposit at the bank that can be used to meet the compensating balance requirement. This means that you will have to put 15 percent of the loan amount from your own personal money (which you had planned to use to help finance the business) in a checking account. What is the cost of the loan now?

**c.** In addition to the compensating balance requirement in (b), you are told that interest will be discounted. What is the effective rate of interest on the loan now?

**18-14B.** (*Cost of financing*) Tanglewood Roofing Supply, Inc., has agreed to finance its working capital by factoring $450,000 in receivables on the following terms: Tanglewood's receivables average $150,000 per month and have a 90-day average collection period (note that the firm offers 90-day credit terms and its accounts receivable average $450,000 because of the 90-day collection period). The factor will charge 13 percent interest paid in advance, will charge a 2 percent factoring fee on all receivables factored, and will maintain a 15 percent reserve. If Tanglewood undertakes the loan, it will reduce its own credit department expenses by $2,000 per month. What is the annual effective rate of interest to Tanglewood on the factoring agreement? Assume that the maximum advance is taken.

**18-15B.** Allergan, Inc., has been striving to improve its management of working capital. Historical data for the firm's sales, accounts receivables, inventories, and accounts payable follow:

| | Jan-96 | Jan-97 | Jan-98 | Jan-99 | Jan-00 |
|---|---|---|---|---|---|
| Sales–Net | 1147.0 | 1149.0 | 1296.1 | 1452.4 | 1562.1 |
| Receivables–Total | 242.5 | 187.0 | 226.1 | 253.2 | 268.5 |
| Accounts Payable | 75.4 | 83.3 | 67.0 | 80.5 | 82.9 |
| Inventories–Total | 130.1 | 147.8 | 123.3 | 130.7 | 135.0 |

**a.** Calculate Allergan's days of sales outstanding and days of sales in inventory for each of the 5 years. What has Allergan accomplished in its attempts to better manage its investments in accounts receivable and inventory?

**b.** Calculate Allergan's cash conversion cycle for each of the 5 years. Evaluate Allergan's overall management of its working capital.

| | Jan-96 | Jan-97 | Jan-98 | Jan-99 | Jan-00 |
|---|---|---|---|---|---|
| Sales–Net | 1,147 | 1,149 | 1,296.1 | 1,452.4 | 1,562.1 |
| Receivables total | 242.5 | 187 | 226.1 | 253.2 | 268.5 |
| Accounts payable | 75.4 | 83.3 | 67 | 80.5 | 82.9 |
| Inventories total | 130.1 | 147.8 | 123.3 | 130.7 | 135 |
| Days of sales outstanding | 77.17 | 59.40 | 63.67 | 63.63 | 62.74 |
| Days of sales in inventory | 41.40 | 46.95 | 34.72 | 32.85 | 31.54 |
| Days of payable outstanding | 23.99 | 26.46 | 18.87 | 20.23 | 19.37 |
| Cash conversion cycle | 94.58 | 79.89 | 79.53 | 76.25 | 74.91 |

## SELF-TEST SOLUTIONS

**ST-1.** The discounted interest cost of the commercial paper issue is calculated as follows:

Interest expense = .10 × \$200,000,000 × 180/360 = \$10,000,000

The effective cost of credit can now be calculated as follows:

$$APR = \frac{\$10{,}000{,}000 + \$125{,}000}{\$200{,}000{,}000 - \$125{,}000 - \$10{,}000{,}000} \times \frac{1}{180/360}$$

$$= .1066, \text{ or } 10.66\%$$

**ST-2.**

**a.** $$APR = \frac{.18 \times \$200{,}000}{\$200{,}000} \times \frac{1}{1}$$

$$= .18 \text{ or } 18\%$$

**b.** $$APR = \frac{.16 \times \$200{,}000}{\$200{,}000 - (.20 \times \$200{,}000)} \times \frac{1}{1}$$

$$= .20 \text{ or } 20\%$$

**c.** $$APR = \frac{.14 \times \$200{,}000}{\$200{,}000 - (.14 \times \$200{,}000) - (.2 \times \$200{,}000)} \times \frac{1}{1}$$

$$= .2121 \text{ or } 21.21\%$$

Alternative (a) offers the lower cost of financing, although it carries the highest stated rate of interest. The reason for this is that there is no compensating balance requirement, and interest is not discounted for this alternative.

# CASH AND MARKETABLE SECURITIES MANAGEMENT

**LEARNING OBJECTIVES**

After reading this chapter, you should be able to

1. Define *liquid assets.*
2. Understand why a firm holds cash.
3. Explain various cash-management objectives and decisions.
4. Describe and analyze the different mechanisms for managing the firm's cash collection and disbursement procedures.
5. Determine a prudent composition for the firm's marketable securities portfolio.

For Harley-Davidson, cash management takes on added importance. After all, it was a cash crisis back in 1985 that left Harley-Davidson only hours away from bankruptcy as one of Harley's largest lenders, Citicorp Industrial Credit, was considering

bailing out on its loan. ● Today, just as with any large corporation, cash management is an important topic at Harley-Davidson, regardless of how sound the firm is. In fact, at the end of the fiscal year 1999, Harley-Davidson held 8.63 percent of its assets in the form of cash and cash equivalents. During 1999, Harley generated sales revenues of $2.453 billion. Based on a 365-day year, this means that Harley-Davidson "produced" $6.72 million in sales revenues each day. ● If the company could have freed up only 1 day's worth of sales and invested it in a money market account yielding 5 percent, the rate prevailing during late 2000, the firm's before-tax profits would have jumped by $336,000. That is a tidy sum and demonstrates why firms like to have efficient treasury management departments in place. Shareholders enjoy the added profits. ● Now, if Harley-Davidson's management felt it could bear a little more risk, then the freed-up cash might be invested in a 1-year certificate-of-deposit (CD) with a 1-year maturity. During late 2000, CDs with 1-year maturities were yielding, on average, 6.53 percent. ● That difference of 153 basis points (i.e., 6.53 − 5.00) may not seem like much, but when put to work on an investment of

$6.72 million, it produces a considerable income. In this case, the increased before-tax profits would total $439,000. So by investing the excess cash in CDs rather than money market accounts, Harley-Davidson's before-tax profits could have been $103,000 greater (i.e., $439,000 − $336,000). ● Managing the cash and marketable-securities portfolio is an important task for financial executives. This chapter teaches you about sophisticated cash management systems and about prudent places to "park" the firm's excess cash balances so they earn a positive rate of return and are liquid at the same time. We also explore sound management techniques that relate to the other asset components of the firm's working capital—accounts receivable and inventory.

**CHAPTER PREVIEW**

Chapter 16 introduced the concept of working-capital management. Now we will consider the various elements of the firm's working capital in some depth. This chapter centers on the formulation of financial policies for management of cash and marketable securities. We explore three major areas: (1) techniques available to management for favorably influencing cash receipts and disbursements patterns, (2) sensible investment possibilities that enable the company to productively employ excess cash balances, and (3) some straightforward models that can assist financial officers in deciding on how much cash to hold.

In this chapter, three principles will be relevant to our study: **Principle 1: The Risk-Return Trade-Off—We won't take on additional risk unless we expect to be compensated with additional returns; Principle 2: The Time Value of Money—A dollar received today is worth more than a dollar received in the future; and Principle 10: Ethical Behavior Is Doing the Right Thing, and Ethical Dilemmas Are Everywhere in Finance.**

You will see the importance of these principles throughout this chapter.

## WHAT ARE LIQUID ASSETS?

OBJECTIVE 1

Before proceeding to our discussion of cash management, it will be helpful to distinguish among several terms. **Cash** is the currency and coin the firm has on hand in petty cash drawers, in cash registers, or in checking or money market accounts. **Marketable securities,** also called *near cash* or *near-cash assets,* are security investments that the firm can quickly convert into cash balances. Generally firms hold marketable securities with very short maturity periods—less than 1 year. Together, cash and marketable securities are known as **liquid assets.**

**Cash**
Currency and coin plus demand deposit accounts.

**Marketable securities**
Security investments (financial assets) the firm can quickly convert to cash balances. Also known as *near cash* or *near-cash assets.*

**Liquid assets**
The sum of cash and marketable securities.

## WHY A COMPANY HOLDS CASH

A thorough understanding of why and how a firm holds cash requires an accurate conception of how cash flows into and through the enterprise. Figure 19-1 depicts the process of cash generation and disposition in a typical manufacturing setting. The arrows designate the direction of the flow—that is, whether the cash balance increases or decreases.

OBJECTIVE 2

### Cash-Flow Process

The firm experiences irregular increases in its cash holdings from several external sources. Funds can be obtained in the financial markets from the sale of securities, such as bonds, preferred stock, and common stock, or the firm can enter into nonmarketable debt contracts with

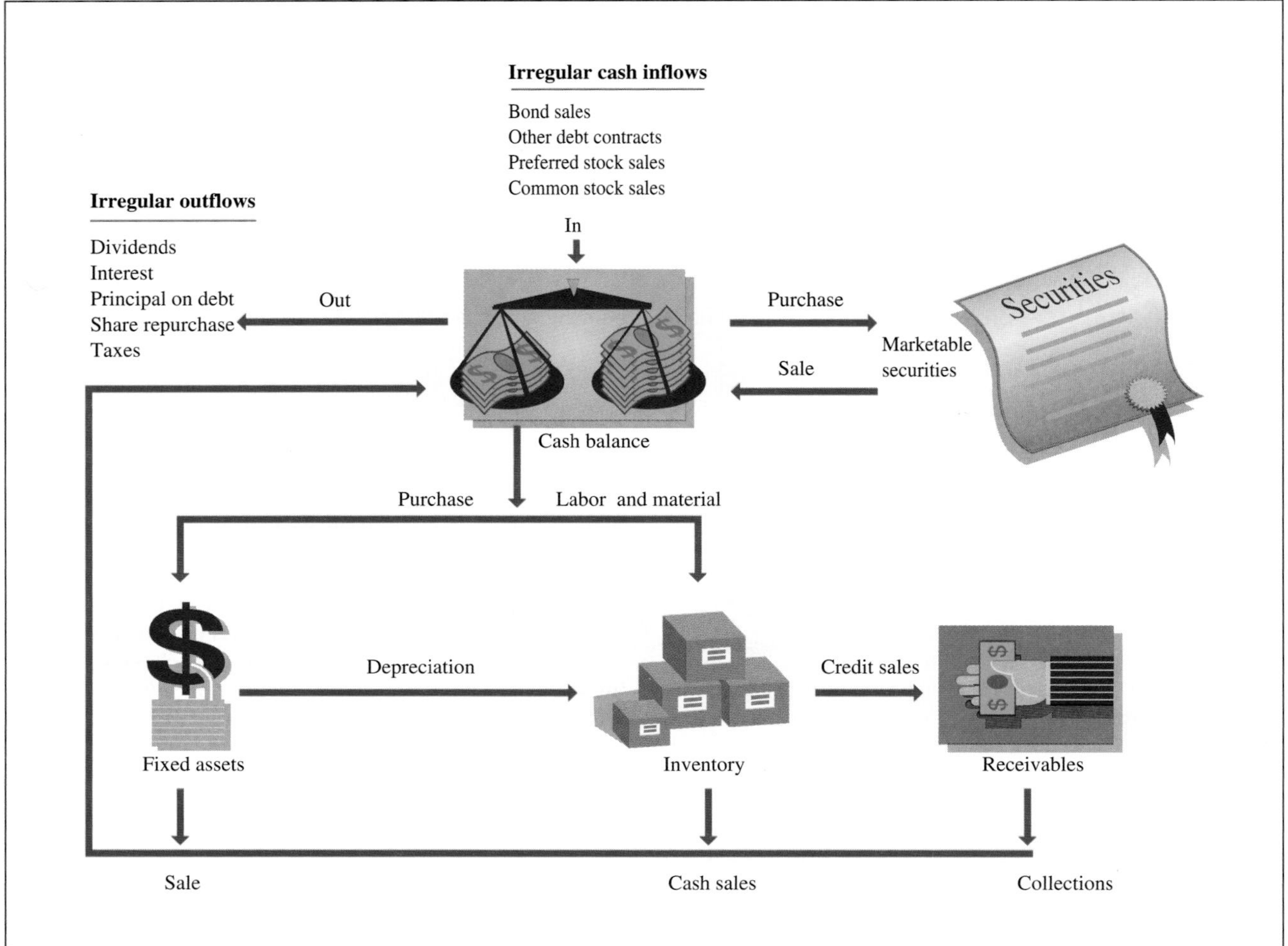


**FIGURE 19-1**
The Cash Generation and Disposition Process

lenders such as commercial banks. These irregular cash inflows do not occur on a daily basis. They tend to be episodic; the financing arrangements that give rise to them are effected at wide intervals. External financing contracts usually involve huge sums of money stemming from a major need identified by the company's management, and these needs do not occur every day. For example, a new product might have moved to the launching stage, or a plant expansion might be required to provide added productive capacity.

In most organizations, the financial officer responsible for cash management also controls the transactions that affect the firm's investment in marketable securities. As excess cash becomes temporarily available, marketable securities are purchased. When cash is in short supply, a portion of the marketable securities portfolio is liquidated.

Whereas the irregular cash inflows are from external sources, the other main sources of cash to the firm arise from internal operations and occur on a more regular basis. Over long periods, the largest receipts come from accounts receivable collections and, to a lesser extent, from direct cash sales of finished goods. Many manufacturing concerns also generate cash on a regular basis through the liquidation of scrap or obsolete inventory. At various times, fixed assets may also be sold, thereby generating some cash inflow. This is not a large source of funds except in unusual situations where, for instance, a complete plant renovation may be taking place.

Apart from the investment of excess cash in near-cash assets, the cash balance experiences reductions for three key reasons. First, on an irregular basis, withdrawals are made to (1) pay cash dividends on preferred and common stock shares; (2) meet interest requirements on debt contracts; (3) repay the principal borrowed from creditors; (4) buy the firm's own shares in the financial markets for use in executive compensation plans, or as an alternative to paying a cash dividend; and (5) pay tax bills. Again, by an *irregular basis,* we mean items *not* occurring on a daily or frequent schedule. Second, the company's capital expenditure program designates that fixed assets be acquired at various intervals. Third, inventories are purchased on a regular basis to ensure a steady flow of finished goods off the production line. Note that the arrow linking the investment in fixed assets with the inventory account is labeled *depreciation.* This indicates that a portion of the cost of fixed assets is charged against the products coming off the assembly line. This cost is subsequently recovered through the sale of the finished goods inventory, because the product selling price will be set by management to cover all the costs of production, including depreciation.

The variety of influences that constantly affect the cash balance held by the firm can be synthesized in terms of the classic motives for holding cash, as identified in the literature of economic theory.

## Motives for Holding Cash

In a classic economic treatise, John Maynard Keynes segmented the firm's, or any economic unit's, demand for cash into three categories: (1) the transactions motive, (2) the precautionary motive, and (3) the speculative motive.[1]

**TRANSACTIONS MOTIVE** Balances held for transactions purposes allow the firm to meet cash needs that arise in the ordinary course of doing business. In Figure 19-1, transactions balances would be used to meet the irregular outflows as well as the planned acquisition of fixed assets and inventories.

The relative amount of cash needed to satisfy transactions requirements is affected by a number of factors, such as the industry in which the firm operates. It is well known that utilities can forecast cash receipts quite accurately, because of stable demand for their services. Computer software firms, however, have a more difficult time predicting their cash flows. New products are brought to market at a rapid pace, thereby making it difficult to project cash flows and balances very precisely.

**THE PRECAUTIONARY MOTIVE** Precautionary balances are a buffer stock of liquid assets. This motive for holding cash relates to the maintenance of balances to be used to satisfy possible, but as yet indefinite, needs.

Cash-flow predictability also has a material influence on the firm's demand for cash through the precautionary motive. The airline industry provides a typical illustration. Air passenger carriers are plagued with a high degree of cash-flow uncertainty. The weather, rising fuel costs, and continual strikes by operating personnel make cash forecasting difficult for any airline. The upshot of this problem is that because of all the things that *might* happen, the minimum cash balances desired by the management of the air carriers tend to be large.

[1]John Maynard Keynes, *The General Theory of Employment, Interest, and Money* (New York: Harcourt Brace Jovanovich, 1936).

In actual business practice, the precautionary motive is met to a large extent by the holding of a portfolio of *liquid assets,* not just cash. Notice in Figure 19-1 the two-way flow of funds between the company's holdings of cash and marketable securities. In large corporate organizations, funds may flow either into or out of the marketable securities portfolio on a daily basis.

THE SPECULATIVE MOTIVE Cash is held for speculative purposes in order to take advantage of potential profit-making situations. Construction firms that build private dwellings will at times accumulate cash in anticipation of a significant drop in lumber costs. If the price of building supplies does drop, the companies that built up their cash balances stand to profit by purchasing materials in large quantities. Generally, the speculative motive is the least important component of a firm's preference for liquidity. The transactions and precautionary motives account for most of the reasons why a company holds cash balances.

**CONCEPT CHECK**

1. Describe the typical cash-flow cycle for a firm.
2. What are the three primary motives for holding cash?

## CASH-MANAGEMENT OBJECTIVES AND DECISIONS

OBJECTIVE 3 

The degree to which a firm invests idle cash into marketable securities will be determined by the amount of insolvency risk the firm is willing to undergo in order to receive additional return on its cash balances. We will see that this trade-off is not easily balanced.

### The Risk-Return Trade-Off

**Insolvency**
The firm is unable to pay its bills on time.

A company-wide cash-management program must be concerned with minimizing the firm's risk of insolvency. In the context of cash management, the term **insolvency** describes the situation where the firm is unable to pay its bills on time. In such a case, the company is *technically insolvent* in that it lacks the necessary liquidity to make prompt payment on its current debt obligations. A firm could avoid this problem by carrying large cash balances to pay the bills that come due.

The financial manager must strike an acceptable balance between holding too much cash and too little cash. This is the focal point of the risk-return trade-off. A large cash investment minimizes the chances of insolvency, but penalizes company profitability. A small cash investment frees excess balances for investment in both marketable securities and longer-lived assets; this enhances company profitability and the value of the firm's common shares, but increases the chances of running out of cash.

**RELATE TO THE BIG PICTURE**

The dilemma faced by the financial manager is a clear example of the application of **Principle 1: The Risk-Return Trade-Off—We won't take on additional risk unless we expect to be compensated with additional return.** To accept the risk of not having sufficient cash on hand, the firm must be compensated with a return on the cash that is invested. Moreover, the greater the risk of the investment into which the cash is placed, the greater the return that the firm demands.

## The Objectives

The risk-return trade-off can be reduced to two prime objectives for the firm's cash-management system:

1. Enough cash must be on hand to meet the disbursal needs that arise in the course of doing business.
2. Investment in idle cash balances must be reduced to a minimum.

Evaluation of these operational objectives, and a conscious attempt on the part of management to meet them, gives rise to the need for some typical cash-management decisions.

## The Decisions

Two conditions or ideals would allow the firm to operate for extended periods with cash balances near or at a level of zero: (1) a completely accurate forecast of net cash flows over the planning horizon and (2) perfect synchronization of cash receipts and disbursements.

Cash-flow forecasting is the initial step in any effective cash-management program. Given that the firm will, as a matter of necessity, invest in some cash balances, certain types of decisions related to the size of those balances dominate the cash-management process. These include decisions that answer the following questions:

1. What can be done to speed up cash collections and slow down or better control cash outflows?
2. What should be the composition of a marketable securities portfolio?

Although the sheer number of cash collection and payment techniques is large, the concepts on which those techniques rest are quite simple. Controlling the cash inflow and outflow is a major theme of treasury management. But, within the confines of ethical management, the cash manager is always thinking (1) "How can I speed up the firm's cash receipts?" and (2) "How can I slow down the firm's cash payments and not irritate too many important constituencies—such as suppliers?"

The critical point is that cash saved becomes available for investment elsewhere in the company's operations, and at a positive rate of return this will increase total profitability. Grasping the elements of cash management requires that you understand the concept of cash "float," to which we now turn.

### CONCEPT CHECK

1. Describe the relationship between the firm's cash-management program and the firm's risk of insolvency.
2. What are the fundamental decisions that the financial manager must make with respect to cash management?

# COLLECTION AND DISBURSEMENT PROCEDURES

The efficiency of the firm's cash-management program can be enhanced by knowledge and use of various procedures aimed at (1) accelerating cash receipts and (2) improving the methods used to disburse cash. We will see that greater opportunity for corporate profit improvement lies with the cash receipts side of the funds flow process, although it would be unwise to ignore opportunities for favorably affecting cash-disbursement practices.

## Managing the Cash Inflow[2]

**Float**
The length of time from when a check is written until the actual recipient can draw upon or use the "good funds."

In order to increase the speed in which we receive cash receipts, it is essential that we understand how to reduce float. **Float** is the length of time from when a check is written until the actual recipient can use the "good funds." Float (or total float) has four elements, as follows:

1. *Mail float* is caused by the time lapse from the moment a customer mails a remittance check until the firm begins to process it.
2. *Processing float* is caused by the time required for the firm to process the customer's remittance checks before they can be deposited in the bank.
3. *Transit float* is caused by the time necessary for a deposited check from a customer to clear through the commercial banking system and become usable funds to the company. Credit is deferred for a maximum of two business days on checks that are cleared through the Federal Reserve System.
4. *Disbursing float* derives from the fact that the customer's funds are available in the company's bank account until the company's payment check has cleared through the banking system. Typically, funds available in the firm's banks *exceed* the balances indicated on its own books (ledgers).

We will use the term *float* to refer to the total of its four elements just described. Float reduction can yield considerable benefits in terms of usable funds that are released for company use and returns produced on such freed-up balances.

THE LOCK-BOX ARRANGEMENT The lock-box system is the most widely used commercial banking service for expediting cash gathering. Banks have offered this service since 1946. Such a system speeds up the conversion of receipts into usable funds by reducing both mail and processing float. Since the Federal Reserve System provides check-clearing facilities for depository institutions, it is possible to reduce transit float if lock boxes are located near Federal Reserve Banks and their branches. For large corporations that receive checks from all parts of the country, float reductions of 2 to 4 days are not unusual.

Figure 19-2 illustrates an elementary, but typical, cash collection system for a hypothetical firm. It also shows the origin of mail float, processing float, and transit float. In this system, the customer places his or her remittance check in the U.S. mail, which is then delivered to the firm's headquarters. This is mail float. On the check's arrival at the firm's headquarters (or local collection center), general accounting personnel must go through the bookkeeping procedures needed to prepare it for local deposit. The checks are then deposited. This is processing float. The checks are then forwarded for payment through the commercial bank clearing mechanism. The checks will be charged against the customer's own bank account. At this point, the checks are said to be "paid" and become "good funds" available for use by the company that received them. This bank clearing procedure represents transit float and, as we said earlier, can amount to a delay of up to two business days.

A lock-box arrangement is based on a simple procedure. The firm's customers are instructed to mail their remittance checks not to company headquarters or regional offices, but to a numbered Post Office box. This replaces step 2 in Figure 19-2, allowing mail to travel a shorter distance and often cutting the mail float by 1 day. The bank that is providing the lock-box service is authorized to open the box, collect the mail, process the checks, and deposit the checks directly into the company's account. The bank, eliminating the processing float entirely, now performs step 3 functions and saves an additional 2 days. Furthermore, transit float (steps 4 to 7) can also be reduced by 1 day as a result of the lock-boxes being located near a Federal Reserve Bank or one of its branches.

[2]The discussions on cash receipt and disbursement procedures draw heavily on materials that were provided by the managements of the Chase Manhattan Bank, Continental Bank, and First National Bank of Chicago.

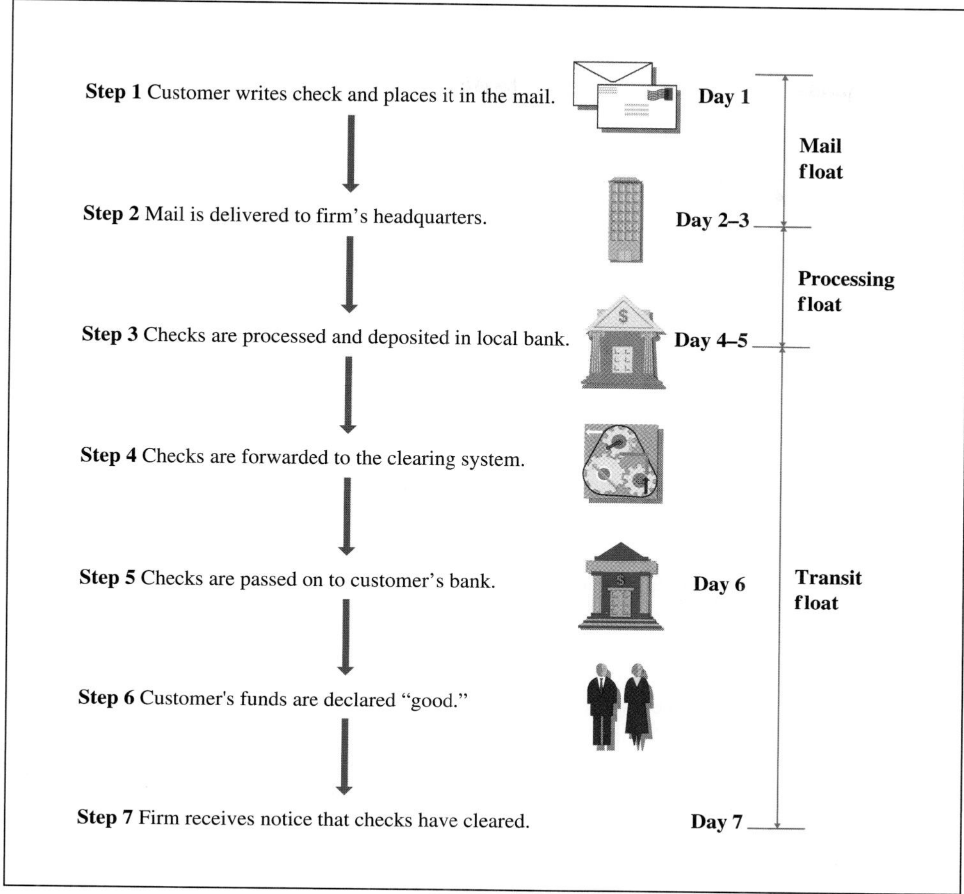


**FIGURE 19-2**
Ordinary Cash-Gathering System

Typically, a large bank will collect payments from the lock box at 1- to 2-hour intervals, 365 days of the year. During peak business hours, the bank may pick up mail every 30 minutes.

Once the mail is received at the bank, the checks will be examined, totaled, photocopied, and scanned. A deposit form is then prepared by the bank, and each batch of processed checks is forwarded to the collection department for clearance. Funds deposited in this manner are usually available for company use in one business day or less.

The same day deposits are made, the bank can notify the firm via some type of telecommunications system as to their amount. At the conclusion of each day, all check photocopies, invoices, deposit slips, and any other documents included with the remittances are mailed to the firm.

Note that the firm that receives checks from all over the country will have to use several lock boxes to take full advantage of a reduction in mail float. The firm's major bank should be able to offer as a service a detailed lock-box study, analyzing the company's receipt patterns to determine the proper number and location of lock-box receiving points.

The installation of the lock-box system can result in funds being credited to the firm's bank account a full 4 working days *faster* than is possible under the ordinary collection system.

In the chapter opening, we calculated the 1999 sales per day for Harley-Davidson to be \$6.72 million and assumed Harley could invest its excess cash in marketable securities yielding 6.53 percent annually. If Harley could speed up its cash collections by 4 days, the results would be dramatic. The gross annual savings to Harley (apart from operating the lock-box system) would amount to \$1.56 million as follows:

(sales per day) × (days of float reduction) × (assumed yield)

\$6.72 million × 4 × .0653 = 1.56 million

These benefits are not free. Usually, the bank levies a charge for each check processed through the system. The benefits derived from the acceleration of receipts must exceed the incremental costs of the lock-box system, or the firm would be better off without it. Companies that find the average size of their remittances to be quite small, for instance, might avoid a lock-box plan. Later in this chapter, we will illustrate how one calculates the costs and benefits of a specific cash-management service.

PREAUTHORIZED CHECKS (PACS) Whereas the lock-box arrangement can often reduce total float by 2 to 4 days, for some firms the use of preauthorized checks (PACs) can be an even more effective way of converting receipts into working cash. A PAC resembles the ordinary check, but it does not contain nor require the signature of the person on whose account it is being drawn. A PAC is created only with the individual's legal authorization.

**Concentration banking**
The selection of a few major banks where the firm maintains significant disbursing accounts.

CONCENTRATION BANKING Both depository transfer checks and wire transfers are used in conjunction with what is known as **concentration banking.** A concentration bank is one in which the firm maintains a major disbursing account.

In an effort to accelerate collections, many companies have established multiple collection centers. Regional lock-box networks are one type of approach to strategically located collection points. Even without lock boxes, firms may have numerous sales outlets throughout the country and collect cash over the counter. This requires many local bank accounts to handle daily deposits. Rather than have funds sitting in these multiple bank accounts in different geographic regions of the country, most firms will regularly transfer the surplus balances to one or more concentration banks.

**Depository transfer checks**
A non-negotiable instrument that provides the firm with a means to move funds from local bank accounts to concentration bank accounts.

**Depository transfer checks** provide a means for moving funds from local bank accounts to concentration accounts. The depository transfer check itself is an unsigned, non-negotiable instrument. It is payable only to the bank of deposit (the concentration bank) for credit to the firm's specific account. The firm files an authorization form with each bank from which it might withdraw funds. This form instructs the bank to pay the depository transfer checks without any signature.

**Wire transfers**
A method of moving funds electronically between bank accounts in order to eliminate transit float. The wired funds are immediately usable at the receiving bank.

WIRE TRANSFERS The fastest way to move cash between banks is by use of **wire transfers,** which eliminate transit float. Funds moved in this manner immediately become usable funds or "good funds" to the firm at the receiving bank. The following two major communication facilities are used to accommodate wire transfers:

1. *Bank Wire.* Bank Wire is a private wire service used and supported by approximately 250 banks in the United States for transferring funds, exchanging credit information, and effecting securities transactions.
2. *Federal Reserve Wire System.* The Fed Wire is directly accessible to commercial banks that are members of the Federal Reserve System. A commercial bank that is not on the Bank Wire or is not a member of the Federal Reserve System can use the wire transfer through its correspondent bank.

## Managing the Cash Outflow

Significant techniques and systems for improving the firm's management of cash disbursements include (1) zero balance accounts, (2) payable-through drafts, and (3) remote disbursing. The first two offer markedly better control over company-wide payments, and as a secondary benefit they *may* increase disbursement float. The last technique, remote disbursing, aims solely to increase disbursement float.

ZERO BALANCE ACCOUNTS Large corporations that operate multiple branches, divisions, or subsidiaries often maintain numerous bank accounts (in different banks) for the purpose of making timely operating disbursements. It does make good business sense for payments for purchased parts that go into, say, an automobile transmission to be made by the Transmission and Chassis Division of the auto manufacturer rather than its central office. The Transmission and Chassis Division originates such purchase orders, receives and inspects the shipment when it arrives at the plant, authorizes payment, and writes the appropriate check. To have the central office involved in these matters would be a waste of company time.

What tends to happen, however, is that with several divisions utilizing their own disbursal accounts, excess cash balances build up in outlying banks and rob the firm of earning assets. Zero balance accounts are used to alleviate this problem. The objectives of a zero balance account system are (1) for the firm to achieve better control over its cash payments, (2) to reduce excess cash balances held in regional banks for disbursing purposes, and (3) to increase disbursing float.

**Zero balance accounts** permit centralized control (at the headquarters level) over cash outflows while maintaining divisional disbursing authority. Under this system, the firm's authorized employees, representing their various divisions, continue to write checks on their individual accounts. Note that the numerous individual disbursing accounts are now *all* located in the same concentration bank. Actually, these separate accounts contain no funds at all, thus their appropriate label, "zero balance." These accounts have all of the other characteristics of regular demand deposit accounts including separate titles, numbers, and statements.

**Zero balance accounts**
A cash-management tool that permits centralized control over cash outflows but also maintains divisional disbursing authority.

PAYABLE-THROUGH DRAFTS **Payable-through drafts** are legal instruments that have the physical appearance of ordinary checks but are *not* drawn on a bank. Instead, payable-through drafts are drawn on and payment is authorized by the issuing firm against its demand deposit account. Like checks, the drafts are cleared through the banking system and are presented to the issuing firm's bank. The bank serves as a collection point and passes the drafts on to the firm. The corporate issuer usually has to return all drafts it does not wish to cover (pay) by the following business day. Those documents not returned to the bank are automatically paid. The firm inspects the drafts for validity by checking signatures, amounts, and dates. Stop-payment orders can be initiated by the company on any drafts considered inappropriate.

**Payable-through drafts**
A payment mechanism that substitutes for regular checks in that drafts are not drawn on a bank, but instead are drawn on and authorized by the firm against its demand deposit account. The purpose is to maintain control over field-authorized payments.

The main purpose of using a payable-through draft system is *to provide for effective control over field payments.* Central office control over payments begun by regional units is provided as the drafts are reviewed in advance of final payment. Payable-through drafts, for example, are used extensively in the insurance industry. The claims agent does not typically have check-signing authority against a corporate disbursement account. This agent can issue a draft, however, for quick settlement of a claim.

## Electronic Funds Transfer

In the purest economic sense, "total" float should equal zero days and therefore should be worth zero dollars to any business firm or other economic unit in the society. Float is really a measure of inefficiency of the financial system in an economy. It is a friction of the business environment that stems from the fact that all information arising from business transactions cannot be instantaneously transferred among the parties involved.

Today the extensive use of electronic communication equipment is serving to reduce float. The central concept of electronic funds transfer (EFT) is simple. If firm A owes money to firm B, this situation ought to be immediately reflected on both the books and the bank accounts of these two companies. Instantaneous transfer of funds would eliminate float. Of course, this ideal within the U.S. financial system has not been reached; the trend toward it, however, is readily observable.

Automated teller machines, like those imbedded in the wall of your supermarket or at the airline terminal, are familiar devices to most consumers. Businesses are now beginning to use even more advanced systems, such as terminal-based wire transfers, to move funds within their cash-management systems.

The heart of EFT is the elimination of the check as a method of transferring funds. The elimination of the check may never occur, but certainly a move toward a financial system that uses fewer checks will. Transit, mail, and processing float become less important as EFT becomes more important. Simultaneously, this also implies that disbursing float becomes trivial.

**RELATE TO THE BIG PICTURE**

All of these collection and disbursement procedures are an illustration of what is meant by **Principle 2: The Time Value of Money—A dollar received today is worth more than a dollar received in the future.** The faster the firm can take possession of the money to which it is entitled, the sooner the firm is able to put the money to work generating a return. Similarly, the longer the firm is able to hold onto the liquid assets in its possession, the greater is the return the firm is able to receive on such funds.

## Evaluation of Costs of Cash-Management Services

A form of break-even analysis can help the financial officer decide whether a particular collection or disbursement service will provide an economic benefit to the firm. The evaluation process involves a very basic relationship in microeconomics:

$$\text{added costs} = \text{added benefits} \tag{19-1}$$

If equation 19-1 holds exactly, then the firm is no better or worse off for having adopted the given service. We will illustrate this procedure in terms of the desirability of installing an additional lock box. Equation 19-1 can be restated on a per-unit basis as follows:

$$P = (D)(S)(i) \tag{19-2}$$

where $P$ = increases in per-check processing cost if the new system is adopted
$D$ = days saved in the collection process (float reduction)
$S$ = average check size in dollars
$i$ = the daily, before-tax opportunity cost (rate of return) of carrying cash

Assume now that check processing cost, *P,* will rise by 18¢ a check if a lock box is used. The firm has determined that the average check size, *S,* that will be mailed to the lock-box location will be \$900. If funds are freed by use of the lock box, they will be invested in marketable securities to yield an *annual* before-tax return of 6 percent. With these data, it is possible to determine the reduction in check collection time, *D,* that is required to justify use of the lock box. That level of *D* is found to be:

$$184 = (D)(\$900)\left(\frac{.06}{365}\right)$$

$$1.217 \text{ days} = D$$

**TABLE 19-1**
Features of Selected Cash-Collection and Disbursal Methods: A Summary

| Method | Objective | How Accomplished |
|---|---|---|
| **CASH-COLLECTION METHODS** | | |
| **1.** Lock-box system | Reduce (1) mail float, (2) processing float, and (3) transit float. | Strategic location of lock boxes to reduce mail float and transit float. Firm's commercial bank has access to lock box to reduce processing float. |
| **2.** Preauthorized checks | Reduce (1) mail float and (2) processing float. | The firm writes the checks (the PACs) for its customers to be charged against their demand deposit accounts. |
| **3.** (Ordinary) Depository transfer checks | Eliminate excess funds in regional banks. | Used in conjunction with concentration banking whereby the firm maintains several collection centers. The transfer check authorizes movement of funds from a local bank to the concentration bank. |
| **4.** Automated depository transfer check | Eliminate the mail float associated with the ordinary transfer check. | Telecommunications company transmits deposit data to the firm's concentration bank. |
| **5.** Wire transfers | Move funds immediately between banks. This eliminates transit float in that only "good funds" are transferred. | Use of Bank Wire or the Federal Reserve Wire System. |
| **CASH-DISBURSAL METHODS** | | |
| **1.** Zero balance accounts | (1) Achieve better control over cash payments, (2) reduce excess cash balances held in regional banks, and (3) possibly increase disbursing float. | Establish zero balance accounts for all of the firm's disbursing units, but in the same concentration bank. Checks are drawn against these accounts, with the balance in each account never exceeding $0. Divisional disbursing authority is thereby maintained at the local level of management. |
| **2.** Payable-through drafts | Achieve effective central office control over field-authorized payments. | Field office issues drafts rather than checks to settle payables. |

Thus, the lock box is justified if the firm can speed up its collections by *more* than 1.217 days. This same style of analysis can be adapted to analyze the other methods of cash management.

Before moving on to a discussion of the firm's marketable securities portfolio, it will be helpful to draw together the preceding material. Table 19-1 summarizes the key features of the cash-collection and disbursal techniques we have considered here.

**CONCEPT CHECK**

1. Define *float* and its origins in the cash management process.
2. What is a lock-box arrangement and how does its use reduce float?
3. Describe the use of zero balance accounts and payable-through drafts as methods for managing cash outflow.
4. How would you estimate the financial benefits of using a lock-box system?

## COMPOSITION OF MARKETABLE SECURITIES PORTFOLIO

Once the design of the firm's cash receipts and payments system has been determined, the financial manager faces the task of selecting appropriate financial assets for inclusion in the firm's marketable securities portfolio.

## General Selection Criteria

Certain criteria can provide the financial manager with a useful framework for selecting a proper marketable securities mix. These considerations include evaluation of the (1) financial risk, (2) interest rate risk, (3) liquidity, (4) taxability, and (5) yields among different financial assets. We will briefly delineate these criteria from the investor's viewpoint.

FINANCIAL RISK *Financial risk* refers to the uncertainty of expected returns from a security attributable to possible changes in the financial capacity of the security issuer to make future payments to the security owner. If the chance of default on the terms of the instrument is high (low), then the financial risk is said to be high (low).

In both financial practice and research, when estimates of risk-free returns are desired, the yields available on Treasury securities are consulted and the safety of other financial instruments is weighed against them.

INTEREST RATE RISK *Interest rate risk* refers to the uncertainty of expected returns from a financial instrument attributable to changes in interest rates. Of particular concern to the corporate treasurer is the price volatility associated with instruments that have long, as opposed to short, terms to maturity. An illustration can help clarify this point.

Suppose the financial officer is weighing the merits of investing temporarily available corporate cash in a new offering of U.S. Treasury obligations that will mature in either (1) 90 days or (2) 1 year from the date of issue. Ninety-day and 1-year Treasury bills are issued at a discount from their maturity price of $1,000. The issue price of these bills is found by discounting at 7 percent, compounded daily.

If after 60 days from the date of purchase, prevailing interest rates rise to 9 percent, the market price of these currently outstanding Treasury securities will fall to bring the yields to maturity in line with what investors could obtain by buying a new issue of a given instrument. The market prices of *both* the 90-day and 1-year obligations will decline. The price of the 1-year instrument will decline by a greater dollar amount, however, than that of the 90-day instrument.

Sixty days from the date of issue, the price obtainable in the marketplace for the original 1-year instrument, which now has 305 days until maturity, can be found by computing $P$ as follows:

$$P = \frac{\$1,000}{\left(1 + \frac{.09}{365}\right)^{305}} = \$926.59$$

If interest rates had remained at 7 percent:

$$P = \frac{\$1,000}{\left(1 + \frac{.07}{365}\right)^{305}} = \$943.19$$

Therefore, the rise in interest rates caused the price of the 1-year bill to fall by $16.60.

$$\$943.19 - \$926.59 = \$16.60$$

Now, what will happen to the price of the bill that has 30 days remaining to maturity? In a similar manner, we can compute its price, $P$:

$$P = \frac{\$1,000}{\left(1 + \frac{.09}{365}\right)^{30}} = \$992.63$$

If interest rates had remained at 7 percent:

$$P = \frac{\$1,000}{\left(1 + \frac{.07}{365}\right)^{30}} = \$994.26$$

Therefore, the price of the Treasury bill falls $1.63:

$$\$994.26 - \$992.63 = \$1.63$$

Thus, the market value of the shorter-term security was penalized much less by the given rise in the general level of interest rates.

If we extended the illustration, we would see that, in terms of market price, a 1-year security would be affected less than a 2-year security, a 5-year security less than a 20-year security, and so on. Equity securities would exhibit the largest price changes because of their infinite maturity periods. To hedge against the price volatility caused by interest rate risk, the firm's marketable security portfolio will tend to be composed of instruments that mature over short periods.

**LIQUIDITY** In the present context of managing the marketable securities portfolio, *liquidity* refers to the ability to transform a security into cash. Should an unforeseen event require that a significant amount of cash be immediately available, then a sizable portion of the portfolio might have to be sold. The financial manager will want the cash *quickly* and will not want to accept a large *price concession* in order to convert the securities. Thus, in the formulation of preferences for the inclusion of particular instruments in the portfolio, the manager must consider (1) the period needed to sell the security and (2) the likelihood that the security can be sold at or near its prevailing market price.

**TAXABILITY** The tax treatment of the income a firm receives from its security investments does not affect the ultimate mix of the marketable securities portfolio as much as the criteria mentioned earlier. This is because the interest income from most instruments suitable for inclusion in the portfolio is taxable at the federal level. Still, some corporate treasurers seriously evaluate the taxability of interest income and capital gains.

The interest income from only one class of securities escapes the federal income tax. That class of securities is generally referred to as *municipal obligations* or more simply as *municipals.* Because of the tax-exempt feature of interest income from state and local government securities, municipals sell at lower yields to maturity in the market than do securities that pay taxable interest. The after-tax yield on a municipal obligation, however, could be higher than the yield from a non-tax-exempt security. This would depend mainly on the purchasing firm's tax situation.

Consider Table 19-2. A firm is analyzing whether to invest in a 1-year tax-free debt issue yielding 6 percent on a $1,000 outlay or a 1-year taxable issue that yields 8 percent on a $1,000 outlay. The firm pays federal taxes at the rate of 34 percent. The yields quoted in the financial press and in the prospectuses that describe debt issues are *before-tax* returns.

The actual *after-tax* return enjoyed by the firm depends on its tax bracket. Notice that the actual after-tax yield received by the firm is only 5.28 percent on the taxable issue versus 6 percent on the tax-exempt obligation. The lower portion of Table 19-2 shows that the fully taxed bond must yield 9.091 percent to make it comparable with the tax-exempt issue.

**YIELDS** The final selection criterion that we mention is a significant one—the yields that are available on the different financial assets suitable for inclusion in the near-cash portfolio. By now it is probably obvious that the factors of (1) financial risk, (2) interest rate risk, (3) liquidity, and (4) taxability all influence the available yields on financial instruments. The yield criterion involves an evaluation of the risks and benefits inherent in all of these factors. If a given risk is assumed, such as lack of liquidity, a higher yield may be expected on the nonliquid instrument.

Table 19-3 summarizes our framework for designing the firm's marketable securities portfolio. The four basic considerations are shown to influence the yields available on

**TABLE 19-2**
Comparison of After-Tax Yields

| | Tax-Exempt Debt Issue (6% Coupon) | Taxable Debt Issue (8% Coupon) |
|---|---|---|
| Interest income | \$ 60.00 | \$ 80.00 |
| Income tax (.34) | 0.00 | 27.20 |
| After-tax interest income | 60.00 | 52.80 |
| After-tax yield | $\frac{60.00}{\$1{,}000.0} = 6\%$ | $\frac{52.80}{\$1{,}000.00} = 5.28\%$ |

Derivation of equivalent before-tax yield on a taxable debt issue:

$$r = \frac{r^*}{1 - t} = \frac{.06}{1 - .34} = 9.091\%$$

**where**
$r$ = equivalent before-tax yield,
$r^*$ = after-tax yield on tax-exempt security,
$t$ = firm's marginal income tax rate.

**Proof:**

| | |
|---|---|
| Interest income [\$1,000 × .09091] = | \$90.91 |
| Income tax (.34) | 30.91 |
| After-tax interest income | \$60.00 |

securities. The financial manager must focus on the risk-return trade-offs identified through analysis. Coming to grips with these trade-offs will enable the financial manager to determine the proper marketable securities mix for the company. Let us look now at the marketable securities prominent in firms' near-cash portfolios.

## Marketable Security Alternatives

Based on the foregoing discussion on the criteria to be used in selecting a security investment, let's now look at the investments that are commonly used.

U.S. TREASURY BILLS *U.S. Treasury bills* are the best-known and most popular short-term investment outlets among firms. A Treasury bill is a direct obligation of the U.S. government sold on a regular basis by the U.S. Treasury. New Treasury bills are issued in denominations of \$1,000 and up.

At present, bills are regularly offered with maturities of 91, 182, and 365 days. The 3-month and 6-month bills are auctioned weekly by the Treasury, and the 1-year bills are offered every 4 weeks. Bids (orders to purchase) are accepted by the various Federal Reserve Banks and their branches, which perform the role of agents for the Treasury. Each Monday, bids are received until 1:30 p.m. eastern time; after that time they are opened, tabulated, and forwarded to the Treasury for allocation (filling the purchase orders).

Treasury bills are sold on a discount basis; for that reason, the investor does not receive an actual interest payment. The return is the difference between the purchase price and the face (par) value of the bill.

Of prime importance to the corporate treasurer is the fact that a very active secondary market exists for bills. After a bill has been acquired by the firm, should the need arise to

**TABLE 19-3**
Designing the Marketable Securities Portfolio

| Considerations | → | Influence | → | Focus Upon | → | Determine |
|---|---|---|---|---|---|---|
| Financial risk<br>Interest rate risk<br>Liquidity<br>Taxability | | Yields | | Risk vs. return preferences mix | | Marketable securities |

turn it into cash, a group of securities dealers stands ready to purchase it. This highly developed secondary market for bills not only makes them extremely liquid, but also allows the firm to buy bills with maturities of a week or even less.

As bills have the full financial backing of the U.S. government, they are, for all practical purposes, risk-free. This negligible financial risk and high degree of liquidity makes the yields lower than those obtainable on other marketable securities. The income from Treasury bills is subject to federal income taxes, but *not* to state and local government income taxes.

**FEDERAL AGENCY SECURITIES** *Federal agency securities* are debt obligations of corporations and agencies that have been created to effect the various lending programs of the U.S. government. Five such government-sponsored corporations account for the majority of outstanding agency debt. The "big five" agencies are the Federal National Mortgage Association, the Federal Home Loan Banks, the Federal Land Banks, the Federal Intermediate Credit Banks, and the Banks for Cooperatives.

It is not true that the "big five" federally sponsored agencies are owned by the U.S. government and that the securities they issue are fully guaranteed by the government. The "big five" agencies are now entirely owned by their member associations or the general public. In addition, it is the issuing agency that stands behind its promises to pay, not the federal government.

These agencies sell their securities in a variety of denominations. The entry barrier caused by the absolute dollar size of the smallest available Treasury bill—$10,000—is not as severe in the market for agencies. A wide range of maturities is also available. Obligations can at times be purchased with maturities as short as 30 days or as long as 15 years.

Agency debt usually sells on a coupon basis and pays interest to the owner on a semiannual schedule, although there are exceptions. Some issues have been sold on a discount basis, and some have paid interest only once a year.

The income from agency debt that the investor receives is subject to taxation at the federal level. Of the "big five" agencies, only the income from FNMA issues is taxed at the state and local level.

The yields available on agency obligations will always exceed those of Treasury securities of similar maturity. This yield differential is attributable to lesser marketability and greater default risk. The financial officer might keep in mind, however, that none of these agency issues has ever gone into default.

**BANKERS' ACCEPTANCES** *Bankers' acceptances* are one of the least understood instruments suitable for inclusion in the firm's marketable securities portfolio. Their part in U.S. commerce today is largely concentrated in the financing of foreign transactions. Generally, an acceptance is a draft (order to pay) drawn on a specific bank by an exporter in order to obtain payment for goods shipped to a customer, who maintains an account with that specific bank.

Because acceptances are used to finance the acquisition of goods by one party, the document is not "issued" in specialized denominations; its dollar size is determined by the cost of the goods being purchased. Usual sizes, however, range from $25,000 to $1 million. The maturities on acceptances run from 30 to 180 days, although longer periods are available from time to time. The most common period is 90 days.

Acceptances, like Treasury bills, are sold on a discount basis and are payable to the holder of the paper. A secondary market for the acceptances of large banks does exist.

The income generated from investing in acceptances is fully taxable at the federal, state, and local levels. Because of their greater financial risk and lesser liquidity, acceptances provide investors a yield advantage over Treasury bills and agency obligations. In fact, the acceptances of major banks are a very safe investment, making the yield advantage over Treasuries worth looking at from the firm's vantage point.

**NEGOTIABLE CERTIFICATES OF DEPOSIT** A *negotiable certificate of deposit, CD,* is a marketable receipt for funds that have been deposited in a bank for a fixed time period. The deposited funds earn a fixed rate of interest. These are not to be confused with ordinary passbook savings accounts or nonmarketable time deposits offered by all commercial banks. CDs are offered by major money-center banks. We are talking here about "corporate" CDs—not those offered to individuals.

CDs are offered by key banks in a variety of denominations running from $25,000 to $10 million. The popular sizes are $100,000, $500,000, and $1 million. The original maturities on CDs can range from 1 to 18 months.

CDs are offered by banks on a basis differing from Treasury bills; that is, they are not sold at a discount. Rather, when the certificate matures, the owner receives the full amount deposited plus the earned interest.

A secondary market for CDs does exist, the heart of which is found in New York City. Even though the secondary market for CDs of large banks is well organized, it does not operate as smoothly as the aftermarket in Treasuries. CDs are more heterogeneous than Treasury bills. Treasury bills have similar rates, maturity periods, and denominations; more variety is found in CDs. This makes it harder to liquidate large blocks of CDs, because a more specialized investor must be found. The securities dealers who "make" the secondary market in CDs mainly trade in $1 million units. Smaller denominations can be traded but will bring a relatively lower price.

The income received from an investment in CDs is subject to taxation at all government levels. In recent years, CD yields have been above those available on bankers' acceptances.

**COMMERCIAL PAPER** *Commercial paper* refers to short-term, unsecured promissory notes sold by large businesses to raise cash. These are sometimes described in the popular financial press as short-term corporate IOUs. Because they are unsecured, the issuing side of the market is dominated by large corporations, which typically maintain sound credit ratings. The issuing (borrowing) firm can sell the paper to a dealer who will in turn sell it to the investing public; if the firm's reputation is solid, the paper can be sold directly to the ultimate investor.

The denominations in which commercial paper can be bought vary over a wide range. At times, paper can be obtained in sizes from $5,000 to $5 million, or even more.

Commercial paper can be purchased with maturities that range from 3 to 270 days. Notes with maturities exceeding 270 days are very rare, because they would have to be registered with the Securities and Exchange Commission—a task firms avoid, when possible, because it is time consuming and costly.

These notes are *generally* sold on a discount basis, although sometimes paper that is interest bearing and can be made payable to the order of the investor is available.

The next point is of considerable interest to the financial officer responsible for management of the firm's near-cash portfolio. For practical purposes, there is *no* active trading in a secondary market for commercial paper. This distinguishes commercial paper from all of the previously discussed short-term investment vehicles. On occasion, a dealer or finance company (the borrower) will redeem a note prior to its contract maturity date, but this is not a regular procedure. Thus, when the corporation evaluates commercial paper for possible inclusion in its marketable securities portfolio, it should plan to hold it to maturity.

The return on commercial paper is fully taxable to the investor at all levels of government. Because of its lack of marketability, commercial paper in past years consistently provided a yield advantage over other near-cash assets of comparable maturity. The lifting of interest rate ceilings in 1973 by the Federal Reserve Board on certain large CDs, however, allowed commercial banks to make CD rates fully competitive in the attempt to attract funds. Over any time period, then, CD yields *may* be slightly above the rates available on commercial paper.

**REPURCHASE AGREEMENTS** *Repurchase agreements (repos)* are legal contracts that involve the actual sale of securities by a *borrower* to the *lender,* with a commitment on the part of the borrower to *repurchase* the securities at the contract price plus a stated interest charge. The securities sold to the lender are U.S. government issues or other instruments of the money market such as those described previously. The borrower is either a major financial institution—most often, a commercial bank—or a dealer in U.S. government securities.

Why might the corporation with excess cash prefer to buy repurchase agreements rather than a given marketable security? There are two major reasons. First, the original maturities of the instruments being sold can, in effect, be adjusted to suit the particular needs of the investing corporation. Funds available for very short time periods, such as 1 or 2 days, can be productively employed. The second reason is closely related to the first. The firm could, of course, buy a Treasury bill and then resell it in the market in a few days when cash was required. The drawback here would be the risk involved in liquidating the bill at a price equal to its earlier cost to the firm. The purchase of a repo removes this risk. The contract price of the securities that make up the arrangement is *fixed* for the duration of the transaction. The corporation that buys a repurchase agreement, then, is protected against market price fluctuations throughout the contract period. This makes it a sound alternative investment for funds that are freed up for only very short periods. For example, mutual funds will buy repos as a way to "park" excess cash flows for a few days.

**MONEY MARKET MUTUAL FUNDS** Money market funds typically invest in a diversified portfolio of short-term, high-grade debt instruments such as those described previously. Some such funds, however, will accept more interest rate risk in their portfolios and acquire some corporate bonds and notes. The portfolio composition of 702 money market funds in 1999 is shown in Table 19-4. We see that commercial paper, repurchase agreements, plus all CDs (both domestic plus Eurodollar) represented 61.1 percent of money fund assets at this point in time. The average maturity period for these same 702 funds stood at 49 days. The interest rate risk contained in this overall portfolio is, therefore, rather small.

The money market funds sell their shares to raise cash, and by pooling the funds of large numbers of small savers, they can build their liquid-asset portfolios. Many of these funds allow the investor to start an account with as little as $1,000. This small initial investment, coupled with the fact that some liquid-asset funds permit subsequent investments in amounts as small as $100, makes this type of outlet for excess cash well suited to the small firm and the individual. Furthermore, the management of a small enterprise may not be highly versed in the details of short-term investments. By purchasing shares in a liquid-asset fund, the investor is also buying managerial expertise.

Money market mutual funds offer the investing firm a high degree of liquidity. By redeeming (selling) shares, the investor can obtain cash quickly. Procedures for liquidation vary among the funds, but shares can usually be redeemed by means of (1) special redemption checks supplied by the fund, (2) telephone instructions, (3) wire instructions, or (4) a letter. When liquidation is ordered by telephone or wire, the mutual fund can remit to the investor by the next business day.

The returns earned from owning shares in a money market fund are taxable at all governmental levels. The yields follow the returns the investor could receive by purchasing the marketable securities directly.

**TABLE 19-4**
Money Market Funds Asset Composition, Year-End 1999

| | Amount ($ billions) | Percent of Total |
|---|---|---|
| U.S. Treasury Bills | $60,054.7 | 7.26 |
| Other Treasury Securities | 46,311.1 | 3.29 |
| U.S. Securities | 195,734.0 | 13.89 |
| Repurchase Agreements | 143,975.3 | 10.22 |
| Certificates of Deposits | 138,984.6 | 9.89 |
| Eurodollar CDs | 42,095.9 | 2.99 |
| Commercial Paper | 535,288.5 | 38.00 |
| Bank Notes | 33,828.2 | 2.40 |
| Bankers Acceptances | 2,884.3 | 0.20 |
| Corporate Notes | 94,010.8 | 6.67 |
| Cash Reserves and other | | 8.20 |
| Other Assets | 115,564.0 | |

**CONCEPT CHECK**

1. What are financial and interest rate risk?
2. Describe each of the following: Treasury bills, federal agency securities, bankers' acceptances, negotiable certificates of deposit, commercial paper, repurchase agreements, and money-market mutual funds.
3. What is meant by the yield structure of marketable securities?

## THE MULTINATIONAL FIRM: THE USE OF CASH AND MARKETABLE SECURITIES

In terms of principles, not much changes for a multinational firm as opposed to a domestic firm. However, just as with other basic financial principles, everything becomes a bit more complicated. No longer can a firm simply look at the operations of its different units and allow those units to make corporate decisions. In fact, more often than not, the global or centralized financial decisions that a firm makes tend to be superior to decisions made by the different subsidiaries.

As we will see in Chapter 22, International Business Finance, when cash management enters the international arena, we are introduced to delaying collections when the currency being collected is strong, or quickly converting those assets into a relatively stronger currency. The bottom line here is that when we introduce multiple currencies we greatly complicate the process of cash management. Your job may be to manage collections from several countries and to make sure that those collections are maintained in as strong a currency as possible. That will mean transferring funds from country to country.

## HOW FINANCIAL MANAGERS USE THIS MATERIAL

Although a company's profitability is important, its ability to manage cash is vital. As a company becomes larger, cash management becomes more difficult and requires sophisticated systems to manage the firm's cash flows. Being effective in managing cash receipts and disbursements can mean thousands of dollars in savings to a larger company over a year's time.

The materials covered in this chapter have addressed many of the techniques used on a daily basis by almost all companies. These include:

- Check clearing mechanisms, electronic funds transfer systems, and float
- Collection (lock-box, preauthorized debits), concentration (branch banking, depository transfers), and disbursement (zero balance accounts, remote and controlled disbursements)
- Use of excess funds through short-term investments, which requires written investment policies and guidelines and deciding where to invest excess cash, be it U.S. Treasury bills, CDs, commercial paper, repurchase agreements, banker's acceptances, money market funds, Munis, or other securities
- Information management systems on deposit and balance reporting
- Selecting the right cash management bank

## SUMMARY

Liquid assets are the summation of cash and marketable securities. Cash is the currency and coin the firm has on hand in cash drawers, cash registers, or checking accounts. Cash balances earn no return. Near-cash assets, also known as marketable securities, are security investments that earn a rate of return and that the firm can quickly convert into cash balances.

The firm experiences both regular and irregular cash flows. Once cash is obtained, the firm will have three motives for holding cash: to satisfy transactions, precautionary needs for liquidity, and speculative needs for liquidity. To a certain extent, such needs can be satisfied by holding readily marketable securities rather than cash.

The financial manager must (1) ensure that enough cash is on hand to meet the payment needs that arise in the course of doing business and (2) attempt to maximize wealth by reducing the firm's idle cash balances to a minimum.

Float is the length of time from when a check is written until the actual recipient can use the "good funds." To reduce float, the firm can benefit considerably through the use of (1) lock-box arrangements, (2) preauthorized checks, (3) special forms of depository transfer checks, and (4) wire transfers. Lock-box systems and preauthorized checks serve to reduce mail and processing float. Depository transfer checks and wire transfers move funds between banks; they are often used in conjunction with concentration banking. Both the lock-box and preauthorized check systems can be employed as part of the firm's concentration banking setup to speed receipts to regional collection centers.

The firm can delay and favorably affect the control of its cash disbursements through the use of (1) zero balance accounts, (2) payable-through drafts, and (3) remote disbursing. Zero balance accounts allow the company to maintain central-office control over payments while permitting the firm's several divisions to maintain their own disbursing authority. Because key disbursing accounts are located in one major concentration bank, rather than in multiple banks across the country, excess cash balances that tend to build up in the outlying banks are avoided. Payable-through drafts are legal instruments that look like checks but are drawn on and paid by the issuing firm rather than its bank. The bank serves as a collection point for the drafts. Effective central-office control over field-authorized payments is the main reason such a system is used; it is not used as a major vehicle for extending disbursing float.

Before any of these collection and disbursement procedures is initiated by the firm, a careful analysis should be undertaken to see if the expected benefits outweigh the expected costs.

The factors of (1) financial risk, (2) interest rate risk, (3) liquidity, and (4) taxability affect the yields available on marketable securities. By considering these four factors simultaneously with returns desired from the portfolio, the financial manager can design the mix of near-cash assets most suitable for a firm.

We looked at several marketable securities. Treasury bills and federal agency securities are extremely safe investments. Bankers' acceptances, CDs, and commercial paper provide higher yields in exchange for greater risk assumption. Unlike the other instruments, commercial paper enjoys no *developed* secondary market. The firm can hedge against price fluctuations through the use of repurchase agreements. Money market mutual funds, a recent phenomenon of our financial market system, are particularly well suited for the short-term investing needs of small firms.

## KEY TERMS

myPHLIP

Go To:
http://www.prenhall.com/keown
for downloads and current events associated with this chapter

**Cash, 635**
**Concentration banking, 642**
**Depository transfer checks, 642**
**Float, 640**
**Insolvency, 638**
**Liquid assets, 635**
**Marketable securities, 635**
**Payable-through drafts, 643**
**Wire transfers, 642**
**Zero balance accounts, 643**

## STUDY QUESTIONS

**19-1.** What is meant by the *cash flow process?*

**19-2.** Identify the principal motives for holding cash and near-cash assets. Explain the purpose of each motive.

**19-3.** What is concentration banking and how may it be of value to the firm?

**19-4.** Distinguish between depository transfer checks and automated depository transfer checks (ADTC).

**19-5.** In general, what type of firm would benefit from the use of a preauthorized check system? What specific types of companies have successfully used this device to accelerate cash receipts?

**19-6.** What are the two major objectives of the firm's cash-management system?

**19-7.** What three decisions dominate the cash-management process?

**19-8.** Within the context of cash management, what are the key elements of (total) float? Briefly define each element.

**19-9.** Distinguish between financial risk and interest rate risk as these terms are commonly used in discussions of cash management.

**19-10.** What is meant when we say, "A money market instrument is highly liquid"?

**19-11.** Which money market instrument is generally conceded to have no secondary market?

**19-12.** Your firm invests in only three different classes of marketable securities: commercial paper, Treasury bills, and federal agency securities. Recently, yields on these money market instruments of 3 months' maturity were quoted at 6.10, 6.25, and 5.90 percent. Match the available yields with the types of instruments your firm purchases.

**19-13.** What two key factors might induce a firm to invest in repurchase agreements rather than a specific security of the money market?

## SELF-TEST PROBLEMS

**ST-1.** (*Costs of services*) Creative Fashion Designs is evaluating a lock-box system as a cash receipts acceleration device. In a typical year, this firm receives remittances totaling \$7 million by check. The firm will record and process 4,000 checks over the same time period. Ocala National Bank has informed the management of Creative Fashion Designs that it will process checks and associated documents through the lock-box system for a unit cost of 25¢ per check. Creative Fashion Designs' financial manager has projected that cash freed by adoption of the system can be invested in a portfolio of near-cash assets that will yield an annual before-tax return of 8 percent. Creative Fashion Designs' financial analysts use a 365-day year in their procedures.

- **a.** What reduction in check collection time is necessary for Creative Fashion Designs to be neither better nor worse off for having adopted the proposed system?
- **b.** How would your solution to (a) be affected if Creative Fashion Designs could invest the freed balances only at an expected annual pre-tax return of 5.5 percent?
- **c.** What is the logical explanation for the differences in your answers to (a) and (b)?

**ST-2.** (*Cash receipts acceleration system*) Artie Kay's Komputer Shops is a large, national distributor and retailer of microcomputers, personal computers, and related software. The company has its central offices in Dearborn, Michigan, not far from the Ford Motor Company executive offices and headquarters. Only recently has Artie Kay's begun to pay serious attention to its cash-management procedures. Last week, the firm received a proposal from the Detroit National Bank. The objective of the proposal is to speed up the firm's cash collections.

Artie Kay's now uses a centralized billing procedure. All checks are mailed to the Dearborn headquarters office for processing and eventual deposit. Remittance checks now take an average of 5 business days to reach the Dearborn office. The in-house processing at Artie Kay's is quite slow. Once in Dearborn, another 3 days are needed to process the checks for deposit at Detroit National.

The daily cash remittances of Artie Kay's average $200,000. The average check size is $800. The firm currently earns 10.6 percent on its marketable securities portfolio and expects this rate to continue to be available.

The cash acceleration plan suggested by officers of Detroit National involves both a lock-box system and concentration banking. Detroit National would be the firm's only concentration bank. Lock boxes would be established in (1) Seattle, (2) San Antonio, (3) Chicago, and (4) Detroit. This would reduce mail float by 2.0 days. Processing float would be reduced to a level of 0.5 days. Funds would then be transferred twice each business day by means of automated depository transfer checks from local banks in Seattle, San Antonio, and Chicago to the Detroit National Bank. Each ADTC costs $20. These transfers will occur all 270 business days of the year. Each check processed through the lock-box system will cost Artie Kay's 25¢.

- **a.** What amount of cash balances will be freed if Artie Kay's adopts the system proposed by Detroit National?
- **b** What is the opportunity cost of maintaining the current banking arrangement?
- **c.** What is the projected annual cost of operating the proposed system?
- **d.** Should Artie Kay's adopt the new system? Compute the net annual gain or loss associated with adopting the system.

**ST-3.** (*Buying and selling marketable securities*) Mountaineer Outfitters has $2 million in excess cash that it might invest in marketable securities. In order to buy and sell the securities, however, the firm must pay a transaction fee of $45,000.

- **a.** Would you recommend purchasing the securities if they yield 12 percent annually and are held for:
  1. 1 month?
  2. 2 months?
  3. 3 months?
  4. 6 months?
  5. 1 year?
- **b.** What minimum required yield would the securities have to return for the firm to hold them for 3 months (what is the break-even yield for a 3-month holding period)?

## STUDY PROBLEMS (SET A)

**19-1A.** (*Concentration banking*) Healthy Herbal Beverage, Inc., produces a very healthy herbal beverage in Tupelo, Mississippi, that is distributed to health-food stores primarily along the Gulf Coast, where many health-food aficionados seem to live. Until now, the company has received collections on its accounts receivable at its Tupelo headquarters. Such collections recently have been $40 million at an annual rate and are expected to remain at that level. The company's bank has suggested to Healthy Herbal's CFO, Wanda Jackson, that the bank could establish a concentration banking system for the company that would save the company 4 days in mail float, 3 days in processing float, and $35,000 in annual clerical costs. The bank would charge a flat fee per year of $40,000 to operate the system for Healthy Herbal. Wanda believes that the funds freed by such an arrangement could be invested at no transaction cost in the company's money market account and could earn an annual rate of return of 5 percent. Should Wanda accept the bank's proposal? Use a 365-day year in your analysis.

**19-2A.** (*Buying and selling marketable securities*) An alternative to investing in a no-transaction-fee money market account under consideration by Wanda Jackson, the CFO at Healthy Herbal Beverage, Inc., (see Problem 19-1A) is direct investment in marketable securities. Assume for this problem that Wanda has determined that adoption of a concentration banking system could make $750,000 available for investment in marketable securities, but such direct investing would result in annual transaction fees of $15,000. Would you recommend that Wanda invest the funds in a money market account (at 5 percent per annum) or purchase the marketable securities directly if such securities yield 7.5 percent per annum and the expected holding period is for:

**a.** 1 month?
**b.** 2 months?
**c.** 6 months?
**d.** 1 year?

**19-3A.** (*Lock-box system*) The Marino Rug Co. is located on the outskirts of Miramar, Florida. The firm specializes in the manufacture of a wide variety of carpet and tile. All of the firm's output is shipped to 12 warehouses, which are located in the largest metropolitan areas nationwide. National Bank of Miami is Marino Rug's lead bank. National Bank has just completed a study of Marino's cash collection system. Overall, National estimates that it can reduce Marino's total float by 3 days with the installation of a lock-box arrangement in each of the firm's 12 regions. The lock-box arrangement would cost each region $325 per month. Any funds freed up would be added to the firm's marketable securities portfolio and would yield 9.75 percent on an annual basis. Annual sales average $6,232,375 for each regional office. The firm and the bank use a 365-day year in their analyses. Should Marino's management approve the use of the proposed system?

**19-4A.** (*Marketable securities portfolio*) Mac's Tennis Racket Manufacturing Company currently pays its employees on a weekly basis. The weekly wage bill is $675,000. This means that on average, the firm has accrued wages payable of ($675,000 + $0)/2 = $337,500.

Jimmy McEnroe works as the firm's senior financial analyst and reports directly to his uncle, who owns all of the firm's common stock. Jimmy McEnroe wants to move to a monthly wage payment system. Employees would be paid at the end of every fourth week. Jimmy is aware that the labor union representing the company's workers will not permit the monthly payments system to take effect unless the workers are given some type of fringe-benefit compensation.

A plan has been worked out whereby the firm will make a contribution to the cost of life insurance coverage for each employee. This will cost the firm $50,775 annually. Jimmy McEnroe expects the firm to earn 8.5 percent annually on its marketable securities portfolio.

**a.** Based on the projected information, should Mac's Tennis Racket Manufacturing Company move to the monthly wage payment system?
**b.** What annual rate of return on the marketable securities portfolio would enable the firm just to break even on this proposal?

**19-5A.** (*Cash receipts acceleration system*) James Waller Nail Corp. is a buyer and distributor of nails used in the home building industry. The firm has grown very quickly since it was established 8 years ago. Waller Nail has managed to increase sales and profits at a rate of about 18 percent annually, despite moderate economic growth at the national level. Until recently, the company paid little attention to cash-management procedures. James Waller, the firm's president, said: "With our growth—who cares?" Bending to the suggestions of several analysts in the firm's finance group, Waller did agree to have a proposal prepared by the Second National Bank in Tampa, Florida. The objective of the proposal is to accelerate the firm's cash collections.

At present, Waller Nail uses a centralized billing procedure. All checks are mailed to the Tampa office headquarters for processing and eventual deposit. Under this arrangement, all customers' remittance checks take an average of 5 business days to reach the Tampa office. Once in Tampa, another 2 days are needed to process the checks for deposit at the Second National Bank.

Daily cash remittances at Waller Nail average $750,000. The average check size is $3,750. The firm currently earns 9.2 percent annually on its marketable securities portfolio.

The cash-acceleration plan presented by the officers of Second National Bank involves both a lock-box system and concentration banking. Second National would be the firm's only concentration bank. Lock boxes would be established in (1) Los Angeles, (2) Dallas, (3) Chicago, and (4) Tampa. This would reduce funds tied up in mail float to 3.5 days. Processing float would be totally eliminated. Funds would then be transferred twice each business day by means of automated depository transfer checks from local banks in Los Angeles, Dallas, and Chicago to the Second National Bank. Each ADTC costs $27. These transfers will occur all 270 business days of the year. Each check processed through the lock box will cost Waller Nail 35¢.

**a.** What amount of cash balances will be freed if Waller Nail adopts the system proposed by Second National Bank?

**b.** What is the opportunity cost of maintaining the current banking arrangement?

**c.** What is the projected annual cost of operating the proposed system?

**d.** Should Waller Nail Corp. adopt the system? Compute the net annual gain or loss associated with adopting the system.

**19-6A.** (*Costs of services*) The Mountain Furniture Company of Scranton, Pennsylvania, may install a lock-box system to speed up its cash receipts. On an annual basis, Mountain Furniture receives $40 million in remittances by check. The firm will record and process 15,000 checks over the year. The Third Bank of Scranton will administer the system at a cost of 35¢ per check. Cash that is freed up by use of the system can be invested to yield 9 percent on an annual before-tax basis. A 365-day year is used for analysis purposes. What reduction in check collection time is necessary for Mountain Furniture to be neither better nor worse off for having adopted the proposed system?

**19-7A.** (*Valuing float reduction*) Griffey Manufacturing Company is forecasting that next year's gross revenues from sales will be $890 million. The senior treasury analyst for the firm expects the marketable securities portfolio to earn 9.60 percent over this same time period. A 365-day year is used in all the firm's financial procedures. What is the value to the company of 1 day's float reduction?

**19-8A.** (*Costs of services*) Mustang Ski-Wear, Inc., is investigating the possibility of adopting a lock-box system as a cash receipts acceleration device. In a typical year, this firm receives remittances totaling $12 million by check. The firm will record and process 6,000 checks over this same time period. The Colorado Springs Second National Bank has informed the management of Mustang that it will expedite checks and associated documents through the lock-box system for a unit cost of 20¢ per check. Mustang's financial manager has projected that cash freed by adoption of the system can be invested in a portfolio of near-cash assets that will yield an annual before-tax return of 7 percent. Mustang financial analysts use a 365-day year in their procedures.

**a.** What reduction in check collection time is necessary for Mustang to be neither better nor worse off for having adopted the proposed system?

**b.** How would your solution to (a) be affected if Mustang could invest the freed balances only at an expected annual return of 4.5 percent?

**c.** What is the logical explanation for the difference in your answers to (a) and (b)?

**19-9A.** (*Valuing float reduction*) The Columbus Tool and Die Works will generate $18 million in credit sales next year. Collections occur at an even rate, and employees work a 270-day year. At the moment, the firm's general accounting department ties up 5 days' worth of remittance checks. An analysis undertaken by the firm's treasurer indicates that new internal procedures can reduce processing float by 2 days. If Columbus Tool invests the released funds to earn 8 percent, what will be the annual savings?

**19-10A.** (*Valuing float reduction*) Montgomery Woodcraft is a large distributor of woodworking tools and accessories to hardware stores, lumber yards, and tradesmen. All its sales are on a credit basis, net 30 days. Sales are evenly distributed over its 12 sales regions throughout the United States. There is no problem with delinquent accounts. The firm is attempting to improve its cash-management procedures. Montgomery recently determined that it took an average of 3.0 days for customers' payments to reach their office from the time they were mailed and another day for processing before payments could be deposited. Annual sales average $5,200,000 for each region, and investment opportunities can be found to return 9 percent per year. What is the opportunity cost to the firm of the funds tied up in mailing and processing? In your calculations, use a 365-day year.

**19-11A.** (*Accounts payable policy and cash management*) Bradford Construction Supply Company is suffering from a prolonged decline in new construction in its sales area. In an attempt to improve its cash position, the firm is considering changes in its accounts payable policy. After careful study, it has been determined that the only alternative available is to slow disbursements. Purchases for the coming year are expected to be $37.5 million. Sales will be $65 million, which represents about a 20 percent drop from the current year. Currently, Bradford discounts approximately 25 percent of its payments at 3 percent 10 days, net 30, and the balance of accounts are paid in 30 days. If Bradford adopts a policy of payment in 45 days or 60 days, how much can the firm gain if the annual opportunity cost of investment is 12 percent? What will be the result if this action causes Bradford Construction suppliers to increase their prices to the company by 0.5 percent to compensate for the 60-day extended term of payment? In your calculations, use a 365-day year and ignore any compounding effects related to expected returns.

**19-12A.** (*Interest rate risk*) Two years ago, your corporate treasurer purchased for the firm a 20-year bond at its par value of $1,000. The coupon rate on this security is 8 percent. Interest payments are made to bondholders once a year. Currently, bonds of this particular risk class are yielding investors 9 percent. A cash shortage has forced you to instruct your treasurer to liquidate this bond.

**a.** At what price will your bond be sold? Assume annual compounding.

**b.** What will be the amount of your gain or loss over the original purchase price?

**c.** What would be the amount of your gain or loss had the treasurer originally purchased a bond with a 4-year rather than a 20-year maturity? (Assume all characteristics of the bonds are identical except their maturity periods.)

**d.** What do we call this type of risk assumed by your corporate treasurer?

**19-13A.** (*Marketable securities portfolio*) Red Raider Feedlots has $4 million in excess cash to invest in a marketable securities portfolio. Its broker will charge $10,000 to invest the entire $4 million. The president of Red Raider wants at least half of the $4 million invested at a maturity period of 3 months or less; the remainder can be invested in securities with maturities not to exceed 6 months. The relevant term structure of short-term yields follows:

| Maturity Period | Available Yield (Annual) |
|---|---|
| 1 month | 6.2% |
| 2 months | 6.4 |
| 3 months | 6.5 |
| 4 months | 6.7 |
| 5 months | 6.9 |
| 6 months | 7.0 |

**a.** What should be the maturity periods of the securities purchased with the excess $4 million to maximize the before-tax income from the added investment? What will be the amount of the income from such an investment?

**b.** Suppose that the president of Red Raider relaxes his constraint on the maturity structure of the added investment. What would be your profit-maximizing investment recommendation?

**c.** If one-sixth of the excess cash is invested in each of the preceding maturity categories, what would be the before-tax income generated from such an action?

**19-14A.** (*Comparison of after-tax yields*) The corporate treasurer of Aggieland Fireworks is considering the purchase of a BBB-rated bond that carries a 9 percent coupon. The BBB-rated security is taxable, and the firm is in the 46 percent marginal tax bracket. The face value of this bond is $1,000. A financial analyst who reports to the corporate treasurer has alerted him to the fact that a municipal obligation is coming to the market with a 5-1/2 percent coupon. The par value of this security is also $1,000.

**a.** Which one of the two securities do you recommend the firm purchase? Why?

**b.** What must the fully taxed bond yield before tax to make it comparable with the municipal offering?

## INTEGRATIVE PROBLEM

New Wave Surfing Stuff, Inc., is a manufacturer of surfboards and related gear that sells to exclusive surf shops located in several Atlantic and Pacific mainland coastal towns as well as several Hawaiian locations. The company's headquarters are located in Carlsbad, California, a small Southern California coastal town. True to form, the company's officers, all veteran surfers, have been somewhat laid back about various critical areas of financial management. With an economic downturn in California adversely affecting their business, however, the officers of the company have decided to focus intently on ways to improve New Wave's cash flows. The CFO, Willy Bonik, has been requested to forgo any more daytime surfing jaunts until he has wrapped up a plan to accelerate New Wave's cash flows.

In an effort to ensure his quick return to the surf, Willy has decided to focus on what he believes is one of the easiest methods of improving New Wave's cash collections—namely, adoption of a cash receipts acceleration system that includes a lock-box system and concentration banking. Willy is well aware that New Wave's current system leaves much room for improvement. The company's accounts receivable system currently requires that remittances from customers be mailed to the headquarters office for processing, then for deposit in the local branch of the Bank of the U.S. Such an arrangement takes a considerable amount of time. The checks take an average of 6 days to reach the Carlsbad headquarters. Then, depending on the surf conditions, processing within the company takes anywhere from 3 to 5 days, with the average from the day of receipt by the company to the day of deposit at the bank being 4 days.

Willy feels fairly certain that such delays are costly. After all, New Wave's average daily collections are $100,000. The average remittance size is $1,000. If Willy could get these funds into his marketable securities account more quickly, he could earn 6 percent at an annual rate on such funds. In addition, if he could arrange for someone else to do the processing, Willy could save $50,000 per year in costs related to clerical staffing.

New Wave's banker was pleased to provide Willy with a proposal for a combination of a lock-box system and a concentration banking system. Bank of the U.S. would be New Wave's concentration bank. Lock boxes would be established in Honolulu, Newport Beach, and Daytona Beach. Each check processed through the lock-box system would cost New Wave 25¢. This arrangement, however, would reduce mail float by an average 3.5 days. The funds so collected would be transferred twice each day, 270 days a year, using automated depository transfer checks from each of the local lock-box banks to Bank of the U.S. Each ADTC would cost $25. The combination of the lock-box system and concentration banking would eliminate the time it takes the company to process cash collections, thereby making the funds available for short-term investment.

1. What would be the average amount of cash made available if New Wave were to adopt the system proposed by Bank of the U.S.?
2. What is the annual opportunity cost of maintaining the current cash collection and deposit system?
3. What is the expected annual cost of the complete system proposed by Bank of the U.S.?
4. What is the net gain or loss that is expected to result from the proposed new system? Should New Wave adopt the new system?

## STUDY PROBLEMS (SET B)

**19-1B.** (*Concentration banking*) Sprightly Step, Inc., produces a line of walking shoes that has become extremely popular with aging baby boomers. The company's recent rapid growth to $80 million in annual credit sales to shoe stores around the country has made consideration of a more advanced billing and collection system worthwhile. Sprightly's bank has proposed a concentration banking system to Sprightly's CFO, Roberto Dylan, that would save the company 3 days in mail float, 2 days in processing float, and $50,000 in annual clerical costs. The bank would charge a flat fee per year of $80,000 to operate the system for Sprightly. Roberto believes that the funds freed by such an arrangement could be invested at no transaction cost in the company's money market account and could earn an annual rate of return of 5.5 percent. Should Roberto accept the bank's proposal? Use a 365-day year in your analysis.

**19-2B.** (*Buying and selling marketable securities*) An alternative to investing in a no-transaction-fee money market account under consideration by Roberto Dylan, the CFO at Sprightly Step, Inc. (see Problem 19-1B), is direct investment in marketable securities. Assume for this problem that Roberto has determined that adoption of a concentration banking system could make $1,100,000 available for investment in marketable securities, but such direct investing would result in annual transaction fees of $15,000. Would you recommend that Roberto invest the funds in a money market account (at 5.5 percent per annum) or purchase the marketable securities directly if such securities yield 8 percent per annum and the expected holding period is for:

**a.** 1 month?
**b.** 2 months?
**c.** 6 months?
**d.** 1 year?

**19-3B.** (*Cash receipts acceleration system*) Kobrin Door & Glass, Inc., is a buyer and distributor of doors used in the home building industry. The firm has grown very quickly since it was established 8 years ago. Kobrin Door has managed to increase sales and profits at a rate of about 18 percent annually, despite moderate economic growth at the national level. Until recently, the company paid little attention to cash-management procedures. Charles Kobrin, the firm's president, said: "With our growth—who cares?" Bending to the suggestions of several analysts in the firm's finance group, Kobrin did agree to have a proposal prepared by the First Citizens Bank in Tampa, Florida. The objective of the proposal is to accelerate the firm's cash collections.

At present, Kobrin Door uses a centralized billing procedure. All checks are mailed to the Tampa office headquarters for processing and eventual deposit. Under this arrangement, all customers' remittance checks take an average of 5 business days to reach the Tampa office. Once in Tampa, another 2 days are needed to process the checks for deposit at the First Citizens Bank.

Daily cash remittances at Kobrin Door average $800,000. The average check size is $4,000. The firm currently earns 9.5 percent annually on its marketable securities portfolio.

The cash-acceleration plan presented by the officers of First Citizens Bank involves both a lock-box system and concentration banking. First Citizens would be the firm's only concentration bank. Lock boxes would be established in (1) Los Angeles, (2) Dallas, (3) Chicago, and (4) Tampa. This would reduce funds tied up in mail float to 3.5 days. Processing float would be totally eliminated. Funds would then be transferred twice each business day by means of automated depository transfer checks from local banks in Los Angeles, Dallas, and Chicago to the First Citizens Bank. Each depository transfer check (ADTC) costs $30. These transfers will occur all 270 business days of the year. Each check processed through the lock box will cost Kobrin Door 40¢.

**a.** What amount of cash balances will be freed if Kobrin Door adopts the system proposed by First Citizens Bank?
**b.** What is the opportunity cost of maintaining the current banking arrangement?
**c.** What is the projected annual cost of operating the proposed system?
**d.** Should Kobrin Door & Glass adopt the system? Compute the net annual gain or loss associated with adopting the system.

**19-4B.** (*Lock-box system*) Regency Components is located in Nashville, Tennessee. The firm manufactures components used in a variety of electrical devices. All the firm's finished goods are shipped to five regional warehouses across the United States.

Tennessee State Bank of Nashville is Regency Components' lead bank. Tennessee State recently completed a study of Regency's cash-collection system. Tennessee State estimates that it can reduce Regency's total float by 3.0 days with the installation of a lock-box arrangement in each of the firm's five regions.

The lock-box arrangement would cost each region $600 per month. Any funds freed up would be added to the firm's marketable securities portfolio and would yield 11.0 percent on an annual basis. Annual sales average $10,000,000 for each regional office. The firm and the bank use a 365-day year in their analyses. Should Regency Components' management approve the use of the proposed system?

**19-5B.** (*Costs of services*) The Hallmark Technology Company of Scranton, Pennsylvania, may install a lock-box system in order to speed up its cash receipts. On an annual basis, Hallmark receives $50 million in remittances by check. The firm will record and process 20,000 checks over the year. The Third Bank of Scranton will administer the system at a cost of 37¢ per check. Cash that is freed up by use of the system can be invested to yield 9 percent on an annual before-tax basis. A 365-day year is used for analysis purposes. What reduction in check collection time is necessary for Hallmark to be neither better nor worse off for having adopted the proposed system?

**19-6B.** (*Valuing float reduction*) Brady Consulting Services is forecasting that next year's gross revenues from sales will be $900 million. The senior treasury analyst for the firm expects the marketable securities portfolio to earn 9.5 percent over this same time period. A 365-day year is used in all the firm's financial procedures. What is the value to the company of one day's float reduction?

**19-7B.** (*Costs of services*) Colorado Communications is investigating the possibility of adopting a lock-box system as a cash receipts acceleration device. In a typical year, this firm receives remittances totaling $10 million by check. The firm will record and process 7,000 checks over this same time period. The Colorado Springs Second National Bank has informed the management of Colorado Comm that it will expedite checks and associated documents through the lock-box system for a unit cost of 30¢ per check. Colorado Comm's financial manager has projected that cash freed by adoption of the system can be invested in a portfolio of near-cash assets that will yield an annual before-tax return of 7 percent. Colorado Comm's financial analysts use a 365-day year in their procedures.

**a.** What reduction in check collection time is necessary for Colorado Comm to be neither better nor worse off for having adopted the proposed system?

**b.** How would your solution to (a) be affected if Colorado Comm could invest the freed balances only at an expected annual return of 4.5 percent?

**c.** What is the logical explanation for the difference in your answers to (a) and (b)?

**19-8B.** (*Valuing float reduction*) Campus Restaurants, Inc. will generate $17 million in credit sales next year. Collections occur at an even rate, and employees work a 270-day year. At the moment, the firm's general accounting department ties up 4 days' worth of remittance checks. An analysis undertaken by the firm's treasurer indicates that new internal procedures can reduce processing float by 2 days. If Campus invests the released funds to earn 9 percent, what will be the annual savings?

**19-9B.** (*Marketable securities portfolio*) Katz Jewelers currently pays its employees on a weekly basis. The weekly wage bill is $500,000. This means that on average the firm has accrued wages payable of $500,000 + $0)/2 = $250,000.

Harry Katz works as the firm's senior financial analyst and reports directly to his father, who owns all of the firm's common stock. Harry Katz wants to move to a monthly wage payment system. Employees would be paid at the end of every fourth week. The younger Katz is fully aware that the labor union representing the company's workers will not permit the monthly payments system to take effect unless the workers are given some type of fringe benefit compensation.

A plan has been worked out whereby the firm will make a contribution to the cost of life insurance coverage for each employee. This will cost the firm $40,000 annually. Harry Katz expects the firm to earn 8 percent annually on its marketable securities portfolio.

**a.** Based on the projected information, should Katz Jewelers move to the monthly wage payment system?

**b.** What annual rate of return on the marketable securities portfolio would enable the firm to just break even on this proposal?

**19-10B.** (*Valuing float reduction*) True Locksmith is a large distributor of residential locks to hardware stores, lumber yards, and tradesmen. All its sales are on a credit basis, net 30 days. Sales are distributed over its 10 sales regions throughout the United States. There is no problem with delinquent accounts. The firm is attempting to improve its cash-management procedures. True Locksmith recently determined that it took an average of 3.0 days for customers' payments to reach their office from the time they were mailed, and another day for processing before payments could be deposited. Annual sales average $5,000,000 for each region, and investment opportunities can be found to return 9 percent per year. What is the opportunity cost to the firm of the funds tied up in mailing and processing? In your calculations, use a 365-day year.

**19-11B.** (*Accounts payable policy and cash management*) Meadowbrook Paving Company is suffering from a prolonged decline in new development in its sales area. In an attempt to improve its cash position, the firm is considering changes in its accounts payable policy. After careful study, it has determined that the only alternative available is to slow disbursements. Purchases for the coming year are expected to be $40 million. Sales will be $65 million, which represents about a 15 percent drop from the current year. Currently, Meadowbrook discounts approximately 25 percent of its payments at 3 percent 10 days, net 30, and the balance of accounts are paid in 30 days. If Meadowbrook adopts a policy of payment in 45 days or 60 days, how much can the firm gain if the annual opportunity cost of investment is 11 percent? What will be the result if this action causes Meadowbrook Paving suppliers to increase their prices to the company by 0.5 percent to compensate for the 60-day extended term of payment? In your calculation, use a 365-day year and ignore any compounding effects related to expected returns.

**19-12B.** (*Interest rate risk*) Two years ago, your corporate treasurer purchased for the firm a 20-year bond at its par value of $1,000. The coupon rate on this security is 8 percent. Interest payments are made to bondholders once a year. Currently, bonds of this particular risk class are yielding investors 9 percent. A cash shortage has forced you to instruct your treasurer to liquidate his bond.

**a.** At what price will your bond be sold? Assume annual compounding.
**b.** What will be the amount of your gain or loss over the original purchase price?
**c.** What would be the amount of your gain or loss had the treasurer originally purchased a bond with a 4-year rather than a 20-year maturity? (Assume all characteristics of the bonds are identical except their maturity periods.)
**d.** What do we call this type of risk assumed by your corporate treasurer?

**19-13B.** (*Marketable securities portfolio*) Spencer Pianos has $3.5 million in excess cash to invest in a marketable securities portfolio. Its broker will charge $15,000 to invest the entire $3.5 million. The president of Spencer wants at least half of the $3.5 million invested at a maturity period of 3 months or less; the remainder can be invested in securities with maturities not to exceed 6 months. The relevant term structure of short-term yields follows:

| Maturity Period | Available Yield (Annual) |
|---|---|
| 1 month | 6.2% |
| 2 months | 6.4 |
| 3 months | 6.5 |
| 4 months | 6.7 |
| 5 months | 6.9 |
| 6 months | 7.0 |

**a.** What should be the maturity periods of the securities purchased with the excess $3.5 million in order to maximize the before-tax income from the added investment? What will be the amount of the income from such an investment?
**b.** Suppose that the president of Spencer relaxes his constraint on the maturity structure of the added investment. What would be your profit-maximizing investment recommendation?
**c.** If one-sixth of the excess cash is invested in each of the preceding maturity categories, what would be the before-tax income generated from such an action?

**19-14B.** (*Comparison of after-tax yields*) The corporate treasurer of Ward Grocers is considering the purchase of a BBB-rated bond that carries an 8.0 percent coupon. The BBB-rated security is taxable, and the firm is in the 46 percent marginal tax bracket. The face value of this bond is $1,000. A financial analyst who reports to the corporate treasurer has alerted him to the fact that a municipal obligation is coming to the market with a 5-1/2 percent coupon. The par value of this security is also $1,000.

**a.** Which one of the two securities do you recommend the firm purchase? Why?
**b.** What must the fully taxed bond yield before tax to make it comparable with the municipal offering?

## SELF-TEST SOLUTIONS

**ST-1. a.** Initially, it is necessary to calculate Creative Fashions's average remittance check amount and the daily opportunity cost of carrying cash. The average check size is

$$\frac{\$7{,}000{,}000}{4{,}000} = \$1{,}750 \text{ per check}$$

The daily opportunity cost of carrying cash is

$$\frac{0.08}{365} = 0.0002192 \text{ per day}$$

Next, the days saved in the collection process can be evaluated according to the general format (see equation 19-1 in the text of this chapter) of

added costs = added benefits

or

$$P = (D)\,(S)\,(i) \quad \text{[see equation 17-2]}$$
$$\$0.25 = (D)(\$1{,}750)(.0002192)$$
$$0.6517 \text{ days} = D$$

Creative Fashion Designs therefore will experience a financial gain if it implements the lock-box system and by doing so will speed up its collections by more than 0.6517 days.

**b.** Here the daily opportunity cost of carrying cash is:

$$\frac{0.055}{365} = 0.0001507 \text{ per day}$$

For Creative Fashion Designs to break even, should it choose to install the lock-box system, cash collections must be accelerated by 0.9480 days, as follows:

$$\$0.25 = (D)(\$1{,}750)(.0001507)$$
$$0.9480 \text{ days} = (D)$$

**c.** The break-even cash-acceleration period of 0.9480 days is greater than the 0.6517 days found in (a). This is due to the lower yield available on near-cash assets of 5.5 percent annually, versus 8.0 percent. Because the alternative rate of return on the freed-up balances is lower in the second situation, more funds must be invested to cover the costs of operating the lock-box system. The greater cash-acceleration period generates this increased level of required funds.

**ST-2. a.** Reduction in mail float:

(2.0 days)($200,000) = $400,000
+ reduction in processing float:
(2.5 days)($200,000) = $500,000
total float reduction = $900,000

**b.** The opportunity cost of maintaining the present banking arrangement is

$$\begin{pmatrix}\text{forecast yield on marketable}\\ \text{securities portfolio}\end{pmatrix} \cdot \begin{pmatrix}\text{total float}\\ \text{reduction}\end{pmatrix}$$
$$(.106)(\$900{,}000) = \$95{,}400$$

**c.** The average number of checks to be processed each day through the lock-box arrangement is

$$\frac{\text{daily remittances}}{\text{average check size}} = \frac{\$200{,}000}{\$800} = 250 \text{ checks}$$

The resulting cost of the lock-box system on an annual basis is

(250 checks)($0.25)(270 days) = $16,875

Next we must calculate the estimated cost of the ADTC system. Detroit National Bank will *not* contribute to the cost of the ADTC arrangement, because it is the lead concentration bank and thereby receives the transferred data. This means that Artie Kay's Komputer Shops will be charged for six ADTCs (three locations @ two checks each) each business day. Therefore, the ADTC system costs:

(6 daily transfers)($20 per transfer)(270 days) = $32,400

We now have the total cost of the proposed system:

| | |
|---|---|
| Lock-box cost | $16,875 |
| ADTC cost | 32,400 |
| Total cost | $49,275 |

**d.** Our analysis suggests that Artie Kay's Komputer Shops should adopt the proposed cash receipts acceleration system. The projected net annual gain is $46,125 as follows:

| | |
|---|---|
| Projected return on freed balances | $95,400 |
| Less: Total cost of new system | 49,275 |
| Net annual gain | $46,125 |

**ST-3.a.** Here we must calculate the dollar value of the estimated return for each holding period and compare it with the transactions fee to determine if a gain can be made by investing in the securities. Those calculations and the resultant recommendations follow:

| | | | | | Recommendation |
|---|---|---|---|---|---|
| **1.** $2,000,000 (.12) (1/12) | = | $ 20,000 | < | $45,000 | No |
| **2.** $2,000,000 (.12) (2/12) | = | $ 40,000 | < | $45,000 | No |
| **3.** $2,000,000 (.12) (3/12) | = | $ 60,000 | > | $45,000 | Yes |
| **4.** $2,000,000 (.12) (6/12) | = | $120,000 | > | $45,000 | Yes |
| **5.** $2,000,000 (.12) (12/12) | = | $240,000 | > | $45,000 | Yes |

**b.** Let (x) be the required yield. With $2 million to invest for 3 months we have

$200,000(x)(3/12) = $ 45,000
$200,000(x) = $180,000
$200,000(x) = $180,000/2,000,000 = 9%

The break-even yield, therefore, is 9 percent.

# ACCOUNTS RECEIVABLE AND INVENTORY MANAGEMENT

If you ever visit Harley-Davidson in Milwaukee, you should not miss the opportunity to tour the parts and accessories division. The facilities are state of the art, but, more important, the people who work there take a tremendous pride and ownership for what happens in their part of the business. They are workers *par excellence.* But it was not always this way. ● In the early 1990s, the company was experiencing tremendous growth in all segments of the business, including parts and accessories. Having come through a turnaround in the 1980s, the distribution and logistics functions in support of this business growth were strained and in need of a strategic change of direction. In mid-1994, a team was formed to develop and implement a new strategy. ● The issues at the time were significant. Harley-Davidson's distribution center was a seven-level facility that was 84 years old. The facility was served by two freight elevators and limited technology support. In addition, the facility contained slightly over half the inventory, requiring off-site storage with daily shuttle runs to replenish stock. ● Symptoms of the situation included inventory turnover rates that were less than two turns per year, inventory accuracy levels in the 75 to 80 percent range; order cycle times from receipt of order to shipment in the 3 to 10 day range; lost inventory; inventory write-offs in the millions of dollars; and extremely low productivity. ● The new strategy was centered on creating a new facility designed around appropriate storage, automation, and technology for each class

**LEARNING OBJECTIVES**

After reading this chapter, you should be able to

1. Discuss the determinants of a firm's investment in accounts receivable and how changes in credit policy are determined.
2. Discuss the reasons for carrying inventory and how inventory management decisions are made.
3. Discuss the changes that TQM and single-sourcing have had on inventory purchasing.

of inventory to create optimum performance against a comprehensive set of metrics for cost, quality, and timing goals. In addition, a new relationship with employees called "partnering" was instituted throughout the firm. The partnering program empowered employees and capitalized on their individual and collective knowledge and skills. • The approach for the facility design began with a Pareto analysis that stratified inventory according to velocity, unit-picked versus case-picked items, hazardous materials, and special items that do not lend themselves to automated picking. For each class of inventory a unique storage and picking method was designed into the facility. • All employees were involved in designing the facilities and inventory processes. During the original design of the facility, 16 employee focus teams were engaged in evaluating all major system and process components. This process created a tremendous sense of ownership by the employees, which produced buy-in for the significant changes recommended by the focus teams. • Additionally, there was a tremendous amount of collaboration across functional lines around the need to significantly improve inventory performance enterprise-wide. This activity included the selection and implementation of a major software solution for forecasting demand and planning inventory. Targets included achieving world-class product availability and inventory turnover performance by shortening the supply lead time and by significantly reducing slow-moving and obsolete inventories. • Brian Smith, Director of Distribution and Logistics at Harley-Davidson, describes the improvements as follows:

> This project was implemented in 1997 and the results have been excellent. Inventory accuracy has been improved to the point where it is no longer an issue. Fill rates have improved dramatically and recovery time on stockouts has been substantially improved. Turnover rates have more than doubled and are approaching world-class. Slow-moving and obsolete inventories have been reduced by over 60 percent. Order cycle times to customers have become world-class, with the majority of orders shipped the same day as they are received with very high levels of reliability.

Smith continues his comments:

> The metrics do not tell the entire story, however. One of the most fascinating aspects of the new environment is the role of the employees. Let me give two examples:
>
> - One employee came up with an idea for better utilizing space in the facility. At first he had a difficult time explaining to the engineers how his idea would work. So he arranged to have a small portion of the distribution center reconfigured to show a prototype of the concept. The engineers immediately saw the benefit and worked with the employee to help develop the business case that eventually led to significant savings.
> - Another employee working in the international shipping area asked for a fairly sizable capital budget to modify the shipping conveyors in her work area to enhance the ability to stage inventory bound for international customers. Her idea was approved and implemented with benefits greater than originally envisioned.

Based on our experience, we have learned that employees are typically the masters of the universe in which they work. They know more about the issues and possible solutions than anyone else possibly could. It is the creation of a culture where every employee is encouraged to contribute ideas for improving the work processes and systems and where resources are made available for them to bring their ideas to fruition. In retrospect, it is evident that this culture may be the most important part of the solution.

In the two previous chapters, we developed a general overview of working-capital management and took an in-depth look at the management of cash and marketable securities. In this chapter, we will focus on the management of two more working-capital items: accounts receivable and inventory. Accounts receivable and inventory make up a large portion of the firm's assets; they actually compose on average 20 and 17 percent, respectively, of a typical firm's assets. Thus, because of their sheer magnitude, any changes in their levels will affect profitability.

In studying the management of these current assets, we first examine accounts receivable management, focusing on its importance, what determines investment in it, what the decision variables are, and how we determine them. Then we turn to inventory management, examine its importance, and discuss order quantity and order point problems, which in combination determine the level of investment in inventory. We also examine the relationship between inventory and total quality management.

As we will see, any changes in levels of accounts receivable and inventory will involve an application of **Principle 1: The Risk-Return Trade-Off—We won't take on additional risk unless we expect to be compensated with additional return.** This chapter will also emphasize **Principle 4: Incremental Cash Flows—It's only what changes that counts,** and **Principle 5: The Curse of Competitive Markets—Why it's hard to find exceptionally profitable projects.**

## ACCOUNTS RECEIVABLE MANAGEMENT

OBJECTIVE 1

All firms by their very nature are involved in selling either goods or services. Although some of these sales will be for cash, a large portion will involve credit. Whenever a sale is made on credit, it increases the firm's accounts receivable. Thus, the importance of how a firm manages its accounts receivable depends on the degree to which the firm sells on credit. Table 20-1 lists, for selected industries, the percentage of total assets made up by accounts receivable. The more that is sold on credit, the higher the proportion of assets that are tied up in accounts receivable. Certainly for firms in the building construction business, managing accounts receivable is important because they make up over 30 percent of a typical firm's assets.

**TABLE 20-1**
Accounts Receivable as a Percentage of Total Assets for Major Industries

| Industry | Accounts Receivable Relative to Total Assets |
|---|---|
| Total construction | 30.23 |
| General merchandising stores—retail | 28.51 |
| Building materials, garden supplies, and mobile home dealers—retail | 12.13 |
| Automotive dealers and service stations—retail | 17.53 |
| Transportation | 11.51 |
| Apparel and accessory stores—retail | 15.07 |
| Agriculture, forestry, and fishing | 8.76 |
| Food stores | 8.08 |
| Hotels and other lodging places | 6.79 |
| All industries | 20.77 |

Source: Internal Revenue Service, U.S. Treasury Department, *Statistics of Income,* 1997, *Corporate Income Tax Returns* (Washington D.C.: Government Printing Office, 1997), 15–167.

From Table 20-1, we can see that accounts receivable typically comprise about 20 percent of a firm's assets. In effect, when we discuss management of accounts receivable, we are discussing the management of one-fifth of the firm's assets. Moreover, because cash flows from a sale cannot be invested until the account is collected, control of receivables takes on added importance; efficient collection determines both profitability and liquidity of the firm.

## Size of Investment in Accounts Receivable

The size of the investment in accounts receivable is determined by several factors. First, the percentage of credit sales to total sales affects the level of accounts receivable held. Although this factor certainly plays a major role in determining a firm's investment in accounts receivable, it generally is not within the control of the financial manager. The nature of the business tends to determine the blend between credit sales and cash sales. A large grocery store tends to sell exclusively on a cash basis, whereas most construction-lumber supply firms make their sales primarily with credit. Actually, most large grocery stores allow you to use your credit card, but they receive immediate payment from the credit card company. Thus, the nature of the business, and not the decisions of the financial manager, tends to determine the proportion of credit sales.

The level of sales is also a factor in determining the size of the investment in accounts receivable. Very simply, the more sales, the greater accounts receivable. As the firm experiences seasonal and permanent growth in sales, the level of investment in accounts receivable will naturally increase. Thus, although the level of sales affects the size of the investment in accounts receivable, it is not a decision variable for the financial manager.

The final determinants of the level of investment in accounts receivable are the credit and collection policies—more specifically, the *terms of sale,* the *type of customer,* and *collection efforts.* The terms of sale specify both the time period during which the customer must pay and the terms, such as penalties for late payments or discounts for early payments. The type of customer or credit policy also affects the level of investment in accounts receivable. For example, the acceptance of poorer credit risks and their subsequent delinquent payments may lead to an increase in accounts receivable. The strength and timing of the collection efforts can affect the period for which past-due accounts remain delinquent, which in turn affects the level of accounts receivable. Collection and credit policy decisions may further affect the level of investment in accounts receivable by causing changes in the sales level and the ratio of credit sales to total sales. However, the three credit and collection policy variables are the only true decision variables under the control of the financial manager. Figure 20-1 shows where the financial manager can—and cannot—make a difference.

To conclude, as we examine the credit decision, try to remember that our goal is not to minimize losses but to maximize profits. Although we will spend a good deal of time trying to sort out those customers with the highest probability of default, this analysis is only an input into a decision based on shareholder wealth maximization. Essentially, a firm with a high profit margin can tolerate a more liberal credit policy than can a firm with a low profit margin.

**Terms of sale**
The credit terms identifying the possible discount for early payment.

TERMS OF SALE—DECISION VARIABLE The **terms of sale** identify the possible discount for early payment, the discount period, and the total credit period. They are generally stated in the form *a/b,* net *c,* indicating that the customer can deduct *a* percent if the account is paid within *b* days; otherwise, the account must be paid within *c* days. Thus, for example, trade credit terms of 2/10, net 30 indicate that a 2 percent discount can be taken if the account is paid within 10 days; otherwise it must be paid within 30 days. What if the customer decides to forgo the discount and not pay until the final payment date? If such a

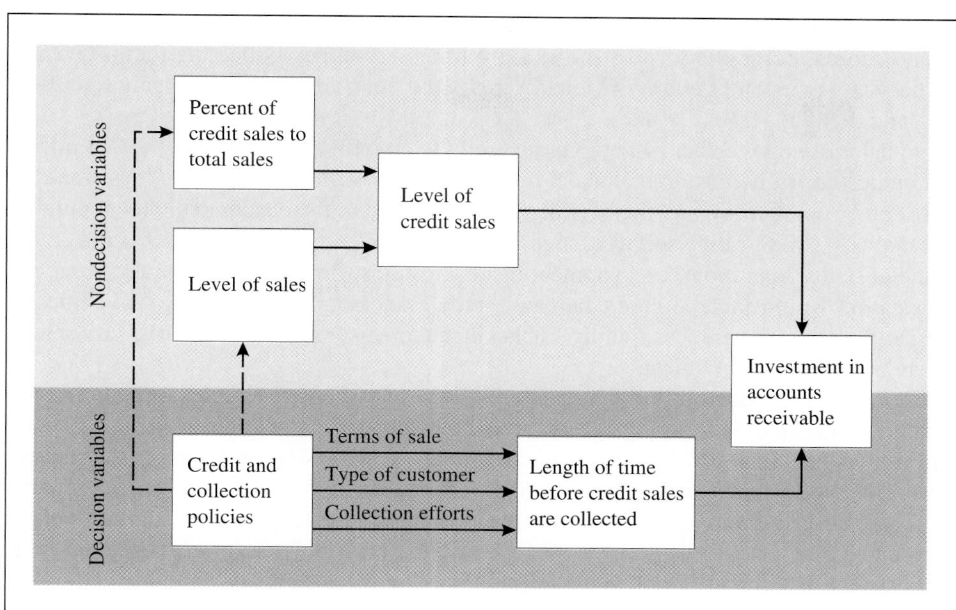


**FIGURE 20-1**
Determinants of Investment in Accounts Receivable

decision is made, the customer has the use of the money for the time period between the discount date and the final payment date. However, failure to take the discount represents a cost to the customer. For instance, if the terms are 2/10, net 30, the annualized opportunity cost of passing up this 2 percent discount in order to withhold payment for an additional 20 days is 36.73 percent. This is determined as follows:

$$\begin{pmatrix}\text{annualized opportunity cost}\\ \text{of forgoing the discount}\end{pmatrix} = \frac{a}{1-a} \times \frac{360}{c-b} \tag{20-1}$$

Substituting the values from the example, we get

$$36.73\% = \frac{.02}{1-.02} \times \frac{360}{30-10} \tag{20-2}$$

The typical discount ranges anywhere from one-half percent to 10 percent, whereas the discount period is generally 10 days and the total credit period varies from 30 to 90 days. Although the terms of credit vary radically from industry to industry, they tend to remain relatively uniform within any particular industry. Moreover, the terms tend to remain relatively constant over time, and they do not appear to be used frequently as a decision variable.

**TYPE OF CUSTOMER—DECISION VARIABLE** A second decision variable involves determining the *type of customer* who is to qualify for trade credit. Several costs always are associated with extending credit to less creditworthy customers (high-risk firms or individuals). First, as the probability of default increases, it becomes more important to identify which of the possible new customers would be a poor risk. When more time is spent investigating the less creditworthy customer, the costs of credit investigation increase.

Default costs also vary directly with the quality of the customer. As the customer's credit rating declines, the chance that the account will not be paid on time increases. In the extreme case, payment never occurs. Thus, taking on less creditworthy customers results in increases in default costs.

Collection costs also increase as the quality of the customer declines. More delinquent accounts force the firm to spend more time and money collecting them. Overall, the decline in customer quality results in increased costs of credit investigation, collection, and default.

In determining whether or not to grant credit to an individual customer, we are primarily interested in the customer's short-run ability and inclination to pay. Thus liquidity ratios, other obligations, and the overall profitability of the firm become the focal point in this analysis. Credit-rating services, such as Dun & Bradstreet, provide information on the financial status, operations, and payment history for most firms. Other possible sources of information would include credit bureaus, trade associations, Chambers of Commerce, competitors, bank references, public financial statements, and, of course, the customer's past relationship with the firm.

**Credit scoring**
The numerical credit evaluation of each candidate.

One way in which both individuals and firms are often evaluated as credit risks is through the use of credit scoring. **Credit scoring** involves the numerical evaluation of each applicant. An applicant receives a score based on his or her answers to a simple set of questions. This score is then evaluated according to a predetermined standard, its level relative to the standard determining whether or not credit should be extended. The major advantage of credit scoring is that it is inexpensive and easy to perform. For example, once the standards are set, a computer or clerical worker without any specialized training could easily evaluate any applicant.

The techniques used for constructing credit-scoring indexes range from the simple approach of adding up default rates associated with the answers given to each question, to sophisticated evaluations using multiple discriminant analysis (MDA). MDA is a statistical technique for calculating the appropriate importance to be given to each question used in evaluating the applicant. Figure 20-2 shows a credit "scorecard" used by a large automobile dealer. The weights or scores attached to each answer are based on the auto dealer's past experience with credit sales. For example, the scorecard indicates that individuals with no telephone in their home have a much higher probability of default than those with a telephone. One caveat should be mentioned: Whenever this type of questionnaire is used to evaluate credit applicants, it should be examined carefully to be sure that it does not contain any illegal discriminatory questions.

Another model that could be used for credit scoring has been provided by Edward Altman, a professor at New York University, who used multiple discriminant analysis to identify businesses that might go bankrupt. In his landmark study, Altman used financial ratios to predict which firms would go bankrupt over a 20-year period. Using multiple discriminant analysis, Altman came up with the following index:

$$Z = 3.3\left(\frac{EBIT}{\text{total assets}}\right) + 1.0\left(\frac{\text{sales}}{\text{total assets}}\right) + .6\left(\frac{\text{market value of equity}}{\text{book value of debt}}\right) + 1.4\left(\frac{\text{retained earnings}}{\text{total assets}}\right) + 1.2\left(\frac{\text{working capital}}{\text{total assets}}\right) \quad \textbf{(20-3)}$$

Altman found that of the firms that went bankrupt over this time period, 94 percent had $Z$ scores of less than 2.7 one year prior to bankruptcy and only 6 percent had scores above 2.7 percent. Conversely, of those firms that did not go bankrupt, only 3 percent had $Z$ scores below 2.7 and 97 percent had scores above 2.7.

Again, the advantages of credit-scoring techniques are low cost and ease of implementation. Simple calculations can easily spot those credit risks that need more screening before credit should be extended to them.

Telephone

| Home | Relative | None | | | | Score |
|---|---|---|---|---|---|---|
| 5 | 1 | 0 | | | | |

Living quarters

| Own home no mortgage | Own home mortgage | Rent a house | Live with someone | Rent an apartment | Rent a room | |
|---|---|---|---|---|---|---|
| 6 | 3 | 2 | 1 | 0 | 0 | |

Bank accounts

| None | 1 | More than 1 | | | | |
|---|---|---|---|---|---|---|
| 0 | 4 | 6 | | | | |

Years at present address

| Under 1/2 | 1/2–2 | 3–7 | 8 or more | | | |
|---|---|---|---|---|---|---|
| 0 | 1 | 3 | 4 | | | |

Size of family including customer

| 1 | 2 | 3–6 | 7 or more | | | |
|---|---|---|---|---|---|---|
| 2 | 4 | 3 | 0 | | | |

Monthly income

| Under $1,600 | $1,601–$1,900 | $1,901–$2,200 | $2,201–$2,800 | More than $2,800 | | |
|---|---|---|---|---|---|---|
| 0 | 1 | 3 | 6 | 8 | | |

Length of present employment

| Under 1/2 year | 1/2–2 years | 3–7 years | 8 years or more | | | |
|---|---|---|---|---|---|---|
| 0 | 1 | 2 | 4 | | | |

Percent of selling price on credit

| Under 50 | 50–69 | 70–84 | 85–99 | | | |
|---|---|---|---|---|---|---|
| 5 | 3 | 1 | 0 | | | |

Interview discretionary points (+5 to –5)

| | |
|---|---|
| | |

Total

| | |
|---|---|
| | |

Credit scorecard

(Customer's name)

(Street address)

(City, State, Zip)

(Home/Office telephone)

(Credit scorer)

Credit scorecard evaluation

Dollar amount of loan: $0–$2,000

| 0–18 | 19–21 | 22 or more |
|---|---|---|
| Reject | Refer to main credit | Accept |

Dollar amount of loan: $2,001–$5,000

| 0–21 | 22–24 | 25 or more |
|---|---|---|
| Reject | Refer to main credit | Accept |

Dollar amount of loan: more than $5,000

| 0–23 | 24–27 | 28 or more |
|---|---|---|
| Reject | Refer to main credit | Accept |

If a previous loan customer, were payments received promptly? Yes ☐ No* ☐

Are you willing to take responsibility for authorizing this loan? Yes ☐ No* ☐

*Refer to main credit if answer to either question is No.

**FIGURE 20-2**
Credit "Scorecard"

**RELATE TO THE BIG PICTURE**

The credit decision is another application of **Principle 1: The Risk-Return Trade-Off—We won't take on additional risk unless we expect to be compensated with additional return.** The risk is the chance of nonpayment whereas the return stems from additional sales. Although it may be tempting to look at the credit decision as a yes or no decision based on some "black-box" formula, keep in mind that simply looking at the immediate future in making a credit decision may be a mistake. If extending a customer credit means that the customer may become a regular customer in the future, it may be appropriate to take a risk that otherwise would not be prudent. In effect, our goal is to ensure that all cash flows affected by the decision at hand are considered, not simply the most immediate cash flows.

COLLECTION EFFORTS—DECISION VARIABLE The key to maintaining control over collection of accounts receivable is the fact that the probability of default increases with the age of the account. Thus, control of accounts receivable focuses on the control and elimination of past-due receivables. One common way of evaluating the current situation is ratio analysis. The financial manager can determine whether or not accounts receivable are under control by examining the average collection period, the ratio of receivables to assets, the ratio of credit sales to receivables (called the *accounts receivable turnover ratio*), and the amount of bad debts relative to sales over time. In addition, the manager can perform what is called an *aging of accounts receivable* to provide a breakdown in both dollars and in percentages of the proportion of receivables that are past due. Comparing the current aging of receivables with past data offers even more control. An example of an *aging account* or *schedule* appears in Table 20-2.

The aging schedule provides you with a listing of how long your accounts receivable have been outstanding. Once the delinquent accounts have been identified, the firm's accounts receivable group makes an effort to collect them. For example, a past-due letter, called a *dunning letter,* is sent if payment is not received on time, followed by an additional dunning letter in a more serious tone if the account becomes 3 weeks past due, followed after 6 weeks by a telephone call. Finally, if the account becomes 12 weeks past due, it might be turned over to a collection agency. Again, a direct trade-off exists between collection expenses and lost goodwill on one hand and noncollection of accounts on the other, and this trade-off is always part of making the decision.

Thus far, we have discussed the importance and role of accounts receivable in the firm and then examined the determinants of the size of the investment in accounts receivable. We have focused on credit and collection policies, because these are the only discretionary variables for management. In examining these decision variables, we have simply described their traits. These variables are analyzed in a decision-making process called *marginal* or *incremental analysis.*

**TABLE 20-2**
Aging Account

| Age of Accounts Receivable (Days) | | Dollar Value (00) | Percent of Total |
|---|---|---|---|
| 0–30 | | $2,340 | 39% |
| 31–60 | | 1,500 | 25 |
| 61–90 | | 1,020 | 17 |
| 91–120 | | 720 | 12 |
| Over 120 | | 420 | 7 |
| | Total | $6,000 | 100% |

## Credit Policy Changes: The Use of Marginal or Incremental Analysis

Changes in credit policy involve direct trade-offs between costs and benefits. When credit policies are eased, sales and profits from customers increase. Conversely, easing credit policies can also involve an increase in bad debts, additional funds tied up in accounts receivable and inventory, and additional costs from customers taking a cash discount. Given these costs, when is it appropriate for a firm to change its credit policy? The answer is when the increased sales generate enough in the way of new profit to more than offset the increased costs associated with the change. Determining whether this is so is the job of **marginal** or **incremental analysis.** In general, there are three categories of changes in credit policy that a firm can consider: a change in the risk class of the customer, a change in the collection process, or a change in the discount terms. To illustrate, let us follow through an example.

**Marginal or incremental analysis**
A method of analysis for credit policy changes in which the incremental benefits are compared to the added costs.

**RELATE TO THE BIG PICTURE**

Marginal or incremental analysis is a direct application of **Principle 4: Incremental Cash Flows—It's only what changes that counts** into the credit analysis decision process. What we are really doing in marginal analysis is looking at all the cash flows to the company as a whole with the change in credit policy versus those cash flows without making the credit policy change. Then, if the benefits resulting from the change outweigh the costs, the change should be made.

**EXAMPLE**

Assume that Denis Electronics currently has annual sales, all credit, of $8 million and an average collection period of 30 days. The current level of bad debt is $240,000 and the firm's pre-tax opportunity cost or required rate of return is 15 percent. Further assume that the firm produces only one product, with variable costs equaling 75 percent of the selling price. The company is considering a change in the credit terms from the current terms of net 30 to 1/30, net 60. If this change is made, it is expected that half of the customers will take the discount and pay on the thirtieth day, whereas the other half will pass the discount and pay on the sixtieth day. This will increase the average collection period from 30 days to 45 days. The major reason Denis Electronics is considering this change is that it will generate additional sales of $1,000,000. Although the sales from these new customers will generate new profits, they will also generate more bad debts; however, it is assumed that the level of bad debts on the original sales will remain constant, and that the level of bad debts on the new sales will be 6 percent of those sales. In addition, to service the new sales, it will be necessary to increase the level of average inventory from $1,000,000 to $1,025,000.

Let's see how to evaluate this. Marginal or incremental analysis involves a comparison of the incremental profit contribution from new sales with the incremental costs resulting from the change in credit policy. If the benefits outweigh the costs, the change should be

**TABLE 20-3**
Denis Electronics: Relevant Information for Incremental Analysis

| | |
|---|---|
| New sales level (all credit) | $9,000,000 |
| Original sales level (all credit) | $8,000,000 |
| Contribution margin | 25% |
| Percent bad debt losses on new sales | 6% |
| New average collection period | 45 days |
| Original average collection period | 30 days |
| Additional investment in inventory | $25,000 |
| Pre-tax required rate of return | 15% |
| New percent cash discount | 1% |
| Percent of customers taking the cash discount | 50% |

made. If not, the credit policy should remain as is. A four-step procedure for performing marginal or incremental analysis on a change in credit policy is:

Step 1: Estimate the change in profit.
Step 2: Estimate the cost of additional investment in accounts receivable and inventory.
Step 3: Estimate the cost of the discount (if a change in the cash discount is enacted).
Step 4: Compare the incremental revenues with the incremental costs.

Table 20-3 provides a summary of the relevant information concerning Denis's proposed credit change, whereas Table 20-4 provides the results of the incremental analysis.

In Step 1 of the analysis, the additional profits less bad debts from the new sales are calculated to be $190,000. In Step 2, the additional investment in accounts receivable and inventory is determined to be $458,340. Because the pre-tax required rate of return is 15 percent, the company's required return on this investment is $72,501. In Step 3, the cost of introducing a cash discount is determined to be $45,000. Finally, in Step 4, the benefits and costs are compared, and the net change in pre-tax profits is determined to be $72,499. Thus, a change in the present credit policy is warranted.

In summary, the logic behind this approach to credit policy is to examine the incremental or marginal benefits from such a change and compare these with the incremental or marginal costs. If the change promises more benefits than costs, the change should be made. If, however, the incremental costs are greater than the benefits, the proposed change should not be made. Figure 20-3 graphs this process: The point where marginal costs equal marginal benefits occurs at credit policy A.

In summary, the calculations associated with the incremental analysis of a change in credit policy illustrate the changes that occur when credit policy is adjusted. On the positive side, a loosening of credit policy should increase sales. On the negative side, bad debts, investment in accounts receivable and inventory, and costs associated with the cash discount all increase. The decision then boils down to whether the incremental benefits outweigh the incremental costs.

## CONCEPT CHECK

1. What factors influence the size of a firm's investment in accounts receivable? Which one(s) of these factors can the financial manager control?
2. What costs are associated with extending credit to high-risk firms or individuals?
3. How can a firm evaluate the credit risk of its customers?
4. Explain the two models of credit scoring. What are the advantages and disadvantages of using these models?
5. Describe the technique of marginal analysis of changing a firm's credit policy.

**TABLE 20-4**
Denis Electronics: Incremental Analysis of a Change in Credit Policy

**Step 1: Estimate the change in profit.** This is equal to the increased sales times the profit contribution on those sales less any additional bad debts incurred.

= (increased sales × contribution margin) − (increased sales × percent bad debt losses on new sales)

= ($1,000,000 × .25) − ($1,000,000 × .06)

= $190,000

**Step 2: Estimate the cost of additional investment in accounts receivable and inventory.** This involves first calculating the change in the investment in accounts receivable. The new and original levels of investment in accounts receivable are calculated by multiplying the daily sales level times the average collection period. The additional investment in inventory is added to this, and the sum is then multiplied by the pre-tax required rate of return.

$$= \begin{pmatrix} \text{additional} & & \text{additional} \\ \text{accounts} & + & \text{inventory} \\ \text{receivable} & & \end{pmatrix} \times \begin{pmatrix} \text{pre-tax required} \\ \text{rate of return} \end{pmatrix}$$

First, calculate the additional investment in accounts receivable.

$$\begin{pmatrix} \text{additional} \\ \text{accounts} \\ \text{receivable} \end{pmatrix} = \begin{pmatrix} \text{new level} \\ \text{of daily} \\ \text{sales} \end{pmatrix} \times \begin{pmatrix} \text{new average} \\ \text{collection} \\ \text{period} \end{pmatrix} - \begin{pmatrix} \text{original level} \\ \text{of daily} \\ \text{sales} \end{pmatrix} \times \begin{pmatrix} \text{original average} \\ \text{collection} \\ \text{period} \end{pmatrix}$$

$$= \left(\frac{\$9{,}000{,}000}{360} \times 45\right) - \left(\frac{\$8{,}000{,}000}{360} \times 30\right)$$

= $458,340

Second, add additional investments in accounts receivable ($458,340) and inventory ($25,000) and multiply this total times the pre-tax required rate of return.

= ($458,340 + $25,000) × .15

= $72,501

**Step 3: Estimate the change in the cost of the cash discount (if a change in the cash discount is enacted).** This is equal to the new level of sales times the new percent cash discount times the percent of customers taking the discount, less the original level of sales times the original percent cash discount times percent of customers taking the discount.

$$= \begin{pmatrix} \text{new} \\ \text{level} \\ \text{of} \\ \text{sales} \end{pmatrix} \times \begin{pmatrix} \text{new} \\ \text{percent} \\ \text{cash} \\ \text{discount} \end{pmatrix} \times \begin{pmatrix} \text{percent} \\ \text{customers} \\ \text{taking} \\ \text{discount} \end{pmatrix} - \begin{pmatrix} \text{original} \\ \text{level} \\ \text{of} \\ \text{sales} \end{pmatrix} \times \begin{pmatrix} \text{original} \\ \text{percent} \\ \text{cash} \\ \text{discount} \end{pmatrix} \times \begin{pmatrix} \text{original} \\ \text{percent} \\ \text{taking} \\ \text{discount} \end{pmatrix}$$

= ($9,000,000 × .01 × .50) − ($8,000 000 × .00 × .00)

= $45,000

**Step 4: Compare the incremental revenues with the incremental costs.**

$$\begin{matrix} \text{net change} \\ \text{in pre-tax} \\ \text{profits} \end{matrix} = \begin{matrix} \text{change} \\ \text{in} \\ \text{profits} \end{matrix} - \begin{pmatrix} \text{cost of new} & & \text{cost of} \\ \text{investment in} & + & \text{change in} \\ \text{accounts receivable} & & \text{cash} \\ \text{and inventory} & & \text{discount} \end{pmatrix}$$

= Step 1 − (Step 2 + Step 3)

= $190,000 − ($72,501 + $45,000)

= $72,499

**FIGURE 20-3**
Credit Policy Changes and Profits

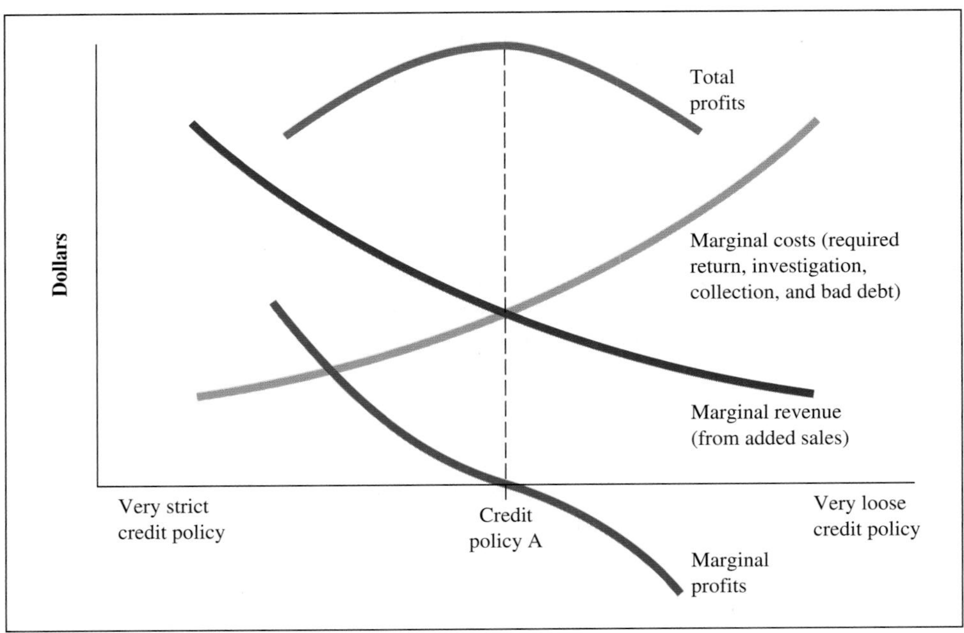


## INVENTORY MANAGEMENT

OBJECTIVE 2 

**Inventory management**
The control of the assets used in the production process or produced to be sold in the normal course of the firm's operations.

**Inventory management** involves the control of the assets that are used in the production process or produced to be sold in the normal course of the firm's operations. The general categories of inventory include raw materials inventory, work-in-process inventory, and finished goods inventory. The importance of inventory management to the firm depends on the extent of the inventory investment. For an average firm, approximately 16.94 percent of all assets are in the form of inventory. However, the percentage varies widely from industry to industry, as Table 20-5 shows. Thus, the importance of inventory management and control varies from industry to industry also. For example, it is much more important in the automotive dealer and service station trade, where inventories make up 41.41 percent of total assets, than in the hotel business, where the average investment in inventory is only 1.22 percent of total assets.

**TABLE 20-5**
Inventory as a Percentage of Total Assets for Major Industries

| Industry | Inventory Relative to Total Assets |
|---|---|
| Automotive dealers and service stations—retail | 41.41% |
| Building materials, garden supplies, and mobile home dealers—retail | 33.85 |
| Apparel and accessory stores | 26.20 |
| Food stores | 19.88 |
| Total construction | 14.33 |
| Agriculture, forestry, and fishing | 7.29 |
| Electrical and electronic equipment | 6.09 |
| Petroleum and coal products | 17.67 |
| Eating and drinking places | 2.91 |
| Hotels and other lodging places | 1.22 |
| All industries | 16.94 |

Source: Internal Revenue Service, U.S. Treasury Department, *Statistics of Income,* 1997 *Corporate Income Tax Returns* (Washington D.C.: Government Printing Office, 1997), 15–167.

## Purposes and Types of Inventory

The purpose of carrying inventories is to uncouple the operations of the firm—that is, to make each function of the business independent of each other function—so that delays or shutdowns in one area do not affect the production and sale of the final product. For example, in the auto industry, a strike or shutdown in a parts plant may shut down several assembly plants. Because production shutdowns result in increased costs, and because delays in delivery can lose customers, the management and control of inventory are important duties of the financial manager. To better illustrate the uncoupling function that inventories perform, we will look at several general types of inventories.

### RELATE TO THE BIG PICTURE

The decision as to how much inventory to keep on hand is a direct application of **Principle 1: The Risk-Return Trade-Off—We won't take on additional risk unless we expect to be compensated with additional return.** The risk is that if the level of inventory is too low, the various functions of business do not operate independently and delays in production and customer delivery can result. The return results because reduced inventory investment saves money. As the size of inventory increases, storage and handling costs as well as the required return on capital invested in inventory rise. Therefore, as the inventory a firm holds is increased, the risk of running out of inventory is lessened, but inventory expenses rise.

RAW MATERIALS INVENTORY **Raw materials inventory** consists of basic materials purchased from other firms to be used in the firm's production operations. These goods may include steel, lumber, petroleum, or manufactured items such as wire, ball bearings, or tires that the firm does not produce itself. Regardless of the specific form of the raw materials inventory, all manufacturing firms by definition maintain a raw materials inventory. Its purpose is to uncouple the production function from the purchasing function—that is, to make these two functions independent of each other, so that delays in shipment of raw materials do not cause production delays. In the event of a delay in shipment, the firm can satisfy its need for raw materials by liquidating its inventory. During the 1991 war with Iraq, many firms that used petroleum as an input in production built up their petroleum inventories in anticipation of a slowdown or possibly a stoppage in the flow of oil from the Middle East. This buildup in raw material inventory would have allowed those firms with adequate inventories to continue production even if the war had severely cut the flow of oil.

**Raw materials inventory** This includes the basic materials purchased from other firms to be used in the firm's production operations.

WORK-IN-PROCESS INVENTORY **Work-in-process inventory** consists of partially finished goods requiring additional work before they become finished goods. The more complex and lengthy the production process, the larger the investment in work-in-process inventory. The purpose of work-in-process inventory is to uncouple the various operations in the production process so that machine failures and work stoppages in one operation will not affect the other operations. Assume, for example, there are 10 different production operations, each one involving the piece of work produced in the previous operation. If the machine performing the first production operation breaks down, a firm with no work-in-process inventory will have to shut down all 10 production operations. Yet if a firm has such inventory, the remaining nine operations can continue by drawing the input for the second operation from inventory rather than directly from the output of the first operation.

**Work-in-process inventory** Partially finished goods requiring additional work before they become finished goods.

**Finished-goods inventory** Goods on which the production has been completed but that are not yet sold.

FINISHED-GOODS INVENTORY The **finished-goods inventory** consists of goods on which the production has been completed but that are not yet sold. The purpose of finished-goods inventory is to uncouple the production and sales functions so that it is not necessary to produce the good before a sale can occur—sales can be made directly out of inventory. In the auto industry, for example, people would not buy from a dealer who made them wait weeks or months, when another dealer could fill the order immediately.

STOCK OF CASH Although we discussed cash management at some length in Chapter 19, it is worthwhile to mention cash again in the light of inventory management. This is because the *stock of cash* carried by a firm is simply a special type of inventory. In terms of uncoupling the various operations of the firm, the purpose of holding a stock of cash is to make the payment of bills independent of the collection of accounts due. When cash is kept on hand, bills can be paid without prior collection of accounts.

As we examine and develop inventory economic ordering quantity (*EOQ*) models, we will see a striking resemblance between the *EOQ* inventory and *EOQ* cash model; in fact, except for a minor redefinition of terms, they will be exactly the same.

## Inventory-Management Techniques

The importance of effective inventory management is directly related to the size of the investment in inventory. Because, on average, approximately 16.94 percent of a firm's assets are tied up in inventory, effective management of these assets is essential to the goal of shareholder wealth maximization. To control the investment in inventory, management must solve two problems: the order quantity problem and the order point problem.

**Order quantity problem** Determining the optimal order size for an inventory item given its usage, carrying costs, and ordering costs.

ORDER QUANTITY PROBLEM The **order quantity problem** involves determining the optimal order size for an inventory item given its expected usage, carrying costs, and ordering costs. Aside from a change in some of the variable names, it is exactly the same as the inventory model for cash management (*EOQ* model) presented in Chapter 19.

The *EOQ* model attempts to determine the order size that will minimize total inventory costs. It assumes that

$$\text{total inventory costs} = \text{total carrying costs} + \text{total ordering costs} \tag{20-4}$$

Assuming that inventory is allowed to fall to zero and then is immediately replenished (this assumption will be lifted when we discuss the order point problem), the average inventory becomes $Q/2$, where $Q$ is inventory order size in units. This can be seen graphically in Figure 20-4.

If the average inventory is $Q/2$ and the carrying cost per unit is $C$, then carrying costs become:

$$\begin{matrix}\text{total} \\ \text{carrying costs}\end{matrix} = \left(\begin{matrix}\text{average} \\ \text{inventory}\end{matrix}\right)\left(\begin{matrix}\text{carrying cost} \\ \text{per unit}\end{matrix}\right) \tag{20-5}$$

$$= \left(\frac{Q}{2}\right)C \tag{20-6}$$

where $Q$ = the inventory order size in units
$C$ = carrying cost per unit

The carrying costs on inventory include the required rate of return on investment in inventory, in addition to warehouse or storage costs, wages for those who operate the warehouse, and costs associated with inventory shrinkage. Thus, carrying costs include both real cash flows and opportunity costs associated with having funds tied up in inventory.

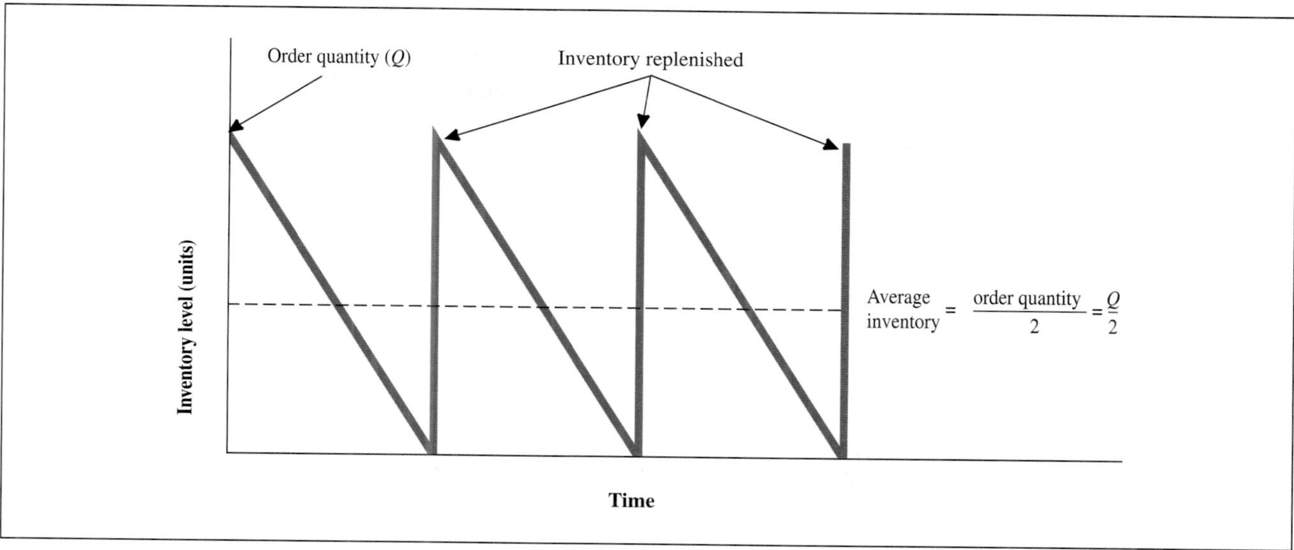


**FIGURE 20-4**
Inventory Level and the Replenishment Cycle

The ordering costs incurred are equal to the ordering costs per order times the number of orders. If we assume total demand over the planning period is *S* and we order in lot sizes of *Q*, then *S/Q* represents the number of orders over the planning period. If the ordering cost per order is *O*, then

$$\text{total ordering costs} = \left(\text{number of orders}\right)\left(\text{ordering cost per order}\right) \tag{20-7}$$

$$= \left(\frac{S}{Q}\right)O \tag{20-8}$$

where $S$ = total demand in units over the planning period
$O$ = ordering cost per order

Thus, total costs in equation 20-4 become

$$\text{total costs} = \left(\frac{Q}{2}\right)C + \left(\frac{S}{Q}\right)O \tag{20-9}$$

Figure 20-5 illustrates this equation graphically. As you can see, as the order size increases, so do the carrying costs, because you are holding more inventory. Eventually, the increased carrying costs outweigh the savings in ordering costs from not placing as many orders. At that point, total costs are minimized.

What we are looking for is the ordering size, $Q^*$, that provides the minimum total costs. By manipulating equation 20-9, we find that the optimal value of *Q*—that is, the economic ordering quantity (*EOQ*)—is

$$Q^* = \sqrt{\frac{2SO}{C}} \tag{20-10}$$

The use of the *EOQ* model can best be illustrated through an example.

**FIGURE 20-5**
Total Cost and *EOQ* Determination

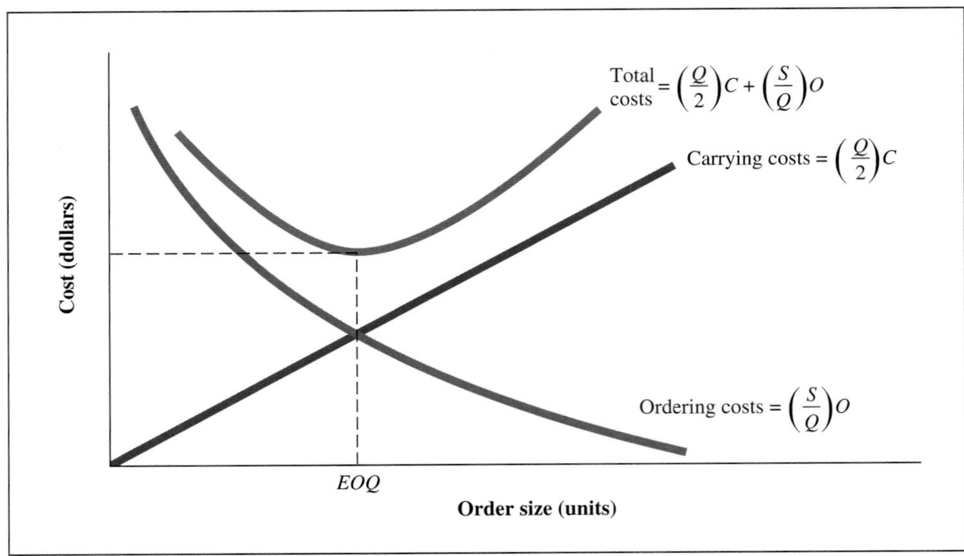


**EXAMPLE**

Suppose a firm expects total demand ($S$) for its product over the planning period to be 5,000 units, whereas the ordering cost per order ($O$) is \$200, and the carrying cost per unit ($C$) is \$2. Substituting these values into equation (20-10) yields

$$Q^* = \sqrt{\frac{2 \times 5{,}000 \times 200}{2}} = \sqrt{1{,}000{,}000} = 1{,}000 \text{ unit}$$

Thus, if this firm orders in 1,000-unit lot sizes, it will minimize its total inventory costs.

Despite the fact that the *EOQ* model tends to yield quite good results, there are weaknesses in the *EOQ* model associated with several of its assumptions. When its assumptions have been dramatically violated, the *EOQ* model can generally be modified to accommodate the situation. The model's assumptions are as follows:

**Safety stock**
Inventory held to accommodate any unusually large and unexpected usage during delivery time.

1. **Constant or uniform demand.** Although the *EOQ* model assumes constant demand, demand may vary from day to day. If demand is stochastic—that is, not known in advance—the model must be modified through the inclusion of a **safety stock,** that is, the inventory held to accommodate any unusually large and unexpected usage during the delivery time.
2. **Constant unit price.** The inclusion of variable prices resulting from quantity discounts can be handled quite easily through a modification of the original *EOQ* model, redefining total costs and solving for the optimum order quantity.
3. **Constant carrying costs.** Unit carrying costs may vary substantially as the size of the inventory rises, perhaps decreasing because of economies of scale or storage efficiency or increasing as storage space runs out and new warehouses have to be rented. This situation can be handled through a modification in the original model similar to the one used for variable unit price.
4. **Constant ordering costs.** Although this assumption is generally valid, its violation can be accommodated by modifying the original *EOQ* model in a manner similar to the one used for variable unit price.

5. **Instantaneous delivery.** If delivery is not instantaneous, which is generally the case, the original *EOQ* model must be modified through the inclusion of a safety stock.
6. **Independent orders.** If multiple orders result in cost savings by reducing paperwork and transportation cost, the original *EOQ* model must be further modified. Although this modification is somewhat complicated, special *EOQ* models have been developed to deal with it.

These assumptions illustrate the limitations of the basic *EOQ* model and the ways in which it can be modified to compensate for them. An understanding of the limitations and assumptions of the *EOQ* model provides the financial manager with more of a base for making inventory decisions.

## Order Point Problem

The two most limiting assumptions—those of constant or uniform demand and instantaneous delivery—are dealt with through the inclusion of safety stock, which is the inventory held to accommodate any unusually large and unexpected usage during delivery time. The decision on how much safety stock to hold is generally referred to as the **order point problem;** that is, how low inventory should be depleted before it is reordered.

**Order point problem**
Determining how low inventory should be depleted before it is reordered.

Two factors go into the determination of the appropriate order point: (1) the procurement or delivery-time stock and (2) the safety stock desired. Figure 20-6 graphs the process involved in order point determination. We observe that the order point problem can be decomposed into its two components, the **delivery-time stock**—that is, the inventory needed between the order date and receipt of the inventory ordered—and the safety stock. Thus, the order point is reached when inventory falls to a level equal to the delivery-time stock plus the safety stock.

**Delivery-time stock**
The inventory needed between the order date and the receipt of the inventory ordered.

Inventory order point can be determined as follows:

$$\begin{bmatrix}\text{order new inventory} \\ \text{when the level of} \\ \text{inventory falls to} \\ \text{this level}\end{bmatrix} = \begin{pmatrix}\text{delivery-time} \\ \text{stock}\end{pmatrix} + \begin{pmatrix}\text{safety} \\ \text{stock}\end{pmatrix} \tag{20-11}$$

As a result of constantly carrying safety stock, the average level of inventory increases. Whereas before the inclusion of safety stock the average level of inventory was equal to *EOQ*/2, now it will be

$$\text{average inventory} = \frac{EOQ}{2} + \text{safety stock} \tag{20-12}$$

In general, several factors simultaneously determine how much delivery-time stock and safety stock should be held. First, the efficiency of the replenishment system affects how much delivery-time stock is needed. Because the delivery-time stock is the expected inventory usage between ordering and receiving inventory, efficient replenishment of inventory would reduce the need for delivery-time stock.

The uncertainty surrounding both the delivery time and the demand for the product affects the level of safety stock needed. The more certain the patterns of these inflows and outflows from the inventory, the less safety stock required. In effect, if these inflows and outflows are highly predictable, then there is little chance of any stockout occurring. However, if they are unpredictable, it becomes necessary to carry additional safety stock to prevent unexpected stockouts.

**FIGURE 20-6**
Order Point Determination

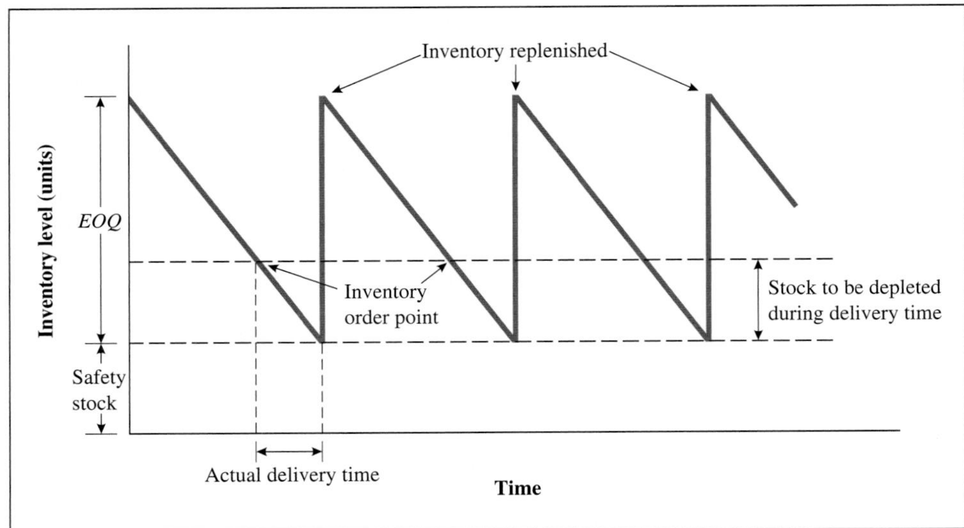


The safety margin desired also affects the level of safety stock held. If it is a costly experience to run out of inventory, the safety stock held will be larger than it would be otherwise. If running out of inventory and the subsequent delay in supplying customers result in strong customer dissatisfaction and the possibility of lost future sales, then additional safety stock is necessary. A final determinant is the cost of carrying additional inventory, in terms of both the handling and storage costs and the opportunity cost associated with the investment in additional inventory. Very simply, the greater the costs, the smaller the safety stock.

The determination of the level of safety stock involves a basic trade-off between the risk of stockout, resulting in possible customer dissatisfaction and lost sales, and the increased costs associated with carrying additional inventory.

## Inflation and EOQ

**Anticipatory buying**
Buying in anticipation of a price increase to secure goods at a lower cost.

Inflation affects the *EOQ* model in two major ways. First, although the *EOQ* model can be modified to assume constant price increases, often major price increases occur only once or twice a year and are announced ahead of time. If this is the case, the *EOQ* model may lose its applicability and may be replaced with **anticipatory buying**—that is, buying in anticipation of a price increase to secure the goods at a lower cost. Of course, as with most decisions, there are trade-offs. The costs are the added carrying costs associated with the inventory. The benefits, of course, come from buying at a lower price. The second way inflation affects the *EOQ* model is through increased carrying costs. As inflation pushes interest rates up, the cost of carrying inventory increases. In our *EOQ* model, this means that $C$ increases, which results in a decline in $Q^*$, the optimal economic order quantity:

$$\downarrow Q^* = \sqrt{\frac{2SO}{C\uparrow}} \tag{20-13}$$

Reluctance to stock large inventories because of high carrying costs became particularly prevalent during the late 1970s and early 1980s, when inflation and interest rates were at high levels.

## Just-in-Time Inventory Control

**Just-in-time inventory control system**
Keeping inventory to a minimum and relying on suppliers to furnish parts "just in time."

The **just-in-time inventory control system** is more than just an inventory control system, it is a production and management system. Not only is inventory cut down to a minimum, but the time and physical distance between the various production operations are also reduced. In addition, management is willing to trade off costs to develop close relationships with suppliers and promote speedy replenishment of inventory in return for the ability to hold less safety stock.

The just-in-time inventory control system was originally developed in Japan by Taiichi Okno, a vice-president of Toyota. Originally, the system was called the *kanban* system, named after the cards that were placed in the parts bins that were used to call for a new supply. The idea behind the system is that the firm should keep a minimum level of inventory on hand, relying on suppliers to furnish parts "just in time" for them to be assembled. This is in direct contrast to the traditional inventory philosophy of U.S. firms, which is sometimes referred to as a "just-in-case" system, which keeps healthy levels of safety stocks to ensure that production will not be interrupted. Although large inventories may not be a bad idea when interest rates are low, they become very costly when interest rates are high.

Although the just-in-time inventory system is intuitively appealing, it has not proved easy to implement. Long distances from suppliers and plants constructed with too much space for storage and not enough access (doors and loading docks) to receive inventory have limited successful implementation. But many firms have been forced to change their relationships with their suppliers. Because firms rely on suppliers to deliver high-quality parts and materials immediately, they must have a close, long-term relationship with them. Despite the difficulties of implementation, many U.S. firms have moved to cut inventory—in some cases, through the use of a just-in-time inventory system. General Motors and NCR are just two of the many firms that have moved at least some of their operations to a just-in-time system. Dell Computer is a classic example of using a just-in-time inventory system for finished-goods inventory. Dell does not carry any finished-goods inventory because it does not assemble any computers until they are ordered. In fact, the average level of inventory relative to total assets for all American corporations has fallen over time, partly because of just-in-time systems.

Although the just-in-time system does not at first appear to bear much of a relationship to the *EOQ* model, it simply alters some of the assumptions of the model with respect to delivery time and ordering costs, and draws out the implications. Actually, it is just a new approach to the *EOQ* model that tries to produce the lowest average level of inventory possible. If we look at the average level of inventory as defined by the *EOQ* model, we find it to be

$$\text{average inventory} = \sqrt{\frac{2SO\downarrow}{C}} + \text{safety stock}\downarrow$$

The just-in-time system attacks this equation in two places. First, by locating inventory supplies in convenient locations, laying out plants in such a way that it is inexpensive and easy to unload new inventory shipments, and computerizing the inventory order system, the cost of ordering new inventory, $O$, is reduced. Second, by developing a strong relationship with suppliers located in the same geographical area and setting up restocking strategies that cut time, the safety stock is also reduced. The philosophy behind the just-in-time inventory system is that the benefits associated with reducing inventory and delivery time to a bare minimum through adjustment in the *EOQ* model will more than offset the costs associated with the increased possibility of stockouts.

Although just-in-time inventory systems seem to do a great job of reducing inventory costs, if there is ever a breakdown in the supply of inventory to the system, the results can be catastrophic. Take, for example, General Motors, which has saved millions of dollars by going to a just-in-time system. In 1996, General Motors was hit by a strike that involved about 3,000 workers at two of its plants that produced brakes for the cars GM makes. As a result of not having brakes to put in cars, GM was forced to stop production and lay off over 177,000 workers. Moreover, because GM used a just-in-time inventory system, it didn't take long for the shutdown of the brake plant to affect all of GM's other operations.

Now let's take a look at exactly how a just-in-time inventory system works. Ford Motor Company's Avon Lake, Ohio, plant, which produces the Mercury Villager and the Nissan Quest minivans, uses a just-in-time inventory system. In fact, some inventory is limited to a supply of only a few hours, whereas other inventory carries supplies up to several days. To allow for this constant resupply of inventory, Ford built the plant with 65 dock doors placed around the plant so that inventory would arrive as close as possible to the location where it was to be used.

In addition, Ford worked with suppliers so that much of the inventory would arrive partially assembled. For example, tires and wheels came pre-assembled by Bridgestone. These arrive several times a day delivered in the order in which they are to be used—with each fifth tire delivered being a spare. Seats also arrived hourly, already preassembled, from a supplier located just 25 miles away. In addition, the seats are arranged in the order they are to be used and arrive on the assembly line by conveyors directly from the delivery trucks ready to use. In effect, the only inventory time for tires and seats is when they are on the delivery truck waiting to be unloaded. Thus, Ford's just-in-time inventory system allows for a dramatically reduced level of investment in inventory by allowing for a continuous flow and resupply of inventory. The end result of all this reduced investment is increased profits.

### CONCEPT CHECK

1. Describe the types of inventory a firm holds and the purpose of each type. How is a firm's stock of cash similar to inventory?
2. What is the objective of the order quantity model? What assumptions are made in developing this model?
3. What is the objective of the order point model? Describe the factors that determine the levels of delivery-time stock and safety stock.
4. Explain the just-in-time inventory system. What factors increase the likelihood of successful implementation of a just-in-time system?

## TQM AND INVENTORY-PURCHASING MANAGEMENT: THE NEW SUPPLIER RELATIONSHIPS

OBJECTIVE 3 

**Total quality management (TQM)**
A company-wide systems approach to quality.

Out of the concept of **total quality management (TQM),** which is a company-wide systems approach to quality, has come a new philosophy in inventory management of "love thy supplier." Under this approach, the traditional antagonistic relationship between suppliers and customers, where suppliers are coldly dropped when a cheaper source can be found, is being replaced by a new order in customer-supplier relationships. In effect, what began as an effort to increase quality through closer supplier relations has turned out to have unexpected benefits. Close customer relationships have helped trim costs, in part, by allowing for the production of higher-quality products. This close customer-supplier relationship has allowed the TQM philosophy to be passed across company boundaries to the supplier, enabling the firm to tap the supplier's expertise in designing higher-quality products. In addition, the interdependence between the supplier and customer has also allowed for the development and introduction of new products at a pace much faster than previously possible.

As we have seen, inventory can make up a rather large percentage of a firm's assets. That by itself lends importance to the role of inventory management and, more specifically, purchasing. In terms of manufacturing costs, purchased materials have historically accounted for 50 percent of U.S. and about 70 percent of Japanese manufacturing costs, and most manufacturers purchase more than 50 percent of their parts. Thus, it is hard to overstate the importance of purchasing to the firm.

The traditional purchasing philosophy is to purchase a part or material from a variety of different suppliers, with the suppliers contracting out to a number of different firms. In fact, many companies put an upper limit of 10 or 20 percent on the purchases of any part from a single supplier. The reasoning behind this is that the company can diversify away the effects of poor quality by any one supplier. Thus, if one supplier is unable to meet delivery schedules, delivers a poor quality batch, or even goes out of business, this affects only a small percent of the total parts or material. However, efforts to raise quality have led to a new approach to the customer-supplier relationship called **single-sourcing.**

**Single-sourcing** Using a single supplier as a source for a particular part or material.

Under single-sourcing, a company uses very few suppliers or, in many cases, a single supplier, as a source for a particular part or material. In this way, the company has more direct influence and control over the quality performance of a supplier because the company accounts for a larger proportion of the supplier's volume. The company and supplier can then enter into a partnership, referred to as *partnering,* where the supplier agrees to meet the quality standards of the customer in terms of parts, material, service, and delivery. In this way, the supplier can be brought into the TQM program of the customer. In return, the company enters into a long-term purchasing agreement with the supplier that includes a stable order and delivery schedule. For example, on General Motor's Quad 4 engine (its first new engine in several decades), every part except the engine block is single-sourced, resulting in only 69 total suppliers—half the normal number for a production engine. In return for the suppliers' assurances of top quality and low cost, GM guaranteed the suppliers their jobs for the life of the engine. In the development of its new LH cars, the Chrysler Concorde, the Dodge Intrepid, and the Eagle Vision, Chrysler trimmed its supplier base from 3,000 to less than 1,000 by the mid-1990s. Single-sourcing clearly creates an environment of cooperation between customers and suppliers where both share the common goal of quality.

Although the partnering relationship results in higher-quality parts, it can also improve the quality of the design process by allowing for the involvement of the supplier in production design. For example, the supplier may be given the responsibility of designing a new part or component to meet the quality standards and features outlined by the company. When Guardian Industries of Northville, Michigan, developed an oversized solar glass windshield for Chrysler's LH cars, its engineers met on almost a daily basis with the Chrysler design team to make sure the quality, features, and cost of the windshield met Chrysler standards. To produce the windshields, Guardian opened a new $35 million plant in Ligonier, Indiana. In a similar manner, Bailey Controls and Boise Cascade entered into a pact in which Bailey was the exclusive provider of control systems for 8 of 10 Boise plants. The two worked together, reviewing and modifying the terms of the arrangement to ensure that they reflected the ever-changing business conditions and that the deal remained fair to both parties. In addition, recognizing the long-term nature of the relationship and that Boise's success would also benefit Bailey, Bailey worked with Boise—in fact, using a Boise plant on which to conduct experiments—to improve the software used to operate the Boise plants.

The concept of partnering has radically changed the way inventory is purchased. Moreover, it has turned the customer-supplier relationship from a formerly adversarial one into a cooperative one. The benefits in terms of increased quality of parts, materials, and design are so dramatic that partnering is not likely to fade away, but rather continue to evolve and take on even more importance in the future.

## The Financial Consequences of Quality—The Traditional View

**Preventive costs**
Costs resulting from design and production efforts on the part of the firm to reduce or eliminate defects.

**Appraisal costs**
Costs of testing, measuring, and analyzing to safeguard against possible defects going unnoticed.

Traditionally, the cost of quality has been viewed as being made up of **preventive costs, appraisal costs,** and failure costs. The costs the firm incurs in running its quality management program include both preventive and appraisal costs. Preventive costs include those resulting from design and production efforts on the part of the firm to reduce or eliminate defects. Whereas preventive costs deal with the avoidance of defects the first time through, appraisal costs are associated with the detection of defects. Thus typical appraisal costs would include the costs of testing, measuring, and analyzing materials, parts, and products, as well as the production operations to safeguard against possible defective inventory going unnoticed. Together, preventive and appraisal costs make up much of what a typical total quality management program does.

**Internal failure costs**
Those costs associated with discovering poor-quality products prior to delivery

**External failure costs**
Costs resulting from a poor-quality product reaching the customers' hands.

Whereas preventive and appraisal costs deal with the costs associated with achieving good quality, *failure costs* refer to the costs resulting from producing poor-quality products. Failure costs can either occur within the firm, called **internal failure costs,** or once the product has left the firm, referred to as **external failure costs.** Internal failure costs are those costs associated with discovering the poor-quality product prior to delivery to the final customer. Internal failure costs include the costs of reworking the product, downtime costs, the costs of having to discount poorer quality products, and the costs of scrapping the product. External failure costs, on the other hand, come as a result of a poor-quality product reaching the customers' hands. Typical external failure costs would include product return costs, warranty costs, product liability costs, customer complaint costs, and lost sales costs.

Traditionally, economists examined the trade-offs between quality and costs looking for the point where costs were minimized. The result of this is that some level of defects should be tolerated. That is because there comes a point when the costs associated with making the product right in the first place are more than the cost of poor quality—the failure costs.

**RELATE TO THE BIG PICTURE**

**Principle 5: The Curse of Competitive Markets—Why it's hard to find exceptionally profitable projects** examines how product differentiation can be used as a means of insulating a product from competition, thereby allowing prices to stay sufficiently high to support large profits. Producing a quality product is one of those ways to differentiate products. This strategy has been used effectively by Caterpillar Tractor, Toyota, and Honda Motors in recent years.

## The Financial Consequences of Quality—The TQM View

In response to this traditional view, the TQM view argues that the traditional analysis is flawed in that it ignores the fact that increased sales and market share result from better-quality products, and that this increase in sales will more than offset the higher costs associated with increased quality. In effect, the TQM view argues that because lost sales resulting from a poor-quality reputation and increased sales resulting from a reputation for quality are difficult to estimate, they tend to be underestimated or ignored in the traditional approach. In addition, the TQM view argues that the cost of achieving higher quality is less than economists have traditionally estimated. In fact, the benefits from quality improvement programs seem to have spillover effects resulting in increased worker motivation, higher productivity, and improved employee relations. Moreover, large increases in quality have been achieved with very low costs when companies focus on training and educating the production workers.

Thus, the TQM view concludes that traditional analysis underestimates the cost of producing a poor-quality product, while it overestimates the cost of producing a high-quality product. As a result, under this new TQM view of the quality-costs trade-offs, the optimal quality level moves much closer to 100 percent quality.

The adoption of total quality management programs by many firms has borne out this TQM view of the quality-cost relationship. For example, after Xerox Corporation introduced TQM, it experienced a decline of 90 percent in defective items. For Xerox, the end result of this was a 20 percent drop in manufacturing costs over that same period.

**CONCEPT CHECK**

1. Define single-sourcing. How does this practice impact the firm purchasing goods and services?
2. Describe the components of the cost of quality.
3. Contrast the traditional analysis of the cost of quality with the TQM view.

## HOW FINANCIAL MANAGERS USE THIS MATERIAL

Given the fact that the total investment in both accounts receivable and inventory represents approximately one-third of a typical firm's assets, it's no surprise that a good deal of time goes into managing them. This includes deciding who should be able to buy on credit, trying to collect on overdue accounts, managing inventory to make sure you don't run out of any products, and overseeing quality control. But more than just managing these accounts and items, inventory and accounts receivable policies are increasingly used as sales tools. In effect, you sell your product, but you make that sale based upon your accounts receivable policy, your inventory policy, or the quality of your goods.

For example, Mitsubishi has an annual sale on its large-screen projection televisions in which prices are not cut. Instead, the projection televisions are offered at zero percent interest with the first payments not due until the following year. In effect, Mitsubishi uses its accounts receivable policy as a marketing tool. If you're working for Mitsubishi, your job may be to set standards as to who qualifies for this deal or to oversee the collection of those accounts.

Inventory policy is also used as a marketing tool. Having the product available for immediate delivery may be your sales gimmick. Other companies don't keep any inventory on hand and pass the savings that are produced on to the customers. For example, Dell computer does not produce any computers until they are sold, which allows it to keep costs down to a minimum and pass those cost savings on to the customers. In fact, this strategy has proved so profitable that, in late 1997, Apple announced it was also going to start selling over the Internet using the same "build-when-ordered" approach. If you took a job for another firm that sells directly out of inventory, your job might be managing that inventory—making sure you don't run out of anything while keeping your investment in inventory down to a minimum. Is inventory management complicated? The answer is yes. Just look at IBM, which has about 1,000 products currently in service with over 200,000 different inventoried parts supporting those products. To provide customers with prompt service, IBM has developed an inventory system that includes 2 central warehouses, 21 field distribution centers, 64 parts stations, and 15,000 outside locations with over 15,000 customer engineers, not to mention all those involved in managing the inventory.

As for quality control, again, for many firms it is a marketing strategy—"Quality is Job 1" touts Ford Motor Company. ITT Electro-Optical Products Division, which manufactures night vision products including pilot's goggles, aviator's night vision imaging systems, and night goggles, is another company to benefit from a TQM approach to business. Complicating ITT's task is the fact that manufacturing these systems is extremely complex, involving over 200 different chemicals and 400 different processes. This production complexity has led to an industry average production level of good units of only 10 to 40 percent. Prior to implementing a TQM program, which involved continuous process involvement, statistical process control, and employee involvement, only 35 percent of the units ITT produced were good. Implementing the TQM approach raised the percent of good units produced to 75 percent. The savings from reducing the proportion of bad units produced were passed on in lower prices, resulting in a 60-fold increase of the number of units sold over 5 years. To say the least, there are an awful lot of people inspecting products and working on ways to improve their quality—and that may be your job.

## SUMMARY

OBJECTIVE 1 

The size of the investment in accounts receivable depends on three factors: the percentage of credit sales to total sales, the level of sales, and the credit and collection policies. However, only the credit and collection policies are decision variables open to the financial manager. The policies that the financial manager has control over include the terms of sale, the type of customer, and the collection efforts.

OBJECTIVE 2 

Although the typical firm has fewer assets tied up in inventory (16.94 percent) than it does in accounts receivable (20.77 percent), inventory management and control is still an important function of the financial manager. The purpose of holding inventory is to make each function of the business independent of the other functions—that is, to uncouple the firm's operations. Inventory-management techniques primarily involve questions of how much inventory should be ordered and when the order should be placed. The answers directly determine the average level of investment in inventory. The *EOQ* model is employed in answering the first of these questions. This model attempts to calculate the order size that minimizes the sum of the inventory carrying and ordering costs. The order point problem attempts to determine how low inventory can drop before it is reordered. The order point is reached when the inventory falls to a level equal to the delivery-time stock plus the safety stock. Determining the level of safety stock involves a direct trade-off between the risk of running out of inventory and the increased costs associated with carrying additional inventory.

The just-in-time inventory control system lowers inventory by reducing the time and distance between the various production functions. The idea behind the system is that the firm should keep a minimum level of inventory on hand and rely on suppliers to furnish parts "just in time" for them to be assembled.

OBJECTIVE 3 

The TQM philosophy affects the way the purchasing portion of inventory management is handled. The traditional adversarial purchaser-supplier relationship has given way to close customer relationships, which have in turn helped trim costs by allowing for the production of higher quality products. This close customer-supplier relationship has allowed the TQM philosophy to be passed across company boundaries to the supplier, and has also allowed the firm to tap the supplier's expertise in designing higher quality products. In addition, this interdependence between the supplier and customer has allowed for the development and introduction of new products much quicker than previously possible. The use of single-sourcing (in which a company uses a very few suppliers or, in many cases, a single supplier, as a source for a particular part or material) has helped align the interests of the supplier and customer.

The movement toward a policy of 100 percent quality has been fueled by the realization that quality can be used as a means of differentiating products. The TQM view concludes that traditional quality-cost analysis underestimates the cost of producing a poor-quality product, while it overestimates the cost of producing a high-quality product. As a result, under this new TQM view of the quality-costs trade-offs, the low point in the total cost curve moves to an optimal quality level of 100 percent quality.

## KEY TERMS

**Anticipatory buying, 682**
**Appraisal costs, 686**
**Credit scoring, 670**
**Delivery-time stock, 681**
**External failure costs, 686**
**Finished-goods inventory, 678**
**Internal failure costs, 686**
**Inventory management, 676**
**Just-in-time inventory control system, 683**
**Marginal or incremental analysis, 673**
**Order point problem, 681**
**Order quantity problem, 678**
**Preventive costs, 686**
**Raw materials inventory, 677**
**Safety stock, 680**
**Single-sourcing, 685**
**Terms of sale, 668**
**Total quality management (TQM), 684**
**Work-in-process inventory, 677**

my**PHLIP**

Go To:
http://www.prenhall.com/keown
for downloads and current events associated with this chapter

## STUDY QUESTIONS

**20-1.** What factors determine the size of the investment a firm makes in accounts receivable? Which of these factors are under the control of the financial manager?

**20-2.** What do the following trade credit terms mean?

- **a.** 1/20, net 50
- **b.** 2/30, net 60
- **c.** net 30
- **d.** 2/10, 1/30, net 60

**20-3.** What is the purpose of an aging account in the control of accounts receivable? Can this same function be performed through ratio analysis? Why or why not?

**20-4.** If a credit manager experienced no bad debt losses over the past year, would this be an indication of proper credit management? Why or why not?

**20-5.** What is the purpose of credit scoring?

**20-6.** What are the risk-return trade-offs associated with adopting a more liberal trade credit policy?

**20-7.** Explain the purpose of marginal analysis.

**20-8.** What is the purpose of holding inventory? Name several types of inventory and describe their purpose.

**20-9.** Can cash be considered a special type of inventory? If so, what functions does it attempt to uncouple?

**20-10.** To control investment in inventory effectively, what two questions must be answered?

**20-11.** What are the major assumptions made by the *EOQ* model?

**20-12.** What are the risk-return trade-offs associated with inventory management?

**20-13.** How might inflation affect the *EOQ* model?

**20-14.** How do single-sourcing and closer customer-supplier relationships contribute to the firm?

**20-15.** What does the TQM view of the quality-cost relationship say is misstated by the traditional economic view of trade-offs between quality and cost?

## SELF-TEST PROBLEMS

**ST-1.** (*EOQ calculations*) A local gift shop is attempting to determine how many sets of wine glasses to order. The store feels it will sell approximately 800 sets in the next year at a price of $18 per set. The wholesale price that the store pays per set is $12. Costs for carrying one set of wine glasses are estimated at $1.50 per year whereas ordering costs are estimated at $25.

**a.** What is the economic order quantity for the sets of wine glasses?

**b.** What are the annual inventory costs for the firm if it orders in this quantity? (Assume constant demand and instantaneous delivery and thus no safety stock is carried.)

**ST-2.** (*EOQ calculations*) Given the following inventory information and relationships for the F. Beamer Corporation:

1. Orders can be placed only in multiples of 100 units.
2. Annual unit usage is 300,000. (Assume a 50-week year in your calculations.)
3. The carrying cost is 30 percent of the purchase price of the goods.
4. The purchase price is $10 per unit.
5. The ordering cost is $50 per order.
6. The desired safety stock is 1,000 units. (This does not include delivery-time stock.)
7. Delivery time is 2 weeks.

Given this information:

**a.** What is the optimal *EOQ* level?

**b.** How many orders will be placed annually?

**c.** At what inventory level should a reorder be made?

## STUDY PROBLEMS (SET A)

**20-1A.** (*Trade credit discounts*) If a firm buys on trade credit terms of 2/10, net 50 and decides to forgo the trade credit discount and pay on the net day, what is the effective annualized cost of forgoing the discount?

**20-2A.** (*Trade credit discounts*) If a firm buys on trade credit terms of 2/20, net 30 and decides to forgo the trade credit discount and pay on the net day, what is the effective annualized cost of forgoing the discount?

**20-3A.** (*Trade credit discounts*) Determine the effective annualized cost of forgoing the trade credit discount on the following terms:

**a.** 1/10, net 20

**b.** 2/10, net 30

**c.** 3/10, net 30

**d.** 3/10, net 60

**e.** 3/10, net 90

**f.** 5/10, net 60

**20-4A.** (*Altman model*) The following ratios were supplied by six loan applicants. Given this information and the credit-scoring model developed by Altman (equation 20-3), which loans have a high probability of defaulting next year?

| | EBIT / Total Assets | Sales / Total Assets | Market Value of Equity / Book Value of Debt | Retained Earnings / Total Assets | Working Capital / Total Assets |
|---|---|---|---|---|---|
| Applicant 1 | .2 | .2 | 1.2 | .3 | .5 |
| Applicant 2 | .2 | .8 | 1.0 | .3 | .8 |
| Applicant 3 | .2 | .7 | .6 | .3 | .4 |
| Applicant 4 | .1 | .4 | 1.2 | .4 | .4 |
| Applicant 5 | .3 | .7 | .5 | .4 | .7 |
| Applicant 6 | .2 | .5 | .5 | .4 | .4 |

**20-5A.** (*Ratio analysis*) Assuming a 360-day year, calculate what the average investment in inventory would be for a firm, given the following information in each case:

**a.** The firm has sales of $600,000, a gross profit margin of 10 percent, and an inventory turnover ratio of 6.

**b.** The firm has a cost of goods sold figure of $480,000 and an average age of inventory of 40 days.

**c.** The firm has a cost of goods sold figure of $1,150,000 and an inventory turnover ratio of 5.

**d.** The firm has a sales figure of $25 million, a gross profit margin of 14 percent, and an average age of inventory of 45 days.

**20-6A.** (*Marginal analysis*) The Bandwagonesque Corporation is considering relaxing its current credit policy. Currently, the firm has annual sales (all credit) of $5 million and an average collection period of 60 days (assume a 360-day year). Under the proposed change, the trade credit terms would be changed from net 60 to net 90 days and credit would be extended to a riskier class of customer. It is assumed that bad debt losses on current customers will remain at their current level. Under this change, it is expected that sales will increase to $6 million. Given the following information, should the firm adopt the new policy?

| | |
|---|---|
| New sales level (all credit) | $6,000,000 |
| Original sales level (all credit) | $5,000,000 |
| Contribution margin | 20% |
| Percent bad debt losses on new sales | 8% |
| New average collection period | 90 days |
| Original average collection period | 60 days |
| Additional investment in inventory | $50,000 |
| Pre-tax required rate of return | 15% |

**20-7A.** (*Marginal analysis*) The Foxbase Alpha Corporation is considering a major change in credit policy. Managers are considering extending credit to a riskier class of customer and extending their credit period from net 30 days to net 45 days. They do not expect bad debt losses on their current customers to change. Given the following information, should they go ahead with the change in credit policy?

| | |
|---|---|
| New sales level (all credit) | $12,500,000 |
| Original sales level (all credit) | $11,000,000 |
| Contribution margin | 20% |
| Percent bad debt losses on new sales | 9% |
| New average collection period | 45 days |
| Original average collection period | 30 days |
| Additional investment in inventory | $75,000 |
| Pre-tax required rate of return | 15% |

**20-8A.** (*EOQ calculations*) A downtown comic shop is trying to determine the optimal order quantity for the reprint of a first issue of a popular comic book. It is expected to sell approximately 3,000 copies in the next year at a price of $1.50. The store buys the comic at a wholesale figure of $1. Costs for carrying the comic are estimated at 10¢ a copy per year, and it costs $10 to order more comics.

**a.** Determine the *EOQ*.
**b.** What would be the total costs for ordering the comics 1, 4, 5, 10, and 15 times a year?
**c.** What questionable assumptions are being made by the *EOQ* model?

**20-9A.** (*EOQ calculations*) The local hamburger fast-food restaurant purchases 20,000 boxes of hamburger rolls every month. Order costs are $50 an order, and it costs 25¢ a box for storage.

**a.** What is the optimal order quantity of hamburger rolls for this restaurant?
**b.** What questionable assumptions are being made by the *EOQ* model?

**20-10A.** (*EOQ calculations*) A local car manufacturing plant has a $75 per-unit per-year carrying cost on a certain item in inventory. This item is used at a rate of 50,000 per year. Ordering costs are $500 per order.

**a.** What is the *EOQ* for this item?
**b.** What are the annual inventory costs for this firm if it orders in this quantity? (Assume constant demand and instantaneous delivery.)

**20-11A.** (*EOQ calculations*) Swank Products is involved in the production of camera parts and has the following inventory, carrying, and storage costs:

1. Orders must be placed in round lots of 200 units.
2. Annual unit usage is 500,000. (Assume a 50-week year in your calculations.)
3. The carrying cost is 20 percent of the purchase price.
4. The purchase price is $2 per unit.
5. The ordering cost is $90 per order.
6. The desired safety stock is 15,000 units. (This does not include delivery-time stock.)
7. The delivery time is 1 week.

Given the preceding information:

**a.** Determine the optimal *EOQ* level.
**b.** How many orders will be placed annually?
**c.** What is the inventory order point? (That is, at what level of inventory should a new order be placed?)
**d.** What is the average inventory level?

**20-12A.** (*EOQ calculations*) Toledo Distributors has determined the following inventory information and relationships:

1. Orders can be placed only in multiples of 200 units.
2. Annual unit usage is 500,000 units. (Assume a 50-week year in your calculations.)
3. The carrying cost is 10 percent of the purchase price of the goods.
4. The purchase price is $5 per unit.
5. The ordering cost is $100 per order.
6. The desired safety stock is 5,000 units. (This does not include delivery-time stock.)
7. Delivery time is 4 weeks.

Given this information:

**a.** What is the *EOQ* level?
**b.** How many orders will be placed annually?
**c.** At what inventory level should a reorder be made?
**d.** Now assume the carrying costs are 50 percent of the purchase price of the goods and recalculate (a), (b), and (c). Are these the results you anticipated?

## INTEGRATIVE PROBLEM

Your first major assignment after your recent promotion at Ice Nine involves overseeing the management of accounts receivable and inventory. The first item that you must attend to involves a proposed change in credit policy that would involve relaxing credit terms from the existing terms of 1/50, net 70 to 2/60, net 90 in hopes of securing new sales. The management at Ice Nine does not expect bad debt losses on its current customers to change under the new credit policy. The following information should aid you in the analysis of this problem.

| | |
|---|---|
| New sales level (all credit) | $8,000,000 |
| Original sales level (all credit) | $7,000,000 |
| Contribution margin | 25% |
| Percent bad debt losses on new sales | 8% |
| New average collection period | 75 days |
| Original average collection period | 60 days |
| Additional investment in inventory | $50,000 |
| Pre-tax required rate of return | 15% |
| New percent cash discount | 2% |
| Percent of customers taking the new cash discount | 50% |
| Original percent cash discount | 1% |
| Percent of customers taking the old cash discount | 50% |

To help in your decision on relaxing credit terms, you have been asked to respond to the following questions:

1. What factors determine the size of investment Ice Nine makes in accounts receivable?
2. If a firm currently buys from Ice Nine on trade credit with the present terms of 1/50, net 70 and decides to forgo the trade credit discount and pay on the net day, what is the effective annualized cost to that firm of forgoing the discount?
3. If Ice Nine changes its trade credit terms to 2/60, net 90, what is the effective annualized cost to a firm that buys on credit from Ice Nine and decides to forgo the trade credit discount and pay on the net day?
4. What is the estimated change in profits resulting from the increased sales less any additional bad debts associated with the proposed change in credit policy?
5. Estimate the cost of additional investment in accounts receivable and inventory associated with this change in credit policy.
6. Estimate the change in the cost of the cash discount if the proposed change in credit policy is enacted.
7. Compare the incremental revenues with the incremental costs. Should the proposed change be enacted?

You have also been asked to answer some questions dealing with inventory management at Ice Nine. Presently, Ice Nine is involved in the production of musical products with its German engineered Daedlufetarg music line. Production of this product involves the following inventory, carrying, and storage costs:

a. Orders must be placed in round lots of 100 units.
b. Annual unit usage is 250,000. (Assume a 50-week year in your calculations.)
c. The carrying cost is 10 percent of the purchase price.
d. The purchase price is $10 per unit.
e. The ordering cost is $100 per order.
f. The desired safety stock is 5,000 units. (This does not include delivery-time stock.)
g. The delivery time is 1 week.

Given the preceding information:

1. Determine the optimal *EOQ* level.
2. How many orders will be placed annually?
3. What is the inventory order point? (That is, at what level of inventory should a new order be placed?)
4. What is the average inventory level?
5. What would happen to the *EOQ* if annual unit sales doubled (all other unit costs and safety stocks remaining constant)? What is the elasticity of *EOQ* with respect to sales? (That is, what is the percent change in *EOQ* divided by the percent change in sales?)
6. If carrying costs double, what would happen to the *EOQ* level? (Assume the original sales level of 250,000 units.) What is the elasticity of *EOQ* with respect to carrying costs?
7. If the ordering costs double, what would happen to the level of *EOQ*? (Again, assume original levels of sales and carrying costs.) What is the elasticity of *EOQ* with respect to ordering costs?
8. If the selling price doubles, what would happen to *EOQ*? What is the elasticity of *EOQ* with respect to selling price?
9. What assumptions are being made by the *EOQ* model that has been used here?
10. How would the results of this model change if carrying cost were to increase, perhaps because of increased inflation?
11. How would an improvement in the relationship that Ice Nine has with its suppliers resulting in a decrease in the average delivery time for replenishment of inventory affect your answer?
12. If Ice Nine could decrease its ordering costs, perhaps by improving its relationship with suppliers, how would this affect your answer?

## STUDY PROBLEMS (SET B)

**20-1B.** (*Trade credit discounts*) If a firm buys on trade credit terms of 2/10, net 60 and decides to forgo the trade credit discount and pay on the net day, what is the effective annualized cost of forgoing the discount?

**20-2B.** (*Trade credit discounts*) If a firm buys on trade credit terms of 2/20, net 40 and decides to forgo the trade credit discount and pay on the net day, what is the effective annualized cost of forgoing the discount?

**20-3B.** (*Trade credit discounts*) Determine the effective annualized cost of forgoing the trade credit discount on the following terms:

**a.** 1/5, net 20
**b.** 2/20, net 90
**c.** 1/20, net 100
**d.** 4/10, net 50
**e.** 5/20, net 100
**f.** 5/30, net 50

**20-4B.** (*Altman model*) The following ratios were supplied by six loan applicants. Given this information and the credit-scoring model developed by Altman (equation 20-3), which loans have a high probability of defaulting next year and thus should be avoided?

| | EBIT / Total Assets | Sales / Total Assets | Market Value of Equity / Book Value of Debt | Retained Earnings / Total Assets | Working Capital / Total Assets |
|---|---|---|---|---|---|
| Applicant 1 | .3 | .4 | 1.2 | .3 | .5 |
| Applicant 2 | .2 | .6 | 1.3 | .4 | .3 |
| Applicant 3 | .2 | .7 | .6 | .3 | .2 |
| Applicant 4 | .1 | .5 | 1.8 | .5 | .4 |
| Applicant 5 | .5 | .7 | .5 | .4 | .6 |
| Applicant 6 | .2 | .4 | .2 | .4 | .4 |

**20-5B.** (*Ratio analysis*) Assuming a 360-day year, calculate what the average investment in inventory would be for a firm, given the following information in each case.

**a.** The firm has sales of $550,000, a gross profit margin of 10 percent, and an inventory turnover ratio of 5.

**b.** The firm has a cost of goods sold figure of $480,000 and an average age of inventory of 35 days.

**c.** The firm has a cost of goods sold figure of $1,250,000 and an inventory turnover ratio of 6.

**d.** The firm has a sales figure of $25 million, a gross profit margin of 15 percent, and an average age of inventory of 50 days.

**20-6B.** (*Marginal analysis*) The Hyndford Street Corporation is considering relaxing its current credit policy. Currently the firm has annual sales (all credit) of $6 million and an average collection period of 40 days (assume a 360-day year). Under the proposed change the trade credit terms would be changed from net 40 days to net 90 days and credit would be extended to a riskier class of customer. It is assumed that bad debt losses on current customers will remain at their current level. Under this change, it is expected that sales will increase to $7 million. Given the following information, should the firm adopt the new policy?

| | |
|---|---|
| New sales level (all credit) | $7,000,000 |
| Original sales level (all credit) | $6,000,000 |
| Contribution margin | 20% |
| Percent bad debt losses on new sales | 8% |
| New average collection period | 90 days |
| Original average collection period | 40 days |
| Additional investment in inventory | $40,000 |
| Pre-tax required rate of return | 15% |

**20-7B.** (*Marginal analysis*) The Northern Muse Corporation is considering a major change in credit policy. Managers are considering extending credit to a riskier class of customer and extending their credit period from net 30 days to net 50 days. They do not expect bad debt losses on their current customers to change. Given the following information, should they go ahead with the change in credit policy?

| | |
|---|---|
| New sales level (all credit) | $18,000,000 |
| Original sales level (all credit) | $17,000,000 |
| Contribution margin | 20% |
| Percent bad debt losses on new sales | 8% |
| New average collection period | 50 days |
| Original average collection period | 30 days |
| Additional investment in inventory | $60,000 |
| Pre-tax required rate of return | 15% |

**20-8B.** (*EOQ calculations*) A downtown bookstore is trying to determine the optimal order quantity for a reprint of a first issue of a popular comic book. It is expected to sell approximately 3,500 copies in the next year at a price of $1.50. The store buys the comic at a wholesale figure of $1. Costs for carrying the comic are estimated at 20¢ a copy per year, and it costs $9 to order more comics.

**a.** Determine the *EOQ*.

**b.** What would be the total costs for ordering the comics 1, 4, 5, 10, and 15 times a year?

**c.** What questionable assumptions are being made by the *EOQ* model?

**20-9B.** (*EOQ calculations*) The local hamburger fast-food restaurant purchases 21,000 boxes of hamburger rolls every month. Order costs are $55 an order, and it costs 20¢ a box for storage.

**a.** What is the optimal order quantity of hamburger rolls for this restaurant?

**b.** What questionable assumptions are being made by the *EOQ* model?

**20-10B.** (*EOQ calculations*) A local car manufacturing plant has a $70 per-unit per-year carrying cost on a certain item in inventory. This item is used at a rate of 55,000 per year. Ordering costs are $500 per order.

**a.** What is the economic order quantity for this item?
**b.** What are the annual inventory costs for this firm if it orders in this quantity? (Assume constant demand and instantaneous delivery.)

**20-11B.** (*EOQ calculations*) Swank Products is involved in the production of camera parts and has the following inventory, carrying, and storage costs:

1. Orders must be placed in round lots of 200 units.
2. Annual unit usage is 600,000. (Assume a 50-week year in your calculations.)
3. The carrying cost is 15 percent of the purchase price.
4. The purchase price is $3 per unit.
5. The ordering cost is $90 per order.
6. The desired safety stock is 15,000 units. (This does not include delivery-time stock.)
7. The delivery time is 1 week.

Given the preceding information:

**a.** Determine the optimal *EOQ* level.
**b.** How many orders will be placed annually?
**c.** What is the inventory order point? (That is, at what level of inventory should a new order be placed?)
**d.** What is the average inventory level?

**20-12B.** (*EOQ calculations*) Toledo Distributors has determined the following inventory information and relationships:

1. Orders can be placed only in multiples of 200 units.
2. Annual unit usage is 500,000 units. (Assume a 50-week year in your calculations.)
3. The carrying cost is 9 percent of the purchase price of the goods.
4. The purchase price is $5 per unit.
5. The ordering cost is $75 per order.
6. The desired safety stock is 5,000 units. (This does not include delivery-time stock.)
7. Delivery time is 4 weeks.

Given this information:

**a.** What is the *EOQ* level?
**b.** How many orders will be placed annually?
**c.** At what inventory level should a reorder be made?
**d.** Now assume the carrying costs are 50 percent of the purchase price of the goods and recalculate (a), (b), and (c). Are these the results you anticipated?

## SELF-TEST SOLUTIONS

**ST-1. a.** The economic order quantity is

$$Q^* = \sqrt{\frac{2SO}{C}}$$

where $S$ = total demand in units over the planning period
$O$ = ordering cost per order
$C$ = carrying costs per unit

Substituting the values given in the self-test problem into the *EOQ* equation we get

$$Q^* = \sqrt{\frac{2 \times 800 \times 25}{1.50}}$$
$$= \sqrt{26{,}667}$$
$$= 163 \text{ units per order}$$

Thus, 163 units should be ordered each time an order is placed. Note that the *EOQ* calculations occur based on several limiting assumptions such as constant demand, constant unit price, and constant carrying costs, which may influence the final decision.

**b.** Total costs = carrying costs + ordering costs

$$= \left(\frac{Q}{2}\right)C + \left(\frac{S}{Q}\right)O$$

$$= \left(\frac{163}{2}\right)\$1.50 + \left(\frac{800}{163}\right)\$25$$

$$= \$122.25 + \$122.70$$

$$= \$244.95$$

Note that carrying costs and ordering costs are the same (other than a slight difference caused by having to order in whole rather than fractional units). This is because the total costs curve is at its minimum when ordering costs equal carrying costs.

**ST-2. a.**

$$Q^* = \sqrt{\frac{2SO}{C}}$$

$$= \sqrt{\frac{2 \times 300{,}000 \times 50}{3}}$$

= 3,162 units, but because orders must be placed in 100-unit lots, the effective *EOQ* becomes 3,200 units

**b.** $\frac{\text{Total usage}}{EOQ} = \frac{300{,}000}{3{,}200} = 93.75$ orders per year

**c.** Inventory order point = delivery-time stock + safety stock

$$= \frac{2}{50} \times 300{,}000 + 1{,}000$$

$$= 12{,}000 + 1{,}000$$

$$= 13{,}000 \text{ units}$$

# RISK MANAGEMENT

This chapter focuses on how financial managers use futures, options, and currency swaps to eliminate risk. Although it looks easy, as many a firm has seen, it is a dangerous undertaking if done incorrectly. It is also an area where understanding is

extremely important. ● What kinds of risks can a firm control with futures, options, and currency swaps? They can be used to lock in prices of commodities used in production, interest rates if they are going to issue debt, or exchange rates for sales abroad. Let's look at Harley-Davidson. About one-fourth of its motorcycles are exported, and many of those exports go to Europe. In fact, in late 2000, Harley moved to strengthen its position in the European market by acquiring its Italian distributor. The new company, Harley-Davidson Italia S.r.l., joins other Harley-Davidson subsidiaries that already exist in Germany, France, the Benelux, and the United Kingdom. In addition, Harley-Davidson also operates a wholly owned subsidiary in Japan. All of that means that Harley sells a lot of motorcycles abroad for Euros, the currency of the European Union, and Japanese Yen. The motorcycles sold in Europe and Japan are made in America, with parts and workers paid in the U.S. dollar. So what happens to profits if the value of the Euro or the Yen drops relative to the dol-

### LEARNING OBJECTIVES

After reading this chapter, you should be able to

1. Explain the difference between a commodity future and a financial future and how they might be used by a financial manager to control risk.
2. Explain what put and call options are and how they might be used by a financial manager to control risk.
3. Explain what a currency swap is and how it might be used to eliminate exchange rate risk.

lar? That means that Harley will be selling its motorcycles for foreign currency that is worth less and less in terms of dollars. Obviously, this is a risk that Harley would rather not be exposed to. How does it eliminate that risk? It eliminates it through the use of foreign exchange futures. As we will see, foreign exchange futures allow us to lock in an exchange rate ahead of time, thus eliminating the problem of currency fluctuations. Is this a real problem? You bet it is. In fact, during 1999 and 2000, the value of the Euro in terms of U.S. dollars fell by about 28 percent! But, as with most other finance tools, the financial manager must have an understanding not only of the proper use of exchange rates, but of their risk potential and limitations.

**CHAPTER PREVIEW**

In this chapter, we examine two financial instruments that are not created by the firm: futures and options. These financial instruments are commonly referred to as "derivative securities" in that their value or price is determined by, or "derived" from, the price of another asset, exchange rate, commodity price, or interest rate. It is important for us to be familiar with them for two reasons. First, these instruments can be used to reduce the risks associated with interest and exchange rate and commodity price fluctuations. Second, as you will see in future finance courses, an understanding of the pricing of options is extremely valuable because many different financial assets can be viewed as options. In fact, risky bonds, common stock, and the abandonment decision can all be thought of as types of options. We also examine currency swaps that are used to hedge exchange rate risk over longer periods of time.

This chapter will emphasize **Principle 1: The Risk-Return Trade-Off—We won't take on additional risk unless we expect to be compensated with additional return.** Be on the lookout for this concept.

## FUTURES

Commodity and financial futures are perhaps the fastest-growing and most exciting new financial instrument today. Financial managers who only a few years ago would not have considered venturing into the futures market are now actively using this market to eliminate risk. As the number of participants in this market has grown, so has the number of items on which future contracts are offered, the old standbys such as coffee and soybeans, to newer ones such as U.S. Treasury bonds, sorghum, municipal bonds, and diammonium phosphate.

**Futures contract**
A contract to buy or sell a stated commodity or financial claim at a specified price at some future, specified time.

A **future,** or **futures contract,** is a contract to buy or sell a stated commodity (such as soybeans or corn) or financial claim (such as U.S. Treasury bonds) at a specified price at some future specified time. They are used by the financial manager to lock in future prices of raw materials, interest rates, or exchange rates. As was mentioned in the introduction to this chapter, if not controlled or understood, there are also dangers associated with their use. It is important to note here that this is a contract that *requires* its holder to buy or sell the asset, regardless of what happens to its value during the interim. The importance of a futures contract is that it can be used by financial managers to lock in the price of a commodity or an interest rate and thereby eliminate one source of risk. For example, if a corporation is planning on issuing debt in the near future and is concerned about a possible rise in interest rates between now and when the debt will be issued, it might sell a U.S. Treasury bond futures contract with the same face value as the proposed debt offering and a delivery date the same as when the debt offering is to occur. Alternatively, with the use of a futures contract, Ralston-Purina or Quaker Oats can lock in the future price of corn or oats whenever they wish. Because a futures contract locks in interest rates or commodity prices, the costs associated with any possible rise in interest rates or commodity prices are completely offset by the profits made by writing the futures contract. In effect, futures contracts allow the financial manager to lock in future interest and exchange rates or prices for a number of agricultural commodities such as corn and oats.

As the use of futures contracts becomes more common in the financial management of the firm, it is important for the financial manager to be familiar with the operation and terminology associated with these financial instruments. Although there are many uses for futures, options, and currency swaps, our interest focuses on how financial managers use them to reduce risk. Keep in mind that the financial manager can use them to effectively offset future movements in the price of commodities or interest rates and thereby eliminate risk.

## An Introduction to Futures Markets

The futures markets originated in medieval times. In fact, England, France, and Japan all developed futures markets of their own. Here in the United States, several futures markets sprang up in the early years, but it was not until the establishment of the Chicago Board of Trade (CBT) in 1848 that the futures markets were provided with their true roots. As we will see, although this market has been in operation for 150 years, it was not until the early 1970s—when the futures markets expanded from agricultural commodities to financial futures—that financial managers began to regularly venture into this market.

To develop an understanding of futures markets, let us examine several distinguishing features of futures contracts. A *futures contract* is distinguished by (1) an organized exchange, (2) a standardized contract with limited price changes and margin requirements, (3) a clearinghouse in each futures market, and (4) daily resettlement of contracts. Remember, a futures contract is legally binding. That means you must buy or sell a commodity some time in the future.

**THE ORGANIZED EXCHANGE** Although the Chicago Board of Trade is the oldest and largest of the futures exchanges, it is certainly not the only exchange. In fact, there are more than 10 different futures exchanges in operation in the United States today. The importance of having organized exchanges associated with the futures market is that they provide a central trading place. If there were no central trading place, then there would be no potential to generate the depth of trading necessary to support a secondary market; in a very circular way, the existence of a secondary market encourages more traders to enter the market and in turn provides additional liquidity.

An organized exchange also encourages confidence in the futures market by allowing for the effective regulation of trading. The various exchanges set and enforce rules and collect and disseminate information on trading activity and the commodities being traded. Together, the liquidity generated by having a central trading place, effective regulation, and the flow of information through the organized exchanges have effectively fostered their development.

**STANDARDIZED CONTRACTS** To develop a strong secondary market in any security, there must be many identical securities—or in this case, futures contracts—outstanding. In effect, standardization of contracts leads to more frequent trades on that contract, leading to greater liquidity in the secondary market for that contract, which in turn draws more traders into the market. This is why futures contracts are highly standardized and very specific with respect to the description of the goods to be delivered and the time and place of delivery. Let's look at a Chicago Board of Trade oats contract, for example. This contract calls for the delivery of 5,000 bushels of No. 2 heavy or No. 1 grade oats to Chicago or to Minneapolis–St. Paul at a 7.5¢ per bushel discount. In addition, these contracts are written to come due in March, May, July, September, and December. Through this standardization of contracts, trading has built up in enough identical contracts to allow for the development of a strong and highly liquid secondary market.

To encourage investors to participate in the futures market, daily price limits are set on most futures contracts (for some contracts coming due in the next 2 months, limits are not imposed). Without these limits, it is thought that there would be more price volatility on most futures contracts than many investors would be willing to accept. These daily price limits are set to protect investors, maintain order on the futures exchanges, and encourage the level of trading volume necessary to develop a strong secondary market. For example, the Chicago Board of Trade imposes a 10¢ per bushel ($500 per contract) price movement limit above and below the previous day's settlement price of oats contracts. This limit protects against runaway price movements. These daily price limits do not halt trading once the limit has been reached, but they do provide a boundary within which trading must occur. The price of an oats contract may rise 10¢ very early in the trading day—"up the limit," in futures jargon. This will not stop trading; it only means that no trade can take place above that level. As a result, any dramatic shifts in the market price of a futures contract must take place over a number of days, with the price of the contract going "up the limit" each day.

**FUTURES CLEARINGHOUSE** The main purpose of the futures clearinghouse is to guarantee that all trades will be honored. This is done by having the clearinghouse interpose itself as the buyer to every seller and the seller to every buyer. Because of this substitution of parties, it is not necessary for the original seller (or buyer) to find the original buyer (or seller) when he or she decides to clear his or her position. As a result, all an individual has to do is make an equal and opposite transaction that will provide a net zero position with the clearinghouse and cancel out that individual's obligation.

Because no trades occur directly between individuals, but between individuals and the clearinghouse, buyers and sellers realizing gains in the market are assured that they will be paid. Because futures contracts are traded with minimal "good faith" money, as we will see in the next section, it is necessary to provide some security to traders so that when money is made, it will be paid. There are other important benefits of a clearinghouse, including providing a mechanism for the delivery of commodities and the settlement of disputed trades, but these benefits also serve to encourage trading in the futures markets and thereby create a highly liquid secondary market.

**DAILY RESETTLEMENT OF CONTRACTS** Another safeguard of the futures market is a margin requirement. Although margin requirements on futures resemble stock margin requirements in that there is an initial margin and a maintenance margin that comes into play when the value of the contract declines, similarities between futures and stock margins end there.

Before we explore margin requirements on futures, it would be helpful to develop an understanding of the meaning of a margin on futures. The concept of a margin on futures contracts has a meaning that is totally different from its usage in reference to common stocks. The margin on common stocks refers to the amount of equity the investor has invested in the stocks. With a futures contract, no equity has been invested, because nothing has been bought. All that has happened is that a contract has been signed obligating the two parties to a future transaction and defining the terms of that transaction. This is an important thought: There is no actual buying or selling occurring with a futures contract; it is merely an agreement to buy or sell some commodity in the future. As a result, the term **futures margin** refers to "good faith" money the purchaser puts down to ensure that the contract will be carried out.

**Futures margin**
Good faith money the purchaser puts down to ensure that the contract will be carried out.

The initial margin required for commodities (deposited by both buyer and seller) is much lower than the margin required for common stock, generally amounting to only 3 to 10 percent of the value of the contract. For example, if September oats contracts on the CBT were selling at $1.65 per bushel, then one contract for 5,000 bushels would be selling for $1.65 × 5,000 = $8,250. The initial margin on oats is $400 per contract, which represents only about 4.85 percent of the contract price. Needless to say, the leverage associated with futures trading is tremendous—both on the up and down sides. Small changes in the price of the underlying commodity result in very large changes in the value of the futures contract, because very little has to be put down to "own" a contract. Moreover, for many futures contracts, if the financial manager can satisfy the broker that he or she is not engaged in trading as a speculator, but as a hedger, the manager can qualify for reduced initial margins. Because of the low level of the initial margin, there is also a *maintenance* or *variation margin* requirement that forces the investor or financial manager to replenish the margin account to a level specified by the exchange after any market loss.

One additional point related to margins deserves mention. The initial margin requirement can be fulfilled by supplying Treasury bills instead of cash. These Treasury bills are valued at 90 percent of their value for margin purposes, so it takes $100,000 worth of Treasury bills to provide a $90,000 margin. The advantage of using Treasury bills as margin is that the investor earns money on them, whereas brokerage firms do not pay interest on funds in commodity cash accounts. Moreover, if the financial manager is going to carry Treasury bills anyway, he or she can just deposit the Treasury bills with the broker and purchase the futures contracts with no additional cash outlay.

Suppose you are a financial manager for Ralston-Purina. You are in charge of purchasing raw materials—in particular, oats. Currently, a September futures contract for the delivery of oats has a price of $1.65 per bushel. You need oats in September, and feel that this is an exceptional price—oats will probably be selling for more than that per bushel in September. Thus you want to lock in this price, and to do this you purchase one contract for 5,000 bushels at 165¢ or $1.65 per bushel. On purchasing the September oats contract, the only cash you would have to put up would be the initial margin of $400. Let's further assume that the price of oats futures then falls to a level of 161¢ per bushel the day after you make your purchase. In effect, you have incurred a loss of 4¢ per bushel on 5,000 bushels, for a total loss on your investment of $200.

At this point, the concept of daily resettlement comes into play. What this means is that all futures positions are brought to the market at the end of each trading day and all gains and losses, in this case a loss, are then settled. You have lost $200, which is then subtracted from your margin account, lowering it to $200 ($400 initially, less the $200 loss). Because the margin account has fallen below the maintenance margin on oats, which is $250, you would have to replenish the account back to its initial level of $400. If on the following day the price of September oats contracts fell another cent to 160¢ per bushel, you would have lost another 1¢ on 5,000 bushels for a loss of $50. This would then be subtracted from your margin account during the daily resettlement at the end of the trading day, leaving $350 in the account. Because your margin account would not be below the maintenance margin requirement of $250, you would not have to add any additional funds to the account. Let's carry our example one day further, this time to the upbeat side, and put some profits in. Let's assume that on the third day, the price of September oats contract is up 5¢ per bushel. This means that you have made 5¢ on 5,000 bushels, for a total profit of $250. This brings your margin account up from $350 to $600, which is $200 above the initial margin of $400. You can withdraw this $200 from your margin account.

Obviously, the purpose of margin requirements is to provide some measure of safety for futures traders; and despite the very small level of margin requirements imposed, they do a reasonable job. They are set in accordance with the historical price volatility of the underlying commodity in such a way that it is extremely unlikely that a trader will ever lose more than is in his or her margin account in any one day.

## Commodity Futures

In general, when people talk about commodities, they are referring to nonfinancial futures. This includes agricultural commodities as well as metals, wood products, and fibers. Although there are several new commodity futures contracts now being traded, such as lumber and orange juice, much of the trading in the commodities futures markets involves such traditional favorites as corn and wheat. For the financial manager, these markets provide a means of offsetting the risks associated with future price changes. Here the financial manager is securing a future price for a good that is currently in production, or securing a future price for some commodity that must be purchased in the future. In either case, the manager is using the futures market to eliminate the effects of future price changes on the future purchase or sale of some commodity.

## Hedging with Futures

Although there are many different futures contracts available, it's not always possible to find what you're looking for. For example, you may have a manufacturing plant that uses petroleum as its primary raw material. However, there may not be futures contracts available on the specific grade of petroleum that you use. If you want to reduce risk by using the futures market to lock in a future price for petroleum, are you out of luck? Not really. Because all petroleum prices tend to move together, you could hedge away the risk of petroleum price rises using futures contracts on other grades of petroleum.

This use of futures contracts on similar but not identical commodities is referred to as *cross hedging.* With cross hedging, you don't actually want the commodity for which you've entered into a futures contract. What you're trying to do is lock in a price on a commodity whose price moves as close to identically as possible with the commodity you're interested in. As a result, you don't want to hold the futures contract to maturity and actually receive delivery of the commodity. The way you reverse your futures position is by taking an opposite and canceling position. That is, if you had earlier bought a futures contract, you would now sell the same contract and allow the two contracts to cancel each other out.

Is there danger in this? Not if it's done correctly. But that doesn't mean that companies haven't been burned when they thought they were using the futures market to hedge away risks. An example of a billion-dollar mistake is Metallgesellschaft AG, a German firm, that lost over $1 billion in 1993. One of its U.S. subsidiaries had entered into 10-year contracts to supply oil and gasoline at fixed prices. That meant that as long as petroleum prices didn't rise, it would make money, but if petroleum prices rose, it would be in trouble. To eliminate the risk from price rises, it turned to the futures market, buying short-term futures contracts. As it turned out, petroleum prices dropped and the subsidiary suffered enormous losses on these futures contracts. Unfortunately, because Metallgesellschaft AG's petroleum contracts were over 10 years, it was not offsetting gains on them. The result was a billion-dollar loss. It hedged the right product, but it didn't hedge for the right maturity. The bottom line here is that although futures contracts can reduce risk, you've got to make sure you know what you're doing with them.

## Financial Futures

Financial futures come in a number of different forms, including futures on Treasury bills, notes and bonds, GMNAs, certificates of deposit, Eurodollars, foreign currencies, and stock indices. These financial newcomers first appeared in 1972, when foreign currencies were introduced; interest rate futures did not appear until 1975. The growth in financial futures has been phenomenal, and today they dominate the futures markets. Our discussion of financial futures will be divided into three sections: (1) interest rate futures, (2) foreign exchange futures, and (3) stock index futures.

**INTEREST RATE FUTURES** Currently, Treasury bond futures are the most popular of all futures contracts in terms of contracts issued. Although Treasury (or T-bond) futures are just one of several interest rate futures contracts, the fact that they are risk-free, long-term bonds with a maturity of at least 15 years has been the deciding factor in making them the most popular of the interest rate futures.

For the financial manager, interest rate futures provide an excellent means for eliminating the risks associated with interest rate fluctuations. As we learned earlier, there is an inverse relationship between bond prices in the secondary market and yields—that is, when interest rates fall bond prices rise, and when interest rates rise bond prices fall. If you think back to the chapter on valuation, you will recall that this inverse relationship between bond prices and yield is a result of the fact that when bonds are issued, their coupon rate is fixed. However, once the bond is issued, it must compete in the market with other financial instruments. Because new bonds are issued to yield the current interest rate, yields on old bonds must adjust to remain competitive with the newer issues. Thus when interest rates rise, the price of an older bond with a lower coupon interest rate must decline to increase the yield on the old bond, making it competitive with the return on newly issued bonds.

Interest rate futures offer investors a very inexpensive way of eliminating the risks associated with interest rate fluctuations. For example, banks, pension funds, and insurance companies all make considerable use of the interest rate futures market to avoid paper losses that might otherwise occur when interest rates unexpectedly increase. Corporations also use interest rate futures to lock in interest rates when they are planning to issue debt. If interest rates rise before the corporation has the opportunity to issue the new debt, the profits on the interest rate futures contracts they have sold will offset the increased costs associated with the proposed debt offering.

**FOREIGN EXCHANGE FUTURES** Of all the financial futures, foreign exchange futures have been around the longest, first appearing in 1972. Foreign exchange futures work in the same way as other futures, but in this case the commodity is the Euro, British pounds, or some other foreign currency. As we will see, the similarities between these futures and the others we have examined are great. Not only do foreign exchange futures work in the same way as other futures, but they also are used by financial managers for the same basic reasons—to hedge away risks, in this case, exchange rate risks. One of the major participants in the foreign exchange futures market is the exporter who will receive foreign currency when its exported goods are finally received and who uses this market to lock in a certain exchange rate. As a result, the exporter is unaffected by any exchange rate fluctuations that might occur before it receives payment. Foreign exchange futures are also used to hedge away possible fluctuations in the value of earnings of foreign subsidiaries.

In the 1990s, fluctuations in exchange rates became common. With exchange rate futures, a financial manager could eliminate the effects—good or bad—of exchange rate fluctuation with a relatively small investment. The extremely high degree of leverage that was available coupled with the dramatic fluctuations in foreign exchange rates encouraged many financial managers to consider entering the exchange rate futures market.

**STOCK INDEX FUTURES** Stock indexes have been around for many years, but it has only been recently that financial managers and investors have had the opportunity to trade them directly. In fact, despite only first appearing in February 1982, by 1984 they became the second most widely traded futures contract of all, exceeded in trading volume only by T-bond futures contracts.

At this point, after looking at other futures contracts, the workings of stock index futures should be clear. They work basically the same way, with one major exception: Stock index futures contracts allow only for cash settlement. There is no delivery, because what is being traded is the *future price* of the index, not the underlying stocks in the index. Currently there are several stock index futures available, with futures on the S&P 500 index clearly dominating in terms of volume. However, in mid-1997, futures trading on the Dow Jones Industrial Average (DJIA) was initiated. Given that the DJIA is perhaps the most recognized stock market index, this is almost certain to be a popular stock index future.

Let's examine exactly what an S&P 500 index futures contract involves. The S&P 500 index is a broad-based index made up of 400 industrials, 40 utilities, 20 transportations, and 40 financial companies. These companies represent about 80 percent of the value of all issues traded on the NYSE. This is a value-weighted index; the weight each stock takes on in the index is determined by the market value of that stock. The contract size or value of each contract is 500 times the S&P 500 index, which puts it at about 663,000 in early 2001.

Just as with currency futures, when there is a major fluctuation in the stock market, entire fortunes can be made or lost in the stock index futures market. Take, for example, trading on October 22, 1987, during the week of the great crash. That day one trader, Albert "Bud" Furman III, made $900,000 in 90 seconds by buying 303 S&P 500 futures contracts at $196.00 a contract and selling 300 futures contracts 90 seconds later at $202.00 per contract (500 × $6/contract × 300 contracts = $900,000).

After the 1987 crash, a system of shock absorber limits and circuit breakers was introduced to most index futures markets. These serve the same purpose as do daily price limits, but they are not as strict. For example, the New York Futures Exchange has 10-minute, 30-minute, 1-hour, and 2-hour trading halts that result from wide swings in the stock market. The purpose of these programmed trading halts is to allow investors to rationally appraise the market during periods of large price swings.

To the financial manager, the great popularity of these financial newcomers lies in their ability to reduce or eliminate systematic risk. When we talked about the variability or risk associated with common stock returns, we said that there were two types of risk: systematic and unsystematic risk. Unsystematic risk, although accounting for a large portion of the variability of an individual security's returns, is largely eliminated in large portfolios through random diversification, leaving only systematic or market risk in a portfolio. As a result, we said that a portfolio's returns are basically determined by market movements, as modified by the portfolio's beta. Before the introduction of stock index futures, a portfolio or pension fund manager was forced to adjust the portfolio's beta if he or she anticipated a change in the direction of the market. Stock index futures allow the portfolio or pension fund manager to eliminate or mute the effects of swings in the market without the large transactions costs that would be associated with the trading needed to modify the portfolio's beta. Unfortunately, although stock index futures allow for the elimination of the unwanted effects of market downswings, they also eliminate the effects of market upswings. In other words, they allow the portfolio or pension fund manager to eliminate as much of the effect of the market as he or she wishes from his or her portfolio.

**RELATE TO THE BIG PICTURE**

The area of risk management has grown rapidly over the last decade. In response to volatile interest rates, commodity prices, and exchange rates of the late 1970s through the 1990s, financial managers turned to the futures, options, and swap markets for relief. Once again, the financial markets demonstrated their dynamic and adaptive nature in finding new ways of reducing risk without affecting return. The inspiration for such behavior, of course, finds its roots in **Principle 1: The Risk-Return Trade-Off—We won't take on additional risk unless we expect to be compensated with additional return.**

**CONCEPT CHECK**

1. What is a futures contract? What are its distinguishing features?
2. How do you hedge with futures contracts?
3. What is a financial future? Give an example of one.

## OPTIONS

OBJECTIVE 2 

**Option contract**
An option contract gives its owner the right to buy or sell a fixed number of shares of stock at a specified price over a limited time period.

An **option,** or **option contract,** gives its owner the right to buy or sell a fixed number of shares of stock at a specified price over a limited time period. Although trading in option contracts has existed for many years, it was not until the Chicago Board Options Exchange (CBOE) began trading in listed options in 1973 that the volume of trading reached any meaningful level. During the years since the CBOE first listed options on 16 stocks, volume has grown at a phenomenal rate, with over 10,000 different active option contracts on over 800 stocks listed today. Trading volume has also grown to such an extent that, on a typical day, trading in options involves numbers equal to half the volume of trading on the NYSE. Still, to many financial managers, options remain a mystery, viewed as closer to something one would find in Las Vegas than on Wall Street.

Clearly, there is too much going on in the options markets not to pay attention to them. Financial managers are just beginning to turn to them as an effective way of eliminating risk for a small price. As we will see, they are fascinating, but they are also confusing—with countless variations and a language of their own. Moreover, their use is not limited to speculators; options are also used by the most conservative financial managers to eliminate unwanted risk. In this section, we will discuss the fundamentals of options, their terminology, and how they are used by financial managers.

### The Fundamentals of Options

**Call option**
A call option gives its owner the right to purchase a given number of shares of stock or some other asset at a specified price over a given time period.

**Put option**
A put option gives its owner the right to sell a given number of shares of common stock or some other asset at a specified price over a given time period.

Although the market for options seems to have a language of its own, there are only two basic types of options: puts and calls. Everything else involves some variation. A **call option** gives its owner the right to purchase a given number of shares of stock or some other asset at a specified price over a given period. Thus, if the price of the underlying common stock or asset goes up, a call purchaser makes money. This is essentially the same as a "rain check" or guaranteed price. You have the option to buy something, in this case common stock, at a set price.

In effect, a call option gives you the right to buy, but it is not a promise to buy. A **put,** on the other hand, gives its owner the right to sell a given number of shares of common stock or some other asset at a specified price over a given period. A put purchaser is betting that the price of the underlying common stock or asset will drop. Just as with the call, a put option gives its holder the right to sell the common stock at a set price, but it is not a promise to sell. Because these are just options to buy or sell stock or some other asset, they do not represent an ownership position in the underlying corporation, as does common stock. In fact, there is no direct relationship between the underlying corporation and the option. An option is merely a contract between two investors.

Because there is no underlying security, a purchaser of an option can be viewed as betting against the seller or *writer* of the option. For this reason, the options markets are often referred to as a *zero sum game.* If someone makes money, then someone must lose money; if profits and losses were added up, the total for all options would equal zero. If commissions are considered, the total becomes negative, and we have a "negative sum" game. As we will see, the options markets are quite complicated and risky. Some experts refer to them as legalized institutions for transferring wealth from the unsophisticated to the sophisticated. However, for the financial manager, they can be tools for eliminating risk.

THE CONTRACT When an option is purchased, it is nothing more than a contract that allows the purchaser to either buy in the case of a call, or sell in the case of a put, the underlying stock or asset at a predetermined price. That is, no asset has changed hands, but the price has been set for a future transaction that will occur *only if and when* the option purchaser wants it to. In this section, we will refer to the process of selling puts and calls as *writing.* Often, selling options is referred to as *shorting* or *taking a short position* in those options, whereas buying an option is referred to as *taking a long position.*

THE EXERCISE OR STRIKING PRICE The **option striking price** is the price at which the stock or asset may be purchased from the writer in the case of a call or sold to the writer in the case of a put.

**Option striking price**
The price at which the stock or asset may be purchased from the writer in the case of a call, or sold to the writer in the case of a put.

OPTION PREMIUM The **option premium** is merely the price of the option. It is generally stated in terms of dollars per share rather than per option contract, which covers 100 shares. Thus, if a call option premium is $2, then an option contract would cost $200 and allow the purchase of 100 shares of stock at the exercise price.

**Option premium**
The price of the option.

EXPIRATION DATE The **option expiration date** is the date on which the option contract expires. An American option is one that can be exercised any time up to the expiration date. A European option can be exercised only on the expiration date.

**Option expiration date**
The date on which the option expires.

COVERED AND NAKED OPTIONS If a call writer owns the underlying stock or asset on which he or she writes a call, the writer is said to have written a *covered call.* Conversely, if the writer writes a call on a stock or asset that he or she does not own, he or she is said to have written a *naked call.* The difference is that if a naked call is exercised, the call writer must deliver stock or assets that he or she does not own.

OPEN INTEREST The term *open interest* refers to the number of option contracts in existence at one point in time. The importance of this concept comes from the fact that open interest provides the investor with some indication of the amount of liquidity associated with that particular option.

IN-, OUT-OF, AND AT-THE-MONEY A call (put) is said to be out-of-the-money if the underlying stock is selling below (above) the exercise price of the option. Alternatively, a call (put) is said to be in-the-money if the underlying stock is selling above (below) the exercise price of the option. If the option is selling at the exercise price, it is said to be selling at-the-money. For example, if Ford Motor's common stock was selling for $22 per share, a call on Ford with an exercise price of $20 would be in-the-money, whereas a call on Ford with an exercise price of $30 would be out-of-the-money.

**Option's intrinsic value** The minimum value of the option.

INTRINSIC AND TIME (OR SPECULATIVE) VALUE The term **intrinsic value** refers to the minimum value of the option—that is, the amount by which the stock is in-the-money. Thus, for a call, the intrinsic value is the amount by which the stock price exceeds the exercise price. If the call is out-of-the-money—that is, the exercise price is above the stock price—then its intrinsic value is zero. Intrinsic values can never be negative. For a put, the intrinsic value is again the minimum value the put can sell for, which is the exercise price less the stock price. For example, a Ford April 20 put—that is, a put on Ford stock with an exercise price of $20 that expires in April—when Ford's common stock was selling for $12 per share would have an intrinsic value of $8. If the put was selling for anything less than $8, investors would buy puts and sell the stock until all profits from this strategy were exhausted. Arbitrage, this process of buying and selling like assets for different prices, keeps the price of options at or above their intrinsic value. If an option is selling for its intrinsic value, it is said to be selling at *parity*.

**Option's time (or speculative) value** The amount by which the option premium exceeds the intrinsic value of the option.

The **time value,** or **speculative value,** of an option is the amount by which the option premium exceeds the intrinsic value of the option. The time value represents the amount above the intrinsic value of an option that an investor is willing to pay to participate in capital gains from investing in the option. At expiration, the time value of the option falls to zero and the option sells for its intrinsic value, because the chance for future capital gains has been exhausted. These relationships are as follows:

$$\text{call intrinsic value} = \text{stock price} - \text{exercise price}$$
$$\text{put intrinsic value} = \text{exercise price} - \text{stock price}$$
$$\text{call time value} = \text{call premium} - (\text{stock price} - \text{exercise price})$$
$$\text{put time value} = \text{put premium} - (\text{exercise price} - \text{stock price})$$

**EXAMPLE**

Perhaps the easiest way to gain an understanding of the pricing of options is to look at them graphically. Figure 21-1 presents a profit and loss graph for the purchase of a call on Ford stock with an exercise price of $20 that is bought for $4. This is termed a "Ford 20 call". In Figure 21-1 and all other profit and loss graphs, the vertical axis represents the profits or losses realized on the option's expiration date, and the horizontal axis represents the stock price on the expiration date. Remember that because we are viewing the value of the option at expiration, the option has no time value and therefore it sells for exactly its intrinsic value. To keep things simple, we will also ignore any transaction costs.

For the Ford 20 call shown in Figure 21-1, the call will be worthless at expiration if the value of the stock is less than the exercise or striking price. This is because it would make no sense for an individual to exercise the call option to purchase Ford stock for $20 per share if he or she could buy the same Ford stock from a broker at a price less than $20. Although the option will be worthless at expiration, if the stock price is below the exercise price, the most that an investor can lose is the option premium—that is, how much he or she paid for the option, which in this case was $4. Although this may be the entire investment in the option, it is also generally only a fraction of the stock's price. Once the stock price climbs above the exercise price, the call option takes on a positive value and increases in a linear one-to-one basis as the stock price increases. Moreover, there is no limit on how high the profits can climb. In the case of the Ford 20 call, once the price of Ford stock rises above $20, the call begins taking on value, and once it hits $24, the investor breaks even. The investor has earned enough in the way of profits to cover the $4 premium he or she paid for the option in the first place.

To the call writer, the profit and loss graph is the mirror image of the call purchaser's graph. As we noted earlier, the options market is a zero sum game in which one individual gains at the expense of another. Figure 21-2 shows the profits and losses at expiration associated with writing a call option. Once again, we will look at the profits and losses at expiration, because at that point in time options have no time value. The maximum profit to the call writer is the premium, or how much the writer received when the option was sold, whereas the maximum loss is unlimited.

Looking at the profit and loss graph presented in Figure 21-3 for the purchase of a Ford 20 put that is bought for $3, we see that the lower the price of the Ford stock, the more the put is worth. Here the put only begins to take on value once the price of the Ford stock drops below the exercise price, which in this case is $20. Then for every dollar that the price of the Ford stock drops, the put increases in value by one dollar. Once the Ford stock drops to $17 per share, the put purchaser breaks even by making $3 on the put, which exactly offsets what was initially paid for the put. Here, as with the purchase of a call option, the most an investor can lose is the premium, which although small in dollar value relative to the potential

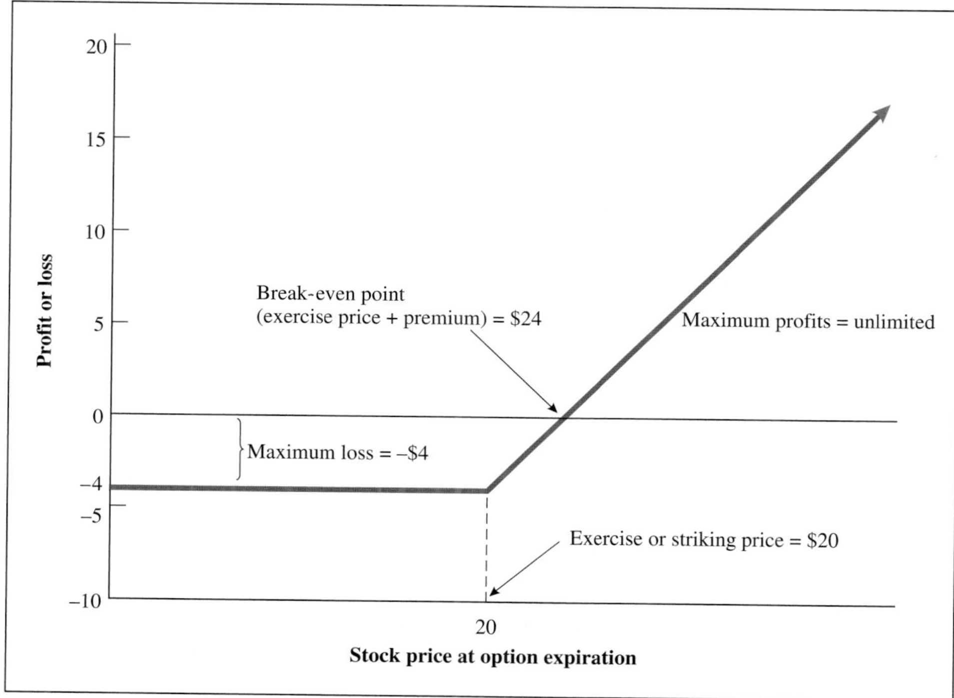


**FIGURE 21-1**
Purchase a Call on Ford Stock with an Exercise Price of $20 for a Premium of $4

gains, still represents 100 percent of the investment. The maximum gain associated with the purchase of a put is limited only by the fact that the lowest a stock's price can fall to is zero.

To a put writer, the profit and loss graph is the mirror image of the put purchaser's graph. This is shown in Figure 21-4. Here the most a put writer can earn is the premium or amount for which the put was sold. The potential losses for the put writer are limited only by the fact that the stock price cannot fall below zero.

All of our graphs have shown the price of the option at expiration. When we reexamine these relationships at a time before expiration, we find that the options now take on some time value. In other words, investors are willing to pay more than the intrinsic value for an option because of the uncertainty of the future stock price. That is, although the stock price may fluctuate, the possible losses on the option are limited, whereas the possible gains are almost unlimited. The most you can ever lose when you purchase a put or call option is the premium, or what you paid for it. Although this may seem rather small relative to the price of the stock, it is still 100 percent of your investment.

**FIGURE 21-2**
Write a Call on Ford Stock with an Exercise Price of $20 for a Premium of $4

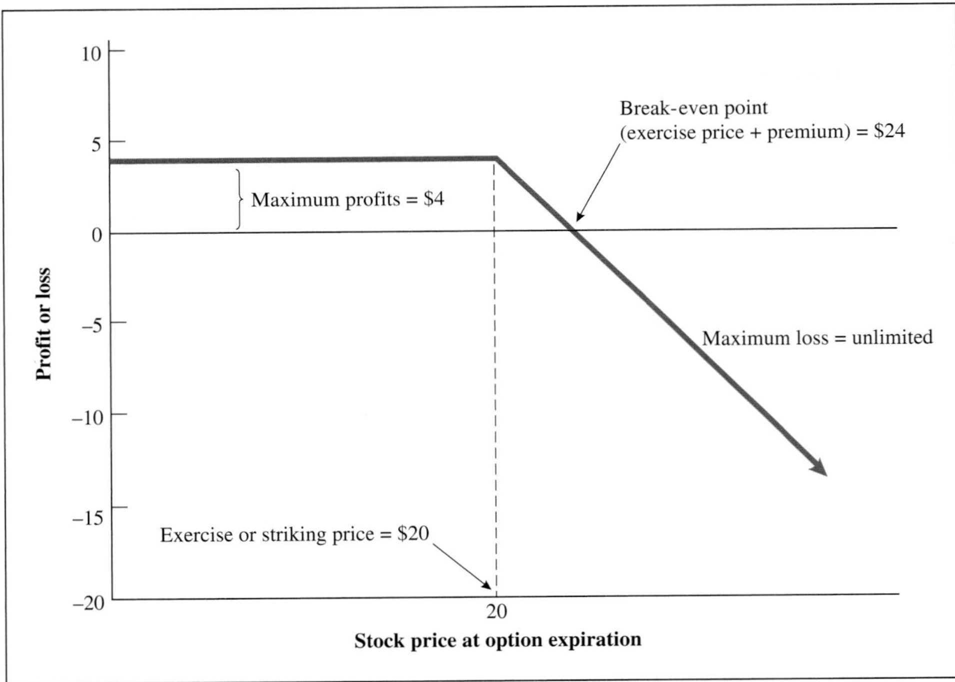


This feature in which the potential loss is limited to the amount invested along with unlimited returns is what draws many speculators to options. Although the biggest corporate losses have been associated with futures contracts, in which losses are not limited to the amount invested, options speculation has produced its share of huge losses for corporations. Look at NatWest, which lost £90 million in interest rate options in February 1997, or

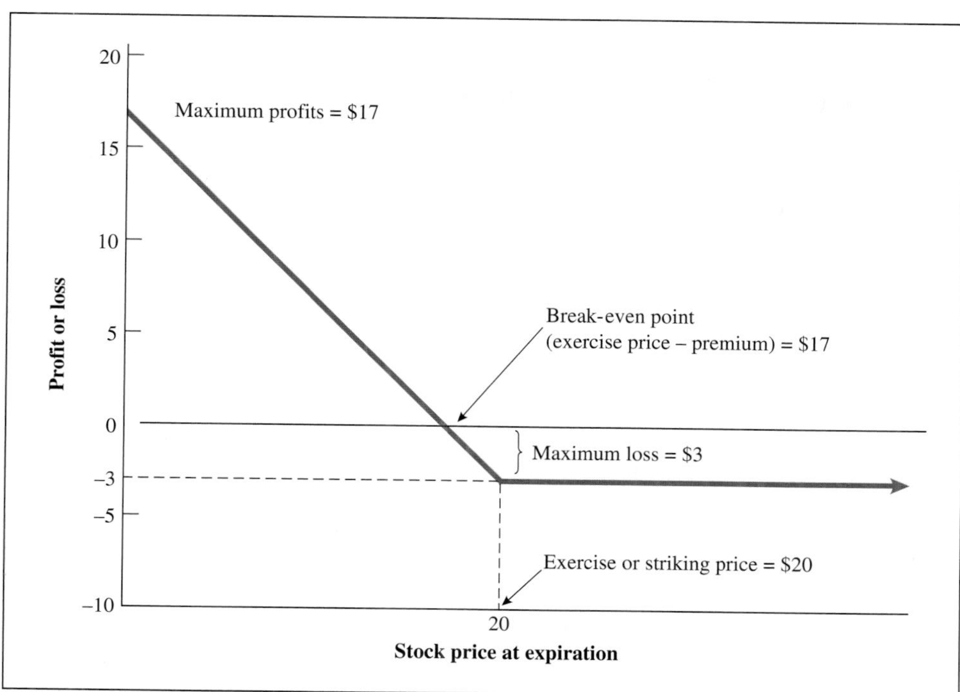


**FIGURE 21-3**
Purchase a Put on Ford Stock with an Exercise Price of $20 for a Premium of $3

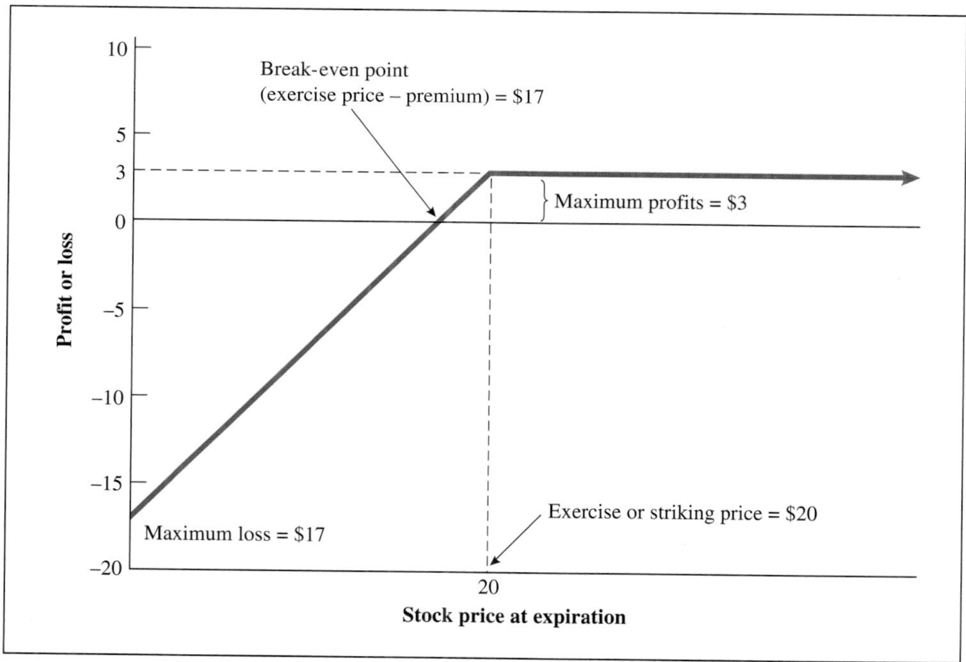


**FIGURE 21-4**
Write a Put on Ford Stock with an Exercise Price of $20 for a Premium of $3

Dell Computer, which lost $8 million in 1992. No doubt, these companies didn't understand the degree of risk that they had exposed themselves to. Keep in mind that options should be used to reduce risk, but if they aren't fully understood or controlled, they can produce results opposite from those intended.

## Characteristics of Options

As we examine options from the viewpoint of the financial manager, we will see that they have some attractive features that help explain their popularity. There are three reasons for the popularity of options:

1. **Leverage.** Calls allow the financial manager the chance for unlimited capital gains with a very small investment. Because a call is only an option to buy, the most a financial manager can lose is what was invested, which is usually a very small percentage of what it would cost to buy the stock itself, whereas the potential for gain is unlimited. As we will see, when a financial manager owns a call, he or she controls or benefits directly from any price increases in the stock. The idea of magnifying the potential return is an example of leverage. It is similar to the concept of leverage in physics, where a small amount of force can lift a heavy load. Here a small investment is doing the work of a much larger investment. Unfortunately, leverage is a double-edged sword: Small price increases can produce a large percentage profit, but small price decreases can produce large percentage losses. With an option, the maximum loss is limited to the amount invested.
2. **Financial insurance.** For the financial manager, this is the most attractive feature of options. A put can be looked on as an insurance policy, with the premium paid for the put being the cost of the policy. The transactions costs associated with exercising the put can then be looked on as the deductible. When a put with an exercise price equal to the current stock price is purchased, it insures the holder against any declines in the stock price over the life of the put. Through the use of a put, a pension fund manager can reduce the risk exposure in a portfolio with little in cost and little change to the portfolio. One dissimilarity between a put and an insurance policy is that with a put an investor does not need to own the asset, in this case the stock, before buying the insurance. A call, because it has limited potential losses associated with it, can also be viewed as an investment insurance policy. With a call, the investor's potential losses are limited to the price of the call, which is quite a bit below the price of the stock itself.
3. **Investment alternative expansion.** From the viewpoint of the investor, the use of puts, calls, and combinations of them can materially increase the set of possible investment alternatives available.

Again, an understanding of the popularity of both puts and calls to the financial manager involves understanding (1) the concept of leverage—in the case of calls unlimited and in the case of puts very large potential gains with limited and relatively small maximum potential losses—and (2) the concept of financial insurance. These two factors combined allow for an expansion of the available investment alternatives. Remember, both puts and calls are merely options to buy or sell the stock at a specified price. The worst that can happen is that the options become worthless and the financial manager loses the investment.

## The Chicago Board Options Exchange

Prior to 1973, when the CBOE opened, there was no central marketplace for put and call options. At that time, put and call options transactions took place on the over-the-counter market through what was called the Put and Call Dealers Association, with only about 20 active brokers and dealers in the market. Through a telephone hookup, these dealers acted as middlemen, matching up potential writers and purchasers of options.

Because the specifics of each option were negotiated directly between the writer and the purchaser of the option, very seldom were any two options alike. Generally, every option written had a different expiration date and a different exercise price. As a result, there was little in the way of a secondary market for these individualized options, and the writers and purchasers generally had to hold their position until expiration or until the options were exercised.

With the creation of the CBOE, all this began to change. In 1973, the CBOE began trading listed options on 16 different stocks. Today there are four different exchanges that list and trade options—the CBOE, the AMEX, the Philadelphia, and the Pacific—with over 800 different stocks having listed options. Although the over-the-counter market run by the Put and Call Association is still in operation for stocks that are not listed on the CBOE or any other exchange, it now handles less than 10 percent of all traded options.

This dramatic growth in the trading of options is almost entirely due to the several developments brought on by exchange-listed trading that the CBOE initiated, including the following:

1. **Standardization of the option contracts.** Today, the expiration dates for all options are standardized. As a result, there is only 1 day per month on which a listed option on any stock can expire. The number of shares that a call allows its owner to purchase, and a put allows its owner to sell, has also been standardized to 100 shares per option contract. In addition, the striking prices have been standardized, generally at five-point intervals, so that there are more identical options. Through this standardization, the number of different option contracts on each stock is severely limited. The result is that more options are identical and the secondary market is made more liquid.
2. **Creation of a regulated central marketplace.** The exchange listing of options provides a central location for continuous trading in options, both newly issued and in the secondary market. The CBOE and the exchanges that followed in listing options also imposed strong surveillance and disclosure requirements.
3. **Creation of the Options Clearinghouse Corporation (OCC).** The OCC bears full responsibility for honoring all options issued on the CBOE. In effect, all options held by individuals have been written by the OCC, and alternatively all options written by individuals are held by the OCC. The purpose of creating a buffer between individual buyers and sellers of options is to provide investors with confidence in the market, in addition to facilitating the clearing and settlement of options. Because of the importance of the OCC, let us look for a moment at its operation.

   When an options transaction is agreed upon, the seller writes an option contract to the OCC, which in turn writes an identical option contract to the buyer. If the buyer later wants to exercise the option, he or she gives the OCC the exercise price associated with the option, which in turn provides the buyer with stock. To get the stock to cover the option, the OCC simultaneously exercises a call option it has on this stock. Because of the operation of the OCC and the strong secondary market created by the CBOE, options are not exercised very frequently but are generally sold. Rather than exercise an option, an investor or financial manager usually just sells the option to another investor and realizes the profits in that manner. Writers of options clear their position by buying an option identical to the one they wrote. As a result, the writer has two identical contracts on both sides of the market with the OCC. These positions then cancel each other out.
4. **Trading was made certificateless.** Instead of issuing certificates, the OCC maintains a continuous record of trader's positions. In addition to making the clearing of positions (the canceling out of an option writer's obligation when an identical option is purchased) easier, it has also allowed for an up-to-date record of existing options to be maintained.
5. **Creation of a liquid secondary market with dramatically decreased transactions costs.** There also has been a self-fulfilling generation of volume adding to the liquidity

of the secondary market. That is, the innovations created a liquid secondary market for options, and this liquid secondary market attracted more investors into the options market, which in turn created even more liquidity in the secondary market.

## Innovations in the Options Market

Recently, five additional variations of the traditional option have appeared: the stock index option, the interest rate option, the foreign currency option, the Treasury bond futures option, and Leaps.

**STOCK INDEX OPTIONS** The options on stock indexes were first introduced on the CBOE in 1983 and have since proved extremely popular. Although there are a variety of different index options, based on several different broad stock market indexes and also industry indexes such as a computer industry index, it has been the broader stock market indexes that have carried the bulk of the popularity of index options. Although the industry-based index options have received a somewhat mixed reception, stock index options, in particular the S&P 100 index on the CBOE, have proved to be extremely popular. In fact, more than 80 percent of all stock index options trading involves the S&P 100 index. Currently it accounts for over half of the volume of all option trading and has made the CBOE the second largest U.S. securities market, with daily trading occasionally reaching nearly 700,000 contracts (remember each contract involves an option on 100 "shares" of the index).

The reason for this popularity is quite simple. These options allow portfolio managers and other investors holding broad portfolios to cheaply and effectively eliminate or adjust the market risk of their portfolios. When we talked about systematic and unsystematic risk, we noted that in a large and well-diversified portfolio, unsystematic risk was effectively diversified away, leaving only systematic risk. Thus, the return on a large and well-diversified portfolio was a result of the portfolio's beta and the movement of the market. As a result, because the movements of the market cannot be controlled, portfolio managers periodically attempt to adjust the beta of the portfolio when they think a change in the market's direction is at hand. Index options allow them to make this change without the massive transaction costs that would otherwise be incurred.

In general, stock index options are used in exactly the same way traditional options are used: for leverage and for investment insurance. However, because of the unusual nature of the "underlying stock," these concepts take on a different meaning. In the case of leverage, the portfolio manager is speculating that the market will head either up or down and is able to cash in on any market volatility with a relatively small investment. In fact, the ability to enjoy the leverage of an option while being concerned with broad market movements has resulted in much of the popularity of stock index options, as small changes in the market can result in very large changes in the price of these options.

In the case of the investment insurance motive for holding index options, the financial manager is really using them to eliminate the effects of a possible downward movement in the market. For example, a portfolio manager who wants to ensure the portfolio against a downturn in the market might purchase a put on the S&P 100 or S&P 500 index. Thus, if the market declines, the put will appreciate in value, offsetting the loss in the investor's portfolio.

In effect, index options can be used in the same way as the more traditional options. The only difference is that here the profits or losses depend on what happens to the value of the index rather than to one stock.

**INTEREST RATE OPTIONS** Options on 30-year Treasury bonds are also traded on the CBOE. Although the trading appeal of interest rate options is somewhat limited, they do open some very interesting doors to the financial manager. In terms of the insurance and leverage traits, they allow the financial manager to insure against the effects of future changes in interest rates. We know that as interest rates rise, the market value of outstanding bonds falls; thus, through the purchase of an interest rate put, the market value of a portfolio manager's bonds can be protected. Alternatively, a financial manager who is about to raise new capital through a debt offering and who is worried about a possible rise in interest rates before the offering occurs may purchase an interest rate put. This would have the effect of locking in current interest rates at the maximum level that the firm would have to pay.

**FOREIGN CURRENCY OPTIONS** Foreign currency options are the same as the other options we have examined, except the underlying asset is the Euro, the British pound, the Japanese yen, or some other foreign currency. Although foreign currency options are limited to the Philadelphia Exchange, there is a considerable amount of interest in them largely because of the wide fluctuations foreign currency has had in recent years relative to the dollar. In terms of the insurance and leverage traits, these options allow multinational firms to guard against fluctuations in foreign currencies that might adversely affect their operations. The leverage trait allows investors to speculate in possible future foreign currency fluctuations with a minimum amount of exposure to possible losses.

Let's look at an example of how foreign currency options might be used. As firms trade more and more internationally, the need to protect sales against undesirable currency fluctuations becomes increasingly important. For example, Cessna might use currency options to protect sales on its Citation V aircraft, which are sold in Europe to Swiss customers. Because the Citation V is built in the United States and sold abroad, its costs in labor and materials are based on the dollar. However, as the dollar fluctuates relative to the Swiss franc, so must the sales price in Swiss francs for Cessna to receive the same amount of dollars on each sale in Switzerland.

Problems surface when the value of the Swiss franc falls relative to that of the dollar. For each sale to bring the same amount of dollars back to Cessna, the selling price in Swiss francs would have to be *increased.* Unfortunately, increasing prices may lead to lost sales. To guard against this situation, Cessna may purchase *put options* on the Swiss franc to cover the anticipated Swiss sales. These puts give Cessna the option to sell or convert Swiss francs into dollars at a preset price. If after the put options are purchased, the Swiss franc falls, Cessna could keep its selling prices constant in terms of the Swiss franc and make up for the loss in the currency exchange with the profits on the puts. Conversely, if the value of the Swiss franc rises relative to the value of the dollar, Cessna could lower its Swiss price, sell more aircraft, and still bring home the same dollars per sale—all that would be lost is the price paid for the put options.

**OPTIONS ON TREASURY BOND FUTURES** Options on Treasury bond futures work the same way as any other option. The only difference between them and other bond options is that they involve the acquisition of a futures position rather than the delivery of actual bonds. To the creative financial manager, they provide a flexible tool to insure against adverse changes in interest rates while retaining the opportunity to benefit from any favorable interest rate movement that might occur. Although a futures contract establishes an obligation for both parties to buy and sell at a specified price, an option only establishes a right. It is therefore exercised only when it is to the option holder's advantage to do so. In effect, a call option on a futures contract does not establish a price obligation, but rather a maximum purchase price. Conversely, a put option on a futures contract is used to establish a minimum selling price. Thus, the buyer of an option on a futures contract can achieve immunization against any unfavorable price movements, whereas the buyer of the futures contract can achieve immunization against any price movements, regardless of whether they are favorable or unfavorable.

In their short history, options on U.S. Treasury bond futures have proved to be extremely popular, with the majority of institutions choosing to trade options on bond futures rather than options on actual bonds. Their extreme popularity can be traced to several important advantages they possess:

1. **Efficient price determination of the underlying instrument.** The U.S. Treasury bond futures contract on the Chicago Board of Trade is the most widely traded futures contract of all. As a result, there is a continuous stream of market-determined price information concerning these contracts. Conversely, price information on most other bonds is generally somewhat sketchy at best, with substantial time between trades and generally a wide gap between existing bid and ask prices.
2. **Unlimited deliverable supply.** Because the Clearinghouse can create as many futures contracts as are needed, the process of exercising an option is made extremely simple. When an option on a futures contract is exercised, the buyer simply assumes a futures position at the exercise price of the option. Because the Clearinghouse can create as many futures contracts as are needed, the market price of these contracts is not affected by the exercise of the options on them. Conversely, if an option holder on an actual bond were to exercise his or her option, he or she would have to take delivery of the underlying bond. Because the supply of any particular bond is limited, a serious price pressure might be placed on that bond, provided the bond does not enjoy sufficient liquidity. Thus, because of the unlimited deliverable supply of futures contracts, the exercise of options on futures does not affect the price of those futures.
3. **Greater flexibility in the event of exercise.** If the option proves to be profitable, the purchaser or writer can settle the transaction in cash by offsetting the futures position acquired by exercise, or do nothing temporarily and assume the futures position and make or take delivery of the actual bonds when the futures contract comes due.
4. **Extremely liquid market.** Because of the other advantages of options on Treasury bond futures, a great number of these options have been created and are traded daily. As a result of the large volume, options on Treasury bond futures have developed a very liquid and active secondary market, which has encouraged other traders to enter this market.

Financial institutions seem to be major participants in the options on Treasury bond futures market, although there are many potential users of financial futures. They use futures options to alter the risk-return structure of their investment portfolios and actually reduce their exposure to downside risk. A common strategy is to purchase put options and thereby eliminate the possibility of large losses while retaining the possibility of large gains. There is a cost associated with this strategy, because the option premium must be paid regardless of whether or not the option is exercised. An additional return is also generated by those who write call options against a bond portfolio. With this strategy, the premium increases the overall return if bond yields remain stable or rise; however, a maximum return is also established for the portfolio, because it is this tail of the distribution that is sold with the option.

**LEAPS—LONG-TERM OPTIONS** Long-term Equity Anticipation Securities or "Leaps" are long-term options—both puts and calls—with expiration dates that go out as far as 3 years in the future. Because they are longer term than traditional options, they can be used to hedge against longer term movements in stocks. Leaps calls allow the investor to benefit from a stock price increase without purchasing the stock, whereas Leaps puts provide a hedge against stock price declines over the long run. As with other options, they expire on the Saturday following the third Friday of the expiration month, with all Leaps expiring in January.

**CONCEPT CHECK**

1. What is an option? Name and explain two basic types of options.
2. What are three reasons for the popularity of options?
3. What are some recent innovations in the options markets?
4. What is a Leap?

## CURRENCY SWAPS

**Currency swap** An exchange of debt obligations in different currencies.

The currency swap is another technique for controlling exchange rate risk. Whereas options and futures contracts generally have a fairly short duration, a currency swap provides the financial manager with the ability to hedge away exchange rate risk over longer periods. It is for that reason that currency swaps have gained in popularity. A **currency swap** is simply an exchange of debt obligations in different currencies. Interest rate swaps are used to provide long-term exchange rate risk hedging. Actually, a currency swap can be quite simple, with two firms agreeing to pay each other's debt obligation.

How does this serve to eliminate exchange rate risk? If I am an American firm with much of my income coming from sales in England, I might enter in a currency swap with an English firm. If the value of the British pound depreciates from 1.90 dollars to the pound to 1.70 dollars to the pound, then each dollar of sales in England will bring fewer dollars back to the parent company in the United States. This would be offset by the effects of the currency swap because it costs the U.S. firm fewer dollars to fulfill the English firm's interest obligations. That is, pounds cost less to purchase, and the interest payments owed are in pounds. The nice thing about a currency swap is that it allows the firm to engage in long-term exchange rate risk hedging, because the debt obligation covers a relatively long time period.

Needless to say, there are many variations of the currency swap. One of the more popular is the interest rate currency swap, where the principal is not included in the swap. That is, only interest payment obligations in different currencies are swapped. The key to controlling risk is to get an accurate estimate on the net exposure level to which the firm is subjected. Then the firm must decide whether it feels it is prudent to subject itself to the risk associated with possible exchange rate fluctuations.

These look like great ideas—enter into a contract that reduces risk—but just as with the other derivative securities, they are dangerous if used by those who don't understand their risks. For example, in 1994 Procter & Gamble Corporation lost $157 million on swaps that involved interest rate payments made in German marks and U.S. dollars. How did this happen? Exchange rates and interest rates didn't go the way Procter & Gamble had anticipated and the costs were a lot more than it thought they might ever be. In effect, Procter & Gamble simply got talked into something it didn't understand.

**CONCEPT CHECK**

1. What is a currency swap?
2. When might a firm use a currency swap?

FINANCE $ MATTERS

### The Risk That Won't Go Away

It has been estimated that the derivatives market has been growing at a rate of about 40 percent per year. Examples of losses in this market abound, with Metallgesellschaft (AG), Germany's 14th largest industrial corporation, which we discussed earlier, leading the way with losses. One of MG's subsidiaries, a U.S. marketing organization and part owner of an oil refinery, reported losses approaching $1.3 billion.

To all generally well-informed business people, a few words of semicomfort about financial derivatives: First, if you don't really understand what these are, don't fret. Most of your colleagues, top brass included, are equally baffled. Second, if ten years from now—despite periodic booster shots from articles like this one—you still can't keep these things in focus, then cheer! That will mean derivatives have not been forcibly brought to your attention by bad, bad news, in which they make headlines as a villain, or even *the* villain, in some financial crisis that sweeps the world.

That possibility must be entertained because derivatives have grown with stunning speed into an enormous, pervasive, and controversial financial force.

Derivatives are contracts whose value is derived—the key word—from the value of some underlying asset, such as currencies, equities, or commodities; from an indicator like interest rates; or from a stock market or other index. The derivative instruments that result—variously called swaps, forwards, futures, puts, calls, swaptions, caps, floors, collars, captions, floortions, spreadtions, lookbacks, and other neverland names—keep bursting into the news as they did recently when the Federal Reserve raised interest rates and share prices sank, costing some traders of derivatives huge amounts that in some cases surely ran into many millions. The "counter-parties" to these contracts customarily use them to hedge some business risk they don't want to bear, such as a jump in interest rates or a fall in the value of a currency.

But transferring such a risk doesn't wipe it away. The risk simply gets passed by the initial contract to a dealer, who in turn may hedge it by a separate contract with still another dealer, who for his part may haul in yet another dealer or maybe a speculator who *wants* the risk. In the words of Roger & Hammerstein's King of Siam: "et cetera, et cetera, et cetera." What results is a tightly wound market of many, many, interconnections—*global* interconnections—that is altogether quite different from anything that has ever existed before.

Most chilling, derivatives hold the possibility of systematic risk—the danger that these contracts might directly or indirectly cause some localized or particularized trouble in the financial markets to spread uncontrollably. An imaginable scenario is some deep crisis at a major dealer that would cause it to default on its contracts and be the instigator of a chain reaction bringing down other institutions and sending paroxysms of fear through a financial market that lives on the expectation of prompt payments. Inevitably, that would put deposit-insurance funds, and the taxpayers behind them, at risk.

Source: Carol J. Loomis, "The Risk That Won't Go Away," *Fortune* (March 7, 1994): 40–57. 

## THE MULTINATIONAL FIRM AND RISK MANAGEMENT

Over the past 10 years, the use of futures and options by corporations has exploded. The primary way they are used is to hedge away risk in commodity markets, foreign exchange rates, and interest rates. How might you become involved in them? Maybe your first job will be working for McDonald's. To say the least, McDonald's, with operations in 91 countries, gets much of its income from its overseas operations. As a result, currency fluctuations can have a dramatic effect on its profits. With profits from abroad coming in currencies such as the baht (Thailand), the won (Korea), and the ringgit (Malaysia), things got pretty scary in late 1997, when all of these currencies collapsed. How does a company such as McDonald's protect itself and take some of the risk out of its international operations? The answer is, by using futures and options to hedge away the interest rate risk.

Given the risks that globalization brings, futures and options are a great tool to use in reducing those risks. It's important to keep in mind that they can also be used by smaller firms. For example, if you have a small specialty bakery with customers in England, France, and Germany, you could easily eliminate your exchange rate risk with currency options. In addition, you could lock in the future price of your raw materials in the futures markets.

## HOW FINANCIAL MANAGERS USE THIS MATERIAL

Most manufacturing firms can use futures to hedge away price fluctuations in their raw materials. For example, Kellogg's may buy futures in rice for Rice Krispies if it feels rice prices are low, and it wants to lock in those prices. USAirways may buy futures on oil to lock in the price of its fuel. In fact, in 2000, when oil prices doubled, USAirways was able to keep its costs down because it had been an active purchaser of oil futures contracts prior to the jump in oil prices. Your job may be making those purchases, analyzing prices to determine if your company should lock in prices of its raw materials, or it may involve determining how many futures and options you should buy. Unfortunately, some firms use futures and options for speculative purposes rather than to hedge away risk. For example, Sumitomo Bank lost $1.8 billion in June 1996 in copper futures.

## SUMMARY

Futures, options, and currency swaps are important for the financial manager due to their ability to reduce risks associated with interest and exchange rate and commodity price fluctuations.

A futures contract is a contract to buy or sell a stated commodity (such as soybeans or corn) or financial claim (such as U.S. Treasury bonds) at a specified price at some future specified time. This contract requires its holder to buy or sell the asset regardless of what happens to its value during the interim. The importance of a futures contract is that it can be used by financial managers to lock in the price of a commodity or an interest rate and thereby eliminate one source of risk. A futures contract is a specialized form of a forward contract distinguished by (1) an organized exchange, (2) a standardized contract with limited price changes and margin requirements, (3) a clearinghouse in each futures market, and (4) daily resettlement of contracts.

A call option gives its owner the right to purchase a given number of shares of stock at a specified price over a given period. Thus, if the price of the underlying common stock goes up, a call purchaser makes money. A put, conversely, gives its owner the right to sell a given number of shares of common stock at a specified price over a given period. Thus, a put purchaser is betting that the price of the underlying common stock will drop. Because these are just options to buy or sell stock, they do not represent an ownership position in the underlying corporation, as does common stock.

A currency swap is an exchange of debt obligations in different currencies. Exchange rate variations are offset by the effects of the swap. One major advantage of a currency swap is that it allows for the hedging of exchange rate risk over a long period of time.

## KEY TERMS

**call option, 706**
**currency swap, 717**
**futures contract, 699**
**futures margin, 701**
**option contract, 706**
**option expiration date, 707**
**option premium, 707**
**option striking price, 707**
**option's intrinsic value, 708**
**option's time (or speculative) value, 708**
**put option, 706**

myPHLIP

Go To: http://www.prenhall.com/keown for downloads and current events associated with this chapter

## STUDY QUESTIONS

**21-1.** What is the difference between a commodity future and financial future? Give an example of each.

**21-2.** Describe a situation in which a financial manager might use a commodity future. Assume that during the period following the transaction the price of that commodity went up. Describe what happened. Now assume that the price of that commodity went down. Now what happened?

**21-3.** Describe a situation in which a financial manager might use an interest rate future. Assume that during the period following the transaction the interest rates went up. Describe what happened. Now assume that interest rates went down following the transaction. Now what happened?

**21-4.** Define a call option.

**21-5.** Define a put option.

**21-6.** What innovative developments were brought on by exchange-listed trading that the CBOE initiated that led to the dramatic growth in the trading of options?

**21-7.** What is an option on a futures contract? Give an example.

**21-8.** Compare the two strategies of buying a call and writing a put. What are the differences between the two?

**21-9.** What is a currency swap and why has it gained so in popularity?

## STUDY PROBLEMS (SET A)

**21-1A.** (*Puts and calls*) Draw a profit or loss graph (similar to Figure 21-1) for the purchase of a call contract with an exercise price of $65 for which a $9 premium is paid. Identify the break-even point, maximum profits, and maximum losses. Now draw the profit or loss graph assuming an exercise price of $70 and a $6 premium.

**21-2A.** (*Puts and calls*) Repeat problem 21-1A, but this time draw the profit or loss graph (similar to Figure 21-2) for the call writer.

**21-3A.** (*Puts and calls*) Draw a profit or loss graph (similar to Figure 21-3) for the purchase of a put contract with an exercise price of $45 for which a $5 premium is paid. Identify the break-even point, maximum profits and maximum losses.

**21-4A.** (*Puts and calls*) Repeat problem 21-3A, but this time draw the profit or loss graph (similar to Figure 21-4) for the put writer.

## INTEGRATIVE PROBLEM

For your job as the business reporter for a local newspaper, you are given the task of putting together a series of articles on the derivatives markets. Much recent local press coverage has been given to the dangers and the losses that some firms have experienced in those markets. Your editor would like you to address several specific questions in addition to demonstrating the use of futures contracts and options and applying them to several problems.

Please prepare your response to the following memorandum from your editor:

TO: Business Reporter

FROM: Perry White, Editor, Daily Planet

RE: Upcoming Series on the Derivative Securities Market

In your upcoming series on the derivative markets, I would like to make sure you cover several specific points. In addition, before you begin this assignment, I want to make sure we are all reading from the same script, as accuracy has always been the cornerstone of the Daily Planet. As such I'd like a response to the following questions before we proceed:

1. What opportunities do the derivative securities markets (i.e., the futures and options markets) provide to the financial manager?
2. When might a firm become interested in purchasing interest rate futures? Foreign exchange futures? Stock index futures?
3. What can a *firm* do to reduce exchange risk?
4. How would Treasury bond futures and options on Treasury bond futures differ?
5. What is an option on a futures contract? Give an example of one and explain why it exists.
6. Draw a profit or loss graph (similar to Figure 21-1) for the purchase of a call contract with an exercise price of $25 for which a $6 premium is paid. Identify the break-even point, maximum profits, and maximum losses.
7. Repeat question 6, but this time draw the profit or loss graph (similar to Figure 21-2) for the call writer.
8. Draw a profit or loss graph (similar to Figure 21-3) for the purchase of a put contract with an exercise price of $30 for which a $5 premium is paid. Identify the break-even point, maximum profits, and maximum losses.
9. Repeat question 8, but this time draw the profit or loss graph (similar to Figure 21-4) for the put writer.
10. What is a currency swap and who might use one?

## STUDY PROBLEMS (SET B)

**21-1B.** (*Puts and calls*) Draw a profit or loss graph (similar to that in Figure 21-1) for the purchase of a call contract with an exercise price of $50 for which a $5 premium is paid. Identify the break-even point, maximum profits, and maximum losses. Now draw the profit or loss graph assuming an exercise price of $55 and a $6 premium.

**21-2B.** (*Puts and calls*) Repeat problem 21-1B, but this time draw the profit or loss graph (similar to Figure 21-2) for the call writer.

**21-3B.** (*Puts and calls*) Draw a profit or loss graph (similar to that in Figure 21-3) for the purchase of a put contract with an exercise price of $60 for which a $4 premium is paid. Identify the break-even point, maximum profits, and maximum losses.

**21-4B.** (*Puts and calls*) Repeat problem 21-3B, but this time draw the profit or loss graph (similar to that in Figure 21-4) for the put writer.

# APPENDIX 21A
# CONVERTIBLE SECURITIES AND WARRANTS

In September of 1997, Costco Companies, Incorporated, issued $900 million of zero coupon bonds that mature in 2017. What made these bonds interesting is that they were zero coupon convertible bonds; that is, each bond could be traded in for 11.3545 shares of Costco's common stock any time on or prior to maturity. In effect, this financing package put together by Costco looked more like options than normal bonds.

In this appendix, we will examine how convertibles and warrants can be used to raise money. Both of these financing methods contain elements of an option in that they can be exchanged at the owner's discretion for a specified number of shares of common stock. In investigating each financing alternative, we look first at its specific characteristics and purpose; then we focus on any special considerations that should be examined before the convertible security or the warrant is issued.

## CONVERTIBLE SECURITIES

**Convertible security**
Preferred stock or debentures that can be exchanged for a specified number of shares of common stock at the will of the owner.

A **convertible security** is a preferred stock or a debt issue that can be exchanged for a specified number of shares of common stock at the will of the owner. In effect, it contains elements of an option. It provides the stable income associated with preferred stock and bonds in addition to the possibility of capital gains associated with common stock. This combination of features has led convertibles to be called *hybrid* securities.

When the convertible is initially issued, the firm receives the proceeds from the sale, less flotation costs. This is the only time the firm receives any proceeds from issuing convertibles. The firm then treats this convertible as if it were normal preferred stock or debentures, paying dividends or interest regularly. If the security owner wishes to exercise an option to exchange the convertible for common stock, he or she may do so at any time according to the terms specified at the time of issue. The desire to convert generally follows a rise in the price of the common stock. Once the convertible owner trades the convertibles in for common stock, the owner can never trade the stock back for convertibles. From then on, the owner is treated as any other common stockholder and receives only common stock dividends.

### Characteristics and Features of Convertibles

**Conversion ratio**
The number of shares of common stock for which a convertible security can be exchanged.

**Conversion Ratio.** The number of shares of common stock for which the convertible security can be exchanged is set out when the convertible is initially issued. On some convertible issues, this **conversion ratio** is stated directly. For example, the convertible may state that it is exchangeable for 15 shares of common stock. Some convertibles give only a conversion price, stating, for example, that the security is convertible at $39 per share. This tells us that for every $39 of par value of the convertible security, one share of common stock will be received.

$$\text{conversion ratio} = \frac{\text{par value of convertible security}}{\text{conversion price}} \tag{21A-1}$$

For example, Union Carbide has $350 million of convertible debentures outstanding that mature in 2012. These convertibles have a $1,000 par value, a 7-1/2 percent coupon interest rate, and a conversion price of $35.50. Thus, the conversion ratio—the number of shares to be received upon conversion—is $1,000/$35.50 = 28.169 shares. The security owner has the option of holding the 7-1/2 percent convertible debenture or trading it in for 28.169 shares of Union Carbide common stock.

**Conversion value**
The total market value of the common stock for which it can be exchanged.

CONVERSION VALUE The **conversion value** of a convertible security is the total market value of the common stock for which it can be exchanged. This can be calculated as follows:

$$\text{conversion value} = \left(\text{conversion ratio}\right) \times \left(\begin{array}{c}\text{market value per share}\\ \text{of the common stock}\end{array}\right) \tag{21A-2}$$

If the Union Carbide common stock were selling for, say, \$24 per share, then the conversion value for the Union Carbide convertible would be (28.169)(\$24.00) = \$676.06; that is, the market value of the common stock for which the convertible could be exchanged would be \$676.06. Thus, regardless of what this convertible debenture was selling for, it could be converted into \$676.06 worth of common stock.

SECURITY VALUE The **security value** (or bond value, as it is sometimes called) of a convertible security is the price the convertible security would sell for in the absence of its conversion feature. This is calculated by determining the required rate of return on a straight (nonconvertible) issue of the same quality and then determining the present value of the interest and principal payments at this rate of return. Thus, regardless of what happens to the value of the firm's common stock, the lowest value to which the convertible can drop should be its value as a straight bond or preferred stock.

**Security value**
The price the convertible security would sell for in the absence of its conversion feature.

CONVERSION PERIOD On some issues, the time period during which the convertible can be exchanged for common stock is limited. Many times conversion is not allowed until a specified number of years have passed, or it is limited by a terminal conversion date. Still other convertibles may be exchanged at any time during their life. In either case, the **conversion period** is specified when the convertible is originally issued.

**Conversion period**
The time period during which the convertible can be exchanged for common stock.

CONVERSION PREMIUM The **conversion premium** is the difference between the convertible's market price and the higher of its security value and its conversion value. It can be expressed as an absolute dollar value, in which case it is defined as:

**Conversion premium**
The difference between the convertible's market price and the higher of its security value and its conversion value.

$$\text{conversion premium} = \left(\begin{array}{c}\text{market price of}\\ \text{the convertible}\end{array}\right) - \left(\begin{array}{c}\text{higher of the security value}\\ \text{and conversion value}\end{array}\right) \qquad \textbf{(21A-3)}$$

In describing convertibles, we have introduced a number of terms. To eliminate confusion, Table 21A-1 summarizes them.

## Why Issue Convertibles?

The major reason for choosing to issue convertibles rather than straight debt, preferred stock, or common stock is the fact that interest rates on convertibles are indifferent to the issuing firm's risk level.

**TABLE 21A-1**
Summary of Convertible Terminology

**Conversion ratio:** The number of shares for which the convertible security can be exchanged.

$$\text{conversion ration} = \frac{\text{par value of convertible security}}{\text{conversion price}}$$

**Conversion value:** The total market value of the common stock for which the convertible can be exchanged.

$$\text{conversion value} = \left(\begin{array}{c}\text{conversion}\\ \text{ratio}\end{array}\right) \times \left(\begin{array}{c}\text{market value per share}\\ \text{of the common stock}\end{array}\right)$$

**Security value:** The price the convertible security would sell for in the absence of its conversion feature.

**Conversion period:** The time period during which the convertible can be exchanged for common stock.

**Conversion premium:** The difference between the convertible's market price and the higher of its security value and its conversion value.

$$\text{conversion premium} = \left(\begin{array}{c}\text{market price of}\\ \text{the convertible}\end{array}\right) - \left(\begin{array}{c}\text{higher of the security value}\\ \text{and conversion value}\end{array}\right)$$

While higher risk and uncertainty bring on higher interest costs in straight debt, this is not necessarily the case with convertibles. If we think about a convertible as a package of straight debt and a convertible feature allowing the holder to purchase common stock at a set price, an increase in risk and uncertainty certainly raises the cost of the straight-debt portion of the convertible. However, the convertibility feature benefits from this increase in risk and uncertainty and the increase in stock price volatility that follows. In effect, the conversion feature only has value if the stock price rises; otherwise it has zero value. The more risk and stock price volatility, the greater the likelihood that the conversion feature will be of value at some point before the expiration date. As a result, more risk and uncertainty increase the value of the conversion feature of the convertible. Thus, the negative effect of an increase in risk and uncertainty on the straight-debt portion of a convertible is partially offset by the positive effect on the conversion feature. The result of all this is that the interest rate associated with convertible debt is, to an extent, indifferent to the risk level of the issuing firm. The coupon rates for medium- and high-risk companies issuing convertibles and straight debt might be as follows:

| | Company Risk | |
|---|---|---|
| | Medium | High |
| Convertible debt | 8% | 8.25% |
| Straight debt | 11 | 13 |

Thus, convertible debt may allow companies with a high level of risk to raise funds at a relatively favorable rate.

## Valuation of a Convertible

The valuation of a convertible depends primarily upon two factors: the value of the straight debenture or preferred stock and the value of the security if it were converted into common stock. Complicating the valuation is the fact that investors are in general willing to pay a premium for the conversion privilege, which allows them to hedge against the future. If the price of the common stock should rise, the investor would participate in capital gains; if it should decline, the convertible security will fall only to its value as a straight debenture or preferred stock.

In examining the Union Carbide convertible debenture, let us assume that if it were selling as a straight debenture, its price would be $785.46. Thus, regardless of what happens to its common stock, the lowest value the convertible can drop to is $785.46. The conversion value, on the other hand, is $676.06, so this convertible is worth more as straight debt than if it were common stock. However, the real question is: Why are investors willing to pay a conversion premium of 16.1 percent over its security or conversion value for this Union Carbide debenture? Quite simply, because investors are willing to pay for the chance for capital gains without the large risk of loss.

Figure 21A-1 graphically depicts the relationship between the value of the convertible and the price of its common stock. The bond value of the convertible serves as a floor for the value of the investment: When the conversion value reaches the convertible's security value (point *A*), the value of the convertible becomes dependent upon its conversion value. In effect, the convertible security is valued as a bond when the price of the common stock is low and as common stock when the price of the common stock rises. Of course, if the firm is doing poorly and in financial distress, both the common stock price and the security value will suffer. In the extreme, when the firm's total value falls to zero both the common stock and any debt that the firm had issued would have no value. Although the minimum price of the convertible is determined by the higher of either the straight bond or preferred stock price or the conversion value, investors also pay a premium for the conversion option. Again, this premium results because convertible securities offer investors stable income from debenture or preferreds—and thus less risk of price decline due to adverse stock conditions—while retaining capital gains prospects from stock price gains. In effect, downside stock price variability is hedged away, whereas upside variability is not.

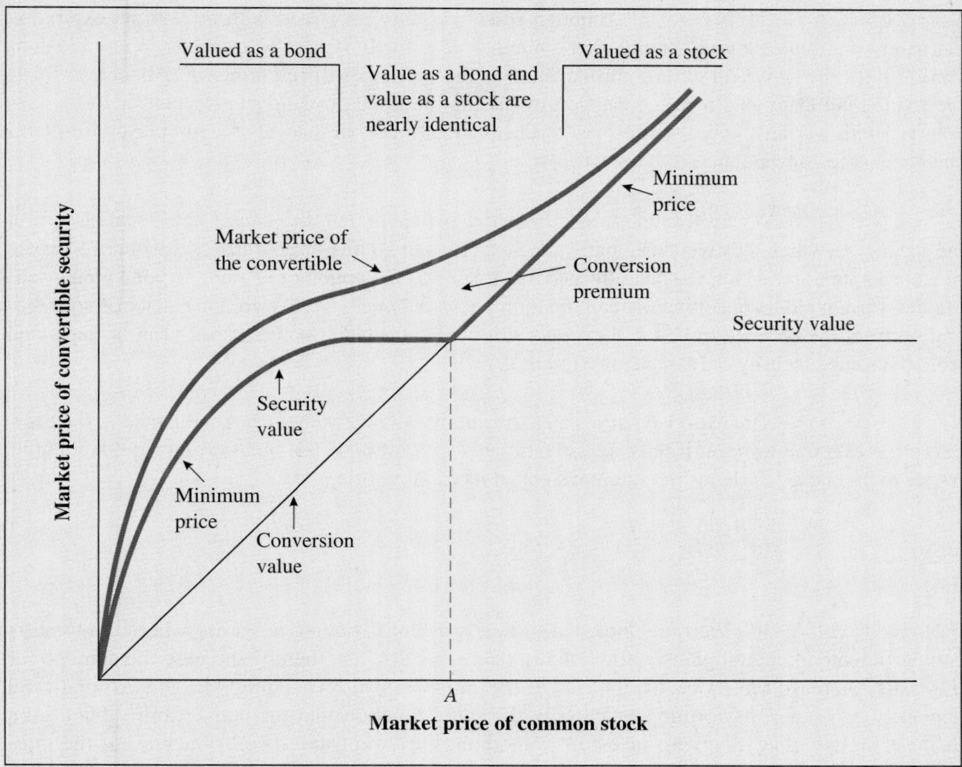


**FIGURE 21A-1**
Relationship Between the Market Price of the Common Stock and the Market Price of the Convertible Security

# WARRANTS

**A warrant** provides the investor with an option to purchase a fixed number of shares of common stock at a predetermined price during a specified time period. Warrants have been used in the past primarily by weaker firms as sweetener attachments to bonds or preferred stock to improve their marketability. However, in April 1970, when AT&T included them as a part of a major financing package, warrants achieved a new level of respectability.

**Warrant**
An option to purchase a fixed number of shares of common stock at a predetermined price during a specified time period.

Only recently have warrants been issued in conjunction with common stock. Their purpose is essentially the same as when they are issued in conjunction with debt or preferred stock—that is, to improve the reception in the market of the new offering or make a tender offer too attractive to turn down.

Although warrants are similar to convertibles in that both provide investors with a chance to participate in capital gains, the mechanics of the two instruments differ greatly. From the standpoint of the issuing firm, there are two major differences. First, when convertibles are exchanged for common stock, debt is eliminated and fixed finance charges are reduced; whereas when warrants are exchanged, fixed charges are not reduced. Second, when convertibles are exchanged, there is no cash inflow into the firm—the exchange is merely one type of security for another. But with warrants, because they are merely an option to buy the stock at a set price, a cash flow accompanies the exchange.

## Characteristics and Features of Warrants

EXERCISE PRICE The **exercise price** is that price at which the warrant allows its holder to purchase the firm's common stock. The investor trades a warrant plus the exercise price for common stock. Typically, when warrants are issued, the exercise price is set above the current market price of the stock. Thus, if the stock price does not rise above the exercise price, the warrant will never be converted. In addition, there can also be a step-up exercise price, where the warrant's exercise price changes over time.

**Warrant exercise price**
The price at which a warrant allows its holder to purchase the firm's common stock.

**WARRANT EXPIRATION DATE** Although some warrants are issued with no warrant expiration date, most warrants are set to expire after a number of years. In issuing warrants as opposed to convertibles, the firm gives up some control over when the warrants will be exercised. With convertibles, the issuing company can force conversion by calling the issue or using step-up conversion prices, whereas with warrants only the approach of the expiration date or the use of step-up exercise prices can encourage conversion.

**DETACHABILITY** Most warrants are said to be *detachable* in that they can be sold separately from the security to which they were originally attached. Thus, if an investor purchases a primary issuance of a corporate bond with a warrant attached, he or she has the option of selling the bond alone, selling the warrant alone, or selling the combination intact. *Nondetachable* warrants cannot be sold separately from the security to which they were originally attached. Such a warrant can be separated from the senior security only by being exercised.

**Exercise ratio**
The number of shares of common stock that can be obtained at the exercise price with one warrant.

**EXERCISE RATIO** The **exercise ratio** states the number of shares that can be obtained at the exercise price with one warrant. If the exercise ratio on a warrant were 1.5, one warrant would entitle its owner to purchase 1.5 shares of common stock at its exercise price.

## Reasons for Issuing Warrants

**SWEETENING DEBT** Warrants attached to debt offerings provide a feature whereby investors can participate in capital gains while holding debt. The firm can thereby increase the demand for the issue, increase the proceeds, and lower the interest costs. Attaching warrants to long-term debt is a sweetener, performing essentially the same function that the convertibility feature on debt performs—that is, giving investors something they want and thereby increasing the marketability and demand for the bonds.

**ADDITIONAL CASH INFLOW** If warrants are added to sweeten a debt offering, the firm will receive an eventual cash inflow when and if the warrants are exercised; a convertibility feature would not provide this additional inflow.

**VALUATION OF A WARRANT** Because the warrant is an option to purchase a specified number of shares of stock at a specified price for a given length of time, the market value of the warrant will be primarily a function of the common stock price. To understand the valuation of warrants, we must define two additional terms, the *minimum price* and the *premium.* Let us look at the Photon Pharmaceutical warrants with an expiration date of December 31, 2004, an exercise ratio of 1.00, and let's assume an exercise price of $80 through the expiration date. This means that any time until expiration on December 31, 2004, an investor with one warrant can purchase one share of Photon Pharmaceutical stock at $80 regardless of the market price of that stock. Let's assume these Photon Pharmaceutical warrants were selling at $5.50, and the Photon Pharmaceutical stock was selling for $56.75 per share.

**MINIMUM PRICE** The *minimum price* of a warrant is determined as follows:

$$\text{minimum price} = \left(\begin{array}{c}\text{market price of}\\ \text{common stock}\end{array}\right) - \left(\begin{array}{c}\text{exercise}\\ \text{price}\end{array}\right) \times \text{exercise ratio} \qquad \textbf{(21A-4)}$$

In the Photon Pharmaceutical example, the exercise price is greater than the price of the common stock ($80 as opposed to $56.75). In this case, the minimum price of the warrant is considered to be zero, because things simply do not sell for negative prices [($56.75 − $80) × 1.00 = −$23.25]. If, for example, the price of the Photon Pharmaceutical common stock rose to $86 per share, the minimum price on the warrant would become ($86 − $80) × 1.00 = $6. This would tell us that this warrant could not fall below a price of $6.00, because if it did, investors could realize immediate trading profits by purchasing the warrants and converting them along with the $80

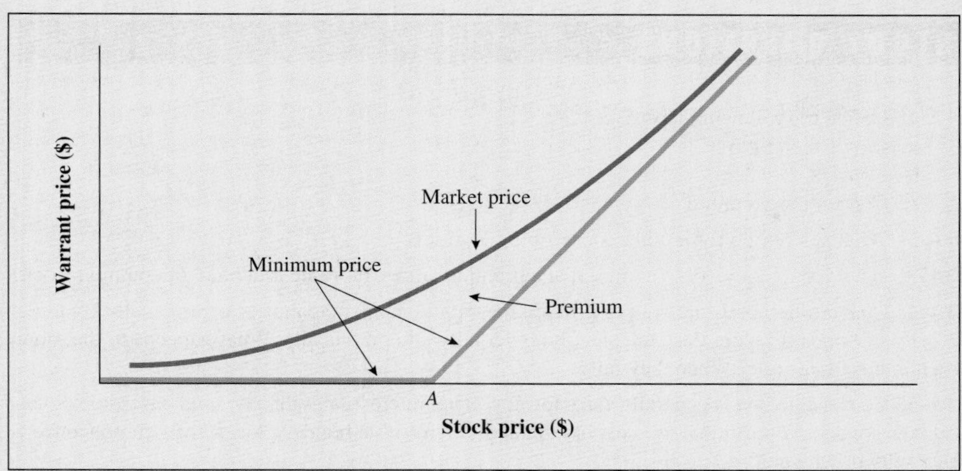


FIGURE 21A-2
Valuation of Warrants

exercise price into common stock until the price of the warrant was pushed up to the minimum price. This process of simultaneously buying and selling equivalent assets for different prices is called *arbitrage.*

PREMIUM The premium is the amount above the minimum price for which the warrant sells:

$$\text{premium} = \begin{pmatrix}\text{market price}\\ \text{of warrant}\end{pmatrix} - \begin{pmatrix}\text{minimum price}\\ \text{of warrant}\end{pmatrix}$$

In the case of the Photon Pharmaceutical warrant, the premium is \$5.50 − \$0 = \$5.50. Investors are paying a premium of \$5.50 above the minimum price for the warrant. They are willing to do so because the possible loss is small although the warrant price is only about 9.69 percent of the common stock; in turn, the possible return is large because, if the price of the common stock climbs, the value of the warrant also will climb.

Figure 21A-2 graphs the relationships among the warrant price, the minimum price, and the premium. Point *A* represents the exercise price on the warrant. Once the price of the stock is above the exercise price, the warrant's minimum price takes on positive or nonzero values.

Although the stock price/exercise price ratio is one of the most important factors in determining the size of the premium, several other factors also affect it. One such factor is the time left to the warrant expiration date. As the warrant's expiration date approaches, the size of the premium begins to shrink, approaching zero. A second factor is investors' expectations concerning the capital gains potential of the stock. If they feel favorably about the prospects for price increases in the common stock, a large warrant premium will result, because a stock price increase will affect a warrant price increase. Finally, the degree of price volatility on the underlying common stock affects the size of the warrant premium. The more volatile the common stock price, the higher the warrant premium. As price volatility increases, so does the probability of and potential size of profits.

## KEY TERMS

**Convertible security, 722**
**Conversion ratio, 722**
**Conversion value, 722**
**Security value, 723**
**Conversion period, 723**
**Conversion premium, 723**
**Warrant, 725**
**Warrant exercise price, 725**
**Exercise ratio, 726**

## STUDY QUESTIONS

**21A-1.** Define the following terms:

**a.** Conversion ratio
**b.** Conversion value
**c.** Conversion premium

**21A-2.** What is a reason for issuing convertible securities?

**21A-3.** Why does a convertible bond sell at a premium above its value as a bond or common stock?

**21A-4.** Convertible bonds are said to provide the capital gains potential of common stock and the security of bonds. Explain this statement both verbally and graphically. What happens to the graph when interest rates rise? When they fall?

**21A-5.** Convertible bonds generally carry lower coupon interest rates than do nonconvertible bonds. If this is so, does it mean that the cost of capital on convertible bonds is lower than on nonconvertible? Why or why not?

**21A-6.** Explain the difference between a convertible security and a warrant.

**21A-7.** Explain the valuation of warrants both verbally and graphically.

**21A-8.** What factors affect the size of the warrant premium? How?

## SELF-TEST PROBLEMS

**ST-1.** (*Convertible terminology*) In 2002, Winky's Cow Paste, Inc., issued $10 million of $1,000 par value, 10 percent semiannual convertible debentures that come due in 2022. The conversion price on these convertibles is $16.75 per share. The common stock was selling for $14-3/4 per share on a given date shortly after these convertibles were issued. These convertibles have a B– rating, and straight B– debentures were yielding 14 percent on that date. The market price of the convertible was $970 on that date. Determine the following:

**a.** Conversion ratio
**b.** Conversion value
**c.** Security value
**d.** Conversion premium

**ST-2.** (*Warrant terminology*) Petro-Tech, Inc., currently has some warrants outstanding that allow the holder to purchase, with one warrant, one share of common stock at $18.275 per share. If the common stock was selling at $25 per share and the warrants were selling for $9.50, what would be the

**a.** Minimum price?
**b.** Warrant premium?

## STUDY PROBLEMS (SET A)

**21A-1A.** (*Convertible terminology*) In 2002, the Andy Fields Corporation of Delaware issued some $1,000 par value, 6 percent convertible debentures that come due in 2022. The conversion price on these convertibles is $40 per share. The price of the common stock is now $27.25 per share. These convertibles have a BBB rating, and straight BBB debentures are now yielding 9 percent. The market price of the convertible is now $840.25. Determine the following (assume bond interest payments are made annually):

**a.** Conversion ratio
**b.** Conversion value

**c.** Security value
**d.** Conversion premium

**21A-2A.** (*Convertible terminology*) The L. Padis, Jr., Corporation has an issue of 5 percent convertible preferred stock outstanding. The conversion price on these securities is $27 per share to 9/30/06. The price of the common stock is now $13.25 per share. The preferred stock is selling for $17.75. The par value of the preferred stock is $25 per share. Similar quality preferred stock without the conversion feature is currently yielding 8 percent. Determine the following:
**a.** Conversion ratio
**b.** Conversion value
**c.** Conversion premium

**21A-3A.** (*Warrant terminology*) The T. Kitchel Corporation has a warrant that allows the purchase of one share of common stock at $30 per share. The warrant is currently selling at $4 and the common stock is priced at $25 per share. Determine the minimum price and the premium of the warrant.

**21A-4A.** (*Warrant terminology*) Cobra Airlines has some warrants outstanding that allow the purchase of common stock at the rate of one warrant for each share of common stock at $11.71 per share.
**a.** Given that the warrants were selling for $3 each and the common stock was selling for $10 per share, determine the minimum price and warrant premium as of that date.
**b.** Given that the warrants were selling for $9.75 each, and the common stock was selling for $16.375 per share, determine the minimum price and warrant premium as of that date.

**21A-5A.** (*Warrant terminology*) International Corporation has some warrants outstanding that allow the purchase of common stock at the price of $22.94 per share. These warrants are somewhat unusual in that one warrant allows for the purchase of 3.1827 shares of common stock at the exercise price of $22.94 per share. Given that the warrants were selling for $6.25 each, and the common stock was selling for $7.25 per share, determine the minimum price and the warrant premium as of that date.

**21A-6A.** (*Warrants and their leverage effect*) A month ago, you purchased 100 Bolster Corporation warrants at $3 each. When you made your purchase, the market price of Bolster's common stock was $40 per share. The exercise price on the warrants is $40 per share whereas the exercise ratio is 1.0. Today, the market price of Bolster's common stock has jumped up to $45 per share, whereas the market price of Bolster's warrants has climbed to $7.50 each. Calculate the total dollar gain that you would have received if you had invested the same dollar amount in common stock versus warrants. What is this in terms of return on investment?

## STUDY PROBLEMS (SET B)

**21A-1B.** (*Convertible terminology*) In 2002, the P. Mauney Corporation of Virginia issued some $1,000 par value, 7 percent convertible debentures that come due in 2022. The conversion price on these convertibles is $45 per share. The price of the common stock is now $26 per share. These convertibles have a BBB rating, and straight BBB debentures are now yielding 9 percent. The market price of the convertible is now $840.25. Determine the following (assume bond interest payments are made annually):
**a.** Conversion ratio
**b.** Conversion value
**c.** Security value
**d.** Conversion premium

**21A-2B.** (*Convertible terminology*) The Ecotosleptics Corporation has an issue of 6 percent convertible preferred stock outstanding. The conversion price on these securities is $28 per share to 9/30/06. The price of the common stock is now $14 per share. The preferred stock is selling for $20. The par value of the preferred stock is $25 per share. Similar quality preferred stock without the conversion feature is currently yielding 8 percent. Determine the following:
**a.** Conversion ratio
**b.** Conversion value
**c.** Conversion premium

**21A-3B.** (*Warrant terminology*) The Megacorndoodles Corporation has a warrant that allows the purchase of one share of common stock at $32 per share. The warrant is currently selling at $5 and the common stock is priced at $24 per share. Determine the minimum price and the premium of the warrant.

**21A-4B.** (*Warrant terminology*) Taco Fever has some warrants outstanding that allow the purchase of common stock at the rate of one warrant for each share of common stock at $11.75 per share.

**a.** Given that the warrants were selling for $4 each, and the common stock was selling for $9 per share, determine the minimum price and warrant premium as of that date.

**b.** Given that the warrants were selling for $7 each, and the common stock was selling for $15.375 per share, determine the minimum price and warrant premium as of that date.

**21A-5B.** (*Warrant terminology*) Fla'vo'phone Corporation has some warrants outstanding that allow the purchase of common stock at the price of $22.94 per share. These warrants are somewhat unusual in that one warrant allows for the purchase of 4.257 shares of common stock at the exercise price of $22.94 per share. Given that the warrants were selling for $6.75 each, and the common stock was selling for $8 per share, determine the minimum price and the warrant premium as of that date.

**21A-6B.** (*Warrants and their leverage effect*) A month ago, you purchased 100 Annie Kay's Corporation warrants at $2.75 each. When you made your purchase, the market price of Annie Kay's common stock was $35 per share. The exercise price on the warrants is $35 per share whereas the exercise ratio is 1.0. Today, the market price of Annie Kay's common stock has jumped up to $40 per share, whereas the market price of Annie Kay's warrants has climbed to $6.75 each. Calculate the total dollar gain that you would have received if you had invested the same dollar amount in common stock versus warrants. What is this in terms of return on investment?

## SELF-TEST SOLUTIONS

**ST-1. a.** conversion ratio = par value of convertible security/conversion price

$$= \frac{\$1{,}000}{\$16.75}$$

$$= 59.70 \text{ shares}$$

**b.** $$\text{conversion value} = \begin{pmatrix}\text{converison}\\ \text{ratio}\end{pmatrix} \times \begin{pmatrix}\text{market value per share}\\ \text{of common stock}\end{pmatrix}$$

$$= 59.70 \text{ shares} \times \$14.75/\text{share}$$
$$= \$880.58$$

**c.** $$\text{security value} = \sum_{t=1}^{40} \frac{\$50}{(1 + .07)^t} + \frac{\$1{,}000}{(1 + .07)^{40}}$$

$$= \$50(13.332) + \$1{,}000(.067)$$

$$= \$666.60 + \$67$$

$$= \$733.60$$

(*Note:* Because this debenture pays interest semiannually, $t$ = 20 years × 2 = 40 and $i$ = 14%/2 = 7% in the calculations.)

**d.** conversion premium $= \begin{pmatrix}\text{market price of}\\ \text{the convertible}\end{pmatrix} - \begin{pmatrix}\text{higher of the security value}\\ \text{and conversion value}\end{pmatrix}$

$= \$970.00 - \$880.58$

$= \$89.42$

**ST-2. a.** minimum price $= \begin{pmatrix}\text{market price of}\\ \text{common stock}\end{pmatrix} - \begin{pmatrix}\text{exercise}\\ \text{price}\end{pmatrix} \times \begin{pmatrix}\text{exercise}\\ \text{ratio}\end{pmatrix}$

$= (\$25.00 - \$18.275) \times (1.0)$

$= \$6.725$

**b.** warrant premium $= \begin{pmatrix}\text{market price}\\ \text{of warrant}\end{pmatrix} - \begin{pmatrix}\text{minimum price}\\ \text{of warrant}\end{pmatrix}$

$= (\$9.50 - \$6.725)$

$= \$2.775$

# INTERNATIONAL BUSINESS FINANCE

Finding new projects doesn't necessarily mean coming up with a new product; it may mean taking an existing product and applying it to a new market. For Harley-Davidson, that could mean taking its heavyweight motorcycles and selling them

abroad. Harley is not just offering these motorcycles for sale, but is also setting up the dealer system and HOG chapters that have proved so effective in America. In October 2000, in a move to strengthen its position in the European market, Harley-Davidson announced the acquisition of its Italian distributor. The new company, Harley-Davidson Italia S.r.l., is the latest sign of Harley-Davidson's growth in Europe, and it will be instrumental in increasing sales performance in the fast-growing Italian market. Harley-Davidson subsidiaries already exist in Germany, France, the Benelux, and the United Kingdom. Harley-Davidson also operates a wholly owned subsidiary in Japan. In fact, if you look at market share, while Harley rules in the United States, it controls only about 7 percent of the European heavyweight market where Honda, Yamaha, Suzuki, and BMW are the leaders, and approximately 20 percent of the Asian/Pacific heavyweight market where only Honda controls more of the market share. Harley's share of both of these markets grew in 1999 and 2000. Harley-Davidson views the fact that it does not control these markets as an opportunity. ● Of course there are the obvious costs associated with going abroad, such as distance, language, distribution, and maintaining inventory abroad, but there are also other, less obvious cultural

**LEARNING OBJECTIVES**

After reading this chapter, you should be able to

1. Discuss the internationalization of business.
2. Explain why foreign exchange rates in two different countries must be in line with each other.
3. Discuss the concept of interest-rate parity.
4. Explain the purchasing-power parity theory and the law of one price.
5. Explain what exchange rate risk is and how it can be controlled.
6. Identify working-capital management techniques that are useful for international businesses to reduce exchange rate risk and potentially increase profits.
7. Explain how the financing sources available to multinational corporations differ from those available to domestic firms.
8. Discuss the risks involved in direct foreign investment.

factors associated with operating a sales outlet outside of the United States that are both different and challenging. In addition, there are the risks associated with the European and Asian/Pacific economies and currencies. ● These risks all materialized in the Asian and Pacific markets in 1998 when those economies crashed, with currencies like Malaysia's Ringgit and Thailand's Baht dropping by about one-third and one-half in value relative to the U.S. dollar. This same problem reappeared over the 1999–2000 period, but this time in Europe, when the value of the Euro, the currency of the European Union, dropped by around 28 percent. Because Harley receives Euros and Yen when it sells its motorcycles in Europe and Japan, the sales value in U.S. dollars is worth less. Unfortunately, Harley makes virtually all of its motorcycles in the United States and pays U.S. dollars to its workers and for its materials. ● All of this goes to show that entering the international markets carries both great opportunities and risks.

**CHAPTER PREVIEW**

This chapter highlights the complications that an international business faces when it deals in multiple currencies. Effective strategies for the reduction of foreign exchange risk are discussed. Working-capital management and capital structure decisions in the international context are also covered. For the international firm, direct foreign investment is a capital-budgeting decision—with some additional complexities.

As you study this chapter on international business finance, you will be reminded of two of the principles that tie this entire text together: **Principle 1: The Risk-Return Trade-Off—We won't take on additional risk unless we expect to be compensated with additional return;** and **Principle 3: Cash—Not Profits—Is King.** Look for them as you work through the several discussions.

## THE GLOBALIZATION OF PRODUCT AND FINANCIAL MARKETS

Today, there is no ducking the global markets. In fact, it has been estimated that the United States exports about one-fifth of its industrial production and that about 70 percent of all U.S. goods compete directly with foreign goods.

There has also been a rise in the global level of international portfolio and direct investment. Both direct and portfolio investment in the United States have been increasing faster than U.S. investment overseas. Direct investment occurs when the **multinational corporation (MNC),** a corporation with holdings and/or operations in more than one country, has control over the investment, such as when it builds an offshore manufacturing facility. Portfolio investment involves financial assets with maturities greater than 1 year, such as the purchase of foreign stocks and bonds. Total foreign investment in the United States now exceeds such U.S. investment overseas.

**Multinational corporation (MNC)**
A corporation with holdings and/or operations in one or more countries.

A major reason for long-run overseas investments of U.S. companies is the high rates of return obtainable from these investments. The amount of U.S. *direct foreign investment (DFI)* abroad is large and growing. Significant amounts of the total assets, sales, and profits of American MNCs are attributable to foreign investments and foreign operations. Direct foreign investment is not limited to American firms. Many European and Japanese firms have operations abroad, too. During the last decade, these firms have been increasing their sales and setting up production facilities abroad, especially in the United States.

Capital flows between countries for international financial investment purposes have also been increasing. Many firms, investment companies, and individuals invest in the capital markets in foreign countries. The motivation is twofold: to obtain returns higher than those obtainable in the domestic capital markets and to reduce portfolio risk through international diversification. The increase in world trade and investment activity is reflected in the recent globalization of financial markets. The Eurodollar market is larger than any domestic financial market. U.S. companies are increasingly turning to this market for funds. Even companies and public entities that have no overseas presence are beginning to rely on this market for financing.

In addition, most national financial markets are becoming more integrated with global markets because of the rapid increase in the volume of interest rate and currency swaps. Because of the widespread availability of these swaps, the currency denomination and the source country of financing for many globally integrated companies are dictated by accessibility and relative cost considerations regardless of the currency ultimately needed by the firm.

The foreign exchange markets have also grown rapidly, and the weekly trading volume in these globally integrated markets (between $4 and $7 trillion) exceeds the annual trading volume on the world's securities markets. Even a purely domestic firm that buys all its inputs and sells all its output in its home country is not immune to foreign competition, nor can it totally ignore the workings of the international financial markets.

**CONCEPT CHECK**

1. Why do U.S. companies invest overseas?
2. What kinds of risks are introduced when a firm invests overseas?

## EXCHANGE RATES

### Recent History of Exchange Rates

OBJECTIVE 2 

Between 1949 and 1970, the exchange rates between the major currencies were fixed. All countries were required to set a specific *parity rate* for their currency vis-à-vis the U.S. dollar. For example, consider the German currency, the deutsche mark (DM). In 1949, the parity rate was set at DM 4.0 per dollar (DM 4.0/$). The actual exchange rate prevailing on any day was allowed to lie within a narrow band around the parity rate. The DM was allowed to fluctuate between DM 4.04 and DM 3.96/$. A country could effect a major adjustment in the exchange rate by changing its parity rate with respect to the dollar. When the currency was made cheaper with respect to the dollar, this adjustment was called a *devaluation.* A *revaluation* resulted when a currency became more expensive with respect to the dollar. In 1969, the DM parity rate was adjusted to DM 3.66/$. This adjustment was a revaluation of the DM parity by 9.3 percent. The new bands around the parity were DM 3.7010 and DM 3.6188/$. The DM strengthened against the dollar because fewer DM were needed to buy a dollar.

**Floating-rate international currency system**
An international currency system in which exchange rates between different national currencies are allowed to fluctuate with supply and demand conditions. This contrasts with a fixed rate system in which exchange rates are pegged for extended periods of time and adjusted infrequently.

Since 1973, a **floating-rate international currency system,** a system in which exchange rates between different national currencies are allowed to fluctuate with supply and demand conditions, has been operating. For most currencies, there are no parity rates and no bands within which the currencies fluctuate.[1] Most major currencies, including the U.S. dollar, fluctuate freely, depending upon their values as perceived by the traders in foreign exchange markets. The country's relative economic strengths, its level of exports and

[1]The system of floating rates is referred to as the "floating-rate regime."

imports, the level of monetary activity, and the deficits or surpluses in its balance of payments (BOP) are all important factors in the determination of exchange rates.[2] Short-term, day-to-day fluctuations in exchange rates are caused by changing supply and demand conditions in the foreign exchange market.

## The Euro: The New Currency of Europe

Beginning January 1, 1999, 11 countries in the European Union introduced a new, single currency, the Euro. These countries, often referred to as Euroland, include Germany, France, Italy, Spain, Portugal, Belgium, the Netherlands, Luxembourg, Ireland, Finland, and Austria. Without question, Germany and France are the big players, accounting for over 50 percent of Euroland's output. Eventually, the Euro will replace the existing national currencies in these countries. The timetable is:

- January 1, 1999: The Euro is introduced in principle only. The foreign exchange rates of the participating national currencies are fixed against each other and the Euro. Even though the currency doesn't exist, consumers and businesses can borrow money, open bank accounts, and write checks in Euros.
- January 1, 2002: Euro currency, both coins and notes, begins circulation.
- July 1, 2002: The national currencies in the 11 countries using the Euro will disappear.

Why has the European Union gone to a single currency? For several reasons: First, it will make it easier for goods, people, and services to travel across national borders. As a result, the economies of the European Union should flourish. A common currency eliminates the exchange costs that occur when you have to trade your German marks for French francs. It also eliminates the uncertainty associated with exchange rate fluctuations. It should also help to eliminate cost differences for goods in different countries. For example, when the Euro was introduced in 1999, "The Classics" Swatch watch was selling for 39.2 Euros ($45.97) in Belgium and only 25.7 Euros ($30.14) in Italy. With the introduction of the Euro, it should be easier to compare prices and eliminate the discrepancies.

What does all this mean for the United States? It means several things: First, it means the competition from abroad will be stronger. It also makes the exchange rate between the Euro and the U.S. dollar a very important exchange rate. If the Euro is strong, it should help U.S. exports by making them cheaper. On the other hand, if the Euro is weak, U.S. exports may suffer. Fortunately, many U.S. multinational firms appear to be in good shape to cash in on any economic surge that may hit Euroland. For example, look at Wal-Mart, which has 21 stores in Germany. In Germany, Wal-Mart is doing just what it does here in the United States: It is wiping out the competition. For the Germans, this is their first sight of wide aisles—bigger than some of the local streets—and discount shopping. The Euro will allow Wal-Mart to offer even more bargains from all over Euroland, and it will allow Wal-Mart to provide a much more diverse selection of goods. That's because in Europe, because of all the exchange rate uncertainties, most goods are regional in nature. That's the bottom line—the Euro should introduce greater choice and greater competition—both good for the consumer.

## The Foreign Exchange Market

The foreign exchange market provides a mechanism for the transfer of purchasing power from one currency to another. This market is not a physical entity such as the New York

[2]The balance of payments for the United States reflects the difference between the import and export of goods (the trade balance) and services. Capital inflows and outflows are tabulated in the capital account.

**FINANCE MATTERS**

### The Euro: A Dismal Failure, a Ringing Success—Yes, It's Sunk Like a Stone, But It Has Cracked Open Europe's Capital Markets

FRANKFURT — The euro has been a surprise in two ways: It has dropped nearly 30% against the dollar in its first 22 months. And it has changed European financial markets, businesses and the economy faster than its founders dared to hope.

The first fact steals the headlines, prompts European Central Bank intervention and makes the common-currency experiment look like a failure. The second likely will have more lasting and profound effects, and will help sustain the euro during troubled times.

Most significantly, the creation of a currency shared by 11 countries is creating bigger and more-liquid European stock and bond markets, including a junk-bond market that is opening global financial markets to companies that were never before welcomed. The maturing capital market is reducing the cost of capital in Europe, liberating corporate borrowers from dependence on banks, and making acquisitions much easier to finance. The value of European mergers and acquisitions this year and last is roughly double that of 1998, the year before the euro was born; the U.S. saw no such increase, according to Thomson Financial Securities Data.

The euro is—as some of its proponents had hoped, and some of its detractors had feared—eroding national economic boundaries, prompting national stock and bond markets to consolidate and pressuring European governments, which now have a common monetary policy, to harmonize other economic policies.

"The euro has been a real revolution," says Isidoro Lucciola, chief financial officer of Grapes Communications NV, a Dutch telecommunications firm based in Italy. "The euro has probably destroyed local capitalism." Grapes, for example, operates in Spain, Portugal and Greece; financing doesn't come just from Italian banks anymore.

"The integration process has started, and much faster than we expected in the very beginning," says Sirkka Haemaelaeinen, a Finnish economist who sits on the six-member European Central Bank's executive board. "It will increase the competitiveness of the European economy."

Apart from the currency's alarming decline, the ramifications of its use are big, and will be unsettling. "The speed of these changes has been breathtaking, their implications far-reaching," says Barry Eichengreen, an international economist at the University of California at Berkeley. "This revolution in European finance implies that the European economy will be market-driven to a far greater extent in the future than in the past. It implies the decline of the national champions on which European industrial policy has long been based."

Source: G. Thomas Sims and David Wessel, "The Euro: A Dismal Failure, a Ringing Success—Yes, It's Sunk Like a Stone, But It Has Cracked Open Europe's Capital Markets," *The Wall Street Journal,* November 6, 2000, page A29. 

Stock Exchange; it is a network of telephone and computer connections among banks, foreign exchange dealers, and brokers. The market operates simultaneously at three levels. At the first level, customers buy and sell foreign exchange (that is, foreign currency) through their banks. At the second level, banks buy and sell foreign exchange from other banks in the same commercial center. At the last level, banks buy and sell foreign exchange from banks in commercial centers in other countries. Some important commercial centers for foreign exchange trading are New York, London, Zurich, Frankfurt, Hong Kong, Singapore, and Tokyo.

An example will illustrate this multilevel trading. A trader in Texas may buy foreign exchange (pounds) from a bank in Houston for payment to a British supplier against some purchase made. The Houston bank, in turn, may purchase the foreign currency (pounds) from a New York bank. The New York bank may buy the pounds from another bank in New York or from a bank in London.

Because this market provides transactions in a continuous manner for a very large volume of sales and purchases, the currency markets are efficient: In other words, it is difficult to make a profit by shopping around from one bank to another. Minute differences in the quotes from different banks are quickly eliminated. Because of the arbitrage mechanism, simultaneous quotes to different buyers in London and New York are likely to be the same.

Two major types of transactions are carried out in the foreign exchange markets: spot and forward transactions.

## Spot Exchange Rates

A typical spot transaction involves an American firm buying foreign currency from its bank and paying for it in dollars. The price of foreign currency in terms of the domestic currency is the **exchange rate**. Another type of spot transaction occurs when an American firm receives foreign currency from abroad. The firm typically would sell the foreign currency to its bank for dollars. These are both **spot transactions** because one currency is traded for another currency today. The actual exchange rate quotes are expressed in several different ways, as discussed later. To allow time for the transfer of funds, the *value date* when the currencies are actually exchanged is 2 days after the spot transaction occurs. Four banks could easily be involved in the transactions: the local banks of the buyer and seller of the foreign exchange, and the money-center banks that handle the purchase and sale in the interbank market. Perhaps the buyer or seller will have to move the funds from one of its local banks to another, bringing even more banks into the transaction. A forward transaction entails an agreement today to deliver a specified number of units of a currency on a future date in return for a specified number of units of another currency.

**Exchange rate**
The price of foreign currency stated in terms of the domestic or home currency.

**Spot transaction**
A transaction made immediately in the marketplace at the market price.

On the spot exchange market, contrasted with the over-the-counter market, the quoted exchange rate is typically called a direct quote. A **direct quote** indicates the number of units of the home currency required to buy one unit of the foreign currency. That is, in New York the typical exchange-rate quote indicates the number of dollars needed to buy one unit of a foreign currency: dollars per pound, dollars per mark, and so on. The spot rates in Table 22-1 are the direct exchange quotes taken from *The Wall Street Journal*. Thus, according to Table 22-1, to buy 1 British pound (£1), $1.6458 was needed. To buy French francs and German marks, $.1763 and $.5912 were needed, respectively.

**Direct quote**
The exchange rate that indicates the number of units of the home currency required to buy one unit of foreign currency.

An **indirect quote** indicates the number of units of foreign currency that can be bought for one unit of the home currency. This reads as francs per dollar, marks per dollar, and so forth. An indirect quote is the general method used in the over-the-counter market. Exceptions to this rule include British pounds, Irish punts, Australian dollars, and New Zealand dollars, which are quoted via direct quote for historical reasons. Indirect quotes are given in the last column of Table 22-1.

**Indirect quote**
The exchange rate that expresses the required number of units of foreign currency to buy one unit of home currency.

In summary, a direct quote is the dollar/foreign currency rate ($/FC), and an indirect quote is the foreign currency/dollar (FC/$). Therefore, an indirect quote is the reciprocal of a direct quote and vice versa. The following example illustrates the computation of an indirect quote from a given direct quote.

### EXAMPLE

Suppose you want to compute the indirect quote from the direct quote of spot rates for pounds given in column 1 of Table 22-1. The direct quote for the pound is $1.6458. The related indirect quotes are calculated as the *reciprocal* of the direct quote as follows:

$$\text{indirect quote} = \frac{1}{\text{direct quote}}$$

Thus,

$$\text{pounds} \qquad \frac{1}{\$1,6458/£} = £.6076$$

Notice that this quote and indirect quote are identical to those shown in the second column of Table 22-1.

**TABLE 22-1**
Foreign Exchange Rates Reported on January 20, 1999

| Country | U.S. $ equiv. | Currency per U.S. $ |
|---|---|---|
| **Argentina** (Peso) | 1.0002 | .9998 |
| **Australia** (Dollar) | .6393 | 1.5642 |
| **Austria** (Schilling) | .08402 | 11.901 |
| **Bahrain** (Dinar) | 2.6525 | .3770 |
| **Belgium** (Franc) | .02866 | 34.890 |
| **Brazil** (Real) | .6329 | 1.5800 |
| **Britain** (Pound) | 1.6458 | .6076 |
| 1-month forward | 1.6444 | .6081 |
| 3-months forward | 1.6429 | .6087 |
| 6-months forward | 1.6416 | .6092 |
| **Canada** (Dollar) | .6572 | 1.5215 |
| 1-month forward | .6564 | 1.5235 |
| 3-months forward | .6566 | 1.5230 |
| 6-months forward | .6560 | 1.5245 |
| **Chile** (Peso) | .002093 | 477.75 |
| **China** (Renminbi) | .1208 | 8.2787 |
| **Colombia** (Peso) | .0006300 | 1587.18 |
| **Czech. Rep.** (Koruna) | | |
| Commercial rate | .03180 | 31.450 |
| **Denmark** (Krone) | .1552 | 6.4425 |
| **Ecuador** (Sucre) | | |
| Floating rate | .0001406 | 7113.00 |
| **Finland** (Markka) | .1945 | 5.1425 |
| **France** (Franc) | .1763 | 5.6734 |
| 1-month forward | .1765 | 5.6644 |
| 3-months forward | .1771 | 5.6465 |
| 6-months forward | .1780 | 5.6185 |
| **Germany** (Mark) | .5912 | 1.6916 |
| 1-month forward | .5921 | 1.6889 |
| 3-months forward | .5940 | 1.6836 |
| 6-months forward | .5969 | 1.6753 |
| **Greece** (Drachma) | .003584 | 279.00 |
| **Hong Kong** (Dollar) | .1291 | 7.7483 |
| **Hungary** (Forint) | .004631 | 215.93 |
| **India** (Rupee) | .02353 | 42.505 |
| **Indonesia** (Rupiah) | .0001183 | 8450.00 |
| **Ireland** (Punt) | 1.4656 | .6823 |
| **Israel** (Shekel) | .2467 | 4.0543 |
| **Italy** (Lira) | .0005971 | 1674.68 |
| **Japan** (Yen) | .008853 | 112.96 |
| 1-month forward | .008853 | 112.96 |
| 3-months forward | .008854 | 112.95 |
| 6-months forward | .008855 | 112.93 |
| **Jordan** (Dinar) | 1.4114 | .7085 |
| **Kuwait** (Dinar) | 3.3124 | .3019 |
| **Lebanon** (Pound) | .0006631 | 1508.00 |
| **Malaysia** (Ringgit-b) | .2632 | 3.8000 |
| **Malta** (Lira) | 2.6378 | .3791 |
| **Mexico** (Peso) | | |
| Floating rate | .09799 | 10.205 |
| **Netherland** (Guilder) | .5247 | 1.9060 |
| **New Zealand** (Dollar) | .5396 | 1.8532 |
| **Norway** (Krone) | .1343 | 7.4443 |

| Country | U.S. $ equiv. | Currency per U.S. $ |
|---|---|---|
| **Pakistan** (Rupee) | .02004 | 49.910 |
| **Peru** (New Sol) | .3078 | 3.2485 |
| **Philippines** (Peso) | .02606 | 38.370 |
| **Poland** (Zloty) | .2857 | 3.5006 |
| **Portugal** (Escudo) | .005767 | 173.40 |
| **Russia** (Ruble) | .04466 | 22.390 |
| **Saudi Arabia** (Riyal) | .2665 | 3.7518 |
| **Singapore** (Dollar) | .5959 | 1.6780 |
| **Slovak Rep.** (Koruna) | .02712 | 36.869 |
| **South Africa** (Rand) | .1670 | 5.9880 |
| **South Korea** (Won) | .0008573 | 1166.50 |
| **Spain** (Peseta) | .006949 | 143.91 |
| **Sweden** (Krona) | .1294 | 7.7253 |
| **Switzerland** (Franc) | .7201 | 1.3887 |
| 1-month forward | .7224 | 1.3842 |
| 3-months forward | .7267 | 1.3762 |
| 6-months forward | .7332 | 1.3639 |
| **Taiwan** (Dollar) | .03100 | 32.263 |
| **Thailand** (Baht) | .02738 | 36.520 |
| **Turkey** (Lira) | .00000311 | 321253.00 |
| **United Arab** (Dirham) | .2723 | 3.6730 |
| **Uruguay** (New Peso) | | |
| Financial | .09066 | 11.030 |
| **Venezuela** (Bolivar) | .001751 | 571.00 |
| **SDR** | 1.4021 | .7132 |
| **Euro** | 1.1562 | .8649 |

Direct and indirect quotes are useful in conducting international transactions, as the following examples show.

**EXAMPLE**

An American business must pay DM 1,000 to a German firm on January 20, 1999. How many dollars will be required for this transaction?

$.5912/DM × DM 1,000 = $591.20

**EXAMPLE**

An American business must pay $2,000 to a British resident on January 20, 1999. How many pounds will the British resident receive?

£.6076/$ × $2,000 = £1,215.50

## Exchange Rates and Arbitrage

The foreign exchange quotes in two different countries must be in line with each other. The direct quote for U.S. dollars in London is given in pounds per dollar. Because the foreign exchange markets are efficient, the direct quotes for the per U.S. dollar rate in London on January 20, 1999, must be very close to the indirect rate prevailing in New York on that date.

**Arbitrageur**
A person involved in the process of buying and selling in more than one market to make riskless profits.

**Simple arbitrage**
Trading to eliminate exchange rate differentials across the markets for a single currency, for example, for the New York and London markets.

**Triangular arbitrage**
Arbitrage across the markets for all currencies.

**Covered-interest arbitrage**
Arbitrage designed to eliminate differentials across currency and interest rate markets.

If the exchange-rate quotations between the London and New York spot exchange markets were out of line, then an enterprising trader could make a profit by buying in the market where the currency was cheaper and selling it in the other. Such a buy-and-sell strategy would involve a zero net investment of funds and no risk bearing yet would provide a sure profit. Such a person is called an **arbitrageur,** and the process of buying and selling in more than one market to make a riskless profit is called *arbitrage.* Spot exchange markets are efficient in the sense that arbitrage opportunities do not persist for any length of time. That is, the exchange rates between two different markets are quickly brought in line, aided by the arbitrage process. **Simple arbitrage** eliminates exchange rate differentials across the markets for a single currency, as in the preceding example for the New York and London quotes. **Triangular arbitrage** does the same across the markets for all currencies. **Covered-interest arbitrage** eliminates differentials across currency and interest rate markets.

Suppose that London quotes £.6200/$ instead of £.6076/$. If you simultaneously bought a pound in New York for £.6076/$ and sold a pound in London for £.6200/$, you would have (1) taken a zero net investment position since you bought £1 and sold £1, (2) locked in a sure profit of £.0124/$ no matter which way the pound subsequently moves, and (3) set in motion the forces that will eliminate the different quotes in New York and London. As others in the marketplace learn of your transaction, they will attempt to make the same transaction. The increased demand to buy pounds in New York will lead to a higher quote there and the increased supply of pounds will lead to a lower quote in London. The workings of the market will produce a new spot rate that lies between £.6076/$ and £.6200/$ and is the same in New York and in London.

## Asked and Bid Rates

**Asked rate**
The rate a bank or foreign exchange trader "asks" the customer to pay in home currency for foreign currency when the bank is selling and the customer is buying.

**Selling rate**
Same as the asked rate.

**Bid rate**
The rate at which the bank buys the foreign currency from the customer by paying in home currency.

**Buying rate**
The bid rate in a currency transaction.

**Bid-asked spread**
The difference between the asked quote and the bid quote.

Two types of rates are quoted in the spot exchange market: the asked and the bid rates. The **asked rate** is the rate the bank or the foreign exchange trader "asks" the customer to pay in home currency for foreign currency when the bank is selling and the customer is buying. The asked rate is also known as the **selling rate** or the *offer rate*. The **bid rate** is the rate at which the bank buys the foreign currency from the customer by paying in home currency. The bid rate is also known as the **buying rate.** Note that Table 22-1 contains only the selling, offer, or asked rates, and not the buying rate.

The bank sells a unit of foreign currency for more than it pays for it. Therefore, the direct asked quote ($/FC) is greater than the direct bid quote. The difference between the asked quote and the bid quote is known as the **bid-asked spread.** When there is a large volume of transactions and the trading is continuous, the spread is small and can be less than –1 percent (.01) for the major currencies. The spread is much higher for infrequently traded currencies. The spread exists to compensate the banks for holding the risky foreign currency and for providing the service of converting currencies.

## Cross Rates

**Cross rate**
The computation of an exchange rate for a currency from the exchange rates of two other currencies.

A **cross rate** is the computation of an exchange rate for a currency from the exchange rates of two other currencies. The following example illustrates how this works.

### EXAMPLE

Taking the dollar/pound and the mark/dollar rates from columns 1 and 2 of Table 22-1, determine the mark/pound and pound/mark exchange rates. We see that

$$(\$/£) \times (DM/\$) = (DM/£)$$

or

$$1.6458 \times 1.6916 = \text{DM } 2.784/£$$

Thus, the pound/mark exchange rate is

$$1/2.7840 = £.3952/\text{DM}$$

Cross-rate computations make it possible to use quotations in New York to compute the exchange rate between pounds, marks, and francs. Arbitrage conditions hold in cross rates, too. For example, the pound exchange rate in Frankfurt (the direct quote marks/pound) must be 2.7840. The mark exchange rate in London must be .3952 pounds/mark. If the rates prevailing in Frankfurt and London were different from the computed cross rates, using quotes from New York, a trader could use three different currencies to lock in arbitrage profits through a process called *triangular arbitrage.*

## Forward Exchange Rates

A **forward exchange contract** requires delivery, at a specified future date, of one currency for a specified amount of another currency. The exchange rate for the forward transaction is agreed on today; the actual payment of one currency and the receipt of another currency take place at the future date. For example, a 30-day contract on March 1 is for delivery on March 31. Note that the forward rate is not the same as the spot rate that will prevail in the future. The actual spot rate that will prevail is not known today; only the forward rate is known. The actual spot rate will depend on the market conditions at that time; it may be more or less than today's forward rate. **Exchange rate risk** is the risk that tomorrow's exchange rate will differ from today's rate.

**Forward exchange contract**
A contract that requires delivery on a specified future date of one currency in return for a specified amount of another currency.

**Exchange rate risk**
The risk that tomorrow's exchange rate will differ from today's.

As indicated earlier, it is extremely unlikely that the future spot rate will be exactly the same as the forward rate quoted today. Assume that you are going to receive a payment denominated in pounds from a British customer in 30 days. If you wait for 30 days and exchange the pounds at the spot rate, you will receive a dollar amount reflecting the exchange rate 30 days hence (that is, the future spot rate). As of today, you have no way of knowing the exact dollar value of your future pound receipts. Consequently, you cannot make precise plans about the use of these dollars. If, conversely, you buy a future contract, then you know the exact dollar value of your future receipts, and you can make precise plans concerning their use. The forward contract, therefore, can reduce your uncertainty about the future, and the major advantage of the forward market is that of risk reduction.

Forward contracts are usually quoted for periods of 30, 90, and 180 days. A contract for any intermediate date can be obtained, usually with the payment of a small premium. Forward contracts for periods longer than 180 days can be obtained by special negotiations with banks. Contracts for periods greater than 1 year can be costly.

Forward rates, like spot rates, are quoted in both direct and indirect form. The direct quotes for the 30-day and 90-day forward contracts on pounds, francs, and marks are given in column 1 of Table 22-1. The indirect quotes for forward contracts, like spot rates, are reciprocals of the direct quotes. The indirect quotes are indicated in column 2 of Table 22-1. The direct quotes are the dollar/foreign currency rate, and the indirect quotes are the foreign currency/dollar rate similar to the spot exchange quotes.

In Table 22-1, the 30-day forward quote for pounds is \$1.6444 per pound. This means that the bank is contractually bound to deliver £1 at this price, and the buyer of the contract is legally obligated to buy it at this price. Therefore, this is the price the customer must pay regardless of the actual spot rate prevailing in 30 days. If the spot price of the pound is less than \$1.6444, then the customer pays *more* than the spot price. If the spot price is greater than \$1.6444, then the customer pays *less* than the spot price.

The forward rate is often quoted at a premium to or discount from the existing spot rate. For example, the 30-day forward rate for the pound may be quoted as .0014 discount (1.6444 forward rate − 1.6458 spot rate). If the British pound is more expensive in the future than it is today, it is said to be selling at a premium relative to the dollar, and the dollar is said to be selling at a discount to the British pound. Notice in Table 22-1 that while the British pound is selling at a discount relative to the dollar, both the French franc and the German mark are selling at a premium to the dollar. This premium or discount is also called the **forward-spot differential.**

**Forward-spot differential** The premium or discount between forward and spot currency exchange rates.

Notationally, the relationship may be written:

$$F - S = \text{premium } (F > S) \text{ or discount } (S > F) \qquad \textbf{(22-1)}$$

where $F$ = the forward rate, direct quote
$S$ = the spot rate, direct quote

The premium or discount can also be expressed as an annual percentage rate, computed as follows:

$$\frac{F - S}{S} \times \frac{12}{n} \times 100 = \text{annualized percentage} \qquad \textbf{(22-2)}$$

premium $(F > S)$ or discount $(S > F)$

where $n$ = the number of months of the forward contract

**EXAMPLE**

Compute the percent-per-annum premium on the 30-day pound.

Step 1: Identify $F$, $S$, and $n$.

$$F = 1.6444,\ S = 1.6458,\ n = 1 \text{ month}$$

Step 2: Because $S$ is greater than $F$, we compute the annualized percentage discount:

$$D = \frac{1.6444 - 1.6458}{1.6458} \times \frac{12 \text{ months}}{1 \text{ month}} \times 100$$

$$= -1.02\%$$

The percent-per-annum discount on the 30-day pound is −1.02 percent. The percent-per-annum discount on the 30-day and 90-day pound and franc contracts are computed similarly. The results are given in Table 22-2.

## Examples of Exchange Rate Risk

The concept of exchange rate risk applies to all types of international businesses. The measurement of these risks, and the type of risk, may differ among businesses. Let us see how exchange risk affects international trade contracts, international portfolio investments, and direct foreign investments.

**TABLE 22-2**
Percent-per-Annum (Discount)

| | 30-Day | 90-Day |
|---|---|---|
| British pound | −1.02% | −2.11% |
| French franc | +1.36% | +5.45% |

**EXCHANGE RATE RISK IN INTERNATIONAL TRADE CONTRACTS** The idea of exchange rate risk in trade contracts is illustrated in the following situations.

**Case I.** An American automobile distributor agrees to buy a car from the manufacturer in Detroit. The distributor agrees to pay \$15,000 on delivery of the car, which is expected to be 30 days from today. The car is delivered on the thirtieth day and the distributor pays \$15,000. Notice that from the day this contract was written until the day the car was delivered, the buyer knew the exact dollar amount of the liability. There was, in other words, no uncertainty about the value of the contract.

**Case II.** An American automobile distributor enters into a contract with a British supplier to buy a car from Britain for £8,800. The amount is payable on the delivery of the car, 30 days from today. From Figure 22-1, we see the range of spot rates that we believe can occur on the date the contract is consummated. On the thirtieth day, the American importer will pay some amount in the range of \$13,699.84(8,800 × 1.5568) to \$15,087.60 (8,800 × 1.7145) for the car. Today, the American firm is not certain what its future dollar outflow will be 30 days hence. That is, the dollar value of the contract is uncertain.

These two examples help illustrate the idea of foreign exchange risk in international trade contracts. In the domestic trade contract (Case I), the exact dollar amount of the future dollar payment is known today with certainty. In the case of the international trade

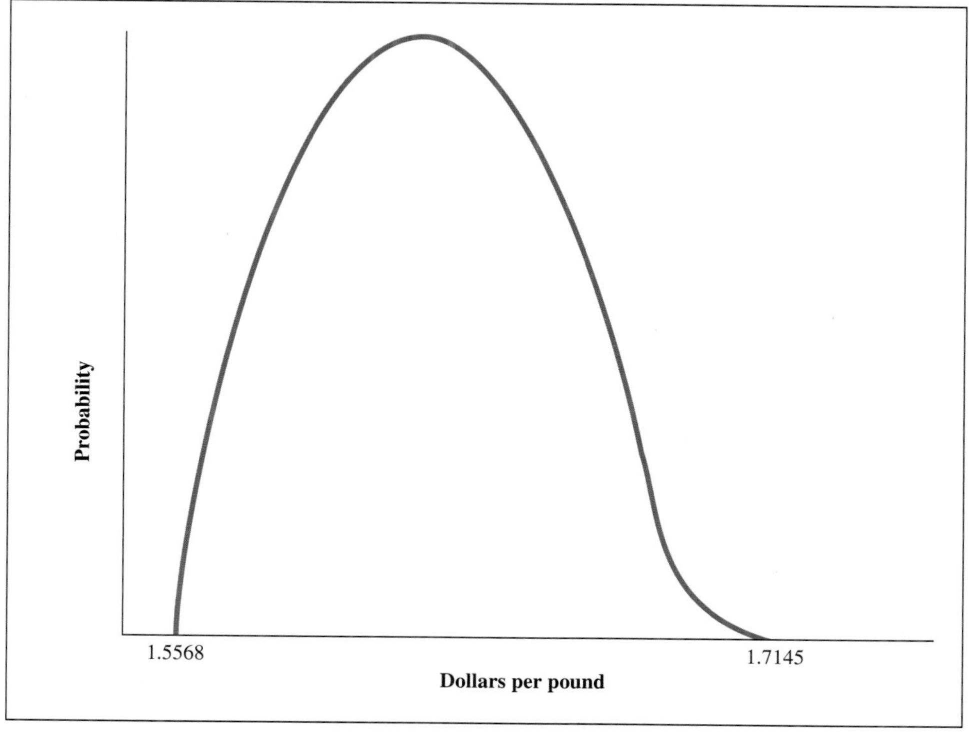


**FIGURE 22-1**
A Subjective Probability Distribution of the Pound Exchange Rate, 30 Days in the Future

contract (Case II), where the contract is written in the foreign currency, the exact dollar amount of the contract is not known. The variability of the exchange rate induces variability in the future cash flow.

Exchange rate risk exists when the contract is written in terms of the foreign currency or *denominated* in foreign currency. There is no direct exchange risk if the international trade contract is written in terms of the domestic currency. That is, in Case II, if the contract were written in dollars, the American importer would face no direct exchange risk. With the contract written in dollars, the British exporter would bear all the exchange rate risk because the British exporter's future pound receipts would be uncertain. That is, the British exporter would receive payment in dollars, which would have to be converted into pounds at an unknown (as of today) pound/dollar exchange rate. In international trade contracts of the type discussed here, at least one of the two parties to the contract always bears the exchange rate risk.

Certain types of international trade contracts are denominated in a third currency, different from either the importer's or the exporter's domestic currency. In Case II, the contract might have been denominated in, say, the deutsche mark. With a mark contract, both importer and exporter would be subject to exchange rate risk.

Exchange rate risk is not limited to the two-party trade contracts; it exists also in foreign portfolio investments and direct foreign investments.

**EXCHANGE RATE RISK IN FOREIGN PORTFOLIO INVESTMENTS** Let us look at an example of exchange rate risk in the context of portfolio investments. An American investor buys a German security. The exact return on the investment in the security is unknown. Thus the security is a risky investment. The investment return in the holding period of, say, 3 months stated in marks could be anything from −2 to +8 percent. In addition, the mark/dollar exchange rate may depreciate by 4 percent or appreciate by 6 percent in the 3-month period during which the investment is held. The return to the American investor, in dollars, will therefore be in the range of −6 to +14 percent.[3] Notice that the return to a German investor, in marks, is in the range of −2 to +8 percent. Clearly, for the American investor, the exchange factor induces a greater variability in the dollar rate of return. Hence, the exchange rate fluctuations may increase the riskiness of the investments.

**EXCHANGE RATE RISK IN DIRECT FOREIGN INVESTMENT** The exchange rate risk of a direct foreign investment (DFI) is more complicated. In a DFI, the parent company invests in assets denominated in a foreign currency. That is, the balance sheet and the income statement of the subsidiary are written in terms of the foreign currency. The parent company receives the repatriated profit stream in dollars. Thus, the exchange rate risk concept applies to fluctuations in the dollar value of the assets located abroad as well as to the fluctuations in the home currency-denominated profit stream. Exchange risk not only affects immediate profits, it may affect the future profit stream as well.

Although exchange rate risk can be a serious complication in international business activity, remember the principle of the risk-return trade-off: Traders and corporations find numerous reasons that the returns from international transactions outweigh the risks.

[3]Example: Assume the spot exchange rate is \$.50/DM. In 3 months, the exchange rate would be $.50 \times (1 - .04) = .48$ to $.50 \times (1 + .06) = .53$. A \$50 investment today is equivalent to a DM 100 investment. The DM 100 investment would return DM 98 to DM 108 in 3 months. The return, in the worst case, is DM $98 \times .48 =$ \$47.04. The return, in the best case, is DM $108 \times .53 =$ \$57.24. The holding-period return, on the \$50 investment, will be between −6 percent (\$47.04 − \$50)/\$50) and +14 percent (\$57.24 − \$50)/\$50).

**RELATE TO THE BIG PICTURE**

In international transactions, just as in domestic transactions, the key to value is the timing and amounts of cash flow spent and received. However, economic transactions across international borders add an element of risk because cash flows are denominated in the currency of the country in which business is being transacted. Consequently, the dollar value of the cash flows will depend on the exchange rate that exists at the time the cash changes hands. The fact remains, however, that it's cash spent and received that matters. This is the point of **Principle 3: Cash—Not Profits—Is King.**

**CONCEPT CHECK**

1. What is a spot transaction? What is a direct quote? An indirect quote?
2. What is an arbitrageur? How does an arbitrageur make money?
3. What is a forward exchange rate?
4. Describe exchange rate risk in direct foreign investment.

## INTEREST-RATE PARITY THEORY

Forward rates generally entail a premium or a discount relative to current spot rates. However, these forward premiums and discounts differ between currencies and maturities (see Table 22-2). These differences depend solely on the difference in the level of interest rates between the two countries, called the *interest-rate differential.* The value of the premium or discount can be theoretically computed from the **interest-rate parity (IRP) theory.** This theory states that (except for the effects of small transaction costs) the forward premium or discount should be equal and opposite in size to the difference in the national interest rates for securities of the same maturity.

**Interest-rate parity (IRP) theory**
States that (except for the effects of small transaction costs) the forward premium or discount should be equal and opposite in size to the differences in the national interest rates for securities of the same maturity.

Stated very simply, what does all this mean? It means that because of arbitrage, the interest-rate differential between two countries must be equal to the difference between the forward and spot exchange rates. If this were not true, arbitrageurs would buy in the forward market and sell in the spot market (or vice versa) until prices were back in line and there were no profits left to be made. For example, if prices in the forward market were too low, arbitrageurs would enter the market, increase the demand for the forward foreign currency, and drive up the prices in the forward market until those prices obeyed the interest-rate parity theory.

**CONCEPT CHECK**

1. In simple terms, what does the interest-rate parity theory mean?

## PURCHASING POWER PARITY THEORY

**Purchasing-power parity (PPP) theory**
In the long run, exchange rates adjust so that the purchasing power of each currency tends to remain the same. Thus exchange rate changes tend to reflect international differences in inflation rates. Countries with high rates of inflation tend to experience declines in the value of their currency.

Long-run changes in exchange rates are influenced by international differences in inflation rates and the purchasing power of each nation's currency. Exchange rates of countries with high rates of inflation will tend to decline. According to the **purchasing-power parity**

**(PPP) theory,** in the long run, exchange rates adjust so that the purchasing power of each currency tends to be the same. Thus, exchange rate changes tend to reflect international differences in inflation rates. Countries with high rates of inflation tend to experience declines in the value of their currency. Thus, if Britain experiences a 10 percent rate of inflation in a year that Germany experiences only a 6 percent rate, the UK currency (the pound) will be expected to decline in value approximately by 3.77 percent (1.10/1.06) against the German currency (the deutsche mark). More accurately, according to the PPP:

$$\text{expected spot rate} = \text{current spot rate} \times \text{expected difference in inflation rate}$$

$$\begin{array}{c}\text{expected spot rate}\\ \text{(domestic currency}\\ \text{per unit of foreign}\\ \text{currency)}\end{array} = \begin{array}{c}\text{current spot rate}\\ \text{(domestic currency}\\ \text{per unit of foreign}\\ \text{currency)}\end{array} \times \frac{(1 + \text{expected domestic inflation rate})}{(1 + \text{expected foreign inflation rate})}$$

Thus, if the beginning value of the mark were £.40, with a 6 percent inflation rate in Germany and a 10 percent inflation rate in Britain, according to the PPP, the expected value of the deutsche mark at the end of that year will be £.40 × [1.10/1.06], or £.4151.

Stated very simply, what does this mean? It means that a dollar should have the same purchasing power anywhere in the world—well, at least on average. Obviously, this is not quite true. However, what the purchasing-power parity theory tells us is that we should expect, on average, that differences in inflation rates between two countries should be reflected in changes in the exchange rates. In effect, the best forecast of the difference in inflation rates between two countries should also be the best forecast of the change in the spot rate of exchange.

## The Law of One Price

**Law of one price**
The proposition that in competitive markets the same goods should sell for the same price where prices are stated in terms of a single currency.

Underlying the PPP relationship is the **law of one price.** This law is actually a proposition that in competitive markets where there are no transportation costs or barriers to trade, the same goods sold in different countries sell for the same price if all the different prices are expressed in terms of the same currency. The idea is that the worth, in terms of marginal utility, of a good does not depend on where it is bought or sold. Because inflation will erode the purchasing power of any currency, its exchange rate must adhere to the PPP relationship if the law of one price is to hold over time.

There are enough obvious exceptions to the concept of purchasing-power parity that it may, at first glance, seem difficult to accept. For example, recently, a Big Mac cost $2.36 in the United States, and given the then existing exchange rates, it cost an equivalent of $2.02 in Mexico, $2.70 in Japan, and $3.22 in Germany. On the surface this might appear to violate the purchasing-power parity theory and the law of one price; however, we must remember that this theory is based upon the concept of arbitrage. In the case of a Big Mac, it's pretty hard to imagine buying Big Macs in Mexico for $2.02, shipping them to Germany, and reselling them for $3.22. But for commodities such as gold and other items that are relatively inexpensive to ship and do not have to be consumed immediately, the law of one price holds much better.

## International Fisher Effect

According to the domestic Fisher effect (FE) (remember our discussion in Chapter 2), nominal interest rates reflect the expected inflation rate and a real rate of return. In other words,

$$\begin{array}{c}\text{nominal}\\ \text{interest rate}\end{array} = \begin{array}{c}\text{expected}\\ \text{inflation rate}\end{array} + \begin{array}{c}\text{real rate}\\ \text{of interest}\end{array}$$

Although there is mixed empirical support for the international Fisher effect (IFE), it is widely thought that, for the major industrial countries, the real rate of interest is about 3 percent when a long-term period is considered. In such a case, with the previous assumption regarding inflation rates, interest rates in Britain and Germany would be (.10 + .03 + .003) or 13.3 percent and (.06 + .03 + .0018) or 9.18 percent, respectively.

In effect, the IFE states that the real interest rate should be the same all over the world, with the difference in nominal or stated interest rates simply resulting from the difference in expected inflation rates. As we look at interest rates around the world, this tells us that we should not necessarily send our money to a bank account in the country with the highest interest rates. That course of action might only result in sending our money to a bank in the country with the highest expected level of inflation.

**CONCEPT CHECK**

1. What does the law of one price say?
2. What is the international Fisher effect?

## EXPOSURE TO EXCHANGE RATE RISK

An asset denominated or valued in terms of foreign-currency cash flows will lose value if that foreign currency declines in value. It can be said that such an asset is exposed to exchange rate risk. However, this possible decline in asset value may be offset by the decline in value of any liability that is also denominated or valued in terms of that foreign currency. Thus, a firm would normally be interested in its net exposed position (exposed assets – exposed liabilities) for each period in each currency.

Although expected changes in exchange rates can often be included in the cost-benefit analysis relating to such transactions, in most cases, there is an unexpected component in exchange rate changes and often the cost-benefit analysis for such transactions does not fully capture even the expected change in the exchange rate. For example, price increases for the foreign operations of many MNCs often have to be less than those necessary to fully offset exchange rate changes, owing to the competitive pressures generated by local businesses.

Three measures of foreign exchange exposure are translation exposure, transaction exposure, and economic exposure. Translation exposure arises because the foreign operations of MNCs have accounting statements denominated in the local currency of the country in which the operation is located. For U.S. MNCs, the *reporting currency* for its consolidated financial statements is the dollar, so the assets, liabilities, revenues, and expenses of the foreign operations must be translated into dollars. International transactions often require a payment to be made or received in a foreign currency in the future, so these transactions are exposed to exchange rate risk. Economic exposure exists over the long term because the value of future cash flows in the reporting currency (that is, the dollar) from foreign operations is exposed to exchange rate risk. Indeed, the whole stream of future cash flows is exposed. The Japanese automaker situation highlights the effect of economic exposure on an MNC's revenue stream. The three measures of exposure now are examined more closely.

### Translation Exposure

Foreign currency assets and liabilities are considered exposed if their foreign currency value for accounting purposes is to be translated into the domestic currency using the currency exchange rate—the exchange rate in effect on the balance sheet date. Other assets and liabilities and equity amounts that are translated at the historic exchange rate—the rate in effect when these items were first recognized in the company's accounts—are not considered to be exposed. The rate (current or historic) used to translate various accounts depends on the translation procedure used.

Although transaction exposure can result in exchange rate change-related losses and gains that are realized and have an impact on both reported and taxable income, translation exposure results in exchange rate losses and gains that are reflected in the company's accounting books, but are unrealized and have little or no impact on taxable income. Thus, if financial markets are efficient and managerial goals are consistent with owner wealth maximization, a firm should not have to waste real resources hedging against possible paper losses caused by translation exposure. However, if there are significant agency or information costs or if markets are not efficient, a firm may indeed find it economical to hedge against translation losses or gains.

## Transaction Exposure

**Transaction exposure**
The net contracted foreign currency transactions for which the settlement amounts are subject to changing exchange rates.

Receivables, payables, and fixed-price sales or purchase contracts are examples of foreign currency transactions whose monetary value was fixed at a time different from the time when these transactions are actually completed. **Transaction exposure** is a term that describes the net contracted foreign currency transactions for which the settlement amounts are subject to changing exchange rates. A company normally must set up an additional reporting system to track transaction exposure, because several of these amounts are not recognized in the accounting books of the firm.

Exchange rate risk may be neutralized or hedged by a change in the asset and liability position in the foreign currency. An exposed asset position (such as an account receivable) can be hedged or covered by creating a liability of the same amount and maturity denominated in the foreign currency (such as a forward contract to sell the foreign currency). An exposed liability position (such as an account payable) can be covered by acquiring assets of the same amount and maturity in the foreign currency (such as a forward contract to buy the foreign currency). The objective is to have a zero net asset position in the foreign currency. This eliminates exchange rate risk, because the loss (gain) in the liability (asset) is exactly offset by the gain (loss) in the value of the asset (liability) when the foreign currency appreciates (depreciates). Two popular forms of hedge are the money-market hedge and the exchange-market or forward-market hedge. In both types of hedge, the amount and the duration of the asset (liability) positions are matched. Note as you read the next two subsections how IRP theory assures that each hedge provides the same cover.

MONEY-MARKET HEDGE In a money-market hedge, the exposed position in a foreign currency is offset by borrowing or lending in the money market. Consider the case of the American firm with a net liability position (that is, the amount it owes) of £3,000. The firm knows the exact amount of its pound liability in 30 days, but it does not know the liability in dollars. Assume that the 30-day money-market rates in both the United States and Britain are, respectively, 1 percent for lending and 1.5 percent for borrowing. The American business can take the following steps:

Step 1: Calculate the present value of the foreign currency liability (£3,000) that is due in 30 days. Use the money-market rate applicable for the foreign country (1 percent in the United Kingdom). The present value of £3,000 is £2,970.30, computed as follows: 3,000/(1 + .01).

Step 2: Exchange dollars on today's spot market to obtain the £2,970.30. The dollar amount needed today is \$4,888.52 (2,970.30 × 1.6458).

Step 3: Invest £2,970.30 in a United Kingdom 1-month money-market instrument. This investment will compound to exactly £3,000 in 1 month. The future liability of £3,000 is covered by the £2,970.30 investment.[4]

*Note:* If the American business does not own this amount today, it can borrow $4,888.52 from the U.S. money market at the going rate of 1.5 percent. In 30 days, the American business will need to repay $4,961.85 [$4,888.52 × (1 + .015)].

Assuming that the American business borrows the money, its management may base its calculations on the knowledge that the British goods, on delivery in 30 days, will cost it $4,961.85. The British business will receive £3,000. The American business need not wait for the future spot exchange rate to be revealed. On today's date, the future dollar payment of the contract is known with certainty. This certainty helps the American business in making its pricing and financing decisions.

Many businesses hedge in the money market. The firm needs to borrow (creating a liability) in one market, lend or invest in the other money market, and use the spot exchange market on today's date. The mechanics of covering a net asset position in the foreign currency are the exact reverse of the mechanics of covering the liability position. With a net asset position in pounds: Borrow in the United Kingdom money market in pounds, convert to dollars on the spot exchange market, invest in the U.S. money market. When the net assets are converted into pounds (i.e., when the firm receives what it is owed), pay off the loan and the interest. The cost of hedging in the money market is the cost of doing business in three different markets. Information about the three markets is needed, and analytical calculations of the type indicated here must be made.

Many small and infrequent traders find the cost of the money-market hedge prohibitive, owing especially to the need for information about the market. These traders use the exchange-market or the forward-market hedge, which has very similar hedging benefits.

**THE FORWARD-MARKET HEDGE** The forward market provides a second possible hedging mechanism. It works as follows: A net asset (liability) position is covered by a liability (asset) in the forward market. Consider again the case of the American firm with a liability of £3,000 that must be paid in 30 days. The firm may take the following steps to cover its liability position:

Step 1: Buy a forward contract today to purchase £3,000 in 30 days. The 30-day forward rate is $1.6444/£.

Step 2: On the thirtieth day pay the banker $4,933.20 (3,000 × $1.6444) and collect £3,000. Pay these pounds to the British supplier.

By the use of the forward contract the American business knows the exact worth of the future payment in dollars ($4,933.20). The exchange rate risk in pounds is totally eliminated by the net asset position in the forward pounds. In the case of a net asset exposure, the steps open to the American firm are the exact opposite: Sell the pounds forward, and on the future day receive and deliver the pounds to collect the agreed-on dollar amount.

The use of the forward market as a hedge against exchange rate risk is simple and direct. That is, match the liability or asset position against an offsetting position in the forward market. The forward-market hedge is relatively easy to implement. The firm directs its banker that it needs to buy or sell a foreign currency on a future date, and the banker gives a forward quote.

The forward-market hedge and the money-market hedge give an identical future dollar payment (or receipt) if the forward contracts are priced according to the interest-rate parity

[4]Observe that £2,970.30 × (1 + .01) = £3,000.

ROAD RULES

## A FOCUS ON HARLEY-DAVIDSON

ROAD RULES

### Managing Foreign Exchange Risk Exposure at Harley-Davidson—The Euro Experience

Harley-Davidson is one of those companies that focus on the long-run growth, and one of the markets that it looks to for future growth is Europe. The potential there for Harley is tremendous. In fact, according to Jim Brostowitz, the Vice President Controller/Treasurer at Harley-Davidson, the number of heavyweight motorcycles registered in Europe is only slightly less than in the United States, with Harley controlling about 7 percent of that market, but growing. As a result, Harley has set its sights on Europe and has set the seeds for a bright future. It has done that by developing dealer networks, H.O.G. (Harley Owners Group) events, and Harley-Davidson events just like the ones that have been so successful in the United States. Things looked bright in Europe.

With much hoopla, on January 1, 1999, the European Union introduced its new currency, the Euro. The idea was that a single currency would make it easier for goods, people, and services to travel across national borders. When the Euro debuted, it was fixed at $1.17. That meant that in January 1999 you could exchange one Euro for $1.17. However, over the next two years, the bottom fell out of the Euro, and by late 2000 each Euro was only worth 84 cents. For Harley-Davidson, and every other multinational company doing business in Europe, the end result was a financial nightmare.

At Harley-Davidson, the job of overseeing this nightmare has fallen in the lap of Jim Brostowitz. One of the problems Harley faces is the fact that virtually all of its motorcycles sold in Europe are made in the United States, and its workers and suppliers are paid in U.S. dollars. However, when most Harleys are sold in Europe, the payment comes in the form of Euros. What happens if the Euro falls by 28 percent between the time the motorcycle is built and payment is received? In that case, Harley receives the purchase price in Euros, but they are worth 28 percent less than expected.

How does Jim Brostowitz go about protecting Harley's bottom line against this exchange rate fluctuation risk? He does it with a combination of hedging in the forward markets, a topic we cover in Chapter 22, and price adjustments. As Brostowitz notes, "Motorcycle prices are set with the introduction of new models, just like car prices are set, and there generally aren't any mid-year price increases. To eliminate short-term exchange rate risk we hedge forward contracts, going out about 6 months. This gives us short-term stability. In the longer-term, you've got to adjust prices. For example, for the 2001 model year, which was introduced in July 2000, the general U.S. price increase was about 1.5 percent, but in Europe, the price increase was between 5 and 10 percent depending on the model." As Harley is well aware, risks from economic and currency problems abroad can be devastating. For that reason, it prepares ahead of time for those risks.

theory. The alert student may have noticed that the dollar payments in the money-market hedge and the forward-market hedge examples were, respectively, $4,888.52 and $4,933.20. Recall from our previous discussions that, in efficient markets, the forward contracts do indeed conform to IRP theory. However, the numbers in our example are not identical because the forward rate used in the forward-market hedge is not exactly equal to the interest rates in the money-market hedge.

**CURRENCY-FUTURES CONTRACTS AND OPTIONS** The forward-market hedge is not adequate for some types of exposure. If the foreign currency asset or liability position occurs on a date for which forward quotes are not available, the forward-market hedge cannot be accomplished. In certain cases, the forward-market hedge may cost more than the money-market hedge. In these cases, a corporation with a large amount of exposure may prefer the money-market hedge. In addition to forward-market and money-market hedges, a company can also hedge its exposure by buying (or selling) some relatively new instruments—foreign currency futures contracts and foreign currency options. Although futures contracts are similar to forward contracts in that they provide fixed prices for the required delivery of foreign currency at maturity, exchange traded options permit fixed (strike) price foreign currency transactions anytime before maturity. Futures contracts and options differ from forward contracts in that, unlike forward contracts, which are customized regarding amount and maturity date, futures and options are traded in standard amounts with standard maturity dates. In addition, although forward contracts are written by banks, futures and options are traded on organized exchanges, and individual traders deal with the exchange-based clearing organization rather than with each other. The purchase of futures requires the fulfillment of margin requirements (about 5 to 10 percent of the face amount), whereas the purchase of forward contracts requires only good credit standing with a bank. The purchase of options requires an immediate outlay that reflects a premium above the strike price and an outlay equal to the strike price when and if the option is executed.

### Economic Exposure

The economic value of a company can vary in response to exchange rate changes. This change in value may be caused by a rate change-induced decline in the level of expected cash flows and/or by an increase in the riskiness of these cash flows. *Economic exposure* refers to the overall impact of exchange rate changes on the value of the firm and includes not only the strategic impact of changes in competitive relationships that arise from exchange rate changes, but also the economic impact of transactions exposure, and if any, translation exposure.

Economic exposure to exchange rate changes depends on the competitive structure of the markets for a firm's inputs and outputs and how these markets are influenced by changes in exchange rates. This influence, in turn, depends on several economic factors, including price elasticities of the products, the degree of competition from foreign markets and direct (through prices) and indirect (through incomes) impact of exchange rate changes on these markets. Assessing the economic exposure faced by a particular firm thus depends on the ability to understand and model the structure of the markets for its major inputs (purchases) and outputs (sales).

A company need not engage in any cross-border business activity to be exposed to exchange rate changes, because product and financial markets in most countries are related and influenced to a large extent by the same global forces. The output of a company engaged in business activity only within one country may be competing with imported products, or it may be competing for its inputs with other domestic and foreign purchasers. For example, a Canadian chemical company that did no cross-border business nevertheless found that its profit margins depended directly on the U.S. dollar/Japanese yen exchange rate. The company used coal as an input in its production process, and the Canadian price of coal was heavily influenced by the extent to which the Japanese bought U.S. coal, which in turn depended on the dollar/yen exchange rate.

Although translation exposure need not be managed, it might be useful for a firm to manage its transaction and economic exposures because they affect firm value directly. In most companies, transaction exposure is generally tracked and managed by the office of the corporate treasurer. Economic exposure is difficult to define in operating terms, and very few companies manage it actively. In most companies, economic exposure is generally considered part of the strategic planning process, rather than a treasurer's or finance function.

#### CONCEPT CHECK

1. Give a simple explanation of translation exposure.
2. Give a simple explanation of transaction exposure.
3. Give a simple explanation of economic exposure.

## MULTINATIONAL WORKING-CAPITAL MANAGEMENT

The basic principles of working-capital management for a multinational corporation are similar to those for a domestic firm. However, tax and exchange rate factors are additional considerations for the MNC. For an MNC with subsidiaries in many countries, the optimal decisions in the management of working capital are made by considering the market as a whole. The global or centralized financial decisions for an MNC are superior to the set of independent optimal decisions for the subsidiaries. This is the control problem of the MNC. If the individual subsidiaries make decisions that are best for them individually, the consolidation of such decisions may not be best for the MNC as a whole. To effect global management, sophisticated computerized models—incorporating many variables for each subsidiary—are solved to provide the best overall decision for the MNC.

Before considering the components of working-capital management, we examine two techniques that are useful in the management of a wide variety of working-capital components.

## Leading and Lagging

Two important risk-reduction techniques for many working-capital problems are called *leading* and *lagging*. Often, forward-market and money-market hedges are not available to eliminate exchange risk. Under such circumstances, leading and lagging may be used to reduce exchange risk.

Recall that a net asset (long) position is not desirable in a weak or potentially depreciating currency. If a firm has a net asset position in such a currency, it should expedite the disposal of the asset. The firm should get rid of the asset earlier than it otherwise would have, or *lead,* and convert the funds into assets in a relatively stronger currency. By the same reasoning, the firm should *lag,* or delay the collection against a net asset position in a strong currency. If the firm has a net liability (short) position in the weak currency, then it should delay the payment against the liability, or lag, until the currency depreciates. In the case of an appreciating or strong foreign currency and a net liability position, the firm should lead the payments—that is, reduce the liabilities earlier than it would otherwise have.

These principles are useful in the management of working capital of an MNC. They cannot, however, eliminate the foreign exchange risk. When exchange rates change continuously, it is almost impossible to guess whether or when the currency will depreciate or appreciate. This is why the risk of exchange rate changes cannot be eliminated. Nevertheless, the reduction of risk, or the increased gain from exchange rate changes, via the lead and lag is useful for cash management, accounts-receivable management, and short-term liability management.

## Cash Management and Positioning of Funds

Positioning of funds takes on an added importance in the international context. Funds may be transferred from a subsidiary of the MNC in country A to another subsidiary in country B such that the foreign exchange exposure and the tax liability of the MNC as a whole are minimized. It bears repeating that, owing to the global strategy of the MNC, the tax liability of the subsidiary in country A may be greater than it would otherwise have been, but the overall tax payment for all units of the MNC is minimized.

**Transfer price**
The price a subsidiary or a parent company charges other companies that are part of the same MNC for its goods or services.

The transfer of funds among subsidiaries and the parent company is done by royalties, fees, and transfer pricing. A **transfer price** is the price a subsidiary or a parent company charges other companies that are part of the MNC for its goods or services. A parent that wishes to transfer funds from a subsidiary in a depreciating-currency country may charge a higher price on the goods and services sold to this subsidiary by the parent or by subsidiaries from strong-currency countries.

**CONCEPT CHECK**

1. Describe the risk-reduction techniques of leading and lagging.
2. How can a parent company use the concept of transfer pricing to move funds from a subsidiary in a depreciating currency country to a strong currency country?

## INTERNATIONAL FINANCING AND CAPITAL-STRUCTURE DECISIONS

An MNC has access to many more financing sources than does a domestic firm. It can tap not only the financing sources in its home country that are available to its domestic counterparts, but also sources in the foreign countries in which it operates. Host countries often provide access to low-cost subsidized financing to attract foreign investment.

In addition, the MNC may enjoy preferential credit standards because of its size and investor preference for its home currency. An MNC may be able to access third-country capital markets—countries in which it does not operate but that may have large, well-functioning capital markets. Finally, an MNC can also access external currency markets: Eurodollar, Eurocurrency, or Asian dollar markets. These external markets are unregulated and, because of their lower spread, can offer very attractive rates for financing *and* for investments. With the increasing availability of interest rate and currency swaps, a firm can raise funds in the lowest-cost maturities and currencies and swap them into funds with the maturity and currency denomination it requires. Because of its ability to tap a larger number of financial markets, the MNC may have a lower cost of capital, and because it may be better able to avoid the problems or limitations of any one financial market, it may have a more continuous access to external finance compared to a domestic company.

Access to national financial markets is regulated by governments. For example, in the United States, access to capital markets is governed by SEC regulations. Access to Japanese capital markets is governed by regulations issued by the Ministry of Finance. Some countries have extensive regulations; other countries have relatively open markets. These regulations may differ depending on the legal residency terms of the company raising funds. A company that cannot use its local subsidiary to raise funds in a given market will be treated as foreign. In order to increase their visibility in a foreign capital market, a number of MNCs are now listing their equities on the stock exchanges of many of these countries.

The external currency markets are predominantly centered in Europe, and about 80 percent of their value is denominated in terms of the U.S. dollar. Thus, most external currency markets can be characterized as Eurodollar markets. Such markets consist of an active short-term money market and an intermediate-term capital market with maturities ranging up to 15 years and averaging about 7 to 9 years. The intermediate-term market consists of the Eurobond and the Syndicated Eurocredit markets. Eurobonds are usually issued as unregistered bearer bonds and generally tend to have higher flotation costs but lower coupon rates compared to similar bonds issued in the United States. A Syndicated Eurocredit loan is simply a large-term loan that involves contributions by a number of lending banks.

In arriving at its capital-structure decisions, an MNC has to consider a number of factors. First, the capital structure of its local affiliates is influenced by local norms regarding capital structure in that industry and in that country. Local norms for companies in the same industry can differ considerably from country to country. Second, the local affiliate capital structure must also reflect corporate attitudes toward exchange rate

FINANCE $ MATTERS

## Ukraine: Not for the Fainthearted

Kiev, Ukraine—S. C. Johnson & Son Inc., the $3 billion family-owned company that makes clothes, floor wax, furniture cleaners, bug killers, and air fresheners, has traditionally been challenged by new frontiers.

When the company opened a plant in Britain 80 years ago, it was one of the first American corporations to go abroad. At the end of the cold war, it trailblazed again this time into the uncertain precincts of the Ukraine.

Johnson Wax's experience since 1990—when the company started to make and bottle detergents and furniture polish in a renovated corner of a ramshackle factory on the outskirts of Kiev—helps explain the reluctance of other consumer-products companies to jump in.

A few months after Ukraine joined Russia and Belarus in leaving the crumbling Soviet Union, it introduced a coupon currency to replace the ruble. In relatively short order, the coupons became all but worthless. By late last year, inflation had reached about 100 percent a month, from almost zero two years before. A fierce credit squeeze by the government left wholesalers little money to buy Johnson's products. And a government that had initially promised to create a friendly environment for Western investors became encrusted with old style—many say corrupt—former Communists.

Last year, Johnson Wax halved its production from that of 1992. And almost half of 1993's 10 million bottles that came off the assembly line had to be sold in Russia, where the economy, however turbulent, is far stronger than Ukraine's.

A major attraction for Western manufacturers here is low wages. Johnson would like to raise the pay of some workers above the monthly $150 that the best get, but a 92 percent tax rate on earned income above $150 makes it impossible to do so.

Some improvements in everyday life make the difficulty of doing business here a little easier. To make an overseas telephone call took two days several years ago. Now they can be made on the spot. And there are more flights in and out of the country.

But unpredictability prevails. In the last six months, the Ukrainian government has raised or lowered the value-added tax rate three times. Now there are worries that the government might impose an excise tax on supplies coming across the border from Russia. And still another currency is expected, prompting further headaches.

Source: Excerpted from Jane Perlez "Ukraine: Not for the Fainthearted," *The New York Times* (June 1, 1994): D1, 5. 

and political risk in that country, which would normally lead to higher levels of local debt and other local capital. Third, local affiliate capital structure must reflect home country requirements with regard to the company's consolidated capital structure. Finally, the optimal MNC capital structure should reflect its wider access to financial markets, its ability to diversify economic and political risks, and its other advantages over domestic companies.

### RELATE TO THE BIG PICTURE

Investment across international boundaries gives rise to special risks not encountered when investing domestically. Specifically, political risks and exchange rate risk are unique to international investing. Once again, **Principle 1: The Risk-Return Trade-Off—We won't take on additional risk unless we expect to be compensated with additional return** provides a rationale for evaluating these considerations. Where added risks are present, added rewards are necessary to induce investment.

### CONCEPT CHECK

1. What factors might an MNC consider in making a capital-structure decision?

# DIRECT FOREIGN INVESTMENT

An MNC often makes direct foreign investments abroad in the form of plants and equipment. The decision process for this type of investment is very similar to the capital-budgeting decision in the domestic context—with some additional twists. Most real-world capital-budgeting decisions are made with uncertain future outcomes. Recall that a capital-budgeting decision has three major components: the estimation of the future cash flows (including the initial cost of the proposed investment), the estimation of the risk in these cash flows, and the choice of the proper discount rate. We will assume that the *NPV* criterion is appropriate as we examine (1) the risks associated with direct foreign investment, and (2) factors to be considered in making the investment decision that may be unique to the international scene.

## Risks in Direct Foreign Investments

Risks in domestic capital budgeting arise from two sources: business risk and financial risk. The international capital-budgeting problem incorporates these risks as well as political risk and exchange risk.

**BUSINESS RISK AND FINANCIAL RISK** International business risk is due to the response of business to economic conditions in the foreign country. Thus, the U.S. MNC needs to be aware of the business climate in both the United States and the foreign country. Additional business risk is due to competition from other MNCs, local businesses, and imported goods. *Financial risk* refers to the risks introduced in the profit stream by the firm's financial structure. The financial risks of foreign operations are not very different from those of domestic operations.

**POLITICAL RISK** Political risk arises because the foreign subsidiary conducts its business in a political system different from that of the home country. Many foreign governments, especially those in the Third World, are less stable than the U.S. government. A change in a country's political setup frequently brings a change in policies with respect to businesses—and especially with respect to foreign businesses. An extreme change in policy might involve nationalization or even outright expropriation of certain businesses. These are the political risks of conducting business abroad. A business with no investment in plant and equipment is less susceptible to these risks. Some examples of political risk are as follows:

1. Expropriation of plants and equipment without compensation.
2. Expropriation with minimal compensation that is below actual market value.
3. Nonconvertibility of the subsidiary's foreign earnings into the parent's currency—the problem of *blocked funds*.
4. Substantial changes in the laws governing taxation.
5. Governmental controls in the foreign country regarding the sale price of the products, wages, and compensation to personnel, hiring of personnel, making of transfer payments to the parent, and local borrowing.
6. Some governments require certain amounts of local equity participation in the business. Some require that the majority of the equity participation belong to their country.

All of these controls and governmental actions introduce risks in the cash flows of the investment to the parent company. These risks must be considered before making the foreign investment decision. The MNC may decide against investing in countries with risks of types 1 and 2. Other risks can be borne—provided that the returns from the foreign investments are high enough to compensate for them. Insurance against some types of political risks may be purchased from private insurance companies or from the U.S. government Overseas Private Investment Corporation. It should be noted that although an MNC cannot protect itself against all foreign political risks, political risks are also present in domestic business.

**EXCHANGE RATE RISK** The exposure of the fixed assets is best measured by the effects of the exchange rate changes on the firm's future earnings stream: that being economic exposure rather than translation exposure. For instance, changes in the exchange rate may adversely affect sales by making competing imported goods cheaper. Changes in the cost of goods sold may result if some components are imported and their price in the foreign currency changes because of exchange rate fluctuations. The thrust of these examples is that the effect of exchange rate changes on income statement items should be properly measured to evaluate exchange risk. Finally, exchange rate risk affects the dollar-denominated profit stream of the parent company, whether or not it affects the foreign-currency profits.

**CONCEPT CHECK**

1. What are some of the risks associated with direct foreign investments?

## HOW FINANCIAL MANAGERS USE THIS MATERIAL

As the magnitude of international trade has expanded over the past two decades, so has the role of the multinational corporation. Firms routinely report their operating results by breaking out revenues *both* from major product lines *and* country-of-origin where direct foreign investment has taken place.

The expanded U.S. multinational presence has made financial executives acutely aware of the problems associated with foreign exchange rate risk. Management of the Walt Disney Company has said: "The Company's objective in managing the exposure to foreign currency fluctuations is to reduce earnings and cash flow volatility associated with foreign exchange rate changes to allow management to focus its attention on its core business issues and challenges."

The preponderance of multinational corporations do indeed focus on their main lines of business and do not, therefore, voluntarily enter into either foreign currency transactions or interest rate transactions for purposes of speculation on possible profit-making opportunities.

International markets have also been fertile grounds for finding new products. In fact, for many firms, finding new projects doesn't necessarily mean coming up with a new product; it may mean taking an existing product and applying it to a new market. That's certainly been the direction that McDonald's has taken in recent years. Today, McDonald's operates in over 70 countries with more than 20,000 restaurants. One of the biggest is a 700-seat McDonald's in Moscow. Was this an expensive venture? It certainly was. In fact, the food plant that McDonald's built to supply burgers, buns, fries, and everything else sold there cost over $60 million. In addition to the costs, there are a number of other factors that make opening an outlet outside of the United States both different and challenging. First, in order to keep the quality of what McDonald's sells identical with what is served at any McDonald's anywhere in the world, McDonald's spent 6 years putting together a supply chain that would provide the necessary raw materials at the quality level McDonald's demands. On top of that, there are the risks associated with the Russian economy and its currency that are well beyond the scope of what is experienced in the United States.

These risks all materialized in 1998 when the Russian economy, along with its currency the ruble, went in the tank. In an attempt to shore up its economy, the Russian government cut its exchange rate from 6,000 rubles for each U.S. dollar to a new rate of 6 rubles per U.S. dollar—in effect, it cut off three zeros. Unfortunately, that didn't solve the problems the Russian economy faced. In May of 1998, the first Russian bank crashed and the value of the ruble started to drop. Then, in the summer of 1998, the Russian economy lost control and, finally, in August the entire banking system failed. When it was all over by the end of 1998, the exchange rate had fallen to 23 rubles per dollar, a drop of over 280 percent. McDonald's sells its burgers for rubles, so when it comes time to trade the rubles in for U.S. dollars, McDonald's won't be worth nearly as much as it was a year prior. In spite of all of this, since it opened, the Moscow McDonald's has proven to be enormously successful. It all goes to show that not all capital-budgeting projects have to be new products—they can be existing domestic products that are introduced into the international markets.

## SUMMARY

The growth of our global economy, the increasing number of multinational corporations, and the increase in foreign trade itself underscore the importance of the study of international finance.

Exchange rate mechanics are discussed in the context of the prevailing floating rates. Under this system, exchange rates between currencies vary in an apparently random fashion in accordance with the supply and demand conditions in the exchange market. Important economic factors affecting the level of exchange rates include the relative economic strengths of the countries involved, the balance-of-payments mechanism, and the countries' monetary policies. Several important exchange rate terms are introduced. These include the asked and the bid rates, which represent the selling and buying rates of currencies. The direct quote is the units of home currency per unit of foreign currency, and the indirect quote is the reciprocal of the direct quote. Cross-rate computations reflect the exchange rate between two foreign currencies.

The forward exchange market provides a valuable service by quoting rates for the delivery of foreign currencies in the future. The foreign currency is said to sell at a discount (premium) forward from the spot rate when the forward rate is greater (less) than the spot rate, in direct quotation. In addition, the influences of purchasing-power parity (PPP) and the international Fisher effect (IFE) in determining the exchange rate are discussed. In rational and efficient markets, forward rates are unbiased forecasts of future spot rates that are consistent with the PPP.

Exchange rate risk exists because the exact spot rate that prevails on a future date is not known with certainty today. The concept of exchange rate risk is applicable to a wide variety of businesses, including export-import firms and firms involved in making direct foreign investments or international investments in securities. Exchange exposure is a measure of exchange rate risk. There are different ways of measuring the foreign exposure, including the net asset (net liability) measurement. Different strategies are open to businesses to counter the exposure to this risk, including the money-market hedge, the forward-market hedge, futures contracts, and options. Each involves different costs.

In discussing working-capital management in an international environment, we find leading and lagging techniques useful in minimizing exchange rate risks and increasing profitability. In addition, funds positioning is a useful tool for reducing exchange rate risk exposure. The MNC may have a lower cost of capital because it has access to a larger set of financial markets than does a domestic company. In addition to the home, host, and third-country financial markets, the MNC can tap the rapidly growing external currency markets. In making capital-structure decisions, the MNC must consider political and exchange rate risks and host and home country capital structure norms.

The complexities encountered in the direct foreign investment decision include the usual sources of risk—business and financial—and additional risks associated with fluctuating exchange rates and political factors. Political risk is due to differences in political climates, institutions, and processes between the home country and abroad. Under these conditions, the estimation of future cash flows and the choice of the proper discount rates are more complicated than for the domestic investment situation.

## KEY TERMS

**myPHLIP**

Go To:
http://www.prenhall.com/keown
for downloads and current events associated with this chapter

**Arbitrageur, 740**
**Asked rate, 740**
**Bid rate, 740**
**Bid-asked spread, 740**
**Buying rate, 740**
**Covered-interest arbitrage, 740**
**Cross rate, 740**
**Direct quote, 737**
**Exchange rate, 737**
**Exchange rate risk, 741**
**Floating-rate international currency system, 734**
**Forward exchange contract, 741**
**Forward-spot differential, 742**
**Indirect quote, 737**
**Interest-rate parity (IRP) theory, 745**
**Law of one price, 746**
**Multinational corporation (MNC), 733**
**Purchasing power parity (PPP) theory, 745**
**Selling rate, 740**
**Simple arbitrage, 740**
**Spot transactions, 737**
**Transaction exposure, 748**
**Transfer price, 752**
**Triangular arbitrage, 740**

## STUDY QUESTIONS

**22-1.** What additional factors are encountered in international as compared with domestic financial management? Discuss each briefly.

**22-2.** What different types of businesses operate in the international environment? Why are the techniques and strategies available to these firms different?

**22-3.** What is meant by *arbitrage profits?*

**22-4.** What are the markets and mechanics involved in generating (a) simple arbitrage profits, (b) triangular arbitrage profits?

**22-5.** How do the purchasing power parity, interest rate parity, and the Fisher effect explain the relationships between the current spot rate, the future spot rate, and the forward rate?

**22-6.** What is meant by (a) exchange risk, (b) political risk?

**22-7.** How can exchange risk be measured?

**22-8.** What are the differences among transaction, translation, and economic exposures? Should all of them be ideally reduced to zero?

**22-9.** What steps can a firm take to reduce exchange risk? Indicate at least two different techniques.

**22-10.** How are the forward market and the money-market hedges affected? What are the major differences between these two types of hedges?

**22-11.** In the New York exchange market, the forward rate for the Indian currency, the rupee, is not quoted. If you were exposed to exchange risk in rupees, how could you cover your position?

**22-12.** Compare and contrast the use of forward contracts, futures contracts, and options to reduce foreign exchange exposure. When is each instrument most appropriate?

**22-13.** Indicate two working-capital management techniques that are useful for international businesses to reduce exchange risk and potentially increase profits.

**22-14.** How do the financing sources available to an MNC differ from those available to a domestic firm? What do these differences mean for the company's cost of capital?

**22-15.** What risks are associated with direct foreign investment? How do these risks differ from those encountered in domestic investment?

**22-16.** How is the direct foreign investment decision made? What are the inputs to this decision process? Are the inputs more complicated than those to the domestic investment problem? If so, why?

**22-17.** A corporation desires to enter a particular foreign market. The DFI analysis indicates that a direct investment in the plant in the foreign country is not profitable. What other course of action can the company take to enter the foreign market? What are the important considerations?

**22-18.** What are the reasons for the acceptance of a sales office or licensing arrangement when the DFI itself is not profitable?

## SELF-TEST PROBLEM

The data for Self-Test Problem ST-1 are given in the following table:

Selling Quotes for the German Mark in New York

| Country-Currency | Contract | $/Foreign Currency |
|---|---|---|
| Germany—mark | Spot | .3893 |
| | 30-day | .3910 |
| | 90-day | .3958 |

**ST-1.** You own $10,000. The dollar rate on the German mark is 2.5823DM/$. The German mark rate is given in the preceding table. Are arbitrage profits possible? Set up an arbitrage scheme with your capital. What is the gain (loss) in dollars?

## STUDY PROBLEMS (SET A)

The data for Study Problems 22-1A through 22-6A are given in the following table:

Selling Quotes for Foreign Currencies in New York

| Country-Currency | Contract | $/Foreign Currency |
|---|---|---|
| Canada—dollar | Spot | .8437 |
| | 30-day | .8417 |
| | 90-day | .8395 |
| Japan—yen | Spot | .004684 |
| | 30-day | .004717 |
| | 90-day | .004781 |
| Switzerland—franc | Spot | .5139 |
| | 30-day | .5169 |
| | 90-day | .5315 |

**22-1A.** An American business needs to pay (a) 10,000 Canadian dollars, (b) 2 million yen, and (c) 50,000 Swiss francs to businesses abroad. What are the dollar payments to the respective countries?

**22-2A.** An American business pays $10,000, $15,000, and $20,000 to suppliers, in, respectively, Japan, Switzerland, and Canada. How much, in local currencies, do the suppliers receive?

**22-3A.** Compute the indirect quote for the spot and forward Canadian dollar, yen, and Swiss franc contracts.

**22-4A.** The spreads on the contracts as a percent of the asked rates are 2 percent for yen, 3 percent for Canadian dollars, and 5 percent for Swiss francs. Show, in a table similar to the preceding one, the bid rates for the different spot and forward rates.

**22-5A.** You own $10,000. The dollar rate in Tokyo is 216.6743£. The yen rate in New York is given in the previous table. Are arbitrage profits possible? Set up an arbitrage scheme with your capital. What is the gain (loss) in dollars?

**22-6A.** Compute the Canadian dollar/yen and the yen/Swiss franc spot rate from the data in the preceding table.

## INTEGRATIVE PROBLEM

For your job as the business reporter for a local newspaper, you are given the assignment of putting together a series of articles on the multinational finance and the international currency markets for your readers. Much recent local press coverage has been given to losses in the foreign exchange markets by JGAR, a local firm that is the subsidiary of Daedlufetarg, a large German manufacturing firm. Your editor would like you to address several specific questions dealing with multinational finance. Prepare a response to the following memorandum from your editor:

TO: Business Reporter

FROM: Perry White, Editor, *Daily Planet*

RE: Upcoming Series on Multinational Finance

In your upcoming series on multinational finance, I would like to make sure you cover several specific points. In addition, before you begin this assignment, I want to make sure we are all reading from the same script, as accuracy has always been the cornerstone of the *Daily Planet.* I'd like a response to the following questions before we proceed:

1. What new problems and factors are encountered in international as opposed to domestic financial management?
2. What does the term *arbitrage profits* mean?
3. What can a firm do to reduce exchange risk?
4. What are the differences between a forward contract, a futures contract, and options?

Use the following data in your response to the remaining questions:

Selling Quotes for Foreign Currencies in New York

| Country-Currency | Contract | $/Foreign |
|---|---|---|
| Canada—dollar | Spot | .8450 |
| | 30-day | .8415 |
| | 90-day | .8390 |
| Japan—yen | Spot | .004700 |
| | 30-day | .004750 |
| | 90-day | .004820 |
| Switzerland—franc | Spot | .5150 |
| | 30-day | .5182 |
| | 90-day | .5328 |

5. An American business needs to pay (a) 15,000 Canadian dollars, (b) 1.5 million yen, and (c) 55,000 Swiss francs to businesses abroad. What are the dollar payments to the respective countries?
6. An American business pays $20,000, $5,000, and $15,000 to suppliers in, respectively, Japan, Switzerland, and Canada. How much, in local currencies, do the suppliers receive?
7. Compute the indirect quote for the spot and forward Canadian dollar contract.
8. You own $10,000. The dollar rate in Tokyo is 216.6752. The yen rate in New York is given in the preceding table. Are arbitrage profits possible? Set up an arbitrage scheme with your capital. What is the gain (loss) in dollars?
9. Compute the Canadian dollar/yen spot rate from the data in the preceding table.

## STUDY PROBLEMS (SET B)

The data for Study Problems 22-1B through 22-6B are given in the following table:

Selling Quotes for Foreign Currencies in New York

| Country-Currency | Contract | $/Foreign Currency |
|---|---|---|
| Canada—dollar | Spot | .8439 |
| | 30-day | .8410 |
| | 90-day | .8390 |
| Japan—yen | Spot | .004680 |
| | 30-day | .004720 |
| | 90-day | .004787 |
| Switzerland—franc | Spot | .5140 |
| | 30-day | .5179 |
| | 90-day | .5335 |

**22-1B.** An American business needs to pay (a) 15,000 Canadian dollars, (b) 1.5 million yen, and (c) 55,000 Swiss francs to businesses abroad. What are the dollar payments to the respective countries?

**22-2B.** An American business pays $20,000, $5,000, and $15,000 to suppliers in, respectively, Japan, Switzerland, and Canada. How much, in local currencies, do the suppliers receive?

**22-3B.** Compute the indirect quote for the spot and forward Canadian dollar, yen, and Swiss franc contracts.

**22-4B.** The spreads on the contracts as a percent of the asked rates are 4 percent for yen, 3 percent for Canadian dollars, and 6 percent for Swiss francs. Show, in a table similar to the previous one, the bid rates for the different spot and forward rates.

**22-5B.** You own $10,000. The dollar rate in Tokyo is 216.6752£. The yen rate in New York is given in the previous table. Are arbitrage profits possible? Set up an arbitrage scheme with your capital. What is the gain (loss) in dollars?

**22-6B.** Compute the Canadian dollar/yen and the yen/Swiss franc spot rate from the data in the preceding table.

## SELF-TEST SOLUTION

**ST-1.** The German rate is 2.5823 marks/$1, while the (indirect) New York rate is 1/.3893 = 2.5687 marks/$.

Assuming no transaction costs, the rates between German and New York are out of line. Thus, arbitrage profits are possible.

Step 1: Because the mark is cheaper in Germany, buy $10,000 worth of marks in Germany. The number of marks purchased would be $10,000 × 2.5823 = 25,823 marks.

Step 2: Simultaneously sell the marks in New York at the prevailing rate. The amount received upon the sale of the marks would be:

25,823 marks × $.3893/mark = $10,052.89

net gain is $10,052.89 − $10,000 = $52.89

# USING A CALCULATOR

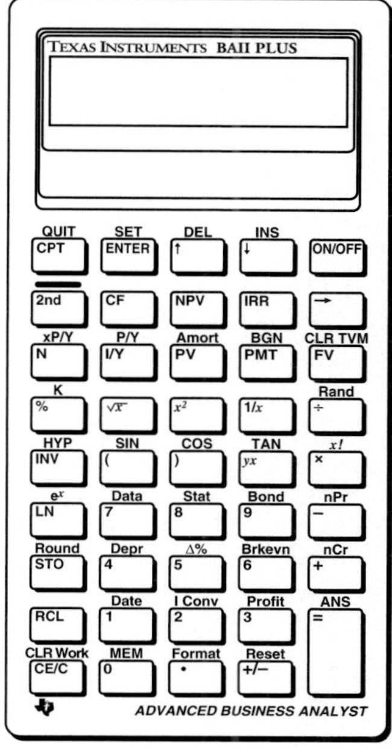


As you prepare for a career in business, the ability to use a financial calculator is essential, whether you are in the finance division or the marketing department. For most positions, it will be assumed that you can use a calculator in making computations that at one time were simply not possible without extensive time and effort. The following examples let us see what is possible, but they represent only the beginning of using the calculator in finance.

With just a little time and effort, you will be surprised at how much you can do with the calculator, such as calculating a stock's beta, or determining the value of a bond on a specific day given the exact date of maturity, or finding net present values and internal rates of return, or calculating the standard deviation. The list is almost endless.

In demonstrating how calculators may make our work easier, we must first decide which calculator to use. The options are numerous and largely depend on personal preference. We have chosen the Texas Instruments BAII Plus.

We will limit our discussion to the following issues:

I. Introductory Comments
II. An Important Starting Point
III. Calculating Table Values for:
  A. Appendix B (Compound sum of $1)
  B. Appendix C (Present value of $1)
  C. Appendix D (Sum on an annuity of $1 for *n* periods)
  D. Appendix E (Present value of an annuity for $1 for *n* periods)
IV. Calculating Present Values
V. Calculating Future Values (Compound sum)
VI. Calculating the Number of Payments or Receipts
VII. Calculating the Payment Amount
VIII. Calculating the Interest Rate
IX. Bond Value
  A. Computing the value of a bond
  B. Calculating the yield to maturity on a bond
X. Computing the Net Present Value and Internal Rate of Return
  A. Where future cash flows are equal amounts in each period (annuity)
  B. Where future cash flows are unequal amounts in each period.

## I. Introductory Comments

In the examples that follow, you are told (1) which keystrokes to use, (2) the resulting appearance of the calculator display, and (3) a supporting explanation.

The keystrokes column tells you which keys to press. The keystrokes shown in an unshaded box tell you to use one of the calculator's dedicated or "hard" keys. For example, if +/− is shown in the keystrokes instruction column, press that key on the keyboard of the calculator. To use a function printed in gray lettering above a dedicated key, always press the gray key 2nd first, then the function key.

**II. AN IMPORTANT STARTING POINT**

Example: You want to display four numbers to the right of the decimal.

| Keystrokes | Display | Explanation |
|---|---|---|
| 2nd | | |
| Format | Dec = | |
| 4 Enter | DEC = 4.0000 | Sets display to show four numbers to the right of the decimal |
| CE/C CE/C | 0.0000 | Clears display |

Example: You want to display two payments per year to be paid at the end of each period.

| Keystrokes | Display | Explanation |
|---|---|---|
| 2nd | | |
| P/Y | P/Y = | |
| 2 Enter | P/Y = 2.0000 | Sets number of payments per year at 2 |
| 2nd | | |
| BGN | END | Sets timing of payment at the end of each period |
| CE/C CE/C | 0.0000 | Clears display |

**III. CALCULATING TABLE VALUES**

**A. The compound sum of $1 (Appendix B)**

Example: What is the table value for the compound sum of $1 for 5 years at a 12 percent annual interest rate?

| Keystrokes | Display | Explanation |
|---|---|---|
| 2nd | | |
| P/Y | P/Y = | |
| 1 Enter | P/Y = 1.0000 | Sets number of payments per year at 1 |
| 2nd | | |
| BGN | END | Sets timing of payment at the end of each period |
| CE/C CE/C | 0.0000 | Clears display |
| 2nd | | |
| CLR TVM | 0.0000 | Clears TVM variables |
| 1 +/− | PV = −1.0000 | Stores initial $1 as a negative present value |
| PV | | Otherwise, the answer will appear as a negative |
| 5 N | N = 5.0000 | Stores number of periods |
| 12 I/Y | I/Y = 12.0000 | Stores interest rate |
| CPT FV | FV = 1.7623 | Table value |

### III. CALCULATING TABLE VALUES (CONTINUED)

**B. The present value of $1 (Appendix C)**

Example: What is the table value for the present value of $1 for 8 years at a 10 percent annual interest rate?

| Keystrokes | Display | Explanation |
|---|---|---|
| 2nd | | |
| P/Y | P/Y = | |
| 1 Enter | P/Y = 1.0000 | Sets number of payments per year at 1 |
| 2nd | | |
| BGN | END | Sets timing of payment at the end of each period |
| CE/C CE/C | 0.0000 | Clears display |
| 2nd | | |
| CLR TVM | 0.0000 | Clears TVM variables |
| 1 +/− | FV = −1.0000 | Stores future amount as negative value |
| FV | | |
| 8 N | N = 8.0000 | Stores number of periods |
| 10 I/Y | I/Y = 10.0000 | Stores interest rate |
| CPT PV | PV = 0.4665 | Table value |

### C. THE SUM OF AN ANNUITY OF $1 FOR *N* PERIODS (APPENDIX D)

Example: What is the table value for the compound sum of an annuity of $1 for 6 years at a 14 percent annual interest rate?

| Keystrokes | Display | Explanation |
|---|---|---|
| 2nd | | |
| P/Y | P/Y = | |
| 1 Enter | P/Y = 1.0000 | Sets number of payments per year at 1 |
| 2nd | | |
| BGN | END | Sets timing of payment at the end of each period |
| CE/C CE/C | 0.0000 | Clears display |
| 2nd | | |
| CLR TVM | 0.0000 | Clears TVM variables |
| 1 +/− | PMT = −1.0000 | Stores annual payment (annuity) as a negative number. Otherwise, the answer will appear as a negative. |
| PMT | | |
| 6 N | N = 6.0000 | Stores number of periods |
| 14 I/Y | I/Y = 14.0000 | Stores interest rate |
| CPT FV | PV = 8.5355 | Table value |

### III. CALCULATING TABLE VALUES (CONTINUED)

**D. The present value of an annuity of $1 for *n* periods (Appendix E)**

Example: What is the table value for the present value of an annuity of $1 for 12 years at 9 percent annual interest rate?

| Keystrokes | Display | Explanation |
|---|---|---|
| 2nd | | |
| P/Y | P/Y = | |
| 1 Enter | P/Y = 1.0000 | Sets number of payments per year at 1 |
| 2nd | | |
| BGN | END | Sets timing of payment at the end of each period |
| CE/C CE/C | 0.0000 | Clears display |
| 2nd | | |
| CLR TVM | 0.0000 | Clears TVM variables |
| 1 +/− PMT | PMT = −1.0000 | Stores annual payment (annuity) as a negative number. Otherwise, the answer answer will appear as a negative. |
| 12 N | N = 12.0000 | Stores number of periods |
| 9 I/Y | I/Y = 9.0000 | Stores interest rate |
| CPT FV | PV = 7.1607 | Table value |

### IV. CALCULATING PRESENT VALUES

Example: You are considering the purchase of a franchise of quick oil-change locations, which you believe will provide an annual cash flow of $50,000. At the end of 10 years, you believe that you will be able to sell the franchise for an estimated $900,000. Calculate the maximum amount you should pay for the franchise (present value) in order to realize at least an 18 percent annual yield.

| Keystrokes | Display | Explanation |
|---|---|---|
| 2nd | | |
| BGN | END | Sets timing of payment at the end of each period |
| CE/C CE/C | 0.0000 | Clears display |
| 2nd | | |
| CLR TVM | 0.0000 | Clears TVM variables |
| 10 N | N = 10.0000 | Stores *n*, the holding period |
| 18 I/Y | I/Y = 18.0000 | Stores *i*, the required rate of return |
| 50,000 PMT | PMT = 50,000,000 | Stores PMT, the annual cash flow to be received |
| 900,000 FV | FV = 900,000.000 | Stores FV, the cash flow to be received at the end of the project |
| CPT PV | PV = −396,662.3350 | The present value, given a required rate of reutrn of 18 percent. (Note: The present value is displayed with a minus sign because it represents cash paid out.) |

**V. CALCULATING FUTURE VALUES (COMPOUND SUM)**

Example: If you deposit $300 a month (at the beginning of each month) into a new account that pays 6.25% annual interested compounded monthly, how much will you have in the account after 5 years?

| Keystrokes | Display | Explanation |
|---|---|---|
| 2nd | | |
| BGN | END | Sets timing of payment at the end of each period |
| 2nd | | |
| SET | BGN | Sets timing of payment at the end of each period |
| 2nd | | |
| P/Y | PY = | |
| 12 Enter | P/Y = 12.0000 | Sets 12 payments per year |
| CE/C CE/C | 0.0000 | Clears display |
| 2nd | | |
| CLR TVM | 0.0000 | Clears TVM variables |
| 60 N | N = 60.0000 | Stores *n*, the number of months for the investment |
| 6.25 I/Y | I/Y = 6.2500 | Stores *i*, the annual rate |
| 300 +/− PMT | PMT = −300.0000 | Stores PMT, the monthly amount invested (with a minus sign for cash paid out) |
| CPT FV | FV = 21,175.7613 | The future value after 5 years |

**VI. CALCULATING THE NUMBER OF PAYMENTS OR RECEIPTS**

Example: If you wish to retire with $500,000 saved, and can only afford payments of $500 each month, how long will you have to contribute toward your retirement if you can earn a 10 percent return on your contributions?

| Keystrokes | Display | Explanation |
|---|---|---|
| 2nd | | |
| BGN | BGN | Verifies timing of payment at the beginning of each period |
| 2nd | | |
| P/Y | P/Y = 12.0000 | |
| 12 Enter | P/Y = 12.0000 | Sets 12 payments per year |
| CE/C CE/C | 0.0000 | Clears display |
| 2nd | | |
| CLR TVM | 0.0000 | Clears TVM variables |
| 10 I/Y | I/Y = 10.0000 | Stores *i*, the interest rate |
| 500 +/− PMT | PMT = −500.0000 | Stores PMT, the monthly amount invested (with a minus sign for cash paid out) |
| 50,000 FV | FV = 500,000.000 | The value we want to achieve |
| CPT N | N = 268.2539 | Number of months (because we considered monthly payments) required to achieve our goal |

**VII. CALCULATING THE PAYMENT AMOUNT**

Example: Suppose your retirement needs were $750,000. If you are currently 25 years old and plan to retire at age 65, how much will you have to contribute each month for retirement if you can earn 12.5% on your savings?

| Keystrokes | Display | Explanation |
|---|---|---|
| 2nd | | |
| BGN | BGN | Verifies timing of payment at the beginning of each period |
| 2nd | | |
| P/Y | P/Y = 12.0000 | |
| 12 Enter | P/Y = 12.0000 | Sets 12 payments per year |
| CE/C CE/C | 0.0000 | Clears display |
| 2nd | | |
| CLR TVM | 0.0000 | Clears TVM variables |
| 12.5 I/Y | I/Y = 12.5000 | Stores *i*, the interest rate |
| 480 N | N = 480.0000 | Stores *n*, the number of periods until we stop contributing (40 years × 12 months/years = 480 months) |
| 750,000 FV | FV = 750,000.000 | The value we want to achieve |
| CPT PMT | PMT = −53.8347 | Monthly contribution required to achieve our utlimate goal (shown as negative because it represents cash paid out) |

**VIII. CALCULATING THE INTEREST RATE**

Example: If you invest $300 at the end of each month for 6 years (72 months) for a promised $30,000 return at the end, what interest rate are you earning on your investment?

| Keystrokes | Display | Explanation |
|---|---|---|
| 2nd | | |
| BGN | BGN | Sets timing of payments to beginning of each period |
| 2nd | | |
| SET | END | Sets timing of payments to end of each period |
| 2nd | | |
| P/Y | P/Y = 12.0000 | |
| 12 Enter | P/Y = 12.0000 | Sets 12 payments per year |
| CE/C CE/C | 0.0000 | Clears display |
| 2nd | | |
| CLR TVM | 0.0000 | Clears TVM variables |
| 72 N | N = 72.0000 | Stores N, the number of deposits (investments) |
| 300 +/− PMT | PMT = −300.0000 | Stores PMT, the monthly amount invested (with a minus sign for cash paid out) |
| 30,000 FV | FV = 30,000.000 | Stores the future value to be received in 6 years |
| CPT I/Y | I/Y= 10.5892 | The annual interest rate earned on the investment |

## IX. BOND VALUATION

### A. Computing the value of a bond

Example: Assume the current date is January 1, 1993, and that you want to know the value of a bond that matures in 10 years and has a coupon rate of 9 percent (4.5% semiannually). Your required rate of return is 12 percent.

| Keystrokes | Display | Explanation |
|---|---|---|
| 2nd | | |
| BGN | END | Verifies timing of payment at the beginning of each period |
| 2nd | | |
| P/Y | P/Y = 12.0000 | |
| 2 Enter | P/Y = 2.0000 | Sets 2 payments per year; end mode (END) assumes cash flows are at the end of each 6-month period |
| CE/C CE/C | 0.0000 | Clears display |
| 2nd | | |
| CLR TVM | 0.0000 | Clears TVM variables |
| 20 N | N = 20.0000 | Stores the number of semiannual periods (10 years × 2) |
| 12 I/Y | I/Y= 12.0000 | Stores annual rate of return |
| 45 PMT | PMT = 45.0000 | Stores the semiannual interest payment |
| 1,000 FV | FV = 1,000.0000 | Stores the bond's maturity or par value |
| CPT PV | PV= −827.9512 | Value of the bond, expressed as a negative number |

**Solution using the bond feature:**

| | | |
|---|---|---|
| CE/C CE/C | 0.0000 | Clears display |
| 2nd | | |
| BOND | STD = 1-01-1970 | (This will be the last date entered) |
| 2nd | | |
| CLR WORK | STD = 1-01-1970 | Clears BOND variables |
| 1.01.93 Enter | STD = 1-01-1993 | Stores the current date (month, day, year) |
| ↓ | CPN = 0.0000 | |
| 9 Enter | CPN = 9.0000 | Stores the coupon interest rate |
| ↓ | RDT = 12-31-1990 | (This will be the last date entered) |
| 1.01.03 Enter | RDT = 1-01-2003 | Stores the maturity date in 10 years |
| ↓ | RV = 100.0000 | Verifies bonds maturity or par value |
| ↓ | ACT | |
| 2nd | | |
| SET | 360 | Sets calculations to be based on 360-day year |
| ↓ | 2/Y | Verifies semiannual compounding rate |
| ↓ | YLD = 0.0000 | |
| 12 Enter | YLD = 12.0000 | Stores the investor's required rate of return |
| ↓ | PRI = 0.0000 | |
| CPT | PRI = 82.7951 | Value of bond as % of par value; i.e., value of bond is $827.95 |

**IX. BOND VALUATION**

**B. Computing the yield to maturity on a bond**

Example: Assume the current date is January 1, 1994, and that you want to know your yield to maturity on a bond that matures in 8 years and has a coupon rate of 12% (6% semiannually). The bond is selling for $1,100.

| Keystrokes | Display | Explanation |
|---|---|---|
| 2nd | | |
| BGN | END | Verifies timing of payment at the beginning of each period |
| 2nd<br>P/Y<br>2 Enter | <br>P/Y = 12.0000<br>P/Y = 2.0000 | Sets 2 payments per year; end mode (END) assumes cash flows are at the end of each 6-month period |
| CE/C CE/C | 0.0000 | Clears display |
| 2nd | | |
| CLR TVM | 0.0000 | Clears TVM variables |
| 16 N | N = 16.0000 | Stores the number of semiannual periods (8 years × 2) |
| 1100 +/− | | |
| PV | PV= −1,100.0000 | Value of the bond, expressed as a negative number |
| 60 PMT | PMT = 60.0000 | Stores the semiannual interest payment |
| 1,000 FV | FV = 1,000.0000 | Stores the bond's maturity or par value |
| CPT I/Y | I/Y= 10.1451 | The yield to maturity, expressed on an annual basis |

**Solution using the bond feature:**

| | | |
|---|---|---|
| CE/C CE/C | 0.0000 | Clears display |
| 2nd | | |
| BOND | SDT = 1-01-1993 | (This will be the last date entered) |
| 2nd | | |
| CLR WORK | SDT = 1-01-1993 | Clears BOND variables |
| 1.03.94 Enter | SDT = 1-03-1994 | Stores the current date (month, day, year) |
| ↓ | CPN = 0.0000 | |
| 12 Enter | CPN = 12.0000 | Stores the coupon interest rate |
| ↓ | RDT = 1-01-2003 | (This will be the last date entered) |
| 1.03.02 Enter | RDT = 1-03-2002 | Stores the maturity date in 8 years |
| ↓ | RV = 100.0000 | Verifies bonds maturity or par value |
| ↓ | 360 | |
| 2nd | | |
| SET | ACT | Sets calculations to be based on 360-day year |
| ↓ | 2/Y | Verifies semiannual compounding rate |
| ↓ | YLD = 0.0000 | |
| ↓ | PRI = 0.0000 | |
| 110 Enter | PRI = 110.0000 | Stores the bond value as a percentage of par value |
| ↑ | YLD = 0.0000 | |
| CPT | YLD = 10.1451 | Bond's yield to maturity |

## X. COMPUTING THE NET PRESENT VALUE AND INTERNAL RATE OF RETURN

### A. Where future cash flows are equal amounts in each period (annuity)

Example: The firm is considering a capital project that would cost $80,000. The firm's cost of capital is 12 percent. The project life is 10 years, during which time the firm expects to receive $15,000 per year. Calculate the NPV and the IRR.

| Keystrokes | Display | Explanation |
|---|---|---|
| 2nd | | |
| BGN | END | Verifies timing of payment at the beginning of each period |
| 2nd<br>P/Y<br>1 Enter | P/Y = 21.0000 | Sets 1 payment per year; end mode (END) assumes cash flows are at the end of each year |
| CE/C CE/C | 0.0000 | Clears display |
| 2nd | | |
| CLR TVM | 0.0000 | Clears TVM variables |
| 15,000 PMT | PMT = 15.0000 | Stores the annual cash flows at $15,000 |
| 10 N | N = 10.0000 | Stores the life of the project |
| 12 I/Y | I/Y = 12.0000 | Stores the cost of capital |
| CPT PV | PV = −84,753.3454 | Calculates present value |
| +/− | PV = 84,753.3454 | Changes PV to positive |
| −80,000 = | 4,753.3454 | Calculates net present value by subtracting the cost of the project |
| 80,000 +/− | −80,000.0000 | |
| PV | PV = −80,000.0000 | |
| CPT I/Y | I/Y = 13.4344 | Calculates the IRR |

### B. WHERE FUTURE CASH FLOWS ARE UNEQUAL AMOUNTS IN EACH PERIOD

Example: The firm is considering a capital project that would cost $110,000. The firm's cost of capital is 15 percent. The project life is 5 years, with the following expected cash flows: $ – 25,000, $50,000, $60,000, $60,000, and $70,000. In addition, you expect to receive $30,000 in the last year from the salvage value of the equipment. Calculate the NPV and IRR.

| Keystrokes | Display | Explanation |
|---|---|---|
| CE/C CE/C | 0.0000 | Clears display |
| CF | $CF_0$ = 0.0000 | |
| 2nd | | |
| CLR WORK | $CF_0$ = 0.0000 | Clears cash flow variables |
| 110,000 +/−<br>Enter | $CF_0$ = 110,000.0000 | Stores $CF_0$, the initial investment (with a minus sign for a negative cash flow) |
| ↓ | C01 = 0.0000 | Stores $CF_1$, the first year's cash flow (with a minus sign for a negative cash flow) |
| 25,000 +/−<br>Enter | C01 = −25,000.0000 | |
| ↓<br>Enter | F01 = 1.0000 | Stores the number of years $CF_1$ is repeated (in this case, 1 year only) |
| ↓ | C02 = 0.0000 | |
| 50,000<br>Enter | C02 = 50,000.0000 | Stores $CF_2$ |
| ↓ | $FO_2$ = 1.0000 | |

**X. COMPUTING THE NET PRESENT VALUE AND INTERNAL RATE OF RETURN (CONTINUED)**

| | | |
|---|---|---|
| Enter | F02 = 1.0000 | Store the number of years $CF_2$ is repeated |
| ↓ | C03 = 0.0000 | |
| 60,000 Enter | C03 = 60,000.0000 | Stores $CF_3$ |
| ↓ 2 Enter | F03 = 2.0000 | Stores the number of years $CF_3$ is repeated (here, 2 years, so our response is 2 to the $FO_3$ prompt) |
| ↓ | C04 = 0.0000 | |
| 100,000 Enter | C04 = 100,000.0000 | Stores $CF_4$, \$70,000 plus expected \$30,000 |
| ↓ Enter | F04 = 1.0000 | Stores the number $CF_4$ is repeated |
| 2nd QUIT | 0.0000 | Ends storage of individual cash flows |
| NPV | I = 0.0000 | |
| 15 Enter | I = 15.0000 | Stores interest rate |
| ↓ | NPV = 0.0000 | |
| CPT | NPV = 25,541.8951 | Calculates the project's NPV at the stated interest rate |
| IRR | IRR = 0.0000 | |
| CPT | IRR = 22.9533 | Calculates the project's IRR |

# COMPOUND SUM OF $1

| n | 1% | 2% | 3% | 4% | 5% | 6% | 7% | 8% | 9% | 10% |
|---|---|---|---|---|---|---|---|---|---|---|
| 1 | 1.010 | 1.020 | 1.030 | 1.040 | 1.050 | 1.060 | 1.070 | 1.080 | 1.090 | 1.100 |
| 2 | 1.020 | 1.040 | 1.061 | 1.082 | 1.102 | 1.124 | 1.145 | 1.166 | 1.188 | 1.210 |
| 3 | 1.030 | 1.061 | 1.093 | 1.125 | 1.158 | 1.191 | 1.225 | 1.260 | 1.295 | 1.331 |
| 4 | 1.041 | 1.082 | 1.126 | 1.170 | 1.216 | 1.262 | 1.311 | 1.360 | 1.412 | 1.464 |
| 5 | 1.051 | 1.104 | 1.159 | 1.217 | 1.276 | 1.338 | 1.403 | 1.469 | 1.539 | 1.611 |
| 6 | 1.062 | 1.126 | 1.194 | 1.265 | 1.340 | 1.419 | 1.501 | 1.587 | 1.677 | 1.772 |
| 7 | 1.072 | 1.149 | 1.230 | 1.316 | 1.407 | 1.504 | 1.606 | 1.714 | 1.828 | 1.949 |
| 8 | 1.083 | 1.172 | 1.267 | 1.369 | 1.477 | 1.594 | 1.718 | 1.851 | 1.993 | 2.144 |
| 9 | 1.094 | 1.195 | 1.305 | 1.423 | 1.551 | 1.689 | 1.838 | 1.999 | 2.172 | 2.358 |
| 10 | 1.105 | 1.219 | 1.344 | 1.480 | 1.629 | 1.791 | 1.967 | 2.159 | 2.367 | 2.594 |
| 11 | 1.116 | 1.243 | 1.384 | 1.539 | 1.710 | 1.898 | 2.105 | 2.332 | 2.580 | 2.853 |
| 12 | 1.127 | 1.268 | 1.426 | 1.601 | 1.796 | 2.012 | 2.252 | 2.518 | 2.813 | 3.138 |
| 13 | 1.138 | 1.294 | 1.469 | 1.665 | 1.886 | 2.133 | 2.410 | 2.720 | 3.066 | 3.452 |
| 14 | 1.149 | 1.319 | 1.513 | 1.732 | 1.980 | 2.261 | 2.579 | 2.937 | 3.342 | 3.797 |
| 15 | 1.161 | 1.346 | 1.558 | 1.801 | 2.079 | 2.397 | 2.759 | 3.172 | 3.642 | 4.177 |
| 16 | 1.173 | 1.373 | 1.605 | 1.873 | 2.183 | 2.540 | 2.952 | 3.426 | 3.970 | 4.595 |
| 17 | 1.184 | 1.400 | 1.653 | 1.948 | 2.292 | 2.693 | 3.159 | 3.700 | 4.328 | 5.054 |
| 18 | 1.196 | 1.428 | 1.702 | 2.026 | 2.407 | 2.854 | 3.380 | 3.996 | 4.717 | 5.560 |
| 19 | 1.208 | 1.457 | 1.753 | 2.107 | 2.527 | 3.026 | 3.616 | 4.316 | 5.142 | 6.116 |
| 20 | 1.220 | 1.486 | 1.806 | 2.191 | 2.653 | 3.207 | 3.870 | 4.661 | 5.604 | 6.727 |
| 21 | 1.232 | 1.516 | 1.860 | 2.279 | 2.786 | 3.399 | 4.140 | 5.034 | 6.109 | 7.400 |
| 22 | 1.245 | 1.546 | 1.916 | 2.370 | 2.925 | 3.603 | 4.430 | 5.436 | 6.658 | 8.140 |
| 23 | 1.257 | 1.577 | 1.974 | 2.465 | 3.071 | 3.820 | 4.740 | 5.871 | 7.258 | 8.954 |
| 24 | 1.270 | 1.608 | 2.033 | 2.563 | 3.225 | 4.049 | 5.072 | 6.341 | 7.911 | 9.850 |
| 25 | 1.282 | 1.641 | 2.094 | 2.666 | 3.386 | 4.292 | 5.427 | 6.848 | 8.623 | 10.834 |
| 30 | 1.348 | 1.811 | 2.427 | 3.243 | 4.322 | 5.743 | 7.612 | 10.062 | 13.267 | 17.449 |
| 40 | 1.489 | 2.208 | 3.262 | 4.801 | 7.040 | 10.285 | 14.974 | 21.724 | 31.408 | 45.258 |
| 50 | 1.645 | 2.691 | 4.384 | 7.106 | 11.467 | 18.419 | 29.456 | 46.900 | 74.354 | 117.386 |

| n | 11% | 12% | 13% | 14% | 15% | 16% | 17% | 18% | 19% | 20% |
|---|---|---|---|---|---|---|---|---|---|---|
| 1 | 1.110 | 1.120 | 1.130 | 1.140 | 1.150 | 1.160 | 1.170 | 1.180 | 1.190 | 1.200 |
| 2 | 1.232 | 1.254 | 1.277 | 1.300 | 1.322 | 1.346 | 1.369 | 1.392 | 1.416 | 1.440 |
| 3 | 1.368 | 1.405 | 1.443 | 1.482 | 1.521 | 1.561 | 1.602 | 1.643 | 1.685 | 1.728 |
| 4 | 1.518 | 1.574 | 1.630 | 1.689 | 1.749 | 1.811 | 1.874 | 1.939 | 2.005 | 2.074 |
| 5 | 1.685 | 1.762 | 1.842 | 1.925 | 2.011 | 2.100 | 2.192 | 2.288 | 2.386 | 2.488 |
| 6 | 1.870 | 1.974 | 2.082 | 2.195 | 2.313 | 2.436 | 2.565 | 2.700 | 2.840 | 2.986 |
| 7 | 2.076 | 2.211 | 2.353 | 2.502 | 2.660 | 2.826 | 3.001 | 3.185 | 3.379 | 3.583 |
| 8 | 2.305 | 2.476 | 2.658 | 2.853 | 3.059 | 3.278 | 3.511 | 3.759 | 4.021 | 4.300 |
| 9 | 2.558 | 2.773 | 3.004 | 3.252 | 3.518 | 3.803 | 4.108 | 4.435 | 4.785 | 5.160 |
| 10 | 2.839 | 3.106 | 3.395 | 3.707 | 4.046 | 4.411 | 4.807 | 5.234 | 5.695 | 6.192 |
| 11 | 3.152 | 3.479 | 3.836 | 4.226 | 4.652 | 5.117 | 5.624 | 6.176 | 6.777 | 7.430 |
| 12 | 3.498 | 3.896 | 4.334 | 4.818 | 5.350 | 5.936 | 6.580 | 7.288 | 8.064 | 8.916 |
| 13 | 3.883 | 4.363 | 4.898 | 5.492 | 6.153 | 6.886 | 7.699 | 8.599 | 9.596 | 10.699 |
| 14 | 4.310 | 4.887 | 5.535 | 6.261 | 7.076 | 7.987 | 9.007 | 10.147 | 11.420 | 12.839 |
| 15 | 4.785 | 5.474 | 6.254 | 7.138 | 8.137 | 9.265 | 10.539 | 11.974 | 13.589 | 15.407 |
| 16 | 5.311 | 6.130 | 7.067 | 8.137 | 9.358 | 10.748 | 12.330 | 14.129 | 16.171 | 18.488 |
| 17 | 5.895 | 6.866 | 7.986 | 9.276 | 10.761 | 12.468 | 14.426 | 16.672 | 19.244 | 22.186 |
| 18 | 6.543 | 7.690 | 9.024 | 10.575 | 12.375 | 14.462 | 16.879 | 19.673 | 22.900 | 26.623 |
| 19 | 7.263 | 8.613 | 10.197 | 12.055 | 14.232 | 16.776 | 19.748 | 23.214 | 27.251 | 31.948 |
| 20 | 8.062 | 9.646 | 11.523 | 13.743 | 16.366 | 19.461 | 23.105 | 27.393 | 32.429 | 38.337 |
| 21 | 8.949 | 10.804 | 13.021 | 15.667 | 18.821 | 22.574 | 27.033 | 32.323 | 38.591 | 46.005 |
| 22 | 9.933 | 12.100 | 14.713 | 17.861 | 21.644 | 26.186 | 31.629 | 38.141 | 45.923 | 55.205 |
| 23 | 11.026 | 13.552 | 16.626 | 20.361 | 24.891 | 30.376 | 37.005 | 45.007 | 54.648 | 66.247 |
| 24 | 12.239 | 15.178 | 18.788 | 23.212 | 28.625 | 35.236 | 43.296 | 53.108 | 65.031 | 79.496 |
| 25 | 13.585 | 17.000 | 21.230 | 26.461 | 32.918 | 40.874 | 50.656 | 62.667 | 77.387 | 95.395 |
| 30 | 22.892 | 29.960 | 39.115 | 50.949 | 66.210 | 85.849 | 111.061 | 143.367 | 184.672 | 237.373 |
| 40 | 64.999 | 93.049 | 132.776 | 188.876 | 267.856 | 378.715 | 533.846 | 750.353 | 1051.642 | 1469.740 |
| 50 | 184.559 | 288.996 | 450.711 | 700.197 | 1083.619 | 1670.669 | 2566.080 | 3927.189 | 5988.730 | 9100.191 |

# COMPOUND SUM OF $1 (CONTINUED)

| n | 21% | 22% | 23% | 24% | 25% | 26% | 27% | 28% | 29% | 30% |
|---|---|---|---|---|---|---|---|---|---|---|
| 1 | 1.210 | 1.220 | 1.230 | 1.240 | 1.250 | 1.260 | 1.270 | 1.280 | 1.290 | 1.300 |
| 2 | 1.464 | 1.488 | 1.513 | 1.538 | 1.562 | 1.588 | 1.613 | 1.638 | 1.664 | 1.690 |
| 3 | 1.772 | 1.816 | 1.861 | 1.907 | 1.953 | 2.000 | 2.048 | 2.097 | 2.147 | 2.197 |
| 4 | 2.144 | 2.215 | 2.289 | 2.364 | 2.441 | 2.520 | 2.601 | 2.684 | 2.769 | 2.856 |
| 5 | 2.594 | 2.703 | 2.815 | 2.932 | 3.052 | 3.176 | 3.304 | 3.436 | 3.572 | 3.713 |
| 6 | 3.138 | 3.297 | 3.463 | 3.635 | 3.815 | 4.001 | 4.196 | 4.398 | 4.608 | 4.827 |
| 7 | 3.797 | 4.023 | 4.259 | 4.508 | 4.768 | 5.042 | 5.329 | 5.629 | 5.945 | 6.275 |
| 8 | 4.595 | 4.908 | 5.239 | 5.589 | 5.960 | 6.353 | 6.767 | 7.206 | 7.669 | 8.157 |
| 9 | 5.560 | 5.987 | 6.444 | 6.931 | 7.451 | 8.004 | 8.595 | 9.223 | 9.893 | 10.604 |
| 10 | 6.727 | 7.305 | 7.926 | 8.594 | 9.313 | 10.086 | 10.915 | 11.806 | 12.761 | 13.786 |
| 11 | 8.140 | 8.912 | 9.749 | 10.657 | 11.642 | 12.708 | 13.862 | 15.112 | 16.462 | 17.921 |
| 12 | 9.850 | 10.872 | 11.991 | 13.215 | 14.552 | 16.012 | 17.605 | 19.343 | 21.236 | 23.298 |
| 13 | 11.918 | 13.264 | 14.749 | 16.386 | 18.190 | 20.175 | 22.359 | 24.759 | 27.395 | 30.287 |
| 14 | 14.421 | 16.182 | 18.141 | 20.319 | 22.737 | 25.420 | 28.395 | 31.691 | 35.339 | 39.373 |
| 15 | 17.449 | 19.742 | 22.314 | 25.195 | 28.422 | 32.030 | 36.062 | 40.565 | 45.587 | 51.185 |
| 16 | 21.113 | 24.085 | 27.446 | 31.242 | 35.527 | 40.357 | 45.799 | 51.923 | 58.808 | 66.541 |
| 17 | 25.547 | 29.384 | 33.758 | 38.740 | 44.409 | 50.850 | 58.165 | 66.461 | 75.862 | 86.503 |
| 18 | 30.912 | 35.848 | 41.523 | 48.038 | 55.511 | 64.071 | 73.869 | 85.070 | 97.862 | 112.454 |
| 19 | 37.404 | 43.735 | 51.073 | 59.567 | 69.389 | 80.730 | 93.813 | 108.890 | 126.242 | 146.190 |
| 20 | 45.258 | 53.357 | 62.820 | 73.863 | 86.736 | 101.720 | 119.143 | 139.379 | 162.852 | 190.047 |
| 21 | 54.762 | 65.095 | 77.268 | 91.591 | 108.420 | 128.167 | 151.312 | 178.405 | 210.079 | 247.061 |
| 22 | 66.262 | 79.416 | 95.040 | 113.572 | 135.525 | 161.490 | 192.165 | 228.358 | 271.002 | 321.178 |
| 23 | 80.178 | 96.887 | 116.899 | 140.829 | 169.407 | 203.477 | 244.050 | 292.298 | 349.592 | 417.531 |
| 24 | 97.015 | 118.203 | 143.786 | 174.628 | 211.758 | 256.381 | 309.943 | 374.141 | 450.974 | 542.791 |
| 25 | 117.388 | 144.207 | 176.857 | 216.539 | 264.698 | 323.040 | 393.628 | 478.901 | 581.756 | 705.627 |
| 30 | 304.471 | 389.748 | 497.904 | 634.810 | 807.793 | 1025.904 | 1300.477 | 1645.488 | 2078.208 | 2619.936 |
| 40 | 2048.309 | 2846.941 | 3946.340 | 5455.797 | 7523.156 | 10346.879 | 14195.051 | 19426.418 | 26520.723 | 36117.754 |
| 50 | 13779.844 | 20795.680 | 31278.301 | 46889.207 | 70064.812 | 104354.562 | 154942.687 | 229345.875 | 338440.000 | 497910.125 |

| n | 31% | 32% | 33% | 34% | 35% | 36% | 37% | 38% | 39% | 40% |
|---|---|---|---|---|---|---|---|---|---|---|
| 1 | 1.310 | 1.320 | 1.330 | 1.340 | 1.350 | 1.360 | 1.370 | 1.380 | 1.390 | 1.400 |
| 2 | 1.716 | 1.742 | 1.769 | 1.796 | 1.822 | 1.850 | 1.877 | 1.904 | 1.932 | 1.960 |
| 3 | 2.248 | 2.300 | 2.353 | 2.406 | 2.460 | 2.515 | 2.571 | 2.628 | 2.686 | 2.744 |
| 4 | 2.945 | 3.036 | 3.129 | 3.224 | 3.321 | 3.421 | 3.523 | 3.627 | 3.733 | 3.842 |
| 5 | 3.858 | 4.007 | 4.162 | 4.320 | 4.484 | 4.653 | 4.826 | 5.005 | 5.189 | 5.378 |
| 6 | 5.054 | 5.290 | 5.535 | 5.789 | 6.053 | 6.328 | 6.612 | 6.907 | 7.213 | 7.530 |
| 7 | 6.621 | 6.983 | 7.361 | 7.758 | 8.172 | 8.605 | 9.058 | 9.531 | 10.025 | 10.541 |
| 8 | 8.673 | 9.217 | 9.791 | 10.395 | 11.032 | 11.703 | 12.410 | 13.153 | 13.935 | 14.758 |
| 9 | 11.362 | 12.166 | 13.022 | 13.930 | 14.894 | 15.917 | 17.001 | 18.151 | 19.370 | 20.661 |
| 10 | 14.884 | 16.060 | 17.319 | 18.666 | 20.106 | 21.646 | 23.292 | 25.049 | 26.924 | 28.925 |
| 11 | 19.498 | 21.199 | 23.034 | 25.012 | 27.144 | 29.439 | 31.910 | 34.567 | 37.425 | 40.495 |
| 12 | 25.542 | 27.982 | 30.635 | 33.516 | 36.644 | 40.037 | 43.716 | 47.703 | 52.020 | 56.694 |
| 13 | 33.460 | 36.937 | 40.745 | 44.912 | 49.469 | 54.451 | 59.892 | 65.830 | 72.308 | 79.371 |
| 14 | 43.832 | 49.756 | 54.190 | 60.181 | 66.784 | 74.053 | 82.051 | 90.845 | 100.509 | 111.120 |
| 15 | 57.420 | 64.358 | 72.073 | 80.643 | 90.158 | 100.712 | 112.410 | 125.366 | 139.707 | 155.567 |
| 16 | 75.220 | 84.953 | 95.857 | 108.061 | 121.713 | 136.968 | 154.002 | 173.005 | 194.192 | 217.793 |
| 17 | 98.539 | 112.138 | 127.490 | 144.802 | 164.312 | 186.277 | 210.983 | 238.747 | 269.927 | 304.911 |
| 18 | 129.086 | 148.022 | 169.561 | 194.035 | 221.822 | 253.337 | 289.046 | 329.471 | 375.198 | 426.875 |
| 19 | 169.102 | 195.389 | 225.517 | 260.006 | 299.459 | 344.537 | 395.993 | 454.669 | 521.525 | 597.625 |
| 20 | 221.523 | 257.913 | 299.937 | 348.408 | 404.270 | 468.571 | 542.511 | 627.443 | 724.919 | 836.674 |
| 21 | 290.196 | 340.446 | 398.916 | 466.867 | 545.764 | 637.256 | 743.240 | 865.871 | 1007.637 | 1171.343 |
| 22 | 380.156 | 449.388 | 530.558 | 625.601 | 736.781 | 865.668 | 1018.238 | 1194.900 | 1400.615 | 1639.878 |
| 23 | 498.004 | 593.192 | 705.642 | 838.305 | 994.653 | 1178.668 | 1394.986 | 1648.961 | 1946.854 | 2295.829 |
| 24 | 652.385 | 783.013 | 938.504 | 1123.328 | 1342.781 | 1602.988 | 1911.129 | 2275.564 | 2706.125 | 3214.158 |
| 25 | 854.623 | 1033.577 | 1248.210 | 1505.258 | 1812.754 | 2180.063 | 2618.245 | 3140.275 | 3761.511 | 4499.816 |
| 30 | 3297.081 | 4142.008 | 5194.516 | 6503.285 | 8128.426 | 10142.914 | 12636.086 | 15716.703 | 19517.969 | 24201.043 |
| 40 | 49072.621 | 66519.313 | 89962.188 | 121388.437 | 163433.875 | 219558.625 | 294317.937 | 393684.687 | 525508.312 | 700022.688 |

# PRESENT VALUE OF $1

| n | 1% | 2% | 3% | 4% | 5% | 6% | 7% | 8% | 9% | 10% |
|---|---|---|---|---|---|---|---|---|---|---|
| 1 | .990 | .980 | .971 | .962 | .952 | .943 | .935 | .926 | .917 | .909 |
| 2 | .980 | .961 | .943 | .925 | .907 | .890 | .873 | .857 | .842 | .826 |
| 3 | .971 | .942 | .915 | .889 | .864 | .840 | .816 | .794 | .772 | .751 |
| 4 | .961 | .924 | .888 | .855 | .823 | .792 | .763 | .735 | .708 | .683 |
| 5 | .951 | .906 | .863 | .822 | .784 | .747 | .713 | .681 | .650 | .621 |
| 6 | .942 | .888 | .837 | .790 | .746 | .705 | .666 | .630 | .596 | .564 |
| 7 | .933 | .871 | .813 | .760 | .711 | .665 | .623 | .583 | .547 | .513 |
| 8 | .923 | .853 | .789 | .731 | .677 | .627 | .582 | .540 | .502 | .467 |
| 9 | .914 | .837 | .766 | .703 | .645 | .592 | .544 | .500 | .460 | .424 |
| 10 | .905 | .820 | .744 | .676 | .614 | .558 | .508 | .463 | .422 | .386 |
| 11 | .896 | .804 | .722 | .650 | .585 | .527 | .475 | .429 | .388 | .350 |
| 12 | .887 | .789 | .701 | .625 | .557 | .497 | .444 | .397 | .356 | .319 |
| 13 | .879 | .773 | .681 | .601 | .530 | .469 | .415 | .368 | .326 | .290 |
| 14 | .870 | .758 | .661 | .577 | .505 | .442 | .388 | .340 | .299 | .263 |
| 15 | .861 | .743 | .642 | .555 | .481 | .417 | .362 | .315 | .275 | .239 |
| 16 | .853 | .728 | .623 | .534 | .458 | .394 | .339 | .292 | .252 | .218 |
| 17 | .844 | .714 | .605 | .513 | .436 | .371 | .317 | .270 | .231 | .198 |
| 18 | .836 | .700 | .587 | .494 | .416 | .350 | .296 | .250 | .212 | .180 |
| 19 | .828 | .686 | .570 | .475 | .396 | .331 | .277 | .232 | .194 | .164 |
| 20 | .820 | .673 | .554 | .456 | .377 | .312 | .258 | .215 | .178 | .149 |
| 21 | .811 | .660 | .538 | .439 | .359 | .294 | .242 | .199 | .164 | .135 |
| 22 | .803 | .647 | .522 | .422 | .342 | .278 | .226 | .184 | .150 | .123 |
| 23 | .795 | .634 | .507 | .406 | .326 | .262 | .211 | .170 | .138 | .112 |
| 24 | .788 | .622 | .492 | .390 | .310 | .247 | .197 | .158 | .126 | .102 |
| 25 | .780 | .610 | .478 | .375 | .295 | .233 | .184 | .146 | .116 | .092 |
| 30 | .742 | .552 | .412 | .308 | .231 | .174 | .131 | .099 | .075 | .057 |
| 40 | .672 | .453 | .307 | .208 | .142 | .097 | .067 | .046 | .032 | .022 |
| 50 | .608 | .372 | .228 | .141 | .087 | .054 | .034 | .021 | .013 | .009 |

| n | 11% | 12% | 13% | 14% | 15% | 16% | 17% | 18% | 19% | 20% |
|---|---|---|---|---|---|---|---|---|---|---|
| 1 | .901 | .893 | .885 | .877 | .870 | .862 | .855 | .847 | .840 | .833 |
| 2 | .812 | .797 | .783 | .769 | .756 | .743 | .731 | .718 | .706 | .694 |
| 3 | .731 | .712 | .693 | .675 | .658 | .641 | .624 | .609 | .593 | .579 |
| 4 | .659 | .636 | .613 | .592 | .572 | .552 | .534 | .516 | .499 | .482 |
| 5 | .593 | .567 | .543 | .519 | .497 | .476 | .456 | .437 | .419 | .402 |
| 6 | .535 | .507 | .480 | .456 | .432 | .410 | .390 | .370 | .352 | .335 |
| 7 | .482 | .452 | .425 | .400 | .376 | .354 | .333 | .314 | .296 | .279 |
| 8 | .434 | .404 | .376 | .351 | .327 | .305 | .285 | .266 | .249 | .233 |
| 9 | .391 | .361 | .333 | .308 | .284 | .263 | .243 | .225 | .209 | .194 |
| 10 | .352 | .322 | .295 | .270 | .247 | .227 | .208 | .191 | .176 | .162 |
| 11 | .317 | .287 | .261 | .237 | .215 | .195 | .178 | .162 | .148 | .135 |
| 12 | .286 | .257 | .231 | .208 | .187 | .168 | .152 | .137 | .124 | .112 |
| 13 | .258 | .229 | .204 | .182 | .163 | .145 | .130 | .116 | .104 | .093 |
| 14 | .232 | .205 | .181 | .160 | .141 | .125 | .111 | .099 | .088 | .078 |
| 15 | .209 | .183 | .160 | .140 | .123 | .108 | .095 | .084 | .074 | .065 |
| 16 | .188 | .163 | .141 | .123 | .107 | .093 | .081 | .071 | .062 | .054 |
| 17 | .170 | .146 | .125 | .108 | .093 | .080 | .069 | .060 | .052 | .045 |
| 18 | .153 | .130 | .111 | .095 | .081 | .069 | .059 | .051 | .044 | .038 |
| 19 | .138 | .116 | .098 | .083 | .070 | .060 | .051 | .043 | .037 | .031 |
| 20 | .124 | .104 | .087 | .073 | .061 | .051 | .043 | .037 | .031 | .026 |
| 21 | .112 | .093 | .077 | .064 | .053 | .044 | .037 | .031 | .026 | .022 |
| 22 | .101 | .083 | .068 | .056 | .046 | .038 | .032 | .026 | .022 | .018 |
| 23 | .091 | .074 | .060 | .049 | .040 | .033 | .027 | .022 | .018 | .015 |
| 24 | .082 | .066 | .053 | .043 | .035 | .028 | .023 | .019 | .015 | .013 |
| 25 | .074 | .059 | .047 | .038 | .030 | .024 | .020 | .016 | .013 | .010 |
| 30 | .044 | .033 | .026 | .020 | .015 | .012 | .009 | .007 | .005 | .004 |
| 40 | .015 | .011 | .008 | .005 | .004 | .003 | .002 | .001 | .001 | .001 |
| 50 | .005 | .003 | .002 | .001 | .001 | .001 | .000 | .000 | .000 | .000 |

# PRESENT VALUE OF $1 (CONTINUED)

| n | 21% | 22% | 23% | 24% | 25% | 26% | 27% | 28% | 29% | 30% |
|---|---|---|---|---|---|---|---|---|---|---|
| 1 | .826 | .820 | .813 | .806 | .800 | .794 | .787 | .781 | .775 | .769 |
| 2 | .683 | .672 | .661 | .650 | .640 | .630 | .620 | .610 | .601 | .592 |
| 3 | .564 | .551 | .537 | .524 | .512 | .500 | .488 | .477 | .466 | .455 |
| 4 | .467 | .451 | .437 | .423 | .410 | .397 | .384 | .373 | .361 | .350 |
| 5 | .386 | .370 | .355 | .341 | .328 | .315 | .303 | .291 | .280 | .269 |
| 6 | .319 | .303 | .289 | .275 | .262 | .250 | .238 | .227 | .217 | .207 |
| 7 | .263 | .249 | .235 | .222 | .210 | .198 | .188 | .178 | .168 | .159 |
| 8 | .218 | .204 | .191 | .179 | .168 | .157 | .148 | .139 | .130 | .123 |
| 9 | .180 | .167 | .155 | .144 | .134 | .125 | .116 | .108 | .101 | .094 |
| 10 | .149 | .137 | .126 | .116 | .107 | .099 | .092 | .085 | .078 | .073 |
| 11 | .123 | .112 | .103 | .094 | .086 | .079 | .072 | .066 | .061 | .056 |
| 12 | .102 | .092 | .083 | .076 | .069 | .062 | .057 | .052 | .047 | .043 |
| 13 | .084 | .075 | .068 | .061 | .055 | .050 | .045 | .040 | .037 | .033 |
| 14 | .069 | .062 | .055 | .049 | .044 | .039 | .035 | .032 | .028 | .025 |
| 15 | .057 | .051 | .045 | .040 | .035 | .031 | .028 | .025 | .022 | .020 |
| 16 | .047 | .042 | .036 | .032 | .028 | .025 | .022 | .019 | .017 | .015 |
| 17 | .039 | .034 | .030 | .026 | .023 | .020 | .017 | .015 | .013 | .012 |
| 18 | .032 | .028 | .024 | .021 | .018 | .016 | .014 | .012 | .010 | .009 |
| 19 | .027 | .023 | .020 | .017 | .014 | .012 | .011 | .009 | .008 | .007 |
| 20 | .022 | .019 | .016 | .014 | .012 | .010 | .008 | .007 | .006 | .005 |
| 21 | .018 | .015 | .013 | .011 | .009 | .008 | .007 | .006 | .005 | .004 |
| 22 | .015 | .013 | .011 | .009 | .007 | .006 | .005 | .004 | .004 | .003 |
| 23 | .012 | .010 | .009 | .007 | .006 | .005 | .004 | .003 | .003 | .002 |
| 24 | .010 | .008 | .007 | .006 | .005 | .004 | .003 | .003 | .002 | .002 |
| 25 | .009 | .007 | .006 | .005 | .004 | .003 | .003 | .002 | .002 | .001 |
| 30 | .003 | .003 | .002 | .002 | .001 | .001 | .001 | .001 | .000 | .000 |
| 40 | .000 | .000 | .000 | .000 | .000 | .000 | .000 | .000 | .000 | .000 |
| 50 | .000 | .000 | .000 | .000 | .000 | .000 | .000 | .000 | .000 | .000 |

| n | 31% | 32% | 33% | 34% | 35% | 36% | 37% | 38% | 39% | 40% |
|---|---|---|---|---|---|---|---|---|---|---|
| 1 | .763 | .758 | .752 | .746 | .741 | .735 | .730 | .725 | .719 | .714 |
| 2 | .583 | .574 | .565 | .557 | .549 | .541 | .533 | .525 | .518 | .510 |
| 3 | .445 | .435 | .425 | .416 | .406 | .398 | .389 | .381 | .372 | .364 |
| 4 | .340 | .329 | .320 | .310 | .301 | .292 | .284 | .276 | .268 | .260 |
| 5 | .259 | .250 | .240 | .231 | .223 | .215 | .207 | .200 | .193 | .186 |
| 6 | .198 | .189 | .181 | .173 | .165 | .158 | .151 | .145 | .139 | .133 |
| 7 | .151 | .143 | .136 | .129 | .122 | .116 | .110 | .105 | .100 | .095 |
| 8 | .115 | .108 | .102 | .096 | .091 | .085 | .081 | .076 | .072 | .068 |
| 9 | .088 | .082 | .077 | .072 | .067 | .063 | .059 | .055 | .052 | .048 |
| 10 | .067 | .062 | .058 | .054 | .050 | .046 | .043 | .040 | .037 | .035 |
| 11 | .051 | .047 | .043 | .040 | .037 | .034 | .031 | .029 | .027 | .025 |
| 12 | .039 | .036 | .033 | .030 | .027 | .025 | .023 | .021 | .019 | .018 |
| 13 | .030 | .027 | .025 | .022 | .020 | .018 | .017 | .015 | .014 | .013 |
| 14 | .023 | .021 | .018 | .017 | .015 | .014 | .012 | .011 | .010 | .009 |
| 15 | .017 | .016 | .014 | .012 | .011 | .010 | .009 | .008 | .007 | .006 |
| 16 | .013 | .012 | .010 | .009 | .008 | .007 | .006 | .006 | .005 | .005 |
| 17 | .010 | .009 | .008 | .007 | .006 | .005 | .005 | .004 | .004 | .003 |
| 18 | .008 | .007 | .006 | .005 | .005 | .004 | .003 | .003 | .003 | .002 |
| 19 | .006 | .005 | .004 | .004 | .003 | .003 | .003 | .002 | .002 | .002 |
| 20 | .005 | .004 | .003 | .003 | .002 | .002 | .002 | .002 | .001 | .001 |
| 21 | .003 | .003 | .003 | .002 | .002 | .002 | .001 | .001 | .001 | .001 |
| 22 | .003 | .002 | .002 | .002 | .001 | .001 | .001 | .001 | .001 | .001 |
| 23 | .002 | .002 | .001 | .001 | .001 | .001 | .001 | .001 | .001 | .000 |
| 24 | .002 | .001 | .001 | .001 | .001 | .001 | .001 | .000 | .000 | .000 |
| 25 | .001 | .001 | .001 | .001 | .001 | .000 | .000 | .000 | .000 | .000 |
| 30 | .000 | .000 | .000 | .000 | .000 | .000 | .000 | .000 | .000 | .000 |
| 40 | .000 | .000 | .000 | .000 | .000 | .000 | .000 | .000 | .000 | .000 |

# SUM OF AN ANNUITY OF $1 FOR n PERIODS

| n | 1% | 2% | 3% | 4% | 5% | 6% | 7% | 8% | 9% | 10% |
|---|---|---|---|---|---|---|---|---|---|---|
| 1 | 1.000 | 1.000 | 1.000 | 1.000 | 1.000 | 1.000 | 1.000 | 1.000 | 1.000 | 1.000 |
| 2 | 2.010 | 2.020 | 2.030 | 2.040 | 2.050 | 2.060 | 2.070 | 2.080 | 2.090 | 2.100 |
| 3 | 3.030 | 3.060 | 3.091 | 3.122 | 3.152 | 3.184 | 3.215 | 3.246 | 3.278 | 3.310 |
| 4 | 4.060 | 4.122 | 4.184 | 4.246 | 4.310 | 4.375 | 4.440 | 4.506 | 4.573 | 4.641 |
| 5 | 5.101 | 5.204 | 5.309 | 5.416 | 5.526 | 5.637 | 5.751 | 5.867 | 5.985 | 6.105 |
| 6 | 6.152 | 6.308 | 6.468 | 6.633 | 6.802 | 6.975 | 7.153 | 7.336 | 7.523 | 7.716 |
| 7 | 7.214 | 7.434 | 7.662 | 7.898 | 8.142 | 8.394 | 8.654 | 8.923 | 9.200 | 9.487 |
| 8 | 8.286 | 8.583 | 8.892 | 9.214 | 9.549 | 9.897 | 10.260 | 10.637 | 11.028 | 11.436 |
| 9 | 9.368 | 9.755 | 10.159 | 10.583 | 11.027 | 11.491 | 11.978 | 12.488 | 13.021 | 13.579 |
| 10 | 10.462 | 10.950 | 11.464 | 12.006 | 12.578 | 13.181 | 13.816 | 14.487 | 15.193 | 15.937 |
| 11 | 11.567 | 12.169 | 12.808 | 13.486 | 14.207 | 14.972 | 15.784 | 16.645 | 17.560 | 18.531 |
| 12 | 12.682 | 13.412 | 14.192 | 15.026 | 15.917 | 16.870 | 17.888 | 18.977 | 20.141 | 21.384 |
| 13 | 13.809 | 14.680 | 15.618 | 16.627 | 17.713 | 18.882 | 20.141 | 21.495 | 22.953 | 24.523 |
| 14 | 14.947 | 15.974 | 17.086 | 18.292 | 19.598 | 21.015 | 22.550 | 24.215 | 26.019 | 27.975 |
| 15 | 16.097 | 17.293 | 18.599 | 20.023 | 21.578 | 23.276 | 25.129 | 27.152 | 29.361 | 31.772 |
| 16 | 17.258 | 18.639 | 20.157 | 21.824 | 23.657 | 25.672 | 27.888 | 30.324 | 33.003 | 35.949 |
| 17 | 18.430 | 20.012 | 21.761 | 23.697 | 25.840 | 28.213 | 30.840 | 33.750 | 36.973 | 40.544 |
| 18 | 19.614 | 21.412 | 23.414 | 25.645 | 28.132 | 30.905 | 33.999 | 37.450 | 41.301 | 45.599 |
| 19 | 20.811 | 22.840 | 25.117 | 27.671 | 30.539 | 33.760 | 37.379 | 41.446 | 46.018 | 51.158 |
| 20 | 22.019 | 24.297 | 26.870 | 29.778 | 33.066 | 36.785 | 40.995 | 45.762 | 51.159 | 57.274 |
| 21 | 23.239 | 25.783 | 28.676 | 31.969 | 35.719 | 39.992 | 44.865 | 50.422 | 56.764 | 64.002 |
| 22 | 24.471 | 27.299 | 30.536 | 34.248 | 38.505 | 43.392 | 49.005 | 55.456 | 62.872 | 71.402 |
| 23 | 25.716 | 28.845 | 32.452 | 36.618 | 41.430 | 46.995 | 53.435 | 60.893 | 69.531 | 79.542 |
| 24 | 26.973 | 30.421 | 34.426 | 39.082 | 44.501 | 50.815 | 58.176 | 66.764 | 76.789 | 88.496 |
| 25 | 28.243 | 32.030 | 36.459 | 41.645 | 47.726 | 54.864 | 63.248 | 73.105 | 84.699 | 98.346 |
| 30 | 34.784 | 40.567 | 47.575 | 56.084 | 66.438 | 79.057 | 94.459 | 113.282 | 136.305 | 164.491 |
| 40 | 48.885 | 60.401 | 75.400 | 95.024 | 120.797 | 154.758 | 199.630 | 295.052 | 337.872 | 442.580 |
| 50 | 64.461 | 84.577 | 112.794 | 152.664 | 209.341 | 290.325 | 406.516 | 573.756 | 815.051 | 1163.865 |

| n | 11% | 12% | 13% | 14% | 15% | 16% | 17% | 18% | 19% | 20% |
|---|---|---|---|---|---|---|---|---|---|---|
| 1 | 1.000 | 1.000 | 1.000 | 1.000 | 1.000 | 1.000 | 1.000 | 1.000 | 1.000 | 1.000 |
| 2 | 2.110 | 2.120 | 2.130 | 2.140 | 2.150 | 2.160 | 2.170 | 2.180 | 2.190 | 2.200 |
| 3 | 3.342 | 3.374 | 3.407 | 3.440 | 3.472 | 3.506 | 3.539 | 3.572 | 3.606 | 3.640 |
| 4 | 4.710 | 4.779 | 4.850 | 4.921 | 4.993 | 5.066 | 5.141 | 5.215 | 5.291 | 5.368 |
| 5 | 6.228 | 6.353 | 6.480 | 6.610 | 6.742 | 6.877 | 7.014 | 7.154 | 7.297 | 7.442 |
| 6 | 7.913 | 8.115 | 8.323 | 8.535 | 8.754 | 8.977 | 9.207 | 9.442 | 9.683 | 9.930 |
| 7 | 9.783 | 10.089 | 10.405 | 10.730 | 11.067 | 11.414 | 11.772 | 12.141 | 12.523 | 12.916 |
| 8 | 11.859 | 12.300 | 12.757 | 13.233 | 13.727 | 14.240 | 14.773 | 15.327 | 15.902 | 16.499 |
| 9 | 14.164 | 14.776 | 15.416 | 16.085 | 16.786 | 17.518 | 18.285 | 19.086 | 19.923 | 20.799 |
| 10 | 16.722 | 17.549 | 18.420 | 19.337 | 20.304 | 21.321 | 22.393 | 23.521 | 24.709 | 25.959 |
| 11 | 19.561 | 20.655 | 21.814 | 23.044 | 24.349 | 25.733 | 27.200 | 28.755 | 30.403 | 32.150 |
| 12 | 22.713 | 24.133 | 25.650 | 27.271 | 29.001 | 30.850 | 32.824 | 34.931 | 37.180 | 39.580 |
| 13 | 26.211 | 28.029 | 29.984 | 32.088 | 34.352 | 36.786 | 39.404 | 42.218 | 45.244 | 48.496 |
| 14 | 30.095 | 32.392 | 34.882 | 37.581 | 40.504 | 43.672 | 47.102 | 50.818 | 54.841 | 59.196 |
| 15 | 34.405 | 37.280 | 40.417 | 43.842 | 47.580 | 51.659 | 56.109 | 60.965 | 66.260 | 72.035 |
| 16 | 39.190 | 42.753 | 46.671 | 50.980 | 55.717 | 60.925 | 66.648 | 72.938 | 79.850 | 87.442 |
| 17 | 44.500 | 48.883 | 53.738 | 59.117 | 65.075 | 71.673 | 78.978 | 87.067 | 96.021 | 105.930 |
| 18 | 50.396 | 55.749 | 61.724 | 68.393 | 75.836 | 84.140 | 93.404 | 103.739 | 115.265 | 128.116 |
| 19 | 56.939 | 63.439 | 70.748 | 78.968 | 88.211 | 98.603 | 110.283 | 123.412 | 138.165 | 154.739 |
| 20 | 64.202 | 72.052 | 80.946 | 91.024 | 102.443 | 115.379 | 130.031 | 146.626 | 165.417 | 186.687 |
| 21 | 72.264 | 81.698 | 92.468 | 104.767 | 118.809 | 134.840 | 153.136 | 174.019 | 197.846 | 225.024 |
| 22 | 81.213 | 92.502 | 105.489 | 120.434 | 137.630 | 157.414 | 180.169 | 206.342 | 236.436 | 271.028 |
| 23 | 91.147 | 104.602 | 120.203 | 138.295 | 159.274 | 183.600 | 211.798 | 244.483 | 282.359 | 326.234 |
| 24 | 102.173 | 118.154 | 136.829 | 158.656 | 184.166 | 213.976 | 248.803 | 289.490 | 337.007 | 392.480 |
| 25 | 114.412 | 133.333 | 155.616 | 181.867 | 212.790 | 249.212 | 292.099 | 342.598 | 402.038 | 471.976 |
| 30 | 199.018 | 241.330 | 293.192 | 356.778 | 434.738 | 530.306 | 647.423 | 790.932 | 966.698 | 1181.865 |
| 40 | 581.812 | 767.080 | 1013.667 | 1341.979 | 1779.048 | 2360.724 | 3134.412 | 4163.094 | 5529.711 | 7343.715 |
| 50 | 1668.723 | 2399.975 | 3459.344 | 4994.301 | 7217.488 | 10435.449 | 15088.805 | 21812.273 | 31514.492 | 45496.094 |

# SUM OF AN ANNUITY OF $1 FOR n PERIODS (CONTINUED)

| n | 21% | 22% | 23% | 24% | 25% | 26% | 27% | 28% | 29% | 30% |
|---|---|---|---|---|---|---|---|---|---|---|
| 1 | 1.000 | 1.000 | 1.000 | 1.000 | 1.000 | 1.000 | 1.000 | 1.000 | 1.000 | 1.000 |
| 2 | 2.210 | 2.220 | 2.230 | 2.240 | 2.250 | 2.260 | 2.270 | 2.280 | 2.290 | 2.300 |
| 3 | 3.674 | 3.708 | 3.743 | 3.778 | 3.813 | 3.848 | 3.883 | 3.918 | 3.954 | 3.990 |
| 4 | 5.446 | 5.524 | 5.604 | 5.684 | 5.766 | 5.848 | 5.931 | 6.016 | 6.101 | 6.187 |
| 5 | 7.589 | 7.740 | 7.893 | 8.048 | 8.207 | 8.368 | 8.533 | 8.700 | 8.870 | 9.043 |
| 6 | 10.183 | 10.442 | 10.708 | 10.980 | 11.259 | 11.544 | 11.837 | 12.136 | 12.442 | 12.756 |
| 7 | 13.321 | 13.740 | 14.171 | 14.615 | 15.073 | 15.546 | 16.032 | 16.534 | 17.051 | 17.583 |
| 8 | 17.119 | 17.762 | 18.430 | 19.123 | 19.842 | 20.588 | 21.361 | 22.163 | 22.995 | 23.858 |
| 9 | 21.714 | 22.670 | 23.669 | 24.712 | 25.802 | 26.940 | 28.129 | 29.369 | 30.664 | 32.015 |
| 10 | 27.274 | 28.657 | 20.113 | 31.643 | 33.253 | 34.945 | 36.723 | 38.592 | 40.556 | 42.619 |
| 11 | 34.001 | 35.962 | 38.039 | 40.238 | 42.566 | 45.030 | 47.639 | 50.398 | 53.318 | 56.405 |
| 12 | 42.141 | 44.873 | 47.787 | 50.895 | 54.208 | 57.738 | 61.501 | 65.510 | 69.780 | 74.326 |
| 13 | 51.991 | 55.745 | 59.778 | 64.109 | 68.760 | 73.750 | 79.106 | 84.853 | 91.016 | 97.624 |
| 14 | 63.909 | 69.009 | 74.528 | 80.496 | 86.949 | 93.925 | 101.465 | 109.611 | 118.411 | 127.912 |
| 15 | 78.330 | 85.191 | 92.669 | 100.815 | 109.687 | 119.346 | 129.860 | 141.302 | 153.750 | 167.285 |
| 16 | 95.779 | 104.933 | 114.983 | 126.010 | 138.109 | 151.375 | 165.922 | 181.867 | 199.337 | 218.470 |
| 17 | 116.892 | 129.019 | 142.428 | 157.252 | 173.636 | 191.733 | 211.721 | 233.790 | 258.145 | 285.011 |
| 18 | 142.439 | 158.403 | 176.187 | 195.993 | 218.045 | 242.583 | 269.885 | 300.250 | 334.006 | 371.514 |
| 19 | 173.351 | 194.251 | 217.710 | 244.031 | 273.556 | 306.654 | 343.754 | 385.321 | 431.868 | 483.968 |
| 20 | 210.755 | 237.986 | 268.783 | 303.598 | 342.945 | 387.384 | 437.568 | 494.210 | 558.110 | 630.157 |
| 21 | 256.013 | 291.343 | 331.603 | 377.461 | 429.681 | 489.104 | 556.710 | 633.589 | 720.962 | 820.204 |
| 22 | 310.775 | 356.438 | 408.871 | 469.052 | 538.101 | 617.270 | 708.022 | 811.993 | 931.040 | 1067.265 |
| 23 | 377.038 | 435.854 | 503.911 | 582.624 | 673.626 | 778.760 | 900.187 | 1040.351 | 1202.042 | 1388.443 |
| 24 | 457.215 | 532.741 | 620.810 | 723.453 | 843.032 | 982.237 | 1144.237 | 1332.649 | 1551.634 | 1805.975 |
| 25 | 554.230 | 650.944 | 764.596 | 898.082 | 1054.791 | 1238.617 | 1454.180 | 1706.790 | 2002.608 | 2348.765 |
| 30 | 1445.111 | 1767.044 | 2160.459 | 2640.881 | 3227.172 | 3941.953 | 4812.891 | 5873.172 | 7162.785 | 8729.805 |
| 40 | 9749.141 | 12936.141 | 17153.691 | 22728.367 | 30088.621 | 39791.957 | 52570.707 | 69376.562 | 91447.375 | 120389.375 |

| n | 31% | 32% | 33% | 34% | 35% | 36% | 37% | 38% | 39% | 40% |
|---|---|---|---|---|---|---|---|---|---|---|
| 1 | 1.000 | 1.000 | 1.000 | 1.000 | 1.000 | 1.000 | 1.000 | 1.000 | 1.000 | 1.000 |
| 2 | 2.310 | 2.320 | 2.330 | 2.340 | 2.350 | 2.360 | 2.370 | 2.380 | 2.390 | 2.400 |
| 3 | 4.026 | 4.062 | 4.099 | 4.136 | 4.172 | 4.210 | 4.247 | 4.284 | 4.322 | 4.360 |
| 4 | 6.274 | 6.362 | 6.452 | 6.542 | 6.633 | 6.725 | 6.818 | 6.912 | 7.008 | 7.104 |
| 5 | 9.219 | 9.398 | 9.581 | 9.766 | 9.954 | 10.146 | 10.341 | 10.539 | 10.741 | 10.946 |
| 6 | 13.077 | 13.406 | 13.742 | 14.086 | 14.438 | 14.799 | 15.167 | 15.544 | 15.930 | 16.324 |
| 7 | 18.131 | 18.696 | 19.277 | 19.876 | 20.492 | 21.126 | 21.779 | 22.451 | 23.142 | 23.853 |
| 8 | 24.752 | 25.678 | 26.638 | 27.633 | 28.664 | 29.732 | 30.837 | 31.982 | 33.167 | 34.395 |
| 9 | 33.425 | 34.895 | 36.429 | 38.028 | 39.696 | 41.435 | 43.247 | 45.135 | 47.103 | 49.152 |
| 10 | 44.786 | 47.062 | 49.451 | 51.958 | 54.590 | 57.351 | 60.248 | 63.287 | 66.473 | 69.813 |
| 11 | 59.670 | 63.121 | 66.769 | 70.624 | 74.696 | 78.998 | 83.540 | 88.335 | 93.397 | 98.739 |
| 12 | 79.167 | 84.320 | 89.803 | 95.636 | 101.840 | 108.437 | 115.450 | 122.903 | 130.822 | 139.234 |
| 13 | 104.709 | 112.302 | 120.438 | 129.152 | 138.484 | 148.474 | 159.166 | 170.606 | 182.842 | 195.928 |
| 14 | 138.169 | 149.239 | 161.183 | 174.063 | 187.953 | 202.925 | 219.058 | 236.435 | 255.151 | 275.299 |
| 15 | 182.001 | 197.996 | 215.373 | 234.245 | 254.737 | 276.978 | 301.109 | 327.281 | 355.659 | 386.418 |
| 16 | 239.421 | 262.354 | 287.446 | 314.888 | 344.895 | 377.690 | 413.520 | 452.647 | 495.366 | 541.985 |
| 17 | 314.642 | 347.307 | 383.303 | 422.949 | 466.608 | 514.658 | 567.521 | 625.652 | 689.558 | 759.778 |
| 18 | 413.180 | 459.445 | 510.792 | 567.751 | 630.920 | 700.935 | 778.504 | 864.399 | 959.485 | 1064.689 |
| 19 | 542.266 | 607.467 | 680.354 | 761.786 | 852.741 | 954.271 | 1067.551 | 1193.870 | 1334.683 | 1491.563 |
| 20 | 711.368 | 802.856 | 905.870 | 1021.792 | 1152.200 | 1298.809 | 1463.544 | 1648.539 | 1856.208 | 2089.188 |
| 21 | 932.891 | 1060.769 | 1205.807 | 1370.201 | 1556.470 | 1767.380 | 2006.055 | 2275-982 | 2581.128 | 2925.862 |
| 22 | 1223.087 | 1401.215 | 1604.724 | 1837.068 | 2102.234 | 2404.636 | 2749.294 | 3141.852 | 3588.765 | 4097.203 |
| 23 | 1603.243 | 1850.603 | 2135.282 | 2462.669 | 2839.014 | 3271.304 | 3767.532 | 4336.750 | 4989.379 | 5737.078 |
| 24 | 2101.247 | 2443.795 | 2840.924 | 3300.974 | 3833.667 | 4449.969 | 5162.516 | 5985.711 | 6936.230 | 8032.906 |
| 25 | 2753.631 | 3226.808 | 3779.428 | 4424.301 | 5176.445 | 6052.957 | 7073.645 | 8261.273 | 9642.352 | 11247.062 |
| 30 | 10632.543 | 12940.672 | 15737.945 | 19124.434 | 23221.258 | 28172.016 | 34148.906 | 41357.227 | 50043.625 | 60500.207 |

# PRESENT VALUE OF AN ANNUITY OF $1 FOR n PERIODS

| n | 1% | 2% | 3% | 4% | 5% | 6% | 7% | 8% | 9% | 10% |
|---|---|---|---|---|---|---|---|---|---|---|
| 1 | .990 | .980 | .971 | .962 | .952 | .943 | .935 | .926 | .917 | .909 |
| 2 | 1.970 | 1.942 | 1.913 | 1.886 | 1.859 | 1.833 | 1.808 | 1.783 | 1.759 | 1.736 |
| 3 | 2.941 | 2.884 | 2.829 | 2.775 | 2.723 | 2.673 | 2.624 | 2.577 | 2.531 | 2.487 |
| 4 | 3.902 | 3.808 | 3.717 | 3.630 | 3.546 | 3.465 | 3.387 | 3.312 | 3.240 | 3.170 |
| 5 | 4.853 | 4.713 | 4.580 | 4.452 | 4.329 | 4.212 | 4.100 | 3.993 | 3.890 | 3.791 |
| 6 | 5.795 | 5.601 | 5.417 | 5.242 | 5.076 | 4.917 | 4.767 | 4.623 | 4.486 | 4.355 |
| 7 | 6.728 | 6.472 | 6.230 | 6.002 | 5.786 | 5.582 | 5.389 | 5.206 | 5.033 | 4.868 |
| 8 | 7.652 | 7.326 | 7.020 | 6.733 | 6.463 | 6.210 | 5.971 | 5.747 | 5.535 | 5.335 |
| 9 | 8.566 | 8.162 | 7.786 | 7.435 | 7.108 | 6.802 | 6.515 | 6.247 | 5.995 | 5.759 |
| 10 | 9.471 | 8.983 | 8.530 | 8.111 | 7.722 | 7.360 | 7.024 | 6.710 | 6.418 | 6.145 |
| 11 | 10.368 | 9.787 | 9.253 | 8.760 | 8.306 | 7.887 | 7.499 | 7.139 | 6.805 | 6.495 |
| 12 | 11.255 | 10.575 | 9.954 | 9.385 | 8.863 | 8.384 | 7.943 | 7.536 | 7.161 | 6.814 |
| 13 | 12.134 | 11.348 | 10.635 | 9.986 | 9.394 | 8.853 | 8.358 | 7.904 | 7.487 | 7.103 |
| 14 | 13.004 | 12.106 | 11.296 | 10.563 | 9.899 | 9.295 | 8.746 | 8.244 | 7.786 | 7.367 |
| 15 | 13.865 | 12.849 | 11.938 | 11.118 | 10.380 | 9.712 | 9.108 | 8.560 | 8.061 | 7.606 |
| 16 | 14.718 | 13.578 | 12.561 | 11.652 | 10.838 | 10.106 | 9.447 | 8.851 | 8.313 | 7.824 |
| 17 | 15.562 | 14.292 | 13.166 | 12.166 | 11.274 | 10.477 | 9.763 | 9.122 | 8.544 | 8.022 |
| 18 | 16.398 | 14.992 | 13.754 | 12.659 | 11.690 | 10.828 | 10.059 | 9.372 | 8.756 | 8.201 |
| 19 | 17.226 | 15.679 | 14.324 | 13.134 | 12.085 | 11.158 | 10.336 | 9.604 | 8.950 | 8.365 |
| 20 | 18.046 | 16.352 | 14.878 | 13.590 | 12.462 | 11.470 | 10.594 | 9.818 | 9.129 | 8.514 |
| 21 | 18.857 | 17.011 | 15.415 | 14.029 | 12.821 | 11.764 | 10.836 | 10.017 | 9.292 | 8.649 |
| 22 | 19.661 | 17.658 | 15.937 | 14.451 | 13.163 | 12.042 | 11.061 | 10.201 | 9.442 | 8.772 |
| 23 | 20.456 | 18.292 | 16.444 | 14.857 | 13.489 | 12.303 | 11.272 | 10.371 | 9.580 | 8.883 |
| 24 | 21.244 | 18.914 | 16.936 | 15.247 | 13.799 | 12.550 | 11.469 | 10.529 | 9.707 | 8.985 |
| 25 | 22.023 | 19.524 | 17.413 | 15.622 | 14.094 | 12.783 | 11.654 | 10.675 | 9.823 | 9.077 |
| 30 | 25.808 | 22.397 | 19.601 | 17.292 | 15.373 | 13.765 | 12.409 | 11.258 | 10.274 | 9.427 |
| 40 | 32.835 | 27.356 | 23.115 | 19.793 | 17.159 | 15.046 | 13.332 | 11.925 | 10.757 | 9.779 |
| 50 | 39.197 | 31.424 | 25.730 | 21.482 | 18.256 | 15.762 | 13.801 | 12.234 | 10.962 | 9.915 |

| n | 11% | 12% | 13% | 14% | 15% | 16% | 17% | 18% | 19% | 20% |
|---|---|---|---|---|---|---|---|---|---|---|
| 1 | .901 | .893 | .885 | .877 | .870 | .862 | .855 | .847 | .840 | .833 |
| 2 | 1.713 | 1.690 | 1.668 | 1.647 | 1.626 | 1.605 | 1.585 | 1.566 | 1.547 | 1.528 |
| 3 | 2.444 | 2.402 | 2.361 | 2.322 | 2.283 | 2.246 | 2.210 | 2.174 | 2.140 | 2.106 |
| 4 | 3.102 | 3.037 | 2.974 | 2.914 | 2.855 | 2.798 | 2.743 | 2.690 | 2.639 | 2.589 |
| 5 | 3.696 | 3.605 | 3.517 | 3.433 | 3.352 | 3.274 | 3.199 | 3.127 | 3.058 | 2.991 |
| 6 | 4.231 | 4.111 | 3.998 | 3.889 | 3.784 | 3.685 | 3.589 | 3.498 | 3.410 | 3.326 |
| 7 | 4.712 | 4.564 | 4.423 | 4.288 | 4.160 | 4.039 | 3.922 | 3.812 | 3.706 | 3.605 |
| 8 | 5.146 | 4.968 | 4.799 | 4.639 | 4.487 | 4.344 | 4.207 | 4.078 | 3.954 | 3.837 |
| 9 | 5.537 | 5.328 | 5.132 | 4.946 | 4.772 | 4.607 | 4.451 | 4.303 | 4.163 | 4.031 |
| 10 | 5.889 | 5.650 | 5.426 | 5.216 | 5.019 | 4.833 | 4.659 | 4.494 | 4.339 | 4.192 |
| 11 | 6.207 | 5.938 | 5.687 | 5.453 | 5.234 | 5.029 | 4.836 | 4.656 | 4.487 | 4.327 |
| 12 | 6.492 | 6.194 | 5.918 | 5.660 | 5.421 | 5.197 | 4.988 | 4.793 | 4.611 | 4.439 |
| 13 | 6.750 | 6.424 | 6.122 | 5.842 | 5.583 | 5.342 | 5.118 | 4.910 | 4.715 | 4.533 |
| 14 | 6.982 | 6.628 | 6.303 | 6.002 | 5.724 | 5.468 | 5.229 | 5.008 | 4.802 | 4.611 |
| 15 | 7.191 | 6.811 | 6.462 | 6.142 | 5.847 | 5.575 | 5.324 | 5.092 | 4.876 | 4.675 |
| 16 | 7.379 | 6.974 | 6.604 | 6.265 | 5.954 | 5.669 | 5.405 | 5.162 | 4.938 | 4.730 |
| 17 | 7.549 | 7.120 | 6.729 | 6.373 | 6.047 | 5.749 | 5.475 | 5.222 | 4.990 | 4.775 |
| 18 | 7.702 | 7.250 | 6.840 | 6.467 | 6.128 | 5.818 | 5.534 | 5.273 | 5.033 | 4.812 |
| 19 | 7.839 | 7.366 | 6.938 | 6.550 | 6.198 | 5.877 | 5.585 | 5.316 | 5.070 | 4.843 |
| 20 | 7.963 | 7,469 | 7.025 | 6.623 | 6.259 | 5.929 | 5.628 | 5.353 | 5.101 | 4.870 |
| 21 | 8.075 | 7.562 | 7.102 | 6.687 | 6.312 | 5.973 | 5.665 | 5.384 | 5.127 | 4.891 |
| 22 | 8.176 | 7.645 | 7.170 | 6.743 | 6.359 | 6.011 | 5.696 | 5.410 | 5.149 | 4.909 |
| 23 | 8.266 | 7.718 | 7.230 | 6.792 | 6.399 | 6.044 | 5.723 | 5.432 | 5.167 | 4.925 |
| 24 | 8.348 | 7.784 | 7.283 | 6.835 | 6.434 | 6.073 | 5.747 | 5.451 | 5.182 | 4.937 |
| 25 | 8.442 | 7.843 | 7.330 | 6.873 | 6.464 | 6.097 | 5.766 | 5.467 | 5.195 | 4.948 |
| 30 | 8.694 | 8.055 | 7.496 | 7.003 | 6.566 | 6.177 | 5.829 | 5.517 | 5.235 | 4.979 |
| 40 | 8.951 | 8.244 | 7.634 | 7.105 | 6.642 | 6.233 | 5.871 | 5.548 | 5.258 | 4.997 |
| 50 | 9.042 | 8.305 | 7.675 | 7.133 | 6.661 | 6.246 | 5.880 | 5.554 | 5.262 | 4.999 |

# PRESENT VALUE OF AN ANNUITY OF $1 FOR n PERIODS (CONTINUED)

| n | 21% | 22% | 23% | 24% | 25% | 26% | 27% | 28% | 29% | 30% |
|---|---|---|---|---|---|---|---|---|---|---|
| 1 | .826 | .820 | .813 | .806 | .800 | .794 | .787 | .781 | .775 | .769 |
| 2 | 1.509 | 1.492 | 1.474 | 1.457 | 1.440 | 1.424 | 1.407 | 1.392 | 1.376 | 1.361 |
| 3 | 2.074 | 2.042 | 2.011 | 1.981 | 1.952 | 1.923 | 1.896 | 1.868 | 1.842 | 1.816 |
| 4 | 2.540 | 2.494 | 2.448 | 2.404 | 2.362 | 2.320 | 2.280 | 2.241 | 2.203 | 2.166 |
| 5 | 2.926 | 2.864 | 2.803 | 2.745 | 2.689 | 2.635 | 2.583 | 2.532 | 2.483 | 2.436 |
| 6 | 3.245 | 3.167 | 3.092 | 3.020 | 2.951 | 2.885 | 2.821 | 2.759 | 2.700 | 2.643 |
| 7 | 3.508 | 3.416 | 3.327 | 3.242 | 3.161 | 3.083 | 3.009 | 2.937 | 2.868 | 2.802 |
| 8 | 3.726 | 3.619 | 3.518 | 3.421 | 3.329 | 3.241 | 3.156 | 3.076 | 2.999 | 2.925 |
| 9 | 3.905 | 3.786 | 3.673 | 3.566 | 3.463 | 3.366 | 3.273 | 3.184 | 3.100 | 3.019 |
| 10 | 4.054 | 3.923 | 3.799 | 3.682 | 3.570 | 3.465 | 3.364 | 3.269 | 3.178 | 3.092 |
| 11 | 4.177 | 4.035 | 3.902 | 3.776 | 3.656 | 3.544 | 3.437 | 3.335 | 3.239 | 3.147 |
| 12 | 4.278 | 4.127 | 3.985 | 3.851 | 3.725 | 3.606 | 3.493 | 3.387 | 3.286 | 3.190 |
| 13 | 4.362 | 4.203 | 4.053 | 3.912 | 3.780 | 3.656 | 3.538 | 3.427 | 3.322 | 3.223 |
| 14 | 4.432 | 4.265 | 4.108 | 3.962 | 3.824 | 3.695 | 3.573 | 3.459 | 3.351 | 3.249 |
| 15 | 4.489 | 4.315 | 4.153 | 4.001 | 3.859 | 3.726 | 3.601 | 3.483 | 3.373 | 3.268 |
| 16 | 4.536 | 4.357 | 4.189 | 4.033 | 3.887 | 3.751 | 3.623 | 3.503 | 3.390 | 3.283 |
| 17 | 4.576 | 4.391 | 4.219 | 4.059 | 3.910 | 3.771 | 3.640 | 3.518 | 3.403 | 3.295 |
| 18 | 4.608 | 4.419 | 4.243 | 4.080 | 3.928 | 3.786 | 3.654 | 3.529 | 3.413 | 3.304 |
| 19 | 4.635 | 4.442 | 4.263 | 4.097 | 3.942 | 3.799 | 3.664 | 3.539 | 3.421 | 3.311 |
| 20 | 4.657 | 4.460 | 4.279 | 4.110 | 3.954 | 3.808 | 3.673 | 3.546 | 3.427 | 3.316 |
| 21 | 4.675 | 4.476 | 4.292 | 4.121 | 3.963 | 3.816 | 3.679 | 3.551 | 3.432 | 3.320 |
| 22 | 4.690 | 4.488 | 4.302 | 4.130 | 3.970 | 3.822 | 3.684 | 3.556 | 3.436 | 3.323 |
| 23 | 4.703 | 4.499 | 4.311 | 4.137 | 3.976 | 3.827 | 3.689 | 3.559 | 3.438 | 3.325 |
| 24 | 4.713 | 4.507 | 4.318 | 4.143 | 3.981 | 3.831 | 3.692 | 3.562 | 3.441 | 3.327 |
| 25 | 4.721 | 4.514 | 4.323 | 4.147 | 3.985 | 3.834 | 3.694 | 3.564 | 3.442 | 3.329 |
| 30 | 4.746 | 4.534 | 4.339 | 4.160 | 3.995 | 3.842 | 3.701 | 3.569 | 3.447 | 3.332 |
| 40 | 4.760 | 4.544 | 4.347 | 4.166 | 3.999 | 3.846 | 3.703 | 3.571 | 3.448 | 3.333 |
| 50 | 4.762 | 4.545 | 4.348 | 4.167 | 4.000 | 3.846 | 3.704 | 3.571 | 3.448 | 3.333 |

| n | 31% | 32% | 33% | 34% | 35% | 36% | 37% | 38% | 39% | 40% |
|---|---|---|---|---|---|---|---|---|---|---|
| 1 | .763 | .758 | .752 | .746 | .741 | .735 | .730 | .725 | .719 | .714 |
| 2 | 1.346 | 1.331 | 1.317 | 1.303 | 1.289 | 1.276 | 1.263 | 1.250 | 1.237 | 1.224 |
| 3 | 1.791 | 1.766 | 1.742 | 1.719 | 1.696 | 1.673 | 1.652 | 1.630 | 1.609 | 1.589 |
| 4 | 2.130 | 2.096 | 2.062 | 2.029 | 1.997 | 1.966 | 1.935 | 1.906 | 1.877 | 1.849 |
| 5 | 2.390 | 2.345 | 2.302 | 2.260 | 2.220 | 2.181 | 2.143 | 2.106 | 2.070 | 2.035 |
| 6 | 2.588 | 2.534 | 2.483 | 2.433 | 2.385 | 2.339 | 2.294 | 2.251 | 2.209 | 2.168 |
| 7 | 2.739 | 2.677 | 2.619 | 2.562 | 2.508 | 2.455 | 2.404 | 2.355 | 2.308 | 2.263 |
| 8 | 2.854 | 2.786 | 2.721 | 2.658 | 2.598 | 2.540 | 2.485 | 2.432 | 2.380 | 2.331 |
| 9 | 2.942 | 2.868 | 2.798 | 2.730 | 2.665 | 2.603 | 2.544 | 2.487 | 2.432 | 2.379 |
| 10 | 3.009 | 2.930 | 2.855 | 2.784 | 2.715 | 2.649 | 2.587 | 2.527 | 2.469 | 2.414 |
| 11 | 3.060 | 2.978 | 2.899 | 2.824 | 2.752 | 2.683 | 2.618 | 2.555 | 2.496 | 2.438 |
| 12 | 3.100 | 3.013 | 2.931 | 2.853 | 2.779 | 2.708 | 2.641 | 2.576 | 2.515 | 2.456 |
| 13 | 3.129 | 3.040 | 2.956 | 2.876 | 2.799 | 2.727 | 2.658 | 2.592 | 2.529 | 2.469 |
| 14 | 3.152 | 3.061 | 2.974 | 2.892 | 2.814 | 2.740 | 2.670 | 2.603 | 2.539 | 2.477 |
| 15 | 3.170 | 3.076 | 2.988 | 2.905 | 2.825 | 2.750 | 2.679 | 2.611 | 2.546 | 2.484 |
| 16 | 3.183 | 3.088 | 2.999 | 2.914 | 2.834 | 2.757 | 2.685 | 2.616 | 2.551 | 2.489 |
| 17 | 3.193 | 3.097 | 3.007 | 2.921 | 2.840 | 2.763 | 2.690 | 2.621 | 2.555 | 2.492 |
| 18 | 3.201 | 3.104 | 3.012 | 2.926 | 2.844 | 2.767 | 2.693 | 2.624 | 2.557 | 2.494 |
| 19 | 3.207 | 3.109 | 3.017 | 2.930 | 2.848 | 2.770 | 2.696 | 2.626 | 2.559 | 2.496 |
| 20 | 3.211 | 3.113 | 3.020 | 2.933 | 2.850 | 2.772 | 2.698 | 2.627 | 2.561 | 2.497 |
| 21 | 3.215 | 3.116 | 3.023 | 2.935 | 2.852 | 2.773 | 2.699 | 2.629 | 2.562 | 2.498 |
| 22 | 3.217 | 3.118 | 3.025 | 2.936 | 2.853 | 2.775 | 2.700 | 2.629 | 2.562 | 2.498 |
| 23 | 3.219 | 3.120 | 3.026 | 2.938 | 2.854 | 2.775 | 2.701 | 2.630 | 2.563 | 2.499 |
| 24 | 3.221 | 3.121 | 3.027 | 2.939 | 2.855 | 2.776 | 2.701 | 2.630 | 2.563 | 2.499 |
| 25 | 3.222 | 3.122 | 3.028 | 2.939 | 2.856 | 2.776 | 2.702 | 2.631 | 2.563 | 2.499 |
| 30 | 3.225 | 2.124 | 3.030 | 2.941 | 2.857 | 2.777 | 2.702 | 2.631 | 2.564 | 2.500 |
| 40 | 3.226 | 3.125 | 3.030 | 2.941 | 2.857 | 2.778 | 2.703 | 2.632 | 2.564 | 2.500 |
| 50 | 3.226 | 3.125 | 3.030 | 2.941 | 2.857 | 2.778 | 2.703 | 2.632 | 2.564 | 2.500 |

# SOLUTIONS FOR SELECTED END-OF-CHAPTER PROBLEMS

*refers to Web site chapter

**CHAPTER 1**

no solutions provided

**CHAPTER 2**

2-1A. Total assets $120,650
Net income $3,360
2-3A. Taxes $469,000
2-5A. Free cash flow ($10,000)
2-7A. Free cash flow (14,000)

**CHAPTER 3**

3-1A. Cash $201,875
Accounts receivable $175,000
Long-term debt $320,000
3-3A. Current ratio 1.75
Operating profit margin 21%
Operating income return on investment 21%
Debt ratio 50%
Return on equity 20%
3-5A. a. Average collection period 30 days
b. Accounts receivable $369,863
c. Inventory $700,000
3-7A. a. Total asset turnover 2.25
Operating profit margin 11.1%
Operating income return on investment 25%
b. 19.5%
c. 14.5%
3-9A. Current ratio 2.51
OIROI 23.2%
Debt ratio 0.26
Return on equity 22.4%

**CHAPTER 4**

4-1A. Discretionary Financing Needed = ($0.5 million)
4-3A. Total Assets = $1.8 million
4-5A. Total Assets = $2 million
4-9A. a. Notes Payable = $1.11 million
b. Current Ratio = 2x and 1.12x
4-11A.

| | January | February | March |
|---|---|---|---|
| Net Monthly Change | $65,500 | (1,000) | (127,500) |
| Cumulative Borrowing | $−0− | −0− | 61,000 |

4-13A. a. Debt to Assets = 61.1%, 61.9%, 59.4%, 50.4%, 44.4%

**CHAPTER 5**

5-1A. a. $12,970
c. $3,019.40
5-2A. a. $n$ = 15 years
5-3A. b. 5%
c. 9%
5-4A. b. $PV$ = $235.20
5-5A. a. $6,289
c. $302.89
5-6A. c. $1,562.96
5-7A. a. $FV_1$ = $10,600
$FV_5$ = $13,380
$FV_{15}$ = $23,970
5-9A. a. $6,690
b. Semiannual: $6,720
Bimonthly: $6,740
5-11A. Year 1: 18,000 books
Year 2: 21,600 books
Year 3: 25,920 books
5-13A. $6,108.11
5-15A. 8%
5-17A. $658,197.85
5-21A. b. $8,333.33
5-26A. $6,509
5-28A. 22%
5-29A. $6,934.81
5-32A. a. $1,989.73
5-35A. $15,912

**CHAPTER 6**

6-3A. $\bar{k}$ = 9.1%: $\sigma$ = 3.06%
6-5A. Security A: $\bar{k}$ = 16.7%; $\sigma$ = 10.12%
Security B: $\bar{k}$ = 9.2%; $\sigma$ = 3.57%
6-7A. About 0.5.
6-11A.

| Time | Asman Return |
|---|---|
| 2 | 20.0% |

6-13A. a. 15.8%
b. 0.95
6-14A. S&P 500: $\bar{k}$ = 0.71%
$\sigma$ = 4.52%
Intel: $\bar{k}$ = 6.07%
$\sigma$ = 9.69%

**CHAPTER 7**

7-1A. $752.52
7-5A. 5.28%
7-7A. a. $863.78
b. Market Value $707.63 when required rate of return is 15%; Market Value $1,171.19 when required rate of return is 8%
7-9A. a. $1,182.57
b. (i) $925.31; (ii) $1,573.50

**CHAPTER 8**

8-1A. $50
8-3A. $116.67
8-5A. a. 8.5%
b. $42.50
8-7A. a. 18.9%
b. $28.57
8-9A. 7.2%
8-11A. $39.96
8-13A. a. 10.91%
b. $36

**CHAPTER 9**

9-1A. a. IRR = 7%
b. IRR = 17%
9-3A. a. IRR = approximately 19%
9-5A. a. Payback Period = $80,000/$20,000 = 4 years
Discounted Payback Period = 5.0 + 4,200/11,280 = 5.37 years.
c. PI = 1.0888
9-7A. Project C:
Payback Period = 3.5 years
Discounted Payback Period = 4.0 + 397/1,242 = 4.32 years
9-9A. Project C: IRR = 16%

**CHAPTER 10**

10-1A. a. $6,800
b. $3,400

c. No taxes
d. $1,020 refund

10-3A. $404,500
10-5A. a. $110,000
b. $33,600
10-7A. a. $230,000
10-11A. b. $NPV_B$ = $12,100
10-13A. a. $EAA_A$ = $9,729

**CHAPTER 11**

11-1A. b. $NPV_A$ = $8,025
$NPV_B$ = $10,112
11-3A. $NPV_A$ = $726,380
11-5A. $NPV_A$ = $24,780

**CHAPTER 12**

12-1A. a. After-tax cost of debt = 6.53%
b. $k_{nc}$ = 14.37%
c. $k_c$ = 15.14%
d. $k_{ps}$ = 8.77%
12-3A. $k_{pc}$ = 12.06%
12-5A. $k_{ps}$ = 7.69%
12-7A. $k_{ps}$ = 14.29%
12-9A. a. $k_{cb}$ = 17.59%
b. $k_{ac}$ = 18.25%
12-11A. a. $V_b$ = $1,063.80
b. $NP_o$ = $952.10
c. 525 bonds
12-13A. $K_d$ = 6.4%

**CHAPTER 13**

13-1A. Stock price = $53.03
13-3A. a. EVA (year 1) = $2,181.82
b. ROI (year 1) = 34.22%
c. Firm value = $30,730.95
Present value of EVAs = $20,912.76

**CHAPTER 14**

no solutions provided

**CHAPTER 15**

15-2A. Breakeven point = 40,000 bottles.
15-4A. a. Jake's EBIT = $154,067.40
Sarasota = 480,000
Jefferson = 28,970
b. Jake's = 8.232
Sarasota = 1.789
Jefferson = 8.310
c. Jake's = 1.78 times
Sarasota = 2.77 times
Jefferson = 4.09 times
d. Jefferson Wholesale would suffer the largest decline in profitability.
15-6A. a. 6,296 pairs of shoes
b. $534,591.19
c. At 7,000, EBIT = $19,000
At 9,000, EBIT = $73,000
At 15,000, EBIT = $235,000
d. 9.95 times; 3.33 times; 1.72 times
15-7A. a. 9,000 units
b. $1,620,000
15-9A. a. $85,416.67
b. 7,030 units; $189,815
15-11A. a. 1.94 times
15-13A. a. 10,000 units
b. $1,800,000
15-15A. a. F = $173,333.33
b. 14,444 units; S* = $288,888.88
15-21. a. 5,000 units
b. $125,000
c. −$10,000; $10,000; $30,000
15-23A. 5 times
15-25A. 1,400,000 units
15-27A. a. 3 times
b. 1.25 times
c. 3.75 times
d. $8 million

**CHAPTER 16**

16-2A. Cash collection from sales = $1,280,000
16-4A. a. EBIT = $2,000,000
b. EPS will be $1.00 for each plan.
d. Plan B
16-6A. a. EBIT = $240,000
b. EPS will be $1.80 for each plan.
16-7. a. EBIT = $220,000
b. Plan B.
16-9A. a. $640,000
b. EPS = $3.20
16-11A. a. $300,000
b. EPS = $3.00
16-13A. a. Plan A = $7.68
b. 10.378
16-17A. a. $20,000,000
b. $k_c$ = 25%; $k_o$ = 25%
16-19A. a. Plan A vs. Plan B = $9,000
Plan A vs. Plan C = $18,000

**CHAPTER 17**

17-2A. 95,238 shares
17-4A. Dividend = $16,000
17-6A. Value of stock both plans = $31.76
17-8A. b. Net gain = $24,500
17-10A. b. 9,615 shares
17-12A. Dividend = $90,000

**CHAPTER 18**

18-1A.

| | Firm A | Firm B |
|---|---|---|
| Working Capital | $500,000 | 550,000 |
| Current Ratio | 1.25x | .917x |

18-3A. APR = 13.79%
18-5A. a. 36.73%
b. 74.23%
c. 37.11%
d. 16.33%
18-7A. a. APR = 16.3%
b. APR = 19.7%
18-9A. a. APR = 16.27%
18-11A. a. APR = 22.85%
18-13A. a. APR = 10%
b. APR = 11.75%
c. APR = 12.5%

**CHAPTER 19**

19-1A. Yes, the projected net annual gain from using the new system is $33,356.

19-4A. a. Yes, the firm will generate $35,288 in net annual savings.
b. 5.01%

19-5A. a. $2,625,000
b. $241,500

19-6A. .5322 days

19-9A. $10,667

**CHAPTER 20**

20-1A. 18.37%

20-3A. a. 36.36%
b. 36.73%

20-5A. a. $90,000
b. $53,333

20-7A. $56,875

20-8A. a. 775 units

20-10A. a. 816 units
b. $61,237

20-12A. b. 35.2 orders per year

**CHAPTER 21**

no solutions provided

**CHAPTER 22**

22-1A. a. $8,437
b. $9,368
c. $25,695

22-3A. Canada: 1,1853; 1,1881; 1,912
Japan: 213,4927; 211,9992; 209,1613
Switzerland: 1,9459, 1,9346: 1,8815

22-5A. Net gain = $149.02

**CHAPTER 23***

Web site 23-1A. Average theoretical value = $12,433

Web site 23-3A. Net present value = $14.87

**CHAPTER 24***

Web site 24-1A. Balloon = $268,160.75

Web site 24-3A. Payment = $31,977.78

Web site 24-5A. a. 15%
b. Payment = $76,359.19
c. 9%

Web site 24-7A. a. NPV(P) = −$2,271
b. NAL = −$874

# GLOSSARY

**Accounts receivable turnover ratio** Accounts receivable turnover ratio indicates how rapidly the firm is collecting its credit, as measured by the number of times its accounts receivable are collected or "rolled over" during the year.

**Acid-test ratio** Acid-test ratio indicates a firm's liquidity, as measured by its liquid assets, excluding inventories, relative to its current liabilities.

**Adjustable rate preferred stock** Preferred stock intended to provide investors with some protection against wide swings in the stock value that occur when interest rates move up and down. The dividend rate changes along with prevailing interest rates.

**Agency costs** The costs, such as a reduced stock price, associated with potential conflict between managers and investors when these two groups are not the same.

**Agency problem** Problem resulting from conflicts of interest between the manager (the stockholder's agent) and the stockholders.

**Amortized loan** A loan paid off in equal installments.

**Analytical income statement** A financial statement used by internal analysts that differs in composition from audited or published financial statements.

**Annual percentage yield (APY) or effective annual rate** The annual compound rate that produces the same return as the nominal or quoted rate.

**Annuity** A series of equal dollar payments for a specified number of years.

**Annuity due** An annuity in which the payments occur at the beginning of each period.

**Anticipatory buying** Buying in anticipation of a price increase to secure goods at a lower cost.

**Appraisal costs** Costs of testing, measuring, and analyzing to safeguard against possible defects going unnoticed.

**Arbitrage-pricing model (APM)** An alternative theory to the capital asset pricing model for relating stock returns and risk. The theory maintains that security returns vary from their expected amounts when there are unanticipated changes in basic economic forces.

**Arbitrageur** A person involved in the process of buying and selling in more than one market to make riskless profits.

**Asked rate** The rate a bank or foreign exchange trader "asks" the customer to pay in home currency for foreign currency when the bank is selling and the customer is buying.

**Asset allocation** Identifying and selecting the asset classes appropriate for a specific investment portfolio and determining the proportions of these assets within the given portfolio.

**Auction rate preferred stock** Variable rate preferred stock in which the dividend rate is set by an auction process.

**Average collection period** Average collection period indicates how rapidly a firm is collecting its credit, as measured by the average number of days it takes to collect its accounts receivable.

**Balance sheet** A statement of financial position at a particular date. The form of the statement follows the balance sheet equation: total assets = total liabilities + owner's equity.

**Beta** A measure of the relationship between an investment's returns and the market returns. This is a measure of the investment's nondiversifiable risk.

**Bid-asked spread** The difference between the asked quote and the bid quote.

**Bid rate** The rate at which the bank buys the foreign currency from the customer by paying in home currency.

**Bird-in-the-hand dividend theory** The belief that dividend income has a higher value to the investor than does capital gains income, because dividends are more certain than capital gains.

**Bond** A type of debt or a long-term promissory note, issued by the borrower, promising to pay its holder a predetermined and fixed amount of interest each year.

**Bondholder's expected rate of return** The discount rate that equates the present value of the future cash flows (interest and maturity value) with the current market price of the bond. It is the rate of return an investor will earn if a bond is held to maturity.

**Book value** The value of an asset as shown on a firm's balance sheet. It represents the historical cost of the asset rather than its current market value or replacement cost.

**Business cycles** A series of commercial adjustments to unanticipated new information accentuated by both public policy decisions and private-sector decisions.

**Business risk** The potential variability in a firm's earnings before interest and taxes resulting from the nature of the firm's business endeavors.

**Buying rate** The bid rate in a currency transaction.

**Call option** A call option gives its owner the right to purchase a given number of shares of stock or some other asset at a specified price over a given time period.

**Call provision** Lets the company buy its preferred stock back from the investor, usually at a premium price above the stock's par value.

**Capital asset pricing model (CAPM)** An equation stating that the expected rate of return on a project is a function of (1) the risk-free rate, (2) the investment's systematic risk, and (3) the expected risk premium for the market portfolio of all risky securities.

**Capital budgeting** The decision-making process with respect to investment in fixed assets.

**Capital gain or loss** As defined by the revenue code, a gain or loss resulting from the sale or exchange of a capital asset.

**Capital market** All institutions and procedures that facilitate transactions in long-term financial instruments.

**Capital rationing** The placing of a limit by the firm on the dollar size of the capital budget.

**Capital structure** The mix of long-term sources of funds used by the firm. Basically, this concept omits short-term liabilities.

**Cash** Currency and coin plus demand deposit accounts.

**Cash breakeven analysis** A variation from traditional breakeven analysis that removes (deducts) noncash expenses from the cost items.

**Cash budget** A detailed plan of future cash receipts and disbursements.

**Cash flows from financing activities** Cash flow that includes proceeds from long-term debt or issuing common stock, and payments made for stock dividends.

**Cash flows from investment activities** Cash flows that include the purchase of fixed assets and other assets.

**Cash flows from operations** Cash flow that consists of (1) collections from customers; (2) payments to suppliers for the purchase of materials; (3) other operating cash flows such as marketing and administrative expenses and interest payments; and (4) cash tax payments.

**Certainty equivalent approach** A method for incorporating risk into the capital-budgeting decision in which the decision maker substitutes a set of equivalent riskless cash flows for the expected cash flows and then discounts these cash flows back to the present.

**Certainty equivalents** The amount of cash a person would require with certainty to make him or her indifferent between this certain sum and a particular risky or uncertain sum.

**Characteristic line** The line of "best fit" through a series of returns for a firm's stock relative to the market returns. The slope of the line, frequently called beta, represents the average movement of the firm's stock returns in response to a movement in the market's returns.

**Clientele effect** The belief that individuals and institutions that need current income will invest in companies that have high dividend payouts. Other investors prefer to avoid taxes by holding securities that offer only small dividend income, but large capital gains. Thus we have a "clientele" of investors.

**Commercial paper** Short-term loans by the most creditworthy borrowers that are bought and sold in the market for short-term debt securities.

**Common stock** Common stock shares represent the ownership in a corporation.

**Compound annuity** Depositing an equal sum of money at the end of each year for a certain number of years and allowing it to grow.

**Compound interest** Interest that occurs when interest paid on the investment during the first period is added to the principal; then, during the second period, interest is earned on this new sum.

**Concentration banking** The selection of a few major banks where the firm maintains significant disbursing accounts.

**Constant dividend payout ratio** A dividend payment policy in which the percentage of earnings paid out in dividends is held constant. The dollar amount fluctuates from year to year as profits vary.

**Contribution margin** Unit sales price minus unit variable cost.

**Conversion period** The time period during which the convertible can be exchanged for common stock.

**Conversion premium** The difference between the convertible's market price and the higher of its security value and its conversion value.

**Conversion ratio** The number of shares of common stock for which a convertible security can be exchanged.

**Conversion value** The total market value of the common stock for which it can be exchanged.

**Convertible preferred stock** Convertible preferred stock allows the preferred stockholder to convert the preferred stock into a predetermined number of shares of common stock, if he or she so chooses.

**Convertible security** Preferred stock or debentures that can be exchanged for a specified number of shares of common stock at the will of the owner.

**Corporation** An entity that *legally* functions separate and apart from its owners.

**Coupon interest rate** A bond's coupon interest rate indicates what percentage of the par value of the bond will be paid out annually in the form of interest.

**Covered-interest arbitrage** Arbitrage designed to eliminate differentials across currency and interest rate markets.

**Credit scoring** The numerical credit evaluation of each candidate.

**Cross rate** The computation of an exchange rate for a currency from the exchange rates of two other currencies.

**Cumulative preferred stock** Requires all past unpaid preferred stock dividends be paid before any common stock dividends are declared.

**Cumulative voting** Each share of stock allows the shareholder a number of votes equal to the number of directors being elected. The shareholder can then cast all of his or her votes for a single candidate or split them among the various candidates.

**Currency swap** An exchange of debt obligations in different currencies.

**Current assets** Current assets consist primarily of cash, marketable securities, accounts receivable, inventories, and prepaid expenses.

**Current ratio** Current ratio indicates a firm's liquidity, as measured by its liquid assets (current assets) relative to its liquid debt (short-term or current liabilities).

**Current yield** The ratio of the annual interest payment to the bond's market price.

**Date of record** Date at which the stock transfer books are to be closed for determining which investor is to receive the next dividend payment.

**Debenture** Any unsecured long-term debt.

**Debt** Consists of such sources as credit extended by suppliers or a loan from a bank.

**Debt capacity** The maximum proportion of debt that the firm can include in its capital structure and still maintain its lowest composite cost of capital.

**Debt ratio** Debt ratio indicates how much debt is used to finance a firm's assets.

**Declaration date** The date upon which a dividend is formally declared by the board of directors.

**Delivery-time stock** The inventory needed between the order date and the receipt of the inventory ordered.

**Depository transfer checks** A non-negotiable instrument that provides the firm with a means to move funds from local bank accounts to concentration bank accounts.

**Depreciation** The means by which an asset's value is expensed over its useful life for federal income tax purposes.

**Direct method** A statement of cash flow that begins with sales and converts the income statement from an accrual basis to a cash basis.

**Direct quote** The exchange rate that indicates the number of units of the home currency required to buy one unit of foreign currency.

**Direct sale** The sale of securities by the corporation to the investing public without the services of an investment banking firm.

**Direct securities** The pure financial claims issued by economic units to savers. These can later be transformed into indirect securities.

**Discount bond** A bond that is selling below its par value.

**Discounted payback period** A variation of the payback period decision criterion defined as the number of years required to recover the initial cash outlay from the discounted net cash flows.

**Discretionary financing** Sources of financing that require an explicit decision on the part of the firm's management every time funds are raised.

**Dividend payout ratio** The amount of dividends relative to the company's net income or earnings per share.

**duPont analysis** The duPont analysis is an approach to evaluate a firm's profitability and return on equity.

**Duration** A measure of how responsive a bond's price is to changing interest rates. Also, it is a weighted average time to maturity in which the weight attached to each year is the present value of the cash flow for that year.

**Earnings before taxes** Operating income minus interest expense.

**EBIT–EPS indifference point** The level of earnings before interest and taxes (EBIT) that will equate earnings per share (EPS) between two different financing plans.

**Economic profit** The difference in a firm's after-tax net operating income and an estimate of the cost of invested capital (invested capital times the firm's weighted average cost of capital).

**Efficient market** A market in which the values of securities at any instant in time fully reflect all available information, which results in the market value and the intrinsic value being the same.

**Equity** Stockholder's investment in the firm and the cumulative profits retained in the business up to the date of the balance sheet.

**Equivalent annual annuity (EAA)** An annual cash flow that yields the same present value as the project's NPV. It is calculated by dividing the project's NPV by the appropriate $PVIFA_{i,n}$.

**Eurobonds** Bonds issued in a country different from the one in whose currency the bond is denominated—for instance, a bond issued in Europe or in Asia by an American company that pays interest and principal to the lender in U.S. dollars.

**Eurodollar loans** Intermediate term loans made by major international banks to businesses based on foreign deposits that are denominated in dollars.

**Exchange rate** The price of a foreign currency stated in terms of the domestic or home currency.

**Exchange rate risk** The risk that tomorrow's exchange rate will differ from today's.

**Ex-dividend date** The date upon which stock brokerage companies have uniformly decided to terminate the right of ownership to the dividend, which is 4 days prior to the record date.

**Exercise ratio** The number of shares of common stock that can be obtained at the exercise price with one warrant.

**Expectations theory** The effect of new information about a company on the firm's stock price depends more on how the new information compares to expectations than on the actual announcement itself.

**Expected rate of return** The weighted average of all possible returns where the returns are weighted by the probability that each will occur.

**Explicit cost of capital** The cost of capital for any funds source considered in isolation from other funds sources.

**External failure costs** Costs resulting from a poor quality product reaching the customer's hands.

**Factoring** The sale of a firm's accounts receivable to a financial intermediary known as a factor.

**Financial assets** Claims for future payment by one economic unit on another.

**Financial lease** A noncancelable contractual commitment on the part of the firm leasing the asset (the lessee) to make a series of payments to the firm that actually owns the asset (the lessor) for the use of the asset over the period of the agreement.

**Financial leverage** Financing a portion of the firm's assets with securities bearing a fixed or limited rate of return.

**Financial markets** Those institutions and procedures that facilitate transactions in all types of financial claims (securities).

**Financial policy** The firm's policies regarding the sources financing and the particular mix in which they will be used.

**Financial ratios** Restating the accounting data in relative terms to identify some of the financial strengths and weaknesses of a company.

**Financial risk** The additional variability in earnings available to the firm's common stockholder, and the additional chance of insolvency borne by the common stockholder caused by the use of financial leverage.

**Financial structure** The mix of all funds sources that appear on the right side of the balance sheet.

**Financial structure design** The management activity of seeking the proper mix of all financing components in order to minimize the cost of raising a given amount of funds.

**Financing costs** Costs incurred by a company that often include interest expenses and preferred dividends.

**Finished-goods inventory** Goods on which the production has been completed but that are not yet sold.

**Firm-specific risk or company-unique risk (diversifiable risk or unsystematic risk)** The portion of the variation in investment returns that can be eliminated through investor diversification. This diversifiable risk is the result of factors that are unique to the particular firm.

**Fixed costs (indirect costs)** Costs that do not vary in total dollar amount as sales volume or quantity of output changes.

**Fixed or long-term assets** Assets comprising equipment, buildings, and land.

**Float** The length of time from when a check is written until the actual recipient can draw upon or use the "good funds."

**Floating rate international currency system** An international currency system in which exchange rates between different national currencies are allowed to fluctuate with supply and demand conditions. This contrasts with a fixed rate system in which exchange rates are pegged for extended periods of time and adjusted infrequently.

**Flotation costs** The underwriter's spread and issuing costs associated with the issuance and marketing of new securities.

**Forward exchange contract** A contract that requires delivery on a specified future date of one currency in return for a specified amount of another currency.

**Forward-spot differential** The premium or discount between forward and spot currency exchange rates.

**Future-value interest factor ($FVIF_{i,n}$)** The value $(1 + i)^n$ used as a multiplier to calculate an amount's future value.

**Future-value interest factor of an annuity ($FVIFA_{i,n}$)** The value $\left[\sum_{t=0}^{n-1}(1 + i)^t\right]$ used as a multiplier to calculate the future value of an annuity.

**Futures contract** A contract to buy or sell a stated commodity or financial claim at a specified price at some future, specified time.

**Futures margin** Good faith money the purchaser puts down to ensure that the contract will be carried out.

**Hedging principle or principle of self-liquidating debt** Financing maturity should follow the cash-flow-producing characteristics of the asset being financed.

**Holding-period return** The return an investor would receive from holding a security for a designated period of time. For example, a monthly holding-period return would be the return for holding a security for a month.

**Implicit cost of debt** The change in the cost of common equity caused by the choice to use additional debt.

**Income statement** The statement of profit or loss for the period is comprised of net revenues less expenses for the period.

**Increasing-stream hypothesis of dividend policy** A smoothing of the dividend stream in order to minimize the effect of company reversals. Corporate managers make every effort to avoid a dividend cut, attempting instead to develop a gradually increasing dividend series over the long-term future.

**Indenture** The legal agreement or contract between the firm issuing the bonds and the bond trustee who represents the bondholders.

**Indirect method** A statement of cash flow that begins with net income and then adds back the non-cash expenses, and other items that affect a company's cash flows.

**Indirect quote** The exchange rate that expresses the required number of units of foreign currency to buy one unit of home currency.

**Indirect securities** The unique financial claims issued by financial intermediaries. Mutual fund shares are an example.

**Information asymmetry** The difference in accessibility to information between management and investors may result in a lower stock price than would occur under conditions of certainty.

**Initial outlay** The immediate cash outflow necessary to purchase the asset and put it in operating order.

**Insolvency** The firm is unable to pay its bills on time.

**Interest-rate parity (IRP)** States that (except for the effect of small transaction costs) the forward premium or discount should be equal and opposite in size to the differences in the national interest rates for securities of the same maturity.

**Interest-rate risk** The variability in a bond's value (risk) caused by changing interest rates.

**Interest tax shield** The savings in taxes resulting from the tax deductibility of the interest expense.

**Internal failure costs** Those costs associated with discovering poor quality products prior to delivery.

**Internal rate of return (IRR)** A capital-budgeting decision criterion that reflects the rate of return a project earns. Mathematically, it is the discount rate that equates the present value of the inflows with the present value of the outflows.

**Intrinsic or economic value** The present value of the asset's expected future cash flows. This value is the amount the investor considers to be a fair value, given the amount, timing, and riskiness of future cash flows.

**Inventory loans** Short-term loans that are secured by the pledge of inventories. The type of pledge or security agreement varies and can include floating liens, chattel mortgage agreements, field warehouse financing agreements, and terminal warehouse agreements.

**Inventory management** The control of the assets used in the production process or produced to be sold in the normal course of the firm's operations.

**Inventory turnover ratio** Inventory turnover indicates the relative liquidity of inventories, as measured by the number of times a firm's inventories are replaced during the year.

**Investment banker** A financial specialist who underwrites and distributes new securities and advises corporate clients about raising external financial capital.

**Investor's required rate of return** The minimum rate of return necessary to attract an investor to purchase or hold a security. It is also the discount rate that equates the present value of the cash flows with the value of the security.

**Joint probability** The probability of two different sequential outcomes occurring.

**Junk or high-yield bonds** Bonds rated BB or below.

**Just-in-time inventory control system** Keeping inventory to a minimum and relying on suppliers to furnish parts "just in time."

**Law of one price** The proposition that in competitive markets the same goods should sell for the same price where prices are stated in terms of a single currency.

**Lease** A contract between a lessee, who acquires the services of a leased asset by making a series of rental payments and the lessor, who is the owner of the asset.

**Lessee and lessor** The user of the leased asset, who agrees to make periodic lease or rental payments to the lessor, who owns the asset.

**Line of credit and revolving credit agreement** A line of credit agreement is an agreement between a firm and its banker to provide short-term financing to meet its temporary financing needs.

**Liquid assets** The sum of cash and marketable securities.

**Liquidation value** The amount that could be realized if an asset were sold individually and not as a part of a going concern.

**Liquidity** The ability of a firm to pay its bills on time, and how quickly a firm converts its liquid assets (accounts receivables and inventories) into cash.

**Majority voting** Each share of stock allows the shareholder one vote, and each position on the board of directors is voted on separately. As a result, a majority of shares has the power to elect the entire board of directors.

**Marginal or incremental analysis** A method of analysis for credit policy changes in which the incremental benefits are compared to the added costs.

**Marginal tax rate** The tax rate that would be applied to the next dollar of income.

**Marketable securities** Security investments (financial assets) the firm can quickly convert to cash balances. Also known as near cash or near-cash assets.

**Market-related risk (nondiversifiable risk or systematic risk)** The portion of variations in investment returns that cannot be eliminated through investor diversification. This variation results from factors that affect all stocks.

**Market value** The observed value for the asset in the marketplace.

**Market Value Added** Market value of a firm's assets minus the sum total of its invested capital.

**Maturity** The length of time until the bond issuer returns the par value to the bondholder and terminates the bond.

**Modified internal rate of return (MIRR)** A variation of the IRR capital-budgeting decision criterion defined as the discount rate that equates the present value of the project's annual cash outlays with the present value of the project's terminal value, where the terminal value is defined as the sum of the future value of the project's cash inflows compounded to the project's termination at the project's required rate of return.

**Money market** All institutions and procedures that facilitate transactions in short-term credit instruments.

**Mortgage bond** A bond secured by a lien on real property.

**Multinational corporation (MNC)** A corporation with holdings and/or operations in one or more countries.

**Mutually exclusive projects** A set of projects that perform essentially the same task, so that acceptance of one will necessarily mean rejection of the others.

**Net and net-net leases** In a net lease agreement, the lessee assumes the risk and burden of ownership over the term of the lease. This means that the lessee must pay insurance and taxes on the asset as well as maintain the operating condition of the asset. In a net-net lease, the lessee must, in addition to the requirements of a net lease, return the asset to the lessor at the end of the lease still worth a preestablished value.

**Net income available to common stockholders (net income)** A figure representing the firm's profit or loss for the period. It also represents the earnings available to the firm's common and preferred stockholders.

**Net operating loss carryback and carryforward** A tax provision that permits the taxpayer first to apply a loss against the profits in the 2 prior years (carryback). If the loss has not been completely absorbed by the profits in these 2 years, it may be applied to taxable profits in each of the 20 following years (carryforward).

**Net present value (NPV)** A capital-budgeting decision criterion defined as the present value of the future net cash flows after tax less the project's initial outlay.

**Net profit margin** Net profit margin measures the net income of a firm as a percent of sales.

**Net working capital** The difference between the firm's current assets and its current liabilities. Frequently when the term working capital is used, it is actually intended to mean net working capital.

**NI approach to valuation** The concept from financial theory that suggests the firm's capital structure has a direct impact upon and can increase its market valuation.

**NOI approach to valuation** The concept from financial theory that suggests the firm's capital structure has no impact on its market valuation.

**Nominal or quoted interest rate** The stated rate of interest on the contract.

**Nominal rate of interest** The observed rate of interest on a specific fixed-income security; no adjustment is made for expected inflation.

**Operating income (earnings before interest and taxes)** Profit from sales minus total operating expenses.

**Operating income return of investment** Operating income return on investment indicates the effectiveness of management at generating operating profits on the firm's assets, as measured by operating profits relative to the total assets.

**Operating lease** A lease agreement (see financial lease) in which the lessee can cancel the agreement at any time after giving proper notice to the lessor.

**Operating leverage** The incurrence of fixed operating costs in the firm's income stream.

**Operating profit margin** Operating profit margin indicates management's effectiveness in managing the firm's income statement, as measured by operating profits relative to sales.

**Opportunity cost of funds** The next best rate of return available to the investor for a given level of risk.

**Optimal capital structure** The unique capital structure that minimizes the firm's composite cost of long-term capital.

**Optimal range of financial leverage** The range of various financial structure combinations that generate the lowest composite cost of capital for the firm.

**Option contract** An option contract gives its owner the right to buy or sell a fixed number of shares of stock at a specified price over a limited time period.

**Option expiration date** The date on which the option expires.

**Option premium** The price of the option.

**Option's intrinsic value** The minimum value of the option.

**Option's time (or speculative) value** The amount by which the option premium exceeds the intrinsic value of the option.

**Option striking price** The price at which the stock or asset may be purchased from the writer in the case of a call, or sold to the writer in the case of a put.

**Order point problem** Determining how low inventory should be depleted before it is reordered.

**Order quantity problem** Determining the optimal order size for an inventory item given its usage, carrying costs, and ordering costs.

**Ordinary annuity** An annuity in which the payments occur at the end of each period.

**Organized security exchanges** Formal organizations involved in the trading of securities. They are tangible entities that conduct auction markets in listing securities.

**Other assets** Assets not included in current assets or fixed assets.

**Over-the-counter markets** All security markets except the organized exchanges.

**Participating preferred stock** Allows the preferred stockholder to participate in earnings beyond the payment of the stated dividend.

**Partnership** An association of two or more individuals joining together as co-owners to operate a business for profit.

**Par value of a bond** The bond's face value that is returned to the bondholder at maturity, usually $1,000.

**Payable-through drafts** A payment mechanism that substitutes for regular checks in that drafts are not drawn on a bank, but instead are drawn on and authorized by the firm against its demand deposit account. The purpose is to maintain control over field-authorized payments.

**Payback period** A capital-budgeting criterion defined as the number of years required to recover the initial cash investment.

**Payment date** The date on which the company mails a dividend check to each investor.

**Percent of sales method** Estimating the level of an expense, asset, or liability for a future period as a percent of the sales forecast.

**Perfect capital markets** Capital markets where (1) investors can buy and sell stock without incurring any transaction costs, such as brokerage commissions; (2) companies can issue stocks without any cost of doing so; (3) there are no corporate or personal taxes; (4) complete information about the firm is readily available; (5) there are no conflicts of interest between management and stockholders; and (6) financial distress and bankruptcy costs are nonexistent.

**Permanent asset investment** An investment in an asset that the firm expects to hold for the foreseeable future, whether fixed assets or current assets. For example, the minimum level of inventory the firm plans to hold for the foreseeable future is a permanent investment.

**Permanent sources of financing** Sources of financing that do not mature or come due within the year, including intermediate term debt, long-term debt, preferred stock, and common stock.

**PIK preferred stock** Investors receive no dividends initially; they merely get more preferred stock, which in turn pays dividends in even more preferred stock.

**Plowback ratio** The percent of a firm's earnings that are reinvested in the firm.

**Portfolio beta** The relationship between a portfolio's returns and the market returns. It is a measure of the portfolio's nondiversifiable risk.

**Preemptive rights** The right of a common shareholder to maintain a proportionate share of ownership in the firm. When new shares are issued, common shareholders have the first right of refusal.

**Preferred stock** A hybrid security with characteristics of both common stock and bonds. It is similar to common stock because it has no fixed maturity date, the nonpayment of dividends does not bring on bankruptcy, and dividends are not deductible for tax purposes. Preferred stock is similar to bonds in that dividends are limited in amount.

**Premium bond** A bond that is selling above its par value.

**Present value** The current value of a future sum.

**Present-value interest factor ($PVIF_{i,n}$)** The value $[1/(1 + i)^n]$ used as a multiplier to calculate an amount's present value.

**Present-value interest factor for an annuity ($PVIFA_{i,n}$)** The value $\left[\sum_{t=1}^{n} \frac{1}{(1+i)^t}\right]$ used as a multiplier to calculate the present value of an annuity.

**Preventive costs** Costs resulting from design and production efforts on the part of the firm to reduce or eliminate defects.

**Primary market** Transactions in securities offered for the first time to potential investors.

**Private placement** A security offering limited to a small number of potential investors.

**Priviliged subscription** The process of marketing a new security issue to a select group of investors.

**Probability tree** A schematic representation of a problem in which all possible outcomes are graphically displayed.

**Profitability index (PI) (or Benefit/Cost Ratio)** A capital-budgeting decision criterion defined as the ratio of the present value of the future net cash flows to the initial outlay.

**Project's contribution-to-firm risk** The amount of risk that a project contributes to the firm as a whole. That is, it is a project's risk considering the effects of diversification among different projects within the firm, but ignoring the effects of shareholder diversification within the portfolio.

**Project standing alone risk** The risk of a project standing alone is measured by the variability of the asset's expected returns. That is, it is the risk of a project ignoring the fact that it is only one of many projects within the firm, and the firm's stock is but one of many stocks within a stockholder's portfolio.

**Protective provisions** Provisions for preferred stock that are included in the terms of the issue to protect the investor's interest.

**Proxy** A proxy gives a designated party the temporary power of attorney to vote for the signee at the corporation's annual meeting.

**Proxy fight** When rival groups compete for proxy votes in order to control the decisions made in a stockholder meeting.

**Public offering** A security offering where all investors have the opportunity to acquire a portion of the financial claims being sold.

**Purchasing-power parity (PPP) theory** In the long run, exchange rates adjust so that the purchasing power of each currency tends to remain the same. Thus exchange rate changes tend to reflect international differences in inflation rates. Countries with high rates of inflation tend to experience declines in the value of their currency.

**Pure play method** A method of estimating a project's beta that attempts to identify a publicly traded firm that is engaged solely in the same business as the project, and uses that beta as a proxy for the project's beta.

**Put option** A put option gives its owner the right to sell a given number of shares of common stock or some other asset at a specified price over a given time period.

**Raw materials inventory** This includes the basic materials purchased from other firms to be used in the firm's production operations.

**Real assets** Tangible assets such as houses, equipment, and inventories.

**Real rate of interest** The nominal rate of interest less the expected rate of inflation over the maturity of the fixed-income security. This represents the expected increase in actual purchasing power to the investor.

**Residual dividend theory** A theory asserting that the dividends to be paid should equal capital left over after the financing of profitable investments.

**Retained earnings** The cumulative earnings that have been retained and reinvested in the firm over its life.

**Return on assets** Return on assets determines the amount of net income produced on a firm's assets by relating net income to total assets.

**Return on common equity** Return on common equity indicates the accounting rate of return on the stockholders' investment, as measured by net income relative to common equity.

**Revolving credit or revolver** A special type of line of credit agreement in which the line of credit is eventually converted into a term loan that requires periodic payments.

**Rights** Certificates issued to shareholders giving them an option to purchase a stated number of new shares of stock at a specified price during a 2- to 10-week period.

**Risk** The prospect of an unfavorable outcome. This concept has been measured operationally as the standard deviation or beta, which will be explained later.

**Risk-adjusted discount rate** A method for incorporating the project's level of risk into the capital-budgeting process, in which the discount rate is adjusted upward to compensate for higher than normal risk or downward to adjust for lower than normal risk.

**Risk-free or riskless rate of return** The rate of return on risk-free investments. The interest rate on short-term U.S. government securities are commonly used to measure this rate.

**Risk premium** The additional rate of return we expect to earn above the risk-free rate for assuming risk.

**Safety stock** Inventory held to accommodate any unusually large and unexpected usage during delivery time.

**Sale and leaseback arrangement** An arrangement arising when a firm sells land, buildings, or equipment that it already owns and simultaneously enters into an agreement to lease the property back for a specified period, under specific terms.

**Scenario analysis** Simulation analysis that focuses on an examination of the range of possible outcomes.

**Secondary market** Transactions in currently outstanding securities.

**Secured and unsecured loans** Secured loans are backed by the pledge of specific assets as collateral whereas unsecured loans are only backed by the promise of the borrower to honor the loan commitment.

**Security market line** The return line that reflects the attitudes of investors regarding the minimal acceptable return for a given level of systematic risk.

**Security value** The price the convertible security would sell for in the absence of its conversion feature.

**Selling rate** Same as the asked rate.

**Selloff** The sale of a subsidiary, division, or product line by one firm to another.

**Semivariable costs (semifixed costs)** Costs that exhibit the joint characteristics of both fixed and variable costs over different ranges of output.

**Sensitivity analysis** The process of determining how the distribution of possible returns for a particular project is affected by a change in one particular input variable.

**Shelf registration** A procedure for issuing new securities where the firm obtains a master registration statement approved by the SEC.

**Simple arbitrage** Trading to eliminate exchange rate differentials across the markets for a single currency, e.g., for the New York and London markets.

**Simulation** The process of imitating the performance of an investment project under evaluation using a computer. This is done by randomly selecting observations from each of the distributions that affect the outcome of the project, combining those observations to determine the final output of the project, and continuing with this process until a representative record of the project's probable outcome is assembled.

**Single-sourcing** Using a single supplier as a source for a particular part or material.

**Sinking fund** A fund that requires the firm periodically to set aside an amount of money for the retirement of its preferred stock. This money is then used to purchase the preferred stock in the open market or through the use of the call provision, whichever method is cheaper.

**Small regular plus year-end extra dividend payout** A dividend payment policy where the firm pays a small regular dividend plus an extra dividend only if the firm has experienced a good year.

**Sole proprietorship** A business owned by a single individual.

**Spinoff** The separation of a subsidiary from its parent, with no change in the equity ownership. The management of the parent company gives up operating control over the assets involved in the spinoff but the stockholders retain ownership, albeit through shares of the newly created spinoff company.

**Spontaneous financing** Sources of financing that arise naturally during the course of business. Accounts payable is a primary example.

**Spot transaction** A transaction made immediately in the market place at the market price.

**Stable dollar dividend payout** A dividend policy that maintains a relatively stable dollar dividend per share over time.

**Standard deviation** A measure of the spread or dispersion about the mean of a probability distribution. We calculate it by squaring the difference between each outcome and its expected value, weighting each squared difference by its associated probability, summing over all possible outcomes, and taking the square root of this sum.

**Statement of cash flows** The statement of cash flow enumerates the cash receipts and cash disbursements for a specified interval of time (usually 1 year).

**Stock dividend** A distribution of shares of up to 25 percent of the number of shares currently outstanding, issued on a pro rata basis to the current stockholders.

**Stock repurchase (stock buyback)** The repurchase of common stock by the issuing firm for any of a variety of reasons resulting in a reduction of shares outstanding.

**Stock split** A stock dividend exceeding 25 percent of the number of shares currently outstanding.

**Subchapter S Corporation** A corporation that, because of specific qualifications, is taxed as though it were a partnership.

**Subordinated debenture** A debenture that is subordinated to other debentures in being paid in the case of insolvency.

**Sustainable rate of growth** The maximum rate of growth in sales that the firm can sustain while maintaining its present capital structure (debt and equity mix) and without having to sell new common stock.

**Syndicate** A group of investment bankers who contractually assist in the buying of a new security issue.

**Systematic risk** The risk of a project measured from the point of view of a well-diversified shareholder. That is, it is a project's risk taking into account the fact that this project is only one of many projects within the firm, and the firm's stock is but one of many stocks within a stockholder's portfolio.

**Target capital structure proportions** The mix of financing sources that the firm plans to maintain through time.

**Tax expenses** Tax liability determined by earnings before taxes.

**Tax shield** The element from the federal tax code that permits interest costs to be deductible when computing the firm's tax bill. The dollar difference (the shield) flows to the firm's security holders.

**Temporary asset investment** Investments in assets that the firm plans to sell (liquidate) within a period no longer than 1 year. Although temporary investments can be made in fixed assets, this is not the usual case. Temporary investments generally are made in inventories and receivables.

**Temporary sources of financing** Another term for current liabilities.

**Tender offer** The formal offer by the company to buy a specified number of shares at a predetermined and stated price.

**Term loans** Loans that have maturities of 1 to 10 years and are repaid in periodic installments over the life of the loan; usually secured by a chattel mortgage on equipment or a mortgage on real property.

**Terms of sale** The credit terms identifying the possible discount for early payment.

**Times interest earned** Times interest earned indicates a firm's ability to cover its interest expense, as measured by its earnings before interest and taxes relative to the interest expense.

**Total asset turnover** Total asset turnover indicates management's effectiveness at managing a firm balance sheet—its assets—as indicated by the amount of sales generated per 1 dollar of assets.

**Total quality management (TQM)** A company-wide systems approach to quality.

**Total revenue** Total sales dollars.

**Trade credit** Accounts payable that arise out of the normal course of business when the firm purchases from its suppliers who allow the firm to make payment after the delivery of the merchandise or services.

**Transaction exposure** The net contracted foreign currency transactions for which the settlement amounts are subject to changing exchange rates.

**Transfer price** The price a subsidiary or a parent company charges other companies that are part of the same MNC for its goods or services.

**Triangular arbitrage** Arbitrage across the markets for all currencies.

**Underwriting** The purchase and subsequent resale of a new security issue. The risk of selling the new issue at a profitable price is assumed (underwritten) by an investment banker.

**Variable costs (direct costs)** Costs that are fixed per unit of output but vary in total as output changes.

**Volume of output** The firm's level of operations expressed either in sales dollars or as units of output.

**Warrant** An option to purchase a fixed number of shares of common stock at a predetermined price during a specified time period.

**Warrant exercise price** The price at which a warrant allows its holder to purchase the firm's common stock.

**Weighted average cost of capital** The average of the after-tax costs of each of the sources of capital used by a firm to finance a project. The weights reflect the proportion of the total financing raised from each source.

**Wire transfers** A method of moving funds electronically between bank accounts in order to eliminate transit float. The wired funds are immediately usable at the receiving bank.

**Working capital** The firm's total investment in current assets or assets which it expects to be converted into cash within a year or less.

**Work-in-process inventory** Partially finished goods requiring additional work before they become finished goods.

**Yield to maturity** The same as the expected rate of return (see above).

**Zero and very low coupon bonds** Bonds issued at a substantial discount from their $1,000 face value that pay no or little interest.

**Zero balance accounts** A cash-management tool that permits centralized control over cash outflows but also maintains divisional disbursing authority.

# ORGANIZATION INDEX

Double numbered entries refer to Web site chapters.


## A

A&P, 21, 249
Abbot Labs, 587, 588
Alcoa, 103
American Airlines, 182
American Express, 21
American Hospital Supply, 209
American Standard, 606
AMF, 10, 32
Apple Computer, 194, 297, 687
Archer Daniels Midland, 468
Armco, 297
Arthur Anderson, 34
AT&T, 543, 23-2

## B

Bailey Controls, 685
Banc of America Securities, 459
BankAmerica, 244
Batterymarch Financial Management, 23-7
Bear Stearns, 459
Beech-Nut Nutrition, 296
Best Buy, 613
Black & Decker, 606
Blanks Engraving, 219
BMW, 21, 732
Boeing, 367
Boise Cascade, 685
Borden, 244
Bridgestone/Firestone, 21, 296, 684
Briggs & Stratton, 188, 381, 382, 394, 395
Bristol-Myers Squibb Co., 19, 189
Brooks Brothers, 21
Burger King, 333, 368
Burlington Northern, 4

## C

Campbell Soup, 15
Canfor Japan Corporation, 297
Caterpillar Tractor, 686
CBS, 209
Chase Manhattan, 459
Chevron Corporation, 469
Chrysler, 685
Cisco Systems, 23-1, 23-13
Citibank, 10, 179
Citicorp Industrial Credit, 1, 634
Citigroup, Inc., 43
Citrix, 11
CNA Financial Corp., 413, 422, 423
Coca-Cola, 21, 179, 295, 333, 350, 366, 413, 423, 468, 492–494, 568, 569, 595
Colgate-Palmolive, 21, 542
Columbia Pictures, 21
CommNet, 215
Compaq, 21, 314
CompUSA, 613
Computer City, 613
Converse, 211
Costco Companies, Incorporated, 722
Credit Suisse First Boston, 459
CUC International, 34

## D

Dana Corporation, 425n
Dell Computer Corporation, 179, 188, 314, 613, 614, 683, 711
Deloitte & Touche, 34
Disney. *See* Walt Disney Company
Dow Chemical, 21, 297
Drexel Burnham Lambert, 296
Dun & Bradstreet, 64, 670
DuPont, 179

## E

Eli Lilly, 23-2
Exxon Corporation, 23-2
Exxon-Mobil, 179, 188

## F

Federal Trade Commission (FTC), 463
Fibreboard Corporation, 544
Firestone Tire & Rubber, 21
Fitch Investor Services, 218
Ford Motor Company, 219, 273, 274, 306, 307, 333, 386, 464, 590, 591, 684, 688, 23-15
Fossil, 188
FTC, 463

## G

General Dynamics Corp., 593
General Electric, 21, 179, 333, 413, 423, 23-14, 23-15
General Foods, 311
General Mills, 543
General Motors (GM), 2, 21, 296, 312, 333, 367, 413, 423, 449, 683, 684, 685, 23-15
General Motors Acceptance Corporation, 620
Georgia-Pacific Corporation, 297, 513, 540
Gerber Products, 296
Gillette, 21
GM. *See* General Motors (GM)
Goldman Sachs, 43, 450, 459
Grapes Communications NV, 736
Great Atlantic and Pacific Tea Co. (A&P), 21, 249

## H

H.J. Heinz, 273, 296, 297
Harley-Davidson, Inc., 1, 2, 10, 27, 29, 32, 34–36, 41–43, 62–79, 127, 182–188, 241, 248, 251, 257, 271, 290, 309, 310, 312, 313, 349, 368, 381, 382, 410, 411, 429, 442, 468, 513, 542, 568, 569, 586, 634, 642, 665, 666, 698, 699, 732, 733, 750, 23-5
Harley-Davidson Italia S.r.I., 698, 732
Heinz, 273, 296, 297
Hewlett Packard, 21, 297
Hoffman-La Roche, 14
Honda, 14, 331–333, 686, 732

## I

IBM, 21, 194, 211, 297, 314, 333, 488, 587, 687
IBP Inc., 22
Intel Corporation, 168, 179, 413, 414, 423, 452
ITT Electro-Optical Products Division, 688

## J

J.C. Penney, 219
J.P. Morgan, 43, 459
John Deere, 426
Johns-Manville, 25
Johnson & Johnson, 352, 426
Johnson Wax, 754

## K

Kellogg's, 311, 719
KKR, 214

## L

Lehman Brothers, 459
Levi's, 14
Loews Corporation, 413, 423

## M

Manitowoc, 424
Mattel Inc., 593
McDonald's, 14, 188, 274, 333, 368, 542, 718, 756, 757
Meade Johnson, 189, 190
Medtronic, 543
Merck, 2, 362, 367
Merrill Lynch, 390, 459
Merrill Lynch Capital Markets, 450
Metallgesellschaft AG, 703, 718
Metropolitan Life Insurance, 25
Microsoft, 168, 179, 413, 423, 452, 23-1
MicroStrategies, 34
Mitsubishi, 297
Mobil Oil, 459
Moody's, 214, 217, 218
Morgan Stanley Dean Witter, 459
Motel 6, 426
Motorola, 297

## N

Nabisco, 413, 423
National Cash Register (NCR), 683
National Semiconductor, 182
NatWest, 710
Navistar, 459
NBC, 179
NCR, 683, 23-2
New York Futures Exchange, 705
New York Stock Exchange (NYSE), 44, 219
New York Yankees, 22
Nissan, 21, 333
Novell, 763
NYSE, 44, 219

## O

Oracle, 168
Oxford Health Plans, 34

## P

Pacific Bell, 211
Parker Pen Co., 249
PCS Health, 763
Penn Central, 609n
PepsiCo, 22, 182, 396, 397, 399
Pfizer, 169
Phar-Mor, 34
Philadelphia Electric, 243
Phillips Petroleum, 468
Pillsbury, 21
Post, 13
Prentice Hall, 64
Procter & Gamble Corporation, 717

## Q

Quaker Oats Co., 22, 245, 273, 699, 23-2

## R

R.J. Reynolds, 360
Radio Corporation of American (RCA), 23-14
Ralston-Purina, 699
Raybestos-Manhattan, 25
RCA, 21, 23-14
Reynolds Metals, 243
Rite-Aid, 34, 37
RJR Nabisco, 214
Robert Morris Associates, 64
Royal Dutch/Shell Group, 23-15

## S

S.C. Johnson & Son Inc., 754
Salomon Smith Barney, 459
Schering-Plough, 14
Smith-Corona, 297
Snapple Beverage, 23-2
Sprint Corporation, 217
Standard & Poor's, 64, 214, 218
Starbucks, 14, 188
Sumitomo Bank, 719
Sunbeam Corporation, 34, 43
Suzuki Motors, 296, 732

## T

Tenneco Corporation, 243
Texaco, 459
Texas Instruments, 543
Texas Power and Light, 242
3Com Corporation, 297, 333
3M, 21
Time Inc., 23-2
Toledo Edison, 242
Toyota, 14, 333, 683, 686
20th Century Fox, 21
21st Century Telecom Group, Inc., 213

## U

U.S. Navy, 24-1
Union Carbide, 722
Union Pacific, 413, 423
Universal Studios, 314
Upjohn, 379
USAirways, 719

## V

Value Line, 390
Virginia State Lottery, 148
Virginia Tech, 22

## W

W.R. Grace & Co., 586, 587
Wal-Mart, 14, 413, 423, 735
Walt Disney Company, 21, 411, 442, 464, 465, 538, 596, 756
Warner Communications, 23-2
Wells Fargo & Co., 43
Western Union, 209
Wordperfect, 23-2

## X

Xerox, 297, 452

Yamaha, 732

# SUBJECT INDEX

Double numbered entries refer to Web site chapters.


## A

Acceptances, 649
Accounting beta technique, 360, 361
Accounting book value, 32
Accounting data, 44
Accounting irregularities, 34
Accounting model of equity valuation, 414, 415
Accounting standards, 44
Accounts payable, 33
Accounts receivable, 31
Accounts receivable loans, 621–623
Accounts receivable management, 667–675
  aging account, 672
  credit scoring, 670
  marginal (incremental analysis), 673, 674
  size of investment in accounts receivable, 668–672
Accounts receivable turnover ratio, 67
Accrual-basis accounting, 39
Accrued expenses, 33
Acid-test ratio, 65
Adjustable rate preferred stock, 244
Agency costs, 526–529, 580
Agency problem, 15, 526
Aging account (schedule), 672
Algebraic analysis (break-even analysis), 477, 478
Altman, Edward, 670
American option, 707
American Stock Exchange (AMEX), 454, 456
Amortization schedule, 149
Amortized loans, 149, 150
Analytical income statement, 478
Anderson, Paul P., 24-15n
Annual percentage rate (APR), 615
Annual percentage yield (APY), 154, 615
Annuity, 140–148
  annuity due, 147, 148
  compound, 141–143
  defined, 140
  infinite, 153
  present value of, 143–147
  types, 141
Annuity due, 141, 147, 148
Anticipatory buying, 682
APM, 208, 209
Appraisal costs, 686
Appraisal value, 23-7
APR, 615
APY, 615
Arbitrage, 727, 739, 740
Arbitrage pricing model (APM), 208, 209
Arbitrageur, 740
*Are the Distinctions between Debt and Equity Disappearing?*, 529
Asbestos, 24–26
Asked rate, 740
Asset allocation, 182
Assets, 30–32
At-the-money, 708
Auction rate preferred stock, 244
Automated depository transfer check, 645
Average collection period, 66
Average tax rate, 39

## B

Balance of payments, 735n
Balance sheet, 30–36
Balance sheet leverage ratios, 538, 539
Bank credit, 617–619
Bank Wire, 642
Bankers' acceptances, 649
Banking Act of 1933, 457
Base pay, 425
Basic security valuation model, 222
Beamer, Frank, 22
Benefit/cost ratio, 280
Bernanke, Ben, 532
Best-efforts basis, 459
Beta, 186–188
Bid rate, 740
Bid-asked spread, 740
Big five federally sponsored agencies, 649
Bird-in-the-hand dividend theory, 574
Black, Fischer, 545
Blanket lien, 623
Bleustein, Jeff, 10, 62, 66
Blocked funds, 755
Blue sky laws, 462
Boesky, Ivan F., 18, 462, 463n
Bond quotations, 225
Bond ratings, 218, 219
Bond valuation, 223–226
Bondholder's expected rate of return, 227
Bonds, 211–240
  claims on assets and income, 216
  coupon interest rate, 216
  current yield, 217
  defined, 212
  duration, 232, 233
  expected rate of return (yield to maturity), 227
  indenture, 216, 217
  interest rate, and, 228–232
  maturity, 216, 230
  par value, 216
  premium/discount, 229, 230
  ratings, 218, 219
  types, 212–215
  valuation, 223–226
Bonus payment, 425–428
Book value, 218, 767
Book, overview, 19–21
Bounded incentive pay programs, 427
Break-even analysis, 472–482
  algebraic analysis, 477, 478
  assumed behavior of costs, 473–475
  BEP in sales dollars, 478, 479
  cash break-even point, 480
  contribution-margin analysis, 476, 477
  finding the break-even point, 476
  formulas (summary), 496
  graphic representation, 479, 480
  limitations, 481, 482
  objective/uses, 472, 473
  total revenue/volume of output, 475
  trial-and-error analysis, 476
  use of, by financial managers, 495
Bressler, Richard, 4
Bribery, 112
Brown, Paul, 37
Brown, Vandivar, 25
Budget, 110
Budget period, 112
Budgeting, 109–112
Buffett, Warren, 250
Burns, Scott, 601
Business cycle, 545, 546
Business risk, 397, 470, 471, 546, 755
Business valuation, 414–419
Bust-up takeover wave, 23-16
Buying rate, 740

## C

Call option, 706
Call provision, 245
Capital account, 735n
Capital asset pricing model (CAPM), 191–193, 353–360, 388–390
Capital budgeting, 271–380
  abandoning the project, 332
  accounting beta techniques, 360, 361
  actual real-world practices, 295
  capital rationing, 324, 325
  certainty equivalent approach, 354–360
  defined, 272
  delaying the project, 331
  depreciation, 316, 317
  differential after-tax cash flow, 316
  EAA, 329, 330
  ethics, 294, 378, 379
  expanding the project, 331, 332
  free cash flows, 314–324
  guidelines for evaluating proposals, 310–314
  initial outlay, 315
  IRR, 281–290, 299
  MIRR, 290–294, 299, 300
  multinational firm, 295–297, 332, 333, 367, 368
  mutually exclusive projects, 326
  NPV method, 277–279, 298, 299
  options, 330–332
  payback period, 274–276, 298
  probability trees, 364–366
  profitability index (benefit/cost ratio), 280, 281, 299
  project ranking, 326–330
  pure play method, 361
  risk, 350–354
  risk-adjusted discount rate, 357–360

Capital budgeting, *(continued)*
scenario analysis, 362
sensitivity analysis, 362, 364
simulation, 361–364
size disparity problem, 326, 327
summary of various methods, 298–300
terminal cash flow, 317
time dependence of cash flows, 366
time disparity problem, 327, 328
unequal lives, 328–330
use of, by financial managers, 297
Capital charge, 421
Capital-expenditure budget, 112
Capital market, 453
Capital rationing, 324, 325
Capital structure, 390, 514
Capital structure management, 515. *See also* Tools of capital structure management
"Capital Structure Puzzle" (Myers), 527n, 528, 530n
Capital structure ratios, 537–540
Capital structure theory, 516–530
agency costs, 526–529
analytical setting, 516–518
dependence hypothesis, 521–523
free cash flow theory, 529
independence hypothesis, 518–521
managerial amplifications, 530, 547–549
moderate position (corporate income taxed/firms fail), 523–525
moderate position (saucer-shaped cost of capital curve), 525, 526
pecking order theory, 528, 529
static trade-off theory, 527
Capital structure weights, 391
CAPM, 191–193, 353, 360, 388–390
Carter, Jimmy, 378, 379
Carty, Lea, 215
Cash, 31, 635
Cash break-even analysis, 481
Cash budget, 110, 111
Cash conversion cycle (CCC), 612–614
Cash flow, 12, 13, 39–43
Cash flow overall coverage ratio, 539
Cash generation and disposition process, 635–637
Cash management
break-even analysis, 644, 645
cash flow process, 635–637
cash inflow, 640–642
cash outflow, 642–644
financial manager's decisions, 639
motives for holding cash, 637, 638
objectives, 639
risk-return trade-off, 638
CBOE, 712, 713
CBT, 700
CCC, 612–614
CD, 650
CEO compensations, 428
Certainty equivalent, 354
Certainty equivalent approach, 354–360
CFO, 7, 8
Chambers, John, 23-13
Characteristic line, 185
Chattel mortgage, 24-2
Chattel mortgage agreement, 623
Chicago Board of Trade (CBT), 700
Chicago Board Options Exchange (CBOE), 712, 713
Chief Financial Officer (CFO), 7, 8
Chop-shop or break-up value, 23-7
Chop-shop valuation approach, 23-5–23-9
Clayton Act, 23-4
Clientele effect, 578, 579
Combinations. *See* Mergers and acquisitions
Combined leverage, 490–493
Commercial paper, 619, 620, 650
Commodity futures, 703
Common equity capital, 33
Common equity ratio, 539
Common stock, 247–256
claim on assets, 248, 249
claim on income, 247, 248
defined, 247
limited liability, 252
preemptive rights, 252
relationship between value and earnings, 267–270
valuation, 252–256
voting rights, 249, 250
Common stockholder's expected rate of return, 258, 259
Common stockholders, 33
Company-unique risk, 180
Comparative leverage ratios, 537–540
Compensation program, 424–429
Competitive bid purchase, 458
Competitive markets, 13
Compound annuity, 141–143
Compound interest, 128–130
Concentration banking, 642
Conditional outcomes, 364
Conditional probabilities, 364, 365
Constant dividend payout ratio, 585
Constant-growth dividend model, 269
Constant-growth valuation model, 268
Contribution margin, 476, 477
Contribution-margin analysis (break-even analysis), 476, 477
Contribution-to-firm risk, 352
Control hypothesis, 529
Controller, 8
Conversion period, 723
Conversion premium, 723
Conversion price, 722
Conversion ratio, 722
Conversion value, 722, 723
Convertible preferred stock, 243
Convertible security, 722–724
Corporate control hypothesis, 580n
*Corporate Debt Capacity* (Donaldson), 528
Corporate debt markets, 445
Corporate executive, 6
Corporate restructuring, 23-1–23-20
combinations, 23-1–23-13. *See also* Mergers and acquisitions
divestitures, 23-14
use of, by financial managers, 23-15
Corporate tax rates, 38
Corporation, 6–8
Cost advantage, 14
Cost of capital, 381–409
CAPM, 388–390
cost of common equity, 386–390
cost of debt, 384
cost of preferred stock, 385, 386
dividend growth model, 386–388
evaluation of new capital investments, 397
example (Briggs & Stratton), 394, 395
formulas (summary), 398
investor's rate of return, contrasted, 382, 383
multiple divisions, 396
use of, by financial managers, 401
weighted average cost of capital, 390–393
Cost of capital-capital structure argument, 516
Cost of common equity, 386–390
Cost of debt, 384
Cost of preferred stock, 385, 386
Cost of quality, 686
Cost of short-term credit, 614, 615
Cotteler, Dave, 290
Coupon interest rate, 216
Coverage ratios, 538, 539
Covered call, 707
Covered-interest arbitrage, 740
Credit scoring, 670
Credit terms, 616, 617, 668
Cross hedging, 703
Cross rate, 740, 741
Cumulative preferred stock, 243
Cumulative voting, 250
Currency swap, 717
Current assets, 30–32
Current debt, 33
Current liabilities, 609
Current ratio, 65
Current yield, 217

## D

Dalkon Shield, 378
Dart throwers/professional money managers, competition, 220
Date of record, 587
Davidson, Pat, 248
Days of payables outstanding (DPO), 613
Days of sales in inventory (DSI), 613
Days of sales outstanding (DSO), 613
Dealer placement, 619
Debenture, 212
Debt, 33
Debt capacity, 525, 545
Debt capital, 33
Debt-equity ratio, 72n
Debt-equity relationship, 36
Debt ratio, 72, 539
Declaration date, 587
Degree of combined leverage ($DCL_s$), 490–492
Degree of financial leverage ($DFL_{EBIT}$), 487–489
Degree of operating leverage ($DOL_s$), 483, 484
Delivery-time stock, 681
Dependence hypothesis, 521–523
Depo-Provera, 378, 379
Depository transfer checks, 642, 645
Depreciation, 37, 38, 316, 317
Derivative securities
currency swap, 717
futures, 699–706. *See also* Futures
options, 706–716. *See also* Options
Detachable warrants, 726
Devaluation, 734

DFI, 744, 755
$DFL_{EBIT}$, 487–489
DFN model, 104, 105
Direct costs, 474
Direct foreign investment (DFI), 744, 755
Direct lease, 24-7
Direct placement, 451
Direct quote, 737
Direct sale, 459
Direct securities, 448
Direct transfer of funds, 450
Disbursing float, 640
Discount bond, 229
Discounted cash-flow valuation model, 414, 415
Discounted payback period, 275
Discretionary financing, 102
Discretionary financing needed (DFN) model, 104, 105
Diversifiable risk, 180
Diversification, 16, 17, 179–182, 220
Divestitures, 23-14
Dividend growth model, 386–388
Dividend irrelevance, 571–574
Dividend payment procedures, 587, 588
Dividend payout ratio, 569
Dividend policy, 567–605
  agency costs, 579, 580
  alternative policies, 585, 586
  bird-in-the-hand theory, 574
  clientele effect, 578, 579
  dividend payment vs. profit retention, 569, 570
  effect of, on stock price, 570–583
  expectations theory, 580, 581
  factors to consider, 584, 585
  general conclusions, 583
  important dates, 587, 588
  information effect, 579
  legal restrictions, 584
  managerial opinion survey on dividends, 582
  payment procedure, 587, 588
  residual dividend theory, 576, 577
  stock dividend, 588–590
  stock repurchase, 590–594
  stock split, 588–590
Dividend rate bond, 244
Dividends, 37
Divisional costs of capital, 396
$DOL_s$, 483, 484
Donaldson, Gordon, 528, 540
Dorrance, John, Jr., 15
DPO, 613
DSI, 613
DSO, 613
Dumping, 378, 379
Dunlap, Al, 34, 81
Dunning letter, 672
DuPont analysis, 77–79
Duration, 232, 233

## E

EAA, 329, 330
Earnings before interest and taxes (EBIT), 29
Earnings before interest, taxes, depreciation, and amortization (EBITDA), 41
Earnings before taxes, 29
Earnings predictability, 584
EBIT, 29
EBIT-EPS analysis, 534–537
EBIT-EPS analysis chart, 535, 536
EBIT-EPS indifference point, 535, 536
EBITDA, 41
Eco-car, 331
Economic exposure, 751
Economic ordering quantity (EOQ) model, 678–683
Economic value, 219
Economic value added (EVA), 421–424
Economies of scale, 106, 107
Effective annual rate, 154
Efficient markets, 14, 15, 219, 220
EFT, 643, 644
Eichengreen, Barry, 736
80/120 bonus plan, 427, 428
Eisner, Michael, 81
Electronic funds transfer (EFT), 643, 644
EOQ model, 678–683
Equity, 33
Equity-based compensation, 428, 429
Equivalent annual annuity (EAA), 329, 330
Escherich, Rick, 43
Ethics
  bribery, 112
  capital budgeting, 294
  importance, 18, 19
  managerial decisions, 395
  overseas dumping, 378, 379
  relevance of, 19
  value of life (Ford Pinto), 306, 307
  *Wall Street Journal* workplace ethics quiz, 20
Euro, 542, 735, 736
Eurobonds, 213
Eurodollar loans, 24-4
European option, 707
EVA, 421–424
Ex-dividend date, 588
Exchange rate risk, 741–744, 747–751, 756
Exchange rates
  arbitrage, and, 739, 740
  asked/bid rates, 740
  cross rates, 740, 741
  defined, 737
  history, 734
  list of, 738, 739
Exercise ratio, 726
Expectations theory, 580, 581
Expected rate of return
  bondholders, 227
  common stockholders, 258, 259
  defined, 175
  preferred stockholders, 258
  stockholders, 258–260
Explicit cost of capital, 520
External capital market, 443, 444
External failure costs, 686

## F

Factor, 622
Factoring, 622, 623
Failure costs, 686
Fair value, 219
Fed Wire, 642
Federal agency securities, 649
Federal funds rate, 439, 441
Federal Reserve System (Fed), 439–442
Federal Reserve Wire System, 642
Field warehouse financing agreement, 623
Financial assets, 446
Financial calculator, 133, 134, 283
Financial forecasting, 99–126
  budgeting, 109–112
  DFN model, 104, 105
  percent of sales method, 101–108
  sales forecast, 101
  steps in process, 100, 101
  sustainable rate of growth, 108, 109
  use of, by financial managers, 112, 113
Financial futures, 703–705
Financial intermediary, 450
Financial lease, 24-6, 24-7
Financial leverage, 472, 482–486
Financial leverage effects, 531–534
Financial management, 2
Financial markets, 445–448. *See also* U.S. financial market system
Financial Modernization Act, 457
Financial policy, 383
Financial principles. *See* Principles
Financial ratios, 62–98
  defined, 63
  DuPont analysis, 77–79
  financing, 71–73
  four question approach, 64–77
  industry norms, 64
  limitations of ratio analysis, 80
  liquidity, 64–68
  operating profits, 68–71
  return on equity, 73, 74
  summary (chart), 75
  use of, by financial managers, 81
Financial risk, 397, 471, 646, 755
Financial statements
  balance sheet, 30–36
  income statement, 28–30
  pro forma statements, 113
  statement of cash flows, 40
Financial structure, 514
Financial structure design, 514
Financing, 33
Financing mix, 445
Financing process, 448, 449
Finished-goods inventory, 678
Fire-retardant children's pajamas, 378
Firm-specific risk, 180
First financial leverage effect, 531–533
Fisher effect, 171, 399, 746
Fisher model, 399
Fixed assets, 30–32
Fixed assets turnover, 75
Fixed costs, 473
Float, 640
Floating lien, 623
Floating-rate international currency system, 734
Flotation costs, 383, 461
Forecasting. *See* Financial forecasting
Foreign Corrupt Practices Act, 112
Foreign currency futures contracts, 750
Foreign currency options, 715, 750
Foreign exchange futures, 704
Foreign exchange market, 735, 736
Foreign exchange rates. *See* Exchange rates
Forms of business organization, 4–7
Forward exchange contract, 741
Forward-market hedge, 749, 750
Forward-spot differential, 742
Four question approach, 64–77
Free cash flow, 529
Free cash-flow approach to merger valuation, 23-10–23-13

Free cash flow theory of capital structure, 529, 532, 533
Free cash flow valuation model, 415–419
Free cash flows, 39–43, 310, 311, 314–324
Friedman, Milton, 6, 395
Furman, Albert "Bud", III, 705
Future value, 128–132
Future-value interest factor ($FVIF_{i,n}$), 131
Future-value interest Factor of an Annuity ($FVIFA_{i,n}$), 141
Futures, 699–706
  commodity, 703
  financial, 703–705
  foreign exchange, 704
  futures markets, 700–703
  hedging, 703
  interest rate, 704
  stock index, 705
Futures clearinghouse, 701
Futures contract, 699, 700
Futures margin, 701
$FVIFA_{i,n}$, 141
$FVIF_{i,n}$, 131

## G

General partnership, 5
Glass-Steagall Act, 457
Globalization. *See* International business finance
Goal of the firm, 3, 4
Going private, 23-14
Golfing points, 427
Goodwill, 23-7
Gramm-Leach-Bliley Act, 457
Gross income, 37
Gross working capital, 31

## H

Hazardous products, 378, 379
Hedging
  cross, 703
  currency-futures contracts and options, 750
  forward-market hedge, 749, 750
  futures, with, 703
  money-market hedge, 748, 749
Hedging principle, 610–612
High-yield bonds, 214
Howrey, M. M., 494
Humanitarian value system, 395
Hybrid securities, 722

## I

Iacocca, Lee, 306
IASC, 44
IFE, 747
Implicit cost of debt, 520
In-the-money, 707
Incentive (performance-based) compensation, 425–429
Income statement, 28–30
Income tax. *See* Taxes
Increasing-stream hypothesis of dividend policy, 585
Incremental analysis, 673, 674
Incremental cash flow, 13
Indenture, 216, 217
Independence hypothesis, 518–521
Indirect costs, 473
Indirect quote, 737
Indirect securities, 448
Indirect transfer of funds, 450
Industry norms, 539, 540
Infinite annuities, 153
Infinite-life replacement chain, 330
Inflation, 585, 682
Inflation rate, 171
Information asymmetry, 579
Information effect, 579
Initial outlay, 315
Initial public offering (IPO), 9, 389
Insider trading, 463
Insolvency, 638
Insolvency risk, 638
Interest expense, 29
Interest rate
  bonds, 228–232
  currency exchange rates, 400
  differences between countries, 399, 400
Interest rate cycles, 439
Interest rate differential, 745
Interest rate futures, 704
Interest rate options, 714, 715
Interest rate parity (IRP) theory, 400, 745
Interest rate risk, 229, 646
Intermediate term financing, 24-1–24-26
  leasing, 24-5–24-19. *See also* Leasing
  term loans, 24-2–24-5. *See also* Term loans
Internal capital market, 444
Internal-external financing choice, 442–444
Internal failure costs, 686
Internal rate of return (IRR), 281–290, 299
International Accounting Standards Committee (IASC), 44
International business finance, 732–761
  direct foreign investment, 755
  exchange rate risk, 741–744, 747–751, 756
  exchange rates. *See* Exchange rates
  interest-rate parity theory, 745
  international Fisher effect, 747
  MNC. *See* Multinational corporation (MNC)
  purchasing power parity, 745, 746
International business risk, 755
International financial-reporting standards, 44
International Fisher effect (IFE), 400, 747
Intrinsic value, 219
Inventory, 32
Inventory loans, 623
Inventory management, 676–687
  anticipatory buying, 682
  defined, 676
  inflation and EOQ, 682
  just-in-time inventory control, 683, 684
  order point problem, 681, 682
  order quantity problem, 678–681
  purpose of carrying inventory, 677
  TQM, 684–687
  types of inventory, 677, 678
Inventory turnover ratio, 67
Invested capital, 413
Investment bankers, 456–459
  advising, 458
  commission/best-efforts basis, 459
  competitive bid purchase, 458
  defined, 457
  direct sale, 459
  distributing, 457, 458
  industry leaders, 459
  negotiated purchase, 458
  privileged subscription, 459
  underwriting, 457
Investment banking firm, 457
Investment banking house, 457
Investment banking syndicate, 450, 457
Investment proposals. *See* Financial forecasting, Capital budgeting
Investor's required rate of return, 190, 191, 382
IPO, 9, 389
IRP, 745
IRR, 281–290, 299
Issue costs, 461
Ivester, M. Douglas, 493, 494

## J

Jensen, Michael C., 529, 532, 533
JIT system, 683, 684
Joint probability, 365
Junk bonds, 214, 215
Just-in-time inventory control, 683, 684

## K

Kampouris, Emmanuel, 606
*Kanban,* 683
Keynes, John Maynard, 637
Kidder, Robert, 424
Kopcke, R. W., 494, 528

## L

La Rouchefoucauld, 212
Lagging, 752
Lanza, Anthony, 25
Law of one price, 746
Leading, 752
Leaps, 716
Lease, 24-6
Lease-purchase algorithm, 24-9–24-11
Lease-versus-purchase decision, 24-8, 24-9
Leasing, 24-5–24-19
  benefits of, 24-13–24-16
  direct lease, 24-7
  economics of leasing versus purchasing, 24-13–24-19
  example (case problem), 24-12–24-14
  financial lease, 24-6, 24-7
  financial reporting, 24-7, 24-8
  lease-purchase algorithm, 24-9–24-11
  lease-versus-purchase decision, 24-8, 24-9
  leveraged, 24-7
  operating lease, 24-6
  sale and leaseback, 24-7
  use of, by financial managers, 24-19
  why firms lease, 24-18, 24-19
Lebaron, Dean, 23-7
Legal forms of business organization, 4–7
Lessee, 24-6
Lessor, 24-6
Leverage analysis, 482–495
  combined leverage, 490–493
  financial leverage, 486–489
  operating leverage, 482–486
  use of, by financial managers, 495
Leverage ratios, 537–540

Leveraged leasing, 24-7
*Liar's Poker* (Lewis), 18
Limited partnership, 5
Line of credit, 617, 618
Lintner, John, 585
Liquid assets, 635
Liquidation, 23-14
Liquidation value, 218
Liquidity, 36
Liquidity position, 584
Loan amortization schedule, 149
Loan participations among banks, 24-4
Loan payment calculation, 24-4, 24-5
Lock-box arrangement, 640–642, 645
Long-term compensation, 425
Long-term debt, 33
Long-term debt to total capitalization, 539
Long-term equity anticipation securities (Leaps), 716
Long-term investment proposals. *See* Capital budgeting
Lotteries, 148
Lumpy assets, 107, 108

## M

M&As. *See* Mergers and acquisitions
Mail float, 640
Majority voting, 250
Malkiel, Burton G., 189
Managerial compensation program, 424–429
Managing for shareholder value, 410–438
  accounting model, 414, 415
  business valuation, 414–419
  compensation program, 424–429
  discounted cash flow model, 414, 415
  EVA, 421–424
  free cash flow valuation model, 415–419
  fundamental paradigm of creating shareholder value, 413
  MVA, 412
  value drivers, 419–421
Marginal (incremental) analysis, 673, 674
Marginal tax rates, 38
Market efficiency, 192n, 220
Market portfolio, 180
Market-related risk, 180
Market value, 219
Market value added (MVA), 412
Marketable securities
  bankers' acceptances, 649
  CDs, 650
  commercial paper, 650
  defined, 635
  federal agency securities, 649
  money market funds, 651, 652
  repurchase agreements, 651
  selection criteria, 646–648
  Treasury bills, 648, 649
Marshall, John, 6
Maturity, 216
Maximization of shareholder wealth, 4
Mayo, Michael, 43
MDA, 670
Medium-term notes (MTNs), 24-2
Mergers and acquisitions, 23-1–23-13
  advantages, 23-2–23-4
  appraisal value, 23-6
  book value, 23-5
  chop-shop approach, 23-4–23-8
  free cash-flow/going concern value, 23-9–23-12
  valuation of acquisition candidate, 23-5–23-12
Microsoft Excel. *See* Spreadsheets
Miller, Merton H., 518n
Miller, Robert, 37
Minority investment positions, 452
Minuit, Peter, 132
MIRR, 290–294, 299, 300
MNC. *See* Multinational corporation (MNC)
Modified accelerated cost recovery system, 37, 316
Modified internal rate of return (MIRR), 290–294, 299, 300
Modigliani, Franco, 518n
Money market, 453
Money market funds, 651, 652
Money-market hedge, 748, 749
Monitoring, 526
Mortgage bond, 213
MTNs, 24-2
Multinational corporation (MNC)
  business risk/global sales, 493, 494
  capital budgeting, 295–297, 332, 333, 367, 368
  cash/marketable securities, 652
  currency risk, 542, 623, 624
  defined, 733
  dividend policy, 594, 595
  finance, 21
  financial markets/intercompany risk, 465, 466
  importance of, 23-15
  international financing/capital-structure decisions, 753, 754
  positioning of funds, 752
  risk management, 718, 719
  time value of money, 154
  working-capital management, 623, 624, 751, 752
Multiple discriminate analysis (MDA), 670
Municipal obligations, 647
Municipals, 647
Mussina, Mike, 22
Mutually exclusive projects, 326
MVA, 412
Myers, Stewart C., 528, 529

## N

Naked call, 707
NAL, 24-9–24-11
NASDAQ, 455, 456
Nasdaq-Amex Market Group, 456
Nasdaq Composite Index, 168
National market system (NMS), 463
Near-cash assets. *See* Marketable securities
Negotiable certificate of deposit (CD), 650
Negotiated purchase, 458
Net advantage of leasing (NAL), 24-9–24-11
Net income, 29
Net income (NI) approach, 521–523
Net lease, 24-7
Net-net lease, 24-7
Net operating income (NOI) approach, 518–521
Net present value (NPV), 277–279, 298
Net present value profile, 288
Net profit margin, 70n
Net value of future dividend growth (NVDG), 268
Net working capital, 35, 418n, 607
New York Stock Exchange (NYSE), 454, 455
New York Stock Exchange Index, 180n
NI theory, 521–523
NMS, 463
NOI theory, 518–521
Nominal interest rate, 153
Nominal rate of interest, 171
Nondetachable warrants, 726
Nondiversifiable risk, 180
Noninterest-bearing current liabilities, 41
NPV, 277–279, 298
NPV method, 277–279, 298, 299
NVDG, 268
NVDG model, 269, 270
NYSE, 454, 455

## O

Observational rights, 451
OCC, 713
Offer rate, 740
Okno, Taiichi, 683
Old-line factor, 622
Open interest, 24-6
Operating income, 29
Operating income return on investment (OIROI), 68–71
Operating lease, 787
Operating leverage, 472, 486–489
Operating profit margin, 69
Opportunity cost, 313
Opportunity cost of funds, 169, 190, 220, 442
Optimal capital structure, 515
Optimal range of financial leverage, 525
Option contract, 706
Option expiration date, 707
Option premium, 707
Option striking price, 707
Option's intrinsic value, 708
Option's speculative value, 708
Option's time value, 708
Options, 706–716
  CBOE, 712–714
  financial insurance, 712
  foreign currency, 715
  fundamentals, 706–711
  interest rate, 714, 715
  Leaps, 716
  leverage, 712
  popularity, 712
  stock index, 714
  Treasury bond futures, on, 715, 716
Options clearinghouse corporation (OCC), 713
Options on Treasury bond futures, 715, 716
Order point problem, 681, 682
Order quantity problem, 678–681
Ordinary annuity, 141
Organized securities exchanges, 454, 455
Other assets, 32
Other payables, 33
Out-of-the-money, 707
Over-the-counter markets, 454–456
Overseas dumping, 378, 379
Overview of book, 19–21
Ownership control, 585

## P

Par value and paid-in capital, 33
Par value of a bond, 216

Partial equilibrium analysis, 516
Participating preferred stock, 244
Partnering, 685
Partnership, 5
Payable-through drafts, 643, 645
Payback period, 274–276, 298
Payment date, 588
Payment-in-kind (PIK) preferred stock, 244
Pecking order theory, 528, 529
Peer group, 66
Percent of sales method, 101–108
Perfect capital markets, 571
Perfect market, 192n
Performance-based compensation, 425–429
Permanent asset investment, 610
Permanent sources of financing, 611
Perpetuity, 153
Persian Golf crisis, 173
PI, 280, 281, 299
PIK preferred stock, 244
Planning period, 415
Pledging, 621, 622
Plowback ratio, 108
Political risk, 755
Portfolio beta, 188
PPP, 745, 746
Preauthorized checks, 645
Precautionary motive, 637, 638
Preemptive right, 252
Preferred stock, 242–247
  adjustable rate, 244
  characteristics, 242
  claims on assets and income, 243
  convertibility, 243
  cumulative feature, 243
  defined, 242
  multiple classes, 243
  participation, 244
  PIK preferred, 244
  protective provisions, 243
  retirement features, 245
  valuation, 245–247
Preferred stockholder's expected rate of return, 258
Preferred stockholders, 33
Preliminary prospectus, 462
Premium bond, 230
Prepaid expenses, 32
Present value, 137–140
Present-value interest factor ($PVIF_{i,n}$), 138
Present-value interest factor for an annuity ($PVIFA_{i,n}$), 145
Present value of annuity, 143–147
Preventive costs, 686
Price takers, 192n
Primary market, 9, 453
Primary market regulations, 462
Prime lending rate, 442
Principle of self-liquidating debt, 610
Principles, 10–19
  agency problem, 15
  cash flow, 12
  competitive markets, 13
  diversification, 16, 17
  efficient markets, 14, 15
  ethical behavior, 18, 19
  incremental cash flow, 13
  risk-return trade-off, 11, 12
  taxes, 16
  time value of money, 12
Private equity market, 451, 452
Private placement, 451, 452, 460, 461
Privileged subscription, 459
Pro forma financial statements, 113
Probability trees, 364–366
Processing float, 640
Product differentiation, 14
Profit and loss statement, 28–30
Profit maximization, 3, 4
Profitability index (PI), 280, 281, 299
Project standing alone risk, 351
Project's contribution-to-firm risk, 352
Prospectus, 462
Protective provisions, 243
Proxy, 250
Proxy fight, 250
Public offering, 451
Public Utility Holding Company Act, 249
Purchasing-power parity (PPP) theory, 745, 746
Pure-play, 23-7
Pure play method, 361
Put option, 706
$PVIFA_{i,n}$, 145
$PVIF_{i,n}$, 138

## Q

Quick ratio, 65
Quoted interest rate, 153

## R

*Random Walk Down Wall Street, A* (Malkiel), 189
Rate of inflation, 171
Ratio analysis. *See* Financial ratios
Raw materials inventory, 677
Real assets, 446
Real rate of interest, 171, 172
Recession, 546, 586
Red herring, 462
Registration statement, 462
Regulation A, 462
Repayment schedules, 24-4, 24-5
Replacement chain, 329
Repos, 651
Repurchase agreements (repos), 651
Repurchasing stock, 590–594
Required rate of return, 190–193
Residual dividend theory, 576, 577
Restrictive covenants, 461, 24-3
Retained earnings, 33
Return on assets (ROA), 69n
Return on common equity, 73
Return on invested capital, 422
Revaluation, 734
Reverse mergers, 23-14
Revolver, 618
Revolving credit, 618
Rights, 252
Rights offerings, 459
Risk, 175–188
  beta, 186–188
  business, 470, 471
  defined, 177, 469
  diversification, 179–182
  investment decision, and, 350–354
  measuring market risk, 182–188
  standard deviation, 177, 178
Risk-adjusted discount rate, 357–360
Risk-free rate of return, 191
Risk management, 698–731. *See also* Derivative securities
Risk premium, 191
Risk-return trade-off, 11, 12
Riskless rate of return, 191
ROA, 69n
Rosengren, E. S., 528

## S

S&P 500 index, 180n
S&P 500 index futures, 705
Safety stock, 680
Sale and leaseback arrangement, 24-7
Sales forecast, 101
Saucer-shaped cost of capital curve, 525
Savings, transfer of, to business firms, 450
Savings-deficit sector, 448, 449
Savings-surplus sector, 449
Scale economics, 106, 107
Scenario analysis, 362
Schulter, F. H., 25
Seasoned new issue, 9
SEC, 462–464
SEC Rule 415, 463
Second financial leverage effect, 533, 534
Secondary market, 9, 447, 453
Secondary market regulations, 463
Secured loans, 616
Securities Act of 1933, 462
Securities Acts Amendments of 1975, 463
Securities Exchange Act of 1934, 463
Securities Exchange Commission (SEC), 462–464
Securities exchanges, 454, 455
Securities market, 9
Securities regulation, 462–464
Security market line, 192
Security value, 723
Sell-off, 23-14
Selling rate, 740
Semifixed costs, 475
Semivariable costs, 475
Sensitivity analysis, 362, 364
Sensitivity coefficients, 209
Share repurchase, 590–594
Shareholder scoreboard, 412n
Shareholder value. *See* Managing for shareholder value
Shelf offering, 463
Shelf registration, 463, 464
Short-term credit
  cost, 614, 615
  sources, 616–623. *See also* Sources of short-term credit
Short-term debt, 609
Short-term liability, 33
Short-term notes, 33
Shorting, 707
Simple arbitrage, 740
Simpson, Sumner, 24, 25
Simulation, 361–364
Single-sourcing, 685
Sinking fund, 245, 536
Size disparity problem, 326, 327
Small-issues exemption, 462
Small, regular dividend plus year-end extra, 585
Smith, Adam, 395
Smith, Brian, 666
Smith, John F., Jr., 296
Smith, Kenneth, 25
Smithian value system, 395
Social responsibility, 6, 19
Social value systems, 395
Sole proprietorship, 5
Solon, 175
Sources of short-term credit, 616–623
  accounts receivable loans, 621–623

accrued wages and taxes, 616
bank credit, 617–619
commercial paper, 619, 620
inventory loans, 623
trade credit, 616, 617
Speculative motive, 638
Speidell, Lawrence, 23-7
Spin-off, 23-14
Spontaneous financing, 102
Spontaneous sources of financing, 611
Spot transactions, 737
Spreadsheets
IRR, 287, 288
MIRR, 293, 294
net present value, 279
time value of money, 134, 135
Stable dollar dividend per share, 585
Standard and Poor (S&P) 500 Index, 180n
Standard deviation, 177, 178
Standby agreement, 459
Statement of cash flows, 40
Static trade-off theory, 527
"Still Searching for Optimal Capital Structure" (Myers), 528
STIP program (Harley-Davidson), 429
Stock
common, 247–256. *See also* Common stock
preferred, 242–247. *See also* Preferred stock
relationship between value and earnings, 267–270
valuation, 245–247, 252–256, 267–270
Stock buyback, 591
Stock dividend, 588–590
Stock index futures, 705
Stock index options, 714
Stock options, 428
Stock quotations, 251
Stock repurchase, 590–594
Stock sensitivity coefficients, 209
Stock split, 588–590
Stock valuation
common stock, 252–256
preferred stock, 245–247
relationship between value and earnings, 267–270
Stockholder's expected rate of return, 258–260
*Stocks, Bonds, Bills and Inflation,* 169
Straight-line depreciation, 38, 316, 317
*Strategy for Financial Mobility* (Donaldson), 528
Stretching trade accounts, 617
Subordinated debentures, 212, 213
Sunk costs, 313
Sustainable rate of growth, 108, 109
Syndicate, 450, 457
Syndicated Eurocredit loan, 753
Synergistic effect, 312
Systematic risk, 180, 352, 360

## T

T-bills, 648, 649
Taking a long position, 707
Taking a short position, 707
Target capital structure proportions, 391
Target debt ratios, 543, 544
Tax-deductible expenses, 37
Tax shield, 524
Taxable income, 37, 38
Taxes, 36–39
business decisions, and, 16
leases, 23-18
marginal/average tax rates, 38, 39
marketable securities, 647
mergers, 23-3
sale of old machine, 315
taxable income, 37, 38
Temporary asset investment, 610
Temporary sources of financing, 611
Tender offer, 593
Term loans, 24-2–24-5
collateral, 24-2
defined, 24-2
Eurodollar loans, 24-4
loan participations among banks, 24-4
loan payment calculation, 24-4, 24-5
maturities, 24-2
repayment schedules, 24-4, 24-5
restrictive covenants, 24-3
Term structure of interest rates, 172, 173
Terminal value, 415
Terminal warehouse agreement, 623
Terms of sale, 668
Texas Instruments BAII Plus financial calculator, 134
Threat hypothesis, 529
TI BAII Plus, 134
Time disparity problem, 327, 328
Time value of money, 127–167
amortized loans, 149, 150
annuity, 140–148. *See also* Annuity
comparing interest rates, 153, 154
compound interest, 128–130
equations (summary), 156
financial calculator, 133, 134
future value, 128–132
multinational firm, 154, 155
nonannual periods, 136, 137
perpetuities, 153
present value, 137–140
present value of complex stream, 150–152
principle, as, 12
spreadsheets, 134, 135
use of, by financial managers, 155
Times burden covered, 539
Times interest earned, 72, 539
Tools of capital structure management, 530–541
companywide cash flows, 540, 541
comparative leverage ratios, 537–540
EBIT-EPS analysis, 534–537
financial leverage effects, 531–534
Total asset turnover, 70
Total fixed costs, 473
Total liabilities to net worth, 539
Total quality management (TQM), 684–687
Total revenue, 475
Total variable costs, 474
TQM, 684–687
Trade credit, 616, 617
Transaction exposure, 748–751
Transaction loans, 619
Transaction motive, 637
Transfer price, 752
Transferring financial capital into economy, 450
Transit float, 640
Translation exposure, 747, 748
Treasurer, 8
Treasury bills, 648, 649
Treasury bond futures, 715, 716
Treasury stock, 33
Trial-and-error analysis (break-even analysis), 476
Triangular arbitrage, 740
Tris-impregnated pajamas, 378
2/10, net 30, 617, 668

## U

U-shaped cost of capital curve, 525
UEPS, 536, 537
Unbounded incentive compensation plan, 427
Uncommitted earnings per share (UEPS), 536, 537
Underwriter's spread, 461
Underwriting, 447, 457
Unit contribution margin, 476, 477
U.S. financial market system
capital market, 453
flotation costs, 461
investment bankers, 456–459
money market, 453
organized securities exchanges, 454, 455
over-the-counter markets, 455, 456
primary market, 453
private placement, 451, 452, 460, 461
public offering, 451
regulation, 462–464
secondary market, 453
U.S. Treasury bills, 648, 649
Unsecured loans, 616
Unsystematic risk, 180, 705
Users of financial information, 45

## V

Valuation
bonds, 223–226
business, 414–419
common stock, 252–256, 267–270
convertibles, 724
determinants of value, 220, 221
mergers, 23-6–23-13
preferred stock, 245–247
steps in process, 222
warrants, 726, 727
Valuation approach to liquidity management, 610n
Valuation ratios, 23-7
Value, 218, 219
Value drivers, 419–421
Variable costs, 474
Venture capitalist, 451
Vice President for Finance, 7, 8
Volume of output, 476

## W

*Wall Street,* 18
Wall Street Journal workplace ethics quiz, 20
Warrant, 725–727
Warrant exercise price, 725
Warrant expiration date, 726
Weighted average cost of capital, 383, 390–393
Weinstein, Jack B., 26
What if analysis, 362
Wire transfers, 642, 645
Work-in-process inventory, 677
Working capital, 607

Working-capital management, 606–633
cash conversion cycle, 612–614
current liabilities, 609
hedging principle, 610–612
multinational firms, 623, 624
risk-return trade-off, 607, 608
short-term credit, 614–623. *See also* Sources of short-term credit
use of, by financial managers, 624
Working-capital requirements, 312
Writing, 707

## Y

Yield curve, 172
Yield to maturity, 172, 227

## Z

Zero and very low coupon bonds, 213
Zero balance accounts, 643, 645
Ziemer, Jim, 32, 23-5

# prentice hall's guide to e-business for finance

2002

marian wood

## *e-business, the Internet . . . and you*

Learn where the e-business wave is headed and how you can ride it. Discover how the Internet can help you in your courses and in your job search. Check out what distance learning may mean for you.

# Prentice Hall's Guide to E-Business

answers your questions...

### ✓*Just what is e-business?*

Learn where e-business has come from and where it's going.
Discover how your business courses tie to the exciting world of e-business.

### ✓*How do I land a job?*

Learn how to research careers and employers.
Find out how to explore job openings online.
Read our tips on creating electronic résumés.

### ✓*How do I learn in cyberspace?*

Learn how to find the distance-learning program that's right for you.

### ✓*So how do I get started exploring the Internet?*

Find out about today's popular search engines.
Get acquainted with advanced search techniques.
Use our wealth of URLs to get the information you need for your business courses.

**Instructors**: Answers to this guide's Cases in Point—short studies that take students online—are available through MyPHLIP, at ***www.prenhall.com/myphlip***. (See the back cover of this guide for more information on MyPHLIP.)

# Prentice Hall's Guide to E-Business for Finance

2002 Edition

Marian B. Wood

Contributors:

Rock Mathis, New Jersey Institute of Technology
Chris Moore
Raymond D. Frost, Ohio University
Judy Strauss, University of Nevada, Reno
Andrew T. Stull

**Prentice Hall**
Upper Saddle River, NJ 07458

**Development:** Steve Deitmer and Melene Kubat
**Manager, Print Production:** Christy Mahon
**Formatter:** Suzanne Duda
**Cover Design:** Michael J. Fruhbeis
**Manufacturer:** Von Hoffman Graphics

Screen shots reprinted with permission from the following companies and organizations:
FreeMarkets
FedCenter.com
eBay, Inc.
Metacrawler/InfoSpace, Inc.
New York State Department of Labor
Monster.com
The College for Financial Planning

The authors and publishers of this manual have used their best efforts in preparing this book. The authors and publisher make no warranty of any kind, expressed or implied, with regard to these programs or the documentation contained in this book. The authors and publisher shall not be liable in any event for incidental or consequential damages in connection with, or arising out of, the furnishing, performance, or use of the programs described in this book.

---

ISBN 0-13-064991-0
10 9 8 7 6 5 4 3 2 1

# What's Inside

**Preface**

**Chapter 1** **Introduction to E-Business and E-Commerce** **1**

E-Business, E-Commerce, and the New Economy
Components of E-Commerce
E-Commerce Around the World
Looking Ahead: Challenges and Opportunities

**Chapter 2** **Searching the Internet** **7**

Advanced Search Techniques
Go Beyond with Metasearch
More Search Engines
Evaluating and Using Search Results

**Chapter 3** **Career Development on the Internet** **13**

How to Research Careers and Employers
How to Find Job Openings
How to Create an Electronic Résumé
For Further Career Surfing
Preparing for a Career in E-Business
Additional Resources

**Chapter 4** **Distance Learning on the Internet** **23**

What is Distance Learning?
Advantages and Disadvantages
A Distance Learning Sampler
10 Questions to Ask Before You Register

**Chapter 5** **E-Business, the Internet, and Your Finance Course** **29**

E-Business Finance Issues
Using the Internet in Your Finance Course
Careers in Finance
The Internet as a Finance Learning Tool

**Glossary** **41**

**Sources** **43**

# Preface

What's going on in the world of e-business today? What will it look like tomorrow? No matter what direction you turn, it seems you'll run into e-business. And although perhaps no one can accurately predict how the world of business will look in the coming year—it's changing every day—it seems certain that e-business will be an increasingly big part of it. This guide introduces you to many aspects of e-business, and it also shows you how to use the Internet to search out information, look for jobs, and take online courses—as the following table of contents promises.

## Chapter 1: Introduction to E-Business and E-Commerce

*An overview of the basic concepts of e-business and e-commerce.* This chapter provides background and perspective on the growth and importance of e-business. We introduce you to the new concepts emerging from the new ways of doing business on the Internet.

## Chapter 2: Searching the Internet

*A discussion of advanced search techniques and descriptions of some popular search engines.* You also learn how to evaluate the credibility of an online source and how to avoid plagiarism.

## Chapter 3: Career Development on the Internet

*An up-to-the-minute look at online job searches and career sites.* We offer tips on how to prepare an electronic résumé, and we annotate hot online job sites. You will also learn about using Web-based self-assessment tools to prepare for a career in e-business.

## Chapter 4: Distance Learning on the Internet

*You will learn what questions to ask to ensure you're taking the right distance-learning course.*

## Chapter 5: E-Business, the Internet, and Your Finance Course

*Information on how e-business and e-commerce are changing the face of finance.* You'll also find mini-cases highlighting important aspects of finance. In addition, we'll give you a wealth of URLs.

## Glossary

*Key terms to help you speak the language of e-business.*

*Instructors:* You will find answers to the Cases in Points at our myPhlip site. Visit us at **www.prenhall.com/myphlip.**

# Chapter One

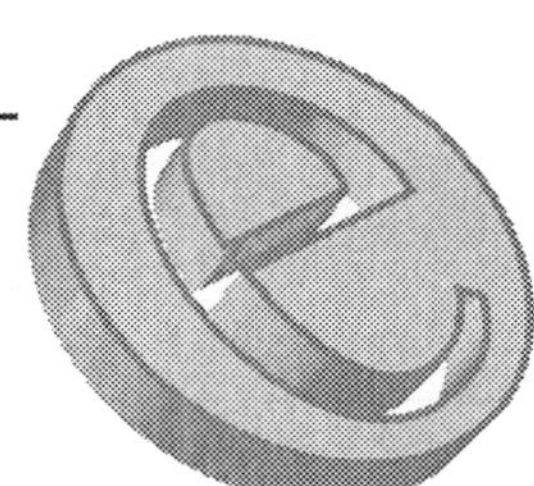

# Introduction to E-Business and E-Commerce

## E-Business, E-Commerce, and the New Economy

When the Internet was in its infancy—little more than a decade ago—words like *e-commerce* and *e-business* had not yet been invented. Now the Internet has become such an integral part of the business world that experts had to create a special phrase—the *new economy*—for its contribution to the economy. The new economy, also known as the *Internet economy*, consists of businesses that generate all or some of their revenues from the Internet or Internet-related goods and services.

Both e-commerce and e-business are part of the new economy. The exchange transactions that take place on the Internet (such as buying, selling, or trading goods, services, and information) are known as *e-commerce*. *E-business* is a broader term covering the combination of business processes, technology, and organizational structure needed for e-commerce.

E-businesses such as Yahoo! (**http://www.yahoo.com**) and Amazon.com (**http://www.amazon.com**) were e-commerce pioneers, attracting the public imagination with their ingenious presentations and innovative use of Internet technology. Yet some of today's most successful—and profitable—e-businesses aren't even "dot-coms" (Internet-based businesses). IBM (**http://www.ibm.com**) and Dell (**http://www.dell.com**) are two of the growing list of traditional firms that now use the Web to improve internal processes, boost sales, and satisfy customers.

## Components of E-Commerce

What comes to mind when you think of e-commerce? Amazon.com, perhaps? Well, e-commerce is much more than *e-tailers* (Internet retailers). It's made up of exchanges among businesses, consumers, and government agencies, which can be classified according to which party initiates and controls the exchange transaction and which party is the target of the exchange. Table 1 shows these components, along with a Web example of each.

In e-commerce jargon, *B2C* means business-to-consumer (initiated by a business, aimed at consumers) transactions, *B2B* means business-to-business transactions, and *B2G* means business-to-government transactions. Similarly, *C2B* means consumer-to-business, *C2C* means consumer-to-consumer, and *C2G* means consumer-to-government. Finally, *G2B* means government-to-business, *G2C* means government-to-consumer, and *G2G* means government-to-government. Here's a closer look at each of these e-commerce components.

***B2B.*** Business-to-business transactions account for most of today's e-commerce sales volume, because they generally involve higher prices and larger quantities than B2C transactions. Within three years, B2B transactions could hit $4 trillion. Taking advantage of the speed and convenience of the Web, companies such as Cisco (**http://www.cisco.com**) now buy nearly all their supplies and sell many of their computer-related products online. The Internet makes business buying so efficient that British Telecom expects to save 11% by moving its purchasing to the Web. E-commerce volume is also growing at *B2B online markets*, Web sites that facilitate the exchange of goods and services among organizational buyers and sellers. One example is FreeMarkets (**http://www.freemarkets.com**), which auc-

| | To Business | To Consumer | To Government |
|---|---|---|---|
| **Initiated by Business** | Business-to-Business (B2B) *FreeMarkets* **http://www.freemarkets.com** | Business-to-Consumer (B2C) *Amazon.com* **http://www.amazon.com** | Business-to-Government (B2G) *FedCenter.com* **http://www.fedcenter.com** |
| **Initiated by Consumer** | Consumer-to-Business (C2B) *Better Business Bureau site* **http://www.bbb.org/** | Consumer-to-Consumer (C2C) *eBay* **http://www.ebay.com** | Consumer-to-Government (C2G) *GovWorks* **http://www.govworks.com** |
| **Initiated by Government** | Government-to-Business (G2B) *Small Business Administration site* **http://www.sba.gov/** | Government-to-Consumer (G2C) *California state site* **http://www.state.ca.us/** | Government-to-Government (G2G) *Fed World site* **http://www.fedworld.gov/** |

**Table 1**

Classifying E-Commerce Sites

tions materials and components, supplies, and services in 70 product categories. See Figure 1.1. These B2B sites help participating businesses reduce buying costs, expand access to more suppliers, and slash the time and paperwork needed to complete purchases.

***B2C.*** Although B2C transactions are a smaller part of e-commerce than B2B transactions, they are capturing an ever-larger share of all retail sales. By 2003, B2C could reach $400 billion in annual sales. Currently, the majority of B2C transactions take

**FIGURE 1.1**

FreeMarkets operates a B2B marketplace that brings together business buyers and sellers of components, raw materials, and services.

place on Amazon.com and a handful of other sites. As this list indicates, dot-coms enjoy an early e-commerce lead over store-based retailers. Why? Barnes and Noble, like so many other firms, dragged its feet in starting an e-business unit (**http://www.bn.com**) out of fear that online sales would cut into the sales of the *legacy business*, the traditional, non-Internet business unit. Meanwhile, start-ups such as Amazon roared ahead, building their brands and their customer bases with aggressive marketing programs. By the time bn.com started clicking, Amazon was way ahead. Amazon's 2000 sales were $2.7 billion, compared with bn.com's sales of $320 million. Online competition is so fierce that as many as 25,000 of today's 30,000 e-tailers may ultimately be driven out of business.

***B2G.*** Government agencies on the local, state, and federal level represent a huge and lucrative market for businesses selling all kinds of goods, services, and information. Government agencies purchase more than $77 billion annually in technology goods and services—and that's only the tip of the procurement iceberg, because it doesn't count non-technology purchasing. That's why B2G sites like FedCenter.com (**http://www.fedcenter.com**) are setting up shop on the Internet (see Figure 1.2). Once government buyers register at FedCenter and receive their passwords, they search the site for goods and services by category and then click to set the purchase in motion. FedCenter offers 3 million items—everything from office furniture to medical supplies—and government buyers can comparison-shop right on the site.

***C2C.*** Consumer-to-consumer transactions are of lower dollar amounts and account for a far smaller piece of the e-commerce pie than B2B, B2C, or B2G transactions. Yet eBay (**http://www.ebay.com**) is one of the highest-profile sites on the Internet because so many people are hopping on the Internet auction bandwagon to buy and sell collectibles and other items online. See Figure 1.3. As another C2C example, the Maryland *Pennysaver* publication (**http://www.mdpennysaver.com/index.cfm**) posts its yard sale and classified listings online to link consumer buyers with consumer sellers.

***C2B.*** In consumer-to-business transactions the consumer, not the business, initiates and controls the exchange. One C2B site is 2001Ideas.com, which helps consumer inventors

**FIGURE 1.2**

FedCenter.com is a B2G one-stop shopping site for government buyers seeking business products and services.

**FIGURE 1.3**

These materials have been reproduced by Prentice Hall Inc. with the permission of eBay Inc. COPYRIGHT EBAY INC. ALL RIGHTS RESERVED.

The eBay site is a C2C auction site that allows consumers (and some businesses) to buy and sell a wide variety of products.

submit ideas for new products and technologies to product development managers at Coca-Cola, DaimlerChrysler, and other corporations. Another C2B site, Respond.com (**http://www.respond.com**), lets consumers post requests for items they want to purchase so businesses can respond with specific offers. The private, nonprofit Better Business Bureau, funded by businesses, also operates a C2B site (**http://www.bbb.org/**). Consumers can search this Web site for free information about problems other consumers have reported with particular businesses, charities, and investment firms.

*C2G.* One of the fastest-growing areas of e-commerce is C2G, which covers consumer-initiated transactions with government agencies. GovWorks (**http://www.govworks.com/**) lets consumers pay government agencies online for traffic fines, real estate taxes, and government licenses and permits. GovWorks makes money by charging consumers a service fee for each payment and by selling site sponsorships. Another C2G site, ezgov.com (**http://www.ezgov.com**), is signing agreements with state and local governments to accept online payments from consumers—again, with service fees paid by consumers. Both sites offer time-pressured consumers the convenience of making payments without having to wait in line at some government office.

*G2C.* More and more government agencies are establishing Web sites to provide information and services to consumers. As one example, the California site (**http://www.state.ca.us/**) contains pages of free data about state services, transportation, public safety, health care, state history, and much more. Some government sites, such as the Washington, D.C., site (**http://www.washingtondc.gov**), allow online transactions such as driver's license renewals as well as business transactions such as permit applications. In addition, Oregon and 11 other states have begun selling seized and surplus property to consumers through eBay auctions. For example, Oregon has sold hundreds of items on eBay, from tools to jewels. These state sales on eBay have been so successful that the federal government is now planning a separate auction site for its own G2C transactions.

***G2B.*** Businesses are another constituency that government agencies want to reach online. The U.S. Small Business Administration site (**http://www.sba.gov/**), for example, is a G2B site offering information and financial assistance to small businesses. The site helps entrepreneurs learn how to establish a business, obtain funding for expansion, buy or sell overseas, and tap other government resources. A number of municipalities also maintain Web sites to solicit business bids on government purchases of goods and services. The Fort Collins, Colorado, purchasing site (**http://www.ci.fort-collins.co.us/purchasing/**) lists current purchasing needs and offers downloadable documents for businesses to use in submitting bids.

***G2G.*** Government-to-government transactions are much less visible to the public than other e-commerce components. One G2G site is the Government Agency Services page on the FedWorld site (**http://www.fedworld.gov/fedservices/fedworld/**), maintained by the National Technical Information Service (NTIS). The NTIS will help any other federal government information agency design a Web site, set up online procurement, sell publications online, or create a database—for a fee. Although this arrangement pits the NTIS against businesses that provide the same services, it also permits the NTIS to generate revenues and offset its operational costs.

## E-Commerce Around the World

U.S. consumers, businesses, and government buyers have been steadily increasing their online purchasing since the early 1990s—a trend that will only accelerate as more people and organizations log on to the Web. According to the U.S. Department of Commerce, U.S. consumers are buying more goods and services online: in the fourth quarter of 2000, e-tail sales totaled $8.7 billion, compared with sales of $5.3 billion in the fourth quarter of 1999. The top product categories for online purchasing are computer hardware and software, travel services, securities investments, collectible items, and music, videos, and books. Meanwhile, U.S.-based giants such as General Electric (**http://www.ge.com**) and General Motors (**http://www.gm.com**) are saving money and time by shifting the bulk of their global business buying and selling to the Web.

The monetary value of European e-commerce is not yet at the U.S. level, but it is growing rapidly, fueled by fast-rising Internet usage, the shift to a single currency (the euro), and new wireless methods of Web access. Eyeing the opportunities, businesses such as Britain's Harrods department store (**http://www.harrods.com**) are promoting their Web sites, even as U.S.-based firms such as E-Loan (**http://www.eloan.com**) launch European Web operations.

E-commerce in Japan is growing more slowly than in the United States and Europe, because far fewer people own personal computers. Still, online purchasing is getting a boost from the wild popularity of wireless Internet access offered by NTT DoCoMo (**http://www.nttdocomo.com/**), the country's largest mobile phone operator. Teens wear the colorful DoCoMo phone like jewelry and use its voice-recognition technology to speed-dial friends and log on to participating Web sites. DoCoMo has already signed 20 million customers and is adding more than 25,000 new subscribers every day. Small wonder that telecommunications providers outside Japan are watching DoCoMo's Internet strategy with great interest.

## Looking Ahead: Challenges and Opportunities

What lies ahead for e-businesses? Here, categorized by business discipline, is a quick overview of key challenges and opportunities facing e-businesses in the new economy.

***MARKETING AND ADVERTISING.*** With so much competition from dot-coms and legacy businesses—and so many new opportunities to reach and satisfy customers—e-businesses are finding new ways of using the four Ps of the marketing mix (product, place, pricing, promotion) to build their brands online for competitive advantage.

***MANAGEMENT AND HUMAN RESOURCES MANAGEMENT.*** How can e-business managers plan, organize, lead, and control in the ever-changing Internet environment?

Meeting this challenge, e-business managers are developing virtual organizations, adding corporate portals (internal Web sites), and offering employee-gripe Web pages. They're also going online to recruit high-tech employees.

***STRATEGY.*** E-commerce has created new challenges and opportunities for managers to consider as they craft strategy. A key decision is determining whether to separate or integrate e-businesses and legacy businesses in the portfolio.

***FINANCE.*** Where do e-businesses get the cash they need to set up shop and pay for marketing to attract and retain customers? Venture capitalists and for-profit incubators are common sources of financing. In addition, the Internet enables e-businesses to offer their stock to online investors.

***LEGAL STUDIES IN BUSINESS.*** Many e-businesses are taking legal steps to protect intellectual property such as Internet domain names and Web patents. Privacy online is another hot legal issue. Information is the lifeblood of e-commerce, yet many consumers and privacy advocates worry that too much personal data is too available on the Web.

***ACCOUNTING, AUDITING, AND TAXATION.*** The explosive growth of e-commerce has put the spotlight on key accounting, auditing, and taxation issues. When and how should an e-business recognize revenues? Should e-businesses capitalize or expense costs? And should Internet sales be taxed?

***ECONOMICS.*** The Internet has opened new business opportunities in four areas: infrastructure, applications, intermediaries, and commerce. It has also cleared the way for cashless payment alternatives such as electronic cash and electronic barter—and for B2B online markets to facilitate the exchange of goods and services among organizational buyers and sellers.

***BUSINESS COMMUNICATION.*** Writing for online readers is a major challenge for business communicators. With more than 569 million e-mailboxes around the world, e-businesses are also able to take advantage of new communication opportunities—if they steer clear of spam (unsolicited e-mail) and comply with rules governing specialized messages.

***MANAGEMENT INFORMATION SYSTEMS.*** E-businesses are using two types of private computer networks—intranets and extranets—to handle the challenge of supporting their e-commerce operations. And the Internet has led to new methods of obtaining specialized application software—as well as to new ways of enhancing online customer service.

***DECISION SCIENCES.*** Sophisticated Internet-based technologies are creating new opportunities for e-businesses to more efficiently and effectively manage all the links in the supply chain. Not only are firms managing inputs by moving procurement to the Web—they're managing outputs by installing computerized systems to optimize production efficiency.

With this background, you're ready for Chapters 2, 3, and 4 of this guide, where you'll learn how to conduct an advanced search over the Internet, how to find—and land—a job on the Internet, and what distance learning could mean for you. Chapter 5 takes a closer look at e-business issues and includes many URLs for you to use to get the information you need for your business course and your business career.

Chapter Two

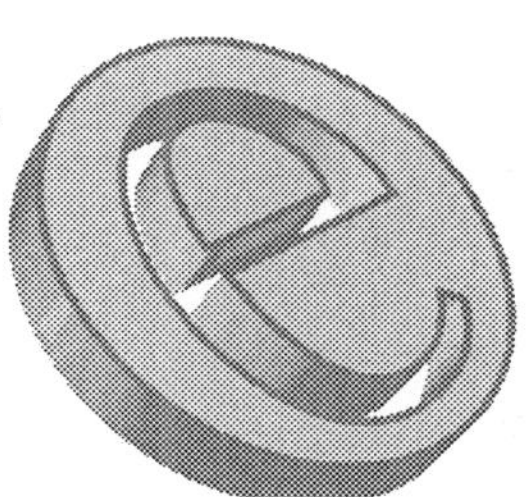

# Searching the Internet

The Internet contains plenty of valuable information, but it's not always easy to find what you want—unless you have a good search strategy, based on an open text search, a subject tree search, or advanced search techniques.

In an *open text search,* the search engine scans the Web looking for a word or group of words you have entered as your search string. The search engine then lists links to Web pages it determines are most relevant to your keyword(s). AltaVista (**http://www.altavista.com**) and Google (**http://www.google.com**) are two of the many open text search engines you can use.

Subject tree searches take a different approach. A *subject tree* is a catalog of a great number of pages on the Web, neatly organized by category, sub-category, sub-sub-category, and so on. Yahoo! (**http://www.yahoo.com**) is one of the most comprehensive subject tree indexes.

## Advanced Search Techniques

Sometimes a simple search turns up rather strange results or a huge number of Web sites. Using advanced search techniques allows you to conduct a more specific open text search and receive more relevant results.

Some of these search techniques are based on the way search engines determine the relevance of a Web page. AltaVista, like many search engines, aims to position the most relevant documents at the top of the list, based on the following criteria:

- the keywords are found in the first few words of the document
- the keywords are found close to one another in the document
- the document contains more than one instance of the keywords

Advanced search techniques include the use of pluses, minuses, quotation marks, and wildcards.

### PLUSES AND MINUSES

During an open text search, you can use plus and minus signs to specify what you want a search engine to include and exclude. On the AltaVista search engine (**http://www.altavista.com**), a plus means that you want the word to appear on a Web page; a minus means that you don't want it to appear. So +inflation -currency gives you all sites containing the word "inflation" but not "currency." Conversely, -inflation +currency gives you all sites without "inflation" but with "currency."

### YOUR TURN

Go to the AltaVista site (**http://www.altavista.com**) and try the inflation and currency searches. Be sure to include a space between the words, or AltaVista will think you are searching for one long word.

| You Type | It Means |
|---|---|
| +inflation -currency | Find all pages that have information on inflation but not currency. |

About how many documents were returned by this first query?

| You Type | It Means |
|---|---|
| -inflation +currency | Find all pages that do not cover inflation but have information on currency. |

About how many documents were returned by this second query?

## KEEP IT IN QUOTES

When you want the search words to appear right next to each other with no words in between, type your keywords in quotes. Use AltaVista for the following two searches.

| You Type | It Means |
|---|---|
| current economic forecast | Find all sites that have the words "current," "economic," and "forecast" (not necessarily right next to each other, not necessarily in that order). |

About how many Web pages did this query find?

Now use quotation marks to find sites where all three words appear right next to each other.

| You Type | It Means |
|---|---|
| "current economic forecast" | Find all sites that have the words "current" and "economic" and "forecast" appearing right next to each other, in that order. |

About how many Web pages did the query find?

Now combine a plus symbol and quotation marks to find just those sites that mention Asia's current economic forecast.

| You Type | It Means |
|---|---|
| +"current economic forecast" + asia | Find all sites that have the words "current economic forecast" appearing right next to each other. Those same pages must also contain the word "asia." |

About how many Web pages did this query find?

As these searches indicate, narrowing a search using quotation marks works best when you want to find a string of three words or more. Sometimes searches for two words reveal the same results with or without using quotes.

## WHEN IN DOUBT, USE LOWERCASE

You may have noticed that in all of the examples above, the keywords were typed in lowercase letters, even when searching for a proper name, such as Asia. The reason for this is that lowercase keywords match both lower and uppercase, but uppercase matches uppercase only. So, if some Webmaster forgets to capitalize Asia, you'll still find that site.

## A STAR FOR THE WILDCARD

What if you are looking for information on European free trade zones? It is reasonable to assume that a search for Europe free trade zones might also produce good results. Rather than run two searches — European free trade zones and Europe free trade zones —you can use the wildcard notation to match all words that start with Europe (that is, both Europe and European) by typing europe*. The keywords you enter would therefore be +europe* +"free trade zones" for this open text search.

### MORE ABOUT ADVANCED SEARCH TECHNIQUES

Most search sites tell users how to conduct advanced searches. For example, you can read AltaVista's Advanced Search Tutorial (**http://doc.altavista.com/adv_search/ast_i_index.shtml**) to learn more about different search engines and the use of symbols and words to narrow your search. Another good starting point is the Search Engines link on About the Web (**http://www.about-the-web.com/**).

You can get more detailed information about various search engines and search strategies on the Search Engine site (**http://searchenginewatch.com/**). Look for ideas on how and where to search by browsing the links on the 4Anything site (**http://4search.4anything.com/**). And you'll find links to search tutorials, search engines, and specialized search strategies on the Search IQ site (**http://www.zdnet.com/searchiq/guide/**).

## Go Beyond with Metasearch

Each search engine uses its own technique or strategy to conduct a search. That's why entering the same keyword on two search engines will usually turn up different results. Want a more comprehensive search? Try a metasearch site, such as Dogpile (**http://www.dogpile.com**), MetaCrawler (**http://www.metacrawler.com**), or Ixquick (**http://www.ixquick.com**).

Metasearch sites send your keyword out to a number of search engines at one time. Within seconds, you get back a listing of results from all the search engines that found sites containing your keyword. This saves you the time and trouble of entering your keyword in one search engine after another.

Dogpile, Ixquick, and Metacrawler work through 14 different search engines, giving you fast access to information across the Web. See Figure 2.1 for a look at the Metacrawler Power Search site. In some cases, you can also specify whether you want the metasearch site to search Web sites, news sites, media sites, or other types of sites. This gives you more flexibility in finding exactly what you want.

**Figure 2.1**



The Metacrawler Power Search site

### YOUR TURN

Compare the results of two searches using the same keywords on different metasearch sites. First go to Dogpile (**http://www.dogpile.com**) and then go to MetaCrawler (**http://www.metacrawler.com**) to search for information on "global business."

| Keywords | Number of Dogpile matches | Number of MetaCrawler matches |
|---|---|---|
| "global business" | | |

Which site turns up more matches? How are the results displayed on each metasearch site? How relevant are most of the matches returned on each site?

## More Search Engines

Here are more good search engines to try.

### About.com http://www.about.com

At About.com, people—called guides—search out information and sites, then post the details on About.com's pages according to category. Type in a keyword and About.com will suggest numerous sites, each recommended by guides who are specialists in their fields and each containing additional links in that area of interest. You can e-mail these guides for more information, too. Guides update their category pages weekly—sometimes daily—and they also host live chats and forum discussions, publish newsletters, and recommend books.

### Excite http://www.excite.com

Excite searches the entire Web not only for your keywords but also for related topics. Clicking on the "zoom in" feature shows you lists of related terms that may help you get closer to what you want. Excite can also conduct searches in eleven languages, a valuable feature if you want to find international data.

### HotBot http://www.hotbot.lycos.com

One nice feature of HotBot is the ability to get more precise by conducting additional searches within your first listing of results. Another nice feature is the "second opinion" button at the bottom of the page, which lets you send your search phrase out to Lycos for another search opportunity.

### Ixquick http://www.ixquick.com

This metasearch site is fast and displays only the most relevant results, listed according to how they are ranked by the various search engines. Because different search engines rank sites according to different criteria, a site that receives high rankings by multiple engines is likely to contain valuable information. In addition, Ixquick eliminates duplicates, so a site appears only once in the listing of results.

### Lycos http://www.lycos.com

When you conduct a search on Lycos, the first set of results consists of popular Web sites that have been reviewed by Lycos editors; the second set consists of other Web sites that were not reviewed; the third set consists of news articles from Internet news sources; and the fourth set consists of shopping sites related to your search term. This site also lets users turn on parental controls to screen out adult and violent sites and sites that are inappropriate in any other way for younger users.

### Yahoo! http://www.yahoo.com

Yahoo! is one of the most popular online search sites. When you enter keywords, Yahoo! will automatically return categories and sites that contain all of those words. You can easily customize your search, and searches on this site are not case-sensitive (that is, it doesn't matter whether words are upper-case or lower-case). Look for the latest site additions under "What's New," or customize your search page using MyYahoo.

## Evaluating and Using Search Results

Just because information is on the Internet doesn't mean that it's complete, accurate, or objective. How can you evaluate sources of information you uncover during an Internet search?

### DETERMINING THE CREDIBILITY OF INTERNET SOURCES

Before you use data from any online source, ask:

- *What do you know about the source?* When in doubt, seek out online sources that have a reputation for reliability. Many Web sites are sponsored by well-known organizations, such as major newspapers, that have earned a reputation for integrity. However, some Web sites don't even identify their sponsors. So be wary if the source is completely unfamiliar or has a questionable reputation.
- *Does the source seem biased?* Think about whether the source is likely to have a definite point of view on certain issues. For example, when you browse the Web site of the American Association of Retired Persons, bear in mind that the information is likely to reflect that group's role as an advocate for people over 50 years old. Knowing the organization's purpose and viewpoint can help you interpret any information you use from that source.
- *What is the original source of the information?* In many cases, Web sites and databases draw their information from other sources, such as government studies. If the original source is noted, take time to evaluate its reputation and potential for bias before you use the data. If no original source is indicated, approach the data with caution.
- *Can you verify the source's information?* Before you use information from an online source, try to find another source to verify the data. You can use another search engine to scan the Internet for the same kind of data provided by at least one other reliable source. The ability to confirm information serves as a valuable check on the data's accuracy—and the accuracy of its source.
- *Does the source's information seem reasonable to you?* As a final check on any online source, use your judgment to evaluate the data and the conclusions. Given the other facts you have uncovered on the subject, does this source's information seem unreasonable or out of line? If so, look further for a more credible source.

### HOW DOES PLAGIARISM APPLY TO INTERNET SOURCES?

Online research is so convenient that you may be tempted simply to copy material from an Internet source and paste it intact within your document. However, unless your sources are properly documented, you will be plagiarizing. Whether you're working on a term paper or researching a business report, you should cite your source when you (1) quote word-for-word, (2) closely paraphrase, or (3) repeat a series of phrases from documents posted on the Internet. This includes news articles, books or excerpts, surveys, speeches, transcripts of online discussions, manuals, and any material on Web pages sponsored by individuals, corporations, schools, nonprofit groups, or government agencies. When in doubt, you can avoid even the hint of plagiarism by fully documenting your sources.

# Chapter Three

# Career Development on the Internet

Whether you're looking for a new job or want to explore an entirely new occupation, you can gather a great deal of information without leaving your keyboard. By launching your Web browser and moving onto the Internet, you will be able to search for career opportunities, find job openings in your chosen field, investigate potential employers, exchange ideas with other job seekers, and enlarge your circle of contacts.

Remember that changes on the Internet occur almost daily, so you are bound to find something new or different every time you log on. From career counseling centers to job-search newsgroups, virtual job fairs to commercial résumé databanks, more and more Internet options are becoming available to help bring employers and potential employees together.

This constant change also means that your favorite Web site may have new features or even a new location next time you go online. As a result, don't be surprised to find a slightly different look or perhaps a new address for the sites mentioned in this chapter.

## How to Research Careers and Employers

A good way to start your online job search is by researching various occupations and industries that sound appealing. This way, you can identify career paths that match your interests, see which have strong potential for future growth, and then focus your search accordingly.

To learn more about specific occupations, bookmark the latest edition of the *Occupational Outlook Handbook*, from the U.S. Department of Labor. This multi-faceted site describes a wide range of occupations, detailing each job's duties, training requirements, employment trends, and future prospects (**http://stats.bls.gov/ocohome.htm**). For the latest news about employment projections, earnings, and the effect of regional economic conditions, check the news releases posted online by the U.S. Bureau of Labor Statistics (**http://stats.bls.gov/newsrels.htm**).

Many state employment offices maintain Web sites bursting with comprehensive information about occupations, industries, wages, and many other topics. You can locate your state's job service site by launching Excite or another search tool and searching for "state employment service" or a similar phrase. Once you find your state's site, be sure to explore each hyperlink—you never know where these connections will lead you.

For example, the Career Resource Library on the New York State Department of Labor Web site (**http://www.labor.state.ny.us/html/library.htm)** contains a wealth of hyperlinks to state and regional employment trends and projections; national, statewide, and local wage rates; industry descriptions; and hyperlinks to dozens of other sites with tips on vital subjects such as résumé preparation, training and education, job applications, and interviewing (see Figure 3.1). Even job seekers outside New York will be interested in the general guidance available on this site.

Be sure to find out about your school's career services, which are often available online through the campus placement office. In addition, you may want to browse other university career counseling Web sites for more information about various occupations. Here are just two samples: The "Career Exploration Links" maintained by the University of California at Berkeley **(http://www.uhs.berkeley.edu/Students/Careerlibrary/links/careerme.htm**) and the "Exploring Occupations" page from the University of Manitoba

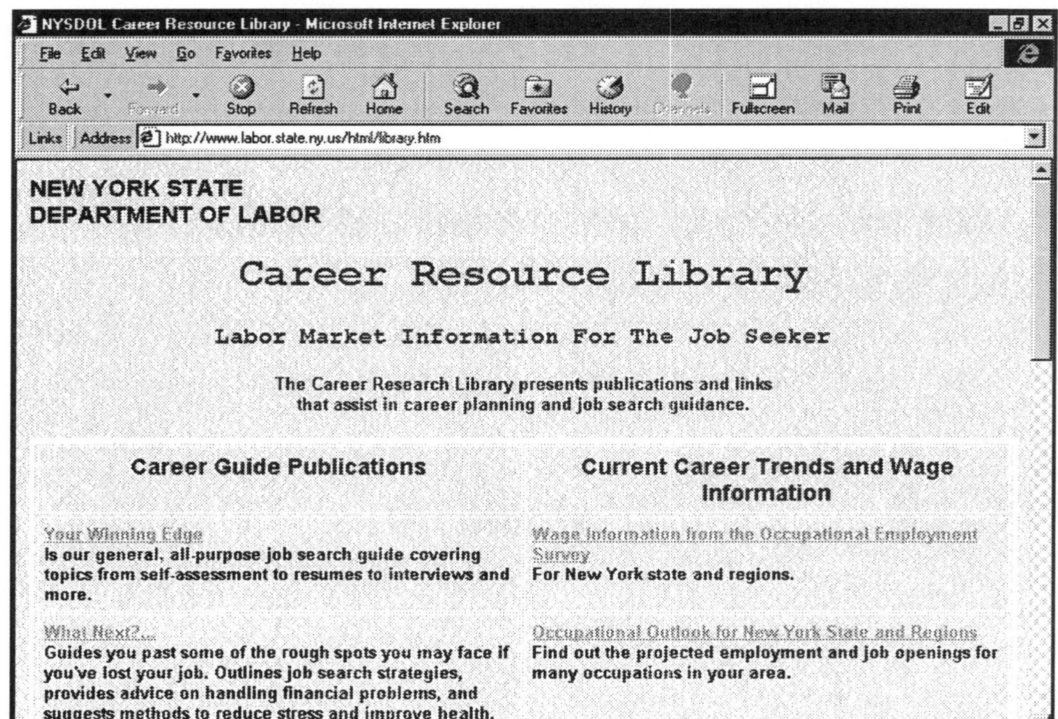


**FIGURE 3.1**

Check out the Career Resource Library at the Web site of the New York State Department of Labor

(**http://www.umanitoba.ca/counselling/careers.html**). Both offer hyperlinks to pages describing dozens of occupations.

Some of the major online services and search tools maintain special areas for job seekers. These areas generally feature career-planning advice, job postings, résumé preparation tips, and other useful information. You may also be able to join a job-search newsgroup, participate in an online chat about how to interview well, or read messages posted by others who are in the job market.

For instance, visit Yahoo's search site and go to its employment area, which is located under the business category (**http://www.yahoo.com/Business/Employment/**). On this page, you can scroll through a variety of help-wanted classified ads, follow links to popular employment Web sites, or drop into an interesting job-related online chat. Events and job openings change daily, so check back often.

Once you have narrowed your search to a particular occupation or industry, you can begin to study potential employers. If you know the names of companies in your targeted field, you can use an Internet search tool to locate their Web sites. Of course, these company sites are designed for promotion, so don't expect them to be objective sources of information. Still, you can get a good idea of what the company does, where it operates, and how it views its business situation.

Another way to locate company Web sites is through hyperlinks on the larger career Web sites such as Career-Index (**http://www.career-index.com**). In some cases, the hyperlink leads to the company's regular Web site. In other cases, the hyperlink leads to a special recruitment page. By reviewing the information on the recruitment page or company Web site, you will get a better idea of what each employer does and the kind of job opportunities it offers.

## How to Find Job Openings

More and more job openings are being posted on the Internet—and not just for high-tech occupations. As you investigate any potential employer's Web site, look carefully for a hyperlink to that company's listing of job vacancies. These hyperlinks may be labeled "career opportunities," "recruitment," or some similar title.

As you might expect, computer makers such as Dell (**http://www.dell.com**) and Internet-based businesses such as Amazon.com (**http://www.amazon.com**) routinely post job openings on their Web sites and invite submission of electronic résumés. But you will also find a wide range of other firms recruiting applicants directly from their Web sites. The retail chain J.C. Penney (**http://www.jcpenney.com/**) and the global household products manufacturer Unilever (**http://www.unilever.com**) are just two of many employers that promote job openings on their Web pages.

Another way to find job openings on the Web is to visit virtual career fairs, where employers and job seekers meet online. As in any career fair, you can find out more about participating employers, explore their immediate and anticipated job openings, submit your résumé for consideration, and (sometimes) have an initial cyberspace interview. Look for career fairs listed on larger career sites such as Monster.com (**http://www.monster.com**) and HotJobs.com (**http://www.hotjobs.com**) and on dedicated job-fair sites such as JobFairs.com (**http://www.jobfairs.com**).

Help-wanted classified ads and job databanks are available on a variety of Web sites. Best Jobs USA (**http://www.bestjobsusa.com**), a Web site maintained by *Employment Review* magazine, invites job seekers to search its listings of jobs by state or job category. You may also want to bookmark the Career Journal, maintained by the Wall Street Journal (**http://www.careerjournal.com**). Here you can search posted job openings by company, industry, job function, and location. If you choose, you can add your name to an e-mail list at this site so you will be alerted when new employers and new features become available.

Newspaper classified ads, a traditional source of leads for new jobs, are increasingly common on the Web. For example, if you live in the Boston area—or if you want to relocate there—you may want to search the Boston Globe's online employment classifieds (**http://bostonworks.boston.com/**). You can use InfoSeek or another search tool to locate the Web sites of newspapers in specific cities. In addition, hyperlinks to leading newspapers are available at US Newspaper Links.com (**http://www.usnewspaperlinks.com**) and at News Directory, which serves as a gateway to dozens of U.S. publications (**http://www.ecola.com/news/press/na/us/**).

Some sites compile listings of help-wanted ads drawn from dozens of newspapers. One good example is the CareerBuilder Web site (**http://www.careerbuilder.com**). This site lets you search more than 75 career sites for job openings. You can also sign up to receive e-mail messages when job openings fitting your specific requirements are posted.

If you want to post your résumé and invite prospective employers to find you, take time to investigate the growing number of résumé databanks available on the Internet. You can find listings of the largest databanks—as well as those that specialize in particular occupations—by checking career Web sites such as The Job Resource Center (**http://www.thejobresource.com**), which was started by students at Stanford University.

Employers that recruit online generally prefer to receive electronic résumés rather than the usual printed résumés. The next section shows how you can prepare your résumé for electronic submission to employers and databanks.

## How to Create an Electronic Résumé

Just as you are using your PC to search for employers and jobs via the Internet, a growing number of employers are using computers to store and search through all the résumés they receive from applicants. Instead of spending hours sifting through a mountain of cover letters and printed résumés, a manager can now enter a few key words or phrases to describe the required skills and qualifications for a particular job opening. In short order, the computer will bring up a listing of all the electronic résumés in the database that fit those exact specifications. Only applicants whose résumés are in the computer system will be considered for such job opportunities—which is why *you* need an electronic résumé.

If you have already created a résumé using a word-processing program, a few simple changes will get it into shape for submission to company computer systems and commercial résumé databanks. Start by opening the file containing your résumé, then saving it as a plain ASCII text file. Change the name, if you want, to distinguish this text-only version from the fully formatted version.

Roberto Cortez
5687 Crosswoods Drive
Falls Church, Virginia 22046
Home: (703) 987-0086 Office: (703) 549-6624
RCortez@silvernet.com

KEY WORDS

Financial executive, accounting management, international finance, financial analyst, accounting reports, financial audit, computerized accounting model, exchange rates, joint-venture agreements, budgets, billing, credit processing, online systems. MBA, fluent Spanish, fluent German, Excel, Access, Visual Basic, team player, willing to travel

OBJECTIVE

Accounting management position requiring a knowledge of international finance

EXPERIENCE

Staff Accountant/Financial Analyst, Inter-American Imports (Alexandria, Virginia)
March 1998 to Present

o Prepare accounting reports for wholesale giftware importer, annual sales of $15 million
o Audited financial transactions with suppliers in 12 Latin American countries
o Created a computerized model to adjust for fluctuations in currency exchange rates
o Negotiated joint-venture agreements with suppliers in Mexico and Colombia
o Implemented electronic funds transfer for vendor disbursements, improving cash flow and eliminating payables clerk position

Staff Accountant, Monsanto Agricultural Chemicals (Mexico City, Mexico)
October 1994 to March 1998

o Handled budgeting, billing and credit-processing functions for the Mexico City branch
o Audited travel/entertainment expenses for Monsanto's 30-member Latin American sales force
o Assisted in launching an online computer system to automate all accounting functions

EDUCATION

MBA with emphasis in international business, George Mason University (Fairfax, Virginia), 1990 to 1994
BBA, Accounting, University of Texas (Austin, Texas) 1986 to 1990

INTERCULTURAL AND TECHNICAL SKILLS

Fluent in Spanish and German
Traveled extensively in Latin America
Excel, Access, HTML, Visual Basic

An attractive and fully formatted hard copy of this document is available upon request.

**Figure 3.2.**

This résumé may serve as a good model for how to prepare an electronic résumé as you use the Web to find job opportunities.

Because text-only files cannot accommodate fancy fonts, be sure your résumé appears in one simple font and one font size. Remove any formatting such as boldface, underlining, and italics. Also remove justification, tables, rules, and columns. If you have tabs in your document, remove them and use the space bar to align your text. Then change every bullet to an asterisk or a lower-case letter o, as shown in Figure 3.2.

The first line of your résumé should contain only your full name. Type your street address, phone and fax numbers, and e-mail address on separate lines below your name. Next, count the number of characters in each line—and create a new line whenever the number of characters (including spaces) exceeds 65. This ensures that your electronic résumé will look neat when a potential employer brings it up on the screen.

Knowing that employers search their résumé databases according to key words, you should include a key word section near the top of your résumé. To do this, compile a list of nouns that describe your job-related skills and abilities. Some of these nouns may already be contained in your résumé, but you will also want to highlight them by positioning them in the key word section.

For example, depending on your work experience, you will want to include appropriate job titles (such as "supervisor" or "team leader") in the key word section. Similarly, if you have experience with a specialized area such as exchange rates, list the phrase "exchange rates" in your key word section. Be sure to highlight your full range of accomplishments, including such skills as fluency in other languages and any official certification courses you have completed.

Once you have completed work on your résumé, be sure to save it again as an ASCII plain text file. If you prepare separate electronic résumés for different employers or job openings, save those in separate ASCII files so you can easily access them when needed. To be sure that your electronic résumé looks good, copy and paste it into an e-mail message to yourself or to a friend. Once the e-mail message has been received, you will be able to spot and correct any formatting errors.

Remember that all the usual rules about writing a good résumé also apply to your electronic résumé: Showcase your strongest qualifications; summarize your work experience with an emphasis on results and achievements; mention relevant activities and talents; and use correct spelling and grammar. Above all, be honest. If you misrepresent your background, you may find yourself out of a job when your new employer finds out.

To get an idea of what other traditional and electronic résumés look like, you may want to browse the career sites, which often feature sample résumés. In addition, you can launch your news reader and access the newsgroup misc.jobs.resumes, where you will find many résumés posted.

Also seek out Web sites that offer general advice about résumés, both traditional and electronic. Among the many academic sites you can browse are the site sponsored by Purdue University (**http://owl.english.purdue.edu/handouts/pw/p_yresum.html**) and the site sponsored by the College of William & Mary (**http://www.wm.edu/csrv/career/**).

Information about electronic résumés is also available at the Riley Guide (**http://www.dbm.com/jobguide/eresume.html**) and at Monster.com (see Figure 3.3) (**http://content.monster.com/resume/**). Both of these sites offer many helpful resources for preparing electronic résumés.

Once you have polished your electronic résumé, should you submit it to one or more résumé databanks? Uploading your résumé to be included in a larger databank of résumés is not the same as sending your résumé to a single employer's résumé database. The employer is going to keep your résumé in its proprietary computer system, to be accessed only by company personnel who are searching for applicants to fill job openings. Commercial résumé databanks, however, are open to many employers, which raises several issues for you to consider.

Be aware that submitting your résumé to a commercial databank makes your private information available to many people. If you have security concerns about publicizing your home address and phone number, you may want to omit these details—or follow the advice of one expert, who recommends arranging for a post office box and answering service with a separate phone number to handle inquiries during the job-search period.

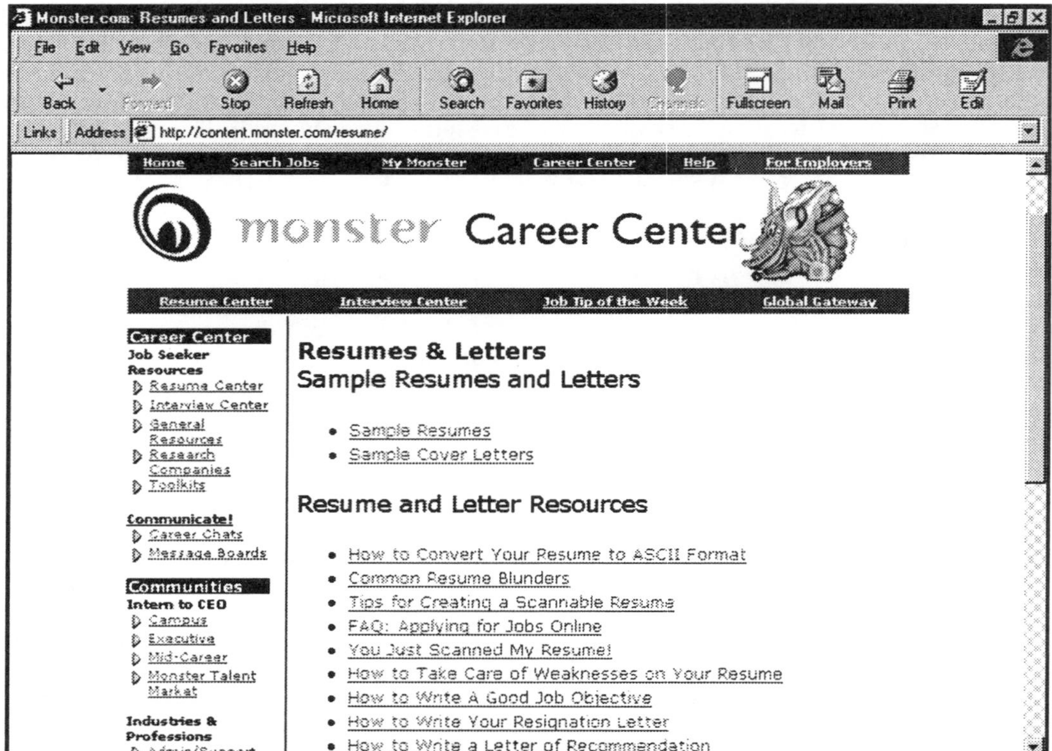


**FIGURE 3.3**



The Career Center at Monster.com offers many helpful tips on how to prepare an electronic résumé.

In addition, before you post your electronic résumé on any databank, find out who is allowed to access the résumés. Also ask whether you will be notified when an employer requests your résumé—and whether you can limit access to prevent specific organizations (such as your current employer) from requesting your résumé.

Another issue to consider is how often you are allowed to update your résumé, and whether you will be charged for doing so. At some point, you may need to correct a spelling error or add a new skill you have recently acquired. Find out whether updates are permitted and if you are expected to pay for updates. If so, continue looking until you find a suitable databank that permits free updates.

Finally, ask each commercial databank how often it removes résumés from its system. Employers want to see only up-to-date résumés, which is why some databanks get rid of older résumés after a certain number of months. So investigate the policy of any commercial databank before you submit your résumé—and, if necessary, plan to submit updated résumés at regular intervals throughout your job search.

Good luck!

## For Further Career Surfing

In addition to the career giants (Monster.com andHotJobs.com) here are some more career sites to check out.

### America's Job Bank http://www.ajb.dni.us/index.html

America's Job Bank (AJB) is operated jointly by the US Department of Labor and by 1,800 local employment Service offices across the US. The listing of jobs is large (more than 1.4 million jobs at last look) partly because this service provides employers with national exposure for their job listings. After searching by keywords, locations, or other options, you can get detailed descriptions of requirements, salaries, and instructions on how to apply.

### Career Magazine  http://www.careermag.com

This site has articles on a host of job hunting topics such as interviewing, networking, and preparing resumes. There are also news items as well as calendars for job fairs and campus recruiting. In addition to job search capabilities, this site offers an e-mail newsletter about career issues and informative columns on employment topics.

### CareerSite  http://www.careersite.com

Instead of posting résumés, job candidates can submit, free of charge, their education, skill sets, and qualifications to create anonymous profiles that can be searched by companies looking for job candidates. CareerSite notifies job-seekers when employers post openings in their fields. This system allows you to protect your privacy while finding out about suitable job openings.

### CareerJournal  http://www.careerjournal.com

Sponsored by the *Wall Street Journal*, CareerJournal is a great resource for career news and job-seeking advice, and to learn what companies are hiring for what jobs. Among the site's many features are "Career Columnists," which offers a variety of articles on career topics, and "Salaries and Hiring Info," which presents an in-depth review of hiring trends and salaries nationwide. You may also use the site to be notified through e-mail about new employers and new jobs posted.

### Catapult on JobWeb  http://www.jobWeb.org/catapult

Catapult describes itself as "the springboard to career- and job-related sites." Catapult has job listings, help guides and career library resources, cyberspace search tools, links to university career offices, college career fairs, job outlook trends, and more.

### College Grad Job Hunter  http://www.collegegrad.com

College Grad is a great place for juniors and seniors to get a start on life after college because it categorizes jobs as internships, entry-level positions, and experienced positions. Job seekers can learn about hiring companies, read up on salaries, and prepare for a job search. There are also pointers for interviews and negotiation techniques.

### JOBTRAK  http://www.jobtrak.com

JOBTRAK, owned by Monster.com, has teamed up with over 1,100 college and university career centers to offer a comprehensive suite of services to both job seekers and employers. Students at member schools obtain a password at their school's career services office and can search the extensive listing of job openings and even sign up for online interviews. Some pages don't require a password. For example, the section on job search tips contains a first-rate job search manual, complete with sample letters and résumés. JOBTRAK also provides a list of its top recruiters so that job seekers can easily obtain company profiles, a guide to applying to graduate schools, and an online resume-posting service.

### Quintessential Careers  http://www.quintcareers.com

This site serves as a career tool kit, with details on how to write cover letters and résumés, how to identify job opportunities through networking, and how to conduct a job search. Try taking one or more of the quizzes to test your knowledge of the job-search process.

### 200 Letters for Job Hunters
### http://www.careerlab.com/letters/link001.htm

Not sure what to put in that letter to a potential employer? Mailing job search letters and no one answers? Want help writing a "thanks for the interview" letter? If so, 200 Free Letters for Job Hunters is divided into two parts. In part one, you will learn the "dos and don'ts" of writing a great letter. There are 239 actual letter samples divided into 20 sections. From announcing job changes, to following up, to negotiating pay, there's a sample letter that will assist in your job hunt.

## Preparing for a Career in E-Business

Start planning your career in e-business (or any business) without leaving your keyboard. The links in this section will lead you to self-assessment tools and online resources for evaluating your interests, values, and competencies and understanding your career options.

Through these self-tests and resources, you'll get a better sense of your personality, values, and goals; see how conventional jobs relate to Internet jobs; gauge your interest in applying technology and other skills; see how your values affect your career goals; and dig into your leadership potential. You'll also find more details about e-business occupations, peek inside the Internet workplace, and hone your job-search techniques.

### Business Interests Quiz (on Fast Company Web site)
### http://www.careerdiscovery.com/fastcompany/

The "Find Your Calling" self-test, posted on the *Fast Company* magazine career pages, offers a series of questions about business-related interests, values, and abilities. These questions fall into eight general categories: using technology, working with numbers, developing theories, using creativity, counseling and mentoring, managing people, controlling resources, and influencing people through language and ideas.

Once you've clicked your way through the quiz and submitted your answers, you get back a ranking of your scores in each category, on a scale of 0 to 7 plus a brief explanation. You can use this self-assessment to gauge your interest in specific areas that apply to e-business careers, such as application of technology.

### Career Questionnaire (on College Board Online site)
### http://cbweb9p.collegeboard.org/career/bin/career.pl

Under the section titled "Has deciding on a career become a job?" this career questionnaire from the College Board features 34 questions about your abilities, interests, temperament, and work preferences. Unlike other self-tests, this one will work even if you don't answer every question.

Once you click to submit your answers, you will see a listing of careers that match your interests and preferences. Click on each career link to see a detailed description of that job's duties, future outlook, and working conditions.

### Preferred Activities Quiz (on MyFuture.com)
### http://myfuture.com/career/interest.html

This 60-question quiz, a sample drawn from a longer self-assessment test, helps you determine the kind of work life you might enjoy, based on your preferred activities. The quiz takes about two minutes, as you read the listing of activities and check off which you like.

Once you submit your answers, the quiz will match you with two of six potential work groups (Realistic, Investigative, Artistic, Social, Enterprising, or Conventional) and show you possible career paths for the two that fit your preferences. While you're on this site, try the personality test, which shows whether you're a Guardian, Artisan, Idealist, or Rational and identifies compatible careers for your type.

### Job Hunting Quiz (on Career Magazine site)
### http://www.careermag.com/jobhunt_iq.html

This 16-question true-false quiz, from *Career* magazine, is a fast and easy way to see whether you've fallen victim to the "three Ms" of job hunting: misinterpretation, misunderstandings, and myths. For example, is the Internet the leading job source in terms of numbers of new employees hired? (Check the quiz to find out.)

After you click to submit your answers, you'll be shown all the right answers. The site highlights your wrong answers so you can jump directly to those sections if you prefer.

### Jobs and Dot.com Jobs (on the Monster dot.com site)
### http://dotcom.monster.com/articles/jobconverter/ie.asp

If you've been researching a particular job outside e-commerce and wonder how that job might apply to the online work world, this is the site for you. Simply highlight the job category that best matches the conventional job you're interested in (or qualified for), and the Job Converter shows you the equivalent job title in e-business. Then you can go on to click on links for ideas about how and where to search for that e-business job.

In addition, click to the main page at **http://dotcom.monster.com/** for job leads and more information about finding and applying for e-business positions. And check the link to Job Seeker Resources at **http://content.monster.com/** to move through self-tests on the "Six Steps to a Better Career" feature.

### Career Key Quiz (on the North Carolina State University site)
### http://www.ncsu.edu/careerkey/

Dr. L. K. Jones developed the online Career Key quiz, which contains a series of questions about the kinds of jobs and tasks you prefer. Based on your answers, the site provides your score on six dimensions: realistic, investigative, artistic, social, enterprising, and conventional. After your scores appear, you can browse listings of occupations well suited to each dimension. Then you can follow links to more detailed descriptions of these jobs, found in the *Occupational Outlook Handbook*.

### Is Your Work Style More Efficient or More Effective? (from Priority Management site)
### http://www.prioritymanagement.com/quiz/efficient.cfm

This quiz's eight questions will help you evaluate your working style. Do you seek to be highly productive? Are you always looking for results? This brief self-test will describe and explain your working style.

### Career Profile Test (on the Princeton Review site)
### http://www.review.com/career/careerQuiz1.cfm?menuID=0&careers=0

The Birkman Method assess individual motivations, interests, styles, and stress behaviors to help fit the right person to the right job and the right work environment. On this site, you can click through a shortened version of the Birkman Method questionnaire by answering just 24 questions.

At the end, you'll see your score, read more about interest categories, and find a listing of suggested careers that fit your category. Then you can follow up on your own, by researching specific jobs in more detail.

### Personality Quiz (on the PersonalityType.com site)
### http://www.personalitytype.com/quiz.html

The compact quiz on this site, based on the Meyers-Briggs Type Indicator, briefly describes the four dimensions of personality and asks you to select among two alternatives for each dimension. Are you an Extravert or an Introvert? Are you a Sensor or an Intuitive? Are you a Thinker or a Feeler? Are you a Judger or a Perceiver?

Once you've made your selections, you'll see a description of your personality type, along with a listing of suggested careers to investigate. Use this test to consider how your personal preferences relate to different career choices.

### High-Tech Office Politics (from High Technology Careers Magazine site)
### http://www.hightechcareers.com/doc899/officepolitics899.html

Office politics are a fact of life in e-businesses as well as in any type of business. Use this self-test to see how politically savvy you are in work settings. After you answer the

15 questions, use the scoring key at the bottom of the page to measure your tendency toward playing office politics.

For extra credit, take a few moments to complete the suggested assignments at the bottom of the page. These will help you look at political activities from both sides and plot a more effective course in politics throughout your career.

## Additional Resources

Check these links for more information about e-business careers and online tools for career management:

**@Brint—Biz Tech Network page http://www.brint.com/jobs.htm**

Articles about information technology occupations, job responsibilities and salaries, required education, certification, advancement and more, plus multiple links to job and résumé sites.

**WetFeet.com http://www.wetfeet.com**

This site offers comprehensive resources for researching industries and companies, plus advice and ideas about interviewing, changing careers, preparing résumés, negotiating salary, and much more.

**ComputerWorld Careers page http://www.computerworld.com/**

Look for the careers link for career articles and a searchable database of jobs in information technology.

**High Technology Careers Magazine page http://www.hightechcareers.com/**

Articles about careers in computer technology, systems, and engineering, with tips about hottest employers, on-the-job strategies, Silicon Valley updates, and more.

**Monster campus page http://campus.monster.com/tools/virtual/**

Practice answering job-interview questions like "What do you do in your spare time?" on Monster's Virtual Interview self-test.

**Siliconvalley.com career page http://www.siliconvalley.com/career/**

Read the latest about jobs, employers, and salary trends in tech-heavy Silicon Valley.

**The Vault Internet/new media page http://www.vault.com**

Follow the link to the Internet/New Media page for the latest industry news, newsletters with job advice, a jobs message center, and listings of job openings.

**SummerJobs.com http://www.summerjobs.com**

Check this site for summer and seasonal jobs. You can search the job database, post your résumé, look at employer profiles, and sign up for an e-mail newsletter with the latest news about jobs and seasonal employment.

**JobTrak Academy http://static.jobtrak.com/academy/skills_students.html**

Detailed information on the basics of using the Internet in a job search, etiquette and ethical issues faced by job-seekers, interviewing techniques, and first-year job jitters.

**Emode.com Career Tests http://www.emode.com/emode/careertests.jsp**

An interesting, ever-changing assortment of timely career tests. One recent example: "Are You A Slacker?" Worth a look.

# Chapter Four

# Distance Learning on the Internet

## What is Distance Learning?

Imagine an educational system in which you can take a course, submit an assignment, even interact with your instructor and classmates without stepping into a real classroom—that's distance learning. As the name implies, students are physically separated from instructors (and often from each other) in a distance learning arrangement. The idea is to bring the learning to the student rather than bring the student to the learning, which provides more flexibility and more options for personal and professional growth.

As a student, you can participate in distance learning in a variety of ways. In some programs, you receive instruction and assignments via the Internet, using e-mail, audio streaming, video clips, group chats, or other techniques. In other programs, you watch your instructor on videotape, videoconference, or television. Your alternatives for distance learning will depend on the provider of the course you select.

Today, some form of distance learning is available at well over half of all four-year colleges and universities in the United States—and many offer degree programs entirely by Internet. For example, the Colorado Electronic Community College (**http://www.ccconline.org**) offers an Internet-only associate degree program. Similarly, the University of Phoenix (**http://www.phoenix.edu**) offers Internet-only undergraduate and graduate degrees. These types of programs allow students to use the Internet for almost everything, from ordering textbooks and filling out financial aid forms to downloading course materials and taking quizzes.

Distance learning is also becoming more popular at colleges and universities around the world, from the University of Leicester in the United Kingdom (**http://www.le.ac.uk/education/courses/distance.html**) to the School of Professional and Continuing Education at the University of Hong Kong (**http://www.hku.hk.space**).

Colleges are not the only sources of distance learning programs. Employers have begun to embrace distance learning in its many forms. As one example, the Tennessee Valley Authority offers career enrichment courses by videotape and by self-paced computer training, in addition to its traditional classroom courses. As another example, employees of GTE Corporation can attend educational videoconferences on personal finance as well as participate in job-related courses.

Professional organizations such as the Illinois Association of Realtors are also using distance learning on the Internet to provide continuing education training to their members. And distance learning is now being developed by companies such as Element K Training (**http://www.elementktraining.com**) as a profit-making venture.

Distance is no object when you are able to access learning materials via the Internet. Whether a course originates in another city, state, or country, all students receive the same lectures, assignments, and attention. As a result, a student in the United States can sign up for a consumer affairs diploma at Halesowen College in the United Kingdom (**http://www.halesowen.ac.uk**), while a student in California can log onto any course offered by Syracuse University Continuing Education OnLine in New York State (**http://www.suce.syr.edu/online/**).

Wherever you are, whatever you want to learn, you can probably find a distance learning course somewhere in the world to meet your needs.

## Advantages and Disadvantages

Distance learning on the Internet has many advantages. At the top of the list is the broad array of choices. You can earn a degree, obtain continuing education credits, sharpen your work skills, prepare for a new job or career, stay abreast of fast-changing technology, even master a new subject for personal enrichment—all without leaving your keyboard.

Easy access is another major advantage. As long as you have the right computer hardware and software as well as a connection to the Internet, you can be a distance learning student. Just log on to the course's Web site to download the latest lecture, or enter the designated chat room for a cyberspace exchange of ideas. If you have a laptop computer with modem, you can easily send in your course assignments from home, office, or almost anywhere.

Most of the time, distance learning on the Internet allows you to work at your own pace, an important advantage for people who are juggling school and work responsibilities and those whose schedules can change from day to day. Rather than having to be in the classroom at a particular time, distance learning students can usually access a Web site at any hour to read new assignments or e-mail the instructor with questions.

Distance learning on the Internet can save you money, though some undergraduate and graduate courses may be more costly than traditional classroom courses. Still, by using the Internet for distance learning, you completely avoid charges for room and board (or the cost of traveling to class), which can represent a significant savings.

Of course, distance learning on the Internet has disadvantages, as well. One key disadvantage is the lack of live interaction with the instructor and with classmates. If you thrive on classroom debate or prefer to have your questions answered immediately, you may not like having to type your comments or wait for an e-mailed response.

Some programs have addressed this issue by arranging for periodic desktop videoconferencing. Students and instructors place small video cameras on their computer monitors and speak into microphones to participate in group discussions during a desktop videoconference session. Students can see the instructor, the instructor can see the students, and everybody can hear every comment.

Of course, you must have an appropriately configured personal computer and an Internet connection to take an online course. To meet these needs, some schools are inviting their distance-learning students to use the computer facilities on campus or at regional satellite centers.

Overall, distance learning is best suited to students who are motivated to assume responsibility for their own learning. You must be willing to log onto the course Web site at regular intervals; download and review instructional materials; and post your questions or ask for additional help.

Remember, some courses require students to visit chat rooms for group discussions. Some courses mandate frequent or lengthy homework projects, while others expect students to read and comment on classmates' reports and projects. You have to be ready to invest sufficient time and effort to meet all these course requirements. You must also have the flexibility to deal with the occasional technical glitches that can crop up. Only you can decide whether distance learning is right for *you.*

## A Distance Learning Sampler

To supplement your search efforts, you may want to take a few minutes to browse the following Web sites, just a small sample of the many distance learning opportunities available on the Internet. Some of these sites contain hyperlinks to other programs or additional sources of information that can be useful as you expand your search.

### GENERAL INFORMATION

- Tips for success: how to get the most from any distance learning opportunity, from the College of DuPage, IL. **http://www.dupage.edu/excel.html**
- Browse distance-learning FAQs (frequently asked questions) and search 24,000 distance learning courses at e-learners.com. **http://elearners.com/**
- Check *Fortune's* e-learning pages for the latest developments in distance learning. **http://www.fortuneelearning.com/**

## ACADEMIC CREDIT

- The National Universities Degree Consortium Web site offers hyperlinks to 9 accredited universities that cooperatively offer distance learning courses for undergraduate and graduate degrees as well as certificate programs. Members include Kansas State University and Colorado State University. **http://www.nudc.org/**
- At the New Jersey Institute of Technology, students can complete bachelor's or master's degrees in computer science and information systems and 10 graduate certificates in their entirety via distance learning. A large number of undergraduate and graduate courses are also offered through distance learning. **http://www.njit.edu/DL/**
- Mindedge is a site that contains a comprehensive listing of distance learning courses and providers with brief descriptions plus hyperlinks to more detailed data. **http://www.mindedge.com**
- University of Minnesota offers undergraduate degrees using a variety of distance learning techniques, including Internet-based instruction. **http://www.cee.umn.edu/dis/**
- Ohio University Independent Study allows students to earn credit toward undergraduate degrees using various distance learning techniques, including e-mail. **http://www.cats.ohiou.edu/~indstu/index.htm**
- University of Phoenix offers numerous undergraduate and graduate courses (and continuing education courses); cyberstudents can earn a bachelor's or master's degree entirely through online study. **http://www.phoenix.edu**

## CAREER DEVELOPMENT

- Certificate programs in telecommunications are available through distance learning programs on the Internet from the University College of the University of Denver; students can also earn undergraduate and graduate degrees in a number of disciplines. **http://www.learning.du.edu/**
- The College for Financial Planning (see Figure 4.1) offers a range of paper-based, audiocassette, and Web-based courses to meet continuing education requirements and enhance professional proficiency. **http://www.fp.edu**.

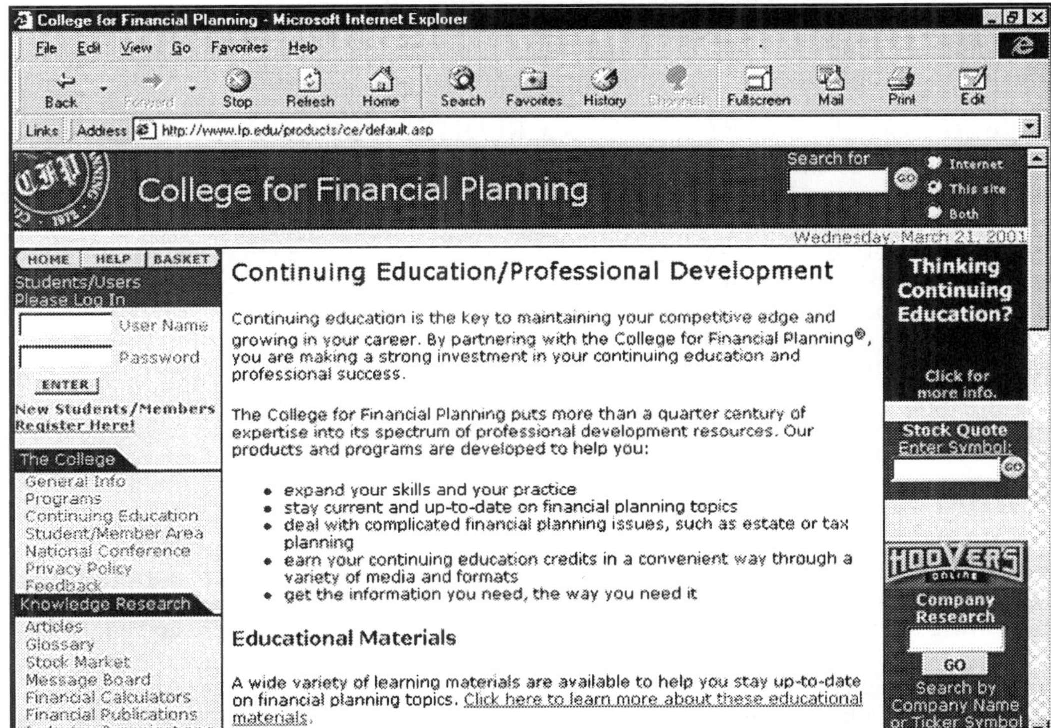


**FIGURE 4.1**
The College for Financial Planning is one of many organizations offering continuing education courses on the Internet.

- The Indiana University School of Continuing Studies offers online certificate programs, credit and noncredit courses in labor studies, workforce development, and other management subjects. **http://www.indiana.edu/~iude/**
- Professional certificates in accounting, business, and management are offered through the Internet by Champlain College Online in Vermont; associate and bachelor's degrees are also available. **http://www.champlain.edu/ccol/index.html**

### PERSONAL ENRICHMENT

- Syracuse University Continuing Education Online offers a variety of non-credit courses, including Investing and Trading on the Internet, Grant Writing, and Textile Ergonomics. **http://www.suce.syr.edu/online/**
- The WhaleNet educational Web site, from Wheelock College in Boston, has everything you want to know about whales and marine life—and more. **http://whale.wheelock.edu/**

## 10 Questions to Ask Before You Register

No matter what goal you want to achieve by taking a distance learning course, you should ask pointed questions before making any commitments. A little advance checking will help you determine the potential benefits and value of each course under consideration. Just as important, these questions will help you recognize potential problems, eliminate inappropriate courses, and narrow your options to identify the courses most suited to your particular needs and situation.

### 1. WHO IS OFFERING THE COURSE?

Find out about the institution, company, or organization offering the course. If the sponsor appears to be an educational institution, is it a real college or university (or a legitimate affiliate)? Names can be deceiving: what sounds like a prestigious university may actually be a front for a rip-off, so do some checking. Similarly, if a company or professional organization is sponsoring the course, you will want to investigate the sponsor's reputation and background before you sign a contract or send money.

The address of the Web site can often provide some clues: **.com** indicates a for-profit site, while **.edu** indicates an educational site. Also look for contact information such as the sponsor or institution's address, phone and fax numbers, affiliations, and other details.

### 2. IS THE COURSE PART OF AN ACCREDITED PROGRAM?

Accreditation is a critical issue for students seeking to earn a recognized degree. If a distance learning course is part of an unaccredited program, you may not be able to transfer the credits to an institution with an accredited program. If you are interested in pursing a degree entirely by distance learning and then continuing to study for even higher degrees, you should be sure that your diploma and coursework will be recognized by other institutions and by potential employers.

Legitimate educational institutions can provide solid information about their accreditation and refer you to the accrediting body for more details. Be especially careful about checking the accreditation of for-profit sponsors—and check on the accrediting body, as well. Accreditation is a complex topic, so you may want to talk with an administrator at a nearby college or university as an initial step.

### 3. WHAT IS THE TIME COMMITMENT?

This is actually a two-part question. First, find out about the time requirements for an individual course. How often must students "meet" for cyberspace discussions (if ever)? How many meetings are required over the entire course? How much time is allowed for submitting assignments? How long can you expect the entire course to last? Must you log on a certain number of times or devote a given amount of time to coursework in order to obtain credit?

Second, if you are planning to take distance learning courses to earn a degree, you will want to ask how many months or years students typically need to complete all their courses and qualify for graduation. In most cases, all courses are not offered year-round, which can slow you down if you are trying to earn a degree quickly. Some institutions schedule courses more frequently, to accommodate students who are in a hurry. In addition, some institutions have regulations regarding the length of time a student can take to complete a degree, so check before you enroll.

## 4. WHAT IS THE COST?

Ask about the tuition per course or per credit as well as any additional charges, such as registration or administration fees. Also ask about payment methods and schedules; nearly every school allows payment by major credit card, and some will accept payments in installments.

If textbooks or other learning materials must be purchased, take these into consideration when calculating the total cost of any distance learning course. Finally, consider the cost of dialing into the Internet to participate in the course.

## 5. WHAT IS THE CONTENT?

Is the course merely an introduction to a topic—or is it an in-depth examination? Is the focus primarily on theory or will you also learn tips for practical application? Is the course covering the latest advances in the field? To answer these questions, you may have to go beyond the course description shown on the screen or in the catalog. In some cases, you will have to contact the institution or sponsoring organization to get more details about the exact content of a particular course. Then ask yourself whether you are really interested in the course content—and whether the coverage will help you meet your goals.

## 6. WHAT ARE THE TEACHER'S CREDENTIALS?

Although some of what you learn in an online course will come from the text—and some from the comments and suggestions of other students—you will also want to look at your teacher's qualifications. How does the teacher's educational and/or work background fit with the course content? Has the teacher had much hands-on experience in applying what is being taught? How long has the teacher been teaching this or similar courses?

Many distance learning programs invite prospective students to read brief biographies of their faculty members. Before you sign up for a course, browse the Web site to read about the teachers so you can make an informed decision.

## 7. WHAT ARE THE ENTRANCE REQUIREMENTS OR PREREQUISITES?

As with traditional college or training programs, many distance learning programs impose entrance requirements or prerequisites. For example, some online master's or doctoral programs are open only to students with extensive work experience, just as some professional courses on the Internet are open only to those who have attained a particular standing or seniority in the industry.

Sometimes students cannot enroll in advanced courses unless they have taken lower-level courses as prerequisites. This is the case in many high-tech courses, where a basic knowledge of a particular programming language is generally required for admission. You should check on any requirements so you can plan to take courses in the appropriate order and at the appropriate point in your career.

## 8. HOW IS THE COURSE CONDUCTED?

Before you sign up, you will want to take time to find out how your course will be conducted. Internet-based courses are often presented via a combination of e-mail, chat, electronic slide shows, and audio- or video-enhanced materials—in addition to a printed text. Some online courses may require a non-Internet component as well (such as teleconferencing).

A few schools allow students to try a sample class or course in advance. For example, Champlain College Online offers a sample course on Vermont history. Students simply sign up (**http://www.champlain.edu/ccol/sample.htm**) and wait for e-mail instructions that explain how to log onto the system to access course materials.

As you investigate the way the course is conducted, also consider the communication between teachers and students. Are you expected to work individually or as part of a team of students to complete one or more class projects? How much e-mail interaction can you expect with the teacher? With other students? The answers to these questions will help you gauge whether a course fits your individual learning style and personal preferences.

## 9. WHAT EQUIPMENT IS REQUIRED?

At the very least, distance learning courses on the Internet require access to a properly configured personal computer with modem, Web browsing software, and a dial-up connection to the Internet. Individual courses may require additional software, such as a word processing program for writing reports or technical software for completing assignments.

You can usually learn about equipment requirements in advance by reading the course description or checking the school's Web site for more information. If all else fails, send an e-mail to the institution or sponsor to inquire about the necessary equipment.

## 10. WHAT ASSISTANCE IS AVAILABLE—AND WHEN?

In distance learning, students bear most of the responsibility for successful learning. However, there will be times when you decide to seek assistance. You may want guidance about courses; you may want help entering the Web site for a scheduled class "chat" session; or you may have some other problem or question. Some colleges and universities offer online assistance through self-guided tutorials or access to experts via e-mail. At Rogers University, for example, students can obtain academic and career counseling from student services at the school's Web site (**http://www.ruonline.edu**).

Be prepared: before you take any class, find out how and when you can obtain help. Although you may be eager to fix a problem at 2 a.m. so you can download an assignment right away, you may not be able to get help at that hour. So play it safe: ask for a name or department to contact and get a telephone number as well as an e-mail address in case you have an urgent request. You may even want to make a request to experience the help system first-hand before you register.

# Chapter Five

# E-Business, the Internet, and Your Finance Course

So what about e-business and the Internet applies to your finance course? We'll look first to some special e-business issues in finance, then turn to a wealth of Internet addresses that can get you to the information you want.

## E-Business Finance Issues

### FINANCING E-BUSINESSES

E-businesses can quickly burn through a mountain of money as they put up Web sites, hire employees, and pay for promotions to establish their brands and attract customers. So how do entrepreneurs fund their e-businesses?

Many Internet start-ups get money from *venture capitalists (VCs)*, investment specialists who provide funding for businesses (ventures) with high, rapid growth potential. For example, eBay (**http://www.ebay.com**), the first online auction site, received its early funding from Benchmark Capital (**http://www.benchmark.com**). Although eBay is one of Benchmark's big successes, not all of its investments provide good returns. Benchmark also backed Living.com, a furniture e-tailer that filed for bankruptcy protection just six months after becoming the exclusive vendor for Amazon.com's Home Living Store (Amazon was an investor, as well). The main problem: lack of additional funding. "Despite our employees' tremendous efforts and the loyalty of our customers, the recent downturn in capital markets has substantially impaired our ability to raise the capital required to achieve profitability," said CEO Shaun Holliday in announcing the shutdown, which idled 275 employees.

Once an e-business is operating, it may raise money by going public through an *initial public offering (IPO)*, selling shares of stock to the public for the first time. Through an IPO, eBay sold 3.5 million shares in 1998 to raise $63 million for aggressive expansion. Here's a closer look at VCs and IPOs.

### WORKING WITH VENTURE CAPITALISTS

Every source of funding carries a cost, including money from VCs. Although the details vary from deal to deal, VCs generally provide funding in exchange for an equity stake. If and when the e-business goes public or is acquired by another company, the VC's stake should appreciate in value. The payoff can be incredibly high. Crosspoint Venture Partners (**http://www.crosspointvc.com**) has returned $29.60 for every $1 invested in funding an Internet business.

A new twist is the *for-profit incubator*, which provides office space, business services, and management resources as well as funding, in exchange for an equity stake of as much as 50%. This set-up gives entrepreneurs more support in the early stages of business formation and growth and improves the e-business's chances of success. Idealab (**http://www.idealab.com**) is a for-profit incubator that has nurtured e-businesses such as CarsDirect (**http://www.carsdirect.com**), a car-shopping site, as well as failures such as eToys. Although CarsDirect has been struggling lately, Idealab stands to profit if and when the firm completes its planned IPO. However, the timing remains unclear as the entire category of online car retailing undergoes consolidation.

## USING THE INTERNET FOR IPOS

The Internet promises to bring major changes to e-business IPOs. Soon, the time-consuming blizzard of paperwork that accompanies traditional IPOs may be replaced by streamlined Web-based procedures for handling the necessary information disclosures and legal filings. Some innovators are already conducting IPO stock sales via the Web. W.R. Hambrecht, a San Francisco investment firm, has developed Open IPO, a Web-based process that allows individual investors to buy IPO stock online. Traditional IPOs attract huge purchases from a concentration of institutional investors, but the Open IPO broadens the investor base by targeting individual investors.

When Andover.Net (**http://www.andover.net/**) went IPO, it raised more than $82 million through Open IPO. Explains Bruce Twickler, Andover's president: "Our biggest asset is Slashdot, a community site, and we needed a vehicle that would allow those community members to have access to the IPO." In fact, strong demand allowed the firm to raise its *offering price*, the price to be paid by investors who receive IPO shares just before the stock starts to trade. Instead of a $15 share price, Andover increased the offering price to $18—raising an additional $9 million from the IPO proceeds. Andover operated as a publicly traded e-business for just two months before being acquired by VA Linux. VA Linux continues to grow revenues, but ongoing losses have forced it to lay off employees and control expenses.

### E-Business Case in Point: Niku ✓

Farzad Dibachi is a seasoned e-business entrepreneur. He sold his first e-business, Diba, to Sun Microsystems in 1997 and stayed on to work for Sun (**http://www.sun.com**) for a short time before starting Niku (**http://www.niku.com**), a multi-faceted e-business. One focus is creating Web-based software to allow consulting firms to automate their internal processes and customer billing. A second focus is iNiku.com, an online marketplace for the consulting industry. A third focus is an Internet job board. And a fourth focus is helping companies expand their internal networks—intranets—for access by partners, customers, and suppliers.

Initially, Dibachi funded Niku with some of his own money plus $60 million from private investors. Although the company still had millions in the bank by the end of 1999—available for acquisitions or operations—it had lost $29 million on 10-month sales of just $12.3 million. Facing competition from Hotjobs.com (**http://www.hotjobs.com)** and other rivals, Dibachi needed more money for growth. With Goldman Sachs as the lead investment bank, Dibachi planned an IPO to sell 8 million shares of common stock, at an offering price between $10 and $12 per share. Farzad Dibachi and his wife, both officers in the company, retained about 17% of the shares.

On February 29, 2000, the stock was scheduled to begin trading with an offering price of $24—raising $192 million for Niku. At the start, the stock sold at $64 per share, and it closed its first day of trading at $69. On the second day, the price zoomed to $100, where it hovered for several days before receding. During the second half of 2000, however, Niku traded close to $30. By early 2001, the stock was hovering below $10, despite new products and services, including plans for customers to access Niku's technology using wireless devices such as Palm Pilot personal digital assistants.

1. How did Niku benefit when its investment bank raised the offering price?
2. Why do you think Dibachi would take Niku public instead of seeking more funding from venture capitalists?

### E-Business Case in Point: eParties and eCompanies ✓

When eParties opened for business in December, 1999, launched by the eCompanies (**http://www.ecompanies.com**) incubator, it was designed as a complete online party store and planning center. Customers could simply sign on, plan their guest lists, and buy hats, plates, invitations, and everything else for birthday bashes and other parties. Within six months, however, eParties fired all its employees and was taken over by online toy retailer eToys. Yet eToys, a company assisted by incubator idealab! (**http://www.idealab.com**) also ran into difficulty and filed for bankruptcy in March, 2001—after selling its BabyCenter unit to Johnson & Johnson for $10 million.

What happened? As the online business environment becomes increasingly competitive, weaker firms are being forced out of business or are having to arrange mergers to gain the strength to continue. Timing is also important. Online rivals such as iparty (**http://www.iparty.com/**) opened for business well ahead of eParties, so they were already established when the newcomer joined the party. In addition, profitability plays a critical role. As eParties learned, the profit margins on party goods are relatively slender. In the end, although incubators such as eCompanies and idealab! can provide valuable support in the form of funding, office space, and other assistance, e-businesses must attract loyal customers and build strong, steady sales to stay alive.

1. Why would an established company such as Johnson & Johnson buy an online business such as eToys' BabyCenter?
2. If you were running an incubator, what characteristics would you look for when screening potential e-businesses?

### E-Business Case in Point: Icebox.com 

Once VC investors fund an e-business, they closely monitor its progress and prospects. Sometimes they put pressure on a company to make changes that will affect financial performance, as Icebox.com has learned. Icebox.com, which develops Web-based creative animated shows, came online in June 2000. Within a few months, both Showtime Networks and Fox Broadcasting had licensed Icebox.com shows as the basis of live-action television comedies. Despite continued interest in its shows, however, Icebox.com recently laid off half of its 100 employees in a bid to achieve profitability more quickly.

> "We're being forced by our investors to take a very rational look at the business and do the things that were the right thing to do — and we've known were the right things to do — for five months, but didn't want to," said CEO Steve Stanford. "We need to be able to do shows a lot less expensively than we've done in the past." Now the company is outsourcing much of its production operations, and it will ask some of the laid-off employees to work as freelancers on selected projects. Stanford says Icebox.com is aiming to be profitable by the end of 2001, which should be good news to the eCompanies incubator and other investors.

1. For what length of time do you think a VC investor or incubator should wait to see results before insisting that an e-business cut costs to move toward profitability?
2. How does its faster movement toward profitability affect Icebox.com's options in raising additional capital?

## Using the Internet in Your Finance Course

Let's turn now to Internet sites that focus on finance topics. An incredible amount of financial information is available on the Internet, which you can use in your Finance class and in making important personal and business decisions. This chapter presents many Internet addresses of finance-oriented Web sites. Each site we present offers at least some of its content free of charge. Some of these sites are broad in their coverage, while others are quite focused. Whenever you find a useful site that you plan to revisit, be sure to bookmark it.

*Remember: The Internet is dynamic, and Web sites often change or even cease to exist. The sites we have selected were accurate when we wrote this guide.*

## FINANCE DIRECTORIES

We begin with a listing of sites that provide a broad spectrum of Finance-related information. The addresses listed in this section include Internet directories and search engines, the Web sites of the major news media, the Web sites of business publications, and directories of financial information maintained by academic institutions and individuals. These sites are great places to begin your exploration.

***INTERNET DIRECTORIES AND SEARCH ENGINES.*** Internet directories and search engines generally have a specific subcategory related to Business and/or Finance. Use these sites to search for information, or visit their Business and Finance subcategories for a comprehensive listing of Finance resources.

| | |
|---|---|
| AltaVista | http://www.altavista.com/ |
| AOL Anywhere | http://search.aol.com/ |
| Excite | http://www.excite.com/ |
| Go Network | http://www.go.com/ |
| HotBot | http://hotbot.lycos.com/ |
| LookSmart | http://www.looksmart.com/ |
| Lycos | http://www.lycos.com/ |
| MetaCrawler | http://www.metacrawler.com/ |
| Netscape Netcenter | http://home.netscape.com/ |
| WebCrawler | http://www.webcrawler.com/ |

***CURRENT NATIONAL AND INTERNATIONAL NEWS.*** The television networks, newspapers, and news magazines typically have a section of their Web sites devoted to Finance news and information.

| | |
|---|---|
| ABC News Online | http://abcnews.go.com/ |
| CBS News | http://www.cbs.com/ |
| CNN Interactive | http://www.cnn.com/ |
| MSNBC | http://www.msnbc.com/news/default.asp |
| New York Times | http://www.nytimes.com/ |
| Newsweek | http://www.newsweek.com/ |
| TIME | http://www.time.com/ |
| USA Today | http://www.usatoday.com/ |
| U.S. News | http://www.usnews.com/ |
| Washington Post | http://www.washingtonpost.com/ |

***CURRENT BUSINESS NEWS.*** The following addresses are the Web sites of Business and Finance publications and news media. Many of these sites provide current business news and market statistics.

| | |
|---|---|
| Bloomberg | http://www.bloomberg.com/ |
| Business Week | http://www.businessweek.com/ |
| CNBC | http://www.cnbc.com/ |
| CNBC Business & The Wall Street Journal | http://www.msnbc.com/news/COM_Front.asp |

| | |
|---|---|
| CNNfn | http://www.cnnfn.com/ |
| Financial Times | http://www.ft.com/ |
| Forbes | http://www.forbes.com/ |
| Fortune | http://www.fortune.com/ |
| Money | http://www.money.com/ |
| Reuters MoneyNet | http://www.moneynet.com/ |
| The Wall Street Journal | http://www.wsj.com/ |

***DIRECTORIES MAINTAINED BY ACADEMIC INSTITUTIONS AND INDIVIDUALS.*** These sites, maintained by universities, Finance departments, and individuals, are great places to begin your search for information to use in your Finance class. Be sure to check out the Financial Data Finder.

| | |
|---|---|
| Financial Data Finder | http://fisher.osu.edu/fin/overview.htm |
| FINWeb Home Page | http://www.finweb.com/ |
| Nijenrode Business Information Services | http://www.library.nijenrode.nl/ |
| OSU Virtual Finance Library | http://fisher.osu.edu/fin/overview.htm |
| The Scout Report for Business and Economics | http://scout.cs.wisc.edu/report/bus-econ/current/index.html |
| Wachowicz's Web World | http://web.utk.edu/~jwachowi/wacho_world.html |

## YOUR TURN

Visit several of the sites listed in the Current Business News section. What's the Dow Jones Industrial Average today? What's the current stock price for a company that you follow or that you live near? What current news articles related to the company can you find?

## FINANCE TOPICS

This section categorizes Web sites according to several important topics in Finance. Remember, though, that the more general sites listed in the previous sections are also important sources of information for these areas.

***CORPORATE FINANCE.*** Important sources of information related to Corporate Finance include the EDGAR database, maintained by the Securities and Exchange Commission (SEC), and the Annual Report Gallery. The EDGAR database provides the filings that public corporations make with the SEC, including their 10K's and 10Q's. In addition, many companies make their annual reports available on the Web, which you can get to through the Annual Report Gallery.

| | |
|---|---|
| Annual Report Gallery | http://www.reportgallery.com/ |
| The Corporate Finance Network | http://www.corpfinet.com/ |
| Corporate Financials Online | http://www.cfonews.com/ |
| EDGAR | http://www.sec.gov/edgarhp.htm |
| FreeEDGAR | http://www.freeedgar.com/ |

***INVESTMENTS.*** Stock prices, bond prices, futures prices, option prices, earnings reports, analysts' opinions, information on initial public offerings (IPOs), credit ratings, trading statistics, and up-to-the-minute business news are all available on the Web. Check out the following sites if you're interested.

## Investment Information

| | |
|---|---|
| BigCharts | http://www.bigcharts.com/ |
| Bonds Online | http://www.bonds-online.com/ |
| Briefing.com | http://www.briefing.com/ |
| Quicken.com | http://www.quicken.com/ |
| Finance.Wat.ch | http://finance.wat.ch/ |
| Futures Online | http://www.futuresmag.com/ |
| Hoover's Online | http://www.hoovers.com/ |
| Inter@ctive Investor | http://www.zdii.com/ |
| INVESTools Homepage | http://www.investools.com/ |
| IPO Central | http://www.hoovers.com/ipo/ 0,1334,23,00.html |
| Morningstar | http://www.morningstar.net/home.html |
| The Motley Fool | http://www.fool.com/ |
| PC Quote Online | http://www.pcquote.com/ |
| PitNews Magazine | http://www.pitnews.com/ |
| Red Herring Investor Center | http://investor.redherring.com/ |
| Silicon Investor | http://www.siliconinvestor.com/ |
| Standard & Poor's Ratings Services | http://www.standardandpoors.com/ ratings |
| Stockpoint | http://www.stockpoint.com/ |
| Technical Analysis of Stocks & Commodities Magazine | http://traders.com/ |
| Yahoo! Finance | http://finance.yahoo.com/ |
| Zacks Investment Research, Inc. | http://my.zacks.com/ |

## Online Brokerages

| | |
|---|---|
| Ameritrade | http://www.ameritrade.com/ |
| CSFB Direct | http://www.csfbdirect.com/ |
| Datek Online | http://www.datek.com/ |
| E*Trade | http://www.etrade.com/ |
| Quick and Reilly | http://www.quickandreilly.com/ |
| Charles Schwab | http://www.schwab.com/ |

### YOUR TURN

Visit **http://www.bigcharts.com/** and chart the stock price for a company that you follow. How has the stock performed over the past year? Do analysts recommend buying, holding, or selling the stock?

***FINANCIAL INSTITUTIONS AND MARKETS.*** The major securities exchanges, financial institutions, and their regulators all maintain sites on the Web. Many of these sites provide extensive information regarding their operations, history, regulation, and the role they play in the economy.

## Securities Exchanges

| | |
|---|---|
| The Chicago Board of Trade | http://www.cbot.com/ |
| The Chicago Board Options Exchange | http://www.cboe.com/ |
| The Chicago Mercantile Exchange | http://www.cme.com/ |
| Chicago Stock Exchange | http://www.chicagostockex.com/ |
| Nasdaq AMEX | http://www.nasdaq.com/ |
| The New York Board of Trade | http://www.nybot.com/ |
| The New York Mercantile Exchange | http://www.nymex.com/ |
| The New York Stock Exchange | http://www.nyse.com/ |
| Pacific Exchange - Stock & Options | http://www.pacificex.com/ |
| Philadelphia Stock Exchange | http://www.phlx.com/ |

### YOUR TURN

The traders on the floor of the futures exchanges communicate through the use of hand signals. Visit **http://www.cme.com/educational/hand1.htm** for a description of the hand signals used on the floor of the Chicago Mercantile Exchange.

## Financial Institutions

| | |
|---|---|
| Bank of America | http://www.bofa.com/ |
| Chase | http://www.chase.com/ |
| Citibank | http://www.citibank.com/ |
| Credit Suisse First Boston | http://www.csfb.com/ |
| Morgan Stanley Dean Witter | http://www.deanwitter.com/ |
| Fidelity Investments | http://www100.fidelity.com/ |
| First Union | http://www.firstunion.com/ |
| Goldman Sachs | http://www.goldmansachs.com/ |
| JP Morgan | http://www.jpmorgan.com/ |
| Merrill Lynch | http://www.ml.com/ |
| MyBank Directory | http://www.mybank.com/ |
| Salomon Smith Barney | http://www.salomonsmithbarney.com/ |
| Vanguard | http://www.vanguard.com/ |

## Regulators and Government Institutions

| | |
|---|---|
| The Federal Reserve Board | http://www.federalreserve.gov/ |
| FASB | http://accounting.rutgers.edu/raw/fasb/ |
| Federal Deposit Insurance Corporation | http://www.fdic.gov/ |
| Federal Reserve Banks | http://www.federalreserve.gov/FRAddress.htm |
| NASD Regulation | http://www.nasdr.com/ |

| | |
|---|---|
| Office of the Comptroller of the Currency | http://www.occ.treas.gov/ |
| Securities and Exchange Commission | http://www.sec.gov/ |
| U.S. Treasury Department | http://www.ustreas.gov/ |

***REAL ESTATE.*** You can easily find mortgage information, real estate prices, and real estate market information on the Web. Most real estate agencies also maintain a Web presence.

| | |
|---|---|
| Better Homes and Gardens/GMAC Real Estate | http://www.gmacrealestate.com/ |
| Century 21 | http://www.century21.com/ |
| Coldwell Banker Online | http://www.coldwellbanker.com/ |
| The Money Page - Real Estate | http://www.moneypage.com/real%20estate/ |
| Mortgage Market Information Services, Inc. | http://www.interest.com/ |
| Prudential Real Estate | http://www.prudential.com/realestate/ |
| Quicken.com Home & Mortgage | http://www.quicken.com/mortgage/ |
| Today's Mortgage Information from HSH Associates | http://www.hsh.com/ |
| Yahoo! – Business and Economy: Companies: Real Estate | http://dir.yahoo.com/Business_and_Economy/Real_Estate |

## YOUR TURN

What is the lowest interest rate available on a 30 year fixed rate mortgage? What does it mean to pay points on a mortgage?

***INSURANCE.*** Information on insurance products and companies is readily available on the Web. Use the following links to enhance your knowledge of the insurance industry.

| | |
|---|---|
| Allstate Insurance Company | http://www.allstate.com/ |
| A.M. Best Company | http://www.ambest.com/ |
| CNA | http://www.cna.com/ |
| Insurance News Network | http://www.insure.com/ |
| Insurance Quote Service | http://www.iquote.com/ |
| John Hancock | http://www.jhancock.com/ |
| MetLife Online | http://www.metlife.com/ |
| Prudential | http://www.prudential.com/ |
| Quicken.com Insurance | http://www.quicken.com/insurance/ |
| State Farm Insurance | http://www.statefarm.com/ |
| Travelers Insurance Online | http://www.travelerspc.com/ |

***INTERNATIONAL FINANCE.*** Today, financial markets around the world are becoming integrated as never before. Corporations are seeking foreign sources of capital, financial institutions are following their clients overseas, and investors are looking to invest in emerging markets. To find what you need to know about International Finance, try these sites.

| | |
|---|---|
| Asia Inc. Online | http://www.asia-inc.com/ |
| Central Banks of the World | http://patriot.net/~bernkopf/ |
| The Economist | http://www.economist.com/ |
| Euronext | http://www.euronext.com/en/ |
| Europa | http://www.europa.eu.int/ |
| Export-Import Bank | http://www.exim.gov/ |
| Financial Times | http://www.ft.com/ |
| FRB: Foreign Central Banks | http://www.federalreserve.gov/centralbanks.htm |
| Hong Kong Exchanges | http://www.hkex.com.hk/ |
| International Monetary Fund | http://www.imf.org/ |
| Korea Stock Exchange | http://www.kse.or.kr/ |
| London International Financial Futures & Options Exchange | http://www.liffe.com/ |
| London Stock Exchange | http://www.londonstockex.co.uk/ |
| Montreal Exchange | http://www.me.org/ |
| Osaka Securities Exchange | http://www.ose.or.jp/ |
| Russia Today | http://www.russiatoday.com/ |
| Sydney Futures Exchange | http://www.sfe.com.au/ |
| Tokyo International Financial Futures Exchange | http://www.tiffe.or.jp/ |
| Tokyo Stock Exchange | http://www.tse.or.jp/ |
| Toronto Stock Exchange | http://www.tse.com/ |
| The World Bank Group | http://www.worldbank.org/ |
| Yahoo! - Stock Exchanges | http://www.yahoo.com/Business_and_Economy/Finance_and_Investment/Exchanges/Stock_Exchanges/ |

## EDUCATIONAL INFORMATION

Information ranging from tutorials for beginners to detailed information for professional investors is available on the Web. You will also find online trading simulations, historical information, and "fun facts" and trivia. Be sure to try one of the trading simulations. After all, it is only play money.

| | |
|---|---|
| Learning to Invest (NASD) | http://www.investor.nasd.com/learn.default.html |
| CBOE – The Basics | http://www.cboe.com/education/ |
| CME Education Center | http://www.cme.com/educational/center/ |

| | |
|---|---|
| EduStock | http://library.thinkquest.org/3088/ |
| Facts & Trivia about the BEP | http://www.moneyfactory.com/facts.cfm |
| FDIC Learning Bank | http://www.fdic.gov/about/learn/learning/index.html |
| Fun Facts about the U.S. Mint | http://www.usmint.gov/about_the_mint/index.cfm?action=fun_facts |
| The Investor's Primer (CBS Marketwatch) | http://cbs.marketwatch.com/news/primer/default.htx? |
| Education, Planning, and Advice (Vanguard) | http://www.vanguard.com/educ/inveduc.html |
| Museum of American Financial History | http://www.financialhistory.org/ |
| Nasdaq Investor Services | http://www.nasdaq-amex.com/services/services.stm |
| The Collegiate Investment Challenge | http://www.ichallenge.net/prenticehall/ |
| Treasury Educational Links | http://www.ustreas.gov/education.html |
| Investor Information (SEC) | http://www.sec.gov/investor.shtml |

### YOUR TURN

See if you can find the answers to the following trivia questions.

- What happened under a buttonwood tree in New York on May 17, 1792?
- What make and model are the cars on the back of a $10 bill?
- Was a three-dollar bill ever used as currency in the U.S.?

## Careers in Finance

So you want a job in Finance? The Web sites in this section describe careers in Finance, present job listings, and offer information on graduate programs. The major securities exchanges listed earlier in this chapter also provide career information. Be sure to visit The Wall Street Journal's excellent site.

| | |
|---|---|
| 4Work.com | http://www.4work.com/ |
| America's Job Bank | http://www.ajb.dni.us/ |
| BLS News Releases | http://stats.bls.gov/newsrels.htm |
| Careers in Business | http://www.careers-in-business.com/ |
| CareerWeb | http://www.cweb.com/ |
| DFN.com Career Information | http://www.dfin.com/dfcareer.htm |
| Internet Career Connection | http://www.iccweb.com/ |
| Jobs.com | http://www.jobs.com/ |
| JOBTRAK | http://www.jobtrak.com/ |
| MBAinfo | http://www.mbainfo.com/ |
| The MBA Scene | http://www.voxcap.com/anon/c214/cover.dhtml |
| The Monster Board | http://www.monster.com/ |

| | |
|---|---|
| Occupational Outlook Handbook | http://stats.bls.gov/ocohome.htm |
| Wall Street Journal - CareerJournal | http://www.careerjournal.com/ |
| What Color is Your Parachute | http://www.jobhuntersbible.com |

### YOUR TURN

Conduct a job search for the Finance career that interests you. Or, if you haven't narrowed your focus yet, search around to determine just what careers are available in Finance. Try to answer the following questions as you conduct your search.

What kind of salary does your chosen career offer? Where are most of the positions in your chosen career located geographically? What are the job requirements? Is a master's degree or an MBA essential?

## The Internet as a Finance Learning Tool

Now that you have an understanding of the breadth of information available on the Internet and know how to locate it, let's see how you can use it. The following assignment illustrates how a Finance professional can use Internet information to solve a business problem.

### YOUR ASSIGNMENT

Let's say that your boss has asked you to investigate three firms within a particular industry as potential acquisition candidates. (If your instructor doesn't assign the particular industry or three specific firms, choose an industry that interests you and pick the three firms yourself.) You are instructed to perform a financial analysis to determine each firm's strengths and weaknesses and to decide which firm, if any, should be acquired. In conducting your analysis, try to accomplish the following:

- Assess the firms' short-term solvency and liquidity, asset management, financial leverage, and profitability.
- Compare their P/E and market-to-book ratios. Identify the average levels of these ratios for the firms' industry.
- Analyze their cash flow. Determine the activities that are generating cash and those that are consuming cash.
- Determine if the firms have made any significant changes in their accounting policies.
- Identify the recent trends in the firms' stock prices.
- Search for recent news and press releases concerning the companies' business activities.
- Assess the conditions in the firms' industry. Determine the growth prospects for the firms and their industry.
- Identify any significant risks the firms may be facing.
- Identify the opinions of other analysts.

### GATHERING THE DATA

Obtain the firms' annual reports (or 10K's) and other public filings from the Annual Report Gallery and the EDGAR database. Search the business news sources listed in this chapter for press releases and current news regarding the firms. Visit Web sites such as Hoover's Online, BigCharts.com, and Briefing.com to obtain analysts' opinions, earnings estimates, price quotes, charts, and so on.

Which of the three firms you have looked into is the best candidate for acquisition? Why?

# Glossary

**advanced planning and scheduling (APS) system**—a computerized system that helps businesses evaluate varying input levels to plan for optimum production efficiency

**application service provider (ASP)**—a business that rents application software via the Internet (or via telecommunications networks) in exchange for usage or monthly fees

**auction pricing**—pricing method in which buyers bid against each other and the highest bidder buys the product

**B2B**—business-to-business transactions

**B2B (business-to-business) online markets**—Web sites that facilitate the exchange of goods and services among organizational buyers and sellers

**B2C**—business-to-consumer transactions

**B2G**—business-to-government transactions

**C2B**—consumer-to-business transactions

**C2C**—consumer-to-consumer transactions

**C2G**—consumer-to-government transactions

**cashless society**—world in which plastic or other cashless payment alternatives replace currency

**cookies**—stored information placed on consumers' hard drives to track their Internet usage

**corporate portal**—a comprehensive internal Web site with company information that employees can personalize and access as needed

**cybersmear**—electronic message that libels a person or company

**cybersquatting**—the practice of claiming a domain name with the intention of reselling it at a profit

**dynamic pricing**—method of pricing in which prices change from transaction to transaction

**e-business**—the combination of business processes, technology, and organizational structure needed for e-commerce

**e-commerce**—exchange transactions (such as buying and selling goods, services, and information) that take place on the Internet

**e-procurement**—purchasing via the Internet

**e-tailers**—Internet retailers

**electronic barter (e-barter)**—an electronic system of barter

**electronic cash (e-cash)**—an electronic cash substitute

**enterprise resource planning (ERP) systems**—sophisticated computer systems that allow comprehensive planning and control of operations throughout the supply chain

**extranet**—a private computer network available to authorized users outside the organization

**for-profit incubator**—a business that provides entrepreneurs with office space, business services, and management resources as well as funding, in exchange for an equity stake

**G2B**—government-to-business transactions

**G2C**—government-to-consumer transactions

**G2G**—government-to-government transactions

**group buying**—pricing method in which the price goes down as more buyers band together to buy an item

**initial public offering (IPO)**—the process a company follows to sell stock to the public for the first time

**Internet telephony**—the transmission of telephone voice conversations via the Internet

**intranet**—an organization's internal computer network based on Internet technology

**legacy business**—a traditional, non-Internet business unit

**marketspace**—an electronic marketplace
**monopsony**—a market consisting of one buyer and many sellers
**name-your-price strategy**—pricing strategy in which buyers state how much they will pay and suppliers decide whether to sell at that price
**new economy**—the economy consisting of businesses that generate all or some of their revenues from the Internet or related goods and services
**nexus**—a physical presence, such as a store, used in determining the tax status of a sales transaction
**offering price**—the price paid by investors who receive an allocation of IPO shares just before the stock starts to trade
**online catalogue**—a Web-based presentation of product information similar to a printed catalogue
**open text search**—a search technique in which someone enters a word or group of words for the search engine to use in scanning the Internet
**opt in**—asking to join an e-mail subscriber list
**opt out**—asking to be removed from an e-mail subscriber list
**profiling**—tracking consumers' online activities and using the data to create a profile of each person's interests
**spam**—unsolicited e-mail messages, also called *junk e-mail*
**spammer**—someone who sends junk e-mail without the audience's consent
**subject tree**—an online catalog of a great number of pages on the Web, organized by categories and sub-categories
**venture capitalists (VCs)**—investment specialists who provide funding for businesses (ventures) with high, rapid growth potential
**viral marketing**—the use of e-mail messages that encourage recipients to send the message to others
**virtual organization**—an organizational structure in which people (employees and, sometimes, non-employees) in different locations use communication technology to work together
**virtual teams**—teams that use technology to link members in different places
**virtual team leader**—person who coordinates the activities of virtual team members

# Sources

## Sources for Chapter 1 Introduction:

"Retail E-Commerce Sales In Fourth Quarter 2000 Were $8.7 Billion, Up 67.1 Percent From Fourth Quarter 1999, Census Bureau Reports," *U.S. Department of Commerce News,* February 16, 2001, **http://www.esa.doc.gov**; "DoCoMo First-Half Profit Rises 22% on I-Mode Growth," *Ringtones News,* November 26, 2000, **http://www.cellular.co.za/news_2000/news-11262000_docomo_profits.htm**; Robert D. Hof, "Shoppers: Take Charge," *Business Week,* May 15, 2000, EB 130; Irene M. Kunii, "Architects: Keiichi Enoki, DoCoMo," *Business Week,* May 15, 2000, EB 44; Virginie Robert, "Who Will Be the Amazons of Europe?" *Connectis,* February 25, 2000, **http://www.ft.com**; "Define and Sell," *The Economist,* February 26, 2000, E-Commerce sec., 6, 11-15; "Something Old, Something New," *The Economist,* February 26, 2000, E-Commerce sec., 15-24; "I-Modest Success," *The Economist,* March 11, 2000, 69-70; Keith Perine, "Making City Hall Obsolete," *The Standard.com,* March 13, 2000, **http://www.thestandard.com**; Robert Conlin, "European E-Commerce Poised For Boom," *E-Commerce Times,* March 28, 2000, **http://www.ecommercetimes.com/ news/articles2000/000328-7.shtml**; "Internet Economics: A Thinkers' Guide," *The Economist,* April 1, 2000, 64-66; "E-Mail Continues To Take Over the World," *Internet.com,* April 4, 2000, **http://www.cyberatlas.internet.com**; "New Study Finds Many E-Retailers Won't Last," *News-Times (Danbury, CT),* April 13, 2000, A14; Jon Caramanica, "The C2G Portal Play," *Wired,* April 2000, 86; "Efficiency.Gov," *Business 2.0,* April 2000, 56; Efraim Turban, Jae Lee, David King, and H. Michael Chung, *Electronic Commerce: A Managerial Perspective* (Upper Saddle River, N.J.: Prentice Hall, 2000), 4-5; Vanessa Richardson, "GovWorks Receives VC Vote," *Redherring.com,* November 8, 1999, **http://www.redherring.com**; Ravi Kalakota and Marcia Robinson, *E-Business: Roadmap for Success* (Reading, MA: Addison Wesley Longman, 1999), xvi.

## Sources for Marketing module:

Erin Kelly, "This Is One Virus You Want To Spread," *Fortune*, November 27, 2000, pp. 297-300; Sofia Javed, "Ethnic E-Tailer Builds Expertise in Untapped Market," *Marketing News*, October 9, 2000, p. 24; David Welch, "Car Dealers Say: Follow That Mouse," *Business Week*, April 10, 2000, pp. 106-110; Timothy M. Laseter, Patrick W. Houston, Joshua L. Wright, Juliana Y. Park, "Amazon Your Industry: Extracting the Value From the Value Chain," *Strategy and Business*, First Quarter 2000, **http://www.strategy-business.com/strategy/00109/page1.html**; Alice Z. Cuneo, "Sears Will Expand Sales to Retooled Hispanic Site," *Advertising Age*, October, 1999, **http://www.adage.com**; Chet Dembeck and Andy Wang, Excite@Home Adds Blue Mountain To Its Arsenal, *E-Commerce Times*, October 25, 1999, **http://www.ecommercetimes.com**; Anne Granfield, "E-Marriage," *Forbes*, January 21, 2000, **http://www.forbes.com**; Penelope Patsuris, "Attention Shoppers," *Forbes*, January 25, 2000, **http://www.forbes.com**; Ralph F. Wilson, "The Six Simple Principles of Viral Marketing," *Web Marketing Today*, February 1, 2000, **http://www.emarketer.com/enews/031300_viral.html**; "Valentine's Day Prompts Surge in Web Traffic," *Reuters*, February 14, 2000, **http://www.emarketer.com/enews/021400_rValentine.html**; "Financial Journalism: Paper Wars," *The Economist*, February 19, 2000, 61-62; Dick Satran, "Sun's Shooting Star," *Business 2.0*, February 2000, 51-53; "Saturday Morning Syndrome," *The Economist*, February 26, 2000, E-Commerce sec., 37; "Sears, Bob Vila to Form Online Joint Venture to Create Definitive Home Improvement Site," Sears news release, March 3, 2000, **http://www.sears.com**; "Kroger to Join Sears, Carrefour and Other Retailers in Global Online Supply Marketplace," Sears news release, March 28, 2000, **http://www.sears.com**; Joann Muller, "A Blue-Light Specialist," *Business Week*, June 19, 2000, 212E8;

## Sources for Management module:

Joan O'C. Hamilton, "The Panic Over Hiring," *Business Week,* April 3, 2000, EB 130-132; "Three Hours with Masayoshi Son: Softbank's Grand Plan," *President Online,* November 1999, **http://www.president.co.jp/pre/9911/e_01_2.html**; William C. Taylor, "Inspired by Work," *Fast Company,* November 1999, 200-208; Emily Fitzloff, "Portal Patrol," *Infoworld.com,* May 17, 1999, **http://www.infoworld.com**; Bill Roberts, "Web Portals Open Doors to One-Stop Services," *HR Magazine,* November 1999, **http://www.shrm.org/hrmagazine/articles/1199roberts.htm**; "Cyberventing: A Site for Sore Employees," *HR Magazine,* November 1999, **http://www.shrm.org/hrmagazine/articles/1199cova.htm**; Bill Leonard, "Cyberventing," *HR Magazine,* November 1999, **http://www.shrm.org/hrmagazine/articles/1199cov.htm**; "Rising Son," *Business Week,* January 10, 2000, 63; Kayte Vanscoy, "The Hiring Crisis," *Smart Business*, July 2000, 85-97; Erick Schonfeld, "The (Electronic) Personal Touch," *Fortune,* March 20, 2000, 214.

## Sources for Strategy module:

Michael Mahoney, "Egghead Executives To Exit," *E-Commerce Times,* March 20, 2001, **http://www.ecommercetimes.com/perl/story/8295.html**; Gene G. Marcial, "Steam for Hoover's," *Business Week,* February 28, 2000, 171; Karen Lake, "Interview with Patrick Spain, Chairman and CEO, Hoover's Inc.," *Strategy Week,* February 19, 1999, **http://www.strategyweek.com**; "Hoover's," *Hoover's Online,* April 4, 2000, **http://www.hoovers.com**; "Egghead.com 2000 Sales May Rise 50%; Sees 2002 Profit," *Boston Herald,* November 23, 1999, **http://www.businesstoday.com/techpages/egg11231999.htm**; Kevin Ferguson, "Onsale.com and Egghead.com Combine," *Forbes,* October 6, 1999, **http://www.forbes.com**; Tom Davey, "What Were Those Eggheads Thinking?" *Redherring.com,* July 15, 1999, **http://www.redherring.com/insider/1999/0715/news-egghead.html**; Gary L. Neilson, Bruce A. Pasternack, and Albert J. Viscio, "Up the (E)Organization!" *Strategy and Business,* First Quarter 2000, **http://www.strategy-business.com/strategy/00106/page1.html**; Diane Brady, "How Barnes & Noble Misread the Web," *Business Week,* February 7, 2000, 63; "Something Old, Something New," *The Economist,* February 26, 2000, E-Commerce sec.,15, 18; Jathon Sapsford, "New Jersey's Commerce Bancorp Stretches Hours, Cuts Service Fees," *Wall Street Journal*, May 17, 2000, p.A1+; Amy Kover, "Why Brandwise Was Brand Foolish," Fortune, November 13, 2000, 201-208.

## Sources for Finance module:

"IPO Bubble Bath of the 1990s: VC Fund Returns," *Forbes.com,* February 23, 2001, **http://www.forbes.com/ipodata/vc_returns.shtml**; Sarah Lai Stirland, "Who Will Incubate the Incubators?" *Redherring.com,* April 10, 2000, **http://www.redherring.com/vc/2000/0410/vc-incubator041000.html**; Khanh T.L. Tran, "Avenue A, Niku Set Brisk Pace With Their Public Offerings," *Wall Street Journal Interactive,* March 1, 2000, **http://www.wsj.com**; "Street Buzzes About Services Firm IPO Share Boost," *Reuters,* February 25, 2000, **http://www.news.cnet.com**; Gracian Mack, "Niku Seeks Friday IPO," *Redherring.com,* February 23, 2000, **http://www.redherring.com**; Penelope Patsuris, "Easy Come, Easy Go," *Forbes,* April 30, 1999, **http://www.forbes.com**; Chris Kraeuter, "European Plan Helps Halt Niku Skid," *CBS MarketWatch,* April 5, 2000, **http://www.cbs.marketwatch.com**; Andrew Osterland, "Wall Street Wired," *CFO Magazine,* February 2000, **http://www.cfonet.com**; Richard A. Shaffer, "These Days, Who Isn't a Venture Capitalist?" *Fortune,* April 17, 2000, 532; Sam Williams, "Open Season: Andover.Net Pounds Gavel With Open IPO," *Upside Today,* January 19, 2000, **http://www.upside.com**; "Eparties Turn Out the Lights," *Red Herring,* June 5, 2000, **http://www.redherring.com/industries/2000/0605/ind-ecompanies060500.html**; Lori Enos, "Etoys Acquires Online Party Site," *E-Commerce Times,* June 12, 2000, **http://www.ecommercetimes.com/news/articles2000/000612-5.shtml;** "EToys Files Chapter 11 Bankruptcy," *CNNfn.com,* March 7, 2001, **http://cnnfn.cnn.com/2001/03/07/technology/etoys/**; Dick Kelsey, "Icebox Sells Series to Fox, But Cuts Staff in Half," *BizReport,* November 30, 2000, **http://www.bizreport.com/daily/2000/11/**

**20001130-2.htm**; Gary Gentile, "Web Entertainment Site Cuts Staff," *Washington Post*, November 28, 2000, **http://www.washingtonpost.com**.

## Sources for Legal Studies module:

Julia King, "Corporate Secrets Up For Grabs At New Exchanges," *Computerworld*, November 15, 2000, **http://www.cnn.com/2000/TECH/computing/11/15/secret.exchanges.idg/**; Lori Enos and Elizabeth Blakey, "Toysmart Will Not Sell Customer Names... For Now," *E-Commerce Times*, July 28, 2000, **http://www.ecommercetimes.com/news/articles2000/000728-2.shtml**; Keith Regan and Clare Saliba, "Privacy Watchdogs Blast Amazon," *E-Commerce Times*, September 14, 2000, **http://www.ecommercetimes.com/news/articles2000/000914-3.shtml**; "Amazon May Share Data," *CNNfn.com*, September 1, 2000, **http://cnnfn.com/2000/09/01/technology/wires/amazon_wg/**; Richard Wolf, "States Move to Protect Online Privacy," *USA Today*, January 19, 2000, 1A, 2A; Heather Green, "Privacy: Outrage on the Web," *Business Week*, February 14, 2000, 38-40; James Gleick, "Patently Absurd," *New York Times Magazine*, March 12, 2000, 44-49; Anna Wilde Mathews, "U.S. Will Give Web Patents More Scrutiny Under New Plan," *Wall Street Journal*, March 29, 2000, **http://www.wsj.com**; Pamela L. Moore, "For Sale: Great Ideas, Barely Used," *Business Week*, April 3, 2000, 78, 80; Tyler Maroney, "The New Online Marketplace of Ideas," *Fortune*, April 17, 2000, 521-522; Timothy J. Mullaney, "Those Web Patents Aren't Advancing the Ball," *Business Week*, April 17, 2000, 62; Sources: Jonathan Ringel, "Federal Circuitry," *American Lawyer Media*, October 2, 2000, **http://www.law.com**; "Digital Firms Urge Changes in Copyright Law," *Reuters*, November 29, 2000, **http://www.reuters.com**; Brad Stone, "The Odd Couple," *Newsweek*, November 13, 2000, pp. 56-57.

## Sources for Accounting module:

Peter Elstrom, "The End of Fuzzy Math?" *Business Week*, December 11, 2000, EB100-102; Joe Firmage, "The New Math," *Business 2.0*, May 2000, 269-279; Catherine Yang, "Earth to Dot-Com Accountants," *Business Week*, April 3, 2000, 40-41; Robert J. Samuelson, "A High-Tech Accounting?" *Newsweek*, April 3, 2000, 37; Howard Gleckman, "The Great Internet Tax Debate," *Business Week*, March 27, 2000, 228-236; Nanette Byrnes and Richard A. Melcher, "Earnings Hocus-Pocus," *Business Week*, October 5, 1998, **http://www.businessweek.com**; Jeremy Kahn, "Presto Chango! Sales Are Huge!" *Fortune*, March 20, 2000, 90-96; Lisa Bertagnoli, "Little Consensus on Net Tax Issues As Vote Deadline Nears," *Marketing News*, March 13, 2000, 6; "SEC's Turner Asks for FASB's Help To Tackle Internet Accounting Issues," *Securities Law Weekly*, January 7, 2000, **http://www.lawnewsnetwork.com**; Jennifer Jones, "Some E-Businesses Lured Overseas: Start-Ups Hope to Take Advantage of Breaks, Benefits Outside the United States," *InfoWorld*, February 28, 2000, pg. 30; Source: Peter Elstrom, "The End of Fuzzy Math?" *Business Week E-Biz*, December 11, 2000, EB100, EB 102.

## Sources for Economics module:

James K. Glassman and Kevin A. Hassett, "Ganging Up," *Standard.com*, December 4, 2000, **http://www.thestandard.com/article/display/0,1151,20421,00.html**; Susan Kuchinskas, "Swap 'Til You Drop," *Business 2.0*, May 2000, 85-87; Paul A. Greenberg, "B2B Marketplaces Face FTC Scrutiny," *E-Commerce Times*, March 29, 2000, **http://www.ecommercetimes.com**; Robert D. Hof, "E-Malls for Business," *Business Week*, March 13, 2000, 32-34; Richard A. Oppel, Jr., "The Higher Stakes of Business-to-Business Trade," *New York Times*, March 5, 2000, sec. 3, 3; "Seller Beware," *The Economist*, March 4, 2000, 61-62; "E-Cash 2.0," *The Economist*, February 19, 2000, 67-69; "Cash Remains King," *The Economist*, February 19, 2000, 21; Philip Kotler, *Marketing Management* 10th edition (Upper Saddle River, N.J.: Prentice Hall, 2000), 9; "What Are the Internet Economy Indicators?" *Center for Research on Electronic Commerce*, (n.d.), **http://www.internetindicators.com**; Susan Moran, "Cash-Free Economy," *Business 2.0*, February 2000, 40-45; Roland Jones, "E-Pay Firms Outpace Banks," *The Street.com*, May 23, 2000, **http://abcnews.go.com/sections/business/thestreet/epay000523.html**; Sources: Thane Peterson, "E-I-E-I-E-Farming," *Business Week*, May 1,

2000, 202; Christina Dyrness, "The New Farmers Market," *Raleigh News & Observer*, April 10, 2000, **http://www.xsag.com/common/news/archive/4-10-2000-no.html**; Source: Roland Jones, "E-Pay Firms Outpace Banks," *The Street.com,* May 23, 2000, **http://abcnews.go.com/sections/business/thestreet/epay000523.html**; Cheryl Rosen, "New Services Let Users Pay Bills Via Cell Phone," *Information Week,* June 19, 2000, **http://www.informationweek.com/791/paypal.htm**.

## Sources for Business Communication module:

Elizabeth Hurt, "Chat Spats," *Business 2.0,* August 25, 2000, **http://www.business2.com/content/channels/ebusiness/2000/08/25/17606**; Amy Gahran, "Major Corporate Web Contender: IBM," *Contentious,* January 6, 2000, **http://www.contentious.com**; Amy Gahran, "A Primer for Print Writers: How Online Is Different," *Content Spotlight,* January 31, 2000, **http://www.content-exchange.com**; Pat Regnier, "Why Your Broker Hates E-Mail," *Money,* October 1999, 154-156; Maxine Lans Retsky, "Spam Getting Trickier For Marketers to Use," *Marketing News,* March 13, 2000, 13; John Sanko, "Senate 'Spam' Bill Cooks Up Debate Over E-Mail," *Rocky Mountain News,* March 17, 2000, **http://www.insidedenver.com/legislature/0317email.shtml**; Elizabeth Crane, "Trip.com," *SmartBusiness Magazine*, August 2000, **http://zdnet.com/smartbusinessmag/stories/all/0,6605,2598240-2,00.html**; Source: Alissa Quart, "How To Cheat the Cheaters," *Time Digital,* November 15, 2000, 70-71.

## Sources for MIS module:

Jim Kerstetter, "Software Shakeout," *Business Week,* March 5, 2001, 72-80; Matthew A. DeBellis, "ASP: Anyone Still Paying?" *Redherring.com,* November 20, 2000, **http://cnnfn.com/2000/11/20/redherring/herring_asp/**; Alan Hall, "ASPing For Trouble," *Business Week,* December 4, 2000, F21-F22; Stephen Baker, "Europe Swoons for Voice-On-the-Net," *Business Week,* May 1, 2000, 196; Steve Rosenbush, "The Talking Internet," *Business Week,* May 1, 2000, 174-188; Wylie Wong, "E-Commerce Customers Chatty With Sites That Talk," *CNET News,* April 24, 2000, **http://www.cnetnews.com**; Michelle V. Rafter, "Back to the Future: San Diego's Scripps Health Is Reinventing Patient Care With a $75 Million Network Linking Doctors and Hospitals," *TheStandard.com*, April 3, 2000, **http://www.thestandard.com**; Corey Grice, "Phone Giants May Gain Most From ASP Market," *CNET News,* March 15, 2000, **http://www.cnetnews.com**; Kim Girard, "The Battle Over Renting Software," *CNET News,* February 1, 2000, **http://www.cnetnews.com**; "Internet Voice Comes to Online Customer Service," *E-Commerce Times,* January 31, 2000, **http://www.ecommercetimes.com/news/articles2000/000131-3.shtml**; Kathleen Ohlson, "New Extranet To Help NYSE Members Execute Orders Faster," *ComputerWorld,* March 17, 2000, **http://www.computerworld.com**; Matt Hamblen, "Shell Protects Brand Via Net," *ComputerWorld,* January 10, 2000, **http://www.computerworld.com**; Melanie Austria Farmer and Kim Girard, "Is the Enterprise Resource Planning Market Dead?" *CNET News,* January 4, 2000, **http://www.cnetnews.com**; Source: Sarah L. Roberts-Witt, "Jam On It," *Business 2.0,* August 22, 2000, 80-83.

## Sources for Decision Sciences module:

Dana Janes, "Request for Cash," *Marketing News,* March 27, 2000, 11; "Internet Enhances RFP/RFQ Process," *Purchasing,* February 10, 2000, 105; "Cincom Lights Up Fern-Howard with Manage:Enterprise," Cincom Systems, August 16, 1999, **http://www.cincom.com**; Ira Sager, "Big Blue Gets Wired," *Business Week,* April 3, 2000, EB 99-100; Scott Leibs, "Think Before You Link," *Industry Week,* April 17, 2000, 23+; George Taninecz, "Value Chain IT Infrastructure," *Industry Week,* April 17, 2000, 32+; Dimitry Elias Léger, "Smokestack Lightning: Eaton Hits the Web," *Fortune,* April 17, 2000, 522, 526; Ed Hess, "Make Advanced Planning and Scheduling Work For Your Company," *Integrated Solutions,* April 2000, **http://www.integratedsolutionsmag.com/articles/2000_04/000408.htm**; Tim Stevens, "Designs in Sync," *Industry Week's The Value Chain,* June 12, 2000, **http://www.iwvaluechain.com/features/articles.asp?article=842**; Jeannette Brown, "Service, Please," *Business Week,* October 23, 2000, EB48-EB50.